APPLICATIONS INCLUDED IN THIS TEXT *continued*

MICROECONOMICS

An Intuitive Approach with Calculus

Thomas J. Nechyba
Duke University

SOUTH-WESTERN
CENGAGE Learning™

Australia • Brazil • Japan • Korea • Mexico • Singapore • Spain • United Kingdom • United States

SOUTH-WESTERN
CENGAGE Learning™

Microeconomics: An Intuitive Approach with Calculus
Thomas J. Nechyba
Print and LiveGraphs: Deborah Antkoviak and John Gross of econweb™

Vice President of Editorial, Business: Jack W. Calhoun

Publisher: Joe Sabatino

Executive Editor: Michael Worls

Supervising Developmental Editor: Jennifer Thomas

Sr. Marketing Manager: John Carey

Marketing Manager: Betty Jung

Marketing Coordinator: Suellen Ruttkay

Editorial Assistant: Lena Mortis

Sr. Content Project Manager: Tamborah Moore

Media Editor: Deepak Kumar

Sr. Marketing Communications Manager: Sarah Greber

Sr. Print Buyer: Sandee Milewski

Production Service and Composition: Integra

Sr. Art Director: Michelle Kunkler

Cover and Internal Designer: Stratton Design

Cover Image: © Mecaleha / iStockphoto

For product information and technology assistance, contact us at
Cengage Learning Customer & Sales Support, 1-800-354-9706

For permission to use material from this text or product, submit all requests online at **cengage.com/permissions**
Further permissions questions can be emailed to
permissionrequest@cengage.com

ExamView® **is a registered trademark of eInstruction Corp.**
© **2011 Cengage Learning. All Rights Reserved.**

Library of Congress Control Number: 2009941965
Package ISBN-13: 978-0-538-45325-7
Package ISBN-10: 0-538-45325-7

Book only ISBN-13: 978-1-439-03999-1
Book only ISBN-10: 1-439-03999-2

South-Western Cengage Learning
5191 Natorp Boulevard
Mason, OH 45040
USA

Cengage Learning products are represented in Canada by Nelson Education, Ltd.

For your course and learning solutions, visit **www.cengage.com**
Purchase any of our products at your local college store or at our preferred online store **www.CengageBrain.com**

Printed in China by RR Donnelley
3 4 5 6 7 13 12 11

BRIEF CONTENTS

CONTENTS

Contents

PREFACE

To Students

As a student, I often felt both alienated and insulted by textbooks: alienated because they seemed to make no attempt to speak *to* rather than *at* me, insulted because they seemed to talk *down* to me by giving me lots of "visuals" (like pictures of monkeys—seriously) to keep me awake and by feeding me endless definitions to memorize—all while never acknowledging the obvious conceptual limits of what was being presented.

I have therefore tried to write a book that is a little different and that I think I might have liked to use when I was a student. Some have commented that you might not like it because it doesn't lend itself to memorizing definitions for exams. Others find it strange that I address you so directly throughout much of the book and that I occasionally even admit that this or that assumption we make is in many ways "silly."

I don't actually have anything against monkeys or definitions or assumptions that seem "silly," but my experience with students over the years tells me that you do not mind being challenged a bit and actually enjoy being part of a conversation rather than committing one to memory. The modern world has few rewards for people who are really good at memorizing but offers much to those who can conceptualize ideas and integrate them with one another. Economics offers a path to practice this—and it does so in a way that can be exciting and interesting, interesting enough to not actually require monkey pictures even if it is sometimes frustrating to get through some of the details.

I will say more about much of this in Chapter 1—so I'll try to avoid repeating myself here and instead just offer a few points on how best to use this text:

1. You may want to review parts of **Chapter 0** (on the accompanying product support web site www.cengage.com/economics/nechyba) to review some basics before proceeding to Chapter 2.
2. Attempt the **within-chapter exercises** as you read—and check your answers with those in the accompanying (web-based) **Study Guide** that contains answers to *all* within-chapter-exercises. (My students who have used drafts of this text have done considerably better on exams when using within-chapter exercises and solutions.)
3. Before you read each chapter, particularly as the book progresses, print out the **Print Graphics** from the accompanying product support web site (www.cengage.com/economics/nechyba).[1] This will reduce frustrations as the discussion of graphs in the text often extends across multiple pages—requiring you to flip back and forth unless you also have the print graphics with you. The print graphs might also prove handy in class as you can take notes directly on them. (And if you really want pictures of monkeys to stay awake, just keep them with your print graphs, or let me know and we'll put some monkey pictures on the web site.)
4. Use the **LiveGraphs** feature of the web site, particularly if the discussion of graphs in the text leaves you with questions. These animated versions of the text graphs come with visual and audio explanations (by yours truly) that you can rewind and fast forward at your own pace. (Some chapters also have additional animated graphs that are not directly related to the print graphs in the text, and you may also access the **Print Graphics** from the LiveGraphs site.)

---

[1] The full site will not go live until Summer of 2010.

5. Look for interesting applications in **end-of-chapter exercises**, but know that some of these are designed to be challenging. Don't get frustrated if they don't make sense at first. It helps to work with others to solve these (assuming your instructor allows this). The [†] symbol denotes exercises with solutions provided in the **Study Guide**, with solutions to the remainder of the exercises provided to instructors. (The symbol * denotes conceptually more challenging exercises, and the symbol ** denotes computationally more intensive exercises.)

6. While you will often feel like you are getting lost in details within chapters, the **Introductions** (to the Parts as well as the Chapters) and the **Conclusions** (in each chapter) attempt to keep an eye on the big picture. Don't skip them!

7. The book has an extensive **Glossary** and **Index** but develops definitions within a narrative rather than pulling them out within the text. Use the Glossary to remind yourself of the meaning of terms and the Index to find where the associated concepts are discussed in detail. But resist the temptation to memorize too much. The terms aren't as important as the concepts.

8. No textbook is without **errors**, and this is particularly true for first editions. In anticipation of this, we have provided a place on the accompanying web site for reporting all errors in real time as they are identified. So if you think there might be an error, check the site and if it is not yet reported, let your instructor know so that it can be passed along to me.

To Instructors

When I was first asked to teach microeconomics, I was surprised to learn that the course had been one of the least popular in my department. It was unclear what the goals of the course were—and without such clarity at the outset, students had come to view the course as a disjointed mess of graphs and math with little real-world relevance and no sense of what value it could add. As I came to define what goals I would like *my* course to develop, I had trouble finding a text that would help my students aim toward these goals without over-emphasizing just one or two to the exclusion of others. So we largely de-emphasized textbooks—but something was working: the course had suddenly become one of the most popular in the department!

I have therefore attempted to build a framework around the five primary goals that I believe any microeconomics course should accomplish:

1. It should present microeconomics not as a collection of unrelated models but *as a way of looking at the world*. People respond to incentives because they try to do the best they can given their circumstances. That's microeconomics in a nutshell—and everything—*everything*—flows from it.

2. It should persuade that microeconomics does not just change the way *we think* about the world—it also tells us a lot about *how and why the world works* (and sometimes doesn't work).

3. It should not only get us to think more clearly about economics but also *to think more clearly in general*—without relying on memorization. Such *conceptual thinking skills* are the very skills that are most sought after and most rewarded in the modern world.

4. It should directly confront the fact that few of us can move from memorizing to conceptual thinking without *applying concepts directly*, but different students learn differently, and instructors need the *flexibility* to target material to *their* students' needs.

5. Finally, it should provide students with a *roadmap for further studies*—a sense of what the most compelling next courses might be given *their* interests.

I am thus trying to provide a flexible framework that keeps us rooted in a *way of thinking* while developing a *coherent overview* to help us better understand the world around us. Half the text builds up to the most fundamental result in all of economics—that self-interested individuals will—*under certain conditions and without intending to*—give rise to a spontaneous order that has great benefits for society. But the second half probes these "certain conditions" and develops insights into how firms, governments, and civil society can contribute to human welfare when markets by themselves "fail." Future courses can then be seen as sub-fields that come to terms with these "certain conditions."

While the material in the full text is more than enough for a two-semester sequence, the text offers a **variety of flexible paths for a one-semester course**. In each chapter, you can emphasize an intuitive A-part or link it to a more mathematical B-part; and, while the last part of the text relies heavily on game theory, the underlying narrative can also be developed through a non-game theoretic approach. Substantive paths include some focused on *theory*, others focused on *policy*, and yet others focused on *business*, with all paths including core material as well as optional topics. Throughout, the models build in complexity, with applications woven into the narrative (rather than being relegated to side-boxes). They are then further developed in an extensive array of exercises that get students—not me or you—to apply concepts to *Everyday*, *Business*, and *Policy* settings.

For more details on how you might use the various parts of the text and its accompanying tools, I hope you will have a look at the **Instructor's Manual** that I have written to go along with the text. Here are just a few examples of how you might weave through the book depending on your focus:

1. **Traditional Theory Emphasis:**
   Ch. 1–23 (with Ch. 3, 8, the latter sections of 9 and 13 optional) plus
   Ch. 29–30 optional

2. **Theory Emphasis with Game Theory:**
   Ch. 1–18 (with 3, 8, the latter sections of 9, 13, and 18 optional) plus
   Ch. 23–27 (with 28 through 30 optional)

3. **Business Focus:**
   Ch. 1–18 (with Ch. 3, 8, 16, the latter sections of 9, 13, and 18 optional) plus
   Ch. 23–26

4. **Policy Focus:**
   Ch. 1–15 (with Ch. 3, 8, and the latter sections of 9 and 13 optional), plus
   Ch. 18–23, 28–30 (with Ch. 24–27 optional depending on level of game theory usage)

Finally, I would like to invite you to **be a partner in shaping the future of this textbook**. No text is perfect the first time around, and this one is no exception. But to achieve serious improvements with future editions, I need feedback on what is working and what is not, what is too much and what is missing. For this reason, we have created a place on the text web site where I can engage with instructors directly, where we can give one another feedback and where I can learn about how things are working out in your classroom. I hope you will make use of this and we will meet on the web site.

Acknowledgments

I never intended to write this textbook and, had it not been for the persuasive pressures applied by Mike Worls (who is formally the executive editor for the project), the book would in fact not have been written. It is for this reason that, during the more trying times of getting this project finished (when, as my kids put it, dad was "grumpy"), Mike became know as "that bad man" in my household. Still, I tell my children that even "bad" people sometimes give rise to good things—and I hope this is the case here. Regardless, I am grateful for Mike's insistence that I give this a shot. The project has taken longer and become more comprehensive than either of us envisioned at first, but Mike continued to believe in it throughout. Jennifer Thomas (the development editor for the project) has been with us since the beginning, and I often wondered whether her children, not yet born when we started, might be in college before the text gets finished. (I think we made it in time.)

Just before launching this project, I had the good fortune to meet John Gross and Deborah Antkoviak of EconWeb. As Director of Undergraduate Studies at Duke, I was interested in their ideas of how to bring graphical analysis alive in animations, and I began to collaborate with them to produce animations that could assist in teaching economics. So it became only natural to extend our partnership to this textbook, with John and Deb producing not only the (299!) graphics that appear in the text but also the LiveGraphs (and related material) that appear on the accompanying web site. I do not believe that the approach taken in this text would be possible without the quality of these graphics, and I know that there would have been no way to produce these without the partnership and friendship that we have developed. I cannot overstate the extent to which I am in their debt.

I am not sure I fully appreciated the challenge of compiling an internally consistent and partially mathematical text when I started typing away in Word, and so I thank my brother (Mike Nechyba) for introducing me to the wonders of LaTeX (while occasionally tutoring me on basics in Mathematica). I also thank Stas Kolenikov for arranging to have the initial Word chapters transferred into LaTeX. Although, much to my regret, the text in your hands was not ultimately laid out using LaTeX, we would not have been able to use pdf drafts of chapters in classrooms over the past few years had it not been for Mike's and Stan's early intervention, nor would I have had the patience to see the process through without the benefit of this approach. I am also grateful to the production team at Cengage. Tamborah Moore diligently kept the content moving throughout, and Michelle Kunkler kept an artist's eye on it as I, lacking any artistic talent whatsoever, was too busy checking subscripts. My thanks to both of them and the entire team.

When I started seriously working on this text, I had just taken over as the new chair of the economics department at Duke. I have had some good ideas in my life, but I suspect that becoming department chair and textbook author at the same time was not one of these. So it seems only appropriate to thank all of my colleagues for their patience when time spent on the book came at the cost of time spent on the department. (Life would be so much better without the need for trade-offs, but then again, that would leave no place for the fascinating area of economics.) I particularly want to thank the department's wonderful staff that helped maintain the illusion of my presence when I was hiding to work on this project, leaving some with the impression that I was actually a competent chair. Above all, I owe them my thanks for keeping me laughing even during the most trying times. Jim Speckart should be particularly acknowledged for processing the many hand-drawn graphs for the solution sets to the exercises in the textbook (while offering his persistently irreverent but unfailingly entertaining "feedback").

Early versions of this text have been patiently endured by many. First and foremost among these, I thank the hundreds of Duke students that have taken microeconomics with me and quasi-voluntarily served as guinea pigs for this text. Their feedback and diligent reporting of errors, sometimes for extra credit, have made this a better book, and it is to all of those students that I therefore dedicate this first edition. Other instructors have also used early drafts of this text, and I thank them and their students as well. And I want to acknowledge in particular the students in the American Economic Association's (AEA) Summer Program who were the first to live through the B-portions of the text when the AEA program was housed at Duke. I am perpetually amazed at the generosity with which all of these students allowed me to teach them from flawed and incomplete pdf documents.

Isaac Linnartz, Jesse Patrone-Werdiger, Suzy Silk, Wendy Wang, and Sejal Shah, all Duke undergraduates some years ago, read patiently through early chapters and gave feedback that helped shape the rest of the book. I should thank my many TAs individually for all their patience as we taught from drafts, but space (and memory problems) keep me from doing so here. I do, however, want to highlight Bethany Peterson, Terry Yang, and Liad Wagman for their comments, encouragement, and contributions. Toward the completion of the text, proof reading and feedback from Chase Wilson, Christina Shin, and Chen Xiaoyan kept many errors from making it into the final text. Naturally, the errors that remain are almost entirely my fault (and, of course, my wife's since she insisted that I actually spend time away from the textbook doing "my share" around the house).

Anyone that has ever tried to undertake a project like this in the midst of a busy family life knows how difficult the burden on family can be at those times when the frustrations of the project seem to outweigh the bright prospect of future royalties. For living through this with me, my thanks to the family that sustains and completes me—Stacy, Ellie, Jenny, Katie, and, most recently, Blake. We will celebrate on our vacation in the Cayman Islands soon.

Thomas J. Nechyba
Durham, NC

FURTHER ACKNOWLEDGMENTS

The author and editorial team at South-Western Cengage Learning would also like to acknowledge the feedback and assistance of many instructors who reviewed this text in various drafts and participated in several focus groups concerning its development and LiveGraphs. Their time and comments have been invaluable in crafting the final product.

J. Ulyses Balderas, *Sam Houston State University*

Klaus G. Becker, *Texas Tech University*

Allen Bellas, *Metropolitan State College of Denver*

Tibor Besedes, *Louisiana State University*

Maharukh Bhiladwalla, *Rutgers University*

Volodymyr Bilotkach, *University of California Irvine*

Benjamin F. Blair, *Mississippi State University*

Victor Brajer, *California State University Fullerton*

Nancy Brooks, *University of Vermont*

James Cardon, *Brigham Young University*

Kalyan Chakraborty, *Emporia State University*

Basanta Chaudhuri, *Rutgers University*

Ben Collier, *Northwest Missouri State University*

Stephen Davis, *Southwest Minnesota State University*

Mary Deily, *Lehigh University*

Wayne Edwards, *University of Alaska*

Adem Y. Elveren, *University of Utah*

Robert M. Feinberg, *American University*

Rhona Free, *Eastern Connecticut State University*

Jaqueline Geoghegan, *Clark University*

Dipak Ghosh, *Emporia State University*

Rajeev K. Goel, *Illinois State University*

Tiffani A. Gottschall, *Washington and Jefferson College*

Chiara Gratton- Lavoie, *California State University Fullerton*

Tom Gresik, *University of Notre Dame*

Philip Grossman, *St. Cloud State University*

Jim Halteman, *Wheaton College*

Vladimir Hlasny, *Michigan State University*

Gary Hoover, *University of Alabama*

Joseph Hughes, *Rutgers University*

Michael Keane, *Yale University*

Farida Khan, *University of Wisconsin Parkside*

Byung-Cheol Kim, *Georgia Institute of Technology*

Felix Kwan, *Maryville University*

Ross LaRoe, *Denison University*

Marc Law, *University of Vermont*

Sang H. Lee, *Southeastern Louisiana University*

Robert J. Lemke, *Lake Forest College*

Anthony M. Marino, *University of Southern California*

Douglas J. Miller, *University of Missouri*

Joshua B. Miller, *University of Minnesota Twin Cities*

Ranganath Murthy, *Bucknell University*

Kathryn Nantz, *Fairfield University*

Tara Natarjan, *Saint Michael's College*

Ronald Nate, *Brigham Young University*

Catherine Norman, *Johns Hopkins University*

Terry Olson, *Truman State University*

Mete Ozcan, *Brooklyn College CUNY*

Ebru Isil Ozturk, *University of Wisconsin*

Silve Parviainen, *University of Illinois at Urbana-Champaign*

Brian Peterson, *Central College*

Jonas Prager, *New York University*

James Prieger *Pepperdine University School of Public Policy*

Salim Rashid, *University of Illinois at Urbana-Champaign*

Tyler R. Ross, *University of Washington Seattle*

Jeremy Sandford, *University of Wisconsin*

Jonathan Sandy, *University of San Diego*

Mustafa Sawani, *Truman State University*

Kwang Soo Cheong, *Johns Hopkins University*

Charles Steele, *Hillsdale College*

Vasant Sukhatme, *Macalester College*

Jeffrey Sundberg, *Lake Forest College*

Jose Vasquez-Cognet, *University of Illinois at Urbana-Champaign*

Richard Vogel, *Farmingdale State College*

Eleanor von Ende, *Texas Tech University*

Rob Wassmer, *California State University Sacramento*

Tetsuji Yamada, *Rutgers University*

Ben Young, *University of Missouri Kansas City*

Sourushe Zandvakili, *University of Cincinnati*

Introduction

Do safer cars necessarily result in fewer traffic deaths? Is it sensible to subsidize domestic U.S. oil drilling in an effort to make the United States less dependent on unstable regions of the world? Would outlawing live Christmas trees help to reduce deforestation? Should we impose laws against "price gouging?" Is boycotting companies that use cheap labor abroad a good way to express our outrage at the dismal working conditions in those countries? Would it be better for workers to require their employers to pay their Social Security taxes rather than taxing the workers directly? Should we tax the sales by monopolies so that these companies don't earn such outrageous profits?

Many people would instinctively answer "yes" to each of these questions. Many economists would say "no," or at least "not necessarily." Why is that?

One possible answer is that economists are social misfits who have different values than "real people." But I don't think that's typically the right answer. By and large, economists are an ideologically diverse group, distributed along the political spectrum much as the rest of the population. Most of us live perfectly normal lives, love our children and empathize with the pain of others. Some of us even go to church. We do, however, look at the world through a somewhat different lens, a lens that presumes *people respond to incentives* and that these responses aggregate in ways that are often surprising, frequently humbling, and sometimes quite stunning. What we think we know isn't always so, and, as a result, our actions, particularly in the policy realm, often have "unintended" consequences.

I know many of you are taking this course with a hidden agenda of learning more about "business," and I certainly hope that you will not be disappointed. But the *social science of economics* in general, and microeconomics in particular, is about much more than that. Through the lens of this science, economists see many instances of remarkable social order emerging from millions of seemingly unconnected choices in the "marketplace," spontaneous cooperation among individuals on different ends of the globe, the kind of cooperation that propels societies out of the material poverty and despair that has characterized most of human history. At the same time, our lens clarifies when individual incentives run counter to the "common good," when private interests unravel social cooperation in the absence of corrective nonmarket institutions. Markets have given rise to enormous wealth, but we also have to come to terms with issues such as economic inequality and global warming, unscrupulous business practices, and racial discrimination. Economics can certainly help us think more clearly about business and everyday life. It can also, however, teach some very deep insights about the world in which we live, a world in which incentives matter.

1.1 What Is Microeconomics?

We will define *microeconomics* as the *science* that investigates the *social consequences* of the interaction of *rational* beings that pursue their *perceived self-interest*.[1] At first glance, this description of human beings as "rational" and "self-interested" sounds a bit naive and vaguely callous. After all, most people would not characterize their fellow citizens as always "rational," and we know first hand that some of our most meaningful experiences derive from stepping outside of our "self." For those who are used to thinking of "scientists" as wearing white coats and protective goggles in research laboratories, the use of the word "science" to characterize what economists do may also seem odd, as may the definition's emphasis on "social" consequences. It's perhaps useful, then, to say a bit more about this definition.

1.1.1 Economics as a *Science*

Let's begin with a few words about *science*. Obviously, economics is not a science in exactly the same way that physics or chemistry are science: we don't generally have laboratories in which we smash atoms into each other or mix fuming chemicals. But in another sense it *is* similar. Science progresses through the formulation and testing of models that generate hypotheses, and in this sense, economics is in fact by and large a science. Most economists, as we will discuss more in Section 1.2, formulate models that are rooted in economic theory and then check to see whether the hypotheses that emerge are rejected by real-world observations. Some economists actually do perform experiments, but most look at data from the real world to see whether our predictions hold. You will learn more about how this *testing* of hypotheses is done if you go on to take statistics and econometrics courses, but in this course, you will mainly learn about the underlying theory and models that most economists use to formulate their hypotheses.

1.1.2 *Rationality, Self-Interest* and Indiana Jones

In these models, we assume that people are *rational* and in pursuit of their *perceived self-interest*. While we will use the term "rational" in other ways once we define tastes in Chapter 4, for now we simply take it to mean that individuals seek to do "the best they can given their circumstances." We don't mean that people are rational in some deeper philosophical sense; all we really mean is that they are deliberative in trying to achieve their goals. Those goals might include improving the welfare of others they care about, and they may include goals that make sense to them but don't make sense to others. Someone who sacrifices personal consumption to improve her children's well-being may be thought of as "unselfish," but improving her children's well-being may still be in her perceived "self-interest" if making her children happy also makes her happy. That seems quite noble, but not everything that one individual finds "worthwhile" might be worthwhile in some deeper sense. The businessman may seek to maximize his own profit when he could be saving starving children instead; the politician may seek to win elections when she could be making a "worthwhile" difference in people's lives by doing something unpopular; the drug addict may seek to get his next fix when he might be "better off" checking himself into a rehab center. Nevertheless, each of these individuals is directing his or her actions toward a goal he or she perceives to be worthwhile and in his or her self-interest.

Some time ago, I watched one of the popular Indiana Jones movies starring Harrison Ford and Sean Connery. Sean Connery plays Harrison Ford's father, and together they find themselves in an unfortunate position. Sean Connery lies in a cave, mortally wounded, and Harrison Ford faces the following dilemma: On the other side of the cave, there are a number of potions in

---

[1]This definition actually applies also to macroeconomics, but *micro*economists are particularly focused on beginning their analysis with *individual* behavior.

different containers. Most of these potions are deadly poisons, but one is a magical elixir that, if consumed by someone mortally wounded, will heal instantly. Harrison Ford runs to the potions and agonizes over which to take. He settles on one and decides to test it himself before giving it to his father.

I guess it seems unselfishly heroic that Harrison Ford would put his own life in jeopardy before subjecting his father to the possible ingestion of a poison, but it also violates what economists think of as rational self-interest. We are not disturbed by the fact that Harrison Ford cares deeply about his father; given that he does, the goal of saving his father falls within the realm of his perceived self-interest. What bothers us is the fact that Harrison Ford appears not to choose rationally given the goal he is attempting to achieve, at least so long as we are willing to assume that preserving his own life, all else being equal, is also in Harrison Ford's perceived self-interest. The rational course of action in this case would have been for Harrison Ford to settle on one of the potions, run with the potion to the other side of the cave where his mortally wounded father lies, and say: "Dad, you are going to die any minute. This potion may kill you, which will happen anyway if you don't take it. But if it's the right potion, it will save your life. So drink the potion and don't think I don't care about you just because I don't first take the risk of killing myself only to watch you also die during my final moments. One of us surviving is better than none, even if both of us surviving is better still."

The example illustrates two points: First, self-interest is not necessarily the same as "selfishness." The latter presumes you care only about yourself; the former leaves open the possibility that others may contribute to your perception of your own well-being. Often, selfishness and self-interest coincide, but not always. Second, "rational" simply means that we pick the best available course of action to achieve our self-interested goal. Harrison Ford does not violate our presumption of self-interest when he cares deeply about his father, but his behavior does violate rationality unless he places no value on his own life. In testing the potion first, Harrison Ford is not doing "the best he can given his circumstances."

1.1.3 *Social Consequences*, Pencils and Global Warming

Ultimately, we don't just try to understand rational, self-interested behavior per se, although that is an important aspect of microeconomics. What we are really after is understanding the *social consequences* of the interaction of rational, self-interested individual behavior. It may be interesting to think about how Robinson Crusoe behaves on an island by himself, but it is more interesting to understand how the world changes as he and his friend Friday interact once Friday comes on the scene. More interesting still is what happens when hundreds, thousands, or even millions of rational, self-interested individuals pursue their individual goals *given that everyone else is doing the same.* Economists call the outcome of these interactions an "equilibrium," and it is in this equilibrium that we find the social consequences of individual behavior.

In his famous PBS series *Free to Choose*, Milton Friedman holds up a pencil and makes the initially preposterous claim that no one in the world knows how to make that pencil. It seems silly at first, but at the same time it is absolutely true if we seriously think about whether anyone knows how to make a pencil *from scratch*. One would have to know which trees to harvest for the wood, how to make the tools to harvest the trees, what chemicals to use to treat the wood once it is cut into the right shape, how to drill the hole to make room for the lead and how to make the tools to drill the hole. That does not begin to scratch the surface, because we also have to know everything about where to get the materials to eventually make the lead (and how to make it and all the necessary tools required for that), how to do the same for the metal cap that holds the eraser, how to make the eraser, and how to create the paint and paintbrushes to coat the outside of the pencil. When you really think about it, tens of thousands of people somehow cooperated across all the continents in the world to make the pencil Friedman was holding, and almost none of those tens of thousands of people were aware that they were participating in a process that would result in a pencil.

Economists are fascinated by the fact that pencils are produced despite the fact that no one knows how to produce them and despite the fact that no one is charged with coordinating all these people and materials into the production of pencils. We are fascinated by the fact that cooperation on such massive scale can simply emerge from the bottom up without the individuals knowing that they are cooperating with one another. We are even more fascinated by the fact that the cooperation emerges purely from the rational, self-interested choices that individuals make along the way, each one simply trying to earn a living, to do the best he or she can given the circumstances. This is a *social consequence* of the interaction of rational, self-interested behavior, one that is guided by the impersonal forces of market prices that tell individuals where to work, what to produce, whom to sell to, etc. If you can see how it might be fascinating that pencils get produced and delivered to my local store for pennies, don't get me started on my fascination about really complicated products that seem to pop up all over the place without anyone really coordinating the millions of people involved.

Of course not all social consequences of rational, self-interested behavior are so rosy. We will see that the same economic lens that explains how people cooperate to make pencils also explains how global warming is not tamed by the same forces, how relative (as opposed to absolute) poverty persists, how concentrated power distorts markets, and how some goods might never get produced unless nonmarket institutions intervene. Understanding when we can rely on individual self-interest to give rise to cooperation—and when such self-interest impedes cooperation—is one of the key themes of this book and one of the central goals of microeconomics. With such an understanding, we can then formulate ways of changing the circumstances in which decisions are made to bring those decisions more in line with social goals: to change the *social consequences* of rational, self-interested behavior by *altering the incentives* people face along the way.

1.2 Economics, Incentives, and Economic Models

When boiled down to its essentials, economics is then all about an exploration of the simple premise that *people respond to incentives* because they generally *attempt to do the best they can given their circumstances*. It is a simple premise but one that leads to a rich framework through which to analyze many small and large debates in the world in a logical and rigorous manner. Yet despite all of my idealistic musings about the important issues that economics can help us to understand better, you will notice that much of this book is devoted to the building of rather cold economic "models" that, at least initially, seem to be starkly disconnected from such grand objectives. In fact, many students initially think of these models as involving *simplistic* and *unrealistic* characterizations of what we are as human beings. And in certain ways, they are undeniably right. Nevertheless, I would like to convince you at the outset that such models represent the only real method through which economists can make any sense at all of the underlying issues we are concerned about. In the process, we also get an "unintended consequence" of learning through economic models: We learn to think more conceptually, to move beyond memorization to a method of linking seemingly unconnected events in ways that translate to life well beyond economics.

1.2.1 Economic Models, *Simplicity*, and Picasso

Consider the way we model consumers in the first section of this book. As you will see in the coming chapters, we will essentially view them as cold individuals who rationally calculate the costs and benefits of different alternatives using a mechanical characterization of "tastes" as a guide. "Economic man," as characterized in many of the models that we start with, boils down to a machine that seems to have little moral standing beyond that of a vacuum cleaner. It is not a full characterization of all the complexity that underlies the human condition, and it omits some of the very aspects of our makeup that make us "human." I have often mentioned in my classes that I would be deeply depressed if I truly thought that my wife was nothing more than "economic woman." The most important factors I considered when proposing marriage to her had virtually nothing to do with our simple model of decision making.

But economics does not attempt to paint a full picture of who we are as human beings. You will no doubt find meaning in your studies of philosophy or psychology or art or religion as you try to complete the picture of what it means to you to say that we are human. Economics simply tries to provide a framework for systematically studying aspects of human decision making that relate to our desire to pursue our perceived self-interest in different institutional settings, and how such self-interested decision making affects society as a whole. For this purpose, it would be maddening to try to come to real conclusions using a fully laid out picture of the complex beings we are, because much of what makes us so complex has little bearing on the questions economists ultimately aim to answer. Simplicity in models therefore becomes a virtue so long as the models can predict well what we are trying to predict.

I often try to illustrate this explicitly to my students by telling them of my ignorance of abstract art and of the insights into such art I have gained from the following example: I am told that, somewhere in a museum, there exists a series of 27 paintings by Picasso. The first of these paintings is one that I could understand: It is a realistic depiction of a particular scene, perhaps a girl holding a watering can in a beautiful garden. The second painting in the series is almost identical to the first but contains somewhat less detail. Similarly, each of the next 25 paintings in the series takes away some more detail, leaving the last painting with nothing but some unrecognizable streaks of paint on a canvas. This last painting, I am told, is Picasso's interpretation of the "essence" of the first painting. I have never seen this series of 27 paintings and am not sure it even exists. But I am told that I would have a much better understanding of what makes the first painting great if I could make the effort to view this series because I would truly see how the last painting captures something profound that gets lost to a simpleton like me as I view the first pretty picture in the series.[2]

Economic models are like the last painting in this series. They are constructed to strip away all the complexity, all the noise that gets in the way of a sound analysis of particular economic problems and leave us with the essence of individual decision making that matters for the questions at hand. They will not tell us whether there is a God or why we like to stare at the stars at night or why we fall in love. But they can be powerful tools that allow us to understand aspects of the world that would remain impenetrable without the use of simplified models. For this reason, I ask you to resist the temptation of dismissing models—in economics or elsewhere—by simply noting that they are simplistic. A measuring tape is simplistic, but it is a useful tool to the carpenter who attempts to build a piece of furniture, much more useful than the more complex microscopic tools a neurosurgeon might use to do his work. In the same way, it is precisely because they are simple that many economic models become useful tools as we try to build an understanding of how individual decision making impacts the world.

1.2.2 Economic Models, *Realism*, and Billiard Players

Here is another analogy (again used by the late economist Milton Friedman) to illustrate a slightly different aspect of economic models. Suppose we were watching an ESPN tournament of the best billiard players in the world. These players are typically not expert physicists who can calculate the precise paths of billiard balls under different circumstances using the latest knowledge of underlying equations that govern the behavior of billiard balls. But suppose we wanted to arrive at a useful model that could predict the next move of each of the billiard players, and suppose I suggested to you that we should model each billiard player as an expert physicist who can instantly access the latest mathematical complexities in physics to predict the best possible next

---

[2]The closest I have actually come to seeing a series of Picasso paintings like the one I described is Picasso's suite of 11 lithographs entitled "Bull" at the Museum of Modern Art in New York. And admittedly I didn't actually see it in the museum (since I have never set foot in it), but Joe Keefer, one of my students, pointed me to some Web sites that picture the 11 lithographs. I am not sure I see the "essence" in the last one, so I am still hoping those 27 paintings are out there somewhere.

move. The model is absurd in the sense that it is completely unrealistic; many of these players have not even completed high school. But my guess is that it would do pretty well at predicting the next move of the best billiard players, better than virtually any other model I could come up with.

Or consider the problem of predicting the growth of a particular plant: which branches will grow leaves this season and in which direction? One possible model would assume that the plant consciously calculates, using the latest knowledge of biologists and other scientists, how to distribute the nutrients it gains from the soil to various branches optimally, taking into consideration the path of the sun (and thus the distribution of resulting sun light), the rotation of the earth, etc. The model is once again absurd in the sense that we are pretty sure there is no conscious mind in the plant that is capable of accessing all the relevant facts and making the appropriate calculations. Nevertheless, a model that assumes the presence of such a mind within the plant may well be a useful model to help us predict how the plant will grow.

Models, regardless of what they aim to predict, thus do not have to be realistic. They can be, and it sometimes might help our understanding if they are. But at the same time, not all aspects of economic models need to be fully realistic. Consider again the case of our consumer model that is introduced in the next several chapters. In these chapters, we seem to be assuming that individuals can map their tastes into complicated graphs or, alternatively, that they use multivariable calculus to analyze choice alternatives using mathematical functions of which few people are aware. This is absurd in the same way as it is absurd to assume that billiard players are expert physicists or plants are expert biologists. But, in the same way that these assumptions help us predict the next moves of billiard players and the next steps in the growth of a plant, our assumptions about consumers allow us to predict their economic choices. Thus, just as I hope you will not dismiss models because of their simplicity, I also hope you will not dismiss them if they appear to be unrealistic in certain ways.

1.2.3 An "Unintended" Consequence of Learning through Economic Models

Economists love to point out "unintended consequences," consequences that don't immediately come to mind when we contemplate doing something. So I can't resist pointing out an unintended consequence of learning to use economic models to think about real-world problems. The models we'll be using are specialized in some sense, but they are general in the sense that each model can be applied to many different real-world problems. In fact, once you get really comfortable with the way economists model behavior, it all really boils down to one single model, or at least one single conceptual approach. And as you internalize this conceptual approach to thinking about the world, you will find that your conceptual thinking skills become much sharper, and that has implications that go far beyond economics.

Our high schools, especially in the United States, seem to focus primarily on developing the ability to memorize and regurgitate, and many students in beginning economics classes often blame instructors for expecting more of them. I urge you to resist that temptation. The modern world expects more than good memorization skills from you. Those who succeed in the modern world have developed higher conceptual thinking skills that have virtually nothing to do with memorization. Memorization does not get us very far these days.

I will never forget my conversations with employers of Duke's economics majors when I first served as Director of Undergraduate Studies. They impressed me with their full understanding of what it is that we can and cannot do in economics classes. We *cannot* prepare you for the details of the tasks you might be asked to perform in the business world. These details vary too much from place to place, and universities are not good places to learn them. Professors are rarely good business people, and most of us spend most of our lives in an academic setting, the proverbial ivory tower. Colleges and universities are therefore typically not good at purely preprofessional training. Employers know this and are more than happy to provide such training on the job.

What we *can* do is train your conceptual muscle, the muscle that allows you to progress beyond viewing each new situation you encounter as a new problem to be solved from scratch and permits you to learn from situations that share some features in common. Put differently, we can use the framework of economics to develop skills that allow you to translate knowledge across time and space. The nightmare employee in the modern world is the person who cannot do this, the person who can memorize a technical handbook but cannot make the leap from one customer to the next and from one computer application to the next. Independent and increasingly complex thinking is rewarded above all else. Employers therefore rely on colleges and universities to prepare you for this, or at the very least to signal to them which of our students have mastered these skills.

Economics is one of the disciplines that can signal mastery of conceptual thinking to employers, and I believe it furthermore provides an interesting platform on which to develop such mastery. Many other college majors, if taught well, can accomplish the same, but economics has a particular appeal to many of you because it concerns itself with issues and problems that young people often care about deeply. Nevertheless, a good economics major can also be complemented by other course work that builds those same skills. Statistics, computer science, and mathematics offer obvious complementary training. You will make a mistake if you pick your course work to avoid classes, both in economics and outside, simply because they are conceptually challenging and difficult. Many of you would tell me, as many of my students have in the past, that you are not a "math person" or a "computer person." Forget about that; someone somewhere along the way made you think that there are "math people" or "computer people," but in the end such people are rare,[3] and few college students are unable to work hard and build their conceptual thinking skills sufficiently to do basic college mathematics, computer science, or statistics.[4] My main message to you in this digression on the unintended consequence of mastering economics is not to neglect the development of your conceptual muscle, to resist the temptation to dismiss the use of models to think about the world just because it seems hard at first. A conceptual approach to life will ultimately make all of your studies, all of your leisure, and all of your work more deeply meaningful.

 ## 1.3 *Predicting* versus *Judging* Behavior and Social Outcomes

Aside from learning to "think better" or "think more conceptually," what is the real point of these models, these simplified versions of reality whose virtue might lie in their simplicity and whose lack of realism should not necessarily disturb us? The point for most economists, as we have already suggested, is to *predict* behavior, and to predict the social consequences of that behavior. For this vast majority of economists, a model is then "good" if it predicts well. The self-interested goals individuals pursue matter in the analysis because they help us predict how behavior will change as circumstances change; but, to the economist interested in prediction, the deeper philosophical question of whether some goals are inherently more "worthwhile" than others is irrelevant. What matters for predicting what you will do if I raise the price of gasoline is how much you desire gasoline, not whether it is morally good or bad to desire gasoline. Whether it might be

---

[3]They do exist. My brother is one of them. We once took a college math course together, and I worked ten times as hard as he did and ended up getting a worse grade. And he thinks math is "fun" just for its own sake. I don't understand it. But I have come to terms with the fact that I will have to struggle some with math while my brother lives happily in his little "math world." I wonder if the colors are the same in that world—or if there even are colors.

[4]This is not to say that you should not also study Shakespeare or Milton or Morrison, Picasso or Mozart, King or Gandhi, Freud or Chesterton or Plato or any number of other works that evoke your passions and interests. Ultimately, much of what makes life worth living involves building a well-rounded foundation that allows you to explore intellectual interests in all areas as you journey through life.

"good" or "bad" to raise the price of gasoline is a very different question, one that presumes some deeper philosophical views about how to *judge* what is "good" and "bad."

The fact that most economists are not in the philosophy business—and therefore not in the business of, as a first priority, telling us what's "good" and what's "bad"—is not to say that each economist has concluded that there are no objective standards for what is ultimately in our best interest, for what is ultimately "good for the soul." As human beings, almost all of us, explicitly or implicitly, hold to such standards and wish that we and the rest of the world would abide by them more frequently. Most of us believe the drug addict would indeed be better off if he or she checked into a treatment center, that the politician ought to care about more than the next election, and that the business person should care about starving children. But most economists, *in their role as economists*, are in the business of predicting how changing incentives will change actual behavior of people who may have quite different ideas about what is worthwhile than the economist who is modeling them. What matters for their behavior is what *they* think is worthwhile, not what I think *should be* worthwhile if only they would have the sense to see it.

1.3.1 Positive Economics: How to *Predict* Real Outcomes

The branch of economics that concerns itself primarily with such predictions is known as *positive economics*, and it is the branch of economics that is in a real sense "value free." In its pursuit to predict what will actually happen as incentives change, the economist does not have the luxury of making value judgments about what people ought to be like; he or she is simply taking people's goals as given and attempting to analyze real behavior that follows from these goals and the incentive structures within which people attempt to translate those goals to real outcomes. If you are a policy maker who is attempting to determine the best way to lower infant mortality or improve low income housing or provide a more equitable distribution of educational opportunities, it is important to get the best *positive* economic analysis of each of the policy alternatives you are considering. After all, it is important to know what the real impact of each policy will be before we attempt to choose the "best" policies. The same is true if you are a business person who tries to price your goods; you need to know how people will actually respond to different prices, not just how you would like them to respond. It's even true for the father of young children who tries to alter incentives to stop the little tykes from screaming so much; if promises of candy will do the trick, it is candy that will be given out even if junior *should* know that broccoli would be so much healthier.

1.3.2 Normative Economics: How to *Judge* Outcomes

There is, however, a second branch of economics known as *normative economics* that goes beyond a value-free analysis of what will happen as incentives change. Once the positive economist tells us his or her best prediction of what will happen as a result of various possible policy alternatives, a normative economist will try to use tools that capture explicit value judgments about what outcomes are "good" and what outcomes are "bad" to determine which of the policies is the best for society. Normative economists thus draw on disciplines such as political philosophy to formalize mechanisms through which to translate particular values into policy recommendations based on a positive analysis of the likely impact of different incentives.

Much of this book concerns itself with positive (rather than normative) economics by attempting to build a framework through which we can predict the impact of different institutions on individual decision making. We will have to be careful along the way, however, because the positive models we develop are often used for policy analysis in ways that allow particular normative value judgments to "slip in." We will treat normative economics more explicitly at the end of the book in Chapter 29.

1.3.3 Efficiency: Positive or Normative?

You will notice the term *efficient* (or *Pareto efficient*) appears throughout the text, often with a normative connotation that efficiency is somehow a good thing. We will define a situation as efficient if there is no way (given the resources available) to change the situation so as to make some people better off without making anyone worse off. And within this definition, we find our "value free" notion of "better off" and "worse off"; i.e., we will consider someone to be better off if *she* thinks she is better off, and we will consider someone as worse off if *he* thinks himself worse off. In that sense, the statement "situation *x* is efficient" is simply a positive statement that could be restated to say "there is no way to make anyone think she is better off without making someone else think he is worse off."

Given this definition of efficiency, you can see how one might tend to be concerned about *inefficiencies*. An *in*efficient situation is one where we can see how to make some people better off without making anyone else worse off. But we should also be careful not to assume immediately that moving toward greater efficiency is always "good" in some bigger philosophical sense. A policy that increases the wealth of the rich by a lot while leaving the wealth of the poor unchanged is probably a policy that moves us to greater efficiency, as is a policy that makes the poor a lot wealthier while leaving the wealth of the rich unchanged. I suspect that most of us think one of these policies is "better" than the other. And some might think that the first policy, because it increases inequality, is actually "bad" even if it really doesn't make anyone worse off. Similarly, as we will see in Chapter 18, allowing a healthy poor person to sell his or her kidney to someone who needs it and can pay a lot for it may indeed make both of them better off, and yet there are many who would have moral concerns over such transactions. We will see other examples of this throughout the text and will return to an explicit discussion of "what is good" and its relation to efficiency in Chapter 29.

1.4 The "Non-Dismal" Science: Some Basic Lessons

Once we get over the initial skepticism of models and the underlying assumptions we make about human behavior, studying microeconomics has a way of changing how we think about ourselves and those we interact with, and the implications for the larger world we occupy. Often economics stands accused of being a "dismal science," a term that goes back to the 19th century.[5] Perhaps this is because people think that, because we study how people respond to incentives, we are trying to "make people selfish." Or perhaps it is because economists engaged in policy discussions often point out that there are trade-offs in life and that politicians too often promise something for nothing. But I actually think that economics provides a rather uplifting, or non-dismal, view of the world. This is something that can be seen in three very basic insights that run counter to predispositions that many of us share before we study economics. If, at the end of this course, these insights have not become part of you, then you have missed the forest for the trees.

1.4.1 Must there Be a Loser for every Winner?

First, psychologists tell me that we appear to be "built" in a way that makes us think that whenever there is a winner, there must be a loser. To the extent that this is true, this colors our view of the world in a way that is neither healthy nor correct. Economists have developed a fundamentally

[5]Originally, the term was introduced by the historian Thomas Carlyle in the mid-1800s. Contrasting economics to Nietzsche's conception of a "gay science" that produces life-enhancing knowledge, Carlyle described economics as "not a 'gay science' . . . no, a dreary, desolate and, indeed, quite abject and distressing one; what we might call . . . the dismal science." His work was in response to Thomas Malthus's admittedly depressing (and erroneous) theories, which actually led Carlyle to advocate a reintroduction of slavery as preferable to the misunderstood forces of supply and demand.

different mind-set because our study began (and begins in this book) with the study of voluntary trade where one party chooses to give up something in exchange for something the other party has to offer. In such trades, there is typically no loser; the fact that I am willing to give up $2 every day to buy a warm, frothy cup of cappuccino at my local coffee shop clearly makes me better off (since I could just stop doing it if I did not think it was worth it). Similarly, the coffee shop owner is better off because she values the cup of cappuccino at less than $2. We trade, and by trading the world has just become a better place because no one was hurt and two of us are better off. Internalizing the lesson that *there are many situations when everyone can win* is part of becoming an economist. In fact, much of the unprecedented wealth that now exists in the world has arisen precisely because individuals continuously identify situations in which voluntary interactions make everyone better off, and in the absence of understanding this, we might often be tempted to restrict such interactions without understanding the negative impact this might have. Of course we will also see many situations that involve winners and losers, and situations when nonmarket institutions are needed to discipline voluntary interactions, but the mere presence of a winner does not imply the offsetting presence of a loser.

1.4.2 Can "Good" People Behave "Badly"?

Second, psychologists also tell me that we are "built" to attribute the nature of actions we observe to the inherent character of the person who is acting. When we see someone do something that is "bad," we tend to think that we are dealing with a "bad" person, and when we see someone do something "good," we tend to think that this implies we are dealing with a "good" person. No doubt there are "bad" people who do "bad things" because of their predispositions, and there are many "good" people who do "good things" for the same reason. But the economist has another view to add to this: *often people do what they do because of the incentives they face, not because of any inherent moral predisposition.* In one of our early end-of-chapter exercises, for instance, I will ask you to think about the incentives faced by someone on welfare under the old welfare system in the United States. You will notice that under this system, those on welfare were taxed at 100% when they worked; that is to say, their welfare benefits were cut by $1 for every $1 that they earned in the labor market. When we notice that individuals under this system do not work (or work primarily in black market activities), is it because they are "lazy" or "bad," or is it because they are facing truly perverse incentives that would make anyone look like they are in fact "lazy" or "bad"? Internalizing this basic skepticism of attributing actions too quickly to moral predispositions sets us up to think about behavior very differently: *Changing behavior for the better suddenly does not necessarily require a remaking of the soul; sometimes all it takes is identifying some really bad incentives and changing those.*

1.4.3 Order: Spontaneous or Created?

Finally, there is a third way in which we seem to be "built" that stands contrary to how economists think: Whenever we see something that is working, something that is creating order in an otherwise disorderly setting, we tend to think that there must be *someone* that deliberately created the order. And, the more complex the order is, the more we tend to think that someone must be in charge of it all. But our study of markets will tell us a different story. Consider the complex "order" that is New York City: millions of people interacting with one another, getting food, going to work, finding a place to live, etc. If you think about it, it is an enormously complex order, even more complex than the order that gives rise to the unplanned existence of pencils. For instance, I am told that on any given day, there is only about two or three days' worth of food left in New York City, yet no one even thinks about this when we take for granted that all sorts of foods will always be available at any time we go to any of the stores in New York. In fact, if the *New York Post* were to publish a large front page headline proclaiming "Only 2 Days of Food Left in City!" we might just see a panic, but that headline would be basically true on any given day.

Is there a "commissioner of food distribution" who makes sure that food continuously flows into the city to just the right places at just the right times? Is there anyone in charge of this process? The answer is no; no one is in charge, but the complex order nevertheless has emerged from the individual actions of millions of people. And, whenever governments have tried to "take charge" of such issues as food distribution, our experience has been that the order breaks down and food disappears from the store shelves. *Under certain circumstances, order can thus emerge spontaneously and without a single planner*, and understanding when this is the case (and when it is not) sets economists apart from others.[6]

Saying that "order" can emerge spontaneously without someone designing it is not, as we will see, the same as saying that the spontaneously emerged order is "good." In some cases, we will identify circumstances when this is the case, circumstances when individual incentives are aligned in such a way as to produce socially desirable outcomes. In other circumstances, however, we will raise serious doubts about the social effects of the spontaneous order of the marketplace and thus suggest nonmarket institutions that are required in order for this order to produce socially desirable outcomes. Put differently, we will identify when individual incentives have to be nudged by nonmarket institutions in order for the order that emerges spontaneously to be "good" in some sense. But the point here, and the point many noneconomists miss, is that the existence of order rather than chaos simply does not imply the existence of an intelligent design of that order.

1.5 The Plan for this Book

As I have indicated in this chapter, I believe that economics and economic models can help us understand big and important questions that intellectuals have struggled with throughout the ages. This will not be immediately apparent as you work your way through the first chapters of this book, chapters that build some basic building blocks of economic models. Many textbook authors do not believe that students will have the patience to sit through tedious details of model building before addressing the important and "hot" topics in microeconomics. You deserve better than this, but you need to have the patience to bear with me. I ask this of all my students in the first class, and I have found students to be quite willing to learn in an intellectually honest way when I tell them from the outset that this is what I am trying to do.

1.5.1 Part 1: Individual Choice

The first chapters of this book, Chapters 2 through 10 lumped together as Part 1, are therefore devoted to building the basic model used by economists to investigate choices made by individuals in their roles as consumers, workers, and people who plan for the future (savers and borrowers).[7] It is one basic underlying model, but it gives rise to somewhat different features as it is applied to the different roles we take as consumers, workers, and savers. Individuals are viewed as having tastes—over different kinds of goods, over leisure and work, over consuming today and making sure they can still consume in the future. In general, they would like to have more of everything, but they are constrained by limited resources such as income and time. As a result, they try to "do the best they can" given the economic circumstances and incentives they face.

---

[6]The "fact" that the existence of "order" necessitates some creator of the order is, of course, often invoked as an argument for the existence of God. I am personally quite religious, believe in God and the potential for us to develop a relationship with God, and often give talks on matters of faith to student groups, but I have never found the argument for the existence of God on the grounds that "someone must have created all this complexity" very persuasive. I think this is because I am an economist, and I know of too many instances when order emerges without a creator.

[7]Some instructors prefer to begin with a review of basic supply and demand graphs, and some review the basic math necessary for a mathematical treatment of material at the beginning of the course. The Web site for this textbook therefore contains a Chapter 0 that provides a review of principles level supply and demand material in part A as well as a review of some of the basic underlying math in part B. This is discussed further in Section 1.6.

Choices that we observe thus result from combining tastes and economic circumstances, and this in turn produces demand curves (or functions) for goods as well as supply curves (or functions) for labor and capital.

1.5.2 Part 2: Competitive Firm Choice

Part 2 of the book then focuses on the choices made by individuals in their roles as producers (or "firms"). You will notice that this section is shorter, encompassing Chapters 11 through 13. This is not because the producer model is in any way less important or less interesting than the consumer/worker/saver model. Rather, in the development of the latter we have already built many of the tools that can then be easily modified and recast into the producer setting. In fact, you could think of consumers as producers: They produce their own individual happiness using as inputs goods, leisure, and future consumption just as a producer of computers uses labor and capital as inputs. Nevertheless, there are important differences between producers and consumers that are explored in this part of the text. The analysis of competitive firm choice then leads to the concepts of supply curves (or functions) for goods as well as demand curves (or functions) for labor and capital.

As we work through these foundational Parts 1 and 2 of the book, we ultimately build from fundamentals to the commonly used supply and demand curves that often appear in the first chapter of an intermediate microeconomics book. These appear only later in our text because it is not possible to fully appreciate what these curves really mean without first knowing what is behind them. Put differently, demand and supply curves follow from individual decision making and can be understood once the process by which they arise is understood. You will probably notice along the way that, for instance, demand curves in consumer goods markets don't always mean what you might have been led to believe in a principles course, nor do supply curves in labor markets mean precisely what you might think. And you will see that one can make fairly big mistakes in using such demand and supply curves incorrectly.[8]

1.5.3 Part 3: Competitive Equilibrium and the Invisible Hand

Part 3 then brings consumers and producers together in competitive market settings where individuals behave non-strategically. When economists use the term "non-strategically," they are thinking of settings in which individuals have no impact on the economic environment in which they make decisions because each individual is a very small part of what generates that environment. When I go to the store to buy milk, I am one of millions of consumers who purchase milk, and my decisions on how much milk to purchase have no impact whatsoever on the milk market. I have no market power in this case, no way to influence how much milk is available or at what price milk will be sold. Similarly, milk may be produced by so many different dairy farmers that each one of them is small relative to the whole market, and no single milk producer can therefore influence the price of milk. We refer to such settings as "perfectly competitive," and within such environments, there is no point for individuals to think a whole lot about how their actions influence the economic environment in which they operate. In this sense, there is no point to thinking "strategically" in perfectly competitive environments.

It is in such idealized settings that economists have arrived at a powerful insight: *Under certain circumstances*, self-interested behavior is not inconsistent with the collective "good," and markets can generate socially desirable outcomes that could not be achieved under government

---

[8]You can test yourself by thinking about the following in light of your previous economics training: Suppose you were told that the labor supply curve is perfectly inelastic (or perfectly vertical), and suppose you were asked whether there is any deadweight loss in this case from taxing labor. Your answer is probably that there is no such deadweight loss because of the inelasticity of labor supply. That answer is almost certainly wrong, as you will see once you become comfortable with what actually lies behind the labor supply curve.

planning. This insight, known as the First Welfare Theorem, lies at the heart of the economist's understanding of the world, both in terms of the positive light in which it casts competitive markets *and* in terms of the limits to competitive markets that it highlights. Put differently, the insight tells us that markets are "efficient" under certain circumstances but may need "correction" under others. (This is sometimes referred to as the "invisible hand" of the market.) When markets are efficient, there is no *efficiency role* for nonmarket institutions (like government). But we might still see a role for nonmarket institutions because, as we will point out, efficiency does not necessarily imply justice or fairness or equity. When markets are efficient but result in outcomes we consider inequitable, for instance, nonmarket institutions have a potential *distributional role* to play. Our understanding of the limits of markets to produce efficient (and equitable) outcomes then motivates the remainder of the text.

1.5.4 Part 4: Distortions of the "Invisible Hand" under Competition

Part 4 focuses on instances when *competitive* markets fail to produce efficient outcomes. As we will see, this can happen when market prices are "distorted" through policies like price controls or taxes. Prices contain information that is necessary for the competitive market to function efficiently, and interference with the price mechanism distorts that information. But inefficiencies can also arise in competitive markets when our actions in markets have direct "externality" costs or benefits for nonmarket participants, as when production decisions result in pollution. And inefficiencies can arise when information relevant to market transactions is not shared equally by buyers and sellers, giving one side the opportunity to take advantage of the other. Thus, in both the case of externalities and asymmetric information, an efficiency role emerges for nonmarket institutions to bring individual incentives in line with the social "good."

1.5.5 Part 5: Distortions of the "Invisible Hand" from Strategic Decision Making

Part 5 then extends our analysis to situations in which *strategic* considerations by individuals create additional reasons why self-interest and the collective "good" may not be fully aligned. Bill Gates is not a "small" producer of operating systems, and his company can directly alter the economic environment in which it operates through the decisions it makes. As a result of this "market power," the potential emerges that those who have such power will strategically use it to gain an advantage over others. We therefore leave the purely competitive environment of the earlier parts of the book as we think about strategic decision making. This can happen not only in monopoly settings but also when industries are dominated by a few small firms (known as oligopolies), and the link from market power to profit can create important strategic business strategies that rely on differentiating products from those of other firms. Such business strategies can lead to extraordinary innovation that drives dynamic modern economies while at the same time conveying market power that, at least in the moment, may give rise to inefficiencies. The game theory lens we develop at the outset of this part of the book not only helps us understand strategic business behavior but can also help us understand behavior in civil society settings, such as when groups try to provide public goods but individuals within groups try to "free-ride" on the contributions by others. Finally, a focus on strategic thinking can help us understand how democratic political processes can be manipulated by individuals who operate within democratic institutions, or how public policy can be captured by concentrated interests at the expense of taxpayers more generally.

1.5.6 Part 6: Stepping Back to Ask "What Is Good?"

Finally, Part 6 concludes with a consideration of how what we have learned can help us think about what is good and how to make the world a better place. We ask how we might think about what is "good" from a social point of view and what tools we have at our disposal to get closer to what we determine to be "good." While economists have developed tools to think about this, we will see that these tools are viewed skeptically from the vantage point of other disciplines like philosophy and psychology. Psychologists have raised doubts about the type of "rationality" that is assumed in many economic models, and philosophers may have more sophisticated notions of "social welfare" than those implicitly used by many economists.

Once we settle on a definition of "the good" and an understanding of the limits of "rationality," government policies provide one possible avenue through which individual incentives can be aligned to allow decentralized decision making to lead to "better" outcomes, but an economic analysis of how governments behave inevitably leads to the conclusion that governments themselves also fail due to individual incentives not being aligned with collective interests. It is therefore not immediately obvious whether government interventions that *could* solve market failures will actually do so when framed within imperfect democratic institutions. A second alternative for addressing market failures lies in what we have and will call "civil society" institutions—institutions that arise from the voluntary cooperation of individuals in such communities as churches and local organizations in which participation is not strictly governed by explicit market prices. However, there is often little reason to believe that these institutions will automatically result in ideal outcomes either as individuals strategically free ride on one another's efforts.

Throughout the text, we develop the insights that can lead us to think about such "big picture" issues more clearly, and we return to them at the end. The text therefore concludes in a final chapter where we ask how the main themes of the book—themes about markets, governments, and civil society—can come together to help us build a framework for thinking about a healthy society. The chapter is not intended to give you "the answer," but rather it is designed to illustrate the considerations that might go into the formation of a coherent view of a balanced society in which the various problems raised throughout the text are addressed as best they can be. Economists, like everyone else, are far from agreement on this, both because our definitions of what is "good" will differ and because we are in many instances only beginning to understand how governments and civil society institutions operate within market settings. Nevertheless, I believe it is the questions we can raise in this final chapter that are among the most interesting for economists to think about.

1.6 Succeeding in this Course

If I have succeeded in writing the kind of book I set out to write, the course you are taking will not be exactly like the courses offered at other universities that also use this text. The material is enough to fill two semesters, giving flexibility to instructors both in terms of *what topics* to emphasize and *how much math* to use. I'll say a bit more in Section 1.6.1 about the structure of the text that facilitates this flexibility before outlining some of the ways that you can use to maximize your chances of succeeding in the course *regardless* of exactly how this textbook is employed in your course.

1.6.1 Part A and B Chapter Structure and Flexibility

Each chapter in this book has two distinct yet closely connecting parts. Part A requires no mathematical sophistication, while part B generalizes the intuitions and graphical approach from the A parts using basic first-semester calculus plus a few additional multivariable calculus tools that are developed as needed. The text in the B parts frequently references graphs and intuition from A parts, and indications are given in A parts as to how the mathematical B parts can help us generalize what we have learned. Still, it is possible to focus solely on the A parts and leave the more mathematical treatment of the material for another time.

A side benefit of this structure lies in the unique flexibility that your instructor has to develop topics in ways that are most appropriate for your school's curriculum. Some, for instance, may choose to use only the A parts, providing you with a full intuitive treatment of microeconomics while also giving you a platform to explore the mathematical side of economics either on your own or in future course work. Others will choose to use only the B parts, allowing those who are struggling with the intuition to use the A parts as a resource. Or your instructor may choose to use both A and B parts for some topics but not for others, or to use some parts in lectures and have others developed in breakout sections led by teaching assistants. Since I am a positive economist who claims no particular insight on what people's tastes should be in different settings, I don't presume to make value judgments about which approach is "best"—my guess is that the answer is (as is so often the case in economics) "it depends" and that your instructor can figure this out better than a textbook writer. At the same time, we should not lose sight of the fact that all the material is rooted in the same underlying conceptual framework, a framework that is supported in a variety of ways not only by the material contained in the text but also by the primarily Web-based supplements that can help you succeed regardless of what precise path through the book you will take.

1.6.2 Preparing for the Course through "Chapter Zero"

The first of these Web-based materials is captured in Chapter 0 (that is not contained in the text version of the book). Like virtually all the text chapters, it contains an A and a B part. The A part reviews some material related to the graphical approach taken in the A parts of the text and applies it to a basic review of supply and demand as you probably encountered it in a previous economics course. Many intermediate microeconomics texts actually begin with an extensive treatment of supply and demand, but we take the view in this book that it makes more sense to focus first on the concepts that lie beneath supply and demand before using the framework extensively. Still, the supply and demand framework allows us to illustrate some of the graphing concepts we use (beginning in Chapter 2) within a setting that is familiar to most of you from previous course work.

Part B of Chapter 0 then serves an analogous function to the B parts in upcoming chapters. It introduces some mathematical analogs of the graphics concepts in part A and reviews the most fundamental pre-calculus and single variable calculus concepts used in the text. Depending on whether or not your course will incorporate part B material from the textbook, it may make sense to review this Web-based portion of Chapter 0 before proceeding.

1.6.3 Within-Chapter Exercises and the Study Guide

Many textbooks come with student study guides, usually written by someone other than the textbook author. In this text, I have taken a different approach. Within-chapter exercises (that I wrote as the text was written) are incorporated throughout the body of the text, and these are intended to get you to confront the concepts immediately rather than simply absorb them through reading. Like any good social scientist, I have experimented on my own students over the years, in some years providing them with the answers to within-chapter exercises so that they can immediately see whether they are understanding the relevant material, in other years holding back and not providing the solutions. The results have been dramatic: When students have access to the solutions to within-chapter exercises as they read the text, their performance on exams is far better. I have therefore written the Web-based Study Guide around solutions to exercises, giving not just "the answer" but also the reasoning behind the answer. My hope is that students who use this textbook at other universities will do what my own students have done: Read the chapter and do the exercises along the way. With the solutions available in the Study Guide, you can immediately check yourself, and then focus on those concepts that are most challenging to you.

The nature of the within-chapter exercises mirrors the nature of each part of the chapters, with exercises in the A parts focusing on intuitive and graphical developments of concepts and exercises in B parts developing the mathematical techniques and linking them to intuitions. Some exercises are *conceptually* more demanding than most, and these are labeled (*). Others are especially *computationally* demanding, and these are labeled (**). You will find that the material may at first "make sense" as you read it, but the exercises are not always as easy as you initially thought. This is because concepts such as those developed in this text can be understood at various levels, and doing these exercises as you read the text gets you to deeper levels of understanding than what you would get from just reading the explanations within the text. Just as Newton's laws of motion become more meaningful as we apply them to particular settings, the economic way of thinking about the world becomes "real" only as we apply it to increasingly complex settings.

1.6.4 End-of-Chapter Exercises

One of the reasons the book is as long as it is can be found at the end of each chapter where you will typically find ten pages or so of end-of-chapter exercises. These differ from the within-chapter exercises in that they take the material to an even deeper level, asking you to integrate concepts you have learned with one another and apply them to new settings. It is one thing to apply Newton's second law of motion to a particular setting but yet another to combine it with Newton's third law. The same is true as we combine concepts within economic models. And just as the text is divided into A and B parts, these exercises have A and B parts, with the A parts not dependent on the B parts but the B parts often benefitting from an initially intuitive way of approaching the problem (in the A part). While the first exercises at the end of each chapter simply develop the concepts more deeply, the later exercises are developed as three types of applications: *Everyday Applications*, *Business Applications*, and *Policy Applications*. As the text progresses, you will notice that these become longer, usually divided into parts that build up to a bigger picture understanding of the application at hand.[9] In many ways, these application exercises take the place of worked-out applications in side-boxes within many textbooks, asking you to engage in the development of the applications rather than simply presenting them without your engagement.

Often the more assertive of my students tell me that some of these exercises "have nothing to do with what was covered in class." That is true only in the narrowest sense. They indeed are not simply reviews of examples covered in the text; rather, they are applications of concepts to new situations. The concepts are the same as those covered in the text, but the settings in which they emerge are indeed new. Our aim in this course should be to gain a sufficiently deep understanding of concepts so that we can not just apply them to examples we have seen but also see them operating all around us. The applications exercises are intended to sharpen that conceptual level of understanding and help develop an understanding of microeconomics that is more than just the sum of its parts. To succeed at these questions, you have to be able to overcome the instinct that you should "just know the answer" as you read the question and develop the confidence that the question contains the ingredients to reason toward an answer.

When students come to see me to work through problems, they are often surprised that I, having written each of the questions, don't "just know the answer," and I suspect they sometimes think that I am just faking "not knowing" the answer. But I genuinely do have to re-reason through the problems to arrive at many of the answers, and you should not think that the answers should always "be obvious." If they were, we would not need all the tools we are developing. My advice to approaching these questions is to work in groups with other students, talking through the questions and helping each other out along the way. Much of the learning happens in this back-and-forth between students rather than just from reading textbooks or listening to lectures.

---

[9]Sometimes, end-of-chapter exercises are written with a view toward applications that will be discussed in future chapters. Using these end-of-chapter exercises along the way will therefore also help in the reading of future chapters.

Your instructor also has fully worked out solutions to all the questions in the text and may decide to make some or all of these available to you as you go through the course, and we have included some of the answers in the Study Guide as well. End-of-chapter exercise solutions are included in the Study Guide for those exercises denoted with a (†).

1.6.5 Accompanying Technology Tools

Both the graphical and the mathematical analysis in the book will challenge you in new directions. In my experience, students are often frustrated in two ways: First, graphs in textbooks and class notes often become so complicated that it is difficult to see exactly how they were built (and how you can use such graphs when you analyze problems on homeworks and exams). Second, few of us come with built-in mathematical intuitions that allow us to easily picture what various functions look like in graphs and how these functions change as elements within the functions change. The graphics technology that is built into the Web site is aimed at addressing these frustrations, as is the development of graphs across panels within the text.

More specifically, all of the graphs in the text have animated counterparts that allow you to bring the book graphics "alive" on your computers. These animations begin with a blank sheet, much like the blank sheet you face when you start on a homework or exam problem. You can then watch as the graph is built—at your own pace, with text accompanying the graph to explain the details of what is happening. Some additional computer graphics also contain options to allow you to explore scenarios that are somewhat different from what is presented in the text. And each of the animations of text graphics can be viewed with an "Audio option" in which I explain what is going on as the graph unfolds.[10]

I use many of these computer animations in my classes when I first present material, and students have almost unanimously reported to me that they have learned much of the material by then spending time on their own with the animations as they study for the course. If your instructor is also using the computer graphics in lectures, you have the added benefit of not having to struggle to keep up in your notes as you feverishly try to replicate graphs on paper because you know you can replay them at any time and at your own pace.

In some of the more mathematical B parts of the chapters, similar graphics are then used to allow you to explore directly how math interacts with the graphical approach. In certain key sections of the book, you can call up a graph on your computer screen and directly enter different elements of particular mathematical functions, and then observe immediately how this affects the graphs to which you have become accustomed. As you build your economic intuitions, the graphs in the B parts therefore simultaneously permit you to strengthen your mathematical intuitions—to become a better mathematician even if you are not a "math person." I will freely admit that my own mathematical intuitions have been strengthened as I have played with some of the graphical tools in the B part of chapters. Since these are contained on the Web site that accompanies the book, I envision that we will create further graphical modules as we hear from you and your instructors about what would be most helpful.

1.7 Onward

I hope that this brief overview of what we are trying to accomplish helps to put the coming chapters into focus. I also hope that it will help you keep an eye on the forest—the big picture of what we are trying to do—as you slog through the trees that often don't look nearly as interesting. Aristotle told us long ago that the higher the pleasure of an activity, the greater the pain as we

[10]If you decide to listen to me as you play the animations, you will detect an accent that I have done my best to suppress but that nevertheless stays with me. Long ago I taught science to second graders, one of whom commented that "he sounds a lot like Arnold Schwarzenegger." (Arnold and I are both originally from Austria.)

develop the skills to find the pleasure. Microeconomics and seeing the world through the lens of an economist can be exhilarating even if getting there is sometimes frustrating.

One final note before moving onward: You have probably noticed that this book is a bit on the long side. The reason for this, as already mentioned earlier, is that it is a book intended to be sufficiently comprehensive for a two-semester microeconomics sequence, with additional space taken up by lots of application exercises. There are many paths through the book, but none of them will get you through in a single semester. So don't let the volume be daunting. Perhaps you can hold on to the book as a reference guide while you make your way through college (and keep it out of the used book market that hurts sales of new books. After all, I only get royalties on new book sales.)

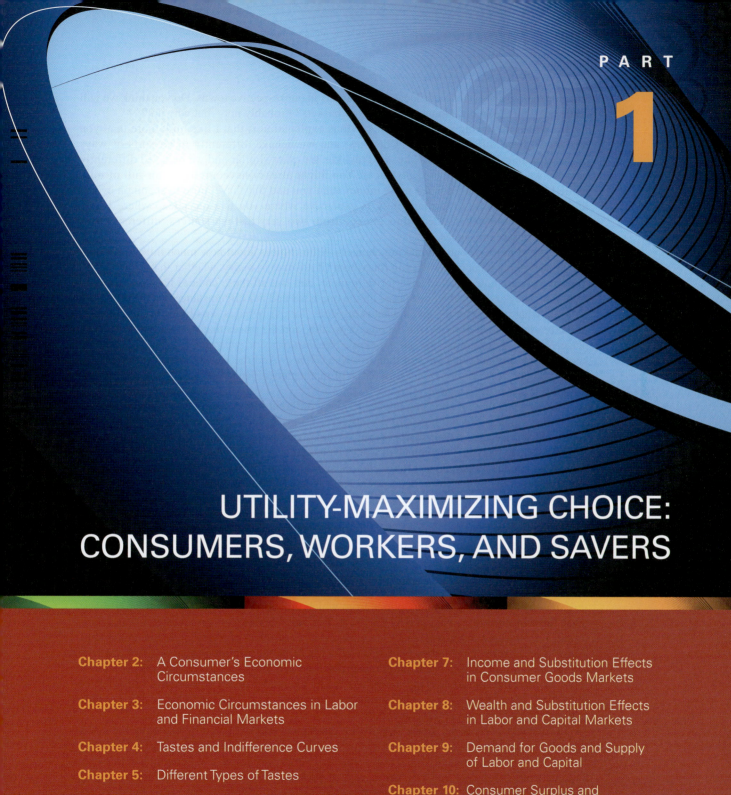

UTILITY-MAXIMIZING CHOICE: CONSUMERS, WORKERS, AND SAVERS

Imagine that you and I go to our local supermarkets in our respective towns. Do you think we will come out with the same amount of milk in our baskets? Probably not—but why not?

If I ended up buying more milk, the obvious explanation is that I like milk more than you do. We all have different likes and dislikes, and we behave differently in all sorts of ways because of that. But maybe our likes and dislikes are quite similar and we behaved differently because we faced different *circumstances*: You might already have a refrigerator full of milk while I am all out; I might make more money than you and thus have more to spend on everything, including milk; or perhaps milk is expensive where you live but cheap where I live. Differences in our behavior can thus emerge from two very distinct sources: different tastes and different circumstances.

We spend much of our life making choices—little choices about how much milk to buy and big choices about what career to train for, whom (if anyone) to marry, whether to borrow money to go to college, how much to save for retirement, etc. But all these choices have one thing in common: They are shaped by our tastes on the one hand and our circumstances on the other. We try to do what is *best* (for us) given what is *possible* (for us). What is possible is limited by a lot of factors such as our abilities, our income or wealth, and the prices that we face in the marketplace. We call these limitations our *economic circumstances* or *constraints*. It is only once we know what is possible that we can then ask *what is best*. And the answer to that question will depend on our *tastes* or *preferences*. In terms of mathematical language, we choose by *optimizing subject to our constraints*.

This basic method of choosing applies to many different settings and lies at the core of how economists think about the behavior we observe. *Consumers* choose the best combination of goods and services given their scarce resources and given the prices they face in stores. *Workers* choose where to work and how much to work given their level of skill and expertise and given the wages that employers pay. *Savers* make choices about how much to consume now and how much to put away for the future given their current and expected future resources and given the rates of return their investments can produce. The choices we make as consumers, workers, and savers are different, but the underlying method of choosing the best option given what is possible is conceptually the same. For this reason, we will develop our model of consumer, worker, and saver choices simultaneously because it really is the same model.

In Chapters 2 and 3, we begin with the first part of choice by modeling the economic circumstances or constraints that consumers (in Chapter 2), workers, and savers (in Chapter 3) face when making choices. We will see the beginning of what we alluded to in Chapter 1: the role that *incentives* play in structuring the options from which individuals can choose. At the most basic level, these incentives are captured by the *prices* that individuals face—prices of goods and services in stores, wages in the workplace, and interest rates (or rates of return) in financial markets. These prices create the fundamental trade-offs we face—determining what we will call the *opportunity cost* of choosing one thing rather than another. We will also see how these opportunity costs and thus our underlying incentives can be altered by *policy* when taxes, subsidies, or regulations alter the economic circumstances individuals face and thus change the possible options from which individuals can choose.

In Chapters 4 and 5, we then proceed with the second part of choice by modeling the tastes that individuals bring to their choice problem. When I first started studying economics, I thought finding ways of modeling individual tastes was really quite intriguing, and I continue to think so. The challenge is for us to find *systematic ways of modeling tastes without falling into the trap of treating everyone's tastes as if they were the same*. Tastes differ in important ways, but there are also some fundamental regularities in tastes that we can use to help us out. In Chapter 4, we discuss these regularities and show how we can capture a wide class of different tastes if we are willing to stipulate some basic (and largely commonsense) characteristics that most people share. In Chapter 5, we then get a little more specific and discuss different types of tastes that might be appropriate in different economic models.

With the two parts that determine choice behavior defined, Chapter 6 then combines these parts and illustrates how individuals make their choice given particular economic circumstances and given their tastes. In this chapter, we get some initial glimpse into two important insights: First, while tastes, and therefore the trade-offs that individuals are willing to make, may differ a lot across individuals, *on the margin* they will be the same if individuals all face the same prices. Put differently, on the way into a store, you and I might be willing to make all sorts of deals with each other because you own different things than I do and we both have different tastes. Coming out of the store, however, we will have altered what we own in such a way that, since our tastes are now the same on the margin, we will no longer be able to find trades that we are willing to make with each other. This implies a second important insight: When we all face the same prices in the marketplace, all gains from trade happen in the marketplace, obviating any need for us to barter with one another. We therefore begin to see the important role that prices play in creating "order" and allocating scarce resources.

Chapters 7 and 8 then illustrate how behavior changes when economic circumstances change. What happens when prices or incomes in an economy are altered, when taxes or subsidies are imposed, when governments introduce incentives to work or save? In Chapter 7, we begin by showing that changes in our economic circumstances can be separated into two different types of changes: those that impact our income or wealth without altering the fundamental trade-offs we face in the market and those that alter these trade-offs without impacting our real income or wealth. We call the former *income effects* and the latter *substitution effects*, and real-world changes in economic circumstances tend to have some of each. In Chapter 8, we extend these concepts to choices of workers and savers. In both cases, we begin to differentiate between *distortionary* and *non-distortionary* policies, between policies that fundamentally alter the trade-offs we face in the world (and thus give rise to substitution effects) and policies that only redistribute wealth without changing trade-offs (and thus only give rise to income effects). The former, we will see, create inefficiencies or deadweight losses while the latter do not.

All this builds up to the final two chapters in this Part 1 of our text: a derivation of *consumer demand* (and *labor supply* as well as *demand and supply for capital*) from the underlying choice problems that individuals solve, and a derivation of *individual welfare in markets*. Chapter 9 illustrates how some common demand and supply curves (and functions) that you have probably encountered in a previous class represent changes in economic behavior induced by changing economic circumstances. When the price of wine goes up, we buy less wine, not because we like wine any less, but rather because our circumstances have changed. In Chapter 10, we then ask how much better off consumers are when given the opportunity to participate in markets, which is a concept known as *consumer surplus*. Here we will see some of the payoff from having done all the preliminary work investigating what underlies demand curves because we will see how some important consumer welfare changes arise from substitution effects but not from income effects. We will see that demand curves are typically not the appropriate curves along which to measure changes in consumer welfare and thus define a related curve (that focuses only on substitution effects), which we will call *marginal willingness to pay* (or compensated demand).

When you have completed this part of the book, you will have developed a conceptual overview of how economists analyze individual choice in a world of scarcity, whether the choice is between apples and oranges, between working and vacationing, or between consuming and investing. You will become comfortable with the idea that people do what they do because of their likes and dislikes (i.e., their tastes) *and* because of the trade-offs and constraints they face. What they do might change because their tastes change, or, probably much more often, because the economic circumstances they face change. Economists do not know much about how and why tastes change, but we do know a lot about how changes in circumstances affect behavior. This knowledge is often summarized in economic relationships like demand curves, but it is important to keep in mind that these are ultimately just short hand ways of depicting what emerges from the interaction of tastes and circumstances. While some business behavior (i.e., marketing and advertising) might be aimed at changing people's tastes, much of business activity is aimed at altering trade-offs (i.e., economic circumstances) in ways that change consumer behavior. And the reason that economists play such a large role in policy making is that most policy making is about changing individual economic circumstances, and thus inducing a change in behavior that is desired by policy makers.

A Consumer's Economic Circumstances

In this chapter, we will begin to formalize what we mean when we say that people make the best choices they can *given their circumstances*.[1] The logical first step is to find ways of describing how our individual circumstances place limits on the kinds of choices that are available to us. Economists refer to these limits as *constraints*, and we refer to all the options we can choose from, given our constraints, as our *choice set*. Most of us would love, for instance, to go on many exotic vacations, to work only when we feel like it, to retire early, and to forget about constantly worrying about the future. But it is simply not possible to do everything we want because our limited resources place constraints on our choice sets. So, we have to determine what kinds of choices are actually possible for us given who we are, and only once we know what choices are *possible* can we decide which of these choices is *best*. This chapter introduces ways of characterizing what choices are possible in our roles as consumers, and Chapter 3 uses the tools introduced here to clarify the choice sets we face as workers and as people who plan for the future by saving or borrowing.

We will begin by focusing entirely on the underlying economic concepts that are relevant for thinking about the individual circumstances consumers face. In the process, we will notice that there are some limits to how easily we can model individual circumstances using only words and graphs, and part B of the chapter will then proceed to demonstrate how economists are using the language of mathematics to generalize intuitions that emerge in the more intuitive and graphical exposition of the material in part A of the chapter. This, as was mentioned in Chapter 1, will characterize many of the chapters throughout this text: a pure focus on economics followed by an exposition of the mathematics that helps economists say more about the world than we otherwise could.

2A Consumer Choice Sets and Budget Constraints

Consumers constantly make decisions about how much to consume of different goods. They are constrained not only by what financial resources they command but also by the prices that they face when they make their choices. Typically, they have little control over these prices since most consumers are individually "small" relative to the market and therefore have no power to influence the prices that are charged within the marketplace. It would, for instance, not even

---

[1]No prior chapter required as background. No calculus required for part B.

occur to most of us to try to haggle about the price of a gallon of milk at the check-out counter of our local supermarket. We will therefore assume for now that consumers are *price takers*, or economic agents who cannot influence the prices in the economy. And while our decisions as workers and investors determine how much money we will have to devote to consumption decisions, we will begin our analysis by assuming that the amount of money we can spend has already been determined by previous decisions. Chapter 3 will then focus on how we can model the circumstances under which these previous decisions are made.

2A.1 Shopping on a Fixed (or "Exogenous") Income

In our role as consumers, we often enter a store with a general idea of what kinds of purchases we would like to make and a fixed income or money budget we can allocate to these purchases. At the beginning of the school year, I might enter Wal-Mart with clear instructions from my wife that I can spend up to $200 on new pants and shirts that I need given my waistline has just expanded during our recent summer vacation. This is my fixed income for purposes of this analysis, and it represents a type of income we will refer to as *exogenous. Income is defined as exogenous if its dollar value is unaffected by prices in the economy.* In this case, regardless of how much Wal-Mart charges for pants and shirts, I will always have exactly $200 available to me.

As I look around the store, I discover that I can purchase shirts for $10 and pants for $20. I now have all the information necessary to determine the *choice set* I face given the *constraints* imposed by my $200 income and the prices of pants and shirts. I could, for instance, purchase 10 pants and no shirts, thus spending my total $200 income. Alternatively, I could purchase 20 shirts and no pants or any combination of pants and shirts such that the total expense does not add up to more than $200.

2A.1.1 Graphing Choice Sets   We can depict this graphically in a two-dimensional picture that has the number of pants on the horizontal axis and the number of shirts on the vertical. Point *A* in Graph 2.1 depicts the choice of 10 pants and no shirts while point *B* depicts the choice of

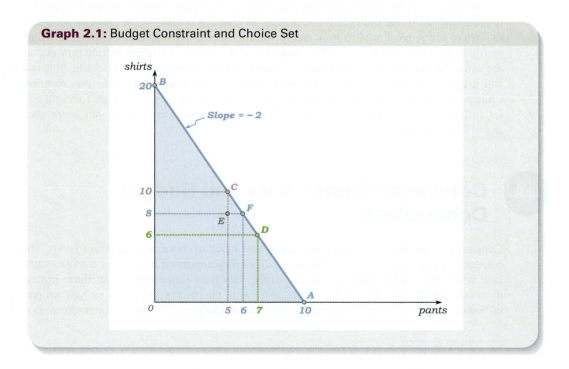

Graph 2.1: Budget Constraint and Choice Set

20 shirts and no pants. The line that connects points *A* and *B* represents other choices that also cost exactly $200. For instance, point *C* represents 5 pants and 10 shirts, which implies a $100 expense on pants (5 times $20) and another $100 expense on shirts (10 times $10). Point *D* represents 7 pants and 6 shirts, which again adds up to a $200 total expenditure.

We will refer to the line connecting points *A* and *B* as the *budget line* or the *budget constraint*. The end points, or intercepts, of the budget line are determined by the fixed income divided by the price of the good on each axis: 200 divided by 20 in the case of pants, and 200 divided by 10 in the case of shirts. For a particular income and a particular set of prices, this *budget line represents all combinations of goods that, if chosen by a particular consumer, would leave no additional money left in his or her budget.* Points below the budget line, on the other hand, represent combinations of goods that, if chosen by the consumer, would still leave some additional unspent money. For instance, point *E* represents 8 shirts and 5 pants, which cost only $180 and would thus leave $20 unspent. Together, the budget line and all shaded points below the budget line represent the choices that are *possible* for a consumer who has a $200 income devoted to spending on pants and shirts that are priced at $20 and $10 respectively. Thanks to my wife's generosity and Wal-Mart's low prices, this is my *choice set* at Wal-Mart.

Now suppose that I currently have 10 shirts and 5 pants (point *C*) in my shopping cart, but I decide that I really would like to have 6 instead of 5 new pants. Since pants are twice as expensive as shirts, I know I will have to put 2 shirts back on the rack to be able to afford one more pair of pants. That's exactly what the budget constraint tells me: As I move to 6 pants, I can only afford 8 shirts rather than the 10 I started with in my shopping cart. Put differently, in going from point *C* to point *F*, I traded 2 shirts on the vertical axis for 1 pair of pants on the horizontal axis, which implies a slope of −2 (since the slope of a line is the change in the variable on the vertical axis (shirts) divided by the change in the variable on the horizontal axis (pants)). You could of course equally well have calculated the slope of this line by simply looking at the end points: In going from point *B* to point *A*, you have to give up 20 shirts to get 10 pants, giving again a slope of −2.

This slope of the budget line arises from the fact that pants cost twice as much as shirts, and it represents the trade-off I face when I chose to buy one more pair of pants. Economists call this trade-off *opportunity cost. The opportunity cost of any action is the next best alternative one gives up by undertaking this action.*[2] In our example, the opportunity cost of buying one more pair of pants is the 2 shirts I have to give up. Of course we can also talk of the opportunity cost of buying one more unit of the good on the vertical axis. In our example, if I want to buy one more shirt, I have to give up half a pair of pants. Given that pants cannot easily be split into two halves, it might sound silly to say that the opportunity cost of one shirt is half a pair of pants, but this statement contains the same information as the statement that the opportunity cost of one pair of pants is 2 shirts: Pants are twice as expensive as shirts. *In general, the opportunity cost of the good on the horizontal axis (in terms of the good on the vertical axis) is the slope of the budget line, whereas the opportunity cost of the good on the vertical axis (in terms of the good on the horizontal axis) is the inverse of the slope of the budget line.*

The slope of the budget constraint can also be determined more directly by simply understanding how the prices a consumer faces translate into opportunity costs. In our example, I face a $20 price for pants and a $10 price for shirts, and the slope of my budget constraint is −2 or, in absolute value, the opportunity cost of one pair of pants in terms of shirts. This opportunity cost arises from the fact that pants are twice as expensive as shirts, with *the slope of the budget*

---

[2]The opportunity cost of you reading this chapter is the next best thing you could be doing with your time right now. The fact that you are still reading means that you must think reading these words is the best possible way to spend your time in this moment. I am flattered.

constraint simply being given by the (negative) ratio of the price of the good on the horizontal axis (pants) divided by the price of the good on the vertical (shirts).[3]

Exercise
2A.1
Instead of putting pants on the horizontal axis and shirts on the vertical, put pants on the vertical and shirts on the horizontal. Show how the budget constraint looks and read from the slope what the opportunity cost of shirts (in terms of pants) and pants (in terms of shirts) is.

2A.1.2 An Increase (or Decrease) in Fixed Incomes

Now suppose that my wife felt particularly generous this year and, instead of the customary $200 money budget for end-of-summer clothing purchases, she has allocated $400 for this purpose. As a result, I could now purchase as many as 20 pants (assuming I buy no shirts) or as many as 40 shirts (assuming I purchase no pants), which means that point *A* shifts to the right by 10 pants and point *B* shifts up by 20 shirts. This results in a parallel shift of my budget constraint from the initial blue to the final magenta budget line in Graph 2.2.

Notice that the set of choices available to me has clearly become larger, but the trade-off I face, the opportunity cost of pants (in terms of shirts) or shirts (in terms of pants), has not changed. This is because my *opportunity cost is determined by Wal-Mart's prices*, not by my wife's generosity. It does not matter whether you, I, or Bill Gates enters Wal-Mart to buy shirts and pants—each of us faces the same trade-offs even though our overall budgets may be quite different.

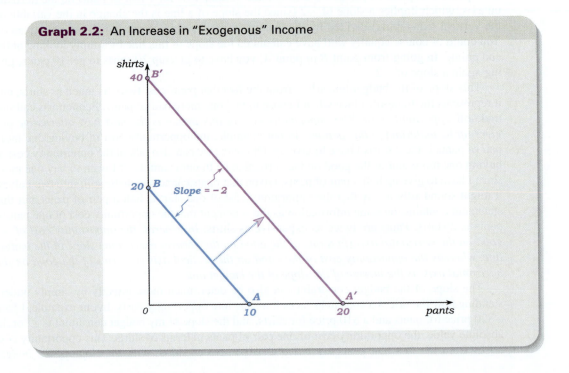

Graph 2.2: An Increase in "Exogenous" Income

---

[3]As explained in more detail in Section B, you can also simply derive this mathematically. Letting income be denoted by I, pants by x_1, shirts by x_2, and the prices of pants and shirts by p_1 and p_2 respectively, any combination of x_1 and x_2 will lie on the budget constraint if all income is spent. Put differently, if $p_1x_1 + p_2x_2 = I$, then the sum of my spending on pants (p_1x_1) and my spending on shirts (p_2x_2) is exactly equal to my income I. Solving this equation for x_2, the good on the vertical axis, the budget constraint can be written as $x_2 = I/p_2 - (p_1/p_2)x_1$, which is an equation with intercept I/p_2 and slope $-(p_1/p_2)$.

To be slightly more precise, the opportunity cost is determined by the *ratio* of Wal-Mart's prices. Suppose, for instance, that instead of giving me an additional $200, my wife had given me a 50% off coupon for shirts and pants. In that case, the real price of a shirt would have dropped to $5 and the real price of pants would have dropped to $10, which would enable me to buy as many as 40 shirts (if I buy no pants) and as many as 20 pants (if I buy no shirts). Thus, a decline in all prices by the same percentage is equivalent to an increase in income; it merely shifts the budget constraint out without changing its slope. In fact, economists would say that in both scenarios—when my fixed income went up by $200 and when all prices fell by 50%—my *real* income doubled (because I could now afford twice as much as before) while relative prices remained unchanged (because the trade-off between the goods as expressed in the slope of the budget constraint did not change).

Demonstrate how my budget constraint would change if, on the way into the store, I had lost $300 of the $400 my wife had given to me. Does my opportunity cost of pants (in terms of shirts) or shirts (in terms of pants) change? What if instead the prices of pants and shirts had doubled while I was driving to the store?

Exercise 2A.2

2A.1.3 A Change in Price

Now suppose that, instead of giving me an extra $200, my wife showed her generosity by giving me a 50% off coupon for pants (but not for shirts) together with my usual $200 money budget. With this coupon, she tells me, I can purchase any number of pants and receive half off. As a result, while the posted price for a pair of pants is $20, each pair only costs me $10 once I present the coupon at the cash register.

To see how this changes my budget line, we can go through the same exercise as before and find the intercepts of the new budget line by asking how much of each good we could buy if we spent nothing on the other good. This is illustrated in Graph 2.3. Since pants now cost only $10 a pair, I can purchase as many as 20 pairs with my $200 money budget (assuming I buy no shirts), and I can similarly buy as many as 20 shirts at $10 each (assuming I buy no pants). Thus point *A*

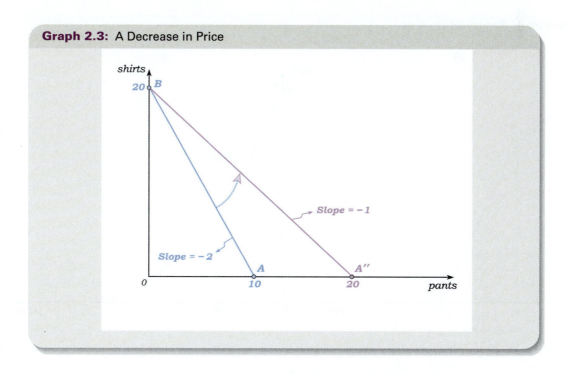

Graph 2.3: A Decrease in Price

shifts from 10 to 20 as a result of the lower price of pants, but point *B* does not change since the price of shirts remains the same and my overall money budget is still $200. My budget line then rotates out from the initial blue budget line to the new magenta budget line, with the slope changing from −2 to −1. This slope again reflects the opportunity cost of one pair of pants (in terms of shirts): Since pants and shirts now both cost $10 each, I have to give up one shirt for every additional pair of pants I would like to purchase.

Exercise 2A.3

How would my budget constraint change if instead of a 50% off coupon for pants, my wife had given me a 50% off coupon for shirts? What would the opportunity cost of pants (in terms of shirts) be?

2A.2 Kinky Budgets

Suppose I now arrive at the store and discover some fine print on the 50% off coupon that limits the discount to the first 6 pants. Thus, rather than facing a price of $10 per pair of pants for any number of pants that I buy, I now know that the $10 price applies only to the first 6 pairs and that each additional pair costs $20. In economics jargon, the *marginal price*—the price of one more pair of pants—changes from $10 to $20 after the sixth pair of pants.

To see what this does to my budget constraint, we can again begin by determining where the intercepts of the new budget constraint lie. If I were to purchase only pants (and no shirts), I would be able to purchase 13 pairs: the first 6 at $10 each (for a total of $60) and another 7 at $20 each (for an additional $140). Thus, point *A* lies at 13 pants on the horizontal axis, as illustrated in Graph 2.4a. Point *B* remains unchanged at 20 shirts on the vertical axis, 20 shirts at $10 each. But because the trade-off between shirts and pants changes once I have 6 pants in my shopping

Graph 2.4: Kinked Budget Constraints

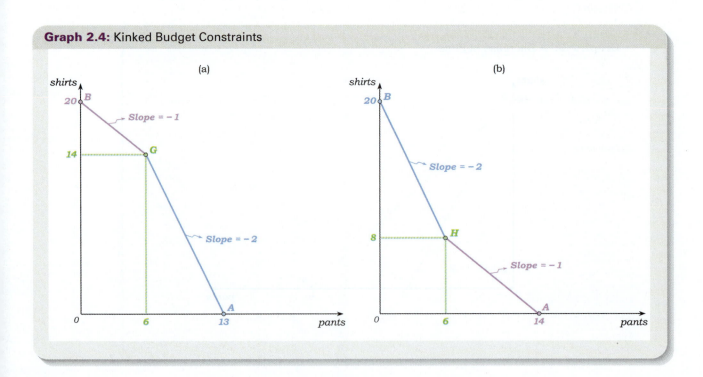

cart, the slope of the budget constraint must change at that point as well. If I purchase exactly 6 pants, I will be able to afford 14 shirts, which implies that point *G* is on my budget constraint. Between point *G* and point *B*, I purchase fewer than 6 pairs of pants and thus face a price of $10 for both pants and shirts. The line segment connecting point *G* and *B* therefore has a slope of −1, indicating an opportunity cost of one shirt for each pair of pants. The line segment connecting *G* and *A*, on the other hand, has a slope of −2, which reflects the higher price of pants for any pair above 6 and the higher opportunity cost (in terms of shirts) I face once I purchase more than 6 pants. My new budget constraint therefore starts at point *B* with a shallow slope of −1, has a kink at point *G* where I have exactly 6 pants in my shopping cart, and then switches to a steeper slope of −2.

Kinked budget constraints of this type occur whenever the price of a good changes as I am purchasing more of it. This can result in a budget constraint like the one we just derived in Graph 2.4a where the kink points out toward the northeast of the graph, but, under different circumstances, it could also result in a kink that points in toward the southwest of the graph. Suppose, for instance, that the 50% off coupon was such that I can only get a discount if I purchase more than 6 pants and that this discount applies to each pair of pants after the initial 6 I purchase. You can verify for yourself that this would result in the budget constraint in Graph 2.4b. Some important real-world examples of kinked budget constraints will appear in end-of-chapter exercises and in Chapter 3 as we think of cases where government policies directly generate such kinks.

Suppose that the two coupons analyzed were for shirts instead of pants. What would the budget constraints look like?

**Exercise
2A.4**

2A.3 Modeling More General Choices

Although two-good examples like the previous ones are useful because they allow us to illustrate budget constraints in a two-dimensional picture easily, they are of course a little artificial since most consumers do not go to stores with the intention of purchasing only two types of goods. (If my wife were not so strict about checking my receipts when I get home, even I might sneak in a candy bar with my pants and shirts.) To generalize such examples beyond choices over two goods, we could use mathematical equations (as is done in part B of this chapter) instead of graphical illustrations. Alternatively, we could illustrate such choice sets in more complicated graphs, although this becomes quite difficult as our illustrations would have to become more than two-dimensional. Or we can employ a technique that treats whole categories of goods as if they were a single good. We will now explore the latter two alternatives.

2A.3.1 Graphing Choice Sets with Three Goods
Throughout the summer, I wear sandals. And, despite the fact that I have to endure endless and merciless mocking from my fashion-conscious wife for this, I always wear socks with my sandals. As a result, I usually need new socks for the fall semester.

Suppose, then, that my wife had sent me to the store to purchase shirts, pants, *and* socks. Our illustrations would then have to become three-dimensional. We would plot pants on one axis, shirts on another, and socks on yet another axis, and we would, just as in the two-good examples, begin by finding the intercepts on each axis illustrating how much of each good we could purchase if we purchased none of the others. Suppose the price of shirts and pants were $10 and $20 and the price of socks were $5, and suppose that my exogenous income or money budget is again $200. On the axis labeled "number of pants," my intercept would be 10: the number of pants I could purchase if I spent all of my money on pants alone. Similarly, the intercept on the shirt axis would be 20, and the intercept on the socks axis would be 40. We could then proceed by

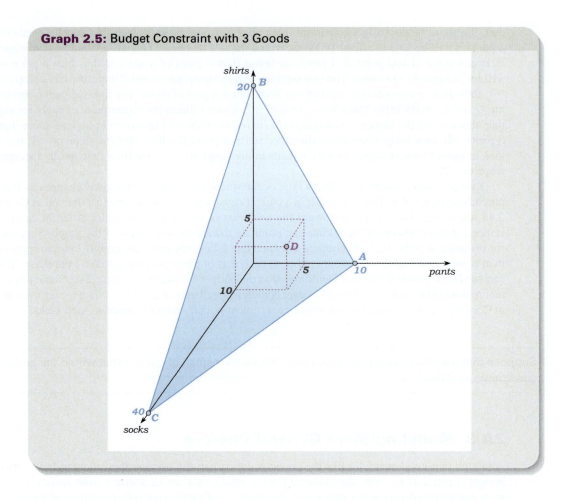

Graph 2.5: Budget Constraint with 3 Goods

illustrating what my budget constraint would look like if I purchased no socks but limited myself to only shirts and pants by connecting *A* and *B*. This budget constraint is equivalent to the one we plotted in Graph 2.1. But we could also illustrate the constraint if I limited myself to only socks and shirts by connecting points *B* and *C*, and the constraint if I limited myself to only socks and pants by connecting points *A* and *C*. Finally, my full budget constraint would be formed by the shaded plane that connects points *A*, *B*, and *C*. For instance, point *D* with 10 pairs of socks, 5 shirts, and 5 pairs of pants would lie on this plane because this combination of goods in my shopping basket would cost exactly $200 ($50 for socks, $50 for shirts, and $100 for pants).

While it is therefore possible to illustrate budget constraints graphically with three goods, you can see that it would become increasingly difficult to graph such constraints for more than three goods because we would have to get comfortable with drawing objects in more than three dimensions. Nevertheless, we are able to analyze more general choice sets graphically by focusing on the choice over a good that we are particularly interested in analyzing and creating, for purposes of the analysis, a second *composite good* that represents all other goods.

2A.3.2 Modeling Composite Goods   Suppose, for instance, that I am going to the store with my $200 to purchase not only pants but also a variety of other goods that I will need to get ready for the academic year (including shirts and socks but also office supplies, drinks for my office refrigerator, and of course flowers for my wife). And suppose further that I am particularly interested in modeling how my budget constraint changes as the price of pants changes. We could reduce our implicit multigood model by putting pants on the horizontal axis and a *composite good representing all other goods I am interested in* on the vertical. We can define this composite good as "dollars spent on goods other than pants." This definition of a composite good then ensures that one dollar spent on goods other than pants costs me exactly one dollar. Implicitly our analysis will have to assume that only the price of pants changes while all other prices remain the same, or alternatively that all other prices change by the same proportion while the price of pants remains the same.[4]

With the aid of the modeling assumption of a composite good, we can then illustrate my choice set over pants and "other goods" exactly as we did in Section 2A.1 when we modeled the choice between pants and shirts. On the horizontal axis, point *A* would again lie at 10 pants because that is the most I can afford if I spend my entire income on pants and I purchase no other goods. Point *B* on the vertical axis would lie at 200 because I can purchase 200 units of the composite good (i.e, $200 worth of "other goods") if I do not purchase any pants. Connecting points *A* and *B* gives me a budget line with slope -20, indicating that the opportunity cost of a pair of pants is 20 units of the composite good or $20 worth of "other good consumption." We could then model how an increase or decrease in my fixed income, a change in the price of pants, or coupons of the kind introduced in Section 2A.3 would affect this budget constraint.

Revisit the coupons we discussed in Section 2A.3 and illustrate how these would alter the choice set when defined over pants and a composite good.

Exercise 2A.5

True or False: When we model the good on the vertical axis as "dollars of consumption of other goods," the slope of the budget constraint is $-p_1$, where p_1 denotes the price of the good on the horizontal axis.

Exercise 2A.6

2A.4 "Endogenous" Incomes that Arise from Endowments

Suppose that I have done my clothes shopping at the original prices (i.e., without coupons) and with my original money budget of $200. I come home with 10 shirts and 5 pants and proudly show them off to my wife who quickly informs me that she thinks I should have gotten more pants and fewer shirts. The problem, however, is that I have lost the receipt and therefore cannot get a refund under Wal-Mart's return policy. But, my wife quickly reminds me, I *can* receive a store credit for the full value of any merchandise at Wal-Mart's posted prices. Thus, as I enter Wal-Mart for the second time, I arrive with no money but rather with an *endowment* of 10 shirts and 5 pants. *An endowment is a bundle of goods owned by a consumer and tradable for other goods.* A defining feature of endowments is that, because the consumer owns the endowment bundle, *he or she can always choose to consume that bundle regardless of what prices of goods in the market happen to be.* In fact, if you are ever unsure of whether a particular bundle is indeed an endowment bundle, you can simply ask yourself whether it is true that the consumer could consume this bundle regardless of what the prices in the economy were. If the answer is yes, then the bundle is an endowment bundle for this consumer.

As I stand in line at the customer service desk, I contemplate what my budget constraint looks like now that I have no money but just an endowment bundle of 10 shirts and 5 pants (labeled

---

[4]The conditions under which it is theoretically sound to aggregate goods into a composite good are well understood but beyond the scope of this text. The interested reader can explore more under the topics of *Hicksian separability* and *functional separability* in a graduate text.

Graph 2.6: Price Change with Endowments

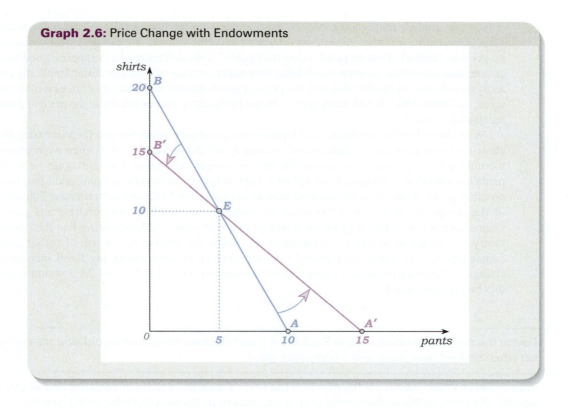

point E in Graph 2.6). I know that I can always stick with my current shirts and pants, so the point "5 pants, 10 shirts" must lie on my budget constraint. What the rest of the constraint looks like depends on what the currently posted prices are at Wal-Mart. If pants still sell for $20 a pair and shirts still sell for $10 each, then I could return my 5 pants, receive $100 in store credit and use it to buy 10 additional shirts, thus ending up with 20 shirts and no pants. Alternatively, I could trade in my 10 shirts for $100 store credit and buy 5 more pants, thus ending up with 10 pants and no shirts. Or I could do something in between. If the price of pants and shirts is unchanged from when I originally purchased the pants and shirts, my budget constraint is therefore exactly the same as it was when I first entered the store with $200 in Graph 2.1 and replicated as the blue line in Graph 2.6.

As I approach the customer service representative, however, I am surprised to see a new poster in the window proclaiming: "All pants on sale at 50% off." As it turns out, pants just went on sale and now only cost $10 a pair rather than the $20 I paid for them. Given Wal-Mart's policy on returns without receipts, I will therefore only get $10 in store credit for each pair of pants. How does this change my choice set?

Well, I still have the option of leaving the store with my 5 pants and 10 shirts, so point E remains on my budget constraint. But if I now return my 5 pants, I only receive a $50 store credit and thus can only get 5 more shirts. Point B therefore shifts down by 5 shirts. At the same time, if I return my 10 shirts, I still get a $100 store credit, but now, because pants are cheaper, I can get as many as 10 extra pairs of pants! So, point A shifts out by 5 pairs of pants, and the new (magenta) budget constraint has a slope of -1 that reflects the new opportunity cost of a pair of pants (given that they now cost the same as shirts). Notice, however, that now the budget line rotates through point E, the endowment point, when the price of pants changes, not through point B as it did when the price changed and I was on a fixed income (in Section 2A.3). This will always be true for budget constraints that arise from endowment bundles rather than fixed incomes.

Notice that when budget constraints arise from endowments, the amount of money available to the consumer is *not* fixed (as it was when my wife simply sent me to the store with $200). Rather, the money available to me depends on the prices of the goods I am endowed with, since I have to sell some of my endowment in order to get money. We will refer to such incomes as *endogenous* to differentiate them from the fixed (or *exogenous*) incomes analyzed earlier.

It may not seem all that common that we find ourselves with a basket of goods (like pants and shirts) as an endowment, and so this exercise might look a little contrived. However, as we will see in Chapter 3, our budget constraints are indeed often determined by endowments when we think of our roles in other sectors of the economy such as the labor market or the financial markets. We are, for instance, endowed with a certain amount of time that we can allocate to various purposes (including gainful employment). We also often accumulate a set of assets (like bank deposits, mutual funds, coin or stamp collections, real estate, etc.), which can be treated like an endowment that can be converted into consumption depending on the value of the endowment.

2A.5 Modeling Constraints Graphically or Mathematically?

We have shown thus far how we can model simple choice sets for consumers facing different circumstances. How much choice a consumer has ultimately depends on (1) the prices of goods and (2) the size of the consumer's available income. The latter can be determined either "exogenously" by a fixed dollar amount that is available to the consumer, or it can arise "endogenously" from the value of some endowment that the consumer can trade for other consumption. A first step to modeling the circumstances that are most relevant to particular choices is therefore simply to identify these two elements, prices and incomes, of the consumer's individual circumstances.

In addition, however, we have to recognize that our models cannot possibly include all the complexity of the real world when we try to analyze individual decisions that consumers make. The point of modeling decisions is, as we suggested in Chapter 1, to draw out the essence of the problem we are investigating in order to better analyze the most essential aspects of the problem. In modeling the circumstances under which consumers make choices, we therefore have to decide which aspects of the complex "real world" are critical for the particular choices we are modeling and which aspects are, for purposes of our model, "noise" that we can abstract away from.

Often, we will conclude that a particular situation can be adequately modeled within the graphical framework we have developed so far. But other times economists will find that, while the graphical framework helps them understand the intuition behind a more complex model, they nevertheless require more complexity to model the essence of a particular situation fully. In those cases, economists turn to mathematics as a language that allows for the introduction of greater complexity. But it is important to understand that this more mathematical approach simply involves a different way of discussing the same underlying economic concepts we have just discussed without the use of math, and it is important for those who use the mathematical approach ultimately to translate their insights back into words that give expression to the underlying economics. Section B therefore turns to a development of the mathematical tools that can help us generalize models in Section 2A while maintaining our focus on the economic choices made by individuals.

2B Consumer Choice Sets and Budget Equations

In the language of mathematics, "doing the best they can" means that consumers solve an "optimization problem," and "given their circumstances" means that this optimization problem is a "constrained optimization problem." In this chapter, we will develop the mathematical language to formalize the notion of choice sets and budget constraints, and later we will proceed to defining the full constrained optimization problem that consumers face. Each section in this part of the chapter corresponds to a similar section in part A; 2B.1, for instance, discusses the mathematics behind the ideas in Section 2A.1. So, if you find yourself losing track of the economic ideas from part A and you discover it is all suddenly looking like "just math," you may find it helpful to turn back to the analogous section in part A and thus create a better link for yourself between the mathematics and the underlying economics.

2B.1 Shopping on a Fixed Income

We began our discussion of choice sets in Section 2A by envisioning me being sent to Wal-Mart to shop for pants and shirts with a fixed, or exogenous, income. Suppose again that this fixed income is $200 and that the price of pants is $20 and the price of shirts is $10. The *choice set* we derived in Graph 2.1 is simply the set of all combinations of pants and shirts that cost no more than $200, and the *budget line* or *budget constraint* is the combination of pants and shirts that cost exactly $200.

2B.1.1 Defining Choice Sets and Budget Lines Mathematically
Letting pants be denoted by the variable x_1 and shirts be denoted by the variable x_2, we can define the choice set formally as

$$\{(x_1,x_2) \in \mathbb{R}^2_+ \mid 20x_1 + 10x_2 \le 200\}. \tag{2.1}$$

The curly brackets "{ }" indicate that we are defining a *set* of points. The vertical line "|" is read as "such that." Everything preceding "|" defines the geometric space within which the points of the set lie, and everything following "|" defines the conditions that must be satisfied in order for a point in that geometric space to lie within the choice set we are defining. More specifically, the symbol $\mathbb{R}^2_+$ is used to represent the two-dimensional space of non-negative real numbers, and the symbol $\in$ is read as "is an element of." Thus, the mathematical expression "$(x_1,x_2) \in \mathbb{R}^2_+$" simply says that the set contains points with 2 components (x_1 and x_2) that are non-negative real numbers. But not all points with 2 components that are non-negative real numbers are in the choice set—only points that represent bundles that cost no more than $200. The mathematical statement following "|" therefore indicates precisely that points that lie in the space defined before "|" are part of the set we are defining only if $20x_1 + 10x_2 \le 200$. We then read the full expression as: "This set contains all combinations of (x_1,x_2) in which both x_1 and x_2 are non-negative real numbers *such that* 20 times x_1 plus 10 times x_2 is less than or equal to 200."

There is a logical structure to this formulation of sets that is worth pointing out even more precisely. The statement preceding "|" provides the *necessary condition* for a point to lie in the set we are defining, while the statement following "|" provides the *sufficient conditions*. In order for you to become President of the United States, it is a necessary condition that you were born a U.S. citizen. As many candidates find out every four years, that is not, however, sufficient to become president; you also have to get a plurality of votes in sufficiently many states to gather the required Electoral College majority. Similarly, in order for a point to lie in my choice set under the circumstances described, it is a necessary condition for that point to consist of two non-negative real numbers. But that is not sufficient because many points that have two non-negative real numbers represent bundles of goods that are not affordable given my exogenous income of $200. The choice set is then fully defined when both necessary and sufficient conditions are stated explicitly.

Exercise 2B.1 What points in Graph 2.1 satisfy the necessary but not the sufficient conditions in expression (2.1)?

To define the set of points that lie *on* the budget line (as opposed to *within* the choice set), we start by recognizing that these points lie within the same geometric space as the choice set, and thus must necessarily consist of points defined by two non-negative real numbers. However, the sufficient condition for such points to be part of the budget line is different from the sufficient condition for such points to be part of the choice set. In particular, the inequality in the constraint $20x_1 + 10x_2 \leq 200$ is replaced with an equality because the budget line represents the set of goods that cost *exactly* \$200. We can thus define the *budget line* as the set of bundles that lie on the boundary of the choice set:

$$\{(x_1, x_2) \in \mathbb{R}_+^2 \mid 20x_1 + 10x_2 = 200\}. \tag{2.2}$$

More generally, we can define choice sets without reference to a particular set of prices or incomes. Rather, we can simply indicate the price of pants as p_1, the price of shirts as p_2, and income as I. With these three pieces of information that constitute the consumer's *economic circumstances*, we defined a consumer's choice set C as

$$C(p_1, p_2, I) = \{(x_1, x_2) \in \mathbb{R}_+^2 \mid p_1 x_1 + p_2 x_2 \leq I\}. \tag{2.3}$$

The notation $C(p_1, p_2, I)$ indicates that the precise nature of my choice set depends on what value is taken by the prices of the goods and by my income level; or, put differently, it indicates that the choice set C *is a function of the prices* (p_1, p_2) *and income level I*. When I plug in the values 20, 10, and 200 for the two prices and my income, I get precisely the set defined in equation (2.1). Similarly, we can define the budget line B as

$$B(p_1, p_2, I) = \{(x_1, x_2) \in \mathbb{R}_+^2 \mid p_1 x_1 + p_2 x_2 = I\}, \tag{2.4}$$

where the inequality in equation (2.3) is replaced with an equality.

We can then examine the mathematical formulation of a budget line and demonstrate how it relates to the graphical intuitions we built in Section 2A. Beginning with the equation $p_1 x_1 + p_2 x_2 = I$ contained within the set defined in (2.4), we can subtract $p_1 x_1$ from both sides and then divide both sides by p_2 to get

$$x_2 = \frac{I}{p_2} - \frac{p_1}{p_2} x_1. \tag{2.5}$$

Notice that in a graph (such as Graph 2.1) with x_1 on the horizontal and x_2 on the vertical axis, this expression of the equation defining a budget line shows an intercept of (I/p_2) on the vertical axis and a slope of $(-p_1/p_2)$, which is precisely what we concluded intuitively in Section 2A. For instance, with the numbers in our example, (I/p_2) is equal to $(200/10)$ or 20, which indicates that I could purchase as many as 20 shirts with my \$200 if all I bought were shirts. Similarly, the slope $(-p_1/p_2)$ is equal to $(-20/10)$ or (-2), which indicates an opportunity cost of 2 shirts for 1 pair of pants.

2B.1.2 An Increase (or Decrease) in the Fixed Income

Our next step in Section 2A was to illustrate what happens as my income increases from \$200 to \$400. Notice that this exogenous income is represented by the variable I in equation (2.5). Thus, when the fixed income changes, only the first term (I/p_2) in equation (2.5) changes. This is the vertical intercept term in the equation, indicating that the intercept on the x_2-axis will shift up as my fixed income increases. The second term in equation (2.5) remains unchanged, indicating that the slope of the budget line $(-p_1/p_2)$ remains the same. A change in the x_2-axis intercept without a change in the slope adds up to a parallel shift outward of the budget line, precisely as we concluded intuitively in Graph 2.2. The choice set has become larger, but the trade-off between the goods as represented by the slope of the budget line has remained the same.

Using equation (2.5), show that the exact same change in the budget line could happen if both prices simultaneously fell by half while the dollar budget remained the same. Does this make intuitive sense?

Exercise 2B.2

2B.1.3 A Change in Price Another scenario explored in Section 2A involved a 50% off coupon for pants, a coupon that effectively lowers the price of pants (p_1) from \$20 to \$10. Going back to equation (2.5), notice that p_1 does not appear in the intercept term (I/p_2) but does appear in the slope term ($-p_1/p_2$). The x_2-axis intercept thus remains unchanged but the slope becomes shallower as p_1/p_2 becomes smaller in absolute value. This is precisely what we concluded intuitively in Graph 2.3.

**Exercise
2B.3**

Using the mathematical formulation of a budget line (equation (2.5)), illustrate how the slope and intercept terms change when p_2 instead of p_1 changes. Relate this to what your intuition would tell you in a graphical model of budget lines.

2B.2 Kinky Budgets

Kinked budget lines of the kind explored in Section 2A.2 are somewhat more difficult to describe mathematically. Consider, for instance, the example of a 50% off coupon for only the first 6 pairs of pants that I purchase. We graphed the choice set that emerges for someone with an income of \$200 facing a (before-coupon) price of \$20 for pants and \$10 for shirts in Graph 2.4a. There, we derived intuitively the result that my budget line will be initially flatter (up to 6 pants) before becoming steeper at the kink point when the effective price of pants changes from \$10 to \$20.

Were we to write down this choice set mathematically, we would simply have to translate the fact that the price of pants changes after the sixth pair into the set notation we developed earlier. And we would need to recognize that, if we buy more than 6 pairs of pants, we in effect have an additional $0.5(6p_1) = 3p_1$ in income because that is how much the coupon gave us back. For instance, when $p_1 = 20$, the coupon was worth \$60 if we buy 6 or more pants. We could, then, define the choice set as

$$C(p_1,p_2,I) = \big\{(x_1,x_2) \in \mathbb{R}^2_+ \,|\, 0.5\,p_1x_1 + p_2x_2 \leq I \text{ for } x_1 \leq 6 \text{ and}$$
$$p_1x_1 + p_2x_2 \leq I + 3p_1 \text{ for } x_1 > 6\big\}. \tag{2.6}$$

Graph 2.4a is a graphical depiction of this set when $p_1 = 20$, $p_2 = 10$, and $I = 200$. The budget line itself is then defined by two line segments, one for $x_1 \leq 6$ and one for $x_1 > 6$; or, stated formally,

$$B(p_1,p_2,I) = \big\{(x_1,x_2) \in \mathbb{R}^2_+ \,|\, 0.5\,p_1x_1 + p_2x_2 = I \text{ for } x_1 \leq 6 \text{ and}$$
$$p_1x_1 + p_2x_2 = I + 3p_1 \text{ for } x_1 > 6\big\}. \tag{2.7}$$

**Exercise
2B.4**

Convert the two equations contained in the budget set (2.7) into a format that illustrates more clearly the intercept and slope terms (as in equation (2.5)). Then, using the numbers for prices and incomes from our example, plot the two lines on a graph. Finally, erase the portions of the lines that are not relevant given that each line applies only for some values of x_1 (as indicated in (2.7)). Compare your graph with Graph 2.4a.

**Exercise
2B.5**

Now suppose that the 50% off coupon applied to all pants purchased after you bought an initial 6 pants at regular price. Derive the mathematical formulation of the budget set (analogous to equation (2.7)) and then repeat the previous exercise. Compare your graph with Graph 2.4b.

2B.3 Choice Sets with More than Two Goods

As we discussed in Section 2A, we are often confronted by the fact that realistic models of economic behavior involve choices over more than two goods. The mathematical formulation of choice sets permits us one way of extending our analysis to settings where choices over many goods can be analyzed. Alternatively, as we noted in Section 2A, we can employ the simplifying assumption that categories of goods can be combined and treated as a composite good.[5] We explore each of these alternatives in turn.

2B.3.1 Choice Sets with 3 or More Goods

When faced with three rather than two goods, we illustrated in Graph 2.5 that our choice sets would now have to be plotted in three dimensions. When faced with more than three goods, we no longer have easy graphical techniques to represent choice sets. With the mathematical tools developed here, however, it becomes quite simple to extend two-good models to many goods.

Suppose, for instance, that we return to the example of me going to Wal-Mart, only now I am sent to purchase pants, shirts, and socks. Let's denote those goods by x_1, x_2, and x_3 and let's similarly denote their prices by p_1, p_2, and p_3. In order for a particular bundle (x_1, x_2, x_3) to lie within the choice set, it must then be true that the total cost of the bundle is no greater than my exogenous income I. The cost of each component of the bundle is simply the price of that component times the quantity, and the sum of these is equal to the full cost $p_1 x_1 + p_2 x_2 + p_3 x_3$. My choice set is then a simple extension of the choice set we defined for two goods in equation (2.3):

$$C(p_1, p_2, p_3, I) = \left\{ (x_1, x_2, x_3) \in \mathbb{R}^3_+ \mid p_1 x_1 + p_2 x_2 + p_3 x_3 \leq I \right\}, \tag{2.8}$$

with the corresponding budget constraint defined by

$$B(p_1, p_2, p_3, I) = \left\{ (x_1, x_2, x_3) \in \mathbb{R}^3_+ \mid p_1 x_1 + p_2 x_2 + p_3 x_3 = I \right\}. \tag{2.9}$$

The equation in this definition of the budget constraint then defines the triangular plane that we graphed in Graph 2.5 for the values $p_1 = 20$, $p_2 = 10$, $p_3 = 5$, and $I = 200$.

By now you can probably quite easily see how the definition of choice sets and budget lines extends when we face choices over more than 3 goods. For the general case of n different goods with n different prices, we would simply extend (2.8) and (2.9) to:

$$C(p_1, p_2, \ldots, p_n, I) = \left\{ (x_1, x_2, \ldots, x_n) \in \mathbb{R}^n_+ \mid p_1 x_1 + p_2 x_2 + \ldots + p_n x_n \leq I \right\}, \tag{2.10}$$

and

$$B(p_1, p_2, \ldots, p_n, I) = \left\{ (x_1, x_2, \ldots, x_n) \in \mathbb{R}^n_+ \mid p_1 x_1 + p_2 x_2 + \ldots + p_n x_n = I \right\}. \tag{2.11}$$

While it is therefore no longer possible to graph these mathematical descriptions of sets, it nevertheless is quite easy to formulate them using equations. As we explore the consumer model in more detail in the upcoming chapters, you will then see how these equations can be used to formulate a quite general model of choice behavior.

2B.3.2 Choice Sets with Composite Goods

We of course also noted in Section 2A that we often find it useful in our graphical models to focus on one good that is of particular interest and to model all other consumption goods as a *composite good* denominated in dollars. We will often refer to this composite good as "dollars of other consumption." One convenient benefit of such a model is that the price of the composite good is by definition 1 ($p_2 = 1$); 1 dollar of

---

[5]As noted in part A, there are several conditions under which it is theoretically sound to aggregate goods into a composite good. One such condition, known as *functional separability*, requires that the prices of the goods to be aggregated always move together in the same proportion. A second condition, known as *Hicksian separability*, involves assumptions about tastes. Either condition allows us to use the concept of a composite good. A detailed discussion of these two conditions is beyond the scope of this text, but the interested reader can learn more by referring to H. Varian, *Microeconomic Analysis*, 3rd ed. (New York: W. W. Norton and Company, 1992).

consumption of other goods costs 1 dollar. This implies that the slope of the budget line simply becomes the price of the good we are concerned with (rather than the ratio of prices that it typically is), and the vertical intercept becomes simply the exogenous income rather than income divided by the price of good 2.

To see this, we could simply write down the equation of a budget line with x_2 as the composite good as

$$p_1 x_1 + x_2 = I, \tag{2.12}$$

leaving out the price for the composite good, which is just 1. Subtracting $p_1 x_1$ from both sides, we get

$$x_2 = I - p_1 x_1, \tag{2.13}$$

with the equation of a line with vertical intercept I and slope $-p_1$. Note that this is simply the same equation as equation (2.5) with p_2 set to 1.

2B.4 Choice Sets that Arise from Endowments

So far, we have assumed that my income level or money budget for my consumption choices is fixed or exogenous. This is a reasonable assumption when we analyze consumer choices where specific amounts have been budgeted for certain categories of goods (like shirts and pants) or when we analyze the consumption choices of someone on a fixed income. In other cases, however, the money that can be devoted to consumption is not *exogenous*; rather it arises *endogenously* from the decisions a consumer makes and from the prices he or she faces in the market. Important examples of this include our choices of selling our time in labor markets and our financial assets in capital markets. These are treated more explicitly in Chapter 3. For now, we simply illustrate the mathematics behind our example from Section 2A in consumer markets.

In particular, we assumed in Section 2A.4 that I returned to Wal-Mart with 10 shirts and 5 pants knowing that Wal-Mart will give me store credit for the value of my returns at the prices Wal-Mart is currently charging. How much of a store credit I will get from Wal-Mart now depends on the prices of shirts and pants that Wal-Mart charges at the time of my return. My income can then be expressed as

$$I = 5p_1 + 10p_2, \tag{2.14}$$

since Wal-Mart will give me its current price for pants, p_1, for each of my 5 pants and its current price for shirts, p_2, for each of my 10 shirts. My choice set is then composed of all combinations of pants and shirts such that my total spending is no more than this income level; i.e.,

$$C(p_1, p_2) = \left\{ (x_1, x_2) \in \mathbb{R}^2_+ \mid p_1 x_1 + p_2 x_2 \leq 5p_1 + 10p_2 \right\}. \tag{2.15}$$

Notice that the set C is now a function of only (p_1, p_2) because my income is "endogenously" determined by p_1 and p_2 as described in equation (2.14). When the inequality in (2.15) is replaced with an equality to get the equation for the budget line, we get

$$p_1 x_1 + p_2 x_2 = 5p_1 + 10p_2. \tag{2.16}$$

Subtracting $p_1 x_1$ from both sides and dividing both sides by p_2, this turns into

$$x_2 = 5\frac{p_1}{p_2} + 10 - \frac{p_1}{p_2} x_1. \tag{2.17}$$

In Graph 2.6, we plotted this budget set for the case where Wal-Mart was charging $10 for both shirts and pants. When these prices are plugged into equation (2.17), we get

$$x_2 = 15 - x_1, \tag{2.18}$$

which represents the equation of a line with vertical intercept 15 and slope -1. This is precisely the magenta budget line we derived intuitively in Graph 2.6.

More generally, we can denote someone's endowment as the number of goods of each kind a consumer has as he or she enters Wal-Mart. For instance, we might denote my endowment of good 1 as e_1 and my endowment of good 2 as e_2. (In our example $e_1 = 5$ and $e_2 = 10$.) We can then define my choice set as a function of my endowment and the prices of the two goods,

$$C(p_1, p_2, e_1, e_2) = \left\{ (x_1, x_2) \mid p_1 x_1 + p_2 x_2 \leq p_1 e_1 + p_2 e_2 \right\}, \tag{2.19}$$

where the left-hand side of the inequality represents my spending on the goods I purchase and the right-hand side represents my endogenous income from returning my endowment goods to Wal-Mart.

Using the equation in (2.19), derive the general equation of the budget line in terms of prices and endowments. Following steps analogous to those leading to equation (2.17), identify the intercept and slope terms. What would the budget line look like when my endowments are 10 shirts and 10 pants and when prices are $5 for pants and $10 for shirts? Relate this to both the equation you derived and an intuitive derivation of the same budget line.

Exercise 2B.6

CONCLUSION

For consumer models in which individuals attempt to "do the best they can" given the "economic circumstances they face," we began in this chapter by deriving ways of modeling "economic circumstances." These circumstances are defined by what consumers bring to the table, whether in the form of an endowment or an exogenous income, and by the prices that they face. Together, these give rise to choice sets and budget constraints that define the set of options from which consumers can choose. These can be modeled graphically when the analysis permits restricting the number of goods to 2 or 3, or they can be represented mathematically for any arbitrary number of goods. The fundamental trade-offs or opportunity costs consumers face are then determined by relative prices, which appear as slopes in our graphs or equations.

Rarely, however, do we have the luxury of acting solely as consumers in the marketplace. In order to consume, we must generally earn income first, either by selling our leisure time in the labor market (i.e., working) or by selling something of value (e.g., a financial asset). And the economist assumes that we attempt to "do the best we can" given our "economic circumstances" whether we act as consumers, workers, or financial planners. We therefore next turn in Chapter 3 to defining choice sets and budget constraints that are relevant for other types of choices we make in the economy before moving on to consider more carefully what it means to "do the best" we can.

END-OF-CHAPTER EXERCISES

2.1 Any good Southern breakfast includes grits (which my wife loves) and bacon (which I love). Suppose we allocate $60 per week to consumption of grits and bacon, and we know that grits cost $2 per box and bacon costs $3 per package.

A. Use a graph with boxes of grits on the horizontal axis and packages of bacon on the vertical to answer the following:

    a. Illustrate my family's weekly budget constraint and choice set.

    b. Identify the opportunity cost of bacon and grits and relate these to concepts on your graph.

----

*conceptually challenging
**computationally challenging
†solutions in Study Guide

    c.   How would your graph change if a sudden appearance of a rare hog disease caused the price of bacon to rise to $6 per package, and how does this change the opportunity cost of bacon and grits?

    d.   What happens in your graph if (instead of the change in (c)) the loss of my job caused us to decrease our weekly budget for Southern breakfasts from $60 to $30? How does this change the opportunity cost of bacon and grits?

B. In the following, compare a mathematical approach to the graphical approach used in part A, using x_1 to represent boxes of grits and x_2 to represent packages of bacon.

    a.   Write down the mathematical formulation of the budget line and choice set and identify elements in the budget equation that correspond to key features of your graph from part 2.1A(a).

    b.   How can you identify the opportunity cost of bacon and grits in your equation of a budget line, and how does this relate to your answer in 2.1A(b)?

    c.   Illustrate how the budget line equation changes under the scenario of 2.1A(c) and identify the change in opportunity costs.

    d.   Repeat (c) for the scenario in 2.1A(d).

2.2†   Suppose the only two goods in the world are peanut butter and jelly.

A. You have no exogenous income, but you do own 6 jars of peanut butter and 2 jars of jelly. The price of peanut butter is $4 per jar, and the price of jelly is $6 per jar.

    a.   On a graph with jars of peanut butter on the horizontal and jars of jelly on the vertical axis, illustrate your budget constraint.

    b.   How does your constraint change when the price of peanut butter increases to $6? How does this change your opportunity cost of jelly?

B. Consider the same economic circumstances described in 2.2A and use x_1 to represent jars of peanut butter and x_2 to represent jars of jelly.

    a.   Write down the equation representing the budget line and relate key components to your graph from 2.2A(a).

    b.   Change your equation for your budget line to reflect the change in economic circumstances described in 2.2A(b) and show how this new equation relates to your graph in 2.2A(b).

2.3   Consider a budget for good x_1 (on the horizontal axis) and x_2 (on the vertical axis) when your economic circumstances are characterized by prices p_1 and p_2 and an exogenous income level I.

A. Draw a budget line that represents these economic circumstances and carefully label the intercepts and slope.

    a.   Illustrate how this line can shift parallel to itself without a change in I.

    b.   Illustrate how this line can rotate clockwise on its horizontal intercept without a change in p_2.

B. Write the equation of a budget line that corresponds to your graph in 2.3A.

    a.   Use this equation to demonstrate how the change derived in 2.3A(a) can happen.

    b.   Use the same equation to illustrate how the change derived in 2.3A(b) can happen.

2.4*   Suppose there are three goods in the world: x_1, x_2, and x_3.

A. On a three-dimensional graph, illustrate your budget constraint when your economic circumstances are defined by $p_1 = 2, p_2 = 6, p_3 = 5$, and $I = 120$. Carefully label intercepts.

    a.   What is your opportunity cost of x_1 in terms of x_2? What is your opportunity cost of x_2 in terms of x_3?

    b.   Illustrate how your graph changes if I falls to $60. Does your answer to (a) change?

    c.   Illustrate how your graph changes if instead p_1 rises to $4. Does your answer to part (a) change?

B. Write down the equation that represents your picture in 2.4A. Then suppose that a new good x_4 is invented and priced at $1. How does your equation change? Why is it difficult to represent this new set of economic circumstances graphically?

2.5   **Everyday Application:** *Watching a Bad Movie:* On one of my first dates with my wife, we went to see the movie *Spaceballs* and paid $5 per ticket.

A.   Halfway through the movie, my wife said: "What on earth were you thinking? This movie sucks! I don't know why I let you pick movies. Let's leave."

    a.   In trying to decide whether to stay or leave, what is the opportunity cost of staying to watch the rest of the movie?

    b.   Suppose we had read a sign on the way into the theater stating "Satisfaction Guaranteed! Don't like the movie half way through—see the manager and get your money back!" How does this change your answer to part (a)?

2.6†   **Everyday Application:** *Renting a Car versus Taking Taxis:* Suppose my brother and I both go on a week-long vacation in Cayman and, when we arrive at the airport on the island, we have to choose between either renting a car or taking a taxi to our hotel. Renting a car involves a fixed fee of $300 for the week, with each mile driven afterward just costing $0.20, which is the price of gasoline per mile. Taking a taxi involves no fixed fees, but each mile driven on the island during the week now costs $1 per mile.

A.   Suppose both my brother and I have brought $2,000 on our trip to spend on "miles driven on the island" and "other goods." On a graph with miles driven on the horizontal and other consumption on the vertical axis, illustrate my budget constraint assuming I chose to rent a car and my brother's budget constraint assuming he chose to take taxis.

    a.   What is the opportunity cost for each mile driven that I faced?

    b.   What is the opportunity cost for each mile driven that my brother faced?

B.   Derive the mathematical equations for my budget constraint and my brother's budget constraint, and relate elements of these equations to your graphs in part A. Use x_1 to denote miles driven and x_2 to denote other consumption.

    a.   Where in your budget equation for me can you locate the opportunity cost of a mile driven?

    b.   Where in your budget equation for my brother can you locate the opportunity cost of a mile driven?

2.7*   **Everyday Application:** *Dieting and Nutrition:* On a recent doctor's visit, you have been told that you must watch your calorie intake and must make sure you get enough vitamin E in your diet.

A.   You have decided that, to make life simple, you will from now on eat only steak and carrots. A nice steak has 250 calories and 10 units of vitamins, and a serving of carrots has 100 calories and 30 units of vitamins. Your doctor's instructions are that you must eat *no more* than 2,000 calories and consume *at least* 150 units of vitamins per day.

    a.   In a graph with "servings of carrots" on the horizontal axis and "servings of steak" on the vertical axis, illustrate all combinations of carrots and steaks that make up a 2,000-calorie-a-day diet.

    b.   On the same graph, illustrate all the combinations of carrots and steaks that provide exactly 150 units of vitamins.

    c.   On this graph, shade in the bundles of carrots and steaks that satisfy both of your doctor's requirements.

    d.   Now suppose you can buy a serving of carrots for $2 and a steak for $6. You have $26 per day in your food budget. In your graph, illustrate your budget constraint. If you love steak and don't mind eating or not eating carrots, what bundle will you choose (assuming you take your doctor's instructions seriously)?

B.   Continue with the scenario as described in part A, letting carrots be denoted by x_1 and steak by x_2.

    a.   Define the line you drew in A(a) mathematically.

    b.   Define the line you drew in A(b) mathematically.

    c.   In formal set notation, write down the expression that is equivalent to the shaded area in A(c).

    d.   Derive the exact bundle you indicated on your graph in A(d).

2.8† **Everyday Application:** *Setting up a College Trust Fund:* Suppose that you, after studying economics in college, quickly became rich, so rich that you have nothing better to do than worry about your 16-year-old niece who can't seem to focus on her future. Your niece already has a trust fund that will pay her a nice yearly income of $50,000 starting when she is 18, and she has no other means of support.

A. You are concerned that your niece will not see the wisdom of spending a good portion of her trust fund on a college education, and you would therefore like to use $100,000 of your wealth to change her choice set in ways that will give her greater incentives to go to college.

   a. One option is for you to place $100,000 in a second trust fund but to restrict your niece to be able to draw on this trust fund only for college expenses of up to $25,000 per year for four years. On a graph with "yearly dollars spent on college education" on the horizontal axis and "yearly dollars spent on other consumption" on the vertical, illustrate how this affects her choice set.

   b. A second option is for you simply to tell your niece that you will give her $25,000 per year for 4 years and you will trust her to "do what's right." How does this impact her choice set?

   c. Suppose you are wrong about your niece's short-sightedness and she was planning on spending more than $25,000 per year from her other trust fund on college education. Do you think she will care whether you do as described in part (a) or as described in part (b)?

   d. Suppose you were right about her: She never was going to spend very much on college. Will she care now?

   e. A friend of yours gives you some advice: Be careful. Your niece will not value her education if she does not have to put up some of her own money for it. Sobered by this advice, you decide to set up a different trust fund that will release $0.50 to your niece (to be spent on whatever she wants) for every dollar that she spends on college expenses. How will this affect her choice set?

   f. If your niece spends $25,000 per year on college under the trust fund in part (e), can you identify a vertical distance that represents how much you paid to achieve this outcome?

B. How would you write the budget equation for each of the three alternatives discussed in part A?

2.9* **Business Application:** *Pricing and Quantity Discounts:* Businesses often give quantity discounts. In the following, you will analyze how such discounts can impact choice sets.

A. I recently discovered that a local copy service charges our economics department $0.05 per page (or $5 per 100 pages) for the first 10,000 copies in any given month but then reduces the price per page to $0.035 for each additional page up to 100,000 copies and to $0.02 per each page beyond 100,000. Suppose our department has a monthly overall budget of $5,000.

   a. Putting "pages copied in units of 100" on the horizontal axis and "dollars spent on other goods" on the vertical, illustrate this budget constraint. Carefully label all intercepts and slopes.

   b. Suppose the copy service changes its pricing policy to $0.05 per page for monthly copying up to 20,000 and $0.025 per page for *all* pages if copying exceeds 20,000 per month. (*Hint*: Your budget line will contain a jump.)

   c. What is the marginal (or "additional") cost of the first page copied after 20,000 in part (b)? What is the marginal cost of the first page copied after 20,001 in part (b)?

B. Write down the mathematical expression for choice sets for each of the scenarios in 2.9A(a) and 2.9A(b) (using x_1 to denote "pages copied in units of 100" and x_2 to denote "dollars spent on other goods").

2.10 **Business Application:** *Supersizing:* Suppose I run a fast-food restaurant and I know my customers come in on a limited budget. Almost everyone that comes in for lunch buys a soft drink. Now suppose it costs me virtually nothing to serve a medium versus a large soft drink, but I do incur some extra costs when adding items (like a dessert or another side dish) to someone's lunch tray.

A. Suppose for purposes of this exercise that cups come in all sizes, not just small, medium, and large; and suppose the average customer has a lunch budget B. On a graph with "ounces of soft drink" on the horizontal axis and "dollars spent on other lunch items" on the vertical, illustrate a customer's budget constraint assuming I charge the same price p per ounce of soft drink no matter how big a cup the customer gets.

a. I have 3 business partners: Larry, his brother Daryl, and his other brother Daryl. The Daryls propose that we lower the price of the initial ounces of soft drink that a consumer buys and then, starting at 10 ounces, we increase the price. They have calculated that our average customer would be able to buy exactly the same number of ounces of soft drink (if that is all he bought on his lunch budget) as under the current single price. Illustrate how this will change the average customer's budget constraint.

b. Larry thinks the Daryls are idiots and suggests instead that we raise the price for initial ounces of soft drink and then, starting at 10 ounces, decrease the price for any additional ounces. He, too, has calculated that, under his pricing policy, the average customer will be able to buy exactly the same ounces of soft drinks (if that is all the customer buys on his or her lunch budget). Illustrate the effect on the average customer's budget constraint.

c. If the average customer had a choice, which of the three pricing systems—the current single price, the Daryls' proposal, or Larry's proposal—would he choose?

B. Write down the mathematical expression for each of the 3 choice sets, letting ounces of soft drinks be denoted by x_1 and dollars spent on other lunch items by x_2.

2.11 Business Application: *Frequent Flyer Perks:* Airlines offer frequent flyers different kinds of perks that we will model here as reductions in average prices per mile flown.

A. Suppose that an airline charges 20 cents per mile flown. However, once a customer reaches 25,000 miles in a given year, the price drops to 10 cents per mile flown for each additional mile. The alternate way to travel is to drive by car, which costs 16 cents per mile.

a. Consider a consumer who has a travel budget of $10,000 per year, a budget that can be spent on the cost of getting to places as well as "other consumption" while traveling. On a graph with "miles flown" on the horizontal axis and "other consumption" on the vertical, illustrate the budget constraint for someone who only considers flying (and not driving) to travel destinations.

b. On a similar graph with "miles driven" on the horizontal axis, illustrate the budget constraint for someone that considers only driving (and not flying) as a means of travel.

c. By overlaying these two budget constraints (changing the good on the horizontal axis simply to "miles traveled"), can you explain how frequent flyer perks might persuade some to fly a lot more than he or she otherwise would?

B. Determine where the air-travel budget from A(a) intersects the car budget from A(b).

2.12* Business Application: *Choice in Calling Plans:* Phone companies used to sell minutes of phone calls at the same price no matter how many phone calls a customer made. (We will abstract away from the fact that they charged different prices at different times of the day and week.) More recently, phone companies, particularly cell phone companies, have become more creative in their pricing.

A. On a graph with "minutes of phone calls per month" on the horizontal axis and "dollars of other consumption" on the vertical, draw a budget constraint assuming the price per minute of phone calls is p and assuming the consumer has a monthly income I.

a. Now suppose a new option is introduced: You can pay $\$P_x$ to buy into a phone plan that offers you x minutes of free calls per month, with any calls beyond x costing p per minute. Illustrate how this changes your budget constraint and assume that P_x is sufficiently low such that the new budget contains some bundles that were previously unavailable to our consumer.

b. Suppose it actually costs phone companies close to p per minute to provide a minute of phone service so that, in order to stay profitable, a phone company must on average get about p per minute of phone call. If all consumers were able to choose calling plans such that they always use exactly x minutes per month, would it be possible for phone companies to set P_x sufficiently low such that new bundles become available to consumers?

c. If some fraction of consumers in any given month buy into a calling plan but make fewer than x calls, how does this enable phone companies to set P_x such that new bundles become available in consumer choice sets?

B. Suppose a phone company has 100,000 customers who currently buy phone minutes under the old system that charges p per minute. Suppose it costs the company c to provide one additional minute of phone service but the company also has fixed costs FC (that don't vary with how many minutes are sold) of an amount that is sufficiently high to result in zero profit. Suppose a second identical phone company has 100,000 customers who have bought into a calling plan that charges $P_x = kpx$ and gives customers x free minutes before charging p for minutes above x.

    a.   If people on average use half their "free minutes" per month, what is k (as a functions of FC, p, c, and x) if the second company also makes zero profit?

    b.   If there were no fixed costs (i.e., $FC = 0$) but everything else was still as stated, what does c have to be equal to in order for the first company to make zero profit? What is k in that case?

2.13   **Policy Application:** *Food Stamp Programs and Other Types of Subsidies:* The U.S. government has a food stamp program for families whose income falls below a certain poverty threshold. Food stamps have a dollar value that can be used at supermarkets for food purchases as if the stamps were cash, but the food stamps cannot be used for anything other than food.

A.   Suppose the program provides $500 of food stamps per month to a particular family that has a fixed income of $1,000 per month.

    a.   With "dollars spent on food" on the horizontal axis and "dollars spent on nonfood items" on the vertical, illustrate this family's monthly budget constraint. How does the opportunity cost of food change along the budget constraint you have drawn?

    b.   How would this family's budget constraint differ if the government replaced the food stamp program with a cash subsidy program that simply gave this family $500 in cash instead of $500 in food stamps? Which would the family prefer, and what does your answer depend on?

    c.   How would the budget constraint change if the government simply agreed to reimburse the family for half its food expenses?

    d.   If the government spends the same amount for this family on the program described in (c) as it did on the food stamp program, how much food will the family consume? Illustrate the amount the government is spending as a vertical distance between the budget lines you have drawn.

B.   Write down the mathematical expression for the choice set you drew in 2.13A(a), letting x_1 represent dollars spent on food and x_2 represent dollars spent on nonfood consumption. How does this expression change in 2.13A(b) through (d)?

2.14   **Policy Application:** *Public Housing and Housing Subsidies:* For a long period, the U.S. government focused its attempts to meet housing needs among the poor through public housing programs. Eligible families could get on waiting lists to apply for an apartment in a public housing development and would be offered a particular apartment as they moved to the top of the waiting list.

A.   Suppose a particular family has a monthly income of $1,500 and is offered a 1,500-square-foot public housing apartment for $375 in monthly rent. Alternatively, the family could choose to rent housing in the private market for $0.50 per square foot.

    a.   Illustrate all the bundles in this family's choice set of "square feet of housing" (on the horizontal axis) and "dollars of monthly other goods consumption" (on the vertical axis).

    b.   In recent years, the government has shifted away from an emphasis on public housing and toward providing poor families with a direct subsidy to allow them to rent more housing in the private market. Suppose, instead of offering the family in part (a) an apartment, the government offered to pay half of the family's rental bill. How would this change the family's budget constraint?

    c.   Is it possible to tell which policy the family would prefer?

B.   Write down the mathematical expression for the budget lines you drew in 2.14A(a) and 2.14A(b), letting x_1 denote hundreds of square feet of monthly housing consumption and x_2 denote dollars spent on non housing consumption.

2.15†   **Policy Application:** *Taxing Goods versus Lump Sum Taxes:* I have finally convinced my local member of Congress that my wife's taste for grits is unnervingly strange and that the world should be protected from too much grits consumption. As a result, my member of Congress has agreed to sponsor new legislation to tax grits consumption, which will raise the price of grits from $2 per box to $4 per box. We carefully observe my wife's shopping behavior and notice with pleasure that she now purchases 10 boxes of grits per month rather than her previous 15 boxes.

A. Putting "boxes of grits per month" on the horizontal and "dollars of other consumption" on the vertical, illustrate my wife's budget line before and after the tax is imposed. (You can simply denote income by I.)

   a. How much tax revenue is the government collecting per month from my wife? Illustrate this as a vertical distance on your graph. (*Hint*: If you know how much she is consuming after the tax and how much in other consumption this leaves her with, and if you know how much in other consumption she would have had if she consumed that same quantity before the imposition of the tax, then the difference between these two "other consumption" quantities must be equal to how much she paid in tax.)

   b. Given that I live in the South, the grits tax turned out to be unpopular in my congressional district and has led to the defeat of my member of Congress. His replacement won on a pro-grits platform and has vowed to repeal the grits tax. However, new budget rules require her to include a new way to raise the same tax revenue that was yielded by the grits tax. She proposes simply to ask each grits consumer to pay exactly the amount he or she paid in grits taxes as a monthly lump sum payment. Ignoring for the moment the difficulty of gathering the necessary information for implementing this proposal, how would this change my wife's budget constraint?

B. State the equations for the budget constraints you derived in A(a) and A(b), letting grits be denoted by x_1 and other consumption by x_2.

2.16 **Policy Application:** *Public Schools and Private School Vouchers:* Consider a simple model of how economic circumstances are changed when free public education is provided.

A. Suppose a household has an after-tax income of $50,000, and consider its budget constraint with "dollars of education services" on the horizontal axis and "dollars of other consumption" on the vertical. Begin by drawing the household's budget line (given that you can infer a price for each of the goods on the axes from the way these goods are defined) assuming that the household can buy any level of school spending on the private market.

   a. Now suppose the government uses its existing tax revenues to fund a public school at $7,500 per pupil; i.e., it funds a school that anyone can attend for free and that provides $7,500 in education services. Illustrate how this changes the choice set. (*Hint*: One additional point will appear in the choice set.)

   b. Continue to assume that private school services of any quantity could be purchased but only if the child does not attend public schools. Can you think of how the availability of free public schools might cause some children to receive more educational services than before they would in the absence of public schools? Can you think of how some children might receive fewer educational services once public schools are introduced?

   c. Now suppose the government allows an option: either a parent can send her child to the public school or she can take a voucher to a private school and use it for partial payment of private school tuition. Assume that the voucher is worth $7,500 per year; i.e., it can be used to pay for up to $7,500 in private school tuition. How does this change the budget constraint? Do you still think it is possible that some children will receive less education than they would if the government did not get involved at all (i.e., no public schools and no vouchers)?

B. Letting dollars of education services be denoted by x_1 and dollars of other consumption by x_2, formally define the choice set with just the public school (and a private school market) as well as the choice set with private school vouchers previously defined.

2.17* **Policy Application:** *Tax Deductions and Tax Credits:* In the U.S. income tax code, a number of expenditures are "deductible." For most tax payers, the largest tax deduction comes from the portion of the income tax code that permits taxpayers to deduct home mortgage interest (on both a primary and a vacation home). This means that taxpayers who use this deduction do not have to pay income tax on the portion of their income that is spent on paying interest on their home mortgage(s). For purposes of this exercise, assume that the entire yearly price of housing is interest expense.

A. *True or False*: For someone whose marginal tax rate is 33%, this means that the government is subsidizing roughly one-third of his or her interest/house payments.

a. Consider a household with an income of $200,000 that faces a tax rate of 40%, and suppose the price of a square foot of housing is $50 per year. With square footage of housing on the horizontal axis and other consumption on the vertical, illustrate this household's budget constraint with and without tax deductibility. (Assume in this and the remaining parts of the question that the tax rate cited for a household applies to all of that household's income.)

b. Repeat this for a household with income of $50,000 that faces a tax rate of 10%.

c. An alternative way for the government to encourage home ownership would be to offer a tax *credit* instead of a tax *deduction*. A tax credit would allow all taxpayers to subtract a fraction *k* of their annual mortgage payments directly from the tax bill they would otherwise owe. (Note: Be careful. A tax credit is deducted from tax *payments* that are due, not from the taxable income.) For the households in (a) and (b), illustrate how this alters their budget if $k = 0.25$.

d. Assuming that a tax deductibility program costs the same in lost tax revenues as a tax credit program, which household would favor which program?

B. Let x_1 and x_2 represent square feet of housing and other consumption, and let the price of a square foot of housing be denoted p.

a. Suppose a household faces a tax rate t for all income, and suppose the entire annual house payment a household makes is deductible. What is the household's budget constraint?

b. Now write down the budget constraint under a tax credit as previously described.

Economic Circumstances in Labor and Financial Markets

As we noted in Chapter 2, the economic choices we make are not limited to the types of choices we face when we visit Wal-Mart on a fixed or "exogenous" dollar budget.[1] After all, where does the money that we can spend on consumer goods come from in the first place? Before we can spend money, we must first generate it through some form of economic activity. For most of us, this activity involves work, or the giving up of our time in return for pay. Alternatively, we might generate money by borrowing or by cashing in savings from savings accounts, mutual funds, real estate investments, or other assets. In each of these scenarios, we are giving up some *endowment*, something whose value is determined by prices in the economy, to get money for consumption. This endowment may be our time when we work, an asset when we cash in our savings or our ability to consume income in the future when we borrow. We are, in effect, trading an endowment in order to generate the money that then can be treated as a fixed budget when we go into Wal-Mart to shop for shirts and pants.

When I returned to Wal-Mart with 5 pants and 10 shirts in Chapter 2, I returned with an endowment, and my *endogenous income* was then determined by the prices at which I could sell this endowment back to Wal-Mart for store credit. In the same way, our economic circumstances in work/leisure and savings/borrowing decisions are shaped by the endowment that we bring to the table as well as the prices that the endowment commands in the market. If the decision involves selling our leisure time for work, the relevant "price" becomes the wage, and when the decision involves postponing consumption (through savings) or borrowing on future income (through taking out a loan), the relevant "price" will be the interest rate that we can earn or that we have to pay. Thus, the choice sets that we derive in this chapter are in essence no different than the choice set we thought about in Chapter 2 when I returned to Wal-Mart with pants and shirts rather than with money; all that is different is that our endowment will not be in terms of pants and shirts, and the prices will involve wage rates and interest rates.

3A Budgets for Workers and Savers

We will begin by analyzing our choice sets as workers and then proceed to choice sets that arise as we think about saving and borrowing. As in the previous chapter, we start by focusing purely on economics and intuition, relying on graphical tools to generate our basic models of choice

---

[1]Chapter 2 is recommended as prior reading for this chapter.

sets. Then, in Section 3B, we will translate some of that intuition into mathematical language in order to demonstrate how to generalize it.

3A.1 Our Choice Sets as Workers

As we have already noted, "work" involves giving up one of our most precious endowments: our time. Depending on our innate talents and characteristics as well as our educational background and work experience, our time may be worth more or less to employers (or to the market more generally if we are self-employed). Let's assume that you are on summer break and have found a job with an employer who is willing to pay you $20 per hour. Your employer is trying to determine how many other summer workers she needs to hire, and so she asks you how many hours per week you would like to work this summer. You now have to determine how much work is best for you given your circumstances. The more you work, the less leisure time you will have this summer but the more consumption goods you will be able to buy with your newfound wealth. The opportunity cost of taking 1 hour of leisure time is how much consumption you implicitly give up by not working during that hour, which is $20 worth of consumption if your wage is $20 per hour. Put differently, *the opportunity cost of an hour of leisure is the wage you could have earned in that hour.*

3A.1.1 Graphing Leisure/Consumption Choice Sets
Illustrating your choice set as you choose between consuming and leisuring is then no different than illustrating your choice set over pants and shirts, except that you begin with a particular endowment of leisure time rather than an exogenous dollar income. Suppose we put "hours of leisure per week" on the horizontal axis and "dollars of consumption per week" on the vertical, as in Graph 3.1. (Notice that we have chosen to make the analysis manageable by lumping all consumption into one composite consumption good as described in Chapter 2.) Let's assume that, given your other obligations (not to mention your need for sleep and personal grooming), you potentially have 60 hours of time available to allocate

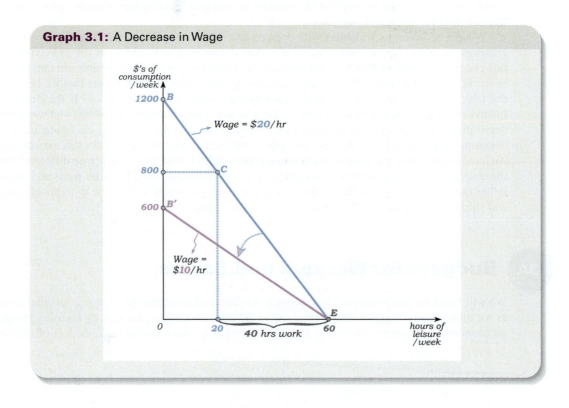

Graph 3.1: A Decrease in Wage

between work and play in any given week. This is your leisure time endowment. The intercept on the leisure axis is then at 60 hours (point E), indicating that one of your possible choices is to hold onto your 60 hours of leisure endowment and thus earn no money for consumption. Notice that you can consume this endowment bundle E *regardless of what prices (including the wage) in the economy are*, a characteristic we said in Chapter 2 is shared by all endowment points.

On the other extreme, you could sell your entire time endowment, i.e., devote all of your time to work, and earn as much as $1,200 per week. This gives you point B as the intercept on the consumption axis. Or you could do something in between, such as selling 40 hours of leisure (leaving you with 20 hours for play) and earning $800 per week for consumption (point C). Connecting these, we get a (blue) budget constraint that illustrates all the possible combinations of consumption and leisure that are available to you per week given your circumstances. Notice that the slope of this line is -20, which is exactly equal to the (negative) wage that we have identified as the opportunity cost of 1 hour of leisure in terms of dollars of consumption.

Now suppose a recession hits prior to the beginning of summer and, as a result, the best wage you can get is $10 rather than $20 per hour. How would this change the budget constraint that illustrates your trade-off between consumption and leisure?

Recall that we noted at the end of Chapter 2 that, when a choice set is derived from an endowment rather than some fixed dollar amount, the budget line will rotate through the endowment point when prices change. The wage in our current example is a price, the price employers have to pay in order to hire workers. The endowment in our example is point E, the point that illustrates the total amount of discretionary leisure time that you have available per week. As we have already noted, regardless of what the wage rate in the economy turns out to be, this point E is *always* available to you since it is your endowment point. Point E therefore does not change when the wage rate declines to $10. Point B, on the other hand, does change; if you decided to sell all of your available leisure time, you could now only earn $600 rather than $1,200 per week for spending on consumption goods. The new (magenta) budget constraint therefore contains the endowment point E and has a slope equal to the new opportunity cost of leisure.

Illustrate what happens to the original budget constraint if your wage increases to $30 per hour. What if your friend instead introduces you to caffeine, which allows you to sleep less and thus take up to 80 hours of leisure time per week?

Exercise 3A.1

3A.1.2 Government Policies and Labor Market Choice Sets

The potential impacts of government policies on labor market decisions are so vast that entire subfields within economics are devoted to studying such impacts. Overtime regulations, mandates regarding benefits for employees, safety regulations, wage taxes, and subsidies: these are all examples of ways in which governments impact the types of choices available to individual employees and employers.

Consider, for instance, a regulation that requires employers to pay 50% overtime for any work done beyond 40 hours per week. One possible outcome of such a regulation is that employers do not permit employees the option of working for more than 40 hours per week. In the example of your summer job, this would not alter point E; if you choose not to work at all (and take 60 hours of leisure), you would still not earn any money for consumption. Similarly, the opportunity cost of leisure would remain unchanged for the first 40 hours of leisure that you give up, implying that the budget constraint would remain the same between points E and C in Graph 3.2a. How the budget changes between points C and B, however, depends on what other labor market opportunities you have given that your current employer is no longer offering you the option of working beyond 40 hours per week. For instance, if your next best labor market opportunity involves a wage of $10 per hour, you could sell your remaining 20 hours of leisure for a total of $200, implying that the most consumption you could obtain by working 40 hours with your first

Graph 3.2: Possible Kinks in Labor Market Choice Sets under Overtime Regulation

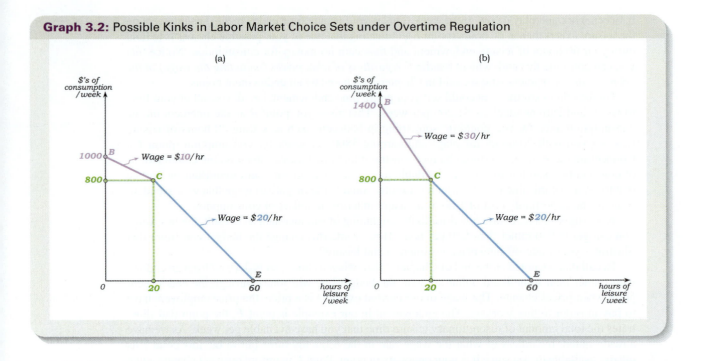

employer and 20 hours in a second job is $1,000. Point *B* therefore shifts down by $200, and the slope of the budget constraint between 0 and 20 hours of leisure becomes -10, reflecting the lower wage in the second job.

Of course, not all employers will choose to respond to overtime regulations by prohibiting work beyond 40 hours a week. If your employer permits you to choose freely the number of hours you work in the presence of overtime regulations, your budget constraint would change differently. While the segment between *E* and *C* would remain unchanged (since it deals with hours of work below 40 per week), the most consumption you could engage in if you worked the full 60 hours would increase to $1,400 because your last 20 hours of leisure could now be sold for $30 per hour: the $20 wage plus the required 50% overtime pay. The resulting budget constraint would again be kinked at *C* but would now point inward rather than outward, as in Graph 3.2b.

Different kinds of taxes and subsidies also have important effects on the choice sets that workers face. Suppose, for instance, the government imposes a 25% tax on all wages and suppose that your employer continues to pay you only $20 per hour.[2] Then your take-home pay is only $15 per hour, and your budget constraint would rotate counterclockwise around the endowment point *E* (with a new consumption intercept of $900 instead of $1,200). While this is an example of a *proportional wage tax*, a tax that collects revenues from workers in strict proportion to their wage income, most real-world taxes are significantly more complicated. Often, tax rates imposed on wage income increase as income rises, but sometimes the reverse is true. For instance, while U.S. federal income tax rates increase with income, U.S. Social Security tax rates decrease (to zero) as income rises. And, for workers in low-income families, the United States has programs to subsidize wages up to a certain level of income through what is known as the Earned Income Tax Credit. These kinds of tax and subsidy systems can create important kinks in leisure/consumption budget sets, kinks that we explore more in end-of-chapter exercises.

---

[2]Under certain assumptions, employers and employees end up sharing the burden of a tax on wages, a scenario we are abstracting away from here. We will discuss this in more detail in later chapters.

3A.2 Constraints We Face in Planning for the Future

In our choices as consumers (Chapter 2), the prices of different goods and the money we have available for spending on these goods combine to form our choice sets. In our choices as workers (Section 3A.1), our available time endowment combined with the wage rates we are able to command in the market form similar choice sets that illustrate the trade-offs we face between working and leisuring. We now turn to a final important set of trade-offs, those involving our planning for the future as we decide whether to delay immediate gratification by saving rather than consuming today or by limiting the degree to which we borrow against our future income. By saving, we generate an asset that, like the time we sell in labor markets, we can later sell in order to consume. By borrowing, on the other hand, we are in effect selling a future asset in order to consume today.

3A.2.1 Planning for Next Year: Intertemporal Budget Constraints   Suppose that you have accepted a summer job for a total of 500 hours at $20 per hour. You therefore know that you will earn a total of $10,000 this summer. Suppose further that you would like not to work next summer because you and your significant other would like to go off to spend a summer exploring the Amazon. Your significant other is a philosopher, steeped in deep thought but utterly unconcerned about money and fully dependent on your financial support during summers. Both of you have full financial aid during the academic year and therefore need money only during summers.

Recognizing that it will be difficult to explore the Amazon on an empty stomach, you decide to plan for next summer with the income you earn this summer. We can illustrate the trade-offs you face by putting "dollars of consumption this summer" on the horizontal axis and "dollars of consumption next summer" on the vertical axis. (Notice that we have chosen to lump all forms of consumption in each summer period together and treat it as a composite good in order to make the analysis manageable in a two-dimensional picture.) You could decide to spend all your income this summer on current consumption, thus obtaining $10,000 worth of consumption for you and your significant other this summer with nothing but your love to sustain you next summer (point E in Graph 3.3a). On the other extreme, you could starve yourselves this summer in anticipation of

Graph 3.3: Different Types of Intertemporal Budget Constraints

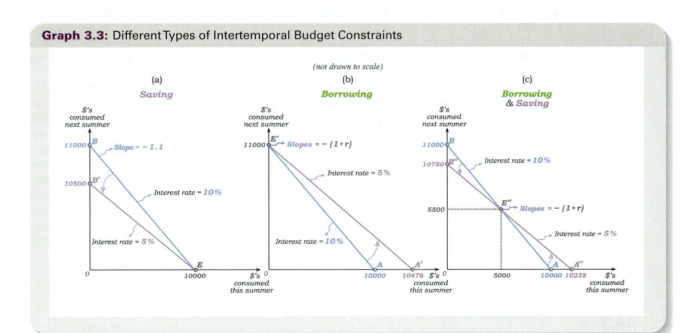

feasting next summer. In that case, you could put the $10,000 in the bank and earn interest for a year. Suppose the annual interest rate is 10%. This would permit you a maximum of $11,000 in consumption next year if you choose to forego all consumption this summer (point *B*). Or you could choose any point on the line connecting points *E* and *B*, a line whose slope of −1.1 illustrates the opportunity cost of consuming a dollar this summer as $1.10 in foregone consumption next summer. More generally, *the opportunity cost of consuming a dollar today is 1 plus the (annual) interest rate (expressed in decimal form) in foregone consumption one year from now.* Such budget constraints that illustrate trade-offs faced over time are often called *intertemporal budget constraints*.

Notice that, for purposes of this model, we are treating this summer's income as your endowment (point *E*). Regardless of what the prices are in the economy (where the interest rate is the important price for our current analysis), you can always choose to consume this endowment; i.e., you can always choose simply to consume all $10,000 now. As the interest rate changes, however, the rest of your budget constraint will rotate through that point. For instance, if the interest rate falls to 5%, the maximum you will be able to consume next summer is $10,500 (point *B'* in Graph 3.3a), and the new slope (of the magenta budget line) illustrates the new opportunity cost of consuming a dollar this year.

Now suppose that your philosopher friend decides the Amazon cannot wait another day and that you must spend this rather than next summer travelling together through the rainforest. Since you have no savings, you can do this only by borrowing against your future income. Your employer agrees to write a note to the bank letting them know that you can work for her next year for a summer salary of $11,000. Let's suppose the interest rate is still 10%. When plotting your budget constraint across the two summers, you know that one possibility would be for you to borrow nothing and thus have the entire $11,000 for consumption next summer (point *E'* in Graph 3.3b). Alternatively, you could borrow the maximum amount the bank will lend you and consume all of it this year. Since the bank knows that you can pay back up to $11,000 next summer, it will lend you up to $10,000 now (knowing that this will mean that you will owe $11,000 next year when the 10% interest has been figured into your debt). Point *A* therefore lies at $10,000 on the "dollars of consumption this summer" axis.

Notice that now we are treating your income next summer as your endowment that you can consume regardless of what the interest rate is, which means that your budget line will rotate through point *E'* as the interest rate changes. Thus, for any given interest rate *r* (expressed in decimal form), the budget line will run through point *E'* with slope −(1 + *r*), which is the opportunity cost of borrowing and consuming a dollar (and then having to pay it back with interest next year). Graph 3.3b illustrates a decrease in the interest rate from 10% to 5% as the change from the initial blue to the new magenta budget line.

Finally, suppose that you are able to convince your philosopher friend that it might be best to split your Amazon trip over two summers and thus to work both half of this summer and half of next summer. Your employer is willing to play along, giving you a $5,000 summer salary this year and promising a $5,500 summer salary next year. In this case, your endowment point—the point that does not depend on the interest rate—is given by a new point *E″* (in Graph 3.3c) where you consume $5,000 this year and $5,500 next year. At an interest rate of 10%, you could save all of your current summer pay and consume a total of $11,000 next summer, or you could borrow $5,000 from the bank and consume as much as $10,000 this summer (with no consumption next summer). As the interest rate changes, your budget line would continue to go through your endowment point *E″* (since you can always just consume what you make when you make it) with a slope −(1 + *r*). Graph 3.3c then illustrates a change in the interest rate from 10% to 5%.

Exercise
3A.2

Verify the dollar quantities on the axes in Graph 3.3a–c.

Exercise 3A.3

In each of the panels of Graph 3.3, how would the choice set change if the interest rate went to 20%?

3A.2.2 Planning for Several Years into the Future

Our analysis becomes a little more complex as we think of planning beyond a year from now. Suppose, for instance, that you and your philosopher friend are required to go to summer school next summer in order to complete your degrees and thus you won't be able to go on your Amazon adventure until two years from now. Since you will be in school next summer, parental and financial aid support will fully cover your expenses between this summer and two summers from now, but you are responsible for covering this summer and your Amazon summer in two years. Again, suppose your summer job this year pays $10,000 and the annual interest rate is 10%.

We can now illustrate your budget constraint across the two summers, with "dollars of consumption this summer" on the horizontal axis and "dollars of consumption two years from now" on the vertical. Point E in Graph 3.3a remains unchanged: You can always just decide to consume everything this summer and nothing two summers from now. But how much could you consume two years from now if you saved everything?

We know that if you put $10,000 in the bank for a year, you will have $11,000 in the bank one year from now. To see what you would have two years from now, we can just repeat the exercise and see how much interest you will get if you keep $11,000 in the bank for one more year. Since 10% of $11,000 is $1,100, we can see that you could have as much as $12,100 in consumption two summers from now if you consume none of your current summer income.

More generally, suppose the annual interest rate is r (expressed in decimal form). Keeping $10,000 in the bank for a year will result in a bank balance of $10,000(1 + r)$. Keeping this new balance of $10,000(1 + r)$ in the bank for an additional year will give you a bank balance of this new amount times $(1 + r)$ two years from now, or $10,000(1 + r)(1 + r)$, or $10,000(1 + r)^2$. The opportunity cost of 1 dollar of consumption this summer is therefore $(1 + r)^2$. Then, if we think yet another summer ahead, we would have $(1 + r)$ times the bank balance after three summers, or $10,000(1 + r)^2(1 + r)$ or $10,000(1 + r)^3$. You can begin to see the pattern: Putting $10,000 in the bank this summer will yield a bank balance of $10,000(1 + r)^n$ if we leave the account untouched for n summers.

Exercise 3A.4

So far, we have implicitly assumed that interest compounds yearly; i.e., you begin to earn interest on interest only at the end of each year. Often, interest compounds more frequently. Suppose that you put $10,000 in the bank now at an annual interest rate of 10% but that interest compounds monthly rather than yearly. Your monthly interest rate is then 10/12 or 0.833%. Defining n as the number of months and using the information in the previous paragraph, how much would you have in the bank after one year? Compare this to the amount we calculated you would have when interest compounds annually.

Graph 3.4 is then a generalized version of the first two panels of Graph 3.3, where instead of thinking about the choice between consuming now and a year from now we are modeling the choice between consuming now and n years from now. In Graph 3.4a, we are assuming that X is earned this summer and a portion of it potentially saved for use n summers later. Thus, the endowment point E lies on the horizontal axis. In Graph 3.4b, on the other hand, we are assuming that Y will be earned n summers from now, and a portion of this may be borrowed for current consumption. Assuming the interest rate for borrowing and saving is the same, we then get two budget constraints with the same slope but with different endowment points.

Graph 3.4: Intertemporal Choice Sets when Planning *n* Years Ahead

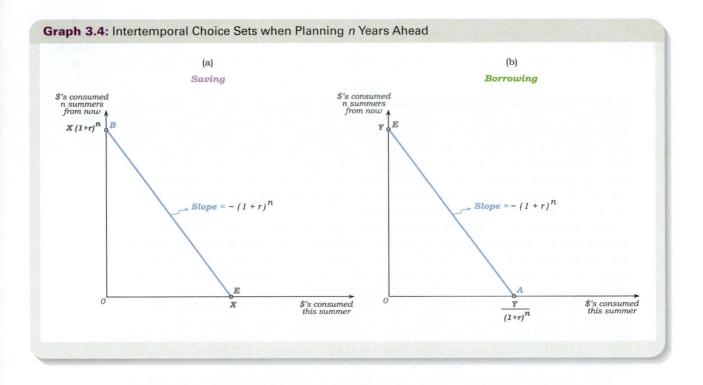

Exercise
3A.5

Suppose you just inherited $100,000 and you are trying to choose how much of this to consume now and how much of it to save for retirement 20 years from now. Illustrate your choice set with "dollars of consumption now" and "dollars of consumption 20 years from now" assuming an interest rate of 5% (compounded annually). What happens if the interest rate suddenly jumps to 10% (compounded annually)?

3A.2.3 More Complex Financial Planning   This two-period model used to analyze financial planning is limiting in the sense that it is difficult to model the full complexity of savings and consumption possibilities as consumers earn income over multiple periods and plan for consumption over those same periods. As we will see throughout this book, we will nevertheless be able to generate substantial intuitions using this two-period model. At the same time, we can use a more mathematical and less graphical approach to investigate choice sets that are difficult to handle in a graphical model. We turn to this more mathematical approach in Section B to this chapter. For those interested in finance applications, we also include end-of-chapter exercises 3.9 through 3.14 that tackle a number of more complex financial planning applications using the basic tools developed here.

3A.3 Putting It All into a Single Model

Between this chapter and Chapter 2, we have now demonstrated how to model choice sets for different types of individuals in the economy: consumers, workers, and financial planners (i.e., borrowers and savers). In the real world, of course, all three types are typically present in the same individual as we work in order to consume and plan for the future by saving or borrowing. While we will demonstrate throughout the book that it is often quite useful to model our choices as workers, consumers, and financial planners separately depending on the type of real-world issue we are trying to address, it is in principle possible also to merge these separate models into a single framework in order to analyze simultaneously the full choice set faced by an individual that undertakes multiple roles within an economy. This is most easily done with the mathematical tools explored in part B of this chapter, but we can also get a glimpse of how this is accomplished in a somewhat more complex graphical model.

Suppose, for example, we return to your decision regarding how much to work this summer. In Section 3A.1, we analyzed the choice set you face when making this decision, but we assumed that your only two options were to consume or leisure *this summer*. Now suppose that your life is more complicated because you are simultaneously planning for the Amazon trip with your philosopher friend next summer. In Section 3A.2, we analyzed your choice set as you are planning for next summer, but we assumed that you had already decided how much you were going to work this summer. Now we can think about what your choice set will look like when you are trying to decide how much to work this summer *and* how you will split your consumption across this and next summer. We thus need a three-dimensional graph such as Graph 3.5, with leisure hours this summer on one axis and consumption this summer and next summer on the other two axes.

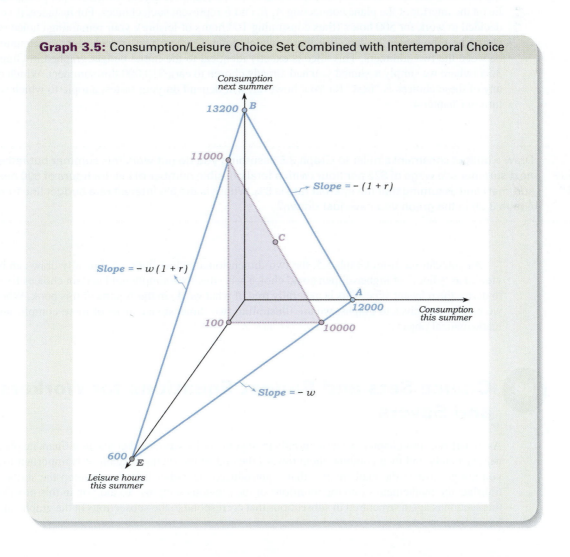

Graph 3.5: Consumption/Leisure Choice Set Combined with Intertemporal Choice

Suppose that you have up to 600 leisure hours this summer, 60 per week for 10 weeks. Also suppose that you can earn a wage of $20 per hour and that the annual interest rate is 10%. Your endowment point, the point that remains in your choice set no matter what wages and interest rates prevail in the economy, is point E at which you simply consume all of your leisure time leaving you with no goods to consume this summer or next. If you decided to consume nothing next summer, your choice set would simply lie on the bottom plane of the graph defined by the budget line that connects A and E. This choice set is much like the choice sets we graphed in Section 3A.1 where you simply considered your trade-off between consuming and leisuring *this summer.* Similarly, if you decided to consume no leisure, your choice set would collapse to a two-dimensional picture in the vertical plane that contains the budget line connecting A and B. This is similar to the types of choice sets we analyzed in Section 3A.2 where you were simply choosing between consuming a given amount now or next year. Finally, in the panel containing E and B, we graph the choice set assuming that you will consume no goods this summer. In that case, for every hour that you work, you will make $20 plus $2 in interest, for a total of $22 of consumption next summer. The opportunity cost of an hour of leisure time is therefore $22 of foregone consumption a year from now, which is your wage w times $(1 + r)$.

Your "best" choice in a choice set such as this will of course most likely involve some leisuring this summer, some consumption now, and some consumption a year from now. All points that lie on the interior of the plane connecting A, B, and E represent such choices. For instance, if you decided to work for 500 hours (thus consuming 100 hours of leisure), your remaining choice set would be represented by the slice that contains point C where you spread your consumption between the two summers. This slice is exactly identical to the initial budget graphed in Graph 3.3a (where we simply assumed you had already chosen to earn $10,000 this summer). Which of any of these choices is "best" for you, however, will depend on your tastes, a topic to which we turn in Chapter 4.

Exercise 3A.6* Draw a budget constraint similar to Graph 3.5 assuming you do not work this summer but rather next summer at a wage of $22 per hour (with a total possible number of leisure hours of 600 next summer) and assuming that the interest rate is 5%. Where is the 5% interest rate budget line from Graph 3.3b in the graph you have just drawn?

As you can see from Graph 3.5, the two-dimensional budget lines we typically draw can be viewed as "slices" of higher-dimensional choice sets where we simply hold certain choices fixed to derive the relevant slice. This is generally true of what we do in the A parts of this book. When we restrict ourselves to graphs, we are illustrating two-dimensional slices of more complicated mathematical objects.

3B Choice Sets and Budget Equations for Workers and Savers

As in part A of this chapter, we will initially treat your choices as a worker and as a financial planner separately and then combine them toward the end of the section. Again, it is important that you not get lost in the mathematics that is introduced but rather that you develop the skills to translate the mathematics into the intuitions of the previous sections. To aid you in this process, this section is again structured in subsections that correspond to the subsections in the graphically based Section 3A.

3B.1 Choice Sets of Workers

In Section 3A, we simplified the choices workers face as leisuring (and thus not working) and consuming a composite good. Taking less leisure implies greater consumption opportunities as income is generated endogenously from reducing leisure hours and thus increasing hours committed to working. This model of worker choice sets can be translated into mathematics straightforwardly using the tools we already developed for consumer choice sets in Chapter 2.

3B.1.1 Translating the Leisure/Consumption Graph into Math

We began in Section 3A.1.1 with an example in which we assumed you had a leisure endowment of 60 hours per week and could earn an hourly wage of $20. Letting c denote "weekly dollars of consumption" and letting ℓ denote "weekly hours of leisure consumption," your choice set was defined as all those combinations of c and ℓ where c is affordable given $20 is earned for each of the 60 hours of leisure endowment that is not consumed. Put differently, you are constrained to a choice set of combinations of c and ℓ such that

$$c \leq 20(60 - \ell). \tag{3.1}$$

The budget line is simply the same equation with the inequality replaced by an equality. Taking this budget line equation and multiplying out the terms, this gives

$$c = 1200 - 20\ell, \tag{3.2}$$

which is exactly the equation we derived intuitively in Graph 3.1.

More generally, we could let our hours of leisure endowment be given by L and the hourly wage by w. Our choice set as a worker would then be given by

$$C(w,L) = \left\{ (c,\ell) \in \mathbb{R}^2_+ \mid c \leq w(L - \ell) \right\}, \tag{3.3}$$

with a budget line given by

$$B(w,L) = \left\{ (c,\ell) \in \mathbb{R}^2_+ \mid c = w(L - \ell) \right\}. \tag{3.4}$$

Notice that only a single price appears in the budget line equation—w, the price of labor. Implicitly we have again taken the price of c to be 1, since $1 of consumption costs exactly $1.

Of course there may be times that economists would like to model the components of c more specifically, perhaps to investigate how particular public policies toward labor income might influence not only our consumption overall but also our consumption of particular goods that might be more or less complementary to leisure. This would clearly be difficult with our graphical models of Section 3A, models that necessarily limit us to two dimensions. But with the mathematical tools developed in the previous chapter, it now becomes quite easy to extend our model of leisure/consumption choice sets to multiple consumption goods.

Suppose, for example, that we are interested in your weekly consumption of n different goods—$x_1, x_2, \ldots, x_n$—and how your consumption of those goods relates to your decisions in the labor market where you have a weekly leisure endowment L that you can sell at wage w. Your choice set is then simply defined as all those combinations of the n different goods that you can afford at their market prices $(p_1, p_2, \ldots, p_n)$ given how much leisure you sold in the labor market; i.e.,

$$C(p_1, p_2, \ldots, p_n, w, L)$$
$$= \left\{ (x_1, x_2, \ldots, x_n, \ell) \in \mathbb{R}^{n+1}_+ \mid p_1 x_1 + p_2 x_2 + \cdots + p_n x_n \leq w(L - \ell) \right\}. \tag{3.5}$$

Graph the choice set in equation (3.5) when $n = 2$, $p_1 = 1$, $p_2 = 2$, $w = 20$, and $L = 60$.

Exercise 3B.1

3B.1.2 Government Policies and Labor Market Choice Sets   As we noted in Section 3A, a variety of government policies have a direct impact on labor markets and thus on our choice sets of workers. We discussed in particular the potential impacts of overtime legislation and the possible kinks in budget lines within the leisure/consumption graph that might result. Such kinks can of course also be formalized within the mathematical framework explored here, as we have already shown for other examples in Section 2B.

Exercise 3B.2   Translate the choice sets graphed in Graph 3.2 into mathematical notation defining the choice sets.

One particular policy that labor economists often focus on relates to wage taxes. Suppose, for instance, that a government tax on wages results in a tax paid by workers of t percent (expressed in decimal form).[3] Then instead of earning w for every hour of leisure that a worker chooses to sell in the labor market, he now only gets to take home $(1 - t)w$ because the government collects tw in wage taxes from the worker. This then changes the budget line in the leisure/consumption model from the equation that appears in (3.4) to

$$c = (1 - t)w(L - \ell). \tag{3.6}$$

As we multiply out some of the terms in parentheses, we can write this same equation as

$$c = (1 - t)wL - (1 - t)w\ell, \tag{3.7}$$

with the first term on the right-hand side representing the intercept term and the second term representing the slope. Graphically, this implies that the intercept term falls from wL—the amount of consumption we could have had before taxes had we consumed no leisure—to $(1 - t)wL$. Similarly, the slope term falls in absolute value, indicating that the slope of the budget line becomes shallower. Finally, we can verify our intuition that the intercept on the leisure axis remains unchanged by setting c to zero and solving for ℓ. Adding $(1 - t)w\ell$ to both sides and dividing by $(1 - t)w$ then gives us the result that $\ell = L$; our leisure when we have no other consumption is simply equal to our leisure endowment.

Exercise 3B.3   Suppose $w = 20$ and $L = 60$. Graph the budget constraint in the absence of taxes. Then suppose a wage tax $t = 0.25$ is introduced. Illustrate how this changes your equation and the graph.

Exercise 3B.4   How would the budget line equation change if, instead of a tax on wages, the government imposed a tax on all consumption goods such that the tax paid by consumers equaled 25% of consumption. Show how this changes the equation and the corresponding graph of the budget line.

3B.2 Choice Sets as We Plan for the Future

The second set of choice sets we introduced in Section 3A of this chapter involved graphical illustrations of trade-offs we face as we plan current and future consumption. Translating these into mathematical formulations involves exactly the same techniques as we have now applied for

---

[3]We will discuss how much of a wage tax is paid by workers rather than employers in Chapter 19.

consumer and worker choice sets, and the more general framework that arises from this again opens possibilities for analyzing significantly more complex decisions guided by the same economic intuitions developed with graphical techniques.

3B.2.1 Planning for Next Year: Intertemporal Budgets

We began our discussion about saving and borrowing in Section 3A within an initially simple example of you and your friend saving some of your earnings from this summer to go on a trip to the Amazon next summer. We then investigated various changes in this scenario, considering the case of borrowing by assuming you will earn income next summer as well as the case where you split both your trip and your summer income between the two summers. These scenarios differed in terms of what endowment point we began with, or which bundle in the model was unaffected by changes in prices such as interest rates.

We can generalize our discussion on planning between two periods by simply letting e_1 and e_2 denote the amount of income you expect to earn this summer and next summer and letting r denote the interest rate in decimal form. (For simplicity, we will continue to assume here that the interest rate for borrowing and saving is the same and that interest compounds annually.) In the initial scenario in Section 3A, we assumed $e_1 = 10,000$ and $e_2 = 0$, whereas in the other scenarios we assumed first $e_1 = 0$ and $e_2 = 11,000$ and then $e_1 = 5,000$ and $e_2 = 5,500$. These are graphed in panels (a), (b), and (c) of Graph 3.3 respectively.

Your consumption set across the two summers is then a pair (c_1, c_2), with c_1 representing consumption this summer and c_2 representing consumption next summer. This pair has to be feasible given the endowments you have and the interest rate you face in the market. We can see most easily how this translates to a budget line equation by first determining how much you *could have* available for consumption next summer *if you consumed nothing this summer*, which is just the sum of the endowments in the two summers $(e_1 + e_2)$ plus the interest you could have earned between the two summers on the first summer's endowment (re_1) for a total of $(1 + r)e_1 + e_2$. Then, for every \$1 you want to consume this year, you will have to decrease your consumption next year by $(1 + r)$. So the most you will actually have for consumption next summer is what you could have had if you had consumed nothing this summer $(1 + r)e_1 + e_2$ minus $(1 + r)$ times your actual consumption this summer (c_1), or

$$c_2 \le (1 + r)e_1 + e_2 - (1 + r)c_1, \tag{3.8}$$

which can also be written as

$$c_2 \le (1 + r)(e_1 - c_1) + e_2. \tag{3.9}$$

When written in this form, the equation should have particular intuitive appeal: The term $(e_1 - c_1)$ is the difference between your period 1 endowment and your period 1 consumption, or just your savings. When you multiply what's in your savings account by $(1 + r)$, that gives you your savings account balance a year from now $(1 + r)(e_1 - c_1)$. Together with your year 2 endowment e_2, that's the most you can consume next year.

Suppose $(e_1 - c_1)$ is negative; i.e., suppose you are borrowing rather than saving in period 1. Can you still make intuitive sense of the equation?

Exercise 3B.5

Using equation (3.8) with $(1 + r)c_1$ added to both sides, we can then define your choice set as a function of your endowments and the interest rate:

$$C(e_1, e_2, r) = \left\{ (c_1, c_2) \in \mathbb{R}_+^2 \mid (1 + r)c_1 + c_2 \le (1 + r)e_1 + e_2 \right\}. \tag{3.10}$$

Note that the budget constraint in equation (3.10) is written in terms of dollars *next* summer. It could equivalently be written in terms of dollars *this* summer by dividing both sides by $(1 + r)$, giving us

$$C(e_1, e_2, r) = \left\{ (c_1, c_2) \in \mathbb{R}^2_+ \mid c_1 + \frac{c_2}{(1 + r)} \leq e_1 + \frac{e_2}{(1 + r)} \right\}. \tag{3.11}$$

Exercise 3B.6 Use the information behind each of the scenarios graphed in Graph 3.3 to plug into equation (3.8) that scenario's relevant values for e_1, e_2, and r. Then demonstrate that the budget lines graphed are consistent with the underlying mathematics of equation (3.8), and more generally, make intuitive sense of the intercept and slope terms as they appear in equation (3.8).

3B.2.2 Planning for Several Years into the Future More generally, we demonstrated intuitively in Section 3A.2.2 that planning over multiple time periods is similar to planning over one period, except that the relevant opportunity cost of consuming a dollar today changes from $(1 + r)$ to $(1 + r)^n$, where n is the number of time periods over which we plan. For instance, if you plan to allocate income you expect to earn this summer and income you plan to earn n summers from now between consumption this summer and consumption n summers from now, your choice set is a simple extension of the choice set derived in the expression (3.10), with $(1 + r)$ replaced by $(1 + r)^n$:

$$C(e_1, e_n, r) = \left\{ (c_1, c_n) \in \mathbb{R}^2_+ \mid (1 + r)^n c_1 + c_n \leq (1 + r)^n e_1 + e_n \right\}. \tag{3.12}$$

3B.2.3 More Complex Financial Planning When looking at the choice set as described in equation (3.12), an immediate question that might occur to us is what happened to all the summers in between the current summer and the summer n years from now? Are we not consuming or earning income in those summers? Should those not be part of our planning as well?

The answer, of course, is that we were limited in Section 3A by our graphical tools: We only had room to graph two dimensions and thus could only graph planning over two periods, whether those were 1 or n years apart. With a more mathematical approach, however, we can easily define much more complex choice sets in which individuals can see their full consumption possibilities across many periods at one time. Suppose, for instance, that I have some expectation about what I will earn not only this year but also for each of the upcoming $(n - 1)$ years. Thus, I have a total of n different "endowments" spread across n years, endowments we can denote $(e_1, e_2, \ldots, e_n)$. Suppose further that I expect the annual interest rate across the next n years to be constant at r. If I consumed nothing until the last year, I would end up having the last year's endowment e_n plus the next to last year's endowment with one year's worth of interest on that endowment $((1 + r)e_{n-1})$, plus the second to last year's endowment (e_{n-2}) with two year's worth of interest on that endowment $((1 + r)^2 e_{n-2})$, etc. Thus, if all my consumption occurred in the last year, I could consume

$$c_n = e_n + (1 + r)e_{n-1} + (1 + r)^2 e_{n-2} + \cdots + (1 + r)^{n-1} e_{n-(n-1)}. \tag{3.13}$$

Now, for every dollar that I consume in the next to last period, the amount left over for my consumption in the last period declines by $(1 + r)$, and for every dollar that I consume in the second to last period, the amount left over for my consumption in the last period declines by $(1 + r)^2$, etc.

Thus, while I *could* consume in the last period as much as indicated in equation (3.13), the *actual* amount I can consume depends on how much I consumed in the previous periods:

$$c_n = e_n + (1 + r)e_{n-1} + (1 + r)^2 e_{n-2} + \cdots + (1 + r)^{n-1} e_1$$
$$- (1 + r)c_{n-1} - (1 + r)^2 c_{n-2} - \cdots - (1 + r)^{n-1} c_1 \qquad (3.14)$$

or, with consumption terms grouped on the left-hand side and two of the subscripts simplified,

$$c_n + (1 + r)c_{n-1} + (1 + r)^2 c_{n-2} + \cdots + (1 + r)^{n-1} c_1$$
$$= e_n + (1 + r)e_{n-1} + (1 + r)^2 e_{n-2} + \cdots + (1 + r)^{n-1} e_1. \qquad (3.15)$$

Our two-period graphical simplification is then a special case of a more complex choice set, a simplification where the consumption and endowment terms for all but two periods are simply assumed to net out to zero. In our framework of individuals attempting to "do the best they can given their circumstances," translating the graphical model into mathematics thus permits us to specify much richer and more realistic circumstances as we investigate how individuals might plan for the future. The basic insights developed here also allow us to investigate some common financial planning issues that are covered in end-of-chapter exercises 3.9 through 3.14 for those with a particular interest in finance-related topics.

Suppose you expect to earn $10,000 this summer, $0 next summer, and $15,000 two summers from now. Using c_1, c_2, and c_3 to denote consumption over these three summers, write down your budget constraint assuming an annual (and annually compounding) interest rate of 10%. Then illustrate this constraint on a three-dimensional graph with c_1, c_2, and c_3 on the three axes. How does your equation and graph change if the interest rate increases to 20%?

Exercise 3B.7*

3B.3 Putting It All in a Single Model

At the conclusion of Section 3A, we briefly explored a three-dimensional graphical example in which a leisure endowment this summer can translate into consumption both this summer and next summer. Specifically, we graphed your choice set under the assumption that you had a particular leisure endowment this summer and you were simultaneously evaluating how much to work this summer and how much to consume over the next two summers, assuming that you would not work any more next summer.

Your income this summer thus depends on how much leisure ℓ you choose to consume this summer, with your income equal to your hourly wage w times the portion of your time endowment L not consumed as leisure, or $w(L - \ell)$. If you choose not to consume any of this income this summer and you put it all in the bank, you would have a total of

$$(1 + r)w(L - \ell) \qquad (3.16)$$

available for consumption next summer. And, for each dollar you do choose to consume this summer, you will have $(1 + r)$ less in consumption next summer. Thus, your consumption c_2 next summer is equal to the most you could have consumed had you not consumed anything this summer minus $(1 + r)$ times what you actually do consume this summer (c_1), or

$$c_2 = (1 + r)w(L - \ell) - (1 + r)c_1. \qquad (3.17)$$

This (with the consumption terms grouped on one side of the equation) then defines the budget constraint as

$$B(L,w,r) = \{(c_1,c_2,\ell) \in \mathbb{R}^3_+ \mid (1 + r)c_1 + c_2 = (1 + r)w(L - \ell)\}. \qquad (3.18)$$

Exercise 3B.8*

When $L = 600$, $w = 20$, and $r = 0.1$, show how equation (3.18) translates directly into Graph 3.5.

It is worth noting once again at this point that whenever we limit ourselves to graphical models in two dimensions, we are essentially holding something in a larger dimensional choice set fixed. For instance, when we graphed your initial choice set between consuming this summer and consuming next summer in Graph 3.3a, we assumed that your labor/leisure decision this summer had already been made and had resulted in 500 hours of labor. When analyzing consumption choices over two periods in a two-dimensional model, we therefore are really operating on a "slice" of a three-dimensional model, a slice where something has been held fixed. In our example, this slice occurs at the fixed leisure consumption of 100 hours (with the 500 remaining hours earning the $10,000 income that makes $10,000 of consumption this summer (or $11,000 in consumption next summer) possible). Mathematically, this slice is simply

$$B(r) = \left\{ (c_1, c_2) \in \mathbb{R}^2_+ \mid (1 + r)c_1 + c_2 = (1 + r)(10{,}000) \right\}, \qquad (3.19)$$

where we have replaced labor income and time endowments with the "exogenous" current summer income of $10,000. This slice is depicted graphically in Graph 3.5

In the same way, the three-dimensional Graph 3.5 is also a "slice" of a yet higher dimensional choice set where something else has been held fixed. For instance, we have assumed in Graph 3.5 that you have decided not to work (i.e., not to sell leisure) next summer, thus permitting us to focus only on three dimensions. Adding the possibility of working next summer is easy to handle mathematically but impossible to graph.

Exercise 3B.9

Define mathematically a generalized version of the budget constraint in expression (3.18) under the assumption that you have both a leisure endowment L_1 this summer and another leisure endowment L_2 next summer. What is the value of L_2 in order for Graph 3.5 to be the correct three-dimensional "slice" of this four-dimensional choice set?

CONCLUSION

We have now concluded our initial modeling of choice sets. The message that emerges from Chapters 2 and 3 is that there are many ways in which we can model such choice sets graphically and mathematically and that the best model for a particular application will depend on the application. In some instances, we are simply interested in the impact on consumer choices of a particular price change, and it may be sufficient simply to model the choice a consumer faces over the good of interest and a composite consumption good under some exogenous income. Other times, we may be interested in situations where both the trade-offs a consumer faces as well as the amount of available money to make choices depends on prices, wages, and/or interest rates as individuals sell endowments to purchase consumption goods. As we discussed in Chapter 1, the key for the economist is often to find the simplest possible model that captures the most important aspects of a particular question we are interested in answering.

We are not, however, yet ready to really analyze choice, only choice sets. To analyze what choices individuals will actually make fully, we need to find ways of modeling not only what choices are available to them but also how these available choices will be evaluated depending on the tastes of the choosing individuals. We will begin our analysis of tastes in Chapter 4.

END-OF-CHAPTER EXERCISES

3.1 In this chapter, we graphed budget constraints illustrating the trade-off between consumption and leisure.

A. Suppose that your wage is $20 per hour and you have up to 60 hours per week that you could work.

    a. Now, instead of putting leisure hours on the horizontal axis (as we did in Graph 3.1), put labor hours on the horizontal axis (with consumption in dollars still on the vertical). What would your choice set and budget constraint look like now?

    b. Where on your graph would the endowment point be?

    c. What is the interpretation of the slope of the budget constraint you just graphed?

    d. If wages fall to $10 per hour, how does your graph change?

    e. If instead a new caffeine drink allows you to work up to 80 rather than 60 hours per week, how would your graph change?

B. How would you write the choice set over consumption c and labor l as a function of the wage w and leisure endowment L?

3.2 In our treatment of leisure/consumption trade-offs, we have assumed that you are deriving income solely from wages.

A. Suppose now that your grandparents set up a trust fund that pays you $300 per week. In addition, you have up to 60 hours of leisure that you could devote to work at a wage of $20 per hour.

    a. On a graph with "leisure hours per week" on the horizontal axis and "weekly consumption in dollars" on the vertical, illustrate your weekly budget constraint.

    b. Where in your graph is your endowment bundle?

    c. How does your graph change when your wage falls to $10?

    d. How does the graph change if instead the trust fund gets raided by your parents, leaving you with only a $100 payment per week?

B. How would you write your budget constraint described in 3.2A?

3.3*† You have $10,000 sitting in a savings account, 600 hours of leisure time this summer, and an opportunity to work at a $30 hourly wage.

A. Next summer is the last summer before you start working for a living, and so you plan to take the whole summer off and relax. You need to decide how much to work this summer and how much to spend on consumption this summer and next summer. Any investments you make for the year will yield a 10% rate of return over the coming year.

    a. On a three-dimensional graph with this summer's leisure (ℓ), this summer's consumption (c_1), and next summer's consumption (c_2) on the axes, illustrate your endowment point as well as your budget constraint. Carefully label your graph and indicate where the endowment point is.

    b. How does your answer change if you suddenly realize you still need to pay $5,000 in tuition for next year, payable immediately?

    c. How does your answer change if instead the interest rate doubles to 20%?

    d. In (b) and (c), which slopes are different than in (a)?

B. Derive the mathematical expression for your budget constraint in 3.3A and explain how elements of this expression relate to the slopes and intercepts you graphed.

3.4* Suppose you are a farmer whose land produces 50 units of food this year and is expected to produce another 50 units of food next year. (Assume that there is no one else in the world to trade with.)

---

*conceptually challenging
**computationally challenging
†solutions in Study Guide

A. On a graph with "food consumption this year" on the horizontal axis and "food consumption next year" on the vertical, indicate your choice set assuming there is no way for you to store food that you harvest this year for future consumption.

   a. Now suppose that you have a barn in which you can store food. However, over the course of a year, half the food that you store spoils. How does this change your choice set?

   b. Now suppose that, in addition to the food units you harvest off your land, you also own a cow. You could slaughter the cow this year and eat it for 50 units of food. Or you could let it graze for another year and let it grow fatter, then slaughter it next year for 75 units of food. But you don't have any means of refrigeration and so you cannot store meat over time. How does this alter your budget constraint (assuming you still have the barn from part (a))?

B. How would you write the choice set you derived in A(b) mathematically, with c_1 indicating this year's food consumption and c_2 indicating next year's food consumption?

3.5 Suppose you are a carefree 20-year-old bachelor whose lifestyle is supported by expected payments from a trust fund established by a relative who has since passed away. The trust fund will pay you \$$x$ when you turn 21 (a year from now), another \$$y$ when you turn 25, and \$$z$ when you turn 30. You plan to marry a rich heiress on your 30th birthday and therefore only have to support yourself for the next 10 years. The bank that maintains the trust account is willing to lend money to you at a 10% interest rate and pays 10% interest on savings. (Assume annual compounding.)

A. Suppose $x = y = z = 100{,}000$.

   a. What is the most that you could consume this year?

   b. What is the most you could spend at your bachelor party 10 years from now if you find a way to live without eating?

B. Define your 10-year intertemporal budget constraint mathematically in terms of x, y, and z, letting c_1 denote this year's consumption, c_2 next year's consumption, etc. Let the annual interest rate be denoted by r.

3.6 **Everyday Application:** *Robots as Labor-Saving Products*: Suppose that you have 60 hours per week of leisure time and that you can earn \$25 per hour in the labor market. Part of the reason you do not have more time to work is that you need to do a variety of household chores: cleaning, shopping for food, cooking, laundry, running errands, etc. Suppose that those chores take 20 hours of your time per week. Suddenly you see an advertisement in the newspaper: "Personal Robot can do the following: clean, shop, cook, do laundry, run errands, etc. Can be rented by the week."

A. Suppose you learn that the weekly rental fee is \$250 and that the robot could indeed do all the things that you currently spend 20 hours per week doing (outside the 60 hours of leisure you could be taking).

   a. Illustrate your new weekly budget constraint assuming you decide to rent the robot. Be sure to incorporate the fact that you have to pay \$250 each week for the robot, but assume that there is no consumption value in having a robot other than the time you are saved doing chores you would otherwise have to be doing. Are you better off with or without the robot?

   b. As it turns out, everyone else wants this robot as well, and so the rental price has increased to \$500 per week. How does this change your answer?

B. Incorporate the impact of the robot into the budget equation and illustrate how it leads to the graph you derived in 3.6A(a).

3.7 **Everyday Application:** *Investing for Retirement*: Suppose you were just told that you will receive a year-end bonus of \$15,000 from your company. Suppose further that your marginal income tax rate is 33.33%, which means that you will have to pay \$5,000 in income tax on this bonus. And suppose that you expect the average rate of return on an investment account you have set up with your broker to be 10% annually (and, for purposes of this example, assume interest compounds annually).

A. Suppose you have decided to save all of this bonus for retirement 30 years from now.

   a. In a regular investment account, you will have to pay taxes on the interest you earn each year. Thus, even though you earn 10%, you have to pay a third in taxes, leaving you with an after-tax return of 6.67%. Under these circumstances, how much will you have accumulated in your account 30 years from now?

b. An alternative investment strategy is to place your bonus into a 401K "tax-advantaged" retirement account. The federal government has set these up to encourage greater savings for retirement. They work as follows: You do not have to pay taxes on any income that you put directly into such an account if you put it there as soon as you earn it, and you do not have to pay taxes on any interest you earn. Thus, you can put the full $15,000 bonus into the 401K account, and you can earn the full 10% return each year for the next 30 years. You do, however, have to pay taxes on any amount that you choose to withdraw after you retire. Suppose you plan to withdraw the entire accumulated balance as soon as you retire 30 years from now, and suppose that you expect you will still be paying 33.33% taxes at that time. How much will you have accumulated in your 401K account, and how much will you have after you pay taxes? Compare this with your answer to (a); i.e., to the amount you would have at retirement if you saved outside the 401K plan.

c. *True or False*: By allowing individuals to defer paying taxes into the future, 401K accounts result in a higher rate of return for retirement savings.

B. Suppose more generally that you earn an amount I now, that you face (and will face in the future) a marginal tax rate of t (expressed as a fraction between 0 and 1), that the interest rate now (and in the future) is r, and that you plan to invest for n periods into the future.

a. How much consumption will you be able to undertake n years from now if you first pay your income tax on the amount I, then place the remainder in a savings account whose interest income is taxed each year. (Assume you add nothing further to the savings account between now and n years from now.)

b. Now suppose you put the entire amount I into a tax-advantaged retirement account in which interest income can accumulate tax-free. Any amount that is taken out of the account is then taxed as regular income. Assume you plan to take the entire balance in the account out n years from now (but nothing before then). How much consumption can you fund from this source n years from now?

c. Compare your answers to (a) and (b) and indicate whether you can tell which will be higher.

3.8 Everyday Application: *Different Interest Rates for Borrowing and Lending*: Suppose we return to the example from the text in which you earn $5,000 this summer and expect to earn $5,500 next summer.

A. In the real world, banks usually charge higher interest rates for borrowing than they will give on savings. So, instead of assuming that you can borrow and lend at the same interest rate, suppose the bank pays you an interest rate of 5% on anything you save but will lend you money only at an interest rate of 10%. (In this exercise, it helps *not* to draw everything to scale much as we did not draw intertemporal budgets to scale in the chapter.)

a. Illustrate your budget constraint with consumption this summer on the horizontal and consumption next summer on the vertical axis.

b. How would your answer change if the interest rates for borrowing and lending were reversed?

c. A set is defined as "convex" if the line connecting any two points in the set also lies in the set. Is the choice set in part (a) a convex set? What about the choice set in part (b)?

d. Which of the two scenarios would you prefer? Give both an intuitive answer that does not refer to your graphs and demonstrate how the graphs give the same answer.

B. Suppose more generally that you earn e_1 this year and e_2 next year and that the interest rate for borrowing is r_B and the interest rate for saving is r_S. Let c_1 and c_2 denote consumption this year and next year.

a. Derive the general expression for your intertemporal choice set under these conditions.

b. Check that your general expression is correct by substituting the values from A(a) and (b) and check that you get a choice set similar to those you derived intuitively.

3.9** Business Application: *Present Value of Winning Lottery Tickets*: The introduction to intertemporal budgeting in this chapter can be applied to thinking about the pricing of basic financial assets. The assets we will consider will differ in terms of when they pay income to the owner of the asset. In order to know how much such assets are worth, we have to determine their *present value*, which is equal to how much *current* consumption such an asset would allow us to undertake.

A. Suppose you just won the lottery and your lottery ticket is transferable to someone else you designate; i.e., you can sell your ticket. In each of the following cases, the lottery claims that you won $100,000. Since you can sell your ticket, it is a financial asset, but depending on how exactly the holder of the ticket receives the $100,000, the asset is worth different amounts. Think about what you would be willing to actually sell this asset for by considering how much *current* consumption value the asset contains assuming the annual interest rate is 10%.

   a.   The holder of the ticket is given a $100,000 government bond that "matures" in 10 years. This means that in 10 years, the owner of this bond can cash it for $100,000.

   b.   The holder of the ticket will be awarded $50,000 now and $50,000 ten years from now.

   c.   The holder of the ticket will receive 10 checks for $10,000: one now, and one on the next 9 anniversaries of the day he/she won the lottery.

   d.   How does your answer to part (c) change if the first of 10 checks arrived one year from now, with the second check arriving two years from now, the third arriving three years from now, etc.?

   e.   The holder of the ticket gets $100,000 the moment he/she presents the ticket.

B. More generally, suppose the lottery winnings are paid out in installments of $x_1, x_2, \ldots, x_{10}$, with payment x_i occurring $(i - 1)$ years from now. Suppose the annual interest rate is r.

   a.   Determine a formula for how valuable such a stream of income is in present day consumption; i.e., how much present consumption could you undertake given that the bank is willing to lend you money on future income?

   b.   Check to make sure that your formula works for each of the scenarios in part A.

   c.   The scenario described in part A(c) is an example of a $10,000 payment followed by an annual "annuity" payment. Consider an annuity that promises to pay out $10,000 every year starting 1 year from now for n years. How much would you be willing to pay for such an annuity?

   d.   How does your answer change if the annuity starts with its first payment now?

   e.   What if the annuity from (c) is one that never ends? (To give the cleanest possible answer to this, you should recall from your math classes that an infinite series of $1/(1 + x) + 1/(1 + x)^2 + 1/(1 + x)^3 + \ldots = 1/x$.) How much would this annuity be worth if the interest rate is 10%?

3.10   **Business Application:** *Picking Savings Accounts*: Suppose you just won $10,000 in the lottery. You decide to put it all in a savings account.

A. Bank A offers you a 10% annual interest rate that compounds annually, while Bank B offers you a 10% annual interest rate compounded every 6 months.

   a.   How much will you have in the bank at the end of the year if you go with Bank A?

   b.   How much will you have if you put your money into Bank B?

   c.   What annual interest rate would Bank A have to offer to make you indifferent between accepting Bank B's and Bank A's offers?

   d.   Would the interest rate you calculated in (c) be sufficient for you to be indifferent between Bank A and Bank B if you planned to keep your money in the savings account for two years?

B. Suppose you place x in a savings account and assume that the account gives an annual interest rate of r compounded n times per year.

   a.   Derive the general formula for how much y you will have accumulated one year from now in terms of x, n, and r. Check the answers you derived in (a) and (b) of part A.

   b.   If $x = 10,000$ and the annual interest rate $r = 0.1$, how much will you have at the end of the year if interest compounds monthly (i.e., $n = 12$)?

   c.   What if interest compounds weekly?

   d.   If you have to choose between an annual interest rate of 10.5% compounded annually or an annual interest rate of 10% compounded weekly, which would you choose?

3.11[†]   **Business Application:** *Compound Interest over the Long Run*: Uncle Vern has just come into some money ($100,000) and is thinking about putting this away into some investment accounts for a while.

A. Vern is a simple guy, so he goes to the bank and asks what the easiest option for him is. The bank tells him he could put it into a savings account with a 10% interest rate (compounded annually).

    a.   Vern quickly does some math to see how much money he'll have 1 year from now, 5 years from now, 10 years from now, and 25 years from now assuming he never makes withdrawals. He doesn't know much about compounding, so he just guesses that if he leaves the money in for 1 year, he'll have 10% more; if he leaves it in 5 years at 10% per year he'll have 50% more; if he leaves it in for 10 years he'll have 100% more and if he leaves it in for 25 years he'll have 250% more. How much does he expect to have at these different times in the future?

    b.   Taking the compounding of interest into account, how much will he really have?

    c.   On a graph with years on the horizontal axis and dollars on the vertical, illustrate the size of Vern's error for the different time intervals for which he calculated the size of his savings account.

    d.   *True/False*: Errors made by not taking the compounding of interest into account expand at an increasing rate over time.

B. Suppose that the annual interest rate is r.

    a.   Assuming you will put x into an account now and leave it in for n years, derive the implicit formula Vern used when he did not take into account interest compounding.

    b.   What is the correct formula that includes compounding?

    c.   Define a new function that is the difference between these. Then take the first and second derivatives with respect to n and interpret them.

3.12   **Business Application:** *Pricing Government Bonds*: A relative sends you a U.S. government savings bond that matures in n years with a face value of $100. This means that the holder of this bond is entitled to collect $100 from the government n years from now.

BUSINESS
APPLICATION

A. Suppose the interest rate is 10%.

    a.   If $n = 1$, how much *current* consumption could this bond finance, and how much do you therefore think you could sell this bond for today?

    b.   Does the bond become more or less valuable if the interest rate falls to 5%?

    c.   Now suppose that $n = 2$. How valuable is the bond if the interest rate is 10%?

    d.   What if $n = 10$?

B. Consider a bond that matures n years from now with face value x when the expected annual interest rate over this period is equal to r.

    a.   Derive the general formula for calculating the current consumption that could be financed with this bond.

    b.   Use a derivative to show what happens to the value of a bond as x changes.

    c.   Show similarly what happens to the value as r changes. Can you come to a general conclusion from this about the relationship between the interest rate and the price of bonds?

3.13* **Business Application:** *Buying Houses with Annuities*: Annuities are streams of payments that the owner of an annuity receives for some specified period of time. The holder of an annuity can sell it to someone else who then becomes the recipient of the remaining stream of payments that are still owed.

BUSINESS
APPLICATION

A. Some people who retire and own their own home finance their retirement by selling their house for an annuity: The buyer agrees to pay $$x$ per year for n years in exchange for becoming the owner of the house after n years.

    a.   Suppose you have your eye on a house down the street someone who recently retired owns. You approach the owner and offer to pay her $100,000 each year (starting next year) for 5 years in exchange for getting the house in 5 years. What is the value of the annuity you are offering her assuming the interest rate is 10%?

    b.   What if the interest rate is 5%?

    c.   The house's estimated current value is $400,000 (and your real estate agent assures you that homes are appreciating at the same rate as the interest rate). Should the owner accept your deal if the interest rate is 10%? What if it is 5%?

    d.   *True/False*: The value of an annuity increases as the interest rate increases.

    e.   Suppose that, after making the second payment on the annuity, you fall in love with someone from a distant place and decide to move there. The house has appreciated in value (from its starting value of $400,000) by 10% each of the past two years. You no longer want the house and therefore would like to sell your right to the house in three years in exchange for having someone else make the last 3 annuity payments. How much will you be able to get paid to transfer this contract to someone else if the annual interest rate is always 10%?

B. In some countries, retirees are able to make contracts similar to those in part A except that they are entitled to annuity payments until they die and the house only transfers to the new owner after the retiree dies.

    a.   Suppose you offer someone whose house is valued at $400,000 an annual annuity payment (beginning next year) of $50,000. Suppose the interest rate is 10% and housing appreciates in value at the interest rate. This will turn from a good deal to a bad deal for you when the person lives n number of years. What's n? (This might be easiest to answer if you open a spreadsheet and you program it to calculate the value of annuity payments into the future.)

    b.   Recalling that the sum of the infinite series $1/(1 + x) + 1/(1 + x)^2 + 1/(1 + x)^3 + \dots$ is $1/x$, what is the most you would be willing to pay in an annual annuity if you want to be absolutely certain that you are not making a bad deal?

3.14**†Business Application: *A Trick for Calculating the Value of Annuities*: In several of the previous exercises, we have indicated that an infinite series $1/(1 + r) + 1/(1 + r)^2 + 1/(1 + r)^3 + \dots$ sums to $1/r$. This can be (and has been, in some of the B-parts of exercises) used to calculate the value of an annuity that pays x per year starting next year and continuing every year eternally as x/r.

A. Knowing this information, we can use a trick to calculate the value of annuities that do not go on forever. For this example, consider an annuity that pays $10,000 per year for 10 years beginning next year, and assume $r = 0.1$.

    a.   First, calculate the value of an annuity that begins paying $10,000 next year and then every year thereafter (without end).

    b.   Next, suppose you are given such an annuity in 10 years; i.e., suppose you know that the first payment will come 11 years from now. What is the consumption value of such an annuity today?

    c.   Now consider this: Think of the 10-year annuity as the difference between an infinitely lasting annuity that starts making payments next year and an infinitely lasting annuity that starts 11 years from now. What is the 10-year annuity worth when you think of it in these terms?

    d.   Calculate the value of the same 10-year annuity without using the trick mentioned in part (c). Do you get the same answer?

B. Now consider more generally an annuity that pays x every year beginning next year for a period of n years when the interest rate is r. Denote the value of such an annuity as $y(x, n, r)$.

    a.   Derive the general formula for valuing such an annuity by using the trick described in part A.

    b.   Apply the formula to the following example: You are about to retire and have $2,500,000 in your retirement fund. You can take it all out as a lump sum, or you can choose to take an annuity that will pay you (and your heirs if you pass away) x per year (starting next year) for the next 30 years. What is the least x has to be in order for you to choose the annuity over the lump sum payment assuming an interest rate of 6%?

    c.   Apply the formula to another example: You can think of banks as accepting annuities when they give you a mortgage. Suppose you determine you would be able to pay at most $10,000 per year in mortgage payments. Assuming an interest rate of 10%, what is the most the bank will lend you on a 30-year mortgage (where the mortgage payments are made annually beginning one year from now)?

    d.   How does your answer change when the interest rate is 5%?

    e.   Can this explain how people in the late 1990s and early 2000s were able to finance increased current consumption as interest rates fell?

3.15   **Policy Application:** *Wage Taxes and Budget Constraints*: Suppose you have 60 hours of leisure that you could devote to work per week, and suppose that you can earn an hourly wage of $25.

    A. Suppose the government imposes a 20% tax on all wage income.

    a.   Illustrate your weekly budget constraint before and after the tax on a graph with weekly leisure hours on the horizontal and weekly consumption (measured in dollars) on the vertical axis. Carefully label all intercepts and slopes.

    b.   Suppose you decide to work 40 hours per week after the tax is imposed. How much wage tax do you pay per week? Can you illustrate this as a vertical distance in your graph? (*Hint*: Follow a method similar to that developed in end-of-chapter exercise 2.15.)

    c.   Suppose that instead of leisure hours on the horizontal axis, you put labor hours on this axis. Illustrate your budget constraints that have the same information as the ones you drew in (a).

B.   Suppose the government imposes a tax rate t (expressed as a rate between 0 and 1) on all wage income.

    a.   Write down the mathematical equations for the budget constraints and describe how they relate to the constraints you drew in A(a). Assume again that the leisure endowment is 60 per week.

    b.   Use your equation to verify your answer to part A(b).

    c.   Write down the mathematical equations for the budget constraints you derived in B(a) but now make consumption a function of labor, not leisure hours. Relate this to your graph in A(c).

3.16   **Policy Application:** *Proportional versus Progressive Wage Taxes*: The tax analyzed in exercise 3.15 is a *proportional* wage tax. The U.S. federal income tax, however, is *progressive*. This means that the *average* tax rate one pays increases the more wage income is earned.

A.   For instance, suppose the government exempts the first $500 of weekly earnings from taxation, then taxes the next $500 at 20% and any earnings beyond that at 40%. Suppose that you again have 60 hours of leisure per week and can earn $25 per hour.

    a.   Graph your weekly budget constraint illustrating the trade-offs between leisure and consumption.

    b.   The *marginal tax rate* is defined as the tax rate you pay for the next dollar you earn, while the *average tax rate* is defined as your total tax payment divided by your before-tax income. What is your average and marginal tax rate if you choose to work 20 hours per week?

    c.   How does your answer change if you work 30 hours? What if you work 40 hours?

    d.   On a graph with before-tax weekly income on the horizontal axis and tax rates on the vertical, illustrate how average and marginal tax rates change as income goes up. Will the average tax rate ever reach the top marginal tax rate of 0.4?

    e.   Some have proposed that the United States should switch to a "flat tax," a tax with one single marginal tax rate. Proponents of this tax reform typically also want some initial portion of income exempt from taxation. The flat tax therefore imposes two different marginal tax rates: a tax rate of zero for income up to some amount x per year, and a single rate t applied to any income earned above x per year. Is such a tax progressive?

B.   Suppose more generally that the government does not tax income below x per week; that it taxes income at t for anything above x and below $2x$, and it taxes additional income (beyond $2x$) at $2t$. Let I denote income per week.

    a.   Derive the average tax rate as a function of income and denote that function $a(I, t, x)$, where I represents weekly income.

    b.   Derive the marginal tax rate function $m(I, t, x)$.

3.17   **Policy Application:** *Social Security (or Payroll) Taxes*: Social Security is funded through a payroll tax that is separate from the federal income tax. It works in a way similar to the following example: For the first $1,800 in weekly earnings, the government charges a 15% wage tax but then charges no payroll tax for all earnings above $1,800 per week.

A.   Suppose that a worker has 60 hours of leisure time per week and can earn $50 per hour.

    a.   Draw this worker's budget constraint with weekly leisure hours on the horizontal axis and weekly consumption (in dollars) on the vertical.

    b.   Using the definitions given in exercise 3.16, what is the marginal and average tax rate for this worker assuming he works 30 hours per week? What if he works 40 hours per week? What if he works 50 hours per week?

    c.   A wage tax is called *regressive* if the average tax rate falls as earnings increase. On a graph with weekly before-tax income on the horizontal axis and tax rates on the vertical, illustrate the marginal and average tax rates as income increases. Is this tax regressive?

    d.   *True or False*: Budget constraints illustrating the trade-offs between leisure and consumption will have no kinks if a wage tax is proportional. However, if the tax system is designed with different tax brackets for different incomes, budget constraints will have kinks that point inward when a wage tax is regressive and kinks that point outward when a wage tax is progressive.

B. Consider the more general case of a tax that imposes a rate t on income immediately but then falls to zero for income larger than x.

    a.   Derive the average tax rate function $a(I, t, x)$ (where I represents weekly income).

    b.   Derive the marginal tax rate function $m(I, t, x)$.

    c.   Does the average tax rate reach the marginal tax rate for high enough income?

3.18*† **Policy Application:** *AFDC versus a Negative Income Tax*: Until the late 1990s, one of the primary federal welfare programs was Aid to Families with Dependent Children (AFDC). The program was structured similarly to the following example: Suppose you can work any number of hours you choose at $5 per hour and you have no income other than that which you earn by working. If you have zero overall income, the government pays you a welfare payment of $25 per day. You can furthermore receive your full welfare benefits so long as you make no more than a total income of $5 per day. For every dollar you earn beyond $5, the government reduces your welfare benefits by exactly a dollar until your welfare benefits go to zero.

A. Suppose you have up to 8 hours of leisure per day that you can dedicate to work.

    a.   Draw your budget constraint between daily leisure and daily consumption (measured in dollars).

    b.   If you define marginal tax rates in this example as the fraction of additional dollars earned in the labor market that a worker does not get to keep, what is the marginal tax rate faced by this worker when she is working 1 hour per day? What if she is working 5 hours per day? What if she is working 6 hours a day?

    c.   Without knowing anything about tastes, how many hours are you likely to work under these trade-offs?

    d.   The late Milton Friedman was critical of the incentives in the AFDC program and proposed a different mechanism for supporting the poor. He suggested a program, known as the negative income tax, that works something like this: Everyone is guaranteed $25 per day that he or she receives regardless of how much he or she works. Every dollar from working, starting with the first one earned, is then taxed at $t = 0.2$. Illustrate our worker's budget constraint assuming AFDC is replaced with such a negative income tax.

    e.   Which of these systems will almost certainly cost the government more for this worker: the AFDC system or the negative income tax? Which does the worker most likely prefer? Explain.

    f.   What part of your negative income tax graph would be different for a worker who earns $10 per hour?

    g.   Do marginal tax rates for an individual differ under the negative income tax depending on how much leisure he or she consumes? Do they differ across individuals?

B. Consider a more general version of the negative income tax, one that provides a guaranteed income y and then reduces this by some fraction t for every dollar earned, resulting eventually in individuals with sufficiently high income paying taxes.

    a.   Derive a general expression for the budget constraint under a negative income tax, a constraint relating daily consumption c (in dollars) to daily leisure hours ℓ assuming that at most 8 hours of leisure are available.

    b.   Derive an expression for how much the government will spend (or receive) for a given individual depending on how much leisure he or she takes.

    c.   Derive expressions for marginal and average tax rates as a function of daily income I, the guaranteed income level y, and the tax rate t. (*Hint*: Average tax rates can be negative.)

    d.   On a graph with daily before-tax income on the horizontal axis and tax rates on the vertical, illustrate how marginal and average tax rates change as income rises.

    e.   Is the negative income tax progressive?

3.19* **Policy Application:** *The Earned Income Tax Credit*: During the Clinton Administration, the Earned Income Tax Credit (EITC) was expanded considerably. The program provides a wage subsidy to low-income families through the tax code in a way similar to this example: Suppose, as in the previous exercise, that you can earn $5 per hour. Under the EITC, the government supplements your first $20 of daily earnings by 100% and the next $15 in daily earnings by 50%. For any daily income above $35, the government imposes a 20% tax.

POLICY APPLICATION

A. Suppose you have at most 8 hours of leisure time per day.

    a.   Illustrate your budget constraint (with daily leisure on the horizontal and daily consumption on the vertical axis) under this EITC.

    b.   Suppose the government ends up paying a total of $25 per day to a particular worker under this program and collects no tax revenue. Identify the point on the budget constraint this worker has chosen. How much is he or she working per day?

    c.   Return to your graph of the same worker's budget constraint under the AFDC program in exercise 3.18. Suppose that the government paid a total of $25 in daily AFDC benefits to this worker. How much is he or she working?

    d.   Discuss how the difference in trade-offs implicit in the EITC and AFDC programs could cause the same individual to make radically different choices in the labor market.

B. More generally, consider an EITC program in which the first x dollars of income are subsidized at a rate $2s$; the next x dollars are subsidized at a rate s; and any earnings above $2x$ are taxed at a rate t.

    a.   Derive the marginal tax rate function $m(I, x, s, t)$ where I stands for labor market income.

    b.   Derive the average tax rate function $a(I, x, s, t)$ where I again stands for labor market income.

    c.   Graph the average and marginal tax functions on a graph with before-tax income on the horizontal axis and tax rates on the vertical. Is the EITC progressive?

3.20*† **Policy Application:** *Three Proposals to Deal with the Social Security Shortfall*: It is widely recognized that the Social Security systems in many Western democracies will face substantial shortfalls between anticipated revenues and promised benefits over the coming decades.

POLICY APPLICATION

A. Various ideas have emerged on how we should prepare for this upcoming shortfall.

    a.   In order to analyze the impact of different proposals, begin with a graph that has "consumption now" on the horizontal and "retirement consumption" on the vertical axes. For simplicity, suppose we can ignore periods between now and retirement. Consider a worker and his or her choice set over these two "goods." This worker earns some current income I and is currently promised a retirement income R from the government. Illustrate how this establishes an "endowment point" in your graph. Then, assuming an interest rate r over the period between now and retirement, draw this worker's choice set.

    b.   Some have proposed that we need to cut expected retirement benefits for younger workers; i.e., we need to cut R to $R' < R$. Illustrate the impact this has on our worker's choice set.

    c.   Others have argued that we should instead raise Social Security taxes; i.e., reduce I to $I' < I$ in order to prepare for the upcoming shortfall. Illustrate how this would impact our worker's budget constraint.

    d.   Assuming that r is not impacted differently by these two policies, could you argue that they are essentially the same policy?

    e.   Yet others have argued that we should lower future retirement benefits R but at the same time subsidize private savings; i.e., increase r through policies like expanding tax deferred savings accounts. Illustrate the impact of lowering R and raising r.

    f.   Which of these policies is the only one that has a chance (although by no means a guarantee) of making some individuals better off?

B. Define I, R, and r as before.

    a.   Write down the mathematical description of the current intertemporal budget for our worker in terms of I, R, and r. Let c_1 denote current consumption and let c_2 denote retirement consumption.

    b.   In your equation, show which parts correspond to the vertical intercept and slope in your graphs from part A.

    c.   Relate your equation to the changes that you identified in the graph from each of the policies.

Tastes and Indifference Curves

Individuals try to do the *best* they can given their circumstances.[1] This was our starting point when we introduced the topic of microeconomics in Chapter 1, and we have devoted the intervening chapters to the question of how to model individual circumstances, what we called choice or budget sets. Choice sets do not tell us what individuals *will* do, only all the possible actions they *could* take. Put differently, knowing what our choice sets are is a *necessary* first step to finding what choices are best, but it is not *sufficient*. To determine what an individual will actually do when presented with a given choice set, we need to know more about the individual and about his or her tastes. This is tricky, both because tastes differ enormously across people and because they are difficult to observe.

I hate peanut butter, but my wife loves it; she hates fish, which I cannot get enough of. Clearly, we will make very different choices when faced with exactly the same choice set over fish and peanut butter, but it is difficult for an economist to look at us and know how much we like different goods without observing our behavior under different circumstances.[2] The good news is that there are some regularities in tastes that we can reasonably assume are shared across most people, and these regularities will lead us to be able to make predictions about behavior that will be independent of what exact tastes an individual has. Furthermore, economists have developed ways of observing choices that individuals make and then inferring from these choices what kinds of tastes they have. We will therefore be able to say a great deal about behavior and how behavior changes as different aspects of an economy change. First, however, we have to get comfortable with what it is that economists mean when we talk about tastes.

 ## 4A The Economic Model of Tastes

In the previous two chapters, we described a choice set as a subset of all possible combinations of goods and services, the subset that is affordable given an individual's particular circumstances. In our example of me going to Wal-Mart to buy shirts and pants, for instance, we used the information we had on the money I had available and the prices for shirts and pants to delineate the

---

[1]No prior chapter required as background for this chapter.
[2]OK, maybe I eat so much fish that I smell a lot like fish, but we probably don't want to build a model about tastes by smelling people.

budget line in the larger space of all combinations of shirts and pants. While I was unable to *afford* bundles of shirts and pants outside the choice set, I may nevertheless dream about bundles outside that set; or put differently, I may nevertheless have tastes for bundles outside the choice set. For instance, I get deeply annoyed at the crammed conditions on commercial airplanes and have long dreamed of getting myself a private plane modeled after Air Force 1. Unless Oprah invites me on her show and then tells everyone to buy this textbook, I doubt I will ever be in a position to be able to afford such a plane and will thus be confined to commercial airlines for the rest of my life. Still, one can dream. Tastes are therefore defined not only over bundles of goods that fall in our choice sets but also over bundles that we may never be able to attain.

4A.1 Two Fundamental Rationality Assumptions about Tastes

While individuals vary widely in how they would rank different bundles of goods, we will argue in this section that there are two basic properties of tastes that must be satisfied in order for us to be able to analyze rational choice behavior. There is some controversy within the broader social sciences regarding these basic properties, but they are nevertheless quite fundamental to much of what we will have to say in the rest of this book.

4A.1.1 Complete Tastes   First, economists assume that individuals are able to compare any two bundles to one another, and this represents our most fundamental assumption about tastes. Put precisely, we assume that economic agents—whether they are workers, consumers, or financial planners—are able to look at any two choice bundles and tell us which they prefer or whether they are indifferent between them. When an economic agent can do this, we say that he or she has *complete tastes (or preferences)*, complete in the sense that the agent is always able to make comparisons between bundles. A statement such as one recently uttered by my wife in a clothing store—"It is impossible for me to compare these two outfits because they are so different"—moves economists like me to despair because they directly violate this assumption of complete preferences. We suspect that such statements are rarely true; human beings indeed do seem to have the ability to make comparisons when confronted with options.

4A.1.2 Transitive Tastes   A second fundamental assumption economists make about tastes is that there is an internal consistency to tastes that makes choosing a *best* bundle possible. Consider, for instance, bundles A, B, and C, each containing different quantities of pants and shirts. If tastes are complete, I should be able to compare any two of these bundles and tell you which I prefer (or whether I am indifferent). But suppose that I tell you that I like A better than B, that I like B better than C, and that I like C better than A. Although my tastes may be complete—I could after all compare each set of two bundles and tell you which is better—there is no *best* alternative. You could present me with a sequence of choices, first A and B, then B and C, then C and A, etc., and we could forever cycle between the three alternatives, never finding one that is best of all (or at least not worse than any other bundle). To rule out this possibility and thus form the foundations of a model of choice, we assume the following: *Whenever an individual likes A at least as much as B and B at least as much as C, it must be the case that she also likes A at least as much as C.*[3] When this holds for all consumption bundles, we say that a person's tastes are *transitive*.

To be honest, it is not clear that people's tastes are indeed always transitive. A friend of mine told me of his experience at a car dealership where he ordered a new car to be custom made. The sales person started with a stripped-down version of the car model he had selected and then offered various special features. For instance, he would offer a choice as to whether to put a CD

---

[3]Similarly, when the individual likes *A strictly more* than *B* and *B strictly more* than *C*, it must be the case that the individual likes *A strictly more* than *C*.

player into the car for an additional $300, or air conditioning for an additional $1,000, etc. Each time, my friend found himself agreeing to the additional feature. At the end, however, he saw the price tag of the car with all the features and decided he liked the stripped-down version better. This certainly seems like a violation of transitivity, although I suspect that my friend in the end had simply not thought carefully along the way whether the various features were really worth the decrease in his other consumption that they implied. After all, in the end he *did* make a decision.[4] Nevertheless, psychologists have sometimes been critical of the economist's transitivity assumption based on experiments in which people seemed to violate the assumption. Economists, however, continue to find the assumption useful in the sense that it permits us to make predictions about people's choice behavior, predictions that seem consistent with the data most of the time (even if there are instances, such as my "friend's" initial behavior in the car dealership, when the assumption might appear to be violated, at least briefly).

4A.1.3 "Rational" Tastes   When an economic agent's tastes satisfy both completeness and transitivity, we will say that the individual has "rational" tastes or preferences. The term "rational" here does not imply any grand philosophical value judgements. Individuals might have tastes that most of us would consider entirely self-destructive (and "irrational", as the term is commonly used), but such individuals might still be able to compare any pair of alternatives and always choose the best one (or one where none of the other alternatives is worse). In that case, we could refer to such individuals as rational when we speak as economists although we may turn around and call them fools behind their backs when we step outside our role as economists. To the economist, rationality simply means the ability to make choices, and economic agents whose tastes violate the two rationality assumptions are incapable of making choices when faced with some types of choice sets.

4A.2 Three More Assumptions

While much of what economists have modeled depends critically only on the validity of the two rationality assumptions discussed in the previous section, some additional assumptions about tastes can simplify our models while remaining true to most real-world applications. One such additional assumption is that, for most goods, "more is better than less" (or, in some instances, "more is no worse than less"). A second additional assumption is that "averages are better than extremes" (or, in some instances, "averages are no worse than extremes"). Finally, we often assume that there are "no sudden jumps" in tastes, that happiness changes gradually as the basket of goods we consume changes only slightly. In what follows, we will explain in more detail what exactly we mean by each of these, and in Section 4A.3 it will become clear how these assumptions simplify our models of tastes in a way that makes our models workable.

4A.2.1 "More Is Better, or at Least not Worse" (Monotonicity)   In most economic applications, we are interested in situations where individuals make choices involving aspects of life that involve scarcity, whether this involves current consumption, future consumption, or leisure. If individuals did not in fact think "more is better" in such choices, scarcity would not be a problem. Everyone would simply be content with what he or she has, and there would be little need for economics as a discipline. The idea of a world in which individuals are just happy with what they have is appealing to many of us, but it is not the world we actually occupy. For better or worse, we always seem to want more, and our choices are often aimed at getting more. The economist's recognition of this is not an endorsement of a philosophy of life focused on materialism or consumerism; rather, it is a simple starting point for better understanding human behavior in a world characterized by scarcity. If an individual has tastes for goods such that "more is

---

[4]All right, I'll confess: The "friend" at the car dealership was actually me, and it took my wife, a noneconomist, to point out the apparent evidence of an intransitivity in my tastes!

better" (or at least that "more is not worse"), we will sometimes call such tastes *monotonic*, or we will say that such tastes satisfy the *monotonicity assumption*.

Consider the five bundles of pants and shirts depicted in Graph 4.1. The monotonicity assumption allows us to conclude that *E* must be better than *C* because *E* contains more pants and shirts than *C*. In cases where we compare two bundles that are the same in terms of one of the goods but differ in terms of the other, we will interpret "more is better" as meaning "more is at least as good." For instance, bundle *C* contains just as many shirts as *D*, but it also contains more pants. Thus, "more is better" implies that *C* is at least as good as *D*. But the "more is better" assumption does *not* make it clear how *A* and *C* relate to each other because neither contains clearly "more"; *A* has more shirts than *C*, but *C* has more pants than *A*. Similarly, the assumption does not clarify how the pairs *A* and *B*, *C* and *B*, or *B* and *D* are ranked.

**Exercise
4A.1**

Do we know from the monotonicity assumption how *E* relates to *D*, *A*, and *B*? Do we know how *A* relates to *D*?

It is worth noting at this point that monotonicity may hold even in cases where it seems at first glance that it does not hold if we conceptualize the model appropriately. For instance, we might think that we would prefer less work over more and thus cite "labor" as a good that violates the "more is better" assumption. But we could equivalently model our choices over how much labor to provide as a choice of how much leisure we choose not to consume (as we did when we constructed choice sets for workers in Chapter 3). By reconceptualizing labor as the amount of leisure we do not consume, we have redefined the choice as one between leisure and consumption rather than between labor and consumption, and leisure is certainly a good that we would like to have more of rather than less. Similarly, consider someone who does not like more consumption beyond some basic subsistence level. For such a person, more consumption may not be

Graph 4.1: Ranking Consumption Bundles

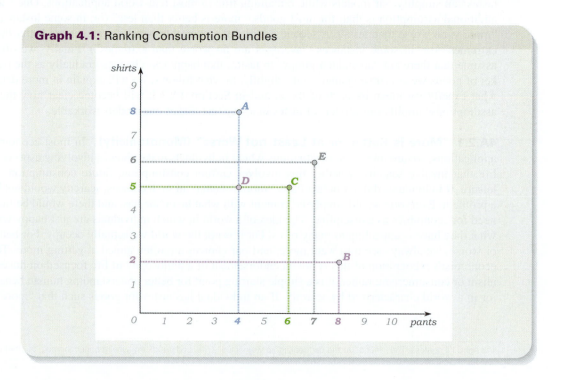

better than less. At the same time, such an individual might care about the well-being of others whose consumption has not reached subsistence levels. The economic scarcity problem such a person faces then involves choices over what to do with money in excess of his or her own subsistence needs, perhaps what charitable causes to support. Once the problem has been reconceptualized in this way, more (charity) is once again better than less. Thus, in many cases we can reconceptualize a choice involving goods we would prefer to have fewer of as a choice involving goods that satisfy the "more is better" assumption.

What other goods are such that we would prefer to have fewer of them than many? How can we reconceptualize choices over such goods so that it becomes reasonable to assume "more is better"?

Exercise
4A.2

4A.2.2 "Averages Are Better than Extremes, or at Least no Worse" (Convexity)

While it may be obvious that the very nature of economic problems arises from the reality that people believe "more is better than less," it is less obvious what we mean by "averages are better than extremes" or why this should be an assumption that is at all reasonable. Consider, for instance, two baskets of goods: the first contains 9 apples and 1 orange while the second contains 9 oranges and 1 apple. If we mixed the two baskets together and then divided them into two identical "average" baskets, we would get baskets with 5 apples and 5 oranges. It certainly seems plausible that this average basket might be preferred to the more extreme baskets we started with, but one could imagine someone who really likes apples and only sort of likes oranges preferring the more extreme basket with 9 apples. Thankfully, the economist's assumption that "averages are better than extremes," when properly defined, does not actually rule out this scenario. Rather, it gives expression to a general tendency by human beings to like variety in consumption choices.

Let's begin by stating what we mean more precisely. We will say that your tastes satisfy the assumption that "averages are better than extremes" whenever it is the case that the average between two baskets *that you are indifferent between* is at least as good as the original two baskets. Thus, *if* you are indifferent between the 9 apples/1 orange basket and the 9 oranges/1 apple basket, *then* you would be willing to trade either of these extreme baskets for a basket with 5 apples and 5 oranges. If someone really likes apples and only sort of likes oranges, he or she would of course not be indifferent between the two extreme baskets. But if you *are* indifferent between the more extreme baskets, it is reasonable to assume that you would be willing to give up some of the good that you have a lot of for some of the good that you have only a little of, and that you would therefore prefer the 5 apples/5 oranges basket or at least not mind taking such a basket instead of one of the extremes. This assumption of "averages being better than extremes" is often called the *convexity assumption*, and tastes that satisfy it are referred to as *convex tastes*.

Consider again the five bundles graphed in Graph 4.1. There is nothing immediate the convexity assumption allows us to say in addition to what we could conclude from applying the monotonicity assumption in the previous section. However, suppose we find out that I am indifferent between bundles A and B. Then the convexity assumption lets us know that I would be at least as happy with an average between A and B. Bundle C is just that; it contains 5 shirts and 6 pants, which is exactly half of bundles A and B added together. (Note that such an average bundle lies halfway between the more extreme bundles on the line segment connecting those bundles.) Thus, convexity implies that C is at least as good as A and B.

Combining the convexity and monotonicity assumptions, can you now conclude something about the relationship between the pairs E and A and E and B if you do not know how A and B are related? What if you know that I am indifferent between A and B?

Exercise
4A.3

**Exercise
4A.4**
Knowing that I am indifferent between *A* and *B*, can you now conclude something about how I rank *B* and *D*? In order to reach this conclusion, do you have to invoke the convexity assumption?

In essence, the "averages are better than extremes" or convexity assumption gives expression to the general human tendency to seek diversity in consumption. No matter how much we like steak, few of us sit down to a meal of only steak, or only salad, only potatoes, only coffee, only dessert, or only wine. We might in fact be able to create all sorts of single-item meals that we are indifferent between: a certain quantity of steak, a certain quantity of salad, a certain quantity of potatoes, etc. However, most of us would prefer a meal with some of each of these, or an average of single-item meals. The "meal" here is of course just an analogy that we don't want to push too far; certain sets of single-item meals (perhaps pancakes and caviar) would, after all, not average well into one meal. Over the course of a week, however, even single-item meals that we may not want to mix in one meal might create welcome variety. Similarly, I may be indifferent between a basket containing 10 blue shirts with matched pants and another containing 10 red shirts with matched pants. My wife would not let me leave the house with mismatched clothes, so she would never let me mix one of the red shirts with one of the pants that matches only blue shirts. But, unless I like wearing the same outfit every day, I probably would prefer to have 5 of each, the average of the more extreme baskets, and then alternate which matched pair I wear on any given day.

These analogies give a sense of what it is that we mean intuitively when we say that often, averages in life are indeed better than extremes. In more life-changing decisions, the same seems to be true. Suppose I am indifferent between, on the one hand, consuming $100,000 a year before retirement and living in poverty afterward and, on the other hand, living in poverty now and consuming $150,000 a year after retirement. It seems reasonable that most of us would prefer an average between these scenarios, one that permits us a comfortable standard of living both before and after retirement. Or suppose that I am equally happy consuming a lot while working almost all the time and consuming very little while working very little. Most of us probably would prefer an average between these two bundles, to work without becoming a workaholic and consume less than we could if we did work all the time.

4A.2.3 "No Sudden Jumps" (or Continuity)

Finally, we will usually assume that a consumer's happiness does not change dramatically if the basket he or she consumes changes only slightly. Perhaps you are currently enjoying a nice cup of coffee so that you can stay awake as you read this chapter. If you like milk in your coffee, our "no sudden jumps" assumption implies that you will become neither dramatically better off nor dramatically worse off if I add one more drop of milk to the coffee. Starting out with coffee that is black, you may become gradually happier as I add milk and, at some point, gradually worse off as even more milk is added,[5] but you will never switch from agony to ecstasy from just one more drop. Tastes that satisfy this assumption are often called *continuous*, and the "no sudden jumps" assumption is referred to as the *continuity assumption*.

The continuity assumption is most appealing for goods that can easily be divided into smaller and smaller units (such as milk) and less appealing for goods that come in very discrete units (such as, perhaps, pants and shirts, or larger goods like cars). For purposes of our models, however, we will treat these other types of goods just as we treat milk: we will assume that you can

---

[5]Note that in this example, your tastes violate the "more is better" assumption if it is indeed the case that you become worse off as I add milk at some stage. Of course this is true only when the situation is viewed very narrowly as one instant in time; you would certainly continue to become better off if, instead of adding the additional milk to your coffee, I put it in the refrigerator for later use.

in fact consume fractions of pants and shirts and cars. We do this not because it is realistic but rather because it simplifies our models in ways that ultimately are not all that critical for any of the analysis we will do with our models. If, for instance, we conclude from our analysis that a 10% drop in the price of pants will result in an increase of your consumption of pants by 3.2, we can simply round this off and know that you will probably end up buying 3 more pants.

Furthermore, in cases where the assumption of continuity becomes particularly problematic, there are often other ways of modeling the behavior such that the assumption once again is reasonable. For instance, we might think of cars or houses as very discrete units; it is, after all, not easy to consume three-quarters of a car or house. At the same time, we could model cars as bundled goods, goods that provide you with varying degrees of speed, safety, comfort, etc. What you are really trying to buy is not a car but rather speed, safety, and comfort on the road, and your tastes over these attributes are probably quite immune to sudden jumps. Similarly, in the case of housing, we can think of your choice as one involving square footage, the age of the house, the quality of the neighborhood, features of the floorplan, etc., and once again it is likely that your tastes over these attributes of housing are not subject to sudden jumps. (We explore this concept of modeling discrete goods as bundles of "attributes" further in the end-of-chapter exercises 4.9.[6])

4A.3 Graphing Tastes

In Chapters 2 and 3, we found ways of graphically representing the constraints on people's choices, or what we called the choice sets from which people can choose given their circumstances. Armed with the assumptions introduced earlier, we will now do the same for people's tastes before demonstrating in Chapter 6 how tastes and constraints combine to result in human behavior we can then observe. More precisely, we will find that it is impossible to graph fully the tastes of any individual, but we will develop ways of graphing the particular portions of individual tastes that are most relevant for the choices that confront individuals at different times.

4A.3.1 An Indifference Curve The basic building block of our graphs of tastes is what we will call an *indifference curve*. Suppose, for instance, that we are back to choosing between pants and shirts, and suppose that I currently have 8 shirts and 4 pants in my shopping basket. This is represented as point *A* in Graph 4.2a. *The indifference curve containing point A is defined as the set of all other consumption bundles (i.e., the set of all other pairs of shirts and pants) that would make me exactly as happy as bundle A.* While it is difficult to know exactly where such bundles lie, our assumptions about tastes allow us to derive the approximate location of this indifference curve.

We can begin by noting some places that could not possibly contain bundles that lie on the indifference curve which contains bundle *A*. Consider, for instance, the shaded magenta area to the northeast of *A*. All bundles in this area contain more pants and more shirts. If "more is better," then bundles that contain more pants and shirts *must be* better than *A* and thus could not be indifferent to *A*. Similarly, consider bundles to the southwest of bundle *A*. All bundles represented by this shaded blue area contain fewer pants and shirts than bundle *A* and must therefore be worse. Thus, the monotonicity assumption allows us to rule out the shaded areas in Graph 4.2a as bundles that could lie on the indifference curve containing bundle *A*. Bundles that lie in nonshaded areas, on the other hand, are not ruled out by the monotonicity assumption. Those to the northwest of *A*, for instance, all have fewer pants but more shirts, while those to the southeast have more pants and fewer shirts than bundle *A*. You therefore know from the monotonicity assumption that my indifference curve containing bundle *A* must be downward sloping through bundle *A*, but you can glean nothing further without knowing more about me.

---

[6]The most common example of tastes that violate the continuity assumption is known as *lexicographic tastes*. An example of such tastes is given in end-of-chapter exercise 4.8.

Graph 4.2: Tastes and Indifference Curves

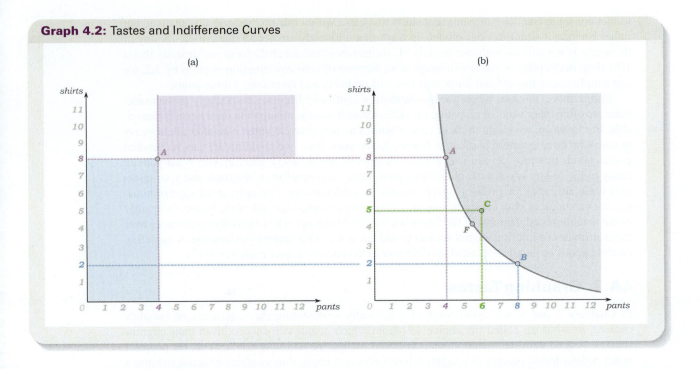

Now suppose that I tell you I am indifferent between the bundles represented by points *A* (4 pants, 8 shirts) and *B* (2 shirts, 8 pants) in Graph 4.2b. This means that you of course immediately know that bundle *B* lies on the indifference curve that contains bundle *A*. You can also now draw some additional shaded areas (to the northeast and southwest of point *B*) that you know could not possibly include further indifferent bundles based on the "more is better" or monotonicity assumption. More importantly, however, you can now employ the "averages are better than extremes" or convexity assumption to come to some additional conclusions about the shape of the indifference curve that contains bundles *A* and *B*.

The convexity assumption simply states that whenever someone is indifferent between two bundles of goods and services, the average bundle (that is created by mixing the two original bundles and dividing them into two equal ones) is judged to be at least as good as the extreme bundles. In our case, the average bundle would be 5 shirts and 6 pants. Graphically, this average bundle is simply the midpoint of the line segment connecting points *A* and *B*, labeled *C* in Graph 4.2b.

Now notice that any bundle to the southwest of *C* has fewer pants and fewer shirts and is thus worse than *C*. Suppose we start at *C* and move a little to the southwest by taking just a tiny bit of each good away (assuming for the moment that it is possible to take away bits of shirts and pants). Then, given our "no sudden jumps" or continuity assumption, the new bundle is just a little worse than *C*. Suppose we keep doing this, each time creating yet another bundle that's just a little worse and moving a little further southwest. If *C* is strictly better than *A* (and *B*), it should be the case that, as we inch our way southwest from *C*, we at some point hit a bundle *F* that is indifferent to *A* and *B*. Without knowing more about me, you can't tell exactly how far southwest of *C* the new indifferent point *F* will lie. All we know is that it lies to the southwest.

Exercise
4A.5   Illustrate the area in Graph 4.2b in which *F* must lie, keeping in mind the monotonicity assumption.

Suppose our tastes satisfy weak convexity in the sense that averages are just as good (rather than strictly better than) extremes. Where does *F* lie in relation to *C* in that case?

Exercise
4A.6

We now have three bundles between which I am indifferent: *A*, *B*, and *F*. We could repeat what we just did for the average between *A* and *F* and the average between *B* and *F*. The intuition that should be emerging already, however, is that the *indifference curve containing bundles A and B must not only be downward sloping (because "more is better") but also must be continuous (because of "no sudden jumps") and bend toward the origin (because "averages are better than extremes").* For someone with tastes like this, all bundles that lie above the indifference curve (in the shaded region) must be better than any of the bundles on the indifference curve because these contain more of everything relative to *some* bundle that lies on the indifference curve. Similarly, all bundles that lie below this indifference curve (in the nonshaded region) are worse because they contain less of everything compared to some bundle that lies on the indifference curve.

4A.3.2 Marginal Rates of Substitution We have just demonstrated how our five assumptions about tastes result in a particular shape of indifference curves. One way of describing this shape is to say that *the slope of indifference curves is negative and becomes smaller in absolute value as one moves to the right in the graph.* The slope of the indifference curve at any given point is, however, more than a mere description of what the indifference curve looks like. It has real economic content and is called the *marginal rate of substitution.*

Consider, for instance, the slope of −3 at point *A* in Graph 4.3. This slope tells us that we could go down by 3 shirts and over to the right by 1 pair of pants and end up roughly on the same indifference curve as the one that contains bundle *A*.[7] Put differently, when I am consuming bundle *A*,

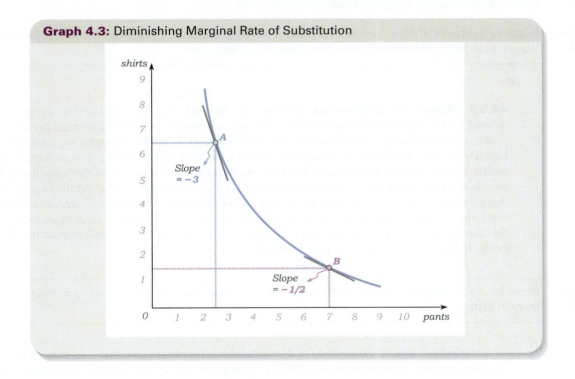

Graph 4.3: Diminishing Marginal Rate of Substitution

---

[7]We would in fact end up slightly below the indifference curve unless we measured shirts and pants in very small units.

I would be *willing to* trade in 3 of my shirts to get 1 more pair of pants because that would leave me roughly as well off as I currently am. Thus, the slope of the indifference curve at point *A* gives us an indication of how much I value 1 more pair of pants in terms of shirts. This *marginal rate of substitution* is therefore *my willingness to trade shirts for 1 more additional (or marginal) pair of pants given what I am currently consuming.*

Since the slope of the indifference curve typically changes as one moves along the indifference curve, the marginal rate of substitution—or how much value we place on an additional good on the horizontal axis in terms of the good on the vertical axis—also changes. Consider, for example, the shallower slope of $-1/2$ at point *B* (in Graph 4.3). This slope tells us that I would be willing to give up only half a shirt for 1 more pair of pants (or 1 shirt for 2 additional pants) when I am already consuming bundle *B*. This makes sense given our discussion about the "averages are better than extremes" assumption. At bundle *A*, I had relatively few pants and relatively many shirts, and I thus placed a high value on additional pants because that would get me to a less extreme bundle (and keep me from having to wash pants all the time or else go without pants). At bundle *B*, on the other hand, I have relatively many pants and few shirts, and thus I would not be willing to give up more shirts very easily given that this would get me to even more extreme bundles (causing me to have to wash shirts all the time or else go shirtless).

In fact, we concluded in the previous section that the shape of the indifference curve pictured in Graph 4.3 is due to the "averages are better than extremes" assumption. This shape implies that marginal rates of substitution begin as large numbers in absolute value and decline (in absolute value) as we move down an indifference curve. This is known as the concept of *diminishing marginal rates of substitution*, and it arises only when averages are indeed better than extremes.

Exercise 4A.7 Suppose extremes are better than averages. What would an indifference curve look like? Would it still imply diminishing marginal rates of substitution?

Exercise 4A.8 Suppose averages are just as good as extremes? What would an indifference curve look like? Would it still imply diminishing marginal rates of substitution?

4A.3.3 "Maps" of Indifference Curves In deriving our first indifference curve, we defined it *with respect to one bundle*. Put differently, we mapped out the indifference curve that contains one arbitrarily selected bundle: bundle *A* in Graph 4.2b. But of course we could have begun with some other arbitrary bundle, for instance bundle *E* in Graph 4.4a. Just as there is an indifference curve that runs through bundle *A*, there is an indifference curve that runs through bundle *E*. Notice that *E* lies to the northeast of the highlighted segment of the indifference curve that contains *A* in Graph 4.4a. This means that *E* contains more shirts and pants than any of the highlighted bundles, which means that it must be the case that *E* is better than those bundles (because of our "more is better" assumption). But this also means that *E* is better than *all* bundles on the indifference curve that contains bundle *A*.

Exercise 4A.9 Show how you can prove the last sentence in the previous paragraph by appealing to the transitivity of tastes.

An important logical consequence of this is that the indifference curve that goes through point *A* can never cross the indifference curve that goes through point *E*. If the two indifference curves did cross, they would share one point in common. This intersection point would be indifferent to *A* (because it lies on the indifference curve that contains *A*), and it would also be indifferent to *E* (since

Graph 4.4: Parallel and Converging Indifference Curves

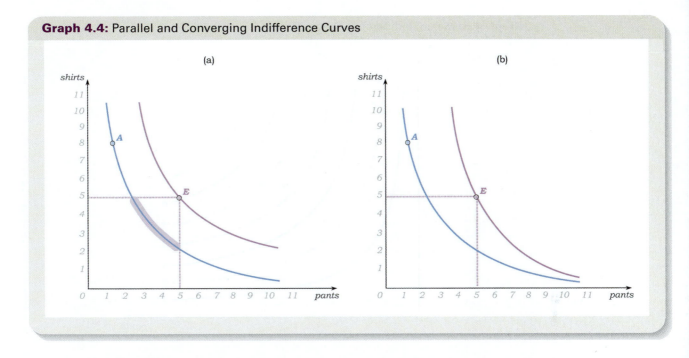

it lies on the indifference curve that contains *E*). Since *E* is preferred to *A*, transitivity implies that the intersection point cannot be indifferent to both *E* and *A* simultaneously. Thus, *as long as tastes are rational (i.e., they satisfy completeness and transitivity), indifference curves cannot cross*. They can be parallel like those in Graph 4.4a, or they can converge like those in Graph 4.4b, or they can relate to each other in any number of other ways, but they can never touch.

Furthermore, if tastes are complete, then *some* indifference curve runs through every bundle. As we showed earlier, the monotonicity assumption implies that indifference curves will be downward sloping; the convexity and continuity assumptions imply that they will bend toward the origin; and the transitivity assumption implies that no two indifference curves can ever cross. Graph 4.5 then illustrates an example of a whole map of indifference curves that represent the tastes over pants and shirts for an individual whose tastes satisfy the rationality assumptions as well as the three additional assumptions outlined in Section 4A.2. This is, of course, only one possible configuration of an indifference "map" that satisfies all these assumptions. While the assumptions we have made about tastes result in particular general shapes for indifference curves, we will see in Chapter 5 that there exist many different types of indifference maps (and thus many different tastes) that can be modeled using these assumptions.

Finally, in order to indicate that indifference curves to the northeast of Graph 4.5 represent bundles that yield greater happiness than indifference curves to the southwest of the graph, each indifference curve is accompanied by a number that indicates how bundles on that particular curve compare with bundles on other curves. For instance, when we compare bundle *A* with bundle *E*, we can read off the number 2 on the indifference curve containing point *A* and the number 4 on the indifference curve containing point *E*, and we can infer from this that bundle *E* is preferred to bundle *A*. If less is better than more, then the ordering of the numbers attached to these indifference curves would be reversed.

Suppose less is better than more and averages are better than extremes. Draw three indifference curves (with numerical labels) that would be consistent with this.

Exercise 4A.10

Graph 4.5: Map of Indifference Curves

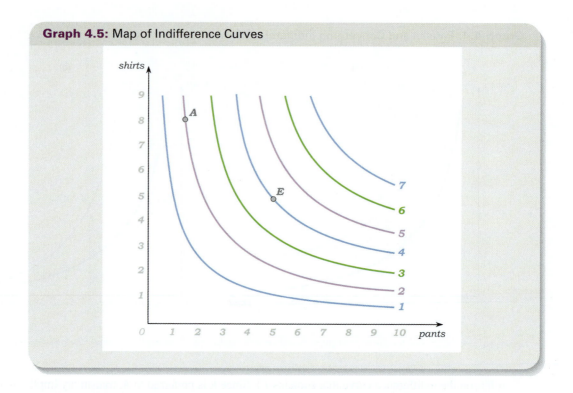

We *cannot*, however, infer from these two numbers that bundles on one indifference curve yield "twice as much happiness" as bundles on the other indifference curve. *Happiness is simply not something that is objectively quantifiable.* While economists in the past had indeed hoped to measure happiness or "utility" in units they called "utils," modern economists have abandoned any such attempts as misguided. To see just how silly the notion of objectively measuring happiness is, try asking a friend the following when you see him or her for the first time after he or she went on a date: "So, how many utils did you get out of that date?"

We *can* say that all bundles on a particular indifference curve yield the same level of utility (and thus must have the same numerical label), and that different utility numbers associated with different indifference curves tell us which are more preferred and which less. But we could change all the numbers in Graph 4.5 by multiplying them by 2 or dividing them by 5 or adding 13 to them because in each case, the *ordering* of indifference curves would remain unchanged. Thus, *so long as the shape of indifference curves and the ordering of the numbers that accompany the curves are unchanged between two graphs, we will say that the maps of indifference curves in the two graphs represent the same tastes.* By changing the numerical labels on indifference curves without changing their order, all we are in effect doing is changing the ruler we use to measure happiness, and since there isn't an agreed upon ruler, any ruler that preserves the ordering of indifference curves will do.

This becomes somewhat clearer if you think of the following analogy (which we expand on in more detail in part B). Consider a two-dimensional map of a mountain (such as that depicted in Graph 4.10), a map in which different heights of the mountain are represented by outlines of the shape of the mountain at that height accompanied by a number that indicates the elevation of that outline. In essence, such maps are depictions of horizontal slices of the mountain at different heights drawn on a single two-dimensional surface. Indifference curves are very much like this. Longitude and latitude are replaced with pants and shirts, and the height of the mountain is replaced with the level of happiness. While real-world mountains have peaks, our happiness mountains generally do not have peaks because of our "more is better" assumption. Indifference curves are then simply horizontal slices of our happiness mountain (such as the one depicted in Graph 4.8), with numbers indicating the height of happiness attained at that slice. And just as the outlines of the different elevations of a real-world mountain don't change whether we measure the height of the elevation in feet or meters, the outlines of the slices of our happiness mountain, i.e., the indifference curves, do not change shapes if we use a different ruler to measure happiness.

We will have much more to say in Chapter 5 about how to interpret different types of indifference maps, what they imply about whether goods are relatively more complementary or substitutable, how to think of relationship of indifference curves to one another, etc. But first, we develop some of the underlying mathematics of the "utility mountains" through the concept of utility *functions*.

4B Tastes and Utility Functions

We have shown in Section 4A how certain basic assumptions about our tastes can enable us to generate graphical ways of representing tastes with the tool of indifference curves. As was true for choice sets in Chapters 2 and 3, these graphical tools are mere representations of more general mathematical formulations of the same economic concepts. And the assumptions we introduced in Section 4A.1 and 4A.2 will translate directly into mathematical properties of functions that we can use to represent tastes.

4B.1 Two Fundamental Rationality Assumptions

When we speak of "bundles" or "baskets" of two goods, we have already defined these as points with two components, each representing the quantity of one of the goods in the basket. The point labeled A in Graph 4.1, for instance, can be expressed as $(x_1^A, x_2^A) = (4,8)$, representing a basket with 4 units of good 1 (pants) and 8 units of good 2 (shirts). In general, we can then express a basket that contains two types of goods as

$$(x_1, x_2) \in \mathbb{R}_+^2, \tag{4.1}$$

where " $\in$ " is read as "is an element of" and "$\mathbb{R}_+^2$" denotes the set of all points with two non-negative (real number) components. Almost all of our graphs of choice sets consist of some subset of points in $\mathbb{R}_+^2$, as do our graphs of indifference curves in Section 4A. When a larger number of different types of goods is included in a basket—shirts, pants, *and* socks, for instance—we can further generalize this by simply denoting a basket with n different types of goods by

$$(x_1, x_2, \ldots, x_n) \in \mathbb{R}_+^n, \tag{4.2}$$

where $\mathbb{R}_+^n$ now represents the set of all points with n non-negative components. In the case of shirts, pants, and socks, $n = 3$.[8]

Tastes, or preferences, involve subjective comparisons of different baskets or different points as denoted in (4.1) and (4.2). We will use the following shorthand notation

$$(x_1^A, x_2^A, \ldots, x_n^A) \succsim (x_1^B, x_2^B, \ldots, x_n^B) \tag{4.3}$$

whenever we want to say that "the basket $(x_1^A, x_2^A, \ldots, x_n^A)$ *is at least as good* as the basket $(x_1^B, x_2^B, \ldots, x_n^B)$." Similarly, we read

$$(x_1^A, x_2^A, \ldots, x_n^A) > (x_1^B, x_2^B, \ldots, x_n^B) \tag{4.4}$$

as "basket $(x_1^A, x_2^A, \ldots, x_n^A)$ *is strictly better than* basket $(x_1^B, x_2^B, \ldots, x_n^B)$," and we will read

$$(x_1^A, x_2^A, \ldots, x_n^A) \sim (x_1^B, x_2^B, \ldots, x_n^B) \tag{4.5}$$

as a person being *indifferent* between these two baskets. The objects "$\succsim$", "$>$" and "$\sim$" are called *binary relations* because they relate two points to each another.

---

[8]You may recall from your math classes that points with such multiple components are referred to as *vectors*.

4B.1.1 Complete Tastes

In Section 4A, we defined tastes as *complete* whenever a person with those tastes can unequivocally compare any two baskets, indicating whether one basket is better than the other or whether he or she is indifferent between the two baskets. We can now write this definition formally as follows: *A person has complete tastes over all baskets with n goods if and only if it is true that for all* $(x_1^A, x_2^A, \ldots, x_n^A) \in \mathbb{R}_+^n$ *and for all* $(x_1^B, x_2^B, \ldots, x_n^B) \in \mathbb{R}_+^n,$

$$(x_1^A, x_2^A, \ldots, x_n^A) \succsim (x_1^B, x_2^B, \ldots, x_n^B) \quad \text{or}$$

$$(x_1^B, x_2^B, \ldots, x_n^B) \succsim (x_1^A, x_2^A, \ldots, x_n^A) \quad \text{or both.} \tag{4.6}$$

All we are saying is that a person can compare any two bundles in $\mathbb{R}_+^n$. Note that logically it has to be the case that if both of the statements in (4.6) are true for a given set of two bundles, then

$$(x_1^A, x_2^A, \ldots, x_n^A) \sim (x_1^B, x_2^B, \ldots, x_n^B). \tag{4.7}$$

Exercise 4B.1 True or False: If only one of the statements in (4.6) is true for a given set of bundles, then that statement's "$\succsim$" can be replaced with "$\succ$".

4B.1.2 Transitive Tastes

While we certainly need tastes in our models to be complete in order for individuals within the models to be able to make choices, we argued in Section 4A that this is not enough: in order for an individual to be able to settle on a "best" choice, there needs to be a certain internal consistency to the tastes that guide the person's choices. We called this internal consistency "transitivity" and said that a person's tastes are *transitive* if, whenever the person likes a bundle A at least as much as a bundle B and he or she likes B at least as much as C, it must be the case that the person likes A at least as much as C. We can now define this more formally using the notation we just developed.

In particular, we will say that *a person's tastes are transitive if and only if it is true that whenever three bundles are evaluated by the person such that*

$$(x_1^A, x_2^A, \ldots, x_n^A) \succsim (x_1^B, x_2^B, \ldots, x_n^B) \quad \text{and} \quad (x_1^B, x_2^B, \ldots, x_n^B) \succsim (x_1^C, x_2^C, \ldots, x_n^C) \tag{4.8}$$

we can conclude that

$$(x_1^A, x_2^A, \ldots, x_n^A) \succsim (x_1^C, x_2^C, \ldots, x_n^C). \tag{4.9}$$

Exercise 4B.2 Does transitivity also imply that (4.8) implies (4.9) when "$\succsim$" is replaced with "$\succ$"?

4B.1.3 "Rational Tastes"

The assumptions of completeness and transitivity of tastes are, as already noted in Section 4A, so fundamental to the economist's modeling of tastes that together they define what we mean by *rational* tastes. An individual's tastes over a particular set of bundles are then said to be rational if they are both complete and transitive.

4B.2 Three More Assumptions

While the two rationality assumptions are quite fundamental for the construction of a model of tastes that can result in individuals choosing "best" alternatives given their circumstances, they do not by themselves tell us very much about what kinds of choices individuals are likely to make. For this reason, we introduced in Section 4A.2 3 additional assumptions that we informally called "more is better," "averages are better than extremes," and "no sudden jumps." In more formal language, these same assumptions were referred to as monotonicity, convexity, and continuity.

4B.2.1 Monotonicity (or "More Is Better or at Least not Worse")

We argued at length in Section 4A.2.1 that the fundamental scarcity that underlies economic decision making implies that more is indeed considered better by most individuals in most economic contexts. Given that bundles of goods and services by definition contain many different types of goods, we have to be clear about what we mean by "more." In Graph 4.1, for instance, bundle E clearly has more of everything than bundle C, but it has more of some and less of other goods when compared with bundles A and B. By "more" we can mean either "more of all goods" or "more of at least some goods and no less of any of the other goods." When a bundle contains "more of all goods" than a second bundle, we will generally assume that a consumer strictly prefers that bundle. When a bundle contains "more of at least some goods and no less of any of the other goods" than a second bundle, on the other hand, we will typically assume that a consumer thinks of this bundle as *at least as good as* the second bundle, thus leaving open the possibility that the consumer might be indifferent between the bundles.

Formally we can then define "more is better," or what we will call monotonic tastes, as follows: *A consumer's tastes are monotonic if and only if*

$$(x_1^A, x_2^A, \ldots, x_n^A) \succsim (x_1^B, x_2^B, \ldots, x_n^B) \text{ whenever } x_i^A \geq x_i^B \text{ for all } i = 1, 2, \ldots, n; \text{ and}$$

$$(x_1^A, x_2^A, \ldots, x_n^A) \succ (x_1^B, x_2^B, \ldots, x_n^B) \text{ whenever } x_i^A > x_i^B \text{ for all } i = 1, 2, \ldots, n. \tag{4.10}$$

The first line of this definition allows for the possibility that some of the goods in the A and B bundles are the same while others are larger for the A bundle than for the B bundle, whereas the second line applies only to pairs of bundles where one contains more of every good than the other. In Graph 4.1, for instance, bundle A contains more shirts but the same number of pants as bundle D, and our definition of monotonic tastes therefore implies that $A \succsim D$, or "A is at least as good as D." Bundle E, on the other hand, contains more of all goods than bundle D, implying that $E \succ D$, or "E is strictly better than D."[9]

4B.2.2 Convexity ("Averages Are Better than (or at Least as Good as) Extremes")

Next we argued in Section 4A.2.2 that it is often reasonable for us to assume that "averages are better than extremes" whenever an individual is indifferent between "extreme" bundles. By an "average" bundle we simply meant the bundle that emerges if we mix 2 more extreme bundles (like bundles A and B in Graph 4.2) and divide them into 2 identical bundles.[10] We could translate this into a more formal statement by saying that

$$(x_1^A, x_2^A, \ldots, x_n^A) \sim (x_1^B, x_2^B, \ldots, x_n^B) \text{ implies}$$

$$\left(\frac{1}{2}\right)(x_1^A, x_2^A, \ldots, x_n^A) + \left(\frac{1}{2}\right)(x_1^B, x_2^B, \ldots, x_n^B) \succsim (x_1^A, x_2^A, \ldots, x_n^A) \text{ and}$$

$$\left(\frac{1}{2}\right)(x_1^A, x_2^A, \ldots, x_n^A) + \left(\frac{1}{2}\right)(x_1^B, x_2^B, \ldots, x_n^B) \succsim (x_1^B, x_2^B, \ldots, x_n^B). \tag{4.11}$$

---

[9]Monotonicity assumptions are sometimes divided into *weak* and *strong* monotonicity, where weak monotonicity requires that each element of a bundle A must be larger than each corresponding element of B for us to be sure that A is strictly preferred to B, while a stronger form of monotonicity would require only some elements of A to be larger than the corresponding elements in B (with all remaining elements the same). Our definition corresponds to the weaker of these definitions of monotonicity. Finally, although we will generally maintain our assumption of monotonicity throughout the text, many of the results that we derive actually hold for a much weaker assumption called *local non-satiation*. This assumption simply requires that there exists no bundle of goods for which there isn't another bundle close by that is strictly better. These concepts are clarified further in the end-of-chapter exercise 4.13.

[10]As in the case of monotonicity, there exist several stronger and weaker versions of the convexity assumption. *Strict* convexity is usually defined as "averages are strictly preferred to extremes" while *weak* convexity is defined as "averages are at least as good as extremens." Note that we will define our convexity notion in line with the latter, although you will see in the coming chapters that most of the tastes we work with actually satisfy the stronger definition of convexity.

Exercise
4B.3

True or False: Assuming tastes are transitive, the third line in expression (4.11) is logically implied by the first and second lines.

More generally, if the literal "average" (as opposed to a weighted average with weights different from 0.5) of two more extreme bundles is better than the extremes, the same logic would suggest that *any weighted average* that emerges from mixing two extremes is preferable to the extremes so long as it is not even more extreme. For instance, suppose again that I am indifferent between bundle A and B in Graph 4.2, where bundle A contains 4 pants and 8 shirts while bundle B contains 8 pairs of pants and 2 shirts. But now, instead of strictly averaging the bundles to yield a bundle with 6 pants and 5 shirts, suppose that we create one bundle that consists of 1/4 of bundle A and 3/4 of bundle B, and a second bundle that consists of 3/4 of A and 1/4 of B. An individual who likes averages better than extremes will then also prefer these two bundles to the more extreme original ones, and these bundles would also lie on the line segment connecting A and B.

Bundles that are created as a weighted average of extremes are called *convex combinations* of the extreme bundles. Put more precisely, any bundle that is created by weighting bundle A by α and bundle B by $(1 - \alpha)$ is a convex combination of A and B so long as α lies between 0 and 1. Our "averages are better than extremes," or convexity, assumption from Section 4A can then be restated in the following way: *Tastes are convex if and only if convex combinations of indifferent bundles are at least as good as the bundles used to create the convex combination.* Or, in terms of the notation we have developed, *tastes over bundles of n goods are convex if and only if, for any α such that $0 \leq \alpha \leq 1$,*

$$(x_1^A, x_2^A, \ldots, x_n^A) \sim (x_1^B, x_2^B, \ldots, x_n^B) \text{ implies}$$

$$\alpha(x_1^A, x_2^A, \ldots, x_n^A) + (1 - \alpha)(x_1^B, x_2^B, \ldots, x_n^B) \succsim (x_1^A, x_2^A, \ldots, x_n^A). \tag{4.12}$$

4B.2.3 Continuity ("No Sudden Jumps")

Finally, we introduced the assumption that tastes generally do not have "sudden jumps" in Section 4A.2.3. We can now formalize this assumption by introducing a mathematical concept called a *converging sequence of points*. This concept is quite intuitive, but it consists of several parts. First, a *sequence of points in $\mathbb{R}_+^n$* is simply a list of points, each with n different non-negative components. This sequence is *infinite* if and only if the list has an infinite number of points in it. An infinite sequence of points then is said to *converge* to a single point in $\mathbb{R}_+^n$ if and only if the distance between the points in the sequence and that single point becomes smaller and smaller (beginning at some point in the sequence).

Suppose for instance that we start in Graph 4.6 at a point B in $\mathbb{R}_+^2$. Then suppose that point B is the first point in an infinite sequence that continues with B^1 lying halfway between point B and some other point A, with B^2 lying halfway between point B^1 and A, with B^3 lying halfway between B^2 and A, and so forth. An example of the first four points of such a sequence is graphed in Graph 4.6. If we now imagine this sequence of points continuing forever, no point in the sequence will ever quite reach point A, but it will get ever closer. In the language of calculus, the *limit of the sequence* is point A, and the sequence itself *converges* to point A.

Now suppose we have two infinite sequences of points: one denoted $\{B^1, B^2, B^3, \ldots\}$ and the other denoted $\{C^1, C^2, C^3, \ldots\}$, with the first sequence converging to point A and the second sequence converging to point D. *If it is the case that $B^i \succ C^i$ for all i's, then the continuity assumption requires that $A \succsim D$.* Thus, if the B bundles are always preferred to the C bundles as we move along the two sequences and if this continues to hold as we get closer and closer to the

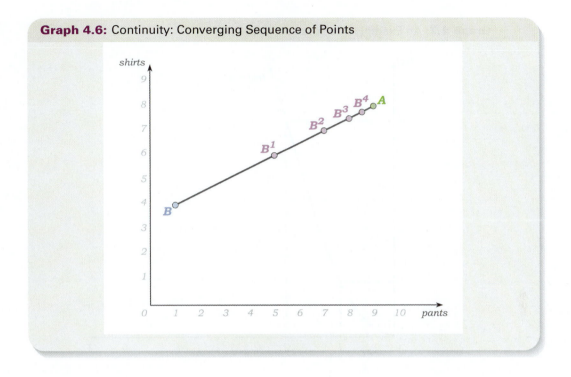

Graph 4.6: Continuity: Converging Sequence of Points

bundles *A* and *D* to which the two sequences converge, we can't suddenly have a "jump" at the end of the sequences that reverses the preference relation and causes *D* to be preferred to *A*.

4B.3 Representing Tastes with Utility Functions

In Section 4A.3, we demonstrated how the assumptions we have made about people's tastes allow us to graph different types of tastes using indifference curves. We will now see that these indifference curves can be interpreted as parts of mathematical functions that summarize tastes more fully. These functions are called *utility functions*, and utility functions are simply mathematical rules that assign numbers to bundles of goods in such a way that more preferred bundles are assigned higher numbers.

Recall from your math classes that a *mathematical function* is just a formula that assigns numbers to points. For instance, the function $f(x) = x^2$ is simply a way of assigning numbers to different points in the space $\mathbb{R}^1$ (the real line), the space consisting of points with only a single component. To the point $x = 1/2$, the function assigns a value of 1/4; to the point $x = 1$, the function assigns a value of 1; and to the point $x = 2$, the function assigns the value 4. The full function is depicted in Graph 4.7.

In mathematical notation, we would indicate by $f: \mathbb{R}^1 \rightarrow \mathbb{R}^1$ that such a function f is a formula that assigns a real number to each point on the real line. We would then read this notation as "the function f takes points on the real line $\mathbb{R}^1$ and assigns to them a value from the real line $\mathbb{R}^1$." Such functions are not, however, of particular use to us as we think about representing tastes because we are generally considering bundles that consist of more than one good, bundles such as those consisting of combinations of shirts and pants. Thus, we might be more interested in a function $f: \mathbb{R}^2_+ \rightarrow \mathbb{R}^1$ that assigns to each point made up of two real numbers (i.e., points that lie in $\mathbb{R}^2_+$) a single real number (i.e., a number in $\mathbb{R}^1$). One example of such a function would be $f(x_1, x_2) = x_1 x_2$, a function that assigns the value 1 to the bundle (1, 1), the value 4 to the bundle (2, 2), and the value 2 to the bundle (2, 1).

Graph 4.7: An Example of a Function $f: \mathbb{R}^1 \to \mathbb{R}^1$

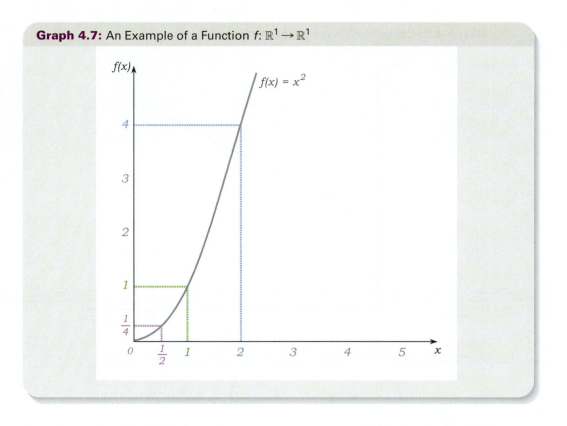

Suppose, for instance, that we are back to choosing between bundles composed of shirts and pants. If I have rational tastes, I can compare any two bundles and tell you which I prefer or whether I am indifferent between them. If I can find a function $f: \mathbb{R}^2_+ \to \mathbb{R}^1$ that assigns to each bundle of shirts and pants (represented by points in $\mathbb{R}^2_+$) a value in such a way that more preferred bundles are assigned higher numbers (and indifferent bundles are assigned the same number), we will say that I have found a utility function that represents my tastes. More formally, a function $f: \mathbb{R}^2_+ \to \mathbb{R}^1$ represents my tastes over pants (x_1) and shirts (x_2) if and only if,

$$(x_1^A, x_2^A) > (x_1^B, x_2^B) \text{ implies } f(x_1^A, x_2^A) > f(x_1^B, x_2^B) \text{ and}$$
$$(x_1^A, x_2^A) \sim (x_1^B, x_2^B) \text{ implies } f(x_1^A, x_2^A) = f(x_1^B, x_2^B). \tag{4.13}$$

We will typically use u instead of f to denote such utility functions.

For the more general case of tastes over bundles with n different goods, we can now define a utility function as follows: $u: \mathbb{R}^n_+ \to \mathbb{R}^1$ *represents tastes* $\succsim$ *over bundles of n goods if and only if, for any* $(x_1^A, x_2^A, \ldots, x_n^A)$ *and* $(x_1^B, x_2^B, \ldots, x_n^B)$ *in* $\mathbb{R}^n_+$

$$(x_1^A, x_2^A, \ldots, x_n^A) > (x_1^B, x_2^B, \ldots, x_n^B) \text{ implies } u(x_1^A, x_2^A, \ldots, x_n^A) > u(x_1^B, x_2^B, \ldots, x_n^B) \text{ and}$$
$$(x_1^A, x_2^A, \ldots, x_n^A) \sim (x_1^B, x_2^B, \ldots, x_n^B) \text{ implies } u(x_1^A, x_2^A, \ldots, x_n^A) = u(x_1^B, x_2^B, \ldots, x_n^B). \tag{4.14}$$

You might notice right away how important our rationality assumptions about tastes are in ensuring that we can indeed represent tastes with utility functions. Functions assign values to all points in the space over which they are defined. Thus, we could not use functions to represent tastes unless we indeed were able to evaluate each bundle in relation to others; i.e., unless our tastes were complete. Similarly, mathematical functions *have to be* logically consistent in the sense that whenever point A is greater than point B and point B is greater than point C, point A

must be greater than point C. Thus, if tastes were not also logically consistent as required by our transitivity assumption, we could not use mathematical functions to represent them.[11]

4B.3.1 Utility Functions and Indifference Curves

Let's return to my tastes over bundles of pants and shirts, with pants represented by x_1 and shirts represented by x_2, and suppose that my tastes can be captured fully by the function $u(x_1, x_2) = x_1^{1/2} x_2^{1/2}$. Graph 4.8a illustrates this function

Graph 4.8: Indifference Curves and Utility Functions

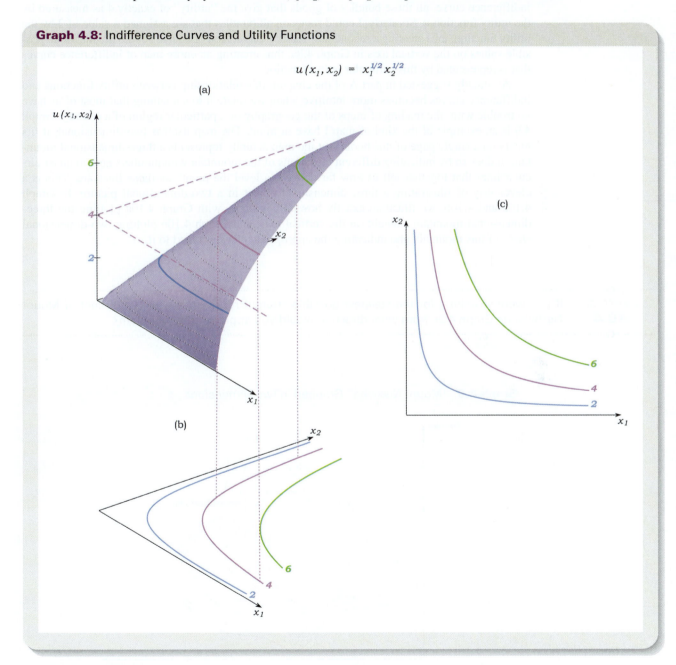

[11] One can formally prove that any tastes that satisfy the rationality and continuity assumptions can be represented by utility functions. See A. Mas-Colell, M. Whinston, and J. Greene, *Microeconomic Theory* (New York, Oxford University Press, 2002). You can also construct a simplified version of this proof in end-of-chapter exercise 4.14.

graphically, with shirts and pants measured on the lower axes and the values $u(x_1, x_2)$ plotted on the vertical axis. Now suppose that I wanted to plot only those bundles that are assigned a value of precisely 4. I would then focus on 1 horizontal (magenta) slice of this function that occurs at a height of 4 and could plot that slice in a two-dimensional picture with just pants and shirts on the axes, as in panels (b) and (c) of Graph 4.8. Since bundles that are assigned the same number are, by the definition of a utility function, valued exactly the same by me, these bundles represent one indifference curve, all those bundles of goods that give me "utility" of exactly 4 as measured by the utility function u. Similarly, I could focus on all bundles that are assigned a value of 2 by the utility function, thus creating a second indifference curve. And of course I could do this for all possible values on the vertical axis in Graph 4.8a, thus creating an entire map of indifference curves that is represented by this particular utility function.

As already suggested in part A of the chapter, this relationship between utility functions and indifference curves becomes more intuitive when we relate it to something that most of us have no trouble with: the reading of maps of the geography of a particular region of a country. Graph 4.9 is an example of the kind of map I have in mind. The map itself is two-dimensional; it fits nicely on a single page of this book. But the map actually represents a three-dimensional mountain. It does so by indicating different elevations of the mountain with numbers next to quasi-circular lines that together tell us how far above sea level the points on those lines are. This is a clever way of illustrating a three-dimensional object in a two-dimensional picture. In Graph 4.10a and 4.10b, we illustrate exactly how this is done, with Graph 4.10a plotting the three-dimensional mountain's height on the vertical axis, and Graph 4.10b plotting two-dimensional slices of this mountain and indicating the appropriate elevation next to it.

Exercise 4B.4   If you were searching for the steepest possible straight route up the last 2,000 feet of Mount Nechyba (in Graph 4.9), from what direction would you approach the mountain?

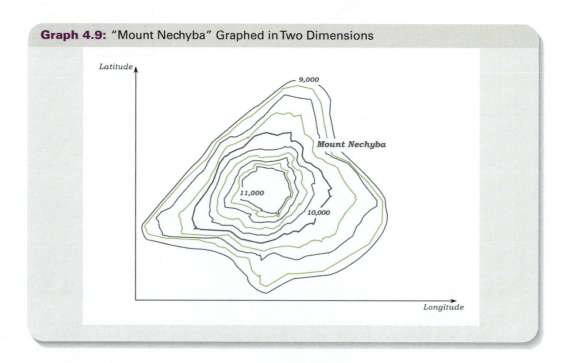

Graph 4.9: "Mount Nechyba" Graphed in Two Dimensions

Graph 4.10: Going from Three to Two Dimensions for "Mount Nechyba"

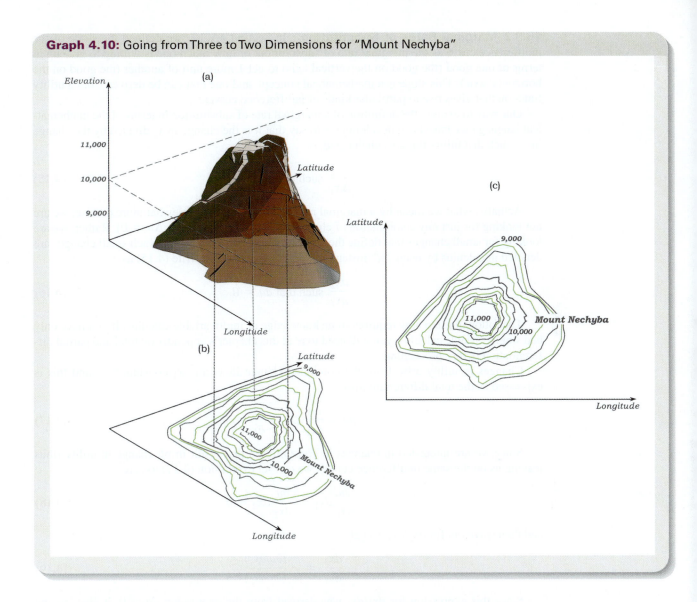

Indifference curves are exactly analogous to these levels of a three-dimensional mountain plotted in two dimensions. Instead of representing the geographical terrain of an area, they illustrate the height of a "utility mountain" that rises as more goods enter a bundle. But unlike real mountains, the utility mountain generally has no peak because our "more is better" assumption implies that we can always climb higher by going to bundles of goods that have more of everything in them. Thus, the slices of our utility mountain are not closed circles like those of mountains with peaks but rather are open ended.

In political science models, politicians are sometimes assumed to choose between bundles of spending on various issues, say military and domestic spending. Since they have to impose taxes to fund this spending, more is not necessarily better than less, and thus most politicians have some ideal bundle of domestic and military spending. How would such tastes over domestic and military spending be similar to the geographic mountain analogy?

Exercise
4B.5

4B.3.2 Marginal Rates of Substitution   In Section 4A.3.2, we defined the slope of the indifference curve as the marginal rate of substitution, or how much one is willing to give up in terms of one good (the good on the vertical axis) to get 1 more unit of another (the good on the horizontal axis). This slope is a mathematical concept, and one that can be derived from a utility function that gives rise to particular kinds of indifference curves.

One way to express the definition of a marginal rate of substitution in terms of the mathematical language we have been developing is to say that it is the change in x_2 divided by the change in x_1 such that utility remains unchanged, or

$$\frac{\Delta x_2}{\Delta x_1} \text{ such that } \Delta u = 0. \tag{4.15}$$

Actually, what we mean by a marginal rate of substitution is somewhat more precise; we are not looking for just *any* combination of changes in x_2 and x_1 (such that $\Delta u = 0$). Rather, we are looking for small changes that define the slope around a particular point. Such small changes are denoted in calculus by using "d" instead of "Δ." Thus, we can rewrite (4.15) as

$$\frac{dx_2}{dx_1} \text{ such that } du = 0. \tag{4.16}$$

The following step now requires some knowledge of multivariable calculus. If you have only had single variable calculus, you will need to read this chapter's appendix on total and partial differentiation before proceeding.

Changes in utility arise from the combined change in x_2 and x_1 consumption, and this is expressed as the total differential (du)

$$du = \frac{\partial u}{\partial x_1} dx_1 + \frac{\partial u}{\partial x_2} dx_2. \tag{4.17}$$

Since we are interested in changes in consumption that result in no change in utility (thus leaving us on the same indifference curve), we can set expression (4.17) to zero

$$\frac{\partial u}{\partial x_1} dx_1 + \frac{\partial u}{\partial x_2} dx_2 = 0 \tag{4.18}$$

and then solve out for dx_2/dx_1 to get

$$\frac{dx_2}{dx_1} = -\frac{(\partial u/\partial x_1)}{(\partial u/\partial x_2)}. \tag{4.19}$$

Since this expression for dx_2/dx_1 was derived from the expression $du = 0$, it gives us the equation for small changes in x_2 divided by small changes in x_1 such that utility remains unchanged, which is precisely our definition of a marginal rate substitution. Thus, if we know that a particular utility function u gives rise to an indifference map that accurately represents someone's tastes, we now know how to calculate the marginal rate of substitution for that person at any consumption bundle (x_1, x_2) with

$$MRS(x_1, x_2) = -\frac{(\partial u/\partial x_1)}{(\partial u/\partial x_2)}. \tag{4.20}$$

Suppose, for instance, your tastes for pants (x_1) and shirts (x_2) can be summarized by the utility function $u(x_1, x_2) = x_1^{1/2} x_2^{1/2}$ (which is graphed in Graph 4.8a), and suppose that we would like to determine the marginal rate of substitution when you are consuming 4 pants and 3 shirts. We can begin by finding the general expression for your marginal rate of substitution given that you have tastes summarized by this utility function. To do this, we have to take the partial derivative of u with respect to each of the two goods,

$$\frac{\partial u}{\partial x_1} = \left(\frac{1}{2}\right)\left(x_1^{-1/2}x_2^{1/2}\right) \quad \text{and} \quad \frac{\partial u}{\partial x_2} = \left(\frac{1}{2}\right)\left(x_1^{1/2}x_2^{-1/2}\right) \tag{4.21}$$

and plug the results into the formula for MRS in equation (4.20) to get:

$$MRS = -\frac{(1/2)(x_1^{-1/2}x_2^{1/2})}{(1/2)(x_1^{1/2}x_2^{-1/2})} = -\frac{x_2}{x_1}. \tag{4.22}$$

This simplified expression, $MRS = -x_2/x_1$, then gives us the formula for the slope of all your indifference curves at every possible bundle in $\mathbb{R}^2_+$ assuming that these indifference curves can indeed be represented by the utility function $u(x_1,x_2) = x_1^{1/2}x_2^{1/2}$. For instance, if you are currently consuming 4 pants (x_1) and 3 shirts (x_2), your marginal rate of substitution is equal to $-3/4$. If you are consuming 10 pants and 1 shirt, your marginal rate of substitution is $-1/10$, and if you are consuming 1 pair of pants and 10 shirts, it is -10.

How does the expression for the marginal rate of substitution change if tastes could instead be summarized by the utility function $u(x_1,x_2) = x_1^{1/4}x_2^{3/4}$?

Exercise 4B.6

4B.3.3 Interpreting Values Assigned to Indifference Curves by Utility Functions
At this point, you may have gotten a little suspicious. After all, we made a big deal in Section 4A.3.3 about the fact that happiness or "utility" cannot be measured objectively and yet we seem to be measuring utility here with utility functions. When discussing the numbers next to indifference curves in Graph 4.5, we indicated that the numbers themselves were not important; it was the ordering of the numbers that mattered because we were simply using the numbers to indicate which indifference curves yield more happiness and which yield less. And we mentioned that we could just as easily have multiplied the numbers in Graph 4.5 by 2 or divided them by 5 or added 13 to them because in each case, the *ordering* of indifference curves would remain unchanged. We concluded that, *so long as the shape of indifference curves and the ordering of the numbers that accompany the curves are unchanged between two graphs, the maps of indifference curves in the two graphs represent the same tastes.*

The same is true of utility functions. You can think of these functions as rulers that use some scale to measure utility. We can adjust the scale: *As long as two functions give rise to the same shapes of indifference curves and as long as the ordering of the numbers assigned to these indifference curves is the same, the two functions represent the same underlying tastes.* All we are doing is using a different ruler. Again, it might be easy to see exactly what we mean here by returning to the mountain analogy. In Graph 4.10a, we used a "ruler" with "feet from sea level" to measure the height of a mountain, and we then translated slices of this mountain into two dimensions, placing the appropriate height of that slice (measured in feet) next to each slice in Graph 4.10b. Suppose that we had instead used a "ruler" with "meters from sea level" in Graph 4.10a. The height of the mountain might now be scaled differently, but the slices of the mountain would continue to exhibit the same shapes in Graph 4.10b, except that they would be accompanied by a different number indicating height since it would be expressed in meters instead of feet. Nothing fundamental changes when we change the units of measurement on our ruler.

Consider the utility function $u(x_1,x_2) = x_1^{1/2}x_2^{1/2}$ that we graphed in Graph 4.8a and that is replicated in Graph 4.11a. Now consider the same function squared; i.e., $v(x_1,x_2) = (x_1^{1/2}x_2^{1/2})^2 = x_1x_2$, which is graphed in Graph 4.11c. The functions certainly look different, but it turns out that they

Graph 4.11: Rescaling Graph 4.8a

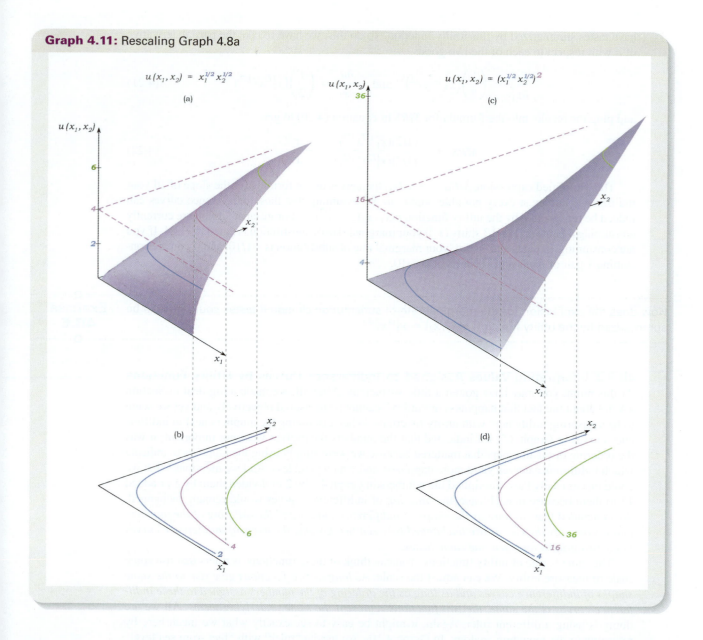

give rise to exactly the same indifference curves in panels (b) and (d) just like the two differently measured versions of the same mountain give rise to the same two-dimensional picture of its levels. To prove this mathematically, all we have to do is check whether the two utility functions give rise to the same expression for the marginal rate of substitution because if the slopes of the indifference curves are the same at all points, the shapes of the indifference curves must be the same. First, we find the partial derivatives of v with respect to each good (as we did for u in (4.21)):

$$\frac{\partial v}{\partial x_1} = x_2 \quad \text{and} \quad \frac{\partial v}{\partial x_2} = x_1. \tag{4.23}$$

These expressions certainly differ from the analogous derivatives for u in equation (4.21). They represent the additional (or marginal) utility you would obtain from 1 more unit of consumption of each of the two goods, and this additional utility differs depending on what ruler we use to measure utility. It therefore makes sense that the two different utility functions, u and v, have different partial derivatives with respect to each of the two goods. (For this reason, we do not think that there is any real content in the concept of "marginal utility.") But when we then plug the results in equation (4.23) into our formula for a marginal rate of substitution in equation (4.20), we get that the marginal rate of substitution implied by the utility function v is again equal to $-x_2/x_1$, just as it was when we calculated the marginal rate of substitution for the utility function u in equation (4.22).

Can you verify that squaring the utility function in exercise 4B.6 also does not change the underlying indifference curves?

Exercise
4B.7

You can see the intuition for what happened by comparing the partial derivatives in equation (4.21) and (4.23). While they are different, they are different only in ways that cancel out when we divide one partial derivative by the other as we calculate the marginal rate of substitution. Put differently, the units that measure marginal utility drop out of the equation when we divide two marginal utilities by each another. Thus, *the concept of a marginal rate of substitution is independent of what scale we use to measure utility*, and is thus meaningful even though we do not think utility itself can be objectively quantified.

Illustrate that the same conclusion we reached with respect to u and v representing the same indifference curves also holds when we take the square root of u; i.e., when we consider the function $w(x_1,x_2) = (x_1^{1/2}x_2^{1/2})^{1/2} = x_1^{1/4}x_2^{1/4}$.

Exercise
4B.8

The idea that a rescaling of a utility function cancels out when we calculate marginal rates of substitution can be seen to hold more generally. Consider a function $f: \mathbb{R}^1 \to \mathbb{R}^1$ that is applied to a utility function $u(x_1,x_2)$ to create a new utility function $v(x_1,x_2) = f(u(x_1,x_2))$. (In our previous example, for instance, we applied the function $f(x) = x^2$ to get $v(x_1,x_2) = f(u(x_1,x_2)) = f(x_1^{1/2}x_2^{1/2}) = (x_1^{1/2}x_2^{1/2})^2 = x_1x_2$.) The partial derivatives of v with respect to the two goods are then

$$\frac{\partial v}{\partial x_1} = \frac{\partial f}{\partial u}\frac{\partial u}{\partial x_1} \quad \text{and} \quad \frac{\partial v}{\partial x_2} = \frac{\partial f}{\partial u}\frac{\partial u}{\partial x_2}. \qquad (4.24)$$

When we divide these two terms by each another as we calculate the marginal rate of substitution, the $(\partial f/\partial u)$ terms cancel and we get

$$-\frac{(\partial v/\partial x_1)}{(\partial v/\partial x_2)} = -\frac{(\partial u/\partial x_1)}{(\partial u/\partial x_2)}. \qquad (4.25)$$

Applying a transformation f to a utility function u therefore does not change the shapes of indifference curves since it does not change their marginal rates of substitutions; it simply relabels indifference curves with different numbers. So long as the ordering of the numbers assigned to indifference curves remains the same, the transformed utility function then represents the same tastes. Such transformations are sometimes called *order preserving* or *positive monotone* functions. Multiplying a utility function by 5, for instance, simply results in a number 5 times as high associated with each indifference curve. Multiplying the same utility function by -5, on the other hand, results in the label of each indifference curve being -5 times what it was before; as a result, the ordering of the indifference curves is reversed, suggesting that indifference curves previously judged better than a particular bundle are now worse than that bundle. The former transformation (multiplying by 5) is therefore order preserving while the latter (multiplying by -5) is not even though both transformations preserve the shapes of the indifference curves. In end-of-chapter exercise 4.5, you will investigate some other possible transformations of utility functions, but it should be clear from our discussion that *once we have found one utility function that represents a particular set of tastes (or indifference curves), we can find a large number of other utility functions that also represent those tastes* by subjecting the original utility function to a variety of different transformations.

Exercise 4B.9

Consider the utility function $u(x_1, x_2) = x_1^{1/2} x_2^{1/2}$. Take natural logs of this function and calculate the *MRS* of the new function. Can the natural log transformation be applied to utility functions such that the new utility function represents the same underlying tastes?

Exercise 4B.10

Consider the utility function $u(x_1, x_2, x_3) = x_1^{1/2} x_2^{1/2} x_3^{1/2}$. Take natural logs of this function and calculate the marginal rates of substitution of each pair of goods. Can the natural log transformation be applied to utility functions of 3 goods such that the new utility function represents the same underlying tastes?

CONCLUSION

In this chapter, we have begun our investigation of how economists can model tastes, sometimes also called *preferences*. By making some basic rationality assumptions that ensure an individual is able to make choices (completeness and transitivity), we are able to graph tastes by illustrating bundles of goods over which an individual is indifferent. By making some additional assumptions that make sense in many economic settings (continuity, convexity, monotonicity), these indifference curves were shown to take on particular shapes. Maps of "indifference curves," accompanied by numbers indicating which bundles are preferred to others, then provide complete descriptions of tastes. These maps can be represented mathematically as levels of utility functions, much as rings on geographic maps are levels of a more general function that represents the height of mountains. Because we do not think that there are objective measures of "utility," we also showed that there are many different utility functions that can represent the same indifference map. While the actual number assigned to each indifference curve by a utility function thus has little meaning, the slope of indifference curves, known as the marginal rate of substitution, does carry real economic meaning because it tells us how easily an individual is willing to trade one good for another (depending on how many of each he or she currently has). As in previous chapters, the mathematical analog to our graphical tools permits us to expand our analysis to more than two goods.

In Chapter 6, we will begin our analysis of how tastes (as represented by indifference curves and utility functions) combine with our economic circumstances (as represented by budget constraints) to lead us to make optimal economic *choices*. Before taking this step, however, we will step back in Chapter 5 to investigate the different types of tastes that can be represented within the model we have introduced here.

APPENDIX: SOME BASICS OF MULTIVARIABLE CALCULUS

Some colleges and universities require a full three-semester calculus sequence for economics majors. If you have taken such a sequence, you will already have covered all the required calculus concepts used in this book and many calculus concepts that are not necessary for what we are trying to do. Often, however, economics majors are required to take only a single semester of calculus. Typically, this means that you will have covered *single-variable differentiation* but not differentiation involving functions of multiple variables.

This appendix is intended to cover the basics of extending single-variable differentiation to functions of multiple variables without going into the level of detail that you would encounter in a full calculus sequence.

Single-variable functions take the form $y = f(x)$ such as the function graphed in Graph 4.7, which graphs $y = f(x) = x^2$. As you know from your first calculus course, the derivative (or slope) of this function is $df/dx = 2x$. Utility functions, however, are typically multivariable functions because we are interested in the trade-offs consumers make among more than 1 type of good. For instance, we graphed in Graph 4.8a the function $u(x_1, x_2) = x_1^{1/2} x_2^{1/2}$. The difference between a single-variable function and a function of multiple variables is simply that the former assigns a number to points on the real line $\mathbb{R}^1$ while the latter assigns numbers to points in a higher dimensional space. A single-variable function is therefore denoted as a rule that assigns a real number to elements of the real line, or $f \colon \mathbb{R}^1 \to \mathbb{R}^1$. A multivariable function $y = f(x_1, x_2, \ldots, x_n)$, on the other hand, is a formula that assigns a real number to points with n components and is therefore denoted $f \colon R^n \to \mathbb{R}^1$.

Partial Derivatives

Any multivariable function becomes a single-variable function if we hold all but 1 variable fixed. Consider, for instance, the utility function $u(x_1, x_2) = x_1^{1/2} x_2^{1/2}$ and suppose that we want to ask how utility

Graph 4.12: A Single-Variable "Slice" of a Multivariable Function

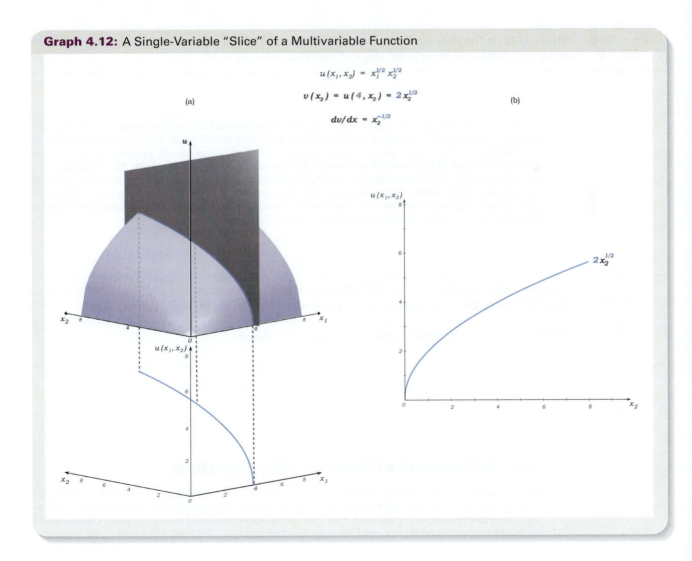

$$u(x_1, x_2) = x_1^{1/2} x_2^{1/2}$$

$$v(x_2) = u(4, x_2) = 2x_2^{1/2}$$

$$dv/dx = x_2^{-1/2}$$

(a)

(b)

(as measured by this function) changes when x_2 changes while $x_1 = 4$. In that case, we are holding the x_1 variable fixed at 4 and are operating on a "slice" of the three-dimensional function depicted in Graph 4.12a. This slice is just a single-variable function $v(x_2) = u(4, x_2) = 2x_2^{1/2}$ (since the square root of 4 is 2) and is depicted in panel (a) of the graph and separately in panel (b).

From your single-variable calculus background, you already know how to take the *derivative* of the function $v(x_2)$ in panel (b) of the graph. This derivative $dv/dx = x_2^{-1/2}$ is then simply the slope of the slice of the two-variable function $u(x_1, x_2)$ depicted in panel (a). It is also called the *partial derivative of u with respect to x_2 when $x_1 = 4$*.

More generally, we can take the partial derivative of u with respect to x_2 by simply treating the x_1 variable as a constant. This partial derivative is denoted $\partial u / \partial x_2$ and is calculated exactly the same way you would calculate a derivative of a single-variable function in which x_1 is just a constant; i.e.,

$$\frac{\partial u}{\partial x_2} = \left(\frac{1}{2}\right) x_1^{1/2} x_2^{-1/2}. \tag{4.26}$$

This then gives us the derivative of a slice of the utility function $u(x_1, x_2)$ that holds x_1 constant at some value. For instance, when $x_1 = 4$ (as we assumed before), the expression reduces to $x_2^{-1/2}$ and represents the slope of the slice in Graph 4.12 at different values of x_2.

Exercise 4B.11 What would be the expression of the slope of the slice of the utility function $u(x_1, x_2) = x_1^{1/2} x_2^{1/2}$ when x_1 is fixed at 9? What is the slope of that slice when $x_2 = 4$?

Such partial derivatives of a utility function give us the *marginal utility* of an additional unit of a consumption good when the quantity of all other consumption goods is held fixed. As we discuss extensively in the main part of the chapter, this concept in and of itself is not economically meaningful because it is expressed in "units of happiness" that we do not believe can be measured objectively. Nevertheless, as we see in Section 4B.3.3, the economically meaningful concept of a marginal rate of substitution is composed of 2 marginal utility values divided by each other (thus canceling out the "units of happiness"). When we get to producer theory where "units of output" are economically meaningful concepts, these partial derivatives themselves will also become economically meaningful.

Exercise 4B.12 Calculate $\partial u / \partial x_1$ for $u(x_1, x_2) = x_1^{1/2} x_2^{1/2}$. What does this reduce to when x_2 is fixed at 4? Where in Graph 4.12 does the slice along which this partial derivative represents the slope lie?

Exercise 4B.13 Calculate $\partial u / \partial x_1$ for the function $u(x_1, x_2) = 10 \ln x_1 + 5 \ln x_2$.

Exercise 4B.14 Calculate $\partial u / \partial x_1$ for the function $u(x_1, x_2) = (2x_1 + 3x_2)^3$. (Remember to use the Chain Rule.)

Total Differential of Multivariable Functions

While a partial derivative of a function like $u(x_1, x_2) = x_1^{1/2} x_2^{1/2}$ tells us the rate at which utility will change if the quantity of one of the two goods in a consumption bundle is increased by a small amount (as the quantity of the other consumption good stays fixed), we might also be interested in how the utility changes when the quantity of both consumption goods changes by small amounts. The *total differential* of the function u

then measures the change in utility resulting from small changes in both x_1 and x_2.[12] Letting dx_1 and dx_2 represent such small changes, the total differential du is expressed mathematically as

$$du = \frac{\partial u}{\partial x_1} dx_1 + \frac{\partial u}{\partial x_2} dx_2 \qquad (4.27)$$

which, for the utility function $u(x_1, x_2) = x_1^{1/2}x_2^{1/2}$, is

$$du = \frac{x_2^{1/2}}{2x_1^{1/2}} dx_1 + \frac{x_1^{1/2}}{2x_2^{1/2}} dx_2. \qquad (4.28)$$

Verify that equation (4.28) is correct.

**Exercise
4B.15**

Notice that if $dx_1 = 0$, i.e., if x_1 does not change and only x_2 changes, equation (4.27) reduces to

$$du = \frac{\partial u}{\partial x_2} dx_2, \qquad (4.29)$$

which is called the *partial differential* of u with respect to x_2.

Calculate the total differential du of $u(x_1, x_2) = 10 \ln x_1 + 5 \ln x_2$.

**Exercise
4B.16**

END-OF-CHAPTER EXERCISES

4.1   I hate grits so much that the very idea of owning grits repulses me. I do, on the other hand, enjoy a good breakfast of Cocoa Puffs cereal.

A. In each of the following, put boxes of grits on the horizontal axis and boxes of cereal on the vertical. Then graph three indifference curves and number them.

   a.   Assume that my tastes satisfy the convexity and continuity assumptions and otherwise satisfy the previous description.

   b.   How would your answer change if my tastes were "non-convex;" i.e., if averages were worse than extremes?

   c.   How would your answer to (a) change if I hated both Cocoa Puffs and grits but we again assumed my tastes satisfy the convexity assumption?

   d.   What if I hated both goods and my tastes were non-convex?

B. Now suppose you like both grits and Cocoa Puffs, that your tastes satisfy our 5 basic assumptions, and that they can be represented by the utility function $u(x_1, x_2) = x_1 x_2$.

   a.   Consider two bundles, $A = (1,20)$ and $B = (10,2)$. Which one do you prefer?

   b.   Use bundles A and B to illustrate that these tastes are in fact convex.

   c.   What is the *MRS* at bundle A? What is it at bundle B?

---

[12]There is a distinction between the *total differential* and the *total derivative* of a multivariable function. For now, we are concerned only with the total differential (which is used in the main part of this chapter).
*conceptually challenging
**computationally challenging
†solutions in Study Guide

    d.   What is the simplest possible transformation of this function that would represent tastes consistent with those described in A(d)?

    e.   Now consider tastes that are instead defined by the function $u(x_1, x_2) = x_1^2 + x_2^2$. What is the *MRS* of this function?

    f.   Do these tastes have diminishing marginal rates of substitution? Are they convex?

    g.   How could you most easily turn this utility function into one that represents tastes like those described in A(c)?

4.2[†]   Consider my wife's tastes for grits and cereal.

A. Unlike me, my wife likes both grits and cereal, but for her, averages (between equally preferred bundles) are worse than extremes.

    a.   On a graph with boxes of grits on the horizontal and boxes of cereal on the vertical, illustrate three indifference curves that would be consistent with my description of my wife's tastes.

    b.   Suppose we ignored labels on indifference curves and simply looked at shapes of the curves that make up our indifference map. Could my indifference map look the same as my wife's if I hate both cereal and grits? If so, would my tastes be convex?

B. Consider the utility function $u(x_1, x_2) = x_1^2 + 4x_2^2$.

    a.   Could this utility function represent the tastes you graphed in part A(a)?

    b.   How could you transform this utility function to be consistent with my tastes as described in A(b)?

4.3   Consider my tastes for consumption and leisure.

A. Begin by assuming that my tastes over consumption and leisure satisfy our 5 basic assumptions.

    a.   On a graph with leisure hours per week on the horizontal axis and consumption dollars per week on the vertical, give an example of 3 indifference curves (with associated utility numbers) from an indifference map that satisfies our assumptions.

    b.   Now redefine the good on the horizontal axis as "labor hours" rather than "leisure hours." How would the same tastes look in this graph?

    c.   How would both of your graphs change if tastes over leisure and consumption were non-convex; i.e., if averages were worse than extremes?

B. Suppose your tastes over consumption and leisure could be described by the utility function $u(\ell, c) = \ell^{1/2} c^{1/2}$.

    a.   Do these tastes satisfy our 5 basic assumptions?

    b.   Can you find a utility function that would describe the same tastes when the second good is defined as labor hours instead of leisure hours? (*Hint*: Suppose your weekly endowment of leisure time is 60 hours. How does that relate to the sign of the slopes of indifference curves you graphed in part A(b)?)

    c.   What is the marginal rate of substitution for the function you just derived? How does that relate to your graph from part A(b)?

    d.   Do the tastes represented by the utility function in part (b) satisfy our 5 basic assumptions?

4.4   Basket *A* contains 1 unit of x_1 and 5 units of x_2. Basket *B* contains 5 units of x_1 and 1 unit of x_2. Basket *C* contains 3 units of x_1 and 3 units of x_2. Assume throughout that tastes are monotonic.

A. On Monday, you are offered a choice between basket *A* and *C*, and you choose *A*. On Tuesday you are offered a choice between basket *B* and *C*, and you choose *B*.

    a.   Graph these baskets on a graph with x_1 on the horizontal and x_2 on the vertical axis.

    b.   If I know your tastes on any given day satisfy a strict convexity assumption, by which I mean that averages are strictly better than extremes, can I conclude that your tastes have changed from Monday to Tuesday?

    c.   Suppose I only know that your tastes satisfy a weak convexity assumption, by which I mean that averages are at least as good as extremes. Suppose also that I know your tastes have not changed from Monday to Tuesday. Can I conclude anything about the precise shape of one of your indifference curves?

B. Continue to assume that tastes satisfy the monotonicity assumption.

    a.   State formally the assumption of "strict convexity" as defined in part A(b).

    b.   Suppose your tastes over x_1 and x_2 were strictly non-convex—averages are strictly worse than extremes. State this assumption formally. Under this condition, would your answer to part A(b) change?

    c.   Consider the utility function $u(x_1, x_2) = x_1 + x_2$. Demonstrate that this captures tastes that give rise to your conclusion about the shape of one of the indifference curves in part A(c).

4.5[†]   In this exercise, we explore the concept of marginal rates of substitution (and, in part B, its relation to utility functions) further.

A. Suppose I own 3 bananas and 6 apples, and you own 5 bananas and 10 apples.

    a.   With bananas on the horizontal axis and apples on the vertical, the slope of my indifference curve at my current bundle is -2, and the slope of your indifference curve through your current bundle is -1. Assume that our tastes satisfy our usual 5 assumptions. Can you suggest a trade to me that would make both of us better off? (Feel free to assume we can trade fractions of apples and bananas.)

    b.   After we engage in the trade you suggested, will our *MRS*'s have gone up or down (in absolute value)?

    c.   If the values for our *MRS*'s at our current consumption bundles were reversed, how would your answers to (a) and (b) change?

    d.   What would have to be true about our *MRS*'s at our current bundles in order for you not to be able to come up with a mutually beneficial trade?

    e.   *True or False*: If we have different tastes, then we will always be able to trade with both of us benefitting.

    f.   *True or False*: If we have the same tastes, then we will never be able to trade with both of us benefitting.

B. Consider the following 5 utility functions and assume that α and β are positive real numbers:

$$1.\ u^A(x_1, x_2) = x_1^\alpha x_2^\beta$$

$$2.\ u^B(x_1, x_2) = \alpha x_1 + \beta x_2$$

$$3.\ u^C(x_1, x_2) = \alpha x_1 + \beta \ln x_2 \qquad\qquad (4.30)$$

$$4.\ u^D(x_1, x_2) = \left(\frac{\alpha}{\beta}\right) \ln x_1 + \ln x_2$$

$$5.\ u^E(x_1, x_2) = -\alpha \ln x_1 - \beta \ln x_2$$

    a.   Calculate the formula for *MRS* for each of these utility functions.

    b.   Which utility functions represent tastes that have linear indifference curves?

    c.   Which of these utility functions represent the same underlying tastes?

    d.   Which of these utility functions represent tastes that do not satisfy the monotonicity assumption?

    e.   Which of these utility functions represent tastes that do not satisfy the convexity assumption?

    f.   Which of these utility functions represent tastes that are not rational (i.e., that do not satisfy the completeness and transitivity assumptions)?

    g.   Which of these utility functions represent tastes that are not continuous?

    h.   Consider the following statement: "Benefits from trade emerge because we have different tastes. If individuals had the same tastes, they would not be able to benefit from trading with one another." Is this statement ever true, and if so, are there any tastes represented by the utility functions in this problem for which the statement is true?

4.6   **Everyday Application:** *Rating Movies on a Numerical Scale*: My wife and I often go to movies and afterward assign a rating ranging from 0 to 10 to the movie we saw.

A. Suppose we go to see a double feature, first *Terminator 2* with the great actor Arnold Schwarzenegger and then the adaptation of Jane Austin's boring novel *Emma*. Afterward, you hear me say that I rated *Terminator 2* as an 8 and *Emma* as a 2, and you hear my wife comment that she rated *Terminator 2* a 5 and *Emma* a 4.

    a.   Do my wife and I agree on which movie is better?

    b.   How would your answer change if my wife's ratings had been reversed?

    c.   Can you tell for sure whether I liked *Terminator 2* more than my wife did?

    d.   Often, my wife and I then argue about our rankings. *True or False*: It makes little sense for us to argue if we both rank one movie higher than the other even if we assign very different numbers.

B. Suppose that the only thing I really care about in evaluating movies is the fraction of "action" time (as opposed to thoughtful conversation) and let the fraction of screen time devoted to action be denoted x_1. Suppose that the only thing my wife cares about when evaluating movies is the fraction of time strong women appear on screen, and let that fraction be denoted x_2. *Terminator 2* has $x_1 = 0.8$ and $x_2 = 0.5$ while *Emma* has $x_1 = 0.2$ and $x_2 = 0.4$.

    a.   Consider the functions $u(x_1) = 10x_1$ and $v(x_2) = 10x_2$ and suppose that I use the function u to determine my movie rating and my wife uses the function v. What ratings do we give to the two movies?

    b.   One day, I decide that I will assign ratings differently, using the function $\bar{u}(x_1) = 5.25x_1^{1/6}$. Will I rank any pair of movies differently using this function rather than my previous function u? What approximate values do I now assign to *Terminator 2* and *Emma*?

    c.   My wife also decides to change her way of assigning ratings to movies. She will now use the function $\bar{v}(x_2) = 590x_2^{6.2}$. Will her rankings of any two movies change as a result? What approximate values does she now assign to the two movies?

    d.   Suppose my wife had instead chosen the function $\underline{v}(x_2) = 10(1 - x_2)$. Will she now rank movies differently?

4.7*   **Everyday Application:** *Did 9/11 Change Tastes?*: In another textbook, the argument is made that consumer tastes over "airline miles travelled" and "other goods" changed as a result of the tragic events of September 11, 2001.

A. Here, we will see how you might think of that argument as true or false depending on how you model tastes.

    a.   To see the reasoning behind the argument that tastes changed, draw a graph with "airline miles travelled" on the horizontal axis and "other goods" (denominated in dollars) on the vertical. Draw an indifference curve from the map of indifference curves that represent a typical consumer's tastes (and that satisfy our usual assumptions).

    b.   Pick a bundle on the indifference curve on your graph and denote it A. Given the perception of increased risk, what do you think happened to the typical consumer's *MRS* at this point after September 11, 2001?

    c.   For a consumer who perceives a greater risk of air travel after September 11, 2001, what is likely to be the relationship of the indifference curves from the old indifference map to the indifference curves from the new indifference map at every bundle?

    d.   Within the context of the model we have developed so far, does this imply that the typical consumer's tastes for air travel have changed?

    e.   Now suppose that we thought more comprehensively about the tastes of our consumer. In particular, suppose we add a third good that consumers care about: "air safety." Imagine a three-dimensional graph, with "air miles travelled" on the horizontal axis and "other goods" on the vertical (as before), and with "air safety" on the third axis coming out at you. Suppose "air safety" can be expressed as a value between 0 and 100, with 0 meaning certain death when one steps on an airplane and 100 meaning no risk at all. Suppose that before 9/11, consumers thought that air safety stood at 90. On the slice of your three-dimensional graph that holds air safety constant at 90, illustrate the pre-9/11 indifference curve that passes through (x_1^A, x_2^A), the level of air miles travelled (x_1^A) and other goods consumed (x_2^A) before 9/11.

f. Suppose the events of 9/11 cause air safety to fall to 80. Illustrate your post-9/11 indifference curve through (x_1^A, x_2^A) on the slice that holds air safety constant at 80 but draw that slice on top of the one you just drew in (e).

g. Explain that while you could argue that our tastes changed in our original model, in a bigger sense you could also argue that our tastes did not change after 9/11, only our circumstances did.

B. Suppose an average traveler's tastes can be described by the utility function $u(x_1, x_2, x_3) = x_1 x_3 + x_2$, where x_1 is miles travelled by air, x_2 is "other consumption," and x_3 is an index of air safety that ranges from 0 to 100.

a. Calculate the *MRS* of other goods for airline miles; i.e., the *MRS* that represents the slope of the indifference curves when x_1 is on the horizontal and x_2 is on the vertical axis.

b. What happens to the *MRS* when air safety (x_3) falls from 90 to 80?

c. Is this consistent with your conclusions from part A? In the context of this model, have tastes changed?

d. Suppose that $u(x_1, x_2, x_3) = x_1 x_2 x_3$ instead. Does the *MRS* of other consumption for air miles travelled still change as air safety changes? Is this likely to be a good model of tastes for analyzing what happened to consumer demand after 9/11?

e. What if $u(x_1, x_2, x_3) = x_2 x_3 + x_2$?

4.8* **Everyday Application:** *Tastes of a Cocaine Addict*: Fred is addicted to cocaine. Suppose we want to model his tastes over cocaine and other goods.

EVERYDAY APPLICATION

A. I propose to model his tastes in the following way: For any two bundles A and B of "grams of cocaine" and "dollars of other consumption," I will assume that Fred always prefers bundle A if it contains more grams of cocaine than bundle B. If bundles A and B contain the same amount of cocaine, then I will assume he prefers A to B if and only if A contains more other consumption than B.

a. On a graph with "grams of cocaine" on the horizontal axis and "other consumption" (denominated in dollars) on the vertical, denote one arbitrary bundle as A. Then indicate all the bundles that are strictly preferred to A.

b. On a separate graph, indicate all bundles that are strictly less preferred than A.

c. Looking over your two graphs, is there any bundle that Fred would say gives him exactly as much happiness as A? Are there any two bundles (not necessarily involving bundle A) that Fred is indifferent between?

d. In order for this to be a useful model for studying Fred's behavior, how severe would Fred's addiction have to be?

e. Are these tastes rational? In other words, are they complete and transitive?

f. Do these tastes satisfy the monotonicity property?

g. Do they satisfy the convexity property?

B. The tastes previously defined are called *lexicographic*. Formally, we can define them as follows: For any $A, B \in \mathbb{R}_+^2$, $A \succ B$ if either "$x_1^A > x_1^B$" or "$x_1^A = x_1^B$ and $x_2^A > x_2^B$."

a. In this formal definition, which good is cocaine, x_1 or x_2?

b. On a graph with x_1 on the horizontal axis and x_2 on the vertical, pick an arbitrary bundle $A = (x_1^A, x_2^A)$. Then pick a second bundle $D = (x_1^D, x_2^D)$ such that $x_1^A = x_1^D$ and $x_2^A > x_2^D$.

c. On your graph, illustrate an infinite sequence of bundles $(B^1, B^2, B^3 \ldots)$ that converges to A from the left. Then illustrate an infinite sequence of bundles $(C^1, C^2, C^3 \ldots)$ that converges to D from the right.

d. *True or False*: Every bundle in the C-sequence is strictly preferred to every bundle in the B-sequence.

e. *True or False*: Bundle A is strictly preferred to bundle D.

f. Based on the answers you just gave to (d) and (e), do lexicographic tastes satisfy the continuity property?

g. Can these tastes be represented by a utility function?

4.9   **Business Application:** *Tastes for Cars and Product Characteristics*: People buy all sorts of different cars depending on their income levels as well as their tastes. Industrial organization economists who study product characteristic choices (and advise firms like car manufacturers) often model consumer tastes as tastes over product characteristics (rather than as tastes over different types of products). We explore this concept here.

A. Suppose people cared about two different aspects of cars: the size of the interior passenger cabin and the quality of handling of the car on the road.

    a.   Putting x_1 = "cubic feet of interior space" on the horizontal axis and x_2 = "speed at which the car can handle a curved mountain road" on the vertical, where would you generally locate the following types of cars assuming that they will fall on one line in your graph: a Chevrolet minivan, a Porsche 944, and a Toyota Camry.

    b.   Suppose we considered three different individuals whose tastes satisfy our 5 basic assumptions, and suppose each person owns one of the three types of cars. Suppose further that each indifference curve from one person's indifference map crosses any indifference curve from another person's indifference map at most once. (When two indifference maps satisfy this condition, we often say that they satisfy the *single crossing property*.) Now suppose you know person A's *MRS* at the Toyota Camry is larger (in absolute value) than person B's, and person B's *MRS* at the Toyota Camry is larger (in absolute value) than person C's. Who owns which car?

    c.   Suppose we had not assumed the "single crossing property" in part (a). Would you have been able to answer the question "Who owns which car" assuming everything else remained the same?

    d.   Suppose you are currently person B and you just found out that your uncle has passed away and bequeathed to you his three children, aged 4, 6, and 8 (and nothing else). This results in a change in how you value space and maneuverability. Is your new *MRS* at the Toyota Camry now larger or smaller (in absolute value)?

    e.   What are some other features of cars that might matter to consumers but that you could not fit easily into a two-dimensional graphical model?

B. Let x_1 denote cubic feet of interior space and let x_2 denote maneuverability as defined in part A. Suppose that the tastes of persons A, B, and C can be represented by the utility functions $u^A(x_1, x_2) = x_1^\alpha x_2$, $u^B(x_1, x_2) = x_1^\beta x_2$, and $u^C(x_1, x_2) = x_1^\gamma x_2$ respectively.

    a.   Calculate the *MRS* for each person.

    b.   Assuming α, β, and γ take on different values, is the "single crossing property" defined in part A(b) satisfied?

    c.   Given the description of the three people in part A(b), what is the relationship between α, β, and γ?

    d.   How could you turn your graphical model into a mathematical model that includes factors you raised in part A(e)?

4.10*†   **Business Application:** *Investor Tastes over Risk and Return*: Suppose you are considering where to invest money for the future.

A. Like most investors, you care about the expected return on your investment as well as the risk associated with the investment. But different investors are willing to make different kinds of trade-offs relative to risk and return.

    a.   On a graph, put risk on the horizontal axis and expected return on the vertical. (For purposes of this exercise, don't worry about the precise units in which these are expressed.) Where in your graph would you locate "safe" investments like inflation indexed government bonds, investments for which you can predict the rate of return with certainty?

    b.   Pick one of these "safe" investment bundles of risk and return and label it *A*. Then pick a riskier investment bundle *B* that an investor could plausibly find equally attractive (given that risk is bad in the eyes of investors while expected returns are good).

    c.   If your tastes are convex and you only have investments *A* and *B* to choose from, would you prefer diversifying your investment portfolio by putting half of your investment in *A* and half in *B*?

    d.   If your tastes are non-convex, would you find such diversification attractive?

B. Suppose an investor has utility function $u(x_1, x_2) = (R - x_1)x_2$ where x_1 represents the risk associated with an investment, x_2 is the expected return, and R is a constant.

    a. What is the *MRS* of risk for return for this investor?

    b. Suppose A is a risk-free investment, with $x_1^A = 0$, and suppose that B is risky but our investor is indifferent between A and B. What must the return x_2^A on the risk-free investment be in terms of x_1^B and x_2^B?

    c. Do this investor's tastes satisfy convexity? Illustrate by considering whether this investor would be willing to switch from A or B in part (b) to putting half his investment in A and half in B.

    d. Suppose $R = 10$ for our investor. Imagine he is offered the following three investment portfolios: (1) a no-risk portfolio of government bonds with expected return of 2 and 0 risk; (2) a high-risk portfolio of volatile stocks with expected return of 10 and risk of 8; (3) or a portfolio that consists half of government bonds and half of volatile stocks, with expected return of 6 and risk of 4. Which would he choose?

    e. Suppose a second investor is offered the same three choices. This investor is identical to the first in every way, except that R in her utility function is equal to 20 instead of 10. Which portfolio will she choose?

    f. *True or False*: The first investor's tastes are convex while the second one's are not.

    g. What value of R would make the investor choose the no-risk portfolio?

4.11* **Policy Application:** *Ideology and Preferences of Politicians*: Political scientists often assume that politicians have tastes that can be thought of in the following way: Suppose that the two issues a politician cares about are domestic spending and military spending. Put military spending on the horizontal axis and domestic spending on the vertical axis. Then each politician has some "ideal point," some combination of military and domestic spending that makes him or her happiest.

POLICY APPLICATION

A. Suppose that a politician cares only about how far the actual policy bundle is from his or her ideal point, not the direction in which it deviates from his or her ideal point.

    a. On a graph, pick any arbitrary "ideal point" and illustrate what 3 indifference "curves" would look like for such a politician. Put numerical labels on these to indicate which represent more preferred policy bundles.

    b. On a separate graph, illustrate how tastes would be different for a political conservative (who likes a lot of military spending but is not as keen on domestic spending), a liberal (who likes domestic spending but is not as interested in military spending), and a libertarian (who does not like government spending in any direction to get very large).

    c. This way of graphing political preferences is a short cut because it incorporates directly into tastes the fact that there are taxes that have to pay for government spending. Most politicians would love to spend increasingly more on everything, but they don't because of the increasing political cost of having to raise taxes to fund spending. Thus, there are really three goods we could be modeling: military spending, domestic spending, and taxes, where a politician's tastes are monotone in the first two goods but not in the last. First, think of this as three goods over which tastes satisfy all our usual assumptions—*including monotonicity* and convexity—where we define the goods as spending on military, spending on domestic goods, and the "relative absence of taxes." What would indifference "curves" for a politician look like in a three-dimensional graph? Since it is difficult to draw this, can you describe it in words and show what a two-dimensional slice looks like if it holds one of the goods fixed?

    d. Now suppose you model the same tastes, but this time you let the third good be defined as "level of taxation" rather than "relative absence of taxes." Now monotonicity no longer holds in one dimension. Can you now graph what a slice of this three-dimensional indifference surface would look like if it holds domestic spending fixed and has taxes on the horizontal and military spending on the vertical axis? What would a slice look like that holds taxes fixed and has domestic spending on the horizontal and military spending on the vertical axis?

    e. Pick a point on the indifference curve you drew for the slice that holds taxes fixed. How does the *MRS* at that point differ for a conservative from that of a liberal?

    f. Pick a point on the slice that holds domestic spending fixed. How would the *MRS* at that point differ for a libertarian compared to a conservative?

B. Consider the following equation $u(x_1, x_2) = P - ((x_1 - a)^2 + (x_2 - b)^2)$.

     a. Can you verify that this equation represents tastes such as those described in this problem (and graphed in part A(a))?

     b. What would change in this equation as you model conservative, liberal, and libertarian politicians?

     c. Do these tastes satisfy the convexity property?

     d. Can you think of a way to write a utility function that represents the tastes you were asked to envision in A(c) and A(d)? Let t represent the tax rate with an upper bound of 1.

4.12 **Policy Application:** *Subsistence Levels of Consumption*: Suppose you are interested in modeling a policy issue involving poor households in an underdeveloped country.

A. The households we are trying to model are primarily worried about survival, with a minimum quantity of certain goods (like food and water) necessary for survival. Suppose that one cannot live without at least 4 liters of water per week and at least 7,500 calories of food per week. These quantities of water and food are then *subsistence levels* of water and food.

     a. Suppose you graph weekly liters of water on the horizontal axis and weekly intake of calories on the vertical. Indicate the bundle required for subsistence.

     b. If life below the subsistence quantities is not sustainable, we might find it reasonable not to model tastes below the subsistence quantities. Illustrate a plausible map of indifference curves that takes this into account.

     c. Subsistence levels are a biological reality for all of us, not just for the poor in developing countries. Why might we nevertheless not worry about explicitly modeling subsistence levels for policy analysis in richer countries?

B. The following utility function is known as the *Stone-Geary utility function*:
$u(x_1, x_2) = (x_1 - \bar{x}_1)^\alpha (x_2 - \bar{x}_2)^{(1-\alpha)}$, where $0 < \alpha < 1$.

     a. When interpreted as a model of tastes such as those described in part A, what are the subsistence levels of x_1 and x_2?

     b. How does this utility function treat tastes below subsistence levels?

     c. What is the *MRS* when consumption is above subsistence levels?

     d. Suppose that instead of water and food for someone poor in the developing world, we modeled calories from food (x_1) and dollars spent on vacations (x_2) for someone in the developed world (taking for granted that he or she is consuming his or her desired quantity of water). How would you modify the Stone-Geary utility function assuming that you still want to recognize the absence of tastes for food levels below subsistence?

4.13*† In this exercise, we will explore some logical relationships between families of tastes that satisfy different assumptions.

A. Suppose we define a strong and a weak version of convexity as follows: Tastes are said to be *strongly convex* if whenever a person with those tastes is indifferent between A and B, the person strictly prefers the average of A and B (to A and B). Tastes are said to be *weakly convex* if whenever a person with those tastes is indifferent between A and B, the average of A and B is at least as good as A and B for that person.

     a. Let the set of all tastes that satisfy strong convexity be denoted as *SC* and the set of all tastes that satisfy weak convexity as *WC*. Which set is contained in the other? (We would, for instance, say that "*WC* is contained in *SC*" if any taste that satisfies weak convexity also automatically satisfies strong convexity.)

     b. Consider the set of tastes that are contained in one and only one of the two sets defined previously. What must be true about some indifference curves on any indifference map from this newly defined set of tastes?

     c. Suppose you are told the following about three people: Person 1 strictly prefers bundle A to bundle B whenever A contains more of each and every good than bundle B. If only some goods are represented in greater quantity in A than in B while the remaining goods are represented in equal quantity, then A is at least as good as B for this person. Such tastes are often said to be *weakly monotonic*. Person 2 likes bundle A strictly better than B whenever at least some goods are represented in greater quantity in A than in B while others may be represented in equal quantity. Such tastes are said to be *strongly monotonic*. Finally, person 3's tastes are such that for every bundle A, there always exists a bundle B very close to A that is strictly better than A. Such tastes are said to satisfy *local nonsatiation*. Call the set of tastes that satisfy strict monotonicity SM, the set of tastes that satisfy weak monotonicity WM, and the set of tastes that satisfy local non-satiation L. Give an example of tastes that fall in one and only one of these three sets.

 d. What is true about tastes that are in one and only one of these three sets?

 e. What is true of tastes that are in one and only one of the sets SM and WM?

B. Here, we will consider the logical implications of convexity for utility functions. For the following definitions, $0 \le \alpha \le 1$. A function $f: \mathbb{R}^2_+ \to \mathbb{R}^1$ is defined to be *quasiconcave* if and only if the following is true: Whenever $f(x_1^A, x_2^A) \le f(x_1^B, x_2^B)$, then $f(x_1^A, x_2^A) \le f(\alpha x_1^A + (1-\alpha)x_1^B, \alpha x_2^A + (1-\alpha)x_2^B)$. The same type of function is defined to be *concave* if and only if $\alpha f(x_1^A, x_2^A) + (1-\alpha) f(x_1^B, x_2^B) \le f(\alpha x_1^A + (1-\alpha)x_1^B, \alpha x_2^A + (1-\alpha)x_2^B)$.

 a. *True or False*: All concave functions are quasiconcave, but not all quasiconcave functions are concave.

 b. Demonstrate that, if u is a quasiconcave utility function, the tastes represented by u are convex.

 c. Do your conclusions imply that if u is a concave utility function, the tastes represented by u are convex?

 d. Demonstrate that if tastes over two goods are convex, any utility functions that represents those tastes must be quasiconcave.

 e. Do your conclusions imply that if tastes over two goods are convex, any utility function that represents those tastes must be concave?

 f. Do the previous conclusions imply that utility functions that are not quasiconcave represent tastes that are not convex?

4.14* In this exercise, you will prove that as long as tastes satisfy rationality, continuity, and monotonicity, there always exists a well-defined indifference map (and utility function) that can represent those tastes.[13]

 A. Consider a two-good world, with goods x_1 and x_2 represented on the two axes in any graphs you draw.

  a. Draw your two axes and pick some arbitrary bundle $A = (x_1^A, x_2^A)$ that contains at least some of each good.

  b. Draw the 45-degree line in your graph. This is a ray that represents all bundles that have equal amounts of x_1 and x_2 in them.

  c. Pick a second bundle $B = (x_1^B, x_2^B)$ such that $x_1^B = x_2^B$ and $x_1^B > \max\{x_1^A, x_2^A\}$. In other words, pick B such that it has equal amounts of x_1 and x_2 and such that it has more of x_1 and x_2 than A.

  d. Is A more or less preferred than the bundle $(0,0)$? Is B more or less preferred than A?

  e. Now imagine moving along the 45-degree line from $(0,0)$ toward B. Can you use the continuity property of tastes we have assumed to conclude that there exists some bundle C between $(0,0)$ and B such that the consumer is indifferent between A and C?

  f. Does the same logic imply that there exists such an indifferent bundle along *any* ray from the origin and not just along the 45-degree line?

  g. How does what you have just done demonstrate the existence of a well-defined indifference map?

 B. Next, we show that the same logic implies that there exists a utility function that represents these tastes.

  a. If you have not already done so, illustrate A(a)-(e).

  b. Denote the distance from $(0,0)$ to C on the 45-degree line as $t_A = t(x_1^A, x_2^A)$, and assign the value t_A to the bundle A.

---

[13]It can actually be demonstrated that this is true as long as tastes satisfy rationality and continuity only, but it is easier to demonstrate the intuition if we also assume monotonicity.

c. Imagine the same procedure for labeling each bundle in your graph; i.e., for each bundle, determine what bundle on the 45-degree line is indifferent and label the bundle with the distance on the 45-degree line from (0,0) to the indifferent bundle. The result is a function $u(x_1, x_2)$ that assigns to every bundle a number. Can you explain how this function meets our definition of a utility function?

d. Can you see how the same method of proof would work to prove the existence of a utility function when there are more than two goods (and when tastes satisfy rationality, continuity and monotonicity)?

e. Could we have picked a ray other than the 45-degree line to construct the utility values associated with each bundle?

Different Types of Tastes

In Chapter 4, we demonstrated how tastes can be represented by maps of indifference curves and how five basic assumptions about tastes result in particular features of these indifference curves.[1] In addition, we illustrated how tastes can be more formally defined and how these can be mathematically represented as utility functions. We now proceed to analyzing how maps of indifference curves can differ in important ways while still satisfying our five basic assumptions. This will tell us much about how different types of tastes can be modeled using our simple graphical framework as well as the more general mathematical framework that builds on our graphically derived intuitions. For instance, if two goods are close substitutes for one another, the indifference map that represents a consumer's tastes for these goods will look very different from one representing tastes for goods that are close complements, even though both types of indifference maps will satisfy our five basic assumptions. Shapes of indifference curves then translate into specific types of functional forms of utility functions.

One of the important insights that should emerge from this chapter is that our basic model of tastes is enormously general and allows us to consider all sorts of tastes that individuals might have. You may like apples more than oranges, but I may like oranges more than apples; you may think peanut butter and jelly go together well, but I may think they can't touch each other; you may see little difference between French wine and California wine, but I may think one is barely drinkable. Often, students that are introduced to indifference curves get the impression that they all look pretty much the same, but we will find here that their shapes and relationships to one another can vary greatly, and that this variation produces a welcome diversity of possible tastes that is necessary to analyze a world as diverse as ours.

5A   Different Types of Indifference Maps

Understanding how different tastes can be graphed will therefore be important for understanding how consumer behavior differs depending on what the consumer's underlying tastes are. We will begin in Section 5A.1 by discussing the shape of *individual* indifference curves for different types of goods. This will give us a way of talking about the degree to which consumers feel that different goods are substitutable for one another and the degree to which goods have their own distinct character. We then proceed in Section 5A.2 with a discussion of *how indifference curves from an indifference map relate to one another* depending on what kinds of goods we are modeling. This will tell us how a consumer's perception of the value of one good relative to others

---

[1]Chapter 4 is necessary as background reading for this chapter.

changes as happiness, or what we will later call "real income," increases. Finally, we conclude in Section 5A.3 by exploring the characteristic of indifference maps that determines how "essential" particular goods are to our perceived well-being, how some goods are the kinds of goods we just can't live without while others are not essential for our happiness.

5A.1 Substitutability along an Indifference Curve: Coke, Pepsi, and Iced Tea

The extent to which two goods are substitutes depends on the nature of the goods we are modeling as well as the types of tastes that individuals have. For instance, Coke and Pepsi are more similar to one another than many other goods. In fact, I personally have trouble telling the difference between Coke and Pepsi. As a result, when my wife and I go to a restaurant and I order Coke, I am not upset if the waiter informs me that the restaurant only serves Pepsi; I simply order a Pepsi instead. My wife, on the other hand, has a strong preference for Coke, and she will switch to iced tea if she finds out that a restaurant serves Pepsi instead of Coke. I think she is nuts for thinking Coke and Pepsi are so different and attribute it to still-unresolved childhood issues. She, on the other hand, thinks my family might have grown up near a nuclear test site whose radiation emissions have destroyed some vital taste buds. (She thinks it might explain some of my other oddities as well.) Be that as it may, it is clear that Coke and Pepsi are less substitutable for her than for me.

5A.1.1 Perfect Substitutes Suppose, then, that we want to model my tastes for Coke and Pepsi. We could begin by thinking about some arbitrary bundle that I might presently consume, say 1 can of Coke and 1 can of Pepsi. We could then ask what other bundles might be of equal value to me given that I cannot tell the difference between the products. For instance, 2 cans of Coke and no cans of Pepsi should be just as good for me, as should 2 cans of Pepsi and no cans of Coke. Thus, each of these three bundles must lie on the same indifference curve for someone with my tastes, as must any other linear combination, such as 1.5 cans of Coke and 0.5 cans of Pepsi. In Graph 5.1, these bundles are plotted and connected by a (blue) line. Each point on this

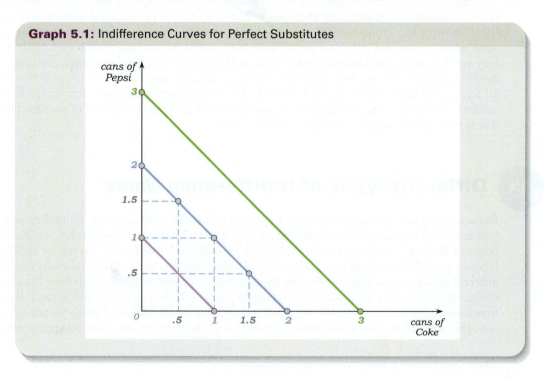

Graph 5.1: Indifference Curves for Perfect Substitutes

line represents some combination of Coke and Pepsi that adds up to 2 cans, which is after all the only thing that matters to someone who can't tell the difference between the products. We could of course construct other indifference curves as well, such as those representing quantities of Coke and Pepsi that add up to 1 can or 3 cans, as also depicted in Graph 5.1.

The tastes we have graphed represent tastes over goods that are *perfect substitutes*. Such tastes are unusual in the sense that one of our five basic assumptions is already "almost" violated. In particular, notice that averages are no longer *better than* extremes; rather, averages are valued *the same as* extremes when two goods are perfect substitutes. (1 can of Coke and 1 can of Pepsi is the average between the more extreme bundles of 2 Cokes or 2 Pepsis, but it is equally valued by a consumer with the tastes we have graphed here.) This also implies that the slope of each indifference curve is constant, giving us constant rather than diminishing marginal rates of substitution. Upon reflection, it should make intuitive sense that marginal rates of substitution are constant in this case. After all, no matter how much or how little Coke I have, I will always be willing to trade 1 Coke for 1 Pepsi.

Students often ask if it has to be true that one is willing to trade goods one-for-one (i.e., that the *MRS* equals -1) in order for goods to be perfect substitutes. Different textbooks give different answers to such questions, but the only answer that makes sense to me is to say no, the defining characteristic of perfect substitute is not that $MRS = -1$ but rather that the *MRS* is the same everywhere. Even when $MRS = -1$ (as in my Coke and Pepsi example), I could change the units with which I measure quantities of Coke and Pepsi and get a different *MRS* without changing a person's tastes. The next within-chapter-exerercise demonstrates this, and the idea is extended in exercise 5A.2.

How would the graph of indifference curves change if Coke came in 8-ounce cans and Pepsi came in 4-ounce cans?

Exercise 5A.1

On a graph with quarters (that are worth 25 cents) on the horizontal axis and dimes (that are worth 10 cents) on the vertical, what might your indifference curves look like? Use the same method we just employed to graph my indifference curves for Coke and Pepsi by beginning with one arbitrary bundle of quarters and dimes (say 4 quarters and 5 dimes) and then asking which other bundles might be just as good.

Exercise 5A.2

5A.1.2 Perfect Complements When my wife orders an iced tea in restaurants (after learning that the restaurant serves Pepsi rather than Coke), I have observed that she adds exactly 1 packet of sugar to the tea before drinking it. If there is less than a packet of sugar available, she will leave the iced tea untouched, whereas if there is more than 1 packet of sugar available, the additional sugar will remain unused unless she gets more iced tea.[2] From this somewhat compulsive behavior, I have concluded that iced tea and sugar are *perfect complements* for my wife: they complement each other to the point that she gets no satisfaction from consuming 1 unit of one without also consuming 1 unit of the other.

We can model my wife's tastes for iced tea and sugar by again starting with an arbitrary point and then asking which other bundles will make her indifferent. Suppose we start with 1 pack of sugar and 1 glass of iced tea. Together, these two represent the ingredients for 1 acceptable beverage. Now suppose I gave my wife another pack of sugar without any additional iced tea, giving her a bundle of 2 sugar packs and 1 glass of iced tea. Since this would still only give her 1 acceptable beverage, she would be no better (and no worse) off; i.e., she would be indifferent. The same

---

[2]Actually that's not quite right: I really like sugar, so when she is not looking, I usually pour the remaining sugar into my mouth. Unfortunately, my wife views such behavior as thoroughly antisocial rather than charmingly quaint, and I usually have to endure a speech about having been raised in a barn whenever she catches me.

is true for a bundle containing any number of sugar packs greater than 1 so long as the bundle included only 1 glass of iced tea, and it would be true for any number of additional glasses of iced tea if only 1 sugar pack were available. The blue indifference curve with a right angle at 1 iced tea and 1 sugar pack in Graph 5.2 then represents all bundles that, given my wife's tastes, result in 1 acceptable beverage for her. Similar indifference curves exist for bundles that add up to 2 or 3 acceptable beverages.

Notice that, as in the case of perfect substitutes, perfect complements represent an extreme case in the sense that some of our five basic assumptions about tastes are almost violated. In particular, more is no longer necessarily better in the case of perfect complements, only more of *both* goods is better. Similarly, averages are not always better than extremes, as for bundles of goods that lie on the linear portions of the indifference curves where averages are just as good as extremes.[3]

Exercise 5A.3   What would my wife's indifference curves for packs of sugar and glasses of iced tea look like if she required 2 packs of sugar instead of 1 for each glass of iced tea?

5A.1.3 Less Extreme Cases of Substitutability and Complementarity   Rarely do goods fall into either of the two extreme cases of perfect complements or perfect substitutes. Rather, goods tend to be relatively more or less substitutable depending on their inherent characteristics and the underlying tastes for the person whose tastes we are modeling. Such less extreme examples will then have shapes falling between the two extremes in Graphs 5.1 and 5.2,

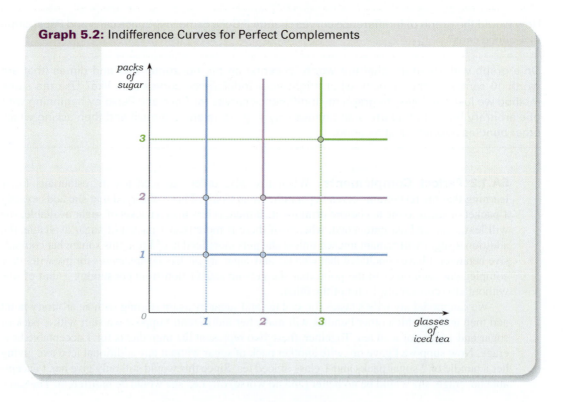

Graph 5.2: Indifference Curves for Perfect Complements

---

[3]Tastes that do not allow for substitutability between goods are sometimes referred to as *Leontief* tastes after Wassily Leontief (1906–1999), who extensively used a similar notion in producer theory. Leontief was awarded the Nobel Prize in Economics in 1973.

Graph 5.3: Indifference Curves for Less Extreme Cases of Substitutability and Complementarity

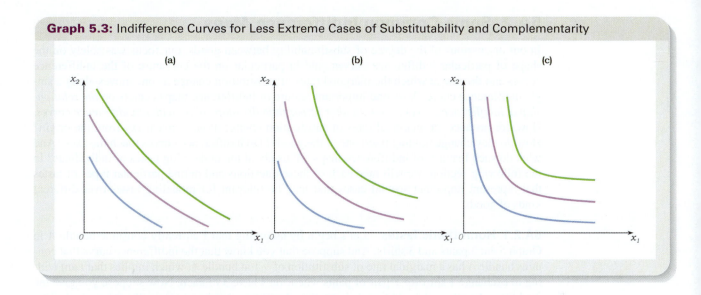

as for instance the tastes for goods x_1 and x_2 graphed in Graph 5.3a through 5.3c. Here, unlike for the case of perfect complements, a person is indeed willing to substitute some of x_2 for some of x_1, but not always in the same proportions as would be true for perfect substitutes. In particular, a person with such tastes would be willing to substitute x_2 for x_1 more easily if the current bundle has a lot of x_2 and little x_1, and this willingness to substitute one for the other decreases as the person moves to bundles that contain relatively more x_1 than x_2. This is of course true because of the embedded assumption that averages are better than extremes, an assumption that, as we showed in the previous chapter, leads to diminishing marginal rates of substitution.

For the tastes modeled in Graph 5.3a, this willingness to substitute x_1 for x_2 changes relatively little as the underlying bundle changes, thus giving rise to indifference curves that are relatively flat and close in shape to those of tastes representing perfect substitutes. Tastes modeled in Graph 5.3c, on the other hand, are such that the willingness to substitute x_1 for x_2 changes relatively quickly along at least a portion of each indifference curve, thus giving rise to indifference curves whose shape is closer to those of perfect complements. Keeping the extremes of perfect substitutes and perfect complements in mind, it then becomes relatively easy to look at particular maps of indifference curves and discern whether they contain a relatively high or a relatively low degree of substitutability. This degree of substitutability decreases as we move from panel (a) to panels (b) and (c) in Graph 5.3.

The degree of substitutability will play an important role in our discussion of consumer behavior and consumer welfare in the next several chapters. It may at first seem like a trivial concept when applied to simple examples like Coke and Pepsi, but it becomes one of the most crucial concepts in controversies surrounding such issues as tax and retirement policy. In such debates, the degree of substitutability between current and future consumption or between consumption and leisure takes center stage, as we will see in later chapters.

Suppose I told you that each of the indifference maps graphed in Graph 5.3 corresponded to my tastes for one of the following sets of goods, which pair would you think corresponds to which map? Pair 1: Levi Jeans and Wrangler Jeans; Pair 2: Pants and Shirts; Pair 3: Jeans and Dockers pants.

Exercise
5A.4

5A.2 Some Common Indifference *Maps*

In our discussions of the degree of substitutability between goods, our focus was solely on the shape of particular indifference curves, and in particular on the curvature of the indifference curves and the rate at which the marginal rates of substitution change as one moves along a single indifference curve. A second important feature of indifference maps centers on *the relationship of indifference curves to one another rather than the shape of individual indifference curves.* How, for instance, do marginal rates of substitution change along a linear ray from the origin? How do they change holding fixed one of the goods? Do indifference curves touch the axes? And what do such features of indifference maps tell us about the underlying tastes of individuals? In the following section, we will take each of these questions and define particular types of tastes that represent important special cases that may be relevant for modeling tastes over different kinds of goods.

5A.2.1 Homothetic Tastes

Let's begin by assuming that I currently consume bundle *A* in Graph 5.4a: 3 pants and 3 shirts. And suppose that you know that the indifference curve that contains bundle *A* has a marginal rate of substitution of −1 at bundle *A*, which implies that I am willing to exchange 1 shirt for 1 pair of pants whenever I have 3 of each. Now suppose you give me 3 additional pants and 3 additional shirts, thus doubling what I had originally at bundle *A*. This will put me on a new indifference curve, one that contains the new bundle *B*. Would it now be reasonable for us to expect that my marginal rate of substitution is still −1 at *B*?

Perhaps it would be reasonable for this particular example. After all, the reason my marginal rate of substitution might be −1 at point *A* is that I like to change pants and shirts roughly at the same intervals *when I have equal numbers of pants and shirts.* If so, the important determinant of my marginal rate of substitution is the number of pants I have *relative to* the number of shirts, which is unchanged between points *A* and *B*. Put differently, if I change pants and shirts at equal intervals when I have 3 of each, I am probably changing them at equal intervals when I have 6 of

Graph 5.4: Homothetic Tastes, Marginal Rates of Substitution, and Indifference Curves

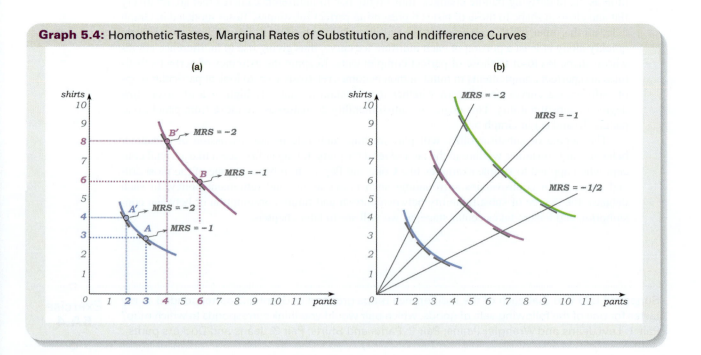

each and am thus willing to trade them off for one another (at the margin) one-for-one. (Remember, however, that when we say that the *MRS* is −1 at *A*, we mean that you are willing to trade very small quantities of pants and shirts one-for-one, not necessarily 1 entire pair of pants for 1 entire shirt. This is what I mean when I say that I am willing to trade them one-for-one *on the margin*. As we noted earlier, while it is awkward to think of pants and shirts as divisible goods, it is a useful modeling simplification and one that usually is not overly restrictive when we talk about bigger examples that matter more than pants and shirts.)

A similar argument could hold for other bundles on the indifference curve that contains bundle *A*. For instance, bundle *A′* contains 4 shirts and 2 pants, and the indifference curve shows a marginal rate of substitution of −2 at *A′*. Thus, I would be willing to give up 2 shirts to get 1 more pair of pants if I were currently consuming bundle *A′* because shirts are not of as much value to me when I have so few pants relative to shirts. But then it sounds plausible for the marginal rate of substitution to remain the same if you doubled *A′* to *B′*: I still have relatively many shirts compared with pants and thus might still be willing to trade 2 shirts for 1 pair of pants at *B′*.

Whenever tastes exhibit the property that marginal rates of substitution at particular bundles depend only on how much of one good relative to the other is contained in that bundle, we will say that tastes are homothetic. This technical term means nothing more than what we have already described for my tastes for pants and shirts: whenever you determine the marginal rate of substitution at one particular bundle, you know that the marginal rate of substitution at all other bundles that lie on a ray connecting the origin and the original bundle is exactly the same. This is true because the amount of one good *relative* to the other is unchanged along this ray. Graph 5.4b illustrates three indifference curves of such a homothetic indifference map.

In Chapter 6, we will see how consumers with homothetic tastes will choose to double their current consumption basket whenever their income doubles. Tastes for certain "big-ticket" consumption goods can thus be quite accurately modeled using homothetic tastes because they represent goods that we consume in rough proportion to our income. For many consumers, for instance, the square footage of housing consumed increases linearly with income. Similarly, as we think of modeling our tastes for consumption across different time periods, it may be reasonable to assume that our tastes are homothetic and that we will choose to increase our consumption this year and next year by the same proportion if our yearly income doubles.

In concluding our discussion of homothetic tastes, it is important to note that when we say that someone's tastes are homothetic, we are making a statement about how different indifference curves relate to one another; we are *not* saying anything in particular about the shape of individual indifference curves. For instance, you should be able to convince yourself that homothetic tastes could incorporate many different degrees of substitutability by thinking about the following:

Are my tastes over Coke and Pepsi as described in Section 5A.1 homothetic? Are my wife's tastes over iced tea and sugar homothetic? Why or why not?

Exercise 5A.5

5A.2.2 Quasilinear Tastes

While the assumption that marginal rates of substitution at different consumption bundles depend only on the relative quantities of goods at those bundles is plausible for many applications, there are also many important instances when the assumption does not seem reasonable. Consider, for instance, my tastes for weekly soft drink consumption and a composite good representing my weekly consumption of all other goods in dollars.

Suppose we begin with a bundle *A* in Graph 5.5a, a bundle that contains 25 soft drinks and $500 in other consumption. My indifference curve has a slope of −1 at that bundle, indicating that, given my current consumption bundle *A*, I am willing to give up $1 in other consumption for 1 additional soft drink. Now suppose that you enabled me to consume at double my current consumption: point *B* with 50 soft drinks and $1,000 in other consumption. Does it seem likely that I would value the 50th soft drink in bundle *B* the same as I valued the 25th soft drink in bundle *A*?

Graph 5.5: Quasilinear Tastes, Marginal Rates of Substitution and Indifference Curves

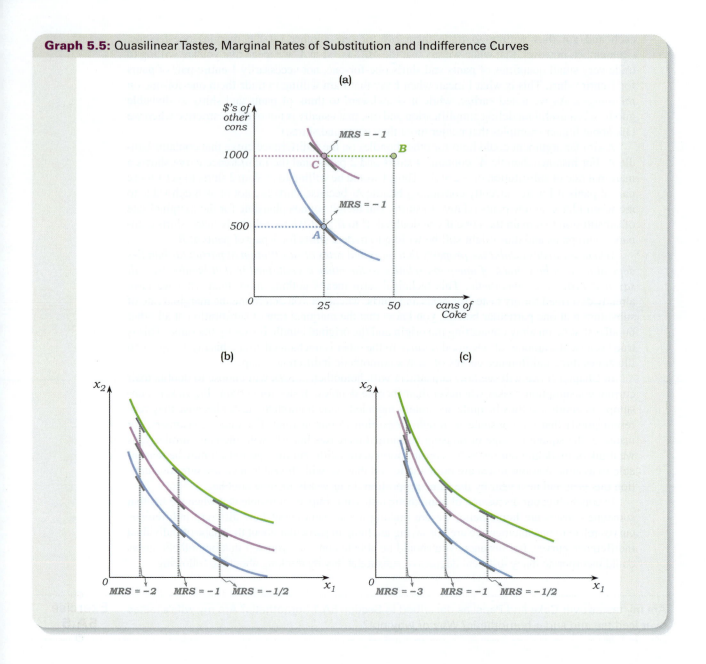

If so, my tastes would again be homothetic. But it is much more likely that there is room for only so many soft drinks in my stomach during any week, and even if you enable me to consume a lot more in other goods, I would still not value additional soft drinks very highly. In that case, my marginal rate of substitution at point B would be less than 1 in absolute value; i.e., I would be willing to consume additional soft drinks at bundle B only if I had to give up less than $1 in additional consumption.

In many examples like this, a more accurate description of tastes might be that my marginal rate of substitution depends *only* on how many soft drinks I am consuming, not on how much in other consumption I have during the same week. Consider, for instance, point C in Graph 5.5a — a bundle containing $1,000 in other consumption and 25 soft drinks. It may well be that my willingness to trade dollars for additional soft drinks does not change at all between points *A* and *C*; whether I am consuming $500 or $1,000 in other goods, I will still only consume any soft drinks beyond 25 if I can get them for less than $1 in other consumption. If this is the case, then my tastes will be such that my marginal rate of substitution is *the same along any vertical line* in Graph 5.5a. Two examples of indifference maps that satisfy this property are depicted in Graphs 5.5b and 5.5c.

Tastes for goods that are valued at the margin the same regardless of how much of the "other good" we are consuming are called *quasilinear* tastes. Goods that are likely to be modeled well using quasilinear tastes tend to be goods that represent a relatively small fraction of our income. They are goods that we tend to consume the same quantity of even if we get a big raise. Many goods that we consume probably fall into this category—milk, soft-drinks, paper clips, etc.—but some clearly do not. For instance, we cited tastes for housing as an example better modeled as homothetic because housing is, at the margin, valued more highly as we become better off. More generally, it will become clearer in Chapter 6 that tastes for many big-ticket consumption items are not likely to be well modeled using the quasilinear specification of indifference maps.

Are my tastes over Coke and Pepsi as described in Section 5A.1 quasilinear? Are my wife's tastes over iced tea and sugar quasilinear? Why or why not?

Exercise 5A.6

5A.2.3 Homothetic versus Quasilinear Tastes   Tastes, then, are quasilinear in a particular good if the marginal rate of substitution between this and "the other" good depends only on the *absolute quantity* of the "quasilinear" good (and is thus independent of how much of "the other" good a consumer has in his or her consumption bundle). Graphically, this means that the marginal rate of substitution is the same along lines that are perpendicular to the axis on which we model the good that is "quasilinear." Tastes are homothetic, on the other hand, if the marginal rate of substitution at any given bundle depends only on the quantity of one good *relative* to the quantity of the other. Graphically, this means that the marginal rates of substitution across indifference curves are the same along rays emanating from the origin of the graph. You will understand the difference between these if you feel comfortable with the following:

Can you explain why tastes for perfect substitutes are the only tastes that are both quasilinear and homothetic?[4]

Exercise 5A.7

5A.3 "Essential" Goods

There is one final dimension along which we can categorize indifference maps: whether or not the indifference curves intersect one or both of the axes in our graphs. Many of the indifference maps we have drawn so far have indifference curves that *converge* to the axes of the graphs without ever touching them. Some, such as those representing quasilinear tastes, however, intersect one or both of the axes. The distinction between indifference maps of the first and second kind will become important in the next chapter as we consider what we can say about the "best" bundle that individuals who are seeking to do the best they can given their circumstances will choose.

For now, we will say little more about this but simply indicate that the difference between these two types of tastes has something to do with how "essential" both goods are to the well-being of an individual. Take, for example, my tastes for Coke and Pepsi. When we model such tastes, neither of

---

[4]In end-of-chapter exercise 5.1, you will work with limit cases of perfect substitutes, cases where the indifference curves become perfectly vertical or perfectly horizontal. For purposes of our discussions, we will treat such limiting cases as members of the family of perfect substitutes.

Graph 5.6: x_2 is "Essential" in (b) but not in (a)

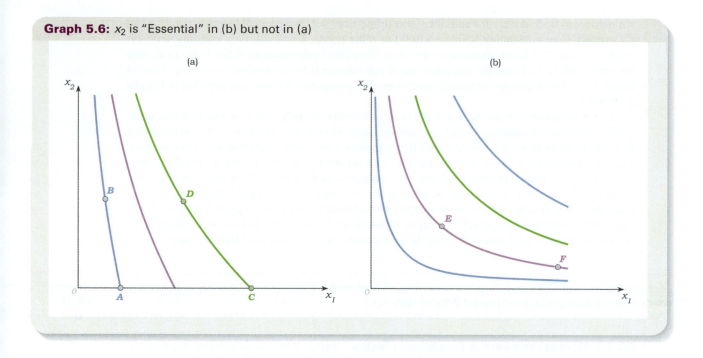

the goods is in and of itself very essential since I am indifferent between bundles that contain both goods and bundles that contain only one of the two goods. This is not true for the case of perfect complements such as iced tea and sugar for my wife. For her, neither iced tea nor sugar are of any use unless she has both in her consumption bundle. In that sense, we could say both goods are "essential" for her well-being, at least so long as our model assumes she consumes only iced tea and sugar.

More generally, suppose we compare the indifference map in Graph 5.6a to that in Graph 5.6b. In the first graph, the indifference curves converge to the vertical axis (without touching it) while they *intersect* the horizontal axis. Therefore, there are bundles that contain no quantity of good x_2 (such as A and C) that are just as good as bundles that contain both x_1 and x_2 (such as B and D). In some sense, x_2 is therefore not as essential as x_1. In the second graph (Graph 5.6b), on the other hand, bundles must always contain some of each good in order for the individual to be happier than he or she is without consuming anything at all at the origin. And, an individual is indifferent to any bundle that contains both goods (like bundle E) *only if* the second bundle (like F) also contains some of both goods. In that sense, both goods are quite essential to the well-being of the individual.

Exercise 5A.8   *True or False*: Quasilinear goods are never essential.

5B Different Types of Utility Functions

The different types of tastes we have illustrated graphically so far can of course also be represented by utility functions, with particular classes of utility functions used to represent different degrees of substitutability as well as different relationships of indifference curves to one another. We therefore now take the opportunity to introduce some common types of utility functions that generalize precisely the kinds of intuitive concepts we illustrated graphically in Section 5A.

5B.1 Degrees of Substitutability and the "Elasticities of Substitution"

In Section 5A.1, we described different shapes of indifference curves that imply different levels of substitutability. For instance, my tastes for Coke and Pepsi were illustrated with linear indifference curves in Graph 5.1, a shape for indifference curves that indicates perfect substitutability between the two goods. The opposite extreme of no substitutability was illustrated using my wife's tastes for sugar and iced tea with L-shaped indifference curves in Graph 5.2. And less extreme indifference curves ranging from those that implied a relatively large degree of substitutability to a relatively small degree of substitutability were illustrated in a sequence of graphs in Graph 5.3. From this discussion, one quickly walks away with the sense that *the degree of substitutability is directly related to the speed with which the slope of an indifference curve changes as one moves along the indifference curve.* The slope, for instance, changes relatively slowly in Graph 5.3a where two goods are relatively substitutable, and much more quickly in Graph 5.3c where goods are less substitutable.

What we referred to informally as the "degree of substitutability" in our discussion of these graphs is formalized mathematically through a concept known as the *elasticity of substitution.*[5] As we will see again and again throughout this book, an *elasticity* is a measure of responsiveness. We will, for instance, discuss the responsiveness of a consumer's demand for a good when that good's price changes as the "price elasticity of demand" in Chapter 18. In the case of formalizing the notion of substitutability, we are attempting to formalize how quickly the bundle of goods on an indifference curve changes as the slope (or marginal rate of substitution) of that indifference curve changes; or, put differently, how "responsive" the bundle of goods along an indifference curve is to the changes in the marginal rate of substitution.

Consider, for instance, point A (with marginal rate of substitution of -2) on the indifference curve graphed in Graph 5.7a. In order for us to find a point B where the marginal rate of substitution

Graph 5.7: Degrees of Substitutability and Marginal Rates of Substitution

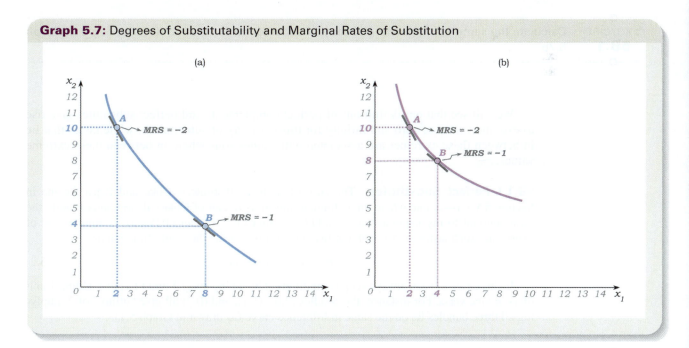

[5]This concept was introduced independently in the early 1930s by two of the major economists of the 20th century, Sir John Hicks (1904–1989) and Joan Robinson (1903–1983). Hicks was awarded the Nobel Prize in Economics in 1972.

is -1 instead of -2, we have to go from the initial bundle $(2,10)$ to the new bundle $(8,4)$. In Graph 5.7b, a similar change from an initial point A with marginal rate of substitution of -2 to a new point B with marginal rate of substitution of -1 implies a significantly smaller change in the bundle, taking us from $(2,10)$ to $(4,8)$. Put differently, the ratio of x_2 over x_1 declines quickly (from 5 to 1/2) in panel (a) as the marginal rate of substitution falls (in absolute value from 2 to 1) while it declines less rapidly (from 5 to 2) in panel (b) for the same change in the marginal rate of substitution.

Economists have developed a mathematical way to give expression to the intuition that the degree of substitutability between two goods is related to the speed with which the ratio of the two goods along an indifference curve changes as the marginal rate of substitution changes. This is done by defining the *elasticity of substitution* (denoted σ) at a particular bundle of two consumption goods as *the percentage change in the ratio of those two goods that results from a 1% change in the marginal rate of substitution along the indifference curve that contains the bundle*, or, put mathematically,

$$\text{Elasticity of substitution} = \sigma = \left| \frac{\%\Delta(x_2/x_1)}{\%\Delta MRS} \right|. \tag{5.1}$$

The "percentage change" of a variable is simply the change of the variable divided by the original level of that variable. For instance, if the ratio of the two goods changes from 5 to 1/2 (as it does in Graph 5.7a), the "percentage change" in the ratio is given by $-4.5/5$ or -0.9. Similarly, the $\%\Delta MRS$ in Graph 5.7a is 0.5. Dividing -0.9 by 0.5 then gives a value of -1.8, or 1.8 in absolute value. This is approximately the elasticity of substitution in Graph 5.7a. (It is only approximate because the formula in equation (5.1) evaluates the elasticity of substitution precisely at a point when the changes are very small. The calculus version of the elasticity formula is treated explicitly in the appendix to this chapter.)

Exercise 5B.1 Calculate the same approximate elasticity of substitution for the indifference curve in Graph 5.7b.

We will see that our definitions of perfect complements and perfect substitutes give rise to extreme values of zero and infinity for this elasticity of substitution, while tastes that lie in between these extremes are associated with values somewhere in between these extreme values.

5B.1.1 Perfect Substitutes

The case of perfect substitutes—Coke and Pepsi for me in Section 5A.1.1—is one where an additional unit of x_1 (a can of Coke) always adds exactly the same amount to my happiness as an additional unit of x_2 (a can of Pepsi). A simple way of expressing such tastes in terms of a utility function is to write the utility function as

$$u(x_1, x_2) = x_1 + x_2. \tag{5.2}$$

In this case, you can always keep me indifferent by taking away 1 unit of x_1 and adding 1 unit of x_2 or vice versa. For instance, the bundles $(2,0)$, $(1,1)$, and $(0,2)$ all give "utility" of 2, implying all three bundles lie on the same indifference curve (as drawn in Graph 5.1).

Exercise 5B.2 What numerical labels would be attached to the three indifference curves in Graph 5.1 by the utility function in equation (5.2)?

Exercise
5B.3

Suppose you measured Coke in 8-ounce cans and Pepsi in 4-ounce cans. Draw indifference curves and find the simplest possible utility function that would give rise to those indifference curves.

Without doing the math explicitly, we can see intuitively that the elasticity of substitution in this case is infinity (∞). This is easiest to see if we think of an indifference map that is close to perfect substitutes, such as the indifference map in Graph 5.8a in which indifference curves are almost linear. Beginning at point A, even the very small percentage change in the *MRS* that gets us to point B is accompanied by a very large change in the ratio of the consumption goods. Considering this in light of equation (5.1), we get an elasticity of substitution that is determined by a large numerator divided by a very small denominator, giving a large value for the elasticity. The closer this indifference map comes to being linear, the larger will be the numerator and the smaller will be the denominator, thus causing the elasticity of substitution to approach ∞ as the indifference map approaches that of perfect substitutes.

Exercise
5B.4

Can you use similar reasoning to determine the elasticity of substitution for the utility function you derived in exercise 5B.3?

5B.1.2 Perfect Complements It is similarly easy to arrive at a utility function that represents the L-shaped indifference curves for goods that represent perfect complements (such as iced tea and sugar for my wife in Section 5A.1.2). Since the two goods are of use to you only when consumed together, your happiness from such goods is determined by whichever of the two goods you have less of. For instance, when my wife has 3 glasses of iced tea but only 2 packs of sugar, she is just as happy with any other combination of iced tea and sugar that contains exactly two units

Graph 5.8: Degrees of Substitutability and the "Elasticities of Substitution"

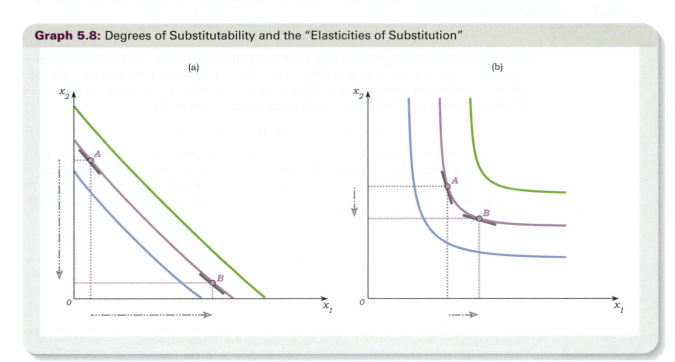

of one of the goods and at least two units of the other. For any bundle, happiness is therefore determined by the smaller quantity of the two goods in the bundle, or

$$u(x_1, x_2) = \min\{x_1, x_2\}. \tag{5.3}$$

Exercise 5B.5 Plug the bundles (3,1), (2,1), (1,1), (1,2), and (1,3) into this utility function and verify that each is shown to give the same utility, thus lying on the same indifference curve as plotted in Graph 5.2. What numerical labels does this indifference curve attach to each of the three indifference curves in Graph 5.2?

Exercise 5B.6 How would your graph and the corresponding utility function change if we measured iced tea in half glasses instead of glasses.

We can again see intuitively that the elasticity of substitution for goods that are perfect complements will be zero. As in the case of perfect substitutes, this is easiest to see if we begin by considering an indifference map that is close to one representing perfect complements, such as the indifference map drawn in Graph 5.8b. Beginning at point A, even the very large percentage change in the *MRS* that gets us to point B implies a small percentage change in the ratio of the inputs. Considering this in light of equation (5.1), this implies a small numerator divided by a large denominator, giving a small number for the elasticity of substitution. As this map comes closer and closer to one that represents perfect complements, the numerator becomes smaller and the denominator rises. This leads to an elasticity of substitution that approaches zero as the indifference map approaches that of perfect complements.

Exercise 5B.7 Can you determine intuitively what the elasticity of substitution is for the utility function you defined in exercise 5B.6?

5B.1.3 The Cobb–Douglas Function Probably the most widely used utility function in economics is one that gives rise to indifference curves that lie between the extremes of perfect substitutes and perfect complements and that, as we will see, exhibits an elasticity of substitution of 1. It is known as the *Cobb–Douglas* utility function and takes the form

$$u(x_1, x_2) = x_1^{\gamma} x_2^{\delta} \text{ where } \gamma > 0, \delta > 0.[6] \tag{5.4}$$

While the exponents in the Cobb–Douglas function can in principle take any positive values, we often restrict ourselves to exponents that sum to 1. But since we know from Chapter 4 that we can transform utility functions without changing the underlying indifference map, restricting the exponents to sum to 1 turns out to be no restriction at all. We can, for instance, transform the function u by taking it to the power $1/(\gamma + \delta)$ to get

$$\left(u(x_1, x_2)\right)^{1/(\gamma+\delta)} = (x_1^{\gamma} x_2^{\delta})^{1/(\gamma+\delta)} = x_1^{\gamma/(\gamma+\delta)} x_2^{\delta/(\gamma+\delta)} =$$
$$= x_1^{\alpha} x_2^{(1-\alpha)} \text{ (where } \alpha = \gamma/(\gamma + \delta)) = \tag{5.5}$$
$$= v(x_1, x_2).$$

---

[6]This function was originally derived for producer theory where it is (as we will see in later chapters) still heavily used. It was first proposed by Knut Wicksell (1851–1926). It is named, however, for Paul Douglas (1892–1976), an economist, and Charles Cobb, a mathematician. They first used the function in empirical work (focused on producer theory) shortly after Wicksell's death. Paul Douglas went on to serve three terms as an influential U.S. senator from Illinois (1949–1967).

Demonstrate that the functions *u* and *v* both give rise to indifference curves that exhibit the same shape by showing that the *MRS* for each function is the same.

Exercise
5B.8

We can therefore simply write the utility function in Cobb–Douglas form as

$$u(x_1, x_2) = x_1^\alpha x_2^{(1-\alpha)} \text{ where } 0 < \alpha < 1. \tag{5.6}$$

In the *n*-good case, the Cobb–Douglas form extends straightforwardly to

$$u(x_1, x_2, \ldots, x_n) = x_1^{\alpha_1} x_2^{\alpha_2} \ldots x_n^{\alpha_n} \text{ with } \alpha_1 + \alpha_2 + \cdots + \alpha_n = 1. \tag{5.7}$$

We will show in the next section that this Cobb–Douglas function is just a special case of a more general functional form, the special case in which the elasticity of substitution is equal to 1 everywhere. Before doing so, however, we can get some intuition about the variety of tastes that can be represented through Cobb–Douglas functions by illustrating how these functions change as α changes in expression (5.6). The series of graphs in Graph 5.9 provide some examples.

While each of these graphs belongs to the family of Cobb–Douglas utility functions (and thus each represents tastes with elasticity of substitution of 1), you can see how Cobb–Douglas tastes can indeed cover many different types of indifference maps. When $\alpha = 0.5$ (as in panel (b) of the graph), the function places equal weight on x_1 and x_2, resulting in an indifference map that is symmetric around the 45-degree line. Put differently, since the two goods enter the utility function symmetrically, the portions of indifference curves that lie below the 45-degree line are mirror images of the corresponding portions that lie above the 45-degree line (when you imagine putting a mirror along the 45-degree line). This implies that the *MRS* on the 45-degree line must be equal to −1; when individuals with such tastes have equal quantities of both goods, they are willing to trade them one-for-one.

When $\alpha \neq 0.5$, on the other hand, the two goods do not enter the utility function symmetrically, and so the symmetry around the 45-degree line is lost. If $\alpha > 0.5$ (as in panel (c) of the graph), relatively more weight is put on x_1. Thus, if a consumer with such tastes has equal quantities of x_1 and x_2, he or she is not willing to trade them one-for-one. Rather, since x_1 plays a more

Graph 5.9: Different Cobb–Douglas Utility Functions

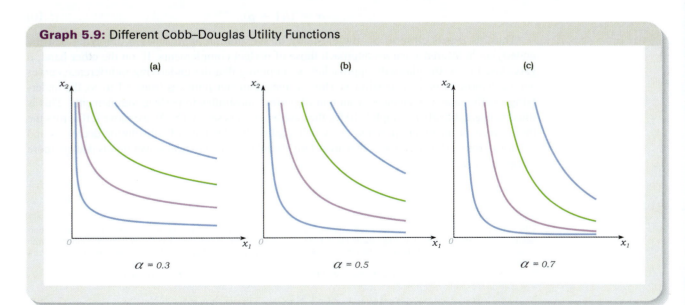

prominent role in the utility function, the consumer would demand more than 1 unit of x_2 to give up 1 unit of x_1 when he or she starts with an equal number of each (i.e., on the 45-degree line), implying an *MRS* greater than 1 in absolute value along the 45-degree line. As α increases above 0.5, the points where $MRS = -1$ therefore fall below the 45-degree line. The reverse is, of course, true as α falls below 0.5 when more emphasis is placed on x_2 rather than x_1 (as in panel (a) of the graph).

Exercise 5B.9

Derive the *MRS* for the Cobb–Douglas utility function and use it to show what happens to the slope of indifference curves along the 45-degree line as α changes.

5B.1.4 A More General Model: Constant Elasticity of Substitution (CES) Utility

So far, we have explored the extremes of perfect substitutes (with elasticity of substitution of ∞) and perfect complements (with elasticity of substitution of 0), and we have identified the Cobb–Douglas case, which lies in between with an elasticity of substitution of 1. Of course there exist other in-between cases where the elasticity of substitution lies between 0 and 1 or between 1 and ∞. And economists have identified a more general utility function that can capture all of these (including the cases of perfect substitutes, Cobb–Douglas tastes, and perfect complements). All utility functions that take this form have one thing in common: the elasticity of substitution is the same at all bundles, and it is for this reason that these functions are called *constant elasticity of substitution utility functions* or just *CES utility functions*.[7]

For bundles that contain two goods, these functions take on the following form:

$$u(x_1,x_2) = \left(\alpha x_1^{-\rho} + (1 - \alpha)x_2^{-\rho}\right)^{-1/\rho}, \tag{5.8}$$

where $0 < \alpha < 1$ and $-1 \le \rho \le \infty$.[8]

It is mathematically intensive to derive explicitly the formula for an elasticity of substitution for utility functions that take this form; if you are curious, you can follow this derivation in the appendix. As it turns out, however, the elasticity of substitution σ takes on the following very simple form for this CES function:

$$\sigma = 1/(1 + \rho). \tag{5.10}$$

Thus, as ρ gets close to ∞, the elasticity of substitution approaches 0, implying that the underlying indifference curves approach those of perfect complements. If, on the other hand, ρ gets close to -1, the elasticity approaches ∞, implying that the underlying indifference curves approach those of perfect substitutes. Thus, as the parameter ρ moves from -1 to ∞, the underlying indifference map changes from that of perfect substitutes to perfect complements. This is illustrated graphically in Graph 5.10 for the case where α is set to 0.5. As we move left across the three panels of the graph, ρ increases, which implies the elasticity of substitution decreases and we move from tastes over goods that are relatively substitutable to tastes over goods that are more complementary.

---

[7]This function was first derived (and explored within the context of producer theory) in 1961 by Ken Arrow (1921–) and Robert Solow (1924–) together with H. B. Cherney and B. S. Minhas. Arrow went on to share the 1972 Nobel Prize in Economics with Sir John Hicks (who had originally developed the concept of an elasticity of substitution). Solow was awarded the Nobel Prize in 1987.

[8]The CES form can also be generalized to more than two goods, with the *n*-good CES function given by

$$u(x_1, x_2, \ldots, x_n) = \left(\sum_{i=1}^{n} \alpha_i x_i^{-\rho}\right)^{-1/\rho} \text{ where } \sum_{i=1}^{n} \alpha_i = 1. \tag{5.9}$$

Graph 5.10: Different CES Utility Functions when $\alpha = 0.5$ and ρ Varies

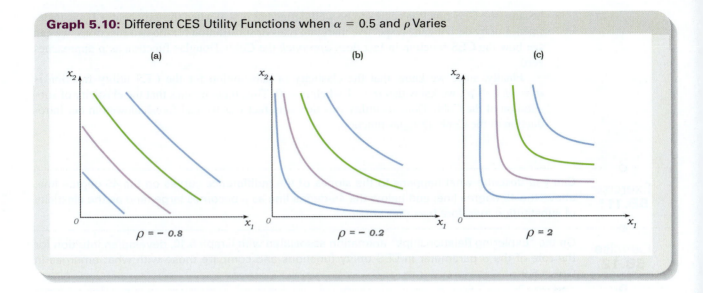

What is the elasticity of substitution in each panel of Graph 5.10?

Exercise
5B.10

The best way to see how the CES function gives rise to different indifference maps is to derive its marginal rate of substitution; i.e.,

$$MRS = -\frac{\partial u/\partial x_1}{\partial u/\partial x_2}$$

$$= -\frac{(\alpha x_1^{-\rho} + (1-\alpha)x_2^{-\rho})^{-(\rho+1)/\rho}\alpha x_1^{-(\rho+1)}}{(\alpha x_1^{-\rho} + (1-\alpha)x_2^{-\rho})^{-(\rho+1)/\rho}(1-\alpha)x_2^{-(\rho+1)}} \qquad (5.11)$$

$$= -\frac{\alpha x_1^{-(\rho+1)}}{(1-\alpha)x_2^{-(\rho+1)}} = -\left(\frac{\alpha}{1-\alpha}\right)\left(\frac{x_2}{x_1}\right)^{\rho+1}.$$

Note, for instance, what happens when $\rho = -1$: the (absolute value of the) MRS simply becomes $\alpha/(1-\alpha)$ and no longer depends on the bundle (x_1, x_2). Put differently, when $\rho = -1$, the slopes of indifference curves are just straight parallel lines indicating that the consumer is willing to substitute perfectly $\alpha/(1-\alpha)$ of x_2 for one more unit of x_1 regardless of how many of each of the two goods the consumer currently has.

We have also indicated that the Cobb–Douglas utility function $u(x_1, x_2) = x_1^\alpha x_2^{(1-\alpha)}$ represents a special case of the CES utility function. To see this, consider the MRS for the Cobb–Douglas function, which is

$$MRS = -\frac{\partial u/\partial x_1}{\partial u/\partial x_2} = -\frac{\alpha x_1^{(\alpha-1)}x_2^{(1-\alpha)}}{(1-\alpha)x_1^\alpha x_2^{-\alpha}} = -\left(\frac{\alpha}{1-\alpha}\right)\left(\frac{x_2}{x_1}\right). \qquad (5.12)$$

Note that the MRS from the CES function in equation (5.11) reduces to the MRS from the Cobb–Douglas function in equation (5.12) when $\rho = 0$. Thus, when $\rho = 0$, the indifference curves of the CES function take on the exact same shapes as the indifference curves of the Cobb–Douglas function, implying that the two functions represent exactly the same tastes. This is not easy to see by simply comparing the actual CES function to the Cobb–Douglas function because the CES function ceases to be well defined at $\rho = 0$ when the exponent $-1/\rho$ is undefined. But by deriving the respective marginal rates of substitution for the two functions, we can see how the CES function in fact does *approach* the Cobb–Douglas function as ρ approaches zero.

Finally, since we know that the elasticity of substitution for the CES utility function is $\sigma = 1/(1 + \rho)$, we know that $\sigma = 1$ when $\rho = 0$. This, then, implies that the elasticity of substitution of the Cobb–Douglas utility function is in fact 1 as we had foreshadowed in our introduction of the Cobb–Douglas function.

Exercise 5B.11* Can you describe what happens to the slopes of the indifference curves on the 45-degree line, above the 45-degree line, and below the 45-degee line as ρ becomes large (and as the elasticity of substitution therefore becomes small)?

Exercise 5B.12 On the "Exploring Relationships" animation associated with Graph 5.10, develop an intuition for the role of the α parameter in CES utility functions and compare those with what emerges in Graph 5.9.

5B.2 Some Common Indifference Maps

In Section 5A, we drew a logical distinction between *shapes* of individual indifference curves that define the degree of substitutability between goods and the *relation* of indifference curves to one another within a single indifference map. We have just formalized the degree of substitutability by exploring the concept of an elasticity of substitution and how tastes that have a constant elasticity of substitution at all consumption bundles can vary and be modeled using CES utility functions. We now turn toward exploring two special cases of indifference maps, those defined as "homothetic" and those defined as "quasilinear" in Section 5A.2.

5B.2.1 Homothetic Tastes and Homogeneous Utility Functions
Recall that we defined tastes as homothetic whenever the indifference map has the property that the marginal rate of substitution at a particular bundle depends only on how much of one good *relative* to the other is contained in that bundle. Put differently, the *MRS* of homothetic tastes is the same along any ray emanating from the origin of our graphs, implying that whenever we increase each of the goods in a particular bundle by the same proportion, the *MRS* will remain unchanged.

Consider, for instance, tastes that can be represented by the Cobb–Douglas utility function in equation (5.6). The *MRS* implied by this function is $-\alpha x_2/(1 - \alpha)x_1$. Suppose we begin at a particular bundle (x_1, x_2) and then increase the quantity of each of the goods in the bundle by a factor t to get to the bundle (tx_1, tx_2) that lies on a ray from the origin that also contains (x_1, x_2). This implies that the new *MRS* is $-\alpha tx_2/(1 - \alpha)tx_1$, but this reduces to $-\alpha x_2/(1 - \alpha)x_1$ since the "t" appears in both the numerator and the denominator and thus cancels. Cobb–Douglas utility functions therefore represent homothetic tastes because the *MRS* is unchanged along a ray from the origin.

More generally, homothetic tastes can be represented by any utility function that has the mathematical property of being *homogeneous*. A function $f(x_1, x_2)$ is defined to be *homogeneous of degree k* if and only if

$$f(tx_1, tx_2) = t^k f(x_1, x_2). \tag{5.13}$$

For instance, the Cobb–Douglas function $u(x_1, x_2) = x_1^\gamma x_2^\delta$ is homogeneous of degree $(\gamma + \delta)$ because

$$u(tx_1, tx_2) = (tx_1)^\gamma (tx_2)^\delta = t^{(\gamma+\delta)} x_1^\gamma x_2^\delta = t^{(\gamma+\delta)} u(x_1, x_2). \tag{5.14}$$

Show that when we normalize the exponents of the Cobb–Douglas utility function to sum to 1, the function is homogeneous of degree 1.

Exercise 5B.13

Consider the following variant of the CES function that will play an important role in producer theory: $f(x_1, x_2) = (\alpha x_1^{-\rho} + (1-\alpha) x_2^{-\rho})^{-\beta/\rho}$. Show that this function is homogeneous of degree β.

Exercise 5B.14

It is then easy to see how *homogeneous utility functions must represent homothetic tastes.* Suppose $u(x_1, x_2)$ is homogeneous of degree k. The *MRS* at a bundle (tx_1, tx_2) is

$$\begin{aligned}
MRS(tx_1, tx_2) &= -\frac{\partial u(tx_1, tx_2)/\partial x_1}{\partial u(tx_1, tx_2)/\partial x_2} = -\frac{\partial(t^k u(x_1, x_2))/\partial x_1}{\partial(t^k u(x_1, x_2))/\partial x_2} = \\
&= -\frac{t^k \partial u(x_1, x_2)/\partial x_1}{t^k \partial u(x_1, x_2)/\partial x_2} = -\frac{\partial u(x_1, x_2)/\partial x_1}{\partial u(x_1, x_2)/\partial x_2} = \\
&= MRS(x_1, x_2).
\end{aligned} \tag{5.15}$$

In this derivation, we use the definition of a homogeneous function in the first line in (5.15), are then able to take the t^k term outside the partial derivative (since it is not a function of x_1 or x_2), and finally can cancel the t^k that now appears in both the numerator and the denominator to end up at the definition of the *MRS* at bundle (x_1, x_2). Thus, the *MRS* is the same when we increase each good in a bundle by the same proportion t, implying that the underlying tastes are homothetic.

Furthermore, *any function that is homogeneous of degree k can be transformed into a function that is homogeneous of degree 1 by simply taking that function to the power $(1/k)$.* We already showed in equation (5.5), for instance, that we can transform the Cobb–Douglas utility function $u(x_1, x_2) = x_1^\gamma x_2^\delta$ (which is homogeneous of degree $(\gamma + \delta)$) into a utility function that is homogeneous of degree 1 (taking the form $v(x_1, x_2) = x_1^\alpha x_2^{(1-\alpha)}$) by simply taking it to the power $1/(\gamma + \delta)$.

Can you demonstrate, using the definition of a homogeneous function, that it is generally possible to transform a function that is homogeneous of degree k to one that is homogeneous of degree 1 in the way we have suggested?

Exercise 5B.15

We can therefore conclude that homothetic tastes *can always be represented* by utility functions that are homogeneous, and since homogeneous functions can always be transformed into functions that are homogeneous of degree 1 without altering the underlying indifference curves, we can also conclude that *homothetic tastes can always be represented by utility functions that are homogeneous of degree 1.*[9] Many commonly used utility functions are indeed

---

[9]Even if a utility function is *not* homogeneous, however, it might still represent homothetic tastes because it is possible to transform a homogeneous function into a nonhomogeneous function by just, for instance, adding a constant term. The function $w(x_1, x_2) = x_1^\alpha x_2^{(1-\alpha)} + 5$, for example, has the same indifference curves as the utility function $u(x_1, x_2) = x_1^\alpha x_2^{(1-\alpha)}$, but w is not homogeneous whereas u is. But given that utility functions are only tools we use to represent tastes (indifference curves), *there is no reason to use nonhomogeneous utility functions when we want to model homothetic tastes because no economic content is lost if we simply use utility functions that are homogeneous of degree 1 to model such tastes.*

homogeneous and thus represent homothetic tastes, including, as you can see from within-chapter exercise 5B.14, *all* CES functions we defined in the previous sections.

5B.2.2 Quasilinear Tastes   In Section 5A.2.2, we defined tastes as quasilinear in good x_1 *whenever the indifference map has the property that the marginal rate of substitution at a particular bundle depends only on how much of x_1 that bundle contains (and thus NOT on how much of x_2 it contains).* Formally, this means that the marginal rate of substitution is a function of only x_1 and not x_2. This is generally not the case. For instance, we derived the *MRS* for a Cobb–Douglas utility function $u(x_1,x_2) = x_1^{\alpha} x_2^{(1-\alpha)}$ to be $-\alpha x_2/((1 - \alpha)x_1)$. Thus, for tastes that can be represented by Cobb–Douglas utility functions, the marginal rate of substitution is a function of both x_1 and x_2, which allows us to conclude immediately that such tastes are *not* quasilinear in either good.

Consider, however, the class of utility functions that can be written as

$$u(x_1,x_2) = v(x_1) + x_2, \tag{5.16}$$

where $v: \mathbb{R}_+ \to \mathbb{R}$ is a function of only the level of consumption of good x_1.

The partial derivative of u with respect to x_1 is then equal to the derivative of v with respect to x_1, and the partial derivative of u with respect to x_2 is equal to 1. Thus, the marginal rate of substitution implied by this utility function is

$$MRS = -\frac{\partial u/\partial x_1}{\partial u/\partial x_2} = -\frac{dv}{dx_1}, \tag{5.17}$$

which is a function of x_1 but *NOT* of x_2. We will then refer to tastes that can be represented by utility functions of the form given in expression (5.16) as *quasilinear in x_1*. While some advanced textbooks refer to the good x_2 (that enters the utility function linearly) as the "quasilinear" good, note that I am using the term differently here; I am referring to the good x_1 as the quasilinear good. This convention will make it much easier for us to discuss economically important forces in later chapters.

The simplest possible form of equation (5.16) arises when $v(x_1) = x_1$. This implies $u(x_1,x_2) = x_1 + x_2$, the equation we derived in Section 5B.1.1 as representing perfect substitutes. The function v can, however, take on a variety of other forms, giving utility functions that represent quasilinear tastes that do not have linear indifference curves. The indifference curves in Graph 5.11, for instance, are derived from the function $u(x_1,x_2) = \alpha \ln x_1 + x_2$, and α varies as is indicated in the panels of the graph.

5B.2.3 Homothetic versus Quasilinear Tastes   It can easily be seen from these graphs of quasilinear tastes that, *in general, quasilinear tastes are not homothetic* because the *MRS* is constant along any vertical line and thus generally not along a ray emanating from the origin. The same intuition arises from our mathematical formulation of utility functions that represent quasilinear tastes. In equation (5.17), we demonstrated that the *MRS* implied by (5.16) is $-(dv/dx_1)$. In order for tastes to be homothetic, the *MRS* evaluated at (tx_1,tx_2) would have to be the same as the *MRS* evaluated at (x_1,x_2), which implies $dv(tx_1)/dx_1$ would have to be equal to $dv(x_1)/dx_1$. But the only way that can be true is if v is a linear function of x_1 where x_1 drops out when we take the derivative of v with respect to x_1.

Thus, if $v(x_1) = \alpha x_1$ (where α is a real number), the marginal rate of substitution implied by (5.16) is just α, implying that the *MRS* is the same for all values of x_1 regardless of the value of x_2. But this simply means that indifference curves are straight lines, as in the case of perfect substitutes. Perfect substitutes therefore represent the only quasilinear tastes that are also homothetic.

5B.3 "Essential" Goods

A final distinction between indifference maps we made in Section 5A is between those that contain "essential" goods and those in which some goods are not essential. Put differently, we defined a good to be "essential" if some consumption of that good was required in order for an

Graph 5.11: The Quasilinear Utility Functions $u(x_1, x_2) = \alpha \ln x_1 + x_2$

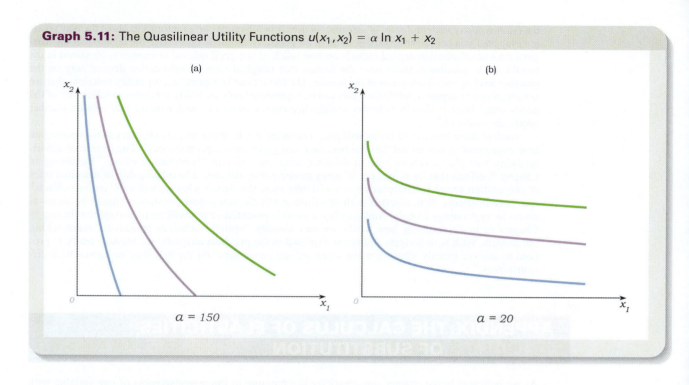

individual to achieve greater utility than he or she does by consuming nothing at all, and we concluded that goods are essential so long as indifference curves do not intersect the axis on which those goods are measured. From our various graphs of CES utility functions, it can be seen that most of these functions implicitly assume that all goods are essential (with the exception of perfect substitutes). From our graphs of quasilinear utility functions, on the other hand, we can easily see that such functions implicitly assume that goods are not essential. This distinction will become important in our discussion in the next chapter.

Use the mathematical expression for quasilinear tastes to illustrate that neither good is essential if tastes are quasilinear in one of the goods.

Exercise 5B.16

Show that both goods are essential if tastes can be represented by Cobb–Douglas utility functions.

Exercise 5B.17

CONCLUSION

This chapter continued our treatment of tastes by focusing on particular features of tastes commonly used in economic analysis. We focused on three main features: First, the *shapes of indifference curves*, whether they are relatively flat or relatively L-shaped, has a lot to do with the degree to which goods are substitutable for the consumer we are analyzing. This degree of substitutability is formalized mathematically as the elasticity of substitution, which simply defines the speed with which the slope of indifference curves changes as one moves along them. Perfect substitutes and perfect complements represent polar opposites of perfect substitutability and no substitutability, with tastes over most goods falling somewhere in between. And a special class of tastes that give rise to indifference curves that have the same elasticity of substitution at every bundle can be represented by the family of constant elasticity of substitution utility functions. Second, the *relationship of marginal rates of substitution across indifference curves* informs us about the way goods are evaluated as a consumer consumes more of all goods. Homothetic tastes have the feature that the marginal rates of substitution depend entirely on how much of one good *relative* to another is contained in the bundle, while quasilinear tastes have the feature that marginal rates of substitution depend only on the *absolute* level of one of the goods in the bundle. The former can be represented by utility functions that are homogeneous of degree 1, while the latter can be represented only by utility functions in which one of the goods enters linearly. Finally, *whether indifference curves intersect one (or more) axis* tells us whether goods are "essential."

Each of these features of tastes will play a prominent role in the coming chapters as we investigate how consumers in our model "do the best they can given their circumstances." The degree of substitutability will play a crucial role in defining what we will call "substitution effects" beginning in Chapter 7, effects that lie at the core of many public policy debates. The relationship of marginal rates of substitution across indifference curves will determine the size of what we will call "income effects" and "wealth effects" that, together with substitution effects, define how consumers change behavior as prices in an economy change. And whether a good is essential or not will be important (beginning in Chapter 6) in determining how easily we can identify "optimal" choices consumers make within our models. With both budgets and tastes explored in the previous chapters, we are now ready to proceed to analyze exactly what we mean when we say consumers "do the best they can given their circumstances."

APPENDIX: THE CALCULUS OF ELASTICITIES OF SUBSTITUTION

As we indicated in the chapter, any elasticity is a measure of the responsiveness of one variable with respect to another. In the case of the elasticity of substitution, we are measuring the responsiveness of the ratio $r = (x_2/x_1)$ to the *MRS* along an indifference curve. Using r to denote the ratio of consumption goods and σ to denote the elasticity of substitution, the formula in equation (5.1) can then be written as

$$\sigma = \left| \frac{\%\Delta r}{\%\Delta MRS} \right| = \left| \frac{\Delta r/r}{\Delta MRS/MRS} \right|. \tag{5.18}$$

Expressing this for small changes in calculus notation, we can rewrite this as

$$\sigma = \left| \frac{dr/r}{dMRS/MRS} \right| = \left| \frac{MRS}{r} \frac{dr}{dMRS} \right|. \tag{5.19}$$

Calculating such elasticities is often easiest using the *logarithmic derivative*. To derive this, note that

$$d \ln r = \frac{1}{r} dr \text{ and}$$

$$d \ln |MRS| = \frac{1}{MRS} dMRS, \tag{5.20}$$

where we have placed *MRS* in absolute values in order for the logarithm to exist. Dividing these by each other, we get

$$\frac{d \ln r}{d \ln |MRS|} = \frac{MRS}{r} \frac{dr}{dMRS}, \tag{5.21}$$

which (aside from the absolute values) is equivalent to the expression for σ in equation (5.19). Expanding out the r term, we can then write the elasticity of substitution as

$$\sigma = \frac{d \ln (x_2/x_1)}{d \ln |MRS|}. \tag{5.22}$$

You can now see more directly why the elasticity of substitution of the CES utility function is indeed $1/(1 + \rho)$. We already calculated in equation (5.11) that the *MRS* of the CES function is $-(\alpha/(1 - \alpha))(x_2/x_1)^{\rho+1}$. Taking absolute values and solving for (x_2/x_1), we get

$$\frac{x_2}{x_1} = \left(\frac{(1 - \alpha)}{\alpha} |MRS| \right)^{\frac{1}{1+\rho}}, \tag{5.23}$$

and taking logs,

$$\ln \frac{x_2}{x_1} = \frac{1}{1 + \rho} \ln |MRS| + \frac{1}{1 + \rho} \ln \left(\frac{(1 - \alpha)}{\alpha} \right). \tag{5.24}$$

We can then just apply equation (5.22) to get

$$\sigma = \frac{1}{1 + \rho}. \tag{5.25}$$

Can you demonstrate similarly that $\sigma = 1$ for the Cobb–Douglas utility function $u(x_1, x_2) = x_1^{\alpha} x_2^{(1-\alpha)}$?

Exercise 5B.18*

END-OF-CHAPTER EXERCISES

5.1   Consider your tastes for right and left shoes.

A. Suppose you, like most of us, are the kind of person who is rather picky about having the shoes you wear on your right foot be designed for right feet and the shoes you wear on your left foot be designed for left feet. In fact you are so picky that you would never wear a left shoe on your right foot or a right shoe on your left foot, nor would you ever choose (if you can help it) not to wear shoes on one of your feet.

   a.   In a graph with the number of right shoes on the horizontal axis and the number of left shoes on the vertical, illustrate three indifference curves that are part of your indifference map.

   b.   Now suppose you hurt your left leg and have to wear a cast (which means you cannot wear shoes on your left foot) for 6 months. Illustrate how the indifference curves you have drawn would change for this period. Can you think of why goods such as left shows in this case are called *neutral goods*?

   c.   Suppose you hurt your right foot instead. How would this change your answer to part (b).

   d.   Are any of the tastes you have graphed homothetic? Are any quasilinear?

   e.   In the three different tastes that you graphed, are any of the goods ever "essential"? Are any not essential?

B. Continue with the description of your tastes given in part A and let x_1 represent right shoes and let x_2 represent left shoes.

   a.   Write down a utility function that represents your tastes as illustrated in A(a). Can you think of a second utility function that also represents these tastes?

   b.   Write down a utility function that represents your tastes as graphed in A(b).

   c.   Write down a utility function that represents your tastes as drawn in A(c).

---

*conceptually challenging
**computationally challenging
†solutions in Study Guide

    d.   Can any of the tastes you have graphed in part A be represented by a utility function that is homogeneous of degree 1? If so, can they also be represented by a utility function that is not homogeneous?

    e.   Refer to end-of-chapter exercise 4.13 where the concepts of "strong monotonicity," "weak monotonicity," and "local non-satiation" were defined. Which of these are satisfied by the tastes you have graphed in this exercise?

    f.   Refer again to end-of-chapter exercise 4.13 where the concepts of "strong convexity" and "weak convexity" were defined. Which of these are satisfied by the tastes you have graphed in this exercise?

5.2   Consider your tastes for $5 bills and $10 bills.

A. Suppose that all you care about is how much money you have, but you don't care whether a particular amount comes in more or fewer bills (and suppose that you could have partial $10 and $5 bills).

    a.   With the number of $5 bills on the horizontal axis and the number of $10 bills on the vertical, illustrate 3 indifference curves from your indifference map.

    b.   What is your marginal rate of substitution of $10 bills for $5 bills?

    c.   What is the marginal rate of substitution of $5 bills for $10 bills?

    d.   Are averages strictly better than extremes? How does this relate to whether your tastes exhibit diminishing marginal rates of substitution?

    e.   Are these tastes homothetic? Are they quasilinear?

    f.   Are either of the goods on your axes "essential"?

B. Continue with the assumption that you care only about the total amount of money in your wallet, and let $5 bills be denoted x_1 and $10 bills be denoted x_2.

    a.   Write down a utility function that represents the tastes you graphed in A(a). Can you think of a second utility function that also represents these tastes?

    b.   Calculate the marginal rate of substitution from the utility functions you wrote down in B(a) and compare it to your intuitive answer in A(b).

    c.   Can these tastes be represented by a utility function that is homogeneous of degree 1? If so, can they also be represented by a utility function that is not homogeneous?

    d.   Refer to end-of-chapter exercise 4.13 where the concepts of "strong monotonicity," "weak monotonicity," and "local non-satiation" were defined. Which of these are satisfied by the tastes you have graphed in this exercise?

    e.   Refer again to end-of-chapter exercise 4.13 where the concepts of "strong convexity" and "weak convexity" were defined. Which of these are satisfied by the tastes you have graphed in this exercise?

5.3   Beer comes in 6- and 12-packs. In this exercise, we will see how your model of tastes for beer and other consumption might be affected by the units in which we measure beer.

A. Suppose initially that your favorite beer is only sold in 6-packs.

    a.   On a graph with beer on the horizontal axis and other consumption (in dollars) on the vertical, depict three indifference curves that satisfy our usual five assumptions assuming that the units in which beer is measured is 6-packs.

    b.   Now suppose the beer company eliminates 6-packs and sells all its beer in 12-packs instead. What happens to the *MRS* at each bundle in your graph if 1 unit of beer now represents a 12-pack instead of a 6-pack.

    c.   In a second graph, illustrate one of the indifference curves you drew in part (a). Pick a bundle on that indifference curve and then draw the indifference curve through that bundle assuming we are measuring beer in 12-packs instead. Which indifference curve would you rather be on?

    d.   Does the fact that these indifference curves cross imply that tastes for beer change when the beer company switches from 6-packs to 12-packs?

B. Let x_1 represent beer and let x_2 represent dollars of other consumption. Suppose that, when x_1 is measured in units of 6-packs, your tastes are captured by the utility function $u(x_1, x_2) = x_1 x_2$.

a. What is the *MRS* of other goods for beer?

b. What does the *MRS* have to be if x_1 is measured in units of 12-packs?

c. Give a utility function that represents your tastes when x_1 is measured in 12-packs and check to make sure it has the *MRS* you concluded it must have.

d. Can you use this example to explain why it is useful to measure the substitutability between different goods using percentage terms (as in the equation for the elasticity of substitution) rather than basing it simply on the absolute value of slopes at different bundles?

5.4† Suppose two people want to see if they could benefit from trading with one another in a two-good world.

A. In each of the following cases, determine whether trade might benefit the individuals:

a. As soon as they start talking with one another, they find that they own exactly the same amount of each good as the other does.

b. They discover that they are long-lost twins who have identical tastes.

c. The two goods are perfect substitutes for each of them, with the same *MRS* within and across their indifference maps.

d. They have the same tastes and own different bundles of goods but are currently located on the same indifference curve.

B*. Suppose that the two individuals have CES utility functions, with individual 1's utility given by $u(x_1, x_2) = (\alpha x_1^{-\rho} + (1 - \alpha)x_2^{-\rho})^{-1/\rho}$ and individual 2's by $v(x_1, x_2) = (\beta x_1^{-\rho} + (1 - \beta)x_2^{-\rho})^{-1/\rho}$.

a. For what values of α, β, and ρ is it the case that owning the same bundle will always imply that there are no gains from trade for the two individuals?

b. Suppose $\alpha = \beta$ and the two individuals therefore share the same preferences. For what values of $\alpha = \beta$ and ρ is it the case that the two individuals are not able to gain from trade regardless of what current bundles they own?

c. Suppose that person 1 owns twice as much of all goods as person 2. What has to be true about α, β, and ρ for them not to be able to trade?

5.5 **Everyday Application:** *Personality and Tastes for Current and Future Consumption*: Consider brothers, Eddy and Larry, who, despite growing up in the same household, have quite different personalities.

EVERYDAY APPLICATION

A. Eddy is known to his friends as "steady Eddy" because he likes predictability and wants to know that he'll have what he has now again in the future. Larry, known to his friends as "crazy Larry," adapts easily to changing circumstances. One year, he consumes everything around him like a drunken sailor; the next, he retreats to a Buddhist monestary and finds contentment in experiencing poverty.

a. Take the characterization of Eddy and Larry to its extreme (within the assumptions about tastes that we introduced in Chapter 4) and draw two indifference maps with "current consumption" on the horizontal axis and "future consumption" on the vertical, one for steady Eddy and one for crazy Larry.

b. Eddy and Larry have another brother named Daryl, who everyone thinks is a weighted average between his brothers' extremes. Suppose he is a lot more like steady Eddy than he is like crazy Larry; i.e., he is a weighted average between the two but with more weight placed on the Eddy part of his personality. Pick a bundle A on the 45-degree line and draw a plausible indifference curve for Daryl through A. Could his tastes be homothetic?

c. One day, Daryl suffers a blow to his head, and suddenly it appears that he is more like crazy Larry than like steady Eddy; i.e., the weights in his weighted average personality have flipped. (If you take this literally in a certain way, you would get a kink in Daryl's indifference curve.) Can his tastes still be homothetic?

d. In end-of-chapter exercise 4.9, we defined what it means for two indifference maps to satisfy a "single crossing property." Would you expect that Daryl's preaccident and postaccident indifference maps satisfy that property?

e. If you were told that either Eddy or Larry saves every month for retirement and the other smokes a lot, which brother is doing what?

B. Suppose that one of the brothers' tastes can be captured by the utility function $u(x_1, x_2)$ = min$\{x_1, x_2\}$, where x_1 represents dollars of current consumption and x_2 represents dollars of future consumption.

a. Which brother is it?

b. Suppose that when people say that Daryl is the weighted average of his brothers, what they mean is that his elasticity of substitution of current for future consumption lies in between those of his brothers. If Larry and Daryl have tastes that could be characterized by one (or more) of the utility functions from end-of-chapter exercise 4.5, which functions would apply to whom?

c. Which of the functions in end-of-chapter exercise 4.5 are homothetic? Which are quasilinear (and in which good)?

d. Despite being so different, is it possible that both steady Eddy and crazy Larry have tastes that can be represented by Cobb Douglas utility functions?

e. Is it possible that all their tastes could be represented by CES utility functions? Explain.

5.6†   **Everyday Application:** *Thinking About Old Age*: Consider two individuals who each take a very different view of life, and consider how this shapes their tastes over intertemporal trade-offs.

A. Jim is a 25-year-old athlete who derives most of his pleasure in life from expensive and physically intense activities: mountain climbing in the Himalayas, kayaking in the Amazon, bungee jumping in New Zealand, lion safaris in Africa, and skiing in the Alps. He does not look forward to old age when he can no longer be as active and plans on getting as much fun in early on as he can. Ken is quite different; he shuns physical activity but enjoys reading in comfortable surroundings. The more he reads, the more he wants to read and the more he wants to retreat to luxurious libraries in the comfort of his home. He looks forward to quiet years of retirement when he can do what he loves most.

a. Suppose both Jim and Ken are willing to perfectly substitute current for future consumption, but at different rates. Given the descriptions of them, draw two different indifference maps and indicate which is more likely to be Jim's and which is more likely to be Ken's.

b. Now suppose neither Jim nor Ken are willing to substitute at all across time periods. How would their indifference maps differ now given the descriptions of them provided?

c. Finally, suppose they both allowed for some substitutability across time periods but not as extreme as what you considered in part (a). Again, draw two indifference maps and indicate which refers to Jim and which to Ken.

d. Which of the indifference maps you have drawn could be homothetic?

e. Can you say for sure if the indifference maps of Jim and Ken in part (c) satisfy the single-crossing property (as defined in end-of-chapter exercise 4.9)?

B. Continue with the descriptions of Jim and Ken as given in part A and let c_1 represent consumption now and let c_2 represent consumption in retirement.

a. Suppose that Jim's and Ken's tastes can be represented by $u^J(c_1, c_2) = \alpha c_1 + c_2$ and $u^K(c_1, c_2) = \beta c_1 + c_2$, respectively. How does α compare with β; i.e., which is larger?

b. How would you similarly differentiate, using a constant α for Jim and β for Ken, two utility functions that give rise to tastes as described in A(b)?

c. Now consider the case described in A(c), with their tastes now described by the Cobb–Douglas utility functions $u^J(c_1, c_2) = c_1^\alpha c_2^{(1-\alpha)}$ and $u^K(c_1, c_2) = c_1^\beta c_2^{(1-\beta)}$. How would α and β in those functions be related to one another?

d. Are all the tastes described by the given utility functions homothetic? Are any of them quasilinear?

e. Can you show that the tastes in B(c) satisfy the single-crossing property (as defined in end-of-chapter exercise 4.9))?

f. Are all the functions in B(a)–(c) members of the family of CES utility functions?

5.7* **Everyday Application:** *Tastes for Paper Clips*: Consider my tastes for paper clips and "all other goods" (denominated in dollar units).

A. Suppose that my willingness to trade paper clips for other goods does *not* depend on how many other goods I am also currently consuming.

a. Does this imply that "other goods" are "essential" for me?

b. Suppose that, in addition, my willingness to trade paper clips for other goods does not depend on how many paper clips I am currently consuming. On two graphs, each with paper clips on the horizontal axis and "dollars of other goods" on the vertical, give two examples of what my indifference curves might look like.

c. How much can the *MRS* vary *within* an indifference map that satisfies the conditions in part (b)? How much can it vary *between* two indifference maps that both satisfy the conditions in part (b)?

d. Now suppose that the statement in (a) holds for my tastes but the statement in part (b) does not. Illustrate an indifference map that is consistent with this.

e. How much can the *MRS* vary *within* an indifference map that satisfies the conditions of part (d)?

f. Which condition do you think is more likely to be satisfied in someone's tastes: that the willingness to trade paper clips for other goods is independent of the level of paper clip consumption or that it is independent of the level of other goods consumption?

g. Are any of the previous indifference maps homothetic? Are any of them quasilinear?

B. Let paper clips be denoted by x_1 and other goods by x_2.

a. Write down two utility functions, one for each of the indifference maps from which you graphed indifference curves in A(b).

b. Are the utility functions you wrote down homogeneous? If the answer is no, could you find utility functions that represent those same tastes and are homogeneous? If the answer is yes, could you find utility functions that are not homogeneous but still represent the same tastes?

c. Are the functions you wrote down homogeneous of degree 1? If the answer is no, could you find utility functions that are homogeneous of degree 1 and represent the same tastes? If the answer is yes, could you find utility functions that are not homogeneous of degree k and still represent the same tastes?

d. Is there any indifference map you could have drawn when answering A(d) that can be represented by a utility function that is homogeneous? Why or why not?

5.8 **Everyday Application:** *Inferring Tastes for "Mozartkugeln"*: I love the Austrian candy Mozartkugeln. They are a small part of my budget, and the only factor determining my willingness to pay for additional Mozartkugeln is how many I already have.

A. Suppose you know that I am willing to give up $1 of "other consumption" to get one more Mozartkugeln when I consume bundle *A*: 100 Mozartkugeln and $500 in other goods per month.

a. What is my *MRS* when my Mozartkugeln consumption remains unchanged from bundle *A* but I only consume $200 per month in other goods?

b. Are my tastes quasilinear? Could they be homothetic?

c. You notice that this month I am consuming bundle *B*: $600 in other goods and only 25 Mozartkugeln. When questioning me about my change in behavior (from bundle *A*), I tell you that I am just as happy as I was before. The following month, you observe that I consume bundle *C*: 400 Mozartkugeln and $300 in other goods, and I once gain tell you my happiness remains unchanged. Does the new information about *B* and *C* change your answer in (b)?

d. Is consumption (other than of Mozartkugeln) essential for me?

B. Suppose my tastes could be modeled with the utility function $u(x_1, x_2) = 20x_1^{0.5} + x_2$, where x_1 refers to Mozartkugeln and x_2 refers to other consumption.

a. Calculate the *MRS* for these tastes and use your answer to prove that my tastes are quasilinear in x_1.

b. Consider the bundles *A*, *B*, and *C* as defined in part A. Verify that they lie on one indifference curve when tastes are described by the previously defined utility function.

c. Verify that the *MRS* at bundle *A* is as described in part A and derive the *MRS* at bundles *B* and *C*.

d. Verify that the *MRS* at the bundle (100,200) corresponds to your answer to A(a).

e. How much "other goods" consumption occurs on the indifference curve that contains (100,200) when my Mozartkugeln consumption falls to 25 per month? What about when it rises to 400 per month?

f. Are Mozartkugeln essential for me?

5.9* **Everday Application:** *Syllabi-Induced Tastes over Exam Grades*: Suppose you are taking two classes, economics and physics. In each class, only two exams are given during the semester.

A. Since economists are nice people, your economics professor drops the lower exam grade and bases your entire grade on the higher of the two grades. Physicists are another story. Your physics professor will do the opposite by dropping your highest grade and basing your entire class grade on your lower score.

a. With the first exam grade (ranging from 0 to 100) on the horizontal axis and the second exam grade (also ranging from 0 to 100) on the vertical, illustrate your indifference curves for your physics class.

b. Repeat this for your economics class.

c. Suppose all you care about is your final grade in a class and you otherwise value all classes equally. Consider a pair of exam scores (x_1, x_2) and suppose you knew before registering for a class what that pair will be, and that it will be the same for the economics and the physics class. What must be true about this pair in order for you to be indifferent between registering for economics and registering for physics?

B. Consider the same scenario as the one described in part A.

a. Give a utility function that could be used to represent your tastes as you described them with the indifference curves you plotted in A(a).

b. Repeat for the tastes as you described them with the indifference curves you plotted in A(b).

5.10* Consider again the family of homothetic tastes.

A. Recall that essential goods are goods that have to be present in positive quantities in a consumption bundle in order for the individual to get utility above what he or she would get by not consuming anything at all.

a. Aside from the case of perfect substitutes, is it possible for neither good to be essential but tastes nevertheless to be homothetic? If so, can you give an example?

b. Can there be homothetic tastes where one of the two goods is essential and the other is not? If so, give an example.

c. Is it possible for tastes to be nonmonotonic (less is better than more) but still homothetic?

d. Is it possible for tastes to be monotonic (more is better), homothetic but strictly non-convex (i.e., averages are worse than extremes)?

B. Now relate the homotheticity property of indifference maps to utility functions.

a. Aside from the case of perfect substitutes, are there any CES utility functions that represent tastes for goods that are not essential?

b. All CES utility functions represent tastes that are homothetic. Is it also true that all homothetic indifference maps can be represented by a CES utility function? (*Hint*: Consider your answer to A(a) and ask yourself, in light of your answer to B(a), if it can be represented by a CES function.)

c. *True or False*: The elasticity of substitution can be the same at all bundles only if the underlying tastes are homothetic.

    d.   *True or False*: If tastes are homothetic, then the elasticity of substitution is the same at all bundles.

    e.   What is the simplest possible transformation of the CES utility function that can generate tastes that are homothetic but nonmonotonic?

    f.   Are the tastes represented by this transformed CES utility function convex?

    g.   So far, we have always assumed that the parameter ρ in the CES utility function falls between -1 and ∞. Can you determine what indifference curves would look like when ρ is less than -1?

    h.   Are such tastes convex? Are they monotonic?

    i.   What is the simplest possible transformation of this utility function that would change both your answers to the previous question?

5.11*†   In this exercise, we are working with the concept of an elasticity of substitution. This concept was introduced in part B of the chapter. Thus, this entire question relates to material from part B, but the A-part of the question can be done simply by knowing the formula for an elasticity of substitution while the B-part of the question requires further material from part B of the chapter. In Section 5B.1, we defined the elasticity of substitution as

$$\sigma = \left| \frac{\%\Delta(x_2/x_1)}{\%\Delta\, MRS} \right|. \tag{5.26}$$

A.   Suppose you consume only apples and oranges. Last month, you consumed bundle $A = (100,25)$ 100 apples and 25 oranges, and you were willing to trade at most 4 apples for every orange. Two months ago, oranges were in season and you consumed $B = (25,100)$ and were willing to trade at most 4 oranges for 1 apple. Suppose your happiness was unchanged over the past two months.

    a.   On a graph with apples on the horizontal axis and oranges on the vertical, illustrate the indifference curve on which you have been operating these past two months and label the *MRS* where you know it.

    b.   Using the formula for elasticity of substitution, estimate your elasticity of substitution of apples for oranges.

    c.   Suppose we know that the elasticity of substitution is in fact the same at every bundle for you and is equal to what you calculated in (b). Suppose the bundle $C = (50,50)$ is another bundle that makes you just as happy as bundles A and B. What is the *MRS* at bundle C?

    d.   Consider a bundle $D = (25,25)$. If your tastes are homothetic, what is the *MRS* at bundle D?

    e.   Suppose you are consuming 50 apples, you are willing to trade 4 apples for 1 orange, and you are just as happy as you were when you consumed at bundle D. How many oranges are you consuming (assuming the same elasticity of substitution)?

    f.   Call the bundle you derived in part (e) E. If the elasticity is as it was before, at what bundle would you be just as happy as at E but would be willing to trade 4 oranges for 1 apple?

B.   Suppose your tastes can be summarized by the utility function $u(x_1, x_2) = (\alpha x_1^{-\rho} + (1 - \alpha)x_2^{-\rho})^{-1/\rho}$.

    a.   In order for these tastes to contain an indifference curve such as the one containing bundle A that you graphed in A(a), what must be the value of ρ? What about α?

    b.   Suppose you were told that the same tastes can be represented by $u(x_1, x_2) = x_1^\gamma x_2^\delta$. In light of your answer, is this possible? If so, what has to be true about γ and δ given the symmetry of the indifference curves on the two sides of the 45-degree line?

    c.   What exact value(s) do the exponents γ and δ take if the label on the indifference curve containing bundle A is 50? What if that label is 2,500? What if the label is 6,250,000?

    d.   Verify that bundles A, B, and C (as defined in part A) indeed lie on the same indifference curve when tastes are represented by the three different utility functions you implicitly derived in B(c). Which of these utility functions is homogeneous of degree 1? Which is homogeneous of degree 2? Is the third utility function also homogeneous?

e. What values do each of these utility functions assign to the indifference curve that contains bundle *D*?

f. *True or False*: Homogeneity of degree 1 implies that a doubling of goods in a consumption basket leads to twice the utility as measured by the homogeneous function, whereas homogeneity greater than 1 implies that a doubling of goods in a consumption bundle leads to more than twice the utility.

g. Demonstrate that the *MRS* is unchanged regardless of which of the three utility functions derived in B(c) is used.

h. Can you think of representing these tastes with a utility function that assigns the value of 100 to the indifference curve containing bundle *A* and 75 to the indifference curve containing bundle *D*? Is the utility function you derived homogeneous?

i. *True or False:* Homothetic tastes can always be represented by functions that are homogeneous of degree *k* (where *k* is greater than zero), but even functions that are not homogeneous can represent tastes that are homothetic.

j. *True or False*: The marginal rate of substitution is homogeneous of degree 0 if and only if the underlying tastes are homothetic.

Doing the "Best" We Can

We began our introduction of microeconomics with the simple premise that economic agents try to do the best they can given their circumstances.[1] For three types of economic agents—consumers, workers, and individuals planning for the future—we showed in Chapters 2 and 3 how choice sets can be used to illustrate the *circumstances* these economic agents face when making choices. We then illustrated in Chapters 4 and 5 how we can model individual tastes, giving us a way of now addressing how individuals will judge which of their available choices is indeed the "best." Chapters 2 through 5 therefore developed our basic *model* of individual choice sets and tastes, the first step in our economic analysis of choice. We now begin the second step, the analysis of how individuals in our basic model *optimize*; i.e., how they would behave if they are indeed doing the best they can.

6A Choice: Combining Economic Circumstances with Tastes

We begin by building some intuition about how tastes and choice sets interact to determine optimal choices. This means that we will essentially combine the graphs of Chapters 2 and 3 with those of Chapters 4 and 5 as we return to some of the examples we raised in those chapters. In the process, we'll begin to get our first glimpse at the important role market prices play in helping us exploit all the potential *gains from trade* that would be difficult to realize in the absence of such prices. Then, in Section 6A.2, we consider scenarios under which individuals may choose not to purchase any quantity of a particular good, scenarios we will refer to as *corner solutions*. And, in Section 6A.3, we will uncover scenarios under which individuals may discover that more than one choice is optimal for them, scenarios that arise when either choice sets or tastes exhibit *non-convexities*.

6A.1 The "Best" Bundle of Shirts and Pants

Suppose we return to my story of me going to Wal-Mart with $200 to spend on shirts and pants, with shirts costing $10 each and pants costing $20 per pair. We know from our work in Chapter 2 that in a graph with pants on the horizontal axis and shirts on the vertical axis, my budget constraint

---

[1]Chapters 2, 4, and 5 are required as reading for this chapter. Chapter 3 is not necessary.

Graph 6.1: Graphical Optimization: Budget Constraint & Indifference Curves

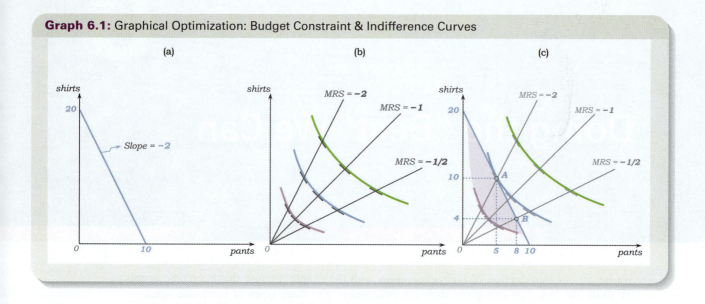

intersects at 20 on the vertical and at 10 on the horizontal. Its slope, which gives expression to the opportunity cost of one more pair of pants in terms of how many shirts I have to give up, is -2. Suppose further that the marginal rate of substitution is equal to -2 at all bundles where I have twice as many shirts as pants, that it is equal to -1 at bundles where I have an equal number of shirts and pants, and that it is equal to $-1/2$ at bundles where I have twice as many pants as shirts. (This is an example of what we called "homothetic" tastes in Chapter 5.) My budget constraint and choice set are then graphed in Graph 6.1a, and some of the indifference curves from the indifference map that represents my tastes are graphed in Graph 6.1b. To determine which of the available choices is "best" given my circumstances, we now have to combine the information from Graphs 6.1a and 6.1b.

This is done in Graph 6.1c where panel (b) is simply laid on top of panel (a). Of the three indifference curves that are graphed, the green curve contains only bundles that are in fact not available to me given my circumstances because the entire curve lies outside my choice set. The magenta indifference curve has many bundles that fall within my choice set, but none of these is "best" for me because there are bundles in the shaded area to the northeast that all lie within my choice set and above this indifference curve, bundles that are "better" for someone with my tastes. We could now imagine me starting at some low indifference curve like this one and pushing northeast to get to higher and higher indifference curves without leaving the choice set. This process would end at the blue indifference curve in Graph 6.1c, an indifference curve that contains 1 bundle that lies in the choice set (bundle A) with no bundles above the indifference curve that also lie in the choice set. Bundle A, then, is the bundle I would choose if indeed I am trying to do the best I can given my circumstances. More precisely, I would consume 5 pair of pants and 10 shirts at my optimal bundle A.[2]

Exercise 6A.1   In Chapter 2, we discussed a scenario under which my wife gives me a coupon that reduces the effective price of pants to \$10 per pair. Assuming the same tastes, what would be my best bundle?

---

[2]This optimal bundle lies at the intersection of the budget line ($x_2 = 20 - 2x_1$) and the ray $x_2 = 2x_1$ representing all the points with MRS of -2. Solving these by substituting the second equation into the first gives us the answer that $x_1 = 5$, and putting that into either of the two equations gives us that $x_2 = 10$.

6A.1.1 Opportunity Cost = Marginal Rate of Substitution

At bundle A in Graph 6.1c, a very particular relationship exists between the slope of the budget constraint and the slope of the indifference curve that contains bundle A: *the two slopes are equal*. This is no accident, and it should make intuitive sense why this is true. The slope of the budget constraint represents the opportunity cost of pants in terms of shirts, which is the number of shirts I *have* to give up to get one more pair of pants (given the prices Wal-Mart charges for pants and shirts). Put differently, the slope of the budget constraint represents the rate at which Wal-Mart is allowing me to change pants into shirts. The slope of the indifference curve, in contrast, represents the marginal rate of substitution, which is the number of shirts I *am willing* to give up to get one more pair of pants. If I have a bundle in my shopping basket at which the value I place on pants (in terms of shirts) differs from the rate at which Wal-Mart is allowing me to change pants into shirts, I can make myself better off by choosing a different bundle. Thus, at the optimal bundle, the rate at which I am *willing* to trade pants for shirt and the rate at which I *have to* trade them must be equal.

Suppose, for instance, that I have B from Graph 6.1c (8 pants, 4 shirts) in my shopping basket. The marginal rate of substitution at B is $-1/2$. This means that I am *willing* to trade 1 pair of pants for half a shirt, but Wal-Mart will give me 2 shirts for every pair of pants that I put back on the rack. If I am willing to trade a pair of pants for just half a shirt and Wal-Mart will give me 2 shirts for a pair of pants, then I can clearly make myself better off by trading pants for more shirts. Put differently, when I have B in my basket, the marginal value I place on pants is lower than the marginal value Wal-Mart is placing on those pants, and Wal-Mart is therefore willing to give me more for pants (in terms of shirts) than I think they are worth. B therefore cannot possibly be a "best" bundle because I can make myself better off by exchanging pants for shirts.

Suppose you and I each have a bundle of 6 pants and 6 shirts, and suppose that my *MRS* of shirts for pants is -1 and yours is -2. Suppose further that neither one of us has access to Wal-Mart. Propose a trade that would make both of us better off.

Exercise 6A.2

6A.1.2 How Wal-Mart Makes Us All the Same *at the Margin*

I am not the only one who rushes to buy shirts and pants right before the school year starts; lots of others do the same. Some of those consumers have tastes very different than mine, so their indifference maps look very different. Others will have more generous wives (and thus more generous budgets); yet others may be poorer and may only be able to spend a fraction of what my wife is permitting me to spend. Imagine all of us—rich and poor, some in more need of pants and some in more need of shirts—all coming to Wal-Mart to do the best we can. Coming into Wal-Mart, we will be very different; but coming out of Wal-Mart, it turns out that we will be quite the same in one important respect: *our marginal rates of substitution of pants for shirts given what we have just purchased will all be the same.*

Consider, for instance, the two consumers whose choice sets and tastes are graphed in Graph 6.2a and 6.2b. Consumer 1 is rich (and thus has a large choice set) whereas consumer 2 is poor (and thus has a small choice set). Consumer 1 and consumer 2 also have very different indifference maps. In the end, however, they both choose an optimal bundle of shirts and pants at which their marginal rate of substitution is equal to the slope of their budget constraint. Since the slope of each consumer's budget constraint is determined by the ratio of prices for shirts and pants at Wal-Mart, and since Wal-Mart charges the same prices to anyone who enters the store, the marginal rates of substitution for both people is thus equal once they have chosen their best bundle. Put differently, *while the two consumers enter the store with very different incomes and tastes, they leave the store with the same tastes for pants and shirts at the margin* (i.e., around the bundle they purchase).

6A.1.3 How Wal-Mart Eliminates Any Need for Us to Trade

An important and unintended side effect of Wal-Mart's policy to charge everyone the same price is that *all gains from trade in pants*

Graph 6.2: Different Choice Sets, Different Tastes: But Same Tastes "at the Margin"

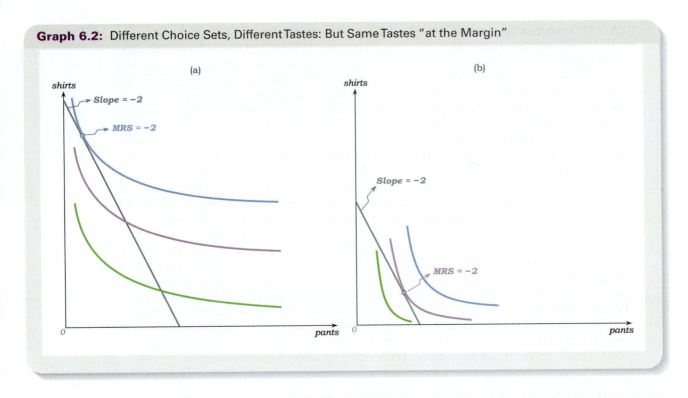

and shirts occur inside Wal-Mart, eliminating any need for us to trade with one another once we leave the store. As we all enter the store, we may have different quantities of pants and shirts at home, and we could probably benefit from trading shirts and pants among us given that some of us might be willing to trade shirts for pants more easily than others. But once we leave Wal-Mart, we value pants and shirts exactly the same at the margin; i.e., we all have the same marginal rate of substitution of pants for shirts. There is therefore no more possibility for us to trade and become better off because we became as well off as we could by simply doing the best we can inside Wal-Mart.

This is an important initial insight into a more general result we will develop later on in this book. Whenever two people have bundles of goods at which they value the goods in the bundle differently on the margin, there is the *potential for gains from trade,* the potential for trade to make both people better off. We already illustrated this in the end-of-chapter exercise 4.5 in Chapter 4 as well as in within-chapter exercise 6A.2, but here is another example. Suppose I am willing to trade 1 can of Coke for 1 can of Pepsi (i.e., my marginal rate of substitution is −1) but my wife is willing to trade 1 can of Coke for 2 cans of Pepsi (i.e., her marginal rate of substitution is −2). Then we can gain from trading with one another so long as we each have both Coke and Pepsi in our bundles. In particular, I could offer my wife 2 Cokes for 3 Pepsis. This will make me better off because I would have been willing to take only 2 Pepsis for 2 Cokes, and it will make my wife better off because she would have been willing to give me as many as 4 Pepsis for 2 Cokes. The fact that our marginal rates of substitution are different, the fact that we value goods differently at the margin, makes it possible for us to trade in a way that makes both of us better off.

Economists say that a situation is efficient if there is no way to change the situation so as to make some people better off without making anyone worse off.[3] A situation is therefore inefficient

---

[3]Sometimes economists refer to this as *Pareto efficient* or *Pareto optimal* after Vilfredo Pareto (1848–1923). Pareto was among the first economists in the late 19th century to realize that economic analysis did not require utility to be objectively measurable, that all that was required was for individuals to be able rank different alternatives. This led him to his definition of efficiency, which stands in contrast to earlier "utilitarian" theories that relied on adding up people's "utils." We will return to some of this in Chapter 29.

if we can think of a way to change the situation and make some people better off without making anyone else worse off. If we find ourselves in a situation where people value goods that they possess differently at the margin, we know there is a way to make everyone better off through trade. Thus, situations where people have different marginal rates of substitution for goods that they possess are inefficient. Since Wal-Mart's policy of charging the same prices to everyone results in a situation where everyone leaves the store with marginal rates of substitution between goods in their baskets identical, *Wal-Mart ensures that the distribution of pants and shirts is efficient among those that purchase pants and shirts at Wal-Mart.*

We keep using the phrase "at the margin" as, for example, when we say that tastes for those leaving Wal-Mart will be the "same at the margin." What do economists mean by this "at the margin" phrase?

Exercise 6A.3

I doubt you have ever thought of approaching someone in the Wal-Mart parking lot to propose a trade of goods in your shopping basket with goods you see in his or her basket. It turns out, there is a very good reason for this: It would be an exercise in futility because all gains from trade have been exhausted within Wal-Mart, and the distribution of goods is already efficient. Put differently, once we leave Wal-Mart, any trade that I propose to you will either leave us just as well off as we would be without trading or would make one of us worse off. So we don't need to bother trying.

6A.2 To Buy or Not to Buy

With the indifference maps and budget sets used above, "doing the best I can" led me to purchase *both* pants and shirts at Wal-Mart. But sometimes our tastes and circumstances are such that doing the best we can implies we will choose *not* to consume any of a particular good. This certainly happens for goods that we consider "bads," goods of which we would prefer less rather than more. Peanut butter is such a good for me. I simply cannot imagine why anyone would ever consume any unless there was an immediate need to induce vomiting. Ketchup is another such good for me. I will never buy peanut butter or ketchup. But there are also goods that I like of which I will consume none. For instance, I like both Coke and Pepsi equally (and in fact cannot tell the difference between the two), but whenever Pepsi is more expensive than Coke, I will buy no Pepsi. My tastes for goods that I like combine, in this case, with my economic circumstances to lead to my "best" choice at a "corner" of my budget constraint.

6A.2.1 Corner Solutions Let's consider the case of me choosing between Coke and Pepsi in the context of our model of tastes and circumstances. Suppose that I get sent to the store with $15 to spend on soft drinks, and suppose that the store sells only Coke and Pepsi. Suppose further that the price of Coke is $1 per can and the price of Pepsi is $1.50 per can. Graph 6.3a then illustrates my choice set and budget constraint. In Chapter 5, we further illustrated my tastes for Coke and Pepsi with an indifference map containing indifference curves that all have a marginal rate of substitution equal to -1 everywhere. Such indifference curves, illustrated again in Graph 6.3b, give expression to the fact that I cannot tell the difference between Coke and Pepsi and therefore am always willing to trade them one for one.

In panel (c) of Graph 6.3, we again overlay my choice set (from panel (a)) and my indifference map (from panel (b)). My goal is to reach the highest indifference curve that contains at least one bundle in the choice set. I could start with the lowest (magenta) indifference curve, note that all bundles on that indifference curve lie in my choice set, then move to the northeast to higher indifference curves. Eventually, I will reach the blue indifference curve in Graph 6.3c, which contains one bundle (bundle *A*) that lies both on the indifference curve and within my choice set.

Graph 6.3: Corner Solutions

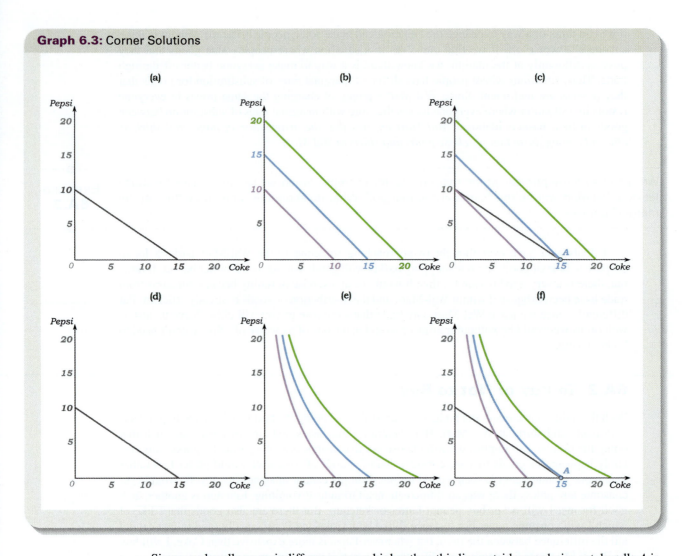

Since any bundle on an indifference curve higher than this lies outside my choice set, bundle *A* is my "best" bundle. It contains 15 Cokes and no Pepsi and is called a "corner solution" because it lies on one corner of my choice set.

Exercise 6A.4*   In the previous section, we argued that Wal-Mart's policy of charging the same price to all consumers ensures that there are no further gains from trade for goods contained in the shopping baskets of individuals who leave Wal-Mart. The argument assumed that all consumers end up at an interior solution, not a corner solution. Can you see why the conclusion still stands when some people optimize at corner solutions where their *MRS* may be quite different from the *MRS*'s of those who optimize at interior solutions?

Exercise 6A.5   Suppose the prices of Coke and Pepsi were the same. Illustrate that now there are many optimal bundles for someone with my kind of tastes. What would be my "best" bundle if Pepsi is cheaper than Coke?

Of course, tastes do not have to be as extreme as those for perfect substitutes in order for corner solutions to arise. Panels (d), (e), and (f) of Graph 6.3, for instance, illustrate a less extreme set of indifference curves that nevertheless results in corner solutions for certain economic circumstances.

6A.2.2 Ruling Out Corner Solutions

In Chapter 5, we discussed how a good is "essential" if indifference curves do not intersect the axes on which the other good is measured, essential in the sense that no utility above that of consuming at the origin of the graph can be attained without at least some consumption of such "essential" goods. If all goods in a particular model of a consumer's tastes are "essential," then corner solutions are not possible; it can never be optimal to choose a bundle with zero quantity of one of the goods because that would be the same as choosing zero quantity of all goods. *Whenever indifference curves intersect an axis, however, some goods are not essential, and there is thus a potential for a corner solution to be the optimal choice under some economic circumstances.*

Consider, for instance, my wife's tastes for iced tea and sugar as described in Chapter 5. Suppose that sugar costs $0.25 per packet and iced tea costs $0.50 per glass, and suppose that my wife has budgeted $15 for her weekly iced tea drinking. Her weekly choice set is illustrated in Graph 6.4a, and her tastes for iced tea and sugar packets are illustrated with three indifference curves in Graph 6.4b (given that these are perfect complements for her). Panel (c) of Graph 6.4 then illustrates her optimal choice as bundle *A*, with equal numbers of glasses of iced tea and sugar packets.

Graph 6.4: Ruling Out Corner Solutions

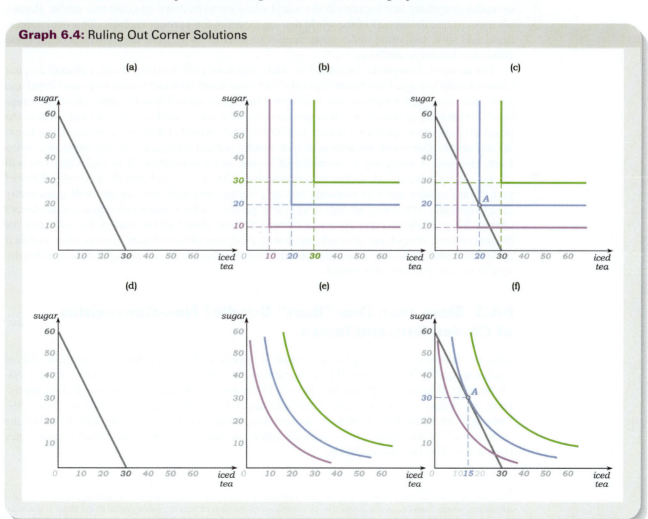

We could now think of changing the prices of iced tea and sugar packets, of making sugar packets really cheap and making iced tea really expensive, for instance. While the total quantity of iced tea and sugar packets that is optimal will be different, it will always be true that my wife will consume equal numbers of iced tea glasses and sugar packets, and never a corner solution.

The case of perfect complements is an extreme case that ensures that no corner solutions will ever be optimal. But the same logic holds for any map of indifference curves that do not intersect either axis, or, put differently, for any set of goods that are all essential. Panels (d) through (f) of Graph 6.4, for instance, model my wife's tastes for iced tea and sugar as less extreme, with some willingness to trade off some sugar for more iced tea and vice versa. Still, the indifference map in panel (e) of the graph is such that no indifference curve ever intersects either axis, ensuring an *interior solution* where the marginal rate of substitution is exactly equal to the slope of the budget constraint.

6A.2.3 Is it Realistic to Rule Out Corner Solutions?

In many of our applications throughout this book, we will assume tastes with indifference maps that rule out corner solutions by assuming that all goods are essential. Our first reaction to this might be that this is highly unrealistic. After all, we are all at corner solutions because there are many goods at Wal-Mart that never end up in our shopping baskets. This is certainly true, but remember that we are not trying to model everything that happens in the world when we write down an economic model. Rather, we try to isolate the aspects of the world that are essential for a proper analysis of particular questions, and so it may often make sense simply to abstract away from the existence of all those goods that we never purchase.

For instance, I might be interested in analyzing how your housing choices change as your circumstances change. I might therefore abstract away from your tastes over Coke and Pepsi and pants and shirts, and simply model your tastes for square feet of housing and "other consumption." In that case, of course, it makes perfect sense to assume indifference maps that exclude the possibility of corner solutions because you will almost certainly choose to consume some housing and some other goods regardless of how much your circumstances change. Similarly, when I am interested in analyzing your choice of leisure and consumption, it is likely that you will always choose some leisure and some consumption. The same is probably the case when I model your choice of how much to consume this year versus next year: Few people will consciously plan to consume only today or only next year regardless of how much individual circumstances change. Thus, while we certainly are at corner solutions almost all the time in the sense that we do not consume many types of goods, economic modeling of the relevant choices often makes it quite reasonable to assume tastes that prohibit corner solutions by assuming that the goods relevant to our analysis are all essential.

6A.3 More than One "Best" Bundle? Non-Convexities of Choice Sets and Tastes

Thus far, almost all our examples have made it appear as if a consumer will always be able to reach a unique optimal decision.[4] It turns out that this "uniqueness" occurs in most of our models because of two assumptions that have held throughout the earlier portions of this chapter: First, all budget constraints were lines, and second, all tastes were assumed to satisfy the "averages are better than extremes" assumption. More generally, we will find next that the "uniqueness" of the "best" choice may disappear as "non-convexities" in choice sets or tastes enter the problem we are modeling.

---

[4]The one exception to this has been the case of indifference curves with linear components such as those for perfect substitutes, where a whole set of bundles may be optimal when the ratio of prices is exactly equal to the slope of the linear component of the budget line (see the within-chapter exercise 6A.5 in Section 6A.2.1.)

6A.3.1 Optimizing with Kinked Budgets

As we illustrated in Chapters 2 and 3, there are two basic types of kinks in budget constraints that may arise under various circumstances: those that point "outward" and those that point "inward." We introduced these in Chapter 2 with two types of coupons for pants. First we considered a coupon that gave a consumer 50% off for the first 6 pairs of pants (Graph 2.4a) and then turned toward thinking about a coupon that gave 50% off for any pair of pants a consumer purchases after buying 6 at regular price. We will demonstrate now that multiple "best" bundles may arise only in the second case but not in the first (assuming for now that our tastes satisfy the basic five assumptions laid out in Chapter 4).

Graph 6.5 considers how three different types of tastes may result in three different optimal bundles on the same "outwardly" kinked budged constraint derived from the first type of coupon (see Section 2A.2). In each case, the general shape of our standard indifference curves guarantees only a single "best" choice because there is no way to draw our usual shapes for indifference curves and get more than one tangency to the outwardly kinked budget constraint.

Graph 6.6, in contrast, considers the "inwardly" kinked budget that arises under the second type of coupon (see also Section 2A.2) and particularly models tastes that lead to two "best" bundles: bundles A and B. You can immediately see how this is possible: Since indifference curves begin steep and become shallower as we move toward the right in the graph, the only way we can have two bundles at which the budget constraint has the same slope at the best indifference curve is for the budget constraint itself also to become shallower as we move to the right. This can happen with an "inward" kink in the budget, but it cannot happen with an "outward" kink such as that in Graph 6.5.

6A.3.2 Non-Convexities in Choice Sets

In fact, a "kink" in the budget is, strictly speaking, not necessary for the possibility of multiple "best" bundles when indifference maps satisfy the "averages better than extreme" assumption. Rather, what is necessary is a property known as "non-convexity" of the choice set.

A set of points is said to be *convex* whenever the line connecting any two points in the set is itself contained within the set. Conversely, a set of points is said to be *non-convex* whenever some part of a line connecting two points in the set lies outside the set. No such non-convexity exists in the choice set of Graph 6.5. Regardless of which two points in the set we pick, the line connecting them always also lies within the set. But in the choice set of Graph 6.6, it is easy to

Graph 6.5: Optimizing along Budget with an "Outward" Kink

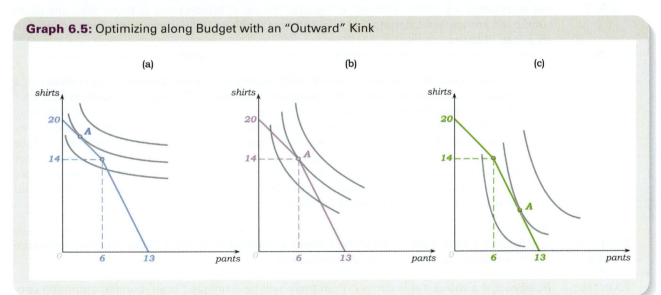

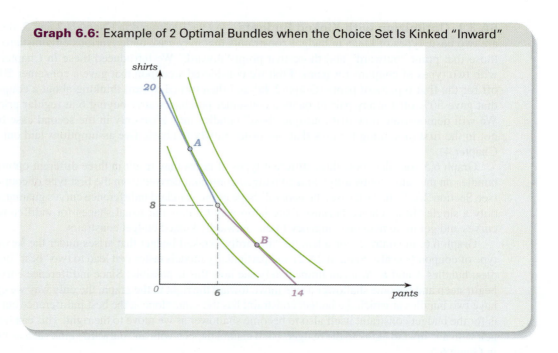

Graph 6.6: Example of 2 Optimal Bundles when the Choice Set Is Kinked "Inward"

find pairs of points where the line connecting those points lies outside the set. For instance, both points *A* and *B* in Graph 6.6 lie in the choice set, but the line connecting the two points lies outside the set. Thus, the choice set in Graph 6.6 is non-convex.

Exercise 6A.6   Consider a set of points that compose a solid sphere. Is this set convex? What about the set of points contained in a donut?

Exercise 6A.7   We have just defined what it means for a set of points to be convex—it must be the case that any line connecting two points in the set is fully contained in the set as well. In Chapter 4, we defined tastes to be convex when "averages are better than (or at least as good as) extremes." The reason such tastes are called "convex" is because the set of bundles that is better than any given bundle is a convex set. Illustrate that this is the case with an indifference curve from an indifference map of convex tastes.

Now, notice that a regularly shaped indifference curve can be tangent to the boundary of a choice set more than once *only if* the choice set is non-convex. The series of graphs in Graph 6.7 attempts to show this intuitively by beginning with a convex choice set (in panel (a)), continuing with a linear budget that is still convex (in panel (b)), and then proceeding to two non-convex choice sets in panels (c) and (d). *The important characteristic of a choice set to produce multiple "best bundles" is therefore* not the existence of a kink but rather *the existence of a non-convexity* (which may or may not involve a kink). While we can think of examples of non-convex choice sets, we will see that convex choice sets are most common in most of the economic applications we will discuss in the remainder of this book.

Exercise 6A.8   *True/False*: If a choice set is non-convex, there are definitely multiple "best" bundles for a consumer whose tastes satisfy the usual assumptions.

Exercise 6A.9   *True/False*: If a choice set is convex, then there will be a unique "best" bundle, assuming consumer tastes satisfy our usual assumptions and averages are strictly better than extremes.

Graph 6.7: The Role of Convexity of Choice Sets in Insuring Unique Optimal Bundles

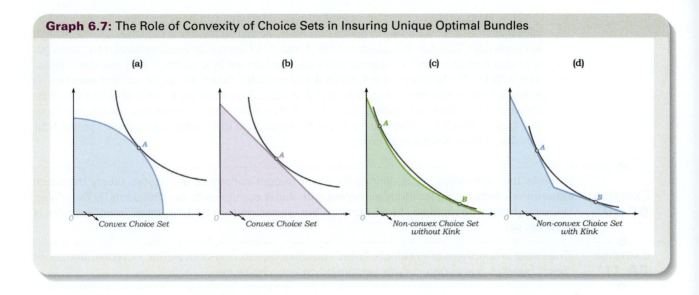

6A.3.3 Non-Convexities in Tastes

Suppose next that an indifference map had indifference curves that looked like those graphed in Graph 6.8a. You can demonstrate that such indifference curves violate the "averages are better than extremes" (or convexity) assumption by considering bundles A and B together with the average between those bundles, labeled C in the graph. Since C falls below the indifference curve that contains A and B, it is worse than A and B; thus the average bundle is not as good as the more extreme bundles. As already suggested in exercise 6A.7, the reason we call such tastes non-convex is that the set of bundles that is better than a given bundle is a non-convex set. In our example, bundle C lies on the line connecting bundles A and B but is worse, not better, than bundles A and B. Thus, the set of bundles that are better than those on the indifference curve containing bundle A (the shaded area in Graph 6.8a) is non-convex.

Graph 6.8: Example of 2 Optimal Bundles when Tastes are Non-Convex

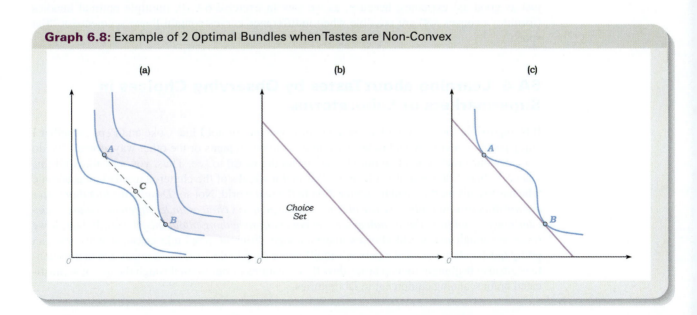

Now suppose we consider an individual with tastes that can be represented by the indifference map in Graph 6.8a trying to do the best he or she can on the linear (and thus convex) budget in Graph 6.8b. This can then result in both A and B in Graph 6.8c being optimal. Our "averages are better than extremes" assumption rules this scenario out by explicitly ruling out non-convexities in tastes. We have argued in Chapter 4 that assuming "averages are better than extremes" is reasonable for most economic models. It makes sense that people are more willing to trade shirts for pants if they have lots of shirts and relatively few pants. In most economic models, we therefore feel comfortable ruling out "non-convex" tastes, and thus ruling out multiple optimal bundles due to non-convexities in tastes.

Exercise 6A.10*

Suppose that the choice set is defined by linear budget constraint and tastes satisfy the usual assumptions but contain indifference curves with linear components (or "flat spots"). *True/False*: There might then be multiple "best" bundles, but we can be sure that the set of "best" bundles is a convex set.

Exercise 6A.11*

True/False: When there are multiple "best" bundles due to non-convexities in tastes, the set of "best" bundles is also non-convex (assuming convex choice sets).

There are instances, however, when we might think that tastes should be modeled as non-convex, and should thus permit multiple optimal solutions. Suppose, for instance, we modeled our tastes for steak dinners versus chicken dinners, and suppose we considered a model in which we are trying to predict whether someone will choose a steak or a chicken dinner, or some combination of the two. It may well be reasonable for someone to have non-convex tastes that allow for both a steak dinner and a chicken dinner to be optimal, with a half steak and half chicken dinner being worse. At the same time, if we instead modeled someone's weekly tastes for steak and chicken dinners (rather than just his or her tastes at a single meal), the non-convexity is less reasonable because, over the course of a week, someone is much more likely to be willing to have some steak and some chicken dinners.

Putting the insights from this and the previous section together, we can conclude that *we can be sure that an individual has a single, unique "best" choice given a particular set of economic circumstances only if neither his or her choice set nor his or her tastes exhibit non-convexities.* More precisely, we need tastes to be *strictly convex*—averages to be strictly better than (and not just as good as) extremes, because, as we saw in exercise 6A.10, multiple optimal bundles (forming a convex set) are possible when indifference curves contain linear segments or "flat spots."

6A.4 Learning about Tastes by Observing Choices in Supermarkets or Laboratories

It is impossible for you to look at me and know whether or not I like Coke and Pepsi, whether I enjoy peanut butter or would rather have more shirts than pants or the other way around. We do not carry our tastes around on our sleeves for all the world to see. Thus, you may think all this "theory" about tastes is a little pie in the sky, that it wreaks of the cluttered mind of an academic who has lost his marbles and his connection to the real world. Not so! *Despite the fact that tastes are not directly observable, we are able to observe people's choices under different economic circumstances, and from those choices we can conclude something about their tastes.* In fact, if we observe enough real-world choices under enough different economic circumstances, we can pretty much determine what a person's indifference map looks like. Economists and neuroscientists are also beginning to map tastes directly to features of our brain through the use of sophisticated brain scanning equipment in laboratories.

6A.4.1 Estimating Tastes from Real-World Choices   It is not difficult to see how we can estimate tastes by observing people's choices in the real world (even though the statistical methods required for an economist actually to determine a consumer's underlying tastes are quite sophisticated and beyond the scope of this text). Take our example of me shopping for pants and shirts at Wal-Mart, for instance, and suppose that you observe that I purchase 10 shirts and 5 pants with my $200 budget when the prices of shirts and pants are $10 and $20 respectively. This tells you that my *MRS* at the bundle (5, 10) is equal to the slope of my budget (-2). Then suppose that my economic circumstances change because Wal-Mart changes the price of pants to $10 and the price of shirts to $20, and suppose you now see me purchasing 10 pants and 5 shirts. You now know that my *MRS* at the bundle (10, 5) is $-1/2$. If you continue to see changes in my economic circumstances and my response to those changes in terms of my choices, you can keep collecting information about the *MRS* at each of the bundles that I purchase under each scenario. The more such choices you observe, the easier it is for you to estimate what my underlying indifference map must look like.

Thus, economists have developed ways to estimate underlying tastes by observing choices under different economic circumstances. Many supermarkets, for instance, provide consumers with cards that can be scanned at the check-out counter and that give consumers some discounts on certain products. Every time I shop in our local supermarket, I give the check-out clerk my card so that I get the discounts on advertised items. The supermarket then automatically collects data on my consumption patterns. It knows what I buy when I shop and how my consumption patterns change with the supermarket's discounts and price changes. Economists can then analyze such data to recover underlying tastes for particular consumers or the "average consumer."

6A.4.2 Learning about the Link from the Brain to Tastes   Over the last few years, a new area has emerged within economics known as *neuroeconomics*. Many neuroeconomists are actually neuroscientists who specialized in understanding how our brain makes decisions, and a small but increasing number have been trained as economists who collaborate with neuroscientists. Their aim is, in part, to unravel the "black box" of tastes: to understand what determines our tastes and how they change over time, to what extent tastes are "hard-wired" into our brain, and how our brain uses tastes to make decisions. In doing their work, neuroeconomists rely on both the economic theory of choice as well as experimental evidence gathered from observing individuals make choices within a laboratory where various aspects of their physiology can be closely monitored. Neuroeconomists can, for instance, see which parts of the brain are active—and how active they are—when individuals confront a variety of choices, and through this they are beginning to be able to infer something about the mapping of features of tastes (such as marginal rates of substitution) to the structure of the brain. They are also able to see how the decision-making process is altered when the brain is altered by such factors as substance abuse. This is fascinating research, but it is beyond the scope of this book. However, within a relatively short period, it is likely that you will be able to take course work in neuroeconomics and should consider doing so if the intersection between economics and neuroscience seems interesting to you.

6B Optimizing within the Mathematical Model

In part 6A, we found ways of depicting mathematical optimization problems in intuitive graphs, and we now turn toward an exposition of the mathematics that underlies this intuition. Specifically, we will see that consumers face what mathematicians call a *constrained optimization problem,* a problem where some variables (the goods in the consumption bundle) are *chosen* so as to *optimize* a function (the utility function), subject to the fact that there are *constraints* (the choice set).

6B.1 Optimizing by Choosing Pants and Shirts

Letting x_1 and x_2 denote pants and shirts, consider once again the example of me choosing a consumption bundle (x_1,x_2) in Wal-Mart given that the price for a pair of pants is $20 and the price for a shirt is $10, and given that my wife gave me a total of $200 to spend. Suppose further that my tastes can be represented by the Cobb–Douglas utility function $u(x_1,x_2) = x_1^{1/2}x_2^{1/2}$, which gives rise to the indifference curves drawn in Graph 6.1 of Section 2A.1. Then the mathematical problem I face is that I would like to choose the quantities of x_1 and x_2 so that they are affordable (i.e., they lie within the choice set) and so that they attain for me the highest possible utility as evaluated by the utility function u. That is, of course, exactly the same problem we were solving graphically in Graph 6.1, where we were finding the "best" bundle by finding the highest indifference curve (and thus the highest level of utility) that contains at least one point in the budget set.

Put differently, I would like to *choose* (x_1,x_2) so as to *maximize* the function $u(x_1,x_2)$ *subject to the constraint* that my expenditures on good x_1 plus my expenditures on good x_2 are no larger than $200. Formally, we write this as

$$\max_{x_1,x_2} u(x_1,x_2) = x_1^{1/2}x_2^{1/2} \text{ subject to } 20x_1 + 10x_2 \leq 200. \tag{6.1}$$

The "max" notation at the beginning of the expression signifies that we are attempting to *maximize* or "get to the highest possible value" of a function. The variables that appear immediately below the "max" notation as subscripts signify those variables that we are choosing, or the *choice variables* in the optimization problem. I am able to choose the quantities of the two goods, but I am not able to choose the prices at which I purchase them or, since my wife determined it, my money budget. Thus, x_1 and x_2 are the only choice variables in this optimization problem. This is then followed by the function that we are maximizing, called the *objective function* of the optimization problem. Finally, if there is a constraint to the optimization problem, it appears as the last item of the formal statement of the problem following the words "subject to." We will follow this general format for stating optimization problems throughout this text.

Since we know that Cobb–Douglas utility functions represent tastes that satisfy our "more is better" assumption, we can furthermore rewrite expression (6.1) with the certainty that the bundle (x_1,x_2) that solves the optimization problem is one that lies *on* the budget line, *not inside* the choice set. When such an inequality constraint holds with equality in an optimization problem, we say that the constraint is *binding*. In other words, we know that I will end up spending all of my allocated money budget, so we might as well write that constraint as an equality rather than as an inequality. Expression (6.1) then becomes

$$\max_{x_1,x_2} u(x_1,x_2) = x_1^{1/2}x_2^{1/2} \text{ subject to } 20x_1 + 10x_2 = 200. \tag{6.2}$$

6B.1.1 Two Ways of Approaching the Problem Mathematically   We begin by viewing the problem strictly through the eyes of a mathematician, and we illustrate two equivalent methods to solving the problem defined in equation (6.2).

Method 1: Converting the Constrained Optimization Problem into an Unconstrained Optimization Problem

One way is to turn the problem from a constrained optimization to an *unconstrained* optimization problem by inserting the constraint into the objective function. For example, we can solve the constraint for x_2 by subtracting $20x_1$ from both sides and dividing both sides by 10 to get $x_2 = 20 - 2x_1$. When we insert this into the utility function for x_2, we get a new function that is simply a function of the variable x_1. We can call this function $f(x_1)$ and rewrite the problem defined in (6.2) as

$$\max_{x_1} f(x_1) = x_1^{1/2}(20 - 2x_1)^{1/2}. \tag{6.3}$$

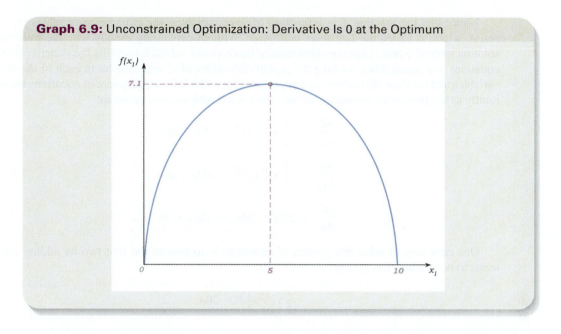

Graph 6.9: Unconstrained Optimization: Derivative Is 0 at the Optimum

Graph 6.9 plots this function, and this graph illustrates that the function f attains a maximum at $x_1 = 5$, which is exactly the same answer we derived graphically in Graph 6.1. Furthermore, the f function attains a value of zero at $x_1 = 10$. Thinking back to the underlying economics, when x_1 (the number of pants) is 10, I have no money left over for shirts. Since the tastes are such that both shirts and pants are "essential," it makes sense that the function returns back to zero when I purchase no shirts.

Rather than plotting the whole function and finding the maximum graphically, we can of course use calculus to find the maximum. More precisely, since the function has a slope of zero when it attains its maximum, all we have to do to find this maximum mathematically is find where the slope (or derivative) of the function is zero. Taking the derivative of f with respect to x_1, we get

$$\frac{df}{dx_1} = \frac{1}{2}x_1^{-1/2}(20 - 2x_1)^{1/2} - x_1^{1/2}(20 - 2x_1)^{-1/2}. \tag{6.4}$$

When we then set this expression to zero and solve for x_1, we get $x_1 = 5$ as the maximum of the function, just as Graph 6.9 illustrated. Thus, we know that I will purchase 5 pairs of pants (costing a total of $100), leaving $100 to purchase 10 shirts (at a price of $10 each). We have found mathematically what we found graphically in Graph 6.1: the "best" choice for me "given my circumstances."

Method 2: The Lagrange Method for Solving the Constrained Optimization Problem

A second (and more general) way to solve problems of the type expressed in (6.2) is to use a method that is known as the *Lagrange Method*. If you have taken a full calculus sequence, you have probably covered this in your last calculus course, but the method is not very complicated and does not require all the material usually covered in the entire calculus sequence. The method does essentially what we did in Method 1: It defines a new function and sets derivatives equal to zero in order to find the maximum of that new function. The function that we define is called the *Lagrange function*, and it is always constructed as a combination of the objective function in the optimization problem plus a term λ multiplied by the constraint (where the terms in the constraint are all collected to one side, with the other side equal to zero). For instance, expression (6.2) results in the *Lagrange function* $\mathcal{L}$ given by

$$\mathcal{L}(x_1, x_2, \lambda) = x_1^{1/2}x_2^{1/2} + \lambda(200 - 20x_1 - 10x_2). \tag{6.5}$$

Notice that the function $\mathcal{L}$ is a function of three variables: the two choice variables (x_1,x_2) and λ, which is called the *Lagrange multiplier*. Without explaining exactly why the following solution method works, Lagrange problems of this type are solved by solving the system of three equations that arises when we take the partial derivatives of $\mathcal{L}$ with respect to each of the three variables and set these derivatives to zero; i.e., we solve the following system of equations known jointly as the *first order conditions* of the constrained optimization problem:

$$\frac{\partial \mathcal{L}}{\partial x_1} = \frac{1}{2} x_1^{-1/2} x_2^{1/2} - 20\lambda = 0,$$

$$\frac{\partial \mathcal{L}}{\partial x_2} = \frac{1}{2} x_1^{1/2} x_2^{-1/2} - 10\lambda = 0, \tag{6.6}$$

$$\frac{\partial \mathcal{L}}{\partial \lambda} = 200 - 20x_1 - 10x_2 = 0.$$

One easy way to solve this system of equations is to rewrite the first two by adding the λ terms to both sides, thus getting

$$\frac{1}{2} x_1^{-1/2} x_2^{1/2} = 20\lambda$$

$$\frac{1}{2} x_1^{1/2} x_2^{-1/2} = 10\lambda \tag{6.7}$$

and then dividing these two equations by each other to get

$$\frac{x_2}{x_1} = 2. \tag{6.8}$$

Multiplying both sides of (6.8) by x_1 then gives us

$$x_2 = 2x_1, \tag{6.9}$$

which we can insert into the third equation in expression (6.6) to get

$$200 - 20x_1 - 10(2x_1) = 0. \tag{6.10}$$

Solving this expression for x_1 then gives the same answer we calculated using our first method: $x_1 = 5$, and substituting that into expression (6.9) gives us $x_2 = 10$. Doing the "best" I can "given my circumstances" in Wal-Mart again means that I will purchase 5 pants and 10 shirts. Intuitively, condition (6.9) tells us that, for the type of tastes we are modeling and the prices that we are facing at Wal-Mart (20 and 10), it will be optimal for me to consume twice as many shirts (x_2) as pants (x_1); i.e., it will be optimal for me to consume on the ray emanating from the origin that contains bundles with twice as many shirts as pants. That is exactly the ray containing point A in Graph 6.1c, where we modeled the same homothetic tastes graphically. In fact, steps (6.9) and (6.10) above are exactly the same as the steps we used to solve for the optimal solutions when all we had to go on was the graphical information in Section 6A.1!

The Lagrange Method of solving constrained optimization problems is the preferred method for economists because it generalizes most easily to cases where we are choosing more than two goods. For instance, suppose that I was at Wal-Mart choosing bundles of pants (x_1), shirts (x_2), and socks (x_3) with the price of socks being equal to 5 (and all other prices the same as before), and suppose one utility function that can represent my tastes is the Cobb–Douglas function $u(x_1,x_2,x_3) = x_1^{1/2} x_2^{1/2} x_3^{1/2}$. Then my constrained optimization problem would be written as

$$\max_{x_1,x_2,x_3} u(x_1,x_2,x_3) = x_1^{1/2} x_2^{1/2} x_3^{1/2} \text{ subject to } 20x_1 + 10x_2 + 5x_3 = 200, \tag{6.11}$$

and the Lagrange function would be written as

$$\mathcal{L}(x_1, x_2, x_3, \lambda) = x_1^{1/2} x_2^{1/2} x_3^{1/2} + \lambda(200 - 20x_1 - 10x_2 - 5x_3). \qquad (6.12)$$

We would then solve a system of 4 equations made up of the partial derivatives of $\mathcal{L}$ with respect to each of the choice variables (x_1, x_2, x_3) and λ.

Solve for the optimal quantities of x_1, x_2, and x_3 in the problem defined in equation 6.11. (*Hint:* The problem will be considerably easier to solve if you take the logarithm of the utility function (which you can do since logarithms are order preserving transformations that do not alter the shapes of indifference curves.))

**Exercise
6B.1**

6B.1.2 Opportunity Cost = Marginal Rate of Substitution: Solving the Problem by Combining Intuition and Math

When we solved my Wal-Mart consumer problem graphically in Graph 6.1, we discovered that once I made my "best" choice "given my circumstances," my *MRS* of shirts for pants (the slope of my indifference curve at the optimal bundle) was exactly equal to the opportunity cost of pants (given by the slope of the budget constraint), at least as long as my tastes are such that I end up buying at least some of each good. The Lagrange Method we have just learned implicitly confirms this.

Specifically, suppose we just write the general constrained optimization problem for a consumer who chooses a bundle (x_1, x_2) given prices (p_1, p_2), an exogenous income I and tastes that can be summarized by a utility function $u(x_1, x_2)$:

$$\max_{x_1, x_2} u(x_1, x_2) \text{ subject to } p_1 x_1 + p_2 x_2 = I. \qquad (6.13)$$

We then write the Lagrange function $\mathcal{L}(x_1, x_2, \lambda)$ as

$$\mathcal{L}(x_1, x_2, \lambda) = u(x_1, x_2) + \lambda(I - p_1 x_1 - p_2 x_2), \qquad (6.14)$$

and we know that, at the optimal bundle, the partial derivatives of $\mathcal{L}$ with respect to each of the three variables is equal to zero. Thus,

$$\frac{\partial \mathcal{L}}{\partial x_1} = \frac{\partial u(x_1, x_2)}{\partial x_1} - \lambda p_1 = 0,$$
$$\qquad (6.15)$$
$$\frac{\partial \mathcal{L}}{\partial x_2} = \frac{\partial u(x_1, x_2)}{\partial x_2} - \lambda p_2 = 0.$$

These first order conditions can then be rewritten as

$$\frac{\partial u(x_1, x_2)}{\partial x_1} = \lambda p_1,$$
$$\qquad (6.16)$$
$$\frac{\partial u(x_1, x_2)}{\partial x_2} = \lambda p_2$$

and the two equations can be divided by one another and multiplied by -1 to give us

$$-\left(\frac{\partial u(x_1, x_2)/\partial x_1}{\partial u(x_1, x_2)/\partial x_2} \right) = -\frac{p_1}{p_2}. \qquad (6.17)$$

Notice that the left-hand side of equation (6.17) is the definition of the *MRS* whereas the right-hand side is the definition of the slope of the budget line. Thus, at the optimal bundle,

$$MRS = -\frac{p_1}{p_2} = \text{opportunity cost of } x_1 \text{ (in terms of } x_2.) \qquad (6.18)$$

Knowing that this condition *has to* hold at the optimum, we can now illustrate a third method for solving the constrained optimization problem defined in (6.2):

Method 3: Using $MRS = -p_1/p_2$ to Solve the Constrained Optimization Problem

Returning to the case of my Wal-Mart problem, we arrived in the previous section at two equivalent methods of solving for my "best" bundle (as evaluated by the utility function $u(x_1,x_2) = x_1^{1/2}x_2^{1/2}$) given my circumstances of facing prices of $20 for pants and $10 for shirts as well as a budget of $200. In each case, the best option for me was to purchase 5 pants and 10 shirts. We could also, however, simply use the fact that we know expression (6.17) must hold at the optimum to get the same solution.

In particular, the left-hand side of equation (6.17) for the utility function $u(x_1,x_2) = x_1^{1/2}x_2^{1/2}$ is simply equal to $-x_2/x_1$ (which we previously derived in Chapter 4 when we derived the *MRS* for such a function). Thus, the full equation (6.17) reduces to

$$-\frac{x_2}{x_1} = -\frac{p_1}{p_2} = -2, \tag{6.19}$$

which can also be written as

$$x_2 = 2x_1. \tag{6.20}$$

The budget constraint must also hold at the optimum, so we can plug (6.20) into the budget constraint $20x_1 + 10x_2 = 200$ to get

$$20x_1 + 10(2x_1) = 200. \tag{6.21}$$

Solving for x_1, we then get $x_1 = 5$, and plugging this back into (6.20) we get $x_2 = 10$; i.e., 5 pants and 10 shirts are once again optimal.

Notice that expressions (6.9) and (6.10) are exactly equivalent to equations (6.20) and (6.21). This is no accident. Method 3 of solving the constrained optimization problem simply substitutes some of our intuition (i.e., $MRS = -p_1/p_2$) to take a shortcut that is implicitly a part of the Lagrange Method (Method 2). Put differently, the two methods are rooted in the same underlying logic, with one using only mathematics and the other using the intuition that $MRS = -p_1/p_2$, an intuition that is based on the graphical logic of Graph 6.1.

This also confirms our intuition from Section 6A.1.2 that when all consumers face the same prices (as they do at Wal-Mart), their tastes are the same *at the margin* after they optimize. This is because the equality $MRS = -p_1/p_2$ holds for *all* consumers who consume both goods, regardless of how different their underlying tastes or money budgets are. Thus, tastes can differ even if tastes *at the margin* are the same after consumers choose their optimal bundles. Our discussion of gains from trade and efficiency in Section 6A.1.3 then follows from this.

6B.2 To Buy or Not to Buy: How to Find Corner Solutions

Although we have assumed throughout our mathematical discussion in this chapter that optimal choices always involve consumption of each of the goods, we had demonstrated in Section 6A.2 that, for certain types of tastes and certain economic circumstances, it is optimal to choose zero consumption of some goods, or, put differently, to choose a *corner solution*. This is important for the three mathematical optimization approaches we have discussed so far because *each of them assumes an interior, not a corner, solution*. We will see in this section what goes wrong with the mathematical approach when there are corner solutions and what assumptions we can make in order to be certain that the mathematical approach in Section 6B.1 does not run into problems due to the possible existence of corner solutions.

6B.2.1 Corner Solutions and First Order Conditions

Consider, for instance, our example of me shopping in Wal-Mart for pants (x_1) and shirts (x_2) when the prices are $20 and $10 and my money budget is $200. Now, however, suppose that my tastes are properly summarized by the quasilinear utility function

$$u(x_1, x_2) = \alpha \ln x_1 + x_2, \tag{6.22}$$

where "ln" stands for the natural logarithm. Notice that tastes that can be represented by this utility function are such that x_2 is not essential and the indifference curves thus cross the x_1 axis. The *MRS* of good x_1 for x_2 for this function is $-\alpha/x_1$. Using our optimization Method 3, this implies that the optimal bundle must be such that $-\alpha/x_1 = -p_1/p_2 = -2$, which implies $x_1 = \alpha/2$. Plugging this into the budget constraint and solving for x_2, we get

$$x_2 = \frac{(200 - 10\alpha)}{10}. \tag{6.23}$$

Set up the Lagrange function for this problem and solve it to see whether you get the same solution.

Exercise 6B.2

Now suppose that $\alpha = 25$ in the utility function (6.22). Then our solution for how much of x_2 is "best" in equation (6.23) would suggest that I should consume a negative quantity of shirts (x_2), negative 5 shirts to be specific! This is of course nonsense, and we can see what went wrong with the mathematics by illustrating the problem graphically.

More specifically, in Graph 6.10a we illustrate the shape of the optimal indifference curve derived from the utility function (6.22) (when $\alpha = 25$) as well as the budget constraint. The optimal bundle, bundle A, contains no shirts and 10 pants. Our mathematical optimization missed this point because we did not explicitly add the constraint that consumption of neither good can be negative and simply assumed an interior solution where $MRS = -p_1/p_2$. At the actual optimum A, however, $MRS \neq -p_1/p_2$.

Our mathematical solution method (without the constraint that consumption cannot be negative) pictured the problem as extending into a quadrant of the graph that we usually do not picture, the quadrant in which consumption of x_2 is negative. This is illustrated in panel (b) of Graph 6.10, where indifference curves represented by the utility function (6.22) are allowed to cross into this new quadrant of the graph, as is the budget constraint. The "solution" found by solving first order conditions is illustrated as the tangency of the higher (magenta) indifference curve with the extended budget line, where $MRS = -p_1/p_2$ as would be the case if the optimum was an interior solution.

The bottom line you should take from this example is that the mathematical methods of optimization we introduced in this chapter *assume that the actual optimum is an interior solution and thus involves a positive level of consumption of all goods.* When this is not the case, the math will give us the nonsensical answer unless we employ a more complicated method that explicitly introduces nonnegativity constraints for all consumption goods.[5] Instead of resorting to more complex methods, however, we can just use common sense to conclude that the true optimum is a corner solution whenever our solution method suggests a negative level of consumption as optimal.

Demonstrate how the Lagrange Method (or one of the related methods we introduced earlier in this chapter) fails even more dramatically in the case of perfect substitutes. Can you explain what the Lagrange Method is doing in this case?

Exercise 6B.3

---

[5]This more complicated method is a generalization of the Lagrange Method known as the "Kuhn Tucker method," but it goes beyond the scope of this chapter. You can find it developed in graduate texts such as that by Mas-Colell, et al. (1992).

Graph 6.10: A Clear Corner Solution (a) with an Economically Nonsensical "Interior Solution" (b)

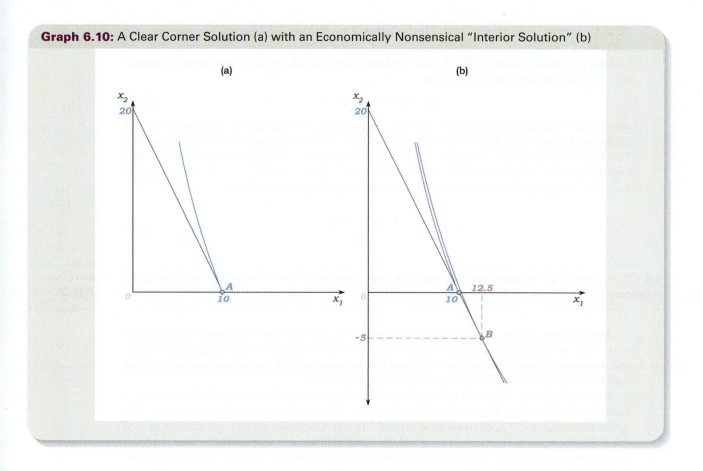

6B.2.2 Ruling Out Corner Solutions

We have already concluded intuitively in Section 6A.2.2 what assumptions on tastes are required in order for us to be sure that the optimum is an *interior* rather than a *corner* solution. Specifically, we argued that all goods that are modeled must be "essential" in the sense we defined in Chapter 5; i.e., indifference curves can converge to each axis but can never cross any axis. This should be even clearer now that we have seen how the mathematics of the Lagrange or related methods fails when indifference curves *do* cross an axis. Since our mathematical solution methods are guaranteed to work only in cases when we assume utility functions that represent tastes for goods that are all essential, the easiest way to model economic circumstances and use only the solution methods we have introduced is to assume only such utility functions. This does, however, rule out the important class of quasilinear tastes unless we simply modify our solution to be zero whenever the Lagrange (or a related) Method indicates a negative optimal consumption level.

The good news is that we will certainly know when we use the Lagrange (or a related) Method and we miss a corner solution because we will get the nonsensical solution of a negative optimal consumption level. *But if we use these methods in models where not all goods are essential and we obtain solutions in which all consumption levels are positive, the methods are still giving us the correct answer.* For instance, if α in equation (6.22) is 10 instead of 25, the answer from equation (6.23) is that I should optimally consume 10 shirts (and five pants with the remainder of my budget). This solution is illustrated graphically in Graph 6.11 where, despite the fact that pants are not essential (and thus my indifference curves cross the shirt axis), my optimal choice is to purchase both shirts and pants under the economic circumstances I am facing at Wal-Mart.

Graph 6.11: The Presence of Nonessential Goods Does not *Have to* Result in a
Corner Solution

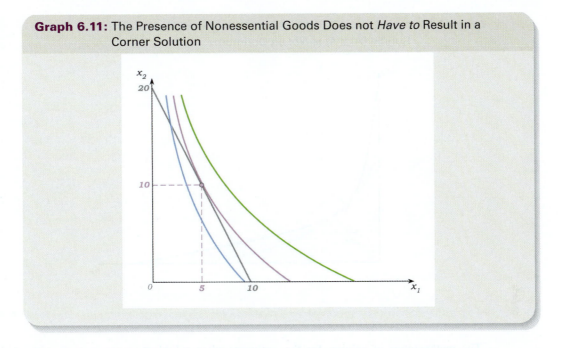

At what value for α will the Lagrange Method correctly indicate an optimal consumption of zero
shirts? Which of the panels of Graph 6.10 illustrates this?

Exercise
6B.4

6B.3 Non-Convexities and First Order Conditions

When all goods in our optimization problem are essential—i.e., when indifference curves do not
cross the axes—we have shown that any optimum of the problem must satisfy the first order conditions of the Lagrange problem. In other words, when all goods are essential, the first order conditions are *necessary conditions* for a point to be optimal. Unless non-convexities are absent from the
optimization problem, however, the system of first order conditions may have multiple "solutions"
(as we demonstrated in Section 6A.3 of the chapter), and not all of these are true optima (as we will
show later). Put differently, in the presence of non-convexities, the first order conditions of the constrained optimization problem are necessary but not *sufficient* for a point to be a true optimum.

For this reason, we can simply solve for the solution of the first order condition equations and
know for sure that the solution will be optimal *only if* we know that the problem has an interior
solution *and* that the model has no non-convexities in choice sets or tastes. In the following section, we briefly explore the intuition of how such non-convexities can in fact result in nonoptimal
solutions to the first order conditions of the Lagrange problem.

In the previous section, we concluded that the first order conditions of the Lagrange problem
may be misleading when goods are not essential. Are these conditions either necessary or sufficient in that case?

Exercise
6B.5

6B.3.1 Non-Convexities in Choice Sets   In Section 6A.3 of the chapter, we motivated the
potential for non-convex choice sets by appealing to one of our coupon examples from an earlier
chapter, an example in which a kink in the budget constraint emerges. Solving optimizations
problems with kinked budgets is a little involved, and so we leave it to be explored in the appendix to this chapter where a problem with an "outward" kink is solved. The same logic can be used
to solve a problem with a non-convex kinked budget, one with an "inward kink."

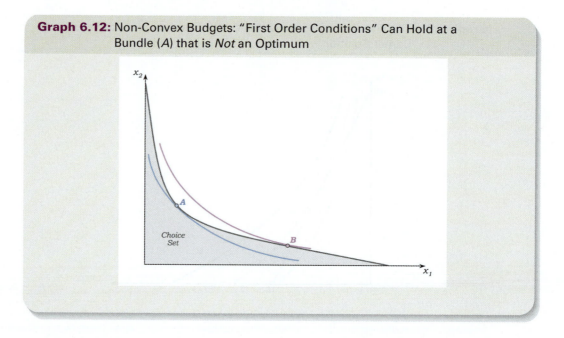

Graph 6.12: Non-Convex Budgets: "First Order Conditions" Can Hold at a Bundle (*A*) that is *Not* an Optimum

The mathematics of solving for the optimum when a budget is non-convex *without the presence of a kink* is somewhat different. We rarely encounter such budget constraints in microeconomic analysis, so we will not spend much time discussing them here. A problem of this type could be formally written as

$$\max_{x_1, x_2} u(x_1, x_2) \text{ subject to } f(x_1, x_2) = 0 \tag{6.24}$$

where the function *f* represents the nonlinear budget constraint. Such a problem could be set up exactly as we set up problems with linear budget constraints using a Lagrange function. The intuition of how just using first order conditions might yield misleading answers is seen relatively clearly with graphical examples. Consider, for instance, the shaded choice set in Graph 6.12 and the indifference curves that are tangent at points *A* and *B*. At both points, the *MRS* is equal to the slope of the budget constraint, and thus both points would be solutions to the system of first derivative equations of the Lagrange function. But it is clear from the picture that only point *B* is truly optimal since it lies on a higher indifference curve than point *A*. Whenever we solve a problem of this kind, we would therefore have to be careful to identify the true optimum from the possible optima that are produced through the Lagrange Method. Put differently, first order conditions are now necessary but not sufficient for identifying an optimal bundle.[6]

6B.3.2 Non-Convexities in Tastes

In Section 6A.3.3, we discussed an example in which non-convex tastes result in multiple optimal solutions to an optimization problem (Graph 6.8). In the presence of such non-convexities in tastes, the Lagrange Method will still identify these optimal bundles, but it will once again also identify nonoptimal bundles. This is again because when non-convexities appear in constrained optimization problems, the first order conditions we use to solve for optimal solutions are necessary but not sufficient.

Graph 6.13 expands Graph 6.8 by adding another indifference curve to the picture, thus giving three points at which the *MRS* is equal to the ratio of prices. We can see immediately in this picture, however, that, while bundles *A* and *B* are optimal, bundle *C* is not (since it lies on

---

[6]You may have learned in your calculus classes about *second order conditions.* These conditions, involving second derivatives, ensure that points identified by first order conditions are indeed optimal. For an exploration of the mathematics of second order conditions, the reader is referred to E. Silberberg and W. Suen, *The Structure of Economics: A Mathematical Analysis, 3d ed.* (Boston: McGraw-Hill, 2001) or other mathematical economics texts.

Graph 6.13: Non-Convex Tastes: "First Order Conditions" Can Hold at a Bundle (*C*) that is *Not* an Optimum

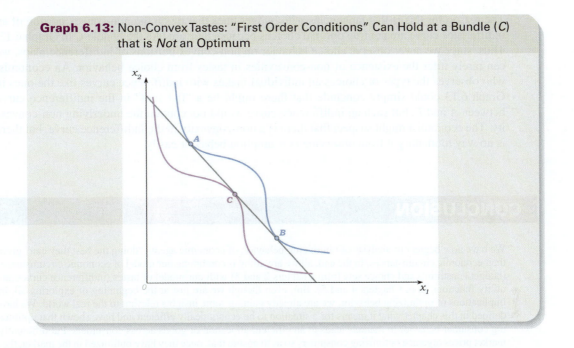

an indifference curve below that which contains bundles *A* and *B*.) The Lagrange Method will offer all three of these points as solutions to the system of first order conditions, which implies that, when we know that the underlying tastes are non-convex, we must check to see which of the points the Lagrange Method suggests are actually optimal. One way to do this is simply to plug the bundles the Lagrange method identifies back into the utility function to see which gives the highest utility. In the example of Graph 6.13, bundles *A* and *B* will give the same utility, but bundle *C* will give less. Thus, we could immediately conclude that only *A* and *B* are optimal.

While this method of plugging in the "candidate" optimal points (identified by the first order conditions) back into the utility function works, there exists a more general method by which to ensure that the Lagrange Method only yields truly optimal points. This method involves checking second derivative conditions, known in mathematics as *second order conditions*. Since we will rarely find a need to model tastes as non-convex, we will not focus on developing this method here. In general, you should simply be aware that we introduce greater complexity to the mathematical approach when we model situations in which non-convexities are important, complexities we do not need to worry about when the optimization problem is convex.

6B.4 Estimating Tastes from Observed Choices

In Section 6A.4, we acknowledged explicitly that tastes in themselves are not observable but also suggested that economists have developed ways of estimating the underlying tastes that are implied by choice behavior that we can observe. Essentially, we saw that the more choices we observe under different economic circumstances, the more information we can gain regarding the marginal rates of substitutions at different bundles that individuals are choosing. One interesting implication of this, however, is that the tastes that choice behavior implies are *always* going to satisfy our convexity assumption *even when the true underlying tastes of a consumer are non-convex*.

To see the intuition behind this, consider the case of a consumer whose indifference map contains the indifference curves drawn in Graph 6.13. We may observe such a consumer choosing bundles *A* and *B*, but we will never observe her choosing a bundle that lies on the non-convex portion of the indifference curve between *A* and *B* (unless the budget sets take on very odd shapes).

The reason for this is that tangencies with budget lines that lie on the non-convex portion of an indifference curve are not true optimal choices because they are like the bundle C in Graph 6.13. Thus, since we never observe choice behavior on non-convex portions of indifference maps, we can rarely infer the existence of non-convexities in tastes from choice behavior. An economist who observes the types of choices an individual makes with indifference curves like the ones in Graph 6.13 could simply conclude that there might be a "flat spot" in the indifference curve between A and B, but such an indifference curve would not contain the underlying non-convexity. The economist might suspect that there is a non-convexity in the indifference curve, but there is no way to identify it from observing consumption behavior easily.

CONCLUSION

We have now begun our analysis of optimizing behavior, of economic agents "doing the best they can" given their economic circumstances. In the end, all we are doing is combining our model of economic circumstances (budget constraints and choice sets from Chapters 2 and 3) with our model of tastes (indifference curves and utility functions from Chapters 4 and 5). But, even though we are just at the beginning of exploring all the implications of optimizing behavior, we are already gaining some insights relevant to the real world. We have defined in this chapter what it means for a situation to be economically efficient and have shown that optimizing consumer behavior in markets leads to an efficient allocation of goods across consumers. Put differently, market prices organize optimizing consumers so as to ensure that, once they have optimized in the market, they all have the same tastes on the margin for the goods that they have purchased. And with the same tastes on the margin, there is no way for consumers to find trades among each other that would make both parties better off; there are no gains from trade that have not already occurred in the market.

Along the way, we have also explored some technical details of optimization. Interior solutions are guaranteed only when tastes are defined such that all goods are "essential," and corner solutions may arise when some goods are not essential. The consumer optimization problem will furthermore have a single unique solution if the optimization problem is in every way convex, with convex choice sets and (strictly) convex tastes (where averages are strictly better than extremes). This "uniqueness" of the solution may disappear, however, when tastes are defined such that averages can be just as good as extremes, or when tastes are non-convex. In the former case, a convex set of bundles may emerge as the solution (tangent to a "flat spot" on an indifference curve), whereas in the latter case a non-convex set of multiple solutions may emerge. Furthermore, when non-convexities in budgets or tastes are part of the consumer choice problem, the Lagrange Method (or derivatives of it) will identify as solutions bundles that are in fact not optimal.

We are not, however, done with our building of conceptual tools in our optimization model. Rather, we now move to Chapter 7 in which we begin to explore how optimizing behavior changes as economic circumstances (income and prices) in the economy change. Chapter 8 will extend this analysis to labor and financial markets, and Chapter 9 will demonstrate how the individual optimizing behavior results in demand curves for goods and supply curves for labor and capital. Finally, we will conclude our analysis of consumer optimization in Chapter 10, where we explore the concept of consumer surplus.

APPENDIX: OPTIMIZATION PROBLEMS WITH KINKED BUDGETS

In Section 6A.3.2, we introduced non-convexities in choice sets by considering budget constraints that have "inward" kinks, budget constraints like that graphed in Graph 6.6. We then discovered that non-convexities in choice sets can also arise without kinks, as in the budget constraint graphed in Graph 6.7c. The mathematics of solving for optimal bundles is now complicated in two ways: First, in budget constraints that have kinks, the optimization problem contains a constraint that cannot be captured in a single equation; and second, in non-convex budgets without kinks, the first order conditions are not sufficient for us to identify optimal bundles.

Graph 6.14: Mathematical Optimization on Kinky Budgets

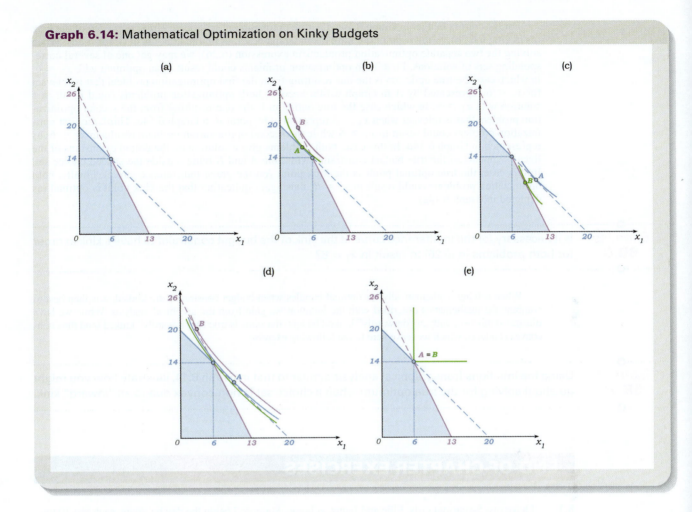

Consider first the shaded kinked (but convex) choice set in Graph 6.14a, which replicates the coupon example graphed initially in Graph 6.5. The budget constraint of this choice set consists of two line segments, with the dotted extension of each line segment indicating the intercepts. The constrained optimization problem can now be written in two parts as

$$\max_{x_1,x_2} u(x_1,x_2) \text{ subject to } x_2 = 20 - x_1 \text{ for } 0 \le x_1 \le 6 \text{ and}$$

$$\max_{x_1,x_2} u(x_1,x_2) \text{ subject to } x_2 = 26 - 2x_1 \text{ for } 6 \le x_1$$

(6.25)

with the true optimum represented by the solution that achieved greater utility.

The easiest way to solve such a problem is to solve two separate optimization problems with the extended line segments in Graph 6.14a representing the budget constraints in those problems; i.e.,

$$\max_{x_1,x_2} u(x_1,x_2) \text{ subject to } x_2 = 20 - x_1 \text{ for } 0 \le x_1 \le 6 \text{ and}$$

$$\max_{x_1,x_2} u(x_1,x_2) \text{ subject to } x_2 = 26 - 2x_1 \text{ for } 6 \le x_1.$$

(6.26)

For the convex budget in Graph 6.14a, the true optimal point will occur either *to the left* of the kink (as in Graph 6.5b), *to the right* of the kink (as in Graph 6.5c), or *on* the kink (as in Graph 6.5d). When solving the two separate optimization problems in expression (6.26), we may get one of several corresponding sets of solutions. First, both optimization problems could result in an optimum with $x_1 < 6$, in which case the true optimum is the one resulting from the first optimization problem that is relevant for $x_1 < 6$ represented by A in Graph 6.14b. Second, both optimization problems could result in a solution with $x_1 > 6$, in which case the true optimum is the one resulting from the second optimization problem that is relevant when $x_1 > 6$ represented by point B in Graph 6.14c. Third, the first optimization problem could result in $x_1 > 6$ while the second optimization problem results in $x_1 < 6$, as represented in Graph 6.14d. In this case, both problems give a solution on the dotted extensions of the linear segments of the true budget constraint, with both A and B lying outside the shaded choice set. In this case, the true optimal point is the kink point (on the green indifference curve). Finally, both optimization problems could result in $x_1 = 6$, thus again indicating that the kink point is optimal (as depicted in Graph 6.14e).

Exercise 6B.6   Is it necessary for the indifference curve at the kink of the budget constraint to have a kink in order for both problems in (6.26) to result in $x_1 = 6$?

When solving mathematically for optimal bundles when budget constraints are kinked, it is then best to combine the mathematics described with the intuition we gain from the graphical analysis. While we have illustrated this here with an "outwardly" kinked budget, the same is true for "inwardly" kinked (and thus non-convex) budgets, which we leave here to the following exercise.

Exercise 6B.7*   Using the intuitions from graphical analysis similar to that in Graph 6.14, illustrate how you might go about solving for the true optimum when a choice set is non-convex due to an "inward" kink.

END-OF-CHAPTER EXERCISES

6.1   I have two 5-year-old girls, Ellie and Jenny, at home. Suppose I begin the day by giving each girl 10 toy cars and 10 princess toys. I then ask them to plot their indifference curves that contain these endowment bundles on a graph with cars on the horizontal and princess toys on the vertical axis.

A.   Ellie's indifference curve appears to have a marginal rate of substitution of −1 at her endowment bundle, whereas Jenny's appears to have a marginal rate of substitution of −2 at the same bundle.

a.   Can you propose a trade that would make both girls better off?

b.   Suppose the girls cannot figure out a trade on their own. So I open a store where they can buy and sell any toy for $1. Illustrate the budget constraint for each girl.

c.   Will either of the girls shop at my store? If so, what will they buy?

d.   Suppose I do not actually have any toys in my store and simply want my store to help the girls make trades between themselves. Suppose I fix the price at which princess toys are bought and sold to $1. Without being specific about what the price of toy cars would have to be, illustrate, using final indifference curves for both girls on the same graph, a situation where the prices in my store result in an efficient allocation of toys.

e.   What values might the price for toy cars take to achieve the efficient trades you described in your answer to (d)?

---

*conceptually challenging
**computationally challenging
†solutions in Study Guide

B. Now suppose that my girls' tastes could be described by the utility function $u(x_1, x_2) = x_1^\alpha x_2^{(1-\alpha)}$, where x_1 represents toy cars, x_2 represents princess toys, and $0 < \alpha < 1$.

    a.   What must be the value of α for Ellie (given the information in part A)? What must the value be for Jenny?

    b.   When I set all toy prices to $1, what exactly will Ellie do? What will Jenny do?

    c.   Given that I am fixing the price of princess toys at $1, do I have to raise or lower the price of car toys in order for me to operate a store in which I don't keep inventory but simply facilitate trades between the girls?

    d.   Suppose I raise the price of car toys to $1.40, and assume that it is possible to sell fractions of toys. Have I found a set of prices that allow me to keep no inventory?

6.2   Suppose Coke and Pepsi are perfect substitutes for me, and right and left shoes are perfect complements.

A. Suppose my income allocated to Coke/Pepsi consumption is $100 per month, and my income allocated to right/left shoe consumption is similarly $100 per month.

    a.   Suppose Coke currently costs $0.50 per can and Pepsi costs $0.75 per can. Then the price of Coke goes up to $1 per can. Illustrate my original and my new optimal bundle with Coke on the horizontal and Pepsi on the vertical axis.

    b.   Suppose right and left shoes are sold separately. If right and left shoes are originally both priced at $1, illustrate (on a graph with right shoes on the horizontal and left shoes on the vertical) my original and my new optimal bundle when the price of left shoes increases to $2.

    c.   *True or False*: Perfect complements represent a unique special case of homothetic tastes in the following sense: Whether income goes up or whether the price of one of the goods falls, the optimal bundle will always lie on a the same ray emerging from the origin.

B. Continue with the assumptions about tastes from part A.

    a.   Write down two utility functions: one representing my tastes over Coke and Pepsi, another representing my tastes over right and left shoes.

    b.   Using the appropriate equation derived in B(a), label the two indifference curves you drew in A(a).

    c.   Using the appropriate equation derived in B(a), label the two indifference curves you drew in A(b).

    d.   Consider two different equations representing indifference curves for perfect complements: $u^1(x_1, x_2) = \min\{x_1, x_2\}$ and $u^2(x_1, x_2) = \min\{x_1, 2x_2\}$. By inspecting two of the indifference curves for each of these utility functions, determine the equation for the ray along which all optimal bundles will lie for individuals whose tastes these equations can represent.

    e.   Explain why the Lagrange Method does not seem to work for calculating the optimal consumption bundle when the goods are perfect substitutes.

    f.   Explain why the Lagrange Method cannot be applied to calculate the optimal bundle when the goods are perfect complements.

6.3   *Pizza and Beer*: Sometimes we can infer something about tastes from observing only two choices under two different economic circumstances.

A. Suppose we consume only beer and pizza (sold at prices p_1 and p_2 respectively) with an exogenously set income I.

    a.   With the number of beers on the horizontal axis and the number of pizzas on the vertical, illustrate a budget constraint (clearly labeling intercepts and the slope) and some initial optimal (interior) bundle A.

    b.   When your income goes up, I notice that you consume more beer and the same amount of pizza. Can you tell whether my tastes might be homothetic? Can you tell whether they might be quasilinear in either pizza or beer?

    c.   How would your answers change if I had observed you decreasing your beer consumption when income goes up?

    d.   How would your answers change if both beer and pizza consumption increased by the same proportion as income?

B. Suppose your tastes over beer (x_1) and pizza (x_2) can be summarize by the utility function $u(x_1, x_2) = x_1^2 x_2$ and that $p_1 = 2, p_2 = 10$ and weekly income $I = 180$.

    a.   Calculate your optimal bundle A of weekly beer and pizza consumption by simply using the fact that, at any interior solution, $MRS = -p_1/p_2$.

    b.   What numerical label does this utility function assign to the indifference curve that contains your optimal bundle?

    c.   Set up the more general optimization problem where, instead of using the prices and income given earlier, you simply use p_1, p_2 and I. Then, derive your optimal consumption of x_1 and x_2 as a function of p_1, p_2 and I.

    d.   Plug the values $p_1 = 2, p_2 = 10$, and $I = 180$ into your answer to B(c) and verify that you get the same result you originally calculated in B(a).

    e.   Using your answer to part B(c), verify that your tastes are homothetic.

    f.   Which of the scenarios in A(b) through (d) could be generated by the utility function $u(x_1, x_2) = x_1^2 x_2$?

6.4† *Inferring Tastes for Roses (and Love) from Behavior*: I express my undying love for my wife through weekly purchases of roses that cost $5 each.

A. Suppose you have known me for a long time and you have seen my economic circumstances change with time. For instance, you knew me in graduate school when I managed to have $125 per week in disposable income that I could choose to allocate between purchases of roses and "other consumption" denominated in dollars. Every week, I brought 25 roses home to my wife.

    a.   Illustrate my budget as a graduate student, with roses on the horizontal and "dollars of other consumption" on the vertical axis. Indicate my optimal bundle on that budget as A. Can you conclude whether either good is not "essential"?

    b.   When I became an assistant professor, my disposable income rose to $500 per week, and the roses I bought for my wife continued to sell for $5 each. You observed that I still bought 25 roses each week. Illustrate my new budget constraint and optimal bundle B on your graph. From this information, can you conclude whether my tastes might be quasilinear in roses? Might they not be quasilinear?

    c.   Suppose for the rest of the problem that my tastes in fact are quasilinear in roses. One day while I was an assistant professor, the price of roses suddenly dropped to $2.50. Can you predict whether I then purchased more or fewer roses?

    d.   Suppose I had not gotten tenure, and the best I could do was rely on a weekly allowance of $50 from my wife. Suppose further that the price of roses goes back up to $5. How many roses will I buy for my wife per week?

    e.   *True or False*: Consumption of quasilinear goods always stays the same as income changes.

    f.   *True or False*: Over the range of prices and incomes where corner solutions are not involved, a decrease in price will result in increased consumption of quasilinear goods but an increase in income will not.

B. Suppose my tastes for roses (x_1) and other goods (x_2) can be represented by utility function $u(x_1, x_2) = \beta x_1^\alpha + x_2$.

    a.   Letting the price of roses be denoted by p_1, the price of other goods by 1, and my weekly income by I, determine my optimal weekly consumption of roses and other goods as a function of p_1 and I.

    b.   Suppose $\beta = 50$ and $\alpha = 0.5$. How many roses do I purchase when $I = 125$ and $p_1 = 5$? What if my income rises to 500?

    c.   Comparing your answers with your graph from part A, could the actions observed in part A(b) be rationalized by tastes represented by the utility function $u(x_1, x_2)$? Give an example of another utility function that can rationalize the behavior described in part A(b).

      d.   What happens when the price of roses falls to \$2.50? Is this consistent with your answer to part A(c)?

      e.   What happens when my income falls to \$50 and the price of roses increases back to \$5? Is this consistent with your answer to part A(d)? Can you illustrate in a graph how the math is giving an answer that is incorrect?

6.5   Assume you have an income of \$100 to spend on goods x_1 and x_2.

    A. Suppose that you have homothetic tastes that happen to have the special property that indifference curves on one side of the 45-degree line are mirror images of indifference curves on the other side of the 45-degree line.

      a.   Illustrate your optimal consumption bundle graphically when $p_1 = 1 = p_2$.

      b.   Now suppose the price of the first 75 units of x_1 you buy is 1/3 while the price for any additional units beyond that is 3. The price of x_2 remains at 1 throughout. Illustrate your new budget and optimal bundle.

      c.   Suppose instead that the price for the first 25 units of x_1 is 3 but then falls to 1/3 for all units beyond 25 (with the price of x_2 still at 1). Illustrate this budget constraint and indicate what would be optimal.

      d.   If the homothetic tastes did not have the symmetry property, which of your answers might not change?

    B.* Suppose that your tastes can be summarized by the Cobb–Douglas utility function $u(x_1, x_2) = x_1^{1/2} x_2^{1/2}$.

      a.   Does this utility function represent tastes that have the symmetry property described in part A?

      b.   Calculate the optimal consumption bundle when $p_1 = 1 = p_2$.

      c.   Derive the two equations that make up the budget constraint you drew in part A(b) and use the method described in the appendix to this chapter to calculate the optimal bundle under that budget constraint.

      d.   Repeat for the budget constraint you drew in A(c).

      e.   Repeat (b) through (d) assuming instead $u(x_1, x_2) = x_1^{3/4} x_2^{1/4}$ and illustrate your answers in graphs.

6.6*   *Coffee, Coke, and Pepsi*: Suppose there are three different goods: cans of Coke (x_1), cups of coffee (x_2), and cans of Pepsi (x_3).

    A. Suppose each of these goods costs the same price, p, and you have an exogenous income, I.

      a.   Illustrate your budget constraint in three dimensions and carefully label all intercepts and slopes.

      b.   Suppose each of the three drinks has the same caffeine content, and suppose caffeine is the only characteristic of a drink you care about. What do "indifference curves" look like?

      c.   What bundles on your budget constraint would be optimal?

      d.   Suppose that Coke and Pepsi become more expensive. How does your answer change? Are you now better or worse off than you were before the price change?

    B. Assume again that the three goods cost the same price, p.

      a.   Write down the equation of the budget constraint you drew in part A(a).

      b.   Write down a utility function that represents the tastes described in A(b).

      c.   Can you extend our notion of homotheticity to tastes over three goods? Are the tastes represented by the utility function you derived in (b) homothetic?

6.7*   *Coffee, Milk, and Sugar*: Suppose there are three different goods: cups of coffee (x_1), ounces of milk (x_2), and packets of sugar (x_3).

    A. Suppose each of these goods costs \$0.25 and you have an exogenous income of \$15.

      a.   Illustrate your budget constraint in three dimensions and carefully label all intercepts.

b. Suppose that the only way you get enjoyment from a cup of coffee is to have at least 1 ounce of milk and 1 packet of sugar in the coffee, the only way you get enjoyment from an ounce of milk is to have at least 1 cup of coffee and 1 packet of sugar, and the only way you get enjoyment from a packet of sugar is to have at least 1 cup of coffee and 1 ounce of milk. What is the optimal consumption bundle on your budget constraint?

c. What does your optimal indifference curve look like?

d. If your income falls to $10, what will be your optimal consumption bundle?

e. If instead of a drop in income the price of coffee goes to $0.50, how does your optimal bundle change?

f. Suppose your tastes are less extreme and you are willing to substitute some coffee for milk, some milk for sugar, and some sugar for coffee. Suppose that the optimal consumption bundle you identified in (b) is still optimal under these less extreme tastes. Can you picture what the optimal indifference curve might look like in your picture of the budget constraint?

g. If tastes are still homothetic (but of the less extreme variety discussed in (f)), would your answers to (d) or (e) change?

B. Continue with the assumption of an income of $15 and prices for coffee, milk, and sugar of $0.25 each.

a. Write down the budget constraint.

b. Write down a utility function that represents the tastes described in A(b).

c. Suppose that instead your tastes are less extreme and can be represented by the utility function $u(x_1, x_2, x_3) = x_1^\alpha x_2^\beta x_3$. Calculate your optimal consumption of x_1, x_2, and x_3 when your economic circumstances are described by the prices p_1, p_2, and p_3 and income is given by I.

d. What values must α and β take in order for the optimum you identified in A(b) to remain the optimum under these less extreme tastes?

e. Suppose α and β are as you concluded in part B(d). How does your optimal consumption bundle under these less extreme tastes change if income falls to $10 or if the price of coffee increases to $0.50? Compare your answers with your answer for the more extreme tastes in A(d) and (e).

f. *True or False*: Just as the usual shapes of indifference curves represent two-dimensional "slices" of a three-dimensional utility function, three-dimensional "indifference bowls" emerge when there are three goods, and these "bowls" represent slices of a four-dimensional utility function.

6.8 *Grits and Cereal*: In end-of-chapter exercise 4.1, I described my dislike for grits and my fondness for Coco Puffs Cereal.

A. In part A of exercise 4.1, you were asked to assume that my tastes satisfy convexity and continuity and then to illustrate indifference curves on a graph with grits on the horizontal axis and cereal on the vertical.

a. Now add a budget constraint (with some positive prices for grits and cereal and some exogenous income, I, for me). Illustrate my optimal choice given my tastes.

b. Does your answer change if my tastes are non-convex (as in part (b) of exercise 4.1A)?

c. In part (c) of exercise 4.1A, you were asked to imagine that I hate cereal as well and that my tastes are again convex. Illustrate my optimal choice under this assumption.

d. Does your answer change when my tastes are not convex (as in part (d) of exercise 4.1A)?

B. In part B of exercise 4.1, you derived a utility function that was consistent with my dislike for grits.

a. Can you explain why the Lagrange Method will not work if you used it to try to solve the optimization problem using this utility function?

b. What would the Lagrange Method offer as the optimal solution if you used a utility function that captured a dislike for both grits and cereal when tastes are non-convex? Illustrate your answer using $u(x_1, x_2) = -x_1 x_2$ and graph your insights.

c.   What would the Lagrange Method offer as a solution if a utility function that captures a dislike for both grits and cereal represented convex tastes? Illustrate your answer using the function $u(x_1, x_2) = -x_1^2 - x_2^2$ and show what happens graphically.

6.9†   **Everyday Application:** *Price Fluctuations in the Housing Market*: Suppose you have $400,000 to spend on a house and "other goods" (denominated in dollars).

A.   The price of 1 square foot of housing is $100, and you choose to purchase your optimally sized house at 2,000 square feet. Assume throughout that you spend money on housing solely for its consumption value (and not as part of your investment strategy).

a.   On a graph with "square feet of housing" on the horizontal axis and "other goods" on the vertical, illustrate your budget constraint and your optimal bundle A.

b.   After you bought the house, the price of housing falls to $50 per square foot. Given that you can sell your house from bundle A if you want to, are you better or worse off?

c.   Assuming you can easily buy and sell houses, will you now buy a different house? If so, is your new house smaller or larger than your initial house?

d.   Does your answer to (c) differ depending on whether you assume tastes are quasilinear in housing or homothetic?

e.   How does your answer to (c) change if the price of housing went up to $200 per square foot rather than down to $50.

f.   What form would tastes have to take in order for you not to sell your 2,000-square-foot house when the price per square foot goes up or down?

g.   *True or False*: So long as housing and other consumption is at least somewhat substitutable, any change in the price per square foot of housing makes homeowners better off (assuming it is easy to buy and sell houses.)

h.   *True or False*: Renters are always better off when the rental price of housing goes down and worse off when it goes up.

B.   Suppose your tastes for "square feet of housing" (x_1) and "other goods" (x_2) can be represented by the utility function $u(x_1, x_2) = x_1 x_2$.

a.   Calculate your optimal housing consumption as a function of the price of housing (p_1) and your exogenous income I (assuming of course that p_2 is by definition equal to 1).

b.   Using your answer, verify that you will purchase a 2,000-square-foot house when your income is $400,000 and the price per square foot is $100.

c.   Now suppose the price of housing falls to $50 per square foot and you choose to sell your 2,000-square-foot house. How big a house would you now buy?

d.   Calculate your utility (as measured by your utility function) at your initial 2,000-square-foot house and your new utility after you bought your new house. Did the price decline make you better off?

e.   How would your answers to B(c) and B(d) change if, instead of falling, the price of housing had increased to $200 per square foot?

6.10   **Everyday Application:** *Different Interest Rates for Borrowing and Lending*: You first analyzed intertemporal budget constraints with different interest rates for borrowing and saving (or lending) in end-of-chapter exercise 3.8.

A.   Suppose that you have an income of $100,000 now and you expect to have a $300,000 income 10 years from now, and suppose that the interest rate for borrowing from the bank is twice as high as the interest rate the bank offers for savings.

a.   Begin by drawing your budget constraint with "consumption now" and "consumption in 10 years" on the horizontal and vertical axes. (Assume for purposes of this problem that your consumption in the intervening years is covered and not part of the analysis.)

b.   Can you explain why, for a wide class of tastes, it is rational for someone in this position not to save or borrow?

c. Now suppose that the interest rate for borrowing was half the interest rate for saving. Draw this new budget constraint.

d. Illustrate a case where it might be rational for a consumer to flip a coin to determine whether to borrow a lot or to save a lot.

B. Suppose that your incomes are as described in part A and that the *annual* interest rate for borrowing is 20% and the *annual* interest rate for saving is 10%. Also, suppose that your tastes over current consumption, c_1, and consumption 10 years from now, c_2, can be captured by the utility function $u(c_1, c_2) = c_1^\alpha c_2^{(1-\alpha)}$.

a. Assuming that interest compounds annually, what are the slopes of the different segments of the budget constraint that you drew in A(a)? What are the intercepts?

b. For what ranges of α is it rational to neither borrow nor save?

6.11* **Business Application:** *Quantity Discounts and Optimal Choices*: In end-of-chapter exercise 2.9, you illustrated my department's budget constraint between "pages copied in units of 100" and "dollars spent on other goods" given the quantity discounts our local copy service gives the department. Assume the same budget constraint as the one described in 2.9A.

A. In this exercise, assume that my department's tastes do not change with time (or with who happens to be department chair). When we ask whether someone is "respecting the department's tastes," we mean whether that person is using the department's tastes to make optimal decisions for the department given the circumstances the department faces. Assume throughout that my department's tastes are convex.

a. *True or False*: If copies and other expenditures are very substitutable for my department, then you should observe either very little or a great deal of photocopying by our department at the local copy shop.

b. Suppose that I was department chair last year and had approximately 5,000 copies per month made. This year, I am on leave and an interim chair has taken my place. He has chosen to make 150,000 copies per month. Given that our department's tastes are not changing over time, can you say that either I or the current interim chair is not respecting the department's tastes?

c. Now the interim chair has decided to go on vacation for a month, and an interim interim chair has been named for that month. He has decided to purchase 75,000 copies per month. If I was respecting the department's tastes, is this interim interim chair necessarily violating them?

d. If both the initial interim chair and I were respecting the department's tastes, is the new interim interim chair necessarily violating them?

B. Consider the decisions made by the three chairs as previously described.

a. If the second interim chair (i.e., the interim interim chair) and I both respected the department's tastes, can you approximate the elasticity of substitution of the department's tastes?

b. If the first and second interim chairs both respected the department's tastes, can you approximate the elasticity of substitution for the department?

c. Could the underlying tastes under which all three chairs respect the department's tastes be represented by a CES utility function?

6.12*† **Business Application:** *Retail Industry Lobbying for Daylight Savings Time*: In 2005, the U.S. Congress passed a bill to extend daylight savings time earlier into the spring and later into the fall (beginning in 2007). The change was made as part of an Energy Bill, with some claiming that daylight savings time reduces energy use by extending sunlight to later in the day (which means fewer hours of artificial light). Among the biggest advocates for daylight savings time, however, was the retail and restaurant industry that believes consumers will spend more time shopping and eating in malls for reasons explored here.

A. Consider a consumer who returns home from work at 6 p.m. and goes to sleep at 10 p.m. In the month of March, the sun sets by 7 p.m. in the absence of daylight savings time, but with daylight savings time, the sun does not set until 8 p.m. When the consumer comes home from work, she can either spend time (1) at home eating food from her refrigerator while e-mailing friends and surfing/shopping on the Internet or (2) at the local mall meeting friends for a bite to eat and strolling through stores to shop. Suppose this consumer gets utility from (1) and (2) (as defined here) but she also cares about x_3, which is defined as the fraction of daylight hours after work.

a. On a graph with "weekly hours at the mall" on the horizontal axis and "weekly hours at home" on the vertical, illustrate this consumer's typical weekly after-work time constraint (with a total of 20 hours per week available, 4 hours on each of the 5 workdays). (For purposes of this problem, assume the consumer gets as much enjoyment from driving to the mall as she does being at the mall.)

b. Consider first the scenario of no daylight savings time in March. This implies only 1 hour of daylight in the 4 hours after work and before going to sleep; i.e., the fraction x_3 of daylight hours after work is 1/4. Pick a bundle A on the budget constraint from (a) as the optimum for this consumer given this fraction of after-work of daylight hours.

c. Now suppose daylight savings time is moved into March, thus raising the number of after-work daylight hours to 2 per day. Suppose this changes the *MRS* at every bundle. If the retail and restaurant industry is right, which way does it change the *MRS*?

d. Illustrate how if the retail and restaurant industry is right, this results in more shopping and eating at malls every week.

e. Explain the following statement: "While it appears in our two-dimensional indifference maps that tastes have changed as a result of a change in daylight savings time, tastes really haven't changed at all because we are simply graphing two-dimensional slices of the same three-dimensional indifference surfaces."

f. Businesses can lobby Congress to change the *circumstances* under which we make decisions, but Congress has no power to change our *tastes*. Explain how the change in daylight savings time illustrates this in light of your answer to (e).

g. Some have argued that consumers must be irrational for shopping more just because daylight savings is introduced. Do you agree?

h. If we consider not just energy required to produce light but also energy required to power cars that take people to shopping malls, is it still clear that the change in daylight savings time is necessarily energy saving?

B. Suppose a consumer's tastes can be represented by the utility function $u(x_1, x_2, x_3) = 12x_3 \ln x_1 + x_2$, where x_1 represents weekly hours spent at the mall, x_2 represents weekly after-work hours spent at home (not sleeping), and x_3 represents the fraction of after-work (before-sleep) time that has daylight.

a. Calculate the *MRS* of x_2 for x_1 for this utility function and check to see whether it has the property that retail and restaurant owners hypothesize.

b. Which of the three things the consumer cares about—x_1, x_2, and x_3—are choice variables for the consumer?

c. Given the overall number of weekly after-work hours our consumer has (i.e., 20), calculate the number of hours per week this consumer will spend in malls and restaurants as a function of x_3.

d. How much time per week will she spend in malls and restaurants in the absence of daily savings time? How does this change when daylight savings time is introduced?

6.13 **Policy Application:** *Food Stamps versus Food Subsidies*: In exercise 2.13, you considered the food stamp programs in the United States. Under this program, poor households receive a certain quantity of "food stamps," stamps that contain a dollar value that is accepted like cash for food purchases at grocery stores.

POLICY APPLICATION

A. Consider a household with monthly income of $1,500 and suppose that this household qualifies for food stamps in the amount of $500.

a. Illustrate this household's budget, both with and without the food stamp program, with "dollars spent on food" (on the horizontal axis) and "dollars spent on other goods" on the vertical. What has to be true for the household to be just as well off under this food stamp program as it would be if the government simply gave $500 in cash to the household (instead of food stamps)?

b. Consider the following alternate policy: Instead of food stamps, the government tells this household that it will reimburse 50% of the household's food bills. On a separate graph, illustrate the household's budget (in the absence of food stamps) with and without this alternate program.

c. Choose an optimal bundle A on the alternate program budget line and determine how much the government is paying to this household (as a vertical distance in your graph). Call this amount S.

d. Now suppose the government decided to abolish the program and instead gives the same amount S in food stamps. How does this change the household's budget?

e. Will this household be happy about the change from the first alternate program to the food stamp program?

f. If some politicians want to increase food consumption by the poor and others just want to make the poor happier, will they differ on what policy is best?

g. *True or False*: The less substitutable food is for other goods, the greater the difference in food consumption between equally funded cash and food subsidy programs.

h. Consider a third possible alternative: giving cash instead of food stamps. *True or False*: As the food stamp program becomes more generous, the household will at some point prefer a pure cash transfer over an equally costly food stamp program.

B.**Suppose this household's tastes for spending on food (x_1) and spending on other goods (x_2) can be characterized by the utility function $u(x_1, x_2) = \alpha \ln x_1 + \ln x_2$.

a. Calculate the level of food and other good purchases as a function of I and the price of food p_1 (leaving the price of dollars on other goods as just 1).

b. For the household described in part A, what is the range of α that makes the $500 food stamp program equivalent to a cash gift of $500?

c. Suppose for the remainder of the problem that $\alpha = 0.5$. How much food will this household buy under the alternate policy described in A(b)?

d. How much does this alternate policy cost the government for this household? Call this amount S.

e. How much food will the household buy if the government gives S as a cash payment and abolishes the alternate food subsidy program?

f. Determine which policy—the price subsidy that leads to an amount S being given to the household or the equally costly cash payment in part (e)—the household prefers.

g. Now suppose the government considered subsidizing food more heavily. Calculate the utility that the household will receive from three *equally funded* policies: a 75% food price subsidy (i.e., a subsidy where the government pays 75% of food bills), a food stamp program, and a cash gift program.

6.14   Policy Application: *Gasoline Taxes and Tax Rebates*: Given the concerns about environmental damage from car pollution, many have proposed increasing the tax on gasoline. We will consider the social benefits of such legislation later on in the text when we introduce externalities. For now, however, we can look at the impact on a single consumer.

A. Suppose a consumer has annual income of $50,000 and suppose the price of a gallon of gasoline is currently $2.50.

a. Illustrate the consumer's budget constraint with "gallons of gasoline" per year on the horizontal axis and "dollars spent on other goods" on the vertical. Then illustrate how this changes if the government imposes a tax on gasoline that raises the price per gallon to $5.00.

b. Pick some bundle A on the after tax budget constraint and assume that bundle is the optimal bundle for our consumer. Illustrate in your graph how much in gasoline taxes this consumer is paying, and call this amount T.

c. One of the concerns about using gasoline taxes to combat pollution is that it will impose hardship on consumers (and, perhaps more importantly, voters). Some have therefore suggested that the government simply rebate all revenues from a gasoline tax to taxpayers. Suppose that our consumer receives a rebate of exactly T. Illustrate how this alters the budget of our consumer.

d. Suppose our consumer's tastes are quasilinear in gasoline. How much gasoline will he consume after getting the rebate?

 e. Can you tell whether the tax/rebate policy is successful at getting our consumer to consume less gasoline than he would were there neither the tax nor the rebate?

 f. *True or False*: Since the government is giving back in the form of a rebate exactly the same amount as it collected in gasoline taxes from our consumer, the consumer is made no better or worse off from the tax/rebate policy.

B. Suppose our consumer's tastes can be captured by the quasilinear utility function $u(x_1, x_2) = 200x_1^{0.5} + x_2$, where x_1 denotes gallons of gasoline and x_2 denotes dollars of other goods.

 a. Calculate how much gasoline this consumer consumes as a function of the price of gasoline (p_1) and income I. Since other consumption is denominated in dollars, you can simply set its price (p_2) to 1.

 b. After the tax raises the price of gasoline to $5, how much gasoline does our consumer purchase this year?

 c. How much of a tax does he pay?

 d. Can you verify that his gasoline consumption will not change when the government sends him a rebate check equal to the tax payments he has made?

 e. How does annual gasoline consumption for our consumer differ under the tax/rebate program from what it would be in the absence of either a tax or rebate?

 f. Illustrate that our consumer would prefer no tax/rebate program but, if there is to be a tax on gasoline, he would prefer to have the rebate rather than no rebate.

6.15*† **Policy Application**: *AFDC and Work Disincentives*: Consider the AFDC program for an individual as described in end-of-chapter exercise 3.18.

A. Consider again an individual who can work up to 8 hours per day at a wage of $5 per hour.

 a. Replicate the budget constraint you were asked to illustrate in 3.18A.

 b. *True or False*: If this person's tastes are homothetic, then he/she will work no more than 1 hour per day.

 c. For purposes of defining a 45-degree line for this part of the question, assume that you have drawn hours on the horizontal axis 10 times as large as dollars on the vertical. This implies that the 45-degree line contains bundles like (1, 10), (2, 20), etc. How much would this person work if his tastes are homothetic and symmetric across this 45-degree line? (By "symmetric across the 45-degree line," I mean that the portions of the indifference curves to one side of the 45-degree line are mirror images to the portions of the indifference curves to the other side of the 45-degree line.)

 d. Suppose you knew that the individual's indifference curves were linear but you did not know the *MRS*. Which bundles on the budget constraint could in principle be optimal and for what ranges of the *MRS*?

 e. Suppose you knew that, for a particular person facing this budget constraint, there are two optimal solutions. How much in AFDC payments does this person collect at each of these optimal bundles (assuming the person's tastes satisfy our usual assumptions)?

B. Suppose this worker's tastes can be summarized by the Cobb–Douglas utility function $u(c, \ell) = c^{\alpha} \ell^{1-\alpha}$, where ℓ stands for leisure and c for consumption.

 a. Forget for a moment the AFDC program and suppose that the budget constraint for our worker could simply be written as $c = I - 5\ell$. Calculate the optimal amount of consumption and leisure as a function of α and I.

 b. On your graph of the AFDC budget constraint for this worker, there are two line segments with slope -5: one for 0–2 hours of leisure and another for 7–8 hours of leisure. Each of these lies on a line defined by $c = I - 5\ell$ except that I is different for the two equations that contain these line segments. What are the relevant Is to identify the right equations on which these budget constraint segments lie?

 c. Suppose $\alpha = 0.25$. If this worker were to optimize using the two budget constraints you have identified with the two different Is, how much leisure would he choose under each constraint?

Can you illustrate what you find in a graph and tell from this where on the real AFDC budget constraint this worker will optimize?

d. As α increases, what happens to the *MRS* at each bundle?

e. Repeat B(c) for $\alpha = 0.3846$ and for $\alpha = 0.4615$. What can you now say about this worker's choice for any $0 < \alpha < 0.3846$? What can you say about this worker's leisure choice if $0.3846 < \alpha < 0.4615$?

f. Repeat B(c) for $\alpha = 0.9214$ and calculate the utility associated with the resulting choice. Compare this to the utility of consuming at the kink point $(7, 30)$ and illustrate what you have found on a graph. What can you conclude about this worker's choice if $0.4615 < \alpha < 0.9214$?

g. How much leisure will the worker take if $0.9214 < \alpha < 1$?

h. Describe in words what this tells you about what it would take for a worker to overcome the work disincentives under the AFDC program.

6.16   **Policy Application**: *Cost of Living Adjustments of Social Security Benefits*: Social Security payments to the elderly are adjusted every year in the following way: The government has in the past determined some average bundle of goods consumed by an average elderly person. Each year, the government then takes a look at changes in the prices of all the goods in that bundle and raises Social Security payments by the percentage required to allow the hypothetical elderly person to continue consuming that same bundle. This is referred to as a cost of living adjustment or COLA.

A. Consider the impact on an average senior's budget constraint as cost of living adjustments are put in place. Analyze this in a two-good model where the goods are simply x_1 and x_2.

a. Begin by drawing such a budget constraint in a graph where you indicate the "average bundle" the government has identified as A and assume that initially this average bundle is indeed the one our average senior would have chosen from his budget.

b. Suppose the prices of both goods went up by exactly the same proportion. After the government implements the COLA, has anything changed for the average senior? Is behavior likely to change?

c. Now suppose that the price of x_1 went up but the price of x_2 stayed the same. Illustrate how the government will change the average senior's budget constraint when it calculates and passes along the COLA. Will the senior alter his behavior? Is he better off, worse off, or unaffected?

d. How would your answers change if the price of x_2 increased and the price of x_1 stayed the same?

e. Suppose the government's goal in paying COLAs to senior citizens is to insure that seniors become neither better nor worse off from price changes. Is the current policy successful if all price changes come in the form of general "inflation"; i.e., if all prices always change together by the same proportion? What if inflation hits some categories of goods more than others?

f. If you could "choose" your tastes under this system, would you choose tastes for which goods are highly substitutable, or would you choose tastes for which goods are highly complementary?

B.**Suppose the average senior has tastes that can be captured by the utility function
$$u(x_1, x_2) = (x_1^{-\rho} + x_2^{-\rho})^{-1/\rho}.$$

a. Suppose the average senior has income from all sources equal to $40,000 per year, and suppose that prices are given by p_1 and p_2. How much will our senior consume of x_1 and x_2? (*Hint*: It may be easiest simply to use what you know about the *MRS* of CES utility functions to solve this problem.)

b. If $p_1 = p_2 = 1$ initially, how much of each good will the senior consume? Does your answer depend on the elasticity of substitution?

c. Now suppose that the price of x_1 increases to $p_1 = 1.25$. How much does the government have to increase the senior's Social Security payment in order for the senior still to be able to purchase the same bundle as he purchased prior to the price change?

d. Assuming the government adjusts the Social Security payment to allow the senior to continue to purchase the same bundle as before the price increase, how much x_1 and x_2 will the senior actually end up buying if $\rho = 0$?

e. How does your answer change if $\rho = -0.5$ and if $\rho = -0.95$? What happens as ρ approaches -1?

f. How does your answer change when $\rho = 1$ and when $\rho = 10$? What happens as ρ approaches infinity?

g. Can you come to a conclusion about the relationship between how much a senior benefits from the way the government calculates COLAs and the elasticity of substitution that the senior's tastes exhibit? Can you explain intuitively how this makes sense, particularly in light of your answer to A(f)?

h. Finally, show how COLAs affect consumption decisions by seniors under general inflation that raises all prices simultaneously and in proportion to one another as, for instance, when both p_1 and p_2 increase from 1.00 to 1.25 simultaneously.

Income and Substitution Effects in Consumer Goods Markets

We have just demonstrated in Chapter 6 how we can use our model of choice sets and tastes to illustrate optimal decision making by individuals such as consumers or workers.[1] We now turn to the question of how such optimal decisions change when economic circumstances change. Since economic circumstances in this model are fully captured by the choice set, we could put this differently by saying that we will now ask how optimal choices change when income, endowments, or prices change.

As we proceed, it is important for us to keep in mind the difference between *tastes* and *behavior*. Behavior, or what we have been calling choice, emerges when tastes confront circumstances as individuals try to do the "best" they can given those circumstances. If I buy less wine because the price of wine has increased, my *behavior* has changed but my *tastes* have not. Wine still tastes the same as it did before, it just costs more. In terms of the tools we have developed, my indifference map remains exactly as it was. I simply move to a different indifference curve as my circumstances (i.e., the price of wine) change.

In the process of thinking about how *behavior* changes with economic circumstances, we will identify two conceptually distinct causes, known as *income* and *substitution* effects.[2] At first it will seem like the distinction between these effects is abstract and quite unrelated to real-world issues we care about. As you will see later, however, this could not be further from the truth. Deep questions related to the efficiency of tax policy, the effectiveness of Social Security and health policy, and the desirability of different types of antipoverty programs are fundamentally rooted in questions related to income and substitution effects. While we are still in the stage of building tools for economic analysis, I hope you will be patient and bear with me as we develop an understanding of these tools.

Still, it may be useful to at least give an initial example to motivate the effects we will develop in this chapter, an example that will already be familiar to you if you have done end-of-chapter exercise 6.14. As you know, there is increasing concern about carbon-based emissions from automobiles, and an increased desire by policy makers to find ways of reducing such emissions. Many economists have long recommended the simple policy of taxing gasoline heavily in order to encourage consumers to find ways of conserving gasoline (by driving less and buying more fuel-efficient cars). The obvious concern with such a policy is that it imposes substantial hardship on households that rely heavily on their cars, particularly poorer households that would be hit pretty hard by such a tax. Some

---

[1]Chapters 2 and 4 through 6 are required reading for this chapter. Chapter 3 is not necessary.
[2]This distinction was fully introduced into neoclassical economics by Sir John Hicks in his influential book, *Value and Capital*, originally published in 1939. We had previously mentioned him in part B of Chapter 5 as the economist who first derived a way to measure substitutability through "elasticities of substitution." Hicks was awarded the Nobel Prize in Economics in 1972 (together with Ken Arrow).

economists have therefore proposed simply sending all tax revenues from such a gasoline tax back to taxpayers in the form of a tax refund. This has led many editorial writers to conclude that economists must be nuts; after all, if we send the money back to the consumers, wouldn't they then just buy the same amount of gasoline as before since (at least on average) they would still be able to afford it? Economists may be nuts, but our analysis will tell us that they are also almost certainly right, and editorial writers are almost certainly wrong, when it comes to the prediction of how this policy proposal would change behavior. And the explanation lies fully in an understanding of substitution effects that economists understand and most noneconomists don't think about. We'll return to this in the conclusion to the chapter.

7A Graphical Exposition of Income and Substitution Effects

There are two primary ways in which choice sets (and thus our economic circumstances) can change: First, a change in our income or wealth might shift our budget constraints without changing their slopes, and thus without changing the opportunity costs of the various goods we consume. Second, individual prices in the economy—whether in the form of prices of goods, wages, or interest rates—may change and thus alter the slopes of our budget constraints and the opportunity costs we face. These two types of changes in choice sets result in different types of effects on behavior, and we will discuss them separately in what follows. First, we will look only at what happens to economic choices when income or wealth changes without a change in opportunity costs (Section 7A.1). Next, we will investigate how decisions are impacted when only opportunity costs change without a change in real wealth (Section 7A.2). Finally, we will turn to an analysis of what happens when changes in income and opportunity costs occur at the same time, which, as it turns out, is typically the case when relative prices in the economy change.

7A.1 The Impact of Changing Income on Behavior

What happens to our consumption when our income increases because of a pay raise at work or when our wealth endowment increases because of an unexpected inheritance or when our leisure endowment rises due to the invention of some time-saving technology? Would we consume more shirts, pants, Coke, housing, and jewelry? Would we consume more of some goods and fewer of others, work more or less, save more or less? Would our consumption of all goods go up by the same proportion as our income or wealth?

The answer depends entirely on the nature of our tastes, and the indifference map that represents our tastes. For most of us, it is likely that our consumption of some goods will go up by a lot while our consumption of other goods will increase by less, stay the same, or even decline. *The impact of changes in our income or wealth on our consumption decisions (in the absence of changes in opportunity costs) is known as the income or wealth effect.*

The economics "lingo" is not entirely settled on whether to call this kind of an effect a "wealth" or an "income" effect, and we will use the two terms in the following way: Whenever we are analyzing a model where the size of the choice set is determined by exogenously given income, as in Chapter 2 and for the remainder of this chapter, we will refer to the impact of a change in income as an *income effect*. In models where the size of the choice set is determined by the value of an endowment, as in Chapter 3 and in the next chapter, we will refer to the impact of changes in that endowment as a *wealth effect*. What should be understood throughout, however, is that by both income and wealth effect we mean *an impact on consumer decisions that arises from a parallel shift in the budget constraint*, a shift that does *not* include a change in opportunity costs as captured by a change in the slope of the budget line.

7A.1.1 Normal and Inferior Goods   During my first few years in graduate school, my wife and I made relatively little money. Often, our budget would permit few extravagances, with dinners heavily tilted toward relatively cheap foods such as potatoes and pasta. When my wife's business began to take off, our income increased considerably, and she observed one night over a nice steak dinner that we seemed to be eating a lot less pasta these days. Our consumption of pasta, it turned out, declined as our income went up, whereas our consumption of steak and other goods increased. How could this happen within the context of the general model that we have developed in the last few chapters?

Consider a simple model in which we put monthly consumption of boxes of pasta on the horizontal axis and the monthly consumption of pounds of steak on the vertical. My wife and I began with a relatively low income and experienced an increase in income as my wife's business succeeded. This is illustrated by the outward shift in our budget constraint (from blue to magenta) in each of the panels of Graph 7.1. As we then add the indifference curves that contain our optimal choices under the two budget constraints, we get less pasta consumption at the higher income only if the tangency on the budget line occurs to the left of our tangency on the lower budget line. This is illustrated in panel (a) of Graph 7.1. Panel (b), on the other hand, illustrates the relationship between the two indifference curves if pasta consumption had remained unchanged with the increase in our income, while panel (c) illustrates the case had our pasta consumption increased with our income. This change in consumer behavior as exogenous income changes is called the *income effect*.

Since my wife observed that our consumption of pasta *declined* with an increase in our income, our preferences must look more like those in panel (a), where increased income has a negative impact on pasta consumption. We will then say that *the income effect is negative whenever an increase in exogenous income (without a change in opportunity cost) results in less consumption*, and goods whose consumption is characterized by negative income effects are called *inferior goods*. In contrast, we will say that *the income effect is positive whenever an increase in exogenous income (without a change in opportunity cost) results in more consumption*, and goods whose consumption is characterized by positive income effects are called *normal goods*. Panel

Graph 7.1: Income Effects for Inferior and Normal Goods

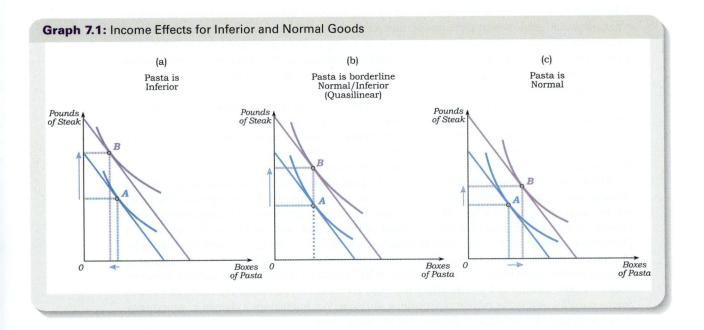

(c) of Graph 7.1 illustrates an example of what our preferences could look like if pasta were in fact a normal good for us.

Finally, panel (b) of Graph 7.1 illustrates an indifference map that gives rise to *no* income effect on our pasta consumption. Notice the following defining characteristic of this indifference map: The marginal rate of substitution is constant along the vertical line that connects points *A* and *B*. In Chapter 5, we called tastes that are represented by indifference curves whose marginal rates of substitution are constant in this way *quasilinear (in pasta)*. The sequence of panels in Graph 7.1 then illustrates how *quasilinear tastes are the only kinds of tastes that do not give rise to income effects for some good, and as such they represent the borderline case between normal and inferior goods.*

It is worthwhile noting that *whenever we observe a negative income effect on our consumption of one good, there must be a positive income effect on our consumption of a different good.* After all, the increased income must be going somewhere, whether it is increased consumption of some good today or increased savings for consumption in the future. In Graph 7.1a, for instance, we observe a negative income effect on our consumption of pasta on the horizontal axis. At the same time, on the vertical axis we observe a positive income effect on our consumption of steak.

Is it also the case that whenever there is a positive income effect on our consumption of one good, there must be a negative income effect on our consumption of a different good?	**Exercise 7A.1**
Can a good be an inferior good at all income levels? (*Hint*: Consider the bundle (0,0).)	**Exercise 7A.2**

7A.1.2 Luxuries and Necessities

As we have just seen, quasilinear tastes represent one special case that divides two types of goods: normal goods whose consumption increases with income and inferior goods whose consumption decreases with income. The defining difference between these two types of goods is how consumption changes in an *absolute* sense as our income changes. A different way of dividing goods into two sets is to ask how our *relative* consumption of different goods changes as income changes. Put differently, instead of asking whether total consumption of a particular good increases or decreases with an increase in income, we could ask whether the fraction of our income spent on a particular good increases or decreases as our income goes up; i.e., whether our consumption increases *relative to our income*.

Consider, for instance, our consumption of housing. In each panel of Graph 7.2, we model choices between square footage of housing and "dollars of other goods." As in the previous graph, we consider how choices will change as income doubles, with bundle *A* representing the optimal choice at the lower income and bundle *B* representing the optimal choice at the higher income. Suppose that in each panel, the individual spends 25% of her income on housing at bundle *A*. If housing remains a constant fraction of consumption as income increases, then the optimal consumption bundle *B* when income doubles would simply involve twice as much housing and twice as much "other good" consumption. This bundle would then lie on a ray emanating from the origin and passing through point *A*, as pictured in Graph 7.2b. If, on the other hand, the fraction of income allocated to housing declines as income rises, *B* would lie to the left of this ray (as in Graph 7.2a), and if the fraction of income allocated to housing increases as income rises, *B* would lie to the right of the ray (as in Graph 7.2c). It turns out that on average, people spend approximately 25% of their income on housing regardless of how much they make, which implies that tastes for housing typically look most like those in Graph 7.2b.

Graph 7.2: Income Effects for Necessities and Luxuries

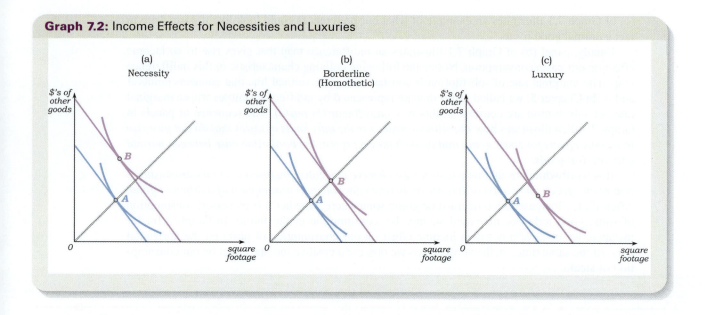

Economists have come to refer to goods whose consumption as a fraction of income declines with income as *necessities* while referring to goods whose consumption as a fraction of income increases with income as *luxuries*. The borderline tastes that divide these two classes of goods are tastes of the kind represented in Graph 7.2b, tastes that we defined as *homothetic* in Chapter 5. (Recall that we said tastes were homothetic if the marginal rates of substitution are constant along any ray emanating from the origin.) Thus, just as quasilinear tastes represent the borderline tastes between normal and inferior goods, *homothetic tastes represent the borderline tastes between necessary and luxury goods.*

Exercise 7A.3 Are all inferior goods necessities? Are all necessities inferior goods? (*Hint:* The answer to the first is yes; the answer to the second is no.) Explain.

Exercise 7A.4 At a particular consumption bundle, can both goods (in a two-good model) be luxuries? Can they both be necessities?

7A.2 The Impact of Changing Opportunity Costs on Behavior

Suppose my brother and I go off on a week-long vacation to the Cayman Islands during different weeks. He and I are identical in every way, same income, same tastes.[3] Since there is no public transportation on the Cayman Islands, you only have two choices of what to do once you step off the airplane: you can either rent a car for the week, or you can take a taxi to your hotel and then rely on taxis for any additional transportation needs. After we returned home from our respective vacations, we compared notes and discovered that, although we had stayed at exactly the same hotel, I had rented a car whereas my brother had used only taxis.

---

[3]This assumption is for illustration only. Both my brother and I are horrified at the idea of anyone thinking we are identical, and he asked for this clarification in this text.

Which one of us do you think went on more trips away from our hotel? The difference between the number of car rides he and I took is what we will call a substitution effect.

7A.2.1 Renting a Car versus Taking Taxis on Vacation

The answer jumps out straight away if we model the relevant aspects of the choice problem that my brother and I were facing when we arrived at the airport in the Cayman Islands. Basically, we were choosing the best way to travel by car during our vacation. We can model this choice by putting "miles travelled" on the horizontal axis and "dollars of other consumption" on the vertical. Depending on whether I rent a car or rely on taxis, I will face different budget constraints. If I rent a car, I end up paying a weekly rental fee that is the same regardless of how many miles I actually drive. I then have to pay only for the gas I use as I drive to different parts of the island. If I rely on taxis, on the other hand, I pay only for the miles I travel, but of course I pay a per mile cost that is higher than just the cost of gas. Translated into budget constraints with "miles driven" on the horizontal axis and "dollars of other consumption" on the vertical, this implies that my budget will have a higher intercept on the vertical axis if I choose to use taxis because I do not have to pay the fixed rental fee. At the same time, the slope of the budget constraint would be steeper if I chose to use taxis because each mile I travel has a higher opportunity cost.

The choice my brother and I faced when we arrived in the Cayman Islands is thus a choice between two different budget constraints, one with a higher intercept and steeper slope than the other, as depicted in Graph 7.3a. (If this looks familiar, it is because you may have done this in end-of-chapter exercise 2.6.) Since my brother and I are identical in every way and faced exactly the same choice, you can reasonably conclude that we were indifferent between these two modes of transportation (and thus between the two budget constraints). After all, if one choice was clearly better than the other, we should have ended up making the same choice.

Thus, although we made different choices, we must have ended up on the same indifference curve. (This statement—that we ended up on the same indifference curve—makes sense only because we know that my brother and I have the same tastes and thus the same map of indifference curves, and we have the same exogenous income.) Graph 7.3b therefore fits a single indifference curve tangent to the two budget constraints, illustrating that our optimal

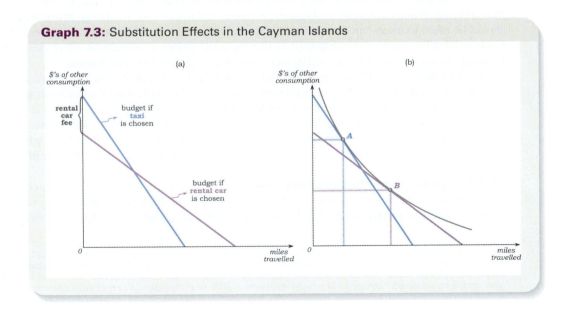

Graph 7.3: Substitution Effects in the Cayman Islands

choices on the two different budget constraints result in the same level of satisfaction. My brother's optimal choice *A* then indicates fewer miles travelled than my optimal choice *B*.

The intuition behind the model's prediction is straightforward. Once I sped off to my hotel in my rented car, I had to pay the rental fee no matter what else I did for the week. So, the opportunity cost or price of driving a mile (once I decided to rent a car) was only the cost of gasoline. My brother, on the other hand, faced a much higher opportunity cost since he had to pay taxi prices for every mile he travelled. Even though our choices made us equally well off, it is clear that my lower opportunity cost of driving led me to travel more miles and consume less of other goods than my brother.

Exercise 7A.5

If you knew only that my brother and I had the same income (but not necessarily the same tastes), could you tell which one of us drove more miles: the one that rented or the one that took taxis?

Economists will often say that the flat weekly rental fee becomes a *sunk cost* as soon as I have chosen to rent a car. Once I have rented the car, there is no way for me to get back the fixed rental fee that I have agreed to pay, and it stays the same no matter what I do once I leave the rental car lot. So, the rental fee is never an opportunity cost of anything I do once I have rented the car. Such sunk costs, once they have been incurred, therefore do not affect economic decisions because our economic decisions are shaped by the trade-offs inherent in opportunity costs. We will return to the concept of sunk costs more extensively when we discuss producer behavior, and we will note in Chapter 29 that some psychologists quarrel with the economist's conclusion that such costs should have no impact on behavior.

7A.2.2 Substitution Effects   The difference in my brother's and my behavior in our Cayman Island example is what is known as a *substitution effect*. Substitution effects arise whenever opportunity costs or prices change. In our example, for instance, we analyzed the difference in consumer behavior when the price of driving changes, but the general intuition behind the substitution effect will be important for many more general applications throughout this book.

We will define a substitution effect more precisely as follows: *The substitution effect of a price change is the change in behavior that results purely from the change in opportunity costs and not from a change in real income.* By *real income*, we mean *real welfare*, so "no change in real income" should be taken to mean "no change in satisfaction" or "no change in indifference curves." The Cayman Island example was constructed so that we could isolate a substitution effect clearly by focusing our attention on a single indifference curve or a single level of "real income."[4]

The fact that bundle *B must* lie to the right of bundle *A* is a simple matter of geometry: A steeper budget line fit tangent to an indifference curve *must* lie to the left of a shallower budget line that is tangent to the same indifference curve. *The direction of a substitution effect is therefore always toward more consumption of the good that has become relatively cheaper and away from the good that has become relatively more expensive.* Note that this differs from what we concluded about income effects whose direction depends on whether a good is normal or inferior.

7A.2.3 How Large Are Substitution Effects?   While the *direction* of substitution effects is unambiguous, the *size* of the effect is dependent entirely on the kinds of underlying tastes a consumer has. The picture in Graph 7.3b suggests a pretty clear and sizable difference between

---

[4]This definition of "real income" differs from another definition you may run into during your studies of economics (one that we also used in an earlier chapter on budget constraints). Macroeconomists who study inflation, or microeconomists who want to study behavior that is influenced by inflation, often define "real income" as "inflation adjusted income." For instance, when comparing someone's income in 1990 to his or her income in 2000, an economist might adjust the 2000 income by the amount of inflation that occurred between 1990 and 2000, thus reporting 2000 "real income" expressed in 1990 dollars.

Graph 7.4: The Degree of Substitutability and the Size of Substitution Effects

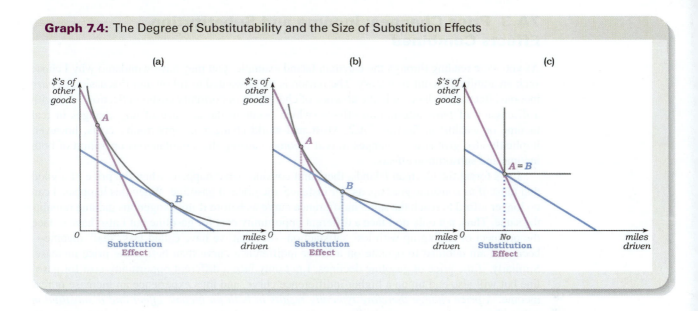

the number of miles I drove and the number of miles my brother drove given that we faced different opportunity costs for driving while having the same level of satisfaction or welfare. But I could have equally well drawn the indifference curve with more curvature, and thus with less substitutability between miles driven and other consumption. *The less substitutability is built into a consumer's tastes, the smaller will be substitution effects arising from changes in opportunity costs.*

For instance, consider the indifference curve in Graph 7.4b, an indifference curve with more curvature than that in Graph 7.4a and thus less built-in substitutability along the portion on which my brother and I are making our choices. Notice that, although the substitution effect points in the same direction as before, the effect is considerably smaller. Graph 7.4c illustrates the role played by the level of substitutability between goods even more clearly by focusing on the extreme case of perfect complements. Such tastes give rise to indifference curves that permit no substitutability between goods, leading to bundles *A* and *B* overlapping and a consequent disappearance of the substitution effect.

True or False: If you observed my brother and me consuming the same number of miles driven during our vacations, then our tastes must be those of perfect complements between miles driven and other consumption.

**Exercise
7A.6**

7A.2.4 "Hicks" versus "Slutsky" Substitution We have now defined the substitution effect as the change in consumption that is due to a change in opportunity cost without a change in "'real income"; i.e., without a change in the indifference curve. This is sometimes called *Hicksian* substitution. A slightly different concept of a substitution effect arises when we ask how a change in opportunity costs alters a consumer's behavior assuming that her ability to purchase the original bundle remains intact. This is called *Slutsky* substitution. It operates very similarly to Hicksian substitution, and we will therefore leave it to end-of-chapter exercise 7.11 to explore this further. We are also using the idea in exercise 7.11 (and its previous companion exercise 6.16) and 7.6 (as well as its previous companion exercise 6.9).

7A.3 Price Changes: Income and Substitution Effects Combined

As you were reading through the Cayman Island example, you may have wondered why I chose such an admittedly contrived story. The reason is that I wanted to follow our discussion of *pure* income effects (which occur in the absence of changes in opportunity costs) in Section 7A.1 with a discussion of *pure* substitution effects (which occur in the absence of any changes in real income or wealth) in Section 7A.2. Most real-world changes in opportunity costs, however, implicitly also give rise to changes in real income, causing the simultaneous operation of both income and substitution effects.

Let's forget the Cayman Islands, then, and consider what happens when the price of a good that most of us consume goes up, as, for instance, the price of gasoline. When this happens, I can no longer afford to reach the same indifference curve as before if my exogenous income remains the same. Thus, not only do I face a different opportunity cost for gasoline but I also have to face the prospect of ending up with less satisfaction—or what we have called less "real" income—because I am doomed to operate on a lower indifference curve than before the price increase. Similarly, if the price of gasoline declines, I not only face a different opportunity cost for gasoline but will also end up on a higher indifference curve, and thus experience an increase in real income. *A price change therefore typically results in both an income effect and a substitution effect.* These can be conceptually disentangled even though they occur simultaneously, and it will become quite important for many policy applications to know the relative sizes of these conceptually different effects. You will see how this is important more clearly in later chapters. For now, we will simply focus on conceptually disentangling the two effects of price changes.

7A.3.1 An Increase in the Price of Gasoline

To model the impact of an increase in the price of gasoline on my behavior, we can once again put "miles driven" on the horizontal axis and "dollars of other consumption" on the vertical. An increase in the price of gasoline then causes an inward rotation of the budget line around the vertical intercept, as illustrated in Graph 7.5a. My optimal bundle prior to the price increase is illustrated by the tangency of the indifference curve at point *A*.

Graph 7.5: Income and Substitution Effects when Gasoline Is a Normal Good

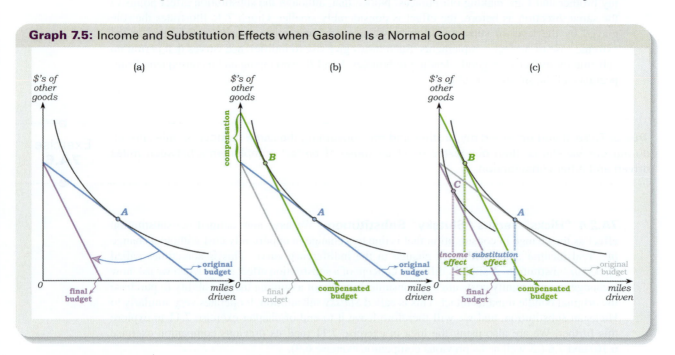

We can now begin our disentangling of income and substitution effects by asking how my consumption bundle would have changed had I only experienced the change in opportunity costs without a change in my real income. Put differently, we can ask how my consumption decision would change if I faced a new budget that incorporated the steeper slope implied by the price change but was large enough to permit me to be as satisfied as I was before the price change, large enough to keep me on my original indifference curve. This budget is illustrated as the green budget tangent to the indifference curve containing bundle A in Graph 7.5b and is called the *compensated budget*. *A compensated budget for a price change is the budget that incorporates the new price but includes sufficient monetary compensation to make the consumer as well off as she was before the price change.* If income is exogenous (as it is in our example), the compensated budget requires positive compensation when prices increase and negative compensation when prices decrease.

Graph 7.5b then looks very much like Graph 7.4b that illustrated a pure substitution effect for our Cayman Islands example. This is because we have imagined that I was provided sufficient compensation at the higher gasoline price to keep my real income constant in order to focus only on the change in my consumption that is due to the change in my opportunity costs along a single indifference curve. As in the Cayman example, we can then quickly see that consumption of gasoline is less at point B than at point A. When real income is unchanged, the substitution effect tells us that I will consume less gasoline because gasoline has become more expensive relative to other goods.

Rarely, however, will someone come to me and offer me compensation for a price change in real life. Rather, I will have to settle for a decrease in my real income when prices go up. In Graph 7.5c, we thus start with the compensated budget and ask how my actual consumption decision will differ from the hypothetical outcome B. Before answering this question, notice that the compensated budget and the final budget in Graph 7.5c have the same slope and thus differ only by the hypothetical compensation we have assumed when plotting the compensated budget. Thus when going from the compensated (green) to the final (magenta) budget, we are simply analyzing the impact of a change in my exogenous money income, or what we called a pure income effect in Section 7A.1.

Whether my optimal consumption of gasoline on my final budget line is larger or smaller than at point B then depends entirely on whether gasoline is a normal or an inferior good for me. We defined a normal good as one whose consumption moves in the same direction as changes in exogenous income, while we defined an inferior good as one whose consumption moved in the opposite direction of changes in exogenous income. Thus, the optimal bundle on the final budget might lie to the left of point B if gasoline is a normal good, and it might lie to the right of B if gasoline is an inferior good. In the latter case, it could lie in between A and B if the income effect is smaller than the substitution effect, or it might lie to the right of point A if the income effect is larger than the substitution effect. In Graph 7.5c, we illustrate the case where gasoline is a normal good, and the optimal final bundle C lies to the left of B. In this case, both income and substitution effects suggest that I will purchase less gasoline as the price of gasoline increases.

7A.3.2 Regular Inferior and Giffen Goods   Notice that we can conclude unambiguously that my consumption of gasoline will decline if its price increases whenever gasoline is a normal good (as is the case if bundle C in Graph 7.5c is my optimal final choice). This is because both the substitution and the income effect suggest declining consumption. If, on the other hand, gasoline is an inferior good for me, then my gasoline consumption could increase or decrease depending on whether my final consumption bundle lies between A and B as in Graph 7.6a or whether it lies to the right of A as in Graph 7.6b. We can therefore divide inferior goods into two subcategories: those whose consumption decreases with an increase in price and those whose consumption increases with an increase in price (when exogenous income remains constant). We will call the former *regular inferior goods* and the latter *Giffen goods*.

When initially introduced to the possibility that a consumer might purchase more of a good when its price goes up, students often misinterpret what economists mean by this. A common example that students will think of is that of certain goods that carry a high level of prestige

Graph 7.6: Income and Substitution Effects When Gasoline Is an Inferior Good

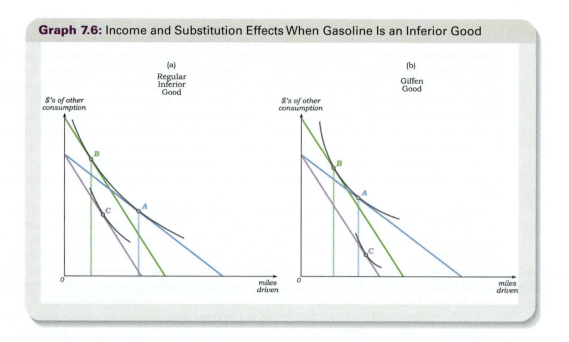

precisely because everyone knows they are expensive. For instance, it may be true that some consumers who care about the prestige value of a BMW will be more likely to purchase BMWs as the price (and thus the prestige value) increases. This is *not*, however, the kind of behavior we have in mind when we think of Giffen goods. The person who attaches a prestige value to the price of a BMW is really buying two different goods when he or she buys this car: the car itself *and* the prestige value of the car. As the price of the BMW goes up, the car remains the same but the quantity of prestige value rises. So, a consumer who is more likely to buy BMWs as the price increases is not buying more of a single good but is rather buying a different mix of goods when the price of the BMW goes up. When the same consumer's income falls (and the price of BMWs remains the same), the consumer would almost certainly be less likely to buy BMWs, which indicates that the car itself (with the prestige value held constant) is a normal good.[5]

Real Giffen goods are quite different, and we rarely observe them in the real world. Economists have struggled for literally centuries to find examples; this is how rare they are. At the end of the 19th century, Alfred Marshall (1842–1924), one of the great economists of that century, included a hypothetical example in his economics textbook and attributed it to Robert Giffen, a contemporary of his.[6] Over the years, a variety of attempts to find credible historical examples that are not hypothetical have been discredited, although a recent paper demonstrates that rice in poor areas of China may indeed be a Giffen good there.[7]

---

[5]While an increase in the price still causes an increase in the consumption of the physical good we observe, such goods are examples of what is known as *Veblen Goods* after Thorstein Veblen (1857–1929) who hypothesized that preferences for certain goods intensify as price increases, which can cause what appear to be increases in consumption as price goes up. You can think through this more carefully in end-of-chapter exercise 7.9, where you are asked to explain an increase in the consumption of Gucci accessories when the price increases. In Chapter 21, we revisit Veblen goods in end-of-chapter exercise 21.5 in the context of network externalities.

[6]To quote from his text: "As Mr. Giffen has pointed out, a rise in the price of bread makes so large a drain on the resources of the poorer labouring families . . . that they are forced to curtail their consumption of meat and the more expensive farinaceous foods: and bread being still the cheapest food which they can get and will take, they consume more, and not less of it." A. Marshall, *Principles of Economics* (MacMillan: London, 1895). While Robert Giffen (1837–1910) was a highly regarded economist and statistician, it appears no one has located a reference to the kinds of goods that are named after him in any of his own writings, only in Marshall's.

[7]R. Jensen and N. Miller, (2007). "Giffen Behavior: Theory and Evidence," National Bureau of Economic Research working paper 13243 (Cambridge, MA, 2007).

A friend of mine in graduate school once told me a story that is the closest example I have ever personally heard of a real Giffen good. He came from a relatively poor family in the Midwest where winters get bitterly cold and where they heated their home with a form of gasoline. Every winter, they would spend a month over Christmas with relatives in Florida. One year during the 1973 energy crisis, the price of gasoline went up so much that they decided they could not afford to go on their annual vacation in Florida. So, they stayed in the Midwest and had to heat their home for one additional month. While they tried to conserve on gasoline all winter, they ended up using more than usual because of that extra month. Thus, their consumption of gasoline went up precisely because the price of gasoline went up and the income effect outweighed the substitution effect. This example, as well as the recent research on rice in China, both illustrate that, in order to find the "Giffen behavior" of increasing consumption with an increase in price, it must be that the good in question represents a large portion of a person's income to begin with, with a change in price therefore causing a large income effect. It furthermore must be the case that there are no very good substitutes for the good in order for the substitution effect to remain small. Given the variety of substitutable goods in the modern world and the historically high standard of living, it therefore seems very unlikely that we will find much "Giffen behavior" in the part of the world that has risen above subsistence income levels.

Can you re-tell the Heating Gasoline-in-Midwest story in terms of income and substitution effects in a graph with "yearly gallons of gasoline consumption" on the horizontal axis and "yearly time on vacation in Florida" on the vertical?

Exercise 7A.7*

7A.3.3 Income and Substitution Effects for Pants and Shirts

Now let's return to our example from Chapter 2: My wife sends me to Wal-Mart with a fixed budget to buy pants and shirts. Since I know how much Wal-Mart charges for pants and shirts, I enter the store already having solved for my optimal bundle. Now suppose that one of the greeters at Wal-Mart hands me a 50% off coupon for pants, effectively decreasing the price of pants I face. We already know that this will lead to an outward rotation of my budget as shown in Graph 7.7a. Armed with the new information presented in this chapter, however, we can now predict how my consumption of pants and shirts will change depending on whether pants and shirts are normal, regular inferior, or Giffen goods.

Graph 7.7: Inferring the Type of Good from Observed Choices

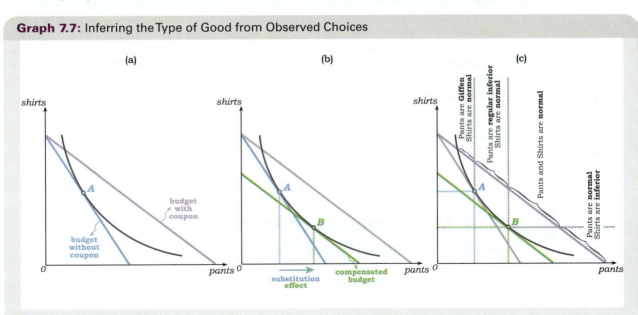

First, we isolate once again the substitution effect by drawing my (green) compensated budget under the new price in Graph 7.7b. Notice that the "compensation" in this case is negative: In order to keep my "real income" (i.e., my indifference curve) constant and concentrate only on the impact of the change in opportunity costs, you would have to take away some of the money my wife had given me. As always, the substitution effect, the shift from A to B, indicates that I will switch away from the good that has become relatively more expensive (shirts) and toward the good that has become relatively cheaper (pants).

In Graph 7.7c, we then focus on what happens when we switch from the hypothetical optimum on the compensated (green) budget to our new optimum on the final (magenta) budget. Since this involves no change in opportunity costs, we are left with a pure income effect as we jump from the optimal point B on the compensated budget line to the final optimum on the final budget constraint. Suppose we know that both shirts and pants are normal goods for me. This would tell me that, when I experience an increase in income from the compensated to the final budget, I will choose to consume more pants and shirts than I did at point B. If shirts are inferior and pants are normal, I will consume more pants and fewer shirts than at B; and if pants are inferior and shirts are normal, I will consume fewer pants and more shirts. Given that I am restricted in this example to consuming only shirts and pants, it cannot be the case that both goods are inferior because this would imply that I consume fewer pants and fewer shirts on my final budget than I did at point B, which would put me at a bundle to the southwest of B. Since "more is better," I would not be at an optimum given that I can move to a higher indifference curve from there.

Now suppose that you know not only that pants are an inferior good but also that pants are a Giffen good. The definition of a Giffen good implies that I will consume less of the good as its price decreases when exogenous income remains unchanged. Thus, I would end up consuming not just fewer pants than at point B but also fewer than at point A. Notice that this is the only scenario under which we would not even have to first find the substitution effect; if we know something is a Giffen good and we know its price has decreased, we immediately know that consumption will decrease as well. In each of the other scenarios, however, we needed to find the compensated optimum B before being able to apply the definition of normal or inferior goods.

Finally, suppose you know that shirts rather than pants are a Giffen good. Remember that in order to observe a Giffen good, we must observe a price change for that good (with exogenous income constant) since Giffen goods are goods whose consumption moves in the same direction as *price* (when income is exogenous and unchanged). In this example, we did not observe a price change for shirts, which means that we cannot usefully apply the definition of a Giffen good to predict how consumption will change. Rather, we can simply note that, since all Giffen goods are also inferior goods, I will consume fewer shirts as my income increases from the compensated budget to the final budget. Thus, knowing that shirts are Giffen tells us nothing more in this example than knowing that shirts are inferior goods.

Exercise 7A.8   Replicate Graph 7.7 for an increase in the price of pants (rather than a decrease).

The Mathematics of Income and Substitution Effects

In this section, we will now begin to explore income and substitution effects mathematically. I say that we will "begin" doing this because our exploration of these effects will become deeper as we move through the next few chapters. For now, we will try to illustrate how to relate the intuitions developed in part A of this chapter most directly to some specific mathematics, and in the process we will build the tools for a more general treatment later on. As you read through this section, you will undoubtedly get lost a bit unless you sit with pencil and paper and follow the calculations we undertake closely on your own. As you do this, you will begin to get a feel for how we can use the various mathematical concepts introduced thus far to identify precisely the points *A*, *B*, and *C* that appear in our graphs of this chapter. It might help you even more to then reread the chapter and construct simple spreadsheets in a program like Microsoft Excel, which is precisely how I kept track of the different numerical answers that are presented in the text as I wrote this section. Setting up such spreadsheets will give you a good feel for how the mathematics of consumer choice works for specific examples.

7B.1 The Impact of Changing Income on Behavior

In Chapter 6, we solved the consumer's constrained optimization problem for specific economic circumstances; i.e., for specific prices and incomes. In Section 7A.1, we became interested in how consumer behavior changes when exogenous income changes, and we discovered that the answer depends on the nature of the underlying map of indifference curves. We will now translate some of this analysis from Section 7A.1 into the mathematical optimization language we developed in Chapter 6.

7B.1.1 Inferior and Normal Goods
Consider, for instance, the example of pasta and steak we introduced in Section 7A.1.1, and suppose my wife and I had discovered that our consumption of pasta remained unchanged as our income increased (as depicted in Graph 7.1b). Suppose that the price of a box of pasta is $2 and the price of a pound of steak is $10, and suppose we let boxes of pasta be denoted by x_1 and pounds of steak by x_2. We know from our discussion in Section 7A.1.1 that pasta consumption can remain constant as income increases only if the underlying tastes are quasilinear in pasta; i.e., when utility functions can be written as $u(x_1,x_2) = v(x_1) + x_2$. For an income level I and for tastes that can be described by a utility function $u(x_1,x_2)$, the constrained optimization problem can then be written as

$$\max_{x_1,x_2} u(x_1,x_2) = v(x_1) + x_2 \text{ subject to } 2x_1 + 10x_2 = I, \tag{7.1}$$

with a corresponding Lagrange function

$$\mathcal{L}(x_1,x_2,\lambda) = v(x_1) + x_2 + \lambda(I - 2x_1 - 10x_2). \tag{7.2}$$

Taking the first two first order conditions, we get

$$\frac{\partial \mathcal{L}}{\partial x_1} = \frac{dv(x_1)}{dx_1} - 2\lambda = 0,$$

$$\frac{\partial \mathcal{L}}{\partial x_2} = 1 - 10\lambda = 0. \tag{7.3}$$

The second of the expressions in (7.3) can then be rewritten as $\lambda = 1/10$, which, when substituted into the first expression in (7.3), gives

$$\frac{dv(x_1)}{dx_1} = \frac{1}{5}. \tag{7.4}$$

Notice that the left-hand side of (7.4) is just a function of x_1, whereas the right-hand side is just a real number, which implies that, when we have a specific functional form for the function v, we can solve for x_1 as just a real number. For instance, if $u(x_1,x_2) = \ln x_1 + x_2$ (implying $v(x_1) = \ln x_1$), expression (7.4) becomes

$$\frac{1}{x_1} = \frac{1}{5} \text{ or } x_1 = 5. \tag{7.5}$$

When the underlying tastes are quasilinear, the optimal quantity of pasta (x_1) is therefore 5 (when prices of pasta and steak are 2 and 10) and is thus always the same regardless of what value the exogenous income I takes in the optimization problem (7.1). Put differently, the variable I simply drops out of the analysis as we solve for x_1. Thus, borderline normal/inferior goods have no income effects.

This is not true, of course, for tastes that cannot be represented by quasilinear utility functions. Consider, for instance, the same problem but with underlying tastes that can be represented by the Cobb–Douglas utility function $u(x_1,x_2) = x_1^\alpha x_2^{(1-\alpha)}$. The Lagrange function is then

$$\mathcal{L}(x_1,x_2,\lambda) = x_1^\alpha x_2^{(1-\alpha)} + \lambda(I - 2x_1 - 10x_2), \tag{7.6}$$

and the first order conditions for this problem are

$$\frac{\partial \mathcal{L}}{\partial x_1} = \alpha x_1^{(\alpha-1)} x_2^{(1-\alpha)} - 2\lambda = 0,$$

$$\frac{\partial \mathcal{L}}{\partial x_2} = (1-\alpha)x_1^\alpha x_2^{-\alpha} - 10\lambda = 0, \tag{7.7}$$

$$\frac{\partial \mathcal{L}}{\partial \lambda} = I - 2x_1 - 10x_2 = 0.$$

Adding 2λ to both sides of the first equation and 10λ to both sides of the second equation, and then dividing these equations by each other, we get $\alpha x_2/(1-\alpha)x_1 = 1/5$ or $x_2 = (1-\alpha)x_1/5\alpha$. Substituting this into the third equation of expression (7.7) and solving for x_1, we get

$$x_1 = \frac{\alpha I}{2}. \tag{7.8}$$

Thus, for the underlying Cobb–Douglas tastes specified here, the optimal consumption of pasta (x_1) depends on income, with higher income leading to greater consumption of pasta. Cobb–Douglas tastes (as well as all other homothetic tastes) therefore represent tastes for normal goods as depicted in Graph 7.1c.

Finally, none of the utility functions we have discussed thus far represent tastes for inferior goods. This is because such tastes are difficult to capture in simple mathematical functions, in part because *there are no tastes such that a particular good is always an inferior good*. To see this, imagine beginning with zero income, thus consuming the origin (0,0) in our graphs. Now suppose I give you $10. Since we cannot consume negative amounts of goods, it is not possible for you to consume less pasta than you did before I gave you $10, and it is therefore not possible to have tastes that represent inferior goods around the origin of our graphs. *All goods are therefore normal or borderline normal/inferior goods at least around the bundle* (0,0). Goods can be inferior only for some portion of an indifference map, and this logical conclusion makes it difficult to represent such tastes in simple utility functions.

7B.1.2 Luxury Goods and Necessities
We also defined in Section 7A.1.2 the terms *luxury goods* and *necessities*, with borderline goods between the two represented by homothetic tastes. We know from our discussion of homothetic tastes in Chapter 5 that such tastes have the feature that the marginal rates of substitution stay constant along linear rays emanating from the origin, and it is this feature of such tastes that ensures that, when exogenous income is increased by $x\%$ (without a change in opportunity costs), our consumption of each good also increases by $x\%$, leaving the ratio of our consumption of one good relative to the other unchanged.

For instance, in equation (7.8), we discovered that my optimal consumption of pasta is equal to $\alpha I/2$ when my tastes are captured by the Cobb–Douglas function $u(x_1,x_2) = x_1^\alpha x_2^{(1-\alpha)}$, when the price of pasta is $2 and the price of steak is $10 and when my income is given by I. When plugging this value into the budget constraint for x_1 and solving for x_2, we can also determine that my optimal consumption of steak is $(1 - \alpha)I/10$. Thus, the ratio (x_1/x_2) of my pasta consumption to my steak consumption under these economic circumstances is $5\alpha/(1 - \alpha)$. Put differently, my consumption of pasta relative to steak is *independent of income*. Since we know that Cobb–Douglas utility functions represent homothetic tastes, this simply confirms what our intuition already tells us: both pasta and steak are borderline luxury/necessity goods when the underlying tastes can be represented by Cobb–Douglas utility functions.

Again, this is not true for all types of tastes. If my tastes could be represented by the quasilinear utility function $u(x_1, x_2) = \ln x_1 + x_2$, we concluded in expression (7.5) that my optimal consumption of pasta would be equal to 5 boxes *regardless of my income level* (assuming, of course, that I had at least enough income to cover that much pasta consumption). Plugging this into the budget constraint for x_1 and solving for x_2, we also get that my optimal steak consumption is $(I - 10)/10$; i.e., my optimal steak consumption is a function of my income whereas my optimal pasta consumption is not. Put differently, my consumption of pasta *relative* to my consumption of steak declines with income, making pasta a necessity (and steak a luxury good).

7B.2 The Impact of Changing Opportunity Costs on Behavior

We introduced the concept of a *substitution effect* in Section 7A.2 by focusing on a particular example in which my brother chose to use taxis for transportation on his Cayman Islands vacation whereas I rented a car. To really focus on the underlying ideas, we assumed that my brother and I were identical in every way, allowing us to infer from the fact that we made two different choices that he and I were indifferent between renting a car and using taxis when we arrived at the airport in Cayman. The choice we made was one of choosing one of two budget constraints between "miles driven" and "other consumption" on our vacation. Renting a car requires a large fixed payment (thus reducing the level of other consumption that is possible if little or no driving occurs) but has the advantage of making additional miles cheap. Using taxis, on the other hand, involves no fixed payment but makes additional miles more expensive. Graph 7.3a illustrated the resulting choice sets, and Graph 7.3b illustrated a substitution effect from the different opportunity costs arising from those choice sets.

7B.2.1 Renting a Car versus Taking a Taxi
Suppose you know that my brother and I came to the Cayman Islands with $2,000 to spend on our vacations and that taxi rides cost $1 per mile. Letting x_1 denote miles driven in Cayman and x_2 "dollars of other consumption in Cayman," we know that my brother's budget line is $2,000 = x_1 + x_2$ given that the price of "dollars of other consumption" is by definition also 1. Suppose we also know that my brother's (and my own) tastes can be summarized by the Cobb–Douglas utility function $u(x_1, x_2) = x_1^{0.1} x_2^{0.9}$. Doing our usual constrained optimization problem, we can then determine that my brother's optimal consumption bundle is $x_1 = 200$ and $x_2 = 1,800$.

....

Set up my brother's constrained optimization problem and solve it to check that his optimal consumption bundle is indeed equal to this.

Exercise 7B.1

....

Now suppose that I had lost my receipt for the rental car and no longer remember how much of a fixed fee I was charged to drive it for the week. All I do remember is that gasoline cost $0.20 per mile. From the information we have, we can calculate what the fixed rental car fee must have been in order for me to be just as well off renting a car as my brother was using taxis.

Specifically, we can calculate the value associated with my brother's optimal indifference curve by simply plugging $x_1 = 200$ and $x_2 = 1,800$ into the utility function $u(x_1, x_2) = x_1^{0.1} x_2^{0.9}$ to get a value of approximately 1,445. While this number has no inherent meaning since we cannot quantify utility objectively, we do know from our analysis in Section 7A.2.1 (and Graph 7.3) that

I ended up on the same indifference curve, and thus with the same utility level as measured by the utility function that my brother and I share. This gives us enough information to find bundle B—my optimal bundle of miles driven and other consumption in Graph 7.3b—using a method that builds on the intuition that comes out of the graph. All we have to do is find the smallest possible choice set with a budget line that has the slope reflecting my lower opportunity cost for miles driven and is tangent to the indifference curve that my brother has achieved; i.e., the indifference curve associated with the utility value 1,445.

This can be formulated mathematically as the following problem: We would like to find the minimum expenditure necessary for achieving a utility value of 1,445 (as measured by the utility function $u(x_1,x_2) = x_1^{0.1}x_2^{0.9}$) given that my price for miles driven is 0.2 (while my price for "other consumption" remains at 1). Letting E stand for expenditure, we can state this formally as a *constrained minimization problem:*

$$\min_{x_1,x_2} E = 0.2x_1 + x_2 \text{ subject to } x_1^{0.1}x_2^{0.9} = 1,445. \tag{7.9}$$

Constrained minimization problems have the same basic structure as constrained maximization problems. The first part of (7.9) lets us know that we are trying to minimize a function by choosing the values for x_1 and x_2. The function we are trying to minimize, or what we call our *objective function,* then follows and is simply the equation for the budget constraint that we will end up with, which reflects the new opportunity cost of driving miles given that I have paid a fixed fee for my rental car and now face a lower opportunity cost for driving each mile. Finally, the last part of (7.9) tells us the *constraint* of our minimization problem: we are trying to reach the indifference curve associated with the value 1,445.

Finding the solution to a minimization problem is quite similar to finding the solution to a maximization problem. The reason for this similarity is most easily seen within the economic examples with which we are working. In our utility maximization problem, for instance, we are taking as fixed the budget line and trying to find the indifference curve that is tangent to that line. This is illustrated graphically in Graph 7.8a where a consumer faces a fixed budget line and tries to get to the highest possible indifference curve that still contains a bundle within the choice set

Graph 7.8: Maximizing Utility with Budgets Fixed (a) versus Minimizing Expenditure with Utility Fixed (b)

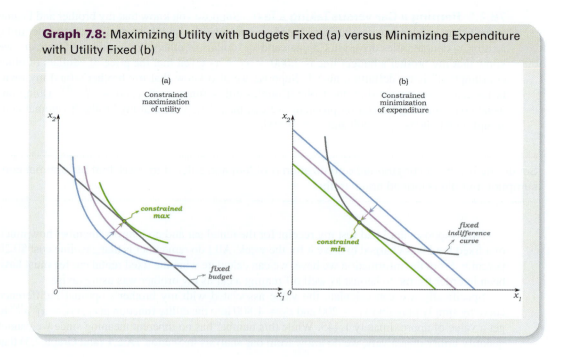

defined by the fixed budget line. In the expenditure minimization problem defined in expression (7.9), on the other hand, we are taking the indifference curve as fixed and trying to find the smallest possible choice set given the opportunity costs of the goods. This is illustrated in Graph 7.8b where we are trying to reach a fixed indifference curve with the smallest possible choice set. In both cases, we are therefore trying to find a solution, a combination of x_1 and x_2, where an indifference curve is tangent to a budget line (assuming the problem does not have non-convexities or corner solutions).

For this reason, the same Lagrange Method that we have employed in solving maximization problems can be employed to solve our newly defined minimization problem. Again, we create the Lagrange function by combining the *objective function* with a second term that is equal to λ times the *constraint* set to zero, only now the objective function is the budget constraint and the constraint is the indifference curve. Thus,

$$\mathcal{L}(x_1, x_2, \lambda) = 0.2x_1 + x_2 + \lambda(1{,}445 - x_1^{0.1}x_2^{0.9}). \tag{7.10}$$

We then again take the first derivatives of $\mathcal{L}$ with respect to the choice variables (x_1 and x_2) and λ to get the first order conditions

$$\frac{\partial \mathcal{L}}{\partial x_1} = 0.2 - 0.1\lambda x_1^{-0.9}x_2^{0.9} = 0,$$

$$\frac{\partial \mathcal{L}}{\partial x_2} = 1 - 0.9\lambda x_1^{0.1}x_2^{-0.1} = 0, \tag{7.11}$$

$$1{,}445 - x_1^{0.1}x_2^{0.9} = 0.$$

Solving the first two equations for x_2 we get

$$x_2 = \frac{0.9(0.2x_1)}{0.1} = 1.8x_1 \tag{7.12}$$

and plugging this into the third equation and solving for x_1, we get $x_1 = 851.34$. Finally, plugging this back into expression (7.12), we get $x_2 = 1{,}532.41$. This is point B in Graph 7.3, which implies that I chose to drive approximately 851 miles in my rental car during my Cayman Island vacation while consuming approximately \$1,532 in other goods.

We can now see how much the bundle B costs by multiplying my optimal levels of x_1 and x_2 by the prices of those goods, 0.2 for x_1 and 1 for x_2, and adding these expenditures together:

$$E = 0.2(851.34) + 1(1{,}532.41) = 1{,}702.68. \tag{7.13}$$

Thus, bundle B costs a total of \$1,702.68. Since you know that I arrived in Cayman with \$2,000, you know that the difference between my total money budget for my vacation and the total I spent on driving and other goods must be what I paid for the fixed rental car fee: \$297.32. This is equal to the vertical distance labeled "rental car fee" in Graph 7.3a.

7B.2.2 Substitution Effects Notice that, in the process of making these calculations, we have identified the size of the substitution effect we treated graphically in Graph 7.3. Put differently, assuming tastes that can be represented by the utility function $u(x_1, x_2) = x_1^{0.1}x_2^{0.9}$, an individual who chooses to drive 200 miles while consuming \$1,800 in other goods when the opportunity cost per mile is \$1 will reduce his other consumption and *substitute* toward 851 miles driven when we keep his real wealth—or his real well-being—fixed and change the opportunity cost for driving a mile to \$0.2.

7B.2.3 The Size of Substitution Effects By using a Cobb–Douglas utility function to represent tastes in the previous example, we have chosen a utility function that we know (from our discussion of Constant Elasticity of Substitution (CES) utility functions in

Chapter 5) has an elasticity of substitution equal to 1. The answers we calculated relate directly to this property of Cobb–Douglas utility functions. In fact, we can verify that the function $u(x_1, x_2) = x_1^{0.1} x_2^{0.9}$ has an elasticity of substitution of 1 using our answers as we determined the bundles associated with points A and B in Graph 7.3. Recall the formula for an elasticity of substitution:

$$\text{Elasticity of Substitution} = \left| \frac{\% \Delta (x_2/x_1)}{\% \Delta MRS} \right|. \tag{7.14}$$

Bundle A, my brother's optimal bundle, is (200, 1800), while bundle B, my optimal bundle, is (851.34, 1532.41). My brother's ratio of x_2/x_1 is therefore equal to 1,800/200, or 9, while my ratio of x_2/x_1 is 1,532.41/851.34 or 1.8. In going from A to B on the same indifference curve, the change in the ratio x_2/x_1, $\Delta(x_2/x_1)$, is therefore equal to -7.2. The $\% \Delta(x_2/x_1)$ is just the change in the ratio (x_2/x_1) divided by the original level of (x_2/x_1) at bundle A; i.e.,

$$\% \Delta \left(\frac{x_2}{x_1} \right) = \frac{\Delta(x_2/x_1)}{x_2^A/x_1^A} = \frac{-7.2}{9} = -0.8. \tag{7.15}$$

Similarly, the MRS at bundle A is equal to the slope of my brother's budget line, which is equal to -1 given that he faces a cost per mile of \$1. My MRS at bundle B, on the other hand, is equal to the slope of my budget line, which is equal to -0.2 given that I face a cost per mile of only \$0.20. The $\% \Delta MRS$ as we go from A to B is therefore the change in the MRS divided by the original MRS at bundle A; i.e.,

$$\% \Delta MRS = \frac{\Delta MRS}{MRS^A} = 0.8. \tag{7.16}$$

Plugging (7.15) and (7.16) into the equation for an elasticity of substitution in expression (7.14), we get an elasticity of substitution equal to 1. Thus, when the marginal rate of substitution of the indifference curve in Graph 7.3 changed by 80% (from -1 to -0.2), the ratio of other consumption (x_2) to miles driven (x_1) also changed by 80% (from 9 to 1.8). *It is the elasticity of substitution that is embedded in the utility function that determined the size of the substitution effect we calculated!*

This relates directly to the intuition we built in Graph 7.4, where we showed how substitution effects get larger as the degree of substitutability, or the elasticity of substitution in our more mathematical language, changes. Were we to substitute utility functions with elasticities of substitution different from those in Cobb–Douglas utility functions, we would therefore calculate substitution effects that were larger or smaller depending on whether the elasticity of substitution imbedded into those utility functions was greater or smaller.

Consider, for instance, the CES utility function with $\rho = -0.5$, which implies an elasticity of substitution of 2 (rather than 1 as in the Cobb–Douglas case where $\rho = 0$). More precisely, suppose that the utility function my brother and I share is

$$u(x_1, x_2) = (0.25 x_1^{0.5} + 0.75 x_2^{0.5})^2, \tag{7.17}$$

and suppose again that our money budget for our Cayman vacation is \$2,000 and the per mile cost is \$1 for taxis and \$0.20 for rental cars.[8] My brother's optimization problem is then

$$\max_{x_1, x_2} (0.25 x_1^{0.5} + 0.75 x_2^{0.5})^2 \text{ subject to } x_1 + x_2 = 2,000, \tag{7.18}$$

which you can verify results in an optimal consumption bundle of $x_1 = 200$ and $x_2 = 1,800$ just as it did in our previous example. Thus, point A remains unchanged. The indifference

---

[8]The exponents in equation (7.17) are positive because ρ is negative and each exponent in the CES utility function has a negative sign in front of it.

curve on which point *A* lies, however, differs substantially from that in the previous example because of the different elasticity of substitution embedded in equation (7.17). When you plug the optimal bundle for my brother back into the utility function (7.17) you can calculate that he operates on an indifference curve giving him utility of 1,250 as measured by this utility function. We could then repeat our analysis of calculating bundle *B* by solving the problem analogous to the one we stated in expression (7.9) but adapted to the model we are now working with:

$$\min_{x_1, x_2} E = 0.2x_1 + x_2 \text{ subject to } (0.25x_1^{0.5} + 0.75x_2^{0.5})^2 = 1,250. \tag{7.19}$$

You can again verify on your own that this results in an optimal bundle *B* of $x_1 = 2,551.02$ and $x_2 = 918.37$, which implies a substitution effect much larger than the one we found with the Cobb–Douglas utility function. This is because we have built a greater elasticity of substitution into the utility function of equation (7.17) than we had in our previous Cobb–Douglas utility function. The difference between the two scenarios is illustrated graphically in Graph 7.9.

How much did I pay in a fixed rental car fee in order for me to be indifferent in this example to taking taxis? Why is this amount larger than in the Cobb–Douglas case we calculated earlier?   **Exercise 7B.2**

Table 7.1 on the next page summarizes the outcome of similar calculations for CES utility functions with different elasticities of substitution. In each case, the remaining parameters of the CES utility function are set to ensure that my brother's optimal choice remains the same: 200 miles driven and $1,800 in other consumption.[9]

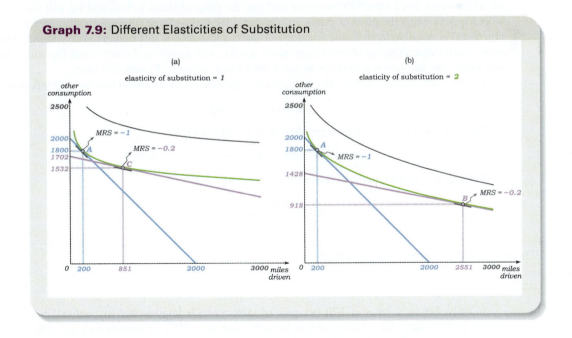

Graph 7.9: Different Elasticities of Substitution

---

[9]More precisely, the utility function $u(x_1, x_2) = (\alpha x_1^{-\rho} + (1 - \alpha)x_2^{-\rho})^{-1/\rho}$ was used for these calculations, with ρ set as indicated in the first column of the table and α adjusted to ensure that point A remains at (200, 1800).

Table 7.1: $u(x_1, x_2) = (\alpha x_1^{-\rho} + (1 - \alpha)x_2^{-\rho})^{-1/\rho}$

	Substitution Effects as Elasticity of Substitution Changes	
ρ	Elasticity of Subst.	Substitution Effect
−0.5	2	2,351.02 More Miles Driven at B than at A
0.0	1	651.34 More Miles Driven at B than at A
0.5	0.67	337.28 More Miles Driven at B than at A
1.0	0.50	222.53 More Miles Driven at B than at A
5.0	0.167	57.55 More Miles Driven at B than at A
10.0	0.091	29.67 More Miles Driven at B than at A
∞	0.000	0.00 More Miles Driven at B than at A

7B.3 Price Changes: Income and Substitution Effects Combined

Finally, we concluded in Section 7A.3 that most price changes involve both income and substitution effects because they involve both a change in our real wealth (or our optimal indifference curve) and a change in opportunity costs. We can then employ all the mathematical tools we have built thus far to identify income and substitution effects when prices change. In the following, we will consider once again the case of me shopping at Wal-Mart for pants (x_1) and shirts (x_2), as we did in Section 7A.3.3, to demonstrate how we can identify these effects separately. Throughout, we will assume that I have $200 to spend and that the price of shirts is $10, and we will focus on what happens when the price of pants, p_1, changes. We will assume (unrealistically) in this section that it is possible to consume fractions of shirts and pants. If this bothers you, you may feel more comfortable thinking of more continuous goods, such as nuts and candy from the bulk food isle where one can scoop as little or as much into a bag, instead of pants and shirts.

Suppose first that my tastes can once again be represented by a Cobb–Douglas utility function

$$u(x_1, x_2) = x_1^{0.5} x_2^{0.5}. \tag{7.20}$$

My constrained maximization problem at Wal-Mart is then

$$\max_{x_1, x_2} x_1^{0.5} x_2^{0.5} \text{ subject to } p_1 x_1 + 10 x_2 = 200. \tag{7.21}$$

Solving this in the usual way gives us the optimal bundle

$$x_1 = \frac{100}{p_1} \text{ and } x_2 = 10. \tag{7.22}$$

Exercise 7B.3   Check to see that this solution is correct.

Initially, I face a price of $20 per pair of pants, which implies that my optimal bundle is 5 pants and 10 shirts. Then I discover that my wife gave me a 50% off coupon for pants, effectively reducing the price of pants from $20 to $10. As a result of this decrease in the price of pants, my optimal consumption bundle changes from (5,10) to (10,10). This is illustrated in Graph 7.10a, with bundle A representing my original optimal bundle and bundle C representing my new optimal bundle.

Graph 7.10: Income and Substitution Effects When Tastes are Cobb–Douglas

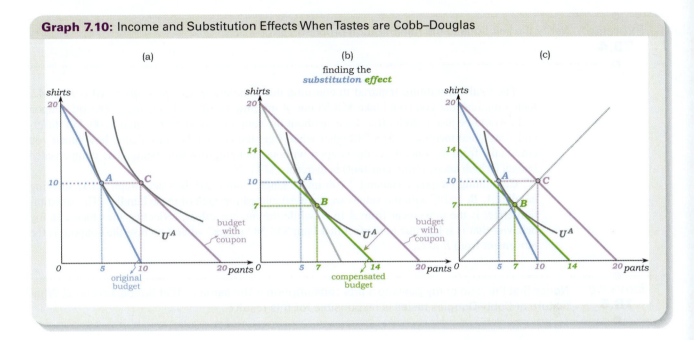

In order to decompose this change in my behavior into income and substitution effects, we have to calculate how my consumption would have changed had I faced the same change in opportunity costs without experiencing an increase in real wealth; i.e., without having shifted to a higher indifference curve. Thus, we need to employ the method we developed in the previous section to identify how much money I would have to give up when I received the coupon to be able to be just as well off as I was originally without the coupon. Notice that this is exactly analogous to our example involving my brother and me in the Cayman Islands where we wanted to identify how much the fixed rental car fee must have been in order for me to be just as well off as my brother was using taxis. In both cases, we have a fixed indifference curve, and we are trying to find the smallest possible choice set that will give me a fixed utility level when my opportunity costs change.

In Graph 7.10b, we illustrate the problem of finding the substitution effect graphically. We begin by drawing the indifference curve U^A that contains bundle A and the (magenta) budget line that I have with the coupon. Then we shift this budget line inward, keeping the slope and thus the new opportunity cost fixed, until only a single point on the indifference curve remains within the choice set. This process identifies bundle B on the compensated (green) budget, the bundle I would choose if I faced the opportunity costs under the coupon but had lost just enough of my money to be just as well off as I was originally when I consumed bundle A.

Mathematically, we state the process graphed in Graph 7.10b as a constrained minimization problem in which we are trying to minimize my total expenditures (or my money budget) subject to the constraint that I would like to consume on the indifference curve that contains bundle A. We can write this as follows:

$$\min_{x_1, x_2} E = 10x_1 + 10x_2 \text{ subject to } x_1^{0.5}x_2^{0.5} = U^A, \tag{7.23}$$

where U^A represents the level of utility I attained at bundle A. This level of utility can be calculated using the utility function $x_1^{0.5}x_2^{0.5}$ by simply plugging the bundle A ($x_1 = 5, x_2 = 10$) into the function, which gives us $U^A \approx 7.071$. Solving this *minimization* problem using the Lagrange Method illustrated in our Cayman example in the previous section, we get

$$x_1 = x_2 \approx 7.071. \tag{7.24}$$

Exercise 7B.4

Verify the solutions to the minimization problem.

The total expenditure required to consume this bundle at prices $p_1 = p_2 = 10$ is $141.42, which implies that you could take $58.58 out of my initial $200 and give me a 50% off coupon and I would be just as well off as I was without the coupon and with my initial $200. Put differently, my "real income" is $58.58 higher when I get the coupon because that is how much you could take from me once I get the coupon without changing my well-being. The compensated budget (which keeps utility constant) is therefore $141.42.

Combining Graphs 7.10a and 7.10b into a single graph, we then get Graph 7.10c showing bundles A, B, and C with the values we have calculated for each of these bundles. The substitution effect is the movement from A to B, while the income effect, reflecting the change in my behavior that is solely due to the fact that I am $58.58 "richer" when I receive the coupon, is the movement from B to C.

Exercise 7B.5

Notice that the ratio of my pants to shirts consumption is the same ($=1$) at bundles B and C. What feature of Cobb–Douglas tastes is responsible for this result?

Just as was true for substitution effects we identified in the Cayman Islands example, the size of the substitution effect here once again arises from the degree of substitutability of the goods as captured by the shape of indifference curves and the form of the utility function. Similarly, the size of the income effect depends on the underlying nature of tastes and the degree to which pants and shirts represent normal or inferior goods.

Suppose, for instance, that my tastes could be represented by the quasilinear utility function

$$u(x_1, x_2) = 6x_1^{0.5} + x_2. \tag{7.25}$$

Setting up the maximization problem analogous to (7.21) gives

$$\max_{x_1, x_2} \ 6x_1^{0.5} + x_2 \text{ subject to } p_1 x_1 + 10x_2 = 200, \tag{7.26}$$

which you can verify solves to

$$x_1 = \frac{900}{p_1^2} \text{ and } x_2 = \frac{20p_1 - 90}{p_1}. \tag{7.27}$$

Thus, when the price of pants is 20, we get an optimal bundle $(2.25, 15.5)$, and when the price falls to 10 due to the coupon, we get an optimal bundle $(9, 11)$. Total utility without the coupon is found by plugging $x_1 = 2.25$ and $x_2 = 15.5$ into equation (7.25), which gives utility equal to 24.5. This then permits us to find the substitution effect by solving the constrained minimization problem

$$\min_{x_1, x_2} E = 10x_1 + 10x_2 \text{ subject to } 6x_1^{0.5} + x_2 = 24.5, \tag{7.28}$$

which gives $x_1 = 9$ and $x_2 = 6.5$. Thus (ignoring the fact that it is difficult to consume fractions of pants) the substitution effect changes my consumption of pants from my original 2.25 to 9, and the income effect causes no additional change in my consumption for pants. This lack of an income effect of course arises because tastes that are quasilinear in a particular good (in this case, pants) do not exhibit income effects for that good; such goods are borderline normal/inferior goods.[10]

---

[10] A small caveat to this is that such tastes *do* exhibit income effects in the quasilinear good when there are corner solutions. This is explored in more detail in end-of-chapter exercise 7.5.

Using the previous calculations, plot graphs similar to Graph 7.10 illustrating income and substitution effects when my tastes can be represented by the utility function $u(x_1, x_2) = 6x_1^{0.5} + x_2$.

Exercise
7B.6

CONCLUSION

We have begun in this chapter to discuss the important concepts of income and substitution effects in the context of consumer goods markets. In our mathematical section, we furthermore began to calculate income and substitution effects for some very specific examples in order to illustrate how the graphs of Section 7A related to the mathematical ideas we have dealt with thus far. A more general theory of consumer behavior will emerge from the building blocks of the optimization model we have laid, but we will not have completed the building of this theory until Chapter 10. Before doing so, we will now first translate the concepts of income and substitution effects in consumer goods markets to similar ideas that emerge in labor and capital markets (Chapter 8). We will then illustrate in Chapters 9 and 10 how our notions of demand and consumer surplus relate directly to income and substitution effects as introduced here.

There is no particular reason why it should be fully apparent to you at this point why these concepts are important. The importance will become clearer as we apply them in exercises and as we turn to some real-world issues later on. We did, however, raise one example in the introduction, and we can now make a bit more sense of it. We imagined a policy in which the government would reduce consumption of gasoline by taxing it heavily, only to turn around and distribute the revenues from the tax in the form of rebate checks. For many, including some very smart columnists and politicians, such a combination of a gasoline tax and rebate makes no sense; on average, they argue, consumers would receive back as much as they paid in gasoline taxes, and as a result, they would not change their behavior.[11] Now that we have isolated income and substitution effects, however, we can see why economists think such a tax/rebate program will indeed curb gasoline consumption: The tax raises the price of gasoline and thus gives rise to income and substitution effects that (assuming gasoline is a normal good) both result in less consumption of gasoline. The rebate, on the other hand, does not change prices back; it simply causes incomes to rise above where they would otherwise have been after the tax. Thus, the rebate only causes an income effect in the opposite direction. The negative income effect from the increase in the price should be roughly offset by the positive income effect from the tax rebate, which leaves us with a substitution effect that unambiguously implies a decrease in gasoline consumption.

END-OF-CHAPTER EXERCISES

7.1 Here, we consider some logical relationships between preferences and types of goods.

A. Suppose you consider all the goods that you might potentially want to consume.

    a. Is it possible for all these goods to be luxury goods at every consumption bundle? Is it possible for all of them to be necessities?

    b. Is it possible for all goods to be inferior goods at every consumption bundle? Is it possible for all of them to be normal goods?

    c. *True or False*: When tastes are homothetic, all goods are normal goods.

    d. *True or False*: When tastes are homothetic, some goods could be luxuries while others could be necessities.

    e. *True or False*: When tastes are quasilinear, one of the goods is a necessity.

---

[11]This argument was in fact advanced by opponents of such a policy advocated by the Carter administration in the late 1970s, a proposal that won only 35 votes (out of 435) in the U.S. House of Representatives. It is not the only argument against such policies. For instance, some have argued that a gasoline tax would be too narrow, and that the goals of such a tax would be better advanced by a broad-based carbon tax on all carbon-emmitting activity.

*conceptually challenging
**computationally challenging
†solutions in Study Guide

    f.   *True or False*: In a two-good model, if the two goods are perfect complements, they must both be normal goods.

    g.*   *True or False*: In a three-good model, if two of the goods are perfect complements, they must both be normal goods.

B. In each of the following cases, suppose that a person whose tastes can be characterized by the given utility function has income I and faces prices that are all equal to 1. Illustrate mathematically how his or her consumption of each good changes with income, and use your answer to determine whether the goods are normal or inferior, luxuries or necessities.

    a. $u(x_1, x_2) = x_1 x_2$

    b. $u(x_1, x_2) = x_1 + \ln x_2$

    c. $u(x_1, x_2) = \ln x_1 + \ln x_2$

    d. $u(x_1, x_2, x_3) = 2 \ln x_1 + \ln x_2 + 4 \ln x_3$

    e.* $u(x_1, x_2) = 2x_1^{0.5} + \ln x_2$

7.2   Suppose you have an income of \$24 and the only two goods you consume are apples (x_1) and peaches (x_2). The price of apples is \$4 and the price of peaches is \$3.

A. Suppose that your optimal consumption is 4 peaches and 3 apples.

    a.   Illustrate this in a graph using indifference curves and budget lines.

    b.   Now suppose that the price of apples falls to \$2 and I take enough money away from you to make you as happy as you were originally. Will you buy more or fewer peaches?

    c.   In reality, I do not actually take income away from you as described in (b), but your income stays at \$24 after the price of apples falls. I observe that, after the price of apples fell, you did not change your consumption of peaches. Can you conclude whether peaches are an inferior or normal good for you?

B. Suppose that your tastes can be characterized by the function $u(x_1, x_2) = x_1^{\alpha} x_2^{(1-\alpha)}$.

    a.   What value must α take in order for you to choose 3 apples and 4 peaches at the original prices?

    b.   What bundle would you consume under the scenario described in A(b)?

    c.   How much income can I take away from you and still keep you as happy as you were before the price change?

    d.   What will you actually consume after the price increase?

7.3   Consider once again my tastes for Coke and Pepsi and my tastes for right and left shoes (as described in end-of-chapter exercise 6.2).

A. On two separate graphs—one with Coke and Pepsi on the axes, the other with right shoes and left shoes—replicate your answers to end-of-chapter exercise 6.2A(a) and (b). Label the original optimal bundles A and the new optimal bundles C.

    a.   In your Coke/Pepsi graph, decompose the change in consumer behavior into income and substitution effects by drawing the compensated budget and indicating the optimal bundle B on that budget.

    b.   Repeat (a) for your right shoes/left shoes graph.

B. Now consider the following utility functions: $u(x_1, x_2) = \min\{x_1, x_2\}$ and $u(x_1, x_2) = x_1 + x_2$. Which of these could plausibly represent my tastes for Coke and Pepsi, and which could represent my tastes for right and left shoes?

    a.   Use the appropriate function to assign utility levels to bundles A, B, and C in your graph from 7.3A(a).

    b.   Repeat this for bundles A, B, and C for your graph in 7.3A(b).

7.4   Return to the case of our beer and pizza consumption from end-of-chapter exercise 6.3.

A. Again, suppose you consume only beer and pizza (sold at prices p_1 and p_2 respectively) with an exogenously set income I. Assume again some initial optimal (interior) bundle A.

    a.   In 6.3A(b), can you tell whether beer is normal or inferior? What about pizza?

    b.   When the price of beer goes up, I notice that you consume less beer. Can you tell whether beer is a normal or an inferior good?

    c.   When the price of beer goes down, I notice you buy less pizza. Can you tell whether pizza is a normal good?

    d.   When the price of pizza goes down, I notice you buy more beer. Is beer an inferior good for you? Is pizza?

    e.   Which of your conclusions in part (d) would change if you knew pizza and beer are very substitutable?

B. Suppose, as you did in end-of-chapter exercise 6.3B, that your tastes over beer (x_1) and pizza (x_2) can be summarize by the utility function $u(x_1, x_2) = x_1^2 x_2$. If you have not already done so, calculate the optimal quantity of beer and pizza consumption as a function of p_1, p_2, and I.

    a.   Illustrate the optimal bundle A when $p_1 = 2$, $p_2 = 10$ and weekly income $I = 180$. What numerical label does this utility function assign to the indifference curve that contains bundle A?

    b.   Using your answer, show that both beer and pizza are normal goods when your tastes can be summarized by this utility function.

    c.   Suppose the price of beer goes up to $4. Illustrate your new optimal bundle and label it C.

    d.   How much beer and pizza would you buy if you had received just enough of a raise to keep you just as happy after the increase in the price of beer as you were before (at your original income of $180)? Illustrate this as bundle B.

    e.   How large was your salary increase in (d)?

    f.   Now suppose the price of pizza (p_2) falls to $5 (and suppose the price of beer and your income are $2 and $180 as they were originally at bundle A). Illustrate your original budget, your new budget, the original optimum A, and the new optimum C in a graph.

    g.   Calculate the income effect and the substitution effect for both pizza and beer consumption from this change in the price of pizza. Illustrate this in your graph.

    h.   *True or False*: Since income and substitution effects point in opposite directions for beer, beer must be an inferior good.

7.5†   Return to the analysis of my undying love for my wife expressed through weekly purchases of roses (as introduced in end-of-chapter exercise 6.4).

A. Recall that initially roses cost $5 each and, with an income of $125 per week, I bought 25 roses each week. Then, when my income increased to $500 per week, I continued to buy 25 roses per week (at the same price).

    a.   From what you observed thus far, are roses a normal or an inferior good for me? Are they a luxury or a necessity?

    b.   On a graph with weekly roses consumption on the horizontal and "other goods" on the vertical, illustrate my budget constraint when my weekly income is $125. Then illustrate the change in the budget constraint when income remains $125 per week and the price of roses falls to $2.50. Suppose that my optimal consumption of roses after this price change rises to 50 roses per week and illustrate this as bundle C.

    c.   Illustrate the compensated budget line and use it to illustrate the income and substitution effects.

    d.   Now consider the case where my income is $500 and, when the price changes from $5 to $2.50, I end up consuming 100 roses per week (rather than 25). Assuming quasilinearity in roses, illustrate income and substitution effects.

    e.   *True or False*: Price changes of goods that are quasilinear give rise to no income effects for the quasilinear good unless corner solutions are involved.

B. Suppose again, as in 6.4B, that my tastes for roses (x_1) and other goods (x_2) can be represented by the utility function $u(x_1, x_2) = \beta x_1^\alpha + x_2$.

    a.   If you have not already done so, assume that p_2 is by definition equal to 1, let $\alpha = 0.5$ and $\beta = 50$, and calculate my optimal consumption of roses and other goods as a function of p_1 and I.

b.   The original scenario you graphed in 7.5A(b) contains corner solutions when my income is $125 and the price is initially $5 and then $2.50. Does your previous answer allow for this?

c.   Verify that the scenario in your answer to 7.5A(d) is also consistent with tastes described by this utility function; i.e., verify that A, B, and C are as you described in your answer.

7.6   **Everyday Application:** *Housing Price Fluctuations: Part 2*: Suppose, as in end-of-chapter exercise 6.9, you have $400,000 to spend on "square feet of housing" and "all other goods." Assume the same is true for me.

A.   Suppose again that you initially face a $100 per square foot price for housing, and you choose to buy a 2,000-square-foot house.

a.   Illustrate this on a graph with square footage of housing on the horizontal axis and other consumption on the vertical. Then suppose, as you did in exercise 6.9, that the price of housing falls to $50 per square foot after you bought your 2,000-square-foot house. Label the square footage of the house you would switch to h_B.

b.   Is h_B smaller or larger than 2,000 square feet? Does your answer depend on whether housing is normal, regular inferior, or Giffen?

c.   Now suppose that the price of housing had fallen to $50 per square foot *before* you bought your initial 2,000-square-foot house. Denote the size of house you would have bought h_C and illustrate it in your graph.

d.   Is h_C larger than h_B? Is it larger than 2,000 square feet? Does your answer depend on whether housing is a normal, regular inferior, or Giffen good?

e.   Now consider me. I did not buy a house until the price of housing was $50 per square foot, at which time I bought a 4,000-square-foot house. Then the price of housing rises to $100 per square foot. Would I sell my house and buy a new one? If so, is the new house size $h_{B'}$ larger or smaller than 4,000 square feet? Does your answer depend on whether housing is normal, regular inferior, or Giffen for me?

f.   Am I better or worse off?

g.   Suppose I had not purchased at the low price but rather purchased a house of size $h_{C'}$ after the price had risen to $100 per square foot. Is $h_{C'}$ larger or smaller than $h_{B'}$? Is it larger or smaller than 4,000 square feet? Does your answer depend on whether housing is normal, regular inferior, or Giffen for me?

B.   Suppose both you and I have tastes that can be represented by the utility function $u(x_1, x_2) = x_1^{0.5} x_2^{0.5}$, where x_1 is square feet of housing and x_2 is "dollars of other goods."

a.   Calculate the optimal level of housing consumption x_1 as a function of per square foot housing prices p_1 and income I.

b.   Verify that your initial choice of a 2,000-square-foot house and my initial choice of a 4,000-square-foot house was optimal under the circumstances we faced (assuming we both started with $400,000).

c.   Calculate the values of h_B and h_C as they are described in A(a) and (c).

d.   Calculate $h_{B'}$ and $h_{C'}$ as they are described in A(e) and (g).

e.   Verify your answer to A(f).

7.7   **Everyday Application:** *Turkey and Thanksgiving*: Every Thanksgiving, my wife and I debate about how we should prepare the turkey we will serve (and will then have left over). On the one hand, my wife likes preparing turkeys the conventional way: roasted in the oven where it has to cook at 350 degrees for 4 hours or so. I, on the other hand, like to fry turkeys in a big pot of peanut oil heated over a powerful flame outdoors. The two methods have different costs and benefits. The conventional way of cooking turkeys has very little set-up cost (since the oven is already there and just has to be turned on) but a relatively large time cost from then on. (It takes hours to cook.) The frying method, on the other hand, takes some set-up (dragging out the turkey fryer, pouring gallons of peanut oil, etc., and then later the cleanup associated with it), but turkeys cook predictably quickly in just 3.5 minutes per pound.

A.   As a household, we seem to be indifferent between doing it one way or another; sometimes we use the oven, sometimes we use the fryer. But we have noticed that we cook much more turkey, several turkeys, as a matter of fact, when we use the fryer than when we use the oven.

a. Construct a graph with "pounds of cooked turkeys" on the horizontal and "other consumption" on the vertical. ("Other consumption" here is not denominated in dollars as it normally is but rather in some consumption index that takes into account the time it takes to engage in such consumption.) Think of the set-up cost for frying turkeys and the waiting cost for cooking them as the main costs that are relevant. Can you illustrate our family's choice of whether to fry or roast turkeys at Thanksgiving as a choice between two "budget lines"?

b. Can you explain the fact that we seem to eat more turkey around Thanksgiving whenever we pull out the turkey fryer as opposed to roasting the turkey in the oven?

c. We have some friends who also struggle each Thanksgiving with the decision of whether to fry or roast, and they, too, seem to be indifferent between the two options. But we have noticed that they only cook a little more turkey when they fry than when they roast. What is different about them?

B. **Suppose that, if we did not cook turkeys, we could consume 100 units of "other consumption," but the time it takes to cook turkeys takes away from that consumption. Setting up the turkey fryer costs c units of consumption and waiting 3.5 minutes (which is how long it takes to cook 1 pound of turkey) costs 1 unit of consumption. Roasting a turkey involves no set-up cost, but it takes 5 times as long to cook per pound. Suppose that tastes can be characterized by the CES utility function $u(x_1, x_2) = (0.5x_1^{-\rho} + 0.5x_2^{-\rho})^{-1/\rho}$ where x_1 is pounds of turkey and x_2 is "other consumption."

a. What are the two budget constraints I am facing?

b. Can you calculate how much turkey someone with these tastes will roast (as a function of ρ)? How much will the same person fry? (*Hint:* Rather than solving this using the Lagrange Method, use the fact that you know the *MRS* is equal to the slope of the budget line and recall from Chapter 5 that, for a CES utility function of this kind, $MRS = -(x_2/x_1)^{\rho+1}$.)

c. Suppose my family has tastes with $\rho = 0$ and my friend's with $\rho = 1$. If each of us individually roasts turkeys this Thanksgiving, how much will we each roast?

d. How much utility will each of us get (as measured by the relevant utility function)? (*Hint:* In the case where $\rho = 0$, the exponent $1/\rho$ is undefined. Use the fact that you know that when $\rho = 0$ the CES utility function is Cobb–Douglas.)

e. Which family is happier?

f. If we are really indifferent between roasting and frying, what must c be for my family? What must it be for my friend's family? (*Hint:* Rather than setting up the usual minimization problem, use your answer to (b) to determine c by setting utility equal to what it was for roasting.)

g. Given your answers so far, how much would we each have fried had we chosen to fry instead of roast (and we were truly indifferent between the two because of the different values of c we face)?

h. Compare the size of the substitution effect you have calculated for my family and that you calculated for my friend's family and illustrate your answer in a graph with pounds of turkey on the horizontal and other consumption on the vertical. Relate the difference in the size of the substitution effect to the elasticity of substitution.

7.8*† **Business Application:** *Sam's Club and the Marginal Consumer:* Superstores like Costco and Sam's Club serve as wholesalers to businesses but also target consumers who are willing to pay a fixed fee in order to get access to the lower wholesale prices offered in these stores. For purposes of this exercise, suppose that you can denote goods sold at superstores as x_1 and "dollars of other consumption" as x_2.

BUSINESS APPLICATION

A. Suppose all consumers have the same homothetic tastes over x_1 and x_2, but they differ in their income. Every consumer is offered the same option of either shopping at stores with somewhat higher prices for x_1 or paying the fixed fee c to shop at a superstore at somewhat lower prices for x_1.

a. On a graph with x_1 on the horizontal axis and x_2 on the vertical, illustrate the regular budget (without a superstore membership) and the superstore budget for a consumer whose income is such that these two budgets cross on the 45-degree line. Indicate on your graph a vertical distance that is equal to the superstore membership fee c.

b. Now consider a consumer with twice that much income. Where will this consumer's two budgets intersect relative to the 45-degree line?

c. Suppose consumer 1 (from part (a)) is just indifferent between buying and not buying the superstore membership. How will her behavior differ depending on whether or not she buys the membership?

d.   If consumer 1 was indifferent between buying and not buying the superstore membership, can you tell whether consumer 2 (from part (b)) is also indifferent? (*Hint*: Given that tastes are homothetic and identical across consumers, what would have to be true about the intersection of the two budgets for the higher income consumer in order for the consumer also to be indifferent between them?)

e.   *True or False*: Assuming consumers have the same homothetic tastes, there exists a "marginal" consumer with income $\bar{I}$ such that all consumers with income greater than $\bar{I}$ will buy the superstore membership and no consumer with income below $\bar{I}$ will buy that membership.

f.   *True or False*: By raising c and/or p_1, the superstore will lose relatively lower income customers and keep high income customers.

g.   Suppose you are a superstore manager and you think your store is overcrowded. You'd like to reduce the number of customers while at the same time increasing the amount each customer purchases. How would you do this?

B.   Suppose you manage a superstore and you are currently charging an annual membership fee of $50. Since x_2 is denominated in dollar units, $p_2 = 1$. Suppose that $p_1 = 1$ for those shopping outside the superstore, but your store sells x_1 at 0.95. Your statisticians have estimated that your consumers have tastes that can be summarized by the utility function $u(x_1, x_2) = x_1^{0.15} x_2^{0.85}$.

a.   What is the annual discretionary income (that could be allocated to purchasing x_1 and x_2) of your "marginal" consumer?

b.   Can you show that consumers with more income than the marginal consumer will definitely purchase the membership while consumers with less income will not? (*Hint*: Calculate the income of the marginal consumer as a function of c and show what happens to income that makes a consumer marginal as c changes.)

c.   If the membership fee is increased from $50 to $100, how much could the superstore lower p_1 without increasing membership beyond what it was when the fee was $50 and p_1 was 0.95?

7.9*   **Business Application:** *Are Gucci Products Giffen Goods?* We defined a Giffen good as a good that consumers (with exogenous incomes) buy more of when the price increases. When students first hear about such goods, they often think of luxury goods such as expensive Gucci purses and accessories. If the marketing departments for firms like Gucci are very successful, they may find a way of associating price with "prestige" in the minds of consumers, and this may allow them to raise the price *and* sell more products. But would that make Gucci products Giffen goods? The answer, as you will see in this exercise, is no.

A.   Suppose we model a consumer who cares about the "practical value and style of Gucci products," dollars of other consumption, and the "prestige value" of being seen with Gucci products. Denote these as x_1, x_2, and x_3 respectively.

a.   The consumer only has to buy x_1 and x_2—the prestige value x_3 comes with the Gucci products. Let p_1 denote the price of Gucci products and $p_2 = 1$ be the price of dollars of other consumption. Illustrate the consumer's budget constraint (assuming an exogenous income I).

b.   The prestige value of Gucci purchases, x_3, is something an individual consumer has no control over. If x_3 is fixed at a particular level $\bar{x}_3$, the consumer therefore operates on a two-dimensional slice of her three-dimensional indifference map over x_1, x_2, and x_3. Draw such a slice for the indifference curve that contains the consumer's optimal bundle A on the budget from part (a).

c.   Now suppose that Gucci manages to raise the prestige value of its products and thus x_3 that comes with the purchase of Gucci products. For now, suppose they do this without changing p_1. This implies you will shift to a different two-dimensional slice of your three-dimensional indifference map. Illustrate the new two-dimensional indifference curve that contains A. Is the new *MRS* at A greater or smaller in absolute value than it was before?

d.*   Would the consumer consume more or fewer Gucci products after the increase in prestige value?

e.   Now suppose that Gucci manages to convince consumers that Gucci products become more desirable the more expensive they are. Put differently, the prestige value x_3 is linked to p_1, the price of the Gucci products. On a new graph, illustrate the change in the consumer's budget as a result of an increase in p_1.

    f.   Suppose that our consumer increases her purchases of Gucci products as a result of the increase in the price p_1. Illustrate two indifference curves: one that gives rise to the original optimum A and another that gives rise to the new optimum C. Can these indifference curves cross?

    g.   Explain why, even though the behavior is consistent with what we would expect if Gucci products were a Giffen good, Gucci products are not a Giffen good in this case.

    h.   In a footnote in the chapter, we defined the following: A good is a *Veblen good* if *preferences* for the good change as price increases, with this change in preferences possibly leading to an increase in consumption as price increases. Are Gucci products a Veblen good in this exercise?

B. Consider the same definition of x_1, x_2, and x_3 as in part A. Suppose that the tastes for our consumer can be captured by the utility function $u(x_1, x_2, x_3) = \alpha x_3^2 \ln x_1 + x_2$.

    a.   Set up the consumer's utility maximization problem, keeping in mind that x_3 is not a choice variable.

    b.   Solve for the optimal consumption of x_1 (which will be a function of the prestige value x_3).

    c.   Is x_1 normal or inferior? Is it Giffen?

    d.   Now suppose that prestige value is a function of p_1. In particular, suppose that $x_3 = p_1$. Substitute this into your solution for x_1. Will consumption increase or decrease as p_1 increases?

    e.   How would you explain that x_1 is not a Giffen good despite the fact that its consumption increases as p_1 goes up?

7.10   **Policy Application:** *Tax Deductibility and Tax Credits*: In end-of-chapter exercise 2.17, you were asked to think about the impact of tax deductibility on a household's budget constraint.

A. Suppose we begin in a system in which mortgage interest is not deductible and then tax deductibility of mortgage interest is introduced.

    a.   Using a graph (as you did in exercise 2.17) with "square feet of housing" on the horizontal axis and "dollars of other consumption" on the vertical, illustrate the direction of the substitution effect.

    b.   What kind of good would housing have to be in order for the household to consume less housing as a result of the introduction of the tax deductibility program?

    c.   On a graph that contains both the before and after deductibility budget constraints, how would you illustrate the amount of subsidy the government provides to this household?

    d.   Suppose the government provided the same amount of money to this household but did so instead by simply giving it to the household as cash back on its taxes (without linking it to housing consumption). Will the household buy more or less housing?

    e.   Will the household be better or worse off?

    f.   Do your answers to (d) and (e) depend on whether housing is normal, regular inferior, or Giffen?

    g.   Under tax deductibility, will the household spend more on other consumption before or after tax deductibility is introduced? Discuss your answer in terms of income and substitution effects and assume that "other goods" is a normal good.

    h.   If you observed that a household consumes more in "other goods" after the introduction of tax deductibility, could that household's tastes be quasilinear in housing? Could they be homothetic?

B.**Households typically spend about a quarter of their after-tax income I on housing. Let x_1 denote square feet of housing and let x_2 denote other consumption.

    a.   If we represent a household's tastes with the Cobb–Douglas function $u(x_1, x_2) = x_1^\alpha x_2^{(1-\alpha)}$, what should α be?

    b.   Using your answer about the value of α, and letting the price per square foot of housing be denoted as p_1, derive the optimal level of housing consumption (in terms of I, p_1, and t) under a tax deductibility program that implicitly subsidizes a fraction t of a household's housing purchase.

    c.   What happens to housing consumption and other good consumption under tax deductibility as a household's tax bracket (i.e., their tax rate t) increases?

    d.   Determine the portion of changed housing consumption that is due to the income effect and the portion that is due to the substitution effect.

    e.   Calculate the amount of money the government is spending on subsidizing this household's mortgage interest.

    f.   Now suppose that, instead of a deductibility program, the government simply gives the amount you calculated in (e) to the household as cash. Calculate the amount of housing now consumed and compare it with your answer under tax deductibility.

7.11   **Policy Application:** *Substitution Effects and Social Security Cost of Living Adjustments*: In end-of-chapter exercise 6.16, you investigated the government's practice for adjusting Social Security income for seniors by ensuring that the average senior can always afford to buy some average bundle of goods that remains fixed. To simplify the analysis, let us again assume that the average senior consumes only two different goods.

A.   Suppose that last year our average senior optimized at the average bundle A identified by the government, and begin by assuming that we denominate the units of x_1 and x_2 such that last year $p_1 = p_2 = 1$.

    a.   Suppose that p_1 increases. On a graph with x_1 on the horizontal and x_2 on the vertical axis, illustrate the compensated budget and the bundle B that, given your senior's tastes, would keep the senior just as well off at the new price.

    b.   In your graph, compare the level of income the senior requires to get to bundle B with the income required to get him back to bundle A.

    c.   What determines the size of the difference in the income necessary to keep the senior just as well off when the price of good 1 increases as opposed to the income necessary for the senior still to be able to afford bundle A?

    d.   Under what condition will the two forms of compensation be identical?

    e.   You should recognize the move from A to B as a pure substitution effect as we have defined it in this chapter. Often this substitution effect is referred to as the *Hicksian substitution effect*, defined as the change in behavior when opportunity costs change but the consumer receives sufficient compensation *to remain just as happy*. Let B' be the consumption bundle the average senior would choose when compensated so as to be able to afford the original bundle A. The movement from A to B' is often called the *Slutsky substitution effect*, defined as the change in behavior when opportunity costs change but the consumer receives sufficient compensation *to be able to afford to stay at the original consumption bundle*. *True or False*: The government could save money by using Hicksian rather than Slutsky substitution principles to determine appropriate cost of living adjustments for Social Security recipients.

    f.   *True or False*: Hicksian and Slutsky compensation get closer to one another the smaller the price changes.

B.   Now suppose that the tastes of the average senior can be captured by the Cobb–Douglas utility function $u(x_1, x_2) = x_1 x_2$, where x_2 is a composite good (with price by definition equal to $p_2 = 1$). Suppose the average senior currently receives Social Security income I (and no other income) and with it purchases bundle (x_1^A, x_2^A).

    a.   Determine (x_1^A, x_2^A) in terms of I and p_1.

    b.   Suppose that p_1 is currently $1 and I is currently $2,000. Then p_1 increases to $2. How much will the government increase the Social Security check given how it is actually calculating cost of living adjustments? How will this change the senior's behavior?

    c.   How much would the government increase the Social Security check if it used Hicksian rather than Slutsky compensation? How would the senior's behavior change?

    d.*   Can you demonstrate mathematically that Hicksian and Slutsky compensation converge to one another as the price change gets small and diverge from each other as the price change gets large?

    e.   We know that Cobb–Douglas utility functions are part of the CES family of utility functions, with the elasticity of substitution equal to 1. Without doing any math, can you estimate the range of how much Slutsky compensation can exceed Hicksian compensation with tastes that lie within the CES family? (*Hint*: Consider the extreme cases of elasticities of subsitution.)

7.12† **Policy Application:** *Fuel Efficiency, Gasoline Consumption, and Gas Prices*: Policy makers frequently search for ways to reduce consumption of gasoline. One straightforward option is to tax gasoline, thereby encouraging consumers to drive less and switch to more fuel-efficient cars.

A.* Suppose that you have tastes for driving and for other consumption, and assume throughout that your tastes are homothetic.

    a.   On a graph with monthly miles driven on the horizontal and "monthly other consumption" on the vertical axis, illustrate two budget lines: one in which you own a gas-guzzling car, which has a low monthly payment (that has to be made regardless of how much the car is driven) but high gasoline use per mile; the other in which you own a fuel-efficient car, which has a high monthly payment that has to be made regardless of how much the car is driven but uses less gasoline per mile. Draw this in such a way that it is possible for you to be indifferent between owning the gas-guzzling and the fuel-efficient car.

    b.   Suppose you are indeed indifferent. With which car will you drive more?

    c.   Can you tell with which car you will use more gasoline? What does your answer depend on?

    d.   Now suppose that the government imposes a tax on gasoline, and this doubles the opportunity cost of driving both types of cars. If you were indifferent before the tax was imposed, can you now say whether you will definitively buy one car or the other (assuming you waited to buy a car until after the tax is imposed)? What does your answer depend on? (*Hint*: It may be helpful to consider the extreme cases of perfect substitutes and perfect complements before deriving your general conclusion to this question.)

    e.   The empirical evidence suggests that consumers shift toward more fuel-efficient cars when the price of gasoline increases. *True or False*: This would tend to suggest that driving and other good consumption are relatively complementary.

    f.   Suppose an increase in gasoline taxes raises the opportunity cost of driving a mile with a fuel-efficient car to the opportunity cost of driving a gas guzzler *before* the tax increase. Will someone who was previously indifferent between a fuel-efficient and a gas-guzzling car now drive more or less in a fuel-efficient car than he did in a gas guzzler prior to the tax increase? (Continue with the assumption that tastes are homothetic.)

B. Suppose your tastes were captured by the utility function $u(x_1, x_2) = x_1^{0.5} x_2^{0.5}$, where x_1 stands for miles driven and x_2 stands for other consumption. Suppose you have $600 per month of discretionary income to devote to your transportation and other consumption needs and that the monthly payment on a gas guzzler is $200. Furthermore, suppose the initial price of gasoline is $0.10 per mile in the fuel-efficient car and $0.20 per mile in the gas guzzler.

    a.   Calculate the number of monthly miles driven if you own a gas guzzler.

    b.   Suppose you are indifferent between the gas guzzler and the fuel-efficient car. How much must the monthly payment for the fuel-efficient car be?

    c.   Now suppose that the government imposes a tax on gasoline that doubles the price per mile driven of each of the two cars. Calculate the optimal consumption bundle under each of the new budget constraints.

    d.   Do you now switch to the fuel-efficient car?

    e.   Consider the utility function you have worked with so far as a special case of the CES family $u(x_1, x_2) = (0.5x_1^{-\rho} + 0.5x_2^{-\rho})^{-1/\rho}$. Given what you concluded in A(d) of this question, how would your answer to B(d) change as ρ changes?

7.13 **Policy Application:** *Public Housing and Housing Subsidies*: In exercise 2.14, you considered two different public housing programs in parts A(a) and (b), one where a family is simply offered a particular apartment for a below-market rent and another where the government provides a housing price subsidy that the family can use anywhere in the private rental market.

A. Suppose we consider a family that earns $1,500 per month and either pays $0.50 per square foot in monthly rent for an apartment in the private market or accepts a 1,500-square-foot government public housing unit at the government's price of $500 per month.

    a.   On a graph with square feet of housing and "dollars of other consumption," illustrate two cases where the family accepts the public housing unit, one where this leads them to consume less housing than they otherwise would and another where it leads them to consume more housing than they otherwise would.

b. If we use the members of the household's own judgment about the household's well-being, is it always the case that the option of public housing makes the participating households better off?

c. If the policy goal behind public housing is to increase the housing consumption of the poor, is it more or less likely to succeed the less substitutable housing and other goods are?

d. What is the government's opportunity cost of owning a public housing unit of 1,500 square feet? How much does it therefore cost the government to provide the public housing unit to this family?

e. Now consider instead a housing price subsidy under which the government tells qualified families that it will pay some fraction of their rental bills in the private housing market. If this rental subsidy is set so as to make the household just as well off as it was under public housing, will it lead to more or less consumption of housing than if the household chooses public housing?

f. Will giving such a rental subsidy cost more or less than providing the public housing unit? What does your answer depend on?

g. Suppose instead that the government simply gave cash to the household. If it gave sufficient cash to make the household as well off as it is under the public housing program, would it cost the government more or less than $250? Can you tell whether under such a subsidy the household consumes more or less housing than under public housing?

B. Suppose that household tastes over square feet of housing (x_1) and dollars of other consumption (x_2) can be represented by $u(x_1, x_2) = \alpha \ln x_1 + (1 - \alpha) \ln x_2$.

a. Suppose that empirical studies show that we spend about a quarter of our income on housing. What does that imply about α?

b. Consider a family with income of $1,500 per month facing a per square foot price of $p_1 = 0.50$. For what value of α would the family not change its housing consumption when offered the 1,500-square-foot public housing apartment for $500?

c. Suppose that this family has α as derived in B(a). How much of a rental price subsidy would the government have to give to this family in order to make it as well off as the family is with the public housing unit?

d. How much housing will the family rent under this subsidy? How much will it cost the government to provide this subsidy?

e. Suppose the government instead gave the family cash (without changing the price of housing). How much cash would it have to give the family in order to make it as happy?

f. If you are a policy maker whose aim is to make this household happier at the least cost to the taxpayer, how would you rank the three policies? What if your goal was to increase the household's housing consumption?

Wealth and Substitution Effects in Labor and Capital Markets

In Chapter 7, we introduced the concepts of income and substitution effects in models where income enters the consumer's optimization problem exogenously; i.e., where consumers are choosing to allocate a fixed money budget across consumption goods.[1] We now turn to cases where income is endogenous; i.e., where our consumption is funded not by a fixed money budget but rather by the sale of something that we own. This can happen in consumer goods markets if we own one of the goods that is part of the analysis. More importantly, as we illustrated in some detail in Chapter 3, it happens in labor markets where we sell our leisure time and in capital markets where we buy and sell financial assets as we plan for the future.

The analysis in this chapter in one sense is no different than that in Chapter 7. We will again look at changes in behavior that result from changes in opportunity costs (i.e., substitution effects) and changes that happen as a result of "real income" having changed. At the same time, some important differences emerge, differences in the analysis that are in the end quite intuitive. When the price of gasoline increases, we would always expect the substitution effect to indicate that we will consume less gasoline. But whether the price increase makes us better off (and thus increases our "real" income) or whether it makes us worse off (and thus decreases our "real" income) depends on whether we own an oil well. Most of us don't, and thus most of us become worse off when gasoline prices increase. In the language of Chapter 7, we experience a negative income effect (that will lead to a further decrease in our gasoline consumption if gasoline is a normal good). But if you own an oil well, the increase in gasoline prices probably makes you better off because what you own just became more valuable. Thus, you would experience a positive income effect, one that will lead you to increase your consumption of gasoline if gasoline is a normal good.

8A   Wealth Effects, Substitution Effects, and Endowments

In Chapter 7, we adopted the term "income effect" for the impact of parallel shifts in budget constraints on consumption behavior. Such effects occurred either because the fixed money income within the models we dealt with changed directly or because the "real" income changed as a result of a price change. We now turn to the case where the change in the price of a good has a

---

[1]Chapters 2 through 7 are required reading for this chapter.

different effect because it changes the value of something we own and thus alters our budget constraint differently than it did in Chapter 7. We will call the new effect that emerges a "wealth effect" because it captures the change in wealth a consumer experiences when prices change and thus affects the value of what the consumer owns. As we will see, the substitution effect remains exactly the same for endogenous choice sets, but the wealth effect can point in different directions depending on what the consumer owns.

8A.1 An Increase in the Price of Gasoline for George Exxon

When we investigated in Chapter 7 the ways in which my consumption of gasoline might change when the price of gasoline increases, two effects emerged: the substitution effect due to the change in the opportunity cost of gasoline, and the income effect due to the fact that my real income (as measured by the indifference curve I am able to reach) declined as a result of the price change. The situation is somewhat different for my imaginary friend George Exxon. George and I are very different in many ways, not the least of which is that he owns large reserves of gasoline. In our following example, we suppose that he finances his entire consumption by selling gasoline. Unlike my income, which we modeled as exogenous, George's income is then more appropriately modeled as arising *endogenously* from the value of his gasoline "endowment."

8A.1.1 The Substitution Effect Revisited   Graph 8.1a then illustrates the impact of an increase in the price of gasoline on George's budget. Point *E* is George's endowment point—the amount of gasoline he owns and can choose to consume if he would like to consume only gasoline and no other consumption. While an increase in the price of gasoline caused my budget constraint to rotate *inward* in Chapter 7, the same increase in price causes George's budget to rotate *outward* around his endowment point until its slope reflects the new opportunity cost. Point *A* denotes George's optimal consumption bundle prior to the increase in price.

We can now divide George's behavioral response to the price change into two distinct parts just as we did for my response in the previous chapter. First, we ask how his behavior would have changed if his real income (as measured by the indifference curve he can reach) were held constant and he only faced a change in the opportunity cost reflected in the steeper slope. Graph 8.1b thus introduces the (green) compensated budget that has the new (magenta) budget's slope and is

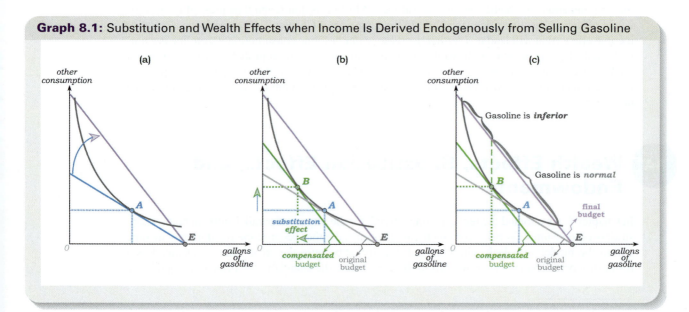

Graph 8.1: Substitution and Wealth Effects when Income Is Derived Endogenously from Selling Gasoline

tangent to the original indifference curve (reflecting no change in real welfare.) As always, the resulting substitution effect from bundle *A* to bundle *B* indicates that George would reduce his consumption of the good that has become relatively more expensive (gasoline) in favor of other goods that have become relatively cheaper.

8A.1.2 The Wealth Effect, and How an Increase in the Price of one Good Can *Look Like* a Decrease in the Price of Another

In Graph 8.1c, we then determine where on the final (magenta) budget line George might consume relative to point *B*. Notice as always that the (green) compensated budget and the final budget are parallel; the only difference is that, in going from the compensated to the final budget, George receives additional income to spend. Unlike me, George is *richer* as a result of the price change because the value of his wealth goes up with an increased price of gasoline. If gasoline is a normal good, an increase in income from the compensated to the final budget should imply an increased level of gasoline consumption, causing the new optimal point on the final budget to lie to the right of *B* and possibly to the right of *A*. If, on the other hand, gasoline is an inferior good, George will consume less gasoline as his income rises from the compensated budget, implying a new optimal point to the left of point *B*. Since we are dealing with a model in which income is determined *endogenously*, we will call the change from *B* to the new optimal point a *wealth effect*. This is analogous to the *income effect* we identified in the previous section in a model with fixed exogenous income.

When the price of gasoline changed for me, we concluded in Chapter 7 that we can be certain that my consumption of gasoline would decline (from the original bundle *A* to the final bundle *C*) so long as gasoline was a normal good, but we could not be certain whether it would increase or decline if gasoline was an inferior good because of offsetting income and substitution effects. The opposite is true in George Exxon's case: We know his consumption of gasoline will definitely decline if gasoline is an inferior good for him, but we cannot be sure whether his gasoline consumption will increase or decrease if gasoline is a normal good. Why the difference between what we can predict for George here and what we could predict for me in Chapter 7?

Despite the fact that both George and I experienced the same increase in price, our situations are vastly different because his income is derived from gasoline and mine is not. In fact, if you knew nothing about the particulars of this example and you simply looked at a change in choice sets like the one graphed in Graph 8.1a, you would conclude that this individual had experienced *a decrease in the price of "other consumption"* (the good on the vertical axis), not an increase in the price of gasoline. That is in fact precisely how we could treat the price change George experienced, and George would feel exactly the same about such a price change (with his income being exogenous) as the one we have analyzed (with income endogenous) because it would alter his budget constraint in exactly the same way. This is also why we cannot identify in George's case any behavior that would lead us to conclude that gasoline is a Giffen good for him, because for him, it is effectively the price of "other consumption" that has changed. In order to identify gasoline as a Giffen good, we would have to observe an effective change in the price of gasoline, as we did for me in Chapter 7.

Since George's situation is equivalent to a decrease in the price of other goods (with exogenous income), illustrate where on his final budget George would consume if other goods are normal, regular inferior, and Giffen.

Exercise 8A.1

8A.2 A Change in Wages

Our analysis of wealth and substitution effects can now be extended from models of consumer choices in goods markets to models of worker choices in labor markets. Recall from Chapter 3 that choices by workers can be analyzed as choices between leisure and consumption. Leisure time is an endowment, much like gasoline was for George Exxon. Its value in the labor market depends on the wage that a worker can earn, which in turn determines how easily a worker can turn leisure hours into goods consumption. As in Chapter 3, we will model these choices by putting hours of leisure on the horizontal axis and dollars of consumption on the vertical.

8A.2.1 Do Higher Wages Make Us Work More or Less?

Suppose we return to an example from Chapter 3 where you were choosing how many hours you will work per week, and suppose again that you have a total of 60 leisure hours per week that you could devote to work. Suppose further that you have no other income, which implies that you will not be able to consume anything (other than leisure) if you do not work. This implies that your endowment point E in Graph 8.2a falls at 60 hours of leisure and no consumption. Furthermore, suppose again that you could earn a wage of $20 per hour, and suppose that you have decided it is optimal for you to work for 40 hours per week under these circumstances. This choice is illustrated as bundle A in Graph 8.2a, a point characterized by 20 hours of leisure, which leaves 40 hours for work given that the total number of hours you can allocate between work and leisure is 60.

Now suppose you are offered a wage increase of $5 per hour, which rotates your budget out through point E as shown in the Graph 8.2a. Will you work more or less as you face this new choice set? On the one hand, you might think that work is really paying off now and therefore you should work more. On the other hand, you are making more every hour you work, so why not work a little less and still end up with more consumption than before? It is not immediately clear which way you might decide to go. *This is because you are most likely facing competing wealth and substitution effects.*

To see this, we begin again by drawing your compensated budget, the budget that keeps your real income the same but has the final budget line's opportunity cost (or slope). This is graphed (in green) in Graph 8.2b and, as always, it indicates that you would consume more of the good that has become relatively cheaper (consumption) and less of the good that has become relatively more expensive (leisure) if all you faced was the new opportunity costs with no change in real income. This is the pure substitution effect, the effect that makes you think that "work is really paying off now and you should thus work more."

In Graph 8.2c, we then isolate the wealth effect, which is the impact of going from bundle B under the (green) compensated budget to the (magenta) final budget. The graph looks identical to George Exxon's Graph 8.1c, and the conclusion is the same for you as a worker as it was for

Graph 8.2: Substitution and Wealth Effects in Leisure/Consumption Choices

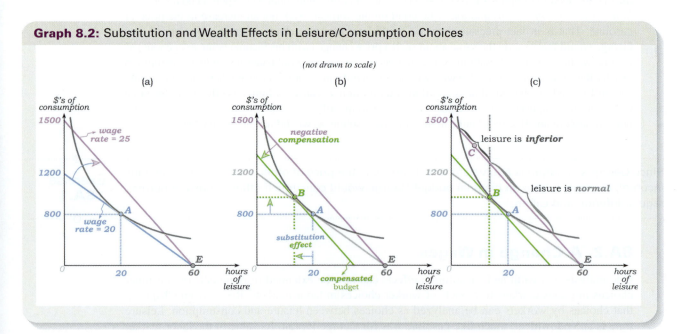

George as an owner of gasoline. If leisure is an inferior good, the wealth effect will reinforce the substitution effect as you consume less leisure when your real income goes up. You would then end at a point like *C* to the left of *B*. It seems, however, unlikely that leisure is really an inferior good; it is probably a normal good for most of us. This implies that you would consume more of it as your real income rises from the compensated budget to the final budget, formalizing our intuition that "you are making more every hour, so why not work a little less."

If leisure is a normal good, it is therefore not clear whether an increase in your wage will cause you to work more or less. The substitution and wealth effects point in opposite directions, leaving us guessing unless we know more about your tastes. Suppose, for instance, that the only way you can enjoy your leisure time is by paying to go parasailing. If your tastes are really that extreme, there is little substitutability in your tastes between leisure hours and consumption—you *must* consume (parasail) in order to enjoy leisure. Your indifference curves would then be those of perfect complements. By doing the following exercise, you can then see that this would eliminate the substitution effect and leave you only with the wealth effect, leading to an unambiguous conclusion that you will work less (consume more leisure) as your wage goes up.

Illustrate substitution and wealth effects; i.e., the initial bundle, the bundle that incorporates a substitution effect from a wage increase, and the final bundle chosen under the wage increase, assuming that your tastes for consumption and leisure are properly modeled as perfect complements.

Exercise 8A.2

On the other hand, suppose that your tastes were properly modeled as quasilinear in leisure. In that case, the only effect of a wage change on your labor supply decision is the substitution effect (because quasilinear tastes do not have income or wealth effects). This would imply that an increase in your wage would cause you to unambiguously work more (consume less leisure).

Replicate the previous exercise under the assumption that your tastes are quasilinear in leisure.

Exercise 8A.3

As it turns out, labor economists who estimate the relationship between labor supply from a worker and that worker's wage have concluded that an average worker responds to wage increases by working more when his or her current wage is relatively low. As wages increase, however, the same average worker eventually will tend to work less as wages increase even further.

Illustrate a set of indifference curves that gives rise to the kind of response to wage changes as described.

Exercise 8A.4

8A.2.2 Taxes on Labor Income Politicians like to convince us that their policies help everyone and hurt no one. Those who propose to cut taxes on wages, for instance, often argue that such tax cuts will not only benefit workers but will also cause an *increase* in government revenue as workers work harder when they get to keep more of their money and thus will pay more in overall taxes even though the tax rates have come down.[2] Is this true?

Our analysis of your labor/leisure choices suggests that it all depends on what we assume about wealth and substitution effects. For workers, a cut in wage taxes is equivalent to an increase in their take-home wages. Thus, our analysis of a wage increase in the previous section applies directly. We have concluded that substitution effects will cause workers to increase their hours when wages go up,

---

[2]The argument made in favor of this position is actually a little more complicated. It generally assumes not only that workers will work more as their after-tax wage increases but also that this will have an effect on the macroeconomy that will cause the economy to grow faster. Since the second part of the argument falls in the area of macroeconomics, we will not treat it here explicitly.

while wealth effects are likely to cause workers to decrease their work hours as their wages rise (assuming that leisure is a normal good). Thus, the politician is more likely to be correct the larger the substitution effect and the smaller the wealth effect. Put differently, politicians who make this argument are either dishonest or they believe one (or both) of the following: (1) that our tastes allow for a great deal of substitutability between consumption and leisure, implying that our indifference curves are relatively flat making substitution effects large, and/or (2) that leisure is an inferior good, which causes wealth effects for wage changes to point in the same direction as the substitution effect. Were they to believe that leisure and consumption are very complementary and that leisure is a normal good, their prediction would almost certainly be false.

Even the combination of substitution and wealth effects leading workers to work more when their after-tax wage increases, however, is not sufficient for the government to increase tax revenue by cutting taxes. To see this, we first have to see how to illustrate tax revenues from a single worker in our leisure/consumption graphs. Consider Graph 8.3 that contains one budget line without taxes and another that shows an effective lower wage because of a wage tax. The worker's optimal choice under the tax is then determined on his after-tax (blue) budget constraint and is denoted by A in the graph. From point A, we can read off directly how much in "dollars of other goods" this worker is consuming after paying taxes: $800. Since the only difference between the two budget lines in Graph 8.3 is the wage tax, we also know that this same worker could have consumed $1,300 in other goods had he not had to pay any taxes and had he worked exactly the same number of hours (40) as he does at bundle A. Thus, the vertical difference between bundle A and bundle "a" is how much the government collected in tax revenue: $500. Note that this does *not* mean that we are assuming this worker would have consumed bundle "a" in the absence of taxes. We are simply using bundle "a" to identify this worker's before-tax income when he is choosing bundle A on his after-tax budget line.

Now consider the case where the government can choose between two different wage taxes, say one of 20% and another of 40%. Suppose further that we are considering two different workers for whom wealth and substitution effects combine to increase the amount they work when they face a higher after-tax wage. Graphs 8.4a and 8.4b then illustrate two different possibilities,

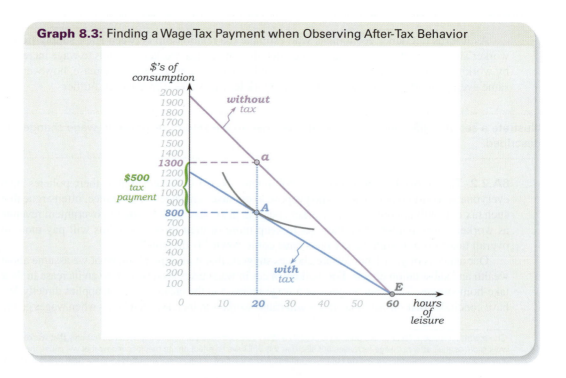

Graph 8.3: Finding a Wage Tax Payment when Observing After-Tax Behavior

Graph 8.4: Tax Revenue Can Rise (a) or Fall (b) with an Increase in Tax Rates

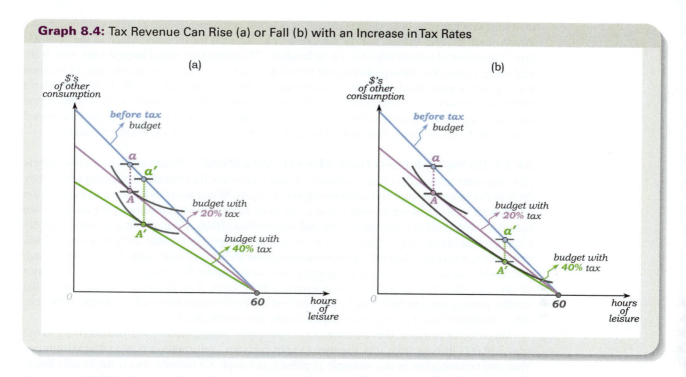

with *A* representing the workers' optimal bundles at a 20% wage tax and *A'* representing their optimal bundles at the 40% wage tax. In the first graph, a decrease in the wage tax from 40% to 20% results in a decrease in tax revenue from the worker (because the distance between *A* and *a* is smaller than the distance between *A'* and *a'*), while in the second graph it results in an increase in tax revenues (because the distance between *A* and *a* is larger than the distance between *A'* and *a'*). We will return to the question of when exactly we might expect the former scenario to hold and when we might expect the latter to hold in later chapters.

For now, it is worth noting one final lesson from understanding substitution and wealth effects in a labor market that is taxed. While it may not always be the case that tax revenues will rise as tax rates fall or vice versa, the presence of substitution effects in labor markets does suggest that we may overpredict how much tax revenues we are likely to get from a given tax increase. This is because substitution effects in the labor market suggest that workers will work less as wage taxes increase. Unless leisure is not only a normal good but also produces a wealth effect sufficiently large to outweigh the substitution effect, workers will work less as taxes increase, which means they will pay less in additional tax revenues than we would predict if we did not take this "substitution" change in behavior into account.

True or False: For decreases in wage taxes, substitution effects put positive pressure on tax revenues while wealth effects typically put negative pressure on revenues.

Exercise
8A.5

8A.3 A Change in (Real) Interest Rates

Just as our choices over consumption and leisure are impacted by the size of the wage we can earn, so our financial planning for the future is impacted by the size of the financial return we receive from saving or the financial cost we incur from borrowing—the real interest rate. We illustrated this in Chapter 3 in simple models in which we saw how our choice sets between current and future consumption change as interest rates change. It is worth emphasizing that, as microeconomists, we always mean the *real* interest rate, or the interest rate adjusted for inflation. Much of the "CNBC-type" discussion of interest rates by talking heads on TV relates to *nominal* interest rates, which are real interest rates plus the expected rate of inflation. You have (or will) discuss the role of nominal interest rates in more detail in your macroeconomics courses, which emphasize the Federal Reserve's ability to affect *nominal* interest rates through monetary policy. Most macroeconomists would agree that monetary policy, at least in the long run, cannot set *real* interest rates, which are determined through the forces of supply and demand in capital markets (as we will see in later chapters).

8A.3.1 Do Higher Interest Rates Make Us Save More?

Wealth and substitution effects play important roles in the choices consumers make regarding their financial planning just as they do in their choices in labor and consumer goods markets. When we asked in the previous section whether an increase in wages will cause us to work more, we were unsure of the answer even before we discussed the relevant wealth and substitution effects. Similarly, it is not immediately clear whether higher interest rates lead to increased savings. On the one hand, you might think that saving now really pays off and thus you might be inclined to save more. On the other hand, you might decide that, since you are getting more in the future for every dollar you put in your savings account, you might as well consume a little more now knowing that the somewhat smaller savings account will grow faster. The first temptation is an informal statement of the substitution effect while the latter gives expression to the wealth effect.

Suppose, for instance, that we return to our example (from Chapter 3) of you choosing to use your $10,000 income from this summer to plan for your consumption now and next summer. Your endowment point in this example is point E in Graph 8.5 because this is the bundle that is always available for you regardless of what the interest rate is. Suppose then that your initial planning is based on the fact that you know you can earn interest at an annual rate of 10%, and suppose that you have concluded that you will consume $5,000 this summer and $5,500 next summer as indicated by point A in Graph 8.5a. Then suppose that you just found a new investment opportunity that will get you a 20% annual return, yielding the larger (magenta) choice set with different opportunity costs depicted in the same graph.

Graph 8.5: The Impact of an Increase in Interest Rates on Savers

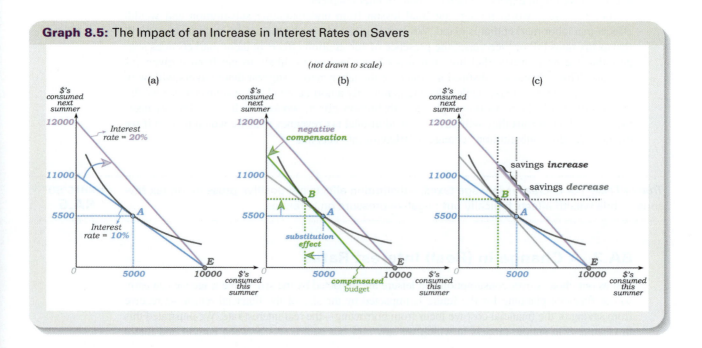

Graph 8.5b then begins by isolating the substitution effect with the hypothetical (green) compensated budget tangent to your original optimal indifference curve. As always, the movement from *A* to *B* results in less consumption of the good that has become relatively more expensive (consumption this summer) and more of the good that has become relatively cheaper (consumption next summer). This substitution effect suggests you will tend to save more because consuming now as opposed to later has just become more expensive.

Whether or how much your wealth effect will counteract this substitution effect then depends on whether consumption this summer and consumption next summer are normal or inferior goods. It seems reasonable to assume that consumption is in fact a normal good in both periods, and so we will restrict ourselves to this assumption in this example. Starting from the optimal point *B* on the compensated budget, we would then expect you to increase your consumption this and next summer as your income rises from the compensated (green) to the final (magenta) budget in Graph 8.5c.

Your new optimal bundle will therefore likely lie somewhere in the darkened segment of your final budget line. All bundles on this segment have higher consumption next summer than the $5,500 you had originally planned, but this does not mean that the increase in the interest rate has led you to save more (in the sense of putting more money into your savings account now). Notice that the darkened segment of the final budget contains some bundles with more consumption *this* summer than at point *A* and some with less. Since your savings—the amount you put away in a savings account—is simply the amount you do not consume *this summer*, we cannot tell whether you will *save* more or less, only that you will consume more next summer. Your increased consumption next summer *may* happen despite lower saving this summer simply because each dollar in your savings account now earns more than before. This happens if your optimal bundle lies on the darkened segment to the right of point *A*. It may also be the case that higher consumption next summer happens in part because of additional savings this summer, if your optimal bundle ends up to the left of point *A*.

Without more information about your tastes, we cannot tell precisely which of these scenarios will come to be. All we know for now is that the more substitutable consumption is across time periods (i.e., the flatter are your indifference curves), the more likely it is that the substitution effect will outweigh the wealth effect and lead to an increase in savings. The opposite is true as consumption becomes more complementary across periods.

Illustrate that your savings will decline with an increase in the interest rate if consumption this summer and next summer are perfect complements.

Exercise 8A.6

8A.3.2 Will an Increase in the (Real) Interest Rate Make Us Borrow Less?
The previous example assumed that your endowment point was consumption this summer because that was the point that you could consume regardless of what happened to interest rates. Suppose instead, however, that your endowment point is future consumption. This would occur if you chose not to work this summer but instead borrowed against income that the bank knows you will earn next summer. In Chapter 3, we used the example of your employer assuring the bank that you will earn $11,000 next summer, which causes the bank to be willing to lend you as much as $10,000 for current consumption when the interest rate is 10%. Thus, the beginning (blue) choice set in this example looks identical to the beginning choice set in the previous example (Graph 8.5a) except that the endowment point occurs on the vertical rather than the horizontal axis. Given that the choice sets are the same across the two examples, the optimal bundle *A* for you is the same.

Now suppose that the interest rate again rises to 20%. While your original (blue) budget is the same across the two examples, your final (magenta) budget after the interest rate change is quite different and is illustrated in Graph 8.6a. In both cases, the slope becomes steeper to reflect the new interest rate, but now it rotates through the new endowment point. Because the slope is the same

Graph 8.6: The Impact of an Increase in Interest Rates on Borrowers

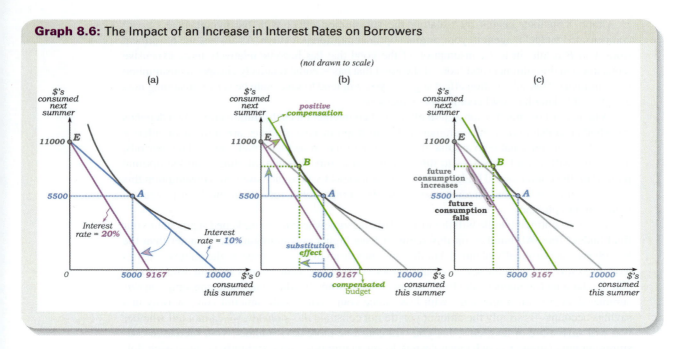

across the two examples, however, the (green) compensated budget will also be the same since it simply assumes a constant real income under the new interest rate. The difference is that the compensated budget now requires *positive* compensation while previously it required *negative* compensation. This should make intuitive sense: If the interest rate rises and you are a saver, you are made better off and thus need less money to be just as well off as you were originally. If, on the other hand, you are a borrower, then an increase in the interest rate makes you worse off, requiring that I give you additional money to make you just as well off as you were originally.

Since your indifference curve that contains point *A* is the same across the two examples and since the original as well as the compensated budgets are the same, it follows that point *B* will be the same. Thus, you again experience a substitution effect that tells us you should consume less now and more later when the interest rate (and thus the cost of consuming now) goes up. The wealth effect, however, now points in the opposite direction from the previous example because, in going from the (green) compensated to the final (magenta) budget, you now lose rather than gain income. If consumption in both periods is a normal good (as we have assumed throughout), you will consume less than at point *B* during both summers as your income falls in going from the compensated to the final budget. In Graph 8.6c, you will therefore end up somewhere on the highlighted portion of the final budget line.

Since both wealth and substitution effects suggest that you will consume less this summer, we can then unambiguously conclude that your consumption this summer will decline, and you will thus unambiguously borrow less. But on the vertical axis of Graph 8.6c, the substitution and wealth effects point in opposite directions, leaving us uncertain about whether consumption next summer will be higher or lower as the interest rate for borrowing increases. Whether you consume more or less next summer thus depends on the degree to which consumption this period and next period are substitutable, and thus whether or not the substitution effect outweighs the wealth effect.

Exercise 8A.7

Illustrate how consumption next summer changes with an increase in the interest rate if consumption this summer and next summer are perfect complements (and all your income occurs next summer).

8A.3.3 "Neither a Borrower nor a Lender Be ..."   Shakespeare advises us in *Hamlet:*
"Neither a borrower nor a Lender be ... " Suppose you had taken this advice to heart and had
decided to arrange your work plans over the next two summers so that you can consume $5,000
this summer and $5,500 next summer without borrowing or saving (which is equivalent to lend-
ing to the bank). Let's suppose that you accomplished this by finding an employer (as you did in
Chapter 3) who is willing to employ you half-time this summer for $5,000 and half-time again
next summer for $5,500. This implies that we have a new endowment bundle in our model, which
is labeled *E* in Graph 8.7. This is your new endowment bundle because it is the bundle that you
can consume regardless of what happens to the interest rate.

   Suppose again that the interest rate was 10% when you made your work arrangements and
then changed to 20% afterward. Your initial (blue) choice set then again looks precisely the way
it did in the previous two examples, but your final budget constraint now rotates through your
new endowment point. Can we tell whether this change in the interest rate will cause you to violate Shakespeare's advice?

   This is one case where it is in fact not necessary to decompose the behavioral change into
substitution and wealth effects. We can simply observe in Graph 8.7a that all the bundles in the
final choice set that lie above your original indifference curve (and are thus preferred) lie to the
left of bundle *E*. Your new optimal choice therefore involves less consumption this period, and
thus some savings. The change in the interest rate thus causes you to violate Shakespeare's advice
by opening a savings account and becoming a "lender" of money to the bank. To see why this is
the case, notice in Graph 8.7b that the (green) compensated budget is quite close to the final
(magenta) budget, implying that almost the entire behavioral change is a substitution effect. The
small wealth effect that remains is not sufficient to overcome the substitution effect *regardless*
of how much substitutability is built into the indifference map. (In fact, the entire effect is a
"Slutsky" substitution effect as discussed in Section 7A.2.4.)

Demonstrate that the only way you will not violate Shakespeare's advice as the interest rate goes   **Exercise**
up is if consumption this summer and next are perfect complements.   **8A.8**

Graph 8.7: From No Saving to Positive Saving when Interest Rates Rise

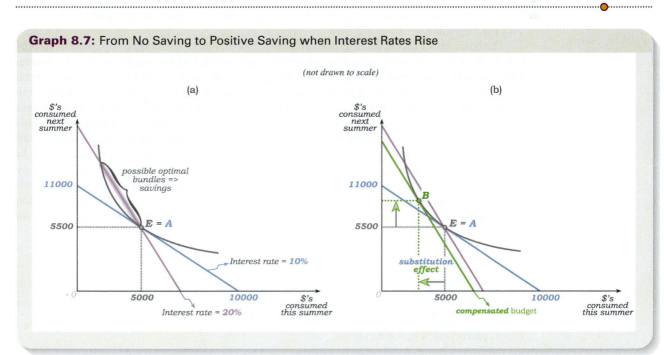

Exercise 8A.9

Illustrate that (unless consumption this summer and consumption next summer are perfect complements) you will violate the first part of Shakespeare's advice—not to be a borrower—if the interest rate fell instead of rose.

8A.3.4 A Policy Example: IRAs, 401ks, and Retirement Policy

For a number of years now, the federal government in the United States has attempted to increase personal savings by providing tax incentives for investing in retirement accounts known as IRAs and 401k plans.[3] Essentially, these accounts work as follows: For each dollar that an individual puts into the account, the individual does not have to pay taxes until he or she takes it out of the account after retirement. This allows individuals to earn interest on money that they otherwise would have had to send to the government as tax payments. For instance, if I earn $1,000 and I face a tax rate of 30%, I typically have to pay $300 in federal income tax, which leaves me with $700 that I can invest for the future. If, on the other hand, I invest the same earnings in an IRA or a 401k account, I can invest the whole $1,000 and defer paying taxes until the future. Suppose the rate of return on my investments is 10% per year. Under the non–tax-deferred savings plan, I will have earned $70 in interest on my $700 investment after 1 year, which is income that I again have to pay 30% tax on. This leaves me $749 in my investment account: my original $700 plus the interest left over after I pay 30% tax on my $70 interest income. Under the tax-deferred savings plan, on the other hand, I will have earned $100 in interest on my $1,000 investment, leaving me with $1,100 that I have to pay taxes on only if I take it out of the account. If I do choose to take it out and consume it after 1 year, I have to pay my usual 30% tax on the whole amount ($1,100), leaving me with $770 rather than $749. While this difference may seem small after 1 year, it accumulates quickly over a longer period. For instance, if I compared the same non–tax-deferred savings plan with the tax-deferred plan over a 30-year period, I would have $12,215 available to me under the latter plan and only $7,423 under the former—a difference of $4,792! You can convince yourself of this by setting up a simple spreadsheet in which you keep track of interest and tax payments over the 30 years.

The basic effect that federal retirement policy has on individual choice sets, then, is to provide individuals with a higher rate of return through deferral of tax payments into the future. This is exactly equivalent to an increase in the interest rate we face, and we have already seen that it is not clear whether such a change in circumstances leads to an increase or a decrease in savings (when savings is defined as current income minus current consumption). To the extent that the aim of federal retirement policy is to increase the amount that we put away for savings today, the policy may therefore not be successful since we know that higher interest rates may lead to less savings. At the same time, to the extent to which federal retirement policy aims to increase our consumption possibilities when we retire, our model would predict that the policy will succeed. After all, we ended Section 8A.3.1 with the conclusion that, while we cannot tell whether savings today will increase when real interest rates rise, we *can* tell that consumption in the future will rise (whether because of higher returns on less savings or higher returns on more savings).

---

[3]IRAs, or Individual Retirement Accounts, are accounts that are set up by individuals. 401k plans, on the other hand, are set up by for-profit corporations who may invest on behalf of their employees and/or give employees opportunities to invest in the account themselves. Non-profit corporations and organizations may set up similar accounts for their employees; these are called 403b accounts rather than 401k accounts. If you have done end-of-chapter exercise 3.7, you will have already done a simpler version of what is done in this section.

8B Constrained Optimization with Wealth Effects

Fundamentally, the mathematics underlying models with endowments is not different from what we already introduced for models with exogenous fixed incomes. Again, we will treat consumers (or workers or investors) as maximizing utility subject to a budget constraint, but now the "income" term in the budget constraint will be replaced with a "wealth" term that depends on the prices in the economy. We illustrated in detail how such budgets can be written in Chapter 3, and we will now merge that treatment of budgets into our mathematical optimization framework.

8B.1 George Exxon and the Price of Gasoline

In Section 8A.1, we introduced my friend George Exxon, who owns large reserves of gasoline and derives all his income from selling gasoline. Letting the number of gallons of gasoline he gets out of the ground each week be denoted by e_1, George's weekly income then depends on the price p_1 he can get for his gasoline. Thus, his weekly income from gasoline extractions is p_1e_1. How much gasoline he is able to extract per week, e_1, is of course different from how much gasoline he *consumes* each week. Letting gallons of weekly gasoline consumption be denoted by x_1 and "Dollars of Other Weekly Consumption" be represented by x_2, we can then write George's weekly budget constraint as

$$p_1x_1 + x_2 = p_1e_1 \text{ or } x_2 = p_1(e_1 - x_1). \tag{8.1}$$

Notice that the second formulation in (8.1) simply has non-gasoline consumption on the left-hand side and income from the sale of gasoline that is not directly consumed by George on the right-hand side. This budget constraint is just the more general budget constraint we derived in Chapter 3 for someone with endowment income,

$$p_1x_1 + p_2x_2 = p_1e_1 + p_2e_2, \tag{8.2}$$

except that the price of "Dollars of Other Weekly Consumption" in our example is by definition equal to 1 (thus making $p_2 = 1$) and George has no endowment of "Dollars of Other Weekly Consumption" (thus making $e_2 = 0$).

Now suppose George's tastes could be captured by the Cobb–Douglas utility function $u(x_1,x_2) = x_1^{0.1}x_2^{0.9}$. Then we can write his constrained optimization problem as

$$\max_{x_1,x_2} u(x_1,x_2) = x_1^{0.1}x_2^{0.9} \text{ subject to } x_2 = p_1(e_1 - x_1). \tag{8.3}$$

The Lagrange function used to calculate the optimal consumption bundle is then

$$\mathcal{L}(x_1,x_2,\lambda) = x_1^{0.1}x_2^{0.9} + \lambda(x_2 - p_1(e_1 - x_1)). \tag{8.4}$$

Solving this in the usual way, we get

$$x_1 = 0.1e_1 \text{ and } x_2 = 0.9(p_1e_1). \tag{8.5}$$

Suppose, for instance, that the price of gasoline p_1 is $2 per gallon and that George's weekly gallons of gasoline extraction e_1 is 1,000. Then expression (8.5) tells us that George's optimal consumption bundle is $x_1 = 100$ and $x_2 = 1,800$; i.e., 100 gallons of gasoline and $1,800 in other consumption.

With the numbers in the previous paragraph, George's income is $2,000 per week. Verify that you would get the same optimal consumption bundle if you modeled this as a constrained optimization problem in which income was exogenously set at $2,000 per week.

Exercise 8B.1

8B.1.1 Revisiting the Substitution Effect

Now suppose an oil shortage caused the price of gasoline to rise to $4 per gallon. We can immediately see from expression (8.5) what the impact on George's consumption will be: He will continue to consume 100 gallons of gasoline each week, but his other consumption will rise from $1,800 to $3,600. This is illustrated in Graph 8.8a, where bundle A represents George's initial optimal consumption under the $2 gasoline price and bundle C represents his new optimal consumption under the $4 price.

This change in behavior from A to C, however, bundles the substitution and wealth effects. In order to isolate the substitution effect from the wealth effect, we first need to calculate how George's consumption would have changed when the price of gasoline increases from $2 to $4 per gallon if we took enough money away from George to make him just as well off as he was originally; i.e., if only his opportunity costs change without a change in real income as measured by his indifference curve.

To find this effect, we defined an expenditure minimization problem in Chapter 7, one that aims to find the lowest possible exogenous money income that George could have at the new $4 price of gasoline and still reach the same indifference curve that contained his original optimal bundle (100, 1800). By plugging this optimal bundle into the utility function $u(x_1, x_2) = x_1^{0.1} x_2^{0.9}$, we find that this indifference curve was assigned a value of approximately 1,348 by George's utility function. We can therefore state the expenditure minimization problem used to identify the substitution effect as

$$\min_{x_1, x_2} E = 4x_1 + x_2 \text{ subject to } x_1^{0.1} x_2^{0.9} = 1,348. \tag{8.6}$$

Notice that this problem makes no reference to George's endowment because that endowment is irrelevant for finding the substitution effect. Put differently, once we know the indifference curve we would like George to reach, identifying the level of exogenous income that it would take to get there has nothing to do with how much stuff George actually owns.

Graph 8.8: Wealth and Substitution Effects for George Exxon: From Math Back to Graphs

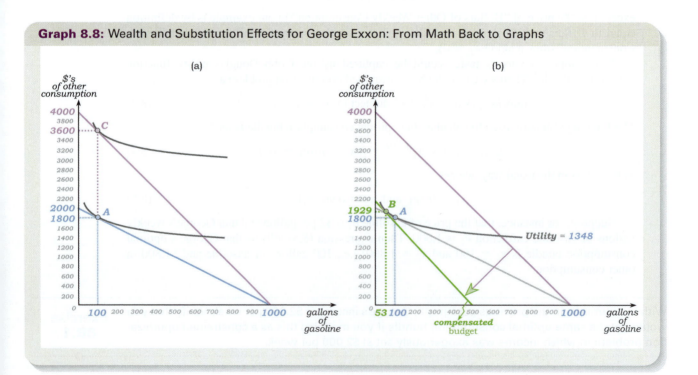

Setting up the Lagrange function and solving for x_1 and x_2, you can verify for yourself that

$$x_1 = 53.59 \text{ and } x_2 = 1,929.19, \tag{8.7}$$

implying that George would consume 53.59 gallons of gasoline and $1,929.19 of other consumption each week.

Verify that the solutions in the previous paragraph are correct.

Exercise
8B.2

Graph 8.8b illustrates what we have just done. Beginning with the optimal bundle A before the price change, we have identified the smallest possible new (green) budget (or what we have called the compensated budget in Chapter 7) that incorporates the new price of gasoline and will still permit George to reach the indifference curve that contains bundle A. The impact of the change in opportunity costs is thus isolated from the impact of the change in wealth that arises from the price change, giving rise to a pure substitution effect. As always, this substitution effect, the change in behavior that takes George from bundle A to bundle B, tells us that the change in opportunity costs causes our consumer to reduce his consumption of the good that has become relatively more expensive (gasoline) in favor of increased consumption of the good that has become relatively cheaper (other consumption).

How much (negative) compensation was required to get George to be equally well off when the price of gasoline increased?

Exercise
8B.3

8B.1.2 The Wealth Effect Given that we have already identified George's final consumption bundle at the $4 gasoline price (and graphed it in Graph 8.8a), we could now combine Graphs 8.8a and 8.8b to illustrate the initial substitution effect (from A to B) and the remaining wealth effect (from B to C). The wealth effect is similar to the income effect in Chapter 7 in that it represents a change of behavior between two budget constraints that exhibit the same opportunity costs (i.e., the same slopes). But the direction of the wealth effect for this example is opposite to the direction of an income effect; as the price of gasoline increased, George's real income went *up* rather than down.

As a result, we computed that George will consume 100 gallons of gasoline at bundle C rather than 53.59 gallons at bundle B. As George's real income goes up (without a change in opportunity costs), George therefore consumes more gasoline. Thus gasoline is a normal good in this example. Similarly, George's consumption of other goods rises from $1,929.19 to $3,600 for the same increase in real income, implying "other goods" are normal goods as well. Of course, from the work we have done in our analysis of Cobb–Douglas utility functions, we already know that goods that are modeled using this function are normal goods.

8B.2 A Change in Wages

In Section 8A.2, we saw that the example of George Exxon is in no fundamental way different from the example of you facing an increase in your wage rate in the labor market while choosing how many hours to devote to leisure as opposed to labor. This analytic similarity holds because, in both examples, income is derived from the sale of a good that we value. In the case of George Exxon, he owns gasoline that he also consumes. Similarly, in the case of you choosing how much to work, you own leisure that you consume just as George consumes gasoline. When the price of gasoline is $2 per gallon, the opportunity cost of consuming one more gallon of gasoline is $2 of other consumption.

When your hourly wage rate is $20, the opportunity cost of consuming one more hour of leisure is similarly $20 of other consumption. The price of gasoline in the George Exxon example is thus exactly analogous to the wage rate in the example of you choosing how much to work.

8B.2.1 Will an Increase in Your Wage Make You Work More or Less?

We have already demonstrated in Graphs 8.2a through (c) how substitution and wealth effects work intuitively in the labor market. Since these effects are exactly analogous to the effects already identified mathematically in the George Exxon example, we have in a sense already demonstrated how one would use our mathematical framework to solve for substitution and wealth effects when wages change in the labor market. We begin by setting up the constrained optimization problem. Suppose again that you have 60 hours per week you can devote to leisure or labor, that your wage rate is w, and that your tastes over consumption (c) and leisure (ℓ) can be represented by a utility function $u(c, \ell)$. The mathematical formulation of the problem is then

$$\max_{c, \ell} u(c, \ell) \text{ subject to } c = w(60 - \ell). \tag{8.8}$$

The budget constraint in expression (8.8) thus simply states that your total spending on consumption goods c is equal to the wage rate w times the hours you work; i.e., the hours you do not take as leisure $(60 - \ell)$.

Suppose that your tastes over consumption and leisure can be modeled using the quasilinear utility function

$$u(c, \ell) = c + 400 \ln \ell. \tag{8.9}$$

Using our usual Lagrange Method, we can compute that the optimal bundle of consumption and leisure is then

$$c = 60w - 400 \text{ and } \ell = \frac{400}{w}. \tag{8.10}$$

Thus, we know that the optimal bundle A in Graph 8.9a when the wage rate is $20 per hour is $800 of weekly consumption and 20 hours of leisure, or, equivalently, 40 hours of labor. If the

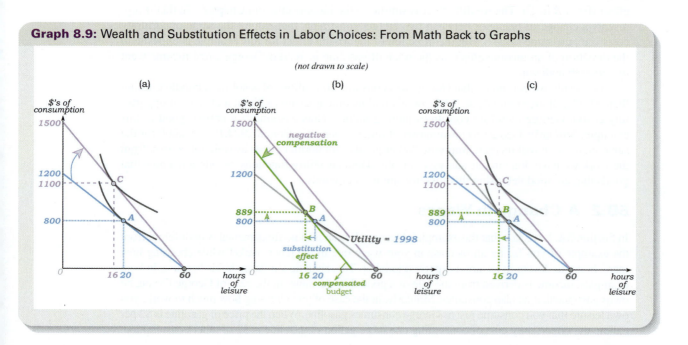

Graph 8.9: Wealth and Substitution Effects in Labor Choices: From Math Back to Graphs

wage rate rises to $25 per hours, your optimal leisure consumption declines to 16 hours (implying 44 hours of work) while other good consumption increases to $1,100 per week. For tastes that can be represented by the utility function (8.9), an increase in the wage thus causes you to work more.

To see why, we can again decompose the total move from A to C in Graph 8.9a into substitution and wealth effects. To find the substitution effect, we follow our previous method by specifying a minimization problem that seeks to find the minimum expenditure necessary to achieve the utility level originally attained at A when the wage rate is $25 (rather than the initial $20) per hour. Plugging the leisure and consumption values at bundle A into the utility function in (8.9), we get a utility level of approximately 1,998. The relevant minimization problem is then

$$\min_{c,\ell} E = c + 25\ell \text{ subject to } c + 400 \ln \ell = 1,998. \tag{8.11}$$

Notice that we are treating the goods "consumption" and "leisure" as we have always treated goods in such minimization problems: We are simply asking how much we would have to spend on these two goods at the market prices in order to reach the indifference curve that contains bundle A. The market price of "consumption" is $1 while the market price of leisure is the market wage (or $25 in our example).

Solve the problem defined in equation (8.11).

Exercise
8B.4

The solution to this minimization problem is $c \approx 889$ and $\ell = 16$. Thus, at bundle B in Graph 8.9b, you would consume 16 hours of leisure per week, or, put differently, you would work for 44 hours. Just as our graphical approach suggested in Section 8A.2, the substitution effect from an increase in the wage leads to less consumption of leisure because consuming leisure has just become more expensive.

Putting panels (a) and (b) of Graph 8.9 together in panel (c), we can depict graphically what we have just calculated mathematically: In terms of its effect on leisure (and labor supply), an increase in your wage from $20 per hour to $25 per hour results in a 4 hour substitution effect away from leisure (and toward labor), and no wealth effect. This arises, of course, from the fact that the underlying utility function (8.9) is quasilinear in leisure, which eliminates income or wealth effects in the consumption of leisure and leaves us only with the substitution effect. For utility functions that model leisure as normal, the wealth effect will point in the opposite direction of the substitution effect (much as was the case in the example of the price of gasoline changing for George Exxon), making it ambiguous as to whether or not you will work more when your wage goes up.

Suppose your tastes were more accurately modeled by the Cobb–Douglas utility function $u(c,\ell) = c^{0.5}\ell^{0.5}$. Determine wealth and substitution effects and graph your answer.

Exercise
8B.5

8B.2.2 Tax Rates and Tax Revenues
We raised in Section 8A.2.2 the issue of whether the labor supply response to a wage tax would ever be sufficiently strong to ensure that tax revenues would actually increase as taxes on wages declined. The intuition of the graphical approach (in Graph 8.4) clearly tells us that, in order for tax revenues to increase with a decrease in the tax rate, it must at a minimum be the case that either leisure is an inferior good or the substitution effect outweighs the wealth effect if leisure is a normal good. These are, however, only necessary conditions; that is, we showed in Graph 8.4 that it is logically possible for work effort to increase as labor taxes decrease but for tax revenue nevertheless to fall. Continuing with our example can shed some further clarity on this.

In particular, suppose that your tastes can be described as in equation (8.9), that you are earning a $25 per hour pre-tax wage, and that you have up to 60 hours per week you can devote to working. Now suppose that you find out that the government will reduce your take home pay by

t percent through a wage tax. Then your effective wage becomes $25(1 − t)$ instead of $25. Replacing w by $25(1 − t)$ in expression (8.10), we then get that your optimal leisure choice is

$$\ell = \frac{400}{25(1 - t)} \tag{8.12}$$

with your optimal labor choice $(60 − \ell)$. Government tax revenue from this worker is simply the tax rate t times the worker's before tax income, $25(60 − \ell)$. Table 8.1 then calculates the number of hours you would work (column 2) under different tax rates (column 1), as well as the tax revenue the government receives (column 3). In addition, column 4 of the table indicates the tax revenue one would expect to receive if you were not going to adjust your labor supply to changing tax rates (and thus always worked 44 hours per week regardless of the tax rate), and column 5 indicates the difference in the predicted tax revenue from the economic analysis of column 3 as opposed to the more naive analysis of column 4.

By specifying your tastes as quasilinear in leisure, we have eliminated any wealth effect from the analysis and thus are left with a pure substitution effect. As a result, your work effort (represented by the number of hours you work) declines as your after-tax wage declines (see column 2). This results in tax revenues initially increasing with the tax rate because, although you work less as the tax increases, each dollar you earn is taxed more heavily. Eventually, however, your work hours decline sufficiently such that tax revenues decline when the tax rate increases further. This happens in the table when the tax rate increases from 50% to 60%, but if you were to fill in tax rates in

Table 8.1: $u(c,\ell) = c + 400 \ln \ell$, $L = 60$, $w = 25$

Impact of Wage Tax on Labor Supply and Tax Revenue				
Tax Rate t	Labor Hours $(60 - \ell)$	Tax Revenue $t(25(60 - \ell))$	Tax Rev. w/o Subst. Effect	Difference
0.00	44.00	$0.00	$0.00	$−0.00
0.05	43.16	$53.95	$55.00	$−1.05
0.10	42.22	$105.56	$110.00	$−4.44
0.15	41.18	$154.41	$165.00	$−10.59
0.20	40.00	$200.00	$220.00	$−20.00
0.25	38.67	$241.67	$275.00	$−33.33
0.30	37.14	$278.57	$330.00	$−51.43
0.35	35.38	$309.62	$385.00	$−75.38
0.40	33.33	$333.33	$440.00	$−106.67
0.45	30.91	$347.73	$495.00	$−147.27
0.50	28.00	$350.00	$550.00	$−200.00
0.55	24.44	$336.11	$605.00	$−268.89
0.60	20.00	$300.00	$660.00	$−360.00
0.65	14.29	$232.14	$715.00	$−482.86
0.70	6.67	$116.67	$770.00	$−653.33
0.75	0.00	$0.00	$825.00	$−825.00

between those in the table, the actual turning point occurs at a tax rate of 48.4%. Thus, if the government were to try to maximize tax revenue from you, it would levy a 48.4% tax rate. Notice, however, that well before this turning point, the tax revenue actually collected (column 3) diverges rather dramatically from the tax revenue predicted without taking the substitution effect into account.

One further thing to note is that were you to solve the maximization problem the usual way when the tax rate equals 75%, your solution would actually indicate that you will take 64 hours of leisure and −$25 of consumption. Since such a bundle is not possible—you cannot, after all, take more than 60 hours of leisure or consume negative amounts of goods—you know immediately that the actual solution to the problem is a corner solution where you simply choose to consume nothing and only take leisure. This, in fact, happens for any tax rate higher than 73.34%.

The relationship between tax rates and tax revenue that emerges from this table is plotted in Graph 8.10a with the tax rate on the horizontal and tax revenue on the vertical. It is a common shape economists expect and is known as the *Laffer Curve*.[4] Simply put, it illustrates that when tax rates become sufficiently high, eventually tax revenue will drop as individuals choose to avoid the tax by consuming less of the taxed good. Furthermore, as illustrated in Graph 8.10b, this Laffer Curve relationship suggests that the difference between actual tax revenues and those predicted without taking changes in economic behavior into account widens as the tax rate increases.

What is the equation for the Laffer Curve in Graph 8.10?

Exercise 8B.6*

Solve for the peak of the Laffer Curve (using the equation you derived in the previous exercise) and verify that it occurs at a tax rate of approximately 48.4%.

Exercise 8B.7**

Graph 8.10: The Laffer Curve: Substitution Effects when Tastes Are Quasilinear in Leisure

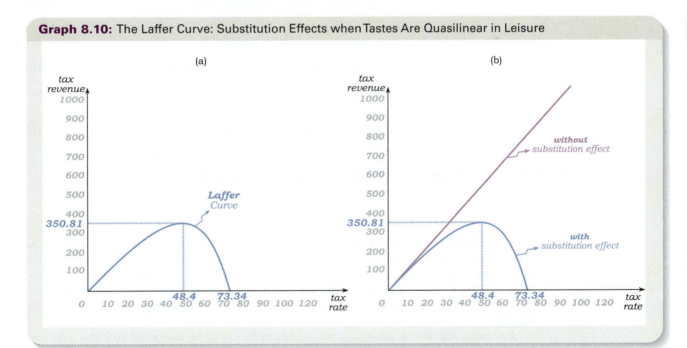

---

[4]This "curve" is named after Arthur Laffer (1940–), an economist who was influential in policy circles during the 1970s and 1980s. Laffer himself admits that the basic idea is not original to him. Jude Wanniski, a writer for the *Wall Street Journal*, appears to be the first to name the curve after Laffer following a 1974 meeting during which Laffer reportedly sketched the curve on a napkin with Wanniski and Dick Cheney, then a deputy assistant to the president.

8B.3 A Change in (Real) Interest Rates

In Section 8A.3, we turned next to the question of how changes in real interest rates affect your consumption, savings and borrowing decisions under different scenarios. We returned in this discussion to an example first raised in Chapter 3, an example in which you chose how to allocate income between consumption this summer and next summer. While the mathematics developed in Chapter 3 allows us to model more complicated savings and borrowing decisions, we will illustrate the basics of substitution and wealth effects in regard to savings and borrowing with just this two-period example. In such a setting, we had denoted the amount of income (or wealth) that you receive this summer as e_1 and the amount of income (or wealth) your receive next summer as e_2. We then wrote your "intertemporal" (or across-time) budget constraint as

$$(1 + r)c_1 + c_2 = (1 + r)e_1 + e_2, \tag{8.13}$$

where c_1 stands for consumption this summer, c_2 for consumption next summer, and r for the real interest rate.

8B.3.1 Do Higher Interest Rates Make Us Save More?   We begin again with the example of you earning $10,000 this summer and choosing how much of it to allocate between consumption this summer and consumption next summer. In Graph 8.5, we illustrated that, without knowing more about tastes, it is unclear whether an increase in the real interest rate from 10% to 20% will cause you to save more or less this summer, although we concluded that you will unambiguously choose to consume more next summer.

In terms of equation (8.13), $e_1 = 10,000$ and $e_2 = 0$ in this example. Thus, equation (8.13) can be written as

$$(1 + r)c_1 + c_2 = 10,000(1 + r). \tag{8.14}$$

Now suppose that your tastes can be described by the Cobb–Douglas utility function $u(c_1,c_2) = c_1^{0.5}c_2^{0.5}$. Then your utility maximization problem is

$$\max_{c_1,c_2} c_1^{0.5}c_2^{0.5} \text{ subject to } (1 + r)c_1 + c_2 = 10,000(1 + r). \tag{8.15}$$

Solving this in the usual way, we get that your optimal consumption levels this summer and next summer are

$$c_1 = 5,000 \text{ and } c_2 = 5,000(1 + r). \tag{8.16}$$

Exercise 8B.8   Verify that this is indeed the solution to the problem defined in (8.15).

Thus, at the initial interest rate of 10% you will choose to consume $5,000 this summer and $5,500 next summer, and at the new interest rate of 20% you will continue to consume $5,000 this summer but will raise your consumption next summer to $6,000. This corresponds to our usual bundles A and C, and we can already tell that the substitution and wealth effects must have exactly offset one another since your savings—the amount you chose not to consume this summer—remained constant.

For many interesting policy questions, however, it will be important to know just how large the substitution effect was. We can calculate this effect using our expenditure minimization approach in which we simply ask how much we would have to give to you (instead of the $10,000 you are making this summer) in order for you to remain just as happy under the new interest rate as you were under the old interest rate when you made $10,000 this summer. Plugging bundle A—$5,000 this summer and $5,500 next summer—into the utility function, we can calculate that you attained a utility level of 5,244 as measured by the Cobb–Douglas function used to represent your tastes. Thus, to calculate our usual bundle B, we need to solve

$$\min_{c_1, c_2} E = (1 + r)c_1 + c_2 \text{ subject to } c_1^{0.5}c_2^{0.5} = 5{,}244, \tag{8.17}$$

with r set to the new interest rate 0.2. Solving this in the usual way, we get that

$$c_1 = 4{,}787.14 \text{ and } c_2 = 5{,}744.56. \tag{8.18}$$

Verify that this is indeed the solution to the problem defined in (8.17).

Exercise 8B.9

Thus, the substitution effect in this example indicates that you would increase your savings this summer by $212.86 if you only faced a change in opportunity costs without a change in real income (as indicated by your initial indifference curve), but this temptation to increase your savings is undone by the wealth effect, by the fact that you are richer as a result of the increase in the interest rate. As we will show in more detail in Chapter 9, this result (that substitution and wealth effects will exactly offset each other) is a special case for Cobb–Douglas tastes and is due to the built-in assumption of an elasticity of substitution equal to 1. In the more general class of constant elasticity of substitution (CES) utility functions (of which the Cobb–Douglas function is a special case), we will see that the substitution effect is outweighed by the wealth effect when the elasticity of substitution falls below 1, leading to a decline in savings with an increase in the real interest rate. Analogously, the wealth effect is outweighed by the substitution effect when the elasticity of substitution is greater than 1, leading to an increase in savings when the real interest rate increases.

Using a set of graphs similar to those depicted in Graph 8.5, label the bundles that we have just calculated.

Exercise 8B.10

8B.3.2 Will an Increase in the (Real) Interest Rate Make Us Borrow Less? We next considered in Section 8A.3.2 how the situation changes if, instead of having a $10,000 income this summer and no income next summer, you had an $11,000 income next summer and no income this summer. In this case, you would have to borrow against your future income in order to consume anything this summer, and the example is structured in such a way that your intertemporal budget across the two summers is the same as it was in our previous example when the interest rate is 10%. The intuition for how your choices are now affected as the interest rate rises to 20% was illustrated in Graph 8.6 where we showed that, while such an increase in the interest rate will certainly make you consume less (and thus borrow less) this summer because of the increased cost of borrowing, it is unclear without knowing more about your tastes whether you will consume more or less next summer.

Suppose, then, that your tastes can continue to be described by the Cobb–Douglas utility function $u(c_1, c_2) = c_1^{0.5}c_2^{0.5}$. The only change in the mathematical analysis from the previous section is then that your budget constraint differs. In terms of equation (8.13), we now have $e_1 = 0$ and $e_2 = 11{,}000$, giving us a new budget constraint of

$$(1 + r)c_1 + c_2 = 11{,}000. \tag{8.19}$$

You should now be able to verify, following exactly the same steps as in the previous section, that bundles A and B will be exactly the same as before (as already indicated by the intuition emerging from Graphs 8.5 and 8.6), but that the new bundle C will be

$$c_1 = 4{,}583.33 \text{ and } c_2 = 5{,}500. \tag{8.20}$$

Thus, for tastes described by the Cobb–Douglas function in this example, your consumption next summer will remain unchanged from your original consumption, indicating that substitution and wealth effects again exactly offset one another on that dimension. But since your consumption this summer declines from \$5,000 at bundle A to \$4,583.33 at bundle C, you have chosen to borrow \$416.67 less as a result of the increase in the interest rate (with \$212.86 of that accounted for by the substitution effect and the remainder by the wealth effect.)

**Exercise
8B.11**

Illustrate what we have just calculated in a graph.

**Exercise
8B.12**

We calculated that consumption next summer is unchanged as the interest rate rises when tastes can be represented by the Cobb–Douglas utility function we used. This is because this function assumes an elasticity of substitution of 1. How would this result change if the elasticity of substitution is larger or smaller than 1?

8B.3.3 "Neither a Borrower nor a Lender Be..." Finally, we considered in Section 8A.3.3 the case where you had put in place plans to earn \$5,000 this summer and \$5,500 next summer knowing that, at an interest rate of 10%, this implied that you would have to neither borrow nor lend in order to consume your optimal bundle: \$5,000 this summer and \$5,500 next summer. Continuing with the Cobb–Douglas tastes from the previous section, you can verify that this is indeed the optimal bundle given a summer income of \$5,000 this summer and \$5,500 next summer by simply recognizing that we are once again solving the exact same maximization problem, except that now $e_1 = 5{,}000$ and $e_2 = 5{,}500$. Thus, the budget constraint (8.13) simply becomes

$$(1 + r)c_1 + c_2 = 5{,}000(1 + r) + 5{,}500. \tag{8.21}$$

Going through the same steps as before, you will find that your new optimal bundle when the interest rate rises to 20% is

$$c_1 = 4{,}791.67 \text{ and } c_2 = 5{,}750, \tag{8.22}$$

with the substitution effect accounting for most of the change in behavior (as suggested by the intuition gained from Graphs 8.7a and 8.7b in Section 8A.3.3). Specifically, point B, the bundle representing just the substitution effect, is

$$c_1 = 4{,}787.14 \text{ and } c_2 = 5{,}744.56, \tag{8.23}$$

just a few dollars off the bundle C of expression (8.22).

**Exercise
8B.13**

Verify that (8.22) and (8.23) are correct.

CONCLUSION

In this chapter, we have extended our treatment of income and substitution effects for models in which incomes are exogenous to those where incomes arise endogenously. In the process, we have defined a new "wealth effect" that arises as prices of endowments change and thus alter a person's wealth. This is particularly important as we discuss the application of our basic model to labor/leisure choices and financial planning choices.

   We are now ready to proceed to an analysis of demand in consumer goods markets (and supply in labor and capital markets). While these concepts are often discussed early in an economics course, they actually derive directly from the optimizing behavior of consumers (and workers and financial planners). Understanding the engine of optimization that underlies demand and supply will become quite important as we apply some of the tools we have learned to real-world issues. Chapter 10 then follows with a discussion of consumer welfare and deadweight loss, and it is in this discussion that we will see further evidence of the importance of understanding the difference between substitution and income (or wealth) effects.

END-OF-CHAPTER EXERCISES

8.1† As we have suggested in the chapter, it is often important to know whether workers will work more or less as their wage increases.

A. In each of the following cases, can you tell whether a worker will work more or less as his or her wage increases?

   a. The worker's tastes over consumption and leisure are quasilinear in leisure.

   b. The worker's tastes over consumption and leisure are homothetic.

   c. Leisure is a luxury good.

   d. Leisure is a necessity.

   e. The worker's tastes over consumption and leisure are quasilinear in consumption.

B. Suppose that tastes take the form $u(c, \ell) = (0.5c^{-\rho} + 0.5\ell^{-\rho})^{-1/\rho}$.

   a. Set up the worker's optimization problem assuming his or her leisure endowment is L and his or her wage is w.

   b. Set up the Lagrange function corresponding to your maximization problem.

   c. Solve for the optimal amount of leisure.

   d.* Does leisure consumption increase or decrease as w increases? What does your answer depend on?

   e. Relate this to what you know about substitution and wealth effects in this type of problem.

8.2 Suppose that an invention has just resulted in everyone being able to cut their sleep requirement by 10 hours per week, thus providing an increase in their weekly leisure endowment.

A. For each of the following cases, can you tell whether a worker will work more or less?

   a. The worker's tastes over consumption and leisure are quasilinear in leisure.

   b. The worker's tastes over consumption and leisure are homothetic.

   c. Leisure is a luxury good.

   d. Leisure is a necessity.

   e. The worker's tastes over consumption and leisure are quasilinear in consumption.

   f. Do any of your answers have anything to do with how substitutable consumption and leisure are? Why or why not?

---

*conceptually challenging
**computationally challenging
†solutions in Study Guide

B. Suppose that a worker's tastes for consumption c and leisure ℓ can be represented by the utility function $u(c, \ell) = c^{\alpha}\ell^{(1-\alpha)}$.

    a.   Write down the worker's constrained optimization problem and the Lagrange function used to solve it, using w to denote the wage and L to denote the leisure endowment.

    b.   Solve the problem to determine leisure consumption as a function of w, α, and L. Will an increase in L result in more or less leisure consumption?

    c.   Can you determine whether an increase in leisure will cause the worker to work more?

    d.   Repeat parts (a) through (c) using the utility function $u(c, \ell) = c + \alpha \ln \ell$ instead.

    e.** Can you show that if tastes can be represented by the CES utility function $u(c, \ell) = (\alpha c^{-\rho}(1 - \alpha)\ell^{-\rho})^{-1/\rho}$, the worker will choose to consume more leisure as well as work more when there is an increase in the leisure endowment L? (Warning: The algebra gets a little messy. You can occasionally check your answers by substituting $\rho = 0$ and checking that this matches what you know to be true for the Cobb–Douglas function $u(c, \ell) = c^{0.5}\ell^{0.5}$.)

8.3   In this chapter, we began by considering the impact of an increase in the price of gasoline on George Exxon, who owns a lot of gasoline. In this exercise, assume that George and I have exactly the same tastes and that gasoline and other goods are both normal goods for us.

    A.   Unlike George Exxon, however, I do not own gasoline but simply survive on an exogenous income provided to me by my generous wife.

        a.   With gallons of gasoline on the horizontal and dollars of other goods on the vertical, graph the income and substitution effects from an increase in the price of gasoline.

        b.   Suppose George (who derives all his income from his gasoline endowment) had exactly the same budget before the price increase that I did. On the same graph, illustrate how his budget changes as a result of the price increase.

        c.   Given that we have the same tastes, can you say whether the substitution effect is larger or smaller for George than it is for me?

        d.   Why do we call the change in behavior that is not due to the substitution effect an *income effect* in my case but a *wealth effect* in George Exxon's case?

    B.   In Section 8B.1, we assumed the utility function $u(x_1, x_2) = x_1^{0.1}x_2^{0.9}$ for George Exxon as well as an endowment of gasoline of 1,000 gallons. We then calculated substitution and wealth effects when the price of gasoline goes up from \$2 to \$4 per gallon.

        a.   Now consider me with my exogenous income $I = 2,000$ instead. Using the same utility function we used for George in the text, derive my optimal consumption of gasoline as a function of p_1 (the price of gasoline) and p_2 (the price of other goods).

        b.   Do I consume the same as George Exxon prior to the price increase? What about after the price increase?

        c.   Calculate the substitution effect from this price change and compare it with what we calculated in the text for George Exxon.

        d.   Suppose instead that the price of "other goods" fell from \$1 to \$0.50 while the price of gasoline stayed the same at \$2. What is the change in my consumption of gasoline due to the substitution effect? Compare this with the substitution effect you calculated for the gasoline price increase.

        e.   How much gasoline do I end up consuming? Why is this identical to the change in consumption we derived in the text for George when the price of gasoline increases? Explain intuitively using a graph.

8.4   **Business Application:** *Merchandise Exchange Policies*: Suppose you have \$200 in discretionary income that you would like to spend on ABBA CDs and Arnold Schwarzenegger DVDs.

    A.   On the way to work, you take your \$200 to Wal-Mart and buy 10 CDs and 5 DVDs at CD prices of \$10 and DVD prices of \$20.

        a.   On a graph with DVDs on the horizontal and CDs on the vertical, illustrate your budget constraint and your optimal bundle A.

        b.   On the way home, you drive by the the same Wal-Mart and see a big sign: "All DVDs half price—only \$10!" You also know that Wal-Mart has a policy of either refunding returned items for the price at which they were bought if you provide them with a Wal-Mart receipt or, alternatively, giving store credit in the amount that those items are currently priced in the store if you have lost your receipt.[5] What is the most in store credit that you could get?

    c.   Given that you have no more cash and only a bag full of DVDs and CDs, will you go back into Wal-Mart and shop?

    d.   On the way to work the next day, you again drive by Wal-Mart and notice that the sale sign is gone. You assume that the price of DVDs is back to $20 (with the price of CDs still unchanged), and you notice you forgot to take your bag of CDs and DVDs out of the car last night and have it sitting right there next to you. Will you go back into Wal-Mart (assuming you still have an empty wallet)?

    e.   Finally, you pass Wal-Mart again on the way home and this time see a sign: "Big Sale—All CDs only $5, All DVDs only $10!" With your bag of merchandise still sitting next to you and your wallet still empty, will you go back into Wal-Mart?

    f.   If you are the manager of a Wal-Mart with this "store credit" policy, would you tend to favor—all else being equal—across the board price changes or sales on selective items?

    g.   *True or False*: If it were not for substitution effects, stores would not have to worry about people gaming their "store credit" policies as you did in this example.

B. Suppose your tastes for DVDs (x_1) and CDs (x_2) can be characterized by the utility function $u(x_1, x_2) = x_1^{0.5} x_2^{0.5}$. Throughout, assume that it is possible to buy fractions of CDs and DVDs.

    a.   Calculate the bundle you initially buy on your first trip to Wal-Mart.

    b.   Calculate the bundle you buy on your way home from work on the first day (when p_1 falls to 10).

    c.   If you had to pay the store some fixed fee for letting you get store credit, what's the most you would be willing to pay on that trip?

    d.   What bundle will you eventually end up with if you follow all the steps in part A?

    e.** Suppose that your tastes were instead characterized by the function $u(x_1, x_2) = (0.5x_1^{-\rho} + 0.5x_2^{-\rho})^{-1/\rho}$. Can you show that your ability to game the store credit policy diminishes as the elasticity of substitution goes to zero (i.e., as ρ goes to ∞)?

8.5*[†] **Policy Application:** *Savings Behavior and Tax Policy*: Suppose you consider the savings decisions of three households: households 1, 2, and 3. Each household plans for this year's consumption and next year's consumption, and each household anticipates earning $100,000 this year and nothing next year. The real interest rate is 10%. Assume throughout that consumption is always a normal good.

POLICY APPLICATION

A. Suppose the government does not impose any tax on interest income below $5,000 but taxes any interest income above $5,000 at 50%.

    a.   On a graph with "Consumption this period" (c_1) on the horizontal axis and "Consumption next period" (c_2) on the vertical, illustrate the choice set each of the three households faces.

    b.   Suppose you observe that household 1 saves $25,000, household 2 saves $50,000, and household 3 saves $75,000. Illustrate indifference curves for each household that would make these rational choices.

    c.   Now suppose the government changes the tax system by exempting the first $7,500 rather than the first $5,000 from taxation. Thus, under the new tax, the first $7,500 in interest income is not taxed, but any interest income above $7,500 is taxed at 50%. Given what you know about each household's savings decisions before the tax change, can you tell whether each of these households will now save more? (*Note*: It is extremely difficult to draw the scenarios in this question to scale, and when not drawn to scale, the graphs can become confusing. It is easiest simply to worry about the general shapes of the budget constraints around the relevant decision points of the households that are described.)

    d.   Instead of the tax change in part (c), suppose the government had proposed to subsidize interest income at 100% for the first $2,500 in interest income while raising the tax on any interest income above $2,500 to 80%. (Thus, if someone earns $2,500 in interest, he or she would receive an additional $2,500 in cash from the government. If someone earns $3,500, on the other hand, he or she would receive the same $2,500 cash subsidy but would also have to pay $800 in a tax.) One of the households is overheard saying: "I actually don't care whether the old policy (i.e., the policy described in part A) or this new policy goes into effect." Which of the three households could have said this, and will that household save more or less (than under the old policy) if this new policy goes into effect?

B. Now suppose that our three households had tastes that can be represented by the utility function $u(c_1, c_2) = c_1^\alpha c_2^{(1-\alpha)}$, where c_1 is consumption now and c_2 is consumption a year from now.

   a. Suppose there were no tax on savings income. Write down the intertemporal budget constraint with the real interest rate denoted r and current income denoted I (and assume that consumer anticipate no income next period).

   b. Write down the constrained optimization problem and the accompanying Lagrange function. Then solve for c_1, current consumption, as a function of α, and solve for the implied level of savings as a function of α, I, and r. Does savings depend on the interest rate?

   c. Determine the α value for consumer 1 as described in part A.

   d. Now suppose the initial 50% tax described in part A is introduced. Write down the budget constraint (assuming current income I and before-tax interest rate r) that is now relevant for consumers who end up saving more than $50,000. (*Note*: Don't write down the equation for the kinked budget; write down the equation for the linear budget on which such a consumer would optimize.)

   e. Use this budget constraint to write down the constrained optimization problem that can be solved for the optimal choice given that households save more than $50,000. Solve for c_1 and for the implied level of savings as a function of α, I, and r.

   f. What value must α take for household 3 as described in part A?

   g. With the values of α that you have determined for households 1 and 3, determine the impact that the tax reform described in (c) of part A would have?

   h. What range of values can α take for household 2 as described in part A?

8.6   Policy Application: *The Negative Income Tax*: Suppose the current tax system is such that the government takes some fixed percentage t of any labor income that you make.

A. Some in Congress have proposed the following alternative type of tax system known as the *negative income tax*: You get a certain guaranteed income x even if you do not work at all. Then, for any income you earn in the labor market, the government takes a certain percentage k in taxes. In order to finance the guaranteed income x, the tax rate on labor income in this alternative system has to be higher than the tax rate under the current system (i.e., $t < k$).[6]

   a. On a graph with leisure on the horizontal axis and consumption on the vertical, illustrate what your budget constraint under the current tax system looks like, and indicate what the intercepts and slopes are assuming a leisure endowment of E and before-tax wage w.

   b. On a similar graph, illustrate what your budget constraint looks like under the alternative system.

   c. You hear me say: "You know what? After looking at the details of the tax proposal, I can honestly say I don't care whether we keep the current system or switch to the proposed one." Without knowing what kind of goods leisure and consumption are for me, can you tell whether I would work more or less under the negative income tax? Explain.

   d. What would your tastes have to look like in order for you to be equally happy under the two systems while also working exactly the same number of hours in each case?

   e. *True or False*: The less substitutable consumption and leisure are, the less policy makers have to worry about changes in people's willingness to work as we switch from one system to the other.

B. Consider your weekly decision of how much to work, and suppose that you have 60 hours of available time to split between leisure and work. Suppose further that your tastes over consumption and leisure can be captured by the utility function $u(c, \ell) = c\ell$ and that your market wage is $w = 20$ per hour.

---

[6]In some proposals, the requirement that $t < k$ actually does not hold because proponents of the negative income tax envision replacing a number of social welfare programs with the guaranteed income x.

   a. Write down the budget constraint under the two different tax policies described; i.e., write down the first budget constraint as a function of c, ℓ, and t and the second as a function of c, ℓ, k, and x.

   b. Derive the optimal choice under the current tax system (as a function of t.) In the absence of anything else changing, do changes in wage taxes cause you to change how much you work? Can you relate your answer (intuitively) to wealth and substitution effects?

   c. Now derive your optimal leisure choice under a negative income tax (as a function of k and x). How is your work decision now affected by an increase in k or an increase in x?

   d. Suppose that $t = 0.2$. Using your utility function to measure happiness, what utility level do you attain under the current tax system?

   e. Now the government wants to set $k = 0.3$. Suppose you are the pivotal voter; if you approve of the switch to the negative income tax, then it will pass. What is the minimum level of guaranteed income x that the negative income tax proposal would have to include in order to win your support?

   f. How much less will you work if this negative income tax is implemented (assuming x is the minimum necessary to get your support)?

8.7 **Policy Application:** *The Earned Income Tax Credit*: Since the early 1970s, the U.S. government has had a program called the Earned Income Tax Credit (previously mentioned in end-of-chapter exercises in Chapter 3.) A simplified version of this program works as follows: The government subsidizes your wages by paying you 50% in addition to what your employer paid you, but the subsidy applies only to the first $300 (per week) you receive from your employer. If you earn more than $300 per week, the government gives you only the subsidy for the first $300 you earned but nothing for anything additional you earn. For instance, if you earn $500 per week, the government would give you 50% of the first $300 you earned, or $150.

POLICY APPLICATION

   A. Suppose you consider workers 1 and 2. Both can work up to 60 hours per week at a wage of $10 per hour, and after the policy is put in place you observe that worker 1 works 39 hours per week while worker 2 works 24 hours per week. Assume throughout that leisure is a normal good.

   a. Illustrate these workers' budget constraints with and without the program.

   b. Can you tell whether the program has increased the amount that worker 1 works? Explain.

   c. Can you tell whether worker 2 works more or less after the program than before? Explain.

   d. Now suppose the government expands the program by raising the cut off from $300 to $400. In other words, now the government applies the subsidy to earnings up to $400 per week. Can you tell whether worker 1 will now work more or less? What about worker 2?

   B. Suppose that workers have tastes over consumption c and leisure ℓ that can be represented by the function $u(c, \ell) = c^{\alpha}\ell^{(1-\alpha)}$.

   a. Given you know which portion of the budget constraint worker 2 ends up on, can you write down the optimization problem that solves for his optimal choice? Solve the problem and determine what value α must take for worker 2 in order for him to have chosen to work 24 hours under the EITC program.

   b. Repeat the same for worker 1 but be sure you specify the budget constraint correctly given that you know the worker is on a different portion of the EITC budget. (*Hint*: If you extend the relevant portion of the budget constraint to the leisure axis, you should find that it intersects at 75 leisure hours.)

   c. Having identified the relevant α parameters for workers 1 and 2, determine whether either of them works more or less than he or she would have in the absence of the program.

   d. Determine how each worker would respond to an increase in the EITC cut off from $300 to $400.

   e. For what ranges of α would a worker choose the kink-point in the original EITC budget you drew (i.e., the one with a $300 cutoff)?

8.8 **Policy Application:** *Advising Congress on Savings Subsidies and Substitution Effects*: Suppose you are asked to model the savings decisions of a household that has an income of $100,000 this year but expects to have no income a period into the future.

POLICY APPLICATION

A. Suppose the interest rate is 10% over this period and we consider the trade-off between consuming now and consuming one period from now.

    a.   On a graph with "Consumption Now" on the horizontal and "Future Consumption" on the vertical axis, illustrate how an increase in the interest rate to 20% over the relevant period would change the household's choice set.

    b.   Suppose that you know that the household's tastes can accurately be modeled as perfect complements over consumption now and consumption in the future period. Can you tell whether the household will save more or less as a result of the increase in the interest rate?

    c.   You are asked to advise Congress on a proposed policy of subsidizing savings in order to increase the amount of money people save. Specifically, Congress proposes to provide 5% in interest payments in addition to the interest households earn in the market. You are asked to evaluate the following statement: "Assuming that consumption is always a normal good, small substitution effects make it likely that savings will actually decline as a result of this policy, but large substitution effects make it likely that savings will increase."

    d.   *True or False*: If the purpose of the policy described in the previous part of the problem is to increase the amount of consumption households have in the future, then the policy will succeed so long as consumption is always a normal good.

B. Now suppose that tastes over consumption now, c_1, and consumption in the future, c_2, can be represented by the Constant Elasticity of Substitution utility function $u(c_1, c_2) = (c_1^{-\rho} + c_2^{-\rho})^{-1/\rho}$.

    a.   Write down the constrained optimization problem assuming that the real interest rate is r and no government programs dealing with savings are in effect.

    b.   Solve for the optimal level of c_1 as a function of ρ and r. For what value of ρ is the household's savings decision unaffected by the real interest rate?

    c.   Knowing the relationship betwen ρ and the elasticity of substitution, can you make the statement quoted in (c) of part A more precise?

8.9[†]   **Policy Application:** *International Trade and Child Labor*: The economist Jagdish Bhagwati explained in one of his public lectures that international trade causes the wage for child labor to increase in developing countries. He then discussed informally that this might lead to more child labor if parents are "bad" and less child labor if parents are "good."

A. Suppose that households in developing countries value two goods: "Leisure time for Children in the Household" and "Household Consumption." Assume that the adults in a household are earning $\$y$ in weekly income regardless of how many hours their children work. Assume that child wages are w per hour and that the maximum leisure time for children in a household is E hours per week.

    a.   On a graph with "weekly leisure time for children in the household" on the horizontal axis and "weekly household consumption" on the vertical, illustrate the budget constraint for a household and label the slopes and intercepts.

    b.   Now suppose that international trade expands and, as a result, child wages increase to w'. Illustrate how this will change the household budget.

    c.   Suppose that household tastes are homothetic and that households require their children to work during some but not all the time they have available. Can you tell whether children will be asked to work more or less as a result of the expansion of international trade?

    d.   In the context of the model with homothetic tastes, what distinguishes "good" parents from "bad" parents?

    e.   When international trade increases the wages of children, it is likely that it also increases the wages of other members of the household. Thus, in the context of our model, y—the amount brought to the household by others—would also be expected to go up. If this is so, will we observe more or less behavior that is consistent with what we have defined as "good" parent behavior?

    f.   In some developing countries with high child labor rates, governments have instituted the following policy: If the parents agree to send a child to school instead of work, the government pays the family an amount x. (Assume the government can verify that the child is in fact sent to school and does in fact not work, and assume that the household views time at school as leisure time for the child.) How does that alter the choice set for parents? Is the policy more or less likely to succeed the more substitutable the household tastes treat child "leisure" and household consumption?

B. Suppose parental tastes can be captured by the utility function $u(c, \ell) = c^{0.5}\ell^{0.5}$. For simplicity, suppose further that $y = 0$.

    a.   Specify the parents' constrained optimization problem and set up the appropriate Lagrange function.

    b.   Solve the problem you have set up to determine the level of leisure the parents will choose for their children. Does w have any impact on this decision?

    c.   Explain intuitively what you have just found. Consider the CES utility function (that has the Cobb–Douglas function you just worked with as a special case). For what ranges of ρ would you expect us to be able to call parents "good" in the way that Bhagwati informally defined the term?

    d.   Can parents for whom household consumption is a quasilinear good ever be "good"?

    e.   Now suppose (with the original Cobb–Douglas tastes) that $y > 0$. If international trade pushes up the earnings of other household members thus raising y, what happens to child leisure?

    f.   Suppose again that $y = 0$ and the government introduces the policy described in part A(f). How large does x have to be in order to cause our household to send its child to school (assuming again that the household views the child's time at school as leisure time for the child)?

    g.   Using your answer to the previous part, put into words what fraction of the market value of the child's time the government has to provide in x in order for the family to choose schooling over work for its child?

8.10* **Policy Application:** *Subsidizing Savings versus Taxing Borrowing*: In end-of-chapter exercise 6.10, we analyzed cases where the interest rates for borrowing and saving are different. Part of the reason they might be different is because of government policy.

POLICY APPLICATION

A. Suppose banks are currently willing to lend and borrow at the same interest rate. Consider an individual who has income e_1 now and e_2 in a future period, with the interest rate over that period equal to r. After considering the trade-offs, the individual chooses to borrow on his or her future income rather than save. Suppose in this exercise that the individual's tastes are homothetic.

    a.   Illustrate the budget constraint for this individual, and indicate his or her optimal choice.

    b.   Now suppose the government would like to encourage this individual to save for the future. One proposal might be to subsidize savings (through something like a 401k plan); i.e., a policy that increases the interest rate for saving without changing the interest rate for borrowing. Illustrate how this changes the budget constraint. Will this policy work to accomplish the government's goal?

    c.   Another alternative would be to penalize borrowing by taxing the interest the banks collect from loans, thus raising the effective interest rate for borrowing. Illustrate how this changes the budget. Will this policy cause the individual to borrow less? Can it cause him or her to start saving?

    d.   In reality, the government often does the opposite of these two policies: Savings (outside qualified retirement plans) are taxed while some forms of borrowing (in particular borrowing to buy a home) are subsidized. Suppose again that initially the interest rate for borrowing and saving is the same, and then suppose that the combination of taxes on savings (which lowers the effective interest rate on savings) and subsidies for borrowing (which lowers the effective interest rate for borrowing) reduce the interest rate to $r' < r$ equally for both saving and borrowing. How will this individual respond to this combination of policies?

    e.   Suppose that instead of taxing or subsidizing interest rates, the government simply "saves for" the individual by taking some of the individual's current income e_1 and putting it into the bank to collect interest for the future period. How will this change the individual's behavior?

    f.   Now suppose that instead of taking some of the person's current income and saving it for him or her, the government simply raises the Social Security benefits (in the future period) without taking anything away from the person now. What will the individual do?

B. Suppose your tastes can be captured by the utility function $u(c_1, c_2) = c_1^{\alpha}c_2^{(1-\alpha)}$.

    a.   Assuming you face a constant interest rate r for borrowing and saving, how much will you consume now and in the future (as a function of e_1, e_2 and r)?

    b.   For what values of α will you choose to borrow rather than save?

    c.   Suppose that $\alpha = 0.5$, $e_1 = 100{,}000$, $e_2 = 125{,}000$ and $r = 0.10$. How much do you save or borrow?

d.   If the government could come up with a "financial literacy" course that changes how you view the trade-off between now and the future by impacting α, how much would this program have to change your α in order to get you to stop borrowing?

e.   Suppose the "financial literacy" program had no impact on α. How much would the government have to raise the interest rate for saving (as described in A(b)) in order for you to become a saver? (*Hint*: You need to first determine c_1 and c_2 as a function of just r. You can then determine the utility you receive as a function of just r, and you will not switch to saving until r is sufficiently high to give you the same utility you get by borrowing.)

f.   Verify your conclusion about the impact of the policy proposal outlined in A(c).

g.   Verify you conclusion to A(d).

h.   Verify your conclusion to A(e); i.e., suppose the government takes x of your current income e_1 and saves it, thus increasing e_2 by $x(1 + r)$.

i.   Finally, suppose the increase in Social Security benefits outlined in A(f) is implemented. How and by how much does your borrowing change?

8.11   **Policy Application:** *Tax Revenues and the Laffer Curve*: In this exercise, we will consider how the tax rate on wages relates to the amount of tax revenue collected.

A.   As introduced in Section B, the *Laffer Curve* depicts the relationship between the tax rate on the horizontal axis and tax revenues on the vertical. (See the footnote in Section 8B.2.2 for background on the origins of the name of this curve.) Because people's decision on how much to work may be affected by the tax rate, deriving this relationship is not as straightforward as many think.

a.   Consider first the extreme case in which leisure and consumption are perfect complements. On a graph with leisure hours on the horizontal and consumption dollars on the vertical, illustrate how increases in the tax on wages affect the consumer's optimal choice of leisure (and thus labor).

b.   Next, consider the less extreme case where a change in after-tax wages gives rise to substitution and wealth effects that exactly offset one another on the leisure axis. In which of these cases does tax revenue rise faster as the tax rate increases?

c.   On a graph with the tax rate (ranging from 0 to 1) on the horizontal and tax revenues on the vertical, how does this relationship differ for tastes in (a) and (b)?

d.   Now suppose that the substitution effect outweighs the wealth effect on the leisure axis as after-tax wages change. Illustrate this and determine how it changes the relationship between tax rates and tax revenue.

e.   Laffer suggested (and most economists agree) that the curve relating tax revenue (on the vertical axis) to tax rates (on the horizontal) is initially upward sloping but eventually slopes down, reaching the horizontal axis by the time the tax rate goes to 1. Which of the preferences we described in this problem can give rise to this shape?

f.   *True or False*: If leisure is a normal good, the Laffer Curve can have an inverted U-shape only if leisure and consumption are (at least at some point) sufficiently substitutable such that the substitution effect (on leisure) outweighs the wealth effect (on leisure).

B.**   In Section 8B.2.2, we derived a Laffer Curve for the case where tastes were quasilinear in leisure. Now consider the case where tastes are Cobb–Douglas, taking the form $u(c, \ell) = c^\alpha \ell^{(1-\alpha)}$. Assume that a worker has 60 hours of weekly leisure endowment that he or she can sell in the labor market for wage w.

a.   Suppose the worker's wages are taxed at a rate t. Derive the worker's optimal leisure choice.

b.   For someone with these tastes, does the Laffer Curve take the inverted U-shape described in Section 8B.2.2. Why or why not? Which of the cases described in A does this represent?

c.   Now consider the more general CES function $(\alpha c^{-\rho} + (1 - \alpha)\ell^{-\rho})^{-1/\rho}$. Again, derive the optimal leisure consumption.

d.   Does your answer simplify to what you would expect when $\rho = 0$?

e.   Determine the range of values of ρ such that leisure consumption increases with t.

f.   When ρ falls in the range you have just derived, what happens to leisure consumption as t approaches 1? What does this imply for the shape of the Laffer Curve?

g.   Suppose $\alpha = 0.25$, $w = 20$, and $\rho = -0.5$. Calculate the amount of leisure a worker would choose as a function of t. Then derive an expression for this worker's Laffer Curve and graph it.

Demand for Goods and Supply of Labor and Capital

If you have ever taken an economics class before, you probably dived right into drawing demand and supply curves.[1] You may be puzzled by the lack of any attention we have given to these concepts thus far. The reason for this is not that demand and supply curves are unimportant. Rather, demand and supply arise from individual decision making, from economic agents choosing to do the best they can given their circumstances. It is difficult to fully appreciate the concepts of demand and supply—to know what they tell us and what they do not tell us—without first understanding how demand and supply arise from such individual optimizing behavior. Having taken a close look at how economists think about individuals doing the best they can given their circumstances, we are now ready to see how such individual decision making leads to some types of demand and supply curves.

In particular, we have analyzed how individuals make choices in three different roles within the economy: as consumers choosing between various goods, as workers choosing between consumption and leisure, and as savers/borrowers choosing how to plan for the future. In their role as consumers, individuals become *demanders of goods and services*, while in their role as workers they become *suppliers of labor*. Finally, as savers they become *suppliers of financial capital*, while as borrowers they become *demanders of financial capital*. We will therefore be able to derive from what we have modeled so far demand curves for goods and supply curves for labor. Depending on whether an individual borrows or saves, we will also be able to derive demand and supply curves for financial capital. In later chapters, we will complete the picture of goods and services markets, labor markets, and capital markets by adding the role played by producers, who supply goods and demand labor and capital.

9A   Deriving Demand and Supply Curves

We begin, as always, with a nonmathematical treatment of demand and supply curves that arise from individual optimizing behavior. Here we will use the graphs we have developed thus far to illustrate how the demand and supply curves you have probably seen in other classes arise from such models. Section 9A.1 will begin with demand relationships for goods and services, while later sections extend the analysis to similar relationships in labor and capital markets.

---

[1]Chapter 2 and Chapters 4 through 7 are required for this chapter. Chapters 3 and 8 are required for Sections 9A.2 and 9A.3 as well as 9B.2 and 9B.3. Those sections can be skipped by students who are not reading Chapters 3 and 8.

9A.1 Demand for Goods and Services

In the previous chapters, we have already analyzed how the quantity of a good that is demanded may change with changes in underlying economic circumstances, whether these are changes in income, wealth, or prices. Our answer has always depended on the underlying tastes that gave rise to sometimes competing income (or wealth) and substitution effects. It became important to know whether, for the particular individual in question, a good was normal or inferior, regular inferior or Giffen. Such distinctions between different types of tastes then become similarly important for understanding demand relationships more generally.

We will distinguish below between three different kinds of demand relationships (or "curves"): *income demand curves, own-price demand curves*, and *cross-price demand curves*. By an "income demand curve" we mean the relationship between (exogenously given) income and the quantity of a good that is demanded; by "own-price demand curve" we mean the relationship between the price of a good and the quantity demanded of *that same* good; and by a "cross-price demand curve" we mean the relationship between one good's price and the quantity demanded of a *different* good. In each of these cases, we will plot demand curves relating the quantity of a good demanded on the horizontal axis and the variable of interest—to income, the good's own price or some other good's price—on the vertical.

9A.1.1 Income Demand Relationships

Of the three types of demand relationships we are interested in, the relationship between income and the quantity of a good demanded is the most straightforward. These income-demand relationships are sometime referred to as *Engel curves*.[2]

Suppose, for instance, that we return to my example from Chapter 5 in which I revealed how, for my wife and me, pasta is an inferior good whereas steak is a normal good. In Graph 9.1, we then derive our income-demand curves for these two goods knowing what kinds of goods these are for my wife and me. Specifically, we begin in Graph 9.1a with an income of $100 and a choice between boxes of pasta per week and "dollars of other consumption per week." Since the good on the vertical axis is denominated in dollars, its price is simply 1 and the slope of the budget is minus the price of pasta. Suppose this price is $4 and that our optimal bundle *A* contains 10 boxes of pasta per week. This then gives us one point on the income-demand graph directly below: at an income of $100 (on the vertical axis), we consume 10 boxes of pasta.

Now suppose our income goes up to $200 (without a change in the price of pasta). Since pasta is an inferior good for us, we know that our pasta consumption will now decline, perhaps to 5 boxes as indicated in the new optimal bundle *B*. This then gives us a second point on the income-demand graph: at an income of $200, we consume 5 boxes of pasta. We can imagine going through these same steps again and again for different levels of income, each time finding the optimal point in the top graph and translating it to the lower graph. The curve connecting these points then forms the complete income-demand curve. For our particular example, the curve has a negative slope because we have assumed pasta is an inferior good, implying a negative relationship between income and consumption. Graph 9.1b then replicates the same analysis for steak when the price of steak is $10 per pound. (In the example, we assume that my wife and I consume only steak and pasta.) As you would expect, this results in a positive income-demand relationship because steak is a normal good for us.

Exercise 9A.1 In an earlier chapter, we mentioned that it is not possible for a good to be inferior for all income levels. Can you see in the lower panel of Graph 9.1a why this is true?

[2]These are named after Ernst Engel (1821–1896), a German statistician and economist who studied how consumption behavior changes with income. He is particularly known for what has become known as "Engel's Law," which states that the proportion of income spent on food falls as income increases (i.e., food is a necessity as we have defined it) even though the overall expenditures on food increase (i.e., food is a normal good as we have defined it).

Graph 9.1: Income-Demand Curves when Pasta Is Inferior (a) and Steak Is Normal (b)

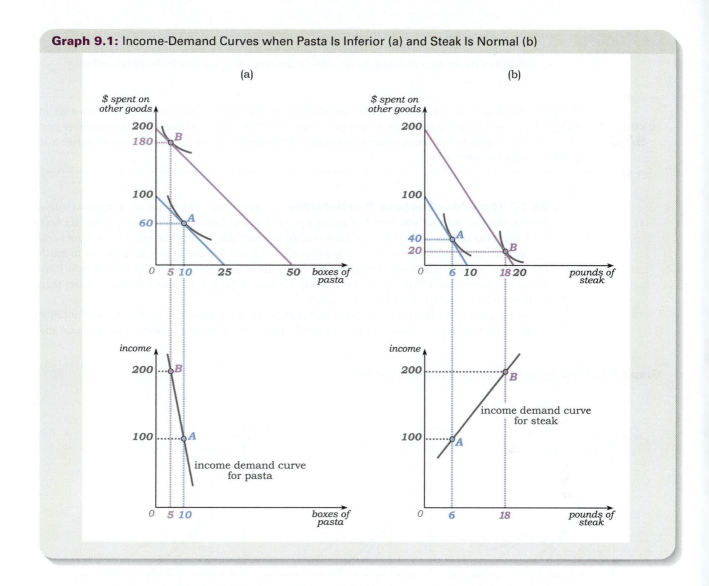

The graphical translation of optimizing choices in the top graphs to income-demand curves in the lower graphs is an intuitive way of accomplishing what can be accomplished straightforwardly with mathematical equations. Thus, in reality economists do not spend their time graphing points again and again as we would have to in order to get the lower relationship just right. Rather, we use the techniques developed in the B-portions of our chapters. Nevertheless, the graphical technique provides us with the intuition of what the mathematics accomplishes for us, and it is a technique we will use repeatedly here and throughout the rest of the book.

The income-demand curves derived in Graph 9.1 are valid for the prices used in the top portions of the graphs: $4 for pasta and $10 for steak. Now suppose that these prices changed. The resulting new optimal bundles in the top portion of the graphs will then translate to different points, and thus different income-demand curves, in the lower portion of the graphs. In particular, for normal and regular inferior goods, an increase in the price of a good will result in less consumption of that good for any given income level. This implies that *for normal or regular inferior goods, the income-demand curve will shift inward for an increase in the price of the good and outward for a decrease in price.* For Giffen goods, on the other hand, an increase in price results in increased consumption for any given income level, while a decrease in the price will result in decreased consumption. Thus, *for Giffen goods, an increase in price results in an outward shift of the income demand curve, while a decrease in price results in an inward shift.*

Exercise 9A.2

Suppose good *x* is an inferior good for an individual. Derive the income-demand curve as in Graph 9.1a. Then graph a decrease in the price for *x* for both income levels in the top panel and show how this affects the income-demand curve in the lower panel depending on whether *x* is Giffen or regular inferior.

9A.1.2 Own-Price Demand Relationships   If you have ever heard of a demand curve before, chances are that you heard of an *own-price demand curve*. An *own-price demand curve for a good (or service) illustrates the relationship between the price of the good (or service) and the quantity demanded by a consumer, holding all else fixed.* We can derive such curves in much the same way that we derived the income-demand curves in Graph 9.1, except that we now have to change prices rather than incomes in the top portion of the graphs (and put prices rather than income on the vertical axis in the lower graph).

In Graph 9.2, we derive the own-price demand curves for a normal good, a regular inferior good, and a Giffen good. In each case, we model the good of interest on the horizontal axis and

Graph 9.2: Three Types of Own-Price Demand Curves

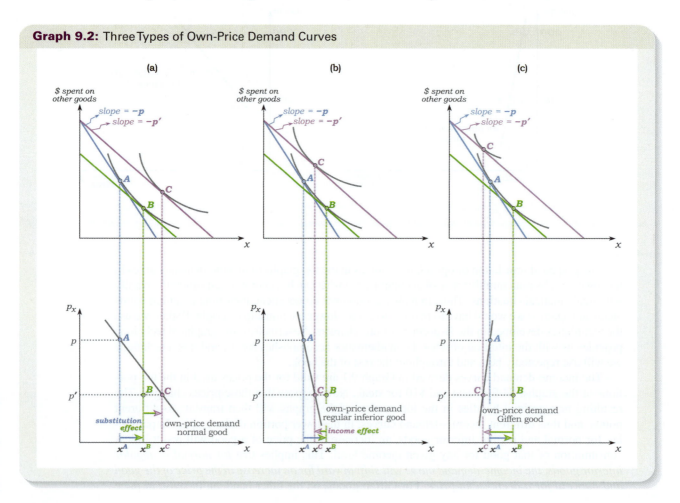

analyze the choices faced by a consumer between that good and a composite good denominated in dollars. We begin in the top panel of each graph with the same initial (blue) budget constraint and the same initial optimal point A, and in each case we analyze a decrease in the price of the good on the horizontal axis from p to p'. To make the illustration as clean as possible, we also assume in each case that the degree of substitutability built into the indifference curve at point A is the same across the three examples, which implies that the substitution effect that gives rise to point B on the compensated (green) budget is the same across the three examples. The only difference, then, lies in the size and direction of the income effect.

Consider first the derivation of the own-price demand curve for a normal good in panel (a) of Graph 9.2. At the initial price p, the consumer consumes x^A in the top graph, a quantity that is translated to the lower graph and placed at the vertical height p. Bundle B, the optimal choice under the compensated budget, is chosen at the lower price p'. Thus, we could translate the quantity x^B to the lower graph and place it at the vertical height p'. This is not, however, a point on the own-price demand curve since it is the hypothetical consumption level at the compensated budget. Still, this will turn out to be an important point in a different relationship we will introduce in Chapter 10.

For now, we want to focus on bundle C in the top graph, the bundle that is chosen on the actual final (magenta) budget. Because we are assuming in panel (a) of this graph that x is a normal good, C falls on the final budget to the right of B. As our income rises from the compensated to the final budget, we consume more of the normal good x. The quantity x^C that is chosen at the final price p' can then again be translated to the lower graph and placed at the height p'. As in the previous section, we can imagine going through this exercise many times to plot the optimal consumption of x at different prices and thus fully trace out the relationship between the price of good x and the quantity of x demanded. For our purposes, it is good enough simply to estimate the remaining points on the own-price demand curve by connecting points A and C on the lower graph.

Next we can see in panel (b) of Graph 9.2 how this analysis differs when x is a regular inferior rather than a normal good. Since bundles A and B are exactly identical to those in panel (a) of the graph, these points translate to the lower graph exactly the same way as they did for a normal good. (This simply reiterates what we have found all along, which is that substitution effects have nothing to do with whether a good is normal or inferior.) As our income rises from the compensated (green) to the final (magenta) budget in the top portion of the graph, however, we will now end up consuming less x rather than more because x is inferior. The quantity x^C therefore now falls to the left of x^B. Because we are assuming that the good is a regular inferior (rather than a Giffen) good, however, we know that the size of the income effect is smaller than the size of the substitution effect, thus causing C to fall in between A and B. When we connect A and C in the lower portion of the graph, we then get a demand curve that is steeper for the inferior good than it was for the normal good. The reason for this is, of course, that income and substitution effects now point in opposite directions.

Repeat the derivation of own-price demand curves for the case of quasilinear tastes and explain in this context again how quasilinear tastes are borderline tastes between normal and inferior goods.

**Exercise
9A.3**

Finally, we can compare this to the own-price demand curve for a Giffen good in panel (c) of Graph 9.2. The difference now is that the income effect not only points in the opposite direction of the substitution effect but now it is also larger in size. As a result, point C in both the top and bottom portions of the graph falls not only to the left of B but also to the left of A. This leads to an own-price demand curve that is upward rather than downward sloping, giving expression to the definition of a Giffen good as a good whose consumption moves in the same direction as its own price.

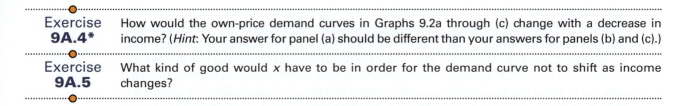

Exercise 9A.4* How would the own-price demand curves in Graphs 9.2a through (c) change with a decrease in income? (*Hint*: Your answer for panel (a) should be different than your answers for panels (b) and (c).)

Exercise 9A.5 What kind of good would x have to be in order for the demand curve not to shift as income changes?

9A.1.3 Cross-Price Demand Relationships Suppose you are a producer of two goods that are used together: razors and razor blades, or printers and toner cartridges, for instance. As you think about how you should price the two different types of goods you produce, you may want to know not only how consumption of each good varies with its own price but also how consumption of one varies with the price of the other. Just as we could derive own-price demand curves in the previous section, we can then also derive cross-price demand curves under different scenarios. We will leave some of this for problems at the end of the chapter and offer only an illustration here.

Suppose, for instance, that you consume goods x_1 and x_2, that your tastes are quasilinear in good x_1, and that we are interested in the cross-price demand curve for good x_1 as the price of good x_2 varies. We would therefore begin in Graph 9.3 by modeling how your choices change as

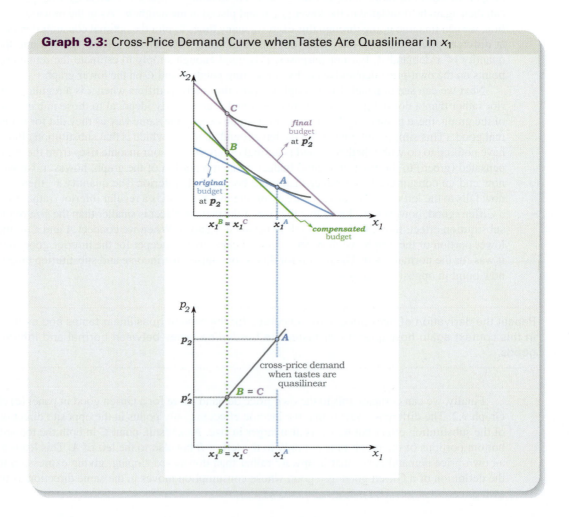

Graph 9.3: Cross-Price Demand Curve when Tastes Are Quasilinear in x_1

the price of good x_2 decreases from p_2 to p_2'. The optimal bundle A at the original price p_2 could then be translated to the lower portion of the graph, where we plot your optimal consumption x_1^A at the initial price p_2. We can similarly translate bundle B but are ultimately interested in where bundle C will fall. Since we have assumed in this example that your tastes are quasilinear in good x_1, we know that your consumption of good x_1 is unchanged as income changes, and thus the same on the compensated and the final budget. Thus bundle C lies directly above bundle B in the top portion of the graph, and exactly on top of the translated B point on the lower portion. The cross-price demand curve that connects A and C is therefore upward sloping. As the price of good x_2 increases, so does your consumption of good x_1.

What kind of good would x_1 have to be in order for this cross-price demand curve to slope down?   **Exercise 9A.6**

9A.2 Labor Supply[3]

Economists and policy makers alike are often interested in how the supply of labor will respond to changes in the wages that workers can earn. Enormous effort has been devoted to determining how different types of workers respond differently to changes in wages, whether women respond differently than men, whether older workers respond differently than younger workers, high wage workers differently than low wage workers. How responsive workers are to changes in their take-home wage impacts the way we think about tax policy as well as labor issues like the minimum wage. At the root of these issues lies once again the question of the direction and relative size of income (or wealth) and substitution effects.

Labor supply curves simply plot the amount of labor an individual chooses to supply to the market at different wage rates. This choice emerges from an individual's choice of how to spend his or her leisure endowment; that is, how much of it to consume as leisure and how much of it to convert into consumption of other goods by selling leisure (i.e., by working). The wage itself is like any other price in the economy, and, while individuals can in the long run affect the wage they command in the market by gaining skills and earning higher levels of education, they typically must accept the wage offered by the market for a given set of skills and education.

Consider again your choice of how much labor to supply this summer given that you have 60 hours of leisure time per week. Suppose first that you can command a wage of $20 per hour. We have previously modeled your choice graphically with weekly hours of leisure on the horizontal axis and dollars of weekly consumption on the vertical. This is done once again in each of the three cases in the top row of Graph 9.4, where in each case we assume that your tastes are such that your optimal level of leisure at the initial $20 wage is equal to 20 hours per week, implying 40 hours of labor supplied. Thus, in each of the three bottom panels of Graph 9.4, point A indicates that you will supply 40 hours of work per week at an hourly wage of $20 per hour. This is one point on the labor supply curve. Note, however, that unlike in the graphs of the previous section, we are not able simply to translate the horizontal axis of the top graph to the horizontal axis of the bottom graph because the bottom graph in each panel contains a different good (labor) on the horizontal axis than the top graph (leisure). Rather, we proceed in two steps: In the middle row of Graph 9.4, we derive the "leisure demand curve" in much the same way we derived demand curves in the previous section. Then we proceed to the lowest graph for each case to derive the corresponding *labor supply curve*, which follows straightforwardly from the leisure demand curve given that labor is equal to 60 minus leisure.

---

[3] Students who did not read Chapters 3 and 8 should skip this and the next section.

Graph 9.4: Leisure Demand (Middle Row) and Labor Supply (Bottom Row) Curves

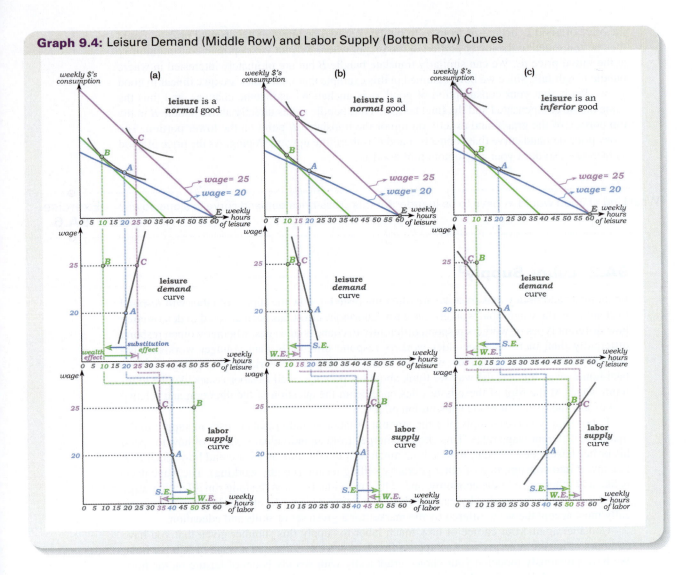

Now suppose that you have gained some additional skills and your market wage increases to $25 per hour. Several scenarios are now possible depending on which direction and what size the wealth effect assumes. In panel (a) of Graph 9.4, leisure is assumed to be normal, implying a wealth effect that points in the direction opposite to that of the substitution effect. In addition, this wealth effect is assumed in panel (a) of the graph to be larger in size than the substitution effect, thus causing an increase in the wage to result in an *increase* in leisure in the top and middle graph and thus a *decrease* in work hours on the bottom graph. As a result, the labor supply curve, estimated by simply connecting A and C in the bottom panel, is downward sloping.

**Exercise
9A.7**

In our analysis of consumer goods, we usually found that income and substitution effects point in the same direction when goods are normal. Why are wealth and substitution effects now pointing in opposite directions when leisure is a normal good?

As we hinted at already in the previous chapter, leisure being a normal good is a *necessary* condition for the labor supply curve to slope down, but it is not sufficient. Panel (b) illustrates this by showing how we can assume that leisure is normal and get the opposite slope for the labor supply curve. The only change from the picture in panel (a) is that the wealth effect, while still pointing in the direction opposite to that of the substitution effect, now is smaller in size than the substitution effect. As a result, the worker takes less leisure at bundle *C* (when the wage is $25) than he or she did at bundle *A* (when the wage was $20 per hour), which results in more labor as the wage increases and thus an upward-sloping labor supply curve.

Finally, panel (c) of the graph illustrates what happens in the event that leisure is an inferior good. In this case, the substitution and wealth effects point in the same direction on the leisure axis, thus unambiguously indicating that leisure will decline as the wage increases and implying that work hours will increase with the wage.

True or False: Leisure being an inferior good is sufficient but not necessary for labor supply to slope up.

Exercise 9A.8

As we have already noted previously, it is not possible to differentiate this case from the case where leisure is a Giffen rather than a regular inferior good. This is because in order to be able to make such a differentiation, we would have to observe the equivalent of a change in the price of leisure with income being exogenous rather than endogenous because a Giffen good is defined relative to price changes of *that* good when income is exogenous. A change in the wage, however, is graphically equivalent to a change in the price of consumption, with an *increase* in the wage being formally equivalent to a *decrease* in the price of consumption. When the wage increased from $20 to $25, for instance, you were unable to consume any more leisure on the horizontal axis but were able to consume more of other goods on the vertical. This is exactly what a decrease in the price of the good "consumption" would look like in a model with exogenous income in which leisure is treated like any other good.

Can you tell which way the labor supply curve will slope in the unlikely event that "other consumption" is a Giffen good?

Exercise 9A.9

9A.3 Demand and Supply Curves for Financial Capital

Finally, we have introduced in Chapter 3 a way of modeling the choices we face as we plan for the future by using graphs of budget constraints known as "intertemporal budgets" that illustrate the trade-offs between consuming now or at some point in the future. And we have demonstrated in Chapter 8 how we can combine such intertemporal choice sets with graphs of indifference curves to illustrate how income and substitution effects operate in our savings and borrowing decisions. We now proceed to show how this analysis can be extended to permit us to derive graphically supply and demand curves for financial capital, curves that illustrate how our behavior in financial markets changes as the real interest rate changes.

9A.3.1 Saving and the "Supply of Capital"   Whenever we save money for the future, we are implicitly supplying financial capital to the market. Typically, we are doing this by putting our savings into a bank account or some other financial institution (like the stock market), which then either lends the bulk of this money to someone else or uses it directly to finance some operation. For instance, when I open a savings account in my local bank, you might come along the next day and ask the bank for a loan to buy a car. In this case, I have indirectly supplied financial capital that you demanded, all at some market interest rate. Or I might invest money by purchasing newly issued stocks or corporate bonds, in which case the firm that is issuing the stocks or bonds is demanding capital that I am supplying. Or I might purchase government treasury bonds, in which case I am lending money directly to the government. In each of these scenarios, "savings" is equivalent to "supplying capital" in the economy.

Consider the case we have raised before where you attempt to decide how much to save for next summer given that you earn $10,000 this summer and expect to have no earnings next summer. As before, let us assume that consumption is always a normal good, whether it happens this summer or next summer, and let's begin by assuming that the annual interest rate is 10% and that, at that interest rate, you find it optimal to save $5,000 for next summer. This "optimum" is illustrated as point A in the top panels of Graphs 9.5a and 9.5b, and this bundle is translated to a lower graph in which we plot the interest rate against the amount of savings you will undertake under this interest rate. Thus, on the lower graphs, point A occurs at the vertical height of the interest rate 0.1 and indicates that you will save $5,000 at that interest rate. Notice that in this case, the quantity on the horizontal axis of the top graph is the same as the quantity on the horizontal axis of the lower graph because you are consuming $5,000 (the quantity on the top graph), which implies you are saving $5,000 because you started out with a $10,000 income. In general, however, the "good" on the horizontal axis in the lower panel is different from the "good" on the horizontal axis in the top panel, much as it was when we had leisure in the consumer diagram and then put labor on the horizontal axis when graphing the labor supply curve. Compared to what we did in Graph 9.4 of the previous section, we are in effect now skipping the intermediate step of illustrating the "consumption now" demand curve before illustrating the savings curve.

Next, suppose the interest rate rises to 20%. As in the previous chapter, the top graph in both panels of Graph 9.5 then illustrates the substitution effect to bundle B, an effect that causes you to consume less this summer (and thus to save more). When translated to the lower graphs, point B thus appears at the higher interest rate and to the right of point A where savings has increased. Notice that point B occurs at less than $5,000 on the horizontal axis of the top graph because your consumption this summer has fallen, but it occurs at greater than $5,000 in the lower graph because you are now saving more than $5,000.

Finally, panels (a) and (b) of Graph 9.5 illustrate two differently sized wealth effects (while assuming that consumption in both summers is a normal good). In panel (a), the wealth effect on this summer's consumption is larger than the substitution effect, thus causing bundle C to lie to the right of bundle A in the top graph, indicating that the increase in the interest rate causes you to consume more this summer. Since this implies less savings, point C on the lower panel of Graph 9.5a therefore falls to the left of point A, giving us a negative relationship between savings and the interest rate. Panel (b) of the graph, however, shows that a smaller wealth effect may lead to the opposite conclusion, with savings and the interest rate exhibiting a positive relationship. Once again, the underlying question is whether consumption this summer is relatively substitutable with consumption next summer, which would give rise to a large substitution effect and cause the positive interest rate/savings relationship in panel (b) of the graph. Alternatively, if consumption across the two time periods is relatively complementary, the substitution effect would be small, giving rise to the negative interest rate/savings relationship in panel (a) of Graph 9.5.

Exercise 9A.10 Would the interest rate/savings curve slope up or down if consumption this period were an inferior good?

Graph 9.5: Supply Curves for Capital from Savers

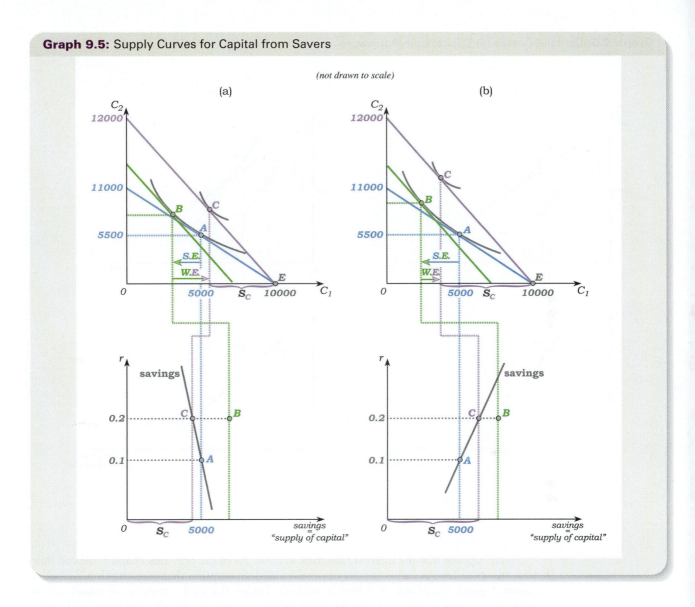

9A.3.2 Borrowing and the "Demand for Capital"
Just as "savings" is equivalent to "supplying capital" to the economy, "borrowing" is equivalent to "demanding capital." When you borrow money to purchase a car or to finance your fancy trip to the Amazon, you are demanding capital that someone else is supplying. We can thus analyze how "borrowers" will respond to changes in the interest rate, and thus how demand for capital changes with the interest rate.

Consider the case we have raised before where you expect to earn $11,000 next summer and you need to decide how much of it to borrow against in order to finance your consumption this summer. Suppose again that you start out facing an annual interest rate of 10% and that, at that interest rate, you have decided it is optimal for you to borrow $5,000 for consumption this summer. This is illustrated as bundle A in both panels of Graph 9.6, and this information is translated to a lower graph relating the interest rate to the amount of borrowing you undertake. Since in this case the amount that you borrow is exactly equal to the amount that you consume this summer, we can simply translate horizontal quantities from the top graphs to horizontal quantities on the lower graphs.

Graph 9.6: Demand Curves for Capital from Borrowers

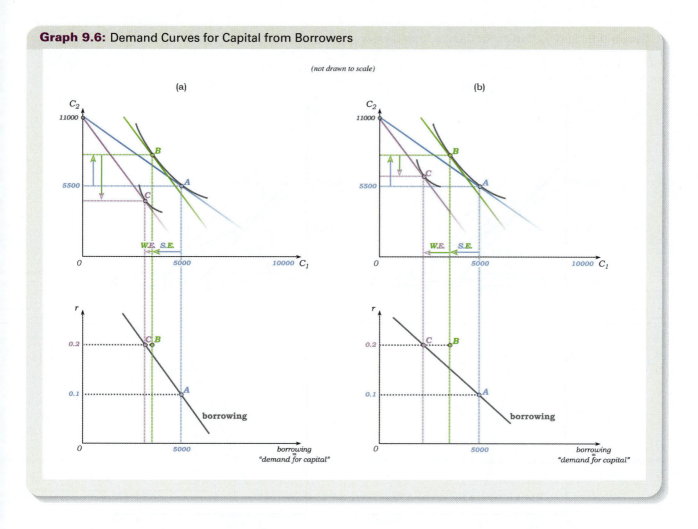

Next, suppose that the interest rate rises to 20%. As in the previous chapter, we can now draw two possible scenarios (under our maintained assumption that consumption is always a normal good regardless of when it occurs). Under the first scenario (in panel (a) of Graph 9.6), consumption next summer declines because the wealth effect outweighs the substitution effect, while under the second scenario, consumption next summer rises because the substitution effect outweighs the wealth effect. In both cases, however, the wealth and substitution effects point in the same direction on the horizontal axis, thus indicating that you will unambiguously consume less this summer (and thus borrow less) as the interest rate rises. Therefore, the relationship between borrowing and the interest rate is negative regardless of which scenario you face; i.e., regardless of how substitutable consumption is across the two time periods. The only impact of having greater substitutability built into the indifference curve that contains bundle A is that it will make the interest rate/borrowing curve in the lower panel shallower.

Exercise 9A.11   What kind of good would consumption this summer have to be in order for the interest rate/borrowing relationship to be positive in Graph 9.6?

9A.3.3 Switching between Borrowing and Savings

In the previous two sections, we have considered the extreme cases when all your income falls either in this summer (Section 9A.3.1) or next summer (Section 9A.3.2). This has allowed us to definitively label you a "saver" or a "supplier of capital" in Section 9A.3.1 and a "borrower" or "demander of capital" in Section 9A.3.2. A more general case would be one in which you earn some income this summer and some next summer, and you choose how much to save or borrow this summer knowing how much you will earn next summer.

Consider, for instance, the two budgets in Graph 9.7. The bundle E indicates the endowment bundle, with I_1 representing income this summer and I_2 representing income next summer. At the high interest rate, bundle S is optimal, indicating an optimal amount of saving of $(I_1 - c_1^S)$. At the low interest rate, on the other hand, bundle B is optimal, with an optimal amount of borrowing equal to $(c_1^B - I_1)$. In this case, then, the consumer will switch between borrowing and saving as the interest rate increases. This is indicated on the lower graph where the interest rate is plotted on the vertical axis, and the vertical axis is placed right underneath the endowment bundle E in the top graph. When the optimal bundle occurs to the right of bundle E in the top graph, the resulting borrowing is then plotted in the positive quadrant of the lower graph. When the optimal bundle occurs to the left of bundle E, on the other hand, the resulting savings (or negative borrowing) is plotted in the negative quadrant of the lower graph.

Graph 9.7: Switching from Borrowing to Saving as the Interest Rate Rises

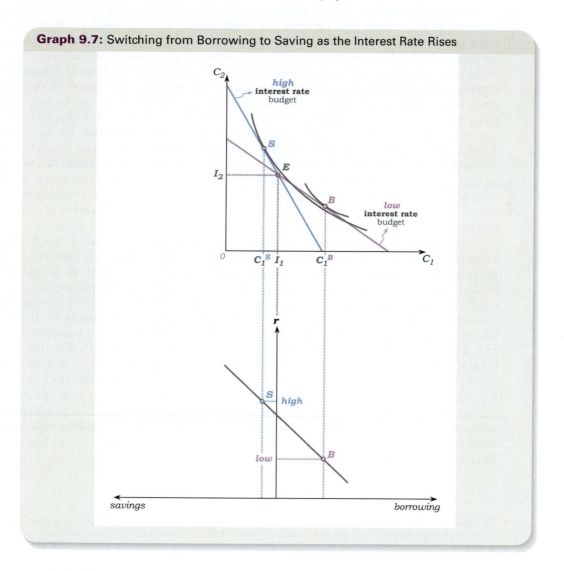

Exercise 9A.12   Is it possible for someone to begin as a saver at low interest rates and switch to become a borrower as the interest rate rises?

Exercise 9A.13   The technique of placing the axis below the endowment point *E* developed in Graph 9.7 could also be applied to the previous two graphs, Graph 9.5 and Graph 9.6. How would those graphs change?

9B   Demand and Supply *Functions*

In Section 9A, we have derived various demand and supply relationships graphically. We will now demonstrate that the "curves" we have graphed are in fact just special cases of more general demand and supply *functions*, cases where all but one of the variables of these functions are held fixed. In that sense, we can think of the curves we derived graphically as two-dimensional "slices" of multidimensional functions.

One peculiar feature of the way we have graphed demand and supply relationships should, however, be pointed out right up front and might already have occurred to you if you are mathematically inclined: Economists have gotten in the habit of graphing these relationships incorrectly, with the independent variable (like income or price) on the vertical axis (instead of the horizontal where it belongs) and the dependent variable (like the quantity demanded or supplied) on the horizontal (instead of the vertical where it belongs.) The number of Twinkies® I buy, for instance, may depend on my exogenous income, but my exogenous income is certainly *not* dependent on the number of Twinkies I buy. Or, in the case of own-price demand curves, the number of Twinkies I demand depends on the price of Twinkies, but the price of Twinkies in the grocery store does not depend on how many Twinkies I buy (given the grocery store barely knows of my individual existence). This would cause a mathematician to put income or price on the horizontal axis and the quantity demanded on the vertical axis, not the other way around as we have done in part A of the chapter. *When we are graphing demand curves with price on the vertical axis, we are therefore graphing the inverse of the demand functions we will be calculating mathematically.*

This tradition of graphing demand curves as *inverse* demand functions dates back to Alfred Marshall's *Principles of Economics* published in 1890.[4] It is only out of sheer habit that economists have never changed the way we graph these economic relationships as the discipline became more mathematical in the second half of the 20th century, and this will require us to be careful at certain stages when we map properties of demand functions into graphs from our intuitive treatment of the material. In particular, slopes that we calculate for demand *functions* will take on the inverse value in our graphs of demand *curves*, with a slope of 1/2 becoming a slope of 2, a slope of −3 becoming −1/3 and so forth. I had briefly contemplated writing this whole book with demand and supply curves graphed the way that mathematicians would do it, but, when I enthusiastically mentioned the idea to my wife (who has taken two economics classes in her whole life), she looked at me with genuine pity and told me to take a year sabbatical to recover my sanity. And, to be honest, I, too, am too brainwashed from years of graphing these curves as the profession has done. So I don't think we'll be able to single-handedly convince the discipline to change its habits, and we'll therefore succumb to the weight of history and simply be careful as we translate math to graphs.

---

[4] In this regard, Marshall's work stood in contrast to the influential work by Leon Walras (1834–1910), who graphed direct (as opposed to inverse) demand curves. Marshall's treatment has, for better or worse, become the standard in economics.

Consider the function $f(x) = x/3$. Graph this as you usually would with x on the horizontal axis and $f(x)$ on the vertical. Then graph the inverse of the function, with $f(x)$ on the horizontal and x on the vertical.

Exercise
9B.1

Repeat the previous exercise for the function $f(x) = 10$.

Exercise
9B.2

9B.1 Demand for Goods and Services

In all the optimization problems that we have computed in the past few chapters, we always restricted ourselves to quite particular examples of tastes and economic circumstances in order to relate particular intuitive concepts to particular mathematical examples. In the process, however, we have set up a much more general approach that gives rise to all of the demand relationships we introduced in Section 9A, and we have already begun to use these in some of the end-of-chapter exercises in the previous chapters. We now move toward a more general specification of our optimization problem by letting the economic circumstances of the consumer be represented by simply I, p_1, and p_2—income, the price of good 1, and the price of good 2—without specifying exact values for these.

Suppose, for instance, that tastes can be represented by the Cobb–Douglas utility function $u(x_1, x_2) = x_1^\alpha x_2^{(1-\alpha)}$. The consumer's utility maximization problem can then be written as

$$\max_{x_1, x_2} x_1^\alpha x_2^{(1-\alpha)} \text{ subject to } p_1 x_1 + p_2 x_2 = I, \tag{9.1}$$

with a corresponding Lagrange function

$$\mathcal{L}(x_1, x_2, \lambda) = x_1^\alpha x_2^{(1-\alpha)} + \lambda(I - p_1 x_1 - p_2 x_2). \tag{9.2}$$

The terms p_1, p_2, and I—the combination of variables that represent an individual's economic circumstances that he or she takes as given and has no control over—are then treated as simple parameters as we solve for the first order conditions, as is the term α which describes tastes that the person also cannot control. The first order conditions, or the first partial derivatives of $\mathcal{L}$ with respect to x_1, x_2 and λ, can then be written as

$$\frac{\partial \mathcal{L}}{\partial x_1} = \alpha x_1^{\alpha-1} x_2^{(1-\alpha)} - \lambda p_1 = 0,$$

$$\frac{\partial \mathcal{L}}{\partial x_2} = (1 - \alpha) x_1^\alpha x_2^{-\alpha} - \lambda p_2 = 0, \tag{9.3}$$

$$\frac{\partial \mathcal{L}}{\partial \lambda} = I - p_1 x_1 - p_2 x_2 = 0.$$

Solving these in the usual way, we get that

$$x_1 = \frac{\alpha I}{p_1} \text{ and } x_2 = \frac{(1 - \alpha) I}{p_2}. \tag{9.4}$$

These functions are called *demand functions* for tastes that can be represented by the Cobb–Douglas utility function $u(x_1, x_2) = x_1^\alpha x_2^{(1-\alpha)}$. More generally, we can leave the functional form of the utility function unspecified, writing the optimization problem as

$$\max_{x_1, x_2} u(x_1, x_2) \text{ subject to } p_1 x_1 + p_2 x_2 = I. \tag{9.5}$$

Solving this, we would then get general expressions for the optimal values of x_1 and x_2 as simply functions of the consumer's economic circumstances; i.e.,

$$x_1 = x_1(p_1, p_2, I) \text{ and } x_2 = x_2(p_1, p_2, I). \tag{9.6}$$

9B.1.1 Income Demand Relationships

Income-demand curves such as those we derived graphically in Graph 9.1 are then simply "slices" of the more general functions we derive mathematically. For instance, for the Cobb–Douglas utility function used to derive the demand functions in expression (9.4), we can now hold fixed the price terms and simply see how the function changes as income changes. Taking the first derivative of each of the two demand functions, we get

$$\frac{\partial x_1}{\partial I} = \frac{\alpha}{p_1} \text{ and } \frac{\partial x_2}{\partial I} = \frac{1-\alpha}{p_2}, \tag{9.7}$$

and, since both α and the price terms are positive, we know immediately that, for the underlying Cobb–Douglas tastes, the income demand relationship for each of the two goods is positive. Furthermore, holding prices fixed, this relationship is constant, implying income-demand curves that are straight lines with positive slope (and zero intercept). Put differently, the second partial derivative of each income-demand function with respect to income is zero, implying no change in the slope.

To map these into the income-demand *curves* from part A of the chapter, we begin by solving the demand functions in expression (9.4) for I to get

$$I_1 = \frac{p_1 x_1}{\alpha} \text{ and } I_2 = \frac{p_2 x_2}{(1-\alpha)} \tag{9.8}$$

and note that the partial derivatives with respect to x_1 and x_2 are

$$\frac{\partial I_1}{\partial x_1} = \frac{p_1}{\alpha} \text{ and } \frac{\partial I_2}{\partial x_2} = \frac{p_2}{(1-\alpha)}. \tag{9.9}$$

These slopes of our income-demand *curves*, which are equal to the slopes of the *inverse* demand functions in expression (9.8), are then the inverse of the slopes of the demand functions in expression (9.7).

For instance, suppose that prices are equal to $p_1 = 1$ and $p_2 = 1$, and suppose that $\alpha = 0.75$. Then the slope of the income demand curve for x_1 is 4/3 while the slope of the income demand curve for x_2 is 4. When $p_1 = 1/2$ and $p_2 = 1/2$, on the other hand, the slopes of the two income-demand curves are 2/3 and 2, and when $p_1 = 1/4$ and $p_2 = 1/4$, the slopes become 1/3 and 1. Thus, for each set of prices, we get a different "slice" of the inverse demand function that becomes an income-demand curve for that particular set of prices. Graph 9.8a and 9.8b then graph these different income-demand curves for the two goods.

The fact that the income-demand curves for Cobb–Douglas tastes have positive slope should not be surprising. After all, we know from the previous chapters that such tastes represent tastes for normal goods, and normal goods are defined as goods that consumers consume more of as income rises. Beyond that, the fact that the income-demand curves in Graph 9.8 depend only on the price of one good is a special case that arises from the Cobb–Douglas specification of tastes. Other types of tastes will have the property (indicated in the functions in expression (9.6)) that demand for each good depends on the prices of both goods.

Exercise 9B.3*

Another special case of tastes that we have emphasized throughout is the case of quasilinear tastes. Consider, for instance, the utility function $u(x_1, x_2) = 100(\ln x_1) + x_2$. Calculate the demand function for x_1 and derive some sample income–demand curves for different prices.

Graph 9.8: Income–Demand Curves when $u(x_1, x_2) = x_1^{0.75} x_2^{0.25}$

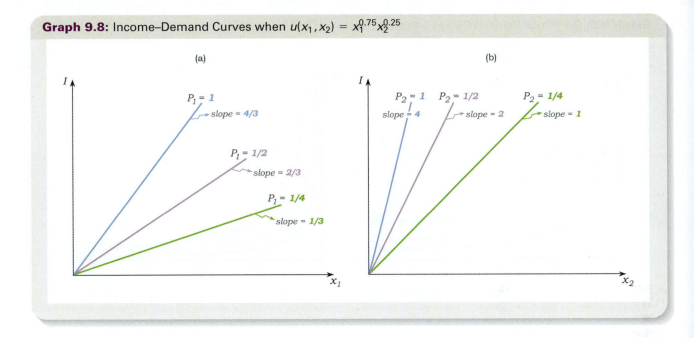

9B.1.2 Own-Price Demand Relationships

The own-price demand curves of the kind derived in Graph 9.2 are similarly just inverse slices of the more general demand functions in expression (9.6). This time, however, we are interested in the relationship between the quantity demanded and that good's price (rather than the quantity demanded and income). The slices of the inverse demand functions that we graph when we graph own-price demand curves then take the form

$$p_1 = p_1(x_1, p_2, I) \quad \text{and} \quad p_2 = p_2(x_2, p_1, I), \tag{9.10}$$

which simply involves solving the demand functions for prices. In the case of the Cobb–Douglas demand functions from expression (9.4), these are

$$p_1 = \frac{\alpha I}{x_1} \quad \text{and} \quad p_2 = \frac{(1 - \alpha)}{x_2}. \tag{9.11}$$

The demand *curves* are then simply slices of these inverse demand functions that hold income and the price of the other good fixed. In the special case of Cobb–Douglas tastes, however, each good's demand is independent of the other good's price, so we only have to hold income fixed as we graph the demand curves. This is done in Graph 9.9a for x_1 and in Graph 9.9b for x_2 for three different income levels. Note that for relatively standard tastes such as those represented by Cobb–Douglas utility functions, these demand curves tend to have relatively nonlinear shapes. This gives us some sense of what is lost when we simply derive such demand curves graphically by estimating them from just two points (as we did in Graph 9.2). Note also that, in each of the panels of Graph 9.9, the demand curve shifts out as income increases. Put differently, holding p_1 fixed, the quantity demanded increases as income rises, implying once again that the tastes are such that each good is a normal good (as we know is the case for Cobb–Douglas tastes). Were one of the underlying goods an inferior good, the demand curve for that good would shift inward as income goes up. And, when tastes are quasilinear in one of the goods, then the demand curve for that good would be unchanged as income rises since such a good would be borderline normal/inferior.

Graph 9.9: Own-Price Demand Curves when $u(x_1, x_2) = x_1^{0.75} x_2^{0.25}$

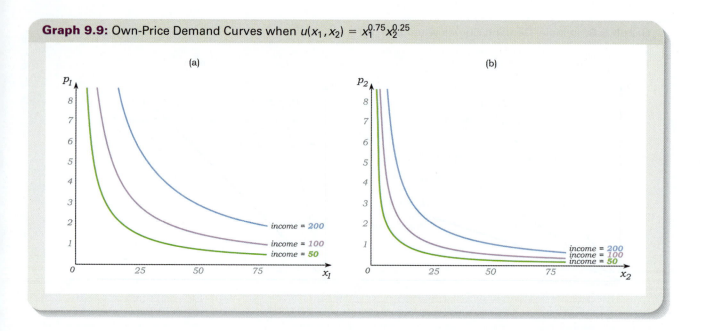

The derivatives of the demand functions (from expression (9.4)) with respect to own-prices are then

$$\frac{\partial x_1}{\partial p_1} = -\frac{\alpha I}{p_1^2} \quad \text{and} \quad \frac{\partial x_2}{\partial p_2} = -\frac{(1-\alpha)I}{p_2^2}, \tag{9.12}$$

and the derivatives of the *inverse* demand functions (in expression (9.11)) with respect to quantities are

$$\frac{\partial p_1}{\partial x_1} = -\frac{\alpha I}{x_1^2} \quad \text{and} \quad \frac{\partial p_2}{\partial x_2} = -\frac{(1-\alpha)I}{x_2^2}. \tag{9.13}$$

Suppose, for instance, that $\alpha = 0.75$ (as it is in the graphs), that $I = 100$, and that $p_1 = p_2 = 1$. The first equation in expression (9.12) then tells us that, when $p_1 = 1$, the slope of the demand function as p_1 changes is $-\alpha I/p_1^2 = -75$. The demand function $x_1 = \alpha I/p_1$ also tells us that $x_1 = 75$ when $p_1 = 1$. Plugging $x_1 = 75$ into the first equation in (9.13) then gives us the slope of the demand *curve* as $-\alpha I/x_1^2 = -1/75$, which is the inverse of what we got from taking the derivative of the demand *function*. More generally, the same steps allow us to write

$$\frac{\partial p_1}{\partial x_1} = -\frac{\alpha I}{x_1^2} = -\frac{\alpha I}{(\alpha I/p_1)^2} = -\frac{p_1^2}{\alpha I} = \left(\frac{\partial x_1}{\partial p_1}\right)^{-1} \tag{9.14}$$

where we use the fact that $x_1 = \alpha I/p_1$ (from equation (9.4)) in the middle of the expression. Once again, our demand *curves* that treat quantities as if they were the independent variable have slopes at every point that are inverses of the slopes of the corresponding slices of the demand *functions* that treat price as the independent variable.

Exercise 9B.4   Can you derive the same result for x_2?

Exercise 9B.5

As in exercise 9B.3, consider again tastes that can be represented by the utility function $u(x_1, x_2) = 100(\ln x_1) + x_2$. Using the demand function for x_1 that you derived in the previous exercise, plot the own-price demand curve when income is 100 and when $p_2 = 1$. Then plot the demand curve again when income rises to 200. Keep in mind that you are actually plotting inverse functions as you are doing this.

Exercise 9B.6

Knowing that own-price demand curves are inverse slices of own-price demand functions, how would the lower panels of Graph 9.2 look if you graphed slices of the actual functions (rather than the inverses); i.e., when you put price on the horizontal and the quantities of goods on the vertical axis?

9B.1.3 Cross-Price Demand Relationships

Finally, we noted in Section 9A.1.3 that the quantity demanded of one good often depends not only on that good's own price but also on the price(s) of other goods. For this reason, the general version of our demand functions in expression (9.6) include both prices as arguments of the function, with $x_1 = x_1(p_1, p_2, I)$ and $x_2 = x_2(p_1, p_2, I)$. Yet another way of "slicing" inverses of these functions then results in what we called "cross-price demand curves" in Section 9A.1.3, curves that illustrate, for a given income and own price, how the quantity demanded varies with changes in the price of a different good.

Cobb–Douglas tastes represent once again a special case in which the demand functions are *not* functions of any prices other than the good's own price. In expression (9.4), we derived those functions as $x_1 = \alpha I/p_1$ and $x_2 = (1 - \alpha)I/p_2$. The partial derivatives of these functions with respect to the other price (i.e., $\partial x_1/\partial p_2$ and $\partial x_2/\partial p_1$) are zero, indicating a zero slope. A slope of zero then becomes a slope of ∞ when we reverse the axes to put price on the vertical axis; i.e., we get cross-price demand curves that are perfectly vertical lines.

For a given taste parameter α and a given income I and own-price p_1, the demand for good x_1 is therefore constant. Take, for example, the case when $\alpha = 0.75, I = 100$, and $p_1 = 1$. Plugging these values into the demand function for x_1, we get that $x_1 = 75$. Similarly, if the price of good x_1 is 3, we get $x_1 = 25$, and if $p_1 = 5$, then $x_1 = 15$. The resulting cross-price demand curves are simply vertical lines at these respective quantities, as illustrated in Graph 9.10a. Similarly, you could derive vertical cross-price demand curves for different levels of income.

Exercise 9B.7

What would the slices of the demand function (rather than the inverse slices in Graph 9.10a) look like?

The reason for this shape of cross-price demand curves in the Cobb–Douglas case lies in the fact that income and substitution effects are exactly offsetting. In Graph 9.3 of Section 9A.1.3, we illustrated a cross-price demand curve for quasilinear tastes, tastes in which the income effect was zero and thus only the substitution effect operated. This substitution effect implied that, whenever p_2 decreases, a consumer would tend to consume more of x_2 and less of x_1, which, in the absence of an income effect, gives rise to the positive slope of the cross-price demand curve. For Cobb–Douglas tastes, however, x_1 is a normal good, implying a positive income effect on x_1 consumption from a decrease in the price of x_2. For a normal good, bundle C in Graph 9.3 would then lie to the right of bundle B (and possibly to the right of bundle A), and our analysis of Cobb–Douglas demand functions tells us that it would lie exactly above A when tastes can be represented by Cobb–Douglas utility functions.

Recall from our discussion of tastes in Chapter 5, however, that Cobb–Douglas tastes are a special case of a more general class of constant elasticity of substitution (CES) tastes, a case in which that elasticity of substitution is equal to exactly 1. The elasticity of substitution determines

Graph 9.10: Cross Price-Demand Curves for CES Utility with different Elasticities of Substitution

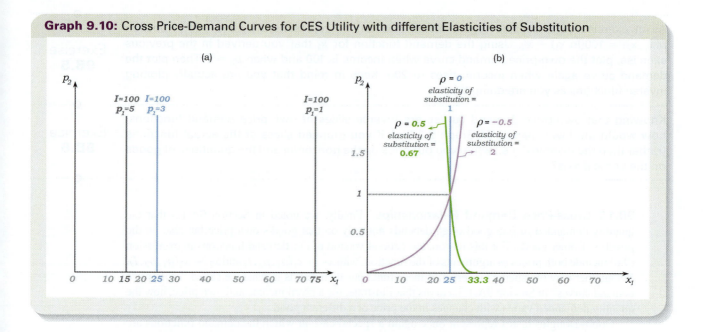

the size of the substitution effect, which implies that, as that elasticity decreases, the substitution effect will fall and will thus be more than offset by the income effect. Similarly, it should be the case that, when the elasticity of substitution is greater than 1, the size of the substitution effect increases and will thus no longer be offset by the income effect.

We can check this intuition by calculating the demand functions for the more general class of CES utility functions $u(x_1,x_2) = (\alpha x_1^{-\rho} + (1 - \alpha)x_2^{-\rho})^{-1/\rho}$, where (as noted in Chapter 5) the elasticity of substitution is equal to $1/(1 + \rho)$. Solving the maximization problem in expression (9.5) using this utility function (and slugging through some algebra), we get that

$$x_1 = \frac{\alpha^{1/(1+\rho)}I}{(\alpha^{1/(1+\rho)}p_1) + ((1 - \alpha)p_1p_2^{\rho})^{1/(1+\rho)}} \quad \text{and}$$

$$x_2 = \frac{(1-\alpha)^{1/(1+\rho)}I}{((1 - \alpha)^{1/(1+\rho)}p_2) + (\alpha p_1^{\rho}p_2)^{1/(1+\rho)}}.$$

(9.15)

Exercise 9B.8** Verify that these are in fact the right demand functions for tastes represented by the CES utility function.

Notice that when $\rho = 0$, these functions collapse down to those in expression (9.4) because when $\rho = 0$, CES utility functions are Cobb–Douglas. We can then graph different (inverse) cross-price demand slices of this function by fixing all parameters and variables other than p_2. Suppose, for instance, we set $\alpha = 0.75, p_1 = 3$, and $I = 100$. Graph 9.10b then graphs the resulting function for x_1 as it varies with p_2 for three different values of ρ (0.5, 0 and −0.5) corresponding to the elasticities of substitution of 0.67, 1 and 2. The middle (blue) curve represents the Cobb–Douglas tastes graphed in panel (a) of Graph 9.10. Notice that an elasticity of substitution below that of Cobb–Douglas tastes leads to a downward-sloping cross-price demand curve, while an elasticity greater than that of Cobb–Douglas tastes leads to an upward slope. You could confirm this by showing that $\partial x_1/\partial p_2 < 0$ when $\rho > 0$ and $\partial x_1/\partial p_2 > 0$ when $\rho < 0$ (recalling again how this translates to inverse slopes). This confirms our intuition that the greater the elasticity of substitution, the larger will be the substitution effect that suggests a positive cross-price relationship. Cobb–Douglas tastes with an elasticity of substitution of 1 represent the boundary case where this substitution effect is just large enough to exactly offset the income effect.

In Graph 9.3, we intuitively concluded that cross-price demand curves slope up when tastes are quasilinear. Verify this for tastes that can be represented by the utility function $u(x_1, x_2) = 100(\ln x_1) + x_2$ for which you derived the demand functions in exercise 9B.3. Draw the cross-price demand curve for x_1 when income is 2,000 and $p_1 = 5$.

Exercise 9B.9

Suppose that income was 500 instead of 2,000 in exercise 9B.9. Determine at what point the optimization problem results in a corner solution (by calculating the demand function for x_2 and seeing when it becomes negative). Illustrate how this would change the cross-price demand curve you drew in exercise 9B.9. (*Hint*: The change occurs in the cross-price demand curve at $p_2 = 5$.)

Exercise 9B.10

9B.2 Labor Supply[5]

As in the case of demand relationships in goods markets, we have already developed the basic technique of deriving labor supply curves of the kind drawn in Graph 9.4. The relevant budget constraint now arises from the fact that the amount spent on consumption c has to be equal to the value of the labor sold by the individual at the market wage w. Given that the individual starts with some particular leisure endowment L, the "hours spent working" is equivalent to "the hours *not* spent leisuring," or $(L-\ell)$. Thus, along the budget constraint, $c = w(L-\ell)$, or written differently,

$$wL = c + w\ell. \tag{9.16}$$

When written in this form, the budget constraint most closely resembles the form we are used to seeing in the goods market, with wL being equal to the wealth endowment (rather than exogenous income), the price of the "c" good equal to 1, and the price (or opportunity cost) of leisure equal to w. The general form of the utility maximization problem that gives rise to labor supply can then be written as

$$\max_{c,\ell} u(c,\ell) \text{ subject to } wL = c + w\ell. \tag{9.17}$$

The solutions to this maximization problem are then of the form

$$\ell = \ell(w,L) \text{ and } c = c(w,L), \tag{9.18}$$

with both the optimal amount of leisure and the optimal amount of consumption a function of the wage rate and the leisure endowment.[6]

Once we have derived the function that tells us, for any wage w and leisure endowment L, the amount of leisure an individual will choose, we are one small step from having derived the

---

[5] Students who did not read Chapters 3 and 8 should skip this and the next section.
[6] Implicitly, of course, these functions are also a function of the price of consumption, but since that is simply equal to 1 given that we defined consumption as "a dollars worth of consumption," it does not formally enter into the previous equations. Were one to use a price for consumption that can vary, then this price would become an argument in the functions in expression (9.18) and would appear in front of the c term in expression (9.17).

labor supply functions. This is because the quantity of labor supplied is simply equal to the quantity of the leisure endowment that is not consumed as leisure, or $(L - \ell)$. Using the equation for optimal leisure consumption in expression (9.18), we can thus simply write the labor supply function as

$$l(w,L) = L - \ell(w,L). \tag{9.19}$$

Now, when we hold the leisure endowment fixed, this labor supply function becomes simply a "slice" of the more general function, a slice in which labor supply is a function of only the wage rate and can thus be represented in a two-dimensional graph as a labor supply curve (when we take its inverse). Notice how the mathematics behind this exactly mirrors the graphical derivation in Graph 9.4. First, holding L fixed at 60, we graphically maximized utility over the budget constraint between consumption and leisure. Then, in order to translate our findings into points on labor supply curves, we subtracted the optimal leisure level from the fixed leisure endowment to plot the labor supply on the lower graphs.

Exercise 9B.11   What function is graphed in the middle portions of each panel of Graph 9.4? What function is graphed in the bottom portion of each panel of Graph 9.4?

As in the section on consumer demand, we can again see how specific tastes now translate into labor supply functions. First, consider tastes that are quasilinear in leisure and can be represented by the utility function $u(c,\ell) = c + \alpha \ln \ell$. Solving the maximization problem defined in expression (9.17) for these tastes, we get

$$\ell = \frac{\alpha}{w} \quad \text{and} \quad c = wL - \alpha, \tag{9.20}$$

with the resulting labor supply function equal to

$$l(w,L) = L - \frac{\alpha}{w}. \tag{9.21}$$

Exercise 9B.12   Verify these results.

Suppose, for instance, that we hold L fixed at 60 hours per week, as we did in Section 9A.2, and suppose tastes are such that $\alpha = 400$. Then the labor supply function becomes $l(w) = 60 - (400/w)$, the inverse of which is graphed as a labor supply curve in Graph 9.11a (and is labeled "$L = 60$" indicating we have assumed a leisure endowment of 60.) Similarly, a second labor supply curve corresponding to a leisure endowment of 40 hours per week is graphed for comparison. (In each case, the labor supply curve asymptotically approaches the leisure endowment as the wage approaches infinity.)

The fact that labor supply is upward sloping for tastes that are quasilinear in leisure should not surprise us given the intuition regarding substitution and wealth effects we built in Section 9A.2. We know that the substitution effect will always suggest that an individual will work more as the wage rises because leisure has become relatively more expensive. When tastes are quasilinear in leisure, we also know that there is no counteracting wealth effect. Thus, the substitution effect is the only effect on the leisure axis, causing consumption of leisure to decline, and work hours to increase, as wage goes up.

Graph 9.11: Labor Supply with Tastes that Are (a) Quasilinear, (b) Cobb–Douglas, and (c) CES

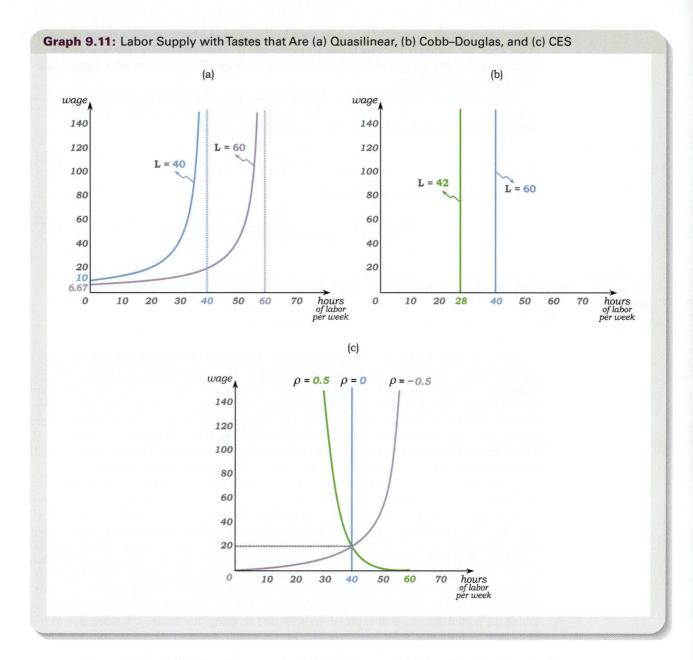

Next, consider Cobb–Douglas tastes that can be represented by the utility function $u(c, \ell) = c^{\alpha} \ell^{(1-\alpha)}$. Solving the maximization problem in expression (9.17) for this utility function, we get that

$$\ell = (1 - \alpha)L \quad \text{and} \quad c = \alpha w L, \tag{9.22}$$

with the resulting labor supply function equal to

$$l(w, L) = L - (1 - \alpha)L = \alpha L. \tag{9.23}$$

Thus, in this special Cobb–Douglas case, the labor supply function in fact does *not* depend on the wage, which implies that the labor supply curves are vertical lines (because $\partial l / \partial w = 0$) with substitution and wealth effects exactly offsetting one another. For instance, suppose that $\alpha = 2/3$ and the leisure endowment L is equal to 60 hours per week. Then weekly labor supply is 40 hours regardless of the wage rate. Similarly, if the leisure endowment were 42 hours instead of 60, the number of hours of labor supplied per week would be 28 regardless of the wage. These different labor supply curves are depicted in Graph 9.11b.

Finally, consider the more general constant elasticity of substitution (CES) utility specification $u(c,\ell) = (\alpha c^{-\rho} + (1-\alpha)\ell^{-\rho})^{-1/\rho}$. Solving the maximization problem in expression (9.17) with this utility function, and doing some tedious algebra, we get

$$\ell = \frac{L(1-\alpha)^{1/(\rho+1)}}{(\alpha w^{-\rho})^{1/(\rho+1)} + (1-\alpha)^{1/(\rho+1)}} \tag{9.24}$$

with corresponding labor supply function

$$l(w,L) = L - \frac{L(1-\alpha)^{1/(\rho+1)}}{(\alpha w^{-\rho})^{1/(\rho+1)} + (1-\alpha)^{1/(\rho+1)}}. \tag{9.25}$$

Exercise 9B.13   Verify this leisure demand and labor supply function for the CES function that is given.

From our work in Chapter 5, we know that the elasticity of substitution, and thus the size of the substitution effect, is decreasing in the parameter ρ. More specifically, as ρ approaches -1, indifference curves approach those of perfect substitutes; when $\rho = 0$, the tastes are Cobb–Douglas; and as ρ approaches positive infinity, indifference curves approach those of perfect complements. From equation (9.23), we also know that substitution and wealth effects are exactly offsetting on the leisure dimension when tastes are Cobb–Douglas; i.e., when $\rho = 0$. This suggests that when $\rho > 0$, the wealth effect will outweigh the substitution effect and will thus result in a negatively sloped labor supply curve, while the opposite holds when $\rho < 0$.

Suppose, for instance, that the weekly leisure endowment L is again set to 60. Graph 9.11c on the previous page then plots the labor supply curves for different levels of ρ, in each case setting α equal to the level required in order to make the optimal labor supply at a wage of 20 equal to 40 hours per week. (This is done so that the resulting labor supply curves have a common labor supply at $w = 20$.[7]) Our intuition regarding the relative sizes of substitution and wealth effects is then confirmed, with tastes that exhibit a high level of substitutability between leisure and consumption ($\rho < 0$) generating substitution effects that outweigh wealth effects, and tastes that exhibit low substitutability between leisure and consumption generating substitution effects that are outweighed by wealth effects. You can formally check that this holds by taking the partial derivative of expression (9.25) and showing that $\partial l/\partial w < 0$ when $\rho > 0$ and that $\partial l/\partial w > 0$ when $\rho < 0$.

9B.3 Demand for and Supply of Financial Capital

Finally, we can show again that the supply and demand curves for financial capital, or the demand curves for savings and borrowing, we derived in Section 9A.3 are simply (inverse) slices of more general functions that arise from general intertemporal optimization problems. In Chapters 3 and 8, we already demonstrated that two-period versions of intertemporal budget constraints can be written as

$$(1 + r)c_1 + c_2 = (1 + r)e_1 + e_2, \tag{9.26}$$

---

[7] The resulting values of α are 0.24025 when $\rho = -0.5$, 2/3 when $\rho = 0$, and 0.9267 when $\rho = 0.5$.

where e_1 and e_2 represent period 1 and 2 endowments (or income), r represents the relevant interest rate over the intervening period, and c_1 and c_2 represent consumption in the two periods. A consumer thus faces the optimization problem

$$\max_{c_1,c_2} u(c_1,c_2) \text{ subject to } (1 + r)c_1 + c_2 = (1 + r)e_1 + e_2. \qquad (9.27)$$

Solving this, we get general demand functions for c_1 and c_2 of the form

$$c_1 = c_1(r,e_1,e_2) \text{ and } c_2 = c_2(r,e_1,e_2). \qquad (9.28)$$

These functions tell us, for any set of economic circumstances faced by the consumer, how much he or she will consume this period and next period. Subtracting $c_1(r,e_1,e_2)$ from e_1 furthermore gives us the difference in period 1 consumption and period 1 income, or the amount of savings the consumer will choose to undertake under different economic circumstances. Thus, we can calculate the savings supply function

$$s(r,e_1,e_2) = e_1 - c_1(r,e_1,e_2). \qquad (9.29)$$

When $s(r,e_1,e_2) > 0$, the consumer chooses to save this period (or supply financial capital), whereas when $s(r,e_1,e_2) < 0$, he or she chooses to borrow (or demand financial capital). A consumer will, of course, switch between saving and borrowing depending on the economic circumstances he or she faces. As we already showed intuitively in Section 9A.3, the consumer will save if $e_1 > 0$ and $e_2 = 0$ (Section 9A.3.1); he or she will borrow if $e_1 = 0$ and $e_2 > 0$ (Section 9A.3.2); and he or she may switch between borrowing and saving as the interest rate changes when $e_1 > 0$ and $e_2 > 0$ (Section 9A.3.3).

Solving the optimization problem in expression (9.27) for Cobb–Douglas tastes represented by the utility function $u(c_1,c_2) = c_1^\alpha c_2^{(1-\alpha)}$, for instance, we get

$$c_1(r,e_1,e_2) = \alpha \left(\frac{(1 + r)e_1 + e_2}{(1 + r)} \right) \text{ and}$$

$$c_2(r,e_1,e_2) = (1 - \alpha)\big((1 + r)e_1 + e_2\big), \qquad (9.30)$$

with a resulting savings function of

$$s(r,e_1,e_2) = e_1 - \alpha \left(\frac{(1 + r)e_1 + e_2}{(1 + r)} \right). \qquad (9.31)$$

Verify that these three equations are correct.

Exercise 9B.14

9B.3.1 Saving and the "Supply of Capital"   Suppose, then, that we return to the example of you earning $10,000 this summer and expecting to earn nothing next summer as you cruise through the Amazon. Suppose further that you place equal value on consumption in both summers, with $\alpha = 0.5$. Then our savings function (9.31) simply becomes

$$s(r) = 5,000. \qquad (9.32)$$

Put differently, your savings are independent of the interest rate in the Cobb–Douglas case, leading to a vertical relationship between savings and the interest rate (when the interest rate appears on the vertical axis and savings appears on the horizontal). We know from our intuitive analysis in Section 9A.3.1 that the substitution effect suggests that savings will increase with the interest rate, and that the wealth effect suggests the opposite (when consumption in period 1 is a normal good as it is under Cobb–Douglas tastes). Thus, the substitution and wealth effects are exactly offsetting for these tastes.

Once again, then, the key to whether the relationship between savings and the interest rate is positive or negative lies in the relative weights of substitution and wealth effects. Thus, as consumption in periods 1 and 2 becomes more substitutable, leading to a greater substitution effect, the relationship becomes positive, whereas when consumption across the periods becomes more complementary, leading to a smaller substitution effect, the relationship becomes negative.

Exercise 9B.15**   Consider the more general CES utility function $u(c_1, c_2) = (0.5c_1^{-\rho} + 0.5c_2^{-\rho})^{-1/\rho}$ and solve for the savings supply function when you earn $10,000 this period and nothing in the future. Then verify that you obtain the vertical relationship between savings and the interest rate when $\rho = 0$ and determine how this slope changes when $\rho > 0$ (implying relatively low elasticity of substitution) and when $\rho < 0$ (implying relatively high elasticity of substitution).

9B.3.2 Borrowing and the "Demand for Capital"

Similarly, we can consider the case in which all your income is earned next summer, with any consumption this summer financed through borrowing against next summer's earnings. Again, suppose that your tastes are Cobb–Douglas with $\alpha = 0.5$, and suppose further that your earnings next summer will be $11,000. We can then again use expression (9.31) to determine your savings this summer by simply plugging in $e_1 = 0$ and $e_2 = 11,000$ to get

$$s(r) = -\frac{5,500}{(1 + r)}. \tag{9.33}$$

Since your income this summer is zero, you will (as we already concluded in Section 9A.3.2) naturally have to borrow in order to consume this summer, and the amount that you will borrow (unlike the amount that you saved in the previous example) will depend on the interest rate. In particular, note that $\partial s/\partial r > 0$, which means that your negative savings become smaller as the interest rate rises. Alternatively, we could phrase your behavior in terms of borrowing (instead of negative saving), in which case we would consider the negative of the savings function in expression (9.33). The partial derivative of that (negative savings) function with respect to the interest rate would be negative, implying that borrowing declines as the interest rate rises. These conclusions are once again consistent with our intuition from Section 9A.3.2 in which we demonstrated that the impact of both the substitution and the wealth effect causes the borrower to lower his or her borrowing as the interest rate rises.

Exercise 9B.16**   Using the CES utility function from exercise 9B.15, verify that the negative relationship between borrowing and the interest rate arises regardless of the value that ρ takes (whenever $e_1 = 0$ and $e_2 > 0$.)

9B.3.3 Switching between Borrowing and Saving

We concluded Section 9A.3 with an example in which a consumer earns income in both periods and chooses to borrow or save depending on the interest rate. This type of savings function is also implicitly possible in our mathematical setup whenever e_1 and e_2 are both positive. In the Cobb–Douglas case, for instance, suppose that $e_1 = 4,600$ and $e_2 = 5,400$, and suppose again that $\alpha = 0.5$. Plugging these values into the savings function (9.31), we get

$$s(r) = 2,300 - \frac{2,700}{(1 + r)}, \tag{9.34}$$

which is -400 at an interest rate of 0% but has positive slope ($\partial s/\partial r = 2700/(1 + r)^2$) and becomes positive at an interest rate of 17.39%.

Graph this function in a graph similar to Graph 9.7 (which is the graph of an inverse borrowing (rather than saving) function).

Exercise 9B.17

CONCLUSION

Having investigated in detail what it means for individuals to "do the best they can given their circumstances," or to "optimize subject to constraints," this chapter took the next step of summarizing the results of such optimizing behavior in various demand relationships. This has allowed us to derive mathematically such concepts as consumer demand functions and labor supply functions, and it has enabled us to derive intuitively the graphical relationships known as demand and supply curves. These curves hold fixed all aspects of a consumer's economic circumstances except one, and then plot the relationship between the remaining variable and the quantity of a good demanded (or the quantity of labor supplied). In that sense, demand (and supply) curves are really just (inverse) "slices" (that hold a number of variables fixed) of multidimensional demand (and supply) functions (that allow all aspects of economic circumstances to vary).

In most undergraduate textbooks, demand curves are then treated as if they tell us something beyond what we have discussed thus far. In particular, it is often claimed that demand curves tell us not only how the quantity demanded of a particular good changes as some economic variable (like price) changes but also that these can be used to measure consumer welfare through notions such as consumer surplus. In the next chapter, we will see to what extent this claim is true and in the process will derive a more general way of thinking about consumer welfare. As it turns out, the claim is true only for one special case of tastes and not for the more general class of tastes that we have treated throughout. This will become important as we think more about policies in upcoming chapters.

END-OF-CHAPTER EXERCISES

9.1 The following is intended to explore what kinds of income-demand relationships are logically possible.

A. For each of the following, indicate whether the relationship is possible or not and explain:

a. A good is a necessity and has a positive income-demand relationship.

b. A good is a necessity and has a negative income-demand relationship.

c. A good is a luxury and has a negative income-demand relationship.

d. A good is quasilinear and has a negative income-demand relationship.

e. Tastes are homothetic and one of the goods has a negative income-demand relationship.

B. Derive the income-demand relationships for each good for the following tastes:

a. $u(x_1, x_2, x_3) = x_1^\alpha x_2^\beta x_3^{(1-\alpha-\beta)}$ where α and β lie between zero and 1 and sum to less than 1.

b. $u(x_1, x_2) = \alpha \ln x_1 + x_2$. (*Note*: To specify fully the income demand relationship in this case, you need to watch out for corner solutions.) Graph the income demand curves for x_1 and x_2, carefully labeling slopes and intercepts.

9.2† The following is intended to explore what kinds of own-price demand relationships are logically possible in a two-good model with exogenous income (unless otherwise specified).

A. For each of the following, indicate whether the relationship is possible or not and explain:

a. Tastes are homothetic and the own-price demand relationship is positive.

b. A good is inferior and its own-price relationship is negative.

---

*conceptually challenging
**computationally challenging
†solutions in Study Guide

c.   In a model with endogenous income, a good is normal and its own-price demand relationship is negative.

d.   In a model with endogenous income, a good is normal and its own-price demand relationship is positive.

B. Suppose that tastes can be represented by the Cobb–Douglas utility function $u(x_1, x_2) = x_1^\alpha x_2^{(1-\alpha)}$.

a.   Derive the demand functions when income is exogenous and illustrate that own-price demand curves slope down.

b.   Now suppose that all income is derived from an endowment (e_1, e_2). If $e_2 = 0$, what is the shape of the own-price demand curve for x_1?

c.   Continuing with part (b), what is the shape of the own price demand curve for x_1 when $e_2 > 0$?

d.   Suppose tastes were instead represented by the more general CES utility function. Without doing any additional math, can you guess what would have to be true about ρ in order for the own-price demand for x_1 to slope up when $e_1 > 0$ and $e_2 = 0$?

9.3   The following is intended to explore what kinds of cross-price demand relationships are logically possible in a two-good model with exogenous income.

A. For each of the following, indicate whether the relationship is possible or not and explain:

a.   A good is normal and its cross-price demand relationship is positive.

b.   A good is normal and its cross-price relationship is negative.

c.   A good is inferior and its cross-price relationship is negative.

d.   Tastes are homothetic and one of the good's cross-price relationship is negative.

e.   Tastes are homothetic and one of the good's cross-price relationship is positive.

B. Now consider specific tastes represented by particular utility functions.

a.   Suppose tastes are represented by the function $u(x_1, x_2) = \alpha \ln x_1 + x_2$. What is the shape of the cross-price demand curves for x_1 and x_2?

b.   Suppose instead tastes are Cobb–Douglas. What do cross-price demand curves look like?

c.   Now suppose tastes can be represented by a CES utility function. Without doing any math, can you determine for what values of ρ the cross-price demand relationship is upward sloping?

d.**   Suppose tastes can be represented by the CES function $u(x_1, x_2) = (0.5x_1^{-\rho} + 0.5x_2^{-\rho})^{-1/\rho}$. Verify your intuitive answer from part (c).

9.4   In Graph 9.4, we illustrated how you can derive the labor supply curve from a consumer model in which workers choose between leisure and consumption.

A. In end-of-chapter exercise 3.1 you were asked to illustrate a budget constraint with labor rather than leisure on the horizontal axis. Do so again, assuming that the most you can work per week is 60 hours.

a.   Now add to this graph an indifference curve that would make working 40 hours per week optimal.

b.   Beginning with the graph you have just drawn, illustrate the same wealth and substitution effects as drawn in the top panel of Graph 9.4a for an increase in the wage.

c.   Then, on a second graph right below it, put weekly labor hours on the horizontal axis and wage on the vertical, and derive the labor supply curve directly from your work in the previous graph. Compare the resulting graph with the lowest panel in Graph 9.4a.

d.   Repeat this for the case where wealth and substitution effects look as they do in Graph 9.4b.

e.   Repeat this again for the case in Graph 9.4c.

f.   *True or False*: We can model the choices of workers either using our five standard assumptions about tastes defined over leisure and consumption, or we can model these choices using tastes defined over labor and consumption. Either way, we get the same answers so long as we let go of the monotonicity assumption in the latter type of model.

B. Now suppose that a worker's tastes over consumption and leisure can be defined by the utility function $u(c, \ell) = c^\alpha \ell^{(1-\alpha)}$ (and again assume that the worker has a leisure endowment of 60 hours per week).

    a.   Derive the labor supply function by first deriving the leisure demand function.

    b.   How would you define a utility function over consumption and *labor* (rather than consumption and *leisure*) such that the underlying tastes would be the same?

    c.   Which of our usual assumptions about tastes do not hold for tastes represented by the utility function you have just derived?

    d.   Using the utility function you have just given, illustrate that you can derive the same labor supply curve as before by making labor (rather than leisure) a choice variable in the optimization problem.

9.5[†]   **Everyday Application:** *Backward-Bending Labor Supply Curve*: We have suggested in this chapter that labor economists believe that labor supply curves typically slope up when wages are low and down when wages are high. This is sometimes referred to as a *backward-bending labor supply curve*.

A. Which of the following statements is inconsistent with the empirical finding of a backward-bending labor supply curve?

    a.   For the typical worker, leisure is an inferior good when wages are low and a normal good when wages are high.

    b.   For the typical worker, leisure is a normal good when wages are low and an inferior good when wages are high.

    c.   For the typical worker, leisure is always a normal good.

    d.   For the typical worker, leisure is always an inferior good.

B. Suppose that tastes over consumption and leisure are described by a constant elasticity of substitution utility function $u(c, \ell) = (0.5c^{-\rho} + 0.5\ell^{-\rho})^{-1/\rho}$.

    a.   Derive the labor supply curve assuming a leisure endowment L.

    b.** Illustrate for which values of ρ this curve is upward sloping and for which it is downward sloping.

    c.   Is it possible for the backward-bending labor supply curve to emerge from tastes captured by a CES utility function?

    d.   For practical purposes, we typically only have to worry about modeling tastes accurately at the margin; i.e., around the current bundles that consumers/workers are consuming. This is because low wage workers, for instance, may experience some increases in wages but not so much that they are suddenly high wage workers, and vice versa. If you were modeling worker behavior for a group of workers and you modeled each worker's tastes as CES over leisure and consumption, how would you assume ρ differs for low wage and high wage workers (assuming you are persuaded of the empirical validity of the backward-bending labor supply curve)?

9.6   **Business Application:** *Price Discounts, Substitutes, and Complements*: A business might worry that pricing of one product might impact demand for another product that is also sold by the same business. Here, we'll explore conditions under which such worries are more or less important before turning to some specific examples.

A. Suppose first that we label the two goods that a firm sells as simply x_1 and x_2. The firm considers putting a discount of δ on the price of x_1, a discount that would lower the price from p_1 to $(1 - \delta)p_1$.

    a.   For a consumer who budgets I for consumption of x_1 and x_2, illustrate the budget before and after the discount is put in place.

    b.   Assuming that tastes are homothetic, derive the relationship between δ on the vertical axis and x_1 on the horizontal axis.

    c.   Now derive the relationship between δ and x_2; can you tell if it slopes up or down? What does your answer depend on?

    d.   Suppose that x_1 is printers and x_2 is printer cartridges produced by the same company. Compare this to the case where x_1 is Diet Coke and x_2 is Zero Coke. In which case is there a more compelling case for discounts on x_1?

B. Suppose that tastes are defined by $u(x_1, x_2) = x_1^\alpha x_2^{(1-\alpha)}$.

    a.   Derive the demand functions for x_1 and x_2 as a function of prices, I and δ.

    b.   Are these upward or downward sloping in δ?

    c.   Under the more general specification of tastes as CES; i.e., $u(x_1, x_2) = (\alpha x_1^{-\rho} + (1 - \alpha)x_2^{-\rho})^{-1/\rho}$, how would your answer change as ρ changes?

9.7   **Business Application:** *Good Apples versus Bad Apples*: People are often amazed at the quality of produce that is available in markets far away from where that produce is grown, and that it is often the case that the average quality of produce is *higher* the farther the place is from where the produce originates. Here we will try to explain this as the result of producers' awareness of relative demand differences resulting from substitution effects.

A. Suppose you own an apple orchard that produces two types of apples: high quality apples x_1 and low quality apples x_2. The market price for a pound of high quality apples is higher than that for a pound of low quality apples; i.e., $p_1 > p_2$. You sell some of your apples locally and you ship the rest to be sold in a different market. It costs you an amount c per pound of apples to get apples to that market.

    a.   Begin with a graph of a consumer who chooses between high and low quality apples in the local store in your town. Illustrate the consumer's budget and optimal choice.

    b.   The only way you are willing to ship apples to a far-away market is if you can get as much for those apples as you can get in your town, which means you will add the per-pound transportation cost c to the price you charge for your apples. How will the slope of the budget constraint for the far-away consumer differ from that for your local consumer, and what does that imply for the opportunity cost of good apples in terms of bad apples?

    c.   Apples represent a relatively small expenditure category for most consumers, which means that income effects are probably very small. In light of that, you may assume that the amount of income devoted to apple consumption is always an amount that gets the consumer to the same indifference curve in the "slice" of tastes that hold all goods other than x_1 and x_2 fixed. Can you determine where consumer demand for high quality apples is likely to be larger: in the home market or in the far-away market?

    d.   Explain how, in the presence of transportation costs, one would generally expect the phenomenon of finding a larger share of high quality products in markets that are far from the production source than in markets that are close.

B. Suppose that we model our consumers' tastes as $u(x_1, x_2) = x_1^\alpha x_2^{(1-\alpha)}$.

    a.   What has to be true about α in order for x_1 to be the good apples?

    b.   Letting consumer income devoted to apple consumption be given by I, derive the consumer's demand for good and bad apples as a function of p_1, p_2, I, and c. (Recall that c is the per-pound transportation cost that is added to the price of apples.)

    c.   What is the ratio of demand for x_1 over x_2?

    d.   Can you tell from this in which market there will be greater relative demand for good versus bad apples: the local market or the far-away market?

    e.   In part A, we held the consumer's indifference curve in the graph fixed and argued that it is reasonable to approximate the consumer's behavior this way given that apple expenditures are typically a small fraction of a consumer's budget. Can you explain how what you just did in part B is different? Is it necessarily the case that consumers in far-away places will consume more high quality apples than consumers (with the same tastes) in local markets? Can we still conclude that far-away markets will have a higher *fraction* of high quality apples?

9.8*   **Policy Application:** *Tax and Retirement Policy*: In Chapter 3, we illustrated budgets in which a consumer faced trade-offs between working and leisuring now as well as between consuming now and consuming in the future. We can use a model of this kind to think about tax and retirement policy.

A. Suppose period 1 represents the period over which a worker is productive in the labor force and period 2 represents the period during which the worker expects to be retired. The worker earns a wage w and has L hours of leisure time that could be devoted to work l or leisure consumption ℓ. Earnings this period can be consumed as current consumption c_1 or saved for retirement consumption c_2 at an interest rate r. Suppose throughout that consumption in both periods is a normal good, as is leisure this period.

a. Illustrate this worker's budget constraint in a three-dimensional graph with c_1, c_2, and ℓ on the axes.

b. For certain types of tastes (as for those used in part B of this question), the optimal labor decision does not vary with the wage or the interest rate in this problem. Suppose this implies that taking ℓ^* in leisure is always optimal for this worker. Illustrate how this puts the worker's decision on a slice of the three-dimensional budget you graphed in part (a).

c. Assume that optimal choices always occur on the two-dimensional slice you have identified. Illustrate how you could derive a demand curve for c_1; i.e., a curve that shows the relationship between c_1 on the horizontal axis and the interest rate r on the vertical. Does this curve slope up or down? What does your answer depend on?

d. Can you derive a similar economic relationship except this time with w rather than r on the vertical axis? Can you be certain about whether this relationship is upward sloping (given that consumption in both periods is a normal good)?

e. Suppose that the government introduces a program that raises taxes on wages and uses the revenues to subsidize savings. Indicate first how each part of this policy—the tax on wages and the subsidy for savings (which raises the effective interest rate)—impacts current and retirement consumption.

f. Suppose the tax revenue is exactly enough to pay for the subsidy. Without drawing any further graphs, what do you think will happen to current and retirement consumption?

g. There are two ways that programs such as this can be structured: Method 1 puts the tax revenues collected from the individual into a personal savings account that is used to finance the savings subsidy when the worker retires; Method 2 uses current tax revenues to support current retirees, and then uses tax revenues from future workers to subsidize current workers when they retire. (The latter is often referred to as "pay-as-you-go" financing.) By simply knowing what happens to current and retirement consumption of workers under such programs, can you speculate what will happen to overall savings under Method 1 and Method 2 (given that tax revenues become savings under Method 1 but not under Method 2)?

B. Suppose the worker's tastes can be summarized by the utility function $u(c_1, c_2, \ell) = (c_1^\alpha \ell^{(1-\alpha)})^\beta c_2^{(1-\beta)}$.

a. Set up the budget equation that takes into account the trade-offs this worker faces between consuming and leisuring now as well as between consuming now and consuming in the future.

b. Set up this worker's optimization problem and solve for the optimal consumption levels in each period as well as the optimal leisure consumption this period. (Using the natural log transformation of the utility function will make this algebraically easier to solve.)

c. In part A, we assumed that the worker would choose the same amount of work effort regardless of the wage and interest rate. Is this true for the tastes used in this part of the exercise?

d. How does consumption before retirement change with w and r? Can you make sense of this in light of your graphical answers in part A?

e. In A(e), we described a policy that imposes a tax t on wages and a subsidy s on savings. Suppose that the tax lowers the wage retained by the worker to $(1 - t)w$ and the subsidy raises the effective interest rate for the worker to $(r + s)$. Without necessarily redoing the optimization problem, how will the equations for the optimal levels of c_1, c_2, and ℓ change under such a policy?

f. Are the effects of t and s individually as you concluded in A(e)?

g. For a given t, how much tax revenue does the government raise? For a given s, how much of a cost does the government incur? What do your answers imply about the relationship between s and t if the revenues raised now are exactly offset by the expenditures incurred next period (taking into account that the revenues can earn interest until they need to be spent)?

h. Can you now verify your conclusion from A(f)?

i. What happens to the size of personal savings that the individual worker puts away under this policy? If we consider the tax revenue the government collects on behalf of the worker (which will be returned in the form of the savings subsidy when the worker retires), what happens to the worker's overall savings—his or her personal savings plus the forced savings from the tax?

j. How would your answer about the increase in actual overall savings change if the government, instead of actually saving the tax revenue on behalf of the worker, were simply to spend current tax revenues on current retirees? (This, as mentioned in part A, is sometimes referred to as a *pay-as-you-go* policy.)

9.9*†   Policy Application: *Demand for Charities and Tax Deductibility:* One of the ways in which government policy supports a variety of activities in the economy is to make contributions to those activities tax deductible. For instance, suppose you pay a marginal income tax rate t and that a fraction δ of your contributions to charity are tax deductible. Then if you give \$1 to a charity, you do not have to pay income tax on \$$\delta$ and thus you end up paying \$$\delta t$ less in taxes. Giving \$1 to charity therefore does not cost you \$1, it only costs you \$$(1 - \delta t)$.

A. In the remainder of the problem, we will refer to $\delta = 0$ as "no deductibility" and $\delta = 1$ as "full deductibility". Assume throughout that giving to charity is a normal good.

  a.   How much does it cost you to give \$1 to charity under no deductibility? How much does it cost under full deductibility?

  b.   On a graph with "dollars given to charity" on the horizontal and "dollars spent on other consumption" on the vertical, illustrate a taxpayer's budget constraint (assuming the taxpayer pays a tax rate t on all income) under no deductibility and under full deductibility.

  c.   On a separate graph, derive the relationship between δ (ranging from zero to 1 on the vertical) and charitable giving (on the horizontal).

  d.   Next, suppose that charitable giving is fully deductible and illustrate how the consumer's budget changes as t increases. Can you tell whether charitable giving increases or decreases as the tax rate rises?

  e.   Suppose that an empirical economist reports the following finding: "Increasing tax deductibility raises charitable giving, and charitable giving under full deductibility remains unchanged as the tax rate changes." Can such behavior emerge from a rationally optimizing individual?

  f.   Shortly after assuming office, President Barack Obama proposed repealing the 2001 tax cuts implemented by President George W. Bush, thus raising the top income tax rate to 39.6%, back to the level it was under President Bill Clinton in the 1990s. At the same time, Obama made the controversial proposal only to allow deductions for charitable giving as if the marginal tax rate were 28%. For someone who pays the top marginal income tax under the Obama proposal, what does the proposal imply for δ? What about for someone paying a marginal tax rate of 33% or someone paying a marginal tax rate of 28%?

  g.   Would you predict that the Obama proposal would reduce charitable giving?

  h.   Defenders of the Obama proposal point out the following: After President Ronald Reagan's 1986 Tax Reform, the top marginal income tax rate was 28%, implying that it would cost high earners 72 cents for every dollar they contribute to charity, just as it would under the Obama proposal. If that was good enough under Reagan, it should be good enough now. In what sense is the comparison right, and in what sense is it misleading?

B. Now suppose that a taxpayer has Cobb–Douglas tastes over charitable giving (x_1) and other consumption (x_2).

  a.   Derive the taxpayer's demand for charitable giving as a function of income I, the degree of tax deductibility δ, and the tax rate t.

  b.   Is this taxpayer's behavior consistent with the empirical finding by the economist in part A(e) of the question?

Consumer Surplus and Deadweight Loss

Economists and policy makers may want to know whether particular policies make people better off or worse off, but sometimes they also need to quantify *how much* better off or worse off different consumers are.[1] At first glance, this may seem an impossible task given what we have said in Chapter 4 about the inherent impossibility of measuring happiness or satisfaction in an objective way. It turns out, however, that the tools we have developed will allow us to measure consumer welfare in objective terms without us having to measure happiness directly. Rather, we will find ways of quantifying how much better off or worse off consumers are in different economic circumstances by asking how much they are willing to pay to avoid particular circumstances or how much compensation would be required to make it up to them when circumstances change.

This way of thinking about welfare effects from institutional or policy changes allows us then to address the following question: Is it at least in principle possible to compensate those who lose from the policy with part of the gains accruing to those who gain from the policy? If the answer is yes, then, at least in principle, there is a way to make the world more *efficient*, to make some people better off without making anyone worse off. If the answer is no, on the other hand, then we know that the new situation will be less *efficient*. Put differently, if the winners from a policy gain more than the losers lose, the policy could *in principle* be accompanid by a compensation scheme that would result in unanimous approval of the policy!

Of course, just because it is *in principle* possible to come up with such a compensation scheme does not mean it is possible *in practice*. Real-world policies come, at best, with imperfect compensation schemes, and thus they rarely enjoy unanimous approval. As a result, it is not immediate that we should in fact favor all policies that create more benefits than costs because in some instances we may in fact place more weight on the decline in welfare of those who lose than on the gains in welfare of those who win. For instance, suppose a group of wealthy citizens would be willing to pay $100 million to have a certain policy implemented, and a group of poor citizens would lose $1 million as a result. If we can't figure out a way to accompany this policy with compensation to those who would otherwise lose, we might decide that the policy is not worth it, that we in essence place more weight on the $1 million loss than on the $100 million gain because the loss would be borne by the most vulnerable among us.

Before we can even begin to think about such trade-offs, however, we need to be able to quantify gains and losses, which is what we will do for the rest of this chapter. The issue of whether it is enough for us to know that overall gains outweigh losses, or whether the distribution of gains and losses should matter, is one that arises in various parts of the book and is dealt with most explicitly in Chapter 29.

---

[1]Chapters 2, 4 through 7, and the first sections (Sections 9A.1 and 9B.1) in 9 are required reading for this chapter. Chapters 3 and 8 as well as the remainder of Chapter 9 (i.e., Sections 9A.2, 9A.3, 9B.2, and 9B.3) are not necessary for this chapter.

10A Measuring Consumer Welfare in Dollars

We will begin our analysis of this measurement of consumer welfare by quantifying how much better off or worse off consumers are for being able to purchase goods voluntarily at given market prices. Put differently, we will ask how much better off a consumer is for being able to participate in a market rather then be excluded from it. This will lead us to define terms like *marginal* and *total willingness to pay* as well as *consumer surplus*. We will then proceed to demonstrate how policy makers might analyze the impact of particular proposals on consumers when those proposals change the relative prices in an economy. In the process, we will see once again the importance of recognizing the difference between income and substitution effects, and how the substitution effect contributes to *deadweight losses* for society while the income effect does not.

10A.1 Consumer Surplus

Let us return to our example of my choices over gasoline and a composite good denominated in dollars. In Graph 10.1, we begin with a particular set of economic circumstances: my choice set determined by the price of gasoline and my current (exogenous) income. My optimal choice A then falls on the indifference curve that is tangent to my choice set (assuming I am not at a corner solution).

Exercise 10A.1 As a way to review material from previous chapters, can you identify assumptions on tastes that are sufficient for me to know for sure that my indifference curve will be tangent to the budget line at the optimum?

Now let's ask the following question: How much better off am I for being able to purchase gasoline at its current price rather than being excluded from the market for gasoline? Or, to be more precise, how much would I be willing to pay for the opportunity to participate in the current market for gasoline?

10A.1.1 Marginal Willingness to Pay   To formulate an answer to this question, we could simply look at each gallon of gasoline that I consume and ask how much I would have been willing to pay for that gallon given that I ended up at my optimal bundle A. For the first gallon, I can measure this willingness to pay by finding the slope of my indifference curve—the marginal rate of substitution—at 1 gallon. Suppose that this slope is -20. This tells me that I was willing to trade $20 worth of other consumption for the first gallon of gasoline. We can then proceed to the second gallon and find the marginal rate of substitution at 2 gallons. Suppose that it is -19. This tells me that I would have been willing to give up $19 of other consumption to get the *second* gallon of gasoline. We could keep doing this for each gallon of gasoline, with the marginal rate of substitution at bundle A being equal to the price of gasoline. At the end of this exercise, we will have identified my *marginal willingness to pay (MWTP)* for each of the gallons of gasoline I consumed and all the additional gallons that I chose not to consume. In the lower panel of Graph 10.1, we simply plot gallons of gasoline on the horizontal axis and dollars on the vertical. The *marginal willingness to pay curve* for a consumer who ends up on the indifference curve containing bundle A is then simply plotted by plotting the dollar values of the *MRS* at each gallon of gasoline.

10A.1.2 Marginal Willingness to Pay Curves and Substitution Effects   There is, however, a slightly different way of deriving marginal willingness to pay curves that builds more directly on material we have covered in the previous chapters and is similar to the way we derived

Graph 10.1: Deriving *MWTP* from *MRS* of Indifference Curve Containing Bundle *A*

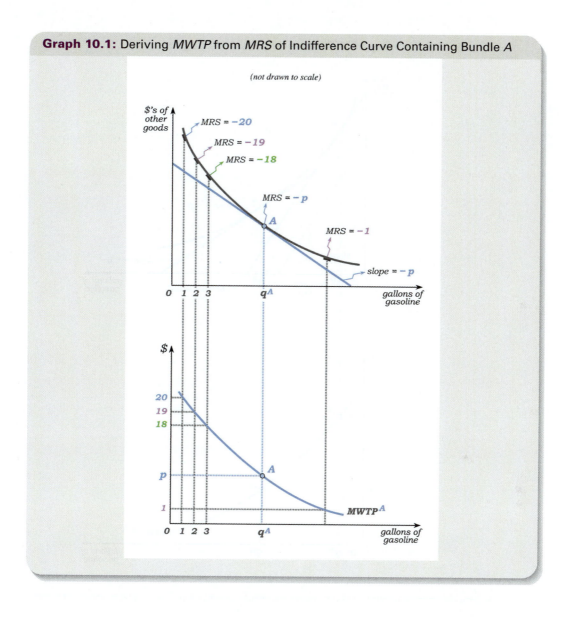

(not drawn to scale)

own-price demand curves in Chapter 9. The top panel of Graph 10.2 begins with the same initial budget and optimal bundle *A* as we started with in Graph 10.1. Instead of directly identifying the marginal rates of substitution on the indifference curve that contains bundle *A*, however, we now imagine a price increase from *p* to *p'* and then illustrate the compensated budget as we have done in previous chapters to get bundle *B* and the substitution effect. In Chapter 9, we then illustrated the final bundle *C* either to the right or left of *B* depending on whether the good on the horizontal axis is a normal or inferior good. Here, we are assuming that gasoline is a normal good and thus place bundle *C* to the left of *B*. In Chapter 9, we then plotted the own-price demand curve on a lower panel by bringing points *A* and *C* down to a graph with price (denominated in dollars) on the vertical and gasoline on the horizontal axis. We simply ignored a similarly derived point *B* in the lower graph as unimportant for purposes of drawing own-price demand curves.

Now, however, we will focus on bundles *A* and *B* rather than bundles *A* and *C*. Specifically, in the lower panel of Graph 10.2, we illustrate the quantity consumed at bundle *A* at the original price *p* and the quantity consumed at bundle *B* at the new price *p'* (when I receive compensation to make

Graph 10.2: Deriving *MWTP* from Compensated Budgets

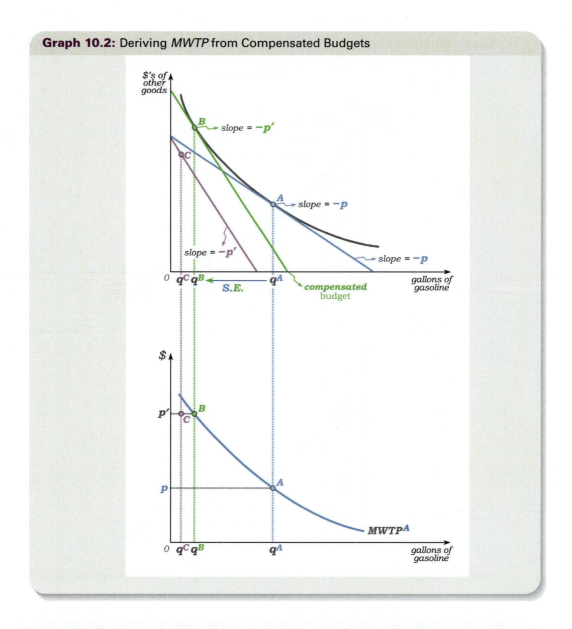

me as well off as I was originally). *But notice that all we are doing is plotting the slope of the indifference curve that contains bundle A at two different quantities,* just as we did in Graph 10.1. We could imagine doing this for many different price changes, each time finding the corresponding *compensated* budget and the new optimal bundle on that compensated budget. In doing so, we would end up plotting the marginal rates of substitution at the different quantities, leaving us with the same marginal willingness to pay curve as in the lower panel of Graph 10.1. For this reason, the marginal willingness to pay curve is often referred to as the *compensated demand curve* whereas the regular demand curve is sometimes referred to as the *uncompensated demand curve.*[2]

In Chapter 9, we translated bundle *B* to the lower graphs but said little more about it. At the time we were concerned with plotting own-price demand curves that connect points *A* and *C*, and we

---

[2]The uncompensated demand curve is also known as the *Marshallian demand* after Alfred Marshall, and the compensated demand curve is also known as the *Hicksian demand* after John Hicks.

merely indicated that point *B* would come in useful later on. Now it has just become useful—it has given us a way to graph the marginal willingness to pay curve and a way to compare it to the own-price demand curve. It is also now clear that the two curves are generally not the same because point *C* is usually different from point *B* since it (unlike point *B*) incorporates both the income and the substitution effect. The only time when the own-price demand curve and the marginal willingness to pay curve are the same is when there are no income effects with respect to the good whose demand curve we are drawing, and that is true only for tastes that are quasilinear in that good.

Demonstrate that own-price demand curves are the same as marginal willingness to pay curves for goods that can be represented by quasilinear tastes.

Exercise 10A.2

Using the graphs in Graph 9.2 of the previous chapter, determine under what condition own-price demand curves are steeper and under what conditions they are shallower than marginal willingness to pay curves.

Exercise 10A.3

What does the *MWTP* or compensated demand curve look like if the two goods are perfect complements?

Exercise 10A.4

Finally, you should note that, since compensated demand curves only include substitution (and not income) effects, and since the direction of the substitution effect is always unambiguously away from the good that has become more expensive, *compensated demand (or MWTP) curves must be downward sloping.* This is at least in principle not true for own-price demand curves that might slope upward when income effects are sufficiently large and in the opposite direction of substitution effects for Giffen goods. (However, as we acknowledged when we introduced Giffen goods in Chapter 7, such circumstances are rare and therefore own-price demand curves rarely actually slope up.)

10A.1.3 Total Willingness to Pay and Consumer Surplus
We began Section 10A.1 by asking how much I might be willing to pay for the opportunity to be able to purchase gasoline at the market price rather than not being able to get access to the gasoline market. The answer can now be read off the marginal willingness to pay curve we have just derived once we have identified two further concepts in the marginal willingness to pay graph. First, we need to identify my *total willingness to pay* for *all* of the gasoline I am purchasing in the market, and second we need to subtract from this the amount that I actually *had* to pay in the market. The difference between these two amounts is how much better off I am for being able to participate in this market—how much more I would have been willing to pay than I actually had to pay.

Graph 10.3 replicates the marginal willingness to pay curve we just derived, illustrating my marginal willingness to pay for each of the gallons of gasoline that I am consuming (and for each of the gallons that I am not consuming), given that I end up consuming at bundle *A* when I face the market price *p*. My total willingness to pay is equal to my marginal willingness to pay for the first gallon plus my marginal willingness to pay for the second gallon, etc., which is roughly equal to the area below the marginal willingness to pay curve (i.e., the green and blue areas together). My total willingness to pay is therefore the area under the marginal willingness to pay curve up to the quantity that I consume.

The amount I *actually* had to pay is simply equal to the price per gallon of gasoline times the number of gallons I chose to consume, which is equal to the shaded (green) rectangle (in Graph 10.3) formed by the vertical distance equal to price and the horizontal distance equal to the number of gallons of gasoline consumed.

Finally, *consumer surplus*, the difference between what I was willing to pay for my gasoline consumption and what I actually paid, is the difference between the two areas we have identified

Graph 10.3: *MWTP*, *TWTP*, and Consumer Surplus

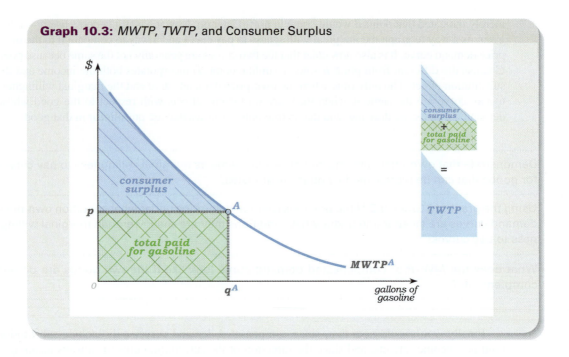

(or the shaded blue area). This is how much better off I am for being able to participate in the gasoline market, and therefore the most I would be willing to pay to get access to a market where gasoline sells at p per gallon.

10A.2 *MWTP* and Own-Price Demand Curves

If you have taken an economics course in the past, chances are that you encountered a graph similar to Graph 10.3. However, you probably graphed consumer surplus along own-price (uncompensated) demand curves, not along the marginal willingness to pay (or compensated demand) curves we just learned to derive.[3] As it turns out, it is correct to use the own-price demand curve to find consumer surplus only in one specific case: when tastes are quasilinear. In all other cases, consumer surplus as we have defined it cannot be identified on own-price demand curves, and policy analysis that uses such curves to identify changes in consumer surplus can give very misleading and incorrect answers. In this section, we will explore in more detail the relationship between demand curves and marginal willingness to pay curves.

10A.2.1 Many *MWTP* and Demand Curves for any Individual

In Section 10A.1, we showed how we can derive a Marginal Willingness to Pay Curve assuming that the consumer currently consumes a particular bundle associated with a particular indifference curve. The curves that we derived in Graphs 10.1 and 10.2 are then labeled $MWTP^A$, with the superscript A indicating that the curve was derived from the indifference curve that contains bundle A. We had picked this as the indifference curve that was relevant for the exercise of deriving *MWTP* in our example because the consumer was assumed to be consuming at A. Of course, had the consumer been

---

[3]When measured along the (uncompensated) own-price demand curve, this area is sometimes called *Marshallian Consumer Surplus*. Many texts in fact still define consumer surplus in this way, and then separately develop measures of welfare changes along uncompensated (or Hicksian) demand curves. We are attempting to be more consistent here by always measuring welfare along compensated curves and behavior along uncompensated curves.

consuming at some other bundle, we would have used a different indifference curve to derive $MWTP$, and thus would have derived a curve different from $MWTP^A$.

In fact, there generally exists a different $MWTP$ curve for each indifference curve. This is quite analogous to the case of own-price demand curves. When we derive an own-price demand curve, we hold income fixed, just as when we derive $MWTP$ curves we hold the indifference curve (or "utility") fixed. If income changes, own-price demand curves shift, just as $MWTP$ curves shift if utility changes.

Consider, for instance, Graph 10.4. In the top panels of parts (a) and (b), we illustrate the same bundles A and B with the same indifference curves. On the left, we indicate two income levels at which A and B are optimal bundles, and on the lower panel of Graph 10.4a we illustrate how these two bundles translate to two points on different (uncompensated) demand curves, one for the higher level of income and one for the lower level. Notice that we are implicitly assuming that x_1 is a normal good, with consumption falling when income falls. Of course we are simply guessing

Graph 10.4: Multiple Demand Curves (for Different Incomes) and Multiple *MWTP* Curves (for Different Utility Levels)

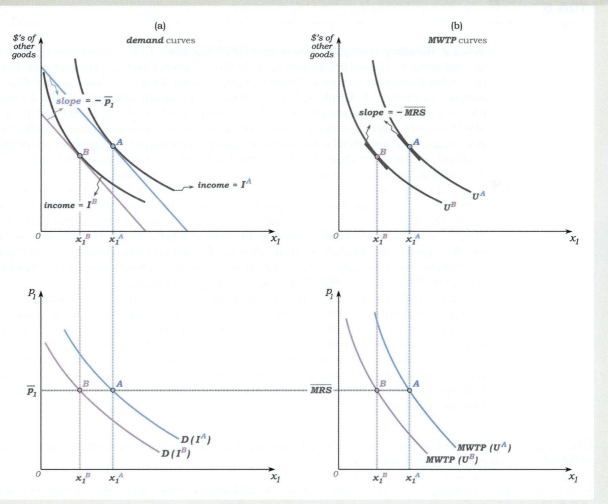

what the rest of the demand curves look like and would have to change the price of x_1 in the top graph to derive the rest of the demand curves formally.

Exercise 10A.5 How would Graph 10.4a change if x_1 were an inferior rather than a normal good?

On part (b) of Graph 10.4, we use points A and B in the top graph to plot the $MWTP$, or the negative MRS, at two different consumption levels. Since the MRS is the same at bundle A and B in the top graph, the derived points on the lower graph happen at the same height. As in the case of the (uncompensated) demand curves in Graph 10.4a, we then simply guess the shape of the rest of the $MWTP$ curves but could formally derive these using either of the methods developed (in Graphs 10.1 and 10.2) in the previous section. The lower part of panel (b) therefore demonstrates shifts in the $MWTP$ curve as utility changes, just as the lower portion of panel (a) demonstrates shifts in the own-price demand curve as income changes.

Exercise 10A.6 How would Graph 10.4b change if x_1 were an inferior rather than a normal good?

10A.2.2 Relating Demand Curves to *MWTP* Curves To understand how the own-price demand curves we derived in Chapter 9 relate to $MWTP$ curves introduced in this chapter, it is useful to relate them to one another on the same graph. Consider, for instance, our example of my consumption of gasoline. In Graph 10.2, we assumed that I currently consumed bundle A when the price of gasoline is p (and when the price of "\$'s of other goods" is simply 1). We then derived the $MWTP$ curve by simply illustrating how my consumption behavior would change when the price of gasoline rises to p' and when I am compensated enough to remain just has happy as I was originally.

Graph 10.2 is then replicated in the top panel of Graph 10.5a. In addition, bundle C, the bundle I actually consume when facing a price increase to p' in the absence of any compensation, is plotted and translated to the lower graph exactly as we would do when deriving my own-price demand curve. This then allows us to plot the demand curve and the $MWTP$ curve on the same graph. The demand curve is the one that is relevant for my *income* level at bundle A, and the $MWTP$ curve is relevant for the *utility* level I attain at bundle A. The $MWTP$ curve, however, only incorporates the substitution effect, while the demand curve incorporates both income and substitution effects. Because we are assuming that gasoline is a normal good, the demand curve ends up shallower than the $MWTP$ curve (i.e., C lies to the left of B).

Panel (b) of Graph 10.5 then repeats the same exercise for a good x_1 that is assumed to be quasilinear, a good that is borderline between normal and inferior and one where my consumption behavior (with respect to x_1) therefore does not exhibit an income effect. Since the only difference between own-price demand and $MWTP$ curves arises from income effects, the disappearance of the income effect then causes the two curves to be identical. *MWTP and (uncompensated) demand curves are thus the same if and only if the tastes for the good we are modeling are quasilinear.* Consequently, the only time the demand curve measures consumer surplus correctly arises when tastes are quasilinear.

Exercise 10A.7 On the lower panel of Graph 10.5b, where does the $MWTP$ curve corresponding to the indifference curve that contains bundle C lie?

Exercise 10A.8 How do the upper and lower panels of Graph 10.5a change when gasoline is an inferior good?

Graph 10.5: Relationship of Demand and *MWTP* Curves

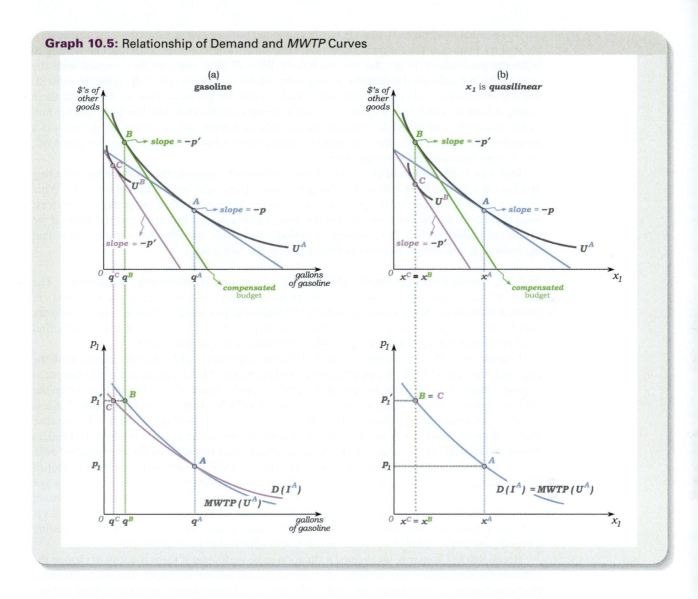

10A.3 What's So Bad About Taxes? Or, Why Is the Bucket Leaking?

Governments use taxes to raise revenues that in turn fund expenditures on a variety of government programs. These programs may have enormous benefits, but, to the extent that they are funded through taxes, they come at an economic cost that economists refer to as the *deadweight loss from taxation*. Often, students think that pointing this out makes all economists raving anarchists, that being an economist means being against all taxes and all government expenditures that are funded through taxes. But recognizing an economic cost of taxation does not mean that one has to oppose all taxes any more than recognizing a cost to going to the movies implies that one is against going to the movies. After all, the benefits from certain government programs may well outweigh these costs just as the enjoyment of the movie might outweigh the cost of watching it. It does, however, lead us to think more carefully about the relative cost of different kinds of taxes, and we can now use the tools we have developed to illustrate how such costs can be measured.

To see what makes a particular tax costly and to see how we can measure this cost objectively, we will try to answer the following question: How much would a taxed individual be willing to bribe the government to get the tax rescinded? We will then compare this amount with the amount that the individual is actually paying in tax. If the maximum size of the bribe the individual is willing to pay is larger than the individual's actual tax payment, then we know that there exists, at least in principle, a way to raise more revenue from the individual without making him or her worse off. The difference between the hypothetical bribe and the actual tax payment is a measure of how much more the government could have raised without making anyone worse off, and it is our measure of deadweight loss.

One way to think of deadweight loss from taxation is to imagine the government collecting taxes in a bucket that has a hole in it; as the government passes the bucket, the bucket leaks. What remains in the bucket is what the government gets to use to provide public programs and services; what leaks from the bucket is the deadweight loss that no one gets but that we could get to if we just found a better bucket. The challenge is to find a bucket—a tax—that has a small hole so that the leakage is minimized. But why is there a hole in the first place?

10A.3.1 Some Intuition on the Deadweight Loss and Inefficiency of Taxation   The question is not rhetorical, and the answer is not immediately obvious. In fact, often students are puzzled at this point. Why would anyone ever be willing to pay more in a bribe to get rid of a tax than he or she is paying in taxes when the tax is in place? Why do we think that we can find another tax that will raise more revenue while not making people worse off?

Consider the following extreme example. I like to drink beer, and I especially like to drink the imported beer Amstel Light. Suppose the domestic beer brewer Miller convinces the government to impose a large tax on imported beers, and suppose that this leads to a sufficient increase in the domestic price of Amstel Light to cause me to switch to Miller Lite (which I like somewhat less because I can't make up my mind about whether it tastes great or is less filling).[4] Notice that because I have substituted away from (the taxed) Amstel Light and toward (the untaxed) Miller Lite, I end up paying no tax at all. At the same time, I have clearly been made worse off by the imposition of a tax on imported beers and would therefore be willing to pay *something* to get the government to abolish this tax, despite the fact that I do not pay *any* of the tax when it is imposed. With the government not raising any revenue and me being made worse off, we have identified a "bucket" that has no bottom; no tax revenue from me is actually reaching the government even though the imposition of the tax is making me worse off. Stated more loftily, society has been made worse off without anyone getting a benefit, and that is called *deadweight loss*. It is also what makes taxes *inefficient*.

Recall that in Chapter 6, we defined a situation to be inefficient if there is a way to change the situation and thus make someone better off without making anyone worse off. The tax on imported beer is *inefficient* because the government could have raised more money from me without making me any worse off (than I am when I drink Miller Lite) by thinking of a different way of raising money—finding a different "bucket" that doesn't leak so much. For instance, they could have just come by my house and taken some money, leaving the price of Amstel Light unchanged and thus not giving me an incentive to switch to Miller Lite just to avoid a tax. The example, though extreme, gives us an initial insight into what it is about taxes that makes taxes costly. *By altering the relative prices in an economy, taxes cause consumers, workers, and savers to substitute away from taxed goods and services and toward untaxed goods and services.* To the extent that this substitution activity happens solely because of a change in opportunity costs, to the extent to which taxes give rise to substitution effects, taxes are distortionary and inefficient ways of raising revenues.

Many real-world examples may be less extreme—they may lead us to consume less of the taxed good and more of other goods without causing us to eliminate our consumption of particular taxed

---

[4]That's a reference to one of the most successful advertising campaigns of the 20th century that featured ads in which various people get into big fights over what's great about Miller Lite: that it tastes great or is less filling.

goods (like Amstel Light) entirely. But the basic intuition remains: To the extent to which taxes change opportunity costs and thus cause us to alter our consumption plans solely because of those changed opportunity costs, we are worse off without contributing to the government's effort to raise revenues, and society has incurred a deadweight loss. We can now use the tools we have developed to show more formally that this entire deadweight loss happens because of substitution effects, which are therefore the underlying cause of the leak in the "bucket."

10A.3.2 Identifying Deadweight Losses in a Consumer Diagram

Suppose that instead of a tax on Amstel Light we considered a tax on housing. We can model such a tax in our usual two-good framework as resulting in an increase in the price of each square foot of housing we consume. Alternatively, we can model removal of such a tax as a decrease in the price of housing. Graph 10.6a illustrates the change in the choice set resulting from such a tax, with bundle A representing a consumer's optimal after-tax choice.

In Chapter 8 (Graph 8.3), we illustrated how one can identify the total tax paid by a consumer in a situation where the good modeled on the horizontal axis is taxed. In particular, we can first identify c^A as the dollars of "other goods consumption" the consumer is able to afford *after the tax* given that she is consuming h^A. Second, we can identify c^α as the dollars of "other goods consumption" had she consumed the same amount of housing in the absence of the tax. The difference between these amounts, labeled T in Graph 10.6a, is the total tax payment the consumer makes under the tax. As explained in Chapter 8, this does not presume that the consumer's optimal consumption bundle without the tax is α. Rather, the bundle α simply helps us identify the magnitude of T.

Graph 10.6b then replicates panel (a) but gives the answer to our second question: How much of this consumer's income could we have taken *without changing opportunity costs* to make the consumer just as well off as she is under the tax on housing? Put differently, how much can we shift the (blue) before-tax budget constraint without changing its slope and still end up on the indifference curve labeled u^A? The answer is that we could shift this budget inward until we get to the (green) budget line that is tangent to u^A at B. The dollar value of this parallel shift can then be measured on the vertical axis (which is denominated in dollar units), and since the two budget

Graph 10.6: Distortionary Tax on Housing

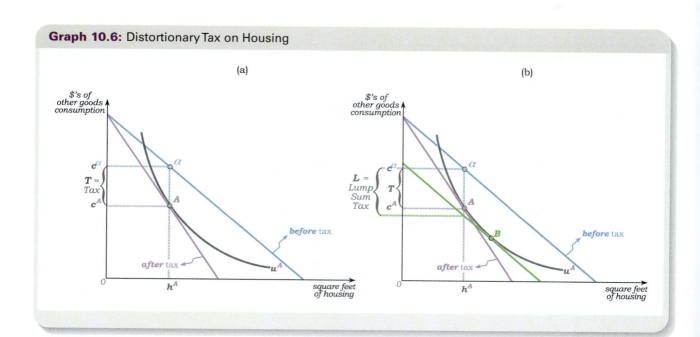

lines are parallel, this distance can equivalently be measured as a vertical distance between the two lines anywhere. In particular, we can measure it as a distance below the bundle α, a distance labeled L in Graph 10.6b.

The distance L is how much we could have taxed this consumer using what is called a *lump sum tax*. A lump sum tax is a tax that *does not change opportunity costs* (i.e., slopes of budget constraints). Graph 10.6b then clearly indicates that this consumer would have been willing to pay a larger amount L in a lump sum tax than the amount T she is paying under the tax on housing, with each tax leaving the consumer exactly on the same indifference curve and thus equally happy. The difference between T and L is the deadweight loss from the tax on housing. Since, beginning with a housing tax, the lump sum tax represents a way to make someone better off (government revenue is higher) without making anyone worse off (our consumer has the same utility in either case), we can equivalently say that the housing tax is *inefficient*.

10A.3.3 Deadweight Losses and Substitution Effects

We can now investigate the reason why most taxes are inefficient and result in deadweight losses. First, consider the same tax on housing we modeled in Graph 10.6, but now assume that the consumer views housing and "other goods" as perfect complements. Graph 10.7a illustrates such tastes, with A representing the consumer's optimal bundle after the tax is imposed and with u^A representing the consumer's indifference curve at bundle A. We can then identify the amount of tax she pays under the housing tax as T just as we did in Graph 10.6a. But when we now ask how much we could have taken from the consumer in a lump sum tax and still ensured that the consumer reaches the indifference curve u^A, we find that the consumer would end up at exactly the same consumption bundle (i.e. $B = A$). Thus, the amount we could have extracted from the consumer in a lump sum tax is exactly equal to the amount we received from the consumer under the tax on housing (i.e., $L = T$). We have therefore identified a case where a tax on housing does *not* produce a deadweight loss and is therefore efficient.

The reason why $B = A$ in Graph 10.7a is that we have given the consumer tastes that eliminate substitution effects. As the substitution effect disappears, so does the deadweight loss from a tax that changes the opportunity cost of housing. Graph 10.7b, on the other hand, assumes tastes

Graph 10.7: Distortionary Taxes and Substitution Effects

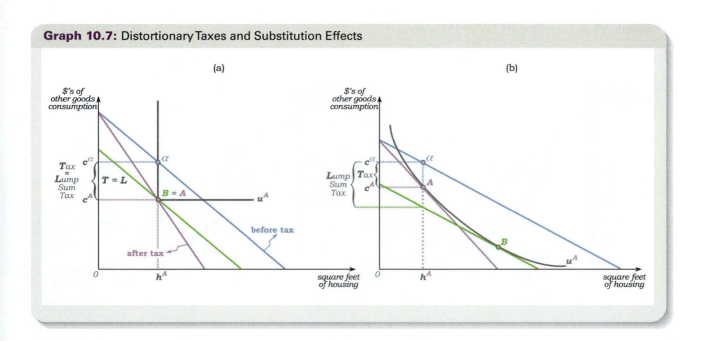

that incorporate a great deal of substitutability, with bundles A and B far from each other. As a result, L is significantly larger than T, implying a large deadweight loss. As the degree of substitutability between housing and other goods consumption increases from zero in Graph 10.7a to some substitutability in Graph 10.6b to a large amount of substitutability in Graph 10.7b, the deadweight loss increases as well. And as the degree of substitutability shrinks, the leak in our tax "bucket" disappears.

Note one other important fact that emerges from this analysis: What makes taxes inefficient is not that consumers respond by consuming less of the taxed good. (After all, the consumer responds to the tax in Graph 10.7a by consuming less than she would at the blue budget, but there is no inefficiency.) Rather, the inefficiency emerges to the extent to which a substitution effect lies behind the change in behavior. As demonstrated in some of the end-of-chapter exercises, this is particularly important in labor markets where income and substitution effects tend to point in opposite direction with respect to the good leisure.

Can you think of a scenario under which a consumer does not change his or her consumption of a good when it is taxed but there still exists an inefficiency from taxation?

Exercise 10A.9

Some years ago, I asked students to comment on a final exam on the following statement: "People hate taxes because of income effects; economists hate taxes because of substitution effects." One student commented that the statement is true because it implies that economists are not people. Be that as it may, the statement is true in another sense: Few taxpayers think about income and substitution effects when they write their check to the tax authorities—they don't like writing these checks because they'd rather have the money for themselves. Economists who care about efficiency, on the other hand, may have no problem with checks going from some people to other people through the government *as long as wealth does not get lost in the process*, or as long as some do not get hurt without someone else at least benefiting. But that is precisely what happens when taxes result in changes of opportunity costs that then result in substitution effects. It is what is causing the "bucket" to leak. Thus, while individual taxpayers may not easily identify a tax that results in Graph 10.7a as better than a tax that results in Graph 10.7b, economists would (all else being equal) tend to have a clear preference for the tax that results in no substitution effects and thus no deadweight losses to society. We may disagree on how big the bucket should be, but we generally agree that it should not have big leaks if we can help it.

10A.3.4 Almost all Real-World Taxes Are Inefficient
From our discussion thus far, we can then identify two scenarios under which a tax may be efficient: (1) if the tax does not change opportunity costs and is thus a lump sum tax; or (2) if the tax does not give rise to substitution effects even though it causes changes in opportunity costs. (In Chapter 21, we will add a third scenario that emerges in the presence of externalities.) Scenario (2) is difficult to count on since we have little control over what kinds of tastes consumers have, although it is possible to identify certain combinations of goods that are less substitutable than others (as we discussed in Chapter 5). And the first scenario (lump sum taxes) rarely represent real-world policy options. As a result, almost all real-world taxes give rise to deadweight losses and are thus inefficient, at least until we get to the topic of externalities in Chapter 21.

Why are lump sum taxes so hard to come by? In order for a tax to truly represent a lump sum tax, it must be such that the consumer cannot engage in any substituting behavior that allows him or her to avoid at least part of the tax. As soon as taxes are imposed differentially on different goods, the possibility of such substituting behavior arises as opportunity costs of different goods are altered. If you think carefully about the implications of this, you will quickly realize how difficult it is in practice to come up with a true lump sum tax. In our example of the tax on housing, for instance, you might think that we can eliminate the "distortionary" (or "deadweight loss–inducing") aspects of the tax by simply taxing "all other consumption" by the same amount, thus keeping the slope of the budget constraint from changing and not causing changes in the opportunity cost of anything. But "all other goods" includes, for instance, "savings." Well, you might say, let's tax savings at the same rate, thus again keeping opportunity costs unchanged. But yet another "other good" that we have not modeled in our two-good diagram is leisure. Can we think of easy ways to tax leisure at the same rate? If not, the "bucket" has sprung a leak.

Exercise
10A.10
On a graph with consumption on the vertical axis and leisure on the horizontal, illustrate the deadweight loss of a tax on all consumption (other than the consumption of leisure).

The most common taxes are taxes on different forms of consumption (sales taxes, value added taxes) or taxes on different forms of income (payroll taxes, wage taxes, income taxes, capital gains taxes). Each of these can be avoided in part through a change in behavior. To truly be a lump sum tax, a tax must be such that consumers can do *nothing* to avoid the tax. In the early 1990s, for instance, Prime Minister Margaret Thatcher attempted to introduce such a tax in Great Britain by imposing what is known as a "head tax." A head tax is a fixed tax payment (say, $2,000 per year) that consumers have to pay as long as they have a head. It is not easy for someone to change the fact that he or she has a head, and so the tax cannot be avoided by changes in behavior and thus is truly a lump sum tax without substitution effects. Yet, despite the efficiency argument in favor of such a tax, few people in Great Britain liked the concept. Margaret Thatcher was out of office within a few weeks, and her successor immediately repealed the head tax.

The British head tax example illustrates why lump sum taxes are rarely considered in the real-world and why, as a result, almost all real-world taxes are inefficient to some degree: Because they must be based on something other than changeable behavior, lump sum taxes usually offend our sense of fairness. It does not seem fair to send everyone the same tax bill, nor does it seem right to base people's tax payments on other unchangeable characteristics such as age, race, sex, or other genetic traits. But something like that is usually necessary in order for a tax not to give rise to substitution effects and the resulting inefficiencies. Sometimes the "bucket" does not leak, but we don't like it for other reasons. (One possible exception to this is a tax on land value, which is explored in Chapter 19.)

While our analysis thus suggests that virtually any tax we might advocate is inefficient and produces deadweight loss, it also suggests that different types of taxes will have different magnitudes of deadweight losses depending on just how big the substitution effects—the leaks in the "bucket"—are that these taxes produce. We will say more about how this might impact tax policy at the end of the next section and again in later chapters.

10A.4 Deadweight Loss Measured on *MWTP* Curves

In Section 10A.2, we have already shown how the concept of consumer surplus can be measured as an area to the left of marginal willingness to pay curves and, under the special case of quasilinear tastes, as the same area to the left of own-price demand curves. We can now show that deadweight loss can be similarly measured along marginal willingness to pay (and, when tastes are quasilinear, own-price demand) curves. We will do this within the context of the example of a housing tax discussed in the previous section.

10A.4.1 *T, L,* and *DWL* on *MWTP* Curves
The top panel in Graph 10.8a is identical to Graph 10.6b and derives, within the consumer diagram, the tax payment T made by a consumer with indifference curve u^A, the largest possible lump sum tax payment L the consumer would have been

Graph 10.8: Translating *DWL* to *MWTP* Curves

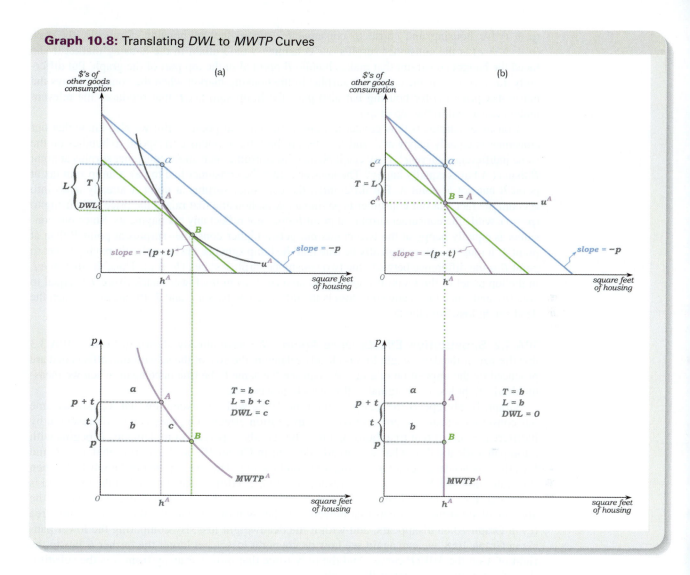

willing to make to not incur the tax on housing, and the deadweight loss $DWL = (L - T)$ from the tax on housing. The lower panel of Graph 10.8a then derives the Marginal Willingness to Pay Curve that corresponds to the indifference curve that includes bundle *A*. This is done by the same process as the derivation of marginal willingness to pay in Graph 10.2, except that we are now deriving the *MWTP* curve corresponding to the optimal indifference curve at the higher (tax-inclusive) price.

We can now identify the distances T, L, and $(L - T)$ from the top graph as areas on the lower graph by carefully thinking about what A and B represent on the lower graph. Point A represents the actual housing consumption this consumer undertakes after a housing tax has been implemented. The difference between the price level $(p + t)$ and the price level p on the vertical axis is just t, or the per square foot tax rate on housing paid by the consumer. Thus, if we multiply the tax paid per square foot of housing t by the square feet of housing (h^A) consumed under the tax, we get the total tax payment this consumer makes under the housing tax. Area (b) in the lower panel of Graph 10.8a is exactly that, which implies that area (b) is equal to distance T in the top graph.

Next, from the work we did in Section 10A.2, we know that area (a) is equal to the consumer surplus this consumer received in the housing market after she paid the tax-inclusive price

$(p + t)$ for housing and chose to consume h^A square feet of housing. Similarly, the area $(a + b + c)$ is the consumer surplus our consumer would attain in the housing market if she faced the budget constraint that makes bundle B optimal in the top part of the graph. Put differently, $(a + b + c)$ is the consumer surplus in the housing market when the consumer pays the before-tax price (p) for housing but also pays the lump sum tax L that produces the relevant budget constraint in the top graph.

Consumer surplus is thus greater at point B than it is at point A. But we also know that our consumer is equally happy at A and B; after all, both these points correspond to bundles on the same indifference curve u^A. How can it be that the consumer gets more consumer surplus at point B than at A but is equally happy? The answer is that the consumer had to pay a lump sum tax at point B but not at point A. Put differently, the consumer surplus at point A already takes into account the fact that our consumer is paying a tax on housing that raised the price of housing to $(p + t)$, while the consumer surplus at point B does not reflect any tax payments. Since our consumer is equally happy at the two points but gets a higher consumer surplus at point B than at point A, it must therefore logically be true that the lump sum tax she is implicitly paying to get to point B is the difference between the two consumer surpluses; i.e., $(b + c)$. Thus, the distance L in the top panel of the graph is equal to the area $(b + c)$ in the lower panel. Since T is equal to area (b), and since the deadweight loss is the difference between L and T, the area (c) is then the deadweight loss from the tax.

10A.4.2 Substitution Effects Once Again
We have already shown in Section 10A.3.3 that the size of the deadweight loss is closely related to the size of the substitution effects that are produced by the imposition of a tax. We can see the same to be true once again when we measure deadweight loss on marginal willingness to pay curves.

Graph 10.8b repeats the analysis in Graph 10.8a with the exception that we now assume our consumer's tastes do not give rise to substitution effects; i.e., they can be represented by indifference curves that treat housing and other goods as perfect complements. It begins with a top panel identical to what we already derived in Graph 10.7a, illustrating that $T = L$ and thus there is no deadweight loss from a tax on housing. The lower panel of Graph 10.8b then illustrates how the *MWTP* curve corresponding to the indifference curve u^A in the top panel is a vertical line: A and B happen at different prices but at the same quantities because of the absence of substitution effects that moved B to the right of A in Graph 10.8a. As a result, area (c) in Graph 10.8a disappears, and with it the deadweight loss. By comparing the lower panels in Graph 10.8, we can again see how deadweight losses get larger the farther B lies to the right of A on the *MWTP* curve. And the only force that moves B away from A is the substitution effect in the top panel of the graphs.

10A.4.3 Measuring the *DWL* on Demand Curves
Most of you have probably seen deadweight loss from taxation in a previous economics course, and chances are you did not bother with marginal willingness to pay curves but simply used areas on own-price demand curves to measure deadweight loss. Whoever was teaching you this implicitly assumed that underlying tastes are quasilinear, which represents the only case under which it is truly legitimate to use own-price demand curves to measure consumer welfare and deadweight loss. Of course, we can approximate the deadweight loss on own-price demand curves as long as we think income effects are small, which is the same as saying that tastes are close to quasilinear. But in cases where income effects are likely to be large, it will be misleading to use the own-price demand curve to approximate consumer surplus and deadweight loss.[5]

---

[5]Historically, the idea of measuring deadweight loss on own-price demand curves dates back to Alfred Marshall's 1895 *Principles of Economics* text. The modern treatment of consumer welfare and deadweight loss, on the other hand, is due to Sir John Hicks, whom we first credited with the related idea of decomposing price changes into income and substitution effects in Chapter 7.

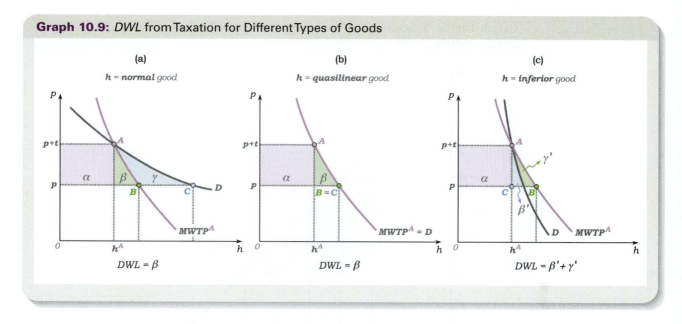

Graph 10.9: *DWL* from Taxation for Different Types of Goods

In Graph 10.9, we extend the lower panel of Graph 10.8a slightly by adding a point *C* that represents the level of housing consumption if the consumer faced neither a housing tax nor a lump sum tax. Panel (a) does this for the case where housing is a normal good, panel (b) does it for the case where housing is a quasilinear good, and panel (c) does it for the (unlikely) case where housing is an inferior good.

Using Graph 10.8a, verify that the relationship between own-price demand and marginal willingness to pay is as depicted in panels (a) through (c) of Graph 10.9.

Exercise
10A.11

It is now easy to read on these graphs whether a measurement of *DWL* approximated on own-price demand curves would over or understate the true *DWL* from the tax on housing. Clearly, there is no difference between using the *MWTP* and using the demand curve to measure deadweight loss when housing is a quasilinear good (panel (b) of Graph 10.9). In this case, the demand curve is exactly equal to the *MWTP* curve, and either can be used for consumer welfare analysis. When housing is a normal good, however, a *DWL* measurement on the demand curve will *overstate* the true *DWL* (by γ in Graph 10.9a), and when housing is an inferior good, it will *understate* it (by γ' in Graph 10.9c). We will see in Chapter 19 that the problem of using uncompensated curves to approximate *DWL* will become much more severe when we discuss taxes on labor or capital, where wealth effects usually mask the very substitution effects that lie at the heart of tax inefficiency.

10A.4.4 Exponential Increases in *DWL* and the Case for Broad Tax Bases   One lesson for tax policy that has emerged from our analysis of taxes and deadweight loss is that taxes give rise to greater deadweight losses the more they give rise to substitution effects. Now that we know how to measure *DWL* along marginal willingness to pay curves, we are ready to derive a second lesson: As tax rates on any given good increase, *DWL* from the tax increases substantially faster; i.e., as tax rates increase, the leak in our "bucket" grows at an increasing rate.

You can see the intuition behind this result in our housing tax example in which we assume that tastes for housing are quasilinear, and the *MWTP* curve is therefore equal to the own-price demand curve. Graph 10.10 depicts a special case of this where the demand (and *MWTP*) curve is

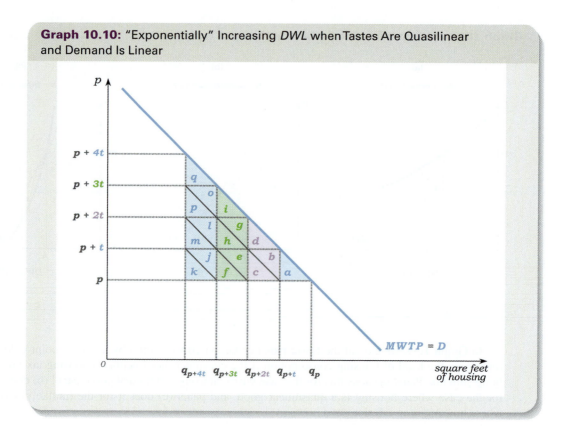

Graph 10.10: "Exponentially" Increasing *DWL* when Tastes Are Quasilinear and Demand Is Linear

linear. Tax-inclusive housing prices for five different levels of housing taxes are indicated on the vertical axis, from no tax (p) going through tax increases starting with t, then $2t$, then $3t$, and finally $4t$. For each level of the housing tax, we can identify the corresponding *DWL*. For instance, when the tax rate is t, the *DWL* is simply a. When it is $2t$, the *DWL* becomes $(a + b + c + d)$. Since each letter corresponds to a triangle with the same area, we can conclude that *doubling the tax led to a quadrupling of the DWL*. When the tax is raised to $3t$, the deadweight loss becomes $(a + b + c + d + e + f + g + h + i)$. Thus, *multiplying the tax rate by 3 leads to a DWL 9 times as large*. And you can verify for yourself that multiplying the tax rate by 4 leads to a *DWL* 16 times as great. While this is a special case since we assumed quasilinear tastes and linear demand curves, the example has led tax economists to use the rule of thumb that *multiplying tax rates by a factor of x leads to an increase of DWL by a factor of approximately x^2!* Put differently, as tax rates go up linearly, *DWL* increases "exponentially."[6]

This has furthermore led to the commonly given advice to policy makers that *it is better from an efficiency perspective to have low tax rates on large tax bases rather than high tax rates on small tax bases*. The *tax base* is the set of goods that are taxed, whereas the tax rate is the rate at which goods are taxed. Suppose, for instance, that there are two markets, single-family housing and condominium housing, and suppose that consumer tastes in both markets lead to exactly the same demand and *MWTP* curves and that these are furthermore as depicted in Graph 10.10. Now suppose that you are a policy maker who has to choose between two tax proposals: One imposes a tax of $2t$ on the single family housing market and no tax on the condominium housing market; the

---

[6]I am using the term "exponentially" in an informal way here and simply mean that it increases by a power of two. I will continue to use the term informally throughout this chapter.

other imposes a tax of t on both markets. The first proposal imposes a high tax rate ($2t$) on a small base (single-family housing), and the second proposal imposes a low tax rate (t) on a large tax base (single-family and condominium housing). The *DWL* of the first proposal is ($a + b + c + d$) while the *DWL* from the second proposal is ($a + a$), which is half the *DWL* of the first proposal. Thus, *because DWL goes up "exponentially" as tax rates rise, imposing low tax rates on broader bases typically results in less DWL.* If topics like this are of interest, you should consider taking a course in public finance.

The two proposals also result in different levels of tax revenue. Which proposal actually results in higher revenue for the government? Does this strengthen or weaken the policy proposal "to broaden the base and lower the rates"?

Exercise
10A.12

 ## The Mathematics of Consumer Welfare and "Duality"

The mathematical generalization of consumer welfare, as introduced intuitively in part A of this chapter, serves two purposes. First, it allows us, as in concepts introduced in previous chapters, to see how the mathematics of the consumer model can help us generalize the graphical analysis and the intuitions that emerge from it. Second, it provides us a forum in which to bring together all the mathematical techniques introduced so far to paint a full picture of consumer theory, a picture that is commonly referred to as the "duality" of utility maximization and expenditure minimization approaches we have used in the past few chapters.

We will depart in this section from our previous practice of following exactly the same order for our mathematical development in part B of chapters as for the graphical development in part A. Rather, we will begin by demonstrating how the intuitive concepts developed in part A help us generate a full picture of how all the intuitive and mathematical aspects of the consumer model fit together. We do this in Section 10B.1 and then proceed to an application of some of the "duality" mechanism to the topic of consumer welfare, taxation, and deadweight loss.

10B.1 Duality of Utility Maximization and Expenditure Minimization

In previous chapters, we have essentially formulated two different ways of solving optimization problems that (typically) lead to a solution that can be graphed as a tangency between an indifference curve and a budget line. Which of these optimization problems we solved at a particular time depended on what we were trying to answer. Whenever we tried to calculate how much a consumer will actually consume as his or her economic conditions (i.e., the consumer's income and the prices in the market) change, we solved the utility maximization problem

$$\max_{x_1,x_2} u(x_1,x_2) \text{ subject to } p_1x_1 + p_2x_2 = I. \tag{10.1}$$

On the other hand, when we attempted to see how much a consumer will change his or her consumption as prices change while being compensated to keep his or her utility from changing, we solved the expenditure minimization problem

$$\min_{x_1,x_2} E = p_1x_1 + p_2x_2 \text{ subject to } u(x_1,x_2) = u \tag{10.2}$$

that gave us the least expenditure necessary for the consumer to reach the same indifference curve u as prices change.

We already showed in Chapter 9 how the solution to problem (10.1) can be written as the (uncompensated) *demand functions*

$$x_1 = x_1(p_1,p_2,I) \text{ and } x_2 = x_2(p_1,p_2,I) \tag{10.3}$$

and how (inverse) slices of these demand functions are related to the various demand curves we have derived graphically. Now consider the solution to problem (10.2), which can be written as

$$x_1 = h_1(p_1,p_2,u) \text{ and } x_2 = h_2(p_1,p_2,u). \tag{10.4}$$

These functions tell us, for any set of prices, how much a consumer will consume of each good *assuming that the consumer is given just enough money to be able to reach utility level u*. For this reason, the functions given in expression (10.4) are often referred to as *compensated demand functions*. They are also known as *Hicksian demand functions* after the economist John Hicks whose work originally identified them, and it is in his honor that we denote the functions in expression (10.4) with "*h*" to distinguish them from the (uncompensated) demand functions in expression (10.3).

10B.1.1 Compensated (or Hicksian) Demand and *MWTP*
In Graph 10.2, we demonstrated how we can derive *MWTP* curves by tracing out the quantity of a good that a consumer would consume at different prices *assuming the consumer gets sufficient compensation to always reach the same indifference curve*. This is exactly what problem (10.2) formalizes mathematically, and the compensated demand functions in expression (10.4) are therefore a simple generalization of the *MWTP* curve derived in Graph 10.2. In fact, when we discussed this derivation in Section 10A.1.2, we mentioned that *MWTP* curves are sometimes referred to as compensated demand curves.

More precisely, note that compensated demand functions are functions of prices and utility. Consider the function $h_1(p_1,p_2',u^A)$ with p_2' set to 1 (as we would do if good x_2 represents "other consumption" denominated in dollars) and utility fixed at the quantity associated with indifference curve u^A. With the other arguments of the function held fixed, this leaves a function of only p_1, a function that tells us how the consumer will change his or her consumption of x_1 as p_1 changes assuming the consumer is compensated sufficiently to permit him or her to reach indifference curve u^A. The inverse of this function is what is derived graphically in the lower panel of Graph 10.2, the marginal willingness to pay curve associated with the indifference curve u^A. The fact that there exist many *MWTP* curves as demonstrated in Graph 10.4b, one corresponding to each indifference curve, then falls straight out of the underlying mathematics: As different utility levels are plugged into the compensated demand function (instead of u^A), different *MWTP* (or compensated demand) curves emerge.

Exercise 10B.1
In Graph 10.5b, we illustrated that *MWTP* curves and own-price demand curves are the same when tastes are quasilinear. Suppose tastes can be modeled with the quasilinear utility function $u(x_1,x_2) = \alpha \ln x_1 + x_2$. Verify a generalization of the intuition from Graph 10.5b that demand functions and compensated demand functions are identical for x_1 in this case.

10B.1.2 Linking Indirect Utility and Expenditure Functions in the Duality Picture
Once we have solved for demand functions (using utility maximization) and compensated demand functions (using expenditure minimization), we can formally define two further functions that we have already used in previous chapters without naming them: the *indirect utility function*, which tells us for any set of economic circumstances (i.e., prices and income) how much utility the consumer will achieve if she does the best she can; and the *expenditure function*, which tells us for any prices and utility level how big a money budget is required for the consumer to reach that utility level.

To find the utility level a consumer can attain under different economic circumstances, all we have to do is plug the demand functions (which tell us how much the consumer will consume of each of the goods under different circumstances) into the utility function. The indirect utility function $V(p_1, p_2, I)$ can then simply be written as

$$V(p_1, p_2, I) = u\Big(x_1(p_1, p_2, I), x_2(p_1, p_2, I)\Big). \tag{10.5}$$

Similarly, the money required to reach a particular utility level u under different prices is found simply by multiplying the compensated demands for the goods (which tell us how much of each good a person will consume if the person always gets just enough money to reach the utility level u) by the prices and adding them up; i.e., the expenditure function $E(p_1, p_2, u)$ can be written as

$$E(p_1, p_2, u) = p_1 h_1(p_1, p_2, u) + p_2 h_2(p_1, p_2, u). \tag{10.6}$$

Consider, for example, the case of a Cobb–Douglas utility function $u(x_1, x_2) = x_1^{\alpha} x_2^{(1-\alpha)}$. The utility maximization and expenditure minimization problems yield demand functions

$$x_1(p_1, p_2, I) = \frac{\alpha I}{p_1} \quad \text{and} \quad x_2(p_1, p_2, I) = \frac{(1 - \alpha)I}{p_2} \tag{10.7}$$

and compensated demand functions

$$h_1(p_1, p_2, u) = \left(\frac{\alpha p_2}{(1 - \alpha)p_1}\right)^{(1-\alpha)} u$$

$$h_2(p_1, p_2, u) = \left(\frac{(1 - \alpha)p_1}{\alpha p_2}\right)^{\alpha} u. \tag{10.8}$$

Verify the solutions given in equations (10.8).

Exercise 10B.2

Plugging (10.7) into the Cobb–Douglas utility function, we get the indirect utility function

$$V(p_1, p_2, I) = \frac{I\alpha^{\alpha}(1 - \alpha)^{(1-\alpha)}}{p_1^{\alpha} p_2^{(1-\alpha)}}. \tag{10.9}$$

and multiplying the equations in (10.8) by the relevant prices and adding, we get the expenditure function

$$E(p_1, p_2, u) = \frac{u p_1^{\alpha} p_2^{(1-\alpha)}}{\alpha^{\alpha}(1 - \alpha)^{(1-\alpha)}}. \tag{10.10}$$

Verify the solutions given in equations (10.9) and (10.10).

Exercise 10B.3

Now notice the following: If you set the left-hand side of (10.9) equal to u and solve for I, you get the right-hand side of (10.10). Similarly, if you set the left-hand side of (10.10) equal to I and solve for u, you get the right-hand side of (10.9). That is because *the indirect utility function is the inverse of the expenditure function and vice versa.* Graph 10.11 shows the intuition behind this by graphing first the indirect utility as a function of income when $p_1 = 4$, $p_2 = 1$, and $\alpha = 0.5$, and then graphing the expenditure function (evaluated at the same prices and the same α) as a function

Graph 10.11: Indirect Utility and Expenditure Function

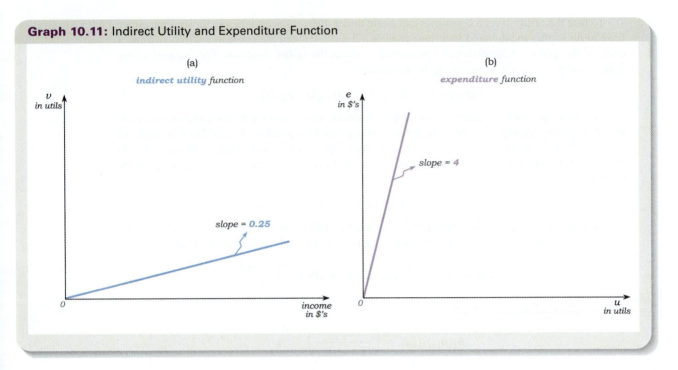

of utility. The only difference between the two graphs is that we have inverted the first graph to get the second, switching the utility and dollar axes in the process!

Other linkages between the utility maximization and the expenditure minimization results can also be identified and should make intuitive sense once you have fully internalized what these functions represent. For instance, suppose we plug the expenditure function in for the income variable I in demand functions. Then, rather than letting income be fixed, we have constructed a new demand function that always provides the consumer sufficient income to reach utility level u. But that is precisely the definition of a compensated demand function. As a result, we can establish the following logical relationship:

$$x_i\big(p_1,p_2,E(p_1,p_2,u)\big) = h_i(p_1,p_2,u). \tag{10.11}$$

Similarly, suppose we plug the indirect utility function in for the utility term u in compensated demands. Then rather than letting utility be fixed, the compensated demand function would give us the optimal consumption level assuming you have enough income to reach the level of utility you would reach with just income I. In other words, the compensated demand function would then tell you the optimal bundle assuming your income (rather than utility) is fixed, which is just the definition of a regular (or uncompensated) demand function:

$$h_i\big(p_1,p_2,V(p_1,p_2,I)\big) = x_i(p_1,p_2,I). \tag{10.12}$$

Exercise 10B.4

Verify that (10.11) and (10.12) are true for the functions that emerge from utility maximization and expenditure minimization when tastes can be modeled by the Cobb–Douglas function $u(x_1,x_2) = x_1^{\alpha}x_2^{(1-\alpha)}$.

Graph 10.12 summarizes the "duality" picture as we have developed it in this section, and indicates through arrows the linkages between the utility maximization and expenditure minimization problems that we have developed thus far. The arrows labeled "Roy's Identity" and

Graph 10.12: "Duality" of Utility Maximization and Expenditure Minimization

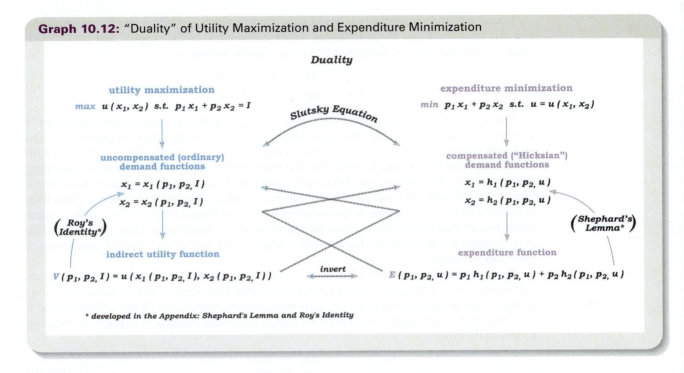

Duality

utility maximization

$max \ u(x_1, x_2) \ s.t. \ p_1 x_1 + p_2 x_2 = I$

Slutsky Equation

expenditure minimization

$min \ p_1 x_1 + p_2 x_2 \ s.t. \ u = u(x_1, x_2)$

uncompensated (ordinary) demand functions

$x_1 = x_1(p_1, p_2, I)$

$x_2 = x_2(p_1, p_2, I)$

compensated ("Hicksian") demand functions

$x_1 = h_1(p_1, p_2, u)$

$x_2 = h_2(p_1, p_2, u)$

$\begin{pmatrix} Roy's \\ Identity* \end{pmatrix}$

$\begin{pmatrix} Shephard's \\ Lemma* \end{pmatrix}$

indirect utility function

expenditure function

$V(p_1, p_2, I) = u(x_1(p_1, p_2, I), x_2(p_1, p_2, I))$

invert

$E(p_1, p_2, u) = p_1 h_1(p_1, p_2, u) + p_2 h_2(p_1, p_2, u)$

* developed in the Appendix: Shephard's Lemma and Roy's Identity

"Shephard's Lemma" are developed in the appendix, and the dotted line labeled "Slutsky Equation" is developed next.

10B.1.3 The Slutsky Equation
There is one final link between the two sides of our duality picture. It is known as the Slutsky equation, and it relates the slopes (with respect to prices) of uncompensated demand curves to the slopes of compensated demand curves.[7] To be more precise, we would like to begin with a point that lies on both the demand and the compensated demand functions and then derive the relationship between the slopes of the two functions at that point. We have already done this intuitively in Graphs 10.5 and 10.9. In those graphs, this common point is point A, and it is at that point that we could say which of the two curves is steeper depending on whether the good is normal or inferior. It is easiest for us to begin our mathematical derivation of the Slutsky equation with expression (10.11), which already relates demand functions to compensated demand functions (but does not relate their slopes to one another). To identify the relationship of the slopes, we simply take the partial derivative (with respect to one of the prices) of each side of equation (10.11). This requires us to invoke the chain rule from calculus since the function on the left-hand side contains the expenditure function E that itself is a function of prices:

$$\frac{\partial x_i}{\partial p_j} + \left(\frac{\partial x_i}{\partial E}\right)\left(\frac{\partial E}{\partial p_j}\right) = \frac{\partial h_i}{\partial p_j}. \tag{10.13}$$

Rearranging terms, and replacing the E term in $(\partial x_i/\partial E)$ with I (since expenditure is the same as income in the consumer model), we can write this equation as

$$\frac{\partial x_i}{\partial p_j} = \frac{\partial h_i}{\partial p_j} - \left(\frac{\partial x_i}{\partial I}\right)\left(\frac{\partial E}{\partial p_j}\right). \tag{10.14}$$

---

[7]The Slutsky Equation is named after the Russian economist and statistician Eugene Slutsky (1880–1948). The equation was so named by John Hicks who also called it the "Fundamental Equation of Value Theory."

Equation (10.14) is written in terms of good x_i and price p_j. To help us investigate precisely how this equation relates to the intuitions we have developed so far, suppose that we focus on good x_1 and a change in p_1. Equation (10.14) can then be written as

$$\frac{\partial x_1}{\partial p_1} = \frac{\partial h_1}{\partial p_1} - \left(\frac{\partial x_1}{\partial I}\right)\left(\frac{\partial E}{\partial p_1}\right). \tag{10.15}$$

The left-hand side of equation (10.15) is the change in the actual quantity demanded of good x_1 when p_1 changes marginally. This is analogous to the move from A to C in Graphs 10.5 and 10.8, although the calculus here corresponds to marginal (or very small) changes. The first term on the right-hand side of equation (10.15) is the change in the quantity of x_1 demanded assuming the consumer has been compensated to keep his or her utility constant. It is analogous to the move from A to B in Graphs 10.5 and 10.9, or the substitution effect. This must mean that the final term in equation (10.15) is analogous to the move from B to C in Graphs 10.5 and 10.9, or the income effect. Indeed, that is precisely what the final term suggests: $(\partial x_1/\partial I)$ is the change in the quantity of x_1 demanded when income changes, and $(\partial E/\partial p_1)$ is the size of the required compensation given that p_1 changes.

First, note that $\partial h_1/\partial p_1 < 0$; when price increases, the substitution effect always suggests we will purchase less of that good when we are compensated. Now suppose that we know that a consumer's tastes are quasilinear in x_1; i.e., x_1 is borderline between a normal and an inferior good. This implies that consumption of x_1 does not change as income changes, or $\partial x_1/\partial I = 0$, reducing equation (10.15) to

$$\frac{\partial x_1}{\partial p_1} = \frac{\partial h_1}{\partial p_1}. \tag{10.16}$$

This is precisely what is illustrated intuitively in Graph 10.5b, where we demonstrated that demand curves and $MWTP$ (or compensated demand) curves are the same for quasilinear goods. The reason for this is that the income effect disappears in this special case, leaving us with only the substitution effect.

Now suppose we knew instead that x_1 was a normal good. In that case, $\partial x_1/\partial I > 0$. Whenever the price of a good we are consuming goes up, it must furthermore be true that the expenditure required to reach the same utility level increases, thus $\partial E/\partial p_1 > 0$. Together, these two statements imply that the second term in equation (10.15) is negative (two positive terms multiplied by each other and preceded by a negative sign). Thus, when x_1 is a normal good, the quantity demanded falls first because of the substitution effect ($\partial h_1/\partial p_1 < 0$) and then again because of the income effect ($-(\partial x_1/\partial I)(\partial E/\partial p_1) < 0$). When x_1 is an inferior good, on the other hand, $\partial x_1/\partial I < 0$, which implies that the second term on the right-hand side of equation (10.15) is positive. Thus, income and substitution effects point in opposite directions. All this is precisely as we have concluded in our graphs of consumer choices.

10B.1.4 Graphs and Inverse Graphs   Sometimes students get confused when looking at a graph like the lower panel of Graph 10.5 and attempting to relate the slopes of the demand and $MWTP$ curves in the graph to the slopes represented by partial derivatives in equation (10.15). For instance, suppose again that x_1 is a normal good. Then it appears that the slope of the demand curve ($\partial x_1/\partial p_1$) is negative because of the negative slope of the $MWTP$ curve ($\partial h_1/\partial p_1$) and because of an additional negative component implicit in the second term of equation (10.15), the income effect. This would mean that the slope of the demand curve at any point is a negative number that is larger in absolute value than the slope of the $MWTP$ curve at that same point. Put differently, it means that the demand curve is downward sloping and steeper than the $MWTP$ curve (which is also downward sloping). But Graph 10.5a suggests the opposite, that the demand curve is downward sloping and *shallower* than the $MWTP$ curve for a normal good.

The reason for the appearance of a discrepancy between the intuition developed in Graph 10.5a and the math implicit in equation (10.15) can once again be found in the unfortunate fact that economists graph demand curves as slices of *inverse* demand functions. Thus, the slopes derived from the mathematics represent the inverse of the slopes derived in our graphs. Taking an inverse of a slope does not change the sign of that slope (i.e., downward-sloping curves remain downward sloping), but it does change whether one curve is relatively steeper than the other (i.e., steep slopes become shallow slopes and vice versa). Graph 10.13 illustrates this relationship by plotting demand curves as inverse slices of demand functions in panel (a) (which illustrate demand and *MWTP* curves as depicted in Graph 10.9) and as simple slices of the same demand functions (with the axes reversed) in panel (b). The arrows in each graph begin with the demand curve representing a normal good and end with the demand curve representing a Giffen good. The slopes in the Slutsky equation correspond to the slopes in the second graph.

10B.2 Taxes, Deadweight Losses, and Consumer Welfare

As suggested in Section 10A, concepts like consumer surplus and deadweight loss can be read off as distances in the consumer diagram or as areas below *MWTP* curves. Areas under curves can be calculated mathematically as integrals, but we do not have to resort to integral calculus to be able to calculate changes in consumer surplus or deadweight loss mathematically. This section thus uses the same example of a housing tax discussed throughout Section A to demonstrate how the relevant concepts can be calculated without any additional calculus and simply using the various parts of our duality picture. (The more mathematically inclined students can turn to the end of the appendix to see an explanation of how areas along compensated demand curves correspond to distances in the consumer diagram.)

10B.2.1 Using Duality Concepts to Calculate Deadweight Loss
We concluded in Section 10A.3 that taxes are inefficient because of substitution effects. We furthermore defined the size of the inefficiency through a measure of deadweight loss (*DWL*)—the difference

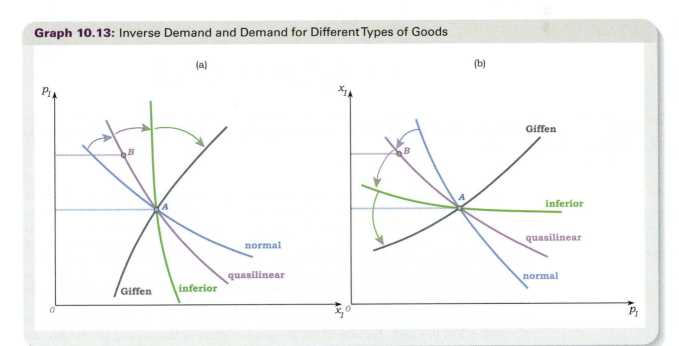

Graph 10.13: Inverse Demand and Demand for Different Types of Goods

between actual tax revenue T and the tax revenue L that could have been raised (without making the consumer worse off) had a lump sum tax been imposed instead.

Suppose, then, that x_1 represents square feet of housing, and t is the tax rate paid by consumers of housing. The tax revenue T raised from a consumer is then just equal to the tax rate t times the square footage $x_1(p_1 + t, p_2, I)$ of housing she consumes when the tax is in place, where x_1 is the demand function for housing and $(p_1 + t)$ is the price of housing faced by consumers under the housing tax. Put in terms of the mathematical functions in our duality picture,

$$T = tx_1(p_1 + t, p_2, I). \tag{10.17}$$

The lump sum tax we could have imposed instead without making the consumer worse off is slightly more challenging to calculate and easiest derived using our graphical intuition from Graph 10.6b. First, we have to determine the value (u^A in Graph 10.6b) associated with the indifference curve the consumer ends up on under the housing tax. This is the utility the consumer receives when she has income I and faces the tax inclusive price $(p_1 + t)$ for housing. The indirect utility function evaluated at the relevant prices and income gives us precisely that utility level. Put differently, u^A in Graph 10.6b is equivalent to $V(p_1 + t, p_2, I)$.

Next, we have to determine the minimum expenditure (or income) necessary for the consumer to reach his or her after-tax utility level $V(p_1 + t, p_2, I)$ if the price of housing is p_1 instead of $(p_1 + t)$. This is given by the expenditure function evaluated at the relevant prices and utility level; i.e., $E(p_1, p_2, u^A)$ or $E(p_1, p_2, V(p_1 + t, p_2, I))$. The lump sum tax we could have taken from the consumer is then simply the difference between the income she starts out with and this expenditure level; i.e.,

$$L = I - E\big(p_1, p_2, V(p_1 + t, p_2, I)\big). \tag{10.18}$$

If the underlying utility function is $u(x_1, x_2) = x_1^\alpha x_2^{(1-\alpha)}$, for instance, we calculated demand, compensated demand, indirect utility, and expenditure functions in Section 10B.1.2 in equations (10.7) through (10.10). Using these and gathering terms, we can get the following expressions for T and L:

$$T = \frac{t\alpha I}{p_1 + t}$$

$$L = I - I\left(\frac{p_1}{p_1 + t}\right)^\alpha = I\left[1 - \left(\frac{p_1}{p_1 + t}\right)^\alpha\right]. \tag{10.19}$$

Exercise 10B.5   Verify that the equations in (10.19) are correct for the Cobb–Douglas utility function $u(x_1, x_2) = x_1^\alpha x_2^{(1-\alpha)}$.

Using these equations, and knowing that $DWL = L - T$, we could calculate the deadweight losses under a variety of taste parameters (α), prices, and incomes, and for a variety of possible tax rates. For instance, suppose the rental price of a square foot of housing is \$10, the price of "other goods" is (by definition) \$1, the taste parameter α is 0.25, and the housing tax raises the price of housing by \$2.50. Then a consumer whose income is \$100,000 will reduce his or her consumption of housing from 2,500 square feet to 2,000 square feet, and, while the consumer pays a total housing tax of \$5,000, she would have been willing to pay \$5425.84 in a lump sum tax to avoid the housing tax. Thus, the tax gives rise to a deadweight loss of roughly \$426, or roughly 8.5% of total tax revenue from the housing tax. Put differently, \$426 of wealth is lost in society because of the substitution effect of the housing tax for this one consumer.

Verify that the numbers calculated in the previous paragraph are correct.

Exercise
10B.6

10B.2.2 Deadweight Loss and Substitution Effects

All our work in Section 10A suggested that deadweight losses from taxation arise from substitution effects, and when tastes are such that substitution effects do not arise (as in Graph 10.8b), there is no deadweight loss from taxation. With the underlying mathematics developed, we can now see how this intuition plays out as elasticities of substitution (and thus substitution effects) get larger.

Suppose, for instance, that tastes can be summarized by the CES utility function

$$u(x_1, x_2) = \left(\alpha x_1^{-\rho} + (1 - \alpha) x_2^{-\rho} \right)^{1/\rho}, \qquad (10.20)$$

where the elasticity of substitution σ, as introduced in Chapter 5, is given by $1/(1 + \rho)$. Suppose further that, as in our example, the rental price of a square foot of housing is \$10, the price of "other goods" is (by definition) \$1, and income is \$100,000. Now we can consider the impact of a tax that raises the price of housing from \$10 to \$12.50 under different assumptions about the underlying elasticity of substitution σ.

Table 10.1 does precisely that, with the column labeled σ varying the elasticity of substitution and with α (in the right-most column) set to ensure that in each case the consumer rents 2,500 square feet of housing in the absence of a tax. The third column in the table then indicates the square footage consumed after the imposition of the tax, and the remaining columns give the resulting values for tax revenue (T), a utility-equivalent lump sum tax (L), the resulting deadweight loss (DWL), and the deadweight loss as a fraction of tax revenue (DWL/T).

Table 10.1: Housing Taxes and the Elasticity of Substitution

Effects of Housing Taxes as the Elasticity of Substitution Rises							
σ	$x_1(p_1, \dots)$	$x_1(p_1 + t, \dots)$	T	L	DWL	DWL/T	α
0.50	2,500	2,172	\$5,430	\$5,650	\$220	0.041	0.01098900
0.75	2,500	2,085	\$5,212	\$5,537	\$325	0.062	0.09688500
1.00	2,500	2,000	\$5,000	\$5,426	\$426	0.085	0.25000000
1.25	2,500	1,917	\$4,794	\$5,316	\$523	0.109	0.39690600
1.50	2,500	1,837	\$4,593	\$5,209	\$616	0.134	0.50878000
1.75	2,500	1,760	\$4,399	\$5,103	\$705	0.160	0.58881600
2.00	2,500	1,684	\$4,211	\$5,000	\$789	0.188	0.64611070
2.50	2,500	1,541	\$3,852	\$4,799	\$947	0.246	0.71952500
3.00	2,500	1,407	\$3,516	\$4,606	\$1,090	0.310	0.76293800
4.00	2,500	1,166	\$2,916	\$4,244	\$1,329	0.456	0.81034997
5.00	2,500	961	\$2,403	\$3,914	\$1,511	0.629	0.83511837
7.50	2,500	580	\$1,450	\$3,215	\$1,766	1.218	0.86402047
10.00	2,500	343	\$856	\$2,674	\$1,817	2.122	0.87679951

The figures in the table provide potential magnitudes for the distortionary effects of a relatively modest tax on housing. When the elasticity of substitution is low, so is the deadweight loss, but the deadweight loss can rise dramatically as the elasticity of substitution (and thus the substitution effect) increases. For the case of housing, empirical estimates of likely elasticities of substitution lie around 1, suggesting that our Cobb–Douglas example in the previous section (which is equivalent to the CES utility example with $\sigma = 1$) may be most relevant. Other goods that we commonly tax, however, may have significantly higher or lower elasticities of substitution.

10B.2.3 *DWL* Rising Faster than Tax Rates

A second lesson from our work in Section 10A relates to the change in *DWL* as tax rates increase. We can now use our Cobb–Douglas example (where $\sigma = 1$) to calculate the changing impact of our housing tax as the tax increases. Table 10.2 does just that—it presents the impact of a tax that raises the price of housing from 10 to $(10 + t)$ as t increases. Notice that the *DWL* of the tax increases much faster than the tax itself, almost quadrupling, for instance, when the tax is doubled from 0.5 to 1.0 and almost increasing nine-fold when the tax is tripled from 0.5 to 1.5. This is in line with the rule of thumb we developed when we used a linear demand curve in Graph 10.10 to conclude that, as the level of a tax is increased by a factor of x, the *DWL* from the tax increases by a factor of x^2. (The increase in *DWL* in Table 10.2 is slightly below what this rule of thumb predicts because compensated demand curves derived from Cobb–Douglas tastes contain some curvature that is not accounted for in Graph 10.10.)

In the last column of Table 10.2, the "exponential" growth in *DWL* results in a steady increase of *DWL* as a fraction of tax revenue. This is a common measure of just how inefficient a particular tax is, because it tells us how much of the revenue that is raised society has lost in wealth along the way.

Table 10.2: Housing Tax Increases under Cobb–Douglas Tastes (with $\alpha = 0.25$)

		Effects of Housing Taxes as Tax Rate Increases				
t	$x_1(p_1, \ldots)$	$x_1(p_1 + t, \ldots)$	T	L	DWL	DWL/T
0.50	2,500	2,381	$1,190	$1,212	$22	0.018
1.00	2,500	2,273	$2,272	$2,355	$82	0.036
1.50	2,500	2,174	$3,261	$3,434	$173	0.053
2.00	2,500	2,083	$4,167	$4,456	$289	0.069
2.50	2,500	2,000	$5,000	$5,426	$426	0.085
3.00	2,500	1,923	$5,769	$6,349	$579	0.101
4.00	2,500	1,786	$7,143	$8,068	$925	0.130
5.00	2,500	1,667	$8,333	$9,640	$1,306	0.157
10.00	2,500	1,250	$12,500	$15,910	$3,410	0.273
25.00	2,500	714	$17,857	$26,889	$9,032	0.506
50.00	2,500	417	$20,833	$36,106	$15,272	0.733
100.00	2,500	227	$22,727	$45,090	$22,363	0.984

CONCLUSION

This chapter has introduced a method by which to measure changes in consumer welfare as the economic environment (i.e., prices faced by consumers) changes. More precisely, we have defined marginal willingness to pay (or compensated demand) curves along which such welfare changes can be measured. In the process, we have identified conditions under which such curves are similar to regular demand curves, and conditions (i.e., in the presence of income effects) when they are different. And this analysis is further extended in the B-portion of the chapter to show a whole series of similarities in the optimization approaches that lead to uncompensated demand and compensated demand curves, similarities that together have painted a "duality" picture that summarizes all the various techniques developed so far as well as their logical connections.

Given the new tool of marginal willingness to pay curves, we can then ask how much is gained by the "winners" and how much is lost by the "losers" of any policy that distorts prices from what they would be in the absence of the policy, and whether it is in principle possible to compensate the losers from the gains experienced by the winners. If the answer to the latter question is yes, then we know we have identified a policy that, at least in principle, could be efficiency enhancing. On the other hand, when we identify a policy as producing more economic losses than economic gains, we know we have a policy that is not efficient.

As emphasized at the outset of the chapter, we need to be cautious not to read too much into this, however. In Chapter 1, we discussed the difference between normative and positive economics, and we noted that there will be times when the line between the two types of analyses becomes blurred. If we conclude from the type of welfare analysis we have introduced in this chapter that a policy produces more economic gains for the "winners" than economic losses for the "losers," that is still a *positive* statement because it is simply a statement of fact (assuming the analysis was done correctly) with no particular value judgments attached to it. However, if we interpret the statement as an endorsement of the policy, we have slipped into *normative* economics and have made some explicit value judgments regarding the desirability of benefitting the winners at the expense of the losers.

Consider, for instance, the chapter's analysis of price-distorting (i.e., non–lump sum) taxes. We concluded that, with a few exceptions, all such taxes are *inefficient* because price-distorting taxes give rise to substitution effects. We also concluded the inefficiency (or deadweight loss) from such taxes increases "exponentially" as tax rates increase linearly, implying that lower tax rates on larger tax bases are generally more efficient than higher tax rates on smaller tax bases. These are *positive* statements so long as they are not interpreted as endorsements of particular policies. All the *positive* economist does is provide the policy maker with estimates of the economic costs of various policy alternatives; it is then up to the policy maker to determine, in light of the relevant costs, what is the best policy option. A policy maker might, for instance, choose a less efficient tax that produces greater deadweight losses because he or she thinks that the burdens of such a tax are more *fairly distributed* than in the case of a more efficient alternative.

This concludes our development of consumer theory for now. We began by modeling economic circumstances and tastes, then put them together in our optimization model, and finally developed the concepts of demand and compensated demand (or *MWTP*) curves. When we return to these in later chapters (after developing basic producer theory in the next section of the book), keep in mind what these two types of demands are used for: Demand curves (or, analogously, labor supply curves) describe *how behavior actually changes with economic circumstances*. Compensated demand (or *MWTP*) curves (or compensated labor supply curves, which we will define in Chapter 19), on the other hand, allow us to measure welfare changes for consumers (and workers). They do not describe actual behavior and thus are useful only when we want to ask what the welfare impact of changing economic circumstances might be.

APPENDIX: SHEPHARD'S LEMMA AND ROY'S IDENTITY

Two further relationships indicated in parentheses in the duality picture of Graph 10.12 are frequently highlighted in more advanced treatments of duality and deserve some supplemental treatment here for those students interested in going a little deeper. The first and more important of these is known as *Shephard's Lemma* and it simply states that

$$\frac{\partial E(p_1, p_2, u)}{\partial p_i} = h_i(p_1, p_2, u).[8]$$ (10.21)

---

[8]This relationship, while expressed for the two-good case here, holds more generally for the *n*-good case as well. The same is true for Roy's Identity, which follows.

The second relationship is known as *Roy's Identity* and states that

$$-\frac{\partial V(p_1, p_2, I)/\partial p_i}{\partial V(p_1, p_2, I)/\partial I} = x_i(p_1, p_2, I). \tag{10.22}$$

Both of these results are a direct application of the *Envelope Theorem* from mathematics. We will briefly state this theorem and then apply it to derive Shephard's Lemma and Roy's Identity.[9] Finally, we can show at the end of the appendix that these insights let us demonstrate quickly how consumer welfare translates into areas on marginal willingness to pay curves.

The Envelope Theorem

Suppose you face a maximization or minimization problem that can be written as one of the following:

$$\max_{x_1, x_2, \ldots, x_n} f(x_1, x_2, \ldots, x_n; \alpha_1, \alpha_2, \ldots, \alpha_m) \text{ subject to } g(x_1, x_2, \ldots, x_n; \alpha_1, \alpha_2, \ldots, \alpha_m) = 0$$

$$\min_{x_1, x_2, \ldots, x_n} f(x_1, x_2, \ldots, x_n; \alpha_1, \alpha_2, \ldots, \alpha_m) \text{ subject to } g(x_1, x_2, \ldots, x_n; \alpha_1, \alpha_2, \ldots, \alpha_m) = 0 \tag{10.23}$$

where $(x_1, x_2, \ldots, x_n)$ are the choice variables (analogous to the consumption bundle in our utility maximization and expenditure minimization problems) and $(\alpha_1, \alpha_2, \ldots, \alpha_m)$ are parameters (such as utility function parameters or prices and income). The Lagrange function for this problem is

$$\mathcal{L}(x_1, x_2, \ldots, x_n, \lambda) = f(x_1, x_2, \ldots, x_n; \alpha_1, \alpha_2, \ldots, \alpha_m) + \lambda g(x_1, x_2, \ldots, x_n; \alpha_1, \alpha_2, \ldots, \alpha_m) \tag{10.24}$$

and the solution to the first order conditions takes the form

$$x_i^* = x_i(\alpha_1, \alpha_2, \ldots, \alpha_m) \text{ for all } i = 1, 2, \ldots, n, \tag{10.25}$$

which is analogous to our uncompensated or compensated demand functions. Finally, suppose we call the function that arises when we plug these solutions into the objective function in (10.23) to get

$$F(\alpha_1, \alpha_2, \ldots, \alpha_m) = f(x_1^*, x_2^*, \ldots, x_n^*). \tag{10.26}$$

Then the Envelope Theorem states that, for all $j = 1, 2, \ldots, m$,

$$\frac{\partial F}{\partial \alpha_j} = \frac{\partial \mathcal{L}}{\partial \alpha_j}\bigg|_{(x_1^*, x_2^*, \ldots, x_n^*)} = \left(\frac{\partial f}{\partial \alpha_j} + \lambda \frac{\partial g}{\partial \alpha_j}\right)\bigg|_{(x_1^*, x_2^*, \ldots, x_n^*)} \tag{10.27}$$

where the "$(x_1^*, x_2^*, \ldots, x_n^*)$" following the vertical lines is read as "evaluated at $(x_1^*, x_2^*, \ldots, x_n^*)$" or "with the derivatives evaluated at the optimum of the choice variables."

The Envelope Theorem Applied to Expenditure Minimization and Utility Maximization

Consider, then, the expenditure minimization problem on the right side of the duality Graph 10.12. In terms of the notation of our definition of the Envelope Theorem, the problem is written with

$(x_1, x_2, \ldots, x_n)$ represented by the goods (x_1, x_2)

$(\alpha_1, \alpha_2, \ldots, \alpha_m)$ represented by the parameters (p_1, p_2, u) (10.28)

$f(x_1, x_2, \ldots, x_n; \alpha_1, \alpha_2, \ldots, \alpha_m)$ represented by $E = p_1 x_1 + p_2 x_2$

---

[9]Shephard's Lemma is named after Ronald Shephard who formally proved the result in 1953 after it had already been used in work by others over the previous two decades. Rene Roy, a French economist, is credited with the proof for Roy's Identity in a paper in 1947.

$$g(x_1, x_2, \ldots, x_n; \alpha_1, \alpha_2, \ldots, \alpha_m) = 0 \text{ represented by } u - u(x_1, x_2) = 0$$

$$x_i^* = x_i(\alpha_1, \alpha_2, \ldots, \alpha_m) \text{ represented by } x_i^* = h_i(p_1, p_2, u) \text{ and}$$

$$F(\alpha_1, \alpha_2, \ldots, \alpha_m) \text{ represented by } E(p_1, p_2, u).$$

We can then apply the Envelope Theorem in equation (10.27) directly to get

$$\frac{\partial E(p_1, p_2, u)}{\partial p_i} = \left(\frac{\partial(p_1 x_1 + p_2 x_2)}{\partial p_i} \right)\Bigg|_{(x_1^*, x_2^*)} + \lambda \left(\frac{\partial(u - u(x_1, x_2))}{\partial p_i} \right)\Bigg|_{(x_1^*, x_2^*)}. \qquad (10.29)$$

Since p_i does not appear in the equation $u - u(x_1, x_2)$, the term following λ is zero. This simplifies the expression in (10.29) to

$$\frac{\partial E(p_1, p_2, u)}{\partial p_i} = x_i|_{(x_1^*, x_2^*)} = h_i(p_1, p_2, u), \qquad (10.30)$$

which is Shephard's Lemma (and can be straightforwardly extended to an expenditure minimization problem with more than 2 goods). In the utility maximization problem on the left side of the duality Graph 10.12, on the other hand, we have

$$(x_1, x_2, \ldots, x_n) \text{ represented by the goods } (x_1, x_2)$$

$$(\alpha_1, \alpha_2, \ldots, \alpha_m) \text{ represented by the parameters } (p_1, p_2, I)$$

$$f(x_1, x_2, \ldots, x_n; \alpha_1, \alpha_2, \ldots, \alpha_m) \text{ represented by } u(x_1, x_2)$$

$$g(x_1, x_2, \ldots, x_n; \alpha_1, \alpha_2, \ldots, \alpha_m) = 0 \text{ represented by } I - p_1 x_1 - p_2 x_2 = 0 \qquad (10.31)$$

$$x_i^* = x_i(\alpha_1, \alpha_2, \ldots, \alpha_m) \text{ represented by } x_i^* = x_i(p_1, p_2, I) \text{ and}$$

$$F(\alpha_1, \alpha_2, \ldots, \alpha_m) \text{ represented by } V(p_1, p_2, I).$$

The Envelope Theorem then implies

$$\frac{\partial V(p_1, p_2, I)}{\partial p_i} = \left(\frac{\partial u(x_1, x_2)}{\partial p_i} \right)\Bigg|_{(x_1^*, x_2^*)} + \lambda \left(\frac{\partial(I - p_1 x_1 - p_2 x_2)}{\partial p_i} \right)\Bigg|_{(x_1^*, x_2^*)}. \qquad (10.32)$$

Since $(\partial u(x_1, x_2)/\partial p_i) = 0$, equation (10.32) reduces to

$$\frac{\partial V(p_1, p_2, I)}{\partial p_i} = -\lambda x_i|_{(x_1^*, x_2^*)} = -\lambda x_i(p_1, p_2, I). \qquad (10.33)$$

The Envelope Theorem also implies

$$\frac{\partial V(p_1, p_2, I)}{\partial I} = \left(\frac{\partial u(x_1, x_2)}{\partial I} \right)\Bigg|_{(x_1^*, x_2^*)} + \lambda \left(\frac{\partial(I - p_1 x_1 - p_2 x_2)}{\partial I} \right)\Bigg|_{(x_1^*, x_2^*)} = \lambda. \qquad (10.34)$$

Dividing equations (10.33) by (10.34) and multiplying both sides by -1, we then get Roy's Identity:

$$-\frac{\partial V(p_1, p_2, I)/\partial p_i}{\partial V(p_1, p_2, I)/\partial I} = x_i(p_1, p_2, I). \qquad (10.35)$$

Intuition behind Shephard's Lemma and the Concavity of the Expenditure Function

Suppose that a consumer initially consumes a bundle A when prices of x_1 and x_2 are p_1^A and p_2^A, and suppose that the consumer attains utility level u^A as a result. This is illustrated in panel (a) of Graph 10.14 with the tangency between the indifference curve and the blue budget line, which involves an overall expenditure level of $E^A = p_1^A x_1^A + p_2^A x_2^A$. This is then one point on the expenditure function $E(p_1, p_2, u)$, in particular the point $E(p_1^A, p_2^A, u^A)$.

Graph 10.14: Substitution Effects, Shephard's Lemma, and the Concavity of $E(p_1, p_2, u)$ in Prices

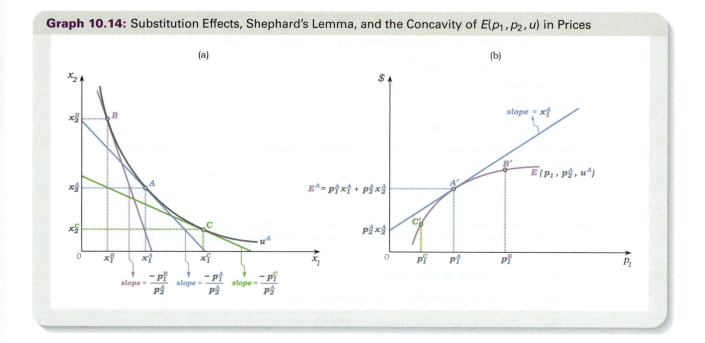

Now suppose we wanted to graph the "slice" of the expenditure function that holds the price of x_2 fixed at p_2^A and utility fixed at u^A; i.e., the slice $E(p_1, p_2^A, u^A)$ that illustrates how expenditure varies with changes in p_1. The point A' in panel (b) of Graph 10.14 is then one point on this slice of the expenditure function, the point $E(p_1^A, p_2^A, u^A)$.

Without knowing about substitution effects, we could then naively assume that a consumer would always have to consume bundle A in order to remain equally happy as p_1 changes. If this were the case, then the slice of the expenditure function would simply be $E = p_1 x_1^A + p_2^A x_2^A$, an equation of a line with intercept $p_2^A x_2^A$ and slope x_1^A when expenditure is graphed on the vertical axis and p_1 on the horizontal. This is illustrated as the blue line in panel (b) of Graph 10.14.

The real expenditure function, however, takes account of the fact that individuals substitute away from goods that become more expensive and toward goods that become cheaper. For instance, suppose the price of x_1 rises from the initial p_1^A to p_1^B, represented in panel (a) of Graph 10.14 in the slope of the magenta budget line tangent to the indifference curve u^A at bundle B. The actual expenditure required to have this individual reach utility level u^A under the prices (p_1^B, p_2^A) is then $p_1^B x_1^B + p_2^A x_2^B$, not $p_1^B x_1^A + p_2^A x_2^A$ as suggested by the blue line in panel (b), and the former amount is smaller than the latter (which you can see in the fact that when the budget line has the steeper (magenta) slope, bundle A lies outside the budget set that contains bundle B). The actual point $E(p_1^B, p_2^A, u^A)$ in panel (b) of the graph therefore lies somewhere below the blue line and is graphed as point B'. The same is true for a decrease in p_1 to p_1^C, which is represented in the slope of the green budget line tangent to the indifference curve u^A at bundle C; the actual expenditure $E(p_1^C, p_2^A, u^A)$ at bundle C is below the expenditure $p_1^C x_1^A + p_2^A x_2^A$ graphed on the blue line in panel (b).

The presence of substitution effects therefore implies that the "slices" of the expenditure function with a price change on the horizontal axis are *concave* with

$$\frac{\partial E(p_1, p_2, u)}{\partial p_i} > 0 \text{ and } \frac{\partial^2 E(p_1, p_2, u)}{\partial p_i^2} \leq 0. \quad (10.36)$$

Exercise 10B.7 What shape must the indifference curves have in order for the second derivative of the expenditure function with respect to price to be equal to zero (and for the "slice" of the expenditure function in panel (b) of Graph 10.14 to be equal to the blue line)?

Panel (b) of Graph 10.14 furthermore is a graphical depiction of Shephard's Lemma (and of the intuition behind the Envelope Theorem): The slope of the actual (magenta) expenditure function at p_1^A is x_1^A, and x_1^A is the expenditure minimizing level of consumption of good 1 to reach the indifference curve u^A when prices are (p_1^A, p_2^A); i.e.,

$$x_1^A = h_1(p_1^A, p_2^A, u^A). \tag{10.37}$$

The fact that the slope of the (magenta) slice of the actual expenditure function at A' is equal to x_1^A can therefore be expressed as

$$\frac{\partial E(p_1^A, p_2^A, u^A)}{\partial p_1} = h_1(p_1^A, p_2^A, u^A), \tag{10.38}$$

which is precisely what Shephard's Lemma tells us. Since we derived this intuition for an arbitrary initial set of prices and utility level, the same intuition applies for any combination of prices and utility levels.

Concavity of the Expenditure Function and the Slope of Compensated Demand Curves

The combination of Shephard's Lemma and the concavity of expenditure functions (that implies the conditions in equation (10.36)) then allows us to conclude

$$\frac{\partial h_i(p_1, p_2, u)}{\partial p_i} = \frac{\partial^2 E(p_1, p_2, u)}{\partial p_i^2} \leq 0, \tag{10.39}$$

which states that the slope of compensated demand curves is always negative; i.e., compensated demand curves that isolate only substitution effects must be downward sloping. This is something we have concluded to be true intuitively already, and it has become mathematically easy to demonstrate given the additional material developed in this appendix.

In a two-panel graph with the top panel containing an indifference curve and the lower panel containing a compensated demand curve for x_1 derived from that indifference curve, illustrate the case when the inequality in equation (10.39) becomes an equality. (*Hint*: Remember that our graphs of compensated demand curves are graphs of the inverse of a slice of the compensated demand functions, with a slope of 0 turning into a slope of infinity.)

Exercise 10B.8

Using Shephard's Lemma to Illustrate Consumer Welfare Changes as Areas on Compensated Demand Curves

At the beginning of Section 10B.2, and in Section 10A.4 before that, we indicated that one can use integral calculus to calculate deadweight loss. Now that we have derived Shephard's Lemma, it is relatively straightforward to demonstrate this mathematically in the context of our example of a tax on housing. In particular, consider the measurement of the lump sum tax L that is equivalent (in terms of utility for the consumer) to a housing tax that raises the price of housing by t. The amount L is the difference between the consumer's actual income and the hypothetical income required to get the consumer to his or her after-tax utility level without changing any of the prices. One way to express a consumer's income is to note that it is equivalent to the consumer's expenditures after the housing tax is put in place; i.e., $I = E(p_1 + t, p_2, u^A)$, where u^A represents the after-tax utility level. The compensated budget that gets the consumer to the same utility level at the pre-tax prices, on the other hand, is $E(p_1, p_2, u^A)$. Thus,

$$L = E(p_1 + t, p_2, u^A) - E(p_1, p_2, u^A). \tag{10.40}$$

Now note that Shephard's Lemma implies

$$\frac{\partial E(p_1, p_2, u)}{\partial p_1} = h_1(p_1, p_2, u). \tag{10.41}$$

We can then use this directly to expand equation (10.40)

$$L = E(p_1 + t, p_2, u^A) - E(p_1, p_2, u^A) = \int_{p_1}^{p_1+t} h_1(p_1, p_2, u^A)dp. \tag{10.42}$$

In other words, the amount L needed to calculate the DWL from a tax can be measured as an integral on the compensated demand function that corresponds to the after-tax utility level u^A, exactly as indicated in Graph 10.8a.

END-OF-CHAPTER EXERCISES

10.1   Consider a good x_1 in a model where a consumer chooses between x_1 and a composite good x_2.

    A. Explain why the following either cannot happen or, if you think it can happen, how:

         a.   Own-price demand for a good is perfectly vertical but taxing the good produces a deadweight loss.

         b.   Own-price demand is downward sloping (not vertical) and there is no deadweight loss from taxing the good.

    B. Now suppose that the consumer's tastes can be summarized by the CES utility function $u(x_1, x_2) = (0.5x_1^{-\rho} + 0.5x_2^{-\rho})^{-1/\rho}$.

         a.   Are there values for ρ that would result in the scenario described in A(a)?

         b.   Are there values for ρ that would result in the scenario described in A(b)?

         c.   Would either of these scenarios work with tastes that are quasilinear in x_1?

10.2[†]   Suppose that both consumption and leisure are always normal goods. Keep in mind the underlying cause for deadweight losses from wage-distorting taxation as you answer the following questions.

    A. Explain why the following either cannot happen or, if you think it can happen, how:

         a.   Labor supply is perfectly vertical, but there is a significant deadweight loss from taxing wages.

         b.   Labor supply is perfectly vertical, and there is no deadweight loss from taxing wages.

         c.   Labor supply is downward sloping, and there is a deadweight loss from taxation of wages.

         d.   Labor supply is upward sloping, and there is a deadweight loss from taxing wages.

         e.   Labor supply is downward sloping, and there is no deadweight loss from taxing wages.

         f.   Labor supply is upward sloping, and there is no deadweight loss from taxing wages.

    B.* Now suppose that tastes can be summarized by the CES utility function $u(c, \ell) = (0.5c^{-\rho} + 0.5\ell^{-\rho})^{-1/\rho}$, where c is consumption and ℓ is leisure.

         a.   Are there values for ρ that would result in the scenario in A(a)?

         b.   Are there values for ρ that would result in the scenario in A(b)?

         c.   Are there values for ρ that would result in the scenario in A(c)?

         d.   Are there values for ρ that would result in the scenario in A(d)?

         e.   Are there values for ρ that would result in the scenario in A(e) and A(f)?

10.3   Suppose that consumption takes place this period and next period, and consumption is always a normal good. Suppose further that income now is positive and income next period is zero.

    A. Explain why the following either cannot happen or, if you think it can happen, how:

         a.   Savings behavior is immune to changes in the interest rate, but taxing interest income causes a deadweight loss.

*conceptually challenging
**computationally challenging
[†]solutions in Study Guide

b. Savings behavior is immune to changes in the interest rate, and taxing interest income causes no deadweight loss.

c. Savings decreases with increases in the interest rate, and there is a deadweight loss from taxation of interest.

d. Savings increases with increases in the interest rate, and there is a deadweight loss from taxation of interest.

e. Savings decreases with an increase in the interest rate, and there is no deadweight loss.

f. Savings increases with an increase in the interest rate, and there is no deadweight loss.

B.* Now suppose that tastes can be summarized by the CES utility function $u(c_1, c_2) = (0.5c_1^{-\rho} + 0.5c_2^{-\rho})^{-1/\rho}$, where c_1 is consumption in the first period and c_2 is consumption in the second period.

a. Are there values for ρ that would result in the scenario in A(a) and A(b)?

b. Are there values for ρ that would result in the scenario in A(c)?

c. Are there values for ρ that would result in the scenario in A(d)?

d. Are there values for ρ that would result in the scenario in A(e) or A(f)?

10.4* Suppose that your tastes do not satisfy the convexity assumption. In particular, suppose the indifference curve corresponding to utility level u^A has a shape like the indifference curves depicted in Graph 6.8, with good x_1 on the horizontal axis and "other consumption" on the vertical. Illustrate what the *MWTP* (or compensated demand) curve corresponding to utility level u^A would look like. How would your answer change if the indifference curve instead satisfied convexity but contained a "flat" portion along which the *MRS* is constant (but not zero or infinite)?

10.5 **Everyday Application:** *Teacher Pay and Professional Basketball Salaries: Do we have our priorities in order?* We trust our school-aged children to be taught by dedicated teachers in our schools, but we pay those teachers only about $50,000 per year. At the same time, we watch professional-basketball games as entertainment, and we pay some of the players 400 times as much!

A. When confronted with these facts, many people throw their hands up in the air and conclude we are just hopelessly messed up as a society, that we place more value on our entertainment than on the future of our children.

a. Suppose we treat our society as a single individual. What is our marginal willingness to pay for a teacher? What is our marginal willingness to pay for a star basketball player?

b. There are about 4 million teachers that work in primary and secondary schools in the United States. What is the smallest dollar figure that could represent our total willingness to pay for teachers?

c. Do you think our *actual* total willingness to pay for teachers is likely to be much greater than that minimum figure? Why or why not?

d. For purposes of this problem, assume there are 10 star basketball players at any given time. What is the least our total willingness to pay for star basketball players could be?

e. Is our actual total willingness to pay for basketball players likely to be much higher than this minimum?

f. Do the facts cited at the beginning of this question really warrant the conclusion that we place more value on our entertainment than on the future of our children?

g. Adam Smith puzzled over an analogous dilemma: He observed that people were willing to pay exorbitant amounts for diamonds but virtually nothing for water. With water essential for sustaining life and diamonds just items that appeal to our vanity, how could we value diamonds so much more than water? This became known as the *diamond-water paradox*. Can you explain the paradox to Smith?

B. Suppose our marginal willingness to pay for teachers (x_1) is given by $MWTP = A - \alpha x_1$ and our marginal willingness to pay for star basketball players (x_2) is given by $MWTP = B - \beta x_2$.

a. Given the previously cited facts, what is the lowest that A and B could be?

b. If A and B were as you just concluded, what would α and β be?

c. What would be our marginal and total willingness to pay for teachers and star basketball players?

d. Suppose $A = B = \$100$ million. Can you tell what α and β must be?

e. Using the parameter values you just derived (with $A = B = \$100$ million), what is our total willingness to pay for teachers and star basketball players?

10.6[†] **Everyday Application:** *Ordering Appetizers*: I recently went out to dinner with my brother and my family. We decided we wanted chicken wings for an appetizer and had a choice of getting 10 wings for $4.95 or 20 wings for $7.95. I thought we should get 10; my brother thought we should get 20 and prevailed.

A. At the end of the meal, we noticed that there were 4 wings left. My brother then commented: "I guess I am vindicated. It really was the right decision to order 20 rather than 10 wings."

a. Is this a correct assessment; i.e., is the evidence of 4 wings at the end of the meal sufficient to conclude that my brother was right?

b. What if no wings were left at the end of the meal?

c. What if 10 wings were left?

d. In order for us to leave wings on the table, which of our usual assumptions about tastes must be violated?

B. Suppose that our *MWTP* for wings (x) can be approximated by the function $MWTP = A - \alpha x$.

a. Given that 4 wings were left at the end of the meal, what must be the relationship between α and A?

b. Suppose $A = 8/3$. Was my brother right to want to order 20 instead of 10 wings?

c. Suppose instead that $A = 2$. Does your answer change? What if $A = 4$?

d. If our tastes were Cobb–Douglas, could it ever be the case that we leave wings on the table?

10.7*[†] **Everyday Application:** *To Trade or Not to Trade Pizza Coupons: Exploring the Difference between Willingness to Pay and Willingness to Accept*: Suppose you and I are identical in every way, same exogenous income, same tastes over pizza and "other goods." The only difference between us is that I have a coupon that allows the owner of the coupon to buy as much pizza as he or she wants at 50% off.

A. Now suppose you approach me to see if there was any way we could make a deal under which I would sell you my coupon. In the following, you will explore under what conditions such a deal is possible.

a. On a graph with pizza on the horizontal axis and "other goods" on the vertical, illustrate (as a vertical distance) the most you are willing to pay me for my coupon. Call this amount P.

b. On a separate but similar graph, illustrate (as a vertical distance) the least I would be willing to accept in cash to give up my coupon. Call this amount R.

c. Below each of the graphs you have drawn in (a) and (b), illustrate the same amounts P and R (as areas) along the appropriate marginal willingness to pay curves.

d. Is P larger or smaller than R? What does your answer depend on? (*Hint*: By overlaying your lower graphs that illustrate P and R as areas along marginal willingness to pay curves, you should be able to tell whether one is bigger than the other or whether they are the same size depending on what kind of good pizza is.)

e. *True or False*: You and I will be able to make a deal so long as pizza is not a normal good. Explain your answer intuitively.

B. Suppose your and my tastes can be represented by the Cobb–Douglas utility function $u(x_1, x_2) = x_1^{0.5} x_2^{0.5}$, and suppose we both have income $I = 100$. Let pizza be denoted by x_1 and "other goods" by x_2, and let the price of pizza be denoted by p. (Since "other goods" are denominated in dollars, the price of x_2 is implicitly set to 1.)

a. Calculate our demand functions for pizza and other goods as a function of p.

b. Calculate our compensated demand for pizza (x_1) and other goods (x_2) as a function of p (ignoring for now the existence of the coupon).

c.   Suppose $p = 10$ and the coupon reduces this price by half (to 5). Assume again that I have the coupon but you do not. How much utility do you and I get when we make optimal decisions?

d.   How much pizza will you consume if you pay me the most you are willing to pay for the coupon? How much will I consume if you pay me the least I am willing to accept?

e.   Calculate the expenditure function for me and you.

f.   Using your answers so far, determine R—the least I am willing to accept to give up my coupon. Then determine P—the most you are willing to pay to get a coupon. (*Hint:* Use your graphs from A(a) to determine the appropriate values to plug into the expenditure function to determine how much income I would have to have to give up my coupon. Once you have done this, you can subtract my actual income $I = 100$ to determine how much you have to give me to be willing to let go of the coupon. Then do the analogous to determine how much you'd be willing to pay, this time using your graph from A(b).)

g.   Are we able to make a deal under which I sell you my coupon? Make sense of this given what you found intuitively in part A and given what you know about Cobb–Douglas tastes.

h.   Now suppose our tastes could instead be represented by the utility function $u(x_1, x_2) = 50 \ln x_1 + x_2$. Using steps similar to what you have just done, calculate again the least I am willing to accept and the most you are willing to pay for the coupon. Explain the intuition behind your answer given what you know about quasilinear tastes.

i.**   Can you demonstrate, using the compensated demand functions you calculated for the two types of tastes, that the values for P and R are in fact areas under these functions (as you described in your answer to A(c))? (*Note:* This part requires you to use integral calculus.)

10.8   **Everyday Application:** *To Join or Not to Join the Local Pool*: Where I live, most people do not have swimming pools despite the fact that it gets very hot in the summers. Thus, families, especially those with children, try to find swimming pools in the area. Our local swimming pool offers two ways in which we can get by the entrance guard: We can either purchase a "family pass" for the whole season, or we can pay an entrance fee for the family every time we want to go swimming.

EVERYDAY APPLICATION

A.   Suppose we have $1,000 to spend on activities to amuse ourselves during the summer, and suppose that there are exactly 100 days during the summer when the swimming pool is open and usable. The family pass costs $750, while the daily passes cost $10 each (for the whole family).

a.   With "days swimming" on the horizontal axis and "dollars spent on other amusements" on the vertical, illustrate our budget constraint if we choose not to buy the season pass.

b.   On the same graph, illustrate the budget constraint we face if we choose to purchase the season pass.

c.   After careful consideration, we decided that we really did not prefer one option over the other, so we flipped a coin with "heads" leading to the season pass and "tails" to no season pass. The coin came up "tails," so we did not buy the season pass. Would we have gone swimming more or less had the coin come up "heads" instead? Illustrate your answer on your graph.

d.   My brother bought the season pass. After the summer passed by, my mother said: "I just can't understand how two kids can turn out so differently. One of them spends all his time during the summer at the swimming pool, while the other barely went at all." One possible explanation for my mother's observation is certainly that I am very different from my brother. The other is that we simply faced different circumstances but are actually quite alike. Could the latter be true without large substitution effects?

e.   On a separate graph, illustrate the compensated (Hicksian) demand curve that corresponds to the utility level u^* that my family reached during the summer. Given that we paid $10 per day at the pool, illustrate the consumer surplus we came away with from the summer experience at the pool.

f.*   Since we would have had to pay no entrance fee had we bought the season pass, can you identify the consumer surplus we would have gotten? (*Hint:* Keep in mind that, once you have the season pass, the price for going to the pool on any day is zero. The cost of the season pass is therefore not relevant for your answer to this part.)

g.*   Can you identify an area in the graph that represents how much the season pass was?

B.   Suppose that my tastes can be represented by the utility function $u(x_1, x_2) = x_1^{\alpha} x_2^{(1-\alpha)}$ with x_1 denoting days of swimming and x_2 denoting dollars spent on other amusements.

a. In the absence of the possibility of a season pass, what would be the optimal number of days for my family to go swimming in the summer? (Your answer should be in terms of α.)

b. Derive my indirect utility as a function of α.

c. Suppose $\alpha = 0.5$. How much utility do I get out of my $1,000 of amusement funds? How often do I go to the swimming pool?

d. Now suppose I had bought the season pass instead (for $750). How much utility would I have received from my $1,000 amusement funds?

e. What is my marginal willingness to pay for days at the pool if I am going 100 times?

f. On a graph with the compensated demand curve corresponding to my utility this summer, label the horizontal and vertical components of the points that correspond to me taking the season pass and the ones corresponding to me paying a per-use fee.

g. Derive the expenditure function for this problem in terms of p_1, p_2, and u (with $\alpha = 0.5$).

h.* In (g) of part A, you identified the area in the *MWTP* graph that represents the cost of the season pass. Can you now verify mathematically that this area is indeed equal to $750? (*Hint*: If you have drawn and labeled your graph correctly, the season pass fee is equal to an area composed of two parts: a rectangle equal to 2.5 times 100, and an area to the left of the compensated demand curve between 2.5 and 10 on the vertical axis. The latter is equal to the difference between the expenditure function $E(p_1, p_2, u)$ evaluated at $p_1 = 2.5$ and $p_1 = 10$ (with $p_2 = 1$ and u equal to the correct utility value associated with the indifference curve in your earlier graph.))

10.9 **Everyday Application:** *To Take, or not to Take, the Bus*: After you graduate, you get a job in a small city where you have taken your sister's offer of living in her apartment. Your job pays you $20 per hour and you have up to 60 hours per week available. The problem is you also have to get to work.

A. Your sister's place is actually pretty close to work, so you could lease a car and pay a total (including insurance and gas) of $100 per week to get to work, spending essentially no time commuting. Alternatively, you could use the city's sparse bus system, but unfortunately there is no direct bus line to your place of work and you would have to change buses a few times to get there. This would take approximately 5 hours per week.

a. Now suppose that you do not consider time spent commuting as "leisure," and you don't consider money spent on transportation as "consumption." On a graph with "leisure net of commuting time" on the horizontal axis and "consumption dollars net of commuting costs" on the vertical, illustrate your budget constraint if you choose the bus and a separate budget constraint if you choose to lease the car.

b. Do you prefer the bus to the car?

c. Suppose that before you get to town you find out that a typo had been made in your offer letter and your actual wage is $10 per hour instead of $20 per hour. How does your answer change?

d. After a few weeks, your employer discovers just how good you are and gives you a raise to $25 per hour. What mode of transportation do you take now?

e. Illustrate in a graph (not directly derived from what you have done so far) the relationship between wage on the horizontal axis and the most you'd be willing to pay for the leased car.

f. If the government taxes gasoline and thus increases the cost of driving a leased cars (while keeping buses running for free), predict what will happen to the demand for bus service and indicate what types of workers will be the source of the change in demand.

g. What happens if the government improves bus service by reducing the time one needs to spend to get from one place to the other?

B. Now suppose your tastes were given by $u(c, \ell) = c^{\alpha} \ell^{(1-\alpha)}$, where c is consumption dollars net of commuting expenses and ℓ is leisure consumption net of time spent commuting. Suppose your leisure endowment is L and your wage is w.

a. Derive consumption and leisure demand assuming you lease a car that costs you $Y per week which therefore implies no commuting time.

b. Next, derive your demand for consumption and leisure assuming you take the bus instead, with the bus costing no money but taking T hours per week from your leisure.

    c.   Express the indirect utility of leasing the car as a function of Y.

    d.   Express your indirect utility of taking the bus as a function of T.

    e.   Using the indirect utility functions, determine the relationship between Y and T that would keep you indifferent between taking the bus and leasing the car. Is your answer consistent with the relationship you illustrated in A(e) and your conclusions in A(f) and A(g)?

    f.   Could you have skipped all these steps and derived this relationship directly from the budget constraints? Why or why not?

10.10† **Business Application:** *Pricing at Disneyland*: In the 1970s, Disneyland charged an entrance fee to get into the park and then required customers to buy tickets separately for each ride once they were in the park. In the 1980s, Disneyland switched to a different pricing system that continues to this day. Now, customers simply pay an entrance fee and then all rides in the park are free.

BUSINESS
APPLICATION

A. Suppose you own an amusement park with many rides (and assume, for the sake of simplicity, that all rides cost the same to operate). Suppose further that the maximum number of rides a customer can take on any given day (given how long rides take and how long the average wait times are) is 25. Your typical vacationing customer has some exogenous daily vacation budget I to allocate between rides at your park and other forms of entertainment (that are, for purposes of this problem) bought from vendors other than you. Finally, suppose tastes are quasilinear in amusement park rides.

    a.   Draw a demand curve for rides in your park. Suppose you charge no entrance fee and only charge your customers per ride. Indicate the maximum price per ride you could charge while ensuring that your consumer will in fact spend all her day riding rides (i.e., ride 25 times).

    b.   On your graph, indicate the total amount that the consumer will spend.

    c.   Now suppose that you decide you want to keep the price per ride you have been using but you'd also like to charge a separate entrance fee to the park. What is the most you can charge your customer?

    d.   Suppose you decide that it is just too much trouble to collect fees for each ride, so you eliminate the price per ride and switch to a system where you only charge an entrance fee to the park. How high an entrance fee can you charge?

    e.   How would your analysis change if x_1, amusement part rides, is a normal good rather than being quasilinear?

B. Consider a consumer on vacation who visits your amusement park for the day. Suppose the consumer's tastes can be summarized by the utility function $u(x_1, x_2) = 10x_1^{0.5} + x_2$ where x_1 represents daily rides in the amusement park and x_2 represents dollars of other entertainment spending. Suppose further that the consumer's exogenous daily budget for entertainment is $100.

    a.   Derive the uncompensated and compensated demand functions for x_1 and x_2.

    b.   Suppose again there is only enough time for a customer to ride 25 rides a day in your amusement park. Suppose further that you'd like your customer to ride as much as possible so he can spread the word on how great your rides are. What price will you set per ride?

    c.   How much utility will your consumer attain under your pricing?

    d.**   Suppose you can charge an entrance fee to your park in addition to charging the price per ride you calculated. How high an entrance fee would you charge? (*Hint*: You should be evaluating an integral, which draws on some of the material from the appendix.)

    e.**   Now suppose you decide to make all rides free (knowing that the most rides the consumer can squeeze into a day is 25) and you simply charge an entrance fee to your park. How high an entrance fee will you now charge to your park? (Note: This part is not computationally difficult. It is designated with ** only because you have to use information from the previous part.)

    f.**   How does your analysis change if the consumer's tastes instead were given by $u(x_1, x_2) = (3^{-0.5})x_1^{0.5} + x_2^{0.5}$?

10.11* **Business Application:** *Negotiating an Endorsement Deal and a Bribe*: Suppose you are an amateur athlete and your uncle owns the cereal company "Wheaties." Your uncle offers you a job working for his company at a wage of w per hour. After looking around for other jobs, you find that the most you could make elsewhere is w', where $w' < w$. You have a weekly leisure endowment of L and can allocate any amount of that to work. Given the higher wage at Wheaties, you accept your uncle's job offer.

BUSINESS
APPLICATION

A. Then you win a gold medal in the Olympics. "Greeties," the makers of grits, ask you for an endorsement. As part of the deal, they will pay you some fixed weekly amount to appear on their boxes of grits. Unfortunately, your uncle (who hates his competitor "Greeties" with the white hot intensity of a thousand suns) will fire you if you accept the deal offered by "Greeties." Therefore, if you accept the deal, your wage falls to w'.

   a. On a graph with Consumption on the vertical and Leisure on the horizontal axis, graph your budget constraint before the "Greeties" offer.

   b. On the same graph, illustrate your budget if you worked for someone other than your uncle prior to your success in the Olympics.

   c. Illustrate the minimum amount that "Greeties" would have to pay you (weekly) for your endorsement in order for you to accept the deal. Call this amount E.

   d. How does this amount E compare to the amount necessary to get you to be able to consume bundle A under a Greeties endorsement deal?

   e. Now suppose that you accepted the endorsement deal from "Greeties" but, unfortunately, the check for the endorsement bounces because "Greeties" goes bankrupt. Therefore the deal is off, but your angry uncle has already fired you. Deep down inside, your uncle still cares about you and will give you back your old job if you come back and ask him for it. The problem is that you have to get past his greedy secretary who has full control over who gets to see your uncle. When you get to the "Wheaties" office, she informs you that you have to commit to pay her a weekly bribe if you want access to your uncle. On a new graph, illustrate the largest possible (weekly) payment you would be willing to make. Call this F.

   f. If your uncle's secretary just asks you for a weekly bribe that gets you to the bundle C that you would consume in the absence of returning to Wheaties, would you pay her such a bribe?

   g. Suppose your tastes are such that the wealth effect from a wage change is exactly offset by the substitution effect; i.e., no matter what the wage, you will always work the same amount (in the absence of receiving endorsement checks or paying bribes). In this case, can you tell whether the amount E (i.e., the minimum endorsement check) is greater than or equal to the amount F (i.e., the maximum bribe)?

B. Suppose that your tastes over weekly consumption c and weekly leisure ℓ can be represented by the utility function $u(c, \ell) = c^{0.5}\ell^{0.5}$ and your weekly leisure endowment is $L = 60$.

   a. If you accept the initial job with Wheaties, how much will you work?

   b. Suppose you accept a deal from Greeties that pays you a weekly amount $\overline{E}$. How much will you work then? Can you tell whether this is more or less than you would work at Wheaties?

   c. Suppose that the wage w at Wheaties is $50 per hour and the wage w' at Greeties (or any other potential employer other than Wheaties) is $25 per hour. What is the lowest possible value for E—the weekly endorsement money from Greeties—that might get you to accept the endorsement deal?

   d. How much will you work if you accept this endorsement deal E?

   e. Suppose you have accepted this deal but Greeties now goes out of business. What is the highest possible weekly bribe F you'd be willing to pay your uncle's secretary in order to get your job at Wheaties back?

   f. How much would you work assuming that the secretary has successfully extracted the maximum amount you are willing to pay to get your Wheaties job back?

   g. Re-draw your graphs from part A but now label all the points and intercepts in accordance with your calculations. Does your prediction from A(g) about the size of the maximum bribe relative to the size of the minimum endorsement hold true?

10.12 **Policy Application:** *Distortionary Taxes*: Suppose that you have tastes for grits and "other goods" (where the price of "other goods" is normalized to 1). Assume throughout (unless otherwise stated) that your tastes are quasilinear in grits.

A. The government decides to place a tax on grits, thus raising the price of grits from p to $(p + t)$.

   a. On a graph with grits on the horizontal axis and "other goods" on the vertical, illustrate the before- and after-tax budget.

   b. Illustrate your optimal consumption bundle after the tax is imposed, then indicate how much tax revenue T the government collects from you.

    c.   Illustrate the most L you would be willing to pay to not have the tax.

    d.   Does your answer depend on the fact that you know your tastes are quasilinear in grits?

    e.   On a graph below the one you have drawn, derive the regular demand curve as well as the *MWTP* curve.

    f.   Illustrate T and L on your lower graph and indicate where in the graph you can locate the deadweight loss from the tax.

    g.   Suppose you only observed the demand curve in the lower graph, and you knew nothing else about tastes. If grits were actually a normal good (rather than a quasilinear good), would you under- or overestimate that deadweight loss by assuming grits are quasilinear?

B. Suppose that your tastes could be represented by the utility function $u(x_1 , x_2) = 10x_1^{0.5} + x_2$, with x_1 representing weekly servings of grits and x_2 representing dollars of other breakfast food consumption. Suppose your weekly (exogenous) budget for breakfast food is $50.

    a.   Derive your uncompensated and compensated demand for grits.

    b.   Suppose the tax on grits raises its price from $1.00 to $1.25 per serving. How does your consumption of grits change?

    c.   How much tax revenue T does the government collect from you per week?

    d.   Use the expenditure function for this problem to determine how much L you would have been willing to pay (per week) to avoid this tax?

    e.** Verify your answer about L by checking that it is equal to the appropriate area on the *MWTP* curve. (For this, you need to take an integral, using material from the appendix.)

    f.   How large is the weekly deadweight loss?

    g.   Now suppose that my tastes were represented by $u(x_1 , x_2) = x_1^{0.5} + x_2^{0.5}$. How would your answers change?

    h.** Under these new tastes, suppose you only observed the regular demand curve and then used it to calculate deadweight loss while incorrectly assuming it was the same as the *MWTP* curve. By what percentage would you be overestimating the deadweight loss? (*Hint*: You again need to evaluate an integral. Note that the integral of $1/(p(1 + p))$ with respect to p is $\ln p - \ln (1 + p)$.)

10.13† **Policy Application:** *Price Subsidies*: Suppose the government decides to subsidize (rather than tax) consumption of grits.

A. Consider a consumer who consumes boxes of grits and "other goods."

    a.   Begin by drawing a budget constraint (assuming some exogenous income) with grits on the horizontal axis and "other consumption" on the vertical. Then illustrate a new budget constraint with the subsidy, reflecting that each box of grits now costs the consumer less than it did before.

    b.   Illustrate the optimal consumption of grits with an indifference curve tangent to the after-subsidy budget. Then illustrate in your graph the amount that the government spends on the subsidy for you. Call this amount S.

    c.   Next, illustrate how much the government could have given you in a lump sum cash payment instead and made you just as happy as you are under the subsidy policy. Call this amount L.

    d.   Which is bigger, S or L?

    e.   On a graph below the one you have drawn, illustrate the relevant *MWTP* curve and show where S and L can be found on that graph.

    f.   What would your tastes have to be like in order for S to be equal to L.

    g.   *True or False*: For almost all tastes, price subsidies are inefficient.

B. Suppose the consumer's tastes are Cobb–Douglas and take the form $u(x_1 , x_2) = x_1^{\alpha}x_2^{(1-\alpha)}$ where x_1 is boxes of grits and x_2 is a composite good with price normalized to 1. The consumer's exogenous income is I.

    a.   Suppose the government price subsidy lowers the price of grits from p to $(p - s)$. How much S will the government have to pay to fund this price subsidy for this consumer?

    b.   How much utility does the consumer attain under this price subsidy?

    c.   How much L would the government have had to pay this consumer in cash to make the consumer equally happy as she is under the price subsidy?

    d.   What is the deadweight loss from the price subsidy?

    e.   Suppose $I = 1,000$, $p = 2$, $s = 1$, and $\alpha = 0.5$. How much grits does the consumer buy before any subsidy, under the price subsidy and under the utility-equivalent cash subsidy? What is the deadweight loss from the price subsidy?

    f.**   Continue with the values from the previous part. Can you calculate the compensated demand curve you illustrated in A(e) and verify that the area you identified as the deadweight loss is equal to what you have calculated? (*Hint:* You need to take an integral and use some of the material from the appendix to answer this.)

10.14 **Policy Application:** *Taxing Interest on Savings:* Suppose I care only about consumption this year and consumption next year, and suppose I earn an income this year but do not expect to earn an income next year.

    A. The government announces an increase in the tax on interest income. Illustrate my before- and after-tax intertemporal budget constraint.

        a.   Suppose I save 50% of my income after the new tax is imposed. Illustrate the amount of the tax the government will collect from me next year. Call this T.

        b.   Illustrate the most I would be willing to pay next year to keep the government from imposing this tax on interest income. Call this amount L.

        c.   Is L larger or smaller than T? What does your answer depend on?

        d.   If consumption is always a normal good, will I consume more or less next year if the tax on interest income is removed?

        e.   If consumption is always a normal good, will I consume more or less *this* year if the tax on interest income is eliminated?

        f.   Can you re-draw your graph but this time indicate how much T' you are paying in taxes in terms of *this* year's consumption, and how much L' you would be willing to pay to avoid the tax in terms of *this* year's consumption?

    B. Now suppose that my tastes over consumption now, c_1, and consumption next period, c_2, can be captured by the utility function $u(c_1, c_2) = c_1^\alpha c_2^{(1-\alpha)}$.

        a.   Suppose the interest rate is r. What does α have to be in order for me to optimally save 50% of my income this year?

        b.   Assume from now on that α is as you calculated and suppose that my current income is $200,000. Suppose the interest rate before the tax increase was 10% and the after-tax interest rate after the tax increase is 5%. How much tax revenue T does the government collect from me? What is the present value of that this period?

        c.   What is the most (L) I would be willing to pay to avoid this tax increase (in either today's dollars or in next period's dollars)?

        d.   Does the amount that I save today change as a result of the tax increase?

        e.   Is the tax efficient? If not, how big is the deadweight loss?

10.15 **Policy Application:** *International Trade and Child Labor:* Consider again the end-of-chapter problem 8.9 about the impact of international trade on child labor in the developing world.

    A. Suppose again that households have non-child income Y, that children have a certain weekly time endowment L, and that child wages are w in the absence of trade and $w' > w$ with trade.

        a.   On a graph with child leisure hours on the horizontal axis and household consumption on the vertical, illustrate the before and after trade household budget constraints.

        b.   Suppose that tastes over consumption and child leisure were those of perfect complements. Illustrate in your graph how much a household would be willing to pay to permit trade; i.e., how much would a household be willing to pay to increase the child wage from w to w'?

        c.   If the household paid the maximum it was willing to pay to cause the child wage to increase, will the child work more or less than before the wage increase?

   d.   Re-draw your graph, assume that the the the same bundle (as at the beginning of part (b)) is optimal, but now assume that consumption and leisure are quite (though not perfectly) substitutable. Illustrate again how much the household would be willing to pay to cause the wage to increase.

   e.   If the household actually had to pay this amount to get the wage to increase, will the child end up working more or less than before trade?

   f.   Does your prediction of whether the child will work more or less if the household pays the maximum bribe to get the higher wage depend on how substitutable consumption and child leisure are?

   g.   Can you make a prediction about the relative size of the payment the household is willing to make to get the higher child wage as it relates to the degree of substitutability of consumption and child leisure? Are "good" parents willing to pay more or less?

B.**Suppose that the household's tastes over consumption and leisure can be represented by the CES utility function $u(c, \ell) = (\alpha c^{-\rho} + (1 - \alpha)\ell^{-\rho})^{-1/\rho}$.

   a.   Derive the optimal household consumption and child leisure levels assuming the household has non-child weekly income Y, the child has a weekly time endowment of L, and the child wage is w.

   b.   Verify your conclusion from end-of-chapter problem 8.9 that parents are neither "good" nor "bad" when $Y = 0$ and $\rho = 0$; i.e., parents will neither increase nor decrease child labor when w increases.

   c.   If international trade raises household income Y, what will happen to child labor in the absence of any change in child wages? Does your answer depend on how substitutable c and ℓ are?

   d.   When $\alpha = 0.5$ and $w = 1$, does your answer depend on the household elasticity of substitution between consumption and child leisure?

   e.   How much utility will the household get when $\alpha = 0.5$ and $w = 1$?

   f.   Derive the expenditure function for this household as a function of w and u. What does this reduce to when $\alpha = 0.5$? (Hint: You can assume $Y=0$ for this part.)

   g.   Suppose non-child income $Y = 0$, child time is $L = 100$, $\alpha = 0.5$, $\rho = 1$, and w is initially 1. Then international trade raises w to 2. How does the household respond in its allocation of child leisure?

   h.   Using your expenditure function, can you determine how much the household would be willing to pay to cause child wages to increase from 1 to 2? If it did in fact pay this amount, how would it change the amount of child labor?

   i.   Repeat the two previous steps for the case when $\rho = -0.5$ instead of 1.

   j.   Are your calculations consistent with your predictions in (f) and (g) of part A of the question?

10.16 Policy Application: *Efficient Land Taxes*: We have argued in this chapter that it is difficult to find taxes that are efficient; i.e., taxes that do not give rise to a deadweight loss. Economists have long pointed to one exception to this proposition: taxation of land.

POLICY APPLICATION

   A. Suppose a particular plot of commercial land generates approximately $10,000 in income for its owner each year into the foreseeable future.

   a.   Assuming an annual interest rate of 10%, what is the most that you would be willing to pay for this land? (*Hint*: Recall from our Chapter 3 exercises that the present discounted value of an annual stream of income of y is y/r where r is the annual interest rate.)

   b.   Now suppose the government announces that, from now on, it will impose a 50% tax on all income derived from land. How does your answer regarding how much you would be willing to pay for this plot of land change?

   c.   If you currently own this land, how are you affected by this tax? Is there any way you can change your behavior and avoid some portion of the tax; i.e., are there any substitution effects that might arise to create a deadweight loss?

   d.   If you currently don't own this land but are about to buy it, how are you affected by the imposition of this land tax?

e.   *True or False*: Regardless of whether the current owner of the land keeps it or sells it to me (after the announcement of the tax), the current owner effectively pays all future taxes associated with income from this land.

f.   In light of your previous answers, how is this an example of an efficient lump sum tax?

B.   Consider the more general case where a particular plot of land yields $\$y$ in annual income.

a.   What is the value of this land assuming an interest rate of r?

b.   Now suppose the government announces a tax rate t (with $0 < t \leq 1$) that will be levied on income obtained purely from land. What happens to the value of the plot of land?

c.   Who is affected by this, current land owners or future land owners?

d.   Suppose the government decides to set $t = 1$; i.e., it announces that it will from now on tax income from land at 100%. What happens to the price of land?

e.   Defend the following statement: A 100% tax on income from land is equivalent to the government confiscating land and asking for annual rental payments, with the present value of all future rental payments equal to the previous price of the land.

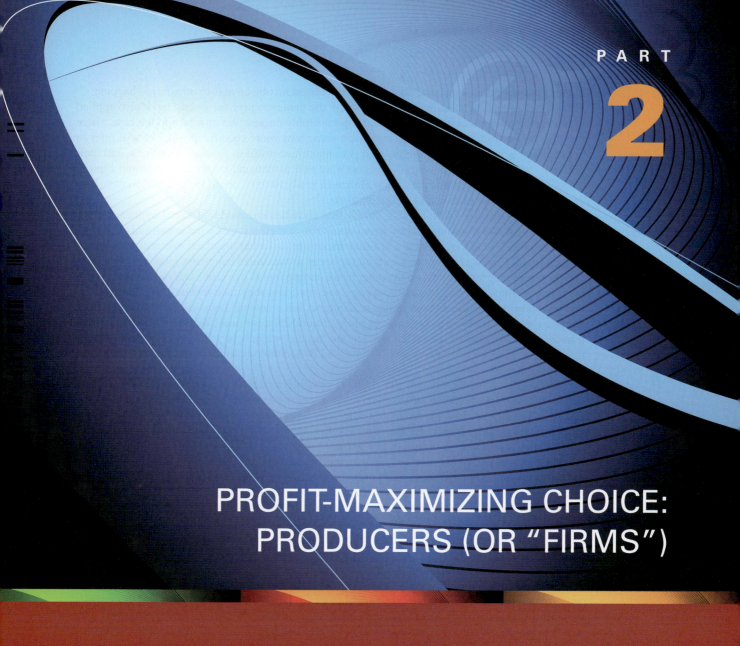

PROFIT-MAXIMIZING CHOICE: PRODUCERS (OR "FIRMS")

In Part 1, we modeled individual choice when the chooser's objective is to maximize "happiness." This model applied to consumers and resulted in the demand curve for goods, but it also applied to workers and savers to give us labor and capital supply curves. We now turn to the case where the chooser's objective is instead to maximize something more specific: profit. We will refer to the individuals in an economy whose goal is to maximize profit as *producers* or *firms*, and their decisions will lead to supply curves for goods as well as demand curves for labor and capital. Once we have completed this part, we will then be ready to think about the interaction of supply and demand in goods, labor, and capital markets.

We will see that the basic logic of choice that underlies our model of Part 1 applies also for producers. Just like consumers, they try to maximize something given the constraints that they face, except that what they choose when they maximize and what they face as constraints is now a bit different. Consumers choose goods and services to maximize happiness given their incomes and the prices they face. Firms, on the other hand, choose *inputs like labor and capital*; they maximize *profit—the difference between revenue and cost*; and they face *technological constraints* that limit how easy it is to convert inputs into outputs and *economic constraints* that emerge from the prices of inputs and outputs. Thus, in place of goods and services, we now choose combinations of inputs; instead of somewhat ambiguous "tastes," we now have the more concrete objective of profit; and we add the constraints imposed by technology to the economic constraints of prices.

We begin in Chapter 11 with the simplest possible model of producers: a model where a single output is produced from a *single input* given a particular technology available to the producer. We then see how the technology that tells us how easy it is to convert the input into the output serves as the constraint for the firm. The firm may want to produce something from nothing, but that is no more an option in our world of scarcity than it is for consumers to consume beyond their means. We can also see easily in this model that the "tastes" for profit are shaped by the prices of the output and input, with more profit possible when output price is high and input price is low. Combining these, we can show how the firm chooses its optimal (or profit-maximizing) level of output using the lowest possible input level under which it is technologically feasible to produce the desired output. From this choice process, we can then illustrate *output supply* and *input demand* relationships, or how output and input decisions are affected by changes in prices in the economy.

The unrealistic simplification in Chapter 11 involves the assumption that only a single input is needed for production. In reality, goods can typically be produced in multiple different ways by combining a little labor with lots of capital or lots of labor with a little capital, and this implies that profit-maximizing producers will typically have to choose the optimal bundle of inputs with which to produce. Put differently, producers have to decide not only *how much* to produce but also *how* to produce, how much to rely on labor versus capital (or some other input). Chapter 12 therefore expands the model of Chapter 11 to include multiple inputs and thus multiple ways of producing any level of output. This allows us to distinguish between *technologically efficient* production that simply involves not wasting any inputs and *economically efficient* production that involves producing output at the least cost possible (given the input prices in the marketplace).

In this expanded model with multiple inputs, we will see that it is often useful to separate the producer's problem into two separate stages: First, we can think of producers as looking only at their technology and the prices of inputs, and using this information to determine the least costly way of producing different levels of output. We will refer to this part of the problem as the firm's *cost minimization* problem. After solving this problem, firms will know how much it costs to produce any level of output, but they will not yet know what level of output is profit maximizing. Thus, they are not done until they compare the cost of producing different levels of output (from their cost minimization problem) to the revenue they can get from different levels of output. Finding the level of output where the gap between revenue and cost is the largest is then equivalent to finding the profit-maximizing level of output (and the accompanying profit-maximizing levels of inputs).

Finally, we introduce in Chapter 13 a distinction between *short-run* and *long-run* decisions by producers. This distinction arises because firms often face short-run constraints that are more binding than long-run constraints. In the short run, for instance, a firm might already have committed to a certain factory space (and thus a certain level of the input "capital"). While this factory space might have been optimal given the circumstances that the producer faced when committing to the space, it may no longer be optimal when prices or technologies change. In the short run, the producer is then locked into the space and is able to decide only how intensively to use the space. In the two-input model, this implies that one input might be fixed in the short run but the other can be changed, so that effectively the short run is characterized by a single-input production process like the one we began with in Chapter 11. When it becomes possible to change the factory space, however, the firm will typically reevaluate its short-run response to changing circumstances and respond some more.

Throughout this part of the text, we will continue to assume that economic agents, consumers and producers alike, are "small" relative to the economic environment; i.e., we will assume that everyone is a "price-taker" who cannot influence the output and input prices in the market. In Part 5 of the text, we will relax this assumption and allow producers to be sufficiently "large" such that they can influence the prices in the economy through their decisions. This will involve a role for strategic thinking that is absent for now as we continue to focus on competitive environments. We will see later, however, that the "cost-minimizing" part of the producer problem that we develop here can be used even in cases where firms become large. We are therefore already also building a foundation for thinking about other economic contexts even as we wait to investigate these contexts until later on in the text.

One Input and One Output: A Short-Run Producer Model

In our exposition of the consumer choice model, we have developed a particular lens through which we can view the actions of economic agents: individuals, whether as consumers, workers, or financial planners, attempt to do *the best they can given their economic circumstances.*[1] Put into the more mathematical language of the B parts of our chapters, we can equivalently say that individuals *optimize subject to constraints.* We will now turn this same lens away from the consumer choice model and toward producers or firms. These are the economic agents who combine "inputs" like labor, raw materials and land to produce "outputs," which are the goods and services that we consume in the marketplace.

As in our development of the consumer model, we will for now maintain the assumption that every economic agent, including producers, is "small" relative to the market and thus lacks the power to influence prices in the economy. In the language we developed in Chapter 1, we will therefore begin our exploration of producers as economic agents in a "nonstrategic" environment, an environment where their actions have no impact on the larger economy and where they, just as consumers, are "price takers." Only after we have fully explored the implications of optimizing behavior in such a nonstrategic environment will we turn in later chapters to considerations that enter our models when firms are sufficiently powerful to have an impact on prices in an economy through their actions.

In some ways, the models of competitive producers and consumers are not all that different: both producers and consumers make choices that are under their control in an attempt to do the best they can given their economic circumstances (that they cannot control). Producers will in fact be a bit more transparent than consumers, because while consumers might have all sorts of tastes that we can't really observe easily, producers, at least as we model them, are pretty shallow: they simply care about profit. But in other ways, we will find that the producer model is more complicated. For this reason, we will start in this chapter with a simple case of a producer who uses a single input to produce a single output. This will permit us to illustrate the idea of profit maximization in two different ways: First, we will show directly how producers maximize profits by choosing the production plan that puts them on their highest "indifference curve," and second, we will show that we can split the profit maximization problem into two steps (that will then form the basis for our analysis of more complex producers in Chapter 12). This latter approach is actually pretty intuitive: We will suppose that producers first analyze their costs, and

---

[1]No material from prior chapters is directly used in this chapter. However, the chapter contains frequent analogies to the consumer model and thus to material covered in Chapter 2 and Chapters 4 through 6. It is therefore highly recommended that material in those chapters be covered prior to Chapter 11.

once they have gotten a good picture of how much different production plans cost, they look at how much revenue can be generated to see which plan results in the most profit. In the end, the two approaches to profit maximization result in exactly the same "solution" for the producer, but sometimes it will be more convenient to use one and sometimes the other.

11A   A Short-Run One-Input/One-Output Model

The simplest possible producer to consider is one that converts a single input into a single output. To be honest, it is not easy to think of many real-world production processes that are that simple; in almost every production process that I know, the producer uses both labor and some other input to produce the output she sells. But it is possible to think of realistic production processes in which some of the inputs simply cannot be varied *in the short run*. Perhaps a certain factory space has been leased for a one-year period, and the lease has to be paid regardless of how much or how little is produced. In that case, a producer might be "locked into" a particular level of the input "factory space" over the next year even though the producer can choose a smaller or larger space after the current lease runs out. However, while it might not be possible for the producer to vary the factory space in the short run, he or she might well be able to vary the intensity with which the space is utilized; i.e., the number of work hours that go into actually using the space for production. In such a scenario, we would say that this producer's input of factory space is *fixed in the short run* while his or her labor input is *variable in the short run*.

Some time ago, for instance, I had a bright idea: I had noticed that children love baseball cards but was disturbed that baseball players had become the object of such intense admiration by the children that will one day have to pay for my Social Security benefits. Would this really make them into productive citizens capable of producing at the level required in order to keep my Social Security checks coming? Why not give them a better mix of heroes to look up to and aspire to be like? So I thought it would be great to replicate the baseball card concept for famous economists—put the picture of the economist in an impressive lecturing pose on the front of the card, and some career statistics like "number of academic publications" and "number of citations by other economists" on the back. Unfortunately, my wife refused to fund my little idea, but that won't keep me from pretending that I went ahead with it anyhow and telling you all about it in this chapter.[2]

So as my children would say, "let's pretend". Suppose I wanted to put my brilliant idea into practice, and suppose that one of my former students (who naturally remains an ardent fan of mine) has arranged for me to have free factory space in one of the old tabacco-processing plants in Durham (where I live). Suppose further that it turns out that the same equipment previously used to make packets of cigarettes is appropriate for making economist cards and that the same paper used to wrap cigarettes can be used as well. So my former student is providing the factory space, the machines, and the raw material for my innovation for free, and all I have to do is decide how many workers to hire to start producing.

11A.1 Technological Constraints Faced by Producers

In my role as a producer, I would love to produce an endless supply of economist cards and sell them to every child in need of a hero, just as I would like to be able to consume without end in my role as a consumer and buy my own Air Force One to avoid commercial air traffic. I can't

---

[2]Some time after I requested spousal funding for this, I actually discovered that I was too late: The University of Michigan undergraduate economics club is already producing such cards, and one of the economics textbook publishers is also making them as a marketing gimmick, mixing cards with their textbook authors in with very famous economists to make their authors seem more distinguished. I missed my chance to get myself on one of those cards when I went with a different publisher for this book.

consume without end because *my finite resources limit my consumer choice set*, and in an exactly analogous way, I cannot produce without end because *the technology available to me as a producer constrains my producer choice set.*

11A.1.1 Production Plans, Producer Choice Sets, and Production Frontiers

Let's begin by defining a *production plan* as *a proposed bundle of inputs and outputs*. This is analogous to the concept of a consumption bundle in consumer theory. In a model in which consumers have only two goods to choose from, we located the set of all possible consumption bundles as points in a two-dimensional space with the good x_1 on the horizontal axis and the good x_2 on the vertical. We can do exactly the same for production plans in models where there is a single input and a single output. For instance, in a model illustrating all possible production plans for economist cards, I can put "hours of labor per day" on the horizontal axis and "packets of economist cards per day" on the vertical, and each point in the resulting two-dimensional space is a production plan that proposes to use a certain number of labor hours to produce a certain number of economist cards per day. Not all of these production plans are, however, technologically feasible given the technology I have available to me, just as not all consumption bundles are feasible choices for consumers on fixed incomes facing a fixed set of prices.

In the consumer model, we then illustrated the set of consumption bundles that are feasible for a particular consumer as the consumer's choice set. In the same way, we can now represent the set of production plans that are technologically feasible as the producer's choice set, as those production plans that propose an input level sufficient to produce the output level called for in the production plan. The *producer choice set is then simply defined as the set of all production plans that are feasible given the technology available to the producer.*

Graph 11.1a illustrates one such possible producer choice set for economist cards as the shaded area under the blue line. It assumes a very particular underlying technology under which every labor hour can always be turned into *at most* four packets of economist cards. For instance,

Graph 11.1: Two Types of Producer Choice Sets and Associated Production Frontiers

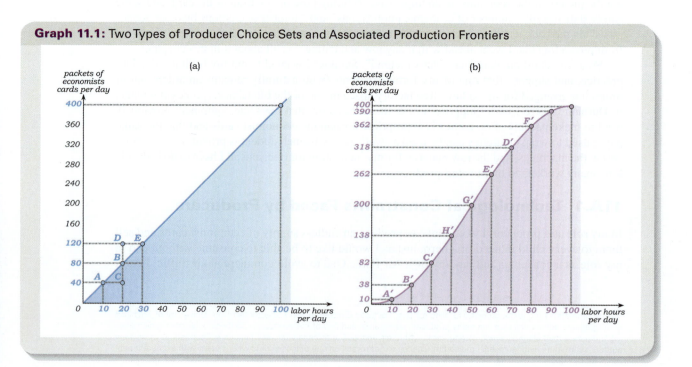

production plan *A* calls for 10 labor hours to be transformed into 40 packets of economist cards, and plan *B* calls for 20 labor hours to be transformed into 80 packets. Of course, this logically implies that plan *C* is feasible as well. At *C*, I would be producing 40 packets with 20 labor hours. Since I know I can produce that many packets with 10 labor hours (under production plan *A*), it should not be hard to hire 10 additional labor hours and still produce 40 packets. Thus the production plan *C* lies *inside* the producer choice set, indicating that we could in fact produce more with the labor input called for in production plan *C*. The production plan *D*, on the other hand, is not feasible under this technology; I need at least 30 worker hours to produce 120 packets of cards (under plan *E*), and it is not possible given the available technology to produce that many cards with only 20 worker hours. Thus, plan *D* lies *outside* the producer choice set.

Notice once again the analogy to consumer choice sets. Consumption bundles that lie within the consumer choice set are bundles that leave some of a consumer's budget unspent, implying that the consumer can do better (assuming "more is better"). Similarly, production plans that lie *inside* the producer choice set are plans under which some of our input stands idle, implying I can produce more with the same level of input. We then defined the boundary of the consumption set as the budget constraint, and we now *define the boundary of the production set as the production frontier*. Only plans along this production frontier represent plans that do not waste inputs. As a result, just as consumers doing the best they can pick consumption bundles on the budget constraint, producers doing the best they can will pick production plans along the production frontier.

Can you model a worker as a "producer of consumption" and interpret his or her choice set within the context of the single input, single output producer model?

Exercise 11A.1

The technology graphed in panel (a) of Graph 11.1 does not, however, seem very realistic. It can't possibly be true that I can keep producing at the same rate in my current factory space regardless of how much I am producing. When I first hire workers for my factory, they would not be able to specialize and probably could not produce as much per worker as when I have more workers. So it would seem more realistic to assume a production frontier along which workers initially become more and more productive as they specialize. At the same time, I have only so much factory floor space and machinery to work with, and adding workers endlessly would seem to eventually lead to lower and lower increases in output as the workers begin to run into each other on the factory floor.

Panel (b) therefore illustrates a more realistic technology for this example: It begins with initial workers not producing nearly as much as initial workers did in the technology represented in panel (a), but as more worker hours are added, each worker hour initially becomes more productive than the last (as workers can begin to specialize in particular tasks). The first 10 worker hours, for instance, result in an output of 10 cards per day (*A′*), while 20 worker hours can produce as many as 38 cards per day (*B′*). The second 10 worker hours therefore add as much as 28 cards per day, 18 more than the first 10 workers. Similarly, the next 10 worker hours add up to 44 more cards to my daily production, allowing me to produce at the production plan *C′*. Eventually, however, this increasing productivity per additional worker hour declines (as my factory workers begin to run into each other on my factory floor). For instance, 70 worker hours can produce as many as 318 cards per day (*D′*), 56 more than I am able to produce at *E′* with just 60 worker hours. But the next 10 worker hours can produce only 44 more cards (to get me to production plan *F′*).

Which of the producer choice sets in Graph 11.1 is non-convex? What makes it non-convex?

Exercise 11A.2

Exercise
11A.3
Suppose my technology was such that each additional worker hour, beginning with the second one, is less productive than the previous. Would my producer choice set be convex? What if my technology was such that each additional worker hour, beginning with the second one, is more productive than the previous?

11A.1.2 Slopes of Production Frontiers: The Marginal Product of Labor

In our development of consumer choice sets, we were then able to give a specific economic interpretation to the slope of the budget constraint (as the opportunity cost of one additional unit of the good on the horizontal axis in terms of the good on the vertical axis). Put differently, we could say that the slope of a consumer's budget constraint represents the *marginal cost* of an additional unit of the good on the horizontal axis in terms of the good on the vertical axis. Slopes of production frontiers turn out to have an analogous economic interpretation.

Consider first the production frontier in Graph 11.1a. The slope of this frontier is 4, indicating that every additional hour of labor results in 4 additional packets of economist cards. In other words, the slope of the production frontier in Graph 11.1a is the *marginal benefit of one more worker hour in terms of increased production*. Turning to panel (b) of Graph 11.1, we can now see how this same interpretation of the slope of the production frontier continues to hold, except that now the marginal benefit of hiring additional workers initially increases but eventually decreases. The slope between production plans A' and B', for instance, is approximately 2.8, indicating that the marginal benefit of 1 additional worker hour is approximately 2.8 packets of economist cards when we have between 10 and 20 labor hours employed already. The approximate slope between G' and E', on the other hand, is 6.2, indicating a marginal benefit of approximately 6.2 additional packets of economist cards for every additional labor hour when I already have 50 to 60 labor hours employed.

Exercise
11A.4
Under the production technology in Graph 11.1b, what is the approximate marginal benefit of hiring an additional labor hour when I already have 95 labor hours employed?

The slope of the production frontier, or the marginal benefit of hiring additional inputs in terms of increased production, is of such economic interest to producers that we frequently graph it separately from the production frontier and call it the *marginal product* curve. The *marginal product of an hour of labor, denoted MP_ℓ, is* thus *the increase in total production that results from hiring one additional labor hour when all other inputs remain fixed*, and it is simply the slope of the single input production frontier (of the type graphed in Graph 11.1) when all other possible inputs (such as factory space) are fixed. Graph 11.2(a) and (b) then plot the marginal product of labor curves for the production frontiers in Graph 11.1(a) and (b). While the marginal product curve in panel (a) is exactly correct, in panel (b) we have plotted the "approximate" marginal product curve by plotting the slope between each of the production plans on the frontier of Graph 11.1b for the input level that occurs halfway in between the input levels of the two relevant production plans. For instance, given that production increases by 28 when labor input rises from 10 to 20, we have plotted a marginal product of 2.8 for the fifteenth labor hour.

Exercise
11A.5
Relate your answer from exercise 11A.4 to a point on the MP_ℓ curve plotted in Graph 11.2b.

Exercise
11A.6
What would the MP_ℓ curves look like for the technologies described in within-chapter exercise 11A.3?

Graph 11.2: The MP_ℓ Associated with the Production Frontiers in Graph 11.1

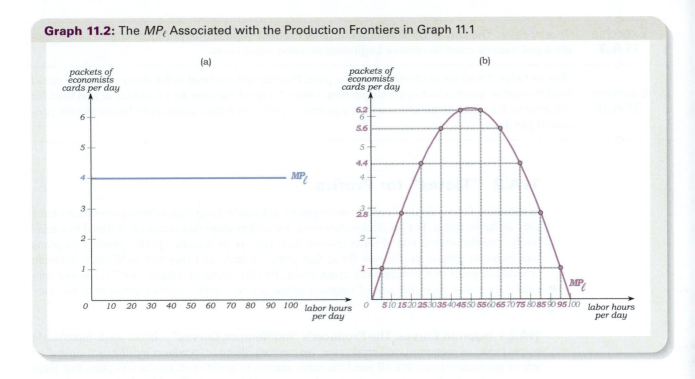

11A.1.3 The Law of Diminishing Marginal Product

Now notice that the marginal product curve derived from the more realistic production frontier in Graph 11.1b is eventually downward sloping. This downward slope is the direct result of the fact that we assumed a production frontier on which each additional labor hour will *eventually* add less to our total output than the previous labor hour. It turns out, however, that this is more than a mere assumption; it is an economic reality that arises directly from the fact that we live in a world governed by scarcity, and it is known as the *Law of Diminishing Marginal Product*.

The easiest way to see this is to consider a case where the marginal product of an input never declines. First, recall the definition of marginal product: It is the *additional* output produced from adding one more unit of the input *assuming all other inputs are held fixed*. Suppose the marginal product of labor in my production process for economist cards never declines in the fixed factory space that my student has provided for me. This would mean that I can keep squeezing more and more workers into my factory and have them use the same amount of paper and ink, and each additional worker I hire will increase my output by at least as much as the previous worker did. Suppose my factory space is 1,000 square feet. How many human beings can I really squeeze into 1,000 square feet and still get them to produce? If the marginal product of labor never declines, I would be able to squeeze the population of the entire world into my 1,000 square feet space, and the last person I squeezed in would have added at least as much to my output of economist cards as any person I hired previously. And not only would I be able to squeeze all these people into my 1,000 square feet but they would also be able to squeeze more and more economist cards out of the same quantity of paper and ink. Perhaps technologies that give rise to such production processes exist in a world beyond ours, but such a world would not be characterized by the scarcity that governs the world we live in, nor would it be a world in which an economist who studies scarcity could find employment. Thus, at least in the world we currently occupy, it *must* be the case that the marginal product of an input like labor at some point declines.

Exercise
11A.7

True or False: The Law of Diminishing Marginal Product implies that producer choice sets in single input models must be convex beginning at some input level.

Exercise
11A.8

True or False: If the Law of Diminishing Marginal Product did not hold in the dairy industry, I could feed the entire world milk from a single cow. (*Hint*: Think of the cow as a fixed input and feed for the cow as the variable input for which you consider the marginal product in terms of milk produced per day.)

11A.2 "Tastes" for Profits

In the case of the consumer model, we began by acknowledging that different consumers have very different tastes. For producers, however, we will assume that tastes are defined in a relatively straightforward way: Producers—in their role as producers—prefer production plans that generate greater profit over those that generate less, and they are indifferent between production plans that generate the same profit. *Profit* is defined simply as *all economic revenue (generated from the sale of outputs) minus all economic cost (incurred from the purchase of inputs)*.

11A.2.1 Isoprofit Curves: The Producer's "Indifference Curves"   In our single input/single output model of economist card production, we can then illustrate "producer indifference curves" as sets of production plans that all yield the same amount of profit, with production plans that yield greater profit valued more than production plans that yield less profit. Consider, for instance, the production plans *A* and *B* in Graph 11.3a. Plan *A* calls for 20 daily hours of labor to be converted into

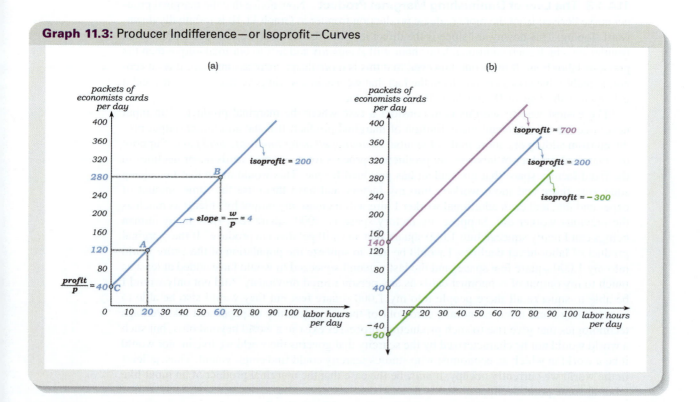

Graph 11.3: Producer Indifference—or Isoprofit—Curves

120 daily packets of economist cards, while plan B calls for 60 daily hours of labor to be converted into 280 daily packets of economist cards. Now suppose that the market wage for the type of labor I need to hire is $20 per hour, and suppose the per packet price of cards such as the ones I am producing is $5. Revenues will then be $600 under plan A and $1,400 under plan B, while costs will be $400 under plan A and $1,200 under plan B. Subtracting costs from revenues, both plans result in a daily profit of exactly $200. For producers who care only about profits, A and B are then equally desirable production plans whenever a packet of cards sells for $5 and an hour of labor costs $20.

But these are not the only production plans that would yield a profit of $200 per day under the assumed price and wage. For instance, the production plan C suggests producing 40 economist cards without using *any* inputs, a feat that might violate the laws of physics but, if one could pull it off, would again result in exactly $200 in profit per day. In fact, since inputs cost 4 times as much as outputs, we can start at the production plan C and find a production plan for any level of input that will yield $200 per day in profit so long as we include four times as much additional output in the production plan. The plan A, for instance, has 20 more labor hours than the plan C *and* 80 more output units, thus keeping profit constant at $200 per day. When we then plot the level of output required for each level of input to keep profit at $200, we get the blue line in Graph 11.3a. Notice that the line has a vertical intercept of 40 (because it takes 40 economist cards to make a $200 profit if there are no costs) and has a slope equal to 4, the wage rate w over price of the output p. If I really care only about profits, then I must be indifferent between all of the production plans on this blue line. An indifference curve such as this for a price-taking producer is called an *isoprofit curve* or, more specifically, the blue indifference curve is the *isoprofit curve corresponding to $200 in daily profit when the wage rate is $20 per hour and the output price is $5.*

As with consumer indifference curves, the full "tastes" of producers are of course not characterized by a single indifference or isoprofit curve. Each profit level carries with it a different isoprofit curve, with the magenta and green isoprofit curves in Graph 11.3b representing production plans that result in $700 and –$300 profit respectively. Notice that, since the slope of isoprofit curves is w/p, all isoprofit lines have the same slope when wages and prices are fixed from the perspective of the producer. The vertical intercept, on the other hand, is simply the profit associated with the particular isoprofit curve divided by the price of the output.

Without knowing what prices and wages are in the economy, can you tell by looking at a single isoprofit curve whether profits for production plans along this curve are positive or negative? What has to be true about an isoprofit curve in order for profit to be zero?

Exercise 11A.9

What would have to be true in order for an isoprofit curve to have a negative slope?

Exercise 11A.10

11A.2.2 The Role of Prices in Consumer and Producer Models

Throughout our development of producer choice sets and tastes (as represented by isoprofit curves), we have thus far emphasized similarities between the consumer and the producer model. For instance, only some consumption bundles are available to consumers because of the budget constraint they face, just as only some production plans are technologically feasible because of production frontiers. Both consumers and producers have tastes that can be represented by points over which they are indifferent: consumption bundles that lie on the same indifference curve in the consumer model, and production plans that lie on the same isoprofit curve in the producer model. And, as we will see in the next section, both consumers and producers generally find their "best" point on the boundary of their choice set.

While these similarities are conceptually important, it is equally worthwhile to point out some of the significant conceptual differences between consumer and producer models. Most importantly, the prices in the economy affect indifference curves and choice sets differently in the two models. In our consumer model, prices (including wages and interest rates) affected the size and shape of the consumer choice set, determining in particular the slopes of budget constraints. But prices have *nothing* whatsoever to do with consumer tastes and the indifference curves that represent consumer tastes. Whether I like peanut butter, how much I like to work rather than leisure, and whether I can tell the difference between Coke and Pepsi: these are internal features that define who I am, features that have arisen in some process that can perhaps be explained by psychologists and biologists but remain outside the area of expertise of most economists.[3] Economists usually just take tastes as given and recognize that, while optimal consumer choices have a lot to do with prices, how a consumer *feels* about the trade-off between different types of goods is a matter of taste, not prices.

In the producer model, on the other hand, things are exactly reversed. Prices have no impact on the producer choice set but have everything to do with what the indifference curves—or isoprofit curves—look like. The producer choice set is the set of production plans that are *technologically* feasible, which implies that the size and shape of the producer choice set is driven by technology. Put differently, whether I am *physically able to* produce 200 economist cards with 10 hours of labor has nothing to do with prices and wages; it is a matter for engineers and factory managers to figure out. The producer's indifference curves, on the other hand, are determined entirely by the prices in the economy, with the intercept a function of prices and the slope a function of both wages and prices. We can see this distinction most clearly by asking the question: What will change in our graphs of producer choice sets and isoprofit curves if prices and wages in the economy change? Since neither prices nor wages entered our development of producer choice sets in Graph 11.1, nothing would change in those graphs (or in the accompanying graphs of marginal product curves). Our graph of isoprofits (in Graph 11.3), on the other hand will change. Consider first a change in the hourly wage rate from $20 to $10. Since the vertical intercept of each isoprofit curve is profit divided by the output price p, a change in the wage w does not change the intercept. Intuitively, the production plans on the intercept give the output level required to attain a particular profit level *assuming the production plan does not envision hiring any labor*. Since labor is not part of the production plan at the vertical intercept of an isoprofit curve, profits for such production plans are therefore unaffected by the wage rate in the economy. The wage rate does become relevant, however, at any other production plan on an isoprofit curve since all production plans other than those located on the vertical axis contain some positive labor input. For a decline in wages from $20 to $10, our slope w/p therefore falls from 4 to 2 (assuming a fixed output price of $p = 5$), leading to a shallower slope for each isoprofit curve. Such an impact of a change in wages is then illustrated graphically in Graph 11.4a.

In Graph 11.4b, on the other hand, the impact of a change in the output price p is illustrated. Suppose, for instance, that p rises from $5 per packet of economist cards to $10 per packet (with the wage rate holding constant at $20). Since the intercept of an isoprofit curve is profit divided by p, the intercept must now fall. Furthermore, given that the slope of each isoprofit curve is w/p, an increase in p will result in a decline in the slope from 4 when $p = 5$ to 2 when $p = 10$. For a particular profit level (such as $200), the isoprofit curve therefore falls at the intercept and becomes shallower as the output price increases. This, too, should make intuitive sense: If I can sell my cards for more, I should be able to make the same profit as before using production plans that contain less output for each level of input. In both panels of the graph, we of course illustrated only what happens to one of the infinite number of isoprofit curves that compose the isoprofit map, with similar changes happening for each of the other isoprofits.

Exercise
11A.11

How would the blue isoprofit curve in Graph 11.3a change if the wage rises to $30? What if instead the output price falls to $2?

---

[3]My wife believes my tastes may more appropriately be explained by Chaos Theory.

Graph 11.4: Isoprofit Curve for $200 Profit as Wages and Prices Change

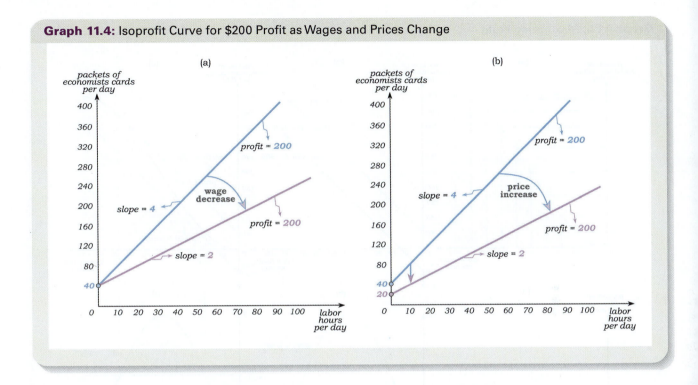

11A.3 Choosing the Production Plan that Maximizes Profit

As soon as we had fully explored consumer choice sets and tastes (in Chapters 2 through 5) *independently*, we proceeded (in Chapter 6) to investigate how choice sets and indifference maps *jointly* allow us to identify the best bundle available to a consumer given her circumstances. We can now follow the same path for single input/single output producers like me. More precisely, in the last 2 sections we have already explored both my producer choice set and tastes *independently*, and we can therefore proceed directly to analyzing how choice sets and producer tastes *jointly* result in profit maximizing producer behavior.

11A.3.1 Combining Production Frontiers with Isoprofit Curves   Graph 11.5a begins by replicating my "realistic" producer choice set from Graph 11.1b, while Graph 11.5b replicates the three isoprofit curves developed in Graph 11.3b under the assumption that I have to purchase labor in the labor market at $20 per hour and can sell my economist cards in the "hero card market" at $5 per packet. Panel (c) of Graph 11.5 then combines the previous two panels into a single graph.

Beginning on the lowest (green) isoprofit curve, we can notice that many production plans that result in profit of –$300 are technically feasible given that they lie within the shaded choice set. However, as a producer I become better off as I move to isoprofit curves that lie to the northwest. Since there are production plans that lie both within my choice set and above (i.e., to the northwest of) the green isoprofit curve, I know I can do better than a daily profit of –$300. I also know from looking at Graph 11.5c that certain levels of profit are not feasible within the current economic and technological environment. For instance, the (magenta) isoprofit curve of production plans that yield $700 in daily profit lies fully outside my choice set, indicating that no production plan that could yield $700 in daily profits is technologically feasible.

My goal as a profit-maximizing producer of economist cards is then to find the highest isoprofit curve that contains at least one technologically feasible production plan, just as my goal as

Graph 11.5: Maximizing Profit

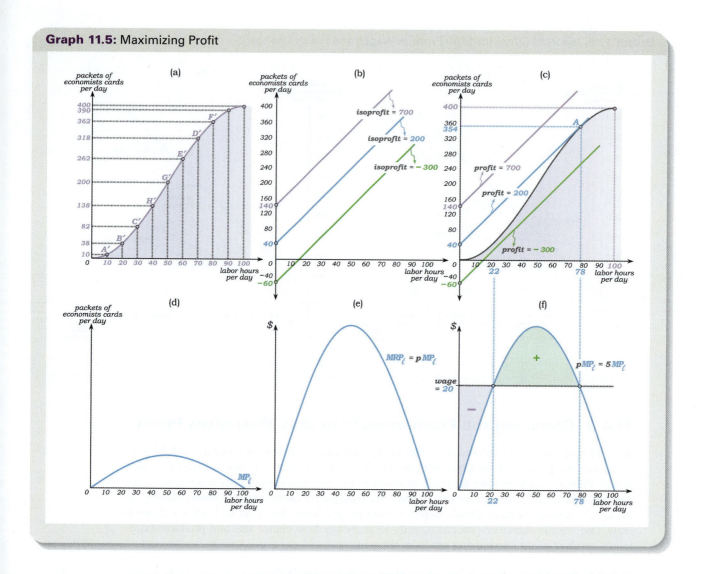

a utility maximizing consumer is to find the highest indifference curve that contains at least one consumption bundle that is feasible given my budget constraint. Beginning on the green isoprofit curve in Graph 11.5c and moving northwest in the direction of the magenta isoprofit curve, we reach this highest possible profit at the production plan A where the (blue) isoprofit curve corresponding to a profit of $200 is tangent to the frontier of my producer choice set. Thus, production plan A is the profit-maximizing plan in this case.

11A.3.2 Marginal Product = w/p (or Marginal Revenue Product = w)

From Graph 11.5c, you can see immediately that, at the profit maximizing production plan A, the slope of the isoprofit curve (w/p) is equal to the slope of the production frontier (which is just the marginal product of labor MP_ℓ). To see how this makes intuitive sense, it is useful for us to see the same profit-maximizing behavior play out in a variant of the marginal product of labor graph that we derived from the production frontier in Graph 11.2b.

Graph 11.5d therefore begins by replicating the MP_ℓ curve from Graph 11.2b with the vertical axis rescaled for graphing convenience (which makes it appear that the curve creates a hill that is "less steep" than before). Recall that this is simply a graph of the slope of the production frontier in panel (a). Panel (e) of the graph then plots a slight variant of the marginal product curve known as the *marginal revenue product* curve. While the marginal product of labor (MP_ℓ) tells us the increase in *output* resulting from one more hour of labor being hired, the marginal revenue product of labor (MRP_ℓ) tells us the increase in *revenue* resulting from one more hour of labor. Since revenue is just output times the price of the output p, $MRP_\ell = pMP_\ell$. Put differently, the MRP_ℓ curve is identical to the MP_ℓ curve when the output price is $1 but is 5 times the MP_ℓ curve when the price of the output is $5 (as in the case of my economist cards). Furthermore, while MP_ℓ is measured in "output" units on the vertical axis in panel (d), MRP_ℓ is measured in dollar units in panel (e).

The final panel (f) in Graph 11.5 then shows how profit maximization first illustrated along the production frontier in panel (c) relates to profit maximization illustrated along the MRP_ℓ curve. Along the production frontier, we noticed that $w/p = MP_\ell$, which we could write differently (by multiplying both sides of the equation by p) as $w = pMP_\ell$ or just $w = MRP_\ell$. In words, at the optimum, the wage I pay for the last labor hour that I hire is just equal to the marginal dollar benefit I get from that labor hour. Because marginal product declines, this means that the MRP_ℓ, or the marginal benefit of labor hours, before the last one I hire is larger than the wage I have to pay. More precisely, Graph 11.5f shows that I actually make a loss on the first 22 labor hours that I hire, in each case paying a wage that is higher than the marginal dollar benefit I get from each labor hour. However, starting with the 23rd labor hour, the marginal dollar benefit of each hour I hire is higher than the wage I have to pay, until I stop hiring when this marginal dollar benefit (the MRP_ℓ) is again equal to the wage rate. I would not want to hire any additional labor hours since, from 78 hours on, the marginal dollar benefit of an additional labor hour is less than the wage I have to pay for that hour. My total profit of $200 (read off the isoprofit curve that contains production plan A in panel (c) of the graph) is then the shaded green area minus the shaded magenta area in panel (f).

It appears from panel (f) of Graph 11.5 that profits are smallest (i.e., most negative) when I stop hiring at 22 labor hours per day. What can you conclude about the slope of the production frontier in panel (c) of the graph at 22 daily labor hours? Explain.

**Exercise
11A.12**

11A.3.3 What's so Special about a $200 Profit? Economic Costs and Revenues

You might pause at this point and question the conclusion that my best possible course of action is to implement the production plan A in Graph 11.5c. After all, if I am only going to make $200 in profit per day, perhaps that's not worth me staying in business. Perhaps there are better opportunities outside the economist card business. It turns out, however, that this is not the case *assuming we have defined all the variables correctly*.

Let's be more precise. When we first defined the term *profit*, we casually mentioned that this is simply equal to all economic revenues (from sales of the output) minus all economic costs (from hiring inputs). The key words that casually slipped twice into this definition of profit are "all" and "economic." Revenue is considered *economic revenue from production* if and only if it is generated from ongoing production and would not exist were the producer to stop production. Similarly, a cost is considered an economic cost incurred in production if and only if it is directly linked to ongoing production and would not arise if the producer chose to discontinue production. These statements may seem trivial at first, but two examples will illustrate how we might understand costs and revenues differently if we talked to boring accountants instead of exciting economists.

First, suppose my business has been running for a while and has paid city taxes in the past. This year, the city has a budget surplus and decides to return the surplus in the form of tax rebate checks to businesses, with the amount of the check each business receives proportional to the tax revenue it paid last year. Is the check I receive in the mail "revenue" for my business? In an accounting sense, it clearly is; after all, I get to deposit money in my business's checking account. The U.S. federal government would also treat this as revenue because, under U.S. tax laws, federal taxes must be paid on any state or local tax rebates. And I am clearly happy to receive the check! But is the check an *economic* revenue from producing economist cards? Put differently, is it revenue that is associated with my ongoing production of economist cards, revenue that would not materialize if I ceased production? When put this way, you can see that the answer is no; the check from the city is based on production decisions I made in the past (which led to my tax payments to the city last year), and the amount of the check will be no different whether I produce 10, 100, 1,000, or no economist cards per day this year. Since this "revenue" has nothing to do with my current economic decisions in my factory, it is not a relevant or "economic" revenue for those decisions.

Next, suppose my little factory had a faulty exhaust valve last year, which caused illegal pollution to escape into the environment. Suppose further that I became aware of the problem at the beginning of the year and quietly fixed it, breathing a sigh of relief that I had not been caught. But then I get a letter from the city telling me that satellite images taken last year reveal excessive pollution emanating from my factory. As a result, I am charged a fine of $10,000 and ordered to fix the problem. Since I have already fixed the problem, I just have to pay the fine, which my tax accountant tells me is considered a current cost for my business. But is it an economic cost of producing? Put differently, does the size of the fine I owe the city depend on my current production decisions? The answer is again no; regardless of whether or how much I produce right now and in the future, the fine is based on something that happened in the past. It is no more an economic cost of producing economist cards than an increase in my children's school tuition because, while neither is good news for my pocketbook, neither has anything to do with the economic choices I currently face in my business. From the perspective of my business, both are what we will call later *sunk costs*, not economic costs.

Exercise 11A.13

Suppose I have already signed a contract with my former student who is providing me with the factory space, machinery, and raw materials for my business, and suppose that I agreed in that contract to pay my former student $100 per month for the coming year. Is this an economic cost with respect to my decision of whether and how much to produce this year?

So what does all this have to do with your concern that it might just not be worth it for me to stay in business for a measly $200 a day, that perhaps it would be optimal for me to put my energies into something else that will make more profit for me? If I were to restate your concern, it would be that you are worried that I have not taken the opportunity cost of my time into consideration, and that my next best alternative to opening my economist cards business, perhaps writing another textbook, for instance, might be more lucrative. But notice that my opportunity cost of time, unlike the city fine for last year's pollution, *is* an economic cost of producing economist cards. Put differently, to the extent that this business takes time away from me, that is an economic cost that must be included in any calculation of economic profit. By not explicitly including it in the model so far, I have merely assumed either (1) that my opportunity cost of time is the market wage of $20 per hour (and my worker hours are thus part of what is hired to produce the cards) or (2) that this business actually takes no time for me at all and will run itself. In the first case, if I spend 8 hours a day at the factory, I am therefore already including in my profit calculations that I am paying myself a wage of $20 per hour, for a total of $160 per day. If that is in fact the opportunity cost of my time, that is the best I could do working anywhere else. But in my little business, I will end up bringing home $360 per day—my $160 paycheck *plus* my $200 profit—and I am therefore doing $200 better in my business than I could doing anything else. In the second case, the business takes no time away from me, which implies that there is no time cost on my part, and the $200 is just free gravy that I would otherwise not have.

The bottom line is that whenever you conclude that someone is making economic profits above zero, you have (assuming you have included everything that should be included in the calculation) by definition concluded that the individual does better in this economic activity than he or she could in any known alternative. No matter what story underlies the statement "I am making $200 in economic profits," it always means that "I am doing $200 better in this economic activity than in the next best alternative."

11A.4 Changing the Economic Environment

Now that we concluded I should produce 354 cards using 78 labor hours per day when the hourly wage is $20 and the output price is $5, we can ask how my profit-maximizing choice will change as either output prices or wages change in the economy. My response to such changes could be (1) to produce more, (2) to produce the same, (3) to produce less, or (4) to shut down and stop producing economist cards.

11A.4.1 A Change in the Market Wage
Suppose first that hourly wages fall from $20 to $10. We have already seen in Graph 11.4a how such a change in wages alters each isoprofit curve: it changes the slopes (w/p) from 4 to 2 without altering the intercept (Profit/p). This implies that the new optimal production plan B *must* lie to the right of the original optimal plan A because a shallower isoprofit line must now be tangent to the production frontier *which becomes shallower to the right of A*. In the top panel of Graph 11.6a, the new optimal production plan then calls for 90 daily labor hours to produce 390 rather than the original 354 packets of economist cards. The intercept of the new optimal isoprofit curve is 209, which implies a profit at production plan B of $1,045.[4]

There are also production plans to the right of *A* where the slope of the production frontier is shallower. Why are we not considering these?

Exercise 11A.14

The lower panel of Graph 11.6a then illustrates the same profit maximization exercise in the marginal revenue product graph that is derived from the production frontier in the top panel.

Which areas in the lower panel of Graph 11.6a add up to the $200 profit I made before wages fell? Which areas add up to the $1,045 profit I make after wages fall?

Exercise 11A.15

Next, suppose the hourly wage rate in the labor market rises to $30. This increases the slope of isoprofit curves (w/p) to 6, implying that the new tangency with the production frontier will lie to the left of A. This is illustrated in the top panel of Graph 11.6b where that tangency occurs at the production plan C, which employs 59 daily labor hours to produce 254 daily packets of economist cards. But notice how this looks on the lower panel of Graph 11.6b along the marginal revenue product curve: Were I to produce according to the production plan C, I would incur losses on each worker I hire up to the 42nd worker hour and only begin to generate marginal benefits above the wage when hiring workers from the 43rd through the 59th worker hour.

---

[4]At first, it may appear that because there is a new intercept on the optimal isoprofit curve, the graph is contradicting what we said at the beginning of the paragraph, that a change in wages changes the slopes but not the intercept of isoprofit curves. The statement that intercepts do not change when wages change, however, applies to *any particular isoprofit curve corresponding to a particular amount of profit*. In panel (a) of the graph, for instance, the original isoprofit curve will indeed change slope without changing intercepts. However, at the new wage, this isoprofit curve is *no longer the optimal isoprofit curve*, and so the producer moves to a higher isoprofit (that is tangent at *B*).

Graph 11.6: The Impact of Changing Wages on Profit-Maximizing Choices

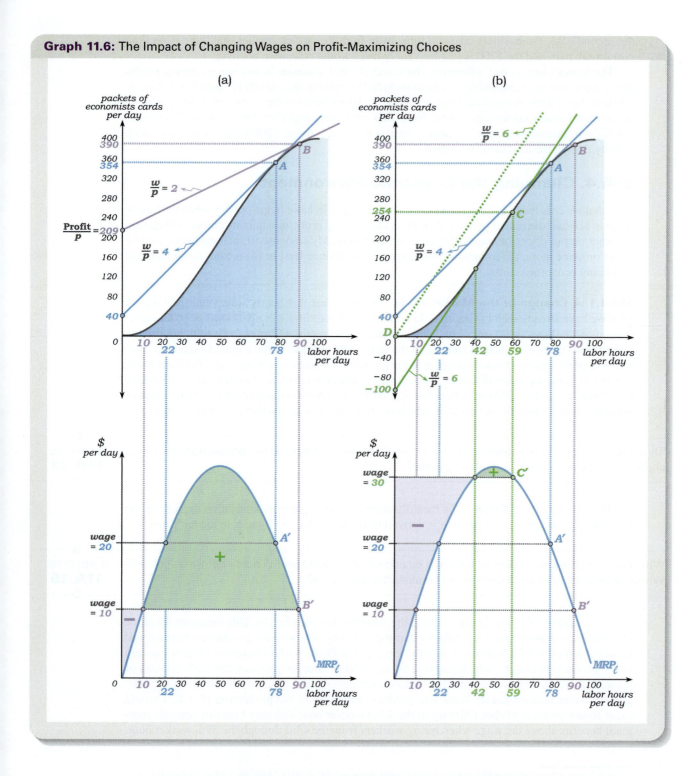

Thus, if I hire 59 hours of labor (as called for in the production plan *C*), my profit is the tiny shaded green area (in the lower right panel of the graph) minus the large shaded magenta area, which appears to be a negative number. Going back to the top panel, we can see that this is indeed the case because the intercept of the isoprofit curve tangent at production plan *C* is −100.

Given an intercept of –100 of this isoprofit curve, what is the value of profit indicated by the shaded green minus the shaded magenta area in the lower panel of Graph 11.6b?

Exercise
11A.16

Thus, for an increase in the wage to $30 per hour, my best course of action is actually not to implement production plan *C* but rather to implement production plan *D*, which calls for no hiring of labor and no production of output and thus zero profit along the dashed green isoprofit curve in Graph 11.6b. Put differently, I should go ahead and engage in the next best alternative economic activity and let the economist card business take a rest. This is an example of a *corner solution* in the producer model.

Had the increase in the market wage been less dramatic, would my best course of action still necessarily have been to shut down production?

Exercise
11A.17

What would have to be true of the production frontier in order for the original optimal production plan *A* to remain optimal as wages either rise somewhat or fall somewhat? (*Hint*: Consider what role kinks in the producer choice set might play.)

Exercise
11A.18*

11A.4.2 The Labor Demand Curve   In Graph 11.6, we have shown how a decrease in the wage I have to pay my employees will cause me to slide down on the MRP_ℓ curve to the new wage rate, and thus to hire more workers (or at least more worker hours). Similarly, an increase in the wage I have to pay will cause me to slide up the MRP_ℓ curve and hire fewer labor hours so long as I can still make a profit, but once the wage goes so high that the best I could do was to make a negative profit, I would simply shut down and hire no labor (as shown in part (b) of Graph 11.6). A portion of the curve thus becomes the *demand curve for labor*; i.e., the curve that shows how many labor hours I will hire at different wage rates.

Graph 11.7 illustrates this more exactly by first determining the wage rate at which the highest profit I could make is zero. More precisely, it plots a MRP_ℓ for a given output price p and then finds the wage rate w^* at which the negative profit I make on the initial workers I hire (the shaded magenta area) is just equal to the positive profit I make on the final workers I hire (the shaded green area). For any $w < w^*$, the magenta area shrinks and the green area gets larger, thus implying a positive overall profit. For any $w > w^*$, on the other hand, the magenta area gets larger while the green area shrinks, which implies a negative overall profit. Thus, I will hire labor along the declining portion of the MRP_ℓ so long as the wage I have to pay is less than (or equal to) w^*, and I will hire no workers for any wage rate above w^*. The darkened two line segments then represent my *labor demand curve*, which, due to the Law of Diminishing Marginal Product, *must slope down*.

Why would it be economically rational for me to still stay open for business when $w = w^*$ where my profit is zero?

Exercise
11A.19

If I had signed a contract and agreed to make monthly payments for the next year to my former student who provided me with my factory space, would w^*—the highest wage at which I will still produce—be any different?

Exercise
11A.20

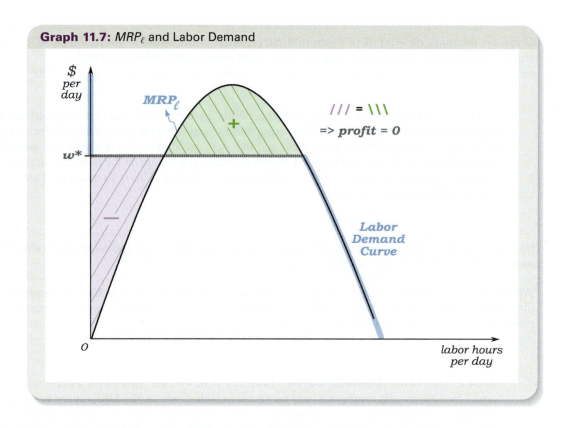

Graph 11.7: *MRP*$_\ell$ and Labor Demand

11A.4.3 A Change in the Output Price

Now suppose that the wage was unchanged at $20 per hour but the market price of "hero cards" (including my economist cards) increases to $10 per packet. Again, we already saw in Graph 11.4b how such an increase in price alters the shape of isoprofit curves. In particular, note that the slope of isoprofit curves is now 2 (instead of 4), just as it was when wages fell to $10 in Graph 11.6a. But if the isoprofits now again have a slope of 2, the tangency of the highest isoprofit curve must again fall exactly at the same production plan *B* as when wages fell to $10! For this reason, the top panel of Graph 11.8 illustrating the change in profit maximization along the production frontier when price increases to $10 *looks exactly the same as the top panel of Graph 11.6a*. Once again, it is optimal to produce 390 packets of economist cards per day using 90 labor hours.

Despite the fact that the profit maximization along the production frontier *looks* exactly identical for an increase in the price from $5 to $10 as it does for a decrease in the hourly wage from $20 to $10, there are underlying differences that emerge in the lower panels of the graphs. First, note that the marginal revenue product curve did not change when the wage changed because *MRP*$_\ell$ is just *pMP*$_\ell$. Since *p* is by definition a part of *MRP*$_\ell$, however, the marginal revenue product curve *does move when price changes*. In particular, since each packet of economist cards now sells for twice what it did before, each worker hour has just become twice as productive in dollar terms (even though it remains unchanged in output terms). Thus, each point on the new (magenta) marginal revenue product curve is twice as high as the corresponding point on the original (blue) marginal revenue product curve. While the optimal production plan is therefore the same when the price of my economist card packets increases to $10 as it is when the wage rate falls to $10, my profit is clearly higher under the former scenario than under the latter.

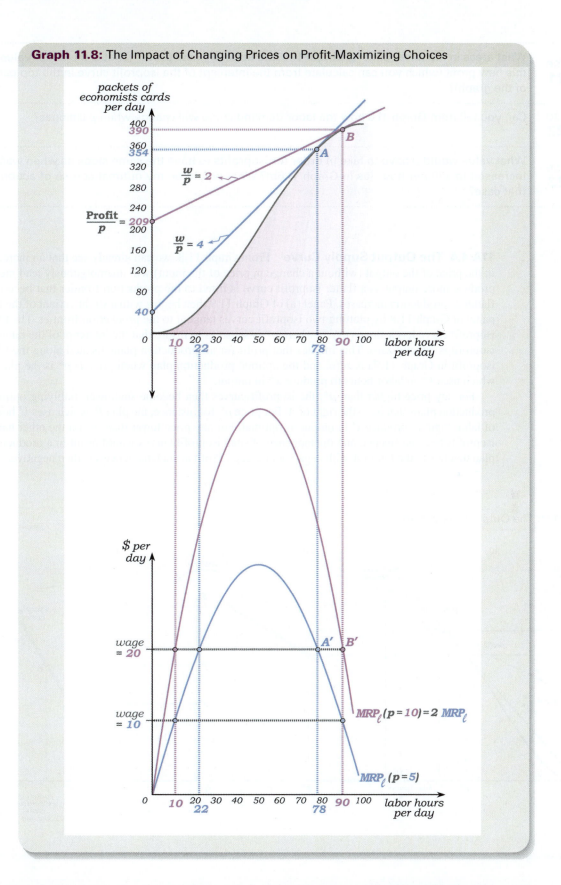

Graph 11.8: The Impact of Changing Prices on Profit-Maximizing Choices

Exercise 11A.21

What areas in the lower panel of Graph 11.8 add up to my new profit? What is the dollar value of this new profit (which you can calculate from the intercept of the isoprofit curve in the top panel of the graph)?

Exercise 11A.22

Can you tell from Graph 11.8 how the labor demand curve will change when p changes?

Exercise 11A.23

What value would p have to take in order for isoprofits to have the same slope as when wages increased to $30 per hour (as in Graph 11.6b)? What would be my optimal course of action in that case?

11A.4.4 The Output Supply Curve   From Graph 11.8, we can already see that an increase in the price of the output (without a change in price of the input) will unambiguously lead me to produce more output as a flatter isoprofit curve is fitted to the production frontier that becomes flatter as production increases. Panel (a) of Graph 11.9 then begins with a slight variant of the top panel of Graph 11.8 by plotting two isoprofit curves tangent to the production frontier. The blue isoprofit curve has a slope (w/p^*) where p^* is set so as to insure that the intercept of the tangent isoprofit is exactly zero. This implies that profit for all production plans located along the blue isoprofit in Graph 11.9a is zero, and the optimal production plan when price is p^* is the plan A which uses ℓ^* in labor hours to produce x^* in output.

For any price higher than p^*, the isoprofit curves then become shallower, implying optimal production plans that lie to the right of A. For price p', for instance, the plan B, which uses ℓ' hours of labor input to produce x' in output, is optimal. For any price lower than p^*, on the other hand, isoprofits become steeper, and the tangency of such isoprofit curves would result in a production plan that lies to the left of A with negative intercept. Profit at such tangencies is then negative, and

Graph 11.9: The Output Supply Curve

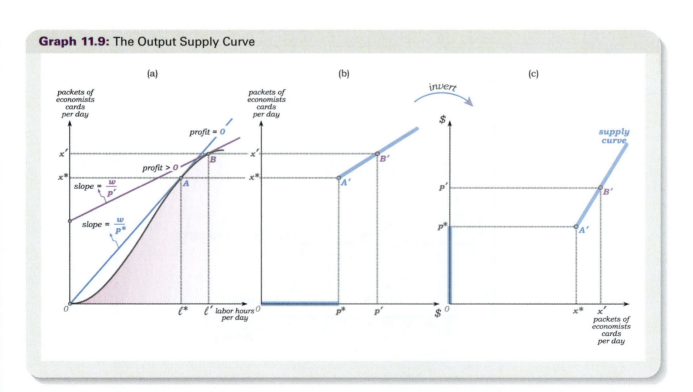

I could do better by just shutting down, producing nothing, and spending all of my time in the company of my lovely wife who will employ me instead. Therefore, if the price of economist cards falls below p^*, my little factory will stand idle.

Panel (b) of Graph 11.9 then translates the output levels at production plans A and B onto the vertical axis and plots the output prices (p^* and p') at which these production plans are optimal on the horizontal axis. By connecting A' and B' in this new graph, we are approximating how my output of economist cards on the vertical axis responds to changes in prices above p^* on the horizontal axis. In addition, the line connecting A' and B' is supplemented by the blue line on the horizontal axis below p^*, which indicates that my optimal output at such prices is simply zero. Panel (c) of the graph then just inverts panel (b) by flipping the axes, putting output on the horizontal and price on the vertical (as we have come to get used to when graphing demand curves). The resulting two line segments in panel (c) then represent the *supply curve* for my factory, which is the curve *illustrating the relationship between the price I can charge for my output and the amount of output I produce.* Just as the labor demand curve unambiguously slopes down, *the output supply curve unambiguously slopes up.*

In Graph 11.9, we implicitly held wage fixed. What happens to the supply curve when wage decreases?

Exercise
11A.24

11A.5 Cost Minimization on the Way to Profit Maximization

So far, we have explored the direct implications of a firm choosing a profit-maximizing production plan. While this is straightforward to graph in the context of the one-input/one-output model, we will see in the next chapter that the approach becomes considerably more difficult when we have two inputs (i.e., labor *and* capital) rather than one (i.e., just labor). Fortunately, there is a second way to conceptualize the firm's profit maximization decision. It gives exactly the same answer, but it generalizes more easily to a graphical treatment when the number of inputs goes to two. We will therefore illustrate this alternative conceptual approach here for the one-input model so that we can begin to get used to some of the underlying ideas as we prepare to expand our discussion to models with multiple inputs.

The approach will begin with the observation that *any profit maximizing producer will choose to produce whatever quantity she produces at minimum cost.* The statement sounds almost trivial. Of course you will produce whatever quantity you do produce at the least cost possible. It is not profit maximizing to waste inputs. But the insight allows us to split the profit maximization problem into two parts: First, we will simply ask how much in terms of costs the firm will incur for all possible quantities of output it might choose to produce. This will permit us to derive *cost curves* that depend on *input prices* but not on the price of the output. We can then proceed to the second step and ask: How much should I produce in order to maximize the difference between my costs (derived in step 1) and my revenues (from selling the output on the market)?

11A.5.1 Total Cost and Marginal Cost Curves
Graph 11.10 derives a series of graphs from the same production frontier we have employed before. The graphs on the left (panels (a) through (c)) are already familiar to us from when we derived the shapes of marginal product of labor (MP_ℓ) and marginal revenue product of labor (MRP_ℓ) curves. In particular, we noted that the initially increasing slope of the production frontier implies that initially each additional labor hour I hire is more productive than the previous labor hour but eventually, after production plan A in Graph 11.10a, the diminishing slope of the frontier implies that each additional hour of labor is becoming less productive than the previous hour. Put differently, *until I reach the production level x^A, production becomes easier and easier* as labor becomes more and more productive, *but once I have reached production level x^A, each additional unit of output becomes harder to produce than the previous unit.*

Graph 11.10: Deriving Total and Marginal Cost from Production Frontiers

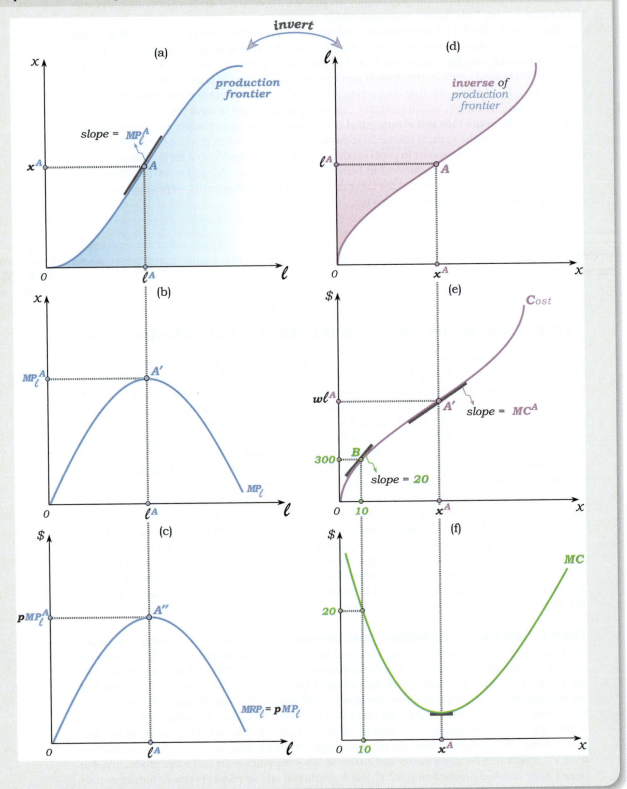

A logical implication of the last statement is that *each additional unit initially (up to x^A) is cheaper to produce than the last unit, but eventually (i.e., for production above x^A) each additional unit is more expensive to produce than the one before it.* This is illustrated in the panels on the right side of Graph 11.10. First, panel (d) simply inverts panel (a), flipping the ℓ axis from the horizontal to the vertical and the x axis from the vertical to the horizontal. As a result, the inverse production frontier graphed in panel (d) has the inverse shape of the production frontier in panel (a), with steep slopes becoming shallow and vice versa. For any quantity of output x, this inverse frontier tells us the minimum number of labor hours required to produce this output level. For the first unit of output, a lot of labor is necessary, but the additional labor necessary for each additional unit of output gets less and less until we reach output level x^A, when the additional labor required for each additional output starts to rise. This is again a reflection of the fact that the production technology is such that production initially gets easier and easier but eventually gets harder and harder.

Panel (e) then simply multiplies the inverse production frontier in panel (d) by the wage rate, converting the units on the vertical axis from labor hours to dollars. While panel (d) gives the total cost of production *in terms of labor hours*, panel (e) thus turns this into the *(total) cost curve*, which tells us how costly any given level of output is assuming I always hire the minimum number of employees necessary to get the job done. As in panel (d), this cost curve tells us that each additional unit initially adds less and less to our total cost up to output level x^A but after that adds more and more to our total cost as we produce more. Notice therefore that both the production frontier and the cost curve contain the same information: They each indicate that it initially becomes easier and easier to produce additional output but eventually it becomes harder and harder. While the production frontier in panel (a) conveys this by showing that labor initially becomes increasingly productive but eventually becomes less and less productive, the cost curve in panel (e) conveys the same information by showing that it initially becomes increasingly cheap to produce additional output but eventually it becomes increasingly expensive to add to production. Since production plan A in panel (a) is the turning point where the slope begins to become shallower (and thus labor begins to become increasingly less productive), the turning point for the cost curve in panel (e) also happens at output level x^A.

Finally, panel (f) plots the slope of the cost curve from panel (e) just as panel (b) plots the slope of the production frontier in panel (a). Earlier in this chapter we argued that the slope of the production frontier is a close approximation for the marginal product of labor because it tells us approximately how much total production increased when I hired the last labor hour. In exactly the same way, the slope of the total cost curve in panel (e) tells us approximately how much my total costs increased from the last output unit I produced or how much it is going to increase for the next output if I produce more. For instance, consider the production plan B in panel (e). The slope of the production frontier at B suggests that my total costs went up by approximately \$20 when I produced 10 rather than 9 units of output and will go up approximately \$20 more when I produce 11 rather than 10 units. This then represents one point on the curve plotted in panel (f) that is called the *marginal cost curve. The marginal cost of a particular unit of output is defined as the increase in (total) cost due to the last unit produced or, alternatively, the increase in total cost from producing one more unit.*

If the wage rate used to construct the panels on the right of Graph 11.10 is \$20, can you conclude what the slope of the production frontier in panel (a) at 10 units of output is? Can you conclude what labor input is required to produce 10 units of output, and then what the vertical values of the curves in panels (b) and (c) are for that level of labor input?

**Exercise
11A.25**

What would be the shape of the MRP_ℓ and MC curves if the entire producer choice set was strictly convex? What would the shape be for the production frontier graphed in Graph 11.1(a)?

**Exercise
11A.26**

11A.5.2 Profit Maximizing with Cost Curves Suppose then that, given my production technology as described by the production frontier and given a wage level w, I have derived the MC curve for my firm as we have just done. We have completed the first step of our new way of profit maximizing; i.e., we have determined how much it will cost us to produce different amounts of output if we do so without wasting inputs. None of this had anything to do with the *output* price; what I can sell my output for has, after all, nothing to do with what it costs me to produce the output. To complete profit maximization in our new two-step approach, we now need to ask how much we should produce *given* we know what it costs us and given that the market has set an output price at which I can sell my goods.

Panel (a) of Graph 11.11 begins by replicating the MC curve from panel (f) of Graph 11.10. Now suppose I face the output price p^* at which I can sell each unit of my output. Since p^* lies below the beginning of my MC curve, I will incur a cost for the first unit of output that exceeds the revenue I am able to make from selling that first unit, known as the *marginal revenue* of the first unit. The same is true for the second unit, with the MC for that unit indicating the increase in total costs when I produce 2 (rather than 1) units. Similarly, I will incur additional losses equal to the distance between the dotted line at p^* and the MC curve for each additional unit I produce until I reach the output level x^C where $MC = p^*$. If I stopped producing at x^C, I would have incurred losses equal to the magenta area in Graph 11.11a. However, if I continue to produce, I will now be able to sell each additional unit that I produce at a price p^* that is higher than the additional cost I incur from producing that unit, until I reach output level x^D. Thus, if I produce x^D units of output, I will have incurred losses summing to the magenta area and gains summing to the green area in Graph 11.11a. Producing any more than that would not make any sense since my MC again rises above the price I am able to charge.

Exercise 11A.27 *True or False*: On a graph with output on the horizontal and dollars on the vertical, the marginal revenue curve must always be a flat line so long as the producer is a price taker.

For the price p^* depicted in the graph, the magenta area is just equal to the green area, indicating that my overall profit from producing x^D units of output is exactly equal to zero. If the price of the output falls below p^*, the magenta area increases and the green area decreases,

Graph 11.11: Deriving the Output Supply Curve from MC

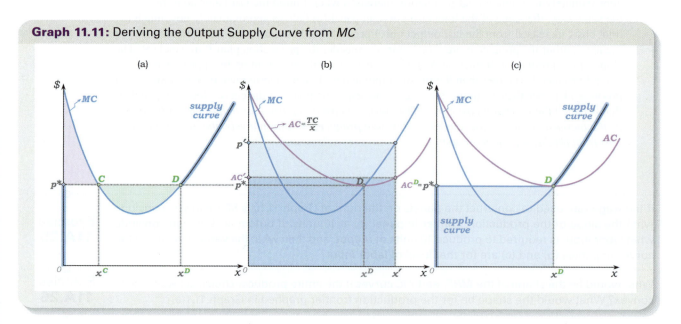

implying that I would incur overall negative profits by producing and thus would choose to shut down production (thereby making zero profit) instead. This is indicated by the blue line segment on the vertical axis below p^*. If, on the other hand, the output price rises above p^*, the magenta area shrinks and the green area increases, implying that my overall profit from producing wherever the price intersects MC is positive. The blue portion of the MC curve that lies above the "break-even" price p^* therefore indicates how much output I will choose to supply to the market when price rises above p^*. The combination of the two blue line segments then represents my output supply curve, which has *exactly the same shape as the output supply curve we derived in Graph 11.9c when we derived the curve directly using isoprofit curves and the production frontier.* That's because it is exactly the same curve. All we have done here is split the profit maximization problem into two parts: First, we asked how much it *costs* to produce all possible output levels, and then we asked which of these output levels creates the largest difference between total revenues (from selling the output) and total production costs (which we identified in step 1).

11A.5.3 Using Average Cost Curves to Locate p^*

Finally, it turns out that there is an easier way than adding magenta and green areas along the MC curve to find the point on the MC curve at which the profit-maximizing producer will choose to shut down. For this, we need to introduce yet another cost curve known as the *average cost curve.*

Average Cost is defined simply as (Total) Cost divided by output. At the production plan B in Graph 11.10e, for instance, the total cost curve indicates that I can produce 10 units of the output at a total cost of $300. This implies that the average cost of producing 1 unit of output when I am producing an overall quantity of 10 units is $30. Notice that this is different from the marginal cost, which is the cost of producing the last unit (or the cost of producing 1 additional unit). The *average cost curve (AC)* then plots the average cost for each quantity of production by simply dividing the total cost by that quantity. This curve has a U-shape for the same reason as the marginal cost curve: because we have assumed a production technology under which it initially becomes easier and easier to produce additional output (thus causing the average cost to fall) while eventually it becomes harder and harder (causing average cost at some point to rise again). In addition, however, the AC curve has a more precise logical relationship to the MC curve in the following two ways: First, *the average cost curve begins at essentially the same vertical intercept as the marginal cost curve and second, it attains its lowest point where the marginal cost curve crosses it.* This is depicted in panel (b) of Graph 11.11.

You can most easily develop the intuition for this relationship between average and marginal cost curves by thinking about average and marginal grades in one of your courses. Suppose you make a 95% on your first assignment in one of your courses. At this point, your marginal grade, the grade on your last assignment, is 95%. Furthermore, since you have had no other assignments, your average grade at this point is also 95%. Thus, when you have had only 1 assignment in the course, your average and marginal grades are the same just as when I have produced only 1 output my marginal and average costs are the same. Now suppose that you are not very ambitious and don't want to get your parents used to such excellent grades. Thus, you want to make sure that your next assignment brings your grade *down.* Your (marginal) grade on the second assignment must then be lower than your average grade going into this assignment, in this case lower than 95%. Suppose you are successful and your second grade is 85%. After 2 assignments, you now have an average grade of 90% because your marginal second grade has brought down your average. Now suppose you want to aim for an even lower course average. You will again have to receive a marginal grade below the average in order to bring the average down further. Going into the final assignment of the course, you have finally reduced your average to 70%, but suppose now that you would like to land with a final grade average above this. In order to accomplish that, you must now get a final marginal grade above your average. Thus *averages are brought down if marginal quantities lie below the average and are brought up if marginal quantities lie above the average.* The same is true for average and marginal costs.

In panel (b) of Graph 11.11, I have therefore plotted the AC curve in such a way that it begins at the same intercept as the MC curve, declines as long as the MC lies below the AC, and increases once the MC lies above the AC. This implies that the MC curve must cross the AC at its lowest point, because as soon as the MC lies above AC, it brings up the average cost (just as when your marginal grade lies above your course average, it will raise your average grade for the course).

Exercise 11A.28* Can *MC* fall while *AC* rises? (*Hint*: The answer is yes.) Can you give an analogous example of marginal test grades falling while the average grade rises at the same time?

In addition, I have plotted the lowest point of the AC curve at point D, which lies at the "break-even" price p^*. This was not an arbitrary choice on my part; *it is logically necessary that this is precisely where the AC reaches its lowest point because overall profits are zero when the output price is exactly equal to the lowest point of the average cost curve.*

This is by no means immediately obvious, but we can reason our way to this conclusion fairly easily. Suppose the price I face is not p^* but rather p' in Graph 11.11b. I would then choose to produce the quantity x' on my output supply curve, which implies that the average cost per unit of output I incur is AC'. If the average cost is AC' and I produce a total output of x', then my *total cost* is AC' times x', or the dark blue shaded area. (You can also see this from the definition of AC as $AC = TC/x$, which directly implies that $TC = x(AC)$.) My *total revenue*, on the other hand, is equal to the quantity I produce (x') times the price I charge for each unit of output (p'), which is equal to the dark blue area plus the light blue area in Graph 11.11b. This implies that my profit is the difference between these two areas, or just the light blue area.

Now we can do the same calculation when the price of the output is p^* in panel (c) of Graph 11.11. In this case, I produce the quantity x^D at average cost AC^D. This implies that my total cost is the blue area. Since the output price is p^*, I can sell each of the x^D goods I produce at p^*, which implies that my total revenue is also equal to the blue area in panel (c). Because $p^* = AC^D$, my total revenue and total cost are therefore exactly equal and my overall profit is zero just as we concluded was true in panel (a) of the graph. The "break-even price" must therefore lie exactly at the lowest point of the AC curve where MC crosses AC. As a result, *if we have a graph with both the average and the marginal cost curves, we can immediately locate the output supply curve as the portion of the MC curve that lies above AC, with zero supply at prices below.*

Exercise 11A.29 How do the marginal and average cost curves look if the producer choice set is convex?

11B The Mathematics of the Short-Run Model

The single input/single output model developed graphically in Section A is easily translated into a mathematical framework, and we will see in upcoming chapters that this mathematical framework can then easily be extended into more complex and more realistic production settings. For now, we will stick with the example (introduced in Section A) of me attempting to produce "packets of economist cards" denoted x using the input "labor hours" denoted ℓ. (I realize we previously used the notation ℓ for "leisure hours" in Chapters 3 and 8, but I don't think it will cause too much confusion to use it to indicate "labor hours" now. After all, I don't know of any firm that would consider leisure hours by their workers as a productive input, although I have questioned myself on occasion as I watched the number of breaks taken by the construction crew that recently built an addition to my house.)

11B.1 Technological Constraints Faced by Producers

When we introduced consumer choice sets in Chapter 2, we did so by defining mathematical notation used to describe sets of points, with the first portion of the definition of a set indicating what geometric space the points occupy (i.e., are they an element of $\mathbb{R}^2_+$, $\mathbb{R}^3_+$, etc.), and the latter part of the definition indicating conditions that such points must satisfy in the form of an equation (i.e., the budget equation). Put differently, the first portion of the definition gave the *necessary conditions* that points must satisfy while the second portion gave the *sufficient conditions* for those points to lie in the set we were describing. We will follow the same practice here when we define producer choice sets and will then work directly with the equations that define producer choice sets to illustrate their mathematical properties.

11B.1.1 Production Plans, Producer Choice Sets, and Production Frontiers
Production plans for single-input/single-output production processes are, as demonstrated already in Section A, simply points in a two-dimensional space just as consumption bundles in a two-good world. More precisely, the producer choice set is given by all production plans that lie below the production frontier that is defined by a *production function*. Defined formally, the producer choice set C defined by the production function $f: \mathbb{R}^1_+ \to \mathbb{R}^1_+$, can be written as

$$C(f: \mathbb{R}^1_+ \to \mathbb{R}^1_+) = \left\{ (x, \ell) \in \mathbb{R}^2 \mid x \le f(\ell) \right\}. \tag{11.1}$$

In principle, this producer choice set could take on all sorts of shapes, but in part A of the chapter we emphasized a particular kind of "sigmoid" shape. There are a number of ways we can derive such a shape of a production function that initially has increasing but eventually decreasing marginal product of labor. (Three such ways are explored in end-of-chapter exercise 11.6.) For instance, consider the function

$$
f(\ell) = \begin{cases} \alpha\left(1 - \cos\left(\beta\ell\right)\right) & \text{for } 0 \le \ell \le \dfrac{\pi}{\beta} \approx \dfrac{3.1416}{\beta} \\[2ex] 2\alpha & \text{for } \ell > \dfrac{\pi}{\beta} \approx \dfrac{3.1416}{\beta}. \end{cases} \tag{11.2}
$$

Since $\cos(0) = 1$, this function begins with zero output for zero labor input (i.e., $f(0) = 0$); and, since $\cos(\pi) = -1$, output reaches 2α when $\ell = \pi/\beta$. In between $\ell = 0$ and $\ell = \pi/\beta$, the function is upward sloping, with initially increasing slope (and thus increasing marginal product of labor) but eventually decreasing slope (and thus decreasing marginal product of labor).[5]

Exercise 11B.1

How would this production function look differently if we did not specify that output levels off at 2α?

The production function graphed in Graph 11.1b (and implicitly used throughout Section A) was derived from this general form, with $\alpha = 200$ and $\beta = 0.031416$ (or $\pi/100$); i.e., we used the production function

$$
f(\ell) = \begin{cases} 200\left(1 - \cos\left(\dfrac{3.1416\ell}{100}\right)\right) & \text{for } 0 \le \ell \le 100 \text{ and} \\[2ex] 400 & \text{for } \ell > 100. \end{cases} \tag{11.3}
$$

---

[5]Note that we are using π to denote the mathematical value of pi (used to calculate the circumference and area of a circle). Elsewhere we use the same Greek letter to denote profit.

Exercise
11B.2   Define the production function generating the production frontier in Graph 11.1a and define the corresponding producer choice set formally.

11B.1.2 Slopes of Production Functions: The Marginal Product of Labor

Now consider the definition of the marginal product of labor (MP_ℓ) as the increase in total output from hiring one more unit of the input. Once we have defined a production function f, we can restate this definition simply as the derivative of the production function with respect to the input; i.e.,

$$MP_\ell = \frac{df}{d\ell}. \tag{11.4}$$

Recalling that the derivative of $(\cos x)$ is $(-\sin x)$, the marginal product of labor for the production function defined in (11.3) is then

$$MP_\ell = 200 \left(\frac{3.1416}{100} \right) \sin \left(\frac{3.1416\ell}{100} \right) = 6.2832 \sin \left(\frac{3.1416\ell}{100} \right), \tag{11.5}$$

which is exactly what is graphed in Graph 11.2b.

Exercise
11B.3   Given that f is really defined as in equation (11.3), how should equation (11.5) be modified to reflect accurately the marginal product of labor for labor hours above 100?

Exercise
11B.4   Derive the marginal product of labor from the production function you derived in exercise 11B.2. Compare this to the graphical derivation in Graph 11.2a.

11B.1.3 Diminishing Marginal Product of Labor

In Section 11A.1.3, we argued that, in a world of scarcity, the marginal product of any input must eventually decline. Knowing that the marginal product is just the derivative of the production function, we can now see how this Law of Diminishing Marginal Product relates directly to the mathematical properties of the production function f. In particular, we can translate the Law of Diminishing Marginal Product into the mathematical statement that "the slope, or the derivative, of MP_ℓ is negative (for sufficiently high levels of labor)." But since the MP_ℓ is the derivative of f, the Law of Diminishing Marginal Product can furthermore be stated as "the second derivative of the production function must be negative (for sufficiently high levels of labor)," or

$$\text{There exists } \ell^* < \infty \text{ such that } \frac{dMP_\ell}{d\ell} = \frac{d^2f}{d\ell^2} < 0 \text{ for all } \ell > \ell^*. \tag{11.6}$$

Of course, this simply means that the production function must at some point begin to get shallower and shallower.

Exercise
11B.5   Check to see that the Law of Diminishing Marginal Product (of labor) is satisfied for the production function in equation (11.3).

11B.2 "Tastes" for Profits

Having defined the technology constraint through producer choice sets, Section 11A.2 proceeded to argue that indifference curves for profit-maximizing (and price-taking) producers must be straight lines of production plans with each yielding the same amount of profit. The intercept of such an indifference curve, or isoprofit, corresponding to the profit level π was then derived as (π/p) and the slope as w/p.

More formally, an isoprofit curve P containing all production plans that result in a particular profit level π when the output price is p and the wage rate is w can be defined as a set

$$P(\pi,w,p) = \{(x,\ell) \in \mathbb{R}^2 \,|\, \pi = px - w\ell\}, \tag{11.7}$$

where the equation contained in the definition of this set is precisely what we derived intuitively in Section 11A.2. More precisely, the equation $\pi = px - w\ell$ can be rewritten (by adding $w\ell$ to both sides and dividing by p) as

$$x = \left(\frac{\pi}{p}\right) + \left(\frac{w}{p}\right)\ell, \tag{11.8}$$

an equation with intercept (π/p) and slope (w/p). The isoprofit curves in Graphs 11.3 and 11.4 are then depictions of equation (11.8) with different values plugged in for π, w, and p.

11B.3 Choosing the Production Plan that Maximizes Profits

In our development of the consumer model, we ultimately set up what we called a constrained optimization problem, which is a problem in which we defined the utility function as the "objective function" to be maximized and the budget line as the "constraint" over which the maximization would happen. In the producer model, on the other hand, we have defined profit π as the objective to be maximized over the technological constraint imposed by a production function that limits the set of production plans that are feasible.

11B.3.1 Setting up the Producer's Optimization Problem
The producer then chooses the production plan (x,ℓ) that will maximize his or her profit $\pi = px - w\ell$ subject to the constraint that (x,ℓ) is technologically feasible. Stated more formally, the producer solves the problem

$$\max_{x,\ell} \pi = px - w\ell \text{ subject to } x = f(\ell). \tag{11.9}$$

In Chapter 6, we described several ways of solving such constrained optimization problems, with Method 1 simply plugging the constraint into the objective function and Method 2 setting up a Lagrange function to differentiate. In the case of the single input/single output model, Method 1 is often the simplest method, allowing us to convert the constrained optimization problem described in equation (11.9) into an unconstrained optimization problem

$$\max_{\ell} \pi = pf(\ell) - w\ell. \tag{11.10}$$

11B.3.2 Marginal Product = w/p (or Marginal Revenue Product = w)
Solving the unconstrained optimization problem (11.10) is then a simple matter of taking the first derivative of the function π and setting it to zero; i.e., the first order condition for the profit maximization problem (11.10) is

$$\frac{d\pi}{d\ell} = p\left(\frac{df(\ell)}{d\ell}\right) - w = 0, \tag{11.11}$$

or, with terms rearranged and substituting MP_ℓ for $df(\ell)/d\ell$,

$$MP_\ell = \frac{w}{p} \text{ or equivalently } pMP_\ell = MRP_\ell = w. \tag{11.12}$$

Thus, for our example of a production process defined by equation (11.3), this implies that the optimal production plan has to satisfy the condition that

$$MP_\ell = 6.2832 \sin\left(\frac{3.1416\ell}{100}\right) = \frac{w}{p}. \tag{11.13}$$

What we concluded from Graphs 11.5c and (f) then falls immediately out of the mathematics behind the graphs: At the optimum, the marginal product of labor is equal to w/p and the marginal revenue product of labor is equal to w. Put in terms of the language used in part A, this simply means that, as a producer, I will hire labor along the declining marginal revenue product curve so long as the marginal benefit of an additional labor hour in terms of revenue is greater than its marginal cost (in terms of the wage). When $w = 20$ and $p = 5$ (as in Graph 11.5), for instance, equation (11.13) simplifies to $\sin(0.031416\ell) = 0.6366$, which is satisfied for $\ell = 22$ and $\ell = 78$. The first of these solutions represents the first point at which wage crosses the marginal revenue product curve in panel (f) of Graph 11.5 and therefore represents a profit "minimum" rather than a maximum. The second solution, $\ell = 78$, then represents the true solution on the downward-sloping part of the marginal revenue product curve.

11B.4 Labor Demand, Output Supply, and "Real Optima"

The optimal solutions in Graphs 11.6 and 11.8 all depict profit-maximizing optima as either w or p changes. Each of these was calculated using the production function (11.3) as the optimization problem (11.10) was solved for these different economic conditions. In fact, the solution to the optimization problem (11.10) implicitly defines a *labor demand function* that gives the quantity of labor ℓ demanded for any wage rate w and price p; i.e.,

$$\ell = \ell(p,w). \tag{11.14}$$

The initial *labor demand curve* derived in Graph 11.7 is then a simple "slice" of the *labor demand function*, with p held fixed at \$5 (i.e., $\ell(5,w)$). To be more precise, just as in the case of consumer demand curves, economists have gotten into the habit of graphing slices of *inverse* functions, and the labor demand *curve* in Graph 11.7 is actually the inverse of $\ell(5,w)$. We then noticed in Graph 11.8b that, as p changes, the MRP_ℓ curve shifts up for an increase in p (and down for a decrease in p). Since the labor demand curve is a part of the MRP_ℓ curve, an outward shift with an increase in p from \$5 to \$10 thus results in a shift in the labor demand curve, going from the slice $\ell(5,w)$ to $\ell(10,w)$. The labor demand function $\ell(p,w)$ can of course be similarly sliced holding w fixed and allowing p to vary, thus providing a curve relating output price to labor demand.

Exercise 11B.6   Without doing the math, can you tell if the curve $\ell(p,20)$ slopes up or down? How does it relate to $\ell(p,10)$?

Once we have a function $\ell(p,w)$ that tells us for each output price and wage rate how many labor hours I will hire in my factory, I can also immediately derive the *output supply function* because the production function f tells me the output produced for any level of labor input. The supply of x from my factory is then a function of p and w given by

$$x(p,w) = f\big(\ell(p,w)\big). \tag{11.15}$$

In Graph 11.6, for instance, we can derive the output quantity $x = 354$ by simply plugging the optimal labor demand (of approximately 78) into the production function.

Thus, the graph of the supply curve that relates the output price to the quantity produced is again a simple (inverse) slice of the supply function in equation (11.15) with wage held fixed. In particular, Graph 11.9b depicts the function $x(p, 20)$ where wage is fixed at $20 per hour, and the graph in Graph 11.9c depicts its inverse called the "supply curve."

Finally, with expressions for output supply and labor demand we can derive a function that tells us, for any price and wage rate, the amount of profit I will earn in my business. This function is known as the *profit function* π and is simply written as:

$$\pi = \pi(p, w) = px(w, p) - w\ell(p, w). \tag{11.16}$$

11B.4.1 Corner Solutions

We have noticed already in our graphs that, for certain combinations of wages and prices, it is optimal for producers to shut down and produce nothing. Our calculus method of finding optimal solutions, however, implicitly assumes a positive level of output is optimal and searches for a tangency between isoprofit curves and the production function. Just as in the consumer model, it will be the case that *if the true optimal solution involves an "interior solution"* (i.e., a positive level of production) then the calculus previously described will indeed find that solution.

Consider, however, the production function depicted in Graph 11.12a with price p and wage w forming isoprofit curves with slopes as depicted in the graph. If I now set the optimization problem up as in expression (11.9) or (11.10) and use any of the calculus-based solution methods we have introduced in this text, the production plan A will be offered as the optimal solution, suggesting production of x^A using labor input ℓ^A. If I then proceed to calculate my profit $\pi = px^A - w\ell^A$, however, I would discover that $\pi < 0$ (as indicated in the graph by the negative vertical intercept). Thus, the corner solution B, which yields zero profit, is better than the production plan A (as indicated by the fact that B lies on a higher isoprofit curve).

Graph 11.12: Non-Convexities in Producer Choice Sets and Negative Profits at Tangencies

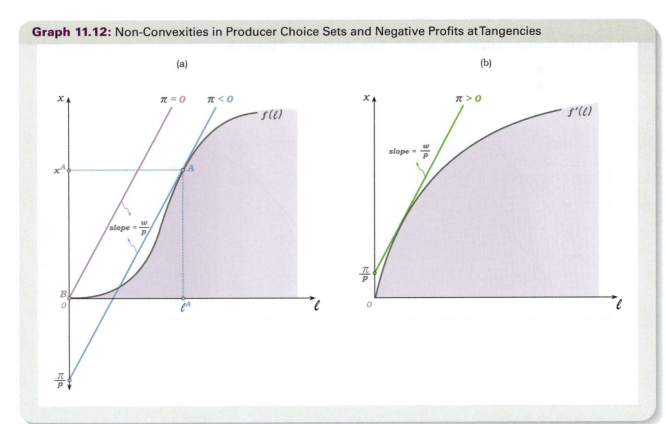

(a)   (b)

When calculating solutions to profit maximization problems, it is then important to be sure that the solutions suggested by our methods are not dominated by corner solutions, especially by the corner solution that implies shutting down. Put differently, before claiming that a particular production plan is profit maximizing, we should check to make sure that profits under that production plan are at least zero. Otherwise, we know that shutting down dominates producing. However, one case in which we do not have to check whether profit for a solution emerging from a tangency between isoprofit and the production function arises is when the producer choice set is convex (as in panel (b) of Graph 11.12).

Exercise 11B.7

Consider a production function that gives rise to increasing marginal product of labor throughout (beginning with the first labor hour). *True or False*: In this case, the mathematical optimization problem will unambiguously lead to a "solution" for which profit is negative.

11B.4.2 Distinguishing a Minimum from Maximum Profit

A second technical problem that could emerge from using our calculus-based solution methods to profit maximization involves the appearance of multiple "candidate" optimal solutions. Consider for instance the production function and isoprofit curves depicted in Graph 11.13a. Recall that our calculus methods identify production plans where the slopes of isoprofit curves w/p are tangent to the production function. In the case depicted here, this method would identify two such plans, A and B, but it is clear from the picture that A is the true optimal production plan (and B in fact generates negative profits).

Graph 11.13: Non-Convexities in Production Sets and Multiple "Solutions"

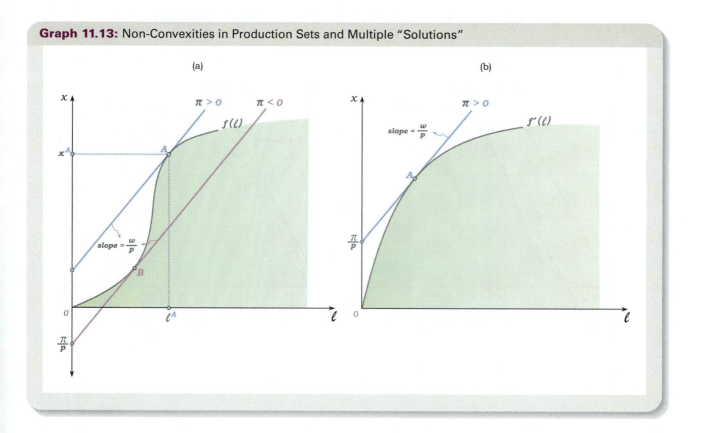

Once again, the culprit of this multiplicity of tangencies lies in the non-convexity of the producer choice set, and when such non-convexities disappear (as in panel (b) of Graph 11.13), the calculus-based optimization methods we use in this text yields a single optimal solution. While more complicated methods for calculating the true optimum in profit maximization problems exist, we can navigate around such methods by being aware of exactly what type of problem we are dealing with (i.e., where are the non-convexities?) and then checking to make sure our calculated optima are truly optimal. Using equation (11.13), for instance, we derived "optimal" labor demand for the production function in equation (11.3) when $w = 20$ and $p = 5$ as $\ell = 22$ and $\ell = 78$. Using Graph 11.6, we realized that the math gave us one incorrect solution because it gave the level of labor where w intersects MRP_ℓ on the upward-sloping portion as well as when it intersects on the downward-sloping part. This is exactly analogous to point B in Graph 11.13a, with the real optimum lying at A.

Consider a production function that gives rise to increasing marginal product of labor throughout (beginning with the first labor hour). *True or False*: In this case, the mathematical optimization problem will give a single solution, albeit one that minimizes rather than maximizes profit.

Exercise 11B.8

11B.4.3 Necessary and Sufficient Conditions for Profit Maximization
The general point illustrated in Section 11B.4.1 is that the *first order condition* (in equation (11.11)) is a *necessary condition* that must be satisfied for profit-maximizing producers so long as the true profit-maximizing plan does not lie at a corner of the producer choice set. There are two such "corners"—one at which production is zero, and another at which it is infinite. As long as the true profit-maximizing plan does not lie at one of these corners, the actual profit-maximizing plan must *necessarily* satisfy the first order condition (11.11).

Give an example of a producer choice set and economic conditions such that infinite production would be "optimal."

Exercise 11B.9

Do you think the scenario you outlined in the previous within-chapter exercise makes sense under the assumption of "price taking" behavior by producers?

Exercise 11B.10

In Section 11B.4.2, however, we showed that just because a production plan satisfies the first order condition (11.11) does not mean it is the true profit maximizing production plan even if none of the "corners" is optimal; i.e., there may be several production plans that satisfy the first order condition, with some yielding more profit than others. The first order conditions are only *sufficient* for us to conclude a production plan is profit maximizing if the producer choice set is convex. Such convexity automatically rules out the potential for corner solutions, and it ensures that there are not multiple production plans that satisfy the first order conditions. Thus, the first order condition from which we derive labor demand and output supply functions is *both* necessary *and* sufficient for profit maximization so long as the underlying producer choice set is convex.

11B.5 Cost Minimization on the Way to Profit Maximization

As we argued in part A, there is a second way to derive the profit-maximizing plan for producers: by splitting profit maximizing into two parts. The first part is concerned simply with how much it costs to produce different output levels; the second part then asks how much we should produce given the costs and given the price at which we can sell the goods in the market.

Cost minimization in a single-input production process is trivial because there exists only one technologically efficient way of producing any level of output: by using the input level that lies on the production frontier for the desired level of output. (Once we have two inputs, this problem will not be nearly as "trivial" because we will then have many different ways in which we can combine labor and capital to produce the same level of output.) We illustrated this one-input cost minimization in Graph 11.10 where the cost of producing x^A of the output required ℓ^A input and thus cost $w\ell^A$. More formally, all we did in going from panel (a) to panel (d) of the graph was to take the inverse of the production function $f(x)$ to get

$$\ell(x) = f^{-1}(x). \tag{11.17}$$

This tells us how many units of labor are required for each level of output. Then, in going from panel (d) to (e), we simply multiplied this function by the cost of labor w to get a cost function

$$C(w,x) = w\ell(x). \tag{11.18}$$

That tells us the total cost of production for any level of output. In fact, panel (e) of Graph 11.10 is a "slice" of the cost function $C(w,x)$ that holds w fixed. From this, we can then derive marginal cost and average cost functions

$$MC(w,x) = \frac{\partial C(w,x)}{\partial x} \quad \text{and} \quad AC(w,x) = \frac{C(w,x)}{x} \tag{11.19}$$

and derive the output supply curve as the portion of the MC curve above the AC curve. More precisely, the supply curve we derived is an inverse "slice" of the more general supply function $x(p,w)$ that tells us how much a producer supplies in any economic environment characterized by some output price p and wage w. To derive this supply function, we recognize that, so long as price is above the lowest point on the AC curve, a price-taking producer will produce until price equals marginal cost; i.e., he or she will produce such that

$$p = MC(w,x) \text{ if } p \geq \min_x \{AC(w,x)\}. \tag{11.20}$$

We can then solve the equation $p = MC(w,x)$ for x to get the supply function $x(p,w)$ that lies above AC, with supply equal to zero below that; i.e.,

$$\begin{aligned} x(p,w) = MC^{-1}(p,w) \text{ if } p \geq \min_x \{AC(w,x)\} \\ 0 \text{ if } p < \min_x \{AC(w,x)\}, \end{aligned} \tag{11.21}$$

where MC^{-1} simply signifies the inverse of the MC function with respect to price. We can furthermore derive the input demand function for labor $\ell(p,w)$ by simply substituting $x(p,w)$ into the inverse production function $\ell(x)$ from equation (11.17).

11B.5.1 Relationship of *MC* and *AC*

Having derived mathematical expressions for total, marginal, and average cost, we can also now easily demonstrate mathematically what we concluded intuitively about the relationship between average and marginal costs. In particular, we concluded that the MC curve crosses the AC curve at its lowest point; i.e., where the derivative of the AC with respect to x is equal to zero. Using the expression for AC from equation (11.19) and taking the derivative with respect to x, we get

$$\frac{\partial AC(w,x)}{\partial x} = \frac{\partial C(w,x)/\partial x}{x} - \frac{C(w,x)}{x^2} = \frac{MC(w,x)}{x} - \frac{C(w,x)}{x^2}. \tag{11.22}$$

Multiplying both sides of this equation by x, this gives

$$\frac{\partial AC(w,x)}{\partial x} x = MC(w,x) - \frac{C(w,x)}{x} = MC(w,x) - AC(w,x). \tag{11.23}$$

When the derivative of AC with respect to x is zero, this can be written as

$$MC(w,x) - AC(w,x) = 0 \text{ or just } MC(w,x) = AC(w,x). \tag{11.24}$$

Thus, when AC reaches its minimum, $MC(w,x) = AC(w,x)$.

11B.5.2 Two Ways of Profit Maximizing: An Example with Strictly Diminishing MP_ℓ

Because of the complexity of production functions with initially increasing and eventually decreasing MP_ℓ (such as the one in equation (11.3)), we have thus far foregone calculating the exact supply and demand functions but have merely indicated the two methods by which these can be calculated. To provide an illustration of these methods in a setting where calculations are more manageable, we will now conclude the chapter by offering an example in which we do not have to worry about corner solutions or multiple potential solutions because we assume from the outset a producer choice set that is strictly convex. Several of the end-of-chapter exercises allow you to investigate the same general methods for more complex production functions.

Suppose the producer choice set and the production frontier are defined by the production function

$$f(\ell) = A\ell^\alpha. \tag{11.25}$$

Exercise 11B.11

What has to be true about α in order for this production function to exhibit diminishing marginal product of labor?

Setting up the profit maximization problem, our first way of calculating input demands and output supplies, we get

$$\max_{x,\ell} \pi = px - w\ell \text{ subject to } x = A\ell^\alpha, \tag{11.26}$$

or, with the constraint placed into the objective function,

$$\max_{\ell} \pi = pA\ell^\alpha - w\ell. \tag{11.27}$$

Taking the first derivative with respect to ℓ, we get the first order condition

$$\alpha A p \ell^{\alpha-1} - w = 0, \tag{11.28}$$

and solving this for ℓ, we find the labor demand function

$$\ell(p,w) = \left(\frac{w}{\alpha A p}\right)^{1/(\alpha-1)}. \tag{11.29}$$

Exercise 11B.12

Suppose $0 < \alpha < 1$ and $A > 0$. Holding price fixed, is the labor demand function downward sloping in the wage? Holding wage fixed, is it upward or downward sloping in price? Can you graphically illustrate why your answers hold?

The output supply function is then simply the production function evaluated at $\ell(p,w)$

$$x(p,w) = f\big(\ell(p,w)\big) = A\left(\frac{w}{\alpha A p}\right)^{\alpha/(\alpha-1)}. \tag{11.30}$$

Exercise 11B.13

Suppose $0 < \alpha < 1$ and $A > 0$. Holding wage fixed, is the supply function upward sloping in price? Holding price fixed, is the supply function upward sloping in wage? Can you graphically illustrate why your answers hold?

Exercise
11B.14*
How do your answers to the previous two exercises change when $\alpha > 1$? Can you make sense of what is going on? (*Hint*: Graph the production function and illustrate the tangencies of isoprofits for different wages and prices.)

Now consider the second method: cost minimization on the way to profit maximization. We begin by taking the inverse of the production function to get $\ell(x)$ as in equation (11.17) and then multiply it by w to get the cost function as in equation (11.18). This gives us

$$\ell(x) = \left(\frac{x}{A}\right)^{1/\alpha} \quad \text{and} \quad C(w,x) = w\left(\frac{x}{A}\right)^{1/\alpha}. \tag{11.31}$$

The marginal and average cost functions then are

$$MC(w,x) = \frac{\partial C(x,c)}{\partial x} = \left(\frac{w}{\alpha A^{1/\alpha}}\right)x^{(1-\alpha)/\alpha} \text{ and}$$

$$AC(w,x) = \frac{C(w,x)}{x} = \left(\frac{w}{A^{1/\alpha}}\right)x^{(1-\alpha)/\alpha}. \tag{11.32}$$

Notice that, in this case, $MC(w,x) = AC(w,x)$ when $x = 0$, and, whenever $0 < \alpha < 1$, $MC(w,x) > AC(w,x)$ for all $x > 0$. Thus, the lowest point of the AC curve occurs at $x = 0$ for this production function when α lies between zero and 1. As a result, we can simply set price equal to MC and solve for x to get (as in equation (11.21)),

$$x(p,w) = \left(\frac{\alpha A^{1/\alpha}p}{w}\right)^{\alpha/(1-\alpha)} A\left(\frac{\alpha Ap}{w}\right)^{\alpha/(1-\alpha)} = A\left(\frac{w}{\alpha Ap}\right)^{\alpha/(\alpha-1)}. \tag{11.33}$$

Note that this is precisely the supply function we calculated in equation (11.30) when we solved the profit maximization problem for the same production function directly rather than solving first for the cost function and then finding the profit-maximizing supply function by setting price equal to marginal cost. Similarly, if we now plug $x(p,w)$ into the function $\ell(x)$ in equation (11.31), we get

$$\ell(p,w) = \left(\frac{w}{\alpha Ap}\right)^{1/(\alpha-1)}, \tag{11.34}$$

just as we did in the profit maximization problem that resulted in equation (11.29).

Exercise
11B.15
Graphically illustrate the way we have just derived the output supply function assuming α lies between 0 and 1. What changes when $\alpha > 1$?

CONCLUSION

This chapter has explored profit-maximizing behavior in the simplest possible producer model: a model in which a single input "labor" is turned into a single output. A production plan is then defined as a plan for converting input into output, and a production frontier divides the set of all production plans into those that are technologically feasible and those that are not. Thus, the production frontier, expressed mathematically as the production function, is the technological constraint under which production occurs. Producers then search for that production plan on the production frontier that results in the highest possible profit, a process we graphed by illustrating a producer's indifference map as a map of isoprofit lines with slopes given by the ratio of input to output prices. We then explored how profit-maximizing choices change as the economic environment—prices and wages—change. This analysis leads to the derivation of labor demand curves (and functions), as well as output supply curves (and functions). Finally, we illustrated that we can also think of profit maximization as a two-step process where the first step involves a focus on determining the cost of producing and the second step brings in the revenue potential of different output levels. This will come in useful in the next chapter.

Much of the intuition behind the producer model emerges from this very simple setting, but some important subtleties are overlooked. Most important among these is the choice producers must make between different inputs like capital and labor. Put differently, given that we have assumed only a single input so far, it was always quite clear how a producer would go about producing a particular quantity of output: he or she would simply take the least amount of labor required to get the job done. But once we introduce a second possible input—like machinery, for instance—the producer must not only choose how much to produce but also with what combination of inputs. We therefore next expand our producer model to focus on issues surrounding this complication.

END-OF-CHAPTER EXERCISES

11.1   Throughout part A of the text, we used the technology we called more "realistic" in panel (b) of Graph 11.1.

  A. Suppose now that the producer choice set was instead strictly convex everywhere.
   a. Illustrate what such a technology would look like in terms of a production frontier.
   b. Derive the output supply curve with price on the vertical and output on the horizontal axis (in graphs analogous to those in Graph 11.9) for this technology.
   c. Derive the labor demand curve for such a technology.
   d. Now suppose the technology were instead such that the marginal product of labor is always increasing. What does this imply for the shape of the producer choice set?
   e. How much should the firm produce if it is maximizing its profits in such a case? (*Hint:* Consider corner solutions.)

  B. Suppose that the production function a firm faces is $x = f(\ell) = 100\ell^\alpha$.
   a. For what values of α is the producer choice set strictly convex? For what values is it non-convex?
   b. Suppose $\alpha = 0.5$ Derive the firm's output supply and labor demand function.
   c. How much labor will the firm hire, and how much will it produce if $p = 10$ and $w = 20$?
   d. How does labor demand and output supply respond to changes in w and p?
   e. Suppose that $\alpha = 1.5$. How do your answers change?

11.2   In the following, we will investigate the profit-maximizing choice in the two steps that first involve a strict focus on the cost side.

  A. Consider again (as in the previous exercise) a production process that gives rise to a strictly convex producer choice set.
   a. Derive the cost curve from a picture of the production frontier.
   b. Derive the marginal and average cost curves from the cost curve.
   c. Illustrate the supply curve on your graph. How does it change if the wage rate increases?
   d. Now suppose the production process gives rise to increasing marginal product of labor throughout. Derive the cost curve and from it the marginal and average cost curves.
   e. Can you use these curves to derive a supply curve?
   f. The typical production process is one that has increasing marginal product initially but eventually turns to one where marginal product is diminishing. Can you see how the two cases considered in this exercise combine to form the typical case?

  B. Consider again (as in the previous problem) the production function $x = f(\ell) = 100\ell^\alpha$.
   a. Derive the firm's cost function.
   b. Derive the marginal and average cost functions, and determine how their relationship to one another differs depending on α.

---

*conceptually challenging
**computationally challenging
†solutions in Study Guide

c.   What is the supply function for this firm when $\alpha = 0.5$? What is the firm's labor demand function?

d.   How do your answers change when $\alpha = 1.5$?

11.3[†]   Consider a profit-maximizing firm.

A.   Explain whether the following statements are true or false:

a.   For price-taking, profit-maximizing producers, the "constraint" is determined by the techno-logical environment in which the producer finds him- or herself, whereas the "tastes" are formed by the economic environment in which the producer operates.

b.   Every profit-maximizing producer is automatically cost minimizing.

c.   Every cost-minimizing producer is automatically profit maximizing.

d.   Price-taking behavior makes sense only when marginal product diminishes at least at some point.

B.   Consider the production function $x = f(\ell) = \alpha \ln (\ell + 1)$.

a.   Does this production function have increasing or decreasing marginal product of labor?

b.   Set up the profit maximization problem and solve for the labor demand and output supply functions.

c.   Recalling that $\ln x = y$ implies $e^y = x$ (where $e \approx 2.7183$ is the base of the natural log), invert the production function and derive from this the cost function $C(w, x)$.

d.   Determine the marginal and average cost functions.

e.   Derive from this the output supply and labor demand functions. Compare them to what you derived directly from the profit maximization problem in part (b).

f.   In your mathematical derivations, what is required for a producer to be cost minimizing? What, in addition, is required for her to be profit maximizing?

11.4   In this exercise, we will explore how changes in output and input prices affect output supply and input demand curves.

A.   Suppose your firm has a production technology with diminishing marginal product throughout.

a.   With labor on the horizontal axis and output on the vertical, illustrate what your production frontier looks like.

b.   On your graph, illustrate your optimal production plan for a given p and w. *True or False*: As long as there is a production plan at which an isoprofit curve is tangent, it is profit maximizing to produce this plan rather than shut down.

c.   Illustrate what your output supply curve looks like in this case.

d.   What happens to your supply curve if w increases? What happens if w falls?

e.   Illustrate what your marginal product of labor curve looks like and derive the labor demand curve.

f.   What happens to your labor demand curve when p increases? What happens when p decreases?

B.   Suppose that your production process is characterized by the production function $x = f(\ell) = 100 \ln (\ell + 1)$. For purposes of this problem, assume $w > 1$ and $p > 0.01$.

a.   Set up your profit maximization problem.

b.   Derive the labor demand function.

c.   The labor demand curve is the inverse of the labor demand function with p held fixed. Can you demonstrate what happens to this labor demand curve when p changes?

d.   Derive the output supply function.

e.   The supply curve is the inverse of the supply function with w held fixed. What happens to this supply curve as w changes? (*Hint*: Recall that $\ln x = y$ implies $e^y = x$, where $e \approx 2.7183$ is the base of the natural log.)

f.   Suppose $p = 2$ and $w = 10$. What is your profit-maximizing production plan, and how much profit will you make?

11.5* When we discussed optimal behavior for consumers in Chapter 6, we illustrated that there may be two optimal solutions for consumers whenever there are non-convexities in either tastes or choice sets. We can now explore conditions under which multiple optimal production plans might appear in our producer model.

A. Consider only profit-maximizing firms whose tastes (or isoprofits) are shaped by prices.

    a.   Consider first the standard production frontier that has initially increasing marginal product of labor and eventually decreasing marginal product of labor. *True or False*: If there are two points at which isoprofits are tangent to the production frontier in this model, the lower output quantity cannot possibly be part of a truly optimal production plan.

    b.   Could it be that neither of the tangencies represents a truly optimal production plan?

    c.   Illustrate a case where there are two truly optimal solutions where one of these does not occur at a tangency.

    d.   What would a production frontier have to look like in order for there to be two truly optimal production plans that both involve positive levels of output? (*Hint*: Consider technologies that involve multiple switches between increasing and decreasing marginal product of labor.)

    e.   *True or False*: If the producer choice set is convex, there can only be one optimal production plan.

    f.   Where does the optimal production plan lie if the production frontier is such that the marginal product of labor is always increasing?

    g.   Finally, suppose that the marginal product of labor is constant throughout. What production plans might be optimal in this case?

B. In the text, we used a cosine function to illustrate a production process that has initially increasing and then decreasing marginal product of labor. In some of the end-of-chapter exercises, we will instead use a function of the form $x = f(\ell) = \beta\ell^2 - \gamma\ell^3$ where β and γ are both greater than zero.

    a.   Illustrate how the profit maximization problem results in two "solutions." (Use the quadratic formula to solve for these.)

    b.   Which of your two "solutions" is unambiguously *not* the actual profit-maximizing solution?

    c.   What else would you have to check to be sure that the other "solution" is profit maximizing?

    d.   Now consider instead a production process characterized by the equation $x = A\ell^\alpha$. Suppose $\alpha < 1$. Determine the profit maximizing production plan.

    e.   What if $\alpha > 1$?

    f.   What if $\alpha = 1$?

11.6 This exercise explores in some more detail the relationship between production technologies and marginal product of labor.

A. We often work with production technologies that give rise to initially increasing marginal product of labor that eventually decreases.

    a.   *True or False*: For such production technologies, the marginal product of labor is increasing so long as the slope of the production frontier becomes steeper as we move toward more labor input.

    b.   *True or False*: The marginal product of labor becomes negative when the slope of the production frontier begins to get shallower as we move toward more labor input.

    c.   *True or False*: The marginal product of labor is positive so long as the slope of the production frontier is positive.

    d.   *True or False*: If the marginal product of labor ever becomes zero, we know that the production frontier becomes perfectly flat at that point.

    e.   *True or False*: A negative marginal product of labor necessarily implies a downward-sloping production frontier at that level of labor input.

B. We have thus far introduced two general forms for production functions that give rise to initially increasing and eventually decreasing marginal product.

    a.**   The first of these was given as an example in the text and took the general form $f(\ell) = \alpha(1 - \cos(\beta\ell))$ for all $\ell \le \pi/\beta \approx 3.1416/\beta$ and $f(\ell) = 2\alpha$ for all $\ell > \pi/\beta \approx 3.1416/\beta$), with α and β assumed to be greater than 0. Determine the labor input level at which the marginal product of labor begins to decline. (*Hint*: Recall that the cosine of $\pi/2 \approx 1.5708$ is equal to zero.)

b.   Does the marginal product of labor ever become negative? If so, at what labor input level?

c.   In light of what you just learned, can you sketch the production function given in (a)? What does the marginal product of labor for this function look like?

d.   The second general form for such a production function was given in exercise 11.5 and took the form $f(\ell) = \beta\ell^2 - \gamma\ell^3$. Determine the labor input level at which the marginal product of labor begins to decline.

e.   Does the marginal product of labor ever become negative? If so, at what labor input level?

f.   Given what you have learned about the function $f(\ell) = \beta\ell^2 - \gamma\ell^3$, illustrate the production function when $\beta = 150$ and $\gamma = 1$. What does the marginal product of labor look like?

g.   In each of the two previous cases, you should have concluded that the marginal product of labor eventually becomes zero and/or negative. Now consider the following new production technology: $f(\ell) = \alpha/(1 + e^{-(\ell-\beta)})$ where $e \approx 2.7183$ is the base of the natural logarithm. Determine the labor input level at which the marginal product of labor begins to decline.

h.   Does the marginal product of labor ever become negative? If so, at what labor input level?

i.   Given what you have discovered about the production function $f(\ell) = \alpha/(1 + e^{-(\ell-\beta)})$, can you sketch the shape of this function when and $\alpha = 150$ and $\beta = 5$? What does the marginal product of labor function look like?

11.7†   We have shown that there are two ways in which we can think of the producer as maximizing profits: Either directly, or in a two-step process that begins with cost minimization.

A.   This exercise reviews this equivalence for the case where the production process initially has increasing marginal product of labor but eventually reaches decreasing marginal product. Assume such a production process throughout.

a.   Begin by plotting the production frontier with labor on the horizontal and output on the vertical axis. Identify in your graph the production plan $A = (\ell^A, x^A)$ at which increasing returns turn to decreasing returns.

b.   Suppose wage is $w = 1$. Illustrate in your graph the price p_0 at which the firm obtains zero profit by using a profit-maximizing production plan B. Does this necessarily lie above or below A on the production frontier?

c.   Draw a second graph next to the one you have just drawn. With price on the vertical axis and output on the horizontal, illustrate the amount the firm produces at p_0.

d.   Suppose price rises above p_0. What changes on your graph with the production frontier, and how does that translate to points on the supply curve in your second graph?

e.   What if price falls below 0?

f.   Illustrate the cost curve on a graph below your production frontier graph. What is similar about the two graphs—and what is different—around the point that corresponds to production plan A.

g.   Next to your cost curve graph, illustrate the marginal and average cost curves. Which of these reaches its lowest point at the output quantity x^A? Which reaches its lowest point at x^B?

h.   Illustrate the supply curve on your graph and compare it with the one you derived in parts (c) and (d).

B** Suppose that you face a production technology characterized by the function $x = f(\ell) = \alpha/(1 + e^{-(\ell-\beta)})$.

a.   Assuming labor ℓ costs w and the output x can be sold at p, set up the profit maximization problem.

b.   Derive the first order condition for this problem.

c.   Substitute $y = e^{-(\ell-\beta)}$ into your first order condition and, using the quadratic formula, solve for y. Then, recognizing that $y = e^{-(\ell-\beta)}$ implies $\ln y = -(\ell - \beta)$, solve for the two implied labor inputs and identify which is profit maximizing (assuming that an interior production plan is optimal).

d.   Use your answer to solve for the supply function (assuming an interior solution is optimal).

e.   Now use the two-step method to verify your answer. Begin by solving the production function for ℓ to determine how much labor is required for each output level assuming none is wasted.

f.   Use your answer to derive the cost function and the marginal cost function.

g.   Set price equal to marginal cost and solve for the output supply function (assuming an interior solution is optimal). Can you get your answer into the same form as the supply function from your direct profit maximization problem?

h.   Use the supply function and your answer from part (e) to derive the labor input demand function (assuming an interior solution is optimal). Is it the same as what you derived through direct profit maximization in part (c)?

11.8   **Everyday Application:** *Workers as Producers of Consumption*: We can see some of the connections between consumer and producer theory by reframing models from consumer theory in producer language.

A.   Suppose we modeled a worker as a "producer of consumption" who can sell leisure of up to 60 hours per week at a wage w.

a.   On a graph with "labor" as the input on the horizontal axis and "consumption" as the output on the vertical, illustrate what the producer choice set faced by such a "producer" would look like.

b.   How is this fundamentally different from the usual producer case where the producer choice set has nothing to do with prices in the economy?

c.   What does the marginal product of labor curve look like for this "producer"?

d.   On the graph you drew for part (a), illustrate what "producer tastes" for this producer would look like assuming the worker's tastes over consumption and leisure satisfy the usual five assumptions for tastes we developed in Chapter 4. How is this fundamentally different from the usual producer case where the producer's indifference curves are formed by prices in the economy?

B.   Suppose the worker's tastes over consumption and leisure are Cobb–Douglas with equal weights on the two variables in the utility function.

a.   Derive an expression for the production function in this model.

b.   Set up the worker's optimization problem similar to a profit maximization problem for producers.

c.   Derive the "output supply" function; i.e., the function that tells us how much consumption the worker will "produce" for different economic conditions.

11.9   **Everyday Application:** *Studying for an Exam*: Consider the problem you face as a student as you determine how much to study for an exam by modeling yourself as a "producer of an exam score" between 0 and 100.

A.   Suppose that the marginal payoff to studying for the initial hours you study increases but that this marginal payoff eventually declines as you study more.

a.   Illustrate, on a graph with "hours studying for the exam" as an input on the horizontal axis and "exam score" (ranging from 0 to 100) as an output on the vertical axis, what your production frontier will look like.

b.   Now suppose that your tastes over leisure time (i.e., non-study time) and exam scores satisfies the usual-assumptions about tastes that we outlined in Chapter 4. What will your producer tastes look like? (Be careful to recognize that the producer picture has "hours studying" and not leisure hours on the horizontal axis.)

c.   Combining your production frontier with graphs of your indifference curves, illustrate the optimal number of hours you will study.

d.   Suppose that you and your friend differ in that your friend's marginal rate of substitution at every possible "production plan" is shallower than yours. Who will do better on the exam?

e.   Notice that the same model can be applied to anything we do where the amount of effort is an input and how well we perform a task is the output. As we were growing up, adults often told us: "Anything worth doing is worth doing well." Is that really true?

B.   Now suppose that you and your friends Larry and Daryl each face the same "production technology" $x = 3\ell^2 - 0.2\ell^3$ where x is the exam grade and ℓ is the number of hours of studying. Suppose further that each of you has tastes that can be captured by the utility function $u(\ell, x) = x - \alpha\ell$.

a.   Calculate your optimal hours of studying as a function of α.

b.   Suppose the values for α are 7, 10, and 13 for you, Larry, and Daryl respectively. How much time will each of you study?

c.   What exam grades will each of you get?

d.   If each of you had 10 hours available that you could have used to study for the exam, could you each have made a 100? If so, why didn't you?

11.10[†] Business Application: *Optimal Response to Labor Regulations*: Governments often impose costs on businesses in direct relation to how much labor they hire. They may, for instance, require that businesses provide certain benefits like health insurance or retirement plans.

A.   Suppose we model such government regulations as a cost c per worker hour in addition to the wage w that is paid directly to the worker. Assume that you face a production technology that has the typical property of initially increasing marginal product of labor that eventually diminishes.

a.   Illustrate the isoprofits for this firm and include both the explicit labor cost w as well as the implicit cost c of the regulation.

b.   Illustrate the profit-maximizing production plan.

c.   Assuming that it continues to be optimal for your firm to produce, how does your optimal production plan change as c increases?

d.   Illustrate a case where an increase in c is sufficiently large to cause your firm to stop producing.

e.   *True or False*: For firms that make close to zero profit, additional labor regulations might cause large changes in behavior.

B   Suppose that your production technology can be represented by the production function $x = 100/(1 + e^{-(\ell-5)})$ where e is the base of the natural logarithm.

a.   Suppose $w = 10$ and $p = 1$. Set up your profit maximization problem and explicitly include the cost of regulation.

b.** Calculate the optimal labor demand and output supply as a function of c. (*Hint*: Solving the first order condition becomes considerably easier if you substitute $y = e^{-(\ell-5)}$ and solve for y using the quadratic formula. Once you have a solution for y, you know this is equal to $e^{-(\ell-5)}$. You can then take natural logs of both sides, recalling that $\ln e^{-(\ell-5)} = -(\ell - 5)$. This follows the steps in exercise 11.7 where we used an almost identical production function.)

c.   What is the profit-maximizing production plan when $c = 0$?

d.   How does your answer change when $c = 2$?

e.   What if $c = 3$? (*Hint*: Check to see what happens to profit.)

11.11   Business Application: *Technological Change in Production*: Suppose you and your friend Bob are in the business of producing baseball cards.

A.   Both of you face the same production technology, which has the property that the marginal product of labor initially increases for the first workers you hire but eventually decreases. You both sell your cards in a competitive market where the price of cards is p, and you hire in a competitive labor market were the wage is w.

a.   Illustrate your profit-maximizing production plan assuming that p and w are such that you and Bob can make a positive profit.

b.   Now suppose you find a costless way to improve the technology of your firm in a way that unambiguously expands your producer choice set. As a result, you end up producing more than Bob (who has not found this technology). Illustrate how the new technology might have changed your production frontier.

c.   Can you necessarily tell whether you will hire more or less labor with the new technology?

d.   Can you say for sure that adopting the new technology will result in more profit?

e.   Finally, suppose p falls. Illustrate how it might now be the case that Bob stops producing but you continue to stay in the business.

B.   You and Bob initially face the production technology $x = 3A\ell^2 - 0.1\ell^3$, and you can sell your output for p and hire workers at a wage w.

a.   Derive the marginal product of labor and describe its properties.

b.   Calculate the profit-maximizing number of baseball cards as a function of A assuming output price is given by p and the wage is $w = 20$. (Use the quadratic formula.)

    c.   How much will you each produce if $A = 1$ and $p = 1$, and how much profit do each of you earn?

    d.   Now suppose you find a better technology, one that changes your production function from one where $A = 1$ to one where $A = 1.1$. How do your answers change?

    e.   Now suppose that competition in the industry intensifies and the price of baseball cards falls to $p = 0.88$. How will you and Bob change your production decisions?

11.12 **Policy Application:** *Politicians as Producers of "Good Feelings"*: Consider a politician who has to determine how much effort to exert in his or her reelection campaign.

  A. We can model such a politician as a "producer of good feelings among voters."

    a.   Begin with a graph that puts "effort" on the horizontal axis and the "good voter feelings" on the vertical axis. Assume that the marginal payoff from exerting effort initially increases with additional effort but eventually declines. Illustrate this politician's feasible "production plans."

    b.   Suppose that the politician dislikes expending effort but likes the higher probability of winning reelection that results from good voter feelings. Assume that tastes are rational, continuous, and convex. Illustrate what indifference curves for this politician will look like.

    c.   Combining your two graphs, illustrate the optimal level of effort expended by a politician during the reelection campaign.

    d.   Now suppose that the politician's opponent in the campaign has the same "production technology." Suppose further that, at any "production plan" in the model, the opponent's indifference curve has a shallower slope than the incumbent's. Assuming the candidate who has produced more good voter feelings will win, will the incumbent or the challenger win this election?

  B. Let effort be denoted by ℓ and "good voter feelings" by x. Suppose that a politician's tastes are defined by $u(x, \ell) = x - \alpha\ell$, and suppose that the production frontier for producing "good feelings" among voters is given by $x = \ell^2 - 0.25\ell^3$.

    a.   When effort ℓ is on the horizontal and x is on the vertical, what is the marginal rate of substitution for this politician?

    b.   What does your answer imply for the shape of indifference curves?

    c.   Setting this up similar to a profit maximization problem, solve for the politician's optimal level of effort.

    d.   Compare the optimal effort level for the politician for whom $\alpha = 1$ and the politician for whom $\alpha = 0.77$.

    e.   Which one will win the election? Explain how this makes sense intuitively.

11.13*† **Policy Application:** *Determining Optimal Class Size*: Public policy makers are often pressured to reduce class size in public schools in order to raise student achievement.

  A. One way to model the production process for student achievement is to view the "teacher/student" ratio as the input. For purposes of this problem, let t be defined as the number of teachers per 1,000 students; i.e., $t = 20$ means there are 20 teachers per 1,000 students. Class size in a school of 1,000 students is then equal to $1000/t$.

    a.   Most education scholars believe that the increase in student achievement from reducing class size is high when class size is high but diminishes as class size falls. Illustrate how this translates into a production frontier with t on the horizontal axis and average student achievement a on the vertical.

    b.   Consider a school with 1,000 students. If the annual salary of a teacher is given by w, what is the cost of raising the input t by 1; i.e., what is the cost per unit of the input t?

    c.   Suppose a is the average score on a standardized test by students in the school, and suppose that the voting public is willing to pay p for each unit increase in a. Illustrate the "production plan" that the local school board will choose if it behaves analogously to a profit-maximizing firm.

    d.   What happens to class size if teacher salaries increase?

    e.   How would your graph change if the voting public's willingness to pay per unit of a decreases as a increases?

f.   Now suppose that you are analyzing two separate communities that fund their equally sized schools from tax contributions by voters in each school district. They face the same production technology, but the willingness to pay for marginal improvements in a is lower in community 1 than in community 2 at every production plan. Illustrate how the isoprofit maps differ for the two communities.

g.   Illustrate how this will result in different choices of class size in the two communities.

h.   Suppose that the citizens in each of the two communities were identical in every way except that those in community 1 have a different average income level than those in community 2. Can you hypothesize which of the two communities has greater average income?

i.   Higher-level governments often subsidize local government contributions to public education, particularly for poorer communities. What changes in your picture of a community's optimal class size setting when such subsidies are introduced?

B.   Suppose the production technology for average student achievement is given by $a = 100t^{0.75}$, and suppose again that we are dealing with a school that has 1,000 students.

a.   Let w denote the annual teacher salary in thousands of dollars and let p denote the community's marginal willingness to pay for an increase in student achievement. Calculate the "profit-maximizing" class size.

b.   What is the optimal class size when $w = 60$ and $p = 2$?

c.   What happens to class size as teacher salaries change?

d.   What happens to class size as the community's marginal willingness to pay for student achievement changes?

e.   What would change if the state government subsidizes the local contribution to school spending?

f.   Now suppose that the community's marginal willingness to pay for additional student achievement is a function of the achievement level. In particular, suppose that $p(a) = Ba^{\beta-1}$ where $\beta \leq 1$. For what values of β and B is the problem identical to the one you just solved?

g.   Solve for the optimal t given the marginal willingness to pay of $p(a)$. What is the optimal class size when $B = 3$ and $\beta = 0.95$ (assuming again that $w = 60$.)

h.   Under the parameter values just specified, does class size respond to changes in teacher salaries as it did before?

12

Production with Multiple Inputs

In Chapter 11, we developed some of the basic building blocks of the competitive producer model, but we limited ourselves to the case of a single input being used to produce a single output.[1] From the outset, we did not hide the fact that such simple production processes rarely exist in the world, except perhaps in the short run where producers can vary only one of their inputs. But restricting ourselves to such short-run settings allowed us to depict the building blocks of the producer model. We did this in two-dimensional graphs of production plans, with producer choice sets forming the technological constraint faced by producers, and with isoprofit curves depicting their "tastes" for profit. We also demonstrated an alternative "indirect" approach to profit maximization, one in which producers first investigate the cost side of their operations before bringing revenues into the analysis.

We will now focus on how we can extend the model to multiple inputs. This will allow us to ask not just how much a competitive firm will produce at different prices but also what *mix of inputs* it will employ. In the short-run model of Chapter 11, we did not have to think about such questions because, so long as firms did not waste inputs, there was only a single way to produce a given output level. But when the firm is using multiple inputs like workers *and* machines, there are typically many different ways of combining these inputs (without wasting any) to produce a particular output level. I can buy a fancy robot to print up my economist cards and fire all my workers, or I can get rid of all the printing presses and have lots of workers stamp the images on the cards by hand, or I can find some in-between solution that uses some machines and some workers. Once we know how to model production processes with such multiple inputs, we can think of how an economist might advise me to choose between these options, or, in my case, how I will advise myself as I hold one of my imaginary discussions between me and myself.[2]

We will find out quickly that the direct "profit maximization" method first employed in Chapter 11 becomes graphically cumbersome, and, in fact, you may skip straight to Section 12A.2 if you already believe me on this point after looking at the daunting Graph 12.1. It is in part for this reason that we will quickly move on to developing the "indirect" approach to profit maximization, the approach that starts by first looking at just costs and only afterward

---

[1]Chapter 11 is required reading for this chapter. No material from chapters prior to Chapter 11 is directly used in this chapter. However, as with Chapter 11, this chapter contains frequent analogies to the consumer model and particularly to material covered in Chapter 2, as well as Chapters 4 through 6. The final part of the B section also draws analogies to Chapter 10.

[2]But, as my wife would say, I am probably revealing too much about myself when I mention the voices in my head. Too much sharing, she tells me. Save it for the therapist, she says.

brings revenues into the picture. As you will see, this approach, even with multiple inputs, ends up looking a lot like the approach developed at the end of Chapter 11 and will be relied on extensively throughout the rest of the book. It is an approach we rely on in part because it lends itself to a more manageable graphical exposition for thinking about competitive firms, but it also gives us a series of *cost curves* that we can use for *all* firms whether they are competitive or not. This is because cost curves are the result of firms thinking about how to produce different levels of output in the least cost way, and that part of the producer problem does not depend on whether the firm is a perfectly competitive price taker in the output market. *All* profit maximizing firms, whether competitive or not, seek to minimize their costs, and the development of cost curves (and functions) therefore builds a basis for our current thinking about price-taking firms as well as our later thinking (in Chapters 23 and 25 through 26) about firms that exercise market power.

12A An Intuitive Development of the Two-Input Model

The basic building block of the producer model extends straightforwardly from the single input to the two-input case. *Production plans*, previously defined as points in two dimensions that indicate how much labor ℓ the plan calls for to produce a certain level of output x, are now defined as points in three dimensions, indicating how much of each of the *two* inputs the plan proposes to use in the production of a certain level of output x. For convenience, we will once again call one input "labor" (denoted ℓ), and we will usually call the other input "capital" (denoted k). Clearly, we are still simplifying the real world a lot, leaving out such important inputs as "land" or "entrepreneurial talent" and neglecting to distinguish between different types of labor and capital.

A production plan A, previously defined as a point (ℓ^A, x^A), is therefore now defined as a point (ℓ^A, k^A, x^A). We will continue to talk about the labor input ℓ as expressed in "hours of labor input" and can thus continue to express its price in the labor market as the hourly wage rate w. Similarly, we can express the output x in terms of those units in which the output is sold, whether as "packets of economist cards" or "bags of oranges" or "computers." This allows us to interpret the output price p as simply the price of a unit of the good that is sold to customers in the output market. Finally, we are left with the input k that is introduced for the first time here and has already been referred to as "capital." In some ways, it is harder to clearly identify a natural unit of measurement for this input, partly because the nature of "capital" will differ across different firms and industries. In some contexts, capital will simply refer to machines such as copiers, as if for instance, we were to analyze the production of photocopies by Kinkos. In other cases, "capital" might lump together all types of nonlabor investments the firm makes in plant and equipment, and might therefore best be thought of as "dollars of capital employed in production." In either case, we will denote the price of a unit of capital as the "rental rate" r.

This *rental rate* of capital is defined as the *opportunity cost of using capital in current production.* To understand what it means intuitively, we have to ask "what is the producer giving up by employing a particular form of capital?" For instance, suppose again that we consider photocopiers at Kinkos, and suppose Kinkos rents all its photocopiers (but pays for its own maintenance, ink, and paper). Then the rental rate is the rent (per week, per day, per hour, or whatever time interval we are trying to model) that Kinkos has to pay for each copier because this is what Kinkos is giving up by employing a photocopier. It gets a little more complicated if we assume that Kinkos has purchased its own photocopiers. What is Kinkos then giving up by employing these copiers? Actually, it is giving up the opportunity to rent the copiers to other users in the same rental market, and thus the rental rate is exactly the same as if Kinkos were renting the photocopier from someone else. If, on the other hand, "capital" simply represents nonlabor investments in current production, then the rental rate of the financial capital required to make these investments is the interest rate the firm has to pay in order to make use of the capital during the period over which we are studying the firm's production.

Exercise
12A.1

Suppose we are modeling all nonlabor investments as capital. Is the rental rate any different depending on whether the firm uses money it already has or chooses to borrow money to make its investments?

12A.1 Profit Maximization with Two-Input Producer Choice Sets

Profit maximization in our one-input/one-output model of Chapter 11 essentially involved three steps: First, we had to identify the technologically feasible production plans known as the producer choice set and its boundary, the production frontier. Second, we had to know the market output price and wage to construct the map of isoprofit curves. Finally, we had to locate the highest possible isoprofit curve that contained at least 1 technologically feasible production plan from the production frontier. This last step typically involved finding a tangency between an isoprofit curve and the production frontier (unless the true profit-maximizing action involved a corner solution).

Panels (a) through (c) of Graph 12.1 replicate these three steps for a convex producer choice set, with the notation π used to denote "profit." This is simply what we did in Chapter 11. Panels (d) through (f) then illustrate the exact same steps for a similarly convex producer choice set in the more complicated two-input case. You may choose to skip forward to Section 12A.2; all I mean to present is an illustration of how the "direct" profit maximization method would look with two inputs. The rest of our development of producer theory, however, relies primarily on material beginning in Section 12A.2.

12A.1.1 Producer Choice Sets and Production Frontiers with Two Inputs   Since production plans with two inputs are now points with the three components ℓ, k, and x, the set of technologically feasible production plans is now a three-dimensional set such as the set of points that lie underneath the production frontier graphed in panel (d) of Graph 12.1. The particular production frontier in this graph is analogous to the two-dimensional production frontier in panel (a) in the sense that it too gives rise to a convex production set (because the line connecting any two production plans in the set is fully contained in the same set.) Furthermore, when we hold capital fixed at some level such as k', the two-dimensional "slice" of the three-dimensional production set becomes a two-dimensional producer choice set such as the one depicted in panel (a). If capital is fixed at k' in the short run, then this slice becomes a one-input production model that can be used to analyze short-run labor demand and output supply decisions by a producer. Thus, even though we stated at the outset of Chapter 11 that most production processes require multiple inputs, the single-input model could still be a useful model in that it might adequately represent the short-run production environment faced by a firm that can vary its multiple inputs only in the long run.

12A.1.2 Isoprofit Curves (or Planes) with Two Inputs   Next, consider what the set of production plans that all yield the same level of profit would look like in this three-dimensional space. Suppose, for instance, we wanted to find all production plans that would generate zero profit when the output price is p and the input prices are w and r. In the one-input model, such production plans simply lie on a line emanating from the origin with slope w/p (depicted as the lowest of the three isoprofit curves in panel (b)). When we restrict ourselves to production plans that make use of no capital in panel (e), we end up with precisely the same isoprofit curve: The line that contains production plan B lies on the two-dimensional plane that holds k fixed at zero and has a slope w/p for precisely the same reasons as in panel (b). It contains all zero profit production plans that make no use of capital. The line emanating from the origin and containing plan C, on the other hand, lies in the two-dimensional plane that holds labor input fixed at zero and represents all zero profit production plans that make no use of labor. This is then once again analogous to the isoprofit curves in the single input model, except that now the slope of the line is r/p since the price of capital is r. Finally, you can imagine forming a three-dimensional plane that contains these two line segments and that contains those production plans that make use of both capital and labor and yield zero profit at wage

Graph 12.1: Profit Maximization in the Single-Input and Two-Input Model

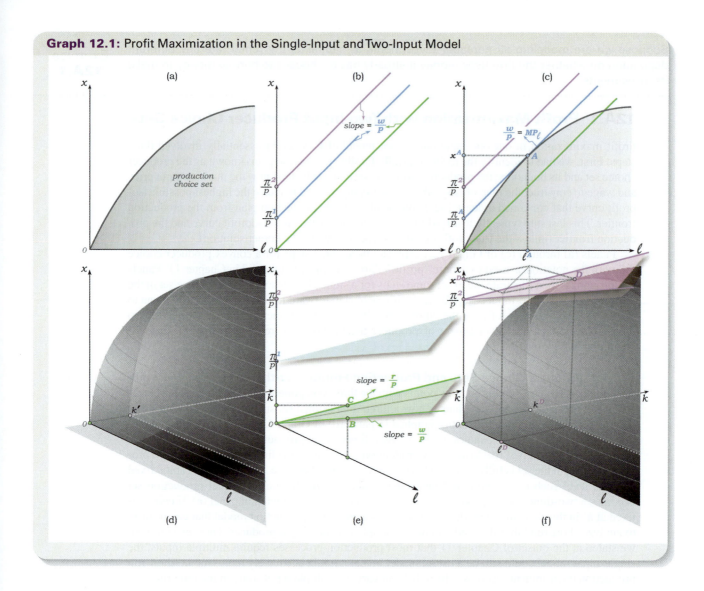

rate w, rental rate r, and output price p. This plane represents the three-dimensional isoprofit "curve" of zero profit production plans. The plane has a vertical intercept at the origin (indicating zero profit when no capital and no labor are used to produce no output), a slope of w/p on any "slice" that holds capital fixed, and a slope of r/p on any "slice" that holds labor fixed.

Just as in the single-input case, we can then think of planes parallel to the zero profit isoprofit plane. When such a parallel plane of production plans lies above the zero profit plane, it results in positive profit; when it lies below, it represents production plans that give rise to negative profits.

Exercise 12A.2 Explain why the vertical intercept on a three-dimensional isoprofit plane is π/p (where π represents the profit associated with that isoprofit plane).

12A.1.3 Profit Maximization
The production frontier in panel (d) and the isoprofits of panel (e) are then combined in panel (f), which graphs the highest possible isoprofit plane that contains at least 1 production plan (D) that is technologically feasible (just as panel (c) did for the single-input

case with production plan A.) The profit-maximizing production plan D lies at a point where an iso-profit plane is tangent to the three-dimensional frontier just as the profit-maximizing production plan A in the single input case lies at a point where the isoprofit curve is tangent to the two-dimensional production frontier. If we then look at the "slice" of panel (f) that holds capital input fixed at its optimal level k^D, we notice that this slice is a two-dimensional picture that looks just like panel (c) of Graph 12.1; i.e., we get a two-dimensional graph in which the slope of the line from the iso-profit plane is tangent to the slope of the short-run (single-input) production frontier (that fixes capital at k^D). The slope of the tangent line is w/p, and the slope of the slice of the production frontier is the marginal product of labor *given that capital is k^D and given that we are currently employing ℓ^D hours of labor*. Thus, just as in the single-input case, $w/p = MP_\ell$ at the profit-maximizing production plan. Similarly, if we were to look at the "slice" of the picture with labor held fixed at ℓ^D, we would conclude that the *marginal product of capital (MP_k)* is exactly equal to r/p at the profit-maximizing production plan. We can then conclude that

$$\text{Profit Maximization implies } MP_\ell = \frac{w}{p} \text{ and } MP_k = \frac{r}{p}. \qquad (12.1)$$

We have just concluded that $MP_k = r/p$ at the profit-maximizing bundle. Another way to write this is that the marginal revenue product of capital $MRP_k = pMP_k$ is equal to the rental rate. Can you explain intuitively why this makes sense?

Exercise 12A.3

Suppose capital is fixed in the short run but not in the long run. *True or False*: If the firm has its long run optimal level of capital k^D (in panel (f) of Graph 12.1), then it will choose ℓ^D labor in the short run. And if ℓ^D in panel (c) is not equal to ℓ^D in panel (f), it must mean that the firm does not have the long-run optimal level of capital as it is making its short-run labor input decision.

Exercise 12A.4

We can of course also write the expression (12.1) in terms of the marginal revenue products of labor and capital,

$$\text{Profit Maximization implies } MRP_\ell = pMP_\ell = w \text{ and } MRP_k = pMP_k = r, \qquad (12.2)$$

a simple extension of our conclusion that $MRP_\ell = pMP_\ell = w$ in the single-input model of Chapter 11 and panel (c) of Graph 12.1. The nice result from the admittedly complicated lower panels of the graph is then that our profit-maximizing conditions from the single-input production model fully generalize to the multi-input production model. The obvious drawback of this depiction of profit-maximization is of course that it is exceedingly difficult for most of us to draw three-dimensional graphs in a way that leads to sound economic analysis.

Fortunately, it turns out that we do not have to do this. Rather, we can develop an alternative graphical approach to profit maximization analogous to the two-step process that begins with "cost minimization" first introduced in Chapter 11. This will enable us to picture the process more easily in two dimensions. Section 12A.3 of the chapter will develop this alternative approach. First, however, we need to do a little more work in exploring what the different shapes of production choice sets tell us about the underlying technology a firm is using when it employs two inputs.

12A.2 Two-Input Production Sets: Isoquants and Returns to Scale

When firms use both labor and capital, production frontiers—as we already saw in Graph 12.1—are three-dimensional. Given that our artistic abilities tend to fail us when we draw in more than two dimensions, this is not very convenient. Fortunately, we already became implicitly familiar with graphing three-dimensional objects in two dimensions when we learned how to graph indifference curves for consumers. In fact, we pointed out in Chapter 4 that our way of drawing indifference curves is a simple extension of how you learned to graph three-dimensional mountains in your grade-school studies of geography, and we now repeat this argument more explicitly here (than we did in part A of Chapter 4) in the context of production frontiers.[3]

Think back to your geography classes where you learned to read two-dimensional maps depicting mountains that are three-dimensional objects. The two-dimensional map provided you with an easy way to represent longitude and latitude but not the vertical elevation of the mountain. So, instead of resorting to three-dimensional graphs, geographers map the elevations (or "levels") of mountains as rings that get smaller and smaller as one approached the peak of the mountain. For instance, Graph 12.2 depicts the shape of a mountain—cleverly named after myself—at different elevations in a three-dimensional picture in panel (a) but then brings those shapes down into a two-dimensional space (with just longitude and latitude on the axes) by mapping out the levels of the

Graph 12.2: Two-Dimensional Level Curves from a Three-Dimensional "Mount Nechyba"

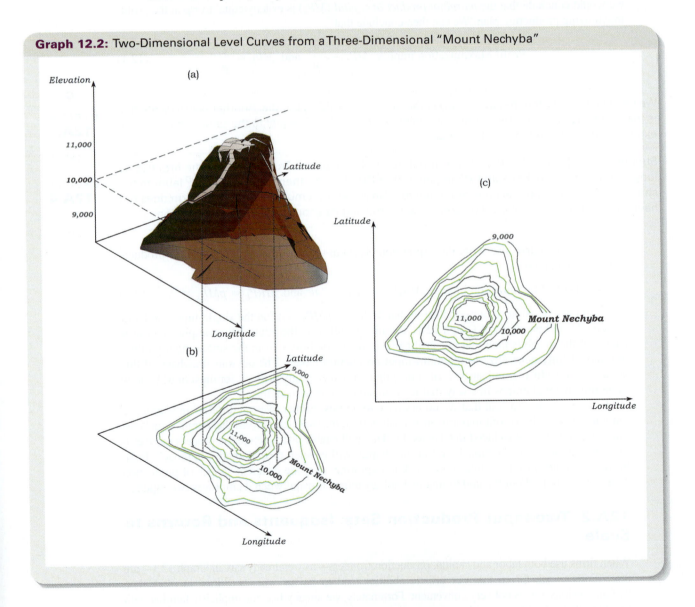

---

[3]If you have read part B of Chapter 4, you have already seen the argument in the next few paragraphs.

mountain and labeling them with the relevant elevation. Moving the axes of panel (b) somewhat, we can then depict the mountain in the two-dimensional picture in panel (c) of Graph 12.2. When we graphed indifference curves, curves that represent "levels" of a three-dimensional "utility mountain" that has no peak (since more is always assumed to yield higher utility), we did exactly the same thing as we just did with our geographical mountain.

In the case of producer theory, we can now do the same with the three-dimensional production frontier in Graph 12.1d. Panel (a) of Graph 12.3 begins by drawing some of the levels of such a three-dimensional production frontier. These levels are then mapped into two dimensions in panel (b), with the axes turned into the usual position in panel (c). The final picture then looks a lot like indifference curves, but each curve, now called an *isoquant*, is interpreted in the context production. More precisely, *an isoquant for some output level x is the set of all combinations of input levels (k and ℓ) that result in this output level assuming no input is wasted in the process.* Points

Graph 12.3: Deriving Two-Dimensional Isoquants from a Three-Dimensional Production Frontier

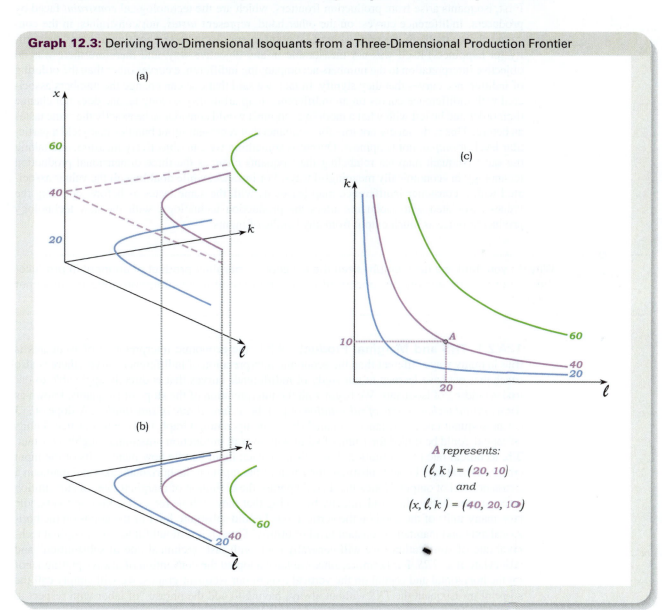

in the two-dimensional isoquant graph can then be interpreted as *input bundles* or, together with the number associated with the isoquant containing the input bundle, as a production plan. Point A in Graph 12.3c, for instance, represents the input bundle $(\ell, k) = (20, 10)$, and it also represents the production plan $(x, \ell, k) = (40, 20, 10)$.

Exercise 12A.5 Apply the definition of an isoquant to the single-input producer model. What does the isoquant look like there? (*Hint:* Each isoquant is typically a single point.)

Given the similarity of the "look" of isoquants to indifference curves, it is worthwhile to recall at the outset that their economic interpretation is quite different in some important ways. First, isoquants arise from production frontiers, which are the technological *constraint* faced by producers. Indifference curves, on the other hand, represent *tastes*, not constraints, in the consumer choice problem. Second, we made a point in our discussion of consumer theory that utility (or happiness) itself was not measurable in any objective way, and therefore there was no objective interpretation to the numbers accompanying indifference curves other than the ordering of indifference curves that they signify. In fact, we said that one can change the numbers associated with indifference curves on an indifference map arbitrarily so long as one does not change their order and be left with what a modern economist would consider to be exactly the same tastes as before. This is decidedly not true for isoquants that represent input bundles that yield a particular level of *output*, not happiness. Output is something we can objectively measure, and taking the same isoquant map but relabeling the isoquants changes the three-dimensional production technology in economically meaningful ways. For instance, while doubling all the values associated with a consumer indifference map leaves us with the same tastes as before, doubling the values associated with isoquants alters the production technology, with the new technology producing twice as much output from any bundle of inputs.

Exercise 12A.6 Why do you think we have emphasized the concept of marginal product of an input in producer theory but not the analogous concept of marginal utility of a consumption good in consumer theory?

12A.2.1 *TRS* and Marginal Product While the economic interpretation of isoquants is thus in many ways different than the economic interpretation of indifference curves, there is also much that we have learned in our study of indifference curves that is directly applicable to our understanding of isoquants. We begin with the interpretation of the slope of isoquants, known as the *marginal technical rate of substitution* or just the *technical rate of substitution*. A slope of -3 on an isoquant (as, for instance, in panel (b) of the upcoming Graph 12.4) indicates that 3 units of capital could be traded for 1 unit of labor with overall production remaining roughly constant. The technical rate of substitution thus tells us at each input bundle how many units of the input on the vertical axis I could substitute for 1 unit of the input on the horizontal axis and maintain a constant level of output. Notice that I could phrase the definition of marginal rates of substitution in consumer theory almost identically by saying that they "tell us for each consumption bundle how many units of the good on the vertical axis I could substitute for 1 of the goods on the horizontal axis and maintain a constant level of utility." Since it is a mouthful to say "marginal technical rate of substitution," we will generally stick with just "technical rate of substitution" and abbreviate it as *TRS*. Furthermore, since we have adopted the convention of always putting labor on the horizontal and capital on the vertical axis in our isoquant graphs, we will simply call the slope of an isoquant the *TRS* without always having to add the phrase "of labor with respect to capital."

Graph 12.4: Relatively More or Less Substitutability of Capital for Labor

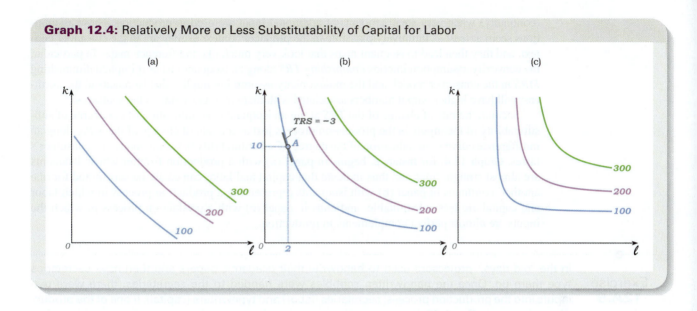

In addition, we can now identify a property of isoquants that we did not emphasize for indifference curves: The relationship between the *TRS* and the marginal products of inputs. We have thus far defined these terms separately, with marginal product representing the slope of a slice of the production frontier along which *one of the inputs* is held fixed and the *TRS* representing the slope of an isoquant along which *output* is held fixed. We will make use later of the following relationship, which is not an assumption but rather a logical implication of the definitions of these concepts:

$$TRS = -\frac{MP_\ell}{MP_k}. \tag{12.3}$$

After a little reflection, this should make intuitive sense: Suppose, for instance, you were currently using the input bundle (ℓ, k) to produce $x = 100$ on the isoquant for 100 units of output, and suppose that $MP_\ell = 4$ and $MP_k = 2$ at that input bundle. This implies that, at your current input bundle, a unit of labor is twice as productive as a unit of capital. If you were then given 1 additional unit of labor, you could let go of approximately 2 units of capital and thereby keep your total output roughly constant at 100 units. But this is just the definition of $TRS = -2$ at this input bundle; we can replace two units of capital on the vertical axis with one additional unit of labor on the horizontal while keeping production constant. Thus, $TSR = (-MP_\ell/MP_k) = -4/2 = -2$.

Repeat this reasoning for the case where $MP_\ell = 2$ and $MP_k = 3$.

Exercise
12A.7

Is there a relationship analogous to equation (12.3) that exists in consumer theory and, if so, why do you think we did not highlight it in our development of consumer theory?

Exercise
12A.8

12A.2.2 Technical Similarities between Isoquants and Consumer Indifference Curves

We can then point out a few more technical similarities between isoquants and consumer indifference curves. First, we assume (1) "more is better" (montonicity) in the sense that more inputs yield more outputs; (2) "averages are better than extremes" (convexity) in the sense that, when two extreme input bundles result in the same output level, an average of these extreme bundles produces at least as much (but typically more) output; and (3) "no sudden jumps in production" (continuity) when very small amounts of additional input are used in production. These assumptions seem at least as intuitively plausible in the producer context as they are in the consumer context, and they then lead to isoquant maps that look very much like indifference maps. In particular, the convexity assumption implies *diminishing TRS* along an isoquant just as it implied diminishing *MRS* in the consumer model, and the monotonicity assumption implies that isoquants to the northeast will have higher output numbers associated with them than isoquants to the southwest.[4]

Second, the rate of change of the *TRS* along an isoquant is an indication of the degree of substitutability of the inputs in the production process just as the rate of change of the *MRS* along an indifference curve is an indication of the degree of substitutability between goods in a consumer's tastes. Graph 12.4, for instance, begins in panel (a) with a production frontier whose isoquants are almost straight lines and thus indicate that capital and labor can easily be substituted for one another, continues in panel (b) with isoquants representing a production process in which labor and capital are less substitutable, and ends in panel (c) with a production process in which the inputs are almost perfect complements in production.

Exercise 12A.9

In the "old days," professors used to handwrite their academic papers and then have secretaries type them up. Once the handwritten scribbles were handed to the secretaries, there were two inputs into the production process: secretaries (labor) and typewriters (capital). If one of the production processes in Graph 12.4 represents the production for academic papers, which would it be?

Finally, we discussed (in Chapter 5) relationships between indifference curves, defining in particular the concepts of quasilinear and homothetic tastes. Recall that we said tastes were quasilinear in the good on the horizontal axis if and only if the *MRS* was the same along any vertical line drawn through the indifference map, and tastes were homothetic if the *MRS* remained constant along any ray emanating from the origin. We can define the very same concepts for maps of isoquants in exactly analogous ways, although homothetic maps of isoquants are more commonly used by economists in producer theory than are quasilinear ones. Just as in consumer theory, the homotheticity property allows for production processes that range from having no substitutability between inputs to those allowing perfect substitutability and thus allows for a wide range of different types of production processes (as illustrated by the three homothetic production processes in Graph 12.4.) We will typically assume that production processes are homothetic because this allows us to most easily define the very useful new concept known as *returns to scale*, a concept we turn to next.

Exercise 12A.10

What would isoquant maps with no substitutability and perfect substitutability between inputs look like? Why are they homothetic?

12A.2.3 Returns to Scale and Convexity of Producer Choice Sets   Before defining formally how we can think of the concept of "returns to scale" in the context of homothetic isoquants, it is useful for us to differentiate briefly between the notion of "convexity" we used in consumer theory and a new notion of "convexity" that becomes economically meaningful for producer choice sets. So far, we have used "convexity" as meaning "averages are better than extremes." We have learned to recognize this notion of convexity in the usual shape of indifference curves and isoquants,

---

[4]We of course implicitly also assume completeness and transitivity; that is, the production frontier can tell me for every combination of inputs the maximum amount of output that is technologically feasible; and if an input bundle A leads to greater output than a second input bundle B which in turn leads to greater output than a third input bundle C, then the input bundle A also leads to greater production than C. In the producer context, these statements are so trivial that they often are not even stated explicitly.

with these curves exhibiting diminishing marginal (or technical) rates of substitution. The set of bundles that lie above an indifference curve or isoquant is sometimes referred to as the "upper contour set," and our use of the term "convexity" arises from the fact that this upper contour set is convex when "averages are better than extremes."

Illustrate the upper contour set for an isoquant that satisfies our notion of "averages being better than extremes." Is it convex?	**Exercise** **12A.11**
Illustrate the upper contour set for an isoquant that does not satisfy our notion of "averages being better than extremes." Is it convex?	**Exercise** **12A.12**

As we now introduce the concept of returns to scale in producer theory, we are implicitly introducing a new notion of convexity that differs from what we have used so far: the convexity of the (three-dimensional) production set (as opposed to the convexity of the upper contour set of a horizontal slice of that production set). Remember that a set is convex if you can pick any two points A and B in the set and know that the line connecting A and B will also lie in the set. For our three-dimensional producer choice set to be convex, it must then certainly be the case that every horizontal slice of the set is convex; otherwise, we could find a point A and B on the non-convex isoquant and know that the line connecting A and B lies outside the producer choice set. But knowing that "averages are better than extremes" is *not* enough for us to be sure that the three-dimensional producer choice set itself is convex because "averages better than extremes" only implies that *horizontal* slices of the producer choice set are convex. The whole producer choice set is not convex unless *vertical* slices are also convex. This is illustrated in Graph 12.5. Both producer choice sets have isoquants that satisfy our old notion of convexity ("averages are better than extremes"), but the

Graph 12.5: Convex and Non-Convex Producer Choice Sets

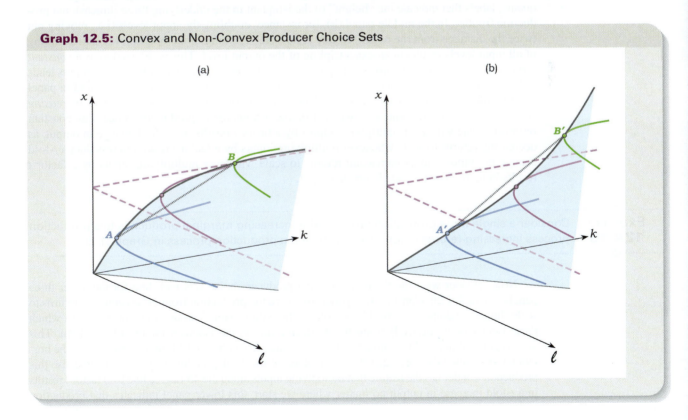

three-dimensional producer choice set in panel (a) is convex while the one in panel (b) is not. This is because, when we slice the producer choice sets vertically along rays from the origin, we get a convex slice in panel (a) but not in panel (b).

Exercise 12A.13*

Consider again a real-world mountain and suppose that the shape of any horizontal slice of this mountain is a perfect (filled in) circle. I have climbed the mountain from every direction, and I have found that the climb typically starts off easy but gets harder and harder as I approach the top because the mountain gets increasingly steep. Does this mountain satisfy any of the two notions of convexity we have discussed?

Exercise 12A.14*

True or False: Convexity in the sense of "averages are better than extremes" is a necessary but not sufficient condition for convexity of the producer choice set.

If x in the two panels of Graph 12.5 represented "utility," the tastes represented in the two panels would be exactly the same because panel (b) simply rescales the utility axis while leaving the shape of indifference curves unchanged. When x represents output, however, rescaling the vertical axis has real economic meaning. Our new notion of convexity therefore has real economic meaning in the context of producer theory even though it had no meaning in consumer theory (where we therefore did not mention it). And we can explore this economic meaning by focusing on the interpretation of *vertical slices of the production frontier along rays from the origin*.

Consider the homothetic isoquant map graphed three times in the upper three panels of Graph 12.6. The only difference between the three panels lies in the labels of the magenta and green isoquants, labels that indicate the "height" of the isoquant in the underlying three-dimensional production frontier. In the middle panel (b), for instance, doubling the input levels (i.e., moving out twice the distance from the origin) results in an exact doubling of the output level, and a tripling of all input levels results in an exact tripling of the output level. This is referred to as a *constant returns to scale* production process. In panel (a), on the other hand, a doubling of the inputs leads to less than double the output, a process referred to as *decreasing returns to scale*, and in panel (c) a doubling of inputs leads to more than twice the output, a process known as *increasing returns to scale*. More generally, we will define a homothetic production process as constant returns to scale whenever multiplying inputs by a factor t results in a t-fold change in output, as decreasing returns to scale whenever multiplying inputs by a factor t results in less than a t-fold change in output, and as increasing returns to scale whenever multiplying inputs by a factor t results in more than a t-fold change in output.

Exercise 12A.15

Consider a single-input production process with increasing marginal product. Is this production process increasing returns to scale? What about the production process in Graph 11.10?

Now consider what the three-dimensional producer choice sets look like for the upper three panels of Graph 12.6. Consider first panel (b) where the production frontier has constant returns to scale. Imagine taking a "vertical" slice of the three-dimensional production frontier (from which these isoquants are derived) along the 45-degree line in the isoquant picture of panel (b). This slice is graphed in panel (e) immediately below panel (b) with ℓ and k both represented on the horizontal axis (since they are equal to one another on the 45-degree line in panel (b)). Because this production frontier has the feature that multiplying inputs along the 45-degree line by a factor t results in a t-fold increase in output no matter where we start, this lower panel indicates that production

Graph 12.6: Homothetic Isoquant Maps Can Represent Increasing, Constant, or Decreasing Returns to Scale Production Processes

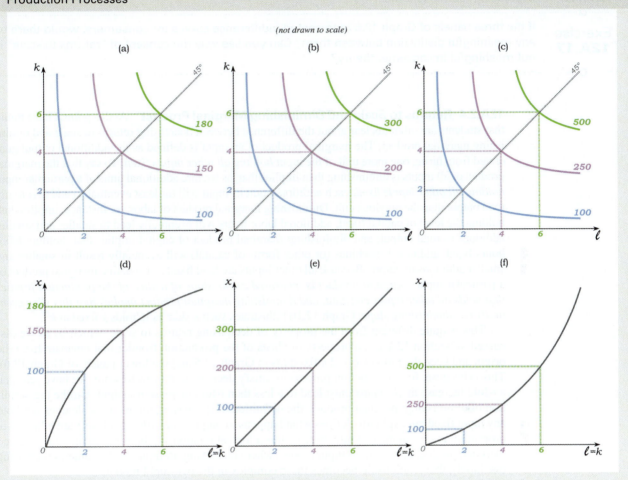

(not drawn to scale)

increases along a straight line on this slice. The same would be true for any other vertical slice of the production frontier along a ray from the origin, causing the producer choice set to be (weakly) convex.[5] In panel (a), on the other hand, the same slice would have the concave shape in panel (d), giving rise to a (strictly) convex producer choice set. Finally, the reverse is true in panel (f) for the production frontier from panel (c), giving rise to a non-convex producer choice set. If you imagine these producer choice sets as three-dimensional "mountains," the first would be a mountain that is initially hard to climb but that becomes easier and easier to climb as we walk up the mountain, while the last producer choice set is a mountain that is initially easy to climb but becomes harder and harder to scale as we approach the top. Put differently, the underlying producer choice set in panel (a) looks like the first picture in Graph 12.5, while the producer choice set in (c) looks like the second picture in Graph 12.5.

---

[5]By "weakly" convex we mean that any combination of production plans in the choice set lies either inside or *on the boundary* of the production set.

Exercise 12A.16*   *True or False*: For homothetic production frontiers, convexity of the producer choice set implies decreasing returns to scale.

Exercise 12A.17   If the three panels of Graph 12.6 represented indifference curves for consumers, would there be any meaningful distinction between them? Can you see why the concept of "returns to scale" is not meaningful in consumer theory?

12A.2.4 Returns to Scale and Diminishing Marginal Product

At this point, I have found that students are often unclear about the difference between decreasing returns to scale and diminishing marginal product. The marginal product of an input is defined as the additional output generated from hiring one more unit of the input *holding all other inputs fixed*. To say that the marginal product of all inputs is diminishing then implies that, as we hire additional units of a particular input *holding all other inputs fixed*, each additional unit of input will (at least eventually) add less to my total output than the previous unit. Diminishing marginal product of labor, for instance, implies that, holding the level of capital fixed, additional labor hours will eventually lead to smaller and smaller additions to total output; and diminishing marginal product of capital implies that, holding labor hours fixed, additional machines (or other forms of capital) will eventually result in smaller and smaller additions to output. Because all other inputs are held fixed as we define marginal product of a particular input, *marginal product is measured as the slope of a slice of the production frontier that holds all other inputs constant, and diminishing marginal product implies that this slice eventually has diminishing slope*. Graph 12.1(f) illustrates such a slice as it holds k fixed at k^D.

This is quite different from the property of decreasing returns to scale, which is, as we discussed in Section 12A.2.3, a property of slices of the production frontier that emanate from the origin and keep the ratio of ℓ and k fixed (as in Graph 12.5 and the lower panels of Graph 12.6). This is because, for a production process to satisfy decreasing returns to scale, we have said that a t-fold increase in *all inputs* must lead to a less than t-fold increase in output. Unlike the definition of diminishing marginal product, the definition of decreasing returns to scale does not hold any input fixed but explicitly defines what happens to output when *all* input levels are adjusted in proportion to one another. While there is thus a logical relationship between returns to scale and marginal product in the single-input model (where increasing *all* inputs is the same as increasing one input), that relationship becomes more complex in the two-input model.

Consider, for instance, the production process for typing services where office assistants use computers to type up academic manuscripts written in long-hand (by really old professors who have not taken the time to figure out how to use word processors). An extreme but not entirely unrealistic model of such a production process would treat capital (computers) and labor hours (of office assistants) as perfect complements in production, with additional output of manuscripts possible only if both capital and labor are added as inputs but not if one is added without the other. To be even more specific, suppose that, for every hour of computer time that is combined with 1 hour of office assistant time, the typing service is able to produce 10 pages of typed manuscripts, but neither computers nor office assistants can produce any typed pages by themselves.

Exercise 12A.18   On a graph with labor hours on the horizontal and computer hours on the vertical axis, illustrate the isoquants for 100, 200, and 300 typed pages of manuscript.

Notice that I have described a constant returns to scale production process in which a doubling of inputs results in an exact doubling of output. But consider the implicit marginal product of labor and capital in this production process. For instance, suppose the typing service currently has rented 10 hours of computer time per day and 10 hours of labor and is thus producing 100 typed pages per day. The marginal product of an hour of labor *given 10 units of capital* is then 10 typed pages for each of the first 10 labor hours because each of the first 10 hours of labor can be matched with an hour on the computer to produce 10 pages. But this marginal product of labor drops to zero for the 11th labor hour because we have used up all our rented computer time and therefore have no way for the 11th labor hour to produce any typed pages. We thus have an extreme form of diminishing marginal product within a constant returns to scale production process.

Suppose there are some gains to specialization in typing manuscripts, with some office assistants specializing in typing mathematical equations, others in typing text, yet others in incorporating graphics. Then, although labor and capital might remain perfect complements in production, the production process becomes increasing rather than constant returns to scale. Could you have diminishing marginal product in both inputs and still increasing returns to scale in production?

Exercise 12A.19

True or False: In a two-input model, if marginal product is increasing for one of the inputs, then the production process has increasing returns to scale.

Exercise 12A.20*

With the tools developed in this section, we are now ready to illustrate how to identify the economically efficient production plans along an isoquant of many technologically efficient plans, and then to show how we can infer profit-maximizing choices from resulting cost curves (as first developed in Section 11A.5 for the single-input model).

12A.3 Cost Minimization on the Way to Profit Maximization

When we derived the total cost curve in the single-input model in Section 11A.5, we were graphically solving a quite trivial problem. In essence, we identified the cheapest possible or *economically most efficient* way to produce each output level (given the input price w) as simply the one production plan on the production frontier that produces this output level in the *technologically efficient way*; i.e., without wasting any resources. In the two-input model, finding the economically efficient way to produce a given output level is not that trivial because *now there are many ways of producing a given output level in a technologically efficient way* as indicated by the many possible input bundles that lie on an isoquant that represents all the ways this output level can be produced without wasting inputs.

12A.3.1 Isocosts and Cost Minimization   Suppose, for instance, we are interested in finding the cheapest possible way of producing 100 units of output in Graph 12.7a. The isoquant in the graph gives us all the technologically efficient input bundles that can result in 100 units of output (with no input going to waste). Given that different inputs are associated with different prices, however, it is not sufficient for a production plan to be *technologically efficient* (in the sense of not wasting inputs) to conclude that the production plan is *economically efficient* (in the sense of being the cheapest).

True or False: In the single-input model, each isoquant is composed of a single point, which implies that all technologically efficient production plans are also economically efficient.

Exercise 12A.21

True or False: In the two-input model, every economically efficient production plan must be technologically efficient but not every technologically efficient production plan is necessarily economically efficient.

Exercise 12A.22

Graph 12.7: Finding the Cheapest Way of Producing Different Units of Output

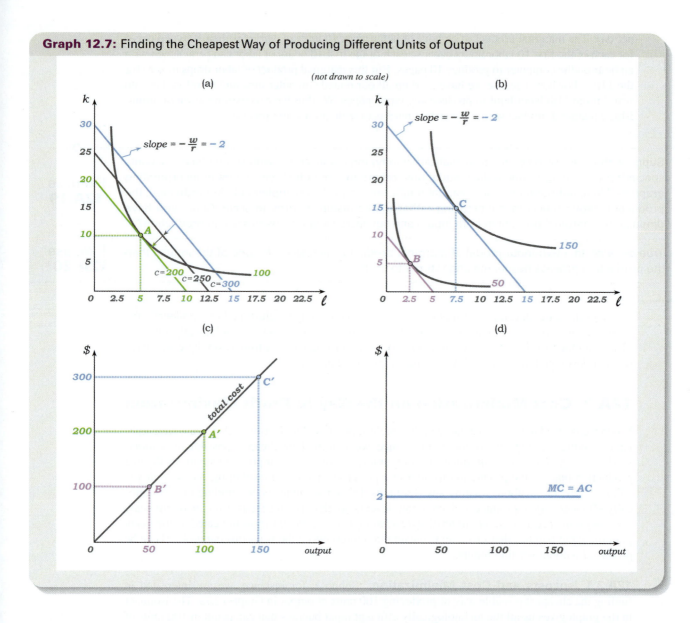

We can then imagine giving the producer a "budget" to work with, a budget with which to buy labor (ℓ) and capital (k) at an hourly wage rate w and a rental rate r. This hypothetical budget is exactly like the budgets we drew for consumers: if, for instance, the wage rate is $20 per hour and the rental rate is $10 per unit of capital, the producer's hypothetical budget could be represented by the blue line in Graph 12.7a if we give the producer a total of $300 to work with. This type of hypothetical budget for producers is called an *isocost curve*, which *represents all the combinations of inputs a producer could afford to purchase at a given set of input prices* (w, r) *and a total allowable cost level C*. While the blue isocost curve certainly makes it possible for this producer to produce 100 units of output, we could reduce the amount of money we give to the producer, thus moving the isocost curve inward. For instance, we could give the producer only $250 to work with, which would put us on the grey isocost curve, but this would still be more than the producer needs to produce 100 units of output. We could thus keep reducing the producer's hypothetical budget until we get to the green isocost curve that represents all input combinations that cost exactly $200. This last isocost curve then contains exactly 1 input bundle—bundle A with 5 hours of labor and 10 units of capital—that can produce

100 units of output. Any less of a hypothetical budget would imply that the producer would not be able to buy sufficiently many inputs to produce 100 units of output. The input bundle A then represents *the least cost way of producing 100 units of output when input prices are $20 for labor and $10 for capital*. Put differently, the production plan $(\ell, k, x) = (5, 10, 100)$ represented by A is the economically efficient way to produce 100 output units given these input prices. Since the slope of the isoquant must equal the slope of the isocost at this cost-minimizing input bundle, we can conclude that

$$\text{Cost Minimization implies } -TRS = \frac{MP_\ell}{MP_k} = \frac{w}{r}. \qquad (12.4)$$

True or False: We have to know nothing about prices, wages, or rental rates to determine the technologically efficient ways of producing different output levels, but we cannot generally find the economically efficient ways of producing any output level without knowing these.

Exercise 12A.23

12A.3.2 Cost Curves with Multiple Inputs

We can then imagine doing this for each possible isoquant; i.e., for each possible output level. For instance, in panel (b) of Graph 12.7, we illustrate the least cost input bundle B for producing 50 units of output as well as the least cost input bundle C for producing 150 units of output. Finally, panel (c) of the graph translates the three production plans represented by the input bundles A, B, and C and their respective isoquants into a new graph illustrating the cost of producing 50, 100, and 150 units of output with output on the horizontal axis and dollars on the vertical. For instance, since the least cost input bundle for producing 100 units of output at input prices $w = 20$ and $r = 10$ involves using 5 labor hours (costing a total of $100) and 10 units of capital (costing an additional $100), the total cost of producing 100 units of output is $200 (point A'). Similarly, the total cost of producing 50 units is $100 (point B') and the total cost of producing 150 units is $300 (point C'). Connecting these points in panel (c) then gives an estimate of the (total) *cost curve, which is the curve illustrating the cost of producing different quantities of output in the economically most efficient way given $w = 20$ and $r = 10$.*

Notice that the underlying technology here has constant returns to scale; i.e., it has the characteristic that multiplying inputs by a factor t leads to a t-fold increase in output. It is for this reason that each additional unit of output always adds exactly the same additional cost to our total cost of production, causing the marginal cost of production to be constant (and equal to $2 per unit of output) and exactly equal to the average cost of producing. Panel (d) of Graph 12.7 then illustrates this with constant MC at $2 that is equal to AC.

Suppose the numbers associated with the isoquants in Graphs 12.7(a) and (b) had been 50, 80, and 100 instead of 50, 100, and 150. What would the total cost, MC, and AC curves look like? Would this be an increasing or decreasing returns to scale production process, and how does this relate to the shape of the cost curves?

Exercise 12A.24

How would your answer to the previous question change if the numbers associated with the isoquants were 50, 150, and 300 instead?

Exercise 12A.25

We implicitly assumed in Graph 12.7 that the underlying production technology is homothetic. If we are then faced with a particular wage w and rental rate r, we immediately know where *all* the economically efficient production plans are as soon as we know where *one* such production plan is because all such cost-minimizing production plans will lie on the same vertical ray from the origin. This is true regardless of whether the production technology has constant returns to scale (as in Graph 12.7) or whether it has some other returns to scale. For instance, consider the homothetic isoquant map in panel (a) of Graph 12.8 and suppose again that $w = 20$ and $r = 10$. If we know that

Graph 12.8: Cost Curves of "Typical" Production Processes

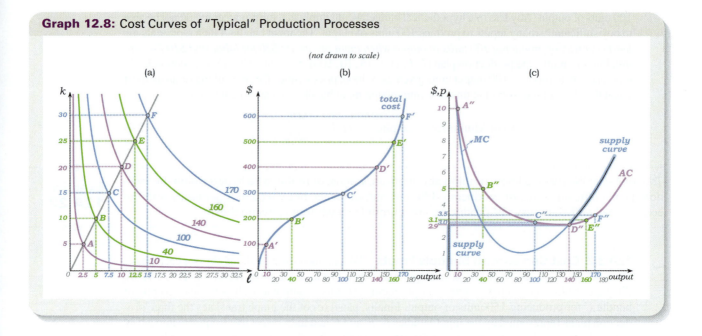

(not drawn to scale)

an isocost with slope $-w/r = -2$ is tangent at D, we know that using 20 units of capital and 10 units of labor is the economically efficient way of producing 140 units of output. But we also know that the slope of *all* the isoquants is -2 along the ray that emanates from the origin and passes through D, and thus we know that *all* the tangencies of isocosts with slope -2 will occur along this ray. Thus, A is the economically efficient input bundle for producing 10 output units, B is the economically efficient input bundle for producing 40 output units, and so on.

Exercise 12A.26 If w increases, will the economically efficient production plans lie on a steeper or shallower ray from the origin (in the isoquant graph)? What if r increases?

The production technology represented by the isoquant map in Graph 12.8 differs from the constant returns to scale technology in Graph 12.7 in that it has one additional feature we often think holds in real-world firms: It initially has increasing returns to scale but eventually assumes decreasing returns. You can tell that this is the case by simply looking at how quickly the labels on the isoquants increase; initially they increase at an increasing rate but eventually they increase at a decreasing rate. Just as for the typical single-input production process we illustrated in Chapter 11, we therefore have an example of a production technology where increased production initially becomes easier and easier but eventually becomes harder and harder.

We can now derive the shape of the (total) cost curve from the points A through F in panel (a) of the graph by simply calculating the cost of of the inputs required to reach each of the isoquants, just as we did in Graph 12.7. For instance, panel (a) of the graph tells us that the least cost way of producing 140 units of output when $w = 20$ and $r = 10$ is to use the input bundle D that contains 20 units of capital and 10 units of labor. The cost of that input bundle is $10w + 20r = 10(20) + 20(10) = 400$. In panel (b) of the graph, we therefore plot D' with 140 units of output (measured on the horizontal axis) costing $400 (measured on the vertical). Repeating this for each of the isoquants in panel (a), we can derive the shape of the (total) cost curve as one that initially increases at a decreasing rate but eventually increases at an increasing rate. This is precisely the shape we derived in Chapter 11 for single-input production processes that have the analogous feature of production initially getting easier and easier but eventually harder and harder.

What is the shape of such a production process in the single-input case? How does this compare to the shape of the vertical slice of the three-dimensional production frontier along the ray from the origin in our graph?

Exercise 12A.27

From this (total) cost curve we can then calculate average and marginal cost curves in exactly the same way we developed in Chapter 11. The *AC* curve in panel (c) arises from plotting the average cost of producing the six different quantities of output, and we can infer the approximate shape of the *MC* curve by knowing that *MC* curves must logically begin where the *AC* curve begins and lie below the *AC* until the *AC* reaches its lowest point (see the discussion in Section 11A.5.3).

12A.3.3 Profit Maximizing with Cost Curves

Finally, the same logic that led us to conclude that profit-maximizing producers in the single-input model will produce where price is equal to *MC* (so long as *MC* lies above *AC*) holds here once again. Rather than repeat this reasoning, you can simply refer to Section 11A.5.3. No step in this argument differs in the two-input case from the argument we already made in the single-input case. As a result, we can derive the producer's output supply curve (for a given set of input prices) directly from the *MC* and *AC* picture and do not need to resort to the three-dimensional graphs of Section 12A.1. For the production frontier illustrated in panel (a) of Graph 12.8, and for the input prices $w = 20$ and $r = 10$, the resulting output supply curve is then graphed in the last panel of Graph 12.8.

True or False: If a producer minimizes costs, he or she does not necessarily maximize profits, but if the producer maximizes profits, he or she also minimizes costs. (*Hint*: Every point on the cost curve is derived from a producer minimizing the cost of producing a certain output level.)

Exercise 12A.28

In filling in the output supply curve in Graph 12.8, we have recognized that the producer will end up at an interior solution (i.e., he or she will produce a positive amount) when the output price is sufficiently high (i.e., above the lowest point of *AC*), and we have implicitly recognized that the producer will end at a corner solution (i.e., produce nothing) if the output price falls too low (i.e., below the lowest point of *AC*). However, there is one additional theoretical possibility that does not emerge when we are working with the type of production frontier that has initially increasing and eventually decreasing returns to scale, which is the theoretical possibility that a producer's optimal choice is to produce an infinite amount of output.

I recognize that this sounds absurd, but bear with me for one minute. Suppose we have a production frontier that has increasing returns throughout. You can verify for yourself that the resulting *MC* curve will always lie below the *AC* curve, which implies that the part of the *MC* curve that lies above *AC* and usually becomes the output supply curve does not exist. Does this mean that a producer for whom it is getting easier and easier to produce should never produce? The answer is no, the producer's optimal choice is to produce either nothing or an infinite amount of the good. You can see this in Graph 12.9 where the *MC* and *AC* curves for a production process that has increasing returns to scale is graphed. Here, both the *MC* and *AC* curves approach (but never quite reach) p^*. If the output price is below p^*, the price always lies below *AC* regardless of how much the producer sends to the market, implying a negative profit no matter how much is produced. In this case, the producer would simply not produce. But if the price rises above p^*, then, although she will make a loss on the initial output she produces, the producer can make a positive profit by producing an infinite amount.

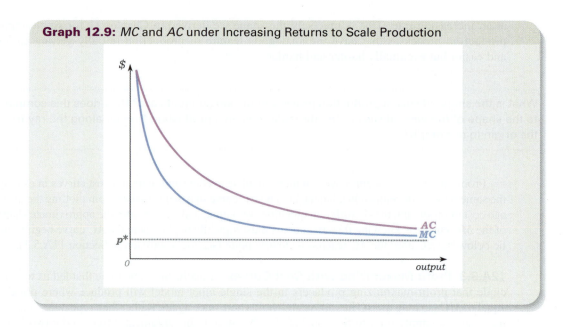

Graph 12.9: *MC* and *AC* under Increasing Returns to Scale Production

·······○·······

Exercise 12A.29* Suppose a production process begins initially with increasing returns to scale and eventually assumes constant returns to scale but never has decreasing returns. Would the *MC* curve ever cross the *AC* curve?

·······○·······

So, do production processes like this exist? Consider the production of operating systems for personal computers. An enormous amount of effort goes into just producing the first operating system and then into getting all the bugs out as one learns where they are. But eventually, producing additional operating systems is just a matter of burning a CD or putting it on a Web site for people to download, which is virtually costless. Such a production process would give rise to *MC* and *AC* curves similar to those in Graph 12.9, perhaps with *MC* actually reaching *p** (the cost of burning a CD) at some point. So yes, such production processes do exist. However, the decisions by producers that face such production processes are not properly modeled with the assumption that such producers are "pricetakers." Examples of such producers include firms like Microsoft that have substantial market power and can influence price. We will therefore postpone further discussion of the profit-maximizing behavior of such producers to Chapter 23 where we will relax the "pricetaking" assumption. It is worth noting here, however, that the cost-minimization part of profit maximization will be exactly the same for such producers; it is only the second step of profit maximization that will differ when producers have market power and no longer take price as given.

·······○·······

Exercise 12A.30 Another special case is the one graphed in Graph 12.7. What are the profit-maximizing supply choices for such a producer as the output price changes?

·······○·······

Exercise 12A.31 Illustrate the output supply curve for a producer whose production frontier has decreasing returns to scale throughout (such as the case illustrated in Graph 12.1).

·······○·······

12A.4 Bringing Cost Minimization and Profit Maximization Together

We have covered a lot in this section, and before moving on, it might pay to pause and take stock of some "bottom lines" that will show up crisply in the math of Section B and will then play an important role in Chapter 13. In particular, it is useful to step back and summarize how profit maximization and cost minimization differ.

A producer that only minimizes costs pays no attention to output prices; all he or she does is determine, for a given set of input prices (w, r), the least cost (or economically efficient) way of producing different levels of output. In our graphical development of the two-input model, this implied that a cost-minimizing producer uses input bundles where the slope of the isoquants is equal to the slope of isocosts (assuming an interior solution is in fact economically efficient); i.e., $TRS = -w/r$. Since we know from Section 12A.2.1 that $TRS = (-MP_\ell/MP_k)$ we can equivalently say that, so long as the least cost production bundle involves at least some of each input,

$$\text{Cost Minimization implies} \quad -TRS = \frac{MP_\ell}{MP_k} = \frac{w}{r}. \tag{12.5}$$

A *profit-maximizing* producer, on the other hand, also thinks about output price and produces where the marginal revenue product of each input is equal to that input's price. In the two-step profit maximization method that begins with cost minimization, this involves comparing marginal costs to marginal revenues, with the latter simply equal to the output price (when producers are price takers). Competitive profit maximizing firms therefore (1) minimize costs and (2) produce where $p = MC$. But this is equivalent to the "direct" profit maximization we discussed in Section 12A.1 where we argued that profit-maximizing firms will produce where the isoprofit planes are tangent to the production frontier, which implied that $MP_\ell = w/p$ and $MP_k = r/p$; i.e.,

$$\text{Profit Maximization implies} \quad MRP_\ell = pMP_\ell = w \quad \text{and} \quad MRP_k = pMP_k = r \tag{12.6}$$

so long as the true profit maximum occurs at an interior solution (and not at output of zero or infinity.)

Dividing the equations in expression (12.6) by one another, we see that profit maximization implies that $MP_\ell/MP_k = w/r$, which is precisely what cost minimization implies. Thus *profit maximizing producers are implicitly cost minimizing.* The reverse, however, is not true because $MP_\ell/MP_k = w/r$ does *not* imply that $pMP_\ell = w$ and $pMP_k = r$.[6] Thus, cost-minimizing producers become profit maximizers only when they set output level such that $p = MC$ (as long as MC is greater than or equal to AC), which turns out to be the same as saying that profit maximizers produce where marginal revenue products are equal to input prices.

12B The Mathematics behind the Multiple-Input Model

Section A essentially began with an illustration of the technical complexity of graphing profit-maximization when production technologies have more than one input and then set up an alternative graphical method that uses cost minimization as a first step to finding the profit-maximizing choices

---

[6]For instance, if $pMP_\ell > w$ and $pMP_k > r$, MP_ℓ/MP_k could still be equal to w/r. Consider the following case: $p = 1$, $MP_\ell = 20$, $MP_k = 10$, $w = 10$ and $r = 5$. Then

$$\frac{w}{r} = 2 = \frac{pMP_\ell}{pMP_k} = \frac{MP_\ell}{MP_k} \tag{12.7}$$

but $pMP_\ell = 20 > 10 = w$ and $pMP_k = 10 > 5 = r$.

made by price-taking producers. When we take a more mathematical approach, the complexity of solving for profit-maximizing choices directly is not as overwhelming and thus the need for an alternative approach is less compelling. However, we will find that the alternative cost minimization approach provides us with a method that is almost identical to the expenditure minimization problem in consumer theory, and it allows us ultimately to derive a "duality" picture such as the one we derived in consumer theory. Cost minimization furthermore builds the basis for deriving the cost functions that apply to *all* producers, whether they are competitive "price takers" or whether they can in fact exercise market power (as will be assumed in chapters beginning with Chapter 23).

12B.1 Producer Choice Sets and Production Functions

In the single-input case of Chapter 11, we represented production frontiers mathematically with production functions of the form $f: \mathbb{R}^1_+ \to \mathbb{R}^1_+$. Production functions in the multiple-input case are then just straightforward extensions, with a production process that uses n inputs represented by a function $f: \mathbb{R}^n_+ \to \mathbb{R}^1_+$. For the case in which labor ℓ and capital k represent the only two inputs, for instance, the function $f: \mathbb{R}^2_+ \to \mathbb{R}^1_+$ tells us the quantity of output $f(\ell, k)$ that can be produced from any input bundle (ℓ, k) assuming no inputs are wasted. The producer choice set is then defined (just as in Chapter 11) as the set of production plans (x, ℓ, k) that are technologically feasible; i.e.,

$$C(f: \mathbb{R}^2_+ \to \mathbb{R}^1_+) = \left\{ (x, \ell, k) \in \mathbb{R}^3 \mid x \le f(\ell, k) \right\}. \tag{12.8}$$

In principle, not only could such a choice set contain some arbitrary number n of inputs but it could also result in a number m of different outputs $(x_1, x_2, ..., x_m)$, with a function $f: \mathbb{R}^n_+ \to \mathbb{R}^m_+$ generating the relevant production frontier. Production processes with multiple outputs may be of two different types: First, it may be the case that a producer *intentionally* uses a given set of inputs to *jointly* produce several different outputs to sell on the market. For instance, the owner of an apple orchard might use the inputs "apple trees" and "bees" (required for cross-pollination) to produce outputs "apples" and "honey" to be sold in the output market. Second, a producer might *unintentionally* produce goods that he or she does not (or is not able to) sell on the market but that impact the lives of others. The apple orchard owner might, for instance, unintentionally provide "cross-pollination" services to a neighboring peach orchard, or the processing of honey might produce the output "water pollution" in a neighboring river. Such unintentionally produced outputs will be referred to as "production externalities" in later chapters. For now, however, we will restrict ourselves to production processes that yield a single, intentionally produced output x.

12B.1.1 Marginal Product and *TRS*
Now consider once again the definition of the marginal product of an input, which is the increase in total output from hiring one more unit of the input while holding all other inputs fixed. This translates directly into the mathematical definition of marginal product as *the partial derivative of the production function with respect to the input*, or

$$MP_\ell = \frac{\partial f(\ell, k)}{\partial \ell} \quad \text{and} \quad MP_k = \frac{\partial f(\ell, k)}{\partial k} \tag{12.9}$$

for the case where the inputs are labor ℓ and capital k. Since k is held fixed in the partial derivative that defines MP_ℓ, this implies that the marginal product of labor is simply the slope of the "slice" of the production function that holds k fixed, while the marginal product of capital is the slope of the "slice" that holds labor input fixed. Examples of such slices are depicted graphically in Graph 12.1.

Exercise 12B.1

Just as we can take the partial derivative of a production function with respect to one of the inputs (and call it the "marginal product of the input"), we could take the partial derivative of a utility function with respect to one of the consumption goods (and call it the "marginal utility from that good"). Why is the first of these concepts economically meaningful but the second is not?

As already discussed extensively in Section A, we can also explore the properties of production functions by considering the horizontal slices of these functions, slices that are known as *isoquants*. In Section A, we argued that it is reasonable to assume that such isoquants will have properties similar to consumer indifference curves (which are just horizontal slices of utility rather than production functions). The slope of an isoquant derived from a production function $f(\ell, k)$, the (marginal) *technical rate of substitution (TRS)*, is then given by

$$TRS = -\left(\frac{\partial f(\ell, k)/\partial \ell}{\partial f(\ell, k)/\partial k}\right), \tag{12.10}$$

which can be derived exactly as the formula for *MRS* in Chapter 4 was derived.

Using the same method employed to derive the formula for *MRS* from a utility function, derive the formula for *TRS* from a production function $f(\ell, k)$.

Exercise 12B.2*

Given the expressions for marginal product in equation (12.9), the technical rate of substitution can then also be expressed as the fraction of the marginal products of the inputs

$$TRS = -\frac{MP_\ell}{MP_k}, \tag{12.11}$$

as we already derived intuitively in Section 12A.2.1.

12B.1.2 "Averages Are Better than Extremes" and Quasiconcavity

A particularly important assumption we typically make about producer choice sets is that "averages are better than extremes" in the sense that an input bundle formed as the average of two input bundles on the same isoquant will produce at least as much (but typically more) than the more extreme bundles. When we made the same assumption in consumer theory, we called it "convexity" because it gives rise to convex upper contour sets of indifference curves. As it turns out, assuming convexity of upper contour sets is equivalent to assuming that the underlying production function is *quasiconcave*. Consider the definition of quasiconcavity of a function: A function $f: \mathbb{R}_+^2 \to \mathbb{R}^1$ is *quasiconcave* if and only if, for any two points $A = (x_1^A, x_2^A)$ and $B = (x_1^B, x_2^B)$ in $\mathbb{R}_+^2$ and any $\alpha \in (0, 1)$,

$$\min\{f(x_1^A, x_2^A), f(x_1^B, x_2^B)\} \leq f(\alpha x_1^A + (1 - \alpha)x_1^B, \alpha x_2^A + (1 - \alpha)x_2^B). \tag{12.12}$$

Now suppose we pick 2 input bundles $A = (\ell^A, k^A)$ and $B = (\ell^B, k^B)$ on an isoquant of the quasiconcave production function $f(\ell, k)$. Since they lie on the same isoquant, we know that $f(\ell^A, k^A) = f(\ell^B, k^B)$, and from our definition of quasiconcavity, we can infer that the output of any weighted average of input bundles A and B will be at least as much as is produced on the isoquant from which A and B were drawn. Thus, quasiconcave production functions represent production processes under which average input bundles produce more than extremes. Similarly, you can convince yourself that, whenever averages are better than extremes in the sense we have defined this, only quasiconcave functions can represent such production processes. As a result, we can conclude that *quasiconcave production functions give rise to isoquants with convex upper contour sets, and production processes in which isoquants have convex upper contour sets must arise from quasiconcave production functions*. Since all the utility functions we worked with in our development of consumer theory had the "averages are better than extremes" feature, we then immediately know that all these utility functions were also quasiconcave.

True or False: Producer choice sets whose frontiers are characterized by quasiconcave functions have the following property: All horizontal slices of the choice sets are convex sets.

Exercise 12B.3

We can note immediately, however, that this does not imply that production (or utility) functions that have the "averages are better than extremes" feature must be *concave*, only that they must be *quasiconcave*. We can clarify this by first stating the definition of a concave function with two inputs: A function $f: \mathbb{R}_+^2 \to \mathbb{R}^1$ is *concave* if and only if, for any two points $A = (x_1^A, x_2^A)$ and $B = (x_1^B, x_2^B)$ in $\mathbb{R}_+^2$ and any $\alpha \in (0,1)$,

$$\alpha f(x_1^A, x_2^A) + (1 - \alpha) f(x_1^B, x_2^B) \le f(\alpha x_1^A + (1 - \alpha) x_1^B, \alpha x_2^A + (1 - \alpha) x_2^B). \quad (12.13)$$

It is easy to see that every concave function is also quasiconcave by noting that, for any $A = (x_1^A, x_2^A)$ and $B = (x_1^B, x_2^B)$ and any $\alpha \in (0,1)$, it is always true that

$$\min\{f(x_1^A, x_2^A), f(x_1^B, x_2^B)\} \le \alpha f(x_1^A, x_2^A) + (1 - \alpha) f(x_1^B, x_2^B) \quad (12.14)$$

as long as f satisfies (12.13). If f is concave, then equations (12.13) an (12.14) together imply that equation (12.12) holds; i.e., f being concave implies f is quasiconcave.

The reverse, however, does not hold. And it is in exploring this through an example that we can get some intuition for the difference between quasiconcavity and concavity of a function. Consider, for instance, the Cobb–Douglas production function $f(\ell, k) = \ell^{1/3} k^{1/3}$, which is graphed in panel (a) of Graph 12.10. The production plans A and B fall on the vertical slice of this function that lies on the 45-degree line in the (ℓ, k) plane. Since the slope on this slice of the function starts out large and declines, the dotted line connecting A and B lies below the function. Points on this dotted line correspond to the left-hand side of equation (12.13), while points on the boundary of the slice correspond to the right-hand side of equation (12.13). The fact that the

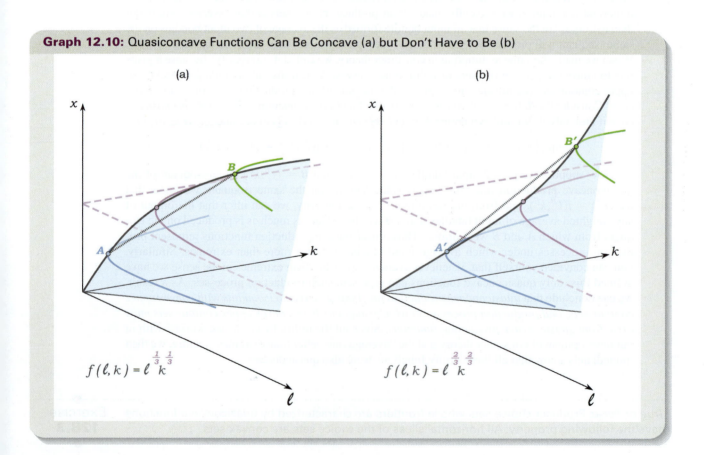

Graph 12.10: Quasiconcave Functions Can Be Concave (a) but Don't Have to Be (b)

former falls below the latter then formally satisfies the definition of concavity. Panel (b) of Graph 12.10, on the other hand, illustrates the same function squared; i.e., $f(\ell, k) = \ell^{2/3}k^{2/3}$, but this time the dotted line connecting A' and B' lies *above* the function, which implies that the definition of concavity is not satisfied.

Therefore, panel (a) of Graph 12.10 represents a production function that is concave while panel (b) represents a production function that is not concave. You can immediately see that this is equivalent to saying that the producer choice set in panel (a) is a convex set, while the producer choice set in panel (b) is a non-convex set. Concave production functions therefore represent convex producer choice sets. At the same time, the shape of the same-colored isoquants in the two panels is identical since, as we learned in the development of consumer theory, a transformation of a function (such as squaring it) does not change the shape of the levels projected into two dimensions even though it does change the three-dimensional function. And these shapes of isoquants give rise to convex upper contour sets, indicating that both functions are quasiconcave.

True or False: All quasiconcave production functions, but not all concave production functions, give rise to convex producer choice sets.

Exercise
12B.4

True or False: Both quasiconcave and concave production functions represent production processes for which the "averages are better than extremes" property holds.

Exercise
12B.5

12B.1.3 Returns to Scale and Concavity Our discussion of concavity of production functions then related directly to the concept of returns to scale. In Section A, we defined a homothetic production process as having *decreasing returns to scale* if multiplying inputs by a factor t will lead to less than t times as much output, *constant returns to scale* if it leads to t times as much output, and *increasing returns to scale* if it leads to more than t times as much output. Notice that the production function graphed in panel (a) of Graph 12.10 has the feature that any vertical slice of the function along a ray from the origin (such as the one that is pictured) has a slope that gets shallower and shallower, implying that multiplying inputs along the ray by a factor t will result in less than t times as much output. The reverse is true for the production function in panel (b) where the slope of the function along any vertical slice emanating from the origin becomes steeper and steeper. Thus, the same feature of homothetic production functions that makes them either concave or not concave determines whether or not they have decreasing returns to scale. Put differently, when isoquant maps are homothetic, *the boundary of convex producer choice sets is represented by a concave production function that has decreasing returns to scale*. Increasing returns to scale, on the other hand, imply a non-convexity in the producer choice set and thus a non-concavity in the production function.

We can, in fact, be even more precise about what returns to scale mean mathematically for the production function if the function is homogeneous. First, recall that all homogeneous functions are homothetic, and a function is homogeneous of degree k if and only if

$$f(t\ell, tk) = t^k f(\ell, k). \tag{12.15}$$

Since a production function is defined to have constant returns to scale when a t-fold increase in inputs causes a t-fold increase in output, it follows that *constant returns to scale production functions are homogeneous of degree 1*. Similarly, *decreasing returns to scale production functions that are homogeneous are homogeneous of degree less than 1*, and *increasing returns to scale production functions that are homogeneous are homogeneous of degree greater than 1*. In the case of two-input Cobb–Douglas production functions, for instance, this implies that the production function is decreasing returns to scale if the exponents sum to less than 1, constant returns to scale if the exponents sum to 1, and increasing returns to scale if they sum to greater than 1. Note, however, that not all homothetic production functions are homogeneous. You could, for instance, have a homothetic production function that has initially increasing and eventually decreasing returns to scale (as will be explored in some end-of-chapter exercises).

Exercise 12B.6   Verify the last statement regarding two-input Cobb–Douglas production functions.

12B.1.4 Returns to Scale and Diminishing Marginal Product
Finally, we can return to our discussion from Section 12A.2.4 in which we argued intuitively that diminishing marginal product of inputs is conceptually quite different from decreasing returns to scale because the first concept holds all inputs but one fixed while the latter varies all inputs in proportion to one another. We can get some further intuition by illustrating the concepts using the homothetic (and homogeneous) Cobb–Douglas production function $f(\ell, k) = \ell^\alpha k^\beta$, which has marginal product of labor and capital equal to

$$MP_\ell = \alpha \ell^{(\alpha-1)} k^\beta \text{ and } MP_k = \beta \ell^\alpha k^{(\beta-1)}. \tag{12.16}$$

The production function has diminishing MP if and only if the derivative of MP is negative, where

$$\frac{\partial MP_\ell}{\partial \ell} = \alpha(\alpha - 1)\ell^{(\alpha-2)} k^\beta \text{ and } \frac{\partial MP_k}{\partial k} = \beta(\beta - 1)\ell^\alpha k^{(\beta-2)}. \tag{12.17}$$

So long as the exponents α and β are positive (as they always are in Cobb–Douglas production functions), this implies that marginal product of labor and capital will be diminishing only if each exponent is less than 1. That's because only when the exponent on the input is less than 1 will the derivative of marginal product in (12.17) be negative.

Graph 12.11 then illustrates two increasing returns to scale Cobb–Douglas production functions, one with diminishing marginal product and the other with increasing marginal product. In particular, panel (a) replicates the production function $f(\ell, k) = \ell^{2/3} k^{2/3}$ from Graph 12.10b but now illustrates the shape of the slice of the production function that holds labor fixed at ℓ^A. Panel (b) of Graph 12.11 then does the same for the production function $f(\ell, k) = \ell^{4/3} k^{4/3}$. From equation (12.17), we would expect the production function in panel (a) to exhibit diminishing marginal product of each input since the exponents on each input in the production function are less than 1, and we would expect the production function in panel (b) to exhibit increasing marginal product since the same exponents are larger than 1. This is precisely what the shapes of the slices of these functions indicate, with $f(\ell^A, k)$ exhibiting a diminishing slope in panel (a) (and thus diminishing MP_k) and an increasingly steep slope in panel (b) (and thus increasing MP_k).

Exercise 12B.7   Can you give an example of a Cobb–Douglas production function that has increasing marginal product of capital and decreasing marginal product of labor? Does this production function have increasing, constant, or decreasing returns to scale?

Exercise 12B.8   *True or False*: It is not possible for a Cobb–Douglas production process to have decreasing returns to scale and increasing marginal product of one of its inputs.

Graph 12.11: Increasing Returns to Scale with (a) Diminishing *MP* and (b) Increasing *MP*

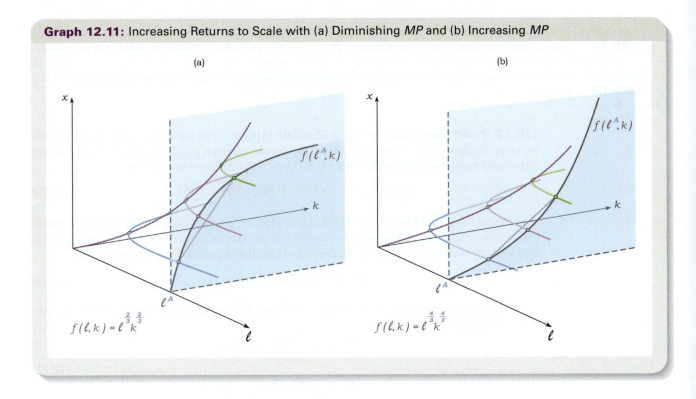

12B.2 Isoprofit Planes and Profit Maximization

In Graph 12.1, we briefly illustrated profit maximization with two-input production frontiers as the tangency of an "isoprofit plane" with the production frontier. Just as in the case of the single-input model in Chapter 11, the production frontier represents the technological constraint faced by producers, and the isoprofit curves represent the "tastes" for profit that arise from the economic environment that the producer takes as given. We will now illustrate the graphical profit maximization of Graph 12.1 mathematically by first defining isopfrofits formally and then setting up and solving the full profit maximization problem.

12B.2.1 Isoprofit Curves with Multiple Inputs   As we already discussed extensively in Chapter 11, we assume that "tastes" for producers are generally quantified straightforwardly in terms of profit. Profit, in turn, is expressed simply as the difference between economic revenue (generated from the sale of goods and services) and economic costs (incurred as inputs are purchased for producing outputs). In the two-input case with labor ℓ and capital k, profit π at a production plan (x, ℓ, k) is then simply

$$\pi = px - w\ell - rk, \qquad (12.18)$$

where the economic environment is characterized by the output price p and the input prices (w, r), all of which our price-taking producer takes as given. An "indifference curve" for price-taking producers, the isoprofit curve P, was then defined in Chapter 11 as the set of production plans that yield the same amount of profit in a given economic environment (p, w, r). This can be defined more formally as

$$P(\pi, p, w, r) = \left\{ (x, \ell, k) \in \mathbb{R}^3 \mid \pi = px - w\ell - rk \right\}. \qquad (12.19)$$

12B.2.2 Profit Maximization with Multiple Inputs   The movement to the highest possible isoprofit plane on the three-dimensional production function graphed in Graph 12.1(f) is then formalized mathematically as the solution to the profit maximization problem

$$\max_{x,\ell,k} \pi = px - w\ell - rk \text{ subject to } x = f(\ell, k). \tag{12.20}$$

This problem could be read as "pick the production plan that lies on the highest isoprofit plane while remaining technologically feasible." It can also be written as an unconstrained maximization problem by substituting the constraint into the objective function and writing

$$\max_{\ell,k} \pi = pf(\ell, k) - w\ell - rk. \tag{12.21}$$

The first order conditions are then simply the partial derivatives of π (with respect to the two choice variables) set to zero; i.e.,

$$\frac{\partial \pi}{\partial \ell} = p\frac{\partial f(\ell, k)}{\partial \ell} - w = 0,$$

$$\frac{\partial \pi}{\partial \ell} = p\frac{\partial f(\ell, k)}{\partial k} - r = 0, \tag{12.22}$$

which can also be written as

$$w = p\frac{\partial f(\ell, k)}{\partial \ell} \quad \text{and} \quad r = p\frac{\partial f(\ell, k)}{\partial k}, \tag{12.23}$$

or simply

$$w = pMP_\ell = MRP_\ell \quad \text{and} \quad r = pMP_k = MRP_k. \tag{12.24}$$

These are of course precisely the conditions that emerge in Graph 12.1(f): At the profit-maximizing production plan A, the slope of the "slice" of the production frontier that holds capital fixed at k^D is equal to the slope of the corresponding "slice" of the isoprofit plane that also holds capital fixed at k^D ($w/p = MP_\ell$); and the slope of the "slice" of the production frontier that holds labor fixed at ℓ^D is equal to the corresponding "slice" of the isoprofit plane that also holds labor fixed at ℓ^D ($r/p = MP_k$).

The two equations in (12.23) can then be solved to give the input demand functions that tell us how much labor and captial the producer will hire in any economic environment (p, w, r) that he or she might face; i.e.,

$$\ell(p, w, r) \quad \text{and} \quad k(p, w, r) \tag{12.25}$$

are the *labor and capital demand functions* for this producer. Plugging these into the production function, we can then derive (the *output supply function*

$$x(p, w, r) = f((\ell(p, w, r), k(p, w, r)) \tag{12.26}$$

that tells me how much output the producer will supply in any economic environment (p,w,r) he or she might face.

12B.2.3 An Example of Profit Maximization

Suppose, for instance, that the technology available to me as a producer can be represented by the function $f(\ell,k) = 20\ell^{2/5}k^{2/5}$. We can then set up the profit maximization problem

$$\max_{x,\ell,k} \pi = px - w\ell - rk \text{ subject to } x = 20\ell^{2/5}k^{2/5}, \tag{12.27}$$

which can also be written as

$$\max_{\ell,k} \pi = p(20\ell^{2/5}k^{2/5}) - w\ell - rk. \tag{12.28}$$

The first order conditions are then

$$\frac{\partial \pi}{\partial \ell} = 8p\ell^{-3/5}k^{2/5} - w = 0,$$

$$\tag{12.29}$$

$$\frac{\partial \pi}{\partial \ell} = 8p\ell^{2/5}k^{-3/5} - r = 0,$$

which can be written as

$$w = 8p\ell^{-3/5}k^{2/5} \quad \text{and} \quad r = 8p\ell^{2/5}k^{-3/5}. \tag{12.30}$$

Solving the second of these two equations for k and plugging it into the first, we get the labor demand function

$$\ell(p,w,r) = \frac{(8p)^5}{r^2 w^3}, \tag{12.31}$$

and plugging this in for ℓ in the second equation, we get the capital demand function

$$k(p,w,r) = \frac{(8p)^5}{w^2 r^3}. \tag{12.32}$$

Finally, we can derive the output supply function by plugging equations (12.31) and (12.32) into the production function $f(\ell,k) = 20\ell^{2/5}k^{2/5}$ to get

$$x(p,w,r) = 20\frac{(8p)^4}{(wr)^2} = 81920\frac{p^4}{(wr)^2}. \tag{12.33}$$

Demonstrate that solving the problem as defined in equation (12.27) results in the same solution.

Exercise 12B.12

Suppose, for instance, the economic environment is characterized by an output price of \$5 for each good I produce, and that I have to pay \$20 per hour for labor and \$10 per hour for the capital equipment I use. Plugging these values into equations (12.31), (12.32), and (12.33), we get that I will choose a production plan that hires 128 worker hours and 256 units of capital to produce 1,280 units of the output. We could then illustrate different "slices" of these functions by varying one price at a time and plotting the resulting economic relationships. For instance, we might be interested to know how output supply responds to output price, in which case we could hold w and r fixed at \$20 and \$10 and plot the function $x(p,20,10)$. Or we might be interested in how labor demand responds to changes in the wage rate and plot $\ell(5,w,10)$, or how labor demand responds to output price changes ($\ell(p, 20, 10)$) or changes in the rental rate ($\ell(5, 20, r)$). The relationships between output supply and price as well as input demand and each input's price are graphed in Graph 12.12. These are commonly known as output supply and input demand curves, and they represent the inverse of the "slices" $x(p, 20, 10)$, $\ell(5, w, 10)$, and $k(5, 20, r)$.

Exercise 12B.13*

Each panel of Graph 12.12 illustrates one of three inverse "slices" of the respective function through the production plan ($x = 1280, \ell = 128, k = 256$). What are the other two slices for each of the three functions? Do they slope up or down?

12B.3 Cost Minimization on the Way to Profit Maximization

So far, we have treated the mathematics of the producer's problem by solving it in one shot as a single profit maximization problem. In deriving the cost curves we used in Section A to illustrate profit maximization, however, we instead imagined that a producer first determines how much it would cost to produce each output level in an economically efficient way and then uses this information to find the profit maximizing output quantity (by setting price equal to marginal cost). We first illustrated this two-step method of profit maximizing in Section 11A.5 for the single-input case and then showed in part A of this chapter how to extend the logic to the two-input case. The defining difference between the single-input and two-input cases was found in the fact that technologically efficient production plans are by default economically efficient in the single-input model but not in the two-input model because when there are two inputs, there are typically many technologically efficient ways of producing each output level, only one of which is usually economically efficient given the relevant prices for labor and capital. We will now show this mathematically.

12B.3.1 Extending Cost Minimization to Multiple Inputs
For the single-input case, we illustrated the steps involved in calculating the output supply function in equations (11.17) through (11.21). The sequence of steps for accomplishing the same in the multiple-input case

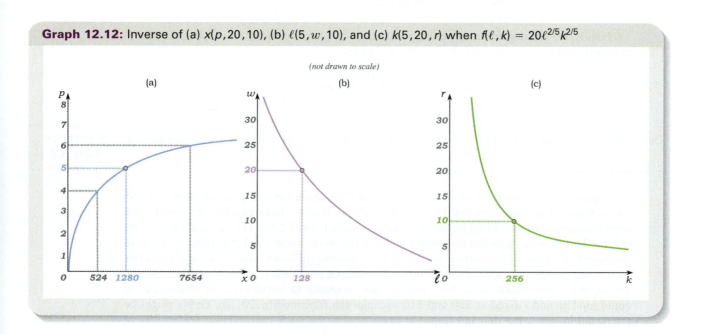

Graph 12.12: Inverse of (a) $x(p, 20, 10)$, (b) $\ell(5, w, 10)$, and (c) $k(5, 20, r)$ when $f(\ell, k) = 20\ell^{2/5}k^{2/5}$

(not drawn to scale)

differs only up to the derivation of the cost function in equation (11.18), with the remaining steps essentially the same. This is analogous to what we concluded graphically in Graph 12.8 where we developed a new way of deriving the (total) cost curve in panel (b) but then derived the supply curve in panel (c) exactly as we would have had the cost curve represented a single-input production process.

More precisely, since there are now many different technologically efficient ways of producing any output level, the derivation of the cost function now requires us to determine the economically most efficient input bundle on each isoquant (rather than simply inverting the production function as we did in Chapter 11 for the single-input case). The process we described in Section A for accomplishing this graphically had us imagine that we try to determine the smallest possible budget under which a producer could produce each level of output; or, in the language of our graphical development, the lowest isocost to reach each isoquant. Put into mathematical language, we can express this process as a constrained minimization problem in which we are attempting to ascertain the minimum cost necessary to reach each of the isoquants from our production function; i.e.,

$$\min_{\ell,k} C = w\ell + rk \text{ subject to } x = f(\ell,k). \tag{12.34}$$

The Lagrange function is then given by

$$\mathcal{L}(\ell,k,\lambda) = w\ell + rk + \lambda(x - f(\ell,k)), \tag{12.35}$$

with first order conditions

$$\frac{\partial \mathcal{L}}{\partial \ell} = w - \lambda \frac{\partial f(\ell,k)}{\partial \ell} = 0,$$

$$\frac{\partial \mathcal{L}}{\partial k} = r - \lambda \frac{\partial f(\ell,k)}{\partial k} = 0, \tag{12.36}$$

$$\frac{\partial \mathcal{L}}{\partial \lambda} = x - f(\ell,k) = 0.$$

Taking the negative terms in the first two equations to the other side and dividing the two equations by each other, we get

$$\frac{w}{r} = \frac{\partial f(\ell,k)/\partial \ell}{\partial f(\ell,k)/\partial k} = -TRS \text{ or } TRS = -\frac{w}{r}, \tag{12.37}$$

precisely what we concluded intuitively in Graph 12.7(a) where we graphically illustrated the process of minimizing the cost of producing 100 units of output and concluded that the economically efficient input bundle A had the property that the slope of the isoquant (or the technical rate of substitution (TRS)) is equal to the slope of the isocost ($-w/r$).

From the three equations in (12.36), we can now calculate the amount of labor and capital input that a cost-minimizing producer will purchase under different economic environments in the input market (w,r) *conditional on* the level of output x the producer wants to reach. Put differently, we can derive the functions

$$\ell(w,r,x) \text{ and } k(w,r,x) \tag{12.38}$$

that are known as *conditional input demand functions*. The name derives from the fact that these functions tell us how much labor and capital a producer will hire at prevailing wage and rental rates *conditional on producing x units of the output*. In Graph 12.8(a), for instance, the conditional labor and capital input demands for producing 40 units of the output when $w = 20$ and $r = 10$ are given by the input bundle B: 5 labor hours and 10 units of capital. A full graphical derivation of conditional input demand is not, however, included in part A of this chapter but is provided in Chapter 13 in Graph 13.2.

Exercise 12B.14* Did we calculate a "conditional labor demand" function when we did cost minimization in the single-input model?

Exercise 12B.15 Why are the conditional input demand functions not a function of output price p?

It is then easy to calculate the lowest possible cost at which a producer can produce 40 units of output at these input prices: simply multiply the input quantities demanded by their respective prices and add up the total expenses for labor and capital. This then gives us a cost of $200 and one point on the cost curve in Graph 12.8(b). More generally, if we know the conditional input demand functions, we can similarly derive the (total) cost function $C(w,r,x)$ that tells us the minimum cost of producing any output level for any set of input prices:

$$C(w,r,x) = w\ell(w,r,x) + rk(w,r,x). \tag{12.39}$$

Once we know the cost function, we can proceed exactly as in the single-input case to calculate the marginal cost function $MC(w,r,x)$ and the average cost function $AC(w,r,x)$ and derive the output supply $x(p,w,r)$ by setting price equal to marginal cost when price is above average cost. Finally, by then plugging this supply function back into the conditional input demands, we can derive the actual (rather than the conditional) input demand functions.

12B.3.2 An Example Continued   Consider, for example, the same production function $f(\ell,k) = 20\ell^{2/5}k^{2/5}$ that we used in Section 12B.2.3 to derive output supply and input demand directly from the profit maximization problem. Using the cost minimization approach, we first define the problem as in equation (12.34)

$$\min_{\ell,k} c = w\ell + rk \text{ subject to } x = 20\ell^{2/5}k^{2/5}. \tag{12.40}$$

The Lagrange function is then given by

$$\mathcal{L}(\ell,k,\lambda) = w\ell + rk + \lambda(x - 20\ell^{2/5}k^{2/5}), \tag{12.41}$$

with first order conditions

$$\frac{\partial \mathcal{L}}{\partial \ell} = w - 8\lambda\ell^{-3/5}k^{2/5} = 0,$$

$$\frac{\partial \mathcal{L}}{\partial k} = r - 8\lambda\ell^{2/5}k^{-3/5} = 0, \tag{12.42}$$

$$\frac{\partial \mathcal{L}}{\partial \lambda} = x - 20\ell^{2/5}k^{2/5} = 0.$$

Taking the negative terms in the first two equations to the other side and dividing the equations by one another, we get

$$\frac{w}{r} = \frac{k}{\ell} \quad \text{or just} \quad k = \frac{w}{r}\ell. \tag{12.43}$$

Substituting the latter into the third first-order condition and solving for ℓ, we then get the conditional labor demand function

$$\ell(w,r,x) = \left(\frac{r}{w}\right)^{1/2}\left(\frac{x}{20}\right)^{5/4}, \tag{12.44}$$

and substituting this back into (12.43), we can solve for the conditional capital demand function

$$k(w,r,x) = \left(\frac{w}{r}\right)^{1/2}\left(\frac{x}{20}\right)^{5/4}.$$

(12.45)

Exercise
12B.16

Suppose you are determined to produce a certain output quantity $\bar{x}$. If the wage rate goes up, how will your production plan change? What if the rental rate goes up?

The cost function is then simply the sum of the conditional input demands multiplied by input prices, or

$$C(w,r,x) = w\ell(w,r,x) + rk(w,r,x) = 2(wr)^{1/2}\left(\frac{x}{20}\right)^{5/4}.$$

(12.46)

Once we have a cost function, we can easily calculate marginal and average costs as

$$MC(w,r,x) = \frac{\partial C(w,r,x)}{\partial x} = \frac{(wr)^{1/2}}{8}\left(\frac{x}{20}\right)^{1/4}, \text{ and}$$

$$AC(w,r,x) = \frac{C(w,r,x)}{x} = \frac{(wr)^{1/2}}{10}\left(\frac{x}{20}\right)^{1/4}.$$

(12.47)

Since the Cobb–Douglas production function we used has decreasing returns to scale, $MC = AC$ when $x = 0$ and $AC < MC$ for all $x > 0$, which implies that both MC and AC curves emanate from the origin and slope up, with MC always lying above AC. Setting MC equal to price and solving for x, we then get

$$x(p,w,r) = 20\frac{(8p)^4}{(wr)^2} = 81920\frac{p^4}{(wr)^2}$$

(12.48)

just as we did in equation (12.33) from the direct profit maximization problem. Similarly, when we now plug $x(p,w,r)$ from equation (12.48) into the conditional input demands in equations (12.44) and (12.45), we get

$$\ell(p,w,r) = \frac{(8p)^5}{r^2w^3} \text{ and } k(p,w,r) = \frac{(8p)^5}{w^2r^3},$$

(12.49)

which we had previously derived as the actual input demand functions in equations (12.31) and (12.32). As expected, the one-step approach that first minimizes costs and then sets price equal to marginal cost yields the same output supply and input demand functions as the direct step profit maximization problem.

12B.4 Duality in Producer Theory

At this point, it has probably become obvious to you that there is a "duality" picture that emerges in producer theory just as there was in consumer theory in Chapter 10. In the case of consumers, the picture (Graph 10.12) had the utility maximization problem on the left-hand side and the expenditure minimization problem on the right. In the producer case, the duality picture presented in Graph 12.13 has profit maximization on the left-hand side and cost minimization on the right.

In comparing the consumer duality picture with the producer duality picture, a striking similarity emerges on the right-hand side: *the consumer expenditure minimization problem is identical to the producer cost minimization problem*, with goods prices (p_1,p_2) replaced by input prices (w,r), the consumer goods bundle (x_1,x_2) replaced by the producer input bundle (ℓ,k), and the utility function u replaced by the production function f. Notice that the

Graph 12.13: "Duality" of Profit Maximization and Cost Minimization

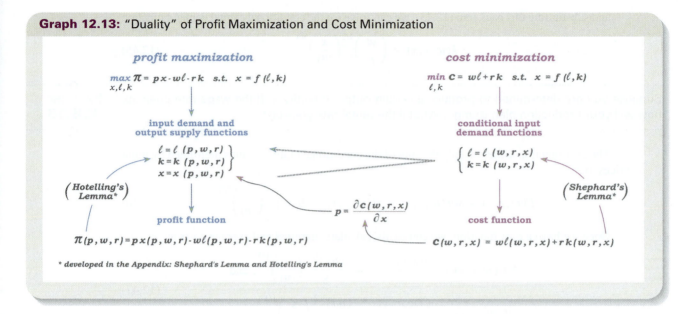

developed in the Appendix: Shephard's Lemma and Hotelling's Lemma

compensated (or Hicksian) demand functions in consumer theory are analogous to conditional input demand functions in producer theory, with the former telling us the consumption bundle a consumer would buy at different output prices assuming he or she always has just enough money to reach a given indifference curve (or utility level) and the latter telling us the input bundle a producer would buy at different input prices assuming he or she always has just enough money to reach a given isoquant (or output level). Similarly, the expenditure function in consumer theory is exactly analogous to the cost function in producer theory, with the former telling us the minimum expenditure necessary at different output prices for a consumer always to reach utility level u and the latter telling us the minimum cost necessary at different input prices for a producer always to reach output level x.

The left-hand side of the duality picture for producers differs, however, from what we developed for consumers. We have now stated the fundamental difference repeatedly: The utility function in consumer theory is the objective function under utility maximization while the production function in producer theory is the constraint under profit maximization. On the right-hand side of the picture, we demonstrated in our development of consumer theory that compensated demand curves incorporated only substitution effects. Since the right-hand side is identical for producers, we will see in the next chapter similar substitution effects for conditional input demands. In addition, consumer theory is complicated by income effects on the left-hand side of the picture, but these only arise because the utility function is maximized subject to a budget constraint. Producers face no such budget constraints; if they can make a profit by producing, the revenues pay for the costs. Thus, income effects will not appear in our discussion of producer theory as these do not emerge on the left-hand side of the producer duality picture.

CONCLUSION

In this chapter, we have moved from single-input production processes to technologies that permit two (or, in terms of the mathematics, multiple) inputs. Just as in Chapter 11, firms are still assumed to choose production plans with the goal of maximizing profit, but, with more than one input, they now face trade-offs between labor and capital depending on how much each costs. The one-step profit maximization problem becomes graphically challenging, but the two-step approach we introduced from Chapter 11 extends naturally to the two-input case. This second method for analyzing profit-maximizing choices by producers views producers as first finding the minimum cost of producing various levels of output and then choosing how much to produce in part based on the results from cost minimization and in part based on the level of output prices. The two methods—direct profit maximization and profit maximization via cost minimization—were also developed mathematically, and we demonstrated that these methods will result in the same ultimate behavioral predictions of what producers will do under different circumstances. Along the way, we developed ways of modeling multi-input production technologies in graphs of isoquants that have much in common with consumer indifference curves but that also have some quite different economic interpretations associated with them. Concepts like marginal product and returns to scale were not meaningful properties of utility functions and consumer indifference curves while they do become meaningful for production functions and isoquants. We will next proceed to a more careful look at how producer choices change as economic circumstances change.

APPENDIX: PROPERTIES OF EXPENDITURE AND PROFIT FUNCTIONS

In our development of the duality picture for producers in Graph 12.13, we have already noted that the right-hand side of this picture is identical (aside from notation) to the right-hand side of the consumer duality picture in Graph 10.12. As a result, the properties of compensated demand functions in consumer theory are identical to the properties of conditional input demand functions in producer theory, and the properties of the expenditure function in consumer theory are identical to the properties of the cost function in producer theory. Thus, the application of the Envelope Theorem to expenditure minimization in the Appendix to Chapter 10 could be repeated almost verbatim here, but we will leave this as an exercise. We can simply note that we know from our work in the Appendix to Chapter 10 that *Shephard's Lemma* holds in producer theory and can be expressed as

$$\frac{\partial C(w,r,x)}{\partial w} = \ell(w,r,x) \text{ and } \frac{\partial C(w,r,x)}{\partial r} = k(w,r,x). \tag{12.50}$$

We furthermore know by analogy to the consumer expenditure minimization problem that the cost function $C(w,r,x)$ is concave in w and r. As a result, we know that conditional input demands always slope down; i.e.,

$$\frac{\partial \ell(w,r,x)}{\partial w} \le 0 \text{ and } \frac{\partial k(w,r,x)}{\partial r} \le 0. \tag{12.51}$$

....

Can you replicate the graphical proof of the concavity of the expenditure function in the Appendix to Chapter 10 to prove that the cost function is concave in w and r?

Exercise 12B.17*

....

What is the elasticity of substitution between capital and labor if the relationships in equation (12.51) hold with equality?

Exercise 12B.18*

....

The left-hand sides of the duality pictures for consumers and producers, however, are different, which means we cannot simply apply what we know from utility maximization to profit maximization.

The Profit Function and Hotelling's Lemma

We can, however, apply the Envelope Theorem once again to prove a relationship analogous to Roy's Identity from the consumer duality picture. Applying this theorem (as we did twice in the Appendix to Chapter 10) to the profit maximization problem on the left side of Graph 12.13 leads to the following, known as *Hotelling's Lemma*:

$$\frac{\partial \pi(p,w,r)}{\partial p} = x(p,w,r), \quad \frac{\partial \pi(p,w,r)}{\partial w} = -\ell(p,w,r) \quad \text{and} \quad \frac{\partial \pi(p,w,r)}{\partial r} = -k(p,w,r), \quad (12.52)$$

where $\pi(p,w,r)$ is the *profit function* that tells us, for any set of prices, how much profit will be made by a profit-maximizing pricetaker. (This profit function, as the one defined in Chapter 11, is simply $\pi = px(p,w,r) - w\ell(p,w,r) - rk(p,w,r)$.)

Exercise 12B.19* Demonstrate how these indeed result from an application of the Envelope Theorem.

As we did in the case of expenditure functions, we can get some of the intuition for why these equations hold from some graphical development. It is easiest to do this in the context of the single-input model, but the same logic holds when there are multiple inputs.

Suppose, for instance, we know that, when I face the economic environment (p^A, w^A), my optimal production plan is (x^A, ℓ^A), giving me profit $\pi(p^A, w^A) = p^A x^A - w^A \ell^A$. In panel (a) of Graph 12.14, we illustrate this using an underlying production function $f(\ell)$, with the optimal production plan A illustrated as the tangency of the (blue) isoprofit containing price p^A and wage w^A with the production function. In panel (b) of the graph, the point A' then represents one point on the "slice" of the profit function $\pi(p, w^A)$ that holds wage fixed at w^A.

Now suppose that the price rises to p^B. If I do not alter my production plan and stick with the plan (x^A, ℓ^A), my profit will be $\pi' = p^B x^A - w^A \ell^A$, which lies on a line (represented by the green line in panel (b) of the graph) with intercept $(-w^A \ell^A)$ and slope x^A. As a producer who is not responding to the changes in my economic environment, I therefore experience an increase in my profit from $\pi(p^A, w^A)$ to π' simply by being able to sell my output at a higher price than before. In addition, however, panel (a) of the graph

Graph 12.14: Convexity (in Output Price) of the Profit Function and Hotelling's Lemma

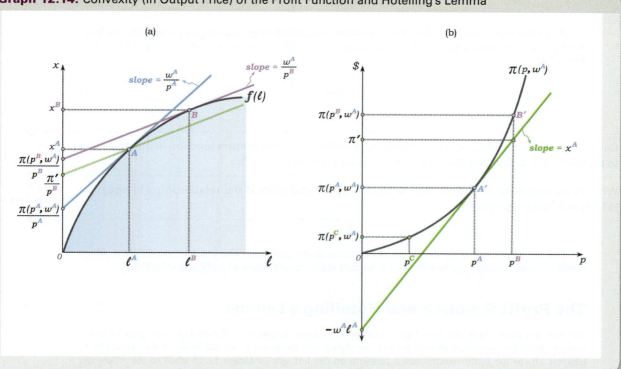

shows that my profit-maximizing production plan does *not* stay the same when the output price rises from p^A to p^B—it changes from (x^A, ℓ^A) to (x^B, ℓ^B), which results in profit $\pi(p^B, w^A) > \pi'$. Thus, at p^B, $\pi(p^B, w^A)$ lies above the green line in panel (b) of Graph 12.14.

How can you tell from panel (a) of the graph that $\pi(x^B, \ell^B) > \pi' > \pi(x^A, \ell^A)$?

Exercise
12B.20*

You can similarly show that, when price falls to p^C, $\pi(x^C, \ell^C)$ is greater than the profit indicated by the green line in panel (b) of Graph 12.14, which represents a producer who does not respond to the price change but continues to produce at the original production plan (x^A, ℓ^A).

The shape of the slice of the profit function $\pi(p, w^A)$ (which holds wage fixed at w^A) that emerges from this analysis is that of a convex function, letting us conclude that *the profit function is convex in the output price.* Furthermore, the slope of this function at p^A is $x^A = x(p^A, w^A)$, or, put differently,

$$\frac{\partial \pi(p^A, w^A)}{\partial p} = x(p^A, w^A), \tag{12.53}$$

exactly consistent with Hotelling's Lemma. The same argument holds more generally for multi-input production processes where we can show that the "slice" $\pi(p, w^A, r^A)$ must be convex in p because producers who respond to changes in price will always make more profit than producers who do not (and whose profit can be illustrated on a line such as the green line in Graph 12.14b).

You can furthermore demonstrate that slices of the profit function $\pi(p^A, w)$ that hold output price constant and vary w are also convex, although, unlike the slice that varies output price (as in Graph 12.14b), $\pi(p^A, w)$ is downward sloping. Suppose again that the economic environment is described by (p^A, w^A) and that the optimal production plan in this environment is (x^A, ℓ^A), giving a profit of $\pi(p^A, w^A) = p^A x^A - w^A \ell^A$. In Graph 12.15, point A' is the same point as A' in Graph 12.14b but viewed from a different angle (with w rather than p on the horizontal axis). Now suppose that wage increases to w^B and the producer does not change behavior. Then profit will be $\pi'' = p^A x^A - w^B \ell^A$, which lies on the blue line in the graph, a line with intercept $p^A x^A$ and slope $-\ell^A$. A producer who responds to changes in the economic environment will make at least as much profit as one who does not (but typically will make more profit). Thus, $\pi(p^A, w^B) \geq \pi''$. The same logic applied to a wage decrease to w^C suggests that

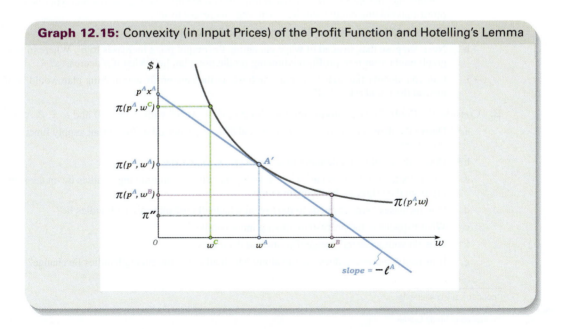

Graph 12.15: Convexity (in Input Prices) of the Profit Function and Hotelling's Lemma

$\pi(p^A, w^C)$ will also lie above the blue line. As a result, the slice of the profit function that holds price constant and varies w is a downward-sloping and convex function, with

$$\frac{\partial \pi(p^A, w^A)}{\partial w} = -\ell(p^A, w^A), \tag{12.54}$$

as suggested by Hotelling's Lemma. Again, the logic extends straightforwardly to multiple inputs.

Exercise 12B.21*   Use a graph similar to that in panel (a) of Graph 12.14 to motivate Graph 12.15.

END-OF-CHAPTER EXERCISES

12.1[†]   In our development of producer theory, we have found it convenient to assume that the production technology is homothetic.

A. In each of the following, assume that the production technology you face is indeed homothetic. Suppose further that you currently face input prices (w^A, r^A) and output price p^A, and that, at these prices, your profit-maximizing production plan is $A = (\ell^A, k^A, x^A)$.

    a.   On a graph with ℓ on the horizontal and k on the vertical, illustrate an isoquant through the input bundle (ℓ^A, k^A). Indicate where all cost-minimizing input bundles lie given the input prices (w^A, r^A).

    b.   Can you tell from what you know whether the shape of the production frontier exhibits increasing or decreasing returns to scale along the ray you indicated in (a)?

    c.   Can you tell whether the production frontier has increasing or decreasing returns to scale around the production plan $A = (\ell^A, k^A, x^A)$?

    d.   Now suppose that wage increases to w'. Where will your new profit-maximizing production plan lie relative to the ray you identified in (a)?

    e.   In light of the fact that supply curves shift to the left as input prices increase, where will your new profit-maximizing input bundle lie relative to the isoquant for x^A?

    f.   Combining your insights from (d) and (e), can you identify the region in which your new profit-maximizing bundle will lie when wage increases to w'?

    g.   How would your answer to (f) change if wage fell instead?

    h.   Next, suppose that, instead of wage changing, the output price increases to p'. Where in your graph might your new profit-maximizing production plan lie? What if p decreases?

    i.   Can you identify the region in your graph where the new profit-maximizing plan would lie if instead the rental rate r fell?

B. Consider the Cobb–Douglas production function $f(\ell, k) = A\ell^\alpha k^\beta$ with $\alpha, \beta > 0$ and $\alpha + \beta < 1$.

    a.**   Derive the demand functions $\ell(w, r, p)$ and $k(w, r, p)$ as well as the output supply function $x(w, r, p)$.

    b.**   Derive the conditional demand functions $\ell(w, r, x)$ and $k(w, r, x)$.

    c.   Given some initial prices (w^A, r^A, p^A), verify that all cost-minimizing bundles lie on the same ray from the origin in the isoquant graph.

    d.   If w increases, what happens to the ray on which all cost-minimizing bundles lie?

    e.   What happens to the profit-maximizing input bundles?

    f.   How do your answers change if w instead decreases?

    g.   If instead p increases, does the ray along which all cost-minimizing bundles lie change?

---

*conceptually challenging
**computationally challenging
[†]solutions in Study Guide

h. Where on that ray will the profit-maximizing production plan lie?

i. What happens to the ray on which all cost-minimizing input bundles lie if r falls? What happens to the profit-maximizing input bundle?

12.2 We have said that economic profit is equal to economic revenue minus economic cost, where cash inflows or outflows are not "real" economic revenues or costs unless they are in fact impacted by the economic decisions of the firm. Suppose that a firm uses both labor ℓ and capital k in its production of x, and that no output can be produced without at least some of each input.

A. In the short run, however, it can only change the level of labor input because it has already committed to a particular capital input level for the coming months. Assume that the firm's homothetic production process is one that has initially increasing but eventually decreasing returns to scale, and that the marginal product of each input is initially increasing but eventually decreasing. (The full production frontier would then look something like what we have plotted in Graph 12.16.)

    a. Suppose the firm is currently implementing the profit-maximizing production plan $A = (\ell^A, k^A, x^A)$. Given input prices w and r and output price p, what is the expression for the profit this firm earns?

    b. Now consider the short run where capital is fixed at k^A. Graph the short-run production function for this firm.

    c. Add to this graph the slice of the isoprofit plane that is tangent to the production frontier at A. Indicate its slope and vertical intercept.

    d. Given that we learned in Chapter 11 that the vertical intercept of the isoprofit is equal to profit (along that isoprofit) divided by output price, what does the vertical intercept in your graph suggest is the profit for this firm when viewed from the short-run perspective?

    e. Explain why the short-run perspective of economic profit differs in this case from the long-run perspective.

    f. *True or False*: It is possible for a firm to be earning zero profit in the long run but positive profit when viewed from a short-run perspective.

B. Suppose that, instead of the production process described in part A, the production frontier is characterized by the Cobb–Douglas production function $x = f(\ell, k) = A\ell^\alpha k^\beta$ with $\alpha + \beta < 1$ and A, α, and β all greater than zero.

Graph 12.16: Production Frontier with Two Inputs

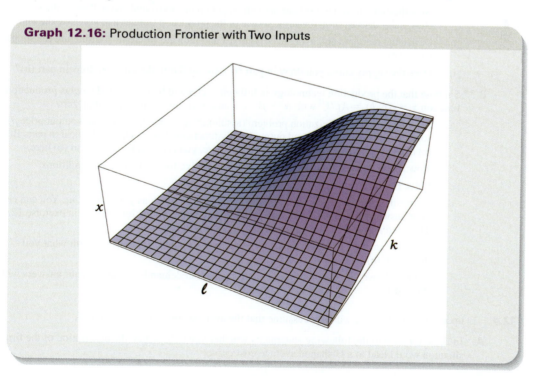

a.   Does this production process have increasing, decreasing, or constant returns to scale?

b.   Set up the profit maximization problem.

c.** Solve this for the optimal production plan.

d.   Now consider the short-run profit maximization problem for the firm that is currently employing $\bar{k}$ of capital. Write down the firm's short-run production function and its short-run profit maximization problem.

e.* Solve for the short-run labor demand and output supply functions.

f.* Suppose that the short-run fixed capital is equal to the long-run optimal quantity you calculated in part (c). Demonstrate that the firm would then choose the same amount of labor in the short run as it does in the long run.

g.   Finally, illustrate that profit is larger from the short-run perspective than the long-run perspective.

12.3   Consider again the two ways in which we can view the producer's profit maximization problem.

A. Suppose a homoethetic production technology involves two inputs, labor and capital, and that its producer choice set is fully convex.

a.   Illustrate the production frontier in an isoquant graph with labor on the horizontal axis and capital on the vertical.

b.   Does this production process have increasing or decreasing returns to scale? How would you be able to see this on an isoquant graph like the one you have drawn?

c.   For a given wage w and rental rate r, show in your graph where the cost-minimizing input bundles lie. What is true at each such input bundle?

d.   On a separate graph, illustrate the vertical slice (of the production frontier) that contains all these cost-minimizing input bundles.

e.   Assuming output can be sold at p^A, use a slice of the isoprofit plane to show the profit-maximizing production plan. What, in addition to what is true at all the cost-minimizing input bundles, is true at this profit-maximizing plan?

f.   If output price changes, would you still profit maximize on this vertical slice of the production frontier? What does the supply curve (which plots output on the horizontal and price on the vertical) look like?

g.   Now illustrate the (total) cost curve (with output on the horizontal and dollars on the vertical axis). How is this derived from the vertical slice of the production frontier that you have drawn before?

h.   Derive the marginal and average cost curves and indicate where in your picture the supply curve lies.

i.   Does the supply curve you drew in part (f) look similar to the one you drew in part (h)?

B. **Suppose that the production technology is fully characterized by the Cobb–Douglas production function $x = f(\ell, k) = A\ell^\alpha k^\beta$ with $\alpha + \beta < 1$ and A, α, and β all greater than zero.

a.   Set up the profit maximization problem (assuming input prices w and r and output price p). Then solve for the input demand and output supply functions. (Note: This is identical to parts B(b) and (c) of exercise 12.2, so if you have solved it there, you can simply skip to part (b) here.)

b.   Now set up the cost minimization problem and solve for the first order conditions.

c.   Solve for the conditional labor and capital demands.

d.   Derive the cost function and simplify the function as much as you can. (*Hint:* You can check your answer with the cost function given for the same production process in exercise 12.4.) Then derive from this the marginal and average cost functions.

e.   Use your answers to derive the supply function. Compare your answer with what you derived in (a).

f.   Finally, derive the (unconditional) labor and capital demands. Compare your answers with those in (a).

12.4   In upcoming chapters, we will often assume that the average cost curve is U-shaped.

A. Indicate for each of the following statements whether you believe that the description of the firm's situation would lead to a U-shaped average cost curve.

a. The firm's production frontier initially exhibits increasing returns to scale but, beginning at some output quantity $\bar{x}$, it exhibits decreasing returns to scale.

b. The firm's production frontier initially exhibits decreasing returns to scale but, beginning at some output quantity $\bar{x}$, it exhibits increasing returns to scale.

c. The firm's production process initially has increasing returns to scale, then, in some interval from $\underline{x}$ to $\bar{x}$, it has constant returns to scale, followed by decreasing returns to scale.

d. The firm's production process initially has increasing returns to scale, then, in some interval from $\underline{x}$ to $\bar{x}$, it has constant returns to scale, followed by once again increasing returns to scale.

e. The production process for the firm has decreasing returns to scale throughout, but, before ever producing the first unit of output, the firm incurs annually a fixed cost FC (such as a large license fee) that must be paid if production is to occur.

f. The firm incurs the same annual FC as in (e), but its production process initially has increasing returns to scale before eventually switching to decreasing returns to scale.

B. We will explore production processes with initially increasing and eventually decreasing returns to scale in exercises 12.5 and 12.6. Here, we instead focus on exploring the impact of recurring fixed costs (like annual license fees) on the shape of cost curves. Consider, as we did in exercises 12.2 and 12.3, the Cobb–Douglas production function $x = f(\ell, k) = A\ell^{\alpha}k^{\beta}$. In exercise 12.3B(d), you should have concluded that the cost function for this production process is

$$C(w, r, x) = (\alpha + \beta)\left(\frac{xw^{\alpha}r^{\beta}}{A\alpha^{\alpha}\beta^{\beta}}\right)^{1/(\alpha+\beta)}. \tag{12.55}$$

a. In problem 12.3, this cost function was derived for the case where $\alpha + \beta < 1$ and A, α, and β are all greater than zero. Is the cost function still valid for the case where $\alpha + \beta \geq 1$?

b. Are marginal and average cost curves for this production process upward or downward sloping? What does your answer depend on?

c. Suppose that the firm incurs a fixed cost FC that has to be paid each period before production starts. How does this change the (total) cost function, the marginal cost function, and the average cost function?

d. Suppose that $\alpha + \beta < 1$. What is the relationship between MC and AC now?

e. How does your answer differ if $\alpha + \beta \geq 1$? What if $\alpha + \beta = 1$?

12.5† In the absence of recurring fixed costs (such as those in exercise 12.4), the U-shaped cost curves we will often graph in upcoming chapters presume some particular features of the underlying production technology when we have more than one input.

A. Consider the production technology depicted in Graph 12.16 where output is on the vertical axis (that ranges from 0 to 100) and the inputs capital and labor are on the two horizontal axes. (The origin on the graph is the left-most corner).

a. Suppose that output and input prices result in some profit-maximizing production plan A (that is not a corner solution). Describe in words what would be true at A relative to what we described as an isoprofit plane at the beginning of this chapter.

b. Can you tell whether this production frontier has increasing, constant, or decreasing returns to scale?

c. Illustrate what the slice of this graphical profit maximization problem would look like if you held capital fixed at its optimal level k^{A}.

d. How would the slice holding labor fixed at its optimal level ℓ^{A} differ?

e. What two conditions that have to hold at the profit-maximizing production plan emerge from these pictures?

f.* Do you think there is another production plan on this frontier at which these conditions hold?

g.* If output price falls, the profit-maximizing production plan changes to once again meet the conditions you derived. Might the price fall so far that no production plan satisfying these conditions is truly profit maximizing?

h.* Can you tell in which direction the optimal production plan changes as output price increases?

B. ** Suppose your production technology is characterized by the production function

$$x = f(\ell, k) = \frac{\alpha}{1 + e^{-(\ell - \beta)} + e^{-(k - \gamma)}} \qquad (12.56)$$

where e is the base of the natural logarithm. Given what you might have learned in one of the end-of-chapter exercises in Chapter 11 about the function $x = f(\ell) = \alpha/(1 + e^{-(\ell - \beta)})$, can you see how the shape in Graph 12.16 emerges from this extension of this function?

a. Set up the profit maximization problem.

b. Derive the first order conditions for this optimization problem.

c. Substitute $y = e^{-(\ell - \beta)}$ and $z = e^{-(k - \gamma)}$ into the first order conditions. Then, with the first order conditions written with w and r on the right-hand sides, divide them by each other and derive from this an expression $y(z, w, r)$ and the inverse expression $z(y, w, r)$.

d. Substitute $y(z, w, r)$ into the first order condition that contains r. Then manipulate the resulting equation until you have it in the form $az^2 + bz + c$ (where the terms a, b, and c may be functions of w, r, α, and p). (*Hint*: It is helpful to multiply both sides of the equation by r.) The quadratic formula then allows you to derive two "solutions" for z. Choose the one that uses the negative rather than the positive sign in the quadratic formula as your "true" solution $z^*(\alpha, p, w, r)$.

e. Substitute $z(y, w, r)$ into the first order condition that contains w and then solve for $y^*(\alpha, p, w, r)$ in the same way you solved for $z^*(\alpha, p, w, r)$ in the previous part.

f. Given the substitutions you did in part (c), you can now write $e^{-(\ell - \beta)} = y^*(\alpha, p, w, r)$ and $e^{-(k - \gamma)} = z^*(\alpha, p, w, r)$. Take natural logs of both sides to solve for labor demand $\ell(w, r, p)$ and capital demand $k(w, r, p)$ (which will be functions of the parameters α, β, and γ.)

g. How much labor and capital will this firm demand if $\alpha = 100$, $\beta = \gamma = 5 = p$, $w = 20 = r$? (It might be easiest to type the solutions you have derived into an Excel spreadsheet in which you can set the parameters of the problem.) How much output will the firm produce? How does your answer change if r falls to $r = 10$? How much profit does the firm make in the two cases.

h. Suppose you had used the other "solutions" in parts (d) and (e), the ones that emerge from using the quadratic formula in which the square root term is added rather than subtracted. How would your answers to (g) be different, and why did we choose to ignore this "solution"?

12.6 We will now reconsider the problem from exercise 12.5 but will focus on the two-step optimization method that starts with cost minimization.

A. Suppose again that you face a production process such as the one depicted in Graph 12.16.

a. What do the horizontal slices—the map of isoquants—of this production process look like? Does this map satisfy our usual notion of convexity as "averages better than extremes"?

b. From this map of isoquants, how would you be able to infer the vertical shape of the production frontier? Do you think the producer choice set is convex?

c. Suppose this production frontier is homothetic. For a given set of input prices (w, r), what can you conclude about how the cost-minimizing input bundles in your isoquant map will be related to one another.

d. What can you conclude about the shape of the cost curve for a given set of input prices?

e. What will the average and marginal cost curves look like?

f. Suppose again that $A = (\ell^A, k^A, x^A)$ is a profit-maximizing production plan at the current prices (and suppose that A is not a corner solution). Illustrate the isoquant that represents the profit-maximizing output quantity x^A. Using the conditions that have to hold for this to be a profit maximum, can you demonstrate that these imply the producer is cost minimizing at A?

g. Where else does the cost-minimizing condition hold? Do the profit-maximizing conditions hold there as well?

h. What happens to output as p falls? What happens to the ratio of capital to labor in the production process (assuming the production process is indeed homothetic)?

B.** Consider the same production function as the one introduced in part B of exercise 12.5.

    a.   Write down the problem you would need to solve to determine the least cost input bundle to produce some output level x.

    b.   Set up the Lagrange function and derive the first order conditions for this problem.

    c.   To make the problem easier to solve, substitute $y = e^{-(\ell-\beta)}$ and $z = e^{-(k-\gamma)}$ into the first order conditions and solve for y and z as functions of w, r, x (and α).

    d.   Recognizing that y and z were placeholders for $e^{-(\ell-\beta)}$ and $e^{-(k-\gamma)}$, use your answers now to solve for the conditional input demands $\ell(w, r, x)$ and $k(w, r, x)$.

    e.   Derive from your answer the cost function for this firm; i.e., derive the function that tells you the least it will cost to produce any output quantity x for any set of input prices. Can you guess the shape of this function when α, β, γ, w, and r are held fixed?

    f.   Derive the marginal cost function. Can you guess its shape when α, w, and r are held fixed?

    g.   Use your expression of the marginal cost curve to derive the supply function. Can you picture what this looks like when it is inverted to yield a supply curve (with input prices held fixed)?

    h.   In (g) of exercise 12.5, you were asked to calculate the profit-maximizing output level when $\alpha = 100, \beta = \gamma = 5 = p$, and $w = r = 20$. You did so using the input demand functions calculated from the profit maximization problem. You can now use the supply function derived from the cost minimization problem to verify your answer (which should have been 91.23 units of output). Then verify that your answer is also the same as it was before (93.59) when r falls to 10.

12.7 **Everyday Application:** *To Study or to Sleep?*: Research suggests that successful performance on exams requires preparation (i.e., studying) and rest (i.e., sleep). Neither by itself produces good exam grades, but in the right combination they maximize exam performance.

A. We can then model exam grades as emerging from a production process that takes hours of studying and hours of sleep as inputs. Suppose this production process is homothetic and has decreasing returns to scale.

    a.   On a graph with hours of sleep on the horizontal axis and hours of studying on the vertical, illustrate an isoquant that represents a particular exam performance level x^A.

    b.   Suppose you are always willing to pay \$5 to get back an hour of sleep and \$20 to get back an hour of studying. Illustrate on your graph the least cost way to get to the exam grade x^A.

    c.   Since the production process is homothetic, where in your graph are the cost-minimizing ways to get to the other exam grade isoquants?

    d.   Using your answer to (c), can you graph a vertical slice of the production frontier that contains all the cost-minimizing sleep/study input bundles?

    e.   Suppose you are willing to pay \$$p$ for every additional point on your exam. Can you illustrate on your graph from (d) the slice of the "isoprofit" that gives you your optimal exam grade? Is this necessarily the same as the exam grade x^A from your previous graph?

    f.   What would change if you placed a higher value on each exam point?

    g.   Suppose a new caffeine/ginseng drink comes on the market, and you find it makes you twice as productive when you study. What in your graphs will change?

B. Suppose that the production technology described in part A can be captured by the production function $x = 40\ell^{0.25}s^{0.25}$, where x is your exam grade, ℓ is the number of hours spent studying, and s is the number of hours spent sleeping.

    a.   Assume again that you'd be willing to pay \$5 to get back an hour of sleep and \$20 to get back an hour of studying. If you value each exam point at p, what is your optimal "production plan"?

    b.   Can you arrive at the same answer using the Cobb–Douglas cost function (given in problem 12.4)?

    c.   What is your optimal production plan when you value each exam point at \$2?

    d.   How much would you have to value each exam point in order for you to put in the effort and sleep to get a 100 on the exam.

    e.   What happens to your optimal production plan as the value you place on each exam point increases?

    f.   What changes if the caffeine/ginseng drink described in A(g) is factored into the problem?

12.8† Everyday and Business Application: *Fast Food Restaurants and Grease*: Suppose you run a fast food restaurant that produces only greasy hamburgers using labor that you hire at wage w. There is, however, no way to produce the hamburgers without also producing lots of grease that has to be hauled away. In fact, the only way for you to produce a hamburger is to also produce 1 ounce of grease. You therefore also have to hire a service that comes around and picks up the grease at a cost of q per ounce.

A. Since we are assuming that each hamburger comes with 1 ounce of grease that has to be picked up, we can think of this as a single-input production process (using only labor) that produces two outputs, hamburgers and grease, in equal quantities.

a. On a graph with hours of labor on the horizontal axis and hamburgers on the vertical, illustrate your production frontier assuming decreasing returns to scale. Then illustrate the profit-maximizing plan assuming for now that it does not cost anything to have grease picked up (i.e., assume $q = 0$.)

b. Now suppose $q > 0$. Can you think of a way of incorporating this into your graph and demonstrating how an increase in q changes the profit-maximizing production plan?

c. Illustrate the marginal cost curves with and without q and then illustrate again how the cost of having grease picked up (i.e., $q > 0$) alters the profit-maximizing production choice.

d. With increasing fuel prices, the demand for hybrid cars that run partially on gasoline and partially on used cooking grease has increased. As a result, fast food chains report that they no longer have to pay to have grease picked up; in fact, they are increasingly being paid for their grease. (In essence, one of the goods you produce used to have a negative price but now has a positive price.) How does this change how many hamburgers are being produced at your fast food restaurant?

e. We have done all our analysis under the assumption that labor is the only input into hamburger production. Now suppose that labor and capital were both needed in a homothetic, decreasing returns to scale production process. Would any of your conclusions change?

f. We have also assumed throughout that producing 1 hamburger necessarily entails producing exactly 1 ounce of grease. Suppose instead that more or less grease per hamburger could be achieved through the purchase of fattier or less fatty hamburger meat. Would you predict that the increased demand for cooking grease in hybrid vehicles will cause hamburgers at fast food places to increase in cholesterol as higher gasoline prices increase the use of hybrid cars?

B. Suppose that the production function for producing hamburgers x is $x = f(\ell) = A\ell^\alpha$ where $\alpha < 1$. Suppose further that for each hamburger that is produced, 1 ounce of grease is also produced.

a. Set up the profit maximization problem assuming that hamburgers sell for price p and grease costs q (per ounce) to be hauled away.

b. Derive the number of hours of labor you will hire as well as the number of hamburgers you will produce.

c. Determine the cost function (as a function of w, q, and x).

d. Derive from this the marginal cost function.

e. Use the marginal cost function to determine the profit-maximizing number of hamburgers and compare your answer with what you got in (b).

f. How many hours of labor will you hire?

g. How does your production of hamburgers change as grease becomes a commodity that people will pay for (rather than one you have to pay to have hauled away)?

12.9* Business and Policy Application: *Investing in Smokestack Filters under Cap-and-Trade*: On their own, firms have little incentive to invest in pollution-abating technologies such as smokestack filters. As a result, governments have increasingly turned to "cap-and-trade" programs. Under these programs, discussed in more detail in Chapter 21, the government puts an overall "cap" on the amount of permissible pollution and firms are permitted to pollute only to the extent to which they own sufficient numbers of pollution permits or "vouchers." If a firm does not need all of its vouchers, it can sell them at a market price p_v to firms that require more.

A. Suppose a firm produces x using a technology that emits pollution through smokestacks. The firm must ensure that it has sufficient pollution vouchers v to emit the level of pollution that escapes the smokestacks, but it can reduce the pollution by installing increasingly sophisticated smokestack filters s.

a. Suppose that the technology for producing x requires capital and labor and, without considering pollution, has constant returns to scale. For a given set of input prices (w, r), what does the marginal cost curve look like?

b. Now suppose that relatively little pollution is emitted initially in the production process, but as the factory is used more intensively, pollution per unit of output increases, and thus more pollution vouchers have to be purchased per unit absent any pollution-abating smokestack filters. What does this do to the marginal cost curve assuming some price p_v per pollution voucher and assuming the firm does not install smokestack filters?

c. Considering carefully the meaning of "economic cost," does your answer to (b) depend on whether the government gives the firm a certain amount of vouchers or whether the firm starts out with no vouchers and has to purchase whatever quantity is necessary for its production plan?

d. Suppose that smokestack filters are such that initial investments in filters yield high reductions in pollution, but as additional filters are added, the marginal reduction in pollution declines. You can now think of the firm as using two additional inputs, pollution vouchers and smokestack filters, to produce output x legally. Does the overall production technology now have increasing, constant, or decreasing returns to scale?

e. Next, consider a graph with "smokestack filters" s on the horizontal and "pollution vouchers" v on the vertical axis. Illustrate an isoquant that shows different ways of reaching a particular output level $\bar{x}$ legally; i.e., without polluting illegally. Then illustrate the least cost way of reaching this output level (not counting the cost of labor and capital) given p_v and p_s.

f. If the government imposes additional limits on pollution by removing some of the pollution vouchers from the market, p_v will increase. How much will this affect the number of smokestack filters used in any given firm assuming output does not change? What does your answer depend on?

g. What happens to the overall marginal cost curve for the firm (including all costs of production) as p_v increases? Will output increase or decrease?

h. Can you tell whether the firm will buy more or fewer smokestack filters as p_v increases? Do you think it will produce more or less pollution?

i. *True or False*: The cap-and-trade system reduces overall pollution by getting firms to use smokestack filters more intensively and by causing firms to reduce how much output they produce.

B. Suppose the cost function (not considering pollution) for a firm is given by $C(w, r, x) = 0.5w^{0.5}r^{0.5}x$, and suppose that the trade-off between using smokestack filters s and pollution vouchers v to achieve legal production is given by the Cobb–Douglas production technology $x = f(s, v) = 50s^{0.25}v^{0.25}$.

a. In the absence of cap-and-trade policies, does the production process have increasing, decreasing, or constant returns to scale?

b. Ignoring for now the cost of capital and labor, derive the cost function for producing different output levels as a function of p_s and p_v, the price of a smokestack filter and a pollution voucher. (You can derive this directly or use the fact that we know the general form of cost functions for Cobb–Douglas production functions from what is given in problem 12.4.)

c. What is the full cost function $C(w, r, p_s, p_v)$? What is the marginal cost function?

d. For a given output price p, derive the supply function.

e. Using Shephard's Lemma, can you derive the conditional smokestack filter demand function?

f. Using your answers, can you derive the (unconditional) smokestack filter demand function?

g. Use your answers to illustrate the effect of an increase in p_v on the demand for smokestack filters holding output fixed as well as the effect of an increase in p_v on the profit-maximizing demand for smokestack filters.

12.10 Policy Application: *Taxes on Firms*: There are several ways in which governments tax firms, including taxes on labor, capital, or profits. As we will see in Chapter 19, it is not at all immediately clear whether taxes on labor or capital are paid by firms even when tax laws specify that firms will pay them. For now, we will simply assume that we know that some share of taxes on inputs are real costs to firms. It is also not clear that governments can easily identify economic profit of firms, or that price-taking firms usually make such profits (as we will see in Chapter 14). Again, we will simply assume these issues away for now.

**POLICY
APPLICATION**

A. Suppose a firm employs labor ℓ and capital k to produce output x using a homothetic, decreasing returns to scale technology.

     a.   Suppose that, at the current wage w, rental rate r and output price p, the firm has identified $A = (x^A, \ell^A, k^A)$ as its profit-maximizing production plan. Illustrate an isoquant corresponding to x^A and show how (ℓ^A, k^A) must satisfy the conditions of cost minimization.

     b.   Translate this to a graph of the cost curve that holds w and r fixed, indicating where in your isoquant graph the underlying input bundles lie for this cost curve.

     c.   Show how x^A emerges as the profit-maximizing production level on the marginal cost curve that is derived from the cost curve you illustrated in (b).

     d.   Now suppose that the government taxes labor, causing the cost of labor for the firm to increase to $(1 + t)w$. What changes in your pictures, and how will this effect the profit-maximizing production plan?

     e.   What happens if the government instead imposes a tax on capital that raises the real cost of capital to $(1 + t)r$?

     f.   What happens if instead the government imposes a tax on both capital and labor, causing the cost of capital and labor to increase by the same proportion (i.e. to $(1 + t)w$ and $(1 + t)r$)?

     g.   Now suppose the government instead taxes economic profit at some rate $t < 1$. Thus, if the firm makes pretax profit π, the firm gets to keep only $(1 - t)\pi$. What happens to the firm's profit maximizing production plan?

B. Suppose your firm has a decreasing returns to scale, Cobb–Douglas production function of the form $x = A\ell^\alpha k^\beta$ for which you may have previously calculated input, and output demands as well as the cost function. (The latter is also given in problem 12.4.)

     a.   If you have not already done so, calculate input demand and output supply functions. (You can do so directly using the profit maximization problem, or you can use the cost function given in problem 12.4 to derive these.)

     b.   Derive the profit function for this firm and check that it is correct by checking whether Hotelling's Lemma works.

     c.   If you have not already done so, derive the conditional input demand functions. (You can do so directly by setting up the cost minimization problem, or you can employ Shephard's Lemma and use the cost function given in problem 12.4.)

     d.   Consider a tax on labor that raises the labor costs for firms to $(1 + t)w$. How does this affect the various functions in the duality picture for the firm?

     e.   Repeat for a tax on capital that raises the capital cost for the firm to $(1 + t)r$.

     f.   Repeat for simultaneous taxes on labor and capital that raise the cost of labor and capital to $(1 + t)w$ and $(1 + t)r$.

     g.   Repeat for a tax on profits as described in part A(g).

Production Decisions in the Short and Long Run

Suppose you are happily profit maximizing in your firm that produces economist cards using labor and capital.[1] Suddenly you realize that a new government regulation has increased your cost of employing workers. If capital is fixed in the short run, then you now find yourself in the world of Chapter 11, making decisions along a short-run production frontier that has output changing solely with the number of workers you employ. As we have seen in Chapter 11, you will now employ fewer workers and will therefore produce fewer economist cards. But as time passes, your firm will have a chance to make some more decisions because it will have the opportunity to change the amount of capital it is using, and then to reevaluate whether it wants to hire more or fewer workers. Now you begin to find yourself in the world of Chapter 12, where both labor and capital can be adjusted to meet the new economic conditions in the labor market. Your firm's short-run problem, it turns out, is a "slice" of the more complex long-run problem you eventually face as time passes. Between this and the next chapter, our focus now turns to how your firm will transition from the short run (of Chapter 11) to the long run (of Chapter 12) as underlying conditions change.

More generally, we will ask how changes in the *economic* or *technological* environment will affect the decisions by producers over time. By the "economic environment," we will continue to mean the output and input prices that price-taking producers take as given as they try to do the best they can, and by the "technological environment" we will mean the technological processes that permit inputs to be converted to outputs as summarized by the production frontier. In the short run, we will typically assume that capital is fixed and labor is variable, but of course this mirrors an analysis where labor is fixed in the short run and capital is variable. And, we will begin to introduce a new type of "fixed" cost for firms, a cost that is not associated with an input like labor or capital. (We actually first such a "recurring fixed cost" in end-of-chapter exercise 12.4.) Our main focus in this chapter, however, remains on a firm's economic response to changing input and output prices, whereas the next chapter will consider the underlying causes of such changes in prices within a competitive industry.

---

[1]This chapter contains some of the most challenging material in the text, and instructors may wish to be selective about which part(s) to use. Chapters 11 and 12 are necessary reading for this chapter. Analogies to substitution effects in the consumer model (Chapter 7) also appear. Upcoming chapters make use mainly of material in Section 13A.1.

Changes in Producer Behavior as Conditions Change

We have already seen that it is often convenient to view profit-maximizing firms initially as cost minimizers that then use information on output prices to determine the production plan at which the difference between revenues and costs is greatest. As we begin to consider how price-taking firms adapt to changing circumstances in both the short and long run, we will therefore often consider how such changes impact the cost curves of firms. We will also find that insights about cost curves will continue to be important as we move through much of the rest of the book, and we therefore begin here (in Section 13A.1) by spending a bit of time on how cost curves are affected in changing environments. In the remainder of the chapter, we will then proceed to illustrate more directly how changes in prices and technologies impact decisions. Upcoming chapters, however, build primarily on the material in Section 13A.1.

13A.1 Different Types of Costs and Expenses in the Short and Long Run

Since we will often use changes in cost curves to arrive at conclusions about a firm's supply responses, it is essential to understand what affects these cost curves in the short and the long run. *If we define costs correctly, then it will always be the case that a price-taking firm's supply curve is that part of the marginal cost curve that lies above its average cost curve, regardless of whether we are talking about the short run or the long run.* The most important insight we will have to keep in mind, however, is that only true *economic* costs can affect a firm's behavior, even if we are tempted to call something a cost when it really isn't one. And "what counts" as a cost will differ depending on whether we are thinking about the short or long run. Section 13A.1.1 therefore explores the distinction between "costs" and "expenditures" and how this distinction relates to short- and long-run cost curves for firms. It is only after gaining some clarity on this that we can then explore the different types of costs (and expenditures) and the impact that changing costs and expenditures have on the firm's short- and long-run supply of output.

13A.1.1 Costs versus Expenses Consider again your economist card business and the increased labor costs that you are experiencing from some new labor regulation. Suppose we would like to use the picture of your short-run cost curves to determine what you will do immediately in response to the increased labor costs. We know that you have committed to a certain amount of capital, say $k = 100$, in the short run, which means you will have to write a check for $100r$ to pay for this capital. There is no doubt that you'd prefer not to have to write this check, but the question we have to confront as we decide whether to include $100r$ as a cost in our analysis is not whether you like writing checks. The question is whether writing this particular check is at all impacted by your decision of whether to produce more or less (or not at all). And the answer is that once you have committed to rent the 100 units of capital in the short run, you have to write the check for $100r$ *regardless* of what decisions you make in your firm, even if you decide not to use any of the capital. This means that your expense on the 100 units of capital is *not* a real cost of doing business in the short run; it is not an *economic* cost that affects your short run decisions in any way. For this reason it is often called a " *sunk* cost," "sunk" in the sense that you have to pay it no matter what you do.

There is much confusion that arises in microeconomics courses because we often slip into the bad habit of using the term "cost" when we don't actually mean "economic cost." We will try to avoid this confusion by adopting the following convention: Whenever the expenses we refer to are 100% true economics costs (such as the short-run cost of labor in our example), we will call them "costs." But if the expenses include sunk "costs" (such as the check you write for the capital you committed to in our example), we will call them "expenditures" or "expenses" (even if some fraction of them represents real costs). Sometimes, textbooks will differentiate between "economic" and "accounting" costs, with "accounting costs" being similar to what we simply call expenses.

So let's return to our example where your current capital is fixed at $k = 100$ but labor can be adjusted as you are free to hire and fire workers in the short run. Panel (a) of Graph 13.1 illustrates the short-run *cost* curve $C_{k=100}$ that is relevant for the short-run decisions your firm makes when it cannot vary the level of capital it is using. If we want to illustrate the total checks you write in your firm, including the wages you pay to your workers as well as the expense of renting the capital, we can do so by showing the fixed expense on capital $FE_{k=100} = \$100r$ on the vertical axis. Even if the firm produces nothing, it will incur this expense, and the expense does not change as you start producing. The rest of the total expenditure curve $TE_{k=100}$ then simply lies exactly $\$100r$ above the $C_{k=100}$ curve, and it includes real economic costs as well as (sunk)

Graph 13.1: Short-Run Expenditure and Cost Curves

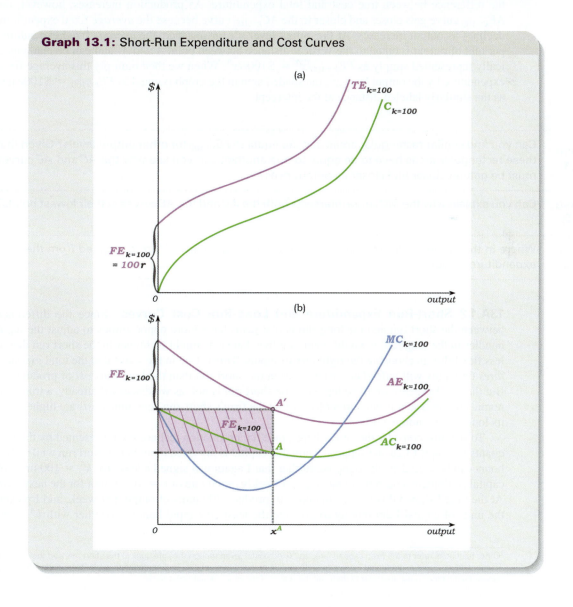

expenditures. For this reason, we call it an "expenditure curve" because it is polluted by expenses that are not real economic costs in the short run and are therefore "sunk" or "irrelevant" as you make short-run decisions.[2]

Panel (b) of Graph 13.1 then translates these curves into marginal and average cost (and expenditure) curves. Since the fixed expenditures have to be paid even if we produce no output, they are never an *additional* cost (or expense) incurred from producing one more unit of the output. The marginal cost curve $MC_{k=100}$, defined as the *additional* cost incurred from producing additional units of output when capital is fixed at 100, thus does *not* include the fixed expenditure of renting the 100 units of capital. It is simply the slope of the $C_{k=100}$ curve (just as it was in previous chapters). Similarly, the *average cost curve* $(AC_{k=100})$ that begins at roughly the intercept of the marginal cost curve represents only true economic costs given that capital is fixed at 100. Finally, the *average expenditure curve* $(AE_{k=100})$, derived from the $TE_{k=100}$ curve in panel (a), has an intercept that lies $FE_{k=100}$ above the intercept of the other 2 curves because at the first unit of output, the difference between the average cost and the average expenditure is exactly equal to the difference between true cost and total expenditure. As production increases, however, the $AE_{k=100}$ curve gets closer and closer to the $AC_{k=100}$ curve because the *average* fixed expenditure declines as output increases. At the output level x^A, for instance, the *average* fixed expenditure per unit of output is equal to the vertical distance between point A and A' and can be mathematically represented simply as $FE_{k=100}/x^A = \$100r/x^A$. When we then multiply this average fixed expenditure by the output level x^A, the shaded area in the graph is equal to $FE_{k=100} = \$100r$ just as the similarly labeled distance at the intercept.

Exercise 13A.1   Can you find similar rectangular areas that are equal to $FE_{k=100}$ for other output levels? Given that these rectangular areas have to be equal to one another, can you see why the AC and AE curves must be getting closer and closer as output rises?

Exercise 13A.2   Can you explain why the MC curve intersects both the AC and the AE curves at their lowest points?

Exercise 13A.3   Where in the graph would you locate the "marginal expenditure" curve (derived from the total expenditure curve)?

13A.1.2 Short-Run Expenditure and Long-Run Cost Curves
Since the difference between the short run and the long run is that firms have more opportunities to adjust the input bundles in the long run, it would seem intuitive that costs might be higher in the short run due to less flexibility in choosing the right mix of inputs. This is true in the sense that the total *expenditures* on inputs will indeed never be lower in the short run than the long run *cost* of production. But the fixed expense on fixed inputs in the short run is not, as we discussed already, a true economic cost, and so it is not correct to say that the firm's short-run economic *costs* are higher than its long-run economic costs.

To see this, consider the case where I face the production technology represented by the isoquants in Graph 13.2a and suppose again that capital is my fixed input in the short run while labor hours can be varied easily. Suppose further that I again just signed a lease for $k^A = 100$ units of capital equipment, committing me to pay a weekly rental rate of $r = 10$ per unit for the next year. At the time I signed this lease, I intended to produce 200 units of output per week, and I picked the units of capital I am renting to give me the least cost input bundle (together with $\ell^A = 50$

---

[2]Other textbooks refer to the fixed expenditures as "fixed costs" even though they are sunk in the short run, and they call our *TE* expenditure curve a "total cost" curve even though it includes sunk costs. To differentiate such "total costs" from the real economic costs, such treatments then call the real cost curve a "variable cost curve."

Graph 13.2: Short-Run Expenditure versus Long-Run Cost Curves

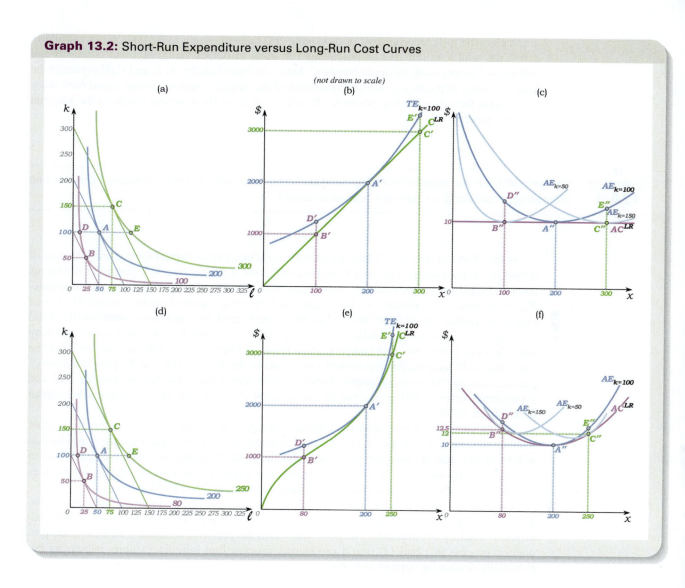

labor hours) for producing 200 output units assuming a wage rate of $w = 20$. This is graphed in panel (a) of Graph 13.2 as the input bundle A on the (blue) isoquant for 200 units of output.

   Now suppose that I change my mind and want to produce 100 instead of 200 units of output. Ideally, I would like to reduce both my labor and capital inputs to reach the least cost way of producing 100 units of output as represented by input bundle B, and in the long run that is precisely what I will do. But in the short run, I have already committed to rent 100 units of capital, which implies that I will use the input bundle D instead of B in the short run. Similarly, if I change my mind again and want to produce 300 units of the output instead, I will choose input bundle E in the short run even through I will choose input bundle C in the long run. Notice that I am constrained in the short run to operate on the slice of my isoquant picture that keeps capital fixed at 100 units.

   In panel (b) of the graph, we then plot the costs and expenditures necessary to pay for the input bundles labeled in panel (a) while continuing to assume that the rental rate of capital is $10 and the wage rate is $20. The input bundle A, for instance, employs 50 hours of labor and 100 units of capital costing a total of $2,000. Since the input bundle A results in output of 200, panel (b) of the graph plots the total long-run cost of producing 200 units of output as $2,000. We can similarly derive the total long-run cost of producing 100 units of output using the input bundle B and 300 units of output using the input bundle C. Since the input bundles A, B, and C all represent the least cost ways of producing different quantities of the output *assuming we can adjust both labor and capital*, the corresponding points A', B', and C' in panel (b) represent points on the long-run (total) cost curve.

Exercise 13A.4   Can you tell from the shape of the long-run (total) cost curve whether the production process has increasing, decreasing, or constant returns to scale?

In the short run, however, I have exactly the right quantity of capital to produce 200 units of output in the least costly way, which means I will incur a greater overall *expense* for the inputs labor and capital if I try to produce more or less than 200 units of output. You can see this immediately in panel (a) of Graph 13.2 by noticing that the input bundle D (which uses 100 units of capital to produce 100 units of output) lies above the isocost line containing input bundle B and thus requires greater overall "budget" to produce 100 units of output than is necessary in the long run. The same is true for input bundle E. As a result, if I have exactly 100 units of capital in the short run, I will incur higher expenditures on inputs in the short run than in the long run unless I produce exactly 200 units of output. Panel (c) then shows the same for the average cost and expenditure curves, with the long-run AC curve below the short-run $AE_{k=100}$ curve when capital is held fixed at 100 units.

I could, of course, derive short-run total and average expenditure curves assuming some other fixed level of capital, and in each case I would conclude that the short-run expense of production will be higher than the long-run cost except for the level of output for which the fixed level of capital is exactly the "right" level in the long run. The lighter-colored average expenditure curves in panel (c) illustrate this for the case when capital is fixed at 50 and 150 units.

The lower set of panels of Graph 13.2 then repeat the same derivation of short-run expenditure and long-run cost curves from a production technology that has the same shapes but different labeling of isoquants. The new labels turn the previous constant returns to scale production process in panel (a) into a production process that initially exhibits increasing but eventually decreasing returns to scale.

Exercise 13A.5   Verify the derivation of cost curves in panels (e) and (f) in Graph 13.2. In what sense is the relationship between short-run expenditure and long-run cost curves similar in this case to the case we derived in the top panels of the graph for constant returns to scale production processes?

Exercise 13A.6   Where would you find the long-run marginal cost curve in panel (f) of the Graph?

Exercise 13A.7*   A textbook author (not me!) once told his publisher to produce a graph such as panel (f) of Graph 13.2 and explained that he wanted the short-run average expenditure curves corresponding to different levels of fixed capital to each be tangent at their lowest point to the U-shaped long-run average cost curve. The graphics artist (who knew nothing about economics) came back to the author and sheepishly explained that such a graph cannot logically be drawn. What was wrong in the author's instructions?

13A.1.3 To Be or Not to Be: Shutting Down versus Exiting the Industry   Using the graphs we have developed so far, we can now determine how low an output price a firm is willing to tolerate and still produce, and at what point the price has just fallen so far that it is not worth going on because profit would be negative. The answer will differ a bit depending on whether we are thinking about the short or the long run because a firm cannot actually disappear entirely in the short run since it is stuck for some period with a fixed level of capital. We will therefore say that a firm "shuts down" production if it stops producing in the short run, and it "exits the industry" if it ceases production in the long run. You can picture "shutting down" as locking the doors of the factory and nailing the sign "Closed for Business" on them, while "exiting the industry" means you have sold the factory (or not renewed your lease) and thus all evidence of your firm has disappeared.

We will see shortly that a firm's "shut down price" is lower than the "exit price" because the firm can more easily cover its economic costs in the short run since these don't include the fixed expense of capital that has to be paid regardless of what the firm does. You may already know that you won't renew the lease to your factory once the lease comes up for renewal, but it may still be worth it to produce in the meantime until you get a chance to unload the factory by not renewing the lease. You'll often see this with new restaurants that try to break into the local restaurant market: Within a few weeks of opening, some restaurants are buzzing with activity and others attract few customers. You can tell pretty quickly which restaurants won't be around a year from now, but often the restaurants continue to stay open for some period even though it is clear that not enough people show up for the restaurant to remain viable. Do the restaurant owners not see what you can see—that their restaurant just isn't going to make it? Probably not; rather, the owner probably had to sign a lease for 6 months or a year and can't get out of the lease, which makes the lease an expense the owner does not have to cover in the short-run in order to justify staying open. Put differently, short-run profit may be positive even though long-run profit is negative, which implies that it is economically rational to remain open in the short run but not to renew the lease in the long run.

In terms of our graphs, we can identify the "shut down" and "exit" prices by simply locating the lowest point of the average cost curves in the short and long run because it is *always* the case that a firm produces so long as price is not below its average cost curve (assuming we have not included expenses that aren't really costs). In the short-run picture of Graph 13.1, this lowest point lies on the $AC_{k=100}$ curve; in our long-run picture of Graph 13.2, it lies on the AC^{LR} curves of panels (c) and (f). We can then combine the insights of the short-run picture (Graph 13.1) and the long-run curves (of Graph 13.2) to see the relationship between the short-run "shut down" price and the long-run "exit" price.

In particular, consider Graph 13.3. In this graph, we assume that the firm is currently producing 200 units of output using the input bundle A from panel (d) of Graph 13.2, precisely the cost-minimizing input bundle for this output level. This implies that the (short-run) average expenditure curve $AE_{k=100}$ touches the long-run average cost curve AC^{LR} at the output level 200 but exceeds it at every other output level (as first derived in panel (f) of Graph 13.2). From our short-run picture in Graph 13.1, we also know that the short-run average cost curve $AC_{k=100}$ lies below the short-run $AE_{k=100}$ curve (because it does not include the fixed expenditure on capital), and we can now include this short-run average *cost* curve as well as the short-run marginal cost ($MC_{k=100}$) curve in Graph 13.3. The bolded portion of the $MC_{k=100}$ curve is then the short-run supply curve, which clearly extends below the lowest point of the AC^{LR} curve. Thus, the short-run "shut down" price $\bar{p}$ lies below the long-run "exit" price (which is $10 in the graph). If the output price falls into the range from $\bar{p}$ to $10, the firm will therefore stay open in the short run but will exit in the long run.

Demonstrate that the firm's (long-run) profit is zero when $p = 10$.

Exercise
13A.8

Graph 13.3: "Shut Down" versus "Exit" Price

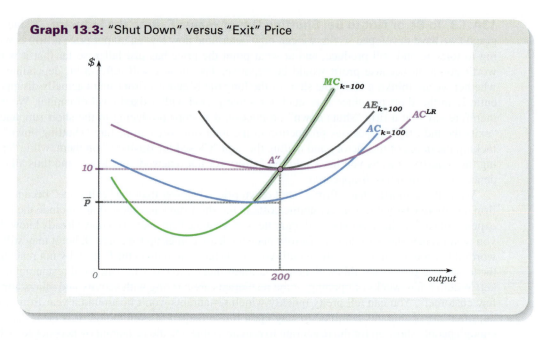

To see a bit more clearly how a firm (like those new restaurants that just don't draw much business) can stay open in the short run but exit in the long run, consider Graph 13.4, which largely replicates the short-run cost and expenditure curves we derived in Graph 13.1b and that are contained in Graph 13.3. Suppose that the price of the output is p^*. If this firm produces at all, it will produce x^* where the additional cost of producing one more unit of output is just equal to the additional revenue from selling that unit. This would generate total revenue of p^*x^*, the shaded blue rectangle in the graph. At the output level x^*, the firm would incur average costs exactly equal to p^*, giving total (short-run) costs equal to the same blue rectangle. Thus, the firm is making enough revenues to cover exactly its short-run economic costs. It does not, however, make enough to cover its fixed expenditure $FE_{k=100}$ (represented by the magenta area) for the

Graph 13.4: Output Supply in the Short Run

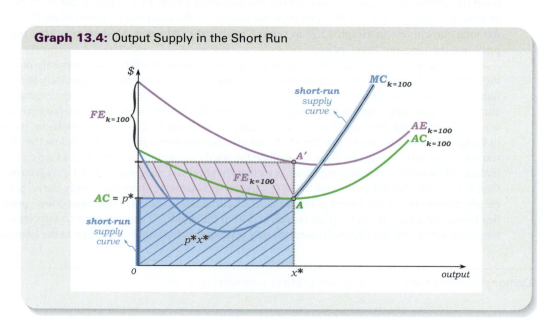

fixed amount of capital it has to rent in the short run. But since the firm has to pay $FE_{k=100}$ regardless of whether or not it produces, it does not have to recover $FE_{k=100}$ in the short run in order to produce. Put differently, it has to write the check for $FE_{k=100}$ whether it produces or not, and so it's no more necessary that you cover this expense with your short-run revenues than it is that you cover your grocery bill with those revenues. It is for this reason that we have said the fixed expenditures associated with inputs that are fixed in the short run are not economic costs: They do not impact economic decisions of the firm in the short run. Since *economic profit* is defined as the difference between economic revenues and economic costs, economic profit is equal to exactly zero in the short run when the output price falls to the lowest point of the short-run $AC_{k=100}$ curve.

Can you illustrate that short-run economic profits will be positive when price falls between the lowest points of the $AC_{K=100}$ and the AC^{LR} curves even though total expenditures exceed total revenues? What will long-run economic profits be in that price range?

Exercise 13A.9

In many beach resorts on the East Coast of the United States, business is brisk in the summers but slow in the winters. In summers, resort rentals are sold out at high weekly rates, but in winters they are only partially rented at much lower rates. If you were to calculate expenses and revenues on a monthly basis, you would almost certainly find these resorts with revenues greater than expenses in the summers and expenses greater than revenues in the winters. How come these resorts don't just shut down in winters?

Exercise 13A.10

13A.1.4 (Long-Run) Fixed Costs

In the short run, we have made a point of using the term "fixed expenditures (*FE*)" for the "costs" of fixed inputs that become variable in the long run. Such fixed expenditures are not true economic costs as long as they have to be paid regardless of any choices the firm makes and thus have no impact on short-run economic behavior. And, since they arise from inputs that can be varied as time goes by, these expenses cease to be "fixed" when they become real economic costs in the long run. Thus, fixed *expenditures* on inputs that cannot be varied in the short run do not become fixed *costs* in the long run so long as these inputs can in fact be varied in the long run. Such costs are then referred to as (long-run) *variable costs* since they "vary with output" in the long run. And all the economic costs we have dealt with so far, including the costs associated with variable labor input, have been of this type. As such, changes in such costs affect both the long-run marginal and average cost curves. There are, however, certain expenses a firm might incur that are "fixed" (in the sense that they do not vary with the level of output) but that actually represent real economic costs that could be avoided in the long run if the firm chose not to produce at all. We will call such costs *fixed costs that are avoidable only by exiting the industry* or simply *long-run fixed costs,* and it is because they are avoidable by exiting the industry that they are real economic costs in the long run.

Suppose, for instance, the government requires an annual payment for a license to produce some output. The license simply allows the firm to produce, but the amount charged for the license does not depend on how much is produced. When you get your hair cut, for instance, you might have noticed your hairdresser's beautician license prominently displayed. Your auto mechanic might have to have a license to do car inspections, and your taxi driver in New York needs to have a license called a medallion to give you a ride, etc. Such licenses are typically renewable on an annual basis, with a license fee charged on, for instance, January 1 of each year. In some instances (like the taxi cab medallions), the cost of such licenses can be quite substantial.

Once you have paid for (or committed to pay for) such an annual license in your business, the expense of the license becomes a sunk "cost." But as January 1 approaches each year, you have a real economic decision to make: Will you renew the license and stay in business next year, or will you exit the business and stop producing? As you make this decision, you will want to look at all your economic costs including the cost of the license. But the only way to avoid paying the license is to abandon your business and stop producing; thus, we have a *fixed cost avoidable only by exiting*. As you approach your decision of whether to renew your license, you will then face cost curves for the coming year that look like those in Graph 13.5, with the *AC* curve having a different intercept than the *MC* curve because of the fixed license fee. The dashed green curve is the average cost curve *excluding* the fixed cost of the license fee, labeled *AVC* for "average variable cost." It is dashed in the graph because it is not a curve of any real relevance for the firm's long-run decision because the firm will produce (as always) along *MC* as long as output price lies above the lowest point of its true average cost curve (which is *AC* in this case).

Exercise 13A.11   Compare Graphs 13.4 and 13.5. Why is the supply curve beginning at the higher average curve in 13.5 and on the lower one in 13.4?

A second type of cost that is a fixed cost in the real world is the cost associated with an input that always remains fixed, in both the short and long run. Different entrepreneurs may, for instance, possess different levels of "entrepreneurial skill" as they manage the various inputs in their firm. Facing the same technology, some producers are simply better at figuring out how to motivate workers or get other organizational objectives accomplished. Yet that entrepreneurial skill, unlike the number of labor hours or units of capital hired by the producer, is in fixed supply within the firm. Bill Gates can double the number of workers in Microsoft and double the equipment and facility space as he increases production, but he cannot replicate himself. His leadership or entrepreneurial skill is a fixed input for Microsoft, and the opportunity cost of hiring this fixed input is a fixed cost. If there is such an input that is simply always fixed as long as the firm is in production, it becomes a fixed cost just like the license fee, with Bill Gates having to decide each year whether to stay in production and employ his talents in Microsoft or to close shop and employ his talents elsewhere. Most real-world production processes probably have some such fixed input, and it is for this reason that

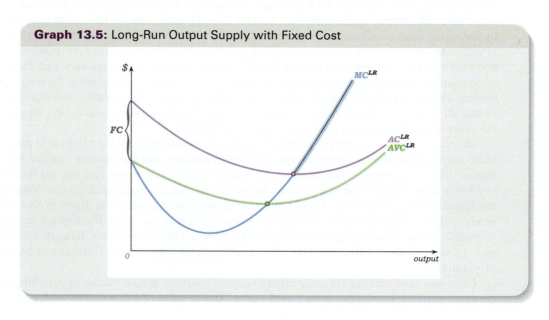

Graph 13.5: Long-Run Output Supply with Fixed Cost

Table 13.1: Examples of Costs and Expenses

EXAMPLE	IMPACT ON FIRM		EFFECT ON *MC* AND *AC*	
	SHORT RUN	LONG RUN	SHORT RUN	LONG RUN
Annual License Fee	Fixed Expense	Fixed Cost	None	*AC*
Cost of Capital	Fixed Expense	(Variable) Cost	None	*AC, MC*
Cost of Labor	(Variable) Cost	(Variable) Cost	*AC, MC*	*AC, MC*

it is usually (although not always) not possible for a firm simply to keep doubling all its inputs to produce twice as much output.[3]

13A.1.5 Overview of Cost and Expense Types
Keeping track of the different types of cost and expenditure changes that might impact firm behavior can get confusing, but in essence, we have really identified only three types of costs that will change what firms do. Table 13.1 identifies examples of each. The first example is the annual license fee that we just discussed in the previous section. It is a fixed *expense* in the short run because there is nothing the firm can do to avoid paying it right now, but it becomes a fixed *cost* in the long run as the firm gets to decide whether to stay in business and renew the license or to exit the industry. Thus, the only cost curves that can possibly be affected by the license fee are those in the long run, but among those, the *MC* curve does not change because the license fee does not actually change the cost of producing additional output, only the cost of staying in business and beginning production. This is illustrated in panel (a) of Graph 13.6; an increase in the license fee raises the long-run average cost curve from *AC* to *AC'* without impacting the (long-run) marginal cost curve. As a result, the long-run supply curve for the firm does not move; it simply becomes "shorter" as the dashed portion disappears.

Graph 13.6: Three Types of Cost Changes

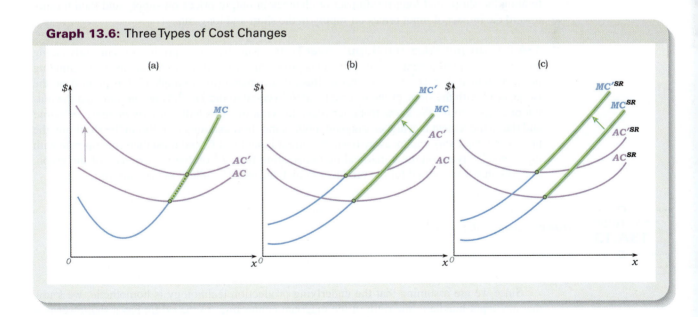

------

[3]Since I am writing these words on a Mac and not a Windows-based PC, I should probably have used Steve Jobs as an example instead of Bill Gates. But Mac folks are generous folks, and occasionally we pretend that there is actual value in the Microsoft world.

The second type of cost listed in the table is the cost of capital, an input we are assuming is fixed in the short run. As we argued in Section 13A.1.1, this is not a real cost in the short run. The only cost curves that can be affected are therefore those in the long run, but this time, the *MC* curve is affected in addition to the (total) cost curve *C* and the average cost curve *AC*. This is because, unlike the license fee, the amount we have to pay for capital will increase as we produce more when capital is variable in the long run. An increase in the cost of capital is then illustrated in panel (b) of Graph 13.6, with the long-run *AC* curve shifting up and the *MC* curve shifting as well.

Finally, the table lists the cost of labor, an input that is assumed to be variable in both the short and long run. Since the amount we must pay for labor depends on how much we produce in both the short and long run, it is always a real cost, with all the cost curves affected in the short and long run. This is illustrated for the short run in panel (c) of Graph 13.6 for an increase in labor costs. (The long-run cost curves are similarly changed.) Whether the lowest point of the long-run *AC* curve shifts to the left or the right will depend on the underlying technology, and the degree to which the firm can substitute capital and labor. We will explore this a bit further in the next section.

Exercise 13A.12 Can we say for sure that the lowest point of the long-run *AC* curve will shift to the right when the license fee increases?

13A.2 Output Supply in the Short and Long Run

In our discussion of short- and long-run cost curves, we have already begun to illustrate how changes in input and output prices affect output supply across time by focusing on the difference between "shutting down" and "exiting." We'll now think about this a bit more directly, first investigating the short- and long-run impact of changes in output prices on supply and then turning toward the impact of input prices on supply in the short and long run.

13A.2.1 Output Price and Supply over Time   Suppose that a producer is currently facing the economic environment (w^A, r^A, p^A) and is producing at his or her long-run profit-maximizing production plan $A = (\ell^A, k^A, x^A)$. This is illustrated in panel (a) of Graph 13.7 as point A on the isoquant x^A with the slope of the isocost $(-w^A/r^A)$ equal to the TRS^A. Now suppose that the output price rises to p'. We know from our previous work that this will cause *an increase in output* and thus a movement to a higher isoquant, both in the short and long run. But in the short run, the producer cannot vary capital away from its current input level k^A and must therefore operate with input bundles lying on the horizontal line emanating from k^A on the vertical axis of the graph. Suppose that it is optimal for the producer to pick the input bundle B in the short run.

Exercise 13A.13 *True or False:* $p' MP_\ell^B = w^A$.

Since we are assuming that the underlying production technology is homothetic, we know that any input bundle to the right of the diagonal connecting to the origin has a shallower isoquant slope than the slope of the isoquant at A (which is equal to $-w^A/r^A$). Thus,

$$TRS^B > -\frac{w^A}{r^A} \tag{13.1}$$

Graph 13.7: Short-Run versus Long-Run Supply Curves

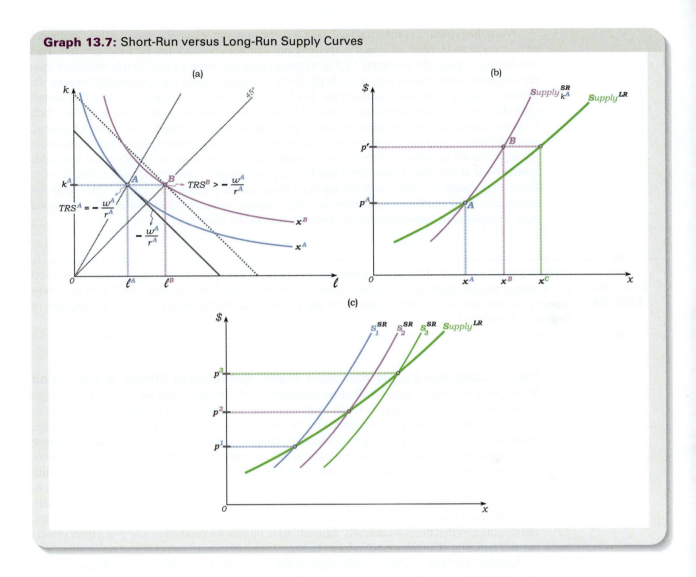

or, given that $-TRS = (MP_\ell/MP_k)$

$$\frac{MP_\ell^B}{MP_k^B} < \frac{w^A}{r^A}. \tag{13.2}$$

Multiplying the denominator and numerator of (MP_ℓ/MP_k) by p' leaves the fraction unchanged, which implies that we can also write what we have concluded as

$$\frac{p'MP_\ell^B}{p'MP_k^B} < \frac{w^A}{r^A}. \tag{13.3}$$

At the same time, since B is the short-run optimum when labor is fully variable, the marginal revenue product of labor at B must be equal to the wage w^A, or $p'MP_\ell^B = w^A$. Thus, the inequality (13.3) can hold only if $p'MP_k^B > r^A$; i.e., the marginal revenue product of capital at B is greater than the rental rate. Put differently, *at the short run optimum B the producer can hire additional capital at a cost that is less than the additional revenue this capital will produce.*

When the producer is able to adjust capital in the long run, he or she will therefore hire more of it, causing an increase in output in the long run that goes beyond the short-run increase. This is reflected in panel (b) of Graph 13.7 in a (green) long-run supply curve that is shallower than the (magenta) short-run supply curve. In particular, the graph shows the relationship between the short-run supply curve that holds capital fixed at k^A and the long-run supply curve that allows capital to vary. The two curves intersect at x^A because that is precisely the output level for which k^A is the correct long-run quantity of capital given the current wage and rental rates. Of course, we could have started out at some other initial price and the corresponding initial profit-maximizing input bundle and derived a similar relationship between the short-run supply curve that holds capital fixed at that initial input level and the long-run supply curve that allows capital to vary. Panel (c) of Graph 13.7 illustrates this for three initial output prices p^1, p^2, and p^3. Thus, *long-run supply curves are shallower than short-run supply curves, indicating that producers will respond more to changes in output price in the long run than in the short run.*

Exercise 13A.14

If the marginal product of labor increases as additional capital is hired in the long run, can you tell whether the producer will hire additional labor (beyond ℓ^B) in the long run?[4] Can you then identify the minimum distance above A on the ray through A the long-run optimal isoquant in Graph 13.7a will lie?

13A.2.2 Long-Run Supply and Input Prices: Substitution Effects in Production

While changes in output prices will cause producers to alter their production behavior *along supply curves*, changes in input prices will *shift supply curves* because such changes cause shifts in cost curves. These shifts are complicated by the fact that, as the relative prices of inputs change, producers will (at least in the long run) adjust the ratio of capital to labor that they use to produce any given level of output. This was an issue that did not arise in the single-input model since there was only a single technologically efficient way of producing any level of output without wasting inputs. Now, however, we have a whole isoquant of possible input combinations that all represent technologically efficient ways of producing a given output level. Which of these technologically efficient input bundles is economically efficient then depends on the relative prices of the inputs, and this implies that the economically efficient input bundle for producing any given level of output will typically change as input prices change.

Suppose, for instance, that we initially face the input prices $w = 20$ and $r = 10$ and the production frontier is represented by the isoquant map in Graph 13.8a (which is the same map we first introduced in Graph 12.8a). Since the isoquant map is homothetic, the economically efficient ratio of inputs will be the same for any output level and can be located along a ray from the origin where isocosts with slope $-w/r = -2$ are tangent to each isoquant. Now suppose that the wage rate falls to $w' = 10$. The new economically efficient input bundles on each of the isoquants in the graph would then lie at tangencies with isocosts that have a slope of -1 rather than -2, causing us to slide down to a new input bundle on each of the isoquants with economically efficient input bundles again lying on a ray from the origin. Put differently, a change in input prices will cause us to *substitute away from the input that has become relatively more expensive and toward the input bundle that has become relatively cheaper.*

The change in isocosts when w falls from \$20 to \$10 is represented in panel (a) of Graph 13.8 along the isoquant labeled 100 as a change in the tangency at the initial isocost at input bundle C

---

[4]At the end of the chapter, we will show that the marginal product of labor does not necessarily increase as more capital is hired. Whether it does or does not depends on the substitutability of capital and labor in production.

Graph 13.8: Costs and Input Substitution Effects

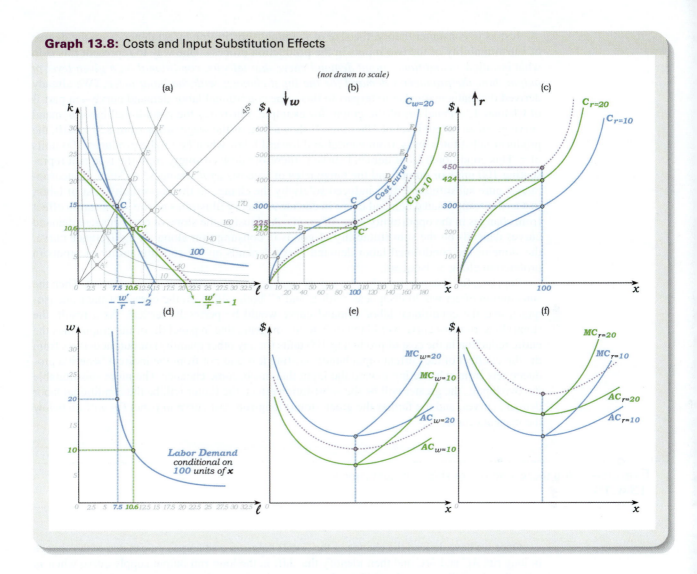

to the tangency at the new isocost at bundle C', with all other economically efficient input bundles for other isoquants lying on the ray connecting the origin with bundle C'. Each of the new input bundles is now cheaper, both because the wage has fallen *and* because we have substituted away from capital and toward the cheaper labor. This is represented in a change in the (total) long-run cost curve in panel (b) from the initial blue curve (which is identical to the one derived in Graph 12.8b) to the final green cost curve. The dotted magenta curve in between represents the change in total costs that would have occurred had the producer not changed input bundles but simply experienced lower costs because the wage had fallen, with the remaining drop in total costs due to the substituting behavior induced by the change in relative input prices.

Can you see in panel (a) of Graph 13.8 the cost of not substituting from C to C'? Can you verify that the numbers in panel (b) are correct?

Exercise 13A.15

Just as in consumer theory, the size of the input substitution effect depends on the degree of substitutability of the two inputs in the production process. One way to represent this is in what is called a *conditional input demand curve that tells us, conditional on a given level of output, how the producer's demand for the input changes with the input price.* (We already derived the mathematical counterpart to this—the conditional labor demand curve—in part B of Chapter 12.) Panel (d) of the graph, for example, illustrates the conditional labor demand curve given an output level of 100 units. It shows that, as the wage drops from \$20 to \$10, the producer substitutes away from capital and toward labor when he or she produces 100 units of x. This conditional labor demand curve is therefore derived solely from the isoquant representing 100 units of output and the tangencies of isocosts as w changes. As such, it incorporates a pure substitution effect induced solely by the change in the opportunity cost of labor, just as the compensated demand curve in consumer theory illustrates a pure substitution effect from changes in the opportunity costs of goods. And just as the slope of compensated demand curves depends on the substitutability of goods in consumption along an indifference curve, the slope of the conditional labor demand curve depends on the substitutability of inputs in production along an isoquant.

Suppose, for instance, that the two inputs were perfect complements in production. Then the substitution effect would disappear, with C and C' both falling on the corner of the same isoquant, and the conditional labor demand curve would be perfectly vertical. As a result, the (total) long-run cost curve would fall only to the magenta line in panel (b) of the graph since the entire reduction in the cost of producing 100 units (or any other quantity) of output derives from the direct effect of the current input bundle costing less and not from the indirect benefit a producer gets from substituting toward the input that has become cheaper. The more substitutable the two inputs, the greater will be the substitution effect, the flatter will be the conditional labor demand curves, and the farther the green (total) long-run cost curve in panel (b) will lie below the magenta curve.

Exercise
13A.16
Are these long-run or short-run cost curves?

Once we have derived the change in the (total) long-run cost curve, we can derive the change in long run AC and MC and then identify the shift in the long-run output supply curve when w falls. Panel (e) illustrates the shift in these curves such that the lowest point of the AC curve remains at the same output level, and thus the portion of the MC curve that is the supply curve begins at the same output level (although at a different price). This is a special case, and there is no particular reason that the lowest point of the long-run AC curve should typically remain at the same output level as input prices change. Depending on the underlying technology, it may be that the lowest point shifts to either the right or the left. Regardless, however, for a fixed price level, the quantity supplied will increase as wage falls because the new (green) supply curve lies to the right of the original (blue) one.

Now suppose that instead of wages falling from \$20 to \$10, the rental rate had increased from \$10 to \$20. In both cases, the ratio w/r changes from -2 to -1, indicating that the slopes of isocosts change in exactly the same way as in Graph 13.8a. Now, however, one of the input prices has gone up, which means that the long-run total cost of producing any quantity of output must be higher than it was originally. This is graphed in panels (c) and (f) of Graph 13.8 as a change in the (total) cost, the AC, and the MC curves from the initial blue to the final green curve. The dotted magenta curves represent how much total and average costs would have increased had the producer not substituted away from capital and toward labor. The conclusion in panel (f) is then that *as the rental rate increases, output supply decreases.*

Can you verify that the numbers in panel (c) are correct?

Exercise 13A.17

Assuming the original cost-minimizing input bundle remains *C*, which of the three curves graphed in Graph 13.8c would be different (and how would it be different) if the inputs in panel (a) of the graph were more substitutable? How would the graph change if the two inputs were perfect complements in productions?

Exercise 13A.18*

In the short run, of course, the substitution effects in Graph 13.8 will not occur when capital is held fixed (just as substitution effects did not arise in the single-input model of Chapter 11). The short-run supply curve then simply appears as the *MC* curve above short-run average cost (as in Graph 13.4), and a change in the price of the variable input simply shifts the short-run *MC* and short-run *AC* as production of any given output level is undertaken with production plans that hold capital constant. It can be shown, however, that *output responses for changes in input prices are at least as large in the long run as in the short run.*

13A.3 Input Demand and Changes in the Economic Environment

Since the distinguishing characteristic of the short run in the two-input model is that one of the inputs is fixed, it must be true (just as in the single-input model of Chapter 11) that the *short-run labor demand decision occurs simply along the marginal revenue product (of labor) curve as* wage changes. As we discussed in detail in Chapter 11, *some portion of the declining part of the MRP_ℓ curve (with capital held fixed at its short-run quantity) is therefore the short-run labor demand curve.* Similarly, short-run labor demand varies with output price as described for the single-input model in Chapter 11, with changes in *p* causing the labor demand curve to shift just as changes in *p* shift the MRP_ℓ curve (see Graph 11.8). In the long run, however, both ℓ and k can be adjusted, which implies that the long-run labor demand curve will be different from the short-run labor demand curve that lies on the MRP_ℓ curve. In the following, we therefore explore how labor demand changes in the long run as input and output prices change.

In Graph 13.8d, we already derived conditional labor demand curves along which capital is allowed to adjust. Explain why these are not long-run labor demand curves.

Exercise 13A.19*

We will again develop the ideas in this section under the assumption that production technologies are homothetic. As demonstrated in part B of the chapter, these ideas hold more generally, but the homotheticity assumption simplifies the graphical approach a bit by giving us a convenient way to narrow the region within the isoquant space where new *cost-minimizing* input bundles will lie as relative input prices change. Suppose, for instance, that the input bundle $A = (\ell^A, k^A)$ in Graph 13.9 is the cost-mimimizing way of producing x^A at input prices (w^A, r^A). If input prices change such that isocosts become steeper, then the new cost-minimizing input bundles must lie to the *left* of the ray connecting *A* to the origin because only in that region could there be a tangency between an isoquant and one of the new (steeper) isocosts. Similarly, if input prices change such that isocosts become shallower, the new cost-minimizing input bundles must lie to the *right* of the same ray.

Can you tell from just seeing the tangency at (ℓ^A, k^A) of the isocost with the isoquant whether the production plan $A = (\ell^A, k^A, x^A)$ is profit-maximizing at prices (w^A, r^A, p^A)?

Exercise 13A.20

Graph 13.9: Changes in Input Prices and New Profit-Maximizing Input Bundles

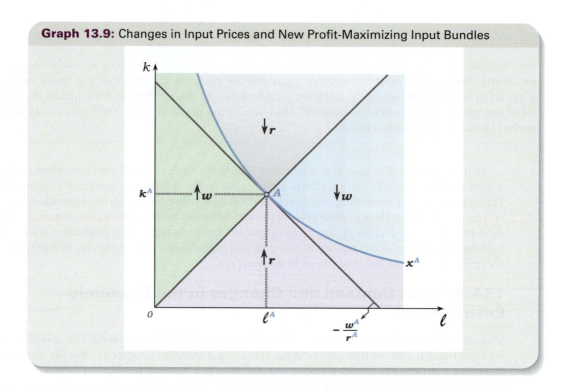

Combined with what we learned in Section 13A.2.2 about the shifting of supply curves induced by changes in input prices, this allows us to be even more precise about narrowing the regions within the isoquant space that must contain the new *profit-maximizing* input bundles as input prices change. Suppose, for instance, that the production plan $A = (\ell^A, k^A, x^A)$ is not only cost-minimizing at input prices (w^A, r^A) but is also long run profit-maximizing given the output price p^A. Now suppose that w decreases, thus causing the isocost curve to become shallower. This implies that the new profit-maximizing input bundle must lie to the *right* of the ray connecting A with the origin (because it is in that region that cost-minimizing input bundles now lie), and it must lie *above* the isoquant corresponding to x^A units of output because, as we saw in Graph 13.8e, output supply increases when w falls. This implies that the new profit-maximizing input bundle lies in the shaded blue area. If, on the other hand, the shallower isocost arose from an increase in r instead of a decrease in w, we saw in Graph 13.8f that output supply will fall, which implies the new profit-maximizing input bundle must lie in the shaded magenta region. Similarly, we can conclude that an increase in w or a decrease in r (both of which cause isocosts to become steeper) will imply that the new input bundle must lie to the *left* of the ray connecting A to the origin, with an increase in w putting us *below* the isoquant containing A and thus into the shaded green region. A decrease in r, on the other hand, puts us *above* the same isoquant into the shaded grey region.

Exercise 13A.21* Do you see from Graph 13.9 that long-run demand curves for labor (with respect to wage) must slope down, as must long-run demand curves for capital (with respect to the rental rate)?

Exercise 13A.22* Does Graph 13.9 tell us anything about whether the cross-price demand curve for labor (with the rental rate on the vertical axis) slopes up or down in the long run?

13A.3.1 An Increase in w: Robots versus Computers

Suppose we run a company that employs labor and capital, and the wage we have to pay our workers goes up. First, note again what we know from our work in Chapter 11: In the short run when capital is fixed, we will simply hire fewer workers, which moves us up the MRP_ℓ curve. Thus, once we have chosen the new short-run optimal number of workers, the marginal product of labor (MP_ℓ) will be higher than it was before the wage increase. This should make sense: Since labor has become more expensive, we will only hire workers so long as their output justifies the higher cost. But what will we do once we can adjust capital? Will we hire more capital or less, and what does that in turn imply for whether we'll let even more workers go in the long run? The answer, it turns out, depends on whether the capital employed in our firm is more like robots or more like computers.

Where in Graph 13.9 will our new production plan fall after we have made our short-run labor adjustment?

Exercise 13A.23*

First, suppose our firm is one that employs both robots and workers to produce cars. In this case, it may be that capital and labor are very substitutable if robots can do many of the same tasks as workers. Since we know that the MP_ℓ has gone up as a result of our decision to have fewer workers in the short run, it would then also be the case that the MP_k has increased. After all, if workers are a lot like robots in our firm, then what happens to the marginal product of one should be roughly equal what happens to the marginal product of the other. But if the MP_k has increased, that means we'll want to hire more robots (that have *not* become any more expensive), and we should let go of more workers (that *have* become more expensive) once we can replace them with robots in the long run. Thus, it is because robots and workers are substitutable that we know the MP_k must have increased when we hired fewer workers in the short run, which in turn means we'll want to hire more robots and replace additional workers with robots in the long run. Our labor demand response is therefore greater in the long run than in the short run, all because we will *increase* capital in the long run due to its substitutability with labor.

We know that we will decrease output in the short run as w increases because we hire fewer workers. In the case of robots and workers, do you think that we will increase or decrease output once we can hire more robots in the long run?

Exercise 13A.24*

Next, suppose that capital and labor were instead quite complementary in production, as perhaps in the case of a computer animations firm that hires computers as capital and computer graphics artists as labor. If the firm we own is of that type, then an increase in w will initially cause a decrease in labor for the same reasons as before. But now labor and capital are more complementary (and less substitutable) because the computer is not of much use without a computer graphics artist. Thus, when we decrease our labor in the short run, the MP_k *falls* (even as the MP_ℓ increases). When I can adjust my capital in the long run, I will therefore let go of some of the computers, which will reduce the marginal product of my workers and cause me to let go of even more of them. Thus, it is because computers and graphic artists are relatively complementary that we know the MP_k *falls* as graphics artists are let go in response to an increase in their wage, which in turn causes a reduction in the number of computers and with it a further reduction in the number of workers, again because the two are complementary. As in the case where labor and capital were substitutable, we therefore again conclude that the long-run reduction in labor exceeds the short-run reduction, but this time it is accompanied by a long-run *reduction* of capital.

The two examples illustrate that regardless of how substitutable capital and labor are in production, the long-run labor demand response to wage changes is always greater than the short-run response. The long-run capital demand response to a wage change, on the other hand, depends on the substitutability of capital and labor. Of course an in-between special case also exists: the case where capital and labor are neither too substitutable nor too complementary, and, as a result, the firm does not change its capital as w increases even when it can in the long run. In that special case, as we will see, the firm's long-run labor demand response is equal to its short-run labor demand response. It is therefore more accurate to restate our conclusion about the long-run labor demand response slightly: *Regardless of how substitutable or complementary capital and labor are in production, the long-run labor response to wage changes will be at least as large as the short-run response.*

13A.3.2 Demand for Labor and Capital as *w* Changes

We can now demonstrate this a little more clearly by applying the fact that two main conditions must hold in order for a producer to be maximizing profits in the short and long run: First, each input's marginal revenue product must equal its price, and second, the negative *TRS* (which is equal to MP_ℓ/MP_k) must equal the ratio of input prices (w/r) in the long run (thus getting us to a new tangency between isocost and isoquant). (Note that the second condition follows logically from the first, but we will proceed in this section as if they were distinct conditions.) Suppose again (as we did in Graph 13.9) that a producer is currently operating at a production plan $A = (\ell^A, k^A, x^A)$ that is his or her long-run profit-maximizing production plan in the economic environment (w^A, r^A, p^A). We then know that

$$p^A MP_\ell^A = w^A, \quad p^A MP_k^A = r^A \quad \text{and} \quad -TRS^A\left(= \frac{MP_\ell^A}{MP_k^A}\right) = \frac{w^A}{r^A}. \tag{13.4}$$

This production plan is depicted as point A in panels (a), (b), and (c) of Graph 13.10.

Now suppose the wage rises to w', thus causing all isocosts to become steeper and implying that the new long-run optimal input bundle C will lie to the left of the ray connecting the origin to A and below the isoquant containing A (as illustrated in Graph 13.9). In the short run, however, the producer cannot adjust capital and therefore must operate with an input bundle B that lies on the horizontal line that holds capital at k^A.

Panel (b) of Graph 13.10 illustrates the special case where the new long-run optimal input bundle C has exactly the same level of capital input as the original input bundle A. In this case, there is nothing to keep the producer from implementing the new long-run optimum even in the short run, which implies that the short-run optimal input bundle B is the same as the long-run optimal bundle C, and the long-run labor and capital demand responses are exactly the same as the short-run responses. Since labor is variable in the short run, $p^A MP_\ell^B = w'$ as the firm adjusts its labor input in exactly the way described in the single-input model of Chapter 11. Since the new isocost happens to be tangent to the isoquant at B,

$$\frac{MP_\ell^B}{MP_k^B} = \frac{w'}{r^A} \quad \text{or, equivalently,} \quad \frac{p^A MP_\ell^B}{p^A MP_k^B} = \frac{w'}{r^A}. \tag{13.5}$$

But, since $p^A MP_\ell^B = w'$, this implies $p^A MP_k^B = r^A$, which, given that $p^A MP_k^A = r^A$, implies $MP_k^A = MP_k^B$. Thus, the fact that we have graphed the new isocost tangent to the isoquant at B implies that we have graphed a technology where the short-run reduction in labor input has left the marginal product of capital unchanged. This in turn implies that the producer reaches his or her long-run optimum in the short-run, causing the short- and long-run labor demand curves to coincide in panel (e) and the cross-price relationship between w and k to be vertical as in panel (h).

Now consider the technology graphed in panel (a). Here, the new optimal input bundle C contains more capital input than the original bundle A, which implies that the producer cannot immediately switch to the long-run optimum when capital is fixed in the short run. Rather, in the

Graph 13.10: Short- and Long-Run Input Demand Responses when w Increases

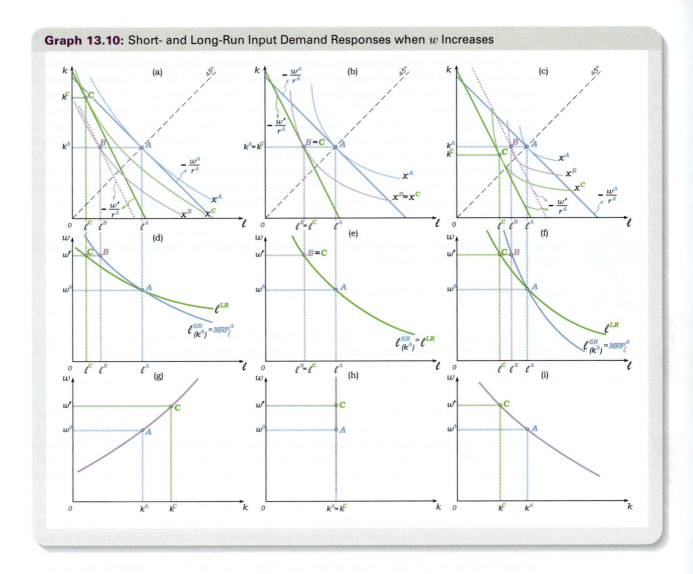

short run the producer switches to input bundle B, which has the characteristic that the isocost containing B cuts the isoquant containing B from above; i.e., $TRS^B > -w'/r^A$ or equivalently

$$\frac{MP_\ell^B}{MP_k^B} < \frac{w'}{r^A}, \text{ which implies } \frac{p^A MP_\ell^B}{p^A MP_k^B} < \frac{w'}{r^A}. \tag{13.6}$$

In the short run, we know the firm will adjust labor until $p^A MP_\ell^B = w'$. The previous equation then implies that $p^A MP_k^B > r^A$ and thus (since $p^A MP_k^A = r^A$) that $MP_k^B > MP_k^A$. Capital is therefore more productive at the margin at B than at A, which causes producers to substitute away from labor and toward capital, causing a decline in labor input beyond the initial decline from ℓ^A to ℓ^B all the way to ℓ^C. This leads the labor demand curve in panel (d) to be shallower in the long run than in the short run and the cross-price relationship between w and k to be upward sloping. As suggested by the relatively flat shape of isoquants in panel (a), this occurs when capital and labor are relatively substitutable in production (as in our example of robots and workers), and when an increase in the cost of labor thus leads to a lot of substitution into capital.

Finally, panel (c) illustrates the opposite case where the producer adjusts to less capital in the long run as wage increases from w^A to w'. Since the producer finds it optimal to adjust capital that is fixed in the short run, his or her long-run response to the wage increase will therefore again differ from her short-run response. In the short run, she switches to input bundle B where the isocost containing B cuts the isoquant containing B from below. Using steps analogous to those in the previous paragraph, this allows us to conclude that $MP_k^B < MP_k^A$; i.e., capital has become less productive at the margin when labor input was adjusted in the short run. As a result, the producer reduces the capital input in the long run and further reduces labor input as well, which leads again to a long-run labor demand curve that is shallower than in the short run (panel (f)) but a cross-price relationship between w and k that is downward sloping (panel (i)). Notice that this is derived from panel (c) where isoquants represent inputs that are relatively complementary (as in our example of computers and workers), and thus an increase in the cost of labor results in less use of both labor and its complementary input capital.

Exercise 13A.25* Suppose labor and capital were perfect complements in production. What would the analogous graph for an increase in w look like?

Exercise 13A.26* Demonstrate that $MP_k^B < MP_k^A$ in panel (c) of Graph 13.10.

Exercise 13A.27* How is the long-run response in output related to the short-run response in output as w increases? What does your answer depend on? (*Hint*: You should be able to see the answer in Graph 13.10.)

We can therefore conclude that, except for the special case in panel (b) of the graph, *the long-run labor demand response to changes in w is larger than the short run labor demand response* (just as we concluded earlier in the chapter that the long-run output supply response to a change in output price is larger in the long run than in the short run). The underlying reasoning is somewhat subtle: In the case where labor and capital are relatively substitutable in production in panel (a) (analogous to our example of capital as "robots"), the marginal product of capital *increases* because of the short-run drop in labor when w increases. As a result, the firm will hire more capital when it can and reduce labor further because capital and labor are relatively substitutable. But in the case where labor and capital are relatively complementary in production in panel (c) (analogous to our example of capital as "computers"), the marginal product of capital *falls* as a result of the short-run drop in labor when w increases. This causes the firm to reduce its capital when it can in the long run, and, because labor and capital are relatively complementary, it will then reduce the labor it hires beyond the short-run reduction. Whether labor and capital are relatively substitutable or relatively complementary, the long-run labor demand response therefore exceeds the short-run response—albeit for somewhat different reasons—and the demand for capital either increases or decreases depending on the degree of substitutability between capital and labor.

13A.3.3 Demand for Labor and Capital as r Changes An analogous set of steps can lead us to an analogous set of conclusions regarding the long-run change in the demand for labor and capital when r rather than w rises. Since we are assuming throughout that capital is fixed in the short run, however, an increase in the cost of capital is a sunk "cost" in the short run and thus does not affect production decisions with respect to labor, capital, or output in the short run.

Suppose again that a producer is currently operating at a production plan $A = (\ell^A, k^A, x^A)$ that is his or her long-run profit-maximizing production plan in the economic environment (w^A, r^A, p^A). Now suppose that r increases, which makes isocosts shallower. We know from our work in Graph 13.9 that this will lead to a new profit-maximizing input bundle that lies below the isoquant containing A and to the right of the ray connecting A to the origin. Graph 13.11 then illustrates three

Graph 13.11: Long-Run Labor Demand Responses when *r* Increases

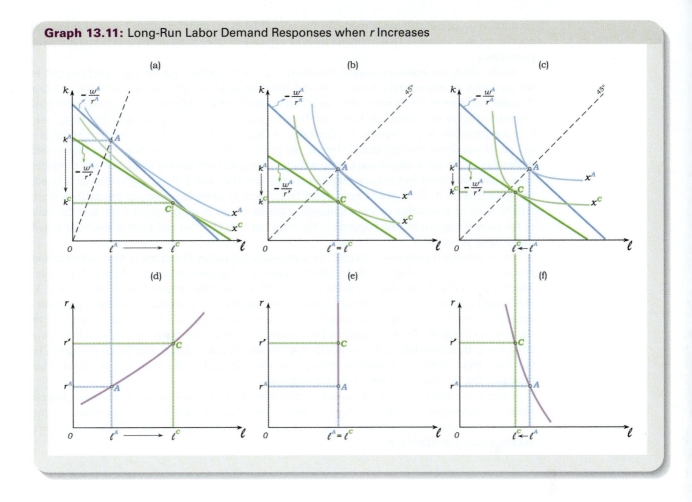

possibilities, with panel (a) once again representing a production process in which capital and labor are relatively substitutable and panel (c) representing the case where capital and labor are relatively complementary in production.

Since capital falls in all three scenarios as *r* increases, we can conclude that *the long-run demand curve for capital is downward sloping (with respect to r)*. The cross-price relationship between *r* and ℓ, however, may slope up when labor and capital are relatively substitutable or down when labor and capital are relatively complementary in production as demonstrated by panels (d) through (f) in Graph 13.11. This happens for reasons exactly analogous to those cited for the potentially upward- or downward-sloping cross-price relationship between *w* and *k* in Graph 13.10.

Can you arrive at these conclusions intuitively using again the examples of robots and computers?

Exercise 13A.28*

13A.3.4 Demand for Labor and Capital as *p* Changes
Finally, we know from our previous work that output supply curves slope up (because the relevant portion of *MC* curves slope up), which implies that output increases when the output price *p* rises. Since a change in output price by itself does not alter the slope of isocosts (which is equal to $-w/r$), this implies that, for

production processes that are homothetic, the ratio of labor to capital employed in production will not change as p changes. Thus, demand for both capital and labor must increase as the output price p increases.

In the short run, however, capital may be fixed, which implies that the increase in output in the short run results entirely from additional labor being hired. Whether the increase in labor demand is higher or lower in the short run then again depends on the relative substitutability of capital and labor in production. Consider, for instance, the case of capital and labor being perfect complements in production, as illustrated in Graph 13.12a where once again A is the initial profit-maximizing input bundle before the price of the output rises. Since it is impossible in this case to produce additional output without adjusting both capital and labor, the producer would have no choice but to keep output unchanged in the short run as long as capital is fixed, resulting in $A = B$. Thus, when capital and labor are very complementary in production, there will be little or no change in labor demand in the short run as output price rises, and the bulk of the increase in production happens in the long run as both labor and capital can be adjusted in the same proportion.

Now consider the opposite extreme, the case where capital and labor are perfect substitutes in production as illustrated in Graph 13.12b. Suppose that capital is relatively cheaper than labor, which implies that the producer is using only capital and no labor at the original input bundle A. When output price increases without a change in input prices, the producer will end up producing more output with an increase in capital in the long run (bundle C), but in the short run he or she cannot change the level of capital in production. As a result, the producer may well hire some labor in the short run (taking him or her to input bundle B) before being able to adjust capital. In this case, then, there is a temporary increase in labor demand in the short-run as output price increases, but this increase vanishes in the long run.

From these extremes, we can conclude that *the short-run labor demand response from a change in output price might be larger or smaller than the long-run response depending on the degree of substitutability between capital and labor in production.* We will illustrate this more mathematically in Section B.

Graph 13.12: Input Demand Responses when p Increases

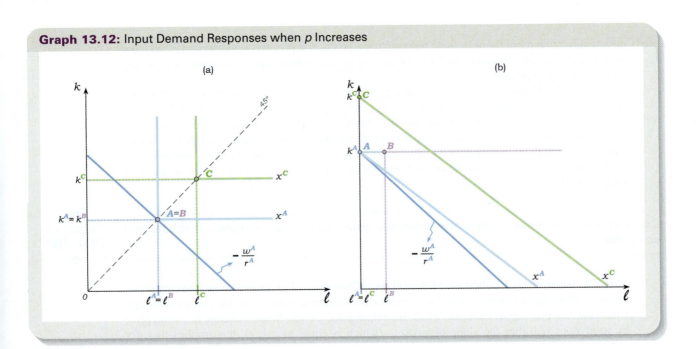

In panel (a) of Graph 13.7, we determined that the firm will once again end up on the steeper ray once it can adjust capital. Call the new (long-run) input bundle at the higher output price C. Can you now tell what will determine whether C lies to the right or left of B?

Exercise
13A.29*

13A.4 Technological Change

A change in the technological rather than the economic environment would manifest itself as a change in the production frontier (and potentially a change in the shape of isoquants). It is not uncommon for such technological change to be modeled as a proportional outward expansion of the three-dimensional production frontier, with the marginal product of labor and capital increasing at all production plans in proportion to one another. Since $-TRS = MP_\ell/MP_k$, such proportional changes in marginal products would leave the TRS unchanged for all input bundles and thus leave the shapes of isoquants (but not the output quantities associated with them) unchanged. At the same time, however, it would cause profit-maximizing producers to hire more labor and capital in order to produce more output.

Suppose, for instance, that the input production plan $A = (100, \ell^A, k^A)$ in Graph 13.13a is the initial profit-maximizing production plan. Then suppose an aerosol spray that I can spray in my factory to cause all my machines and workers to become more productive has just been invented, and suppose that this technological change is of the kind described in the previous paragraph. Then, since technical rates of substitution are unaffected by this change, the shapes of isoquants remain the same *but the labels on the isoquants increase,* with the label on the blue isoquant increasing from 100 to 200, on the magenta isoquant from x^B to $\tilde{x}^B$, and on the green isoquant from x^C to $\tilde{x}^C$. Put differently, the rate at which labor and capital can be substituted for one another in production remains unchanged, but each input bundle now produces more than before.

Since A was initially profit-maximizing, we know that $pMP_\ell^A = w$ and $pMP_k^A = r$. But with the technological change, the new marginal products of labor and capital ($\widetilde{MP}_\ell$ and $\widetilde{MP}_k$) are higher at every input bundle, which means that, were the producer to continue to use input bundle A, $p\widetilde{MP}_\ell^A > w$ and $p\widetilde{MP}_k^A > r$. Thus, the producer would increase labor in the short run until

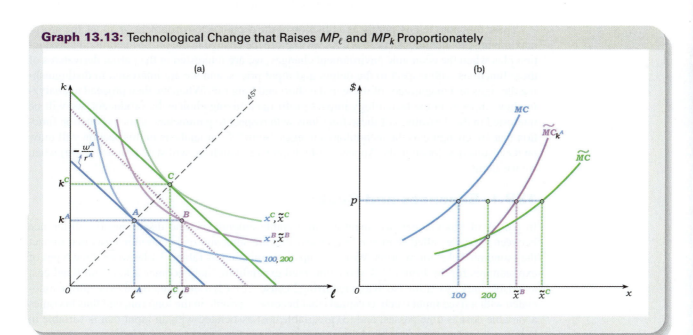

Graph 13.13: Technological Change that Raises MP_ℓ and MP_k Proportionately

capital can be adjusted in the long run, moving from the initial blue isoquant to the short-run magenta and the long-run green isoquants. This increase in production can also be illustrated in our graph with *MC* curves in panel (b) of Graph 13.13, with an initial shift in the *MC* from the blue to the magenta and a long-run shift to the green curve. Since output price is unchanged, we can then simply read off the change in output along these *MC* curves.

Exercise 13A.30*	Why do the magenta and green marginal cost curves intersect at the output level 200?
Exercise 13A.31*	Where would points *A*, *B*, and *C* lie if labor and capital were perfect complements?
Exercise 13A.32*	What feature of the production technology determines whether *C* lies to the right or left of *B* in panel (a) of Graph 13.13?

Of course, this is an illustration of a very particular type of technological change, and other types of technological change may well alter the shape of isoquants in ways that make it more difficult to predict precisely how producers would react. Nevertheless, it will generally be true that technological change reduces marginal cost in ways similar to those graphed in panel (b) of Graph 13.13.

13B Transitioning From Short to Long Run Mathematically

In the duality picture in Graph 12.13, the profit maximization problem on the left-hand side yields output supply and input demand functions

$$x(p,w,r), \ell(p,w,r) \text{ and } k(p,w,r). \tag{13.7}$$

These functions tell us, purely as a function of the economic environment (p,w,r), the profit-maximizing production plan (x,ℓ,k). As we explore the change in the profit-maximizing production plan when the economic environment changes, we are interested in the partial derivatives of these functions with respect to the output and input prices, and we are interested in distinguishing the signs and magnitudes of these in the short and long run. When we then proceed to analyzing how changes in the technology impact profit-maximizing choices by producers, we will be interested in the derivatives of these functions with respect to parameters of the production function that are changing as the technology changes. Some of our analysis in this section will draw on the results developed in the Appendix of Chapter 12, which we will state (but not prove) when we use them.

13B.1 Expenses and Costs

In part A of this chapter, we spent a considerable amount of time discussing the difference between what we called short-run "expenses" that are sunk and real economic costs that impact the economic behavior of firms. We ended up distinguishing in Table 13.1 between three types of expenditures for the firm: (1) A short-run fixed expenditure that becomes a long-run fixed cost avoidable only by exiting (such as a recurring license fee); (2) a short-run fixed expenditure associated with a fixed input (such as capital) that becomes variable in the long run, and thus becomes a variable cost as time passes; and (3) a variable cost associated with an input that is variable in both the short and long run (like labor).

13B.1.1 Short-Run Expenses and Long-Run Costs without Fixed Costs

Suppose, for instance, that k^A is the economically efficient level of capital to employ when input prices are (w^A, r^A) if one wants to produce the output level x^A. If capital is fixed at that level in the short-run, the short-run cost-minimizing input bundle for producing any given level of output x is then $(\ell_{k^A}(x), k^A)$, where $\ell_{k^A}(x)$ is just the minimum amount of labor necessary to produce output x given that capital is fixed at k^A. We would arrive at this in exactly the same way that we used in Chapter 11, with the relevant production function in the short run simply being the slice of the long-run production function that holds capital fixed at k^A. We can denote this slice as $f_{k^A}(\ell)$. For instance, if the full (long-run) production function is $f(\ell, k) = A\ell^\alpha k^\beta$, the short-run production function when the firm is restricted to keep capital at k^A is $x = f_{k^A} = [A(k^A)^\beta]\ell^\alpha$, with the term in brackets being treated as a constant. To find the cost-minimizing labor input level for producing x in the short run, we would simply invert this to get

$$\ell_{k^A}(x) = \left(\frac{x}{[A(k^A)^\beta]} \right)^{1/\alpha}. \tag{13.8}$$

Suppose the long-run production function were a function of three inputs, labor, capital, and land, and suppose that both labor and capital were variable in the short run but land is only variable in the long run. How would we now calculate the short-run cost-minimizing labor and capital input levels conditional on some (short-run) fixed level of land?

Exercise 13B.1

When input prices are (w^A, r^A), the short-run *expense* associated with producing x is then

$$E_{k^A}(x, w^A, r^A) = w^A \ell_{k^A}(x) + r^A k^A \tag{13.9}$$

while the short run *cost* is

$$C_{k^A}(x, w^A) = w^A \ell_{k^A}(x). \tag{13.10}$$

Can you use these expressions to justify the difference in the (total) cost and total expenditure curves in panel (a) of Graph 13.1 as well as the difference between *AC* and *AE* in panel (b) of that graph?

Exercise 13B.2

The long-run cost, however, is derived from solving the cost minimization problem

$$\min_{\ell, k} w\ell + rk \text{ subject to } x = f(\ell, k) \tag{13.11}$$

with the underlying assumption that both capital and labor can be adjusted. As we saw in Chapter 12 (and in the intuitive exposition of Graph 13.2), this results in conditional input demands $\ell(x, w, r)$ and $k(x, w, r)$ and the long-run cost function $C(x, w, r) = w\ell(x, w, r) + rk(x, w, r)$. When input prices are (w^A, r^A), the long-run cost is therefore

$$C(x, w^A, r^A) = w^A \ell(x, w^A, r^A) + r^A k(x, w^A, r^A). \tag{13.12}$$

Saying that x^A is the output level for which k^A is the long-run optimal quantity of capital is then the same as saying $k^A = k(x^A, w^A, r^A)$. If the firm starts with k^A in the short run and decides to produce x^A, it can then set labor (which is variable in the short run) to its (long-run) cost-minimizing level, resulting in $\ell_{k^A}(x^A) = \ell(x^A, w^A, r^A)$, which implies that the firm's short-run expenses are equal to its long-run costs; i.e., $E_{k^A}(x^A, w^A, r^A) = C(x^A, w^A, r^A)$. For any other output level, however, k^A is not generally the long-run optimal level, which implies that

$$E_{k^A}(x, w^A, r^A) \geq C(x, w^A, r^A) \tag{13.13}$$

with the expression holding with equality only when $x = x^A$. This is precisely what we showed graphically in Graph 13.2.

Exercise 13B.3 Can you derive from this the relationship between long-run average cost and short-run average expenses as illustrated graphically in Graph 13.2?

The short-run supply curve would then be calculated by setting price equal to short-run marginal cost derived from $C_{k^A}(x, w^A)$ while the long-run supply curve would be calculated by setting price equal to long-run marginal cost derived from $C(x, w^A, r^A)$.

Exercise 13B.4 In the case of U-shaped average cost curves, how can you use the previous mathematical expressions to argue that the short-run "shut down" price is lower than the long-run "exit" price?

13B.1.2 An Example   Consider, for instance, our example of a decreasing returns to scale production process modeled by the production function $f(\ell, k) = 20\ell^{2/5}k^{2/5}$. In Chapter 12 (equations (12.44) and (12.45)), we derived the conditional input demands for this production function as

$$\ell(w, r, x) = \left(\frac{r}{w}\right)^{1/2}\left(\frac{x}{20}\right)^{5/4} \quad \text{and} \quad k(w, r, x) = \left(\frac{w}{r}\right)^{1/2}\left(\frac{x}{20}\right)^{5/4}, \tag{13.14}$$

and the (long-run) cost function (in equation (12.46)) as

$$C(w, r, x) = w\ell(w, r, x) + rk(w, r, x) = 2(wr)^{1/2}\left(\frac{x}{20}\right)^{5/4}. \tag{13.15}$$

If we were to produce 1,280 units of output at input prices $(w, r) = (20, 10)$, for instance, these functions imply that we would want to choose the cost-minimizing input bundle $(\ell, k) = (128, 256)$ incurring a (long-run) cost of \$5,120.

Exercise 13B.5 Verify that these numbers are correct.

Suppose this is the current input bundle employed by a producer facing input prices $(w, r) = (20, 10)$, and the producer now considers producing a different level of output. In the long run, the cost of producing other levels of output at these input prices is given by the cost function in equation (13.15) with $w = 20$ and $r = 10$ plugged into the equation, which results in

$$C(x, 20, 10) = 0.66874x^{5/4}. \tag{13.16}$$

In the short run, however, demand for labor is given by the inverse of the short-run production function $f_{k^A=256} = [20(256)^{2/5}]\ell^{2/5}$, which is

$$\ell_{k^A=256}(x) = \left(\frac{x}{20(256)^{2/5}}\right)^{5/2} = \frac{x^{5/2}}{20^{5/2}(256)}. \tag{13.17}$$

This gives a short-run expense function of

$$E_{k^A=256}(x, 20, 10) = 20\ell_{k^A=256}(x) + (10)256 = \frac{x^{5/2}}{20^{3/2}256} + 2{,}560. \tag{13.18}$$

Exercise 13B.6

What is the short-run cost (as opposed to expenditure) function?

The cost function in equation (13.16) and the short-run expense function in (13.18) are then graphed in panel (a) of Graph 13.14, with panel (b) graphing the corresponding average cost and expense functions. As we concluded intuitively, these functions are related in that average short-run expenses are never lower than average long-run costs.

Exercise 13B.7

Verify that when $x = 1{,}280$, the short-run expense is equal to the long-run cost.

13B.1.3 Adding a (Long-Run) Fixed Cost

So far, we have included in our analysis the expenses and costs associated with inputs, with the expense on fixed inputs not showing up as an economic cost in the short run and showing up as a variable cost in the long run. In part A of the chapter, we also introduced a new type of cost that we called a "fixed cost avoidable only by exiting" or a "long-run fixed cost." We gave two examples of such a cost: the cost associated with recurring license fees that do not vary with the level of output and the cost associated with an input (such as the management skills of the firm's CEO) that remains fixed even in the long run. These are fixed expenses in the short run and therefore do not affect short-run costs (and thus short-run supply decisions), but they are real economic costs in the long run. We can include them in our usual cost function $C(x,w,r)$ by simply adding them as a fixed cost FC term. Thus, the new cost function becomes

$$\overline{C}(x,w,r) = C(x,w,r) + FC = w\ell(x,w,r) + rk(x,w,r) + FC. \qquad (13.19)$$

You can then see immediately that the addition of such a fixed cost has no impact on the marginal cost function because, when we take the derivative of $\overline{C}(x,w,r)$ with respect to x, the FC term simply drops out. The average cost function, however, changes to

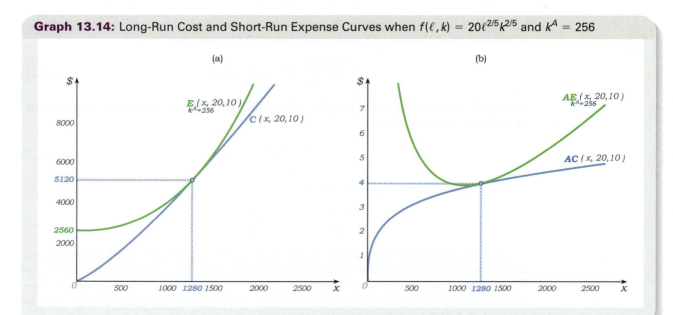

Graph 13.14: Long-Run Cost and Short-Run Expense Curves when $f(\ell,k) = 20\ell^{2/5}k^{2/5}$ and $k^A = 256$

$$AC(x,w,r) = \frac{C(x,w,r)}{x} + \frac{FC}{x} = AVC(x,w,r) + \frac{FC}{x} \qquad (13.20)$$

where AVC denotes the average *variable* cost associated with the variable inputs of capital and labor. Since the term FC/x declines as x increases, the new average cost AC converges to the average variable cost as illustrated in Graph 13.5. This implies that the long-run supply curve is not shifted by the addition of such a fixed cost; it merely becomes "shorter" because its starting point (at the lowest point of AC) moves up with an upward shift in the AC curve.

Exercise 13B.8   Does the inclusion of a fixed cost cause any change in conditional input demands? What about unconditional input demands?

Exercise 13B.9   Does the inclusion of a fixed cost change either the (short-run) "shut down" price or the (long-run) "exit" price?

13B.2 Output Supply and Changes in the Economic Environment

We now turn more directly to the output supply function $x(p,w,r)$, asking why it slopes up and how short- and long-run supply curves relate to one another (as we did graphically in Graph 13.7). We then proceed to investigate how changes in input prices shift these supply curves. Note that a "supply curve" is simply a "slice" of the supply function $x(p,w,r)$ that holds the input prices (w,r) fixed and illustrates how output supply changes with output price p. To be more precise, the output supply curves we graphed in Section A are *inverse* slices of supply functions (just as consumer demand curves were inverse slices of demand functions) because output is a function of price and therefore would appear on the vertical rather than on the horizontal axis unless we took inverses.

13B.2.1 Supply Curves always Slope Up   In the appendix to Chapter 12, we developed two concepts relating to output supply that we will simply take as given in this chapter. First, part of what we called Hotelling's Lemma in equation (12.52) states that

$$\frac{\partial \pi(p,w,r)}{\partial p} = x(p,w,r), \qquad (13.21)$$

and one of our conclusions from Graph 12.14 was that the profit function $\pi(p,w,r)$ in our duality picture is convex in p; i.e.,

$$\frac{\partial^2 \pi(p,w,r)}{\partial p^2} \geq 0. \qquad (13.22)$$

Combining these two equations, we get

$$\frac{\partial x(p,w,r)}{\partial p} = \frac{\partial^2 \pi(p,w,r)}{\partial p^2} \geq 0; \qquad (13.23)$$

i.e., the output supply curve is upward sloping in price. Since Hotelling's Lemma holds for production functions of any number of inputs, it also holds for short-run production functions (in which some inputs are held fixed); thus *all output supply curves, both in the short and long run, slope up*. Notice furthermore that none of this requires assumptions like homotheticity, which we used in part A of the chapter simply for convenience.

13B.2.2 Short-Run Supply Curves are Steeper than Long-Run Supply Curves

Next, suppose that capital is fixed at quantity k^A in the short-run (as it was in our development of Graph 13.7). Then, while our long-run supply function is $x(p, w, r)$, our short-run supply function $x_{k^A}(p, w)$ is derived from the single-input production function that is given by the "slice" of the two-input production function, which holds capital fixed at k^A. For instance, as we already discussed in the example of Section 13B.1.2, if the long-run production function is $f(\ell, k) = 20\ell^{2/5}k^{2/5}$, the short-run production function with capital fixed at k^A is $f_{k^A}(\ell) = [20(k^A)^{2/5}]\ell^{2/5}$ where the bracketed term is simply a constant parameter. While $x(p, w, r)$ is derived from the profit maximization problem using the function $f(\ell, k)$, $x_{k^A}(p, w)$ is derived from the profit maximization problem using $f_{k^A}(\ell)$. As will become clear in a minute, the short-run supply function will then not be a function of r because the expense on the fixed amount of capital k^A is not an economic cost in the short run.

To be more precise, the short-run profit maximization problem is

$$\max_{x, \ell} px - w\ell \quad \text{such that} \quad x = f_{k^A}(\ell), \tag{13.24}$$

which can be written as the unconstrained optimization problem

$$\max_{\ell} pf_{k^A}(\ell) - w\ell. \tag{13.25}$$

Exercise 13B.10

Would including the fixed expense rk^A in the short-run profit maximization problem (so that the objective function becomes $px - w\ell - rk^A$) make any difference as the problem is solved?

Solving this exactly as we solved the single-input profit maximization problem in Chapter 11, we then get the short-run labor demand function $\ell_{k^A}(p, w)$, and plugging this back into the short-run production function, we get the short-run output supply function $x_{k^A}(p, w)$. At this short run optimum, the marginal revenue product of labor is equal to the wage, but the marginal revenue product of capital is not typically equal to the rental rate because we are unable to adjust capital away from its fixed quantity k^A in the short run. The short-run profit function is equal to $\pi_{k^A}(p, w) = px_{k^A}(p, w) - w\ell_{k^A}(p, w)$, which does not include a term rk^A for the expense on capital because this expense is a sunk "cost" in the short run.

Now suppose that input and output prices are such that k^A happens to be equal to the long-run optimal quantity of capital; i.e., suppose that we happen to have just the right quantity of capital that results in the marginal revenue product of capital being equal to the rental rate. In that case, the short-run profit *minus* the expense on fixed capital is exactly equal to the long-run profit, which takes the cost of capital as a real economic cost; i.e., $\pi(p, w, r) = \pi_{k^A}(p, w) - rk^A$. This emerges directly from the insight that the short-run total *expenditure* is exactly equal to the (total) *cost* in the long-run when capital is at its long-run optimum, an insight we first developed in Graph 13.2 and then developed mathematically in Section (13B.1.1). But if k^A is not equal to the long-run optimal level of capital, the short-run profit *minus* rk^A must be less than the long-run profit because in the long run we would adjust capital to the optimal quantity. This again emerges directly from Graph 13.2 and from equation (13.13) where we showed that the short-run total *expenditure* exceeds the long-run (total) cost whenever capital is not at its long-run optimal level. We can therefore conclude that

$$\pi(p, w, r) \geq \pi_{k^A}(p, w) - rk^A, \tag{13.26}$$

with this equation holding with equality only when k^A is in fact at its long-run optimal level.

Suppose next that the input prices are currently fixed at (w^A, r^A). We can then define $g(p)$ as the difference between long-run profit and short-run profit adjusted for the expense on capital; i.e.,

$$g(p) = \pi(p, w^A, r^A) - \pi_{k^A}(p, w^A) + r^A k^A, \tag{13.27}$$

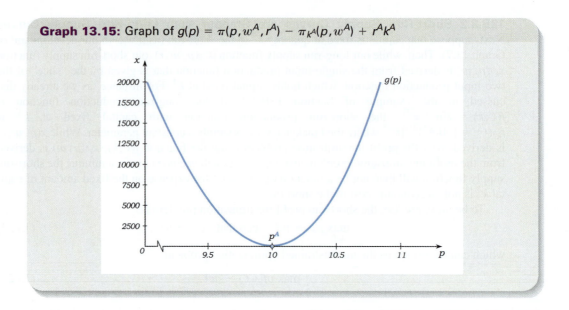

Graph 13.15: Graph of $g(p) = \pi(p, w^A, r^A) - \pi_{k^A}(p, w^A) + r^A k^A$

and we know from what we have concluded so far that $g(p)$ will be equal to zero when k^A is the long-run optimal level of capital for the output price p, but $g(p)$ is greater than zero when this is not the case. This function is sketched out in Graph 13.15 where p^A is the price at which k^A is the long-run optimal quantity of capital (when input prices are held at (w^A, r^A)).

As is apparent from this graph, $g(p)$ attains its minimum at p^A, which implies that the second derivative of g is positive at p^A. Thus,

$$\frac{\partial^2 g(p^A)}{\partial p^2} = \frac{\partial^2 \pi(p^A, w^A, r^A)}{\partial p^2} - \frac{\partial^2 \pi_{k^A}(p^A, w^A)}{\partial p^2} \geq 0. \tag{13.28}$$

Hotelling's Lemma is valid for both short-run and long-run profit functions, and so, when we apply Hotelling's Lemma to both these profit functions in equation (13.28), we can rewrite the equation as

$$\frac{\partial x(p^A, w^A, r^A)}{\partial p} - \frac{\partial x_{k^A}(p^A, w^A)}{\partial p} \geq 0, \tag{13.29}$$

or simply

$$\frac{\partial x(p^A, w^A, r^A)}{\partial p} \geq \frac{\partial x_{k^A}(p^A, w^A)}{\partial p}. \tag{13.30}$$

This then simply states what we showed graphically in Graph 13.7: the long-run supply response is larger than the short-run supply response from a change in output price. Note that, while we showed this for homothetic production processes in our graphical development, the mathematical proof again required no such restrictions on production. Thus, the result holds generally for all production processes.

Exercise 13B.11

Equation (13.30) can also be read as "the slope of the long-run output supply function is larger than the slope of the short-run output supply function (with respect to price)." But the long-run supply curve in Graph 13.7 appears to have a shallower (and thus smaller) slope than that of the short-run supply curve. How can you reconcile what the math and the graphs seem to be telling us?

13B.2.3 An Example (continued) In our example of the long-run production function $f(\ell,k) = 20\ell^{2/5}k^{2/5}$, for instance, we determined in Chapter 12 that the long-run output supply and input demand functions are

$$x(p,w,r) = 81{,}920 \frac{p^4}{(wr)^2} \;,\; \ell(p,w,r) = 32{,}768 \frac{p^5}{r^2w^3} \text{ and } k(p,w,r) = 32{,}768 \frac{p^5}{w^2r^3}. (13.31)$$

Suppose the economic environment is given by $(p,w,r) = (5,20,10)$ for which we concluded in Chapter 12 that the long-run optimal production plan is $(x,\ell,k) = (1280,128,256)$. Now suppose capital is fixed at 256 in the short-run. The short-run production function is then given by $f_{k=256}(\ell) = 20(256^{2/5})\ell^{2/5} = 183.79\ell^{2/5}$. When this production function is used to define the short-run profit maximization problem

$$\max_{\ell} p(183.79\ell^{2/5}) - w\ell, (13.32)$$

the resulting short-run output supply and input demand functions are

$$x_{k=256}(p,w) = 3{,}225\left(\frac{p}{w}\right)^{2/3} \text{ and } \ell_{k=256}(p,w) = 1{,}290\left(\frac{p}{w}\right)^{5/3}. (13.33)$$

Verify that these are truly the short-run output supply and input demand functions by checking to see if the short-run functions give the same answers as the long-run functions when $(p,w,r) = (5,20,10)$.

Exercise 13B.12

Taking derivatives of the long-run and short-run output supply functions with respect to p, we get

$$\frac{\partial x(p,w,r)}{\partial p} = 327{,}680 \frac{p^3}{(wr)^2} \text{ and } \frac{\partial x_{k=256}(p,w)}{\partial p} = \frac{2{,}150}{p^{1/3}w^{2/3}}. (13.34)$$

Evaluated at the $(p,w,r) = (5, 20,10)$, this gives a partial derivative of the long-run supply function of 1,024 and a partial derivative of the short-run supply function of 170.67, indicating the predicted larger change in output in the long run than in the short run when we begin at a production plan that is long-run profit-maximizing and experience a change in output price. If p, for instance, were to rise from \$5.00 to \$7.50, the long-run profit-maximizing production plan given by equations (13.31) would go from $(x,\ell,k) = (1280,128,256)$ to $(x,\ell,k) = (6480,972,1944)$, but the new short-run production plan (holding k fixed at 256) would be given by equations (13.33) as $(x,\ell,k) = (1677,252,256)$, implying that production will rise from 1,280 to 1,677 output units in the short run and to 6,480 in the long run when capital can be adjusted.

13B.2.4 Substitution Effects in Production In Graph 13.8, we illustrated that, as input prices fall, the cost of production falls both because the *direct effect* of current cost-minimizing input bundles becoming cheaper and because of the *substitution effect* leading to less intensive use of relatively more expensive inputs. We can illustrate this with our example of a production process represented by the production function $f(\ell,k) = 20\ell^{2/5}k^{2/5}$ for which we have calculated the various functions in our producer duality picture. In particular, we recall again the conditional input demands (from equation (13.14))

$$\ell(w,r,x) = \left(\frac{r}{w}\right)^{1/2}\left(\frac{x}{20}\right)^{5/4} \text{ and } k(w,r,x) = \left(\frac{w}{r}\right)^{1/2}\left(\frac{x}{20}\right)^{5/4}, (13.35)$$

which explicitly incorporate the substitution effect, with the slice of the conditional labor demand curve in Graph 13.8d derived explicitly from a single isoquant. The corresponding cost function, previously given in equation (13.15), then incorporates both the direct and the substitution effect from input price changes and is given by

$$C(w,r,x) = 2(wr)^{1/2}\left(\frac{x}{20}\right)^{5/4}. \tag{13.36}$$

Suppose we begin with input prices of $(w,r) = (20,10)$ and w falls to \$10. Then the slice of the cost function at the original input prices is $C(x,20,10) = 0.66874x^{5/4}$ while the slice at the new input prices becomes $C(x,10,10) = 0.47287x^{5/4}$. Thus the (total) long-run cost curve shifts down by $0.19587x^{5/4}$. Taking the derivative of these functions with respect to x, we can also calculate the corresponding marginal cost curves $MC(x,20,10) = 0.83593x^{1/4}$ and $MC(x,10,10) = 0.59109x^{1/4}$, and dividing the total cost curves by x we can calculate the average cost curves $AC(x,20,10) = 0.66874x^{1/4}$ and $AC(x,10,10) = 0.47287x^{1/4}$. The shift in the total and marginal cost curves are illustrated in Graph 13.16 as a shift from blue to green curves.

Now let's suppose we isolate the direct effect of an input price change by assuming that the producer does not substitute away from capital and into labor when w falls from \$20 to \$10. When input prices are $(20,10)$, the conditional labor demand for different output levels x is given by $\ell(20,10,x) = 0.01672x^{5/4}$ and $k(20,10,x) = 0.03344x^{5/4}$. If the producer does not alter his or her behavior as a result of a decline in the wage to \$10, this would imply that his or her (total) costs are given by $10\ell(20,10,x) + 10k(20,10,x) = 0.5016x^{5/4}$, which is higher than the (total) cost including the substitution effect $(C(x,10,10) = 0.47287x^{5/4})$ we calculated. The magenta curves in Graph 13.16 represent the change in cost curves that is due to this direct effect, with the remainder due to the substitution effect.

Exercise 13B.13

Panels (a) and (b) of Graph 13.16 are analogous to panels (b) and (e) of Graph 13.8. Now calculate the relevant curves and graph them for the case that is analogous to panels (c) and (f) of Graph 13.8 where, instead of wage falling from \$20 to \$10, the rental rate of capital rises from \$10 to \$20.

Graph 13.16: Change in Cost Curves as w Falls when $f(\ell,k) = 20\ell^{2/5}k^{2/5}$

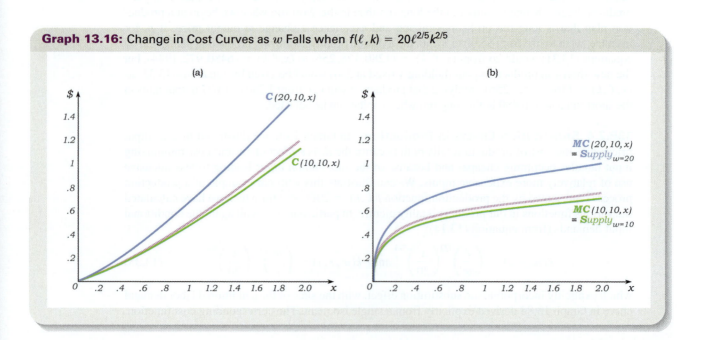

Table 13.2: Declining Substitution Effects with Declining Substitutability (as w falls from 10 to 5)

ρ	$\ell(5,10,5000)$	$k(5,10,5000)$	Change in Cost	Direct Effect	Substitution Effect
\multicolumn{6}{c}{Producing 5,000 Units of Output When w Falls and $f(\ell,k) = 100(0.5\ell^{-\rho} + 0.5k^{-\rho})^{-0.5/\rho}$}
−1.00	5,000	0	−$25,000	−$12,500	−$12,500
−0.90	5,388	5	−$23,004	−$12,500	−$10,504
−0.75	5,384	336	−$19,715	−$12,500	−$7,215
−0.50	4,444	1,111	−$16,667	−$12,500	−$4,167
0.00	3,536	1,768	−$14,645	−$12,500	−$2,145
1.00	3,018	2,134	−$13,572	−$12,500	−$1,072
5.00	2,617	2,379	−$12,855	−$12,500	−$365
25.00	2,538	2,472	−$12,582	−$12,500	−$82
∞	2,500	2,500	−$12,500	−$12,500	$0

It should be clear to you by this point that the size of the substitution effect is captured in the downward slope of the conditional input demands.[5] Thus, as the elasticity of substitution in production increases, the input demand curves become flatter causing the substitution effect to become relatively more important. Table 13.2 illustrates this with an example in which the production function is a generalized CES production function with decreasing returns to scale. The general form of this function is

$$f(\ell,k) = A(\alpha\ell^{-\rho} + (1-\alpha)k^{-\rho})^{-\beta/\rho}, \qquad (13.37)$$

where, as in the case of CES utility functions, ρ can take on values between -1 and ∞ with the elasticity of substitution given by $1/(1+\rho)$. Thus, when $\rho = -1$, the isoquants are straight lines with perfect substitutability between labor and capital, while when $\rho = \infty$, labor and capital are perfect complements in production. The only difference between this family of CES production functions and the family of CES utility functions we defined in Chapter 5 is that we have included the additional β and A terms in the producer version, terms we will see used later in this chapter. For now we can simply note that β indicates the returns to scale of the function (with $\beta < 1$ indicating decreasing returns to scale and $\beta > 1$ indicating increasing returns to scale) and A scales the function up or down. We will explore the properties of this family of production functions in some more detail at the end of the chapter.[6]

---

[5]In the Appendix to Chapter 10, we proved formally that compensated demand curves always slope down in consumer theory, and, since we have seen that compensated demand curves are exactly analogous to conditional input demand curves in producer theory, the same argument can be used to prove formally that conditional input demand curves slope down; i.e., the substitution effect always points in the same direction.

[6]While it is algebraically tedious, you can calculate the various functions in the duality picture that arise from the generalized CES function. For instance, the input demand and output supply functions are

$$\ell(p,w,r) = \left(\frac{w + r\gamma}{\beta Ap(\alpha + (1-\alpha)\gamma^{-\rho})^{-(\beta/\rho)}}\right)^{1/(\beta-1)},$$

$$k(p,w,r) = \gamma\left(\frac{w + r\gamma}{\beta Ap(\alpha + (1-\alpha)\gamma^{-\rho})^{-(\beta/\rho)}}\right)^{1/(\beta-1)}, \qquad (13.38)$$

$$x(p,w,r) = (Ap)^{-1/(\beta-1)}\left(\frac{w + r\gamma}{\beta(\alpha + (1-\alpha)\gamma^{-\rho})^{-(\beta/\rho)}}\right)^{\beta/(\beta-1)}\left(\alpha + (1-\alpha)\gamma^{-\rho}\right)^{-\beta/\rho}.$$

where

$$\gamma = \left(\frac{(1-\alpha)w}{\alpha r}\right)^{1/(\rho+1)} \qquad (13.39)$$

**Exercise
13B.14**   If the generalized CES function was used as a utility function instead of the version where A and β are set to 1, would the underlying tastes represented by that function be changed?

The particular version of this production function selected for the derivation of results in Table 13.2 has the property that, when w and r are set to \$10 and p is set to \$20, the profit-maximizing production plan is $(x, \ell, k) = (5000, 2500, 2500)$ regardless of what value ρ takes. Table 13.2 then presents the conditional input demand for labor and capital when wage drops to \$5 and production remains at 5,000 units of output, and it reports the overall change in the cost of producing 5,000 units of output as well as the portion of the overall drop in costs that is due to the direct effect and the portion that is due to the substitution effect. Notice that, as the production process becomes one of declining substitutability between capital and labor (as one goes down the table), the direct effect of the drop in w on cost (equivalent to moving from the blue to the magenta curves in our graphs) remains constant while the effect due to the substitution effect (equivalent to moving from the magenta to the green curves in our graphs) declines dramatically.

**Exercise
13B.15**   Explain why the direct effect in the table does not depend on the degree of substitutability between capital and labor in production.

13B.3 Input Demand and Changes in the Economic Environment

In Section A, we demonstrated that input demand curves slope down and that short-run input demand curves are steeper than long-run input demand curves. We also showed that the "cross-price" relationship between one input's price and demand for another input is ambiguous and depends on the relative substitutability of the inputs in production. Similarly, we showed that short-run and long-run labor responses to output price changes may differ with the relative substitutability of the inputs. In this section, we will demonstrate some of these results mathematically and illustrate others by using specific production functions.

13B.3.1 Input Demand Curves Slope Down   In Graph 13.10 (and implicitly in Graphs 13.9 and 13.11), we illustrated the impact of input price changes on input demand and for both labor and capital found that the *own price input demand curves slope down*; that is, the quantity of labor demanded falls with increases in w and the quantity of capital demanded falls with increases in r. While our graphical illustrations were for the case of homothetic production processes, the result turns out to hold more generally, with no possibility of upward-sloping input demand curves (unlike in consumer theory where a sufficiently large income effect—absent from producer theory—could lead to upward-sloping consumer demand curves). And like our proof that output supply curves slope down (in Section 13B.2.1), this can be illustrated quickly from Hotelling's Lemma and the fact that profit functions are convex (as developed in the appendix to Chapter 12). First, Hotelling's Lemma states that

$$\frac{\partial \pi(p, w, r)}{\partial w} = -\ell(p, w, r) \text{ and } \frac{\partial \pi(p, w, r)}{\partial r} = -k(p, w, r). \tag{13.40}$$

The convexity of the profit function implies that

$$\frac{\partial^2 \pi(p, w, r)}{\partial w^2} \geq 0 \text{ and } \frac{\partial^2 \pi(p, w, r)}{\partial r^2} \geq 0. \tag{13.41}$$

Combining these, we can conclude that

$$\frac{\partial \ell(p,w,r)}{\partial w} = -\frac{\partial^2 \pi(p,w,r)}{\partial w^2} \leq 0 \quad \text{and} \quad \frac{\partial k(p,w,r)}{\partial r} = -\frac{\partial^2 \pi(p,w,r)}{\partial r^2} \leq 0; \quad (13.42)$$

i.e., labor and capital demand curves slope down with respect to their own prices. Since the properties of profit functions and Hotelling's Lemma apply regardless of how many inputs a production function has when the optimization problem is solved, this implies that the result holds for both short-run and long-run input demand curves (since short-run supply curves are derived simply from smaller dimensional slices of larger dimensional production frontiers).

Show that the short- and long-run input demand curves calculated for the production function $f(\ell,k) = 20\ell^{2/5}k^{2/5}$ in equation (13.33) and (13.31) are downward sloping.

Exercise 13B.16

13B.3.2 Labor Demand Curves are Steeper in the Long Run than in the Short Run

Next, we illustrated in Graph 13.10 that short-run labor demand curves are steeper than long-run labor demand curves; or, put differently, as wage changes, the quantity of labor adjusts more in the long run than in the short run. This result is similar to the result in Section 13B.2.2 that output supply is more responsive in the long run than in the short run. In fact, the steps are virtually identical to those in equations (13.26) through (13.30), except that derivatives are with respect to w rather than p. I will therefore leave it to you as an end-of-chapter exercise to demonstrate that labor demand responses to wage changes are stronger in the long run than in the short run.

13B.3.3 Substitutability of ℓ and k and Slopes of Cross-Price Input Demand

In some of the same graphs (particularly Graphs 13.10 and 13.11), we also demonstrated that cross-price input demand relationships may be upward or downward sloping depending on the substitutability of capital and labor in production. More specifically, we showed that demand for capital may increase or decrease with the wage rate, and demand for labor may increase or decrease with the rental rate of capital. And we demonstrated that *a positive cross-price input demand relationship emerges when inputs are relatively substitutable, while a negative relationship emerges when they are relatively complementary.*

We will forego demonstrating this formally but will rather return to our example of a generalized CES production function $f(\ell,k) = A(\alpha\ell^{-\rho} + (1-\alpha)k^{-\rho})^{-\beta/\rho}$. Specifically, we will again let $A = 100$, $\alpha = 0.5$, and $\beta = 0.5$ and present in Table 13.3 how input demands change as the substitutability of the inputs (captured by the parameter ρ) changes. And, as in the previous table, we begin in the economic environment $(p,w,r) = (20,10,10)$. For this particular configuration of economic and technological parameters, the profit-maximizing production plan is invariant to changes in ρ. With $(x,\ell,r) = (5000,2500,2500)$ optimal for all degrees of substitutability of inputs.[7]

Beginning with the economic environment $(p,w,r) = (20,10,10)$, we then ask how the behavior of the producer changes in the short and long run as w increases from 10 to 11. In particular, Table 13.3 reports the new short- and long-run labor demand, the new long-run demand for capital, and the new short- and long-run output supply for this wage increase as we vary the

---

[7]This is very much a special case, with optimal production plans ordinarily varying a great deal with the degree of input substitutability. The special case arises from the fact that we have set α equal to 0.5 *and* because we have set the initial wage and rental rates to be equal to one another. You should be able to convince yourself that $\alpha = 0.5$ implies that all isoquants have slope -1 along the 45-degree line. Similarly, isocosts have slope -1 when wages and rental rates are equal to one another. Thus, all cost-minimizing bundles lie on the 45-degree line, and changing ρ simply changes the curvature of isoquants without changing the slope along the 45-degree line. Furthermore, changing ρ does not alter the vertical slice of the production choice set along the 45-degree line, which implies that the cost-minimizing bundle that is also profit-maximizing will remain unchanged by changes in ρ. We will explore this in some more detail in one of the end-of-chapter exercises that employs a computer simulation.

Table 13.3: Cross-Price Input Demands when w Increases (from 10 to 11) and $\bar{k} = 2,500$

ρ	$\ell(20,10,10)$	$\ell_{\bar{k}}(20,11,10)$	$\ell(20,11,10)$	$k(20,11,10)$	$x_{\bar{k}}(20,11,10)$	$x(20,11,10)$
-0.99	2,500	1,652	0.36	4,965	4,556	4,965
-0.80	2,500	1,891	1,767	2,845	4,681	4,789
-0.60	2,500	2,021	2,016	2,558	4,749	4,775
-0.50	2,500	2,066	2,066	2,500	4,773	4,773
-0.25	2,500	2,147	2,133	2,422	4,815	4,769
0.00	2,500	2,201	2,167	2,384	4,843	4,767
0.50	2,500	2,271	2,200	2,345	4,880	4,766
1.00	2,500	2,314	2,217	2,326	4,902	4,765
5.00	2,500	2,425	2,250	2,287	4,961	4,763
50.00	2,500	2,490	2,266	2,270	4,995	4,762

The header of the table reads: SR and LR Production Plans When w Increases and $f(\ell,k) = 100(0.5\ell^{-\rho} + 0.5k^{-\rho})^{-0.5/\rho}$

input substitutability (as captured by ρ) beginning with virtually perfect substitutes in the first row to virtually perfect complements in the final row. First, notice that labor demand falls (from the initial 2,500), both in the short run and the long run, for all rows, and it always falls more in the long run than in the short run. This is consistent with our conclusions about labor demand thus far.

Exercise 13B.17   Can you make sense of the fact that the demand for labor falls less (both in the short and long run) the more complementary labor and capital are in production?

Second, consider the column that illustrates demand for capital at the higher wage $(k(20,11,10))$ and recall that the optimal production plan before w increased contained 2,500 units of capital. When ρ lies between -1 and -0.5 and the inputs are therefore relatively substitutable, demand for capital increases as wage increases, whereas when ρ rises above -0.5 and inputs become less substitutable, demand for capital falls when wage increases. This is precisely the result we derived intuitively in Graph 13.10 where the relationship between capital and wage was upward sloping in panel (g) when it was derived from relatively flat isoquants in panel (a), while the relationship was downward sloping in panel (i) when it was derived from isoquants with relatively little substitutability in panel (c). Panel (h) of Graph 13.10 then gives the "in between case" where the quantity of capital demanded as the wage changes is the same as the original quantity at the initial wage. In this special case, the producer is therefore able to go immediately to the long-run profit-maximizing production plan because there is no need to change how much capital is used.

Exercise 13B.18   What value of ρ, and what implied elasticity of substitution between capital and labor, corresponds to the "in between case"?

Lastly, notice one other feature of Table 13.3: While output always falls, both in the short and long run, from the 5,000 units of output before the wage increased, it *increases* from the short to the long run when labor and capital are relatively substitutable and *decreases* from the short to the long run when labor and capital are relatively complementary. This, too, is consistent with Graph 13.10 where long-run output x^C falls on a higher isoquant than short-run output x^B in panel (a) but not in panel (c). The dividing line between these two cases is once again the case where capital input remains unchanged as w rises, with short-run and long-run production plans coinciding in panel (b).

13B.3.4 Demand for Labor as p Changes

Finally, we used two extreme sets of isoquants in Graph 13.12 to argue that the relationship between the short- and long-run labor demand response to changes in output price also depends on the relative substitutability of labor and capital. The intuition behind this result is relatively straightforward. Whenever output price rises, we know from our results on output supply curves that producers will want to produce more in the short run and even more in the long run. Suppose capital and labor are relatively substitutable and capital is relatively cheap compared to labor. Then producers would rely primarily on capital in their production processes, but if capital is fixed in the short run, they might initially hire additional labor to increase production in response to an output price increase. In the long run, however, they would substitute away from this additional labor and into more capital. Thus, it may well be the case that labor demand increases in the short run with an increase in output price but that some of that increased labor is laid off as the producer enters the long run. At the same time, if capital and labor are relatively more complementary, short-run increases in labor may be supplemented with additional increases in labor as capital is adjusted in the long run.

We again illustrate this with the CES production function we previously used in Table 13.3 and with an initial economic environment $(p, w, r) = (20, 10, 10)$. Table 13.4 then once again varies ρ in the first column, going from virtually perfect substitutes in the first row to virtually perfect complements in the last row. The table differs from Table 13.3 in that now we are changing the output price from 20 to 25 rather than changing the wage. Note that since the ratio of wage to rental rate

Table 13.4: Substitutability and Responses to a Change in p (from 20 to 25) when $\bar{k} = 2{,}500$

ρ	$\ell(20,10,10)$	$\ell_{\bar{k}}(25,10,10)$	$\ell(25,10,10)$	$k(25,10,10)$	$x_{\bar{k}}(25,10,10)$	$x(25,10,10)$
\multicolumn{7}{l}{SR and LR Production Plans When p Increases and $f(\ell,k) = 100(0.5\ell^{-\rho} + 0.5k^{-\rho})^{-0.5/\rho}$}
−0.99	2,500	5,270	3,906	3,906	6,230	6,250
−0.80	2,500	4,584	3,906	3,906	5,925	6,250
−0.60	2,500	4,088	3,906	3,906	5,707	6,250
−0.50	2,500	3,906	3,906	3,906	5,625	6,250
−0.25	2,500	3,579	3,906	3,906	5,480	6,250
0.00	2,500	3,366	3,906	3,906	5,386	6,250
0.50	2,500	3,116	3,906	3,906	5,275	6,250
1.00	2,500	2,975	3,906	3,906	5,212	6,250
5.00	2,500	2,666	3,906	3,906	5,074	6,250
50.00	2,500	2,520	3,906	3,906	5,009	6,250

therefore does not change in this table, the long-run profit-maximizing input bundle will have the same ratio of labor to capital at any output price, but in the short run this ratio changes as we hold capital fixed.

Exercise 13B.19

Can you identify in Table 13.4 the relationship of the substitutability of capital and labor to the degree of short- versus long-run response in labor demand from an increase in output price? Is this consistent with what emerges in Graph 13.12?

13B.4 Technological Change: The Role of β and A in the Generalized CES Production Function

In Section A, we described the impact of a particular type of technological change, one that keeps isoquants unchanged while relabeling them. With our generalized CES production function, we could in principle permit technology to change in a variety of other ways, but we will restrict ourselves here to investigating changes in producer choices when technological change takes the form it did in Section A, which occurs when β or A change but not when ρ or α change in the function $f(\ell, k) = A(\alpha \ell^{-\rho} + (1 - \alpha)k^{-\rho})^{-\beta/\rho}$.

To see this, it is relatively straightforward to first derive the *TRS* of the generalized CES function as

$$TRS = -\frac{\alpha k^{(\rho+1)}}{(1 - \alpha)\ell^{(\rho+1)}}. \tag{13.43}$$

Exercise 13B.20

Can you use equation (13.43) to demonstrate that generalized CES production functions take on the Cobb–Douglas form when $\rho = 0$?

Since the parameters A and β do not appear in the expression for *TRS*, we can conclude immediately that these parameters do not affect the shapes of isoquants, only their labeling. The parameters α and ρ, on the other hand, alter the shapes of isoquants, with ρ changing the elasticity of substitution and α altering the slope of isoquants at each input bundle. Graph 5.10 in Chapter 5, for instance, graphs indifference curves for different values of ρ with α set to 0.5 for a CES utility function, while Graph 5.9 illustrates three indifference maps with different values for α (when ρ is set to zero). Since A and β do not alter shapes of isoquants, these graphs look exactly the same for any value of A and β.

Exercise 13B.21

How does what you have just learned explain why we did not have an A or β parameter in CES utility functions?

The parameter β is, as we indicated before, a measure of returns to scale. To be more precise, *the generalized CES production function is homogeneous of degree β*, implying that it has decreasing returns to scale when $\beta < 1$, constant returns to scale when $\beta = 1$, and increasing returns to scale when $\beta > 1$. This is easily demonstrated in the usual way by illustrating that when inputs are multiplied by a factor t, output rises by t^β:

$$
\begin{aligned}
f(t\ell, tk) &= A(\alpha(t\ell)^{-\rho} + (1 - \alpha)(tk)^{-\rho})^{-\beta/\rho} \\
&= A(t^{-\rho}(\alpha \ell^{-\rho} + (1 - \alpha)k^{-\rho}))^{-\beta/\rho} \\
&= t^\beta A(\alpha \ell^{-\rho} + (1 - \alpha)k^{-\rho})^{-\beta/\rho} = t^\beta f(\ell, k).
\end{aligned}
\tag{13.44}
$$

The parameter A, on the other hand, simply scales the production function up or down without changing returns to scale, causing the marginal products of the inputs at any input bundle to increase in proportion to one another (as we assumed in our discussion of technological change in Section A).

Given that the CES production function is homothetic, cost-minimizing choices occur along rays in our isoquant pictures, and as technological change alters the labeling of isoquants without altering their shapes, profit-maximizing producers therefore change input bundles along the relevant ray (so long as input prices remain the same). As β and A rise, the ratio of input bundles at the optimum production plan is therefore unchanged, but the optimal plan entails greater demand for capital and labor, and greater output.

Table 13.5 illustrates changes in output levels for different combinations of A and β, holding $\rho = 1$ and $\alpha = 0.5$. First, note that output increases in the parameter A with the exception of the last column where β is set greater than 1. Since we know how β is related to returns to scale, we know that this last column models a production process that has increasing returns to scale, which implies that production becomes easier and easier the more inputs are thrown into the production process. If this is the case, however, then it ought to be the case that a price-taking producer will produce an infinite amount of the output, a case we briefly investigated in Graph 12.9 where we concluded that it makes little sense to model producers whose production process has increasing returns to scale as price-takers.

The case of $\beta > 1$ is also a case where our Lagrange solution method (that results in equations (13.38)) yields an incorrect answer, because the actual optimum is a corner solution (involving an infinite amount of capital and labor to produce an infinite level of output). We can picture this in a 2-dimensional graph because we know (from the homotheticity of the CES function) that, for a given set of input prices (w, r), all cost-minimizing plans for any output level x always involve the same ratio of $\ell(x, w, r)$ to $k(x, w, r)$ regardless of the value of β (since TRS is not affected by β). Thus, for a given set of input prices (w^A, r^A), we can graph simply the vertical slice of the production function along the ray from the origin with slope $\ell(x, w^A, r^A)/k(x, w^A, r^A)$; i.e., the ray that contains all input bundles that have $-TRS = w^A/r^A$. This is pictured in Graph 13.17 for two values of β when $A = 100$ and when the input prices are $(w, r) = (10, 10)$ and all cost-minimizing input bundles lie on the 45-degree line of our usual isoquant map. Both ℓ and k appear on the same horizontal axis (since they are equal to one another along the 45-degree line of our usual isoquant map), while output is graphed on the vertical axis. The line tangent to the slice of the production set is then a slice of the isoprofit plane that results in A being the profit-maximizing production plan in panel (a) where β is set to 0.5 and the production function therefore has decreasing returns to scale. In panel (b), on the other hand, β is set to 1.1, resulting in a non-convex production choice set with increasing

Table 13.5: (Long-Run) Changes in Production with Changes in Technology

Optimal x for $f(\ell, k) = A(0.5\ell^{-1} + 0.5k^{-1})^{-\beta}$ when $(p, w, r) = (20, 10, 10)$						
A	$\beta = 0.1$	$\beta = 0.25$	$\beta = 0.5$	$\beta = 0.75$	$\beta = 0.9$	$\beta = 1.1$
5	4.629	5.386	12.5	263.7	3,783,403	$3.589(10^{-8})$
10	10	13.52	25	4,219	$3.874(10^{10})$	$3.505(10^{-11})$
25	27.68	46.05	312.5	164,794	$3.695(10^{13})$	$3.675(10^{-15})$
50	59.79	116.0	1,250	2,636,718	$3.783(10^{16})$	$3.589(10^{-19})$
100	129.2	292.4	2,500	42,187,500	$3.874(10^{19})$	$3.505(10^{-21})$

Graph 13.17: Profit Maximization with (a) $\beta = 0.5$ and (b) $\beta = 1.1$

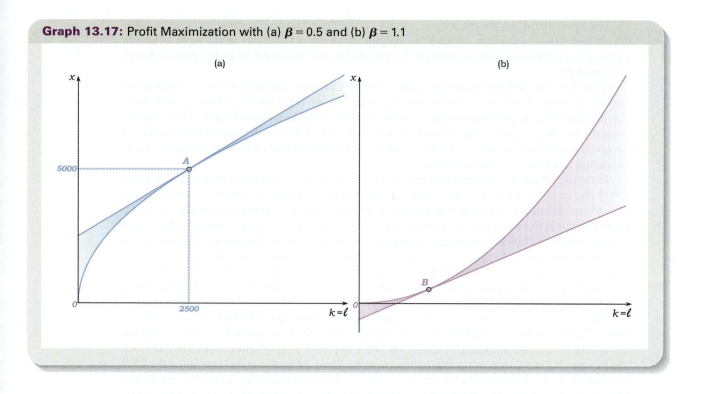

returns to scale. The Lagrange Method then finds the production plan B that lies at a tangency of the isoprofit curve with the production function, but because the increasing returns to scale of the production process results in a non-convex production choice set, this tangency is not the true optimum, with all shaded production plans yielding higher profit. In fact, profit at the production plan B is negative.

Exercise 13B.22 Can you confirm using the last equation in (13.38) that output will increase with a change in A so long as $\beta < 1$? (*Hint*: While the equation is messy, taking the derivative with respect to A is straightforward.)

Exercise 13B.23 What values could the optimal production plans take if $\beta = 1$?

We can also get a sense of how output changes with changes in β (rather than A) by reading across Table 13.5: output is increasing in β (i.e., as returns to scale increase) as long as β remains below 1 (or as long as we remember that the "solutions" derived for $\beta = 1.1$ are actually not correct since the firm would want to produce an infinite amount). This should strike an intuitive cord; when it becomes easier and easier to produce (as β increases), output goes up. Since the shapes of isoquants are again unaffected by changes in β, we could plot vertical slices of the production function similar to those we graphed in Graph 13.17 to illustrate profit maximization.

CONCLUSION

This chapter concludes our treatment of production by a price-taking firm in isolation. We began the chapter by tracing out the impact of changes in input prices on cost curves, and we emphasized that care must be taken to include in these curves only those expenditures by the firm that are true economic costs. When we do this correctly, it is *always* the case that the price-taking firm's supply curve, whether in the short or long run, is equal to the portion of the marginal cost curve that lies above average cost. Because some expenses (such as those on inputs that are fixed in the short run) are not real economic costs in the short run, we found that firms will often stay open in the short run even if they have decided that they will exit the industry in the long run. This is because short-run profit can be positive even when long-run profit is negative when certain long-run costs are not real economic costs in the short run, and it implies that the short-run supply curve extends "below" the long run supply curve. We furthermore found that output supply responses to price changes are greater in the long run than in the short run, and that labor demand responses to wage changes are similarly greater in the long run than in the short run.

Much of the remainder of the chapter focused on the role of substitution effects in production. When one input price changes relative to another, we found that firms will, conditional on producing some output quantity, substitute away from the input that has become relatively more expensive and toward the input that has become relatively cheaper. The degree of substitutability between inputs in the production process was then found to determine whether "cross-price" input demands slope up or down—whether long-run labor demand increases or decreases with an increase in the price of capital, and whether long-run capital demand increases or decreases with an increase in the price of labor. We similarly determined that the degree of substitutability of inputs determines whether changes in labor demand are greater or less in the short run than in the long run when output price changes. Finally, we discussed briefly how technological change impacts firm decisions, or how this impacts cost curves as well as optimal production plans. In general, technological change reduces costs and increases output.

We will now leave behind some of the details we uncovered in this chapter and move toward discussing the interaction of the demand and supply sides of markets. This implies that we will combine the insights from consumer theory with those from producer theory, putting consumer demand together with producer supply in output markets, and combining consumer supply and producer demand in input markets. Put differently, we will now move from the world of "optimization" where we consider an individual's choices in isolation toward the world of "equilibrium" where we investigate the aggregate implications of individual optimizing behavior. What happens when lots of price-taking individuals who try to do the best they can on all sides of a market interact with one another? And how does our answer to this change when underlying conditions change?

END-OF-CHAPTER EXERCISES

13.1 The following problem explores the relationship between maximizing profit in the short and long run when capital is fixed in the short run.

A. Suppose you have a homothetic production technology and you face output price p and input prices (w, r).

a. On a graph with labor ℓ on the horizontal and capital k on the vertical axis, draw an isoquant and label a point on that isoquant as $(\bar{\ell}, \bar{k})$.

b. Suppose that the point in your graph represents a profit-maximizing production plan. What has to be true at this point?

c. In your graph, illustrate the slice along which the firm must operate in the short run.

d. Suppose that the production technology has decreasing returns to scale throughout. If p falls, can you illustrate all the possible points in your graph where the new profit-maximizing production plan might lie in the long run? What about the short run?

e. What condition that is satisfied in the long run will typically not be satisfied in the short run?

f. What qualification would you have to make to your answer in (d) if the production process had initially increasing but eventually decreasing returns to scale?

---

*conceptually challenging
**computationally challenging
†solutions in Study Guide

B. Consider the Cobb–Douglas production function $x = f(\ell, k) = A\ell^\alpha k^\beta$.

    a.** For input prices (w, r) and output price p, calculate the long-run input demand and output supply functions assuming $0 < \alpha, \beta \leq 1$ and $\alpha + \beta < 1$.

    b.   How would your answer change if $\alpha + \beta \geq 1$?

    c.   Suppose that capital is fixed at $\bar{k}$ in the short run. Calculate the short-run input demand and output supply functions.

    d.   What has to be true about α and β for these short-run functions to be correct?

    e.   Suppose $\bar{k} = k(w, r, p)$ (where $k(w, r, p)$ is the long-run capital demand function you calculated in part (a)). What is your optimal short-run labor demand and output supply in that case?

    f.   How do your answers compare to the long-run labor demand function $\ell(w, r, p)$ and the long-run supply function $x(w, r, p)$ you calculated in part (a)? Can you make intuitive sense of this?

13.2   The following problem explores issues similar to those in exercise 13.1, but instead of thinking directly about profit maximization, we will think about cost minimization on the way to profit maximization.

A. Suppose you have a homothetic production technology and you face input prices (w, r).

    a.   On a graph with labor ℓ on the horizontal and capital k on the vertical axis, illustrate a ray along which all cost-minimizing production plans might lie for a given set of input prices. Does your answer depend on whether the production technology has increasing or decreasing returns to scale (or some combination of these)?

    b.   Illustrate in your graph an isoquant corresponding to some output level $\bar{x}$. What has to be true at the intersection of the ray and the isoquant?

    c.   Show what happens to the ray of cost-minimizing input bundles if w increases to w'. Then illustrate how you would derive the conditional labor demand curve for producing $\bar{x}$.

    d.   From this point forward, suppose that the production technology has decreasing returns to scale. Illustrate how you would derive the firm's long-run cost curve for the original input prices.

    e.   What happens to the cost curve when w increases to w'?

    f.   Suppose that you are initially producing at the intersection of your original isoquant (corresponding to $\bar{x}$) and the original ray. If w remained unchanged, where would your (short-run) *expenditure* curve fall on your graph with the long-run cost curve?

    g.   Translate your cost/expenditure curve graph to a graph with the average (long-run) cost and average (short-run) expenditure curves.

    h.   How does the average (long-run) cost curve change when w increases to w'? If you also graphed a cost curve that removed the substitution effect, where would it generally lie relative to the original and final cost curve? What would its precise location depend on?

    i.   Now suppose that instead of wage increasing, the rental rate on capital r fell to r'. What happens to the conditional labor demand curve that you graphed in part (c)?

    j.   Repeat (h) for the change in the rental rate.

B. Suppose again (as in exercise 13.1) that the production process is defined by the Cobb–Douglas production function $x = f(\ell, k) = A\ell^\alpha k^\beta$.

    a.** For input prices (w, r), calculate the long-run conditional input demand functions.

    b.   Do you need to assume $0 < \alpha, \beta \leq 1$ and $\alpha + \beta < 1$ in order for these to be valid?

    c.   Derive the long-run total, marginal, and average cost functions.

    d.   Suppose output price is p. Use your answer to derive the firm's (long-run) profit-maximizing output supply function. Do you need to assume $0 < \alpha, \beta \leq 1$ and $\alpha + \beta < 1$ for this to be valid? (If you have done exercise 13.1, check to make sure your answer agrees with what you concluded in part (a) of that exercise.)

    e.   From your answer, derive the firm's profit-maximizing long-run labor and capital demand functions. (You can again check your answers with those you derived through direct profit maximization in exercise 13.1.)

    f.   Now suppose capital is fixed in the short-run at $\bar{k}$. Derive the short-run conditional input demand for labor.

g.   Derive the short-run (total) cost function as well as the short-run marginal and average cost functions.

h.   Derive the short-run supply curve.

i.   *True or False*: As long as the production function has decreasing returns the scale, the (short-run) average *expenditure* curve will be U-shaped even though the short-run average cost curve is not.

j.   What is the shape of the long-run average cost curve? Can the Cobb–Douglas production function yield U-shaped long-run average cost curves?

13.3   In this exercise, we add a (long-run) fixed cost to the analysis.

A.   Suppose the production process for a firm is homothetic and has decreasing returns to scale.

a.   On a graph with labor ℓ on the horizontal and capital k on the vertical axis, draw an isoquant corresponding to output level $\bar{x}$. For some wage rate w and rental rate r, indicate the cost-minimizing input bundle for producing $\bar{x}$.

b.   Indicate in your graph the slice of the production frontier along which all cost-minimizing input bundles lie for this wage and rental rate.

c.   In two separate graphs, draw the (total) cost curve and the average cost curve with the marginal cost curve.

d.   Suppose that, in addition to paying for labor and capital, the firm has to pay a recurring fixed cost (such as a license fee). What changes in your graphs?

e.   What is the firm's exit price in the absence of fixed costs? What happens to that exit price when a fixed cost is added?

f.   Does the firm's supply curve shift as we add a fixed cost?

g.   Suppose that the cost-minimizing input bundle for producing $\bar{x}$ that you graphed in part (a) is also the profit-maximizing production plan before a fixed cost is considered. Will it still be the profit-maximizing production plan after we include the fixed cost in our analysis?

B.   As in exercises 13.1 and 13.2, suppose the production process is again characterized by the production function $x = f(l, k) = A\ell^{\alpha}k^{\beta}$ with $0 < \alpha, \beta \le 1$ and $\alpha + \beta < 1$.

a.   If you have not already done so in a previous exercise, derive the (long-run) cost function for this firm.

b.   Now suppose that, in addition to the cost associated with inputs, the firm has to pay a recurring fixed cost of FC. Write down the cost minimization problem that includes this FC. Will the conditional input demand functions change as a result of the FC being included?

c.   Write down the new cost function and derive the marginal and average cost functions from it.

d.   What is the shape of the average cost curve? How does its lowest point change with changes in the FC?

e.   Does the addition of a FC term change the (long-run) marginal cost curve? Does it change the long-run supply curve?

f.   How would you write out the profit maximization problem for this firm including fixed costs? If you were to solve this problem, what role would the FC term play?

g.   Considering not just the math but also the underlying economics, does the addition of the FC have any implications for the input demand and output supply functions?

13.4   Repeat exercise 13.3 assuming increasing rather than decreasing returns to scale. What changes in the analysis, and what does not change?

13.5[†]   We will often assume that a firm's long-run average cost curve is U-shaped. This shape may arise for two different reasons that we explore in this exercise.

A.   Assume that the production technology uses labor ℓ and capital k as inputs, and assume throughout this problem that the firm is currently long-run profit-maximizing and employing a production plan that is placing it at the lowest point of its long-run AC curve.

a. Suppose first that the technology has decreasing returns to scale but that, in order to begin producing each year, the firm has to pay a fixed license fee F. Explain why this causes the long-run AC curve to be U-shaped.

b. Draw a graph with the U-shaped AC curve from the production process described in part (a). Then add to this the short-run MC and AC curves. Is the short-run AC curve also U-shaped?

c. Next, suppose that there are no fixed costs in the long run. Instead, the production process is such that the marginal product of each input is initially increasing but eventually decreasing, and the production process as a whole has initially increasing but eventually decreasing returns to scale. (A picture of such a production process was given in Graph 12.16 of of the previous chapter.) Explain why the long-run AC curve is U-shaped in this case.

d. Draw another graph with the U-shaped AC curve. Then add the short-run MC and AC curves. Are they also U-shaped?

e.* Is it possible for short-run AC curves to *not* be U-shaped if the production process has initially increasing but eventually decreasing returns to scale?

B. Suppose first that the production process is Cobb–Douglas, characterized by the production function $x = f(\ell, k) = A\ell^\alpha k^\beta$ with $\alpha, \beta > 0$ and $\alpha + \beta < 1$.

a. In the absence of fixed costs, you should have derived in exercise 13.2 that the long-run cost function for this technology is given by

$$C(w, r, x) = (\alpha + \beta)\left(\frac{w^\alpha r^\beta x}{A\alpha^\alpha \beta^\beta}\right)^{1/(\alpha+\beta)}. \tag{13.45}$$

If the firm has long-run fixed costs F, what is its long-run average cost function? Is the average cost curve U-shaped?

b. What is the short-run cost curve for a fixed level of capital $\bar{k}$? Is the short-run average cost curve U-shaped?

c. Now suppose that the production function is still $f(\ell, k) = A\ell^\alpha k^\beta$ but now $\alpha + \beta > 1$. Are long-run average and marginal cost curves upward or downward sloping? Are short-run average cost curves upward or downward sloping? What does your answer depend on?

d.** Next, suppose that the production technology were given by the equation

$$x = f(\ell, k) = \frac{\alpha}{1 + e^{-(\ell-\beta)} + e^{-(k-\gamma)}} \tag{13.46}$$

where e is the base of the natural logarithm. (We first encountered this in exercises 12.5 and 12.6.) If capital is fixed at $\bar{k}$, what is the short-run production function and what is the short-run cost function?

e.** What is the short-run marginal cost function?

f. You should have concluded in exercise 12.6 that the long-run MC function is $MC(w, r, x) = \alpha(w + r)/(x(\alpha - x))$ and demonstrated that the MC curve (and thus the long-run AC curve) is U-shaped for the parameters $\alpha = 100$, $\beta = 5 = \gamma$ when $w = r = 20$. Now suppose capital is fixed at $\bar{k} = 8$. Graph the short-run MC curve and use the information to conclude whether the short-run AC curve is also U-shaped.

g. What characteristic of the this production function is responsible for your answer in part (f)?

13.6* In Graph 13.3, we illustrated the relationship between short-run average expenditure AE_k, short-run average cost AC_k, and long-run average cost AC^{LR} curves for a particular level of capital. The particular level of capital chosen in Graph 13.3 is that level which makes the AE_k curve tangent to the AC^{LR} at its lowest point.

A. Consider a firm whose technology has decreasing returns to scale throughout and who faces a recurring fixed cost. Denote the level of capital chosen in the long run at the lowest point of the long run AC as k^*.

a. Replicate the short-run MC and long-run AC curves from Graph 13.3. Where in your graph does the long-run MC curve lie?

b. Draw a separate graph with the AC^{LR} curve. Suppose that $k < k^*$ in the short run. Illustrate where the AE_k must now lie.

c. Next illustrate where the AC_k and MC_k curves lie. Is the long-run MC curve now different than in part (a)?

d. On a separate graph, repeat (b) and (c) for $k' > k^*$.

e. Illustrate the short-run MC curves you drew in parts (c) and (d) in the graph you first drew in part (a). How is this graph similar to Graph 13.7 in the text?

f. *True or False*: The MC_k curve crosses the AC^{LR} curve at the lowest point of the AE_k curve *only* if $k = k^*$.

g. How would your answer to (f) change if the sentence had started with the words "If the production technology has constant returns to scale and there are no fixed costs, ..."?

h. *True or False*: Unless the production technology has constant returns to scale and no long-run fixed costs, the short-run AE curves are tangent at the lowest point of the long-run AC curve only if $k = k^*$.

B. Suppose that a firm's production function is $x = f(\ell, k) = A\ell^\alpha k^\beta$ with $\alpha, \beta > 0$ and $\alpha + \beta < 1$. Suppose further that the firm incurs a recurring (long-run) fixed cost FC.

a. In equation (13.45) from exercise 13.5, we already provided the long-run cost function for such a firm in the absence of fixed costs. What are this firm's long-run marginal and average cost functions?

b. Derive the output level x^* at which the lowest point of the long-run average cost curve occurs.

c. From here on, suppose that $\alpha = 0.2$, $\beta = 0.6$, $A = 30$, $w = 20$, $r = 10$, and $FC = 1,000$. Given these values, what is x^*? How much capital k^* does the firm hire to produce x^*? (Note: The conditional input demand functions for a Cobb–Douglas production process are given in equation (13.47) of exercise 13.7.)

d. What is the long-run marginal cost of production at x^*? What about the long-run average cost? Interpret your answer.

e. For a fixed level of capital k, what are the short-run MC, AC, and AE functions?

f. What is the short-run AE, AC, and MC for $x = x^*$ when capital is fixed at k^*? How do these compare to long-run AC and MC of producing x^*?

g. Now suppose capital is fixed in the short run at $k = 200$. How does your answer to (f) change? What if capital were instead fixed at $k = 400$? Interpret your answer.

13.7*† **Business Application:** *Switching Technologies*: Suppose that a firm has two different homothetic, decreasing returns to scale technologies it could use, but one of these is patented and requires recurring license payments F to the owner of the patent. In this exercise, assume that all inputs, including the choice of which technology is used, are viewed from a long-run perspective.

BUSINESS APPLICATION

A. Suppose further that both technologies take capital k and labor ℓ as inputs but that the patented technology is more capital intensive.

a. Draw two isoquants, one from the technology representing the less capital intensive and one representing the more capital intensive technology. Then illustrate the slice of each map that a firm will choose to operate on assuming the wage w and rental rate r are the same in each case.

b. Suppose that the patented technology is sufficiently advanced such that, for any set of input prices, there always exists an output level $\bar{x}$ at which it is (long-run) cost effective to switch to this technology. On a graph with output x on the horizontal and dollars on the vertical, illustrate two cost curves corresponding to the two technologies and then locate $\bar{x}$. Then illustrate the cost curve that takes into account that a firm will switch to the patented technology at $\bar{x}$.

c. What happens to $\bar{x}$ if the license cost F for using the patented technology increases? Is it possible to tell what happens if the capital rental rate r increases?

d. At $\bar{x}$, which technology must have a higher marginal cost of production? On a separate graph, illustrate the marginal cost curves for the two technologies.

e. At $\bar{x}$, the firm is cost-indifferent between using the two technologies. Recognizing that the marginal cost curves capture all costs that are not fixed and that total costs excluding fixed costs can be represented as areas under marginal cost curves, can you identify an area in your graph that represents the recurring fixed license fee F?

f. Suppose output price p is such that it is profit-maximizing *under the nonpatented technology* to produce $\bar{x}$. Denote this as $\bar{p}$. Can you use marginal cost curves to illustrate whether you would produce more or less if you switched to the patented technology?

g. Would profit be higher if you used the patented or nonpatented technology when output price is $\bar{p}$. (*Hint*: Identify the total revenues if the firm produces at $\bar{p}$ under each of the technologies. Then identify the total cost of using the nonpatented technology as an area under the appropriate marginal cost curve and compare it to the total costs of using the patented technology as an area under the other marginal cost curve and add to it the fixed fee F.)

h. *True or False*: Although the total cost of production is the same under both technologies at output level $\bar{x}$, a profit-maximizing firm will choose the patented technology if price is such that $\bar{x}$ is profit maximizing under the nonpatented technology.

i. Illustrate the firm's supply curve. (*Hint*: The supply curve is not continuous, and the discontinuity occurs at a price below $\bar{p}$.)

B. Suppose that the two technologies available to you can be represented by the production functions $f(\ell, k) = 19.125\ell^{0.4}k^{0.4}$ and $g(\ell, k) = 30\ell^{0.2}k^{0.6}$, but technology g carries with it a recurring fee of F.

a. In exercise 13.2, you derived the general form for the two-input Cobb–Douglas conditional input demands and cost function.[8] Use this to determine the ratio of capital to labor (as a function of w and r) used under these two technologies. Which technology is more capital intensive?

b. Determine the cost functions for the two technologies (and be sure to include F where appropriate).

c. Determine the output level $\bar{x}$ (as a function of w, r and F) at which it becomes cost effective to switch from the technology f to the technology g. If F increases, is it possible to tell whether $\bar{x}$ increases or decreases? What if r increases?

d. Suppose $w = 20$ and $r = 10$. Determine the price $\bar{p}$ (as a function of F) at which a firm using technology f would produce $\bar{x}$.

e. How much would the firm produce with technology g if it faces $\bar{p}$? Can you tell whether, regardless of the size of F, this is larger or smaller than $\bar{x}$ (which is the profit-maximizing quantity when the firm uses technology f and faces $\bar{p}$)?

f. The (long-run) profit function for a Cobb–Douglas production function $f(\ell, k) = A\ell^{\alpha}k^{\beta}$ is

$$\pi(w, r, p) = (1 - \alpha - \beta)\left(\frac{Ap\alpha^{\alpha}\beta^{\beta}}{w^{\alpha}r^{\beta}}\right)^{1/(1-\alpha-\beta)}. \tag{13.48}$$

Can you use this to determine (as a function of p, w and r) the highest level of F at which a *profit-maximizing* firm will switch from f to g? Call this $\overline{F}(w, r, p)$.

g. From your answer to (f), determine (as a function of w, r and F) the price p^* at which a profit-maximizing firm will switch from technology f to technology g.

h. Suppose again that $w = 20$, $r = 10$. What is p^* (as a function of F)? Compare this to $\bar{p}$ you calculated in part (d) and interpret your answer in light of what you did in A(i).

i. Suppose (in addition to the values for parameters specified so far) that $F = 1,000$. What is $\bar{p}$ and p^*? At the price at which the profit-maximizing firm is indifferent between using technology f and technology g, how much does it produce when it uses f and how much does it produce when it uses g?[9]

---

[8]For the Cobb–Douglas production function $x = f(\ell, k) = A\ell^{\alpha}k^{\beta}$, you should have derived the conditional input demands

$$\ell(w, r, x) = \left(\frac{\alpha r}{\beta w}\right)^{\beta/(\alpha+\beta)}\left(\frac{x}{A}\right)^{1/(\alpha+\beta)} \quad \text{and} \quad k(w, r, x) = \left(\frac{\beta w}{\alpha r}\right)^{\alpha/(\alpha+\beta)}\left(\frac{x}{A}\right)^{1/(\alpha+\beta)}. \tag{13.49}$$

The cost function was previously provided in equation (13.45).

[9]Recall from your previous work in exercise 13.1 that the supply function for a Cobb–Douglas production process $f(\ell, k) = A\ell^{\alpha}k^{\beta}$ is

$$x(w, r, p) = \left(\frac{Ap^{(\alpha+\beta)}\alpha^{\alpha}\beta^{\beta}}{w^{\alpha}r^{\beta}}\right)^{1/(1-\alpha-\beta)}.$$

j. Continuing with the values we have been using (including $F = 1,000$), can you use your answer to (a) to determine how much labor and capital the firm hires at p^* under the two technologies? How else could you have calculated this?

k. Use what you have calculated in (i) and (j) to verify that profit is indeed the same for a firm whether it uses the f or the g technology when price is p^* (when the rest of the parameters of the problem are as we have specified them in (i) and (j)). (Note: If you rounded some of your previous numbers, you will not get exactly the same profit in both cases, but if the difference is small, it is almost certainly just a rounding error.)

13.8* Business Application: *Switching Technologies: Short Run versus Long Run*: In exercise 13.7, we viewed all inputs (including the technology that is chosen) as variable, which is to say we viewed these inputs from a long-run perspective.

A. Now consider the same set-up as in exercise 13.7 but assume throughout that labor is instantaneously variable, that capital is fixed in the short run and variable in the *intermediate* run, and that the choice of technology is fixed in the short and intermediate run but variable in the long run.

a. Suppose you are currently long-run profit-maximizing. Graph the (long-run) supply curve you derived in part A(i) of exercise 13.7 and indicate a price p and quantity x combination that is consistent with using the nonpatented technology.

b. Next suppose that output price increases to $\bar{p}$ and that this increase is sufficient for you to wish that you in fact had rented the patented technology instead. Illustrate how your output level will adjust in the intermediate run to x^{IR}.

c. In the short run, your firm cannot change its level of capital. Where would your short-run optimal output level x^{SR} (at the new $\bar{p}$) lie relative to x and x^{IR}? How is your answer impacted by the relative substitutability of capital and labor in the nonpatented technology?

d. In the long run, where will your optimal output level x^{LR} lie?

e. Suppose price had fallen to p instead of rising to $\bar{p}$. Indicate where your short, intermediate- and long-run output levels would lie.

f. On a new graph, illustrate the short-, intermediate-, and long-run supply curves for your firm given you started at the original price p and the original optimal output level x.

g. What would your last graph look like if you had originally started at price $\bar{p}$ and had originally produced at the long-run optimal output level x^{LR}?

B. Suppose, as in exercise 13.7, that the two technologies available to you can be represented by the production functions $f(\ell, k) = 19.125\ell^{0.4}k^{0.4}$ and $g(\ell, k) = 30\ell^{0.2}k^{0.6}$, but technology g carries with it a recurring fee of F. Suppose further that $w = 20$, $r = 10$, and $F = 1,000$.

a. If $p = 2.25$ and the firm is currently long-run optimizing, how much does it produce? (You can use what you learned from exercise 13.7 and employ equation (13.49).)

b. Now suppose the output price increases from 2.25 to 2.75. How much will the firm adjust output in the short run (where neither capital nor technology can be changed)?[10]

c. How much will it increase output in the intermediate run (where capital can adjust but technology remains fixed)?

d. How much will it adjust output in the long run?

e. What happens to the quantity of labor and capital hired in the short, intermediate, and long run?

f. Suppose that instead of increasing, the output price had fallen from 2.25 to 2.00. What would have happened to output in the short, intermediate, and long run?

g. Suppose that the firm has fully adjusted to the higher output price of 2.75. Then price falls to 2.25. What happens to output in the short, intermediate, and long run?

---

[10]It may be helpful to know that for Cobb–Douglas functions that take the form $f(\ell, k) = A\ell^{\alpha}k^{\beta}$, the input demand functions are

$$\ell(w, r, p) = \left(\frac{pA\alpha^{(1-\beta)}\beta^{\beta}}{w^{(1-\beta)}r^{\beta}}\right)^{1/(1-\alpha-\beta)} \quad \text{and} \quad k(w, r, p) = \left(\frac{pA\alpha^{\alpha}\beta^{(1-\alpha)}}{w^{\alpha}r^{(1-\alpha)}}\right)^{1/(1-\alpha-\beta)} \quad (13.50)$$

13.9*   **Business and Policy Application:** *Fixed amount of Land for Oil Drilling:* Suppose that your oil company is part of a competitive industry and is using three rather than two inputs—labor ℓ, capital k, and land L—to produce barrels of crude oil denoted by x. Suppose that the government, due to environmental concerns, has limited the amount of land available for oil drilling, and suppose that it has assigned each oil company $\bar{L}$ acres of such land. Assume throughout that oil sells at a market price p; labor, at a market wage of w; and capital, at a rental rate r, and these prices do not change as government policy changes.

A. Assume throughout that the production technology is homothetic and has constant returns to scale.

   a.   Suppose that, once assigned to an oil company, the company is not required to pay for using the land to drill for oil (but it cannot do anything else with it if it chooses not to drill). How much land will your oil company use?

   b.   While the three-input production frontier has constant returns to scale, can you determine the effective returns to scale of production once you take into account that available land is fixed?

   c.   What do average and marginal cost curves look like for your company over the time frame when both labor and capital can be varied?

   d.   Now suppose that the government begins to charge a per-acre rental price q for use of land that is assigned to your company, but an oil company that is assigned $\bar{L}$ acres of land only has the option of renting all $\bar{L}$ acres or none at all. Given that it takes time to relocate oil drilling equipment, you cannot adjust to this change in the short run. Will you change how much oil you produce?

   e.   In the long run (when you can move equipment off land), what happens to average and marginal costs for you company? Will you change your output level?

   f.   Suppose the government had employed a different policy that charges a per-acre rent of q but allowed companies to rent any number of acres between 0 and $\bar{L}$. What do long-run average and marginal cost curves look like in that case? Would it ever be the case that a firm will rent fewer than $\bar{L}$ acres? (*Hint:* These curves should have a flat as well as an upward-sloping portion.)

   g.   How much will you produce now compared to the case analyzed in (d)?

   h.   Suppose that under this alternative policy the government raises the rental price to q'. Will your company change its output level in the short run?

   i.   How do long-run average and marginal cost curves change? If you continue to produce oil under the higher land rental price, will you increase or decrease your output level, or will you leave it unchanged?

   j.   *True or False:* The land rental rate q set by the government has no impact on oil production levels so long as oil companies do not exit the industry. (*Hint:* This is true.)

B. Suppose that your production technology for oil drilling is characterized by the production function $x = f(\ell, k, L) = A\ell^{\alpha}k^{\beta}L^{\gamma}$ where $\alpha + \beta + \gamma = 1$ (and all exponents are positive).

   a.   Demonstrate that this production function has constant returns to scale.

   b.   Suppose again that the government assigns $\bar{L}$ acres of land to your company for oil drilling, and that there is no rental fee for the land but you cannot use the land for any other purpose. Given the fixed level of land available, what is your production function now? Demonstrate that it has decreasing returns to scale.

   c.   In exercise 13.2, you were asked to derive the (long-run) cost function for a two-input Cobb–Douglas production function. Can you use your result, which is also given in equation (13.45) of exercise 13.5, to derive the cost function for your oil company? What is the marginal cost function associated with this?

   d.   Next, consider the scenario under which the government charges a per-acre rental fee of q but only gives you the option of renting all $\bar{L}$ acres or none at all. Write down your new (long-run) cost function and derive the marginal and average cost functions. Can you infer the shape of the marginal and average cost curves?

   e.   Does the (long-run) marginal cost function change when the government begins to charge for use of the land in this way?

   f.   Now suppose that the government no longer requires your company to rent all $\bar{L}$ acres but instead agrees to rent you up to $\bar{L}$ acres at the land rental rate q. What would your conditional input demands and your (total) cost function be in the absence of the cap on how much land you can rent?

g. From now on, suppose that $A = 100$, $\alpha = \beta = 0.25$, $\gamma = 0.5$, $\bar{L} = 10{,}000$. Suppose further that the weekly wage rate is $w = 1{,}000$, the weekly capital rental rate is $r = 1{,}000$, and the weekly land rent rate is $q = 1{,}000$. At what level of output $\bar{x}$ will your production process no longer exhibit constant returns to scale (given the land limit of $\bar{L}$)? What is the marginal and average cost of oil drilling prior to reaching $\bar{x}$ (as a function of x)?

h. After reaching this $\bar{x}$, what is the marginal and average long-run cost of oil drilling (as a function of x)? Compare the marginal cost at $\bar{x}$ to your marginal cost answer in (g) and explain how this translates into a graph of the marginal cost curve for the firm in this scenario.

i. What happens to $\bar{x}$ as q increases? How does that change the graph of marginal and average cost curves?

j. If the price per barrel of oil is $p = 100$, what is your profit-maximizing oil production level?

k. Suppose the government now raises q from 1,000 to 10,000. What happens to your production of oil? What if the government raises q to 15,000?

13.10 Policy and Business Application: *Minimum Wage Labor Subsidy*: Suppose you run your business by using a homothetic, decreasing returns to scale production process that requires minimum wage labor ℓ and capital k where the minimum wage is w and the rental rate on capital is r.

A. The government, concerned over the lack of minimum wage jobs, agrees to subsidize your employment of minimum wage workers, effectively reducing the wage you have to pay to $(1 - s)w$ (where $0 < s < 1$). Suppose your long-run profit-maximizing production plan before the subsidy was (ℓ^*, k^*, x^*).

a. Begin with an isoquant graph that contains the isoquant corresponding to x^* and indicate on it the cost-minimizing input bundle as A. What region in the graph encompasses all possible production plans that could potentially be long run profit-maximizing when the effective wage falls to $(1 - s)w$?

b. On your graph, illustrate the slice of the production frontier to which you are constrained in the short run when capital is fixed. Choose a plausible point on that slice as your new short-run profit-maximizing production plan B. What has to be true at this point?

c. Can you conclude anything about how the marginal product of capital changes as you switch to its new short-run profit-maximizing production plan?

d. Will you hire more workers in the long run than in the short run?

e. Will you hire more capital in the long run than in the short run?

f. Once you have located B in part (b), can you now use this to narrow down the region (that you initially indicated in part (a)) where the long-run profit-maximizing production plan must lie?

B. Suppose, as in previous exercises, that your production function is $f(\ell, k) = 30\ell^{0.2}k^{0.6}$.

a. Suppose that $w = 10 = r$ and $p = 5$. What is your profit-maximizing production plan before the labor subsidy?

b. What is the short-run profit-maximizing plan after a subsidy of $s = 0.5$ is implemented.

c. What is the new long-run profit-maximizing plan once capital can be adjusted?

d. For any Cobb–Douglas function $f(\ell, k) = A\ell^{\beta\alpha}k^{\beta(1-\alpha)}$, the CES production function $g(\ell, k) = A(\alpha\ell^{-\rho} + (1 - \alpha)k^{-\rho})^{-\beta/\rho}$ converges to f as ρ approaches 0. What values for A, α, and β will do this for the production function $x = 30\ell^{0.2}k^{0.6}$?

e.** Using a spreadsheet to program the output supply and input demand equations for a CES production function given in equation (13.38) in a footnote in the text, verify that your long-run production plans mirror those you calculated for the Cobb–Douglas function when ρ approaches 0 and α and β are set appropriately.

f.** Finally, derive the first order condition for the short-run profit maximization problem with fixed capital using the CES production function. Then, using your spreadsheet, check to see whether those first order conditions hold when you plug in the short-run profit-maximizing quantity of labor that you calculated in (b).

POLICY APPLICATION

BUSINESS APPLICATION

13.11† Policy and Business Application: *Business Taxes*: In this exercise, suppose that your hamburger business "McWendy's" has a homothetic decreasing returns to scale production function that uses labor ℓ and capital k to produce hamburgers x. You can hire labor at wage w and capital at rental rate r but also have to pay a fixed annual franchise fee F to the McWendy parent company in order to operate as a McWendy's restaurant. You can sell your McWendy's hamburgers at price p.

A. Suppose that your restaurant, by operating at its long-run profit-maximizing production plan (ℓ^*, k^*, x^*), is currently making zero long-run profit. In each of the policy proposals in parts (b) through (h), suppose that prices w, r, and p remain unchanged.[11] In each part, beginning with (b), indicate what happens to your optimal production plan in the short and long run.

    a. Illustrate the short-run AC and MC curves as well as the long-run AC curve. Where in your graph can you locate your short-run profit, and what is it composed of?

    b. Suppose the government determined that profits in your industry where unusually high last year and imposes a one-time "windfall profits tax" of 50% on your business's profits from last year.

    c. The government imposes a 50% tax on short-run profits from now on.

    d. The government instead imposes a 50% tax on long-run profits from now on.

    e. The government instead taxes franchise fees causing the blood-sucking McWendy's parent company to raise its fee to $G > F$.

    f. The government instead imposes a tax t on capital used by your restaurant, causing you to have to pay not only r but also tr to use one unit of capital.

    g. Instead of taxing capital, the government taxes labor in the same way as it taxed capital in part (f).

    h. Finally, instead of any of these possibilities, the government imposes a "health tax" t on hamburgers, charging you $\$t$ for every hamburger you sell.

B. In previous exercises, we gave the input demand functions for a a firm facing prices (w, r, p) and technology $f(\ell, k) = A\ell^{\alpha}k^{\beta}$ (with $\alpha, \beta > 0$ and $\alpha + \beta < 1$) in equation (13.50) and the long-run output supply function in equation (13.49). They were both given in footnotes to earlier end-of-chapter exercises in this chapter.

    a. When you add a recurring fixed cost F, how are these functions affected? (*Hint*: You will have to restrict the set of prices for which the functions are valid, and you can use the profit function given in exercise (13.7) to do this strictly in terms of A, α, β, and the prices (w, r, p).) What are the short-run labor demand and output supply functions for a given $\bar{k}$?

    b. For each of (b) through (h) in part A of the exercise, indicate whether (and how) the functions you derived in part (a) are affected.

---

[11]This is only an assumption for now, which will in fact often not hold, as we will see in Chapter 14.

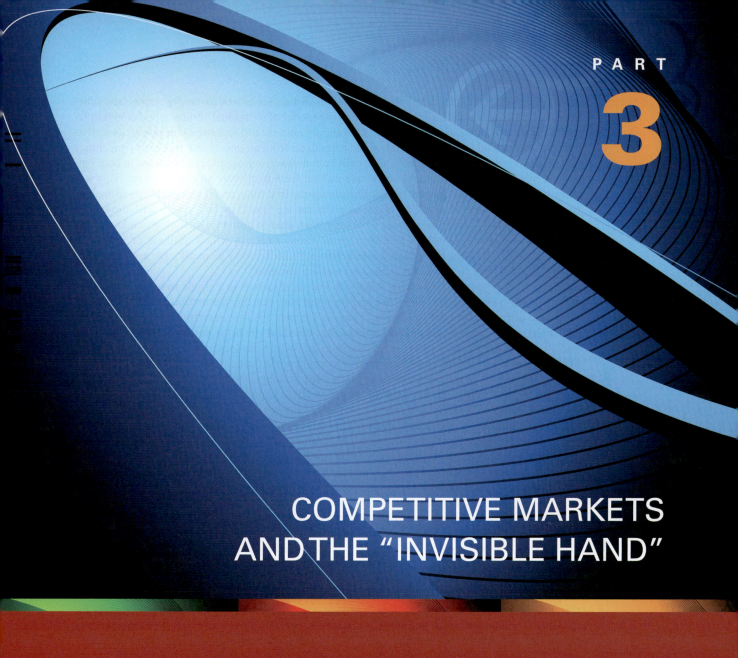

COMPETITIVE MARKETS AND THE "INVISIBLE HAND"

In Part 1, we derived demand curves (and functions) for goods as well as supply curves (and functions) for labor and capital, all from an underlying model of individual choice aimed at maximizing happiness. In Part 2, we similarly derived supply curves (and functions) for goods, as well as demand curves (and functions) for labor and capital, all from an underlying model of firm choice aimed at maximizing profit. We thus have built both demand and supply relationships in both output and input markets and are now ready to combine them to analyze an entire market. This will allow us to talk about the concept of *equilibrium* for the first time, and it will enable us to analyze *how prices form* rather than taking prices as given (as we have thus far). And it will allow us to illustrate more fully some insights we have only been able to hint at: namely that, under certain conditions, competitive markets lead to a *spontaneous order* in which millions of individual choices combine to form prices that guide behavior in such a way as to allocate resources efficiently. We will refer to this result as the *first welfare theorem*.

Chapter 14 begins by combining supply and demand curves in a single industry. Again, we will distinguish between the *short run* and the *long run*, but this distinction arises for reasons somewhat different from (but related to) those in Chapter 13. In *competitive industries that are characterized by the presence of many small firms*, the short run is the period over which it is not easily possible for firms to *enter or exit* the industry, while the long run arises when firms can freely enter and exit. Given our definition of economic profit (with its implication that a producer is doing the best he or she can by being in an industry so long as the producer makes at least zero profit), we can be confident that long-run profits in any competitive industry will always be zero for the last firm that entered (or the next firm that would exit) the industry. Thus, while short-run supply in an industry is determined by the individual supply curves of the firms that already exist in this industry, long-run supply is determined by the entry and exit decisions of firms that will drive price to a level at which profits will be zero for the marginal firm in the industry. In both the short and long run, we will see the logic behind the fact that market prices will settle at the intersection of market demand and supply, and the logic behind the process by which a "spontaneous order" emerges from the interaction of many individuals in the market.

Chapter 15 then proceeds to an evaluation of the order that emerges in a competitive industry through the interaction of supply and demand and the resulting prices that guide individual decision making. We will see how the voluntary trade, guided by individual incentives, can result in winners on all sides of the market, and how the prices that form in markets provide all the information necessary for individuals to make decisions that produce the maximum surplus. In particular, we will be able to show how an omniscient and benevolent social planner who is seeking to maximize overall surplus would often distribute scarce resources in an industry in exactly the way that an unplanned or decentralized market does. For this reason, economists sometimes talk of markets as guided by *an invisible hand*, as if a social planner were moving the pieces underneath, but this invisible hand is simply the sum of all individuals in the market responding to the incentives that arise from prices.

But we immediately point out in Chapter 15 that this result, known as the first welfare theorem, is predicated on several implicit assumptions that, when violated, would cause a divergence between what markets do on their own and what our mythical social planner would want to do. First, the theorem assumes that *prices are allowed to form without interference*; second, that there are *no externalities* or effects from individual choices that directly impact others who are not participating in the market; third, that there are *no informational asymmetries* that put one side of the market in the position of taking advantage of the other; and fourth, that everyone is "small" and thus *no one has market power*. Parts 4 and 5 of the text will examine closely how markets on their own will "fail" when these assumptions are violated, and how nonmarket institutions can reign in markets by aligning individual incentives with some notions of the "common good."

Put differently, an understanding of the first welfare theorem and its underlying assumptions provides a framework for us to think about the role of nonmarket institutions in society. When the assumptions are satisfied, there is in fact no "efficiency" role for nonmarket institutions because markets already allocate resources in a way that maximized the social pie. Even then, however, we may be dissatisfied with the outcome of markets because *saying that something is efficient is not the same as saying that it is "good."* It may, for instance, be the case that sometimes we believe that resources should be allocated more equally than what markets accomplish even though markets create the biggest possible overall level of social surplus. Thus, even if all the assumptions underlying the first welfare theorem are satisfied, there may be a *distributional role* for nonmarket institutions to aim at greater "fairness." And as the underlying assumptions of the first welfare theorem are violated in particular instances in the real world, an additional *efficiency role* emerges for nonmarket institutions since markets on their own will no longer maximize the social surplus.

The bulk of the remaining parts of the text is therefore devoted to an analysis of what goes wrong in markets when the assumptions underlying the first welfare theorem are violated, and what role this creates for nonmarket institutions that we will refer to as civil society and government. Before proceeding to these parts, however, we revisit the first welfare theorem in two additional settings.

In Chapter 16, we will present the basics of a more general model than the one used in Chapters 14 and 15 where we looked simply at a single industry in isolation. We will distinguish the single industry model as a *partial equilibrium* model that does not consider interactions across markets. Put differently, in our analysis of Chapters 14 and 15, we did not view the economy as a closed system but rather looked at one segment of the economy. Under certain circumstances, this is perfectly appropriate, but in other cases there are important spillovers from what happens in one industry into what happens in other industries. A full treatment of this is not possible in this text, but Chapter 16 attempts to give you a sense of how *general equilibrium* models that look at interactions across markets arrive at some results similar to what we illustrated in the partial equilibrium model of Chapter 15. While our examples in Chapter 16 will look quite restrictive, we will point out that the same results hold in much more general settings and that, in fact, the first welfare theorem (and related results) have been fully developed in quite general settings that build on our examples. We will also be able to demonstrate more clearly in this context how "efficiency" may well imply outcomes that many of us would consider "unfair," and that this gives rise to a distributional function of nonmarket institutions. More precisely, the *second welfare theorem* will tell us that, so long as nonmarket institutions (like governments) can redistribute resources without cost, markets can be fine-tuned to give more "equitable" but still "efficient" outcomes. At the same time, we will note that governments rarely have costless ways of redistributing, which then implies that a fundamental trade-off between efficiency and certain notions of equity will emerge.

Finally, we conclude this part of the text with a demonstration of how markets deal with *risk*, a prevalent feature of life that we have until this point not introduced into our models. I waited until this point to introduce risk into our model because it is at this point that we can show how modeling risk can build directly on our models of individual choice and general equilibrium. Chapter 17 thus develops a model of risky choice and introduces markets (such as insurance markets) that can serve to distribute risk efficiently in ways analogous to the efficient allocation of resources in markets in the absence of risk. Again, of course, this iteration of the first welfare theorem has the caveat that it is built on assumptions that, when violated, open a potential efficiency role for nonmarket institutions.

14

Competitive Market Equilibrium

We have spent the bulk of our time up to now developing relationships between economic variables and the behavior of agents such as consumers, workers, and producers.[1] To be more precise, we began by developing "models," simplified versions of reality, in which we then assumed that economic agents "do the best they can given their economic circumstances." This process of "optimizing" results in the relationships between prices and behavior, such as demand curves, supply curves, and cross-price demand and supply curves. And it is these relationships we can now use to take the economic analysis to its final step: describing how the economic environment (that agents take as given) arises within the model as many individuals optimize. This economic environment is called a *competitive equilibrium*.

In this and the next chapter, we will focus on a "market" or an "industry," terms we will use interchangeably. Firms are considered to operate in the same market (or industry) if they produce the same goods, and the market (or industry) is considered "competitive" if all firms are sufficiently small such that they cannot individually manipulate the economic environment. We will discover the important role played by equilibrium market prices in such competitive industries. Perhaps the most fascinating aspect of such prices is that they emerge "spontaneously" without anyone planning the process. Thus, the equilibrium we are about to analyze is a "decentralized market equilibrium" in the sense that it comes into being without central planning and only from the decentralized decisions of individuals who have no control over, or even awareness of, the process. In fact, production, *guided by self-interest and the emergence of market prices*, occurs in many cases without most of the participants in the process even knowing the nature of the final product they are producing. And we will see in Chapter 15 that the "spontaneous order" that is generated by this combination of self-interest and prices can create enormous benefits for society.

The insights emerging from the analysis in Chapters 14 and 15 are perhaps the most significant to come out of the discipline of economics. They derive from an internally consistent model in which the counterintuitive happens: *order emerges without planning, and self-interest does not (necessarily) conflict with the "social good."* The same model, as we will see in upcoming chapters, also illustrates that real-world frictions may create circumstances in which the order that emerges entails conflict between private self-interest and the social good. We will thus *begin the process of defining a role for non-market institutions in society*. Put differently, the insights that we will discuss in this and the next chapter have come to define most aspects of the discipline of economics as it searches for nonmarket institutions that harness self-interest for the social good when market forces by themselves do not adequately do so.

---

[1]This chapter requires a good understanding of consumer theory as exposited in Chapters 2, 4 through 6, and Sections 9A.1 and 9B.1 of Chapter 9 while making only a brief reference to consumer theory as it pertains to labor and capital markets. It also relies on a good understanding of cost curves as covered in Sections 13A.1 and 13B.1 of Chapter 13.

Equilibrium: Combining Demand and Supply Curves

We will begin by illustrating the concept of a competitive equilibrium in the context of one industry that is composed of many small producers who compete with one another for the business of many consumers. We therefore continue to assume that each economic agent is "small" relative to the industry and the economy and that, as a result, no economic agent has sufficient power to, by him- or herself, alter the equilibrium. Rather, it is rational for each economic agent to simply take the world as given and do the best he or she can within that world, even though it is from the combination of all the individual optimizing decisions that the equilibrium and thus the economic environment springs. In later chapters, we will investigate how our understanding of an equilibrium changes when some economic agents are "large" in the sense that their behavior influences the economic environment in a significant way. While there is no need for "small" economic agents to think strategically about the impact of their behavior on the economic environment, such strategic thinking will become central to understanding the behavior of "large" agents.

14A.1 Equilibrium in the Short Run

As we will see shortly, an equilibrium in an industry will be defined by the intersection of market (or industry) demand and supply curves. Deriving these curves for a particular industry *in the short run* is easy in that it simply involves adding up the individual demand and supply curves that are generated from individual optimization problems. For instance, in panel (a) of Graph 14.1, we plot two individual demand curves D^1 and D^2 and a third *market demand curve* D^M that would result if these were the only two consumers in the market. At a price above \$90, individual 2 demands

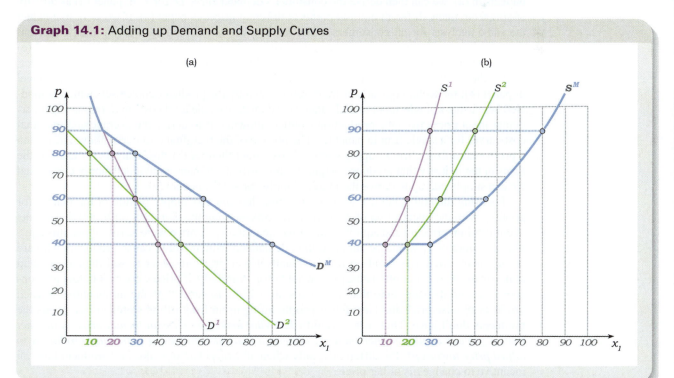

Graph 14.1: Adding up Demand and Supply Curves

none of the output x_1, which implies that individual 1 is the only consumer in the market, and this individual's demand curve therefore represents the market demand curve (for $p > 90$). For prices below $90, however, both consumers demand some of the output. For instance, at a price of $80, consumer 1 demands 20 units of x_1 while consumer 2 demands 10 units, for an overall market demand of 30 units. A similar process for adding up individual supply curves to get a *short-run market supply curve* S^M is illustrated in Graph 14.1b, with only firm 2 supplying output for prices below $40 and both firms supplying output for prices above $40. The process of adding up more than two demand or supply curves is a straightforward extension of this.

We will see a little later in this chapter that market supply is derived somewhat differently in the long run, and that "adding up supply curves" is the correct way of finding market supply curves only in the short run. For now, however, we will stick with the short-run curves and investigate the resulting short-run equilibrium. We will also see in Chapter 15 that we have to be careful about what precise interpretations we give to market demand curves.

14A.1.1 Short-Run Equilibrium in the Goods Market

Market (or industry) demand and supply curves are powerful tools that help us predict the terms under which consumers and producers will interact in a competitive world, and how these terms will change as underlying institutional and technological constraints change. Put differently, these curves help us predict the economic environment that governs individual behavior. If you have ever taken an economics course before, you have almost certainly been exposed to this as demand and supply curves were used in your course to describe equilibrium price and quantity in a market. Our work leading up to this chapter has informed us about what is behind this type of analysis, and this work will help us determine what we can and cannot say from economic analysis that relies on market demand and supply curves.

Consider, for instance, the sequence of graphs in Graph 14.2. In panel (a), we begin with the basic building blocks of the consumer model: indifference curves (representing tastes) and budgets (representing different economic environments as the price for good x_1 changes). From the budgets in (a), we can then derive the consumer's demand curve D^i for x_1 in panel (d) as directly arising from many different optimal points at different prices in panel (a). If we were to conduct the same analysis for all consumers in the market, we would then be deriving many different demand curves, which we could add up to arrive at the market demand curve D^M in panel (e) (with $\sum D^i$ in the graph simply read as "the sum of all individual D^i demand curves").

On the producer side, we are similarly starting with the fundamentals of the producer model in panel (b): the technological constraint represented by the producer choice set (which is modeled here using a single-input model). Panel (c) then derives the total cost curve (assuming a particular input price) from the production frontier, allowing us to derive the average and marginal cost curves for a single firm in panel (f). The portion of the marginal cost curve above AC is then a profit-maximizing firm's supply curve S^j. We could then repeat this analysis for each of the firms in the industry that produces output x_1, thus arriving at many individual supply curves that we can simply add up to derive the market supply curve S^M in panel (e).

Focusing then on panel (e), we have a simple demand and supply picture of the market for good x_1, with the intersection of the two curves representing the market equilibrium that results in equilibrium price p^* and equilibrium output quantity X_1^*. If price were to rise above this equilibrium, more of x_1 would be supplied than demanded, which would cause producers who are seeing their inventories build up to individually lower prices in order to sell their goods and make themselves better off. Thus, price would drop. Similarly, if price were ever below p^*, consumers would demand more than producers are willing to supply, giving an incentive to each producer to raise price and have fewer people lining up in front of the stores to buy goods the producers don't have. Thus, price would rise. *What makes p^* an equilibrium price is the fact that, if price is anything other than p^*, there is a natural tendency of individual producers to adjust price toward p^*.* Put differently, only when all firms charge p^* does no producer have an incentive to change his or her price.

Graph 14.2: Equilibrium, and What's Behind It

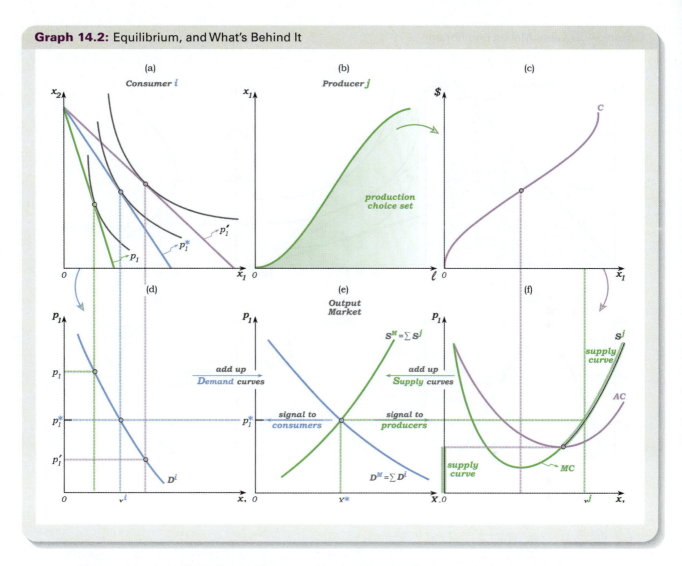

Without any particular individual intentionally directing the formation of p^*, the natural tendency is in place for p^* to emerge as individual consumers and producers simply try to do the best for themselves. Once p^* is formed, it then directs individual actions, telling each consumer how much to consume and each producer how much to produce. Thus, the market signals consumers and producers through the equilibrium price, coordinating their actions in a decentralized way that, as we will see in Chapter 15, is "efficient" under some circumstances. In the case graphed here, the signal p^* tells the consumer we modeled to consume x_1^i and the producer we modeled to produce x_1^i, with the market as a whole producing X_1^*.

14A.1.2 Short-Run Equilibrium in Input Markets In an analogous way, a decentralized market equilibrium also emerges in the labor market when different producers in many different industries compete for workers. Graph 14.3 illustrates this, with producers facing production choice sets in panel (a) that result in marginal revenue product curves in panel (d), and with a portion of this marginal revenue product curve composing the short-run labor demand curve for each producer. Workers, on the other hand, begin with preferences over leisure and consumption in panel (b), with different wages resulting in different optimal leisure choices. Panel (c) then illustrates a typical "leisure demand" curve, with panel (f) representing the implied labor supply curve

Graph 14.3: Labor Market Equilibrium

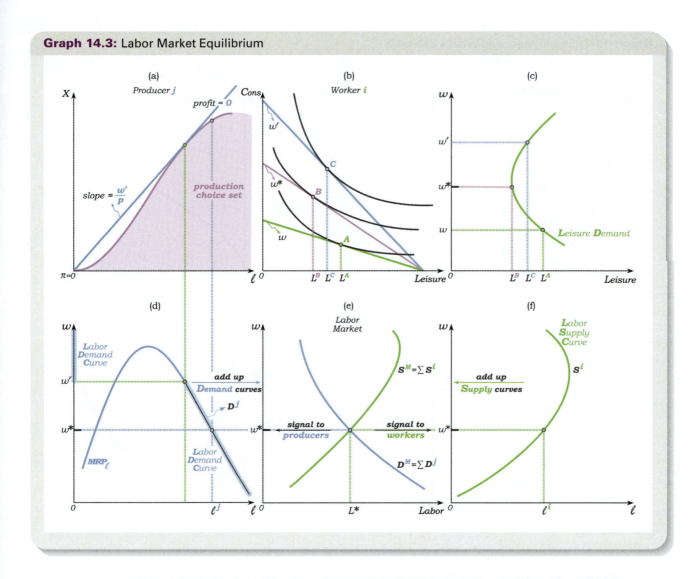

for this consumer. Adding up the individual labor demand curves of firms and labor supply curves of workers, we arrive at a market demand and supply curve for the particular type of labor modeled here, with the intersection of the two resulting in an *equilibrium wage rate* w^* that sends a signal back to workers and producers. This signal causes the producer we modeled to hire ℓ^j worker hours and the worker we modeled to sell ℓ^i labor hours, with the market as a whole trading L^* labor hours across the many industries that hire the types of workers modeled in the series of graphs.

Note that while the demand curve in output markets comes from all those *consumers* who consume the output we are modeling, the demand curve in labor markets comes from all those *producers* who hire the kind of labor we are modeling. Thus, in our labor market graph, we are adding up labor demand curves from firms that could potentially be producing very different outputs but are all demanding the same kind of labor input. On the supply side, we considered in our output market only those firms that produce the particular output we are modeling, just as in the labor market we only consider those workers who supply the type of labor we are modeling.

Can you explain why there is always a natural tendency for wage to move toward the equilibrium wage if all individuals try to do the best they can?

Exercise
14A.1

In the capital market, we could similarly derive a demand curve for capital by producers except that it would be a more long-run demand curve if capital for firms is fixed in the short run. The supply curve would emerge from consumers making trade-offs between consuming now or consuming in the future—and thus saving for future consumption—and the equilibrium price that emerges in the market is the equilibrium interest rate.

14A.2 A Market (or Industry) in Long-Run Equilibrium

As we glance at Graphs 14.2 and 14.3, we might at first think that not all that much changes in the graphs when we think of the long run rather than the short run. After all, in our exploration of the difference between short- and long-run producer behavior in Chapter 13 we simply concluded that output supply and input demand curves will tend to be shallower in the long run than in the short run (with higher "exit" prices than short-run "shut down" prices), and it might therefore seem that we just have to draw our producer pictures a little bit differently to turn our previous two graphs into long-run equilibrium pictures. This is, however, not the case because, in addition to changing their input mix more in the long run than in the short run, firms have the opportunity to *enter or exit industries in the long run.* This implies that while the number of firms in an industry is fixed in the short run (even if some of them perhaps shut down), that number is *variable* in the long run as more or fewer firms might exist in response to changing market conditions.

Formally, we thus define the "long run" for a firm as the time it takes for a firm to adjust the input levels that are fixed in the short run, and we define the "long run" for an industry as the time it takes for firms to be able to enter or exit the industry. Notice, however, that the fundamentals that underlie these two definitions of "long run" derive from a similar source. A firm may have a fixed level of capital (such as a fixed factory size) in the short run, and this keeps it from adjusting its capital as conditions change until the long run. That same firm also cannot exit an industry, or enter a new industry, in the short run for exactly the same reason: It is currently locked into a fixed level of capital that can only be changed in the long run. Thus, when we think of the "long run" for an industry as the time it takes for firms to enter or exit, we are usually thinking of the time it takes to adjust capital, to dispose of the factory if a firm exits or acquire one if a firm enters. In this sense, there is usually a nice symmetry between what we think of as the "long run" for a firm and for an industry. The only difference is that some firms might be locked into their current capital for shorter periods than others, and the "long run" for an industry does not truly emerge until sufficient numbers of firms have had the opportunity to enter or exit.

14A.2.1 Revisiting the Entry/Exit Decision In Chapter 13, we drew the distinction between a firm "shutting down" in the short run and "exiting an industry" in the long run. The short run was defined as the time during which one of the firm's inputs (capital, in particular) is fixed, and during which the cost associated with the fixed input is a fixed expenditure and a sunk cost. The firm's decision whether to produce in the short run depended on the firm's ability to cover its short-run economic costs, which don't include the expense on fixed inputs or other types of fixed expenditures (like license fees). The firm's short-run supply curve then arises from the (short-run) MC curve above the short-run AC^{SR} curve. In the long run, however, the firm needs to cover all its economic costs, which will now include the costs of inputs that are fixed in the short run as well as other fixed costs (like license fees); therefore, the firm will enter an industry if it can do so and make some profit and will exit an industry if it cannot cover these costs. Thus, in the long run, a firm will exit the industry if price falls below the long-run AC curve.

Suppose, for instance, that we consider the case in which one of the inputs is fixed in the short run or, alternatively, there is a fixed cost associated with an annual license to operate my business. Graph 14.4 then illustrates the resulting AC^{SR} curve representing all my economic costs in the short run when the fixed input or license expense is sunk, and the AC curve that represents my long-run economic costs that take into account the cost of fixed inputs or of renewing my annual license. In the short run, I will operate my business so long as price is not below p', the lowest point of the short-run AC^{SR} curve, while in the long run I will exit if price falls below p, the lowest point of my long-run AC curve. In between these prices, there exists a range of prices that allow me to cover my short-run costs but not my fixed expenses, sufficient to keep me open in the short run but not sufficient to keep me from exiting in the long run. If price is above p, on the other hand, I can make (long-run) positive profits, which implies that I will produce and will enter the industry if I am not already in it.

Exercise 14A.2 Suppose your firm only used labor inputs (and not capital) and that labor is always a variable input. If your firm had to renew an annual license fee, would the AC^{SR} and the long-run AC curves ever cross in this case?

Exercise 14A.3* Why might the AC^{SR} and the long-run AC curves cross when the difference emerges because of an input (like capital) that is fixed in the short run? (*Hint:* Review Graphs 13.2 and 13.3.)

Exercise 14A.4 Explain why the MC curve in Graph 14.4 would be the same in the long and short run in the scenario of exercise 14A.2 but not in the scenario of exercise 14A.3.

14A.2.2 Long-Run Equilibrium Price when All Producers Are Identical Now suppose there are many producers of "hero cards" like me. Each one of us wants to make as much profit as possible, and so we constantly look around for the best opportunities. In the short run,

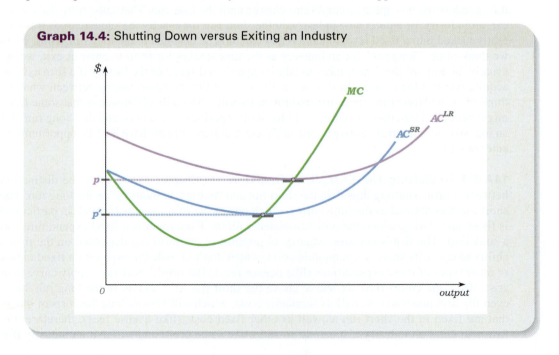

Graph 14.4: Shutting Down versus Exiting an Industry

we are stuck in the particular industries in which we are currently producing, but in the long run we can switch if new opportunities open up. Put differently, we can keep track of the AC curves in many different industries, and when we notice that AC is below output price in some industry, we know there is profit to be made, and we enter. Some of us might be a little faster at doing this than others, or some of us might notice opportunities a bit sooner than others. But whatever determines the sequence of which one of us pounces on new opportunities first, the fact that we all eventually will pounce on these opportunities means that together we will shift the market supply curve as we enter, and we will keep shifting it as long as there are profits to be made.

Consider, for instance, Graph 14.5. Suppose that the market for good x finds itself in the short-run equilibrium represented by the intersection of the blue market demand and supply curves with equilibrium price p' in panel (a). This price signal tells each producer to produce x' of output along her (green) supply curve as illustrated in panel (b), which generates a long-run profit equal to the shaded blue area in panel (b) for each firm (assuming we have included all the costs relevant for the long run in the AC curve). Remember from our discussion of economic profit in Chapter 11 that positive profit, no matter how small, means that a producer is doing better here than she could do anywhere else. Thus, since we are assuming for now that all producers are identical, there are producers who currently operate in a different industry and see that they could make positive profits in the industry that produces x, which logically implies that they are making negative profit in their current industry.

Given the current price p', there is thus an incentive in place for additional firms to enter the industry, with each entry shifting the short-run market supply curve just a little bit in panel (a). The incentive for firms to enter remains as long as (long-run) profits in the industry are positive and thus as long as price remains above p^*. Thus, the shift in short-run supply curves in panel (a) of the graph will not stop until we arrive at the green short-run supply curve when the price has reached the lowest point of each individual producer's long-run AC curve. Once we have reached this new short-run equilibrium, each producer in the industry makes zero (long-run) profit, eliminating any incentive for any new producers to enter and stopping short of giving an incentive to current producers to exit.

We could have drawn a similar sequence of shifts in short-run supply curves but in the opposite direction if we had drawn the original intersection of the blue supply and demand curves in

Graph 14.5: Moving from Short-Run to Long-Run Equilibrium

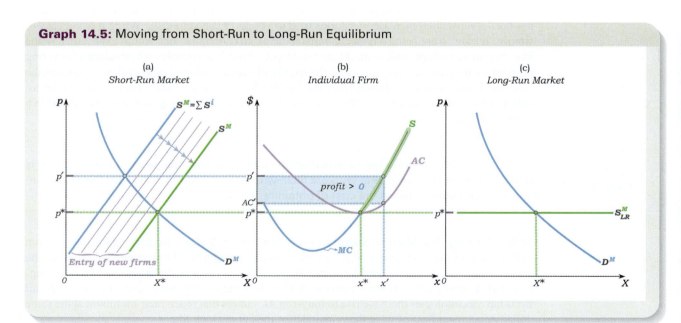

panel (a) at an equilibrium price below p^*. In that case, the shift in short-run supply curves would have resulted from the exiting of firms from the industry in which firms were experiencing negative profits; i.e., where firms could be doing better elsewhere. Thus, *whenever producers face identical costs and the short-run equilibrium output price lies anywhere other than the lowest point of (long-run) AC, entry and exit of firms will drive the long-run price of output to that lowest point*. In panel (c) of the graph, *the long-run market supply curve is then horizontal and lies at the lowest point of AC.* Put differently, the market will, in the long run when firms can enter and exit, supply any quantity that is demanded at the price p^* that falls at the lowest point for AC. This implies that the long-run market (or industry) supply curve arises not from adding up individual supply curves but rather from the entry and exit decision of firms that will drive price to the point where long-run profit is equal to zero; i.e., where price settles at the lowest point of the long-run AC curve for individual firms.

Exercise 14A.5   Can you draw the analogous sequence of graphs for the case when the short-run equilibrium price falls below p^*?

Exercise 14A.6   How does the full picture of equilibrium in Graph 14.2 look different in the long run?

14A.2.3 Long-Run Equilibrium in Labor Markets   While entry and exit of firms shape the difference between long- and short-run equilibrium in the output market for a particular industry's good, the same is generally not true of labor market equilibria, at least not when a particular industry is small relative to the whole economy. This is because the "labor market" in Graph 14.3 is composed of firms from many different industries, and conditions that affect one particular industry will tend not to have an impact on the economy-wide labor market when an industry is small relative to the economy as a whole. Thus, whether some firms are entering or exiting a particular industry will not be perceptible as causing a shift in labor demand.

Entry and exit may play a role on the labor supply curve if an increase or decrease of wages for a particular type of labor alters perceptions sufficiently to cause workers to retrain or new workers to choose training differently from in the past. For instance, over the past 10 years, there has been a substantial increase in salaries paid to young PhD economists. While it is not easy to simply "retrain" from being a noneconomist to being an economist, one would expect that, in the long run, more college seniors might choose to get a PhD in economics when salaries for young economists have risen, thus increasing the supply of economists and driving down wages in the long run. Long-run wages in each labor market thus have to have a relationship with the relevant opportunity costs of workers, a topic you can (if it interests you) study in much more detail in a labor economics course.

Exercise 14A.7   How would you think the time-lag between short- and long-run changes in labor markets is related to the "barriers to entry" that workers face, where the barrier to entry into the PhD economist market, for instance, lies in the cost of obtaining a PhD?

14A.2.4 Long-Run Market Supply when Producers Differ   In deriving the flat long-run industry supply curve in Graph 14.5c, we explicitly assumed that all producers had access to the same technology, and thus faced the same AC and MC curves. For the argument (that the long-run market supply curve is horizontal) to hold, it is actually only necessary to assume that all firms have technologies that give rise to long-run AC curves that reach their minimum at the same dollar value, regardless of what the remainder of the curves look like.

Can you explain why the previous sentence is true?

Exercise
14A.8

Now suppose that different producers have access to very different technologies. It might then be true that, at a given output price, some producers are able to make a profit while others are not. This in turn has implications for who will enter and who will exit an industry as market conditions change, and it has implications for the shape of the long-run market supply curve.

Consider, for instance, the short-run market equilibrium pictured in panel (a) of Graph 14.6 as the intersection of the blue demand and supply curves at point A (with p^* as the equilibrium price). Suppose further that there are many potential firms for this industry, and to keep the graph manageable, suppose that each of these firms has a (long-run) AC curve that reaches its minimum at output level x^*, but some AC curves are lower everywhere than others. Six such AC curves are pictured in panel (b) of the graph, and we can imagine that there are many firms whose similarly shaped AC curves fall in between these. At the price p^*, firms 1, 2, and 3 all make at least zero profit, while firms 4, 5, and 6 would make negative long-run profit if they produced. Thus, those firms with lower average cost curves—those that are "better" at producing x—will choose to be in the industry while those with higher cost curves will not.

Next, suppose that there is a shift in market demand (from D^M to $D^{M'}$) that causes the (short-run) equilibrium price in panel (a) to rise above p^* to p'. Producer 4 would then notice that he or she is now able to make a positive profit in this industry, and thus would therefore have an incentive to enter the industry, as would other firms that previously would have made negative profit. This entry of new firms then shifts the short-run supply curve in panel (a) as new firms enter the market, but the process will stop *before* the price falls back to the original p^* because the firms that are entering have higher costs than the firms that originally composed the industry. In our graph, producer 5 is the last one to enter, with all producers whose costs fall below p'' also entering but no producer whose costs are higher than those of producer 5 entering. The shift in market demand from D^M to $D^{M'}$ thus causes a short-run shift in the equilibrium from A to B and a long-run shift to C in panel (a) of the graph, with a short-run increase in the price from p^* to p' and a

Graph 14.6: Long-Run Market Supply when Firms Differ

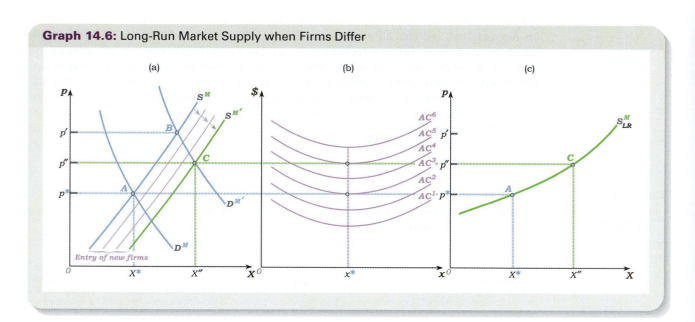

long-run change to p''. Panel (c) then simply graphs the long-run market supply relationship from A to C, indicating an upward-sloping long-run market supply curve when producers have different cost curves. Once again, the long-run market supply curve is not determined by the shape of individual firm supply curves, only by the distribution of the lowest point of the AC curves for firms. Industries like this, with upward-sloping (long-run) industry supply curves, are called *increasing cost industries*.

Exercise 14A.9   Suppose market demand shifts inward instead of outward. Can you illustrate what would happen in graphs similar to those of Graph 14.6?

Exercise 14A.10   *True or False:* The entry and exit of firms in the long run ensures that the long-run market supply curve is always shallower than the short-run market supply curve.

It is in principle also possible for long-run market supply curves to slope down in industries where firm costs fall as the industry expands. This may occur if, for instance, the expansion of an industry leads to greater competition in one of the input markets unique to that industry, and thus to a decline in costs for all firms. Such industries are called *decreasing cost industries*. Since this is relatively rare for industries that are appropriately modeled as perfectly competitive, we will not focus on this case here and only mention it for the sake of completeness.[2]

Exercise 14A.11*   *True or False:* While long-run industry supply curves slope up (in increasing cost industries) because firms have different cost curves, long-run industry supply curves in decreasing cost industries slope down even if firms have identical cost curves.

14A.2.5 Zero Profit for Marginal Firms in the Long Run   Finally, notice that entry and exit of firms into markets always continues until the *marginal producer makes zero (long-run) profit.* By "marginal producer," I mean the producer who has the highest costs within an industry. In the case where all producers have the same costs (as in Graph 14.5), all producers are marginal, and thus all producers make zero (long-run) profit. In the case where producers have access to different technologies and thus face different cost curves (as in Graph 14.6), on the other hand, all producers other than the marginal producer make positive (long-run) profit. Similarly, if all potential producers have the same costs as all those within the industry, then all producers who are not in the industry are also marginal and would make zero (long-run) profit if they entered. When producers face different costs, however, those who are outside the industry in long-run equilibrium would make negative profits if they entered because their costs are greater than the costs of the marginal producer in the industry (who is making zero profit).

Exercise 14A.12   *True or False:* In the presence of fixed costs (or fixed expenditures), short-run profit is always greater than zero in long-run equilibrium.

---

[2]In Chapter 21, where we develop the concept of externalities, we provide in end-of-chapter exercise 21.9 another example of a decreasing cost industry that arises from positive production externalities. We similarly illustrate in this example that we can get upward-sloping industry supply curves from negative production externalities even when all firms have identical production technologies.

14A.3 Changing Conditions and Changing Equilibria

In the real world, conditions facing particular industries change constantly as new competing products enter the larger market, labor and capital input prices change, and government tax and regulatory policies are altered. The concepts of short- and long-run equilibria are useful, however, not only for those industries that find themselves in relatively stable economic environments for long periods but also for those industries that experience constantly changing conditions. Whether we remain in any particular equilibrium for very long or whether we even reach a static equilibrium before conditions change once again, knowing what the ultimate equilibrium in an economy is lets us know which way an economy is headed, and that is useful even if conditions change once again before the economy reaches the new equilibrium. It is a bit like predicting the weather: It is never quite in equilibrium, but the forces of nature are constantly aiming to get toward an equilibrium. Thus, if we know that a new high pressure system is moving into our area, we can predict what will happen to the weather because we understand how the weather will adjust in an "attempt" to head toward a new equilibrium. So it is with an economy: When a new force is introduced, we can predict which way things are headed by knowing the equilibrium the economy is aiming for.

In our model of a competitive industry, a "change in conditions" translates in some way into a change in demand or supply curves, and thus a change in short-run and/or long-run equilibrium. In the remainder of this chapter, we will run through some of the types of changes that might have short- and long-run impacts on a particular industry. On the producer side, changing conditions might result from (1) a change in variable costs (like those associated with labor), (2) a change in fixed expenditures associated with an input that is fixed in the short run, or (3) a change in a fixed cost that is avoidable only by exiting the industry. On the consumer side, changes in consumer tastes or the appearance of new products on the market may cause shifts in market demand. For each of these cases, we will begin our analysis with the assumption that the market was in long-run equilibrium prior to the change in underlying conditions faced by the industry.

14A.3.1 Short-Run Equilibrium within a Long-Run Equilibrium
Suppose that our industry is currently in long-run equilibrium, which implies that the marginal producer is making zero (long-run) profits and thus producing at a price that falls at the lowest point of the producer's (long-run) AC curve. This is illustrated in Graph 14.7 where the market demand and market supply curves, both consisting simply of individual demand and supply curves added up, cross in panel (a) at price p^*, which falls at the lowest point of the (long-run) AC curve of the marginal firm in the industry in panel (b). Since panel (b) illustrates the "marginal firm" in the industry, we know that all firms outside the industry have costs that are at least as high as this firm's. Thus, all firms outside the industry would make zero (long-run) profit or less if they entered the industry. Similarly, we know that the firms inside the industry have costs that are no higher than the marginal firm's. Thus, all the firms inside the industry make at least zero (long-run) profit. The industry finds itself in long-run equilibrium because no firm has an incentive to enter or exit this industry unless conditions change.

At the same time, note that each firm in the industry makes positive short-run profits. This is because short-run economic costs are fully contained in the short-run average cost curve whose lowest point lies below the lowest point of the long-run AC curve because certain expenses (associated with fixed inputs or recurring long-run fixed costs) are not economic costs in the short run. It is for this reason that the green (short-run) supply curve in panel (b) of the graph extends below the lowest point of the (long-run) AC curve as we illustrated before in Graph 14.4.

Can you illustrate graphically the short- and long-run profits of the marginal firm in long-run equilibrium? (*Hint:* You can do this by inserting into the graph the AC^{SR} curve as previously pictured in Graph 14.4.)

Exercise 14A.13

Graph 14.7: An Industry in both Short- and Long-Run Equilibrium

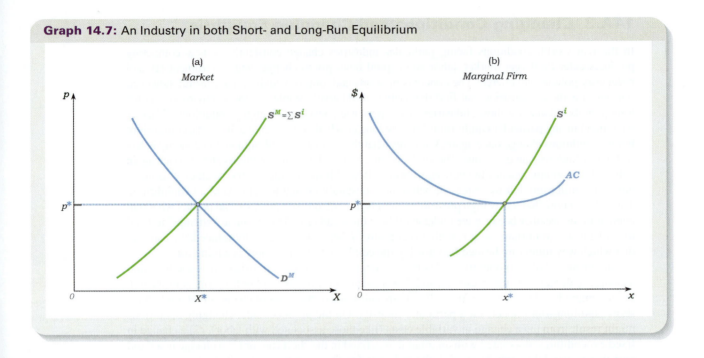

This will then be the starting point for our analysis of the impact of changing conditions on short- and long-run equilibrium. In each case, we will need to ask ourselves which curves in our graph are affected by the change, and this will permit us to come to a conclusion about how changing firm behavior results in changes in the equilibrium. For purposes of illustration, we will also assume for the remainder of this chapter that all firms face the same cost curves, and all firms are therefore marginal firms. I will leave it to you as an end-of-chapter exercise to think about how the graphs would differ if firms had different cost curves. Before proceeding, notice that we have stripped the firm side of our pictures to only those curves that actually matter for our analysis: the short-run supply curve and the long-run AC curve, with the short-run supply curve extending below AC. We should keep in mind throughout, however, that the short-run supply curve is really a portion of the MC curve and is thus moved by changes in (short-run) marginal costs.

14A.3.2 A Change in a Long-Run Fixed Cost
Suppose first that producers in an industry incur some annual fixed cost that is not associated with an input. An annual license fee charged by the government is one example of this type of cost; each year, in order to continue producing, a firm has to pay a fee to the government. Another example might involve annual insurance premiums, premiums that might insure the firm against damage to its property or liability suits from its consumers or workers. Once paid, such fees are sunk costs in the short run and thus do not enter the short-run cost curves. In the long run, however, such fees are a real economic cost of staying in the industry and thus become part of the long-run cost curve AC.

Now suppose that this fee goes up, a scenario considered in Graph 14.8. Since it is not a part of the short-run average or marginal curves, it is not part of any of the cost curves that are relevant for the firm's short-run decisions. Thus the firm's short-run supply curve (which is not pictured in panel (b)) remains unchanged. Since the (blue) short-run market supply curve S^M is simply composed of the sum of all firm supply curves, this also implies that the market supply curve does not change in the short run. This further implies that the equilibrium price in the market remains at p^* in the short run. As a result, the increase in the fee causes no changes in the industry in the short run.

The increased fee does, however, cause the (long-run) AC curve to move up as depicted in the green curve in Graph 14.8b. While short-run profit for the firms is unchanged, long-run

Graph 14.8: An Increase in a Long-Run Fixed Cost

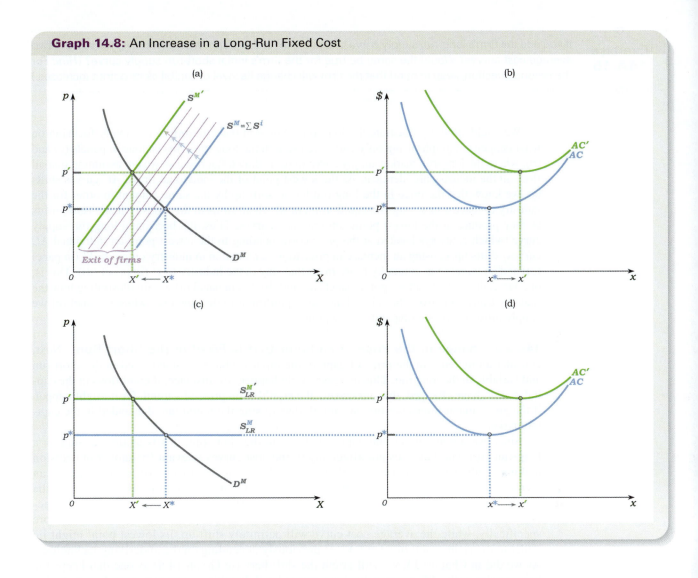

profit therefore falls and, since it was zero in the initial equilibrium, it now becomes negative. This causes some firms to exit the market in the long run, which in turn causes the (short-run) market supply curve S^M to shift inward. More specifically, as individual firms exit, the magenta market supply curves in panel (a) drive up the market price, and firms will continue to exit so long as the market price remains below the new lowest point of the green AC' curve in panel (b). Only when the market price has increased all the way to p' will the firms that remain in the industry make zero profits again, eliminating any further incentive for firms to exit (or enter). The short-run market supply curve then stops shifting when it has reached the green $S^{M'}$ curve in panel (a). The firms that remain in the industry then produce x', which is more than they produced initially (x^*), but the industry as a whole produces less (X' rather than X^* in panel (a)).

Why does the increase in the fee result in a new (green) AC' curve that converges to the original (blue) AC curve?

Exercise
14A.14

Exercise
14A.15

Exercise 14A.15 If you add the firm's long-run supply curve into panel (b) of the graph, where would it intersect the two average cost curves? Would the same be true for the firm's initial short-run supply curve? (*Hint:* For the second question, keep in mind that the firm will change its level of capital as its output increases.)

We could similarly illustrate the long-run change in the equilibrium by simply focusing on what happens in graphs using only curves relevant in the long run. This is done in panels (c) and (d), where the long-run market supply curve in (c) is drawn flat because we are assuming that all firms in the industry are identical. As the lowest point of the individual firms' AC curves shifts up, we know that the price in the long run has to shift up by the same amount in order for the industry to reach a new long-run equilibrium in which all firms in the industry make zero profits as they produce at the lowest points on their AC curves. Thus, the horizontal long-run supply curve (which is always located at the price corresponding to the lowest point on individual AC curves) shifts up, causing an increase in price to p', a reduction in industry output to X' (in panel (c)) and an increase in output by those firms that stay in the industry to x' (in panel (d)). This is, of course, the same result we got in panels (a) and (b), but in panel (a) we are illustrating how the industry transitions from the initial long-run equilibrium to the new one, while in panel (c) we simply illustrate the starting and ending points.

14A.3.3 Change in the Price of an Input that Is Fixed in the Short Run

Next, consider an increase in the price of capital, the input we have assumed fixed in the short run and variable in the long run. This increase might happen, for instance, if conditions in the capital market have changed, thus increasing the equilibrium price of capital. Or it might happen if the government imposes a tax on capital, thus raising the rental rate demanded in the capital market.

Since we are assuming that capital is fixed in the short run, this is again a change in a long-run cost and thus does not affect any of the cost curves relevant for short-run decision making. Unlike the increase in a fixed fee, a long-run (recurring) fixed cost, this is an increase in a long-run *variable cost*, not a long-run fixed cost. As a result, the shift in the (long-run) AC curve for each firm will look a little different than it did in the previous section where the new (green) AC' curve converges to the original (blue) AC curve. More specifically, while the average cost curve will definitely shift up, its lowest point might lie either to the right or left of where it was previously depending on the underlying technology. As we did in Chapter 13, we will graph the shift here (in Graph 14.9) as one that keeps the lowest point of the AC curve at the same output level, but this is simply a special case of what might happen more generally.

Exercise
14A.16

Exercise 14A.16 Could the AC curve shift similarly in the case where the increase in cost was that of a long-run fixed cost?

This can get a little confusing at first because it seems to involve a logical contradiction: How can it be that the lowest point of the AC curve can remain at the same output quantity when we know that the short-run MC curve has to cross the (long-run) AC curve at its lowest point in the new long-run equilibrium? After all, doesn't the short-run MC curve include only the cost of labor and not the cost of capital that has just increased? The apparent contradiction is resolved, however, if we recognize that the firm will shift away from capital and toward labor when r increases. This implies that, from a short-run perspective (in the new long-run equilibrium), costs will be higher since more labor will be involved in producing each unit of output. It is for

Graph 14.9: An Increase in the Rental Rate of Capital

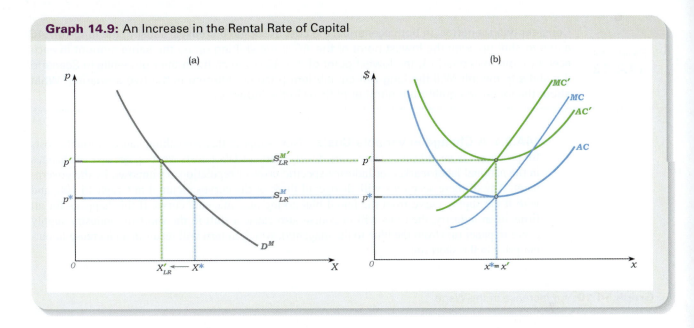

this reason that the short-run *MC* curve shifts as a result of moving to the new long-run equilibrium, but that shift only happens in the long run when firms substitute away from capital and toward labor.

This is illustrated in panel (b) of Graph 14.9 where the blue curves represent the original cost curves and the green curves represent the new cost curves. The (long-run) *AC* is drawn as shifting up with its lowest point remaining at the same output level x^*. Once the firm has been able to adjust its level of capital in the long run, it will now face a new (green) short-run *MC'* curve that is higher than the original *MC* because the firm has substituted away from capital and toward labor, and the short-run *MC* curve considers only the cost of labor since capital is now once again fixed in the short run. Thus, even though the cost of labor has not increased and the short-run *MC* curve only includes the cost of labor, the short-run *MC* curve in the new long-run equilibrium has shifted up because each producer is now using more labor and less capital for each input he or she produces.

The rest of the story of how the equilibrium changes is then similar to what we discussed in the previous section for an increase in a fixed fee. Nothing changes in the short run (since none of the short-run curves are affected *in the short run* by an increase in the cost of an input that is fixed in the short run). However, each firm in the industry now makes negative profits, which means that some firms will exit. As firms exit, the equilibrium price rises, and this continues until all firms in the industry once again make zero profits. Thus, the long-run supply curve in the industry shifts up, with industry output falling to X' in panel (a) of Graph 14.9 and price settling at the new lowest point of the *AC'* curve p'. The only difference between the increased fee and the increased cost of capital is that, because of the different shifts in the *AC* curve, we can no longer be sure whether each firm will produce more or less in the new equilibrium than it did originally. When the shift in the *AC* curve is drawn as in Graph 14.9, each firm in the industry will now produce the same as it did before.

How would you illustrate the transition from the short run to the long run using graphs similar to those in panels (a) and (b) in Graph 14.8?

Exercise
14A.17

Exercise
14A.18
Consider two scenarios: In both scenarios, the cost of capital increases, causing the long-run *AC* curve to shift up, with the lowest point of the *AC* curve shifting up by the same amount in each scenario. But in Scenario 1, the lowest point of the *AC* curve shifts to the right while in Scenario 2 it shifts to the left. Will the long-run equilibrium price be different in the two scenarios? What about the long-run equilibrium number of firms in the industry?

14A.3.4 A Change in Variable Costs

Now suppose that something causes variable costs for producers in an industry to rise immediately. Perhaps labor costs went up because of changes in the national labor market, or industry-specific taxes or regulation are imposed by the government. Any of these scenarios will change all three of the curves pictured in Graph 14.10b, and with it the supply curve from the initial blue to the new magenta curve. If this happens for all firms in an industry, then this will of course also cause a shift in the short-run industry supply curve in panel (a) (from the blue to the magenta), which in turn will result in an increase in output price in the short run.

Graph 14.10: An Increase in the Wage

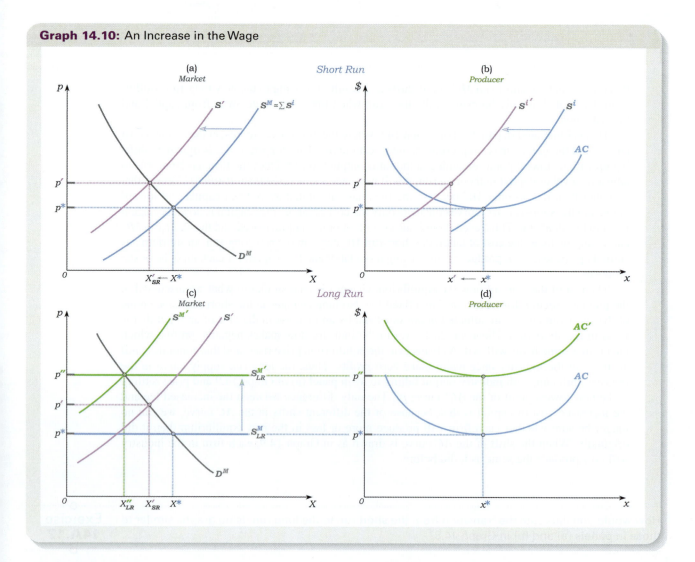

In the short run, the industry as a whole will therefore produce less, X'_{SR} instead of X^*. Since all firms are assumed to be identical, each firm will continue to produce in the short run, with each firm producing less (x' rather than x^* in panel (b)). Thus, price in the short run rises sufficiently (to p') to ensure that short-run profit remains above zero. (If we assumed instead that some firms had lower cost curves than others, some higher cost firms might shut down in the short run if they can no longer make non-negative short-run profits.)

In the long run, price has to adjust to the new lowest point of AC', which implies that the long-run market supply curve in panel (c) rises from the initial blue horizontal line to the new green line at price p''. If we stick with our assumption that the lowest point on the long-run average cost curve remains at the same output level, each firm that remains in the industry will therefore again produce as much as it did before costs increased (panel (d)), but since the overall market output falls at higher prices, some firms must have exited as we transition from the short run to the long run. It is for this reason that we can place the magenta short-run shift in the market supply curve (that resulted from an increase in short-run MC for all firms) in panel (c) intersecting the demand curve at a price below the long run price p'', with the shift from this magenta curve to the new (green) final short-run supply curve resulting from the exit of firms that experienced negative long-run profits at the price p'. Thus, even though each firm that remains in the industry will end up producing as much as it did before costs increased, the market produces less (X''_{LR}) as the industry has shrunk.[3] The long-run effect of an increase in labor costs, for instance, is therefore similar to the long-run increase in the price of capital, with the difference between the two cases emerging in the short run because labor is assumed to be variable in the short run while capital is not.

How can it be that firms are making short-run profit (and thus remain open in the short run) while simultaneously making negative long-run profit (causing some of them to exit and thus price to rise further)?

Exercise 14A.19

Note again, however, that the upward shift in the AC curve in Graph 14.10 could involve either a rightward or a leftward shift in the lowest point of the curve when the wage increases. If it shifted to the right, we could similarly conclude that the number of firms in the industry has fallen as a result of the increase in the wage (just as when the lowest point of AC shifts vertically up). This is because we know the industry produces less (at the higher price) and *each firm* produces more when the lowest point of the AC curve shifts to the right. But if that lowest point shifts to the left instead, then it is no longer as clear whether the number of firms in the industry will increase or decrease. While the total industry output would fall just as before (because consumers demand less when prices are higher), it may still take more firms to produce that lower industry output if each firm produces sufficiently less than before. In this case, p'' and p' in panel (c) of Graph 14.10 would be reversed, with the short-run increase in price being sufficiently high to attract new firms into the industry.

What would happen if (instead of wage increasing) the government imposed a per unit tax for each packet of economist cards?

Exercise 14A.20

---

[3]In fact, there are some additional subtle changes that we are not picturing because the short-run MC itself will shift again in the long run as firms substitute away from labor and into capital.

14A.3.5 A Change in Demand   As we already demonstrated in Graph 14.6 when we considered the shape of long-run market supply when firm costs differ, an industry may be impacted not only by changing costs but also by changing market demand. The market for standard portable music players, for instance, may be affected when the demand curve for such players shifts in as new MP3 players gain in popularity. The market demand for MP3 players, on the other hand, might be affected as it becomes easier to purchase music via the Internet by the song rather than in standard tape or CD formats. Such shifts in market demand may result from changing tastes (that change individual demand curves that compose the market demand curve), from the introduction of new products in a related market, or from new consumers entering a market. Such shifts in demand have no impact on the cost curves of firms, which implies that we will not need to change any of the firm cost curves.

Consider, for instance, the increase in demand for the good x graphed in panel (a) of Graph 14.11, and let's stick with the assumption that all firms are identical in terms of their cost structure. We begin at the initial industry equilibrium, with the industry producing X^* at the equilibrium price p^*. When demand shifts from the blue demand curve to the green, there is an immediate increase in price

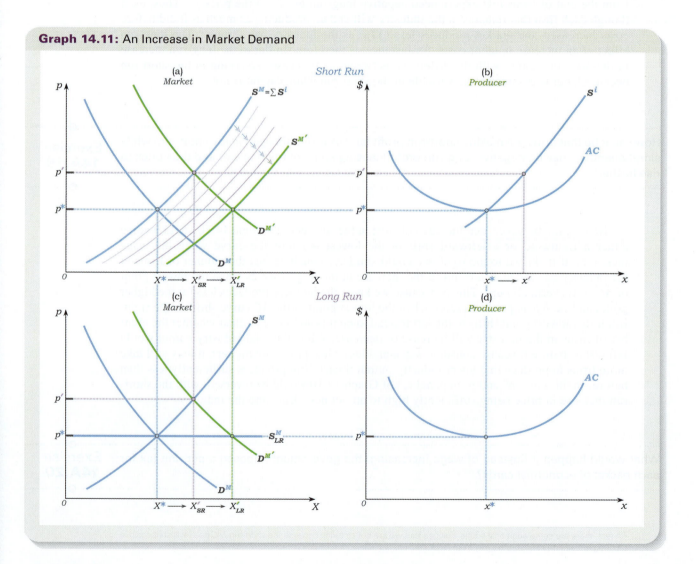

Graph 14.11: An Increase in Market Demand

to p' as the existing firms in the industry meet the new demand along the existing individual supply curves that sum to the market supply curve. But, since firms were initially making zero long-run profits, the increase in price now allows them to earn positive long-run profits. This provides new firms an incentive to enter the industry, and the (short-run) market supply curve therefore shifts out with each new entrant. This in turn puts downward pressure on price, with that pressure continuing so long as firms in the industry are making positive long-run profits. Thus, entry into the industry will stop (assuming all firms have identical costs) only when price falls back to the original p^* where all firms once again make zero long-run profits. The final short-run market supply curve therefore settles at the green curve $S^{M'}$.

While panel (a) of the graph illustrates the transition from the initial change in the short-run equilibrium to the final long-run equilibrium by showing the shifting (magenta) supply curves as new firms enter, panel (c) illustrates the change from the initial long-run equilibrium to the final long-run equilibrium by focusing on the long-run supply curve S_{LR}^{M} that does not shift (because the lowest point of the AC curve for firms does not shift). In both panels (a) and (c), we see that industry output rises to X'_{SR} in the short run and ultimately settles at the larger industry output X'_{LR}. In panel (b), we furthermore see that each firm in the industry initially increases its production, but panel (d) illustrates that each firm will ultimately end up producing the same as it did before the increase in demand. The larger industry output therefore arises solely from the fact that the industry as a whole has expanded through the entry of new firms.

14A.3.6 Changes Affecting a Single Firm versus Changes Affecting the Industry

In everything we have done thus far in this section, we have assumed that the change we are analyzing affects every firm in the industry. Sometimes, however, only a single firm in the industry might experience a change. The analysis of what happens for such firm-specific changes is then considerably simpler because each firm in a competitive industry is sufficiently small so that any change in behavior by that firm will not affect the short- or long-run market equilibrium.

Suppose, for instance, that I am one of many producers who produces trading cards with heroes (economists, in my case) pictured on them. I am only one of many producers of "hero cards," and so what I do has no impact on the market. Now suppose the government gets upset at me because economists are critical of government policy and, in the view of the government, therefore do not represent legitimate heroes for children. As a result, the government raises my annual license fee for operating in the hero card market, but it does not raise the fees for anyone else. In that case, I'll continue to produce in the short run as if nothing happened until my license fee for next year comes due. Since I (as every other firm in the industry) was initially making zero profits, I would now make negative long-run profits if I paid the license fee again and continued to produce. So, I will exit the industry, leaving the market equilibrium unchanged (since I am one of many producers and therefore can't by myself shift the market supply curve).

Sometimes, the change in costs that affect a single firm are less obvious than the simple example of the government imposing a fee or tax on just me. Suppose, for instance, that I discovered that the economist card factory I owned sits on land that contains substantial oil reserves underneath. This new information would imply that the value of the land under my factory is considerably higher than I initially thought, and thus the opportunity cost of using this land for my factory has gone up. Thus, my AC shifts up, implying that I will now make negative profits if I continue to produce economist cards. I will therefore exit the industry and either go into the oil business or sell the land to an oil company. The increase in my costs has thus driven me out of the hero card business, even though I am better off since I get to make more money in the oil business (or make more money by selling the land). If, on the other hand, I had rented the land rather than owned it, the rent for the land would have increased, thus again raising my AC and driving me out of business, but now the owner of the land would have benefitted rather than me. In either case, though, the increase in opportunity costs for me as a hero card producer increased and drove me out of the industry.

Exercise 14A.21

True or False: Regardless of what cost it is, if it increases for only one firm in a competitive industry, that firm will exit in the long run but it might not shut down in the short run.

14A.4 An Overview of Changes Affecting Firms and Industries

In this chapter, we have—for the first time—aggregated both the consumer and producer sides of a competitive market. By understanding what moves the supply side of the goods market, we have then been able to trace the short- and long-run impacts of changes in several types of market conditions on prices and output levels within affected industries. Table 14.1 summarizes our main conclusions.

The table gives an example for each of the four general market conditions we have covered: (1) changes in (long-run) fixed costs (e.g., license fees); (2) changes in costs associated with inputs that are fixed in the short run but variable in the long run (e.g., the price r of capital); (3) changes in costs associated with inputs that are immediately variable (e.g., the price w of labor); and (4) changes in consumer demand for the product produced in the industry. For each of these, the table first indicates which of the key cost curves are affected in firms in both the short and long run. It then indicates short- and long-run movements in equilibrium prices, industry output levels, and individual firm output levels. Single arrows (such as $\uparrow$) indicate a smaller change than a double arrow (such as $\Uparrow$) when variables are expected to move in the same direction in both the short and long run; a horizontal line ($-$) indicates no change from the initial equilibrium; and a question mark (?) indicates that the theory, absent additional assumptions, allows for changes in either direction. Finally, the last column indicates whether the change causes the overall number of firms in the industry to increase or decrease in the long run, indicating whether firms are expected to enter or exit the industry as a result of the change.[4]

Exercise 14A.22*

Replicate Table 14.1 for the cases where the demand and the various cost examples decrease rather than increase.

Table 14.1: The Impact of Changing Conditions of Firms and Industries (assuming Identical Firms)

Example	Affected Costs SR	Affected Costs LR	Market Price	Industry Output	Firm Output	LR # of Firms
$\uparrow$ License Fee	None	AC	$-SR\uparrow LR$	$-SR\downarrow LR$	$-SR\uparrow LR$	$\downarrow$
$\uparrow r$	None	AC, MC	$-SR\uparrow LR$	$-SR\downarrow LR$	$-SR?LR$	?
$\uparrow w$	AC, MC	AC, MC	$\uparrow SR\uparrow LR$	$\downarrow SR\downarrow LR$	$\downarrow SR?LR$	?
$\uparrow$ Demand	None	None	$\uparrow SR-LR$	$\uparrow SR\Uparrow LR$	$\uparrow SR-LR$	$\uparrow$

[4]See Graphs 14.8, 14.9, 14.10, and 14.11 and surrounding discussion for details on each of the rows in Table 14.1.

14B The Mathematics of Industry (or Market) Equilibrium

Given that we have derived demand and supply for various scenarios quite carefully, there is little in terms of new mathematics that has to be added at this point to further our understanding of the intuitive concepts related to industry or market equilibrium in Section A. I will therefore use Section B in this chapter to simply run through an example illustrating how we use all we have learned to calculate an industry equilibrium from knowing some basics about an economy. This is obviously going to be a stylized example, not one meant in any way to approximate any real-world industry. Nevertheless, it is often the case that understanding the full implications of what one learns is more than understanding the sum of all the parts. It is for this reason that I think we benefit from fully developing an industry equilibrium from the ground up.

We will begin with consumers who all have tastes over the good x and "all other goods" y that can be represented by the quasilinear utility function

$$u(x,y) = 50x^{1/2} + y. \tag{14.1}$$

You can check for yourself that such consumers have the demand function

$$x^d(p) = \left(\frac{25}{p}\right)^2 = \frac{625}{p^2}, \tag{14.2}$$

where we assume a price of 1 for the composite good y and let p denote the price of good x.

Why is the demand function not a function of income?

Exercise
14B.1

Suppose further that producers operate in competitive input markets in which labor costs $w = 20$ and capital costs $r = 10$, and that all producers (and potential producers) for the good x face the same technology that can be captured by the production function

$$f(\ell,k) = 20\ell^{2/5}k^{2/5}. \tag{14.3}$$

Note that this is the same decreasing returns to scale technology for which we calculated the various functions in the duality picture in Chapter 12. Suppose that in addition to the inputs ℓ and k, however, the firm must purchase a recurring operating license that costs \$1,280 from the government. As you should have concluded if you did end-of-chapter exercise 12.4, an addition of a fixed cost such as this to a decreasing returns to scale production process results in a U-shaped long-run average cost curve for the producer.

We can demonstrate this here by combining results we already derived (for the most part) elsewhere. In Chapter 12 (equation (12.46)), we derived the cost function for the production function (14.3) as $C(w,r,x) = 2(wr)^{1/2}(x/20)^{5/4}$. With the additional recurring fixed cost of 1,280, this implies a long-run cost function for the production process in equation (14.3) of

$$C(w,r,x) = 2(wr)^{1/2}\left(\frac{x}{20}\right)^{5/4} + 1,280 \tag{14.4}$$

or, when $w = 20$ and $r = 10$,

$$C(x) = 0.66874x^{5/4} + 1,280. \tag{14.5}$$

This implies an AC function (when $w = 20$ and $r = 10$) of

$$AC(x) = 0.66874x^{1/4} + \frac{1,280}{x} \tag{14.6}$$

which is U-shaped and attains its minimum at $x = 1,280$ at an average cost of \$5 per unit.

Exercise 14B.2

Demonstrate that the average cost of production is U-shaped and reaches its lowest point at $x = 1,280$ where $AC = 5$. (*Hint:* You can illustrate the U-shape by showing that the derivative of AC is zero at 1,280, negative for output less than 1,280, and positive for output greater than 1,280.)

14B.1 Industry Equilibrium in the Short Run

Short-run industry equilibrium is then determined solely by the intersection of market demand and supply curves, where demand and supply curves are represented by the sum of all individual demand curves from consumers and supply curves from producers who are currently operating in the industry. Adding up demand curves in our example is particularly easy because the demand functions (equation (14.2)) of *all* consumers are exactly identical (since they share the same quasilinear tastes and thus their income does not matter for demand). "Adding up" demand curves for all consumers therefore simply means "multiplying" equation (14.2) by the number of consumers in the market for good x. For instance, suppose the total number of consumers in the market is 64,000. Then the market demand function $D^M(p)$ is

$$D^M(p) = 64,000x^d(p) = 64,000\left(\frac{625}{p^2}\right) = \frac{40,000,000}{p^2}. \tag{14.7}$$

14B.1.1 Short-Run Industry Supply

To calculate the market supply curve, we need to first know the individual short-run supply function for each producer and then similarly "add up" these functions. In equation (11.33) of Chapter 11, we concluded that the supply function for a producer with technology $f(\ell) = A\ell^\alpha$ is

$$x(p, w) = A\left(\frac{w}{\alpha A p}\right)^{\alpha/(\alpha-1)} \tag{14.8}$$

If capital is fixed at k^A in the short run, then our production function from equation (14.3) is simply

$$f(\ell) = A\ell^\alpha \text{ where } A = 20(k^A)^{2/5} \text{ and } \alpha = 2/5. \tag{14.9}$$

Suppose, for instance, that $k^A = 256$, which we will show shortly in Section 14B.2 is the case in long-run equilibrium. Then, using the values for A and α specified in equation (14.9) and plugging them into equation (14.8), we get a short-run supply function

$$x(p, w) = 3,225.398\left(\frac{p}{w}\right)^{2/3} \text{ or } x^s(p) = 437.754p^{2/3} \text{ when } w = 20. \tag{14.10}$$

Since we are assuming all producers are identical, "adding up" these supply functions to get short-run market supply is again equivalent to "multiplying" them by the number of firms *that are currently operating in the industry.* Suppose that number is 1,250 (which we will shortly show is the correct number of firms in long-run equilibrium). Then the short-run industry supply function $S^M(p)$ is

$$S^M(p) = 1,250x^s(p) = 1,250(437.754)p^{2/3} = 547,192p^{2/3}. \tag{14.11}$$

14B.1.2 Short-Run Industry Equilibrium

With market demand and market supply given by equations (14.7) and (14.11) respectively, we can now calculate the short-run equilibrium by setting the two equations equal to one another and solving for the equilibrium price; i.e., solve

$$S^M(p) = 547,192p^{2/3} = \frac{40,000,000}{p^2} = D^M(p), \tag{14.12}$$

which gives $p = 5$. Thus, with 64,000 consumers and 1,250 producers, with tastes and technologies described by equations (14.1) and (14.3), with short-run capital k^A fixed at 256 units and with the wage rate given by $w = 20$, market demand and supply intersect at an equilibrium price $p^* = 5$. Plugging this back into the individual consumer and producer equations, this implies that each consumer in the market consumes 25 units of x, and each producer produces 1,280 units of output by hiring 128 labor hours.

Verify these individual production and consumption quantities.

Exercise 14B.3

    To make sure that each firm is in fact making non-negative short-run profits, we can compare total revenues to total short-run economic costs. Total revenues are simply given by the output quantity (1,280) times price ($5), for a total of $6,400. Short-run economic costs in this case include only labor costs: 128 labor hours at a wage of $20, or $2,560. Thus, short-run profit for each producer is $3,840. At the same time, the producer also incurs fixed short-run *expenses* of $10 for each of the 256 units of capital that are fixed in the short run *and* the recurring fixed license fee of $1,280, for a total of $3,840 in total expenditures that are not costs in the short run.

We have already indicated that $k = 256$ is in fact the optimal long-run quantity of capital when $(p, w, r) = (5, 20, 10)$. Can you then conclude that the industry is in long-run equilibrium from the information in the previous paragraph? (*Hint:* This can only be true if no firm has an incentive to enter or exit the industry.)

Exercise 14B.4

14B.2 An Industry in Long-Run Equilibrium

We already concluded after equation (14.6) that the long-run AC curve for each of the firms (assuming $w = 20$ and $r = 10$) is U-shaped and attains its lowest point of $5 at output quantity 1,280. We also know that *in the long run, the number of firms in the market will adjust to keep the equilibrium price at this lowest point of the AC curve*; i.e., in the long run, equilibrium price is $5. With market demand given by equation (14.7), this implies that the industry will produce a total of 1,600,000 units of x, which is the quantity demanded by the market when price is $5. And, since each firm will produce at the lowest point of its AC curve in long-run equilibrium, we know that each individual firm will produce 1,280 units of x, implying that there will be exactly 1,250 producers in the industry.

    The short-run equilibrium we calculated in the previous section is therefore also the long-run equilibrium, with the short-run fixed quantity of capital (256 units per firm) exactly equal to how much capital each firm desires to utilize given the current prices. The industry equilibrium is pictured in Graph 14.12, with panel (b) illustrating the short-run industry demand curves whose intersection signals prices to the typical consumer in panel (a) and the typical producer in panel (c). Note that the supply and demand curves are once again actually plotted as inverse supply and demand curves given that they are functions of prices but prices appear on the vertical axes.

Graph 14.12: A Graphical Representation of the Industry Equilibrium

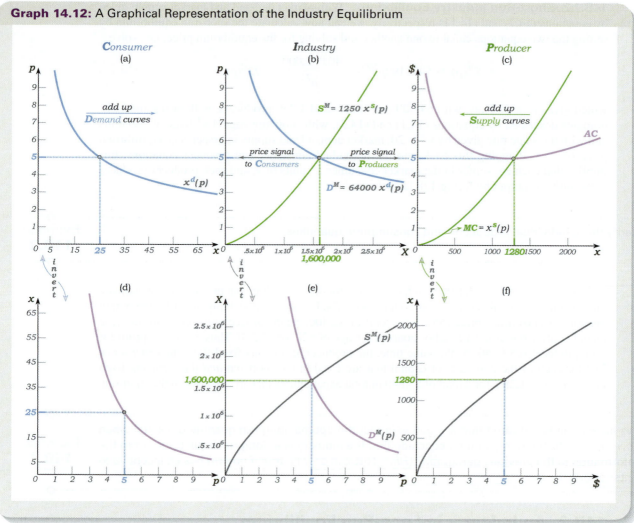

The graph looks similar to those we are used to seeing from Section A except for the fact that short-run firm supply curves begin at the origin in panel (b) whereas we drew them as beginning at the lowest point of short-run average cost AC^{SR} in our graphs in Section A. When you think about the underlying assumptions in Graph 14.12, however, the reasons for this difference should become apparent. The short-run production function (given in equation (14.9)) has decreasing returns to scale throughout, implying increasing MC throughout. In our graphs of Section A, on the other hand, we implicitly assumed a sigmoid shaped short-run production function of the type we introduced in Chapter 11, with an initial portion that has increasing returns to scale before becoming decreasing returns to scale. This assumption then led to a U-shaped AC^{SR}, with the portion of the MC above AC^{SR} forming the short-run firm supply curve. In the case of our short-run production function that has decreasing returns to scale throughout, however, the AC^{SR} is not U-shaped and has its lowest point at the origin.

Exercise 14B.5   Can you graph the AC^{SR} into panel (c) of Graph 14.12?

14B.3 Changing Conditions and Changing Equilibrium

At this point in Section A, we proceeded to demonstrate how the short- and long-run equilibrium changes as different parts of the economic environment change. We began by noting that our starting point will always be an industry in long-run equilibrium, and we can think of a short-run equilibrium lying embedded in this long-run equilibrium. This is what we in fact have just calculated and graphed in Graph 14.12: The industry is in long-run equilibrium because each firm is producing at the lowest point of (long-run) AC, and this lowest point lies on the short-run supply curve that is formed from assuming that each firm currently has the long-run optimal quantity of capital given its current production of 1,280 units of output. The total number of firms in the industry is then exactly sufficient to cause the short-run industry demand curve to intersect the market demand curve at $5, which keeps the industry in long-run equilibrium with no incentive for any firm to enter or exit.

We can then illustrate, beginning at this equilibrium, the impact of changes in long-run fixed costs (represented in our example by the recurring license fee), changes in cost associated with inputs that are fixed in the short run but variable in the long run (represented in our example by the cost of capital), changes in costs associated with variable inputs (represented in our example by the cost of labor) and, finally, changes in demand for the industry's output. As in Section A, we will consider positive changes in each of these and will leave it to you to investigate what happens when these changes are in the opposite direction.

14B.3.1 An Increase in a Long-Run Fixed Cost Suppose, then, that the government seeks to cover a deficit by raising all license fees by 75%, implying an increase in the recurring license fee for our firms from $1,280 to $2,240. Since the license fee does not appear in the short-run firm supply functions in equation (14.10), the short-run market supply does not shift and nothing changes in the short run. In the long run, however, firms would experience a negative profit of $960 each period, giving an incentive for some of them to exit the industry. This will cause an upward shift in the market supply curve until profits are once again zero in the industry.

Why does the long-run profit become negative $960 if nothing changes?

**Exercise
14B.6**

To see at what output price profits will be zero, we simply have to see where the new lowest point of each producer's AC curve lies. Instead of the AC in equation (14.6), the increase in the license fee causes the new AC' curve to be

$$AC'(x) = 0.66874x^{1/4} + \frac{2,240}{x}, \tag{14.13}$$

which is once again U-shaped but now has its lowest point at approximately $x = 2,000$ where average cost is approximately $5.59 per unit. We therefore know that the new long-run equilibrium will have an output price of approximately $5.59 (up from the previous price of $5.00 per unit), with each firm that remains in the industry producing approximately 2,000 units of output each period (up from the previous 1,280 units produced by each firm in the industry). Plugging this new price into the market demand curve in equation (14.7), we find that consumers will demand approximately 1,280,000 units of output each period at this new long-run equilibrium price. With each firm in the industry producing approximately 2,000 units, this implies that the new long-run equilibrium will have approximately 640 firms, down from 1,250 before the increase in the license fee. Finally, we can insert the new price into the individual demand curves in equation (14.2) to conclude that each consumer will lower his or her consumption from 25 to approximately 20 units of x each period.

Exercise 14B.7   Verify these calculations.

Exercise 14B.8   Compare the changes set off by an increase in the license fee to those predicted in Graph 14.8.

14B.3.2 An Increase in the Cost of Capital

Next, suppose that, instead of an increase in the license fee, the cost of capital r increases from $10 per unit to $15 per unit. Since capital is a fixed input in the short run, this change once again does not alter the short-run supply curve of firms (equation (14.10)) and thus has no impact on the short-run market equilibrium. However, as capital becomes a variable input in the long run, it becomes an economic cost, and profit for each firm becomes negative unless output price rises. Thus, firms have an incentive to exit the industry, causing price to rise until long-run profit is zero for all firms that remain in the industry.

How high the price rises again depends on how far up the lowest point of the producers' (long-run) AC curve has shifted. Plugging in the wage $w = 20$ and the new rental rate $r' = 15$ into the general cost function in equation (14.5), we get cost as a function of output given by

$$C(x) = 0.819036x^{5/4} + 1{,}280 \qquad (14.14)$$

with accompanying average cost given by

$$AC'(x) = 0.819036x^{1/4} + \frac{1{,}280}{x}. \qquad (14.15)$$

This new AC' curve reaches its lowest point at approximately $x = 1{,}088$ where average cost is approximately $5.88 per unit, up from $5.00 per unit before the increase in r. Thus, the new long-run equilibrium price has to be approximately $5.88, with each firm that remains in the industry producing 1,088 units of x each period. At this price, the market demand function tells us that consumers will demand approximately 1,156,925 units of x, which implies that the new long-run equilibrium will have approximately 1,063 producers, down from the initial 1,250.

Exercise 14B.9   Verify these calculations.

Exercise 14B.10   Are these results consistent with Graph 14.9?

Exercise 14B.11   How much capital and labor are hired in the industry before and after the increase in r?

14B.3.3 An Increase in the Cost of Labor

The most complicated cost change we analyzed in Section A was that of an increase in the wage rate w because labor can be adjusted in both the short and long run. Suppose, for instance, that the wage rate increases from $20 to $30 (with the cost of capital remaining at $10 and the license fee remaining at $1,280). From equation (14.10), we know that the short-run supply function for each producer is $x(p, w) = 3{,}225.398(p/w)^{2/3}$, which implies that the supply curve shifts from $x^s(p) = 437.754p^{2/3}$ when $w = 20$ to

$$x^{s'}(p) = 334.069p^{2/3}. \qquad (14.16)$$

With 1,250 producers in the industry, this implies that short-run industry supply shifts from $S^M(p) = 547,192p^{2/3}$ to

$$S^{M'}(p) = 417,586p^{2/3}. \tag{14.17}$$

When set equal to the (unchanged) market demand $D^M(p) = 40,000,000/p^2$, we get a short-run equilibrium price of approximately \$5.53 (up from the initial equilibrium price of \$5.00 before the wage increase). At this price, each firm produces approximately 1,045 units of output (down from 1,280), earning revenue of approximately \$5,782 each period.

Verify these calculations.

Exercise 14B.12

In the short run, expenses associated with capital and license fees are not economic costs, and labor costs are the only short-run economic costs. With each firm's capital fixed at 256 units, approximately 77 units of labor are hired by each firm to produce the 1,045 units of output, implying that short-run economic costs are approximately \$2,310. Given \$5,782 in revenue, this leaves a short-run economic profit of \$3,472.

How much does the industry production change in the short run?

Exercise 14B.13

In the long run, however, license costs and costs associated with capital become economic costs. Were each firm to continue to produce as it does in short-run equilibrium, total costs would therefore include \$2,560 for capital inputs and \$1,280 for the license to operate, implying that each firm would earn a long-run economic profit of −\$367 each period. Thus, firms have an incentive to exit until long-run profit is once again zero for all firms that remain in the industry. This will occur when price reaches the lowest point of the new (long-run) AC' curve, which happens when long-run output price settles at approximately \$5.88 (up from \$5.53 in the short run). At this long-run equilibrium price, each producer that remains in the market will produce approximately 1,088 units of output (up from 1,045 in the short run) while the market demand for output falls to approximately 1,156,925 (from 1,306,395 in the short run). This leaves room for approximately 1,063 producers in the industry (down from 1,250).

Verify these calculations and compare the results with our graphical analysis of an increase in the wage rate in Graph 14.10.

Exercise 14B.14

14B.3.4 An Increase in Market Demand Finally, we concluded Section A with a brief analysis of how the industry changes in the short and long run when there is an increase in market demand. Suppose, for instance, that some unexpected news coverage of the health benefits of consuming our mythical x good increases the number of consumers in our market from 64,000 to 100,000. Market demand, initially equal to $D^M(p) = 64,000x^d(p) = 40,000,000/p^2$ then shifts to the new $D^{M'}(p)$ given by

$$D^{M'}(p) = 100,000x^d(p) = 100,000\left(\frac{625}{p^2}\right) = \frac{62,500,000}{p^2}. \tag{14.18}$$

The short-run market supply function $S^M(p) = 547{,}192p^{2/3}$ remains unchanged (since each firm's cost curves remain unchanged). Setting this equal to the new demand function, we then get a new short-run equilibrium price of approximately $5.91 (up from $5.00). At this price, each of the 1,250 existing firms produce (given their short-run supply curves from equation (14.10)) approximately 1,431 units of output (up from 1,280), with industry supply rising to approximately 1,789,234 (from 1,600,000).

Exercise 14B.15 How much does individual consumption by consumers who were originally in the market change in the short run?

At the new short-run equilibrium price, each firm earns positive economic profits, thus providing an incentive for new firms to enter the industry until price is driven back to $5.00 when all firms in the industry make zero profits. At $5, the new market demand curve tells us that consumers demand 2,500,000 units of x. With each firm once again producing at the lowest point of its average cost curve (where $x = 1{,}280$), this implies that there will be approximately 1,953 producers in the new long-run equilibrium (up from 1,250).

Exercise 14B.16 Verify these calculations and compare the results with Graph 14.11, where we graphically illustrated the impact of an increase in market demand.

CONCLUSION

In this chapter, we have combined for the first time the results from consumer and producer models to illustrate how competitive or decentralized market equilibria arise. These equilibria are based on the assumption that individuals—producers and consumers—are "small" relative to the economy and thus cannot individually influence the economic environment in which they operate. Put differently, competitive equilibrium arises when individuals are price-takers with no incentive to think strategically about how their own actions influence prices. Later on, we will see how the notion of an equilibrium changes when some individuals in an economy are not "small."

While the difference between the short and long run for firms is defined by the time it takes for all inputs to become variable, the difference between the short and long run for the industry is defined by the time it takes for new firms to enter or old ones to exit. Firms can exit once they can release the inputs that are fixed in the short run, which implies that the time horizon for the short run to turn into the long run is the same from the firm's and the industry's perspective (if the fixed input is fixed for the same time period for all firms). Firms can enter once they can release their fixed inputs in other industries and convert them to inputs in the industry they wish to enter, and it is convenient as well as plausible to assume that this, too, is similar to the period during which inputs are fixed in the industry we are analyzing. The most important insight to emerge from all this is that the short-run equilibrium emerges from the intersection of demand and supply *of existing firms* in the industry, while the long-run equilibrium is entirely derived from the entry/exit decisions that drive long-run profits (of marginal firms) to zero.

The competitive equilibrium that we have described is, as we noted at the beginning of the chapter, remarkable in that it describes a "spontaneous order." By "order" we mean that a mechanism is put in place to signal, through market prices, to millions of individual actors in the market how they should cooperate with others in that market. By "spontaneous" we mean that the order arises without anyone planning it; each individual simply considers his or her own economic circumstances and makes the best decision he or she can. We will now turn to another remarkable result: Under certain conditions, this spontaneous order turns out to maximize the overall gains to society from the scarce resources that are available to the society.

END-OF-CHAPTER EXERCISES

14.1[†] In Table 14.1, the last column indicates the predicted change in the number of firms within an industry when economic conditions change.

A. In two cases, the table makes a definitive prediction, whereas in two other cases it does not.

  a. Explain first why we can say definitively that the number of firms falls as a recurring fixed cost (i.e., license fee) increases. Relate your answer to what we know about firm output and price in the long run.

  b. Repeat (a) for the case of an increase in demand.

  c. Now consider an increase in the wage rate and suppose first that this causes the long-run AC curve to shift up without changing the output level at which the curve reaches its lowest point. In this case, can you predict whether the number of firms increases or decreases?

  d. Repeat (c) but assume that the lowest point of the AC curve shifts up and to the right.

  e. Repeat (c) again but this time assume that the lowest point of the AC curve shifts up and to the left.

  f. Is the analysis regarding the new equilibrium number of firms any different for a change in r?

  g. Which way would the lowest point of the AC curve have to shift in order for us not to be sure whether the number of firms increases or decreases when w *falls*?

B. Consider the case of a firm that operates with a Cobb–Douglas production function $f(\ell, k) = A\ell^\alpha k^\beta$ where $\alpha, \beta > 0$ and $\alpha + \beta < 1$.

  a. The cost function for such a production process, assuming no fixed costs, was given in equation (13.45) of exercise 13.5. Assuming an additional recurring fixed cost F, what is the average cost function for this firm?

  b.** Derive the equation for the output level x^* at which the long-run AC curve reaches its lowest point.

  c. How does x^* change with F, w, and r?

  d. *True or False*: For industries in which firms face Cobb–Douglas production processes with recurring fixed costs, we can predict that the number of firms in the industry increases with F but we cannot predict whether the number of firms will increase or decrease with w or r.

14.2 Table 14.1 was constructed under the assumption that all firms in the industry are identical.

A. Suppose that all firms in an industry have U-shaped long-run average cost curves.

  a. Leaving aside the column labeled "Firm Output," what would change in the table if firms have different cost structures; i.e., some firms have lower marginal and average costs than others?

  b. Industries such as those described in (a) are sometimes called *increasing cost industries* compared with *constant cost industries* where all firms are identical. Can you derive a rationale for these terms?

  c. It has been argued that, in some industries, the average and marginal costs of *all* firms decline as more firms enter the market. For instance, such industries might make use of an unusual labor market skill that becomes more plentiful in the market as more workers train for this skill when many firms demand it. How would the long-run industry supply curve differ in this case from that discussed in the text as well as that described in (a)?

  d. Industries such as those described in (c) are sometimes referred to as *decreasing cost industries*. Can you explain why?

14.3 **Everyday and Business Application:** *Fast Food Restaurants and Grease (cont'd):* In exercise 12.8, you investigated the impact of hybrid vehicles that can run partially on grease from hamburger production on the number of hamburgers produced by a fast food restaurant. You did so, however, in the absence of considering the equilibrium impact on prices and assumed instead that prices for hamburgers are unaffected by the change in demand for grease.

EVERYDAY APPLICATION

BUSINESS APPLICATION

---

*conceptually challenging
**computationally challenging
[†]solutions in Study Guide

A. Suppose again that you use a decreasing returns to scale production process for producing hamburgers using only labor and that you produce 1 ounce of grease for every hamburger. In addition, suppose that you are part of a competitive industry and that each firm also incurs a recurring fixed cost F every week.

    a.   Suppose that the cost of hauling away grease is $q > 0$ per ounce. Illustrate the shape of your marginal and average cost curve (given that you also face a recurring fixed cost).

    b.   Assuming all restaurants are identical, illustrate the number of hamburgers you produce in long-run equilibrium.

    c.   Now suppose that, as a result of the increased use of hybrid vehicles, the company you previously hired to haul away your grease is now willing to pay for the grease it hauls away. How do your cost curves change?

    d.   Describe the impact this will have on the equilibrium price of hamburgers and the number of hamburgers you produce in the short run.

    e.   How does your answer change in the long run?

    f.   Would your answers change if you instead assumed that restaurants used both labor and capital in the production of hamburgers?

    g.   In exercise 12.8, you concluded that the cholesterol level in hamburgers will increase as a result of these hybrid vehicles if restaurants can choose more or less fatty meat. Does your conclusion still hold?

B. Suppose, as in exercise 12.8, that your production function is given by $f(\ell) = A\ell^{\alpha}$ (with $0 < \alpha < 1$) and that the cost of hauling away grease is q. In addition, suppose now that each restaurant incurs a recurring fixed cost of F.

    a.   Derive the cost function for your restaurant.

    b.   Derive the marginal and average cost functions.

    c.   How many hamburgers will you produce in the long run?

    d.**   What is the long-run equilibrium price of hamburgers?

    e.   From your results, determine how the long-run equilibrium price and output level of each restaurant changes as q changes.

14.4†   **Business Application:** *Brand Names and Franchise Fees*: Suppose you are currently operating a hamburger restaurant that is part of a competitive industry in your city.

A. Your restaurant is identical to others in its homothetic production technology, which employs labor ℓ and capital k and has decreasing returns to scale.

    a.   In addition to paying for labor and capital each week, each restaurant also has to pay recurring weekly fees F in order to operate. Illustrate the average weekly long-run cost curve for your restaurant.

    b.   On a separate graph, illustrate the weekly demand curve for hamburgers in your city as well as the short-run industry supply curve assuming that the industry is in long-run equilibrium. How many hamburgers do you sell each week?

    c.   As you are happily producing burgers in this long-run equilibrium, a representative from the national MacWendy's chain comes to your restaurant and asks you to convert your restaurant to a MacWendy's. It turns out, this would require no effort on your part; you would simply have to allow the MacWendy's company to install a MacWendy's sign, change some of the furniture, and provide your employees with new uniforms, all of which the MacWendy's parent company is happy to pay for. MacWendy's would, however, charge you a weekly franchise fee of G for the privilege of being the only MacWendy's restaurant in town. When you wonder why you would agree to this, the MacWendy's representative pulls out his marketing research that convincingly documents that consumers are willing to pay $\$y$ more per hamburger when it carries the MacWendy's brand name. If you accept this deal, will the market price for hamburgers in your city change?

    d.   On your average cost curve graph, illustrate how many hamburgers you would produce if you accepted the MacWendy's deal.

    e.   Next, for a given y, illustrate the largest that G could be in order for you to accept the MacWendy's deal.

f.   If you accept the deal, will you end up hiring more or fewer workers? Will you hire more or less capital?

g.   Does your decision on how many workers and capital to hire under the MacWendy's deal depend on the size of the franchise fee G?

h.* Suppose that you accepted the MacWendy's deal and, because of the increased sales of hamburgers at your restaurant, one hamburger restaurant in the city closes down. Assuming that the total number of hamburgers consumed remains the same, can you speculate whether total employment (of labor) in the hamburger industry went up or down in the city? (*Hint*: Think about the fact that all restaurants operate under the same decreasing returns to scale technology.)

B. Suppose all restaurants in the industry use the same technology that has a long-run cost function $C(w, r, x) = 0.028486(w^{0.5}r^{0.5}x^{1.25})$, which, as a function of wage w and rental rate r, gives the weekly cost of producing x hamburgers.[5]

a.   Suppose that each hamburger restaurant has to pay a recurring weekly fee of \$4,320 to operate in the city in which you are located and that $w = 15$ and $r = 20$. If the restaurant industry is in long-run equilibrium in your city, how many hamburgers does each restaurant sell each week?

b.   At what price do hamburgers sell in your city?

c.   Suppose that the weekly demand for hamburgers in your city is $x(p) = 100,040 - 1,000p$. How many hamburger restaurants are there in the city?

d.   Now consider the MacWendy's offer described in A(c) of this exercise. In particular, suppose that the franchise fee required by MacWendy's is $G = 5,000$ and that consumers are willing to pay 94 cents more per hamburger when it carries the MacWendy's brand name. How many hamburgers would you end up producing if you accept MacWendy's deal?

e.   Will you accept the MacWendy's deal?

f.   Assuming that the total number of hamburgers sold in your city will remain roughly the same, would the number of hamburger restaurants in the city change as a result of you accepting the deal?

g.   What is the most that the MacWendy's representative could have charged you for you to have been willing to accept the deal?

h.   Suppose the average employee works for 36 hours per week. Can you use Shephard's Lemma to determine how many employees you hire if you accept the deal? Does this depend on how high a franchise fee you are paying?

i.   How does this compare with the number of employees hired by the competing non-MacWendy's hamburger restaurants? In light of your answer to (f), will overall employment in the hamburger industry increase or decrease in your city as a result of you becoming a MacWendy's restaurant?

14.5 **Business Application:** *"Economic Rent" and Profiting from Entrepreneural Skill*: Suppose, as in exercise 14.4, that you are operating a hamburger restaurant that is part of a competitive industry. Now you are also the owner, and suppose throughout that the owner of a restaurant is also one of the workers in the restaurant and collects the same wage as other workers for the time he/she puts into the business each week. (In addition, of course, the owner keeps any weekly profits.)

BUSINESS
APPLICATION

A. Again, assume that all the restaurants are using the same homothetic decreasing returns to scale technology, but now the inputs include the level of entrepreneural capital c in addition to weekly labor ℓ and capital k. As in exercise 14.4, assume also that all restaurants are required to pay a recurring weekly fixed cost F.

a.   First, assume that all restaurant owners possess the same level of entrepreneural skill c. Draw the long-run AC curve (for weekly hamburger production) for a restaurant and indicate how many weekly hamburgers the restaurant will sell and at what price assuming that the industry is in long-run equilibrium.

---

[5]For those who find unending amusement in proving such things, you can check that this cost function arises from the Cobb–Douglas production function $f(\ell, k) = 30\ell^{0.4}k^{0.4}$.

b.   Suppose next that you are special and possess more entrepreneural and management skill than all those other restaurant owners. As a result of your higher level of c, the marginal product of labor and capital is 20% greater for any bundle of ℓ and k than it is for any of your competitors. Will the long-run equilibrium price be any different as a result?

c.   If your entrepreneural skill causes the marginal product of capital and labor to be 20% greater for any combination of ℓ and k than for your competitors, how does your isoquant map differ from theirs? For a given wage and rental rate, will you employ the same labor to capital ratio as your competitors?

d.   Will you produce more or less than your competitors? Illustrate this on your graph by determining where the long-run MC and AC curves for your restaurant will lie relative to the AC curve of your competitors.

e.   Illustrate in your graph how much weekly profit you will earn from your unusually high entrepreneural skill.

f.   Suppose the owner of MacroSoft, a new computer firm, is interested in hiring you as the manager of one of its branches. How high a weekly salary would it have to offer you in order for you to quit the restaurant business assuming you would work for 36 hours per week in either case and assuming the wage rate in the restaurant business is $15 per hour?

g.   The benefit that an entrepreneur receives from his or her skill is sometimes referred to as the *economic rent* of that skill because the entrepreneur could be renting that skill out (to someone like MacroSoft) instead of using it in his or her own business. If the economic rent of entrepreneurial skill is included as a cost to the restaurant business you run, how much profit are you making in the restaurant business?

h.   Would counting this economic rent on your skill as a cost in the restaurant business affect how many hamburgers you produce? How would it change the AC curve in your graph?

B.   Suppose that all restaurants are employing the production function $f(\ell, k, c) = 30\ell^{0.4}k^{0.4}c$ where ℓ stands for weekly labor hours, k stands for weekly hours of rented capital and c stands for the entrepreneurial skill of the owner. Note that, with the exception of the c term, this is the same production technology used in exercise 14.4. The weekly demand for hamburgers in your city is, again as in exercise 14.4, $x(p) = 100{,}040 - 1{,}000p$.

a.   First, suppose that $c = 1$ for all restaurant owners, that $w = 15$ and $r = 20$, that there is a fixed weekly cost $4,320 of operating a restaurant, and the industry is in long-run equilibrium. Determine the weekly number of hamburgers sold in each restaurant, the price at which hamburgers sell, and the number of restaurants that are operating. (If you have done exercise 14.4, you should be able to use your results from there.)

b.   Next, suppose that you are the only restaurant owner who is different from all the others in that you are a better manager and entrepreneur and that this is reflected in $c = 1.24573$ for you. Determine your long-run AC and MC functions. (Be careful not to use the cost function given in exercise 14.4 since c is no longer equal to 1. You can instead rely on the cost function derived for Cobb–Douglas technologies given in equation (13.45) in exercise 13.5 (and remember to add the fixed cost).)

c.   How many hamburgers will you produce in long-run equilibrium?

d.   How many restaurants will there be in long-run equilibrium given your higher level of c?

e.   How many workers (including yourself) and units of capital are you hiring in your business compared with those hired by your competitors? (Recall that the average worker is assumed to work 36 hours per week.)

f.   How does your restaurant's weekly long-run profit differ from that of the other restaurants?

g.   Suppose MacroSoft is interested in hiring you as described in part A(f). How high a weekly salary would MacroSoft have to offer you in order for you to quit the restaurant business and accept the MacroSoft offer?

h.   If you decide to accept the MacroSoft offer and you exit the restaurant business, will total employment in the restaurant business go up or down?

14.6   **Business and Policy Application:** *Capital Gains Taxes*: Taxes on capital gains are applied to income earned on investments that return a profit or "capital gain" and not on income derived from labor. To the extent that such capital gains taxes are taxes on the return on capital, they will impact the rental rate of capital in ways we will explore more fully in a later chapter. For now, we will simply investigate the impact of a capital-gains-tax-induced increase in the rental price of capital on firms within an industry.

A. Suppose you are running a gas station in a competitive market where all firms are identical. You employ weekly labor ℓ and capital k using a homothetic decreasing returns to scale production function, and you incur a weekly fixed cost of F.

    a.   Begin with your firm's long-run weekly average cost curve and relate it to the weekly demand curve for gasoline in your city as well as the short-run weekly aggregate supply curve assuming the industry is in long-run equilibrium. Indicate by x^* how much weekly gasoline you sell, by p^* the price at which you sell it, and by X^* the total number of gallons of gasoline sold in the city per week.

    b.   Now suppose that an increase in the capital gains tax raises the rental rate on capital k (which is fixed for each gas station in the short run). Does anything change in the short run?

    c.   What happens to x^*, p^* and X^* in the long run? Explain how this emerges from your graph.

    d.   Is it possible for you to tell whether you will hire more or fewer workers as a result of the capital gains tax-induced increase in the rental rate? To the extent that it is not possible, what information could help clarify this?

    e.   Is it possible for you to be able to tell whether the number of gasoline stations in the city increases or decreases as a result of the increase in the rental rate? What factors might your answer depend on?

    f.   Can you tell whether employment of labor in gasoline stations increases or decreases? What about employment of capital?

B. Suppose that your production function is given by $f(\ell, k) = 30\ell^{0.4}k^{0.4}$, $F = 1{,}080$ and the weekly city-wide demand for gallons of gasoline is $x(p) = 100{,}040 - 1{,}000p$. Furthermore, suppose that the wage is $w = 15$ and the current rental rate is 32.1568. Gasoline prices are typically in terms of tenths of cents, so express your answer accordingly.

    a.   Suppose the industry is in long-run equilibrium in the absence of capital gains taxes. Assuming that you can hire fractions of hours of capital and produce fractions of gallons of gasoline, how much gasoline will you produce and at what price do you sell your gasoline? (Use the cost function derived for Cobb–Douglas technologies given in equation (13.45) in exercise 13.5 (and remember to add the fixed cost).)

    b.   How many gasoline stations are there in your city?

    c.   Now suppose the government's capital gains tax increases the rental rate of capital by 24.39% to $40. How will your sales of gasoline be affected in the new long-run equilibrium?

    d.   What is the new price of gasoline?

    e.   Will you change the number of workers you hire? How about the hours of capital you rent?

    f.   Will there be more or fewer gasoline stations in the city? How is your answer consistent with the change in the total sales of gasoline in the city?

    g.   What happens to total employment at gasoline stations as a result of the capital gains tax? Explain intuitively how this can happen.

    h.*   Which of your conclusions do you think is qualitatively independent of the production function used (so long as it is decreasing returns to scale), and which do you think is not?

    i.*   Which of your conclusions do you think is qualitatively independent of the demand function, and which do you think is not?

14.7   **Business and Policy Application:** *Using License Fees to Make Positive Profit:* Suppose you own one of many identical pharmaceutical companies producing a particular drug x.

A. Your production process has decreasing returns to scale but you incur an annually recurring fixed cost F for operating your business.

    a.   Begin by illustrating your firm's average long-run cost curve and identify your output level assuming that the output price is such that you make zero long-run profit.

    b.   Next to your graph, illustrate the market demand and short-run market supply curves that justify the zero-profit price as an equilibrium price.

    c.   Next, suppose that the government introduces an annually recurring license fee G for any firm that produces this drug. Assume that your firm remains in the industry. What changes in your firm and in the market in both the short and long run as a result of the introduction of G and assuming that long-run profits will again be zero in the new long-run equilibrium?

d.   Now suppose that G is such that the number of firms required to sustain the zero-profit price in the new long-run equilibrium is not an integer. In particular, suppose that we would require 6.5 firms to sustain this price as an equilibrium in the market. Given that fractions of firms cannot exist, how many firms will actually exist in the long run?

e.   How does this affect the long-run equilibrium price, the long-run production level in your firm (assuming yours is one of the firms that remains in the market), and the long-run profits for your firm?

f.   *True or False*: Sufficiently large fixed costs may in fact allow identical firms in a competitive industry to make positive long-run profits.

g.   *True or False*: Sufficiently large license fees can cause a competitive industry to become more *concentrated*, by which we mean fewer firms are competing for each customer.

B. Suppose that each firm in the industry uses the production function $f(\ell, k) = 10\ell^{0.4}k^{0.4}$ and each incurs a recurring annual fixed cost of $175,646.

a.   Determine how much each firm produces in the long-run equilibrium if $w = r = 20$. (You can use the cost function derived for Cobb–Douglas technologies given in equation (13.45) in exercise 13.5 (and remember to add the fixed cost).)

b.   What price are consumers paying for the drugs produced in this industry?

c.   Suppose consumer demand is given by the aggregate demand function $x(p) = 1,000,000 - 10,000p$. How many firms are in this industry?

d.   Suppose the government introduces a requirement that each company has to purchase an annual operating license costing $824,354. How do your answers to (a), (b), and (c) change in the short and long run?

e.   Are any of the firms that remain active in the industry better or worse off in the new long-run equilibrium?

f.   Suppose instead that the government's annual fee were set at $558,258. Calculate the price at which long-run profits are equal to zero.

g.   How many firms would this imply will survive in the long run assuming fractions of firms can operate?

h.   Since fractions of firms cannot operate, how many firms will actually exist in the long run? Verify that this should imply an equilibrium price of approximately $48.2. (*Hint*: Use the supply function given for a Cobb–Douglas production process in equation (13.49) found in the footnote to exercise 13.7.)

i.   What does this imply for how much profit each of the remaining firms can actually make?

14.8   **Policy and Business Application:** *Business Taxes (cont'd)*: In exercise 13.11, we introduced a number of possible business taxes and asked what a firm's response would be *assuming that prices w, r, and p remained unchanged*. Now that we have introduced the notion of equilibrium price formation, we can revisit the exercise.

A. Suppose the restaurant industry is in long-run equilibrium, all restaurants use the same homothetic decreasing returns to scale technology, and all have to pay a fixed annual franchise fee F.

a.   Illustrate the average cost curve for a restaurant and the related (short-run) supply and demand graph for the industry.

b.   Revisit parts A(b) through A(h) of exercise 13.11 and explain whether the assumption that prices remained unchanged was warranted and, if not, why not.

B. Consider the same technology as the one used in exercise 13.11 as well as the recurring fixed cost F.

a.**   Determine the long-run equilibrium price p^* and output level x^* as a function of A, α, β, w, and r. (You can use the cost function given in equation (13.45) in exercise 13.5 as well as the profit function given equation (13.48) in exercise 13.7.)

b.   In exercise 13.11, we focused on the impact of policies from A(b) through A(h) on output supply and input demand functions. Now use your result from (a) to determine the impact of each of these policies on the long-run equilibrium price and firm output level.

14.9 **Policy and Business Application:** *Minimum Wage Labor Subsidy (cont'd):* In exercise 13.10, we investigated the firm's decisions in the presence of a government subsidy for hiring minimum wage workers. Implicitly, we assumed that the policy has no impact on the prices faced by the firm in question.

POLICY APPLICATION

BUSINESS APPLICATION

A. Suppose again that you operate a business that uses minimum wage workers ℓ and capital k. The minimum wage is w, the rental rate for capital is r, and you are one of many identical businesses in the industry, each using a homothetic, decreasing returns to scale production process and each facing a recurring fixed cost F.

  a. Begin by drawing the average cost curve of one firm and relating it to the (short-run) supply and demand in the industry assuming we are in long-run equilibrium.

  b. Now the government introduces a wage subsidy s that lowers the effective cost of hiring minimum wage workers from w to $(1 - s)w$. What happens in the firm and in the industry in the short run?

  c. What happens to price and output (in the firm and the market) in the long run compared with the original quantities?

  d. Is it possible to tell whether there will be more or fewer firms in the new long-run equilibrium?

  e. Is it possible to tell whether the long-run price will be higher or lower than the short-run price? How does this relate to your answer to part (d)?

B. Suppose that the firms in the industry use the production technology $x = f(\ell, k) = 100\ell^{0.25}k^{0.25}$ and pay a recurring fixed cost of $F = 2,210$. Suppose further that the minimum wage is $10 and the rental rate of capital is $r = 20$.

  a. What is the initial long-run equilibrium price and firm output level?

  b. Suppose that $s = 0.5$, implying that the cost of hiring minimum wage labor falls to $5. How does your answer to (a) change?

  c. How much more or less of each input does the firm buy in the new long-run equilibrium compared with the original one? (The input demand functions for a Cobb–Douglas production process were previously derived and given in equation (13.50) of exercise 13.8.)

  d. If price does not affect the quantity of x demanded very much, will the number of firms increase or decrease in the long run?

  e. Suppose that demand is given by $x(p) = 200,048 - 2,000p$. How many firms are there in the initial long-run equilibrium?

  f. Derive the short-run market supply function and illustrate that it results in the initial long-run equilibrium price.

  g. Verify that the short-run equilibrium price falls to approximately $2.69 when the wage is subsidized.

  h. How much does each firm's output change in the short run?

  i. Determine the change in the long-run equilibrium number of firms when the wage is subsidized and make sense of this in light of the short-run equilibrium results.

14.10† **Policy Application:** *School Vouchers and the Private School Market:* In the United States, private schools charge tuition and compete against public schools that do not. One policy proposal that is often discussed involves increasing demand for private schools through *school vouchers*. A school voucher is simply a piece of paper with a dollar amount V that is given to parents who can pay for some portion of private school tuition with the voucher if they send their child to a private school. (Private schools can then redeem the vouchers for a payment of V from the government.) Assume throughout that private schools strive to maximize profit.

POLICY APPLICATION

A. Suppose private schools have U-shaped average (long-run) cost curves, and the private school market in a metropolitan area is currently in long-run equilibrium (in the absence of private school vouchers).

  a. Begin by drawing a school's average long-run cost curve (with the number of private school seats on the horizontal axis). Then, in a separate graph next to this, illustrate the city-wide demand curve for seats in private schools as a function of the tuition price p. Finally, include the short-run aggregate supply curve that intersects with demand at a price that causes the private school market to be in long-run equilibrium.

b.   Illustrate what happens to the demand curve as a result of the government making available vouchers in the amount of V to all families that live in the city. What happens to the number of seats made available in each existing private school, and what happens to the tuition level p in the short run?

c.   Next, consider the long run when additional private schools can enter the market. How does the tuition level p, the number of seats in each school, and the overall number of children attending private schools change?

d.   Opponents of private school vouchers sometimes express concern that the implementation of vouchers will simply cause private schools to increase their tuition level and thus cause no real change in who attends private school. Evaluate this concern from both a short- and long-run perspective.

e.   Proponents of private school vouchers often argue that the increased availability of private schools will cause public schools to offer higher quality education. If this is true, how would your answers to (b) and (c) change as a result?

f.   If private school vouchers are made available to anyone who lives within the city boundaries (but not to those who live in suburbs), some families who previously chose to live in suburbs to send their children to suburban public schools might choose instead to live in the city and send their children to private schools. How would this affect your answers to (b) and (c)?

B. In the following, all dollar values are expressed in thousands of dollars. Suppose that the total city-wide demand function for private school seats x is given by $x(p) = 24{,}710 - 2{,}500p$ and each private school's average long-run cost function is given by $AC(x) = 0.655x^{1/3} + (900/x)$.

a.   Verify that $AC(x)$ arises from a Cobb–Douglas production function $x = f(\ell, k) = 35\ell^{0.5}k^{0.25}$ when $w = 50$ and $r = 25$ and when private schools face a fixed cost of 900. One unit of x is interpreted as one seat (or one child) in the school, and ℓ is interpreted here as a teacher. Since dollar values are expressed in thousands, $w = 50$ represents a teacher's salary of \$50,000 and the fixed cost of 900 represents a recurring annual cost of \$900,000.

b.   In order for the private school market to be in long-run equilibrium, how many children are served in each private school? What is the tuition (per seat in the school) charged in each private school?

c.   Given that you know the underlying production function, can you determine the class size in each private school? (*Hint*: You already determined the total number of children in part (a) and now need to determine the number of teachers in each private school.[6])

d.   How many private schools are operating?

e.   Now suppose that the government makes private school vouchers in the amount of 5.35 (i.e., \$5,350) per child available to parents. How will this change the demand function for seats in private schools? (*Hint*: Be careful to add the voucher in the correct way; i.e., to make the demand *curve* shift up.)

f.*   Given this change in demand, what will happen to tuition and the number of children served in existing private schools in the short run assuming the number of schools is fixed and no new schools can enter in the short run? (*Hint*: You will need to know the current level of capital, derive the short-run supply function for private schools, then aggregate them across the existing private schools.)

g.   What happens to private school class size in the short run?

h.   How do your answers change in the long run when new schools can enter?

14.11* Policy Application: *Public School Teacher Salaries, Class Size, and Private School Markets*: In exercise 14.10, we noted that private schools that charge tuition operate alongside public schools in U.S. cities. There is much discussion in policy circles regarding the appropriate level of public school teacher salaries (which are set by the local or state government) as well as the appropriate number of public school teachers (that determines class size in public schools).

POLICY APPLICATION

A. Suppose again that private schools face U-shaped long-run AC curves for providing seats to children and that the private school market is currently in long-run equilibrium.

---

[6]It may be helpful to check equation (13.50) in exercise 13.8.

a.   Begin by drawing two graphs, one with the long-run AC curve for a representative private school and a second with the demand and (short-run) aggregate supply curves (for private school seats) that are consistent with the private school market being in long-run equilibrium (with private school tuition p on the vertical axis).

b.   Now suppose the government initiates a major investment in public education by raising public school teacher salaries. In the market for private school teachers (with private school teacher salaries on the vertical and private school teachers on the horizontal), what would you expect to happen as a result of this public school investment?

c.   How will this impact private school tuition levels, the number of seats in private schools and the overall number of children attending private schools in the short run?

d.   How does your answer change in the long run as private schools can enter and exit the industry?

e.   Suppose that instead of this teacher salary initiative, the city government decides to channel its public school investment initiative into hiring more public school teachers (as the city government is simply recruiting additional teachers from other states) and thus reducing class size. Assuming that this has no impact on the equilibrium salaries for teachers but does cause parents to feel more positively about public schools, how will the private school market be impacted in the short and long run?

f.   How will your long-run answer to (e) be affected if the government push for more public school teachers also causes equilibrium teacher salaries to increase?

B. As in exercise 14.10, assume a total city-wide demand function $x(p) = 24{,}710 - 2{,}500p$ for private school seats and let each private school's average long-run cost function be given by $AC(x) = 0.655x^{1/3} + (900/x)$. Again, interpret all dollar values in thousands of dollars.

a.   If you have not already done so, calculate the initial long-run equilibrium size of each school, what tuition price each charges, and how many private schools there are in the market.

b.   If you did B(a) in exercise 14.10, you have already shown that this $AC(x)$ curve arises from the Cobb–Douglas production function $x = f(\ell, k) = 35\ell^{0.5}k^{0.25}$ when $w = 50$ and $r = 25$ and when private schools face a fixed cost of 900. If you have not already done so, use this information to determine how many teachers and how much capital each school hires.

c.   Suppose that the increased pay for public school teachers drives up the equilibrium wage for private school teachers from 50 to 60 (i.e., from $50,000 to $60,000 per year). What happens to the equilibrium tuition price in the short run?

d.   What happens to school size and class size?

e.   How will your answers on school size, tuition level, and class size change in the long run? (*Hint*: You can use the cost function given in equation (13.45) of exercise 13.5 to derive the AC function; just make sure you keep track of the fixed cost of 900!)

f.   How many private schools will remain in the market in the long run?

14.12 Policy Application: *Pollution Taxes on Output*: Suppose you are one of many firms that refine crude oil into gasoline. Not surprisingly, this process creates pollution. The government therefore announces a new tax of $\$t$ on each gallon of gasoline that leaves a refinery (to be paid by the refinery).

A. For purposes of this exercise, assume that the refinement process of crude oil into gasoline has decreasing returns to scale but entails a recurring fixed cost.

a.   Begin by illustrating the industry in pre-tax equilibrium, showing one firm's average cost curve as well as the (short-run) market supply and demand that supports an industry in long-run equilibrium.

b.   What changes for each firm and in the industry in the short run when the tax is introduced?

c.   What changes in the long run?

d.   *True or False*: While refineries bear some of the burden of this tax in the short run, they will pass all of the tax on to consumers in the long run.

e.   I recently heard the following comment on one of the TV news shows (regarding a tax similar to the one we are analyzing here): "Regulators are particularly concerned about reports that companies in the industry managed to pass the pollution tax fully onto consumers and view this as a sign that the industry is not competitive but is rather engaged in strategic manipulation of gasoline prices." What do you make of this TV wisdom?

f. Will refineries change the mix of labor and capital in the long run (assuming they continue operating)?

g. Here is another quote from a recent TV analysis: "In talking to this refinery's owner, it seems that there are no plans in place to lay off any workers in response to the pollution tax on refined gasoline. Jobs in the industry therefore appear to be safe for now." Do you agree?

B. Once again, suppose that the production function used by firms in the gasoline refinery industry is $f(\ell, k) = A\ell^{\alpha}k^{\beta}$ with $\alpha, \beta > 0$ and $\alpha + \beta < 1$, and suppose that each refinery pays a recurring fixed cost F.

a. If you did not already do so in exercise 14.1, derive the expression for the output level x^* at which the long-run AC curve reaches its lowest point. (This should be a function of A, α, β, w, and r.)

b. How does x^* change under the per-gallon tax on gasoline leaving the refinery?

c. Can you use your answer to determine whether the number of gasoline refineries will increase or decrease as a result of the tax?

d. If you have not already done so in exercise 14.1, determine the long-run equilibrium price p^* before the tax (a function of A, α, β, w, and r). How does this change under the tax?

e. Can you use your answer to determine who actually pays the tax?

f. Will the tax result in less pollution? If so, why?

The "Invisible Hand" and the First Welfare Theorem

In Chapter 14, we combined all of the pieces of the consumer and producer models to arrive at a definition of market or industry equilibrium.[1] We saw how tastes and budget constraints result in individual output demand and input supply curves that, when added up, result in output market demand and input market supply curves. On the producer side, we similarly saw how production frontiers combine with prices to form individual firm supply and input demand curves that, when added up, result in short-run market supply curves and input market demand curves. Furthermore, we saw how the entry and exit of firms results in long-run market supply curves that differ from short-run curves in goods markets.

The individual demand and supply relationships were derived by considering how changing economic environments—changing input and output prices—would cause consumers, workers and firms to change their behavior. The economic environment itself, however, arises in equilibrium from the many individual decisions that are made in the economy, giving rise to equilibrium prices that consumers and producers in a competitive world take as given when they decide how to behave. The prices that arise in equilibrium therefore serve the purpose of coordinating the many individuals in the market, signaling to consumers how much they should consume, to workers how much they should work, and to producers how much they should produce. No one plans this; it happens "spontaneously" as everyone in the economy simply tries to do the best he or she can. The resulting equilibrium is therefore sometimes referred to as a "spontaneous order" created by market forces.

This insight that order can emerge without anyone planning it is quite remarkable in and of itself. What is even more remarkable, however, is that, under certain conditions, the spontaneous order generated in a decentralized market precisely mimics what a central planner might wish to implement if he or she knew everything there was to know about the individuals in the market. Put differently, not only do the incentives in a decentralized market generate a predictable equilibrium but also, under certain conditions, there is no way that the resulting situation could be altered to make some people better off without making anyone worse off. In the language we developed earlier in this book, the spontaneous order of the decentralized market is, under certain conditions, fully efficient. This chapter, and much of the remainder of the book, is devoted to demonstrating this important result. We will demonstrate the conditions necessary for the result to hold as well as the real-world conditions that might cause the result to break down, making room for civil society or government institutions to improve on the spontaneous order of the market.

---

[1]This chapter builds on Chapter 14 and uses the concept of marginal willingness to pay and consumer surplus introduced in Chapter 10.

15A Welfare Analysis in Equilibrium

In order to demonstrate the welfare properties of markets, we will need to measure the benefit each economic agent derives from being able to participate in markets. In output markets, this requires us to measure the benefit to consumers and producers, whereas in input markets we need to measure the benefit to workers, to firms, and to those supplying capital. The suppliers of capital are often individuals who are lending financial capital by saving, and the demanders of capital are often firms that invest in order to produce goods and services.

Fortunately, we have already defined the basic building blocks for conducting this analysis. For consumers, we developed in Chapter 10 the notion of "consumer surplus," which we defined as the benefit consumers derive from being able to participate in a market. We can straightforwardly extend this concept to workers, with "worker surplus" defined as the benefit workers derive from being able to sell their labor in labor markets, and we can similarly define the surplus that those who provide capital to the market derive from being able to plan for the future. On the producer side, defining a measure for how much better off producers are for being able to operate in markets is more straightforward: Since producers care about profit, we will simply use profit, which we can also call "producer surplus," as the relevant measure for producers. We will discuss each of these in turn before illustrating how markets, under certain conditions, maximize the sum of producer and consumer surplus.

15A.1 Consumer and Worker Surplus

In Chapter 10, we illustrated that individual consumer surplus can be measured as the area underneath the compensated demand (or marginal willingness to pay) curve and above the price at which a consumer consumes. However, unless consumer tastes for the good that we are analyzing are borderline between normal and inferior (and tastes are thus quasilinear in the good of interest), the compensated demand curves for individual consumers are different from their regular demand curves that we added up in Chapter 14 to derive market demand. This tells us immediately that we cannot, in general, illustrate the total consumer surplus for all the consumers in a market along the market demand curve that we use to derive the equilibrium. (Keep in mind, however, that the market demand curve that is derived from the regular demand curves of consumers is still the correct demand curve to predict the equilibrium because it is the demand curve that tells us how consumers respond to changing incentives.)

Since we know how to measure consumer surplus on individual demand and compensated demand curves, the easiest way to measure consumer (as well as worker and saver) surplus in market demand and supply graphs is to treat all the consumers (as well as workers and savers) in a market as a single "representative agent." This sounds strange at first since we have made a big point of the fact that the equilibrium that arises in a competitive market results from the decentralized actions of many individuals that simply take the economic environment as given. Nevertheless, we will see that there exist circumstances under which we can simply think of all these individuals as a single individual who also takes the economic environment as given. When these conditions hold, we have the luxury of assuming that the market demand curve has all the same properties as an individual demand curve, that we can treat it as if it had arisen from a single consumer doing the best he or she can given the economic circumstances he or she faces. And we can assume that the representative consumer's compensated demand curve can accurately measure aggregate consumer surplus.

15A.1.1 "Representative Consumers"   We can thus begin by asking under what conditions a market demand curve that simply adds up all the individual demand curves might have the same properties as an individual demand curve. To develop some intuition, suppose first that the "market" is composed of only me and my wife, with the market demand curve simply being our "household demand curve" that results from summing our individual demand curves that in turn arise from the assumption that my wife and I always *individually* do the best we can given our *individual* economic circumstances. To be even more specific, suppose that my wife, the true master of our household, has exogenous disposable income $I^1 = 800$ and she has generously permitted me to have exogenous disposable income $I^2 = 400$ as we go to Wal-Mart to buy clothes (denoted x_1) and "other goods" (denoted x_2). Within Wal-Mart, we face the same prices (p_1 and p_2) and end up at two different check-out counters with two different baskets of goods (A^1 and A^2). The composition of these baskets depends on our individual tastes, our individual incomes, and the common prices we face.

If we truly meant what we said at our wedding, that the two of us henceforth are a single unit, we might think that our "household demand" really is as if it had arisen from a single consumer doing the best she can. Put differently, if our household jointly behaves like a single individual, it should not matter how our household's exogenous income is divided between me and my wife. Thus, if a streak of righteous indignation at the inequity of our exogenous incomes led you to take $200 out of my wife's purse and put it into my wallet so that each of us now has $600 as we walk into Wal-Mart, we would jointly come out of Wal-Mart with the same number of clothes and other goods as if we had gone in with our original budgets. Our individual baskets at the check-out counters would be different (with more stuff in mine and less in hers), but when we put it in the trunk of our car, we would end up having exactly the same as if you had never interfered. Only if this is true do we really behave as if we were the single mystical unit we forged on that fateful wedding day.

This does not, however, have to imply that my wife and I have exactly the same tastes. Suppose, for instance, that my wife and I initially faced the blue and magenta budget lines in Graph 15.1. She arrives at the check-out counter with bundle A^1 as her optimal basket, and I arrive with bundle A^2 in my basket. Then let's imagine that instead you had pulled off your righteous transfer of $200 from her purse into my wallet before we entered Wal-Mart, causing both of us to face the green budget rather than the initial blue and magenta. In order for us to end up putting the same overall basket into our family car's trunk, it must be that the change in my

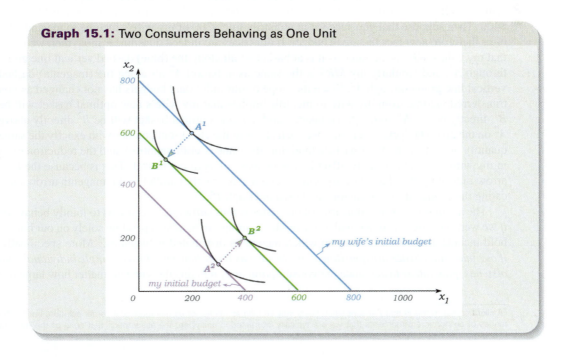

Graph 15.1: Two Consumers Behaving as One Unit

wife's optimal basket from her initial blue to her new green budget is exactly offset by the change in my optimal basket as I move from my initial magenta to my new green budget. Put differently, the blue arrow linking my wife's original optimum A^1 to her new optimum B^1 must be exactly parallel to the magenta arrow from my original optimum A^2 to my new optimum B^2. Our individual tastes may therefore be quite different, but the change in our individual behavior as income is redistributed between us keeps our overall consumption bundle constant. As long as this holds over the relevant range of economic environments that is of interest to us, our mystical union is complete and we behave as a single "representative agent." This implies that we behave in the aggregate as if we were a single individual with rational tastes, tastes that give rise to demand and compensated demand curves that have exactly the interpretation we developed in Part 1 of the text for a single consumer.

Exercise 15A.1   Suppose that my tastes and my wife's tastes are exactly identical. If our tastes are also homothetic, does our household behave like a single representative agent? What if our tastes are quasilinear and neither individual is at a corner solution?

Exercise 15A.2   Can you illustrate a case where our tastes are identical but we do not behave as a representative agent?

Exercise 15A.3   Suppose both my wife and I have homothetic tastes but they are not identical. Does this still imply that we behave like a single representative agent?

15A.1.2 Consumer Surplus and the Special Case of Quasilinear Tastes

In Section B of this chapter, we formalize the intuition we have just developed and specify exactly what range of individual tastes can permit us to assume that a group of consumers can be treated as a single consumer. For our purposes here, however, it is enough for us to focus on one special case: The case when both my tastes and my wife's tastes are quasilinear in the good x_1.

Consider exactly the same budget lines for me and my wife as we did in Graph 15.1 with the same initially optimal baskets for my wife (A^1) and me (A^2) when our incomes are $800 and $400. Then suppose that you succeed in redistributing $200 of my wife's income to me and both of us therefore now face the green budget. If our tastes are indeed quasilinear in x_1, then we know that my wife's *MRS* is the same as it is at basket A^1 all along the (blue) dashed vertical line going through A^1, and similarly my *MRS* is the same as at basket A^2 all along the (magenta) dashed vertical line going through A^2. Since the slope of our individual budgets has not changed as you transferred income from my wife to me, this implies that my wife's new optimal basket will be B^1 directly below A^1 on the green budget, and my new optimal basket will be B^2 directly above A^2 on the green budget. As a result, we each arrive at the check-out counter with exactly the same quantity of x_1 in each of our baskets (and thus the same overall quantity), and the reduction of x_2 in my wife's basket is exactly offset by the increase of x_2 in my basket. This is because the blue arrow indicating the change in my wife's behavior is exactly parallel to the magenta arrow indicating the change in my behavior (as shown in Graph 15.2).

The assumption of quasilinearity of our tastes is thus sufficient to cause us to jointly behave *as if* we were a single consumer, with our overall consumption bundle depending solely on our household income and not on the way in which income is distributed between us.[2] More specifically, *if our individual tastes are quasilinear, we behave as if our household was a single individual who also has quasilinear tastes* since our consumption of x_1 remains the same no matter how large our

---

[2]A slight caveat to this is that the conclusion holds only so long as neither of us has reached a corner solution, but for the ranges of economic environments that we are typically interested in analyzing, the assumption that none of the relevant economic agents is at a corner solution is often fine.

Graph 15.2: Aggregating Consumers with Quasilinear Tastes

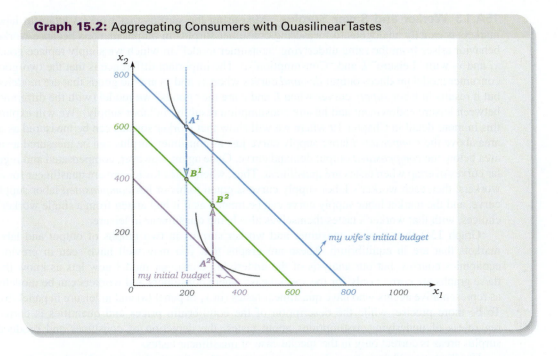

household income gets (so long as the prices we face remain the same). This should make intuitive sense: The whole challenge in aggregating consumers and treating them as if they were a single consumer arises from the fact that individual consumers change their consumption bundles when we redistribute income within a group. Put differently, the challenge arises from the presence of *income effects* that cause people to change their consumption. When income effects are assumed away, as they are when we assume quasilinearity of tastes, then the problem of aggregating consumers goes away.

True or False: As long as everyone has quasilinear tastes, the group will behave like a representative agent even if all the individuals do not share the same tastes (assuming no one is at a corner solution). The same is also true if everyone has homothetic tastes.

Exercise 15A.4

Suppose, then, that we move beyond the simple example of my household and we consider all the consumers in a particular output market. If we can assume that all consumers have tastes that are quasilinear in the output, then we can, by the same logic we just used for my household, treat the market demand curve (that sums all the individual demand curves) as if it had arisen from a single representative consumer who also has quasilinear tastes. Since the only difference between compensated and regular demand curves arises from income effects, and since quasilinear tastes do not give rise to income effects, we can furthermore assume that the regular demand curve is also the compensated demand curve, and that this demand curve therefore also represents the marginal willingness to pay curve along which we can measure consumer surplus. We have therefore identified the conditions that individual tastes have to satisfy in order for us to use the (uncompensated) market demand curve for measuring aggregate consumer surplus.

Suppose that my wife and I share identical homothetic tastes (that are not over perfect substitutes). Will our household demand curve be identical to our marginal willingness to pay curve?

Exercise 15A.5

15A.1.3 Worker and Saver Surplus   Measuring the surplus that workers attain in labor markets is exactly analogous to measuring consumer surplus in output markets because worker behavior arises from the same underlying "consumer model" in which we simply replace goods x_1 and x_2 with "Leisure" L and "Consumption" c. The important difference is that the two-good consumer model produces output *demand* curves when x_1 and x_2 are the goods that are modeled, but it results in labor *supply* curves when L and c are the "goods" we model (with the difference between leisure endowment and leisure consumption resulting in labor supply). We will explore this in more detail in Chapter 19 where we will show that worker surplus can be measured as an area above the *compensated* labor supply curve just as consumer surplus can be measured as an area below the *compensated* output demand curve. Once again, however, compensated and regular curves overlap when tastes are quasilinear. Thus, when tastes for leisure are quasilinear for all workers, then each worker's labor supply curve is equal to his or her *compensated* labor supply curve, and the market labor supply curve can be treated as if it had arisen from a single worker's choices, with that worker's tastes themselves also being quasilinear in leisure.

Graph 15.3 then depicts consumer and worker surplus in two graphs of output and labor markets that are in equilibrium. These are graphs that you may well have seen in previous economics courses, but our analysis of the underlying consumer model now lets us know that these graphs are correct only for the special case where consumers and workers can be modeled as representative agents who have quasilinear tastes (in x_1 in panel (a) and in leisure in panel (b)). To be more precise, while the description of the equilibrium prices and quantities is correct regardless of underlying assumptions about tastes, the depiction of consumer and producer surplus areas is correct only in the special case of quasilinear tastes.

Finally, we could draw an analogous graph representing the surplus attained by those who save financial capital (and therefore lend it to others at the market interest rate). Note that it becomes particularly problematic, however, to assume that the underlying tastes that result in capital supply curves are quasilinear. Recall that these curves arise from choices in the consumer model where consumption this period is put on the horizontal axis and consumption in some future period is put on the vertical. It seems relatively implausible that tastes are indeed quasilinear in consumption in either period, with consumption in that period being neither a normal nor an inferior good but

Graph 15.3: Aggregate Consumer and Worker Surplus when Tastes Are Quasilinear

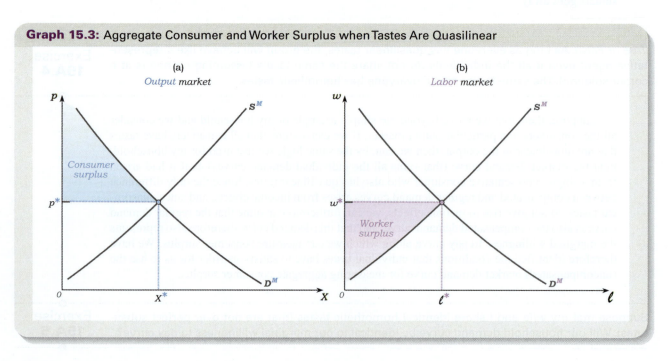

consumption in the other period being normal. Consumption, one would think, is likely to be a normal good regardless of when it takes place. We will therefore need to be particularly cautious with welfare analysis involving those who plan for the future by saving in financial markets.

15A.2 "Producer Surplus" or Profit

While it was not immediately obvious at first how we would arrive at a dollar value for the benefit a consumer derives from being able to participate in a market, it is much easier to arrive at such a dollar value for producers. After all, producers are in business to make profit, and if a producer is able to earn positive economic profit, the producer has by definition been made better off by the amount of that profit by being able to participate in this market (rather than pursue his or her next best alternative). Economic profit is then our measure of the "surplus" producers derive from being able to participate in markets. We will therefore use the terms *producer surplus* and *economic profit* interchangeably.[3]

15A.2.1 Measuring Producer Surplus on the Supply Curve
In our development of producer theory, we ran into two ways of illustrating profit (in the absence of fixed costs) graphically, using either the MC curve or the AC curve. As it turns out, we can now combine these methods of illustrating profit to demonstrate that profit can also be measured as an area above the producer's supply curve.

Consider first the AC curve pictured in panel (a) of Graph 15.4. Suppose that the equilibrium price was p^* and that you initially think about producing quantity x^A corresponding to the lowest point of the AC curve. In that case, your total revenues would be p^* times x^A while your total costs would be AC_{min} times x^A, and the difference between those two areas in the graph would be equal to the shaded blue area.

Of course, we know from our previous work that a profit-maximizing producer would produce more than x^A if facing the conditions in panel (a) of Graph 15.4. In particular, the producer

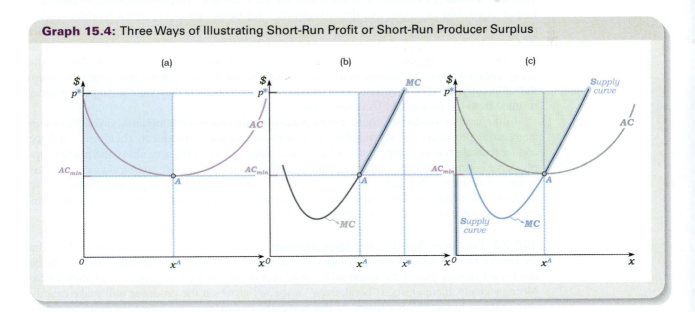

Graph 15.4: Three Ways of Illustrating Short-Run Profit or Short-Run Producer Surplus

---

[3]Some textbooks make a distinction between the term "producer surplus" and "economic profit," using the former to refer to what we have called short-run economic profit and the latter to what we called long-run economic profit.

would produce until price is equal to MC. In panel (b) we therefore graph the MC curve, with the portion of the MC that lies above AC (and thus above point A from panel (a)) highlighted. We already know that we can measure the profit a producer makes by producing x^A units of output as the blue area in panel (a), and so we are now interested in how much *additional* profit the producer will make by producing x^* rather than x^A. This *additional* profit is simply equal to the difference between the *additional* revenue and the *additional* cost the producer incurs. The additional revenue is represented by the area formed by the vertical distance p^* times the horizontal distance $(x^* - x^A)$, while the additional cost is represented as the area below the MC curve in the interval between x^A and x^*. The difference between these areas, representing the additional profit from producing x^* rather than x^A, is then the shaded magenta area in panel (b).

Since the blue area in panel (a) is the profit the producer makes when producing x^A and the magenta area in panel (b) is the *additional* profit the producer makes when producing x^* rather than just x^A, the two areas summed together are equal to total profit from producing x^* at price p^*. This is depicted as the green area in panel (c) of the graph, and you can see that this green area is simply the area to the left (or "above") the firm's supply curve up to the equilibrium price.

The argument that *profit can be measured as the area above the producer's supply curve* then applies to both short-run and long-run profit. In the case of short-run profit, the blue area in panel (a) is measured along the short-run AC curve, while in the case of long-run profit it is measured along the long-run AC curve. Similarly, the magenta area in panel (b) is measured along the short-run MC curve for short-run profit and along the long-run MC curve for long-run profit. In panel (c), profit is measured either along the short-run or the long-run firm supply curve depending on whether we want to measure short-run or long-run profit.

Exercise 15A.6   Does this measure of long-run profit apply also when the firm encounters long-run (recurring) fixed costs?

15A.2.2 Treating Producers in an Industry as a Single "Representative Producer"
In our discussion of "representative consumers," we noted the difficulty of treating market demand *as if* it had arisen from a single representative agent. This difficulty arose from the fact that in order for a group of consumers to be treated as a single consumer, it was necessary to know that individual tastes are such that any redistribution in income among the individuals in the group does not result in a change in the overall demand for the good of interest from that group. Put differently, the difficulty in treating groups of consumers as if they were a single consumer resulted from the presence of income effects.

In the case of producers, there are no analogous income effects to cause any difficulty in aggregating producers and treating them as a single representative producer. Therefore, when we add individual producer supply curves into market supply curves, the area above the market supply curve is simply the sum of the areas above individual supply curves, and *producer surplus as measured on the market supply curve is simply the sum of the individual producer surpluses of the firms in the industry*. In other words, we can simply treat the market supply curve as if it was the supply curve of a single representative producer.

15A.2.3 Producer Surplus in Labor Markets   We can make a similar argument about the area *under* a firm's demand curve for labor. Recall that short-run demand for labor arises from the downward-sloping part of the marginal revenue product of labor curve pictured in Graph 15.5a. More precisely, there exists a "break-even" wage w^A at which the producer will make exactly zero profit by hiring ℓ^A labor hours. At that wage, the loss incurred for hiring the first ℓ' workers is exactly offset by the gain from hiring the remaining workers. (You should be able to find the areas on the graph corresponding to this gain and loss.) If the equilibrium wage falls below this break-even wage, the firm will then hire along the blue portion of the MRP_ℓ curve in panel (a) of Graph 15.5, which corresponds to the firm's short-run labor demand curve D^i.

Graph 15.5: Producer Surplus in Labor Markets

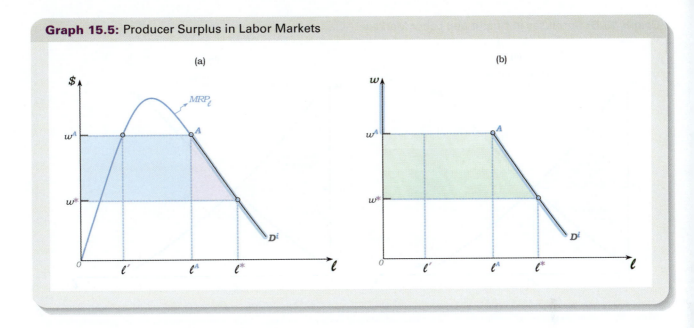

Suppose, for instance, that the market wage is w^* and that the firm stopped hiring at ℓ^A. We can then ask how much additional profit the firm makes from what it would have made had the wage been the break-even wage w^A where profit was zero. Since the firm has to pay $(w^A - w^*)$ *less* per worker hour, this becomes surplus (or profit) for the firm for each of the ℓ^A worker hours. Summing over all ℓ^A worker hours, the total surplus from being able to hire ℓ^A worker hours at the market wage w^* is therefore equal to the shaded blue area in the panel (a) of Graph 15.5.

Of course, the producer would not stop hiring at ℓ^A if the market wage was w^* but would hire ℓ^* worker hours instead. For each *additional* worker hour the firm hires beyond ℓ^A, the *additional* surplus would be the difference between the MRP_ℓ for that worker hour and the wage w^*. Thus, the *additional* profit made on the worker hours hired beyond ℓ^A is equal to the shaded magenta area in panel (a) of the graph, and the *total* surplus for the producer is the sum of the blue and magenta areas.

In panel (b) of the graph, we then simply graph the entire short-run labor demand curve for the producer, which includes the bold segment from the MRP_ℓ curve in panel (a) and the vertical blue line segment at $\ell = 0$ for wages above the break-even wage w^A. The green area in panel (b) is then exactly equal to the sum of the blue and magenta areas in panel (a) and represents short-run producer surplus. Note that this *producer surplus is equal to the area below the firm's labor demand curve down to the market wage*. The treatment of long-run labor demand curves and firm surpluses is somewhat more complicated and we will therefore not get into it here.

15A.2.4 Putting all Surpluses Together

Graph 15.6 completes what we started in Graph 15.3. Panel (a) depicts the output market in equilibrium, with the industry producing X^* output and selling it at price p^*. Under the assumption of quasilinear tastes on the part of consumers, we previously concluded that the blue area represents aggregate consumer surplus. And from our work in this section, we have concluded that we can measure producer surplus (or profit) as the area above the industry supply curve up to the equilibrium price. Thus, the green area represents producer surplus, and the two areas together represent the total surplus gained by producers and consumers from the existence of the market for good X.

How would the picture be different if we were depicting an industry in long-run equilibrium with all firms facing the same costs? What would long-run producer surplus be in that case?

Exercise 15A.7

Graph 15.6: Surpluses in Output and Labor Markets

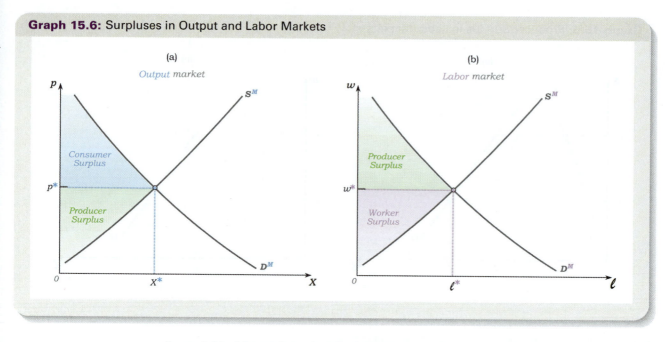

In panel (b) of the graph, on the other hand, we previously concluded that the magenta area above the market supply curve for labor up to the equilibrium wage is the aggregate worker surplus under the assumption that tastes are quasilinear in leisure. From what we have done in this section, we can now furthermore conclude that the area below the market demand curve for labor down to the equilibrium wage is equal to the producer surplus. Note that the blue area in panel (a) and the magenta area in panel (b) are derived from the consumer model while the green areas are derived from the producer model. Thus, the blue and magenta areas require our assumption of quasilinearity in tastes because this assumption is required for us to be able to treat the market curves as if they depicted an economic relationship derived from a single "representative agent" doing the best he or she can in the absence of income effects. The green areas, on the other hand, do not require any particular assumptions since they are derived from the producer model that is not subject to the income effects that make aggregating individual economic relationships and interpreting welfare measures along them problematic.

Exercise 15A.8 Suppose we were not concerned about identifying producer and worker surplus but instead wanted to only predict the equilibrium wage and the number of workers employed. Would we then also have to assume that leisure is quasilinear for workers?

15A.3 The Invisible Hand and the First Welfare Theorem

We are now ready to consider seriously the question of how well decentralized market forces do in maximizing the total surplus for society. To do this, we have to come up with some ideal benchmark of what could be accomplished for society and compare to this benchmark how the market measures up. Economists establish this ideal by imagining that, instead of market forces determining how much is produced in each industry, a fictional all-knowing and benevolent "social planner" was in charge and dictated how much of each good is produced in the economy, which firms produce what, and how much each consumer gets to consume.

15A.3.1 "Barney" as the Benevolent Social Planner
I have young children and therefore have to endure hours of "Barney," the purple PBS dinosaur who gets my children to annoyingly sing "I love you, you love me, we're a happy family" until I can no longer stand it and use

my earphones to listen to the soothing sounds of ABBA on my iPod. I imagine the fictional "social planner" employed by economists as an omniscient version of "Barney," a dinosaur that knows all our desires and dreams, knows all the different production technologies of all the possible firms in the world, and desires to create the greatest possible surplus for the world. What would this benevolent and omniscient Barney do?

Let's begin with the simplest possible world in which Barney knows that all our tastes for good x are quasilinear (and thus Barney does not have to consider income effects). Barney would then try to calculate how much of x should be produced by finding those firms that can produce x at the lowest possible cost and try to match what these firms produce with those consumers who value x the most. In particular, Barney would try to begin by finding the consumer who values the first good x more than anyone else, and is thus willing to pay more than anyone else for it. Similarly, he would try to find the producer who can produce that first good at the lowest possible cost. Suppose that this first consumer has a marginal willingness to pay $MWTP^A$ and this first producer has a marginal cost MC^B for that first unit of x. These quantities are graphed for the first x in Graph 15.7. Then, after getting this first unit produced and channeling it to the right consumer, Barney would move to the next unit, finding the consumer who has the highest marginal willingness to pay for the next unit and matching the consumer with the producer who can produce this unit at the lowest marginal cost. By continuing to do this for each additional unit of output, Barney would slowly plot the *marginal social benefit MSB* and the *marginal social cost MSC* for all levels of output as depicted in Graph 15.7.

For the first unit of x, the total surplus for society would be the difference between how much society has benefitted from this unit of x and how much it has cost society. So long as the only beneficiary of a unit of x is the person who consumes that unit, $MWTP^A$ is a measure of the marginal social benefit, and so long as the only costs society incurs are those incurred by the producer of x, MC^B is a measure of the marginal social cost (since the value of the resources employed in production could have been used elsewhere in society). Thus, the dashed blue line connecting A to B is society's surplus from the first unit of output. The same is then true for each additional unit of output, with society's surplus for each *additional* output represented by the vertical difference

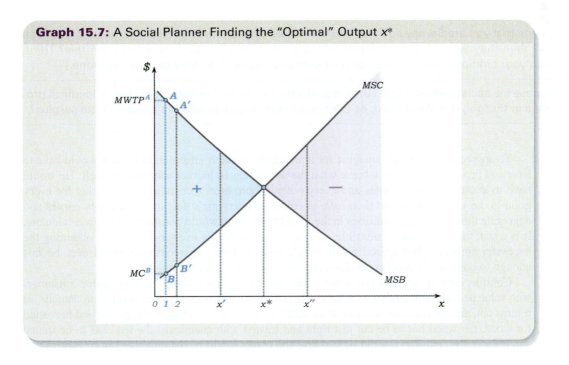

Graph 15.7: A Social Planner Finding the "Optimal" Output x^*

between the *MSB* and the *MSC* curves. As long as that difference is positive, Barney would decide it is worth it to continue producing. And this difference remains positive so long as Barney produces less than x^*, the output level at which *MSB* and *MSC* intersect, but the difference becomes negative for any output level beyond x^*.

The *total surplus for society is therefore maximized at the output level x^**, with the blue area representing this maximum level of surplus. For instance, were Barney to stop producing at x' before x^* is reached, society would be left with only the portion of the blue area to the left of x' and would therefore give up the blue area to the right of x'. Similarly, were Barney to produce x'' above x^*, society would get all of the blue area but would *lose* the magenta area to the left of x''.

15A.3.2 The Market versus Barney

By now you have surely guessed where all this is headed. As long as consumers gain all the benefits of consuming the output, the *MSB* curve in Graph 15.7 is the aggregate *MWTP* curve for all the consumers in the market, and if all the consumers have tastes that are quasilinear in x, the aggregate *MWTP* curve is the market demand curve. Similarly, as long as producers bear all of the costs of producing, the *MSC* curve in Graph 15.7 is the industry supply curve. The decentralized market in which consumers and producers just selfishly try to do the best they can given their circumstances therefore produces where market demand and supply intersect which is, under the assumptions we have made, exactly the same intersection as that of the *MSB* and *MSC* curves in Graph 15.7. *The decentralized market therefore produces exactly the quantity the social planner would have chosen to produce if the planner's objective was to maximize the total surplus for society!*

This result is probably the most important result ever derived by economists, and it is a result that is considerably more general than might be apparent at this point. It states that, *under certain conditions, decentralized markets maximize total surplus for society, leaving no possible way for anyone, even an omniscient social planner, to change the situation and make someone better off without making anyone else worse off*. Put differently, the first welfare theorem states that, *under certain conditions, markets are efficient*. Of course, the social planner could decide to distribute the overall surplus differently than the market does, giving more to consumers or more to producers than the market does, but omnicient Barney *cannot increase the total pie*.

Exercise 15A.9

Imagine that you are Barney and that you would like consumers to get a bigger share of the total "pie" than they would get in a decentralized market. How might you accomplish this? (*Hint*: Given your omnipotence, you are not restricted to charging the same price to everyone.)

Exercise 15A.10

Suppose the social marginal cost curve is perfectly flat, as it would be in the case of identical producers in the long run. Would you, as Barney, be able to give producers a share of the surplus?

To appreciate this result, imagine for a minute how much information Barney would have to have and process in order to achieve what the decentralized market achieves by itself. He would have to know everyone's tastes and every potential producer's costs in every market for every good in the world. He would then have to calculate everyone's demand and supply curves and aggregate these. And, as conditions in the world change, he would constantly have to recalculate. It is a task that is absurdly infeasible; no one in the world can ever come close to obtaining the necessary information required for Barney's task, and no supercomputer could ever be fast enough to continually process this information as it continually changes.

Consider even the simplest task, one we mentioned already in Chapter 1: ensuring that consumers who value pencils sufficiently much have access to No. 2 pencils when they need them. Pencils, as it turns out, are not that easy to make from scratch. The right trees have to be grown and harvested for wood; the wood has to be cut just right and treated with chemicals; the lead has to be mined and refined, then cut into just the right shape; the eraser has to be manufactured from various raw materials; the metal holding the eraser on the pencil has to be produced and shaped; the yellow paint, and the black lettering on the paint indicating what kind of pencil it is, has to be produced and applied, then coated with a finish to make it stick. Literally hundreds of thousands of steps are involved, with each step requiring different expertise, and raw materials from literally all corners of the world have to come together in just the right way. It is not an exaggeration to say that no one in the world actually knows how to make a No. 2 pencil. Rather, thousands of individuals are somehow coordinated in just the right way, motivated at each turn by their own desire to do the best they can given their circumstances, and somehow, almost *as if guided by an invisible hand*,[4] their actions result in cheap pencils available in abundance in our stores. Most of these individuals have no idea that they are participating in a sequence of events that leads to the availability of pencils, and yet it happens. And because of the complexity of the process involved in getting it to happen, the world has seen in centrally planned economies that when a single individual is put in charge of planning the process, it almost always results in a vast shortage of pencils.

15A.3.3 The Crucial Role of Information Contained in Prices How on earth can a decentralized and unplanned market then do what no planner in the world could ever accomplish? The answer lies in the information contained in market prices. Prices, whether in input or output markets, signal to consumers and producers what they need to do in order to "do the best they can." If milk in New York City is running low, prices will rise, signaling to suppliers of milk that they can make a profit by shipping milk to New York. Lead for pencils is running short thus driving up the price of lead, signaling to mining companies across the world that profit can be made by increasing production. Miners themselves may be needed to get to more lead, causing wages for miners to go up as mining companies compete with other firms for labor, which signals to workers that they might want to switch to mining lead. Prices everywhere therefore capture the information Barney so desperately needs and thus coordinate the actions of millions across thousands of different markets around the world.

It is because of the information implicitly contained in prices that individuals do not need to know anything beyond their individual circumstances to determine what their next step should be as they try to do the best they can. It is not necessary for any individual actor in the market to know how his or her actions fit into the bigger picture because prices ensure that our actions fit together. This is one of the great advantages of decentralized markets: Markets do not require anyone to have information that is not easily at their fingertips. Relying on central planning, on the other hand, requires us to rely on the central planner, our mythical Barney, to gather and process vast amounts of information. The success of decentralized market economies in their competition with centrally planned economies in the 20th century has much to do with this insight.[5]

15A.3.4 The Crucial Role of Self Interest A second advantage in decentralized markets is that the emergence of efficient market equilibria does not presume any benevolence on anyone's part as the implementation of Barney's social planning does. Rather, markets explicitly rely on individuals, consumers, workers, and producers alike, to be guided purely by their own perceptions of what is in their self-interest.

Adam Smith (1723–1790), who was one of the earliest economists to focus sharply on the spontaneous order generated by decentralized market forces, gives the example of a consumer purchasing bread from a baker. He asks rhetorically: Do we appeal to the baker's benevolence when we come to get his bread? Do we present our "need" for bread and ask him to consider this carefully in deciding whether to give us bread? Or do we instead rely on his self-interest, proposing to pay him an amount

---

[4]The reference to the market process operating "as if guided by an invisible hand" is from Adam Smith (1723–1790) who coined the phrase in *The Wealth of Nations*.

[5]The case for the informational content in prices was made eloquently by F. A. Hayek (1899–1992) (who would go on to win the Nobel Prize in Economics in the 1970s) during the great debate about planned versus decentralized economies in the 1940s. It is summarized in the following (quite readable) article: F. A. Hayek, "The Use of Knowledge in Society," *American Economic Review* 35(4), (1945) 519–30. It is well worth reading for anyone interested in the role of markets in the world.

that is larger than the value he places on the bread? Does he in turn ask for our benevolence when he appeals to us to pay him? Does he give us a list of all the reasons why he needs or deserves some money so that he can buy clothing and shelter for his family? Or does he simply appeal to our self-interest as he agrees to accept payment that is lower than the value we place on the bread? The answer, of course, is that we interact in markets with a clear understanding that each of us is trying to do the best we can for ourselves, and it is from this self-interested behavior that market demand and supply curves emerge and generate the equilibrium that maximizes the social surplus.

Decentralized markets therefore generate outcomes that maximize social surplus not only because they process information efficiently but also because they rely on the aspect of human nature that governs most of our actions. Centralized planning runs into difficulty not only because it faces enormous hurdles in gathering and processing the required information but also because it relies on powerful central planners to be benevolent in ways that appear not to happen when such planners are put in place. While there are many real-world limits (which we will discuss shortly) to this result, it remains, as we have said, central to an understanding of much that the economist does.

15A.3.5 Extending the First Welfare Theorem to Include All Rational Tastes

Before we move on to the limitations of the first welfare theorem, however, we need to note that while the assumption of quasilinear tastes will make policy analysis significantly easier in some of the upcoming chapters, it is *not* a necessary condition for the result that competitive markets result in efficient output levels. Suppose, for instance, that the good x is normal. In this case, we would find the market equilibrium exactly as we did before: by adding up all the individual (regular) demand curves and finding where the market demand curve intersects with the market supply curve. In panel (b) of Graph 15.8, this results in the intersection of the market supply curve S^M with the blue market demand curve D^M at price p^A. The market demand curve is composed of individual demand curves such as the blue curve D^i in panel (a).

If tastes for good x are normal, then we know that there exists a *MWTP* curve for each consumer that intersects the individual's regular demand curve at the equilibrium price p^A from above; i.e., a *MWTP* curve that is steeper than the demand curve. This is the *MWTP* curve that is formed from the indifference curve that the individual finds him- or herself on in equilibrium, and it is plotted as the magenta curve in panel (a) of the graph. These curves, just like the individual demand curves, can then be added up and placed in the market picture in panel (b), and consumer surplus is now appropriately measured on this "aggregate MWTP" curve as the shaded blue area. Without assuming

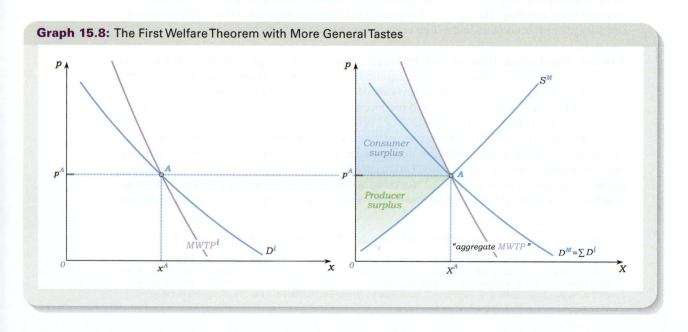

Graph 15.8: The First Welfare Theorem with More General Tastes

that individual income effects exactly offset each other, we cannot treat the market demand and aggregate MWTP curves as if they came from a single representative consumer. But notice that, just as in the case where the demand and *MWTP* curves were the same under quasilinear tastes, it is still the case that each good that is produced has lower social marginal cost (as represented by the supply curve) than social marginal benefit (as measured by the magenta *MWTP* curve), and if any additional goods were produced, the marginal social value would fall below the marginal social cost. Thus, once again the market produces where the total surplus in the x market is maximized, and the validity of the first welfare theorem is not contingent on any particular assumption about individual consumer tastes. In the absence of quasilinearity, we simply have to be careful if we want to determine the precise size of the consumer surplus, but the efficiency result remains.

How would Graph 15.8 look if good *x* were an inferior good for all consumers?

Exercise 15A.11

True or False: If goods are normal, we will underestimate the consumer surplus if we measure it along the market demand curve, and if goods are inferior we will overestimate it.

Exercise 15A.12

There is, however, an important wrinkle that is added by introducing income effects through tastes in ways that do not permit the market demand to be modeled by a representative consumer. In the absence of income effects, Barney's choice of the overall output level of *x* remains the same regardless of how Barney decides to distribute income across individuals. But in the presence of income effects, the overall level of *x* production chosen by Barney will depend on how other resources in the economy are distributed. Put differently, if Barney's ideal income distribution across individuals is different than the actual income distribution, Barney may choose a different output level for *x* than the market will choose if tastes are not quasilinear in *x*. He will do so not because the market's output level is inefficient; rather, he will do so because he prefers a *different* efficient output level that satisfies his desire for a different distribution of overall resources in the economy. Markets still give rise to efficiency and the first welfare theorem still holds in the presence of income effects, but the market outcome may violate some notions of "equity". This is explored further in end-of-chapter exercises 15.5 and 15.6. The possible existence of different efficient allocations of resources, with some striking us as more equitable than others, will also be further discussed in Chapter 16 as well as Chapter 29. In fact, we will be able to show that Barney could achieve his preferred outcome by simply redistributing income first and then letting the market find the efficient level of *x*.

As we will see in some upcoming chapters, the first welfare theorem is indeed quite general, extending well beyond the model we have illustrated thus far. For now, however, we will conclude by stating some of the limits of this theorem, and in the process we will set the stage for many of the remaining chapters in this book.

15A.4 Conditions Underlying the First Welfare Theorem

At this point, some of you are getting a little worried and are asking yourself if all this isn't getting a bit too ideological. It appears so far that we are saying that if we just leave everything to markets, we can enter the wonderful world of Barney and leave our worries behind. The benefit of using rigorous models to investigate the role of decentralized markets in dealing with self-interested individuals, however, is that it takes ideology out of it and allows us to investigate the issue through the logical lens of the models. Yes, so far our models appear to point to an important role played by competitive markets in organizing economies to allocate resources to their most efficient uses. But within these models are also the built-in assumptions, some explicit and some implicit, that are crucial for markets to have the wonderful properties we have just discussed. By knowing what these assumptions are, we will understand better both the benefits *and* the costs of decentralized markets. Put differently, by understanding the conditions that generate the first welfare theorem in our models, we can judge when these conditions are violated in the real world, and when there might be government or civil society institutions that can improve on a purely decentralized market outcome.

Much of the remainder of the book is therefore devoted to an exploration of the real-world conditions that undermine the first welfare theorem. After all, we see many problems in the real world that appear to not be adequately addressed by decentralized market forces: excessive pollution, too much poverty and human suffering, exploitation of certain natural resources, corporate abuses, etc. Our model so far does not give any particular explanation for such phenomena because it excludes some of the real-world frictions that chip away at the first welfare theorem. It is these frictions that occupy many economists whose research is aimed at discovering the real-world institutions that might act as a lubricant to permit decentralized markets to work with less friction, and produce better results. We will mention these only briefly here and point to the upcoming chapters that deal with these issues more comprehensively.

15A.4.1 Policy Distortions of Prices

The first implicit assumption we have made is that market prices actually operate as modeled, that they are permitted to form in such a way as to send an undistorted signal to the various actors in the market. A primary cause for this signal to become distorted lies in deliberate government policies such as taxes, price regulation, wage controls, subsidy programs, or, in some instances, the explicit prohibition of a market. Saying that such policies can distort market prices and therefore move the market away from the situation where it maximizes social surplus is, however, *not necessarily* the same as saying that we should not have these policies. As I will try to suggest throughout, there may be circumstances when policy makers are perfectly aware of the fact that price-distorting policies will shrink the total social surplus as we have measured it thus far but nevertheless believe that some other sufficiently useful purpose is served by the policy. Other times, the loss in social surplus seems so stark—and the distortionary policy so contrary to its stated purpose once we consider the impact on markets—that it becomes difficult to believe policy makers truly thought that a sufficiently useful *social* purpose was served by the policy to justify its social cost.[6] We will consider a number of common price-distorting policies in Chapters 18 through 20.

15A.4.2 Externalities, Social Costs, and Property Rights

In arguing that the marginal social benefit (*MSB*) and marginal social cost (*MSC*) curves in Graph 15.7 are the same as the market demand and supply curves, we made a very crucial assumption: The only individuals whose welfare is affected by the production of a particular unit of x are the producer and the consumer of that unit. This is not, however, always the case. Consider, for instance, the greenhouse gases that are produced by firms in certain industries; literally everyone in the world might be affected by this pollution through global warming. The *MSC* is therefore higher than the producers' costs that result in the market supply curve. Similarly, my consumption of certain goods, travelling in my polluting car, for instance, may affect others in ways that are not captured in demand (or even *MWTP*) curves for cars. Whenever this is the case, we will say that there exists an *externality*, and whenever an externality exists, the intersection of *MSC* and *MSB* will be different from the intersection of market demand and supply. Thus, in the presence of externalities, the decentralized market does *not* produce the efficient quantity, and the market price signals sent to consumers and producers coordinate their behavior in ways that do not maximize social surplus. We will discuss these issues in more detail in Chapters 21 and 27. In Chapter 21, we will also uncover explicitly the most important efficiency-enhancing role of governments: to ensure that property rights are well established and enforced so as to minimize the inefficiencies from externalities that arise when property is "commonly" owned.

---

[6]In such cases, economists tend to search for explanations that treat policy makers themselves as self-interested individuals who are (at least in part) attempting to make policy with their individual welfare in mind. We will have more on this to say in Chapter 28.

15A.4.3 Asymmetric Information   In addition to an absence of externalities, we have implicitly assumed that all economic agents have the same information about the relevant aspects of the market. Consumers and producers can look at good x and both fully know its uses and quality; employers can fully discern the qualification of workers and those selling used cars know just as much about the cars as the potential buyers. But this is, of course, not always so, and when it isn't, new issues enter the analysis as more informed parties can use their information to take advantage of less informed parties. We will consider this in more detail in Chapter 22.

15A.4.4 Market Power   Throughout this text so far, we have always assumed that economic agents—consumers, workers, financial planners, and producers—are "small" relative to the market. Thus, we have assumed that each economic agent takes his or her economic environment as exogenously given, with no one able to control prices in the economy. Put differently, we have assumed that no one in the economy has *market power*, which is the power to influence the economic environment itself. But when an industry is composed of a single or only a few firms, each firm may well be large enough to impact the economic environment in the industry. (The same is true when one or only a few consumers make up all the demand for a particular good.) What we have concluded in this chapter in the form of the first welfare theorem thus does not necessarily hold when the assumption of competitive behavior is relaxed. We have also not paid much attention to the surplus created by innovative activities that create new goods and new markets, and the role of the profit motive in generating new surplus rather than simply producing surplus within existing markets. We will deal with instances of this in more detail in Chapters 23 through 26.

15A.4.5 Efficiency versus Alternative Social Objectives   Finally, we have made an implicit assumption that attaining efficient outcomes is the most desirable objective for society. In some sense, this has some intuitive appeal: If we find a way of organizing society so that the total "pie" is as large as possible, then there is more pie to go around, so why not get it to be as large as possible? But of course most of us care not only about the size of the pie but also about its distribution. If the pie is huge but only one person gets to eat it while everyone else starves, few of us would think we have reached a "good society." And the market not only maximizes the total pie (under certain conditions) but it also divides this pie between producers and consumers, firms and workers in ways that may not be as appealing to us as we might like. We will mention this concern at various times and return to an explicit treatment of considerations other than efficiency in Chapter 29.

15B Equilibrium Welfare Analysis: Preliminaries and an Example

The fully generalized version of the first welfare theorem is quite general, and quite mathematically involved. Chapter 16 will contain some indications of how this theorem was actually developed and how it relates to other important results. For now, I will simply illustrate some of the intuitions of the current model in more mathematical detail.

15B.1 Consumer Surplus

We already developed in Section A the point that market demand functions cannot automatically be treated as if they had the same properties as individual demand functions; i.e., as if they fit nicely into a duality picture derived from a single set of rational tastes. For the special case of quasilinear tastes, however, we illustrated that we *can* treat market demand as if it had arisen from the optimization of rational (and quasilinear) tastes by a single "representative consumer." And we developed the intuition in Graph 15.1 that market demand has the properties of individual demand curves more generally so long as individual tastes are such that income can be redistributed among individual consumers with no overall change in demand; i.e., with changes in demand resulting from such redistributions exactly offsetting one another. We can now treat these topics a little more formally and demonstrate more precisely how the intuitions of Section A translate into the mathematics of the consumer model.

15B.1.1 "Representative Consumers"
Consider again the example of the aggregated household demand for me and my wife, and whether this household demand can be treated as if it had arisen from rational "household tastes." Intuitively, we argued in Graph 15.1 that my household's demand can indeed be treated as if it was an individual demand function if and only if my household's demand for each good is independent of who controls the money in my family. Put differently (and in terms easily seen in Graph 15.1), the change in my demand for good x_i when my income changes must be exactly the same as the change in the demand when my wife's income changes *regardless of how income is initially divided*. Letting me be denoted by the superscript n and my wife by the superscript m, this implies that

$$\frac{\partial x_i^m}{\partial I^m} = \frac{\partial x_i^n}{\partial I^n} \quad \text{and} \quad \frac{\partial^2 x_i^m}{\partial (I^m)^2} = \frac{\partial^2 x_i^n}{\partial (I^n)^2} = 0. \tag{15.1}$$

The first derivative of our demands with respect to income must be the same in order for the changes in demand from income redistribution to offset one another, and the second derivative must be zero in order for changes to always offset one another regardless of where we start. In order for the second derivative of a demand function with respect to income to be zero, income cannot enter the function in any way other than linearly (so that it drops out when we take the first derivative). With a little work (that you are asked to do in the upcoming within-chapter exercises), we can then see that the demand functions must take the form

$$x_i^m(p_1, p_2, I^m) = a_i^m(p_1, p_2) + I^m b_i(p_1, p_2),$$
$$x_i^n(p_1, p_2, I^n) = a_i^n(p_1, p_2) + I^n b_i(p_1, p_2), \tag{15.2}$$

where a_i^m denotes a function specific to good i and individual m while b_i denotes a function specific to good i but the same for all individuals.

Exercise 15B.1
Demonstrate that the conditions in equation (15.1) are satisfied for the demand functions in (15.2).

Exercise 15B.2
Can you see why equation (15.2) represents the most general way of writing demands that satisfy the conditions in equation (15.1)?

Demand functions of this type are known in microeconomics as satisfying the *Gorman Form*, and it is whenever individual demand functions are of the Gorman Form that aggregate demand functions can be treated as if they arose from the utility maximization of a representative consumer.[7]

15B.1.2 The Special Case of Quasilinear Tastes
In Section A, we focused on the special case of quasilinear tastes, demonstrating in Graph 15.2 that changes in individual demand (for both x_1 and x_2) exactly offset one another as income is redistributed. Suppose, for instance, that we know both my wife and I have tastes that are quasilinear in x_1, with her tastes represented by the utility function $u^n(x_1, x_2) = v^n(x_1) + x_2$ and mine represented by $u^m(x_1, x_2) = v^m(x_1) + x_2$. From our work in earlier chapters, we then know that both of our demand functions for x_1 are *not*

---

[7]This condition is often expressed in terms of conditions on the indirect utility function, with tastes (for individual m) that satisfy the Gorman Form leading to indirect utility functions of the form $V^m(p_1, p_2, I^m) = \alpha^m(p_1, p_2) + \beta(p_1, p_2)I^m$, where α and β are functions.

a function of income while our demand for x_2 is simply determined by the income left over after we purchase the amount of x_1 (that does not depend on our income); i.e.,

$$x_1^m = x_1^m(p_1,p_2) \quad \text{and} \quad x_2^m = \frac{I^m}{p_2} - \frac{p_1 x_1^m(p_1,p_2)}{p_2}$$

$$x_1^n = x_1^n(p_1,p_2) \quad \text{and} \quad x_2^n = \frac{I^n}{p_2} - \frac{p_1 x_1^n(p_1,p_2)}{p_2}$$

(15.3)

You can check for yourself that these demand functions satisfy the Gorman Form, and thus the first and second derivative conditions in equation (15.1). It is furthermore the case that the aggregate (household) demand then takes the form it would take if it had been derived from a single quasilinear utility function.

What are my household demand functions (for x_1 and x_2) if my wife's and my individual demands are those in equation (15.3)? Do the household demand functions also satisfy the Gorman Form?

Exercise 15B.3

15B.1.3 Aggregate Consumer Surplus
We already know from our work in Chapter 10 that individual consumer surplus in the market for the good x can be measured as the area below the *MWTP* (or Hicksian or compensated demand) curve down to the price (where the relevant *MWTP* curve is derived from the indifference curve that contains the consumption bundle the individual has chosen). This can be expressed mathematically using an integral as

$$\text{Consumer Surplus in } x_1 \text{ Market} = \int_{p_1}^{\infty} h_1(p_1,p_2,u)dp,$$

(15.4)

where $h_1(p_1,p_2,u)$ is the compensated (or Hicksian) demand function. If you have not yet taken integral calculus, $\int_{p_1}^{\infty}$ is the "integral" of the function above p_1, which simply means "the area underneath the function above the price p_1." In many cases, we might approximate this function with a strictly linear function, in which case Consumer Surplus can be calculated simply as the area of the triangle that is equivalent to this integral. And when all individual tastes are quasilinear, we can replace the compensated demand function $h_1(p_1,p_2,u)$ with the uncompensated demand function $x_1(p_1,p_2,I)$ in equation (15.4).

Finally, when individual demands satisfy the Gorman Form, we know we can treat aggregate market demand as if it had arisen from a single representative consumer. Thus, since quasilinear demand functions satisfy the Gorman Form, we can avoid having to calculate aggregate consumer surplus by going to all individual demand functions and adding up individual consumer surpluses. Instead, we can treat the *aggregate* demand function as if it had arisen from the optimization problem of a representative consumer whose tastes are quasilinear. Thus, applying the formula in equation (15.4) with $h_1(p_1,p_2,u)$ replaced by the (uncompensated) aggregate demand function will give consumer surplus for the fictional representative consumer, which in turn is the same number we would get if we added up individual consumer surpluses.

In our example of the equilibrium we calculated in Chapter 14 and depicted graphically in Graph 14.12, for instance, the underlying individual tastes are assumed to be quasilinear, implying that individual demand curves are equivalent to *MWTP* curves and that aggregate demand curves can be interpreted as if they had arisen from a single representative consumer with quasilinear tastes. In Graph 15.9a, we replicate panel (b) from Graph 14.12—the picture of market equilibrium with the numerical example we have been using. To this picture, we have added the labels (*a*), (*b*), and (*c*) to indicate areas, and our work in Part A of this chapter suggests that the blue area (*a*) is equal to consumer surplus and the magenta area (*b*) is equal to producer surplus (or profit).

Graph 15.9: $S^M(p) = 547{,}192p^{2/3}$ and $D^M(p) = 40{,}000{,}000/p^2$ from Graph 14.12

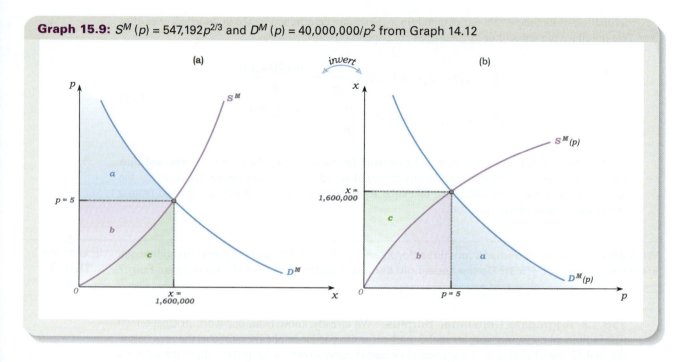

As noted in Chapter 14, however, this picture graphs the *inverse* of the underlying demand and supply functions. Panel (b) of Graph 15.9 then inverts panel (a) to get a picture of the actual demand and supply functions we have calculated mathematically. Area (*a*) now clearly shows up as the area *underneath* the demand function beginning at the equilibrium price $p = 5$, or the integral identified in equation (15.4). For the numerical example we used in Chapter 14, the market demand function was $D^M(p) = 40{,}000{,}000/p^2$. Thus, if you are comfortable with the concept of computing an integral, consumer surplus can be calculated as

$$\text{Consumer Surplus} = \int_5^\infty \frac{40{,}000{,}000}{p^2}\,dp = 8{,}000{,}000. \tag{15.5}$$

15B.2 Producer Surplus

We have demonstrated in Graph 15.4 that profit (or producer surplus) can be measured as an area on individual (as well as aggregate) supply curves. In Graph 15.9, this is equivalent to area (*b*) in the two panels of the graph. Using the supply function in panel (b) (as opposed to the inverse supply function in panel (a)), we can then see that this is equivalent to the area *underneath* the supply function up to the market price measured either on the short-run supply function (for short-run producer surplus) or the long-run supply function (for long-run producer surplus). Put into equations for a single firm,

$$\text{Short-Run Producer Surplus} = \int_0^p x_{k^A}(w,p)\,dp \text{ and}$$

$$\text{Long-Run Producer Surplus} = \int_0^p x(w,r,p)\,dp, \tag{15.6}$$

where $x_{k^A}(\ell,p)$ and $x(\ell,r,p)$ are the short-run and long-run supply functions (with capital assumed to be fixed at k^A in the short run). Since cost functions (which make up supply functions) can be aggregated (into market supply functions), and since the market supply function can then be interpreted as if it had arisen from a single representative firm, aggregate producer surplus can also be measured using the same formulas as those in equation (15.6), with individual supply functions replaced by aggregate market supply functions.

In the short-run equilibrium depicted graphically in Graph 15.9, for instance, we assumed an underlying production function of $f(\ell, k) = 20\ell^{2/5}k^{2/5}$ for each firm in the market, with each firm also incurring a recurring fixed license fee of $1,280 and a short-run fixed level of capital $k_A = 256$. Using equations in (13.31) and (13.33) from Chapter 13, we derived the following short- and long-run input demand and output supply functions for each of the firms:

$$\text{Short Run: } x_{k^A=256}(p,w) = 3,225\left(\frac{p}{w}\right)^{2/3} \text{ and } \ell_{k^A=256}(p,w) = 1,290\left(\frac{p}{w}\right)^{5/3}$$

(15.7)

$$\text{Long Run: } x(p,w,r) = 81,920\frac{p^4}{(wr)^2}, \quad \ell(p,w,r) = \frac{(8p)^5}{w^3 r^2} \text{ and } k(p,w,r) = \frac{(8p)^5}{w^2 r^3}$$

Given that the firms encounter a recurring fixed cost of $1,280, which of the previous functions should actually be qualified to take account of this fixed cost?

Exercise 15B.4

When prices are $(p,w,r) = (5, 20, 10)$, we furthermore concluded in Chapter 14 that there are 1,250 firms. At these prices, each firm produces 1,280 units for an overall output level of 1,600,000 and industry revenue (at $p = 5$) of $1,250(1,280)(5) = \$8,000,000$. In equation (14.11) of Chapter 14, we used this information to calculate the short-run market supply function at $w = 20$ as $S^M(p) = 547{,}192p^{2/3}$. The long-run market supply curve, on the other hand, is horizontal at the lowest point of the firm AC curves, which happens at 5 in our example. Using again the notion of an integral to calculate the area below a function, we can then calculate short- and long-run producer surplus as

$$\text{Short-Run Producer Surplus} = \int_0^5 547{,}192p^{2/3}dp = 4{,}800{,}000 \text{ and}$$

(15.8)

$$\text{Long-Run Producer Surplus} = 0,$$

with zero long-run surplus simply arising from the fact that the long-run supply curve is horizontal at $p = 5$.

We can check to see that this is correct by calculating the short-run and long-run profits of each firm in equilibrium more directly—simply subtracting the appropriate economic costs from revenue—and then adding these up across the number of firms that exist in equilibrium. Plugging prices $(p,w,r) = (5, 20, 10)$ into equations in (15.7), we get that each firm uses 128 units of labor and 256 units of capital to produce 1,280 units of output. In the short run, the firm then incurs a cost for labor equal to $2,560 while earning revenue of $6,400. Since the fixed license fee and the cost of capital are not economic costs in the short run, each firm therefore earns producer surplus equal to $3,840, and since there are 1,250 firms in equilibrium, the aggregate (short-run) producer surplus is $4,800,000 just as we calculated by taking the integral in equation (15.8). In the long run, each firm incurs an additional license fee of $1,280 and a cost for capital of $2,560, which results in a long-run profit of $0 for each firm.

15B.3 The First Welfare Theorem

We will postpone more formal treatments of the first welfare theorem to the next chapter but can for now demonstrate its applicability to the example we have used in Graph 15.9. To do this, we can consider once again the optimization problem faced by the fictional benevolent social planner, the benevolent "Barney" from Section A.

In essence, we could view Barney as both the representative consumer and producer who is simply attempting to maximize his own well-being. He knows the long-run cost of producing x, which we have assumed in our example to be \$5 per unit. This allows him to draw a social *production possibilities frontier*, which is a society-wide budget constraint that illustrates the trade-offs faced as we produce more x in terms of a composite good y. Since the composite good y is denominated in dollars, 1 unit of x costs society 5 units of y, and the most y we could produce is simply equal to the total income I of all the consumers in the society.

If we now know a utility function $U(x,y)$ that can represent the "representative consumer's" tastes, we could write Barney's problem of attempting to maximize social surplus in the world as

$$\max_{x,y} \ U(x,y) \text{ subject to } I = 5x + y. \tag{15.9}$$

Exercise 15B.5

Draw the production possibility frontier previously described. How would it look differently if the long-run market supply curve slopes up? (*Hint:* With an upward-sloping supply curve, society is facing an increasing cost of producing x, implying that the trade-off in the society-wide production possibility frontier must reflect that increasing cost.)

As it turns out, it is possible to recover a utility function that would indeed give rise to the demand function $D^M(p) = 40{,}000{,}000/p^2$ from our example in Chapter 14. For instance, you can check for yourself that the utility function $U(x,y) = 12{,}649.11x^{1/2} + y$ accomplishes this. Solving the problem in equation (15.9) using this utility function for Barney gives the solution that Barney should produce 1,600,000 units of x, which is precisely the equilibrium quantity produced in the market.

Exercise 15B.6

Verify that this is indeed the case.

Exercise 15B.7

One way to verify that the representative consumer's utility function is truly "representative" is to calculate the implied demand curve and see whether it is equal to the aggregate demand curve $D^M(p) = 40{,}000{,}000/p^2$ that we are trying to represent. Illustrate that this is the case for the utility function $U(x,y) = 12{,}649.11x^{1/2} + y$.

CONCLUSION

In this chapter, we have moved from *predicting* (a competitive equilibrium) to *evaluating* (it), from what we called "positive" economics to something that has a much more "normative" flavor. We have done so by imagining how the outcome of decentralized market competition would differ if the economy instead were managed by an omniscient and benevolent "social planner," a social planner whose goal it was to achieve the highest possible overall "surplus" for society. And we have concluded that, under the stark conditions assumed so far, the social planner would in fact choose centrally what the market produces through the decentralized choices made by individuals who simply know their own circumstances and whose self-interested actions are guided by the signals they receive through market prices. Put differently, the "spontaneous order" of the market is, at least under certain conditions, "efficient," which is not to say that it is necessarily "good," a judgment that requires a deeper grounding in philosophy than what a simple economist can offer (at least for now). Still, it is a remarkable result—one that we have already suggested has its limits, but remarkable nonetheless.

Along the way, we have stumbled into a few issues that will appear throughout the remainder of this book. First, we saw that it is not trivial to simply think about groups as if they were individuals, that tastes do not "aggregate" easily and that we cannot treat the choices made by groups as if they were made by an individual unless we restrict the kinds of tastes that members of the group have. This is a theme we will see reappear in a somewhat different form in Chapter 28 when we think about political decisions made by groups. Second, we reintroduced the importance of income effects in evaluating welfare changes for individuals, the fact that, in the presence of income effects, we cannot simply measure consumer (or worker or investor) surplus along the usual demand (or supply) curves. This point will reappear in a number of applications throughout the text as we think through policies where making the mistake of forgetting about income effects can lead to the wrong conclusions. Third, we ended Part A of the chapter by listing the implicit underlying conditions of the "first welfare theorem" and pointed out that much of the remainder of the text is organized around the fact that these conditions are often violated in the real world. Finally, we have already mentioned that "efficient" is not the same as "good," but that the "good" is something that most economists are not particularly great at talking about. We will return to this issue at the end of the text in Chapter 29.

We will begin our analysis of what happens when the underlying conditions of the first welfare theorem are violated in the real world in Part 4 of the text with Chapter 18. But before getting to this, we now turn to a somewhat different way of thinking about the first welfare theorem and related results (Chapter 16) and a discussion of how economists think about the inclusion of risk in our models (Chapter 17).

END-OF-CHAPTER EXERCISES

15.1   **Everyday Application:** *Labor-Saving Technologies*: Consider inventions such as washing machines or self-propelled vacuum cleaners. Such inventions reduce the amount of time individuals have to spend on basic household chores, and thus in essence increase their leisure endowments.

A.   Suppose that we wanted to determine the aggregate impact such labor-saving technologies will have on a particular labor market in which the wage is w.

   a.   Draw a graph with leisure on the horizontal axis and consumption on the vertical and assume an initially low level of leisure endowment for worker A. For the prevailing wage w, indicate this worker's budget constraint and his or her optimal choice.

   b.   On the same graph, illustrate the optimal choice for a second worker B who has the same leisure endowment and the same wage w but chooses to work more.

   c.   Now suppose that a household labor-saving technology (such as an automatic vacuum cleaner) is invented and both workers experience the same increase in their leisure endowment. If leisure is quasilinear for both workers, will there be any impact on the labor market?

   d.   Suppose instead that tastes for both workers are homothetic. Can you tell whether one of the workers will increase his or her labor supply by more than the other?

   e.   How does your answer suggest that workers in an economy cannot generally be modeled as a single "representative worker" even if they all face the same wage?

B.* Consider the problem of aggregating agents in an economy where we assume individuals have an exogenous income.

   a.   In a footnote in this chapter, we stated that when the indirect utility for individual m can be written as $V^m(p_1, p_2, I^m) = \alpha^m(p_1, p_2) + \beta(p_1, p_2)I^m$, then demands can be written as in equation (15.2). Can you demonstrate that this is correct by using Roy's Identity?

   b.   Now consider the case of workers who choose between consumption (priced at 1) and leisure. Suppose they face the same wage w but different workers have different leisure endowments. Letting the two workers be superscripted by n and m, can you derive the form that the leisure demand equations $l^m(w, L^m)$ and $l^n(w, L^n)$ would have to take in order for redistributions of leisure endowments to not impact the overall amount of labor supplied by these workers (together) in the labor market?

   c.   Can you rewrite these in terms of labor supply equations $\ell^m(w, L^m)$ and $\ell^n(w, L^n)$?

   d.   Can you verify that these labor supply equations have the property that redistributions of leisure between the two workers do not affect overall labor supply?

15.2†   **Business Application:** *Disneyland Pricing Revisited*: In end-of-chapter exercise 10.10, we investigated different ways that you can price the use of amusement park rides in a place like Disneyland. We now return to this example. Assume throughout that consumers are never at a corner solution.

A.   Suppose again that you own an amusement park and assume that you have the only such amusement park in the area; i.e., suppose that you face no competition. You have calculated your cost curves for operating the park, and it turns out that your marginal cost curve is upward sloping throughout. You have also estimated the downward-sloping (uncompensated) demand curve for your amusement park rides, and you have concluded that consumer tastes appear to be identical for all consumers and quasilinear in amusement park rides.

    a.   Illustrate the price you would charge per ride if your aim was to maximize the overall surplus that your park provides to society.

    b.*   Now imagine that you were not concerned about social surplus and only about your own profit. Illustrate in your graph a price that is slightly higher than the one you indicated in part (a). Would your profit at that higher price be greater or less than it was in part (a)?

    c.   *True or False*: In the absence of competition, you do not have an incentive to price amusement park rides in a way that maximizes social surplus.

    d.   Next, suppose that you decide to charge the per-ride price you determined in part (a) but, in addition, you want to charge an entrance fee into the park. Thus, your customers will now pay that fee to get into the park, and then they will pay the per-ride price for every ride they take. What is the most that you could collect in entrance fees without affecting the number of rides consumed?

    e.   Will the customers who come to your park change their decision on how many rides they take? In what sense is the concept of "sunk cost" relevant here?

    f.   Suppose you collect the amount in entrance fees that you derived in part (d). Indicate in your graph the size of consumer surplus and profit assuming you face no fixed costs for running the park.

    g.   If you do face a recurring fixed cost FC, how does your answer change?

    h.   *True or False*: The ability to charge an entrance fee in addition to per-ride prices restores efficiency that would be lost if you could only charge a per-ride price.

    i.   In the presence of fixed costs, might it be possible that you would shut down your park if you could not charge an entrance fee but you keep it open if you can?

B.   Suppose, as in exercise 10.10, tastes for your consumers can be modeled by the utility function $u(x_1, x_2) = 10x_1^{0.5} + x_2$, where $x_1 = x$ represents amusement park rides and x_2 represents dollars of other consumption. Suppose further that your marginal cost function is given by $MC(x) = x/(250,000)$.

    a.   Suppose that you have 10,000 consumers on any given day. Calculate the (aggregate) demand function for amusement park rides.

    b.   What price would you charge if your goal was to maximize total surplus? How many rides would be consumed?

    c.   In the absence of fixed costs, what would your profit be at that price?

    d.   Suppose you charged a price that was 25% higher. What would happen to your profit?

    e.   Derive the expenditure function for your consumers.

    f.*   Use this expenditure function to calculate how much consumers would be willing to pay to keep you from raising the price from what you calculated in (b) to 25% more. Can you use this to argue that raising the price by 25% is inefficient even though it raises your profit?

    g.**   Next, determine the amount of an entrance fee that you could charge while continuing to charge the per-ride price you determined in (b) without changing how many rides are demanded.

    h.   How much is your profit now? What happens to consumer surplus? Is this efficient?

    i.   Suppose the recurring fixed cost of operating the park is $200,000. Would you operate it if you had to charge the efficient per-ride price but could not charge an entrance fee? What if you could charge an entrance fee?

15.3   **Business and Policy Application:** *License Fees and Surplus without Income Effects*: In previous chapters, we explored the impact of recurring license fees on an industry's output and price. We now consider their impact on consumer and producer surplus.

    A.   Suppose that all firms in the fast food restaurant business face U-shaped average cost curves prior to the introduction of a recurring license fee. The only output they produce is hamburgers. Suppose throughout that hamburgers are a quasilinear good for all consumers.

        a.   First, assume that all firms are identical. Illustrate the long-run market equilibrium and indicate how large consumer and long-run producer surplus (i.e., profit) are in this industry.

b.   Illustrate the change in the long-run market equilibrium that results from the introduction of a license fee.

c.   Suppose that the license fee has not yet been introduced. In considering whether to impose the license fee, the government attempts to ascertain the cost to consumers by asking a consumer advocacy group how much consumers would have to be compensated (in cash) in order to be made no worse off. Illustrate this amount as an area in your graph.

d.   Suppose instead that the government asked the consumer group how much consumers would be willing to pay to avoid the license free. Would the answer change?

e.   Finally, suppose the government simply calculated consumer surplus before and after the license fee is imposed and subtracted the latter from the former. Would the government's conclusion of how much the license fee costs consumers change?

f.   What in your answers changes if, instead of all firms being identical, some firms had higher costs than others (but all have U-shaped average cost curves)?

B.   Suppose that each firm's cost function is given by $C(w, r, x) = 0.047287 w^{0.5} r^{0.5} x^{1.25} + F$ where F is a recurring fixed cost.[8]

a.   What is the long-run equilibrium price for hamburgers x (as a function of F) assuming wage $w = 20$ and rental rate $r = 10$?

b.   Suppose that prior to the imposition of a license fee, the firm's recurring fixed cost F was $1,280. What is the pre-license fee equilibrium price?

c.   What happens to the long-run equilibrium price for hamburgers when a $1,340 recurring license fee is introduced?

d.   Suppose that tastes for hamburgers x and a composite good y can be characterized by the utility function $u(x, y) = 20x^{0.5} + y$ for all 100,000 consumers in the market, and assume that all consumers have budgeted $100 for x and other goods y. How many hamburgers are sold before and after the imposition of the license fee?

e.   Derive the expenditure function for a consumer with these tastes.

f.*   Use this expenditure function to answer the question in A(c).

g.*   Use the expenditure function to answer the question in A(d).

h.** Take the integral of the demand function that gives you the consumer surplus before the license fee and repeat this to get the integral of the consumer surplus after the license fee is imposed.

i.   How large is the change in consumer surplus from the price increase? Compare your answer with what you calculated in parts (f) and (g).

15.4   **Business and Policy Application:** *License Fees and Surplus with Income Effects:* In this exercise, assume the same set-up as in exercise 15.3 except that this time we will assume that hamburgers are a normal good for all consumers.

A.   As in exercise 15.3, we'll consider the long-run impact of a license fee for fast food restaurants on consumer surplus. In (a) and (b) of exercise 15.3, you should have concluded that the long-run price increases as a result of the license fee.

a.   Consider your graph from part (c) of exercise 15.3. Does the area you indicated over- or underestimate the amount consumers would have to be compensated (in cash) in order to accept the license fee?

b.   Does the area over- or underestimate the amount consumers are willing to pay to avoid the license fee?

c.   How would your answers to (a) and (b) differ if hamburgers were instead an inferior good for all consumers?

d.   Do any of your conclusions depend on the assumption (made explicitly in exercise 15.3) that all firms are identical?

---

[8]You can check for yourself that this is the cost function that arises from the production function $f(\ell, k) = 20\ell^{0.4} k^{0.4}$.

B. Suppose that tastes by consumers are characterized by the utility function $u(x, y) = x^{0.25}y^{0.75}$ and that each consumer had \$100 budgeted for hamburgers x and other goods y.

   a.   Calculate how many hamburgers each consumer consumes—and how much utility (as measured by this utility function) each consumer obtains—when the price of hamburgers is \$5 (and the price of "other goods" is \$1).

   b.   Derive the expenditure function for a consumer with such tastes.

   c.   Suppose that the license fee causes the price to increase to \$5.77 (as in exercise 15.3). How does your answer to (a) change?

   d.* Using the expenditure function, calculate the amount the government would need to compensate each consumer in order for them to agree to the imposition of the license fee.

   e.* Calculate the amount that consumers would be willing to pay to avoid the license fee.

   f.** Suppose you used the demand curve to estimate the change in consumer surplus from the introduction of the license fee. How would your estimate compare to your answers in (d) and (e)?

   g.** Can you use integrals of compensated demand curves to arrive at your answers from (d) and (e)?

15.5† Policy Application: *Redistribution of Income without Income Effects*: Consider the problem a society faces if it wants to maximize efficiency while also ensuring that the overall distribution of "happiness" in the society satisfies some notion of "equity."

A. Suppose that everyone in the economy has tastes over x and a composite good y, with all tastes quasilinear in x.

   a.   Does the market demand curve (for x) in such an economy depend on how income is distributed among individuals (assuming no one ends up at a corner solution)?

   b.   Suppose you are asked for advice by a government that has the dual objective of maximizing efficiency as well as ensuring some notion of "equity." In particular, the government considers two possible proposals: Under proposal A, the government redistributes income from wealthier individuals to poorer individuals before allowing the market for x to operate. Under proposal B, on the other hand, the government allows the market for x to operate immediately and then redistributes money from wealthy to poorer individuals after equilibrium has been reached in the market. Which would you recommend?

   c.   Suppose next that the government has been replaced by an omniscient social planner who does not rely on market processes but who shares the previous government's dual objective. Would this planner choose a different output level for x than is chosen under proposal A or proposal B in part (b)?

   d.   *True or False*: As long as money can be easily transferred between individuals, there is no tension in this economy between achieving many different notions of "equity" and achieving efficiency in the market for x.

   e.   To add some additional realism to the exercise, suppose that the government has to use distortionary taxes in order to redistribute income between individuals. Is it still the case that there is no trade-off between efficiency and different notions of equity?

B. Suppose there are two types of consumers: Consumer type 1 has utility function $u^1(x, y) = 50x^{1/2} + y$, and consumer type 2 has utility function $u^2(x, y) = 10x^{3/4} + y$. Suppose further that consumer type 1 has income of 800 and consumer type 2 has income of 1,200.

   a.   Calculate the demand functions for x for each consumer type.

   b.   Calculate the aggregate demand function when there are 32,000 of each consumer type.

   c.   Suppose that the market for x is a perfectly competitive market with identical firms that attain zero long-run profit when $p = 2.5$. Determine the long-run equilibrium output level in this industry.

   d.   How much x does each consumer type consume?

   e.   Suppose the government decides to redistribute income in such a way that, after the redistribution, all consumers have equal income; i.e., all consumers now have income of 1,000. Will the equilibrium in the x market change? Will the consumption of x by any consumer change?

f. Suppose instead of a competitive market, a social planner determined how much x and how much y every consumer consumes. Assume that the social planner is concerned about both the absolute welfare of each consumer as well as the distribution of welfare across consumers, with more equal distribution more desirable. Will the planner produce the same amount of x as the competitive market?

g. *True or False*: The social planner can achieve his or her desired outcome by allowing a competitive market in x to operate and then simply transferring y across individuals to achieve the desired distribution of happiness in society.

h. Would anything in your analysis change if the market supply function were upward sloping?

i. Economists sometimes refer to economies in which all individuals have quasilinear tastes as "transferable utility economies," which means that in economies like this, the government can transfer happiness from one person to another. Can you see why this is the case if we were using the utility functions as accurate measurements of happiness?

15.6 **Policy Application:** *Redistributing Income with Income Effects*: Consider again, as in exercise 15.5, the problem faced by a society that wants to both maximize efficiency and achieve some notion of "equity."

POLICY APPLICATION

A. Suppose again that everyone has tastes over x and a composite good y, but now suppose that tastes are homothetic.

a. Does the market demand curve (for x) depend on how income is distributed among individuals?

b. Would your answer to (a) be different if you thought that everyone had identical (homothetic) tastes?

c. Suppose you are again asked for the same advice as in exercise 15.5A(b). What is your answer now?

d. Repeat part A(c) from exercise 15.5 for this economy.

e. Recall that we defined a situation as "efficient" if there is no way to change the situation and make someone better off without making someone else worse off. In general (i.e., not just within the context of the example in this exercise), is it possible to have two efficient outcomes where some individuals prefer the first outcome while others prefer the second?

f. *True or False*: If the government redistributes income between individuals prior to the market for x operating, the outcome is efficient so long as income can be redistributed without cost.

g. *True or False*: In the quasilinear example of exercise 15.5, all efficient outcomes (excluding those that involve corner solutions) will involve the same level of production of x, but in the example of the current exercise this is no longer the case.

h. *True or False*: Assuming redistribution takes place before the market opens, a trade-off between efficiency and equity only emerges in this economy if redistributing money between individuals involves the use of distortionary taxes.

i. Does your conclusion in (h) hold more generally for nonhomothetic tastes as well?

B. Suppose again, as in exercise 15.5, that there are two types of individuals in the economy. Type 1 has utility function $u^1(x, y) = x^\alpha y^{(1-\alpha)}$ and type 2 has utility function $u^2(x, y) = x^\beta y^{(1-\beta)}$ (with both α and β falling between 0 and 1). Suppose further that type 1 individuals have income I and type 2 individuals have income I'.

a. What is each type's demand function for x assuming price p for x and a price of 1 for y?

b. What is the market demand function for x if there is an equal number N of each type in the economy?

c. Suppose $\alpha = \beta$ and money can be transferred across individuals without cost. Will the equilibrium output level in the x market be affected by income redistribution policies? Will individual consumption levels of x be affected by such policies?

d. Next, suppose $\alpha \neq \beta$. Will the equilibrium output level in the x market be affected by income redistribution policies?

e. Suppose again that you are asked for your advice on the two alternative policies described in exercise 15.5A(b) (assuming again that the government has the dual objective of maximizing efficiency and achieving some notion of "equity"). What is your advice now assuming that individuals cannot trade goods with one another after they have purchased x?

f.   Assume again that the government is replaced with an omniscient social planner who shares
      the previous government's dual objective. Will the social planner's decision on how much x to
      produce mirror the outcome of either of the two policies you considered in part (e)?

15.7   Policy Application: *Deadweight Loss from Subsidy of Mortgage Interest*: The U.S. tax code subsidizes
housing through a deduction of mortgage interest. For new homeowners, mortgage interest makes up the
bulk of their housing payments, which tend to make up about 25% of a household's income. Assume
throughout that housing is a normal good.

A. For purposes of this problem, we will assume that all housing payments made by a household
represent mortgage interest payments. If a household is in a 25% tax bracket, allowing the household
to deduct mortgage interest on its taxes then is equivalent to reducing the price of $1 worth of housing
consumption to $0.75.

   a.   Illustrate a demand curve for a consumer, indicating both the with- and without-deductibility
        housing price.

   b.   On the same graph, illustrate the compensated (or *MWTP*) curve for this consumer assuming
        that housing costs are deductible.

   c.   On your graph, indicate where you would locate the amount that a consumer would be willing
        to accept in cash instead of having the subsidy of housing through the tax code.

   d.   On your graph, indicate the area of the deadweight loss.

   e.   If you used the regular demand curve to estimate the deadweight loss, by how much would
        you over- or underestimate it?

B. Suppose that a household earning $60,000 (after taxes) has utility function $u(x, y) = x^{0.25}y^{0.75}$,
where x represents dollars worth of housing and y represents dollars worth of other consumption.
(Thus, we are implicitly setting the price of x and y to $1.)

   a.   How much housing does the household consume in the absence of tax deductibility?

   b.   If the household's marginal tax rate is 25% (and if all housing payments are deductible), how
        much housing will the household consume?

   c.   How much does the implicit housing subsidy cost the government for this consumer?

   d.   Derive the expenditure function for this household (holding the price of other consumption at
        $1 but representing the price of housing as p).

   e.   Suppose the government contemplates eliminating the tax deductibility of housing expendi-
        tures. How much would it have to compensate this household for the household to agree to this?

   f.** Can you derive the same amount as an integral on a compensated demand function?

   g.* Suppose you only knew this household's (uncompensated) demand curve and used it to
        estimate the change in consumer surplus from eliminating the tax deductibility of housing
        expenditures. How much would you estimate this to be?

   h.   Are you over- or underestimating the deadweight loss from the subsidy if you use the
        (uncompensated) demand curve?

   i.   Suppose that all 50,000,000 homeowners in the United States are identical to the one you have
        just analyzed. What is the annual deadweight loss from the deductibility of housing expenses?
        By how much would you over- or underestimate this amount if you used the aggregate demand
        curve for housing in this case?

15.8   Policy Application: *Markets, Social Planners, and Pollution*: One of the conditions we identified
as important to the first welfare theorem is that there are no *externalities*. One of the most important
externalities in the real world is pollution from production (which we will explore in detail in
Chapter 21).

A. Suppose that we consider the production of some good x and assume that consumers have tastes over
x and a composite good y where x is quasilinear.

   a.   Illustrate the market equilibrium in a graph with x on the horizontal and the price p of x on the
        vertical axis. Assume that the supply curve is upward sloping, either because you are consider-
        ing the short run in the industry or because the industry is composed of firms that differ in
        their cost curves.

    b. On your graph, indicate the consumer surplus and producer profit (or producer surplus).

    c. In the absence of externalities, why is the market equilibrium output level the same as the output level chosen by a social planner who wants to maximize social surplus?

    d. Now suppose that for every unit of x that is produced, an amount of pollution that causes social damage of δ is emitted. If you wanted to illustrate not just the marginal cost of production (as captured in supply curves) but also the additional marginal cost of pollution (that is not felt by producers), where would that "social marginal cost" curve lie in your graph?

    e. In the absence of any nonmarket intervention, do firms have an incentive to think about the marginal cost of pollution? Will the market equilibrium change as a result of the fact that pollution is emitted in the production process?

    f. Would the social planner who wishes to maximize social surplus take the marginal social cost of pollution into account? Illustrate in your graph the output quantity that this social planner would choose and compare it to the quantity the market would produce.

    g. Redraw your graph with the following two curves: the demand curve and the marginal social cost curve (that includes both the marginal costs of producers and the cost imposed on society by the pollution that is generated). Also, indicate on your graph the quantity x^* that the social planner wishes to produce as well as the quantity x^M that the market would produce. Can you identify in your graph an area that is equal to the deadweight loss that is produced by relying solely on the competitive market?

    h. Explain how pollution-producing production processes can result in inefficient outcomes under perfect competition. How does your conclusion change if the government forces producers to pay δ in a per-unit tax?

B. In exercise 15.2, you should have derived the aggregate demand function $X^D(p) = 250{,}000/p^2$ from the presence of 10,000 consumers with tastes that can be represented by the utility function $u(x, y) = 10x^{0.5} + y$. Suppose that this accurately characterizes the demand side of the market in the current problem. Suppose further that the market supply curve is given by the equation $X^S(p) = 250{,}000p$.

    a. Derive the competitive equilibrium price and quantity produced in the market.

    b.** Derive the size of consumer surplus and profit (or producer surplus).

    c. Consider a social planner who wants to maximize the social surplus. How would this planner arrive at the same output quantity as the market?

    d. Now suppose that each unit of x that is produced results in a pollution cost to society of $0.61. What would be the market outcome in the absence of any nonmarket intervention?

    e. Verify that, when each unit of x results in $0.61 pollution cost, the social planner would choose $x = 160{,}000$ as the optimal output quantity.

    f. Calculate the total social cost of pollution under the competitive market outcome. How much is social surplus reduced from what it would be in the absence of pollution?

    g.** Calculate the overall social surplus (including the cost of pollution) under the social planner's preferred outcome.

    h. What deadweight loss is produced as a result of the market's overproduction?

15.9† **Policy Application:** *Anti-Price-Gauging Laws*: As we will discuss in more detail in Chapter 18, governments sometimes interfere in markets by placing restrictions on the price that firms can charge. One common example of this is so-called "anti-price-gauging laws" that restrict profits for firms when sudden supply shocks hit particular markets.

POLICY APPLICATION

A. A recent hurricane disrupted the supply of gasoline to gas stations on the East Coast of the United States. Some states in this region enforce laws that prosecute gasoline stations for raising prices as a result of natural disaster–induced drops in the supply of gasoline.

    a. On a graph with weekly gallons of gasoline on the horizontal and price per gallon on the vertical, illustrate the result of a sudden leftward shift in the supply curve (in the absence of any laws governing prices).

    b. Suppose that gasoline is a quasilinear good for consumers. Draw a graph similar to the one in part (a) but include only the post-hurricane supply curve (as well as the unchanged demand curve). Illustrate consumer surplus and producer profit if price is allowed to settle to its equilibrium level.

c.   Now consider a state that prohibits price adjustments as a result of natural disaster–induced supply shocks. How much gasoline will be supplied in this state? How much will be demanded?

d.   Suppose that the limited amount of gasoline is allocated at the pre-crisis price to those who are willing to pay the most for it. Illustrate the consumer surplus and producer profit.

e.   On a separate graph, illustrate the total surplus achieved by a social planner who ensures that gasoline is given to those who value it the most and sets the quantity of gasoline at the same level as that traded in part (c). Is the social surplus different than what arises under the scenario in (d)?

f.   Suppose that instead the social planner allocates the socially optimal amount of gasoline. How much greater is social surplus?

g.   How does the total social surplus in (f) compare to what you concluded in (b) that the market would attain in the absence of anti-price-gauging laws?

h.   *True or False*: By interfering with the price signal that communicates information about where gasoline is most needed, anti-price-gauging laws have the effect of restricting the inflow of gasoline to areas that most need gasoline during times of supply disruptions.

B.**Suppose again that the aggregate demand function $X^D(p) = 250,000/p^2$ arises from 10,000 local consumers of gasoline with quasilinear tastes (as in exercise 15.8).

a.   Suppose that the industry is in long-run equilibrium and that the short-run industry supply function in this long-run equilibrium is $X^S(p) = 3,906.25p$. Calculate the equilibrium level of (weekly) local gasoline consumption and the price per dollar.

b.   What is the size of the consumer surplus and (short-run) profit?

c.   Next suppose that the hurricane-induced shift in supply moves the short-run supply function to $\overline{X}^S = 2,000p$. Calculate the new (short-run) equilibrium price and output level.

d.   What is the sum of consumer surplus and (short-run) profit if the market is allowed to adjust to the new short-run equilibrium?

e.   Now suppose the state government does not permit the price of gasoline to rise above what you calculated in part (a). How much gasoline will be supplied?

f.   Assuming that the limited supply of gasoline is bought by those who value it the most, calculate overall surplus (i.e., consumer surplus and (short-run) profit) under this policy.

g.   How much surplus is lost as a result of the government policy to not permit price increases in times of disaster-induced supply shocks?

General Equilibrium

Our analysis of competitive markets has thus far focused on a single market. It has not treated the entire economy as an interrelated system in which there are equilibrium forces that cross markets, and for this reason the model is often called a *partial equilibrium model*.[1] With the assumption of quasilinear tastes, the model gives not only a convenient way of illustrating equilibrium in a single market but it also allows us to measure welfare along market demand and supply curves in a manner consistent with how the material is typically presented in introductory economics texts. The simplicity of the model makes it a powerful tool for economists to develop insights about markets, and, as we have suggested in the last chapter, it provides a convenient benchmark for us to think about economic forces that may "distort" markets.

At the same time, the partial equilibrium model is restrictive in a number of ways. We have already illustrated that a deviation from quasilinearity in tastes creates complications for the simple "introductory economics" approach because of the emergence of income or wealth effects. In addition, we have to assume that the single market that is being analyzed is "small" relative to other markets, thus not impacting prices in those other markets. But often markets are fundamentally interrelated, with changes in one market spilling over into others through changes in input prices, through substitution effects as consumers switch between products and through the creation of wealth effects (due to nonquasilinear tastes). *General equilibrium models* therefore view the economy as a closed system of related markets, explicitly taking into account the effects that are assumed away in partial equilibrium analysis. Such models can be particularly important in policy analysis because policies represent institutional changes that affect many markets and create feedback effects that are ignored if we consider only a single market at a time.

Over the past 50 years, economists have therefore developed a large number of increasingly sophisticated models of this "general equilibrium" kind, with different models making different simplifying assumptions depending on the particular application for which they are designed.[2] These models now show up in different forms in virtually all subfields in economics. It is beyond the scope of this text to provide a thorough review of these approaches, and you will encounter them in different forms in a variety of future classes. For now, we will simply illustrate some very simple examples, and show how the first welfare theorem remains fully intact as we move away from the assumptions of the partial equilibrium model. Within these simple general equilibrium models, we can further illustrate some other important general equilibrium concepts: the "second

---

[1]This chapter is built on the foundations of consumer theory as illustrated in Chapter 6 as well as a basic understanding of producer theory as illustrated in Chapter 11.
[2]The pioneers in this area were Ken Arrow (1921–), Gerard Debreu (1921–2004) and Lionel McKenzie (1919–). In 1972, Arrow was awarded the Nobel Prize in economics, followed by a 1983 Nobel award to Debreu.

welfare theorem," a notion of stability of resource allocations known as the "core," and the result that this "core" in fact converges to what emerges through decentralized market forces. At the end of the chapter, we will then discuss some more general examples of the importance of general equilibrium effects, examples that go beyond the analytic tools we can illustrate here.

16A A Graphical Exposition of General Equilibrium

There are three basic economic activities that occur in a market economy: production, exchange, and the consumption that results from these. Rich general equilibrium models in which large numbers of firms and consumers engage in economic activity have been developed mathematically with the basic tools we have introduced in this text, but some of the underlying concepts and ideas that emerge from these models can be illustrated in small examples that lend themselves to a graphical approach, with the same insights generalizing to a much richer setting.

We will introduce these ideas in two steps: In 16A.1, we begin by introducing what we will call a pure exchange economy in which no production occurs and two consumers simply engage in trade of two types of goods that they already own. We can then demonstrate some of the fundamental general equilibrium ideas and results that also hold in settings with many consumers and many goods (in Section 16A.2). In Section 16A.3, we will then move on to consider production in an economy in which a single agent acts as both a producer and a consumer.

16A.1 A Pure Exchange Economy

We begin with a treatment of what is known as a *pure exchange economy* defined as *an economy in which there is no production and in which consumers are endowed with different bundles of goods*. Obviously, a model of an economy without production is not one that aims to be a fully realistic model. Rather, it offers us the simplest possible setting in which to illustrate the basic insights and methods of general equilibrium theory.

The simplest possible version of an exchange economy is one with two consumers and two goods. Suppose, for instance, we consider my wife and me on a weekend getaway in a secluded cottage on a remote island in the Bahamas. In the rush to catch our flight, we grabbed a few fruits to sustain us over the weekend. Suppose she grabbed a basket with 10 oranges and 4 bananas and I took a basket with 3 oranges and 6 bananas. As we consider our situation over the weekend, we therefore have a total of 13 oranges and 10 bananas to sustain us, and each of us is interested in exploring a trade that would make us both better off.

More formally, our little economy is defined simply by (1) the individuals in the economy (me and my wife), (2) our tastes over goods, and (3) the endowments of goods that we own in the economy (our baskets of oranges and bananas). If all we do is consume our individual endowments, we can each get to a certain indifference curve on our indifference map. These indifference curves are illustrated in panels (a) and (b) of Graph 16.1, with the bundle E_2 denoting my wife's endowment bundle in panel (a) and the bundle E_1 denoting my endowment bundle in panel (b). My wife and I are now interested in exploring whether there are other feasible distributions of our joint endowment that could make both of us better off and thus lead to a mutually beneficial trade.

It is not easy to see whether such trades are possible when my wife's and my situation are depicted separately as they are in panels (a) and (b). Economists, beginning with the 19th-century economist Francis Edgeworth (1845–1926), have therefore developed a graphical technique that allows us to see the fundamentals of this exchange economy within a single picture.[3] In panel (c), we simply take the picture from panel (a) by the origin and "flip it over" so that the origin now

---

[3]It is generally believed that Edgeworth was also the first person to draw an indifference curve in his 1881 book entitled *Mathematical Psychics*, where he also developed the idea of the "core" as well as the idea of "core convergence," both introduced later in this chapter and developed further in the appendix.

Graph 16.1: Deriving a Graphical Depiction of a Two-Person, Two-Good Exchange Economy

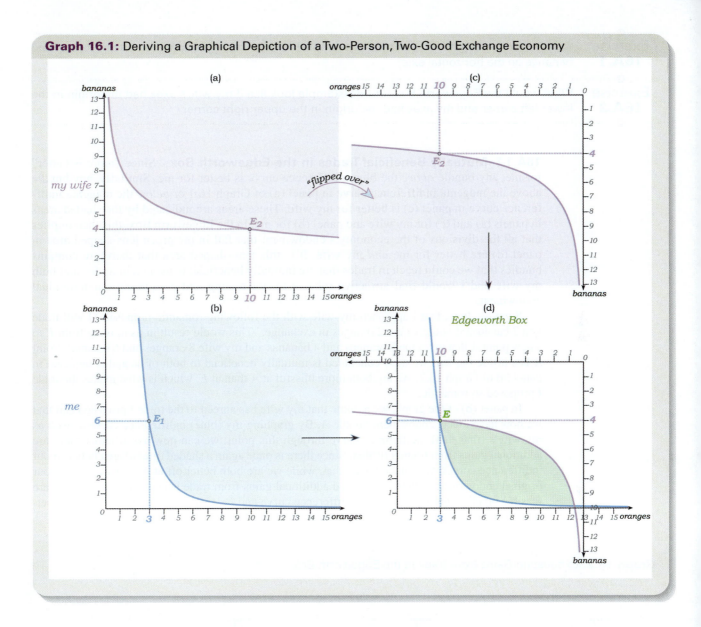

lies on the northeast (i.e., upper right) rather than the southwest (i.e., lower left) corner. Then, we replicate panel (b) in panel (d) and move the "flipped" graph in panel (c) on top of this graph in such a way that point E_2 lies exactly on top of point E_1. Although points E_1 and E_2 now appear to be the same point, they remain distinct points with the relevant levels of oranges and bananas read off the axis with the origin at the lower left corner for me and off the axis with the origin on the upper right corner for my wife.

The box in panel (d) of the graph is known as the *Edgeworth Box*. Notice that by moving point E_2 on top of point E_1, we have caused the width of the box to be equal to 13 oranges and the height of the box to be 10 bananas, with 13 oranges and 10 bananas representing the total endowment that my wife and I jointly have. All the points inside the box therefore represent different ways of dividing the total endowment in our little economy between me and my wife. The endowment point $E = E_1 = E_2$ thus represents one possible way of dividing the total endowment in the economy: 3 oranges and 6 bananas for me and 10 oranges and 4 bananas for my wife.

Exercise 16A.1   What would the Edgeworth Box for this example look like if oranges appeared on the vertical and bananas on the horizontal axis?

Exercise 16A.2   What would the Edgeworth Box for this example look like if my wife's axes had the origin in the lower left corner and my axes had the origin in the upper right corner?

16A.1.1 Mutually Beneficial Trades in the Edgeworth Box

Since "more is better" for me, any bundle *above* the blue indifference curve is better for me. Similarly, any bundle above the magenta indifference curve in panel (a) of Graph 16.1 or *below* the magenta indifference curve in panel (c) is better for my wife. These areas are indicated by the shaded areas in panels (a) and (c) for my wife and panel (b) for me. In the Edgeworth Box, this then implies that all the divisions of the economy's endowment that fall in the green lens-shaped area in panel (d) are better for me *and* my wife. It is this lens-shaped area that therefore contains bundles that we could reach in trades that are mutually beneficial to us; i.e., in trades that both my wife and I would find attractive relative to not trading and consuming our individual endowments.

Suppose, then, that I approach my wife with the following romantic proposal: "I will trade you 2 bananas if you give me 2 oranges in exchange." This would result in us moving from *E* to a new point *A* that gives me 5 oranges and 4 bananas and my wife 8 oranges and 6 bananas. Point *A* lies inside the lens we have concluded is mutually beneficial to both of us and is depicted in panel (a) of Graph 16.2. We are both more blissful at *A* than at *E*, which is what makes the trade I proposed so romantic.

In panel (b) of the graph, we assume that my wife has agreed to the trade I proposed and that we now have a new endowment bundle *A*. By graphing my (blue) indifference curve as well as my wife's (magenta) indifference curve through this point, we can now ask whether there are additional gains from trading further. Since there is once again a shaded (green) area between our indifference curves, we can conclude that, while we are both better off at *A* than we were at our original endowment *E*, there are indeed additional gains from trade because whenever there are feasible bundles that lie *above* my indifference curve and *below* my wife's, we can both do better by trading more. There is still room for more romantic trading!

Graph 16.2: Exhausting Gains from Trade in the Edgeworth Box

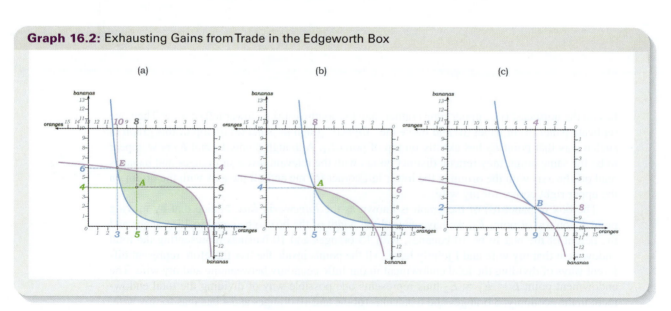

Exercise
16A.3

True or False: Starting at point *A*, any mutually beneficial trade will involve me trading bananas for oranges, and any trade of bananas for oranges will be mutually beneficial. (*Hint*: Part of the statement is true and part is false.)

It is therefore reasonable to assume that my wife and I will continue to trade until we reach a point in the Edgeworth Box that does *not* give rise to a lens-shaped area between our indifference curves through that point. Panel (c) of the graph illustrates such a point: point *B* that contains 9 oranges and 2 bananas for me and 4 oranges and 8 bananas for my wife. If we trade to the point *B* (where I have given up 4 bananas in exchange for 6 oranges from the original endowment *E*), we will find that any further trade that is proposed will make either me or my wife worse off. Put differently, if we reach point *B* in the Edgeworth Box, we will have exhausted all gains from trade and have thus reached an efficient division of our economy's endowment. With no further gains from trade, we will now have to find other ways of expressing our romantic inclinations toward one another.

Exercise
16A.4

In Chapter 6, we argued that consumers leave Wal-Mart with the same tastes "at the margin," i.e. with the same marginal rates of substitution between goods that they have purchased, and that this fact implies that all gains from trade have been exhausted. How is this similar to the condition for an efficient distribution of an economy's endowment in the exchange economy?

16A.1.2 The Contract Curve: Pareto Efficient Points in the Edgeworth Box

Recall that a situation is *efficient*, or what is often referred to as *Pareto efficient*, if there is no way to make someone better off without making anyone else worse off. The division of our little economy's endowment at point *B* in Graph 16.2c is an example of such a situation: No matter what direction we move within the Edgeworth Box from point *B*, someone will be worse off. Points *E* and *A*, on the other hand, are not efficient because we found ways to move within the box such that both my wife and I became better off.

Point *B* is by no means, however, the only Pareto efficient distribution of the economy's endowment. Think of it this way: Suppose my wife gets all of the endowment, all 13 oranges and all 10 bananas, and, as a result, I get nothing. In the Edgeworth Box, this point lies at the lower left corner of the box, or the origin of the axes that refer to me. This point is also Pareto efficient because any movement away from this point, while making me better off, will make my wife worse off. Of course, despite my infatuation with my wife, I would never agree to move to this point if I start out with the endowment *E*, but that does not mean that, were we somehow to reach that point, it would not be Pareto efficient.

Exercise
16A.5

Starting at the point where my wife gets the entire endowment of the economy, are there points in the Edgeworth Box that make my wife worse off without making me better off (assuming that bananas and oranges are both essential goods for me)?

Exercise
16A.6

Is the point on the upper right-hand corner of the Edgeworth Box Pareto efficient?

Exercise
16A.7*

If bananas and oranges are essential goods for both me and my wife, can any points on the axes (other than those at the upper right and lower left corners of the Edgeworth Box) be Pareto efficient?

Now suppose that we consider an arbitrary blue indifference curve for me, such as that depicted in panel (a) of Graph 16.3. We can then start at a relatively low indifference curve (such as the grey

Graph 16.3: The Contract Curve: Pareto Efficient Allocations in the Edgeworth Box

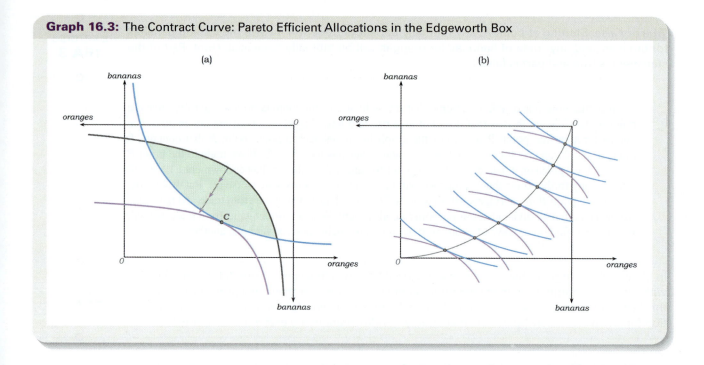

curve) for my wife and ask if we can make her better off without pushing me below the blue indifference curve we have picked. As long as there is a lens-shaped area between the blue curve and the grey curve, the answer is yes, we can move to higher and higher indifference curves for my wife. This process stops when we reach the magenta indifference curve in the graph, a curve that is just tangent to the blue curve at point C. Once we reach C, any higher indifference curve for my wife implies that I will end up below the blue indifference curve.

Point C then represents another Pareto efficient point, an allocation of the economy's endowment where it is not possible to make one of us better off without making the other worse off. But of course we could have picked any other arbitrary indifference curve for me and gone through exactly the same process to find a tangency with an indifference curve for my wife, thus again arriving at a Pareto efficient allocation. Panel (b) of the graph then illustrates that there is a whole range of Pareto efficient points, beginning at the lower left corner of the Edgeworth Box and extending to the upper right corner. Points B (in Graph 16.2c) and C (in Gaph 16.3a) are simply two examples of such points. Because it is reasonable to assume that, regardless of where the initial endowment in the economy falls, individuals will find trades (or "contracts") that lead to efficient allocations of the economy's endowment, *the entire set of Pareto efficient allocations of the economy's endowment is called the contract curve.*

Exercise 16A.8* What would the contract curve look like if bananas and oranges were perfect complements for both me and my wife? (*Hint*: It is an area rather than a "curve.") What if they were perfect complements for me and perfect substitutes for my wife?

Exercise 16A.9* What does the contract curve look like if bananas and oranges are perfects substitutes (one for one) for both me and my wife? (*Hint*: You should get a large area within the Edgeworth Box as a result.

16A.1.3 Mutually Beneficial Efficient Trades and the "Core"
We have already noted that the mere fact that a particular allocation of bananas and oranges is Pareto efficient does not imply that we would expect that allocation to emerge from mutually agreed upon trades by me and my wife. After all, I already know that I can be guaranteed a minimum level of utility by simply consuming my endowment E_1, and similarly my wife knows she can be guaranteed a minimum level of utility by consuming her endowment E_2. No matter how good or bad we are at negotiating with one another, there is no reason to expect that either one of us will agree to trades that make us worse off than we were before we started trading. At the same time, we also saw that we both have an incentive to trade with one another so long as the allocation of bananas and oranges is not Pareto efficient.

As a result, it would be reasonable to predict that we will (1) trade until we have reached an efficient allocation that lies on the contract curve and (2) that neither one of us will be worse off than we were at our respective endowment points (E). In Graph 16.4, we therefore draw the indifference curves that my wife and I would attain were we to simply consume our endowment, the shaded (green) lens-shaped area that indicates the set of allocations that make both of us better off, and the (grey) line representing efficient allocations where our indifference curves are tangent to one another. Predicting that we will (1) exhaust all gains from trade and (2) agree only to trades that improve our well-being then implies that the set of possible allocations we might agree on will lie on the green portion of the contract curve.

Without knowing more about our relative bargaining skills, it is difficult to say much beyond that. My wife is clearly the better negotiator in our marriage, which would lead me to predict that we would probably end up on the lower portion of the green segment where my wife ends up enjoying more of the gains from trade than I do. If I am completely incompetent at bargaining, my wife might even end up convincing me to trade to the very lowest point on this green segment where I end up just as well off as I was at point E and she becomes much better off. But even my meager negotiating skills are sufficient to keep me from agreeing to anything less than that.

This green segment on the contract curve is then often referred to as the *core* of the two-person exchange economy. *An allocation lies in the core if and only if no subset of individuals in the*

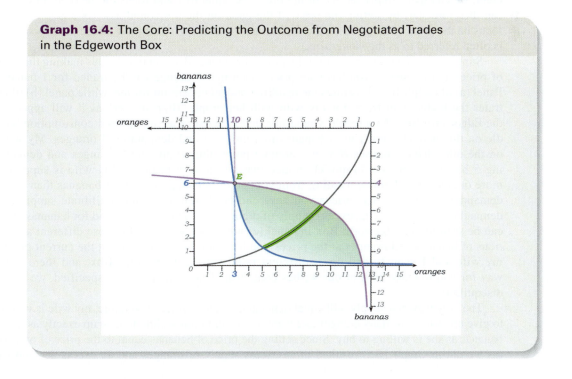

Graph 16.4: The Core: Predicting the Outcome from Negotiated Trades in the Edgeworth Box

economy can make themselves better off by trading among one another. In our example of an exchange economy with only two individuals, this implies that, for an allocation of the endowment to lie in the core, there is no way the two individuals can figure out a means for both to become better off. In the two-person case, the core is then equivalent to the set of Pareto efficient allocations that lies within the lens-shaped mutually beneficial region. As we will discuss shortly, however, when the economy is composed of more than two individuals, the core will typically be a subset of this (green) portion of the contract curve.

16A.1.4 Competitive Equilibrium in the Edgeworth Box

Now suppose that you find yourself on the same secluded island and you agree to spare my wife and me the pain of negotiating with one another. To minimize marital conflict (and maximize marital bliss), you propose the following: You will try to find a set of prices for oranges and bananas such that I will agree to sell you some of my bananas and my wife will sell you some of her oranges, and you in turn will sell me some of the oranges you bought from my wife (and sell her some of the bananas you bought from me) at those same prices. My wife and I in turn promise to take the prices you quote as given and trade based on those prices; i.e., we agree to be "price-takers." Your problem, however, is that, since you have no bananas or oranges of your own, you have to find prices such that what I am selling you is what my wife will agree to buy and what I am buying from you is what my wife will agree to sell. Put differently, you will try to find prices such that demand for both goods is equal to supply.

First, remember from our development of budget constraints in Chapters 2 and 3 how such constraints arise when income is based solely on endowments (and not on some exogenous money income). Since it is always possible, regardless of what prices are quoted, for me to consume my endowment E_1 and not trade anything at those prices, E_1 will always lie on my budget constraint. The prices you quote will then determine the slope at which my budget line passes through point E_1. More precisely, the ratio $-p_1/p_2$, or the price of good 1 (oranges) *relative to* the price of good 2 (bananas), determines the slope of my budget through my endowment E_1. Since the *ratio* of prices is what matters when income is defined by an endowment, we can then simply let one of the prices be equal to 1 and focus on the other price. We can therefore start by setting the price of the good on the horizontal axis (oranges) to 1 and focus on the price of the good on the vertical axis (bananas). (The good whose price is set to 1 is often referred to as the *numeraire*.)

Suppose that you start by setting the price of bananas also equal to 1, thus making the ratio of prices 1. In essence, you have set prices such that 1 orange can be traded for 1 banana. Panel (a) of Graph 16.5 illustrates the resulting budget constraint for me, while panel (b) illustrates the budget constraint for my wife with her graph "flipped over" as it will appear in the Edgeworth Box. As a result, you notice that I choose A as my optimal consumption bundle on this budget, supplying 3 bananas to your store and demanding 3 oranges. My wife, on the other hand, chooses B as her optimal point, thus supplying 5 oranges and demanding 5 bananas. You should quickly notice that you have a problem: My wife is supplying more oranges than I am demanding from you, and I am supplying fewer bananas than she is demanding from you. The prices you have chosen therefore do not equilibrate supply and demand but rather cause an excess supply of oranges and an excess demand for bananas. This can be seen in the Edgeworth Box in panel (c) where my wife and I choose different allocations of bananas and oranges at the prices you have set. Put differently, at the current prices, my wife and I want to end up at different points in the Edgeworth Box, and there is no way for you to make both of our wishes come true. Under the prices as specified, we are in disequilibrium.

The only way that supply will equal demand is if, at the prices you quote, my wife is willing to give up exactly as many oranges as I want to buy and I am willing to give up exactly as many bananas as she is willing to buy. Since setting the price of bananas equal to the price of oranges (as we did in Graph 16.5) resulted in an excess supply of oranges and an excess demand for

Graph 16.5: A Disequilibrium Price: Supply Is not Equal to Demand

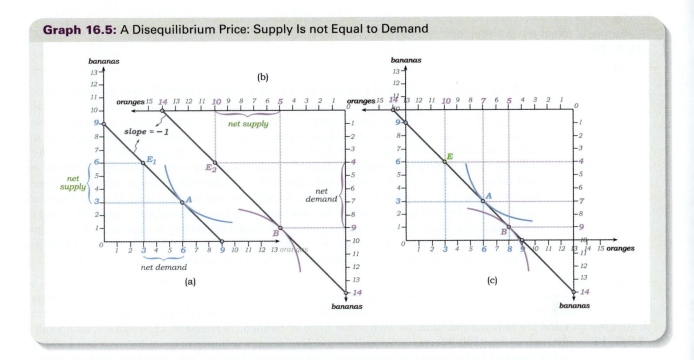

bananas, it would seem reasonable that you have set the price of bananas too low relative to the price of oranges. So suppose you next try to raise the price of bananas to 1.5 (leaving the price of oranges at 1). The resulting price ratio is then 2/3, forming the budget constraint in the Edgeworth Box of Graph 16.6.

Graph 16.6: Competitive Equilibrium Prices: Supply Equals Demand

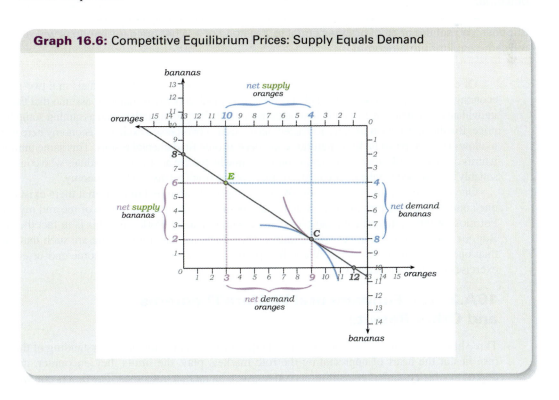

Exercise 16A.10 What are the intercepts of this budget on my wife's axes for oranges and bananas?

Since oranges have become relatively cheaper and bananas relatively more expensive, I end up choosing to demand more oranges while my wife decides to demand fewer bananas. If you have raised the price of bananas by just the right amount, this will result in the quantities demanded and supplied by my wife and me to exactly equal one another, which in turn results in both of us choosing the same point in the Edgeworth Box as our optimal point. Of course, this does not mean that we will consume identical bundles since my wife's consumption bundle is read off of a different axis than mine. In Graph 16.6, my wife sells 6 oranges (earning $6) and buys 4 bananas (for $6) while I sell 4 bananas (earning $6) and buy 6 oranges (for $6). Demand equals supply and we end up choosing the allocation C. You have therefore successfully found a set of prices that result in both me and my wife individually optimizing in such a way that we end up at C. Since these prices then result in demand equaling supply when my wife and I act as price-takers, they are *competitive equilibrium prices* for our economy.

Exercise 16A.11 Suppose both oranges and bananas are normal goods for both me and my wife. Draw separate graphs for me and my wife, with the initial budget constraint when the prices were both equal to 1 and the new budget constraint when the price of bananas is raised to 1.5. Illustrate, using substitution and wealth effects, why my demand for oranges will unambiguously increase and my wife's demand for bananas will unambiguously decrease. Can you say unambiguously what will happen to my demand for bananas and my wife's demand for oranges?

Exercise 16A.12 Suppose you had decided to leave the price of bananas at 1 and to rather change the price of oranges. What price (for oranges) would you have to set in order to achieve the same equilibrium outcome?

Exercise 16A.13 Suppose you set the price of oranges equal to 2 instead of 1. What price for bananas will result in the same equilibrium outcome?

Of course, there is something artificial in this exercise: Why would individuals in a two-person economy ever be price-takers? In such a setting, it is much more reasonable to assume that the two individuals find their way to an efficient outcome through bargaining rather than assuming some fixed price. But the only reason we have restricted ourselves to a two-person exchange economy here is that it allows us to graph some basic intuitions and derive some fundamental results. This same intuition, it turns out, then works for much larger economies in which there are many individuals who could reasonably be assumed to take prices as given since each is small relative to the economy.

One final note before we move on: We have implicitly assumed thus far that there exists only one competitive equilibrium in an exchange economy like the one composed of me and my wife. For most of the mathematical examples that we would usually work with, this is in fact the case. But one can imagine instances where indifference maps for me and my wife are such that more than one equilibrium is possible. We will explore scenarios of this type in some end-of-chapter exercises (such as exercise 16.7).

16A.2 The Fundamental Welfare Theorems and Other Results

Three basic results lie at the heart of general equilibrium theory, and an understanding of these in turn lies at the heart of appreciating the role markets play, the limits they encounter, and the degree to which nonmarket institutions can improve on market outcomes. The first is one we have already encountered in our partial equilibrium model of competitive markets. It is the *first welfare theorem* that provides conditions under which market outcomes are efficient. The second, known as the *second welfare theorem*, is in some sense the inverse of the first: It states that, as long as the government can redistribute endowments in a lump sum way, any efficient allocation can in fact be a market equilibrium. Thus, if initial endowments result in an equilibrium that gives rise to unacceptable levels of inequality (for instance), then, in the presence of lump sum redistribution, the government can rely on markets to produce more equitable outcomes once it redistributes some endowments. Finally, it has been shown that, as economies become large, the core of an economy shrinks down to just the set of market equilibrium outcomes, a result we will refer to as *core convergence*. This is perhaps the most abstract of the results, but it provides some real reason as to why we think the concept of a competitive market equilibrium is such a powerful one for predicting outcomes. Since it is reasonable to expect that individuals, using their bargaining skills, will trade with one another until they reach an allocation in the core, the result suggests that when individual bargaining power is diluted as many consumers enter an economy, the competitive equilibrium outcome is in fact the only one we should expect to arise. We will discuss each of these results in sequence.

16A.2.1 The First Welfare Theorem

In the previous chapter's "partial equilibrium" model where we investigated a single market at a time, we derived our first version of what we called the "First Welfare Theorem." This theorem states simply that, under certain conditions, the competitive equilibrium in a market is efficient. We can now see in the "general equilibrium" model of an exchange economy (where we are analyzing equilibrium across several markets such as the market for oranges and for bananas) that the same theorem holds (again under the conditions outlined at the end of the previous chapter).

In the two-person, two-good exchange economy of the Edgeworth Box, the insight is almost instantly obvious in Graph 16.6: Since an equilibrium price results in the two consumers optimizing along their budgets at the same point in the Edgeworth Box, and since their indifference curves are tangent to identically sloped budget constraints, the indifference curves are tangent to one another. As we saw earlier, when an allocation in the Edgeworth Box is such that the indifference curves through that allocation are tangent to one another and therefore do not give rise to a lens-shaped area in between the indifference curves, the allocation is Pareto efficient. This insight holds for exchange economies with many individuals and many goods as well, with the intuition virtually identical to what emerges from the simple Edgeworth Box.

True or False: When the First Welfare Theorem holds, competitive equilibria in an exchange economy result in allocations that lie on the contract curve but not necessarily in the core.

**Exercise
16A.14**

16A.2.2 The Second Welfare Theorem

While, as we discussed in some detail in Chapter 15, the First Welfare Theorem contains remarkable insights, it does not imply that we necessarily have to believe that the allocation of goods that results from competitive market prices is "good." Rather, the theorem simply tells us that, under the conditions outlined in Chapter 15, the market allocation of goods will be efficient. As we have seen in our derivation of the contract curve, however, there are many different "efficient" allocations, and most of us would probably judge some of these to be more desirable than others. For instance, under many notions of "equity" or "fairness," we might be disturbed if the allocation in the economy is such that one person gets almost everything while everyone else gets little to nothing, even if that allocation is Pareto efficient.

Thinking along these lines leads us to a second general equilibrium insight known as the *Second Welfare Theorem*. This theorem is in some sense a mirror image of the first. It states that *any Pareto efficient allocation can result from a competitive equilibrium so long as the initial endowments are redistributed appropriately.* Thus, while the First Welfare Theorem says that competitive equilibria are efficient, the Second Welfare Theorem says that any efficient allocation can be a competitive equilibrium allocation *so long as the government can redistribute endowments without shrinking the economy in the process.*

Again, the intuition for this is easily seen in the Edgeworth Box for two-person, two-good exchange economies. Suppose, as before, that *E* in Graph 16.7 is the initial endowment point for this economy but that, for some reason, we wanted to get the efficient allocation *D* to be the competitive equilibrium allocation. It should be clear that no set of prices for bananas and oranges could possibly result in my wife and me trading from *E* to *D*; after all, the magenta indifference curve that contains *D* lies *below E*, which implies that my wife would prefer to consume her initial endowment rather than agree to trade to *D*.

If *D* were to become an equilibrium allocation, it would have to be the case that we could draw a budget constraint into the Edgeworth Box such that this constraint passes through *D* and has exactly the slope of the blue and magenta indifference curves at point *D*. The green line in Graph 16.7 satisfies these conditions and would therefore have to be the equilibrium budget constraint for me and my wife in order for *D* to be an equilibrium allocation. But, since budget lines always pass through endowment points, the only way this line can be a budget constraint for us is if our endowment point lies on that line. For instance, were our initial endowment at *E′* rather than *E*, then *D* would be an equilibrium allocation.

The Second Welfare Theorem as stated at the beginning of this section says that any efficient allocation can be an equilibrium allocation so long as the initial endowments are redistributed appropriately. In our example in Graph 16.7, one "appropriate" redistribution from the initial endowment *E* would be to redistribute 5 oranges and 2 bananas from my wife to me, which would make the new endowment point *E′*.

Exercise 16A.15   Can you think of other redistributions of oranges and bananas that would be "appropriate" for ensuring that *D* is the competitive equilibrium outcome?

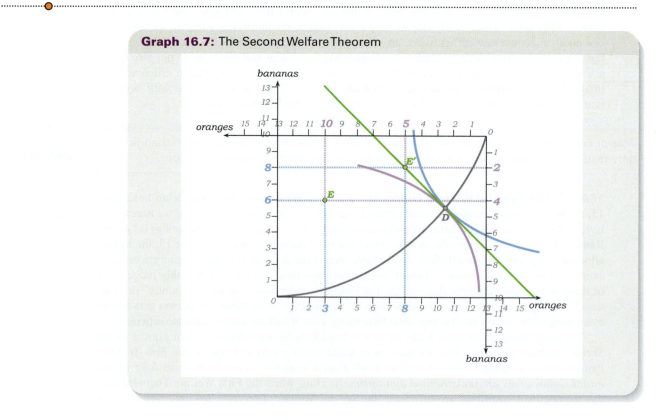

Graph 16.7: The Second Welfare Theorem

At first glance, this Second Welfare Theorem seems very powerful because it appears to suggest that, if we find the competitive market outcome inequitable, we can redistribute the endowments of individuals in the economy in a more "equitable" manner and then allow the market to find a new equilibrium that will once again be efficient. Thus, the theorem appears to suggest that there is no trade-off between equity and efficiency, that we can achieve more equitable market outcomes through redistribution of endowments and then rest assured that the market will preserve efficiency.

Given what we have learned in earlier chapters, however, we need to be very cautious in not reading too much into this "first glance" impression of what the Second Welfare Theorem states. The hidden assumption in the theorem is that we can undertake redistribution without cost, that we can redistribute without shrinking the size of the economy. Put differently, the Second Welfare Theorem assumes that "lump sum redistribution"—redistribution through the use of lump sum taxes and subsidies—is possible. However, as we have argued in previous chapters, lump sum taxes and subsidies are exceedingly rare in the real world, and almost all real-world taxes and subsidies give rise to deadweight losses. Put differently, redistribution achieved through real-world (distortionary) taxes and subsidies shrinks the economy (or the Edgeworth Box). Thus, it isn't really possible to "redistribute appropriately" as the Second Welfare Theorem envisions because real-world redistributions will result in inefficiencies. As a result, if endowments in an economy are inequitably distributed, leading to an efficient but inequitable market outcome, a trade-off between equity and efficiency emerges, with redistribution leading to inefficiency but potentially more equity (depending on how one defines what is equitable). We will return to this issue more explicitly in Chapter 29.

16A.2.3 Equilibrium and the Core

We began our discussion of the simple Edgeworth Box exchange economy by asking where trade by two individuals (like my wife and me) might take them. Our conclusion was that it would be reasonable to assume that individuals would continue to trade until no further mutually beneficial trades were possible and that this implies that they will end up with some allocation of the economy's endowment that lies in the core (i.e., on the contract curve and between the indifference curves through the original endowment). Where exactly they would end up in the core depended on assumptions about the individuals' relative bargaining skills, but nothing outside the core was likely to last since individuals would still have an incentive to find mutually beneficial trades.

We then defined a much stricter (and seemingly unrelated) tool for predicting where individuals in Edgeworth Box exchange economies would end up: competitive prices. We acknowledged at the outset that, with only two individuals in the economy, the assumption of competitive, or "price-taking," behavior is silly, but we foreshadowed that terms of trade arising from competitive prices (rather than relative bargaining skills) would be more realistic and important in general equilibrium economies with many individuals.

As it turns out, however, the core and the set of competitive equilibrium allocations in an exchange economy are quite related. You should be able to easily convince yourself from what we have done that the competitive equilibrium allocation *must* lie in the set of core allocations but that the latter is typically a much larger set than the former. What is not obvious from what we have done so far, however, is that, as an exchange economy gets "larger," the set of core allocations shrinks; and as the size of the economy becomes really large, the core shrinks to just the set of competitive equilibrium allocations. Thus, were we to predict who gets what in a large exchange economy by simply finding allocations that lie in the "core" of the economy, it would be exactly the same exercise as finding the set of allocations that can be supported by competitive market prices. Put differently, in large economies, only stable allocations in which no subgroup can find a way to make itself better off can arise as a competitive equilibrium, and no allocation that cannot arise as a competitive equilibrium has that stability property.

If this sounds interesting to you, you can explore the intuition behind this result in much more detail in the appendix to this chapter. But the basic intuition behind the result goes as follows: We know that when it is only me and my wife in the economy, I have bargaining power because the only way my wife is ever going to be able to make a trade is to make it with me. But as we envision larger economies with other consumers who are a lot like me, my wife suddenly has options: If I don't trade with her, she can find someone else who is pretty similar to me to trade with. Thus, the increasing competition from others like me reduces my bargaining power. Similarly, as the economy gets large there are others like my wife, and her bargaining power is decreasing for the same reason as mine. What is remarkable is that the competition between me and consumers like me as we all try to make bargains without any reference to any prices leads to the exact same outcome as if we were in a competitive equilibrium in which market prices (rather than competition with others in bargaining) governed everyone's behavior.

Think of it this way: Suppose you compare two countries that are identical in all ways except that in one there are shopping malls in which stores post their prices (with "no haggling" allowed or tolerated) and in the other the stores post no prices but each merchant tries to get you to bargain about the price. In the first country, we would predict that who gets what is determined by a competitive market process in which individual behavior is guided by the posted prices. In the second country, on the other hand, we would predict that who gets what depends on bargaining skills of individuals as everyone tries to haggle toward the best possible deal. But if there are many similar shops along the street, our results suggest that the competition between similar merchants will lead to exactly the same outcome as the price mechanism produces in the first country.

16A.3 A Simple "Robinson Crusoe" Production Economy

Suppose that on the way to the island in the Bahamas, my wife and I encountered unexpected turbulence and I was accidentally ejected from the airplane as I panicked and pressed the "eject" button. Fortunately, I always travel with a parachute strapped to my back, and so I was able to land safely on one of the many islands in the Bahamas. But the love of my life, who has a pilot's license and does not panic as easily, ended up landing the plane safely on another island, leaving me to fend for myself on my island without any of the provisions of oranges and bananas we had packed.

If I am going to survive, I will therefore have to expend some effort to find food. Suppose I find that the only food that grows on this island is bananas. You could then think of me as a producer and a consumer: I am a producer who uses labor to produce bananas, and I am a consumer who gives up leisure in order to be able to eat. I am just like the fictional character Robinson Crusoe, which is why the "economy" I find myself in is often referred to by economists as a *Robinson Crusoe economy*.[4] It is the simplest possible economy that contains both a producer and a consumer.

If you thought an exchange economy with me and my wife trading oranges and bananas was silly, you will surely find the Robinson Crusoe economy in which I act as both a producer and consumer of bananas silly. And, taken at face value, both these types of economies are silly. But, as we have now said repeatedly, they illustrate, within a simple setting in which we can use graphs, the very insights that continue to hold up in much more complicated economies. So, if the idea of a single consumer and a single producer behaving competitively really bothers you, just remember that the analysis holds equivalently for a large number of identical consumers and producers. And the broader results further apply to economies with many different types of consumers and producers.

16A.3.1 Robinson Crusoe Doing the Best He Can   We can imagine my search for bananas as being characterized by a set of feasible production plans inside a simple production frontier such as the one depicted in Graph 16.8a. Here, the only input into production is labor

---

[4]Daniel Defoe published the novel *Robinson Crusoe* in 1719. The novel explores the fictional life of an English castaway (named Robinson Crusoe) stranded on a remote tropical island. While Robinson Crusoe initially finds himself alone, he eventually encounters natives, most notably a man he names "Friday," and escapes our "Robinson Crusoe production economy."

Graph 16.8: Robinson Crusoe Choosing His Optimal Bundle

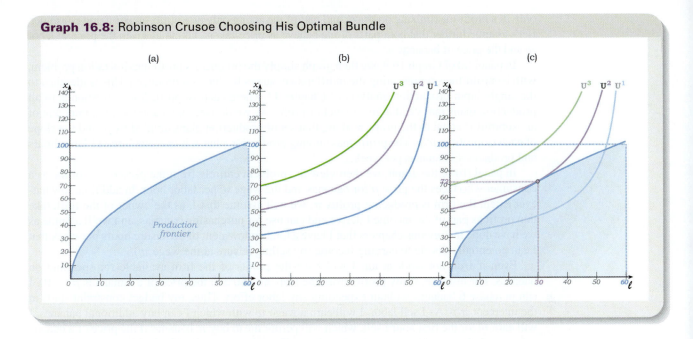

hours per week ℓ on the horizontal axis, and the only output is the number of bananas harvested per week x on the vertical axis. We assume that the production choice set ends at $\ell = 60$ and thus assume that I have a total leisure endowment of 60 hours per week.

Exercise 16A.16

Does this production frontier exhibit increasing, decreasing, or constant returns to scale? Is the marginal product of labor increasing, constant, or decreasing?

In panel (b) of the graph, we illustrate a set of indifference curves for me on a graph that again has labor hours on the horizontal and bananas on the vertical axis. Since we are illustrating these indifference curves with *labor* rather than *leisure* on the horizontal axis, I become better off as my consumption bundle shifts to the northwest of the graph, with less labor (i.e., more leisure) and more consumption.

Exercise 16A.17

As drawn, which of our usual assumptions about tastes—rationality, convexity, monotonicity, continuity—are violated?

The production frontier then describes the set of feasible consumption bundles from which I can choose, and panel (c) of the graph combines the first two panels to illustrate the optimal decision for me on this island. Once I reach the bundle that has me working 30 hours per week and consuming 72 bananas, I have reached the highest possible indifference curve that still contains at least 1 bundle that lies within my production choice set.

16A.3.2 Robinson Crusoe with a Split Personality So far, there isn't much of a market here; I am simply choosing my optimal bundle from my choice set, with no one trading anything at any particular prices. But now let's imagine that I have a split personality, with part of me acting only as a profit-maximizing producer and part of me acting only as a utility-maximizing consumer. Let's assume further that both parts of me behave as price-takers, taking as given the price of labor w and the price of bananas p.

In panel (a) of Graph 16.9, we then graph simply the producer's profit maximization problem, with isoprofit lines representing the indifference curves for me as a producer. This is identical to the single-input production analysis of Chapter 11 where each isoprofit line corresponds to all production plans that yield a given level of profit. As we derived in Chapter 11, the intercept of an isoprofit is equal to the profit π along that set of production plans divided by p, and the slope of each isoprofit is w/p. The profit-maximizing production plan A is one that hires 11 labor hours and produces 43 bananas per week.

In panel (b) of the graph, we then view the problem entirely from the perspective of me as a consumer who faces the price p for bananas and the wage w per labor hour. In addition, to whatever extent the firm is producing profits π, we will assume that I, as the owner of the firm, take that profit as part of the income I derive and can use for purchasing bananas, and we'll assume as we have done in previous chapters that I have a total endowment of 60 leisure hours per week that I can potentially devote to earning income (by selling leisure at the wage w).

Even if I do not work at all, I will have the profits of the firm available for spending on bananas. For instance, if my profits from the firm are $60 and the price of a banana is $p = 10$, I can purchase 6 bananas without expending any labor effort. Thus, my budget constraint starts at the intercept π/p. As I sell labor, I will earn a wage w with which I can buy additional bananas. I will earn w for the first hour I sell, which will permit me to buy w bananas if the price of a banana is $1 or w/p bananas if the price is given by p. Thus, the slope of my budget, starting at the intercept π/p, is w/p, and my budget constraint ends when I have sold all my 60 available leisure hours.

We can then add the indifference curves from Graph 16.8b to panel (b) of Graph 16.9 to find the optimal consumption bundle B given this budget constraint: 36 hours of labor and 94 bananas per week.

Graph 16.9: Robinson Crusoe as Price-Taking Producer and Consumer

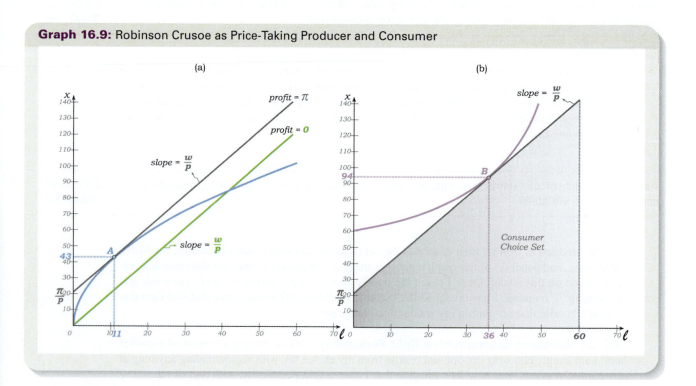

16A.3.3 Disequilibrium and Equilibrium in the Robinson Crusoe Economy

It should be immediately obvious from the two panels of Graph 16.9 that the wage and price that are being taken as given by me as a producer and me as a consumer are *not* equilibrium prices. As a producer, I want to hire 11 hours of labor to produce 43 bananas per week, but as a consumer I want to sell 36 hours of labor to consume 94 bananas per week. There is thus an *excess supply of labor* and an *excess demand for bananas* under this wage and price.

We can illustrate this disequilibrium in a single graph once we notice that the budget constraint in panel (b) of Graph 16.9 is exactly identical to the optimal isoprofit line in panel (a). Moving the two panels on top of each another, we get panel (a) of Graph 16.10, with the producer choosing bundle *A* that is feasible and the consumer choosing bundle *B* that is not feasible in this economy. In order for this economy to be in equilibrium, p and w have to change such that the optimal production plan for the producer coincides with the optimal consumption plan for the consumer.

Panel (b) then illustrates a combination of w^* and p^* that result in such an equilibrium. Here, both the producer and the consumer, taking w^* and p^* as given, choose optimal plans (point *C*) that result in demand equaling supply in both the labor and output markets.

16A.3.4 First and Second Welfare Theorems

Recall that a first welfare theorem is a theorem that specifies the conditions under which a competitive equilibrium is (Pareto) efficient. In an economy with a single individual, Pareto efficiency simply means that the single individual, our Robinson Crusoe, is doing the best he can given his circumstances. In Section 16A.3.1, we illustrated how I would choose the best possible bundle available to me on this deserted island: I simply found the highest indifference curve that still contained a consumption bundle that was feasible (in Graph 16.8). In panel (b) of Graph 16.10, on the other hand, we illustrated a competitive market equilibrium in which I maximize profits as a producer and maximize utility as a consumer, subject to market prices p^* and w^*. If you simply remove the isoprofit line (which doubles as the consumer budget constraint) in Graph 16.10b, you are left with exactly Graph 16.8c that illustrated

Graph 16.10: Disequilibrium and Equilibrium in the Robinson Crusoe Economy

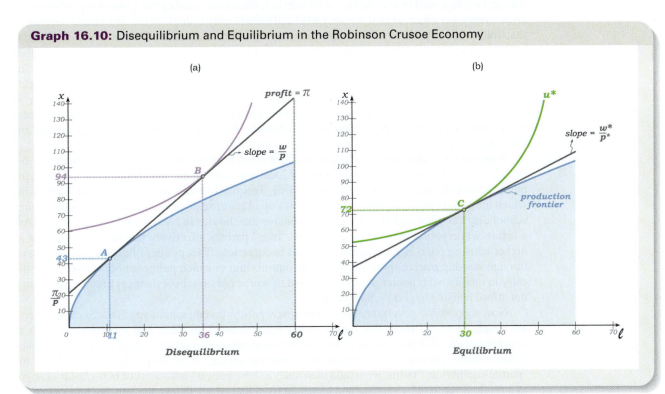

how I "do the best I can given my circumstances." Thus, *the competitive equilibrium in the Robinson Crusoe economy is Pareto efficient* and the first welfare theorem holds. Similarly, we can quickly see that the second welfare theorem holds in the Robinson Crusoe economy. Recall that a second welfare theorem says that any Pareto optimum in an economy can be supported as an equilibrium. A Pareto optimum simply looks like Graph 16.8c with an indifference curve tangent to the production frontier. But this means that we can fit a line that is tangent to both the production frontier and the optimal indifference curve, a line that defines a ratio w/p which results in this optimum being an equilibrium so long as the producer and consumer both take w and p as given. In end-of-chapter exercise 16.5, we will illustrate a caveat to this conclusion: The second welfare theorem is guaranteed to hold only if the production choice set and tastes are convex. (The same caveat applies to the second welfare theorem for exchange economies.)

16A.4 General Equilibrium Analysis and Policy

Public policy is often all about making large institutional changes in an economy, changes that alter the budget constraints faced by consumers, the production constraints faced by producers, and/or the prices faced by both. The first welfare theorem suggests that such policy changes will generate inefficiencies unless there are already distortionary forces at work and the policy is designed to combat the impact of these forces. Much of the remainder of the book is devoted to carefully analyzing the types of distortionary forces that invalidate the conclusions of the first welfare theorem and thus give rise to the possibility of nonmarket institutions improving efficiency.

But there is also a more general lesson that emerges from taking a general equilibrium view of policy analysis. As we will see in upcoming chapters, for instance, taxes and subsidies change the prices in particular markets. Sometimes, these changes happen in such a way that we can isolate a market and analyze it fruitfully without considering the general equilibrium in an economy, but often, even if a policy explicitly alters only a single price, individual decisions that follow then "spill over" in important ways into other markets. This complicates policy analysis considerably, but economists have shown that the general equilibrium effects (or the *unintended* consequences) that follow from a policy change are frequently more important than the initial partial equilibrium effects (or the *intended* consequences) that a policy maker might have at the forefront of his or her mind. Although the tools we have developed will not always allow us to demonstrate this to the extent to which more complex models can, we will see hints of this basic theme repeatedly in upcoming chapters. For now, however, I want to just offer an example of a case that has been important in some of my own research.

Suppose we want to analyze the way in which schools are financed. In the United States, public schools are financed by a combination of local and state taxes, and children are admitted to public schools based on where their parents live. This has resulted in a particular equilibrium in which the quality of local public schools shows up in housing prices, with houses in good public school districts often significantly more expensive than houses in bad public school districts. As a result, while public schools are nominally "free," parents effectively pay tuition by paying a higher housing price in good districts than in bad districts. This pricing of public school access through housing markets in turn supports an equilibrium in which public schools differ dramatically in quality, with poorer parents relegated to worse public school districts because they cannot afford housing in good school districts.

Now suppose the government considers a new policy: private school vouchers. Such vouchers are simply pieces of paper that have a dollar figure printed on them, and the holder of such a voucher can take this piece of paper and use it toward tuition in a private school (which the private school can then present to the government for reimbursement). If we simply think of this policy in "partial equilibrium" terms, we would then analyze how budget constraints of households change as a result of receiving a voucher and conclude from that who will take the voucher and switch to a private school. (This was done in end-of-chapter exercise 14.10.) But it turns out that such a partial equilibrium analysis will miss what are likely the most important effects resulting from the introduction of government-funded private school vouchers.

Think of it this way: Consider the "marginal" family that is stretching its budget to buy a relatively small house in a good school district in order to send the children to good public schools. Now this family receives a voucher that makes private schooling a real option. If the family chooses to use the voucher, why would it continue to pay the high premium on housing in the good public school district? The answer is that it would not, and that this family can likely find real housing bargains in a bad public school district now that it no longer cares about the public school in that district. Using the voucher for this family therefore implies a move to a larger house in another district, which in turn drives up demand for such housing and therefore causes an increase in housing prices in bad school districts (and a corresponding decrease in prices for houses in good school districts). This in turn implies that those who own houses in bad school districts will see an increase in their wealth (because their houses are worth more) while those who own houses in good school districts will see a decline in their wealth (as their housing prices fall). The introduction of private school vouchers, aimed at altering individual decisions about schooling, therefore causes general equilibrium price effects in housing markets, which in turn cause wealth effects that alter decisions individuals make. Research on this suggests that most families will be impacted more by these general equilibrium changes in housing markets than by the change in school markets, which implies that an analysis of school vouchers that ignores general equilibrium effects will lead to incorrect predictions about who benefits and who is hurt by this policy.[5]

In votes on referenda on school vouchers, researchers have found that renters vote differently than homeowners. Consider a renter and homeowner in a bad public school district. Who do you think will be more likely to favor the introduction of school vouchers and who do you think will be more likely to be opposed?

Exercise 16A.18

How do you think the elderly (who do not have children in school but who typically do own a home) will vote differently on school vouchers depending on whether they currently live in a good or bad public school district?

Exercise 16A.19

If you were considering opening up a private school following the introduction of private school vouchers, would you be more likely to open your school in poor or in rich districts?

Exercise 16A.20

Suppose two different voucher proposals were on the table: The first proposal limits eligibility for vouchers only to families below the poverty line, while the second limits eligibility to those families who live in bad public school districts. Which policy is more likely to lead to general equilibrium effects in housing markets?

Exercise 16A.21

This is just one example of how policy analysis that focuses too narrowly on partial equilibrium effects can be misleading. At this point, a general lesson from our example is simply that, after thinking through the partial equilibrium effects of a policy, we should ask carefully: Are there other markets that are likely to be impacted in significant ways by this policy? If so, how are these effects likely to change our predictions?

---

[5]See, for instance, T. Nechyba, "Mobility, Targeting and Private School Vouchers," *American Economic Review* 90, no. 1 (2000), 130–46.

16B The Mathematics of Competitive General Equilibrium

General equilibrium theory is one of the more mathematical branches of modern economics, and we will here only scratch the surface of a rich literature that evolved over the latter half of the 20th century. At its heart lie the basic insights developed intuitively in part A of this chapter—the nature of competitive equilibrium prices, the first and second welfare theorems and the idea that the "core" of an economy converges to the set of competitive equilibria if the economy gets large. We will show in this section how the basic model of an exchange economy can be formalized for many individuals and many goods, and we will prove somewhat more formally the first welfare theorem. But our main focus will be on demonstrating how we can use the basic tools we learned so far to calculate an equilibrium in both an exchange economy and a Robinson Crusoe economy.

16B.1 A Pure Exchange Economy

When we introduced the concept of an exchange economy in Section 16A.1, we defined it as *an economy in which there is no production and in which consumers are endowed with different bundles of goods.* More formally, we can define an exchange economy as a collection of consumers with preferences and endowments. Suppose, for instance, that the economy contains N consumers (denoted by $n = 1, 2, \ldots, N$) who choose among M goods (denoted by $m = 1, 2, \ldots, M$). An exchange economy is then fully defined by

$$(\{(e_1^n, e_2^n, \ldots, e_m^n)\}_{n=1}^N, \{u^n : \mathbb{R}^M \to \mathbb{R}^1\}_{n=1}^N), \tag{16.1}$$

where $(e_1^n, e_2^n, \ldots, e_m^n)$ gives the endowment of each of the M goods for individual n and $u^n : \mathbb{R}^M \to \mathbb{R}^1$ is individual n's utility function over the M goods. The notation $\{\ \}_{n=1}^N$ then simply indicates that whatever appears in the curly brackets is listed for each of the N different consumers in the economy.[6] It will be our convention in this chapter to let individuals appear as superscripts and goods as subscripts; thus e_m^n is read as "individual n's endowment of good m."

Suppose we returned to the example (from Section 16A.1) of me and my wife on a weekend getaway with oranges and bananas on a deserted island. In this case, $N = 2$ (since there are only two consumers) and $M = 2$ (since the only goods are oranges and bananas). In this example, I am endowed with 3 oranges and 6 bananas while my wife is endowed with 10 oranges and 4 bananas. Letting oranges be denoted by x_1 and bananas by x_2, and letting me be denoted by the superscript 1 and my wife by the superscript 2, we can then denote our endowments as $(e_1^1, e_2^1) = (3, 6)$ and $(e_1^2, e_2^2) = (10, 4)$. Furthermore, our tastes are represented by a utility function $u^1 : \mathbb{R}^2 \to \mathbb{R}^1$ for me and $u^2 : \mathbb{R}^2 \to \mathbb{R}^1$ for my wife, and in many of the graphs in Section A we have implicitly assumed that $u^1(x_1, x_2) = x_1^{3/4} x_2^{1/4}$ and $u^2(x_1, x_2) = x_1^{1/4} x_2^{3/4}$.

The endowment point in such an economy is, as we have seen in the Edgeworth Box, only one possible way of dividing the economy's endowment among the individuals in the economy. Any other allocation of goods between the individuals in the economy is *feasible* so long as we are not allocating more of each good than what is available overall. For any good m, we can define the economy's overall endowment E_m by simply adding up all the individual endowments; i.e.,

$$E_m = e_m^1 + e_m^2 + \ldots + e_m^N. \tag{16.2}$$

We can then define the *set of feasible allocations FA* in an exchange economy as

$$FA = \{\{(x_1^n, x_2^n, \ldots, x_M^n)\}_{n=1}^N \in \mathbb{R}_+^{NM} \mid x_m^1 + x_m^2 + \ldots + x_m^N = E_m \text{ for all } m = 1, 2, \ldots, M\}. \tag{16.3}$$

---

[6]An even "purer" form of defining an exchange economy would simply specify a preference ordering rather than a utility function representing that preference ordering for each consumer.

The statement to the left of the "|" sign simply states that the allocation has to specify how much of each of the M goods each individual is allocated. Since there are M goods and N individuals, this implies that we have to specify NM quantities, and thus a point in $\mathbb{R}_+^{NM}$. The statement following the "|" sign indicates that the sum of what is given out for each of the M goods must be equal to the overall endowment (of that good) that is available in the economy. We can then read the full statement in equation (16.3) as "the set of feasible allocations of goods to individuals is such that the total amount of each good that is allocated between the individuals is equal to the economy's endowment of that good." When $M = N = 2$ in our example, this set is equivalent to what we have drawn as the allocations in the Edgeworth Box and can be written formally as

$$FA = \{(x_1^1, x_2^1, x_1^2, x_2^2) \in \mathbb{R}_+^4 \mid x_1^1 + x_1^2 = 13 \text{ and } x_2^1 + x_2^2 = 10\}. \qquad (16.4)$$

Can you see how the Edgeworth Box we drew in Section A contains all the allocations in this set?

Exercise 16B.1

True or False: The Edgeworth Box represents a graphical technique that allows us to graph in a two-dimensional picture points that lie in four dimensions.

Exercise 16B.2

16B.1.1 Mutually Beneficial Trades

Before we engage in any trade, my wife and I can already achieve some level of "utility" by simply consuming our endowments. We can refer to the level of utility that we can attain on our own as our *reservation utility*. In order for trade to be mutually beneficial, it must be that the division of the economy's endowment that emerges from trade gives each one of us at least our reservation utility. Letting individual n's reservation utility be denoted by U^n, we can calculate the appropriate reservation utility value by simply evaluating utility at the endowment; i.e.,

$$U^n = u^n(e_1^n, e_2^n, \ldots, e_M^n). \qquad (16.5)$$

What are the reservation utilities for me and my wife in our example (given the utility functions previously specified)?

Exercise 16B.3

The set of allocations (of the economy's endowment) that is mutually beneficial for everyone in the economy (denoted MB) is then simply the set of feasible allocations that give each consumer at least his or her reservation utility; i.e.,

$$MB = \{\{(x_1^n, x_2^n, \ldots, x_M^n)\}_{n=1}^N \in FA \mid u^n(x_1^n, x_2^n, \ldots, x_M^n) \geq U^n \text{ for all } n = 1, 2, \ldots, N\}. \qquad (16.6)$$

The statement to the left of the "|" sign simply states that the allocation has to be a feasible allocation, while the statement after the "|" sign states that, given what each of the N individuals is given, it must be the case that everyone achieves at least his or her reservation utility. We can then read the full statement in equation (16.6) as "the set of mutually beneficial allocations is equal to the set of feasible allocations of goods to individuals such that each individual attains at least his or her reservation utility." This is equivalent to the set of allocations in the lens-shaped area between the indifference curves that pass through the endowment point in an Edgeworth Box.

For the example of me and my wife, write the set of mutually beneficial allocations in the form of equation (16.6). Can you see that the lens-shaped area identified in the Edgeworth Box in Graph 16.2 is equivalent to this set?

Exercise 16B.4

16B.1.2 The Contract Curve

As we saw in our development of the Edgeworth Box in Section A, not all mutually beneficial trades necessarily lead to a Pareto efficient allocation nor is it the case that all efficient allocations lie in the lens-shaped region of mutually beneficial trades. In Graph 16.2, for instance, my wife and I initially trade from our endowment to point E, but our indifference curves through point A still formed a lens-shaped area in which both of us could be made better off. Viewed from our initial endowment, point A was therefore mutually beneficial, but it was not efficient because we could still think of ways of making both of us better off. The allocation where my wife is given the entire endowment of the economy, on the other hand, is efficient because there is no way to make one of us better off without making the other worse off. At the same time, such an allocation is not mutually beneficial when viewed from our initial endowment.

To calculate the set of Pareto efficient allocations, or what we called the *contract curve*, we therefore had to find allocations in the Edgeworth Box where indifference curves are tangent to one another and thus no lens-shaped area of mutually beneficial trades is possible. We can define this set PE (for the more general setting of N individuals and M goods) as

$$PE = \{\{(x_1^n, x_2^n, \ldots, x_M^n)\}_{n=1}^N \in FA \mid \text{there does not exist } \{(y_1^n, y_2^n, \ldots, y_M^n)\}_{n=1}^N \in FA$$

$$\text{where } u^n(y_1^n, y_2^n, \ldots, y_M^n) \geq u^n(x_1^n, x_2^n, \ldots, x_M^n) \text{ for all } n = 1, 2, \ldots, N \quad (16.7)$$

$$\text{and } u^n(y_1^n, y_2^n, \ldots, y_M^n) > u^n(x_1^n, x_2^n, \ldots, x_M^n) \text{ for some } n\}.$$

Again, the statement to the left of the "|" sign simply states that the allocation has to be a feasible allocation. The statement following the left of the "|" sign then states that there does not exist another feasible allocation that makes everyone at least as well off and at least one person better off.

Exercise 16B.5

Can you see that no allocation in the set PE of an Edgeworth Box could have indifference curves pass through it in a way that creates a lens-shaped area between them?

Returning to the example of me and my wife with oranges and bananas, suppose again that our tastes can be represented by the utility functions $u^1(x_1, x_2) = x_1^{3/4} x_2^{1/4}$ and $u^2(x_1, x_2) = x_1^{1/4} x_2^{3/4}$ and our endowments by $(e_1^1, e_2^1) = (3, 6)$ and $(e_1^2, e_2^2) = (10, 4)$. Within the Edgeworth Box, if a consumption bundle (x_1^1, x_2^1) is given to me, it means that my wife received the remaining available goods; i.e., $(x_1^2, x_2^2) = (13 - x_1^1, 10 - x_2^1)$ (since the economy as a whole is endowed with 13 of the x_1 good and 10 of the x_2 good). A Pareto efficient allocation then occurs wherever our indifference curves are tangent to one another in the Edgeworth Box; i.e., wherever my marginal rate of substitution $MRS^1(x_1^1, x_2^1)$ is equal to my wife's $MRS^2(13 - x_1^1, 10 - x_2^1)$. For the utility functions specified for me and my wife, this tangency of our indifference curves then implies that

$$MRS^1(x_1^1, x_2^1) = \frac{3x_2^1}{x_1^1} = \frac{(10 - x_2^1)}{3(13 - x_1^1)} = MRS^2(13 - x_1^1, 10 - x_2^1). \quad (16.8)$$

Solving the middle part of expression (16.8) for x_2^1, we get

$$x_2^1 = \frac{10x_1^1}{(117 - 8x_1^1)}. \quad (16.9)$$

This equation represents all my consumption bundles for oranges and bananas where my indifference curve is exactly tangent to my wife's in the Edgeworth Box. In other words, equation (16.9) is the contract curve identified in Graph 16.3. More formally, we can use this equation to define the set PE for this exchange economy as

$$PE = \left\{ (x_1^1, x_2^1, x_1^2, x_2^2) \in \mathbb{R}_+^4 \mid x_2^1 = \frac{10x_1^1}{(117 - 8x_1^1)}, x_1^2 = 13 - x_1^1 \text{ and } x_2^2 = 10 - x_2^1 \right\}. \quad (16.10)$$

Exercise
16B.6

Verify that the contract curve we derived goes from one corner of the Edgeworth Box to the other.

A different way to find the contract curve would be to maximize my utility subject to the constraint that my wife's utility is held constant at utility level u^* and that her consumption bundle is whatever is left over after I have been given my consumption bundle. Put mathematically, this problem can be written as

Exercise
16B.7*

$$\max_{x_1, x_2} x_1^{3/4} x_2^{1/4} \text{ subject to } u^* = (13 - x_1)^{1/4}(10 - x_2)^{3/4}$$

(where we drop the superscripts given that all variables refer to my consumption). Demonstrate that this leads to the same solution as that derived in equation (16.9).

16B.1.3 The Core

The *core* of a two-person exchange economy was then defined in Section A as the set of Pareto efficient allocations that is also mutually beneficial given the endowments that individuals in the economy have. Put differently, the core in the two-person case is then simply the intersection of the set *MB* and *PE*; i.e.,

$$Core = MB \cap PE. \tag{16.11}$$

For the example of me and my wife, we can then define the core as the subset of the contract curve *PE* that contains allocations yielding utility above our reservation utilities. Our reservation utilities are simply found by plugging our endowments $(3, 6)$ and $(10, 4)$ into our utility functions, which gives reservation utilities of $U^1 = 3^{3/4}6^{1/4} = 3.57$ and $U^2 = 10^{1/4}4^{3/4} = 5.03$. The core can then be written as

$$Core = \{(x_1^1, x_2^1, x_1^2, x_2^2) \in PE \mid (x_1^1)^{3/4}(x_2^1)^{1/4} \geq 3.57 \text{ and } (x_1^2)^{1/4}(x_2^2)^{3/4} \geq 5.03\}. \tag{16.12}$$

This corresponds to the core allocations we derived graphically in Graph 16.4. Note, however, that this definition of the core as the intersection of *MB* and *PE* holds only for the case of two-person exchange economies. More generally, the core is defined as the set of allocations under which no "coalition" of individuals can do better on their own. With only two individuals, this is equivalent to saying that an allocation lies in the core when the two individuals cannot reallocate goods such that both are better off, leaving us with the intersection of *MB* and *PE*. In the appendix, we will treat the more general case of how the core of an exchange economy evolves when there are more than two individuals in the economy.

16B.1.4 Competitive Equilibrium

In our development of consumer theory, we drew a distinction between models in which income was *exogenously* given and models where income arose *endogenously* as the consumer sold some endowment. When income is exogenously given, the (uncompensated) demand function for some good m took the form $x_m(p_1, p_2, \ldots, p_M, I)$ where p_m represents the price of good m and I represents the exogenous income. When income is derived endogenously from endowments, the I term is replaced by the market value of the consumer's endowment, or $p_1 e_1 + p_2 e_2 + \ldots + p_M e_M$. In a two-good exchange economy in which trade is governed by prices, for instance, the demand for good m by individual n can then be expressed as $x_m^n(p_1, p_2, (p_1 e_1^n + p_2 e_2^n))$. To cut down on notation, we will assume a two-good, two-person exchange economy for the rest of this section, but you should be able to see that everything we are doing can be written more generally with additional notation.

In equilibrium, the market prices for goods have to then be such that supply is equal to demand. A consumer n becomes a *net supplier* of a good m if his or her demand at the market prices is less than his or her endowment (i.e., $x_m^n(p_1, p_2, (p_1 e_1^n + p_2 e_2^n)) - e_m^n < 0$), and the consumer becomes a *net demander* if his or her demand is greater than his or her endowment (i.e., $x_m^n(p_1, p_2, (p_1 e_1^n + p_2 e_2^n)) - e_m^n > 0$). Supply is then equal to demand whenever the amount supplied by net suppliers is cancelled out exactly by the amount demanded by net demanders. A set of equilibrium prices for a two-person, two-good exchange economy can therefore be defined as a set of prices (p_1, p_2) such that

$$(x_1^1(p_1, p_2, (p_1 e_1^1 + p_2 e_2^1)) - e_1^1) + (x_1^2(p_1, p_2, (p_1 e_1^2 + p_2 e_2^2)) - e_1^2) = 0$$
$$(x_2^1(p_1, p_2, (p_1 e_1^1 + p_2 e_2^1)) - e_2^1) + (x_2^2(p_1, p_2, (p_1 e_1^2 + p_2 e_2^2)) - e_2^2) = 0. \tag{16.13}$$

Alternatively, we can rewrite this same condition for equilibrium prices by adding the endowment terms to both sides to get

$$x_1^1(p_1, p_2, (p_1 e_1^1 + p_2 e_2^1)) + x_1^2(p_1, p_2, (p_1 e_1^2 + p_2 e_2^2)) = e_1^1 + e_1^2$$
$$x_2^1(p_1, p_2, (p_1 e_1^1 + p_2 e_2^1)) + x_2^2(p_1, p_2, (p_1 e_1^2 + p_2 e_2^2)) = e_2^1 + e_2^2; \tag{16.14}$$

i.e., aggregate demand for each good (on the left-hand side of the equations) is equal to the aggregate endowment of that good (on the right-hand side).

Suppose, for instance, that we return to the example of me and my wife, with my endowment $(e_1^1, e_2^1) = (3, 6)$, my wife's endowment $(e_1^2, e_2^2) = (10, 4)$, and with our tastes represented by the utility functions $u^1(x_1, x_2) = x_1^{3/4} x_2^{1/4}$ and $u^2(x_1, x_2) = x_1^{1/4} x_2^{3/4}$. Solving our optimization problems (using the value of our endowments as our "income"), we get demands

$$x_1^1(p_1, p_2) = \frac{3(3p_1 + 6p_2)}{4p_1} \text{ and } x_2^1(p_1, p_2) = \frac{(3p_1 + 6p_2)}{4p_2}$$
$$x_1^2(p_1, p_2) = \frac{(10p_1 + 4p_2)}{4p_1} \text{ and } x_2^2(p_1, p_2) = \frac{3(10p_1 + 4p_2)}{4p_2}. \tag{16.15}$$

....

**Exercise
16B.8**
     Verify that these are the correct demands for this problem.

....

We concluded in our discussion of the Edgeworth Box that a set of equilibrium prices in this exchange economy cannot be determined unless we normalize one of the prices because the budget constraints of each individual always go through the endowment point with slope $-p_1/p_2$. Put differently, if we find one set of equilibrium prices that give rise to the "right" slope to get both individuals to optimize at the same point in the Edgeworth Box, any other set of prices that give rise to the same ratio of prices will also work. Thus, all we can do is determine the *relative prices* that can create an equilibrium.

Consider the first of the two equations in expression (16.14): demand equal to supply for good 1. Plugging in the relevant expressions from (16.15), we get that

$$\frac{3(3p_1 + 6p_2)}{4p_1} + \frac{(10p_1 + 4p_2)}{4p_1} = 3 + 10, \tag{16.16}$$

which reduces to

$$p_2 = \frac{3}{2} p_1. \tag{16.17}$$

This implies that, in order for the good 1 market to be in equilibrium, the price of good 2 has to be 1.5 times the price of good 1. Normalizing p_1 to be equal to 1, p_2 then has to be equal to 3/2 in equilibrium.

....

**Exercise
16B.9**
     Write down the equilibrium condition in the x_2 market (from the second equation in expression (16.14)) using the appropriate expressions from (16.15) and solve for the equilibrium price ratio. You should get the same answer.

....

To determine what my wife and I will consume in equilibrium, we can then simply plug in the equilibrium prices $p_1 = 1$ and $p_2 = 3/2$ into the demand functions in expression (16.15) to get

$$(x_1^1, x_2^1) = (9, 2) \text{ and } (x_1^2, x_2^2) = (4, 8); \quad (16.18)$$

i.e., I end up consuming 9 oranges and 2 bananas while my wife ends up consuming 4 oranges and 8 bananas in equilibrium, precisely the equilibrium we depicted graphically in Graph 16.6.

The reason we can find only a price ratio (and not precise prices) without normalizing one of the prices first can be seen intuitively in our graphs of budget constraints with endowments in which the price ratio determines the slope of the budget and the endowment point determines its location in each consumer's optimization problem. Mathematically, this arises from the fact that *demand functions are homogeneous of degree 0 in prices*. So long as all prices rise by the same proportion, the consumer is just as well off because, while goods are more expensive, endowments are worth more. Thus, for any individual n and good m, $x_m^n(p_1, p_2, (p_1 e_1^n + p_2 e_2^n)) = x_m^n(t p_1, t p_2, (t p_1 e_1^n + t p_2 e_2^n))$ for any $t > 0$.

Demonstrate that the same equilibrium allocation of goods will arise if $p_1 = 2$ and p_2 is 1.5 times p_1; i.e., $p_2 = 3$.

Exercise 16B.10

A *competitive equilibrium* for an exchange economy is then defined as a set of prices and a set of allocations such that, at those prices, each individual in the economy will choose the equilibrium allocation and supply is equal to demand.[7]

Can you demonstrate that the equilibrium allocation we derived for me and my wife lies in the core that we defined in equation (16.12)?

Exercise 16B.11

16B.1.5 Walras' Law In our calculation of the competitive equilibrium for the two-person, two-good economy, you might have wondered why it is that we do not need to solve the system of the two equations in expression (16.14) to solve for the equilibrium price ratio. Rather, each of the two equilibrium equations individually yielded the same result. The reason for this is that we implicitly have a third equation that is a natural consequence of individuals optimizing.

To be more precise, we know that the budget constraint for each individual *binds* at the optimum; i.e. that at the optimum a consumer's indifference curve is tangent to the budget constraint. Mathematically, this can be stated for consumer n simply as $p_1 x_1^n + p_2 x_2^n = p_1 e_1^n + p_2 e_2^n$; i.e., spending (on the left-hand side) for consumer n is equal to income (on the right-hand side). But if this holds for each individual consumer, it also holds for the economy as a whole: *the aggregate budget constraint for the economy binds*. In the two-person, two-good economy, this aggregate budget constraint for the economy simply becomes

$$p_1(x_1^1 + x_1^2) + p_2(x_2^1 + x_2^2) = p_1(e_1^1 + e_1^2) + p_2(e_2^1 + e_2^2). \quad (16.19)$$

---

[7]Several technical issues related to competitive equilibria in exchange economies are not discussed here. One issue relates to the *existence* of such equilibria. A formal proof of the conditions under which competitive equilibria in fact exist can be found in graduate texts such as MasColel, Whinston, and Green (1996). The main condition that is required is that tastes are convex, and one of the end-of-chapter exercises will demonstrate that such equilibria might not exist when tastes are non-convex. A second issue relates to *uniqueness* of equilibria. Under what condition is there only a single competitive equilibrium allocation? Again, you can find formal treatments of this in graduate texts, but in general there might be more than a single such equilibrium allocation. However, with the functional forms for utility that we use in this text, there will generally be a single equilibrium in our examples. Finally, economists have worried about conditions under which equilibria are *stable*, and again you will find treatments of the conditions under which stability arises in graduate texts. For examples in this text, the equilibrium is always stable.

The condition is known as *Walras' Law*.[8] Since it follows directly from individual optimizing behavior, it is implicit that when we write down the first equation in expression (16.14), the second equation will hold; i.e., demand equals supply in the good 1 market necessarily implies that demand equals supply in the good 2 market. It is for this reason that we can simply solve one of the two equations in expression (16.14) to solve for the equilibrium price ratio.

More generally, if we are dealing with an N-person, M-good exchange economy, we can write down M different "demand equals supply" equations such as those in expression (16.14), but because of Walras' Law, we only need to solve $(M-1)$ equations to find the relative prices for the M goods because if "demand equals supply" holds in $(M-1)$ markets, it necessarily holds in the last market.

16B.2 The Fundamental Welfare Theorems and Other Results

As in Section A of this chapter, we will now turn to some of the main results of general equilibrium theory, results that establish a benchmark for when we can think of market economies as efficient. These results include the first welfare theorem, the second welfare theorem, and the core convergence theorem.

16B.2.1 The First Welfare Theorem

The first welfare theorem simply states that (under certain conditions) the competitive equilibrium is efficient. We saw the result intuitively for a two-person, two-good exchange economy within the context of the Edgeworth Box. We will now prove it a bit more formally using the notation we have developed thus far and will again confine ourselves to the case of a two-person, two-good exchange economy in order to keep the notation to a minimum. The exact same logic, however, can be used to demonstrate the first welfare theorem for an N-person, M-good exchange economy, although the notation gets a little more involved.

Suppose, then, that $\{p_1, p_2, x_1^1, x_2^1, x_1^2, x_2^2\}$ is a competitive equilibrium for an exchange economy defined by $\{e_1^1, e_2^1, e_1^2, e_2^2, u^1, u^2\}$, where u^1 and u^2 are utility functions that represent the two individuals' tastes. We will use what is known as a *proof by contradiction* (also known in Latin as *reductio ad absurdum*) to illustrate that the equilibrium allocation $(x_1^1, x_2^1, x_1^2, x_2^2)$ must be Pareto efficient. A "proof by contradiction" is a logical method of proving a statement to be true by assuming that it is not true and showing how that assumption leads to a logical contradiction. If we can show that assuming the statement to be untrue leads to a logical contradiction, we have then shown that the statement must be true.

So, suppose the equilibrium allocation $(x_1^1, x_2^1, x_1^2, x_2^2)$ is *not* efficient. This would imply that there must exist another feasible allocation of the economy's goods that makes no one worse off and at least one person better off. Let's call that allocation $(y_1^1, y_2^1, y_1^2, y_2^2)$. Suppose that in fact both individuals are better off under this allocation (as opposed to the equilibrium allocation). Since each individual did the best he or she could at the equilibrium prices (p_1, p_2) to get to the equilibrium allocation, it must be that (y_1^1, y_2^1) is not affordable for individual 1 at the equilibrium prices and (y_1^2, y_2^2) is not affordable for individual 2 under those prices. Thus

$$p_1 y_1^1 + p_2 y_2^1 > p_1 x_1^1 + p_2 x_2^1 \text{ and } p_1 y_1^2 + p_2 y_2^2 > p_1 x_1^2 + p_2 x_2^2. \tag{16.20}$$

Adding each side of these inequalities together then implies

$$p_1(y_1^1 + y_1^2) + p_2(y_2^1 + y_2^2) > p_1(x_1^1 + x_1^2) + p_2(x_2^1 + x_2^2). \tag{16.21}$$

The right-hand side of this equation is the same as the left-hand side of equation (16.19), which is Walras' Law. Thus, equations (16.19) and (16.21) imply

---

$$p_1(y_1^1 + y_1^2) + p_2(y_2^1 + y_2^2) > p_1(e_1^1 + e_1^2) + p_2(e_2^1 + e_2^2), \tag{16.22}$$

which can be rewritten as

$$p_1(y_1^1 + y_1^2 - e_1^1 - e_1^2) + p_2(y_2^1 + y_2^2 - e_2^1 - e_2^2) > 0. \tag{16.23}$$

Since prices are positive, this then implies that $(y_1^1 + y_1^2 - e_1^1 - e_1^2)$ or $(y_2^1 + y_2^2 - e_2^1 - e_2^2)$ or both are greater than zero, which in turn implies that $(y_1^1 + y_1^2) > (e_1^1 + e_1^2)$ and/or $(y_2^1 + y_2^2) > (e_2^1 + e_2^2)$. But that implies that the allocation $(y_1^1, y_2^1, y_1^2, y_2^2)$ is not feasible because it allocates more than the economy has of at least one of the goods. So, assuming that there exists a feasible allocation $(y_1^1, y_2^1, y_1^2, y_2^2)$ that is preferred by everyone to the equilibrium allocation $(x_1^1, x_2^1, x_1^2, x_2^2)$ leads to a logical contradiction, which implies that there cannot be such a universally more preferred allocation. Thus, the equilibrium allocation $(x_1^1, x_2^1, x_1^2, x_2^2)$ must in fact be efficient.

In our proof, we began by assuming that there exists an allocation $(y_1^1, y_2^1, y_1^2, y_2^2)$ that is strictly preferred by everyone to $(x_1^1, x_2^1, x_1^2, x_2^2)$ and showed that there cannot be such an allocation within this economy. Can you see how the same logic also goes through if we assume that there exists an allocation $(z_1^1, z_2^1, z_1^2, z_2^2)$ that is strictly preferred by one of the individuals while leaving the other indifferent to $(x_1^1, x_2^1, x_1^2, x_2^2)$?

Exercise 16B.12*

For the more complicated setting of N individuals and M goods, the same steps we just went through will lead to the conclusion that any allocation that is at least as good as the equilibrium for everyone and better for at least one person will similarly lead to the conclusion that this alternative allocation will not be feasible given the economy's endowment.

Can you demonstrate that this is in fact the case for an N-person, M-good economy?

Exercise 16B.13*

16B.2.2 The Second Welfare Theorem

The formal proof of the second welfare theorem, which states that there always exists a redistribution of the economy's endowment such that any point on the contract curve can be supported as a competitive equilibrium after the redistribution, is somewhat more difficult. It furthermore assumes that tastes are convex (which the first welfare theorem does not require).[9] We will forego a formal demonstration of this here,[10] but the intuition is relatively straightforward. For instance, one could redistribute the endowment so that it coincides with the Pareto efficient allocation on the contract curve and then demonstrate that there exists a set of prices such that each individual would in fact choose to remain at this new endowment point. (Of course any other endowment allocation on the budget lines formed in this way would also work.)

The first welfare theorem is powerful in that it tells us that there are conditions under which a competitive equilibrium is efficient. The second welfare theorem, as we discussed in Section A, is somewhat less powerful because it assumes that we can redistribute endowments without cost; i.e., that there exist what we have previously called "lump sum taxes" that do not give rise to substitution effects. It furthermore assumes that we have enough information about the individuals in the economy to be able to redistribute in just the right way to get our preferred point on the contract curve to emerge as an equilibrium. Nevertheless, the second welfare theorem suggests that, so long as redistribution of endowments is possible, competitive markets can be used to

---

[9]In end-of-chapter exercise 16.5, you will be asked to investigate why convexity of tastes is not necessary for the first welfare theorem but is necessary for the second welfare theorem in an Edgeworth Box setting of a two-person, two-good economy.
[10]The interested reader is referred to graduate texts such as MasColel, Whinston, and Green (1996).

achieve a "fairer" equilibrium outcome than the one that might emerge from the initial distribution of endowments in an economy. Put differently, the mere fact that we might think endowments are "unfairly" distributed does not imply that markets cannot still play an important efficiency role after redistribution has taken place.

16B.2.3 Equilibrium and the Core

Once we are convinced of the first welfare theorem in an exchange economy, it is almost immediately obvious that the competitive equilibrium of a two-person exchange economy must lie within the "core" of the economy. Remember that when the economy has only two consumers, the core is just the subset of the Pareto efficient allocations that is mutually preferred by each individual to his or her endowment. The first welfare theorem guarantees that the competitive equilibrium is Pareto efficient. Furthermore, the logic of individual optimization implies that each individual willingly agrees to give up his or her endowment to move to the equilibrium allocation under the equilibrium prices. After all, each individual always has the option of simply not trading and consuming his or her endowment regardless of what the prices in the economy are. Therefore, it must be the case that the equilibrium allocation is at least as good for each individual as that individual's endowment. Thus, the equilibrium allocation lies in the Pareto efficient set PE (i.e., on the contract curve) *and* is mutually agreed as better than the endowment allocation by all market participants.[11]

The second result involving competitive equilibria and the core is that, as an economy expands in the sense of having many individuals of each type, the core shrinks to the set of competitive equilibria. This is known as the *core convergence theorem*. We leave an intuitive demonstration of this result to the appendix of this chapter. Since the set of core allocations is the set of allocations that might feasibly arise from bargaining by individuals and groups, the core convergence theorem then tells us that when competition in bargaining becomes sufficiently intense because of the large number of consumers, each person's bargaining power is reduced sufficiently for the outcome of any bargaining process to become identical to the outcome of competitive behavior in markets.

16B.3 A Simple "Robinson Crusoe" Production Economy

In Section A, we illustrated graphically how we can think of a simple economy in which I am the only person choosing to use some of my leisure time to produce bananas. As suggested there, this is once again not an economy that is meant to be realistic, but it represents the simplest possible way of introducing production into a general equilibrium model and allows us to generate the basic insights that continue to hold in more complex settings.

16B.3.1 Robinson Crusoe "Doing the Best He Can"

In Graph 16.8, we illustrated how I would arrive at my optimal consumption plan—the optimal amount of labor effort to expend in order to generate banana consumption—given the circumstances I encounter on the deserted island. Suppose, for instance, that the production frontier is defined by the production function

$$x = f(\ell) = A\ell^\beta, \tag{16.24}$$

and suppose that my tastes can be summarized by the utility function

$$u\big(x, (L - \ell)\big) = x^\alpha (L - \ell)^{(1-\alpha)}. \tag{16.25}$$

Note that we are denoting *labor hours* by ℓ but defining utility over leisure which is the difference between a leisure endowment L and labor hours ℓ. My optimization problem is then to maximize utility subject to the production constraint that I face and can be written as

---

[11]The logic in this paragraph holds for two-person exchange economies. In larger economies, the result that the equilibrium lies in the core still holds, but the logic behind the result is more involved. The reason for this is that the core is the set of allocations such at any *subgroup* in the economy cannot do better with their endowment by segregating from the larger economy. Subgroups in two-person economies are just individuals, which implies that the core requirement reduces to the requirement that each person cannot do better by going off on his or her own with his or her endowment.

$$\max_{x,\ell} x^\alpha (L - \ell)^{(1-\alpha)} \text{ subject to } x = A\ell^\beta. \tag{16.26}$$

Setting up the corresponding Lagrange function, taking first order conditions and solving these in the usual way, we get

$$\ell = \frac{\alpha\beta L}{1 - \alpha(1 - \beta)} \text{ and } x = A\left(\frac{\alpha\beta L}{1 - \alpha(1 - \beta)}\right)^\beta. \tag{16.27}$$

Verify the results in equation (16.27).

Exercise 16B.14

In Graphs 16.8 through 16.10, for instance, we used these functional forms, with $A = 13.15, \beta = 0.5, \alpha = 2/3$ and $L = 60$. Plugging these into equation (16.27), we get the result that I would choose 30 hours of work and banana consumption of 72 (as illustrated in Graph 16.9).

16B.3.2 Robinson Crusoe as Consumer and Producer

In Section A, we next considered a competitive economy in which I determine how many bananas to produce separately from how many I will consume based on market prices for labor and bananas. As a producer, I therefore take the price of bananas p and the wage w as given and solve the profit maximization problem

$$\max_{x,\ell} px - w\ell \text{ subject to } x = f(\ell) = A\ell^\beta, \tag{16.28}$$

which can alternatively be written (by substituting the constraint into the objective function) as

$$\max_{\ell} pA\ell^\beta - w\ell. \tag{16.29}$$

Solving this, we get optimal input demand ℓ^D for the profit-maximizing firm as

$$\ell^D(w,p) = \left(\frac{\beta pA}{w}\right)^{1/(1-\beta)}, \tag{16.30}$$

and plugging this into the production function in equation (16.24), we get output supply

$$x^S(w,p) = A\left(\frac{\beta pA}{w}\right)^{\beta/(1-\beta)}. \tag{16.31}$$

Verify that this is the correct solution.

Exercise 16B.15

The supply side of the labor market and the demand side of the banana market are then determined by my behavior as a consumer. Since I own the firm, I not only generate income by selling leisure but I also receive the weekly profits of the firm. We can calculate these profits by simply subtracting labor costs $w\ell^D(w,p)$ from revenues $px^S(w,p)$ to get the profit function

$$\pi(w,p) = (1 - \beta)(Ap)^{1/(1-\beta)}\left(\frac{\beta}{w}\right)^{\beta/(1-\beta)}. \tag{16.32}$$

The income I have as a consumer to spend on bananas is therefore equal to $\pi(w,p)$ plus the labor income I derive from giving up leisure. Assuming a total of L leisure hours are available per week, this allows us to write my consumer utility maximization problem as

$$\max_{x,\ell} u\left(x,(L - \ell)\right) = x^\alpha (L - \ell)^{(1-\alpha)} \text{ subject to } px = w\ell + \pi(w,p). \tag{16.33}$$

Solving this in the usual way (which requires some tedious algebra), we can derive my labor supply as

$$\ell^S(w,p) = \alpha L - \frac{(1-\alpha)\pi(w,p)}{w} = \alpha L - \frac{(1-\alpha)(1-\beta)}{\beta}\left(\frac{\beta pA}{w}\right)^{1/(1-\beta)}, \quad (16.34)$$

and my demand for bananas as

$$x^D(w,p) = \frac{\alpha}{p}\Big(wL + \pi(w,p)\Big) = \frac{\alpha w}{p}\left(L + \frac{(1-\beta)}{\beta}\left(\frac{\beta pA}{w}\right)^{1/(1-\beta)}\right). \quad (16.35)$$

Exercise 16B.16 Verify that these solutions for labor supply and banana demand are correct.

We have thus derived demand and supply equations for both the labor and the banana market. These presume that I behave as a price-taker in both markets in both my roles as consumer and producer, and in general there is no reason to think that supply will equal demand for some arbitrarily chosen w and p. For instance, in Graph 16.9, we illustrate a set of prices in the economy at which I will choose to produce 43 bananas per week using 11 labor hours (production plan A in the graph), but in my role as a consumer I will demand 94 bananas and supply 36 hours of labor (consumption plan B in the graph). You can check for yourself that this is the approximate outcome when $A = 13.15, \beta = 0.5, \alpha = 2/3$ and $L = 60$ and when the output price p is 10 and the wage is 20 (as was assumed when drawing the graph).[12]

16B.3.3 Equilibrium in the Robinson Crusoe Economy

In order to calculate equilibrium prices for this simple economy, we then have to ensure that demand is equal to supply in the labor and output markets. Since the two markets are related to one another, it should however be intuitive that equilibrium in one of the markets necessarily implies that the other market is also in equilibrium (much as we found in the exchange economy). This is most easily seen in our graphical depiction of an equilibrium in Graph 16.10 where we illustrated how the optimal isoprofit line for the firm is also the budget constraint for the consumer, with the equilibrium arising from the simultaneous tangency of the isoprofit line and the optimal indifference curve with the production frontier.

By setting ℓ^D from equation (16.30) equal to ℓ^S from equation (16.34), we can then solve for the equilibrium wage w^* in terms of the output price p. This gives us

$$w^* = \beta A\left(\frac{1-\alpha(1-\beta)}{\alpha\beta L}\right)^{(1-\beta)} p. \quad (16.36)$$

Alternatively, we can solve for the equilibrium relationship between w and p in the banana market by setting x^S from equation (16.31) equal to x^D from equation (16.35) and, if we do the math right, we get exactly the same expression as we did by solving for equilibrium prices in the labor market.

Exercise 16B.17** Verify that the same equilibrium relationship between prices and wages arises by solving $x^S = x^D$.

---

[12]These solutions are approximate. The actual solutions are 10.81 for labor demand, 43.23 for output supply, 36.40 for labor supply, and 94.41 for output demand.

As in the case of exchange economies, we therefore can only solve for the equilibrium price ratio, and any set of w and p that satisfies this ratio can support an equilibrium in the economy. For the values $A = 13.15, \beta = 0.5, \alpha = 2/3$ and $L = 60$ used in the graphs of Section A, equation (16.37) then becomes

$$w^* = 1.2004p, \tag{16.37}$$

implying that any set of prices such that wage is approximately 1.2 times price will result in an equilibrium in the labor and banana market. For instance, if $p = 10$ and $w = 12$, you can verify that labor demand and supply will be equal to 30 hours per week and banana supply and demand will be 72 bananas per week. Similarly, you can verify that the same holds whether $p = 1$ and $w = 1.2$ or $p = 2$ and $w = 2.4$ (subject to some small rounding error).

Can you tell from the graph of an equilibrium in Graph 16.10 that any combination of w and p that satisfies a particular ratio will generate the same equilibrium in the labor and banana markets?

Exercise 16B.18

Can you tell from the graph of an equilibrium in Graph 16.10 whether profit will be affected by different choices of w and p that satisfy the equilibrium ratio? Verify whether your intuition holds mathematically.

Exercise 16B.19

16B.3.4 Welfare Theorems in the Robinson Crusoe Economy

We have already illustrated in Section A the intuition behind the first and second welfare theorems in the context of our Robinson Crusoe economy and therefore won't add much more here. You should notice with great glee, however, that our mathematical example already illustrates this for the particular functional forms we have chosen. In particular, we solved (in Section 16B.3.1) for the optimum, or the Pareto efficient outcome, when we simply asked how I would choose to optimize in the absence of looking separately at production and consumption decisions. This resulted in the labor and banana consumption bundle described in equation (16.27), with $\ell = 30$ and $x = 72$ when $A = 13.15, \beta = 0.5, \alpha = 2/3$ and $L = 60$ (as is the case for the graphs in Section A). Plugging the expression for w^* from equation (16.37) into the expression for labor demand ℓ^D from equation (16.30) (or alternatively plugging w^* into the expression for labor supply ℓ^S from equation (16.34)), we can quite easily derive the equilibrium labor supply and demand as

$$\ell = \frac{\alpha \beta L}{1 - \alpha(1 - \beta)}, \tag{16.38}$$

which is exactly what we concluded in equation (16.27) is the efficient level of labor. You can similarly verify that the equilibrium wage w^* results in the optimal level of banana consumption. Thus, the Pareto efficient allocation in this problem is the same as the equilibrium allocation, and the equilibrium is the same as the Pareto optimum.

Demonstrate that the equilibrium banana consumption (and production) is equal to the optimal level of banana consumption.

Exercise 16B.20

CONCLUSION

We have now extended—from a partial equilibrium to a general equilibrium setting—the result from Chapter 15 that, when there are no distorting forces in place, a competitive equilibrium results in an efficient allocation of scarce resources. As suggested repeatedly in this chapter, this result is considerably more general than may be apparent at first. It holds for economies with many goods, many consumers, and many producers. While we have demonstrated the result in simple settings, the more general results typically involve simply additional notation. The insight furthermore extends to settings that involve consumption over different time periods, with a simple addition of time subscripts on consumption goods leading to very similar proofs. What we are left with is the general result that, assuming no distortionary forces mentioned at the end of Chapter 15, competitive markets allocate scarce resources efficiently. In addition, the relationship between the core and the set of competitive equilibrium allocations suggests that, when economies are large, subgroups of individuals will never be able to bargain their way to outcomes that are better for them than what they get under competitive markets. The "price-taking" assumption required for competitive equilibrium is therefore quite sound as economies get large.

We have also indicated throughout that efficiency is not necessarily the only standard by which we want to judge an economy. Efficient allocations of resources may be judged to be "unfair" under many ethical standards if they result in large inequalities across individuals. The second welfare theorem, however, suggests that even when this is the case, an important role for competitive markets remains. In particular, to the extent to which governments can redistribute endowments efficiently (in a lump sum way), a more equitable redistribution of endowments will allow markets to reach "fairer" allocations of scarce resources that will once again be efficient. To the extent to which governments create inefficiencies by redistributing, however, a trade-off between equity and efficiency emerges. But even then, the efficiency role of markets remains— with distortionary redistribution shrinking the "pie," but with market prices once again getting us to an efficient outcome within the now smaller pie.

We will now turn to a final issue individuals face in real-world markets in which there are no distortionary forces in place. So far, throughout this book, we have assumed that individuals operate in a world without risk. In the real world, of course, individuals often have to make decisions in risky environments. Having developed our theory of individual decision making as well as our theory of competitive markets in the absence of risk, we can now turn in the next chapter to an investigation of how the introduction of risk introduces additional complexity to our models. We will find that, once again, so long as there are no distortionary forces in place, a new set of competitive markets (that deal with risk) will ensure efficiency.

APPENDIX: CORE CONVERGENCE

We have shown within this chapter that the competitive equilibrium of a two-person exchange economy lies inside the set of core allocations. We also stated a second result: As exchange economies get "large," the set of core allocations shrinks to the set of competitive equilibrium allocations. Thus, *in the limit, the set of core allocations is equivalent to the set of competitive equilibrium allocations*, a result known as *core convergence* or *core equivalence*.

A core allocation has the property that there is no way any individual *or any coalition of individuals* can improve their well-being by separating from the larger economy with their endowment. If we expect that individuals will always search for ways to make themselves better off, we would therefore expect core allocations to be the ones that emerge in economies where voluntary trade among individuals is permitted. The core convergence result then states that, for large economies, the *only* set of allocations that we would expect to emerge are those that arise under trades governed by competitive prices.

We can begin to get some intuition for why the set of core allocations in an economy shrinks as the economy grows by beginning with a two-person, two-good exchange economy just like the ones we have discussed throughout the chapter. In Graph 16.11, point E represents the endowment of the two individuals, and the grey indifference curves labeled U^1 and U^2 represent the reservation utility levels of the two individuals respectively. The grey curve connecting the two origins of the Edgeworth Box represents the contract curve, and the darkened region between points A and B represents the set of core allocations.

Now suppose that we "replicate" the economy; i.e., we consider a four-person, two-good exchange economy in which we have two individuals of "type 1" and two individuals of "type 2." Individuals of the same type are assumed to have the same tastes and the same endowments. A core allocation in this replicated economy has to have the property that there does not exist a coalition of several individuals in the economy that can, by trading with one another, do better than the individuals do under the core allocation.

We can now check whether a point like A which is a core allocation in the two-person economy is still a core allocation in the four-person (replicated) economy. Suppose allocation A is proposed, with each of the individuals getting the number of goods indicated by A as read off the relevant axes. Now suppose that as they consider whether to agree to move from E to A, the two "type 1" individuals get together with one of the "type 2" individuals to see if together they can make each other better off than they would be at A. For instance, starting at E, the "type 1" individuals might propose terms of trade under which they give up one x_1

Graph 16.11: End Points of Core no Longer in the Core as the Economy Expands

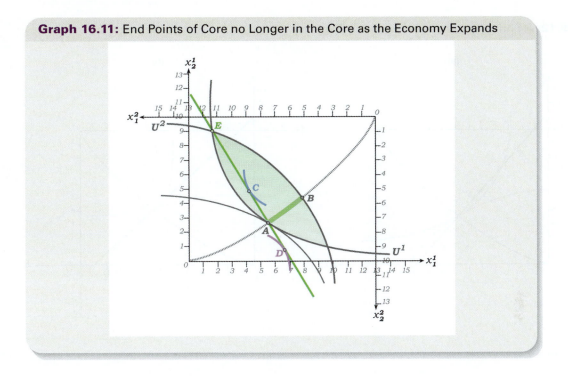

good for every one x_2 good they each receive. This implies that individual 2 would agree to accept 2 x_1 goods in exchange for two x_2 goods because there are two of "type 1" and one of "type 2". Any trade that is made under these terms then implies that the new "type 2" allocation (after the trade) is twice as far from E on the budget line (that incorporates the proposed terms of trade) as the new "type 1" allocation.

Suppose, then, that the subgroup composed of two "type 1" and one "type 2" individuals agrees to trade in such a way that "type 1" individuals end up at C and the "type 2" individual ends up at D (which is twice as far from E as C) in Graph 16.11. Again, this is logically possible for this three-person coalition; they are simply reallocating what they had at point E. But this means that the "type 1" individuals will end up moving to the blue indifference curve while the one "type 2" individual moves to the magenta indifference curve; i.e., all three individuals in the coalition are better off after trading with each other than than they would be at point A. Thus, the allocation at point A is *not* in the core for the four-person economy even though it is in the core for the two-person economy. Economists would say that "the coalition of two 'type 1' individuals and one 'type 2' individual *blocks* the proposed allocation A," and they would refer to this coalition as a *blocking coalition*.

Why is there no coalition to block A in the two-person version of this economy?

Exercise
16B.21

Can you demonstrate that a coalition of two of the "type 2" individuals with one "type 1" individual will block the allocation B?

Exercise
16B.22*

Now suppose you made the line through E a little shallower, as in panel (a) of Graph 16.12. This moves the intersection of the line further into the core of the two-person economy to point A' (which therefore lies on the blue indifference curve above E for "type 1" individuals). You should be able to convince yourself that it will still be possible for the coalition of two "type 1" consumers and one "type 2" consumer to continue blocking the core allocation that lies on this shallower line. The distance between E and C' represents a trade that the two "type 1" individuals would be willing to make, while the distance from E to D' represents the corresponding trade the one individual of "type 2" would be willing to accept. Thus, the coalition of two "type 1" individuals and one "type 2" individual will block the allocation A' in the four-person exchange economy.

Graph 16.12: A Shrinking Core as the Economy Expands

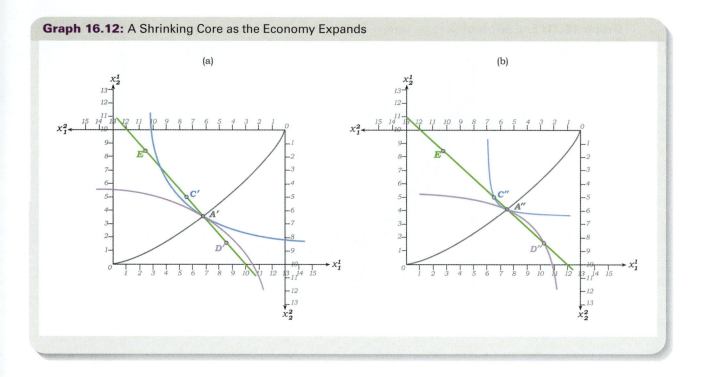

Exercise 16B.23*
Why must the distance between E and D' be twice the distance from E to C'?

If, however, the line becomes sufficiently shallow, it will no longer be possible for this coalition to block the two-person core allocation on that line. This is illustrated in panel (b) of Graph 16.12. Here, a trade from E to C'' leaves "type 1" individuals just as well off as they are under the allocation A'' on the contract curve, and the corresponding trade from E to D'' for the "type 2" individual leaves him or her also just as well off as under A''. Any smaller trade would make the "type 1" individuals worse off than at A'', while any larger trade would make the "type 2" individual worse off than at A''. Thus, there are no trades from the two "type 1" individuals to the one "type 2" individual that will make anyone in the coalition better off without making someone else worse off, which implies that the coalition will no longer block A'', and A'' is therefore in the core of the four-person exchange economy. The core is thus shrinking but not disappearing. In particular, the core is (as we have just shown) shrinking from below, and it is shrinking from above for analogous reasons. However, I will leave it as an exercise for you to demonstrate that the equilibrium allocation remains in the new, smaller core.

Exercise 16B.24*
Demonstrate that the competitive equilibrium allocation must lie in the core of the replicated exchange economy.

As the economy is replicated further, with additional "type 1" and "type 2" individuals joining the economy, the number of possible blocking coalitions increases. The coalition previously discussed still exists, which implies that the core is no larger than it was when we had two consumers of each type. But the increase in the number of other possible coalitions implies that further allocations that were previously in the core are blocked by some new coalition. You should be able to see, however, that the equilibrium allocation always remains in the core. While we won't demonstrate this formally here, the important result that can be proven rigorously is that, as the economy becomes larger, the set of core allocations ultimately shrinks down to just the set of equilibrium allocations.

END-OF-CHAPTER EXERCISES

16.1 Consider a two-person, two-good exchange economy in which person 1 is endowed with (e_1^1, e_2^1) and person 2 is endowed with (e_1^2, e_2^2) of the goods x_1 and x_2.

A. Suppose that tastes are homothetic for both individuals.

    a. Draw the Edgeworth Box for this economy, indicating on each axis the dimensions of the box.

    b. Suppose that the two individuals have identical tastes. Illustrate the contract curve; i.e., the set of all efficient allocations of the two goods.

    c. *True or False*: Identical tastes in the Edgeworth Box imply that there are no mutually beneficial trades.

    d.* Now suppose that the two individuals have different (but still homothetic) tastes. *True or False*: The contract curve will lie to one side of the line that connects the lower left and upper right corners of the Edgeworth Box; i.e., it will never cross this line inside the Edgeworth Box.

B. Suppose that the tastes for individuals 1 and 2 can be described by the utility functions $u^1 = x_1^\alpha x_2^{(1-\alpha)}$ and $u^2 = x_1^\beta x_2^{(1-\beta)}$ (where α and β both lie between 0 and 1). Some of the following questions are notationally a little easier to keep track of if you also denote $E_1 = e_1^1 + e_1^2$ as the economy's endowment of x_1 and $E_2 = e_2^1 + e_2^2$ as the economy's endowment of x_2.

    a. Let $\bar{x}_1$ denote the allocation of x_1 to individual 1, and let $\bar{x}_2$ denote the allocation of x_2 to individual 1. Then use the fact that the remainder of the economy's endowment is allocated to individual 2 to denote individual 2's allocation as $(E_1 - \bar{x}_1)$ and $(E_2 - \bar{x}_2)$ for x_1 and x_2 respectively. Derive the contract curve in the form $\bar{x}_2 = x_2(\bar{x}_1)$; i.e., with the allocation of x_2 to person 1 as a function of the allocation of x_1 to person 1.

    b. Simplify your expression under the assumption that tastes are identical; i.e., $\alpha = \beta$. What shape and location of the contract curve in the Edgeworth Box does this imply?

    c. Next, suppose that $\alpha \neq \beta$. Verify that the contract curve extends from the lower left to the upper right corner of the Edgeworth Box.

    d. Consider the slopes of the contract curve when $\bar{x}_1 = 0$ and when $\bar{x}_1 = E_1$. How do they compare to the slope of the line connecting the lower left and upper right corners of the Edgeworth Box if $\alpha > \beta$? What if $\alpha < \beta$?

    e. Using what you have concluded, graph the shape of the contract curve for the case when $\alpha > \beta$ and for the case when $\alpha < \beta$.

    f. Suppose that the utility function for the two individuals instead took the more general constant elasticity of substitution form $u = (\alpha x_1^{-\rho} + (1 - \alpha)x_2^{-\rho})^{-1/\rho}$. If the tastes for the two individuals are identical, does your answer to part (b) change?

16.2 Consider again, as in exercise 16.1, a two-person, two-good exchange economy in which person 1 is endowed with (e_1^1, e_2^1) and person 2 is endowed with (e_1^2, e_2^2) of the goods x_1 and x_2.

A. Suppose again that tastes are homothetic, and assume throughout that tastes are also identical.

    a. Draw the Edgeworth Box and place the endowment point to one side of the line connecting the lower left and upper right corners of the box.

    b. Illustrate the contract curve (i.e., the set of efficient allocations) you derived in exercise 16.1. Then illustrate the set of mutually beneficial trades as well as the set of core allocations.

    c. Why would we expect these two individuals to arrive at an allocation in the core by trading with one another?

    d. Where does the competitive equilibrium lie in this case? Illustrate this by drawing the budget line that arises from equilibrium prices.

    e. Does the equilibrium lie in the core?

    f. Why would your prediction when the two individuals have different bargaining skills differ from this?

---

*conceptually challenging
**computationally challenging
†solutions in Study Guide

B. Suppose, as in exercise 16.1, that the tastes for individuals 1 and 2 can be described by the utility functions $u^1 = x_1^\alpha x_2^{(1-\alpha)}$ and $u^2 = x_1^\beta x_2^{(1-\beta)}$ (where α and β both lie between 0 and 1).

a. Derive the demands for x_1 and x_2 by each of the two individuals as a function of prices p_1 and p_2 (and as a function of their individual endowments).

b. Let p_1^* and p_2^* denote equilibrium prices. Derive the ratio p_2^*/p_1^*.

c. Derive the equilibrium allocation in the economy; i.e., derive the amount of x_1 and x_2 that each individual will consume in the competitive equilibrium (as a function of their endowments).

d. Now suppose that $\alpha = \beta$; i.e., tastes are the same for the two individuals. From your answer in (c), derive the equilibrium allocation to person 1.

e. Does your answer to (d) satisfy the condition you derived in exercise 16.1B(b) for Pareto efficient allocations (i.e., allocations on the contract curve)?[13]

16.3† Suppose you and I have the same homothetic tastes over x_1 and x_2, and our endowments of the two goods are $E^M = (e_1^M, e_2^M)$ for me and $E^Y = (e_1^Y, e_2^Y)$ for you.

A. Suppose throughout that, when $x_1 = x_2$, our MRS is equal to -1.

a. Assume that $e_1^M = e_2^M = e_1^Y = e_2^Y$. Draw the Edgeworth Box for this case and indicate where the endowment point $E = (E^M, E^Y)$ lies.

b. Draw the indifference curves for both of us through E. Is the endowment allocation efficient?

c. Normalize the price of x_2 to 1 and let p be the price of x_1. What is the equilibrium price p^*?

d. Where in the Edgeworth Box is the set of all efficient allocations?

e. Pick another efficient allocation and demonstrate a possible way to reallocate the endowment among us such that the new efficient allocation becomes an equilibrium allocation supported by an equilibrium price. Is this equilibrium price the same as p^* calculated in (c)?

B. Suppose our tastes can be represented by the CES utility function $u(x_1, x_2) = (0.5x_1^{-\rho} + 0.5x_2^{-\rho})^{-1/\rho}$.

a. Let p be defined as in A(c). Write down my and your budget constraint (assuming again endowments $E^M = (e_1^M, e_2^M)$ for me and $E^Y = (e_1^Y, e_2^Y)$).

b. Write down my optimization problem and derive my demand for x_1 and x_2.

c. Similarly, derive your demand for x_1 and x_2.

d. Derive the equilibrium price. What is that price if, as in part A, $e_1^M = e_2^M = e_1^Y = e_2^Y$?

e. Derive the set of Pareto efficient allocations assuming $e_1^M = e_2^M = e_1^Y = e_2^Y$. Can you see why, regardless of how we might redistribute endowments, the equilibrium price will always be $p^* = 1$?

16.4* Suppose, as in exercise 16.3, that you and I have the same homothetic tastes over x_1 and x_2, and our endowments of the two goods are $E^M = (e_1^M, e_2^M)$ for me and $E^Y = (e_1^Y, e_2^Y)$ for you.

A. Suppose also, again as in exercise 16.3, that whenever $x_1 = x_2$, $MRS = -1$.

a. First, consider the case where $e_1^M + e_1^Y = e_2^M + e_2^Y$. *True or False*: As long as the two goods are not perfect substitutes, the contract curve consists of the 45-degree line within the Edgeworth Box.

b. What does the contract curve look like for perfect substitutes?

c. Suppose next, and for the rest of part A of this question, that $e_1^M + e_1^Y > e_2^M + e_2^Y$. Where does the contract curve now lie? Does your answer depend on the degree of substitutability between the two goods?

d. Pick some arbitrary bundle (on either side of the 45-degree line) in the Edgeworth Box and illustrate an equilibrium price. Where will the equilibrium allocation lie?

e. If you move the endowment bundle, will the equilibrium price change? What about the equilibrium allocation?

f. *True or False*: As the economy's endowment of x_1 grows relative to its endowment of x_2, the equilibrium price p^* falls.

---

[13]You should have derived the equation describing the contract curve as $\bar{x}_2(x_1) = (E_2/E_1)x_1$.

g. *True or False*: As the goods become more complementary, the equilibrium price falls in an economy with more x_1 endowment than x_2 endowment.

B. Suppose, as in exercise 16.3, that our tastes can be represented by the CES utility function $u(x_1, x_2) = (0.5x_1^{-\rho} + 0.5x_2^{-\rho})^{-1/\rho}$.

   a. Derive the contract curve and compare it to your graphical answer in part A(c). Does the shape of the contract curve depend on the elasticity of substitution?

   b. If you have not done so already in exercise 16.3, derive my and your demand functions, letting p denote the price of x_1 and letting the price of x_2 equal 1. Then derive the equilibrium price.

   c. Does the equilibrium price depend on *how* the overall endowment in the economy is distributed?

   d. What happens to the equilibrium price as the economy's endowment of x_1 grows? Compare this to your intuitive answer in A(f).

   e. Suppose $e_1^M + e_1^Y = e_2^M + e_2^Y$. Does the equilibrium price depend on the elasticity of substitution?

   f. Suppose $e_1^M + e_1^Y > e_2^M + e_2^Y$. Does this change your answer to (e)?

16.5*† In this exercise, we explore some technical aspects of general equilibrium theory in exchange economies and Robinson Crusoe economies. Unlike in other problems, parts A and B are applicable to both those focused on A-Section material and those focused on B-Section material. Although the insights are developed in simple examples, they apply more generally in much more complex models.

A. *The role of convexity in Exchange Economies:* In each of the following parts, suppose you and I are the only individuals in the economy, and pick some arbitrary allocation E in the Edgeworth Box as our initial endowment. Assume throughout that your tastes are convex and that the contract curve is equal to the line connecting the lower left and upper right corners of the box.

   a. Begin with a depiction of an equilibrium. Can you introduce a non-convexity into my tastes such that the equilibrium disappears (despite the fact that the contract curve remains unchanged)?

   b. *True or False*: Existence of a competitive equilibrium in an exchange economy cannot be guaranteed if tastes are allowed to be non-convex.

   c. Suppose an equilibrium does exist even though my tastes exhibit some non-convexity. *True or False*: The first welfare theorem holds even when tastes have non-convexities.

   d. *True or False*: The second welfare theorem holds even when tastes have non-convexities.

B. *The role of convexity in Robinson Crusoe Economies:* Consider a Robinson Crusoe economy. Suppose throughout that there is a tangency between the worker's indifference curve and the production technology at some bundle A.

   a. Suppose first that the production technology gives rise to a convex production choice set. Illustrate an equilibrium when tastes are convex. Then show that A may no longer be an equilibrium if you allow tastes to have non-convexities even if the indifference curve is still tangent to the production choice set at A.

   b. Next, suppose again that tastes are convex but now let the production choice set have non-convexities. Show again that A might no longer be an equilibrium (even though the indifference curve and production choice set are tangent at A).

   c. *True or False*: A competitive equilibrium may not exist in a Robinson Crusoe economy that has non-convexities in either tastes or production.

   d. *True or False*: The first welfare theorem holds even if there are non-convexities in tastes and/or production technologies.

   e. *True or False*: The second welfare theorem holds regardless of whether there are non-convexities in tastes or production.

   f. Based on what you have done in parts A and B, evaluate the following statement: "Non-convexities may cause a non-existence of competitive equilibria in general equilibrium economies, but if an equilibrium exists, it results in an efficient allocation of resources. However, only in the absence of non-convexities can we conclude that there always exists some lump-sum redistribution such that any efficient allocation can also be an equilibrium allocation." (Note: Your conclusion on this holds well beyond the examples in this problem for reasons that are quite similar to the intuition developed here.)

16.6†   **Everyday Application:** *Children, Parents, Baby Booms, and Baby Busts*: Economists often think of parents and children trading with one another across time. When children are young, parents take care of children; but when parents get old, children often come to take care of their parents. We will think of this in a two-period model in which children earn no income in period 1 and parents earn no income in period 2. For purposes of this problem, we will assume that parents have no way to save in period 1 for the future and children have no way to borrow from the future when they are in period 1. Thus, parents and children have to rely on one another.

A. Suppose that, during the periods when they earn income (i.e., period 1 for parents and period 2 for children), parents and children earn the same amount y. Suppose further that everyone has homothetic tastes with $MRS = -1$ when $c_1 = c_2$.

   a.   Suppose first that there is one parent and one child. Illustrate an Edgeworth Box with current consumption c_1 on the horizontal and future consumption c_2 on the vertical axes. Indicate where the endowment allocation lies.

   b.   Given that everyone has homothetic tastes (and assuming that consumption now and in the future are not perfect substitutes), where does the region of mutually beneficial trades lie?

   c.   Let p be the price of current consumption in terms of future consumption (and let the price of future consumption be normalized to 1). Illustrate a competitive equilibrium.

   d.* Suppose that there are now two identical children and one parent. Keep the Edgeworth Box the same dimensions as in (a). However, because there are now two children, every action on a child's part must be balanced by twice the opposite action from the one parent that is being modeled in the Edgeworth Box. Does the equilibrium price p^* go up or down? (*Hint:* An equilibrium is now characterized by the parent moving twice as far on the equilibrium budget as each child.)

   e.* What happens to child consumption now and parent consumption in the future?

   f.* Instead, suppose that there are two parents and one child. Again show what happens to the equilibrium price p^*.

   g.* What happens to child consumption now and parent consumption in the future?

   h.   Would anything have changed in the original one-child, one-parent equilibrium had we assumed two children and two parents instead?

   i.* While it might be silly to apply a competitive model to a single family, we might interpret the model as representing generations that compete for current and future resources. Based on your analysis, will parents enjoy a better retirement if their children were part of a baby boom or a baby bust? Why?

   j.* Will children be more spoiled if they are part of a baby boom or a baby bust?

   k.* Consider two types of government spending: (1) spending on social security benefits for retirees, and (2) investments in a clean environment for future generations. When would this model predict will the environment do better: During baby booms or during baby busts? Why?

B. Suppose the set-up is as described in A and A(a), with $y = 100$, and let tastes be described by the utility function $u(c_1, c_2) = c_1 c_2$.

   a.   Is it true that, given these tastes, the entire inside of the Edgeworth Box is equal to the area of mutually beneficial allocations relative to the endowment allocation?

   b.   Let p be defined as in A(c). Derive the parent and child demands for c_1 and c_2 as a function of p.

   c.   Derive the equilibrium price p^* in the case where there is one parent and one child.

   d.   What is the equilibrium allocation of consumption across time between parent and child?

   e.   Suppose there are two children and one parent. Repeat (c) and (d).

   f.   Suppose there are two parents and one child. Repeat (c) and (d).

   g.   Suppose there are two children and two parents. Repeat (c) and (d).

16.7   **Everyday Application:** *Parents, Children, and the Degree of Substitutability across Time*: Consider again exactly the same scenario as in exercise 16.6.

A. This time, however, suppose that parent and child tastes treat consumption now and consumption in the future as perfect complements.

   a.   Illustrate in an Edgeworth Box an equilibrium with a single parent and a single child.

b.   Is the equilibrium you pictured in (a) the only equilibrium? If not, can you identify the set of all equilibrium allocations?

c.* Now suppose that there were two children and one parent. Keep the Edgeworth Box with the same dimensions but model this by recognizing that, on any equilibrium budget line, it must now be the case that the parent moves twice as far from the endowment E as the child (since there are two children and thus any equilibrium action by a child must be half the equilibrium action by the parent). Are any of the equilibrium allocations for parent and child that you identified in (b) still equilibrium allocations? (*Hint*: Consider the corners of the box.)

d.* Suppose instead that there are two parents and one child. How does your answer change?

e.   Repeat (a) through (d) for the case where consumption now and consumption in the future are perfect substitutes for both parent and child.

f.   Repeat for the case where consumption now and consumption in the future are perfect complements for parents and perfect substitutes for children.

g.* *True or False*: The more consumption is complementary for the parent relative to the child, and the more children there are per parent, the more gains from trade will accrue to the parent.

B. Suppose that parent and child tastes can be represented by the CES utility function $u(c_1, c_2) = (0.5c_1^{-\rho} + 0.5c_2^{-\rho})^{-1/\rho}$. Assume that the income earned by parents in period 1 and by children in period 2 is 100.

a.   Letting p denote the price of consumption now with price of future consumption normalized to 1, derive parent and child demands for current and future consumption as a function of ρ and p.

b.   What is the equilibrium price, and what does this imply for equilibrium allocations of consumption between parent and child across time? Does any of your answer depend on the elasticity of substitution?

c.   Next, suppose there are two children and only one parent. How does your answer change?

d.   Next, suppose there are two parents and only one child. How does your answer change?

e.   Explain how your answers relate to the graphs you drew for the extreme cases of both parent and child preferences treating consumption as perfect complements over time.

f.   Explain how your answers relate to your graphs for the case where consumption was perfectly substitutable across time for both parents and children.

16.8 **Business Application:** *Valuing Land in Equilibrium*: Suppose we consider a Robinson Crusoe economy with one worker who has preferences over leisure and consumption and one firm that uses a constant returns to scale production process with inputs land and labor.

A. Suppose that the worker owns the fixed supply of land that is available for production. Throughout the problem, normalize the price of output to 1.

a.   Explain why we can normalize one of the three prices in this economy (where the other two prices are the wage w and the land rental rate r).

b.   Assuming the land can fetch a positive rent per unit, how much of it will the worker rent to the firm in equilibrium (given his or her tastes are only over leisure and consumption)?

c.   Given your answer to (b), explain how we can think of the production frontier for the firm as simply a single-input production process that uses labor to produce output?

d.   What returns to scale does this single input production process have? Draw the production frontier in a graph with labor on the horizontal and output on the vertical axis.

e.   What do the worker's indifference curves in this graph look like? Illustrate the worker's optimal bundle if the worker took the production frontier as his or her constraint.

f.   Illustrate the budget for the worker and the isoprofit for the firm that lead both worker and firm to choose the bundle you identified in (e) as the optimum. What is the slope of this budget/isoprofit? Does the budget/isoprofit have a positive vertical intercept?

g.* In the text, we interpreted this intercept as profit which the worker gets as part of his or her income because the worker owns the firm. Here, however, the worker owns the land that the firm uses. Can you reinterpret this positive intercept in the context of this model (keeping in mind that the true underlying production frontier for the firm has constant returns to scale)? If land had been normalized to 1 unit, where would you find the land rental rate r in your graph?

B.* Suppose that the worker's tastes can be represented by the utility function $u(x, (1 - \ell)) = x^{\alpha}(1 - \ell)^{(1-\alpha)}$ (where x is consumption, ℓ is labor, and where the leisure endowment is normalized to 1). Suppose further that the firm's production function is $f(y, \ell) = y^{0.5}\ell^{0.5}$ where y represents the number of acres of land rented by the firm and ℓ represents the labor hours hired.

   a. Normalize the price of output to be equal to 1 for the remainder of the problem and let land rent and the wage be equal to r and w. Write down the firm's profit maximization problem, taking into account that the firm has to hire both land and labor.

   b. Take the first order conditions of the firm's profit maximization problem. The worker gets no consumption value from his or her land and therefore will rent his or her whole unit of land to the firm. Thus, you can replace land in your first order conditions with 1. Then solve each first order condition for ℓ and from this derive the relationship between w and r.

   c. The worker earns income from his or her labor and from renting his or her land to the firm. Express the worker's budget constraint in terms of w and then solve for the worker's labor supply function in terms of w.

   d. Derive the equilibrium wage in your economy by setting labor supply equal to labor demand (which you implicitly derived in (b) from one of your first order conditions).

   e. What's the equilibrium rent of the land owned by the worker?

   f. Now suppose we reformulate the problem slightly: Suppose the firm's production function is $f(y, \ell) = y^{(1-\beta)}\ell^{\beta}$ (where y is land and ℓ is labor) and the worker's tastes can be represented by the utility function $u(x, (L - \ell)) = x^{\alpha}(L - \ell)^{(1-\alpha)}$, where L is the worker's leisure endowment. Compare this to the way we formulated the Robinson Crusoe economy in the text. If land area is in fixed supply at 1 unit, what parameter in our formulation in the text must be set to 1 in order for our problem to be identical to the one in the text?

   g. *True or False*: By turning land into a fixed input, we have turned the constant returns to scale production process into one of decreasing returns to scale.

   h. Suppose that, as in the earlier part of the problem, $\beta = 0.5$ and the worker's leisure endowment is again normalized to $L = 1$. Use the solution for the equilibrium wage in the text to derive the equilibrium wage now, again normalizing the output price to 1.

   i. Use the profit function in equation (16.32) of the text to determine the profit of the firm (given the equilibrium wage and given the parameter values used here). Compare this to the equilibrium land rent you derived in (e). Explain your result intuitively.

16.9 Business Application: *Hiring an Assistant*: Suppose you are a busy CEO with lots of consumption but relatively little leisure. I, on the other hand, have only a part-time job and therefore lots of leisure with relatively little consumption.

A. You decide that the time has come to hire a personal assistant, someone who can do some of the basics in your life so that you can have a bit more leisure time.

   a. Illustrate our current situation in an Edgeworth Box with leisure on the horizontal and consumption on the vertical axis. Indicate an endowment bundle that fits the description of the problem and use indifference curves to illustrate a region in the graph where both of us would benefit from me working for you as an assistant.

   b. Next, illustrate what an equilibrium would look like. Where in the graph would you see the wage that I am being paid?

   c. Suppose that anyone can do the tasks you are asking of your assistant, but some will do it cheerfully and others will do it with attitude. You hate attitude and therefore would prefer someone who is cheerful. Assuming you can read the level of cheerfulness in me, what changes in the Edgeworth Box as your impression of me changes?

   d. How do your impressions of me—how cheerful I am—affect the region of mutually beneficial trades?

   e. How does increased cheerfulness on my part change the equilibrium wage?

   f.* Your graph probably has the new equilibrium (with increased cheerfulness) occurring at an indifference curve for you that lies below (relative to your axes) the previous equilibrium (where I was less cheerful). Does this mean that you are worse off as a result of me becoming more cheerful?

B. Suppose that my tastes can be represented by $u(c, \ell) = 200 \ln \ell + c$ while yours can be represented by $u(c, \ell, x) = 100x \ln \ell + c$ where ℓ stands for leisure, c stands for consumption, and x stands for cheerfulness of your assistant. Suppose that, in the absence of working for you, I have 50 leisure hours and 10 units of consumption while you have 10 leisure hours and 100 units of consumption.

    a.   Normalize the price of c to 1. Derive our leisure demands as a function of the wage w.

    b.   Calculate the equilibrium wage as a function of x.

    c.   Suppose $x = 1$. What is the equilibrium wage, and how much will I be working for you?

    d.   How does your *MRS* change as my cheerfulness x increases?

    e.   What happens to the equilibrium wage as x increases to 1.2? What happens to the equilibrium number of hours I work for you? What if I get grumpy and x falls to 0.4?

16.10*†Policy Application: *Distortionary Taxes with Redistribution*: Consider a two-person exchange economy in which I own 200 units of x_1 and 100 units of x_2 while you own 100 units of x_1 and 200 units of x_2.

POLICY
APPLICATION

A. Suppose you and I have tastes that are quasilinear in x_1, and suppose that I sell x_1 to you in the competitive equilibrium without taxes.

    a.   Illustrate the no-tax competitive equilibrium in an Edgeworth Box.

    b.   Suppose the government imposes a per-unit tax t (paid in terms of x_2) on all units of x_1 that are traded. This introduces a difference of t between the price sellers receive and the price buyers pay. How does the tax result in kinked budget constraints for us?

    c.   *True or False*: The tax can never be so high that I will turn from being a seller to being a buyer.

    d.   Illustrating the tax in the Edgeworth Box will imply we face different budget lines in the box, but demand and supply of x_1 still has to equalize. Illustrate this and show how a difference between the economy's endowment of x_2 and the amounts consumed by us emerges. What's that difference?

    e.   Suppose the government simply takes the x_2 revenue it collects, divides it into two equal piles, and gives it back to us. In a new Edgeworth Box, illustrate our indifference curves through the final allocation that we will consume. How can you tell that the combination of the tax and transfer of x_2 is inefficient?

B. Suppose that our endowments are as specified at the beginning. My tastes can be represented by the utility function $u^M(x_1, x_2) = x_2 + 50 \ln x_1$ and yours by the utility function $u^Y(x_1, x_2) = x_2 + 150 \ln x_1$.

    a.   Derive our demand functions and use them to calculate the equilibrium price p defined as the price of x_1 given that the price of x_2 is normalized to 1.

    b.   How much of x_1 do we trade among each other?

    c.   Now suppose that a per-unit tax t (payable in terms of x_2) is introduced. Let p be the price buyers will end up paying, and let $(p - t)$ be the price sellers receive. Derive the equilibrium levels of p and $(p - t)$ as a function of t. (*Hint*: You will need to solve a quadratic equation using the quadratic formula, and the larger of the two solutions given by the formula is the correct one.)

    d.   Consider the case of $t = 0.25$. Illustrate that the post-tax allocation is inefficient.

    e.   Suppose the government distributes the x_2 revenue back to us, giving me half of it and you the other half. Does your previous answer change?

    f.**   Construct a table relating t to tax revenues, buyer price p, seller price $(p - t)$, my consumption level of x_1, and your consumption level of x_1 in 0.25 increments from 0 to 1.25. (This is most easily done by putting the relevant equations into an excel spreadsheet and changing t.)

    g.   Would anything in the table change if the government takes the x_2 revenue it collects and distributes it between us in some way?

16.11 Policy Application: *Distortionary Taxes in General Equilibrium*: Consider, as in exercise 16.10, a two-person exchange economy in which I own 200 units of x_1 and 100 units of x_2 while you own 100 units of x_1 and 200 units of x_2.

POLICY
APPLICATION

A. Suppose you and I have identical homothetic tastes.

    a.   Draw the Edgeworth Box for this economy and indicate the endowment allocation E.

    b.   Normalize the price of good x_2 to 1. Illustrate the equilibrium price p^* for x_1 and the equilibrium allocation of goods in the absence of any taxes. Who buys and who sells x_1?

c.   Suppose the government introduces a tax t levied on all transactions of x_1 (and paid in terms of x_2). For instance, if one unit of x_1 is sold from me to you at price p, I will only get to keep $(p - t)$. Explain how this creates a kink in our budget constraints.

d.   Suppose a post-tax equilibrium exists and that price increases for buyers and falls for sellers. In such an equilibrium, I will still be selling some quantity of x_1 to you. (Can you explain why?) How do the relevant portions of the budget constraints you and I face look in this new equilibrium, and where will we optimize?

e.   When we discussed price changes with homothetic tastes in our development of consumer theory, we noted that there are often competing income (or wealth) and substitution effects. Are there such competing effects here relative to our consumption of x_1? If so, can we be sure that the quantity we trade *in equilibrium* will be less when t is introduced?

f.   You should see that, in the new equilibrium, a portion of x_2 remains not allocated to anyone. This is the amount that is paid in taxes to the government. Draw a new Edgeworth Box that is adjusted on the x_2 axes to reflect the fact that some portion of x_2 is no longer allocated between the two of us. Then locate the equilibrium allocation point that you derived in your previous graph. Why is this point not efficient?

g.   *True or False*: The deadweight loss from the distortionary tax on trades in x_1 results from the fact that our marginal rates of substitution are no longer equal to one another after the tax is imposed and *not* because the government raised revenues and thus lowered the amounts of x_2 consumed by us.

h.   *True or False*: While the post-tax equilibrium is not efficient, it does lie in the region of mutually beneficial trades.

i.   How would taxes that redistribute endowments (as envisioned by the Second Welfare Theorem) be different than the price distorting tax analyzed in this problem?

B.   Suppose our tastes can be represented by the utility function $u(x_1, x_2) = x_1 x_2$. Let our endowments be specified as at the beginning of the problem.

a.   Derive our demand functions for x_1 and x_2 (as functions of p – the price of x_1 when the price of x_2 is normalized to 1).

b.   Derive the equilibrium price p^* and the equilibrium allocation of goods.

c.   Now suppose the government introduces a tax t as specified in A(c). Given that I am the one that sells and you are the one that buys x_1, how can you now rewrite our demand functions to account for t? (*Hint*: There are two ways of doing this: either define p as the pre-tax price and let the relevant price for the buyer be $(p + t)$ or let p be defined as the post-tax price and let the relevant price for the seller be $(p - t)$.)

d.   Derive the new equilibrium pre- and post-tax prices in terms of t. (*Hint*: You should get to a point where you need to solve a quadratic equation using the quadratic formula that gives two answers. Of these two, the larger one is the correct answer for this problem.)

e.   How much of each good do you and I consume if $t = 1$?

f.   How much revenue does the government raise if $t = 1$?

g.   Show that the equilibrium allocation under the tax is inefficient.

16.12   Policy Application: *The Laffer Curve in General Equilibrium*: Consider, as in exercise 16.11, an exchange economy in which I own 200 units of x_1 and 100 units of x_2 while you own 100 units of x_1 and 200 units of x_2.

A.   Suppose again that we have identical homothetic tastes.

a.   In exercise 16.11, you illustrated the impact of a tax t (defined in A(c) of exercise 16.11) in the Edgeworth Box. Begin now with a graph of just my endowment and my budget constraint (outside the Edgeworth Box). Illustrate how this constraint changes as t increases assuming that equilibrium price falls for sellers and rises for buyers.

b.   Repeat (a) for you.

c.   *True or False*: As t increases, you will reduce the amount of x_1 you buy, and, for sufficiently high t, you will stop buying x_1 altogether.

d.   *True or False*: As t increases, I will reduce the amount of x_1 I sell and, for sufficiently high t, I will stop selling altogether.

   e.   Can you explain from what you have done how a Laffer curve emerges from it? (Recall that the Laffer curve plots the relationship of t on the horizontal axis to tax revenue on the vertical, and Laffer's claim is that this relationship will have an inverse U-shape.)

   f.   *True or False*: The equilibrium allocation in the Edgeworth Box will lie in the core so long as t is not sufficiently high to stop trade in x_1.

   g.   If you have done exercise 16.10, can you tell whether the same inverse U-shaped Laffer curve also arises when tastes are quasilinear?

B.** Assume, as in exercise 16.11, that our tastes can be represented by the utility function $u(x_1, x_2) = x_1 x_2$ and that our endowments are as specified at the beginning of the problem.

   a.   If you did not already do so in exercise 16.11, derive the equilibrium pre- and post-tax prices as a function of t.

   b.   Construct a table relating t to tax revenues, buyer price p, seller price $(p - t)$, my consumption level of x_1 and your consumption level of x_1 in 0.25 increments. (This is easiest done by putting the relevant equations into an excel spreadsheet and changing t.)

   c.   Can you see the Laffer curve for this example within your table?

   d.   Does the inverse U-shaped Laffer curve also emerge in the case where we assumed quasilinear tastes such as those in exercise 16.10?

Choice and Markets in the Presence of Risk

Life is full of risk, yet in everything we have done thus far, we have assumed that individuals operate in an economic environment that involves no risk.[1] Sometimes the risks we face are personal: the increased risk of lung disease a coal miner faces or the risk of dying in a car crash when we get on the road. As I am writing this, I face the risk of investing a lot of my time in a book that I think is great only to find out that no one will read it, not to mention having to admit to my wife that no one actually cares about my brilliant thoughts. Other times, the risk is strictly financial: when we purchase a house whose value may rise or fall, when we make investment decisions in our retirement portfolio, or when we buy a new computer without knowing for sure whether it will break down in three months. If I don't care about the humiliation of writing a book that no one reads, I still face a financial risk of having spent time I could have used to make money in other ways rather than spend that time on a project that does not pay off financially as I had hoped.

Where there is risk, however, there is also a potential market for products that reduce risk. In many instances, such products take the form of insurance—like health, disability, or life insurance—but they can also come in the form of extended warranty agreements on the computer I buy or through financial planning strategies that balance different forms of risky assets. My publishers have provided me with some insurance for writing this book by giving me an advance on future royalties, an advance that they will recoup if the book sells but not otherwise.

We will find in this chapter that some tweaking of the tools we have already developed will allow us to extend our analysis of choice (and markets) to circumstances where risk is central to the concerns of the individual who is choosing. In much of the chapter, we will use the example of life insurance to illustrate a model that can be used to address all sorts of situations that involve risk. Again, it will be a combination of tastes and constraints that will determine choice, with different individuals having different attitudes (or tastes) toward risk, and with prices in markets determining the options that individuals have for dealing with the risks they face. And again we will find that, in the absence of distorting forces such as those listed at the end of Chapter 15, competitive markets result in efficient outcomes. In Chapter 22, however, we will discover that markets that deal with risk often face, almost by definition, distortions arising from asymmetric information, and it is from these distortions that we will later see a role for nonmarket institutions to improve on market outcomes that involve risk.[2]

---

[1]Most of this chapter builds on a basic understanding of consumer theory as captured in Chapter 6, with some brief references to material from Chapter 11. Only toward the end in Sections 17A.3 and 17B.3 do we build on general equilibrium theory from Chapter 16. These sections can (and should) be skipped if you have not yet gone through Chapter 16.

[2]One of the reasons for choosing life insurance as the example throughout this chapter is that this market is less likely than others to face substantial problems arising from asymmetric information.

17A An Intuitive Model of Choice in the Presence of Risk

Whenever we face risk, we are essentially facing a choice over gambles in which there are better and worse outcomes and we can't be sure which of the outcomes will ultimately materialize. Insurance offers a means of changing the gamble, improving the bad outcomes while giving something up in the good outcomes. The simplest cases to analyze are those where the only thing that matters about the outcomes is money. When we invest in the stock market, for instance, we care about how much of a return we will ultimately get on our investment. The degree to which the investment pays off simply determines the budget constraint we will face, but our tastes (or indifference map) over the goods we consume are unaffected by how well our stock portfolio is doing. When we consider investing in disability insurance, on the other hand, we probably care about a lot more than how much money we have depending on whether we become disabled or not; the disability itself, apart from its financial implications, is something that we probably have strong feelings about. Put differently, when we think about the appropriate level of disability insurance, we face a situation in which our tastes (or indifference map) over the goods we consume may well depend on whether we are disabled or not.

We will begin in Section 17A.1 with the simpler of the situations where risky choices involve only money. Later on, we will refer to these types of situations as involving "state-independent utility" because our tastes (or utility) are independent of what "state of the world" we end up facing. We will then outline (in Section 17A.2) a more complicated model in which we evaluate consumption differently depending on what risky outcome happens, and we will see that our first model (where only money matters) is a special case of the second. The latter model is one that allows for "state-dependent utility", i.e., cases where tastes (or utility) depend on what "state of the world" occurs. After investigating how individuals make choices in these models, we then use the tools we have developed in Chapter 16 to investigate how competitive market equilibria emerge in situations involving risk (Section 17A.3). Finally, while we will develop all of these ideas in the context of life insurance markets, we will conclude Section A of this chapter with a brief discussion of how the model can also deal with risk in financial markets.

17A.1 Risky Choices Involving Money

We begin, then, with a model in which individual tastes over consumption are independent of what risky outcome we end up facing. Put differently, we will assume in this section that the consumer uses the same rule for evaluating the value of consumption regardless of whether the "good" outcome or the "bad" outcome happens. While we will restrict ourselves to gambles in which there are only two possible outcomes, the model can in principle be extended to include a large number of possible outcomes.

17A.1.1 Utility and Expected Utility
Suppose my wife and I have made the decision that I will specialize in earning income to support our household while my wife will specialize in running the household, rearing children, keeping me in line, etc. For my wife, this is a somewhat risky decision that might leave her in a precarious financial position were anything to happen to me. For simplicity, let's suppose that there is some chance (or "probability") δ (where $0 < \delta < 1$) that I will die and leave my wife with a significantly reduced standard of living and some chance $(1 - \delta)$ that I will live to hold up my end of the bargain.[3]

---

[3]We will assume that these are the only two possibilities and abstract away from such possibilities as divorce. In my case, this is quite realistic since my wife, a Roman Catholic, has explained to me that divorce is never an option, and if I ever thought it was, she would quickly speed my transition to the "life beyond."

We will now think about how my wife's well-being is affected by the introduction of the risk of my premature demise, and for now we will make the assumption (to be relaxed later in this chapter) that the only way I contribute to my wife's well-being is through my paycheck. We will also assume something a little stronger than we did in our treatment of choice in the absence of risk—that my wife is able to measure utility of different consumption levels. This does not mean that we are assuming that utility itself is objectively measurable, only that my wife, in her own thinking, can measure her own utility in quantifiable (rather than just "ordinal") terms. (In Section B, we will show that even this is too strong an assumption for what we actually need, that nothing about what we are doing here is actually in any way "cardinal," but we will need access to some of the underlying math to make that case.) This allows us to model my wife's utility like a single-input production process (Chapter 11) where the input is annual consumption (measured in dollars) and the output is "utility." As depicted in Graph 17.1a, the resulting "production frontier" implies *diminishing marginal utility of consumption*; i.e., each additional dollar of consumption yields a smaller increase in utility than the previous dollar. This is analogous to "diminishing marginal product of labor" in Chapter 11 where labor (instead of consumption) appeared on the horizontal axis. Note that, for simplicity, we are lumping all consumption goods together as one composite good.

Exercise 17A.1 If the relationship depicted in Graph 17.1a were a single input production function, would it have increasing, decreasing, or constant returns to scale?

Now suppose that I am doing pretty well financially and bringing home an annual paycheck of $250,000. If I bite the dust, however, my household will be left with a meager $10,000 in annual income (from some savings that my wife will inherit). Suppose further, for illustration, that I am not very popular at work and that there is a 25% chance that someone there will arrange

Graph 17.1: Relation of "Utility" to "Consumption"

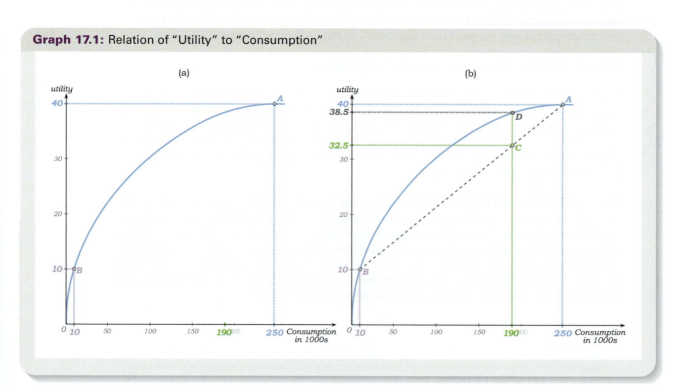

for my early demise (i.e., $\delta = 0.25$), and, again for illustration, let's suppose my wife is looking ahead one year as she thinks about the risk she is taking by relying so heavily on me to bring home the bacon.

From my wife's perspective, she knows she can count on $250,000 in consumption with a probability of 0.75 and $10,000 in consumption with a probability of 0.25. Her *expected consumption* (defined as the probability of the good outcome times $250,000 plus the probability of the bad outcome times $10,000) is then $190,000. We will sometimes also refer to this as the *expected value* of the gamble she is taking.

Verify that my wife's expected household consumption is $190,000.

Exercise
17A.2

From Graph 17.1a, we can also read off my wife's utility under each scenario. If I survive the year to bring home the $250,000 paycheck, her utility is read off A as 40, but if I die and she is left with only $10,000, her utility is read off point B as only 10. Looking ahead toward next year, then, my wife's *expected utility*—defined as the probability of the good outcome times 40 plus the probability of the bad outcome times 10—is 32.5.

The geometry of this is relatively straightforward and illustrated in panel (b) of Graph 17.1. The dashed line connecting A and B is the set of points in the graph that average points A and B using different weights. For instance, the mid-point of this line simply takes the average of A and B. Point C, on the other hand, lies three-quarters of the way toward point A and thus represents the weighted average of A and B where A is given weight of 0.75 and B is given weight 0.25. Point C then places the same weight on the good and bad outcome as my wife does given that she knows I have a 75% chance of surviving the year, and it is at point C that we can then read off my wife's expected utility of 32.5.

17A.1.2 Different Attitudes about Risk

If I had simply given you panel (a) of Graph 17.1 and asked you to determine my wife's expected utility, you might have been tempted to do the following: First, calculate that her expected consumption is $190,000, and then rely on the fact that my wife's utility of having $190,000 is 38.5 to answer my question. The problem with this reasoning is that my wife's utility of having $190,000 *with certainty* is 38.5, but what we really want to know is what her utility of getting $250,000 with probability 0.75 and $10,000 with probability of 0.25 is. In panel (b) of Graph 17.1 (and in our calculations), we find that my wife's expected utility from facing this risk (read off point C) is less than the utility she would get by receiving $190,000 with certainty (read off point D). The reason for this is that, in drawing the relationship between income and utility as we have, we have implicitly assumed that my wife is *risk averse* and would prefer to have $190,000 with certainty rather than face the risk of perhaps receiving a higher amount and perhaps receiving a lower amount even though in expectation she is receiving the same. Put differently, *a risk-averse person's utility of the expected value of a gamble is always higher than the expected utility of the gamble*.

Of course, different people have different attitudes toward risk, and not everyone may be as risk averse as my wife. In Graph 17.2, we illustrate three different cases, with panel (a) replicating the graph that we just developed for my wife and thus representing the case of a risk-averse person who prefers a "sure thing" to a gamble that has the same expected value but involves risk. In panel (b), we consider the case of *risk-neutral* tastes, or a person who is indifferent between a "sure thing" and a gamble with the same expected value; and in panel (c) we consider a person who is *risk loving* and would prefer to take a gamble rather than get the expected value of the gamble for sure.

Graph 17.2: Risk Aversion, Risk Neutrality, and Risk Loving

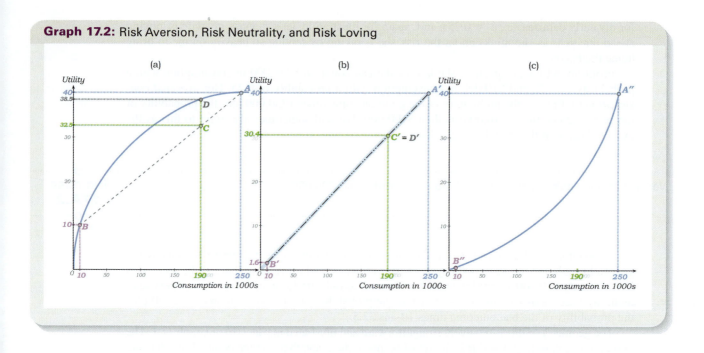

........●........

Exercise
17A.3

What is the relationship between increasing, constant, and decreasing marginal utility of consumption to risk-loving, risk-neutral, and risk-averse tastes?

........●........

Exercise
17A.4

We said that "a risk-averse person's utility of the expected value of a gamble is always higher than the expected utility of the gamble." How does this statement change for risk-neutral and risk-loving tastes?

........●........

Suppose first that my wife's tastes were accurately graphed as in panel (b). At point A', her utility of getting \$250,000 is 40, while (at point B') her utility of getting \$10,000 is just 1.6. Given that she will attain utility of 40 with probability of 0.75 and utility of 1.6 with probability of 0.25, this implies her expected utility is 30.4. As before, this is read off graphically at point C' on the line connecting points A' and B' three-quarters of the way toward point A', only now this line lies right on top of the consumption/utility relationship. Were we to ask how much utility my wife would get by receiving \$190,000 with certainty, we would read this off at exactly the same point as 30.4. Put differently, as the curvature of the consumption/utility relationship in the risk-averse case of panel (a) is reduced, point D comes closer and closer to point C, and when the consumption/utility relationship becomes linear, the two points overlap as they do in panel (b). In this case, my wife would be indifferent between getting \$190,000 with certainty as opposed to facing the risk of getting \$250,000 with probability 0.75 and \$10,000 with probability 0.25. She simply does not care about the risk and only cares about the expected value of the gamble she is facing.

........●........

Exercise
17A.5

Illustrate that if tastes are as described in panel (c), my wife prefers the "risky gamble" (of getting \$250,000 with probability 0.75 and \$10,000 with probability 0.25) over the "sure thing" (\$190,000 with certainty) that has the same expected value.

........●........

17A.1.3 The Certainty Equivalent and Risk Premium   So far, we have shown that a risk-averse person who is asked to take a chance would prefer to get the expected value of the gamble for sure rather than have to face the risk of the gamble. In panel (a) of Graph 17.2, for instance, my wife would prefer to get $190,000 for sure rather than face a gamble that has an expected value of $190,000. But some people are more risk averse than others, which raises the question of how we might quantify the degree of risk aversion that we can compare across individuals (rather than just identifying some as risk averse and some as risk loving or risk neutral).

One way to do this is to begin by asking the following question: What's the least I have to give the person (for sure) in order for her to agree not to participate in the gamble at all? Put into the context of the gamble my wife takes on me, how much would we have to give her so that she would agree to simply run off and get neither $250,000 (if I survive the year) nor $10,000 (if I don't)? In Graph 17.3, we answer this question by once again illustrating my wife's risk-averse tastes. We know from what we have done so far that we can read off her utility of taking the gamble at point C as 32.5. If we want to buy her out of this gamble, we would have to offer her an amount that makes her indifferent to facing the gamble; i.e., an amount that will give her utility of 32.5. We can then simply check to see how much consumption it would take to accomplish this by finding the point E where the dashed horizontal line at utility of 32.5 intersects the consumption/utility relationship. Point E lies at $115,000 on the consumption axis, which implies that my wife will get utility of 32.5 if she receives $115,000 with certainty. She would therefore be indifferent between betting on me and receiving $115,000 without risk.

The lowest possible amount that someone is willing to take (for sure) in order not to participate in a gamble is called the *certainty equivalent of the gamble*. My wife's certainty equivalent of facing the gamble of getting $250,000 with probability of 0.75 and $10,000 with probability 0.25 is therefore $115,000. The *risk premium* of a gamble is the difference between the expected value of a gamble and its certainty equivalent. My wife's risk premium is therefore $75,000, which represents the amount she is willing to sacrifice in expected value in order to eliminate the risk she faces.

Graph 17.3: Certainty Equivalent and Risk Premium

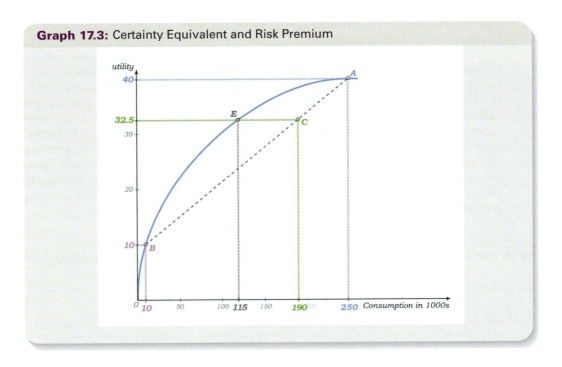

**Exercise
17A.6**

What is the certainty equivalent and the risk premium for my wife if she had tastes that can be summarized as in panel (b) of Graph 17.2?

**Exercise
17A.7**

In panel (c) of Graph 17.2, is the risk premium positive or negative? Can you reconcile this with the fact that the tastes in this graph represent those of a risk lover?

**Exercise
17A.8**

True or False: As an individual becomes more risk averse, the certainty equivalent for a risky gamble will fall and the risk premium will rise.

17A.1.4 "Actuarily Fair" Insurance Markets   Since my wife is risk averse, she might be interested in finding an arrangement under which she pays some amount in order to reduce or eliminate the risk that she faces. Put differently, she might be interested in investing in life insurance on me. This, of course, is precisely the point of insurance: to pay something up front in order to reduce risks that we face.

More precisely, an *insurance contract* or an *insurance policy* is composed of two parts: an *insurance premium* that the consumer agrees to pay before knowing what outcome she faces, and an *insurance benefit* that the insured consumer is entitled to if she ends up facing the "bad" outcome. For instance, if my wife agrees to take out a $100,000 life insurance policy on me for a premium of $10,000, she in essence agrees to reduce her consumption if she faces the "good outcome" by $10,000 (because she will have had to pay the $10,000 insurance premium without getting anything back from the insurance company) in exchange for increasing her consumption by $90,000 if she faces the "bad" outcome (because, although she will have paid a $10,000 insurance premium, she will end up collecting a $100,000 insurance benefit from the policy).

Suppose, then, that there is a competitive insurance industry that has full information about the risks that individuals face.[4] For simplicity, suppose that many other consumers find themselves in a position similar to my wife's, and insurance companies compete for the business of these consumers. And suppose that the risks are not "correlated" across individuals, which implies that in any given year, 25% of those who are insured will be owed payments by an insurance company and 75% will find themselves facing the "good outcome" and thus will not require payment from an insurance company.

Insurance companies might then offer a variety of insurance contracts, some with high premiums and high benefits, others with lower premiums and lower benefits. Since each insurance company covers many consumers, it can be reasonably certain that it will have to pay benefits to 25% of its customers while collecting the premium from all of them. Put differently, an insurance company that offers a policy with benefit b and premium p to 100 customers will receive $100p$ in revenues and incur $25b$ in costs. Thus, if b is less than or equal to $4p$, the insurance company will make a profit (assuming it has negligible costs of collecting premiums and paying benefits). Under perfect competition, each insurance company will make zero profit, which implies that the long-run equilibrium insurance contract will have benefits that are four times as high as premiums. More generally, if the probability of the "bad" outcome is δ, $b = (p/\delta)$ in equilibrium.

**Exercise
17A.9**

Verify that the zero-profit relationship between b and p is as described in the previous sentence.

---

[4]As we will see in Chapter 22, insurance companies do not always have such full information, and this gives rise to problems of asymmetric information in insurance markets that we glance over here. However, for reasons we will discuss in Chapter 22, this is likely to be a minor issue for life insurance markets.

The type of insurance contract that we have just described is known as *actuarily fair*. An *actuarily fair insurance contract reduces the risk a consumer faces without changing the expected value of the gamble for which the consumer buys insurance. In expectation,* a consumer who buys an actuarily fair insurance policy therefore pays an amount equal to what she receives back (which therefore causes the insurance company to make zero profit). As we will see shortly, such an actuarily fair life insurance contract in our example might, for instance, have a premium of $20,000 and a benefit of $80,000, or a premium of $40,000 and a benefit of $160,000, or a premium of $60,000 and a benefit of $240,000.

Suppose my wife purchases the first policy with a premium of $20,000 and a benefit of $80,000. This would imply that if I survive the year and bring home a $250,000 check, my wife will have only $230,000 left given that she had to pay the $20,000 premium. If I do not survive to bring home a paycheck, on the other hand, my wife would still have paid the $20,000 premium but would receive a benefit of $80,000, thus leaving her with $60,000 more than the $10,000 she would have had in the absence of insurance. By purchasing this policy, my wife would therefore have a 0.75 probability of facing a "good" outcome with $230,000 and a 0.25 probability of facing a "bad" outcome with $70,000. Her *expected consumption,* however, remains unchanged at $190,000. She has thus reduced her risk without changing her expected consumption level.

Verify that my wife's expected income is still $190,000 under this insurance policy.

Exercise
17A.10

Would my wife be interested in such an insurance policy? To analyze this, we can return again to the graph of my wife's consumption/utility relationship and find her expected utility under this insurance policy. In panel (a) of Graph 17.4, we begin with the picture as before, with point A indicating the relevant point under the "good" outcome and B indicating the relevant point under the "bad" outcome assuming my wife has bought no life insurance on me. If she buys the insurance policy with $b = \$80,000$ and $p = \$20,000$, the "good" outcome shifts to point A_1 while the "bad" outcome shifts to point B_1. We can now once again read off my wife's expected

Graph 17.4: Buying Actuarily Fair Insurance

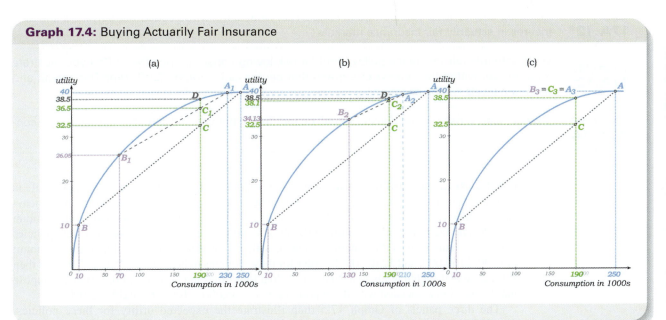

utility under this insurance policy by drawing the line connecting points A_1 and B_1 and finding the utility level (36.5) associated with the point that lies 3/4 of the way toward point A_1 at the consumption level $190,000. Since my wife's expected utility without insurance is 32.5 and her expected utility with this insurance policy is 36.5, we can conclude that she would prefer to hold this insurance rather than no insurance at all. It should be intuitive that this is the case given my wife is risk averse: The actuarily fair insurance policy does not change the expected value ($190,000) of the gamble she faces, but it does reduce the risk.

Panel (b) of the graph then illustrates points A_2 and B_2 associated with the good and bad outcomes under the second insurance policy that has a $40,000 premium a $160,000 benefit. The $40,000 premium reduces my wife's consumption in the good outcome to $210,000, and the premium combined with the benefit raises her consumption in the bad outcome by $120,000 to $130,000. Once again, you can check that the expected value of my wife's situation remains unchanged, but this policy further reduces the risk my wife faces. As a result, you can read off the graph (in the same way as before) that my wife's expected utility under the second policy is 38.1, which is higher than under the first insurance policy where the expected utility was 36.5.

Finally, consider the third insurance policy that provides a benefit of $240,000 in exchange for a premium of $60,000. The premium would reduce my wife's consumption if I survive to $190,000, and the combination of the premium and the benefit would raise her consumption if I do not survive by $180,000, from $10,000 to $190,000. Thus, under this policy, my wife is *fully insured* in the sense that she has eliminated all risk by equalizing the good and bad outcomes to exactly the expected value of the initial gamble she faced. Her expected utility is then simply the utility from having an income of $190,000 read off the consumption/utility relationship. Since this is higher than any of the other insurance contracts, we can conclude that she will choose to insure fully.

Exercise 17A.11 What are some examples of other actuarily fair insurance contracts that do not provide full insurance? Would each of these also earn zero profit for insurance companies? Can you see why none of them would ever be preferred to full insurance by my wife?

Exercise 17A.12* Referring back to what you learned in Graph 17.3, what is my wife's consumer surplus if she fully insures in actuarily fair insurance markets?

Exercise 17A.13* What actuarily fair insurance policy would a risk-loving consumer purchase? Can you illustrate your answer within the context of a graph that begins as in Graph 17.2c? (*Hint:* The benefit and premium levels will be negative.)

Exercise 17A.14 *True or False:* A risk-neutral consumer will be indifferent between all actuarily fair insurance contracts.

17A.1.5 Actuarily Unfair Insurance

Now suppose that the insurance policies my wife is offered are not actuarily fair; i.e., my wife's expected consumption falls as she insures more heavily. Consider again three policies, the first with premium $20,000, the second with premium $40,000, and the third with premium $60,000. In the previous section, we saw that such policies would be actuarily fair if the benefit associated with each was four times as high as the premium: $80,000, $160,000, and $240,000. In order for these policies to be actuarily "unfair," it must then be the case that each has a benefit that is less than four times the premium. For instance, suppose that the benefits associated with these policies were $65,000, $100,000, and $122,000.

The three panels of Graph 17.5 then illustrate the expected utility for these policies. Notice that the first policy (in panel (a)) gives my wife an expected consumption of $186,250,

Graph 17.5: Actuarily Unfair Insurance

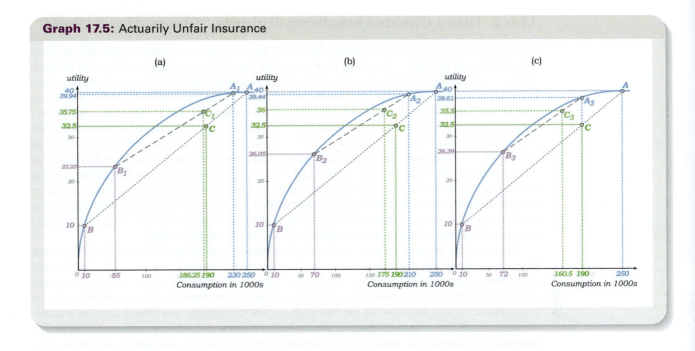

and the next two policies cause this expected consumption to fall to $175,000 and $160,500 respectively. The expected utility of the first insurance policy is then read off as 35.75, three-quarters of the way toward point A_1 on the line connecting B_1 and A_1 at the expected consumption value of $186,250. Similarly, we can read the expected utility of the second and third policies as 36 and 35.5.

Each of the policies is therefore preferred to no insurance at all because each gives higher utility than 32.5. But the insurance policy with premium $40,000 and benefit $100,000 yields the highest utility. Thus, when faced with these choices, my wife would choose not to buy the policy that comes closest to full insurance.

Verify the numbers on the horizontal axis of Graph 17.5.

Exercise 17A.15

This is an example of a more general result: *While we found in the previous section that risk-averse individuals will choose to fully insure when insurance markets are actuarily fair, this is not the case when insurance markets are actuarily unfair.*

True or False: If firms in a perfectly competitive insurance industry face recurring fixed costs and marginal administration costs that are increasing, risk-averse individuals will not fully insure in equilibrium.

Exercise 17A.16*

Suppose only full insurance contracts were offered by the insurance industry; i.e., only contracts that insure that my wife will be equally well off financially regardless of what happens to me. What is the most actuarily unfair insurance contract that my wife would agree to buy? (*Hint*: Refer back to Graph 17.3.)

Exercise 17A.17*

17A.2 Risky Choices Involving Multiple "States of the World"

Our discussion so far is a little distasteful and (I hope) a little unrealistic. After all, we have assumed that all my wife cares about is money, with my existence adding no utility to her consumption and my untimely death causing her no pain to detract from the pleasure of consumption. Let's face it: For my wife, the air smells sweeter and the birds chirp more melodiously when I am around, and a dark cloud descends on everything if I disappear. For her, it might not at all be very easy to replace me with money, and I know she is priceless to me. In terms of the economist's language, we would say that life with me and life without me therefore represent two very different *states of the world* for my wife. And in the "good" state in which I am around, each dollar of consumption means more than it does in the "bad" state when I am not around. Put differently, my wife gets utility from consumption in part because we consume in each other's presence, and when I am not around, consumption (or income) means less to her (just as consumption would mean less to me if my wife were not there to share it). It is therefore not true that, so long as my wife's income is the same in the two states of the world, she will be equally happy.

The example illustrates the limits of the simple model of the previous section, and it suggests that the model is useful only in some circumstances. For instance, if the gamble we are analyzing involves an investment opportunity that is risky, we may think the model is perfectly appropriate because nothing fundamentally changes (aside from our income) when an investment pays off more or less. But in circumstances where the cause of the bad state is itself undesirable and affects how we evaluate money, we need a more general model of choice in the presence of risk. As we will see, the model we introduce now contains the model we discussed in the previous section as a special case but also permits a more realistic analysis of situations like my wife's decision to buy life insurance on me.

17A.2.1 Modeling Consumption in Different "States of the World"   This more general model bears strong resemblance to the model of consumer choice in a two-good world when the consumer is endowed with different amounts of each good but has no other source of income. In panel (a) of Graph 17.6, we put "consumption in the good state" (denoted x_G) on the horizontal axis and "consumption in the bad state" (denoted x_B) on the vertical, in each case denominating consumption in (thousands of) dollar units (and thus implicitly assuming that consumption of goods can be modeled as a single composite good in each state). In the absence of insurance, my wife's consumption if I survive the year is $250,000, and her consumption if I do not survive is $10,000. This is illustrated by her endowment point E.

The 45-degree line in this graph represents points under which consumption in the "good" and "bad" states is exactly equal, with points below the 45-degree line representing situations where consumption in the good state is higher than consumption in the bad state, and where the consumer therefore faces financial risk that is absent on the 45-degree line. My wife's endowment point E lies in this region precisely because she faces such a financial risk in the absence of insurance.

17A.2.2 Choice Sets under Actuarily Fair Insurance   We can now determine what my wife's choice set looks like when insurance markets offer actuarily fair insurance policies. Recall that such contracts leave the expected value of my wife's finances unchanged (at $190,000) while increasing her consumption in the "bad" state and decreasing it in the "good" state. In order for the expected value of her consumption (before she knows in which state she will find herself) to remain unchanged, we have determined that the benefit offered by the insurance contract must be four times as high as the premium. For instance, we illustrated three such policies in the previous section: policy A with a premium of $20,000 and a benefit of $80,000, policy B with a premium of $40,000 and a benefit of $160,000, and policy C with a premium of $60,000 and a benefit of $240,000.

Under policy A, my wife's consumption in the "good" state will fall to $230,000 while her consumption in the "bad" state will rise to $70,000. Point A in Graph 17.6b illustrates this outcome. Similarly, points B and C correspond to the consumption levels my wife would attain in the good and bad states under policies B and C, with policy C representing full insurance that

Graph 17.6: Consumption in Different "States"

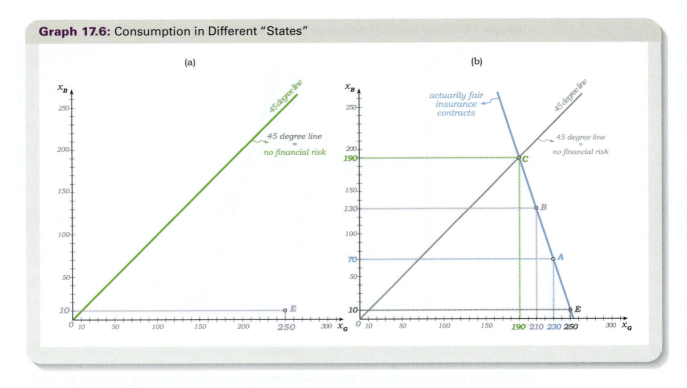

equalizes consumption in both states and thus removes all financial risk. Of course, there exist a number of other actuarily fair insurance contracts, with each having the feature that consumption in the bad state rises by $3 for every $1 paid in a premium. The line with slope -3 through E, A, B, and C then represents all possible actuarily fair insurance policies.

Why does consumption in the bad state rise only by three times the premium amount when actuarily fair insurance benefits are four times as high as the premium?

Exercise
17A.18

Note that all insurance policies that fall below the 45-degree line represent policies under which consumers do not fully insure and thus are left with less consumption in the "bad" state than in the "good" state, while policies above the 45-degree line result in "overinsurance" under which the consumer ends up with more consumption in the "bad" state than in the "good" state.

17A.2.3 Indifference Curves when Only Money Matters

Now suppose we consider indifference curves with the usual shape. As in our previous models of consumer choice, the consumer's optimal choice will then involve a point of tangency between an indifference curve and the budget line that is created by the set of actuarily fair insurance contracts. Where will this tangency occur?

Let's begin with the special case in which my wife only cares about money and could not care less about whether I am around or not; i.e., consider the case we treated in the previous section. We demonstrated in that section that when money is all that matters, any risk-averse consumer will choose to fully insure against risk when given a choice between all possible actuarily fair insurance contracts. Thus, in this special case, we know that the tangency between the optimal indifference curve and the budget set will lie on the 45-degree line at point C as illustrated in Graph 17.7. This implies that the marginal rate of substitution at point C (and similarly all along the 45-degree line) is exactly equal to -3, the slope of the budget set created by the menu of

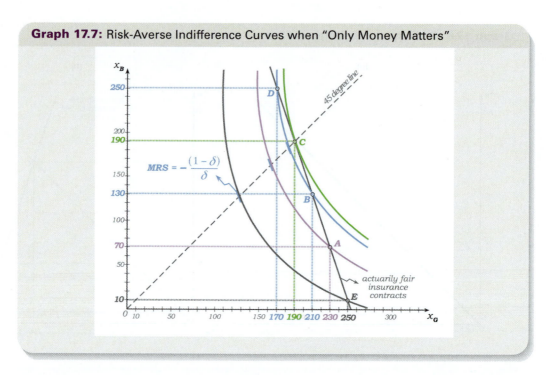

Graph 17.7: Risk-Averse Indifference Curves when "Only Money Matters"

actuarily fair insurance contracts. Adding indifference curves that go through points A, B, and C, we see that my wife moves to higher and higher indifference curves as she purchases increasing levels of insurance up to the point where she is fully insured.

More generally, if the probability of the "bad" state is denoted by δ and the probability of the "good" state by $(1 - \delta)$, the slope of the budget constraint will be $-(1 - \delta)/\delta$. For the special case when there is no difference between the two "states of the world," when only money matters, this implies that the marginal rate of substitution for the risk-averse consumer is also equal to $-(1 - \delta)/\delta$ along the 45-degree line.

Exercise 17A.19 Why is the slope of the budget constraint $-(1 - \delta)/\delta$?

Before leaving this special case, you can see how the convexity property embedded in the usual shape of indifference curves has a particularly intuitive interpretation within this model. Convexity means that when we have extreme bundles like B and D that lie on the same indifference curve, an average of those bundles (like C) is preferred. Since the expected consumption level remains the same along the line through B, C, and D, this implies that less risk (C) is better than more risk (B or D) so long as the expected value of the gamble remains unchanged. But that is precisely the definition of risk aversion. Thus, when indifference curves in this model satisfy convexity, the consumer is risk averse.

Exercise 17A.20 What would indifference curves look like for a risk-neutral consumer? What insurance policy would he or she purchase?

Exercise 17A.21 What would indifference curves look like for a risk-loving consumer? What insurance policy would he or she purchase?

Indifference curves for risk-averse consumers in this model therefore look very much like the indifference curves over consumption bundles that we are used to seeing from models without risk, and the budget constraint formed by the set of actuarily fair insurance contracts also looks very much like our usual budget constraints. There is, however, an important difference to keep in mind: In our previous consumer model without risk, a bundle (x_1, x_2) was a bundle of x_1 units of the first good *together with* x_2 units of the second good. A point (x_G, x_B) in our model with risk, on the other hand, represents two *separate* consumption levels that are *never* consumed together. Rather, if the "good" state hits, x_G is the quantity of consumption available, while if the "bad" state hits, x_B of the consumption good is available.

17A.2.4 Indifference Curves and Choices when the "States" Are Different

We have now established that if there is no inherent difference between the "good" and "bad" states (aside from the different levels of income associated with each state), indifference curves for risk-averse consumers will have the usual convexity property and a *MRS* equal to $-(1 - \delta)/\delta$ along the 45-degree line. But now suppose that the two states are inherently different, that money is not all that matters.

At the beginning of this section, I made the statement that consumption simply does not mean as much to my wife when I am not around. We enjoy each other's company, enjoy nice vacations, car rides in comfortable settings, and good dinners out together, but my wife might just choose to search for new meaning in the Peace Corps if it is no longer possible to consume with me. In that case, there is no reason for her to "fully insure"—to equalize her income in the good and bad states—even though she does not like risk. Rather, because consumption is so much more meaningful with me around, she would not want to give up too much of it in order to insure greater consumption when I am not around.

In Graph 17.8, we depict what her optimal decision on life insurance might look like in this case. The endowment point is just as it was before, as is the set of actuarily fair insurance contracts that forms my wife's choice set. Unlike the case where only money mattered to my wife

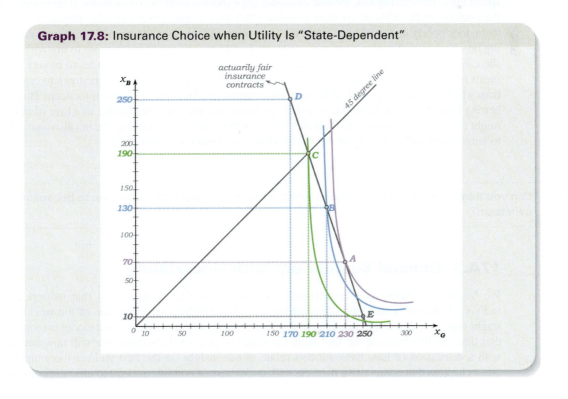

Graph 17.8: Insurance Choice when Utility Is "State-Dependent"

and where she therefore chooses to fully insure where her budget constraint intersects the 45-degree line, we have now drawn an indifference curve tangent at point *A* where my wife purchases an $80,000 life insurance policy on me in exchange for a premium of $20,000, thus reducing her consumption in the the good state to $230,000 and raising her consumption in the bad state to $70,000. While risk aversion implies full insurance in a "state-independent" model where only money matters, this illustrates that risk aversion is consistent with less than full insurance in the "state-dependent" model. *When we observe an individual not insuring fully, it may therefore be because insurance markets are not actuarily fair and/or because the individual has state-dependent utility.*

Exercise 17A.22

We concluded previously that when the two states are the same (aside from the income level associated with each state), $MRS = -(1 - \delta)/\delta$ along the 45-degree line. In the case we just discussed, can you tell whether the MRS is greater or less than this along the 45-degree line?

Exercise 17A.23

Suppose my wife was actually depressed by my presence and tolerates me solely for the paycheck I bring. Due to this depression, consumption is not very meaningful in the "good" state when I am around, but if I were not around, she would be able to travel the world and truly enjoy life. Might this cause her to purchase more than "full" life insurance on me? How would you illustrate this in a graph?

Here is another example that we will develop more fully in end-of-chapter exercise 17.4: Sports fans often bet on their favorite team. How can we explain this? If the fan agrees with the bookies on the odds of his team winning, we would have to assume that the fan is risk loving to explain his betting behavior if money were all that mattered. (After all, by betting on the game, the sports fan is introducing risk without changing the expected level of consumption if he agrees with the bookies on the odds of his team winning.) But for the true sports fan who despairs when his team does poorly and celebrates when his team wins, the "state of the world" is different depending on whether his favorite team wins or loses. Just as money might mean more to my wife when she can enjoy consuming it with me than when she has to consume in solitude, so money might mean more to the sports fan when his team wins and he wants to go out on the town to celebrate than when his team loses and all he wants is to crawl into bed and cry himself to sleep. Thus, the betting behavior of the sports fan who bets on his own team might not be due to a love of risk but might rather be explained by the fact that the event that leads to his winning the bet also causes him to enter a very different state of the world where consumption means more.

Exercise 17A.24

Can you think of a different scenario in which it makes sense for the sports fan to bet against his own team?

17A.3 General Equilibrium with Uncertainty

We began by developing a model with the assumption that money is all that matters when individuals face risk and then illustrated a second model in which the state of the world itself might matter in addition to the money associated with each state. The second model is more general than the first because the first model is a special case of the second. We will now conclude with a discussion of how these models relate to our insight (in the first welfare theorem) from other chapters that competitive markets will, under certain conditions, lead to efficient outcomes.

As in the previous chapter, we will illustrate this for very simple "economies" that lend themselves to graphical representation, but the basic insights hold for much more general economies with many individuals and many goods.

17A.3.1 Efficiency without Aggregate Risk

Suppose that you and I are the only individuals on a deserted island. I own half the island, and you own the other half, and in any given season, we might face rainy weather or drought. It just so happens that my part of the island has a variety of banana plant that yields much more fruit in rainy conditions, and your part of the island has a variety that yields more fruit under drought conditions. We therefore have two "states of the world," rain and drought, and our endowments depend on which state occurs. For now, however, we'll assume that the total crop of bananas on the entire island is always the same, with the weather determining only where the bananas grow. This assumption implies that there is *no aggregate risk* because in the aggregate, the economy always produces the same regardless of which state occurs. Putting consumption in the rainy state on the horizontal axis and consumption in the drought state on the vertical, we can then illustrate my "endowment" in a graph similar to that of the previous section. Specifically, Graph 17.9a illustrates the point E^1, with e_d^1 bananas in the dry state and e_r^1 bananas in the rainy state, and u^1 represents the level of utility I can get by simply accepting the hand I am dealt by nature. We can similarly illustrate your endowment E^2 in the same type of graph, only your endowment will lie above the 45-degree line as in panel (b) of the graph. Using our trick of illustrating both of these cases in a single Edgeworth Box, we get panel (c).

Which assumption in our example results in the square shape of this Edgeworth Box?

**Exercise
17A.25**

Panel (c) of Graph 17.9 then looks exactly like our usual Edgeworth Box, with the lens shape between our respective indifference curves suggesting that our situation is inefficient if we simply accept nature's outcome and eat our bananas when we grow them. Instead, we might wish to make a contract that specifies how many bananas I will give you if the rainy state happens in

Graph 17.9: A Simple Economy with Risk

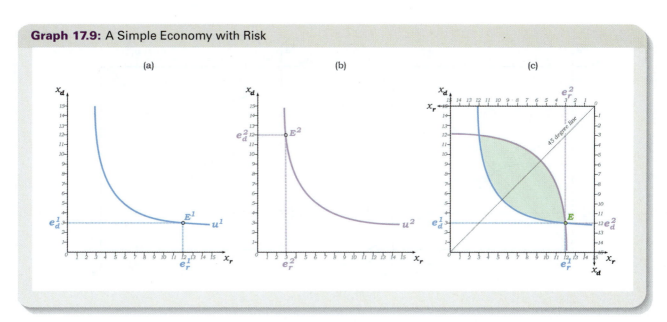

exchange for some set of bananas you will give me if we face the dry state. The terms of this contract can be denoted p_r/p_d, with this ratio telling us how much consumption in the drought state we can buy by giving up one banana in the rainy state. This is no different than the role prices play in forming budgets in the absence of risk and will therefore result in a budget line (much like the terms of insurance contracts for my wife created a budget line for her). And we will reach an efficient outcome when we have found contract terms such that we both end up optimizing at the same point in the Edgeworth Box. As we have seen in the previous chapter, such a point must have the feature that our indifference curves in the Edgeworth Box will have exactly the same slope.

First, suppose our utilities are not state-dependent; i.e., we get just as much enjoyment from each banana whether it rains or shines. We know from our work in the previous section that along the 45-degree line, our indifference curves have marginal rates of substitution equal to the probability of the rainy state divided by the probability of the dry state. Suppose the probability of drought is δ (and the probability of rain is $(1 - \delta)$). Then this implies that $MRS^1 = MRS^2 = (1 - \delta)/\delta$ along the 45-degree line of the Edgeworth Box.

Exercise
17A.26

True or False: The 45-degree line is, in this case, the contract curve.

To find the competitive equilibrium terms p_r^*/p_d^* of the contract we will strike, we therefore need to find terms that will create a budget line going through E with slope $(-(1 - \delta)/\delta)$; i.e., $-p_r^*/p_d^* = -(1 - \delta)/\delta$. This is illustrated in panel (a) of Graph 17.10, and, from our work with Edgeworth Boxes in the previous chapter, you should see immediately that any resulting equilibrium allocation A must be efficient; i.e., the first welfare theorem holds. In the case of tastes that are not state-dependent, the equilibrium terms of our contract also have the feature that they are "actuarily fair."

Graph 17.10: Equilibrium Contracts with No Aggregate Risk

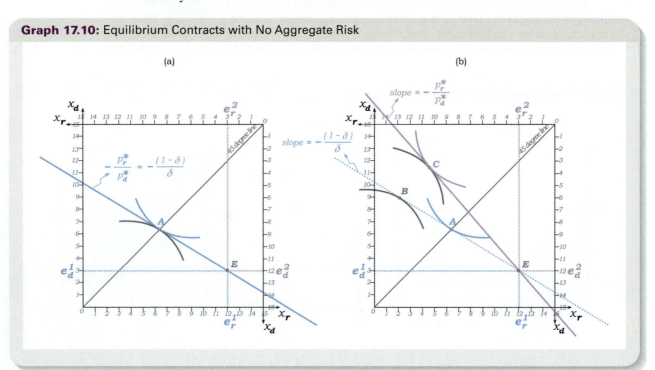

Next, suppose that my tastes continue to be "state-independent" but you place more value on consuming bananas when it rains than when it shines. Under the "actuarily fair" contract terms that give rise to budgets with slope $(-(1-\delta)/\delta)$, this would imply that I would choose to locate on the 45-degree line at A but you would not. This is illustrated along the dashed blue budget in panel (b) of Graph 17.10 where you would choose B, and it implies that these contract terms are no longer a competitive equilibrium. Rather, the equilibrium contract would now involve a ratio of prices p_r^*/p_d^* more favorable to me $(p_r^*/p_d^* > (1-\delta)/\delta)$, and would result in an equilibrium allocation C above the 45-degree line as illustrated along the magenta budget. Still, the first welfare theorem continues to hold.

What would the contract curve look like in this case?	**Exercise 17A.27**
Suppose you liked bananas more when it rains than when it shines. Where would the equilibrium be?	**Exercise 17A.28**
Suppose you were the one who had state-independent tastes and I was the one who values consuming bananas more when it shines than when it rains. Where would the equilibrium be?	**Exercise 17A.29**

17A.3.2 Introducing Aggregate Risk Now suppose that our little economy faces *aggregate risk* in addition to the *individual risk* you and I face. In particular, suppose that the overall yield of bananas on our island is twice as large when it rains than when it shines. Panel (a) of Graph 17.11 then illustrates the resulting Edgeworth Box, which now is twice as long as it is high because in the rainy state the economy produces twice as many bananas. The point E again represents the endowment point, with e_r^1 and e_d^1 representing the bananas that grow on my side of the island in the two states, and e_r^2 and e_d^2 representing the bananas that grow on your side of the island.

Since our Edgeworth Box is no longer a square, the 45-degree line emanating from my (lower left) origin is now not the same as the 45-degree line emanating from your (upper right) origin. If our tastes are state-independent, we know that our marginal rates of substitution

Graph 17.11: Equilibrium with Aggregate Risk

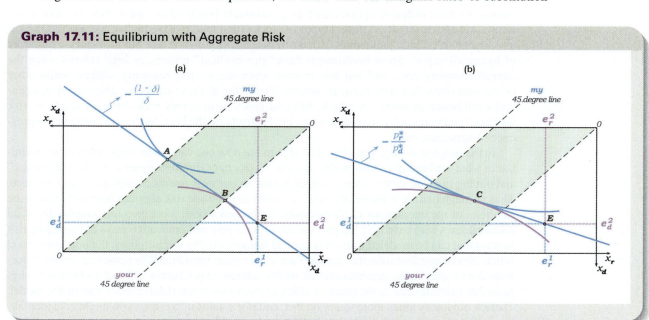

along our 45-degree lines are equal to $(-(1 - \delta)/\delta)$. But this implies immediately that there is no way we can have competitive equilibrium contracts that have actuarily fair terms of $(p_r/p_d) = (1 - \delta)/\delta$. More precisely, if the blue budget through E has slope $(-(1 - \delta)/\delta)$, I would choose to optimize at point A while you would choose to optimize at point B.

Now notice that the only region in which our indifference curves could ever be tangent to one another is the region that lies between our two 45-degree lines. This is because above my 45-degree line, the slopes of my indifference curves are steeper than $(-(1 - \delta)/\delta)$, which is true for your indifference curves only below your 45-degree line. Any equilibrium allocation must therefore fall in the shaded region where both your and my indifference curves are *shallower* than $(-(1 - \delta)/\delta)$. This allows us to conclude that (p_r^*/p_d^*) must be less than $((1 - \delta)/\delta)$. Put differently, it must be the case that I will not be able to get as many bananas in the drought state by giving up one banana in the rainy state as I could when there was no aggregate risk (in Graph 17.10a). A resulting equilibrium is then pictured in panel (b) of the graph.

This result can be generalized as follows: *In the presence of aggregate risk, the good in the "bad" state is relatively more valuable the larger the aggregate risk.* We will see shortly how this relates to important themes in finance.

Exercise 17A.30

Given that there are more bananas in the aggregate in the rainy state of the world, consider an endowment that has relatively more bananas in the dry state and another that has relatively more bananas in the rainy state. If you could choose your endowment, which endowment would you be more likely to want (assuming we both have state-independent tastes and the overall endowments are not too different)?

17A.3.3 Financial Asset Markets   Much of our discussion of risk has centered around insurance markets since insurance is all about us attempting to reduce the risks that life hands to us. Insurance markets are interesting for a number of reasons, some of which will not become clear until we get to the topic of asymmetric information in Chapter 22. But insurance markets are not the only markets that center around attempts to deal with risk. Another important example arises in financial markets. For instance, when we look for places to invest our money, we have different options such as government bonds (that tend to have relatively low returns but also low risk), different types of stocks (that tend to have higher average returns but also higher risk), and "junk bonds" (that promise a really high return but also carry a high risk of losing all value). Some investments have "pro-cyclical" returns, or high returns when the overall economy does well but low returns when the overall economy suffers, while other investments have "counter-cyclical" returns. Prices for all these assets are determined in a general equilibrium economy in which different types of investors with different levels of risk aversion (and potentially state-dependent tastes) try to do the best they can, usually in the presence of aggregate risk.

In the simplest setting, you should be able to see how one can model such assets in ways similar to what we have described in this section. Assets have different returns in different "states," and trading in assets changes the expected return on our investments as well as the risk we face. Thus, through trading in financial assets, investors can manage risk at prices determined from the sum total of the interactions of all investors. In the real world, most investors employ financial intermediaries who have over the past decades found new and innovative ways of managing risk in ways that can be modeled using this general framework. For our purposes, the important point is that, absent any distortion that we have not at this point introduced (in particular absent distortions due to asymmetric information that will be addressed in Chapter 22), our analysis here suggests that markets once again result in efficient outcomes when risk becomes part of the model. There is obviously much more to say on this, and if it sounds interesting, you might consider taking further course work in financial economics.

In modeling equilibrium terms of trade that might emerge in financial markets, would you likely assume state-dependent or state-independent tastes?

Exercise 17A.31

Suppose the two "states" of the world are recessions and economic booms. If you put consumption in economic booms on the horizontal axis, will the height of the Edgeworth Box be larger or smaller than its width?

Exercise 17A.32

17B The Mathematics of Choice in the Presence of Risk

Introducing the mathematics to go along with our graphs from Section A will illustrate some subtleties that are not immediately apparent from our intuitive treatment. In particular, we will see in some clearer detail what is assumed and what is not assumed in expected utility theory, and we will be able to illustrate with numerical examples some of the basic insights of the previous section. We will depart from our usual practice of employing the functional forms used to construct the graphs in the corresponding section of part A and instead leave this as an exercise at the end of the chapter (end-of-chapter exercise 17.1) in order to give you some additional practice in relating graphs to mathematics. We will, however, return to the context of our example of my wife's choice over life insurance policies and this time will ask you in the within-chapter exercises to sketch out the graphs that result in the mathematical solutions we derive.

17B.1 "Utility" and Expected Utility

In Section A, we began with an underlying "consumption/utility" relationship in Graph 17.1. We likened this to a single-input production process that takes "consumption" as an input and "utility" as an output, and we illustrated how the shape of this function relates to the concept of risk aversion when my wife potentially faces a "bad" and a "good" outcome, x_B and x_G. We then developed a more general model in which we illustrated indifference curves in a graph with x_G on the horizontal and x_B on the vertical axis. We will now see that it is really the indifference curves in this more general model (which allows for both state-independent and state-dependent utility) that represent tastes over risky gambles and that the underlying "consumption/utility" relationship is simply a by-product of modeling these indifference curves.

Suppose that we are again concerned about the case where my wife faces the possibility of low consumption x_B with probability δ and high consumption x_G with probability $(1 - \delta)$ depending on whether or not I survive. For now, let's again assume that all my wife cares about is money (and not whether or not I am around, aside from the implications this has on her consumption levels). We would then like to represent my wife's tastes over the various possible combinations of x_G and x_B with a utility function $U(x_G, x_B)$ that gives rise to her indifference curves in a graph like Graph 17.7. As with any particular indifference map over pairs (x_G, x_B), there exist many utility functions that will give rise to that particular indifference map. John von Neumann (1903–1957) and Oskar Morgenstern (1902–1977),[5] however, derived a condition

---

[5]Von Neumann made foundational contributions to fields as varied as quantum mechanics, computer science, statistics, and mathematics and served as a key member of the Manhattan Project (that developed the first nuclear bomb). Together with his Princeton colleague Oskar Morgenstern, he also wrote the first classic in game theory, *Games and Economic Behavior*, in 1944.

under which *an underlying function u(x) exists such that we can represent my wife's indifference map over pairs of x_G and x_B using a utility function that takes the form*

$$U(x_G, x_B) = \delta u(x_B) + (1 - \delta)u(x_G); \qquad (17.1)$$

i.e., a utility function that is simply the "expected utility" *if we interpret the function u(x) as measuring the utility of consumption.* (There actually exist many such functions that will work for any given individual, a fact we demonstrate in end-of-chapter exercise 17.2.) The condition under which we can find such a function $u(x)$ is known as the *independence axiom*, which is explained in some detail in Appendix 1. It is not a very strong assumption, and we will simply take it as given much as we have taken as given the rationality axioms in our development of consumer theory in the absence of risk. (At the same time, we should acknowledge that there are some famous "paradoxes" that appear to illustrate violations of the independence axiom, one of which is explored in Appendix 2 and another in end-of-chapter exercise 17.7.) The utility function $U(x_G, x_B)$ that takes the expected utility form and represents a consumer's underlying indifference curves over risky gambles is often called a *von Neumann-Morgenstern expected utility function.*

The "consumption/utility" relationship in Graph 17.1 of Section A is then simply the graph of such an underlying function $u(x)$; i.e., it is a graph of the "utility function over consumption" that allows us to write my wife's utility over risky gambles as an *expected utility.* Thus, this "consumption/utility" relationship is not some "real" underlying relationship between my wife's consumption level and her happiness. It is simply a mathematical function that permits us to represent her "real" preferences over risky gambles in the form of an "expected utility function" $U(x_G, x_B)$. Put differently, we do not have to assume that my wife actually has some internal production function for utility that allows her to measure her happiness in some quantifiable way (as we implicitly assumed early on in Section A). We simply have to assume that she has indifference curves over risky gambles (such as those in Graph 17.7), just as we assumed that people have indifference curves over consumption bundles in our earlier development of consumer theory in the absence of risk.

Suppose, then, that the function that allows us to represent my wife's tastes over gambles involving x_G (with probability $(1 - \delta)$) and x_B (with probability δ) with an expected utility function $U(x_G, x_B)$ is

$$u(x) = 0.5 \ln x. \qquad (17.2)$$

Exercise 17B.1   Letting x denote consumption measured in thousands of dollars, illustrate the approximate shape of my wife's consumption/utility relationship in the range from 1 to 250 (interpreted as the range from \$1,000 to \$250,000).

Exercise 17B.2   What does the graph of the utility function look like in the range of consumption between 0 and 1 (corresponding to 0 to \$1,000)?

Using the "ruler" $u(x) = 0.5 \ln x$ as a tool to measure utility, we can then say that my wife's utility of consuming x_B is $u(x_B) = 0.5 \ln x_B$ and her utility of consuming x_G is $u(x_G) = 0.5 \ln x_G$. Again, this does not mean that we think we are in any way objectively measuring my wife's happiness at consumption levels x_B and x_G, but we have chosen the "ruler" with which to measure her happiness in such a way that we can now express her utility of facing a particular gamble (x_G, x_B) (with probabilities $(1 - \delta, \delta)$) using the von Neumann-Morgenstern expected utility function

$$U(x_G, x_B) = E(u) = \delta u(x_B) + (1 - \delta)u(x_G) = 0.5\delta \ln x_B + 0.5(1 - \delta) \ln x_G. \qquad (17.3)$$

Following our discussion in Section A, suppose then that my wife's consumption is $250,000 if I survive and $10,000 if I do not survive. Expressing x in thousands of dollars, $x_B = 10$ and $x_2 = 250$. Suppose further, again as in Section A, that the probability I do not survive is 25%; i.e., $\delta = 0.25$. My wife's expected consumption level is therefore

$$E(x) = \delta x_B + (1 - \delta)x_G = 0.25(10) + 0.75(250) = 190, \qquad (17.4)$$

and, using equation (17.3), her expected utility is

$$E(u) = 0.5(0.25) \ln(10) + 0.5(0.75) \ln(250) \approx 2.358. \qquad (17.5)$$

What is the utility of receiving the expected income, denoted $u(E(x))$? Illustrate $E(x)$, $E(u)$, and $u(E(x))$ on a graph of equation (17.2).

**Exercise
17B.3**

True or False: If u is a concave function, then $u(E(x))$ is larger than $E(u)$, and if u is a convex function, then $u(E(x))$ is smaller than $E(u)$.

**Exercise
17B.4**

17B.1.1 Risk Aversion and Concavity of *u(x)* In within-chapter-exercise (17B.3), you should have concluded that my wife's utility of receiving the expected value of the gamble she faces is approximately 2.624. Since we determined in equation (17.5) that her expected utility of facing the gamble is only 2.358, we know that she would prefer to collect 190 with certainty rather than take her chances and have 250 with probability of 0.75 but only 10 with probability 0.25. In other words, my wife would prefer to eliminate the risk of facing the gamble if she can keep the expected value of the gamble without risk. If a consumer prefers to reduce risk when offered the chance to do so without giving up consumption in expectation, we say that the consumer is *risk averse*.

Another way of saying the same thing is to say that *an individual is risk averse if and only if the utility of the expected value of the gamble is greater than the expected utility of the gamble;* i.e., if and only if $u(E(x)) > U(x_G, x_B)$. This can be expanded to read

$$u\Big(\delta x_B + (1 - \delta)x_G\Big) = u\Big(E(x)\Big) > U(x_G, x_B) = \delta u(x_B) + (1 - \delta)u(x_G). \qquad (17.6)$$

Now recall that, as we first saw in Chapter 12, a concave function can be defined as a function f such that, for all $x_1 \neq x_2$ and all δ between zero and 1,

$$f\Big(\delta x_1 + (1 - \delta)x_2\Big) > \delta f(x_1) + (1 - \delta)x_2. \qquad (17.7)$$

Equation (17.6) defines risk aversion of tastes using the expected utility function (and the appropriate function $u(x)$ that allows us to represent tastes with the expected utility form). Equation (17.7) defines concavity of a function. Looking at these side-by-side, you can quickly see that equation (17.6) implies that the function $u(x)$ is concave. Thus, *if tastes over gambles involving x_B and x_G exhibit risk aversion, then any function $u(x)$ that permits us to represent these tastes using an expected utility function $U(x_G, x_B)$ must be concave.* While our discussion in Section A may lead one to believe that risk aversion derives from the concavity of some underlying utility function $u(x)$, the real story is that an individual's risk aversion implies that any function $u(x)$ that allows us to represent such tastes with an expected utility function must be concave. Put differently, we are not assuming concavity of $u(x)$ to get risk-averse tastes; rather, we are deriving that $u(x)$ *must be* concave if underlying tastes over risky gambles exhibit risk aversion and u can be used to represent indifference curves over (x_G, x_B) in the expected utility form.

While it is at first confusing to keep in mind the difference between the expected utility $E(u)$ of a gamble and the utility of the expected value of the gamble $u(E(x))$, it is straightforward to show that the only way these can ever be the same is if $u(x)$ is linear. Suppose, for instance, that $u(x) = \alpha x$. Then

$$E(u) = \delta \alpha x_B + (1 - \delta)\alpha x_G = \alpha\big(\delta x_B + (1 - \delta)x_G\big) = \alpha E(x) = u\big(E(x)\big); \quad (17.8)$$

i.e., my wife would be indifferent between accepting a risky gamble and the expected value of the gamble with certainty. This is the definition of *risk-neutral* tastes.

Exercise 17B.5 What would $E(u)$ and $u(E(x))$ be for my wife if her utility of consumption were given instead by the convex function $u(x) = x^2$? Illustrate your answer in a graph.

Exercise 17B.6 The convexity of a function f is defined analogously to concavity, with the inequality in equation (17.7) reversed. Can you show that tastes that exhibit risk loving (as opposed to risk aversion) necessarily imply that any $u(x)$ used to define an expected utility function must be convex?

17B.1.2 Concavity of $u(x)$ and Convexity of Tastes

So far, we have shown that if my wife's tastes exhibit risk aversion, then any function $u(x)$ we use to measure her utility of consumption *must* be concave if we are to use it to represent her indifference curves over bundles of (x_G, x_B) using an expected utility function $U(x_G, x_B) = \delta u(x_B) + (1 - \delta)u(x_G)$. With a little work, we can now furthermore show that this in turn implies the convex shape of indifference curves that we concluded in Section A must be associated with risk aversion.

Remember from our development of consumer theory that indifference curves exhibit the usual convexity property if "averages are better than extremes." By this, we meant that if a consumer is indifferent between two bundles, she would prefer any weighted average of the those two bundles to either of the more extreme bundles we started with. In the context of our model of outcome bundles (x_G, x_B), suppose we begin with two such bundles, (x_G^1, x_B^1) and (x_G^2, x_B^2), over which we are indifferent; i.e., two bundles such that

$$U(x_G^1, x_B^1) = U(x_G^2, x_B^2) = \overline{U}. \quad (17.9)$$

Now consider a weighted average (x_G^3, x_B^3) of these two bundles of outcomes; i.e., for some α that lies between 0 and 1, consider (x_G^3, x_B^3) such that

$$x_G^3 = \alpha x_G^2 + (1 - \alpha)x_G^1 \text{ and } x_B^3 = \alpha x_B^2 + (1 - \alpha)x_B^1. \quad (17.10)$$

By simply using the definition of the expected utility function $U(x_G, x_B)$ and the concavity of $u(x)$, we can then conclude the following:

$$
\begin{aligned}
U(x_G^3, x_B^3) &= \delta u(x_B^3) + (1 - \delta)u(x_G^3) \\
&= \delta u(\alpha x_B^2 + (1 - \alpha)x_B^1) + (1 - \delta)u(\alpha x_G^2 + (1 - \alpha)x_G^1) \\
&> \delta[\alpha u(x_B^2) + (1 - \alpha)u(x_B^1)] + (1 - \delta)[\alpha u(x_G^2) + (1 - \alpha)u(x_G^1)] \\
&= \alpha[\delta u(x_B^2) + (1 - \delta)u(x_G^2)] + (1 - \alpha)[\delta u(x_B^1) + (1 - \delta)u(x_G^1)] \\
&= \alpha U(x_G^2, x_B^2) + (1 - \alpha)U(x_G^1, x_B^1) \\
&= \alpha \overline{U} + (1 - \alpha)\overline{U} = \overline{U}.
\end{aligned}
\quad (17.11)
$$

The first line simply plugs the average bundle (x_G^3, x_B^3) into the expected utility function $U(x_G, x_B) = \delta u(x_B) + (1 - \delta)u(x_G)$; the second substitutes the equations from (17.10) for x_B^3 and x_G^3; the third (inequality) is a direct application of the definition of concavity of $u(x)$; the fourth simply rearranges terms; the fifth line derives from the fact that the terms in the parentheses in the fourth line are just the expected utilities of the original more extreme bundles; and the last line uses the fact that both the original bundles were on the same indifference curve $\overline{U}$. Taken together, we conclude that

$$U(x_G^3, x_B^3) > \overline{U} = U(x_G^2, x_B^2) = U(x_G^1, x_B^1); \tag{17.12}$$

i.e., the average bundle created from the more extreme bundles that lie on the same indifference curve is preferred to the more extreme bundles of outcomes. Thus, we have now shown that risk aversion implies concavity of $u(x)$ and concavity of $u(x)$ implies convexity of the indifference curves over pairs (x_G, x_B) of outcomes.

Can you show in analogous steps that convexity of $u(x)$ must imply non-convexity of the indifference curves over outcome pairs (x_G, x_B)?

Exercise 17B.7*

17B.1.3 Certainty Equivalents and Risk Premiums
The *certainty equivalent* of a gamble is the minimum amount an individual would accept in order to give up participating in the gamble. For my wife, for instance, we calculated the expected utility of participating in the gamble (of relying on my income but facing the possibility of me not surviving to bring home an income) as, $U(250, 10) = E(u) = 2.358$. To determine her certainty equivalent to facing this gamble, we need to find the value x_{ce} such that her utility of getting this amount is equal to the expected utility of facing the gamble; i.e., we need to find for what value of x_{ce} the equation $u(x_{ce}) = 2.358$ holds. Using the function $u(x) = 0.5 \ln x$ as we have earlier, this implies we need to solve the equation $0.5 \ln x_{ce} = 2.358$ or, written slightly differently, $\ln x_{ce} = 2.358/0.5$, which solves to approximately $x_{ce} \approx 111.8$.[6]

Thus, my wife would take an amount roughly equal to $111.8 thousand in exchange for having me around and thus facing a 0.75 probability of a $250 thousand income and a 0.25 probability of a $10 thousand income. The *risk premium* of a gamble is then defined as the difference between the expected value $(E(x))$ of the gamble and the certainty equivalent (x_{ce}) of the gamble. For our example, this is the difference between $E(x) = 190$ and $x_{ce} = 111.8$, or $78.2 thousand dollars.

Illustrate x_{ce} and the risk premium on a graph with my wife's utility function $u(x) = 0.5 \ln x$.

Exercise 17B.8

17B.1.4 Actuarily Fair Insurance Markets
Now suppose my wife is offered a choice of different insurance contracts (or policies). Such contracts are composed of two parts: an *insurance benefit b* that my wife receives in the event that I do not survive, and an *insurance premium p* that she has to pay prior to knowing whether or not I survive. Regardless of what happens to me, my wife has to pay p, which implies that her *net benefit* from buying insurance is $(b - p)$ in the event that I do not survive. Thus, her income if I survive will be $(x_G - p)$, and her income if I do not survive will be $(x_B + b - p)$.

Now suppose that the set of insurance contracts she is offered is the full set of *actuarily fair* policies; i.e., policies that reduce her risk without changing her expected income. (In Section A, we argued that this would be the expected set of contracts that a competitive insurance industry with negligible costs would offer in equilibrium.) Since, under any given contract (b, p) she gets a (net) payment of $(b - p)$ with probability δ but has to pay p with probability $(1 - \delta)$, her expected income will remain unchanged so long as $\delta(b - p) = (1 - \delta)p$, or, solving for b, as long as $b = p/\delta$. Thus, *an insurance contract (b, p) is actuarily fair if and only if $b = p/\delta$*.

---

[6]Recall that the natural logarithm ln is defined with respect to base $e \approx 2.7182818$, and thus $x_{ce} = e^{2.358/0.5}$.

We can then ask which type of actuarily fair insurance policy my wife would choose if she could choose from a full set of policies, some with low premiums and low benefits, others with higher premiums and higher benefits. Her expected utility from an actuarily fair policy (b,p) is

$$U(x_G,x_B) = \delta u(x_B + b - p) + (1 - \delta)u(x_G - p) \text{ where } b = \frac{p}{\delta}, \qquad (17.13)$$

or, substituting $b = p/\delta$,

$$U(x_G,x_B) = \delta u\left(x_B + \frac{(1 - \delta)p}{\delta}\right) + (1 - \delta)u(x_G - p). \qquad (17.14)$$

Choosing among a full set of actuarily fair insurance contracts then simply involves my wife maximizing $U(x_G,x_B)$ from equation (17.14) by choosing the optimal premium p (and thus the optimal benefit $b = p/\delta$). When $u(x) = \alpha \ln x$ (as in equation (17.2) where $\alpha = 0.5$), we can write this optimization problem as

$$\max_{p} \delta\alpha \ln\left(x_B + \frac{(1 - \delta)p}{\delta}\right) + (1 - \delta)\alpha \ln(x_G - p). \qquad (17.15)$$

Taking the first derivative of the expression in (17.15), setting it to zero and solving for p, we get the optimal premium

$$p^* = \delta(x_G - x_B) \qquad (17.16)$$

and then, substituting this into the condition for actuarily fair insurance ($b = p/\delta$), the implied optimum insurance benefit

$$b^* = x_G - x_B. \qquad (17.17)$$

Exercise 17B.9   Verify the expressions for p^* and b^*.

In Section A, we concluded that when facing actuarily fair insurance markets, a risk-averse person in this model will always choose to fully insure, that is, to insure to the point where income is the same no matter what happens. Under the insurance policy (b^*, p^*), my wife's consumption is either $(x_B + b^* - p^*)$ or $(x_G - p^*)$ depending on whether or not I survive, and you can check that both these reduce to

$$x = \delta x_B + (1 - \delta)x_G. \qquad (17.18)$$

For instance, when $x_B = 10$, $x_G = 250$, and $\delta = 0.25$ (as in our life insurance example throughout this chapter), my wife's optimal insurance policy has her paying a premium of $60 thousand in exchange for an insurance benefit of $240 thousand, which implies that whether I survive or not, my wife will have $190 thousand available for consumption. Put differently, she will choose the actuarily fair insurance contract that insures her fully against the risk of my premature demise.

Exercise 17B.10   Even though we did not use the same underlying utility function as the one used to plot graphs in Section A, we have gotten the same result for the optimal actuarily fair insurance policy. Why is this?

17B.2 Risky Choices Involving Multiple "States of the World"

So far, we have illustrated a model in which my wife takes a gamble on two different "states of the world": one with me in it, the other without me. But the model presumes that, aside from the paycheck I produce if I am around, my presence in the world is entirely ornamental and has no direct impact on how my wife evaluates consumption. If consumption for my wife is more or less pleasurable when I am around than when I am not around, then the two states of the world differ in ways that are not captured by the model in which the gamble my wife takes is solely about money.

17B.2.1 Modeling Consumption in Different "States of the World" Suppose, then, that the state B of the world (where I am no longer around) differs from state G of the world (where I am around) in the sense that my wife evaluates the benefits of consumption differently in the two states. This implies that the indifference curves over outcome bundles (x_G, x_B) will now differ from the case where the state of the world was irrelevant to how my wife views consumption. However, an extension of von Neumann and Morgenstern's result implies that there will now exist two functions of x, $u_B(x)$ and $u_G(x)$, such that these indifference curves can be represented by an expected utility function of the form

$$U(x_G, x_B) = \delta u_B(x_B) + (1 - \delta)u_G(x_G). \tag{17.19}$$

The only difference between this and our previous expected utility function is that the functions used to measure utility in the two different states of the world take on different forms whereas before, when the state of the world was irrelevant to how my wife feels about consumption, a single function $u(x)$ was used in the expected utility function $U(x_G, x_B)$. State-dependent tastes can therefore be modeled as if my wife uses the function $u_G(x)$ to evaluate consumption in state G and $u_B(x)$ to evaluate consumption in state B. When tastes are state-independent, $u_G(x) = u_B(x)$, which is why the state-independent case is simply a special case of the state-dependent model.

Extending the model to the functional form for u that we used in the previous section, my wife might now have tastes such that $u_B(x) = \alpha \ln x$ and $u_G(x) = \beta \ln x$ can be used to formulate the expected utility function in equation (17.19). The expected utility function that represents her indifference curves over outcome pairs (x_G, x_B) then becomes

$$U(x_B, x_G) = \delta\alpha \ln x_B + (1 - \delta)\beta \ln x_G. \tag{17.20}$$

Derive the expression for the marginal rate of substitution for equation (17.20). Now suppose $\alpha = \beta$. What is the *MRS* along the 45-degree line on which $x_B = x_G$? Compare this to the result we derived graphically in Graph 17.7.

Exercise 17B.11

Can you see that the indifference curves generated by $U(x_G, x_B)$ in equation (17.20) are Cobb–Douglas? Write the function as a Cobb–Douglas function and derive the *MRS*. Does the property that must hold along the 45-degree line when tastes are not state-dependent hold?

Exercise 17B.12

True or False: The expected utility function $U(x_G, x_B)$ can be transformed in all the ways that utility functions in consumer theory can usually be transformed without changing the underlying indifference curves, but such transformations will imply a loss of the expected utility form.

Exercise 17B.13*

17B.2.2 Choice Sets under Actuarily Fair Insurance

Now that we know how indifference curves in the (x_G, x_B) space are formed, we can next ask how budget constraints arise when individuals have opportunities to insure against risk in an actuarily fair way. We can begin with the analog to what we called the endowment point in our discussion of budgets in Chapter 3, which in our example is simply the point (e_G, e_B) that my wife faces in the absence of buying insurance. Letting consumption be denominated in thousands of dollars, $(e_G, e_B) = (250,10)$ since my wife's consumption (in the absence of insurance) is $10,000 in state B and $250,000 in state G.

An insurance contract is then a contract for which my wife pays a premium p regardless of what state she ends up facing in exchange for receiving a benefit b if state B occurs. As we discussed already, this contract is actuarily fair if and only if $b = p/\delta$. Beginning at the endowment point (e_G, e_B), this implies that for every dollar my wife gives up in the state G, she will get $(1 - \delta)/\delta$ in state B.[7] The slope of the budget emanating from the point (e_G, e_B) is therefore $(-(1 - \delta)/\delta)$. Were my wife to pay a premium of e_G (thus giving up all consumption in state G), she would receive a net benefit of $(1 - \delta)e_G/\delta$ in state B, which implies her overall consumption in state B (including her state B endowment e_B and her net benefit from the insurance) would be $e_B + ((1 - \delta)e_G/\delta)$, which can be rewritten as $(\delta e_B + (1 - \delta)e_G)/\delta$. This is then the vertical intercept of the budget line formed by the availability of actuarily fair insurance (where we graph state B on the vertical axis to be consistent with our graphs from Section A).

We can then use the intercept and slope we have just calculated to express the budget line arising from actuarily fair insurance as the equation

$$x_B = \frac{\delta e_B + (1 - \delta)e_G}{\delta} - \frac{(1 - \delta)}{\delta} x_G, \tag{17.21}$$

or, multiplying through by δ and collecting terms, as

$$\delta e_B + (1 - \delta)e_G = \delta x_B + (1 - \delta)x_G. \tag{17.22}$$

Exercise 17B.14

On a graph with x_G on the horizontal and x_B on the vertical axis, illustrate this budget constraint using values derived from the example of my wife's choices over insurance contracts. Compare it with Graph 17.6b.

17B.2.3 Choice over Actuarily Fair Insurance Contracts

With tastes represented by the state-dependent expected utility function $U(x_G, x_B)$ as in equation (17.19) and budgets specified as in equation (17.22), we can now write down the optimization problem that a consumer who faces a complete set of actuarily fair insurance contracts faces as

$$\max_{x_G, x_B} U(x_G, x_B) = \delta u_B(x_B) + (1 - \delta)u_G(x_G) \tag{17.23}$$

$$\text{subject to } \delta e_B + (1 - \delta)e_G = \delta x_B + (1 - \delta)x_G,$$

or, using the functional form for $U(x_G, x_B)$ from equation (17.20),

$$\max_{x_G, x_B} \delta \alpha \ln x_B + (1 - \delta)\beta \ln x_G \text{ subject to } \delta e_B + (1 - \delta)e_G = \delta x_B + (1 - \delta)x_G. \tag{17.24}$$

Solving this in the usual way, we get

$$x_B^* = \frac{\alpha(\delta e_B + (1 - \delta)e_G)}{\delta \alpha + (1 - \delta)\beta} \text{ and } x_G^* = \frac{\beta(\delta e_B + (1 - \delta)e_G)}{\delta \alpha + (1 - \delta)\beta}. \tag{17.25}$$

---

[7]To be more precise, she will get a benefit of $1/\delta$ but she still has to pay the $1 premium. Thus, her net benefit in state B is $((1/\delta) - 1)$, which can also be expressed as $(1 - \delta)/\delta$.

Exercise
17B.15

Verify the result in equation (17.25).

We argued at the beginning of this section that the model in which "only money matters" is a special case of the model in which different states are associated with different ways in which consumption contributes to welfare. You can now see this in the context of our example by assuming that $\alpha = \beta$, which would make $u_G(x) = u_B(x)$. Replacing β with α in the equations for x_B^* and x_G^*, we get

$$x_B^* = \delta e_B + (1 - \delta)e_G = x_G^*. \qquad (17.26)$$

Put differently, when utility is not "state-dependent," my wife will choose an actuarily fair insurance policy that equalizes her consumption in the "good" and "bad" states of the world.

Exercise
17B.16

Using the values of $10 and $250 as the consumption level my wife gets in state B and state G in the absence of insurance, what level of consumption does she get in each state when she chooses her optimal actuarily fair insurance policy (assuming, as before, that state B occurs with probability 0.25 and state G occurs with probability 0.75)?

Now suppose that $\beta > \alpha$, which implies that the marginal contribution of each dollar to my wife's well-being is greater in state G when I am around than in state B when I have disappeared. You should see immediately by inspecting the equations for x_B^* and x_G^* that this implies $x_B^* < x_G^*$ under my wife's optimal insurance contract. The reverse is true when $\alpha > \beta$.

Using the example we have employed throughout, with $e_B = 10$, $e_G = 250$, and $\delta = 0.25$, Table 17.1 then gives the results for different ratios of α/β. Put differently, the table illustrates how insurance behavior changes when utility is state-dependent, with the ratio α/β describing by how much utility of consumption differs in the two states. When $\alpha/\beta = 1$, utility is not state-dependent and the consumer fully insures. When $\alpha/\beta < 1$, consumption is more meaningful in state G (when my wife can consume with me) than in state B, and the first four rows of the table illustrate different scenarios under which my wife will "underinsure" because of the state-dependence of

Table 17.1: "Over" and "Under" Insurance

Optimal Insurance Contracts when "States" Differ				
α/β	x_B	x_G	p	b
1/10	$ 24,516	$245,161	$ 4,839	$ 19,355
1/4	$ 58,462	$233,846	$ 16,154	$ 64,615
1/2	$108,571	$217,143	$ 32,857	$ 131,429
3/4	$152,000	$202,667	$ 47,333	$ 189,333
1/1	$190,000	$190,000	$ 60,000	$240,000
4/3	$233,846	$175,385	$ 74,615	$298,462
2/1	$304,000	$152,000	$ 98,000	$392,000
4/1	$434,286	$108,571	$141,429	$565,714
10/1	$584,615	$ 58,462	$191,538	$766,154

her tastes. When $\alpha/\beta > 1$, on the other hand, consumption is more meaningful in state B (when my wife is finally rid of me and can truly enjoy life), with the last four rows in the table illustrating different scenarios under which my wife chooses to "overinsure" as a result of this type of state-dependence.

Exercise 17B.17* Using an Excel spreadsheet, can you verify the numbers in Table 17.1?

Exercise 17B.18 Using a graph similar to Graph 17.8, illustrate the case of $\alpha/\beta = 1/4$ (row 2 in the table).

Exercise 17B.19 Using a graph similar to Graph 17.8, illustrate the case of $\alpha/\beta = 2/1$ (row 7 in the table).

17B.3 General Equilibrium with Risk

We have thus far introduced a model of risk in which we define different "states" of the world, and, to go along with each state, we define a *state contingent consumption level*. In principle, this could be extended to multiple types of consumption, with state contingent consumption levels for each good specified in each of the states of the world. This is merely a matter of complicating the notation of the model (and making it impossible to develop graphical versions), but it is important to keep in mind that what we are doing is much more general than may be apparent at first.

Insurance contracts represent particular ways of selling state contingent consumption in one state in order to purchase state contingent consumption in another state. And, as noted at the end of Section A, other types of contracts, such as those involving investments in financial assets, can serve a similar purpose. We can then model all of these types of markets as markets in *state-contingent assets*, markets in which individuals trade across "states of the world" at prices that are determined within the market. General equilibrium models of risk allow us to investigate how these prices are determined in equilibrium. As we already saw in Section A, the mechanics of this are no different than those already developed in the previous chapter's treatment of exchange (or Edgeworth Box) economies.

We will mathematically illustrate the basic insights introduced intuitively in Section A by using a two-consumer model in which consumer utility can be state-dependent, in which consumers might differ in their beliefs about the *individual* risk that they face, and in which there might be *aggregate* risk for the whole economy. More precisely, each consumer is endowed with some consumption level in each state, with e_i^j representing consumer j's endowment of consumption in state i. Consumer 1's utility in states 1 and 2 is given by $u_1^1(x) = \alpha \ln x$ and $u_2^1(x) = (1 - \alpha) \ln x$, while consumer 2's utility in these states is given by $u_1^2(x) = \beta \ln x$ and $u_2^2(x) = (1 - \beta) \ln x$.

Exercise 17B.20 For what values of α and β is utility state-independent for each of these consumers?

Finally, we will allow for the possibility that the two consumers have different beliefs about the likelihood of each of the two states actually transpiring, with consumer 1 placing probability δ on state 1 and consumer 2 placing probability γ on state 1. We can then write consumer 1's expected utility as

$$U^1(x_1, x_2) = \delta\alpha \ln x_1 + (1 - \delta)(1 - \alpha) \ln x_2 \tag{17.27}$$

and consumer 2's expected utility as

$$U^2(x_1, x_2) = \gamma\beta \ln x_1 + (1 - \gamma)(1 - \beta) \ln x_2. \quad (17.28)$$

Are we imposing any real restrictions by assuming that the utility weights placed on log consumption in the two states sum to one for each of the two consumers?

Exercise 17B.21

17B.3.1 Calculating Equilibrium Prices for State-Contingent Consumption Trades

In equilibrium, the terms of trade for changing consumption from one state into consumption in the other are determined by the price ratio (p_2/p_1) that specifies how much consumption in state 1 a consumer can get by giving up one unit of consumption in state 2. But in order for this ratio to support an equilibrium, it must be the case that demand for each state-contingent consumption good is equal to supply in exactly the same way that this had to hold in our treatment of exchange economies in the previous chapter. The mathematics of calculating this equilibrium ratio is then exactly the same as it is for exchange economies without risk.

We can begin by solving each consumer's optimization problem given prices p_1 and p_2. For consumer 1, this can be written as

$$\max_{x_1^1, x_2^1} \delta\alpha \ln x_1^1 + (1 - \delta)(1 - \alpha) \ln x_2^1 \text{ subject to } p_1 e_1^1 + p_2 e_2^1 = p_1 x_1^1 + p_2 x_2^1. \quad (17.29)$$

How would you write the analogous optimization problem for individual 2?

Exercise 17B.22

Solving this (and solving the analogous problem for consumer 2), we can derive each consumer's demand for x_1 as

$$x_1^1(p_1, p_2) = \frac{\alpha\delta(p_1 e_1^1 + p_2 e_2^1)}{(\alpha\delta + (1 - \alpha)(1 - \delta))p_1} \text{ and } x_1^2(p_1, p_2) = \frac{\beta\gamma(p_1 e_1^2 + p_2 e_2^2)}{(\beta\gamma + (1 - \beta)(1 - \gamma))p_1}. \quad (17.30)$$

In equilibrium, prices have to be such that demand is equal to supply, with demand given above and supply given by the sum of endowments in the economy. Demand equals supply in state 1 then implies

$$x_1^1(p_1, p_2) + x_1^2(p_1, p_2) = e_1^1 + e_1^2. \quad (17.31)$$

From our work in the previous chapter (and the intuition from the Edgeworth Box), we know that we can only calculate an equilibrium price *ratio* and that any two prices that satisfy that ratio will result in exactly the same equilibrium. We can therefore let $p_1^* = 1$ and simply solve for p_2^* by plugging the demands from (17.30) into equation (17.31). Some tedious algebra then gives us

$$p_2^* = \frac{(1 - \alpha)(1 - \delta)(\beta\gamma + (1 - \beta)(1 - \gamma))e_1^1 + (1 - \beta)(1 - \gamma)(\alpha\delta + (1 - \alpha)(1 - \delta))e_1^2}{\alpha\delta(\beta\gamma + (1 - \beta)(1 - \gamma))e_2^1 + \beta\gamma(\alpha\delta + (1 - \alpha)(1 - \delta))e_2^2}. \quad (17.32)$$

Suppose that the overall endowment in the economy is the same in each of the two states (i.e., $e_1^1 + e_1^2 = e_2^1 + e_2^2$); suppose that each consumer has state-independent utility (i.e., $\alpha = (1 - \alpha)$ and $\beta = (1 - \beta)$); and suppose that both consumers evaluate risk in the same way (i.e., $\delta = \gamma$). Can you then demonstrate that equilibrium terms of trade will be actuarially fair; i.e., $p_2^*/p_1^* = (1 - \delta)/\delta$?

Exercise 17B.23

Exercise
17B.24

Exercise 17B.24 For the scenario described in the previous exercise, can you use individual demand functions to illustrate that each consumer will choose to equalize consumption across the two states? Where in the Edgeworth Box does this imply the equilibrium falls?

Deriving the equilibrium price p_2^* (while setting p_1^* to 1) is tedious, but the payoff is that we now have an easy way to illustrate how the equilibrium changes as aggregate risk, the perception of individual risk, endowments, and individual tastes change. In the following sections, we will therefore employ a simple Excel spreadsheet in which we specify endowments, parameters in utility functions, and levels of risk, and then use equation (17.32) to calculate the equilibrium price. Finally, we can then plug equilibrium prices back into demands (equation (17.30)) to determine the equilibrium consumption levels for each consumer in each of the two states.

17B.3.2 General Equilibrium with Individual (but no Aggregate) Risk

We begin with the case where the economy as a whole faces no aggregate risk and where the individuals in the economy agree on the likelihood of each of the two states arising. This is analogous to our example from Section A in which you and I owned different parts of an island and each of us is aware of the likelihood of rain or drought; where the total level of banana production is the same regardless of whether it rains or not, but where the fraction of the banana crop that grows on our respective parts of the island does depend on weather conditions. No aggregate risk then implies that $e_1^1 + e_1^2 = e_2^1 + e_2^2$, and each of us of knowing the chance of rain and drought implies $\delta = \gamma$.

Exercise 17B.25 What is the shape of the Edgeworth Box representing an economy in which $e_1^1 + e_1^2 = e_2^1 + e_2^2$?

In exercise 17B.23, you were asked to make these assumptions and to assume in addition that utility for each of the two consumers is state-independent. You should have been able to demonstrate that this would result in an equilibrium price $p_2^* = (1 - \delta)/\delta$, and in exercise 17B.24 you should have concluded that this results in each individual fully insuring and the equilibrium falling on the 45-degree line in the Edgeworth Box (as in Graph 17.10a).

Now suppose that utility for our two consumers is state-dependent. Table 17.2 then provides three sets of predictions about the nature of the resulting equilibrium. In each case, $\delta = 0.25 = \gamma$; i.e., both individuals agree that the probability that they will face state 1 is 0.25 and the probability that they will face state 2 is 0.75. The endowments of the two individuals are symmetrically opposite, with $e_1^1 = 250$, $e_2^1 = 10$, $e_1^2 = 10$ and $e_2^2 = 250$. Thus, in the absence of trading state-contingent consumption, individual 1 ends up with a lot of consumption in state 1 but not in state 2, and the reverse is true for individual 2.

The first three rows keep consumer 1's utility state-independent, with the middle row ($\alpha = \beta = 0.5$) representing the case where consumer 2's utility is state-independent as well and where, as a result, both consumers fully insure at the actuarially fair price $p_2^* = (1 - \delta)/\delta = 3$. We can tell that both fully insure because $x_1^1 = x_2^1$ and $x_1^2 = x_2^2$; i.e., after trading state contingent consumption, each individual ends up consuming the same regardless of which state he or she faces.

Exercise 17B.26 Why do you think individual 1 ends up with less consumption than individual 2 once they fully insure?

The top row introduces state-dependent utility for individual 2, with that individual now placing less of a weight on state 1 consumption and more on state 2 consumption. The equilibrium price p_2^* now more than doubles, making it more costly to shift consumption from state 1 to state 2. As a

Table 17.2: $\delta = 0.25 = \gamma$, $e_1^1 = 250$, $e_2^1 = 10$, $e_1^2 = 10$ and $e_2^2 = 250$

		Equilibrium with State-Dependent Utility				
α	β	p_2^*	x_1^1	x_2^1	x_1^2	x_2^2
0.50	0.25	7.15	80.36	33.74	179.64	226.26
0.50	0.50	3.00	70.00	70.00	190.00	190.00
0.50	0.75	1.51	66.27	131.69	193.73	128.31
0.75	0.75	1.00	130.00	130.00	130.00	130.00
0.75	0.60	1.49	132.45	88.86	127.55	171.14
0.75	0.40	2.64	138.20	52.35	121.80	207.65
0.75	0.25	4.47	147.33	32.99	112.67	227.01
0.25	0.25	9.00	34.00	34.00	226.00	226.00
0.25	0.40	5.02	30.02	53.82	229.98	206.18
0.25	0.60	2.75	27.75	90.91	232.25	169.09
0.25	0.75	1.83	26.83	132.26	233.17	127.74

result, individual 1 (whose tastes we have not changed) keeps more of his consumption in state 1 and therefore "underinsures." Individual 2 similarly underinsures because she does not care as much about consuming in state 1. The third row then conducts the opposite simulation, with individual 1 now placing *more* weight on state 1 consumption. Individual 1 (whose tastes we have still not changed) now "overinsures" because the equilibrium price of shifting consumption to state 2 has fallen by about half from the actuarily fair rate. Individual 2 similarly "overinsures" because she values state 1 consumption so much more.

....

Can you draw out the equilibrium in rows 1 and 3 in Edgeworth Boxes?   **Exercise**
17B.27

....

The second and third set of results in Table 17.2 then illustrate cases where both consumers have state-dependent utility. As you can see, the equilibrium price can differ greatly depending on the nature of the state-dependence of tastes and their relation to the distribution of endowments. In the first row of the second set of results, for instance, both individuals place heavy weight on state 1 consumption, resulting in a relatively low price p_2^* for shifting consumption from state 1 to state 2. We then see that both individuals happen to be fully insuring, with individual 1 shifting a lot of consumption from state 1 to state 2 because it is cheap (and despite such a heavy utility weight on state 1 consumption), and individual 2 shifting a lot of consumption from state 2 to state 1 despite it being expensive because so much utility weight is placed on consuming in state 1. As individual 1 places less weight on state 1 consumption (with β falling over the next three rows), the price p_2^* increases because state 2 consumption is in greater demand. Individual 1 therefore reduces his state 2 consumption in favor of keeping more consumption in state 1 because of the higher price, and individual 2 increases her state 2 consumption (despite the increase in price) because it is becoming more desirable as β falls.

**Exercise
17B.28***
Can you offer a similar intuitive explanation for the third set of results in Table 17.2?

17.B.3.3 Introducing Differing Beliefs about Risk

So far, we have assumed that both individuals hold the same beliefs about the probability of each state occurring; i.e., $\delta = \gamma$. Now suppose that they hold different opinions about these probabilities. From looking at the equations for each consumer's expected utility, $U^1(x_1, x_2)$ and $U^2(x_1, x_2)$ in equations (17.27) and (17.28), it should then be immediately apparent that this will result in effects similar to those that arise when consumers place different value on each of the two states (i.e., when $\alpha \neq \beta$). For instance, the actual weight placed on state 1 in consumer 1's expected utility function U^1 is $\delta\alpha$ while the actual weight placed on state 1 in consumer 2's expected utility function U^2 is $\gamma\beta$. When their beliefs about the probability associated with state 1 are the same ($\delta = \gamma$), the only way consumer 1 will place less weight on state 1 is if $\alpha < \beta$, but the same difference in weights can arise if $\alpha = \beta$ and $\delta < \gamma$; i.e., if consumer 1 believes state 1 is less likely to occur than consumer 2 believes.

**Exercise
17B.29***
Suppose $\alpha = \beta = 0.25$. For what values of δ and γ will the equilibrium be the same as the one in the first row of Table 17.2? (*Hint*: This is harder than it appears. In row 1 of the table, $\beta\gamma = 1/16$ and $(1 - \beta)(1 - \gamma) = 9/16$. Thus, the overall weight placed on state 2 is 9 times the weight placed on state 1. When you now change β from 0.25 to 0.5, you need to make sure when you change γ that the the overall weight placed on state 2 is again 9 times the weight placed on state 1.)

Table 17.3 then replicates Table 17.2 but now assumes state-independent utilities ($\alpha = \beta = 0.5$) and instead generates the same equilibria through different beliefs on the part of the two consumers.

Table 17.3: $\alpha = 0.5 = \beta$, $e_1^1 = 250$, $e_2^1 = 10$, $e_1^2 = 10$ and $e_2^2 = 250$

δ	γ	p_2^*	x_1^1	x_2^1	x_1^2	x_2^2
		State-Independent Utility with Differing Beliefs				
0.25	0.1000	7.15	80.36	33.74	179.64	226.26
0.25	0.2500	3.00	70.00	70.00	190.00	190.00
0.25	0.5000	1.51	66.27	131.69	193.73	128.31
0.50	0.5000	1.00	130.00	130.00	130.00	130.00
0.50	0.3333	1.49	132.45	88.86	127.55	171.14
0.50	0.1818	2.64	138.20	52.35	121.80	207.65
0.50	0.1000	4.47	147.33	32.99	112.67	227.01
0.10	0.1000	9.00	34.00	34.00	226.00	226.00
0.10	0.1818	5.02	30.02	53.82	229.98	206.18
0.10	0.3333	2.75	27.75	90.91	232.25	169.09
0.10	0.5000	1.83	26.83	132.26	233.17	127.74

17B.3.4 Introducing Aggregate Risk

Finally, we can introduce aggregate risk by changing our assumption that the overall endowment in the economy is the same regardless of which state arises (i.e., $e_1^1 + e_1^2 = e_2^1 + e_2^2$). Put differently and in the context of the example in Section A, rather than assuming that rain simply changes the distribution of banana production on the island, we can assume that rain increases or decreases the total banana crop (while also changing its relative distribution on the island).

Suppose, for instance, that I have the land that does better with rain (in "state 1") and you have the land that does better with drought (in "state 2"). If there is no aggregate risk, I have to do as much better under rain as you do under drought. Our example so far has assumed that the endowment for consumer 1 (me, in this example is $(e_1^1 = 250, e_2^1 = 10)$, and the endowment for consumer 2 (you, in this example) is the mirror image $(e_1^2 = 10, e_2^1 = 250)$, which implies that the aggregate endowment in the economy is the same in the two states. Now suppose that only half as many bananas grow on the island during droughts as during rainy seasons, with my endowment changing to $(e_1^1, e_2^1) = (250, 5)$ and your endowment changing to $(e_1^2, e_2^2) = (10, 125)$. This introduces aggregate risk because now the economy as a whole has 260 bananas in rainy seasons (state 1) and only 130 bananas during droughts (state 2). We'll assume in this example that we agree that the probability of the rainy season occurring is 0.25 (i.e., $\delta = \gamma = 0.25$) and our tastes are state-independent (i.e., $\alpha = \beta = 0.5$).

The resulting equilibrium is given in the first row of Table 17.4 and can be compared to the equilibrium without aggregate risk that is given in the second row. The price for trading state 1 consumption for state 2 consumption is now higher as a result of the fact that the banana crop in state 2 has fallen by half (in row 1 relative to row 2). My endowment is not much different in the two rows because most of it comes from the rainy season (state 1), but the increase in p_2^* causes my consumption of bananas in the drought season (state 2) to fall by half. You are similarly forced to cut back on consumption of bananas in the drought season because your crop has fallen.

Table 17.4: $\alpha = 0.5 = \beta$, $\delta = 0.25 = \gamma$

Aggregate Risk (with State Independence and Identical Beliefs)								
e_1^1	e_2^1	e_1^2	e_2^2	p_2^*	x_1^1	x_2^1	x_1^2	x_2^2
250	5	10	125	6.00	70.00	35.00	190.00	95.00
250	10	10	250	3.00	70.00	70.00	190.00	190.00
250	20	10	500	1.50	70.00	140.00	190.00	380.00
250	10	5	125	5.67	76.67	40.59	178.33	94.41
250	10	10	250	3.00	70.00	70.00	190.00	190.00
250	10	20	500	1.59	66.47	125.56	203.53	384.44
125	5	10	250	1.59	33.24	62.68	101.76	192.22
250	10	10	250	3.00	70.00	70.00	190.00	190.00
500	20	10	250	5.67	153.33	81.18	356.67	188.82
250	10	250	10	75.00	250.00	10.00	250.00	10.00
250	10	130	130	8.14	82.86	30.53	297.14	109.47
250	10	10	250	3.00	70.00	70.00	190.00	190.00

**Exercise
17B.30**   Can you see from the demand equations why consumption in the rainy season remains unchanged?

Suppose next that a new fertilizer is discovered, a fertilizer that quadruples banana output in drought seasons but has no impact on banana output in rainy seasons. The endowments now change to those in the third row of Table 17.4, and, because of the increased abundance of bananas in the drought season (state 2), the price of shifting consumption from state 1 to state 2 now falls. Both of us end up increasing our banana consumption in the rainy season.

**Exercise
17B.31***   Can you depict the equilibria in rows 1 and 3 in two Edgeworth Boxes?

The second set of simulations in Table 17.4 keeps the productivity of my land constant and varies solely your land productivity while still keeping your land relatively more productive in the drought season (state 2). As your land becomes more productive, the supply of bananas in the drought season increases relative to the supply of bananas in the rainy season, thus driving down the price of shifting consumption from the rainy season (state 1) to the drought season (state 2). Since the productivity of my land remains unchanged, I am only affected through this change in p_2^* and I therefore substitute away from consumption in the rainy season and toward consumption in the drought season. You, on the other hand, also become wealthier as your land becomes more productive, and so you end up increasing consumption in both states. The results are also examples of the general principle introduced in Section A that, *when there is aggregate risk, the terms of trade will be less favorable for consumers intending to trade consumption from the high aggregate output state to the low aggregate output state.* In the first row of the second set of simulations, the high output state is the rainy season (state 1) and as a result it is expensive to buy state contingent consumption during droughts (i.e., p_2^* is high). These are not favorable terms of trade for me (individual 1) because I want to trade consumption in rainy seasons for consumption in dry seasons, but the terms are quite favorable to you because you want to trade in the other direction. The reverse is true in the last row of the second set of simulations where the drought state (state 2) is the high productivity state.

**Exercise
17B.32***   In the third set of results of Table 17.4, we hold your land productivity constant while varying mine. Can you make sense of the results?

Finally, in the last set of simulations, we again hold the productivity of my land fixed and vary your land productivity, but this time we start initially with your land being identical to mine and then alter the relative productivity during rainy and dry seasons in the direction of increasing productivity during droughts (state 2) and decreasing it during rain (state 1). When our land is identical, the equilibrium price is so high that neither of us alters our consumption from our endowments and thus no insurance through trades in state-contingent commodities takes place. Thus, *despite enormous aggregate risk, there is no way we can insure each other because our individual risk is the same.* This is an important insight: In order for insurance markets to enable individuals to protect one another against *individual risk*, risk cannot be so similarly distributed. It is not easy to insure fully against recessions because recessions hit the whole economy, but it is possible to insure against fire damage to our homes because such damage does not hit everyone at once. As we increase your land productivity during drought seasons relative to rainy seasons, gains from trade across states emerge, for much the same reason as we can insure one another against fire damage.

CONCLUSION

In this chapter, we have developed a framework that allows us to extend the theory of individual choice as well as our theory of general equilibrium to cases where individuals face risk. We have done this both for the narrow case where individuals evaluate consumption the same way regardless of what happens to them (state-independent tastes) as well as the more general case where tastes over consumption are state-dependent. In the case of state-independent tastes, we have shown that risk-averse individuals will always wish to fully insure so long as the terms of insurance contracts are actuarially fair, but individuals may over- or underinsure in cases where their tastes are state-dependent. As we introduced risk into a general equilibrium setting, we furthermore discovered that competitive markets once again lead to an efficient allocation of resources, and an efficient distribution of risk. This does not imply that all risk can be eliminated (any more than efficiency in the absence of risk implies everyone gets everything they want), and this is particularly true in the case of aggregate risk (like recessions) as opposed to individual risk (like house fires) that is distributed more randomly across the population.

Once again, we have therefore found another version of the first welfare theorem; but, as before, this result on market efficiency is again subject to the caveats first mentioned in Chapter 15: We are still assuming that property rights are well established, that there are no price distortions or restrictions on the terms of trade that can emerge, that there are no externalities and no market power, and no asymmetric information. As we will see in Chapter 22, the assumption of no asymmetric information will be particularly problematic for certain insurance markets and is thus especially relevant here where much of our treatment of risk has been in the context of insurance.

This concludes our treatment of the efficiency of markets. We now turn in the next section to instances when the assumptions of the first welfare theorem are violated and, because of these violations, the conclusion of the first welfare theorem no longer holds. Put differently, we now turn our attention to instances when markets, in the absence of corrective action from government or civil society institutions, will not result in efficient outcomes. However, while the mere existence of inefficiencies in markets is a *necessary* condition for nonmarket institutions to play an efficiency enhancing role, it is not *sufficient* unless we can identify how such nonmarket intervention will improve on market outcomes. Furthermore, as we have said repeatedly, the mere absence of inefficiencies in markets does not negate a socially useful role for nonmarket institutions unless efficiency is the sole value of a society.

APPENDIX 1: EXPECTED UTILITY AND THE INDEPENDENCE AXIOM

Expected utility theory as developed in this chapter is based on an assumption that we have not thus far dealt with explicitly aside from mentioning it in Section B. This assumption is known as the *Independence Axiom*, and it builds the foundation to expected utility theory in much the same way as some of our assumptions about tastes in Chapter 4 built the foundation to choice theory in the absence of risk. Whenever individuals face risk, they are (as we have said throughout) facing a gamble. But individuals have choices over which gamble to play, with institutions like insurance contracts offering ways of choosing gambles that are different from what nature has dealt us. Choice in the presence of risk therefore essentially involves choices over gambles that have different risks and expected values. And expected utility theory begins with the assumption that individuals have "tastes" or "preferences" over gambles in much the same way they have tastes over consumption goods. In the chapter, we have illustrated these as indifference curves over outcome pairs (x_G, x_B), but we can take a further step back and simply think of them as preference relations. Adopting our notation from Chapter 4, we can read a statement like "$G_1 \succsim G_2$" as "Gamble 1 is preferred to (or at least as good as) Gamble 2" and a statement like "$G_1 \succ G_2$" as "Gamble 1 is strictly better than Gamble 2." The Independence Axiom is then an assumption about individual preference relations over gambles.

Before we can state this assumption, we need to define what it means to "mix" two different gambles. Suppose, for instance, that Gamble 1 places 0.60 probability on outcome 1 and 0.40 probability on outcome 2 while Gamble 2 places 0.20 probability on outcome 1 and 0.80 probability on outcome 2. Now suppose that half the time I end up playing Gamble 1 and half the time I end up playing Gamble 2.

Overall, I will then reach outcome 1 with probability 0.60 half the time and with probability 0.20 half the time, for an overall probability 0.40 of reaching outcome 1.[8]

Exercise 17B.33 What is the probability of reaching outcome 2 if we play Gamble 1 half the time and Gamble 2 half the time?

In this case, we would say that we created a third gamble by averaging Gamble 1 and Gamble 2, and we would denote the new gamble as $(0.5G_1 + 0.5G_2)$. Of course, there are many ways to mix gambles by taking different *weighted* averages of the two gambles. For instance, if we place weight α (where $0 < \alpha < 1$) on Gamble 1, we would get a new gamble denoted as $(\alpha G_1 + (1 - \alpha)G_2)$.

Exercise 17B.34 What weights would I have to put on Gambles 1 and 2 in order for the mixed gamble to result in a 0.50 probability of reaching outcome 1 and a 0.50 probability of reaching outcome 2?

The Independence Axiom then assumes the following: Suppose there are three gambles, G_1, G_2, and G_3. Then

$$G_1 \succsim G_2 \text{ if and only if } \left(\alpha G_1 + (1 - \alpha)G_3\right) \succsim \left(\alpha G_2 + (1 - \alpha)G_3\right). \tag{17.33}$$

In words, what we are saying is both simple and subtle: Gamble 1 is preferred to Gamble 2 if and only if a mixture of Gamble 1 with a third Gamble 3 is also preferred to the same mixture of Gamble 2 with Gamble 3. Thus, an individual's tastes over two gambles remain the same when those gambles are mixed with any other gamble or, put differently, an individual's tastes over two gambles are *independent* of what other gambles are mixed in (so long as they are mixed the same way).

This axiom has a lot of intuitive appeal. Suppose I like playing roulette better than playing poker. Suppose you then invite me to come to one of two game nights at a local casino and you ask me to choose which night to come. On the first night, we will flip a coin and play roulette if the coin comes up heads and slot machines if the coin comes up tails, and on the second night we will play poker if the coin comes up heads and slot machines if it comes up tails. If I like roulette better than poker, then I should come to the first night. The fact that there is a 50 percent chance that I will end up playing slots on either night does not take anything away from the fact that the night with a chance at roulette should be better than the night with an equal chance at poker (given that I like roulette better than poker).

The following result then forms the basis for using expected utility theory to analyze choice in the presence of risk: *If an individual's tastes over gambles satisfy the independence axiom, then these tastes can be represented by an expected utility function.* Put differently, so long as tastes over gambles satisfy the independence axiom, we will be able to find a function $u(x)$ over consumption such that we can represent indifference curves over outcome pairs (x_G, x_B) that happen with probabilities $((1 - \delta), \delta)$ with a von Neumann-Morgenstern expected utility function $U(x_G, x_B) = \delta u(x_B) + (1 - \delta)u(x_G)$ when tastes are not state-dependent.[9] We will not prove this result here formally but refer you to a graduate text in microeconomics for a formal proof.

---

[8]All we are doing is multiplying the probability that we are playing a particular gamble times the probability that outcome 1 is reached in that gamble. We do that for each gamble we might face and then add up the probabilities. For instance, in this case we find the probability of outcome 1 if we play Gamble 1 half the time and Gamble 2 half the time as $0.5(0.60) + 0.5(0.2) = 0.40$.

[9]When tastes are state-dependent, an extension of the independence axiom will similarly imply that we can find functions $u_G(x)$ and $u_B(x)$ such that indifference curves over outcome pairs (x_G, x_B) that occur with probabilities $((1 - \delta), \delta)$ can be represented by an expected utility function $U(x_G, x_B) = \delta u_B(x_B) + (1 - \delta)u_G(x_G)$. Furthermore, the result extends to more than two outcome pairs: For instance, if there are three possible consumption outcomes—x_1, x_2, and x_3—that will occur with probabilities δ_1, δ_2, and δ_3 respectively, we will be able to find a function $u(x)$ (when tastes are state-independent) such that $U(x_1, x_2, x_3) = \delta_1 u(x_1) + \delta_2 u(x_2) + \delta_3 u(x_3)$. Or, when tastes are state-dependent, we can find three u functions that will allow us to again express indifference curves with an expected utility function.

APPENDIX 2: THE ALLAIS PARADOX AND "REGRET THEORY"

Almost since the conception of expected utility theory, certain paradoxical examples that violate the predictions of the theory have been studied, and more recently, such examples have given rise to an interest in behavioral economics (which we discuss in Chapter 29), a branch of economics that attempts to resolve such paradoxes by introducing principles from psychology and neurobiology into economic models.

The oldest and most famous of these paradoxes—dating back to at least 1953—is known as the *Allais Paradox*.[10] Like other paradoxes, it deviates from the examples in this chapter in that it begins with three (rather than two) possible outcomes. Suppose, for instance, you are in a game show where the host presents you with three closed doors that appear identical. He tells you that behind one of the doors is a pot of $5 million, behind another door there is a pot of $1 million, and behind a third door there is an empty pot.

You are then asked to choose between two different games: Game 1 has a 100% chance of you finding the door with $1 million behind it, while game 2 has a 10% chance of you finding the $5 million door, an 89% chance of you finding the $1 million door and a 1% chance of you finding the door with no money. Which option would you choose? It turns out that most people would choose to play Game 1.

Now suppose that you were instead asked to choose between two other games: Game 3 has an 11% chance of you discovering the $1 million door and an 89% chance of you discovering the door with no money. Game 4, on the other hand, has a 10% chance of you finding the $5 million door and a 90% chance of you finding the door with no money. Which would you choose now? Most people end up choosing to play Game 4 rather than Game 3.

It turns out, however, that it is not possible for an individual to behave in a way predicted by expected utility theory and choose Game 1 in the first case and Game 4 in the second. Suppose we have identified an underlying function $u(x)$ that permits us to represent a person's indifference curves over risky outcomes with an expected utility function, and suppose the utilities of getting $5 million, $1 million and $0 are denoted (by this function $u(x)$) as u_5, u_1 and u_0 respectively. The expected utility of each game is then simply the sum of the probabilities of each outcome times the utility level associated with that outcome. If an individual chooses Game 1 over Game 2, it implies that her expected utility of Game 1 is greater than her expected utility of Game 2, or

$$u_1 > 0.1u_5 + 0.89u_1 + 0.01u_0. \tag{17.34}$$

If you add $0.89u_0$ to both sides of this equation and subtract $0.89u_1$, equation (17.34) becomes

$$0.11u_1 + 0.89u_0 > 0.1u_5 + 0.9u_0. \tag{17.35}$$

Now notice that the left-hand side of equation (17.35) is the expected utility of Game 3, and the right-hand side is the expected utility of Game 4. Thus, expected utility theory implies that anyone who chooses Game 1 over Game 2 should choose Game 3 over Game 4, yet the very people who choose Game 1 over Game 2 tend to choose Game 4 over Game 3. However reasonable the independence axiom that builds the foundation for expected utility theory is, it simply does not appear to hold for people who behave this way.

Does the paradox still hold if people's tastes are state-dependent? (*Hint:* The answer is yes.)

Exercise 17B.35*

Examples like this have led some to develop what is known as *regret theory*. Perhaps the reason that Game 1 is preferred to Game 2 is that it is difficult for anyone to face the possibility of getting nothing when the individual could have had $1 million dollars with certainty, even if getting nothing is a very low probability event. Thus, looking ahead to the regret one would face, the individual might just go for the sure thing. When choosing between Games 3 and 4, on the other hand, there is a large probability of getting nothing in either game, so regret might be less of a factor, thus permitting individuals to go for the chance to have $5 million even though it increases the chance of having nothing slightly.

---

[10]The paradox is named after Maurice Allais (1911–) who was awarded the Nobel Prize in Economics in 1988 for his work on the theory of markets.

An alternative view of the Allais Paradox is that we should not worry about its implications for real-world choices too much because the paradox arises only in examples where very small probability events are considered (such as the 1% probability of getting nothing in Game 2). Yet another explanation offered by behavioral economics is explored in end-of-chapter exercise 29.2.[11]

END-OF-CHAPTER EXERCISES

17.1 In this exercise, we review some basics of attitudes toward risk when tastes are state-independent and, in part B, we also verify some of the numbers that appear in the graphs of part A of the chapter.

A. Suppose that there are two possible outcomes of a gamble: Under outcome A, you get $\$x_1$ and under outcome B you get $\$x_2$ where $x_2 > x_1$. Outcome A happens with probability $\delta = 0.5$ and outcome B happens with probability $(1 - \delta) = 0.5$.

   a. Illustrate three different consumption/utility relationships: one that can be used to model risk-averse tastes over gambles, one for risk-neutral tastes, and one for risk-loving tastes.

   b. On each graph, illustrate your expected consumption on the horizontal axis and your expected utility of facing the gamble on the vertical. Which of these—expected consumption or expected utility—does not depend on your degree of risk aversion?

   c. How does the expected utility of the gamble differ from the utility of the expected consumption level of the gamble in each graph?

   d. Suppose I offer you $\$\bar{x}$ to not face this gamble. Illustrate in each of your graphs where $\bar{x}$ would lie if it makes you just indifferent between taking $\bar{x}$ and staying to face the gamble.

   e. Suppose I come to offer you some insurance; for every dollar you agree to give me if outcome A happens, I will agree to give you y dollars if outcome B happens. What's y if the deal I am offering you does not change the expected value of consumption for you?

   f. What changes in your three graphs if you buy insurance of this kind, and how does it impact your expected consumption level on the horizontal axis and the expected utility of the remaining gamble on the vertical?

B. Suppose we can use the function $u(x) = x^\alpha$ for the consumption/utility relationship that allows us to represent your indifference curves over risky outcomes using an expected utility function. Assume the rest of the set-up as described in A.

   a. What value can α take if you are risk averse? What if you are risk neutral? What if you are risk loving?

   b. Write down the equations for the expected consumption level as well as the expected utility from the gamble. Which one depends on α and why?

   c. What's the equation for the utility of the expected consumption level?

   d. Consider $\bar{x}$ as defined in A(d). What equation would you have to solve to find $\bar{x}$?

   e. Suppose $\alpha = 1$. Solve for $\bar{x}$ and explain your result intuitively.

   f. Suppose that, instead of two outcomes, there are actually three possible outcomes: A, B, and C, with associated consumption levels x_1, x_2, and x_3 occurring with probabilities δ_1, δ_2, and $(1 - \delta_1 - \delta_2)$. How would you write the expected utility of this gamble?

   g. Suppose that u took the form

   $$u(x) = 0.1x^{0.5} - \left(\frac{x}{100,000}\right)^{2.5} \tag{17.36}$$

   This is the equation that was used to arrive at most of the graphs in part A of the chapter, where x is expressed in thousands but plugged into the equation as its full value; i.e., consumption of 200 in a graph represents $x = 200,000$. Verify the numbers in Graphs 17.1 and 17.3. (Note that the numbers in the graphs are rounded.)

---

[11] Another famous paradox is known as Machina's Paradox, and it also deals with low probability events. We develop this in detail in end-of-chapter exercise 17.7.
*conceptually challenging
**computationally challenging
†solutions in Study Guide

17.2*† In our development of consumer theory, we made a big point about the fact that neoclassical economics does not put much stock in the idea of "cardinally" measuring utility (in terms of units of happiness or "utils"). Rather, our theory of consumer behavior is based only on the assumption that individuals can simply "order" pairs of bundles in terms of which they prefer or whether they are indifferent between the two. In this sense, we said *neoclassical consumer theory was ordinal and not cardinal*. We now ask whether the same continues to hold for our theory of choice in the presence of risk.

A. Return to the example from exercise 17.1, where consumption levels differ depending on whether outcome A or outcome B occurs (where A occurs with probability δ and B with probability $(1 - \delta)$). In the absence of insurance, these outcomes are x_1 and x_2 respectively (with $x_1 < x_2$).

   a. Draw a graph with consumption x_A in outcome A on the horizontal and consumption x_B in outcome B on the vertical axis. Then locate (x_1, x_2)—the consumption levels you will enjoy in the absence of insurance depending on which outcome occurs.

   b. Calculate, as you did in part A(e) of exercise 17.1, how much I would have to give you in outcome A if you agree to give me \$1 in outcome B assuming we want your expected consumption level to remain unchanged.

   c. Now identify in your graph all bundles that become available if we assume that you and I are willing to make trades of this kind on these terms; i.e., on terms that keep your expected consumption unchanged. Indicate the slope (in terms of δ) of the line you have just drawn.

   d. If you are risk neutral, would you strictly prefer any particular bundle on the line you just drew?

   e. We can define someone as risk averse if, when faced with two gambles that give rise to the same expected consumption level, she prefers the one that has less risk. Using this definition, which bundle on our line should a risk-averse individual prefer? Could the same bundle be optimal for someone that loves risk?

   f. Now suppose that we assume individuals can make ordinal comparisons between bundles; i.e., when faced by two bundles in your graph, they can tell us which they prefer or whether they are indifferent. Suppose these rankings are "rational," that "more is better," and that there are "no sudden jumps" as we defined these in our development of consumer theory earlier in the text. Is this sufficient to allow us to assume there exist downward-sloping indifference curves that describe an individual's tastes over the risky gambles we are graphing?

   g. What does your answer to (d) further imply about these indifference curves when tastes are risk neutral?

   h. Now consider the case of risk aversion. Pick a bundle C that lies off the 45-degree line on the "budget line" you have drawn in your graph. In light of your answer to (e), is the point D that lies at the intersection of your "budget line" with the 45-degree line more or less preferred? What does this imply for the shape of the indifference curve that runs through C?

   i. What does your answer to (e) imply about the *MRS* along the 45-degree line in your graph?

   j. *True or False*: Risk aversion implies strict convexity of indifference curves over bundles of consumption for different outcomes, with all risk-averse tastes sharing the same *MRS* along the 45-degree line if tastes are state-independent.

   k. *True or False*: As the probability of each outcome changes, so do the indifference curves.

   l. Have we needed to make any appeal to being able to measure utility in "cardinal" terms? *True or False*: Although risk aversion appears to arise from how we measure utility in our graphs of consumption/utility relationships (such as those in exercise 17.1), the underlying theory of tastes over risky gambles does not in fact require any such cardinal measurements.

   m. Repeat (h) for the case of someone who is risk loving.

B. Consider again the case of the consumption/utility relationship described by $u(x) = x^\alpha$ with $\alpha > 0$. In exercise 17.1B(a), you should have concluded that $\alpha < 1$ implies risk aversion, $\alpha = 1$ implies risk neutrality, and $\alpha > 1$ implies risk loving because the first results in a concave relationship, the second in an upward-sloping line, and the third in a convex relationship.

   a. Let x_A represent consumption under outcome A (which occurs with probability δ) and x_B consumption under outcome B (which occurs with probability $(1 - \delta)$). Suppose we can in fact use $u(x)$ to express tastes over risky gambles as expected utilities. Define the expected utility function $U(x_A, x_B)$.

b.   Next, consider the shape of the indifference curves that are represented by the expected utility function U. First, derive the MRS of $U(x_A, x_B)$.

c.   What is the MRS when $\alpha = 1$? How does this compare to your answer to A(g)?

d.   Regardless of the size of α, what is the MRS along the 45-degree line? How does this compare to your answer to A(i) for risk-averse tastes?

e.   Is the MRS diminishing, giving rise to convex tastes? Does your answer depend on what value α takes? How does your answer compare to your answer to A(h)?

f.   What do indifference curves look like when $\alpha > 1$?

g.   Do the slopes of indifference curves change with δ? How does your answer compare to your answer to A(k)?

h.   Suppose we used $u(x) = \beta x^\alpha$ (instead of $u(x) = x^\alpha$) to calculate expected utilities. Would the indifference map that arises from the expected utility function change?

i.   Suppose we used $u(x) = x^{\alpha\beta}$ (instead of $u(x) = x^\alpha$) to calculate expected utilities. Would the indifference map that arises from the expected utility function change?

j.   *True or False*: The tastes represented by expected utility functions are immune to *linear* transformations of the consumption/utility relationship $u(x)$ that is used to calculate expected utility but are not immune to all types of positive transformations.

k.   Consider the expected utility function $U(x_A, x_B)$ that uses $u(x) = x^\alpha$. Will the underlying indifference curves change under any order-preserving transformation?

l.   *True or False*: Expected utility functions can be transformed like all utility functions without changing the underlying indifference curves, but such transformations can then no longer be written as if they were the expected value of two different utility values emerging from an underlying function u.

m.   In light of all this, can you reconcile the assertion that expected utility theory is not a theory that relies on cardinal interpretations of utility?

17.3   We have illustrated in several settings the role of actuarily fair insurance contracts (b, p) (where b is the insurance benefit in the "bad state" and p is the insurance premium that has to be paid in either state). In this problem, we will discuss it in a slightly different way that we will later use in Chapter 22.

A.   Consider again the example, covered extensively in the chapter, of my wife and life insurance on me. The probability of me not making it is δ, and my wife's consumption if I don't make it will be 10 and her consumption if I do make it will be 250 in the absence of any life insurance.

a.   Now suppose that my wife is offered a full set of actuarily fair insurance contracts. What does this imply for how p is related to δ and b?

b.   On a graph with b on the horizontal axis and p on the vertical, illustrate the set of all actuarily fair insurance contracts.

c.   Now think of what indifference curves in this picture must look like. First, which way must they slope (given that my wife does not like to pay premiums but she does like benefits)?

d.   In which direction within the graph does my wife have to move in order to become unambiguously better off?

e.   We know my wife will fully insure if she is risk averse (and her tastes are state-independent). What policy does that imply she will buy if $\delta = 0.25$?

f.   Putting indifference curves into your graph from (b), what must they look like in order for my wife to choose the policy that you derived in (e)?

g.   What would her indifference map look like if she were risk neutral? What if she were risk-loving?

B.   Suppose $u(x) = \ln (x)$ allows us to write my wife's tastes over gambles using the expected utility function. Suppose again that my wife's income is 10 if I am not around and 250 if I am, and that the probability of me not being around is δ.

a.   Given her incomes in the good and bad state in the absence of insurance, can you use the expected utility function to arrive at her utility function over insurance policies (b, p)?

b.   Derive the expression for the slope of an indifference curve in a graph with b on the horizontal and p on the vertical axis.

c.   Suppose $\delta = 0.25$ and my wife has fully insured under policy $(b, p) = (240, 60)$. What is her MRS now?

d.   How does your answer to (c) compare to the the slope of the budget formed by mapping out all actuarily fair insurance policies (as in A(b))? Explain in terms of a graph.

17.4   **Everyday Application:** *Gambling on Sporting Events*: Some people gamble on sporting events strictly to make money while others care directly about which teams win quite apart from whether or not they gambled on the game.

A.   Consider your consumption level this weekend and suppose that you have $1,000 available. On Friday night, Duke is playing UNC in an NCAA basketball tournament, and you have the opportunity to bet an amount $\$X \leq \$1,000$ on the game. If you bet $\$X$, you will only have $(\$1,000 - \$X)$ if you lose the bet, but you will have $(\$1,000 + \$X)$ if you win. We would say in this case that you are being given even odds (since your winnings if you win are as big as your losses if you lose). Suppose that you believe that each team has a 50% chance of winning (and that, if a game is tied, it goes into overtime until the tie is broken).

a.   First, suppose you don't care about sports and only care which team wins to the extent to which it increases your consumption. I offer you the opportunity to place a bet of $X = \$500$ on either team. Will you take the bet?

b.   Suppose you got a little inebriated and wake up in the middle of the game to find that you did place the $500 bet on Duke. You notice the game is tied, and you ask me if you can get out of the bet. How much would you be willing to pay to get out?

c.   Suppose that, just as you come to realize that alcohol had made you place the bet, Duke scores a series of points and you now think that the probability of Duke winning is $\delta > 0.5$. Might you choose to stay in the bet even if I give you a chance to get out for free?

d.   Suppose you were actually a risk lover. If you could choose to place any bet (that you can afford), how much would you bet on the game (assuming you again think each team is equally likely to win)?

e.   Illustrate your answer to (a) and (c) again, but this time in a graph with x_D on the horizontal and x_{UNC} on the vertical (with the two axes representing consumption in the "state" where Duke wins (on the horizontal) and where UNC wins (on the vertical)). (*Hint:* The "budget constraint" in the picture does not change as you go from reanswering (a) to reanswering (c).)

f.   Suppose that you love Duke and hate UNC. When Duke wins, everything tastes better, and if UNC wins, there is little you want to do other than lie in bed. Might you now enter my betting pool (prior to the start of the game) even if you are generally risk averse and not at all drunk? Illustrate your answer.

g.   *True or False:* Gambling by risk-averse individuals can arise if the gambler has a different probability estimate of each outcome occurring than the "house." Alternatively, it can also arise from state-dependent tastes.

h.   *True or False:* If you are offered a bet with even odds and you believe that the odds are different, you should take the bet.

B.   Consider again the types of bets described in part A, and suppose the function $u(x) = x^\alpha$ allows us to represent your indifference curves over gambles using an expected utility function.

a.   Suppose $\alpha = 0.5$. What is your expected utility of betting $500 on one of the teams, and how does this compare to your utility of not gambling?

b.   Consider the scenario in A(b). How much would you be willing to pay to get out of the bet?

c.   Consider the scenario in A(c). For what values of δ will you choose to stay in the bet?

d.   Suppose $\alpha = 2$. How much will you bet?

e.   Consider what you were asked to do in A(e). Can you show how the MRS changes as δ changes? (*Hint:* Express the expected utility function in terms of x_{UNC} and x_D and derive the MRS.) For what value of δ is the $500 bet on Duke the optimal bet to place?

f.   Suppose that $u_D(x) = \alpha x^{0.5}$ and $u_{UNC}(x) = (1 - \alpha)x^{0.5}$ are two functions that allow us to represent your tastes over bets like this using an expected utility function. What is the equation for the MRS in your indifference map assuming that you think the probability of each team winning is in fact 0.5? For what value of α will the $500 bet be the optimal bet.

17.5†   **Everyday Application:** *Teenage Sex and Birth Control:* Consider a teenager who evaluates whether she should engage in sexual activity with her partner of the opposite sex. She thinks ahead and expects to have a present discounted level of life time consumption of x_1 in the absence of a pregnancy interrupting her educational progress. If she gets pregnant, however, she will have to interrupt her education and expects the present discounted value of her lifetime consumption to decline to x_0, considerably below x_1.

A.   Suppose that the probability of a pregnancy in the absence of birth control is 0.5 and assume that our teenager does not expect to evaluate consumption any differently in the presence of a child.

a.   Putting the present discounted value of lifetime consumption x on the horizontal axis and utility on the vertical, illustrate the consumption/utility relationship assuming that she is risk averse. Indicate the expected utility of consumption if she chooses to have sex.

b.   How much must the immediate satisfaction of having sex be worth in terms of lifetime consumption in order for her to choose to have sex?

c.   Now consider the role of birth control, which reduces the probability of a pregnancy. How does this alter your answers?

d.   Suppose her partner believes his future consumption paths will develop similarly to hers depending on whether or not there is a pregnancy, but he is risk neutral. For any particular birth control method (and associated probability of a pregnancy), who is more likely to want to have sex assuming no other differences in tastes?

e.   As the payoff to education increases in the sense that x_1 increases, what does the model predict about the degree of teenage sexual activity assuming that the effectiveness and availability of birth control remains unchanged and assuming risk neutrality?

f.   Do you think your answer to (e) also holds under risk aversion?

g.   Suppose that a government program makes daycare more affordable, thus raising x_0. What happens to the number of risk-averse teenagers having sex according to this model?

B.*   Now suppose that the function $u(x) = \ln(x)$ allows us to represent a teenager's tastes over gambles involving lifetime consumption using an expected utility function. Let δ represent the probability of a pregnancy occurring if the teenagers engage in sexual activity, and let x_0 and x_1 again represent the two lifetime consumption levels.

a.   Write down the expected utility function.

b.   What equation defines the certainty equivalent? Using the mathematical fact that $\alpha \ln x + (1 - \alpha)\ln y = \ln(x^\alpha y^{(1-\alpha)})$, can you express the certainty equivalent as a function x_0, x_1, and δ?

c.   Now derive an equation $y(x_0, x_1, \delta)$ that tells us the least value (in terms of consumption) that this teenager must place on sex in order to engage in it.

d.   What happens to y as the effectiveness of birth control increases? What does this imply about the fraction of teenagers having sex (as the effectiveness of birth control increases) assuming that all teenagers are identical except for the value they place on sex?[12]

e.   What happens to y as the payoff from education increases in the sense that x_1 increases? What does this imply for the fraction of teenagers having sex (all else equal)?

f.   What happens to y as the government makes it easier to continue going to school; i.e., as it raises x_0? What does this imply for the fraction of teenagers having sex?

g.   How do your answers change for a teenager with risk-neutral tastes over gambles involving lifetime consumption that can be expressed using an expected utility function involving the function $u(x) = x$.

h.   How would your answers change if $u(x) = x^2$?

---

[12]It will be helpful to recall the mathematical fact that the derivative of x^α *with respect to* α is equal to $x^\alpha \ln x$.

17.6 **Everyday Application:** *Gambling with Different Beliefs*: Suppose you and I consider the following game: We both put $y on the table, then flip a coin. If it comes up heads, I get everything on the table, and if it comes up tails, you get everything on the table.

A. Suppose we both have an amount $z > y$ available for consumption this week and both of us are risk averse.

    a. Draw my (weekly) consumption/utility relationship given that I am risk averse. On your graph, indicate the expected value of the gamble and the expected utility of the gamble assuming that we are playing with a fair coin; i.e., a coin that comes up heads half the time and tails the other half.

    b. Will I agree to participate in the gamble if I think the coin is fair?

    c. Now suppose that I exchanged the game coin for a weighted coin that comes up heads more often than tails. Illustrate in your graph how, if the coin is sufficiently unfair, I will now agree to participate in the gamble.

    d. Now consider both of us in the context of an Edgeworth Box, and suppose again that the coin is fair. Draw an Edgeworth Box with consumption x_H under "heads" on the horizontal and consumption x_T under "tails" on the vertical axis. Illustrate our "endowment" bundle E before the gamble and the outcome bundle A if we do gamble.

    e. Illustrate the indifference curves through E and A. Will we gamble? Is it efficient not to gamble?

    f.* Suppose next that I have an unfair coin that is weighted toward coming up heads with probability $\delta > 0.5$. How do my indifference curves change as a result?

    g.* You do not know about the unfair coin, but you are delighted to hear that I have just sweetened the gamble for you: If the coin comes up heads, I agree to give you a fraction k of my winnings. Draw a new Edgeworth Box with the endowment bundle E and the outcome bundle B implied by the change I have made to the gamble.

    h.* Can you illustrate how both of us engaging in the gamble might now be an efficient equilibrium?

    i. *True or False*: If individuals have different beliefs about the underlying probabilities of different states occurring, then there may be gains from state-contingent consumption trades that would not arise if individuals agreed on the underlying probabilities.

B.* Suppose that the function $u(x) = \ln x$ allows us to represent both of our preferences over gambles using the expected utility function. Suppose further that z and y (as defined in part A) take on the values $z = 150$ and $y = 50$.

    a. Calculate the expected utility of entering this gamble (assuming a fair coin) and compare it to the utility of not entering. Will either of us agree to play the game?

    b. Suppose that I paid you a fraction k of my winnings in the event that heads comes up. What is the minimum that k has to be for you to agree to enter the game (assuming you think we are playing with a fair coin)?

    c. If I agreed to set k to the minimum required to get you to enter the game, determine the lowest possible δ that an unbalanced coin must imply in order for *me* to want to enter the game.

    d. Suppose my unbalanced coin comes up heads 75% of the time. Define the expected utility function for me and you as a function of x_T and x_H given that I know that the coin is unbalanced and you do not.

    e. Define p as the price for $1 worth of x_H consumption in terms of x_T consumption. Suppose you wanted to construct a linear budget (with price p for x_H and price of 1 for x_T) that contains our "endowment" bundle as well as the outcome bundle from the gamble (in which I return k of my winnings if the coin comes up heads). Derive p as a function of k.

    f. Using our expected utility functions and the budget constraints (as a function of k), derive our demands for x_H and x_T as a function of k.

    g. Determine the level of k that results in an equilibrium price and then verify that the resulting equilibrium output bundle is the one associated with the gamble we have been analyzing. Call this $k*$ and illustrate what you have done in an Edgeworth Box.

    h. Is the allocation chosen through the gamble efficient when $k = k*$?

    i. Suppose I had offered the lowest possible k that would induce you to enter the game instead; i.e., the one you derived in (b). Would the allocation chosen through the gamble be efficient in that case? Could it be supported as an equilibrium outcome with some equilibrium price?

    j. Illustrate in an Edgeworth Box what is different in part (i) compared to part (g).

17.7 **Everyday Application:** *Venice and Regret*: Suppose that you can choose to participate in one of two gambles: In Gamble 1 you have a 99% chance of winning a trip to Venice and a 1% chance of winning tickets to a movie about Venice; and in Gamble 2, you have a 99% of winning the same trip to Venice and a 1% chance of not winning anything.

A. Suppose you very much like Venice, and, were you to be asked to rank the three possible outcomes, you would rank the trip to Venice first, the tickets to the movie about Venice second, and having nothing third.

   a. Assume that you can create a consumption index such that getting nothing is denoted as 0 consumption, getting the tickets to the movie is $x_1 > 0$ and getting the trip is $x_2 > x_1$. Denote the expected value of Gamble 1 by $E(G_1)$ and the expected value of Gamble 2 by $E(G_2)$. Which is higher?

   b. On a graph with x on the horizontal axis and utility on the vertical, illustrate a consumption/utility relationship that exhibits risk aversion.

   c. In your graph, illustrate the expected utility you receive from Gamble 1 and from Gamble 2. Which gamble will you choose to participate in?

   d. Next, suppose tastes are risk neutral instead. Redraw your graph and illustrate again which gamble you would choose. (*Hint*: Be careful to accurately differentiate between the expected values of the two gambles.)

   e. It turns out (for reasons that become clearer in part B) that risk aversion (or neutrality) is irrelevant for how individuals whose behavior is explained by expected utility theory will choose among these gambles. In a separate graph, illustrate the consumption/utility relationship again, but this time assume risk loving. Illustrate in the graph how your choice over the two gambles might still be the same as in parts (c) and (d). Can you think of why it in fact *has to be* the same?

   f. It turns out that many people, when faced with a choice of these two gambles, end up choosing Gamble 2. Assuming that such people would indeed rank the three outcomes the way we have, is there any way that such a choice can be explained using expected utility theory (taking as given that the choice implied by expected utility theory does not depend on risk aversion)?

   g. This example is known as *Machina's Paradox*.[13] One explanation for it (i.e., for the fact that many people choose Gamble 2 over Gamble 1) is that expected utility theory does not take into account *regret*. Can you think of how this might explain people's paradoxical choice of Gamble 2 over Gamble 1?

B. Assume again, as in part A, that individuals prefer a trip to Venice to the movie ticket, and they prefer the movie ticket to getting nothing. Furthermore, suppose there exists a function u that assigns u_2 as the utility of getting the trip, u_1 as the utility of getting the movie ticket and u_0 as the utility of getting nothing, and suppose that this function u allows us to represent tastes over risky pairs of outcomes using an expected utility function.

   a. What inequality defines the relationship between u_1 and u_0?

   b. Now multiply both sides of your inequality from (a) by 0.01, and then add $0.99u_2$ to both sides. What inequality do you now have?

   c. Relate the inequality you derived in (b) to the expected utility of the two gambles in this example. What gamble does expected utility theory predict a person will choose (assuming the outcomes are ranked as we have ranked them)?

   d. When we typically think of a "gamble," we are thinking of different outcomes that will happen with different probabilities. But we can also think of "degenerate" gambles; i.e., gambles where one outcome happens with certainty. Define the following three such "gambles": Gamble A results in the trip to Venice with probability of 100%; Gamble B results in the movie ticket with probability of 100%; and Gamble C results in nothing with probability of 100%. How are these degenerate "gambles" ranked by someone who prefers the trip to the ticket to nothing?

   e. Using the notion of *mixed gambles* introduced in Appendix 1, define Gambles 1 and 2 as mixed gambles over the degenerate "gambles" we have just defined in (d). Explain how the *Independence Axiom* from Appendix 1 implies that Gamble 1 must be preferred to Gamble 2.

---

[13]The paradox is named after Mark Machina (1954–), who first identified it.

f.   *True or False*: When individuals who rank the outcomes the way we have assumed choose Gamble 2 over Gamble 1, expected utility theory fails because the independence axiom is violated.

g.   Would the paradox disappear if we assumed state-dependent tastes? (*Hint*: As with the Allais Paradox in Appendix 2, the answer is no.)

17.8   **Business Application:** *Choosing a Mafia for Insurance*: Consider Sunny, who is committed to a life of crime. Sunny is risk averse, and he knows that he will enjoy consumption level x_1 if he does not get caught and consumption level of x_0 (very much below x_1) if he gets caught and goes to jail. He estimates the probability of getting caught as δ.

A.   Suppose there are various mafia organizations that have connections in the District Attorney's office and can affect the outcomes of court cases. Suppose initially that Sunny's tastes are state-independent.

a.   First, consider a really powerful mafia that can ensure that any of its members who is caught is immediately released. Can you illustrate how much such a mafia would be able to charge Sunny if Sunny is risk averse? What about if Sunny is risk loving?

b.   Next, suppose that the local mafia is not quite as powerful and can only get jail sentences reduced, thus in effect raising x_0. It approaches Sunny to offer him a deal: Pay us p when you don't get caught, and we'll raise your consumption level if you do get caught by b. If the local mafia insurance business is perfectly competitive (and faces no costs other than paying for increased consumption in jail), what is the relationship between b and p? (*Hint*: Note that this is different than the insurance example in the text where my wife had to pay p *regardless* of whether she was in the good or bad outcome.)

c.   Suppose that Sunny can choose any combination of b and p that satisfies the relationship you derived in (b). What would he choose if he is risk averse? What if he is risk loving?

d.   Why does Sunny join the mafia in (a) but not in (c) if he is risk loving (and if "negative" insurance is not possible)?

e.   How much consumer surplus does Sunny get for buying his preferred (b, p) package when he is risk averse; i.e., how much more would Sunny be willing to pay to eliminate risk than he has to pay?

f.   Construct a graph with x_G, defined as consumption when not caught, on the horizontal and x_B, defined as consumption when caught, on the vertical axis. Illustrate, in the form of a budget line, all the combinations of insurance contracts that Sunny is offered by the local mafia.

g.   Illustrate his optimal choice when he is risk averse and his tastes are still state-independent. How does this change if the corrupt jailer takes a fraction k of every dollar that the mafia makes available to Sunny in jail?

h.   Can you show in this type of graph where Sunny would optimize if he is risk-loving?

i.   Finally, suppose Sunny's utility from consumption is different when he is forced to consume in jail than when he consumes on the outside. Can you tell an intuitive story for how this might cause Sunny to pick a (b, p) combination that either over- or underinsures him?

B.   Suppose we express consumption in thousands of dollars per year and that $x_0 = 20$ and $x_1 = 80$. Suppose further that $\delta = 0.25$ and that the function $u(x) = x^\alpha$ is the utility function over consumption that allows us to express tastes over gambles through an expected utility function.

a.   Consider first the powerful mafia (from part A(a)) that can eliminate any penalties from getting caught. How much would Sunny be willing to pay to join this mafia if $\alpha = 0.5$? What if $\alpha = 2$?

b.   One of these cases represents risk-averse tastes, the other risk-loving. In light of this, can you explain your answer intuitively?

c.   Next, consider the weaker mafia that can raise consumption in jail. Suppose this mafia asks Sunny to pay p during times when he is not caught in exchange for getting an increase of b in consumption when he finds himself in jail. If you have not already done so in part A of the question, derive the relationship between p and b if the mafia insurance market is perfectly competitive (and faces no costs other than paying b to members who are in jail).

d.   Using the function $u(x) = x^\alpha$, set up the optimization problem for Sunny, who is considering which combination of b and p he should choose from all possible combinations that satisfy the relationship you derived in (c). Then derive his optimal insurance contract with the mafia.

e. If $\alpha = 0.5$, what is Sunny's consumer surplus from participating in the mafia?

f. Why does your solution to (d) give the wrong answer when $\alpha > 1$? Explain using the example of $\alpha = 2$.

g. Suppose again that $\alpha = 0.5$. What changes when the jailer takes a fraction $k = 0.25$ of every dollar that is smuggled into the jail?

h. Finally, suppose that tastes are state-dependent and that the functions $u_B(x) = 0.47x^{0.5}$ and $u_G(x) = 0.53x^{0.5}$ (where u_B applies in jail and u_G applies outside) allow us to represent Sunny's tastes over gambles using an expected utility function. Assuming that Sunny still chooses from the insurance contracts that satisfy the relationship between b and p you derived in (c), what contract will he pick? What if $u_B(x) = 0.53x^{0.5}$ and $u_G(x) = 0.47x^{0.5}$ instead? Can you make intuitive sense of your answers?

17.9 Business Application: *Diversifying Risk along the Business Cycle:* Suppose you own a business that does well during economic expansions but not so well during recessions, which happen with probability δ. Let x_E denote your consumption level during expansions and let x_R denote your consumption level during recessions. Unless you do something to diversify risk, these consumption levels are $E = (e_E, e_R)$ where e_E is your income during expansions and e_R your income during recessions (with $e_E > e_R$). Your tastes over consumption are the same during recessions as during expansions and you are risk averse. For any asset purchases described here, assume that you pay for these assets from whatever income you have depending on whether the economy is in recessions or expansion.

A.* Suppose I own a financial firm that manages asset portfolios. All I care about as I manage my business is expected returns, and any asset I sell is characterized by (p, b_R, b_E) where p is how much I charge for 1 unit of the asset, b_R is how much the asset will pay you (as, say, dividends) during recessions, and b_E is how much the asset will pay you during expansions.

a. Is someone like me—who only cares about expected returns—risk averse, risk loving, or risk neutral?

b. Suppose that all the assets I offer have the feature that those who buy these assets experience no change in their expected consumption levels as a result of buying my assets. Derive an equation that expresses the price p of my assets in terms of δ, b_R and b_E.

c. What happens to my expected returns when I sell more or fewer of such assets?

d. Suppose you buy 1 asset (p, b_R, b_E) that satisfies our equation from (b). How does your consumption during expansions and recessions change as a result?

e. At what rate do assets of the kind I am offering allow you to transfer consumption opportunities from expansions to recessions? On a graph with x_E on the horizontal and x_R on the vertical axis, illustrate the "budget line" that the availability of such assets creates for you.

f. Illustrate in your graph your optimal choice of assets.

g. Overall output during recessions is smaller than during expansions. Suppose everyone is risk averse. Is it possible for us to all end up doing what you concluded you would do in (f)? (We will explore this further in exercise 17.10.)

B. Suppose that the function $u(x) = x^\alpha$ is such that we can express tastes over gambles using expected utility functions.

a. If you have not already done so in part A, derive the expression $p(\delta, b_R, b_E)$ that relates the price of an asset to the probability of a recession δ, the dividend payment b_R during recessions, and the dividend payment b_E during economic expansions assuming that purchase of such assets keeps expected consumption levels unchanged.

b. Suppose you purchase k units of the same asset (b_E, b_R), which is priced as you derived in part (a) and for which $(b_R - b_E) = y > 0$. Derive an expression for x_R defined as your consumption level during recessions (given your recession income level of e_R) assuming you purchase these assets. Derive similarly an expression for your consumption level x_E during economic expansions.

c. Set up an expected utility maximization problem where you choose k—the number of such assets that you purchase. Then solve for k.

d.   How much will you consume during recessions and expansions?

e.   For what values of α is your answer correct?

f.   *True or False*: So long as assets that pay more dividends during recessions than expansions are available at "actuarily fair" prices, you will be able to fully insure against consumption shocks from business cycles.

g.   Could you accomplish the same outcome by instead creating and selling assets with $(b_E > b_R)$?

17.10*† **Business Application:** *Diversifying Risk along the Business Cycle in General Equilibrium*: In exercise 17.9, we considered the case of me trading assets that allow you to transfer consumption from good times to bad times. Suppose again that your income during economic expansions is e_E and your income during recessions is e_R, and that the probability of a recession is $\delta < 0.5$.

BUSINESS APPLICATION

A.   Also, suppose again that my tastes are risk neutral while yours are risk averse and that $e_E > e_R$. My consumption opportunity endowment, however, is the reverse of yours, with e_R equal to my income during economic expansions and e_E equal to my income during recessions.

a.   Draw an Edgeworth Box representing the economy of you and me.

b.   Illustrate the equilibrium in this economy. Will you do in equilibrium what we concluded you would do in exercise 17.9?

c.   Next, suppose that there was a third person in our economy: your identical twin who shares your tastes and endowments. Suppose the terms of trade for transferring consumption in one state to the other remain unchanged, and suppose an equilibrium exists in which everyone ends up at an interior solution. Illustrate what this would look like, given that there are now two of you and only one of me. (*Hint*: It should no longer be the case that our indifference curves within the box are tangent to one another because equilibrium now implies that two of your trades have to be exactly offset by one of mine.)

d.   Is anyone fully insured against consumption swings in the business cycle? Is everyone?

e.   Now continue with the example but suppose that my tastes, instead of being risk neutral, were also risk averse. Would the same terms of trade still produce an equilibrium?

f.   How do the terms of trade now have to change to support an equilibrium when all of us are risk averse?

g.   Will anyone be fully insured; i.e., will anyone enjoy the same level of consumption during recessions as during expansions?

h.   Relate your conclusion to the existence of aggregate risk in economies that experience expansions and recessions. Who would you rather be: me or you?

B.*** Suppose that the function $u(x) = \ln x$ allows us to express your tastes over gambles as expected utilities. Also, suppose again that your income during expansions is e_E and your income during recessions is e_R, with $e_E > e_R$.

a.   Let p_R be defined as the price of \$1 of consumption in the event that a recession occurs and let p_E be the price of \$1 of consumption in the event that an economic expansion occurs. Explain why we can simply normalize $p_R = 1$ and then denote the price of \$1 of consumption in the event of expansions as $p_E = p$.

b.   Using these normalized prices, write down your budget constraint and your expected utility optimization problem.

c.   Solve for your demand for x_R and x_E.

d.   Repeat parts (b) and (c) for me, assuming I share your tastes but my income during *recessions* is e_E and my income during *expansions* is e_R, exactly the mirror image of your incomes over the business cycle.

e.   Assuming we are the only ones in this economy, derive the equilibrium price, or terms of trade across the two states.

f.   How much do each of us consume during expansions and recessions at this equilibrium price?

g.   Now suppose that there are two of you and only one of me in this economy. What happens to the equilibrium price?

h.   Do you now consume less during recessions than during expansions? Do I?

17.11 **Business Application:** *Local versus National Insurance*: Natural disasters are local phenomena, impacting a city or a part of a state but rarely impacting the whole country, at least if the country is geographically large. To simplify the analysis, suppose there are two distinct regions that might experience local disasters.

A. Define "state 1" as region 1 experiencing a natural disaster, and define "state 2" as region 2 having a natural disaster. I live in region 2 whereas you live in region 1. Both of us have the same risk-averse and state-independent tastes, and our consumption level falls from y to z when a natural disaster strikes in our home region. The probability of state 1 is δ and the probability of state 2 is $(1 - \delta)$.

   a. Putting consumption x_1 in state 1 on the horizontal axis and consumption x_2 in state 2 on the vertical, illustrate an Edgeworth Box assuming you and I are the only ones living in our respective regions. Illustrate our "endowment" bundle in this box.

   b. Suppose an insurance company wanted to insure us against the risks of natural disasters. Under actuarily fair insurance, what is the opportunity cost of state 2 consumption in terms of state 1 consumption? What is the opportunity cost of state 1 consumption in terms of state 2 consumption? Which of these is the slope of the acuarily fair budget in your Edgeworth Box?

   c. Illustrate the budget line that arises from the set of all actuarily fair insurance contracts within the Edgeworth Box. Where would you and I choose to consume assuming we are risk averse?

   d. How does this outcome compare to the equilibrium outcome if you and I were simply to trade state-contingent consumption across the two states?

   e. Suppose there were two of me and two of you in this world. Would anything change?

   f. Now suppose that the two of me living in region two go to a local insurance company that operates only in region 2. Why might this company not offer us actuarily fair insurance policies?

   g. Instead of insurance against the consequences of natural disasters, suppose we instead considered insurance against noncommunicable illness. Would a local insurance company face the same kind of problem offering actuarily fair insurance in this case?

   h. How is the case of local insurance companies insuring against local natural disasters similar to the case of national insurance companies insuring against business cycle impacts on consumption? How might international credit markets that allow insurance companies to borrow and lend help resolve this?

B. Suppose that, as in exercise 17.10 the function $u(x) = \ln x$ allows us to represent our tastes over gambles as expected utilities. Assume the same set-up as the one described in A.

   a. Let p_1 be defined as the price of $1 of consumption if state 1 occurs and let p_2 be the price of $1 of consumption in the event that state 2 occurs. Set $p_2 = 1$ and then denote the price of $1 of consumption in the event of state 1 occurring as $p_1 = p$ and write down your budget constraint.

   b. Solve the expected utility maximization problem given this budget constraint to get your demand x_1 for state 1 consumption as well as your demand x_2 for state 2 consumption.

   c. Repeat (a) and (b) for me.

   d. Derive the equilibrium price. Is this actuarily fair?

   e. How much do we consume in each state?

   f. Does the equlibrium price change if there are two of you and two of me?

   g. Finally, suppose that the two of me attempt to trade state-contingent consumption between just the two of us. What will be the equilibrium price?

   h. Will we manage to trade at all?

   i. Can you illustrate this in an Edgeworth Box? Is the equilibrium efficient?

17.12 **Policy Application:** *More Police or More Jails? Enforcement versus Deterrence*: Consider a person who is thinking about whether to engage in a life of crime. He knows that, if he gets caught, he will be in jail and will sustain a consumption level of x_0, but if he does not get caught, he will be able to consume x_1 considerably above x_0.

A. Suppose that this person cares only about his consumption level (i.e., he has state-independent tastes).

   a. On a graph with consumption x on the horizontal axis and utility on the vertical, illustrate this person's consumption/utility relationship assuming he is risk averse.

b. Suppose the probability δ of getting caught is 0.25. Illustrate the expected utility of choosing a life of crime. What if $\delta = 0.75$?

c. Redraw the consumption/utility graph and suppose $\delta = 0.5$. Let $\bar{x}$ indicate the income this person would need to be able to make honestly in order for him to be indifferent between an honest living and a life of crime.

d. Senator C believes the criminal justice system spends too much effort on identifying criminals but not enough effort on punishing them harshly. He proposes an *increased deterrence policy* under which penalties for committing crimes are raised while less is spent on law enforcement. This implies a drop in both x_0 as well as δ. Suppose the expected consumption level for a person engaged in a life of crime remains unchanged under this policy. Will the person who was previously indifferent between an honest living and a life of crime still be indifferent?

e. Senator L believes we are treating criminals too harshly. He proposes an *increased enforcement policy* that devotes more resources toward catching criminals but then lowers the penalties that criminals face if caught. The policy thus increases x_0 as well as δ. Suppose that the expected consumption level of a person engaged in a life of crime is again unchanged under this policy. Will the person who was previously indifferent between an honest living and a life of crime still be indifferent?

f. *True or False*: If criminals are risk averse, the increased deterrence policy is more effective at reducing crime than the increased enforcement policy.

g. How would your answers change if criminals were risk loving?

B. Suppose that $x_0 = 20$ and $x_1 = 80$ (where we can think of these values as being expressed in terms of thousands of dollars), and suppose the probability of getting caught is $\delta = 0.5$.

a. What is the expected consumption level if the life of crime is chosen?

b. Suppose the potential criminal's tastes over gambles can be expressed using an expected utility function that evaluates the utility of consumption as $u(x) = \ln(x)$. What is the person's expected utility from a life of crime?

c. How does the expected utility compare with the utility of the expected value of consumption? Can you tell from this whether the criminal is risk averse?

d. Consider the level of consumption this person could attain by not engaging in a life of crime. What level of consumption from an honest living would make the person be indifferent between a life of crime and an honest living? Denote this consumption level $\bar{x}$.

e. Now consider the *increased deterrence policy* described in A(d). In particular, suppose that the policy increases penalties to the point where x_0 falls to 5. How much can δ drop if the expected consumption level in a life of crime is to remain unchanged?

f. What happens to $\bar{x}$ as a result of this increased deterrence policy?

g. Now consider the *increased enforcement policy* described in A(e). In particular, suppose that δ is increased to 0.6. How much can x_0 increase in order for the expected consumption in a life of crime to remain unchanged?

h. What happens to $\bar{x}$ as a result of this increased enforcement policy?

i. Which policy is more effective at reducing crime assuming potential criminals are risk averse?

j. Suppose that the function $u(x)$ that allows us to represent this individual's tastes over gambles with an expected utility function is $u(x) = x^2$. How do your answers change?

17.13† **Policy Application:** *More Police or More Teachers? Enforcement versus Education*: Suppose again (as in exercise 17.12) that the payoff from engaging in a life of crime is x_1 if you don't get caught and x_0 (significantly below x_1) if you end up in jail, with δ representing the probability of getting caught. Suppose everyone has identical tastes but we differ in terms of the amount of income we can earn in the (legal) labor market, with (legal) incomes distributed uniformly (i.e., evenly) between x_0 and x_1.

POLICY APPLICATION

A. Suppose there are two ways to lower crime rates: spend more money on police officers so that we can make it more likely that those who commit crimes get caught, or spend more money on teachers so that we increase the honest income that potential criminals could make. The first policy raises δ; the second raises individual (honest) incomes through better education.

a. Begin by drawing a risk averse individual's consumption/utility relationship and assume a high δ. Indicate the corresponding $\bar{x}$ that represents the (honest) income level at which a person is indifferent between an honest life and a life of crime.

b. Consider a policy that invests in education and results in a uniform increase in all (honest) incomes by an amount $\tilde{x}$. On the horizontal axis of your graph, indicate which types of individuals (identified by their pre-policy income levels) will now switch from a life of crime to an honest life.

c. Next, consider the alternative policy of investing in more enforcement, thus increasing the probability δ of getting caught. Indicate in your graph how much the expected consumption level of a life of crime must be shifted in order for the policy to achieve the same reduction in crime as the policy in part (b).

d. If it costs the same to achieve a \$1 increase in everyone's income through education invest- ments as it costs to achieve a \$1 reduction in the expected consumption level of a life of crime, which policy is more cost effective at reducing crime given we started with an already high δ.

e. How does your answer change if δ is very low to begin with?

f. *True or False*: Assuming people are risk averse, the following is an accurate policy conclusion from our model of expected utility: The higher current levels of law enforcement, the more likely it is that investments in education will cause greater reductions in crime than equivalent investments in additional law enforcement.

B. Now suppose that, as in exercise 17.12, $x_0 = 20$ and $x_1 = 80$ (where we can think of these values as being expressed in terms of thousands of dollars).

a. Suppose, again as in exercise 17.12, that expressing utility over consumption by $u(x) = \ln x$ allows us to express tastes over gambles using the expected utility function. If $\delta = 0.75$, what is the income level $\bar{x}$ at which an individual is indifferent between a life of crime and an honest life?

b. If an investment in eduction results in a uniform increase of income of 5, what are the pre- policy incomes of people who will now switch from a life of crime to an honest life?

c. How much would δ have to increase in order to achieve an equivalent reduction in crime? How much would this change the expected consumption level under a life of crime?

d. If it is equally costly to raise incomes by \$1 through education investments as it is to reduce the expected value of consumption in a life of crime through an increase in δ, which policy is the more cost effective way to reduce crime?

e. How do your answers change if $\delta = 0.25$ to begin with?

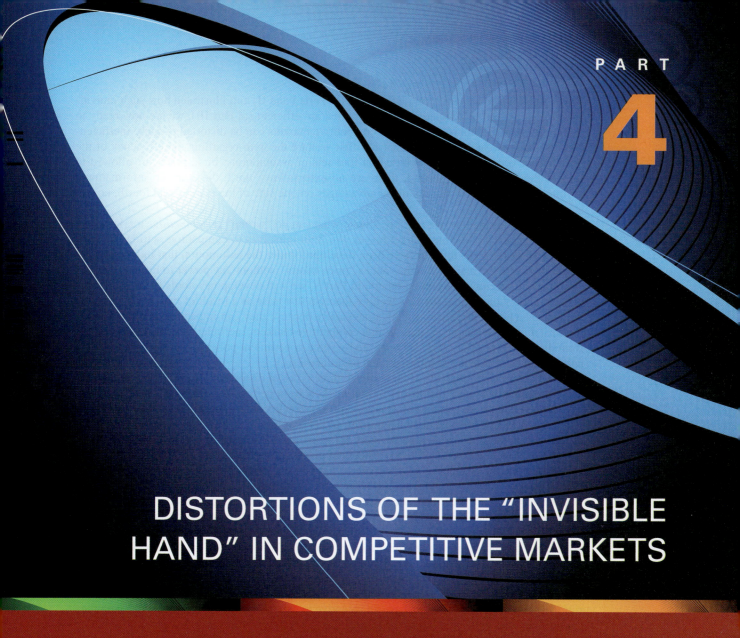

PART 4

DISTORTIONS OF THE "INVISIBLE HAND" IN COMPETITIVE MARKETS

Having built our models of individual choice (in Parts I and II) and illustrated how such individual choice can lead to competitive equilibria that are efficient (in Part III), we are now ready to investigate how the "invisible hand" of competitive markets can be distorted to cause inefficiencies. We have already mentioned that our first welfare theorem regarding the efficiency of the spontaneous order of markets is based on four sets of assumptions: First, prices are allowed to form without distortions; second, there are no externalities; third, there are no informational asymmetries that bestow informational advantages on one side of the market; and fourth, no one has market power.

In this part of the text, we will investigate what can go "wrong" in *competitive* markets; i.e., in markets where no one has market power. We limit ourselves to competitive settings for now because all of the tools thus far have been developed under the assumption that individuals are small relative to the market and thus act as "price-takers" without any power to influence prices (and thus the incentives) faced by others. In Part V, we will develop new tools (from game theory) to tackle violations of the first welfare theorem that arise as a result of market power when individuals have an incentive to think strategically because they can impact the economic environment directly by shaping prices. Within competitive markets, inefficiencies can therefore arise from distortions of prices (typically caused by some government policy), the existence of externalities and the existence of informational asymmetries.

In Chapters 18 through 20, we investigate three types of distortions of prices and the mechanism through which these distortions inhibit markets from performing efficiently. Recall that we have argued that prices contain information, information necessary for individuals to make individual choices in a manner that maximizes social surplus. It is therefore not surprising that distortions of these prices distort the very information that causes prices to guide individual behavior in an efficient manner. In the process of investigating the impact of price distortions, we will also define the concept of *price elasticity* that you may have encountered in a previous economics course.

Chapter 18 begins with the most obvious and direct types of price distortions. For a variety of reasons, governments may choose to limit how high prices for particular goods may rise or how low prices are allowed to fall. Such policies, known as *price ceilings* and *price floors*, prohibit voluntary exchange at prices at which markets would otherwise trade. In the absence of some other mechanism, we will see that this will lead to *disequilibrium shortages* or *surpluses* of goods. But we will also discover that there is no particular reason that such shortages or surpluses will persist. For instance, if a price ceiling artificially lowers price below its undistorted equilibrium level, individual consumers have an incentive to expend additional effort to make sure they are the ones who will get to buy at the lower price. They may, for instance, have to line up before stores open, thus spending their time as well as their money in pursuit of the goods. In the new equilibrium, a new *non-price rationing* mechanism will therefore arise to once again cause demand to equal supply at the mandated price. The important insight here is that the market price mechanism is one of many ways in which scarce goods are rationed: they are rationed to those who are willing to pay the most. If this rationing mechanism is disturbed and price cannot be used to ration fully, a new non-price mechanism has to emerge to determine who gets what. And this non-price mechanism, we will demonstrate, will introduce inefficiencies.

Our analysis will allow us to identify winners and losers from the imposition of price floors and price ceilings, and it will give us some insight about how such policies may arise in democratic policy making even though they are inefficient. In particular, for many such policies, it is the case that the "winners" are a concentrated few for whom it is easy to organize politically while the "losers" are a diffuse many who may barely notice why it is that they are losing. At the same time, we will also discover circumstances in which price ceilings or price floors are motivated by ethical concerns, such as in the case of human kidney markets where the government has in most countries set a price ceiling of zero that permits individuals to donate one of their kidneys but not to sell it (at a price above zero).

In Chapter 19, we revisit *taxes* and *subsidies*, which are by far the most common ways in which market prices are distorted through policy. We have previously discussed in Chapter 10 how taxes cause substitution effects and create deadweight losses. Now that we have built models of markets, however, we can see more clearly how taxes (and subsidies) translate into price changes, whether consumers or producers are affected more depending on relative price elasticities, and which types of taxes (and subsidies) are likely to result in greater or lesser inefficiencies. Throughout, we will emphasize that recognizing inefficiencies introduced through taxes (and subsidies) is not the same as arguing that taxes (and subsidies) should not be used. Government expenditures need to be funded somehow, and many expenditure programs may carry benefits that outweigh the efficiency cost of the taxes that are required to fund them. Nevertheless, it is important to be aware of the cost that taxes impose on society, and to understand how such costs are related to the types of taxes that are considered.

We then turn in Chapter 20 to markets that extend across geographic regions or across time, markets that are connected through the activities of *exporters* and *speculators* who look for opportunities to buy low and sell high. Such activities have the effect of equalizing prices across regions and time, but sometimes governments interfere with this process by taxing trades across markets (through *tariffs* or imposing particular *quotas* that limit the amount of trade). We will see how such policies once again distort prices and cause inefficiencies, whether in goods markets were explicit trade is limited or in labor markets where policies are often aimed at restricting worker or firm *migration*.

We do not, however, want to give the impression that government tax and price policies are the only factors that contribute to inefficiencies in competitive markets. Chapter 21 introduces the topic of *externalities*—impacts of individual actions that affect others who are not participating in a given market transaction. Pollution generated in the production of goods is a prime example, but other types of externalities, both positive and negative, are pervasive in the real world. Within competitive settings, Chapter 21 illustrates how such externalities can cause markets to over- or underproduce relative to what is efficient because individual actors within those markets no longer face the full costs or reap the full benefits of their actions. While taxes and subsidies in competitive markets are inefficient in the absence of such externalities, they can now become efficiency enhancing when applied in the right way. Alternatively, we will see that there exist policies that involve the creation of new markets that can in turn cause externality-emitters to face the full costs of their actions. Our main example in this regard is the establishment of *pollution voucher markets*.

The fact that the establishment of new markets can, in some instances, represent a solution to the efficiency problem faced by markets under externalities then points to a deeper issue regarding externalities. In particular, while we often call the inefficiencies arising from the presence of externalities in a competitive market a *market failure*, we could similarly say that the existence of an externality is evidence of a *failure of markets to exist*. Put differently, externalities arise because important markets are "missing." Although it is not always technologically possible to establish such missing markets, understanding the root cause of inefficiencies arising from externalities can then help us think more creatively of nonmarket institutions that can address such inefficiencies.

In addition, we will see that the problem of *missing markets* is not confined to externalities. In Chapter 22, we turn to informational asymmetries that result in opportunities for the more informed parties in a market to "take advantage" of the less informed. When such informational asymmetries become sufficiently pronounced, entire markets might in fact cease to exist at all since the less informed are too skeptical to engage in trades with the more informed. The phenomenon that leads to such problems for markets is known as *adverse selection*, with insurance markets providing a good example. In such markets, the person seeking insurance might have more information about the likely risk he or she faces than the insurance company can observe, with the insurance company as a result not offering certain types of insurance contracts. Put differently, if insurance companies have reason to believe that they are recipients of an adverse selection of high cost customers, they may not be able to offer insurance packages that low cost customers are willing to buy. While we had shown in Chapter 17 that complete sets of competitive insurance markets lead to an efficient allocation of risk, informational asymmetries might in fact cause such markets to be less than "complete," and thus result in something less than an efficient allocation of risk.

The problem of informational asymmetries is not, however, confined to insurance markets. One important example involves labor markets and, in particular, the emergence of racial and gender discrimination in such markets. While such discrimination might exist under competition if "bigots" in an economy derive utility from discriminating, we will see that asymmetric information may cause even "non-bigots" to discriminate as they infer individual characteristics from average characteristics of populations. Understanding how asymmetric information can lead to problems of missing markets and related problems of discrimination can then help us understand better how nonmarket institutions might aid in resolving problems created by asymmetric information. In some cases, we will see that market-like institutions might in fact emerge "spontaneously" to deal with the problem, and in other cases we will see how government policies might be able to play a role.

Elasticities, Price-Distorting Policies, and Non-Price Rationing

We have demonstrated in the last few chapters how prices form in competitive markets.[1] Prices, we have argued, send important signals to all the relevant actors in an economy, allowing each individual actor to then choose how to behave in the market while ensuring that the market produces output at the lowest possible cost and channels it to those that value the output the most. In a world defined by scarcity, prices therefore represent one way of *rationing* scarce resources, a way of determining who gets to consume what, how much everyone works, how much consumption will occur now as opposed to in the future, and how much risk each individual faces.

We may not always like the way in which the competitive price system rations scarce goods in the world. Maybe we do not like the fact that, in an unregulated labor market, some individuals will be able to earn only very low wages, at least until they get more experience or acquire more skills or education. We may not like the fact that housing in some areas is so expensive as to preclude the poor from consuming it, or that innovations in agriculture are pushing aside the traditional small family farm. As a result, we often ask the government to tinker with the price system, to come up with ways of getting toward outcomes that we like better. Examples of this include minimum wage laws, milk price regulations, rent control, and a variety of other policies aimed at improving in some way on the market outcome.

In the end, there may be good reasons why people disagree on the wisdom of such policies. But much of the disagreement comes from not understanding sufficiently the economics behind markets and policy interventions, and to the extent to which this is the cause of differing opinions, the economist has a role in clarifying the trade-offs involved. The most fundamental of these trade-offs rests on an understanding of the fact that, in a world of scarcity, *something* will always lead to rationing of goods. Put differently, there will always be some mechanism that determines who gets what goods and who is left out. Market prices represent one such rationing mechanism, and when we add other institutions in attempts to improve on market mechanisms, we will explicitly or implicitly add other rationing mechanisms on top of it. As some economists have put it, there is no "free lunch," no magic wand that eliminates the problem of scarcity, at least not in the world we occupy.

The goal of this chapter is then to use some commonly talked about policies that aim to improve on market outcomes to illustrate how such policies "distort" prices and thus change the rationing of scarce goods in the world. This is done most easily within the "partial equilibrium" model of Chapters 14 and 15. As we will see in this and upcoming chapters, the

---

[1]This chapter is built on a basic understanding of demand and supply as treated in Chapter 14. It furthermore uses the ideas of consumer and producer surplus as developed in Chapter 15, with distinctions between marginal willingness to pay and demand assumed away (through quasilinearity).

magnitude of the various impacts of price distortions will depend on the responsiveness of consumers and producers to price changes, on the *elasticity* of their behavior. We have waited to introduce the concept of elasticity until now as we will now begin to see it in action.

With some of the policies we discuss, it is then indeed the case that many economists end up on one side of the debate because they are persuaded that the *unintended consequences* of well-intentioned policies outweigh the intended benefits. But the point here is not to argue for or against particular policies; rather, we will try to simply use the logic of our models to illustrate trade-offs that we should be aware of in these policy debates, and then everyone can decide for themselves whether what we have learned leads them to favor or oppose particular policies. And by identifying the "winners" and "losers" from such policies, we will find that we can get a sense of why democratic political processes will sometimes implement certain policies over others, even if an economic analysis of those policies suggests that alternative policies should dominate.

Interactions of Markets and Price-Distorting Policies

This chapter begins our analysis of policy in competitive markets with two general classes of policies: those that aim to lower prices for the benefit of consumers, and those that aim to raise prices for the benefit of producers. We will see that such policies give rise to deadweight losses that can be quite large, but they may also make some individuals in the economy better off while making others worse off. There are many real-world examples of such policies, some of which you will be asked to analyze in end-of-chapter exercises. Within the chapter itself, I will simply focus on providing a framework within which you can conduct policy analysis on your own.

Before proceeding to these, however, I want to first revisit our picture of a competitive market equilibrium to illustrate how the benefits of market interactions are distributed by the market process between producers and consumers (or workers and employers). To keep the analysis as simple as possible, we will in this chapter focus on the special case where individual tastes are quasilinear in the good on which we are focusing. This will permit us for purposes of illustration to abstract away from the difference between marginal willingness to pay curves and demand curves and from general equilibrium considerations, and simply measure consumer and worker surpluses on output demand and labor supply curves. In the next chapter, we will then return to more general cases where we will have to be more careful as we measure consumer (and worker) surpluses.

18A.1 Elasticities and the Division of Surplus

Markets do more than just allocate scarce goods and services. They also, without anyone controlling the process so long as all economic agents are "small," determine how large a benefit from interacting in markets accrues to different economic agents.

Consider, for instance, the market demand and supply picture in Graph 18.1a which we developed in Chapter 15. Here we have the equilibrium price p^* emerging from the intersection of a demand and supply curve, and because we are assuming that tastes are quasilinear in the good x, we can interpret the demand curve as an aggregate marginal willingness to pay curve. The shaded areas representing consumer and producer surplus then represent the aggregate size of consumer and producer surplus that emerges in this market. Put differently, these areas represent how much of a benefit from the market interactions accrues to consumers and producers, or how total surplus in the market is divided among producers and consumers. Within each of these areas, there are of course some consumers and some producers who benefit relatively more; in particular, those consumers who value the good highly and those producers who can produce the good at very low cost.

Graph 18.1: Different Distributions of Consumer and Producer Surplus in a Market

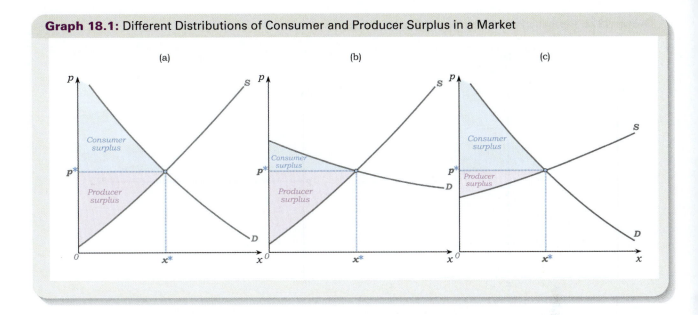

Panel (a) of Graph 18.1 illustrates a case where it appears that the overall social benefits created in this market are divided pretty evenly between consumers and producers. But that's just because of the particular way we have drawn these curves. Panels (b) and (c) illustrate how it is equally plausible that benefits are distributed very differently when demand and supply curves have different shapes. In panel (b), most of the benefits accrue to producers because the demand (and marginal willingness to pay) curve is relatively shallow, while in panel (c) the opposite is true because the demand curve is steep relative to the supply curve.

Knowing what you do from previous chapters, how would the social benefits from market interactions be distributed between producers and consumers in a long-run competitive equilibrium in which all producers face the same costs?

Exercise 18A.1

At first glance, it would appear from Graph 18.1 that the relative division of society's surplus between consumers and producers depends on the relative slopes of demand and supply curves. This is correct, but economists have developed a somewhat better way of talking about this by using a concept known as "price elasticity."

The problem with focusing solely on slopes of such curves is that slopes depend on the units we use to measure quantities on the horizontal and vertical axes. Do we measure prices, for instance, in dollars or cents, in French francs or the British pound? If the x good represents beer, do we measure it in cans or in liters or in six-packs? As we change these units, we change the slopes without changing the fundamental underlying economic content of the curves. *Elasticities* get around this by converting changes in behavior from absolute changes to percentage changes.

18A.1.1 The Price Elasticity of Linear Demand
Economists use the term "elasticity" to mean "responsiveness." My Econ 1 instructor would illustrate this quite graphically in his lecture by bringing into the lecture a pair of old and new underwear, with the old underwear having lost its "elasticity" and the new underwear being quite elastic. While the old underwear was no longer responsive to changes in waist size, the new underwear was quite responsive (or elastic). In economics, elasticity refers to responsiveness in behavior to changes in price

Graph 18.2: Perfectly Price Inelastic and Elastic Demand

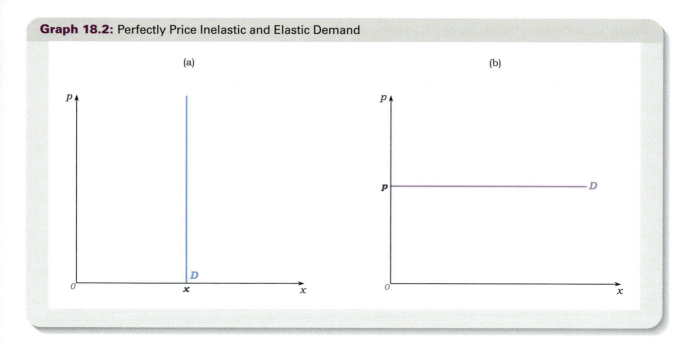

(or some other economic variable) just as elasticity in my Econ 1 instructor's example refers to the responsiveness of waistbands to changes in stretch tensions.

Consider first some very extreme linear demand curves in Graph 18.2. In panel (a), it does not matter what happens to the price of good x; the consumer will always buy exactly the same quantity. This is of course not an economic relationship that can persist for all levels of prices because it would imply that even as price goes to infinity the consumer would continue to purchase the same quantity of the good. Scarcity implies that eventually this demand curve must have a negative slope. But over the range of prices we have graphed, this consumer is extremely *unresponsive* to price changes, or we will say that the consumer's price elasticity of demand is zero and demand is *perfectly price inelastic*. In panel (b), on the other hand, even a miniscule increase in price from p will cause the consumer to no longer consume any of good x. Again, it can't be that this perfectly horizontal relationship between price and quantity persists forever because that would imply that the consumer is willing to buy an infinite amount of x at price p. Eventually, the demand curve must again have a negative slope. But over the range of quantity graphed in panel (b), this consumer is extremely responsive to increases in price. We will say that the consumer's price elasticity is minus infinity or his or her demand is *perfectly price elastic*.[2]

Exercise 18A.2

True or False: If an individual consumer's demand curve is perfectly inelastic, the good is border-line between regular inferior and Giffen.

Real demand curves are of course not this extreme, and the concept of price elasticity becomes a little more subtle along less extreme demand curves. Consider, for instance, the particular linear demand curve in Graph 18.3. With the units we are using in the graph, this demand

---

[2]When I teach the concept of price elasticity to my young children, I tell them a little trick to remember these extreme examples: You can remember that the demand curve in panel (a) is perfectly *I*nelastic by noticing that it represents the letter *I*, while you can remember that the demand curve in panel (b) is perfectly *E*lastic by noticing that it can be turned into a capital *E* by simply adding a horizontal line at the top of the graph.

Graph 18.3: Price Elasticity along a Linear Demand Curve

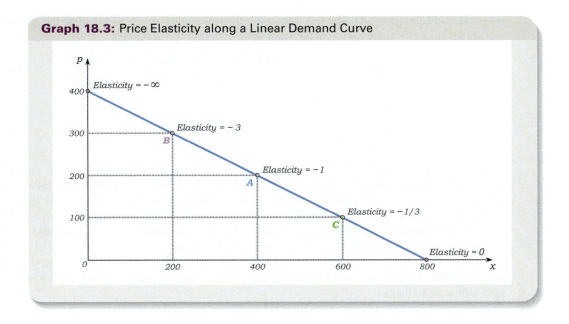

curve has a slope of $-1/2$ everywhere, indicating that whenever price goes up by \$1, the quantity demanded falls by 2. But now suppose we asked: With a 1% change in price, how responsive is demand to a change in price?

Suppose first that price is currently \$200, which implies consumption of 400 units (at point A in the graph). A 1% increase in price is equivalent to a \$2 increase to \$202, which would imply that the quantity demanded falls by 4 to 396. That is a 1% drop in quantity (from the original 400). Thus, when the price starts at 200, a 1% change in the price leads to a 1% change in the quantity demanded. If we had instead started at a price of \$300 (point B), a 1% increase in the price would be equal to a \$3 increase, which would lead to a drop in the quantity demanded from 200 to 194, or a 3% drop. Had we started at a price of \$100, on the other hand, a 1% increase in price would be equivalent to a \$1 increase leading to a drop in the quantity demanded from 600 to 598, or only 1/3% drop in quantity.

The *price elasticity of demand is defined as the percentage change in quantity resulting from a 1% change in price*. Thus, based on what we just calculated, the price elasticity of demand for the demand curve in Graph 18.3 is -1 at point A, -3 at point B, and $-1/3$ at point C. While the absolute response to a \$1 price change is the same at all of these points, in each case leading to a 2 unit drop in quantity, the *percentage change* in the quantity demanded differs depending on where along the demand curve we are measuring it. Because we are measuring price elasticity in percentage changes, it is immune to any change in the units we use to measure either quantity or price.

The price in Graph 18.3 is measured in dollars. What would the demand curve look like if instead we measured price in terms of pennies? Can you recalculate price elasticity at 200, 400, and 600 units of output and demonstrate that you get the same answers we just derived?

**Exercise
18A.3**

More generally, you can calculate approximate price elasticities for particular portions of demand curves whenever you are given at least two points on the demand curve. Suppose, for instance, that you did not know the full demand curve in Graph 18.3 but only knew that consumers demand 600 units of x when price is \$100 (point C) and that they demand 200 units of x

when price is $300 (point *B*). You can then apply the following formula to calculate the approximate price elasticity at the midpoint between the two points you are given:

$$\text{Price elasticity at Midpoint} = \frac{\text{(Change in } x)/\text{(Average } x)}{\text{(Change in } p)/\text{(Average } p)} = \frac{\Delta x/x_{avg}}{\Delta p/p_{avg}}. \qquad (18.1)$$

In our example, this translates to

$$\text{Price elasticity at \$200} = \frac{(600 - 200)/(400)}{(100 - 300)/(200)} = -1. \qquad (18.2)$$

The negative sign on the elasticity measure indicates that quantity and price move in opposite directions (as they do whenever demand curves slope down). Knowing that the price elasticity of demand is equal to -1 at a price of $200 means that, when price is equal to $200, a 1% increase in price leads to a 1% decline in quantity, or alternatively, a 1% decline in price leads to a 1% increase in quantity. Notice that this is exactly what we calculated when we knew the whole demand curve and calculated the elasticity of demand at point *A* at the price $200. (The reason that the answer is *exactly* the same for our approximation formula is that the underlying demand curve is linear. The formula would give only an approximate answer whenever demand curves have curvature to them.)

Exercise 18A.4 *True or False*: Unless a good is a Giffen good, price elasticity of demand is negative.

You can then convince yourself that, *for any linear demand curve, the price elasticity of demand is −1 at the midpoint of the demand curve, less than −1 above the midpoint, and greater than −1 below the midpoint.* In fact, as we will try to clarify more in end-of-chapter exercise 18.1, the price elasticity of demand approaches zero as we approach the horizontal axis and minus infinity as we approach the vertical axis.

18A.1.2 Price Elasticity and Consumer Spending Whether a consumer *spends* more or less on her consumption of a particular good when price increases then depends on how responsive she is to changes in price. If she is relatively unresponsive, she may end up buying less of the good but still *spend more* than before because she pays a higher price for those units of the good she continues to buy. If, on the other hand, she is very responsive to the price change, she will end up buying sufficiently less so as to make her overall spending on the good decline despite the fact that each unit of the good costs her more.

Put differently, the impact of price changes on consumer spending depends on the price elasticity of demand. Consider, for instance, the three panels of Graph 18.4 that each replicate the linear demand curve we first graphed in Graph 18.3. In each panel, we consider an increase in the price of good *x* by $50, but in panel (a) the consumer finds herself on the portion of her demand curve that has price elasticity between −1 and 0, in panel (b) she finds herself on the portion that has price elasticity of approximately −1, and in panel (c) she finds herself on the portion that has price elasticity of less than −1. Her total spending at any given price is simply the price times the quantity she consumes, or the rectangle formed by the vertical distance of the price and the horizontal distance of her quantity. The shaded blue area represents the decrease in her spending that results from her purchasing less of *x* as price increases, while the shaded magenta area represents the increase in her spending on those units of *x* that she continues to buy. Thus, the difference between the magenta and blue areas is the increase in her overall spending.

Now notice that the two shaded areas are of equal size in panel (b) (indicating no net change in her spending), but the magenta area is bigger than the blue area in panel (a) (indicating a net

Graph 18.4: Price Elasticity and Changes in Consumer Spending

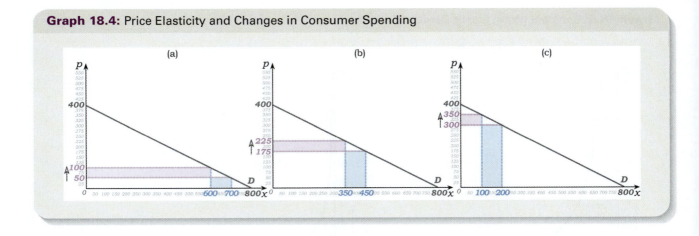

increase in spending) while the reverse is true in panel (c) (indicating a net decrease in spending). Given the numbers in the graph, you can even calculate these areas and make sure that your eyes are not deceiving you.

Calculate the total spending this consumer undertakes at each of the two prices in panels (a) through (c) of Graph 18.4 and identify the magnitude and direction of the change in overall spending on good *x*.

Exercise 18A.5

Thus, we are finding that *consumer spending on a good increases with an increase in price when the price elasticity is between −1 and 0, stays the same when the price elasticity is −1, and decreases when the price elasticity is less than −1.* This should make intuitive sense: If quantity drops by 1% whenever price increases by 1%, the consumer buys 1% fewer goods but pays 1% more on those she buys, leaving her overall spending constant. It then follows that a larger drop in her quantity demanded will cause her spending to decline and a smaller drop will cause her spending to increase. It is for this reason that we will say that *demand is relatively inelastic* or relatively unresponsive to price changes *when the price elasticity lies between −1 and 0,* and *demand is relatively elastic* or relatively responsive to price changes *when the price elasticity of demand is below −1.*

Suppose I notice that when long-distance telephone rates came down, our monthly long-distance phone bill went up. What can you conclude about our price elasticity of demand for long-distance telephone calls?

Exercise 18A.6

18A.1.3 Price Elasticities for Non-linear Demand Curves

Since price elasticity varies between 0 and negative infinity along linear demand curves that have the same (negative) slope everywhere, it is not surprising that price elasticity in general will be quite different at different points on demand curves more generally. We already illustrated two exceptions to this in Graph 18.2 where we illustrated demand curves that have price elasticity of 0 and minus infinity everywhere. A third example of a demand curve that has the same price elasticity everywhere is the demand curve depicted in panel (a) of Graph 18.5, which has price elasticity of −1 everywhere. The easiest way to convince yourself of this is to see whether it is true that an increase in price will cause no change in consumer spending regardless of where on the demand curve we start. For

Graph 18.5: Constant (Price) Elastic Demand Curves

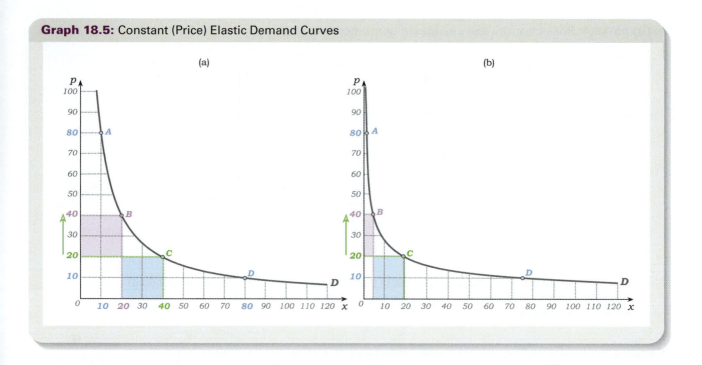

instance, at all the four points A, B, C, and D, total consumer spending is $800. Such a demand curve is sometimes referred to as having the property of *unitary price elasticity*.

Of course the set of constant elasticity demand curves is not limited to demand curves that have 0, minus infinity, or -1 as the constant elasticity. The constant elasticity could be any negative number. For instance, panel (b) of the graph illustrates a demand curve with constant price elasticity of -2.

Exercise 18A.7 The diamond industry's marketing efforts have convinced many of the convention that an engagement ring should always cost the lucky groom exactly 3 months' salary. What does this imply about the price elasticity of demand for diamond size that the diamond industry is attempting to persuade us we should have?

18A.1.4 Other Elasticities Elasticities are measures of responsiveness to changes in economic variables. So far, we have looked at one particular type of responsiveness: the change in a consumer's demand for a good when that good's price changes. We can similarly define the responsiveness of a consumer's demand with respect to changes in other prices, and we refer to such measures as "cross-price elasticities." Similarly, we can define "income elasticities of demand," or how much the quantity demanded changes as income changes by 1%. You can practice with some of these concepts in end-of-chapter exercises 18.2 and 18.3.

Exercise 18A.8 Is the income elasticity of demand positive or negative? (*Hint*: Does your answer depend on whether the good is inferior or normal?)

Exercise 18A.9 What kind of good does x have to be in order for the demand for x to be perfectly income inelastic?

In a two-good model, is the cross-price elasticity of demand for good x_1 positive or negative if x_1 is a regular inferior good? (*Hint*: Is the cross-price demand curve for good x_1 upward or downward sloping?)

Exercise
18A.10

Of course, consumers are not the only economic agents in an economy that respond to changes in economic variables. The responsiveness of *producers* to changes in prices can similarly be illustrated using the concept of price elasticity in exactly the same way using exactly the same formula. We could again begin by illustrating perfectly elastic and perfectly inelastic supply curves that would look exactly the same way as the perfectly elastic and inelastic demand curves in Graph 18.2. We could then proceed to analyzing the price elasticity of supply along a linear, upward-sloping supply curve, and we would once again find that the price elasticity (in general) will vary along such a curve. Unlike price elasticities of demand (when the underlying good is not a Giffen good), however, price elasticities of supply are positive numbers because an increase in price causes producers to produce *more* (whereas it causes consumers to typically consume *less*).

Given what you learned in Chapter 13, is the price elasticity of supply for a competitive firm larger or smaller in the long run (than in the short run).

Exercise
18A.11

Given what you learned in Chapter 14, what is the price elasticity of industry supply in the long run when all firms have identical costs?

Exercise
18A.12

Suppose a supply curve is linear and starts at the origin. What is its price elasticity of supply?

Exercise
18A.13*

Finally, we could of course also consider the responsiveness of workers to changes in wages, or the responsiveness of savers to changes in interest rates. This gives us the concepts of "wage elasticity of labor supply" and "interest rate elasticity of capital supply," concepts that are further explored in end-of-chapter exercises 18.3 and 18.4. And we could similarly talk of concepts like "wage elasticity of labor demand" and "rental rate elasticity of capital demand" on the producer side.

If labor supply curves are "backward bending" (in the sense that they are upward sloping for low wages and downward sloping for high wages), how does the wage elasticity of labor supply change as wage increases?

Exercise
18A.14

True or False: The wage elasticity of labor demand is always negative.

Exercise
18A.15

18A.2 Price Floors

We can now begin to investigate some common government policies that are aimed directly at altering the price used for trading between buyers and sellers in the market. One such policy involves the setting of a price floor. *A price floor is a minimum legal price the government mandates in a particular market, making all trades at prices below this price floor illegal.* Such a price floor will have no impact at all on the market if it is set below the equilibrium price because the market would automatically set a price above the floor with trading between buyers and sellers occurring at that market price. For instance, if the market price for "hero cards" is $10 per pack and the government sets a price floor of $5, the policy has no impact since the market "wants to" trade above $5 anyhow. It will, however, have an impact if the price floor is set *above* the equilibrium price because then the market price becomes illegal, with buyers and sellers forced to trade at a price above the price that would otherwise have arisen in the market.

As a result of the imposition of a price floor above the equilibrium price, a *surplus* of goods will emerge until some *non-price rationing* mechanism allocates the quantity of the good that is produced among the consumers who demand *less than* that quantity at the price floor. This is depicted in Graph 18.6 where the (green) price floor p^f is set above the intersection of the (blue) market demand and (magenta) market supply curve. Reading the quantity demanded x_d off the demand curve and the quantity supplied x_s off the supply curve, we see that $x_s > x_d$ at p^f. Put differently, because the government has interfered with the price mechanism that ensures $x_d = x_s$ at the equilibrium price p^*, producers are willing to supply more of the good at the higher price p^f than consumers are willing to buy at that price. The price floor has thus caused the market to enter a state of *disequilibrium*.

It cannot, however, be the case that suppliers will perpetually produce more than they can sell simply because the government has set a price above the equilibrium price. After all, this would mean that producers are perpetually producing goods they cannot sell, which is inconsistent with the requirement that economic agents will do the best they can given their circumstances. Thus, *an equilibrium is not reached until some non-price mechanism emerges that ensures that the quantity demanded is equal to the quantity supplied once again.* Such a mechanism could be constructed on purpose by a government that recognizes the disequilibrium caused by the imposition of the price floor, or, in the absence of government action, it will arise independently through some other form of non-price rationing that restores the market to a new equilibrium.

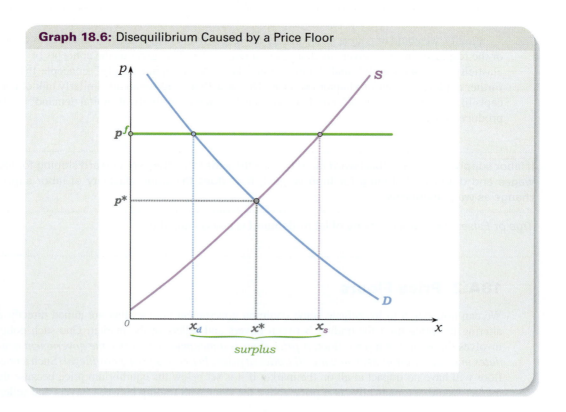

Graph 18.6: Disequilibrium Caused by a Price Floor

How does the size of the disequilibrium surplus change with the price elasticity of supply and demand?

Exercise
18A.16

18A.2.1 Non-Price Rationing in the Market under Price Floors

Consider first the case where the government does not explicitly attempt to solve the disequilibrium created by the price floor. Given that producers now know that all producers together will attempt to sell more goods at the price floor than consumers demand, each individual producer then has an incentive to expend additional effort attempting to convince consumers to buy from him. This additional effort represents an additional cost to producers, whether it takes the form of aggressive advertising or lobbying the government for special advantages that will cause consumers to purchase from one producer rather than from another. Thus, whatever form the additional effort takes, the MC and AC curves for producers will shift up, which in turn causes the market supply curve to shift up until it intersects market demand at the quantity x_d. If producers in the market initially face different cost curves, we would then expect those producers who face lower costs to be the ones who can most easily absorb the additional cost of expending effort to attract consumers, with other producers exiting the market.

Using the combination of industry and firm curves we employed in Chapter 14, illustrate what happens to each firm's cost curves as a result of the imposition of a price floor.

Exercise
18A.17

Panel (a) of Graph 18.7 then depicts a shift in market supply resulting from the shifts in individual cost curves, with the blue supply curve representing the pre-price floor supply and the magenta supply curve representing the post-price floor market supply. Any less of a shift in the supply curve will still result in more being supplied than is demanded at the price floor, implying the market continues to be in disequilibrium with producers producing goods that they cannot sell. In the new equilibrium, it therefore has to be the case that costs shift up by the distance of the green arrow in Graph 18.7a, a distance equal to $(p^f - p')$. This is a new equilibrium because

Graph 18.7: Restoring Equilibrium through Increased Costs for Producers

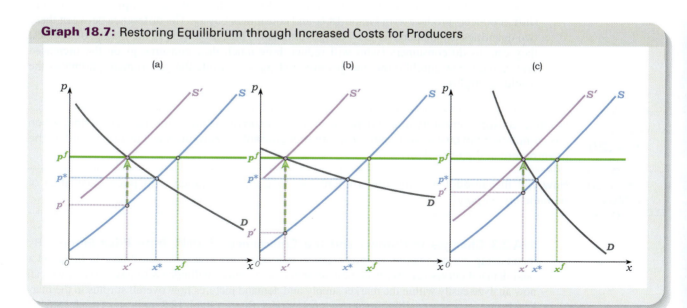

demand is once again equal to supply, with both producers and consumers once again doing the best they can given their changed circumstances. Put differently, consumers are buying bundles on their new budget constraints (that incorporate the increase in price) where their marginal willingness to pay (i.e., their MRS) is equal to the new price (or where they are at a corner solution at which they no longer purchase x), while producers produce where the new price intersects with their new MC (or they exit the market altogether).

The reduction in market output then depends not only on how high the government sets the price floor but also on the price elasticity of demand. In panel (b), for instance, the price floor is set exactly the same as in panel (a) but demand is depicted as more responsive to price—more price elastic—than in panel (a). As a result, x_d falls significantly more, causing more firms to exit the market as a substantially larger shift in supply is required to bring the market back to an equilibrium where producers do not produce a surplus quantity. In panel (c), on the other hand, demand is depicted as more price inelastic, resulting in a significantly smaller decrease in output in the market as producers do not have to expend as much effort to attract the remaining consumers.

Exercise 18A.18 Depict the impact of a price floor on the quantity produced by the market when demand is perfectly price elastic. Repeat for the case when demand is perfectly price inelastic.

Exercise 18A.19 What is p' in long-run equilibrium when all firms face the same costs?

18A.2.2 Non-Price Rationing by Government under Price Floors

Alternatively, the government is often quite aware of the fact that setting price floors will result in reductions in market output and therefore accompanies price floor policies with additional government programs to counteract the market's response. This has, for instance, been common in government programs known as "farm price supports," programs under which the government not only sets a price floor for certain farm products but then also guarantees that it will purchase any surplus that producers cannot sell at the price floor.

When such a program is implemented, producers no longer have an incentive to expend additional effort to attract consumers because they know they can always sell whatever remains on the shelves to the government at the price p^f. As a result, the market supply curve does not shift, producers produce x_s in Graph 18.6, and consumers buy x_d. The difference between these two quantities is then purchased by the government. Thus, producers in the market do the best they can, as do consumers (who will reduce how much they consume given the increased price), and a new equilibrium emerges in which $x_d < x_s$ while the government purchases the resulting surplus.

Exercise 18A.20 Would you expect any entry or exit of producers as a result of the imposition of a price floor when it is complemented by a government program that guarantees surpluses will be purchased by the government at the price floor?

Exercise 18A.21 How will the amount that the government has to purchase change with price elasticities of demand and supply?

18A.2.3 Changes in Surplus and the Emergence of *DWL* from Price Floors

By maintaining our assumption (in this chapter) that consumer tastes are quasilinear in the good x (and demand curves can therefore be interpreted as marginal willingness to pay curves), we can now analyze easily within the market supply and demand pictures how overall surplus in the market changes as a new equilibrium emerges under price floors. Graph 18.8 replicates Graph 18.6 but

Graph 18.8: Changes in Costs and Surplus when Price Floors Are Imposed

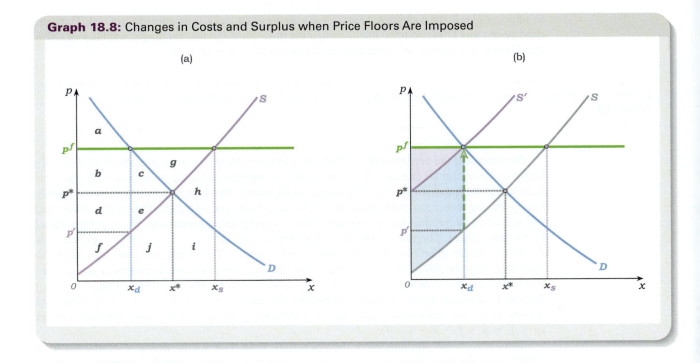

then labels different areas within the graph in order to help us identify the various surpluses that emerge under the two types of equilibria that may emerge under price floors. For instance, we can begin by identifying the surpluses that exist in the absence of a price floor when x^* is produced in the market and sold at p^*. Consumer surplus is then given by the area $(a + b + c)$ and producer surplus by the area $(d + e + f)$.

Now consider the new equilibrium under the price floor when the government does not supplement the imposition of a price floor with any additional programs and the supply curve therefore shifts as producers face higher costs when expending effort to attract the smaller number of consumers. Consumers will then purchase only x_d, leaving them with a surplus of area (a). Without explicitly drawing in the shifted supply curve, it is a little trickier to see what happens to producer surplus, but once you see it, the picture is a lot more manageable without explicitly shifting the supply curve.

As we illustrated in panel (a) of Graph 18.7 and again in panel (b) of Graph 18.8, the shift in supply is caused by an increase of $(p^f - p')$ (i.e., the length of the green arrow) in marginal costs. In panel (b) of Graph 18.8, the shaded magenta area then represents the new producer surplus while the shaded blue area represents the additional costs that producers incur. But we can find these same quantities in panel (a) without drawing in the new supply curve by simply recognizing that, once we subtract the additional costs producers incur, they really receive a price p' for each of the goods they produce. By netting out the additional cost this way, we can then measure the remaining marginal costs (that have not changed due to the imposition of the price floor) along the original supply curve. Area (f) is therefore exactly identical to the shaded magenta area in panel (b), and area $(b + d)$ is equivalent to the shaded blue area in panel (b).

We have then concluded that the sum of consumer and producer surplus shrinks from the initial $(a + b + c + d + e + f)$ to $(a + f)$. What happens to $(b + d)$, the increased costs faced by producers, depends on what exact form these costs take. For instance, it could be spent on advertising that provides little information to consumers and is thus socially wasteful, or it could represent transfers to individuals in the economy who benefit from receiving payment. It is therefore likely that some of $(b + d)$ is socially wasteful but some represents a transfer from producers to someone else in the economy. Area $(c + e)$, on the other hand, is unambiguously lost. Thus, the deadweight loss DWL from the imposition of the price floor and the resulting emergence of a new equilibrium is at least $(c + e)$ but may be as large as $(b + c + d + e)$.

Exercise 18A.22
How does the deadweight loss change as the price elasticity of demand changes?

Now consider the new equilibrium that emerges when the government attempts to deal directly with the disequilibrium that the price floor creates by supplementing the price floor with a government purchasing program that buys any surplus in the market. Consumers in the market will still only buy x_d, leaving them again with consumer surplus (a). Producers, on the other hand, now produce x_s and sell all of the product that is produced, with x_d going to consumers and $(x_s - x_d)$ purchased by the government. The new producer surplus then rises to $(b + c + d + e + f + g)$, which is the area under the price floor and above the supply curve S. This is not, however, the end of the story since now the government also incurs costs that are costs to society. In particular, the government purchases the quantity $(x_s - x_d)$ at the price p^f, which results in a total cost of $p^f(x_s - x_d)$ that can be depicted as the rectangle formed by the areas $(c + e + g + h + i + j)$. Summing the new consumer and producer surpluses and subtracting the government costs we therefore get $(a + b + d + f - h - i - j)$.

Thus, the overall surplus before the price floor is $(a + b + c + d + e + f)$ and the total surplus after the price floor is $(a + b + d + f - h - i - j)$ assuming the government simply throws away the goods it purchased. In that case, a deadweight loss of $(c + e + h + i + j)$ emerges from the price floor. Instead of throwing the goods it purchases into the ocean, however, it might be that the government finds a way to get the goods it has purchased to those consumers that place the highest value on those goods. Since those who value x more than the price floor p^f have already purchased x_d in the market, the set of consumers who value the next $(x_s - x_d)$ goods the most are those that compose the portion of the market demand curve that lies between x_d and x_s, and, since in our example we can interpret the demand curve as the marginal willingness to pay curve, the value these consumers place on the quantity of x the government has purchased can be read off the graph as the area below the demand curve between the quantities x_d and x_s. This area is given by $(c + e + i + j)$. So, if the government finds a way to get the goods it purchased to those who value them most rather than throw those goods into the ocean, the government can recover $(c + e + i + j)$ in surplus. Subtracting this from the deadweight loss we calculated when the government throws away the goods it purchased, we would then be left with a deadweight loss of area (h). Depending on how good the government is at getting the surplus it purchases to consumers who value x, the deadweight loss may therefore be as little as (h) or as high as $(c + e + h + i + j)$.

Exercise 18A.23
How does the deadweight loss change in size as the price elasticity of demand and supply changes?

The most common example of a price floor that is often discussed in beginning economics classes is the minimum wage. The *minimum wage* is a price floor that has an impact on labor markets where the equilibrium wage falls below the minimum wage the government requires employers to pay to employees. Such labor markets are typically those involving relatively low skilled labor. Using the tools developed in this section, you can now analyze the impact of minimum wage laws on workers and producers in such labor markets, an exercise we leave for end-of-chapter exercise 18.7.

18A.3 Price Ceilings

While price floors represent attempts by the government to impose prices above the equilibrium price, *price ceilings* are intended to place a cap on prices below the equilibrium price. More specifically, *price ceilings are legally mandated maximum prices*, with any trades made at prices above the price ceiling illegal. If the price ceiling is set above the equilibrium price, it will have no effect since the market would simply set the normal equilibrium price below the price ceiling. As a result, the price ceiling only has an effect on the equilibrium if it is set *below* the market equilibrium price.

Consider, for instance, the case of a (green) price ceiling set at p^c below the market equilibrium p^* in Graph 18.9. This price ceiling makes the initial equilibrium price p^* illegal and forces producers to exchange goods with consumers at the legal maximum price p^c. But of course at that price, producers in the market are only willing to produce x_s, a quantity below x_d that consumers would like to purchase. As a result, a *shortage* emerges in the market, with $(x_d - x_s)$ more demanded than supplied. Put differently, the market is in disequilibrium with less produced than is demanded.

How does the shortage that emerges in disequilibrium change as price elasticities of demand and supply change?

**Exercise
18A.24**

However, whenever a shortage of goods emerges in disequilibrium, some form of non-price rationing must take the place of market price rationing to allocate the existing goods among consumers who want them. Non-price rationing can then again be the result of some deliberate mechanism designed by the government, or it can emerge without central direction. In either case, something or someone has to decide who gets the limited quantity of goods that is produced under the price ceiling, and a new equilibrium in which the quantity demanded is equal to the quantity supplied must emerge.

Graph 18.9: Disequilibrium when Price Ceilings Are Imposed

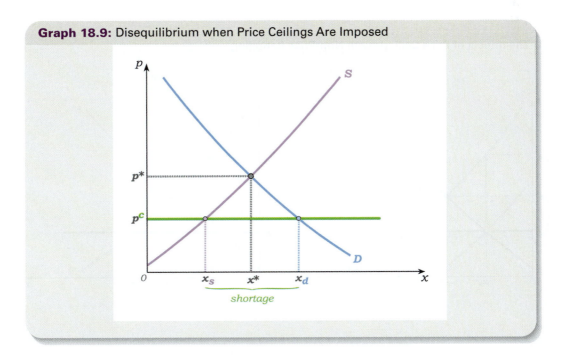

18A.3.1 Non-Price Rationing under Price Ceilings

In the case of surpluses generated by price floors, we said that producers will need to expend some additional effort to convince consumers to buy from them rather than from someone else. This caused the marginal costs of producers to increase, thus shifting the market supply curve until the new equilibrium was reached. In the case of shortages generated by price ceilings, on the other hand, consumers are the ones who will have to expend some additional effort since there are too few goods produced to meet demand. This additional effort will therefore impose costs on consumers who, as a result, will have a lower marginal willingness to pay for each of the goods produced. This means that the demand curve will shift down as consumers take into account the additional cost of effort expended to get the limited quantity of goods produced. This effort may take a variety of forms, including standing in line, getting on waiting lists, or even bribing producers or government officials to ensure that you are high enough on the waiting list to get the goods you would like.

Consider, for instance, Graph 18.10a. In order for the market to reach a new equilibrium in which all economic agents do the best they can given their economic circumstances, the initial demand curve D must shift down (as consumers expend effort) to the new demand curve D' where the quantity demanded is once again exactly equal to the quantity supplied. The per-unit cost of the effort that is expended in the new equilibrium is then equal to the vertical distance of the green arrow.

We can once again determine how surplus in this market changes from the initial equilibrium formed by the intersection of S and D and the new equilibrium that emerges under the price ceiling. Rather than shifting the demand curve as we do in panel (a), we could instead analyze this in a less cluttered graph such as the one depicted in panel (b). Here, we simply recognize that an underlying shift in demand causes consumers to have to expend effort that costs $(p' - p^c)$, the length of the green arrow in panel (a). Saying that consumers will end up paying the price p^c along the new demand curve D' in panel (a) plus the cost of effort indicated by the green arrow is the same as saying that consumers will end up paying the higher price p' along their original

Graph 18.10: The Impact of Price Ceilings with Non-Price Rationing

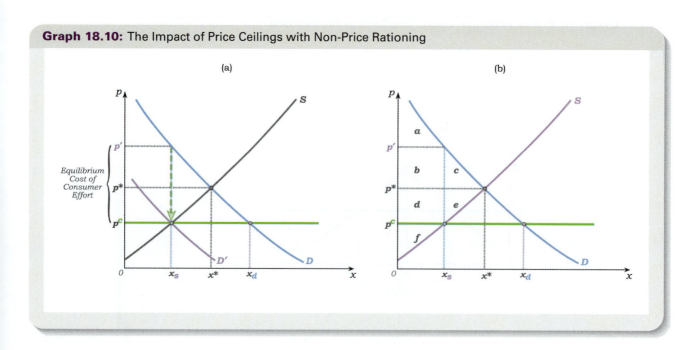

demand curve. Put differently, the real price that consumers will end up paying when the new equilibrium emerges is p'.

Consumer surplus then shrinks from the initial $(a + b + c)$ to just (a), and producer surplus shrinks from the initial $(d + e + f)$ to just (f). Whether someone in the economy gets the area $(b + d)$ now depends on the exact nature of the non-price rationing that results in the new equilibrium. For instance, suppose that goods are allocated by individuals spending time standing in line. Then the cost of standing in line is of no benefit to anyone else in the economy and $(b + d)$ becomes a deadweight loss. If, on the other hand, side payments (or bribes) are permitted to ensure someone who really wants the goods gets them, the per unit cost of the green arrow is a cost to the consumer but a benefit for whoever gets the bribe. In that case, the additional cost to the consumer is a benefit to someone else in the economy and thus not a deadweight loss. The area $(c + e)$, however, cannot be recovered by anyone in the economy because the goods that created this surplus are no longer produced. Thus, the overall deadweight loss from the price ceiling will lie between $(c + e)$ and $(b + c + d + e)$ depending on the precise form of non-price rationing that supports the new equilibrium.[3]

How does the size of deadweight losses from price ceilings vary with the price elasticities of demand and supply?

Exercise 18A.25

18A.3.2 Government Programs to Address Shortages under Price Ceilings   It is, of course, also possible that the government introduces some program designed explicitly to address the disequilibrium shortage that results from the imposition of a price ceiling. In end-of-chapter exercise 18.5, for instance, we explore the impact of a government program in which the government purchases goods that are traded at price ceilings on the world market (where there is no price ceiling), then sells them at the price ceiling to domestic consumers. You will see in that exercise that such a program introduces yet additional deadweight losses.

In the case of price ceilings, however, it is more likely that the government designs some more explicit rationing mechanism that determines who gets the limited quantity of the goods that are produced. For instance, some city governments have "rent control" programs that set a price ceiling on rents that can be charged in the housing market. Often, the shortages that emerge under such programs are addressed not only by rationing through the use of waiting lists but also through some explicit criteria that those who can get on the waiting lists have to satisfy. No such program can, however, alter the fact that interference with the market price mechanism results in deadweight losses, as you can conclude on your own in end-of-chapter exercise 18.11. (We will also see in end-of-chapter exercise 18.6 that price ceilings are sometimes imposed by institutions other than governments.)

18A.3.3 Ethical Considerations in Some "Markets" with Price Ceilings of Zero
There are also some very interesting examples of price ceilings in markets that most noneconomists don't think of as markets at all, examples where the government sets a price ceiling of zero. Consider, for instance, the "market for kidneys." As you probably know, there are large numbers of individuals who are currently waiting for a donated kidney to replace their own kidneys that

---

[3]It is actually possible that the deadweight loss gets even larger than that if the non-price rationing mechanism is, for instance, waiting in line and it is not permitted that people can pay for someone else to wait in line for them. This can occur if those who have the highest marginal willingness to pay for good x also have a high opportunity cost of time and therefore are not willing to spend the time waiting in line, thus causing individuals whose marginal willingness to pay is lower to be the ones standing in line.

are failing as a result of some kidney disease. Some have advocated that the government should permit healthy individuals to sell one of their kidneys (since it is in most cases quite possible for someone to function with only a single kidney). Others have advocated a system in which healthy individuals could sell the "right to their kidneys" to organizations who could then channel those kidneys to those in need in the event that the healthy individual dies unexpectedly. Instead, the government has placed a price ceiling of zero in the kidney market, allowing individuals to donate a kidney but not to sell one. Since such a price ceiling leads to a shortage of kidneys, a complex, dynamically adjusting wait list system has been developed, with those in need of a kidney moving up on the list as their own kidneys functions less and less well.

We will explore the case of kidney "markets" further in end-of-chapter exercise 18.13 but raise it here merely to point out something that may already have occurred to many of you: While price ceilings inevitably create often significant deadweight losses, they are sometimes motivated by ethical considerations that lie well outside the sphere of competence of an economist. In the kidney market, for instance, huge deadweight losses result from the zero price ceiling imposed by the government. In this case, those deadweight losses literally involve the unnecessary death of many who spend years on waiting lists but never get the kidney they need. Yet, even knowing that this is the case, ethical considerations may cause many of you to favor the current system (or some variant of it) over the creation of a kidney market in which kidneys are either explicitly sold or the "right to kidneys" is sold.

Should individuals be permitted to sell their own organs? I really don't know and leave it to others to think about such deep philosophical issues. I do know as an economist that, if a market price would emerge for kidneys, those who would sell their kidneys would disproportionately come from poor backgrounds where an additional $50,000 or even $10,000 that healthy kidneys might fetch in the market could be quite tempting. Is that bad given that real lives will be saved in the process? Again, all the economist can do is say how behavior will change as institutions change, but it is left to us in our role as noneconomists to make some of the deeper ethical judgments. Similar issues emerge in other areas, such as the sale of human eggs and sperm for reproductive purposes; the sale of frozen human embryos created in fertility clinics but no longer desired by the couples from whom they derived; the sale of embryos for research; or explicit pricing in "adoption markets" for children.

18A.4 The Politics of "Concentrated Benefits and Diffuse Costs"

While sometimes there are clear ethical considerations that motivate the imposition of price ceilings (such as in the case of kidney markets that we just discussed), in many cases such ethical considerations do not appear to be the main motivators of price floors and price ceilings in the real world, especially if the full impact of such policies is analyzed. Rather, there may be cases where such policies emerge as different interest groups capture a part of the political process and thereby gain surplus they otherwise would not gain in the market. We will treat this more explicitly in Chapter 28, but for now I want to introduce a way that some economists and political scientist have developed for thinking about why certain policies that create clear deadweight losses are implemented and others are not. Throughout the remainder of this book, we will see how this basic "model" of political behavior can explain many of the policies we see implemented in the real world.

The basic idea is that, in political processes that can be influenced by interest groups that expend effort to change policy, *it is easier for particular interest groups to be effective when the benefits of the policy are concentrated among a small number of individuals while the costs are diffused over a large number*. Consider, for instance, a farm price support system modeled along the lines of a price floor accompanied by a government purchasing program that buys any surplus that is produced at the price floor. Who benefits from such a program, and who pays the costs? The beneficiaries are relatively concentrated: farmers who will be able to sell more goods at higher prices (whether to consumers or the government) and perhaps some who will end up getting the products purchased by the government (if the government sells the products at a reduced price to them). Those paying the costs, on the other hand, include essentially everyone: all those who purchase farm products (who now pay higher prices) and all taxpayers who must fund the additional purchases made by the government.

It may appear initially counterintuitive that, when the beneficiaries of a policy include only a few and the "losers" from the policy include many, a democratic process is more likely to implement such a policy. But if the policy-making process is impacted by interest group efforts, and if such efforts require interest groups to organize and lobby, it becomes much easier to organize the few who will benefit a lot from a policy than the many who suffer a little bit. Food prices may be only slightly higher as a result of farm price support policies, causing all of us to pay just a little bit more while often not even being aware of why it is that we are paying more. It will not be easy to organize all of us, but it may be much easier to organize a small number of farmers who benefit a lot if the policy is put in place. The politics of "concentrated benefits and diffuse costs" can therefore explain how policies that benefit a few by a lot but hurt many by a little can be implemented even when the sum total of all the costs is significantly larger than the sum total of all the benefits.

This furthermore points out a major challenge to policy makers: Whenever the sum total of benefits of a program is outweighed by the sum total of the costs, it should in principle be possible to make everyone better off by eliminating the program and compensating the beneficiaries of the program. In other words, *whenever there is a deadweight loss from a policy, it should in principle be possible to eliminate the policy in such a way as to make some people better off without making anyone worse off, or even to do it so that everyone is better off.* Doing so, however, and then keeping the policy from coming back when interest groups organize once again to lobby, is often a difficult political challenge when benefits are concentrated and costs diffuse.[4]

18A.5 A Note on General Equilibrium Considerations

Our analysis of price distortions in this chapter is entirely within a partial equilibrium framework where we are implicitly assuming that the effects of price ceilings and price floors in one market do not "spill over" into other markets. It is worth noting, however, that a fuller analysis of such policies would ask whether such spillovers are likely to happen, and if so, how this would change our analysis of the impact of the policy. A full treatment of this is beyond the scope of this text, but a quick example might clarify how such general equilibrium considerations might be important.

Consider, for instance, the minimum wage, which you are asked to analyze in a partial equilibrium context in end-of-chapter exercise 18.7. In this exercise, you will illustrate the standard prediction—that the minimum wage will lead to a decline in employment in labor markets that are affected by it, a possible increase in surplus for minimum wage workers who remain employed (and a decrease in surplus for those who lose their jobs as a result), and an increase in costs for firms that employ minimum wage workers.[5] Some economists, however, have argued that a full analysis of the effects of minimum wage laws must include a general equilibrium analysis of how the increased costs faced by firms get translated into other price changes in the economy. It is true,

---

[4]In 1996, for instance, a large farm bill passed Congress and was signed by the president. The purpose of the farm bill was to make large payments to farmers now to compensate them for a reduction in farm price supports over the coming years. It was an example of a policy that aimed at eliminating deadweight losses of a policy in such a way as to ensure that those who were benefitting from the policy were not made worse off. Farm interest groups supported the policy change. However, a few years later, farm price supports were reintroduced.
[5]There has been some controversy surrounding this result because of a study in the 1990s that claimed to have found an increase in employment resulting from an increase in the minimum wage. Still, most economists have taken the view that this study is an anomaly, perhaps due to bad measurement on the part of the researchers or perhaps due to some effects that are generally not present when minimum wages are increased.

for instance, that minimum wage workers tend to work in industries whose goods and services are disproportionately consumed by low income households. Since costs increase disproportionately for such firms, prices of their products will tend to increase disproportionately. Some households may therefore benefit in the labor market from increased earnings only to turn around and face higher prices for the goods they purchase. It is obviously quite complex to trace all general equilibrium price effects from an increase in the minimum wage through the economy and then conclude something about who ultimately benefits by how much, but in some cases we will miss important economic effects of price-distorting policies unless we engage in such an analysis.[6]

Exercise 18A.26*

Consider our Robinson Crusoe Economy from Chapter 16 and suppose that the economy is currently in equilibrium with wage w^* and price p^*. Now suppose that a government requires that no wage lower than kw^* (with $k > 1$) be paid in this economy. What will happen in order for this economy to return to equilibrium?

18B The Mathematics of Elasticities and Price Distortions

The mathematics of price elasticities is relatively straightforward and involves a simple conversion of our elasticity formula to calculus notation. Similarly, once we understand the underlying economic forces unleashed by price-distorting policies such as price ceilings and price floors, the mathematical description of these changes follows straightforwardly from the graphs in Section A. For these reasons, this section of the chapter will be somewhat shorter, highlighting the basic techniques and then leaving you to practice with them in end-of-chapter exercises.

18B.1 Elasticities

As we discussed in Section A, elasticities are measures of responsiveness of economic behavior to some economic variable. When we use the term "price elasticity of demand," for instance, we simply mean the responsiveness of demand to changes in price. When we say "income elasticity of demand," we mean the responsiveness of demand to changes in income, and when we say "cross-price elasticity of demand," we mean the responsiveness of demand for one good with respect to changes in the price of another good.

18B.1.1 The Price Elasticity of Demand   In Section A, we gave the noncalculus-based formula for deriving price elasticity of demand (denoted as ε_d here) from two points on the demand curve as

$$\varepsilon_d = \frac{\Delta x/x_{avg}}{\Delta p/p_{avg}} = \frac{\Delta x}{\Delta p}\frac{p_{avg}}{x_{avg}}. \tag{18.3}$$

In the special case of linear demand, this formula gives a precise estimate of the price elasticity, but in cases where demand is not linear, it only gives an approximation. The precise formula for deriving the price elasticity of demand at a given point on the demand curve is then simply

[6]One general equilibrium study on the impact of minimum wages, for instance, suggests that, while 1 in 4 low income workers gains from an increase in the minimum wage, 3 in 4 low income workers lose due to higher prices resulting from the minimum wage (T. MaCurdy, and F. McIntyre, "Winners and Losers of Federal and State Minimum Wages," Public Policy Institute of California, 2001).

calculated for small changes in price and quantity, which in calculus notation means a simple change of the Δ's in equation (18.3) to d's; i.e.,

$$\varepsilon_d = \frac{dx}{dp}\frac{p}{x(p)}, \tag{18.4}$$

where the "average" variables in the approximation formula are replaced by the actual levels of these variables at the point (with price p and quantity $x(p)$) at which we are trying to evaluate the price elasticity.

Consider, for instance, the linear demand curve graphed in Graph 18.3, which is given by the equation $p = 400 - (1/2)x$ or, written in terms of x,

$$x(p) = 800 - 2p. \tag{18.5}$$

Taking the derivative $dx/dp(= -2)$ and plugging it into the formula for price elasticity, we get a general expression for the price elasticity as

$$\varepsilon_d = -2\left(\frac{p}{800 - 2p}\right) = \frac{-p}{400 - p}, \tag{18.6}$$

where we have used the demand function $x = 800 - 2p$ in the denominator. This allows us to express the price elasticity simply as a function of price.

Could you also express the price elasticity as a function of only quantity? (*Hint*: Think of replacing the numerator rather than the denominator.)

**Exercise
18B.1**

When price is 300, this equation then tells us that the price elasticity at $p = 300$ is -3; when price is 200, the equation gives us a price elasticity of -1; and when price is 100, it gives us a price elasticity of $-1/3$. These values are identical to the ones we derived for points B, A, and C in Graph 18.3.

Using the formula for price elasticity you derived in exercise 18B.1, verify that you get the same price elasticity for x equal to 200, 400, and 600 (corresponding to points B, A, and C in Graph 18.3.)

**Exercise
18B.2**

We can also show formally now that *when demand curves are linear, price elasticity will be equal to exactly -1 at the midpoint of the demand curve.* Suppose the demand curve is given by $p = A - \alpha x$; i.e., suppose that on our graph of the linear demand curve, the price intercept is A and the slope is $-\alpha$. We can rewrite this as a function $x(p) = (A - p)/\alpha$, and, employing our price elasticity formula, this implies $\varepsilon_d = -p/(A - p)$. Setting ε_d to -1, we can then solve for the price at which price elasticity is equal to -1 as $p = A/2$; i.e., the price halfway between the vertical intercept A and 0, or simply the midpoint of the demand curve.

18B.1.2 Price Elasticity and Consumer Spending

We next argued in Section A that consumer spending increases as price rises when price elasticity lies between -1 and 0, and consumer spending decreases as price rises when price elasticity is less than -1. This is easy to verify mathematically.

Let the demand function take the general form $x(p)$.[7] Total consumer spending on x is then simply price times quantity, or $TS = px(p)$, and the change in consumer spending that results

----

[7]Of course demand functions are, as we saw in our development of consumer theory, generally functions of all prices as well as income. In a model of M different consumption goods, for instance, the general expression of the demand function for good x_i takes the form $x_i(p_1, p_2, \ldots, p_M, I)$. By denoting the demand function for good x as simply $x(p)$, we are implicitly just looking at a slice of the more general demand function that holds all prices other than the price for x as well as income fixed.

from a small increase in price is given by the derivative of TS with respect to price. Using the chain rule, this can be written as

$$\frac{d(TS)}{dp} = x(p) + p\frac{dx}{dp}. \tag{18.7}$$

Whenever this expression is equal to zero—i.e., whenever $p(dx/dp) = -x(p)$—consumer spending does not change when price increases by a small amount. We can rewrite $p(dx/dp) = -x(p)$ as

$$\frac{p}{x(p)}\frac{dx}{dp} = -1, \tag{18.8}$$

where the left-hand side is our formula for price elasticity ε_d. Thus, consumer spending remains unchanged with a small change in price whenever $\varepsilon_d = -1$.

Similarly, consumer spending will increase with a small increase in price whenever $p(dx/dp) > -x(p)$, or, dividing both sides by $x(p)$, whenever

$$\frac{p}{x(p)}\frac{dx}{dp} = \varepsilon_d > -1. \tag{18.9}$$

Thus, when demand is *price inelastic* ($\varepsilon_d > -1$), consumer spending rises with an increase in price and falls with a decrease in price.

Exercise 18B.3* Demonstrate that $\varepsilon_d < -1$ implies that consumer spending will fall with an increase in price and rise with a decrease in price.

18B.1.3 Demand Curves with Constant Price Elasticity
For many types of tastes, the demand curves that result from individual optimizing behavior have constant price elasticity throughout rather than price elasticities that vary along the demand curve. Consider, for instance, quasilinear tastes that can be represented by the utility function $u(x_1,x_2) = \alpha \ln x_1 + x_2$. You can check for yourself that the demand function for x_1 will then have the form

$$x_1(p_1,p_2) = \frac{\alpha p_2}{p_1}. \tag{18.10}$$

Using our formula for calculating price elasticity of demand ε_d, we get

$$\varepsilon_d = \frac{dx_1}{dp_1}\left(\frac{p_1}{x_1(p_1,p_2)}\right) = \left(\frac{-\alpha p_2}{p_1^2}\right)\left(\frac{p_1}{\alpha p_2/p_1}\right) = -\left(\frac{\alpha p_2}{p_1^2}\right)\left(\frac{p_1^2}{\alpha p_2}\right) = -1. \tag{18.11}$$

Thus, the tastes captured by this utility function give rise to a *unitary elastic* demand curve for the quasilinear good x_1.

Exercise 18B.4 What is the price elasticity of demand for x_1 and x_2 when tastes are Cobb–Douglas; i.e., when tastes can be represented by the utility function $u(x_1,x_2) = x_1^\alpha x_2^{(1-\alpha)}$? (*Hint*: Recall that the demand functions in this case are $x_1(p_1,I) = \alpha I/p_1$ and $x_2(p_2,I) = (1 - \alpha)I/p_2$.)

While unitary elastic demand curves are an example of demand curves that have the same elasticity throughout, it is also possible to have demand curves that have constant elasticity different from -1. Consider, for instance, the quasilinear tastes represented by the utility function $u(x_1,x_2) = \alpha x_1^\beta + x_2$. The demand function for x_1 can be derived as

$$x_1(p_1,p_2) = \left(\frac{\alpha\beta p_2}{p_1}\right)^{1/(1-\beta)}. \tag{18.12}$$

Applying the elasticity formula, we then get that $\varepsilon_d = -1/(1-\beta)$. For instance, if $\beta = 0.5$, the demand curve for x_1 has constant price elasticity of -2 throughout. Examples of demand curves with constant price elasticity of -1 and -2 are given in Graph 18.5.

18B.1.4 Other Price Elasticities
As we have noted already, elasticities represent a general concept that can refer to any change in economic behavior resulting from a change in some economic variable. We will introduce some other types of elasticities in end-of-chapter exercise 18.2. For instance, the "income elasticity of demand"—or the percentage change in quantity demanded from a 1% change in income—is given by

$$\varepsilon_I = \frac{dx}{dI}\frac{I}{x(I)}, \tag{18.13}$$

and the "cross-price elasticity of demand" of x_i with respect to the price p_j of some other good x_j is given by

$$\varepsilon_{x_i,p_j} = \frac{dx_i}{dp_j}\frac{p_j}{x_i(p_j)}. \tag{18.14}$$

Similarly, we can write the "price elasticity of supply" as

$$\varepsilon_s = \frac{dx_s}{dp}\frac{p}{x_s(p)}. \tag{18.15}$$

In each of these equations, we have again used shorthand notation for the x function, implicitly holding fixed the various other variables that enter this function.

Can you see from the expression for income elasticities that the sign of the elasticity will depend on whether the good x is normal or inferior?

Exercise 18B.5

Can you see that the sign of the cross-price elasticity depends on the slope of the cross-price demand curve?

Exercise 18B.6

18B.2 Calculating Equilibria under Price Floors and Price Ceilings

Once we understand the graphs surrounding the impact of price floors and price ceilings, it is not difficult to calculate the various components of these graphs so long as demand and supply curves are linear. In what follows, we will quickly illustrate this for one example and leave others to end-of-chapter exercises. It does, however, become a little more challenging to do this when demand and supply curves are not linear. In essence, we will have to use integral calculus to derive consumer and producer surpluses (rather than adding up simple geometric areas as we can do for linear demand and supply curves). For those of you comfortable with integral calculus, we will therefore provide a second example with nonlinear demand curves. Our examples will deal with price floors, and you will be asked to undertake similar calculations for price ceilings in end-of-chapter exercises.

18B.2.1 Price Floors and Ceilings when Demand and Supply Are Linear

Suppose, then, that the demand curve is $p = A - \alpha x_d$ and the supply curve is described by $p = B + \beta x_s$. These curves are illustrated in panel (a) of Graph 18.11, with intercepts and slopes labeled accordingly. Writing these equations in terms of quantities as functions of prices, the demand and supply functions are

$$x_d(p) = \frac{A - p}{\alpha} \quad \text{and} \quad x_s(p) = \frac{p - B}{\beta}. \tag{18.16}$$

In equilibrium (in the absence of price distortions), $x_d(p) = x_s(p)$. Setting the two equations above equal to one another and solving for price, we therefore get the equilibrium price p^*:

$$p^* = \frac{\beta A + \alpha B}{\alpha + \beta}. \tag{18.17}$$

<hr />

Exercise 18B.7 Can you express x^* in Graph 18.11 in terms of the demand and supply parameters A, α, B, β?

<hr />

Now suppose the government sets a *price floor* p^f above p^*. The quantity transacted in the market will then be determined by consumer demand at the higher price, and can be derived by simply plugging the price floor p^f into x_d to get $x_d(p^f) = (A - p^f)/\alpha$.

<hr />

Exercise 18B.8 What is the surplus of x that exists in the initial disequilibrium?

<hr />

Graph 18.11: Linear Demand and Supply

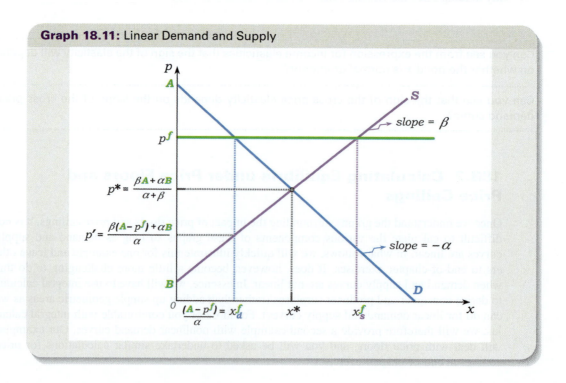

From our work in Section A, we know that, in the absence of any other programs, producers will now expend additional effort in order to sell their goods to the smaller number of consumers that are interested at the higher price. This additional effort is a cost to producers and thus shifts up the supply curve until it intersects the demand curve at p^f and at the quantity $(A - p^f)/\alpha$ demanded by consumers. Or, put differently, the actual price p' that producers will receive (net of the additional costs incurred) in the new equilibrium has to satisfy the equation

$$\frac{A - p^f}{\alpha} = \frac{p' - B}{\beta}. \tag{18.18}$$

Solving for p', we get

$$p' = \frac{\beta(A - p^f) + \alpha B}{\alpha}. \tag{18.19}$$

By how much does the supply curve shift up? Express your answer purely in terms of demand and supply parameters and p^f.

Exercise 18B.9

Once we have identified the pre- and post-price floor equilibrium, the various consumer and producer surplus areas are easily calculated given the linear nature of demand and supply curves (since these areas are simply rectangles and squares). In Table 18.1, we then put some numbers to this example by setting $A = 1,000$, $B = 0$, and $\alpha = 10 = \beta$. As the price floor p^f increases, the quantity demanded (and therefore the quantity transacted in the new equilibrium) x_d^f falls, the price (net of effort costs) p' received by producers falls, as does consumer and producer surplus (CS_{p^f} and PS_{p^f}). Finally, a lower and upper bound on how big the deadweight loss would be under each price floor is reported in the final columns, with the upper bound including the effort cost of producers.

Can you graphically illustrate why the lower and upper bounds of *DWL* ultimately converge as the price floor increases?

Exercise 18B.10

Can you express the total effort cost incurred by producers as a function of demand and supply parameters and p^f?

Exercise 18B.11

Table 18.1: $A = 1,000$, $B = 0$, $\alpha = \beta = 10$

			Equilibrium under Price Floors with Linear Demand and Supply Curves					
p^f	x_d^f	p'	CS_{p*}	CS_{p^f}	PS_{p*}	PS_{p^f}	DWL_{low}	DWL_{high}
$500	50	$500	$12,500	$12,500	$12,500	$12,500	$0	$0
$600	40	$400	$12,500	$8,000	$12,500	$8,000	$1,000	$9,000
$700	30	$300	$12,500	$4,500	$12,500	$4,500	$4,000	$16,000
$800	20	$200	$12,500	$2,000	$12,500	$2,000	$9,000	$21,000
$900	10	$100	$12,500	$500	$12,500	$500	$16,000	$24,000
$1,000	0	$0	$12,500	$0	$12,500	$0	$25,000	$25,000

In the example of Table 18.1, demand and supply curves have the same slopes in absolute value, which accounts for the symmetry of the impact of price floors on producer and consumer surplus. Table 18.2 then reports the impact of a price floor of $p^f = \$600$ for differently sloped demand and supply curves but with the pre-price floor equilibrium always having $p^* = \$500$ and $x^* = 50$. In the first section of the table, the demand curve is unchanged (with intercept $A = 1{,}000$ and slope $-\alpha = -10$) but the supply curve becomes shallower as the slope β falls (while the intercept B is adjusted to keep the pre-price floor equilibrium unchanged). In the second part of the table, the supply curve is unchanged (with intercept $B = 0$ and slope $\beta = 10$) while the slope α of the demand curve becomes shallower (and the intercept A is adjusted to keep the pre-price floor equilibrium unchanged). Finally, both demand and supply curves become shallower at the same time in the third part of the table.

Table 18.2: Demand and Supply Parameters set to keep $p^* = 500$ and $x^* = 50$; $p^f = 600$

Equilibrium under Price Floors as Price Elasticities Change							
				$A = 1{,}000$ $\alpha = 10$			
β	B	x_d^f	CS_{p^*}	CS_{p^f}	PS_{p^*}	PS_{p^f}	DWL_{low}	DWL_{high}
10	0	40	$12,500	$8,000	$12,500	$8,000	$1,000	$9,000
8	100	40	$12,500	$8,000	$10,000	$6,400	$900	$8,100
6	200	40	$12,500	$8,000	$7,500	$4,800	$800	$7,200
4	300	40	$12,500	$8,000	$5,000	$3,200	$700	$6,300
2	400	40	$12,500	$8,000	$2,500	$1,600	$600	$5,400
0	500	40	$12,500	$8,000	$0	$0	$500	$4,500
				$B = 0$ $\beta = 10$			
α	A	x_d^f	CS_{p^*}	CS_{p^f}	PS_{p^*}	PS_{p^f}	DWL_{low}	DWL_{high}
10	1,000	40	$12,500	$8,000	$12,500	$8,000	$1,000	$9,000
8	900	37.50	$10,000	$5,625	$12,500	$7,031	$1,406	$9,844
6	800	33.33	$7,500	$3,333	$12,500	$5,556	$2,222	$11,111
4	700	25.00	$5,000	$1,250	$12,500	$3,125	$4,375	$13,125
2	600	0	$2,500	$0	$12,500	$0	$15,000	$15,000
				$B = 0 + \gamma$ $A = 1{,}000 - \gamma$			
$\alpha = \beta$	γ	x_d^f	CS_{p^*}	CS_{p^f}	PS_{p^*}	PS_{p^f}	DWL_{low}	DWL_{high}
10	0	40	$12,500	$8,000	$12,500	$8,000	$1,000	$9,000
8	100	37.50	$10,000	$5,625	$10,000	$5,625	$1,250	$8,750
6	200	33.33	$7,500	$3,333	$7,500	$3,333	$1,667	$8,333
4	300	25.00	$5,000	$1,250	$5,000	$1,250	$2,500	$7,500
2	400	0	$2,500	$0	$2,500	$0	$5,000	$5,000

For each of the three sections of Table 18.2, graphically illustrate the third row using the information in the table to label everything on the axes that you can label.   **Exercise 18B.12**

Why do the lower and upper bounds for *DWL* converge in the lower two sections of Table 18.2 but not in the top portion?   **Exercise 18B.13***

8B.2.2 Non-linear Demands
Calculating the impact of price ceilings and price floors when market demand and supply are not linear is quite similar to calculating these effects when the underlying functions are linear. The only exception is that we will have to employ integrals in order to precisely calculate consumer and producer surpluses. If you are not comfortable with integral calculus, you can simply skip this section.

Consider, for instance, the market demand and supply functions

$$x_d(p) = \frac{40{,}000{,}000}{p^2} \quad \text{and} \quad x_s(p) = 547{,}192 p^{2/3}, \tag{18.20}$$

which are identical to the demand and supply curves we worked with in Chapters 14 and 15 where demand was derived explicitly from quasilinear tastes and supply represents a short-run market supply curve derived from a particular production technology. These are graphed in panels (a) and (b) of Graph 18.12, with panel (a) graphing the inverse demand and supply functions and panel (b) graphing the actual functions.

What is the price elasticity of demand? What is the price elasticity of supply?   **Exercise 18B.14**

Graph 18.12: Non-linear Demand and Supply

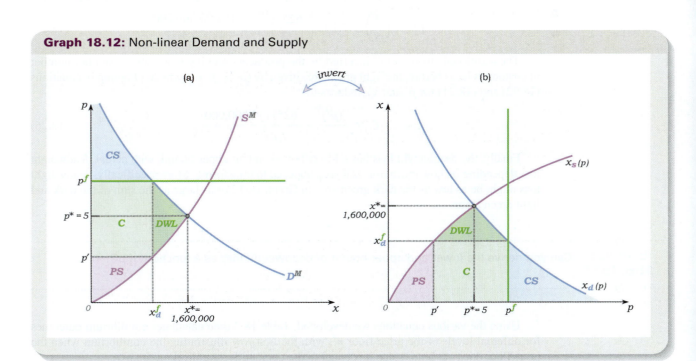

You can verify again (as we already did in past chapters) that the market equilibrium for these supply and demand functions is $p^* = \$5$ and $x^* = 1{,}600{,}000$. Now suppose the government imposes a price floor of $p^f > \$5$ (indicated by the green horizontal line in panel (a) and the green vertical line in panel (b)). Then the quantity transacted in the market will be determined by the reduced demand from consumers, with

$$x_d(p^f) = \frac{40{,}000{,}000}{(p^f)^2}. \tag{18.21}$$

In order for producers to supply this quantity, their effective price p' (taking into account their effort cost to get the smaller number of customers to pay attention) must satisfy the condition $x_d(p^f) = 547{,}192(p')^{2/3}$. Substituting equation (18.21) into this condition and solving for p', we get

$$p' = \frac{625}{(p^f)^3}. \tag{18.22}$$

In panel (b) of Graph 18.12, it is easy to see that consumer surplus after the imposition of the price floor p^f is the blue area *underneath* the demand function $x_d(p)$ above p^f. Put differently, consumer surplus is

$$CS = \int_{p^f}^{\infty} x_d(p)dp = \int_{p^f}^{\infty} \frac{40{,}000{,}000}{p^2} dp = \frac{40{,}000{,}000}{p^f}. \tag{18.23}$$

Producer surplus, on the other hand, can be seen in Graph 18.12b as the magenta area *underneath* the supply function $x_s(p)$ up to the producer's price p' (with effort costs having been subtracted from the transactions price p^f); i.e.,

$$PS = \int_{0}^{p'} x_s(p)dp = \int_{0}^{p'} 547{,}192 p^{2/3} dp = \left(\frac{3}{5}\right)547{,}192(p')^{5/3}, \tag{18.24}$$

which can be written in terms of the price floor p^f by substituting equation (18.22) for p'; i.e.,

$$PS = \left(\frac{3}{5}\right)547{,}192 \left(\frac{625}{(p^f)^3}\right)^{5/3} \approx \frac{15{,}000{,}000{,}000}{(p^f)^5}. \tag{18.25}$$

The additional effort cost C incurred by the producers seeking to attract the smaller number of customers is, as before, the light green area given by $(p^f - p')x_d^f$, which, plugging in equations (18.22) and (18.21) for p' and x_d^f, reduces to

$$C = \frac{((p^f)^4 - 625)(40{,}000{,}000)}{(p^f)^5}. \tag{18.26}$$

Finally, the deadweight loss has a lower bound and an upper bound, with actual deadweight loss depending on how much of C is lost as opposed to transferred. More specifically, deadweight loss might be as low as the dark green area in Graph 18.12 or as large as the sum of the dark and light green areas.

Exercise 18B.15** Can you derive the lower and upper bound of deadweight loss as a function of p^f?

Using the various equations we developed, Table 18.3 then calculates equilibrium outcomes for different levels of the price floor p^f, with the first row illustrating the equilibrium when the price floor does not bind (since it is equal to the competitive equilibrium price).

Table 18.3: All Values Other than p^f and p' are in 1,000s

			Equilibrium under Price Floors with Non-linear Demand and Supply				
p^f	x_d^f	p'	CS	PS	C	DWL_{low}	DWL_{high}
$5	1,600	$5.00	$8,000	$4,800	$0	$0	$0
$6	1,111	$2.89	$6,667	$1,929	$3,452	$753	$4,204
$7	816	$1.82	$5,714	$892	$4,227	$1,966	$6,193
$8	625	$1.22	$5,000	$458	$4,237	$3,105	$7,342
$9	494	$0.86	$4.444	$254	$4,021	$4,080	$8,102
$10	400	$0.63	$4.000	$150	$3,750	$4,900	$8,650
$15	178	$0.19	$2,667	$20	$2,634	$7,480	$10,114
$20	100	$0.08	$2,000	$5	$1,992	$8,803	$10,795

CONCLUSION

This chapter is the first in a series of chapters that investigate how competitive markets may result in inefficient outcomes when some of the conditions underlying the first welfare theorem do not hold. One of these conditions is that the price signal is not distorted by government policy, and we have seen above that explicit distortions through the setting of price ceilings or price floors will indeed result in deadweight losses (or inefficiencies). The presence of such deadweight losses implies that, at least in principle, there should be a way to eliminate the price-distorting policy and make everyone better off because the sum of the individual losses from price-distorting policies is larger than the sum of the individual gains. At the same time, we have noted that there might be instances when the motivation for price-distorting policies lies outside the framework we have developed, involving complex ethical considerations that noneconomists may have much to say about. And you should keep in mind that our analysis applies to *competitive* markets that face *no other distortions*. As we will see later, policies that create inefficiencies in the absence of other distortions may *reduce* inefficiencies in the presence of other distortions.

Of course, the size of the inefficiency from price distortions depends on the particulars of markets. It is for this reason that we have waited until now to introduce the concept of price elasticity, with price elasticities playing a large role in determining how different market participants are affected by price-distorting policies. The same will hold in the next chapter, where we will consider a less explicit form of price distortion and revisit some of the issues raised initially in our development of consumer theory. In particular, we will see how prices are distorted by tax and subsidy policies, and how price elasticities once again play a crucial role in determining the impact of such policies.

END-OF-CHAPTER EXERCISES

18.1   Consider, as we did in much of the chapter, a downward-sloping linear demand curve.

    A. In what follows, we will consider what happens to the price elasticity of demand as we approach the horizontal and vertical axes along the demand curve.

        a.   Begin by drawing such a demand curve with constant (negative) slope. Then pick the point A on the demand curve that lies roughly three-quarters of the way down the demand curve. Illustrate the price and quantity demanded at that point.

---

*conceptually challenging

**computationally challenging

†solutions in Study Guide

  b. Next, suppose the price drops by half and illustrate the point B on the demand curve for that lower price level. Is the percentage change in quantity from A to B greater or smaller than the absolute value of the percentage change in price?

  c. Next, drop the price by half again and illustrate the point C on the demand curve for that new (lower) price. The percentage change in price from B to C is the same as it was from A to B. Is the same true for the percentage change in quantity?

  d. What do your answers imply about what is happening to the price elasticity of demand as we move down the demand curve?

  e. Can you see what will happen to the price elasticity of demand as we get closer and closer to the horizontal axis?

  f. Next, start at a point A' on the demand curve that lies only a quarter of the way down the demand curve. Illustrate the price and quantity demanded at that point. Then choose a point B' that has only half the consumption level as at A'. Is the percentage change in price from A' to B' greater or less than the absolute value of the percentage change in quantity?

  g. Now pick the point C' (on the demand curve) where the quantity demanded is half what it was at B'. The percentage change in quantity from A' to B' is then the same as the percentage change from B' to C'. Is the same true of the percentage change in price?

  h. What do your answers imply about the price elasticity of demand as we move up the demand curve? What happens to the price elasticity as we keep repeating what we have done and get closer and closer to the vertical intercept?

B. Consider the linear demand curve described by the equation $p = A - \alpha x$.

  a. Derive the price elasticity of demand for this demand curve.

  b. Take the limit of the price elasticity of demand as price approaches zero.

  c. Take the limit of the price elasticity as price approaches A.

18.2 In this exercise, we explore the concept of elasticity in contexts other than own-price elasticity of (uncompensated) demand. (In cases where it matters, assume that there are only two goods).

A. For each of the following, indicate whether the statement is true or false and explain your answer:

  a. The income elasticity of demand for goods is negative only for Giffen goods.

  b. If tastes are homothetic, the income elasticity of demand must be positive.

  c. If tastes are quasilinear in x, the income elasticity of demand for x is zero.

  d. If tastes are quasilinear in x_1, then the cross-price elasticity of demand for x_1 is positive.

  e. If tastes are homothetic, cross-price elasticities must be positive.

  f. The price elasticity of *compensated* demand is always negative.

  g. The more substitutable two goods are for one another, the greater the price elasticity of *compensated* demand is in absolute value.

B. Consider first the demand function $x = \alpha I/p$ that emerges from Cobb–Douglas tastes.

  a. Derive the income elasticity of demand and explain its sign.

  b. We know Cobb–Douglas tastes are homothetic. In what way is your answer to (a) simply a property of homothetic tastes?

  c. What is the cross-price elasticity of demand? Can you make sense of that?

  d. Without knowing the precise functional form that can describe tastes that are quasilinear in x, how can you show that the income elasticity of demand must be zero?

  e. Consider the demand function $x_1(p_1, p_2) = (\alpha p_2/p_1)^\beta$. Derive the income and cross-price elasticities of demand.

  f. Can you tell whether the tastes giving rise to this demand function are either quasilinear or homothetic?

18.3† In the labor market, we can also talk about responsiveness—or elasticity—with respect to wages on both the demand and supply sides.

A. For each of the following statements, indicate whether you think the statement is true or false (and why):

    a.   The wage elasticity of labor supply must be positive if leisure and consumption are normal goods.

    b.   In end-of-chapter exercise 9.5, we indicated that labor supply curves are often "backward-bending." In such cases, the wage elasticity of labor supply is positive at low wages and negative at high wages.

    c.   The wage elasticity of labor demand is always negative.

    d.   In absolute value, the wage elasticity of labor demand is at least as large in the long run as it is in the short run.

    e.*   (The compensated labor supply curve, which we will cover more explicitly in Chapter 19, is the labor supply curve that would emerge if we always ensured you reached the same indifference curve regardless of the wage rate.) The wage elasticity of compensated labor supply must always be negative.

    f.*   The (long-run) rental rate (of capital) elasticity of labor demand (which is a cross-price elasticity) is always positive.

    g.*   The output price elasticity of labor demand is positive and increases from the short to the long run.

B.** Suppose first that tastes over consumption and leisure are Cobb–Douglas.

    a.   Derive the functional form of the labor supply function.

    b.   What is the wage elasticity of labor supply in this case? Explain how this relates to the implicit elasticity of substitution in Cobb–Douglas tastes.

    c.   Next, suppose that the decreasing returns to scale production process takes labor and capital as inputs and is also Cobb–Douglas. Derive the long-run wage elasticity of labor demand.[8]

    d.   Derive the rental rate elasticity of labor demand. Is it positive or negative?

    e.   Derive the long-run output price elasticity of labor demand. Is it positive or negative?

    f.   In the short run, capital is fixed. Can you derive the short-run wage elasticity of labor demand and relate it to the to long-run elasticity you calculated in part (c)?

    g.   Can you derive the short-run output price elasticity of labor demand and compare it to the long-run elasticity you calculated in part (e)?

18.4 In this exercise, treat the real interest rate r as identical to the the rental rate on capital.

A. We will now consider the responsiveness—or elasticity—of savings and borrowing behavior with respect to changes in the interest rate (and other prices). Suppose that tastes over consumption now and in the future are homothetic, and further suppose that production frontiers (that use labor and capital as inputs) are homothetic.

    a.   Can you tell whether the interest rate elasticity of savings (or capital supply) is positive or negative for someone who earns income now but not in the future?

    b.   Can you tell whether the interest rate elasticity of borrowing (or capital demand) is positive or negative for someone who earns no income now but will earn income in the future?

    c.   Is the interest rate elasticity of demand for capital by firms positive or negative?

    d.   Is the wage elasticity of demand for capital by firms positive or negative?

    e.   Is the output price elasticity of demand for capital positive or negative?

---

[8]It may be helpful to recall that, for Cobb–Douglas functions that take the form $f(\ell, k) = A\ell^\alpha k^\beta$, the labor demand function is

$$\ell(w, r, p) = \left(\frac{pA\alpha^{(1-\beta)}\beta^\beta}{w^{(1-\beta)}r^\beta} \right)^{1/(1-\alpha-\beta)}. \tag{18.27}$$

B.** Suppose that intertemporal tastes over consumption are Cobb–Douglas. Furthermore, suppose that production technologies (which take capital and labor as inputs) have decreasing returns to scale and are Cobb–Douglas.

    a. Suppose that your income this period is e_1 and your income in he future is e_2. Set up your intertemporal utility maximization problem and derive your demand for consumption c_1 now.

    b. Suppose all your income occurs now (i.e., $e_2 = 0$). What is your savings (or capital supply) function, and what is the interest rate elasticity of savings?

    c. Suppose instead that all your income happens next period (i.e., $e_1 = 0$). What is the interest rate elasticity of borrowing (or capital demand)?

    d. Next, derive the interest rate elasticity of capital demand by firms. Is it positive or negative?[9]

    e. Repeat this for the wage elasticity of capital demand as well as the output price elasticity of capital demand for firms.

18.5 In our treatment of price floors, we illustrated the case of a government program that purchases any surplus produced in the market. Now consider a price ceiling, and the analogous case of the government addressing disequilibrium shortages through purchases on international markets.

A. Suppose, for instance, that the U.S. demand and supply curves for coffee intersect at p^*, which is also the world price of coffee.

    a. Suppose that the government imposes a price ceiling p^c below p^* for domestic coffee sales. Illustrate the disequilibrium shortage that would emerge in the domestic coffee market.

    b. In the absence of any further interference in the market, what would you expect to happen?

    c. Next, suppose that as part of the price ceiling policy, the government purchases coffee in the world market (at the world market price p^*) and then sells this coffee at p^c domestically to any consumer that is unable to purchase coffee from a domestic producer. What changes in your analysis?

    d. Illustrate in a graph with the domestic demand and supply curves for coffee the deadweight loss from this government program (assuming that your demand curve is a good approximation of marginal willingness to pay).

B. Suppose demand and supply are given by $x_d = (A - p)/\alpha$ and $x_s = (p - B)/\beta$ (and assume that demand is equal to marginal willingness to pay).

    a. Derive the equilibrium price p^* that would emerge in the absence of any interference.

    b. Suppose the government imposes a price ceiling p^c that lies below p^*. Derive an expression for the disequilibrium shortage.

    c. Suppose, as in part A, that the government can purchase any quantity of x on the world market for p^* and it implements the program described in A(c). How much will this program cost the government?

    d. What is the deadweight loss from the combination of the price ceiling and the government program to buy coffee from abroad and sell it domestically at p^c?

18.6[†] **Everyday Application:** *Scalping College Basketball Tickets*: At many universities, college basketball is intensely popular and, were tickets sold at market prices, many students who wish to attend games would not be able to afford to do so. As a result, universities have come up with non-price rationing mechanisms to allocate basketball tickets.

A. Suppose throughout this exercise that demand curves are equal to marginal willingness to pay curves and no one would ever pay more than $250 for a basketball ticket.

    a. First, suppose only students care about basketball. Draw a demand and supply curve for basketball tickets (to one game) assuming the stadium capacity is 5,000 seats and assuming that supply and (student) demand intersect at $100.

---

[9]It will be helpful to know that, for Cobb–Douglas functions that take the form $f(\ell, k) = A\ell^\alpha k^\beta$, the capital demand function is

$$k(w, r, p) = \left(\frac{pA\alpha^\alpha \beta^{(1-\alpha)}}{w^\alpha r^{(1-\alpha)}} \right)^{1/(1-\alpha-\beta)} .$$

(18.28)

b. Suppose students have an opportunity cost of time equal to $20 per hour. The university gives away tickets to the game for free to anyone with a valid student ID, but only the first 5,000 students who line up will get a ticket. In equilibrium, how long will the line for basketball tickets be; i.e., how long will students have to wait in line to get a ticket?

c. What is the deadweight loss from the free ticket policy in (b)? (You can show this on your graph as well as arrive at a dollar figure.)

d. Now suppose that faculty care about basketball every bit as much as students. Unlike students, however, faculty have an opportunity cost of time equal to $100 per hour. Will any faculty attend basketball games under the policy in (b) (assuming students are not allowed to sell tickets to the faculty)?

e.* Now suppose anyone can sell, or "scalp," his ticket at any price if he obtained one standing in line. Draw a new supply and demand graph, but this time let this be the market for tickets *after* the university has allocated them using their zero price/waiting-in-line policy. The suppliers are therefore those who have obtained tickets by standing in line, and the supply curve is determined by the willingness of those people to sell their tickets. What would this supply curve look like? Who would be the demanders?

f.* A market such as the one you have just illustrated is called a *secondary market*; i.e., a market where previous buyers now become sellers. The common policy (often enshrined into law) of not permitting "scalping" of tickets is equivalent to setting a price ceiling of zero in this market. Under this policy, how many tickets will be sold in the secondary market?

g. How much surplus is being lost through the "no scalping" policy? Is anyone made worse off by allowing scalping of tickets?

h. In the absence of this policy, how would the mix of people attending the game change?

B. Suppose that the students' aggregate demand curve for tickets x is $p = 250 - 0.03x$ and assume throughout that there are no relevant income effects to worry about. Suppose further that the aggregate demand for tickets by faculty is the same as that for students and, as in part A, 5,000 seats are available.

a. What is the aggregate demand function for students and faculty jointly? If the tickets were allocated through a market price, what would be the price?

b. Suppose that the university only sold tickets to students. What would the equilibrium price be then?

c. Now suppose the tickets were allocated to those students who waited in line. Do you have to know anything about students' value of time to calculate the deadweight loss from this allocation mechanism?

d.* Suppose again that students are the only ones who are allocated tickets, and suppose they are prohibited from selling, or "scalping," them to faculty. Derive the demand and supply curves in the secondary market where students are potential suppliers and faculty are potential demanders.

e. What would be the price for tickets in this secondary market if it were allowed to operate?

f. What fraction of the attendees at the game will be faculty?

g. How large is the deadweight loss from the no-scalping policy? Does this depend on whether students bought the tickets as in (c) or waited in line as in (d)?

h. Compare the outcome in (a) and (e). Would the composition of the crowd at the basketball game differ between the scenario in which everyone can buy tickets at the market price as opposed to the scenario where students get tickets by waiting in line but can then sell them?

18.7 **Business and Policy Application:** *Minimum Wage Laws*: Most developed countries prohibit employers from paying wages below some minimum level $\underline{w}$. This is an example of a price floor in the labor market, and the policy has an impact in a labor market so long as $\underline{w} > w^*$ (where w^* is the equilibrium wage in the absence of policy-induced wage distortions).

BUSINESS APPLICATION

POLICY APPLICATION

A. Suppose $\underline{w}$ is indeed set above w^*, and suppose that labor supply slopes up.

a. Illustrate this labor market and the impact of the minimum wage law on employment.

b. Suppose that the disequilibrium unemployment caused by the minimum wage gives rise to more intense effort on the part of workers to find employment. Can you illustrate in your graph the equilibrium cost of the additional effort workers expend in securing employment?

   c. If leisure were quasilinear (and you could therefore measure worker surplus on the labor supply curve), what's the largest that deadweight loss from the minimum wage might become?

   d. How is the decrease in employment caused by the minimum wage (relative to the nonminimum wage employment level) related to the wage elasticity of labor demand? How is it related to the wage elasticity of labor supply?

   e. Define unemployment as the difference between the number of people willing to work at a given wage and the number of people who can find work at that wage. How is the size of unemployment at the minimum wage affected by the wage elasticities of labor supply and demand?

   f.* How is the equilibrium cost of effort exerted by workers to secure employment affected by the wage elasticities of labor demand and supply?

B. Suppose that labor demand is given by $\ell_D = (A/w)^\alpha$ and labor supply is given by $\ell_S = (Bw)^\beta$.

   a. What is the wage elasticity of labor demand and labor supply?

   b. What is the equilibrium wage in the absence of any distortions?

   c. What is the equilibrium labor employment in the absence of any distortions?

   d. Suppose $A = 24,500$, $B = 500$, and $\alpha = \beta = 1$. Determine the equilibrium wage w^* and labor employment ℓ^*.

   e. Suppose that a minimum wage of $10 is imposed. What is the new employment level ℓ^A and the size of the drop in employment $(\ell^* - \ell^A)$?

   f. How large is unemployment under this minimum wage, with unemployment U defined as the difference between the labor that seeks employment and the labor that is actually employed at the minimum wage?

   g. If the new equilibrium is reached through workers expending increased effort in securing employment, what is the equilibrium effort cost c^*?

   h. Create a table with w^*, ℓ^*, ℓ^A, $(\ell^* - \ell^A)$, U, and c^* along the top. Then fill in the first row for the case you have just calculated; i.e., the case where $A = 24,500$, $B = 500$, and $\alpha = \beta = 1$.

   i. Next, consider the case where $A = 11,668$, $B = 500$, $\alpha = 1.1$, and $\beta = 1$. Fill in the second row of the table for this case and explain what is happening in terms of the change in wage elasticities.

   j. Finally, consider the case where $A = 24,500$, $B = 238.1$, $\alpha = 1$, and $\beta = 1.1$. Fill in the third row of the table for this case and again explain what is happening in terms of the change in wage elasticities.

18.8† **Business and Policy Application:** *Usury Laws:* The practice of charging interest on money that is lent by one party to another, while commonplace now, has been historically controversial. Major religions have prohibited the charging of interest in the past (and some do so today), and governments have often codified this moral objection to interest in what is known as *usury laws* that limit the amount of interest that individuals can charge one another.

A. Usury laws are thus simply an example of a price ceiling in the market for financial capital.

   a. Illustrate a demand and upward-sloping supply curve in the market for financial capital (with the interest rate on the vertical axis). Denote the equilibrium interest rate in the absence of distortions as r^*.

   b. If usury laws prohibit interest rates above r^*, will they have any impact?

   c. Suppose the highest legal interest rate $\bar{r}$ is set below r^*. Explain what will happen to the amount of financial capital provided by suppliers of such capital.

   d. In light of the fact that financial capital is essential for an economy to grow, what would you predict will happen to economic growth as a result of such a usury law?

   e. How is the decrease in financial capital from usury laws related to the interest rate elasticity of demand? How is it related to the interest rate elasticity of supply?

   f.* Consider how a new equilibrium is likely to be reached in the financial market after the imposition of such a usury law. In addition to the dampening effect of less capital on economic growth, can you think of another related factor that may dampen such growth?

   g.* How is this factor (relating to the effort expended on securing financial capital) affected by the interest rate elasticity of demand and supply?

B. Suppose that demand and supply curves are similar to those used in exercise 18.7, with demand given by $k_D = (A/r)^\alpha$ and supply by $k_S = (Bw)^\beta$.

    a.   Derive the interest rate elasticity of capital demand and supply.

    b.   What is the equilibrium interest rate in the absence of price distortions?

    c.   What is the equilibrium level of financial capital transacted in the absence of any price distortions?

    d.   Suppose $A = 24{,}500$, $B = 500$, and $\alpha = \beta = 1$. Determine the equilibrium interest rate r^* and the equilibrium level of financial capital k^*.

    e.   Suppose the usury law sets a maximum interest rate $\bar{r} = 5$. What is the new level of financial capital k' transacted, and how big is the drop $(k^* - k')$ in financial capital as a result of the usury law?

    f.   If the new equilibrium is reached by investors expending additional effort to get to financial capital, what is the equilibrium effort cost c^*?

    g.   Create a table with r^*, k^*, k', $(k^* - k')$, and c^* at the top. Then fill in the first row for the case you just calculated; i.e., $A = 24{,}500$, $B = 500$, and $\alpha = \beta = 1$.

    h.   Next, consider the case where $A = 11{,}668$, $B = 500$, $\alpha = 1.1$, and $\beta = 1$. Fill in the second row of the table for this case and explain what is happening in terms of the change in interest rate elasticities.

    i.   Finally, consider the case where $A = 24{,}500$, $B = 238.1$, $\alpha = 1$, and $\beta = 1.1$. Fill in the third row of the table for this case and again explain what is happening in terms of the change in interest rate elasticities.

18.9   **Business and Policy Application:** *Subsidizing Corn through Price Floors*: Suppose the domestic demand and supply for corn intersects at p^*, and suppose further that p^* also happens to be the world price for corn. (Since the domestic price is equal to the world price, there is no need for this country to either import or export corn.) Assume throughout that income effects do not play a significant role in the analysis of the corn market.

BUSINESS APPLICATION

POLICY APPLICATION

    A.   Suppose the domestic government imposes a price floor $\bar{p}$ that is greater than p^* and it is able to keep imports of corn from coming into the country.

        a.   Illustrate the disequilibrium shortage or surplus that results from the imposition of this price floor.

        b.   In the absence of anything else happening, how will an equilibrium be reestablished and what will happen to producer and consumer surplus?

        c.   Next, suppose the government agrees to purchase any corn that domestic producers cannot sell at the price floor. The government then plans to turn around and sell the corn it purchases on the world market (where its sales are sufficiently small to not affect the world price of corn). Illustrate how an equilibrium will now be reestablished, and determine the change in domestic consumer and producer surplus from this government program.

        d.   What is the deadweight loss from the price floor with and without the government purchasing program?

        e.   In implementing the purchasing program, the government notices that it is not very good at getting corn to the world market, and all of it spoils before it can be sold. How does the deadweight loss from the program change depending on how successful the government is at selling the corn on the world market?

        f.   Would either consumers or producers favor the price floor on corn without any additional government programs?

        g.   Who would favor the price floor combined with the government purchasing program? Does their support depend on whether the government succeeds in selling the surplus corn? Why might they succeed in the political process?

        h.   How does the deadweight loss from the price floor change with the price elasticity of demand and supply?

    B.   Suppose the domestic demand curve for bushels of corn is given by $p = 24 - 0.00000000225x$ while the domestic supply curve is given by $p = 1 + 0.00000000025x$. Suppose there are no income effects to worry about.

a.   Calculate the equilibrium price p^* (in the absence of any government interference). Assume henceforth that this is also the world price for a bushel of corn.

b.   What is the quantity of corn produced and consumed domestically? (Note: The price per bushel and the quantity produced is roughly equal to what is produced and consumed in the United States in an average year.)

c.   How much is the total social (consumer and producer) surplus in the domestic corn market?

d.   Next, suppose the government imposes a price floor of $\bar{p} = 3.5$ per bushel of corn. What is the disequilibrium shortage or surplus of corn?

e.   In the absence of any other government program, what is the highest possible surplus after the price floor is imposed, and what does this imply about the smallest possible size of the deadweight loss?

f.   Suppose next that the government purchases any amount that corn producers are willing to sell at the price floor $\bar{p}$ but cannot sell to domestic consumers. How much does the government have to buy?

g.   What happens to consumer surplus? What about producer surplus?

h.   What happens to total surplus assuming the government sells the corn it buys on the world market at the price p^*?

i.   How much does deadweight loss jump under just the price floor as well as when the government purchasing program is added if $\bar{p} = 4$ instead of 3.5? What if it is 5?

18.10 Business and Policy Application: *Corn Subsidies through Price Floors (continued):* Consider the same set-up as in exercise 18.9.

A. Suppose again that a price floor $\bar{p}$ greater than the equilibrium price p^* has been imposed and that the government has committed to purchase the difference between what is supplied at the price floor and what is demanded.

a.   If you have not done so in exercise 18.9, illustrate the smallest possible deadweight loss in the absence of the government purchasing program as well as the deadweight loss if the government purchases the excess corn and then sells it at the world price p^*.

b.   How would the deadweight loss change if the government found a way to give the corn it purchases to those consumers that place the highest value on it?

c.   What happens to the deadweight loss if the government instead sets a price at which all the excess corn gets sold assuming it can keep those who purchased at the price floor from buying at the lower government price?

d.   Compare your answers to (b) and (c). They should be the same. Can you explain intuitively why this is the case?

e.*   Consider the policy as described in (c). After the initial set of consumers purchase corn at the price floor, illustrate the demand curve for the remaining consumers and the supply curve for corn from the government. What's the elasticity of supply of government corn, and at what price must this supply curve cross the demand curve of the consumers who did not buy at the price floor?

f.*   Finally, suppose that everyone (including those with marginal willingness to pay the exceeds the price floor) wants to buy at the lower government price but the government still agrees to buy any amount of corn that producers are willing to supply at the price floor. What will happen and how will it affect the deadweight loss?

g.   Why is your answer again the same as under the previous policies?

B. Consider again, as in exercise 18.9, a demand curve $p = 24 - 0.00000000225x$ and a supply curve that is given by $p = 1 + 0.00000000025x$.

a.   Calculate consumer surplus, producer surplus, and deadweight loss under the scenario described in A(b) assuming a price floor of $\bar{p} = 3.5$.

b.   Consider the scenario described in A(c). Derive the demand curve that remains once the consumers who are willing to purchase at the price floor have done so.

c.   Given the quantity supplied to the remaining demanders by the government, what is the price the government has to charge to sell all the excess corn? Calculate consumer and producer surplus and verify that the deadweight loss is the same as in (a).

d.   Finally, consider the scenario in A(f). Verify that the price the government has to charge to sell all its corn is the same as in (c). Then calculate consumer surplus, producer surplus, and deadweight loss.

18.11 Policy Application: *Rent Control*: A portion of the housing market in New York City (and many other cities in the world) is regulated through a policy known as *rent control*. In essence, this policy puts a price ceiling (below the equilibrium price) on the amount of rent that landlords can charge in the apartment buildings affected by the policy.

A.   Assume for simplicity that tastes are quasilinear in housing.

a.   Draw a supply and demand graph with apartments on the horizontal axis and rents (i.e., the monthly price of apartments) on the vertical. Illustrate the "disequilibrium shortage" that would emerge when renters believe they can actually rent an apartment at the rent-controlled price.

b.   Suppose that the NYC government can easily identify those who get the most surplus from getting an apartment. In the event of excess demand for apartments, the city then awards the right to live (at the rent-controlled price) in these apartments to those who get the most consumer surplus. Illustrate the resulting consumer and producer surplus as well as the deadweight loss from the policy.

c.   Next, suppose NYC cannot easily identify how much consumer surplus any individual gets and therefore cannot match people to apartments as in (b). So instead, the mayor develops a "pay-to-play" system under which only those who pay monthly bribes to the city will get to "play" in a rent-controlled apartment. Assuming the mayor sets the required bribe at just the right level to get all apartments rented out, illustrate the size of the monthly bribe.

d.   Will the identity of those who live in rent-controlled apartments be different in (c) than in (b)? Will consumer or producer surplus be different? What about deadweight loss?

e.   Next, suppose that the way rent-controlled apartments are allocated is through a lottery. Whoever wants to rent a rent-controlled apartment can enter his or her name in the lottery, and the mayor picks randomly as many names as there are apartments. Suppose the winners can sell their right to live in a rent-controlled apartment to anyone who agrees to buy that right at whatever price they can agree on. Who do you think will end up living in the rent-controlled apartments (compared to who lived there under the previous policies)?

f.*   The winners in the lottery in part (e) in essence become the suppliers of "rights" to rent-controlled apartments while those that did not win in the lottery become the demanders. Imagine that selling your right to an apartment means agreeing to give up your right to occupy the apartment in exchange for a monthly check q. Can you draw a supply and demand graph in this market for "apartment rights" and relate the equilibrium point to your previous graph of the apartment market?

g.*   What will be the equilibrium monthly price q^* of a "right" to live in one of these apartments compared to the bribe charged in (c)? What will be the deadweight loss in your original graph of the apartment market? How does your answer change if lottery winners are not allowed to sell their rights?

h.   Finally, suppose that instead the apartments are allocated by having people wait in line. Who will get the apartments and what will deadweight loss be now? (Assume that everyone has the same value of time.)

B.   Suppose that the aggregate monthly demand curve is $p = 10,000 - 0.01x$ while the supply curve is $p = 1,000 + 0.002x$. Suppose further that there are no income effects.

a.   Calculate the equilibrium number of apartments x^* and the equilibrium monthly rent p^* in the absence of any price distortions.

b.   Suppose the government imposes a price ceiling of $1,500. What's the new equilibrium number of apartments?

c.   If only those who are willing to pay the most for these apartments are allowed to occupy them, what is the monthly willingness to pay for an apartment by the person who is willing to pay the least but still is assigned an apartment?

d.   How high is the monthly bribe per apartment as described in A(c)?

e.* Suppose the lottery described in A(e) allocates the apartments under rent control, and suppose that the "residual" aggregate demand function by those who did not win in the lottery is given by $x = 750,000 - 75p$. What is the demand function for y—the "rights to apartments" (described in A(f))? What is the supply function in this market? (*Hint*: You will have to determine the marginal willingness to pay curves for those who did not win to get the demand for y and for those who did win to get the supply for y. And remember to take into account the fact that occupying an apartment is more valuable than having the right to occupy an apartment at the rent controlled price.)

f. What is the equilibrium monthly price of a right y to occupy a rent-controlled apartment? Compare it to your answer to (c).

g. Calculate the deadweight loss from the rent control for each of the scenarios you analyzed.

h. By how much would the deadweight loss increase if the rationing mechanism for rent-controlled apartments were governed exclusively by having people wait in line? (Assume that everyone has the same value of time.)

18.12 Policy Application: *NYC Taxi Cab Medallions*: In New York City, you are allowed to operate a taxi cab only if you carry a special taxi "medallion" made by the Taxi Commission of New York. Suppose 50,000 of these have been sold, and no further ones will be put into circulation by the Taxi Commission. We will see that restricting supply in this way is another way in which governments can inefficiently distort price.

A. Suppose for simplicity that there are no income effects of significance in this problem. We will analyze the demand and supply of a day's worth of cab rides, which we will call "daily taxi rides."

a. On a graph with daily taxi rides on the horizontal axis and dollars on the vertical, illustrate the daily aggregate demand curve for NYC taxi rides. Given the fixed supply of medallions, illustrate the supply curve under the medallion system.

b. Illustrate the daily revenue a cab driver will make. (Since we are denoting quantity in terms of "daily cab rides," the price of one unit of the output is equal to the daily revenue.)

c. In the absence of the medallion system, taxi cabs would be free to enter and exit the cab business. Assuming that everyone faces the same cost to operating a cab, what would the long-run supply curve of cabs look like? Illustrate this on your graph under the assumption that removal of the medallion system would result in an increase in the number of cab rides. Indicate the long-run daily price of a cab and the number of cabs operating in the absence of the medallion system.

d. Suppose you own a medallion and you can rent it out to someone else. Indicate in your graph the equilibrium daily rental fee you could charge for your medallion. How much profit are those who rent a medallion in order to operate a cab making? Is that different from how much profit those who own a medallion and use it to operate a cab are making?

e. *True or False*: The only individuals who would be made worse off if medallions were no longer required to operate a cab are the owners of medallions.

f. Illustrate in your graph the daily deadweight loss from the medallion system. Can you think of a policy proposal that would make everyone better off?

B. Let x denote a day's worth of cab rides and suppose the demand curve for x was given by $p = 2,500 - (x/100)$.

a. Given the fixed supply of 50,000 medallions, what is the price of a day's worth of cab rides?

b. Suppose that the daily cost of operating a cap is $1,500 (in the absence of having to pay for a medallion). What is the equilibrium daily rental fee for a medallion?

c. Suppose that everyone expects the rental value of a medallion to remain the same into the future. How much could you sell a medallion for, assuming a daily interest rate of 0.01%?

d. How many more cabs would there be on NYC streets if the medallion system were eliminated (and free entry and exit into the cab business is permitted)?

e. What is the daily deadweight loss of the medallion system?

f. What do you think is the biggest political obstacle to eliminating the system?

18.13† Policy Application: *Kidney Markets*: A large number of patients who suffer from degenerative kidney disease ultimately require a new kidney in order to survive. Healthy individuals have two kidneys but usually can live a normal life with just a single kidney. Thus, kidneys lend themselves to "live donations"; i.e., unlike an organ like the heart, the donor can donate the organ while alive (and live a healthy life with a high degree of likelihood). It is generally not permitted for healthy individuals to sell a kidney; kidneys can only be donated for free (with only the medical cost of the kidney transplant covered by the recipient or his insurance). In effect, this amounts to a price ceiling of zero for kidneys in the market for kidneys.

A. Consider, then, the supply and demand for kidneys.

    a.   Illustrate the demand and supply curves in a graph with kidneys on the horizontal axis and the price of kidneys on the vertical. Given that there are some that in fact donate a kidney for free, make sure your graph reflects this.

    b.   Illustrate how the prohibition of kidney sales results in a "shortage" of kidneys.

    c.   In what sense would permitting the sale of kidneys eliminate this shortage? Does this imply that no one would die from degenerative kidney disease?

    d.   Suppose everyone has the same tastes but people differ in terms of their ability to generate income. What would this imply about how individuals of different income levels line up along the kidney supply curve in your graph? What does it imply in terms of who will sell kidneys?

    e.   How would patients who need a kidney line up along the demand curve relative to their income? Who would not get kidneys in equilibrium?

    f.   Illustrate in your graph the lowest that deadweight loss from prohibiting kidney sales might be assuming that demand curves can be used to approximate marginal willingness to pay. (*Hint*: The lowest possible deadweight loss occurs if those who receive donated kidneys under the price ceiling are also those that are willing to pay the most.)

    g.   Does the fact that kidneys might be primarily sold by the poor (and disproportionately bought by well-off patients) change anything about our conclusion that imposing a price ceiling of zero in the kidney market is inefficient?

    h.   In the absence of ethical considerations that we are not modeling, should anyone object to a change in policy that permits kidney sales? Why do you think that opposition to kidney sales is so widespread?

    i.   Some people might be willing to sell organs—like their heart—that they cannot live without in order to provide financially for loved ones even if it means that the seller will die as a result. Assuming that everyone is purely rational, would our analysis of deadweight loss from prohibiting such sales be any different? I think opposition to permitting such trade of vital organs is essentially universal. Might the reason for this also, in a less extreme way, be part of the reason we generally prohibit trade in kidneys?

B. Suppose the supply curve in the kidney market is $p = B + \beta x$.

    a.   What would have to be true in order for the phenomenon of kidney donations (at zero price) to emerge?

    b.   Would those who donate kidneys get positive surplus? How would you measure this, and how can you make intuitive sense of it?

18.14 **Policy Application:** *Oil Shocks and Gasoline Prices*: In 1973, the OPEC countries sharply reduced the supply of oil in the world market, which raised the price of oil and thus the marginal cost of producing gasoline in domestic refineries. In 2008, uncertainties over the stability of oil supplies and increasing demand from developing countries (as well as from oil speculators) also caused sharp increases in the price of oil, which again dramatically increased the marginal cost of producing gasoline in domestic refineries. While the causes of higher oil prices differed, the impact on domestic gasoline refineries was similar. Yet in 1973, vast gasoline shortages emerged, leading cars to line up for miles at gasoline stations and causing governments to ration gasoline, but in 2008 no such shortages emerged. In this exercise, we explore the difference between these experiences.

POLICY APPLICATION

A. The difference is attributable to the following policy intervention used in 1973: In 1973, the government imposed price controls—i.e., price ceilings—in order to combat inflationary pressures, but in 2008 the government did no such thing.

    a.   Consider first the experience of 1973. Begin by drawing the equilibrium in the gasoline market prior to the oil shock.

    b.   Now illustrate the impact of the OPEC countries' actions on the domestic gasoline market.

  c. As gasoline prices began to rise, the government put in place a price ceiling between the pre-crisis price and the price that would have emerged had the government not interfered. Illustrate this price ceiling in your graph.

  d. If we take into account the cost of time spent in gasoline lines, what was the effective price of gasoline that consumers faced?

  e. Now consider 2008, when the government did not impose a price ceiling as gasoline prices nearly quadrupled over a short period. Illustrate the change in equilibrium and the reason no shortage emerged.

  f. Suppose that the 1973 and 2008, shocks to the marginal costs of refineries were identical as were initial supply and demand curves. If we take into account the cost of waiting in lines for gasoline in 1973, in which year did the real price of gasoline faced by consumers rise more?

  g. When the government compiles statistics on inflation, in which year would it have shown a larger jump in inflation due to the increase in the price of gasoline?

B. Suppose that the demand curve for gasoline in both years is given by $p = A - \alpha x$ while the pre-crisis supply curve is given by $p = B + \beta x$.

  a. Derive the pre-crisis equilibrium price p^*.

  b. Suppose the crises in both years cause the supply curve to change to $p = C + \beta x$ where $C > B$. Derive the new equilibrium price p' that emerged in 2008.

  c. Now consider 1973, when the government imposed a price ceiling $\bar{p}$ between p^* and p'. Derive the real price p'' paid by consumers (taking into account the effort cost of waiting in line).

  d. Can you show that $p'' > p'$?

Distortionary Taxes and Subsidies

In Chapter 18, we began our discussion of how policies that alter or "distort" market prices in a competitive market can create deadweight losses.[1] But such policies are not limited to those that explicitly set price floors above the equilibrium price or price ceilings below the equilibrium price. In fact, the most common government policies that distort market prices involve tax and subsidy policies rather than explicit regulatory policies aimed at setting prices directly. With federal, state, and local governments funded primarily through taxes, and with all government spending combined making up more than 40 percent of most economies, tax policy then becomes a particularly important area for understanding how price distortions impact welfare.

Because of the important role taxes play in most economies, we have already developed many of the concepts that are crucial to understanding tax policy in earlier chapters, particularly in the chapters leading up to and including Chapter 10. We already understand from this development that, on the consumer (or worker or saver) side of markets, taxes result in deadweight losses or inefficiencies to the extent to which they give rise to *substitution effects*. Now that we have added producers to the model, however, we are able to talk much more explicitly about how taxes affect economic behavior *in equilibrium* when all sides of the market respond to changes in incentives. This makes it possible to now become explicit about who is affected most by particular taxes—who ends up paying taxes in equilibrium, and how this translates to welfare changes for consumers, producers, and workers as well as society overall.

Again, it is worth noting that, in pointing out the logic behind the emergence of deadweight losses from taxation, the economist is not voicing opposition to taxes per se. Rather, the economist is in the business of identifying costs and benefits, leaving it up to others to judge whether particular policies with particular costs and benefits are good or bad. Taxes have hidden costs that policy makers should understand, and some taxes have greater hidden costs than others. Similarly, some taxes may appear to affect one group on the surface while in fact economic analysis suggests that they will actually affect a different group much more. Understanding issues of this kind is the point of this chapter, with later chapters identifying more clearly why we might indeed need to use taxes despite their hidden costs. As in the previous chapter, it is also important to note that the inefficiencies from taxes (and subsidies) are identified here in a *competitive* setting in which *there are no other distortions*. We will see in upcoming chapters that, in noncompetitive settings or in the

---

[1]In addition to the usual consumer theory material, this chapter includes material on labor and capital markets, material that draws on our development of models in Chapters 3 and 8 as well as the later sections of Chapter 9. Students who have not read this material can skip Sections 19A.2.2, 19A.2.3, and 19B.3. The chapter also presumes a basic understanding of producer theory from Chapter 11, partial equilibrium as developed in Chapters 14 and 15, and elasticity as developed in the first part of Chapter 18.

presence of other distortions, taxes and subsidies *may* become efficiency enhancing. Finally, we will develop the main ideas in this chapter within our partial equilibrium framework (focusing on a single market), but at the end we will offer an example to illustrate how general equilibrium effects may also be important in many settings. This theme will then carry forward into Chapter 20.

19A   Taxes and Subsidies in Competitive Markets

As we have pointed out before, almost all taxes change some opportunity costs in the economy. Put differently, almost all taxes distort some of the market prices that, at least under certain circumstances, coordinate all sides of a market to an efficient outcome. As a result, almost all taxes result in deadweight losses and are thus, to one degree or another, inefficient. But not all taxes are equally inefficient, nor do all taxes impact all groups in the same way. We therefore begin our intuitive analysis of taxes with an analysis of who actually ends up paying taxes in equilibrium before we revisit the issue of deadweight loss and the potential for real-world taxes that might actually be efficient.

One note before we start: Taxes and subsidies are very similar in that both change the prices individuals face in an economy. In fact, we can think of subsidies as simply negative taxes. For instance, a government might impose a 10% tax on every good that is sold in a market, or it might impose a 10% subsidy. The 10% tax will cause an increase in the price of the good sold in the market, while the 10% subsidy will cause a decrease in the price. Taxes raise revenues for the government, while "negative taxes" (or subsidies) cause increases in government expenditures. Thus, even when we don't explicitly treat taxes and subsidies separately in this chapter, you should always be able to conduct a particular economic analysis for both positive and negative taxes.

19A.1 Who Pays Taxes and Receives Subsidies?

Since there are always two sides to a market, buyers and sellers, a government that wants to tax the good sold in a market can in principle do so by writing many different types of tax laws. In particular, the government might write the law in such a way as to make the buyers be the ones that pay the tax and send a check to the government whenever they purchase the taxed good. Alternatively, the government might write the law so as to make sellers send the tax payment to the government. Or the government might do some combination of the two. For instance, in the case of U.S. payroll taxes that fund expenditures in the Social Security system, the government requires workers to pay half of the overall tax and employers to pay the other half. Thus, on every pay stub that accompanies your paycheck, you will notice that your employer has deducted some payroll taxes and sent that amount to the government on your behalf. What you do not see on your pay stub is that the employer sent a separate check for his or her share of your payroll taxes.

19A.1.1 Statutory versus Economic Incidence   It turns out that it ends up not mattering at all which way the government writes tax laws, whether it requires the bulk of the tax to be paid by buyers or sellers. Economists use the term *statutory incidence of a tax* to refer to the way in which the legal (or "statutory") obligation to pay a tax is phrased in tax laws. In the case of U.S. payroll taxes, for instance, the statutory incidence of the tax falls equally on employers and employees. We will distinguish this from the *economic incidence of a tax* by which we will mean how the tax burden is *actually* divided among buyers and sellers when a new equilibrium under the tax has emerged.

Consider, for instance, a tax law that imposes a statutory incidence of a per-unit tax t on the producers of good x. In other words, for every unit of x that is produced, the firm producing it owes a tax of amount t. This raises the marginal cost of production by t, shifting up the MC (and AC) curves for each firm in the market. Since market supply in the short run is simply the combination of all MC curves (above AC), this implies that the short-run market supply curve will shift up by t. Similarly, since the long-run market supply curve is determined by the lowest points of (long-run) AC curves, the long-run market supply curve will shift up by t. This shift in the market supply curve is illustrated in Graph 19.1a by the upward shift (equal to the vertical distance of the green arrow) of the market supply curve from the initial (blue) supply curve S to the new (magenta) supply curve S'. This causes an increase in the market price from p^* to p', and it reduces the quantity of x transacted in the market from x^* to x'.

Will the increase in price from the tax be larger or smaller in the long run? (*Hint:* How is the price elasticity of supply in the long run usually related to the price elasticity of supply in the short run?)

Exercise 19A.1

Now suppose that instead the government imposed the statutory incidence of an equally sized per-unit tax on consumers of x. In this case, costs would remain unchanged for producers, but each consumer who was previously willing to pay a price p will now only be willing to pay $(p - t)$ given that he or she knows he or she must still send t per unit to the government. Thus, the demand curve will shift down by t, a distance indicated by the size of the green arrow in Graph 19.1b, causing a new equilibrium to emerge at price p''. At first glance, it certainly appears that panels (a) and (b) look quite different due to the different statutory incidence of the same per-unit tax.

If you think about what information is contained in panels (a) and (b), however, you will notice that the two graphs actually end up being identical in the underlying predicted impact of the two taxes on buyers and sellers. In panel (a), good x is traded at price p', but sellers do not get to keep this price for each unit they sell. Rather, they still have to pay the government a tax t for each unit they sell, leaving them with a net-of-tax price $(p' - t)$ while buyers pay price p'. In panel (b), on the other hand, good x is traded at the lower price p'', but buyers still need to pay the tax t. Thus, buyers in panel (b) actually pay a price $(p'' + t)$ while sellers receive the lower price p''. *In both cases, sellers end up receiving a price that is exactly t below the price buyers pay, with the difference going to the government.*

Once we recognize this, we can graph the economic incidence of a tax *regardless of the statutory incidence* in a less complicated graph depicted in panel (c). Here, we simply insert a vertical green line that is equal to the per-unit tax to the left of the pre-tax equilibrium and label the price read off the demand curve as p_d and the price read off the supply curve as p_s. Since the green line

Graph 19.1: Statutory versus Economic Incidence of Taxes

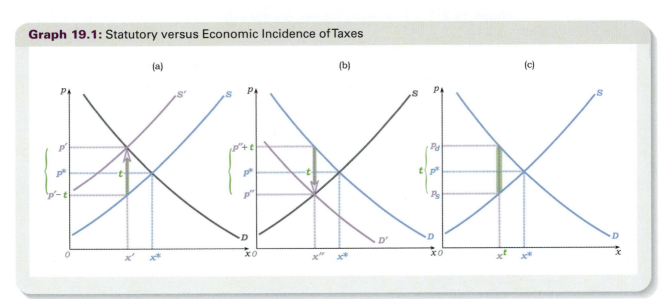

segment in panel (c) has exactly the same height as the green arrows in panels (a) and (b), it logically follows that p' in panel (a) is equal to p_d in panel (c) and p'' in panel (b) is equal to p_s in panel (c). The price p_d is then the price paid by buyers after the tax is imposed, and p_s is the price received by sellers, with the difference t going to the government. Notice further that x^t in panel (c) is logically equal to x' and x'' in panels (a) and (b).

Exercise 19A.2

Using a pencil, redraw the graphs in panel (a) and (b) but this time label clearly which price buyers end up paying and sellers end up receiving, taking into account that sellers have to pay the tax in panel (a) and buyers have to pay the tax in panel (b). Then, erase the shifted curves in your two graphs. Do the two graphs now look identical to each other and to the graph in panel (c)? (The answer should be yes.)

Regardless of which way tax laws are phrased and who is legally responsible for paying a tax, the economic analysis of Graph 19.1 therefore suggests that the economic incidence of the tax will always be exactly the same: Buyers and sellers will share the burden of the tax, with buyers paying higher prices and sellers receiving lower prices than they did before the imposition of the tax. The exact same is true for negative taxes known as subsidies. Graph 19.2 illustrates the impact of a per-unit subsidy s, with the new price received by sellers p_s now higher than the new price paid by buyers p_d.

Exercise 19A.3

Illustrate how the equilibrium changes when the subsidy is paid to sellers (thus reducing their *MC*). Compare this to how the equilibrium changes when the subsidy is paid to buyers (thus shifting the demand curve). Can you see how both of these types of subsidies will result in an economic outcome summarized in Graph 19.2?

19A.1.2 Economic Incidence and Price Elasticity   Our analysis so far may lead one to incorrectly conclude that the economic burden of taxes (and the economic benefit of subsidies) is shared equally between buyers and sellers. This has been true so far only because of the way we

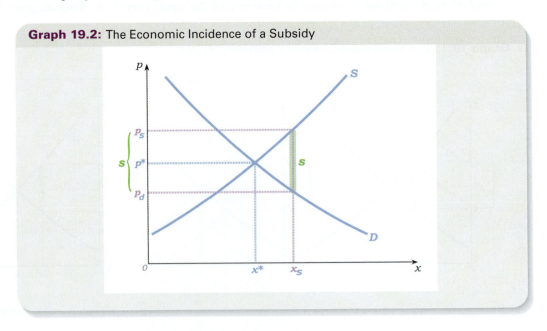

Graph 19.2: The Economic Incidence of a Subsidy

happened to graph demand and supply curves in Graphs 19.1 and 19.2. The actual economic incidence of taxes and subsidies, however, depends on the relative responsiveness of buyers and sellers to price changes.

Consider, for instance, a tax on cigarettes. The evidence suggests that most smokers are relatively unresponsive to changes in the price of cigarettes and will continue to smoke roughly as much at higher prices as they do at lower prices. A tax imposed on cigarettes will therefore tend to primarily be passed onto consumers regardless of who is legally responsible for paying the tax. This is depicted in Graph 19.3a where demand is relatively inelastic. A tax t will raise the price paid by buyers by a lot while lowering the price received by cigarette companies relatively little.

Now consider a tax on the sale of oil. Oil is, at least in the short run, in relatively fixed supply, leaving the oil market with a relatively steep supply curve. Panel (b) of Graph 19.3 then illustrates that a tax will cause a sharp decline in the price received by sellers while causing only a small increase in the price paid by buyers. Thus, *the economic incidence of a tax falls disproportionately on those who are less responsive to price changes; i.e., those whose behavioral response to price is more inelastic.*

During the 2008 presidential campaign in the United States, oil prices increased sharply. Some candidates advocated a "tax holiday" on gasoline taxes to help consumers. Others argued that this would have little effect on gasoline prices in the short run. Assuming each side was honest, how must they have disagreed on their estimates of underlying price elasticities?

Exercise 19A.4

In graphs with demand and supply curves similar to those in Graph 19.3, illustrate the economic impact on buyers and sellers of subsidies. How does the benefit of a subsidy relate to relative price elasticities?

Exercise 19A.5

Graph 19.3: Price Elasticities and the Relative Burden of Taxes on Buyers and Sellers

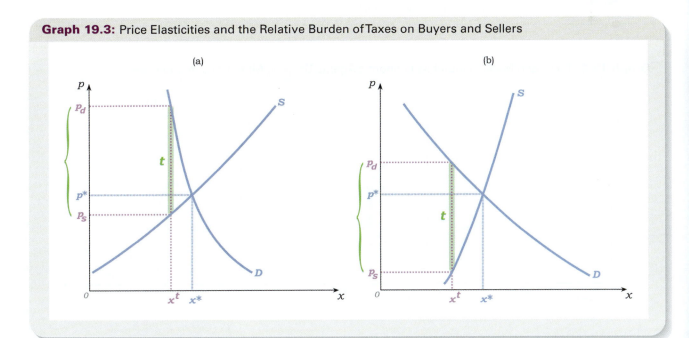

19A.1.3 The Impact of Taxes on Market Output and Tax Revenue

Just as price elasticities determine who bears disproportionately more of the burden of a tax (or gains a disproportionate share of the benefit of a subsidy), price elasticities determine how much market output will respond to changes in taxes and consequently how much tax revenue will be raised. This is illustrated in Graph 19.4 where the impact on market output is illustrated for three different scenarios. In each panel of the graph, buyers and sellers are assumed to be similarly responsive to price changes, and the relative burden of a tax is therefore similar for both sides of the market. The size of the tax imposed in each of the panels is exactly the same. However, panel (a) of the graph begins with relatively elastic market demand and supply curves that become increasingly more inelastic in panels (b) and (c). As a result, market output drops a lot in panel (a), less in panel (b), and even less in panel (c). Thus, *as buyers and sellers become more unresponsive to price changes, taxes have a smaller impact on market output.*

Exercise 19A.6 Does the impact of subsidies on market output also rise with the price-responsiveness of buyers and sellers?

In addition, each panel of Graph 19.4 illustrates the total tax revenue collected by the government (using the same per unit tax t) as the shaded green area. These areas are simply the vertical distance (which represents the per unit tax rate) multiplied by the horizontal distance that represents output after the tax is imposed. Note how tax revenue changes as demand and supply become more inelastic. This should, of course, make intuitive sense: If consumers and producers are very responsive to price changes, their large response to a tax will undermine efforts to raise revenue.

Exercise 19A.7 Suppose the government has already imposed the taxes graphed in Graph 19.4 and is now considering raising this tax. Can you see in these graphs under what circumstances this would result in a decrease in overall tax revenues?

Graph 19.4: Taxes and Market Output as Economic Agents Become More Price-Responsive

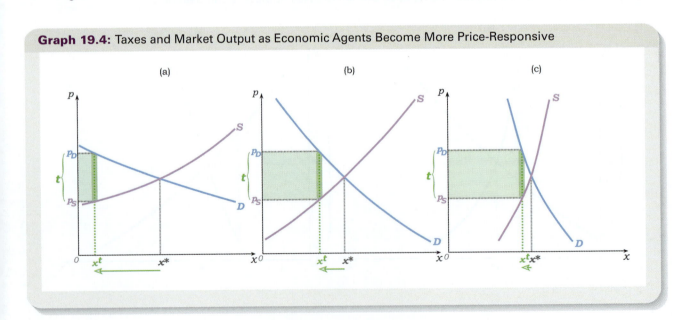

19A.1.4 Differential Impact of Taxes on Other Markets   Whenever we use the partial equilibrium model that focuses on a single market in isolation, we are implicitly assuming that all other prices in the economy are moving in lock-step and thus all other goods in the economy can be modeled as one big composite good. We are also treating our analysis of a tax change as if it occurred in an environment where other goods are not taxed. However, it is often the case that taxes imposed in one market cause differential effects in other markets and that taxes already exist and may be impacted in these other markets. For instance, suppose the government imposes a large tax on gasoline. Then it is likely that markets for more fuel-efficient cars are affected differently from markets for less fuel-efficient cars, while markets for paperclips may not be impacted very much at all.

   This then creates further complications for tax policy analysts. Suppose, for instance, that the government is already taxing car sales when it contemplates the imposition of a new tax on gasoline. Tax revenue in the market for fuel-efficient cars is likely to increase as a result of an increase in the tax on gasoline as demand for such cars increases, while tax revenue is likely to decrease in markets for less fuel-efficient cars where demand drops. When new taxes or increases in existing taxes are contemplated in economies that already have many preexisting taxes, a full treatment of the economic impact of the new tax thus involves tracing the effect of the new tax through other markets that are affected. The secondary effects in these other markets may, in some cases, end up being of larger significance than the primary effect in the market for the taxed goods, which in turn can mean that a tax that looks "good" when analyzed in isolation looks "bad" in a fuller economic analysis. The reverse is, of course, also possible.[2]

Suppose the tax on fuel-efficient cars is low and the tax on gas-guzzling cars is high. Is it likely that our partial equilibrium estimate of a tax on gasoline will cause us to over- or underestimate the full impact on government revenues?

**Exercise
19A.8**

19A.2 Deadweight Loss from Taxation Revisited

Market demand and supply curves are full descriptions of predicted behavioral changes induced by price changes. As such, they are the appropriate tools with which to predict the economic incidence of taxes and subsidies; i.e., how much prices paid by buyers and received by sellers will change, as well as the impact of such policies on market output. However, as we already began to discuss in Chapter 10, these are not necessarily the appropriate curves to use for an analysis of changes in welfare.

   In particular, we know that consumer surplus (and changes in consumer surplus) can be measured as areas underneath marginal willingness to pay (or compensated demand) curves. Only when these curves are the same as regular (uncompensated) demand curves can the market demand curves be used to measure consumer surplus. And we furthermore know from our work in Chapter 10 that compensated and uncompensated demand curves are the same only when tastes for the underlying good are quasilinear. It is for this reason that we assumed quasilinear tastes in the previous chapter where we identified consumer surplus along (uncompensated) market demand curves. If we know that tastes for the underlying good are either normal or inferior, we have already demonstrated in Graph 10.9 how deadweight loss on the consumer side will be over or underestimated if welfare changes are measured on uncompensated demand curves.

   We will then begin our analysis of the full welfare impact on both buyers and sellers by initially once again assuming that tastes are quasilinear, and thus the market demand curve can be

---

[2]An analysis of the types of effects hinted at is often referred to as "second best" analysis. While we are implicitly assuming that our analysis starts in a "first best" world of full efficiency, a "second best" analysis starts with a model in which new taxes are introduced into a "second best" world where there already exist tax distortions elsewhere.

used to calculate consumer surplus in goods markets. We will then proceed to demonstrate cases in which quasilinearity is clearly the wrong assumption, and we will show how an analysis of welfare changes from taxation will necessarily lead to large policy mistakes if conducted as if tastes were indeed quasilinear.

19A.2.1 Deadweight Loss from Taxes and Subsidies when Tastes Are Quasilinear

Graph 19.5 illustrates the economic effect of a tax t in panel (a) and of a subsidy s in panel (b) along the lines discussed in the previous section. Assuming for now that tastes are quasilinear and demand curves can therefore be interpreted as compensated demand curves, changes in consumer and producer surplus are then easily identified much as we identified such changes in the previous chapter.

In panel (a), an initial consumer surplus of $(a + b + c)$ shrinks to (a) as consumers face the higher after-tax price p_d while producer surplus shrinks from $(d + e + f)$ to (f) as producers face the lower after-tax price p_s. The government earns no tax revenue before the tax but gets area $(b + d)$ after it is imposed. The overall surplus in society therefore falls from the initial $(a + b + c + d + e + f)$ to an after-tax $(a + b + d + f)$, leaving us with a deadweight loss of $(c + e)$ represented by the shaded blue area in Graph 19.5a.

For the subsidy in panel (b), on the other hand, both consumers and producers are better off after the subsidy but the government incurs a cost that we also have to take into account. Consumer surplus rises from the initial $(g + h)$ to the final $(g + h + i + n + m)$ as consumers now face a lower price, while producer surplus rises from the initial $(i + j)$ to the final $(h + i + j + k)$ as producers now sell goods at a higher price. The cost of the subsidy, however, is the per-unit subsidy rate times the number of units transacted, or (sx^s), which is represented by the area $(h + i + k + l + m + n)$. Adding consumer and producer surpluses and subtracting the cost of the subsidy (which is zero before its imposition), we then get an overall surplus that falls from an initial $(g + h + i + j)$ to a final $(g + h + i + j - l)$, giving a deadweight loss of area (l) represented by the magenta triangle in Graph 19.5b. Once we know we can identify deadweight loss from taxation or subsidies as triangles to the left and right of the pure market equilibrium, we can then easily see how the size of the deadweight loss is impacted by price elasticities of demand and supply. For instance, looking across the three panels of Graph 19.4,

Graph 19.5: Deadweight Loss when Tastes Are Quasilinear

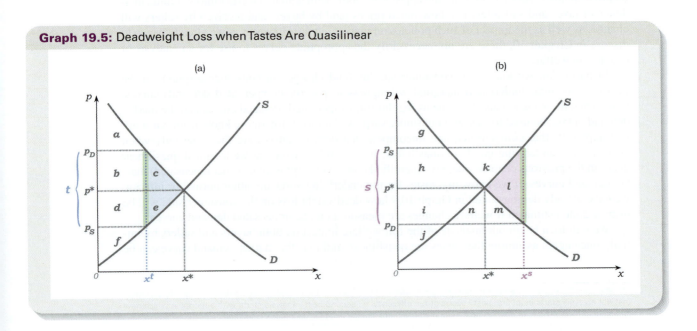

the deadweight loss triangle represented as the triangle next to the shaded rectangles clearly shrinks as demand and supply become more price inelastic. In fact, were one of the two market curves completely inelastic, the deadweight loss triangle would disappear entirely and the tax would be efficient. The same is true for deadweight losses from subsidies.

If you have covered deadweight losses from taxation in a previous economics course, chances are that you learned to read deadweight loss exactly as we just described. Remember, however, that the analysis we have just done is valid only if the tastes for the underlying goods are quasi-linear because only then are compensated and uncompensated demand curves the same. As we already demonstrated in Chapter 10, we will either over or underestimate deadweight loss if we use uncompensated demand curves when goods are either inferior or normal. Awareness of the difference between compensated and uncompensated curves becomes even more important, however, as we analyze taxes in labor and capital markets where the way we have just illustrated deadweight loss is almost certainly quite incorrect.

19A.2.2 Deadweight Loss from Taxes in Labor and Capital Markets   Most of the tax revenue raised by governments comes from taxation of income derived either from labor or from investments (i.e., savings). Such taxes alter the opportunity cost of leisure (in the case of taxes on labor income) or the opportunity cost of consuming now or in the future (in the case of taxation of savings). And we have demonstrated before that such taxes (typically) give rise to opposing wealth and substitution effects for labor or capital supply, thus causing (uncompensated) labor and capital supply curves to at least partially hide the substitution effects that give rise to deadweight losses from taxation.

Suppose, for instance, that you were told that all workers are unresponsive to changes in their wage; i.e., as wage changes, they continue to work the same number of hours. This would imply that the market supply curve for labor is perfectly inelastic as depicted by the vertical supply curve S in Graph 19.6a. Inserting the market labor demand curve D then yields an equilibrium wage w^*. If the government now imposes a per labor hour tax of t in this market, there would be no impact on the number of hours workers worked, nor would there be any change in the wage that employers had to pay workers per hour. However, because of the inelasticity of labor supply, workers would end up bearing the entire burden of the tax and would receive an after-tax wage $(w^* - t)$. And the government would raise revenues equal to the blue shaded area in panel (a) of the graph. All of this is sound economic analysis using exactly the right market curves to predict the economic impact of the tax.

But notice that there is no triangle next to the box that indicates tax revenue, which would lead many to conclude that there is no deadweight loss. It is at this point, however, that the market demand and supply curves become misleading because there is almost certainly a deadweight loss that is obscured in Graph 19.6a. And, if there is a deadweight loss, it has to lie on the worker (or supply) side of the labor market since the wage rate paid by producers is unaffected by the tax.

Consider, then, the underlying consumer choice picture that gives rise to individual labor supply curves and, when aggregated across all workers, to market labor supply. This picture is depicted in Graph 19.6b where leisure hours are on the horizontal and dollars of consumption on the vertical axis. The fact that the entire economic incidence of the tax falls on workers in this case (as seen from panel (a)) implies that worker budget constraints shrink from the initial blue budget with slope $-w^*$ to the new magenta budget with slope $-(w^* - t)$.

If workers are indeed unresponsive to changes in wages, then the worker depicted in panel (b) of the graph will make the same leisure choice on the initial and the final budget. Panel (b) labels the after-tax choice as A and the before-tax choice as C, with C lying exactly above A due to the inelasticity of the worker's behavior. When we then add the indifference curve u^A (that makes point A optimal after the imposition of the tax) and introduce the green compensated budget (that keeps utility at u^A but leaves the wage at the before-tax level), we see that the lack of change in worker behavior is due to fully offsetting substitution and wealth effects.

Now notice the following: The green compensated budget is equivalent to a lump sum tax that makes the worker just as well off at B as the wage tax does at point A. However, the lump sum tax raises revenue equal to the distance between the parallel blue and green budgets, while the wage tax raises revenue equal to the vertical distance between A and C. Put differently, the lump sum tax raises revenue L while the wage tax raises only revenue T, implying a deadweight loss equal to the difference between the two quantities illustrated as DWL in the graph.

Why is there a deadweight loss in panel (b) for the individual worker we are modeling but no deadweight loss triangle in panel (a)? It is because deadweight losses on the worker side of the market arise only from substitution effects that are obscured by the counteracting wealth effect when (uncompensated) labor supply is derived as perfectly inelastic. Panel (c) then presents the uncompensated and compensated labor supply curves for these workers within the same graph, illustrating a perfectly inelastic (uncompensated) labor supply curve but an upward sloping compensated labor supply (that represents the change in labor choices for workers whose utility is kept at u^A). The former includes both the wealth and substitution effect, while the latter includes only the substitution effect (much as marginal willingness to pay—or compensated demand—curves for consumers only contain substitution effects).

Under the wage tax, the workers settle at point A in Graph 19.6c and receive a wage of $(w^* - t)$. With worker surplus measured along the compensated supply curve (just as consumer surplus is measured along compensated demand curves), this gives an after-tax surplus of (b). Under the lump sum tax that leaves the workers just as well off, they would end up at point B earning a wage w^*. This would give them a worker surplus of $(a + b + c)$, $(a + c)$ greater than the surplus at point A. However, at point A the workers had already paid the wage tax (a) (equal to the shaded blue area), while at point B we have not yet taken into account the fact that the workers have paid a lump sum tax that makes them just as happy as they would be at A. Since workers are equally happy at the two points (as seen in panel (b)) but have a surplus $(a + c)$ greater at B than at A, it must be that the lump sum tax raises $(a + c)$ in revenue. This leaves a difference (c) between the wage tax revenue and the lump sum tax revenue that both leave the workers equally well off, implying $DWL = c$.

Of course, labor supply is not always perfectly inelastic and may even be downward sloping for some workers, but notice that the direction of the substitution effect always implies that the

Graph 19.6: Deadweight Loss from Wage Taxes when Labor Supply Is Perfectly Inelastic

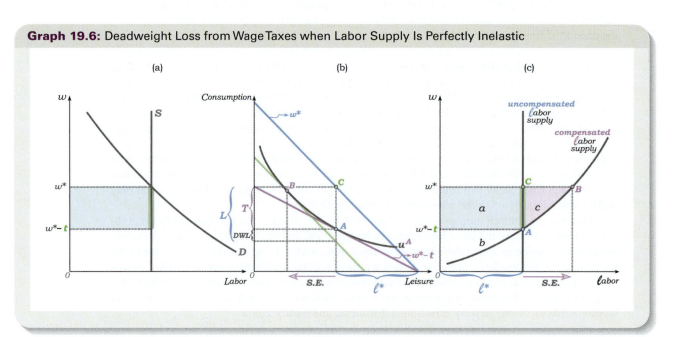

compensated labor supply curve is upward sloping. As a result, whether one can see it or not in a picture of market equilibrium in the labor market, wage taxes will have deadweight losses so long as there is any substitutability at all between leisure and consumption (which there almost certainly is).

Illustrate, using an analogous set of steps we just used as we worked our way through Graph 19.6, how wage subsidies are inefficient even when workers are completely unresponsive to changes in wages. (*Hint:* If you get stuck, read the next section and come back.)

Exercise 19A.9*

19A.2.3 Deadweight Losses from Subsidies in Labor or Capital Markets

We can show a similar error that may arise when we use the (uncompensated) savings-interest rate relationship, which represents the supply curve for financial capital, to predict the welfare effect of savings subsidies. Consider, for instance, the case where individuals are completely unresponsive to changes in the rate of return to savings—they always put the same amount into the savings account. This gives a perfectly inelastic supply curve for capital as presented in panel (a) of Graph 19.7. When a subsidy for saving is now introduced, the entire benefit of the subsidy accrues to savers as their rate of return jumps from the initial equilibrium interest rate r^* to the new interest rate $(r^* + s)$ that includes the per unit subsidy s.[3] The shaded blue area is then the cost incurred by the government, with no change in the capital saved given the inelastic response by savers.

Once again it appears as if there is no deadweight loss triangle and the subsidy is therefore efficient. But again this is not true because the capital supply curve obscures the very substitution effects that are responsible for the inefficiencies of subsidies. We can show this most easily by

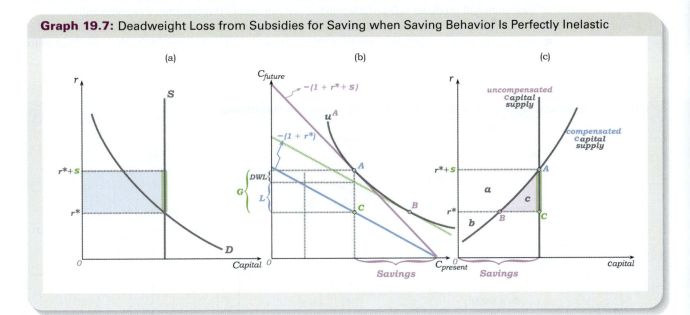

Graph 19.7: Deadweight Loss from Subsidies for Saving when Saving Behavior Is Perfectly Inelastic

---

[3]If you have trouble seeing why this economic incidence of the subsidy emerges, try first graphing the impact of a subsidy (as we did earlier in this chapter) for the case where the supply curve is almost but not quite perfectly inelastic. Then make the supply curve increasingly inelastic until you see Graph 19.7a emerge.

illustrating the case of a single saver who exhibits inelastic saving behavior in panel (b) of the graph. The subsidy changes the budget from the original blue to the final magenta, with A optimal after the subsidy and C optimal before (and with both bundles exhibiting exactly the same level of savings). Next, we can put in the indifference curve u^A that makes point A optimal after the subsidy raises the rate of return to savings, and we can put in the compensated green budget that results in the same utility as this saver gets at A but at the before-tax interest rate. The reason for the inelastic behavioral response for this worker is that the substitution effect is fully covered up by an equally large and opposite wealth effect.

But we can also see in this graph that this subsidy is inefficient. The total government cost of paying the subsidy to this one saver can be measured as the vertical distance between A and C and is labeled G. At the same time, we can see from the difference between the blue and green budgets that a lump sum subsidy of L would make this individual exactly as well off as the distortionary subsidy that cost G. The difference between G and L is the deadweight loss for this one saver.

Translating points A, B, and C to a graph with capital on the horizontal axis and the rate of return on the vertical, we can then see what goes wrong when we try to find this deadweight loss in panel (a) of the graph. More specifically, in panel (c) of the graph we illustrate the vertical (uncompensated) capital supply curve that is formed from points A and C in panel (b), but we also illustrate the *compensated* capital supply curve (derived from A and B in panel (b)) that corresponds to the utility level u^A. Using this compensated curve, we can identify the saver surplus as $(a + b)$ under the distortionary subsidy and as just (b) under the lump sum subsidy (at point B). Since this saver is equally happy at A and B, the lump sum subsidy at B must be equal to (a). But the distortionary subsidy cost $(a + c)$, which is (c) more than the lump sum subsidy that made the saver just as well off. Thus, the DWL distance in panel (b) is analogous to the magenta area (c) in panel (c).

19A.2.4 DWL and Revenue as Tax Rates Rise

In Chapter 10, we illustrated the idea that, on the consumer side of the market, as tax rates rise by a factor of k, deadweight loss increases by approximately k^2. Now that we are familiar with the process by which taxes affect both the consumer and producer sides of the market, we can extend this intuition more generally.

Consider, for instance, the market demand and supply curves in Graph 19.8a, and, to keep the analysis as simple as possible, suppose that tastes for good x are quasilinear, thus allowing us to

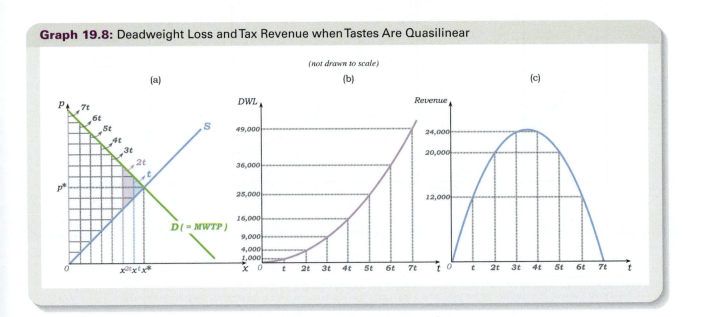

Graph 19.8: Deadweight Loss and Tax Revenue when Tastes Are Quasilinear

assume that the market demand curve is equivalent to the aggregate marginal willingness to pay curve. The market price in the absence of taxes is then $p*$. If a per-unit tax of t is imposed, the market output drops from $x*$ to x^t, with prices for consumers rising and prices for producers falling. The deadweight loss from this tax would be equivalent to the blue triangle, with half of the deadweight loss falling on the consumer side of the market and half falling on the producer side. Then suppose that the tax is doubled to $2t$, thus raising the price for consumers, decreasing the price for producers, and leading to the output x^{2t}. Now the deadweight loss increases by the shaded magenta area.

Suppose that each triangle, such as the two triangles that form the initial blue deadweight loss when the tax is t, is equal to $500. This implies that each square, such as the squares contained in the magenta area, is equal to $1,000. Adding these up, we then get that the deadweight loss associated with the initial tax t is $1,000, while the deadweight loss associated with the tax $2t$ is $4,000. A doubling of the tax leads to a quadrupling of the deadweight loss. We can then keep increasing the tax, to $3t$, $4t$, going all the way to $7t$, and by adding up the relevant deadweight loss areas, we can derive the relationship between the tax rate and the deadweight loss in panel (b) of Graph 19.8. The graph illustrates that it is indeed still the case that, with the linear demand and supply curves graphed in panel (a), deadweight loss rises by a factor of k^2 whenever the tax rate increases by a factor of k.

How large does deadweight loss get if the tax rate rises to $3t$? What if it rises to $4t$?	**Exercise 19A.10**

We can similarly trace out the tax revenue collected by the government as the tax increases. When the tax rate is set at t, the tax revenue is tx^t, which is equal to 12 squares in panel (a) or equivalent to $12,000 when each square represents $1,000. Similarly, when the tax rate is $2t$, the tax revenue is $2tx^{2t}$ or $20,000. The relationship between the tax rate and tax revenue that then emerges in panel (c) of the graph has an inverse U-shape, with tax revenue equal to zero when there is no tax and equal to zero once again when the tax becomes sufficiently high. This is another version of what we previously called the *Laffer Curve* that suggests governments will ultimately lose revenue if tax rates get too high.

While we are illustrating this in a stylized graph of linear demand and supply curves that lead to an equal sharing of economic tax incidence between consumers and producers, the intuitions are applicable more generally (even if the precise relationship between tax rates, deadweight loss, and tax revenue will differ somewhat). As a result, the simple intuition (first discussed in Chapter 10) emerging from these graphs has often led to the general advice from economists to governments that it is more efficient to levy low rates on large tax bases rather then high tax rates on small tax bases.

Illustrate the relationship between subsidy rates, the deadweight loss from a subsidy, and the cost of the subsidy using the same initial graph of supply and demand as in Graph 19.8a in graphs analogous to panels (b) and (c) of Graph 19.8.	**Exercise 19A.11**

19A.3 Taxing Land: An Efficient Real-World Tax

At this point, you may have given up your search for a fully efficient tax. As we have demonstrated, it is not sufficient for demand or supply relationships in general to be fully inelastic for a tax to be efficient, because inelastic behavioral relationships with respect to price may well mask underlying substitution effects that make taxes inefficient. There is, however, a tax that economists have identified as an efficient tax because of the existence of a price-inelastic relationship that does not mask such substitution effects. This tax is a tax on land value or on land rents.

Land value is simply the market price of land, while a *land rent* is the income (or utility) one can derive from a particular quantity of land over a particular time period. While land value and land rents are therefore different concepts, they are closely connected. After all, the reason land has value is that the owner of the land can derive land rents every year. It is easiest to discuss this in terms of farm land, but the general lesson applies more generally to all forms of land whether the land is used for farming, production of non-farm goods, or housing. What makes land special is that it is not itself something that is produced, and it therefore exists in essentially fixed supply.[4]

19A.3.1 The Relationship between Land Value and Land Rents

Sometimes I get sick of talking about economics all the time and yearn to reconnect with the land in ways that my wife does not fully appreciate. Suppose, however, that I convince her to move to Iowa and buy 100 acres of farm land. I can now derive annual income from this land by either producing potatoes directly or by renting it out to someone else who will produce potatoes. For it to be worth it to farm the land myself, I have to receive compensation that covers the opportunity cost of my time and the opportunity cost of the land that I will be using. The opportunity cost of my time is determined by what other market opportunities I have; perhaps my other alternative is teaching economics, which carries with it a certain level of compensation. The opportunity cost of using the land, on the other hand, is the income I could derive from the land by just renting it to someone else. How much I can rent the land for in the market of course depends on the quality of the land and on how much someone else would be able to make with it.

Suppose, for instance, I could rent the 100 acres in the market for $10,000 per year and my time is worth $100,000 per year. Then in order for me to farm the land myself, I will have to be able to generate at least $110,000 in income by farming the land; otherwise, I am better off making $100,000 elsewhere and collecting $10,000 in rent. In equilibrium, only those who are relatively good at farming will end up making the choice to be farmers and the rest of us will do something else. And if farming is a competitive industry, those who engage in farming will make zero profits and thus exactly an amount equal to their opportunity cost of time plus the rent they have to pay for the land (whether they are paying it explicitly or whether they simply forego collecting rents from others if they own the land themselves).

Put differently, the land itself produces an income stream of $10,000 per year: the annual land rent, which we will assume that we collect at the end of each year. But the *value* of the land, how much I could sell it for in the market, is based on not only this year's income stream but also all future income streams that can be produced from this land. In Chapter 3, we discussed how such future income streams are evaluated in the presence of interest rates. If, for instance, the annual interest rate is r (expressed in decimal form), then $10,000 one year from now is worth ($10,000/(1 + r)$) and $10,000 n years from now is worth ($10,000/(1 + r)^n$). The *value of land is then the present discounted value of all future land rents*, or simply ($10,000/(1 + r)$) (from the rent derived a year from now for this year's rent) plus ($10,000/(1 + r)^2$) (from the rent derived two years from now) and so forth. It turns out that when all land rents into the future are added up in this way, the resulting land value is equal to ($10,000/r$). Or, put more generally, land value LV is related to land rents LR according to the formula

$$LV = \frac{LR}{(1 + r)} + \frac{LR}{(1 + r)^2} \cdots = \frac{LR}{r}. \tag{19.1}$$

---

[4]There are instances when land is actually "produced," such as in The Netherlands where significant amounts of land have been "reclaimed" from the sea in a complex system of dams and levies, or in the Florida Everglades where marsh land is converted to usable land for housing. Even in these instances, however, the land itself simply existed before "improvements" of that land made it usable for production or consumption.

19A.3.2 Taxation of Land Rents   Now suppose that the government requires landowners to pay 50% of their land rents as a tax. We will call this here a 50% land rent tax. Graph 19.9 illustrates the market for renting a particular type of land, say land of a particular quality in Iowa. Such land is in fixed supply, which implies that the supply curve is completely inelastic. As a result, the economic incidence of the tax is fully on land owners who are renting the land to farmers (or to themselves if they themselves are farming), with the annual rental value that land owners get to keep dropping by 50% (while the rent paid by renters remains unchanged).

As the current owner of the land, I will have no choice but to accept a lower (after-tax) rental price for my land. I may get very upset at this, and I may try to instead sell the land, but remember that the value of land is simply equal to the present discounted value of all future land rents. Since all future (after-tax) land rents have just fallen by 50%, this implies that the value of my land has just fallen from ($LR*/r$) to ($0.5LR*/r$). In other words, the 50% tax on land rents has caused the value of an asset that I own to decline by 50%, and I have no way to substitute to anything else and avoid the tax. If I continue to hold on to the land, I will make 50% less on it every year, and if I decide to sell it I will make 50% less now and forego any future rents. In present value terms, I am equally well off whether I hold on to the land, whether I sell it, or whether I hold on to it for a little while and then sell it.

You might think that perhaps I can make myself better off by turning around and using the land for something else, but if the tax is truly on (unimproved) land rents, it is independent of what exactly is being done with the land because only the value of the unimproved land is taxed. Whether I use it for farming or for producing paperclips or for housing, a land rent tax still taxes the rental value of the land itself. So there is literally nothing I can do to prevent paying this tax in one form or another, and thus no possibility for a substitution effect to emerge and make the tax inefficient. A tax on land rent is therefore a simple transfer of wealth from landowners to the government. Land owners are worse off, but the government captures all the wealth that landowners lost. It is in part for this reason that a writer by the name of Henry George suggested over 100 years

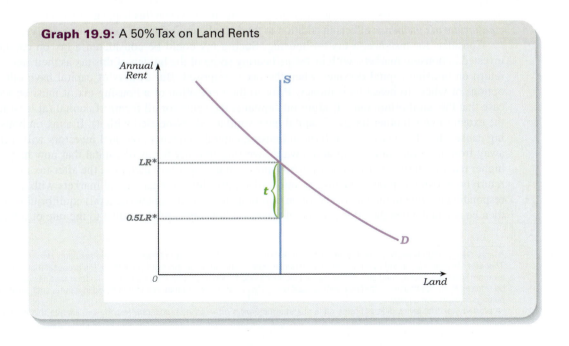

Graph 19.9: A 50% Tax on Land Rents

ago that all government expenditures should be financed by taxes on land rents. In fact, Henry George went even further and suggested that all land rents should be taxed at 100%.[5]

Exercise 19A.12   What would be the economic impact of a 100% tax on land rents (levied on owners)?

The proposal to tax land rents is a policy option that is increasingly considered in the United States by local governments that rely for much of their revenue on property taxes. Property taxes are not land rent taxes because they tax both land rents and the improvements on land (such as housing). Thus, to the extent that property taxes change the opportunity cost of improving land, such taxes may give rise to substitution effects that create inefficiencies (by diverting capital away from housing and into other uses), and local governments can move toward more efficient taxes by lowering the tax on improvements on land and increasing the tax on land itself.[6] In developing countries where much wealth is often concentrated in the hands of relatively few landowners, taxes on land rents are similarly discussed for purposes of funding government expenditures and redistributing wealth. You can learn more about land taxes and their relations to other types of taxes (such as property taxes) in courses such as Urban Economics and Public Finance.

19A.4 General versus Partial Equilibrium Tax Incidence

Our analysis of the economic incidence of a tax has thus far focused solely on partial equilibrium models where we have implicitly assumed that the incidence of a tax is confined solely within the market in which the tax is imposed. As we have seen, it does not matter whether the tax is statutorily imposed on one party or the the other—on buyers or sellers—because who ends up paying the tax within this partial equilibrium framework will depend on the relative elasticities of demand and supply curves. Put differently, we have seen that taxes are *shifted* from buyers to sellers and vice versa depending on whose economic behavior is more inelastic.

Tax shifting, however, is not always confined solely to actors within a particular market. In many instances, taxes (and tax incidence) is shifted outside the market in which a tax is imposed and onto actors in other markets that face no legal tax obligations. When this happens, there are *general equilibrium tax incidence* effects in addition to the partial equilibrium effects we have analyzed.

Consider, for instance, a tax on housing. Such a tax could be considered a tax on capital invested in housing markets, with investors bearing some of the burden of this tax as their rate of return on housing capital declines when the tax is imposed. But owners of capital have other options of where to invest their money. Prior to the imposition of a housing tax, it must be the case that the equilibrium rate of return on capital is the same for all forms of capital (at least to the extent to which other forms of capital have similar risk associated with it). If a tax on housing causes the after-tax rate of return on housing capital to decline, rational investors will shift away from investing in housing and toward investing in other forms of capital that now have a higher rate of return. An inward shift in housing capital supply will then raise the after-tax rate of return on housing capital and cause an outward supply shift in other capital markets with a corresponding decline in the rate of return on non-housing capital. A new (general) equilibrium will then be reached when the after-tax rate of return on housing capital is equal to the rate of return

---

[5]Henry George (1839–1897) made this argument in 1879 in his book *Progress and Poverty*, and the resulting *Henry George Theorem* has been formalized by a number of local public finance and urban economists since then. His proposal that all government functions be financed by a 100% tax on land rents was based in part on the philosophical notion that has come to be referred to as "Georgism"—that everyone should own what they create but that everything found in nature, such as land, belongs to everyone equally.

[6]A property tax that levies different rates on land and structures is often called a *split-rate tax*. You can analyze this in more detail in end-of-chapter exercise 19.12.

on non-housing capital. Thus, some of the incidence of the housing tax is shifted away from owners of housing capital to owners of all capital.[7]

We will see other examples of this in Chapter 20 where we will investigate the role of taxes imposed in one geographic region but not in another. As in the case of the housing tax where some of the incidence is shifted away from the housing market and toward other capital markets, we will see that taxes are also shifted from one region (where a tax is imposed) to another. Such general equilibrium effects of taxes can be extremely important and thus add a substantial layer of complexity to tax policy. If this topic is of interest to you, you should consider taking a course on public finance or public economics in your future studies of economics. For now, you should merely begin to gain some intuition for the insight that *to the extent to which taxed inputs or goods are mobile across markets, the imposition of a tax in one market will generate general equilibrium tax incidence in other markets.* This is analogous to the role of price elasticity in determining tax incidence in a partial equilibrium model: Market actors who are more "responsive" bear less of the tax burden because they can shift that burden to actors who are less "responsive." In the same way, market actors who are more "mobile" across markets are able to shift tax burdens to market actors that are less "mobile" across markets.

19B The Mathematics of Taxes (and Subsidies)

In this section, we continue our exploration of tax incidence and deadweight loss from taxation (leaving the analogous case of subsidies for end-of-chapter exercises). We begin in Section 19B.1 with a general demonstration of the relationship between tax incidence and price elasticities, proving more formally that the degree to which market participants bear the burden of a tax is increasing in the relative inelasticity of their response to price changes. In Sections 19B.2 and 19B.3, we then continue by illustrating how deadweight losses are calculated, first for the quasilinear case and then, in an application to wage taxes, more generally. While tax incidence depends on uncompensated demand and supply curves, we will see once again that deadweight loss calculations depend on compensated curves. Finally, we conclude with a very simple example of tax incidence in a more general equilibrium setting where a tax on housing is shifted to other forms of capital when capital is mobile between different sectors in the economy.

19B.1 Tax Incidence and Price Elasticities

Consider the general case where demand is given by $x_d(p)$, supply is given by $x_s(p)$, and the pre-tax equilibrium has price p^* and quantity x^*. Now suppose a small tax t (to be paid by consumers for each unit of x that is purchased) is introduced. This implies that the price p_d paid by buyers is t higher than the price p_s at which the good is purchased from suppliers; i.e., $p_d = p_s + t$. Taking the differential of this, we get

$$dp_d = dp_s + dt; \tag{19.2}$$

---

[7]The property tax, which is a tax on both land and housing, is therefore often viewed as a tax on land (which is efficient) and a tax on housing capital, which translates in general equilibrium to a tax on all capital. An alternative view of the property tax, known as the "benefit view," argues that when combined with strict zoning laws, housing becomes much more like land, and the housing portion of the property tax therefore has some of the properties of a land tax. Again, you can learn much more about these different views of the property tax in a local public finance course.

i.e., the change in the consumer price p_d is equal to the change in the producer price p_s plus the change in t. In the new equilibrium, demand has to equal supply, with each evaluated at the relevant price; i.e.,

$$x_d(p_d) = x_s(p_s). \tag{19.3}$$

Taking the differential of this, we can write

$$\frac{dx_d}{dp_d} dp_d = \frac{dx_s}{dp_s} dp_s \tag{19.4}$$

and substituting equation (19.2) into equation (19.4), this becomes

$$\frac{dx_d}{dp_d}(dp_s + dt) = \frac{dx_s}{dp_s} dp_s. \tag{19.5}$$

Rearranging terms in this equation, we can write it as

$$\left(\frac{dx_d}{dp_d} - \frac{dx_s}{dp_s} \right) dp_s = -\frac{dx_d}{dp_d} dt. \tag{19.6}$$

Before the tax is introduced, the equilibrium was at the intersection of supply and demand at p^* and x^*, which is a point on both the supply and demand curve. Multiplying equation (19.6) by p^*/x^*, it becomes

$$\left(\frac{dx_d}{dp_d} \frac{p^*}{x^*} - \frac{dx_s}{dp_s} \frac{p^*}{x^*} \right) dp_s = -\frac{dx_d}{dp_d} \frac{p^*}{x^*} dt, \tag{19.7}$$

which you should notice contains several price elasticity terms (evaluated at the pre-tax equilibrium). Rewriting the equation in terms of these price elasticities, it becomes

$$(\varepsilon_d - \varepsilon_s)dp_s = -\varepsilon_d dt, \tag{19.8}$$

where ε_d is the price elasticity of demand and ε_s is the price elasticity of supply. Rearranging terms, we can also then write this as

$$\frac{dp_s}{dt} = -\frac{\varepsilon_d}{\varepsilon_d - \varepsilon_s}. \tag{19.9}$$

What does this tell us? Suppose that supply is perfectly inelastic with $\varepsilon_s = 0$. Then the equation says that $dp_s/dt = -1$ or $dp_s = -dt$. Put into words, the producer's price adjusts by exactly the change in the tax, with the producers therefore bearing the entire burden (or incidence) of the tax. If, on the other hand, demand is perfectly inelastic ($\varepsilon_d = 0$), $dp_s/dt = 0$ or $dp_s = 0$. The producer's price does not change and the producers bear none of the incidence of the tax. This conforms entirely to the intuition we get from simple graphs. Finally, suppose that, at the initial (pre-tax) equilibrium, consumers and producers were equally responsive to price changes with price elasticities of demand and supply equal to each other in absolute value, or $\varepsilon_s = -\varepsilon_d$. Plugging this into equation (19.9), we get $dp_s/dt = 0.5$ or $dp_s = 0.5dt$; producers bear half the incidence of the tax. The equation therefore implies that *the incidence of the tax will fall disproportionately on the side of the market that is relatively less price elastic* as we concluded intuitively in Graph 19.3.

Exercise 19B.1* Demonstrate that whenever ε_d is less in absolute value than ε_s, consumers will bear more than half the incidence of the tax, and whenever the reverse is true, they will bear less than half of the incidence of the tax.

Can you show that $dp_d/dt = \varepsilon_s/(\varepsilon_s - \varepsilon_d)$? (*Hint:* Note that equation (19.2) implies $dp_d/dt = (dp_s/dt) + 1$.)

Exercise
19B.2*

One can derive similar conclusions regarding the economic incidence of subsidies, which we leave for end-of-chapter exercise 19.1.

19B.2 Deadweight Loss from Taxation when Tastes Are Quasilinear

Tax incidence in a partial equilibrium model then depends on the relative price elasticities of uncompensated demand and supply curves. Deadweight loss calculations, however, depend on elasticities of *compensated* demand and supply curves. As we know from our development of consumer theory, the difference between uncompensated and compensated relationships disappears when income effects disappear, and income effects disappear when tastes are quasilinear. We therefore begin our discussion of the mathematics of deadweight loss from taxation for the case when tastes are indeed quasilinear. As we will see, you can do this by calculating areas under demand and supply curves (as we did in part A of the chapter), but you can also employ the expenditure function we derived in Chapter 10 and thus avoid using integral calculus.

In the previous chapter, we demonstrated that when $u(x,y) = \alpha \ln x + y$, demand for the quasilinear good x is $x_d(p_x, p_y) = \alpha p_y/p_x$. You can also verify for yourself that the demand for y is given by $y_d(p_y, I) = (I - \alpha p_y)/p_y$. To focus on just good x within a partial equilibrium model, we can treat y as a composite good with $p_y = 1$, which allows us to write the demands for the two goods as

$$x_d(p) = \frac{\alpha}{p} \quad \text{and} \quad y_d(I) = I - \alpha, \tag{19.10}$$

where p now simply denotes the price of good x.

What is the price elasticity of demand for x? What is the cross-price elasticity of demand for y?

Exercise
19B.3

Suppose, then, that the demand side of the market for x can be modeled as arising from the optimization problem of a representative consumer with the above tastes and some income level I. Suppose further that the supply side of the market can be represented by the supply curve $x_s = \beta p$.

What is the price elasticity of supply?

Exercise
19B.4

Setting supply equal to demand and solving for p, we then get that the equilibrium price under no taxation is $p^* = (\alpha/\beta)^{1/2}$ and the equilibrium quantity transacted is $x^* = (\alpha\beta)^{1/2}$.

Now suppose the government imposes a per unit tax t on producers, implying that producers will receive a price $(p_d - t)$ when consumers pay p_d. The new equilibrium then requires that supply evaluated at the producer price equals demand evaluated at the consumer price; i.e., $\beta(p_d - t) = \alpha/p_d$. Multiplying both sides of this equation by p_d and subtracting α, we get

$\beta p_d^2 - \beta t p_d - \alpha = 0$, which, by the quadratic formula,[8] implies a new equilibrium price paid by consumers of

$$p_d = \frac{\beta t + \sqrt{(\beta t)^2 + 4\beta\alpha}}{2\beta} = \frac{t + \sqrt{t^2 + 4(\alpha/\beta)}}{2} \tag{19.11}$$

with corresponding equilibrium price for producers (net of tax obligations) of

$$p_s = p_d - t = \frac{-t + \sqrt{t^2 + 4(\alpha/\beta)}}{2}. \tag{19.12}$$

Suppose, for instance, that $\alpha = 1{,}000$ and $\beta = 10$. The resulting demand and supply curves (and their inverses) are then drawn in Graph 19.10, with before and after tax prices and quantities calculated using the previous equations and assuming $t = 10$. From what we have done in Section A, we know that (since tastes for x are quasilinear), consumer surplus shrinks from the original area $(a + b + c)$ to just (a) while producer surplus shrinks from $(d + e + f)$ to just (f) while tax revenue grows from zero to area $(b + d)$, leaving a deadweight loss of $(c + e)$.

19B.2.1 Calculating Deadweight Loss Using Integrals
If you are comfortable with basic integral calculus, we can then calculate changes in consumer and producer surpluses using integrals to calculate the appropriate areas under the curves. (If you are not comfortable with integral calculus, you can skip to Section 19B.2.2.) Using the functions graphed in panel (b) of Graph 19.10, the change in consumer surplus $(b + c)$ is

$$\Delta CS = \int_{p^*}^{p_d} x_d(p)dp = \int_{p^*}^{p_d} \frac{\alpha}{p}\, dp \tag{19.13}$$

$$= \alpha(\ln p_d - \ln p^*) = 1{,}000(\ln (16.18) - \ln (10)) \approx 481$$

Graph 19.10: Welfare Changes with Quasilinear Demand

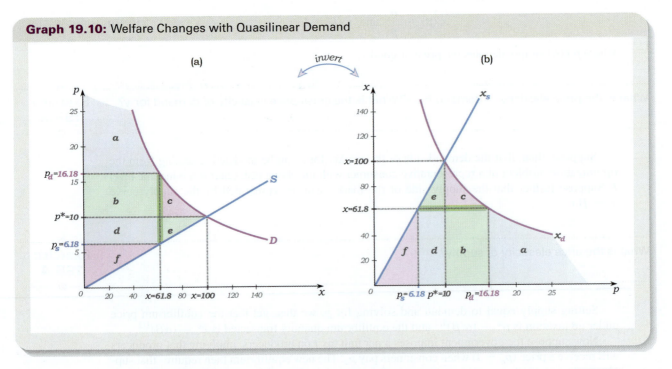

---

[8]Recall that the quadratic formula gives two solutions to the equation $ax^2 + bx + c = 0$: $x = (-b - \sqrt{b^2 - 4ac})/2a$ and $x = (-b + \sqrt{b^2 - 4ac})/2a$. It is the latter that is relevant for our particular problem.

and the change in producer surplus ($d + e$) as

$$\Delta PS = \int_{p_s}^{p^*} x_s(p)dp = \int_{p_s}^{p^*} (\beta p)dp = \frac{\beta}{2}((p^*)^2 - p_s^2) = 5(10^2 - 6.18^2) \approx 309. \quad (19.14)$$

Exercise 19B.5 Can you verify that our answer for ΔPS is correct by simply calculating the area of the rectangle (d) and the triangle (e) in Graph 19.10?

Summing the change in producer and consumer surplus, we then get a total loss of surplus equal to approximately $790. The tax revenue collected by the government is equal to the $10 per unit tax times the 61.8 units sold under the tax, or approximately $618. This gives us a dead-weight loss of approximately $172.

19B.2.2 Calculating Deadweight Loss Using the Expenditure Function

In Chapter 10, we also developed an alternative way of calculating the change in consumer surplus using the expenditure function. In particular, we concluded that the ΔCS (area ($b + c$)) is equal to the maximum lump sum tax the representative consumer would be willing to pay to avoid having the distortionary tax imposed. Plugging the demands $x_d(p)$ and $y_d(I)$ from equation (19.10) into the utility function $u(x,y) = \alpha \ln x + y$, we can derive the indirect utility function $V(p,I) = \alpha \ln (\alpha/p) + I - \alpha.$[9] Inverting this and replacing V with a utility value u, we can then get the expenditure function

$$E(p,u) = u + \alpha - \alpha \ln \frac{\alpha}{p}. \quad (19.15)$$

Exercise 19B.6 Can you derive this expenditure function more directly through an expenditure minimization problem?

The representative consumer's utility under the distortionary tax is

$$u_t = V(p_d,I) = \alpha \ln x_d(p_d) + y_d(I) = \alpha \ln \frac{\alpha}{p_d} + (I - \alpha), \quad (19.16)$$

and the expenditure necessary to reach that utility level u_t without distorting prices is

$$E(p^*,u_t) = u_t + \alpha - \alpha \ln \frac{\alpha}{p^*} = \alpha\left(\ln \frac{\alpha}{p_d} - \ln \frac{\alpha}{p^*} \right) + I$$
$$= \alpha(\ln \alpha - \ln p_d - (\ln \alpha - \ln p^*)) + I = \alpha(\ln p^* - \ln p_d) + I \quad (19.17)$$
$$= \alpha \ln \left(\frac{p^*}{p_d}\right) + I,$$

where we use the property of logarithms that $\ln (a/b) = \ln a - \ln b$.

Exercise 19B.7 Can you verify that the expenditure necessary to reach the after-tax utility at the pre-tax price is always less than (or equal to) I?

Exercise 19B.8 What has to be true for $E(p^*,u_t) = I$ to hold?

[9]Because of the underlying quasilinearity in x, it does not matter in this case what income level we pick so long as it does not result in a corner solution. In our case, there is an interior solution so long as $I > \alpha$.

Finally, the maximum lump sum amount our representative consumer is willing to give up to avoid the distortionary tax (area $(b + c)$ in Graph 19.10) is the difference between the consumer's income and $E(p^*, u_t)$; i.e.,

$$\Delta CS = I - E(p^*, u_t) = I - \left(\alpha \ln \left(\frac{p^*}{p_d} \right) + I \right)$$

$$= -\alpha \ln \left(\frac{p^*}{p_d} \right) = -1{,}000 \ln \left(\frac{10}{16.18} \right) \approx 481.$$

(19.18)

Exercise 19B.9

Can you show that in general, before substituting in specific pre- and post-tax prices, equation (19.13) (which we derived using integral calculus) and equation (19.18) (which we derived using the expenditure function) yield identical results?

The representative consumer is therefore willing to pay $481 in a lump sum amount in order to avoid the tax. The consumer's share of tax revenue, however, is only $6.18(61.8) \approx 382, implying a deadweight loss of approximately $99 on the consumer side of the market. On the producer side, we could similarly calculate profit before and after the tax and then compare the change in profit to the tax actually paid by producers. In our example, however, the supply curve is linear, and we can see in Graph 19.10 that the deadweight loss on the producer side is simply the triangle (e), which is $(100 - 61.8)(10 - 6.18)/2 \approx 73. Summing the deadweight losses from the two sides of the market, we get an overall deadweight loss of approximately $172 (just as we did when we used integrals in the previous section).

Table 19.1 then illustrates the impact of different levels of per unit taxes for this example. Notice that, as we have noted numerous times before, deadweight loss increases at a significantly faster rate than the tax rate. However, because the price elasticity of demand is -1 everywhere (as you should have concluded in exercise 19B.3), no tax rate is ever high enough to fully shut down the market. In fact, given what we learned about the relationship between price elasticity of demand and consumer spending, we know that a price elasticity of -1 implies that consumers

Table 19.1: $x_d(p) = 1{,}000/p$, $x_s(p) = 10p$

			Welfare Changes from Per-Unit Tax				
t	p_d	p_s	$x_d = x_s$	ΔCS	ΔPS	Revenue	DWL
0	$10.00	$10.00	100.00	$0.00	$0.00	$0.00	$0.00
1	$10.51	$9.51	95.12	$49.98	$47.56	$95.12	$2.42
2	$11.05	$9.05	90.50	$99.83	$90.50	$181.00	$9.34
3	$11.61	$8.61	86.12	$149.44	$129.18	$258.36	$20.27
4	$12.20	$8.20	81.98	$198.69	$163.96	$327.92	$34.73
5	$12.81	$7.81	78.08	$247.47	$195.19	$390.39	$52.27
10	$16.18	$6.18	61.80	$481.21	$309.02	$618.08	$172.19
25	$28.51	$3.51	35.08	$1,047.59	$438.48	$876.95	$609.12
50	$51.93	$1.93	19.26	$1,647.23	$481.46	$962.91	$1,165.76
100	$100.99	$0.99	9.90	$2,312.44	$495.10	$990.20	$1,817.34
1000	$1,000.10	$0.10	1.00	$4,605.27	$499.95	$999.90	$4,105.32

will always spend the same amount on their consumption of x regardless of price, which further implies that tax revenue always increases with higher tax rates.

Does the Laffer Curve in this example have a peak? Why or why not?

Exercise 19B.10

When the tastes are not quasilinear, substitution effects will cause the compensated demand curve to differ from the uncompensated demand, implying that welfare changes (and deadweight loss) cannot be measured along the market demand curve. We will encounter this in the next section in our example of labor markets, and we treat it in the context of goods markets in end-of-chapter exercise 19.2. In cases like this, you can, however, use the same expenditure function method we developed here to calculate the change in consumer surplus.

19B.3 Deadweight Loss from Taxes in Labor (and Capital) Markets

Now suppose we return to the example of workers with Cobb–Douglas tastes over leisure and consumption (as introduced in Chapter 9) represented by the utility function $u(c,\ell) = c^{\alpha}\ell^{(1-\alpha)}$. Given leisure endowment L, this implies demand for leisure and consumption of

$$\ell = (1 - \alpha)L \text{ and } c = \alpha wL. \tag{19.19}$$

Since labor supply is simply leisure endowment minus leisure consumption, this then implies a perfectly inelastic labor supply function

$$l_s = L - (1 - \alpha)L = \alpha L. \tag{19.20}$$

Verify that this labor supply function has zero wage elasticity of supply.

Exercise 19B.11

Suppose, for instance, that a worker has 60 leisure hours per week ($L = 60$) and that $\alpha = 2/3$. Then the labor supply function implies that the worker will work 40 hours per week regardless of wage. If there are 1,000 workers in this labor market, with each having the same leisure endowment and the same tastes, this further implies a vertical market supply of labor at 60,000 hours per week. Suppose further that the market demand for labor is given by $l_d(w) = 25{,}000{,}000/w^2$. Setting this equal to the inelastic labor supply of 60,000, we can derive an equilibrium wage of $w^* = 25$.

What is the wage elasticity of labor demand?

Exercise 19B.12

19B.3.1 Calculating Deadweight Loss in the Labor Market
Now suppose a wage tax of \$10 per labor hour is imposed as an additional cost on producers. Given the perfectly inelastic labor supply in this market, this drives the equilibrium wage down to \$15, leaving producers entirely unaffected (given that they now pay a wage of \$15 plus a \$10 tax for a total of \$25 per worker hour as before). We can then focus entirely on the worker side of the market to determine deadweight loss from the tax.

Consider an individual worker who continues to work 40 hours per week under the lower wage. To determine the deadweight loss from the tax for this particular worker, we can ask the question (as we have throughout this book): How much could we have taken from this worker in a lump sum way and left him just as well off as he is when his wage drops from \$25 to \$15? Or, more generally, how much could we have taken in a lump sum way to make the worker just as well off as he is when his wage declines from w^* to $(w^* - t)$?

To answer this question, we first have to determine how happy the worker is under the tax t. Since the worker will always consume $(1 - \alpha)L$ in leisure, his consumption is given by $\alpha(w^* - t)L$. Plugging these values into his utility function, we get utility u_t under a tax t of

$$u_t = \Big(\alpha(w^* - t)L\Big)^\alpha\Big((1 - \alpha)L\Big)^{(1-\alpha)} = \alpha^\alpha(1 - \alpha)^{(1-\alpha)}(w^* - t)^\alpha L. \qquad (19.21)$$

Next, we have to determine how much expenditure would be necessary to achieve this utility level u_t if the wage were still w^*. The expenditure function emerges from the worker's expenditure minimization problem

$$\min_{c,\ell} E = w\ell + c \text{ subject to } u_t = c^\alpha\ell^{(1-\alpha)}. \qquad (19.22)$$

Solving this in the usual way, we first get the compensated leisure and consumption demands

$$\ell^c(w) = \left(\frac{1 - \alpha}{\alpha w}\right)^\alpha u_t \text{ and } c^c(w) = \left(\frac{\alpha w}{1 - \alpha}\right)^{(1-\alpha)} u_t, \qquad (19.23)$$

and, plugging these back into $E = w\ell + c$, the expenditure function

$$E(w, u_t) = \frac{w^{(1-\alpha)}u_t}{\alpha^\alpha(1 - \alpha)^{(1-\alpha)}}. \qquad (19.24)$$

Exercise 19B.13 Verify this.

For instance, in our example of a worker with $\alpha = 2/3$ and $L = 60$ facing a tax that decreases his wage from $w^* = 25$ to $(w^* - t) = 15$, we can use equation (19.21) to calculate his after-tax utility as $u_t \approx 193.1$. Plugging this into equation (19.24), we get that the expenditure necessary to achieve this utility level in the absence of taxes is $E(w^*, u_t) \approx 1{,}067.07$. Since the value of the worker's leisure endowment is \$1,500 (i.e., his leisure endowment of 60 hours times the wage of \$25), this implies we could have raised approximately \$432.93 from the worker in a lump sum way and kept him just as happy as he was under the \$10 tax. But under the \$10 wage tax, we raised only \$400 from him, implying a deadweight loss of approximately \$32.93. With 1,000 workers in this market, the overall deadweight loss is therefore approximately \$32,930.

More generally, we can then write the expression for deadweight loss per worker as

$$DWL(t) = [w^*L - E(w^*, u_t)] - \Big(tl_s(w - t)\Big) \qquad (19.25)$$

where the term in brackets is the amount we could have raised in a lump sum way without making the worker worse off than he is under the tax and the term outside the brackets is the actual tax revenue from the wage tax.

Exercise 19B.14 Can you find in a graph such as panel (b) of Graph 19.6 the various numbers we just calculated?

Table 19.2 then illustrates the welfare and revenue effects of different levels of wage taxes for this example.

19B.3.2 Using Compensated Labor Supply to Calculate Deadweight Loss
In panel (c) of Graph 19.6, we argued that there was an alternative way of identifying deadweight loss as an area on the compensated labor supply curve. This will, however, once again involve the use of integral calculus, and if you are not comfortable with this approach, you can once again

Table 19.2: $u(c, \ell) = c^{\alpha}\ell^{(1-\alpha)}$, $\alpha = 2/3$, $\ell = 60$

				Per Worker Welfare Changes from Per-Hour Wage Tax				
t	$(w^* - t)$	$l_s(w^* - t)$	$l_s^c(w^*)$	u_t	$E(w^*, u_t)$	Δ Surplus	Revenue	DWL
0	$25.00	40.00	40.00	271.44	$1,500.00	$0.00	$0.00	$0.00
1	$24.00	40.00	40.53	264.15	$1,459.73	$40.27	$40.00	$0.27
2	$23.00	40.00	41.08	256.76	$1,418.89	$81.11	$80.00	$1.11
3	$22.00	40.00	41.63	249.27	$1,377.46	$122.54	$120.00	$2.54
4	$21.00	40.00	42.19	241.66	$1,335.40	$164.60	$160.00	$4.60
5	$20.00	40.00	42.76	233.92	$1,292.66	$207.34	$200.00	$7.34
10	$15.00	40.00	45.77	193.10	$1,067.07	$432.93	$400.00	$32.93
15	$10.00	40.00	49.14	147.36	$814.33	$685.67	$600.00	$85.67
20	$5.00	40.00	53.16	92.83	$512.99	$987.01	$800.00	$187.01
25	$0.00	40.00	60.00	0.00	$0.00	$1,500	$1,000.00	$500.00

skip to the next section (since we already found a way to calculate deadweight loss by simply using the expenditure function).

Just as the uncompensated labor supply curve is simply the uncompensated leisure demand subtracted from the leisure endowment, the compensated labor supply curve l_s^c is the compensated leisure demand (from equation (19.23)) subtracted from leisure endowment L; i.e.,

$$l_s^c(w, u_t) = L - \ell^c(w) = L - \left(\frac{1-\alpha}{\alpha w}\right)^{\alpha} u_t. \qquad (19.26)$$

In panel (b) of Graph 19.11, this function is graphed (for $u_t = 193.1$, $L = 60$, and $\alpha = 2/3$) together with the inelastic uncompensated labor supply curve, and panel (a) graphs the inverses of these functions to facilitate comparison to Graph 19.6 where we first argued that deadweight loss can be measured on the compensated labor supply curve.

Areas under the compensated labor supply curve are defined by the integral

$$\int l_s^c(w, u_t)dw = \left(Lw - \frac{w^{(1-\alpha)}u_t}{\alpha^{\alpha}(1-\alpha)^{(1-\alpha)}}\right), \qquad (19.27)$$

which, when evaluated from w of 15 to 25 (with $u_t = 193.1$, $L = 60$, and $\alpha = 2/3$), gives area $(a + c)$ as

$$\text{Area}(a + c) = \int_{15}^{25} l_s^c(w, u_t)dw \approx 432.93. \qquad (19.28)$$

Note that this is exactly equal to the lump sum tax that would get the worker to the same utility level as the wage tax $t = 10$. Subtracting from that the actual tax revenue collected (area (a) in the graph), we once again get deadweight loss of approximately $32.93 per worker, which is equal to area (c).

19B.3.3 Taxation of Capital
A similar example analogous to Graph 19.7 involving savings decisions and deadweight loss from taxation of interest is explored in end-of-chapter exercises 19.4 and 19.5, and the case of subsidies is further considered in end-of-chapter exercise 19.3.

Graph 19.11: Deadweight Loss from a Wage Tax

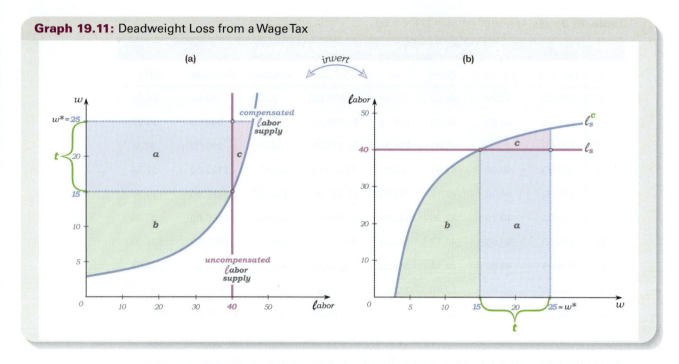

19B.3.4 DWL and Revenue as Tax Rates Rise

In Graph 19.8, we illustrated for linear demand and supply curves the impact of raising tax rates on tax revenue and deadweight loss (under the assumption that uncompensated and compensated demand are equivalent). For tax revenue, we derived an inverted U-shape for the "Laffer Curve," indicating the existence of a tax rate that maximizes revenue. For deadweight loss, we argued that, as in earlier chapters, increasing a tax by a factor of k will often increase the deadweight loss by a factor of approximately k^2.

Consider, for instance, the demand and supply functions given by $x_d(p) = (A - p)/\alpha$ and $x_s(p) = (p - B)/\beta$ (and assume that there are no income effects). You should be able to derive the equilibrium consumer price p_d and the equilibrium producer price $p_s = (p_d - t)$ as

$$p_d = \frac{\beta A + \alpha B + \alpha t}{\alpha + \beta} \quad \text{and} \quad p_s = \frac{\beta A + \alpha B - \beta t}{\alpha + \beta}, \tag{19.29}$$

and the equilibrium quantity x_t as

$$x_t = \frac{A - B - t}{\alpha + \beta}. \tag{19.30}$$

Exercise 19B.15   Verify these.

Tax revenue is then simply the per unit tax rate t times the quantity transacted x_t, which reduces to

$$TR = \frac{(A - B)t - t^2}{\alpha + \beta}. \tag{19.31}$$

This is the functional form graphed in panel (b) of Graph 19.8, and it attains its peak when its derivative with respect to the tax rate is zero. You can verify for yourself that this occurs when $t = (A - B)/2$.

It is somewhat more tedious to derive the equation for deadweight loss, but if you are careful in the various algebra steps involved, you can verify that

$$DWL(t) = \Delta CS + \Delta PS - TR = \frac{t^2}{2(\alpha + \beta)}. \qquad (19.32)$$

Verify the expression for deadweight loss. (*Hint:* There are two ways of doing this: You can either take the appropriate integrals of the supply and demand functions evaluated over the appropriate ranges of prices, or you can add rectangles and triangles in a graph.)

Exercise 19B.16**

Thus, if a tax rate t is multiplied by k, the resulting deadweight loss will be k^2 the original deadweight loss; i.e.,

$$DWL(kt) = \frac{(kt)^2}{2(\alpha + \beta)} = k^2 \frac{t^2}{2(\alpha + \beta)} = k^2 DWL(t). \qquad (19.33)$$

Both the Laffer Curve and the result about increases in deadweight loss with increases in tax rates therefore arise straightforwardly in a partial equilibrium model with linear demand and supply curves, and these results form the basis for much intuition that guides tax policy. As we can see from our example in Table 19.1 of the previous section, however, these are only rules of thumb, and they do not necessarily arise the same way in all models. With unitary price elastic demand in Table 19.1, for instance, the Laffer Curve does not attain a peak but only converges to a maximum tax revenue as the tax rate rises. This is a direct consequence of the unitary price elasticity of demand, which implies consumer spending on the taxed good never declines. In the real world, of course, it is unlikely that any demand curve truly has price elasticity of -1 regardless of how high the price goes, and we would therefore expect an eventual downward slope to the Laffer Curve. Similarly, in Table 19.2, tax revenue for a wage tax continues to rise with the tax rate because of the perfectly inelastic labor supply curve.

You might also have noticed that deadweight loss in Table 19.1, while increasing at an increasing rate, does not increase in the same way as it does in the linear case. The rule of thumb that an increase in a tax rate by a factor k will lead to an increase in deadweight loss by a factor k^2 is therefore just that: a rule of thumb derived from the linear case. In Table 19.2, on the other hand, deadweight loss from multiplying the wage tax by a factor k increases by more than k^2. Even though the rule of thumb about the relationship between increases in tax rates and increases in deadweight losses does not hold precisely in all cases, it is typically the case that deadweight loss increases at an increasing rate as tax rates rise, leading to the common policy recommendation that it is more efficient to raise tax revenues through low tax rates on large tax bases rather than high tax rates on small tax bases.

19B.4 Taxing Land

We argued in Section A that a tax on land rents is one real-world tax that does not give rise to deadweight losses and is therefore efficient. The mathematics behind this was already explored somewhat in Section A, and you can practice it further in the context of end-of-chapter exercises 19.7 and 19.12.

19B.5 A Simple Example of General Equilibrium Tax Incidence

In Section A, we also briefly introduced the notion that tax burdens may not only be shifted between buyers and sellers within the taxed market (as in the partial equilibrium models of this chapter) but may also be shifted to agents outside the taxed market through general equilibrium effects. We mentioned in particular a tax on housing that leads to a reallocation of capital away from housing and into other uses, thereby reducing the rate of return to non-housing capital and thus shifting a portion of the tax burden to owners of non-housing capital.

We can illustrate the basic intuition behind this in a very simple setting. Suppose we modeled owners of capital as a "representative investor" who chooses to allocate K units of capital between the housing sector and all other sectors that make use of capital. Letting capital invested in housing be denoted by k_1 and capital invested in other uses by k_2, let's assume that the before-tax rate of return in the housing sector is determined by the production function $f_1(k_1) = \alpha k_1^{1/2}$, and the rate of return in the untaxed remaining sector is determined by the production function $f_2(k_2) = \beta k_2^{1/2}$. But suppose the government imposes a tax of $t\%$ on housing.

Our representative investor then wants to maximize her total after-tax return by optimally choosing the allocation of her capital K across the two sectors. Put differently, she wants to solve the maximization problem

$$\max_{k_1, k_2} (1 - t)f_1(k_1) + f_2(k_2) \text{ subject to } k_1 + k_2 = K. \tag{19.34}$$

The solution to this problem is

$$k_1^* = \frac{(1 - t)^2 \alpha^2 K}{(1 - t)^2 \alpha^2 + \beta^2} \text{ and } k_2^* = \frac{\beta^2 K}{(1 - t)^2 \alpha^2 + \beta^2}. \tag{19.35}$$

Table 19.3 then demonstrates how the tax t on housing is partially shifted to other forms of capital when 1,000 units of capital are available to the representative investor and when $\alpha = \beta = 100$ (which implies that equal amounts are invested in housing and other forms of capital in the absence of taxes). The last column of the table represents the marginal product of a unit of capital in the untaxed sector, and in equilibrium this has to be equal to the after-tax marginal product of a unit of capital in the taxed sector (which is reported in the second to last column). In the absence of taxes (first row), these marginal products are equal to 2.24. As the tax on housing is increased (going down in the table), this marginal product declines as capital is shifted out of the taxed sector (where its after-tax return is falling) and into the untaxed sector. Thus, even though the tax is imposed on housing, the burden of the tax falls equally on all capital. Implicitly, we are assuming that capital is perfectly mobile between sectors.

Exercise 19B.17   For $t = 0.5$, verify that the marginal product columns of the table report the correct results.

Exercise 19B.18   If capital is "sector-specific" and cannot move from one use to another, would you still expect the housing tax to be shifted? Explain.

In addition to the degree of capital mobility between sectors, the degree to which owners of capital in other sectors are affected by a tax on housing also depends on the pre-tax size of the housing sector relative to the non-housing sector. In Table 19.3, we set values for the example

Table 19.3: $K = 1,000$, $\alpha = \beta = 100$

			Shifting of Housing Tax to Other Forms of Capital		
t	k_1^*	k_2^*	$MP_1(k_1^*)$	$(1 - t)MP_1(k_1^*)$	$MP_2(k_2^*)$
0	500.00	500.00	2.24	2.24	2.24
0.1	447.51	552.49	2.36	2.13	2.13
0.2	390.24	609.76	2.53	2.02	2.02
0.3	328.86	671.14	2.76	1.93	1.93
0.4	264.71	735.29	3.07	1.84	1.84
0.5	200.00	800.00	3.54	1.77	1.77
0.6	137.93	862.07	4.26	1.70	1.70
0.7	82.57	917.43	5.50	1.65	1.65
0.8	38.46	961.54	8.06	1.61	1.61
0.9	9.90	990.01	15.89	1.59	1.59

so that the two sectors are initially of equal size. In Table 19.4, on the other hand, we keep α plus β at 200 but reduce the ratio of alpha/beta below 1, which has the effect of reducing the housing sector relative to the non-housing sector. The final column of this table then reports the percentage drop in the marginal product of capital that results from a 50% tax on housing.

Why is the relative size of the housing sector relevant for determining how much owners of capital in other sectors are affected by a tax on housing capital?

Exercise 19B.19

Table 19.4: $K = 1,000$, $t = 0.5$, $\alpha + \beta = 200$

			Tax Shifting Depends on Relative Size of Housing Sector		
α/β	$(k_1/k_2)_{before}$	$(k_1/k_2)_{after}$	MP_{before}	MP_{after}	%Change
1	1.0000	0.2500	2.236	1.768	−26.471%
1/2	0.2500	0.0625	2.357	2.173	−8.466%
1/3	0.1111	0.2778	2.500	2.404	−3.972%
1/4	0.0625	0.0156	2.608	2.550	−2.275%
1/5	0.0400	0.0100	2.687	2.648	−1.473%
1/10	0.0100	0.0025	2.889	2.878	−0.373%
1/50	0.0004	0.0001	3.101	3.100	−0.015%

CONCLUSION

The first welfare theorem guarantees efficiency of market outcomes so long as a number of conditions are satisfied. In this (and the previous) chapter, we have explored how inefficiencies are introduced (and the first welfare theorem "fails") when prices are distorted, in Chapter 18 because of explicit price ceilings and floors and now because of taxes (and subsidies). In both cases, we have seen that the group that bears the burden of the price distortion is not necessarily the one we might think of first, that the *economic incidence* of price distortions is determined in equilibrium and usually depends critically on the relative price responsiveness of different actors in the market. The cost of price regulations as well as the cost of taxes can thus be passed from one side of the market to the other in ways that our partial equilibrium framework can clarify. We have similarly seen that not all price regulation or tax/subsidy policies are equally inefficient, and that the relative inefficiency of different price-distorting policies once again often depends on the price-responsiveness of those in the market. And we rediscovered in this chapter the fact that inefficiencies arise from substitution effects that may be masked by income or wealth effects that prohibit us from relying solely on (uncompensated) market demand and supply curves for purposes of welfare (and efficiency) analysis. Finally, we have at least briefly pointed out that the impact of price regulations or taxes and subsidies can extend beyond a particular market through general equilibrium effects that cross from one market to another. We will explore this latter notion more explicitly in Chapter 20 where we investigate the consequences of taxation or regulation in one of multiple connected markets where such policies erect barriers to unfettered trade.

As before, we should caution again to not misinterpret the lessons of these chapters: While economists unapologetically point out that there is an efficiency cost to using distortionary taxes to raise revenue, this does not imply that economists are uniformly opposed to the use of such taxes to raise revenues for expenditures considered to be socially valuable. Similarly, we make no apology for pointing out the efficiency cost of using distortionary subsidies while not necessarily judging all such subsidies to lack social value if they foster activities that are important to policy makers. The economist's role is to clarify how taxes and subsidies affect individuals in an economy, how costly they are, and how they might be redesigned to become less costly.

END-OF-CHAPTER EXERCISES

19.1   In our discussion of economic versus statutory incidence, the text has focused primarily on the incidence of taxes. This exercise explores analogous issues related to the incidence of benefits from subsidies.

A.   Consider a price subsidy for x in a partial equilibrium model of demand and supply in the market for x.

    a.   Explain why it does not matter whether the government gives the per-unit subsidy s to consumers or producers.

    b.   Consider the case where the slopes of demand and supply curves are roughly equal in absolute value at the no-subsidy equilibrium. What does this imply for the way in which the benefits of the subsidy are divided between consumers and producers?

    c.   How does your answer change if the demand curve is steeper than the supply curve at the no-subsidy equilibrium?

    d.   How does your answer change if the demand curve is shallower than the supply curve at the no-subsidy equilibrium?

    e.   Can you state your general conclusion—using the language of price elasticities—on how much consumers will benefit relative to producers when price subsidies are introduced. How is this similar to our conclusions on tax incidence?

    f.   Do any of your answers depend on whether the tastes for x are quasilinear?

B.* In Section 19B.1, we derived the impact of a marginal per-unit tax on the price received by producers; i.e., dp_s/dt.

    a.   Repeat the analysis for the case of a per-unit subsidy and derive dp_s/ds where s is the per-unit subsidy.

---

*conceptually challenging
**computationally challenging
†solutions in Study Guide

    b.   What is dp_d/ds?

    c.   What do your results in (a) and (b) tell you about the economic incidence of a per-unit subsidy when the price elasticity of demand is zero? What about when the price elasticity of supply is zero?

    d.   What does your analysis suggest about the economic incidence of the subsidy when the price elasticities of demand and supply are equal (in absolute value) at the no-subsidy equilibrium?

    e.   More generally, can you show which side of the market gets the greater benefit when the absolute value of the price elasticity of demand is less than the price elasticity of supply?

19.2   In the chapter, we discussed the deadweight loss from taxes on consumption goods when tastes are quasilinear in the taxed good, and we treated deadweight loss when tastes are not quasilinear for the case of wage taxes. In this exercise, we will consider deadweight losses from taxation on consumption goods when tastes are not quasilinear.

A.   Suppose that x is a normal good for consumers.

    a.   Draw the market demand and supply graph for x and illustrate the impact on prices (for consumers and producers) and output levels when a per-unit tax t on x is introduced.

    b.   Would your answer to (a) have been any different had we assumed that all consumers' tastes were quasilinear in x?

    c.   On a consumer diagram with x on the horizontal and "all other goods" (denominated in dollars) on the vertical axes, illustrate the impact of the tax on a consumer's budget.

    d.   In your graph from (c), illustrate the portion of deadweight loss that is due to this particular consumer.

    e.   On a third graph, depict the demand curve for x for the consumer whose consumer diagram you graphed in (d). Then illustrate on this graph the same deadweight loss that you first illustrated in (d).

    f.   Now return to your graph from (a). Illustrate where deadweight loss lies in this graph. How does it compare to the case where the original market demand curve arises from quasilinear tastes rather than the tastes we are analyzing in this exercise?

    g.   *True or False*: We will overestimate the deadweight loss if we use market demand curves to measure changes in consumer surplus from taxation of normal goods.

B.   Suppose that consumers all have Cobb–Douglas tastes that can be represented by the utility function $u(x, y) = x^\alpha y^{(1-\alpha)}$ and each consumer has income I. Assume throughout that the price of y is normalized to 1.

    a.   Derive the uncompensated demand for x by a consumer.

    b.   Suppose income is expressed in thousands of dollars and each consumer has income $I = 2.5$ (i.e., income of \$2,500). There are 1,000 consumers in the market. What is the market demand function?

    c.   Suppose market supply is given by $x_s = \beta p$. Derive the market equilibrium price and output level.

    d.   Suppose $\alpha = 0.4$ and $\beta = 10$. Determine the equilibrium p_d, p_s, and x_t when $t = 10$. How do these compare to what we calculated for the quasilinear tastes in Section 19B.2.1 (where we assumed $\alpha = 1,000$ and $\beta = 10$) graphed in Graph 19.10?

    e.   What is the before-tax and after-tax quantity transacted?

    f.   If you used the market demand and supply curves to estimate deadweight loss, what would it be?

    g.   Calculate the real deadweight loss in this case, and explain why it is different than in Section 19B.2.1 where market demand and supply curves were the same as here.

19.3†   In the text, we discussed deadweight losses that arise from wage *taxes* even when labor supply is perfectly inelastic. We now consider wage *subsidies*.

A.   Suppose that the current market wage is w^* and that labor supply for all workers is perfectly inelastic. Then the government agrees to pay employers a per-hour wage subsidy of \$$s$ for every worker hour they employ.

    a.   Will employers get any benefit from this subsidy? Will employees?

    b.   In a consumer diagram with leisure ℓ on the horizontal and consumption c on the vertical axes, illustrate the impact of the subsidy on worker budget constraints.

    c.   Choose a bundle A that is optimal before the subsidy goes into effect. Locate the bundle that is optimal after the subsidy.

    d.   Illustrate the size of the subsidy payment S as a vertical distance in the graph.

    e.   Illustrate how much P we could have paid the worker in a lump sum way (without distorting wages) to make him just as well off as he is under the wage subsidy. Then locate the deadweight loss of the wage subsidy as a vertical distance in your graph.

    f.   On a separate graph, illustrate the inelastic labor supply curve as well as the before and after-subsidy points on that curve. Then illustrate the appropriate compensated labor supply curve on which to measure the deadweight loss. Explain where this deadweight loss lies in your graph.

    g.   *True or False*: As long as leisure and consumption are at least somewhat substitutable, compensated labor supply curves always slope up and wage subsidies that increase worker wages create deadweight losses.

B. Suppose that, as in our treatment of wage taxes, tastes over consumption c and leisure ℓ can be represented by the utility function $u(c, \ell) = c^\alpha \ell^{(1-\alpha)}$ and that all workers have leisure endowment of L (and no other source of income). Suppose further that, again as in the text, the equilibrium wage in the absence of distortions is $w^* = 25$.

    a.   If the government offers an \$11 per hour wage subsidy for employers, how does this affect the wage costs for employers and the wages received by employees?

    b.   Assume henceforth that $\alpha = 0.5$. What is the utility level u_s attained by workers under the subsidy (as a function of leisure endowment L)?

    c.*   What's the least (in terms of leisure endowment L) we would need to give each worker in a lump sum way to get them to agree to give up the wage subsidy program?

    d.*   What is the per worker deadweight loss (in terms of leisure endowment L) of the subsidy?

    e.** Use the compensated labor supply curve to verify your answer.

19.4   This exercise reviews some concepts from earlier chapters on consumer theory in preparation for exercise 19.5.

A. Consider an individual saver who earns income now but does not expect to earn income in a future period for which she must save.

    a.   Draw a consumer diagram with current consumption c_1 on the horizontal axis and future consumption c_2 on the vertical. Illustrate an intertemporal budget constraint assuming an interest rate r, then draw an indifference curve that contains the optimal bundle A.

    b.   Now suppose the interest rate increases to r'. Illustrate the new budget constraint and indicate where the new optimal bundle C will lie given that the individual does not change her savings decision when interest rates change.

    c.   How much, in terms of future dollars, would this person be willing to pay to get the interest rate to change from r to r'? If she pays that amount, will she end up saving more or less?

    d.   Suppose instead that the interest rate starts at r' and then falls to r. Illustrate how much I would have to give this individual to compensate her for the drop in the interest rate. If this is done, will she save more or less than she did at the high interest rate?

    e.   On a new graph, illustrate the individual's inelastic savings supply curve. Then illustrate the compensated savings supply curves that correspond to the utility levels the individual has at the interest rates r and r'.

    f.   *True or False*: Compensated savings supply curves always slope up.

B. Suppose your tastes over current consumption c_1 and future consumption c_2 can be modeled through the utility function $u(c_1, c_2) = c_1^\alpha c_2^{(1-\alpha)}$, your current income is I, and you will earn no income in the future. The real interest rate from this period to the future is r.

    a.   Derive your demand functions $c_1(r, I)$ and $c_2(r, I)$ for current and for future consumption.

    b.   Define "savings" as the difference between current income and current consumption. Derive your savings—or capital supply—function $k_s(r, I)$. (*Note*: It turns out that this function is not actually a function of r.)

    c.   Derive the indirect utility function $V(r, I)$; i.e., the function that gives us your utility for any combination of (r, I).

    d.   Next, derive your compensated demand functions $c_1^c(r, u)$ and $c_2^c(r, u)$ for current and future consumption.

    e.   Define the expenditure function $E(r, u)$; i.e., the function that tells us the current income necessary for you to reach utility level u at interest rate r.

    f.   Can you verify your answers by comparing $V(r, I)$ with $E(r, u)$?

    g.   Finally, suppose that we begin with an interest rate $\bar{r}$ and derive from it $V(\bar{r}, I)$. Define the *compensated savings* or *compensated capital supply* function as $k_s^c(r, \bar{r}) = I - c_1^c(r, V(\bar{r}, I))$.

    h.   What is the interest rate elasticity of savings? Without deriving it precisely, can you tell whether the interest rate elasticity of compensated savings is positive or negative?

19.5   (This exercise builds on exercise 19.4, which you should do before proceeding.) Through the income tax code, governments typically tax most interest income; but, through a variety of retirement programs, they often subsidize at least some types of interest income.

  A. Suppose all capital is supplied by individuals that earn income now but don't expect to earn income in some future period, and who therefore save some of their current income. Suppose further that these individuals do not change their current consumption (and thus the amount they put into savings) as interest rates change.

    a.   What is the economic incidence of a government subsidy of interest income? What is the economic incidence of a tax on interest income?

    b.   In the text, we illustrated the deadweight loss from a subsidy on interest income when savings behavior is unaffected by changes in the interest rate. Now consider a tax on interest income. In a consumer diagram with current consumption c_1 on the horizontal and future consumption c_2 on the vertical axis, illustrate the deadweight loss from such a tax for a saver whose (uncompensated) savings supply is perfectly inelastic.

    c.   What does the size of the deadweight loss depend on? Under what special tastes does it disappear?

    d.   On a separate graph, illustrate the inelastic savings (or capital) supply curve. Then illustrate the compensated savings supply curve that allows you to measure the deadweight loss from the tax on interest income. Explain where in the graph this deadweight loss lies.

    e.   What happens to the compensated savings supply curve as consumption becomes more complementary across time, and what happens to the deadweight loss as a result?

    f.   Is the special case when there is no deadweight loss from taxing interest income compatible with a perfectly inelastic *uncompensated* savings supply curve?

  B. Suppose everyone's tastes and economic circumstances are the same as those described in part B of exercise 19.4, with $\alpha = 0.5$ and $I = 100{,}000$.[10]

    a.   Suppose further that there are 10,000,000 consumers like this, and they are the only source of capital in the economy. How much capital is supplied regardless of the interest rate?

    b.   Suppose next that demand for capital is given by $K_d = 25{,}000{,}000{,}000/r$. What is the equilibrium real interest rate r^* in the absence of any price distortions?

    c.   Suppose that, for any dollar of interest earned, the government provides the person who earned the interest a 50-cent subsidy. What will be the new (subsidy-inclusive) interest rate earned by savers, and what will be the interest rate paid by borrowers? What if the government instead taxed 50% of interest income?

    d.   Consider the subsidy introduced in (c). How much utility V will each saver attain under this subsidy?

---

[10]Among other functions, you should have derived uncompensated and compensated savings function as

$$k_s(r, I) = (1 - \alpha)I \text{ and } k_s^c = \left[1 - \alpha\left(\frac{1 + \bar{r}}{1 + r}\right)^{(1-\alpha)}\right]I. \tag{19.36}$$

e. How much current income would each saver have to have in order to obtain the same utility V at the pre-subsidy interest rate r^*? In terms of future dollars, how much would it therefore cost the government to make each saver as well off in a lump sum way as it does using the interest rate subsidy?

f. How much interest will the government have to pay to each saver (in the future) under the subsidy? Use this and your previous answer to derive the amount of deadweight loss per saver in terms of future dollars. Given the number of savers in the economy, what is the overall deadweight loss?

g. Derive the compensated savings function (as a function of r) given the post-subsidy utility level V.

h.** Use your answer to (g) to derive the aggregate compensated capital supply function, and then find the area that corresponds to the deadweight loss. Compare this with your answer in part (f).

i.** Repeat parts (d) through (h) for the case of the tax on interest income described in part (c).

j.** You have calculated deadweight losses for interest rates that are reasonable for 1-year time horizons. If we consider distortions in people's decisions over longer time horizons (such as when they plan for retirement), a more reasonable time frame might be 25 years. With annual market interest rates of 0.05 in the absence of distortions, can you use your compensated savings function (given in the footnote to the problem) to estimate again what the deadweight losses from a subsidy that raises the effective rate of return by 50% and from a tax that lowers it by 50% would be?

19.6 **Business and Policy Application:** *City Wage Taxes*: In the United States, very few cities tax income derived from wages, whereas the national government imposes considerable taxes on wages (through both payroll and income taxes) and then passes some of those revenues back to city governments.

A. In this exercise, we will consider the reason for this difference in local and national tax policy and why city governments might in fact be "employing" the national government to levy wage taxes and then have the national government return them to cities.

a. Consider first a national labor market. While workers and firms can move across national boundaries to escape domestic taxes, suppose that this is prohibitively costly for the labor market that we are analyzing. Illustrate demand and supply curves for domestic labor (assuming that supply is upward sloping). Indicate the no-tax equilibrium wage and and employment level and then show the impact of a wage tax.

b. Next, consider a city government that faces a revenue shortfall and considers introducing a wage tax. Why might you think that labor demand and supply are more elastic from the city's perspective than they are from a national government perspective?

c. Given your answer to (b), draw two Laffer Curves: one for tax revenue raised in a city when the tax is imposed nationally and one for tax revenues raised in the same city when it is imposing the tax on its own. Explain where the peaks of the two Laffer Curves are relative to one another.

d. How do your answers to (b) and (c) most likely contain the answer to why cities do not typically use wage taxes to raise revenues?

e. Suppose you are a mayor of a city and would like to impose a wage tax but understand the problem so far. How might it make sense for you to ask the federal government to increase the wage tax nationwide and then to give cities the additional revenue collected in each city?

f. Of those cities that do have wage taxes, most are relatively large. Why do you think it is exceedingly rare for small cities to impose local wage taxes?

g. Does any of this analysis depend on whether there are wealth (or income) effects in the labor market?

B. Suppose that labor demand and supply are linear, with $l_d = (A - w)/\alpha$ and $l_s = (w - B)/\beta$.

a. For a given per-unit wage tax t, calculate the employment level and tax revenue.

b. Consider two scenarios: scenario 1 in which $(A - B)$ is large and scenario 2 in which $(A - B)$ is small. What has to be true about $(\alpha + \beta)$ in scenario 1 relative to scenario 2 if the no-tax equilibrium employment level is the same in both cases?

c. Suppose one scenario is relevant for predicting tax revenue from your city when it is collected nationwide and the other is relevant for predicting tax revenue when the wage tax is collected just in your city. Which scenario belongs to which tax analysis?

    d.   Find the tax rate $\bar{t}$ at which government revenue is maximized.

    e.   Demonstrate that the scenario appropriate for the tax analysis when only your city imposes the wage tax leads to a Laffer Curve that peaks earlier.

    f.   As cities get small, what happens to $(A - B)$ in the limit? What happens to the peak of the Laffer Curve for a local city tax in the limit?

19.7† **Business and Policy Application:** *Land Use Policies*: In most Western democracies, it is settled law that governments cannot simply confiscate land for public purposes. Such confiscation is labeled a "taking," and even when the government has compelling reasons to "take" someone's property for public use, it must compensate the landowner. But, while it is clear that a "taking" has occurred when the government confiscates private land without compensation, constitutional lawyers disagree on how close the government has to come to literally confiscating private land before the action constitutes an unconstitutional "taking."

BUSINESS APPLICATION

POLICY APPLICATION

A. Any restriction that alters the way land would otherwise be used reduces the annual rental value of that land and, from the owner's perspective, can therefore be treated as a tax on rental value.

    a.   Explain why this statement is correct.

    b.   Suppose a land use regulation is equivalent (from the owner's perspective) to a tax of $t\%$ on land rents to be statutorily paid by landowners (where $0 < t < 1$). How does it affect the market value of the land?

    c.   I am about to buy an acre of land from you in order to build on it. Right before we agree on a price, the government imposes a new zoning regulation that limits what I can do on the land. Who is definitively made worse off by this?

    d.   Suppose you own 1,000 acres of land that is currently zoned for residential development. Then suppose the government determines that your land is home to a rare species of salamander, and that it is in the public interest for no economic activity to take place on this land in order to protect this endangered species. From your perspective, what approximate tax rate on land rents that you collect is this regulation equivalent to? Do you think this is a "taking"?

    e.   Suppose that, instead of prohibiting all economic activity on your 1,000 acres, the government reduces your ability to build residential housing on it to a single house. How does your answer change? What if it restricts housing development to 500 acres? Do you think this would be a "taking"?

B.* Suppose that people gain utility from housing services h and other consumption x, with tastes described by the utility function $u(x, h) = \ln x + \ln h$. Consumption is denominated in dollars (with price therefore normalized to 1). Housing services, on the other hand, are derived from the production process $h = k^{0.5}L^{\alpha}$, where k stands for units of capital and L for acres of land. Suppose $0 < \alpha < 1$. Let the rental rate of capital be denoted by r, and assume each person has income of 1,000.

    a.   Write down the utility maximization problem and solve for the demand function for land assuming a rental rate R for land.

    b.   Suppose your city consists of 100,000 individuals like this, and there are 25,000 acres of land available. What is the equilibrium rental rate per acre of land (as a function of α)?

    c.   Using your answers, derive the amount of land each person will consume.

    d.   Suppose the government imposes zoning regulations that reduce the coefficient α in the production function from 0.5 to 0.25. What happens to the equilibrium rental value of land?

    e.   Suppose that what you have calculated so far is the monthly rental value of land. What happens to the total value of an acre of land as a result of these zoning regulations assuming that people use a monthly interest rate of 0.5% to discount the future?

    f.   Suppose that, instead of lowering α from 0.5 to 0.25 through regulation, the government imposes a tax t on the market rental value of land and statutorily requires renters to pay. Thus, if the market land rental rate is R per acre, those using the land must pay tR on top of the rent R for every acre they use. Set up the renters' utility maximization problem, derive the demand for land, and aggregate it over all 100,000 individuals. Then derive the equilibrium land rent per acre as a function of t (assuming $\alpha = 0.5$).

    g.   Does the amount of land consumed by each household change?

    h.   Suppose you own land that you rent out. What level of t makes you indifferent between the zoning regulation that drove α from 0.5 to 0.25 and the land rent tax that does not change α?

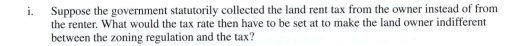

i.   Suppose the government statutorily collected the land rent tax from the owner instead of from the renter. What would the tax rate then have to be set at to make the land owner indifferent between the zoning regulation and the tax?

19.8   Business and Policy Application: *Price Floors for Corn: Is it a Tax or a Subsidy?* In exercises 18.9 and 18.10, we investigated policies that imposed a price floor in the corn market.

A. We will now see whether some of the price regulation proposals we considered are equivalent to taxes or subsidies. For simplicity, assume that tastes are quasilinear in corn.

a.   In exercise 18.9, we began by considering a price floor without any additional government program. Illustrate the equilibrium impact of such a price floor on the price of corn paid by consumers as well as the price of corn received by producers.

b.   If you were to design a tax or subsidy policy that has the same impact as the standalone price floor, what would it be?

c.   In exercise 18.10, we considered the combination of a price floor and a government purchasing program under which the government guaranteed it would purchase any surplus corn at the price ceiling and then sell it at a price sufficiently low for all of it to be bought. Illustrate the impact of this program, including the deadweight loss.

d.   If you were to design a tax or subsidy policy with the aim of achieving the same outcome for the marginal consumer and producer as the policy in (c), what would you propose?

e.   Would your proposal result in the same level of consumer and producer surplus? Would it result in the same deadweight loss?

B. Suppose, as in exercises 18.9 and 18.10, that the domestic demand curve for bushels of corn is given by $p = 24 - 0.00000000225x$ while the domestic supply curve is given by $p = 1 + 0.00000000025x$.

a.   Suppose the government imposes a price ceiling of $\bar{p} = 3.5$ (as in exercise 18.9). In the absence of any other program, how much will consumers pay (per bushel) and how much will sellers keep (per bushel) after accounting for the additional marginal costs incurred by producers to compete for consumers?

b.   If you wanted to replicate this same outcome using taxes or subsidies, what policy would you propose?

c.   Suppose next that the government supplemented its price floor from (a) with a government purchasing program that buys all surplus corn, and then sells it at the highest possible price at which all surplus corn is bought. What is that price?

d.   If you were to design a tax or subsidy policy that has the same impact on the marginal consumer and producer, what would it be?

19.9   Policy Application: *Rent Control: Is it a Tax or a Subsidy?* In exercise 18.11, we analyzed the impact of rent control policies that impose a price ceiling in the housing rental market. The stated intent of such policies is often to make housing more affordable. Before answering this question, you may wish to review your answers to exercise 18.11.

A. Begin by illustrating the impact of the rent control price ceiling on the price received by landlords and the eventual equilibrium price paid by renters.

a.   Why is it not an equilibrium for the price ceiling to be the rent actually paid by renters?

b.   If you wanted to implement a tax or subsidy policy that achieves the same outcome as the rent control policy, what policy would you propose?

c.   Could you credibly argue that the alternative policy you proposed in (b) was designed to make housing more affordable?

d.   If you did actually want to make housing more affordable (rather than trying to replicate the impact of rent control policies), would you choose a subsidy or a tax?

e.   Illustrate your proposal from (d) and show what would happen to the rental price received by landlords and the rents paid by renters. What happens to the number of housing units available for rent under your new policy?

   f.   *True or False*: Policies that make housing more affordable must invariably increase the equilibrium quantity of housing, and rent control policies fail because they reduce the equilibrium quantity of housing while subsidies succeed for the opposite reason.

   g.   *True or False*: Although rental subsidies succeed at the goal of making housing more afford-able (while rent control policies fail to do so), we cannot in general say that deadweight loss is greater or less under one policy rather than the other.

B. Suppose, again as in exercise 18.11, that the aggregate monthly demand curve is $p = 10,000 - 0.01x$ while the supply curve is $p = 1,000 + 0.002x$. For simplicity, suppose again that there are no income effects.

   a.   Calculate the equilibrium number of apartments x^* and the equilibrium monthly rent p^* in the absence of any price distortions.

   b.   In exercise 18.11, you were asked to consider the impact of a $1,500 price ceiling. What housing tax or subsidy would result in the same economic impact?

   c.   Suppose that you wanted to use tax/subsidy policies to actually reduce rents to $1,500 the stated goal of the rent control policy. What policy would you implement?

   d.   Consider the policies you derived in (b) and (c). Under which policy is the deadweight loss greater?

19.10† **Policy Application:** *Incidence of U.S. Social Security Taxes*: In the United States, the Social Security system is funded by a payroll (wage) tax of 12.4% that is split equally between employer and employee; i.e., the statutory incidence of the Social Security tax falls half on employers and half on employees.

A. In this exercise, we consider how this split in statutory incidents impacts the labor market. Assume throughout that labor supply is upward sloping.

   a.   Illustrate the labor supply and demand graph and indicate the market wage w^* and employ-ment level l^* in the absence of any taxes.

   b.   Which curve shifts as a result of the statutory mandate that employers have to pay the government 6.2% of their wage bill? Which curve shifts because of the statutory mandate that employees pay 6.2% of their wages in Social Security tax?

   c.   Suppose the wage elasticity of labor demand and supply are equal in absolute value at the pre-tax equilibrium. Can you illustrate how the market wage at the post-tax equilibrium, when both parts of the Social Security tax are taken into account, might be unchanged from the initial equilibrium wage w^*?

   d.   In your graph, illustrate what the imposition of the two-part Social Security tax means for the take-home wage w_w for workers. What does it mean for the real cost of labor w_f that firms incur?

   e.   How would the equilibrium wage in the market change if the government imposed the entire 12.4% tax on workers (and let employers statutorily off the hook)? How would it change if the government instead imposed the entire tax on employers?

   f.   What happens to the take-home wage for workers and the real labor cost of firms as a result of the two statutory tax reforms raised in part (e)?

   g.   Does any of this analysis depend on whether there are wealth effects in the labor market?

B. Suppose, as in exercise 19.6, that labor demand and supply in the absence of taxes are given by $l_d = (A - w)/\alpha$ and $l_s = (w - B)/\beta$.

   a.   Determine the equilibrium employment level l^* and the equilibrium wage w^*.

   b.   Now suppose the government imposes a per-unit tax t on workers and a second per-unit tax t on employers. Derive the new labor demand and supply curves that incorporate these (as you would when you shift demand and supply curves in response to statutory tax laws).

   c.   Determine the new equilibrium wage and employment level. Under what condition is the new observed equilibrium wage unchanged as a result of the two-part wage tax? Is there any way that employment will not fall?

d.   Determine the take-home wage w_w for workers and the real labor cost w_f for firms.

e.   Suppose you did not know the statutory incidence of the wage tax but simply knew the total tax was equal to $2t$. How would you calculate the economic incidence; i.e., how would you calculate w_w and w_f?

f.   Compare your answers to (e) with your answers to (d). Can you conclude from this whether statutory incidence matters?

19.11 Policy Application: *Mortgage Interest Deductibility, Land Values, and the Equilibrium Rate of Return on Capital*: In the text, we suggested that the property tax can be thought of in part as a tax on land and in part as a tax on capital invested in housing. In the United States, property taxes are typically levied by local governments, while the major piece of federal housing policy is contained in the federal income tax code that allows individuals to deduct (from income) the interest they pay on home mortgages prior to calculating the amount of taxes owed.

A. Whereas we can think of the property tax as a tax on both land and housing structures, we can think of the homeownership subsidy in the federal tax code as a subsidy on land and housing structures.

a.   If your marginal federal income tax rate is 25% and you are financing 100% of your home value, how much of your housing consumption is being subsidized through the tax code? What if you are only financing 50% of the value of your home?

b.   Suppose homeowners are similar to one another in terms of their marginal tax rate and how much of their home they are financing, and suppose that this implies a subsidy of s for every dollar of housing/land consumption. How would you predict the value of suburban residential land (assumed to be in fixed supply) is different as a result of this than it would have been in the absence of this policy?

c.   When s was first introduced, who benefitted from the implicit land subsidy: current homeowners or future homeowners?

d.   Now consider s as a subsidy on housing capital. Do you think houses are larger or smaller as a result of the federal income tax code?

e.   Suppose that the overall amount of capital in the economy is fixed and that capital is mobile across sectors. Thus, any given unit of capital can be invested in housing or alternatively in some other non-housing sector where it earns some rate of return. If the overall amount of capital in the economy is fixed, what happens to the fraction of capital invested in the housing sector?

f.   What would you predict will happen to the rate of return on capital in the non-housing sector? Explain.

g.   *True or False*: Even though only housing capital is statutorily subsidized, the economic incidence of this subsidy falls equally on all forms of capital (so long as capital is mobile between sectors).

B. Suppose we model owners of capital as a "representative investor" who chooses to allocate K units of capital between the housing sector and other sectors of the economy. With k_1 representing capital invested in housing and k_2 representing capital invested in other sectors, suppose $f_1(k_1) = \alpha k_1^{0.5}$ and $f_2(k_2) = \beta k_2^{0.5}$ are the production functions of the two sectors.

a.   In the absence of any policy distortions, calculate the fraction of total capital (K) that is invested in the housing sector.

b.   What changes as a result of the federal income tax code's implicit housing subsidy s?

c.   What happens to the marginal product of capital in the non-housing sector?

d.   What happens to the equilibrium rate of return on capital?

e.   *True or False*: The general equilibrium subsidy incidence of the implicit subsidy of housing capital falls equally on all forms of capital.

19.12† Policy Application: *The Split-Rate Property Tax*: As we have mentioned several times, the usual property tax is really two taxes: one levied on land value (or on land rents) and the other levied on the value of the "improvements" of land, or the rents from capital investments. The typical property tax simply sets the same tax rate for each part, but in an increasing number of places, governments are reforming property taxes to levy a higher rate on land than on improvements. Such a tax is called a *split-rate property tax*.

A. Suppose you are in a locality that currently taxes rental income from capital at the same rate as rental income from land. Assume throughout that the amount of land in the community is fixed.

    a.   Which portion of your local tax system is distortionary and which is non-distortionary?

    b.   Next, suppose that your community lowers the tax on capital income and raises it on land rents, and suppose that overall tax revenues are unchanged as a result of this reform. Do you think the tax reform enhances efficiency?

    c.   Your community has a fixed amount of land, but capital can move in and out of your community and therefore changes depending on economic conditions. Do you think the land in your community will be more or less intensively utilized as a result of the tax reform; i.e., do you think more or less capital will be invested on it?

    d.   What do you think happens to the marginal product of land in your community under this tax reform? What must therefore happen to the rental value of land (before land rent taxes are paid)?

    e.   Suppose half of your community has land that is relatively substitutable with capital in production, and the other half of your community has land that is relatively complementary to capital in production. Might it be the case that land values go up in part of your community and go down in another part of your community as a result of the tax reform? If so, which part experiences the increase in land values *despite an increase in the tax on land rents*?

    f.   Will overall output in your community increase or decrease as a result of the tax reform? Under what extreme assumption about the degree of substitutability of land and capital in production would local production remain unchanged?

    g.   *True or False*: The more substitutable land and capital are in production, the more likely it is that the tax reform toward a split-rate property tax (that taxes land more heavily) will result in a Pareto improvement.

B.* Suppose we normalize units of land so that the entire land area of a particular locality equals one unit. Economic activity is captured by the constant elasticity of substitution production function $y = f(k, L) = (0.5L^{-1} + 0.5k^{-1})^{-1}$. The government collects revenues through a property tax that taxes land rents at a rate t_L and the rental value of capital at a rate t_k, resulting in total tax revenue of $TR = t_L R + t_k \bar{r} K$, where R is the rental value of the 1 unit of land in the locality, $\bar{r}$ is the interest rate in the local economy, and K is the total capital employed in the locality. (Note that we have defined capital units such that the interest rate is equal to the rental rate of capital).

    a.   Suppose that this locality is sufficiently small so that nothing it does can affect the global economy's rental rate r; i.e., the supply of capital is perfectly elastic. If the locality taxes the rental value of capital at rate t_k, at what local interest rate $\bar{r}$ would investors be willing to invest here?

    b.   Suppose that land is utilized optimally given the local tax environment, which implies that the marginal product of capital must equal $\bar{r}$. Define the equation that you would have to solve in order to calculate the level of capital invested in this locality.

    c.   Suppose $r = 0.06$. Solve for the level of capital K invested on the one unit of land of this locality (as a function of t_k).

    d.   Can you determine the rental value of land? (*Hint*: Derive the marginal product of land and evaluate it at the level of capital you calculated in the previous part and the one unit of land that is available.)

    e.   Now consider the case where the local tax system is $(t_L, t_k) = (0, 0.5)$. Derive the total capital K invested in the locality, the land rental value R, the value of land P (assuming that future income is discounted at the interest rate $r = 0.06$), the production level y, and the tax revenue TR. (You may find it convenient to set up a simple spreadsheet to do the calculations for you.)

f.** Repeat this for the tax system $(t_L, t_k) = (0.05, 0.3637)$, the tax system $(t_L, t_k) = (0.1, 0.1748)$, and the tax system $(t_L, t_k) = (0.1353, 0)$. Present your results for K, R, P, y, and TR in a table (and keep in mind that $\bar{r}$ changes with t_k even though r remains at 0.06). (*Hint*: All three systems should give the same tax revenue.)

g.   Use your table to discuss how the shift from a tax solely on capital (i.e., structures) toward a revenue-neutral tax system that increasingly relies on taxing land rents impacts the local economy. Which of the rows in your table could look qualitatively different under different elasticity of substitution assumptions?

Prices and Distortions across Markets

So far, we have usually treated a market as if it was literally that: a place where buyers and sellers come together, compete with one another, and trade goods at the prices that emerge in equilibrium.[1] But markets are of course quite a bit more complicated, with goods being traded across geographic markets, from city to city, region to region, and country to country. With lower and lower transportation costs in growing sectors such as information technology, services are often performed in one country for customers across the world.[2] And goods are traded as much across time as they are across space, with some purchasing now in order to sell in the future and others selling now what they bought in the past; or, as we will see, what they intend to buy in the future.

In each of these cases, we can think of trade as occurring both within and across markets. When goods are shipped between cities, we don't usually pay much attention to such trades, but when goods cross international boundaries, we refer to those that bring the goods into a country as *importers* and those that ship them out of a country as *exporters*. When someone buys in today's market with the intention of selling when price rises in the future, on the other hand, we refer to this person as a *speculator*. We will demonstrate in this chapter that exporters, importers, and speculators can play an important efficiency role in markets. Policies that disturb this interconnection of markets once again disturb price signals that contain information that coordinates markets and, for this reason, such policies often again cause deadweight losses.

This chapter therefore represents the third (and final) chapter investigating violations of the first welfare theorem due to government policy distorting prices. We began in Chapter 18 by looking at direct attempts by governments to control prices through price ceilings and price floors and continued in Chapter 19 by looking at indirect price distortions arising from government taxes and subsidies within a single market. We now conclude by investigating policies that interfere with prices that govern trade *across* interacting markets. This will require us to take a somewhat more "general equilibrium" view, something we began to hint at in Chapter 19 when we briefly discussed the shifting of tax burdens from taxed sectors (like housing) to untaxed markets (like nonhousing capital) through capital mobility. We will see the same phenomenon here: a shifting of taxes across markets when a tax is imposed in only one of multiple markets that are connected by some form of mobility of goods or inputs. We will draw

---

[1]This chapter presumes a basic understanding of partial equilibrium as developed in Chapters 14 and 15 and uses the concept of elasticity as developed in the first part of Chapter 18. It also uses the concept of tax incidence covered in Section 19A.1 of Chapter 19.

[2]When I recently called the support line for my local cell phone company, for instance, I had a hunch that the person I was speaking to was not living just down the street. I asked him, and sure enough, my phone call had gone all the way to India to be answered by someone there.

some connections between the material in this chapter and our treatment of housing taxes in the previous chapter's end-of-chapter exercises. We will furthermore see in this chapter's end-of-chapter exercises that the insights from this chapter extend far beyond just the most obvious examples that are covered in the text.

20A Exporters, Importers, and Speculators

Just as market competition results in an equilibrium in which stores that are next to one another charge the same prices, competition across neighboring *markets* results in the equalization of prices across these markets as long as trade between them is relatively costless. In the former case, this happens because consumers themselves will seek out lower prices and thus provide a "disciplining force" in the market. In the case of competition across markets, on the other hand, new economic agents that are neither producers nor consumers will emerge if prices differ because when prices differ, money can be made by "buying low and selling high." We will then see that these new economic agents impose the same kind of "disciplining force" across markets as consumers impose within markets.

20A.1 Buying Low and Selling High

Suppose, for instance, we consider two markets for our "hero cards," one in Florida and another in New York, and suppose the market demand and supply curves of consumers and producers in these two markets are as depicted in Graph 20.1. If these markets operate in complete isolation, this would result in the quantity x^{FL} produced and sold at a price p^{FL} in Florida and the quantity x^{NY} produced and sold at a price p^{NY} in New York. Suppose, then, that on a recent cross-country

Graph 20.1: Equilibrium across 2 Markets

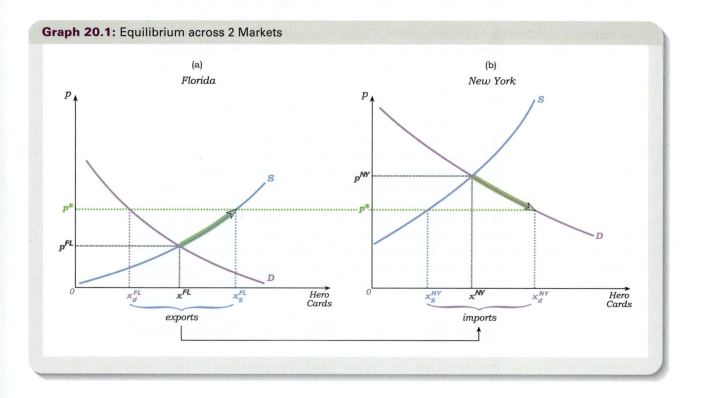

trip I notice the difference in prices across these markets. I turn to my wife with unbridled excitement at the prospect of becoming rich, ignoring for the moment the condescending way in which she tells me to "just keep driving." The cause for my excitement, of course, is that I can see in the regional price differences an opportunity to make money by simply buying hero cards in Florida where prices are low and selling them in New York where prices are high. In other words, I can make money by *exporting* cards from Florida and *importing* them to New York, an insight apparently not yet fully appreciated by my impatient companion.

Of course, it is unlikely that I am the only one who is in search of money-making opportunities. There are individuals in every economy who make it their business to find opportunities to buy low and sell high, and each one of them could find this same opportunity. Thus, exporters will go into the Florida market and shift the demand curve as they buy hero cards, thus causing prices in Florida to rise. When they then sell the same cards in New York, they will shift the supply curve, thus driving prices in New York down. So long as there exist price differences that are larger than the cost of transporting the cards from one market to the other, this process will continue. If we abstract away from such transportation costs, the process of buying low and selling high will continue until prices are just equal in the two markets, with the green arrows in the graphs indicating the shifts in equilibrium that result from the export of hero cards from Florida to New York.

If we then start in an initial equilibrium in which trade is not permitted between Florida and New York, the opening up of trade between the markets will result in a new equilibrium in which the same price p^* governs all trades in both Florida and New York. This implies that producers in Florida will increase their production from x^{FL} to x_s^{FL} while consumers in Florida will lower their consumption from x^{FL} to x_d^{FL} as both face higher prices after trade is permitted than before. The blue difference between what is produced and what is consumed is then exported to New York where consumers increase their consumption from x^{NY} to x_d^{NY} and producers decrease their production from x^{NY} to x_s^{NY} as both face lower prices than before. The magenta difference between what is consumed and produced in New York is then what has been imported from Florida.

20A.1.1 Profits for Exporters and Importers

As we transition from the "no-trade" equilibrium to the trade equilibrium, exporters and importers are clearly able to make economic profits by buying low and selling high. But notice that, in the new equilibrium, the model suggests that exporters buy at the same price in Florida at which they sell in New York. Why would they do this in equilibrium?

The answer is that the model gives us an approximation of the new equilibrium. Exporters and importers, just like everyone else in the world, face opportunity costs, which include the cost of their own time as well as the cost of shipping goods from one place to another. In equilibrium, they have to make enough to cover their opportunity costs. If they did not, they would be making negative economic profits, which tells us they could be doing better by undertaking another activity. Thus, prices will not fully equalize because some difference needs to remain to allow exporters and importers to cover their economic costs. However, the difference that remains will tend to be small in most markets given that exporters and importers ship large quantities of goods and therefore only need a tiny difference in price per unit in order to continue shipping goods from one place to another.

The fact that exporters and importers can make positive profits during the transition from a "no-trade" equilibrium to one with trade is consistent with our earlier work where producers often were able to make positive profits during the transition period from one equilibrium to another when economic conditions changed. This is the period over which entry and exit into an industry takes place, and it is that entry and exit that ultimately drives individual profits to zero. If the export/import business is also competitive (in the sense that each economic agent in the business is small relative to the whole business), we therefore know from what we have done previously that economic profits will be zero for each of them in the new equilibrium. So long as profits are positive, additional economic agents would enter the export/import business because they could be doing better here than in any other business.

For purposes of our discussion, we will then continue to illustrate an equilibrium with trade across regions as one in which the prices fully equalize as goods are exported from low-priced markets and imported into high-priced markets. But we will do so with an implicit understanding that this is an approximation of the new equilibrium and that, in reality, prices might still differ slightly between markets as trade is unfolding.

20A.1.2 Winners and Losers from Trade across Regions

Without doing much further analysis, it is already possible to identify the winners and losers from permitting trade across markets that were previously closed to one another. Consumers of hero cards in Florida will be unhappy with the new equilibrium as they now have to pay higher prices than they did before. Producers in Florida, on the other hand, get to produce more at a higher price and therefore end up on the winning side.[3] Similarly, consumers in New York are better off as their prices drop, while producers in New York are worse off as they face lower prices.

Exercise 20A.1 During the transition from the initial to the new equilibrium, which producers make positive profits and which might make negative (long-run) profits?

20A.1.3 Changes in Overall Surplus when Trade Is Permitted

While we might indeed be quite interested in the changes in welfare for different groups, and while this almost certainly has an impact on the political decisions that are made about trade, the relevant issue from a pure efficiency perspective is whether trade makes the pie overall grow larger or smaller. Put differently, does trade across regions increase or decrease overall surplus?

To illustrate how surplus changes, it is easiest for us to assume once again that tastes over hero cards are quasilinear because that allows us to interpret market demand curves as aggregate willingness to pay curves along which we can measure consumer surplus. The conclusion remains the same when tastes are not quasilinear, but the graphs would become more complex as we would have to introduce additional curves into the analysis.

Consider, then, Graph 20.2 in which we replicate market demand and supply curves from Graph 20.1. In the absence of trade across the two regions, initial consumer surplus in Florida is given by the area $(a + b)$, which is the area above the price paid by Florida consumers up to their marginal willingness to pay curve. Initial producer surplus in Florida is given by area (c), the area below the price received by producers down to their supply curve. Once trade has unfolded, consumer surplus shrinks to area (a) as consumers face higher prices, while producer surplus increases to area $(b + c + d)$. Thus, overall surplus in Florida increases by the blue area (d) because producer surplus increases more than consumer surplus shrinks. In New York, on the other hand, consumer surplus increases from (e) to $(e + f + h)$, while producer surplus falls from $(f + g)$ to (g). Thus, overall surplus in New York also increases—by the magenta area (h)—because in New York consumers gain more than producers lose.

The shaded areas in Graph 20.2 therefore represent the equilibrium increase in overall surplus that is generated by the activities of exporters and importers across the two markets. Notice that nowhere in the analysis have we had to say anything about surplus for exporters and importers because we know that, so long as the export/import industry is competitive, economic profit for exporters and importers will be zero. Trade makes both regions better off in the aggregate even though it causes some economic agents to be hurt (consumers in Florida and producers in

---

[3]Of course, if all producers face the same costs, they would end up making zero profit once again in the new equilibrium. In that case, the long-run market supply curve would be perfectly elastic. The picture in Graph 20.1 implicitly assumes that producers face different costs, which results in an upward-sloping long-run supply curve. This was covered in more detail in Chapter 14.

Graph 20.2: Changes in Surplus when Trade Is Permitted

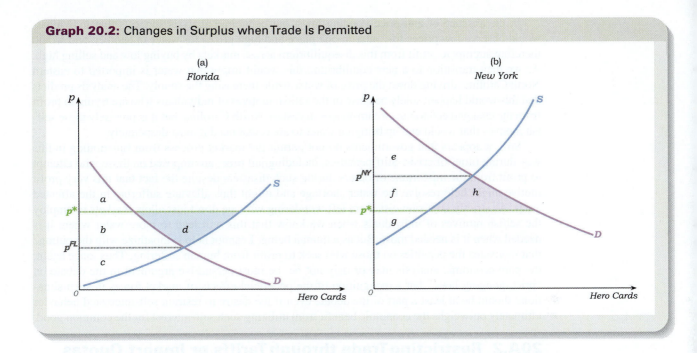

(a)
Florida

(b)
New York

New York) while others benefit (producers in Florida and consumers in New York). But because the overall surplus from trade increases, it is at least in principle possible to compensate the losers from trade with some of the gains from the winners of trade, thus leading to a strict Pareto improvement from the no-trade equilibrium to the new equilibrium.

20A.1.4 Restricting Trade and "Price Gouging"

You have no doubt heard trade discussed often in political debates, with one side arguing for the benefits of restricting trade and the other arguing for the benefits of allowing expanded trade. Since World War II, the world community has made enormous efforts to lower barriers to trade across countries, in large part because of the general recognition that, in the aggregate, all countries benefit from trade. At the same time, we have clearly seen in our analysis (and we will see further in some of the analysis in the remainder of the chapter) that lowering barriers to trade does produce winners and losers. While those who advocate restricting trade may in some cases do so because they are not aware that trade will produce overall benefits for all regions, it may also be the case that arguments in favor of restricting trade are based on a concern for those parties that are hurt when trade is expanded. While it is in principle possible to compensate those parties and still leave others better off, such compensation would have to involve additional efforts beyond just lowering trade barriers.

There are, however, cases where restrictions of trade by governments arise from an even deeper concern about the ethics of trade in particular circumstances. Consider, for instance, the change in economic circumstances for a particular region that emerges from a natural disaster striking that region. For example, suppose a hurricane hits eastern North Carolina and temporarily restricts the supply of drinkable water in that region. In the absence of trade, this shift in the supply curve for water in eastern North Carolina could dramatically raise water prices. Most states, however, have strict "anti-price gouging" laws that prohibit those who have drinkable water from selling that water at a significantly higher price. Such laws are, in effect, laws restricting trade because they keep individuals from taking advantage of the opportunity to buy water at low prices in western North Carolina in order to sell it at high prices in eastern North Carolina. As a result, the price ceiling on water prices imposed by "anti-price gouging" laws results in water shortages and the unfolding of some non-price rationing of the type we discussed in Chapter 18.

In the absence of anti-price-gouging laws, our economic analysis suggests that individuals would observe low prices for water in one place and high prices for water in another, and would therefore attempt to profit from this disequilibrium across markets by buying low and selling high. As we then transition to a new equilibrium, this would imply that water is imported to eastern North Carolina, driving down the price of water while increasing the supply. The analysis predicts that this would happen solely because of the selfish motives of individuals who are trying to profit from the changed economic circumstances in eastern North Carolina, but it is precisely these selfish motives that would end up bringing water to areas that need it most desperately.

Still, it appears that governments do not permit the market process from functioning in this way during times of crisis. Stiff penalties, including jail time, are imposed on those who attempt to profit from the misfortune of others during such disasters despite the fact that this very profit motive might help resolve the water shortage and might thus alleviate suffering in the affected areas. As strictly an economist, I am left wondering why we don't just allow markets to employ the selfish motives of individuals when we know that this will lead to more water where it is needed when it is needed most. But as a human being, I cannot help sympathize with the outrage that motivates the penalties on those who seek to profit from human suffering. Thus, once again, the pure economic analysis may or may not be the most persuasive argument in the debate on "price-gouging laws," but a recognition of the beneficial effects of market forces in such situations should be at least a part of the debate even if the desire to restrain self-interested behavior ultimately outweighs the economic benefit from utilizing such self-interest for the common good.

20A.2 Restricting Trade through Tariffs or Import Quotas

Often the debate about trade is not about whether or not to permit trade across countries but rather at what terms such trade will be permitted. The government has two options when contemplating restrictions (as opposed to the prohibition) of trade: It can either use taxes on traded goods to limit the flow of goods across borders by affecting the price of such goods, or it can impose quantity restrictions that limit the volume of trade directly. In principle, taxes or quotas could be imposed on exports and imports, although in practice government policy is usually focused on imports.[4] A tax levied on imports is called a *tariff*, while a quota restricting imports is called an *import quota*.

20A.2.1 Tariffs on Imports
Since taxes on imports, or tariffs, raise revenue for the government, the imposition of such taxes could be motivated by a desire to raise revenues in order to cover government expenditures. In fact, the bulk of revenues for the federal government in the United States at the time of the country's founding was raised through tariffs. Today, however, the motivation for the imposition of tariffs rarely derives primarily from a desire to raise revenues and typically involves a desire to protect certain domestic industries from foreign competition. Regardless of the motivation, a tariff remains a tax, and our analysis of taxes thus far suggests that, to the extent that they distort a price signal in a competitive market, they lead to inefficiencies.

In the context of trade across countries, the main effect of a tax on imports is to restrict the activities of exporters and importers. While exporters and importers are often also producers of goods, it is convenient for purposes of our analysis to simply treat them as if they were separate individuals. As we discussed in the previous section, these economic agents are attempting to buy low and sell high, and the imposition of a tariff is essentially an imposition of an additional economic cost imposed on this activity. Thus, if such an economic agent sees an opportunity to buy at a low price in one country and sell the same good at a high price in a different country, he will be less able to take advantage of such an opportunity if, upon importing the good, he has to pay a significant tax for each unit of the good that is imported.

---

[4]In the United States, there are actually constitutional barriers that limit the government's ability to tax exports.

Suppose, for instance, that Florida and New York are different countries, that they are currently trading without any barriers to trade, and that New York now imposes a per-unit tariff t on all "hero cards" that are imported from Florida. Prior to the imposition of the tariff, prices for hero cards in the two markets are equal because of the activity of exporters and importers who make zero profits in the trade equilibrium. This is what we illustrated in Graph 20.1 where consumers and producers in both markets faced the equilibrium price p^*, and this initial equilibrium is replicated in Graph 20.3.

When the tariff t is now imposed, exporters and importers no longer make zero profits because they have to pay this tax for each good that is imported. As a result, they will reduce the quantity that they demand in Florida and the quantity they supply in New York, thus causing prices in Florida to fall and prices in New York to increase as the equilibrium moves down along the supply curve in Florida and up along the demand curve in New York as indicated by the green arrows. This process continues until exporters and importers once again make zero profit, and this in turn will happen once the price in Florida is t dollars below the price in New York. At that point, exporters and importers are able to buy at price p_t^{FL} in Florida and sell at p_t^{NY} in New York, with the difference covering the tax they owe for each good that they are importing. Understanding again that this is an approximation and that prices in the two regions will differ by a bit more in order for exporters and importers to be able to cover their other economic costs, we have reached a new equilibrium where exporters are making zero profits once again. In this new equilibrium, the quantity that is imported to New York is the (magenta) difference between what New York producers manufacture (x_s^{NY}) and what New York consumers demand (x_d^{NY}).

It is then again fairly easy to identify the winners and losers from the imposition of the tariff by just looking at the new prices in Florida and New York. Since prices fall in Florida, consumers there will be better off while producers will be worse off, and the reverse is true in New York where prices increase as a result of the tariff. But in order to identify the deadweight loss from the tariff, we have to compare the change in overall surplus. Once again,

Graph 20.3: The Imposition of a Tariff on Hero Cards

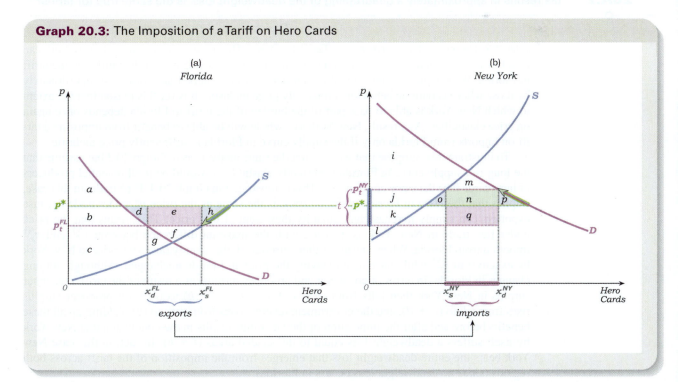

the analysis is easiest if we simply assume that tastes for hero cards are quasilinear, thus allowing us to measure consumer surplus along the market demand curve.

Consider first the changes in surplus in Florida. Before the tariff, consumers and producers traded at price p^*, resulting in a consumer surplus of (a) and a producer surplus of $(b + c + d + e + f + g + h)$. Once the new equilibrium with the tariff has been reached, consumers and producers in Florida face the lower price p_t^{FL}, giving rise to a consumer surplus of $(a + b)$ and a producer surplus of $(c + g + f)$. Total surplus therefore shrinks by the shaded magenta and blue areas $(d + e + h)$, which then represents deadweight loss in Florida.

In New York, on the other hand, prices rise as a result of the tariff, causing consumer surplus to shrink from $(i + j + m + n + o + p)$ to $(i + m)$ and producer surplus to rise from $(k + l)$ to $(k + l + j)$. Thus, overall surplus among producers and consumers shrinks by the area $(n + o + p)$. But New York gets one additional benefit from the tariff: the tax revenue generated by the tariff. This tax revenue is equal to the tax rate times the quantity of imports, where the former is represented by the blue vertical distance on the vertical axis (i.e., the difference between the price in Florida and New York) and the latter is represented by the magenta horizontal distance on the horizontal axis. Multiplying these results in a tax revenue equal to $(n + q)$, the shaded green and magenta areas. Thus, while consumers and producers jointly lose $(n + o + p)$, the government gains $(n + q)$, leaving New York overall better off by the area $(q - o - p)$.

Notice, however, that the magenta areas in our two graphs are exactly equal to one another. The area (e) in the Florida graph is exactly equal to the area (q) in the New York graph. Florida incurs a loss of $(d + e + h)$ whereas New York benefits by $(q - o - p)$, which implies that New York and Florida together lose $(d + h + o + p)$ because the benefit (q) in New York is exactly canceled by the loss of (e) in Florida. The overall deadweight loss across Florida and New York is then equal to the shaded blue areas in the two graphs.

Exercise 20A.2   In our treatment of taxes within a single market in Chapter 19, we concluded that a doubling of a tax results in approximately a quadrupling of the deadweight loss. Is the same true for tariffs?

20A.2.2 Passing the Burden of a Tariff to Other Regions

In Graph 20.3, New York can benefit overall from the imposition of a tariff because it is shifting part of the burden of the tariff to Florida. We saw in Chapter 19 that tax burdens within a market are borne disproportionately by those whose economic behavior is relatively price inelastic. It is for this reason that the extent to which New York is able to pass part of the burden of the tariff to Florida depends once again on price elasticities. As a result, New York as a whole will be able to benefit from imposing a tariff on imports from Florida only if the supply curve in Florida is sufficiently price inelastic.

To illustrate this, suppose that we conduct the same analysis as in Graph 20.3 but assume that the long-run supply curve in Florida is perfectly elastic (as it would be if all potential producers of hero cards face the same cost curves). This is illustrated in Graph 20.4. Free trade, in this case, implies that the price in Florida under no trade is the same as the price p^* under trade because exporters can simply purchase any quantity they want at that price. This means that the price under free trade in New York is also p^*, with the magenta difference between x_d^{NY} and x_s^{NY} imported from Florida. When a tariff t is then introduced, this simply raises the price in New York by exactly t to p_t^{NY} while once again leaving the price in Florida unchanged. Although nothing changes in Florida (in terms of consumer and producer surplus) as a result of the tariff, consumer surplus in New York then falls from $(b + c + e + f + g + h)$ to $(b + e)$; producer surplus rises from (d) to $(c + d)$; and the government revenue rises from zero to (g). Adding up all these benefits before and after the imposition of the tariff thus results in the conclusion that New York by itself suffers a deadweight loss equal to the shaded areas $(f + h)$. In fact, in this case New York bears the entire deadweight loss that emerges from the imposition of the tariff across both regions (since no deadweight loss occurs in Florida).

Graph 20.4: A Tariff when Supply Is Perfectly Elastic in the Exporting Region

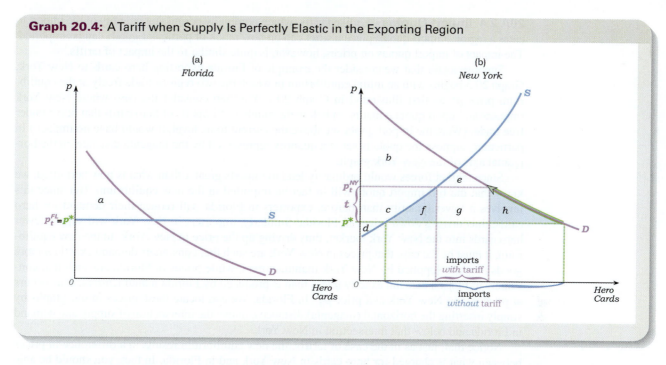

Thus, *New York is more likely to suffer a loss in surplus from the imposition of a tariff the more elastic the supply curve is in the market from which it is importing.* This is because *as Florida's supply curve becomes more elastic, it becomes increasingly difficult to pass on a portion of the tariff to Floridians.*

How would the analysis change if supply were perfectly elastic in both regions (with the supply curve lying at a higher price in New York than in Florida)?

Exercise 20A.3

20A.2.3 Trade Deals between Regions or Countries We have thus shown in Graph 20.3 that there may be instances in which it is economically efficient *for a region* to impose tariffs on imports even if this causes deadweight loss across both regions combined. At the same time, if supply curves in the exporting region are sufficiently elastic, the importing region will suffer a deadweight loss (Graph 20.4). Even when New York can gain in overall surplus, however, the exporting region (Florida) loses more than the importing region (New York) gains, which makes it possible at least in principle for the two regions to reach a trade agreement under which Florida compensates New York for reducing or eliminating its tariffs. Thus, negotiated trade agreements between regions (or countries) can always raise surplus for both regions (or countries).

More generally, it is important to remember that all countries and regions are exporting as well as importing. Thus, while Florida may be exporting hero cards to New York, New York may be exporting frozen pizza to Florida. This implies that while New York might in principle benefit from the imposition of a tariff in the hero card market, Florida might similarly benefit from an imposition of tariffs on frozen pizza. Both tariffs, however, will be inefficient when Florida and New York are considered simultaneously, and both regions will benefit from negotiated agreements that bring down multiple tariffs simultaneously. Thus, in practice, trade deals such as the North American Free Trade Agreement (NAFTA) typically reduce many tariffs simultaneously.

20A.2.4 Import Quotas Unlike tariffs, which nominally permit any quantity of the import to enter a region, import quotas place a strict cap on how much of particular goods can be imported. The impact of import quotas on prices, however, is quite similar to the impact of tariffs.

Suppose again that we consider the example of Florida exporting hero cards to New York. Graph 20.5 begins with an initial equilibrium in which the two regions trade freely at the equilibrium price p^* as first illustrated in Graph 20.1. We then consider the case where New York imposes an import quota q that is set below the number of imports of hero cards that occur under free trade. (Were the import quota set above the current trade level, it would have no impact.) In particular, suppose the quota is set at a quantity represented by the magenta distance on the horizontal axis of the New York graph.

Since market forces would ordinarily lead to imports greater than what is now permitted, we know that the full import quota will in fact be imported in the new equilibrium. But since this involves a lower quantity than before, exporters in Florida will reduce their demand for hero cards, thus driving down prices in Florida. Similarly, importers in New York will supply fewer hero cards into the New York market, thus driving up the price in New York. In the new equilibrium, it must be the case that prices in New York are such that consumers demand exactly q more goods than are supplied by New York manufacturers, while prices in Florida are such that consumers in Florida demand exactly q less than is produced by Florida manufacturers. This occurs at price p_q^{NY} in New York and price p_q^{FL} in Florida. We can locate these prices in our graphs by simply inserting the horizontal (magenta) distance q above the intersection of supply and demand in Florida and below that intersection in New York.

Notice that, just as in the case of tariffs, the new equilibrium results in a difference in prices between what is charged for hero cards in New York and in Florida. In fact, you should be able to convince yourself that *for every quota there exists a tariff that would have exactly the same impact on prices in Florida and New York.* And, since the impact of a quota on prices is exactly the same as the impact of a tariff on prices, consumer and producer surplus change in exactly the same way. From our work in Graph 20.3 (which labels the areas in the graph with the same letters) we then know that the joint consumer and producer surplus in Florida falls by $(d + e + h)$, while the joint producer and consumer surplus in New York falls by $(n + o + p)$.

Graph 20.5: The Imposition of an Import Quota

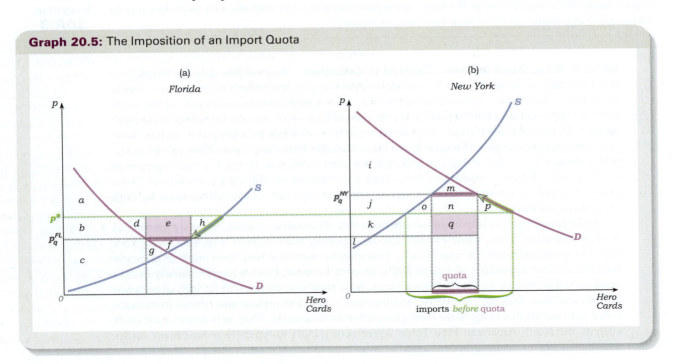

Exercise 20A.4
Identify separately consumer and producer surplus in both regions both before and after the import quota, and check that the previous sentence is correct.

In the case of the tariff, we next needed to consider the tax revenue that is raised under the tariff as another social benefit. But under an import quota, there is no tax revenue. However, since hero cards are bought at a lower price in Florida than the price at which they are sold, the exporters and importers are now making profit where they were not able to make a profit before. In particular, the area we identified as tax revenue in our analysis of tariffs now becomes the profit earned by exporters and importers under the import quota. This is area $(n + q)$ or, since $(e) = (q)$, $(n + e)$. If we assume that the area e is gained by exporters in Florida while the area n is gained by importers in New York, we can then conclude that the deadweight loss from the imposition of the quota is the sum of the blue rectangles: $(d + h + o + p)$.

Exercise 20A.5
What is the economic effect of an import quota in New York when the supply curve for hero cards in Florida is perfectly elastic?

This analysis is not quite right in the sense that we have not yet explained how it is determined which exporters and importers now find themselves in the nice position of earning positive profits in equilibrium. Presumably, every exporter and importer would like to be in this game, which implies that exporters and importers will need to exercise additional effort (and thus incur additional costs) to be among those that operate under the import quota. (The idea is analogous to our analysis of price floors in Chapter 18 where producers exerted effort to compete to be the ones to sell at the artificially high price.) To the extent to which such effort is socially wasteful, a portion of the areas (e) and (n) may in fact also be deadweight loss.

20A.3 Immigration versus Outsourcing

We have thus far discussed trade solely in terms of *goods* being traded across regions. But trade can also occur in the labor market, and it is arguments relative to the impact of trade on labor that often dominate the debate about free trade in general. Using the tools developed so far, we can now take a look at the economic issues related to this debate.

In order to focus our analysis, we will consider in particular two ways in which labor might be traded across regions. In one case, which we will call "outsourcing," firms in high-wage countries send a portion of the labor intensive work abroad before shipping back the goods to be sold in the domestic market (or elsewhere). It sounds like this might involve excessive transportation costs, but it has become common in many manufacturing sectors (like textiles) for U.S. firms to shift much of the labor-intensive portion of production abroad. It is even easier to do for firms that are engaged in businesses such as telephone marketing or computer processing where direct-marketing phone calls can be made to the United States directly from abroad or computer processing results can be wired back to the United States via the Internet.

The second case we will consider is one where, rather than production moving abroad to take advantage of low wages elsewhere, workers move to where wages are high. Migration flows like this are obviously restricted by immigration laws, but some countries are increasingly focused on reducing barriers to the mobility of labor by forming common labor markets across national boundaries. Even in countries that are not joining common labor markets, temporary migration permits for "guest workers" from other countries are widely discussed, as are special visas for immigrants with special skills.

Throughout, we will implicitly be assuming that skill levels of workers, and thus worker productivity, is the same across countries. This is of course not generally true; U.S. workers, for instance, are typically more productive (due to higher levels of education) than workers in developing countries where wages are low in part because of low levels of human capital (from lower levels of education). It is important to keep this in mind, because our stark prediction that trade or immigration will erase wage differences depends on the artificial assumption of equal worker productivity across countries. In exercise 20.2, we will give an example of how the insights from this section change as differences in skill levels across countries are introduced.

20A.3.1 Outsourcing

Outsourcing labor-intensive parts of production is attractive to profit-maximizing firms that use labor that is relatively more expensive in the domestic market than it is in other countries. Thus, in order for outsourcing to emerge, wage rates across countries must differ. Consider, then, an example in which a relatively high wage country like the United States has production sectors that can benefit from employing workers in a relatively low wage country like India. As we did in our example of trade in goods, we can thus begin with a state in which the labor markets are separate, with the U.S. market for a particular type of labor characterized by a high wage w^{US} while the same market in India is characterized by a low wage w^I. This initial equilibrium in which the two labor markets function independently is depicted in Graph 20.6.

Now suppose that outsourcing becomes an economically viable option for U.S. producers, and suppose further that the additional nonlabor costs of outsourcing (like transportation of goods) are negligible. U.S. producers would then demand less labor in the United States while increasing demand for labor in India. This creates downward pressure on wages in the U.S. labor market while creating upward pressure on wages in India, and if sufficiently many producers can make use of outsourcing, these pressures would continue until a new equilibrium emerges in which wages for this particular type of labor are equalized across the two countries at wage w^*. At this wage, U.S. producers demand L_d^{US} hours of labor, but U.S. workers are willing to supply only L_s^{US} hours while Indian producers demand L_d^I and Indian workers supply L_s^I. A new equilibrium is reached when the blue difference in the hours of labor supplied and

Graph 20.6: Outsourcing of Labor-Intensive Jobs from High to Low Wage Countries

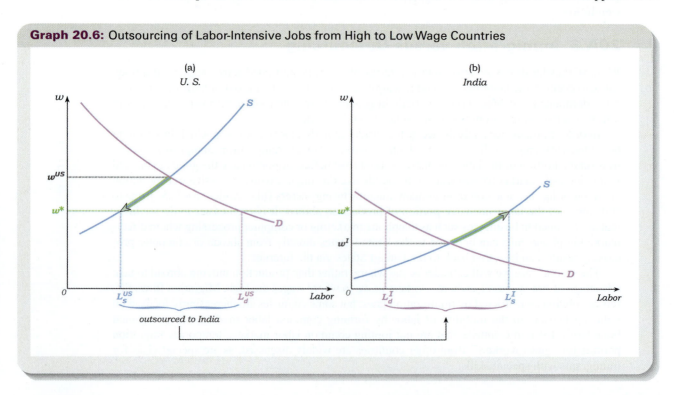

demanded in the United States is exactly equal to the magenta difference in hours of labor demanded and supplied in India.[5]

It is once again not difficult to see who will benefit and who will be hurt by this practice of outsourcing. Workers in the U.S. labor market experience falling wages, while workers in India experience rising wages, thus making workers in the United States worse off while making workers in India better off. The reverse is true for producers, with U.S. producers experiencing lower labor costs while Indian producers face increasing wages.

20A.3.2 Immigration   Now consider the alternative way in which trade in labor may occur, with labor rather than production moving from one country to the other. Suppose that outsourcing is not an option but that workers can freely move across borders. Since production is not shifting from one country to another, labor demand will now remain constant in the two countries but labor supply will shift as workers in India immigrate to the United States to take advantage of higher wages. This increases the supply of labor in the United States and reduces the supply of labor in India, thus once again putting downward pressure on wages in the United States and upward pressure on wages in India. Assuming that migration of labor is relatively costless, such migration would continue until wages across the two labor market are fully equalized at wage w^*, with the difference in the hours of labor demanded and supplied in the United States representing the number of hours provided in the United States by Indian workers who have immigrated to the United States. Similarly, the difference in labor supplied and labor demanded in India at the new wage w^* represents the hours of labor provided by Indian workers in the United States.

The process I have just described is then depicted in Graph 20.7. Notice that this graph is almost exactly identical to Graph 20.6 for outsourcing. The only exception is that the downward

Graph 20.7: Migration from High to Low Wage Countries

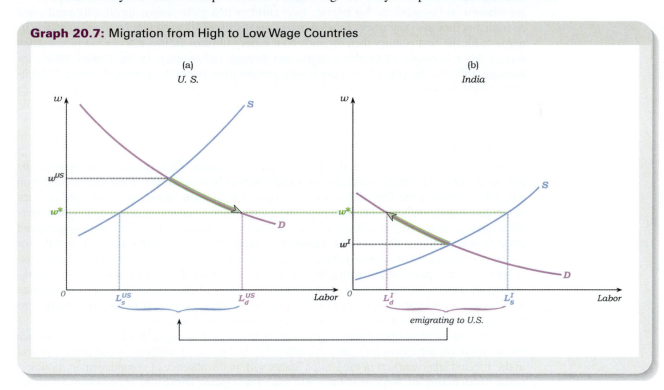

[5]From our discussion of labor supply in Chapter 9, you might recall that labor economists typically estimate labor supply curves to bend backward at sufficiently high wages. Outsourcing, however, tends to happen in relatively low wage markets where workers are on the upward-sloping portion of their labor supply curve, thus allowing us to simply assume an upward-sloping market labor supply curve in both markets. In addition, aggregate labor supply curves will tend to slope up because of the attraction of new workers into the labor market as wages rise.

pressure on wages in the United States and the simultaneous upward pressure on wages in India (represented by the green arrows) arises along supply curves under outsourcing and along demand curves under migration. This is because the pressures on market wages arise from shifts in labor demand in the two countries when firms move jobs, while it arises from shifts in labor supply in the two countries when workers themselves move between countries. The end effect, however, is exactly the same once the new equilibrium has been reached.

20A.3.3 Moving Goods or Moving People?

In our example of a high wage country competing with a low wage country, we can then characterize "outsourcing" as requiring the movement of goods, while immigration requires the movement of people. Outsourcing requires low barriers to trading goods, so that companies from the high wage country can move operations to the low wage country and then transport goods back to the high wage country where they are disproportionately demanded. Immigration, on the other hand, requires low barriers to labor mobility so that workers can move where wages are high. Graphs 20.6 and 20.7 then illustrate our model's prediction that both "moving goods" (as a result of outsourcing) and "moving people" (through migration of labor) have the same ultimate impact on wages because both mechanisms offer ways of integrating two labor markets. In both cases, people in the high wage country in essence employ workers from the low wage country to produce goods for them.

The difference between these two ways of integrating markets is, of course, that the workers from the low wage country who are employed to produce for the high wage country remain in their country of origin under outsourcing but physically move to the high wage country under immigration. This may then raise other concerns related to the integration of different cultures and languages in the host (i.e., the high-wage) country. It may also raise issues of other potential government costs—workers that migrate have children that go to school, health care needs, and so forth, but they also pay taxes. To what extent the net fiscal effect of immigration is positive or negative for the host country then depends on a variety of other factors that are not raised when foreign labor is employed (without migration) through outsourcing. In the United States, for instance, this may be part of the reason why immigration policy is more welcoming to high-skilled foreign workers than to low-skilled workers (who may make more use of public services in the United States while paying less in income, consumption, and payroll taxes). Thus, while there are indeed important similarities between trade in goods and migration of labor, the difference between the two may explain the balance of trade and immigration policy that emerges in the real world.

Having said this, the reality is that both trade and migration, while increasing the overall surplus in all countries, brings with it winners and losers in both countries. There is a good reason why labor unions in the United States tend to oppose both open immigration laws and policies that reduce barriers to trade. The challenge for policy makers is then to realize the increased overall surplus in such a way that those who are likely to lose from such policies are compensated through other policies that are implemented as barriers to trade come down. You will, for instance, often see debates about job retraining programs at the same time as trade policy is discussed in high wage countries, with policy makers seeking to find ways of retraining those workers that are adversely affected by trade. Our analysis suggests that, since overall surplus increases with trade, it is at least in principle possible to make everyone better off by lowering barriers to trade and migration when such policies are implemented simultaneously.

From a more global perspective, of course, it is difficult to argue that high wage countries should maintain barriers to trade and migration for the benefit of workers. While some workers in the affected labor markets in the United States will, in the absence of complementary policies, suffer losses in surplus, workers in India will experience gains. Those who are concerned with the suffering of people in less-developed countries might therefore argue for increased trade and more open immigration laws precisely because such policies will raise the material well-being of those who are suffering the most in the world. At the same time, as trade barriers are lowered, we may be outraged by the working conditions and wages that workers in less-developed countries are experiencing even in those production facilities set up by U.S. companies that are outsourcing some of their labor-intensive production. Terms like "sweatshops" have frequently been used to express such outrage, and it is argued that it is unethical for us to lower trade barriers that will result in U.S. firms setting up such "sweatshops" abroad. Nevertheless, the logic of economics gives the unambiguous prediction that, while worker conditions abroad may still be poor relative to what we expect in the United States, they will be better than they otherwise would have been had trade barriers not come down. Put differently, the economic analysis allows us to separate our instinctive reaction against "sweatshops" from the logical implication of the economic forces that are unleashed by trade. It diverts us from asking the nonsensical question of whether foreign workers in "sweatshops" are worse off than U.S. workers and instead gets us to ask the question: Are foreign workers better off than they would have been in the absence of U.S. companies increasing demand for foreign labor?

Suppose that the U.S. government attempts to alleviate suffering abroad by requiring that out-sourcing firms apply some fraction of U.S. labor standards (i.e., good working conditions, health benefits, etc.) in any production facility abroad. Illustrate the impact this will have in Graph 20.6. Does the logic of the model suggest that this will improve the fortunes of workers abroad? Will it benefit domestic U.S. workers?

Exercise 20A.6

20A.3.4 A Final General Equilibrium Caveat to Results on Outsourcing

What we have presented are the consequences of outsourcing and immigration in high wage and low wage countries *assuming all else remains equal*. When applying these results to real-world policy discussions, however, we have to be careful about that assumption and would want to consider some general equilibrium changes in behavior that might result from outsourcing. If U.S. firms save on labor costs, will they invest these savings in new innovations? Will these new innovations increase demand for other types of labor? Will these innovations result in lower production costs in other industries? Will the general decrease in production costs translate to cheaper consumption goods that in turn make real wages increase? If so, then the overall impact of outsourcing or immigration on wages in the United States might well be positive in the aggregate even as some sectors might experience decreased wages.

20A.4 Trading across Time

All of our examples of trade thus far have involved trading across two markets at a given point in time. But trade in the real world also happens *across* time. Those who are looking for opportunities to buy low and sell high across markets may identify opportunities when the price of a particular good happens to be low right now while they anticipate that the price will rise in the future. This may permit them to purchase goods now, store them, and then sell them in the future when price increases. Such behavior is often referred to as "speculation" because it requires individuals to speculate that prices will in fact rise in the future. In the real world, there are entire divisions of some firms that are occupied by market forecasters who try to identify such opportunities. And, just as the impact of trade across regions has the effect of equalizing prices across regions at any given time, trade across time initiated by *speculators* can have the tendency to stabilize prices over time in markets that would otherwise experience price fluctuations.

We should, however, not overemphasize this tendency as there are circumstances under which "trade across time"—unlike "trade across space"—can lead to *less* stability. The important difference between trade *across space* and trade *across time* is that the former occurs in an environment of relative *certainty* while the latter may occur in an environment of relative *uncertainty*. Exporters and importers can see the difference in prices across regions and thus buy low and sell high at any given time, but speculators have to guess about price differences across time. When speculators are on average correct in their guesses, their behavior will tend to have the stabilizing influence on prices across time that export/import behavior has across space; but when speculators "get it wrong," the same will not be true. A detailed exploration of such circumstances is beyond the scope of this text, but in end-of-chapter exercise 20.6 we take you through an example of assumptions that lead to such instability.

20A.4.1 Seasonal Demand for Gasoline

Consider the market for gasoline in the United States. This market has predictable seasonal changes in consumer demand, with consumers demanding significantly more gasoline in summer months due to holiday travel. A variant of gasoline used for home heating in the colder regions of the United States has similar predictable seasonal fluctuations in demand. You may have noticed that we tend to hear news reports of increasing gasoline prices as the summer months approach, often accompanied by dire predictions that gasoline prices will reach unprecedented levels "if the current trends" continue into the summer months as demand increases. Yet almost invariably, these dire predictions never materialize, with gasoline prices stabilizing just as demand increases in the summer. The same goes for predictions of increasing home heating oil prices as the winter months approach.

We can model the gasoline market at two points in time (just as we modeled the hero card market at two points in "space"): in the spring and the summer. This is done in Graph 20.8 where the intersection of market demand and supply results in the relatively low gasoline price p^{Spr} in the spring and the relatively high gasoline price p^{Sum} in the summer in the absence of trade across time. Thus, an opportunity has arisen for someone to buy low and sell high so long as the costs of storing gasoline in the meantime are relatively low. Suppose, for purposes of illustration, that such storage costs are negligible. Speculators will then purchase low-priced gasoline in the spring and sell it in the summer, leading to increased demand in the spring and increased supply in the summer. This then causes upward pressure on gasoline prices in the spring and downward pressure in the summer as indicated by the green arrows, with the blue quantity indicated in the first graph stored for sale in the summer (and equal to the magenta quantity in the summer graph). Just as in our analysis of trade

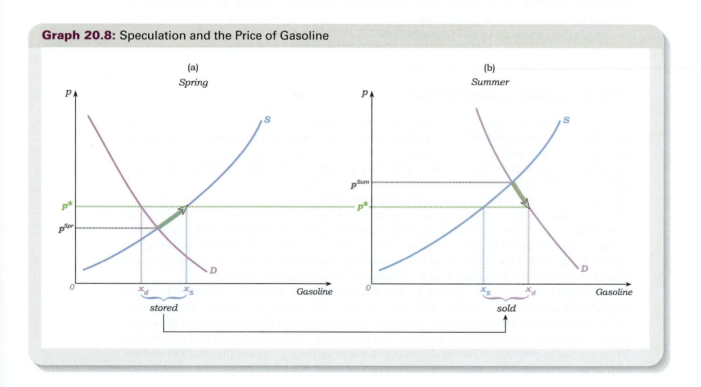

Graph 20.8: Speculation and the Price of Gasoline

across regions, prices are thus equalized through trade, with speculators ensuring that gasoline is plentiful when it is most needed.

The fact that gasoline prices do in fact rise as the summer months approach is then an indication that the costs of storing gasoline are in fact not negligible. As the summer months approach, more and more gasoline gets stored away as it has to be held in storage for shorter and shorter periods of time. Thus, gasoline prices rise as the summer approaches, leading to the dire prediction that, "if current trends continue as demand increases in the summer," prices will go through the roof. But just as consumer demand increases in the summer, speculators open their reserve in order to cash in, causing the price increase to come to an end just as consumer demand increases.

Exercise 20A.7 Illustrate how Graph 20.8 changes as the cost to storing gasoline is introduced. Can you see how price fluctuations across time will worsen as the cost of storing gasoline increases?

20A.4.2 "Long" versus "Short" Positions by Speculators In our previous example of speculators expecting gasoline prices to increase, it is easy to see how the speculator makes money by buying low now and selling high in the future. In financial markets, this type of speculation (which involves betting on prices rising and thus buying now) is known as *taking a long position* in the market. But what if you notice a price that you think is high now and is likely to drop in the future? Can speculators play a role in equalizing prices in this case if they don't currently hold any of the good that is priced high?

It turns out that the answer is yes. So long as anyone in the economy is holding reserves of gasoline that you think is currently priced too high, you could ask to borrow some of their gasoline reserves (in exchange for some interest payment), and sell it at the current (high) price. Then, when the price falls, you can buy an amount equal to what you borrowed and return it to the person who had the reserves of gasoline. You are in essence "selling high" now and "buying low" in the future (as long as you are right about the price falling in the future). In financial markets, this is known as *selling gasoline short* or *taking a short position*.

Exercise 20A.8 Illustrate in a graph similar to Graph 20.8 how this can contribute to stabilization of gasoline prices across time.

More generally, consider your options as an investor in any asset or commodity market, say for instance the market for hero cards. If you believe that we are at the beginning of a hero card fad and the price of these cards will therefore rise, you will simply take a "long position" by buying hero cards now with a plan of selling them in the future. But suppose you think instead that we are at the end of a fad, that hero cards, for instance, are currently priced at $10 a pack but will fall to $5 a pack in the next three months. You might then come to me (a producer of hero cards) and ask to borrow 1,000 packs of such cards for a charge of, say, $1,000 per month (or $1 per pack per month). Since you believe the hero card market is about to experience a downturn, you will then immediately sell those borrowed cards at the current price of $10 per pack, raising a total of $10,000.

Suppose you were right and three months from now the price of hero cards is only $5 per pack. At this point, you have paid me $3,000 in interest, leaving you with only $7,000 of your original $10,000. But now that the price of hero cards is only $5 per pack, you can buy 1,000 packs for $5,000, return what you borrowed (and cease paying interest to me), and be left with a profit of $2,000!

Selling assets or commodities "short" is a mysterious concept to most people, but the simple hero card example illustrates the essence of what it means. Because of the possibility of short selling, it is possible for speculators to profit anytime that they correctly identify a situation in which prices are out of balance. And it is not a mere theoretical construct: There exist markets for short selling virtually any asset or commodity you can think of. Of course, whenever speculators trade based on their hunches about price imbalances, the speculators stand to lose money if they turn out to be incorrect in their hunches. And, as you can see in end-of-chapter exercise 20.7, the risks faced by speculators can be much higher when they take short rather than long positions in financial or commodities markets.

In addition, there are many ways in which investors can take long and short positions in asset and commodities markets, and all we have done is to show the essence of each. You may, for example, have heard about *options*, which are *contracts giving the owner of the contract the right but not the obligation to buy or sell an asset or a commodity at a set price on or before a particular date.* A *call* option gives the owner of the option the right to buy, while a *put* option gives the owner a right to sell. Call options present another way to take a long position in the market, while put options are another way to take a short position. You can explore these, and the pricing of such *futures contracts*, in end-of-chapter exercise 20.8.

Exercise 20A.9   Can you see why investors would want to hold a call option if they believe the price of the asset is likely to go up, and why they would want to hold a put option if they believe prices are likely to fall?

If topics such as these interest you, you might consider taking further courses in financial economics or finance. Here, we were only able to scratch the surface of what is a fascinating and quite complicated topic. Before leaving the topic, we once again note that, while our treatment suggests that the behavior of speculators will lead to stabilization of prices across time, there are clearly real-world examples of financial "bubbles" (such as the run-up in stock prices prior to the Great Depression, the run-up of "dot-com" stocks in the late 1990s, or the run-up in real estate values leading up to the 2008 financial crisis) in which speculator behavior may have aggravated price instability. In further studies of these topics, you will be able to identify more clearly the circumstances where speculation leads to stabilization and the anomalies where speculation can lead to instability.

20B The Mathematics of Trading across Markets

There is little new in the way of the underlying mathematics to the graphs in Section A, and we will therefore not have much new to add in this section and will leave much of the details to end-of-chapter exercises. Just to get you started, we will simply go through one exercise to illustrate how one sets these kinds of problems up mathematically. More in-depth treatments of trade across markets would involve an extension of our general equilibrium models, a topic that goes beyond the scope of this text. (If the topic is of interest, you might consider taking a course on international trade.)

20B.1 Trade, Tariffs, and Quotas

Consider the case of linear demand and supply functions in two different regions, with regional variables denoted by superscripts 1 and 2 (for regions 1 and 2); i.e.,

$$x_d^1(p) = \frac{A - p}{\alpha} \quad \text{and} \quad x_s^1(p) = \frac{B + p}{\beta} \tag{20.1}$$

for region 1 and

$$x_d^2(p) = \frac{C - p}{\gamma} \quad \text{and} \quad x_s^2(p) = \frac{D + p}{\delta} \tag{20.2}$$

for region 2.

In the absence of trade across the two regions, equilibrium prices within each region can be found as in previous chapters by simply setting supply and demand within each region equal to one another and solving for price, giving

$$p^1 = \frac{\beta A - \alpha B}{\alpha + \beta} \quad \text{and} \quad p^2 = \frac{\delta C - \gamma D}{\gamma + \delta}. \tag{20.3}$$

If p^1 and p^2 are not equal to one another, then trade between the regions should occur until prices are equalized. Suppose $p^2 > p^1$. Then, in an equilibrium with trade, region 1 will export some amount X to region 2, causing demand in region 1 and supply in region 2 to increase by X; i.e.,

$$\tilde{x}_d^1(p) = \frac{A - p}{\alpha} + X \quad \text{and} \quad \tilde{x}_s^2(p) = \frac{D + p}{\delta} + X. \tag{20.4}$$

Letting $\tilde{x}_d^1(p) = x_s^1(p)$ and $x_d^2(p) = \tilde{x}_s^2(p)$ and solving once again for price in each region, we get

$$\tilde{p}^1 = \frac{\beta A - \alpha B + \alpha \beta X}{\alpha + \beta} \quad \text{and} \quad \tilde{p}^2 = \frac{\delta C - \gamma D - \gamma \delta X}{\gamma + \delta}. \tag{20.5}$$

The equilibrium level of exports X from region 1 to region 2 must equalize these two prices. Thus, setting $\tilde{p}^1 = \tilde{p}^2$ and solving for X, we get the equilibrium level of exports as

$$X^* = \frac{(\alpha + \beta)(\delta C - \gamma D) - (\gamma + \delta)(\beta A - \alpha B)}{(\gamma + \delta)\alpha \beta + (\alpha + \beta)\gamma \delta}. \tag{20.6}$$

Can you verify that, when exports are X^*, prices in the two regions are equal?

**Exercise
20B.1**

One can then calculate the impact of tariffs and quotas in a straightforward way. Suppose first that the importing region 2 imposes a per unit tariff of t on all imports. Rather than $\tilde{p}^1 = \tilde{p}^2$, the resulting equilibrium will then have $\tilde{p}^1 = \tilde{p}^2 - t$. Solving this equation, the equilibrium level of exports under a tariff of t becomes

$$X^*(t) = \frac{(\alpha + \beta)(\delta C - \gamma D) - (\gamma + \delta)(\beta A - \alpha B) - (\alpha + \beta)(\gamma + \delta)t}{(\gamma + \delta)\alpha \beta + (\alpha + \beta)\gamma \delta}. \tag{20.7}$$

Taking the derivative of $X^*(t)$ with respect to t, we get the decrease in exports from region 1 to region 2 for a 1 unit increase in the tariff t; i.e.,

$$\frac{dX^*(t)}{dt} = -\left(\frac{(\alpha + \beta)(\gamma + \delta)}{(\gamma + \delta)\alpha \beta + (\alpha + \beta)\gamma \delta} \right). \tag{20.8}$$

Now suppose that instead of a tariff, the government in region 2 imposed an import quota $\overline{X} < X^*$. The prices in the two regions will then not equalize, with

$$p^1(\overline{X}) = \frac{\beta A - \alpha B + \alpha \beta \overline{X}}{\alpha + \beta} \quad \text{and} \quad p^2(\overline{X}) = \frac{\delta C - \gamma D - \gamma \delta \overline{X}}{\gamma + \delta}. \tag{20.9}$$

Subtracting $p^1(\overline{X})$ from $p^2(\overline{X})$ then tells us how much of a price difference between the two regions is created by the import quota $\overline{X}$, with

$$p^2(\overline{X}) - p^1(\overline{X}) = \frac{\delta C - \gamma D}{\gamma + \delta} - \frac{\beta A - \alpha B}{\alpha + \beta} - \frac{((\gamma + \delta)\alpha \beta + (\alpha + \beta)\gamma \delta)\overline{X}}{(\alpha + \beta)(\gamma + \delta)}. \tag{20.10}$$

which can be rewritten in terms of the no-trade equilibrium prices p^1 and p^2 from equation (20.3) as

$$p^2(\bar{X}) - p^1(\bar{X}) = p^2 - p^1 - \frac{((\gamma + \delta)\alpha\beta + (\alpha + \beta)\gamma\delta)\bar{X}}{(\alpha + \beta)(\gamma + \delta)}. \tag{20.11}$$

Put differently, the difference between the prices in the 2 regions will shrink in proportion to the size of the import quota.

Exercise 20B.2 Can you demonstrate that a tariff $t = p^2(\bar{X}) - p^1(\bar{X})$ will result in the same level of exports from region 1 as the import quota $\bar{X}$, as well as the same equilibrium prices (in the two regions)?

20B.2 A Numerical Example

To add some numbers to this example, suppose that $A = 1,000 = C$, $\alpha = \beta = 1 = \gamma = \delta$, $B = 0$, and $D = -400$. Demand and supply curves in the two regions are therefore identical except for the intercept term of the supply curves. Plugging these values into equation (20.3), we get $p^1 = 500$ and $p^2 = 700$, with resulting equilibrium quantities in the absence of trade $x^1 = 500$ and $x^2 = 300$. Plugging the appropriate values into equation (20.6), we get an equilibrium export level $X^* = 200$ under free trade, with the equations in (20.5) then implying an equalized price under trade of $p* = 600$.

Exercise 20B.3 Illustrate demand and supply curves in the two regions (with price on the vertical and quantity on the horizontal axes). Carefully label each intercept as well as the no-trade equilibrium prices and quantities. Then illustrate the equilibrium under free trade.

Exercise 20B.4 Assuming that demand curves are also marginal willingness to pay curves, calculate the deadweight loss from prohibiting trade.

We could then ask how trade is affected by different levels of tariffs and quotas. Suppose, for instance, that a per unit tariff of $100 is imposed on all imports to region 2. Equation (20.7) then tells us that exports will fall to 100.

Exercise 20B.5 Illustrate the impact of a $100 per unit tariff on the equilibrium you have graphed in exercise 20B.3.

Exercise 20B.6 Assuming again that demand curves are marginal willingness to pay curves, what happens to surplus in regions 1 and 2 when considering each in isolation? What happens to overall deadweight loss when considering both regions jointly?

We will work more with this and related numerical examples in the end-of-chapter exercises.

CONCLUSION

This chapter concludes our series of three chapters that deal with government-induced price distortions in markets that would otherwise allocate resources efficiently. The chapter differs from the previous two in that it considers actions by economic agents who neither produce nor consume but instead find opportunities to "buy low" and "sell high." Despite the fact that such individuals do not produce anything, their activity can be socially beneficial by equilibrating prices across markets. In equilibrium, such individuals will then earn zero economic profit (so long as there are many of them competing with one another) while increasing surplus in both markets.

Policies that disturb the resulting prices *across* markets then create deadweight losses every bit as much as policies that distort prices *within* markets. Two common ways in which governments distort prices across markets are taxes on imports (known as tariffs) and restrictions on import quantities (known as import quotas). And, as with other policies, tariffs and quotas create "winners" and "losers," with the deadweight losses arising from the fact that the winnings of the winners are smaller than the losses of the losers. This makes it in principle possible to make everyone better off through the removal of tariffs and import quotas so long as additional policies assist those who would otherwise lose surplus. We also showed that the burden of tariffs (and quotas) will shift to those regions in which consumers and producers behave more inelastically (relative to price), just as taxes within a market are shifted to the more inelastic side of the market.

Finally, we extended our insights on trade across markets to two other settings. First, we showed a symmetry in outcomes between "trade in goods" and "migration of labor." Outsourcing of production to low wage countries arises in environments where goods can be traded freely and firms therefore move to where labor costs are cheapest, and immigration of labor to high wage countries arises when labor is freely mobile and moves where firms locate to produce output. In both cases, the high wage country essentially employs workers from the low wage country to produce goods, but workers stay in their home country under outsourcing while moving to the high wage country under labor mobility. Second, we illustrated how trading *across time* is quite similar to trading across regions, with the exception that price differences are directly observed in the latter (by exporters and importers) but only guessed (by speculators) in the former. Still, just as trade across regions causes prices to equalize across these regions, so trade across time can cause prices to stabilize across time, at least when speculators guess correctly about the future or when seasonal demand or supply fluctuations are relatively predictable.

END-OF-CHAPTER EXERCISES

20.1 In the text, we argued that the burden of tariffs is shifted across markets in ways that are analogous to how tax burdens are shifted between consumers and producers.

   A. Consider two countries: country 1 in which product x would sell at p^1 and country 2 in which it would sell at p^2 in the absence of any trade between the countries. Suppose throughout that $p^2 > p^1$.

   a. Begin by illustrating the free trade equilibrium assuming negligible transportation costs.

   b. Illustrate how the imposition of an import tax (or tariff) of t per unit of x by country 2 changes the equilibrium.

   c. What in your answer to (b) would change if, instead of country 2 imposing a per unit import tax of t, country 1 had imposed a per unit *export* tax of the same amount t?

   d. In your graph, illustrate the economic incidence of the tax t on trade; i.e., illustrate how much of the overall tax revenue is raised from country 1 and how much is raised from country 2.

   e. How would your answer change if you made the supply curve in country 1 more elastic while keeping p^1 unchanged? What if you made the demand curve more elastic?

*conceptually challenging
**computationally challenging
†solutions in Study Guide

      f.   In Chapter 19, we argued that it does not matter whether a per-unit tax is imposed on producers or on consumers within a market—the economic impact will be the same. How is what you have found in this exercise analogous to this result?

      g.   If the supply curve in country 1 were perfectly inelastic, would any of the tariff be paid by country 2?

B. Now consider demand and supply functions $x_d^1(p) = (A - p)/\alpha$ and $x_s^1(p) = (B + p)/\beta$ for country 1 and $x_d^2(p) = (C - p)/\gamma$ and $x_s^2(p) = (D + p)/\delta$ for country 2 (as in part B of the text).

      a.   Set up an Excel spreadsheet that calculates production and consumption levels in each country as a function of the demand and supply parameters A, B, α, β, C, D, γ, and δ as well as the per-unit tariff t imposed by country 2. Would any of your spreadsheet differ if instead we analyzed a per-unit export tax in country 1?

      b.   Let $A = 1{,}000 = C$, $\alpha = \beta = 1 = \gamma = \delta$, $B = 0$, and $D = -400$. Verify that you get the same result as what is reported in part B of the text for the same parameters when $t = 0$ and when $t = 100$.

      c.   Set up a table in which the rows correspond to scenarios where we change the parameters B and β from $(49\,500, 100)$ in the first row to $(12\,000, 25)$, $(2\,000, 5)$, $(500, 2)$, $(0, 1)$, $(-250, 0.5)$, $(-375, 0.25)$, $(-450, 0.1)$, and $(-495, 0.01)$ in the next 8 rows. Then report in each row p^1 and x^1, which are the price and quantity in country 1 in the absence of trade; $p^* = \widetilde{p}^1 = \widetilde{p}^2$, which is the world price under free trade; X^*, which is the level of exports under free trade; $X^*(t)$, which is the level of exports when $t = 100$ is imposed; $\widetilde{p}^1(t)$ and $\widetilde{p}^2(t)$, which are the prices when a per unit tariff of $t = 100$ is imposed; and the fraction k of the tariff that is shifted to country 1.

      d.   Explain what is happening as we move down the rows in your table.

      e.   Next, set up a table in which the rows correspond to scenarios where we change the parameters A and α from $(50\,500, 100)$ in the first row to $(13\,000, 25)$, $(3\,000, 5)$, $(1\,500, 2)$, $(1000, 1)$, $(750, 0.5)$, $(625, 0.25)$, $(550, 0.1)$, and $(505, 0.01)$ in the next 8 rows. (Keep the remaining parameters as originally specified in (b).) Then report the same columns as you did in the table you constructed for part (c).

      f.   Are there any differences between your two tables? Explain.

20.2†   The prediction that unrestricted trade causes a convergence of wages across the trading countries seems quite stark: Is it really the case that U.S. wages will converge to the wages in the developing world if trade is unrestricted? We will consider this here.

A. Workers in the United States have significantly more *human capital*—education, skills, etc.—than workers in Bangladesh. As a result, workers in the United States have a higher marginal product of labor.

      a.   Begin by illustrating the United States and the Bangladesh labor markets side-by-side, with demand and supply in Bangladesh intersecting at a lower wage in the absence of trade and migration than in the United States.

      b.   Suppose workers in the United States are 20 times as productive per hour as workers in Bangladesh. To account for this, interpret the wage in your U.S. graph as the "wage per hour" and interpret the wage in Bangladesh as the "wage per 20 hours" of work. What will happen when trade between the United States and Bangladesh opens and U.S. companies outsource production?

      c.   Does your graph look any different than our outsourcing graphs in the text? Does it still imply that wages for U.S. workers will converge to wages of Bangladeshi workers?

      d.   *True or False*: In order for true convergence of wages to emerge from trade and outsourcing, countries in the developing world will have to first invest in schooling and other forms of human capital accumulation.

      e.   *True or False*: Under a full free trade regime across the world, differences in wages across countries will arise entirely from differences in skill and productivity levels of workers.

B. Consider the case where U.S. workers are k times as productive as Bangladeshi workers. Suppose labor demand and supply in Bangladesh are given by $l_d^B(w) = (A - w)/\alpha$ and $l_s^B(w) = (B + w)/\beta$, while labor supply in the United States is given by $l_s^{US}(w) = (D + w)/\delta$. Since firms care about both wage costs as well as labor productivity, suppose that labor demand in the United States is given by $l_d^{US}(w) = (C - (w/k))/\gamma$.

   a.   Derive the wage w^{US} in the United States and the wage w^B in Bangladesh if there is no trade or migration.

   b.   Suppose trade between the United States and Bangladesh opens, and U.S. firms outsource some production that used to take place in the United States to Bangladesh. Suppose that the impact in labor markets is equivalent to immigration of X Bangladeshi workers to the United States. Determine the new wage $w^B(X)$ in Bangladesh and $w^{US}(X)$ in the United States.

   c.   At the equilibrium level of migration X^*, what is the relationship between $w^{US}(X^*)$ and $w^B(X^*)$?

   d.   Use this relationship to calculate the equilibrium level of migration that the outsourcing of U.S. production is equivalent to.

   e.   Suppose that $A = 16,000$, $B = -1,000$, $C = 160250$, $D = -10,000$, $\alpha = 0.00018$, $\beta = 0.00002$, $\gamma = 0.0007$, and $\delta = 0.0002$. Suppose further that $k = 20$; i.e., U.S. workers are 20 times as productive as Bangladeshi workers. What is w^B and w^{US} in the absence of trade? What is the employment level in the United States and in Bangladesh?

   f.   When trade is opened up and we determine the migration level X^* that free trade is equivalent to, what is X^*?

   g.   What are the equilibrium wages in the United States and in Bangladesh in the new equilibrium? What are employment levels in the two countries?

20.3   **Everyday Application:** *Quality of Life Indexes*: Every year, various magazines publish lists of "The 10 Best Cities for Living" or "The 10 Worst Cities." These lists are constructed by magazines weighting various factors such as climate, public amenities (like school quality and crime rates), local taxes, and housing prices. Economists often sneer at these lists. Here is why.

A.   Consider two cities that are identical in every way: same climate, same public amenities, same housing prices. Suppose for simplicity, unless otherwise stated, that everyone rents housing and everyone has the same tastes and income.

   a.   Begin by drawing two side-by-side graphs of the housing markets in city A and city B.

   b.   Suppose city A elects a new mayor who is superb at what he does. He finds ways of improving the schools, lowering crime, and building better public parks, all while lowering local tax rates. What will happen to the demand for housing in city A? What about in city B?

   c.   Depict the new equilibrium. Will housing prices still be the same in the two cities? Why or why not?

   d.   Last year, two magazines independently ranked the quality of life in city A and city B as equal. This year, one magazine ranks the quality of life in city A higher than in city B and the other does the reverse. When pressed for an explanation, the first magazine highlights all the wonderful improvement in city A, while the second one highlights the "excessively high" housing prices in city A and the "housing bargains" in city B. Which magazine is right?

   e.   What happens to the population size in cities A and B? What happens to the average house and lot sizes in cities A and B?

   f.   *True or False*: If city A is large relative to the national housing market, the mayor's actions make everyone in the country better off; i.e., not all of the benefits of the mayor's ingenuity stay in city A.

   g.   If you like public amenities more than the average person, will you be better off? What if you like them less than the average person?

   h.   *True or False*: If city A is small relative to the national housing market, the primary beneficiaries of the mayor's actions are landlords in city A (i.e., those who owned land and housing in city A prior to the mayor's actions).

B. Suppose that individuals have tastes over housing h, consumption x, and public amenities y, and these tastes can be represented by the utility function $u(h,x,y) = h^{0.25}x^{0.75}y$. Suppose everyone rents rather than owns housing.

    a.   In city A, the average resident earns \$50,000 in income, faces a rental price for housing equal to \$5 per square foot, and enjoys amenity level $y = 10$. Assuming everyone maximizes utility, what utility level does the average resident attain? (*Hint*: Note that y is not a choice variable.)

    b.   Suppose the housing market across the nation is in equilibrium. If households can move across cities to maximize utility, can you tell what this implies about the utility level households attain in city B?

    c.   Now suppose the new mayor in city A is able to increase the public amenity level y from 10 to 11.25. If utility for residents remains unchanged because of an increase in housing prices, how much will housing consumption have to fall for each household?

    d.   Suppose that city A is small relative to the nation and thus does not affect housing price elsewhere. Can you tell how much the rental price of housing must have increased from the initial price of 5 as a result of the mayor's innovation?

    e.   Are renters in city A better off as a result of the mayor's innovations? What about landlords who own land and housing?

20.4* **Everyday Application:** *Trade, Migration, and the Price of a Haircut*: In the text, we discussed the similarities between outsourcing and immigration, and with this the similarity between trading goods and moving workers. The implicit assumption in our discussion, however, was that it was in fact possible to produce the "goods" anywhere and sell them anywhere else. Dramatic drops in transportation costs have made this assumption reasonable in many, but not all, cases. In this exercise, we consider a case where the assumption does not hold: haircuts.

A. Suppose haircuts are considerably cheaper in Mexico than they are in the United States.

    a.   When barriers to the flow of goods between the United States and Mexico are removed (but barriers to migration remain), why might you not expect the price of haircuts in the United States to converge to the price of haircuts in Mexico but you might expect the price of apples in Mexico to converge to the price of apples in the United States?

    b.   Suppose the barriers to migration instead of the barriers to trade had come down. How would your answer to (a) differ?

    c.   Now consider this a bit more carefully. Begin by considering two sectors in the Mexican economy: The sector for tradable goods (like apples) and the sector for nontradable goods (like haircuts). Before any trade or migration between Mexico and the United States, suppose the labor market in Mexico is in equilibrium, with wages in the two Mexican sectors equal to one another. Illustrate the initial labor market equilibrium in Mexico in two graphs: one with demand and supply in the tradable sector, the other with demand and supply in the nontradable sector.

    d.   Suppose trade in goods opens between the United States and Mexico. As a result, some U.S. companies that produce tradable goods relocate to Mexico, hire the lower-wage workers in Mexico, and then export the goods to the United States (and other countries). What happens to the Mexican wage in the tradable sector?

    e.   Suppose workers can move across sectors; i.e., someone who cuts hair for a living can also work in an apple processing plant. If this is the case, what will happen in the Mexican labor market? What will happen to the price of haircuts in Mexico?

    f.   *True or False*: Even when migration of labor across national boundaries is not permitted, we would expect a drop in the barriers to trade in goods to result in wage movements that are similar in tradable and nontradable sectors of both economies so long as labor is substitutable across sectors within an economy.

    g.   Does an analogous process happen between the tradable and nontradable sector in the United States? Might you expect the price of haircuts to converge across Mexico and the United States after all?

B. Consider two sectors in the Mexican and U.S. economies: tradable goods (like apples) and nontradable goods (like haircuts). Suppose that Mexican labor demand and supply in the tradable sector is characterized by the equations $l_d(w) = (A - w)/\alpha$ and $l_s(w) = (B + w)/\beta$. Suppose the same holds in the nontradable sector, and suppose that initially there is no trade or migration between Mexico and the United States, with wages across the two sectors in Mexico equal.

    a.   Let $A = 100,000$, $B = -1,000$, $\alpha = 0.01$, and $\beta = 0.001$. What is the equilibrium wage in Mexico, and what is the employment level in each sector?

    b.   Suppose next that trade in goods opens between the United States and Mexico. As a result, demand for labor in the tradable sector increases, with A increasing to 210,000 in the tradable sector. If there is no labor mobility across sectors in Mexico, what wage emerges in the tradable goods sector in Mexico?

    c.   Suppose that labor can easily cross sectors within Mexico. What is the equilibrium Mexican wage that emerges?

    d.   What is the employment level in each sector in the new equilibrium from part (c)?

20.5*† Everyday and Business Application: *Compensating Wage Differentials and Increased Worker Safety*: Why would any worker choose to work in a profession (like coal mining) that is risky for the worker's health and safety? The answer is that such jobs tend to pay more than other jobs that require similar skill levels. The difference in wages between such "safe" jobs and risky jobs is what labor economists call a *compensating wage differential*. In the following exercise, suppose that it takes similar skills to work in coal mines as it does to work on oil rigs, and that workers in industries other than these two cannot easily switch to these industries.

A. Suppose that initially the wages in coal mines and oil rigs are the same.

    a.   Illustrate demand and supply in the labor markets for oil workers and coal miners in two separate graphs. What does the fact that wages are identical in the two sectors tell you about the level of risk a worker takes on by working in coal mining relative to the level of risk he or she takes on by working on oil rigs?

    b.   Suppose a new mining technology has just been invented, a technology that makes working in coal mines considerably safer than it was before. (For simplicity, suppose it is essentially costless to coal mining firms to put this technology in place.) What will happen to the supply of workers in the oil industry, and what will happen to the supply of workers in the coal industry?

    c.   What happens to wages in the two industries? How does this relate to the idea of compensating wage differentials?

    d.   Are workers in either industry better off?

    e.   Suppose next that the oil industry if very large compared to the coal industry, so large that the change in wages in the oil industry is imperceptibly small. Are any workers better off as a result of the safety innovation in coal mines?

    f.   In the case of the very large oil industry (relative to the coal industry), are any producers better off?

    g.   *True or False*: The more competitive the labor market is across industries, the greater is the incentive for a producer in a competitive industry to find ways of improving employment safety conditions.

B. Suppose all workers' annual utility can be given by the function $u(s, w) = (\alpha s^{-\rho} + (1 - \alpha)w^{-\rho})^{-1/\rho}$, where s is a work safety index that ranges from 0 to 10 (with 0 the least safe and 10 the most safe) and w is the annual wage denominated in tens of thousands of dollars.

    a.   Suppose that workers of the skill type of coal miners are currently getting utility u^* in all sectors of the economy in which they are employed. Determine the relationship of the current wages offered to such workers in the economy as it relates to safety conditions; i.e., find $w(s)$ (which will itself be a function of u^*, α, and ρ).

    b.   Suppose that $\alpha = 0.5$ and $\rho = 0.5$, and suppose that workers in the coal mining and in the oil rigging industries currently face safety conditions 5 and earn an annual wage (in tens of thousands) of 8. What level of utility u^* do workers like coal miners achieve in the economy?

    c.   Suppose that school teachers—who face safety of 10—could equally well have chosen to become coal miners. What is their wage? How much of the coal miners' salary is therefore equilibrium compensation for the risk they face?

d. Suppose that safety conditions in coal mines improve to a safety index level of 6. Assuming the coal industry employs a small fraction of workers of this skill type, what will be the new equilibrium wage for coal miners? Are they better or worse off?

e. Next, construct a table that shows how compensating wage differentials vary with the elasticity of substitution of safety for wage. Let the first column of your table give ρ and let the next 4 columns give u^*, the wage of workers on oil rigs, the wage of workers in coal mines (after the safety improvements have been made), and the wage of teachers, all in tens of thousands of dollars. (Continue to assume $\alpha = 0.5$ and an initial annual wage of 8 in the coal and oil rigging industries (before the safety improvements in coal mining).) Fill in the table for the following values of ρ: –0.99, 0.01, 0.5, 5, 10.

f. Interpret the results in your table.

g. How do you think each row of the table would change if α is lowered or increased? Check your intuition in a table identical to the previous table except that you now fix ρ at 0.5 and let α take on the following values: 0.1, 0.25, 0.5, 0.75, 0.9.

20.6 **Everyday and Business Application:** *Adaptive Expectations and Oil Price Instability*: We mentioned in the text that trading across time is similar to trading across space in that individuals find opportunities to buy low and sell high. Unlike the case where individuals trade across space, however, speculators who trade across time have to guess what future prices will be. If they guess correctly, they will introduce greater price stability over time (just as exporters equalize prices across regions). We now ask what might happen if this is not the case. More precisely, we will assume that individuals form *adaptive expectations*. Under such expectations, people expect prices in the future to mimic price patterns in the past.

A. Consider first the case of the oil industry. It takes some time to get additional capacity for oil production, so oil companies have to project where future oil prices will be in order to determine whether it is economically prudent to pay the large fixed costs of increasing their ability to pump more oil. They are, in essence, speculators trying to see whether to expend resources now to raise oil production in the future or whether to allow existing capacity to depreciate in anticipation of lower oil prices in the future.

a. Begin by drawing a demand and supply graph for oil, with linear supply steeper than linear demand, and label the equilibrium price as p^*.

b. Suppose that unexpected events have caused price to rise to p_1. Next, suppose that oil companies have adaptive expectations in the sense that they believe future price will mirror the current price. Will they invest in additional capacity?

c. If the demand curve remains unchanged but the oil industry in the future produces an amount of oil equal to the level it would produce were the price to remain at p_1, indicate the actual price that would emerge in the future as p_2. (*Hint*: After identifying how much the oil industry will produce on its supply curve at p_1, find what price will have to drop to in order for oil companies to be able to sell their new output level.)

d. Suppose again that firms have adaptive expectations and believe the price will now remain at p_2. If they adjust their capacity to this new "reality" and demand remains unchanged, what will happen to price the next period? If you keep this going from period to period, will we eventually converge to p^*?[6]

e. Repeat (b) through (d), but this time do it for the case where demand is steeper than supply. How does your answer change?

f. How would your answer change if demand and supply were equally steep?

g. While this example offers a simple setting in which speculative behavior can result in price fluctuations rather than price stability, economists are skeptical of such a simple explanation (which is not to say that they are skeptical of all explanations that involve psychological factors on how people might form incorrect expectations). To see why, imagine you are a speculator (who is not an oil producer) and you catch onto what's going on. What will

---

[6]This model is often referred to as the *Cobweb Model*. You might be able to see why if you begin to draw a horizontal line at p_1, then drop the line down to the demand curve, then draw a horizontal line at p_2 over to the supply curve, then connect it up to the demand curve where p_3 lies, etc.

you do? What will happen to the patterns of oil prices that you identified in the different scenarios?

B. Suppose again that the demand function for oil x is given by $x_d(p) = (A - p)/\alpha$ and the supply function by $x_s(p) = (B + p)/\beta$. Suppose throughout that $B = 0$ and $\beta = 0.00001$.

    a.   What is the equilibrium price p^* if $A = 80$ and $\alpha = 0.000006$?

    b.   Next, suppose that some unexpected events led to a price of $p_1 = 75$, but the underlying fundamentals—supply and demand curves—remain unchanged. If oil suppliers expect the price to remain at \$75 in period 2, how much will they produce in period 2? What will the actual price p_2 in period 2 be?

    c.   Suppose period 2 unfolds as you derived in part (b), and now oil suppliers expect prices to remain at p_2. How much will they produce in period 3? What will price p_3 be in period 3?

    d.   If the same process continues, what will price be in period 10? In period 20?

    e.   Next, suppose instead that $A = 120$ and $\alpha = 0.000014$. What is the equilibrium price p^*?

    f.   Suppose that p_1 is unexpectedly 51 but the fundamentals of the economy remain unchanged. What are p_2 and p_3 (as defined in (b) and (c)) now? What about the prices in periods 10 and 11?

    g.   Finally, suppose that $A = 100$ and $\alpha = 0.00001$? What will be the price pattern over time if p_1 is unexpectedly 75? What if it is unexpectedly 51?

    h.   If you were a speculator of the type described in A(g), what would you do in period 2 in each of the three scenarios we have explored? What would be the result of your action?

20.7   **Business Application:** *The Risks of Short Selling*: In the text, we mentioned that short selling can entail a lot more risk if the investor's guesses are wildly incorrect than taking the more conventional long position of buying and holding an asset.

BUSINESS APPLICATION

A. Suppose oil currently sells for \$50 a barrel. Consider two different investors: Larry thinks that oil prices will rise, and Darryl thinks they will fall. As a result, Larry will take a long position in the oil market, while Darryl will take a short position. Both of them have enough credit to borrow \$10,000 in cash or an equivalent amount (at current prices) in oil. (For purposes of this exercise, do not worry about any opportunity costs associated with the interest rate; simply assume an interest rate of 0 and suppose oil can be stored without cost.)

    a.   Consider Larry first. How much will he have one year from now if he carries through with his strategy of investing all his money in oil and oil one year from now stands at \$75 a barrel?

    b.   Now consider the worst-case scenario: A new energy source is found, and oil is no longer worth anything one year from now. Larry's guess about the future was wildly incorrect. How much has he lost?

    c.   Next, consider Darryl. How much will he have one year from now (if he carries through with his strategy to sell oil short) if the price of oil one year from now stands at \$25 a barrel?

    d.   Suppose instead that Darryl's prediction about the future was wildly incorrect and the price of oil stands at \$100 a barrel next year. How much will he have lost if he leaves the oil market at that point?

    e.   Was the scenario in (d) the worst-case scenario for Darryl? Is there a limit to how much Darryl might lose by "going short"? Is there a limit to the losses that Larry might incur?

    f.   Can you explain intuitively, without referring to this example, why short selling entails inherently more risk for investors who are very wrong in their predictions than going long in the market does?

B.* Suppose more generally that a barrel of oil sells at price p_0 on the current "spot market," which is defined as the market for oil that is currently being sold. Suppose further that you expect the price of a barrel of oil on the spot market n years from now to be p_n. Suppose the annual interest rate is r.

    a.   Can you write down an equation $\pi_n^L(p_0, p_n, r, q)$ that gives the profit (expressed in current dollars) from going long in the oil market for n years by buying q barrels of oil today?

    b.   How high does the ratio p_n/p_0 have to be in order to justify going long in the oil market in this way? Can you make intuitive sense of this?

    c.   Next, can you write down the equation for $\pi_n^S(p_0, p_n, r, q)$ that gives the profit from selling q barrels of oil short by borrowing them now and repaying them in n years? (Assume that the person you are borrowing the oil from expects you to return $(1 + r)^n$ times as much oil; i.e., she is charging the interest to be paid in terms of barrels of oil.)

    d.   How high can p_n/p_0 be to still warrant a short selling strategy of this type? Can you make intuitive sense of this?

20.8*† **Business Application:** *Pricing Call and Put Options*: In the text, we mentioned contracts called "call" and "put" options as examples of somewhat more sophisticated ways in which one can take a short or long position in the market.

    A.   Suppose, as in exercise 20.7, that the current price of oil is $50 a barrel. There are two types of contracts one can buy: The owner of contract 1 has the right to sell 200 barrels of oil at the current price of $50 a barrel one year from now. The owner of contract 2 has the right to buy 200 barrels of oil at the current price of $50 a barrel a year from now. Assume in this exercise that the annual interest rate is 5%.

        a.   Suppose, as in exercise 20.7, that Larry thinks the price of oil will rise while Darryl thinks it will fall. Consider Larry first and suppose he feels quite certain that oil will sell for $75 a barrel one year from now. What's the most he is willing to pay to buy contract 1? What is the most he is willing to pay to buy contract 2?

        b.   Next consider Darryl, who is quite certain that oil will be trading at $25 a barrel one year from now. What is the most that he is willing to pay for the two contracts?

        c.   Which contract allows you to take a short position and which allows you to take a long position in the oil futures market?

        d.   Suppose that contract 1 currently sells for $6,000. What does that tell us about the market's collective prediction about the price of a barrel of oil one year from now?

        e.   Suppose instead that contract 2 currently sells for $6,000. What does that tell us about the market's prediction of oil prices one year from now?

    B.   In part A, we considered only a single call or put option at a time. In reality, a much larger variety of such futures contracts can exist at any given time.

        a.   Suppose that a call option gives the owner the right to buy 200 barrels of oil at $50 one year from now. You observe that this futures contract is selling for $3,000 in the market. What is the market's prediction about the price of oil one year from now? (Assume again an interest rate of 0.05.)

        b.   Suppose someone else has just posted another call option contract for sale. This one entitles the owner to buy 200 barrels of oil at a price of $43 one year from now. How much do you predict this contract will sell for (given your answer to (a))?

        c.   Then a put option is posted for sale that allows the owner to sell 200 barrels of oil at a price of $71 one year from now. What do you think this option will be priced at by the market?

        d.   Let $P^C(\bar{p}, p, q, r, n)$ be the price of a call option to buy q barrels of oil n years from now at price $\bar{p}$ when the market interest rate is r and the market expectation of the actual price of oil n years from now is p. What is the equation that defines P^C?

        e.   Let $P^P(\bar{p}, p, q, r, n)$ be the price of a put option to sell q barrels of oil n years from now at price $\bar{p}$ when the market interest rate is r and the market expectation of the actual price of oil n years from now is p. What is the equation that defines P^P?

        f.   The price p at which oil actually sells at any given time is called the *spot price*. Illustrate what you have just found in a graph with the future spot price p on the horizontal axis and dollars on the vertical. First, graph the relationship of P^C to p (holding fixed $\bar{p}$, q, n, and r). Label intercepts and slopes. Then graph the same for P^P. Where must these intersect? Explain.

        g.   Illustrate the same thing in a second graph, except this time put the call or put price $\bar{p}$ on the horizontal axis. Where do the P^C and P^P lines now intersect? Explain.

20.9* **Business and Policy Application:** *General Equilibrium Effects of a Property Tax*: In Chapter 19, we introduced the idea that the property tax is really composed of two taxes: a tax on land, and a tax on improvements of land, which we can think of as capital invested in housing.

A. For purposes of this problem, we focus only on the part of the property tax that is effectively a tax on housing capital. Assume, unless otherwise stated, that capital can move freely between housing and other uses.

    a.   Begin by drawing a graph with housing capital h on the horizontal axis and the rental rate of housing capital r_h on the vertical. Draw demand and supply curves that intersect at r_h^* and illustrate the impact of the property tax t on the rental rate $r_h^s(t)$ earned by suppliers of capital when considering this market in isolation.

    b.   Next to your graph from part (a), illustrate the demand and supply curves for nonhousing capital prior to the imposition of the property tax on the housing market. Where must the equilibrium rental rate r^* be in relation to the pre-tax equilibrium housing capital rental rate r_h^*? Given that capital is mobile between the two sectors, can the after-tax "partial" equilibrium you identified for the housing market in (a) be the "general" equilibrium for the housing market once we take into account the mobility of capital across sectors?

    c.   What does your answer to (b) imply for what will happen to the supply curve for capital in the housing and nonhousing sectors?

    d.   Illustrate the new general equilibrium that takes into account the movement of capital across sectors in response to the property tax. What happens to the rental rate of capital in the nonhousing sector?

    e.   In what sense is a portion of the property tax burden shifted to nonhousing capital?

    f.   Are renters of housing capital better or worse off as a result of the general equilibrium shifting of some portion of the tax burden across sectors? Will they consume more or less housing compared to the initial partial equilibrium prediction?

    g.   *True or False*: The property tax will result in smaller houses and more investment in business machinery, but if we do not take the general equilibrium effect of the tax into account, we will underestimate how much smaller the houses will be and overestimate how many more business machines there will be.

B. Suppose that demand and supply for capital are identical in the housing and nonhousing sector, taking the form $k_d(r) = (A - r)/\alpha$ and $k_s(r) = (B + r)/\beta$ (as in the example of part B of the text). In this example, let $A = 1$, $B = 0$, $\alpha = 0.00000015$, and $\beta = 0.00000001$.

    a.   Begin by determining the equilibrium rental rates r^* and r_h^* for nonhousing capital and housing capital, and think of these as interest rates. How much capital is being transacted in each sector?

    b.   Next, suppose that a tax of $t = 0.04$ is imposed through the property tax in the housing sector. If you assumed that there was no connection of the housing sector to any other sector of the economy, what would happen to the interest rate r_h^s received by suppliers of housing capital and the interest rate r_h^d paid by demanders of housing capital.

    c.   Next, suppose that capital is freely mobile across the two sectors. How much capital will flow out of the housing sector? (*Hint*: You can treat this just like any other problem involving trade between two sectors where the starting prices are not equal to one another. The flow of capital is then just defined exactly like X^* derived in the text. To apply this formula, you need to redefine the demand (or supply) curve in the housing sector to include the tax $t = 0.04$, which simply shifts A down (or B up) by 0.04.)

    d.   What happens to the new equilibrium interest rate that suppliers of capital can get in the economy? In what sense has a portion of the property tax been shifted to all forms of capital?

    e.   What happens to the rental rate of capital paid by consumers in the housing sector?

    f.   Describe the general equilibrium economic incidence of the tax.

20.10* Business and Policy Application: *Local Differences in Property Taxes*: Since property taxes are set locally in the United States, they differ across communities, with different communities therefore facing different taxes on housing capital. (Note: This exercise presumes you have already gone through exercise 20.9.)

A. Consider the "general equilibrium" effect of the property tax; i.e., the effect that results from the mobility of capital across sectors and is in addition to the initial "partial equilibrium" effect you predicted in part (a) of exercise 20.9.

    a.   Does this general equilibrium effect become larger or smaller as the supply of nonhousing capital becomes more elastic?

b.   Compare the following two cases: In case 1, only the local community i imposes a property tax t, while in case 2, a national property tax t (of the same magnitude) is imposed across the whole country. Given your answer to (a), in which case are renters of housing capital in community i more affected?

c.   Now consider the case where all communities are imposing property taxes, but some are imposing higher property tax rates than others. We can then think of the national property tax system as having two components: First, there is an average property tax rate $\bar{t}$ that is imposed across the country, and second, each community i has a supplemental local tax that may be positive or negative depending on whether its property tax rate lies above the national average or below. Treating the national average tax rate like case 2 in part (b), what do you think is the general equilibrium incidence of this portion of the U.S. property tax system?

d.   Now consider community i and suppose this community taxes property more heavily than the national average. Using your insight from case 1 in part (b), what do you think is the incidence of the portion of community i's tax that lies above the national average?

e.   How would your answer change for community j that taxes property at a rate below the national average?

f.   *True or False*: All else equal, community j will have larger houses than community i.

g.   *True or False*: The U.S. property tax system (in which local property tax rates vary across communities) results in a uniform decrease in the return on all forms of capital, with business decisions regarding nonhousing capital being affected the same way across the country.

B.   Suppose that the demand and supply for housing capital and nonhousing capital are the same as in part B of exercise 20.9.

a.   Suppose that the local property tax system in the United States has resulted in an *average* property tax rate of $\bar{t} = 0.04$. Use what you calculated in exercise 20.9 to determine the impact of this property tax system on the rate of return on capital for owners of capital.

b.   Suppose community i deviates from the national average and sets a local property tax rate of $t_i = 0.05$. What will be the rental rate received by housing capital suppliers, and what will be the rental rate paid by renters of housing capital in community i?

c.   Suppose community j deviates from the national average by setting a local property tax rate of only $t_j = 0.03$. What will be the rental rate received by housing capital suppliers, and what will be the rental rate paid by renters of housing capital in community j?

d.   *True or False*: The entire difference in local tax rates between community i and community j is borne by renters; i.e., renters in community j pay a local rental rate that is less than the rate paid by renters in community i, with the difference equal to the difference in the local property tax rates.

20.11 Policy Application: *U.S. Immigration Policy*: U.S. immigration law is based on a quota system; i.e., a system under which there is a maximum number of immigrants allowed for each country, with different quotas set for different countries. In this exercise, we consider an alternative way of achieving the same level of immigration from each country. To make the exercise tractable, assume that all workers around the world are identical.[7]

A.   Assume throughout that the primary motivation for migration is a search for higher wages.

a.   Begin by drawing the U.S. supply and demand curves for workers and, next to it, the supply and demand curves in the rest of the world. Assume that the equilibrium wage (in the absence of trade or migration) is higher in the United States.

b.   Illustrate the equilibrium in which there are no restrictions to migration, assuming migration is relatively costless.

---

[7]In reality, of course, workers have different skill and education levels, and immigration law specifies preference classes for some skills over others.

    c.   Now suppose the United States introduces an immigration quota that allows less migration than would naturally occur in the absence of restrictions. Illustrate the impact of such a quota on the labor markets in the United States and in the rest of the world.

    d.   Suppose that the United States had not imposed the immigration quota but instead rations access to the United States from the rest of the world by charging an immigration tax of T per worker. Illustrate how large T would have to be to result in the same level of immigration from the rest of the world.

    e.   *True or False*: Within the context of this example, country-specific immigration quotas are equivalent to country-specific immigration taxes.

B. Now consider labor demand and supply functions $l_d^1(w) = (A - w)/\alpha$ and $l_s^1(w) = (B + w)/\beta$ for the rest of the world and $l_d^2(w) = (C - w)/\gamma$ and $l_s^2(w) = (D + w)/\delta$ for the United States.

    a.   Let $A = C = 100{,}000$, $B = -1{,}000$, $D = 0$, $\alpha = 0.002$, and $\beta = \gamma = \delta = 0.001$. What would be the equilibrium wage in the the United States and in the rest of the world if they were isolated from one another?

    b.   What would be the equilibrium wage if labor was fully and costlessly mobile? How high would immigration to the United States be?

    c.   Suppose the U.S. government sets a 1,000,000 quota for immigration from the rest of the world. How will the equilibrium wage in the United States and the rest of the world be affected by this?

    d.   How high would the United States have to set an immigration tax in order to achieve the same outcome?

20.12[†] **Policy Application:** *Trade Barriers against "Unfair" Competition*: Some countries subsidize some of their industries heavily, which leads U.S. producers to lobby for tariffs against products from such industries. It is argued that countries with lower subsidies, like the United States, need to impose such tariffs in order to protect the United States from unfair foreign competition.

A. Suppose that initially the domestic demand and supply curves for steel intersect at the same price in the United States as in Europe.

    a.   Begin by illustrating this in side-by-side graphs.

    b.   Next, suppose Europe introduces a subsidy for each ton of steel. Illustrate the impact this has on the price paid by buyers of steel in Europe before any trade with the United States emerges.

    c.   Suppose the United States does not introduce any tariffs on steel to counter the subsidy given in Europe. What will happen to steel prices in the United States? Why?

    d.   In your U.S. graph, illustrate the change in consumer and producer surplus (and assume for simplicity that there are no income effects in the steel market). Are U.S. steel producers rational when they lobby for steel tariffs in response to European steel subsidies?

    e.   What happens to total surplus in the United States? On purely efficiency grounds, would you advocate for U.S. tariffs in response to European subsidies on steel?

    f.   Without pinpointing areas in the graph, do you think trade increases or reduces the deadweight loss from the subsidy in Europe?

    g.   How much of a tariff would the United States have to impose in order to eliminate any effect of the European steel subsidies on U.S. markets?

    h.   Suppose the steel industry is perfectly competitive in both Europe and the United States. *True or False*: The European steel subsidy, if not followed by a U.S. tariff on European steel, would in the long run eliminate the U.S. steel industry while at the same time increasing U.S. overall surplus.

B. Now consider demand and supply functions $x_d^1(p) = (A - p)/\alpha$ and $x_s^1(p) = (B + p)/\beta$ for Europe and $x_d^2(p) = (C - p)/\gamma$ and $x_s^2(p) = (D + p)/\delta$ for the United States. Let $\alpha = \gamma = 0.00006$, $\beta = \delta = 0.0001$, $A = C = 800$, and $B = D = 0$.

    a.   Calculate the prices and quantities in Europe and the United States in the absence of trade. Is there any reason for trade to emerge?

b. Suppose next that Europe puts a $250 per ton subsidy for steel in place. In the absence of any trade, what happens to the purchase price of a ton of steel? What happens to the price received by sellers?

c. If there are no trade barriers in place, how much steel will now be exported from Europe to the United States? What will be the equilibrium price of steel in the United States?

d. How much of a tariff on steel would the United States have to impose to prevent the European steel subsidy from affecting the U.S. market for steel?

e. What is the deadweight loss in the United States of such a tariff (assuming no income effects)?

21

Externalities in Competitive Markets

At this point, you may have gotten the impression that economists believe markets always and unambiguously result in efficient outcomes, with total surplus maximized when markets operate without interference from other institutions.[1] If this were the case, there would be no efficiency role for nonmarket institutions in society, and their only justification would lie in concerns about the *distribution* of surplus, concerns about equity and fairness as these relate to the market allocation of scarce resources. But, while such equity issues do play an important role in justifying nonmarket institutions (including government), we will in this and the coming chapters investigate conditions under which nonmarket institutions are motivated by *efficiency* rather than equity concerns. These conditions include all the possible violations of the assumptions underlying the first welfare theorem (Chapter 15), including the presence of market power and asymmetric information.

Before we get to asymmetric information and market power, however, we will first take a look at yet a third set of conditions that lead to dead weight losses in the absence of other institutions, even when markets are perfectly competitive. These conditions are called *externalities*, and they arise whenever decisions of some parties in the market have a direct impact on others in ways that are not captured by market prices. When a firm's production process emits pollution into the air, for instance, this pollution potentially has a direct impact on many. Put differently, the emission of pollution imposes on society costs that are typically not priced by the market and thus are not taken into account by producers unless some other institution imposes those costs on them. When I decide to get in the car and enter a congested road, I am similarly contributing to the overall congestion and thus am delaying others from getting to where they want to go, but I don't think about others when I make the decision of whether to get in the car. When I play loud music on my patio at home, my neighbors get to "enjoy" the music as well. These are all examples of externalities, of "external costs or benefits" that markets do not internalize because the market participants do not have to pay for them.

21A The Problem of Externalities

The essential feature of an externality is then that either costs or benefits of production or consumption are directly imposed on nonmarket participants. Since nonmarket participants are neither demanders nor suppliers of goods, neither market demand nor market supply curves are

---

[1]This chapter builds once again on a basic understanding of the partial equilibrium model from Chapters 14 and 15. Section 21B.3 also builds on the discussion of exchange economies in Chapter 16 but can be skipped if you have not yet read Chapter 16.

affected by such externality costs or benefits. Thus, a competitive market composed of price-taking consumers and producers continues to produce in equilibrium where demand intersects supply. However, while the aggregate marginal willingness to pay curve still allows us to measure the benefits consumers receive from participating in markets and the supply curve still allows us to measure costs incurred by producers, there are now nonmarket participants that also incur benefits or costs. Thus, we can no longer simply use consumer and producer surplus to measure the net-gains for society from the existence of markets. Put differently, we have to include the externality costs and benefits that a competitive market ignores in our calculation of overall surplus.

Before we get started, I should note that we will treat consumers and producers as strictly separate *in their roles as consumers and producers* from their roles as individuals who may incur some damage or benefit from an externality. We generally lose nothing by making this assumption. Even if, for instance, a producer whose production causes pollution incurs health problems from pollution, no individual producer will take those costs into account in his or her production choices because, in competitive markets, each producer is so small relative to the market that his or her contribution to overall pollution is negligible. Thus, we will simply treat all producers as considering only their own production costs when making decisions, and then lump them in separately with all economic agents who are hurt by the aggregate level of pollution produced by the industry. In other words, we will treat producers as individuals who consider their own cost of production when making supply decisions, and then we will treat the part of that producer that is hurt by the overall level of pollution as a separate person.

21A.1 Production Externalities

Suppose, then, that we return to the example of an industry that produces "hero cards" but now we assume that the least-cost production process for producers involves the emission of greenhouse gases that contribute to environmental problems. Thus, in addition to the costs of production that are faced by each of the producers of hero cards, costs of pollution are imposed on others in society. We will then reconsider how many hero cards would be produced by a social planner who knows all the relevant costs and benefits and who seeks to maximize social surplus—how much production would take place if our omniscient and benevolent "Barney" from Chapter 15 would allocate resources. In our Chapter 15 analysis that excluded production externalities like pollution, it turned out that "Barney" could do no better than the competitive market. We will now see that this is no longer true when externalities become part of the analysis.

21A.1.1 "Barney" versus the Market

In Graph 21.1, we begin with the market demand and supply graph for hero cards in panel (a). Whether there are production externalities or not, the market will then produce x^M at price p^M, with all consumers and all producers doing the best they can in equilibrium. Assuming tastes are quasilinear in hero cards, consumers then get the shaded blue area in surplus, while producers get the shaded magenta area. If the production of hero cards produces pollution, however, each hero card that is produced imposes a pollution cost on society, a cost that is borne neither by those who consume nor those who produce hero cards.

Panel (b) of the graph then inserts a green curve labeled "*SMC.*" This curve represents the *social marginal cost of producing* hero cards. It includes the producers' marginal costs that are captured in the market supply curve, but it also includes the additional cost of pollution that is imposed on others. Thus, the social marginal cost curve must lie above the supply curve since it includes costs *in addition to* those incurred by producers. It may be that the *SMC* curve is parallel to the supply curve, implying a constant marginal cost of pollution for each hero card produced, or that it diverges from the supply curve, implying that each additional hero card results in a greater additional pollution cost than the last one. Regardless of how exactly it is related to supply, however, it is this curve that accurately reflects the society-wide cost of production.

Graph 21.1: Maximizing Social Surplus in the Presence of a Negative Production Externality

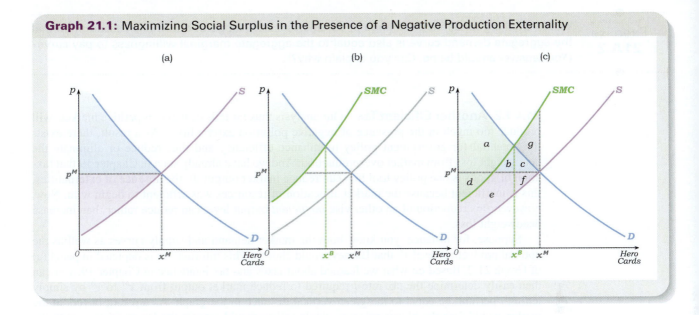

As a result, our omniscient and benevolent "Barney" would then decide to continue to produce so long as the benefits from production as represented by the marginal willingness to pay of consumers outweighs the overall cost of additional production for society. Put differently, Barney would certainly produce the first hero card because there is some consumer to whom this card is worth more than all the costs incurred by society as measured by SMC, and he would continue to produce until the green SMC crosses the blue marginal benefit curve. He would not, however, produce any more than that because once SMC is higher than the marginal willingness to pay of consumers, the society-wide cost of additional hero cards is larger than the benefit. Barney then would choose to produce x^B, resulting in an overall surplus for society represented by the shaded green area.

We can already see that the social planner who seeks to maximize overall surplus will therefore choose less production than will occur in the market. This implies that the market will produce an inefficiently high level of output in the absence of any nonmarket institutions that curtail production. This is clarified even further in panel (c) where we have labeled some areas in the graph that can now be used to calculate the deadweight loss society incurs under market production. Area $(a + b + c)$ is equal to the blue consumer surplus (assuming the uncompensated demand is equal to marginal willingness to pay) in panel (a) while area $(d + e + f)$ is equal to the magenta producer surplus from panel (a). Producers and consumers are, in their roles as producers and consumers, unaffected by the pollution and therefore receive the same surplus as if there was no pollution. However we also know that, in the presence of pollution, we have to take into account the overall cost of the pollution that is produced when the market quantity x^M is produced. That area is the difference between the costs incurred by producers and the costs as represented in the SMC curve, an area equal to $(b + c + e + f + g)$. Thus, we have to subtract that from consumer and producer surplus to get overall social surplus $(a + d - g)$ under market production. Under Barney's benevolent dictatorship, on the other hand, society gets an overall surplus of $(a + d)$ equal to the green area in panel (b). The market therefore produces a deadweight loss equal to (g).

Suppose that the "pollution" emitted in the production of hero cards is of a kind that has no harmful effects for humans but does have the benefit of killing the local mosquito population; i.e., suppose the pollution is good rather than bad. Would the market produce more or less than Barney?

**Exercise
21A.1**

Exercise 21A.2

Would anything fundamental change in our analysis if we let go of our implicit assumption that the aggregate demand curve is also equal to the aggregate marginal willingness to pay curve? (Your answer should be no. Can you explain why?)

21A.1.2 Another Efficient Tax   Our analysis thus far tells us that competitive markets will produce too much in the presence of negative pollution externalities. As a result, there exists the potential for government policy to enhance efficiency and thus reduce or eliminate the deadweight loss from market overproduction. And we have already seen in Chapter 19 that taxation of goods is one policy tool that can reduce market output. In the absence of externalities, this is inefficient because the market allocation of resources was efficient to begin with. Now, however, this reduction of an otherwise *inefficient* output level can reduce rather than increase deadweight loss.

Suppose, for instance, you knew both the market demand and supply curves as well as the optimal production level x^B that Barney would choose. This information is depicted in panel (a) of Graph 21.2. Based on what we learned about taxes and tax incidence in Chapter 19, you can then easily determine the tax rate t required to reduce market output from x^M to x^B by simply letting t per unit be equal to the green vertical distance in the graph. As a result, buyers in the market would face the higher price p_B, while sellers would receive the lower price p_S with the difference between the two prices representing the payment t per unit in taxes. A tax such as this that is intended to reduce market output to its efficient quantity because of the presence of a negative production externality is called a *Pigouvian tax*.[2]

In panel (b) of the graph, we can then analyze more directly how this tax is efficient. In the absence of the tax, the market produces output x^M at price p^M. You can check for yourself, in a

Graph 21.2: An Efficient Pigouvian Tax

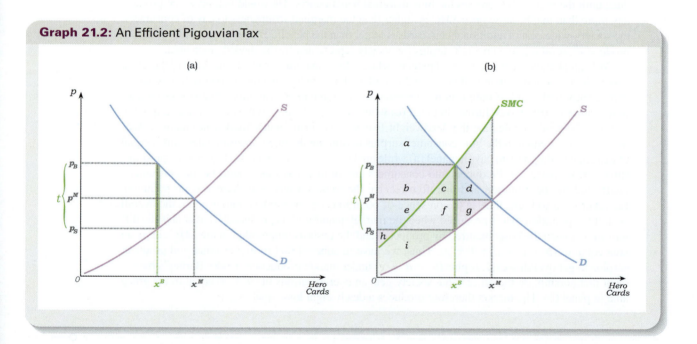

[2]The tax is named after Arthur Cecil Pigou (1877–1959), a British economist and student of Alfred Marshall (who succeeded Marshall as Professor of Political Economy at Cambridge University). Pigou developed the distinction between private and social marginal cost in his most influential work entitled *Wealth and Welfare*.

way exactly analogous to what we did in panel (c) of Graph 21.1, that the competitive market on its own will produce overall surplus equal to $(a + b + e + h - j)$, with the triangle (j) once again representing deadweight loss. Under the tax t, however, consumer surplus (a) and producer surplus $(h + i)$ combine with a positive tax revenue $(b + c + e + f)$ and a social cost from pollution $(c + f + i)$ to produce an overall surplus $(a + b + e + h)$. This is exactly equal to the green maximum surplus achieved by benevolent Barney in Graph 21.1b and eliminates the deadweight loss (j). Put differently, the reason we found taxes to be inefficient in Chapter 19 was that they distorted the price signal that coordinated efficient cooperation between producers and consumers, but, *in the presence of externalities, the price signal is already distorted* insofar as it does not efficiently coordinate production and consumption. The tax then removes the distortion and causes the market to "internalize the externality."

In order for the government to be able to impose an efficient Pigouvian tax t, it must however know the optimal quantity x^B it wants the market to reach *and* it must know the difference between the market demand and supply curve at that quantity. Put differently, the government must know the *marginal social damage caused by pollution at the optimum quantity*. If it possesses this information, the government can achieve the maximum social surplus by simply setting the per-unit tax on output equal to this marginal social damage of pollution.

What if the government only knows the marginal social damage of pollution at the equilibrium output level x^M and sets the tax rate equal to this quantity? Will this result in the optimal quantity being produced? If not, how do the the *SMC* and the supply curve have to be related to one another in order for this method of setting the tax to work?

Exercise 21A.3

It may in principle not look too difficult for the government to gather sufficient information to implement a Pigouvian tax that causes markets to once again produce efficiently. However, suppose that there are now many different industries, each causing pollution. In order to set optimal Pigouvian taxes, the government now has to know this same information for each industry and set the per unit tax in each industry, letting taxes vary across polluting industries as the marginal social damage of pollution at the optimum is different everywhere. This would then result in a complex system of different Pigouvian taxes across all polluting industries. As technology changes, these rates would have to be continuously adjusted. And, perhaps worst of all, unless the government adjusts Pigouvian taxes whenever firms find ways of reducing pollution on their own, individual firms in each industry would gain no benefit from applying pollution-abating technologies in their own firms because they would still face the same taxes. Thus, while it may look easy in principle to impose Pigouvian taxes on output in polluting industries, it is much more difficult to do so in practice and to simultaneously encourage those industries for whom it is easy to reduce pollution to do so in ways other than simply cutting production due to the tax.

It is for this reason that economists have largely turned away from recommending Pigouvian taxes *on output* and have instead turned to alternatives that focus more directly on forcing producers to confront the trade-off between reducing pollution (through less production or through the development of pollution-abating technologies) and paying for its social costs. This shift in focus has also been made possible by new technologies that allow governments to pinpoint who is producing pollution, and thus to require polluters to pay for pollution directly. This can be done either through a *pollution tax* (as opposed to a Pigouvian tax on output), or through the design of market-based environmental policy. We will discuss the latter first and then briefly compare it with the former.

In Chapter 18, we discussed the efficiency losses from government-mandated price ceilings or price floors. Could either of these policies be efficiency enhancing in the presence of pollution externalities (assuming the government has sufficient information to implement these policies)?

Exercise 21A.4

21A.1.3 Market-based Environmental Policy

The most common market-based environmental policy works as follows: The government determines an overall level of pollution (of each kind) that it finds acceptable and then issues pieces of paper that permit the owner to emit a certain quantity of different types of pollutants per week (or month or year). These pieces of paper, known as *pollution vouchers* or *tradable pollution permits*, thus represent the "right to pollute" by some amount. Then the government releases these rights, either by auctioning them off or by simply giving them to different firms in different industries. It turns out that it does not matter which precise way the government uses to distribute such permits; the important feature for our analysis is that individuals who own such permits can sell them to others if they so choose (and thus transfer the "right to pollute" to someone who is willing to pay more than it is worth to the original owner). In essence, the policy therefore "caps" the overall pollution level by fixing the number of pollution permits and then allows "trade" in permits to determine who uses them. For this reason, it has come to be known as a *cap-and-trade* policy.

Pollution vouchers have value to producers because they permit producers to emit pollution in their production process. At the same time, whenever a producer chooses to use such a voucher, she incurs an economic (or opportunity) cost because she could have chosen to sell (or rent) the voucher to someone else instead. Each producer therefore has to weigh the costs and benefits of using a pollution voucher, and each producer knows that she will have to use fewer vouchers the less she produces and the more she takes advantage of pollution-abating technologies. Since some production processes lend themselves to pollution-abating technologies more easily than others, firms in some industries will have a greater demand for such vouchers than firms in other industries. As a result, by introducing pollution vouchers into an economy (and prohibiting the emission of pollution when firms do not own such vouchers), the government has created a new market: the market for pollution vouchers.

Exercise 21A.5   Explain how firms face a cost for pollution regardless of whether the government gives them tradable pollution vouchers or whether firms have to purchase these.

This market is depicted in Graph 21.3 where pollution vouchers appear on the horizontal axis and the price per voucher appears on the vertical. By introducing only a limited quantity of such vouchers, the government has set a perfectly inelastic supply at precisely that quantity which results in the level of overall pollution across all industries. Firms that emit pollution in their production processes are the demanders of such vouchers, with demand depending on how much pollution is involved in producing different types of goods and how easy it is for firms to find ways of reducing the pollution emitted in production. Put differently, those firms that find it difficult to reduce their pollution will be willing to pay more for the right to pollute than those that can easily put a filter on their smokestacks. In equilibrium, pollution vouchers will then sell at price p^*.

Assuming the government can monitor polluting industries effectively (which is becoming increasingly easy as pollution monitors are widely distributed by the Environmental Protection Agency across different regions and as satellite technology is becoming increasingly effective at detecting pollution emissions from very precise locations), a system of pollution vouchers then achieves the following: First, it imposes a cost on polluters by requiring that they purchase sufficient pollution rights for the pollution they emit. This, then, causes an upward shift in firm MC curves as pollution vouchers become an input into the production process, and with it a shift in the market supply curve in polluting industries. Such a shift will result in less production of output in such polluting industries. Second, the system introduces an incentive for firms to search for (and invest in) pollution-abating technologies. So long as it costs less to reduce pollution from my firm than the pollution vouchers would cost me, I now have an incentive to reduce my pollution emissions. Third, the system creates an incentive for new firms to arise and to independently invest in research and development of pollution-abating technologies because the system has increased the demand for such technologies in light of the fact that polluters would otherwise have to pay for vouchers in order to produce.

Graph 21.3: A Market for Pollution Vouchers

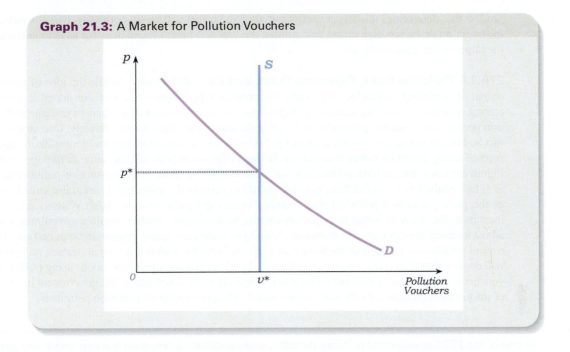

As a result, the system *achieves an overall reduction in pollution at the least social cost and without the government adjusting any policy to changing conditions.* The government does not have to be in the business of picking which industry reduces which type of pollution by how much, and it does not have to adjust those policies as pollution-abating technologies (that are more applicable to some industries than to others) are produced. All the government has to do is to set an overall pollution target and print a corresponding quantity of pollution vouchers. The newly created pollution voucher market then rations who gets the vouchers and who does not get them, with those for whom reductions in pollution are most costly choosing to use vouchers and others choosing to reduce pollution cheaply. Put differently, *pollution vouchers are government interventions that harness the power of a newly created market to generate the information required to reduce pollution at the lowest possible cost without any further government interference.*

If the government, after creating the pollution voucher market, decides to tax the sale of pollution vouchers, will there be any further reduction in pollution? (*Hint:* The answer is no.)

Exercise 21A.6

And there is one final check on the system: While we have said thus far that polluters are the ones who will form the demand curve in the pollution voucher market, it is in principle possible to allow anyone at all to participate in that market. If, for instance, a group of deeply concerned citizens feels that the government is permitting too much pollution to be emitted into the air, they could pool resources and purchase some quantity of the vouchers, thus increasing the price (and raising the cost to polluting) while lowering the supply (if they simply store away the pollution vouchers). As we will see in a later chapter on public goods, such groups face a difficult free rider problem that they need to overcome, but if they can, they are able to impact the overall level of pollution without lobbying the government.

One last clarifying caveat, however: While pollution vouchers offer a mechanism to reduce pollution to a target level in the least costly way, there is nothing in a pollution voucher system that guarantees we will have set the socially optimal target for pollution to begin with. If the political process that determines this target is efficient, then the target will be set optimally. But otherwise, the target might be too high or too low; all that the cap-and-trade system does for us is to get us to the target in the least costly way.

21A.1.4 Pollution Taxes, Pigouvian Taxes, and Cap-and-Trade

While the idea of taxing *output* in polluting industries—as originally proposed by Pigou—has lost considerable favor among economists, the very technology that allows the establishment of markets in tradable pollution permits now enables governments to tax *pollution* (rather than output) directly. One suspects that had Pigou thought it possible to detect pollution where it is emitted, he would most likely have favored taxing pollution rather than output. Taxing pollution directly has the same advantages over Pigouvian taxes that we have pointed out for cap-and-trade systems, and a per-unit-of-pollution tax is in fact equivalent to establishing tradable pollution permits if the tax rate is set at the same level as the price-per-unit-of-pollution that emerges in cap-and-trade systems. Both systems provide incentives for firms to invest in pollution-abating technologies; neither requires governments to adjust industry tax rates as circumstances change (as is the case under Pigouvian taxes on output); overall pollution is reduced in the least cost ways as firms for which it is easy to reduce pollution will do so rather than incur the cost of pollution (by either paying a pollution tax or using pollution vouchers); and neither system automatically results in full efficiency unless the government has lots of information on what the efficient tax rate or the efficient number of pollution permits is.

Exercise 21A.7

In one of the 2008 presidential primary debates, one candidate advocated the cap-and-trade system over a carbon tax on the grounds that the carbon tax would be partially passed on to consumers in the form of higher prices. Another candidate who also supported the cap-and-trade system corrected this assertion by suggesting that to whatever extent a carbon tax would be passed on to consumers, the same is true of costs (of tradable permits) under the cap-and trade system. Who was right?[3]

While pollution taxes and cap-and-trade systems are therefore quite similar, environmental policy makers nevertheless debate their relative merits. Some consider it important to set precise target levels for pollution, with cap-and-trade systems allowing an easy way of establishing such targets while then letting the market for tradable permits determine the per-unit-of-pollution price required to implement the target. Others believe it is more important to specify the per-unit-of-pollution cost directly through a tax in order to allow firms to plan accordingly, leaving the level of pollution reduction that results to arise from firm responses to the tax. Again, if the per-unit-of-pollution tax is set at the same rate as the per-unit-of-pollution price that emerges under a particular "cap" in a cap-and-trade system, the two policies have identical effects, but one gets there by being precise about the target pollution level up front while the other gets there by being precise about the per-unit-pollution cost up front.

A second issue that is raised in policy debates regarding cap-and-trade versus pollution taxes relates to politics and implementation. Some fear that a nationwide, or even worldwide, cap-and-trade system would involve excessive government bureaucracy to administer the various markets for different types of pollution vouchers while others argue that administering pollution taxes would involve similar issues. In practice, however, there appears to be one important political reason for environmental policy makers to favor the cap-and-trade system: It has a built-in mechanism for overcoming concentrated opposition from industries that are particularly affected. Such industries would face increased marginal costs under both the pollution tax and the cap-and-trade system, but pollution vouchers could be given away for free to some industries in order to "buy" their political

---

[3]The exchange took place in the January 5, 2008, Democratic presidential primary debate held at St. Anselm College. The first candidate was New Mexico Governor Bill Richardson; the second was then-Senator Barack Obama.

support. In essence, this involves a transfer of wealth (in the form of pollution vouchers that can be traded) without a change in the increased opportunity cost of emitting pollution. Under pollution taxes, one could similarly "buy off" industry opposition through transfers of taxpayer money, but this appears to be politically more controversial.[4]

Suppose that advocates of pollution taxes proposed a reduction in such taxes for key industries that would otherwise be opposed to the policy. How is this different than giving pollution vouchers away for free to such key industries in a cap-and-trade system?

Exercise 21A.8

Finally, to the extent to which the pollution problem to be addressed is global (as in the case of greenhouse gases) rather than local (as in the case of acid rain), policy makers may favor the cap-and-trade system as it permits the establishment of global markets in tradable pollution permits to achieve global reductions in pollution while allowing an initial establishment of country-specific "caps" through negotiated international agreements. Such a system does not enshrine country-specific caps because permits could be traded across national boundaries, but much as support from particular industries can be gained by giving some pollution permits away, international support for such agreements could be facilitated by initially allocating relatively more pollution permits to some countries rather than other countries.

Less-developed countries often point out that countries like the United States did not have to confront the fact that they caused a great deal of pollution during their periods of development, and thus suggest that developed countries should disproportionately incur the cost of reducing worldwide pollution now. Can you suggest a way for this to be incorporated into a global cap-and-trade system?

Exercise 21A.9

21A.2 Consumption Externalities

We have thus far considered only externalities generated in the production of goods and, with the exception of the externality considered in within-chapter-exercise 21A.1, we have limited ourselves to externalities that have negative impacts on others, or what we have referred to as *negative externalities*. Externalities can, however, arise in production and consumption, and they can be positive or negative. We will now illustrate the impact of an externality on the consumer side, and, to differentiate it further from what we have done so far, we will consider a positive rather than a negative externality.

Suppose, for instance, that production of hero cards entails no pollution whatsoever but, whenever a consumer purchases hero cards for children, the world becomes a better place. In particular, suppose that for each child who is exposed to hero cards, future crime falls and good citizens emerge. This may sound silly because of the context of the example, but such arguments are often made in markets like children's programming on television or markets involving the arts. The essential nature of the argument is always the same: In addition to the private benefits that consumers obtain directly from consumption, others in society benefit indirectly in ways that are not priced by the market.

21A.2.1 Positive Externalities from Consumption
Graph 21.4 then presents a series of graphs for positive externalities that is exactly analogous to the series of graphs in Graph 21.1 for negative externalities. Panel (a) simply illustrates consumer and producer surplus along market

---

[4]As this textbook goes to press, a cap-and-trade bill has passed the U.S. House of Representatives and awaits action in the Senate. The bill indeed provides politically powerful industries with "free" pollution permits for a number of years, with some representatives supporting the bill only after the inclusion of such wealth transfers.

Graph 21.4: Underproduction in the Presence of a Positive Externality

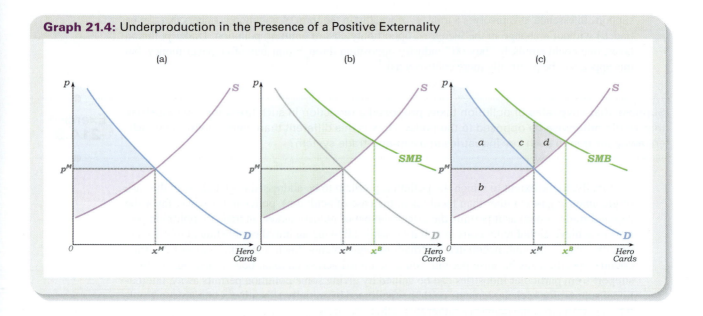

supply and demand curves (once again under the assumption that demand can be interpreted as marginal willingness to pay). Panel (b) introduces a new curve called "*SMB*" or *social marginal benefit*. This curve includes all the benefits society gains from each unit of consumption. It therefore includes all the private benefits that consumers get (and that are measured by the demand curve), plus it includes additional social benefits that are gained by others. As in the case of *SMC* and supply, *SMB* and demand can be related to each other in a variety of ways, but under positive externalities *SMB* must certainly lie above demand (or private marginal willingness to pay).

Our benevolent social planner would then use this *SMB* to measure the marginal benefit of each hero card that is produced (while measuring the marginal cost along the supply curve in the absence of negative externalities). He would therefore choose the production level x^B in panel (b) of the graph, giving the shaded green area as overall social surplus. Thus, the market produces an inefficiently low quantity of a good that exhibits a positive consumption externality. We can derive the exact deadweight loss from the areas labeled in panel (c) of Graph 21.4. At the competitive market equilibrium, consumer surplus is simply area (*a*) (equivalent to the blue area in panel (a)) and producer surplus is area (*b*) (equivalent to the magenta area in panel (a)). Since the market produces an output level x^M, the additional social benefit from the externality is given by area (*c*). Thus, the market achieves an overall social gain equal to area (*a* + *b* + *c*). Our social planner, on the other hand, achieves that *plus* area (*d*), implying that society incurs a deadweight loss of (*d*) in the absence of nonmarket institutions that induce additional production.

21A.2.2 Pigouvian Subsidies

One nonmarket institution that we already know from our previous work can raise the level of output in the market is a government price subsidy. Suppose that the government knows it wants to raise output in the hero card market to x^B above the market quantity x^M. In panel (a) of Graph 21.5, this implies that the government can accomplish its goal by imposing a subsidy *s* equal to the green vertical distance, thus lowering the price for buyers to p_B and raising the price for sellers to p_S. Our discussion of the economic incidence of a subsidy in Chapter 19 treats this in more detail and illustrates that the degree to which prices faced by buyers and sellers change depends on the relative price elasticities of market demand and supply curves. When such a subsidy is used to "internalize a positive externality," it is known as a Pigouvian subsidy. As in the case of a Pigouvian tax, it can restore efficiency by removing the externality-induced distortion in market prices.

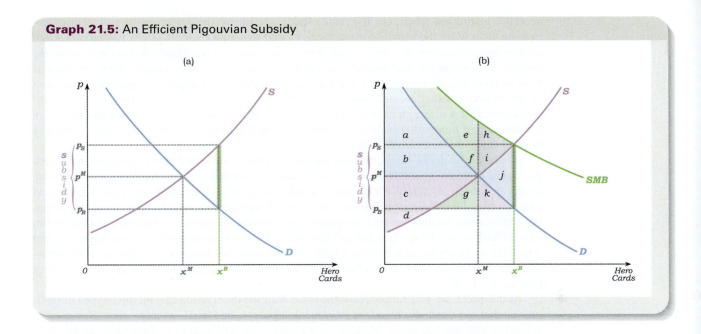

Graph 21.5: An Efficient Pigouvian Subsidy

Suppose again (for simplicity) that tastes for hero cards are quasilinear and that we can therefore treat the market demand curve as the aggregate marginal willingness to pay curve for consumers. In panel (b) of the graph, we can then calculate the areas that make up total surplus before and after the subsidy. Before the subsidy, consumer and producer surplus simply sum to $(a + b + c + d)$, and nonmarket participants gain additional surplus of $(e + f)$. Thus, total surplus under pure market allocations is $(a + b + c + d + e + f)$. Under the subsidy, consumer surplus is $(a + b + c + g + k)$, producer surplus is $(b + c + d + f + i)$, and surplus for nonmarket participants is $(e + f + h + i + j)$. From the sum of these areas, we then need to subtract the cost of the subsidy, which is $(b + c + f + g + i + j + k)$, giving us a total surplus of $(a + b + c + d + e + f + h + i)$. Thus, total surplus under the subsidy is now equal to the green area in Graph 21.4b, which we concluded was the maximum social gain possible, with the subsidy having eliminated the deadweight loss $(h + i)$ that occurred under a pure market allocation.

Suppose that, instead of generating positive consumption externalities, hero cards actually divert the attention of children from studying and thus impose negative consumption externalities. Can you see how such externalities can be modeled exactly like negative production externalities?

**Exercise
21A.10**

21A.2.3 Charitable Giving, Government Policy, and Civil Society

In the case of a negative production externality of pollution, we illustrated next how government could, instead of attempting to calculate all the "right" Pigouvian taxes each year, create a new market of pollution vouchers that can efficiently reduce pollution to some level set by the government. In the case of positive consumption externalities, I can't offer a similar market-based policy that is currently under discussion, but we should note that the market outcome we have predicted in the model may not necessarily be the actual outcome if markets operate within the context of nongovernmental and nonmarket institutions that we referred to in Chapter 1 as *civil society*. The words "civil society" do not have a clear definition and are often used to mean many different things. In this text, I will refer to an institution as a "civil society" institution whenever it is not clearly set up by the government and it does not operate strictly on the self-interested motives that generate explicit prices in markets. *Civil society institutions are then the sets of interactions among individuals that occur outside the context of government and outside the context of explicit market prices.* Such institutions tend to arise as individuals try to use persuasion rather than the political process to address issues of concern that are not addressed in the market. The existence of positive consumption externalities offers an example because, as we have seen, it is a case when the market in the absence of nonmarket institutions produces too little of goods that are valued in society beyond their simple consumption value.

As you are no doubt aware, many organizations spend substantial energy trying to make people aware of many social concerns in an attempt to persuade them to voluntarily contribute money or time to organized efforts aimed at addressing such concerns. In the case of television programming for children, for instance, we have all seen appeals on television for private donations to increase funding for such programs. Such efforts to appeal for charitable donations run into difficulties involving "free riding" that we will address more explicitly in Chapter 27 and thus offer no guarantee of achieving a fully efficient outcome, but they appear to play an important role in many circumstances where positive externalities would make markets by themselves produce too little.

At this point, we will simply leave the issue with the observation that all three types of institutions that we have discussed—government, markets, and civil society—face obstacles in achieving efficient outcomes. Markets, as we have seen, will tend to underproduce in the presence of positive externalities and overproduce in the presence of negative externalities; governments may face difficulties in ascertaining the information necessary for implementing optimal outcomes through taxes or subsidies (or other means), especially as circumstances within societies change, and they face political hurdles that we will treat more explicitly in Chapter 28. And civil society efforts that rely on strictly voluntary engagement of nonmarket participants face difficulties in engaging those nonmarket participants fully as each will tend to rely on others to address the problem. Yet each appears to play a role in the real world.

Finally, just as the case of pollution vouchers represents an effort by government to engage market forces in finding efficient solutions to excessive pollution, government policies are often aimed at engaging civil society institutions more. The most obvious example of this can be found in the U.S. income tax code, which offers tax deductions to individuals who voluntarily give to charitable causes, thus subsidizing such causes without the government making the explicit decision of which charities will end up engaging nonmarket participants. Thus, when the government faces too many hurdles in designing explicit subsidies for each industry that generates positive externalities, it can offer such general subsidies aimed at reducing the hurdles faced by civil society organizations in finding nonmarket, nongovernmental solutions.

Exercise 21A.11   In what sense does the tax-deducibility of charitable contributions represent another way of subsidizing charities?

Exercise 21A.12   In a progressive income tax system (with marginal tax rates increasing as income rises), are charities valued by high income people implicitly favored over charities valued by low income people? Would the same be true if everyone could take a tax credit equal to some fraction k of their charitable contributions?

Exercise 21A.13   We did not explicitly discuss a role for civil society institutions in correcting market failures due to negative externalities. Can you think of any examples of such efforts in the real world?

21A.3 Externalities: Market Failure or Failure of Markets to Exist?

Thus far, we have seen that markets by themselves will produce inefficient quantities of goods that exhibit positive or negative consumption and production externalities. In the absence of government intervention, civil society efforts may contribute to greater efficiency. Alternatively, government policies can be designed to change market output directly (as in the case of Pigouvian taxes and subsidies) or to indirectly harness the advantages of market forces (as in the case of cap-and-trade policies) or civil society institutions (as in the case of the tax deductibility of charitable contributions) to increase efficiency and lower deadweight losses. After we have explored more fully (in the upcoming chapters) the many hurdles faced by markets, governments, and civil society institutions in implementing optimal outcomes for society, we will return in Chapter 30 of the book to a general approach for considering how we can ascertain the appropriate balance of markets, government, and civil society depending on the particulars of the social problem that is to be solved.

In the meantime, however, we can see yet another efficiency-enhancing policy tool the government has at its disposal by exploring a little more deeply the fundamental problem created by the presence of externalities. We have seen that markets by themselves will tend to "fail" in the presence of externalities, and this has often led economists to refer to externalities as one (of several) potential *market failures*. In this section, we will see how this market failure arises because of the fact that whenever there is an externality generated in competitive markets, *we can trace the over or underproduction that arises from this externality to the lack of a market or the nonexistence of a market somewhere else.*

21A.3.1 Pollution and Missing Markets
Consider again the case of a market in which pollution is a by-product of production. The fundamental reason that a market will overproduce in this case (relative to the efficient quantity) is that producers are not forced to face the full costs they impose on societies when making production decisions. In particular, if the pollution that is generated is air pollution, the producer escapes paying for the input "clean air" that is used in the production process unless some mechanism (like Pigouvian taxes, pollution taxes, or pollution vouchers) is implemented. Were there a market for each of the inputs used in production, including the input "clean air," the producers would have to fully pay for all the costs they impose. *Air pollution therefore arises as a problem that keeps markets from producing efficiently because one of the inputs into production is not bought and sold.*

I know that this sounds rather silly—how could there possibly be a "market for clean air" when no one owns the air and therefore no one can sell clean air to firms that use it in the production process. It sounds silly because it is silly. Nevertheless, if we can suspend disbelief for a moment, we can see the conceptual point that the externality is a problem precisely because we have not found a way to create a market in clean air. If there was such a market, and if all air was owned by different people, then each user of clean air would have to pay for it as it is being used. Consumers of clean air, including producers who use clean air as an input, would have to pay for clean air just as firms have to pay for labor and capital. Such a market for clean air would therefore result in a market price that would, in the absence of any other externalities, result in maximum social surplus in the clean air market. As producers contemplate production that involves pollution, they would then face a price for clean air, shifting their marginal cost curves up and thus shifting market supply up to be equal to the social marginal cost (*SMC*) of production rather then the marginal private cost that excludes the social cost of pollution. This would then result in the efficient quantity of the pollution-generating output, with social surplus once again maximized purely by market forces.[5]

---

[5]It is noteworthy that it does not actually matter for efficiency purposes who owns the right to clean air. Whether individuals or firms own this right, a market that prices the use of clean air in production would form. If the polluter owns the right to the air, he is still facing the cost of polluting because his opportunity cost of using the clean air in his own production is to sell the clean air to someone else in the market. We will say more on this later on.

In an abstract conceptual sense, the market failure generated by the presence of externalities can then be traced to the failure of a market to exist. Does recognizing this get us any closer to solving the problem? In the case of pollution, it is that recognition that has led economists to come up with the proposal for creating markets in pollution vouchers. Pollution voucher markets are not the same as markets in clean air, but they represent an attempt to resolve a problem created by the nonexistence of a market (for clean air) through the creation of a different type of market that can help. Recognizing the market failure generated by externalities as a failure of a market to exist can therefore create the opportunity for innovative government interventions that may, at least in some cases, work better than other government solutions we might otherwise implement.

21A.3.2 The Tragedy of the Commons

This insight then points toward a huge role that governments more generally have to play in order for markets to function efficiently. Throughout our treatment of the efficiency of markets in Chapters 15, 16, and 17, for instance, we made the implicit assumption that markets for all sorts of inputs such as labor and capital actually exist. Presuming that such markets exist presumes that individuals own resources that they can trade, and *this presumes that there is some mechanism in place that protects the property rights of owners of resources*. Firms cannot just take my leisure and use it for labor inputs; they are required to persuade me to sell my leisure to them by offering me a wage that I consider sufficient. Similarly, they cannot just take my savings or retirement account and use the money to buy labor, land, and equipment; they have to pay for using my financial capital by paying me interest. All this requires a well-established *system of legally enforced property rights*, and such a system has in practice typically required government protection and a well-functioning court system to enforce property rights.[6]

Externalities, as we have seen, arise when such property rights have not been established. Pollution is a problem because there does not exist a system of property rights to clean air that forces firms to pay for using clean air as an input into production. In effect, without some other institution in place, firms are simply able to take clean air for free as they produce goods, something we do not permit for inputs like labor and capital. Were they to similarly be able to take my leisure and capital, were there no legal system of property rights in those input markets, we would have even worse externality issues to deal with. Whenever a resource is not clearly owned by someone, it therefore becomes possible for economic agents to take those resources without incurring a cost, even though this imposes costs on society. It is then a logical consequence that, if it is feasible for the government to establish a system of property rights in resources that are not currently owned by anyone, such government interference can create additional markets that reduce the problem of externalities by forcing market participants to face the true social cost of what they are doing.

For this reason, economists have come to refer to externality problems that arise from the nonexistence of markets as the " *Tragedy of the Commons*," the "tragedy" of *social losses that emerges when resources are "commonly" rather than privately owned*. We could say, for instance, that clean air is owned by everyone, but that simply means it is owned by no one in particular. Parents know this tragedy well. When we give toys to our children as common property to be shared without any guidance or rules, our children tend to fight like cats and dogs as they try to get those toys for themselves. Most parents therefore quickly learn that conflict is reduced if clear ownership of toys is established, with each child knowing (to the extent that children fully internalize this) that they have to get permission from the other child when seeking to use that child's toys. When parents realize this, they act as economists who understand the tragedy of the commons.

More generally, much human suffering in the world can be directly traced to societies not heeding the lessons of the Tragedy of the Commons. Entire societies have been set up in attempts

---

[6]Most of us, including me, take for granted that such protection of property rights must be provided by government. And it usually is. But there are contrarian voices among some economists and philosophers that maintain government is not necessary for protection of private property to emerge. We will say a bit more about this in Chapter 30.

to abolish private property and replace the mechanism of markets with some alternative mechanism. It takes only a quick glance at 20th-century history, for instance, to see how much societies that have protected private property (and thus established markets) have economically thrived, while societies that have attempted to do the opposite have failed. A full understanding of externalities suggests that such societies failed because they created huge externalities by eliminating markets without finding an alternative government or civil society mechanism to generate social surplus. In short, by not supporting markets, they have created large "tragedies of the commons."

Large portions of the world's forests are publicly owned and not protected from exploitation. Identify the Tragedy of the Commons, and the externalities associated with it, that this creates.

Exercise 21A.14

Why do you think there is a problem of over fishing in the world's oceans?

Exercise 21A.15

21A.3.3 Congestion on Roads We do not, however, have to dig into historical examples of nonmarket-based societies or reach for the pie in the sky of "markets in clean air" to see the relevance of an understanding of the Tragedy of the Commons in thinking about solutions to externality problems. Economists who have estimated the social cost of externalities in the United States, for instance, have found that the social cost of time wasted on congested roads rivals the social cost of environmental damage from pollution. Think of your own experiences being stuck in traffic. It is mind-numbing to be stuck in traffic even for short periods of time because the opportunity cost of our time is large. In some of our larger cities, commuters routinely spend significant amounts of time in precisely such a position.

The problem of congested roads is an example of a Tragedy of the Commons. Roads, by and large, are commonly or publicly owned, which is to say that they are not owned by anyone. As you and I get on the road, we may think about the cost of taking the drive into the city, the cost of our time, the gasoline we use, and the depreciation of our car. We do not, however, think about the cost we are imposing on everyone else who is also taking a trip. Put differently, there is a negative externality each of us imposes on everyone else who is on the road as we add to the congestion of the road. In the absence of a mechanism that makes us face this social cost of our private actions, we therefore will tend to take too many trips, and we will be on the road at the "wrong" times. You may say that surely my own contribution to the congestion of the roads is minor, but all of us together are causing the congestion problem that wastes billions of dollars worth of time each week on the congested roads of larger cities. If my entry onto the road causes thousands of others to take even one more second to get to where they are going, I am imposing quite a social cost on others without paying any attention to it.

Can you think of any other costs that we do not think about as we decide to get onto public roads?

Exercise 21A.16

Solutions for this particular Tragedy of the Commons are still evolving, and changes in technology are playing a large part in shaping these solutions just as new technologies that permit detection of pollution have shaped new environmental policies (such as pollution taxes and cap-and-trade systems). The difficulty in finding a way for individuals to internalize the social cost they are imposing on others on the road lies in the difficulty of establishing a market that will price that social cost. In the past, economists have often proposed somewhat blunt policies falling into two general categories: First, we can impose a tax on gasoline that will raise the cost of driving and therefore reduce the amount of driving individuals will undertake; and second, when there are sufficiently many individuals in sufficiently dense geographic areas, governments can design public transportation systems like subways that are expensive to build but that, once built, can offer attractive alternative means of transportations within cities.

The building of public transportation may alleviate congestion, but it does not in itself address the Tragedy of the Commons that remains on public roads, and it may create a different Tragedy of the Commons if public transportation is priced in such a way as to cause congestion in buses, subways, and so forth. Nevertheless, it has represented an important element of addressing crowding on roads in some urban areas. Taxation of gasoline is appealing in that it does raise the cost of driving and brings it more into line with the social cost of individual decisions during peak traffic hours, but it also raises the cost of driving during off-peak hours when congestion is not a problem, thus creating deadweight losses during those hours just as it reduces deadweight losses during peak hours.

Exercise 21A.17   Are there other externality-based reasons to tax gasoline?

In recent years, however, it has become possible to price driving on congested roads more directly through tolls. Before the advent of electronic equipment that has made this easier, such tolls have involved toll booths, which themselves can contribute to congestion around the booths as traffic slows down even as they keep individuals off the roads. As technology improves, however, we are beginning to see increasingly efficient mechanisms for tolls to be imposed, mechanisms that do not require individuals to stop, reach into their wallets, and pay a toll-booth attendant. As a result, we are seeing cities increasingly use electronic tolls that can vary with the time of day that individuals choose to use roads. User fees in the form of tolls then represent an attempt to make individuals face the social cost of driving during peak hours. At least in principle, such technology also permits the more direct establishment of markets in roads, markets in which road networks are privately owned and the use of the road is priced within markets. As technology and our understanding of the underlying causes of externalities on roads is changing, we therefore see the emergence of new ways for government policy to interact with markets to reduce the social costs of an important externality. If such topics are of interest to you, you might consider taking an urban or transportation economics course at some point.

Exercise 21A.18   Some have argued against using tolls to address the congestion externality on the grounds that wealthier individuals will have no problem paying such tolls while the poor will. Is this a valid argument against the efficiency of using tolls?

21A.4 Smaller Externalities, the Courts, and the Coase Theorem

We have thus far focused primarily on externalities that affect many individuals, such as pollution and congestion. But many of the externalities that we are most aware of in our daily lives are much less grand: the loud music in the dorm room next to yours, the odor from the student who insists on sitting next to you in class but who also insists on showering infrequently, the insensitivity of the person on the bus who appears to be talking loudly to himself but is actually speaking on his well-hidden cell phone, or that baby that just stopped screaming only to have switched from an externality that affects the auditory nerve to one that affects our sense of smell. These are all negative externalities, but we could think of positive ones as well. When I smile in the hallway at work, a few people a day might derive direct benefits from my cheerful disposition, or when I open the door for a student carrying heavy books (such as the one you are reading—sorry, I don't know how to be brief!), that student's life might be just a bit better today, even more so if I happen at the moment to be offering a rousing rendition of "O Sole Mio." If you think about it, externalities are everywhere that people operate within close proximity to one another: in the workplace, in restaurants, in neighborhoods. And sometimes these externalities cause us to take each other to court.

21A.4.1 The Case of the Shadow on Your Swimming Pool

Consider, for instance, the following example: You and I live next to each other in peace and harmony. Suddenly, I win some money in the lottery and decide that I want to add to my house. So I draw up some plans to add an additional floor to my existing house. Normally, you would not care about this, but it turns out that the additional floor will cast a long shadow onto your property, and in particular the area of your property that currently contains a beautiful (and sunny) swimming pool. You get very upset that your swimming pool will suddenly be in the shade all the time, and so you go to court and ask the judge to stop my building plans. Your legitimate argument is that I am imposing a negative externality that I am not taking into account. "He must be stopped," you insist to the judge.

The judge sees your point but he wants to be careful and is trying to figure out whether it would or would not be efficient to build the addition to my house despite the adverse effect this will have on you. Maybe I get a lot more enjoyment from the addition than you lose from the shade on your swimming pool, or maybe it's the other way around. Maybe it would cost you very little to move to a different house and have someone who does not care about the shade on the swimming pool move into your house (thereby eliminating the very externality we are worried about). Or maybe it would be easy for me to find a bigger house elsewhere and relatively costless for me to move. It's hard to tell without the judge figuring out a lot of details about the case. And one might argue that there isn't an easy way to judge this on a basis other than efficiency. After all, we both are equally to blame for the existence of the externality: It would not exist if I were not trying to build an addition, but it also would not exist if you were not so insistent on having the sun shining on your silly pool!

21A.4.2 The Coase Theorem

Ronald Coase, an economist at the University of Chicago, came along and had a neat insight that might, under certain conditions, make the judge's life a lot easier.[7] Coase thought that the reason you are taking me to court is that we are confused about who has what "property rights," and this ambiguity is making it difficult for us to come up with the optimal solution to our problem on our own. Suppose, for instance, you *knew* the judge would rule that I had the right to build regardless of the damage this does to you. You might then invite me for coffee and ask if there is a way you could convince me to not build my addition. If the damage that is done to you is greater than the pleasure I get from my addition—if it would be efficient for me not to build the addition—you would in fact be willing to pay me an amount that will make me stop the addition. Perhaps I would find another way to add to my house, or perhaps I would move with the money you gave me to make me stop. If, on the other hand, your pain from the addition is less (in dollar terms) than my pleasure—if it is efficient for me to go ahead with the addition—you would discover over coffee that you aren't willing to pay me enough to stop the addition. Perhaps you will just stay and suffer in a shaded pool, or perhaps you'll move elsewhere. But notice that once you *know* that I have every right to build the addition, you have an incentive to figure out whether you can pay me to stop, and once you figure this out, you will ensure that the efficient outcome happens.

---

[7]Ronald Coase (1910–), who won the 1991 Nobel Prize in part for his contribution to this area, has the rare quality of being both an economist and a person so averse to math that it has been said of him (which is probably not true) that he will not number the pages of his manuscripts. The article in which he put forth the Coase Theorem ("The Problem of Social Cost," *The Journal of Law and Economics* 3 (1960), 1–44) is therefore quite readable by those with math phobias, and incidentally is one of the most cited articles in all of economics.

The same is true in the case where I know that *you* have the "property right"; that is, that you have a right to block my addition. In that case, I have an incentive to have you over for coffee to my house to see if I could persuade you to let me go ahead. If the addition means more to me than the pain it causes you, then you will be willing to accept a payment that I am willing to pay in order to get you to drop your objections. If, on the other hand, my gain from the addition is less than your pain, then I won't be willing to pay you enough to get you to stop your objections. Thus, if the initial "property right" rests with you, then I am the one who has an incentive to figure out whether my gain is greater than your pain, and in the process get us to do what is efficient. Note that neither one of us actually cares about efficiency, but, once we know who has what rights, our private incentives make it in our interest to find the efficient outcome.

Exercise
21A.19

True or False: While it might not matter for efficiency which way the judge rules, you and I nevertheless care about the outcome of his ruling.

To the extent to which we find this reasoning persuasive, Coase has just gotten the judge who cares only about efficiency off the hook: *No matter what the judge decides, you and I will arrive at the efficient outcome; the most important thing is that the judge needs to define the property rights so that we can have coffee and know what we are negotiating about.* I know this problem well in my house where I am frequently called upon to be the judge that adjudicates cases of property rights disputes involving my two eight-year-old daughters. Knowing about Coase, I don't even listen to their arguments. I just flip a coin to decide who gets the property rights this time and then send them off to negotiate with each other.[8]

21A.4.3 Bargaining, Transactions Costs, and the Coase Theorem The Coase Theorem then says it is essential *that* property rights be clearly defined in cases when there are negative externalities but it is *not* necessarily essential *how* those rights are defined. This should have a familiar ring because we just emphasized in the previous section that the absence of "markets" for the externality is the real underlying problem with externalities. Coase's argument is similar, except that he does not insist that we have to have a *competitive* "market" in the externality; all we need to do is establish who has what rights and then let people solve the problem on their own by bargaining with one another. In our example of me building an addition to my house that will then cast a shadow on your swimming pool, there is no hope of establishing a real (competitive) market, but we can clarify property rights sufficiently to give us an incentive to figure out how to solve the externality problem.

Coase was not, however, naive, and he recognized that there might be barriers that keep people from getting together to bargain their way out of an externality problem once property rights are fully defined. These barriers are called *transactions costs*, and if they are sufficiently high, you and I might never have that coffee to talk about how to proceed. If we just can't stand each other's presence in the same room, then there is a transactions cost to getting together, and when this is the case, the judge's decision suddenly matters a great deal more. If the efficient outcome is for me to build my addition and the judge rules in your favor, these transactions costs would keep me from getting together with you to offer you the payment necessary to let me proceed. Similarly, if the efficient outcome is for me to not build the addition and the judge rules in my favor, transactions costs again keep us from getting together in order for you to offer me the payment necessary not to build. Thus, in the presence of sufficiently high transactions costs, the judge needs to figure out what the efficient outcome is and then rule accordingly so that it is not necessary for us to get together to solve the problem through side payments between each other.

---

[8]My wife thinks this makes me a bad parent. Weird.

The full Coase Theorem can then be stated as follows: *If transactions costs are sufficiently low the efficient outcome will arise in the presence of externalities so long as property rights are sufficiently clear.*

We can then see that the Coase Theorem offers us a decentralized way out of externality problems so long as transactions costs are low, and transactions costs will tend to be lower the fewer individuals are affected by an externality. If it's just you and me arguing about whether I should or should not build an addition that only affects the two of us, we might think that transactions costs are in fact sufficiently low and we will bargain our way to a solution if the assignment of property rights requires such bargaining. For this reason, we might not worry about all the everyday externalities that affect only small numbers of people. Chances are probably better that individuals themselves will figure out the efficient outcome than that a government with limited information can dictate the efficient outcome. Put differently, as long as people in "small externality settings" have reasonable expectations about how the law will treat externality issues if such issues were to be adjudicated in a court room, such problems are best handled in the "civil society" in which people interact voluntarily outside the usual price-governed market setting.

Use the Coase Theorem to explain why the government probably does not need to get involved in the externality that arises when I play my radio sufficiently loud that my neighbors are adversely affected, but it probably does need to get involved in addressing pollution that causes global warming.

Exercise 21A.20

21A.4.4 Bees and Honey: The Role of Markets and Civil Society

The Coase Theorem applies to all types of externalities, positive or negative. So far, we have been sticking with the example of the negative externality of the shadow cast on your pool by the addition to my house. A classic example of *positive* externalities involves beekeepers and apple orchard owners. It turns out, however, that although the example was originally given as motivation for Pigouvian subsidies, this is a case where Coase's insights, as well as our more general insights on markets and property rights, have held true in the real world, and there appears to be no need for further Pigouvian interventions.[9]

Externalities in the case of bees and apple orchards abound. In order for apple trees to produce fruit, bees need to travel from tree to tree to carry pollen from "male" to "female" trees. And in order for bees to produce honey, they need some blossoms to visit. (You probably remember all this from the "birds and the bees" talk that I recently had to have with my children.) Beekeepers that let their bees roam therefore impose a positive externality on apple orchard growers (who benefit from the cross-polination services), and apple orchard growers bestow a positive externality on bee keepers (by providing them with the means for apple honey production). Even if we can figure out a way for markets to solve this problem in general, there is the second problem: Bees have a way of not staying on the precise properties on which they were released. So if one orchard owner hires cross-polination services (or invests in her own bees), the bees will cross into neighboring orchards and provide services there, while also contributing to honey production.

In the absence of markets that can price all these externalities, our theory predicts that there would be too few bees on apple orchards, resulting in too little cross-polination and too little honey. As it turns out, however, none of this is a surprise to beekeepers and orchard growers. Fairly sophisticated markets for beekeepers to release their bees on orchards have emerged "spontaneously," markets that established "themselves" in an environment where government's

---

[9]This externality between beekeepers and orchard growers was pointed out by the economist James Meade (1907–1995), who argued in 1952 that Pigouvian subsidies were needed to remedy the problem. Meade shared the Nobel Prize in 1977 for contributions to the theory of international trade, which only goes to prove that even Nobel Laureates can get it wrong (as Meade did in the case of subsidies in the beekeeping business). To his credit, Meade wrote eight years before Coase published his insights that came to be known as the Coase Theorem.

only role has been to guarantee the integrity of contracts and thus the property rights that are defined in those contracts. The flowers on apple trees, it turns out, do not produce much honey, causing the externality to go almost entirely from beekeepers to apple orchard growers. (The "apple honey" that you can find on your supermarket shelves has precious little honey produced from apple trees—it's mainly the product of wild flowers that grow in the area of the orchards.) Clover, on the other hand, produces tons of honey. Thus, growers of clover produce a net-positive externality for beekeepers. While apple growers pay beekeepers to release their bees on the orchard, beekeepers pay clover growers for permitting them to release their bees on the clover farms. This is an example of competitive markets resolving an externality problem when property rights are well established.

Exercise 21A.21 In what sense do you think the relevant property rights in this case are in fact well established?

This does not, however, resolve the more "local" externalities between orchard owners. If one owner hires bee-services, those same bees cross over into other orchards, benefitting those growers (while also benefitting the beekeepers). Another economist has looked at this closely, and he identifies a social custom that has emerged within the civil society, that is to say, outside the realm of explicit market-based transactions and outside the realm of government intervention.[10] This has been dubbed the "custom of the orchards," and it takes the form of an implicit understanding among orchard owners in the same area that each owner will employ the same number of bee hives per acre as the other owners in the area. While the Coase Theorem literally interpreted suggests that individuals will resolve these "local" externalities through bargaining, this illustrates another possible way for the theorem to unfold: Sometimes it is easier to converge on some local understanding of appropriate behavior that can be sustained among small groups within the civil society rather than negotiate all the time about how many beehives everyone is going to hire this time around. (In part B of exercise 24.17, we investigate a game theoretic explanation for the "custom of the orchards.")

21B The Mathematics of Externalities

We will begin our mathematical exploration of externalities in competitive markets (as in Section A) with the motivating example of a polluting industry in partial equilibrium. Using linear supply and demand curves, we can demonstrate how to calculate the optimal Pigouvian tax. Furthermore, we will explore how the establishment of pollution permit markets can in principle achieve the same efficiency gains as an optimally set Pigouvian tax and that, in fact, there exists a cap-and-trade policy that is equivalent to any Pivouvian tax policy in the absence of pollution-abating technologies. In the presence of such technologies, however, we will suggest, as we have in Section A, that pollution voucher markets (as well as direct pollution taxes) have an inherent advantage over Pigouvian taxes on output. While we won't cover positive externalities (and accompanying Pigouvian subsidies) in detail, the mathematics is virtually identical to that underlying Pigouvian taxes and is therefore left as an end-of-chapter exercise.

We then turn to a more in-depth analysis of how externalities and the inefficiencies they give rise to are fundamentally problems of missing markets. In particular, we'll demonstrate how new markets can be defined in an exchange economy that contains consumption externalities and how

---

[10]The economist is Steven Cheung, who was also the one who uncovered the contracts made by clover and apple growers with beekeepers. This is discussed in considerably more detail in "The Fable of the Bees: An Economic Investigation," *Journal of Law and Economics* 17 (1973), 53–71.

establishment of these new markets should in principle resolve the inefficiency from externalities. We then demonstrate this in an extension of our example of a two-person exchange economy from Chapter 16 before concluding with a discussion of the Coase Theorem.

21B.1 Production Externalities

In the presence of sufficient information, it is not mathematically difficult to determine the extent of deadweight losses from pollution or to arrive at an optimal Pigouvian tax. We will demonstrate this here briefly with an example in which we use linear demand, supply, and social marginal cost SMC curves, and we will assume for convenience that the (uncompensated) market demand curve is in fact also the appropriate marginal willingness to pay curve along which to measure consumer surplus.

21B.1.1 "Barney" versus the Market
We can begin with linear market demand and supply functions we have used in previous chapters with

$$x_d = \frac{A - p}{\alpha} \quad \text{and} \quad x_s = \frac{B + p}{\beta}, \tag{21.1}$$

and we have previously calculated the competitive market equilibrium in this case as

$$p^M = \frac{\beta A - \alpha B}{\alpha + \beta} \quad \text{and} \quad x^M = \frac{A + B}{\alpha + \beta}. \tag{21.2}$$

Now suppose that each unit of output x produces δ units of carbon dioxide pollution, and suppose that the damage from this pollution increases quadratically with additional pollution dumped into the air. In particular, suppose the externality cost is given by $C_E(x) = (\delta x)^2$. Then the *marginal* externality cost for each unit of x is the derivative of $C_E(x)$ with respect to x, or $MC_E = 2\delta^2 x$. The inverse of the supply curve in equation (21.1) is the industry's marginal cost curve; i.e., $MC_S = -B + \beta x$. Added together, these two curves make up the social marginal cost curve

$$SMC = -B + (\beta + 2\delta^2)x. \tag{21.3}$$

Suppose $A = 1,000$, $\alpha = 1$, $\beta = 0.5$, $\delta = 0.5$, and $B = 0$. Illustrate the market demand and supply as well as the SMC curves in a graph with x on the horizontal axis.

Exercise 21B.1

The efficient or optimal output level x^{opt}, the output our mythical "Barney" would choose, then occurs at the intersection of the SMC and the inverse demand curve $p = A - \alpha x$. Solving the equation $-B + (\beta + 2\delta^2)x = A - \alpha x$ for x, we get

$$x^{opt} = \frac{A + B}{\alpha + \beta + 2\delta^2}, \tag{21.4}$$

which you can immediately see is less than the competitive equilibrium quantity x^M in equation (21.2).

Suppose the "pollution" emitted is actually not harmful and simply kills the mosquito population in the area. The SMC of the pollution might then be negative; i.e., this kind of pollution might actually produce social benefits. Will the efficient quantity now be greater or less than the market quantity? Show this within the context of the example.

Exercise 21B.2

21B.1.2 The Efficient Pigouvian Tax

We can now determine the optimal Pigouvian tax t^{opt} that will ensure that the market produces the efficient level of output. In order for consumers to want to buy x^{opt}, they must face a price p_d such that $x^{opt} = x_d(p_d) = (A - p_d)/\alpha$. Similarly, in order for producers to supply x^{opt} in equilibrium, they must face a price p_s such that $x^{opt} = x_s(p_s) = (B + p_s)/\beta$. Solving these equations and plugging in our solution for x^{opt} from equation (21.4), we then get

$$p_d = \frac{(\beta + 2\delta^2)A - \alpha B}{\alpha + \beta + 2\delta^2} \text{ and } p_s = \frac{\beta A - (\alpha + 2\delta^2)B}{\alpha + \beta + 2\delta^2}, \tag{21.5}$$

and subtracting p_s from p_d gives us the optimal Pigouvian tax t^{opt} required to get this difference in consumer and producer prices; i.e.,

$$t^{opt} = p_d - p_s = \frac{2\delta^2(A + B)}{\alpha + \beta + 2\delta^2}. \tag{21.6}$$

Exercise 21B.3 Complete exercise 21B.1 by illustrating and labeling the Pigouvian tax for this example.

Exercise 21B.4 Using the graph from the previous exercise, calculate consumer surplus, producer surplus, the externality cost, and overall surplus in the absence of the Pigouvian tax. Then calculate these again under the Pigouvian tax, taking into account the tax revenue raised. What is the deadweight loss from not having the Pigouvian tax?

21B.1.3 Cap-and-Trade

Now suppose that instead of imposing a tax t on output, the government requires that producers hold a pollution voucher for each unit of carbon dioxide emitted in the production process. Since every unit of output x produces δ units of pollution, a producer must therefore hold δ pollution vouchers for every unit of output he or she produces. If the rental price of a voucher is r, this implies that the industry marginal cost goes from $(-B + \beta x)$ to

$$MC = -B + \beta x + \delta r. \tag{21.7}$$

Exercise 21B.5 Illustrate how this shifts the supply curve in your graph (where you assume $A = 1,000$, $\alpha = 1$, $\beta = 0.5$, $\delta = 0.5$, and $B = 0$.).

Setting this equal to the (inverse) demand curve (which is $p = A - \alpha x$) and solving for x, we get the new equilibrium quantity (given a voucher rental rate of r) as

$$x^*(r) = \frac{A + B - \delta r}{\alpha + \beta}. \tag{21.8}$$

It is immediately clear from this equation, as it should be from the graph you drew in exercise 21B.5, that the market will produce less so long as the rental price of vouchers is greater than zero. But this does not yet answer the question of how the rental price of vouchers is determined in the first place. This price is, as demonstrated in Graph 21.3, determined in the new market for pollution vouchers that the government creates when it limits the quantity of vouchers to some level V.

Every unit of output causes δ in pollution and thus requires δ pollution vouchers. In the absence of any new introduction of pollution-abating technologies, a total voucher level of V then implies that the market will reduce its output to $(1/\delta)V$. Substituting this into equation (21.8) on the left-hand side and solving for r, we get the equilibrium rental price for vouchers (given an overall supply of vouchers fixed at V) as

$$r(V) = \frac{\delta(A + B) - (\alpha + \beta)V}{\delta^2}. \qquad (21.9)$$

Now notice what happens if the government provides exactly enough vouchers to allow the market quantity $x^M = (A + B)/(\alpha + \beta)$ to be produced; i.e., suppose the government sets $V = \delta(A + B)/(\alpha + \beta)$. Plugging this into equation (21.9), we get an equilibrium voucher price of zero: the voucher giving me the right to pollute ceases to be worth anything. For any level of V below this, equation (21.9) tells us we will have a positive rental price for vouchers.

We can then relate this directly to Graph 21.3 in which we argued that firms will form a demand curve in the market for vouchers while the government will set a perfectly inelastic supply by setting a fixed voucher (and thus a fixed pollution) amount. In fact, equation (21.9) *is* the demand curve (or the inverse demand function) for vouchers by polluting firms, and the inverse of this equation,

$$v(r) = \frac{\delta(A + B) - \delta^2 r}{\alpha + \beta}, \qquad (21.10)$$

is the demand function that relates the rental price r to the quantity demanded by producers.

Verify that a voucher price of zero results in the market output according to this demand function. **Exercise 21B.6**

Illustrate the demand curve for pollution vouchers and label its slope and intercept. **Exercise 21B.7**

Here is an alternative (and perhaps more intuitive) derivation of the demand for pollution vouchers: The maximum amount that a firm is willing to pay to be allowed to produce one more unit of output depends on how much the firm thinks it can sell its output for and what the firm's other costs are. In panel (a) of Graph 21.6, for instance, if the government limited the quantity in the market to x_1, the marginal firm would be willing to pay an amount equal to the blue distance in order to produce because this is the difference between the marginal cost of production for this firm and the marginal willingness to pay for the output by the marginal consumer. Similarly, if the government limited total output to x_2, the marginal firm would be willing to pay at most an amount equal to the magenta distance.

Now suppose we converted the units in which we measure x to voucher units, knowing that we will have to have δ vouchers for 1 unit of output x. The marginal benefit (or inverse demand) function when units are measured in terms of x is just the demand curve $MB = A - \alpha x$. If we now measure x in $1/\delta$-units, for instance, then the vertical intercept term of this function will have to be divided by δ, giving a vertical intercept of A/δ for our new marginal benefit curve. The horizontal intercept of our original marginal benefit curve, on the other hand, has to change from A/α to $\delta A/\alpha$. From this, we can calculate the slope of our new marginal benefit curve as the (negative) vertical intercept divided by the horizontal intercept, or $(-(A/\delta)/(\delta A/\alpha)) = -\alpha/\delta^2$. Thus, the marginal benefit curve when output is expressed in voucher-units is

$$MB(v) = \frac{A}{\delta} - \frac{\alpha}{\delta^2} v = \frac{\delta A - \alpha v}{\delta^2}, \qquad (21.11)$$

Graph 21.6: Going from the Market for x to the Pollution Voucher Market

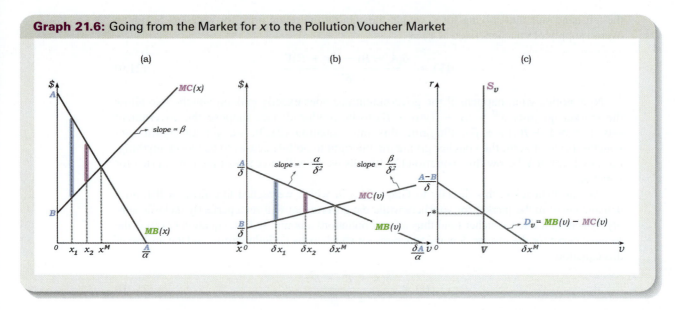

and, applying similar logic to the producers' marginal cost curve $MC = -B + \beta x$, the marginal cost curve when output is expressed in voucher units is

$$MC(v) = \frac{-\delta B + \beta v}{\delta^2}. \qquad (21.12)$$

Panel (b) of Graph 21.6 illustrates these marginal benefit and cost curves, which are equivalent to those in panel (a) except that the units on the horizontal axis are $1/\delta$ the units in panel (a).

Exercise 21B.8   What is the relationship between the length of the blue and magenta lines in panels (a) and (b)?

Exercise 21B.9   Implicitly, we are assuming $\delta = 2$ in panel (b) of Graph 21.6. How would this graph change if $\delta < 1$, i.e., if each unit of output produces less than one unit of pollution?

The most that the marginal firm is willing to pay for a voucher is then simply the difference between $MB(v)$ and $MC(v)$,

$$MB(v) - MC(v) = \frac{\delta(A + B) - (\alpha + \beta)v}{\delta^2}, \qquad (21.13)$$

exactly the expression for the voucher demand curve in equation (21.9). This function is graphed in panel (c) of Graph 21.6, and the equilibrium price r^* in the voucher market is then simply determined by the intersection of this demand curve with the inelastic supply set at V by the government or, mathematically, by substituting V for v in equation (21.13).

Exercise 21B.10   If $V = \delta x_2$, which distance in panels (a) or (b) of Graph 21.6 is equal to r^*?

Exercise 21B.11   For the case when $A = 1,000$, $\alpha = 1$, $\beta = 0.5$, $\delta = 0.5$, and $B = 0$ (as you have assumed in previous exercises), what is the rental rate of the pollution voucher when $V = 250$? What is the price of a pollution voucher if the interest rate is 0.05?

21B.1.4 Pollution Vouchers versus Taxes In Section A, we drew a distinction between Pigouvian taxes (that are levied on *output*) and pollution taxes, which are levied on *pollution* that a firm emits. In our mathematical example here, there is a one-to-one relationship between taxing output and taxing pollution because we have assumed that each unit of output produces δ units of pollution. Thus, in our simplified example, the Pigouvian tax on output is not that different from a pollution tax, and, as a result, we can illustrate that, for every pollution voucher cap under a cap-and-trade policy, there exists a tax that achieves the same outcome. Keep in mind, however, that the real world introduces complexities that create a real distinction between Pigouvian and pollution taxes, an issue we return to after demonstrating the equivalence of tax and cap-and-trade policies for our example.

Suppose the government knows the optimal level of output x^{opt} in equation (21.4) as well as the amount δ of pollution emitted by each unit of production. The information, combined with our knowledge of supply and demand curves, is then sufficient to set the optimal voucher level at

$$V^{opt} = \delta x^{opt} = \frac{\delta(A + B)}{\alpha + \beta + 2\delta^2}. \tag{21.14}$$

Plugging V^{opt} into equation (21.9), this implies an equilibrium rental rate for vouchers of

$$r^*(V^{opt}) = \frac{2\delta(A + B)}{\alpha + \beta + 2\delta^2}. \tag{21.15}$$

In order to produce one unit of output, we have to rent δ vouchers, which implies that the marginal cost of production has increased by

$$\delta r^*(V^{opt}) = \frac{2\delta^2(A + B)}{\alpha + \beta + 2\delta^2}. \tag{21.16}$$

Note that this is exactly equal to the optimal Pigouvian tax t^{opt} we derived in equation (21.6); i.e.,

$$t^{opt} = \delta r^*(V^{opt}). \tag{21.17}$$

Thus, so long as the government sets the number of pollution vouchers correctly, the market for these vouchers will result in a price equal to the tax the government would have liked to impose had it chosen to use a Pigouvian tax instead. In fact, as illustrated in Table 21.1 for the example that you have worked with in many of the within-chapter exercises, *for any tax imposed on outputs, there exists an equivalent voucher level that will result in a voucher rental rate that has the same impact on producers as the tax.*

Suppose the government simply gives away the pollution vouchers. Why is the deadweight loss the same under tax and cap-and-trade policies that satisfy $t = \delta r^*(V)$ (even though one makes revenue for the government while the other does not)? **Exercise 21B.12**

Illustrate on a graph where the deadweight loss falls when $t = 400$ in Table 21.1. What about when it falls at $t = 100$? **Exercise 21B.13**

As noted, however, our mathematical example obscures within its simplicity a difference between taxing output in polluting industries and taxing pollution emissions directly. This is because we illustrated the case of a single industry, ignoring the fact that many industries engage in pollution, *and* we have not introduced the potential for pollution-abating technologies to play a role. Even within a single industry, a Pigouvian tax on output differs from a pollution tax in that

Table 21.1: $A = 1,000$, $\alpha = 1$, $\beta = 0.5$, $\delta = 0.5$, and $B = 0$

		Equivalent Tax and Pollution Voucher Policies			
t	V	$r^*(V)$	x	x^{opt}	DWL
$0	333	$0	667	500	$27,778
$50	317	$100	633	500	$17,778
$100	300	$200	600	500	$10,000
$150	283	$300	567	500	$4,444
$200	267	$400	533	500	$1,111
$250	250	$500	500	500	$0
$300	233	$600	467	500	$1,111
$350	217	$700	433	500	$4,444
$400	200	$800	400	500	$10,000
$450	183	$900	367	500	$17,778
$500	167	$1,000	333	500	$27,778

the latter allows firms to reduce their tax obligations by introducing pollution-abating technologies while the former does not (unless it is constantly re-assessed). Thus, the equivalence of a Pigouvian tax to a pollution tax within an industry only survives if we assume that the government will adjust the Pigouvian tax on output as firms introduce pollution-abating technologies. When considering pollution across industries, this is further complicated by the fact that industries will differ in terms of the ease with which they can introduce pollution abating technologies, with any equivalence between Pigouvian taxes and pollution taxes then assuming that the government continuously adjusts Pivougian per-unit taxes as pollution-abating technologies are introduced in different settings. The equivalence between cap-and-trade and pollution taxes, on the other hand, is robust to the introduction of such real-world complications.

21B.2 Consumption Externalities

The mathematics behind our graphical development of consumption externalities is almost identical to that behind production externalities. As a result, we will treat this in end-of-chapter exercise 21.1 rather than developing it fully here. Instead, we will proceed next to considering the problem of consumption externalities in a general equilibrium setting where we will be able to illustrate more precisely what we mean when we say that the presence of an externality necessarily implies the absence of a market that, if established, would eliminate the inefficiency that arises from the externality.

21B.3 Externalities and Missing Markets

The idea of using (pollution voucher) markets to solve the externality problems created by pollution is closely linked to a more general understanding of externalities as a problem of "missing markets" (or, as we put it in Section A, of a failure of markets to exist). The intuition behind this is not difficult to see once we see how the missing markets could be defined, and how pricing within those markets will then lead those who emit externalities to face the costs (or benefits) they impose on others. Using our tools from Chapter 16, however, we can be a little more precise about what we mean by missing markets and how an establishment of those markets resolves the inefficiency from externalities under competition. We will do so here for the case of externalities in an exchange economy, but one could similarly illustrate this in an economy with production.[11]

21B.3.1 Introducing Consumption Externalities into an Exchange Economy

In Chapter 16, we defined an exchange economy as a set of consumers denoted $n = 1, 2, ..., N$, with each consumer characterized fully by her endowments of each of M different goods as well as her tastes summarized by utility functions defined over M goods (denoted $m = 1, 2, ..., M$). An exchange economy was then given simply by

$$\left(\{(e_1^n, e_2^n, ..., e_m^n)\}_{n=1}^N, \{u^n : \mathbb{R}^M \to \mathbb{R}^1\}_{n=1}^N \right).^{12} \tag{21.18}$$

Because each consumer cares only about her own consumption of each of the goods (and because there are no other agents like producers), there is no externality in this exchange economy. *An externality (in the absence of production) then arises when one consumer's consumption directly enters the utility function of another consumer.* In principle, such consumption externalities in an exchange economy could arise in every direction, with every consumer's consumption of each good entering every other consumer's utility function.

We could then think of consumer n as consuming some of each of the M goods *and* being affected by her "impression" of each other consumer's consumption of each of the M goods. Suppose, for instance, that we let x_{ij}^n denote "person n's impression of person j's consumption of good i". If x_{ij}^n enters person n's utility function, then person j is generating a consumption externality when consuming good i. But if each person's consumption of each good potentially enters each person's utility function, then each person is in essence consuming NM different goods rather than M goods as before. For instance, if $N = 2$ and $M = 2$, consumer 1 consumes $(x_{11}^1, x_{21}^1, x_{12}^1, x_{22}^1)$.

Exercise 21B.14

Which two of these four goods represent the consumption levels x_1^1 and x_2^1 that exist for person 1 in an exchange economy without externalities?

We have therefore taken an economy with M goods and defined, for each person, NM goods that enter his or her utility function. The exchange economy defined in equation (21.18) can then be rewritten with consumption externalities as

$$\left(\{(e_1^n, e_2^n, ..., e_m^n)\}_{n=1}^N, \{u^n : \mathbb{R}^{NM} \to \mathbb{R}^1\}_{n=1}^N \right). \tag{21.19}$$

21B.3.2 The Missing Markets in an Exchange Economy with Externalities

We have now introduced "impressions of other individuals' consumption" explicitly as new goods. But this implies that we have implicitly introduced production into the exchange economy because *each time a consumer makes a decision to consume some of the M goods, he or she is "producing" $(N - 1)$ of these newly defined goods.* When I consume good 1, I am producing an impression of

---

[11]This approach to illustrating the "missing market" aspect of externalities was introduced by Kenneth Arrow (1921–) (whom we previously mentioned in Chapter 16 as the 1972 Nobel Laureate who co-founded modern general equilibrium theory) in "The Organization of Economic Activity: Issues Pertinent to the Choice of Market versus Non-Market Allocations," in *Public Expenditure and Policy Analysis,* R. Havenman, and J. Margolis, eds. (Chicago: Markham, 1970). A subsequent literature that we allude to in the Appendix to this chapter points out a technical problem in this way of modeling externality markets, a problem we will for now glance over.

[12]If you are uncomfortable with this notation, please review the discussion surrounding expression (16.1) in Chapter 16.

my consumption of good 1 that now potentially enters everyone else's utility function. But our exchange economy has no markets that set prices for such goods and thus no market mechanism to govern my production decisions!

Suppose, for instance, that person j's consumption of good i enters individual n's utility function in a positive way. In this case, person j is a producer of an output x_{ij}^n, an output that consumers like n would be willing to pay for but don't since there is no market and no price. Alternatively, suppose that x_{ij}^n enters person n's utility function negatively, implying consumer j emits a *negative* consumption externality by consuming good i. In this case, we can view consumer j as using x_{ij}^n as an *input* into the production of her own consumption of good i. But, once again because there is no market for this input and thus no price, consumer j does not need to purchase the input x_{ij}^n when deciding how much of the good i to consume.

Exercise 21B.15

If there are two consumers and two goods, how many missing markets are there potentially? More generally, how many missing markets could there be when there are M goods and N consumers?

In some cases, externalities will take a form where the externality affects every consumer whereas in other cases the externality may affect only some consumers. Suppose, for instance, that consumer j is choosing good i that represents the number of car rides she takes, and each car ride emits pollution that contributes to global warming. In that case, her car rides enter each consumer's utility function in the same quantity (even though different consumers will feel differently about how bad this externality is). Put differently, in this example

$$x_{ij}^n = x_{ij} \text{ for all } n \neq j; \tag{21.20}$$

i.e., each individual other than j experiences the impact of j's car rides in the same quantity. In other cases, an externality is more "local," affecting some individuals differently than others. For instance, if j chooses good i that represents music played in the backyard, her immediate neighbors are affected more than more distant neighbors. In this case, x_{ij}^n will differ depending on the distance between individual j and n.

21B.3.3 Introducing Property Rights and New Markets
In order to establish the new markets that can price the externality effects within this exchange economy, we have to begin by specifying a set of new property rights. If my car rides cause pollution, do I have the right to pollute, or do others have the right not to have pollution inflicted on them? If I play loud music on my patio, do I have the right to do as much of this as I want to, or do others have the right to not be bothered by my music? For efficiency purposes, however, it turns out that what matters most is that property rights be established so that markets can form. For now, we will illustrate in a simple example how markets price externalities when markets are established, and we will return to a discussion of the extent to which it matters how property rights are assigned in Chapter 27.

One way to think of how property rights are established in the new markets is to extend the endowments for individuals to include endowments of the new goods. In this way, rights could be distributed in a variety of ways, although we will typically think of rights being established strictly one way or another; i.e., either someone has the right to pollute or the polluters have the right not to be bothered by pollution unless they sell their rights. But once we have established a system of property rights, we have arrived at an exchange economy that simply has more goods than before. And none of the goods now appears in more than one utility function, which means there is technically no more externality in the economy with the expanded set of markets. Since we know that exchange economies without externalities are such that competitive equilibria are efficient regardless of how many goods and consumers there are in the economy, the establishment of these new markets therefore leads to an economy in which competitive equilibria are efficient, with prices of the newly defined goods causing the emitters of externalities to take full account of the marginal (social) costs and benefits of their actions.

21B.3.4 A Numerical Example

In Chapter 16, we worked through an example of a two-person, two-good exchange economy in which $(e_1^1, e_2^1) = (3, 6)$, $(e_1^2, e_2^2) = (10, 4)$, $u^1(x_1, x_2) = x_1^{3/4} x_2^{1/4}$ and $u^2(x_1, x_2) = x_1^{1/4} x_2^{3/4}$. Given that only each individual's own consumption appears in his or her utility function, this represents an exchange economy without externalities. Suppose now, however, that consumption of good 1 by individual 1 enters individual 2's utility function. Using our notation, this implies that the good x_{11}^2, individual 2's perception of individual 1's consumption of good 1, enters u^2. To keep our notation in this example as simple as possible, let's define $x_3 = x_{11}^2$, and let individual 2's utility function be redefined as

$$u^2(x_1, x_2, x_3) = x_1^{1/4} x_2^{3/4} x_3^{\gamma}. \qquad (21.21)$$

Depending on whether γ is greater or less than zero, individual 1 is therefore now imposing a positive or negative consumption externality on individual 2. When $\gamma = 0$, the example reduces to our example from Chapter 16 with no externality.

We can first ask what the competitive equilibrium of this exchange economy will be. In the absence of a market for x_3, however, nothing fundamental has changed from the way we calculated the equilibrium of this economy in Chapter 16: Individual 1 will maximize the same utility function subject to the same budget constraint as before and will thus have the same demand equations. Individual 2 will maximize the new utility function in equation (21.21) subject to the same constraints as before, but x_3^{γ} will simply cancel out as we solve for her demand equations, resulting in the same demands as in Chapter 16. With both individuals exhibiting the same demands, we get the same competitive equilibrium as before, with $p^2/p^1 = 3/2$, $(x_1^1, x_2^1) = (9, 2)$ and $(x_1^2, x_2^2) = (4, 8)$.

Verify that individual 2's demand functions for x_1 and x_2 are unchanged as a result of the inclusion of x_3 in her utility function.

Exercise 21B.16

Do you think the conclusion (in exercise 21B.16) that demands for x_1 and x_2 do not change will hold regardless of what form the utility function takes?

Exercise 21B.17

But now suppose that a market is introduced for the good x_3 (with price p_3). Let's begin by thinking of the externality as negative (i.e., $\gamma < 0$), and suppose that property rights are assigned such that individual 2 has the right to not experience the externality unless she agrees voluntarily to do so. This implies that individual 1 will have to pay not only p_1 for each unit of x_1 he consumes but also p_3 (since $x_1^1 = x_3$). The optimization problem for consumer 1 then becomes

$$\max_{x_1, x_2} u^1(x_1, x_2) = x_1^{\alpha} x_2^{(1-\alpha)} \text{ subject to } p_1 e_1^1 + p_2 e_2^1 = (p_1 + p_3) x_1 + p_2 x_2. \qquad (21.22)$$

Solving this in the usual way, we get

$$x_1^1 = \frac{\alpha(p_1 e_1^1 + p_2 e_2^1)}{p_1 + p_3} \text{ and } x_2^1 = \frac{(1-\alpha)(p_1 e_1^1 + p_2 e_2^1)}{p_2}. \qquad (21.23)$$

Individual 2, on the other hand, will receive p_3 for every unit of x_3 that individual 1 emits, but, since individual 2 is given the "property rights" to x_3, individual 2 chooses how much of x_3 to sell. The optimization problem for individual 2 then becomes

$$\max_{x_1,x_2,x_3} u^2(x_1,x_2,x_3) = x_1^\beta x_2^{(1-\beta)} x_3^\gamma \text{ subject to } p_1 e_1^2 + p_2 e_2^2 + p_3 x_3 = p_1 x_1 + p_2 x_2. \quad (21.24)$$

Solving this, we get

$$x_1^2 = \frac{\beta(p_1 e_1^2 + p_2 e_2^2)}{(1+\gamma)p_1}, \quad x_2^2 = \frac{(1-\beta)(p_1 e_1^2 + p_2 e_2^2)}{(1+\gamma)p_2} \text{ and } x_3 = \frac{-\gamma(p_1 e_1^2 + p_2 e_2^2)}{(1+\gamma)p_3}. \quad (21.25)$$

Exercise 21B.18 Verify these demand functions. (*Hint*: It becomes significantly easier algebraically to first take natural logs of the utility function.)

Exercise 21B.19 Do the demand functions converge to those we derived in the absence of an externality as the externality approaches zero (i.e., as γ approaches zero)?

We can now solve for equilibrium prices. As in Chapter 16, we will be able to solve only for *relative* prices and can therefore set one of the prices to 1. Suppose, then, we set

$$p_1 = 1. \quad (21.26)$$

Setting demand equal to supply in the market for good 2, i.e., setting $x_2^1 + x_2^2 = e_2^1 + e_2^2$, we can then solve for p_2 as

$$p_2 = \frac{(1-\alpha)(1+\gamma)e_1^1 + (1-\beta)e_1^2}{\alpha(1+\gamma)e_2^1 + (\beta+\gamma)e_2^2}. \quad (21.27)$$

In addition, it must be true that demand is equal to supply in the x_3 market, where the amount of x_3 consumer 2 is willing to sell must be equal to the amount of x_1 that consumer 1 wants to consume; i.e., $x_1^1 = x_3$. Solving this, we can get p_3 in terms of p_2 (with p_1 again set to 1),

$$p_3 = \frac{-\gamma(e_1^2 + p_2 e_2^2)}{\alpha(1+\gamma)(e_1^1 + p_2 e_2^1) + \gamma(e_1^2 + p_2 e_2^2)}. \quad (21.28)$$

In Table 21.2, we then calculate the competitive equilibrium prices and quantities when the market for good x_3 has been established. The table begins with negative values for γ, i.e., with the case where individual 1's consumption of good 1 imposes a negative externality on individual 2. As you move down the table, the externality becomes less severe, with no externality when $\gamma = 0$. Finally, the table moves into positive values for γ, implying a positive externality on individual 2 from the consumption of good 1 by individual 1. Notice that p_3 is positive whenever the consumption externality is negative, implying that the presence of a negative externality results in individual 2 receiving compensation for suffering the negative effects of individual 1's consumption. But when the externality becomes positive, p_3 becomes negative, implying that now individual 2 compensates individual 1 for the positive effect x_1^1 has on individual 2. Thus, *the establishment of the missing market results in individual 2 imposing a "tax" on individual 1's consumption of good 1 when the externality is negative and a "subsidy" when the externality is positive.*

Of course, just as in Chapter 16, it would not be reasonable to expect market prices to govern exchange—either in the presence or in the absence of externalities—when there is literally only one individual on each side of the market. The two-person exchange economy simply provides a useful tool with which to illustrate how markets set prices in general equilibrium. But the previous analysis continues to hold exactly the same way if we assume that there are many "type 1" and many "type 2" individuals when competitive price-taking behavior becomes more realistic. And for the "two-person case" we have the Coase Theorem to fall back on, a theorem already mentioned in Section A and one we now examine a bit more closely.

Table 21.2: $\alpha = 3/4$, $\beta = 1/4$, $(e_1^1, e_2^1) = (3,6)$, $(e_1^2, e_2^2) = (10,4)$

			Equilibrium with "Missing Market" Established				
γ	p_1	p_2	p_3	x_1^1	x_2^1	x_1^2	x_2^2
−0.4	$1.00	$3.79	$6.64	2.52	1.70	10.48	8.30
−0.3	$1.00	$2.72	$1.61	5.54	1.76	7.46	8.22
−0.2	$1.00	$2.13	$0.64	7.21	1.85	5.79	8.15
−0.1	$1.00	$1.76	$0.23	8.27	1.93	4.73	8.07
0.0	$1.00	$1.50	$0.00	9.00	2.00	4.00	8.00
0.1	$1.00	$1.31	-$0.15	9.54	2.07	3.46	7.93
0.2	$1.00	$1.17	-$0.25	9.94	2.14	3.06	7.86
0.3	$1.00	$1.05	-$0.32	10.27	2.21	2.73	7.79
0.4	$1.00	$0.96	-$0.38	10.53	2.28	2.47	7.72

21B.4 Small "Markets" and the Coase Theorem

In Section A, we introduced the insight of Ronald Coase with respect to the types of externalities that make us mad enough to take each other to court. We gave the example of me building an addition to my house and you taking me to court because my addition would cast a shadow on your beautiful swimming pool. It is precisely in such "small" settings that, even if we established "markets" of the types we have discussed, there would not be much of a "market" since only one or a few people would be operating on each side of the market. And, while we can theoretically investigate what market prices would look like if they in fact arose, it is more realistic to think of "bargaining" as the way in which externality issues would be resolved in such "markets."

21B.4.1 Bargaining under Complete and Incomplete Information
Bargaining by definition does not happen in competitive settings, since in competitive settings each consumer and producer is a price-taker. We are therefore jumping a bit ahead of ourselves as we think about bargaining under the Coase Theorem. You and I are decidedly not price-takers during our coffee as we discuss the level of compensation that you have to offer me to stop building (if the judge ruled in my favor) or the level of compensation I will pay you to let me build (if the judge ruled in your favor). Put differently, we are jumping ahead because we are thinking of a "strategic" setting, one in which you and I have some real control over our economic environment.

Economists (and particularly game theorists) have, over the past few decades, arrived at a well-defined theory of bargaining, some of which was directly inspired by Coase's confidence that bargaining in an atmosphere in which property rights have been fully clarified will lead to efficient outcomes when externalities are involved. Some of that theory (just as some of the development of game theory in Chapter 24) assumes that you and I have perfect information about each other's costs and benefits of my addition to my house. And under such circumstances, Coase appears to be on solid ground: The theory predicts that you and I will in fact reach a bargain that will lead to the efficient outcome under the conditions envisioned by Coase.[13] Intuitively, this is not hard to see: If

---

[13]In cases where income (or endowment) effects are important (as when tastes are not quasilinear), we have to be slightly more careful because "the" efficient outcome may differ depending on how property rights are assigned. This is explored further in exercise 21.4.

the story I told in Section A about how we will bargain our way to efficiency made sense, you have the basic intuition. We can demonstrate this more formally once we have developed some game theory tools and illustrate how two individuals arrive at bargains under complete information in end-of-chapter exercise 24.9.

21B.4.2 Bargaining under Incomplete Information

In Section A, however, we implicitly assumed what we have just made explicit: that you and I *both* know what the costs to you are (relative to you solving your shaded pool problem in other ways) of me adding to my house in a way that casts a shadow on your swimming pool and what the benefits (relative to other ways of solving my need for additional housing) are to me of building the addition in this way. Let's denote your costs as c and my benefit as b. Efficiency dictates that I go ahead with my addition if $b > c$, and we argued that, so long as property rights have been specified and transactions costs are low, the efficient outcome will happen.

But suppose that you are not sure what b is and I am not sure what c is. Rather, you have beliefs about b and I have beliefs about c. Let my beliefs be represented by $0 \leq \rho(c) \leq 1$ for any $c > 0$, with $\rho(c)$ equal to the probability I place on your costs being less than or equal to c. Similarly, let your beliefs be represented by $0 \leq \delta(b) \leq 1$ for any $b > 0$, with $\delta(b)$ equal to the probability that you place on my benefits being less than or equal to b. Now suppose the judge rules in your favor; i.e., you now have the right to a shadow-free pool and I cannot build my addition unless you agree to it.

I will therefore come to coffee and offer you compensation based on my beliefs of what your costs are. To arrive at an offer I make to you, I will have to calculate the offer p that maximizes my expected payoff. My expected payoff from any offer p is the probability that the offer will be accepted times the benefit I receive from having my offer accepted. For any offer p, I believe that the probability that your true costs are less than or equal to p is $\rho(p)$, which implies that I believe that the probability of you accepting my offer is $\rho(p)$. The benefit I receive if the offer is accepted is my benefit b from having the addition built minus the payment p I have to make to you; i.e., the benefit I receive if the offer is accepted is $(b - p)$. I therefore solve the following optimization problem as I calculate my optimal offer given the beliefs I have:

$$\max_{p} \rho(p)(b - p). \tag{21.29}$$

I will obviously not make an offer $p > b$, and you will not accept an offer $p < c$. But, depending on what my beliefs are, I may well make an offer p^* that maximizes my expected payoff but where $p^* < c$ even though $b > c$. Thus, depending on my beliefs about your true underlying costs, the addition may not get built if the judge rules in your favor despite the fact that building the addition is efficient.[14]

Exercise 21B.20

Suppose the judge rules in my favor instead. What optimization problem do you solve as you come over to have coffee in order to offer me a payment for not building the addition? Can it again be the case that the efficient outcome does not happen for certain beliefs δ you might have about my true benefit from the addition?

Depending on how we define what we mean by "transactions costs," we now may or may not have to amend the Coase Theorem. As stated in Section A, the theorem says that so long as property rights are sufficiently specified in the presence of externalities, the efficient outcome will occur from decentralized decisions if transactions costs are sufficiently low. As we have just seen,

---

[14]In Section B of Chapter 24, you will learn more about the equilibrium concept that we have implicitly just applied, which we will call a Bayesian Nash Equilibrium. An example of this is also presented in end-of-chapter exercise 21.2.

strategic bargaining between individuals who understand the assignment of property rights in the presence of externalities may not result in efficiency even when there are no transactions costs keeping the individuals from getting together and bargaining. But the cost of obtaining information about the relative costs and benefits from the externality may in itself be considered a transactions cost, in which case we can leave the Coase Theorem as stated before.

CONCLUSION

This chapter is the first to have introduced an economic force that causes our First Welfare Theorem to break down: Markets, by themselves, cease to be efficient maximizers of social surplus in the presence of externalities. While previous chapters may have given the impression that microeconomists see all forms of government intervention as inherently inefficient, we have now seen that markets cannot operate efficiently in isolation. First, the very existence of markets presumes an underlying system of property rights that, in practice, has almost always required the explicit involvement of government. In the absence of such property rights, we are faced with what we have called the "Tragedy of the Commons" where individual incentives lead to overuse of resources. And where externalities arise, it is precisely because of the "Tragedy of the Commons": We all "own" the air (or, alternatively, none of us own it), and as a result no one makes sure we pay for the pollution we cause. We all "own" the roads, and so no one is charging us for the congestion we contribute when we drive during peak hours. The market failure that arises from externalities is therefore caused by the "failure of a market to exist."

This is not to say that markets themselves can always solve externality problems. Air pollution is a problem because no market for air exists, but it is not exactly easy to establish such markets. But policies aimed at correcting inefficiencies from externalities must ultimately do what markets would do if they could be established fully: They must cause individual actors in the economy to face the full marginal costs (and benefits) of their actions. We saw that this could in principle be done through Pigouvian taxes and subsidies that force individuals to confront the larger social costs and benefits of their private choices. We saw it could be done through the creative establishment of markets like those for pollution vouchers that, this time through the need to purchase a voucher if one intends to pollute, again forces polluters to pay for at least some of the social cost of their production choices. Or it could be done through such policies as electronic tolls on roads or direct taxation of pollution. Or, as Coase tells us, it could be done in the case of smaller externalities simply by clarifying through property rights cases who in fact has a right to do what, and then relying on interested individuals to bargain their way to efficiency. The key in all these policies, however, is to bring private and social marginal costs in line with one another. Government policies (such as Pigouvian taxes and subsidies), fostering of new markets (such as pollution vouchers), and clarifications of property rights in the civil society (that can have individuals bargain outside the price-based market system) can thus all contribute to greater efficiency in the presence of externalities.

In the upcoming chapter, we will see another important instance when competitive markets by themselves will not result in efficient outcomes: the wide spread case where information is not shared uniformly by market participants. We will see that such asymmetric information results in a new form of externality that can prevent important markets from forming and that offer opportunities for nonmarket institutions to enhance efficiency.

APPENDIX: FUNDAMENTAL NON-CONVEXITIES IN THE PRESENCE OF EXTERNALITIES

In our treatment of how the establishment of missing markets can restore efficiency in the presence of externalities, we glanced over a technical problem that has become known as the problem of *fundamental non-convexities*. The essence of the problem is this: Suppose we reconsider our numerical example of an exchange economy with a negative consumption externality from consumer 1's consumption of good 1 (as we did in the chapter). Suppose further that we take the assumption that consumer 2 has a right to not experience the externality and must be persuaded to sell that right by accepting payment in proportion to the externality that is emitted. We know that if the price p_3 is zero, consumer 2 will not sell any rights to consume good 1 to consumer 1 (since consumer 2 would then experience a negative externality without compensation). Now suppose that $p_3 > 0$ (as in the equilibria we described in Table 21.2). What is to keep consumer 2 from wanting to sell an infinite number of rights to pollute, thus making an infinite income to spend on consumption of goods 1 and 2? Put differently, if there is no limit on the number of rights that individual 2 can sell, a positive price will cause the consumer to want to sell an infinite quantity of x_3 while a non-positive price will cause her to want to sell zero. No matter what p_3 is set at, consumer 2 therefore prefers a corner solution.[15]

But if consumer 2 will sell only zero or an infinite amount of x_3, no equilibrium in the x_3 market exists, and the establishment of the x_3 market with all rights assigned to the victim of the negative externality does not in fact lead to a competitive equilibrium that eliminates the inefficiency from the externality. In order for the equilibria that we discuss in Table 21.2 to emerge, there *must* therefore be some limit to the number of rights that consumer 2 can sell.

The solution to this fundamental non-convexity problem lies in finding ways of "bounding" the property rights in externality markets such that, for instance, victims of pollution cannot in fact sell large or infinite amounts of these rights when the price is positive. While this is not easily done in the context of defining externality markets in the way that we have done in our exchange economy example, we have already shown how this in fact can be done when "rights" are defined along the lines of pollution vouchers. Here, a limited number of these rights are allocated in the economy, thus eliminating the problem of fundamental non-convexities.[16]

Exercise 21B.21   Why did our mathematical methods of solving for consumer 2's demand for x_3 not uncover this problem?

END-OF-CHAPTER EXERCISES

21.1[†]   Consider the case of a positive consumption externality.

A.   Suppose throughout this exercise that demand and supply curves are linear, that demand curves are equal to marginal willingness to pay curves, and that the additional social benefit from each consumption unit is k and is constant as consumption increases.

   a.   Draw two graphs with the same demand curve but one that has a fairly inelastic and one that has a fairly elastic supply curve. In which case is the market output closer to the optimal output?

   b.   Does the Pigouvian subsidy that would achieve the optimal output level differ across your two graphs in part (a)?

   c.   Draw two graphs with the same supply curve but one that has a fairly inelastic demand curve and one that has a fairly elastic demand curve. In which case is the market output closer to the optimal output?

   d.   Does the Pigouvian subsidy that would achieve the optimal output level differ across your two graphs in part (c)?

   e.   *True or False*: While the size of the Pigouvian subsidy does not vary as the slopes of demand and supply curves change, the level of under-production increases as these curves become more elastic.

   f.   In each of your graphs, indicate who benefits more from the Pigouvian subsidy: producers or consumers.

---

[15]This is referred to as a "fundamental non-convexity" because it represents a non-convexity in the production set for pollution rights. The problem of fundamental non-convexities in externality markets was first pointed out by D. Starrett, "Fundamental Nonconvexities in the Theory of Externalities," *Journal of Economic Theory* 4 (1972), 180–99.
[16]This is explored in some detail by J. Boyd and J. Conley, "Fundamental Nonconvexities in Arrovian Markets and a Coasian Solution to the Problem of Externalities," *Journal of Economic Theory* 72 (1997), 388–407.
*conceptually challenging
**computationally challenging
†solutions in Study Guide

B. Suppose demand is given by $x_d = (A - p)/\alpha$ and supply is given by $x_s = (B + p)/\beta$.

   a.   Derive the competitive equilibrium price and output level.

   b.   Suppose that the marginal positive externality benefit is k per unit of output. What is the function for the social marginal benefit SMB curve?

   c.   What is the optimal output level?

   d.   What is the Pigouvian subsidy? Show the impact it has on prices paid by consumers and prices received by producers, and illustrate that it achieves the optimal outcome.

   e.   Next, suppose that the total externality social benefit is given by $SB = (\delta x)^2$. Does the market outcome change? What about the optimal outcome?

   f.   Derive the Pigouvian subsidy now, and illustrate again that it achieves the social optimum.

21.2   The Coase Theorem is often applied in court cases where the parties seek to clarify who has the right to do what in the presence of externalities. Consider again (as in the text discussion) the case of the addition to my house that will then cast a shadow on your swimming pool. Suppose that my benefit from the addition is b, and the cost you incur from my shadow is c. Suppose throughout this exercise that transactions costs are zero.

   A.   In this part of the exercise, suppose that you and I both know what b and c are.

   a.   If we both know b and c, why don't we just get together and try to settle the matter over coffee rather than ending up in court?

   b.   If the judge (who has to decide whether I have a right to build my addition) also knows b and c, propose a sensible and efficient rule for him to use to adjudicate the case.

   c.   Judges rarely have as much information as plaintiffs and defendants. It is therefore reasonable for the judge to assume that he cannot easily ascertain b and c. Suppose he rules in my favor. What does Coase predict will happen?

   d.   What if he instead rules in your favor?

   e.   In what sense will the outcome always be the same as it was in part (b), and in what sense will it not?

   B.   Next, assume that I know b and you know c, but I do not know c and you do not know b.

   a.   Suppose the judge rules in your favor, and I now attempt to convince you to let me build the addition anyhow. I will come to your house and make an offer based on my belief that your cost is less than $\bar{c}$ with probability $\rho(\bar{c}) = \bar{c}/\alpha$. What offer will I make?

   b.   For what combinations of b and c will the outcome be inefficient?

   c.   Suppose instead that the judge ruled in my favor. You therefore come to my house to convince me not to build the addition even though I now have the right to do so. You will make me an offer based on your belief that my benefit from the addition is less than or equal to $\bar{b}$ with probability $\delta(\bar{b}) = \bar{b}/\beta$. What offer will you make?

   d.   For what combinations of b and c will the outcome be inefficient?

   e.   Explain how the cost of obtaining information might be considered a transactions cost, and the results you derived here are therefore consistent with the Coase Theorem.

21.3[†]   We discussed in the text that the "market failure" that emerges in the presence of externalities can equally well be viewed as a "failure of markets to exist," and we discussed the related idea that establishing property rights may allow individuals to resolve externality issues even when markets are not competitive.

   A.   We will explore this idea a bit further by asking whether there is a "right way" to establish property rights in the case of pure consumption externalities.

   a.   Suppose we consider the case where your consumption of music in your dorm room disturbs me next door. Let x denote the number of minutes you choose to play music each day, and let e be the number of minutes you are allowed to play music. If e is set at 0, who is given the "property rights" over the air on which the soundwaves travel from your room to mine?

   b.   What if e is set to 1,440 (which is equal to the number of minutes in a day)?

   c.   Draw a graph with minutes of music per day on the horizontal axis, ranging from 0 to 1,440. Draw a vertical axis at 0 minutes and another vertical axis at 1,440 minutes. Then illustrate your marginal willingness to pay for minutes of music (measured on the left vertical axis) and my marginal willingness to pay for reductions in the number of minutes of music (measured on the right axis) and assume that these are invariant to how e is set. What is the efficient number of minutes m^*?

   d.   The assignment of e in part (a) represents the extreme case where you have no right to play your music, while the assignment in (b) represents the polar opposite extreme where I have no right to peace and quiet. Review the logic behind the Coase Theorem that suggests the efficient outcome will be reached regardless of whether $e = 0$ or $e = 1,440$ so long as transaction costs are low.

   e.   Since $e = 0$ and $e = 1,440$ are two extreme assignments of property rights, we can now easily think of many cases in between. Does the Coase Theorem apply also to these in between cases? Why or why not?

   f.   From a pure efficiency standpoint, if the Coase Theorem is right, is there any case for any particular assignment of e?

B.   Suppose that your tastes can be described by the utility function $u(x, y) = \alpha \ln x + y$, where x is the number of minutes per day of music and y is a composite consumption good. My tastes, on the other hand, can be described by $u(x, y) = \beta \ln (1440 - x) + y$, with $(1440 - x)$ representing the number of minutes per day without your music. Both of us have some daily income level I, and the price of y is 1 given that y is a composite good denominated in dollars.

   a.   Let e be the allocation of rights as defined in part A; i.e., e is the number of minutes that you are permitted to play music without my permission. When $x < e$, I am paying you $p(e - x)$ to play less than you are allowed to, and when $x > e$, you are paying me $p(x - e)$ for the minutes above your "rights." What is your budget constraint?

   b.   What is my budget constraint?

   c.   Set up your utility maximization problem using the budget constraint you derived in (a), then solve for your demand for x.

   d.   Set up my utility maximization problem and derive my demand for x.

   e.   Derive the p^* we will agree to if transaction costs are zero and derive the number of minutes of music you will play. Does your answer depend on the level at which e was set?

   f.   According to your results, how much music is played if I don't care about peace and quiet (i.e., if $\beta = 0$)? How much is played if you don't care about music (i.e., $\alpha = 0$)?

   g.   *True or False*: The total number of minutes of music played does not depend on e, but you and I still care how e is assigned.

21.4*   In exercise 21.3, we began to investigate different ways of assigning property rights in the presence of externalities.

A.   Consider again the case of you playing music that disturbs me.

   a.   Begin with the assumptions in exercise 21.3 that led to the graph you drew in part (c) of that exercise. Then suppose that the transaction cost of getting together is k. In your graph, indicate for what range of e such a transaction cost will prohibit the efficient outcome from being reached.

   b.   If e is assigned outside that range, what will be the outcome?

   c.   Next, suppose income (or wealth) effects are important; i.e., tastes are not quasilinear. Did we allow for that in exercise 21.3?

   d.   Suppose in particular that such endowment effects matter for you but not for me, with music a normal good for you. Illustrate in a graph what happens to the amount of music as e increases. What happens to p, the price we agree to?

   e.   If endowment effects matter similarly for you and me, might it be the case that the agreed upon level of music is once again unaffected by e?

   f.   Is the Coase Theorem wrong in cases where endowment effects impact the amount of music that is played as property rights are assigned differently?

   g.   *True or False*: As long as transactions costs are zero, we will reach an efficient outcome, but that outcome (i.e., the amount of music played) might differ depending on whether income effects are important.

B.**Suppose first that our tastes are again those given in part B of exercise 21.3.

    a.   If you have not done exercise 21.3, do so now and check whether the level of music played will depend on the assignment of property rights e in the absence of transactions costs.

    b.   Next, suppose that instead of the tastes in exercise 21.3, your tastes can be described by the utility function $u(x,y) = x^{\alpha}y^{(1-\alpha)}$ (where α lies between 0 and 1). My tastes remain unchanged. How much music will be played? Does your answer depend on e and does the equilibrium price p^* depend on e?

    c.   Next, suppose that my utility function is also Cobb–Douglas, taking the form $u(x,y) = (1440 - x)^{\beta}y^{(1-\beta)}$. Derive again the amount of music that will be played (assuming zero transactions costs). Does your answer depend on e? Does the equilibrium price depend on e?

    d.   Explain your results intuitively.

    e.   In Section 21B.3.4, we went through a numerical exercise to illustrate how the establishment of property rights in the presence of externalities will resolve the "market failure" in a simple exchange economy. Review the example in the text prior to proceeding. Note that in the text we assigned the property rights in the new market to person 2, the victim of the externality. But we could have assigned property rights in many other ways (as suggested in our music example). Define x_3 once again as the impression of person 1's consumption of x_1 on person 2; i.e., $x_3 = x_{11}^2$. We can establish a market for the good x_3 by endowing individual 1 with e_3 units of x_3. This means that individual 1 can produce up to e_3 units of x_3, which is the same as saying that individual 1 can consume up to e_3 units of x_1 without having to pay the market price p_3. But if he wants to produce any more x_3, he must pay individual 2 the price p_3 for each additional unit above e_3. Similarly, under the endowment of e_3 for individual 1, individual 2 must pay p_3 per unit to individual 1 for any amount of x_3 that falls below e_3, and receives p_3 for any amount of x_3 above e_3. In the numerical example of the text, what did we implicitly set e_3 to?

    f.   Write down individual 1's budget constraint when he is assigned e_3 in property rights. (*Hint*: If $x_1 < e_1$, individual 1 will earn $p_3(e_3 - x_1)$ but if $x_1 > e_1$, he will have to pay $p_3(x_1 - e_3)$ which is equivalent to saying he will earn $p_3(e_3 - x_1)$.)

    g.   Next, write down individual 2's budget constraint.

    h.   If you substitute your answer to (e) into the budget constraints in (f) and (g), you should end up with the budget constraints we used in the numerical example of the text. Do you?

    i.   Now suppose that $u^1 = x_1^{\alpha}x_2^{(1-\alpha)}$ and $u^2 = (1440 - x_3)^{\beta}x_2^{(1-\beta)}$. Suppose further that $p_1 = 0$, $p_2 = 1$, and $p_3 = p$, and that $e_2^1 = e_2^2$. Can you now interpret the general equilibrium model as modeling our case of you (person 1) bothering me (person 2) with music?

    j.   Solve for p and x_3 (which is equal to x_1^1). Do you get the same answer as you got when you assumed Cobb–Douglas tastes for both of us in part (c)?

21.5   **Everyday Exercise:** *Children's Toys and Gucci Products*: In most of our development of consumer theory, we have assumed that tastes are independent of what other people do. This is not true for some goods. For instance, children are notorious for valuing toys more if their friends also have them, which implies their marginal willingness to pay is higher the more prevalent the toys are in their peer group. Some of my snooty acquaintances, on the other hand, like to be the center of attention and would like to consume goods that few others have. Their marginal willingness to pay for these goods thus falls as more people in their peer group consume the same goods.[17]

    A.   The two examples we have cited are examples of positive and negative *network externalities*.

        a.   Consider children's toys first. Suppose that, for a given number N of peers, demand for some toy x is linear and downward sloping, but that an increase in the "network" of children (i.e., an increase in N) causes an upward parallel shift of the demand curve. Illustrate 2 demand curves corresponding to network size levels $N_1 < N_2$.

        b.   Suppose every child at most buys 1 of these toys, which are produced at constant marginal cost. For a combination of p and x to be an equilibrium, what must be true about x if the equilibrium lies on the demand curve for network size N_1?

---

[17]Such goods are examples of *Veblen goods*. We previously mentioned these in an exercise in Chapter 7 as goods whose demand can slope up without being Giffen goods.

c. Suppose you start in such an equilibrium and the marginal cost (and thus the price) drops. Economists distinguish between two types of effects: a *direct* effect that occurs along the demand curve for network size N_1, and a *bandwagon effect* that results from increased demand due to increased network size. Label your original equilibrium A, the "temporary" equilibrium before network externalities are taken into account as B, and your new equilibrium (that incorporates both effects) as C. Assume that this new equilibrium lies on the demand curve that corresponds to network size N_2.

d. How many toys are sold in equilibrium C? Connect A and C with a line labeled $\overline{D}$. Is $\overline{D}$ the true demand curve for this toy? Explain.

e. If you were a marketing manager with a limited budget for a children's toy company, would you spend your budget on aggressive advertising early as the product is rolled out or wait and spread it out? Explain.

f. Now consider my snooty acquaintances who like Guuci products more if few of their friends have them. For any given number of friends N that also have Gucci products, their demand curve is linear and downward sloping, but the intercept of their demand curve falls as N increases. Illustrate two demand curves for $N_1 < N_2$.

g. Assume for convenience that everyone buys at most 1 Gucci product. Identify an initial equilibrium A under which N_1 Gucci products are sold at some initial price p and then a second equilibrium C at which N_2 Gucci products are sold at price $p' < p$. Can you again identify two effects: a *direct* effect analogous to the one you identified in (c) and a *snob effect* analogous to the bandwagon effect you identified for children's toys? How does the snob effect differ from the bandwagon effect?

h. *True or False*: Bandwagon effects make demand more price elastic while snob effects make demand less price elastic.

i.* In exercise 7.9, we gave an example of an upward-sloping demand curve for Gucci products, with the upward slope emerging from the fact that utility was increasing in the price of Gucci products. Might the demand that takes both the direct and snob effects into account also be upward sloping in the presence of the kinds of network externalities modeled here? (*Hint*: The answer is no.)

B. Consider again the positive and negative network externalities previously described.

a. Consider first the case of a positive network externality such as the toy example. Suppose that, for a given network size N, the demand curve is given by $p = 25N^{1/2} - x$. Does this give rise to parallel linear demand curves for different levels of N, with higher N implying higher demand?

b. Assume that children buy at most 1 of this toy. Suppose we are currently in an equilibrium where $N = 400$. What must the price of x be?

c. Suppose the price drops to \$24. Isolate the direct effect of the price change; i.e., if child perception of N remained unchanged, what would happen to the consumption level of x?

d. Can you verify that the real equilibrium (that includes the bandwagon effect) will result in $x = N = 576$ when price falls to \$24? How big is the direct effect relative to the bandwagon effect in this case?[18]

e. Consider next the negative network externality of the Gucci example. Suppose that, given a network of size N, the market demand curve for Gucci products is $p = (1000/N^{1/2}) - x$. Does this give rise to parallel linear demand curves for different levels of N, with higher N implying lower demand?

f. Assume again that no one buys more than 1 Gucci item. Suppose we are currently in equilibrium with $N = 25$. What must the price be?

g. Suppose the price drops to \$65. Isolate the direct effect of the price change; i.e., if people's perception of N remained unchanged, what would happen to the consumption level of x?

h. Can you verify that the real equilibrium (that includes the snob effect) will result in $x = N = 62$? How big is the direct effect relative to the snob effect in this case?

i. Although the demand curves for a fixed level of N are linear, can you sketch the demand curve that includes both direct and snob effects?

---

[18]For a more detailed analysis of the quite interesting demand curve that arises under this network externality, see a similar example in exercise 21.8.

21.6† **Business Application:** *Fishing in the Commons*: In the text, we introduced the notion of the *Tragedy of the Commons* and found its source in the emergence of externalities when property rights are not well established. This exercise demonstrates the same idea in a slightly different way.

A. Consider a self-contained lake that is home to fish that are sold on the market at price p. Suppose the primary input into fishing this lake is nets that are rented at a weekly rate of r, and suppose the single input production frontier for fish has decreasing returns to scale.

   a.   Draw a graph with fishing nets on the horizontal axis and fish on the vertical. Illustrate the marginal product of fishing nets.

   b.   Recalling the relationship between "marginal" and "average" quantities, add the *average* product curve to your graph.

   c.   If you own the lake, what is the relationship between the marginal product of fishing nets and prices (p, r) assuming you maximize profit?

   d.   Illustrate the profit-maximizing quantity of nets n^* on your graph. Then, on a graph below it that plots the production frontier for fish, illustrate the number of fish x^* that are brought to market.

   e.* Suppose you instead charge a weekly fee for every fishing net that fishermen bring to your lake. Does the number of fish produced and nets used change?

   f.   Next, consider a nearby lake that is identical in every way except that it is publicly owned, with no one controlling who can come onto the lake to fish. Assuming all nets are used with the same intensity, each fishing net that is brought onto the lake can then be expected to catch the *average* of the total weekly catch. Illustrate on your graphs how many nets $\overline{n}$ will be brought onto this lake and how many fish $\overline{x}$ this implies will be brought to market each week.

   g.   Which lake yields more fish per week? Which lake is being harvested for fish efficiently?

   h.   Suppose that what matters is not just the current crop of fish but also its implication for the future fish population of the lake. Explain how the privately owned lake is likely to house a relatively constant population of fish over time, while the publicly owned lake is likely to run out of fish as time passes.

   i.   The trade in elephant trunks, or ivory, has decimated much of the elephant population in some parts of Africa but not in others, with hunters often slaughtering entire herds, removing the trunks, and leaving the rest. In some parts of Africa, the land on which elephants roam is public property; in other parts it is privately owned with owners allowed to restrict access. Can you guess from our lake example what is different about the parts of Africa where elephant herds are stable compared with those parts where they are nearing extinction?

   j.   Why do you think that wild buffalo in the American West are nearly extinct but domesticated cattle are plentiful in the same region?

B. Let n again denote the fishing nets used in the lake and assume that r is the weekly rental cost per net. The number of fish brought out of the lake per week is $x = f(n) = An^\alpha$ where $A > 0$ and $0 < \alpha < 1$, and fish sell on the market for p.

   a.   Suppose you own the lake and you don't let anyone other than yourself fish. How many fish will you pull out each week assuming you maximize profit?

   b.   Suppose instead you allow others to fish for a fee per net and you want to maximize your fees. Will more or fewer fish be pulled out each week?

   c.   Next, consider the identical lake that has just been discovered near yours. This lake is publicly owned, and anyone who wishes to can fish there. How many fish per week will be pulled out from that lake?

   d.   Suppose $A = 100$, $\alpha = 0.5$, $p = 10$, and $r = 20$. How many fish are harvested per week in (a), (b), and (c)? How many nets are used in each case?

   e.   What is the weekly rental value of the lake? If we count all your costs, including the opportunity cost of owning the lake, how much weekly profit do you make if you are the only one to fish on your lake?

   f.   How much profit (including the opportunity cost of fishing on the lake yourself) do you make if you allow others to fish on your lake for a per-net fee? How much profit do the fishers who pay the fee to fish on your lake make?

   g.* How much profit do the fishers who fish on the publicly owned nearby lake make?

  h.   If the government auctioned off the nearby lake, what price do you think it would fetch if the weekly interest rate is 0.12% or 0.0012?

  i.   If the government auctioned off the nearby lake with the condition that the same number of fish per week needs to be brought to market as before, what price would the lake fetch?

21.7 **Business and Policy Application:** *The Externality when Fishing in the Commons*: In exercise 21.6, we showed that free access to a fishing lake causes overfishing because fishers will continue to fish until the cost of inputs (i.e., fishing nets, in our example) equals *average* rather than *marginal* revenue product.

A. Suppose that the lake in exercise 21.6 is publicly owned.

  a.   What is the externality that fishers impose on one another in this lake?

  b.   Seeing the problem as one involving this externality, how would you go about setting a Pigouvian tax on fishing nets to remedy the problem? What information would you have to have to calculate this?

  c.   Suppose instead that the lake is auctioned off to someone who then charges per-net fees to fishers who would like to fish on the lake (as in A(e) of exercise 21.6). How do you think the fees charged by a profit-maximizing lake owner compare to the optimal Pigouvian tax?

  d.   Do you think it is easier for the government to collect the information necessary to impose a Pigouvian tax in part (b) or for a lake owner to collect the information necessary to impose the per-net fees in part (c)? Who has the stronger incentive to get the correct information?

  e.   How would the price of the lake that the government collects in (c) compare to the tax revenues it raises in (b)?

  f.   Suppose instead that the government tries to solve the externality problem by simply setting a limit on per-net fishing licenses that fishers are now required to use when fishing on the public lake. If the government sets the optimal cap on licenses and auctions these off, what will be the price per license?

  g.   What do each of the previous solutions to the Tragedy of the Commons share in common?

  h.   Legislators who represent political districts (such as members of Congress in the U.S. House of Representatives) can be modeled as competing for pork-barrel projects to be paid for by the government budget. Could you draw an analogy between this and the problem faced by fishers competing for fish in a public lake? (This is explored in more detail in end-of-chapter exercise 28.2 in Chapter 28.)

B.* Let N denote the total number of fishing nets used by everyone and $X = f(N) = AN^{\alpha}$ the total catch per week. As in exercise 21.6, let r be the weekly rental cost per net, let p be the market price for fish, and let $A > 0$ and $0 < \alpha < 1$.

  a.   The lake is freely accessible to anyone who wants to fish. How much revenue does each individual fishers make when he or she uses one net?

  b.   What is the loss in revenue for everyone else who is fishing the lake when one fisher uses one more net?

  c.   Suppose that each fisher took the loss of revenue to others into account in his or her own profit maximization problem when choosing how many nets n to bring. Write down this optimization problem. Would this solve the externality problem?

  d.   A Pigouvian tax is optimally set to be equal to the marginal social damage an action causes when evaluated at the optimal market level of that action. Evaluate your answer to (b) at the optimal level of N to derive the optimal Pigouvian tax on nets.

  e.   Suppose that all fishers just consider their own profit but that the government has imposed the Pigouvian per-net tax you derived in (d). Write down the fisher's optimization problem and illustrate its implications for the overall level of N. Does the Pigouvian tax achieve the efficient outcome?

  f.   Suppose the government privatized the lake and allowed the owners to charge per-net fees. The owner might do the following: First, calculate the maximum profit (not counting the rental value of the lake) he or she would be able to make by simply fishing the lake him or herself with the optimal number of nets, then set the fee per net at this profit divided by the number of nets he or she would have used. What per-net fee does this imply?

g. Compare your answer to (f) with your answer to (d). Can you explain why the two are the same?

h. Suppose $A = 100, \alpha = 0.5, p = 10$, and $r = 20$. What is the optimal Pigouvian (per-net) tax and the profit-maximizing per-net fee that an owner of the lake would charge?

21.8 **Business Application:** *Network Externalities and the Battle between Microsoft and Apple:* Many markets related to technology products operate in the presence of *network externalities* because the value of such products to consumers depends on how many other consumers are in the "network" of consumers. For instance, an Internet connection would not be nearly as useful if no one else in the world was connected to the Internet; a telephone becomes more useful the more other people also have telephones; and a computer operating system becomes more useful the more others use it because then the market for software that runs on this operating system increases, which in turn fosters greater software innovation for that platform. Assume throughout that we are analyzing the consumer market for computers and that a consumer buys at most one computer.

A. Consider the market for PCs when the Microsoft Windows system first competed with the Apple Macintosh platform in the 1980s. Microsoft and Apple pursued very different strategies: Microsoft licensed the Windows platform to lots of PC makers who competed with one another and thus drove down the price of PCs. Apple, on the other hand, did not license its Macintosh operating system and sold it only with its own Apple computers that were more expensive.

a. Suppose that people vary greatly in their interest for buying a personal computer, but their willingness to pay for a computer increases with the square root of the size of the "network" of others who use a computer with the same operating system; i.e., if someone's willingness to pay for a computer is B when no one else is in the "network," the person's willingness to pay for the same computer is $BN^{1/2}$ when the network has N people. Pick three different levels of N, with $N_1 < N_2 < N_3$, and illustrate the linear aggregate demand curves, D_1, D_2, and D_3, that correspond to these levels of N for a computer with a particular operating system.

b. Suppose the demand curve D_1 tells us that N_1 computers are demanded at price p. In what sense is this an equilibrium in which consumers are taking into account the network externality in their decision making?

c. Now suppose the price drops from p to p'. If everyone assumes that the network size remains fixed at N_1, illustrate how many more computers will be sold. Why can this not be an equilibrium in the same way that our previous situation was an equilibrium?

d. Now take into account that people will realize that the network is growing as price falls. What will happen if the number of computers demanded at p' on D_3 is N_3? Illustrate the new equilibrium, and explain why some economists say that network externalities give rise to a *bandwagon effect* in addition to a *direct price effect*.

e. How do you think the process of moving from our initial equilibrium to the final equilibrium unfolds over time as price falls from p to p'? *True or False:* Network externalities of this kind cause demand to become more price elastic.

f. Microsoft got a head start with its licensing policy that created competition and thus sharply falling prices in the PC market, while Apple's computers were perpetually priced above PCs. Can you use this model to explain how Microsoft's Windows operating system became the dominant operating system?

g. Suppose that the quality of Apple computers is now far better than any competing PCs and that it can be priced competitively. Why is this not enough for Apple to gain dominance in the computer market? How might you argue that the network externality you analyzed has led to an inefficient market outcome?

h. Explain the following statement made by a technology company executive: "In the quickly moving tech market, it is usually better to be first rather than best."

i. In a recent update to its operating system, Apple introduced a new feature that allows users to switch between the traditional Macintosh operating system and the Microsoft Windows operating system. Do you think this was a good move in light of what this exercise has told us about network externalities?

B. Now consider the type of network externality described in part A more carefully. Suppose that the aggregate demand function for computers is given by $x = (AN^{1/2} - p)/\alpha$.

   a. Does this demand function give rise to the parallel demand curves (for different levels of network size) you analyzed in part A?

   b. The consumer side of the market is in equilibrium if the network size N is equal to the number of computers sold. Use this to derive the actual demand curve $P(x)$ that takes the network externality fully into account.

   c. Suppose $A > 2\alpha$. What is the shape of this demand curve? Explain.

   d. Check your answer to (c) by graphing the demand function when $A = 100$ and $\alpha = 1$. Continue with these parameter values for the rest of the exercise.

   e. In models like this, we say that an equilibrium is *stable* if it does *not* lie on an upward-sloping portion of the demand curve. Can you guess why? (*Hint*: Suppose that x^* is the equilibrium quantity on the upward sloping part of demand for some price p^*. Imagine what would happen if slightly more than x^* were bought, and what would happen if slightly less than x^* would be bought.)

   f. Suppose the supply curve is horizontal at $p = 2,000$. Our model implies there are three equilibria: two that are stable and one that is not stable. What network sizes are associated with each of these equilibria?

   g. Suppose that we begin in the equilibrium in which no one owns a computer and the marginal cost of producing computers is $2,000. Why might firms launch an aggressive campaign in which they give away computers before selling them in stores? How many might they give away to "jump-start" the market?

21.9† **Business Application:** *Pollution that Increases Firm Costs—The Market Outcome*: In the text, we assumed for convenience that the ill effects of pollution are felt by people other than producers and consumers. Consider instead the following case: An entire competitive industry is located around a single lake that contains some vital property needed for the production of x. Each unit of output x that is produced results in pollution that goes into the lake. The only effect of the pollution is that it introduces a chemical into the lake, a chemical that requires firms to reinforce their pipes to keep them from corroding. The chemical is otherwise harmless to the population as well as to all wildlife in the area.

A. We have now constructed an example in which the only impact of pollution is on the firms that are creating the pollution. Suppose that each unit of x that is produced raises every firm's (recurring) fixed cost by δ.

   a. Suppose all firms have identical decreasing returns to scale production processes, with the only fixed cost created by the pollution. For a given amount of industry production, what is the shape of an individual firm's average cost curve?

   b. In our discussion of long-run competitive equilibria, we concluded in Chapter 14 that the long-run industry supply curve is horizontal when all firms have identical cost curves. Can you recall the reason for this?

   c. Now consider this example here. Why is the long-run industry supply curve now upward sloping despite the fact that all firms are identical?

   d. In side-by-side graphs of a firm's cost curves and the (long-run) industry supply and demand curves, illustrate the firm and industry in long-run equilibrium.

   e. Usually we can identify producer surplus, or firm profit, as an area in the demand and supply picture. What is producer surplus here? Why is your answer different from the usual?

   f. In Chapter 14, we briefly mentioned the term *decreasing cost industries*, industries in which the long-run industry supply curve is downward sloping despite the fact that all firms might have identical production technologies. Suppose that in our example the pollution causes a decrease rather than an increase in (recurring) fixed costs for firms. Would such a positive externality be another way of giving rise to a decreasing cost industry?

B.* Suppose that each firm's (long-run) cost curve is given by $c(x) = \beta x^2 + \delta X$, where x is the firm's output level and X is the output level of the whole industry. Note that x is contained in X, and thus we could write the cost function as $c(x) = \beta x^2 + \delta x + \delta \overline{X}$, where $\overline{X}$ is the output produced by all other firms. When each firm is small relative to the industry, however, the impact of a single firm's pollution output on its own production cost is negligible, and it is a good approximation (that makes the problem a lot easier to solve) to simply write a single firm's cost curve as $c(x) = \beta x^2 + \delta X$ and treat X as a fixed amount that the firm cannot influence. Furthermore, if all firms are identical, it is reasonable to assume that all firms produce the same output level $\bar{x}$. Letting N denote the number of firms in the industry, we can therefore write $X = N\bar{x}$ and rewrite the cost function for an individual firm as $c(x) = \beta x^2 + \delta N\bar{x}$.

a. How is our treatment of a producer's contribution to her own costs similar to our "price-taking" assumption for competitive firms?

b. Derive the marginal and average cost functions for a single firm (using the final version of our approximate cost function). (Be careful to realize that the second part of the cost function is, from the firm's perspective, simply a fixed cost.)

c. Assuming the firm is in long-run equilibrium, all firms will make zero profit. Use your answer to (b) to derive the output level produced by each firm as a function of δ, β, N, and $\bar{x}$.

d. Since all firms are identical, in equilibrium the single firm we are analyzing will produce the same as each of the other firms; i.e., $x = \bar{x}$. Use this to derive a single firm's output level $x(N)$ as a function of δ, N, and β. What does this imply about the equilibrium price $p(N)$ (as a function of δ and N) given that firms make zero profit in equilibrium?

e. Since each firm produces $x(N)$, multiply this by N to get the aggregate output level $X(N)$, then invert it to get the number of firms $N(X)$ as a function of β, δ, and X.

f. Substitute $N(X)$ into $p(N)$ to get a function $p(X)$. Can you explain why this is the long-run industry supply curve with free entry and exit?

g. Suppose the aggregate demand for X is given by the demand curve $p_D(X) = A/(X^{0.5})$. Set the industry supply curve equal to the demand curve to get the equilibrium market output X^* (as a function of A, δ, and β).[19]

h. Use your answer to (g) to determine the equilibrium price level p^* (as a function of A, δ, and β).

i. Use your answer to (g) to determine the equilibrium number of firms N^* (as a function of A, δ, and β).

j. Suppose that $\beta = 1$, $\delta = 0.01$, and $A = 10,580$. What are X^*, p^* and N^*? How much does each individual firm produce? (Do exercise 21.10 to compare these to what is optimal.)

21.10 **Policy Application:** *Pollution that Increases Firm Costs—Barney's Solution:* Consider the same situation as the one described in exercise 21.9.

POLICY APPLICATION

A. Assume again that the only impact of pollution is that it increases firm fixed costs by δ for every unit of x that is produced in the industry.

a. Suppose there are N firms in the equilibrium you described in exercise 21.9. What is the pollution-related cost of firm i producing one more unit of x?

b. How much of this pollution-related cost does firm i *not* take into account? If firm i is one of a large number of firms, is it a good approximation to say that firm i does not take any of the pollution-related cost into account? How is this similar to our "price-taking" assumption for competitive firms?

c. Suppose that our benevolent social planner Barney can tell firms what to count as costs. Illustrate how Barney's suggestion for each firm's marginal cost curve is related to the marginal cost curve firms would otherwise use (given a fixed number N of firms in the industry)?

d. What does your answer imply about the relationship between the firm's AC curve and Barney's suggestion for what the firm's AC curve should be?

e. *True or False:* If firms used Barney's suggested cost curves, the long-run industry supply curve would be upward sloping, as you should have concluded in exercise 21.9 it is in the absence of Barney, but now it would lie above where it was in exercise 21.9.

f. *True or False:* Under the efficient outcome, the industry would produce less at a higher price.

g. If a single corporation acquired all the firms around the lake, would that corporation take the costs of pollution into account more like Barney or more like the individual competitive firms? (In parts of exercise 23.11, you'll be asked to revisit this in the context of such a monopoly.)

[19]Note that the demand function is one that would emerge from utility maximization of the utility function $U(x, y) = 2Ax^{0.5} + y$ (where y is a composite good). Thus, it can be viewed as emerging from a representative agent with tastes that are quasilinear in x, and thus represents a true aggregate marginal willingness to pay as well as an uncompensated demand curve. See Chapter 15 for a review of this.

B.* Consider the same set-up as in part B of exercise 21.9. In the previous case where we derived the market equilibrium, we said that in a model with many firms it was reasonable to model each individual firm as not taking its own impact of pollution into account and to simply model the cost function as $c(x) = \beta x^2 + \delta N \bar{x}$ (where the latter entered as a fixed cost).

    a.   Now consider the cost function that benevolent Barney would use for each firm: From the social planner's perspective, the firm's variable costs (captured by βx^2) would still matter, as would the fixed cost from pollution (captured by $\delta N \bar{x}$ where $\bar{x}$ is the amount produced by each firm and N is the number of firms in the industry). But Barney also cares about the following: each unit of x produced by firm i causes an increase in costs of δ for each of the N firms, which implies that the pollution cost Barney would consider firm i as imposing on society is $\delta N x$. This implies that Barney's cost function for each firm is $c_B(x) = \beta x^2 + \delta N \bar{x} + \delta N x$. Derive from this the marginal and average cost functions that Barney would use for each firm (being sure to not treat the last term as a fixed cost).

    b.   Repeat parts (c) through (i) from exercise 21.9 using the cost functions Barney would use for each firm to arrive at N^*, p^*, and X^*.

    c.   Compare your answers to those from exercise 21.9. How do they differ?

    d.   Suppose, as in part (j) of exercise 21.9, that $\beta = 1$, $\delta = 0.1$, and $A = 10,580$. What are X^*, p^*, and N^*? How much does each individual firm produce?

    e.   Compare these to your answers in exercise 21.9. Can you give an intuitive explanation for why these answers differ despite the fact that pollution only affects the firms in the industry?

    f.   What is the Pigouvian tax that is required in order for competitive firms to implement the equilibrium you just calculated in (d)? What price does this imply consumers would pay and what price does it imply producers would receive?

    g.   Verify that your Pigouvian tax in fact results in prices for consumers and the industry that lead them to demand and supply the output level you calculated in part (d). (Note: You will need to refer back to your answers to exercise 21.9 to do this part.)

21.11 Policy Application: *Pollution that Increases Firm Costs—Policy Solutions*: This exercise continues to build on exercises 21.9 and 21.10. Assume the same basic set-up of firms located around a lake producing pollution that causes the (recurring) fixed costs of all firms to increase.

A. Continue to assume that each output unit that is produced results in an increase of fixed costs of δ for all firms in the industry.

    a.   Begin by illustrating the market demand and long-run industry supply curves, labeling the market equilibrium as A.

    b.   Next, without drawing any additional curves, indicate the point B in your graph where the market would be producing if firms were taking the full cost of the pollution they emit into account.

    c.   Illustrate the Pigouvian tax that would be necessary to get the market to move to equilibrium B.

    d.   Suppose N^* is the number of firms in the industry in the market outcome, N^{opt} is the optimal number of firms and δ continues to be as defined throughout. What does the government have to know in order to implement this Pigouvian tax? Is what the government needs to know easily observable prior to the tax?

    e.   Where in your graph does consumer surplus before and after the tax lie?

    f.   Keeping in mind what you concluded in exercise 21.9, has (long-run) producer surplus, or long-run industry profit, changed as a result of the tax?

    g.   *True or False*: The pollution cost under the Pigouvian tax is, in this example, equal to the tax revenue that is raised under the tax.

    h.   Is there *additional pollution damage* under the market outcome (in the absence of the tax)?

    i.   Is there a deadweight loss from not using the tax?

    j.   Suppose the government instead wanted to impose a cap-and-trade system on this lake, with pollution permits that allow a producer to produce the amount of pollution necessary to produce one unit of output. What is the "cap" on pollution permits the government would want to impose to achieve the efficient outcome? What would be the rental rate of such a permit when it is traded?

    k.   What would the government have to know to set the optimal cap on the number of pollution permits?

B. Continue with the functional forms for costs and demand as given in exercises 21.9 and 21.10. Suppose, as you did in parts of the previous exercises, that $\beta = 1$, $\delta = 0.1$, and $A = 10,580$ throughout this exercise.

    a.   If you have not already done so in part B(f) of exercise 21.9, determine the Pigouvian tax that would cause producers to behave the way the social planner would wish for them to behave. What price will consumers end up paying and what price will firms end up keeping under this tax?

    b.** Calculate (for our numerical example) consumer surplus with and without the Pigouvian tax. (Skip this if you are not comfortable with integral calculus.) Why is (long-run) producer surplus, or long-run profit in the industry, unchanged by the tax?

    c.   Determine the total cost of pollution before and after the tax is imposed.

    d.   Determine tax revenue from the Pigouvian tax.

    e.   What is the total surplus before and after the tax, and how much deadweight loss does this imply in the absence of the tax?

    f.   Suppose next that the government instead creates a tradable pollution permit, or voucher, system in which one voucher allows a firm to produce the amount of pollution that gets emitted from the production of 1 unit of output. Derive the demand curve for such vouchers.

    g.   What is the optimal level of vouchers for the government to sell, and what will be the rental rate of the vouchers if the government does this?

21.12 **Policy Application:** *Social Norms and Private Actions*: When asked to explain our actions, we sometimes simply respond by saying "it was the right thing to do." The concept of "the right thing to do" is one that is often formed by observing others, and the more we see others "do the right thing," the more we believe it is in fact "the right thing to do." In such cases, my action "to do the right thing" directly contributes to the social norm that partially governs the behavior of others, and we therefore have an example of an externality.

POLICY APPLICATION

A. Consider for instance the use of observably "green" technology, such as driving hybrid cars. Suppose there are two types of car-buyers: (1) a small minority of "greenies" for whom green technology is attractive regardless of what everyone else does, and whose demand for green cars is therefore independent of how many others are using green cars; and (2) the large majority of "meanies" who don't care that much about environmental issues but do care about being perceived as "doing the right thing."

    a.   Draw a graph with the aggregate demand curve D_0 for the "greenies." Assume that green cars are competitively supplied at a market price p^*, and draw in a perfectly elastic supply curve for green cars at that price.

    b.   There are two types of externalities in this problem. The first arises from the positive impact that green cars have on the environment. Suppose that the social marginal benefit associated with this externality is an amount k per green car and illustrate in your graph the efficient number of cars x_1 that this implies for "greenies." Then illustrate the Pigouvian subsidy s that would eliminate the market inefficiency.

    c.   The second externality emerges in this case from the formation of *social norms*, a form of *network externality*. Suppose that the more green cars the "meanies" see on the road, the more of them become convinced that it is "the right thing to do" to buy green cars even if they are somewhat less convenient right now. Suppose that the "meanies'" linear demand D_1 for green cars when x_1 green cars are on the road has vertical intercept below $(p^* - k)$. In a separate graph, illustrate D_1, and then illustrate a demand curve D_2 that corresponds to the demand for green cars by "meanies" when $x_2 (> x_1)$ green cars are on the road. Might D_2 have an intercept above p^*?

    d.   Does the subsidy in (b) have any impact on the behavior of the "meanies"? In the absence of the network externality, is this efficient?

    e.   How can raising the subsidy above the Pigouvian level have an impact far larger than one might initially think from the imposition of the original Pigouvian tax? If the network externalities are sufficiently strong, might one eventually be able to eliminate the subsidy altogether and see the majority of "meanies" use green cars anyhow?

    f.   Explain how the imposition of a larger initial subsidy has changed the "social norm," which can then replace the subsidy as the primary force that leads people to drive green cars.

g. Sometimes people advocate for so-called "sin taxes," taxes on such goods as cigarettes or pornography. Explain what you would have to assume for such taxes to be justified on efficiency grounds in the absence of network externalities.

h. How could sin taxes like this be justified as a means of maintaining social taboos and norms through network externalities?

B. Suppose you live in a city of 1.5 million potential car owners. The demand curves for green cars x for "greenies" and "meanies" in the city are given by $x_g(p) = (D - p)/\delta$ and $x_m(p) = (A + BN^{1/2} - p)/\alpha$, where N is the number of green cars on the road and p is the price of a green car. Suppose throughout this exercise that $A = 5,000$, $B = 100$, $D = 100,000$, $\alpha = 0.1$, and $\delta = 5$.

a. Let the car industry be perfectly competitive, with price for cars set to marginal cost. Suppose the marginal cost of a green car x is $25,000. How many cars are bought by "greenies"?

b. Explain how it is possible that no green cars are bought by "meanies"?

c. Suppose that the purchase of a green car entails a positive externality worth $2,500. For the case described in (a), what is the impact of a Pigouvian subsidy that internalizes this externality? Do you think it is likely that this subsidy will attract any of the "meanie" market?

d. Would your answer change if the subsidy were raised to $5,000 per green car? What if it were raised to $7,500 per green car?

e.** Suppose that a subsidy of $7,500 per green car is implemented, and suppose that the market adjusts to this in stages as follows: First, "greenies" adjust their behavior in period 0. Then, in period 1 "meanies" purchase green cars based on their observation of the number of green cars on the road in period 0. From then on, in each period n, "meanies" adjust their demand based on their observation in period $(n - 1)$. Create a table that shows the number of green cars x_g bought by "greenies" and the number x_m bought by "meanies" in each period from period 1 through 20.

f. Explain what you see in your table in the context of network externalities and changing social norms.

g.* Now consider the same problem from a slightly different angle. Suppose that the number of green cars driven by "greenies" is $\bar{x}$. Then the total number of green cars on the road is $N = \bar{x} + x_m$. Use this to derive the equation $p(x_m)$ of the demand *curve* for green cars by "meanies," and illustrate its shape assuming $\bar{x} = 16,000$.

h. Relate this to the notion of "stable" and "unstable" equilibria introduced in exercise 21.8B(e). Given that you can calculate $\bar{x}$ for different prices, what are the stable equilibria when $p = 25,000$? What if $p = 22,500$? What if $p = 17,500$?

i. Explain now why the $2,500 and $5,000 subsidies would be expected to cause no change in behavior by "meanies" while a $7,500 subsidy would cause a dramatic change.

j. Compare your prediction for x_m when the subsidy is $7,500 to the evolution of x_m in your table from part (e). Once we have converged to the new equilibrium, what would you predict will happen to x_m if the subsidy is reduced to $2,500? What if it is eliminated entirely?

22

Asymmetric Information in Competitive Markets

In our treatment of externalities in Chapter 21, we introduced into our model for the first time an economic force (other than government-induced price distortions) that causes a competitive market to allocate scarce resources inefficiently in the absence of some other market or nonmarket institution.[1] We furthermore illustrated that the problems raised by externalities are problems related to the nonexistence of some market, necessitating either the establishment of a new market or the fine-tuning of market forces by some nonmarket institution. In this chapter, we will see another example of an economic force that can result in the nonexistence of certain markets—and in an inefficient allocation of scarce resources in existing markets. This economic force arises from certain types of information being distributed asymmetrically across potential market participants and, as we will see, it relates closely to a particular type of externality that is generated in the process.

Information is, of course, always different for buyers and sellers, with buyers knowing about the tastes and economic circumstances that underlie their demand for a good and sellers knowing the costs of production that underlie their supply decisions. One of the great advantages of markets is that, through the formation of market prices, such information is utilized in an efficient manner as the price sends just the "right" signal to buyers and sellers about how scarce goods should be allocated in the market. Information asymmetries that cause externality problems in markets, however, are different from simply different sets of knowledge about our own individual tastes and costs. They involve *hidden information that impacts others adversely* because the information can be used to "take advantage" of the person on the other side of the market.

We will then say that *information asymmetries* occur whenever buyers and sellers have different information regarding the nature of the product (or service) that is being traded or the true costs of providing that product (or service). A common example of this occurs in insurance markets. Suppose, for instance, I approach a health insurance company about my interest in purchasing health insurance. I have inherently more information than the insurance company. In particular, I know more about my own health status, and thus the likelihood that I will need health care, than the insurance company, and I know more about how my lifestyle might change if I know that I am insured. This is information the insurance company would very much like to have in order to ascertain the likely cost of providing insurance to me. The worse my health is and the more likely I am to engage in risky behavior if I am insured, the more costly it is likely to be for the insurance company to provide health insurance to me. And I have every incentive to hide bad

---

[1]This chapter presumes a good understanding of the partial equilibrium model from Chapters 14 and 15 and makes conceptual references to material on externalities from Chapter 21. Section B of the chapter also builds on the non-general equilibrium parts of Chapter 17.

health or a tendency toward risky behavior as I approach the insurance company to get a good deal on health insurance. If the insurance company cannot distinguish between people who are hiding information about their health and those who simply want insurance but have nothing to hide, it may end up finding it impossible to provide insurance packages that healthy individuals would be willing to buy. Thus, the problem of asymmetric information, and the associated problem of those with hidden information "adversely selecting" into insurance markets, can lead to missing markets.

Similar problems arise in other markets. In the used car market, for instance, the owner of a used car may have significantly more information about the quality of the car than do potential buyers. In labor markets, workers know more about their real qualifications than employers may be able to ascertain. In mortgage markets, potential homeowners may know more about their real ability to make mortgage payments in the future than do the banks that lend money. In pharmaceutical markets, drug companies may know much more about the real effectiveness of particular drugs than do patients or even doctors. And in financial markets, corporate officers know more about the true financial health of a corporation than does the average shareholder. Each of these cases shares some of the characteristics of insurance markets in that one side of the market has inherently more information that is relevant for the market transaction than does the other side, which then may make the other side hesitate about entering a transaction. And in each case there may exist other market mechanisms, civil society institutions, or government policies that can alleviate the problems markets face in dealing with such information asymmetries.

This chapter is organized somewhat differently from other chapters in that Section A is written without requiring that you have covered the topic of risk in Chapter 17. You can gain an appreciation for the problems markets encounter under asymmetric information without understanding fully how we model risk, and Section A attempts to provide such an understanding. However, since information asymmetries represent particular problems for insurance markets that deal with risk (as described in Chapter 17), Section B of the chapter builds on the framework for insurance under risk that we introduced in Chapter 17. If you have covered only the intuitive first part of Chapter 17, you can still read the subsections (of Section B) that focus on a graphical exposition of the impact of asymmetric information in insurance markets. For this reason, the mathematical exposition in Section B is confined to separate subsections.

 ## Asymmetric Information and Efficiency

We will discover in this section that the presence of hidden information on one side of the market can generate inefficiencies by resulting in externality problems. In some cases, this will lead to the nonexistence of markets that, if information were more generally available, would make everyone better off. In other cases, it will lead to market distortions in which we can see in principle how more information will lead to greater efficiency. We will develop these ideas initially through a treatment of one hypothetical insurance market before illustrating the deadweight losses in a set of more familiar graphs. Then, in the final two sections of Part A of this chapter, we will discuss some other real-world examples of adverse selection problems unrelated to insurance markets.

22A.1 Grade Insurance Markets

Let's begin with a somewhat silly example. Suppose I approached your professor the day before the beginning of the semester and told him I wanted to sell "grade insurance" in your class. Here is how it would work: If a student wants to insure that he gets at least a grade x in the class, he can purchase insurance that guarantees him grade x as a minimum grade for a price p_x. Higher grade guarantees will carry with it a higher price. At the end of the semester, the professor and I will sit down and look at the legitimate grade distribution and particularly at the grades earned by those who bought insurance from me. If an earned grade falls below x for which a student bought insurance at the beginning of the semester, I have to pay the professor to overcome his scruples and raise the grade, with the size of the payment depending on how much the grade needs to be raised in order to get to the grade for which the student had bought insurance. If, on the other hand, a student who bought insurance for grade x actually earned a grade at or above x, no grade adjustment is necessary and no cost is incurred by my grade insurance company—I just get to keep what the student paid me without dishing out anything to the professor.

To make this example more concrete, let's suppose that the grade insurance business is perfectly competitive (which implies that each grade insurance company will end up making zero economic profit in equilibrium), and let's suppose that grades in your course are curved (prior to me paying off the instructor to raise some grades) around a C, with 10% of all students earning an A, 25% earning a B, 30% earning a C, 25% earning a D and 10% earning an F.[2] Finally, let's suppose that your professor's scruples are such that it costs a minimum of c for her to raise your grade by 1 letter grade (and $2c$ to raise it by 2 letter grades, $3c$ to raise it 3 letter grades, etc.).

22A.1.1 *A*-Insurance and the Adverse Selection Problem

To focus on one particular problem that the grade insurance market faces, suppose first that only A-insurance can be offered and that student behavior will be exactly the same whether or not a student has insurance. Students who buy insurance at the beginning of the semester thus study and work just as hard in the class as they would have in the absence of having insurance. Students themselves have a pretty good idea whether they are likely to do well or poorly in the class, but as an outsider coming in, I don't know anything about any individual student and only know the distribution of grades that will emerge at the end.

If everyone were forced to buy the A-insurance, it would not be difficult to determine the equilibrium insurance premium p_A if we know that everyone in the grade insurance business makes zero profit in equilibrium. We would know that I would have to pay $4c$ for everyone in the 10% of the class that earns an F, $3c$ for everyone in the 25% of the class that earns a D, $2c$ for everyone in the 30% of the class that earns a C, and c for everyone in the 25% of the class that earns a B. The insurance premium would then be

$$p_A = 0.1(4c) + 0.25(3c) + 0.3(2c) + 0.25c = 2c. \tag{22.1}$$

The price of A-insurance would thus simply be determined by how much it takes to pay off your professor to raise a grade by 1 level. If that price is \$100, the premium would be equal to \$200 per student.

What would be the equilibrium insurance premium if, in a system that forced all students to buy insurance, the only insurance policy offered were one that guarantees a B? What if the only policy that were offered was one that guaranteed a C?

Exercise 22A.1

Suppose, however, that we do not force everyone to buy a particular policy but simply left it up to individual students to determine whether or not to buy insurance. If it were reasonable to expect the set of students who choose to buy insurance to be a random sample of the class, the exact same logic that we used earlier would result in exactly the same premium.[3] It seems likely, however, that those students choosing to buy insurance will not represent a random sample, with students who are expecting an A in the class anyhow uninterested in purchasing insurance. Thus, if I charged the insurance premium in equation (22.1), I would lose money.

---

[2]Note to my students at Duke: I understand that we have grade inflation at Duke, so please don't write me e-mails telling me that this is not a "Duke" curve.

[3]It is true that this would involve some risk for the insurance company since a random sample will sometimes contain relatively more good students and other times relative bad students, but if the insurance company sells many of these types of contracts in different classrooms, that risk would disappear.

Now suppose that all students are willing to pay as much as $2c$ to raise their grade by one level and $0.5c$ for any additional increase in the grade by another level. Put differently, an *F* student is willing to pay $2c$ to raise his grade to a *D*, $2.5c$ to raise his grade to a *C*, $3c$ to raise his grade to a *B*, and $3.5c$ to raise his grade to an *A*.

Exercise 22A.2

In an efficient allocation of grade insurance (when only *A*-insurance is offered), who would have *A*-insurance? (*Hint*: Compare the total cost of raising each student type's grade to the total benefit that this would yield for each student type.)

Exercise 22A.3

If all types of insurance policies were available—*A*-insurance, *B*-insurance, etc.—who would have what type of insurance under efficiency? (*Hint*: Compare the marginal cost of raising each student type's grade by each level to the marginal benefit of doing so.)

This would imply that 90% of the class would be willing to buy the *A*-insurance if it were offered at a premium of $2c$. But my insurance company would now incur higher costs. If the class has 100 students in it, I would incur a cost of c for the 25 *B* students, a cost of $2c$ for the 30 *C* students, a cost of $3c$ for the 25 *D* students, and a cost of $4c$ for the 10 *D* students, for an overall cost of $200c$ or an average cost of $2.22c$ for each of the 90 students that buy the insurance. In order for me to make zero profit, I therefore have to now charge a premium of $2.22c$ for the *A*-insurance. But at that price, the *B* students would no longer be willing to pay for the *A*-insurance because the price is above what they are willing to pay for a 1 letter grade increase in their grade. This means that I would have to charge a premium of approximately $2.69c$ for the same insurance policy in order to break even if only *C*, *D*, and *F* students bought my insurance.

Exercise 22A.4

Verify that my break-even insurance premium for *A*-insurance would have to be approximately $2.69c$ if only the 65 *C*, *D*, and *F* students bought the insurance.

But now the *C* students are no longer willing to pay for the insurance since they are willing to pay only $2.5c$ to raise their grade by two levels: $2c$ for the first level and $0.5c$ for the second. Thus, only *D* and *F* students are willing to pay $2.69c$ for my *A*-insurance. But if they are the only ones buying, you can verify that my premium has to go up to approximately $3.29c$—sufficient to get only *F* students to be interested in the *A* insurance, which would then necessitate a premium of $4c$ that not even *F* students are willing to pay. Thus, *if students are allowed to choose whether or not to buy A-insurance, I will not be able to sell any insurance in equilibrium if the students know what kind of students they are and I do not.* This is an example of a more general problem known as the *adverse selection problem* that can arise in markets with asymmetric (or hidden) information.

The adverse selection problem arises in our example because each student has more information than my insurance company about how much of a cost I will incur if I sell her grade insurance. As a result, students will "adversely" select into buying insurance from me, with "high cost" students more likely to demand insurance than "low cost" students. It would be efficient (as you should have concluded in exercise 22A.2) for *B* and *C* students to hold *A*-insurance in our example, but neither does.[4] As in the case of the externalities in Chapter 21, the competitive equilibrium is inefficient. Even if students cannot perfectly predict what grade they will earn in the absence of

---

[4]It is efficient for *B* and *C* students to hold *A*-insurance (when only *A*-insurance is an option) because the cost of raising their grades is c and $2c$ respectively while their benefit from getting an *A* is $2c$ and $2.5c$ respectively. The benefit is equal to the cost for *D* students, and it is therefore efficient for them to have or not have insurance. But *F* students benefit by $3.5c$ and cost $4c$.

insurance, they will have more information than I do about the probability that they will earn a good grade. Thus, even if students that end up earning an A in the absence of insurance are willing to buy insurance at the beginning of the term, they will still be willing on average to pay less than those who end up with a worse grade. Because of the adverse selection problem, students who line up to buy insurance from me therefore impose a negative externality in the market by raising the average cost of insurance (and thus the premium I have to charge). Their decision to enter the market "adversely" impacts the other students. It is this negative externality that arises from asymmetric information, and it is because of the presence of this externality that a market equilibrium does not exist in our example.

Would I be able to sell A-insurance if students were always willing to pay $2c$ for every increase in their letter grade? Would the resulting equilibrium be efficient?	**Exercise 22A.5**

22A.1.2 Information, Adverse Selection, and Statistical Discrimination

We have seen how the asymmetry of information in the A-insurance market can lead to a nonexistence of the insurance market due to the negative externality generated through adverse selection. To focus a little further on how asymmetric information causes this, we can consider how the equilibrium (or lack thereof) will change if I am able to obtain the information that we have so far assumed only students possess.

Suppose first that I can observe student transcripts at the beginning of the semester and, from them, I can perfectly infer what grade each student will make at the end of the term in the absence of insurance. I could then offer each student a menu of insurance policies and price them with that information in mind. For a B student, for instance, I could offer the A-insurance at a price of c, which the student would be more than willing to pay (with me making zero profit). For C, D, and F students, I could similarly price A-insurance at $2c$, $3c$, and $4c$ respectively, with C and D students willing to pay the price but F students unwilling (since such insurance is worth only $3.5c$ to them). We have thus restored the market for A-insurance by eliminating the informational asymmetry. We have furthermore done so in an *efficient* way, with insurance sold only to students whose willingness to pay is above the cost of the insurance product.

The real world, of course, is never that certain, and neither students nor I can perfectly predict what grade they will end up earning at the end of the term in the absence of insurance. Suppose, then, that I observe from transcripts what grades a student has made "on average" and am therefore able to classify students into "A students," "B students," "C students," and "D students." Suppose I also know by looking at the past performance of students in your course that "A students" earn an A 75% of the time and a B 25% of the time, and all other students earn a grade one level above their usual grade 25% of the time, their usual grade 50% of the time, and a grade below their usual grade 25% of the time. Assuming that students have no more information than I do, I could then again offer the different insurance policies to each type of students at a premium that will result in an expected zero profit for me.

For instance, since I know that I will incur a cost of c with 25% probability for an "A student," I can price an A-insurance policy for an "A student" at $0.25c$. Similarly, since I know a "B student" who purchases an A-insurance will cost me nothing with 25% probability, c with 50% probability, and $2c$ with 25% probability, I can price an A-insurance for a "B student" at c. You can verify on your own that the equilibrium price for an A-insurance would again be $2c$ for a "C student" and $3c$ for a "D student."

What would be the equilibrium price p_A^F for an F student if that student will earn an F with 75% probability and a D with 25% probability?	**Exercise 22A.6**

Notice that nothing has fundamentally changed if the grade outcome is uncertain *so long as it is equally uncertain from the student's perspective as it is from mine*. As long as the student has no more information than I do, whether that information involves uncertainty or not, no adverse selection problem will arise and an equilibrium price will emerge for *A*-insurance but will differ depending on what type of student is purchasing the insurance. When I have perfect information about each student and can perfectly predict the type of grade he will earn in the absence of insurance, I will discriminate based on the *individual* characteristics of the student. In the case where both I and the students are somewhat uncertain about what the semester will hold, however, I end up discriminating based on the statistical evidence I have regarding the probabilities that a particular student will earn particular grades. Such price discrimination that is based on the underlying characteristics *of the group* to which an individual belongs is called *statistical discrimination*.

22A.1.3 The Moral Hazard Problem

Throughout our discussion of the problems in our silly *A*-insurance market, we have made the heroic assumption that students will study just as hard and diligently if they have grade insurance as if they did not. But would they? Or would the knowledge of the guarantee of a certain grade offered by my insurance company cause some students to blow off the material, stop coming to class, stop studying, and perhaps even skip exams? If you have stuck with this course all the way through Chapter 22, chances are you are the kind of student who gets at least some satisfaction from actually learning rather than just getting a grade on a transcript. Perhaps you are even that rare student who would work just as hard if there were no exams and no grades given. But students will vary in terms of how much value they place on the grade relative to the actual learning in a course, which implies that the degree to which students will change behavior under my grade insurance will differ across students. The problem of individuals changing behavior in this way after entering a contract is known as the *moral hazard problem*, and it makes executing the contract more expensive for the other party to the contract.

If all students react the same to being insured, then I can at least predict how much more they will cost me than they would if they continued to behave as if they were not insured. If, for instance, a random selection of half the class buys *A*-insurance from me, we calculated earlier that a premium of $2c$ would make my expected profit zero in the absence of moral hazard. But, if each of the students who bought insurance then changes behavior sufficiently to end up with one letter grade below where she would have ended up otherwise, I would have to charge a premium of $3c$ to have an expected profit of zero. The anticipation of moral hazard behavior by those I insure therefore implies I must charge more than I otherwise would, and it arises in insurance markets whenever individuals engage in riskier behavior when insured.

If students differ in their change in behavior once they have insurance, however, we have a bigger problem than simply higher insurance premiums *assuming students know themselves better than I know them*. Once again, I would possess less information about the student than the student himself possesses, and this will *reinforce the adverse selection problem* that we discussed in the absence of moral hazard. Even if I could identify the *A*, *B*, *C*, *D*, and *F* students from their transcripts and knew precisely what grade each will earn in the absence of insurance, I would now have to worry about the fact that some of each type of student will exhibit greater moral hazard once they are insured than others. The *B* student that knows she can earn a *B* in the course and knows that she will work just as hard if she is insured will not, for instance, be willing to pay as much for *A*-insurance as the *B* student who knows he can enjoy the beach a whole lot more if he has *A*-insurance. Thus, students will "adversely select" into my insurance pool based on the level of moral hazard they will exhibit once insured. As long as they know this information and I do not, we can get the same kind of unraveling of the insurance market we saw in our initial example of adverse selection.

Adverse selection, then, causes problems for insurance companies because of the "adverse" externality that "high cost" customers impose on "low cost" customers as they drive up the price of insurance and may cause insurance markets to no longer function in equilibrium. Moral hazard by itself, on the other hand, is a problem that insurance companies can, in our example, deal with through pricing of premiums. However, if moral hazard creates informational asymmetries because insurance companies cannot identify how different individuals will engage in different levels of risky behavior once insured, this creates another adverse selection problem that can once again undermine the existence of markets. Much has been written by economists about the optimal ways in which insurance companies (and others facing moral hazard problems on the other side of the market) can arrange contracts so as to minimize moral hazard behavior. Although we will not develop this formally in this chapter, you can think of some possible conditions my insurance company might place on those who buy grade insurance. For instance, I might require as part of the contract that your professor certifies at the end of the term that students who will benefit from owning grade insurance have in fact attended class, handed in assignments, and taken exams. (Issues like this are often covered in courses on the economics of contracting.) For now, we can simply note that to the extent to which insurance companies can find ways of minimizing moral hazard through contractural arrangements as they sell insurance, they limit the adverse selection problem that accompanies the existence of moral hazard.

22A.1.4 Less Extreme Equilibria with Adverse Selection
So far, we have demonstrated that the adverse selection problem may cause certain markets *not to exist*. This is an extreme manifestation of the problem of adverse selection, and not all markets that are subject to adverse selection will cease to exist entirely. Suppose, for instance, that your professor will not permit me to sell *A*-insurance but only agrees to let me sell *B*-insurance; i.e., insurance that guarantees a student will earn at least a *B* in the course. To make the example as simple as possible, let's assume that there is no moral hazard problem, that students know exactly what grade they will earn, that I have no information about any individual student, and that it is prohibitively costly for me to gather any useful information on individual students.

We know right away, of course, that no *A* or *B* student would then be interested in buying insurance from me. In a class of 100 students, only the 65 *C*, *D*, and *F* students are therefore potential customers. If they all end up buying the insurance from me, I know that I will incur a cost of *c* for the 30 *C* students, $2c$ for the 25 *D* students, and $3c$ for the 10 *F* students. My average cost per customer is then $110c/65$ or approximately $1.69c$. Since students are willing to pay $2c$ for a one-level increase in their grade and $0.5c$ for each additional level increase, we know that *C*, *D*, and *F* students would be willing to pay $2c$, $2.5c$, and $3c$ for *B*-insurance and thus are all willing to pay my break-even premium of $1.69c$. In this case, *the adverse selection problem is therefore not sufficiently large to eliminate the equilibrium in the B-insurance market.*

Conditional on only *B*-insurance being allowed, is this equilibrium efficient?

Exercise 22A.7

Now suppose that student demand for grade insurance was slightly different: Suppose a student is willing to pay $1.5c$ for a one-level increase in his grade and *c* for each additional increase. This implies that *C* students would only be willing to pay $1.5c$ for *B*-insurance, less than the premium of $1.69c$ I have to charge to break even when all *C*, *D*, and *F* students buy insurance. If I therefore end up providing *B*-insurance to only the 35 *D* and *F* students, you can verify that I would have to charge a break-even premium of approximately $2.29c$. Since this is less than the value *D* and *F* students place on *B*-insurance, the equilibrium would involve 35 *B*-insurance policies sold to just those students. Now, *the externality of adverse selection causes fewer policies to be sold, but an equilibrium still exists.*

Conditional on only *B*-insurance being allowed, is this equilibrium efficient?

Exercise 22A.8

The example can, of course, get a lot more complex if the professor allows me to sell all forms of insurance; i.e., A, B, C, D insurance. In end-of-chapter exercise 22.1, we will investigate this more closely under the assumption that individuals are uncertain about exactly the grade they will get and are willing to pay $1.5c$ to get their typical grade but only $0.5c$ more for each grade above their usual. In this case, it is inefficient for anyone to buy insurance other than insurance to guarantee his usual grade. This is because the cost of insuring your usual grade is c, while the benefit is $1.5c$, but raising your grade each level above the usual is valued at only $0.5c$ but costs c. As we will demonstrate in the exercise, adverse selection will result in inefficiency once again.

22A.1.5 Signals and Screens to Uncover Information

At this point, we have shown how asymmetric information can cause problems in our grade insurance market. It should be clear from our example, however, that good—or "low cost"—students have an incentive to find ways of credibly revealing information to my insurance company so that I can give them a better deal. Similarly, my insurance company has an incentive to invest in ways of uncovering information, by getting access to transcripts, interviewing students, etc. Put differently, students have an incentive to *signal* information to me, and I have an incentive to *screen* the applicant pool. You can explore in end-of-chapter exercises 22.2 through 22.4 how such signals and screens can be efficiency enhancing—and how they can be wasteful—under different assumptions about the grade insurance market. We will furthermore revisit the issue in the next section after exploring a more graphical model that frames the ideas we have explored thus far in a different (and more realistic) setting.

22A.2 Revealing Information through Signals and Screens

Let's now move away from the artificial grade insurance market and consider the case for insurance more generally. While our treatment in this section can be applied to all types of insurance, we'll frame our discussion in terms of car insurance. Suppose that there are two types of potential consumers: "high cost" consumers that are likely to get into accidents, and "low cost" consumers that drive safely and are less likely to call on insurance companies to pay for damages. We can then think of car insurance for type 1 consumers carrying an expected marginal cost of MC^1 and car insurance for type 2 consumers carrying an expected marginal cost of MC^2, with $MC^1 > MC^2$. To make the example as simple as possible, let's suppose further that demand curves are equal to marginal willingness to pay curves and that the aggregate demand curve D^1 for type 1 consumers is the same as the aggregate demand curve D^2 for type 2 consumers.

Panel (a) of Graph 22.1 then illustrates what the car insurance market would be like if there were only type 1 consumers, and panel (b) illustrates what it would be like if there were only type 2 consumers. In each case, it is straightforward to predict how the competitive market would allocate resources (assuming there are no substantial recurring fixed costs to running insurance companies): In panel (a), the equilibrium price p^1 would cause consumers of type 1 to purchase x^1, the efficient quantity that maximizes social surplus. In panel (b), the equilibrium price p^2 would similarly cause type 2 consumers to buy x^2 insurance policies, once again allocating resources efficiently. And if a competitive insurance industry can tell type 1 consumers apart from type 2 consumers, this is exactly the outcome that will emerge, with all insurance policies priced at the marginal cost relevant for the type of consumer who is purchasing insurance.

Panel (c) of Graph 22.1 then merges panels (a) and (b) into a single picture. If insurance companies can tell safe drivers apart from unsafe drivers, type 1 consumers will get consumer surplus equal to area (a) while consumers of type 2 will get consumer surplus equal to area $(a + b + c + d + e + f)$. Since insurance firms are making zero profit, the overall social surplus would then be equal to $(2a + b + c + d + e + f)$.

Graph 22.1: Adverse Selection in Car Insurance Market

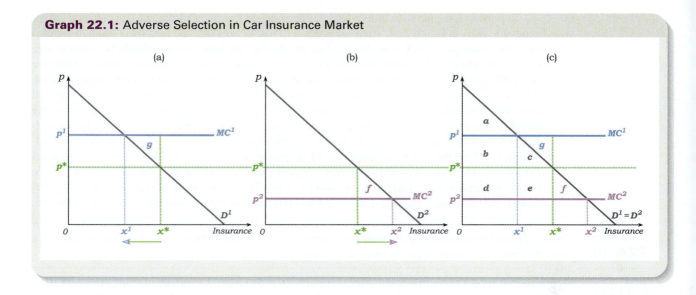

22A.2.1 Deadweight Loss from Asymmetric Information

Now suppose that firms cannot distinguish between type 1 and type 2 drivers and thus cannot price car insurance based on the expected marginal cost of each consumer who walks through the door. Rather, the only information that firms have is that half of all drivers are of type 1 and half are of type 2. Each insurance company then gets a random selection of drivers to insure and thus knows that half their customers are high cost and half are low cost. Under perfect competition that drives profits for insurance companies to zero, this implies that the single price charged for car insurance will lie halfway between MC^1 and MC^2, indicated by $p*$ in panel (c) of Graph 22.1.

Suppose the current market price for car insurance were less than $p*$. What would happen under perfect competition with free entry and exit? What if instead the market price for car insurance were greater than $p*$?

Exercise
22A.9

It is easy to see immediately that high cost consumers will benefit from the information asymmetry we have introduced: Their price for car insurance drops from p^1 under full information to $p*$. Consumers of type 2 will analogously be hurt by the informational asymmetry, seeing their price increase from p^2 to $p*$. The fact that some consumers are better off and some are worse off does not, however, itself raise an efficiency problem. Rather, the efficiency problem emerges from the fact that *overall consumer surplus falls as a result of the informational asymmetry*.

To be more precise, we can see in panel (c) of Graph 22.1 that consumer surplus for type 1 consumers increases to $(a + b + c)$, while consumer surplus for type 2 consumers falls to $(a + b + c)$, giving us an overall surplus of $(2a + 2b + 2c)$. Note that area (b) is equal in size to area (d), which means we can rewrite this overall surplus as $(2a + b + 2c + d)$. Note further that the triangle (c) is equal in size to triangle (f), which means we can further rewrite the overall surplus as $(2a + b + c + d + f)$. Comparing this to the full information surplus of $(2a + b + c + d + e + f)$, we have lost area (e), which is therefore the size of the deadweight loss from introducing asymmetric information that keeps firms from pricing insurance policies differently for consumers of type 1 and 2.[5]

---

[5]It may seem that our analysis relies too heavily on symmetries that emerge from the assumption that type 1 and 2 consumers do not differ in overall number or demand. End-of-chapter exercise 22.5 illustrates that the analysis, while notationally more complex, is similar when these assumptions are relaxed.

To provide some intuition as to where this deadweight loss comes from, we can note two further geometric facts in Graph 22.1: Area (g) is equal to half of area (e), and area (f) is equal to area (g) (and thus also equal to half of area (e)). Thus, the deadweight loss can equivalently be stated as area $(f + g)$. Panel (a) of the graph places area (g) into the graph for just consumers of type 1 where we originally said that consumers would buy x^1 insurance policies when they are priced at marginal cost. All the way up to x^1, the marginal benefit (as indicated by the demand curve) exceeds the marginal cost, and it is therefore efficient to provide policies up to x^1. For policies after x^1, however, the marginal cost of providing additional insurance policies exceeds the marginal benefit, making it inefficient to provide policies beyond x^1. When x^* policies are bought by type 1 consumers, the deadweight loss from this "over-consumption" of insurance is then area (g). The reverse holds in panel (b) for low cost consumers whose marginal benefit exceeds marginal cost until x^2 but who reduce their consumption to x^* under the uniform price p^*. Thus, consumers of type 2 are now "under-consuming" insurance, with the deadweight loss (f) emerging directly from this under-consumption.

Exercise 22A.10 *True or False:* The greater the difference between MC^1 and MC^2, the greater the deadweight loss from the introduction of asymmetric information.

Exercise 22A.11 Suppose that type 1 consumers valued car insurance more highly, implying D^1 lies above D^2. Can you illustrate a case where the introduction of asymmetric information causes type 2 consumers to no longer purchase any car insurance? What price would type 1 consumers then pay?

Notice that the adverse selection problem in our car insurance market is very much like the problem we first encountered in the grade insurance market of the last section: Consumers that cost less to insure—safer drivers or better students—are driven out of the insurance market by rising premiums due to the adverse selection of consumers who cost more to insure. The result in Graph 22.1 is less extreme in the sense that not all low cost consumers are driven out of the market, and not all high cost consumers come into the market. But the basic economic forces are the same.

22A.2.2 Screening Consumers The asymmetric information equilibrium in Graph 22.1 (which is replicated in panel (a) of Graph 22.2) is called a *pooling equilibrium* because all consumer types end up in the same insurance "pool" with the same insurance contract, while the full information equilibrium in which the different types are charged based on their marginal cost is called a *separating equilibrium* (because the types end up in separate insurance contracts). When asymmetric information leads to pooling of different types, however, it would be to the advantage of an insurance company to find a way of "screening" out high cost customers and providing insurance to only "low cost" types.

Given that there is a demand for "screening services" that identify who the safe drivers are, we might then imagine that a "screening industry" will form, a competitive industry that screens consumers and sells information to insurance companies. Suppose first that this screening industry becomes very good at gathering information on consumers, so good, in fact, that the marginal cost of gathering information on any particular driver is virtually zero. In that case, competition in the screening industry will drive the price of screening services (paid by insurance companies) to zero. Put differently, if the screening industry becomes very good at gathering information on drivers, information will be revealed to insurance companies at roughly zero cost. This then leads us back to the full information separating equilibrium in which high cost drivers are charged a price p^1 and low cost drivers are charged p^2. The emergence of a screening industry that screens consumers at low cost therefore restores the efficient equilibrium and recovers the deadweight loss from the pooling equilibrium.

Exercise 22A.12 How much do type 1 consumers lose? How much do type 2 consumers gain? What is the net effect on overall consumer surplus?

Graph 22.2: Insurance Companies Screening Drivers

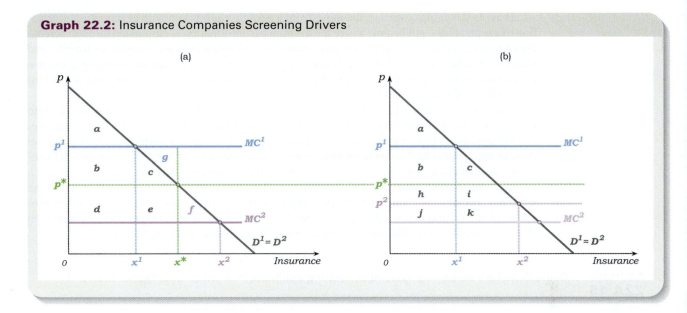

But now suppose that information is not all that easy to gather. In particular, suppose it costs q per driver to gather sufficient information to allow the screening firms to tell type 1 drivers apart from type 2 drivers. If insurance companies buy this information for all drivers that apply for policies, insurance companies will have to pass this screening cost on to consumers in order to maintain zero profits. But they can't pass it on to type 1 consumers because if the price for high cost insurance policies rose above p^1, a new insurance company could emerge and simply sell insurance at p^1. So, in order for insurance companies to make zero profit, they will have to price the policies of low cost customers above MC^2 to pay for the screening price charged by the screening firms for both type 1 and type 2 consumers. Thus, the new separating equilibrium will have $p^1 = MC^1$ and $p^2 = MC^2 + \beta$ where $\beta > q$ and sufficient to cover all the screening costs for both types of consumers.

Suppose, then, that the screening cost q per driver is such that $\beta = (p^* - MC^2)$ is required in order for insurance companies to make zero profit in the separating equilibrium where they charge $p^1 = MC^1$ to type 1 consumers. This implies that $p^2 = p^*$; i.e., the insurance premiums for low cost drivers remain unchanged from the pooling equilibrium because of the screening cost. But the premiums for high cost drivers rise to MC^1 because insurance companies can now tell who the unsafe drivers are and thus will no longer insure them below marginal cost. In panel (a) of Graph 22.2, consumer surplus for type 1 drivers then falls by $(b + c)$ (from $(a + b + c)$ to just (a)), while consumer surplus for type 2 drivers remains unchanged. Overall consumer surplus therefore falls by $(b + c)$, raising the deadweight loss that already existed in the initial pooling equilibrium. But wait—it gets worse! The cost of screening customers is paid to screening firms who make zero profit and thus is not a benefit to anyone. In panel (a) of Graph 22.2, this cost is equal to area $(d + e)$, which means that the increase in deadweight loss from moving to the separating equilibrium is $(b + c + d + e)$.

Why is the screening cost equal to area $(d + e)$?

Exercise 22A.13

Why do firms in this case pay a screening cost that does not allow them to lower any premiums? (*Hint*: Think about whether, given that everyone else pays for the screening costs and discovers who are the safe and unsafe drivers, an individual firm can do better by not discovering which of its potential customers are type 1 and which are type 2.)

Exercise 22A.14*

Thus, as screening costs rise, the move from a pooling equilibrium with asymmetric information to a separating equilibrium (where the asymmetric information is eliminated through screening) becomes inefficient. This is because gathering information is itself costly to society, and someone will have to bear that cost. While the pooling equilibrium without screening gives rise to deadweight losses, these deadweight losses can be reduced through screening only if the cost of gathering information is relatively low.

Panel (b) of Graph 22.2 illustrates a less extreme case where the separating equilibrium price p^2 lies below the pooling equilibrium price p^* because screening costs are lower than previously assumed. Type 1 consumers still lose $(b + c)$ in consumer surplus as their premium rises to MC^1, but type 2 consumers now gain $(h + i)$ in consumer surplus. Thus, overall consumer surplus changes by $(h + i - b - c)$. Screening costs are furthermore equal to $(j + k)$, implying an overall change in social surplus of $(h + i - b - c - j - k)$ as we move to the screening equilibrium. Note that as screening costs fall toward zero, $(j + k)$ approaches zero while $(h + i)$ approaches $(d + e + f)$. Since $(d + e + f)$ is unambiguously greater than $(b + c)$, overall surplus therefore increases for sufficiently low screening costs.

Exercise 22A.15 Could there be a screening-induced separating equilibrium in which p^2 is higher than p^*?

Exercise 22A.16 Would your analysis be any different if the insurance companies did the screening themselves rather than hiring firms in a separate industry to do it for them?

22A.2.3 Consumer Signals
Suppose next that insurance companies find it too costly to screen consumers, and we are therefore in our pooling equilibrium where p^* is charged to all drivers. As we have already shown, this implies that low cost drivers are paying "too much," and high cost drivers are paying "too little." It is therefore in the interest of low cost drivers to find a way to *signal* insurance companies that they are a safe bet and, if they succeed in signaling their type, it becomes in the interest of high cost types to falsely signal that they, too, are safe drivers. Whether a separating equilibrium can emerge in the insurance market through consumer signals then depends on the cost of signaling your true type, as well as the cost of falsely signaling that you are a different type than you actually are.

Consider first the extreme case where it is costless for type 2 drivers to signal that they are safe but it is very costly for type 1 drivers to falsely signal that they too are safe drivers. Because it is easy for type 2 drivers to reveal information that can then not easily be obscured by type 1 drivers, a full information separating equilibrium with insurance premiums $p^1 = MC^1$ and $p^2 = MC^2$ will emerge, and the deadweight loss from pooling will be eliminated through consumer signaling. If, on the other hand, it is equally costless for type 1 drivers to pretend to be type 2 drivers, this cannot happen, and we simply remain in the pooling equilibrium where no useful information is conveyed to the insurance companies.

Exercise 22A.17 *True or False*: When it is costless to tell the truth and very costly to lie, consumer signaling will unambiguously eliminate the inefficiency from adverse selection.

Now suppose that things get a little murkier in that it costs δ for type 2 consumers to signal that they are safe drivers, and it costs γ for type 1 consumers to pretend to be safe drivers. If the industry is currently pooling all drivers into a single insurance contract with price p^*, type 2 drivers would be able to reduce their premiums to MC^2 if they can credibly signal that they are safe drivers, thus each getting a benefit of $(p^* - MC^2)$. So long as $\delta < (p^* - MC^2)$, it therefore makes sense for a type 2 consumer who is currently paying p^* to absorb the cost of signaling his type and get his premium lowered to MC^2.

Suppose, then, that the type 2 consumers successfully signal their type and induce a separating equilibrium where the industry charges MC^2 to type 2 consumers and MC^1 to type 1 consumers. The only way this can truly be an equilibrium is if it is too costly for the type 1 consumers to falsely signal that they, too, are safe drivers, and a type 1 consumer in a separating equilibrium would be willing to pay as much as $(MC^1 - MC^2)$—the difference between the low and high insurance premiums— to pretend to be a safe type! Thus, we can get a separating equilibrium if $\delta < (p^* - MC^2)$ and $\gamma > (MC^2 - MC^1)$; i.e., if the signaling cost plus the low cost insurance premium is less than the pooling insurance premium for safe drivers, *and* if the cost of lying is greater than the difference between the low and high cost insurance rates. Is this outcome necessarily efficient? Just as in the case of screening, the answer again depends on how high δ—the cost of revealing information—is.

Suppose $\delta = (p^* - MC^2)$ and $\gamma > (MC^1 - MC^2)$. What is the increase in deadweight loss in going from the initial pooling equilibrium to the separating equilibrium?

Exercise 22A.18

True or False: If δ and γ are such that a separating equilibrium emerges from consumer signaling, the question of whether the resulting resolution of asymmetric information enhances efficiency rests only on the size of δ, not the size of γ.

Exercise 22A.19

But there is another possibility: Suppose $\delta < (p^* - MC^2)$ and $\gamma < (MC^1 - p^*)$; i.e., suppose the cost of truthfully signaling that you are a safe driver is less than the amount that safe drivers are overpaying in our initial pooling equilibrium *and* the cost of lying is less than the amount that unsafe drivers are underpaying. It is then possible to get a *pooling equilibrium with signaling* where both types send signals that they are safe drivers, but because both types send these signals, no actual information is conveyed to the insurance companies that therefore continue to price all policies at p^*. Given that everyone is sending an "I am safe" signal, not sending such a signal might be interpreted as you being "unsafe," and thus everyone will send them because everyone else is sending them.[6] This is of course unambiguously inefficient: Consumers are sending costly signals without revealing any actual information and thus without changing anything in the insurance industry.

Is it possible under these conditions for there to also be a pooling equilibrium in which no one sends any signals? (*Hint*: What would insurance companies have to believe in such an equilibrium if they did see someone holding up the "I am safe" sign?)

Exercise 22A.20*

Suppose $(p^* - MC^2) < \delta = \gamma < (MC^1 - p^*)$. Will there be a separating equilibrium?

Exercise 22A.21*

Why is it possible for a signaling equilibrium to result in a pooling equilibrium in which no information is revealed, but it is not possible to have such a pooling equilibrium emerge when firms screen?

Exercise 22A.22

22A.2.4 Information Costs and Deadweight Losses under Asymmetric Information

Our example of car insurance has illustrated two fundamental points: First, as already shown in our grade insurance examples, the presence of asymmetric information may cause pooling equilibria in which behavior is based on average characteristics rather than individual characteristics. This will lead to the emergence of deadweight losses as some will over-consume while others will

---

[6]It is not clear what insurance companies should believe in this case about someone who deviates from the behavior of everyone else and does not send an "I am safe" signal, but it is certainly possible that insurance companies would believe such individuals to be of type 1. We will discuss how economists might think about such "out-of-equilibrium" beliefs in Section B of Chapter 24.

under-consume (relative to the efficient level) or, if the problem is sufficiently severe, entire markets will cease to exist. Second, it may be possible for information asymmetries to be remedied through the revelation of information, either because the informed side of the market "signals" or because the uninformed side of the market "screens." But this only leads to greater efficiency if the cost of transmitting information is relatively low *and* if the information that is exchanged is actually informative (and thus leads to a separating equilibrium). We will explore these ideas further in end-of-chapter exercises, including some where we will investigate the possible outcomes of signals and screens within our grade insurance markets. But now we turn to a discussion of some of the most prevalent real-world situations in which asymmetric information plays an important role. As you will see, many of these have nothing to do with insurance even though they can be understood with the tools we have developed within the insurance context.

22A.3 Real-World Adverse Selection Problems

In our development of the basic demand and supply model of markets earlier in the book, we distinguished between three different types of markets: output markets in which consumers demand goods supplied by producers, labor markets in which producers demand labor supplied by workers, and financial markets in which producers demand capital from investors (or savers). Asymmetric information can appear in any of these markets, and we will therefore treat each of these separately in the following sections. As before, we will point to three types of institutions that can then ameliorate the externality problem created by adverse selection. New *markets*, like the screening firms in our car insurance example, might appear and facilitate the exchange of hidden information; nonmarket *civil society* institutions might play a similar role, or *government* policy might be crafted to address the problem. And in many instances a combination of these approaches is utilized in the real world.

22A.3.1 Adverse Selection in Output Markets
We have already discussed extensively the problems of adverse selection in one particular output market where the "output" is insurance. In some insurance markets, there is much that insurance companies can observe about individuals (thus giving rise to a relatively small adverse selection problem), while in other insurance markets much remains hidden information. In the case of life insurance, for instance, the chances of a consumer "using" the insurance can be predicted reasonably well so long as the insurance company knows a few basics such as the consumer's age, gender, health condition, and whether or not the consumer smokes. (For life insurance policies with high benefits, they might also require a basic health exam.) While some consumers might behave more recklessly if their life is insured (thus giving rise to a moral hazard problem that can strengthen adverse selection), most consumers probably will not change behavior significantly just because their heirs will receive a payment if they die.[7] Life insurance companies can therefore use relatively costless "screens" to categorize consumers into different "risk types" and then price life insurance policies accordingly. As a result, we rarely hear of calls for government intervention in life insurance markets, with insurance providers employing an army of "actuaries" who predict the probability of premature death for different types of consumers.

Exercise
22A.23

Another factor that lessens the adverse selection problem in life insurance markets is that the bulk of demand for life insurance comes from people who are young to middle aged and not from the elderly. How does this matter?

---

[7]An exception to this involves individuals contemplating suicide, and suicide is therefore typically excluded as a cause of death that would trigger an insurance payment.

In the case of unemployment insurance, on the other hand, markets may face considerably more difficulty in overcoming the adverse selection problem. As someone approaches an insurance company to inquire about unemployment insurance policies, it is difficult for the insurance company to tell whether the consumer is asking for this insurance because she knows that she is about to get laid off. Age or health exams do not provide a useful screen (as they do in the case of life insurance) because the hidden knowledge is much more difficult to unearth. Consumers themselves may also not find easy ways to signal their "type." It may therefore be the case that signaling and screening are too costly for widespread unemployment insurance markets to form without some nonmarket institution to spur such a market. Before governments became involved in insuring everyone, certain civil society institutions, for instance, utilized local knowledge of individual reputations to provide insurance within small communities where individual reputations were relatively well known. In most developed countries, such institutions disappeared when governments instituted mandatory unemployment insurance for everyone, using compulsory unemployment insurance taxes to fund the system. Tenured professors with lifetime job security (who would not voluntarily purchase unemployment insurance) as well as workers in industries whose fortunes fluctuate greatly with the business cycle then all pay into the system in hopes that overall consumer surplus is increased even as some are paying for a service they do not require, all because the adverse selection problem may be sufficiently severe for private markets and civil society institutions to offer "too little" insurance.

Exercise 22A.24 In our car insurance example, asymmetric information caused the market to create a pooling equilibrium in which some over-consumed and others under-consumed. Why might this not be the case in the unemployment insurance market where those with high demand are much more likely to be those with high probability of being laid off? (*Hint*: Can you imagine an unraveling of the market for reasons similar to what we explored in the grade insurance case?)

Exercise 22A.25 Is mandatory participation in government unemployment insurance efficient, or do you think it might just be more efficient than market provision?

In yet other insurance markets, a combination of approaches has emerged. For instance, in the United States, health insurance for the non-elderly is provided largely by private insurance companies. However, the government covers some segments of the population (the elderly and the poor) directly through Medicare and Medicaid which pays for most of the health care bills for these populations as they are treated in privately run hospitals and doctor's offices. For veterans, on the other hand, the U.S. government has set up a separate system of hospitals that it directly operates and funds. It also subsidizes employers to provide private health insurance to their employees, with large employers operating with the advantage of providing insurance for a large "pool" of workers that is less risky to insure than individuals or smaller groups. And an ethical "civil society" standard (often also codified into laws) in the medical profession requires doctor's in emergency rooms to treat uninsured patients, thus effectively providing at least some form of implicit insurance to the formally uninsured. Debates over whether this is the right balance of markets, civil society, and government in the health insurance market, particularly as the number of uninsured Americans has increased, have intensified in the United States as this book goes to press, and it may well be that health care legislation will pass shortly and will alter the way health care is regulated and funded for many. In other countries governments have approached health insurance more like the United States has approached unemployment insurance, in some cases (as in Canada) directly insuring everyone in ways similar to the Medicare system that is restricted to the elderly in the U.S., and in other cases (such as the U.K.) directly employing doctors and running hospitals (which is done only for veterans in the U.S.). My goal is not to offer an answer as to what the best approach to a fairly complicated set of issues is but merely to point out that adverse selection (and moral hazard) has something to do with the policy debates surrounding this issue. You can learn more about this in public finance and health economics courses and in end-of-chapter exercises 22.7, 22.8, and 22.9.

Exercise 22A.26   What is the adverse selection problem in health insurance markets? What is the moral hazard problem for such markets?

Exercise 22A.27   It is often proposed that health insurance companies not be allowed to discriminate based on "preexisting health conditions." Does this ameliorate or aggravate the adverse selection problem? Can you see why such proposals are usually accompanied by proposals that everyone be required to carry health insurance?

Insurance markets, however, are not the only output markets that might suffer from adverse selection problems. The *used car market*, for instance, is plagued by adverse selection, but this time the hidden information resides with the supplier rather than the consumer. You may have heard that when you buy a new car, its value drops by several thousand dollars the moment you drive it off the lot. Why? Because if you were to try to sell this car to someone else the week after you bought it, potential buyers would (rightfully) wonder whether you have discovered something about the car that is not observable to them and whether you might not be adversely selecting (as a seller) into the used car market. Consumers in the used car market can then employ various "screens" to try to get to the potentially hidden information, screens such as taking the used car to a trusted mechanic who can give an independent *third party certification* of quality. Or used car dealerships might offer *warranties* that signal to consumers the quality of the used car. Some brands of cars are known to have fewer problems, and so *brand names* can signal quality. *Brand names, warranties, and third party certifications* therefore all represent ways that hidden information can be unearthed and at least partially overcome the adverse selection problem.

Exercise 22A.28   Consider used car dealerships in small towns. How might *reputation* play a role similar to brand names in addressing the asymmetric information problem?

In a world with increasingly complex products, the issue of product quality that is potentially hidden from consumers of course extends far beyond the used car market. The quality of much of what I see in stores—from computers to televisions to kitchen appliances to over-the-counter medications—is difficult for me to evaluate. Again, warranties can signal quality, as can the brand names that have good reputations. Third party certification groups (such as the magazine *Consumer Reports*) have emerged. They routinely test products and *sell the information* to me in a separate market (through, for instance, the *Consumer Reports* magazine or Web site), and consumer advocacy groups outside the market provide similar services. The American Heart Association puts its seal of approval on certain foods. And industry groups have often established *industry standards*, sometimes requiring third party certification to ensure quality. Even my underwear has stickers that try to signal quality, informing me that "Inspector 10" had done his job. While all these signals are costly and thus use some of society's resources, they nevertheless *can be* (and often are) socially beneficial if they are not "too costly" and if they lead to more widespread information that can overcome adverse selection externalities in markets. At the same time, some producers might be able, at least in the short run, to signal that their products are of higher quality than they actually are, expending wasteful effort to hide their true type in order to end up in a "pooling equilibrium" with high quality producers. Thus, just as in the example of car insurance, signals may in some instances represent a socially wasteful use of resources aimed at deceiving rather than informing, or they may be too costly even when they result in a resolution of the information asymmetry.

Exercise 22A.29   What is *Consumer Reports* analogous to in our discussion of car insurance?

Finally, as in insurance markets, the government often steps in as well. Cigarette packages contain dire warnings required by law, and my barber has a sign on his mirror telling me that he is licensed to cut hair. We will see in later chapters that there may be other, less benign reasons why my barber had to get a license to operate, and we therefore might be careful in interpreting such government involvement as solely serving the purpose of reducing adverse selection. Our goal here, however, is not to sort out which of the various signals and screens aimed at adverse selection problems are "good" and which are "bad," which truly raise social surplus and which are socially wasteful. Rather, I simply want to persuade you that a variety of market, civil society, and government-supported signals and screens in fact operate at least in part because markets by themselves might not perform optimally in the presence of adverse selection.

22A.3.2 Adverse Selection in Labor and Capital Markets   There is only so much that an employer can ascertain about a potential employee before hiring her. The adverse selection problem in labor markets therefore occurs when workers have hidden information about their own productivity. Education, work experience, and letters of reference offer ways for us to signal information to our employers, but workers with identical resumes may still be quite different on the job. Additional information might be signaled less formally in job interviews aimed at screening applicants. Depending on the cost of the signal relative to the benefit, such efforts may once again be socially productive in the sense that they convey true information or socially wasteful if they signal false information or are simply too costly.

We are often led to believe, for instance, that more education is always "better." This may be true if the only reason for someone to get more education is to truly increase productivity on the job (and if the marginal cost of additional education is greater than the marginal benefit for the student). But in some instances, education may simply serve as a signal masking the underlying productivity of a worker. If the cost of getting the "signal" of having attained a certain level of education is sufficiently low, then low-productivity workers might get an education simply to end up in a pooling equilibrium with truly high-productivity workers. While this may make the unproductive worker better off, it dilutes the information of the signal and does not serve to convey the information that employers seek.[8] If you take a course on the economics of education or in labor economics, you will probably find yourself debating the issue of whether your college increases your real productivity or simply serves as a screening institution that signals something about you that was already there when you started as a freshman. (This is explored in more detail in exercise 24.14.)

Which of the following possibilities makes it more likely that widespread college attendance is efficient: (1) colleges primarily provide skills that raise marginal product, or (2) colleges primarily certify who has high marginal product?

Exercise 22A.30

The same issues arise in financial markets. Banks and mortgage companies have less information than those who apply for loans. Applicants therefore seek ways of signaling their creditworthiness and banks seek ways of screening applicants. In the past, when individuals moved less often and resided more within small communities, one's informal *reputation* was an important signal; if everyone knows Joe is a liar and a cheat, there is not much point to lending him money. In today's world, such informal mechanisms are less effective, but other institutions have taken their place. Credit companies keep detailed records on anyone who has ever had a credit card or a loan or a bank account. We are often told to be sure to "build a credit history" precisely because this signals something about us that may come in handy when the time comes to apply for a mortgage.

---

[8]Note that the adverse selection problem is less severe if it is easy for firms to fire workers who prove less productive than they initially appeared, but many laws and regulations as well as union protections for workers often make firing workers costly for firms.

Thus, as informal reputations became less effective, new markets formed, markets that gather and sell information about our creditworthiness. In many ways, our credit report has become our reputation in credit markets.

We face similar information problems when we try to decide where to invest our money. Companies try to get us to buy their stocks, and banks try to sell us various types of savings instruments with different risks and returns. Often, the places we consider investing have much more information about their true value than we do, and we therefore have to expend effort, or hire someone to expend effort in our place, to gather information that might be hidden. Again, there exist many different financial advising firms that now specialize in gathering such information and selling it to us for a price (or a commission), and nonprofit ("civil society") institutions provide information on firms (often on Web sites accessible to potential investors). In addition, the government has created its own oversight mechanism, requiring financial disclosure statements by publicly traded companies and offering their "seal of approval" in terms of deposit insurance to banks. (This, too, is in somewhat of a state of flux as this book goes to press, with the 2008 financial crisis having led to legislative proposals to restructure the regulatory framework underpinning the financial sector.)

22A.4 Racial and Gender Discrimination

Many societies, including the U.S., continue to struggle with overcoming social problems arising from the legacy of racial and gender discrimination. Such discrimination has deep historical roots, dating back to some of the darker periods in history when prejudice was endemic and often explicitly supported by government policy. Despite legislation that now outlaws such discrimination, studies continue to suggest instances when applicants for employment (in labor markets) or credit (in financial markets) are offered different wages or interest rates despite identical observable qualifications, with less favorable deals offered to women and minorities. We will see in this section that such discrimination may persist in markets *even when old prejudices have died out* if markets are characterized by asymmetric information of the type discussed throughout this chapter.

22A.4.1 Statistical Discrimination and Gender   Consider first a case where gender discrimination characterizes market transactions in the life insurance market. We have already discussed how life insurance companies calculate the expected probability of premature death for individuals. Smokers, for instance, are required to pay higher life insurance premiums than nonsmokers because, *on average*, smokers die earlier than nonsmokers. At the same time, many of us know of people who smoked all their life and ended up living to a ripe old age. Smoking appears to be more damaging to some than to others, with some individuals being fortunate to have genes that protect them from the adverse consequences of smoking. Even if I know that my family tends to be able to smoke like chimneys and still survive to an old age, insurance companies will discriminate against me in their pricing policies if they know that I smoke. Because they lack information on my individual probability of being affected by smoking, they discriminate *based on the statistical evidence on smokers as a group*; they engage in *statistical discrimination* because of the informational asymmetry that keeps them from knowing fully my individual characteristics.

The same reason that causes statistical discrimination against smokers in life insurance markets then also causes statistical discrimination *against men* in these markets. Women *on average* live longer than men, and so my wife, despite the fact that her family seems more predisposed to cancer and heart disease than mine, ends up getting a better deal on life insurance than I do. The same is true of young people in car insurance markets: You might be a much better driver than I am, but because I am older and *on average* people my age get into fewer accidents, you end up having to pay a higher car insurance premium than I do. *Statistical discrimination—discrimination based on the average statistics of the demographic groups to which individuals belong*—is therefore economically rational in insurance markets that are characterized by asymmetric information.

Exercise
22A.31

What are we implicitly assuming about the costs of screening applicants in these markets?

While we may not see a big moral issue arising from such statistical discrimination in certain insurance markets, we might be considerably more disturbed when the same type of discrimination emerges in other markets. *On average*, for instance, women are more likely to exit the labor force for some period in order to raise children. This is not at all true for *some* women, and an increasing number of men are also taking larger responsibility for child rearing. Employers, however, have a difficult time identifying which women and men are *individually* more likely to exit the labor force for child rearing, but it is easy for them to identify whether employees or potential employees are men or women. As a result of this *asymmetric information*, employers may therefore use the underlying statistics of average behavior by men and women to infer the likelihood that a particular employee will be with the company for a long period. As a result, they may *statistically discriminate* against female employees, offering them lower wages or less job training in anticipation of the greater likelihood that they will leave the company. Notice that, from a purely economic perspective, this is no different than the insurance company statistically discriminating against me when my wife and I apply for life insurance; because the company does not have full information, it uses the available statistical evidence to infer information that is true *on average* but may be false for any given individual. And, just as in the case of life insurance, the discrimination that results in equilibrium may have nothing to do with companies inherently preferring one gender over another.

Exercise
22A.32

True or False: Statistical discrimination leads to equilibria that have both "separating" and "pooling" features.

22A.4.2 Gender Discrimination Based on Prejudice versus Statistical Discrimination

When we observe incidences of gender discrimination, it is therefore difficult to know whether the discrimination arises from inherent prejudices or from economic considerations due to asymmetric information. *Discrimination based on prejudice is defined as discrimination that arises from tastes that inherently prefer one group over another*, while *statistical discrimination arises from asymmetric information*. Life insurance companies that charge lower premiums to women do not do so because they like women more than men; they do so because women *on average* live longer than men. Similarly, employers who discriminate against women in labor markets *may* be motivated solely by economic considerations rooted in asymmetric information. Let me be clear: I am not arguing that such discrimination may not be due to more pernicious causes related to good-old-boys on corporate boards feeling uncomfortable about allowing women more economic opportunities. I am simply pointing out that the same logic that causes life insurance companies to discriminate in favor of women (and against smokers) may also lie behind *some* of the discrimination against women we might observe in labor markets. Nor am I saying that only taste discrimination based on prejudice should disturb us, but understanding the root causes of discrimination may help us better formulate solutions that eliminate all forms of gender discrimination.

Exercise
22A.33

Suppose public schools invested more resources into gender sensitivity training in hopes of lessening gender discrimination in the future. Would you recommend this if you knew that gender discrimination was purely a form of statistical discrimination?

Markets, for instance, tend to "punish" employers for discriminating based on prejudice. Suppose that companies *A* and *B* in a competitive market are identical in every way except for the fact that company A is governed by a corporate board that is prejudiced against working with women while company B is not. This implies that company B has a larger pool of talent to draw from and will be able to gain a competitive advantage over company A by employing qualified women. Both companies may operate in equilibrium, but the prejudiced company will earn lower dollar profits because part of its "profit" comes in the form of prejudiced corporate leaders getting "utility" from excluding women. Shareholders should prefer to invest in company B that makes more "dollar profits," which implies that the stock of company B will have higher market value than the stock of company A.[9]

Now consider a third company C that is just like company B but suppose that C is willing to engage in statistical discrimination while B is not. If the labor market is characterized by asymmetric information and if women *on average* are more likely to leave the labor force to rear children, then company C will engage in statistical discrimination that will likely make it more profitable. While the market thus tends to "punish" companies that engage in taste discrimination based on prejudice, it will *reward* companies that engage in statistical discrimination. Finally, suppose there exists yet a fourth company D that has developed an effective screening tool that can differentiate *individually* among applicants (of both genders), between those that are likely to leave the labor force and those that are not. This company can, of course, do even better than company C by using its information and eliminate all forms of discrimination.

Exercise 22A.34

In the past, gender discrimination was often enshrined in statutory laws, making it illegal for firms to hire women into certain roles or schools to admit women as students. If you are one of the corporate board members in company A, why might you favor such laws even if all you care about is not having women in your own company? If you are one of the corporate board members in company C, would you similarly favor such a law?

As societies consider ways of eliminating all forms of gender discrimination in labor markets, the appropriate strategies then differ depending on what form the discrimination takes. Both taste discrimination (due to prejudice) and statistical discrimination (due to asymmetric information) can persist in markets, but markets tend to "punish" the former while "rewarding" the latter. Taste discrimination disappears as old prejudices disappear from people's tastes, but statistical discrimination persists so long as companies are economically rewarded by discriminating in the presence of asymmetric information. Statistical discrimination will therefore tend to persist so long as underlying statistical differences between the genders persist unless other institutions are put in place to make statistical discrimination less profitable. If, for instance, men *on average* demand equal amounts of time away from the labor force in order to rear children, the root cause of statistical gender discrimination in labor markets disappears. Alternatively, some governments have instituted *mandatory* parental leave for both genders when children enter a household, some have focused on subsidizing child care to make it easier for women to return to the labor force, and some have instituted rigorous antidiscrimination laws that offset the "rewards" from statistical discrimination with government sanctions. Finally, there exists an incentive for companies (such as company D in our example) to figure out more effective ways of differentiating between potential employees of both genders, and for potential employees to signal whether they are likely to leave the labor force or not. Again, the goal here is not to advocate one form of institutional solution over another but simply to suggest that there are a variety of government and nongovernment institutions that might emerge to address the asymmetric information problem that results in statistical gender discrimination in labor markets.

---

[9]This presumes, of course, that not all shareholders are similarly prejudiced. But even if some shareholders are prejudiced and get "utility" from owning stock in companies that discriminate against women, the stock market will reward the nondiscriminating company with higher stock values so long as not all shareholders are prejudiced.

22A.4.3 Racial Discrimination   Just as gender discrimination in labor markets can result from either inherent prejudice or from asymmetric information, persistent racial discrimination can have the same two root causes. We began our discussion of gender discrimination in the context of life insurance markets where insurance companies price discriminate against men because of the higher *average* life expectancy of women. For a variety of complex reasons, it turns out that African Americans have shorter *average* life expectancy in the United States than whites. Gender discrimination in insurance markets, however, is legal, while racial discrimination is not. Thus, the statistical discrimination that would tend to make life insurance premiums higher for African Americans is not permitted, causing insurance companies not to explicitly price-discriminate against African Americans as they do against men. Even in the absence of legal barriers, the bad publicity from explicit racial discrimination in the pricing of life insurance premiums might be sufficient to keep this from happening so long as large numbers of potential customers would be offended by seeing insurance premium tables that have separate columns for different races. At the same time, it may well be the case that insurance companies discriminate "below the radar screen" by being less aggressive in advertising their life insurance products to African Americans.

Despite the legal barriers to racial discrimination and despite much progress over the past decades, however, it appears that such racial discrimination continues to persist in other markets. But it again becomes difficult to ascertain what fraction of the observed discrimination in those markets is due to taste discrimination based on prejudice as opposed to statistical discrimination based on asymmetric information. In the case of racial discrimination, such statistical discrimination may well be due to *average* differences between groups that emerge from the historical legacy of past (and present) racial discrimination elsewhere.

It is well-documented, for instance, that African American children *on average* attend worse public schools than nonminority children. In the past, this resulted from explicit public policy that, at least in the American South, set up different school systems for African Americans, systems that were funded at vastly different levels and, as the Supreme Court stated explicitly (in 1954) in *Brown v. Board of Education*, resulted in *separate and unequal* education for African-American children. But even today, entry into public schools is determined by where a child's parents live, with schools that serve disproportionate numbers of minority children (on average) systematically worse than schools that serve primarily nonminority children. A variety of economic factors therefore continue to cause minority children on average to attend worse public schools than nonminority children even as the public school system overall has become officially more integrated.

Now suppose that an employer is faced with identical high school transcripts from two applicants, one nonminority and one African American. For all the employer knows, the African-American applicant has many unobservable characteristics that will make him a much better employee than the nonminority applicant. But the employer also knows that *on average*, African-American children attend worse public schools and thus have not had the same opportunity to gain skills as nonminority children. The employer then faces the same asymmetric information problem we have discussed throughout this chapter and will be tempted to *statistically discriminate* against the African-American applicant *even if she has no prejudice (derived from pernicious tastes) in her heart.* Recognizing that it may thus be "economically rational" for her to discriminate does not imply moral approval for such discrimination. Whether racial discrimination in labor markets results from inherent prejudice or from asymmetric information, it is deeply disturbing to many of us. Rather, recognizing that such discrimination can persist even in the absence of explicit taste discrimination simply suggests that market forces by themselves may be insufficient to stamp out racial discrimination when underlying *average* group differences arise from discrimination elsewhere. It furthermore suggests that, even if all forms of racial discrimination are illegal, it is likely that subtle and difficult-to-detect racial discrimination may persist in markets so long as these markets are characterized by such asymmetric information.

Exercise
22A.35 *True or False*: In the previous example, the asymmetric information that leads to statistical discrimination against African Americans is still rooted in discrimination based on prejudice, but it may be rooted primarily in prejudice-based discrimination from the past.

In the short run, societies can combat such discrimination through a variety of civil society and government institutions. For instance, if a decline in inherent prejudice due to pernicious tastes leads to an increasing number of individuals placing explicit value on diversity, employers might overcome their temptation to statistically discriminate because their nonminority employees gain "utility" from knowing that they are working in a diverse environment and because their customers are offended if civil society advocacy groups advertise that a particular company has a homogeneous labor force. Alternatively, governments have instituted a variety of different forms of affirmative action policies to explicitly encourage more diverse work environments. In the long run, however, the temptation to engage in statistical discrimination of the kind we have raised here subsides only when more equal access to educational opportunities is offered to all irrespective of race and ethnicity. A society that successfully equalizes such opportunities will therefore eliminate the very statistical group differences that lead to informational asymmetries that in turn lead to statistical discrimination. The tendency of racial discrimination to persist in markets is therefore not fully eliminated until attitudes in people's tastes are nondiscriminatory *and* opportunities for different groups are truly equal.

22B Insurance Contracts with Two Risk Types

As noted at the beginning, we deviate in this chapter somewhat from our usual practice of formalizing mathematically in Section B what we did intuitively in Section A. Section A was written without the presumption that you have covered the sometimes optional topic of risk (from Chapter 17), and this constrained us to thinking only about whether or not a consumer will buy insurance, not how much insurance coverage each consumer might buy. But now we will build a model of adverse selection directly on the topics related to insurance markets that we introduced in Chapter 17, models in which we considered a whole menu of actuarily fair insurance contracts ranging from no insurance to full insurance. If you have previously covered only Section A of Chapter 17, you can focus solely on the nonmathematical parts of this section to build adverse selection into the graphical insurance models you have previously seen. For this reason, the mathematical Sections 22B.1.2, 22B.2.2, and 22B.3.3 are put in separate subsections, allowing you simply to skip them if you'd prefer to focus on just the graphical exposition. While we will develop some new intuitions and insights with this model, we should note however that the car insurance model in the previous section could in fact be reinterpreted to yield similar insights. We leave you to do this in the context of health insurance in end-of-chapter exercises 22.7 and 22.8.

Suppose, then, that consumers (like my wife in Chapter 17) face the possibility of a "bad" outcome in which their consumption is x_1 and the possibility of a "good" outcome in which their consumption is x_2. Suppose further that there are two consumer types, with consumers of type δ facing outcome x_1 with probability δ (and outcome x_2 with probability $(1 - \delta)$), and consumers of type θ facing outcome x_1 with probability θ (and outcome x_2 with probability $(1 - \theta)$). We will adopt the convention that $\delta < \theta$, implying that the δ types face less risk than the θ types. Otherwise, the two consumer types are identical in every way, with $x_1 < x_2$ the same for both types and with each type having the same underlying tastes, which we will assume throughout are independent of which "state" of the world occurs. As in Chapter 17, we will furthermore assume that each individual's tastes over risky gambles can be expressed as an expected utility. And we will assume that each type knows the risk he or she faces but that insurance companies do not necessarily know which type any given individual represents. In most of what follows, the insurance companies only know that a fraction γ of the population is of type δ and the remaining fraction $(1 - \gamma)$ is of type θ.

Insurance companies offer insurance contracts that are defined (as in Chapter 17) by an insurance premium p and an insurance benefit b. If a consumer purchases an insurance contract (p, b), his or her consumption in the good state falls to $(x_2 - p)$ while his or her consumption in the bad state rises to $(x_1 + b - p)$. As we showed in Chapter 17, since we assume that tastes over consumption are state-independent, each consumer type would then choose to fully insure so long as he or she faced complete and actuarially fair insurance markets.

22B.1 Equilibrium without Adverse Selection

In Chapter 17, we graphed indifference curves in graphs with x_2 on the horizontal and x_1 on the vertical axis, and we graphed the menu of actuarially fair insurance contracts in the same graphs. We will return to this way of modeling insurance in end-of-chapter exercises 22.4, 22.5, and 22.8. In end-of-chapter exercise 17.3, however, we showed that we can alternatively graph indifference curves on a graph with the insurance benefit b on the horizontal and the insurance premium p on the vertical. And, if insurance companies were able to offer actuarially fair (and thus zero-profit) contracts to each type separately, these contracts could similarly be graphed in such a graph. From our work in Chapter 17, we know that such contracts would have the feature that $p = \delta b$ for consumer type δ and $p = \theta b$ for consumer type θ.

Explain why such contracts are actuarially fair.

**Exercise
22B.1**

22B.1.1 A Graphical Depiction of Equilibrium without Adverse Selection   Panel (a) of Graph 22.3 does this for a consumer of type δ where $x_1 = 10$, $x_2 = 250$, and $\delta = 0.25$ as it was for the example of my wife deciding on life insurance in Chapter 17. Notice that this consumer

Graph 22.3: Equilibrium Insurance Policies in the Absence of Asymmetric Information

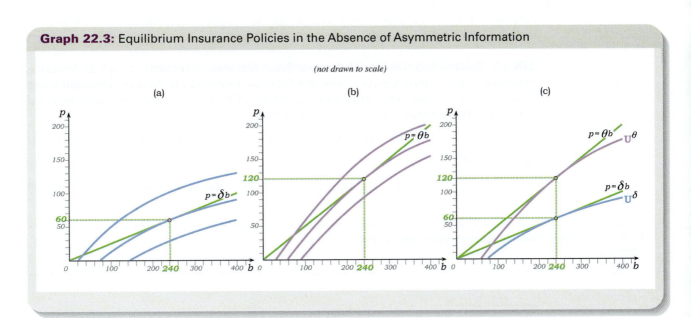

becomes better off as she moves southeast on the graph because moving southeast implies greater insurance benefits and lower insurance premiums. The graph also contains the line $p = \delta b$ that represents the menu of actuarily fair insurance contracts for this consumer type. Since tastes are state-independent in this example, our work in Chapter 17 implies that our risk averse consumer will fully insure, purchasing a policy $(b,p) = (240,60)$ at which her indifference curve must be tangent to the line representing her insurance options.

Exercise 22B.2   Why is $(b,p) = (240,60)$ an insurance contract that provides full insurance to a δ type consumer?

Exercise 22B.3   What would indifference curves look like for risk-neutral consumers? What about risk-loving consumers?

Panel (b) of the graph then illustrates exactly the same for consumer type θ assuming that $\theta = 0.5$, i.e., assuming that this consumer type is twice as likely to encounter the "bad" state. Risk aversion again implies that the consumer will choose to fully insure when faced with a menu of actuarily fair insurance contracts, but such contracts are twice as expensive for type θ since the insurance company is twice as likely to have to pay out benefits.

Exercise 22B.4   Demonstrate that full insurance for type θ implies the same benefit level as for type δ.

If insurance companies can tell which consumer type they are facing when they enter an insurance contract, then panel (c) depicts the competitive equilibrium in which the full insurance contract $(b^\delta, p^\delta) = (240,60)$ is sold to type δ and the full insurance contract $(b^\theta, p^\theta) = (240,120)$ is sold to type θ, with insurance companies earning zero profit. This equilibrium is efficient. There is no way to make anyone, consumers or firms, better off without making someone else worse off.

22B.1.2 Calculating the Equilibrium without Adverse Selection
Graph 22.3 (and the remaining graphs in this chapter) assume that the (state-independent) utility of consumption can be described by the function $u(x) = \alpha \ln x$ (again as in Chapter 17). This results in an *expected utility* from the insurance contract (b,p) for type δ of

$$U^\delta(b,p) = \delta \alpha \ln(x_1 + b - p) + (1 - \delta)\alpha \ln(x_2 - p), \qquad (22.2)$$

and for type θ

$$U^\theta(b,p) = \theta \alpha \ln(x_1 + b - p) + (1 - \theta)\alpha \ln(x_2 - p).^{10} \qquad (22.3)$$

Exercise 22B.5   Are these consumer types risk averse?

---

[10] If you have trouble seeing how we arrive at this as the expected utility, you should review the concepts in Chapter 17.

If consumer type δ faces an actuarily fair menu of insurance contracts described by $p = \delta b$, she will choose (b, p) to maximize equation (22.2) subject to $p = \delta b$. Solving this problem results in an optimal choice of

$$b = x_2 - x_1 \text{ and } p = \delta(x_2 - x_1), \qquad (22.4)$$

which fully insures the consumer.

Set up the expected utility maximization problem for θ types and derive the optimal choice assuming they face an actuarily fair insurance menu.

Exercise 22B.6

How do these results relate to the values in Graph 22.3?

Exercise 22B.7

22B.2 Self-Selecting Separating Equilibria

Now suppose that insurance companies cannot tell the low risk type δ consumers apart from high risk type θ consumers unless some information is revealed through signaling or screening. In part A of the chapter, we investigated how consumers can send explicit signals to try to reveal their "type" and how firms can invest in screens that reveal information, and we implicitly assumed that such signals and screens could be bought at some cost. But there is another way that consumers of insurance can identify themselves when multiple different insurance contracts are offered to all customers: They could simply choose different contracts depending on which risk type they are and thus *self-select* into different insurance pools. Firms may therefore want to design the set of contracts that are offered in such a way that consumers reveal their type through their actions. Note that we could not investigate this possibility in our car insurance example of part A because we assumed there that the decision to insure was a discrete decision—either you bought insurance or you did not—and not one that involved choices over *how much* insurance to buy.

The full information equilibrium depicted in Graph 22.3c can then no longer be an equilibrium when firms do not know who is what type. Under full information, there was no problem having insurance companies offer all actuarily fair insurance contracts $p = \delta b$ to δ types because they knew who the θ types were and could simply prevent them from buying insurance contracts intended for low cost δ types. But if insurance companies cannot tell who the high cost types are, they can no longer offer all the $p = \delta b$ contracts because type θ consumers would end up buying one of those contracts rather than those intended for them. Insurance companies would then make negative profits as they incur higher costs on type θ consumers while selling them low cost insurance. In the absence of knowing who is what type, the insurance industry will therefore have to restrict what types of contracts it offers.

22B.2.1 A Graphical Exposition of Self-Selecting Separating Equilibrium We can then ask which insurance contracts will *not* be offered in an equilibrium in which insurance companies achieve the outcome that individuals self-select into different insurance pools based on their risk types. First, note that it must be the case that high risk types still get fully insured at actuarily fair rates in such an equilibrium. If this were not the case, there would be room for new insurance companies to enter and offer such actuarily fair full insurance to high risk types. This implies that the insurance contracts that will be restricted are those for low risk types. Since those types face less risk, it is less costly for them to forego *some* insurance in order to be able to get a better deal on their insurance contract than they could if they chose from contracts intended for high risk types. This then opens the door for low risk types to *signal* that they are in fact low risk types by choosing an insurance contract that is actuarily fair for them but does not fully insure, with insurance companies simply not making actuarily fair full insurance available for low risk types.

This is illustrated in panel (a) of Graph 22.4 where we again have two (green) actuarily fair contract lines, one for high risk θ types and another for low risk δ types. The high risk θ types once again optimize along the actuarily fair set of insurance contracts aimed at them, settling at the full insurance contract A. All the contracts that lie in the shaded area below the magenta U^θ, however, are preferred by high risk types to their actuarily fair full insurance contract A. They would therefore much prefer to choose an insurance contract from the portion of the $p = \theta b$ line that lies within the shaded region, with any contract on that line to the right of B strictly preferred by them to A. Thus, if insurance companies want to induce high and low risk types to self-select into separate actuarily fair insurance contracts, they cannot offer any of the $p = \delta b$ contracts to the right of B.

In a *separating equilibrium* in which risk types identify themselves through the insurance contracts that they purchase, the only actuarily fair insurance contracts that can then be offered are those that are located on the bold portion of the $p = \delta b$ line in Graph 22.4a. And of these, risk-averse consumers of type δ will demand only the contract represented by point B since all other contracts that are offered involve greater risk (without a change in the expected value of the outcome).

Exercise 22B.8 Suppose insurance companies offer all actuarily fair insurance contracts to type θ. Can you identify in panel (b) of Graph 22.4 the area representing all insurance contracts that consumers of type δ would purchase rather than choosing from the menu of contracts aimed at type θ?

Exercise 22B.9 From the area of contracts you identified in exercise 22B.8, can you identify the subset that insurance companies would be interested to offer assuming they are aware that high risk types might try to get low cost insurance?

Exercise 22B.10 From the contracts identified in exercise 22B.9, can you identify which of these contracts could not be offered in equilibrium when the insurance industry is perfectly competitive?

Graph 22.4: Self-Selecting Separating Equilibrium with Asymmetric Information

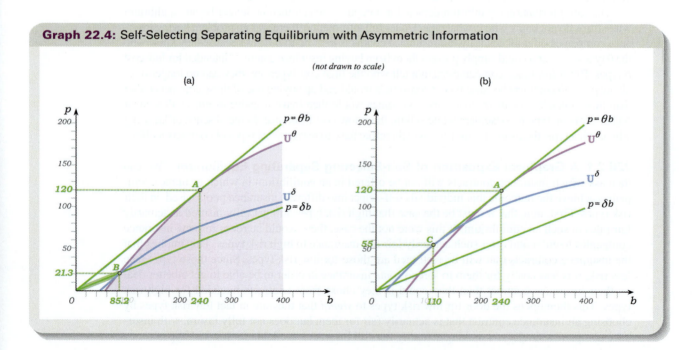

You should be able to see straight away that the competitive separating equilibrium in this example is inefficient. In particular, the competitive equilibrium in the absence of asymmetric information (depicted in Graph 22.3c) has low risk types δ with higher utility without anyone else doing worse (since high risk θ types do equally well and firms make zero profits in either case). The inefficiency arises from the fact that there are *missing markets*—not all the actuarially fair insurance contracts for δ types are offered under asymmetric information. And the missing markets arise from the adverse selection problem, i.e., the problem that high risk types would adversely select into the low risk insurance market if the missing market for fuller insurance targeted at low risk customers emerged.

22B.2.2 Calculating the Separating Equilibrium

The mathematics behind Graph 22.4a is in principle relatively straightforward: The insurance contract B is identified as the intersection of the indifference curve of high risk θ types who fully insure under actuarily fair insurance with the line representing all actuarially fair insurance contracts for the low risk δ types. Full insurance for a θ type implies a consumption level of $((1 - \theta)x_2 + \theta x_1)$ in each state with certainty, which implies that the full insurance utility for type θ is

$$U_f^\theta = u\big((1 - \theta)x_2 + \theta x_1\big) = \alpha \ln \big((1 - \theta)x_2 + \theta x_1\big). \tag{22.5}$$

Can you verify that full insurance implies consumption of $((1 - \theta)x_2 + \theta x_1)$?

Exercise
22B.11

The indifference curve that gives all combinations of b and p such that a θ type is indifferent to the full insurance outcome is then given by all (b,p) under which her *expected* utility $U^\theta(b,p)$ is equal to U_f^θ from equation (22.5); i.e.,

$$U^\theta(b,p) = \alpha\theta \ln (x_1 + b - p) + \alpha(1 - \theta) \ln (x_2 - p)$$
$$= \alpha \ln \big((1 - \theta)x_2 + \theta x_1\big) = U_f^\theta. \tag{22.6}$$

We can then cancel the α terms and use the rules of logarithms to rewrite the middle part of this equation as

$$(x_1 + b - p)^\theta (x_2 - p)^{(1-\theta)} = (1 - \theta)x_2 + \theta x_1, \tag{22.7}$$

which we can solve for b to get

$$b = \left(\frac{(1 - \theta)x_2 + \theta x_1}{(x_2 - p)^{(1-\theta)}} \right)^{1/\theta} + p - x_1. \tag{22.8}$$

Although Graph 22.4 is not drawn using this precise function, this is the (inverse of the) equation for the magenta indifference curve in Graph 22.4a when we substitute in $\theta = 0.5$, $x_2 = 250$ and $x_1 = 10$; i.e., the equivalent to the magenta indifference curve in our graph is described by the equation

$$b = \left(\frac{(1 - 0.5)250 + 0.5(10)}{(250 - p)^{(1-0.5)}} \right)^{1/(0.5)} + p - 10 = \frac{130^2}{250 - p} + p - 10. \tag{22.9}$$

Our logic told us that the highest actuarily fair insurance policy for the low risk δ types that can exist in a separating equilibrium is given by the intersection of this indifference curve with the line $p = \delta b$ that represents the menu of all actuarially fair insurance contracts for low risk types. Written in terms of b, this line is $b = p/\delta$ or $b = 4p$ when $\delta = 0.25$ (as we assumed in our graph). Thus the premium at point B in the graph is given by the intersection of equation (22.9) and the actuarily fair insurance menu $b = 4p$ (represented by the lower green line in Graph 22.4a). This means we need to solve the equation

$$4p = \frac{130^2}{250 - p} + p - 10, \tag{22.10}$$

which can be rewritten as

$$3p^2 - 740p + 14{,}400 = 0. \tag{22.11}$$

Applying the quadratic formula, we get $p = 225.37$ and $p = 21.30$, which represent the two premiums at which the magenta indifference curve crosses the lower green line in Graph 22.4a. Point B in our graph lies at the lower of these premiums, with $p = 21.30$ and corresponding $b = 4p = 85.20$. In a competitive separating equilibrium, we therefore have two insurance contracts that are sold, $(b^\theta, p^\theta) = (240, 120)$ and $(b^\delta, p^\delta) = (85.2, 21.3)$, with high risk θ types fully insuring under the former and low risk δ types revealing their type by purchasing less than full insurance under the latter contract.

Exercise 22B.12 Can you show mathematically (by evaluating utilities) that this equilibrium is inefficient relative to the equilibrium identified in Graph 22.3c?

Exercise 22B.13 *True or False*: Under perfect competition (and assuming that insurance companies incur no costs other than the benefits they pay out), risk-averse individuals with state-independent tastes will fully insure in the absence of asymmetric information but may insure less than fully in its presence.

Exercise 22B.14 Can you verify the intercepts for point C in Graph 22.4b?

Table 22.1 then presents the equilibrium insurance contracts for low risk δ types as the high risk type becomes "riskier", i.e., as θ increases. For our particular example, low risk types continue to find some insurance regardless of how risky the θ types are (unless θ reaches 1), but low risk types clearly purchase less insurance in separating equilibria as high risk types become riskier. Put differently, the externality from adverse selection increases in severity as high risk types become riskier. In cases where insurance can only be sold in "discrete" units, such as cases like those in Section A where "grade insurance" was not continuous, low risk types might be frozen out of the insurance market altogether.

Table 22.1: $\delta = 0.25$, $x_1 = 10$, $x_2 = 250$

		Equilibrium Insurance for Low Risk δ Types		
θ	p	b	$x_1 + b - p$	$x_2 - p$
0.25	60.00	240.00	190.00	190.00
0.33	31.05	124.20	102.10	219.30
0.50	21.30	85.20	73.90	228.70
0.75	12.19	48.76	46.57	237.81
0.90	5.77	23.08	27.31	244.23
0.99	0.68	2.70	12.03	249.32
1.00	0.00	0.00	10.00	250.00

Draw a graph, with *b* on the horizontal and *p* on the vertical axis, illustrating the separating equilibrium in row 4 of Table 22.1.

Exercise
22B.15

22B.3 Pooling Contracts with Asymmetric Information

In our treatment of self-selecting separating equilibria, we have implicitly assumed that insurance companies cannot earn positive profit by offering an insurance contract that attracts *both* high and low risk types into the same insurance pool. We will now explore how such a possibility might emerge, and how it might make the self-selecting equilibrium we have analyzed so far impossible to achieve. And we will see shortly that this possibility depends crucially on the number of high risk types relative to the number of low risk types in the economy.

Suppose an insurance company were to offer a contract that was more attractive for *both* risk types than the separating equilibrium contracts we previously identified. If a fraction γ of the population is of type δ (and the remaining fraction $(1 - \gamma)$ is of type θ), then such an insurance company would expect on average to pay δb for the fraction γ of its customers that are low risk types and θb to the fraction $(1 - \gamma)$ of its customers who are high risk types. Thus, the insurance company would expect to make zero profits when

$$p = \gamma \delta b + (1 - \gamma)\theta b = [\gamma \delta + (1 - \gamma)\theta]b. \tag{22.12}$$

22B.3.1 Pooling Contracts that Eliminate Self-Selecting Separating Equilibria

Note that, when $\gamma = 0$, this simply reduces to the equation $p = \theta b$ that defines the zero profit line for high risk types, and when $\gamma = 1$ it reduces to the zero profit line for low risk types. As γ increases from zero to 1, the zero profit line from having both types buy the same policy therefore rotates from the high-risk zero profit line to the low-risk zero profit line. In Graph 22.5a, for instance, the zero profit pooling line is depicted for the case where $\gamma = 0.5$, with this (green) line lying exactly midway between the zero profit lines for the individual risk types.

Graph 22.5: A Pooling Equilibrium Does Not Exist

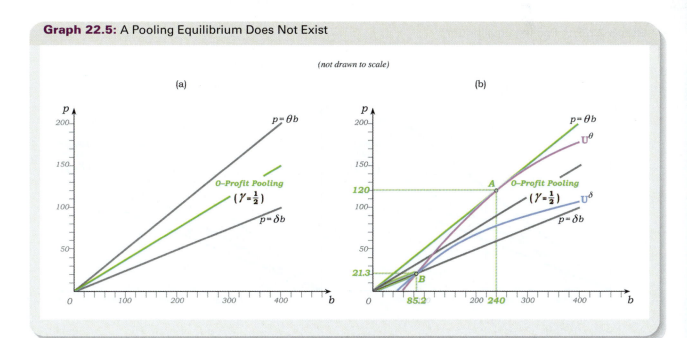

(not drawn to scale)

We can now think about the possibility of a pooling insurance contract that breaks the self-selection separating equilibrium in this example. Panel (b) of Graph 22.5 replicates panel (a) from Graph 22.4 and illustrates the contracts A and B that would be bought by types θ and δ in a separating equilibrium. In addition, panel (b) of Graph 22.5 includes the set of zero-profit pooling contracts that emerges when half the consumers are of type δ and half the consumers are of type θ (i.e., when $\gamma = 0.5$). Note that in this case, the (blue) indifference curve for δ types that goes through contract B lies to the southeast of the (grey) zero profit pooling line, which implies that the low-risk δ types prefer to identify themselves as low risk types by choosing the contract B over any possible zero-profit pooling contract. Thus, there is no pooling contract that would attract both risk types *and* result in non-negative profit for insurance companies when B is currently offered. The self-selecting separating equilibrium stands.

But now suppose that γ is equal to 2/3 instead of 1/2; i.e., suppose that 2/3 of the population was low risk and 1/3 of the population was high risk. What changes as a result in Graph 22.5b? The zero-profit lines aimed at the two types individually are given by $p = \delta b$ and $p = \theta b$ and thus are unaffected by changes in γ. Similarly, the tastes of the two types are unchanged (since individual tastes have nothing to do with how many others of each type there are in the economy), which implies the blue and magenta indifference curves remain unchanged. The only thing that changes is the (grey) line representing the possible pooling contracts that give insurance companies zero profit! In particular, as γ increases, this line becomes shallower (without a change in the intercept), and as it becomes shallower, it will eventually cross the blue indifference curve for δ types.

Exercise 22B.16 Can you show, using equation (22.12), that the last sentence is correct?

Panel (a) of Graph 22.6 then illustrates the zero-profit pooling line for $\gamma = 2/3$, and it illustrates the (blue) indifference curve for δ types that is tangent to this line at point D. Point B, the best possible contract that would allow δ types to identify themselves without θ types wanting to imitate them, now lies slightly to the northwest of this indifference curve, implying that low risk

Graph 22.6: A Pooling Equilibrium?

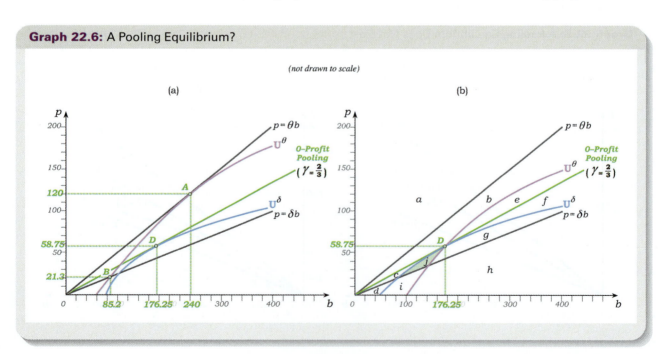

δ types would (slightly) prefer D even though this contract is not actuarily fair from their perspective. Similarly, θ types prefer D to the actuarily fair full insurance contract A; i.e., while the contract D does not fully insure them, it represents terms that are better (from their perspective) than actuarial fairness. Thus, we have identified a contract D that is strictly preferred by both risk types to the contracts B and A in the previous separating equilibrium, and the same is true for contracts slightly to the northwest of D, which would result in positive profits for insurance companies. This then makes it impossible to sustain the separating equilibrium we were able to sustain when γ was 0.5: By raising γ to 2/3, we have made it sufficiently easy to find pooling contracts that everyone prefers. And this of course becomes even easier as γ increases further.

What is the expected value of consumption for θ types at point D? Is it higher or lower than under full insurance? Explain.

**Exercise
22B.17**

What is the expected value of consumption for δ types at point D? Is it higher or lower than the expected value of consumption without insurance? Explain.

**Exercise
22B.18**

22B.3.2 Almost a Pooling Equilibrium   We have so far shown that the separating equilibrium breaks down when there are sufficiently many low risk types relative to high risk types in the economy because this allows firms to offer pooling contracts that are both preferred to the separating equilibrium contracts by all types and result in positive profit. To check whether there exists a pooling *equilibrium*, however, is trickier. Not only would we have to identify a zero-profit contract (such as D in Graph 22.5) that breaks the separating equilibrium, but we would further need to demonstrate that no other contract could result in positive profits for a firm that offers such a contract when all other firms offer D.

Why must any potential pooling equilibrium contract D lie on the zero-profit pooling line?

**Exercise
22B.19**

Panel (b) of Graph 22.6 illustrates once again point D on the zero-profit pooling line but this time shows both the (magenta) indifference curve for high risk types and the (blue) indifference curve for low risk types that contain point D. We can then ask whether there exist insurance contracts in each of the areas (labeled by lower case letters) that would earn an individual insurance company positive profits given that all other companies offer the contract D.

First, note that all insurance contracts that fall in the regions $(a),(b),(c)$, or (d) lie to the northeast of both the blue and the magenta indifference curves, and thus any company that offers a contract in those regions would attract no customers. Second, contracts that lie in the regions (e) and (f) lie to the northeast of the blue indifference curve and to the southeast of the magenta indifference curve, which implies that such contracts would attract only high risk θ types and thus yield negative profit (given that all these contracts lie below the zero-profit line for high risk types). Third, contracts that fall in the regions (g) and (h) lie to the southeast of both the blue and the magenta indifference curves, which implies they will attract both high and low risk types. But all such contracts lie below the zero-profit pooling line, which implies that an insurance company would earn negative profits when offering such contracts. Finally, this leaves regions (i) and (j) that lie to the southeast of the blue indifference curve and the northeast of the magenta indifference curve, implying that such contracts would attract only low risk δ types. Those contracts falling in region (i), however, lie below the zero-profit line for δ types and would thus earn negative profit.

We are then left with only contracts in the shaded region (j) that could potentially earn positive profit for a firm that offers insurance contracts in this region while other companies all offer the policy D. Without some friction in the market, everyone offering policy D is therefore not a competitive equilibrium. However, there are several ways in which we might still have D emerge as a pooling equilibrium: First, it might be that there are some start-up costs to offering an insurance policy different from what the market offers, costs of advertising and alerting consumers about the new policy. If those costs are sufficiently high, it may well be that contracts in region (j) will not result in positive profits for individual insurance companies (when all others are offering D). Second, it might be that there is some "search" cost that consumers incur when looking for something other than the prevalent market policy, and if this cost is sufficiently high, the policies in region (j) might not lie to the southeast of the blue indifference curve once the search cost is taken into account.

Finally, if firms in the market adjust quickly to changing circumstances, it might be that firms who currently offer D know that, as soon as they make a positive profit in region (j), other firms will offer policies closer to the zero-profit line $p = \delta b$ and will thus drive profits to zero. If the firms anticipate this, they may not offer policies in regions (j). This, however, begins to get us into the area of "strategic" thinking on the part of firms, a topic for later chapters.

Exercise 22B.20* Can you think of what would have to be true about how the blue and magenta indifference curves relate to one another at D in order for the problematic area (j) to disappear? Explain why this would then imply that D is a competitive equilibrium pooling contract.

Exercise 22B.21 For the case where $\gamma = 1/2$ and where a pooling equilibrium therefore does not exist (as shown in Graph 22.5b), can you divide the set of possible insurance contracts into different regions and illustrate that no firm would have an incentive to offer any contracts other than those that are provided in the separating equilibrium?

22B.3.3 Calculating the "Almost" Pooling Equilibrium

From our graphical exposition, it is clear that a competitive pooling equilibrium can arise only if the optimal insurance contract for low risk δ types from the set of zero-profit pooling contracts (given in equation (22.12)) yields greater utility for δ types than the insurance contract that allows δ types to separate from high risk θ types. Thus, we can begin by calculating the optimal contract from the set of contracts (b,p) satisfying $p = [\gamma\delta + (1 - \gamma)\theta]b$; i.e., we can solve the optimization problem

$$\max_{b,p} U^{\delta}(b,p) = \alpha\delta \ln (x_1 + b - p) + \alpha(1 - \delta) \ln (x_2 - p) \text{ subject to}$$

$$p = [\gamma\delta + (1 - \gamma)\theta]b. \tag{22.13}$$

Solving this in the usual way, we get

$$b = \frac{(1 - \delta)x_1}{\gamma\delta + (1 - \gamma)\theta - 1} + \frac{\delta x_2}{\gamma\delta + (1 - \gamma)\theta} \tag{22.14}$$

and

$$p = \frac{(\gamma\delta + (1 - \gamma)\theta)(1 - \delta)x_1}{\gamma\delta + (1 - \gamma)\theta - 1} + \delta x_2. \tag{22.15}$$

In Graph 22.6a, we assumed $\gamma = 2/3$ (with $\delta = 0.25$, $\theta = 0.5$, $x_1 = 10$, and $x_2 = 250$). Plugging these into equations (22.14) and (22.15), we get $(b,p) = (176.25, 58.75)$, which is point D in the graph. Substituting these back into the utility function for δ types, we get utility of 5.1522α. Low risk δ types could alternatively purchase the contract $(b,p) = (85.2, 21.3)$

(represented by point B) that allows them to separate from high risk types, but plugging this contract into the expected utility function for δ types gives utility of 5.1500α, which is just below what the same types can attain by pooling with high risk types. Thus, δ individuals prefer D to B when $\gamma = 2/3$, and by implication for all $\gamma > 2/3$.

Can you demonstrate mathematically that θ types also prefer D to their separating contract A (which has $(b,p)=(240,120)$)?

Exercise 22B.22

Can you demonstrate mathematically that θ types also prefer D to their separating contract A (which has $(b,p)=(240,120)$)?

When $\gamma = 0.5$ (as in Graph 22.5), equations (22.14) and (22.15) give $(b,p) = (154.67,58)$. Can you demonstrate that the indifference curve containing this point lies "below" the indifference curve that δ types can attain by purchasing the contract B that allows them to separate?

Exercise 22B.23

Table 22.2 then reports results for higher values of γ, with the insurance contract approaching that of actuarily fair full insurance for the low risk δ types as the fraction of δ types in the population approaches 1.

Can you explain intuitively the change in pooling contracts as you move down Table 22.2? What happens to the problematic (j) region from our graph as we go down the table?

Exercise 22B.24

22B.4 Nonexistence of a Competitive Equilibrium

In Graph 22.6b, we gave an example of how competitive markets may have difficulty sustaining a pooling equilibrium when γ is sufficiently high such that a separating equilibrium does not exist. In particular, we illustrated for a particular set of indifference curves that, unless there are some "frictions" that make it difficult for individual insurance companies in competitive markets to deviate from the commonly offered "pooled" insurance contract, there exists an incentive for firms to find contracts in the region denoted (j) that is preferred by low risk types to the pooled contract D and that would earn the deviating firm a positive profit. But none of the policies in the (j) region of the graph represent policies that can be sustained as an equilibrium either. Thus, if γ is sufficiently high to make the potential pooling preferable to separating for low risk types, a competitive equilibrium may in fact not exist in this set-up. (For other sets of indifference curves, such an equilibrium does exist, as you might have already worked out in within-chapter-exercise 22B.20.)

Table 22.2: $\delta = 0.25$, $\theta = 0.5$, $x_1 = 10$, $x_2 = 250$

	Pooling Contracts			
γ	p	b	$x_1 + b - p$	$x_2 - p$
2/3	58.75	176.25	127.50	191.25
0.80	59.29	197.62	148.33	190.71
0.85	59.47	206.86	157.39	190.52
0.90	59.66	216.93	167.27	190.34
0.95	59.83	227.93	178.10	190.17
1.00	60.00	240.00	190.00	190.00

How should we interpret such a nonexistence of an equilibrium? It may lead us to conclude that insurance markets like this will simply shift back and forth, with firms moving policies around to attract customers, earning profits briefly before shifting policies again to adjust to changing market conditions. It may imply that markets will search for other ways—more explicit signals and screens—to separate different risk types into different insurance pools. As we have argued in Section A, there may be instances when firms can gain only "noisy" information that can lead to *statistical discrimination*. The insurance industry may also develop particular "norms" or industry standards that constrain the set of insurance contracts that can be offered. Alternatively, you can see how the government could, in principle, solve the nonexistence (or instability) problem by simply offering a single insurance contract (like *D*) and not permitting an insurance industry to operate in this market, or it could regulate the insurance market and mandate that only *D* is offered within that market. None of these "solutions," however, will implement efficiency unless they find ways of costlessly revealing the asymmetric information to all parties and thus allowing the industry to reach the full information competitive equilibrium.

CONCLUSION

The primary problem raised by asymmetric information is what we have called the adverse selection problem. High cost consumers, for instance, "adversely" select into markets with low cost consumers and thus impose a negative externality on low cost consumers by driving up price; or low quality producers "adversely select" into markets with high quality producers, thus lowering price and making it difficult to sustain high quality. We have shown that such adverse selection—sometimes aggravated by moral hazard—will cause over-consumption by some and under-consumption by others, with deadweight losses for society overall. In some instances, we have even seen that asymmetric information can cause entire markets to disappear. Our primary application has been the insurance market where the concept of adverse selection can be presented in a variety of different ways, as can the pooling equilibira that arise in the absence of a resolution to the asymmetric information problem—and separating equilibria that may emerge through signals and screens (or, as discussed in Section B, through self-selection when firms restrict the set of contracts they offer). But we have also seen how understanding adverse selection and information asymmetries can help us understand some fundamental struggles that societies experience, struggles like overcoming the legacy of discrimination. In some of the end-of-chapter exercises, we will further illustrate some tensions between efficiency goals (which have been the focus of the chapter) and other societal priorities (such as those advocated by proponents of universal health insurance based on the premise that everyone is in some moral sense "entitled" to such insurance).

This chapter concludes our treatment of inefficiencies that may arise in *competitive* markets. In Chapters 18 through 20, such inefficiencies resulted from policy-induced distortions of market prices; in Chapter 21, they arose from market prices not fully capturing all marginal social benefits or costs due to the presence of externalities; and in this chapter, inefficiencies emerged from the presence of asymmetric information, with one side of the market able to potentially "take advantage" of the other side because of more knowledge that is directly relevant to the market transaction. In the case of policy-induced price distortions, we suggested that an understanding of how these distortions arise may allow governments to find less distortionary ways to accomplish their goals. In the case of externalities or asymmetric information, on the other hand, we discussed ways in which additional markets, nonmarket "civil society" institutions, and governments may find ways of improving (in terms of efficiency) on market outcomes.

We will now move to Part V where we will begin to think about how to model behavior in economic settings where individuals are not "small" and where strategic thinking becomes important. To some extent, we have already begun to head down this road: In our treatment of adverse selection, for instance, we thought about whether individual firms might be able to benefit by deviating from the equilibrium behavior of other firms, and in our treatment of the Coase Theorem in the previous chapter, we thought about individuals negotiating after courts assign property rights. But from now on, we will let go of any notion of perfectly competitive behavior and focus more squarely on the strategic element of economic life. In the settings we will investigate, individuals can no longer take their economic environment as "given" because their actions help shape the economic environment in discernable ways. This will introduce the concept of "market power" into our thinking and will lead us away from thinking of "price-taking" behavior. It will also open another way in which markets fail to achieve efficient outcomes: when markets are no longer perfectly competitive and thus some agents employ market power to advance their own interests.

END-OF-CHAPTER EXERCISES

22.1† Consider again the example of grade insurance. Suppose students know whether they are typically *A*, *B*, *C*, *D*, or *F* students, with *A* students having a 75% chance of getting an *A* and a 25% chance of getting a *B*; with *B*, *C*, and *D* students having a 25% chance of getting a grade above their usual, a 50% chance of getting their usual grade and a 25% chance of getting a grade below their usual; and with *F* students having a 25% chance of getting a *D* and a 75% chance of getting an *F*. Assume the same bell-shaped grade distribution as in the text; i.e., in the absence of grade insurance, 10% of grades are *A*'s, 25% are *B*'s, 30% are *C*'s, 25% are *D*'s, and 10% are *F*'s.

A. Suppose, as in the text, that grade insurance companies operate in a competitive market and incur a cost *c* for every level of grade that is changed for those holding an insurance policy. And suppose that *A* through *D* students are willing to pay $1.5c$ to insure they get their usual grade and $0.5c$ for each grade level above the usual; *F* students are willing to pay $2c$ to get a *D* and $0.5c$ for each grade level above that.

   a. Suppose first that your instructor allows me only to sell *A* insurance in your classroom. Will I be able to sell any?

   b. Suppose next that your professor only allowed me to sell *B*-insurance. Would I be able to sell any?

   c. What if I were only allowed to sell *C*- or *D*-insurance?

   d.* If they were the only policies offered, could policies *A* and *D* attract customers in a competitive equilibrium at the same time? In equilibrium, who would buy which policy? (*Hint*: Only *C*, *D*, and *F* students buy insurance in equilibrium.)

   e.* If they were the only policies offered, could policies *A* and *C* attract customers in a competitive equilibrium at the same time? (*Hint*: The answer is no.)

   f.* If they were the only policies offered, could policies *B* and *D* attract customers in a competitive equilibrium at the same time? (*Hint*: The answer is again no.)

   g. Without doing any further analysis, do you think it is possible to have an equilibrium in which more than two insurance policies could attract customers?

   h. Are any of the equilibria you identified efficient? (*Hint*: Consider the marginal cost and marginal benefit of each level of insurance above insuring that each student gets his or her typical grade.)

B. In A(d), you identified a particular equilibrium in which *A*- and *D*-insurance are sold when it was not possible to sell just *A*-insurance.

   a. How is this conceptually similar to the self-selecting separating equilibrium we introduced in Section B of the text?

   b. How is it different?

22.2 Suppose that everything in the grade insurance market is as described in exercise 22.1. But instead of taking the asymmetric information as fixed, we will now ask what can happen if students can transmit information. Assume throughout that no insurance company will sell *A*-insurance to students other than *A* students, *B*-insurance to students other than *B* students, etc. whenever they know what type students are.

A. Suppose that a student can send an accurate "signal" to me about the type of student he is by expending effort that costs *c*. Furthermore, suppose that each student can signal that he is a better student than he actually is by expending additional effort *c* for each level above his true level. For instance, a "*C* student" can signal his true type by expending effort *c* but can falsely signal that he is a "*B* student" by expending effort $2c$ and that he is an "*A* student" by expending $3c$.

   a. Suppose everyone sends truthful signals to insurance companies and that insurance companies know the signals to be truthful. What will be the prices of *A*-insurance, *B*-insurance, *C*-insurance, and *D*-insurance?

   b. How much surplus does each student type get (taking into account the cost *c* of sending the truthful signal)?

   c. Now investigate whether this "truth-telling" can be part of a real equilibrium. Could *B* students get more surplus by sending a costlier false signal? Could *C*, *D*, or *F* students?

---

*conceptually challenging
**computationally challenging
†solutions in Study Guide

   d.   Would the equilibrium be any different if it was costless to tell the truth but it costs c to
        exaggerate the truth by each level? (Assume F-students would be willing to pay $1.5c$ for
        getting an F just as other students are willing to pay $1.5c$ to get their usual grade.)

   e.   Is the equilibrium in part (d) efficient? What about the equilibrium in part (c)? (*Hint*: Think
        about the marginal cost and marginal benefit of providing more insurance to any type.)

   f.   Can you explain intuitively why signaling in this case addresses the problem faced by the
        insurance market?

B.   In Section B of the text, we considered the case of insurance policies (b, p) in an environment where
         the "bad outcome" in the absence of insurance is x_1 and the "good" outcome in the absence of
         insurance is x_2. We further assumed two risk types: δ types that face the bad outcome with probability
         δ and θ types that face the bad outcome with probability θ, where $\theta > \delta$.

   a.   Suppose that both types are risk averse and have state-independent tastes. Show that, under
        actuarially fair insurance contracts, they will choose the same benefit level b but will pay
        different insurance premiums.

   b.   Suppose throughout the rest of the problem that insurance companies never sell more than full
        insurance; i.e., they never sell policies with b higher than what you determined in (a). In
        Section B, we focused on self-selecting equilibria where insurance companies restrict the
        contracts they offer in order to get different types of consumers to self-select into different
        insurance policies. In Section A, as in part A of this question, we focused on explicit signals
        that consumers might be able to send to let insurance companies know what type they are.
        How much would a θ type be willing to pay to send a credible signal that she is a δ type if this
        will permit her access to the actuarially fair full insurance contract for δ types?

   c.   Suppose for the rest of the problem that $u(x) = \ln x$ is a function that permits us to represent
        everyone's tastes over gambles in the expected utility form. Let $x_1 = 10$, $x_2 = 250$,
        $\delta = 0.25$, and $\theta = 0.5$ as in the text. Suppose further that we are currently in a self-selecting
        equilibrium of the type that was discussed in the text (where not all actuarily fair policies are
        offered to δ types).[11] How much would a δ type be willing to pay to send a credible signal to
        an insurance company to let them know she is in fact a δ type?

   d.   Suppose we are currently in the separating equilibrium, but a new way of signaling your type
        has just been discovered. Let c_t be the cost of a signal that reveals your true type and let c_f
        be the cost of sending a false signal that you are a different type. For what ranges of c_t and c_f will
        the efficient allocation of insurance in this market be restored through consumer signaling?

   e.   Suppose c_t and c_f are within the ranges you specified in (d). Has efficiency been restored?

22.3   In exercise 22.2, we showed how an efficient equilibrium with a complete set of insurance markets can
           be reestablished with truthful signaling of information by consumers. We now illustrate that signaling
           might not always accomplish this.

   A.   Begin by once again assuming the same set-up as in exercise 22.1. Suppose that it costs c to truthfully
            reveal who you are and $0.25c$ more for each level of exaggeration; i.e., for a C student, it costs c to
            reveal that he is a C student, $1.25c$ to falsely signal that he is a B student, and $1.5c$ to falsely signal
            that he is an A student.

      a.   Begin by assuming that insurance companies are pricing A-, B-, C-, and D-insurance competi-
           tively under the assumption that the signals they receive are truthful. Would any student wish
           to send false signals in this case?

      b.* Could A-insurance be sold in equilibrium (where premiums have to end up at zero-profit rates
           given who is buying insurance)? (*Hint*: Illustrate what happens to surplus for students as
           premiums adjust to reach the zero-profit level.)

      c.* Could B-insurance be sold in equilibrium? What about C- and D-insurance?

      d.* Based on your answers to (b) and (c), can you explain why the equilibrium in this case is to
           have only D-insurance sold, and bought by both D and F students? Is it efficient?

---

[11]Recall from the text that, in this separating equilibrium, δ types bought the insurance policy $(b, p) = (85.2, 21.3)$. While the
u function in the text is multiplied by α, we showed that the indifference curves are immune to the value α takes, and so we
lose nothing in this problem by setting it to 1.

e. Now suppose that the value students attach to grades is different: They would be willing to pay as much as $4c$ to guarantee their usual grade and $0.9c$ more for each level of grade above that. Suppose further that the cost of telling the truth about yourself is still c but the cost of exaggerating is $0.1c$ for each level of exaggeration about the truth. How much surplus does each student type get from signaling that he is an A student if A-insurance is priced at $2c$?

f. Suppose that insurance companies believe that any applicant for B-insurance is a random student from the population of B, C, D, and F students; that any applicant for C-insurance is a random student from the population of C, D, and F students; and any applicant for D-insurance is a random student from the population of D and F students. How would they competitively price B-, C-, and D-insurance?

g. Suppose that, in addition, insurance companies do not sell insurance to students who did not send a signal as to what type they are. Under these assumptions, is it an equilibrium for everyone to signal that they are A students?

h. There are two sources of inefficiency in this equilibrium. Can you distinguish between them?

B. In exercise 22.2B, we introduced a new "signaling technology" that restored the efficient allocation of insurance from an initially inefficient allocation in a self-selecting separating equilibrium. Suppose that insurance companies believe anyone who does not send a signal that she is a δ type must be a θ type.

a. Suppose that c_f is below the range you calculated in B(d) of exercise 22.2. Can you describe a pooling equilibrium in which both types fully insure and both types send a signal that they are δ types?

b. In order for this to be an equilibrium, why are the beliefs about what a nonsignal would mean important? What would happen if companies believed that both types are equally likely not to signal?

c. *True or False*: For an equilibrium like the one you described in part (a) to be an equilibrium, it matters what firms believe about events that never happen in equilibrium.

22.4† Assume again the basic set-up from exercise 22.1.

A. We will now investigate the role of firm *screens* as opposed to consumer signals.

a. Suppose that an insurance company can *screen* students. More precisely, suppose an insurance company can, for a fee of c, obtain a student's transcript and thus know what type a student is. If insurance companies will only sell insurance of type i to students who have been screened as type i, what would be the equilibrium insurance premium for each insurance assuming perfect competition (and no recurring fixed costs)?

b. Would each insurance type be offered and bought in equilibrium?

c. How high would the cost of obtaining transcripts have to be in order for the insurance market to collapse?

d. In the case of *signaling*, we had to consider the possibility of "pooling equilibria" in which the same insurance is sold to different types of students who care sufficiently for the higher grade to each be willing to pay the zero-profit premium as well as, for some, to pay the cost of falsely signaling their type. If insurance companies can *screen* for the relevant information, could it ever be the case, assuming that individuals care sufficiently much about higher grades, that several types will get the same insurance? (*Hint*: Suppose an insurance company attempted to price a policy such that several types would get positive surplus by buying this policy. Does another insurance company have an incentive to compete some of the potential customers for that policy away?)

e. Does the separating equilibrium that results from screening of customers depend on how many of each different type are in the class, and what exactly the curve is that is imposed in the class?

f. Suppose we currently have a market in which a large number of insurers sell the different insurance types at the zero-profit price after screening customers to make sure insurance of type i is only sold to type i. Now suppose a new insurance company enters the market and devises "B-insurance for C students." Will the new company succeed in finding customers?

g. Would your answer to (f) change if students are willing to pay $1.5c$ to insure their usual grade and c (rather than $0.5c$) for each grade above the usual?

h. *True or False*: When insurance companies screen, the same insurance policy will never be sold to different student types at the same price, but it may be the case that students of different types will insure for the same grade.

B.* Now consider the introduction of screening into the self-selection separating equilibrium of Section B of the text. As in the text, suppose that consumption in the absence of insurance is 10 in the bad state and 250 in the good state and that δ types have a probability of 0.25 of reaching the bad state while θ types have a probability of 0.5 of reaching that state. Suppose further that individuals are risk averse and their tastes are state-independent.

  a.   Instead of graphing b on the horizontal and p on the vertical axis, begin by graphing x_2 (consumption in the good state) on the horizontal and x_1 (consumption in the bad state) on the vertical. Indicate with an "endowment" point E where consumption would be in the absence of insurance.

  b.   Illustrate the actuarily fair insurance contracts for the two types of consumers, and indicate the two insurance policies that are offered in a self-selection separating equilibrium.

  c.   Suppose a "screening industry"—an industry of firms that can identify what type an insurance applicant is for a cost of k per applicant—emerges. If an insurance firm gives applicants the option of paying k (as an application fee) to enable the company to pay a screening firm for this information, would θ types pay it?

  d.   What is the highest that k can be in order for δ types to agree to pay the fee? Illustrate this in your graph.

  e.   The applicant's decision of whether or not to pay the fee is really a decision of whether to send a signal. How is this different from the type of signal we analyzed in exercise 22.3? In particular, why does θ's signaling behavior matter in exercise 22.3 but not here?

  f.   Suppose that instead of asking applicants to pay the screening fee, the insurance company paid to get the information from the screening firms for *all* applicants before determining the terms of the insurance contract they offered. Will the highest that k can be to change the self-selection separating equilibrium differ from what you concluded in part (d)?

  g.   Will the insurance allocation be efficient if the screening industry ends up selling information to insurance firms?

22.5* We developed our first graphical model of adverse selection in the context of car insurance in Section 22A.2 where we assumed that the marginal cost MC^1 of providing car insurance to unsafe drivers of type 1 is greater than the MC^2 of providing insurance to safe drivers of type 2.

  A. Continue with the assumption that $MC^1 > MC^2$. In this exercise, we will investigate how our conclusions in the text are affected by altering our assumption that $D^1 = D^2$, i.e., our assumption that the demand (and marginal willingness to pay) curves for our two driver types are the same.

  a.   Suppose demand curves continue to be linear with slope α, but the vertical intercept for type 1 drivers is A^1 while the intercept for type 2 drivers is A^2. Suppose first that $A^1 > A^2 > MC^1 > MC^2$. Illustrate the equilibrium. Would p^* still be halfway between MC^1 and MC^2 as was the case in the text?

  b.   Identify the deadweight loss from asymmetric information in your graph.

  c.   What is the equilibrium if instead $A^2 > A^1 > MC^1 > MC^2$? How does p^* compare to what you depicted in (a)?

  d.   Identify again the deadweight loss from asymmetric information.

  e.   What would have to be true about the relationship of A^1, A^2, MC^1, and MC^2 for safe drivers not to buy insurance in equilibrium?

  f.   What would have to be true about the relationship of A^1, A^2, MC^1, and MC^2 for unsafe drivers not to buy insurance in equilibrium?

  B. In our model of Section B, we assumed that the same consumption/utility relationship $u(x)$ can be used for high cost θ and low cost δ types to represent their tastes over risky gambles with an expected utility function.

  a.   Did this assumption imply that tastes over risky gambles were the same for the two types?

  b.   Illustrate the actuarily fair insurance contracts in a graph with x_2 (the consumption in the good state) on the horizontal and x_1 (the consumption in the bad state) on the vertical. Then illustrate the choice set created by a set of insurance contracts that all satisfy the same terms; i.e., insurance contracts of the form $p = \beta b$ (where b is the benefit level and p is the premium).

  c.   Can you tell whether θ or δ types will demand more insurance along this choice set?

    d.   *True or False*: Our θ types would be analogous to the car insurance consumers of type 1 in part A of the exercise while our δ types would be analogous to consumers of type 2.

    e.   Suppose there are an equal number of δ and θ types and suppose that the insurance industry for some reason offered a single full set of insurance contracts $p = \beta b$ and that this allowed them to earn zero profits. Would the $p = \beta b$ line lie halfway between the actuarily fair contract lines for the two risk types?

    f.   Suppose instead that the insurance industry offered a single insurance policy that provides full insurance, and that firms again make zero profits. Would the contract line that contains this policy lie halfway between the two actuarily fair contract lines in your graph? What is different from the previous part?

22.6   **Everyday Application:** *Non-Random "Selection" Is Everywhere*: The problem in our initial discussion of A-grade insurance markets was that adverse selection led to non-randomness in the insurance pool: Although almost everyone was willing to pay the insurance premium that would have made zero expected profit for insurance companies with a randomly selected insurance pool, no one was willing to pay as higher cost students adversely selected into the pool. This kind of *non-random selection* is, however, not confined to insurance markets but lies at the heart of much that we see around us.[12] (Both part A and part B of this exercise can be done without having done Section B in the chapter.)

EVERYDAY APPLICATION

A. Consider the following examples and describe the non-random selection that can cause observers to reach the wrong conclusion just as insurance companies would charge the "wrong" premiums if they did not take into account the effect of non-random selection.

    a.   Suppose I want to know the average weight of fish in a lake. So you take out a boat and fish with a net that has 1-inch holes. You fish all day, weigh the fish, take the average, and report back to me.

    b.   A TV report tells us the following: A recent study revealed that people who eat broccoli twice a week live an average of 6 years longer than people who do not. The reporter concludes that eating broccoli increases live expectancy.

    c.   A cigarette company commissions a study on the impact of smoking on fitness. To compare the average fitness of smokers to that of nonsmokers, they recruit smokers and nonsmokers at a fitness center. In particular, they recruit smokers from the aerobics program and they recruit nonsmokers from a weight-loss class. They find the "surprising result" that smokers are more fit than nonsmokers.

    d.   "Four out of five dentists" recommend a particular toothbrush, from a sample of dentists that are provided free dental products by the company that makes the toothbrushes.

    e.   When surveyed after one year of buying and using a facial cream, 95% of women attest to its effectiveness at making their skin look younger.

    f.   Children in private schools perform better than children in public schools. Thus, concludes an observer, private schools are better than public schools. (Careful: The selection bias may go in either direction!)

    g.   A study compares the test scores of children from high income and low income households and demonstrates that children from high income households score significantly higher than children from low income households. An observer concludes that we can narrow this test score gap by redistributing income from high income families to low income families.

B. It is often said that the "gold standard" of social science research is to have a randomized experiment where some subjects are assigned to the "treatment" group while others are randomly assigned to the "control" group. Here is an example: A school voucher program is limited to 1,000 voucher participants, but 2,000 families apply, with each having their child tested on a standard exam. The administrators of the program then randomly select 1,000 families that get the voucher—or the "treatment"—and treat the remaining 1,000 families as the "control" group. One year later, they test the children again and compare the change in average test scores of children from the two groups. They find that those who were randomly assigned to the "treatment" group have, on average, significantly higher test scores.

---

[12]Research studies often refer to the erroneous conclusions one might draw as a result of such non-random selection as *selection bias*. If you take an econometrics course, you will learn much about how to statistically adjust for such biases. Many of the these techniques emanate from work by Nobel Laureate James Heckman (1944–).

a.   Suppose that all 1,000 children in each group participated in the testing that led to the computation of average score changes for each group. Would you be comfortable concluding that it was likely that access to the voucher program *caused* an increase in student performance?

b.   Suppose that only 800 students in each group participated in the testing at the end of the first year of the program, but they were randomly selected within each group. Would your answer to (a) change if only the average change in test scores for these students were used?

c.   Suppose that families had a choice in terms of whether to participate in the testing at the end of the year. But families in the "treatment" group were told that the only way they can continue using the voucher for another year is to have their child tested; and families in the "control" group were told that some new slots in the voucher program would open up (because some of the voucher families have dropped out of the program) but the only way the families in the "control" group get another chance to be picked to receive a voucher is to have their child tested. In the "treatment" group, who do you think is more likely to self-select to have their child tested: families that had a good experience with their voucher, or families that had a bad experience?

d.   In the "control" group, who do you think is more likely to self-select to have their child tested: families that had a good experience the previous year outside the voucher program, or families that had a bad experience?

e.   Suppose again that 800 students from each group participated in the testing, but now you know about the incentives that families have for showing up to have their child tested. How does this affect your answer to (b)?

f.   From a researcher's perspective, how can the non-random selection into testing be described as "adverse" selection that clouds what you can conclude from looking at average test score differences between the two groups? How is this example similar to part A(c)?

22.7   **Business Application:** *Competitive Provision of Health Insurance*: Consider the challenge of providing health insurance to a population with different probabilities of getting sick.

A.   Suppose that, as in our car insurance example, there are two consumer types: consumers of type 1 that are likely to get sick, and consumers of type 2 that are relatively healthy. Let x represent the level of health insurance, with $x = 0$ implying no insurance and higher levels of x indicating increasingly generous health insurance benefits. Assume that each consumer type has linear demand curves (equal to marginal willingness to pay), with d^1 representing the demand curve for a single consumer of type 1 and d^2 representing the demand curve for a single consumer of type 2. Suppose further that the marginal cost of providing additional health coverage to an individual is constant, with $MC^1 > MC^2$.

a.   For simplicity, suppose throughout that d^1 and d^2 have the same slope. Suppose further, unless otherwise stated, that d^1 has higher intercept than d^2. Do you think it is reasonable to assume that type 1 has higher demand for insurance?

b.   Begin by drawing a graph with d^1, d^2, MC^1, and MC^2 assuming that the vertical intercepts of both demand curves lie above MC^1. Indicate the efficient level of insurance $\bar{x}^1$ and $\bar{x}^2$ for the two types.

c.   Suppose the industry offers any level of x at price $p = MC^1$. Illustrate on your graph the consumer surplus that type 1 individuals will get if this were the only way to buy insurance and they buy their optimal policy A. How much consumer surplus will type 2 individuals get?

d.   Next, suppose you want to offer an additional insurance contract B that earns zero profit if bought only by type 2 consumers, is preferred by type 2 individuals to A, and makes type 1 consumers just as well off as they are under the options from part (c). Identify B in your graph.

e.   Suppose for a moment that it is an equilibrium for the industry to offer only contracts A and B (and suppose that the actual B is just slightly to the left of the B you identified in part (d)). *True or False*: While insurance companies do not know what type consumers are when they walk into the insurance office to buy a policy, the companies will know what type of consumer they made a contract with after the consumer leaves.

f.   In order for this to be an equilibrium, it must be the case that it is not possible for an insurance company to offer a "pooling price" that makes at least zero profit while attracting both type 1 and 2 consumers. (Such a policy has a single price p^* that lies between MC^1 and MC^2.) Note that the demand curves graphed thus far were for only one individual of each type. What additional information would you have to know in order to know whether the zero-profit price p^* would attract both types?

   g.   *True or False*: The greater the fraction of consumers that are of type 1, the less likely it is that such a "pooling price" exists.

   h.   Suppose that no such pooling price exists. Assuming that health insurance firms cannot observe the health conditions of their customers, would it be a competitive equilibrium for the industry to offer contracts A and B? Would this be a pooling or a separating equilibrium?

   i.   Would you still be able to identify a contract B that satisfies the conditions in (d) if $d^1 = d^2$? What if $d^1 < d^2$?

B. Part A of this exercise attempts to formalize a key intuition we covered in Section B of the text with a different type of model for insurance.

   a.   Rather than starting our analysis by distinguishing between marginal costs of different types, our model from Section B starts by specifying the probabilities θ and δ that type 1 and type 2 individuals will find themselves in the "bad state" that they are insuring against. Mapping this to our model from part A of this exercise, with type 1 and 2 defined as in part A, what is the relationship between δ and θ?

   b.   To fit the story with the model from Section B, we can assume that what matters about bad health shocks is the impact they have on consumption, and that tastes are state independent. (We will relax this assumption in exercise 22.8.) Suppose we can, for both types, write tastes over risky gambles as von-Neumann Morgenstern expected utility functions that employ the same function $u(y)$ as "utility of consumption" (with consumption denoted y). Write out the expected utility functions for the two types.

   c.   Does the fact that we can use the same $u(y)$ to express expected utilities for both types imply that the two types have the same tastes over risky gambles, and thus the same demand for insurance?

   d.   If insurance companies could tell who is what type, they would (in a competitive equilibrium) simply charge a price equal to each type's marginal cost. How is this captured in the model developed in Section B of the text?

   e.   In the separating equilibrium we identified in part A, we had insurance companies providing the contract A that is efficient for type 1 individuals but providing an inefficient contract B to type 2. Draw the model from Section B of the text and illustrate the same A and B contracts. How are they exactly analogous to what we derived in part A?

   f.   In part A we also investigated the possibility of a potential pooling price, or pooling contract, breaking the separating equilibrium in which A and B are offered. Illustrate in the different model here how the same factors are at play in determining whether such a pooling price or contract exists.

   g.   Evaluate again the *True/False* statement in part A(g).

22.8*† Policy Application: *Expanding Health Insurance Coverage*: Some countries are struggling with the problem of expanding the fraction of the population that has good health insurance.

**POLICY
APPLICATION**

A. Continue with the set-up first introduced in exercise 22.7 including the definition of x as the amount of insurance coverage bought by an inidividual. Assume throughout that demand for health insurance by the relatively healthy (type 2) is lower than demand for health insurance by the relatively sick (type 1); i.e., $d^1 > d^2$.

   a.   Illustrate d^1, d^2, MC^1, and MC^2 and identify the contracts A and B from exercise 22.7.

   b.   Suppose that the fraction of relatively sick (type 2) consumers is sufficiently high such that no pooling contract can keep this from being an equilibrium. On the MC^1 line, indicate all the contracts that can be offered in this equilibrium (even though only A is chosen). Similarly, indicate on the MC^2 line all the contracts that can be offered in this equilibrium (even though only B is chosen).

   c.   *True or False*: Insurance companies in this equilibrium restrict the amount of insurance that can be bought at the price $p = MC^2$ in order to keep type 1 consumers from buying at that price.

   d.   Why is the resulting separating equilibrium inefficient? How big is the deadweight loss?

   e.   Suppose that the government regulates this health insurance market in the following way: It identifies the zero-profit pooling price p^* and requires insurance companies to charge p^* for each unit of x but does not mandate how much x every consumer consumes. Illustrate in your graph how much insurance type 1 and type 2 consumers will consume under this policy. Does overall insurance coverage increase or decrease?

    f.   How much does consumer surplus for each type change as a result of this regulation? Does overall surplus increase?

    g.   *True or False*: This policy is efficiency enhancing but does not lead to efficiency.

    h.   It may be difficult for the government to implement the above price regulation p^* because it does not have enough information to do so. Some have suggested that the government instead set the insurance level to some $\bar{x}$ and then let insurance companies compete on pricing this insurance level. Could you suggest, in a new graph, a level of $\bar{x}$ that will result in greater efficiency than regulating price? (You need to do this on a new graph for the following reason: If the government sets $\bar{x}$ between the amounts consumed by type 1 and 2 under the zero-profit price regulation p^*, the resulting competitive price $\bar{p}$ should be lower than p^*.)

B. Now consider again whether we can find analogous conclusions in the model from Section B as modified in exercise 22.7.

    a.   Interpreting the model as in exercise 22.7, illustrate the separating equilibrium in a graph with the insurance benefit b on the horizontal axis and the insurance premium p on the vertical. Include in your graph a zero-profit pooling contract line that makes the separation of types an equilibrium outcome.

    b.   How would you interpret the price regulation proposed in A(e) in the context of this model?

    c.   Illustrate in your graph how insurance coverage will increase if the government implements this policy.

    d.   Now consider the same problem in a graph with y_2, the consumption level when healthy, on the horizontal axis and y_1, the consumption level when sick, on the vertical. Illustrate the "endowment point" $E = (\bar{y}_1, \bar{y}_2)$ that both types face in the absence of insurance.

    e.   Illustrate the actuarily fair insurance contracts for type 1 and 2 consumers. Then indicate where the separating equilibrium contracts A and B lie in the graph assuming state-independent tastes.

    f.   Introduce into your graph a zero-profit pooling contract line such that the separating equilibrium is indeed an equilibrium. Then illustrate how the proposed government regulation affects the choices of both types of consumers.

    g.   Suppose that, instead of regulating price, the government set an insurance benefit level $\bar{b}$ (as in part A(h)) and then allowed the competitive price to emerge. Where in your graph would the resulting contract lie if it fully insures both types?

    h.   Suppose next that tastes were state-dependent, with $u_1(y)$ and $u_2(y)$ the functions (for evaluating consumption when sick and when healthy) that we need to use in order to arrive at our expected utility function. If u_1 and u_2 are the same for both consumer types, does our main conclusion that the price regulation will cause an increase in insurance coverage change?

22.9 **Policy Application:** *Moral Hazard versus Adverse Selection in Health Care Reform*: We mentioned moral hazard only briefly, and primarily in the context of how this might aggravate the adverse selection problem. In this exercise, we explore moral hazard a bit more in the context of health insurance. (Both part A and part B of this exercise can be done without having done Section B in the chapter.)

A. Suppose throughout that individuals do not engage in riskier life-styles as a result of obtaining health insurance.

    a.   How does this assumption eliminate one form of moral hazard that we might worry about?

    b.   Suppose that a unit of health care x is such that it can be provided at constant marginal cost that is the same for all patients. Illustrate a patient's demand curve for x as well as the MC curve for providing x.

    c.   Suppose demand for health care services is equal to marginal willingness to pay. If the patient pays out-of-pocket for health care, how much would he or she consume assuming that health care services are competitively priced (with health care providers facing negligible recurring fixed costs)?

    d.   Suppose next that the patient has insurance coverage that pays for all health-related expenses. How much x does he or she consume now?

    e.   Moral hazard refers to the change in behavior that arises once a person enters a contract. Have you just uncovered a source of moral hazard in the health insurance market? Explain how this results in inefficiency.

f.   Now replicate your picture two times: Once for a patient where the moral hazard problem is small, and once for a patient where it is large. If insurance companies cannot tell the difference between these two individuals, how does this asymmetric information potentially give rise to adverse selection?

B. Consider two alternative proposals for health care reform: Under proposal *A*, the government mandates that everyone must buy health insurance, restricts insurance companies to provide a single type of policy with generous benefits, and then lets the companies compete for customers to sell that policy. Under proposal *B*, the government sets up "health care savings accounts" for everyone and allows insurance companies to offer only policies with high "deductibles." Under this latter policy, consumers would then pay for most health-related expenditures using funds in their health care savings accounts and could convert any balance to retirement accounts when they reach the age of 65 (and thus become eligible for government health care for the elderly, called Medicare in the United States). Insurance under policy *B* is therefore aimed only at "catastrophic" events that cost more than the deductible of the policy.

    a.   Suppose you were concerned about excessive health care costs. How would the two different proposals aim at addressing this?

    b.   If you thought the primary problem arose from the moral hazard analyzed in part A of this exercise, which policy would you favor?

    c.   Suppose instead that you thought the primary problem arose from the rising cost of health insurance linked to increasingly severe adverse selection (unrelated to the moral hazard problem analyzed in part A) and a growing pool of uninsured people. Which policy might you more likely favor?

22.10 Policy Application: *Statistical Profiling in Random Car Searches*: Local law enforcement officials sometimes engage in "random" searches of cars to look for illegal substances. When one looks at the data of who is actually searched, however, the pattern of searches often does not look random.

POLICY APPLICATION

A. In what follows, assume that random searches have a deterrent effect; i.e., the more likely someone believes he or she is going to be searched, the less likely he or she is to engage in transporting illegal substances.

    a.   Suppose first that it has been documented that, *all else being equal*, illegal substances are more likely to be transported in pick-up trucks than in passenger cars. Put differently, if pick-up truck owners are searched with the same probability as passenger car owners, law enforcement officials will be more likely to find illegal substances when they randomly search a pick-up truck than when they randomly search a passenger vehicle. If the objective by police is to find the most illegal substances given that they have limited resources (and thus cannot search everyone), is it optimal for them to search randomly?

    b.   Suppose the police force decides to allocate its limited resources by searching pick-up trucks with probability δ and passenger cars with probability γ (where $\delta > \gamma$). After a few months of this policy, the police discover that they find on average 2.9 grams of illegal substances per pick-up-truck search and 1.5 grams of illegal substances per passenger vehicle. Given their limited resources, how would you advise the police to change their search policy in order to increase the amount of drugs found?

    c.   Given your answer to (b), what has to be true about the probability of finding illegal substances in pick-up trucks and passenger cars *if* the search probabilities for the two types of vehicles are set optimally (relative to the police's objective to find the most illegal substances)?

    d.   If you simply observe that $\delta > \gamma$, can you conclude that the police are inherently biased against pick-up trucks owners? Why or why not?

    e.   What would have to be true about the average yield of illegal substances per search for the different types of vehicles for you to argue that the police were inherently biased against pick-up trucks?

    f.   Could it be the case that $\delta > \gamma$ *and* the police show behavior inherently biased against passenger cars?

    g.   We have used the emotionally neutral categories of "pick-up trucks" and "passenger vehicles." Now consider the more empirically relevant case of "minority neighborhoods" and "nonminority neighborhoods," with law enforcement often searching cars in the former with significantly higher probability than in the latter. Can you argue that such behavior by law enforcement officials is not inherently racist in the sense of being motivated by animosity against one group, but that instead it could be explained simply as a matter of *statistical discrimination* that maximizes the effectiveness of car searches in deterring the trafficking in illegal substances? What evidence might you look for to make your case?

B. Suppose that the police force has sufficient resources to conduct 100 car searches per day and that half of all vehicles are pick-up trucks and half are passenger cars. The probability of finding an illegal substance in a pick-up truck is $p_t(n_t) = 9/(90 + n_t)$ where n_t is the number of pick-up truck searches conducted. The probability of finding an illegal substance in a passenger car is $p_c(n_c) = 1/(10 + n_c)$ (where n_c is the number of car searches conducted).

a. Suppose that the objective of the police is to maximize the number of interdictions of illegal substances. Write down the optimization problem, with n_t and n_c as choice variables and the constraint that $n_t + n_c = 100$.

b. According to the police's objective function, how many trucks should be searched per day? How many passenger vehicles?

c. If law enforcement conducts searches as calculated in (b), what is the probability of interdicting illegal substances in pick-up trucks? What is the probability of interdicting such substances in passenger cars?

d. If law enforcement officials search trucks and cars at the rates you derived in (b), how many illegal substance interdictions would on average occur every day?

e. How many of each type of car would on average be searched each day if the police instead searched vehicles randomly?

f. If the police conducted random searches, what would be the probability of finding illegal substances in each of the two vehicle types? How does this compare to your answer to (c)?

g. How many illegal substance interdictions per day would on average occur if the police conducted random searches instead of what you derived in (d)?

h. Why is your answer to (d) different than your answer to (g)?

i. Insurance companies charge higher insurance rates to young drivers than to middle-aged drivers. How is their behavior similar to the behavior by law enforcement that searches pick-up trucks more than passenger cars in (b)?

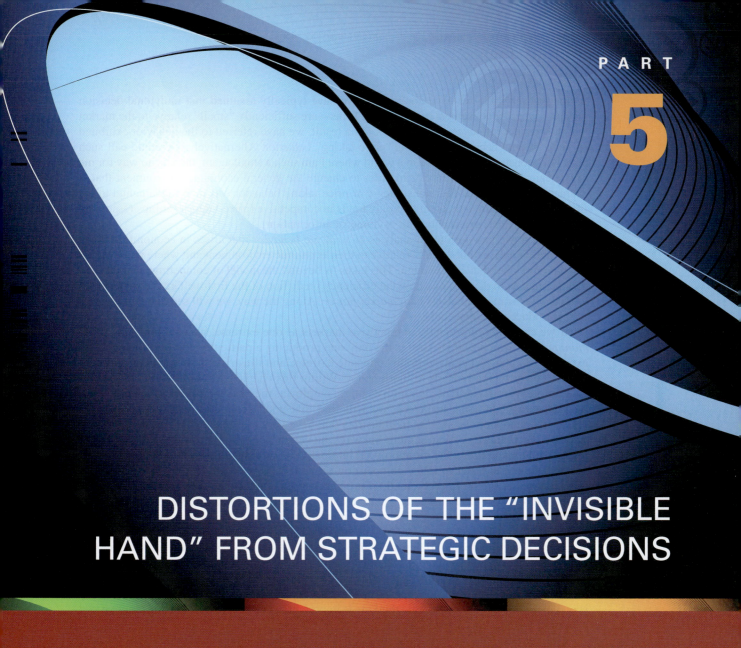

DISTORTIONS OF THE "INVISIBLE HAND" FROM STRATEGIC DECISIONS

In almost everything we have done so far, we have typically assumed that individual decision makers—whether consumers or workers or firms—are sufficiently "small" relative to the market that they cannot influence market prices. As a result, we have referred to the behavior exhibited by such "small" decision makers as "price-taking" behavior. Alternatively, we could call such behavior "nonstrategic" because in a world where I am such a small agent, there is no way for me to strategically alter my behavior in order to change the general economic environment that is characterized by prices. This nonstrategic or price-taking behavior was then fundamental to the first welfare theorem, a theorem that only holds in competitive (price-taking) settings (assuming no price distortions, externalities, or asymmetric information).

In Part 5, we now turn to an analysis of *strategic behavior* that arises in economic settings where individuals are not "small" relative to their economic environment and where their actions can therefore alter that environment. This takes us beyond the model of competitive markets and then permits us to demonstrate how the efficiency prediction of the first welfare theorem ceases to hold when some individuals gain *market power*. Along the way, we will see that this requires us to introduce some new tools.

If we can think of perfectly competitive markets as one extreme, we can think of perfect *monopoly* (in which a single firm is the only one producing a particular good) as the opposite extreme. Chapter 23 begins with this opposite extreme and illustrates how such concentrated market power typically leads to inefficiency. Within this chapter, we will be able to investigate different strategies that monopolists might employ as they use their market power to their own advantage. In some instances, we will find that good economic reasons exist for the presence of a monopoly, such as in industries that have very high fixed costs. In such circumstances, the policy question centers on ways in which policy might alleviate deadweight losses while maintaining the monopoly or, alternatively, on ways in which fixed costs can be publicly shared in order to allow competition on variable costs. In other cases, we will find that monopolies are more problematic if not checked by at least the threat of outside competition, but we will also find that governments face informational problems that make it nontrivial to determine in any given case what policy is most desirable from an efficiency perspective.

As we discuss different pricing strategies by monopolists, we begin to use some of the reasoning that underlies *game theory* without yet calling it that or being explicit about it. Much of game theory is common sense, which is why we can begin to use it (and in fact have used it a few times quite informally in earlier chapters) without fully defining it first. But as we get deeper into economic situations where strategic thinking is important, it is useful to develop this intuitive tool a bit first. We do so in Chapter 24.

Over the past 50 or so years, game theory has emerged in economics and other social sciences as the primary tool for thinking about strategic behavior. It models economic situations in the form of games in which players face incentives similar to those that individuals with market power face in the real world. Within a game theory model, we can therefore investigate how strategic behavior impacts the equilibrium that emerges. The competitive model can be reframed as a game theory model in which individuals simply have no incentive to think strategically, but as the economic environment becomes less competitive, strategic considerations become increasingly important. One particular type of game, known as the *Prisoner's Dilemma*, will become particularly important in some upcoming chapters.

While we will be able to give some economic examples within the context of our development of game theory in Chapter 24, we will investigate more well-defined problems in the remaining chapters of Part 5. Chapters 25 and 26 consider market structures that fall in between the extremes of perfect competition and perfect monopoly, market structures where competitors with market power have to think about what others do before determining what the best course of action is. Chapter 25 begins with a treatment of a market structure known as *oligopoly*. Oligopolies are industries in which firms produce identical (or, in some instances, somewhat differentiated) products, but high barriers to entry keep the number of firms small. For instance, if firms face sufficiently high recurring fixed costs of production, then the market cannot be reasonably assumed to sustain many small firms (as under perfect competition). If the resulting small number of firms (that compose the "oligopoly") were to merge into a single firm, they would be a perfect monopolist of the kind we discuss in Chapter 23, but because there are several firms in the industry, no one firm has the kind of perfect monopoly power that a monopolist enjoys. We will then be able to show that strategic incentives are such that oligopolists may find it difficult to enforce collusive agreements among themselves (because of incentives captured in the Prisoner's Dilemma game). The resulting oligopoly competition can then lead to pricing and production levels that fall in between those of perfect competition and perfect monopoly. In our conclusion of Chapter 25, we will note that the existence of oligopolies may not in itself always be a policy concern, but the potential for collusion in such markets is of great interest to both governments and potential competitors as such collusion limits oligopolistic competition and generates deadweight loss.

In Chapter 26, we then introduce the idea of more fully differentiated product markets, markets that serve a particular demand from consumers but in which firms find ways of producing somewhat different products that target somewhat different consumer tastes. *Monopolistic competition* occurs when many firms produce such differentiated products, with each firm having some market power given that each firm's output is just a bit different from every other firm's output. While there are barriers to entry, these are lower in monopolistically competitive markets, leading to a greater number of firms than we would observe in oligopolies. Each firm's market power is then limited by the competition it faces from other firms that produce similar (though not identical) products. Many industries in the real world can be modeled in this way, with each firm in the industry constantly searching for new ways of differentiating its product from that of competitors. This type of market structure is particularly interesting because, while the market power held by each individual firm may cause inefficiently low production by that firm, the prospect of gaining market power (and thus increasing profit) through product *innovation* results in increased product variety and the formation of new products to meet consumer needs more and more effectively. Thus it is far from clear that monopolistic competition truly gives rise to inefficiencies even though at any given moment the argument can certainly be made that, were innovation to stop, such inefficiencies are indeed present.

While different types of imperfect competition certainly represent the most obvious cases where strategic choices become important, there are other interesting topics that involve such strategic thinking. We will conclude Part 5 with two chapters that investigate such topics. In Chapter 27, we will return to the problem of externalities (first covered in Chapter 21) but will focus our attention on a special type of externality problem that arises when markets, civil society, or government provides *public goods*. Up to this point in the text, we have focused primarily on *private* goods, goods that can only be consumed by a single individual. But there are many goods that can be consumed by multiple individuals: swimming pools, fireworks, police protection, schools, and national defense, to name a few. When we attempt to provide such goods in a decentralized way, institutions have to grapple with another version of the Prisoner's Dilemma known as the *free-rider problem*, which is the tendency of individuals to "free ride" on the production of such goods by others. This is because of the fundamental externalities that are often involved in public good production, externalities that lead to strategic underprovision of such goods. At the same time, we will see that individuals also often have incentives to misrepresent their true preferences for public goods, making it difficult to even determine what the optimal level of public good provision is.

While we will illustrate in Chapter 27 instances in which one can cleverly design a "mechanism" that aligns private incentives with social goals (so that individuals will not free ride on others and will reveal their true tastes for public goods), the most common way in which we reveal our preferences for public goods is through the ballot box. Chapter 28 therefore concludes our discussion of strategic choices by looking inside the black box of democratic political processes.

We will illustrate that politics is messy, and that, in some sense, it is asking way too much of political processes to provide us with coherent aggregate preferences to be used in making social choices. Instead, we will see that political processes are typically subject to strategic manipulation by those who can influence the agenda of what is to be voted on. Strategic thinking therefore extends from (noncompetitive) markets into the formation of government policy by self-interested politicians and public interest groups.

Monopoly

We will now turn to an analysis of the polar opposite of the extreme assumption of perfect competition that we have employed thus far.[1] Under perfect competition, we have assumed that industries are composed of so many small firms that each firm has no impact on the economic environment in which decisions are made. As a result, we could assume that individual firms in an industry simply take the market price as given as they determine how much to produce in order to maximize profits. In the case of a monopoly, on the other hand, the firm must make a decision not only on *how much* to produce but also on *what price* to charge. There is, in the case of monopoly, no "market" to set the price. In this sense, the monopolist has some control over his or her economic environment (i.e., prices) that the competitive producer lacks.

While we will often talk about a "monopoly" as if it was a fixed concept, it is important to keep in mind that monopoly power comes in more and less concentrated doses. Under perfect competition, the demand that a firm faces for *its* product is perfectly elastic because of the existence of many firms that produce the same product at the market price. Whenever a firm faces a demand curve for *its* product that is not perfectly elastic, it has *some* market power. For instance, I might produce a particular soft drink in a largely competitive market for soft drinks, but my soft drink is nevertheless a bit distinctive. In a sense, my soft drink is therefore a separate product with a separate market, but in another sense it is part of a larger market in which other firms produce close but imperfect substitutes. The demand curve for my soft drink may then not be perfectly elastic, which gives me *some* market power, but that power is limited by the fact that there are close substitutes in the larger soft drink market. If, on top of the existence of close substitutes, there is free entry into the soft-drink market, my market power is limited even more. We will treat this type of market in Chapter 26 as one characterized by "monopolistic competition."

In other settings, of course, there is less of an availability of substitutes for a particular firm's product. If there are market entry barriers that keep potential competitors from producing substitutes, my monopoly power would then be considerably more pronounced, and the demand for my product considerably less elastic. For now, we will simply treat monopolies as firms that face downward-sloping demand curves in an environment where barriers to entry keep other firms from entering to produce substitute goods, and we will keep in mind that the elasticity of demand for the monopoly's product is closely connected to just how powerful a monopoly we are dealing with. When we get to Chapter 26, it will become clear that the stark model of monopoly in this chapter is an extreme model that rarely holds fully in the real world, but it gives us a good starting point to talk about market power, just as perfect competition gives us a useful starting point to talk about competition.

---

[1]This chapter presumes a basic understanding of demand and makes frequent references to the partial equilibrium models of Chapters 14 and 15. It furthermore presumes a basic understanding of cost curves as derived in Chapter 11 and summarized in Section 13A.1 of Chapter 13.

23A   Pricing Decisions by Monopolist

We begin our analysis of monopoly power by analyzing how the profit-maximizing condition of marginal revenue being equal to marginal cost translates into optimal firm decision making when a firm faces a downward sloping demand curve. At first, we'll assume that the firm is restricted in its pricing policy in the sense that it can only set a single price per unit of output, a single price that is charged to every consumer. We then proceed to think about how a monopoly might want to differentiate the price it charges to different consumers, and under what conditions that is possible. Finally, we will talk explicitly about what kinds of barriers to entry might in fact result in real-world monopolies, and how the nature of the barrier to entry might determine the extent to which we think monopoly power is a problem that requires government intervention.

Before moving on, however, recall the two ways in which we thought about profit maximization for price-taking firms in Chapter 11. We first set up the profit maximization problem under the assumption that the competitive firm takes price as fixed and solves for the profit-maximizing production plan by finding the tangency between isoprofit curves with production frontiers. This method no longer holds for monopolists because the method presumes a fixed price that the price-taking firm simply takes as given. We then developed a two-step profit maximization method, with the first step focusing solely on the cost side (where firms attempt to minimize cost) and the second step adding revenue considerations (given the price that competitive firms take as given). Since output price plays no role in the cost-minimizing problem where the firm simply asks "what is the least cost way of producing different levels of output," this step is the same for monopolists. The difference enters in the second step where we compare revenue to cost, with revenue for the monopolist depending on the price that the monopolist chooses (rather than the price that is set by the market). We can therefore use everything we learned about *cost curves*—marginal costs, average costs, recurring fixed costs, etc.—and will thus focus on step 2 of the two-step profit maximization method in analyzing monopoly decisions.

23A.1 Demand, Marginal Revenue, and Profit

For competitive producers, price is the same as marginal revenue. Put differently, the competitive producer knows that she can sell any amount of the good she could feasibly produce at the market price, and so the marginal revenue she receives for each good she produces is simply the price set by the interactions of producers and consumers in market equilibrium. She could, of course, choose to sell her goods at a lower price, but that would not be profit maximizing. If, on the other hand, she tries to sell her goods at a price above the market price, consumers will simply shop at a competitor. *While the market demand curve in competitive markets is therefore downward sloping, the demand curve for each competitive producer is perfectly elastic at the market price.*

For a monopolist, however, the market demand is the same as the firm's demand since the monopolist is the only producer in the market. As a result, the monopolist gets to choose a point on the market demand curve, which involves a simultaneous choice of how much to produce and how much to charge. When a monopolist decides to increase output, she therefore confronts the following trade-off: On the one hand, she gets to sell more goods to consumers, but on the other hand she sells *all* her goods at a lower price than before. Thus, as a monopolist increases output, her marginal revenue is *not* equal to the price she charged initially because she will have to lower price in order to sell the additional output.

23A.1.1 Marginal Revenue along a Market Demand Curve   Suppose we consider a demand curve first illustrated in Graph 18.3 in Chapter 18 and replicated here as Graph 23.1a. The first unit produced by a monopolist facing such a market demand for her goods can be sold for approximately $400. Thus, the marginal revenue for the first unit of output is approximately

Graph 23.1: Linear Demand and Marginal Revenue

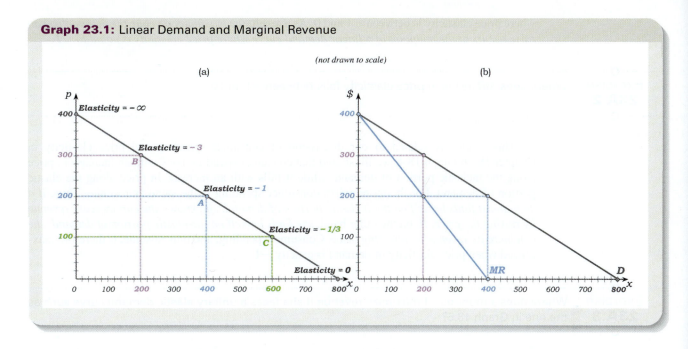

(not drawn to scale)

$400. Next, suppose the monopolist was currently producing 199 units of the output for $300.50 each. Were this monopolist to produce two additional units of output, she would have to lower her price to $299.50 in order to sell all 201 goods. She would therefore experience a $599 increase in her total revenues from the 200th and 201st good, but she would simultaneously lose $1 on each of the first 199 goods she is producing. Her marginal revenue from producing two additional units is therefore $400, or approximately $200 for each of the two units.

Next, suppose that the monopolist was producing 399 units and selling each at $200.50, and suppose she considered producing two additional units. She would then have to lower the price to $199.50 in order to sell the additional two units, earning an additional revenue of $399 on those units but losing $399 on the units she previously produced because she had to lower the price by $1 for each of the 399 units. Thus, her marginal revenue from producing two additional units is 0.

The *marginal revenue curve* for this monopolist is then depicted in panel (b) of Graph 23.1. It begins at the same point as the demand curve because the marginal revenue of the first good is approximately $400. When the monopolist is at approximately point B on the market demand curve, we demonstrated that her marginal revenue from producing an additional unit is approximately $200, and when the monopolist is at approximately point A on her demand curve, her marginal revenue from producing an additional unit is approximately 0. Connecting these gives us the blue line that shares the intercept of the demand curve but has twice the slope.

What is the marginal revenue of producing an additional good if the producer is at point C on the demand curve in Graph 23.1?

Exercise
23A.1

23A.1.2 Price Elasticity of Demand and Revenue Maximization

You can already see in Graph 23.1 that marginal revenue is positive when price elasticity is below -1 and becomes zero as the price elasticity of demand approaches -1 (and becomes negative when price elasticity lies between -1 and 0). This implies that total revenue for the monopolist increases as she moves down the demand curve until she reaches the midpoint where price elasticity is equal to -1, and total revenue falls if she moves beyond that midpoint into the range of the demand curve where price elasticity is between -1 and 0. As a result, *the maximum revenue the monopolist can raise occurs at the midpoint of a linear demand curve where price elasticity is equal to -1.*

Exercise 23A.2   Where does *MR* lie when price elasticity falls between -1 and 0?

This is closely related to our discussion of consumer spending and price elasticity in Chapter 18. In Graph 18.4, we illustrated that consumer spending rises with an increase in price along the inelastic portion of demand, while it falls with an increase in price along the elastic portion of demand. For the monopolist, consumer spending is the same as revenue. Thus, *if a monopolist finds herself on the inelastic portion of demand, she knows she can increase revenue by raising the price. If,* on the other hand, *she finds herself on the elastic portion of demand, she can increase revenue by lowering price.* Consumer spending, and thus revenue, is therefore maximized when price elasticity of demand is exactly -1.

Exercise 23A.3   Where does a monopolist maximize revenue if she faces a unitary elastic demand curve such as the one in Graph 18.5?

23A.1.3 Profit Maximization for a Monopolist
Like all producers, however, monopolists do not maximize revenue—they try to maximize *profit*, which is economic revenue minus economic costs. Thus, in order for us to see what combination of price and quantity a monopolist will choose (assuming she produces at all), we need to know not only marginal revenue but also marginal cost.

First, suppose that the marginal cost of producing is zero. In that case, the monopolist's *MC* curve is a flat line that lies on the horizontal axis on Graph 23.1b, intersecting the *MR* curve at 400 units of output. If the monopolist has no variable costs, maximizing revenue and maximizing profit is exactly the same thing, and so the monopolist would simply choose point *A* on the demand curve where price elasticity is exactly equal to -1. By selling 400 units at $200 each, revenue and profit (not counting recurring fixed costs) is then equal to $80,000. So long as recurring fixed costs are not larger than $80,000, the monopolist would then choose to produce 400 units of output in both the short and the long run.

Exercise 23A.4   *True or False*: If recurring fixed costs are $40,000, then the monopolist will earn $80,000 in short-run economic profit and $40,000 in long-run economic profit.

Next, suppose that the monopolist has the more common U-shaped *MC* curve depicted in Graph 23.2a. If this monopolist produces a positive quantity, she will choose the quantity x^M where *MC* intersects *MR* and charge the price p^M that allows her to sell everything she is producing. So long as the short-run average (variable) cost at x^M is less than p^M, this implies the monopolist will in fact produce in the short run, and so long as average long-run cost (including recurring fixed costs) at the quantity x^M lies below p^M, she will produce in the long run.

Exercise 23A.5   Suppose *MC* is equal to $200 for all quantities for a monopolist who faces a market demand curve of the type in Graph 23.1. At what point on the demand curve will she choose to produce?

Graph 23.2: Profit Maximization for a Monopolist

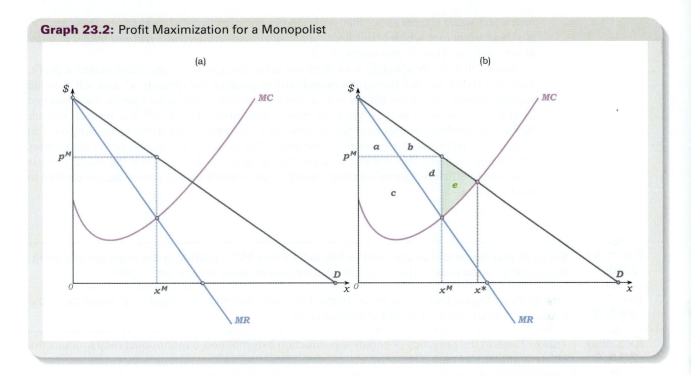

The first thing we can then observe is that, *whenever MC is positive, a monopolist will choose to produce on the elastic part of demand*. This is because, for any positive *MC*, the intersection of *MC* and *MR* must lie to the left of the intercept of *MR* with the horizontal axis, which in turn occurs where price elasticity is exactly equal to -1. This should make intuitive sense: We know that, if a monopolist ever finds herself on the inelastic portion of demand, she can raise revenue by increasing price and producing less. If producing costs something, this implies that whenever a monopolist is on the inelastic portion of demand, she can raise revenue *and* reduce costs by producing less and charging a higher price. As a result, it makes no sense for a monopolist to produce on the inelastic portion of demand.

Exercise 23A.6

Suppose a deep freeze causes the Florida orange crop to be reduced by 50%, which causes the price for oranges to increase. As a result, we observe that the total revenues of Florida orange growers increases. Could the Florida orange industry be a monopoly? (*Hint:* The answer is no.)

Second, the concept of a "supply curve" that we developed for competitive firms does not make any sense when we talk about monopolists. A supply curve illustrates the relationship between the price set by the market and the quantity of output produced by a profit-maximizing firm. But a monopolist does not have a "market" that sets price; the monopolist herself sets the price. Thus, for any given demand curve and any technology that results in cost curves, the monopolist simply picks a *supply point*.

23A.1.4 Monopoly and Deadweight Loss   Finally, we can see in Graph 23.2 that the profit-maximizing monopolist will produce an *inefficiently low quantity*. In panel (b) of the graph, consumer surplus (assuming no income effects) can be identified as area ($a + b$) and monopolist surplus (in the short run, or in the absence of recurring fixed costs) as area ($c + d$). But there are additional units of output that could be produced at a marginal cost below the value consumers place on that output. Such additional output could be produced all the way up to the intersection of *MC* and demand at output x^*, and additional surplus of (e) could be produced if a benevolent social planner rather than a monopolist were in charge of production. Thus, area (e) is a *deadweight loss, which arises because the monopolist strategically restricts output in order to raise price to its profit-maximizing level.*

Notice that the deadweight loss does *not* arise because the monopolist makes a profit. Even if a social planner forced the monopolist to produce the quantity x^* and sell it at the appropriate price along the demand curve, the monopolist might make a profit; the profit just would not be as large as it is when the monopolist raises price to p^M and restricts output. Rather, the deadweight loss emerges from the fact that the monopolist is using her power to strategically restrict output in order to raise price. The monopolist's market power then causes self-interest to come into conflict with the "social good"—at least when the social good is measured in efficiency terms—unless something else interferes and causes the monopolist to produce more.

Exercise 23A.7   Suppose that demand is as depicted in Graph 23.1 and $MC = 0$. What is the monopolist's profit-maximizing output level and what is the efficient output level? What if $MC = 300$?

Exercise 23A.8   *True or False*: Depending on the shape of the MC curve, the efficient output level might lie on the elastic or the inelastic portion of the demand curve.

Exercise 23A.9   *True or False*: In the presence of negative production externalities, a monopolist may produce the efficient quantity of output.

Exercise 23A.10   *True or False*: If demand were not equal to marginal willingness to pay (due to the presence of income effects on the consumer side), the deadweight loss area may be larger or smaller but would nevertheless arise.

23A.1.5 Monopoly Rent-Seeking Behavior and Deadweight Loss

We have demonstrated that monopolists are able to achieve economic profits if they have indeed secured monopoly power in some way. We have furthermore demonstrated that this economic profit comes at a social cost as the monopolist produces below the socially optimal level in order to raise price above marginal cost, and we have denoted that social cost as deadweight loss. The actual deadweight loss may, however, be larger than what we have derived thus far because firms may engage in socially wasteful activity in order to secure and maintain the monopoly power that gives them the opportunity to generate economic profits.

There are a variety of ways in which barriers to entry that lead to monopoly power can arise, and we will say more about this later on in this chapter. One possibility, for instance, is that monopoly power is granted through government intervention, with governments granting to a single firm the exclusive right to produce a certain product. In such circumstances, firms may compete for such government favor, in the process expending resources on lobbying politicians. The maximum amount that a firm would be willing to invest in order to secure a government-granted monopoly is then equal to the present discounted value of the future profits the firm can expect to make from exercising its monopoly power. It is therefore conceivable that firms will expend resources equal to their monopoly profits in order to get the monopoly power, and it is similarly conceivable that many of these resources are spent in socially wasteful ways. This is referred to as political "rent seeking", i.e., the seeking of "rents" or "profits" in the political arena. To the extent to which the resources spent on political rent seeking are socially wasteful, this would add to deadweight loss beyond what we have derived in our graphs thus far.

23A.2 Market Segmentation and Price Discrimination

So far, we have assumed that the monopolist is constrained in the sense that she can only charge a single price to all of her customers. This is the case when a monopolist cannot effectively differentiate between consumers and their marginal willingness to pay for her product, or when charging different prices to different consumers is illegal. In this section, we will suppose that charging different prices to different consumers, a practice known as *price discrimination*, is permitted *and* that the monopolist can *segment* the set of consumers into those who are willing to pay relatively more and those who are willing to pay relatively less. Even when a monopolist can segment the market into different types of consumers, however, she must also have some way of *preventing resale* to keep those consumers who purchase the product at a low price from selling to those who are being offered the same product at a higher price.

In the following, we will illustrate three different ways in which monopolists may price discriminate under different circumstances. We will begin with the case where monopolists can perfectly identify each consumer's demand and can offer each consumer a particular quantity at a particular overall price for that quantity. One way to achieve this is to charge each consumer both a fixed fee for the right to purchase and a per unit price for each unit that is purchased, with both the fee and the per unit price potentially differing across consumers. This is known as perfect (or "first degree") price discrimination. Then, we will consider a case where the monopolist, while still being able to identify each consumer's demand perfectly, can offer different *per-unit prices* (but no fixed fees) to different customers who potentially want to buy multiple units of the good. We will call this imperfect (or "third degree") price discrimination. Finally, we will consider the case where a monopolist knows that there are different types of consumers with different demands, but she does not know what type each particular consumer is. We will see that the monopolist can then construct price/quantity packages, or combinations of fixed fees and per-unit prices, that cause customers to "reveal their type." This is known as "second degree" price discrimination.

23A.2.1 Perfect (or "First Degree") Price Discrimination

We can begin with another extreme assumption: Suppose that the monopolist knows all of her customers extremely well and can thus perfectly ascertain each consumer's willingness to pay for her product. For example, suppose that I am an artist who has his own studio and gallery. I am the only one who produces my unique type of art, and I know my customers personally and invite them individually to sip snooty wine while pretentiously gazing at my art. To make the analysis as simple as possible, let's further suppose that each of my clients will buy a single piece of art from me. (After all, my art is so special that owning a single piece produces complete intoxication as my clients spend all their time simply gazing at their wall to view it.)

The demand curve for my art is then composed of many different individuals who each place a certain value on one of my pieces of art. As I produce my art, I can therefore invite first the individual who places the most value on my art, and who therefore sits at the very top of the demand curve that I face. Suppose this individual of impeccable taste places a value of $10,000 on my art. In that case, I will charge that individual exactly $10,000. Next, I invite my second biggest fan who might place a value of only $9,900 on my art. I can then sell a piece of art to this individual for exactly $9,900. My marginal revenue for the first piece was $10,000, and my marginal revenue for the second piece was $9,900. Since I can charge different prices to each of my clients, I can therefore produce a second piece of art without foregoing any profit on the first piece. As a result, *the demand curve becomes my marginal revenue curve when I can price discriminate perfectly* between all my clients.

Graph 23.3 illustrates the behavior by a profit-maximizing producer who can perfectly price discriminate in this way. Since demand is equal to *MR*, this producer simply chooses to produce x^M where *MC* intersects demand. No single price is charged because each consumer is charged exactly what she is willing to pay along the market demand curve. Consumers therefore attain no surplus, and all the surplus, equal to the shaded area, accrues to the monopolist. In the process, the efficient quantity is supplied, with any additional quantity costing more than the level at which it is valued in society.

Graph 23.3: Perfect Price Discrimination

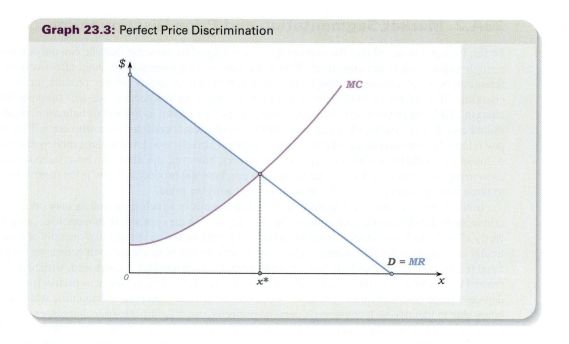

This form of *perfect price discrimination*, when extended to cases in which consumers might purchase multiple units and are thus charged their exact marginal willingness to pay for *each* unit they purchase, is also referred to as *first degree price discrimination*. While it leads to an efficient quantity of output, it clearly leaves consumers worse off than the non-price discriminating outcome in the previous section. This is because consumers now attain no consumer surplus while they do attain some consumer surplus (albeit at a lower output level) when there is no price discrimination. Efficiency is, as we know, a statement about the maximum overall surplus and says nothing about whether the *distribution* of the surplus is desirable.

Exercise 23A.11* We simplified the analysis by assuming that each person will buy only one piece of art. How would you extend the idea of perfect price discrimination (resulting in demand being equal to marginal revenue) to the case where consumers bought multiple pieces? (The answer is provided in the next section.)

23A.2.2 Imperfect or "Third Degree" Price Discrimination

Perfect price discrimination assumes that a monopolist can not only identify perfectly each consumer type's demand but can also charge an amount that is exactly equal to each consumer's total willingness to pay. In our hypothetical example of my art studio, we assumed that each consumer only demands one piece of art (implicitly assuming that the marginal value of the second piece is zero for each consumer). As a result, perfect price discrimination meant that I simply arrived at an individualized price equal to exactly each consumer's willingness to pay for one piece of art.

More generally, consumers have downward-sloping demand curves and thus place value on more than one unit of output. Consider, for instance, two types of consumers whose demands are given as D^1 and D^2 in panels (a) and (b) of Graph 23.4. Suppose further that the producer faces a constant marginal cost of $10 per unit of output. Under perfect price discrimination, the producer would sell 200 units of the output to type 1 consumers and 100 units of the output to type 2 consumers, and he or she would charge type 1 consumers the entire shaded blue area in panel (a) and type 2 consumers the entire shaded magenta area in panel (b). Thus, when

Graph 23.4: Imperfect ("Third Degree") Price Discrimination

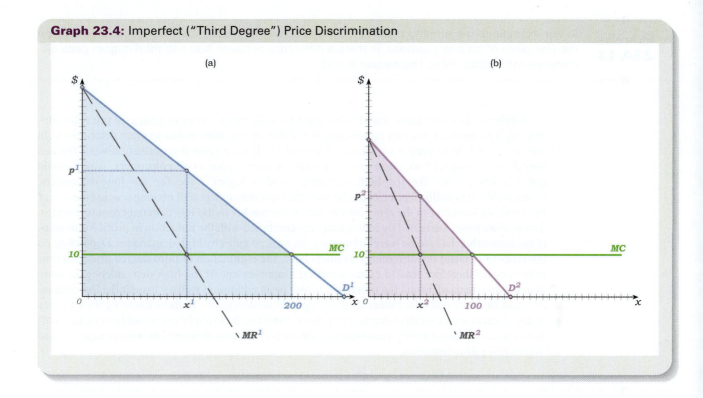

consumers place value on more than one good, perfect price discrimination implies that the monopolist will not charge a per unit price but rather a single price for all the units sold to a consumer together or, equivalently, a fixed fee plus a per-unit price.

The practice of charging a fixed fee plus a per unit price is called a "two-part tariff." It consists of a fixed payment that is independent of the quantity a consumer buys and a per-unit price for each unit the consumer chooses to purchase. Can you identify in the Graph 23.4 which portion would be the fixed payment and what would be the per-unit price for each of the two consumers if the two-part tariff is implemented by a perfectly price-discriminating monopolist?

Exercise 23A.12

In many situations, this seems rather unrealistic. Instead, it might be that a monopolist who can identify different types of consumers is restricted to charging a per-unit price for the goods, a price that can differ across different types of consumers but remains constant for any amount a particular consumer chooses to purchase. If this is the case, the monopolist can typically no longer perfectly price discriminate (in the sense of capturing all consumer surplus) but will rather price discriminate "imperfectly." Such price discrimination is also known as *third degree price discrimination*.

For our example in Graph 23.4, this would imply that the monopolist determines the marginal revenue curve for each of the two types of consumers and then sets output where the constant MC intersects MR. This leads the monopolist to charge the price p^1 to type 1 consumers, with those consumers choosing to consume x^1 (in panel (a)). Similarly, a potentially different price p^2 would be charged to type 2 consumers who would then consume x^2 (in panel (b)). Thus, when monopolists can charge a per unit price that differs across identifiable consumer types, they will restrict output below what it would be under efficient first degree price discrimination. As a result, a deadweight loss will arise under imperfect (or third degree) price discrimination.

Exercise
23A.13

In our example of me running my art studio and selling to consumers who place value only on the first piece of art they purchase, is there a difference between first and third degree price discrimination? Explain. (*Hint*: The answer is no.)

While we therefore know that deadweight loss will emerge under third degree price discrimination, it is not clear whether eliminating the ability by the monopolist to price discriminate in this way will lead to greater or less deadweight loss. If such price discrimination were deemed illegal, the monopolist would revert to charging a single price to all consumers, which would entail a lower price for the high demanders and a higher price for the low demanders. Conceivably, this uniform price could be such that low demanders will no longer consume *any* of the good, thus leading to the effective closing of the market in the low demand consumer sector. The welfare losses sustained by low demanders combined with the reduction in profit for monopolists would then have to be weighed against the welfare gains by high demanders. Depending on the types of demand the different consumers have, the elimination of third degree price discrimination could therefore lead to either a welfare improvement (if the high demanders gain more than the low demanders and the monopolist lose) or an additional welfare loss (if the low demanders and the monopolist lose more than the high demanders gain). Without knowing the specifics in any particular case of third degree price discrimination, it is simply not possible to make a uniform efficiency-based policy recommendation on how to treat monopolists who engage in third degree price discrimination.

Exercise
23A.14

Why do we not run into similar problems of ambiguity in thinking about the welfare effects of first degree price discrimination?

23A.2.3 Nonlinear Pricing and "Second Degree" Price Discrimination

Sometimes there are external signals that a firm can use to infer the type of consumer it is facing. Movie theaters know that students will generally have different demands than adults in the labor force, and they may therefore offer student prices that are different from regular prices (and not available to nonstudents). This is an example of third degree price discrimination. But in many real-world circumstances, firms do not have such external signals and therefore are unsure of what types of consumers they face at any given moment. Put differently, it is often difficult to tell by just looking at someone whether that person is a "high demander" or a "low demander," even if a firm knows how many high demanders there are relative to low demanders.

Even in such cases, however, the monopolist can try to find ways of increasing profit through strategic pricing. But since the monopolist cannot tell what type of consumer she is facing, she has to structure her pricing in such a way as to give the incentive to consumers to self-identify who they are. This involves the setting of *a single nonlinear price schedule, or offering different quantities of the good at different prices.* Such a pricing strategy does not explicitly discriminate between different consumers because all consumers are offered the same price schedule for different quantities of the good. Rather, consumers end up paying different average prices *based on their choices* once they see the nonlinear price schedule the monopolist posts.

Suppose, for instance, that the monopolist knows that she has two types of customers, just as in Graph 23.4 in the previous section. But now suppose she cannot tell in any particular instance which type of consumer has entered her store; all she knows is that there is an equal number of both types of consumers in the economy. In Graph 23.5a, we then illustrate the blue type 1 demand curve D^1 and the magenta type 2 demand curve D^2 within the same picture and again assume a constant marginal cost of $10 per unit of output. If the monopolist could price discriminate

Graph 23.5: "Second Degree" Price Discrimination

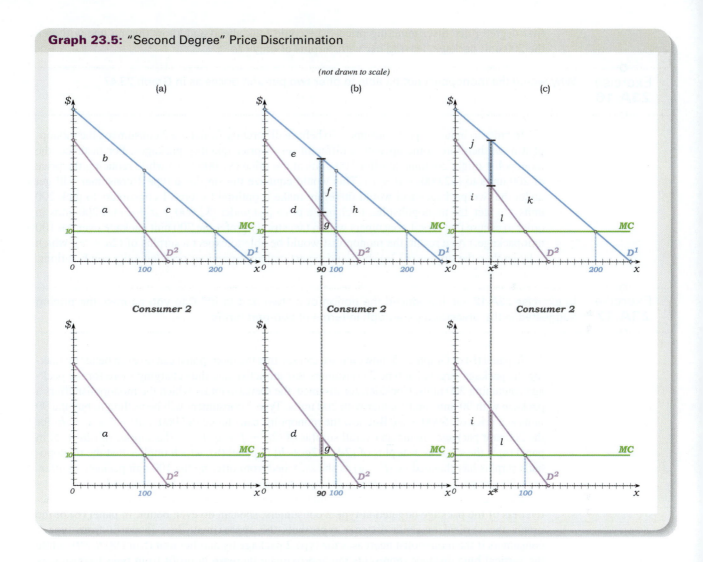

(not drawn to scale)

perfectly, she would want to offer 200 units of output to type 1 consumers and charge the entire area under D^1 (i.e., \$2,000 + a + b + c). Similarly, she would want to offer 100 units of the output to type 2 consumers and charge the entire area under D^2 (i.e., \$1,000 + a). This would result in no consumer surplus and a surplus for the monopolist of ($2a$ + b + c) assuming there is one consumer of each type.

Explain how this represents separate "two-part tariffs" for the two consumer types (as defined in exercise 23A.12).

Exercise 23A.15

When the monopolist cannot tell which consumers are type 1 and which are type 2, she cannot implement this perfect price discrimination (nor can she implement the third degree price discrimination from Graph 23.4). This is because type 1 consumers now have an incentive to simply pretend to be type 2 consumers, purchase 100 units at the price (\$1,000 + a), and get consumer surplus of (b). Were the monopolist to offer the 100 and 200 unit packages at the first-degree price discriminating prices, she could look ahead and know that no one will pick the 200 unit package, leaving her with surplus of only $(2a)$.[2]

----------●----------

Exercise
23A.16

----------●----------
Why would the monopolist not be able to offer two per-unit prices as in Graph 23.4?

In order to induce type 1 consumers to behave differently from type 2 consumers, the monopolist must therefore come up with a different set of price/quantity packages. For instance, the monopolist might continue to offer 100 units at the price ($1,000 + a) while reducing the price of 200 units to ($2,000 + a + c). This would equalize the surplus a type 1 consumer will get under the two packages and would therefore make it optimal for type 1 consumers to pick 200 units. (In fact, the monopolist has to charge a price just under ($2,000 + a + c) for 200 units in order to ensure that type 1 consumers will in fact strictly prefer the 200 unit package over the 100 unit package.) As a result, the monopolist would be able to expect a surplus of ($2a$ + c), which is larger than the surplus of ($2a$) she could expect under the previous price/quantity combinations.

----------●----------

Exercise
23A.17

----------●----------
In exercise 23A.12, we introduced the notion of a "two-part tariff." Can you express the pricing suggested in the preceding paragraph in terms of two-part tariffs?

In panel (b) of Graph 23.5, however, we can see that the monopolist can do even better by making the package targeted at type 2 consumers less attractive and thus charging more for the package containing 200 units. Consider, for instance, the scenario under which the monopolist offers a package with 90 units and another with 200 units. Type 2 consumers will be willing to buy the 90 units at a price of ($900 + d). But now the monopolist can charge ($2,000 + d + f + g + h) for the 200 unit package, giving an overall surplus of ($2d$ + f + g + h). The surplus of ($2a$ + c) in panel (a) is the same as a surplus of ($2d$ + $2g$ + h) in panel (b), which implies that the monopolist's surplus has changed by (f − g) as she switched from offering the 100 unit package to offering a 90 unit package instead. Area (f) is larger than area (g), so profit has increased.

But once the monopolist recognizes that she can earn higher profit by reducing the attractiveness of the package targeted at type 2 consumers, she can do even better. In panel (b) of the graph, the vertical magenta distance represents the approximate loss in profit from type 2 consumers if the monopolist decreases the type 2 package by another unit (from 90 to 89), while the vertical blue distance represents the approximate increase in profit from type 1 consumers that can now be charged a higher price for the 200 unit package. The monopolist can increase profit by reducing the type 2 package so long as the vertical magenta distance is shorter than the vertical blue distance. Thus, a forward-looking monopolist would reduce the type 2 package to a quantity x^* (where the two distances are equal to one another). This is represented in panel (c) of the graph.

----------●----------

Exercise
23A.18

----------●----------
What price will the profit-maximizing monopolist charge for x^* and for 200 units in panel (c) of Graph 23.5?

----------●----------

Exercise
23A.19*

----------●----------
We have assumed in our example that there is an equal number of type 1 and type 2 consumers in the economy. How would our analysis change if the monopolist knew that there were twice as many type 1 consumers as type 2 consumers?

---

[2]In Chapter 24, we will introduce the idea of a "sequential game" in which some players move first. We could then say that the monopolist plays such a sequential game with consumers, setting her pricing schedule in stage 1 knowing that consumers will optimize in stage 2.

In Chapter 22, we analyzed situations in which there is asymmetric information between consumers and producers (as in the insurance market). Can you see how the problems faced by an insurance company that does not know the risk-types of its consumers are similar to the problem faced by the monopolist who is trying to second degree price discriminate?

Exercise 23A.20

This example is just one of many that might arise for a monopolist who seeks to price-discriminate among different customers whose type she cannot identify. We will see further examples later on. In the real world, the "packages" offered to different types of consumers may also vary in ways that are related to quality and not just quantity. For instance, in the airline industry, fares for the same flights are often priced quite differently for business travelers and leisure travelers, with business travelers facing fewer restrictions on when and how they can change their tickets. If these topics are of interest, you should consider taking a course in industrial organization.

23A.3 Barriers to Entry and Remedies for Inefficient Monopoly Behavior

So far, we have simply assumed that a particular firm has a monopoly in the market for good x. But how does a firm get such monopoly status in the first place? And how does it hold onto it? We began to discuss this a bit in our brief section on political rent seeking and its implications for deadweight loss. We will now try to dig a bit deeper and point out more explicitly that *there must exist some barrier to entry* of new firms in order for a monopoly to be able to earn long-run positive profits. Such a barrier might emerge simply from the technological nature of production, from different types of legal barriers to entry that we introduced when thinking about political rent seeking, or through other channels.

23A.3.1 Technological Barriers to Entry and Natural Monopolies
In our discussion of perfectly competitive firms, we never considered the case of a firm that has increasing returns to scale for all output quantities. Rather, we focused on firms that may have increasing returns to scale in their production process for low levels of output but eventually face decreasing returns to scale as output increases. It is because of this assumption that MC and AC curves eventually sloped up. But, while we argued in Chapter 11 that the logic of scarcity requires that marginal product of each input eventually diminishes, there is no particular reason that the production process itself cannot have increasing returns to scale over very large ranges of inputs.

Review the logic of how a production process can have diminishing marginal product of all inputs while still exhibiting increasing returns to scale.

Exercise 23A.21

Now suppose the production process for good x always has increasing returns to scale. This implies, as we illustrated in Graph 12.9, that the MC curve is always downward sloping and always lies below AC, which further implies that any price-taking firm will either produce nothing at a particular price or will produce an infinite quantity of the good. But, in a world of scarcity, consumers will not demand an infinite quantity of the good at a positive price, which implies that the assumption of price-taking behavior on the part of the firm is not reasonable under increasing returns to scale. It is for this reason that no competitive industry can have firms whose production process always has increasing returns to scale.

Similar logic applies when a production process has a large initial or a significant recurring fixed cost together with a constant marginal cost, a case that is illustrated in Graph 23.6a. This can arise in many different contexts. For instance, a large investment in research and development

Graph 23.6: A Natural Monopoly

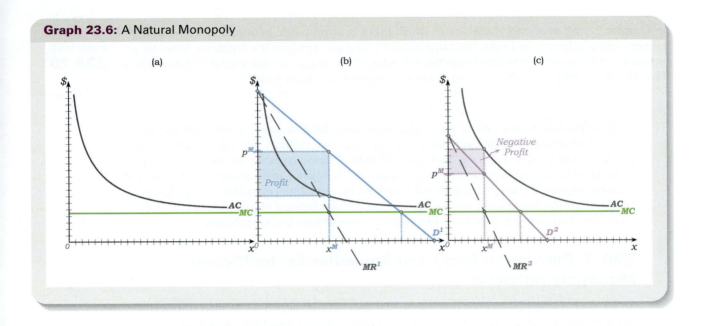

may be required prior to the production of a vaccine, but once the research is complete, the vaccine can be produced easily at constant MC. Or a utility company might have to invest a large amount in laying electricity lines within a city in order to then be able to provide electricity to everyone at a constant MC. Or a software company might work for years to produce a piece of software that can then be offered at virtually no marginal cost by having customers download it from the Internet.

A *natural monopoly* is then defined as *a firm that faces an AC curve that declines at all output quantities*. This declining AC curve can be due to increasing returns to scale everywhere or due to the presence of a recurring fixed cost with constant marginal cost. In either case, we cannot identify a "supply curve" that is equal to the MC curve above AC because MC never lies above AC. It is therefore "natural" for a single firm to emerge as a monopoly.

Exercise 23A.22 Can you see in Graph 23.6a that a price-taking firm facing a downward-sloping AC curve would produce either no output or an infinite amount of the output depending on what the price is?

Exercise 23A.23 Suppose the technology is such that AC is U-shaped but the upward-sloping part of the U-shape happens at an output level that is high relative to market demand. Can the same "natural monopoly" situation arise?

Panels (b) and (c) of Graph 23.6 then add demand and MR curves to the cost curves from panel (a). In panel (b), demand is relatively "high," and the usual profit-maximizing single price p^M (read off the demand curve at quantity x^M where MC and MR intersect) results in a positive profit for the monopoly firm (assuming no recurring fixed costs). In panel (c), on the other hand, demand is relatively "low," causing the monopoly to make a loss if it simply produced where MR intersects MC.

In order for a firm facing the situation in panel (c) to make a positive profit, it would therefore have to price output differently, employing some variant of the price discrimination strategies discussed in the previous section. In the absence of being able to identify different consumer types, this implies that, in order to produce, the firm would have to engage in a form of pricing that involves more than just a single per-unit price. The most common such strategy for natural monopolists (in the absence of price regulation) is to charge a fixed fee plus a per unit price, which we referred to as a "two-part tariff" in exercise 23A.12. In the case of utility companies, for instance, there might be a fixed service fee per month plus a price per unit of electricity consumed.

Because the technological constraints are such that multiple firms in such industries would entail higher per unit costs, governments have often favored *regulation* of natural monopolies over alternative policies to address the deadweight loss from monopoly pricing. Such regulation typically focuses on pricing policies that guarantee a "fair market return" for the natural monopolist while moving production closer to the socially optimal level. Given that the fixed cost is a sunk cost once the monopolist is operating, efficiency would require output where MC crosses the demand curve. But because AC lies above MC, forcing the natural monopolist to price the output at MC would imply negative profits for the monopolist.

In a graph similar to Graph 24.6b, illustrate the negative profit that arises when the monopolist is forced to price at MC.

Exercise 23A.24

Suppose the fixed cost is a one-time fixed entry cost that is sufficiently large to result in a picture like panel (c). *True or False*: If the government pays the fixed cost for the firm, it will not have to regulate the firm in order to make sure the firm makes a profit, but the monopoly outcome will be inefficient.

Exercise 23A.25

For instance, suppose the monopolist faces high recurring fixed costs. Then regulators who attempt to achieve efficient output levels in natural monopolies might aim to set price at MC and allow monopolists to charge an additional "fixed fee" that each customer has to pay independent of the level of consumption. For instance, an electricity provider might charge a fixed "hook up" fee for connecting a household to the service and then a per unit price for each unit of electricity consumed, or a phone company might charge a fixed monthly fee plus a per minute charge for phone calls made. The fixed fees can then be set in such a way as to make the natural monopoly profitable even though the per-unit prices do not cover any of the fixed costs.

Is this an example of a two-part tariff? Does it result in efficiency?

Exercise 23A.26

While it is easy to see how this type of regulation works in principle, in practice the regulator unfortunately does not have all the required information to implement the optimal two-part pricing. In particular, the regulator does not typically know the cost functions of the natural monopoly, and the natural monopolist has every incentive to inflate her costs to the regulator in order to obtain higher fixed fees and higher per-unit prices. There are examples in the real world of natural monopolists devising clever schemes involving fake billing from secondary firms in order to show higher costs than they actually incur, and it is not always easy for regulators to identify such falsifications of cost records. The monopolist furthermore has no particular incentive to find innovative ways of lowering costs through technological innovations even if she is perfectly honest in how she reports the costs she actually incurs.

For some of these reasons, more recent policy approaches have made an effort to introduce competition into some industries that face these cost curves by having the government pay the fixed costs that cause AC curves to be downward sloping. In the utility industry, for instance, the government could lay (and maintain) the electricity lines to all the houses in a city and then allow any utility company to use these lines in order to "ship" electricity to individual houses. It is much like the government laying a system of roads that different trucking companies can use to deliver goods. With the fixed costs paid by the government, individual electricity suppliers then have only variable costs, and thus flat or upward-sloping *MC* curves. It then becomes once again possible for many different electricity providers to compete for households, with households choosing a provider based on quality of service and price.

Exercise 23A.27   Suppose that instead a private company is charged with laying all the infrastructure and then charges competing electricity firms to use the electrical grid. How might this raise a different set of efficiency issues related to monopoly pricing? Would these issues still arise if the government auctioned off the right to build an electricity grid to a single private company?

23A.3.2 Legal Barriers to Entry

While monopoly power can certainly arise from *technological* barriers that prevent several firms from operating simultaneously, it may alternatively arise from *legal* barriers. Such legal barriers might derive from general patent and copyright laws that grant the exclusive right to produce particular products (for a certain number of years) to those firms that were awarded the patent or copyright. The motivation behind such laws is not to encourage the formation of monopolies but rather to provide incentives for innovations by ensuring that innovators can profit from their activities for some period. We will discuss the role of patents and copyrights in more detail in Chapter 26.

Patent and copyright laws are not, however, the only legal barriers to entry. As we have seen, free entry (in the absence of technological barriers) tends to drive economic profits to zero. Thus, if a firm can successfully lobby the government to protect it from competitors, it will invest resources to accomplish this if the required resources are smaller than the present discounted value of the monopoly profits the firm can expect to earn if legal barriers to entry were erected. As we have already mentioned, to the extent to which such lobbying involves socially wasteful activities, the deadweight loss from government-created monopolies may therefore exceed the loss due to the decline in production that results under monopoly profit maximization.

Monopoly power has been granted by governments to a variety of firms throughout history. In the 15th and 16th centuries, for instance, the British Crown awarded exclusive rights to shipping companies to establish trade routes in the West Indies and other parts of the world. More recently, airlines routes were regulated in a similar manner, with airlines being assigned exclusive rights to certain routes within the United States (prior to airline deregulation). The same was true until the 1970s in the trucking industry and the phone industry. Today, the United States Postal Service continues to hold the exclusive right to deliver first class mail, although the government now permits carriers like UPS and FedEx to deliver express packages and large ground packages. In each of these cases, you should be able to see how the firm that attained the exclusive rights to serve a particular market benefits from the governments' entry barriers, and how it might have a vested interest in engaging in socially wasteful lobbying activities in order to retain its monopoly power.

23A.3.3 Restraining Monopoly Power

While governments have, as we have mentioned, been prime culprits—for better or worse—of granting monopoly power to certain firms, the increasing awareness of potential social losses from the exercise of monopoly power has also led to government policies aimed at restraining monopolies. The question of when and under what circumstances government intervention is desirable is a complicated one. The tendency of monopolies to limit output in order to raise price has the clear deadweight loss implications that we have discussed. At the same time, patent-protection of innovation may have led to the emergence of products that might otherwise never have seen the light of day, implying the creation of social surplus despite the fact that, at any given moment, more surplus could be gained by forcing monopolies to produce more. (We will have more to say about this in Chapter 26.) And the existence of increasing returns to scale in certain industries implies that natural monopolies may lower per-unit costs even as they attempt to use their monopoly status to raise price above marginal cost.

We will show in end-of-chapter exercise 23.9 that some of the potential remedies that one might think of applying to monopolies are either ineffective or counterproductive. These include per-unit taxes and profit taxes. We have already discussed (in our treatment of regulation of natural monopolies) that attempts to directly regulate the pricing of monopoly goods run into informational constraints because regulators typically do not know the real costs of firms and because such regulation would give little incentive for cost innovations by monopolies. This does not imply that regulation in some circumstances is not the appropriate policy, but it does imply that regulation is no panacea in all cases. In some instances, governments have forced the break-up of monopolies (as in the case of large oil companies many years ago or large phone companies more recently), and in other cases they have found ways of addressing the root causes of natural monopolies by disconnecting the fixed cost infrastructure from the marginal cost provision of services. And in other cases, governments have actively blocked mergers of large companies that might have resulted in excessive monopoly power. Finally, there has been an increasing trend toward deregulation of industries where regulation itself (such as in the airline industry) created monopolies to begin with. If these topics seem interesting to you, you might consider taking a course on antitrust economics or law and economics.

In many circumstances, however, the most effective tool for restraining monopoly power has little to do with direct government actions and more to do with the fact that when a monopoly does exercise its power to create profit, there is a powerful incentive for entrepreneurs to find new ways to challenge that monopoly power. A firm may, for instance, have captured a large portion of the market, perhaps for no other reason than being first and making early, strategically smart decisions (as in the case of Microsoft and its Windows operating system). There is no doubt that such firms will use their monopoly power to their advantage, but they may also be more cognizant of the threat of competitors (that may find ways of producing substitutes) than our simple static models of monopoly behavior predict. The more a firm exercises its monopoly power, the greater is the incentive for others to find ways of producing such substitutes, and a forward looking monopolist should take that into account when setting current prices, as we will see in upcoming chapters. Sometimes barriers to entry that may seem rock-solid at one time can fall quickly with new technological innovations, as, for instance, with the sudden emergence of cell phone technology, Internet calling, and cable provision of telephone service that are challenging traditional phone companies. In such environments, governments can play an important role in ensuring that existing firms (such as traditional phone companies) do not successfully erect barriers of entry through legislation or regulation (by prohibiting, for instance, cable companies or Internet providers from providing telephone service). Just as there exists a powerful incentive for innovators to find ways of breaking barriers to entry by existing firms, there is a similarly powerful incentive on the part of existing firms to find other ways of shoring up these barriers to entry in order to preserve market power.

In the 1970s when OPEC countries raised world prices for oil substantially by exercising their market power, the Saudi oil minister is said to have warned them: "Remember, the Stone Age did not end because we ran out of stones." Explain what he meant and how his words relate to constraints that monopolies face.

Exercise 23A.28

The Mathematics of Monopoly

From a mathematical point of view, monopolies engage in the same optimization problem that competitive firms undertake except that monopolies have additional choice variables. Both types of firms face some cost function that emerges from the cost minimization problem and tells them the total cost $c(x)$ of producing any quantity x. We should note at the outset that for much of this section we will assume that $dc(x)/dx = c$; i.e., the firm faces a constant marginal cost. This simplifies some of the analysis in convenient ways, and we will explore different marginal cost schedules in some of the end-of-chapter exercises.

Exercise 23B.1   Explain why the cost minimization problem in the firm's duality picture of Chapter 13 is identical for firms regardless of whether they are monopolies or perfect competitors.

A monopoly that is restricted to charging a single per-unit price then solves the problem

$$\max_{x,p} \pi = px - c(x) \text{ subject to } p \le p(x), \tag{23.1}$$

where the price the monopolist charges when trying to sell the quantity x cannot be greater than the price for that quantity given by the inverse demand function $p(x)$. The perfect competitor's problem could be written in exactly the same way, except that for the perfect competitor the inverse demand function is simply $p(x) = p^*$, where p^* is the market price. Thus, price ceases to be a choice variable when price is set by the competitive market, but it is a choice variable for a monopolist who faces a downward-sloping demand curve.

Since the monopolist will set price as high as she can while still selling all the goods she produces, the inequality in equation (23.1) will bind; i.e., $p = p(x)$. The monopolist's problem can therefore be rewritten as

$$\max_{x} \pi = p(x)x - c(x). \tag{23.2}$$

Note that by choosing the optimal quantity x^M, the monopolist implicitly chooses the optimal price $p^M = p(x^M)$ once we have substituted the constraint into the objective function of the optimization problem. And because of the resulting one-to-one mapping from quantity to price, the monopolist's problem could alternatively be written as

$$\max_{p} \pi = px(p) - c(x(p)), \tag{23.3}$$

where $x(p)$ is the market demand function (as opposed to the inverse market demand function $p(x)$ in the previous problem). Whether we view the monopolist as choosing quantity as in equation (23.1) or price as in equation (23.3), the same monopoly quantity and price will emerge.

When a monopolist is not restricted to charging a single per-unit price, she has additional decisions to make as we have seen in our discussion of price discrimination in Section A. The exact nature of that choice problem depends on what the firm knows and what pricing strategies are available to the firm. If the firm can identify consumer types prior to consumption choices by consumers, first and third degree price discrimination become possible (assuming resale can be prevented), and if the firm only knows the distribution of consumer types in the population, second degree price discrimination becomes possible. Different forms of such discrimination are furthermore restricted by the types of pricing schedules that firms are permitted to post, as we will see a little later in the chapter. Fundamentally, however, the firm is still just maximizing profit by making production choices and potentially by engaging in strategic price differentiation.

23B.1 Demand, Marginal Revenue, and Profit

Suppose that the market demand facing a monopolist is of the form

$$x(p) = A - \alpha p, \tag{23.4}$$

which gives rise to an inverse market demand

$$p(x) = \frac{A}{\alpha} - \frac{1}{\alpha}x. \tag{23.5}$$

For consistency, we will use this market demand specification repeatedly, both in this chapter as well as in the following chapters that deal with other market structures within which firms might operate.

23B.1.1 Marginal Revenue and Price Elasticity

For the monopolist, total revenue is then equal to price times output, where price is determined by the inverse market demand (or what we usually call the market demand curve); i.e.,

$$TR = p(x)x = \left(\frac{A}{\alpha} - \frac{1}{\alpha}x\right)x = \frac{A}{\alpha}x - \frac{1}{\alpha}x^2. \tag{23.6}$$

In Section A, we argued verbally that the marginal revenue curve for a monopolist has the same intercept as the demand curve but twice the slope. This is easily verified mathematically, with marginal revenue simply the derivative of TR with respect to output

$$MR = \frac{dTR}{dx} = \frac{A}{\alpha} - \frac{2}{\alpha}x. \tag{23.7}$$

More generally, we can write the inverse demand function as $p(x)$ and total revenue as $TR = p(x)x$. Using this expression, we can differentiate TR with respect to x to get

$$MR = p(x) + \frac{dp}{dx}x. \tag{23.8}$$

Now suppose we multiply the second term in equation (23.8) by $(p(x)/p(x))$. Then we can write the expression for MR as

$$MR = p(x)\left(1 + \frac{dp}{dx}\frac{x}{p(x)}\right). \tag{23.9}$$

Recall that the price elasticity of demand for an inverse demand function $p(x)$ is given by $\varepsilon_D = (dx/dp)(p(x)/x)$, which is just the inverse of the second term in parentheses in equation (23.9). Thus, we can write the expression for MR as

$$MR = p(x)\left(1 + \frac{1}{\varepsilon_D}\right). \tag{23.10}$$

Suppose, for instance, that we are currently at the mid-point of a linear demand curve (such as the one in Graph 23.1a) where the price elasticity of demand is equal to -1. Equation (23.10) then tells us that marginal revenue at that point is equal to 0, precisely as we derived in panel (b) of Graph 23.1.

....

Use equation (23.10) to verify the vertical intercept of the marginal revenue curve in Graph 23.1b. **Exercise 23B.2**

....

23B.1.2 Revenue Maximization

In order to maximize total revenue TR, the monopolist would simply set MR equal to zero. Using equation (23.10) for MR, it follows immediately that revenue is maximized when $\varepsilon_D = -1$. With the linear demand specified in equation (23.4), this implies an output level of $A/2$.

Exercise 23B.3 Set up a revenue maximization problem for the firm. Then verify that this is indeed the revenue-maximizing output level and that, at that output, $\varepsilon_D = -1$.

23B.1.3 Profit Maximization

The monopolist's profit maximization problem differs from revenue maximization in that costs are taken into account. This problem, already introduced at the beginning of this section, can be written as

$$\max_x \pi = p(x)x - c(x), \tag{23.11}$$

where $c(x)$ is the total cost function (that is derived from the production function as described in our producer theory chapters earlier in the text).[3] Taking first order conditions, we get

$$MR = p(x) + \frac{dp}{dx}x = \frac{dc(x)}{dx} = MC. \tag{23.12}$$

Exercise 23B.4 Can you use equation (23.10) to now prove that, so long as $MC > 0$, the monopolist will produce where $\varepsilon_D < -1$?

For instance, suppose that market demand is linear as specified in equation (23.4) and $c(x) = cx$. Then our $MR = MC$ condition implies

$$\frac{A}{\alpha} - \frac{2}{\alpha} = c, \tag{23.13}$$

which further implies a monopoly output x^M and price p^M of

$$x^M = \frac{A - \alpha c}{2} \quad \text{and} \quad p^M = \frac{A + \alpha c}{2\alpha}. \tag{23.14}$$

Exercise 23B.5 Illustrate that profit maximization approaches revenue maximization as $MC = c$ approaches zero.

Exercise 23B.6 Verify for the example of our linear demand curve and constant marginal cost c that it does not matter whether the firm maximizes profit by choosing x or p (as in the problems defined in equations (23.2) and (23.3)).

---

[3]Recall that the cost function is really a function of output x as well as input prices. We are suppressing the input price notation since input markets are not a focus for us here.

23B.1.4 Constant Elasticity Demand and Monopoly Markups

Another way to write the optimal monopoly price emerges from substituting our elasticity-based expression for *MR* from equation (23.10) into the $MC = MR$ condition of equation (23.12); i.e.,

$$p\left(1 + \frac{1}{\varepsilon_D}\right) = MC. \qquad (23.15)$$

Rearranging terms, we then get

$$\frac{p - MC}{p} = \frac{-1}{\varepsilon_D}. \qquad (23.16)$$

The difference between price and *MC*—i.e., $(p - MC)$—is called the *monopoly markup* because it represents how much the monopolist "marks its price up" above marginal cost where we would expect competitive firms to produce. The left-hand side of equation (23.16) is called the *monopoly markup ratio*, which is simply the markup relative to the price charged by the monopolist. (The markup ratio is also called the *Lerner Index*.) Since the price elasticity term ε_D is negative, this cancels the negative sign on the right-hand side and makes the markup ratio itself positive.

Suppose, then, that instead of facing a linear demand curve for which price elasticity differs at each point, a monopolist faces a constant-elasticity demand curve of the form $x = \alpha p^{-\varepsilon}$ for which the price elasticity of demand is $-\varepsilon$ everywhere. Equation (23.16) then tells us that the monopolist's markup ratio is inversely proportional to the price elasticity of demand. This implies that the markup ratio (and the markup itself) approaches zero as the price elasticity of demand approaches minus infinity. That certainly makes intuitive sense: As the price elasticity of demand approaches minus infinity, the monopolist faces a demand curve that increasingly looks like the demand curve a perfect competitor faces. When working with the family of constant elasticity demand curves, the price elasticity of demand is therefore a nice measure of the degree of monopoly power that the firm actually has.

23B.2 Price Discrimination when Consumer Types Are Observed

In Section A of the chapter, we differentiated between three different types of price discrimination that monopolists might employ depending on what they know about their consumers and the degree to which the monopolist can prevent consumers from undermining the price discrimination. In cases where monopolists can identify demand by each consumer, the firm can perfectly (or first degree) price discriminate and capture the consumers' entire surplus *as long as something prevents consumers from selling the goods to each other*. When monopolists are restricted to charging per-unit prices but are not restricted to charging the *same* per unit price to all consumers (whose demand they can again identify), we illustrated how they can employ third degree price discrimination, again assuming that consumers cannot engage in resale. Finally, if monopolists know that different consumers have different demands but cannot identify which consumer is which type, we saw that the firm can second degree price discriminate by designing (nonlinear) price/quantity combinations that cause consumers to self select into packages based on their type. We will begin in this section with the mathematically easier cases of first and third degree price discrimination where we assume that firms observe consumer types prior to setting pricing policies.

23B.2.1 Perfect or First Degree Price Discrimination

As we illustrated in Section A, first degree price discrimination implies that the firm will charge the consumer his marginal willingness to pay for each of the goods he purchases. Suppose that a monopolist faces a constant marginal cost *MC* and let $p^c = MC$ represent the per-unit price we would expect under perfect competition. For a particular consumer *n*, let CS^n represent the consumer surplus *n* would receive under competitive pricing, with the consumer choosing to consume where p^c crosses his demand curve D^n. As we suggested in

Section A, one way to think of perfect price discrimination is to think of the monopolist as continuing to charge a per-unit price of p^c but supplementing this with a fixed fee that the consumer has to pay before he can purchase anything at all. Notice that this fixed fee is a sunk cost for the consumer once it is paid and therefore has no impact on the quantity the consumer will purchase once the fee is paid.

The only question for the consumer is then whether he wants to pay the fixed fee in order to be able to purchase from the monopolist. Since he expects a consumer surplus of CS^n when he faces a per-unit price of p^c in the absence of a fixed fee, he will be willing to pay any fixed fee that is less than or equal to CS^n. The monopolist can therefore set a *two-part tariff*, with the overall payment P^n charged to consumer n equal to

$$P^n(x) = CS^n + p^c x. \tag{23.17}$$

Under this two-part tariff, the monopolist has set a price policy for consumer n that will leave the consumer with no surplus but results in the efficient level of consumption by consumer n. The fixed portion of the price policy is different for each type of consumer, which implies the monopolist must know each consumer's type in order to implement the first degree price discrimination if consumers have different demands.

Exercise 23B.7   Illustrate graphically the two different parts of the two-part tariff in equation (23.17).

23B.2.2 Third Degree Price Discrimination   Suppose now that the monopolist is selling to two different distinct markets but is limited to charging per-unit prices in each market (and thus cannot implement a two-part tariff of the type in equation (23.17)). With knowledge of the two inverse demand functions $p^1(x)$ and $p^2(x)$ for the two markets, the monopolist will then try to maximize her profit across the two markets by choosing how much to produce in each market (and thus also how much to charge in each market); i.e., the monopolist will solve the problem

$$\max_{x^1, x^2} \pi = p^1(x^1)x^1 + p^2(x^2)x^2 - c(x^1 + x^2), \tag{23.18}$$

where c is the firm's total cost function. Taking first order conditions, we get

$$\frac{\partial \pi}{\partial x^1} = p^1(x^1) + \frac{dp^1}{dx^1}x^1 - \frac{dc}{dx} = 0,$$
$$\frac{\partial \pi}{\partial x^2} = p^2(x^2) + \frac{dp^2}{dx^2}x^2 - \frac{dc}{dx} = 0, \tag{23.19}$$

which can simply be rewritten as

$$MR^1 = MC = MR^2, \tag{23.20}$$

where MR^i is the marginal revenue function derived from the ith market's inverse demand function. Since we know from equation (23.10) how to write MR functions in price elasticity terms, we can write this as

$$p^1\left(1 + \frac{1}{\varepsilon_{D^1}}\right) = MC = p^2\left(1 + \frac{1}{\varepsilon_{D^2}}\right), \tag{23.21}$$

which simply extends equation (23.15) to two separate markets, with the "mark-up" in each market reflecting the price elasticity in each market. This then implies

$$\frac{p^1}{p^2} = \frac{(\varepsilon_{D^2} + 1)\varepsilon_{D^1}}{(\varepsilon_{D^1} + 1)\varepsilon_{D^2}}. \tag{23.22}$$

Put into words, regardless of what the *MC* of production is, the price charged in one market *relative to* that charged in the other market depends only on the price elasticities of demand in the two markets when *MC* is constant.

Suppose, for instance, that a monopoly faces constant marginal cost equal to c and that the demand functions in two different markets are $x^1 = A - \alpha p$ and $x^2 = B - \beta p$. These demand functions give rise to inverse demand functions (or demand curves)

$$p^1 = \frac{A - x^1}{\alpha} \text{ and } p^2 = \frac{B - x^2}{\beta}, \qquad (23.23)$$

and the first order conditions requiring marginal revenue to be equal to marginal cost in both markets imply

$$x^1 = \frac{A - \alpha c}{2} \text{ and } x^2 = \frac{B - \beta c}{2} \qquad (23.24)$$

and

$$p^1 = \frac{A + \alpha c}{2\alpha} \text{ and } p^2 = \frac{B + \beta c}{2\beta}. \qquad (23.25)$$

Verify that equation (23.22) holds for this example. (Be sure to evaluate elasticities at the profit maximizing output levels.)

Exercise 23B.8

True or False: The higher-priced market under (third degree) price discrimination is more price inelastic.

Exercise 23B.9*

As we noted in our Section A discussion of third degree price discrimination, the welfare effect of eliminating such discrimination is ambiguous and requires an analysis of the gains by low elasticity consumers relative to the losses by high elasticity consumers (and the monopolist).

23B.3 Discrimination when Consumer Types Are Not Observable

First and third degree price discrimination are relatively straightforward since firms are assumed to know the types of consumers they face. When they do not know the consumer types but are only aware of the fraction of the population that falls into each category, the monopolist's problem becomes more difficult and involves more strategic considerations. In particular, since the monopolist has no external signal about the consumer types she is facing, she must design her pricing policy in such a way that consumers themselves choose to reveal what type they are through the types of purchases they make. As you may have noticed already in Section A, all the various ways of thinking about monopoly pricing involve the firm choosing two-part tariffs of the form

$$P^n(x) = F^n + p^n x \text{ for } n = 1, 2. \qquad (23.26)$$

In other words, we can express each of the pricing strategies as separate two-part tariffs aimed at the two types of consumers. The difference in all these strategies is that in some cases we are restricting fixed charges F^n to be zero and in some cases we are restricting the monopolist to only a single pricing schedule. Table 23.1 illustrates this for the forms of price discrimination we have treated and those we are about to discuss. For instance, we began the chapter in Section 23B.1 with a monopolist who was restricted to charging a single per-unit price to all consumers, effectively assuming $F^1 = F^2 = 0$ and $p^2 = p^1$ as in the first column

Table 23.1: F^n = type n's fixed charge; p^n = type n's per-unit price

	Two-Part Tariff Restrictions for Different Forms of Price Discrimination				
	None	1st Degree	3rd Degree	Two-Part Tariff	2nd Degree
F^1	= 0		= 0		
F^2	= 0		= 0	= F^1	
p^1					
p^2	= p^1			= p^1	

of the table. Under first degree price discrimination, on the other hand, we make no restrictions on the fixed and per-unit prices that the monopolist can use. Under third degree price discrimination, no fixed fees are permitted (i.e., $F^1 = F^2 = 0$) but no restrictions are placed on the per-unit prices the monopolist can charge. We will shortly revisit the case where no restrictions are placed on fixed fees or per-unit prices (as in first degree price discrimination) but under the informational constraint that the firm cannot observe consumer type prior to consumers making their purchasing decisions. This is second degree price discrimination, represented in the last column of Table 23.1. But we will build up to this full second degree price discrimination by first considering the case where a firm does not observe consumer type and is restricted to posting a single two-part tariff (rather than separate two-part tariffs aimed at different consumer types). This is represented in the second-to-last column in Table 23.1 and represents a case we did not treat in Section A of the chapter.

To simplify the analysis to its essentials, we will also allow a single preference parameter to differentiate the different consumer types in this section.[4] In particular, suppose that consumer n has tastes for the monopoly good x that can be represented by the utility function

$$U^n = \theta_n u(x) - P(x), \tag{23.27}$$

where $P(x)$ is the total charge for consuming quantity x.[5] Differences in consumer tastes are then captured by differences in the value of θ_n. Note that this is not the typical type of utility function we have worked with given that it is defined over only a single good. However, as we demonstrate in a short appendix, this type of "reduced form" utility function can be justified as arising from preferences that are separable (between other consumption and the good x) when the overall spending on the good x represents only a small portion of the consumer's income. (In fact, we demonstrate in the appendix that we can assume identical underlying (separable) preferences where consumers differ only in their income, and that the differences in the value of θ_n in the reduced form utility function above are simply related to underlying differences in consumer income.)

23B.3.1 Second Degree Price Discrimination with a *Single* Two-Part Tariff   As already mentioned, we begin our consideration of second degree price discrimination with a restricted version that we did not discuss in Section A of the chapter, a version in which the monopolist is limited to using a *single* two-part tariff for both consumer types (rather than two different two-part tariffs aimed at the two different types). If the monopolist is so constrained, $P(x)$ has to take the form

$$P(x) = F + px, \tag{23.28}$$

---

[4]Previously, we have allowed different consumer types to differ in both the intercept and the slope of their demand curves.
[5]This exposition draws on similar exposition in J. Tirole, *The Theory of Industrial Organization*, (Cambridge, MA: The MIT Press, 2001). For the interested student, this text is an excellent reference for matters related to market power, but it is quite advanced.

where F is the fixed charge and p the per-unit price, with neither being superscripted by n (since the same price schedule applies to both types). Maximizing consumer utility from equation (23.27) given the two-part tariff from equation (23.28) entails the simple optimization problem

$$\max_{x} \theta_n u(x) - F - px \tag{23.29}$$

and gives us the first order condition

$$\theta_n \frac{du(x)}{dx} = p. \tag{23.30}$$

The analysis becomes particularly clean if we assume the following functional form for $u(x)$:

$$u(x) = \frac{1 - (1 - x)^2}{2}, \tag{23.31}$$

which has a first derivative with respect to x that is just $(1 - x)$. Plugging this into equation (23.30) and solving for x, we then get the consumer's demand function as

$$x^n(p) = \frac{\theta_n - p}{\theta_n}. \tag{23.32}$$

Notice that we therefore have specified underlying preferences in such a way as to once again have linear demand curves of the form $x(p) = A - \alpha p$ where $A = 1$ and $\alpha = 1/\theta_n$.

Intuitively, why does the fixed charge F from the two-part tariff not show up in the demand function?

Exercise 23B.10

Derive the price charged to consumer n by a third-degree price discriminating monopolist with constant marginal cost c.

Exercise 23B.11

In Graph 23.7, we depict the inverse of this demand function and illustrate the consumer surplus triangle CS^n that, for a particular per-unit price p with $F = 0$, is of size

$$CS^n(p) = \frac{(\theta_n - p)x^n(p)}{2} = \frac{(\theta_n - p)^2}{2\theta_n}. \tag{23.33}$$

Now suppose that a monopolist faces two types of consumers, type 1 and type 2 with preference parameters θ_1 and θ_2 respectively and with $\theta_1 < \theta_2$. Suppose further that the monopolist knows that a fraction $\gamma < 1$ of the consumers are of type 1, with the remaining fraction $(1 - \gamma)$ made up of consumers of type 2. Finally, suppose the monopolist faces a constant marginal cost of c. Whatever per-unit price the monopolist chooses, she then has to respect the constraint that the lower demand consumer 1 will not choose to consume any of the good if the fixed charge F is set above $CS^1(p) = (\theta_1 - p)^2/(2\theta_1)$.[6] Thus, for a given per-unit price p, the monopolist's optimal fixed charge is $CS^1(p)$.

Knowing this, the monopolist needs to determine the optimal per-unit charge in the two-part tariff. One way to think of this is as a process in which the monopoly maximizes the expected profit from each encounter with a consumer, knowing the fractions of the consumer pool that fall into one type or the other. This expected profit takes the form

$$E(\pi) = CS^1(p) + \gamma(p - c)x^1(p) + (1 - \gamma)(p - c)x^2(p). \tag{23.34}$$

---

[6]This constraint is often referred to as the *individual rationality constraint*.

Graph 23.7: Consumer n's Inverse Demand Function

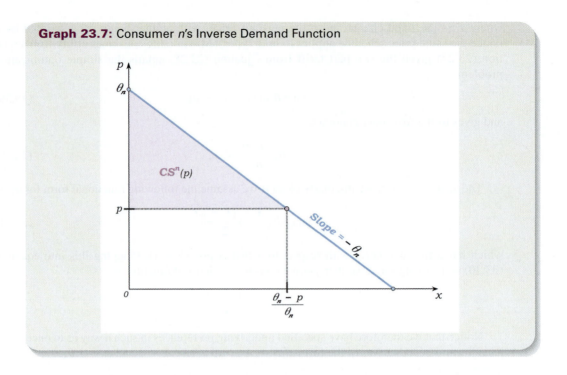

The $CS^1(p)$ term is simply the fixed charge that we have concluded the firm will set in its two-part tariff, a charge that will be paid by both types of consumers. Thus, the firm receives that amount for sure each time a customer shows up. With probability γ, the firm faces a consumer of type 1 who will purchase $x^1(p)$ at price p. When multiplied by the difference between price p and marginal cost c, we get the expected additional profit from facing this type of consumer. Similarly, with probability $(1 - \gamma)$ the firm will face a consumer of type 2 and with it an additional profit of $(p - c)x^2(p)$.

Substituting in for what we derived for $CS^1(p)$, $x^1(p)$, and $x^2(p)$ (in equations (23.33) and (23.32)) and rearranging terms, the expected profit can then be expressed as

$$E(\pi) = \frac{(\theta_1 - p)^2}{2\theta_1} + (p - c)\left[1 - \left(\frac{\gamma}{\theta_1} + \frac{(1 - \gamma)}{\theta_2}\right)p\right] \tag{23.35}$$

Exercise 23B.12   Verify that this equation is correct.

The only choice variable for the monopolist in this expected profit equation is p. Thus, maximizing the expected profit subject to the implicit constraint that only a two-part tariff can be employed is simply maximizing $E(\pi)$ by choosing p. Solving the first order condition from this maximization problem for p, we get the optimal per-unit price p^*

$$p^* = \frac{c(\gamma\theta_2 + (1 - \gamma)\theta_1)}{2(\gamma\theta_2 + (1 - \gamma)\theta_1) - \theta_2} \tag{23.36}$$

Exercise 23B.13**   Verify that this equation is correct.

Graph 23.8: Second Degree Price Discrimination with Two-Part Tariffs

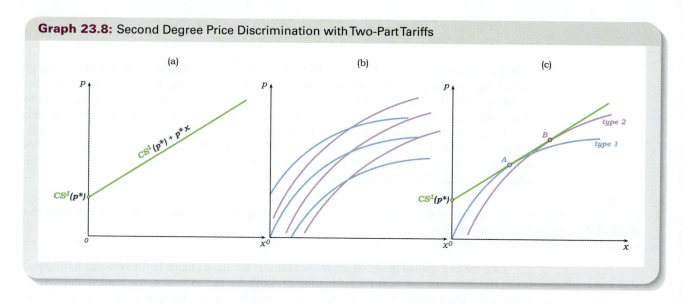

In panel (a) of Graph 23.8, the line $CS^1(p^*) + p^*x$ represents the two-part tariff $P(x)$ that indicates, for any quantity x, the total price charged to consumers. What makes this a two-part tariff is that the line has a vertical intercept, which puts in place a fixed cost to the consumer for purchasing from the firm. Were the line to go through the origin, we would have a simple per-unit price.

In panel (b) of the graph, we illustrate the shape of indifference curves for the two types of consumers, with the blue indifference curves representing type 1 and the magenta indifference curves representing type 2. Consumers prefer to have more of x and less of P and thus become better off as they move toward indifference curves to the southeast of the graph.

Are these preferences convex?

Exercise
23B.14

Note that each set of blue and magenta indifference curves cross once, with the magenta indifference curve having a steeper slope at that point than the blue indifference curve. Can you give an intuitive explanation for this?

Exercise
23B.15

Finally, in panel (c) of the graph, we put indifference curves and the two-part tariff-induced constraint into a single graph to illustrate the consumers' optimal choices, with type 1 consumers optimizing at point A and type 2 consumers optimizing at point B. Note that the optimal blue indifference curve for type 1 crosses the origin, which implies that type 1 consumers are as well off at point A as they are at point $(0,0)$ where they consume no x and pay no price. Put differently, consumers of type 1 attain zero consumer surplus at point A under the two-part tariff that has been set by the firm.

Given that you know how the firm constructed the two-part tariff, can you give an intuitive explanation for this?

Exercise
23B.16

While the firm that is implementing the two-part tariff does not know what type of consumer it faces prior to a consumption decision, the graph illustrates that the two-part tariff allows the firm to know what type of consumer it faced *after* the decision has been made. Put differently and in the language of Chapter 22, the firm has induced a separating equilibrium, with the consumer types signaling their type through their consumption choices.

23B.3.2 Second Degree Price Discrimination More Generally

In our definition of second degree price discrimination in Section A, we did not limit the monopolist to using a *single* two-part tariff but allowed her to create price/quantity packages that in effect allowed her to charge different fixed fees and different per-unit prices. In order to reconcile our treatment here with the graphs we drew in Section A, particularly Graph 23.5, we can again consider the problem using demand curves rather than indifference curves. Panel (a) of Graph 23.9 then illustrates the demand curves for type 1 (blue) and type 2 (magenta) as well as the per-unit price p^* in the single two-part tariff that we just derived.

Exercise 23B.17   Explain why, for the preferences we have been working with, the two demand curves have the same horizontal intercept.

Since the monopolist in our example thus far sets the fixed charge in the two-part tariff equal to the consumer surplus type 1 would get under only the per-unit price, the shaded blue area is equal to the fixed charge F. This implies zero consumer surplus for type 1 consumers and consumer surplus equal to the magenta area for type 2 consumers.

We began our exploration of second degree price discrimination in Section A, however, by proposing that the firm set a per-unit price at $MC = c$ (instead of p^*), that it charge type 1 consumers the maximum possible fixed fee and that it charge type 2 consumers the highest possible fee that would still cause those consumers to behave differently from type 1 consumers. We replicate this in panel (b) of Graph 23.9 for the demand curves we are working with, taking the liberty of drawing these in a particular way so as to minimize the number of

Graph 23.9: Two-Part Tariff Illustrated with Demand Curves

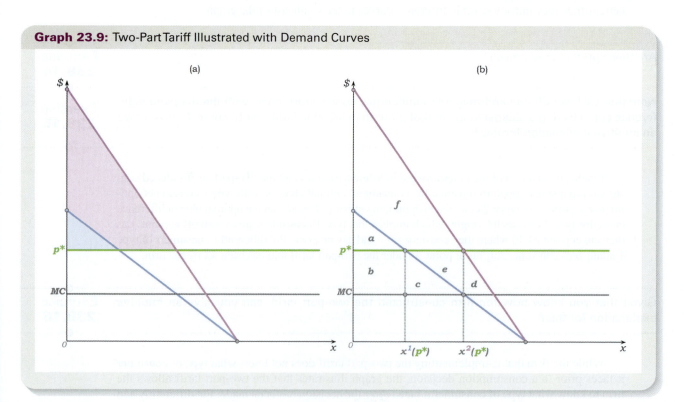

areas we have to keep track of. After setting per-unit price at MC, the firm then charges a fee $F^1 = (a + b + c)$ to type 1 (thereby capturing all of type 1's consumer surplus) and a fee $F^2 = (a + b + c + d)$ to type 2 consumers. The expected profit from a consumer of unknown type is then $(a + b + c + (1 - \gamma)d)$ under this pricing policy, while it is $(a + b + (1 - \gamma)(c + e))$ under the single two-part tariff we calculated in the previous section.

Why is $F^2 = (a + b + c + d)$ the highest possible fixed fee the firm can charge to type 2 consumers given that it sets per unit prices at MC and charges type 1 $F^1 = (a + b + c)$?

Exercise 23B.18

Why is the expected profit from the single two-part tariff developed in the previous section $(a + b + (1 - \gamma)(c + e))$?

Exercise 23B.19

It is easy to see in this example that charging the proposed different fixed fees (combined with per-unit prices equal to MC) might in fact result in more profit for the monopolist than the single two-part tariff from the previous section. Suppose, for instance, that $\gamma = 0.5$. Then the expected profit from a given consumer of unknown type under different fixed fees and marginal cost pricing is $(a + b + c + 0.5d)$, while it is $(a + b + 0.5(c + e))$ under the single two-part tariff with per-unit price p^*. Since areas c and e are equal to each other, the profit from the two-part tariff can also be written as $(a + b + c)$, which is lower than the profit from charging two different fixed fees and pricing at marginal cost.

Can you think of alternative scenarios under which the single two-part tariff yields more profit?

Exercise 23B.20

But then we also illustrated in Graph 23.5 that, when allowed to design fixed fee and per unit pricing packages that differ in both dimensions, the monopolist can do even better by raising the per-unit price on the low demand consumer and thus increasing the fixed fee for the high demand consumer. Complete freedom in designing pricing when faced with different consumer types then results in high demand consumers purchasing the socially optimal quantity but paying a higher fixed fee, and the lower demand consumers purchasing suboptimal quantities and paying a lower fixed fee.

A potentially profit maximizing level of second degree price discrimination (analogous to what we derived in Section A) is pictured once again in Graph 23.10. It can be viewed as consisting of *two* separate two-part tariffs, with consumers free to choose which one to select. The two-part tariff targeted at low-demand consumers consists of a per unit price $\bar{p}$ accompanied by a fixed fee equal to that consumer type's consumer surplus $CS^1(\bar{p})$ under the per unit price $\bar{p}$. Under this two-part tariff, type 1 consumers will choose $x^1(\bar{p})$ and pay a total tariff

$$P^1 = CS^1(\bar{p}) + \bar{p}x^1(\bar{p}), \qquad (23.37)$$

which is equal to the shaded blue area in the graph plus the rectangle $cx^1(\bar{p})$ underneath the shaded blue area. The tariff aimed at high demand consumers, on the other hand, consists of a per-unit price c equal to marginal cost and the highest possible fixed fee that will keep type 2 consumers from taking the two-part tariff aimed at type 1 consumers. This will result in type 2 consumers purchasing the quantity $x^2(c)$, leaving them with consumer surplus equal to the shaded blue, green, and magenta areas in the absence of a fixed fee. Since type 2 consumers can obtain consumer surplus equal to the shaded green area by accepting the two-part tariff aimed at low demand consumers, the most that the firm can then charge in a fixed fee is equal to the shaded

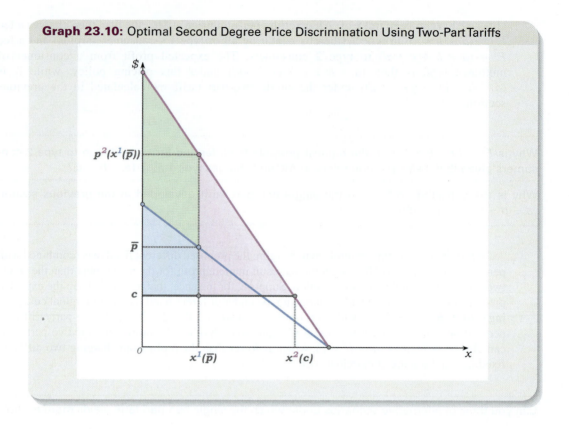

Graph 23.10: Optimal Second Degree Price Discrimination Using Two-Part Tariffs

blue plus the shaded magenta areas. The resulting two-part tariff P^2 aimed at type 2 consumers is then given by

$$P^2 = \left\{ \left[CS^1(\bar{p}) + (\bar{p} - c)x^1(\bar{p}) \right] + \left[\frac{\left(p^2(x^1(\bar{p})) - c\right)\left(x^2(c) - x^1(\bar{p})\right)}{2} \right] \right\} + cx^2(c), \quad (23.38)$$

where the first bracketed term represents the shaded blue area and the second bracketed term represents the shaded magenta area, which together compose the fixed fee charged to type 2 consumers.

This implies that the firm can expect profit of

$$\pi^1(\bar{p}) = CS^1(\bar{p}) + (\bar{p} - c)x^1(\bar{p}) \quad (23.39)$$

from type 1 consumers and

$$\pi^2(\bar{p}) = CS^1(\bar{p}) + (\bar{p} - c)x^1(\bar{p}) + \left[\frac{\left(p^2(x^1(\bar{p})) - c\right)\left(x^2(c) - x^1(\bar{p})\right)}{2} \right] \quad (23.40)$$

from type 2 consumers. The expected profit from encountering a consumer of unknown type is then $E(\pi) = \gamma\pi^1(\bar{p}) + (1 - \gamma)\pi^2(\bar{p})$ or

$$E(\pi) = CS^1(\bar{p}) + (\bar{p} - c)x^1(\bar{p}) + (1 - \gamma)\left[\frac{\left(p^2(x^1(\bar{p})) - c\right)\left(x^2(c) - x^1(\bar{p})\right)}{2} \right]. \quad (23.41)$$

The only variable in the expression for $E(\pi)$ that is under the control of the monopolist is the price $\bar{p}$ because the setting of $\bar{p}$ determines the fixed charges that can be levied on the two types of consumers and we already know that the per-unit price for type 2 consumers is c. Thus, the monopolist's problem is to choose $\bar{p}$ to maximize $E(\pi)$ and then to define the two-part tariffs for the two consumer types accordingly.

For the preferences we have used in this section, we can substitute in for the various functions in $E(\pi)$ and write the firm's problem as

$$\max_{\bar{p}} E(\pi) = \frac{(\theta_1 - \bar{p})^2}{2\theta_1} + (\bar{p} - c)\frac{(\theta_1 - \bar{p})}{\theta_1}$$
$$+ \frac{(1 - \gamma)}{2}\left[\frac{\theta_2\bar{p}}{\theta_1} - c\right]\left[\frac{(\theta_2 - c)}{\theta_2} - \frac{(\theta_1 - \bar{p})}{\theta_1}\right] \quad (23.42)$$

With a bit of careful math, the first order condition for this maximization problem can then be solved for $\bar{p}$ to yield

$$\bar{p} = \left(\frac{\theta_1\gamma}{\theta_1 - (1 - \gamma)\theta_2}\right)c \quad (23.43)$$

from which the two-part tariffs P^1 and P^2 can be derived.

We have thus derived full second degree price discrimination in the form of two separate two-part tariffs, with different fixed fees and different per-unit prices targeted at the two consumer types in such a way as to get each consumer type to utilize the two-part tariff intended for him while maximizing the monopolist's profit (conditional on the monopolist not being able to a priori identify the consumer types).

There is one final caveat for the monopolist who is contemplating this pricing policy: If there are sufficiently many high demand consumers (i.e., if γ is sufficiently low) or if the high demanders have sufficiently greater demand than low demanders (i.e., θ_2 is sufficiently above θ_1), it may be better for the monopolist to write off the type 1 market and simply set a single two-part tariff intended to extract the most possible surplus from type 2 consumers. You can see this clearly in Graph 23.10. Suppose, for instance, that $\gamma = 0.5$, implying an equal number of type 1 and type 2 consumers. By choosing second degree price discrimination, the monopolist chooses to forego capturing the shaded green area in type 2's consumer surplus in exchange for instead getting the shaded blue area of type 1's consumer surplus. The alternative is for the firm to capture the green area of type 2's surplus and not offer anything that type 1 consumers would choose, thus foregoing the shaded blue area. Note that in our graph, the green area is larger than the blue area. Thus, with $\gamma = 0.5$, the monopolist is better off engaging in first degree price discrimination with respect to type 2 consumers (and not sell to type 1 consumers) than to engage in second degree price discrimination.

If the monopolist is restricted to offering a single two-part tariff (rather than two separate tariffs intended for the two consumer types), is she more or less likely to forego second degree price discrimination in favor of first degree price discrimination with respect to the high demand type?

**Exercise
23B.21**

23B.3.3 Comparing Different Monopoly Pricing: An Example

We noted at the beginning of our discussion of second-degree price discrimination that we can think of each of the pricing strategies we have covered as different personalized two-part tariffs of the form $P^n(x) = F^n + p^n x$. Under some strategies, we assume fixed charges F^n to be zero; under others, we require them to be equal for the different consumer types (as summarized in Table 23.1). This then gives us a convenient way of comparing the different forms of price discrimination.

Table 23.2 undertakes this comparison for a particular example in which $\theta_1 = 100$, $\theta_2 = 150$, $\gamma = 0.5$, and the marginal cost $c = 25$. The first column begins by presenting the outcome of monopoly behavior when no price discrimination takes place, with the next two columns presenting

Table 23.2: $\theta_1 = 100$, $\theta_2 = 150$, $\gamma = 0.5$, $c = 25$

	Different Forms of Monopoly Price Discrimination				
	None	1st Degree	3rd Degree	Two-Part Tariff	2nd Degree
F^1	$0	$28.13	$0	$23.63	$12.50
F^2	$0	$52.08	$0	$23.63	$33.33
p^1	$72.50	$25.00	$62.50	$31.25	$50.00
p^2	$72.50	$25.00	$87.50	$31.25	$25.00
x^1	0.2750	0.7500	0.3750	0.6875	0.5000
x^2	0.5167	0.8333	0.4167	0.7917	0.8333
CS^1	3.7813	0	7.0313	0	0
CS^2	20.0208	0	13.0208	23.3724	18.7500
$E(\pi)$	18.8021	40.1042	20.0521	28.2552	29.1667
TS	30.7031	40.1042	30.0781	39.9414	38.5417

the outcome for first and third degree price discrimination where the firm knows each consumer's type and the final two columns presenting the outcome when the firm does not know each consumer's type and is at first restricted to using a single two-part tariff and then permitted to employ separate two-part tariffs aimed at the two consumer types. In each case, we begin with the fixed fees and the per-unit prices charged to the two consumer types and then report the consumption levels, consumer surpluses, and the firm's expected profit per consumer. The final row of the table then sums the consumer surpluses and the firm's profit to arrive at the total surplus.

We know from our work that first degree price discrimination results in full efficiency, with the entire surplus accruing to the firm. It is therefore not surprising to see that the firm's profit and the total surplus are the largest under first degree price discrimination, nor is it surprising that this is the least preferred outcome for consumers whose entire surplus is taken in fixed fees by the monopolist. It should also not be surprising that the firm's profit is the lowest when it is not permitted to engage in any price discrimination. After all, we can see from Table 23.1 that the firm is most restricted in its pricing policy in that case, with no possibility of charging a fixed fee and no possibility of differentiating between the consumer types in terms of the per-unit price charged. These restrictions are lifted partially under third degree price discrimination, resulting in higher firm profit, and fully lifted under first degree price discrimination. It is therefore natural to expect the firm's profit from third degree price discrimination to fall in between the no-discrimination and full (first degree) discrimination scenarios.

In the case where firms can discriminate but do not know the consumer types (represented in the last two columns), it is again not surprising that the firm makes more profit than it does in the no-discrimination case, nor should it be surprising that firm profit is higher when the firm can charge two separate two-part tariffs (in the last column) than when it is restricted to a single two-part tariff (in the second-to-last column). The only case that is theoretically ambiguous with respect to firm profit is the comparison between third degree price discrimination and the two forms of second degree price discrimination in the last two columns. For our particular example, it turns out that both forms of second degree price discrimination result in greater profit than third degree price discrimination, but for other examples the reverse could be true.

Exercise
23B.22

From looking at Table 23.1, it seems that the firm is unambiguously less restricted in its pricing under second degree price discrimination than under third degree price discrimination. So how could it theoretically be the case that profit is higher under third degree price discrimination?

We can summarize these implications in two sets of equations, with

$$\pi(\text{None}) \leq \pi(\text{two-part tariff}) \leq \pi(\text{2nd Degree}) \leq \pi(\text{1st degree}) \qquad (23.44)$$

comparing profit under the second degree price discrimination scenarios to the extremes of no discrimination and perfect discrimination, and with

$$\pi(\text{None}) \leq \pi(\text{3rd Degree}) \leq \pi(\text{1st degree}) \qquad (23.45)$$

comparing third degree price discrimination to these same extremes.

Exercise
23B.23*

Can you think of a scenario under which all the inequalities turn to equalities in equations (23.44) and (23.45)? (*Hint:* Think of goods for which consumers demand only 1 unit.)

Turning from profit to consumer surplus, we can derive the following implications for the low demand consumers:

$$0 = CS^1(\text{1st Degree}) = CS^1(\text{two-part tariff}) = CS^1(\text{2nd Degree}) \qquad (23.46)$$
$$\leq CS^1(\text{None}) \leq CS^1(\text{3rd Degree}).$$

Exercise
23B.24

Can you give an intuitive explanation for why this has to hold?

For the high demand consumers, however, the implications for consumer surplus are not nearly as unambiguous. We can definitively conclude that

$$0 = CS^2(\text{1st Degree}) \leq CS^2(\text{3rd Degree}) \leq CS^2(\text{None}) \qquad (23.47)$$

and

$$CS^2(\text{1st Degree}) \leq CS^2(\text{2nd Degree}) \leq CS^2(\text{two-part tariff}), \qquad (23.48)$$

but we again cannot be certain about how consumer surplus for the high demand type under no and third degree price discrimination compares to consumer surplus under the two forms of second degree price discrimination. In our example, third degree price discrimination happens to be worse for high demand consumers than either of the forms of second degree price discrimination, but no discrimination is better than second degree price discrimination.

The theoretical ambiguities with respect to profit and consumer surplus of high demand consumers then create theoretical uncertainty about the overall efficiency (or total surplus) under different monopoly behavior. The only conclusions that hold regardless of the types of demand are that total surplus is largest under first degree price discrimination. For instance, by simply changing γ in our example from 0.5 to 0.4, the ranking of total surplus changes from one in which second degree price discrimination is more efficient than no discrimination which is more efficient than third degree price discrimination (as illustrated in Table 23.2) to one where no discrimination is more efficient than third degree price discrimination which is more efficient than second degree price discrimination. It is therefore important from an efficiency-focused policy perspective to know as much as possible about underlying demands before intervening in monopoly pricing behavior. Furthermore, it may be that policy makers are less concerned about monopoly profit and more concerned about consumer welfare, in which case overall surplus is not the relevant outcome to consider.

Exercise 23B.25 Can you think of any definitive policy implications if the goal of policy is to maximize consumer welfare (with no regard to firm profit)?

Exercise 23B.26 Explain all the zeros in Table 23.2.

Exercise 23B.27 In Table 23.1, we note that there are no restrictions on per-unit prices for the two consumer types under either first or second degree price discrimination, with firms being able to tell consumer types apart in the former case but not the latter. Yet in Table 23.2, the firm appears to be charging exactly the same per unit prices to the two consumers under first degree price discrimination when it can tell the consumers apart and *different* per-unit prices under second-degree price discrimination when the firm cannot tell the consumer types apart. Explain this intuitively.

23B.4 Barriers to Entry and Natural Monopoly

In Section A, we concluded with a discussion of barriers to entry that create monopolies and particularly focused on the case of natural monopolies that are characterized by downward-sloping average cost curves. The mathematical treatment of such monopolies is relatively straightforward, and we therefore leave its development to end-of-chapter exercise 23.8. We will also return to the role of barriers to entry in creating market power in Chapters 25 and 26.

CONCLUSION

In this chapter, we have begun exploring market power by focusing on the extreme case in which a single firm controls the entire market for a particular good and thus faces the market demand curve rather than the perfectly elastic demand curve that arises for a firm's output under perfect competition. We noted at the beginning that "market power" is a relative concept that is closely linked to the price elasticity of demand that the firm is facing, with infinite price elasticity representing the extreme case of no market power. We then illustrated how monopolies can take advantage of market power to increase profit, whether it is by charging a single per-unit price to all consumers or by price discriminating in various ways that depend on which pricing strategies are available to the firm, whether it is possible to prevent resale, and how much information regarding consumer types the firm has. Unless a firm is able to perfectly price discriminate, we concluded that monopoly behavior results in deadweight loss because monopolies will strategically restrict output in order to raise price. This deadweight loss might be even higher in cases where firms engage in socially wasteful activities in order to attain or maintain monopoly power. At the same time, we noted that our models probably overpredict the size of deadweight losses in many circumstances in which a single firm might in fact control the market for a particular good but in which its monopoly power is disciplined by fear of the possible entry of future competitors. In the case of government-induced monopolies, however, our models may underestimate the deadweight loss if monopolists expend resources to lobby for government protection.

The emergence of deadweight loss from the existence of market power raises the possibility that government intervention in markets characterized by market power might result in efficiency enhancements. But whether such intervention is possible and will in fact lead to increased efficiency depends on the precise nature of the monopoly and the information available to policy makers. In some cases, monopolies might exist for good reasons, such as in the case of natural monopolies that have cost curves that make the presence of multiple firms in the market inherently inefficient. Government intervention in such cases might require information about cost curves that is not readily available to regulators, with the added problem that firms have an explicit incentive to misrepresent their true costs and a possible incentive to not innovate if regulation simply guarantees a "fair market return." At the same time, we discussed market-based interventions, such as the public provision of the fixed cost infrastructure that might open up the possibility of multifirm competition along the infrastructure that would otherwise result in a natural monopoly.

Often, monopolies exist because governments create market power. Governments might, as we will see more clearly in Chapter 26, offer market power in the form of copyrights and patents in order to provide powerful incentives for innovations that might otherwise not occur, and the surplus from such innovation may well outweigh the deadweight losses from underproduction that arises due to the granted market power. At the same time, governments might grant market power as a result of lobbying efforts by firms that seek profit, thus bestowing "concentrated benefits" on owners of the firm while creating "diffuse costs" that nevertheless exceed the benefits. In such circumstances, efficiency and consumer welfare would clearly be enhanced by the removal of such market power. Finally, when faced with a monopoly exercising its market power through price discrimination, we found that it is not always obvious whether the mere tempering of price discrimination through government intervention will necessarily increase social welfare. In such circumstances, much depends on the underlying specifics of the case. As a result, courts that are asked to adjudicate in antitrust law suits that challenge monopoly pricing will typically need to take great care to understand the specifics of the case at hand.

Our focus in this chapter has been exclusively on the ways in which monopolists can use pricing to exercise market power and generate profit. There are, however, a variety of other ways in which a monopoly might exercise market power. These include differentiating the quality of its output across different consumer types and strategically bundling different goods so as to extend monopoly power from one market to another. An entire course can easily be taught on such topics, and probably is taught in your department under the heading of antitrust economics or industrial organization. If this chapter has been interesting to you, you might want to consider taking such a course in your future studies.

We will proceed in Chapters 25 and 26 by investigating market structures that lie in between the extremes of perfect competition and monopoly. Before doing so, however, we need to develop some concepts that assist economists in thinking about strategic behavior, concepts that come under the heading of game theory. It turns out that we have implicitly begun to use some of these concepts in this chapter as we thought through the strategic choices made by monopolists under different pricing strategies (as we illustrate in end-of-chapter exercise 24.11 in the next chapter). We will now formalize these and other concepts and then return to the topic of market power and its impact on efficiency in a wider array of settings.

APPENDIX: DERIVING A "REDUCED FORM" UTILITY FUNCTION FROM SEPARABLE PREFERENCES

In Section 23B.3, we introduced what we called a "reduced form" utility function representing preferences for the monopoly good x that took the form

$$U^n = \theta_n u(x) - P(x), \tag{23.49}$$

where θ_n became our preference parameter that distinguished consumer types and $P(x)$ was the total charge to the consumer for consuming the quantity x of the monopoly good. We indicated at the time that this way of representing preferences for a single good can be derived from a more typical utility function over x and a composite good y. We furthermore indicated that one can assume that consumers in fact have identical underlying preferences and that the parameter θ_n is simply a measure of consumer income, with consumer demands therefore differing solely because of underlying income differences. We will now illustrate this more fully.

Suppose that consumers have underlying preferences that can be represented by the utility function

$$\bar{U}(x, y) = u(x) + v(y). \tag{23.50}$$

If spending on the monopoly good x represents a relatively small fraction of the consumer's income I, we can approximate this utility function by writing it as

$$\bar{U}(x, I) \approx u(x) + v(I) - P(x)\frac{dv(I)}{dI}. \tag{23.51}$$

When we then choose x to maximize $\bar{U}(x, I)$, the term $v(I)$ plays no role in the first order conditions, leaving only the portion $(u(x) - P(x)dv(I)/dI)$ as relevant for the optimization problem. We can then define $\theta = 1/(dv(I)/dI)$ and multiply this relevant portion of the utility function by θ to get

$$\tilde{U}(x, \theta) = \theta u(x) - P(x) \text{ with } \theta = \frac{1}{dv(I)/dI}. \tag{23.52}$$

The term θ is then simply the inverse of the "marginal utility of income." To the extent to which we place meaning in the concept of marginal utility of income, it is common to assume that marginal utility of income declines in income; i.e., $dv(I)/dI < 0$. Since θ is the inverse of marginal utility of income, this implies that θ is increasing in income; i.e., $d\theta/dI > 0$.

Suppose, then, that we have two consumers with identical preferences that can be represented by the separable utility function in equation (23.50) but their incomes are $I_1 < I_2$. Then we can represent their preferences for purposes of determining demand for the monopoly good x by the equation

$$U(x) = \theta_n u(x) - P(x) \text{ with } \theta_1 < \theta_2. \tag{23.53}$$

Thus, low demand consumers will be those with less income than high demand consumers. This then implies that, for instance, under full second degree price discrimination, lower income consumers purchase the monopoly good at a higher per-unit price but are charged a lower fixed fee than high demand consumers.

END-OF-CHAPTER EXERCISES

23.1[†] Suppose that the demand curve for a product x provided by a monopolist is given by $p = 90 - x$ and suppose further that the monopolist's marginal cost curve is given by $MC = x$.

    A. In this part, we will focus on a graphical analysis, which we ask you to revisit with some simple math in part B. (It is not essential that you have done Section B of the chapter in order to do (a) through (d) of part B of this question.)

       a.   Draw a graph with the demand and marginal cost curves.

       b.   Assuming that the monopolist can only charge a single per-unit price for x, where does the marginal revenue curve lie in your graph?

       c.   Illustrate the monopolist's profit-maximizing "supply point."

       d.   In the absence of any recurring fixed costs, what area in your graph represents the monopolist's profit? (There are actually two areas that can be used to represent profit. Can you find both?)

       e.   Assuming that the demand curve is also the marginal willingness to pay curve, illustrate consumer surplus and deadweight loss.

       f.   Suppose that the monopolist has recurring fixed costs of an amount that causes her actual profit to be zero. Where in your graph would the average cost curve lie? In particular, how does this average cost curve relate to the demand curve?

       g.   In a new graph, illustrate again the demand, MR, and MC curves. Then illustrate the monopolist's average cost curve assuming the recurring fixed costs are half of what they were in part (f).

       h.   In your graph, illustrate where profit lies. *True or False*: Recurring fixed costs only determine *whether* a monopolist produces, not how much she produces.

    B. Consider again the demand curve and MC curve as specified at the beginning of this exercise.

       a.   Derive the equation for the marginal revenue curve.

       b.   What is the profit-maximizing output level x^M? What is the profit-maximizing price p^M (assuming that the monopolist can only charge a single per-unit price to all consumers)?

       c.   In the absence of recurring fixed costs, what is the monopolist's profit?

------

*conceptually challenging
**computationally challenging
[†]solutions in Study Guide

      d.   What is consumer surplus and deadweight loss (assuming that demand is equal to marginal willingness to pay)?

      e.   What is the cost function if recurring fixed costs are sufficiently high to cause the monopolist's profit to be zero?

      f.   Use this cost function to set up the monopolist's optimization problem and verify your answers to (b).

      g.   Does the average cost curve relate to the demand curve as you concluded in part A(f)?

      h.   How does the profit maximization problem change if the recurring fixed costs are half of what we assumed in part (e)? Does the solution to the problem change?

23.2   **Everyday and Business Application:** *Diamonds Are a Girl's Best Friend*: Historically, most of the diamond mines in the world have been controlled by a few companies and governments. Through clever marketing by diamond producers, many consumers have furthermore become convinced that "diamonds are a girl's best friend" because "diamonds are forever." In fact, the claim is that the only way to show true love is to give a diamond engagement ring that costs the equivalent of three months of salary. (We will refer to this throughout the exercise as "the claim.")

EVERYDAY APPLICATION

BUSINESS APPLICATION

  A. For purposes of this question, assume that diamonds are only used for engagement rings, that there is no secondary market for engagement rings, and that the diamond industry acts as a single monopoly.

      a.   Let x be the size of diamonds (in karats). Draw a demand curve for x (with the price per karat on the vertical axis) and make the shape of this demand curve roughly consistent with the claim at the beginning of the question.

      b.   If this claim is true, what is the price elasticity of demand for diamonds?

      c.   What price per karat would be consistent with the diamond monopoly maximizing its *revenues* (assuming the claim accurately characterizes demand)?

      d.   What price is consistent with *profit* maximization?

      e.   How large would the diamonds in engagement rings be if the marketing campaign to convince us of the claim at the beginning of the question was fully successful and if the diamond industry really has monopoly power?

      f.   *True or False*: By observing the actual size of diamonds in engagement rings, we can conclude that either the market campaign has not yet fully succeeded or the diamond industry is not really a monopoly.

  B. Suppose that demand for diamond size is $x = (A/p)^{(1/(1-\beta))}$.

      a.   What value must β take in order for the claim to be correct?

      b.   How much *revenue* will the diamond monopoly earn if the claim holds? Does this depend on what price it sets?

      c.   Derive the marginal revenue function (assuming the claim holds). Assuming $MC > 0$, does MR ever cross MC?

      d.   If $MC = 0$, how large a diamond size per engagement ring is consistent with profit maximization (assuming the claim holds)?

      e.   Suppose the diamond monopoly has recurring fixed costs that are sufficiently high to cause its profits to be zero. If marginal costs were zero, what would be the relationship between the demand curve and the average cost curve?

      f.   Suppose $\beta = 0.5$ and $MC = x$. What is the profit-maximizing diamond size now?

      g.   What if instead $\beta = -1$?

23.3[†]   **Business and Policy Application:** *Monopoly Pricing in Health Insurance Markets*: In Chapter 22, we worked with models in which high and low cost customers compete for insurance. Consider the level x of health insurance that consumers might choose to buy, with higher levels of x indicating more comprehensive insurance coverage.

BUSINESS APPLICATION

POLICY APPLICATION

  A. Suppose that there are relatively unhealthy type 1 consumers and relatively healthy type 2 consumers. The marginal cost of providing additional insurance coverage is MC^1 and MC^2, with $MC^1 > MC^2$. Unless otherwise stated, assume that $d^1 = d^2$; i.e., the individual demand curves for x are the same for the two types. Also, suppose that the number of type 1 and type 2 consumers is the same, and some portion of each demand curve lies above MC^1.

a.   Begin by drawing a graph with the individual demands for the two types, d^1 and d^2, as well as the marginal costs. Indicate the efficient levels of health insurance x_*^1 and x_*^2 for the two types.

b.   Suppose the monopolist cannot tell consumers apart and can only charge a single price to both types. What price will it be, and what level of insurance will each type purchase?

c.   How does your answer change if the monopolist can first degree price discriminate?

d.   What if she can third degree price discriminate?

e.   Suppose you worked for the U.S. Justice Department's antitrust division and you only cared about efficiency. Would you prosecute a first degree price discriminating monopolist in the health insurance market? What if you cared only about consumer welfare?

f.   In the text, we suggested that it is generally not possible without knowing the specifics of a case whether third degree price discrimination is more or less efficient than no price discrimination by a monopolist. For the specifics in this case, can you tell whether type 1 consumers are better off without this price discrimination? What about consumer type 2?

g.   Would it improve average consumer surplus to prohibit the monopolist from third-degree price discriminating? Would it be more efficient?

B.   Suppose next that we normalize the units of health insurance coverage such that the demand function is $x^n(p) = (\theta_n - p)/\theta_n$ for type n. You can interpret $x = 0$ as no insurance and $x = 1$ as full insurance. Let $\theta_1 = 20$ and $\theta_2 = 10$ for the two types of consumers, and let $MC^1 = 8$ and $MC^2 = 6$.

a.   Determine the efficient level of insurance for each consumer type.

b.   If a monopolist cannot tell who is what type and can only charge a single per-unit price for insurance, what will she do assuming there are γ type 1 consumers and $(1 - \gamma)$ type 2 consumers, with $\gamma < 0.5$? (*Hint*: Define the monopolist's expected profit and maximize it.)

c.   What would the monopoly price be if $\gamma = 0$? What if $\gamma = 2/7$? What is the highest that γ can be and still result in type 2 consumers buying insurance?

d.   Suppose that the monopolist first degree price discriminates. How much insurance will each consumer type purchase? How much will each type pay for his coverage?

e.   How do your answers to (d) change if the monopolist third degree price discriminates?

f.   Let the payment that individual n makes to the monopolist be given by $P^n = F^n + p^n x^n$. Express your answers to (c), (d), and (e) in terms of F^1, F^2, p^1, and p^2.

g.   Suppose $\gamma = 0.5$; i.e., half of the population is type 1 and half is type 2. Can you rank the three scenarios in (c), (d), and (e) from most efficient to least efficient?

h.   Can you rank them in terms of their impact on consumer welfare for each type? What about in terms of population weighted average consumer welfare?

23.4*   **Business and Policy Application:** *Second Degree Price Discrimination in Health Insurance Markets*: In exercise 23.3, we analyzed the case of a monopoly health insurance provider. We now extend the analysis to second degree price discrimination, with x again denoting the degree of health insurance coverage.

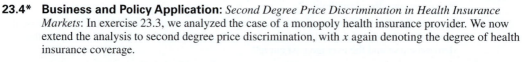

A.   Consider the same set-up as in part A of exercise 23.3, and assume there is an equal number of type 1 and type 2 consumers.

a.   Begin again by drawing a graph with the individual demands for the two types, d^1 and d^2, as well as the marginal costs. Indicate the efficient levels of health insurance x_*^1 and x_*^2 for the two types.

b.   Under second degree price discrimination, the monopolist does not know who is what type. What two packages of insurance level x and price P (that can have a per-unit price plus a fixed charge) will the monopolist offer? (*Hint*: You can assume that, if consumers are indifferent between two packages, they each buy the one intended for them.)

c.   Is the outcome efficient? Are consumers likely to prefer it to other monopoly pricing strategies?

    d.   Suppose next that the demand from type 1 consumers is greater than the demand from type 2 consumers, with d^1 intersecting MC^1 to the right of where d^2 intersects MC^2. Would anything fundamental change for a first degree or third degree price discriminating monopolist?

    e.   Illustrate how a second degree price-discriminating monopolist would now structure the two health insurance packages to maximize profit. Might relatively healthy individuals no longer be offered health insurance?

    f.   *True or False*: Under second degree price discrimination, the most likely to not buy any health insurance are the relatively healthy and the relatively young.

B. **Consider again the set-up in part B of exercise 23.3. Suppose that a fraction γ of the population is of type 1, with the remainder $(1 - \gamma)$ of type 2. In analyzing second degree price discrimination, let the total payment P^n made by type n be in the form of a two-part tariff $P^n = F^n + p^n x^n$.

    a.   Begin by assuming that the monopolist will set $p^2 = \bar{p}$ and $p^1 = MC^1 = 8$. Express the level of insurance x^2 for type 2 consumers as a function of $\bar{p}$. Then express consumer surplus for type 2 consumers as a function of $\bar{p}$ and denote it $CS^2(\bar{p})$.

    b.   Why would a second degree price-discriminating monopolist set F^2 equal to $CS^2(\bar{p})$ once she has figured out what $\bar{p}$ should be? What would the payment $P^2(\bar{p})$ made by type 2 consumers to the monopolist be under $\bar{p}$ and $F^2(\bar{p})$?

    c.   Suppose $MC^2 < \bar{p} < MC^1$. For $\bar{p}$ in that range, what is the largest possible F^1 that the monopolist can charge to type 1 consumers if she sets $p^1 = MC^1 = 8$? (*Hint:* Draw the graph with the two demand curves and then ask how much consumer surplus type 1 consumers could get by simply pretending to be type 2 consumers and accepting the package designed for type 2 consumers.)

    d.   Suppose instead that $MC^1 < \bar{p} < 10$. What would now be the largest possible F^1 that is consistent with type 1 consumers not buying the type 2 insurance (assuming still that $p^1 = MC^1 = 8$?) (*Hint:* Use another graph as you did in the previous part to determine the answer.)

    e.   Given that the fraction of type 1 consumers is γ (and the fraction of type 2 consumers is $(1 - \gamma)$), what is the expected profit $E(\pi(\bar{p}))$ per customer from setting $p^2 = \bar{p}$ when $MC^2 < \bar{p} < MC^1$? What if $MC^1 < \bar{p} < 10$?

    f.   For both cases, i.e., for $MC^2 < \bar{p} < MC^1$ and when $MC^1 < \bar{p} < 10$, set up the optimization problem the second degree price-discriminating monopolist solves to determine $\bar{p}$. Then solve for $\bar{p}$ in terms of γ. (*Hint:* You should get the same answer for both cases.)

    g.   Determine the value for $\bar{p}$ when $\gamma = 0$. Does your answer make intuitive sense? What about when $\gamma = 0.1$, when $\gamma = 0.2$, and when $\gamma = 0.25$? *True or False*: As the fraction of type 1 consumers increases, health insurance coverage for type 2 consumers falls.

    h.   At what value for γ will type 2 consumers no longer buy insurance? If we interpret the difference in types as a difference in incomes (as outlined in the appendix), can you determine which form of price discrimination is best for low income consumers?

23.5   **Business and Policy Application:** *Labor Unions Exercising Market Power*: Federal antitrust laws prohibit many forms of collusion in price setting between firms. Labor unions, however, are exempt from antitrust laws and are allowed to use market power to raise wages for their members.

BUSINESS APPLICATION

POLICY APPLICATION

A.   Consider a competitive industry in which workers have organized into a union that is now renegotiating the wages of its members with all the firms in the industry.

    a.   To keep the exercise reasonably simple, suppose that each firm produces output by relying solely on labor input. How does each firm's labor demand curve emerge from its desire to maximize profit? Illustrate a single firm's labor demand curve (with the number of workers on the horizontal axis). (Note: Since these are competitive firms, this part has nothing to do with market power.)

    b.   On a graph next to the one you just drew, illustrate the labor demand and supply curves for the industry as a whole prior to unionization.

    c.   Label the competitive wage w^* and use it to indicate in your first graph how many workers an individual firm hired before unionization.

d.* Suppose that the union that is negotiating with the firm in your graph is exercising its market power with an aim of maximizing the overall gain for its members. Suppose further that the union is sufficiently strong to be able to dictate an outcome. Explain how the union would go about choosing the wage in this firm and the size of its membership that will be employed by this firm. (*Hint*: The union here is assumed to have monopoly power, and the marginal cost of a member is that member's competitive wage w^*.)

e. If all firms in the industry are becoming unionized, what impact will this have on employment in this industry? Illustrate this in your market graph.

f. Suppose that those workers not chosen to be part of the union migrate to a nonunionized industry. What will be the impact on wages in the nonunionized sector?

B.* Suppose that each firm in the industry has the same technology described by the production function $f(\ell) = A\ell^\alpha$ with $\alpha < 1$, and suppose that there is some recurring fixed cost to operating in this industry.

a. Derive the labor demand curve for each firm.

b. Suppose that the competitive wage for workers of the skill level in this industry is w^*. Define the optimization problem that the labor union must solve if it wants to arrive at its optimal membership size and the optimal wage according to the objective defined in A(d). (It may be more straightforward to set this up as a maximization problem with w rather than ℓ as the choice variable.)

c. Solve for the union wage w^U that emerges if the union is able to use its market power to dictate the wage. What happens to employment in the firm?

d. Can you verify your answer by instead finding MR and MC from the perspective of the union and then setting these equal to one another?

e. Given the fixed cost to operating in the industry, would you expect the number of firms in the industry to go up or down?

23.6* **Business and Policy Application:** *Monopsony: A Single Buyer in the Labor Market*: The text treated extensively the case where market power is concentrated on the *supply* side, but it could equally well be concentrated on the *demand* side. When a buyer has such market power, he is called a *monopsonist*. Suppose, for instance, the labor market in a modest-sized town is dominated by a single employer (like a large factory or a major university). In such a setting, the dominant employer has the power to influence the wage just like a typical monopolist has the power to influence output prices.

A. Suppose that there is a single employer for some type of labor, and to simplify the analysis, suppose that the employer only uses labor in production. Assume throughout that the firm has to pay the same wage to all workers.

a. Begin by drawing linear labor demand and supply curves (assuming upward-sloping labor supply). Indicate the wage w^* that would be set if this were a competitive market and the efficient amount of labor ℓ^* that would be employed.

b. Explain how we can interpret the labor demand curve as a marginal revenue curve for the firm. (*Hint*: Remember that the labor demand curve is the marginal revenue product curve.)

c. How much does the first unit of labor cost? Where would you find the cost of hiring a second unit of labor if the firm could pay the second unit of labor more than the first?

d. We are assuming that the firm has to pay all its workers the same wage; i.e., it cannot wage discriminate. Does that imply that the marginal cost of hiring the second unit of labor is greater or less than it was in part (c)?

e. How does the *monopsony* power of this firm in the labor market create a divergence between labor supply and the firm's marginal cost of labor, just as the *monopoly* power of a firm causes a divergence between the output demand curve and the firm's marginal revenue curve?

f. Profit is maximized where $MR = MC$. Illustrate in your graph where marginal revenue crosses marginal cost. Will the firm hire more or fewer workers than a competitive market would (if it had the same demand for labor as the monopsonist here)?

g. After a monopolist decides how much to produce, she prices the output at the highest possible level at which all the product can be sold. Similarly, after a monopsonist decides how much to buy, he will pay the lowest possible price that will permit him to buy this quantity. Can you illustrate in your graph the wage w^M that our dominant firm will pay workers?

h. Suppose the government sets a minimum wage of w^* (as defined in (a)). Will this be efficiency enhancing?

i. We gave the example of a modest-sized town with a dominant employer as a motivation for thinking about monopsonist firms in the labor market. As it becomes easier to move across cities, do you think it is more or less likely that the monopsony behavior we have identified is of significance in the real world?

j. Labor unions allow workers to create market power on the supply side of the labor market. Is there a potential efficiency case for the existence of labor unions in the presence of monopsony power by firms in the labor market? Would increased mobility of workers across cities strengthen or weaken this efficiency argument?

B. Suppose that the firm's production function is given by $f(\ell) = A\ell^\alpha$ (with $\alpha < 1$) and the labor supply curve is given by $w_s(\ell) = \beta\ell$.

a. What is the efficient labor employment level ℓ^*? (*Hint:* You should first calculate the marginal revenue product curve.)

b. At what wage w^* would this efficient labor supply occur?

c. Define the firm's profit maximization problem, keeping in mind that the wage the firm must pay depends on ℓ.

d. Take the first order condition of the profit maximization problem. Can you interpret this in terms of marginal revenue and marginal cost?

e. How much labor ℓ^M does the monopsonist firm hire, and how does it compare to ℓ^*?

f. What wage w^M does the firm pay, and how does it compare to w^*?

g. Consider the more general case of a monopsonist firm with production function $f(\ell)$ facing a labor supply curve of $w(\ell)$. Derive the $MR = MC$ condition (which is the same as the condition that the marginal revenue product equals MC) from the profit maximization problem.

h. Can you write the MC side of the equation in terms of the wage elasticity of labor supply?

i. *True or False*: As the wage elasticity of labor supply increases, the monopsonist's decision approaches what we would expect under perfect competition.

23.7 Business and Policy Application: *Taxing Monopoly Output*: Under perfect competition, we found that the *economic* incidence of a tax (i.e. who ends up paying a tax) has nothing to do with *statutory* incidence (i.e. who the law said should pay the tax).

BUSINESS
APPLICATION

POLICY
APPLICATION

A. Suppose the government wants to tax the good x, which is exclusively produced by a monopoly with upward-sloping marginal cost.

a. Begin by drawing the demand, marginal revenue, and marginal cost curves. On your graph, indicate the profit-maximizing supply point (x^M, p^M) chosen by the monopolist in the absence of any taxes.

b. Suppose the government imposes a per-unit tax of t on the *production* of x, thus raising the marginal cost by t. Illustrate how this changes the profit-maximizing supply point for the monopolist.

c. What happens to the price paid by consumers? What happens to the price that monopolists get to keep (given that they have to pay the tax)?

d. Draw a new graph as in (a). Now suppose that the government instead imposes a per-unit tax t on *consumption*. Which curves in your graph are affected by this?

e. In your graph, illustrate the new marginal revenue curve and the impact of the consumption tax for the monopolist's profit-maximizing output level.

f. What happens to the price paid by consumers (including the tax)? What happens to the price received by monopolists?

g. In terms of who pays the tax, does it matter which way the government imposes the per-unit tax on x?

h. By how much does deadweight loss increase as a result of the tax? (Assume that demand is equal to marginal willingness to pay.)

i. Why can't monopolists just use their market power to pass the entire tax on to the consumers?

B. Suppose the monopoly has marginal costs $MC = x$ and faces the demand curve $p = 90 - x$ as in exercise 23.1.

    a.   If you have not already done so, calculate the profit-maximizing supply point (x^M, p^M) in the absence of a tax.

    b.   Suppose the government introduces the tax described in A(b). What is the new profit-maximizing output level? How much will monopolists charge?

    c.   Suppose the government instead imposed the tax described in A(d). Set up the monopolist's profit maximization problem and solve it.

    d.   Compare your answers to (b) and (c). Is the economic incidence of the tax affected by the statutory incidence?

    e.   What fraction of the tax do monopolists pass on to consumers when monopolists are statutorily taxed? What fraction of the tax do consumers pass on to monopolists when consumers are statutorily taxed?

23.8   **Business and Policy Application:** *Two Natural Monopolies: Microsoft versus Utility Companies:* We suggested in the text that there may be technological reasons for the barriers to entry required for the existence of a monopoly. In this exercise, we consider two examples.

A. Microsoft and your local utilities company have one thing in common: They both have high fixed costs with low variable costs. In the case of Microsoft, the fixed cost involves producing software which, once produced, can be reproduced cheaply. In the case of your local utility company, the fixed cost involves maintaining the infrastructure that distributes electricity to homes, with the actual delivery of that electricity costing relatively little if the infrastructure is in good shape.

    a.   Let's begin with Microsoft. Draw a graph with low constant marginal costs and a downward-sloping demand curve. Add Microsoft's marginal revenue curve and indicate which point on the demand curve Microsoft will choose (assuming, until later chapters, that it is not worried about potential competitors). Then draw a second and similar graph for your local utilities company.

    b.   There is one stark difference between Microsoft and your local utilities company: Microsoft has not asked the government for help to allow it to operate but has instead been under strict scrutiny by governments around the world for potential abuse of its market power. Utility companies, on the other hand, have often asked for government aid in regulating prices in such a way that the companies can earn a reasonable profit. What is missing from your two graphs that can explain this difference?

    c.   Put into words the "problem" in the two cases from a government's perspective (assuming the government cares about efficiency).

    d.   In the case of Microsoft, how can the granting of a copyright on the software explain the existence of "the problem"? How much is Microsoft willing to pay for this copyright?

    e.   Now consider the "problem" in the utilities industry. How would setting a two-part tariff allow the utilities company to produce at zero profit? If properly structured, might its output level be efficient?

    f.   Explain how the alternative of having the government lay and maintain the infrastructure on which electricity is delivered could address the same "problem."

    g.   What would be the analogous government intervention in the software industry, and why might you think that this was not a very good idea there? (*Hint:* Think about innovation.) Could you think of a way to offer a similar criticism regarding the proposal of having the government provide the infrastructure for electricity delivery?

B. We did not develop the basic mathematics of natural monopolies in the text and therefore use the remainder of this exercise to do so. Suppose demand for x is characterized by the demand curve $p(x) = A - \alpha x$. Suppose further that x is produced by a monopolist whose cost function is $c(x) = B + \beta x$.

    a.   Derive the monopolist's profit-maximizing supply point, i.e., the price and quantity (p^M, x^M) under the implicit assumption of no price discrimination.

    b.   At the output level x^M, what is the average cost paid by the monopolist?

    c.   How high can fixed costs be and still permit the monopolist to make non-negative profit by choosing the supply point you calculated in (a)?

    d.   How much is Microsoft willing to pay its lawyers to get copyright protection?

    e.   Suppose Microsoft and your local utility company share the same demand function. They also share the same cost function except for the fixed cost B. Given our description of the "problem" faced by Microsoft versus your utility company, whose B is higher?

    f.   Suppose B for the utility company is such that it cannot make a profit by behaving as you derived in (a) and suppose there are N households. Suggest a two-part tariff that will allow the utility company to earn a zero profit while getting it to produce the efficient amount of electricity.

    g.   Suppose the government were to build and maintain the infrastructure needed to deliver electricity to people's homes. It furthermore allows any electricity firm to use the infrastructure for a fee δ (per unit of electricity that is shipped). Can the electricity industry be competitive in this case? What has to be true about the fee for using the infrastructure in order for this industry to produce the efficient level of electricity?

23.9† **Policy Application:** *Some Possible "Remedies" to the Monopoly Problem*: At least when our focus is on efficiency, the core problem with monopolies emanates from the monopolist's strategic under-production of output, not from the fact that monopolists make profits. But policy prescriptions to deal with monopolies are often based on the presumption that the problem is that monopolies make excessive profits.

A. Suppose the monopoly has marginal costs $MC = x$ and faces the demand curve $p = 90 - x$ as in exercise 23.1. Unless otherwise stated, assume there are no recurring fixed costs. In each of the policy proposals that follow, indicate the impact the policy would have on consumer welfare and deadweight loss.

    a.   The government imposes a 50% tax on all economic profits.

    b.   The government imposes a per-unit tax t on x. (In problem 23.7, you should have concluded that it does not matter whether the tax is levied on production or consumption.)

    c.   The government sets a price ceiling equal to the intersection of MC and demand. (*Hint*: How does this change the marginal revenue curve?)

    d.   The government subsidizes production of the monopoly good by s per unit.

    e.   The government allows firms to engage in first degree price discrimination.

    f.   Which of these analyses might change if the firm also has recurring fixed costs?

    g.   *True or False*: In the presence of distortions from market power, price distorting policies *can* be efficient.

B. Suppose demand and marginal costs are as specified in part A. Unless otherwise stated, assume no recurring fixed costs.

    a.   Determine the monopolist's optimal supply point (assuming no price discrimination). Does it change when the government imposes a 50% tax on economic profits?

    b.   Suppose the government imposes a $6 per-unit tax on the production of x. Solve for the new profit-maximizing supply point.

    c.   Is there a price ceiling at which the monopolist will produce the efficient output level?

    d.   For what range of recurring fixed costs would the monopolist produce prior to the introduction of the policies in (a), (b), and (c) but not after their introduction?

    e.   What is the profit-maximizing output level if the monopolist can perfectly price discriminate?

    f.   How high a per-unit subsidy would the government have to introduce in order for the monopolist to produce the efficient output level?

    g.   For what range of recurring fixed costs does the monopolist not produce in the absence of a subsidy from part (f) but produces in the presence of the subsidy? If recurring fixed costs are in this range, will the monopolist produce the efficient quantity under the subsidy?

23.10 **Policy Application:** *Pollution and Monopolies*: In Chapter 21, we discussed the externality from pollution-producing industries within a competitive market.

A. Suppose now that the polluting firm is a monopolist.

    a.   Begin by illustrating a linear (downward-sloping) demand curve and an upward-sloping MC curve for the monopolist. Indicate the efficient level of production in the absence of any externalities.

    b.   Draw the marginal revenue curve and illustrate the monopolist's profit-maximizing "supply point."

    c.   Suppose that the monopolist pollutes in the process of producing, with the social marginal cost curve SMC therefore lying above the monopolist's marginal cost curve. Does this change anything in terms of the monopolist's profit-maximizing decision?

    d.   Illustrate a SMC curve with sufficient pollution costs such that the monopoly's output choice becomes efficient.

    e.   *True or False*: In the presence of negative production externalities, the per-unit tax that would cause the monopolist to behave efficiently might be positive or negative (i.e., it might take the form of a tax or a subsidy).

    f.   Suppose that the production externality were positive instead of negative. *True or False*: In this case, the monopolist's output level will be inefficiently low.

B. Suppose a monopolist faces the cost function $c(x) = \beta x^2$, but production of each unit of x causes pollution damage B.

    a.   What is the marginal cost function for the monopolist? What is the social marginal cost function?

    b.   Suppose the demand curve is equal to $p(x) = A - \alpha x$. Determine the monopolist's output level x^M (assuming no price discrimination).

    c.   What is the monopoly price?

    d.   For what level of B is the monopolist's output choice efficient?

23.11 **Policy Application:** *Regulating Market Power in the Commons*: In exercises 21.9 and 21.10, we investigated the case of many firms emitting pollution into a lake. We assumed the only impact of this pollution was to raise the marginal costs for all firms that produce on the lake.

A. Revisit part A(g) of exercise 21.10.

    a.   How does a merging of all firms around the lake (into one single firm) solve the externality problem *regardless* of how large the pollution externality is?

    b.   Suppose you are an antitrust regulator who cares about efficiency. You are asked to review the proposal that all the firms around this lake merge into a single firm. What would you decide if you found that, despite being the only firm that produces output x *on this lake*, there are still plenty of other producers of x such that the output market remains competitive?

    c.   Suppose instead that by merging all the firms on the lake, the newly emerged firm will have obtained a monopoly in the output market for x. How would you now think about whether this merger is a good idea?

    d.   How would your answers to (c) and (d) change if the externality emitted by firms on the lake *lowered* rather than raised everyone's marginal costs?

B. Suppose, as in exercises 21.9 and 21.10, that each of the many firms around the lake has a cost function $c(x) = \beta x^2 + \delta X$, where x is the firm's output level and X is the total output by all firms around the lake.

    a.   In exercise 21.10B(a), we discussed how a social planner's cost function for each firm would differ from that of each individual firm. Review this logic. How does this apply when all the firms merge into a single company that owns all the production facilities around the lake?

    b.   Will the single company make decisions different from that of the social planner in exercise 21.10? What does your answer depend on?

Strategic Thinking and Game Theory

For most of the book, we have assumed that individuals are "small," that they are unable to alter the economic environment that emerges from individual decisions in a competitive equilibrium and therefore have no reason to think about their role in the world "strategically."[1] In Chapter 23, we began to deviate from this assumption by considering the case of "large" firms that constitute monopolies, and we found that such firms become "price setters" that deliberately manipulate the economic environment in which they operate. But the case of monopolies is just one example of a large set of possible economic settings in which such deliberate—or "strategic"—thinking becomes important, and strategic considerations can become considerably more complex than those we encountered in Chapter 23.

Before we can proceed to a more general analysis of strategic behavior, we therefore have to develop some new tools. Known collectively as *game theory*, these tools find their roots in the pioneering work of John Nash (1928–) in the 1940s and 1950s and have become integrated into a variety of social sciences over the following decades.[2] For economic situations in which strategic thinking matters, the game theory approach models the most salient features of such situations as a "game" in which fictional "players" face incentives that are similar to those faced by the real-world actors in the underlying economic setting. In 1994, this approach received the full recognition of the economics community when John Nash and two succeeding game theorists, John Harsanyi (1920–2000) and Reinhard Selten (1930–), were awarded the Nobel Prize in Economics. Nash's compelling life story has since been immortalized in the movie *A Beautiful Mind* (which takes some artistic liberties with game theory as explored further in end-of-chapter exercise 24.1).

While game theory thus opens the door to incorporating strategic thinking into economic models, the models still follow the same path that we have seen in our development of competitive markets: First, a model is defined; second, we analyze how individuals "do the best they can" within the context of the model; and finally, we investigate how an "equilibrium" emerges, an equilibrium in which we discover the economic environment that arises when everyone is doing the best he or she can *given what everyone else is doing*. The only difference from our competitive models is that there is now an incentive for individuals to strategically consider how their own behavior impacts the equilibrium, a consideration that is absent when individuals are too small to have such an impact. Our goal in this chapter is then to begin to appreciate how one can model equilibria that emerge from such strategic thinking in a systematic way, leaving many of the applications to exercises and later chapters.

---

[1]This chapter introduces a new set of tools and does not directly build on any previous material.
[2]You will also find these same tools have found their way into evolutionary biology, where scientists have modeled biological evolution as if it were guided by the strategic behavior of genes.

Before we begin, however, we point out two basic distinctions between different types of games, distinctions that give rise to four types of games. In some settings, it is reasonable to assume that all economic agents (that are modeled as "players") have *complete information*. By complete information we mean that all players know the economic benefits that all the other players will receive as the game unfolds in different ways. In other situations, economic agents do not have such complete information; i.e., they do not fully know how other players fare as the game unfolds in different ways and therefore cannot as easily put themselves in their opponents' shoes. Such games are then characterized by *incomplete information*. In an auction in which you and I bid for a $100 bill, for instance, both of us can be pretty sure how much the other values the prize. But in an auction where you and I bid on a painting, we can't be sure how much the painting is valued by the other unless we know each other really well.

The second important distinction between games is whether all players in a game have to decide on the actions they will take at the same time or whether some players take actions before others do. We will call a game in which all players move at the same time *a simultaneous move game*, while we will call a game in which players move in sequence *a sequential move game*. In the latter, some players therefore know at least a bit about how the other player is playing the game when the time comes to make a move. Simultaneous move games are sometimes referred to as "static," while sequential move games are often called "dynamic." The game "Rock, Paper, Scissors" played by my children on long car trips, for instance, is a simultaneous move game, but the game of chess is a sequential move game.[3]

Combining these two distinctions, we have four basic types of games: (1) complete information, simultaneous move games; (2) complete information, sequential move games; (3) incomplete information, simultaneous move games; and (4) incomplete information, sequential move games. These games become increasingly complex to analyze as one proceeds from (1) to (4), and we will focus in Section A solely on (1) and (2)—games of complete information. In Section B, we then expand our discussion to games of incomplete information—games of type (3) and (4).[4] In addition, many games have both sequential and simultaneous stages, as we will see in our treatment of repeated simultaneous move games—games in which players meet repeatedly and, at each meeting, play a simultaneous move game. Such repeated interactions will have important implications for what kinds of behavior we can expect to observe in equilibrium. Similarly, we will see in Section B that some games have some players that have complete information and other players that have incomplete information. In such games, less informed individuals may attempt to gain information about the more informed players through their own strategic choices. We have in fact already encountered examples in our Chapter 22 treatment of asymmetric information (where, for instance, insurance companies have less information than clients) and in our Chapter 23 treatment of second degree price discriminating monopolists (who had less information about what type of consumer they were dealing with than the consumers themselves).

Game Theory under Complete Information

In this section, we will introduce the basics of game theory under complete information. In Section 24A.1, we define what we mean by a complete information game theory model, specifying in particular the players, the actions available to each player, and the payoffs they can receive depending on how the game is played. In Section 24A.2, we then expand our notion of an "equilibrium" to one that incorporates the strategic element that has been absent from our definition of

---

[3]If the game "Rock, Paper, Scissors" is unfamiliar to you, it is described in end-of-chapter exercise 24.7A(a).

[4]For the interested student who becomes fascinated by game theory, this categorization of games into four types is treated more comprehensively by John Gibbons in *Game Theory for Applied Economists* (Princeton, NJ: Princeton University Press, 1992). The basic structure of this chapter, as well as some of the examples and exercises, is based on the structure of Gibbons's book. Some end-of-chapter exercises are furthermore motivated by examples in Martin J. Osborne, "An Introduction to Game Theory" (New York: Oxford University Press 2004).

a competitive equilibrium. This will require us to specify what we mean by a "strategy" in order to describe an outcome in which everyone's equilibrium strategy is a "best response" to everyone else's equilibrium strategy. In the process, we will give some examples of games in which the strategic element does not result in any efficiency problems and other examples in which strategic behavior leads to inefficient outcomes (or, in our previous language, to violations of the first welfare theorem). We then focus in Section 24A.3 on a particular game of the latter type: the Prisoner's Dilemma. In this game, all players agree they would be better off if they cooperated with each other, but their individual incentives are such that they will not choose to cooperate in equilibrium. This game is one that has many real-world applications and has therefore become a work horse of sorts for social scientists interested in problems involving voluntary cooperation. We will also use the example of the Prisoner's Dilemma to illustrate how to think about repeated simultaneous move games, games in which players interact more than once and each time play the same (simultaneous move) game, and we will show that the repeated nature of certain strategic interactions can fundamentally alter the type of equilibrium we might observe. Finally we will introduce in Section 24A.4 the notion of a "mixed strategy" in which players decide on probabilities with which they will take particular actions rather than arriving at a plan that involves settling on actions with probability 1. This last section is somewhat optional as we will make limited use of it in the remainder of the book, but it nevertheless represents an important way in which game theorists model strategic behavior, particularly in models where there does not exist a "pure strategy" equilibrium.

24A.1 Players, Actions, Sequence, and Payoffs

We begin then by defining the basic structure of complete information games. This structure is given by specifying who the players are, what actions they can take, in what sequence they move, and what their payoffs are depending on the combination of moves made by the different players. In the rest of the chapter, we will sometimes also refer to players as "agents" or "actors."

24A.1.1 Players and Actions Each of N different players in a given game is often permitted to take one of M possible *actions*. We will denote the set of possible actions for player n as a set $A^n = \{a_1^n, a_2^n, \ldots, a_M^n\}$. Often, the actions that different players of the game can take are the same for all players, in which case we can dispense with the superscript notation and simply denote the (common) set of possible actions for all players by the same set $A = \{a_1, a_2, \ldots, a_M\}$. Sometimes, as we will see in end-of-chapter exercises and upcoming chapters, the set of possible actions will instead be continuous. For instance, it might be that a player n can choose any number on the interval $[0,1]$ as an action, in which case we simply denote the set of possible actions for player n as $A^n = [0,1]$.

Consider, for instance, a simple game in which two individuals in a small town are the only ones that drive cars. They might choose to drive on the left side of the road or on the right side of the road. In this case, the two players have the same common set of actions $A = \{Left, Right\}$. Alternatively, we might have a game involving a single consumer and a single producer, where the producer can set a high price or a low price for his or her product, and the consumer can decide to buy the product or not buy it. In that case, the set of actions available to the producer would be $A^p = \{High, Low\}$ whereas the set of actions available to the consumer would be $A^c = \{Buy, Don't Buy\}$. Or an employer might offer either a high wage or a low wage to a worker, and the worker has the option of accepting or rejecting the offer, resulting in $A^e = \{High Wage, Low Wage\}$ and $A^w = \{Accept, Reject\}$.

For which of these examples might it be more appropriate to assume that the set of possible actions is continuous?

Exercise 24A.1

24A.1.2 Sequence of Actions

As already mentioned at the beginning of this chapter, a further feature of a game involves the *sequencing* of moves by the different players. In some cases, we might model an economic situation as one where all players have to decide what action to take *simultaneously*, while in other cases we might model a situation where some players will make *sequential* moves, with the actions of players who move early observable to the players who decide on their actions later on. The first is a *simultaneous move game*, while the second is a *sequential move game*. For instance, as two gasoline station owners on opposite sides of a street come to work in the morning, they might face a simultaneous choice of what gasoline price to post as rush hour traffic is about to start. Alternatively, one gasoline station owner might show up a half hour later to work, in which case she might be able to observe what her competitor has posted prior to deciding what she will post. *Players in a game are therefore defined not only by the set of actions they have available to choose from but also by whether or not they are able to observe the other players' moves prior to determining their own.*

24A.1.3 The Payoff Matrix for a Simultaneous Move Game

Once we have defined the set of possible actions and the sequence of moves for the relevant players in a game, we have to settle on what the consequences of different combinations of actions will be for each player. These "consequences" are referred to as *payoffs*, and the payoff for player n may depend on both his or her own action as well as the action(s) taken by others.

Exercise 24A.2*

Suppose that for every player n in a game, the payoffs for player n depend on player n's action as well as the sum of all the other players' actions, but no single other player has, alone, a perceptible influence on player n's payoff. Would such a game characterize a setting in which strategic thinking was important?

Payoffs for two-player, simultaneous move games in which both players have a discrete number of possible actions they can take are typically represented in a *payoff matrix* such as that depicted in Table 24.1. In the game that is depicted, each player has two possible actions, with the actions for player 1 appearing on the left as a_1^1 and a_2^1 and actions for player 2 appearing at the top as a_1^2 and a_2^2. The *payoffs* for player 1 then appear as either utility values or dollars in the matrix, with $u^1(a_1^1, a_1^2)$ denoting the utility (or dollar) payoff player 1 receives when both she and player 2 take action a_1, $u^1(a_1^1, a_2^2)$ denoting her payoff when she plays action a_1 but her opponent plays action a_2, and so on. Similarly, player 2's payoffs appear as $u^2(a_1^1, a_1^2)$ when both players take action a_1, as $u^2(a_2^1, a_1^2)$ when player 1 takes action a_2 and she plays a_1 and so forth.

Suppose, for instance, that we again considered the simple game in which two individuals in a small town have to decide on which side of the road they should drive. In the end, neither individual cares much about which side of the road is ultimately chosen so long as cars don't crash into each other when the two individuals choose different actions. The payoffs from this game might then be represented in a payoff matrix such as the one depicted in Table 24.2 in which both individuals receive a payoff of 10 when they pick the same action but a payoff of 0 when they pick different actions.

Table 24.1: Payoffs in a Two-Player Simultaneous Move Game

		Player 2	
		a_1^2	a_2^2
Player 1	a_1^1	$u^1(a_1^1, a_1^2)$, $u^2(a_1^1, a_1^2)$	$u^1(a_1^1, a_2^2)$, $u^2(a_1^1, a_2^2)$
	a_2^1	$u^1(a_2^1, a_1^2)$, $u^2(a_2^1, a_1^2)$	$u^1(a_2^1, a_2^2)$, $u^2(a_2^1, a_2^2)$

Table 24.2: Driving on the Left or Right Side of the Road

		Player 2	
		Left	*Right*
Player 1	*Left*	**10 , 10**	**0 , 0**
	Right	**0 , 0**	**10 , 10**

As we will see in later applications (within end-of-chapter exercises as well as in upcoming chapters), payoffs in games where players have a continuous set of possible actions, such as $A = [0,1]$, are instead represented in payoff *functions* that specify a player n's payoffs for any combination of actions taken by all the players. In a two-player game, we would then find player n's payoff as a function $u^n(a^1, a^2)$ where u^n is a function that assigns a payoff value for n to any combination of player 1 and player 2 actions, both of which are drawn from the interval $[0,1]$ (when $A = [0,1]$ for both players).

24A.1.4 Game Trees for Sequential Move Games   Sequential move games are often represented in *game trees* that clearly specify the sequence of moves prior to indicating the payoff each player receives as different actions are taken. Graph 24.1 presents an example of such a game tree for the case where two players each have two possible actions to choose from, with player 1 moving before player 2. For player 2, two possible "information nodes"—or just *nodes*—emerge depending on which action player 1 has taken. If player 1 chooses action a_1, player 2 has sufficient information to know that she is making her decision at the left node, whereas if player 1 chooses action a_2, player 2 knows she is making her decision at the right node in the game tree. At the end of the game tree, the payoffs that result from each possible sequence of actions are indicated as utility values for each player.

Graph 24.1: Example of a Two-Player Sequential Move Game

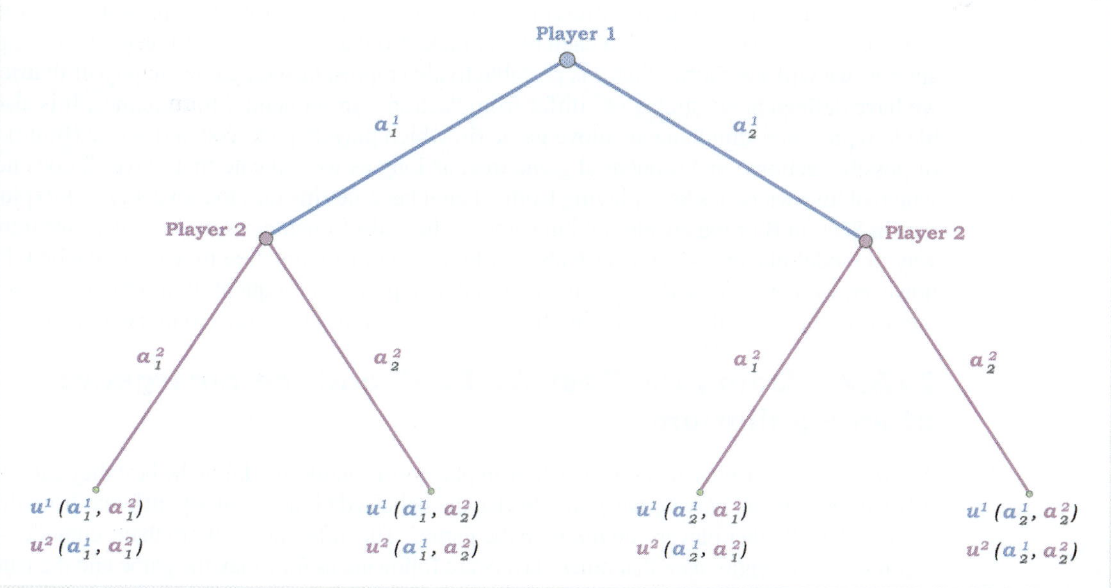

Graph 24.2: Driving on the Left or Right Side of the Road with Sequential Moves

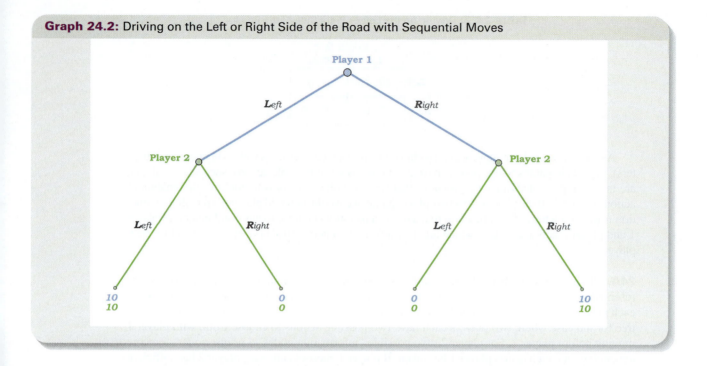

Consider, for instance, the same game as we did in Table 24.2 in which each player has a choice of driving on either the right or the left. But instead of assuming that the players choose simultaneously on which side of the road to drive, player 1 gets on the road first and player 2 gets to observe player 1's choice prior to making her own choice. Graph 24.2 then displays the game tree for this sequential move game. The payoffs at the bottom of the game tree are the same as those we see in the payoff matrix in Table 24.2, with both players receiving a payoff of 10 if they choose the same side of the road and a payoff of 0 when they crash into each other because they chose different sides of the road.

While game trees indeed represent a very convenient way for us to present the structure of sequential move games in which each player picks from a discrete (and finite) number of possible actions, we will see shortly that it is possible to also represent such games in payoff matrices once we have defined how "strategies" differ from "actions" in sequential form games. It is also possible to represent a simultaneous move game (in which players pick from a discrete (finite) number of possible actions) in a sequential game tree, as long as we indicate that player 2 does not know which of his own nodes he is playing from when it becomes his turn to move. (This is explored further in Section B of the chapter and in some of the end-of-chapter exercises where we introduce a way to model players being unsure about which node in a game tree they have reached. For now, however, we will assume throughout Section A that players in sequential move games can identify precisely what node they are playing from when it becomes their turn to make a move.)

24A.2 "Doing the Best We Can" and the Emergence of an Equilibrium

An *equilibrium* emerges in our game when all players of a game are doing the best they can *given how all other players are playing the game*. Notice the italicized phrase is subtly different from the phrase "given what all other players are *doing* in the game." The difference is more than semantic—the former refers to the entire *plan* that other players are following as they play the game and the latter refers to the observable *actions* that other players are taking as the game unfolds. As we will see, this is the difference between "strategies" and "actions," and it is a difference that will become particularly important in sequential move games where early players will need to know what later players are *planning* to do at each of their decision nodes in the game tree in order to know which action early on in the game has them "doing the best they can." We will therefore first define *strategies* as *plans of action* for each player, and we will then say that an equilibrium has been reached when each player is playing a strategy that is the *best response* to the strategies played by the other player(s).

24A.2.1 Strategies Strategies are most straightforwardly defined in simultaneous move games in which all players have to choose a plan of action at the same time. Each player in such a game can either settle on a particular action to take or decide to play particular actions with some probability. A strategy that involves picking a particular action with probability 1 is called a *pure strategy*, while a strategy that places probabilities of less than 1 on more than one action is called a *mixed strategy*. In most of the chapter, we will focus only on pure strategies, but we will conclude Section A with an optional discussion of mixed strategies and their role in the development of game theory models. In fact, all strategies can be viewed as mixed strategies, with pure strategies simply special cases that assign probability 0 to all but one action.

In sequential move games, strategies are a little more complicated because some players will already know what other players are doing when they decide on their own actions. Thus, a complete plan of action for a player other than the one who moves first involves a plan for what to do *at each possible node at which a player might find him- or herself in the game tree*. A pure strategy for player 2 in the game depicted in Graph 24.2, for instance, involves a plan for what to do in case player 1 has chosen the action *Left* and what to do if player 1 has chosen the action *Right*. Pure strategies in simultaneous move games therefore involve simply picking one action, while pure strategies in sequential move games involve picking one action at each node in the game tree. (Just as in simultaneous move games, a mixed strategy in a sequential setting involves playing different pure strategies with probabilities that sum to 1, but we will limit our discussion of mixed strategies to simultaneous move games.)

When we restrict ourselves to considering pure strategies, player 2 in the game in Graph 24.2 then has *four possible strategies even though she only has two possible actions available*. These strategies are:

> <u>Strategy 1</u>: Always play *Left*.
> <u>Strategy 2</u>: Always play *Right*.
> <u>Strategy 3</u>: Play *Left* if player 1 plays *Left* and play *Right* if player 1 plays *Right*.
> <u>Strategy 4</u>: Play *Right* if player 1 plays *Left* and play *Left* if player 1 plays *Right*.

We can denote these four strategies as (*Left, Left*), (*Right, Right*), (*Left, Right*), and (*Right, Left*), with the first action in each pair indicating the plan of action if player 2 ends up on the left node in the game tree and the second action in each pair indicating the plan of action if player 2 finds herself on the right node in the game tree.

True or False: In simultaneous move games, the number of pure strategies available to a player is necessarily equal to the number of actions a player has available.

Exercise
24A.3

Once we recognize that players who move later in the sequence within a sequential move game have more pure strategies than actions available to them, we can see how we can represent the structure of such games in payoff matrices rather than game trees. All we have to do is list the payoffs that each player will receive for each combination of pure *strategies*. For the game in which players choose the right or left side of the road sequentially, this implies that player 1 has only 2 pure strategies (equal to the actions she is able to take), while player 2 has four pure strategies. The sequential move game represented in Graph 24.2 can then also be represented in the payoff matrix in Table 24.3.[5]

---

[5]Representing a game in a payoff matrix is often referred to as the game's *normal form*, whereas representing the game in a game tree is often referred to as the game's *extensive form*.

Table 24.3: A Sequential Move Game Represented in a Payoff Matrix

		Player 2			
		(Left, Left)	*(Right, Right)*	*(Left, Right)*	*(Right, Left)*
Player 1	*Left*	10 , 10	0 , 0	10 , 10	0 , 0
	Right	0 , 0	10 , 10	10 , 10	0 , 0

Exercise 24A.4   Verify that the payoffs listed in Table 24.3 are consistent with those given in the game tree of Graph 24.2.

24A.2.2 Pure Strategy Nash Equilibrium in Simultaneous Move Games
John Nash was the first to formalize the notion of an equilibrium in games, and what we explore next has therefore come to be called a *Nash equilibrium.* The definition of such an equilibrium is best given in terms of "best responses," where *a best response for player n to a set of strategies played by other players is* simply *a strategy that will result in the highest possible payoff for player n given the strategies played by others.* A *Nash equilibrium is* reached whenever *each player in the game is playing a best response strategy relative to the strategies played by all other players*; i.e., whenever everyone's plan is the best possible plan given the plans that all the others have adopted. In some cases, we will see that it is very clear what Nash equilibrium will emerge as individual players try to do the best they can given how others are playing the game. Sometimes, a single equilibrium will emerge, while other times multiple different equilibria are possible. Depending on the structure of the game, we will find instances when only pure strategies are employed in equilibrium, but many games also have mixed strategy equilibria. In fact, in games where there are no pure strategy equilibria, there generally exists a mixed strategy equilibrium.[6] And in games in which there are multiple pure strategy equilibria, there generally also exist mixed strategy equilibria (as we will see in Section 24A.4).

Let's begin by considering again the game represented in the payoff matrix in Table 24.2. Suppose you are player 1 and I am player 2, and suppose you contemplate what pure strategy to play. If I choose to drive on the left side of the road, you know that you will get a payoff of 10 if you also choose the left side but will receive a payoff of 0 if you choose the right side. Your best response to my strategy of playing *Left* is therefore to play *Left* as well. Similarly, if I choose the right side of the road, your best response is to also choose *Right*. It is clear in this example that you will do the best you can if you mimic what I do. I of course face exactly the same incentives.

We can then look at each of the four possible outcomes and check to see if the outcome could be a Nash equilibrium supported by strategies that are best responses. The two outcomes that result in 0 payoff for each player cannot possibly be an equilibrium outcome because, if we find ourselves crashing into each other as we are choosing different sides of the road, there is a way for you to improve your fortunes by changing what you do. The two outcomes that result in payoffs of 10, on the other hand, can be equilibrium outcomes. Whenever one of us chooses *Left*, the other's best response is to also choose *Left*, and whenever one of us chooses *Right*, the best response of the other is to also choose *Right*. Put differently, if we end up in the upper left corner of the payoff matrix, neither one of us has an incentive to change what we are doing, implying that we have reached an equilibrium. The same holds for the lower right corner of the payoff matrix.

In this example, it is unclear whether both of us driving on the right side or both of us driving on the left side will emerge as an equilibrium. In the real world, conventions arise and are often

---

[6]In the original investigation by Nash on the existence of Nash equilibria, it was in fact proven that such equilibria generally exist so long as the equilibrium concept includes mixed strategies.

formalized in laws that ensure everyone knows which equilibrium is to be expected. As you know, in some societies the convention of driving on the left side of the road has become the equilibrium, while in other societies the convention of driving on the right side has emerged. Games like this are sometimes called *coordination games* because the key for the players is to *coordinate* their actions to get to one of the possible pure strategy equilibria.

Are the two pure strategy Nash equilibria we have identified efficient?

Exercise
24A.5

It might appear at this point that an equilibrium will necessarily entail both sides achieving the maximum possible payoffs. If this were always the case, the first welfare theorem would still hold in the sense that decentralized decision making by individuals is resulting in efficient outcomes. But this is not necessarily the case. Suppose we changed the payoff matrix in Table 24.2 by assuming that each of us has an innate preference for driving on the left side of the road and thus we only receive a payoff of 5 each if we end up driving on the right side. In this case, both of us driving on the right side of the road is still an equilibrium of the game; if one of us chooses to play *Right*, it remains a best response for the other to also choose *Right*. *Games with multiple equilibria might therefore have some equilibria that are better for everyone than others*. In such cases, a role for nonmarket institutions emerges to try to get individuals to switch from the suboptimal equilibrium to the more efficient one.

24A.2.3 Dominant Strategy Equilibria in Simultaneous Move Games Even in games where there is a single pure strategy Nash equilibrium, however, there is no guarantee that the Nash equilibrium will achieve the maximum possible payoffs for the players. Consider the games defined by the payoff matrices in Tables 24.4 and 24.5. In the first game, a clear optimal strategy for each player is to always play the action *Up* because *regardless of what the other player does*, each individual player is better off playing *Up* rather than *Down*. This is an example of a game with a clear *dominant strategy, a strategy where a player always has the incentive to play a single action regardless of what the opponent does*. Even if you think your opponent will play the action *Down*, it is best for you to play *Up* because that will give you a payoff of 7 rather than 5. Since both players face the same incentives, a single pure strategy equilibrium emerges in which both players play *Up* and thus receive a payoff of 10. The game in Table 24.4 therefore unambiguously leads to an equilibrium in which both players receive the highest possible payoff; i.e., the Nash equilibrium is efficient and is particularly compelling since it is both the only equilibrium *and* it involves each player playing a strategy that is the best for that player regardless of what the other player does.

True or False: If a simultaneous move game gives rise to a dominant strategy for a player, then that strategy is a best response for any strategy played by the other players.

Exercise
24A.6

Table 24.4: A Game with a Single
Efficient Pure Strategy Nash Equilibrium

		Player 2	
		Up	*Down*
Player 1	*Up*	10 , 10	7 , 7
	Down	7 , 7	5 , 5

Table 24.5: A Game with a Single Inefficient
Pure Strategy Nash Equilibrium

		Player 2	
		Up	*Down*
Player 1　*Up*		10 , 10	0 , 15
Down		15 , 0	5 , 5

Now consider the game in Table 24.5 and suppose that you and I are playing this game. If I play *Up*, you will receive a payoff of 10 by also choosing *Up* and a payoff of 15 if you choose *Down*. Your best response to me playing *Up* is therefore to play *Down*. If, on the other hand, I choose to play *Down*, you will receive a payoff of 0 if you play *Up* and a payoff of 5 if you play *Down*. Thus, playing *Down* is also your best response to me playing *Down*. Put differently, playing *Down* is a *dominant strategy* for you because it is your best response to any strategy I play. Since I face the same incentives, we will both end up playing *Down*, resulting in the equilibrium outcome represented by the payoffs (5, 5) in the lower right corner of the payoff matrix. Thus, *even though we would both prefer the payoffs (10, 10) in the upper right corner of the matrix, the incentives in the game are such that we will end up in the lower right corner with payoffs (5, 5)*. The unique Nash equilibrium of this game is therefore inefficient, and it is just as compelling an equilibrium as the one we found in Table 24.4 in that it is the only pure strategy equilibrium *and* it involves only dominant strategies.

In Section 24A.3, we will discuss this game—known as the "Prisoner's Dilemma"—in much more detail because it will represent an important game that can be used to analyze many economic situations in the real world. For now, however, it should be clear that we will be unable to come up with something analogous to the First Welfare Theorem we derived for competitive economies when individual players have an incentive to be strategic in their decision making. Put differently, we will not be able to say in general that equilibria that rely on decentralized decision making by individuals are always efficient in economic circumstances that can be modeled by game theory. Sometimes they are, and sometimes they are not.

Exercise 24A.7　Suppose that player 2 has payoffs as in Table 24.4, while player 1 has payoffs as in Table 24.5. Write out this payoff matrix. Is there a dominant strategy equilibrium? Is there a unique Nash equilibrium? If so, is it efficient?

Exercise 24A.8　Suppose both players' payoffs are as in Table 24.5 except that player 1's payoff when both players play *Up* is 20. Is there a dominant strategy equilibrium? Is there a unique Nash equilibrium? If so, is it efficient?

Exercise 24A.9　Suppose payoffs are as in exercise 24A.8 except that player 2's payoff from playing *Down* is 10 less than before (regardless of what player 1 does). Is there a dominant strategy equilibrium? Is there a unique Nash equilibrium? If so, is it efficient?

24A.2.4 Nash Equilibrium in Sequential Move Games　The notion of a Nash equilibrium can then be straightforwardly applied in sequential move games if we represent the structure of such games within a payoff matrix in which we specify the set of payoffs for each combination of strategies. In Table 24.3, for instance, we depicted the structure of the game in which two players sequentially choose on which side of the road to drive.

Exercise 24A.10　Can you find which strategies in the game depicted in Table 24.3 constitute a Nash equilibrium? (*Hint*: You should be able to find four combinations of strategies that constitute Nash equilibria.)

A slightly more interesting version of this game arises when we assume again that the players have an innate preference for driving on the left side of the road, resulting in payoffs of 10 if they both choose *Left*, payoffs of 5 when they both choose *Right*, and payoffs of 0 when they choose different sides of the road. In the case when the players move simultaneously, we discovered that two pure strategy equilibria emerge: one in which both players drive on the left side of the road and one in which both players drive on the right side of the road. Thus, we discovered a simultaneous move game in which one of the equilibria was inefficient. When player 2 makes her choice after player 1 moves, the payoff matrix (analogous to the one we derived in Section 24A.2.1), is given in Table 24.6.

There are now several Nash equilibria in this game, with the accompanying equilibrium outcomes shaded in Table 24.6. One of these equilibria involves player 1 playing *Right* and player 2 playing (*Right, Right*). Given that player 2 always plays *Right*, it is a best response for player 1 to play *Right*, and given that player 1 plays *Right*, player 2's (*Right, Right*) strategy is a best response. Thus, the (inefficient) outcome of both players driving on the right side of the road continues to be possible in a Nash equilibrium in the sequential move game.

Is it also a Nash equilibrium for player 1 to play *Right* and player 2 to play (*Left, Right*)? If not, why was it a Nash equilibrium before when players were indifferent between coordinating on the left or the right side of the road?

Exercise 24A.11

In the case where player 1 gets to decide first which side of the road to pick, however, this equilibrium seems very counterintuitive. The only reason this is a Nash equilibrium is that player 2 is in effect threatening to drive on the right side of the road regardless of what player 1 chooses to do. But this threat is fundamentally noncredible because player 1 knows that player 2 is better off driving on the left side of the road once she sees that player 1 has chosen to drive on the left. For this reason, game theorists have developed a more refined notion of Nash equilibrium for sequential move games, a refinement that eliminates the possibility that noncredible threats are taken seriously in equilibrium. This refinement is known as *subgame perfection*.

24A.2.5 Subgame Perfect Equilibria in Sequential Move Games It is reasonable to assume that players who move early in a sequential move game will look down the game tree and determine what strategies by players that follow are *credible*, and that only credible strategies can emerge in an equilibrium. This implies that player 1 will look at each node in the game tree of the sequential move game to determine what is optimal for player 2. Player 1 can then infer something about what player 2 plans to do once player 2 has observed the action of player 1.

Consider the game tree in Graph 24.3 that depicts the game we represented in the payoff matrix in Table 24.6. Player 1 can now view each of the 2 nodes that player 2 could face as a separate *subgame* in which player 2 is the only player. If the left node is reached (as a result of player 1 playing *Left*), it is optimal for player 2 to also play *Left*, which we indicate in the graph by highlighting this action. Thus, player 1 can infer that she will receive a payoff of 10 if she moves *Left*. If the right

Table 24.6: The Sequential *Right/Left* Game with *Left* Preferred by All

		Player 2			
		(*Left, Left*)	(*Right, Right*)	(*Left, Right*)	(*Right, Left*)
Player 1	Left	10 , 10	0 , 0	10 , 10	0 , 0
	Right	0 , 0	5 , 5	5 , 5	0 , 0

Graph 24.3: Game Tree for the Game Represented in Table 24.6

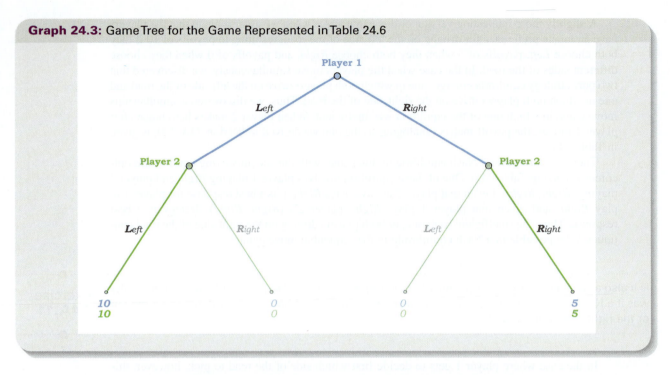

node is reached (as a result of player 1 playing *Right*), on the other hand, player 1 knows it will be optimal for player 2 to play *Right*, leading to a payoff of 5 for player 1. We again indicate this in the graph by highlighting that action. Thus, in choosing between *Left* and *Right*, player 1 knows that she is choosing between a payoff of 10 and a payoff of 5 and will therefore choose to play *Left*. The only rational response for player 2 is to also play *Left*, which leads to a unique equilibrium in which both players drive on the left side of the road.

While the outcome in which both players drive on the right side can therefore arise from a Nash equilibrium in which player 2 plays the strategy (*Right, Right*), this outcome cannot emerge as an equilibrium in which player 1 does not pay attention to noncredible threats. The elimination of Nash equilibria that are supported by noncredible threats then results in *subgame perfect equilibria.*[7]

Exercise 24A.12   *True or False*: In sequential move games, all pure strategy subgame perfect equilibria are pure strategy Nash equilibria, but not all pure strategy Nash equilibria are subgame perfect.

Now suppose that one of our players is from the United States and the other is from the U.K. and the players therefore do not share the same preferences over which side of the road to choose. In particular, player 1 now receives a payoff of 10 if both end up driving on the left and 5 when both end up driving on the right side, and player 2 receives a payoff of 5 when both end up driving on the left and 10 when both end up driving on the right. The only feature of the game tree in Graph 24.3 that then changes is that the 10 and the 5 on the last line in the graph reverse positions. But player 1 still knows that player 2 will choose the left side of the road if player 2 has to make a decision from the left node in the game tree and the right side of the road if she has to

---

[7]The notion of subgame perfection is due to Reinhard Selten who was awarded the Nobel Prize together with John Nash. As we will note in Section 24A.3.2, subgame perfect equilibria can equivalently be defined as Nash equilibria under which the equilibrium strategies represent Nash equilibria *for every subgame* of the actual sequential game.

make a decision on the right node. Thus, player 1 again knows that she will earn a payoff of 10 from choosing *Left* and a payoff of 5 from choosing *Right*, which again results in a unique sub-game perfect equilibrium in which both players end up driving on the left side of the road. While player 2 might threaten to always drive on the right side in order to get to the Nash equilibrium in which both players drive on the right, player 1 would be rational not to pay any attention to such a noncredible threat. As a result, player 1 enjoys a *first mover advantage* because by moving first, she gets the outcome most favorable to her.

What are the Nash equilibria and the subgame perfect equilibria if player 2 rather than player 1 gets to move first in this version of the game?

Exercise 24A.13

As we will see in later chapters, however, it is not the case that a *first mover* in a game will always get his or her way. Suppose, for example, we consider a firm that currently has a monopoly in a particular market but worries about a potential second firm entering the market and competing. To keep the game simple, let's suppose that the existing firm can set a *Low* or a *High* price for the product and that the potential firm can choose to *Enter* or *Not Enter* after observing the price set by the existing firm. Suppose further that the payoffs (or profits) in this game are as depicted in Graph 24.4.

If the potential firm does not enter, it receives a profit of 0, but if it enters, it earns a positive profit when the current price is high and a negative profit when the current price is low. The existing firm, on the other hand, earns the highest profit under a high price and no competition and the lowest profit if it announces a high price and the competitor enters (and undercuts that price in order to steal customers). The existing firm then looks down the game tree at each node faced by its potential competitor and determines what the competitor will do at each node. When price is set low by the existing firm, the competitor will not enter (because he or she would make a profit of -10 by entering) but when price is set high, he or she will enter. In choosing between *Low* and

Graph 24.4: Facing Potential Competition

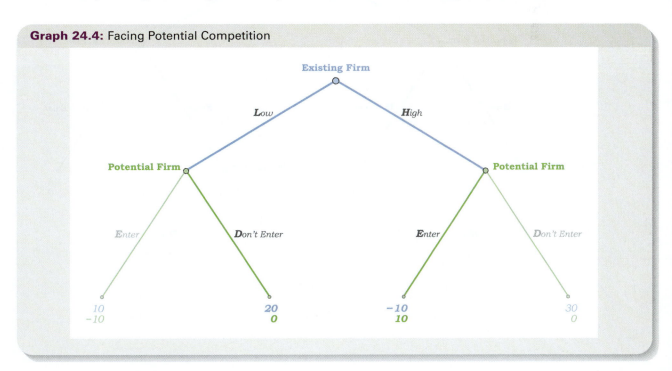

High, the existing firm is therefore choosing between a payoff of 20 and a payoff of −10 and will choose the low price in order to keep the potential firm from entering. This results in the subgame perfect equilibrium in which the existing firm sets a low price and the potential firm does not enter. Notice that in this case, the subgame perfect equilibrium does not result in the most preferred outcome for the first mover, and it is supported by a credible threat that the potential firm will enter if the price is set high by the existing firm.

Exercise 24A.14

Suppose the game had a third stage in which the existing firm gets a chance to re-evaluate its price in the event that a new firm has entered the market. This would imply that the game tree in Graph 24.4 continues as depicted in Graph 24.5. What is the subgame perfect equilibrium in this case?

Finally, we can note from the sequential move game in Graph 24.4 that, just as we found in simultaneous move games, there is no guarantee that equilibria in game theory are efficient; i.e., there is no general first welfare theorem. The efficient outcome (from the perspective of the two players) is the outcome that maximizes the sum of the profits (or payoffs). In our example, that occurs when the existing firm earns a profit of 30 and faces no competition from potential entrants. But, at least as the game is specified in Graph 24.4, this is not a subgame

Graph 24.5: An Extension of the Game in Graph 24.4

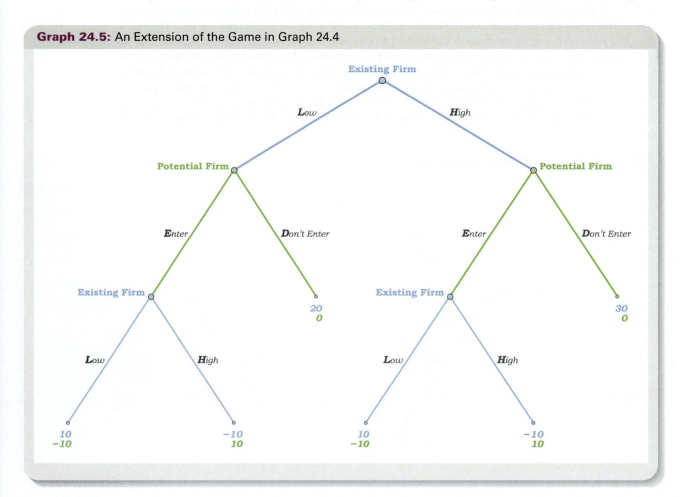

perfect equilibrium. Rather, the subgame perfect equilibrium results in a profit of 20 for the existing firm and a profit of zero for the potential entrant. From the perspective of the two firms, a move to the outcome in which the existing firm gets to set a high price and the potential firm does not enter makes one player better off without making the other worse off, but it is not an outcome that can be sustained as an equilibrium in the game without some nonmarket institution altering the incentives of the game.

In our example in Graph 24.4, we say that the subgame perfect equilibrium is not efficient from the perspective of the two players. Could it be efficient from the perspective of "society"?

Exercise
24A.15

24A.2.6 Solving for (Pure Strategy) Nash and Subgame Perfect Equilibria

While we have already solved for the equilibria in several games, it might be useful to briefly review the method by which we solve for these. *In the case of Nash equilibria in which 2 players have a finite number of actions to choose from, we start with the payoff matrix*, whether this represents a simultaneous move game or a sequential move game. Let's refer to the player whose strategies appear in the rows of the matrix as the "row player" and the player whose strategies appear in the columns of the matrix as the "column player." To solve for pure strategy Nash equilibria, we can then simply start with the first strategy of the row player and ask which strategy (or strategies) the column player would play as a best response. For each of these best response strategies by the column player, we then ask whether the first row strategy is a best response by the row player. When we find a case where the first row strategy is a best response to one of the column player's best responses, we have identified a Nash equilibrium. Doing this for each row, we end up finding all the pure strategy Nash equilibria.

When the set of possible actions for players in a simultaneous move game are not finite, such as when the set A is a continuum like the line segment $[0,1]$ from which the player can choose any point, we cannot use payoff matrices as just described (because such matrices would have to specify the payoffs from an infinite number of combinations of actions). We will encounter some examples of this in some of the end-of-chapter exercises, and we will develop the method for solving such games explicitly in the next chapter. For now, we just note that the logic of a strategy and an equilibrium remains exactly the same; all we will do is define "best-response functions" that must then intersect in an equilibrium. This is similar to how we solve games with discrete numbers of possible actions for mixed strategy equilibria in Section 24A.4.

In the case of subgame perfect (Nash) equilibria to sequential games in which players have a finite number of actions to choose from, *we have to start with the game tree rather than the payoff matrix of the game*. In particular, we start at the bottom of the game tree and ask which action is optimal at each node of the last player. These actions are the only actions that could be planned in a credible strategy for that player, and we then assume that these are in fact the actions that would be played at the respective nodes. We then move to the second-to-last player and ask which action (at each of the player's nodes) is optimal given that the player assumes the final player will play rationally at each of his or her nodes in the next stage. This then allows us to identify the optimal actions for the second-to-last player, which can be taken as given by the third-to-last player. In this way, we can solve the game backward to the top and derive the full set of subgame perfect equilibrium strategies. It is important to keep in mind, however, that the equilibrium is defined by best response *strategies*, and not just by the path along which the game unfolds in equilibrium. Put differently, the players' plans "off the equilibrium path" are often crucial to keeping other players "on the equilibrium path." We will again encounter games in which some players have a continuum of possible actions they can choose from, and we will see in end-of-chapter exercises as well as upcoming chapters that the basic logic for solving such games will again mirror that for games with a finite set of possible actions.

24A.3 The Prisoner's Dilemma

In Table 24.6, we illustrated a simultaneous move game in which each player has a dominant strategy, and in which the resulting Nash equilibrium is inefficient. This type of game is often referred to as the "Prisoner's Dilemma," and it occupies a particularly important place in microeconomics because it so starkly illustrates how strategic behavior can lead to outcomes that can be improved on through some type of nonmarket institution.

The name "Prisoner's Dilemma" has its origins in the 1950s when Albert Tucker (1905–1995), a mathematician and dissertation advisor to the young John Nash, attempted to find an accessible way of illustrating the basic incentives of the game with a "story" that made sense to psychology undergraduates at Stanford.[8] The story goes something like this: A prosecutor knows that two individuals he has in custody have committed armed robbery but he does not have enough evidence to convict them on anything other than a relatively minor charge of illegal possession of firearms. So he puts them in separate rooms and tells each of them that they can choose to confess or deny the armed robbery. If one confesses and the other does not, then he will let the confessor out on parole while using his testimony to go for the maximum sentence of 20 years in prison for the one that remains silent. If they both confess, they will each get a plea agreement that will put them in jail for 5 years. If neither confesses, all the prosecutor can do is press the illegal firearms convictions and get them 1-year prison sentences each.

Table 24.7 then illustrates the payoff matrix that the prosecutor has created for the two prisoners. You should be able to see that confessing is a dominant strategy for each of the players, implying a unique Nash equilibrium outcome in which both confess and get 5-year prison terms. Of course, both prisoners would have preferred the outcome in which they only go to prison for 1 year. This, however, would require both of them to deny the armed robbery, and this would require that each play a strategy that is not a best response. After all, *regardless* of what the other prisoner does, each prisoner is better off confessing. From the perspective of the prisoners, the prosecutor's game has set up incentives that will result in an inefficient outcome. (It will also cause them to falsely confess if they happen to be innocent.)

Exercise 24A.16   Why is this outcome inefficient from the perspective of the two players? Could it be efficient from the perspective of "society"?

As we will see in upcoming chapters, many economic circumstances have similar incentives. We may all wish to live in a society in which we smile and are courteous to one another. But smiling and being courteous requires effort, and so regardless of whether others smile and show courtesy, it might be a dominant strategy to individually behave like an ass. We may all want to live in a world in which we look out for our neighbors and provide them with help when they are in need, but helping others requires effort and it might just be a dominant strategy to not bother and just hope others will take care of it. Once you have internalized the incentive structure of the

Table 24.7: The Prisoner's Dilemma
(with Years in Prison as Payoffs)

		Prisoner 2	
		Deny	*Confess*
Prisoner 1	*Deny*	1 , 1	20 , 0
	Confess	0 , 20	5 , 5

---

[8]The underlying game was already known at the time and played a large role in the Rand Corporation's investigation of game theory as part of its federally sponsored project to research incentives in global nuclear strategy.

Prisoner's Dilemma game, you'll see these incentives all around you. We want to live in a world in which we cooperate with one another for the common good but in which it is often in our self-interest to not cooperate and hope everyone else will. The fact that individuals inadvertently cooperate in competitive markets and maximize overall social surplus (as illustrated by the First Welfare Theorem) simply does not mean they cooperate purposefully when put in situations where they have an incentive to behave strategically.

Once you understand the incentives in Prisoner's Dilemma games, observing a lack of cooperation in the world is not surprising. What is surprising is how much cooperation we actually do observe in the real world despite the predictions of the Prisoner's Dilemma. While it may not happen to the extent to which we would hope, we see neighbors helping one another, individuals holding open doors for strangers, charities successfully raising money to combat hunger and disease, and soldiers dying in battle to save another's life. We also see prisoners denying crimes when faced with the incentives in Table 24.7 and firms colluding to set prices even when it appears that they would individually benefit by producing more than their collusive agreement permits (as we will discuss in detail in our treatment of cartels in Chapter 25). In some sense, once we understand the Prisoner's Dilemma, the question becomes not "Why don't we observe people cooperating more with one another?" but rather "Why do we see any cooperation in many situations at all?"

24A.3.1 Repeated Prisoner's Dilemma Games and the "Unraveling of Cooperation"
You might think that one possible explanation for cooperation in the real world is that, at least in some circumstances, players run into each other repeatedly and therefore develop a cooperative relationship. It turns out, however, that repeated interaction in circumstances that can be described by the Prisoner's Dilemma is not enough for game theory to predict cooperation.

Suppose you and I face the payoffs (in, say, dollar terms) in Table 24.8 every time we meet.

Why is this a Prisoner's Dilemma game?

Exercise 24A.17

Now suppose you and I know that we will run into each other 100 times, and each time we will face the incentives in Table 24.8. This means we are now playing a *sequential move game* in the sense that we encounter each other (after the first time) knowing what we did in previous encounters, but in each encounter we play a *simultaneous move game*. We can then apply the logic of *subgame perfection* to see what would happen. Subgame perfection requires that we start at the very bottom of the game tree that, in this case, consists of 100 different simultaneous move games. We can then ask: What would we expect will happen when we encounter each other for the 100th (and last) time?

Since we will know that we will not encounter each other again, it will be exactly as if we simply played the game one time, with each one of us facing a dominant strategy of not cooperating in that last encounter. When we meet each other the 99th time, it is therefore not credible for either one of us to promise or threaten any action other than not cooperating in the 100th round. Put differently, we will both know in the 99th round that we will not cooperate in the 100th round. But then there is no particular reason to cooperate in the 99th round; once again, regardless of what you do in the 99th round, I will do better by not cooperating. So we both realize when we play the 98th

Table 24.8: Another Prisoner's Dilemma (with Payoffs in $'s)

		You	
		Cooperate	Don't Cooperate
Me	Cooperate	100 , 100	0 , 200
	Don't Cooperate	200 , 0	10 , 10

round that we will not cooperate in the 99th or 100th rounds, which, by the same logic, implies we won't cooperate in the 98th round or in any round before that. *The prediction from subgame perfection is that we will not cooperate in the Prisoner's Dilemma even if we know we will interact repeatedly n different times.* This holds true regardless how large n is (assuming it is finite).

Notice what is going on in this argument for why cooperation will not arise even under repeated interactions: We might think that if I know we will run into each other 100 times, I could say to you "Why don't we cooperate since we will run into each other repeatedly and we both know we'll be better off by cooperating?" You would presumably see that what I said is true. I might even try a carrot-and-stick approach by telling you that I will cooperate so long as you cooperate but if I see you not cooperating, I will punish you and never cooperate again. The problem is that my promise to cooperate is not credible because as you look down the game tree, you know I will not cooperate in the 100th round, which means that there is no incentive to cooperate in the 99th round, which means there is no incentive to cooperate in the 98th round, and so on.

Exercise 24A.18*   Does the same logic hold for any repeated simultaneous game in which the simultaneous game has a single pure strategy Nash equilibrium? Put differently, does subgame perfection require that players in such games always simply repeat the simultaneous game Nash equilibrium?

24A.3.2 Infinitely Repeated Games, Trigger Strategies, and Cooperation

The reason why cooperation unravels in the repeated Prisoner's Dilemma is that both of us can look toward the last time we interact and work backward to realize that there is no credible (i.e., subgame perfect) way of sustaining any cooperation. But what if there was no "last time"? What if we keep running into each other without end? Or more realistically, what if we are never sure whether we'll run into each other again but each time we run into each other we know there is a good chance we'll see each other again under similar circumstances?

Exercise 24A.19   *True or False*: In an infinitely repeated Prisoner's Dilemma game, every subgame of the sequential game is identical to the original game.

Before answering this question, we need to briefly address what the concept of "subgame perfection" means in the case of a game that has no end. So far, we have simply thought of subgame perfection as eliminating noncredible strategies by solving the game "from the bottom up," but now there is no "bottom"! The basic idea of subgame perfection can, however, be expressed a little differently and in a way that then allows us to apply it to infinitely repeated games: When we solve the game backward in a finite sequential game, we are actually making sure that the Nash equilibrium is such that each *subgame* of the whole game—i.e., each game that begins at one of the nodes in the game tree—is also in equilibrium. Put differently, we are requiring that the subgames that are "off the equilibrium path" and are never reached still involve strategies that are best responses to each other in the hypothetical case that such subgames were reached. We can then restate the concept of a subgame perfect equilibrium by defining it as follows: *A Nash equilibrium in a sequential move game of complete information is subgame perfect if all subgames of the sequential game, whether they are reached in equilibrium or not, also involve Nash equilibrium strategies.*

Now let's return to our question: What could be a subgame perfect equilibrium in a repeated Prisoner's Dilemma game in which there is no definitive end to our interactions? Robert Axelrod (1943–), a political scientist, has written a famous series of papers in which precisely this question was analyzed theoretically and experimentally. Consider the case in which you and I meet repeatedly, and each time we meet we know that we will meet again with probability γ. At the beginning of our interactions, we decide on our strategies. Remember that a "strategy" for me is a complete plan for what I will do each time we run into each other, a plan in which I can make my actions dependent on how we interacted in the past. Axelrod distinguished between two kinds of such plans or strategies we might adopt: those that are "nice" and those that are "not nice." "Nice" strategies are those in which an individual will not stop cooperating first, while "not nice" strategies are those in which an individual is the first to stop cooperating.

True or False: If two players play "nice" strategies in the repeated Prisoner's Dilemma, they will always cooperate with one another every time they meet.

Exercise 24A.20

Suppose, for instance, I play a strategy in which I plan to cooperate the first time I see you and then plan to continue to cooperate every time I see you as long as all our previous interactions have been characterized by both of us cooperating, but if at some point we do not cooperate, I will punish you by never cooperating again. One act of noncooperation, according to this strategy, will "trigger" my noncooperation at every meeting thereafter, which is why this type of a strategy is sometimes called a *trigger strategy*.

Explain why this type of trigger strategy is "nice."

Exercise 24A.21

What is your best response to this strategy? One possible best response might well be for you to play the same strategy, resulting in us always cooperating. This is because the cost of being punished with noncooperation from now on is too high to justify the gain from not cooperating one time while I am still cooperating. Whether it's worth it to you to cheat me at our current encounter by not cooperating (despite knowing that I will never cooperate again thereafter) then depends on two things: the probability γ that we will meet again and the degree to which you discount the future. If γ is sufficiently high and you do not discount the future too much, you will value future cooperation more than the one-time payoff you could get by cheating me at our present meeting.

Would you playing "Cooperate Always" also potentially be a best response for you to my trigger strategy? Would my trigger strategy then be a best response to your "Cooperate Always" strategy?

Exercise 24A.22

If you playing the trigger strategy is a best response to me playing this strategy, then it is of course also a best response for me to play this strategy if you play it. And when both of us play this strategy, we will always cooperate with one another. It is certainly possible, then, to have Nash equilibria in which cooperation is sustained in repeated relationships that are characterized by Prisoner's Dilemma incentives if those relationships have no clear end. But is such a Nash equilibrium subgame perfect? Given our restated definition of subgame perfection as involving only strategies that are Nash equilibrium strategies to every subgame, we have to ask whether the Nash equilibrium strategies we have proposed are also Nash equilibrium strategies in every subgame of the infinitely repeated game. Every such subgame is, of course, once again an infinitely repeated game identical to the original game, but subgames have different "histories" of previous interactions between us that led up to them. Thus, unlike the first time we meet, I know something about how you are playing the game every time we meet thereafter, and you know something about how I play the game.

When we reach a particular subgame, there are then two possible histories that have brought us there: either we have gotten there by always cooperating, or we have gotten there by not cooperating at some point. Suppose first that we had always cooperated previously. Then, given that we are playing our trigger strategies, we are starting this subgame in exactly the same way as we started the first time we interacted: We both cooperate and plan to continue cooperating unless one of us deviates at some point. If the proposed trigger strategy played by both of us was a Nash equilibrium to the original game, it must therefore be a Nash equilibrium to this subgame. This leaves us to consider the ("off-the-equilibrium path") case where cooperation broke down at some point in a previous meeting. In this case, our trigger strategies for the next subgame are both to "Never Cooperate." Given that you will never cooperate, it is a best response for me to never cooperate and the other way around. Thus, we are best-responding to each other in this kind of a subgame, and we have therefore shown that both of us playing the proposed trigger strategy represents a Nash equilibrium in every subgame of our infinitely repeated game. These strategies are therefore subgame perfect.

Put differently, the "threats" required to sustain our cooperation are credible in our example. In fact, as we demonstrate in the appendix, *anything between no cooperation and full cooperation* can be part of a subgame perfect equilibrium through similar trigger strategies in an infinitely repeated Prisoner's Dilemma. Thus, when Prisoner's Dilemma games are repeated infinitely, many possible subgame perfect equilibria emerge even though there is only a single subgame perfect equilibrium when such games are repeated a large but finite number of times.

Exercise 24A.23 Why can't the same type of "trigger strategy" sustain cooperation in a repeated Prisoner's Dilemma that has a definitive end?

Exercise 24A.24 If you model the decision about whether to be friendly to someone you run into as part of a Prisoner's Dilemma, why might you expect people in small towns to be friendlier than people in big cities?

24A.3.3 The "Evolution" of Cooperation and the Emergence of "Tit-for-Tat"

Axelrod, however, was interested in more than just demonstrating that cooperation could in principle emerge in repeated relationships—he wanted to know what kinds of strategies individuals might use to in fact sustain such cooperation. The answer is far from obvious. Once relationships have no clear end (and cooperation in the repeated Prisoner's Dilemma does not unravel from the bottom), many different strategies, some sustaining cooperation and others not, can be part of a subgame perfect Nash equilibrium. So which will people actually choose?

To answer this question, Axelrod did several very clever experiments.[9] First, he asked the world's most eminent game theorists to submit strategies that they think might do well in repeated Prisoner's Dilemmas that have no definitive end. He placed no limit on how complex these strategies could be and included them all in a computer simulation in which different strategies encountered each other randomly. The strategy that consistently outperformed all others was remarkably simple and has become known as the "tit-for-tat" strategy.

Under the *tit-for-tat strategy*, a player begins at a first encounter with someone by cooperating and from then on mimics what the opposing player did at the last meeting. Thus, if the other player also cooperates, then the tit-for-tat player will cooperate again next time. If the other player does not cooperate, the tit-for-tat player punishes him at the next meeting by not cooperating and will continue to not cooperate at each successive meeting unless the other player shows good will by cooperating at some point. If so, the tit-for-tat player will begin cooperating again. The strategy reminds me of what my mother told me when I was a child and she sent me to the

---

[9]If you are interested to learn more about these, you may want to read R. Axelrod, *The Evolution of Cooperation* (New York: Basic Books, 1984).

playground to play with other kids. "Play nice with the other kids," she would say, "but if some-one hits you, you hit them back until they start being nice again."

Axelrod also took the same strategies submitted by game theorists and did another simulation in which strategies "reproduced" if they achieved high average payoffs and decreased in the pop-ulation if they received relatively low payoffs. As the computer simulation continued, unsuccess-ful strategies would therefore die out while successful strategies would increase in number. Eventually, he found, only one strategy survived this evolutionary process and was left standing: you guessed it—tit-for-tat. Eventually Axelrod showed that strategies that were "evolutionarily stable" had to have properties similar to the tit-for-tat strategies.[10] Put differently, strategies that would do well in evolutionary settings had to (1) attempt cooperation and sustain it if it is recip-rocated (i.e., the strategies have to be "nice"), (2) punish noncooperation, but (3) leave the door open for forgiving noncooperation if a player signals that he or she is ready to cooperate again.

24A.3.4 Sustaining Cooperation (in Prisoner's Dilemmas) through Institutions

As we have seen, it is possible for cooperation in Prisoner's Dilemma games to emerge if the same players meet repeatedly without any definitive end of the repetitions. Even in such settings, however, equilibria without cooperation are also possible, and in settings other than that, cooper-ation unravels under subgame perfection. As we will see throughout the remainder of this text, there are, however, other ways in which market and nonmarket institutions might emerge to help sustain cooperation when the incentives in each interaction are themselves insufficient.

One possibility is for the individuals in a Prisoner's Dilemma to write a contract that imposes sufficient penalties for not cooperating. If there is a way to enforce the penalties, such a contract in essence changes the payoffs in the matrix to eliminate the "Dilemma." The prisoners in our game depicted in Table 24.6, for instance, might be part of a "mafia" or a "gang" that has the rule that those who cooperate with prosecutors will be severely punished. In joining the mafia, indi-viduals implicitly sign a contract that imposes penalties for not cooperating with the goals of the mafia (i.e., cooperating with prosecutors). Getting out of jail early loses some of its appeal if the prisoner knows he will be killed in some particularly gruesome way as soon as he is out.

But not all institutions that solve Prisoner's Dilemma problems are as sinister as the mafia. Religious institutions might, for instance, persuade individuals that there are eternal benefits from cooperating, thus changing the way in which we evaluate the payoffs in a Prisoner's Dilemma because we get "utility" from the act of cooperating. Private fund-raisers have devel-oped ways of "personalizing" our participation in large efforts to help the poor, and thus making us view the payoffs from helping others differently. For instance, you may have seen how organ-izations that help poor children in developing countries offer the opportunity for individuals to "sponsor" particular children whose pictures and stories are shared with the donors. There is no particular reason to believe that the children whose pictures are sent to sponsors would not have been helped had the particular sponsor not decided to contribute to the organization, but the use of pictures personalizes the contribution in a way that appears to move people to give more.

And in some cases, government policy can alter the payoffs in Prisoner's Dilemma games, sometimes achieving positive and sometimes, as we will see, achieving less desirable out-comes. If individuals face Prisoner's Dilemma incentives in their decision to give to charitable organizations, tax breaks for charitable contributions (or other forms of more explicit govern-ment subsidies for giving to charitable causes) might change behavior in the direction of greater efficiency. (We will say more about this in Chapter 27.) At the same time, if large cor-porations in concentrated industries face Prisoner's Dilemma incentives when trying to collude on setting high prices, they might also look to government to act as the enforcer of their collu-sion. (We will discuss this at greater length in our discussion of oligopolies in Chapter 25.) For

---

[10]The concept of evolutionary stability has precise meaning in a subfield of game theory known as evolutionary game theory (which is beyond the scope of this chapter).

now, I simply want to convince you that government policies and civil society institutions often look for ways to alter payoffs in situations in which Prisoner's Dilemma incentives arise.

Exercise 24A.25   *True or False*: Whenever individuals find themselves in a Prisoner's Dilemma game, there is profit to be made if someone can determine a way to commit players to change behavior.

Exercise 24A.26   How might your answer to the previous exercise help explain why we see more cooperation in real-world Prisoner's Dilemma games than we expect from the incentives contained in the game?

24A.3.5 Sustaining Cooperation (in Prisoner's Dilemmas) through "Reputations"

Another way in which cooperation might emerge is if there is a way for individuals to credibly establish a reputation for cooperating. This is, however, far from trivial and requires the introduction of uncertainty on the part of one player with respect to the type of player he or she is facing in a (finitely) repeated setting. In other words, it requires the modeling of repeated interactions as sequential games of *incomplete* information, a topic we take up in Section B. We will therefore return to the role of reputations in finitely repeated Prisoner's Dilemmas in Section 24B.3.

24A.4 Mixed Strategies

The distinction between "strategies" and "actions" has been most apparent for the case of sequential games where a plan for the game is different (for at least some players) than just picking an action. In simultaneous move games, however, *pure strategies* have involved simply picking an action, but this is not true for *mixed strategies*, which we now explore.

Consider the following game: You and I are both asked to put a penny on the table. If our pennies "match" in the sense that they both have the same side of the penny showing, I end up getting your penny. If, on the other hand, the pennies do not "match" (in the sense that one shows "heads" and the other "tails"), you get my penny. This simple game, known as *matching pennies*, is illustrated in Table 24.9.

You should be able to convince yourself fairly quickly that there is no pure strategy Nash equilibrium to this game; my best response to any move of yours is to match it while your best response to any move of mine is to contradict it. In such a game, there is no way to predict for sure what will happen because the very structure of the game prohibits such predictability. A common way to think of this formally is then through the use of "mixed strategies."

A *mixed strategy* for a player is simply a *probability distribution over the pure strategies*. (Even though we will only explore mixed strategies for simultaneous move games, the same definition holds for sequential move games.) For instance, I have two pure strategies in the matching pennies game: *Heads* and *Tails*. A mixed strategy is a set of two probabilities $(\rho, 1 - \rho)$ such that $0 \le \rho \le 1$. If I decide to play the mixed strategy $(0.5, 0.5)$, it simply means that I will play *Heads* with probability 0.5 and *Tails* with probability 0.5. More generally, if a player has n different pure strategies available to him or her, a mixed strategy is a list of n probabilities $(\rho_1, \rho_2, ..., \rho_n)$ (with $\rho_i \ge 0$ for all $i = 1, 2, ..., n$ and the sum of all ρ_i's equal to 1).

Table 24.9: Matching Pennies

		You	
		Heads	*Tails*
Me	*Heads*	1, −1	−1, 1
	Tails	−1, 1	1, −1

Exercise
24A.27

Note that it is always possible to write a pure strategy in the form of a mixed strategy with one probability set to 1 and the others set to zero. How would you write my pure strategy of *Heads* in the form of a mixed strategy?

24A.4.1 Best Responses to Mixed Strategies

Now suppose that I have some belief about the probability λ with which you will play *Heads* and I am trying to determine how best to respond by setting my own probability ρ of playing *Heads*. My goal is to match your penny. So if I think $\lambda > 0.5$, I will do best by simply playing *Heads* all the time, i.e., by setting $\rho = 1$. Similarly, if I think $\lambda < 0.5$, I should just play *Tails*, which implies setting $\rho = 0$. But if I think you are setting $\lambda = 0.5$, I could always play *Heads* (i.e., $\rho = 1$) or always play *Tails* (i.e., $\rho = 0$), and my expected payoff would be exactly the same in either case.

Exercise
24A.28

What would be my expected payoff if I play *Heads* all the time when you play the mixed strategy that places probability 0.5 of *Heads*?

Furthermore, if you set $\lambda = 0.5$, I could play any mixed strategy in between and get the same payoff. To see this, note that if you end up playing *Heads* (which you will do with probability 0.5), I will get your penny with probability ρ and will lose my penny with probability $(1 - \rho)$. In expectation, I will therefore get $\rho - (1 - \rho) = (2\rho - 1)$ in the event that you put down *Heads*. If, on the other hand, you put down *Tails* (which you will do half the time), I will win a penny with probability $(1 - \rho)$ and lose a penny with probability ρ. In expectation, I will therefore get $(1 - \rho) - \rho = (1 - 2\rho)$. Each of these expectations is equally likely, which means my expected payoff from playing the mixed strategy that places probability ρ on *Heads* when I believe you are playing a mixed strategy that places probability 0.5 on *Heads* is $0.5(2\rho - 1) + 0.5(1 - 2\rho) = 0$, exactly the same expected payoff as if I chose to simply always play *Heads* or always *Tails* (when you play *Heads* with probability 0.5).

In panel (a) of Graph 24.6, we then graph my best response mixed strategy to all possible mixed strategies you might be playing. On the horizontal axis, we plot λ, which is the probability

Graph 24.6: Mixed Strategy Nash Equilibrium for Matching Pennies

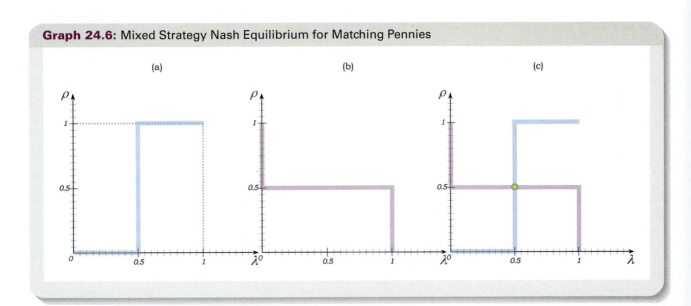

you assign to *Heads*, while on the vertical axis we plot ρ. For any $\lambda < 0.5$, my best response is $\rho = 0$, and for any $\lambda > 0.5$, my best response is $\rho = 1$. Finally, for $\lambda = 0.5$, my best response can set ρ anywhere between 0 and 1.

Panel (b) does the same from your perspective, illustrating your best response in terms of setting λ to any possible ρ that I might set. Finally, we put the two panels together in panel (c) of the graph and note that our best responses intersect at $\lambda = \rho = 0.5$.

24A.4.2 Mixed Strategy Nash Equilibrium

Recall that a Nash equilibrium requires each player to play a strategy that is a best response to the strategy played by the opposing player. This is no different for the case of mixed strategies: The only way we are in a Nash equilibrium is if you are "best responding" to my ρ when you set λ just as I am "best responding" to your λ when I set my ρ. Put differently, the only time we are at a Nash equilibrium is if our best responses in Graph 24.6c intersect. In our "matching pennies" game, there is then only a single Nash equilibrium, one in which both you and I play mixed strategies in which we place probability 0.5 on each of our two possible pure strategies.

The matching pennies game is a natural game to use to motivate the notions of mixed strategies and mixed strategy equilibrium because the game does not give rise to any pure strategy equilibria. But even in games with pure strategy equilibria, there may exist separate mixed strategy equilibria. Consider, for instance, our *Left/Right* game pictured in Table 24.2. In Graph 24.7, we again plot out the best responses for me and you to different mixed strategies by the other. It turns out that my best response function in panel (a) looks exactly like the one we plotted for me in the matching pennies game. This is because I am trying to match your action in both games. But *your* best response in panel (b) differs across the two games because you are trying to contradict my action in the matching pennies game while trying to match it in the *Left/Right* game. As a result, when we put the two best response functions together in panel (c), they now intersect three times: at $\rho = \lambda = 0$, at $\rho = \lambda = 0.5$, and at $\rho = \lambda = 1$.

Notice that two of the intersections of the best response functions involve both of us playing one of our pure strategies with probability 1. These are simply the pure strategy Nash equilibria we identified earlier. In addition, however, we have now discovered a third Nash equilibrium in mixed strategies, one in which both of us play each of our two possible pure strategies with probability 0.5.

Graph 24.7: Nash Equilibria for *Left/Right* Game from Table 24.2

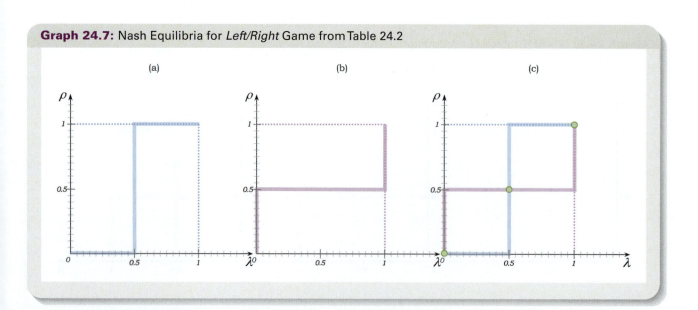

Is the mixed strategy equilibrium more or less efficient than the pure strategy equilibria in the *Left/Right* game?

Exercise
24A.29

Because of the particular payoff values we have chosen so far, the two mixed strategy equilibria that we have found both involve each player placing equal weight on each of his or her pure strategies. But one can easily identify games where a mixed strategy equilibrium involves other weights. For instance, in the version of the *Left/Right* game in which the payoffs for both players choosing *Right* are 5 rather than 10, you should be able to convince yourself that the mixed strategy equilibrium involves $\rho = \lambda = 1/3$. We can also think of settings in which the two players will place different probabilities on their pure strategies, such as, for instance, when the payoff from both choosing left is 10 for player 1 but 5 for player 2 and the payoff from both choosing right is 5 for player 1 and 10 for player 2. (This game is sometimes referred to as the "Battle of the Sexes" game for reasons explained in exercise 24.8.)

Determine the mixed strategy Nash equilbrium for the game described in the previous sentence.

Exercise
24A.30*

24A.4.3 A Quick Note on the Existence of Nash Equilibria   John Nash proved in 1950 that all well-defined games have at least one Nash equilibrium. The proof makes use of fixed point theorems that are beyond the scope of this text, but the intuition for it is simple: In graphs plotting best response functions to mixed strategies, each player's best response function must cross the 45-degree line at some point, and this ensures that the two players' best response functions must cross at least once (though not necessarily on the 45-degree line). When they cross, we have a Nash equilibrium. As we have already seen in the matching pennies game, not all games have pure strategy equilibria. Similarly, you should be able to convince yourself that the Prisoner's Dilemma is a game in which there does not exist a mixed strategy equilibrium and we are therefore left with only the single pure strategy equilibrium. As a general rule, you can remember the following: If there are no pure strategy equilibria in a game you are asked to analyze, there is sure to be a mixed strategy equilibrium. If there is a single pure strategy equilibrium, you won't find a mixed strategy equilibrium to the same game. But if there are two pure strategy equilibria, there will also be at least one mixed strategy equilibrium.

Plot the best response functions to mixed strategies for the Prisoner's Dilemma game and illustrate that there exists only a single, pure strategy equilibrium.

Exercise
24A.31

24A.4.4 How Should We Interpret Mixed Strategies?   It is often a little difficult for students to figure out what to make of the concept of a "mixed strategy." Taken literally, it means that players just randomize over pure strategies in some fashion. But there is another interpretation that many game theorists think makes more sense. In particular, it can be shown that if we change a game of complete information (in which all the players know everyone's payoffs) to a very similar game with just a little bit of incomplete information (in which there is some uncertainty on the part of some players about the payoffs of other players), a mixed strategy equilibrium in the complete information game can be interpreted as a pure strategy Nash equilibrium in the incomplete information game. Put differently, the "mixing" might arise from a little uncertainty about other players' payoffs. In Section B, we turn toward games of incomplete information, and in end-of-chapter exercise 24.4 you can explore how mixed strategies in games of complete information are in fact related to pure strategy equilibria in similar games with incomplete information. Exercise 24.7 also provides some real-world examples where you might find the idea of mixed strategy equilibria somewhat persuasive (as it is in the matching pennies game).

24B Game Theory under Incomplete Information

As noted in the introduction to this chapter, we can distinguish between *complete information* games in which the payoffs of all the players are known to all players and *incomplete information* games in which some players do not know the payoffs of other players. So far, we have dealt only with complete information games. But there are economically important situations in which players don't in fact have such complete information. Think, for example, of a sealed-bid auction in which you and I are bidding on a painting. I know what the painting is worth to me, but I have no idea what it is worth to you. I therefore know only my own payoff from winning the auction. Or think of two firms (in an industry that is not perfectly competitive) competing without knowing quite what costs the other is facing. Each firm will know its own profit under different output prices, but not the other firm's. We now turn to such games of incomplete information and will distinguish once again between simultaneous move games and sequential games. Games of incomplete information are also often called *Bayesian games*.

24B.1 Simultaneous Bayesian Games

When we first introduced games of complete information, we began by specifying the set of N players, their possible actions and the payoffs each player receives from different combinations of actions. In particular, we assumed that a player n could take an action from a set of possible actions denoted A^n. Player n's payoff was then given by a function $u^n:\mathbb{R}^N \to \mathbb{R}^1$ that specifies a payoff value $u^n(a^1, a^2, ..., a^N)$ for all possible combinations of actions that the N players might take. In games of incomplete information, we similarly need to specify the set of N players and their possible actions A^n, but the payoffs are now no longer common knowledge. We therefore have to introduce *beliefs* on the part of players about other players' payoffs.

24B.1.1 "Types" and Beliefs   This is typically accomplished by assuming that players could be one of several (or many) *types*, and that player n's payoff depends on her type t as well as on the set of actions $(a^1, a^2, ..., a^N)$ taken by everyone in the game. If a player n could be one of T different types, she now has T different possible payoff functions $(u_1^n, u_2^n, ..., u_T^n)$, with $u_t^n:\mathbb{R}^N \to \mathbb{R}^1$ giving the payoff $u_t^n(a^1, a^2, ..., a^N)$ when n is type t. We will assume that each player knows his or her own payoff function (which is equivalent to saying that each player knows her own type) before he or she has to make a move in the game, but at least some players in the game only have *beliefs* about what type other players are. The set of types, as we will see in the following examples, could be a finite number of possible types (as in Section 24B.1.5) or a continuum of types (as in Section 24B.1.6).

To be more precise, beliefs are simply probability distributions that players have over the set of possible types that other players might be. Suppose there are two players, me and you, and that each of us could be one of three types. If I know my own type, then there are three possible scenarios I am facing: you could be type 1, 2, or 3. My beliefs about the game can then be characterized by the probability distribution (ρ_1, ρ_2, ρ_3), where $0 \le \rho_i \le 1$ for all i and $\sum_i \rho_i = 1$. This means that I believe you are a type 1 player with probability ρ_1, a type 2 player with probability ρ_2, and a type 3 player with probability ρ_3. If there are three players and three possible types, then I face six possible scenarios (assuming I know my own type) with beliefs given by the probability distribution $(\rho_{11}, \rho_{12}, \rho_{13}, \rho_{21}, \rho_{22}, \rho_{23})$ where ρ_{ij} is the probability that the first player is of type i and the second player is of type j. And if an opposing player can take on types from a continuous interval such as $T = [0,1]$, we will see in the example of Section 24B.1.6 that the probability distribution is given in terms of a function $\rho: T \rightarrow \mathbb{R}^1$, with $\rho(t)$ equal to the probability that the player is a type less than or equal to t.

If there are N players and T possible types, how many probabilities constitute my beliefs about the other players in the game?

Exercise 24B.1

Note that this structure of beliefs as probability distributions makes it possible for some player n's payoffs to be known with certainty by everyone; the other players' beliefs would simply assign probability zero to player n being of a different type. We therefore do not require that everyone is equally uncertain about what type everyone else in the game is but, even if one player is uncertain about another one's type, we will call this a Bayesian game (of incomplete information).

24B.1.2 The Role of "Nature" For reasons that will become clearer shortly, it has become common to introduce into Bayesian games a nonstrategic fictional player called "Nature" (that has no payoffs) that moves prior to any other move. Thus, even simultaneous move Bayesian games have a sequential structure in the sense that Nature goes first and then everyone else moves at the same time. The only role played by Nature is that it assigns a type to each player, with knowledge of one's own type becoming private information for each individual. In some games, Nature might also share some information about other players' types with some of the players, perhaps leaving some players more informed than others. Only if all information about player types were shared with everyone in the game would the game cease to be one of incomplete information. In this sense, we can think of games of complete information as a special case of games of incomplete information. The crucial assumption we will make throughout is that *all players know the probability distribution Nature uses to assign types to players, and each player is assigned his or her type independently of others.* Put differently, all players in the game begin (prior to Nature moving) with the same initial beliefs about types.

24B.1.3 Strategies Recall from our discussion of complete information games that a strategy is a *complete* plan of action *prior to the beginning of the game.* In the case of simultaneous move games with complete information, this implied that a pure strategy for player n involves picking an action from the set A^n, but in the sequential move case, it meant something more than simply choosing an action for those players that moved later in the game. Specifically, in a sequential game, a strategy involved specifying an action for each possible prior history of the game. In the two-player case, this meant that player 2's strategy involved a plan for what to do for each possible action that player 1 might have taken in the first stage of the game, even if player 1 never chooses a particular action in equilibrium.

This is relevant for our discussion of simultaneous move Bayesian games because we have embedded the simultaneous moves that the players make into a sequential structure in which the fictional player Nature moves first. Since the game begins with Nature's move, and since a strategy is a complete plan for how to play the game prior to the beginning of the game, a strategy now involves each player settling on what action he or she will take *for each possible type Nature might assign to him or her.* Put differently, by introducing the fictional player Nature as the first player in the game, we implicitly require that every actual player determines a plan for how to play the game *before finding out what type of player he or she is.*

At first glance, this may seem silly. After all, the player "Nature" is just a fiction, so why can't we just assume that each player will simply decide on a a plan of action once he or she finds out his or her type? But think of it this way: Suppose you and I are in a simultaneous Bayesian game and I know what type Nature has assigned to me. Now I want to figure out what my best course of action is. In order to do that, I have to think about what your strategy will be, and your strategy will depend on what you think I will do. Since only I know my true type, you will have to use your beliefs to infer what I will do, which means you will need to think about what I would do depending on what type I am and then appropriately weight each of the possibilities by the probability your beliefs assign to me being a particular type. Thus, you have to be thinking about what I would do for each possible type that I could in fact have been assigned. And that in turn means that I need to think about what I would have done had I been assigned another type because this goes into your thinking about what you will do in the game.

A *strategy* in a simultaneous Bayesian game is therefore a plan of action for each possible type that a player might be assigned by Nature. If a player's type is drawn from the set of possible types T and this player can choose from actions in the set A, her strategy is then a function $s:T \rightarrow A$, i.e., a function that assigns to every possible type in T an action from A. Such a strategy might have a player choosing the same action regardless of what type he or she was assigned, or it might have the player choose a different action for each type he or she might be assigned. We will later refer to the first type of strategy as a "separating strategy" and the second as a "pooling strategy." Regardless, however, it is important to remember that we will no more be able to find an equilibrium in a Bayesian game without fully specified strategies than we would be able to find an equilibrium in a sequential complete information game without specifying full strategies. Put differently, plans for what to do "off the equilibrium path" can, in either case, affect the nature of the equilibrium.

Exercise 24B.2 In what sense does the distinction between Nash and subgame perfect equilibrium illustrate how "off the equilibrium path" plans—i.e., plans that are never executed in equilibrium—can be important?

24B.1.4 Bayesian Nash Equilibrium   Once we have fully understood the set-up of a simultaneous move Bayesian game and its implications for what a strategy is for each player, the definition for a Nash equilibrium is then exactly the same as it has always been, with one twist at the end: A *(Bayesian) Nash equilibrium* in a simultaneous move game of incomplete information occurs when each player's strategy is a best response to every other player's strategy *given the player's beliefs that are consistent with how the game is being played*.

The "twist at the end," the part that extends the concept of a Nash equilibrium to incomplete information games, is important in simultaneous games for the following reason: As we have already noted, we assume that everyone knows the probabilities with which the player Nature assigns types to players in the stage of the game that precedes the simultaneous move game. Unless new information is revealed in the course of the game, which does not happen when the rest of the game is a simultaneous move game, each person's beliefs are therefore just the probabilities with which types are assigned. (This will change in a sequential game of incomplete information where information may be revealed in the actions taken by players that move early in the game.) In simultaneous move Bayesian games, having beliefs be "consistent with how the game is being played" therefore means that equilibrium beliefs have to be consistent with how the player Nature plays the game.

Exercise 24B.3 Do you agree or disagree with the following statement: "Both complete and incomplete information simultaneous move games can be modeled as games in which Nature moves first, but Nature plays only pure strategies in complete information games while it plays mixed strategies in incomplete information games."

Graph 24.8: Incomplete Information about Player 2's Payoffs

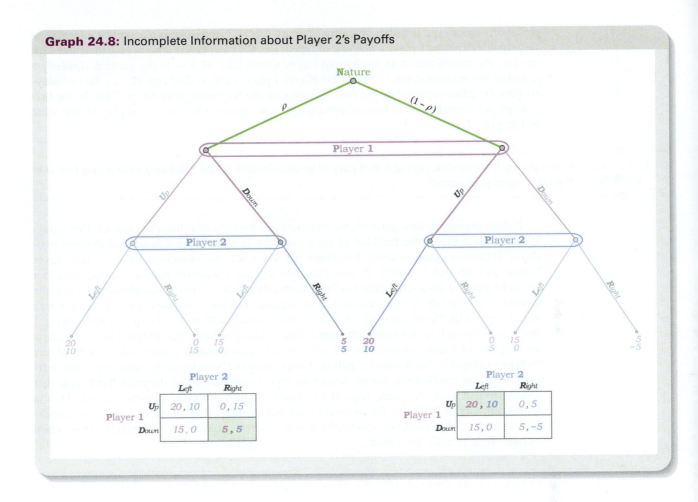

24B.1.5 A Simple Example Suppose, for instance, that we consider the two (complete information) games from exercises 24A.8 and 24A.9, which are depicted at the bottom of Graph 24.8. These games differ only in terms of player 2's payoffs, with payoffs for playing R being 10 more in the first game than in the second. In both games, player 2 has a dominant strategy, but player 1's best response will depend on player 2's strategy. In particular, player 1's best response to L is U (giving a payoff of 20 instead of 15), and his best response to R is D (giving payoff 5 instead of 0). Since player 1's payoffs are the same in both games, these best responses to strategies played by player 2 are the same in both games.

What is player 2's dominant strategy in each of the two games?

Exercise
24B.4

Now suppose that there is a probability ρ that player 2 will be of type I (with payoffs as in the first game) and a probability $(1 - \rho)$ that player 2 will be of type II (with payoffs as in the second game). Player 2 knows what type he is before the game starts, but player 1 does not know what type he is facing in player 2. This is then a simultaneous move Bayesian game in which player 2 could be one of two possible types. To model this, we introduce a third player—"Nature"—that moves before the simultaneous game begins, assigning type I to player 2 with probability ρ and type II with probability $(1 - \rho)$. If $\rho = 1$, the game is a complete information game in which player 1 plays a player 2 of type I; i.e., the two players simply play the game captured by the payoff matrix in the bottom left of Graph 24.8. If $\rho = 0$, the game is similarly a complete information game, but this time player 1 plays a player 2 of type II; i.e., the two players play the game captured by the payoff matrix on the bottom right of Graph 24.8. In the first case, player 1 would play D in equilibrium, and in the second case, he would play U. But what will he play if $0 < \rho < 1$?

Exercise 24B.5 How can we be sure that player 1 will play D in equilibrium in the left-hand side game but U in the right-hand side game?

Before answering this question, we need to show how we can illustrate, using either a payoff matrix or a game tree, the kind of game we have just introduced. Note first that our two-player Bayesian game actually has three players once we introduce the fictional player Nature, and this makes it difficult to depict such a game in a payoff matrix. Second, note that this third player adds a sequential structure to the simultaneous game, which suggests that the resulting game might best be illustrated in a game tree (or "extensive form"). Such a tree would begin with Nature moving first, as is done in the game tree in Graph 24.8. If player 1 then moves second, we have to furthermore find a way to indicate that player 1 does not know the outcome of Nature's move when it is his turn to play because Nature only reveals player 2's type to player 2. We do this by pulling both of player 1's nodes in the game tree—the left-hand node that results from Nature assigning type I to player 2 and the right-hand node that results from Nature assigning type II to player 2—into a single *information set*. This is depicted in Graph 24.8 with the magenta oval that contains both of these nodes, and it indicates that player 1 is uncertain about which of his two possible nodes he is playing from when it comes time to make his move.

Exercise 24B.6 Since all players know the probabilities with which types are assigned, how would you characterize player 1's beliefs about which node he is playing from once the game reaches his information set?

Next, note that the two players play the (complete information) game depicted in the payoff matrix on the lower left of the graph if they are playing from player 1's left-hand side node, and they play the (complete information) game depicted in the payoff matrix on the lower right of the graph if they are playing from player 1's right-hand side node. In order for us to depict the Bayesian game (that includes Nature's move) in a game tree, we therefore have to find a way to depict the complete information games from these payoff matrices in game tree format. In Section A, when we showed how a sequential game can be depicted in a payoff matrix, we hinted at the fact that it was possible to represent a simultaneous move (complete information) game in a game tree, but we postponed illustrating this because there was no particular need to do so at the time and because we were still missing a key ingredient—the concept of an *information set*—which we just introduced.

Given this new tool, all we have to do is to make sure that the information sets over the nodes following Nature's move are such that no new information is conveyed through the actions of any player because all players following Nature's move are playing simultaneously. Thus, player 2 does not know whether player 1 moved *Up* or *Down*, which means both actions by player 1 must end in the same information set for player 2. Put differently, we cannot allow player 2 to infer anything from the fact that player 1 has taken a particular action, because player 2 is acting at the same time as player 1 even though the game tree shows her making a decision farther down the game tree. But player 2 *does* know whether Nature assigned type I or type II, and thus whether she is playing the left-hand side or the right-hand side game. As a result, the information sets for player 2 do not cross from one side of the tree into the other.

True or False: If we depict a simultaneous move (complete information) game in a game tree, each player only has one information set.

Exercise 24B.7

How would you depict the complete information game from either of the payoff matrices in the graph if you had player 2 rather than player 1 at the top of the game tree?

Exercise 24B.8

Notice that the game tree in Graph 24.8 now fully captures all aspects of a simultaneous move Bayesian game: the actions that each player has available, the types that players might be assigned by Nature, the beliefs captured by the probability ρ, and the payoffs for each player and type. Reading the game tree from the top down, we see that Nature begins by moving left with probability ρ and right with probability $(1 - \rho)$. We then see from player 1's information set that player 1 cannot tell what Nature did when the time comes for him to choose between the actions *Up* and *Down*. We can furthermore note from player 2's two information sets that player 2 can never tell whether player 1 has decided to go *Up* or *Down* but she *can* tell whether Nature moved left or right. Player 2 therefore has more information than player 1.

You could also draw the game tree in Graph 24.8 with player 2 going first and player 1 going second. What do the information sets look like if you depict the game in this way?

Exercise 24B.9

While (pure) strategies in each of the games at the bottom of Graph 24.8 are simply actions, strategies in the Bayesian game depicted in the graph are now more complicated for player 2 *because they have to represent complete plans of action prior to the beginning of the game,* prior to Nature's move. Put differently, player 2's strategy must specify an action for each of her information sets; i.e., for the case where Nature assigns her type I and for the case where Nature assigns her type II. Player 1, on the other hand, has only a single information set in the game, which implies that a pure strategy for player 1 is simply an action for that one information set.

True or False: Player 2 has four possible strategies while player 1 has two possible strategies.

Exercise 24B.10

Now, since each of the two simultaneous move games at the bottom of Graph 24.8 has a dominant strategy for player 2, we know that player 2 will play *R* if she is assigned type I and *L* if she is assigned type II. Player 1 knows this and knows that she is at the first node in her information set with probability ρ and at the second node with probability $(1 - \rho)$. This implies that her expected payoff from playing *U* is $0\rho + 20(1 - \rho)$ while her expected payoff from playing *D* is $5\rho + 15(1 - \rho)$. The former is larger than the latter so long as $\rho < 0.5$. Thus, if $\rho < 0.5$, player 1 will play *U* and if $\rho > 0.5$, she will play *D*. (If $\rho = 0.5$, she is indifferent between her two possible actions and could play either.)

How would the outcome be different if the two games at the bottom of Graph 24.8 were the games in Table 24.5 and exercise 24A.7 (with player 2's actions labeled *L* and *R* instead of *U* and *D*)?

Exercise 24B.11

24B.1.6 Another Example: Sealed Bid Auctions

One of the most common applications for simultaneous games of incomplete information is in the area of auctions. In a *sealed bid auction*, for instance, different players bid on the same item at the same time by submitting sealed bids, with none of the players knowing exactly what the item is worth to the other players. Consider such an auction in which the player who bids the most ends up getting the item and has to pay the price that he or she bid. This type of auction is called a *first-price sealed bid auction* (which you can compare to a *second-price sealed bid auction* described in end-of-chapter exercise 24.10).

Suppose, for instance, that you and I are bidding on a painting. I know that the painting is worth at most t^i to me, and you know that it is worth at most t^j to you. But I do not know how much the painting is worth to you and you do not know how much it is worth to me. Suppose that all we know is that, for any potential bidder n, the private value t^n is drawn randomly (and independently) from the uniform distribution on the interval $[0,1]$.[11] Thus, the set of possible types is $T = [0,1]$, and the probability that Nature assigns to a player a type t less than $\bar{t}$ (for any $0 \le \bar{t} \le 1$) is simply $\bar{t}$.

Exercise 24B.12   What is the probability that Nature assigns a type greater than $\bar{t}$ to a player?

Each player n has to choose an action a^n that is just her bid for the painting. If a player wins the auction, her payoff is her consumer surplus $(t^n - a^n)$. If a player loses the auction, on the other hand, she does not get the painting and does not have to pay anything, leaving her with payoff of 0. Finally, we will assume that, when both players bid the same amount, the auctioneer will flip a coin, which gives each player a 50% chance of winning the auction and thus an expected payoff of $(t^n - a^n)/2$. (We will, however, be able to ignore the possibility of ties in our example because they happen with probability zero.)

Exercise 24B.13   What is the set of possible actions A for this game?

A *strategy* for each of the bidders in this auction has to once again be a complete plan of action for every possible type that a player might be assigned. A *type* in this game is determined by the valuation t^n that a player was assigned by Nature, which could lie anywhere on the continuum between 0 and 1. Thus, a strategy must be a function $s^n: [0,1] \to \mathbb{R}^1$ that specifies a bid for each possible value that a player might place on the painting. It is possible to formally demonstrate that such strategies in this setting will, in equilibrium, take on a linear form; i.e., $s^n(t^n) = \alpha_n + \beta_n t^n$.[12]

Suppose, then, that you play the strategy $s^j(t^j) = \alpha_j + \beta_j t^j$. My best response to this strategy is to maximize my expected payoff, which is (ignoring the possibility of a tie)

$$\max_{a^i} (t^i - a^i)\text{Prob}\{a^i > \alpha_j + \beta_j t^j\}. \tag{24.1}$$

---

[11]Assuming that individual valuations are drawn *independently* means that you cannot infer something about my valuation of the painting from knowing your valuation. Assuming that the distribution is *uniform* simply means that each value on the interval $[0,1]$ is equally likely to be drawn.

[12]Demonstrating this involves the use of differential equations and is thus beyond the scope of this text. The mathematically inclined reader is referred to Gibbons's text.

Simply by rearranging the terms in the previous inequality, we can write the probability term as

$$\text{Prob}\left\{a^i > \alpha_j + \beta_j t^j\right\} = \text{Prob}\left\{t^j < \frac{a^i - \alpha_j}{\beta_j}\right\} \tag{24.2}$$

But recall that, given the underlying uniform probability distribution on the interval $[0,1]$ with which Nature assigns types, the probability that $t^j < \bar{t}$ is simply $\bar{t}$, which implies

$$\text{Prob}\left\{t^j < \frac{a^i - \alpha_j}{\beta_j}\right\} = \frac{a^i - \alpha_j}{\beta_j}. \tag{24.3}$$

We can then rewrite equation (24.1) as

$$\max_{a^i} (t^i - a^i) \frac{a^i - \alpha_j}{\beta_j}, \tag{24.4}$$

which solves to

$$a^i = \frac{t^i + \alpha_j}{2}. \tag{24.5}$$

Verify that this is correct.

Exercise 24B.14

Thus, my best response to you playing $s^j(t^j) = \alpha_j + \beta_j t^j$ is $s^i(t^i) = \alpha_i + \beta_i t^i$, where $\alpha_i = \alpha_j/2$ and $\beta_i = 1/2$. If I play $s^i(t^i) = \alpha_i + \beta_i t^i$, then the exact same steps imply that your best response is $s^j(t^j) = \alpha_j + \beta_j t^j$, where $\alpha_j = \alpha_i/2$ and $\beta_j = 1/2$. But $\alpha_i = \alpha_j/2$ and $\alpha_j = \alpha_i/2$ can both hold only if $\alpha_i = \alpha_j = 0$, which implies that our equilibrium strategies are

$$s^i(t^i) = \frac{t^i}{2} \quad \text{and} \quad s^j(t^j) = \frac{t^j}{2}. \tag{24.6}$$

In other words, in equilibrium we will each bid half of the value that we attach to the painting.

Suppose that both bidders know how much each of them values the painting; i.e., suppose the game was one of complete information. What would be the Nash equilibrium bidding behavior then? How does it differ from the incomplete information game?

Exercise 24B.15

This is, of course, a very simple auction setting, and there exist many different types of auctions and different economically relevant beliefs that might be introduced in different settings. In fact, over the past two decades, an extensive literature on auctions has developed (and an entire course could now be taught simply about auctions), all based on game theoretic modeling of the underlying incentives. This literature has guided the design of large auctions, such as auctions for rights to harvest timber on federal land or for rights to broadcast on particular frequencies. Many of these auctions, however, have a sequential structure that goes beyond the simultaneous Bayesian games we have defined so far.

24B.2 Sequential Bayesian Signaling Games

While we can think of economically interesting applications of simultaneous games of incomplete information, the set of potential applications of *sequential* games of incomplete information is much richer. Such games have the feature that some players not only have *private information* but, *through their actions in the early part of the game, they can reveal some, all, or none of that information to the other players.* In our chapter on asymmetric information, we already dealt with situations of this kind, situations where buyers had less information than sellers (as in the used car market) or workers had more information (about their productivity) than potential employers or insurance clients had more information (about their risk type) than the insurance company. These instances of asymmetric information are precisely the kinds of economic situations that can be represented in sequential games of incomplete information, games in which the more informed party can *signal* something about him- or herself or in which the less informed party can set up incentives so as to extract information.

Just as we needed to extend the concept of Nash equilibrium to that of *subgame perfect* Nash equilibrium in the sequential complete information case, we now need to extend the concept of a Bayesian Nash equilibrium to that of a (subgame) *perfect* Bayesian Nash equilibrium in the sequential incomplete information case. And we need to do so for exactly the same reason as before: to eliminate implausible Nash equilibria that rely on noncredible behavior off the equilibrium path. To do so, however, we will again *need to make beliefs, and not just strategies, part of the equilibrium.* More precisely, we will need to specify what beliefs players hold on *and off* the equilibrium path in order to be sure the equilibrium strategies are in fact part of an equilibrium, and we need to make sure that players *update their beliefs* (from those they hold at the beginning of the game) if new information is revealed by the actions taken early on in the game. We will return to these issues more formally after first illustrating them in concrete settings where we will simply use the logic of subgame perfection to find sensible equilibria in sequential Bayesian games. By the "logic of subgame perfection," we will simply mean attacking the sequential game from the "bottom up" as we did in the complete information games of Section A.

24B.2.1 Simple Signaling when Beliefs Don't Matter

We will use one of the most common families of games of incomplete information to fix ideas. This family of games is known as *signaling games*, games in which a person first finds out (from Nature) what type he or she is, then sends a "signal" to the other player before that other player takes an action that impacts both players. Thus, the signaling player initially has private information that he or she might choose to reveal before the other player makes a move.

The simplest such setting is one in which one player (whom we will call the *sender*) might be one of two possible types and can send one of two possible signals. The other player (whom we will call the *receiver*) then has to choose between two actions. Consider, for example, a sequential version of the simultaneous game we introduced in Graph 24.8. In that game, player 2 was one of two possible types, with her payoff depending on which type she was. To turn this game into a signaling game, player 2 would first find out her type, would then be able to play the actions L or R before player 1, *after observing player 2's signal*, gets a chance to undertake her action of either U or D. Thus, player 2 becomes the sender who signals through her choice of L or R, and player 1 becomes the receiver. A convenient way to represent the new structure of this game is then given in Graph 24.9.

Unlike the game trees we have looked at so far, this tree begins in the center with Nature revealing the sender's type, assigning type I with probability ρ and type II with probability $(1 - \rho)$. After finding out her type, the sender can then play L or R (going either left or right in the graph). The receiver only observes the sender's actions, not her type. Thus, the receiver's two nodes on the left (following L by the sender) are in the same information set, as are the receiver's two nodes on the right (following R by the sender). Note that the person we called "player 2" in the simultaneous version of the game gets the private information and thus moves *first* in the

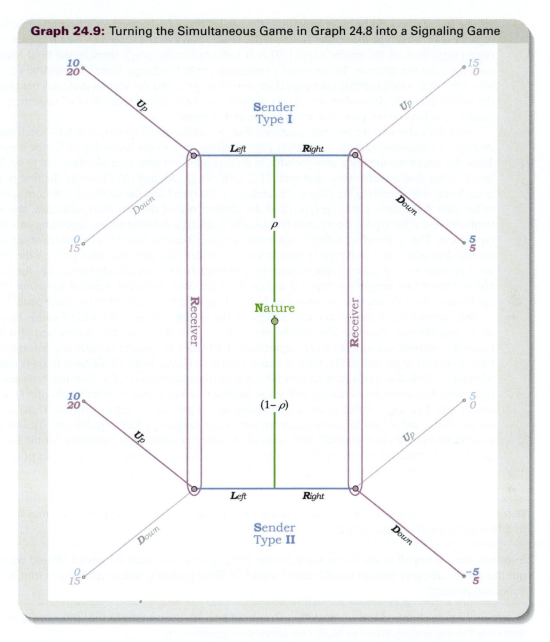

Graph 24.9: Turning the Simultaneous Game in Graph 24.8 into a Signaling Game

signaling game. As you compare payoffs in Graph 24.9 with those in Graph 24.8, keep in mind that the first payoff at each terminal point in the sequential game should therefore correspond to player 2's payoff in the previously graphed simultaneous game.

Check that the payoffs listed in Graph 24.9 correspond to the payoffs in Graph 24.8.

Exercise
24B.16

First, note that the receiver's (subgame perfect) strategy is particularly easy to figure out in this game because, once the receiver observes which action the sender has taken, she knows exactly what she wants to do even if she is uncertain about which of the nodes in her information set she has reached. To be more precise, if the sender plays L, the receiver's best response is U regardless of what type the sender is, and if the sender plays R, the receiver's best response is D (again regardless of the sender's type). This is indicated in the graph through the bold lines at each node for the receiver. The receiver's (subgame perfect) strategy therefore must be (U,D), where the first action indicates her plan if the sender plays L and the second indicates her plan if the sender plays R. Since this strategy is optimal for the receiver *regardless of what type the sender is*, beliefs do not play an important role in this game.

Next, let's consider the possible strategies that the sender could employ and let's recall that a strategy in a Bayesian game is a complete plan of action prior to the beginning of Nature's move. Thus, the sender has to have a plan for what to do depending on what type she turns out to be. She therefore has four possible pure strategies: (L,L), (R,R), (L,R), and (R,L), where the first action in each pair corresponds to her plan if she turns out to be type I and the second action corresponds to her plan if she turns out to be type II. If she chooses one of the two latter strategies, she will implicitly reveal her type to the receiver because she is taking a different action depending on which type she is. This is therefore called a *separating strategy* because it involves separate observable actions depending on which type is assigned to the sender. The first two strategies, on the other hand, provide no information to the receiver beyond what the receiver already knows, i.e., the probabilities that nature assigns one type rather than the other. Such a strategy is called a *pooling strategy* because the different types of sender end up looking as if they came from the same pool.[13]

We can then begin to look at each strategy for the sender and see if it could plausibly be part of an equilibrium. Suppose the sender plays (L,L). We have already determined that the receiver's optimal strategy is (U,D) regardless of whether the sender reveals any information through her strategy, and so (U,D) is a best response to (L,L). Now all we have to do is check whether (L,L) is also a best response for the sender to the receiver's (U,D). Note that both sender types would do worse by switching to R given that the receiver would respond by playing D, with sender type I getting 5 rather than 10 and sender type II getting -5 rather than 10. Thus, (L,L) for the sender and (U,D) for the receiver are part of a (subgame perfect) equilibrium. You should also be able to convince yourself that none of the other possible pure strategies for the sender could be a (subgame perfect) equilibrium because in each case at least one of the types of sender would have an incentive to deviate given that the receiver is playing (U,D).

Exercise 24B.17   Determine for each of the three remaining sender pure strategies why the strategy cannot be part of a (subgame perfect) equilibrium.

Exercise 24B.18   Suppose the -5 payoff in the lower right corner of the game tree were 0 instead. Would we still get the same subgame perfect equilibrium? Could (R,R) be part of a Nash equilibrium that is not subgame perfect?

Exercise 24B.19   Suppose that we changed the -5 payoff in Graph 24.9 to 20. Demonstrate that this would imply that only the separating strategy (L,R) can survive in equilibrium.

Since the equilibrium we have identified involves both sender types playing the same "signal" L, the receiver gets no information about the sender's type from observing the sender's action, and therefore the receiver cannot update her beliefs from those she held at the beginning of the game when she knew that Nature would assign type I to the sender with probability ρ and type II with probability $(1 - \rho)$. These are, then, the equilibrium beliefs for the receiver. But in this game, the receiver's beliefs play no role because her response to either action on the part of the sender is clear cut and independent of her beliefs. This is not generally true in signaling games, and when it is not true, beliefs take on a much more critical role.

---

[13]When there are more than two types, we might get hybrid strategies in which some types pool and some separate.

24B.2.2 Signaling Games where Beliefs Matter Now suppose we change the game in Graph 24.9 slightly by changing the payoff for the receiver in the upper right of the graph (where type I sender plays R and the receiver plays U) from 0 to 10. This is depicted in Graph 24.10, and as a result of this change, the receiver's optimal action when she observes R from the sender is no longer the same irrespective of her beliefs about which node within her information set she occupies when choosing the action. To be more precise, the optimal receiver action after the sender plays R is U if the sender is of type I and D if the sender is of type II (as indicated again through the bold lines in the graph). If the receiver observes L from the sender, she will still unambiguously play U.

Recall that we extended the concept of a Nash equilibrium to a subgame perfect Nash equilibrium by insisting that a Nash equilibrium in a sequential game also consists of a Nash equilibrium in each *subgame* of the sequential game. Subgames were defined as beginning at a particular node

Graph 24.10: A Small Change to the Previous Game and Beliefs Matter

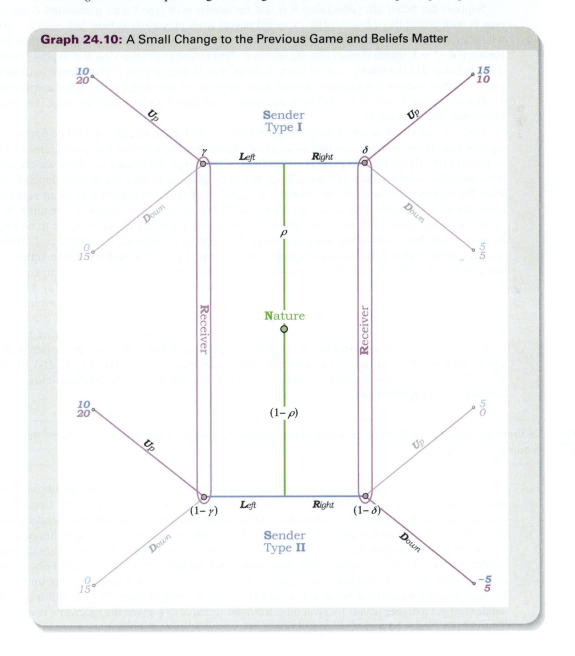

that had been reached in the game tree. The problem we now face is that such subgames may not be readily available in games of the type depicted in Graphs 24.9 and 24.10. When the receiver gets to move after receiving a signal from the sender, she does not find herself at a particular node; rather, she finds herself at an information set that contains two nodes, with some *belief* about which of two nodes she might actually be playing from. Those beliefs now become important for determining what the best response for the receiver should be if she observes R.

Exercise 24B.20

In the previous section, we talked about subgame perfect strategies in ways that we cannot do here. What is different?

Suppose her belief after observing R is that the sender is of type I with probability δ and of type II with probability $(1 - \delta)$. Her expected payoff from playing U is then $10\delta + 0(1 - \delta)$, while her expected payoff from playing D is $5\delta + 5(1 - \delta) = 5$. The latter is greater than the former if $\delta < 0.5$, which implies that the receiver's best response to observing R is to play D *only if* her belief is that the sender is more likely to be of type II than of type I. The receiver will then play U if she observes L regardless of what type she believes the sender to be, but she will play U after observing R only if she believes the sender is of type I with probability of at least 0.5. Otherwise, she will play D.

Now we can check to see if the pooling strategy (L,L) for the sender can still be part of an equilibrium. If the sender plays that strategy, we know that the receiver will play U, resulting in payoff $(10, 20)$ for the two players (regardless of what type the sender is). Now we can ask whether either of the sender types could do better by playing R, and the answer depends on what the receiver would do if she ever saw a signal R. If (L,L) is indeed part of an equilibrium, the receiver will in fact never see the signal R, but a full plan of action still requires her to have a plan in case she does see R, and we need to know what that plan is in order to be able to answer whether either of the sender types could do better by sending R rather than L. If the receiver were to plan U following a signal R, then a type I sender would indeed be better off sending R rather than L, which in turn would imply that (L,L) cannot be part of an equilibrium. And we just concluded in the previous paragraph that the receiver will play U after observing R only if $\delta > 0.5$. In order for the pooling strategy (L,L) to be an equilibrium strategy, the receiver must therefore believe that the sender is more likely to be type II if a signal R is observed. Put differently, *the receiver's beliefs have to be appropriately specified as part of the pooling equilibrium.* And we see in this example that beliefs "off the equilibrium path" can be critical for sustaining an equilibrium; that is, in the equilibrium $\{(L,L), (U,D)\}$ where $\delta < 0.5$, it matters what the receiver believes in the event that R is observed *even though R is not observed in equilibrium.*

Exercise 24B.21

Is there any way for (R,R) to be an equilibrium sender strategy? (Your answer should be no. Can you explain why?)

We can also ask whether there is a *separating equilibrium* in this case; i.e., an equilibrium that involves the sender playing either (L,R) or (R,L). Consider first the strategy (L,R). Under this strategy, the receiver knows with certainty which type the sender is because different sender types play different actions observable to the receiver. As a result, the receiver will update her beliefs; i.e., γ, the probability that the sender is type I if L is observed, is 1 and δ, the probability that the sender is of type I if R is observed, is 0. That means that the receiver will play U after observing L and D after observing R. Given this response by the receiver, a type I sender cannot do better by changing her signal to R because that would reduce her payoff from 10 to 5. But a type II sender *can* get a higher payoff by switching from the signal R to L given the receiver's response. Thus, (L,R) cannot be part of an equilibrium.

**Exercise
24B.22**

How much higher a payoff would a type II sender get by switching her signal in this way?

Next, consider the other separating strategy: (R,L). If the sender plays this strategy, the receiver will know that the sender is of type I if she observes R (i.e., $\delta = 1$), and she will know that the sender is of type II if she observes L (i.e., $\gamma = 0$). Either way, her best response is to play U. For this to be an equilibrium, we now have to again make sure that neither of the two sender types could do better (given that the receiver will always play U). If type I switched, her payoff would fall from 15 to 10, and if type II switched, her payoff would fall from 10 to 5. Thus, neither type can benefit from deviating from the strategy (R,L), which means we have found a separating equilibrium $\{(R,L) , (U,U)\}$ with equilibrium beliefs $\delta = 1$ and $\gamma = 0$. (The initial probability ρ with which Nature assigned types no longer matters because all information is revealed in the separating strategy played by the sender.)

**Exercise
24B.23***

For the game in Graph 24.10, we have therefore found both a separating and a pooling equilibrium, but for the pooling equilibrium we needed to place a restriction on out-of-equilibrium beliefs. Do you find this restriction "reasonable" in this example?[14]

24B.2.3 Signaling Games where Beliefs and Nature's Probabilities Matter

In the previous example, we have seen that out-of-equilibrium beliefs on the part of the receiver might be critical in sustaining a pooling equilibrium. This was because the optimal action differed across the two nodes in the information set that is not reached in equilibrium. Beliefs along the pooling equilibrium path have not yet played a crucial role because so far we have had examples in which the optimal action from each node in the information set that is reached in the pooling equilibrium is the same.

Now suppose we change the game in Graph 24.10 a little more by changing the receiver's payoff from playing U when she faces a type I sender who plays L from 20 to 10. This new game is depicted in Graph 24.11, with the optimal receiver actions from each node again highlighted. Note that now we have a game in which the receiver's optimal action differs across the nodes in each of her two information sets.

First, we can begin with the receiver and ask which way she will play from each of her information sets. If she observes L and thus plays from her left information set, her payoff from U is $10\gamma + 20(1 - \gamma) = 20 - 10\gamma$, while her payoff from D is $15\gamma + 15(1 - \gamma) = 15$. The former is larger than the latter so long as $\gamma < 0.5$, which means the receiver will play U following L if she believes the probability that the sender is of type I is less than 0.5 and D if she believes that probability is greater than 0.5. Similarly, from what we did in the previous section, we know that the receiver will play U following R if $\delta > 0.5$ and D if $\delta < 0.5$.

Next, we can begin again with the pooling strategy (L,L) and see whether it can still be part of an equilibrium. The receiver's response would (as we just argued) depend on her belief γ, but if the two sender types both always play L, the receiver's belief about the probability that she is facing each type after observing L should be unaltered from what it was at the beginning of the game. Since we assume that all players know the probability ρ with which Nature assigns types, this means that, under the sender strategy (L,L), $\gamma = \rho$. Since we determined that the receiver will play U from her left information set if $\gamma < 0.5$, this means that we know she will play U under the pooling strategy (L,L) so long as $\rho < 0.5$ and D so long as $\rho > 0.5$. But if the receiver

---

[14]This is far from a trivial question and it has concerned game theorists a great deal. After all, what does it mean for beliefs related to events that do not happen in equilibrium to be reasonable? An approach to this, known as the "Intuitive Criterion" has been derived. You can read more about this in Section 4.4 of Gibbons.

Graph 24.11: Beliefs Matter Even More

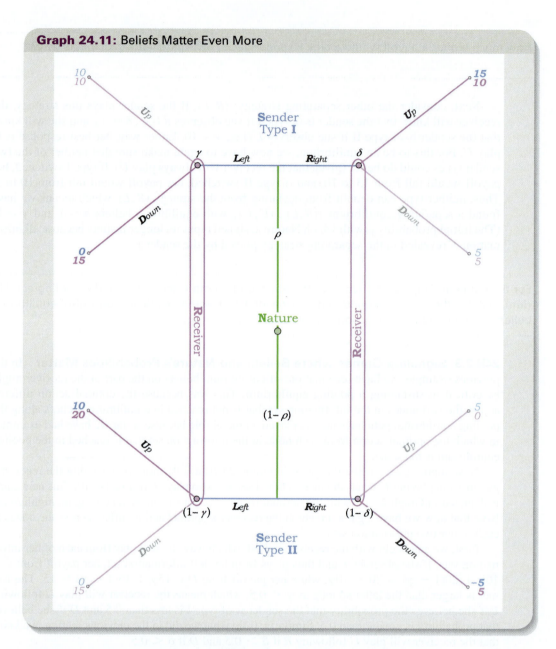

were to play D, type I senders can make themselves better off by playing R since their payoff would be greater than 0 regardless of what the receiver planned in that event. So (L,L) cannot be a pooling equilibrium if $\rho > 0.5$, only if $\rho \leq 0.5$.

Exercise 24B.24   What has to be true about δ in order for (L,L) to be an equilibrium pooling strategy when $\rho < 0.5$?

We can also check again if the second pooling strategy (R,R) could be part of an equilibrium. If (R,R) is played, the sender again reveals nothing about herself, which means that the receiver should not change her beliefs about what sender type she is facing if she observes R. Thus, $\delta = \rho$.

Since the receiver will play U from her right information set if $\delta > 0.5$ and D if $\delta < 0.5$, we then know she will play U if $\rho > 0.5$ and D if $\rho < 0.5$. But if the receiver were to play D, type II senders can do better by deviating and playing L since both possible payoffs for her would then be larger than -5. So (R,R) cannot be part of an equilibrium if $\rho < 0.5$.

To ensure that (R,R) can be an equilibrium pooling strategy with the receiver playing U after seeing R when $\rho > 0.5$, we now need to make sure that type II senders can't do better by deviating. Since such senders would get a payoff of 5 under the proposed equilibrium, this means they can't think that the receiver would play U if she observed L (since that would result in a payoff for type II players of 10). We concluded before that the receiver would in fact play D following L if she believed $\gamma > 0.5$. Thus, (R,R) and (D,U) are pooling equilibrium strategies so long as $\rho > 0.5$ and $\gamma > 0.5$. Since L is never played in this equilibrium, any belief γ is an out-of-equilibrium belief, and thus could take on any form including $\gamma > 0.5$. But still, despite the fact that L is not played in this pooling equilibrium, we can have an equilibrium only if the receiver thinks an L signal (that is never sent) is most likely indicative of a type I sender. We therefore have a pooling equilibrium $\{(R,R),(D,U)\}$ with beliefs $\delta = \rho > 0.5$ and $\gamma > 0.5$.

Finally, consider the separating equilibrium strategy (R,L). If the sender plays this strategy, the receiver will best respond by playing (U,U), which results in payoffs of 15 and 10 for type I and II senders respectively. Neither sender type can do better by deviating, which means we have found a separating equilibrium $\{(R,L),(U,U)\}$ with $\delta = 1$ and $\gamma = 0$, an equilibrium where the sender reveals her type and the receiver therefore knows with certainty which type the sender is by the time she has to choose an action.

Could the separating strategy (L,R) be part of an equilibrium in this case?

Exercise 24B.25

Suppose that, in the game in Graph 24.10, we had changed the receiver's payoff from playing U when facing a sender of type II who plays left from 20 to 5 instead. Could there be a separating equilibrium in that game? Is there a pure strategy equilibrium for all values of ρ?

Exercise 24B.26*

24B.2.4 Perfect Bayesian Nash Equilibria in Signaling (and Other) Games
So far, we have talked through several different signaling games, illustrating the possibility of separating and pooling equilibria and demonstrating the role that beliefs play in supporting such equilibria. Given the intuition we have developed, we can now be a little more precise about what we mean by an equilibrium in a sequential game of incomplete information such as a signaling game.

Recall that a game of incomplete information (or a Bayesian game) has the following components: (1) actions for each player; (2) types for each player; (3) beliefs about other players' types; and (4) payoffs that depend on which types are actually in the game and what actions they take. Furthermore, recall that we have assumed throughout that all players know the probabilities with which Nature assigns types to individuals, and that these probabilities therefore form everyone's initial beliefs. In simultaneous move games, those initial beliefs are the same throughout the game since no new information about other players' types is revealed before an action has to be taken. But in sequential move games, individuals will *update their beliefs* if actions by others reveal new information.

We have seen such updating of beliefs in the signal game when we considered separating strategies by the sender. In that case, the sender fully revealed her type through the signals she sent, allowing the receiver to update her beliefs. In the case where the sender did not reveal additional information (because of the use of a pooling strategy), no updating had to be done once the receiver reached her information set, leaving her with the same beliefs she had at the beginning of the game. Off the equilibrium path, we did not restrict the receiver's beliefs because it is not clear how one forms beliefs in circumstances that happen with zero probability. (We did hint in one of the exercises, however, that game theorists have developed reasonable restrictions (that are beyond the scope of this text) on such out-of-equilibrium beliefs.)

More generally, updating of beliefs in sequential Bayesian games satisfies what is known as *Bayes rule*. Bayes rule in the context of sequential Bayesian games simply means the following: Suppose that a particular information set I contains nodes $N_1, N_2, \ldots, N_k$, with $P(N_i)$ giving the probability that node N_i is reached (and the probability of the information set I being reached therefore equal to $\sum_{i=1}^{k} P(N_i)$). Now suppose that, as the game progresses, the information set I is actually reached. Then the updated probability that N_i has been reached *given that the information set I has been reached* is

$$P(N_i|I) = \frac{P(N_i)}{P(I)}. \tag{24.7}$$

Suppose, for instance, that player 1 in a game moves first and has three available actions: $a_1, a_2,$ and a_3. Suppose player 1 is playing a mixed strategy that places equal weight of 1/4 on a_1 and a_2 and 1/2 on a_3, and suppose that player 2 can tell whether player 1 has played a_1 but cannot tell the difference between player 1 having played a_2 and a_3. Thus, player 2 has two information sets $I_1 = \{a_1\}$ and $I_2 = \{a_2, a_3\}$. Now suppose that player 2 faces a decision after reaching information set I_2; i.e., suppose player 2 knows that player 1 did not play a_1. Then, according to Bayes rule, player 2 now believes that player 1 has played actions a_2 and a_3 with probabilities 1/3 and 2/3 because

$$P(a_2|I_2) = \frac{P(a_2)}{P(I_2)} = \frac{1/4}{3/4} = \frac{1}{3} \quad \text{and} \quad P(a_3|I_2) = \frac{P(a_3)}{P(I_2)} = \frac{1/2}{3/4} = \frac{2}{3}, \tag{24.8}$$

with $P(a_1|I_2) = 0$. If, on the other hand, player 2 reaches information set I_1, then Bayes rule says the updated probabilities are $P(a_1|I_1) = \frac{1/4}{1/4} = 1$ and $P(a_2|I_1) = P(a_3|I_1) = 0$.

Note that implicitly we have applied Bayes rule a number of times as we updated beliefs in our signaling games. Suppose the sender played a pooling strategy L, thus taking the receiver to the information set on the left of our game trees with probability 1. Let's denote that information set as I_L which contains two nodes defined by whether the sender was a type I or a type II. To make the upcoming notation a bit easier to read, let's denote type I as T_1 and type II as T_2. The receiver knows that Nature, at the beginning of the game, assigned T_1 to the sender with probability ρ and T_2 with probability $(1 - \rho)$. If the sender then plays a pooling strategy that results in the receiver making decisions from the information set I_L, Bayes rule implies that the receiver should have beliefs $P(T_1|I_L) = P(T_1)/P(I_L) = \rho/1 = \rho$ and $P(T_2|I_L) = P(T_2)/P(I_L) = (1 - \rho)/1 = (1 - \rho)$. Put differently, since the sender's pooling strategy adds no information, no updating of beliefs occurs. Under a separating strategy where the sender plays L if type I and R if type II, Bayes rule implies $P(T_1|I_L) = P(T_1)/P(I_L) = \rho/\rho = 1$, $P(T_2|I_R) = P(T_2)/P(I_R) = (1 - \rho)/(1 - \rho) = 1$, and $P(T_2|I_L) = 0 = P(T_1|I_R)$.

Exercise 24B.27 If the sender plays a pooling strategy (L,L), why is the receiver's belief about nodes in the information set I_R undefined according to Bayes rule?

Earlier, we said a Bayesian Nash equilibrium occurs when each player's strategy is a best response to every other player's strategy *given the player's beliefs that are consistent with how the game is being played*. We can now extend this formally to say that, in a sequential Bayesian game, a *(subgame) perfect Bayesian Nash equilibrium* is a Bayesian Nash equilibrium in which all the strategies and beliefs in all "subgames" (that begin at each information set) also constitute a Bayesian Nash equilibrium for each "subgame". (We are putting *subgame* in quotation marks here because subgames are usually defined as beginning at one node. For this reason, the equilibrium concept we are now defining is usually referred to simply as a perfect (rather than subgame perfect) Bayesian Nash equilibrium.) This is exactly analogous to the relationship between Nash equilibria and subgame perfect Nash equilibria in a complete information game, where subgame perfection in sequential settings required all subgames to be in equilibrium as well (and thus eliminated Nash equilibria that relied on noncredible strategies down the game tree). The difference in sequential Bayesian games is that at least some "subgames" now begin with information sets that contain more than a single node, and this in turn requires the specification of beliefs.

All such beliefs have to be "consistent with how the game is played," which simply meant that all players shared beliefs consistent with Nature's probabilities in our initial simultaneous move game where no new information could arise for players to update their beliefs. In a sequential setting, however, it means that beliefs have to be updated using Bayes rule wherever it applies (beginning with initial beliefs consistent with the probabilities employed by Nature). And Bayes rule applies at information sets that are reached with positive probability under the equilibrium strategies. At information sets that are reached with probability 0, however, Bayes rule does not apply and beliefs are therefore unrestricted, which is not the same as saying they can remain *unspecified*. In order to sustain an equilibrium, these "off-the-equilibrium-path" beliefs have to be structured so as to make the equilibrium strategies best responses to one another in all "subgames" that are not reached.

Is every Bayesian Nash equilibrium also a perfect Bayesian Nash equilibrium? Is every perfect Bayesian Nash equilibrium also a Bayesian Nash equilibrium? Explain.

Exercise 24B.28

True or False: When a game tree is such that all information sets are single nodes, then subgame perfect Nash equilibrium is the same as perfect Bayesian Nash equilibrium.

Exercise 24B.29

24B.3 "Reputations" in Finitely Repeated Prisoner's Dilemmas

In Section A of this chapter, we placed a lot of emphasis on the Prisoner's Dilemma because, as we will see in the remainder of the text, it is a game that has particular relevance in many economic settings. We solved the simultaneous Prisoner's Dilemma and found that there exists a single Nash equilibrium that involves both parties in the game choosing not to cooperate with one another *despite the fact that the cooperative outcome is preferred by both to the non-cooperative outcome*. We also found that if two players face each other repeatedly a finite number of times, then the only subgame perfect Nash equilibrium again involves a lack of cooperation in every stage of the repeated game. But we noted that in experimental settings as well as in many real-world settings, we see significantly more cooperation than what the model predicts, and we discovered a way to think about repeated Prisoner's Dilemma games in which the players are uncertain about whether they will meet again each time that they meet or in which players expect to interact an infinite number of times. In such a setting, we argued, it is plausible that cooperation can emerge, and we show in the appendix that anything between no cooperation and full cooperation can in fact emerge in infinitely repeated Prisoner's Dilemma games (assuming players do not discount the future too heavily).

This set of results is, in some ways, quite odd. In finitely repeated Prisoner's Dilemma games, not the slightest bit of cooperation can emerge under subgame perfection, while in the infinitely repeated game (or a game in which individuals are uncertain about whether they will meet again but think it sufficiently likely each time), all levels of cooperation can be sustained under subgame perfection. In some sense, one model seems to predict too little cooperation; the other potentially predicts too much.

We will now introduce a Bayesian element to repeated Prisoner's Dilemma games in which players are uncertain about what type they face (and not about whether they will interact again). What we will find is that the introduction of uncertainty of a certain kind can result in equilibrium cooperation even in finitely repeated Prisoner's Dilemma settings. In particular, we will see that the introduction of uncertainty on the part of one player about the type of player he is facing opens the possibility for the opposing player to establish a "reputation" for cooperation, a reputation that will cause cooperation to persist for some time even among rational players in finitely repeated Prisoner's Dilemmas.

24B.3.1 Introducing the Possibility of a "Tit-for-Tat" Player   Suppose that Nature moves before the beginning of a finitely repeated Prisoner's Dilemma game involving me and you (with me being player 1 and you being player 2), and suppose that the payoffs in each stage of this game (after Nature moves) are as in Table 24.10. Nature's move determines my type, assigning me with probability ρ the "Tit-for-Tat" type t_1 and with probability $(1 - \rho)$ the "rational player" type t_2. If I am assigned the Tit-for-Tat type, I will play the Tit-for-Tat strategy, "begin by playing C and then mimic for the rest of the game the last action played by the opposing player in the previous period." If, on the other hand, I am assigned the "rational player" type, I simply maximize my own utility as we have assumed throughout. As in our signaling games, we assume that I learn my own type but you do not.

Note that this is a little different than previous incomplete information introduced into our Bayesian games in which Nature assigned different *payoffs* to different types. Here, Nature is rather assigning me a particular strategy (Tit-for-Tat) with probability ρ, thus removing choice about the strategy that I adopt in the event that I am assigned this type. One could argue that we are assuming Nature is making me "irrational" with probability ρ, but irrational in a particular way. One could also model this more in line with our previous models as a change in payoffs for the first type such that Tit-for-Tat is the optimal strategy.[15]

24B.3.2 Considering a Twice-Repeated Prisoner's Dilemma Game   Suppose first that we know we are going to play the Prisoner's Dilemma twice and, to keep things as simple as possible, let's suppose we do not discount the future. From our earlier discussion, we know that a typical rational player will choose D the second time we play. If I end up being a t_2 ("rational") player, I know this when we play the first time and will therefore choose D each time we meet. If I am a t_1 type, I have no choice and will play the Tit-for-Tat strategy. But this leaves an open question for you: Should you play C the first time we meet in the hope of me being a Tit-for-Tat type, which would mean you could get the cooperative payoff 10 the first time we meet *and* then get 15 the second time we meet (by playing D when the Tit-for-Tat type will play C)? Playing C followed by D then gives you a combined payoff across the two periods of 25 if you face a Tit-for-Tat type, but it gives you a payoff of only 5 if you end up facing me as a "rational" t_2. Put differently, playing

Table 24.10: Prisoner's Dilemma

		Player 2	
		*C*ooperate	*D*on't Cooperate
Player 1	*C*ooperate	*10 , 10*	*0 , 15*
	*D*on't Cooperate	*15 , 0*	*5 , 5*

---

[15]For instance, we could simply assume that there is a chance that I was raised to believe Tit-for-Tat is the correct moral path in life, that I am deeply committed to this path, and that I would suffer greatly if I chose a different path.

C first followed by D gives you an *expected* payoff of $25\rho + 5(1 - \rho) = 20\rho + 5$, while your *expected* payoff from playing D both periods is $10\rho + 10$.

Verify the last sentence.

Exercise 24B.30

Thus, your expected payoff from playing C followed by D is larger than your expected payoff from playing D always if $\rho > 0.5$. If I am therefore more likely to be a Tit-for-Tat player than a "rational" t_2 player, the perfect Bayesian Nash equilibrium has you playing (C, D), with me playing (C, C) if I am a Tit-for-Tat player and (D, D) if I am not.

What are the beliefs that support this as a perfect Bayesian equilibrium?

Exercise 24B.31

24B.3.3 Considering a Thrice-Repeated Prisoner's Dilemma Game

Now suppose that we instead know at the beginning that we are going to play the game three times and suppose that $\rho > 0.5$. I learn at the very beginning whether I am a Tit-for-Tat player or not, but you learn it only if I choose to reveal it by violating the Tit-for-Tat strategy when I am a type t_2.

Suppose, then, that I learn I am t_2 (and thus do not have to play the Tit-for-Tat strategy). If I play D in the first game, I will have revealed to you that I am not a Tit-for-Tat type, and Bayesian updating of your beliefs will imply that you now place probability 1 on me being a t_2 type by the time we begin the second game. Knowing that, it will be best for you to play D in the second and third game. If, on the other hand, I play C in the first game after finding out that I am a t_2 type, I am at this point acting as if I was a Tit-for-Tat player by beginning the game with a pooling strategy. Bayes Rule then tells us that you have no information to update your beliefs about what type I am, which means we enter game 2 with the same information that we had at the beginning of the twice-repeated game we have just analyzed. This implies that, if you also played C in the first round and thus a Tit-for-Tat type would begin playing game 2 with C, the beginning of game 2 is identical to the Twice-Repeated Prisoner's Dilemma and our previous analysis holds for the rest of the game. Put differently, if both of us cooperate in the first stage, we know that you will play C followed by D in the second and third game while I will play C for the rest of the game if I am a Tit-for-Tat type and D for the rest of the game if I am not. If you observe me playing D in the first stage, however, you will plan to play D for the rest of the game. The question we now want to think about is whether the following strategies are part of a perfect Bayesian Nash equilibrium:

Strategy for Me if I am Type t_2: Play C in the first game and D in the second and third games.

Strategy for You: Play C in the first game. If you observe me also playing C in the first game, play C in the second game. Otherwise, play D in the second game. Finally, play D in the last game.

Verify that if we play these strategies, your expected payoff will be $35\rho + 15(1 - \rho) = 20\rho + 15$, and my payoff as a t_2 type will be 30.

Exercise 24B.32

Suppose, then, that I in fact play this strategy. Can you do better by playing D in the first game? Since we know that you will do best playing D in the third (i.e., the last) game, you will play either $D - D - D$ or $D - C - D$ over the three games if you choose D in the first stage. By playing $D - D - D$, your payoffs will be $15 + 5 + 5 = 25$ if you face a Tit-for-Tat t_1 type (who will mimic your D's in the second and third games), exactly the same as if you faced a "rational" t_2 type who plays the suggested equilibrium strategy $C - D - D$. Your expected payoff from playing $D - D - D$ is then 25. By playing $D - C - D$, on the other hand, you will get payoffs $15 + 0 + 15 = 30$ if you face a Tit-for-Tat t_1 opponent (who will respond with $C - D - C$) and payoffs $15 + 0 + 5 = 20$ if you face a "rational" t_2 opponent, giving expected payoff $30\rho + 20(1 - \rho) = 20 + 10\rho$ from playing $D - C - D$. Since we are assuming $\rho > 0.5$ throughout, your expected payoff from $D - D - D$ (i.e., 25) then falls short of your expected payoff from $D - C - D$ (i.e., $20 + 10\rho$), implying that *if you were to deviate from playing C in the first stage, you would play $D - C - D$*. But your payoff from playing the suggested equilibrium strategy is $20\rho + 15$, which exceeds your expected payoff from the deviation $D - C - D$ given that $\rho > 0.5$. The suggested equilibrium strategy is therefore a best response to the t_2 strategy suggested for me (given that there is a probability $\rho > 0.5$ that I am a Tit-for-Tat player).

Next, we can check if I have an incentive to deviate from the proposed strategy. We know from our work on the twice-repeated game that if I do not deviate in the first stage by playing D, I cannot benefit from deviating in the second and third stage by playing C (since the game starting in the second stage is identical to the twice-repeated game if both of us play C in the first stage). So the only question is if I can benefit by playing D rather than C in the first stage, thereby revealing in the first game that I am a t_2. If I do so, I will get a payoff of 15 in the first game followed by payoffs of 5 in the next two stages for a total payoff of 25. But by playing the proposed strategy, my payoff is 30. I therefore cannot benefit from deviating from the proposed strategy, which means the proposed strategy is a best response to your proposed strategy.

We have therefore demonstrated that your suggested strategy is a best response to mine and mine is a best response to yours. In the "Thrice-Repeated" Prisoner's Dilemma, both of us cooperating in the first game can therefore emerge as part of a perfect Bayesian Nash equilibrium so long as the probability of me being a Tit-for-Tat player is sufficiently high. The reason for this is that it is now in my interest as a rational player to try to establish a "reputation" for being a Tit-for-Tat player (or, more generally, for being a cooperative player) in order to get you to cooperate with me for a while.

24B.3.4 *N*-Times Repeated Prisoner's Dilemma and the Role of Reputations

It should be intuitive that if we are trying to show that a perfect Bayesian Nash equilibrium exists for N-Times Repeated Prisoner's Dilemma games with players cooperating up to some point in the game, such an equilibrium with early cooperation will also exist for an $(N + 1)$-Times Repeated Prisoner's Dilemma. Thus, by demonstrating that you and I (as a t_2 type) might choose to cooperate in the first game of a thrice-repeated Prisoner's Dilemma if the probability of me being a Tit-for-Tat player is high enough, we have picked an unlikely game for which to demonstrate our result. As N becomes larger, cooperation in the early part of the game becomes easier to sustain and can emerge for smaller probabilities of me being a Tit-for-Tat player. In fact, for large but finite N, this probability can get very close to zero, meaning that we will observe cooperation in Finitely Repeated Prisoner's Dilemma games even if there is only a small chance that one of the players is a Tit-for-Tat player.

It is furthermore the case that, for the payoffs in the game of Table 24.10, there is a perfect Bayesian Nash equilibrium under which cooperation will persist (between you and me when I am a type t_2 player) in all games prior to the second to last game in an N-Times Repeated Prisoner's Dilemma so long as $\rho > 0.5$. Thus, for a sufficiently high probability that one of the players is a Tit-for-Tat player, cooperation in an N-Times Repeated Prisoner's Dilemma can persist for long periods, $(N - 2)$ periods to be exact. Such cooperation will of course persist for a shorter period as ρ falls.

If you have thought a bit about this problem, these results for the N-Times Repeated Prisoner's Dilemma may seem intuitive, but it takes a little doing to prove formally. We will therefore forego formal proofs and simply note that we have, using the concept of perfect Bayesian Nash equilibrium, arrived at one possible explanation for why we see cooperation in finitely repeated settings when subgame perfection suggests that such cooperation should not occur among rational players.

That explanation essentially says that, in environments where there is some uncertainty about the type of opponents that players face, players (like me) may want to establish a *reputation* for being cooperative in order to sustain cooperation over some period of time.

CONCLUSION

In this chapter, we have developed a number of tools to help us think about economic situations in which individuals have an incentive to think strategically because their actions can influence the equilibrium that defines the economic environment we face. We had already begun doing this in Chapter 23 for the case of a monopolist, but the game theory tools developed here will now help us to extend our analysis of strategic thinking into a variety of other areas in which individuals are "large" relative to their economic environment.

In some ways, however, what we are doing is not different than what we have been doing all along: We are assuming that individuals seek to do the best they can given what everyone else is "doing," or, more accurately, what others are "planning to do." In strategic situations, this implies that individuals have to arrive at complete plans of actions—or strategies—and that doing the best they can given what everyone else is planning is the same as playing "best response strategies" to the strategies played by other players. When all players are "best responding" to all other players in this way, we have reached a Nash equilibrium (or a Bayesian Nash equilibrium in games involving incomplete information). And when such best responses involve players giving no credence to noncredible threats in sequential move games, it means that we have reached a subgame perfect Nash equilibrium (or a perfect Bayesian Nash equilibrium in incomplete information games). (In Bayesian games, we have seen that these equilibrium strategies must be accompanied by equilibrium beliefs that allow players to calculate their expected payoffs from different strategies.)

One of the fundamental insights from this chapter is that such equilibria in game theory models may not result in efficiency. Put differently, the equilibrium that emerges in a game might be such that there are alternative outcomes that all players would in fact prefer but that their rational individual (decentralized) decisions cannot reach without intervention by nonmarket institutions. Put into language developed earlier, decentralized decision making in strategic settings may violate the efficiency prediction of the First Welfare Theorem.

In the context of markets in which producers supply goods to consumers, strategic incentives derive from the market power of producers that are "large" relative to the market, which implies that producers may have the power to influence prices through their choice of how much to supply to the market (as we have already seen for monopolists). In the next two chapters, we will focus a bit more on this type of market power, but in cases that are less extreme than those for monopolists in Chapter 24. In the process we will see strategic thinking play a large role in choices made by producers, and we will see how such strategic choices may result in deadweight losses (and thus violations of the First Welfare Theorem). Throughout, we will draw on the game theory tools developed in this chapter. Strategic incentives may also arise from the existence of externalities and aymmetric information. Following our treatment of market power on the part of producers, we will therefore proceed to other cases in which strategic thinking plays important roles, such as in market provision of public goods (Chapter 27) that will cause us to revisit the topic of externalities, and in the choices made by politicians (Chapter 28).

APPENDIX: INFINITELY REPEATED GAMES AND THE FOLK THEOREM

Consider the Prisoner's Dilemma in Table 24.5, which is again depicted here in panel (a) of Graph 24.12 (with the actions relabeled *C* for "Cooperate" and *D* for "Don't Cooperate"). The four possible payoff combinations are then graphed in panel (b). Each of these is of course a possible *average* (per-period) payoff in the infinitely repeated game if the two players were to always play the actions that lead to those payoffs in the simultaneous game. But by alternating different combinations of actions in different stages of

Graph 24.12: Average Payoffs under Infinite Repetition of the Prisoner's Dilemma

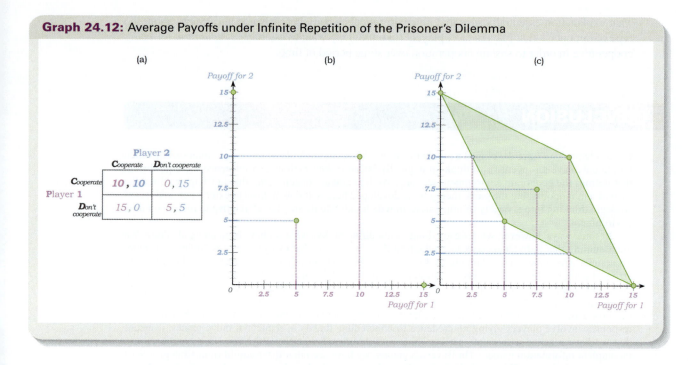

the sequential game, other combinations of average payoffs per game become possible. For instance, if we alternated between both playing C and both playing D, we would alternate between payoffs of 5 and 10, thus getting an average payoff of 7.5 each. If we alternated between both playing C and player 1 playing D while player 2 plays C, player 1 would get an average payoff of 10 while player 2 would get an average payoff of 2.5.

Exercise
24B.33

Propose a way that average payoffs could be 5 for player 1 and 12.5 for player 2.

You should be able to see that, by combining different ways of playing the game in different periods, *any* payoff combination in the shaded region in panel (c) of the graph can then arise in the infinitely repeated game as the *average* payoffs for the two players. The question we would like to turn to now is which of these average payoff combinations could arise in a subgame perfect Nash equilibrium.

The answer is relatively easy to see.[16] We will begin by showing that the fully cooperative average payoff outcome (10,10) can emerge under subgame perfection and will then discuss how the same logic can lead to many other average equilibrium payoffs.

Suppose each player in the game plays what we previously called a *trigger strategy* of the following kind: Play C in the first stage of the infinitely repeated game and continue to do so as long as both players cooperated in all previous stages; otherwise, play D. We can first check that these are best responses to one another. Suppose player 1 plays this strategy. If player 2 also plays the same strategy, she will receive a payoff of 10 in every stage of the game. Recall that, for $0 < \delta < 1$, $1 + \delta + \delta^2 + \ldots = 1/(1 - \delta)$, which implies that the present discounted value of receiving a payoff of 10 in every period from now on is

$$10 + 10\delta + 10\delta^2 + \ldots = \frac{10}{(1 - \delta)}, \qquad (24.9)$$

---

[16]This was first proposed for repeated games more generally by J. Friedman, "A Non-cooperative Equilibrium for Supergames," *Review of Economic Studies* 38 (1971), 1–12.

where $1 one period from now is worth $\delta < 1$. If player 2 decides to deviate from this trigger strategy, she will play D now knowing that this will get her a payoff of 15 this period but then relegate her future payoffs to 5 per period as no more cooperation takes place. Thus, her present discounted value from deviating is

$$15 + 5\delta + 5\delta^2 + \ldots = 15 + 5\delta(1 + \delta + \delta^2 + \ldots) = 15 + \frac{5\delta}{(1 - \delta)}. \qquad (24.10)$$

As long as $\delta > 0.5$, equation (24.9) is greater than (24.10) and deviation from the trigger strategy does not pay in expected value terms. Put differently, as long as the players do not excessively discount the future (to the point where $1 next period is worth less than 50 cents this period), the proposed trigger strategies are best responses to each other and thus constitute Nash equilibrium strategies.

To check whether these strategies are also subgame perfect, we need to check that they represent Nash equilibrium strategies for every subgame of the infinitely repeated game. Every subgame is identical to the original game (since it, too, is an infinitely repeated Prisoner's Dilemma), and one of two possible histories of the game could have led up to any particular subgame: Either all previous meetings between the players have resulted in both players playing C, or in at least one previous game at least one of the players played D. In the first case, we are still playing the same trigger strategy in the subgame, which is identical to the original game for which we already demonstrated these trigger strategies to be a Nash equilibrium. In the second case, we are simply playing the strategy "Always D." Given the other player i plays this strategy, it is a best response for player j to do the same, and so again we have a Nash equilibrium in the subgame. We can therefore conclude that the proposed trigger strategies are subgame perfect, and they result in full cooperation with average per period payoffs of 10 for each player.

The *Folk Theorem*, however, says more than this; not only is full cooperation possible through the use of the particular trigger strategy we specified, but partial cooperation is also possible. By *partial cooperation*, we mean sequences of equilibrium actions that result in payoffs for the two players that give more than the non-cooperative average payoff of 5 to each player. This corresponds to the average payoff combinations that lie in the shaded region in Graph 24.13.

It should not be too difficult to see how any of these payoffs could in fact emerge in a subgame perfect Nash equilibrium of the infinitely repeated game. Pick any payoff combination in the shaded area of Graph 24.13. By definition, these payoffs are greater than what a player could get under non-cooperation. Determine

Graph 24.13: The Folk Theorem for the Infinitely Repeated Prisoner's Dilemma

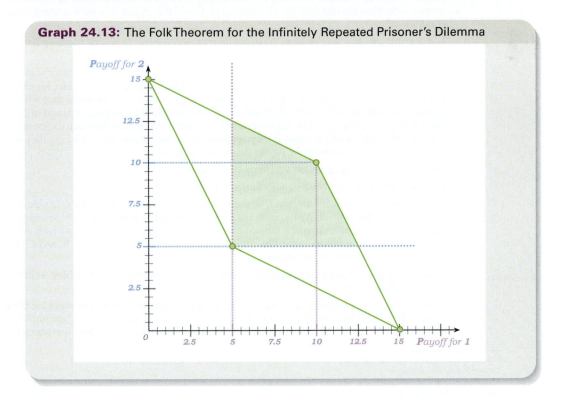

the sequence of actions necessary to ensure the average payoff combination you chose and then define a trigger strategy that says "Play this sequence as long as the other player plays his or her part; otherwise switch forever to D." You should be able to see that, as long as δ is sufficiently close to 1 (and we therefore do not discount the future too much) it is a subgame perfect equilibrium for both players to play this trigger strategy.

You should also see that similar logic can be extended to games other than the Prisoner's Dilemma where average payoffs above any simultaneous Nash equilibrium payoffs can arise under subgame perfection through the use of similar trigger strategies. Thus, the Folk Theorem is considerably more general than simply applying to repeated Prisoner's Dilemmas, and in fact it has been extended in ways that will become relevant when we discuss oligopoly behavior in Chapter 25.

END-OF-CHAPTER EXERCISES

24.1[†] In the Hollywood movie *A Beautiful Mind,* Russel Crowe plays John Nash, who developed the Nash equilibrium concept in his PhD thesis at Princeton University. In one of the early scenes of the movie, Nash finds himself in a bar with three of his fellow (male) mathematics PhD students when a group of five women enters the bar.[17] The attention of the PhD students is focused on one of the five women, with each of the four PhD students expressing interest in asking her out. One of Nash's fellow students reminds the others of Adam Smith's insight that pursuit of self-interest in competition with others results in the socially best outcome, but Nash, in what appears to be a flash if insight, claims "Adam Smith needs revision."

   A. In the movie, John Nash then explains that none of them will end up with the woman they are all attracted to if they all compete for her because they will block each other as they compete, and that furthermore they will not be able to go out with the other women in the group thereafter (because none of them will agree to a date once they know they are at best everyone's second choice). Instead, he proposes, they should all ignore the woman they are initially attracted to and instead ask the others out. It's the only way they will get a date. He quickly rushes off to write his thesis, with the movie implying that he had just discovered the concept of Nash equilibrium.

      a. If each of the PhD students were to play the strategy John Nash suggests, each one selects a woman other than the one they are all attracted to. Could this in fact be a pure strategy Nash equilibrium?

      b. Is it possible that any pure strategy Nash equilibrium could result in no one pursuing the woman they are all attracted to?

      c. Suppose we simplified the example to one in which it was only Nash and one other student encountering a group of two women. We then have two pure strategies to consider for each PhD student: Pursue woman A or pursue woman B. Suppose that each viewed a date with woman A as yielding a "payoff" of 10 and a date with woman B as yielding a payoff of 5. Each will in fact get a date with the woman who is approached *if* they approach different women, but neither will get a date if they approach the same woman, in which case they both get a payoff of 0. Write down the payoff matrix of this game.

      d. What are the pure strategy Nash equilibria of this game?

      e. Is there a mixed strategy Nash equilibrium in this game?

      f. Now suppose there is also a woman C in the group of women, and a date with C is viewed as equivalent to a date with B. Again, each PhD student gets a date if he is the only one approaching a woman, but if both approach the same woman, neither gets a date (and thus both get a payoff of zero). Now, however, the PhD students have three pure strategies: A, B, and C. Write down the payoff matrix for this game.

      g. What are the pure strategy Nash equilibria of this game? Does any of them involve woman A leaving without a date?

      h. In the movie, Nash explains that "Adam Smith said the best result comes from everyone in the group doing what's best for themselves." He goes on to say " . . . incomplete . . . incomplete . . . because the best result will come from everyone in the group doing what's best for themselves

---

[17]Nash is actually with four others, but the rest of the scene unfolds as if there were four of them in total.
*conceptually challenging
**computationally challenging
[†]solutions in Study Guide

and the group ... Adam Smith was wrong." Does the situation described in the movie illustrate any of this?

    i.   While these words have little to do with the concept of Nash equilibrium, in what way does game theory—and in particular games like the Prisoner's Dilemma—challenge the inference one might draw from Adam Smith that self-interest achieves the "best" outcome for the group?

B. Consider the two-player game described in part A(c). (Note: Parts (a) and (b) can be done without having read Section B of the chapter.)

    a.   Suppose that the players move sequentially, with player 1 choosing A or B first and player 2 making his choice after observing player 1's choice. What is the subgame perfect Nash equilibrium?

    b.   Is there a Nash equilibrium in which player 2 goes out with woman A? If so, is there a noncredible threat that is needed to sustain this as an equilibrium?

    c.   Next, consider again the simultaneous move game from A(c). Draw a game tree for this simultaneous move game, with player 1's decision on the top. (*Hint*: Use the appropriate information set for player 2 to keep this game a simultaneous move game). Can you state different beliefs for player 2 (when player 2 gets to his information set) such that the equilibria you derived in A(d) and A(e) arise?

    d.   Continue to assume that both players get payoff of 0 if they approach the same woman. As before, player 1 gets a payoff of 10 if he is the only one to approach woman A and a payoff of 5 if he is the only one to approach woman B. But player 2 might be one of two possible types: If he is type 1, he has the same tastes as player 1, but if he is of type 2, he gets a payoff of only 5 if he is the only one to approach woman A and a payoff of 10 if he is the only one to approach woman B. Prior to the beginning of the game, Nature assigns type 1 to player 2 with probability δ (and thus assigns type 2 to player 2 with probability $(1 - \delta)$.) Graph the game tree for this game, using information sets to connect nodes where appropriate.

    e.   What are the pure strategy equilibria in this game? Does it matter what value δ takes?

24.2 Consider a sequential game that is known as the *Centipede Game*. In this game, each of two players chooses between *Left* and *Right* each time he or she gets a turn. The game does not, however, automatically proceed to the next stage unless players choose to go *Right* rather than *Left*.

A. Player 1 begins, and if he plays *Left,* the game ends with payoff of $(1,0)$ (where here, and throughout this exercise, the first payoff refers to player 1 and the second to player 2). If, however, he plays *Right,* the game continues and it's player 2's turn. If player 2 then plays *Left,* the game once again ends, this time with payoffs $(0,2)$, but if she plays *Right,* the game continues and player 1 gets another turn. Once again, the game ends if player 1 decides to play *Left,* this time with payoffs of $(3,1)$, but if he plays *Right* the game continues and it's once again player 2's turn. Now the game ends regardless of whether player 2 plays *Left* or *Right,* but payoffs are $(2,4)$ if she plays *Left* and $(3,3)$ if she plays *Right*.

    a.   Draw out the game tree for this game. What is the subgame perfect Nash equilibrium of this game?

    b.   Write down the 4 by 4 payoff matrix for this game. What are the pure strategy Nash equilibria in this game? Is the subgame perfect Nash equilibrium you derived in (a) among these?

    c.   Why are the other Nash equilibria in the game not subgame perfect?

    d.   Suppose you changed the $(2,4)$ payoff pair to $(2,3)$. Do we now have more than one subgame perfect Nash equilibrium?

    e.   How does your answer to (b) change?

    f.   Consider again the original game but suppose I came as an outsider and offered to change the payoff pairs in the final stage from $(2,4)$ and $(3,3)$ to $(2,2)$ and $(4,4)$. How much would each of the two players be willing to pay me to change the game in this way (assuming we know that players always play subgame perfect equilibria)?

B. Consider the original Centipede game described in part A. Suppose that, prior to the game being played, Nature moves and assigns a type to player 2, with type 1 being assigned with probability ρ and type 2 with probability $(1 - \rho)$. Throughout, type 1 is a rational player who understands subgame perfection.

    a.   Suppose type 2 is a super-naive player who simply always goes *Right* whenever given a chance. For what values of ρ will player 1 go *Right* in the first stage?

    b.   Suppose instead that type 2 always goes *Right* the first time and *Left* the second time. How does your answer change?

    c.   (Note: This (and the next) part requires that you have read Chapter 17.) We have not explicitly mentioned this in the chapter, but game theorists often assume that payoffs are given in utility terms, with utility measured by a function u that allows gambles to be represented by an expected utility function. Within the context of this exercise, can you see why?

    d.   Suppose the payoffs in the Centipede game are in dollar terms, not in utility terms. What do your answers to (a) and (b) assume about the level of risk aversion of player 1?

24.3   Consider a simultaneous game in which both players choose between the actions "Cooperate," denoted by C, and "Defect," denoted by D.

A.   Suppose that the payoffs in the game are as follows: If both players play C, each gets a payoff of 1; if both play D, both players get 0; and if one player plays C and the other plays D, the cooperating player gets α while the defecting player gets β.

    a.   Illustrate the payoff matrix for this game.

    b.   What restrictions on α and β would you have to impose in order for this game to be a Prisoner's Dilemma? Assume from now on that these restrictions are in fact met.

B.*   Now consider a repeated version of this game in which players 1 and 2 meet two times. Suppose you were player 1 in this game, and suppose that you knew that player 2 was a "Tit-for-Tat" player; i.e., a player who does not behave strategically but rather is simply programed to play the Tit-for-Tat strategy.

    a.   Assuming you do not discount the future, would you ever cooperate with this player?

    b.   Suppose you discount a dollar in period 2 by δ where $0 < \delta < 1$. Under what condition will you cooperate in this game?

    c.   Suppose instead that the game was repeated three rather than two times. Would you ever cooperate with this player (assuming again that you don't discount the future)? (*Hint*: Use the fact that you should know the best action in period 3 to cut down on the number of possibilities you have to investigate.)

    d.   In the repeated game with three encounters, what is the intuitive reason why you might play D in the first stage?

    e.   If player 2 is strategic, would he ever play the "Tit-for-Tat" strategy in either of the two repeated games?

    f.   Suppose that each time the two players meet, they know they will meet again with probability $\gamma > 0$. Explain intuitively why "Tit-for-Tat" can be an equilibrium strategy for both players if γ is relatively large (i.e., close to 1) but not if it is relatively small (i.e., close to 0).

24.4[†]   *Interpreting Mixed Strategies in the Battle of the Sexes*: One of the most famous games treated in early game theory courses is known as the "Battle of the Sexes," and it bears close resemblance to the game in which you and I choose sides of the street when you are British and I am American. In the "Battle of the Sexes" game, two partners in a newly blossoming romance have different preferences for what to do on a date, but neither can stand the thought of not being with the other. Suppose we are talking about you and your partner. You love opera and your partner loves football.[18] Both you and your partner can choose to go to the opera and today's football game, with each of you getting 0 payoff if you aren't at the same activity as the other, 10 if you are at your favorite activity with your partner, and 5 if you are at your partner's favorite activity with him/her.

A.   In this exercise, we will focus on mixed strategies.

    a.   Begin by depicting the game in the form of a payoff matrix.

---

[18]Since this game dates back quite a few decades, you can imagine which of the two players was referred to as the "husband" and which as the "wife" in early incarnation. I will attempt to write this problem without any such gender (or other) bias and apologize to the reader if he/she is not a fan of opera.

    b.   Let ρ be the probability you place on going to the opera, and let δ be the probability your partner places on going to the opera. For what value of δ are you indifferent between showing up at the opera or showing up at the football game?

    c.   For what values of ρ is your partner indifferent between these two actions?

    d.   What is the mixed strategy equilibrium to this game?

    e.   What are the expected payoffs for you and your partner in this game assuming the mixed strategy equilibrium is played?

B.* In the text, we indicated that mixed strategy equilibria in complete information games can be interpreted as pure strategy equilibria in a related incomplete information game. We will illustrate this here. Suppose that you and your partner know each other's ordinal preferences over opera and football, but you are not quite sure just how much the other values the most preferred outcome. In particular, your partner knows your payoff from both showing up at the football game is 5, but he thinks your payoff from both showing up at the opera is $(10 + \alpha)$ with some uncertainty about what exactly α is. Similarly, you know your partner gets a payoff of 5 if both of you show up at the opera, but you think his/her payoff from both showing up at the football game is $(10 + \beta)$, with you unsure of what exact value β takes. We will assume that both α and β are equally likely to take any value in the interval from 0 to x; i.e., α and β are drawn randomly from a uniform distribution on $[0, x]$. We have thus turned the initial complete information game into a related incomplete information game in which your type is defined by the randomly drawn value of α and your partner's type is defined by the randomly drawn value of β, with $[0, x]$ defining the set of possible types for both of you.

    a.   Suppose that your strategy in this game is to go to the opera if $\alpha > a$ (and to go to the football game otherwise), with a falling in the interval $[0, x]$. Explain why the probability (evaluated in the absence of knowing α) that you will go to the opera is $(x - a)/x$. What is the probability you will go to the football game?

    b.   Suppose your partner plays a similar strategy: go to the football game if $\beta > b$ and otherwise go to the opera. What is the probability that your partner will go to the football game? What is the probability that he/she will go to the opera?

    c.   Given you know the answer to (b), what is your expected payoff from going to the opera for a given α? What is your expected payoff from going to the football game?

    d.   Given your partner knows the answer to (a), what is your partner's expected payoff from going to the opera? What about the expected payoff from going to the football game?

    e.   Given your answer to (c), for what value of α (in terms of b and x) are you indifferent between going to the opera and going to the football game?

    f.   Given your answer to (d), for what value of β (in terms of a and x) is your partner indifferent between going to the opera and going to the football game?

    g.   Let a be equal to the value of α you calculated in (e), and let b be equal to the value of β you calculated in (f). Then solve the resulting system of two equations for a and b (using the quadratic formula).

    h.   Why do these values for a and b make the strategies defined in (a) and (b) pure (Bayesian Nash) equilibrium strategies?

    i.** How likely is it in this equilibrium that you will go to the opera? How likely is it that your partner will go to the football game? How do your answers change as x approaches zero, and how does this compare to the probabilities you derived for the mixed strategy equilibrium in part A of the exercise? (*Hint*: Following the rules of taking limits, you will in this case have to take the derivative of a numerator and a denominator before taking the limit.)

    j.   *True or False*: The mixed strategy equilibrium to the complete information Battle of the Sexes game can be interpreted as a pure strategy Bayesian equilibrium in an incomplete information game that is almost identical to the original complete information game, allowing us to interpret the mixed strategies in the complete information game as arising from uncertainty that players have about the other player.

24.5   **Everyday Application:** *Splitting the Pot*: Suppose two players are asked to split $100 in a way that is agreeable to both.

    A. The structure for the game is as follows: Player 1 moves first, and he is asked to simply state some number between zero and 100. This number represents his "offer" to player 2; i.e., the amount player 1 offers for player 2 to keep, with player 1 keeping the rest. For instance, if player 1 says "30," he is offering player 2 a split of the $100 that gives $70 to player 1 and $30 to player 2. After an offer has been made by player 1, player 2 simply chooses from two possible actions: either "Accept" the offer or "Reject" it. If player 2 accepts, the $100 is split in the way proposed by player 1; if player 2 rejects, neither player gets anything. (A game like this is often referred to as an *ultimatum game*.)

    a.   What are the subgame perfect equlibria in this game assuming that player 1 is restricted to making his "offer" in integer terms; i.e., assuming that player 1 has to state a whole number.

    b.   Now suppose that offers can be made to the penny; i.e., offers like $31.24 are acceptable. How does that change the subgame perfect equilibria? What if we assumed dollars could be divided into arbitrarily small quantities (i.e., fractions of pennies)?

    c.   It turns out that there are at most two subgame perfect equilibria to this game (and only 1 if dollars are assumed to be fully divisible), but there is a very large number of Nash equilibria regardless of exactly how player 1 can phrase his offer (and an infinite number when dollars are assumed fully divisible). Can you, for instance, derive Nash equilibrium strategies that result in player 2 walking away with $80? Why is this not subgame perfect?

    d.   This game has been played in experimental settings in many cultures, and while the average amount that is "offered" differs somewhat between cultures, it usually falls between $25 and $50, with players often rejecting offers below that. One possible explanation for this is that individuals across different cultures have somewhat different notions of "fairness," and that they get utility from "standing up for what's fair." Suppose player 2 is willing to pay $30 to stand up to "injustice" of any kind, and anything other than a 50-50 split is considered by player 2 to be unjust. What is now the subgame perfect equilibrium if dollars are viewed as infinitely divisible? What additional subgame perfect equilibrium arises if offers can only be made in integer amounts?

    e.   Suppose instead that player 2 is outraged at "unfair" outcomes in direct proportion to how far the outcome is removed from the "fair" outcome, with the utility player 2 gets from rejecting an unfair offer equal to the difference between the amount offered and the "fair" amount. Suppose player 2 believes the "fair" outcome is splitting the $100 equally. Thus, if the player faces an offer $x < 50$, the utility she gets from rejecting the offer is $(50 - x)$. What are the subgame perfect equilibria of this game now under the assumption of infinitely divisible dollars and under the assumption of offers having to be made in integer terms?

B.   Consider the same game as that outlined in A and suppose you are the one who splits the $100 and I am the one who decides to accept or reject. You think there is a pretty good chance that I am the epitome of a rational human being who cares only about walking away with the most I can from the game. But you don't know me that well, and so you think there is some chance ρ that I am a self-righteous moralist who will reject any offer that is worse for me than a 50-50 split. (Assume throughout that dollars can be split into infinitesimal parts.)

    a.   Structure this game as an incomplete information game.

    b.   There are two types of pure strategy equilibria to this game (depending on what value ρ takes). What are they?

    c.   How would your answer change if I, as a self-righteous moralist (which I am with probability ρ) reject all offers that leave me with less than $10?

    d.   What if it's only less than $1 that is rejected by self-righteous moralists?

    e.   What have we implicitly assumed about risk aversion?

24.6   **Everyday Application:** *Another Way to Split the Pot*: Suppose again, as in exercise 24.5, that two players have $100 to split between them.

A.   But now, instead of one player proposing a division and the other accepting or rejecting it, suppose that player 1 divides the $100 into two piles and player 2 then selects his preferred pile.

    a.   What is the subgame perfect equilibrium of this game?

    b.   Can you think of a Nash equilibrium (with an outcome different than the subgame perfect outcome) that is not subgame perfect?

    c.   In exercise 24.5, we considered the possibility of restricting offers to be in integer amounts, to be in pennies, etc. Would our prediction differ here if we made different such assumptions?

     d.   Suppose that the pot was $99 and player 1 can only create piles in integer (i.e., full dollar) amounts. Who would you prefer to be: player 1 or 2?

     e.   Suppose that player 2 has three possible actions: pick up the smaller pile, pick up the larger pile, and set all of it on fire. Can you now think of Nash equilibria that are not subgame perfect?

B. In exercise 24.5, we next considered an incomplete information game in which you split the $100 and I was a self-righteous moralist with some probability ρ. Assuming that the opposing player is some strange type with some probability can sometimes allow us to reconcile experimental data that differs from game theory predictions.

     a.   Why might this be something we introduce into the game from exercise 24.5 but not here?

     b.   If we were to introduce the possibility that player 2 plays a strategy other than the "rational" strategy with probability ρ, is there any way that this will result in player 1 getting less than $50 in this game?

24.7 **Everyday Application:** *Real-World Mixed Strategies*: In the text, we discussed the "Matching Pennies" game and illustrated that such a game only has a mixed strategy equilibrium.

    A. Consider each of the following and explain (unless you are asked to do something different) how you might expect there to be no pure strategy equilibrium, and how a mixed strategy equilibrium might make sense.

     a.   A popular children's game, often played on long road trips, is "Rock, Paper, Scissors." The game is simple: Two players simultaneously signal through a hand gesture one of three possible actions: *Rock*, *Paper*, or *Scissors*. If the two players signal the same, the game is a tie. Otherwise, *Rock* beats *Scissors*, *Scissors* beats *Paper*, and *Paper* beats *Rock*.

     b.   One of my students objects: "I understand that *Scissors* can beat *Paper*, and I get how *Rock* can beat *Scissors*, but there is no way *Paper* should beat *Rock*. What ... *Paper* is supposed to magically wrap around *Rock* leaving it immobile? Why can't *Paper* do this to *Scissors*? For that matter, why can't *Paper* do this to people? I'll tell you why: Because *Paper* can't beat anybody!"[19] If *Rock* really could beat *Paper*, is there still a mixed strategy Nash equilibrium?

     c.   In soccer, penalty kicks often resolve ties. The kicker has to choose which side of the goal to aim for, and, because the ball moves so fast, the goalie has to decide simultaneously which side of the goal to defend.

     d.   How is the soccer example similar to a situation encountered by a professional tennis player whose turn it is to serve?

     e.   For reasons I cannot explain, teenagers in the 1950's sometimes played a game called "chicken." Two teenagers in separate cars drove at high speed in opposite directions on a collision course toward each other and whoever swerved to avoid a crash lost the game. Sometimes, the cars crashed and both teenagers were severely injured (or worse). If we think behavior in these games arose within an equilibrium, could that equilibrium be in pure strategies?

    B. If you have done part B of exercise 24.4, appeal to incomplete information games with almost complete information to explain intuitively how the mixed strategy equilibrium in the chicken game of A(e) can be interpreted.

24.8* **Everyday Application:** *Burning Money, Iterated Dominance, and the Battle of the Sexes*: Consider again the "Battle of the Sexes" game described in exercise 24.4. Recall that you and your partner have to decide whether to show up at the opera or a football game for your date, with both of you getting a payoff of 0 if you show up at different events and therefore aren't together. If both of you show up at the opera, you get a payoff of 10 and your partner gets a payoff of 5, with these reversed if you both show up at the football game.

    A. In this part of the exercise, you will have a chance to test your understanding of some basic building blocks of complete information games whereas in part B we introduce a new concept related to dominant strategies. Neither part requires any material from Section B of the chapter.

---

[19]My student continues (with some editing on my part to make it past the editorial censors): "When I play "Rock, Paper, Scissors," I always choose *Rock*. Then, when someone claims to have beaten me with *Paper*, I can punch them in the face with my already clenched fist and say, 'Oh, sorry—I thought paper would protect you, moron'."

a. Suppose your partner works the night shift and you work during the day and, as a result, you miss each other in the morning as you leave for work just before your partner gets home. Neither of you is reachable at work, and you come straight from work to your date. Unable to consult one another before your date, each of you simply has to individually decide whether to show up at the opera or at the football game. Depict the resulting game in the form of a payoff matrix.

b. In what sense is this an example of a "coordination game"?

c. What are the pure strategy Nash equilibria of the game?

d. After missing each other on too many dates, you come up with a clever idea: Before leaving for work in the morning, you can choose to burn $5 on your partner's nightstand, or you can decide not to. Your partner will observe whether or not you burned $5. So we now have a sequential game where you first decide whether or not to burn $5, and you and your partner then simultaneously have to decide where to show up for your date (after knowing whether or not you burned the $5). What are your four strategies in this new game?

e. What are your partner's four strategies in this new game (given that your partner may or may not observe the evidence of the burnt money depending on whether or not you chose to burn the money)?

f. Illustrate the payoff matrix of the new game assuming that the original payoffs were denominated in dollars. What are the pure strategy Nash equilibria?

B. In the text, we defined a *dominant strategy* as a strategy under which a player does better *no matter what his opponent does* than he does under any other strategy he could play. Consider now a weaker version of this: We will say that a strategy *B* is *weakly dominated* by a strategy *A* for a player if the player does at least as well playing *A* as he would playing *B* regardless of what the opponent does.

a. Are there any weakly dominated strategies for you in the payoff matrix you derived in A(f)? Are there any such weakly dominated strategies for your partner?

b. It seems reasonable that neither of you expects the other to play a weakly dominated strategy. So take your payoff matrix and strike out all weakly dominated strategies. The game you are left with is called a *reduced game*. Are there any strategies for either you or your partner that are weakly dominated in this reduced game? If so, strike them out and derive an even more reduced game. Keep doing this until you can do it no more. What are you left with in the end?

c. After repeatedly eliminating weakly dominated strategies, you should have ended up with a single strategy left for each player. Are these strategies an equilibrium in the game from A(f) that you started with?

d. Selecting among multiple Nash equilibria to a game by repeatedly getting rid of weakly dominated strategies is known as applying the idea of *iterative dominance*. Consider the initial game from A(a) (before we introduced the possibility of you burning money). Would applying the same idea of iterative dominance narrow the set of Nash equilibria in that game?

e. *True or False*: By introducing an action that ends up not being used, you have made it more likely that you and your partner will end up at the opera.

24.9*† Everyday and Business Application: *Bargaining over a Fixed Amount*: Consider a repeated version of the game in exercise 24.5. In this version, we do not give all the proposal power to one person but rather imagine that the players are *bargaining* by making different proposals to one another until they come to an agreement. In part A of the exercise we analyze a simplified version of such a bargaining game, and in part B we use the insights from part A to think about an infinitely repeated bargaining game. (Note: Part B of the exercise, while conceptually building on part A, does not require any material from Section B of the chapter.)

A. We begin with a three-period game in which $100 gets split between the two players. It begins with player 1 stating an amount x_1 that proposes she should receive x_1 and player 2 should receive $(100 - x_1)$. Player 2 can then accept the offer, in which case the game ends with payoff x_1 for player 1 and $(100 - x_1)$ for player 2; or player 2 can reject the offer, with the game moving on to period 2. In period 2, player 2 now has a chance to make an offer x_2 that proposes player 1 gets x_2 and player 2 gets $(100 - x_2)$. Now player 1 gets a chance to accept the offer—and the proposed payoffs—or to reject it. If the offer is rejected, we move on to period 3 where player 1 simply receives x and player 2 receives $(100 - x)$. Suppose throughout that both players are somewhat impatient and they value $1 a period from now at $\delta(< 1)$. Also suppose throughout that each player accepts an offer whenever he/she is indifferent between accepting and rejecting the offer.

    a.   Given that player 1 knows she will get x in period 3 if the game continues to period 3, what is the lowest offer she will accept in period 2 (taking into account that she discounts the future as described)?

    b.   What payoff will player 2 get in period 2 if he offers the amount you derived in (a)? What is the present discounted value (in period 2) of what he will get in this game if he offers less than that in period 2?

    c.   Based on your answer to (b), what can you conclude player 2 will offer in period 2?

    d.   When the game begins, player 2 can look ahead and know everything you have thus far concluded. Can you use this information to derive the lowest possible period 1 offer that will be accepted by player 2 in period 1?

    e.   What payoff will player 1 get in period 1 if she offers the amount you derived in (d)? What will she get (in present value terms) if she offers an amount higher for her (and lower for player 2)?

    f.   Based on your answer to (e), can you conclude how much player 1 offers in period 1, and what this implies for how the game unfolds in subgame perfect equilibrium?

    g.   *True or False*: The more player 1 is guaranteed to get in the third period of the game, the less will be offered to player 2 in the first period (with player 2 always accepting what is offered at the beginning of the game).

B.   Now consider an infinitely repeated version of this game; i.e., suppose that in odd-numbered periods, beginning with period 1, player 1 gets to make an offer that player 2 can accept or reject, and in even-numbered periods the reverse is true.

    a.   *True or False*: The game that begins in period 3 (assuming that period is reached) is identical to the game beginning in period 1.

    b.   Suppose that, in the game beginning in period 3, it is part of an equilibrium for player 1 to offer x and player 2 to accept it at the beginning of that game. Given your answer to (a), is it also part of an equilibrium for player 1 to begin by offering x and for player 2 to accept it in the game that begins with period 1?

    c.   In part A of the exercise, you should have concluded that when the game was set to artificially end in period 3 with payoffs x and $(100 - x)$, player 1 ends up offering $x_1 = 100 - \delta(100 - \delta x)$ in period 1, with player 2 accepting. How is our infinitely repeated game similar to what we analyzed in part A when we suppose, in the infinitely repeated game beginning in period 3, the equilibrium has player 1 offering x and player 2 accepting the offer?

    d.   Given your answers, why must it be the case that $x = 100 - \delta(100 - \delta x)$?

    e.   Use this insight to derive how much player 1 offers in period 1 of the infinitely repeated game. Will player 2 accept?

    f.   Does the first mover have an advantage in this infinitely repeated bargaining game? If so, why do you think this is the case?

24.10 **Everyday and Business Application:** *Auctions*: Many items are sold not in markets but in auctions where bidders do not know how much others value the object that is up for bid. We will analyze a straightforward setting like this here, which technically means we are analyzing (for much of this exercise) an incomplete information game of the type covered in Section B of the chapter. The underlying logic of the exercise is, however, sufficiently transparent for you to be able to attempt the exercise even if you have not read Section B of the chapter. Consider the following, known as a *second-price sealed bid auction*. In this kind of auction, all people who are interested in an item x submit sealed bids (simultaneously). The person whose bid is the highest then gets the item x at a price equal to the second highest bid.

EVERYDAY APPLICATION

BUSINESS APPLICATION

A.   Suppose there are n different bidders who have different marginal willingness to pay for the item x. Player i's marginal willingness to pay for x is denoted v_i. Suppose initially that this is a complete information game; i.e., everyone knows everyone's marginal willingness to pay for the item that is auctioned.

    a.   Is it a Nash equilibrium in this auction for each player i to bid v_i?

    b.   Suppose individual j has the highest marginal willingness to pay. Is it a Nash equilibrium for all players other than j to bid zero and player j to bid v_j?

    c.   Can you think of another Nash equilibrium to this auction?

d. Suppose that players are not actually sure about the marginal willingness to pay of all the other players, only about their own. Can you think of why the Nash equilibrium in which all players bid their marginal willingness to pay is now the most compelling Nash equilibrium?

e. Now consider a *sequential first price auction* in which an auctioneer keeps increasing the price of x in small increments and any potential bidder signals the auctioneer whether she is willing to pay that price. (Assume that the signal from bidders to auctioneer is not observable by other bidders.) The auction ends when only a single bidder signals a willingness to pay the price, and the winner then buys the item x for the price equal to his winning bid. Assuming the increments the auctioneer uses to raise the price during the auction are sufficiently small, approximately what will each player's final bid be?

f. In equilibrium, approximately what price will the winner of the sequential auction pay?

g. *True or False*: The outcome of the sealed bid second price auction is approximately equivalent to the outcome of the sequential (first price) auction.

B. This part provides a real-world example of how an auction of the type analyzed in part A can be used. When I became Department Chair in our economics department at Duke, the chair was annually deciding how to assign graduate students to faculty to provide teaching and research support. Students were paid a stipend by the department, but their services were free to the faculty member to whom they were assigned.

a. Under this system, faculty complained perpetually of a "teaching assistant shortage." Why do you think this was?

b. I replaced the system with the following: Aside from some key assignments of graduate students as TAs to large courses, I no longer assigned any students to faculty. Instead, I asked the faculty to submit dollar bids for the right to match with a graduate student. If we had N graduate students available, I then took the top N bids, let those faculty know they had qualified for the right to match with a student and then let the matches take place (with students and faculty seeking each other out to create matches). Every faculty member who had a successful bid was then charged (to his/her research account) a price equal to the lowest winning bid, which we called the "market price." (Students were still paid by the department as before. The charges to faculty accounts simply came into the chair discretionary account and were then redistributed in a lump sum way to all faculty.) Given that we have a large number of faculty, should any individual faculty member think that his/her bid would appreciably impact the "market price"?

c. In my annual e-mail to the faculty at the beginning of the auction for rights to match with students, I included the following line: "For those of you who are not game theorists, please note that it is a dominant strategy for you to simply bid the actual value you place on the right to match with a student." Do you agree or disagree with this statement? Why?

d. Would it surprise you to discover that for the rest of my term as chair, I never again heard complaints that we had a "TA shortage"? Why or why not?

e. Why do you think I called the lowest winning bid the "market price"? Can you think of several ways in which the allocation of students to faculty might have become more efficient as a result of the implementation of the new way of allocating students?

24.11 Business Application: *Monopoly and Price Discrimination*: In Chapter 23, we discussed first, second, and third degree price discrimination by a monopolist. Such pricing decisions are strategic choices that can be modeled using game theory, which we proceed to do here. Assume throughout that the monopolist can keep consumers who buy at low prices from selling to those how are offered high prices.

A. Suppose a monopolist faces two types of consumers: a high demand consumer and a low demand consumer. Suppose further that the monopolist can tell which consumer has low demand and which has high demand; i.e., the consumer types are observable to the monopolist.

a. Can you model the pricing decisions by the monopolist as a set of sequential games with different consumer types?

b. Suppose the monopolist can construct any set of two-part tariffs, i.e., a per-unit price plus fixed fee for different packages. What is the subgame perfect equilibrium of your games?

c. *True or False*: First degree price discrimination emerges in the subgame perfect equilibrium but not in other Nash equilibria of the game.

    d.   How is this analysis similar to the game in exercise 24.5?

    e.   Next, suppose that the monopolist cannot charge a fixed fee but only a per-unit price, but he can set different per-unit prices for different consumer types. What is the subgame perfect equilibrium of your games now?

B. Next, suppose that the monopolist is unable to observe the consumer type but knows that a fraction ρ in the population are low demand types and a fraction $(1 - \rho)$ are high demand types. Assume that firms can offer any set of price/quantity combinations.

    a.   Can you model the price-setting decision by the monopolist as a game of incomplete information?

    b.   What is the perfect Bayesian equilibrium of this game in the context of concepts discussed in Chapter 23? Explain.

24.12* **Business Application:** *Carrots and Sticks: Efficiency Wages and the Threat of Firing Workers*: In our treatment of labor demand earlier in the text, we assumed that firms could observe the marginal revenue product of workers, and thus would hire until wage is equal to marginal revenue product. But suppose a firm cannot observe a worker's productivity perfectly, and suppose further that the worker himself has some control over his productivity through his choice of whether to exert effort or "shirk" on the job. In part A of the exercise, we will consider the subgame perfect equilibrium of a game that models this, and in part B we will see how an extension of this game results in the prediction that firms might combine "above market" wages with the threat to fire the worker if he is not productive. Such wages, known as *efficiency wages*, essentially have firms employing a "carrot-and-stick" approach to workers: Offer them high wages (the carrot), thus making the threat of firing more potent. (Note: It is recommended that you only attempt this problem if you have covered the whole chapter.)

BUSINESS APPLICATION

A. Suppose the firm begins the game by offering the worker a wage w. Once the worker observes the firm's offer, he decides to accept or decline the offer. If the worker rejects the offer, the game ends and the worker is employed elsewhere at his market wage w^*.

    a.   Suppose the worker's marginal revenue product is $MRP = w^*$. What is the subgame perfect equilibrium for this game when marginal revenue product is not a function of effort?

    b.   Next, suppose the game is a bit more complicated in that the worker's effort is correlated with the worker's marginal revenue product. Assuming he accepted the firm's wage offer, the worker can decide to exert effort $e > 0$ or not. The firm is unable to observe whether the worker is exerting effort, but it does observe how well the firm is doing overall. In particular, suppose the firm's payoff from employing the worker is $(x - w)$ if the worker exerts effort, but if the worker shirks, the firm's payoff is $(x - w) > 0$ with probability $\gamma < 1$ and $(-w)$ with probability $(1 - \gamma)$. For the worker, the payoff is $(w - e)$ if the worker exerts effort and w if he does not. What is the firm's expected payoff if the worker shirks?

    c.   How must w^* be related to γ and x in order for it to be efficient for the worker *not* to be employed by the firm if the worker shirks?

    d.   Suppose the worker exerts effort e if hired by the firm. Since e is a cost for the worker, how must w^* be related to $(x - e)$ in order for it to be efficient for non-shirking workers to be hired by the firm?

    e.   Suppose w^* is related to γ, x, and e such that it is efficient for workers to be hired by the firm only if they don't shirk, i.e., if the conditions you derived in (c) and (d) hold. What is the subgame perfect equilibrium? Will the firm be able to hire workers?

    f.   The subgame perfect equilibrium you just derived is inefficient. Why? What is the underlying reason for this inefficiency?

B. The problem in the game defined in part A is that we are not adequately capturing the fact that firms and workers do not typically interact just once if a worker is hired by a firm. Suppose, then, that we instead think of the relationship between worker and firm as one that can potentially be repeated infinitely. Each day, the firm begins by offering a wage w to the worker; the worker accepts or rejects the offer, walking away with a market wage w^* (and ending the relationship) if he rejects. If he accepts, the worker either exerts effort e or shirks, and the firm observes whether it ends the day with a payoff of $(x - w)$ (which it gets for sure if the worker exerts effort but only with probability $\gamma < 1$ if the worker shirks) or $(-w)$ (which can happen only if the worker shirks). Everyone goes home at the end of the day and meets again the next day (knowing how all the previous days turned out).

a. Consider the following strategy for the firm: Offer $w = \overline{w} > w^*$ on the first day; then offer $w = \overline{w}$ again every day so long as all previous days have yielded a payoff of $(x - \overline{w})$; otherwise offer $w = 0$. Is this an example of a *trigger strategy*?

b. Consider the following strategy for the worker: Accept any offer w so long as $w \geq w^*$; reject offers otherwise. Furthermore, exert effort e upon accepting an offer so long as all previous offers (including the current one) have been at least $\overline{w}$; otherwise shirk. Is this another example of a trigger strategy?

c. Suppose everyone values a dollar next period at $\delta < 1$ this period. Suppose further that P_e is the present discounted value of all payoffs for the worker assuming that firms always offer $w = \overline{w}$ and the worker always accepts and exerts effort. Explain why the following must then hold: $P_e = (\overline{w} - e) + \delta P_e$.

d. Use this to determine the present discounted value P_e of the game (as a function of $\overline{w}$, e, and δ) for the worker assuming it is optimal for the worker to exert effort when working for the firm.

e. Suppose the firm offers $w = \overline{w}$. Notice that the only way the firm can ever know that the worker shirked is if its payoff on a given day is $(-\overline{w})$ rather than $(x - \overline{w})$, and we have assumed that this happens with probability $(1 - \gamma)$ when the worker exerts no effort. Thus, a worker might decide to take a chance and shirk, hoping that the firm will still get payoff of $(x - \overline{w})$ (which happens with probability γ). What is the worker's immediate payoff (today) from doing this?

f. Suppose that the worker gets unlucky and is caught shirking the first time and that he therefore will not be employed at a wage other than the market wage w^* starting on day 2. In that case, what is the present discounted value of the game that begins on day 2? (Note: The infinite sum $\delta + \delta^2 + \delta^3 + \dots$ is equal to $\delta/(1 - \delta)$.)

g. Suppose that the worker's expected payoff from always shirking is P_s. If the worker does not get caught the first day he shirks, he starts the second day exactly under the same conditions as he did the first, implying that the payoff from the game beginning on the second day is again P_s. Combining this with your answer to parts (e) and (f), explain why the following equation must hold:

$$P_s = \overline{w} + \delta\left[\gamma P_s + (1 - \gamma)\frac{w^*}{1 - \delta}\right]. \qquad (24.11)$$

Derive from this the value of P_s as a function of δ, γ, $\overline{w}$, e, and w^*.

h. In order for the worker's strategy in (b) to be a best response to the firm's strategy in (a), it must be that $P_e \geq P_s$. How much of a premium above the market wage w^* does this imply the worker requires in order to not shirk? How does this premium change with the cost of effort e? How does it change with the probability of getting caught shirking? Does this make sense?

i. What is the highest that $\overline{w}$ can get in order for the firm to best respond to workers (who play the strategy in (b)) by playing the strategy in (a)? Combining this with your answer to (h), how must $(x - e)$ be related to w^*, δ, γ, and e in order for the strategies in (a) and (b) to constitute a Nash equilibrium? Given your answer to A(d), will it always be the case that firms hire non-shirking workers whenever it is efficient?

24.13 Policy Application: *Negotiating with Pirates, Terrorists (and Children):* While we often think of pirates as a thing of the past, piracy in international waters has been on the rise. Typically, pirates seize a commercial vessel and then demand a monetary ransom to let go of the ship. This is similar to some forms of terrorism where, for instance, terrorists kidnap citizens of a country with which the terrorists have a grievance and then demand some action by the country in exchange for the hostages.

A. Often, countries have an explicit policy that "we do not negotiate with terrorists," but still we often discover after the fact that a country (or a company that owns a shipping vessel) paid a ransom or took some other action demanded by terrorists in order to resolve the crisis.

a. Suppose the ships of many countries are targeted by pirates. In every instance of piracy, a country faces the decision of whether or not to negotiate, and the more likely it is that pirates find victims amenable to negotiating a settlement, the more likely it is that they will commit more acts of piracy. Can you use the logic of the Prisoner's Dilemma to explain why so many countries negotiate even though they say they don't? (Assume pirates cannot tell who owns a ship before they board it.)

    b.   Suppose that only a single country is targeted by terrorists. Does the Prisoner's Dilemma still apply?

    c.   If you had to guess, do you think small countries or large countries are more likely to negotiate with pirates and terrorists?

    d.   Children can be like terrorists: screaming insanely to get their way and implicitly suggesting that they will stop screaming if parents give in. In each instance, it is tempting to just give them what they want, but parents know that this will teach children that they can get their way by screaming, thus leading to an increased frequency of outbursts by the little terrors. If a child lives with a single parent, is there a Prisoner's Dilemma?

    e.   What if the child lives in a two-parent household? What if the child is raised in a commune where everyone takes care of everyone's children?

    f.   All else being equal, where would you expect the most screaming per child: in a single-parent household, a two-parent household, or in a commune?

24.14[†] **Everyday, Business, and Policy Application:** *Education as a Signal*: In Chapter 22, we briefly discussed the signaling role of education; i.e., the fact that part of the reason many people get more education is not to learn more but rather to signal high productivity to potential employers (in hopes of getting a higher wage offer). We return to this in part B of this exercise in the context of an incomplete information game (built on concepts from Section B of the chapter), but first consider the lack of a role for signaling in a complete information game. Throughout, suppose that there are two types of workers, type 1 workers with low productivity and type 2 workers with high productivity, with a fraction δ of all workers being type 2 and a fraction $(1 - \delta)$ being type 1. Both types can earn education by expending effort, but it costs type 1 workers e to get education level $e > 0$, while it costs type 2 workers only $e/2$. An employer gets profit $(2 - w)$ if she hires a type 2 worker at wage w and $(1 - w)$ if she hires a type 1 worker at wage w. (Employers get zero profit if they do not hire a worker.) We then assume that the worker decides in stage 1 how much education to get; then, in stage 2, he approaches two competing employers who decide simultaneously how much of a wage w to offer; and finally, in stage 3, he decides which wage offer to accept.

EVERYDAY
APPLICATION

BUSINESS
APPLICATION

POLICY
APPLICATION

A.   Suppose first that worker productivity is directly observable by employers; i.e., firms can tell who is a type 1 and who is a type 2 worker by just looking at them.

    a.   Solving this game backwards, what strategy will the worker employ in stage 3 when choosing between wage offers?

    b.   Given that firms know what will happen in stage 3, what wage will they offer to each of the two types in the simultaneous move game of stage 2 (assuming that they best respond to one another)? (*Hint*: Ask yourself if the two employers could offer two different wages to the same worker type, and, if not, how competition between them impacts the wage that they will offer in equilibrium.)

    c.   Note that we have assumed that worker productivity is not influenced by the level of education e chosen by a worker in stage 1. Is there any way that the level of e can then have any impact on the wage offers that a worker gets in equilibrium?

    d.   Would the wages offered by the two employers be any different if the employers moved in sequence, with employer 2 being able to observe the wage offer from employer 1 before the worker chooses an offer?

    e.   What level of e will the two worker types then get in any subgame perfect equilibrium?

    f.   *True or False*: If education does not contribute to worker productivity and firms can directly observe the productivity level of job applicants, workers will not expend effort to get education, at least not for the purpose of getting a good wage offer.

B.   Now suppose that employers cannot tell the productivity level of workers directly; all they know is the fraction δ of workers that have high productivity and the eduction level e of job applicants.

    a.   Will workers behave any differently in stage 3 than they did in part A of the exercise?

    b.   Suppose that there is a *separating equilibrium* in which type 2 workers get education $\bar{e}$ that differs from the education level type 1 workers get, and thus firms can identify the productivity level of job applicants by observing their education level. What level of education must type 1 workers be getting in such a separating equilibrium?

    c.   What wages will the competing firms offer to the two types of workers? State their complete strategies and the beliefs that support these.

    d.   Given your answers so far, what values could $\bar{e}$ take in this separating equilibrium? Assuming $\bar{e}$ falls in this range, specify the separating perfect Bayesian Nash equilibrium, including the strategies used by workers and employers as well as the full beliefs necessary to support the equilibrium.

    e.   Next, suppose instead that the equilibrium is a *pooling equilibrium*; i.e., an equilibrium in which all workers get the same level of education $\bar{e}$ and firms therefore cannot infer anything about the productivity of a job applicant. Will the strategy in stage 3 be any different than it has been?

    f.   Assuming that every job applicant is type 2 with probability δ and type 1 with probability $(1 - \delta)$, what wage offers will firms make in stage 2?

    g.   What levels of education $\bar{e}$ could in fact occur in such a perfect Bayesian pooling equilibrium? Assuming $\bar{e}$ falls in this range, specify the pooling perfect Bayesian Nash equilibrium, including the strategies used by workers and employers as well as the full beliefs necessary to support the equilibrium.

    h.   Could there be an education level $\bar{e}$ that high productivity workers get in a separating equilibrium and that all workers get in a pooling equilibrium?

    i.   What happens to the pooling wage relative to the highest possible wage in a separating equilibrium as δ approaches 1? Does this make sense?

24.15 Everyday, Business, and Policy Application: *To Fight or Not to Fight*: In many situations, we are confronted with the decision of whether to challenge someone who is currently engaged in a particular activity. In personal relationships, for instance, we decide whether it is worthwhile to push our own agenda over that of a partner; in business, potential new firms have to decide whether to challenge an incumbent firm (as discussed in one of the examples in the text); and in elections, politicians have to decide whether to challenge incumbents in higher level electoral competitions.

A.   Consider the following game that tries to model the decisions confronting both challenger and incumbent: The potential challenger moves first, choosing between staying out of the challenge, preparing for the challenge and engaging in it, or entering the challenge without much preparation. We will call these three actions O (for "out"), P (for "prepared entry"), and U (for "unprepared entry"). The incumbent then has to decide whether to fight the challenge (F) or give in to the challenge (G) if the challenge takes place; otherwise, the game simply ends with the decision of the challenger to play O.

    a.   Suppose that the payoffs are as follows for the five potential combinations of actions, with the first payoff indicating the payoff to the challenger and the second payoff indicating the payoff to the incumbent: (P,G) leads to $(3,3)$; (P,F) leads to $(1,1)$; (U,G) leads to $(4,3)$; (U,F) leads to $(0,2)$; and O leads to $(2,4)$. Graph the full sequential game tree with actions and payoffs.

    b.   Illustrate the game using a payoff matrix (and be careful to account for all *strategies*).

    c.   Identify the pure strategy Nash equilibria of the game and indicate which of these is subgame perfect.

    d.   Next, suppose that the incumbent only observes whether or not the challenger is engaging in the challenge (or staying out) but does not observe whether the challenger is prepared or not. Can you use the logic of subgame perfection to predict what the equilibrium will be?

    e.   Next, suppose that the payoffs for (P,G) changed to $(3,2)$, the payoffs for (U,G) changed to $(4,2)$, and the payoffs for (U,F) changed to $(0,3)$ (with the other two payoff pairs remaining the same). Assuming again that the incumbent fully observes both whether he is being challenged and whether the challenger is prepared, what is the subgame perfect equilibrium?

    f.   Can you still use the logic of subgame perfection to arrive at a prediction of what the equilibrium will be if the incumbent cannot tell whether the challenger is prepared or not as you did in part (d)?

B.   Consider the game you ended with in part A(f).

    a.   Suppose that the incumbent believes that a challenger who issues a challenge is prepared with probability δ and not prepared with probability $(1 - \delta)$. What is the incumbent's expected payoff from playing G? What is his expected payoff from playing F?

    b.   For what range of δ is it a best response for the incumbent to play G? For what range is it a best response to play F?

c. What combinations of strategies and (incumbent) beliefs constitute a pure strategy perfect Nash equilibrium? (Be careful: In equilibrium, it should not be the case that the incumbent's beliefs are inconsistent with the strategy played by the challenger!)

d. Next, suppose that the payoffs for (P,G) changed to $(4,2)$ and the payoffs for (U,G) changed to $(3,2)$ (with the remaining payoff pairs remaining as they were in A(f)). Do you get the same pure strategy perfect equilibria?

e. In which equilibrium—the one in part (c) or the one in part (d)—do the equilibrium beliefs of the incumbent seem more plausible?

24.16* Everyday and Policy Application: *Reporting a Crime*: Most of us would like to live in a world where crimes are reported and dealt with, but we'd prefer to have others bear the burden of reporting a crime. Suppose a crime is witnessed by N people, and suppose the cost of picking up the phone and reporting a crime is $c > 0$.

EVERYDAY APPLICATION

POLICY APPLICATION

A. Begin by assuming that everyone places a value $x > c$ on the crime being reported, and if the crime goes unreported, everyone's payoff is 0. (Thus, the payoff to me if you report a crime is x, and the payoff to me if I report a crime is $(x - c)$.)

a. Each person then has to simultaneously decide whether or not to pick up the phone to report the crime. Is there a pure strategy Nash equilibrium in which no one reports the crime?

b. Is there a pure strategy Nash equilibrium in which more than one person reports the crime?

c. There are many pure strategy Nash equilibria in this game. What do all of them have in common?

d. Next, suppose each person calls with probability $\delta < 1$. In order for this to be a mixed strategy equilibrium, what has to be the relationship between the expected payoff from not calling and the expected payoff from calling for each of the players?

e. What is the payoff from calling when everyone calls with probability $\delta < 1$?

f. What is the expected payoff from not calling when everyone calls with probability δ? (*Hint*: The probability that one person does not call is $(1 - \delta)$, and the probability that $(N - 1)$ people don't call is $(1 - \delta)^{(N-1)}$.)

g. Using your answers to (d) through (f), derive δ as a function of c, x, and N such that it is a mixed strategy equilibrium for everyone to call with probability δ. What happens to this probability as N increases?

h. What is the probability that a crime will be reported in this mixed strategy equilibrium? (*Hint*: From your work in part (f), you should be able to conclude that the probability that no one else reports the crime—i.e., $(1 - \delta)^{(N-1)}$—is equal to c/x in the mixed strategy equilibrium. The probability that no one reports a crime is then equal to this times the probability that the last person also does not report the crime.) How does this change as N increases?

i. *True or False*: If the reporting of crimes is governed by such mixed strategy behavior, it is advantageous for few people to observe a crime, whereas if the reporting of crime is governed by pure strategy Nash equilibrium behavior, it does not matter how many people witnessed a crime.

j. If the cost of reporting the crime differed across individuals (but is always less than x), would the set of pure Nash equilibria be any different? Without working it out, can you guess how the mixed strategy equilibrium would be affected?

B. Suppose from here on out that everyone values the reporting of crime differently, with person n's value of having a crime reported denoted x_n. Assume that everyone still faces the same cost c of reporting the crime. Everyone knows that c is the same for everyone, and person n discovers x_n prior to having to decide whether to call. But the only thing each individual knows about the x values for others is that they fall in some interval $[0,b]$, with c falling inside that interval and with the probability that x_n is less than x given by $P(x)$ for all individuals.

a. What is $P(0)$? What is $P(b)$?

b. From here on out, suppose that $P(x) = x/b$. Does what you concluded in (a) hold?

c. Consider now whether there exists a Bayesian Nash equilibrium in which each player n plays the strategy of reporting the crime if and only if x_n is greater than or equal to some critical value y. Suppose that everyone other than n plays this strategy. What is the probability that at least one person other than individual *n* reports a crime? (*Hint*: Given this strategy, the probability that person *k* will *not* report a crime is equal to the probability that x_k is less than *y*, which is equal to $P(y)$. The probability that *K* individuals do *NOT* report the crime is then $(P(y))^K$.)

    d.   What is the expected payoff of not reporting the crime for individual *n* whose value is x_n? What is the expected payoff of reporting the crime for this individual?

    e.   What is the condition for individual *n* to not report the crime if $x_n < y$? What is the condition for individual *n* to report the crime when $x_n \geq y$?

    f.   For what value of *y* have we identified a Bayesian Nash equilibrium?

    g.   What happens to the equilibrium probability of a crime being reported as *N* increases?

    h.   How is the probability of a crime being reported (in this equilibrium) affected by *c* and *b*? Does this make sense?

24.17 **Policy Application:** *Some Prisoner's Dilemmas*: We mentioned in this chapter that the incentives of the Prisoner's Dilemma appear frequently in real-world situations.

A. In each of the following, explain how these are Prisoner's Dilemmas and suggest a potential solution that might address the incentive problems identified in such games.

    a.   When I teach the topic of Prisoner's Dilemmas in large classes that also meet in smaller sections once a week, I sometimes offer the following extra credit exercise: Every student is given 10 points. Each student then has to decide how many of these points to donate to a "section account" and convey this to me privately. Each student's payoff is a number of extra credit points equal to the number of points they did *not* donate to their section *plus* twice the average contribution to the section account by students registered in their section. For instance, if a student donates 4 points to his section and the average student in the section donated 3 points, then this student's payoff would be 12 extra credit points: 6 because the student only donated 4 of his 10 points, and 6 because he gets twice the average donated in his section.

    b.   People get in their cars without thinking about the impact they have on other drivers by getting on the road, and at certain predictable times, this results in congestion problems on roads.

    c.   Everyone in your neighborhood would love to see some really great neighborhood fireworks on the next national independence day, but somehow no fireworks ever happen in your neighborhood.

    d.   People like downloading pirated music for free but would like to have artists continue to produce lots of great music.

    e.   Small business owners would like to keep their businesses open during "business hours" and not on evenings and weekends. In some countries, they have successfully lobbied the government to force them to close in the evening and on weekends. (Laws that restrict business activities on Sunday are sometimes called *blue laws*.)

B. In Chapter 21, we introduced the *Coase Theorem*, and we mentioned in Section 21A.4.4 the example of bee keeping on apple orchards. Apple trees, it turns out, don't produce much honey (when frequented by bees), but bees are essential for cross-pollination.

    a.   In an area with lots of apple orchards, each owner of an orchard has to ensure that there are sufficient numbers of bees to visit the trees and do the necessary cross-pollination. But bees cannot easily be kept to just one orchard, which implies that an orchard owner who maintains a bee hive is also providing some cross-pollination services to neighboring orchards. In what sense to orchard owners face a Prisoner's Dilemma?

    b.   How does the Coase Theorem suggest that orchard owners will deal with this problem?

    c.   We mentioned in Chapter 21 that some have documented a "custom of the orchards," an implicit understanding among orchard owners that each will employ the same number of bee hives per acre as the other owners in the area. How might such a custom be an equilibrium outcome in a repeated game with indefinite end?

Oligopoly

We have thus far covered two extreme market structures: *perfect competition*, where a large number of small firms produce identical products, and *monopoly*, where a single firm is isolated from competition through some form of barrier to entry (and through a lack of close substitutes that could be produced by someone else).[1] The models that represent these polar opposites are incredibly useful because they allow us to develop intuition about important economic forces in the real world. At the same time, few markets in the real world really fall on either of these extreme poles, and so we now turn to some market structures that fall in between.

The first of these is the case of *oligopoly*. An oligopoly is a market structure in which a small number of firms is collectively isolated from outside competition by some form of barrier to entry. Just as in the case of monopolies, this barrier to entry may be technological (as, for instance, when there are high fixed costs) or legal (as when the government regulates competition). We will assume in this chapter's analysis of oligopoly that the firms produce the same identical product and will leave the case where firms can differentiate their products to Chapter 26. Were the firms in the oligopoly to combine into a single firm, they would therefore become a monopoly just like the one we analyzed in Chapter 23. Were the barriers to entry to disappear, on the other hand, the oligopoly would turn into a competitive market as new firms would join so long as positive profits could be made.

Since there are only a few firms in an oligopoly, my firm's decision about how much to produce will have an impact on the price the other firms can charge, or my decision about what price to set may determine what price others will set. Firms within an oligopoly therefore find themselves in a *strategic* setting, a setting in which their decisions have a direct impact on the economic environment in which they operate. You can see this in how airlines behave as they watch each other to determine what fares to set or how many planes to devote to particular routes, or in how the small number of large car manufacturers set their financing packages for new car sales. In the following sections, we will develop a few different ways of looking at the limited and strategic competition that such oligopolistic firms face.

---

[1] This chapter builds primarily on Chapter 23 and Section A of Chapter 24. Only Section 25B.3 of this chapter requires knowledge of Section B from Chapter 24, and this section can be skipped if you only read Section A of Chapter 24. The chapter also presumes an understanding of the different types of costs covered in the earlier chapters on producer theory (as summarized in the first section of Chapter 13) as well as a basic understanding of demand and elasticity as covered in the first section of Chapter 18.

25A Competition and Collusion in Oligopolies

While we could think of oligopolies with more than two firms, we will focus here primarily on the case where two firms operate within the oligopoly market structure (which is then sometimes called a "duopoly"). The basic insights extend to cases where there are more than two firms in the oligopoly, but as the number of firms gets large, the oligopoly becomes more and more like a perfectly competitive market structure. We will also simplify our analysis by assuming that the two firms are identical (in the sense of facing identical cost structures) and that the marginal cost of production is constant. In end-of-chapter exercises, we then explore how our results are affected by changing these baseline assumptions.

To fix ideas, let's think of the following concrete situation: I am a producer of economist cards, but I recently discovered that you are also producing identical cards. Suppose both of us applied for a copyright on this idea and, since we both applied at the same time, the government has granted both of us the copyright but will not grant it to anyone else. For some inexplicable reason that suggests a general lack of sophistication on the part of the general public, the only people who buy these cards are economists who attend the annual American Economic Association (AEA) meetings every January, and you and I therefore have to determine our strategy for selling cards at these meetings.

Each of our firms in this oligopoly then has, essentially, two choices to make: (1) how much to produce and (2) how much to charge. It might be that it's really easy to duplicate the cards at the AEA meetings, in which case we might decide to simply post a price at our booth and produce the cards as needed. In this case, *price* is the strategic variable that we are setting prior to getting to the meetings as we advertise to the attendees to try to get them to come to our booth. Alternatively, it might be that we have to produce the cards before we get to the AEA meetings because it's not possible to produce them on the spot as needed. In that case, *quantity* is the strategic variable since we have to decide how many cards to bring prior to getting to the meetings, leaving us free to vary the price depending on how many people actually want to buy cards when we get there. Whether price or quantity is the right strategic variable to think about then depends on the circumstances faced by the firms in an oligopoly, on what we will call the "economic setting" in which the firms operate. We will therefore develop two types of models: models of *quantity competition* and models of *price competition*.

The other feature of oligopoly models is that they either assume that the firms in the oligopoly make their strategic decision *simultaneously* or *sequentially*. Maybe it takes me longer to get my advertising materials together and I therefore end up posting my price after you do, or maybe I work in a local market where I have to set the capacity for producing a certain quantity of cards before you do. As we have seen in our discussion of game theory, we can employ the concept of Nash equilibrium for the case of simultaneous decision making while we use the concept of subgame perfect (Nash) equilibrium in the case of sequential decisions. Sometimes, as we will see, it matters who moves first.

We therefore have four different types of models we will discuss: (1) *price competition*, where firms make strategic decisions about price *simultaneously*; (2) *price competition*, where firms make strategic decisions about price *sequentially*; (3) *quantity competition*, where firms make strategic decisions about quantity *simultaneously*; and (4) *quantity competition*, where firms make strategic decisions about quantity *sequentially*. We will begin with price competition and then move to quantity competition, each time considering both the simultaneous and the sequential case, and we will see that firms could in principle do better by simply combining forces and behaving like a single monopoly. Following our discussion of oligopoly price and quantity competition, we will therefore consider the circumstances under which oligopoly firms might succeed in forming *cartels* that behave like monopolies by eliminating competition between the firms in the oligopoly.

25A.1 Oligopoly Price (or "Bertrand") Competition

Competition between oligopoly firms that strategically set price (rather than quantity) is often referred to as *Bertrand competition* after the French mathematician Joseph Louis Francois Bertrand (1922–1900). Bertrand took issue with another French mathematician, Antoine Augustin Cournot (1801–1877), whose work on quantity competition (which we discuss in the next section) had suggested that oligopolies would price goods somewhere between where price would fall under perfect competition and perfect monopoly. Bertrand came up with a quite different and striking conclusion: He suggested that Cournot had focused on the wrong strategic variable—quantity—and that his result goes away when firms instead compete on price. In particular, Bertrand argued that such price competition will result in a price analogous to what we would expect to emerge under perfect competition (price equal to marginal cost) even if only two firms are competing with one another.

25A.1.1 *Simultaneous* Strategic Decisions about Price   Bertrand's logic is easy to see in a model with two identical firms that make decisions simultaneously and face a constant marginal cost of production (with no recurring fixed cost). Suppose we face no real fixed costs and we can easily adjust the quantity of cards we produce on the spot at the AEA meetings. We therefore decide to advertise a *price* and produce whatever quantity is demanded by consumers at that price. But as we think about announcing a price, we have to think about what price the other might announce and how consumers might react to different price combinations. One conclusion is pretty immediate: If we announce different prices, then consumers will simply flock to the firm that announced the lower price, and the other firm won't be able to sell anything.

I will therefore want to avoid two scenarios: First, I don't want to set a price that is so low that it would result in negative profits if I managed to attract consumers at this price. Since we are assuming no recurring fixed costs and constant marginal costs, this means I don't want to set a price below marginal cost. Second, assuming your firm similarly won't set a price below marginal cost, I don't want to set a price higher than what you set because then I don't get any customers. Put differently, whatever price you set, it cannot be a "best response" for me to set a higher price or a price below marginal cost. The same is true for you, which means that, in any Nash equilibrium in which we both do the best we can given the strategy played by the other, we will charge identical prices that do not fall below marginal cost.

But we can say more than that. Suppose that the price announced by both of us is above marginal cost. Then I am not playing a "best response" because, given that you have announced a price above marginal cost, I can do better by charging a price just below that and getting all the customers. The only time this is not true is if both firms are announcing the price equal to marginal cost. Given that you are charging this price, I can do no better by charging a lower price (which would result in negative profit) or a higher price (which would result in me getting no customers). The same is true for your firm given that I am charging a price equal to marginal cost. Thus, by each announcing a price equal to marginal cost, we are both playing "best response" strategies to the other, and the outcome is a Nash equilibrium.

Can you see how this is the only possible Nash equilibrium? Is it a dominant strategy Nash equilibrium?

Exercise 25A.1

Is there a single Nash equilibrium if more than two firms engage in Bertrand competition within an oligopoly?

Exercise 25A.2

25A.1.2 Using "Best Response Functions" to Verify Bertrand's Logic   While the logic behind Bertrand's conclusion that price competition leads oligopolistic firms to behave competitively is straightforward, this is a good time to develop a tool that will be useful throughout our discussion of oligopoly: *best response functions*. These functions are simply plots of the best response of one player to particular strategic choices by the other. They are useful when players have a continuum of possible actions they can take in a simultaneous move game rather than a discrete number of actions as in most of our game theory development in Chapter 24. When best response functions for both players are then plotted on the same graph, they can help us identify the Nash equilibria easily.

Suppose I am firm 1 and you are firm 2. Consider panel (a) of Graph 25.1. On the horizontal axis, we plot p_1 (the price set by me), and on the vertical axis we plot p_2 (the price charged by you). We then plot your *best responses* to different prices I might announce. We already know that you will never want to set a price below marginal cost (*MC*), and if I were to ever be stupid enough to set a price below *MC*, any $p_2 > p_1$ would be a best response for you (since it would simply result in you not selling anything and letting me get all the business). For purposes of our graph, we can then simply let your best response to $p_1 < MC$ be $p_2 = MC$. If I announce a price p_1 above *MC*, we know that you will want to charge a price just below p_1 to get all consumers away from my booth. Thus, for $p_1 > MC$, your best response is $p_2 = p_1 - \epsilon$ (where ϵ is a small number close to zero). Since $p_1 = p_2$ on the 45-degree line in the graph, this means that your best response in panel (a) will lie just below the 45-degree line for $p_1 > MC$.

In panel (b) of Graph 25.1, we do the same for my firm, only now p_2 (on the vertical axis) is taken as given by firm 1, and firm 1 finds its best response to different levels of p_2. If you set your price below *MC*, my best response can then be taken to simply be $p_1 = MC$, and if you set your price p_2 above *MC*, my best response is $p_1 = p_2 - \epsilon$ (which lies just above the 45-degree line).

We defined a Nash equilibrium in Chapter 24 as a set of strategies for each player that are best responses to each other. In order for an equilibrium to emerge in our price setting model, *my price therefore has to be a best response to your price, and your price has to be a best response to my price*. Put differently, when we put the two best response functions onto the same graph in panel (c), the equilibrium happens where the two best response functions intersect. This happens at $p_1 = p_2 = MC$ just as we derived intuitively.

25A.1.3 *Sequential* Strategic Decisions about Price

In the real world, it is often the case that one firm has to make a decision about its strategic variable before the other, with the second firm being able to observe the first firm's decision when its turn to act comes. As we argued in our chapter on game theory, sometimes this makes a big difference, with the first mover

Graph 25.1: Best Response Functions for Simultaneous Bertrand Competition

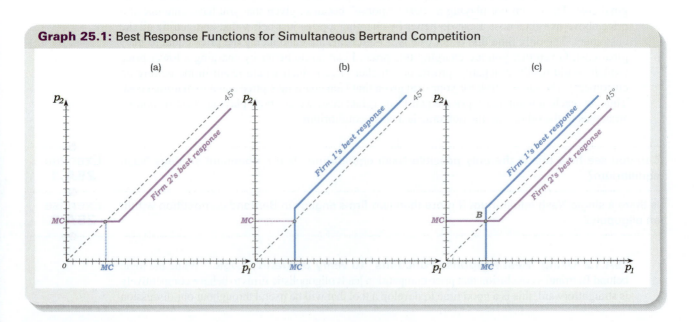

gaining an advantage (or disadvantage) from having to declare its intentions in advance of the second mover. It's easy to see that this is not, however, the case for our two firms engaging in Bertrand competition.

Suppose I move first and you get to observe my advertised price before you advertise your own. Remember that in such *sequential* settings, subgame perfection requires that I will have to think through what you will do for any action I announce. But our previous discussion already tells us the answer: You will choose a price just below p_1 whenever $p_1 > MC$, leaving me with no consumers. Since I will not choose a price below MC, this implies that I will set $p_1 = MC$ and you will follow suit, with our two firms splitting the market by charging prices exactly equal to MC.

How would you think about subgame perfect equilibria under sequential Bertrand competition with three firms (where firm 1 moves first, firm 2 moves second, and firm 3 moves third)?

Exercise 25A.3

25A.1.4 Real-World Caveats to Bertrand's Price Competition Result

While Bertrand's logic is intuitive, few economists believe that his result is one that truly characterizes many real-world oligopoly outcomes. There are several real-world considerations that considerably weaken the Bertrand prediction regarding price competition in oligopolies, and here we will briefly mention some of them. (In end-of-chapter exercises, we also explore how the Bertrand predictions change with different assumptions about firm costs.)

First, the pure Bertrand model assumes that firms are able to produce *any* quantity demanded at the price that they announce. This might in fact be true in some markets but typically does not hold. As a result, real-world firms have to set some "capacity" of production as they think about announcing a price, and this capacity choice, as we will again mention in Section 25A.2.2, then introduces *quantity* as a strategic variable. In cases where capacity choices are in fact binding on the Bertrand competitors, the model predicts that each firm will again announce the same price but that this price will be above marginal cost in much the way that it is under strict quantity competition (as we will demonstrate in the next section).[2] Second, we have assumed throughout that the two firms in our oligopoly interact only once, whether simultaneously or sequentially. But in the real world, firms typically interact repeatedly, which implies that price competition of the type envisioned by Bertrand occurs in a *repeated game context*. Again, we would expect an equilibrium in which the firms in the oligopoly announce the same price in each period. In the non-repeated game, we concluded that the only such equilibrium price has to be equal to marginal cost because, were this not the case, neither firm is "best responding" to the strategic choice of the other. But now suppose that firms are engaged in repeated price competition and consider whether $p > MC$ could emerge in a given period. A "strategy" for each firm must then specify a price *for any possible previous price history*, which opens the possibility of "trigger strategies" of the following form: I will begin our repeated interactions by charging a price $p > MC$ and will continue to do so in future periods as long as that price has been played by both of us in all previous periods; otherwise, I will charge $p = MC$ forever. Suppose we both play this strategy. Then, in any given period, I have to weigh whether the short-run gain from charging a price slightly below p (which results in me getting all the customers this period) outweighs the long-run cost of reverting to $p = MC$ in all future periods. It is quite plausible that this short-run benefit is smaller than the long-run cost, which would make my strategy a best response to yours (and yours a best response to mine). In infinitely repeated interactions, or in interactions where there is a good chance we will meet again, we can therefore see how $p > MC$ can emerge as an equilibrium under price competition.

---

[2] This "solution" to the Bertrand "Paradox" of $p = MC$ was first developed by Francis Edgeworth (1845–1926) at the end of the 19th century and has since been formalized using modern economic tools.

Exercise 25A.4

Suppose our two firms know that we will encounter each other *n* times and never again there-after. Can $p > MC$ still be part of a subgame perfect equilibrium in this case assuming we engage in pure price competition?

Finally, Bertrand assumed that firms are restricted to producing *identical* products. If we allow for the possibility that consumers differ somewhat in their tastes for how economist cards look and what exactly they say on the back, we might however decide to produce slightly differ-ent versions of economist cards—and through such product differentiation become able to charge $p > MC$. This is because consumers who have a strong preference for my type of card will still buy from me at a somewhat higher price, and similarly those with a preference for your type of card will continue to buy yours at a somewhat higher price. Product differentiation therefore also introduces the possibility of $p > MC$ emerging under price competition. We will develop this more in Chapter 26.

25A.2 Oligopoly Quantity Competition

The implicit assumption that underlies Bertrand competition is that firms can easily adjust quan-tity once they set price. In our example, we assumed that we can both just produce the required cards on the spot at the AEA meetings. But, as we just mentioned, many firms have to set capac-ity for their production and, once they have done so, cannot easily deviate from this in terms of how much they will produce. It might be hard for us to have our card factory at our booth at the AEA meetings, which means we will have to produce our cards ahead of time and bring them with us to our booths. In such circumstances, it is more reasonable to assume that firms choose capacity (or "quantity") first and then sell what they produce at the highest price they can get. This is the scenario that Cournot had in mind when he investigated competition between oligop-olistic firms, and it is the scenario we turn to next. As we will see, this model, known as the *Cournot model*, has very different implications regarding the equilibrium price at which oligop-olistic firms produce. As in the previous section, we will continue by assuming that firms in our oligopoly are identical and face constant marginal cost.

25A.2.1 *Simultaneous* Strategic Decisions about Quantity: Cournot Competition

We can again use best response functions to see what Nash equilibrium will emerge when two firms in an oligopoly choose capacity simultaneously. In panel (a) of Graph 25.2, we begin by considering firm 2's best response to different quantities x_1 set by firm 1. If I set $x_1 = 0$, then you would know that you will have a monopoly on economist cards at the AEA meetings. From our work in Chapter 23, we can then easily determine the optimal quantity for you by solving the monopoly problem. This is depicted in panel (b) of the graph where D is the market demand curve and MR is your monopoly's marginal revenue curve that has the same intercept (as D) but twice the slope. Your firm, firm 2, would then produce the monopoly quantity x^M where $MR = MC$ (and charge the monopoly price p^M). The quantity x^M therefore becomes your best response to $x_1 = 0$ and determines the intercept of your best response function in panel (a).

Now suppose I set $x_1 = \bar{x}_1 > 0$. You then know that you no longer face the entire market demand curve because I have committed to filling $\bar{x}_1$ of the market demand. Put differently, you now face a demand curve that is equal to the market demand curve D *minus* $\bar{x}_1$. In panel (c) of Graph 25.2, we therefore shift the demand D by $\bar{x}_1$ to get the new "residual" demand D^r that remains given that I will satisfy a portion of market demand. From this, we can calculate the residual marginal revenue curve MR^r that now applies to your firm. Once again, you will maxi-mize profit where marginal revenue equals marginal cost; i.e., $MR^r = MC$. This results in a new optimal quantity *given* $\bar{x}_1$—denoted $x_2(\bar{x}_1)$, which in turn becomes your best response to me hav-ing set $x_1 = \bar{x}_1$. Note that $x_2(\bar{x}_1)$ necessarily lies below x^M; i.e., your best response quantity

Graph 25.2: The Best Response Function for Firm 2 under Simultaneous Cournot Competition

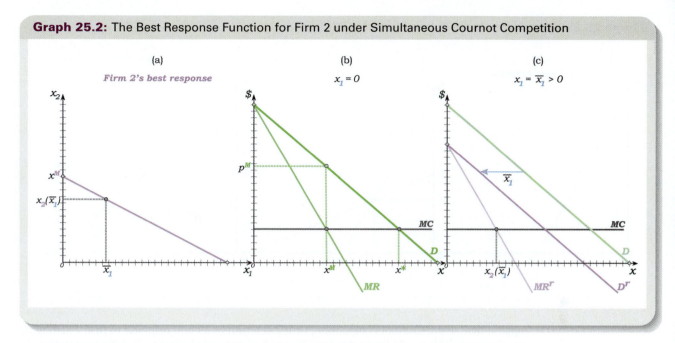

decreases as x_1 increases. We can imagine doing this for all possible quantities of x_1 to get the full best response function for your firm 2 as depicted in panel (a).

Can you identify in panel (b) of Graph 25.2 the quantity that corresponds to the horizontal intercept of firm 2's best response function in panel (a)?

Exercise 25A.5

What is the slope of the best response function in panel (a) of Graph 25.2? (*Hint*: Use your answer to exercise 25A.5 to arrive at your answer here.)

Exercise 25A.6

We can then do what we did for Bertrand competition by putting the best response functions of the two firms together into one graph to see where they intersect. Since our two firms are identical, my best response function can be similarly derived. This is done in panel (a) of Graph 25.3, which is just the mirror image of the best response function for your firm that we derived in the previous graph. The two best response functions then intersect at $x_1 = x_2 = x^C$ in panel (b), with x^C the Cournot-Nash equilibrium output for each of our firms in the oligopoly.

25A.2.2 Comparing and Reconciling Cournot, Bertrand, and Monopoly Outcomes
In panel (c) of Graph 25.3 we can then see how the quantities produced under monopoly, Cournot, and Bertrand competition compare. As illustrated in panel (b), C represents each firm's output under Cournot (or quantity) competition. From constructing the best response functions, we know that the vertical intercept of firm 2's best response function is the monopoly quantity, as is the horizontal intercept of firm 1's best response function. When we connect these (with the dashed magenta line in panel (c)), we get all combinations of firm 1 and firm 2 production that sum to the monopoly quantity. Were the two firms to collude, for instance, and simply split the monopoly quantity, they would produce half of x^M at the point labeled M. Thus, *production is unambiguously higher under Cournot competition than it would be under monopoly production.*

We can also see how Cournot production compares to Bertrand production. From our work in the last section, we know that Bertrand or price competition results in both firms charging a price equal to MC. At such a price, market demand will be equal to x^* in panel (b) of Graph 25.2. Now

Graph 25.3: Simultaneous Move Cournot-Nash Equilibrium

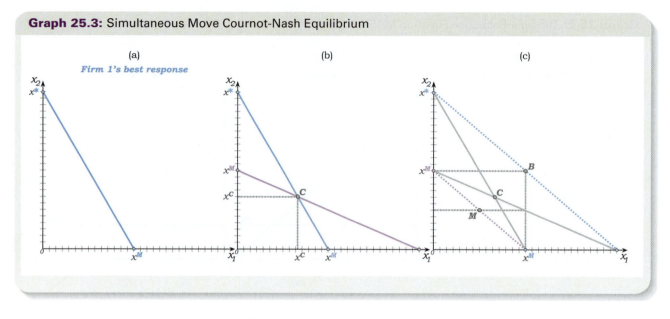

suppose that, under Cournot competition, firm 2 determines its best response to firm 1 setting its quantity to x^*. This would imply that firm 2's residual demand is equal to D shifted inward by x^*, leaving it with a residual demand curve that has a vertical intercept at MC. Thus any output that firm 2 would produce *given that firm 1 is producing x^** would have to be sold at a price below MC, which implies firm 2's best response is to produce $x_2 = 0$. This implies that firm 2's best response function reaches zero at $x_1 = x^* = 2x^M$; i.e., the horizontal intercept of firm 2's best response function lies at x^*. (Note: This is the answer to within-chapter-exercise 25A.5.) Since the two firms are identical, the same is true for firm 1's vertical intercept.

If we connect the horizontal intercept of firm 1's best response function with the vertical intercept of firm 2's best response function (with the dashed blue line) in panel (c), we then get all the different ways in which the two firms could split production and produce x^*, the quantity that would be sold when $p = MC$ as happens under Bertrand competition. If we assume that, when both firms charge the Bertrand price of $p = MC$, the two firms split overall output, each firm would produce half of x^* as indicated at point B in the graph. Thus, *Bertrand competition leads to unambiguously higher output than Cournot competition.*

Exercise 25A.7 Which type of behavior under simultaneous decision making within an oligopoly results in greater social surplus: quantity or price competition?

Exercise 25A.8 *True or False:* Under Bertrand competition, $x_1^B = x_2^B = x^M$.

As we will note again in Chapter 26, the dramatic difference between Bertrand and Cournot competition seems quite strange, and it is not easy to choose between the two models on intuitive grounds: On the one hand, it seems that firms in the real world often set prices (when they are not in perfectly competitive settings), and this seems to speak in favor of the Bertrand model. (In Chapter 26, for instance, I give the example of Apple coming out with a new computer and immediately setting its price long before it finds out how much it will have to produce.) On the other hand, the Bertrand prediction of price being set equal to marginal cost even when only two firms are competing seems a stretch, which speaks in favor of the Cournot model, which not only arrives at the intuitively reasonable prediction that price falls between the monopoly and the competitive level when there are only two firms but also predicts (as we will show in Section B) that oligopoly prices converge to competitive prices as the number of firms in the oligopoly becomes large. Much work has, as a result, been done by economists to reconcile these models of oligopoly competition.

One of the most revealing results, which we already mentioned in our discussion of Bertrand competition, is the following: Suppose that firms really do set prices (as the Bertrand model assumes) but they set capacities for production (which sounds a lot like the quantity setting of the Cournot model) before announcing prices. Then under plausible conditions, it has been shown that this Bertrand equilibrium outcome of price competition results in Cournot quantities and prices.[3] Economists have therefore often come to view oligopoly competition as guided in the long run by production capacity competition (as envisioned by Cournot) equilibrated through price competition (as envisioned by Bertrand) in the short run when capacities are fixed. Both models appear to have their place, and both play important roles in how we think of oligopoly competition.

25A.2.3 *Sequential* Strategic Decisions about Quantity: The "Stackelberg" Model

Under Bertrand competition, we concluded that it does not matter whether firms determine their price simultaneously or sequentially; in either case, firms end up charging $p = MC$ in equilibrium. The same is not true for quantity competition, as we will see now.

The sequential quantity competition model is known as the *Stackelberg model*,[4] and the firm designated to "move first" is called the *Stackelberg leader* while the firm that moves second is called the *Stackelberg follower*. In sequential move games, we concluded in Chapter 24 that noncredible threats are eliminated by restricting ourselves to Nash equilibria that are subgame-perfect; i.e., to equilibria in which early movers look forward and determine the best responses by their opponents later on in the game. When she decides how much capacity to set, the Stackelberg leader will then take into account the entire best response function of the follower because that function tells the leader exactly how the follower will respond once she finds out how much the leader will be producing. Thus, rather than "guessing" about the quantity the opposing firm will set (as is the case under simultaneous quantity competition), the leader now has the luxury of *inducing* how much the follower will set by her own actions in the first stage.

Suppose, then, that you (firm 2) are the follower and I (firm 1) am the leader. I already know your best response function for any quantity that I might set; we derived this in Graph 25.2a, which we now replicate in panel (a) of Graph 25.4. In deciding how much capacity to set, I then simply have to determine my residual demand curve *given your best response function*. The grey demand curve D in panel (b) is simply the market demand curve. For any output level $x_1 \geq x^*$, we know that your best response is simply not to produce, which implies that I know I will "own" the market demand curve if I choose to produce above x^*. Thus, my residual demand is equal to market demand for quantities greater than x^*.

If I set capacity below x^*, however, I know that you will produce along your best response function once you find out how much capacity I set. To arrive at my residual demand, I therefore have to subtract the quantity that I know you will produce for any $x_1 < x^*$. If I set my capacity close to x^*, you will choose to produce relatively little, but as x_1 falls, your best response quantity rises and reaches x^M, the monopoly quantity, when $x_1 = 0$. My residual demand curve D^r therefore begins at the monopoly price p^M (which would be charged by you if I set $x_1 = 0$) and reaches the market demand curve D when it crosses MC.

Once we have figured out firm 1's residual demand, we can now do what we always do to identify my firm's optimal capacity: simply plot out the MR^r curve that corresponds to D^r and find its intersection with MC. Because all the relationships are linear, this intersection occurs at half the distance between x^* and zero, which happens to be the monopoly quantity x^M. Thus, the

---

[3] This was demonstrated by D. Kreps and J. Scheinkman, "Quantity Precommitment and Bertrand Competition Yield Cournot Outcomes," *Rand Journal of Economics* 14(1983), 326–37.
[4] The model is named after Heinrich Freiherr von Stackelberg (1905–46), a German economist.

Graph 25.4: Stackelberg Equilibrium

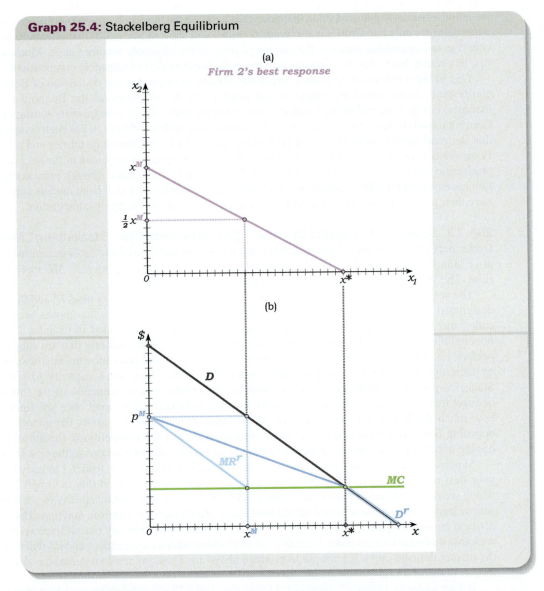

(a)
Firm 2's best response

(b)

Stackelberg leader, firm 1, will set $x_1 = x^M$, and the Stackelberg follower will produce half this amount as read off its best response function. Given what I as the leader have done in the first stage, you as the follower are doing the best you can, and given your predictable output decisions in the second stage (as summarized in your best response function), I have done the best I can. We have reached a subgame perfect equilibrium.

Exercise 25A.9   Determine the Stackelberg price in terms of p^M—the price a monopolist would charge—and *MC*.

Adding this outcome to our predicted outputs for Bertrand, Cournot, and monopoly settings from Graph 25.3, we can then see that the Stackelberg quantity competition results in greater overall output than simultaneous Cournot competition but less overall output than Bertrand price competition.

Where is the predicted Stackelberg outcome in Graph 25.3c?

Exercise
25A.10

25A.2.4 The Difference between Sequential and Simultaneous Quantity Competition

We can now step back a little and ask why the Stackelberg model differs fundamentally from the Cournot model. Why, for instance, don't I threaten to act like a Stackelberg leader when you and I are competing simultaneously?

Suppose you and I set quantity simultaneously before we arrive at the AEA meetings, but I call you ahead of time and tell you that I will produce the Stackelberg leader quantity. Would you have any reason to believe me when I threaten to do this? The answer is that you should not take my threat seriously. After all, if you thought that I thought you would produce $x^M/2$, my best response (according to my best response function in Graph 23.5) would be to produce less than x^M! (You can see this in panel (c) of the graph where the horizontal (dashed) grey line that passes through M at an output level of $x^M/2$ for you crosses my best response function to the left of x^M.) Your best response to me producing less than x^M would then be to produce more than $x^M/2$. My threat to produce x^M is therefore simply not credible when I try to bully you over the phone.

When the game assumes a sequential structure, however, the threat becomes real because you *know* how much I have produced by the time that you have to decide how much to produce. It's no longer an idle threat for me to say I will produce the Stackelberg leader quantity; I have just done so. Now it is indeed a best response for you to produce the Stackelberg follower quantity, and given that you will do so it is best for me to have produced the Stackelberg leader quantity. It is the sequential structure of the game that results in the difference in equilibrium behavior, and without that sequential structure, there is no way for me to credibly threaten to do anything other than produce the Cournot quantity.

25A.3 Incumbent Firms, Fixed Entry Costs, and Entry Deterrence

The insight that the sequential structure of the oligopoly quantity competition changes the outcome of that competition can then get us to think of other ways in which sequential decision making might matter. An important case is the case in which one firm is the *incumbent firm* that currently has the whole market but is threatened by a second firm that might potentially enter the market and turn its structure from a monopoly to an oligopoly. Is there anything (aside from sending someone with a baseball bat) the incumbent firm can do to prevent the potential entrant from coming into the market? The answer depends on two factors: (1) how costly is it for the potential entrant to actually enter the market and begin production, and (2) to what extent can the incumbent firm credibly threaten the potential entrant.

25A.3.1 Case 1: Incumbent Quantity Choice Follows Entrant Choice
Suppose the potential entrant has to pay a one-time fixed entry cost FC in order to be able to begin production. Now consider the case in which the potential entrant makes its decision on whether to enter the market before either firm makes a choice about how much to produce. Panels (a) and (b) in Graph 25.5 picture two such scenarios. In both panels, firm 2 first decides whether or not to enter, and if it does not enter, firm 1 sets its quantity x_1. If firm 2 does enter, the firms are assumed to choose their production quantities simultaneously in panel (a) and sequentially in panel (b).

Recall that we solve games of this kind from the bottom up in order to find subgame perfect equilibria. If firm 2 does not enter, we know that firm 1 will optimize by simply producing the monopoly quantity and thus will make the monopoly profit π^M while firm 2 will make zero profit. If firm 2 enters, on the other hand, the two firms will engage in simultaneous Cournot competition

Graph 25.5: Possible Sequences of Entry and Quantity Choices

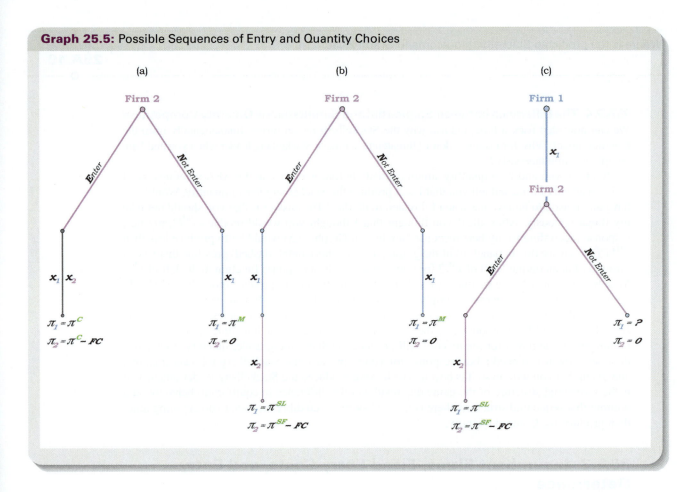

in panel (a), with each firm making the Cournot profit π^C but with firm 2 paying the fixed entry cost FC. Firm 2 therefore looks ahead and makes its entry decision based on whether or not $(\pi^C - FC)$ is greater than zero. Put differently, so long as the profit from producing the Cournot quantity at the Cournot price is greater than the fixed cost of entering, firm 2 will enter the market. Similarly, in panel (b), firm 2 knows that it will be a Stackelberg follower if it enters, and so it will enter so long as the profit π^{SF} from producing the Stackelberg follower quantity at the Stackelberg price is greater than the fixed cost of entering.

Exercise 25A.11   *True or False*: Once the entrant has paid the fixed entry cost, this cost becomes a sunk cost and is therefore irrelevant to the choice of how much to produce.

Exercise 25A.12   Is the smallest fixed cost of entering that will prevent firm 2 from coming into the market greater in panel (a) or in panel (b)?

Notice that in neither of these cases can the incumbent firm (firm 1) do anything to affect firm 2's entry decision because the entry decision happens before quantities are set. This implies that firm 2's entry decision is entirely dependent on the size of the fixed entry cost FC. The problem (from firm 1's perspective) is once again that there is no way it can credibly threaten firm 2, a problem that can disappear if firm 1 gets to *commit* to an output quantity *before* firm 2 makes its entry decision (as we will see next).

25A.3.2 Case 2: Entry Choice Follows Incumbent Quantity Choice   Now consider

the sequence pictured in panel (c) of Graph 25.5 where the incumbent (firm 1) chooses its quantity x_1 before the potential entrant (firm 2) makes its decision on whether to enter the market and produce. Again, we can solve the resulting game from the bottom up, beginning with the case in which firm 2 has decided to enter the market. Firm 2's optimal quantity is then simply given by its best response function (derived in Graph 25.2) to the quantity set by firm 1 (which is known to firm 2 at the time it makes its quantity decision). Firm 1 knows firm 2's best response function, which implies that *if firm 2 enters the market*, firm 1 is simply a Stackelberg leader. Thus, if firm 2 enters, the equilibrium payoffs are the Stackelberg profits, π^{SL} and π^{SF}, minus the fixed entry cost for firm 2.

The incumbent firm, however, would very much like to remain the only firm in the market. Short of sending in big guys with baseball bats to beat up firm 2, the only way to persuade firm 2 to stay out of the incumbent's (monopoly) market is for the incumbent to ensure that firm 2 cannot make a positive profit by entering. And the only way to do that is to commit to producing a larger quantity in order to drive the price down sufficiently to keep firm 2 from wanting to come into the market. Whether it is possible for firm 1 to do this and thereby to make a profit higher than that of a Stackelberg leader depends on just how big the fixed entry cost FC is for firm 2.

This is illustrated in the two panels of Graph 25.6. In panel (a), we plot the profit that the incumbent can expect from different output levels *if it remains the only firm in the market*. The highest possible profit occurs at the monopoly quantity x^M (which, as we have seen, is also the Stackelberg leader quantity x^{SL}). *If the fixed entry cost is very high*, the incumbent can simply produce x^M and rest assured in its monopoly given that it is simply too costly for any potential entrant to enter the market. This is illustrated in panel (b) where, for $FC \geq \overline{FC}$, firm 1 produces x^M (as indicated by the blue line) while firm 2 stays out of the market (and thus produces zero, as indicated by the magenta line). *If the fixed entry cost is very low*, on the other hand, there is little that firm 1 can do to keep the entrant out of the market, and so firm 1 simply produces the Stackelberg leader quantity x^{SL} and accepts firm 2's production of the Stackelberg follower quantity x^{SF}. This is illustrated in panel (b) for $FC \leq \underline{FC}$.

The interesting case of *entry deterrence* arises for fixed entry costs between $\underline{FC}$ and $\overline{FC}$. Suppose, for instance, that FC is just below $\overline{FC}$; i.e., suppose that firm 2 would make a slightly

Graph 25.6: Setting Quantity to Deter Entry

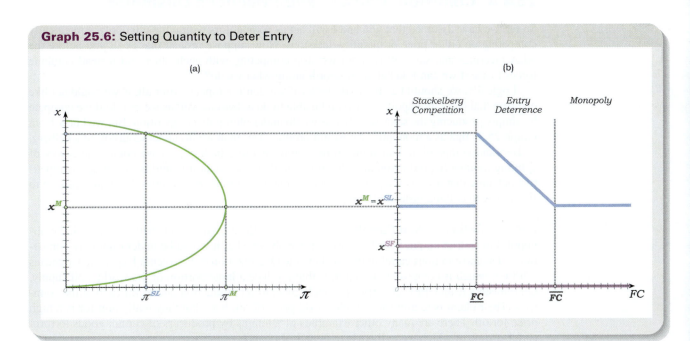

positive profit by entering if firm 1 behaved like a Stackelberg leader and produced x^{SL}. If firm 1 then produces just a little more than x^{SL}, this will ensure that firm 2 can no longer make a positive profit by entering. The incumbent firm can therefore *deter entry* by producing above x^{SL}. While this will mean that firm 1's profit falls below the monopoly profit, it is preferable to engaging in Stackelberg competition with firm 2 (in which case firm 1 would only get π^{SL}). As the fixed entry cost falls, it becomes harder and harder for firm 1 to do this, necessitating higher and higher levels of output to deter entry. But it's worth it as long as the incumbent's profit remains above the Stackelberg leader profit π^{SL}. Thus, the highest quantity that firm 1 would ever be willing to produce to deter entry, x^{ED}_{max}, is the quantity that will ensure π^{SL}. When fixed entry costs fall below $\underline{FC}$, it is too costly for the incumbent to deter entry, and firm 1 reverts back to producing simply the Stackelberg leader quantity.

This is, then, a more rigorous treatment of an idea that we raised in Chapter 23 when we discussed the possibility that a monopoly might be restrained in its behavior (and might produce more than the monopoly quantity) if it feels threatened by potential competitors. Notice that, if it could, the incumbent firm would like to reduce its output back to the monopoly quantity x^M once it has successfully deterred an entrant, but the only way that deterrence could succeed is if the incumbent was able to *commit* to not doing so by setting output prior to firm 2's entry decision. It is this commitment that made the threat to the entrant credible; were it possible to then go back on the commitment, the threat would not be credible and entry could not be deterred. In the real world, incumbent firms can make such credible commitments by raising observable production capacity (in forms like factory size) above the monopoly level.

It is a little like the general that would like to strike fear into the opposing army on the battlefield by telling them that his army will fight to the death. Of course just saying "We will fight to the death!" is not credible—anyone can *say* it. So the general might cross a bridge into the battlefield and then burn the bridge down, thus cutting off any possibility of retreat. This would certainly make the threat to fight to the death more credible, just as the incumbent firm's threat to increase production to prevent entry becomes credible when the firm actually does it and thus cuts off any possibility of retreat.

25A.4 Collusion, Cartels, and Prisoner's Dilemmas

So far, we have assumed that you and I will act as competitors within the oligopoly, strategically competing on either price or quantity decisions. Now suppose instead that I call you before the AEA meetings and say: "Why don't we stop competing with each other and instead combine forces to see if we can't do better by coordinating what we do?"

Logically, we should be able to do better if we don't compete. After all, if we could act like one firm that has a monopoly, we would be able to do at least as well as we can do if we compete by simply producing the same quantity as we do under oligopoly competition. But we know from Graph 25.3c that as a monopoly we would produce less than we do under Cournot, Stackelberg, or Bertrand competition. Our joint profit would therefore be higher if we could find a way of splitting monopoly production and charging a higher price than it would be under any competitive outcome that results in a price below the monopoly price. We therefore have an incentive to find a way to collude instead of compete.

25A.4.1 Collusion and Cartels   A *cartel* is a collusive agreement (between firms in an oligopoly) to restrict output in order to raise price above what it would be under oligopoly competition. The most famous cartel in the world is the Organization of Petroleum Exporting Countries (OPEC), which is composed of countries that produce a large portion of the world's oil supply. Oil ministers from OPEC countries routinely meet to set production quotas for each of the countries. Their claim is to aim for a stable world price of oil, but what they really aim for is a high price for oil. There are many other examples of attempts by producers of certain goods to form cartels, some of which we will analyze in end-of-chapter exercises.

Suppose our two little firms are currently engaged in Cournot competition, with each of us producing x^C as depicted in Graph 25.3b. It's then easy to see how we can do better: All we have to do is figure out what the monopoly output level x^M would be and agree to each limit our own production to half of that. This would allow us to sell our economist cards at the AEA meetings at the monopoly price p^M, with each of us making half the profit we would if our individual firm was the sole monopoly. The same cartel agreement would make each of us better off if we currently engaged in Bertrand competition.

How might the cartel agreement have to differ if we were currently engaged in Stackelberg competition? (*Hint*: Think about how the cartel profit compares to the Stackelberg profits for both firms, and use the Stackelberg price you determined in exercise 25A.9 along the way.)

**Exercise
25A.13***

25A.4.2 A Prisoner's Dilemma: The Incentive of Cartel Members to Cheat

Suppose, then, that you and I enter a collusive cartel agreement and decide to each produce half of x^M in order to maximize our joint profit. It is certainly in our interest to sign such an agreement. But is it optimal for us to stick by our agreement as we prepare to come to the AEA meetings with our economist cards?

Suppose I believe you will stick by the agreement. We can then ask what I would have to gain from producing one additional set of economist cards above the quota we set in our cartel. In panel (a) of Graph 25.7, we assume that we we have agreed to behave as a single monopolist, jointly producing x^M, which allows us to sell all our cards at price p^M. Were we, as a monopoly, to produce one more set of cards, we would have to drop the price in order to sell the larger quantity. This would result in a loss of profit equal to the magenta area since we can no longer sell the initial x^M goods at the price p^M. It would also result in an increase in profit equal to the blue area since we get to sell one more set of cards. For a monopoly, the quantity x^M is profit maximizing because the magenta area is slightly larger than the blue area; i.e., our monopoly profit would fall if we produced one more set of cards.

But now think of the question of whether to produce one more set of cards from the perspective of one of the members of the cartel that has agreed to behave as a single monopolist. In our

Graph 25.7: The Incentive to Cheat on a Cartel Agreement

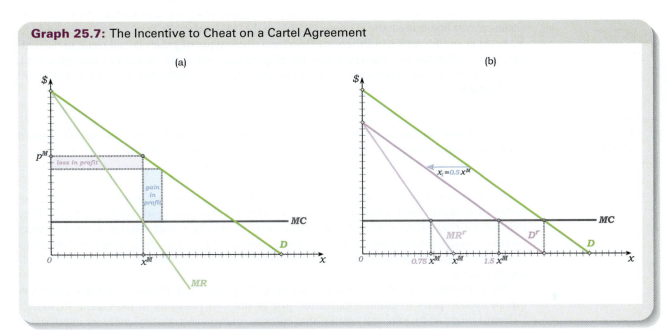

cartel agreement, we agreed that I would produce half of the monopoly output level x^M and you would produce the other half. If you produce one more set of cards, you will therefore lose only *half* the magenta area in profit from having to accept a price slightly lower than p^M for the half of x^M you are producing under the cartel agreement, but you would get *all* of the blue area in additional profit from the additional unit you produce. Since the magenta area is only slightly larger than the blue area, half of the magenta area is certainly smaller than all of the blue area in the graph, which means *your profit will increase if you cheat* and produce one more set of cards than you agreed to in the cartel.

Panel (b) looks at this another way and asks not only whether it would be in your best interest to produce one unit of output beyond the cartel agreement but also *how much* more you would in fact want to produce assuming you believe that I will be a sucker and stick by the agreement to produce only half of x^M. The residual demand D^r that you would face given that I produce $x_1 = 0.5x^M$ is equal to the market demand D minus $0.5x^M$, which intersects MC at the quantity $1.5x^M$. The corresponding residual marginal revenue curve MR^r has twice the slope and therefore intersects MC at $0.75x^M$, implying that it would be optimal for you to produce $0.75x^M$ rather than $0.5x^M$ as called for in your cartel agreement. Put differently, if you believe I will produce $0.5x^M$, your best response is to produce $0.75x^M$.

Exercise 25A.14 Can you verify the last sentence by just looking at the best response functions we derived earlier in Graph 25.2?

Now, if you are smart enough to figure out that it is in your best interest to cheat on the cartel agreement, chances are that I am smart enough to figure this out as well. But that means that, unless we can find a way to enforce the cartel agreement, the cartel will unravel as each of us cheats. And if each of us knows that the other will cheat, we are right back to Cournot competition and will end up behaving as if there was no cartel agreement at all.

Put in terms of the game theory language we developed earlier, we face a classic Prisoner's Dilemma: We would both be better off colluding and producing in accordance with the agreement than we would be by competing with one another (either in Bertrand or Cournot competition), but we also both have a strong incentive to cheat on the agreement (whether the other party cheats or not) and bring more economist cards to the AEA meetings than we had promised. As we noted in our discussion of Prisoner's Dilemmas, these types of games do not result in the optimal outcome for the two players unless the players can find a way to enforce the agreement. Inconveniently for us, cartel agreements are usually illegal. (Usually, but not always, as we will see shortly.)

Exercise 25A.15 The Prisoner's Dilemma you and I face as we try to maintain a cartel agreement works toward making us worse off. How does it look from the perspective of society at large?

While the incentives of cartel members therefore contain seeds that undermine cartel agreements, there are real-world examples of cartel agreements that have lasted for long periods. They may not always be successful at maintaining exactly monopoly output, but they often do restrict output beyond what Cournot competition would predict. This raises the question of how firms can overcome the Prisoner's Dilemma incentives that would, if unchecked, lead to a full unraveling of a cartel.

We can think of two possible ways of accomplishing this: First, firms might find ways of hiring an outside party to enforce the cartel, just as our two prisoners in the classic Prisoner's Dilemma might do by joining a "mafia" that enforces silence when the prisoners are interrogated by the prosecutor. Second, in our discussion of repeated Prisoner's Dilemmas in Chapter 24, we found that, if the game is repeated an infinite number of times or, more realistically, if the players know that there is a decent chance that they will meet again each time that they meet, cooperation in the Prisoner's Dilemma can emerge as part of a subgame perfect equilibrium strategy. We will now briefly discuss each of these paths that can lead to successful cartel cooperation among oligopolists.

25A.4.3 Enforcing Cartel Agreements through Government Protection

In 1933, in the midst of the Great Depression, Congress passed the National Industrial Recovery Act (NIRA) at the urging of newly inaugurated President Franklin D. Roosevelt who proclaimed it "the most important and far-reaching" legislation "ever enacted by the American Congress." The act represented a stark departure from laissez-faire attitudes toward industry, envisioning a more planned economy in which industrial leaders would coordinate production and prices to "foster fair competition," with compliance enforced by the newly created National Recovery Administration (NRA). In essence, the act legalized cartels in major manufacturing sectors, thus putting the force of law behind oligopolists' efforts to set price and quantity within particular markets. It generally received strong support from large corporations but was opposed by smaller firms.[5] The NIRA has become the clearest example in the United States of how oligopolists can employ the government as an enforcer of cartel agreements to limit quantity and raise price. Less than two years after its enactment, the U.S. Supreme Court unanimously declared the portion of the NIRA that established cartels as unconstitutional.

Why would oligopolists who cannot voluntarily sustain cartel agreements want to have such agreements enforced?

Exercise 25A.16

While this large-scale establishment of cartels vanished in the United States with the demise of the NIRA, similar legislation often governs industry in other countries. And there continue to be more modest attempts to establish cartels through government action, typically with the stated purpose of benefitting the "general welfare" but the actual consequence of restricting quantity and raising price. In the 1990s, for instance, Congress authorized the Northeast Interstate Dairy Compact that permitted the setting of minimum wholesale prices of milk across six New England states (amending extensive federal price regulation of milk that predated the establishment of the Compact) and the implementation of restrictions of competition from milk producers in other regions. Other regional milk cartels were similarly authorized in other regions. The stated intent of such legislation was to "assure the continued viability of dairy farming in the Northeast and to assure consumers of an adequate, local supply of pure and wholesome milk" at "a fair and equitable price." The cooperative suggested that "dramatic price fluctuations, with a pronounced downward trend, threaten the viability of the Northeast dairy region" and that "cooperative, rather than individual state action, may address more effectively the market disarray." But the ultimate aim of the cartel was the same as that of all cartels: to curtail competition and raise price. Predictably, such legislation tends to be fought vigorously by consumer groups and is advocated by firms producing the cartel good.[6]

In some cases, it is generally recognized that the purpose of government sponsored cartels is to limit competition in order to raise price. Few, for instance, would argue that this is not the prime mission of OPEC, which meets frequently to set production quotas for each of its 13 member

---

[5]The act also encouraged collective bargaining through unions, set maximum work hours and minimum wages, and forbade child labor.

[6]To the extent to which milk cartels are intended to support the viability of small, family-owned dairy farmers, they appear not to be very successful. Most of the economic benefits accrue to larger corporate dairy farms, with little evidence that cartels slow the disappearance of smaller, less efficient farms.

countries. Yet one would not be able to tell this from OPEC's official mission statement, which states: "OPEC's mission is to coordinate and unify the petroleum policies of Member Countries and to ensure the stabilization of oil prices in order to secure an efficient, economic and regular supply of petroleum to consumers, a steady income to producers and a fair return on capital to those investing in the petroleum industry." The words sound similar to those used to advocate for the NIRA in 1933 and continue to be similar to those articulated whenever government enforcement for cartel agreements is sought by firms.

25A.4.4 Self-Enforcing Cartel Agreements in Repeated Oligopoly Interactions

Alternatively, we can turn to the case where oligopolists that seek to establish a cartel agreement know that they will meet repeatedly. From our game theory chapter, we know that this is not sufficient for cooperation to emerge: If the firms know they will interact repeatedly but that this interaction will end at some definitive point in the future, subgame perfection leads to an unraveling of cooperation from the bottom of the repeated game tree upward. The firms know that, in their final interaction, neither will have an incentive to stick by the cartel agreement. But that means that in the second-to-last period, there will also be no incentive to cooperate since there is no credible way to punish noncooperation in the final interaction. But that then means that there is no way to enforce cooperation in the third-to-last interaction given that both firms know that noncooperation will take place in the last two periods. And by the same logic, cooperation cannot emerge in any period.

But the real world is rarely quite as definitive as setting up a finitely repeated set of interactions with a clear end-point. Rather, firms will know that they are likely to interact again each time that they meet, and for our purposes, we can therefore treat such interactions as infinitely repeated. Again, as we saw in our discussion of repeated Prisoner's Dilemmas in Chapter 24, this removes the "unraveling" feature of finitely repeated games because there is no definitive final interaction. And it opens the possibility of simple "trigger strategies" under which firms begin by complying with the cartel agreement, continue to do so as long as everyone complied in previous interactions, and revert to oligopoly competition if someone deviates from the agreement. Such strategies can sustain cartel cooperation so long as the immediate payoff from violating the cartel agreement is not sufficiently large to overcome the long-run loss from the disappearance of the cartel and the reversion to oligopoly competition.

Real-world strategies of this type are complicated by the fact that firms might not in fact be able to tell for sure whether another firm has violated the agreement. For instance, suppose that oil producers cannot observe how much oil is produced by any given company but they can only see the price that oil sells for in the market. Suppose further that oil price in any given period depends on both the overall quantity of oil supplied by the oligopoly firms *and* unpredictable (and unobservable) demand shocks to the oil market. If a firm then observes an unexpectedly low price in a given period, it might be because a member of the cartel has cheated and has produced more oil than the agreement specified, but it might also be because of an adverse demand shock in the oil market. Firms in such markets may then find it difficult to be certain about whether cartel members are cheating and run the risk of misinterpreting an unexpectedly low price as a sign of cheating. Economists have introduced such complicating factors into economic models of oligopolies and cartels, and it becomes plausible to observe equilibria in which cartel agreements break down and reemerge in repeated oligopoly interactions. This corresponds well to observed cartel behaviors in some industries.

Exercise 25A.17

In circumstances where firms are not certain about demand conditions in any given period, why might a more forgiving trigger strategy (like Tit-for-Tat) that allows for the reemergence of cooperation be better than the extreme trigger strategy that forever punishes perceived noncooperation in one period?

The Mathematics of Oligopoly

Throughout most of this section, we will assume for simplicity that firms face a constant marginal cost $MC = c$ (with no recurring fixed costs) and that the market demand for the oligopoly good x is linear and of the form

$$x = A - \alpha p. \qquad (25.1)$$

In some of our end-of-chapter exercises, we will explore how the various oligopoly models are affected by different assumptions, including different marginal costs and the presence of recurring fixed costs for the firms. For now, note that, under our current assumptions, were the oligopoly to function as a single monopoly, we know from our work in Chapter 23 (equation (23.14)) that, assuming no price discrimination, the firm would produce the monopoly quantity x^M and sell it at the monopoly price p^M where

$$x^M = \frac{A - \alpha c}{2} \quad \text{and} \quad p^M = \frac{A + \alpha c}{2\alpha}. \qquad (25.2)$$

Verify x^M and p^M in equation (25.2).

Exercise 25B.1

25B.1 Bertrand Competition

From our work in part A, we know that Bertrand competition, whether simultaneous or sequential, will result in both firms setting price equal to marginal cost. It is therefore quite easy to determine the overall Bertrand oligopoly output level by simply substituting $MC = c$ for price in the market demand function to get the joint output level $x = A - \alpha c$. Assuming that the consumers will come to our two firms in equal numbers when we charge the same price, this implies Bertrand output levels for our two firms of

$$x_1^B = x_2^B = \frac{A - \alpha c}{2} \qquad (25.3)$$

sold at the Bertrand price of $p^B = c$. Thus, for the linear demand and constant MC model we are using, the Bertrand model predicts that *each* of the two firms will produce the quantity that a single monopolist would choose to produce on its own, because the "competitive" quantity is twice the monopoly quantity.

The Bertrand model becomes more interesting, as we will see in Chapter 26, when firms can differentiate their products; i.e., when firms are not producing identical products but are still part of an oligopoly. We will also demonstrate in end-of-chapter exercise 25.1 how the inclusion of recurring fixed costs and differences in marginal costs across firms can alter the stark Bertrand predictions.

25B.2 Quantity Competition: Cournot and Stackelberg

Next we briefly describe the mathematics behind Cournot and Stackeberg competition as treated in Section A before covering some other aspects of quantity competition in Section 25B.3.

25B.2.1 Cournot Competition
In order to calculate the best (quantity) response functions for our two firms in the economist card oligopoly described in part A, we begin (as we did in Graph 25.2c) by calculating my *residual demand given I assume you produce* $\bar{x}_2$. If the market demand is given by equation (25.1), then my residual demand if you produce $\bar{x}_2$ is simply

$$x_1^r = A - \alpha p - \bar{x}_2. \qquad (25.4)$$

To make this analogous to the residual demand curve graphed in Graph 25.2c, we need to put it in the form of an inverse demand function; i.e.,

$$p_1^r = \left(\frac{A - \bar{x}_2}{\alpha}\right) - \left(\frac{1}{\alpha}\right)x_1. \tag{25.5}$$

Exercise 25B.2   Verify that p_1^r is in fact the correct inverse demand function.

We know from our work in Chapter 23 that the marginal revenue curve for any linear inverse demand function is itself a linear function with the same intercept as the inverse demand function but twice the slope; i.e., the relevant marginal revenue function for my firm given that I assume you will produce $\bar{x}_2$ is

$$MR_1^r = \left(\frac{A - \bar{x}_2}{\alpha}\right) - \left(\frac{2}{\alpha}\right)x_1. \tag{25.6}$$

Exercise 25B.3   Derive this *MR* function using calculus.

Given this residual marginal revenue for my firm, I can now determine the optimal quantity to produce (assuming I think you are producing $\bar{x}_2$) by setting equation (25.6) equal to marginal cost $MC = c$. Solving this for x_1, I get

$$x_1 = \frac{A - \bar{x}_2 - \alpha c}{2}. \tag{25.7}$$

Since our two firms are identical, your best response to thinking that I produce some quantity $\bar{x}_1$ is symmetric. Put differently, for any quantity x_1 that I am producing, we can now write down the best response for you in terms of x_1, and for any quantity of x_2 that you are producing, we can write down my best response in terms of x_2. This gives us the best response functions $x_1(x_2)$ and $x_2(x_1)$ as

$$x_1(x_2) = \frac{A - x_2 - \alpha c}{2} \quad \text{and} \quad x_2(x_1) = \frac{A - x_1 - \alpha c}{2}. \tag{25.8}$$

In a Nash equilibrium, the quantity $\bar{x}_2$ that I predict you will be producing has to be your best response to what I am producing; i.e., $\bar{x}_2 = x_2(x_1)$. We can therefore substitute $x_2(x_1)$ into our expression for $x_1(x_2)$ and solve for x_1, which then gives us the Cournot output level for me as

$$x_1^C = \frac{A - \alpha c}{3}. \tag{25.9}$$

Since our two firms are identical, your Nash equilibrium quantity should then be the same.

Exercise 25B.4   Verify that this is correct.

Exercise 25B.5   Verify that these quantities are in fact the Nash equilibrium quantities; i.e., show that, given you produce this amount, it is best for me to do the same, and given that I produce this amount, it is best for you to do the same.

Note that this implies that together we will produce $2(A - \alpha c)/3$, which is larger than the monopoly quantity $(A - \alpha c)/2$ we derived in equation (25.2) and smaller than the competitive and Bertrand quantities $(A - \alpha c)$.

How does the monopoly price p^M (derived in equation (25.2)) compare to the price that will emerge in the Cournot equilibrium? How does it compare to the Bertrand price?

Exercise
25B.6

25B.2.2 Cournot Competition with More than Two Firms

We can also demonstrate how Cournot competition changes as the number of firms increases. To be a bit more general, suppose that the inverse market demand function is $p(x)$ and that all firms have the same cost function $c(x_i)$ that gives the total cost of production as a function of the firm's production level x_i. Suppose there are N firms in the oligopoly, and let's denote the output levels of all firms other than firm i as $x_{-i} = (x_1, x_2, \ldots, x_{i-1}, x_{i+1}, \ldots, x_N)$. Firm i's profit maximization problem given $\bar{x}_{-i}$ is then

$$\max_{x_i} \pi_i = p(x_i, \bar{x}_{-i})x_i - c(x_i)$$

$$= p(\bar{x}_1 + \bar{x}_2 + \ldots + \bar{x}_{i-1} + x_i + \bar{x}_{i+1} + \ldots + \bar{x}_N)x_i - c(x_i). \quad (25.10)$$

The first order condition

$$\frac{dp(x_i, \bar{x}_{-i})}{dx} x_i + p(x_i, \bar{x}_{-i}) - \frac{dc(x_i)}{dx_i} = 0 \quad (25.11)$$

can then be written as

$$MR_i = \frac{dp(x_i, \bar{x}_{-i})}{dx} x_i + p(x_i, \bar{x}_{-i}) = \frac{dc(x_i)}{dx_i} = MC_i. \quad (25.12)$$

As we did in our work on monopoly in equation (23.9), we can express the MR_i as

$$MR_i = p\left(1 + \frac{dp}{dx} \frac{x_i}{p}\right). \quad (25.13)$$

Since we are assuming all firms are identical, in equilibrium they will produce the same quantity. This means that $Nx_i = x$, and this in turn means we can write the MR_i equation as

$$MR_i = p\left(1 + \frac{dp}{dx} \frac{x_i}{p} \frac{N}{N}\right) = p\left(1 + \frac{dp}{dx} \frac{x}{p} \frac{1}{N}\right) = p\left(1 + \frac{1}{N\varepsilon_D}\right), \quad (25.14)$$

where $\varepsilon_D = (dx/dp)(p/x)$ is the price elasticity of market demand. Using this as the expression for MR_i, and recognizing that in equilibrium marginal costs will be the same for all our firms (even though we are allowing MC to be non-constant by expressing costs as $c(x)$), we can write equation (25.12) as

$$MR_i = p\left(1 + \frac{1}{N\varepsilon_D}\right) = MC. \quad (25.15)$$

Note that, as N becomes large, this implies that price approaches MC just as it does under perfect competition. Thus, as oligopolies with identical firms become large, Cournot competition approaches perfect competition (as well as Bertrand competition).

Compare this equation with equation (23.15) in our chapter on monopolies. How are they related?

Exercise
25B.7

Can you make a case for why the Cournot model gives intuitively more plausible predictions than the Bertrand model for oligopolies in which identical firms produce identical goods?

Exercise
25B.8

25B.2.3 Stackelberg Competition Now suppose we return to our linear demand and constant *MC* example and suppose that we set quantity sequentially, with me (firm 1) being the Stackelberg leader and you (firm 2) being the Stackelberg follower. Subgame perfection requires that I first figure out what your optimal response will be for any x_1 I might set in the first stage of the game. But this is simply your best response function, which we already calculated (in equation (25.8)) to be

$$x_2(x_1) = \frac{A - x_1 - \alpha c}{2}. \tag{25.16}$$

I can then determine the residual demand for my goods by subtracting what I know you will produce from the market demand; i.e.,

$$x_1^r = A - \alpha p - x_2(x_1) = A - \alpha p - \frac{A - x_1 - \alpha c}{2}. \tag{25.17}$$

To get the inverse residual demand curve D^r that we graphed in Graph 25.4b, we solve this for p to get

$$p_1^r = \frac{A + \alpha c}{2\alpha} - \frac{1}{2\alpha} x_1. \tag{25.18}$$

Exercise 25B.9 Verify that this is the correct inverse residual demand function for me.

Exercise 25B.10 In Graph 25.4b, the residual demand curve has a kink at the level of *MC*. Verify that the function we previously derived in fact meets the market demand curve at $p = MC$. How would you fully characterize the residual demand curve mathematically (taking into account the fact that it is kinked)?

From p_1^r we can now derive my residual marginal revenue curve by once again recognizing that it will have the same intercept but twice the slope; i.e.,

$$MR_1^r = \frac{A + \alpha c}{2\alpha} - \frac{1}{\alpha} x_1. \tag{25.19}$$

We can then set this equal to $MC = c$ and solve for my optimal Stackelberg leader (*SL*) quantity

$$x_1^{SL} = \frac{A - \alpha c}{2}. \tag{25.20}$$

Given this output level for firm 1, firm 2's best response function implies the optimal Stackelberg follower (*SF*) quantity of

$$x_2^{SF} = \frac{A - \alpha c}{4}. \tag{25.21}$$

Exercise 25B.11 How does the overall level of Stackelberg output relate to the monopoly quantity and the Cournot quantity? What is more efficient in this setting (from society's vantage point): Cournot or Stackelberg competition?

Exercise 25B.12 What will be the output price under Stackelberg competition, and how does this relate to the Cournot and monopoly prices?

Can you draw a graph analogous to Graph 25.3c, indicating the monopoly outcome (assuming the two firms would split the monopoly output level), the Cournot outcome, the Stackelberg outcome, and the Bertrand outcome? Carefully label all the points.

Exercise
25B.13

25B.3 Oligopoly Competition with Asymmetric Information

So far we have assumed that firms always know the costs of other firms, but this is not generally true in the real world. Suppose, for instance, we have a relatively new oligopoly, with firm 1 having lost its monopoly status given the successful entry of firm 2 into the industry. It might then be reasonable to assume that firm 1's costs are well known (given it's history as a monopolist) but firm 2's costs might not be known. Or suppose that it is known that firm 2 invented a new manufacturing process but it is not yet known how costly that process is. Either of these scenarios results in an oligopoly in which firm 2 knows firm 1's costs but firm 1 does not know firm 2's costs. Put differently, we now have asymmetrically informed firms, and thus one player (firm 1) with incomplete information. The resulting oligopoly quantity setting game is an example of a simultaneous Bayesian game. (If you have not done Section B of Chapter 24, you can skip to Section 25B.4.)

To be more concrete, suppose that the oligopoly once again faces the same market demand $x = A - \alpha p$, with inverse market demand of $p = (A/\alpha) - x/\alpha$. In a two-firm oligopoly, this inverse demand can then again be written as $p = (A - x_1 - x_2)/\alpha$, with x_i simply indicating firm i's production level. Firm 1 is assumed to have marginal cost of c as before, but firm 2 might have either "high" marginal costs of c^H or "low" marginal costs of c^L, with $c^H > c^L$. The high cost "type" in firm 2 occurs with probability ρ while the low cost "type" occurs with probability $(1 - \rho)$. Firm 2 knows its type but firm 1 only has beliefs about firm 1's type (based on the probability with which each type occurs). We will consider Cournot competition in this setting (and explore Bertrand competition briefly in two within-chapter exercises at the end of the section).

It seems intuitive that firm 2 will produce a different level of output depending on whether its costs are high or low. A "strategy" for firm 2 therefore involves settling on a quantity depending on whether the firm is a high or a low cost type.[7] But firm 1 does not have the luxury of setting its quantity with the knowledge of firm 2's cost structure; it has to settle on a single quantity given its beliefs about the likelihood of firm 2 being a high cost rather than low cost type. Put differently, firm 1 needs to solve the optimization problem

$$\max_{x_1}\left[\rho\left(\frac{A - x_1 - x_2^H}{\alpha} - c\right)x_1 + (1 - \rho)\left(\frac{A - x_1 - x_2^L}{\alpha} - c\right)x_1\right], \qquad (25.22)$$

where x_2^H and x_2^L are the firm 2 production levels of high and low cost types. Depending on which type i firm 2 is assigned (by "Nature"), it solves the optimization problem

$$\max_{x_2^i}\left(\frac{A - x_1 - x_2^i}{\alpha} - c^i\right)x_2^i. \qquad (25.23)$$

The first order condition of the optimization problem in (25.22) solves to

$$x_1 = \frac{A - \alpha c - \rho x_2^H - (1 - \rho)x_2^L}{2} \qquad (25.24)$$

---

[7]Remember from Chapter 24 that a simultaneous Bayesian game involves Nature assigning types first, and a strategy for each player therefore involves a plan of action for each possible type that might be assigned.

for firm 1, and the first order conditions for the optimization problems (for the two types) in (25.23) solve to

$$x_2^H = \frac{A - x_1 - \alpha c^H}{2} \quad \text{and} \quad x_2^L = \frac{A - x_1 - \alpha c^L}{2} \tag{25.25}$$

for firm 2.

Exercise 25B.14

Show that the first order condition for firm 1 approaches an expression similar to the first order condition for each of the firm 2 types as firm 1's uncertainty diminishes; i.e., as ρ approaches zero or 1.

Substituting the first order conditions for firm 2 into equation (25.24) and solving for x_1, we get firm 1's optimal quantity x_1^* as

$$x_1^* = \frac{A - 2\alpha c + \alpha(\rho c^H + (1 - \rho)c^L)}{3}. \tag{25.26}$$

Now suppose that firm 1 actually knew firm 2's type. This would imply that it would produce $(A - 2\alpha c + \alpha c^H)/3$ if it knew it was facing a high cost firm and $(A - 2\alpha c + \alpha c^L)/3$ if it knew it was facing a low cost firm. But since it does not know what type it is facing, firm 1 produces a quantity in between these, thus producing less than it would under complete information when it faces a high cost opponent and more when it faces a low cost opponent.

Firm 2 has an informational advantage and will, we we will see shortly, try to use that to its advantage. Suppose, for instance, it has high marginal costs c^H. Substituting firm 1's output level from equation (25.26) into x_2^H in expression (25.25), we can solve for the output level of firm 2 when it has high costs. This gives us

$$x_2^{H*} = \frac{2A + 2\alpha c - \alpha(3 + \rho)c^H - \alpha(1 - \rho)c^L}{6}, \tag{25.27}$$

which, by adding and subtracting $\alpha\rho c^H$, can be written as

$$x_2^{H*} = \frac{A + \alpha c - 2\alpha c^H}{3} + \frac{\alpha(1 - \rho)}{6}(c^H - c^L). \tag{25.28}$$

In the absence of informational asymmetries, the high cost firm 2 would produce only the first term in this expression, which implies that it will produce *more* than it would under complete information when it knows it has high costs but its opponent does not. We just saw that firm 1 will produce *less* than it would under complete information when it faces a high cost opponent. Firm 2 is therefore using its informational advantage to its advantage.

We can similarly solve for x_2^{L*} to get

$$x_2^{L*} = \frac{A + \alpha c - 2\alpha c^L}{3} - \frac{\alpha\rho}{6}(c^H - c^L), \tag{25.29}$$

and we can now see that firm 2 will produce *less* than it would under complete information when it knows it is a low cost type, allowing firm 1 to produce more.

Exercise 25B.15**

Verify the last equation.

Can you tell whether the Cournot price will be higher or lower under this type of asymmetric information than it would be under complete information? (*Hint:* For both the case of a high cost and a low cost type, can you see if overall production is higher or lower in the absence of asymmetric information?)

Exercise
25B.16*

Suppose the two firms engage in price (Bertrand) competition, and suppose $c > c^H$. What price do you expect will emerge?

Exercise
25B.17*

Suppose again the two firms engage in price (Bertrand) rather than quantity competition, and suppose $c^L < c < c^H$. This case is easier to analyze if we assume sequential Bertrand competition, with firm 1 setting its price first and firm 2 setting it after it observes p_1 (and after it finds out its cost type). What equilibrium prices would you expect? Does your answer change with ρ?

Exercise
25B.18*

25B.4 Fixed Entry Costs and Entry Deterrence

We showed in Section 25A.3 that, for particular fixed costs of entry, it is possible for an incumbent firm to deter entry by a new firm *if the incumbent firm is able to set quantity prior to the potential entrant's entry decision*. Given our previous work, we can now show exactly the range of fixed costs for which the intuition we developed in part A is correct. Recall that the sequence of moves required for entry deterrence has the incumbent firm setting quantity first, followed by an entry and quantity decision by the potential entrant. (That sequence is pictured in panel (c) of Graph 25.5.)

First, we can begin by asking how high fixed entry costs FC would have to be in order for the incumbent firm to not have to worry about challenges from an entrant. Suppose firm 1 produces the monopoly quantity x^M (in equation (25.2)), which we have shown is exactly equal to the Stackelberg leader quantity x^{SL} (in equation (25.20)) under our linear assumptions about demand and costs. The best firm 2 could then do if it did enter is to produce the Stackelberg follower quantity x^{SF} (in equation (25.21)) and to sell that quantity at the Stackelberg price, which you should have calculated in exercise 25B.12 to be

$$p^S = \frac{A + 3\alpha c}{4\alpha}. \tag{25.30}$$

The profit π_2 for firm 2 from entering is then equal to revenue minus the cost of production minus the fixed cost of entry FC; i.e.,

$$\pi_2 = p^S x^{SF} - c x^{SF} - FC = \frac{(A - \alpha c)^2}{16\alpha} - FC. \tag{25.31}$$

Verify that this equation is correct.

Exercise
25B.19

We can therefore say that, so long as $FC > (A - \alpha c)^2/16\alpha$, the profit from entering if the incumbent firm is producing the monopoly output level is negative and firm 2 would choose to not enter while firm 1 would produce x^M without feeling the threat of competition from the potential entrant. In terms of the notation in Graph 25.6b, this implies

$$\overline{FC} = \frac{(A - \alpha c)^2}{16\alpha}. \tag{25.32}$$

Next, we can ask at what fixed entry cost the incumbent firm would be better off accepting the Stackelberg outcome rather than attempting to raise quantity in order to keep the entrant from coming into the market. To answer this, we first have to determine, for any given FC, how much firm 1 would have to produce in order to keep firm 2 from entering. Whatever x_1 is produced, firm 2 will respond (if it enters) by producing according to its best response function $x_2(x_1)$ (in equation (25.8)). This allows us to calculate the price that firm 1 can expect to emerge for any quantity x_1 conditional on firm 2 entering the market

$$p(x_1) = \frac{A}{\alpha} - \frac{x_1 + x_2(x_1)}{\alpha} = \frac{A - x_1 + \alpha c}{2\alpha}. \tag{25.33}$$

Exercise 25B.20 Verify that this derivation of $p(x_1)$ is correct.

Firm 2 will enter if $(p(x_1)x_2(x_1) - cx_2(x_1)) > FC$. Substituting in for $x_2(x_1)$ and $p(x_1)$, this implies firm 2 will enter so long as

$$\frac{(A - x_1 - \alpha c)^2}{4\alpha} > FC. \tag{25.34}$$

Exercise 25B.21 Again, verify that this derivation is correct.

Firm 1 is in full control of what x_1 will be when firm 2 has to make its entry decision, which implies that firm 1 has to make sure that the inequality in (25.34) goes in the other direction (if it wants to keep firm 2 out). Firm 1 therefore has to solve

$$\frac{(A - x_1 - \alpha c)^2}{4\alpha} \le FC \tag{25.35}$$

for x_1. Doing so, we get the minimum output for firm 1 to deter firm 2 from entering as

$$x_1^{ED} = A - \alpha c - 2(\alpha FC)^{1/2}. \tag{25.36}$$

When fixed entry costs are below $\overline{FC} = (A - \alpha c)^2/(16\alpha)$, the incumbent firm now has a choice: It can either produce the *entrance deterrent quantity* x_1^{ED} and keep firm 2 from entering, or it can produce the *Stackelberg leader quantity* and accept firm 2's competition. If the incumbent settles into Stackelberg leadership and accepts firm 2 entry, its profit π_1^{SL} will be

$$\pi_1^{SL} = \frac{(A - \alpha c)^2}{8\alpha}. \tag{25.37}$$

Exercise 25B.22 Verify that this is correct. Does it make sense that profit for the Stackelberg leader is exactly twice the profit of the Stackelberg follower (which we calculated in equation (25.31)) when $FC = 0$?

The profit from producing a quantity x as the sole producer in the market (graphed in panel (a) of Graph 25.6) is

$$\pi = \left(p(x) - c\right)x = \left(\frac{A - x}{\alpha} - c\right)x = \left(\frac{A - x - \alpha c}{\alpha}\right)x \tag{25.38}$$

Since the incumbent can always just decide to be Stackelberg leader, the most it is ever willing to produce to deter entry is an amount that sets equations (25.37) and (25.38) equal. Doing so and solving for x (using the quadratic formula), we get the highest quantity that would ever be produced to deter entry as[8]

$$x_{max}^{ED} = \frac{(2 + 2^{1/2})(A - \alpha c)}{4}. \tag{25.39}$$

As noted in the footnote, the quadratic formula also gives a second solution, namely $x = (2 - 2^{1/2})(A - \alpha c)/4$. Can you locate this solution in panel (a) of Graph 25.6?

Exercise 25B.23

Setting this equal to equation (25.36), we can calculate the lowest fixed cost $\underline{FC}$ at which entry deterrence is still optimal for firm 1 as

$$\underline{FC} = \left(\frac{(2 - 2^{1/2})(A - \alpha c)}{8} \right)^2. \tag{25.40}$$

Thus, if the fixed entry cost falls below $\underline{FC}$, the incumbent firm will make no effort to deter firm 2 from entering, and the two firms simply play the Stackelberg game. If the fixed entry cost falls between $\underline{FC}$ and $\overline{FC}$ (from equation (25.32)), the incumbent firm will raise its output to x_1^{ED} (from equation (25.36)) and will thereby successfully deter firm 2 from entering the market. Finally, if the fixed entry cost is higher than $\overline{FC}$, the incumbent can safely produce the monopoly quantity x^M without worrying about firm 2 entering.

25B.5 Dynamic Collusion and Cartels

The mathematics behind our Section A discussion of cartels and collusion is relatively straightforward. We will briefly illustrate mathematically the temptation by members of cartels to cheat on cartel agreements before illustrating how dynamic collusion can nevertheless emerge under the right conditions.

25B.5.1 The Temptation to Cheat on a One-Period Cartel Agreement
Continuing with the assumption that market demand is given by $x = A - \alpha p$, we already calculated that a monopolist facing this market demand will produce $x^M = (A - \alpha c)/2$ and sell at $p^M = (A + \alpha c)/2\alpha$. Two identical firms in an oligopoly facing the same market demand would therefore maximize their joint profit if they agree to each produce half the monopoly quantity; i.e., $x_i^{Cartel} = x^M/2 = (A - \alpha c)/4$.[9] If both parties to a cartel agreement abide by the agreement, this implies that profit for each cartel member i would be

$$\pi_i^{Cartel} = (p^M - c)\frac{x^M}{2} = \left(\frac{A + \alpha c}{2\alpha} - c \right)\frac{A - \alpha c}{4} = \frac{(A - \alpha c)^2}{8\alpha}. \tag{25.41}$$

---

[8]The quadratic formula gives two solutions for x. However, one of these is less than the Stackelberg leader quantity and we can therefore discard that solution as economically irrelevant.

[9]Of course other production quotas for the two firms can also maximize joint profits so long as the quotas add up to the monopoly quantity. End-of-chapter exercise 25.9 explores how unequal the quotas could be in principle.

Now suppose that firms i and j have entered such a cartel agreement but firm i, rather than blindly following the agreement, asks itself if it could produce a different quantity and do better. If firm j sticks by the agreement to produce $x^M/2$, this means firm i would choose x_i to solve

$$\max_{x_i} \pi_i = \left(\frac{A - (x^M/2) - x_i}{\alpha} - c \right) x_i = \left(\frac{3(A - \alpha c) - 4x_i}{4\alpha} \right) x_i. \tag{25.42}$$

Solving the first order condition, we can then calculate the optimal quantity for firm i conditional on firm j sticking by the cartel agreement. Denoting this quantity as x_i^D,

$$x_i^D = \frac{3(A - \alpha c)}{8}, \tag{25.43}$$

which is 50% greater than half the monopoly quantity assigned to firm i in the cartel agreement. The profit from deviating, π_i^D, conditional on firm j not deviating from the cartel agreement can then be calculated to be

$$\pi_i^D = \frac{9(A - \alpha c)^2}{64\alpha}. \tag{25.44}$$

Exercise 25B.24   Verify π_i^D. Is it unambiguously larger than π_i^{Cartel}?

25B.5.2 Collusion in Finitely Repeated Oligopoly Quantity Setting

It is clear from what we just derived that, unless there is some outside enforcement mechanism that can get the two firms to abide by the cartel agreement, it is not possible to sustain the agreement in equilibrium once the firms meet. As we pointed out in Section A, the two firms are caught in a classic Prisoner's Dilemma: They both know that an enforced cartel agreement makes both of them better off, but without enforcement, it is rational for both of them to cheat. The equilibrium continues to be the Cournot equilibrium despite the cartel agreement. And, as explained in Section A, this does not change when the firms interact repeatedly a finite number of times (since cooperation of repeated Prisoner's Dilemma games unravels from the bottom up under subgame perfection).

As we noted in Section A, however, there are many real-world instances of collusion in oligopolies, which casts doubt on the real-world relevance of the result that collusion cannot arise under subgame perfection in finitely repeated oligopoly interactions. We already discussed in Section A some of the real-world considerations that might in fact be responsible for instances of firm collusion despite this theoretical result. It may, for instance, be that firms found a way to enforce their cartel agreement, perhaps by employing government in some fashion. Or it may, as we discussed in Chapter 24, be the case that there is a Bayesian dimension to the game that we have not considered. For instance, there may be firms that will always play Tit-for-Tat even if it is not in their best interest to do so, and that firm 1 might be uncertain about whether it is in fact playing such an opponent. We have shown that, even if the probability of encountering an "irrational" Tit-for-Tat opponent is small, the mere possibility that one of the players might be such an opponent may be enough for "rational" players to want to establish a reputation for cooperating. Or it may be the case that firms are uncertain about whether they will interact again, which in essence turns the finitely repeated game into one that can, in some sense, be modeled like a game of infinitely repeated interactions.

25B.5.3 Infinitely Repeated Oligopoly Interactions

As we saw in Chapter 24, the unraveling of cooperation in finitely repeated Prisoner's Dilemmas is due to the fact that there is a definitive end to the interactions of the players. In the real world, we rarely know when the last time is that we interact with someone, and so it might be with firms in an oligopoly. We could model this directly as a probability that firms will interact again when they find themselves interacting. Or we can model the game as an infinitely repeated game in which the firms discount the future. We will do the latter here, assuming that $1 next period is worth δ this period, where $\delta < 1$. Recall that this means that a stream of income of y per period starting this period is worth $y/(1 - \delta)$, and a stream of income of y per period starting next period is worth $\delta y/(1 - \delta)$.

We will now show that, assuming firms do not discount the future too much, collusion between firms in an oligopoly can emerge in infinitely repeated settings. One possibility that we raised in Chapter 24 is that players employ "trigger strategies," strategies that presume cooperation initially but that "trigger" eternal noncooperation if noncooperation ever enters the game. In the context of oligopolies in cartel agreements that assign to each of two identical firms half of the monopoly output in each period, such a strategy would be: "Produce $(x^M/2)$ in the first period; every period thereafter, produce $(x^M/2)$ if everyone in previous periods has stuck by the cartel agreement but produce the Cournot quantity x^C otherwise." One instance of noncooperation therefore "triggers" the Cournot equilibrium from then on.

Such a trigger strategy, if adopted by both players, is a subgame perfect equilibrium of the infinitely repeated oligopoly game so long as one of the firms cannot make enough additional profit immediately by deviating this period to compensate for the loss of cartel profits in the future. Put differently, when firm i considers whether to deviate, it knows that it can get π_i^D from equation (25.44) this period at the cost of settling for the Cournot profit π_i^C for every period thereafter; i.e., deviating results in profit of $\pi_i^D + \delta\pi_i^C/(1 - \delta)$. Not deviating, on the other hand, implies a profit of π^{Cartel} (from equation (25.42)) every period starting now or, in present value terms, $\pi_i^{Cartel}/(1 - \delta)$. Deviating from the trigger strategy therefore does not pay so long as

$$\frac{\pi_i^{Cartel}}{(1 - \delta)} > \pi_i^D + \frac{\delta\pi_i^C}{(1 - \delta)}. \tag{25.45}$$

We previously calculated (in equation (25.9)) the Cournot quantity to be $x^C = (A - \alpha c)/3$, and in exercise 25B.6 you should have derived the Cournot price as $p^C = (A + 2\alpha c)/3\alpha$. This implies a Cournot profit for each firm of $\pi_i^C = (A - \alpha c)^2/(9\alpha)$.

Verify that this is the correct per-period profit in the Cournot equilibrium.

**Exercise
25B.25**

Plugging the relevant quantities into the inequality (25.45), we get

$$\frac{(A - \alpha c)^2}{8\alpha(1 - \delta)} > \frac{9(A - \alpha c)^2}{64\alpha} + \frac{\delta(A - \alpha c)^2}{9\alpha(1 - \delta)}. \tag{25.46}$$

Solving for δ, we then get that

$$\delta > \frac{9}{17} \approx 0.53. \tag{25.47}$$

Thus, so long as $1 next period is worth more than $0.53 this period, neither firm will want to deviate from the proposed trigger strategy, which implies the two firms will collude in accordance with their cartel agreement.

This is, of course, as our discussion of the Folk Theorem in the appendix to Chapter 24 illustrated, not the only way to sustain collusion in infinitely repeated oligopoly games. Furthermore, in a world where there is less certainty than what we have assumed here, the trigger strategy we proposed here seems far too severe since it eternally punishes deviations. Consider, for instance, a world in which firms in an oligopoly cannot observe the output of other firms but only see what the equilibrium price turned out to be in every period. In a two-firm oligopoly, this is enough to infer the other firm's output, but only if firms know market demand perfectly. If there is some uncertainty in each period about what exactly market demand looks like—if there are, as we put it in Section A, unobservable market demand "shocks"—then it becomes more difficult to know whether an unexpectedly low price was due to unexpectedly low market demand in a given period or whether it was due to the other firm cheating on its cartel agreement. A number of economists have investigated such settings closely and have concluded that more forgiving trigger strategies are likely to be optimal from the cartel's perspective, strategies where a price below some level "triggers" punishment for some period but eventually collusion is restored. Our only point here is that, when firms interact without knowing that their interactions will end at some point, collusion may well be sustainable despite the incentives to deviate from cartel agreements in finitely repeated games.

CONCLUSION

We have now moved from a model of perfect competition in which firms could behave non-strategically (since their actions had no influence on price) to models of perfect monopoly in Chapter 23 to the intermediate case of oligopoly. Any deviation from perfect competition introduces strategic considerations and eliminates the possibility of modeling firms as price-takers. In the monopoly setting, we illustrated different types of pricing policies that monopolists might employ to strategically shape their economic environment, and in the oligopoly case we have illustrated how less-than-perfect competition results in pricing and output in between the extremes of perfect competition and monopoly so long as oligopolists do not form cartels and are not perfect Bertrand competitors. In the process, we have also illustrated that the potential threat of competition can, assuming sufficiently low entry costs, alter the quantities produced by monopolists (or "incumbent" firms) in a socially desirable direction.

The welfare implications of different forms of oligopoly competition are relatively straightforward, but the policy question of how to deal with oligopoly markets to enhance efficiency runs into complications similar to some of those we discussed in our chapter on monopolies. There are often very good underlying economic reasons for the existence of oligopolies, reasons that mirror those for the existence of natural monopolies. For instance, a firm has to pay a relatively large fixed cost before it can begin producing cars, which results in U-shaped average cost curves for which the bottom of the "U" occurs at large quantities relative to market demand. In such instances, the nature of production does not permit the existence of many small firms that can all act as price-taking competitors, nor would such a market arrangement be efficient if it could be forced (since it would result in high average costs for cars as each firm needs to recoup its fixed costs). The loss of efficiency from pricing above marginal cost by Cournot competitors can therefore easily be outweighed by the gain in efficiency from having a small number of firms produce at lower points of their average cost curves.

As a result, the thrust of antitrust policy in oligopoly markets is focused on attempts to detect and deter collusion by oligopoly firms that seek to escape oligopoly competition by forming cartels that behave more like monopolies. Without knowing the cost functions of firms in an oligopoly (as well as demand conditions on the consumer side), however, it is not always easy for regulators charged with fostering competitive behavior in oligopolistic markets to detect collusion, and firms in an oligopoly (just as natural monopolists) have no particular incentive to reveal their true cost functions to regulators. Suspected colluders are then often taken to court for alleged violations of antitrust laws (that make such anticompetitive collusion illegal), and courts are then charged with investigating the underlying economics of the relevant market to determine the extent to which collusion has in fact taken place and what damages have resulted from such collusion.[10] To the extent to which colluding firms can be shown to have had explicit interactions in which they discussed and coordinated pricing and production decisions, evidence of collusion can be found in records that do not require explicit knowledge of cost functions, but the assessment of damages requires such information in order to determine the extent to which the observed prices and production levels deviated from what one would have expected under oligopoly competition. But one can easily envision instances where firms are quite clever in how they engineer their collusive relationship without making explicit cartel agreements that can be entered as evidence in court. Again, these complications lead to quite interesting ways in which courts have successfully or mistakenly dealt with allegations of collusion, and if this is interesting to you, a course in antitrust economics (or law and economics) should be fascinating.

Oligopoly market structures are not, however, the only market structures that fall in between the extremes of perfect competition and perfect monopoly. Perfect competition involves the assumption of no barriers to entry, while monopoly and oligopoly markets require significant barriers to such entry of new firms. In Chapter 26, we will therefore introduce a final type of market structure known as "monopolistic competition" in which barriers to entry are low (unlike for oligopoly and monopoly market structures) but firms can engage in innovation that differentiates their product (unlike in the case of perfect competition where we have assumed all firms produce identical products). The potential for product differentiation through innovation also exists in oligopoly markets (or, for that matter, for monopolists who fear innovative potential competitors), and we will treat this explicitly in Chapter 26 as well.

END-OF-CHAPTER EXERCISES

25.1*† In the text, we demonstrated the equilibrium that emerges when two oligopolists compete on price when there are no fixed costs and marginal costs are constant. In this exercise, continue to assume that firms compete solely on price and can produce whatever quantity they want.

A. We now explore what happens as we change some of these assumptions. Maintain the assumptions we made in the text and change only those referred to in each part of the exercise. Assume throughout that costs are never so high that no production will take place in equilibrium, and suppose throughout that price is the strategic variable.

   a. First, suppose both firms paid a fixed cost to get into the market. Does this change the prediction that firms will set $p = MC$?

   b. Suppose instead that there is a recurring fixed cost FC for each firm. Consider first the sequential case where firm 1 sets its price first and then firm 2 follows (assuming that one of the options for both firms is to not produce and not pay the recurring fixed cost). What is the subgame perfect equilibrium? (If you get stuck, there is a hint in part (f).)

   c. Consider the same costs as in (b). Can both firms produce in equilibrium when they move simultaneously?

   d. What is the simultaneous move Nash equilibrium? (There are actually two.)

   e. *True or False*: The introduction of a recurring fixed cost into the Bertrand model results in $p = AC$ instead of $p = MC$.

   f. You should have concluded that the recurring fixed cost version of the Bertrand model leads to a single firm in the oligopoly producing. Given how this firm prices the output, is this outcome efficient, or would it be more efficient for both firms to produce?

---

[10]Such court cases may arise from federal regulators initiating lawsuits, or they often arise from firms that charge competitors with collusive behavior in civil court. Damages to both consumers and competitors who did not participate in the collusion are then assessed.

*conceptually challenging
**computationally challenging
†solutions in Study Guide

g.   Suppose next that, in addition to a recurring fixed cost, the marginal cost curve for each firm is upward sloping. Assume that the recurring fixed cost is sufficiently high to cause AC to cross MC to the right of the demand curve. Using logic similar to what you have used thus far in this exercise, can you again identify the subgame perfect equilibrium of the sequential Bertrand game as well as the simultaneous move pure strategy Nash equilibria?

B. Suppose that demand is given by $x(p) = 100 - 0.1p$ and firm costs are given by $c(x) = FC + 5x^2$.

a.   Assume that $FC = 11,985$. Derive the equilibrium output x^B and price p^B in this industry under Bertrand competition.

b.   What is the highest recurring fixed cost FC that would sustain at least one firm producing in this industry? (*Hint*: When you get to a point where you have to apply the quadratic formula, you can simply infer the answer from the term in the square root.)

25.2   In exercise 25.1, we checked how the Bertrand conclusions (that flow from viewing *price* as the strategic variable) hold up when we change some of our assumptions about fixed and marginal costs. We now do the same for the case where we view *quantity* as the strategic variable in the simultaneous move Cournot model.

A. Again, maintain all the assumptions in the text unless you are asked to specifically change some of them.

a.   First, suppose both firms paid a fixed cost to get into the market. Does this change the predictions of the Cournot model?

b.   Let x^C denote the Cournot equilibrium quantities produced by each of two firms in the oligopoly as derived under the assumptions in the text. Then suppose that there is a recurring fixed cost FC for each firm (and FC does not have to be paid if the firm does not produce). Assuming that both firms would still make non-negative profit by each producing x^C, will the presence of FC make this no longer a Nash equilibrium?

c.   Can you illustrate your conclusion from (c) in a graph with best response functions that give rise to a single pure strategy Nash equilibrium with both firms producing x^C? (*Hint*: You should convince yourself that the best response functions are the same as before for low quantities of the opponent's production but then, at some output level for the opponent, jump to 0 output as a best response.)

d.   Can you illustrate a case where FC is such that both firms producing x^C is one of three different pure strategy Nash equilibria?

e.   Can you illustrate a case where FC is sufficiently high such that both firms producing x^C is no longer a Nash equilibrium? What are the two Nash equilibria in this case?

f.   *True or False*: With sufficiently high recurring fixed costs, the Cournot model suggests that only a single firm will produce and act as a monopoly.

g.   Suppose that, instead of a recurring fixed cost, the marginal cost for each firm was linear and upward sloping, with the marginal cost of the first unit the same as the constant marginal cost assumed in the text. Without working this out in detail, what do you think happens to the best response functions, and how will this affect the output quantities in the Cournot equilibrium?

B. Suppose that both firms in the oligopoly have the cost function $c(x) = FC + (cx^2/2)$, with demand given by $x(p) = A - \alpha p$ (as in the text).

a.   Derive the best response function $x_1(x_2)$ (of firm 1's output given firm 2's output) as well as $x_2(x_1)$.

b.   Assuming that both firms producing is a pure strategy Nash equilibrium, derive the Cournot equilibrium output levels.

c.   What is the equilibrium price?

d.   Suppose that $A = 100$, $c = 10$, and $\alpha = 0.1$. What is the equilibrium output and price in this industry, assuming $FC = 0$?

e.   How high can FC go with this remaining as the unique equilibrium?

f.   How high can FC go without altering the fact that this is at least one of the Nash equilibria?

g.   For what range of FC is there no pure strategy equilibrium in which both firms produce but two equilibria in which only one firm produces?

h.   What happens if FC lies above the range you calculated in (g)?

25.3 In exercise 25.2, we considered *quantity* competition in the simultaneous Cournot setting. We now turn to the sequential Stackelberg version of the same problem.

A. Suppose that firm 1 decides its quantity first and firm 2 follows after observing x_1. Assume initially that there are no recurring fixed costs and that marginal cost is constant as in the text.

    a. Suppose that both firms have a recurring *FC* (that does not have to be paid if the firm chooses not to produce). Will the Stackelberg equilibrium derived in the text change for low levels of *FC*?

    b. Is there a range of *FC* under which firm 1 can strategically produce in a way that keeps firm 2 from producing?

    c. At what *FC* does firm 1 not have to worry about firm 2?

    d. Could *FC* be so high that no one produces?

    e. Suppose instead (i.e., suppose again $FC = 0$) that the firms have linear, upward-sloping *MC* curves, with *MC* for the first output unit equal to what the constant *MC* was in the text. Can you guess how the Stackelberg equilibrium will change?

    f. Will firm 1 be able to engage in entry deterrence to keep firm 2 from producing?

B.* Consider again the demand function $x(p) = 100 - 0.1p$ and the cost function $c(x) = FC + 5x^2$ (as you did in exercise 25.1 and implicitly in the latter portion of exercise 25.2).

    a. Suppose first that $FC = 0$. Derive firm 2's best response function to observing firm 1's output level x_1.

    b. What output level will firm 1 choose?

    c. What output level does that imply firm 2 will choose?

    d. What is the equilibrium Stackelberg price?

    e. Now suppose there is a recurring fixed cost $FC > 0$. Given that firm 1 has an incentive to keep firm 2 out of the market, what is the highest *FC* that will keep firm 2 producing a positive output level?

    f. What is the lowest *FC* at which firm 1 does not have to engage in strategic entry deterrence in order to keep firm 2 out of the market?

    g. What is the lowest *FC* at which neither firm will produce?

    h. Characterize the equilibrium in this case for the range of *FC* from 0 to 20,000.

25.4 **Business Application:** *Entrepreneural Skill and Market Conditions*: We often treat all firms as if they must inherently face the same costs, but managerial or entrepreneural skill in firms can sometimes lead to a decrease in the marginal cost of production. We investigated this in the competitive setting in exercise 14.5 of Chapter 14 and now investigate the extent to which effective managers can leverage their skill in oligopolies depending on the market conditions they face.

BUSINESS APPLICATION

A. Suppose two firms in an oligopoly face a linear demand curve, constant marginal costs MC_1 and MC_2, and no recurring fixed costs. Assume $MC_1 < MC_2$.

    a. Suppose first that the market conditions are such that firms compete on price and can easily produce any quantity that is demanded at their posted prices. If the firms simultaneously choose price, what happens in equilibrium?

    b. Does your answer change if the firms post prices sequentially, with firm 1 posting first?

    c. When firms face the same costs, we concluded that the Bertrand equilibrium is efficient. Does the same still hold when firms face different marginal costs?

    d. Next, suppose that instead firms have to choose capacity and they therefore are engaged in quantity competition. What happens in equilibrium compared to the situation where both firms face the same marginal cost equal to the average of MC_1 and MC_2 we assume in this exercise?

    e. Could it be that firm 2 does not produce in the Cournot equilibrium? If so, how much does firm 1 produce?

    f. If firms set quantity sequentially, do you think it matters whether firm 1 or firm 2 moves first?

    g.* In (b) you were asked to find the subgame perfect equilibrium in a sequential Bertrand pricing market where firm 1 moves first. How would your answer change if firm 2 moved first? Is there a subgame perfect equilibrium in which the efficient outcome is reached? What is the subgame perfect equilibrium that results in the least efficient outcome? (*Hint*: Think about firm 2's payoffs for all its possible strategies in stage 1, given it predicts firm 1's response.)

B. The two oligopoly firms operate in a market with demand $x = A - \alpha p$. Neither firm faces any recurring fixed costs, and both face a constant marginal cost. But firm 1's marginal cost c_1 is lower than firm 2's; i.e., $c_1 < c_2$.

    a.   In a simultaneous move Bertrand model, what price will emerge, and how much will each firm produce?

    b.   Does your answer to (a) change if the Bertrand competition is sequential, with firm 1 moving first? What if firm 2 moves first? (Assume subgame perfection.)

    c.   How does your answer change if the two firms are Cournot competitors (assuming that both produce in equilibrium)?

    d.   What if the two firms are engaged in Stackelberg competition, with firm 1 as the first mover? What if firm 2 is the first mover?

    e.   How would each firm behave if it were a monopolist?

    f.** Suppose $A = 1000$, $\alpha = 10$, $c_1 = 20$, and $c_2 = 40$. Use your results from parts (a) through (e) to calculate the equilibrium outcome in each of those cases. Illustrate your answer in a table with p, x_1, and x_2 for each of the cases. Do the results make intuitive sense?

    g.** Add a column to your table in which you calculate profit in each case. What market conditions are most favorable in this example for the good manager to leverage his or her skills?

    h.   What would be the efficient outcome? Add a row to your table illustrating what would happen under the efficient outcome.

    i.   Which of the oligopoly/monopoly scenarios in your table is most efficient? Which is best for consumers?

    j.** Are there any scenarios in your table that would result in the same level of overall production if the marginal costs for each of the two firms were the same and equal to the average we have assumed for them (i.e., $c_1 = c_2 = 30$)?

25.5* **Business Application:** *Quitting Time: When to Exit a Declining Industry:*[11] We illustrated in the text the strategic issues that arise for a monopolist who is threatened by a potential entrant into the market, and in Chapter 26, we will investigate firm entry into an industry where demand increases. In this exercise, suppose instead that an industry is in decline in the sense that demand for its output is decreasing over time. Suppose there are only two firms left: a large firm L and a small firm S.

A. Since our focus is on the decision of whether or not to exit, we will assume that each firm i has fixed capacity k^i at which it produces output in any period in which it is still in business; i.e., if a firm i produces, it produces $x = k_i$. Since L is larger than S, we assume $k^L > k^S$. The output that is produced is produced at constant marginal cost $MC = c$. (Assume throughout that once a firm has exited the industry, it can never produce in this industry again.)

    a.   Since demand is falling over time, the price that can be charged when the two firms together produce some output quantity $\bar{x}$ declines with time; i.e., $p_1(\bar{x}) > p_2(\bar{x}) > p_3(\bar{x}) > \ldots$ where subscripts indicate the time periods $t = 1,2,3,\ldots$. If firm i is the only firm remaining in period t, what is its profit π_t^i? What if both firms are still producing in period t?

    b.   Let t^i denote the last period in which demand is sufficiently high for firm i to be profitable (i.e., to make profit greater than or equal to zero) if it were the only firm in the market. Assuming they are in fact different, which is greater: t^L or t^S?

    c.   What are the two firms' subgame perfect strategies beginning in period $(t^S + 1)$?

    d.   What are the two firms' subgame perfect strategies in periods $(t^L + 1)$ to t^S?

[11]This exercise is derived from Martin J. Osborne, An *Introduction to Game Theory* (New York: Oxford University Press, 2004).

e. Suppose both firms are still in business at the beginning of period t^L before firms make their decision of whether to exit. Could both of them producing in this period be part of a subgame perfect equilibrium? If not, which of the two firms must exit?

f. Suppose both firms are still in business at the beginning of period $(t^L - 1)$ (before exit decisions are made). Under what condition will both firms stay? What has to be true for one of them to exit, and if one of them exits, which one will it be?

g. Let $\bar{t}$ denote the last period in which $(p_t(k^S + k^L) - c) \geq 0$. Describe what happens in a subgame perfect equilibrium, beginning in period $t = 1$, as time goes by, i.e., as $\bar{t}$, t^L, and t^S pass. Is there ever a time when price rises as the industry declines?

h. Suppose that the small firm has no access to credit markets and therefore is unable to take on any debt. If the large firm knows this, how will this change the subgame perfect equilibrium? *True or False*: Although the small firm will not need to access credit markets in order to be the last firm in the industry, it will be forced out of the market before the large firm exits if it does not have access to credit markets.

i. How does price now evolve differently in the declining industry (when the small firm cannot access credit markets)?

B. Suppose $c = 10$, $k^L = 20$, $k^S = 10$, and $p_t(\bar{x}) = 50.5 - 2t - \bar{x}$ until price is zero.

a. How does this example represent a declining industry?

b. Calculate t^S, t^L, and $\bar{t}$ as defined in part A of the exercise.

c. Derive the evolution of output price as the industry declines.

d. How does your answer change when firm S has the credit constraint described in A(h), i.e., when the small firm has no access to credit markets?

e. How would your answer change if the large rather than the small firm had this credit constraint?

f. Suppose firm S can only go into debt for n time periods. Let $\bar{n}$ be the smallest n for which the subgame perfect equilibrium without credit constraints holds, with $n < \bar{n}$ implying the change in equilibrium you described in part A(h). What is $\bar{n}$? (Assume no discounting.)

g. If $n < \bar{n}$, how will output price evolve as the industry declines?

25.6† **Business Application:** *Financing a Strategic Investment under Quantity Competition*: Suppose you own a firm that has invented a patented product that grants you monopoly power. Patents only last for a fixed period of time, as does the monopoly power associated with the patent. Suppose you are nearing the end of your patent and you have the choice of investing in research that will result in a patented technology that reduces the marginal cost of producing your product.

BUSINESS APPLICATION

A. The demand for your product is linear and downward sloping and your current constant marginal cost is MC. There is one potential competitor who faces the same constant MC. Neither of you currently faces any fixed costs, and the competitor observes your output before he or she decides whether and how much to produce.

a. If this is the state of things when the patent runs out, will you change your output level? What happens to your profit?

b. Suppose you can develop an improved production process that lowers your marginal cost to $MC' < MC$. Once developed, you will have a patent on this technology, implying that your competitor cannot adopt it. You would finance the fixed cost of this new technology with a payment plan that results in a recurring fixed cost FC for the life of the patent. If you do this, what do you think will happen to your output?

c. If MC' is relatively close to MC, will you be able to keep your competitor out? In this case, might it still be worth it to invest in the technology?

d. If the technology reduces marginal costs by a lot, might it be that you can keep your competitor from producing? If so, what will happen to output price?

e. Do you think that investments like this—intended to deter production by a competitor—are efficiency enhancing?

f. Suppose the potential competitor could also invest in this technonlogy. Might there be circumstances under which your firm will invest and your competitor does not?

B.* Suppose again that demand is given by $x = A - \alpha p$, that there are currently no fixed costs, that all firms face a constant marginal cost c, and that you are about to face a competitor (because your patent on the good you produce is running out).

    a.   What will happen to your output level if you simply engage in the competition by producing first? What will happen to your profit?

    b.   If you lower your marginal cost to $c' < c$ by taking on a recurring fixed cost FC, what will be your profit assuming that your competitor still produces? (If you have done exercise 25.4, you can use your results from there to answer this.)

    c.   Suppose that $A = 1,000$, $c = 40$, and $\alpha = 10$. What is the highest FC can be for you to decide to go ahead with the investment if the new marginal cost is $c' < c$ and assuming the competitor cannot get the same technology? Denote this $\overline{FC}_1(c')$.

    d.   Now consider the competitor. Suppose he or she sees that firm 1 has invested in the technology (and thus lowered its marginal cost to c'). Firm 2 finds out that the patent on firm 1's technology has been revoked, making it possible for firm 2 to also adopt the technology at a recurring fixed cost FC. What is the highest FC at which firm 2 will adopt the technology in equilibrium? Denote this $\overline{FC}_2$.

    e.   Suppose $c' = 20$. For what range of FC will firm 1 adopt and firm 2 not adopt the technology even if it is permitted to do so?

25.7   **Business Application:** *Financing a Strategic Investment under Price Competition*: In exercise 25.6, we investigated the incentives of firms to finance technologies that lower marginal costs. We did so in a sequential setting where firms compete by setting quantity, with the incumbent firm moving first. Can you repeat the exercise under the assumption that firms are sequentially competing on price (with firm 1 moving first)?

25.8†   **Business Application:** *Deal or No Deal—Acquisitions of Upstart Firms by Incumbents*: Large software companies often produce a variety of different software, and sometimes a small upstart develops a competing product. The large firm then faces a decision of whether to compete with the upstart or whether to "acquire" it. Acquiring an upstart firm implies paying its owners to give up and join your firm. Since the two firms will jointly make less money than the merged firm can make on this product, the two parties have to negotiate an acquisition price. What price will emerge will depend on the market conditions the firms face as well as the way the bargaining unfolds. In end-of-chapter exercises 24.5 and 24.9, we discussed two bargaining models that we apply here. In the first, known also as an *ultimatum game*, one firm would make a take-it-or-leave-it offer, and the other either accepts or rejects. In the second, the parties make alternating offers until an offer is accepted.[12]

A.   Suppose that the firms face a linear, downward-sloping demand curve, the same constant marginal cost, and no recurring fixed costs.

    a.   Let Y denote the overall gain in profit to the industry if an acquisition deal is cut. How is Y divided between the firms under three bargaining environments: An ultimatum game in which the incumbent firm proposes an acquisition price, an ultimatum game in which the upstart firm proposes the price, and an alternating offer game?

    b.   Which of your answers in (a) might change if firm 2 is very impatient while firm 1 can afford to be patient?

    c.   Let Y^B represent the overall gain in profit when the alternative to a deal is Bertrand competition, let Y^C represent the same when the alternative is Cournot competition, and let Y^S represent the same when the alternative is Stackelberg competition. Which is biggest? Which is smallest?

    d.   Let π^M denote monopoly profit, let π^C denote one firm's Cournot profit, and let π^{SL} and π^{SF} denote the Stackelberg leader and follower profits. In terms of these, what will be the acquisition price under the three bargaining settings if the alternative is Bertrand

---

[12]In exercise 24.5 you should have concluded that the proposing party gets all the gains in a subgame perfect equilibrium, and in exercise 24.9 you should have concluded that they will split the gains equally. Assume these bargaining outcomes throughout this exercise.

competition? What about if the alternative is Cournot competition or Stackelberg competition?

    e.   Which of these acquisition prices is largest? Which is smallest?

    f.   Do you think acquisition prices for a given bargaining setting will be larger under Cournot competition than under Stackelberg competition? Does your answer depend on which bargaining setting we are using?

    g.   If part of the negotiations involves laying the groundwork to set expectations about what kind of economic environment will prevail in the absence of a deal, what would you advise the up-start firm to say at the first meeting with the incumbent? Does your answer depend on what kind of bargaining environment you expect?

    h.   Would your advice be any different for the incumbent?

B. Let firm 1 be the large incumbent firm and firm 2 the upstart firm. Assume they have no recurring fixed costs and both face the same constant marginal cost c. The demand for the product is given by $x(p) = A - \alpha p$.

    a.   Suppose the firms expect to be Bertrand competitors if they cannot agree on an acquisition price. If firm 1 is the proposer in the ultimatum bargaining game, what is the subgame perfect acquisition price? What if firm 2 is the proposer?

    b.   What is the acquisition price if the two firms engage in the alternating offer game?

    c.   Repeat (a) for the case where the two firms expect to be Cournot competitors.

    d.   Repeat (b) if the two firms expect to be Cournot competitors. How does it compare with the answer you arrived at in (b)?

    e.   Repeat (a) if the two firms expect firm 1 to be a Stackelberg leader.

    f.   Repeat (b) if the two firms expect firm 1 to be the Stackelberg leader.

    g.   Suppose $A = 1,000$, $c = 20$, and $\alpha = 40$. What is the acquisition price in each of the cases you previously analyzed? Can you make intuitive sense of these?

25.9   **Business and Policy Application:** *Production Quotas under Cartel Agreements*: In exercise 25.8, we investigated the acquisition price that an incumbent firm might pay to acquire a competitor under different bargaining and economic settings. Instead of one firm acquiring or merging with another, two firms in an oligopoly might choose to enter a cartel agreement in which they commit to each producing a quota of output (and no more).

BUSINESS APPLICATION

POLICY APPLICATION

  A. Suppose again that both firms face a linear, downward-sloping demand curve, the same constant marginal cost, and no recurring fixed costs.

    a.   Under the different bargaining settings and economic environments described in exercise 25.8,[13] what are the profits that the two firms in the cartel will make in terms of π^M, π^C, π^{SL}, and π^{SF} (as these were defined in A(d) of exercise 25.8)? (If you have already done this in A(d), skip to (b).)

    b.   It turns out that $\pi^C = (4/9)\pi^M$, $\pi^{SL} = (1/2)\pi^M$, and $\pi^{SF} = (1/4)\pi^M$ for examples like this. Using this information, can you determine the relative share of profit that each firm in the cartel will get for each of the bargaining and economic settings from (a)?

    c.   Assuming the cartel agreement sets x^M—the monopoly output level—as the combined output quota across both firms, what fraction of x^M will be produced by firm 1 and what fraction by firm 2 under the different bargaining and economic settings we are analyzing?

    d.   Assume that any cartel agreement results in x^M being produced, with each firm producing a share depending on what was negotiated. *True or False*: For any such cartel agreement, the payoffs for firms could also have been achieved by one firm acquiring the other at some price.

    e.   Explain why the firms might seek government regulation to force them to produce the prescribed quantities in the cartel agreement.

---

f.   In the early years of the Reagan administration, there was a strong push by the U.S. auto industry to have Congress impose protective tariffs on Japanese car imports. Instead, the administration negotiated with Japanese car companies directly and got them to agree to "voluntary export quotas" to the United States, with the U.S. government ensuring that companies complied. How can you explain why Japanese car companies might have agreed to this?

g.   Suppose the firms cannot get the government to enforce their cartel agreement. Explain how such cartel agreements might be sustained as a subgame perfect equilibrium if, each time the firms produce, they expect there is a high probability that they will again each produce as the only firms in the industry in the future.

h.   If you are a lawyer with the antitrust division of the Justice Department and are charged with detecting collusion among firms that have entered a cartel agreement, and if you thought that these agreements were typically sustained by trigger strategies, in which market setting (Bertrand, Cournot, or Stackelberg) would you expect this to happen most frequently?

B.   Suppose again that firms face the demand function $x(p) = A - \alpha p$, that they both face marginal cost c, and neither faces a recurring fixed cost.

a.   For each of the bargaining and economic settings discussed in exercise 25.8, determine the output quotas x_1 and x_2 for the two firms.

b.   Verify that the fraction of the overall cartel production undertaken by each firm under the different scenarios is what you concluded in A(c).

c.   Suppose $A = 1,000$, $c = 20$, and $\alpha = 40$. What is the cartel quota for each of the two firms under each of the economic and bargaining settings you have analyzed?

d.   In terms of payoffs for the firms, is the outcome from the cartel agreement any different than the outcome resulting from the negotiated acquisition price in exercise 25.8?

e.*   Suppose the two firms enter a cartel agreement with a view toward an infinite number of interactions. Suppose further that $\$1$ one period from now is worth $\$\delta < \$1$ now. What is the lowest level of δ for each of the bargaining settings such that the cartel agreement will be respected by both firms if they would otherwise be Cournot competitors?

f.*   Repeat (e) for the case of Bertrand and Stackelberg competitors.

g.   Assuming that cartel quotas are assigned using alternating offer bargaining, which cartels are most likely to hold: those that revert to Bertrand, Cournot, or Stackelberg? Can you explain this intuitively? Which is second most likely to hold?

25.10 Policy Application: *Mergers, Cartels, and Antitrust Enforcement*: In exercises 25.8 and 25.9, we illustrated how firms in an oligopoly can collude through mergers or through the formation of cartel agreements. We did this for different bargaining and economic environments and concluded that payoffs for the firms might differ dramatically depending on the environments in which the negotiations between firms take place. Suppose now that you are a lawyer in the antitrust division of the Justice Department, and you are charged with limiting the efficiency costs from collusive activities by oligopolists.

A.   Suppose that cartel agreements are always negotiated through alternating offers; i.e., suppose the firms always split the gains from forming a cartel 50-50. Suppose further, unless otherwise stated, that demand curves are linear and firms face the same constant marginal costs and no recurring fixed costs.

a.   Suppose you have limited resources to employ in pursuing antitrust investigations. Given that breaking up some forms of collusion leads to greater efficiency gains than breaking up others, which firms would you focus on: those that would revert to Bertrand, Cournot, or Stackelberg environments?

b.   Given that some cartels are more likely than others to last, which would you pursue if you wanted to catch as many as possible?

c.   Given the likelihood that one form of collusion is more likely to last than the other, would you focus more on collusion through mergers and acquisitions or on collusion through cartel agreements?

    d.   Suppose that you were asked to focus on collusion through mergers and acquisitions. In what way would the size of recurring fixed costs figure into your determination of whether or not to pursue an antitrust case against firms that have merged? What trade-off do you have to consider?

B. Suppose that demand is given by $x(p) = 1{,}000 - 10p$ and is equal to marginal willingness to pay. Firms face identical marginal costs $c = 40$ and identical recurring fixed cost FC.

    a.   Suppose two Cournot oligopolists have merged. For what range of FC would you decide that there is no efficiency case for breaking up the merger?

    b.   Repeat (a) for the case of Stackelberg oligopolists.

    c.*   Repeat (a) for the case of Bertrand oligopolists.

    d.   It is often argued that antitrust policy is intended to maximize consumer welfare, not efficiency. Would your conclusions change if you cared only about consumer welfare and not efficiency?

25.11 Policy Application: *Subsidizing an Oligopoly*: It is common in many countries that governments subsidize the production of goods in certain large oligopolistic industries. Common examples include aircraft industries and car industries.

POLICY APPLICATION

  A. Suppose that a two-firm oligopoly faces a linear, downward-sloping demand curve, with each firm facing the same constant marginal cost and no recurring fixed cost.

    a.   If the intent of the subsidy is to get the industry to produce the efficient output level, what should be the subsidy for Bertrand competitors?

    b.*   How would your answer to (a) change if each firm faced a recurring fixed cost?

    c.   What happens (as a result of the subsidy) to best response functions for firms that are setting quantity (rather than price)? How does this impact the Cournot equilibrium?

    d.   How would you expect this to impact the Stackelberg equilibrium?

    e.   Suppose policy makers can either subsidize quantity-setting oligopoly firms in order to get them to produce the efficient quantity or invest in lowering barriers to entry into the industry so that the industry becomes competitive. Discuss how you would approach the trade-offs involved in choosing one policy over the other.

    f.   How would your answer be affected if you knew that it was difficult for the government to gather information on firm costs?

    g.   Suppose there are recurring fixed costs that are sufficiently high for only one firm to produce under quantity competition. Might the subsidy result in the entry of a second firm?

  B. Suppose demand is given by $x(p) = A - \alpha p$, that all firms face constant marginal cost c, and that there are no recurring fixed costs.

    a.   If the government introduces a per-unit subsidy $s < c$, what happens to the marginal costs for each firm?

    b.   How do the monopoly, Bertrand, Cournot, and Stackelberg equilibria change as a result of the subsidy?

    c.** Suppose $A = 1{,}000$, $c = 40$, and $s = 15$. What is the economic incidence of the subsidy in each economic environment; i.e., what fraction of the subsidy is passed on to consumers and what fraction is retained by producers?

    d.** How would your answer to (c) change if the government instead imposed a per-unit tax $t = 15$?

    e.   How much of a tax or subsidy has to be set in order to get the efficient level of output under each of the four market conditions?

    f.   Suppose you are advising the government on policy and you have two choices: Either you subsidize the firms in the oligopoly, or you lower the barriers to entry that keep the industry from being perfectly competitive. For each of the four market conditions, determine what cost you would be willing to have the government incur to make the industry competitive rather than subsidize it.

g.*   Suppose that pollution was produced in this industry, emitting a constant level of pollution per unit of output, with a cost of b per unit of output imposed on individuals outside the market. How large would b have to be under each of the market conditions in order for the outcome to be efficient (without any government intervention)?

25.12   Policy Application: *Government Grants and Cities as Cartels*: In exercise 19.6, we explored the idea of city wage taxes and noted that these were exceedingly rare and occurred primarily in very large cities. We explained this by noting that labor demand and supply are more wage elastic locally than they are nationally because firms and workers can move from one city to another more easily than they can move from one country to another. We then suggested that it would make sense for a mayor of a city (that wants to raise revenues by taxing wages) to ask the national government to increase wage taxes nationally and pass back the revenues to cities and other communities in the form of grants. Review the logic behind this. If cities persuaded the national government to do this, in what way are they overcoming a Prisoner's Dilemma? Have they found a way to successfully collude (in a way similar to cartels)?

Product Differentiation and Innovation in Markets

In all our discussions of different market structures, we have so far assumed that there is such a thing as "the market" for "the good" that is being discussed.[1] This has made markets appear to be quite *static* in the sense that something in the past has led up to the existence of certain markets for certain well-defined goods, but nothing is currently happening to change this. All that is happening is that different market structures satisfy existing consumer demand in one way or another, dividing total potential surplus between consumers, producers, and possibly deadweight loss. In this static world, firms are relegated to simply producing goods that someone else invented at some point, making sure to not waste any resources in the process while looking for some strategic pricing advantage from which to profit.

But the real world appears to be constantly changing, with firms attempting to "get an edge" by finding new and better technologies for production, by changing features of existing products and inventing new ones, and by changing the image of products through aggressive marketing and advertising. The real world does not have the *static* flavor of our models from the previous chapters; rather, it is *dynamic*, constantly changing and adapting to new circumstances. Firms often do not take "as given" that their choice is to produce or not produce some combination of existing goods; they try to differentiate what they do and innovate toward creating new markets in which they can meet consumer demand more effectively while also establishing just a bit of market power from which to profit. It is to this process of *product differentiation* and *innovation* that we now turn.[2]

From the outset, however, we should acknowledge that modeling "innovation" is not something that comes naturally in models that aim to characterize "equilibrium" behavior. As soon as we focus on the notion of an equilibrium in a typical model, we are in fact focused on describing a state of the world in which everyone is "doing the best they can given what everyone else is doing." Still, by introducing product differentiation *within* a market into our models, we can begin to talk about the incentives firms have to innovate and set themselves apart from the pack.

26A Differentiated Products and Innovation

In this section, we will proceed in several steps. We will first look at the implications of moving away from the assumption that oligopolists are producing identical products and instead assume that oligopoly firms produce differentiated products in an attempt to lessen price

---

[1]This chapter builds on Chapters 23 through 25 but no use of part B of Chapter 24 is made.
[2]The underlying structure of the material developed in this chapter follows in many ways the development of Chapter 7 in J. Tirole, *The Theory of Industrial Organization* (Cambridge MA: The MIT Press, 1992).

competition. We begin this in Section 26A.1 by considering how the stark Bertrand prediction of price equaling marginal cost under price competition changes when products are differentiated. We then introduce two ways of thinking about differentiated products within a market, one appropriate for thinking about oligopolists strategically choosing product characteristics (Section 26A.2) and the other appropriate for thinking about more competitive markets with product differentiation (Section 26A.3). These models will allow us to identify product differentiation not only as a means by which firms can soften price competition but also as a way in which consumer demand is met more effectively through differentiation and innovation. It will lead us to a model of *monopolistic competition*, which is a market structure in which each of many firms produces a somewhat differentiated product and thus has *some* market power (Section 26A.4). At the same time, we will see how this is compatible with the equilibrium result that such firms will in fact make zero expected profit when entering the market so long as there are fixed costs to entering. Monopolistic competition then represents a market structure in between oligopoly and perfect competition, a structure that permits relatively free entry and exit (almost as under perfect competition) while allowing firms to gain small monopolies through differentiation and innovation. This will permit us to discuss in some more detail the dynamic real-world story of innovation as one in which firms seek market power through finding new ways of satisfying consumer demand, and we will argue that it is often the case that the apparent deadweight loss from market power in such markets is outweighed by the generation of large amounts of additional surplus from innovation. Finally, we will conclude by discussing advertising and marketing as strategies firms use to differentiate products to gain market power (Section 26A.5).

26A.1 Differentiated Products in Oligopoly Markets

Remember that we had two different types of competition in which oligopolistic firms could engage when they made decisions simultaneously: *price* or Bertrand competition and *quantity* or Cournot competition. But Bertrand competition seemed kind of trivial when the two firms produced identical products (at constant *MC* and in the absence of fixed costs) because as soon as there were two firms in the oligopoly, this type of competition resulted in price being set equal to marginal cost. Put differently, it did not matter whether there were only two firms or many firms in the industry; as long as there were at least two firms, the oligopoly would price as if it was engaged in perfect competition. Under Cournot competition, on the other hand, firms in oligopolies produced equilibrium quantities that resulted in a price between that under monopoly and that under competition (with price converging to the competitive price as the number of firms in the oligopoly got large).

Given the much more realistic predictions of the Cournot model, one might wonder why we even talk about the Bertrand model. At the same time, the Bertrand model often seems more intuitive in terms of how it defines the strategic variables for firms in oligopolies. Do we really think that firms set quantities and then wait for prices to emerge magically once all the firms in the oligopoly have brought their goods to market, or do we think that, at least sometimes, firms advertise prices and then meet demand through production? I am writing this book on a Macintosh Power Book G4. When Macintosh unveiled this computer, it immediately advertised a price from which it did not deviate over the coming year. It then produced and shipped Power Book G4 computers as demand revealed itself in different parts of the country. Put differently, it did not produce a quantity just to sit back and wait for a price to "emerge"; it set the price the moment it unveiled the computer.

As we foreshadowed in Chapter 25, it turns out that the Bertrand model is not as silly in its predictions once we allow firms to differentiate their products (as Macintosh certainly does). And it is in part for this reason that the model continues to play a large role in economics, not because we take its initial prediction of price equal to *MC* all that seriously, but rather because we think it is intuitively more plausible in many settings that firms set prices for products while trying to differentiate them from the products of competitors.[3]

26A.1.1 Coke and Pepsi

Despite the fact that many of us cannot tell the difference between Coke and Pepsi in blind taste tests, most consumers have a preference for one over the other. In other words, most consumers do not view Coke and Pepsi as the same product, although most do consider them somewhat substitutable. One way to think of an oligopoly like the soft drink industry where differentiated products are produced is to then think of demand for Coke as dependent on both the price of Coke and the price of Pepsi, with demand for Coke rising as the price of Coke falls *and as the price of Pepsi rises*. We will shortly demonstrate how specifying demand in this way leads to Bertrand competition in which the prices charged by the oliogopolistic firms are above marginal cost.

The intuition for this is straightforward: If Coke and Pepsi were identical in the minds of all consumers, then everyone would always buy from the lower priced producer, which in turn drives prices down to *MC* as Bertrand predicted. But if some consumers prefer Coke to Pepsi when they are equally priced, Coke will not lose all of its market share if it charges a price above Pepsi's. In fact, it may well be the case that some consumer will purchase Coke at $p > MC$ even if Pepsi hands its soft drinks out for free. The fact that Coke and Pepsi are different in the eyes of consumers therefore implies that demand does not shift so radically as the price of Coke rises above the price of Pepsi, giving room for producers to raise price above *MC*.

This then has implications for what the best response functions under price competition look like when Coke and Pepsi are somewhat different products in the minds of consumers. In Graph 25.1, we illustrated such best response functions in the case where consumers do not perceive a difference in the two products, and we concluded that the only equilibrium is one in which both oligopolists set $p = MC$. If we put the price of Pepsi on the horizontal axis and the price of Coke on the vertical assuming that consumers *can* tell the difference between the two goods, however, Coke's best response to a price of 0 by Pepsi might still be to set a price above *MC*. Thus, Coke's best response function has a positive intercept, and it will have a positive slope given that any increase in the price of Pepsi will make it easier to increase the price of Coke and retain consumer demand. You can then easily see how the best price response functions for Coke and Pepsi can intersect at $p > MC$. If this is not yet entirely clear, it will become clearer once we discuss Graph 26.3.

True or False: Suppose that Coke knows that it has positive consumer demand if it sets $p = MC$. Then it must be the case that Coke will price above *MC*.

Exercise 26A.1

26A.1.2 Modeling Choice of Product Characteristics

In markets where producers engage in price competition but where they can differentiate their products, we therefore have a more complicated oligopoly setting because both price and product characteristics become strategic variables. During our discussion of Coke and Pepsi, we have not yet made this leap because we have simply taken it as given that Coke and Pepsi produce somewhat different products but have not yet thought about how they came to choose the product characteristics to begin with. To make our analysis of product characteristic choice in an environment of price competition more tractable, we will develop a new model to deal with this complication and will illustrate how product differentiation emerges within oligopolies as firms attempt to soften the harsh price competition envisioned by Bertrand.

---

[3]As we also mentioned in Chapter 25, the Bertrand model similarly produces more plausible predictions when it is placed in a repeated game setting or when it is combined with a choice of productive capacity prior to the announcement of a price.

We will begin with a setting in which products vary in terms of one characteristic that can take on a value on the interval from 0 to 1. Firms will choose where on this interval to locate their product, and thus how much to differentiate their products from one another. To keep the analysis as simple as possible, we will also assume that each consumer demands only one good in this market, and that consumers are characterized by an "ideal point" on the interval [0,1]. Thus, a consumer $n \in [0,1]$ is defined as a consumer whose ideal product has the characteristic n. If the consumer ends up consuming a product with characteristic $y \neq n$, we will then assume that the consumer incurs a cost in addition to the price he or she pays for the product, with that additional cost increasing the farther away n is from y. We will also assume that consumer ideal points are equally spread across the interval [0,1], or put differently, we will assume that consumer ideal points are *uniformly distributed* on the interval [0,1].

This type of model of product differentiation is called the *Hotelling model* and is useful in analyzing product differentiation for oligopolies with two firms.[4] Panel (a) of Graph 26.1 represents the set of possible product characteristics (as well as the set of possible ideal points for consumers) for this model. Panel (b) of Graph 26.1 then represents an alternative way of modeling product characteristics along a circle rather than a line.[5] This way of representing the possible product characteristics is more useful as we consider markets with more than two firms as well as markets in which firms can enter after paying a fixed entry cost. The basic idea, however, is similar to the Hotelling model in that product characteristics can fall anywhere along the circle, as can consumer ideal points, with a consumer n once again paying a cost (in addition to the price of the product) that increases as the distance along the circle between the characteristic of the good y and his or her ideal point n increases. Note that in panel (a) there are "better" and "worse" places to locate in the sense that more consumers are close to the firm at the center than at the extremes. In panel (b), on the other hand, no particular point on the circle is "better" or "worse" in this sense so long as consumer ideal points are distributed uniformly around the circle.

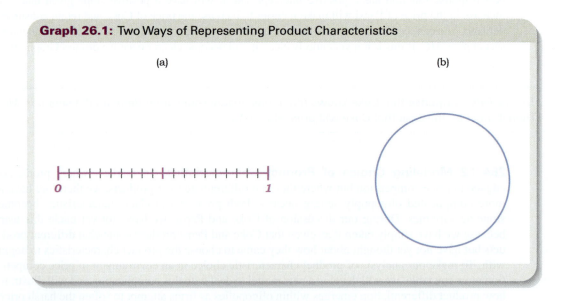

Graph 26.1: Two Ways of Representing Product Characteristics

[4]The model originated with Harold Hotelling (1895–1973), a mathematical statistician and economic theorist. Aside from his many academic contributions, Hotelling is also sometimes credited with persuading Ken Arrow, a future Nobel Laureate, to switch from math and statistics to economics.
[5]This model is due to Steven Salop, "Monopolistic Competition with Outside Goods," *Bell Journal of Economics* 10 (1979), 141–56.

**Exercise
26A.2**

We have said that under product differentiation we would expect the quantity of Coke that is demanded to be affected by both the price of Coke and the price of Pepsi. Can you see how the models of product differentiation result in firms facing precisely this kind of demand when they locate at different points in the product characteristics interval (or circle)?

We will begin our discussion in Section 26A.2 with an oligopoly that consists of two firms and with the product characteristics modeled as in panel (a) of Graph 26.1. In Section 26A.3 we then consider the model from panel (b) in the context of oligopolies that emerge when firms can choose whether to enter a market and produce differentiated goods. This will begin our discussion of entry into differentiated product markets that we then revisit in Section 26A.4 as markets characterized by monopolistic competition.

26A.2 The Hotelling Model of Oligopoly Product Differentiation

Suppose that there is a single characteristic of the good that can be differentiated, perhaps the sweetness of the soft drink, and suppose we think of this characteristic as ranging from 0 to 1 as in panel (a) of Graph 26.1. Suppose further that consumers have "ideal points" along that interval, with each consumer attempting to get a soft drink that is as close as possible to his or her ideal point. And suppose that consumer ideal points are uniformly distributed along the interval $[0,1]$ and that each consumer demands just one unit of the good. While this is not the most natural assumption in the soft drink market, the assumption becomes more natural in markets such as cars or computers in which most consumers in fact only purchase one unit at a time. We can then ask how much product differentiation we should expect by two firms that can each choose to produce a product that has a "sweetness characteristic" somewhere on that interval.

26A.2.1 Product Differentiation in the Absence of Price Competition   Suppose first that the soft drink industry is regulated and the two firms are required to charge some fixed price $p \geq MC$ and are therefore not permitted to engage in price competition. Put differently, suppose the only strategic variable is the product characteristic that can fall between 0 and 1 and that price is not a strategic variable at all. We can then derive each firm's best response to the other firm's product characteristic. If Coke sets its product characteristic y_1 below 0.5, Pepsi's best response is to choose a product characteristic $y_2 = y_1 + \epsilon$ where ϵ is small enough so that there exists no consumer with ideal point between y_1 and y_2. This way, Pepsi captures all consumers to the right of $y_1 < 0.5$, and since consumers are uniformly distributed along the interval $[0,1]$, this implies Pepsi gets more than half the market. The reverse is true if Coke sets $y_1 > 0.5$; Pepsi's best response is then to choose $y_2 = y_1 - \epsilon$ where ϵ is again small enough so that no consumer's ideal point falls between y_2 and y_1. Finally, suppose Coke sets $y_1 = 0.5$. Then, Pepsi would get less than half the market if it set y_2 below or above y_1, which means that, as long as we can assume that the two firms will split the market equally when $y_1 = y_2$, Pepsi's best response to $y_1 = 0.5$ is to set $y_2 = 0.5$.

   Graph 26.2a then plots this best response function for firm 2 (Pepsi), with $y_2 = y_1 + \epsilon < 0.5$ if $y_1 < 0.5$, $y_2 = y_1 - \epsilon > 0.5$ if $y_1 > 0.5$ and $y_2 = y_1 = 0.5$ if $y_1 = 0.5$. Coke's best response to Pepsi's choice of y_2 is similarly derived and plotted in blue in panel (b) of the graph (with Pepsi's best response in magenta). The two best response functions intersect at 0.5, implying a unique Nash equilibrium in which both firms set their product characteristic to exactly 0.5. Put differently, *in the absence of price competition, the model predicts that there will be no product differentiation.*

Graph 26.2: Best Response Product Differentiation without Price Competition

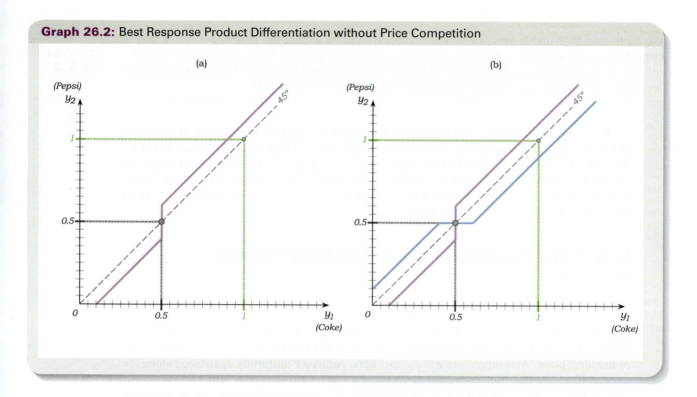

········○········
Exercise
26A.3
········○········

Would the equilibrium outcome be different if one firm announced its product characteristic prior to the other one having to do so?

26A.2.2 The Impact of Product Differentiation on (Bertrand) Price Competition

Now suppose that instead the firms have chosen extreme product differentiation, with firm 1 locating at $y_1 = 0$ and firm 2 at $y_2 = 1$. We can then ask what impact this will have on the nature of Bertrand price competition between the two firms.

We can do this again by thinking about what the best response functions for each firm will be to actions taken by the other firm. Unlike in the previous section where price was fixed and product characteristics were the strategic variables, we now have a situation where product characteristics are fixed (with $y_1 = 0$ and $y_2 = 1$) and prices become the strategic variables. Thus, we begin in panel (a) of Graph 26.3 by plotting firm 1's price on the horizontal axis and firm 2's price on the vertical. We then ask what the best price response for firm 2 might be for different prices chosen by firm 1.

Suppose that firm 1 sets its price to 0. Then it might well be the case that there are still consumers whose ideal point lies close to 1 and who would prefer to purchase from firm 2 at a price above *MC* rather than get a good with "worse" characteristics from firm 1 for free. Assuming consumer preferences distinguish sufficiently between the two product characteristics, firm 2's best price response to $p_1 = 0$ might therefore have an intercept as shown in panel (a). Furthermore, as firm 1 increases its price, firm 2 will be able to also increase its price and retain consumers. Thus, firm 2's best response function must have a positive slope.

········○········
Exercise
26A.4
········○········

Suppose the demand for firm 2's output is zero for any p_2 at or above *MC* when firm 1 sets price p_1 to zero. Furthermore, suppose that demand for firm 2's output becomes positive at $p_2 = MC$ when firm 1 sets a price $\overline{p}$ that lies between 0 and *MC*. What would firm 2's best response function look like?

Graph 26.3: Best Response Prices with Extreme Product Differentiation

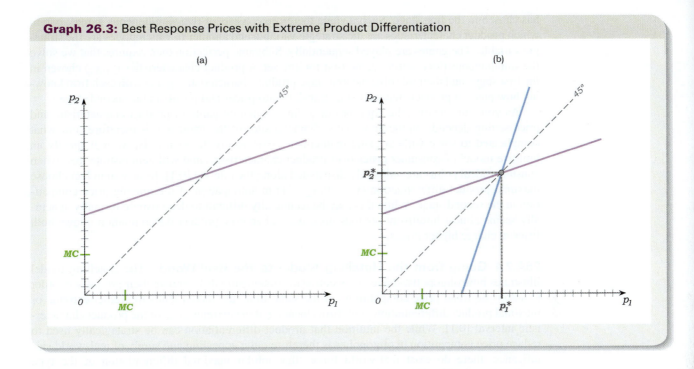

The problem is symmetric for firm 1, and its best response function is then plotted in blue in panel (b) of the graph. In equilibrium, each firm's price must be a best response to the other firm's price, which occurs when the blue and magenta best response functions intersect. Again, because of the symmetry of the two firms, that intersection must lie on the 45-degree line, with both firms in equilibrium charging equal prices for their differentiated goods. But these prices now lie above MC; i.e., above the prices predicted by the Bertrand price competition model when products are not differentiated.

Consider the case described in exercise 26A.4 and assume the two firms are symmetric relative to one another. Will it still be the case that $p > MC$? Can you see how decreasing product differentiation in the minds of consumers will lead to a result that approaches $p = MC$? (*Hint*: As $\bar{p}$ gets closer to MC, product differentiation diminishes.)

Exercise 26A.5

We have therefore demonstrated that, under maximal product differentiation, firm profits will be higher than under no product differentiation, thus giving firms an incentive to differentiate their products from one another when they are engaged in price competition. In Graph 26.2, on the other hand, we illustrated that there is no incentive to differentiate products in the absence of price competition. The incentive for product differentiation therefore arises directly from price competition *because strategic product differentiation allows the oligopoly firms to soften the price competition they face.*

26A.2.3 Choosing Product Characteristics *and* Prices Strategically
We have not, at this point, analyzed the full game that oligopolistic firms in the Hotelling model face. A reasonable way of specifying such a game is in two stages: In the first stage firms choose product characteristics, and in the second stage they set prices knowing the product characteristics that each

has chosen in the first stage. Such a game therefore consists of two simultaneous games, one in which product characteristics are the strategic variable and another in which prices are the strategic variable. The games are played sequentially. Subgame perfection then requires that we solve the simultaneous price setting game first for any set of product characteristics (y_1, y_2) chosen in the first stage, and then we solve the first stage product characteristics game with each firm knowing how pairs of product characteristics translate into prices and profits in the second stage.

As you can imagine, the equilibrium of this sequential game of product characteristic and price setting depends on the underlying characteristics of the game and is therefore somewhat complicated to solve without using mathematics extensively. In Section B, we will specify an intuitive model of consumer tastes over product characteristics and will demonstrate that, when consumer ideal points are uniformly distributed along the interval [0,1], firms will in fact choose maximal product differentiation $(y_1 = 0, y_2 = 1)$ in anticipation of minimizing price competition in the second stage. While this may be technically difficult to demonstrate formally, it actually seems almost intuitively obvious once we realize how product differentiation allows both firms to charge higher prices.

26A.2.4 Going from the Hotelling Model to the Real World

The Hotelling model illustrates how oligopolists have an incentive to strategically differentiate their products in order to soften Bertrand price competition. At the same time, the model tends to predict extreme or maximal product differentiation, with firms locating at the extreme ends of the product characteristic interval [0,1]. While the intuition that product differentiation can be strategically used to reduce price competition in oligopolies is therefore quite appealing and surely of real-world significance, there do exist real-world forces that inhibit maximal differentiation of the type predicted by the Hotelling model. First, we already illustrated that the incentive for product differentiation disappears when price competition is eliminated. If, for instance, prices within oligopolies are regulated by governments, firms have no incentive to engage in product differentiation. This has been true in the past in certain heavily regulated industries such as the airline industry prior to deregulation in the 1970s. A potential cost from government attempts to regulate prices within oligopolies is therefore the loss of product differentiation within the regulated industry, a cost that becomes more severe the more diverse consumer tastes are. A related cost of price regulation is a decreased incentive on the part of oligopolists to innovate further in order to achieve even greater product differentiation.

Second, the Hotelling model assumes that consumer tastes (or ideal points) are uniformly distributed along the product characteristic interval. Often, however, it might be much more reasonable to assume that consumer tastes are clustered around the middle of that interval, with most consumers having "in between" ideal points and fewer consumers having more extreme tastes. Introducing such distributions of consumer tastes into the Hotelling model then introduces a force against extreme product differentiation because, while firms want to soften price competition through differentiation, they also would like to locate their product characteristics where there is relatively more demand. As a result, one can construct Hotelling models in which strategic product differentiation is balanced against clustering of demand on particular product characteristics, with firms still differentiating their products (i.e., $y_1 < y_2$) but doing so in a less extreme way than we might otherwise predict (i.e., $0 < y_1$ and $y_2 < 1$).

Third, when we think of product differentiation as spatial differentiation in terms of where firms physically locate within, say, a city, it may be that firms gain other benefits from being near one another. For instance, in some markets consumers might have to invest a great deal of time searching over the different goods that are offered and thus are more likely to shop in places where multiple firms have settled. A firm might therefore gain a sufficient advantage from locating near another firm because of increased consumer demand from such clustering to outweigh the hardening of price competition that such a location entails. (You may have noticed, for instance, that car dealerships tend to cluster near one another.) Or there may be other externalities between firms that foster clustering. When high-tech firms locate near one another, for instance, they may have access to a more qualified pool of workers who in turn share important information that helps the individual firms. (The most obvious U.S. example of this is Silicon Valley in California.)

26A.3 Entry into Differentiated Product Markets

As we mentioned before, the Hotelling model is useful for thinking about product differentiation in oligopolies with two firms, and it helps illustrate the incentive to differentiate products in order to avoid the intense price competition of the simple Bertrand model. The model becomes less useful as we think about competition between more than two firms and as we think about how the number of firms in an oligopoly arises when product differentiation is possible. We therefore now turn to the second model of product differentiation that we introduced in panel (b) of Graph 26.1, a model in which product characteristics lie on a circle that we can normalize to have circumference of 1.

Suppose that firms can enter this market by paying a fixed set-up cost FC and that, once they have paid this cost, they face a constant marginal cost of production. The existence of a fixed cost is then the only "barrier to entry," and firms will enter this market so long as profit once in the market is sufficient to cover the fixed set-up cost. Once again, we will assume that consumer ideal points are equally (or "uniformly") distributed around the circle that represents different product characteristics. And we again assume that consumers pay (in addition to the price they are charged for a product) a cost that increases with the distance between their ideal point and the actual product characteristic y that is produced by the firm from which the consumers purchase. Thus, a consumer with ideal point n on the circle will purchase from the firm whose product characteristic y lies closest to n (assuming all firms charge equal prices).

We can then consider the following two-stage (sequential) game, which involves two sequentially played simultaneous games. In stage 1, a large number of potential firms decide whether to pay the fixed cost FC to enter this market, and in stage 2 the firms that chose to enter in stage 1 strategically choose an output price knowing where on the circle they as well as all their competitors have located their product characteristic. Since this is a sequential game, subgame perfection requires that we solve the game beginning in Stage 2 by determining what prices the firms will charge given the outcome of stage 1. We then proceed to stage 1, with firms choosing whether to enter the market knowing what prices will emerge in stage 2 for different entry decisions. Since all the firms are identical prior to making their product characteristic choice, it is reasonable to assume that, in any equilibrium, those firms that enter in stage 1 will choose to locate their product characteristics at equal distances from one another along the circle that represents all possible product characteristics. We will therefore operate under this assumption as we begin by thinking about price setting in stage 2.

26A.3.1 Stage 2: Strategic Price Setting
Suppose N firms entered in the first stage and are now located at equal distances from one another along the product characteristic circle. The second stage of the game therefore begins with an oligopoly that has N firms producing differentiated products as they engage in Bertrand price competition. We already know from our work on the Hotelling model that such product differentiation softens price competition, and that the equilibrium price that emerges under Bertrand competition will lie above MC when firms produce differentiated products.

Since the N firms all face the same constant MC and are located at equal distances from one another, in equilibrium we should expect them to end up choosing the same price. Each firm's best price response function to the price charged by all other firms will in fact be identical to every other firm's best price response function. We will formally derive these in Section B, but the prediction that emerges from the formal analyses is straightforward and intuitive: For a given number of equally spaced firms N, each firm will choose the same price $p^*(N)$ in the Bertrand equilibrium, with $p^*(N) > MC$ so long as N is finite. Furthermore, the larger the number of firms that entered in stage 1, the closer $p^*(N)$ will get to MC, with price converging to MC as the number of firms becomes large and product differentiation between neighboring firms diminishes.

Exercise
26A.6
If there is no first stage entry decision and the number of firms is simply fixed as in an oligopoly with barriers to entry, can you see how this represents the full equilibrium of the game?

This conforms precisely to our intuition from the Hotelling model: The greater the product differentiation between any two adjacent firms, the more this will soften Bertrand price competition. As the number of firms that enter in the first stage increases, firms will necessarily be closer to one another on the product characteristic circle. And while N can be large, in equilibrium each firm actually only faces two competitors: those adjacent to the firm on both sides of the product characteristic circle. When these competitors are nearer to one another (as N increases), the relevant competitors are producing products more similar to one another, with the firms therefore facing greater price competition due to less product differentiation with their direct competitors. This greater price competition then results in lower prices.

26A.3.1 Stage 1: The Entry Decision

The number of firms, however, is only fixed in the second stage because it emerges from the entry decisions of potential firms in the first stage. We thought about the price-setting stage among a fixed number of firms first only because subgame perfection requires that firms contemplate their entry decision without taking seriously noncredible threats by other firms about prices they might charge in the second stage. Entry decisions are therefore made with credible expectations about prices that will emerge under price competition once firms have committed to entering by paying the fixed entry cost FC.

Since we are assuming that this fixed entry cost is the only barrier to entry, it must be the case that, in equilibrium, firms enter so long as expected profits (given credible equilibrium pricing expectations) once a firm has entered are at least as high as the fixed entry cost. The equilibrium number of firms N^* that then emerges in stage 1 is a number sufficient to drive the profit from entering (which includes fixed entry costs) to zero. More precisely, the equilibrium number will stop just short of the number of firms that would make the profit from entering negative.

Exercise
26A.7
In the context of this model, why is the last sentence slightly more correct than the second to last sentence in the previous paragraph?

It is therefore the case that the higher the fixed entry cost, the smaller will be the equilibrium number of firms, and the smaller the equilibrium number of firms going into stage 2, the higher will be the price charged by firms that enter. On the other hand, lower fixed entry costs imply more firms will enter in stage 1, which in turn implies prices will be lower, and as fixed costs fall to zero, the number of firms becomes large and price converges to MC as one would expect in a model of perfect competition (with no barriers to entry).

Exercise
26A.8
True or False: As long as the fixed entry cost $FC > 0$, firms in the industry will make positive profits while firms outside the industry would make negative profits by entering the industry.

The "circle model" of product differentiation then allows us to fully fill in the gap between perfect competition and monopoly through the use of industry fixed entry costs. For very high fixed costs, we only have a single firm entering; i.e., we have a monopoly. As fixed costs fall, we may still only have one firm, but it will begin to lower its price as it engages in strategic entry deterrence (as covered in Chapter 25). At some point, fixed entry costs fall sufficiently for strategic entry deterrence to no longer be worthwhile, and a second firm enters (on the opposite side of the circle). We now have a Bertrand model with differentiated products, with each firm using price as its strategic variable and each firm setting price above MC as illustrated first in Graph 26.3. And, as fixed entry costs fall further, we get increasing numbers of firms with market power declining, until fixed entry costs disappear entirely and we have a perfectly competitive industry with no barriers to entry.

True or False: While we needed a model of product differentiation to allow for Bertrand competition to be able to fully fill the gap between perfect competition and monopoly, we do not need anything in addition to what we introduced in Chapter 25 to do the same for Cournot competition.

Exercise 26A.9

26A.4 Monopolistic Competition and Innovation

In our discussion of firm entry followed by price competition in a market characterized by product differentiation (along a circle of possible product characteristics), we have seen the emergence of a possible market structure in which firms have some market power (which allows them to set $p > MC$) but new firms cannot enter and earn positive profits. Existing firms for which the fixed entry cost has become a sunk cost make positive profits from pricing above MC, but potential entrants for which fixed entry costs are still real economic costs would make negative profits if they chose to enter. The simultaneous existence of positive economic profits for firms and a lack of entry of new firms is therefore quite plausible in the presence of fixed entry costs.

This idea is one that predates game theoretic models of product differentiation.[6] In the absence of game theory, however, economists thought about the issue a bit differently and in ways that link nicely to our previous discussion of monopoly. Their model of *monopolistic competition* also allows us to tell a story of dynamic innovation even if it does not itself capture this directly.

26A.4.1 Fixed Costs and Average Cost Pricing Suppose a firm i is one of many that produces in a market in which each producer is producing a slightly different output. Think, for example, of your most recent trip down the supermarket isle that contains breakfast cereals or shampoos or toilet paper. You probably noticed a large number of different cereals or shampoos or toilet paper varieties, each differing from the other a bit. Or think of restaurants in larger cities, each providing a menu a bit different from the others. Many consumers have tastes that distinguish between these goods, which gives rise to downward-sloping demand curves for each of the types of goods that is produced despite the fact that they are close substitutes. As we discussed at the beginning of our treatment of monopoly, the degree of market power that an individual firm in such a market has is then dependent on the price elasticity of demand of its demand curve.

We can illustrate firm i's output and pricing decision (assuming no price discrimination) exactly as we did at the beginning of our discussion of monopoly because each firm in such a market has some monopoly power since it faces a downward-sloping demand curve. This is done in panel (a) of Graph 26.4 where D^i represents firm i's demand curve and MR^i is the marginal revenue curve derived from D^i. When profit is defined as the difference between total revenues and variable costs, it can be seen in panel (a) as the shaded area.

Where in panel (a) of Graph 26.4 is the firm's total revenue given that it charges p^i? Where is its variable cost given that it produces x^i?

Exercise 26A.10

---

[6]The idea is credited to the American economist Edward Chamberlin (1899–1967) and the British economist Joan Robinson (1903–1983) who simultaneously (and independently) worked on the topic. Their work in many ways gave rise to the economics of imperfect competition. Robinson's contributions to economics extended far beyond the topic of imperfect competition, and many believe she deserved to win the Nobel Prize for her accomplishments. Had she done so, she would have been the only woman to receive the prize until the 2009 Nobel Prize was awarded as this book goes to press. The 2009 prize was shared between Oliver Willimson and Elinor Olmsrtom (who is actually a political scientist.) Given the quick rise of prominent women economists in academic institutions around the world, this will no doubt be the first of many Nobel prizes awarded to women in the profession over the coming years.

Graph 26.4: Zero Profit for a Monopoly that Sets $p = AC$

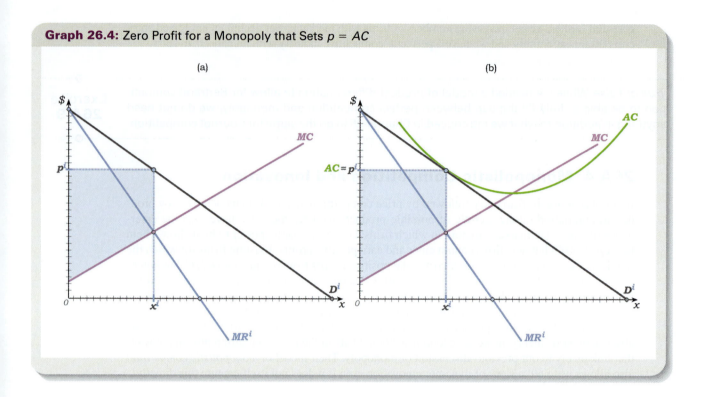

In monopolistically competitive markets, however, firms enter so long as the profit *from entering* is positive and stops when profit from entering becomes zero. Thus, in order for firm i to operate in equilibrium, it must be that its profit as depicted in panel (a) is exactly offset by the fixed entry cost faced by potential entrants. This is because, just as in our "circle model," such fixed costs are in fact real economic costs for entrants and thus figure into the calculation of the expected profit *from entering* the market for those who currently are outside the market. Put differently, for potential entrants, the relevant definition of profit is total revenue minus variable costs *minus fixed costs*, and in equilibrium it must be that this profit is equal to zero. But that simply means that, in equilibrium, it must be that the total revenue minus variable costs is equal to fixed entry costs.

In panel (b) of the graph, we illustrate the one circumstance under which this is true. The graph is identical to that in panel (a) in every way except that we have now added the marginally entering firm's average total cost curve (which includes variable and fixed costs) as AC. When this curve is tangent to D^i at p^i, the *total* cost (including fixed entry costs) is exactly equal to the revenue the firm makes when it enters. You can see this by simply recognizing that total cost is average cost times output, $AC \times x^i$, while total revenue is price times output, $p^i \times x^i$. Since $p^i = AC$ when the average cost curve is tangent to D^i at p^i, revenue is equal to total cost. Put differently, with the average cost curve as represented in panel (b), the fixed entry cost is exactly equal to the shaded area in panels (a) and (b).

Exercise 26A.11

True or False: With economic profit appropriately defined for each firm, the profit of firms in the industry is positive while the profit of a firm outside the industry would be zero or negative if it entered the monopolistically competitive market in equilibrium.

26A.4.2 A "Story" of Innovation in Monopolistically Competitive Markets
On my way home yesterday, I listened to the radio and heard a story of an innovation in the egg market. That market already has some product differentiation, with some producers selling only brown eggs, some selling larger eggs, some selling eggs from farm raised chickens, some selling eggs from chickens fed with only organically grown grain, etc. The new innovation I heard about on the radio, however, is really neat: It involves a treatment of eggs such that the egg itself tells you (as you boil it) when it is a perfectly soft-boiled egg (with the yolks soft and the whites solid) and when it has turned into a perfectly hard-boiled egg. (This is similar to an innovation from some years past in the turkey market where some turkeys now have a "pop-up" thermometer that tells you when the turkey is done.)[7] My wife won't care about this innovation at all; she only eats scrambled and fried eggs and mainly cares about whether the chickens from which the eggs came were treated humanely. I, on the other hand, was raised in Austria on soft-boiled eggs but I hate it if the egg is too soft (with the whites still runny) or too hard (with the yolks partially hardened). So I am pretty excited about this new innovation. Who knows—if the radio story was really true, perhaps I am already buying these new types of eggs once this book finds its way into your hands and you are reading it. If so, I am a happy man.

Because of people like me, whoever ends up producing these self-timing eggs will have carved out a new market niche and will have some monopoly power in that niche. Since the producer is, at least at first, the only one serving this niche, he or she will probably be able to more than recoup the fixed cost of having invented the process of producing these self-timing eggs and therefore will enjoy a positive profit from entering the market. Put differently, the producer's AC curve probably falls below p^i at x^i as pictured in panel (a) of Graph 26.5.

But, given that there is free entry in monopolistic markets (aside from the fact that entrants have to pay a fixed entry cost), it cannot be that this is where the story ends. Perhaps the self-timing egg company is protected in the short run from competitors because the firm obtained a patent that keeps others from imitating the product, and perhaps this slows down the process by which new

Graph 26.5: A New Product Enters the Market

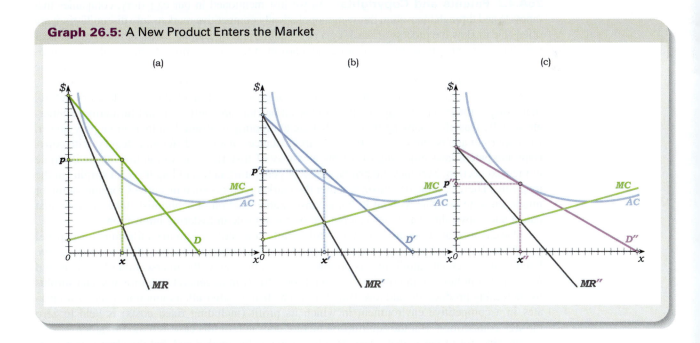

firms will challenge the self-timing egg company. But if this egg really works the way they said on the radio, I bet other potential firms that smell profit in the air will find other production processes that will achieve similar products or will perhaps innovate in ways that I haven't thought of. (After all, I would have never thought of the self-timing egg either before hearing about it on the radio.)

What will change for the self-timing egg firm as other firms find ways of challenging it? The firm's costs are what they are (in the absence of other innovations), so the cost curves probably won't move. What will change, however, is the demand faced by the firm when new entrants will chip away at demand as they produce competing products. In particular, it would be reasonable to assume that both the intercept and the slope of D in panel (a) of Graph 26.5 will change, with the intercept falling (as even the most enthusiastic consumers are willing to pay less for the self-timing egg) and the slope becoming shallower (as all consumers become more price sensitive). This process should continue as long as the profit from entering is greater than zero and should stop when the profit from entering becomes zero.

In panel (b) of Graph 26.5, the "chipping away" at the self-timing egg company's market power has begun as demand has changed to D' resulting in a lower price p' and a lower per-unit profit (where profit is defined to include fixed costs). In panel (c), the process has run its course, with D'' now tangent to AC at the profit-maximizing quantity x'' and with per-unit profit (where profit is defined to include fixed costs) reaching zero. The innovation of the self-timing egg therefore introduced disequilibrium into the monopolistically competitive egg market in panel (a) by generating the opportunity for new firms to make positive profit from entering (or for existing firms changing their egg production to take advantage of additional profit opportunities). The transition to panel (c) through panel (b) then represents the process by which equilibrium in the monopolistically competitive egg market reemerges, ending in a market in which existing firms make positive profits (that don't count fixed, or sunk, costs) but potential entrants cannot make positive profits from entering (in the absence of new innovations).

26A.4.3 Patents and Copyrights

As we just mentioned in our egg story, companies that innovate and through innovation throw monopolistically competitive markets into disequilibrium are often able to slow the process of reaching a new equilibrium by gaining patent or copyright protection that keeps other firms from imitating the innovation for some period of time. And, as we mentioned in our chapter on monopoly, such government-granted patents and copyrights represent one way in which governments erect temporary barriers to entry that establish temporary monopolies.

I have expressed skepticism about the value of government-erected barriers to entry before, indicating in the previous chapters that often such barriers are inefficient and furthermore generate socially wasteful lobbying by firms that are attempting to strengthen their monopoly power. But copyright and patent laws are in many circumstances in a very different category, with copyright and patent laws emerging over time as a way of fostering innovation that, as I will argue in the next section, becomes the primary way of generating new and larger social surplus in the long run. (There is some debate on whether the market requires such incentives for innovation or might innovate just fine without it, but a considerable fraction of economists take the view that patent and copyright protections can play in important role in fostering innovation.)

One can look at our picture of a monopolistically competitive firm in equilibrium (as in panel (b) of Graph 26.4 and panel (c) of Graph 26.5), however, and come to a very different conclusion. Each firm in such an equilibrium is producing a quantity below the intersection of demand and MC, which implies that in principle we could force the firm to generate additional social surplus by increasing production (and lowering price). The firm is, after all, a monopoly even as it operates in a competitive environment in which its profit (including fixed costs) is held to zero through competition. But the equilibrium picture does not, in this case, tell the full story.

Imagine, for instance, that a new drug has come on the market and that this drug is considerably more effective than existing drugs at treating a particular disease for some patients. By granting the pharmaceutical company a patent on this drug, we are granting it some monopoly power, and this will result in a level of production that looks suboptimal in our graphs. The temptation is great, then, to tell the firm it has to lower price and increase output in order to treat more patients whose benefits from using the drug outweigh the marginal cost of producing it. But if we do this, we are lowering the incentive for firms to engage in innovations that lead to new and better drugs because such firms would reasonably expect that they will similarly be forced into lower profits than they can obtain under patent protection. As a result, patent and copyright laws attempt to strike a balance between (1) providing an incentive for new innovations through the establishment of monopoly power for n years and (2) the "underproduction" that takes place during those n years (in the absence of other innovations that supercede the initial innovation). Increasing n provides greater incentives for innovations but also increases the period of time during which too little of the good is produced. As a result, there must exist some n between zero (where no patent is granted) and infinity (where the patent protection lasts forever) that makes the trade-off in an optimal way. Some recent work on patents and innovation suggests that the patent laws that have evolved over time do a pretty good job of striking the right balance by setting n in the range of 14 to 20 years in most cases in the United States. Not everyone, however, agrees, with some proposing that n could be set much closer to zero without any appreciable decline in product innovation.

Many of the advocates for lowering n in patent laws draw on the burst of innovation in open source software communities. Can you see why?

Exercise 26A.12

26A.4.4 Innovation in Real-World Markets

As we have mentioned before in this book, the concept of "equilibrium" is useful in the sense that it gives us a benchmark toward which the market is striving in the absence of new changes, just as the concept of "equilibrium" in meteorology is useful in the sense that it gives us a benchmark toward which current weather patterns are striving in the absence of new weather disturbances. At the same time, we know that weather never actually reaches a stable equilibrium from which it no longer deviates because it is subject to new variables constantly entering the mix. And so it is in many of the most interesting real-world markets in which innovation plays an important role.

I used the egg market to tell my story just because I am currently enamored by the possibility that the radio story is true and I will actually be able to have a self-timing egg produce the perfect soft-boiled egg at breakfast from now on. But think of some of the most interesting markets that are currently subject to major innovations. The software industry, for instance, is made up of many producers who are constantly attempting to gain an edge in an intensely competitive environment by producing the next software package that will bring just a bit more market power. New firms come out with new software that chips away at demand for existing software, and existing firms find new innovations to their products that chip away at the demand for products produced by competitors. In terms of our model, these firms are constantly engaged in ways of trying to get their demand curves to have higher intercepts and steeper slopes to get more market power, but competitors and new firms are doing the same thing. The software market is not in a static equilibrium in which an existing set of firms produce an existing set of products, with potential new firms unable to make positive profits from entering. Rather, the market is, from a static perspective, in disequilibrium as new innovations move demand curves for each firm's products and some firms gain temporary market power while others are left behind. Successful firms in this dynamic environment are those that keep innovating and thus keep finding better ways of meeting consumer demand (or lower cost ways of producing existing products).

There are, to be sure, markets that are considerably more mature and stable, markets in which the likely gains from innovation are small and which therefore have settled into a state that resembles our static equilibrium models much more. Some of these are perfectly competitive, with each firm producing essentially the same product and pricing at MC as our perfectly competitive model predicts. Low fat milk is, after all, just low fat milk, and most of us cannot tell the difference between different 2% low fat milk regardless of which company produces it.[8] Other markets are monopolistically competitive with little new innovation to disturb the static equilibrium. Cereal comes in many different forms and shapes, with limited prospect for innovation disturbing the equilibrium, at least to the extent to which parents can keep children from thinking that a picture of "Dora the Explorer" or "Barney" on the cereal box makes for a truly different product worthy of special attention. Yet other markets might be more appropriately characterized as relatively stable oligopolies with high fixed entry costs and some product differentiation. Only a handful of companies are producing cars, and these differ in the features they offer consumers. Innovation does take place, and sometimes these innovations (such as the invention of the minivan) are quite dramatic and might truly disturb the static equilibrium our models predict. But other times the innovations are, perhaps, sufficiently minor to allow us to continue to think of the industry as being in a roughly stable equilibrium.

All markets, as we have seen, add to human welfare (at least as economists think of welfare) by producing social surplus—sometimes at efficient levels and other times not—for consumers, workers, and owners of firms. Mature markets that have reached a state that can be approximated by our static equilibrium models do so in a way in which a constant amount of surplus is produced. Markets that are characterized by innovations, however, add *additional* surplus through the creation of new products that change the way we live. I remember well the fascination with which I watched *Good Morning America* in the mid-1980s when Luciano Pavarotti came on to show off a new way of listening to music on compact discs (rather than cassettes that degrade or LPs that can easily be scratched or 8-tracks that seemed just plain silly). But now I have converted all my CDs to digital format and carry thousands of songs on my iPod. Because of innovation, we can now carry more high-quality music in our pockets than people used to be able to listen to in a lifetime. The same iPod contains thousands of pictures and home movies I have taken of my children, all of which I watch frequently in near-perfect contentment as I listen to Luciano Pavarotti. The world has truly changed since I watched *Good Morning America* in the mid-1980s.

And of course this little personal story only scratches the surface. New medical innovations are extending our life while improving our quality of life; new ways of transporting goods allow me to experience aspects of the world I could previously only experience through costly travelling; the Internet is creating constantly new ways of accessing information previously contained only in distant libraries. Even this book, as I think about it, would simply have been impossible for me to write without the multitude of innovations that led to my nifty Macintosh PowerBook that allows me to write as I sit on a bench in the beautiful gardens outside my office. Just a decade or two ago, not a single supercomputer in the world could do as much as this little laptop.

The point here is not to be overly dramatic but to illustrate the powerful force that innovation represents in the real world, and to further point out that our equilibrium models of different market structures suffer from not really being able to capture this innovative process very well. We are good at finding ways of representing stable equilibria that have emerged in mature industries with low marginal gains from innovation, but we need to think beyond the static models to understand less mature industries with large marginal gains from innovation. Well-managed firms in mature industries maintain surplus generated by previous innovations, but innovative entrepreneurial firms generate new ways of producing surplus, both now and in the future. Put differently, in many ways the disequilibrium generated from innovation is the engine of growth and provides a topic for an entire class on innovation and economic growth that you might want to take.

26A.5 Advertising and Marketing

So far, we have always assumed that consumers are aware of the types of goods offered in the market and the prices that firms are charging for those goods. We have also assumed that consumers understand how they themselves feel about the physical characteristics of goods that they

---

[8]Even this is not entirely correct, as some producers of milk are differentiating their product as, for instance, "organic."

consider consuming. When these assumptions are violated, firms have reason to think about not only producing goods but also engaging in advertising and marketing.

We can then distinguish between two views of advertising, which we will call *informational advertising* and *image marketing*. The informational advertising view emerges from the economist's typical assumption that consumers are "rational" (as we defined the term in our discussion of consumer preferences) but may lack information. The image marketing view, on the other hand, finds its roots more in psychology where consumer rationality is called into question and the possibility of firms manipulating the "irrational" aspect of consumers by altering the "image" of the product (rather than what we might call the product itself) becomes a real possibility. Drawing this distinction of views as one arising from the economist's and the other arising from the psychologist's perspective is not to say that there are not economists who in fact take the psychology view of advertising. Famous and highly regarded economists such as Paul Samuelson (1915–), one of the first winners of the Nobel Prize in Economics, and John Kenneth Galbraith (1908–2006), one of the most influential economists and public intellectuals of the 20th century, have in fact taken the latter view. I suspect it is similarly true that there exist psychologists who place emphasis on the former view. But we can nevertheless say that the informational advertising view comes from the consumer rationality assumption, which tends to be emphasized by economists, and the image marketing view comes from the consumer irrationality assumption, which tends to be emphasized by psychologists. And it is the image marketing view of advertising that fits well into this chapter because it views advertising as a way for firms to create "artificial" product differentiation when the products themselves are really not all that different. We will briefly discuss this view after saying a bit more about informational advertising.

26A.5.1 Informational Advertising

Suppose that consumers in fact are "rational" in the sense that they have complete and transitive preferences over differentiated goods, but suppose that consumers do not have perfect information about the prices and the types of goods that are offered by firms. Without introducing a formal model, we can easily see how advertising under these assumptions might in fact play a socially useful purpose. In the absence of such advertising, firms enjoy protection from competition to the extent to which some consumers are unaware of the existence of competitors or the prices charged by competitors. If advertising is prohibited (as it is, at least to some extent, for goods like cigarettes and hard liquor in the United States), the market is less competitive than it could be and thus leaves firms with more market power than they otherwise would have. Such market power, as we have seen, can result in deadweight losses as firms restrict output to raise price.

When advertising is permitted in such markets, individual firms have an incentive to advertise because, regardless of what other firms do, my firm will gain more customers if I make sure more consumers know about my products and prices. But if each firm individually has an incentive to engage in informative advertising, all firms will do so and, in the end, we will again split the market in roughly the same proportion we did in the absence of advertising, only now we face more competition because consumers are more aware of competitors' products. Of course, the advertising itself is costly and therefore gets incorporated into prices, but it is quite conceivable in many circumstances that the upward pressure on prices from increased costs will be outweighed by the downward pressure from increased competition. *Informational advertising of this kind can therefore, at least in principle, generate additional social surplus.* Formal models have confirmed this, with some in fact predicting that the equilibrium amount of advertising in such settings is socially optimal (as we will see in a special case discussed in Section B).

Consider an oligopoly with consumers being only partially aware of each firm's products and prices, and suppose that firms in the oligopoly decide to engage in informational advertising. In what sense might they be facing a Prisoner's Dilemma?

Exercise 26A.13

Exercise 26A.14

Suppose that you hear that an industry group is attempting to persuade the government to ban advertising in its industry. Given your answer to exercise 26A.13, might you be suspicious of the industry group's motives?

26A.5.2 Image Marketing: Advertising as a Means to Manipulate Preferences

Now suppose that advertising is not used to convey information but rather to manipulate preferences by shaping the image of what we consider the real underlying product. While we have just seen that informational advertising can increase competition in markets that are not perfectly competitive, the alternative of "image marketing" can do the reverse: restrain competition in markets that are quite competitive. For this reason, those who believe this is the correct view of advertising generally believe it is socially wasteful.

The logic behind their argument is straightforward: Suppose firms in a particular industry face intense competition. Perhaps the industry is perfectly competitive, or perhaps it consists of only two firms that are engaged in fierce Bertrand price competition with undifferentiated products. Each firm in such settings has an incentive, as we have seen in this chapter, to "set its goods apart" from the crowd through product differentiation. In the rest of the chapter, we have assumed that such product differentiation means actually producing a product with different characteristics. But a firm might instead find it more cost effective (if consumers exhibit some "irrationality") to artificially differentiate its product by shaping its image rather than changing its underlying characteristics. Cereal companies are famous for this in their marketing to children: Take the same cereal and stick it in a box that has the latest cartoon character on it, and children suddenly go nuts for it when previously they could not have cared less. The product that is ingested, the cereal inside the box, has not changed, but the way that the relevant consumers feel about the cereal has been "artificially" altered. In the process, the cereal company has gained some market power as it has deputized an army of children to pester their parents to buy its product even at a higher price. Social losses arise from both the decrease in competition and the cost incurred by the cereal company to engage in this form of advertising.

Many economists feel quite conflicted when reading a paragraph such as the previous one, and I admit to not being an exception. On the one hand, I can certainly see how this form of advertising—putting the cartoon character on the cereal box without changing anything about the actual cereal—leaves the actual product unchanged while increasing market power and creating socially wasteful advertising expenditures. On the other hand, I recognize that this view assumes that I know better than the consumers what "the product" actually is. Who am I to say that the product has not changed when the cartoon character appears on the cereal box; it clearly *has* changed in the eyes of the children who suddenly want it. These children care about not only the type of cereal inside the box but also the box itself, giggling in delight as the box with "Dora the Explorer" on it shows up on the breakfast table.[9] By taking the view that the appearance of "Dora the Explorer" on the box does not change the product unless the cereal itself is different, we are taking the paternalistic view that what is on the cereal box *should not* change the way children feel about the product. But economists have a tendency to respect consumer "sovereignty" in the sense of accepting consumer tastes without making value judgments.

If, therefore, we carry the economist's respect for consumer sovereignty to its extreme, the distinction between informational advertising and advertising intended to "manipulate preferences" largely disappears. Consider two different ways in which a cereal company might differentiate its product. First, the company might increase the amount of raisins in the cereal, thus altering the physical characteristics of the cereal itself, and it might then launch an informational

---

[9]This has given me another great idea for a new marketing campaign analogous to my previous idea of producing economist cards: Why not put famous economists on cereal boxes? If the kids go nuts over "Dora the Explorer," just think how they'll react to having Hotelling's picture on the box!

advertising campaign that informs consumers that its cereal now has two scoops of raisins rather than one. Second, the company might instead put "Dora the Explorer" on its cereal box and advertise that its product now displays this popular cartoon character. Both advertising campaigns provide information about a change in the product to consumers, with "the product" defined as the cereal inside the box under the first campaign and as the combination of the cereal and the box in the other. Saying that the latter conveys no useful information while the former does is the same as saying that we take the position that the box itself is not a legitimate product characteristic for consumers to consider in their decision process while the quantity of raisins is. But both advertising campaigns will succeed only to the extent to which consumers themselves believe the emphasized product characteristics are in fact legitimate to consider in decision making. If no one cares about raisins in cereal but many people care about the appearance of the cereal box, consumers are telling us that the box is an important characteristic for them while the raisins are not. Thus, if we take this less paternalistic view about what product characteristics are legitimate means for product differentiation, we should place social value on the enthusiastic giggling that the appearance of "Dora the Explorer" generates at my breakfast table. And if so, it is far from obvious that advertising that shapes the image of the cereal is necessarily more socially wasteful than advertising that informs consumers of the fact that the cereal now has two rather than one scoop of raisins in it.

Again, I admit to being conflicted, and I certainly sympathize with the view that the unseemly marketing of cereal to children through the altering of cereal boxes is socially wasteful (not to mention annoying for parents). But I also see that the distinction between what we call "informational advertising" and "image marketing" is quite blurry and involves normative judgment calls about what "should be." The study of such image marketing, while traditionally not part of the economics tradition, has recently become important in an evolving branch of economics known as "behavioral economics." Behavioral economics attempts to blend traditional economic modeling with insights from psychology and neuroscience. We will say a bit more about this in Chapter 29.

26A.5.3 Distinguishing Informational Advertising from Image Marketing in the Real World
To the extent to which we admit to a difference between informational advertising and image marketing, is there a way to tell what kind of advertising is actually taking place? I think there is, at least to some extent. Consider what we typically see advertised in newspapers versus what we typically see advertised on television. In the newspaper advertisements that I see in my local paper, stores are advertising that they have particular products at particular prices. This conveys real information to me, information on which I sometimes act. Knowing that Wal-Mart is selling a particular digital camera I have been looking for and offering it at an attractive price tells me something useful, particularly if the same newspaper has an ad from K-Mart that tells me the same product is being sold there at a higher price. Much of newspaper advertising appears to have at least some informational content for consumers who cannot possibly be aware of all the choices they have in their local market.

Now consider the typical television advertisement. I rarely see any information about price in such advertisements, and a lot of the ads are telling me about products such as Coke and Pepsi, products that I am quite familiar with already, as is virtually everyone on the planet. What possible reason is there for Coke to advertise its product (without announcing any new price or some new Coke variety) unless it is to shape the image of Coke in a way that makes me more likely to choose it over Pepsi? Does knowing that LeBron James (who quite successfully plays professional basketball in the NBA) drinks Coke or Pepsi make any difference to the way Coke and Pepsi tastes, or does it convey any useful information about the taste of Coke and Pepsi, particularly when I know perfectly well that LeBron James was paid millions of dollars to appear in the commercial? (Actually, it *might* convey useful information in some circumstances, as we will explore in end-of-chapter exercise 26B.5 where we find that seemingly frivolous but conspicuous advertising expenditures may signal something about the unobserved quality of products.)

Exercise 26A.15   In my experience, car advertisements on television are different. Can you argue that they are more in the category of informational advertising than the Coke and Pepsi ads we just discussed?

Coke and Pepsi ads on television represent, for me at least, a pretty easy case in which to argue that the purpose of the ads is primarily to shape the image of the product that people consume, and newspaper ads are often pretty easily put into the informational advertising category. And then there are the cases that lie in between, with information and image being melded by creative marketing firms. I just mentioned that I am not sure what informational content there could possibly be in knowing that LeBron James agreed to say he likes Coke on TV after getting paid a few million dollars for doing so. But what if I learn that LeBron James has agreed to say on TV that he likes a particular athletic shoe (again after getting paid millions to do so), and that part of his contract is that he will wear that shoe in all the basketball games he plays? There is certainly image marketing going on here, but there is also some real information being conveyed since LeBron James presumably would not agree easily to wear a shoe that handicaps his basketball playing. As is often the case in the real world, our abstract categories (of, in this case, informational advertising and image marketing) often flow together in practice.

26B Mathematical Modeling of Differentiated Product Markets

It makes intuitive sense, as I hope you have seen in Section A, that firms have an incentive to differentiate their products in order to gain market power, and that such differentiation "works" for a firm to the extent to which it is successfully addressing some segment of consumer demand through differentiation. We'll begin our analysis of this here the same way we did in Section A, initially simply illustrating mathematically (in Section 26B.1) how existing product differentiation in an oligopoly softens price competition and leads to a Bertrand equilibrium with $p > MC$. We then formally develop the Hotelling model with a particular specification of consumer utility that allows us to solve the full two-stage model in which firms choose the degree of product differentiation in the first stage while anticipating the Bertrand price equilibrium that emerges in the second stage when prices are announced (Section 26B.2). In Section 26B.3, we then move to the "circle model" of product differentiation and consider a game in which firms initially choose whether to enter a differentiated product market before settling on a price to charge. In this model, we will be able to derive an equilibrium in which firms in the industry have market power and earn positive profits but firms outside the industry have no incentive to enter the market because of fixed entry costs. Section 26B.4 then develops a more modern version of a monopolistically competitive market that differs from the notion of monopolistic competition in Section A in that consumers explicitly value product diversity, with the restaurant market serving as our motivating example. Finally, we will revisit our discussion of advertising in Section 26B.5. We will present a model of informational advertising in which advertising provides the optimal level of information to consumers, and we will use a variant of the Hotelling model to illustrate how image marketing *can* result in socially wasteful advertising.

26B.1 Differentiated Products in Oligopoly Markets

In Section A, we discussed briefly the example of Coke and Pepsi, which, in the minds of many consumers, are sufficiently differentiated products that many consumers prefer one over the other (all else being equal) while at the same time being willing to substitute one for the other if the prices are sufficiently different. When Coke and Pepsi serve a similar market but nevertheless are somewhat distinct goods in the minds of consumers, the demand for each of the two products depends on both the price for Coke and the price for Pepsi. We can then represent the demand for good x_i by $x_i(p_i, p_j)$ if there are two firms in the oligopoly. Firm i (which produces x_i) will have to take p_j as given when it selects its price p_i to solve the optimization problem

$$\max_{p_i} \pi_i = (p_i - c)x_i(p_i, p_j), \tag{26.1}$$

where c again represents constant marginal cost of production. Suppose firm i sets $p_i = c$. If the resulting demand for its goods, $x_i(c, p_j)$, is greater than zero, we know that it can do better by setting a price higher than marginal cost. This is because we know the firm's profit will be zero if $p_i = c$ but strictly higher (assuming $x_i(p_i, p_j)$ is continuously downward sloping in p_i) if price is raised just a bit above marginal cost.

To make things a bit more concrete, suppose that Coke and Pepsi face demands for their products that take the form

$$x_i = A - \alpha p_i + \beta p_j \text{ where } \alpha > \beta. \tag{26.2}$$

Exercise 26B.1

Can you think of why it is reasonable to assume $\alpha > \beta$?

Then demand for Coke falls as Coke increases its price but rises if Pepsi increases its price, and similarly, the demand for Pepsi falls as the price of Pepsi increases but rises as the price of Coke increases. Each firm then faces a profit maximization problem of the form

$$\max_{p_i} \pi_i = (p_i - c)(A - \alpha p_i + \beta p_j). \tag{26.3}$$

Solving the first order conditions for p_i, we get firm i's best response function given p_j,

$$p_i(p_j) = \frac{A + \alpha c + \beta p_j}{2\alpha}. \tag{26.4}$$

Exercise 26B.2

Suppose $p_j = 0$. Interpret the resulting best price response for firm i in light of what we derived as the optimal monopoly quantity and price when $x = A - \alpha p$.

Since the two firms are symmetric, firm j's best response to p_i, $p_j(p_i)$, is the same (with i and j in equation (26.4) reversed). Substituting $p_j(p_i)$ into $p_i(p_j)$ and solving for p_i, we get

$$p_i^* = \frac{A + \alpha c}{2\alpha - \beta} = p_j^*, \tag{26.5}$$

which is larger than marginal cost c so long as $c < A/(\alpha - \beta)$.

Exercise 26B.3*

Before going to our concrete example, we argued that Bertrand competition will lead to prices above marginal cost when $x_i(c, p_j) > 0$. In our example, we find that, in equilibrium, $p > c = MC$ so long as $c < A/(\alpha - \beta)$. Can you reconcile the general conclusion with the conclusion from the example?

26B.2 Hotelling's Model with Quadratic Costs

We have shown that price competition in oligopolies does not reach the initially predicted ferocity that leads to prices being equal to marginal cost when products produced by the firms in the oligopoly are differentiated. In light of this, it may be more realistic to model oligopolists who engage in price competition as having two strategic variables: price and product characteristics. The model we began to develop in Section A for this purpose is the Hotelling model that is aimed at investigating precisely such situations.

Recall that this model assumes product characteristics y could take on any value in the interval $[0,1]$ and that each consumer $n \in [0,1]$ had some ideal product characteristic n. Suppose that the cost a consumer n pays for consuming the product with characteristic y is $\alpha(n - y)^2$ in addition to the price the consumer has to pay for the product. Put differently, suppose that the cost a consumer incurs for consuming away from his or her ideal product is quadratic in the distance of the product from his or her ideal point. We will now ask what equilibrium to expect in a two-stage game in which two firms simultaneously choose their product characteristics y_1 and y_2 followed by a second stage in which they simultaneously choose the product prices p_1 and p_2 (knowing the product characteristics that were chosen in the first stage.)

Before we begin, note that demand for each firm's output can be calculated in this case for any combination of prices and product characteristics by simply identifying the consumer $\bar{n}$ who is indifferent between purchasing from firm 1 and firm 2, with everyone to the left of $\bar{n}$ purchasing from the firm whose product characteristic lies to the left of $\bar{n}$ and everyone to the right of $\bar{n}$ purchasing from the other firm. Suppose, for instance, that $y_1 \leq y_2$. Then the consumer $\bar{n}$ who is indifferent between the firms is that consumer for whom the effective price of purchasing from firm 1 is equal to his or her effective price of purchasing from firm 2; i.e., $\bar{n}$ is such that

$$p_1 + \alpha(\bar{n} - y_1)^2 = p_2 + \alpha(\bar{n} - y_2)^2, \tag{26.6}$$

which we can solve to get

$$\bar{n} = \frac{(p_2 - p_1) + \alpha(y_2^2 - y_1^2)}{2\alpha(y_2 - y_1)} = \frac{y_2 + y_1}{2} + \frac{(p_2 - p_1)}{2\alpha(y_2 - y_1)}. \tag{26.7}$$

Since everyone in the interval $[0, \bar{n}]$ will consume from firm 1, expression (26.7) then also represents the fraction of consumer demand that goes to firm 1. Adding y_1 and substracting $2y_1/2$ from the right-hand side, we can rewrite this as

$$D^1(p_1, p_2, y_1, y_2) = y_1 + \frac{y_2 - y_1}{2} + \frac{(p_2 - p_1)}{2\alpha(y_2 - y_1)} \tag{26.8}$$

with the remaining demand $(1 - \bar{n})$ from interval $[\bar{n}, 1]$ equal to demand for firm 2's output. After some algebraic manipulation (similar to what we did to derive D^1), we can then write demand for firm 2's output as

$$D^2(p_1, p_2, y_1, y_2) = 1 - \bar{n} = (1 - y_2) + \frac{y_2 - y_1}{2} + \frac{(p_1 - p_2)}{2\alpha(y_2 - y_1)}. \tag{26.9}$$

Exercise 26B.4   Derive the right-hand side of equation (26.9).

26B.2.1 Stage 2: Setting Prices (Given Product Characteristics)

To solve for the subgame perfect equilibrium, we begin in the second stage when firms already know the product characteristic chosen by each firm in the first stage. Let these product characteristics be denoted by y_1 and y_2 respectively, and (without loss of generality) assume that $y_1 \leq y_2$. In the simultaneous price setting game of the second stage, we then need to calculate the best response functions for each firm to the price set by the other firm. To calculate firm 1's best price response function to prices set by firm 2, for instance, we need to choose p_1 to maximize firm 1's profit $\pi^1 = (p_1 - c)D^1(p_1; p_2, y_1, y_2)$, where c is constant marginal cost and where p_2, y_2, and y_1 are taken as fixed by the firm. Substituting equation (26.8) in for D^1, we can the write the problem as

$$\max_{p_1} (p_1 - c)\left(y_1 + \frac{y_2 - y_1}{2} + \frac{(p_2 - p_1)}{2\alpha(y_2 - y_1)}\right). \qquad (26.10)$$

Solving the first order condition for this problem, we get firm 1's best response function

$$p_1(p_2) = \frac{p_2}{2} + \frac{c + \alpha(y_2^2 - y_1^2)}{2}. \qquad (26.11)$$

Going through the same steps for firm 2, we can similarly derive firm 2's best response function to p_1 as

$$p_2(p_1) = \frac{p_1}{2} + \frac{c - \alpha(y_2^2 - y_1^2) + 2\alpha(y_2 - y_1)}{2}. \qquad (26.12)$$

Set up firm 2's optimization problem and verify the best response function $p_2(p_2)$.

Exercise 26B.5

In order for the price setting game to be in equilibrium, these best response functions have to intersect. Substituting equation (26.12) into (26.11), we can then solve for the equilibrium price for firm 1

$$p_1^*(y_1, y_2) = c + \alpha\left(\frac{y_2^2 - y_1^2 + 2(y_2 - y_1)}{3}\right), \qquad (26.13)$$

and plugging this into equation (26.12) we get the equilibrium price for firm 2

$$p_2^*(y_1, y_2) = c + \alpha\left(\frac{y_1^2 - y_2^2 + 4(y_2 - y_1)}{3}\right). \qquad (26.14)$$

26B.2.2 Stage 1: Selecting Product Characteristics

In stage 1 of the game, firms then know the prices that will emerge in stage 2 conditional on the product characteristics that are set in stage 1. Firm 1 thus chooses y_1 taking as given firm 2's choice of y_2 as well as $p_1^*(y_1, y_2)$ and $p_2^*(y_1, y_2)$ that will result in stage 2 of the game. Put differently, to obtain firm 1's (subgame perfect) best response function in stage 1, we solve

$$\max_{y_1} \pi^1 = \left(p_1^*(y_1, y_2) - c\right)D^1\left(y_1; y_2, p_1^*(y_1, y_2), p_2^*(y_1, y_2)\right), \qquad (26.15)$$

which can, given equation (26.8), be written as

$$\max_{y_1} \pi^1 = \left(p_1^*(y_1, y_2) - c\right)\left[y_1 + \frac{y_2 - y_1}{2} + \frac{\left(p_2^*(y_1, y_2) - p_1^*(y_1, y_2)\right)}{2\alpha(y_2 - y_1)}\right]. \qquad (26.16)$$

An implicit constraint given the model we have defined is that $0 \le y_1 \le y_2 \le 1$, and this constraint complicates the mechanics of undertaking the optimization problem because of the presence of inequality constraints that make our usual Lagrange method inapplicable. But it is easy to set up an Excel spreadsheet and calculate different profits for firm 1 depending on the level of y_2 and what choice firm 1 makes regarding y_1. This is done in Table 26.1 where, for different levels of $y_2 \ge 0.5$ in the top row, we report the profit firm 1 makes for different choices of y_1. (We do not have to consider the cases for $y_2 < 0.5$ since we have assumed $y_1 \le y_2$ and that is not compatible with $y_2 < 0.5$.)

Table 26.1: Firm 1's Profit when $c = 5$, $\alpha = 10$ (Assuming $y_1 \leq y_2$)

	Setting Product Characteristics in First Stage					
y_1	$y_2 = 0.5$	$y_2 = 0.6$	$y_2 = 0.7$	$y_2 = 0.8$	$y_2 = 0.9$	$y_2 = 1.0$
1.0						0.0000
0.9					0.0000	0.8450
0.8				0.0000	0.7606	1.6044
0.7			0.0000	0.6806	1.4400	2.2817
0.6		0.0000	0.6050	1.2844	2.0417	2.8800
0.5	0.0000	0.5339	1.1378	1.8150	2.5689	3.4028
0.4	0.4672	1.0000	1.6017	2.2756	3.0250	3.8533
0.3	0.8711	1.4017	2.0000	2.6694	3.4133	4.2350
0.2	1.2150	1.7422	2.3361	3.0000	3.7372	4.5511
0.1	1.5022	2.0250	2.6133	3.2706	4.0000	4.8050
0.0	1.7361	2.2533	2.8350	3.4844	4.2050	5.0000

Exercise 26B.6 Explain the last sentence in parentheses.

Since firm 1's only choice variable in stage 1 is its own product characteristic y_1, we can then trace out firm 1's best response function in stage 1 of the game by looking down each column to see where firm 1 makes its highest profit. What you will quickly notice is that, regardless of what product characteristic y_2 is chosen by firm 2, firm 1 "best responds" by choosing $y_1 = 0$. Were we to trace out a symmetric table for firm 2's profits given choices of y_1 by firm 1, we would similarly find that firm 2's best response (given that we are assuming $y_1 \leq y_2$) is always to set $y_2 = 1$. Thus, the equilibrium product characteristics that emerge are characterized by *maximal product differentiation*; the two firms choose to select product characteristics that are as far apart as possible because they know that this will serve to minimize price competition in the second stage.

Exercise 26B.7 Suppose we do not restrict y_1 to be less than y_2. Given what we have done, can you plot the two firms' best response functions to the product characteristics chosen by the other firm and illustrate the stage 1 pure strategy equilibria? How many such equilibria are there? (*Hint:* Once the restriction that $y_1 \leq y_2$ is removed, there are two pure strategy equilibria.)

Now that we know that the firms choose $y_1 = 0$ and $y_2 = 1$ in the first stage, we can plug these into equations (26.13) and (26.14) to calculate the equilibrium prices that emerge as

$$p_1^* = p_2^* = c + \alpha. \qquad (26.17)$$

Recall the only place α enters the problem: It defines how large a cost $\alpha(n - y)^2$ (in addition to price) a consumer pays when consuming a product that is not her ideal. As α goes to zero, the cost consumers incur from not consuming their ideal disappears, as does the firms' ability to make profit from differentiating their products. As α increases, on the other hand, consumers care more about being close to their ideal point, and firms are able to take advantage of this through product differentiation that allows them to charge price above marginal cost.

Exercise 26B.8

Can you plot the two firms' best response functions in stage 2 of the game given that $y_1 = 0$ and $y_2 = 1$ were chosen in the first stage? Carefully label slopes and intercepts. Are these prices the same for the two pure strategy equilibria in stage 1 that you identified in exercise 26B.7?

26B.2.3 Comparing Oligopoly Product Innovation to Optimal Differentiation

In the Hotelling model with quadratic costs of deviating from the ideal product characteristic for consumers, we can then ask how the oligopoly equilibrium compares to what a social planner would do if he or she were limited to only selecting two product characteristics to be produced. Note that quadratic costs of the type we have modeled imply that the *marginal* cost of deviating from a consumer's ideal point is increasing with distance from the ideal point. This makes it easy to determine the optimal level of product differentiation when consumer ideal points are uniformly distributed along the interval [0,1].

In particular, the social planner would want to minimize the *average* distance between consumers' ideal points and their closest product characteristic. This is done when the social planner locates product characteristics halfway in between the midpoint and the extremes of the interval [0,1] to both sides of the midpoint; i.e., when the social planner sets $y_1 = 0.25$ and $y_2 = 0.75$. To see how this is more efficient than the equilibrium outcome, compare the situation where $(y_1, y_2) = (0,1)$ to the situation where $(y_1, y_2) = (0.25, 0.75)$ assuming there exists a consumer at every point in the interval [0,1]. In both cases, consumers in the interval [0,0.5) buy from firm 1 and consumers in the interval (0.5,1] buy from firm 2 (with consumer 0.5 indifferent between the two firms), but the overall cost incurred by consumers is lower when there is less than extreme product differentiation. In what follows, we use a simple integral to illustrate this, but, if you are not comfortable with integrals, you can simply skip to Section 26B.3 on the next page.

When $(y_1, y_2) = (0,1)$, consumer $n \in [0,0.5)$ incurs a cost αn^2 when shopping at $y_1 = 0$. Since the first and second halves of the [0,1] interval are symmetric, we can derive the overall cost incurred by consumers when $(y_1, y_2) = (0,1)$ as

$$2 \int_0^{0.5} \alpha n^2 dn = \frac{\alpha}{12}. \tag{26.18}$$

When $(y_1, y_2) = (0.25, 0.75)$, on the other hand, consumers in the interval [0, 0.25] incur costs symmetric to consumers in each of the other three quarters of the [0,1] interval, implying that we can express the total cost to consumers as

$$4 \int_0^{0.25} \alpha n^2 dn = \frac{\alpha}{48}. \tag{26.19}$$

Thus, the oligopolists engage in socially *excessive product differentiation* because they strategically use product differentiation to dampen price competition.

Exercise 26B.9

Suppose that, instead of being quadratic as we have modeled them here, the cost that consumer n pays for consuming a product with characteristic $y \neq n$ is linear; i.e., suppose that this cost is $\alpha|n - y|$ where $|n - y|$ represents the distance between y and n. If the two oligopolists engage in maximal product differentiation (i.e., $y_1 = 0$ and $y_2 = 1$), is that product differentiation still socially excessive?[10]

---

[10]Note that in this exercise we are *assuming* that firms still choose $y_1 = 0$ and $y_2 = 1$ in the first stage. This is, as it turns out, not an equilibrium under the linear cost model. In fact, the reason we assumed quadratic costs is because under the linear cost model there does not exist a pure strategy equilibrium (but only a mixed strategy equilibrium).

26B.3 Firm Entry and Product Differentiation

The Hotelling model works well for thinking about competition between two firms in an oligopoly when such firms have the opportunity to engage in product differentiation. But many markets in the real world are not oligopolistic because there are no strict barriers to entry of potential firms other than a fixed entry cost. We now turn toward considering such markets and will assume that the only barrier to entry that exists is a fixed set-up cost FC. Once that cost is paid, it is a sunk cost, but potential entrants consider this cost as they consider whether it is worth entering a particular market in which product differentiation is possible.

We therefore again assume that consumers have different tastes as represented by different ideal points in terms of a product characteristic. However, once we proceed to cases where there might be more than two firms, it is more natural to define the product characteristic space in such a way that there is no natural advantage to any particular location within that space. The line segment [0,1] in the Hotelling model does not satisfy this requirement since locations near the center naturally grant more access to consumers than locations at the extremes. For this reason, we now define product characteristics to lie on a circle and assume, without loss of generality, that the circumference of the circle is 1 (as first illustrated in Graph 26.1b).

As discussed in Section A, we can then think of the following two-stage game: In the first stage, potential firms that face a fixed entry cost of FC and a marginal production cost of c decide whether or not to enter. It seems reasonable to assume that the firms that enter will locate along the circle of product characteristics equally distant from one another, and we therefore assume this from the start (rather than modeling both the entry decision and the location decision on the circle).[11] Then, in the second stage, firms strategically choose the price they charge for their product knowing where within the product characteristic circle all competitors have located. As in the Hotelling model, we will make the further simplifying assumption that consumers whose ideal points are uniformly distributed around the circle are only interested in purchasing a single unit of the good. And we will assume that the effective price that consumers pay for a good is equal to the price that is charged plus a linear function of the distance of the consumer's ideal point from the product's characteristic; i.e., the effective price for a consumer with ideal point n consuming from a firm with product characteristic y_i that charges p_i is $p_i + \alpha|n - y_i|$ where $|n - y_i|$ represents the distance along the circle between n and y_i. This is in contrast to our treatment of the Hotelling model where we assumed quadratic costs of consuming away from one's ideal point, a case we will leave for you to solve in end-of-chapter exercise 26.7.

26B.3.1 Stage 2: Setting Prices

In order to determine the equilibrium prices that emerge once the number of firms and their locations have been determined in stage 1, we need to specify the demand for a firms product as a function of the price it sets. In equilibrium, it will have to be the case that all firms charge the same price. So consider firm i's best response to all other firms charging a price p, and consider firm j that is adjacent on the circle to firm i in terms of product characteristics. A consumer whose ideal point $\bar{n}$ lies between y_i and y_j is then indifferent between consuming from firm i and firm j if its effective price is the same for products from the two firms, i.e., if

$$p_i + \alpha|\bar{n} - y_i| = p + \alpha|y_j - \bar{n}|. \tag{26.20}$$

Suppose we let, without loss of generality, $y_i = 0$. Then, if there are N firms in the market and all neighboring firms are equally distant from one another along the circle with circumference 1, $y_j = 1/N$. Substituting these into equation (26.20), the equation becomes

$$p_i + \alpha\bar{n} = p + \alpha\left(\frac{1}{N} - \bar{n}\right). \tag{26.21}$$

---

[11]This is actually not a trivial matter. A fuller game might consist of three stages in which firms first decide *whether* to enter the market, then decide *where* to locate in terms of product characteristics and finally decide what price to charge. For the quadratic cost case considered in end-of-chapter exercise 26.7, it has been demonstrated that firms will in fact locate equidistant from one another.

Solving this for $\bar{n}$, we get

$$\bar{n} = \frac{p - p_i}{2\alpha} + \frac{1}{2N}. \tag{26.22}$$

Thus, given firm i's choice of p_i (and given all other firms choose p), all consumers whose ideal points along the circle are located between y_i and $\bar{n}$ will consume from firm i. Because of the symmetry along the circle, the same is true for consumers whose ideal point lies to the other side of y_i, which implies that demand for firm i's output is $2\bar{n}$; i.e.,

$$D^i(p_i, p) = 2\bar{n} = \frac{p - p_i}{\alpha} + \frac{1}{N}. \tag{26.23}$$

To determine firm i's best response price to other firms choosing p, we therefore simply have to solve the problem

$$\max_{pi} \pi^i = (p_i - c)D^i(p_i, p) = (p_i - c)\left(\frac{p - p_i}{\alpha} + \frac{1}{N} \right). \tag{26.24}$$

Why does the fixed entry cost *FC* not enter this problem? If you did include it in the definition of profit, would it make any difference?

Exercise 26B.10

Taking the first order condition and solving for p_i, we then get firm i's best response function to other firms charging p as

$$p_i(p) = \frac{p + c}{2} + \frac{\alpha}{2N}. \tag{26.25}$$

Verify $p_i(p)$.

Exercise 26B.11

In equilibrium, all firms have to be best responding to each other, with $p_i(p) = p$. Thus, substituting p for $p_i(p)$ and solving for p, we get the equilibrium price

$$p^*(N) = c + \frac{\alpha}{N}. \tag{26.26}$$

Put into words, firms will charge prices above marginal cost in the price competition stage, with the "markup" proportional to the degree to which consumers care about consuming near their ideal point (i.e., α) and inversely proportional to the number of firms in the market. As the number of firms gets large, the markup goes to zero and firms charge price equal to *MC*, and as consumers lose the taste for product differentiation (by α going to zero), firms engage in the usual Bertand competition that drives price to *MC*.

26B.3.2 Stage 1: Firm Entry Decisions
Knowing what prices $p^*(N)$ to expect in the second stage, firms decide in the first stage whether or not to enter the market. Firms will enter so long as the profit from entering (including fixed entry cost *FC*) is not negative, which implies that entry should drive profit (including fixed entry costs) to zero. Thus, the equilibrium number of firms that enter in the first stage is such that each firm makes zero profit when fixed costs are included in the profit calculation; i.e., for every firm i that enters,

$$\pi^i = (p^* - c)D^i(p^*, p^*) - FC = 0. \tag{26.27}$$

With demand D^i from equation (26.23) collapsing to $1/N$ when p_i is set equal to all other firm's prices, we can then plug p^* from equation (26.26) into this profit function and write the zero-profit condition as

$$\left(c + \frac{\alpha}{N} - c \right) \frac{1}{N} - FC = 0, \tag{26.28}$$

which in turn implies that the equilibrium number of entering firms N^* is

$$N^* = \left(\frac{\alpha}{FC} \right)^{1/2} \tag{26.29}$$

and the equilibrium price from the second stage of the game becomes

$$p^* = c + (\alpha FC)^{1/2}. \tag{26.30}$$

Exercise 26B.12   Verify p^* and N^*.

In equilibrium, we therefore expect the number of firms to increase as the fixed entry cost falls and as consumers care more about consuming close to their ideal point (i.e., as α increases). Furthermore, the markup above marginal cost will increase as consumers care more about being close to their ideal point and as fixed entry costs go up. If fixed entry costs disappear, all barriers to entry have been removed and the market becomes perfectly competitive. The result is exactly what our perfectly competitive model predicts: a large number of small firms, each charging $p = MC$. Just as described in Section A, this "circle" model therefore allows us to fully fill in the gap between perfect monopoly and perfect competition when price is the strategic variable for firms in the industry.

26B.3.3 Comparing the Number of Firms to the Optimal

As in the Hotelling model, we therefore predict that firms will engage in strategic product differentiation. We found in the Hotelling model that, in the case of two oligopolistic firms differentiating their products, we predict socially excessive product differentiation, with a social planner (who is restricted to using only two firms) producing products that are more similar to one another than what occurs in equilibrium. In the case of differentiated firm entry as analyzed in this section, it is similarly true that a socially excessive degree of product differentiation emerges, but this time because too many firms enter the market.

To demonstrate this, we need to ask what our benevolent social planner would want to consider as he or she chooses the number of firms for this industry. First, the planner would consider the fact that a fixed cost FC has to be paid for every one of the firms that enters the market, for a total of $N(FC)$ in fixed costs when the number of firms is set to N. Second, he or she would want to consider the cost consumers incur from not consuming their ideal product. When there are N firms equally spaced on our circle of product characteristics, each firm serves a fraction $1/N$ of customers, half of whom will come from the firm's "left" and half from the firm's "right." Since we have normalized the circumference of the circle to 1, this implies that the farthest a customer's ideal point will lie from his or her firm's product y_i is $1/(2N)$ and the closest is 0, with the *average* customer's ideal point lying $1/(4N)$ from y_i. The same is true for customers to the "right" of y_i. In choosing N, the social planner therefore sets the average cost for consumers at $\alpha/(4N)$ (since we have assumed a consumer's cost is α times the distance from his or her ideal point). And when we assume that there is a consumer located at every point on the circle of circumference 1, this implies we have normalized the population size to 1, and thus the total cost to consumers (from not consuming at their ideal points) is just this average cost of $\alpha/(4N)$. Taking these two factors—the consumer costs and the fixed costs of setting up firms—into account, the social planner who seeks to find the efficient number of firms then faces the problem

$$\min_{N} \left(N(FC) + \frac{\alpha}{4N} \right), \qquad (26.31)$$

which solves to

$$N^{opt} = \frac{1}{2} \left(\frac{\alpha}{FC} \right)^{1/2}. \qquad (26.32)$$

Note that this is exactly half of what equation (26.29) tells us the actual number of firms N^{*} will be in equilibrium. Only when fixed costs approach zero and the market becomes perfectly competitive (with the number of firms approaching infinity) does the social planner solution N^{opt} approach the market solution N^{*}. We therefore have another model where market power leads to a violation of the first welfare theorem, and the elimination of market power (through the elimination of the fixed entry cost) implies the first welfare theorem holds (under the perfectly competitive conditions that arise from free entry). From a practical standpoint, of course it is not clear how much policy relevance this has since governments are far from omniscient social planners. However, if governments impose additional fixed costs to entry, such as the costs involved in obtaining copyright or patent protections, such costs might in fact move the market closer to the social optimum.

In both the Hotelling case and the "circle model," we have assumed for convenience that each consumer always just consumes one good from the firm that produces a product closest to his or her ideal. How does this assumption alleviate us from having to consider the price of output in our efficiency analysis (even though we know that firms end up pricing above MC)?

Exercise 26B.13

26B.4 Monopolistic Competition and Product Diversity

The model of monopolistic competition outlined in Section A is useful in that it helped us tell a story about innovation and product differentiation in a quasi-formal way. As we mentioned at the time, the model dates back to the 1930s and represents an early attempt to model market structures in which firms have market power (and set $p > MC$) but no potential entrant can make positive profits by entering (because of fixed costs of entry).

More recently, monopolistic competition has received a more modern treatment that will be the focus of this section.[12] It differs somewhat from the models in the previous two sections where we began by defining a set of possible product characteristics (either along an interval of a line or along a circle) on which firms choose to locate their product. In those models, we could talk about the "degree of product differentiation" between two products as the distance between the product characteristics, and we assumed that consumers can only choose one of the products and will choose the one whose product characteristic is closest to their "ideal point." But in many markets, consumers actually do not choose just one product type but rather have a "taste for diversity." Think, for instance, of restaurants. Few of us go to the same restaurant every time we go out but instead prefer areas with lots of different restaurants we can frequent over time. Product differentiation in such a market cannot really be modeled with the tools we have explored thus far since those tools assumed each consumer will simply always pick his or her "favorite" restaurant.

---

[12]Different models of monopolistic competition have been developed over the past few decades. The model described here is due to Avinash Dixit (1944–) and Joseph Stiglitz (1943–) as well as Michael Spence (1943–). Stiglitz and Spence have both won the Nobel Prize in Economics, albeit primarily for their contributions to the economics of asymmetric information and not the work we are featuring here.

The model we will present next therefore departs from the assumption that consumers consume only one good and thus choose the one that is closest to their ideal. Rather, we will model consumers as becoming better off the more choices within a market (like restaurants) they have. They will then choose to spread their consumption in the differentiated product market across the different types of products offered. A firm i is assumed to produce a single type of product, denoted y_i, and all we will say is that this product is "different" but somewhat substitutable with other products y_j produced by other firms in the same market. Firm i might, for instance, offer Northern Italian food, while firm j might offer Chinese food. We will therefore abstract away from "degrees of product differentiation" between two products in the same market and instead consider the entire market more "diversified" the more firms it contains. As in the previous sections, we continue to assume that there are many potential firms that could in principle enter the market, but that entry entails payment of a fixed entry cost FC.

26B.4.1 Consumer Preferences for Diversified Products

We will denote all the products in the market for y by y_i, with i denoting the firm that produces y_i. Our working assumption will be that the number of firms in the y market is N, and we will then find out exactly what N will be in equilibrium. We will also assume that there are many other goods that consumers consume, goods outside the differentiated product market y, and we will represent these with a single composite good x denominated in dollar units (as we did in our consumer theory chapters). Finally, we will assume that we can represent the consumer side of the economy with a "representative consumer" whose preferences can be captured by a utility function of the form

$$u\Big((x,v(y_1,\ldots,y_N))\Big) = u\Big(x,[y_1^{-\rho} + y_2^{-\rho} + \ldots + y_N^{-\rho}]^{-1/\rho}\Big) = u\left(x,\left[\sum_{i=1}^{N}y_i^{-\rho}\right]^{-1/\rho}\right) \quad (26.33)$$

where $-1 < \rho < 0$.[13] You may recall from our consumer theory work that a utility function of the form $v(y_1,y_2,\ldots,y_N) = [y_1^{-\rho} + y_2^{-\rho} + \ldots + y_N^{-\rho}]^{-1/\rho}$ represents preferences over the y goods that exhibit constant elasticity of substitution (CES) and that the elasticity of substitution σ is given by $\sigma = 1/(1 + \rho)$. We have therefore constructed preferences in such a way that there exists a CES subutility function v over the y goods, and by restricting ρ to lie between -1 and 0, we are assuming that the elasticity of substitution of that subutility function lies between ∞ and 1. An infinite elasticity of substitution represents goods that are perfect substitutes, while an elasticity of substitution of 1 represents Cobb–Douglas preferences. We are therefore purposefully restricting the complementarity of the y goods because, after all, we are attempting to model a differentiated product market y in which the products are relatively substitutable.

Some of what we will demonstrate will be true for any utility function that takes the form in equation (26.33) (as we explore further in end-of-chapter exercise 26.2), but to make the analysis a bit more concrete, we will now work with the following special case:

$$u\Big(x,v(y_1,y_2,\ldots,y_N)\Big) = x^{\alpha}\left(\left[\sum_{i=1}^{N}y_i^{-\rho}\right]^{-1/\rho}\right)^{(1-\alpha)} = x^{\alpha}\left(\sum_{i=1}^{N}y_i^{-\rho}\right)^{-(1-\alpha)/\rho} \quad (26.34)$$

From the first way in which this equation is written, you can see that we have embedded the CES subutility over the y goods into a Cobb–Douglas specification, with x taken to the power α and the CES subutility to the power $(1 - \alpha)$.[14]

....

Exercise 26B.14   What is the elasticity of substitution between x and the subutility over the y goods?

....

---

[13]Functions of this form, which can also be defined using integrals instead of summation signs, are often called *Dixit-Stiglitz utility functions*.

[14]The astute reader might notice that this utility function does not quite satisfy the conditions for representative consumer utility functions derived in Chapter 15. We will address this in end-of-chapter exercise 26.2.

Cobb–Douglas preferences have the feature that, when the exponents sum to 1, these exponents represent the share of the consumer's budget that will be spent on the good. Thus, if $\alpha = 0.9$, we know that the consumer will spend $\$0.9I$ on the composite x good and $\$0.1I$ on all of the y goods together (with I denoting the representative consumer's exogenous income). Furthermore (as we will work out shortly), since each of the y_i goods enters exactly the same way into the subutility function for y goods, the consumer will divide his or her consumption on the y goods equally among all available N alternatives if these alternatives are equally priced at price $\bar{p}$. Thus, the consumer would choose

$$x = \alpha I \quad \text{and} \quad y_i = \frac{(1-\alpha)I}{\bar{p}N} \quad \text{(for all } i\text{)}, \tag{26.35}$$

which would give utility

$$u = (\alpha I)^\alpha \left[N \left(\frac{(1-\alpha)I}{\bar{p}N} \right)^{-\rho} \right]^{-(1-\alpha)/\rho} = (\alpha I)^\alpha N^{-(1-\alpha)(1+\rho)/\rho} \left[\frac{(1-\alpha)I}{\bar{p}} \right]^{(1-\alpha)}. \tag{26.36}$$

Differentiating this with respect to N gives us

$$\frac{\partial u}{\partial N} = \frac{-(1-\alpha)(1+\rho)}{\rho} (\alpha I)^\alpha N^{-[(1-\alpha)(1+\rho)+\rho]/\rho} \left[\frac{(1-\alpha)I}{\bar{p}} \right]^{(1-\alpha)}, \tag{26.37}$$

which is greater than zero when $-1 < \rho < 0$. Thus, consumer utility increases as y good expenditures are spread across more differentiated products.

To get a sense of the magnitude of the potential importance of product diversity in this model, Table 26.2 illustrates the impact on the representative consumer's utility as N goes up when we assume (as we do in the example in Section 26B.4.5) that consumers have disposable income of $\$1$ billion, $\alpha = 0.9$ (which implies consumers will spend 10% of their income in the differentiated product market) and the price charged by each firm in the differentiated product market is $\bar{p} = 100$. In addition, we assume an elasticity of substitution across the y goods of 2 (by setting $\rho = -0.5$).

The first row in the table sets the number of differentiated firms N, with the second row deriving the implied number of output units of y_i the representative consumer purchases given a price of 100 and given the consumer devotes 10% of his or her income to all the y goods together. The third row then calculates the subutility in the y good market, and the fourth row presents the overall utility for the representative consumer. Finally, the last row derives the percentage reduction in overall income that the consumer would be willing to accept in exchange for the increased diversity in the y market from the baseline case of no product variation (when $N = 1$ in the first column). As you can see, despite the fact that the consumer continues to spend only 10% of income in the y market, the mere increase in the diversity of offerings in that market is worth a lot to this consumer. In particular, the consumer is willing to give up over 20% of income to have 10 rather than 1 firm in the y market, 37% to have 100 rather than 1 firm, 50% to have 1,000 rather than 1 firm, and 60% to have 10,000 rather than 1. Frequenting many restaurants makes the consumer better off than frequenting only a few even if his or her overall budget for going to restaurants is the same in both cases!

Table 26.2: $\alpha = 0.9$, $\rho = -0.5$, $I = \$1$ billion, $\bar{p} = 100$

	Utility as N Changes				
N	1	10	100	1,000	10,000
y_i (in 10,000's)	10,000	1,000	100	10	1
$(v(y_1, \ldots y_N))^{(1-\alpha)}$	3.981	5.012	6.310	7.943	10.000
$u(x, y_1, \ldots y_N)$ (in millions)	455.85	573.88	722.47	909.53	1,145.03
% Equivalent Income	100%	79.43%	63.10%	50.12%	39.81%

26B.4.2 Utility Maximization and Demand   The representative consumer faces a budget constraint

$$x + p_1y_1 + p_2y_2 + \ldots + p_Ny_N = x + \sum_{i=1}^{N} p_iy_i = I, \qquad (26.38)$$

where I again represents the representative consumer's (exogenous) income. We can then write the consumer's utility maximization problem as an unconstrained optimization problem in which he or she chooses only the y goods if we simply assume that the remaining income goes toward the x good by solving equation (26.38) for x and substituting it into the utility function. The resulting optimization problem for the representative consumer can then be written as

$$\max_{y_1, y_2, \ldots, y_N} u = \left(I - \sum p_iy_i \right)^{\alpha} \left(\sum y_i^{-\rho} \right)^{-(1-\alpha)/\rho}, \qquad (26.39)$$

where we have simplified notation a bit by taking it as given that the summations are from $i = 1$ to N. The problem becomes a lot easier to solve if we take a positive monotone transformation of u by taking natural logs, thus rewriting u as $\bar{u}$ in the form

$$\bar{u} = \alpha \ln \left(I - \sum p_iy_i \right) - \frac{(1 - \alpha)}{\rho} \ln \left(\sum y_i^{-\rho} \right). \qquad (26.40)$$

The first order conditions for the resulting optimization problem then simply set the partial derivatives of u (with respect to each y_j) to zero; i.e.,

$$\frac{-\alpha p_j}{I - \sum p_iy_i} + \frac{(1 - \alpha)\rho y_j^{-(\rho+1)}}{\rho \sum y_i^{-\rho}} = 0 \ \text{ for all } \ j = 1, 2, \ldots, N. \qquad (26.41)$$

We can re-arrange this to write

$$y_j = \left[\frac{(1 - \alpha)(I - \sum p_iy_i)}{\alpha \sum y_i^{-\rho}} \right]^{1/(\rho+1)} p_j^{-1/(\rho+1)}. \qquad (26.42)$$

Because we are assuming that N is large, y_j has no major impact on the value of the terms in the summation signs, which then allows us to approximate equation (26.42) as

$$y_j(p_j) \approx \beta p_j^{-1/(\rho+1)} \ \text{ where } \ \beta = \left[\frac{(1 - \alpha)(I - \sum p_iy_i)}{\alpha \sum y_i^{-\rho}} \right]^{1/(\rho+1)}. \qquad (26.43)$$

which represents the representative consumer's approximate demand for good y_j as a function of p_j.

Exercise 26B.15   Demonstrate that the price elasticity of demand for y_j is $-1/(\rho + 1)$.

26B.4.3 Firm Pricing   Recall that each of the goods in the y-market is produced by a single firm, which means that firm j knows that the demand for *its* output is given by equation (26.43). When determining what price to charge, firm j therefore solves the problem

$$\max_{p_j} \pi^j = (p_j - c)y_j(p_j) \approx (p_j - c)\beta p_j^{-1/(\rho+1)}. \qquad (26.44)$$

Why do fixed entry costs not enter this problem?

Exercise
26B.16

Taking first order conditions by setting the partial derivative of π^j (with respect to p_j) to zero, we can then solve for p_j charged by firm j for output y_j as

$$p_j = -\frac{c}{\rho}. \tag{26.45}$$

Recall that we have assumed that the y goods are relatively substitutable by assuming $-1 < \rho < 0$, which implies that p_j in the previous equation is positive and $p_j > c$. Firms therefore charge above marginal cost, but as the elasticity of substitution goes to ∞ (i.e., as ρ approaches -1), price approaches marginal cost. This complies well with the intuition we have developed earlier in this chapter: As product differentiation goes to zero (with the y goods becoming perfect substitutes), price competition becomes more intense and approaches the undifferentiated products Bertrand result of price equal to marginal cost.

Since each of the firms in the y market faces a similar problem, this price is then the price that is charged by all firms in the market; i.e., the equilibrium price p^* is

$$p^* = p_1 = p_2 = \ldots = p_N = -\frac{c}{\rho}. \tag{26.46}$$

26B.4.4 Firm Entry Equilibrium But in equilibrium it must furthermore be the case that no potential entrant could enter the y market and make a positive profit, and no firm would have entered the market had that meant it made negative profit by entering. Thus, the profit from entering the market (which includes the fixed entry cost FC) must be zero (even though, once in the market, firms make positive profits because entry costs have become sunk costs).[15] This zero (entry) profit condition can be written as

$$(p^* - c)y_i = \left(-\frac{c}{\rho} - c\right)y_i = -\left(\frac{1 + \rho}{\rho}\right)cy_i = FC, \tag{26.47}$$

which implies that, in full equilibrium,

$$y_i = \frac{-\rho}{1 + \rho}\left(\frac{FC}{c}\right) = y^* \quad \text{for all } i = 1, 2, \ldots, N. \tag{26.48}$$

The zero profit condition that emerges from entry of firms into the y market therefore implies that firms must supply y^* in the full equilibrium in which there is no further incentive for firms to enter the market. Since we are restricting ρ to lie between 0 and -1, the term $-\rho/(1 + \rho)$ lies between 0 (as ρ approaches 0) and ∞ (as ρ approaches -1). Each firm in the y market therefore produces a positive quantity, with production increasing (1) as the y goods become more substitutable for consumers (i.e., as ρ moves from 0 to -1), (2) as fixed entry cost FC increases, and (3) as marginal production costs c decrease.

Can you give an intuitive explanation for each of the three factors that causes firm output in the y market to increase?

Exercise
26B.17

---

[15]In representative consumer models of this kind, it is typically assumed that the representative consumer is also the owner of all the firms in the economy and thus derives income from firm profits. Since firm profits are zero, however, we can conveniently ignore firm profits as a source of consumer income in the consumer's optimization problem.

If y^* is produced by each firm and sold at p^* in equilibrium, it must then also be the case that the representative consumer demands exactly y^* at p^* for each of the y goods produced in equilibrium. Put differently, it must be that demand is equal to supply.

The consumer demand (in equation (26.42)) for each of the y goods was derived from the consumer's optimization problem and thus has to satisfy the first order condition of that problem in equation (26.41). Since all firms charge the same price p^* and produce the same quantity y^*, we can then replace all the p_i and y_i terms in that first order condition by p^* and y^*. This allows us to simplify the summation terms, with

$$\sum p_i y_i = N p^* y^* \quad \text{and} \quad \sum y_i^{-\rho} = N y^{*-\rho}. \tag{26.49}$$

Replacing these summations and substituting in p^* for the remaining p_j terms and y^* for the remaining y_j terms, the first order condition (26.41) then simplifies to

$$\frac{\alpha p^*}{I - N p^* y^*} = \frac{(1 - \alpha)}{N y^*}, \tag{26.50}$$

which can be solved to yield

$$N = \frac{(1 - \alpha)I}{p^* y^*}. \tag{26.51}$$

Substituting equations (26.46) and (26.48) in for p^* and y^*, this gives us the equilibrium number of firms in the market,

$$N^* = \frac{(1 - \alpha)(1 + \rho)I}{FC}. \tag{26.52}$$

Thus, once we determined the equilibrium prices p^* charged by firms from the firm optimization problem (that takes the consumer's approximate demand function $y_j(p_j)$ as given), we used this to determine the equilibrium quantity y^* produced by each firm by making sure that the zero (entry) profit condition holds. Then, to ensure that demand is equal to supply, we substituted these into the first order condition from the consumer problem to solve for the equilibrium number of firms, N^*.

The number of firms in the y market (and thus the amount of product diversity) therefore increases (1) as consumers place more value on y goods (i.e., as $(1 - \alpha)$ increases), (2) as the y goods become less substitutable (i.e., as ρ moves from -1 to 0), (3) as disposable income I increases, and (4) as the fixed entry cost FC falls.

Exercise 26B.18   Can you give an intuitive explanation for each of the four factors that increase product diversity in the y market?

A final observation about the model before we look at a brief example: You may have noticed that only ρ and the cost parameters c and FC enter the expressions for y^* and p^*. This suggests that these might in fact be independent of the Cobb–Douglas functional form we assumed and might hold for the more general utility function (with CES subutility for the y goods) we introduced at the beginning of our discussion of monopolistic competition. That is, in fact, correct, as you can explore for yourself in end-of-chapter exercise 26.2. The equilibrium number of firms N^* that we calculated does, however, depend on the Cobb–Douglas specification, although the basic intuitions it brings to light are more general.

26B.4.5 An Example Suppose, for instance, that the y goods represent tables served in restaurants in a city and that consumers in the city have $1 billion in disposable income to allocate between "other consumption" and "eating out in restaurants." Suppose further that we know our consumers spend 10% of disposable income on eating out. We know from our work with Cobb–Douglas preferences that, when the Cobb–Douglas exponents sum to 1, the exponent on each good represents the share of a consumer's budget that will be allocated to consumption of that good. Thus, knowing that consumers will spend 10% of their disposable income on "eating out" means that $(1 - \alpha) = 0.1$, or $\alpha = 0.9$, in the utility function in equation (26.34). On the firm side, suppose that it costs $100,000 to set up a restaurant and that the marginal cost of serving an average table in a restaurant is $100; i.e., suppose $FC = \$100,000$ and $c = \$100$.

Table 26.3 then uses the equations we derived to calculate the monopolistically competitive equilibrium under different assumptions about the elasticity of substitution between restaurants. In particular, the first row assumes different values of ρ that are translated into elasticity of substitution values σ in the second row, where we know from our understanding of CES utility functions that $\sigma = 1/(1 + \rho)$. The remaining rows then report the resulting values for the equilibrium price p^* charged per table in each restaurant, the equilibrium number of tables y^* served in each restaurant, and the equilibrium number of restaurants N^* in the city.

Verify the values for the column $\rho = -0.5$.

Exercise 26B.19

What values in the table change if consumer income rises? What if consumers develop more of a taste for "eating out"; i.e., what if α falls? What if the fixed cost of setting up restaurants increases?

Exercise 26B.20

This model of monopolistic competition, with consumer preferences that include a "taste for diversity," has come to play an important role in the area of urban economics in which economists attempt to understand the characteristics of modern cities. An understanding of cities requires some appreciation for why it is that people might, all else being equal, want to live toward the center of cities and why, in equilibrium, only some choose to actually live there. One way to think of this is to think of consumers as wanting, all else being equal, to consume the greater diversity of products that can be offered in geographically dense areas, with people who live farther away from dense areas having less access to diversified product markets (because of, say, fewer restaurants in suburbs) and having to pay a commuting cost to gain access to products offered in the city. Such models will then predict that land prices fall with distance away from the diversified product market in the city, with people trading off more land (and housing) consumption in the suburbs against less access to diversified consumption possibilities (like restaurants). Of course there are other factors that are important as well, such as

Table 26.3: $\alpha = 0.9$, $I = \$1$ billion, $FC = 100,000$, $c = 100$

	Equilibrium Prices, Quantities, and Number of Firms				
ρ	−0.05	−0.25	−0.50	−0.75	−0.95
σ	1.05	1.33	2.00	4.00	20.00
p^*	$2,000.00	$400.00	$200.00	$133.33	$105.26
y^*	52.63	333.33	1,000.00	3,000.00	19,000.00
N^*	950.00	750.00	500.00	250.00	50.00

access to better schools or lower crime rates in many U.S. suburbs. Combining these factors with models of "tastes for diversity" can then help explain why people might pay higher housing prices to live in cities until they have children, at which time they might choose to move to suburbs to get access to better schools and larger houses while decreasing the number of times they go out to nice restaurants.

26B.5 Advertising and Marketing

In Section 26A.5, we distinguished between two types of advertising that we called "informational advertising" and "image marketing." Informational advertising is aimed at providing consumers with information about the existence of products and their prices, while image marketing is aimed at differentiating identical underlying "products" by altering consumer perceptions. Although we concluded in Section 26A.5 that this distinction is in fact far from crisp, we will now illustrate each in specialized settings.

26B.5.1 Informational Advertising

Let us consider the simplest possible setting in which to think about informational advertising.[16] Suppose that a market is perfectly competitive with many identical firms producing the same undifferentiated product x at marginal cost c in the absence of any fixed costs. Suppose further that there are n consumers who are also identical, with each willing to pay up to $s > c$ for one unit of x but less than c for any additional units. Since no firm will sell below marginal cost c, this implies that each consumer will demand exactly one unit of x so long as price p is less than s. In the absence of any informational constraints on the part of consumers, the competitive equilibrium in this market would therefore have firms setting price equal to marginal cost and each consumer purchasing one unit of x.

Exercise 26B.21 What is the equilibrium if $s < c$? What if $s = c$?

But suppose that consumers are unaware of the existence of firms and their prices unless they receive an ad in the mail that informs them that a particular firm is producing x and selling at p. Suppose further that firms can send out any number of advertisements randomly to consumers, with each ad costing c_a. Given that there are n consumers in the market, the probability that any given ad will reach a particular consumer i is therefore equal to $1/n$.

A consumer will not purchase any x if he or she receives no ad from any firm because without an ad, the consumer is unaware that the product is available. If the consumer receives one ad, he or she will buy from that firm at the firm's price so long as $p \leq s$. If the consumer receives multiple ads, he or she will purchase from the lowest priced firm (again assuming that this firm charges a price below s). Since it is pointless for firms to send out ads announcing prices above s, we know that all ads will announce prices no higher than s, and since firms would lose money at prices below marginal cost plus the cost of sending the ad, we know that no firm will announce a price below $c + c_a$. Thus, any price p featured in an ad will satisfy

$$c + c_a \leq p \leq s, \tag{26.53}$$

which means, for the problem to remain interesting, $s > c + c_a$.

Exercise 26B.22 What is the equilibrium if $c \leq s < c + c_a$?

[16]This was considered by Gerald Butters, "Equilibrium Distribution of Prices and Advertising," *Review of Economic Studies* 44 (1977), 465–92.

Without doing much math, we can now reason our way to what must emerge in equilibrium assuming the existence of a large number of firms (as we have done) and a large number of consumers. Since there are no barriers to entry into this market, it must mean that all firms expect to make zero profit. The only way in which a firm can make a sale is to advertise, but advertising is no guarantee that a sale is made since the consumer who receives the ad might have received an ad from another firm that advertised a lower price. Let $x(p)$ denote the probability that an ad announcing price p results in the consumer purchasing the product at that price from the advertising firm. The expected revenue from sending out an ad announcing p is then $(p - c)x(p)$, while the cost of sending out the ad is c_a. The only way that expected profits are zero (as the free entry assumption implies must hold in equilibrium) is if the expected profit from each ad that is sent out is zero, i.e., if

$$(p - c)x^*(p) - c_a = 0, \qquad (26.54)$$

where $x^*(p)$ is the equilibrium probability that an ad announcing p will result in a sale. Notice that $x(p)$ looks a lot like a downward-sloping demand function: It tells us for any given price that might appear in an ad how likely it is that the consumer will respond to receiving the ad by buying the advertised good. The lower the advertised price, the higher is the probability of a sale; i.e., $dx(p)/dp < 0$.

The interesting conclusion that then follows is that there is no particular reason to expect a single price to appear on every ad that is sent out. Higher priced ads have a lower probability of resulting in a sale but a higher profit if they do result in a sale. We would then expect many prices that satisfy expression (26.53) to appear on ads with free entry of firms ensuring that the expected profit from each ad remains at zero. For instance, even when a firm sends out an ad with $p = s$, there is some probability $x(s)$ that the receiving consumer did not receive any other ads and will therefore purchase from the firm. From the zero profit condition (26.54), we know that in the free entry equilibrium it must then be that

$$x^*(s) = \frac{c_a}{s - c}. \qquad (26.55)$$

No matter how many ads are sent by firms, there is always a chance that a particular consumer will not receive an ad since all ads are sent out randomly. If that probability is greater than $x^*(s)$, a firm could enter and make a positive expected profit by sending out an ad that announces price $p = s$. Thus, in equilibrium, the probability that a given consumer does not receive an ad (and therefore does not consume x) is equal to $x^*(s)$; i.e., in equilibrium

$$(\text{Probability that a consumer does not consume } x) = \frac{c_a}{s - c}. \qquad (26.56)$$

We have arrived, then, at a market in which firms price above marginal cost but end up making zero expected profit because of the cost of informing consumers of the existence of their products. Put differently, the competitive market takes on the characteristics of a monopolistically competitive market because of the need to convey information through costly advertising.

We can then ask how the equilibrium outcome under this monopolistic competition relates to the efficient outcome that a social planner would dictate if the planner faced the same constraint of having to inform consumers of the existence of products through the same form of advertising. The planner does not have to bother with thinking about prices; he or she can simply give the product to the consumer who has been made aware of its existence due to the receipt of an ad. The planner will therefore keep sending out ads so long as the cost of sending out the ad is no greater than the probability that the recipient has not yet received an ad times the social surplus that would be gained by getting the good to a consumer who does not yet have one. This social gain is $(s - c)$, and the cost of sending the ad is c_a. Let the probability that an ad reaches a consumer who has not yet received an ad be $P(a)$, where a is the number of ads that have already gone out. The planner then keeps sending ads until $P(a)(s - c) = c_a$, or until

$$P(a) = \frac{c_a}{s - c}. \tag{26.57}$$

Notice that $P(a)$ is exactly equal to the probability that a consumer will not be reached by an ad under monopolistic competition (as derived in equation (26.56))! The social planner therefore chooses an amount of advertising that results in exactly the same probability that a given consumer will not be informed of the existence of the product x, thus leaving exactly as many consumers without x as the monopolistically competitive market. Put differently, *we have illustrated a model in which informational advertising results in the socially optimal level of information being conveyed through advertising.* While this is not a general "first welfare theorem" for informational advertising (because the result does not hold in other types of plausible models), it makes the case that informational advertising *can* be socially optimal and certainly does convey socially useful information.

Exercise 26B.23

Suppose the social planner decides to sell goods at $p = c$. Is consumer surplus the same in the market with advertising as under this social planner's solution? If not, how is overall surplus the same?

One final note: In Section 26A.5, we discussed informational advertising in the context of a market where consumers are aware of some but not all firms and where the emergence of advertising creates increased awareness of competitors and thus increases competition. We could build this into a model such as the one presented here by assuming that consumers initially know of one firm (which, in the absence of advertising, then has market power). This would then result in the intuitions from Section 26A.5; i.e., advertising would lead to greater competition as consumers become aware of competitors, with firms themselves potentially preferring a ban on advertising.

26B.5.2 Image Marketing

As we mentioned in Section 26A.5, the idea behind "image marketing" is at once easy and difficult to grasp. It is easy to grasp from a gut-level perspective; we can all see how the typical Superbowl ad for Coke is shaping the image of the product, not the product (i.e., what's in the can) itself. At the same time, if consumers respond to this "image marketing," there is something that they value in what Coke is doing; there is something about the association of, say, LeBron James endorsing Coke that makes at least some consumers think of Coke as more differentiated from, say, Pepsi. So it's not all that clear that the product itself has not changed when viewed as consisting of not only what's in the can. Economists do not have a comparative advantage in modeling something of this kind. But we can try to do a bit just to illustrate how such image marketing might in fact be socially wasteful.

Suppose we think back to the Hotelling model and suppose that now the interval [0,1] does not represent true product differentiation but rather marketing-induced product differentiation in the minds of consumers. In particular, let's assume exactly as in our Hotelling model that consumers are spread uniformly along the interval [0,1] and demand only a single unit of y output so long as they receive non-negative surplus from doing so. As in our previous treatment of the Hotelling model, consumer $n \in [0,1]$ incurs a utility cost of $\alpha(n - y)^2$ for consuming a product $y \in [0,1]$, except now we will make α a function of the level of adversing taking place in the industry; i.e., $\alpha = f(a_1, a_2)$ where a_i represents units of advertising purchased by firm i. If we choose f such that $f(0,0) = 0$, we have defined a model in which the firms' products are perfectly substitutible in the absence of advertising, with consumer n incurring no utility loss from consuming a good $y \neq n$.

Now consider a three-stage game: In the first stage, each firm chooses its level of advertising a_i, which it can purchase at a per-unit cost of c_a. At the conclusion of the first stage, the parameter α that indicates the degree to which consumers care about a product's location on the $[0,1]$ interval relative to their ideal points will then have been determined, with $\alpha = f(a_1, a_2)$. In the second stage, the firms then choose their locations y_1 and y_2 on the $[0,1]$ interval, and in the final stage they engage in price competition and set their prices p_1 and p_2.

Subgame perfection requires us to begin in stage 3 and work backward. But from our work in Section 26B.2, we already know that equilibrium prices in stage 3 (equation (26.17)) will take the form

$$p_1 = p_2 = c + \alpha, \tag{26.58}$$

where c is again the marginal production cost. Since α is determined solely from the advertising choices in stage 1, we can write this as

$$p_1 = p_2 = p(a_1, a_2) = c + f(a_1, a_2). \tag{26.59}$$

We also know from our work in Section 26B.2 that, as soon as $\alpha > 0$, the firms will locate their products at $y_1 = 0$ and $y_2 = 1$ in stage 2. If $\alpha = 0$, i.e., in the absence of advertising in the first stage, it does not matter to the firms where they locate their outputs since consumers view all locations on the interval $[0,1]$ as perfectly substitutable.

So all that remains is to consider what will take place in the first stage of the game. To make our example concrete, suppose that the technology for differentiating products through advertising requires both firms to advertise their "image differences" and takes the Cobb–Douglas form

$$\alpha = f(a_1, a_2) = a_1^{1/3} a_2^{1/3}. \tag{26.60}$$

Firm i will then choose its level of advertising a_i taking as given firm j's advertising choice a_j, solving the problem

$$\max_{a_i} \pi^i = (p(a_1, a_2) - c)\frac{1}{2} - c_a a_i, \tag{26.61}$$

where the per-unit profit $(p(a_1, a_2) - c)$ is multiplied by 1/2 because the two firms will each get half the consumers in equilibrium (assuming all consumers still purchase the good in equilibrium) and where $c_a a_i$ is the cost of advertising incurred by the firm. The solution to the first order condition for this problem is

$$a_i(a_j) = \frac{a_j^{1/2}}{6^{3/2} c_a^{3/2}} = \left(\frac{a_j}{216 c_a^3} \right)^{1/2}. \tag{26.62}$$

Verify that this best response function is correct.

Exercise 26B.24

This, then, is firm i's best response to firm j's advertising level a_j. Since the two firms are identical, their best response functions are symmetric and we can solve for the equilibrium level of advertising

$$a^* = a_1^* = a_2^* = \frac{1}{216 c_a^3}, \tag{26.63}$$

which implies an equilibrium level of "image differentiation" of

$$\alpha^* = f(a_1^*, a_2^*) = \left(\frac{1}{216 c_a^3} \right)^{1/3} \left(\frac{1}{216 c_a^3} \right)^{1/3} = \frac{1}{36 c_a^2}. \tag{26.64}$$

Exercise
26B.25

Can you determine whether firms are making positive profits in equilibrium? What happens as the cost of image advertising gets large? What happens as it approaches zero? Can you make sense of this within the context of the model?

The firms, then, engage in strategic image marketing in the first stage in order to position their otherwise identical products at different ends of the interval [0,1], with the intent of softening price competition and raising profits. In the absence of such image marketing, there is nothing in the model to prevent fierce Bertrand price competition, with price ending at marginal cost and profits being zero. While profits increase as price rises above marginal cost, consumer welfare falls both because consumers pay higher prices and because consumers incur utility losses when $\alpha > 0$. The higher prices paid by consumers are, in this model, simple transfers from consumers to firms and thus carry no efficiency losses (since we are assuming that consumers always end up buying 1 unit of the good). But the utility loss benefits no one, and the adversing costs incurred by firms are similarly socially wasteful. This is precisely the result predicted by skeptics of image marketing.

But the inefficiency result is also an artifact of the modeling. To be more precise, we can change the model slightly, get exactly the same equilibrium prediction about behavior but the reverse prediction about welfare. Suppose we assume that consumer n incurs a utility change of $\gamma\alpha - \alpha(n - y)^2$ when he or she consumes a good of type y, with $\gamma \geq 0$. The model above is just a special case of this where $\gamma = 0$ and a deviation from a consumer's ideal point therefore entails a pure utility loss of $\alpha(n - y)^2$. Assuming $\gamma > 0$ is equivalent to assuming that image marketing makes y goods more attractive (by adding $\gamma\alpha$ to the utility of consuming the good) while also imposing a utility cost on n to the extent to which n is far from y. If $\gamma > 1/4$, the utility gain from image marketing is at least as large as the utility loss so long as the distance $|n - y|$ is no greater than $1/2$ (which, in an equilibrium in which the two firms locate at $y_1 = 0$ and $y_2 = 1$, is the case for all consumers).

Exercise
26B.26

Suppose boys tend to like "Fred Flintstone" and girls tend to like "Dora the Explorer." Interpret our model in terms of a cereal company placing "Dora the Explorer" on a cereal box with the intent of differentiating the cereal from otherwise identical cereal by a second firm that instead places "Fred Flintstone" on its cereal box. Do you think $\gamma > 0$ for the intended consumers (i.e., children)?

Allowing γ to be greater than 0, however, changes nothing in terms of the equilibrium behavior of firms and consumers. Firms will still set prices as in equation (26.59) in the third stage of the game, will still choose $y_1 = 0$ and $y_2 = 1$ so long as $\alpha > 0$, and will still choose equilibrium advertising levels of a^* as derived in equation (26.63). This is because what matters for firm pricing is not the absolute utility level that all consumers get from consuming one y good (which is what is affected when $\gamma > 0$) but rather the degree to which the products have been differentiated. This differentiation drives the softening of price competition, the location choice on the interval [0,1], and the optimal advertising levels. Similarly, consumers will still shop at firm 1 if $n < 0.5$ and at firm 2 if $n > 0.5$ because their decision depends on where they can get *more* utility, not whether all y locations have become more attractive.

While equilibrium *behavior* is therefore independent of the value of $\gamma \geq 0$, the welfare predictions of the model are not. With γ sufficiently high and the cost of advertising c_a sufficiently low, it is easy to generate a scenario under which the image marketing is in fact welfare enhancing. And since the behavioral predictions of the welfare enhancing scenario are exactly the same as the behavioral predictions of the welfare loss scenario, it's not possible to use behavioral observations to differentiate between the two, at least not within this model. In

Table 26.4: $c = 1$, $c_a = 0.1$

	Welfare from "Image Marketing" as γ Changes				
γ	0	0.1	0.25	0.5	1
$a*$	4.623	4.623	4.623	4.623	4.623
$\alpha*$	2.778	2.778	2.778	2.778	2.778
$p*$	3.778	3.778	3.778	3.778	3.778
π^i	0.926	0.926	0.926	0.926	0.926
Utility Change	−0.232	0.046	0.463	1.157	2.546
Total Ad Cost	0.926	0.926	0.926	0.926	0.926
Social Gain (Loss)	(1.157)	(0.880)	(0.463)	0.231	1.620

such a case, welfare analysis makes little sense even when behavioral predictions do. Put differently, our model tells us that, at least under our particular assumptions, image marketing decreases price competition and raises firm profits, but it cannot tell us whether this raises or lowers social welfare.

This is illustrated in Table 26.4 where different equilibrium variables are calculated for increasing values of γ (when we assume $c = 1$ and $c_a = 0.1$). The first four variables—equilibrium advertising levels ($a*$), product image differentiation (α), prices ($p*$), and firm profits (π^i)—are all unchanged as γ increases. The table then reports the overall "utility change" induced by advertising across all consumers, with the utility change from the price increase above marginal cost not counted (since it is merely a transfer to firms without efficiency loss). When added to the total cost of advertising, we get the social gain or loss from advertising in the last row. As you can see, increasing γ changes the welfare implications of image advertising, with larger γ entailing lower social costs or, for sufficiently large γ, net social benefits.

CONCLUSION

We have now come a long way from our initial model of perfectly competitive markets in which a large number of firms produce identical products in the absence of barriers to entry. The perfectly competitive model served as our benchmark for the First Welfare Theorem in which the market outcome was unambiguously efficient. In Chapter 23, we took a dramatic turn when we introduced the opposite extreme by assuming that a single firm that we called a monopoly had to itself the entire market for a good due to the presence of high barriers to entry that kept out potential competitors. In Chapter 25, we considered the case of oligopolies that continued to benefit from large barriers to entry but competed with one another, either by setting quantity in the Cournot model or by setting price in the Bertrand model. But not until this chapter have we considered the role of product differentiation (and product innovation).

The real world is characterized by an almost unimaginable level of such product differentiation that can, in principle, arise under any market structure. We have focused here on such differentiation in the two market structures that lie in between the extremes of perfect competition and perfect monopoly; i.e., in oligopolies and in monopolistically competitive markets. The difference between these two market structures often arises endogenously from the size of fixed entry costs, with markets that exhibit high fixed entry costs relative to demand resulting in oligopolies that contain a few firms, and with markets that exhibit low fixed entry costs relative to demand resulting in monopolistic competition with many firms. In each case, in the absence of other barriers to entry, firms within the industry earn positive profits (when fixed entry costs are taken to be sunk), while firms outside the industry would earn negative expected profits by entering the industry (because fixed entry costs for them are real economic costs).

We have furthermore emphasized in this chapter that the drive to gain market power (in the absence of artificial barriers to entry) carries some social cost as successful firms use market power to raise price by restricting production, but it also generates social surplus as firms can succeed only if they find new and better ways of satisfying consumer demand. In many monopolistically competitive settings, the latter outweighs the former, with innovation aimed at generating market power providing an engine for economic growth while held in check by competition. This insight is often lost in static models of oligopoly behavior where it is easy to see the social loss from the exercise of market power at any given time but difficult to see, without thinking a bit outside the equilibrium models, the social gain from the innovations that result in this market power.

As I have mentioned repeatedly, the economics literature on market structures and strategic firm behavior outside the perfectly competitive case is extensive, and if the topics we have covered in the past few chapters are of interest to you, you should take further course work in industrial organization and related courses. We have only scratched the surface of a fascinating set of insights that have arisen in models we have introduced. For instance, we have not even considered (and will do so only briefly in end-of-chapter exercise 26.5) the issues raised by *vertical* rather than *horizontal* product differentiation. To be more precise, we have in this chapter assumed that firms simply aim to differentiate their products to appeal to some segments of the market by making the product a bit "different," but firms also engage in "vertical" differentiation in which they aim to appeal to consumers who are willing to pay more for the same product if it is of higher quality.

We will now leave our analysis of firm behavior and market structure, but we will not leave our consideration of *strategic* decision making. In the next chapter, we will revisit the case of externalities, which we previously treated in a competitive market in Chapter 21, and will focus on a particular type of externality that arises from *public goods*. As in the case of inefficiencies that arise from market power, we will see yet another example where governments *might* be able to enhance social welfare. Put differently, we will again be able to *in principle* identify ways in which benevolent governments that have sufficient information can alter the institutions within which markets operate and thereby bring decentralized decisions by firms and consumers more in line with the "common good." But, as we have noted repeatedly, governments do encounter informational constraints and, even if entirely benevolent, are limited in their ability to bring private incentives in line with social goals to the extent to which the necessary information is costly to obtain. In Chapter 28, we will furthermore see ways in which we can model government decision makers themselves as strategic actors. The strategic decision making by politicians in democratic settings then creates additional hurdles for efficiency-enhancing government action.

END-OF-CHAPTER EXERCISES

26.1[†]   We introduced the topic of differentiated products in a simple two-firm Bertrand price setting model in which each firm's demand increases with the price of the other firm's output. The specific context we investigated was that of imperfect substitutes.

   A.   Assume throughout that demand for each firm's good is positive at $p = MC$ even if the other firm sets its price to 0. Suppose further that firms face constant MC and no fixed costs.

   a.   Suppose that instead of substitutes, the goods produced by the two firms are complements; i.e., suppose that an increase in firm j's price causes a decrease rather than an increase in the demand for firm i's good. How would Graph 26.3 change assuming both firms end up producing in equilibrium?

   b.   What would the in-between case look like in this graph; i.e., what would the best response functions look like if the price of firm j's product had no influence on the demand for firm i's product?

   c.   Suppose our three cases—the case of substitutes (covered in the text), of complements (covered in (a)), and of the in-between case (covered in (b))—share the following feature in common: When $p_j = 0$, it is a best response for firm i to set $p_i = \bar{p} > MC$. How does $\bar{p}$ relate to what we would have called the monopoly price in Chapter 23?

---

    d. Compare the equilibrium price (and output) levels in the three cases assuming both firms produce in each case.

    e. In which of the three cases might it be that there is no equilibrium in which both firms produce?

B. Consider identical firms 1 and 2, and suppose that the demand for firm i's output is given by $x_i(p_i, p_j) = A - p_i - \beta p_j$. Assume marginal cost is a constant c and there are no fixed costs.

    a. What range of values correspond to goods x_i and x_j being substitutes, complements, and in-between goods as defined in part A of the exercise.

    b. Derive the best response functions. What are the intercepts and slopes?

    c. Are the slopes of the best response functions positive or negative? What does your answer depend on?

    d. What is the equilibrium price in terms of A, α, β, and c. Confirm your answer to A(d).

    e. Under what conditions will only one firm produce when the two goods are relatively complementary?

26.2** In Section B of the text, we developed a model of tastes for diversified goods and then applied a particular functional form for such tastes to derive results, some of which we suggested hold for more general cases.

B. We first introduced a general utility function representing such tastes in equation (26.33) before working with a version that embeds the subutility for y goods into a Cobb–Douglas functional form in equation (26.34). Consider now the more general version from equation (26.33).

    a. Begin by substituting the budget constraint into the utility function for the x term (as we did in the Cobb–Douglas case in the text).

    b. Derive the first order condition that differentiates utility with respect to y_i.

    c. Assume that the number of firms is sufficiently large such that terms in which y_i plays only a small role can be approximated as constant. Then use your first order condition from (b) to derive an approximate demand function that is just a function of p_i and a constant. What is the price elasticity of demand of this (approximate) demand function?

    d. Set up firm i's profit maximization problem given the demand function you have derived. Then solve for the price p_i that the firm will charge.

    e. *True or False*: The equilibrium price $p^* = -c/\rho$ we derived in the text for the Cobb–Douglas case does not depend on the Cobb–Douglas specification.

    f. Recalling our Chapter 15 discussion of treating groups of consumers as if they behaved like a "representative consumer," what form for the utility function might you assume if you were concerned that the Cobb–Douglas version we used in the text might technically not satisfy the conditions for a representative consumer? Would the implied equilibrium price differ from the Cobb–Douglas case?

26.3 **Everyday Application:** *Cities and Land Values*: Some of the models that we introduced in this chapter are employed in modeling the pattern of land and housing values in an urban areas.

A. One way to think about city centers is as places that people need to come to in order to work and shop.

    a. Consider the Hotelling line [0,1] that we used as a product characteristics space. Suppose instead that this line represents physical distance, with a city located at 0 and another city located at 1. Think of households as locating along this line, with a household that locates at $n \in [0,1]$ having to commute to one of the two cities unless $n = 0$ or $n = 1$. What does this imply for the distribution of consumer "ideal points"?

    b. If land along the Hotelling line were equally priced, where would everyone wish to locate? If the city at 0 is larger than the city at 1, and if bigger cities offer greater job and shopping opportunities, how would this affect your answer?

    c. What do your answers imply for the distribution of land values along the Hotelling line if land at each location is scarce and only one household can locate at each point on the line?

   d.   Suppose instead that more than one household can potentially locate at each point on the line, but if multiple households locate at a point, each consumes less land. (For instance, 100 families might share a high-rise apartment building.) Suppose this results in unoccupied farm land toward the middle of the Hotelling line. How would you expect population density to vary along the line?

   e.   In recent decades, a new phenomenon called "edge cities" has emerged, with smaller cities forming in the vicinity of larger cities, and land values adjusting accordingly. How would the distribution of land values change as edge cities appear on the Hotelling line?

   f.   What do you think will happen to the distribution of land values along the Hotelling line if commuting costs fall? What would happen to population density along the line?

   g.   Could you similarly see how land values are distributed in our "circle" model if cities are located at different points on the circle?

B. Now consider the model of tastes for diversified product markets in Section 26B.4.

   a.   Can you use the intuitions from this model to explain why larger cities on the Hotelling line (or the circle) in part A of the exercise will have higher land values?

   b.   Consider two cities in the same general area (but sufficiently far apart that consumers would rarely commute from one to the other). Suppose the model used to derive Table 26.2 in the text was the appropriate model for representing consumer tastes in this state, and suppose that city A had 100 restaurants and city B had 1,000. If the typical household in this economy has an annual income of $60,000 and a typical apartment in city A rents for $6,000 per year, what would you estimate this same apartment would rent for in city B?

26.4 **Business and Policy Application:** *Mergers and Antitrust Policy in Related Product Markets*: In exercise 26.1, we investigated different ways in which the markets for good x_i (produced by firm i) and good x_j (produced by firm j) may be related to each other under price competition. We now investigate the incentives for firms to merge into a single firm in such environments, and the level of concern that this might raise among antitrust regulators.

A. One way to think about firms that compete in related markets is to think of the externality they each impose on the other as they set price. For instance, if the two firms produce relatively substitutable goods (as described in (a)), firm 1 provides a positive externality to firm 2 when it raises p_1 because it raises firm 2's demand when it raises its own price.

   a.   Suppose that two firms produce goods that are relatively substitutable in the sense that, when the price of one firm's good goes up, this increases the demand for the other good's firm. If these two firms merged, would you expect the resulting monopoly firm to charge higher or lower prices for the goods previously produced by the competing firms? (Think of the externality that is not being taken into account by the two firms as they compete.)

   b.   Next, suppose that the two firms produce goods that are relatively complementary in the sense that an increase in the price of one firm's good *decreases* the demand for the other firm's good. How is the externality now different?

   c.   When the two firms in (b) merge, would you now expect price to increase or decrease?

   d.   If you were an antitrust regulator, which merger would you be worried about: the one in (a) or the one in (c)?

   e.   Suppose that instead the firms were producing goods in unrelated markets (with the price of one firm not affecting the demand for the goods produced by the other firm). What would you expect to happen to price if the two firms merge?

   f.   Why are the positive externalities we encountered in this exercise good for society?

B. Suppose we have two firms, firm 1 and 2, competing on price. The demand for firm i is given by $x_i(p_i, p_j) = 1,000 - 10p_i + \beta p_j$.

   a.   Calculate the equilibrium price p^* as a function of β.

   b.   Suppose that the two firms merged into one firm that now maximized overall profit. Derive the prices for the two goods (in terms of β) that the new monopolist will charge, keeping in mind that the monopolist now solves a single optimization problem to set the two prices. (Given the symmetry of the demands, you should of course get that the monopolist will charge the same price for both goods).

    c.   Create the following table: Let the first row set different values for β ranging from minus 7.5 to 7.5 in 2.5 increments. Then, derive the equilibrium price (for each β) when the two firms compete and report it in the second row. In a third row, calculate the price charged by the monopoly (that results from the merging of the two firms) for each value of β.

    d.   Do your results confirm your intuition from part A of the exercise? If so, how?

    e.   Why would firms merge if, as a result, they end up charging a lower price for both goods than they were able to charge individually?

    f.   Add two rows to your table, calculating first the profit that the two firms together make in the competitive oligopoly equilibrium and then the profit that the firms make as a monopoly following a merger. Are the results consistent with your answer to (e)?

26.5*   **Business Application:** *Advertising as Quality Signal*: In the text, we have discussed two possible motives for advertising, one focused on providing information (about the availability of goods or the prices of goods) and another focused on shaping the image of the product. Another possible motive might be for high quality firms to signal that they produce high quality goods to consumers who cannot tell the difference prior to consuming a good. Consider the following game that captures this: In each of two periods, firms get to set a price and consumers get to decide whether or not to buy the good. In the first period, consumers do not know if a firm is producing high or low quality goods; all they observe is the prices set by firms and whether or not firms have advertised. But if a consumer buys from a firm in the first period, the consumer experiences the quality of the firm's product and thus knows whether the firm is a high or low quality firm when he or she makes a decision of whether to buy from this firm in the second period. Assume throughout that a consumer who does not buy from a firm in the first period exits the game and does not proceed to the second period.

A.   Notice that firms and consumers play a sequential game in each period, with firms offering a price first and consumers then choosing whether or not to buy. But in the first period, firms also have the option to advertise in an attempt to persuade consumers of the product's value.

    a.   Consider the second period first. Given that the only way a consumer enters the second period is if he or she bought from the firm in the first period, and given that he or she then operates with the benefit of having experienced the good's quality, would any firm choose to advertise in the second period if it could?

    b.   Suppose that both firms incur a marginal cost of MC for producing their goods. High quality firms produce goods that are valued at $v_h > MC$ by consumers and low quality firms produce goods that are valued at $v_\ell > MC$ (with $v_h > v_\ell$). In any subgame perfect equilibrium, what prices will each firm charge in the second period, and what will consumer strategies be (given they decide whether to buy after observing prices)?

    c.   Now consider period 1. If consumers believe that firms that advertise are high quality firms and firms that don't advertise are low quality firms, what is their subgame perfect strategy in period 1 (after they observe prices and whether a firm has advertised)?

    d.   What is the highest cost a_h (per output unit) of advertising that a high quality firm would be willing to undertake if it thought that consumers would interpret this as the firm producing a high quality good?

    e.   What is the highest cost a_ℓ that a low quality firm would be willing to incur if it thought this would fool consumers into thinking that it produced high quality goods (when in fact it produces low quality goods)?

    f.   Consider a level of advertising that costs a^*. For what levels of a^* do you think that it is an equilibrium for high quality firms to advertise and low quality firms to not advertise?

    g.   Given the information asymmetry between consumers and firms in period 1, might it be efficient for such advertising to take place?

    h.   We often see firms sponsor sporting events, and it is difficult to explain such sponsorships as "informational advertising" in the way we discussed such advertising in the text. Why? How can the model in this exercise nevertheless be rationalized as informational advertising (rather than simply image marketing)?

B.   Suppose that a firm is a high quality firm h with probability δ and a low quality firm ℓ with probability $(1 - \delta)$. Firm h produces an output of quality that is valued by consumers at 4, while firm ℓ produces an output of quality 1 (that is valued by consumers at 1), and both incur a marginal cost equal to 1 per unit of output produced. (Assume no fixed costs.)

a.   Derive the level of a^* of advertising (as defined in part A) that could take place in equilibrium.

b.   What is the most efficient of the possible equilibria in which high quality firms advertise but low quality firms do not advertise?

c.   Do your answers thus far depend on δ?

d.   The equilibria you have identified so far are *separating equilibria* because the two types of firms behave differently in equilibrium, thus allowing consumers to learn from observing advertising whether or not a firm is producing a high or low quality good. Consider now whether both firms choosing (p, a), and firms thus playing a *pooling* strategy, could be part of an equilibrium. Why is period 2 largely irrelevant for thinking about this?

e.   If the firms play the pooling strategy (p, a), what is the consumer's expected payoff from buying in period 1? In terms of δ, what does this imply is the highest price p that could be part of the pooling equilibrium?

f.   Suppose consumers believe a firm to be a low quality firm if it deviates from the pooling strategy. If one of the firms has an incentive to deviate from the pooling strategy, which one would it be? What does this imply about the lowest that p can be relative to a in order for (p, a) to be part of a pooling equilibrium?

g.   Using your answers from (b) and (c), determine the range of p in terms of δ and a such that (p,a) can be part of a Bayesian Nash pooling equilibrium.

h.   What equilibrium beliefs do consumers hold in such a pooling equilibrium when they have to decide whether or not to buy in period 1? What out-of-equilibrium beliefs support the equilibrium?

i.   Can advertising in a pooling equilibrium ever be efficient?

26.6   **Business Application:** *Price Leadership in Differentiated Product Markets*: We have considered how oligopolistic firms in a differentiated product market price output when the firms simultaneously choose price. Suppose now that two firms have maximally differentiated products on the Hotelling line [0,1] and that the choice of product characteristics is no longer a strategic variable. But let's suppose now that your firm gets to move first, announcing a price that your opponent then observes before setting his or her own price. This is similar to the Stackelberg quantity-leadership model we discussed in Chapter 25 except that firms now set price rather than quantity.

A.   Suppose you are firm 1 and your opponent is firm 2, with both firms facing constant marginal cost (and no fixed costs).

a.   Begin by reviewing the logic behind sequential pricing in the pure Bertrand setting where the two firms produce undifferentiated products. Why does the sequential (subgame perfect) equilibrium price not differ from the simultaneous price setting equilibrium?

b.   Now suppose that you are producing maximally differentiated products on the Hotelling line. When firm 2 sees your price p_1, illustrate its best response in a graph with p_2 on the horizontal and p_1 on the vertical axis.

c.   Include in your graph the 45-degree line and indicate where the price equilibrium falls if you and your competitor set prices simultaneously.

d.   Let $\bar{p}$ be the price that results in zero demand for your goods assuming that your competitor observes $\bar{p}$ before setting his or her own price. Indicate $\bar{p}$ in a plausible place on your graph. Then, on a graph next to it, put p_1 on the vertical axis and x_1, the good produced by your firm, on the horizontal. Where does your demand curve start on the vertical axis given that you take into account your competitor's response?

e.   Draw a demand curve for x_1 and let this be the demand for x_1 given you anticipate your competitor's response to any price you set. Include MC and MR in your graph and indicate p_1^*, the price you will choose given that you anticipate your competitor's price response once he or she observes your price.

f.   Finally, find your competitor's price p_2^* on your initial graph. Does it look like p_1^* is greater or less than p_2^*?

g.   Who will have greater market share on the Hotelling line: you as the price leader, or your competitor?

B. Suppose that the costs (other than price) that consumers incur is quadratic as in the text; i.e., a consumer n whose ideal point is $n \in [0,1]$ incurs a cost $\alpha(n - y)^2$ from consuming a product with characteristic $y \in [0,1]$. Continue to assume that firm 1 has located its product at 0 and firm 2 has located its product at 1; i.e., $y_1 = 0$ and $y_2 = 1$. Firms incur constant marginal cost c (and no fixed costs).

    a. For what value of α is this the Bertrand model of Chapter 25? In this case, does the equilibrium price differ depending on whether one firm announces a price first or whether they announce price simultaneously? (Assume subgame perfection in the sequential case.)

    b. Now suppose $\alpha > 0$. If the firms set price simultaneously, what is the equilibrium price?

    c. Next, suppose firm 1 announces its price first, with firm 2 then observing firm 1's price before setting its own price. Using the same logic we used in the Stackelberg model of quantity competition, derive the price firm 1 will charge (as a function of c and α). (*Hint*: You can use the best response function for firm 2 derived in the text, substituting $y_1 = 0$ and $y_2 = 1$, to set up firm 1's optimization problem.)

    d. What price does this imply firm 2 will set after it observes p_1? Which price is higher?

    e. Derive the market shares for firms 1 and 2. In the Stackelberg quantity setting game, the firm that moved first had greater market share. Why is that not the case here?

    f. Derive profit for the two firms. Which firm does better: the leader or the follower? *True or False*: The quantity leader in the Stackelberg model has a first mover advantage, while the price leader in the Hotelling model has a first mover *disadvantage*.

    g. *True or False*: Both firms prefer sequential pricing in the Hotelling model over simultaneous pricing (given maximal product differentiation).

26.7 **Business Application:** *The Evolution of the Fashion Industry*: Consider the market for clothes and suppose there exist 100 different styles that can be produced and can be arranged (and equally spaced) on a circle. Among the billions of consumers of clothes, each has an ideal style somewhere on that circle (either at one of the 100 styles that can potentially be produced or in between two of those). Styles become less appealing the farther they are from the consumer's ideal. For simplicity, suppose that the marginal cost of producing clothes of any style is constant (once the fixed cost of starting production has been paid), and suppose that a firm that comes into the industry must pay the fixed entry cost for each style it wants to produce.

BUSINESS APPLICATION

A. Suppose first that only a single firm operates in the industry (and produces one of the 100 styles) and that the fixed cost of starting production is sufficiently high for no second firm to wish to enter.

    a. Explain how the firm in the industry can be making positive economic profit but the firms outside would make negative economic profit by entering.

    b. Over the decades, the price of the equipment necessary for producing clothes has fallen, thus lowering the fixed entry cost into the clothing industry. When the costs fall to the point where the second firm enters, where on the circle would you expect that firm to locate its clothes?

    c. What would happen to the price of clothing assuming the two firms are price competitors?

    d. Suppose entry costs have fallen sufficiently for 100 different firms to be in the clothing industry. Now suppose entry costs fall further and firms continue to be price competitors. How low would entry costs have to fall for another firm to enter the market (assuming only 100 clothing styles can potentially be produced)?

    e. Suppose that an avalanche of new ideas has made all clothing styles on the circle, not just the initial 100, possible to produce. As entry costs fall, how many new entrants would you expect when the next firm finds it profitable to enter?

    f. Beginning with the case where the industry first consists of 100 firms, would you expect price to fall as entry costs fall even before any additional competitors enter the industry (assuming that existing firms can credibly announce their price before new firms have to make a decision on whether or not to enter)?

    g. Suppose entry costs disappear altogether. What happens to price?

B. (Part B of this exercise is not directly related to part A but rather offers you a chance to go through solving the "circle model" with a slight modification from the version used in the text.) In our treatment of the "circle model" in Section 26B.3, we assumed that the cost consumer $n \in [0,1]$ incurs from consuming a product with characteristic $y \in [0,1]$ (rather than his or her ideal of n) increases linearly with the distance between n and y; i.e., the cost was $\alpha|n - y|$. In our treatment of the Hotelling "line" model, we instead assumed that this cost increases with the square of the distance; i.e., the cost was $\alpha(n - y)^2$.

   a. Consider the second stage of the "circle model" game; i.e., the stage at which N firms have entered in the first stage having equally spaced their products on the product characteristic circle (of circumference 1). Assume that every point y on the circle contains one consumer n whose ideal point is y. What is the farthest that any consumer n's ideal point will lie from the closest firm's product?

   b. Suppose that all firms other than firm i charge a price p and suppose firm i's product characteristic is $y_i = 0$. Denote by $\bar{n}$ the consumer who is indifferent between consuming from firm i and adjacent firm j (with firm j producing y_j) assuming firm i charges price p_i. Given that the consumer's total cost from consuming a particular product includes both the price he or she has to pay and the cost of consuming away from his or her ideal, what has to be true about the total cost $\bar{n}$ incurs when shopping at firm i versus firm j? Express this in an equation and solve it for $\bar{n}$.

   c. Given that there are N (equally spaced) firms in the industry, what is y_j (when $y_i = 0$)? Substitute this into your expression for $\bar{n}$. What is the demand $D^i(p_i, p)$ that firm i faces? Explain.

   d. Using your expression for $D^i(p_i, p)$, derive firm i's best (price) response function to all other firms setting price p (with all firms facing constant marginal cost c).

   e. Since all firms end up charging the same price in equilibrium, what is the equilibrium price $p^*(N)$ in terms of c, α, and N given that N firms have entered in stage 1 of the "circle game"?

   f. Assuming that firms have to pay a fixed cost FC to enter the circle market in stage 1 of the game, how many will enter (given they forecast p^* in the second stage)? Denote this as N^*. What is the equilibrium price that will emerge as a result?

   g.** Now consider the problem a social planner who wants to maximize efficiency faces when deciding how many firms to set up on the circle. Suppose the planner sets the number of firms at N. Explain why the cost consumers incur from not consuming at their ideal is $2N\int_0^{1/(2N)} x^2 dx$.

   h.** What is the socially optimal number of firms N^{opt} that the planner would set up? How does it compare to the equilibrium number of firms N^*, and what has to be true for the two to converge to one another?

26.8† **Business Application:** *Deterring Entry of Another Car Company:* Suppose that there are currently two car companies that form an oligopoly in which each faces constant marginal costs. Their strategic variables are price and product characteristics.

   A. Use the Hotelling model to frame your approach to this exercise and suppose that the two firms have maximally differentiated their products, with company 1 selecting characteristic 0 and company 2 selecting characteristic 1 from the set of all possible product characteristics [0,1].

   a. Explain why such maximal product differentiation might in fact be the equilibrium outcome in this model.

   b. Next, suppose a new car company plans to enter the market and chooses 0.5 as its product characteristic, and suppose existing companies can no longer vary their product characteristics. If the new company enters in this way, what happens to car prices? In what way can we view this as two distinct Hotelling models?

   c. How much profit would the new company make relative to the original two?

   d. Suppose that the existing companies announce their prices prior to the new company making its decision on whether or not to enter. Suppose further that the existing companies agree to announce the same price. If the new company has to pay a fixed cost prior to starting production, do you think there is a range of fixed costs such that companies 1 and 2 can strategically deter entry?

   e. What determines the range of fixed costs under which the existing companies will successfully deter entry?

    f.   If the existing companies had foreseen the potential of a new entrant who locates at 0.5, do you think they would have been as likely to engage in maximum product differentiation in order to soften price competition between each other?

    g.   We have assumed throughout that the entrant would locate at 0.5. Why might this be the optimal location for the entrant?

B.   Consider the version of Hotelling's model from Section 26B.2 and suppose that two oligopolistic car companies, protected by government regulations on how many firms can be in the car industry, have settled at the equilibrium product characteristics of 0 and 1 on the interval [0,1]. Suppose further that $\alpha = 12{,}000$ and $c = 10{,}000$ and assume throughout that car companies cannot change their product characteristics once they have chosen them.

    a.   What prices are the two companies charging? How much profit are they making given that they do not incur any fixed costs (and given that we have normalized the population size to 1)?

    b.   Now suppose that the government has granted permission to a third company to enter the car market at 0.5. But the company needs to pay a fixed cost FC to enter. If the third company enters, we can now consider the intervals [0,0.5] and [0.5,1] separately and treat each of these as a separate Hotelling model. Derive $D^1(p_1, p_3)$. Then derive $D^3(p_1, p_3)$ (taking care to note that the relevant interval is now [0,0.5] rather than [0,1].)

    c.   Determine the best response functions $p_1(p_3)$ and $p_3(p_1)$. Then calculate the equilibrium price.

    d.   How much profit will the three companies make (not counting the FC that any of them had to pay to get into the market)?

    e.   If company 3 makes its decision of whether to enter and what price to set at the same time as companies 1 and 2 make their pricing decisions, what is the highest FC that will still be consistent with the new car company entering?

    f.   Suppose instead that companies 1 and 2 can commit to a price before company 3 decides whether to enter. Suppose further that companies 1 and 2 collude to deter entry and agree to announce the same price prior to company 3's decision. What is the most that companies 1 and 2 would be willing to lower price in order to prevent entry?

    g.   What is the lowest FC that would now be consistent with company 3 not entering? (Be careful to consider firm 3's best price response and the implications for market share.)

26.9* **Policy Application:** *Lobbying for Car Import Taxes:* In exercise 26.8, we investigated the incentives of existing car companies to deter entry of new companies through lowering of car prices. When the potential new car company is a foreign producer that wants to enter the domestic car market, an alternative way in which such entry might be prevented or softened is through government import fees and/or import tariffs.

    A.   Suppose throughout that the foreign car company has product characteristic 0.5 while the domestic companies are committed to the maximally differentiated product characteristics of 0 and 1 in the Hotelling model.

        a.   Suppose first that the government requires the foreign car company to pay a large fee for the right to import (as many cars as it would like) into the domestic market. If the government makes any revenue from this policy, will it have any impact on the car market when all decisions are made simultaneously?

        b.   For a given fee F, why might the domestic car industry expend zero lobbying effort on behalf of this policy? Why might it expend a lot?

        c.   Suppose domestic firms can collude on setting a price in anticipation of entry (and can credibly commit to that price). *True or False*: There is now a range of F under which the foreign company does not enter when it would have entered given conditions in (a). (Assume that if entry occurs, the industry plays the simultaneous Nash pricing equilibrium.)[17]

        d.   Under the conditions in (c), does your answer to (a) change? Is there now a range of fees under which the foreign company does not enter the market but domestic companies lobby for higher fees?

---

[17]We are therefore not considering the case where domestic firms become price leaders, a case we analyze separately in exercise 26.6.

   e.   Suppose that instead the government imposes a per-unit tax t on all imported cars. Compared to what would happen in the absence of any government interference, how do you think domestic and foreign car prices will be affected?

   f.   How will market share of domestic versus foreign cars differ under the tariff?

   g.* Suppose the government imposes the lowest tariff that results in no foreign cars being sold. Do you think that domestic car companies can now charge the same price they would if foreign cars were prohibited from the domestic market outright?

   h.   Based on your answer to (g), might domestic firms lobby for higher import tariffs even if no cars are imported at current tariff levels?

B.   Consider again, as in exercise 26.8, the version of the Hotelling model from Section 26B.2 with the domestic car companies having settled at the equilibrium product characteristics of 0 and 1 on the interval [0,1]. Suppose again that $\alpha = 12,000$ and $c = 10,000$. Assume throughout that domestic companies cannot change their product characteristics.

   a.   If you have not already done so, do parts (a) through (e) of exercise 26.8.

   b.   Suppose that the government required the foreign company to pay a fee F in order to access the domestic market (without placing any restrictions on how many cars may be imported). Suppose there is no way for domestic firms to credibly commit to prices prior to the foreign firm deciding whether or not to enter. What is the lowest F that the domestic industry would lobby for assuming there are no other fixed entry costs? Would lobbying efforts be more intense for imposition of a higher fee?

   c.   How would your answer change if the domestic firms could credibly commit to a price prior to the foreign firm deciding on whether or not to enter? (Assume that the domestic firms agree to announce the same price.) For what range of F will domestic firms push to increase F? (Note: It is helpful to reason through (f) and (g) of exercise 26.8 prior to attempting this part.)

   d.   Next, suppose that instead the government imposed a per-unit tariff of t on all car imports. Treat this as an increase in the marginal cost for importing firms, from c to $(c + t)$. Derive the equilibrium prices charged by domestic firms and importing firms as a function of t. (Follow the same steps as in B(c) and (d) of exercise 26.8.) What can you say about the tax incidence of this tariff?

   e.   Derive the market share for firm 1 (and thus also firm 2) as a function of t. What level of t will restrict foreign imports to the same level as an import quota that limits foreign cars to one third of the market (assuming no fixed entry costs)?

   f.   What is the lowest level of $t = \bar{t}$ that guarantees no foreign cars will be sold in the domestic market (assuming no fixed entry costs)?

   g.   What prices will domestic car companies charge if t is set to $\bar{t}$?

   h.   Explain why setting $\bar{t}$ differs from the case where the import of foreign cars is prohibited.

   i.   What level of $t > \bar{t}$ is equivalent to prohibiting the entry of the foreign firm?

26.10† Business and Policy Application: *The Software Industry*: When personal computers first came onto the scene, the task of writing software was considerably more difficult than it is today. Over the following decades, consumer demand for software has increased as personal computers became prevalent in more and more homes and businesses at the same time as it has become easier to write software. Thus, the industry has been one of expanding demand and decreasing fixed entry costs.

A.   In this part of the exercise, analyze the evolution of the software industry using the monopolistic competition model from Section 26A.4 as well as insights from our earlier oligopoly models.

   a.   Begin with the case where the first firm enters as a monopoly, i.e., the case where it has just become barely profitable to produce software. Illustrate this in a graph with a linear downward-sloping demand curve, a constant MC curve, and a fixed entry cost.

   b.   Suppose that marginal costs remain constant throughout the problem. In a separate graph, illustrate how an increase in demand impacts the profits of the monopoly and how a simultaneous decrease in fixed entry costs alters the potential profit from entering the industry.

   c.   Given the possibility of strategic entry deterrence, what might the monopolist do to forestall entry of new firms?

d. Suppose the time comes when strategic entry deterrence is no longer profitable and a second firm enters. Would you expect the entering firm to produce the same software as the existing firm? Would you expect both firms to make a profit at this point?

e. As the industry expands, would you expect strategic entry deterrence to play a larger or smaller role? In what sense is the industry never in equilibrium?

f. What happens to profit for firms in the software market as the industry expands? What would the graph look like for each firm in the industry if the industry reaches equilibrium?

g. If you were an antitrust regulator charged with either looking out for consumers or maximizing efficiency, why might you not want to interfere in this industry despite the presence of market power? What dangers would you worry about if policy makers suggested price regulation to mute market power?

h. In what sense does the emergence of open-source software further weaken the case for regulation of the software industry? In what sense does this undermine the case for long-lasting copyrights on software?

B. In this part of the exercise, use the model of monopolistic competition from Section 26B.4. Let disposable income I be \$100 billion, $\rho = -0.5$, and marginal cost $c = 10$.

a. What is the assumed elasticity of substitution between software products?

b. Explain how increasing demand in the model can be viewed as either increasing I or decreasing α. Will either of these change the price that is charged in the market? Explain.

c. We noted in part A of the exercise that fixed entry costs in the software industry have been declining. Can that explain falling software prices within this model?

d. *True or False*: As long as the elasticity of substitution between software products remains unchanged, the only factor that could explain declining software prices in this model is declining marginal cost. (Can you think of real-world changes in the software industry that might be consistent with this?)

e. Now consider how increases in demand and decreases in costs translate to the equilibrium number of software firms. Suppose $\alpha = 0.998$ initially. What fraction of income does this imply is spent on software products? How many firms does this model predict will exist in equilibrium under the parameters of this model, assuming fixed entry costs are \$100 million? What happens to the number of firms as FC falls to \$10 million, \$1 million, and \$100,000?

f. Suppose that FC is \$1,000,000. What happens as α falls from 0.998 to 0.99 in 0.002 increments as demand for software expands through changes in representative tastes when more consumers have computers?

g. Suppose FC is \$1,000,000 and $\alpha = 0.99$. What happens if demand increases because income increases by 10%?

26.11 Policy Application: *To Tax or Not to Tax Advertising*: In the text, we discussed two different views of advertising. One arises primarily from an economist's perspective, while the other emerges primarily from a psychologist's. The nature of public policy toward the advertising industry will depend on which view of advertising one takes.

A. Consider the two views: *informational advertising* and *image marketing*.

a. In what sense does information advertising potentially address a market condition that represents a violation of the first welfare theorem?

b. In what sense does image marketing result in potentially negative externalities? Might it result in positive externalities?

c. If you wanted to make an efficiency case for taxing advertising, how would you do it? What if you wanted to make an efficiency case for subsidizing it?

d. Suppose a public interest group lobbies for regulatory limits on the amount of advertising that can be conducted. Explain how this might serve the interests of firms.

B. Consider the three-stage image marketing model in Section 26B.6 but assume that $f(a_1,a_2) = a_1^{1/2} + a_2^{1/2}$. Suppose further that the cost for consumer n from consuming y is $\alpha(n - y)^2 - \gamma\alpha$, with $\gamma = 0$ unless otherwise stated.

a. Solving the game backwards (in order to find subgame perfect equilibria), does anything change in stages 2 and 3 of the game?

b. What would be the advertising levels chosen by each firm?

c. Suppose the two firms can collude on the amount of advertising each undertakes (but the rest of the game remains the same). Would they choose different levels of a_1 and a_2?

d. For what level of $\gamma = \bar{\gamma}$ is there no efficiency case for either subsidizing or taxing advertising? What if $\gamma > \bar{\gamma}$? What if $\gamma < \bar{\gamma}$?

e. Is there any way to come to a conclusion about the level of γ from observing consumer and firm behavior?

CHAPTER
27

Public Goods

A *public good* is a good that can be consumed by more than one individual at a time, while a *private good* is a good that can be consumed by only a single individual.[1] When I take out my lunch sandwich, I can take a bite or I can let you take a bite, but there is no way that both of us can take the same bite (unless we want to think of some really gross scenarios). The sandwich bite is what economists call "rivalrous," and this rivalry is what characterizes private goods. When I launch some fireworks out of my backyard, on the other hand, both you and I can enjoy the same fireworks display without either of us taking away from the enjoyment of the other. The fireworks display is therefore what economists call "non-rivalrous," and this non-rivalry is what characterizes public goods. As we will see, this gives rise to particular kinds of *externalities* because I might not consider the benefits you get from my fireworks as I decide how big to make them. In our discussion of public goods, we therefore return to a topic we partially covered in Chapter 21, but we do so now with the benefit of some game theory tools from Chapter 24.

While we will often consider the extreme cases of non-rivalry and rivalry, we should start by pointing out that it is actually more appropriate to think of goods as lying somewhere on a continuum between complete rivalry and complete non-rivalry. Complete non-rivalry would mean that we can keep adding additional consumers, and no matter how many we add, each new consumer can enjoy the same level of the good without taking away from the enjoyment of others. National defense is a good example of such an extreme: The national defense system of the United States protects the entire population, and as new immigrants join the population or as new citizens are born, these additional "consumers" can enjoy the same level of protection that current citizens enjoy without making current citizens less safe from external threats. But if my city's population increases, we will need to get more police officers to keep public safety constant, which means that local public safety is not as non-rivalrous as national defense. Or you and I can probably enjoy the same large swimming pool without taking away from each other's enjoyment, but as more people join, things will get "crowded" and our enjoyment falls when new consumers come on board. Even my TV in my living room is non-rivalrous to some extent, but my living room gets crowded even more quickly than our local swimming pool.

The degree of non-rivalry then characterizes the degree to which we think of a good as being a public good. My sandwich bite is on one extreme end of the spectrum, with even one other person crowding my consumption to a point where it is no longer meaningful. National defense might be on the other extreme, with no limit to the number of people who can be protected by the same national security umbrella without "crowding" the protection enjoyed by everyone else.

---

[1]This chapter employs basic game theory concepts from Section A of Chapter 24 and refers frequently to our analysis of externalities in Chapter 21. Chapters 25 and 26 are *not* required for this chapter.

And then there are all the in-between goods, goods that can be consumed by more than one person at a time but that are subject to crowding in the sense that, at least at some point, each individual's enjoyment of the public good falls when more people consume it. Within the class of public goods, there are of course those that are quite *local*, like my TV or my local swimming pool, and some that allow consumption over a wider geographic area, like national defense or reductions in greenhouse gas emissions. The former are sometimes referred to as *local public goods*, and these, like local public safety, in turn are typically (though not always) subject to some crowding within the area in which they are provided.

While the degree of rivalry of a good is thus one dimension along which we can distinguish between different goods (and the geographic reach of non-rivalrous goods is another), it will furthermore become important for us to distinguish between goods based on whether or not we can *exclude others* from consuming the good. If you are my neighbor, I can't exclude you from enjoying my fireworks (unless I clobber you over the head and knock you unconscious), but I can exclude you from my living room and thus from watching my TV. This will play an obvious role in how public goods can be provided: If exclusion is possible, it is in principle (and often in practice) the case that firms can charge consumers for their consumption of public goods and consumers can decide, much as they do for private goods, whether it's worth it to pay the price of admission. But if the good is non-excludable, that option is not typically open to us. Firms are therefore much more likely to provide excludable public goods than they are to provide non-excludable public goods.

Table 27.1 then illustrates four stylized types of goods that emerge from distinguishing goods along the dimensions of rivalry and excludability. So far, we have almost always assumed that goods are rivalrous, and thus we have dealt almost exclusively with *private goods* from the first column of the table. Usually the private goods we have dealt with were excludable, with consumers who were not willing to pay for such goods priced out of the market. In Chapter 21, however, we discussed the case of private (rivalrous) goods to which multiple people have access. Such goods included wood in a public forest or fish in the ocean, goods not owned by anyone, goods that are part of the "commons." And we illustrated that lack of ownership (or "property rights") of such private goods results in the "Tragedy of the Commons," where individuals overuse the private good as they do not consider the impact their actions have on others who also wish to make use of the good. Overconsumption then resulted from the non-excludability of private goods in the "commons."

We now turn to the second column in the table: public goods that are (at least to some extent) non-rivalrous. When consumers cannot easily be excluded from consumption of such public goods (as in the case of national defense or my backyard fireworks), we will call them simply "public goods" or, if their consumption is limited to small geographic areas, "local public goods." Such public goods might be "pure" in the sense that new consumers can always engage in consumption without taking away from the consumption of current consumers (i.e., national defense and fireworks) or they can be "crowded" (i.e., public safety in cities and public swimming pools). When there exists a mechanism for excluding consumers (such as the case of the swimming pool or my TV), we will sometimes refer to such goods as "club" goods. Again, the real world is much richer than this table suggests because there are many cases in between the extremes, but this categorization will become useful as we think about different ways in which goods can be provided by markets, governments, and civil society.

Table 27.1: Different Kinds of Public and Private Goods

Types of Goods		
	Rivalrous (Private)	Non-Rivalrous (Public)
Excludable	(Pure) Private Good	Club Good
Non-Excludable	Common (Private) Good	Public (or Local Public) Good

27A Public Goods and Their Externalities

We will begin with the case of fully non-rivalrous goods in the absence of excludability, or what we just referred to as "pure" public goods in Table 27.1. In Section 27A.1, we will illustrate the conditions that would have to be met in order for such public goods to be produced in optimal quantities. We will see that decentralized behavior by individuals results in a fundamental externality problem, known as the "free-rider problem," that keeps individuals on their own from providing optimal quantities of the public good. And we will see that this fundamental problem is yet another incarnation of the Prisoner's Dilemma. Put differently, for the case of such "pure" public goods, the first welfare theorem does not hold—decentralized individual behavior does not result in optimal outcomes—because of the strategic considerations that guide individual behavior in the presence of externalities.

For the remainder of part A of this chapter, we will then investigate different approaches for solving this free-rider problem. The classic solution is to look toward government intervention, which we will investigate in Section 27A.2. In Section 27A.3, we then ask, given our understanding of externalities as a problem of "missing markets," to what extent market forces could assist in the provision of some types of public goods, in particular those that are excludable (which we referred to as "club goods" in Table 27.1) and those that are local. In the process we will identify a second fundamental problem that plagues both government and market solutions to the free-rider problem: the problem that individuals often have an incentive to misrepresent their tastes for public goods. In Section 27A.4, we discuss a possible role of civil society institutions and, in the process, we will refer back to the Coase Theorem from Chapter 21 while also thinking of how individuals might partially overcome the free-rider problem through the evolution of tastes that include a particular taste for giving. Finally, we will return to the problem of the incentive to misrepresent tastes for public goods in Section 27A.5 and will ask to what extent it might be possible for government or private institutions to overcome this problem through the clever design of incentive mechanisms that make it in people's best interest to tell the truth.

27A.1 Public Goods and the Free-Rider Problem

In panel (a) of Graph 27.1, we begin by replicating panel (a) from Graph 14.1 in Chapter 14. In that graph, we had illustrated how we add up individual demand curves in the case of a private good. Since private goods are rivalrous and can be consumed by only one person, this addition of demand curves was "horizontal" in nature; for every additional consumer, we simply added that consumer's demand at each price level to the previous demand curves. Public goods are different because they are non-rivalrous; that is, they can be consumed by more than one person at a time. Thus, in order to derive the aggregate marginal willingness to pay for 1 unit of the public good, we have to add how much that good is worth to the first consumer to how much it is worth to the second consumer and so forth. When tastes are quasilinear, we can equivalently say that this amounts to adding demand curves "vertically." This is done in panel (b) of Graph 27.1.

27A.1.1 The Optimal Level of Public Goods

Now suppose that the good on the horizontal axis can be produced at constant marginal cost. In the private good case, the efficient level of production then occurs where marginal cost intersects the aggregate (or "market") demand curve D^M in panel (a) of Graph 27.1 (as we showed in Chapter 15). At that intersection point, it was then the case that each consumer's marginal willingness to pay was equal to the marginal cost of production, and when the private good represented a composite good denominated in dollar units, this is equivalent to saying that each consumer's marginal rate of substitution (*MRS*) was equal to the marginal cost of production.

Now consider a public good that can similarly be produced at constant marginal cost. It is still the case that efficiency requires that the good be produced so long as the marginal benefit of the

Graph 27.1: Aggregate Demand Curves for Private and Public Goods

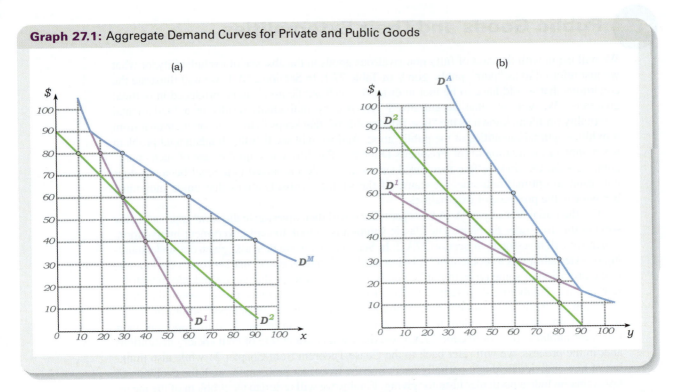

good is greater than the marginal cost, but now all the consumers who consume the same public good are receiving a marginal benefit from doing so. To say that the efficient level of production of the public good occurs where marginal benefit is equal to marginal cost is therefore the same as saying that production occurs where the *sum* of the marginal benefits of all consumers equals the marginal cost. In a sense, exactly the same is true in the private goods case, except there the sum of the marginal benefits is only the marginal benefit of a single consumer since no good can be consumed by more than one person.

Exercise 27A.1 *True or False:* The efficient level of public good production therefore occurs where marginal cost crosses the aggregate demand for public goods as drawn in Graph 27.1b.

Exercise 27A.2* Can you explain how there is a single efficient level of the public good when tastes for public goods are quasilinear, but there are multiple levels of efficient public good provision when this is not the case? (*Hint:* Consider how redistributing income (in a lump-sum way) affects demand in one case but not the other.)

There is another way we can derive this optimality condition for public good production. Remember that a situation is "(Pareto) optimal" or "efficient" if there is no way to change the situation and make some people better off without making anyone else worse off. Suppose then that we consider the case of two consumers with preferences over a composite private good x and a public good y and with private good endowments e_1 and e_2. Suppose further that there exists a concave production technology that converts private goods x into public goods y. We can then depict the trade-offs that our "society" of two individuals faces with the green "production possibilities frontier" in panel (a) of Graph 27.2 where the two consumers could have only private consumption (equal to $e_1 + e_2$) on the vertical axis, or they could devote some of their private goods to producing a public good that they can both consume. A concave production technology

Graph 27.2: Optimal Provision of Public Goods

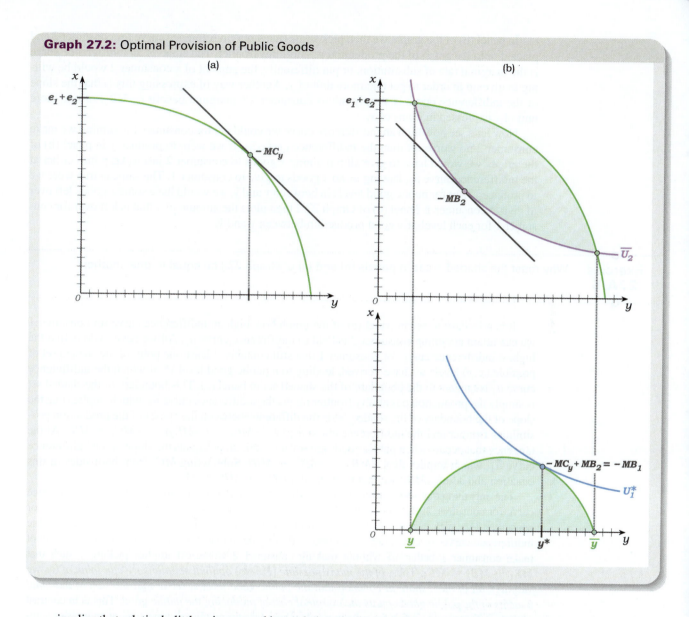

implies that relatively little private good is needed to produce the first units of the public good but that it takes increasingly more private goods to produce each additional unit of the public good. As a result, the trade-off that emerges takes on the shape depicted in the graph, with an initially shallow slope that becomes increasingly steep as more public goods are produced. The slope of this graph represents the number of x units required to produce one more unit of y, or the (negative) marginal cost $(-MC_y)$ in terms of x goods for producing another unit of public good.

Does this production technology exhibit increasing or decreasing returns to scale?

Exercise 27A.3

What would the relationship in the graph look like if the technology had the opposite returns to scale as what you just concluded?

Exercise 27A.4

In panel (b) of the graph, we then pick some (magenta) indifference curve for consumer 2 and place it onto the graph of the production possibilities frontier. The slope of an indifference curve is the marginal rate of substitution, or put differently, the amount of x consumer 2 would be willing to give up in order to get one more unit of y. Another way of expressing this is that the slope of the indifference curve is simply minus consumer 2's marginal benefit $(-MB_2)$ of one more unit of y expressed in terms of x.

Now let's see how high an indifference curve we could get for consumer 1 assuming we make consumer 2 no worse off than the indifference curve $\bar{u}_2$. If we were to produce $\underline{y}$ in panel (b) of the graph, we would have to give all remaining x goods to consumer 2 just to keep him or her at the indifference curve $\bar{u}_2$, leaving us no x goods to give to consumer 1. The same is true were we to produce $\bar{y}$. But for public good levels in between $\underline{y}$ and $\bar{y}$, we would have some x goods left over to give to consumer 1. Panel (c) of Graph 27.2 then plots the amount of x that is left over for consumer 1 for each level of y good production between $\underline{y}$ and $\bar{y}$.

Exercise 27A.5   Why must the shaded areas in panels (b) and (c) of Graph 27.2 be equal to one another?

It is now easy to see in panel (c) of the graph how high an indifference curve for consumer 1 we can attain assuming consumer 2 is held to indifference curve $\bar{u}_2$. All we have to do is find the highest indifference curve for consumer 1 that still contains at least one point of the shaded set of possible (x, y) levels we have derived, leading to a public good level y^* at which the indifference curve u_1^* is tangent to the boundary of the shaded set in panel (c). This boundary of the shaded set is simply the production possibility frontier minus the indifference curve $\bar{u}_2$, which implies that the slope of the boundary of the shaded set is the difference between the slopes of the production possibilities frontier and the indifference curve $\bar{u}_2$; i.e., $-MC_y - (-MB_2) = -MC_y + MB_2$. At the tangency that occurs when public goods are set at y^*, this slope equals the slope of the indifference curve u_1^*, which implies that $-MB_1 = -MC_y + MB_2$. Subtracting MC_y from both sides of this equation and adding MB_1, we therefore get that $MB_1 + MB_2 = MC_y$.

The only thing that seems arbitrary about what we just did is that we just picked some indifference curve for consumer 2. But notice that the reasoning does not depend on what indifference curve for consumer 2 we pick in panel (b) as long as some shaded area remains. Thus, no matter what feasible indifference curve for consumer 2 we choose, finding the public good level that ensures we cannot make consumer 1 better off without making consumer 2 worse off implies picking y such that $MB_1 + MB_2 = MC_y$. Thus, *of the many possible (Pareto) optimal solutions we can think of* (as we vary $\bar{u}_2$), *all of them share in common that the public good level is set so that the sum of marginal benefits of the public good equals the marginal cost of producing the public good.* This is in contrast with the efficiency condition for private goods where (assuming all consumers are at an interior solution) *each* individual MB_i equals the marginal cost.

Exercise 27A.6*   Is there any reason to think that y^*, the optimal level of the public good, will be the same regardless of what indifference curve for consumer 2 we choose to start with? How does your answer change when tastes are quasilinear in the public good? And how does this relate to your answer to exercise 27A.2?

27A.1.2 Decentralized Provision of Fireworks   Suppose now that we consider a particular example. A national holiday is approaching, and you and I are planning to celebrate by launching fireworks in our backyards. The resulting fireworks are a public good: My enjoyment as I glance up into the evening sky does not take away from your enjoyment, and I will get to enjoy the fireworks you launch just as you will enjoy the ones launched from my backyard. We should probably get together and pool our resources in order to arrive at the Pareto opitmal level of fireworks y^*, which, as we just derived, implies that y^* would be set such that the sum of our marginal benefits equals the marginal cost of launching an additional firework. But instead, we go about our business and determine the number of fireworks we launch independently of one another knowing that the other is also doing so.

To estimate how many fireworks will be launched by each one of us, we then have to figure out the Nash equilibrium of the game we are playing as we try to anticipate how many fireworks the other will launch. In a Nash equilibrium, my level of firework production must be a best response to your level of firework production and vice versa. We therefore begin by thinking about my best response to any quantity of fireworks you might launch.

If I thought you were not going to launch any fireworks (i.e., $y_2 = 0$), I would invest in my own fireworks until the marginal cost of launching one more firework is equal to the marginal benefit I receive; i.e., I will set $y_1(0)$ such that $MB_1 = MC$. If I think you will produce some quantity $\bar{y}_2$, I will have to rethink how many fireworks I will launch because I know I already get to enjoy $\bar{y}_2 > 0$ of your fireworks. You purchasing fireworks is a lot like me having additional disposable income because I could now simply enjoy your fireworks and spend all my income on private goods. If all goods are normal goods, the additional income I now have will be split between all goods, which means I will not spend all the effective additional income on the public good. Put differently, while I will end up *consuming* more fireworks if you buy some, I will *purchase* less myself.

In a graph with y on the horizontal axis and a composite private good x on the vertical, illustrate my budget constraint assuming that $\bar{y}_2 = 0$. How does this budget constraint change when $\bar{y}_2 > 0$? Show that, if tastes are homothetic, I will end up consuming more y when $\bar{y}_2 > 0$ but will myself purchase less y. Does this hold whenever y and x are both normal goods? Does it hold if y is an inferior good?

Exercise 27A.7

In panel (a) of Graph 27.3, we can then illustrate my best response function to different values of y_2 that you might choose on a graph with y_2 on the horizontal axis and y_1 on the vertical. Our reasoning implies that this best response function has a positive intercept $y_1(0)$ when $y_2 = 0$

Graph 27.3: Private Provision of Public Goods

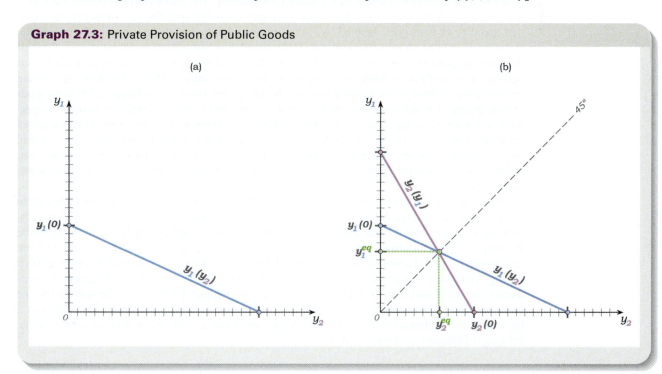

(i.e., I will purchase fireworks until $MB_1 = MC$) but negative slope (i.e., as y_2 increases, I buy fewer fireworks). In panel (b), we put your best response function on top of mine assuming that you are just like me, with the two best response functions therefore crossing on the 45-degree line. That intersection then represents the levels of fireworks (y_1^{eq}, y_2^{eq}) that we will buy in equilibrium when we both best respond to the other's actions.

Exercise 27A.8 If you and I have identical tastes but I have more income than you, would the equilibrium fall above, on, or below the 45-degree line (assuming all goods are normal goods)?

We can now ask if the total quantity of fireworks $y^{eq} = y_1^{eq} + y_2^{eq}$ is efficient. In equilibrium, I am doing the best I can if I continue to buy fireworks as long as, given that you are purchasing y_2^{eq}, my own marginal benefit of additional fireworks was greater than the MC; i.e., I would stop when $MB_1 = MC$. Since you also get a benefit from the fireworks I launch in my backyard, this implies that I stop buying fireworks when $MB_1 + MB_2 > MC$, which implies that the equilibrium quantity of fireworks is less than the efficient quantity y^* for which we concluded before $MB_1 + MB_2 = MC$. Thus, $y^{eq} < y^*$; in equilibrium we are producing an inefficiently low quantity of fireworks.

The intuition for the result is straightforward and easy to understand given our work on externalities in Chapter 21. When I make my choice on how many fireworks to buy, I am generating a *positive externality* for you but I have no incentive to take that into account. The same is true for you. Because we have no incentive to take into account the benefits we are producing for others, we will underconsume fireworks. This is often referred to as the *free-rider problem*: Each of us is "free riding" on the public good produced by the other.

27A.1.3 The Free-Rider Problem: Another Prisoner's Dilemma
This free rider problem is yet another example of a Prisoner's Dilemma. You and I could, after all, have gotten together before going to the fireworks store and agreed to split the cost of buying the optimal quantity of fireworks. Instead, we acted independently and did not explicitly cooperate. But even if we had chosen to coordinate beforehand and had agreed to each buy our share of the optimal quantity of fireworks, we would not have had an incentive to actually abide by our agreement regardless of what we thought the other was doing. This is because our private incentive is to behave in accordance with our best response functions in Graph 27.3, setting our private marginal benefit equal to the marginal cost we incur. Thus, in order to sustain cooperation when we get to the store, we need a mechanism to enforce our agreement. Our incentives are exactly like those of the oligopolists who make a cartel agreement in Chapter 25; abiding by the agreement would in fact make both of us better off than we are by going at it alone, but, if there is no one to make sure we actually abide by the agreement, it is in our individual incentive to cheat.

In our fireworks example, we might easily be able to imagine that we could in fact think of an enforcement mechanism. All we have to do is have one of us buy the optimal number of fireworks, have the other pay half the bill and then get together in one of our backyards and blast off all the fireworks. Even in the absence of being so explicit about enforcing our agreement, we might think it's enough for us to know that we are likely to be neighbors for a long time and that we will keep having occasions to cooperate on the fireworks we launch. As we have seen in Chapter 24, introducing the likelihood that we will interact repeatedly (without knowing a definitive end to the game) can in fact be enough for us to sustain cooperation in repeated interactions. We will think a bit more about circumstances under which private actors are likely to find ways out of the Prisoner's Dilemma in Section 27A.4.

More generally, however, there are many circumstances involving public goods where it is unlikely that it will be so easy to figure out ways of overcoming the incentives of the one-shot Prisoner's Dilemma. Many public goods involve many players, and it is difficult for large numbers of players to cooperate the way that you and I might when we prepare for our fireworks. Not only is it more difficult to enforce cooperation, but the incentives to free ride on the contributions of others get worse the more "others" there are. (You can explore this further in end-of-chapter exercise 27.1.) We all benefit from investments in cancer research, but the American Cancer Association cannot easily get us all to consider the larger social benefits of cancer research when it appeals to individuals to contribute to the cause. We all benefit from an effective police force that keeps us relatively safe, but it's not easy to see how the police can simply walk around and collect the optimal level of donations for its worthwhile work. For this reason, we often look to nonmarket institutions like governments to bring our private incentives in line with socially desirable levels of investments in public goods.

27A.2 Solving the Prisoner's Dilemma through Government Policy

As we have already seen in previous chapters, governments are often employed as nonmarket institutions that enforce ways out of Prisoner's Dilemmas. There are at least two possible avenues for governments to do so: First, in many cases governments simply take on the responsibility of providing public goods and use the power to tax individuals to finance those goods. Second, in some cases governments do not directly provide public goods but instead subsidize private consumption of public goods. Each can, assuming governments have sufficient information, result in optimal levels of public good provision.

27A.2.1 Government Provision and "Crowd-Out"   Perhaps the most straightforward solution to the public goods/free-rider problem is for the government to simply provide the public good directly. This happens in most countries for goods such as national defense or the establishment of an internal police force. But the argument for government provision of public goods has also been used to justify income redistribution programs in most Western democracies where it is assumed that most citizens place some value on making sure the least well off are taken care of to some extent. Assuming that this is the case, contributions to the alleviation of poverty are in fact contributions to a public good because everyone who cares about the issue benefits from less poverty.[2]

When governments do not know exactly what the optimal level of a particular good is (and thus do not fund the optimal level), or alternatively, if political processes are not efficient and therefore do not result in optimal economic decision making, a particular issue called "crowd-out" may arise. Consider, for instance, government financing for public radio. In the United States the federal government in fact finances part of the cost of operating public radio stations, but radio stations attempt to get listeners to add private contributions on top of the funds received from the government. The government is, as a result, just one of many contributors to the provision of the public good "public radio," and public radio listeners will presumably think about their own level of voluntary contribution in light of how much others are giving, with "others" including the government's contribution.

---

[2]End-of-chapter exercise 27.8 explores this argument in some more detail. Of course, an alternative explanation for the existence of redistributive programs arises from a desire by voters to establish insurance markets when private markets are missing due to adverse selection. We discussed this in Chapter 22 for cases such as unemployment insurance.

The resulting "game" is then not at all unlike the game in which you and I are trying to decide how much to contribute to our local fireworks except that now there is just another player called the government. We derived in the previous section an individual's best response function in such a game as a function of how much others are giving to the public good, and we noticed that as others give more, each individual's best response is to give less. When the government therefore contributes to a public good (such as public radio) that also relies on private contributions, game theory predicts that private contributions will decline as government contributions increase, or, to use the economist's language, government contributions to the public good "crowd out" private contributions. In fact, as we will see more formally in Section B, if the government taxes individuals in order to finance its contribution to a public good, the model would predict that individuals who are giving to the public good will reduce their contributions by exactly the amount that the government has taken from them in order to finance the same public good. Thus, so long as individuals are giving on their own, we would expect increased government contributions to be exactly offset by decreases in private contributions.

Exercise 27A.9

True or False: If everyone is currently giving to a public good, including the government, then this model would predict that the government's involvement has not done anything to alleviate the inefficiency of private provision of public goods.

In the case of public radio, of course, not every taxpayer is also giving voluntarily to public radio stations. The tax revenues raised for public radio from individuals who are not giving therefore do not result in decreased private contributions since those individuals are already at a "corner solution" where they do not give anything to public radio. In part for this reason, we do not see government contributions to public goods in the real world accompanied by dollar-for-dollar decreases in private contributions. In the case of public radio, it appears that an increase of $1 in government contributions is accompanied by a decrease in the range of 10 to 20 cents in private contributions.[3]

Exercise 27A.10

Could it be that an increase of government support for a public good causes someone who previously chose to give to that public good to cease giving? How would such a person's best response function look?

27A.2.2 Government Provision under Distortionary Taxes

Another real-world problem governments face is that, as we have emphasized earlier in this book, governments are rarely able to use non-distortionary taxes to raise revenues. If a government does find a non-distortionary or efficient tax (that generates no deadweight loss), it would in fact be optimal for it to provide the public good level y^* at which the sum of individual marginal benefits is equal to the marginal cost of providing the public good. But if distortionary taxes have to be used in order to raise revenues for public good provision, the social marginal cost of government provision is higher than simply the cost of producing the public good because each dollar in tax revenues raised is accompanied by a deadweight loss. Thus, the optimal level of government-provided public goods decreases the more distortionary the taxes used to finance public goods are. (This is explored further in end-of-chapter exercise 27.9.)

Exercise 27A.11

Given what we have learned about the rate at which deadweight loss increases as tax rates rise, what would you expect to happen to the optimal level of government provision of a particular public good as the number of public goods financed by government increases?

---

[3]See Bruce Kingma, "An Accurate Measurement of the Crowd-out Effect, Income Effect, and Price Effect for Charitable Contributions," *Journal of Political Economy* 97, no. 5 (1989), 1197–1207.

Exercise
27A.12

If a particular public good is subject to some partial "crowd-out" when governments contribute to its provision, might it be optimal for the government not to contribute to the public good in the presence of distortionary taxation?

27A.2.3 Subsidies for Voluntary Giving

An alternative policy to government provision of a public good involves the government subsidizing the private production of the good. This, too, should be intuitive as soon as we recognize the free-rider problem as arising from the presence of a positive externality. In our Chapter 21 treatment of externalities, we in fact illustrated that the underprovision of goods due to positive externalities can be corrected through what we called Pigouvian-subsidies.

Suppose, for instance, that our local city government finds it just silly that you and I keep falling victim to Prisoner's Dilemma incentives when we put up our annual fireworks display. So the government decides to make it cheaper for each of us to buy fireworks by paying for some portion s of each firework we purchase. You and I will still be playing the same game we did before, except that our best response functions will now shift up. Remember that my best response to any public good level y_2 that you purchase is determined by the condition that my marginal benefit from the last unit of public good I purchase will be equal to the marginal cost of making the purchase. If the government pays for a portion of each firework I buy, my marginal cost falls, which implies I will purchase more fireworks for any expectation I have of y_2 than I did before. Graph 27.4 then illustrates how both of our best response functions (and thus the Nash equilibrium) change as the subsidy increases from panel (a) through (c). In panel (a), we have no subsidy and we each purchase less than half the efficient quantity y^*. In panel (b), a modest subsidy shifts our purchases closer to the efficient level, and in panel (c) the subsidy is exactly the size it needs to be in order for both of us to purchase half the efficient quantity (and together we therefore purchase y^*).

Exercise
27A.13

In Section B, we show mathematically that the optimal subsidy will involve the government paying for half the cost of the fireworks if you and I have the same preferences. By thinking about the size of the externality (or how much of the total benefit is not taken into account by an individual consumer), does this make intuitive sense?

Graph 27.4: The Changing Nash Equilibrium under Subsidies

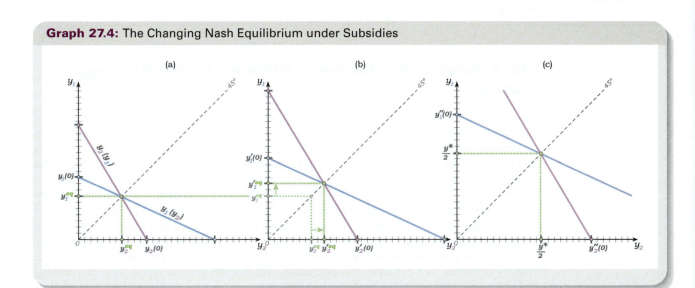

Exercise 27A.14   Could the government induce production of the efficient level of fireworks if it only subsidized the purchases of one of the consumers?

In the real world, the most common way in which governments fund private giving for public goods is through tax deductions. The U.S. income tax code, for instance, allows individuals to give to charitable institutions and not pay taxes on the amount that they give to such institutions. Thus, if I give $100 of my income to the American Cancer Society, I get to deduct this from the income on which I would otherwise have to pay taxes. If my marginal income tax rate is 30%, I then have a choice of either paying $30 of the $100 in income taxes and spending the remaining $70 on stuff I like to consume, or I can give $100 to the American Cancer Society. Giving $100 to the American Cancer Society therefore costs me only $70 in private consumption. Thus, by making my charitable contribution tax deductible, the government has subsidized my contributions by 30%.

Exercise 27A.15   *True or False*: Under an income tax that has increasing marginal tax rates as income goes up, the rich get a bigger per-dollar subsidy for charitable giving than the poor when charitable giving is tax deductible.

Americans make heavy use of this subsidy for giving to charitable organizations that, at least to some extent, provide public goods. Organizations that receive such subsidized contributions include churches, hospitals, organizations (like the American Cancer Society) that fund research, art galleries, museums, etc. Chances are, if you are taking this course in an American university, your university has received substantial private contributions from individuals who deduct these contributions from their income taxes, and your university is providing public goods such as contributing to the creation of knowledge through the research activities supported by the faculty at your university.

Exercise 27A.16   If the only way to finance the subsidy for private giving is through distortionary taxation, would you expect the optimal subsidy to be larger or smaller than if the subsidy can be financed through efficient lump sum taxes?

27A.3 Solving the Prisoner's Dilemma by Establishing Markets

In Chapter 21, we saw that, at a fundamental level, the "market failure" that arises from the existence of externalities is really a "failure of markets to exist." And we argued that, hypothetically, if sufficient numbers of markets were established, the externality would disappear and with its disappearance, the first welfare theorem would reappear. We will therefore investigate next the extent to which we can think of markets as a possible solution to the public goods problem.

We could apply this at a purely abstract level to our fireworks example. The fundamental public goods (and free-rider) problem emerges from the fact that, when I *consume* fireworks, I am also *producing* fireworks consumption for you. But there is no market that prices the production of fireworks consumption for you; i.e., there is no price that you have to pay me when I produce something that you value. As a result, I do not take into consideration the benefit that you incur from my fireworks. There is a positive externality, which is the same as saying there is a missing market for goods that are being produced as I make my consumption decision. It is not at all clear how we would establish the missing market for my fireworks production, nor would there be much of a "market" with only two of us involved. The point is therefore not to argue that such markets could generally be established. But neither does the difficulty of establishing the abstract "missing markets" mean, as we saw in the example of negative pollution externalities and pollution voucher markets, that we cannot consider some form of market solution to the problem.

We therefore want to think about the conditions under which decentralized market provision of public goods *could* emerge if certain types of markets were appropriately set up. In order for us to have any chance of public goods being provided in such a decentralized market setting, it would seem that at the very least we have to assume that consumption of the public good is *excludable*; that is, we would have to assume that the producer of the public good can keep people from consuming the good if they do not pay what the producer demands. This does not take away from the *non-rivalry* of the good; that is, the public good can still be consumed by multiple people at the same time. For instance, a large swimming pool can be enjoyed by a large number of families at the same time, but the provider of the swimming pool can keep people out if they don't pay an entrance fee.

Can you think of other goods that are non-rivalrous (at least to some extent) but also excludable?

Exercise 27A.17

27A.3.1 Lindahl Price Discrimination and the Incentive to Lie

Decentralized market exchanges are governed by prices, and in our typical competitive equilibrium, this means that everyone faces the same market price and each consumer gets to choose his or her optimal quantity at that price. *Same price, different quantities.* Now let's ask how a "market" for a typical pure public good would have to look. A pure public good is a good that all consumers can consume at the very same time in the same quantity. So in a "market" for public goods, individuals would consume the same quantity of the public good. But, in order for that quantity to be something the consumer actually chooses given his or her budget constraint, different consumers would have to face different prices. *Different prices, same quantity*, which is the exact opposite of the decentralized market equilibrium for private goods.

Consider the case of fireworks and suppose that a producer of fireworks displays owns a sufficiently large land area such that the only way to see the fireworks is to actually step onto the producer's land. Suppose further that the producer has put up barbed wire around his land with, just to be mean, a sufficiently strong electrical current flowing through the wire to instantly knock any potential trespasser unconscious. The only way to step onto the land is to go through an entrance booth at which the producer can charge individuals an entry fee.

Now suppose the producer knows each consumer's demand curve for the intensity of firework displays, and we can thus determine the optimal number of fireworks y^* to launch into the air during a particular holiday. Recall that we can calculate y^* by simply adding the demands vertically and finding where the resulting aggregate demand curve intersects marginal cost. Our producer of fireworks can then determine *individualized prices* for each consumer such that each consumer would in fact choose y^* as part of her optimal consumption bundle at her own individual price. The individualized price for consumer i would then simply be her marginal benefit of the public good y^*, and since the marginal benefits sum to marginal cost at y^*, the individualized prices sum to marginal cost.

Illustrate, using a graph of two different demand curves for two different consumers, how a producer would calculate y^* and what prices she would charge to each individual in order to get him to in fact choose y^* as his most preferred bundle.

Exercise 27A.18

Does the producer collect enough revenues under such individualized pricing to cover marginal costs?

Exercise 27A.19

The resulting equilibrium would be one in which a single producer of the public good charges *different prices* to consumers in such a way that each consumer chooses the *same quantity* of the public good. This is the public good analog to the private good competitive equilibrium, and it is known as a *Lindahl equilibrium*.[4] The prices that emerge in this equilibrium are known as *Lindahl prices*. Note that it involves *price discrimination* by the producer, with higher prices charged to consumers that have greater demand for the public good. But in order to implement the price discrimination, the producer has to know the demands (or preferences) of individual consumers. And therein lies the problem with the Lindahl equilibrium.

Since I know that the price I will be charged as I enter the land on which I can view the fireworks is directly related to the producer's impression of my tastes for fireworks, I have every incentive to play down how much I actually like fireworks. "I can't believe I am going to see another stupid fireworks display," I will mutter on my way toward the gate, just loud enough for the fireworks producer to hear me. Put differently, I have an incentive to lie about my preferences. And, what's worse, that incentive increases the more people are lining up to get onto the land from which the fireworks can be enjoyed. If you and I are the only ones to see the fireworks, I face a trade-off when I decide on how much to lie about my enthusiasm for fireworks: On the one hand, any lie will reduce the number of fireworks that will be launched (because it will affect the calculation of y^*), but, on the other hand, I will not have to pay as much to get in if I lie. So I'll lie a little bit but won't claim that I don't care about fireworks at all. If, however, there are 10,000 people lined up to get onto the land from which the fireworks display can be enjoyed, I am suddenly only one of many. This means that the impact of my lie on y^* becomes very small, but the impact of my lie on the price I'll get charged continues to be big. As the number of consumers goes up, the incentive to lie therefore increases because the impact of a lie on y^* diminishes with more consumers but the impact of the lie on the price I get charged does not. *Unless producers of public goods already know a lot about the preferences of their consumers*, a Lindahl equilibrium under which consumers choose the optimal quantity of the public good at individualized prices therefore cannot emerge because the consumers have a strong incentive to misrepresent their preferences for the public good.

Exercise 27A.20

Consider the entrance fees to movie theaters on days when not every seat in the movie theater fills up. If it is generally true that older people and students have lower demand for watching new releases in movie theaters, can you explain entrance discounts for the elderly and for students as an attempt at Lindahl pricing?

One could argue that private goods markets also face such incentive problems; that is, when you and I negotiate over the price I will pay you for a gallon of milk, I also have an incentive to pretend that the milk is not worth that much to me so that you'll give it to me at a lower price. That's true, but the difference is that my incentive to lie about my tastes for milk get weaker and weaker the more milk consumers there are because if I claim to not like milk that much, you'll just go to someone that isn't such a pain. Thus, in private goods markets the incentive to misrepresent our preferences disappears as the market becomes large, while in public goods markets that incentive gets bigger and bigger the larger the market. I doubt it has ever even occurred to you to try to tell the local supermarket owner that you really don't care for milk that much in order to get a better price, but if I came to you and told you that your taxes will increase the more you tell me you like national defense but the increased tax payments from you will have little perceptible impact on the level of national defense, you'd probably pretend to be a pacifist singing "Give Peace a Chance" pretty quickly.[5]

---

[4]This is named after Erik Lindahl (1891–1960), a Swedish economist, who first proposed the idea in 1919.

[5]In Chapter 16, we argued that the concept of a competitive equilibrium becomes particularly compelling once we realize that the set of stable allocations in the world, formalized in the concept of the "core" set of allocations, converges to the set of competitive equilibrium allocations as an economy becomes large. It can be shown that the opposite is true for public goods economies: As the economy becomes large, the set of core allocations explodes far beyond just the allocations that could be supported in a Lindahl equilibrium. The reason for this is closely related to the reason why the incentive to misrepresent one's preferences increases as the economy gets large.

27A.3.2 "Clubs," Local Public Goods Markets, and "Voting with Feet" The concept of a Lindahl equilibrium, while academically interesting, is therefore of limited real-world usefulness given the necessity for producers to know consumer preferences that consumers themselves have every incentive to misrepresent. That does not, however, mean that other forms of market forces might not play an important role in shaping the kinds and varieties of *excludable* public goods we can choose. Homeowners' associations offer public security, swimming pools, and golf courses; a variety of "clubs" offer access to public spaces to paying customers; and local governments of all kinds offer a variety of public services. The goods offered by such institutions are not "pure" public goods that are fully "non-rivalrous," but each can still be consumed by multiple consumers at the same time. And in each case, market forces play an important role.

This was pointed out by Charles Tiebout (1924–68) in the 1950s and has given rise to one of the largest academic literatures in all of economics.[6] Tiebout proposed a simple and intuitive hypothesis: When there are goods that are neither fully rivalrous nor fully non-rivalrous, and when there exists a mechanism for excluding consumers who do not pay the required fee for using the good, one can derive conditions under which multiple providers of such goods will compete in a market-like setting and provide efficient levels of the goods. Tiebout was thinking of local communities as being the providers, with local public services restricted to those who reside within the boundaries of local communities. Just as different malls and shopping centers provide different varieties of stores and different levels of characteristics (such as lighting in parking lots, a private security force to protect the mall, etc.) that consumers might care about, we can think of different communities providing different mixes of public services with different mixes of local fees and taxes for residents of those communities. Just as malls compete with one another for customers who will decide to frequent one mall or shopping center more than others, communities then compete for residents. Successful malls find sufficient numbers of consumers with similar tastes to create a sufficiently large clientele, as do successful communities.

To the extent to which there is enough competition between shopping centers, each center will make roughly zero profits in equilibrium and consumers can choose from the optimal number of different centers to find those that most closely match their tastes given their budgets. And to the extent to which there is sufficient competition between local communities, such communities similarly offer a variety of bundles of goods and services for consumers to choose from, with each community's choices disciplined by competitive market forces. In the case of communities, *land* then serves as the exclusionary device since only those who own or rent land (and housing) in a particular community have access to the public services offered. Such communities could be privately operated (as are, for instance, homeowners' associations) or publicly administered (as, for instance, local school districts). And even when local governments are operated through political processes, politicians have to confront market pressures to ensure that the mix of public services and local taxes attracts a sufficient clientele of local residents.

Why do consumers not face the same incentive to lie about their tastes in such a "Tiebout" equilibrium as they do in a Lindahl equilibrium?

Exercise 27A.21

Clubs that are not tied to land offer another application of Tiebout's insight. One can think, for instance, of churches as clubs providing public goods such as religious services, with churches competing for parishoners who have different tastes for the types of music, sermons,

---

[6]The argument was presented in a quite accessible article: see C. Tiebout, "A Pure Theory of Local Expenditures," *Journal of Political Economy* 64 (1956), 416–24, which has become one of the most cited articles in economics. It was written while Tiebout was a graduate student at the University of Michigan. He died suddenly at a relatively young age, and his relatives appear not to have realized the importance of his contributions. I know this from personal experience: I once gave a paper at a university workshop and was afterward approached by an elderly man who told me he had no real idea what on earth I had been talking about in my 90-minute presentation, but he just wondered whether my reference to the "Tiebout Model" in the title of my paper had anything to do with his "cousin Charles." Turns out it did.

and denominational affiliations that are offered. While churches typically do not charge an entrance fee, they find other ways of enforcing expectations about contributing to the church in financial and nonfinancial ways (as we will discuss more a little later). Or one can think of private schools that offer a service that has at least some public goods characteristics, with such schools competing on both the types of curricula they offer and the level of tuition they charge. Or we can think of private operators of swimming pools and health clubs who charge for uses of their somewhat non-rivalrous goods and compete with others that do the same.

Exercise 27A.22   In recent years, gated communities that provide local security services privately have emerged in many metropolitan areas that are growing quickly. Can you think of these from "club" perspective?

For a much richer treatment of these topics, you should consider taking a course on local public finance or a course on urban economics where Tiebout's insights are typically discussed at length. As with many economic theories, the insights rarely hold perfectly in the real world but they do play an important role in the bigger picture of how public goods are provided. For now, our main point is just that in speaking as if there is a crass distinction between "private goods" and "public good," we are implicitly ignoring a whole set of important goods that lie in between the extremes, and the in-between cases are often provided by a rich combination of civil society, market, and government actions.

27A.3.3 The Lighthouse: Another Look at Excludability and Market Provision

In our discussion of market provision of public goods, we have placed some emphasis on the importance of "excludability" of public goods if such goods are to be provided through market forces. After all, if a provider cannot exclude those who attempt to free ride, how can the provider ever expect to collect sufficient revenues to provide anything close to the optimal level of the public good?

There is much truth in the intuitive insight that providers (other than governments that can use taxes) must find ways to finance public goods, and that this typically involves some mechanism for excluding nonpayers. But we sometimes underestimate the extent to which providers might find creative ways of doing this. In a famous article, Ronald Coase studied the particularly revealing case of lighthouses in the 18th century. Until Coase's case study, the lighthouse was often given as a motivating example in textbooks to illustrate the difficulty of providing a vital public good without the government doing so directly. Before the invention of the current navigational technologies used on ships, lighthouses played a pivotal role in guiding ships safely along dangerous shores where, in the absence of the guidance offered by lighthouses, ships could easily run aground. The services offered by lighthouses are classically non-rivalrous; no matter how many ships are safely guided toward the shores by a lighthouse, additional ships can similarly make use of the light that is emitted. And economists writing about the problem of providing lighthouses could not see an easy way for private lighthouse operators to exclude those who do not pay.

Coase, however, looked to see how lighthouses were actually provided in many instances, and what he found was that private providers had indeed found ways of financing lighthouses by charging those who benefitted most from them. It turns out that providers *bundled* the public good provided by the lighthouses with private goods, in particular the rights to dock a ship in the harbor to which the lighthouses guided ships.[7] While it is true that lighthouses offered additional positive externalities to ships that simply used the light to navigate the shore without docking in

---

[7]The "light dues" that funded lighthouses across England, Scotland, and Wales were collected by customs officials in ports, which created the effective bundling of port use to use of lighthouses. For a detailed discussion of this, see R. Coase, "The Lighthouse in Economics," *The Journal of Law and Economics* 17, no. 2 (1974), 357–76.

the harbor, it appears that these externalities were small relative to the benefits that could be priced for those who used the local harbors. While the British government played a role in the protection of property rights and the collection of light fees, it was not necessary to have the government directly provide lighthouses.

....

Can you think of the provision of free access to swimming pools in condominium complexes in a way that is analogous to Coase's findings about lighthouses?

**Exercise
27A.23**

....

27A.4 Civil Society and the Free-Rider Problem

When we introduced the Prisoner's Dilemma in Chapter 24, we pointed out that the model's prediction of complete non-cooperation is often contradicted by experimental and real-world evidence. In the real world, people simply do not seem to free ride nearly as much as our model predicts. As a result, our model does not successfully predict the *level* of voluntary contributions to public goods that we observe in the world. Nor does the model make sense of the *distribution* of charitable giving; or, to be more precise, the model cannot make sense of the fact that the same person is often observed to give to *many* different charities.

Think of it this way: To one extent or another, most of us care about large public goods such as finding cures to diseases, alleviating poverty, saving the environment, etc. But, aside from people like Bill Gates, most of us have modest resources to contribute to solving these very large problems. If all we care about as we contemplate how much and to whom to give, the rational course of action would be to find the public good that we care about most and where we think our contribution can have the biggest impact. We should then give the entire amount that we decide to devote to charitable purposes to one *and only one* cause. Suppose, for example, I care most about poor children in the developing world and I want to make as much of a difference there as I can. Once I have given $1,000 or $10,000 to that effort, it is hard for me to think that I have now made enough of a difference in alleviating poverty in the developing world to move on to contribute my next dollar to a different public good, say Alzheimer's research or the local Girl Scouts. I am simply too small a part of the world for my contribution to make a large enough marginal impact in the area I care about most to think I have "solved" that problem sufficiently to move on to the next one.

But in most cases, we actually see individuals giving their time and money to multiple causes. A model of giving that assumes we only take into account the difference our giving makes in the world cannot rationalize this behavior. So when I see others (or myself) giving to multiple causes, there must be something else that explains this pattern of giving, just as there must be something else that explains why we give as much as we do. And that "something else" often has to do with the way that civil society institutions persuade us to give. In some instances, as we will see, we might be seeing the Coase Theorem (that we introduced in Chapter 21) at work, and in other cases civil society institutions persuade us that we in fact get *private* benefits in addition to the *public* benefit from our giving. In this section, we'll further explore these ways in which the civil society engages, and why it sometimes succeeds so much more than other times. Finally, civil society institutions might design creative incentive schemes that overcome the Prisoner's Dilemma incentives. In end-of-chapter exercise 27.5, we give an example of this in the context of a particular type of fundraising campaign that some civil society institutions employ.

27A.4.1 Small Public Goods and the Coase Theorem   In Chapter 21, we introduced the Coase Theorem in the broader context of externalities, and we illustrated Coase's argument that, as long as property rights are sufficiently well defined and transactions costs are sufficiently low, decentralized bargaining would result in optimal outcomes. We developed the theorem for the case of negative externalities, but the same argument holds for positive externalities (such as those produced by public goods).

Suppose we think again of you and me launching fireworks. In this case, the property rights are pretty settled: You have the right to enjoy my fireworks without paying for them (and I have the right to enjoy yours). If I take you to court to demand compensation for the enjoyment you get from my fireworks, the court will probably give me a swift kick and tell me to go away. I therefore have an incentive to go over to your house for coffee to discuss the whole fireworks issue and to see if we can't find a way for you to contribute so that we can jointly find a way out of our little Prisoner's Dilemma. If transactions costs, including the costs of enforcing our agreement, are sufficiently low, we should be able to solve our dilemma.

This might help explain why we often voluntarily provide for multiple public goods in our immediate vicinity, especially when we combine our understanding of the Coase Theorem with the intuitions from our game theory chapter that suggest cooperation between players with Prisoner's Dilemma incentives can emerge in settings where the players interact repeatedly (and each time believe there is a good chance they will meet again). But it cannot get us very far toward explaining why we give to larger public goods the way we do: to museums, universities, hospitals, and perhaps even economics departments.

27A.4.2 Private Benefits from Public Giving: The "Warm Glow Effect"   Suppose that I write checks to support Alzheimer's research not only because I believe that my check will have a positive marginal impact on the probability that a cure will be found but also because, whenever I write such a check, I remember my grandmother who passed away from this dreadful disease and I take pleasure in remembering (and honoring) her through my contribution. In such cases, economists say that I am deriving a "warm glow" from giving to a public good. I feel good even if my contribution actually does nothing to get us closer to a cure for Alzheimer's. Put differently, I get a *private benefit* from my public giving. And to the extent to which our purpose for giving to charitable causes fulfills a private need, we do not encounter the free-rider problem any more than we do when we think of my "contribution" to buying my lunch. While the free-rider problem is still present to the degree to which Alzheimer's research is a public good, it is counteracted by the private benefit I receive from writing my check. And the more the Alzheimer's Research Foundation can get me to view my contribution as honoring my grandmother rather than contributing to the big public good of finding a cure, the smaller is the free-rider problem that remains to be overcome.

In the case of my contributions to Alzheimer's research, there are particular reasons for my "warm glow," but in other cases charitable organizations deliberately manufacture such reasons in the way they market themselves. In a previous chapter, we mentioned the case of relief organizations that help poor families and communities in developing countries. You have almost certainly seen such agencies advertise that, with a monthly contribution of $20, you can change a *particular* child's life. Not only that, the organization will match you with a particular child and establish contact with the family, send you pictures and yearly updates, etc. It seems highly unlikely that such organizations will actually stop helping a particular family if you stop sending checks, which means that your contribution is actually a contribution to a larger "public good" of alleviating poverty in the developing world. But by framing their fundraising efforts in a way that personalizes your contributions, the organizations in essence attempt to convert what is a fairly abstract public good to a concrete private good: helping one particular family that you end up caring about. It is, in the language we used in Chapter 26, an example of "image marketing" in which the organization changes the image of what it is asking you to contribute to in order to make it more likely that you will view your contribution as a private rather than a public good.

Exercise 27A.24   Explain how it is rational for me to give to both relieving poverty in the developing world and to Alzheimer's research in the presence of "warm glow" but not in its absence.

Non-profit organizations can therefore make use of image marketing just as for-profit firms do, except that we tend to think of successful image marketing that leads to greater charitable giving as a socially positive outcome given that it helps individuals overcome Prisoner's Dilemma incentives. Churches appeal to a sense that we are working toward a reward in the next life as we give "selflessly" in this life; local relief organizations offer individuals a chance to build meaningful relationships as they volunteer to build houses for the homeless; universities put names of large donors on buildings to give a private reward for giving to a public good; and public radio stations give bumper stickers to contributors so that they can proudly display these on their cars. There is nothing in any of these efforts to guarantee an "optimal" level of public goods provision within the civil society, but all of them appear to succeed in overcoming Prisoner's Dilemma incentives to some extent through providing contributors with a "warm glow" from giving.

From Coase we learn that it is important to have individuals "take ownership" of externalities, and that it is similarly important to ensure that transactions costs of people taking such ownership are low. One way to think of civil society efforts to provide public goods is to then think of such organizations as finding creative ways of getting individuals to "take ownership" and reducing the transactions costs of participating in the lowering of externality inefficiencies when such ownership has been established. Linking your contribution to the alleviation of poverty in the developing world to a particular family you are supposedly helping is a way of establishing ownership in the presence of a desire by individuals to "make a difference." It is also a way of having an organization take on the task of coordinating the efforts of many individuals and thereby reduce the transactions costs individuals would face in the absence of such civil society institutions.

Can you use the "warm glow effect" to explain why government contributions to public goods (such as public radio) do not fully crowd out private contributions?

Exercise 27A.25

27A.4.3 Civil Society, Warm Glows, and "Tipping Points"

And then there are the occasional episodes in history when very large public goods appear to emerge quite spontaneously from civil society interactions outside government or market mechanisms. We can think, for example, of the big social movements of the past century: civil rights marches in the 1960s when white and black Americans gave up their time (often at considerable risk) to demand social change, for example. Or one can think of the Solidarity movement in Poland that laid the foundation for the fall of the Iron Curtain in Eastern Europe. Or the demonstration of "people power" that drove dictators in places like the Philippines into exile. Such large social movements often aim at social change that affects us all, and as such they represent attempts to provide large public goods (like more democracy, more human rights, etc.). But most of our models would suggest that such movements are unlikely to gain much momentum because the larger they get, the deeper the free-rider problem they encounter. Does it really make sense for me to skip work or a day in the park with my family to go to a rally in which millions are already participating? Is there any chance that my contribution to the rally will make any difference whatsoever?

And yet, under some circumstances, individuals seem to be willing to risk almost anything to be a part of such movements, and on occasion, such movements have established public goods (such as greater civil rights) quite successfully without (and often in spite of) government action (or inaction). One theory that explains such phenomena is based on an assumption that we derive increased private benefits from participating in such movements the more of our friends participate. (We previously encountered this idea in some of our Chapter 21 end-of-chapter exercises where we modeled such *network externalities* in business and policy settings.) Someone who feels really strongly about a particular issue might start standing on a street corner, and most of the time that's pretty much where it ends. Maybe a few others who feel strongly about the issue (or who just feel sorry for the guy) show some support and stand there with him. But sometimes, as others join, yet others join and the movement builds into an avalanche that can't be stopped. At a critical point, such movements cross a "tipping point" where they gain a self-perpetuating momentum, while movements that don't cross the "tipping point" quickly fizzle and become remembered as quaint fads.

Suppose individuals in some group (like a church congregation) differ in their demand for a public good y (like helping the poor), but all individuals receive a greater warm glow from giving to the public good the more others gave in the previous period (where you can think of a period as a day or a week or a month, depending on the application). Such models tend to have at least two pure strategy Nash equilibria. In one equilibrium, few people contribute and, because so few people contribute, most people do not get much of a "warm glow" from contributing. In a second equilibrium, most people contribute and, because so many contribute, people get substantial "warm glow" from contributing. Social entrepreneurs (like the young idealistic minister that takes over a congregation) therefore often have the challenge of starting in a low contribution equilibrium and finding ways of getting sufficiently many individuals energized to cross a tipping point that takes them to the high contribution equilibrium. They must first find those who are most deeply committed and then hope that such individuals have sufficient social contacts with others who care less about the public good at hand but who care more as the number of other people engaged in the movement increases.[8]

Exercise 27A.26*

Suppose my warm glow from demonstrating in the streets (for some worthy cause) depends on how much you demonstrate in the streets and vice versa. Letting the fraction of our time spent demonstrating go from 0 to 1, suppose that I do not get enough of a warm glow from demonstrating unless you spend at least half your time on the streets, and you feel similarly (about your warm glow and my participation). Illustrate our best response functions to each other's time on the streets. Where are the two stable pure strategy Nash equilibria, and where is the tipping point?

27A.5 Preference Revelation Mechanisms

The problem of providing public goods optimally could, as we saw at the beginning of the chapter, be easily solved if we just knew people's preferences for public goods. We would then simply add up individual demands and find where the aggregate demand for public goods crosses the marginal cost of providing such goods. We could then also implement Lindahl prices for public goods, which would ensure that individuals are charged appropriately for the marginal benefits they receive from the optimal level of public goods we provide. But, as we saw in our discussion of Lindahl pricing, we face a fundamental underlying problem: Individuals typically have an incentive to misrepresent their preferences for public goods if their contributions to the public good are linked to their stated preferences for public goods. Economists have therefore thought hard about how to overcome this problem, and they have proposed "mechanisms" that take into account this incentive problem. The general study of creating mechanisms that provide individuals with the incentive to truthfully reveal private information (like their preferences for public goods) is called *mechanism design*.

The fundamental problem faced by mechanism designers is the following: The designer has a clear idea of what he would like to do if he could magically know people's preferences. But since he does not know those preferences, he needs to come up with an incentive scheme that makes it in people's best interest to tell the mechanism designer their true preferences. And this

---

[8]This theory of multiple equilibria and tipping points applies to more than just social movements and related contributions to public goods. For a fascinating discussion of how tipping points between low and high equilibria emerge in all sorts of interesting circumstances, I highly recommend reading the recent best-seller by Malcom Gladwell, *Tipping Point: How Little Things Can Make Big Difference* (New York, NY: Little Brown and Company, 2000).

scheme has to be such that individuals think it is in their best interest to reveal information truthfully as they take into account what the mechanism designer will do with the information he collects. In the public goods context, the mechanism designer would like to know people's preferences over public goods in order to implement the optimal public goods level. So what he needs to do is define "messages" that individuals can send him and that contain the information he needs to determine optimal public good provision, and then he needs to define a method by which he uses these "messages" to determine how much public good to produce. That "method" in turn needs to have the property that it provides individuals the incentive to send true messages about their tastes for public goods.

Suppose you have a piece of art that you would like to give to the person who values it the most but you do not know people's tastes. Explain how a second-price sealed bid auction (as described in exercise 27.10) represents a mechanism that accomplishes this while eliciting truthful messages from all interested parties.

**Exercise
27A.27**

27A.5.1 A Simple Example of a Mechanism

Suppose that you and I live at the end of a cul-de-sac that currently has no streetlight. At night it gets very dark in front of our houses and we therefore approach the city government about putting up a light. The city would like to help but only if the value that you and I place on the streetlight actually exceeds the cost of the $1,000 it will cost to put it up. We do our best to use artful prose to verbalize our deep desire to have light, punctuated by an occasional reference to our phobias of darkness. But the city knows we have every incentive to exaggerate our desire for light and fear of the dark in order to get the taxpayers to fund the light on our street. The city therefore needs to figure out a way for us to reveal our true desires.

So, the mayor proposes the following. To begin with, he splits the $1,000 cost in two and asks us each to write him a check for $500. He then asks us to tell him how much value above (or below) $500 we each place on the streetlight. In other words, he asks us to send him a "message" that is simply a number, which could be negative (if we want to tell him we place less that $500 value on the light) or positive (if we want to tell him we place more than $500 of value on the light). Let's denote the message that you and I send as m_1 and m_2 respectively. The city will only build the light if we indicate the value we place on the light is at least $1,000. Since the messages we send are messages about how much each of us values the light *above $500*, this means the city will only build the streetlight if $m_1 + m_2 \geq 0$. The mayor furthermore tells us that if the city ends up building the streetlight, he will refund me an amount equal to the message m_1 that you sent while refunding you an amount equal to the message m_2 that I sent. If you send a message $m_1 > 0$, I will therefore get a partial refund, but if you send a message $m_1 < 0$, I will have to write another check for the amount $(-m_1)$. If, on the other hand, the city does not build the streetlight (because $m_1 + m_2 < 0$), the mayor will refund our $500 checks.

The city has therefore set up a simultaneous move "message sending" game in which each of us now has to decide what message to send about our true underlying preference for the streetlight. Let v_1 and v_2 denote your and my true valuation of the light above $500. If the light is built, you will therefore get your true value v_1 from enjoying the streetlight beyond the $500 payment you have made plus you will get a check from the mayor equal to m_2 if $m_2 > 0$ or you will have to write another check equal to $(-m_2)$ if $m_2 < 0$. Your total "payoff" if the streetlight is built is therefore $(v_1 + m_2)$, while your total "payoff" if the streetlight is not built is 0 (since your $500 will be refunded).

At the time you decide what m_1 message to send to the mayor, you do not know what m_2 message I am sending. It may be that $-m_2 \leq v_1$ or it may be that $-m_2 > v_1$. If $-m_2 \leq v_1$, we can add m_2 to both sides of the inequality and get $v_1 + m_2 \geq 0$. Thus, if you send a truthful message of $m_1 = v_1$, $m_1 + m_2 \geq 0$ and the streetlight will be built. Your resulting payoff is then

$v_1 + m_2 \geq 0$, which is at least as good as getting a payoff of 0 that would occur if you sent a false message that caused the light not to be built. Thus, if $-m_2 \leq v_1$, you should send a truthful message $m_1 = v_1$. Now suppose the other scenario is true; i.e., $-m_2 > v_1$. If, under that scenario, you again sent a truthful message $m_1 = v_1$, then $m_1 + m_2 < 0$, the streetlight does not get built, and you get a payoff of 0. If you instead sent a false message that is high enough to get the streetlight built, your payoff will be $v_1 + m_2 < 0$, so again it's best to send the truthful message $m_1 = v_1$. Thus, *regardless of what message m_2 I send, it is your best strategy to send a truthful message about your own preferences.* Put differently, truth telling in this game is a dominant strategy. Since I face the same incentives as you, we will both send truthful messages and the streetlight gets built only if we value the light more than what it costs.

If there are $N > 2$ people at the end of the cul-de-sac, the city can design analogous mechanisms that will similarly result in truth telling. Instead of beginning with a charge of $500 for each person, the city would instead charge each person $1,000/N$ at the beginning and build the light only if the sum of the messages is at least zero. It would then refund to each person an amount equal to the sum of the other people's messages.

Exercise 27A.28*

Suppose three people lived at the end of the cul-de-sac and suppose the mayor proposes the same mechanism except that he now asks you for a $333.33 check at the start (instead of $500) and you are told (as player 1) that you will get a refund equal to $m_2 + m_3$ if $(m_1 + m_2 + m_3) \geq 0$ and the light is built. (Otherwise, you just get your $333.33 back and no light is built.) Can you show that truth telling is again a dominant strategy for you?

27A.5.2 Truth-telling Mechanisms and their Problems

We have therefore given a simple example of a mechanism in which the government elicits the necessary information to determine whether a public good should be built. The trick for doing this was that the payoff to each of the people does not depend on the message they send except to the extent that each person's message might be pivotal in determining whether or not the public good is provided. Remember, your payoff was constructed to be equal to $v_1 + m_2$ if the streetlight is built and 0 otherwise. Nowhere in your payoff does your own message m_1 appear; it only matters in the sense that it enters the city's decision on whether or not to put up the streetlight. So all you had to think about was whether it made sense to tell the truth knowing that this will determine whether the streetlight is built, and in making that decision the city forced you to consider the messages sent by others about how much they value the streetlight. Put differently, the mechanism we designed forces you to consider in your own decision how much others value the streetlight by making a payment to you that equaled the sum of how much (above $500) other people said they valued the light.

Of course, the typical public goods decision is not *whether* to provide a public good but also *how much* of the public good to provide. A city, for instance, has to decide how much police to hire to ensure public safety, and a higher-level government has to decide how much to spend on national defense. In Section B, we will illustrate a different version of the simple mechanism we just discussed, a version that will permit the determination of the optimal quantity of a more continuous public good, and again we will find a way to get people to tell the truth about their preferences.[9]

A second problem with our simple mechanism is that it will generally not yield sufficient revenues to fund the public good. Thus, while the mechanism elicits truthful information for the city to determine whether or not to invest in the public good, it does not provide sufficient funds

---

[9]Our discussion of the more elaborate mechanism in Section B is relatively nonmathematical and can be understood solely based on the graphs in that section. The interested reader can therefore investigate this mechanism further without the mathematical background that is generally presumed for B portions of our chapters.

for actually paying the cost. This, too, is a problem that is addressed in the somewhat more elaborate mechanism introduced in Section B where we will present a mechanism that elicits truthful information *and* generates at least as much revenue as will be necessary to fund the optimal public good level.

Can you think of a case where our simple mechanism generates sufficient revenues to pay for the streetlight?	**Exercise** **27A.29**
Can you think of a case where the mechanism results in an outcome under which the city needs to come up with more money than the cost of the streetlight in order to implement the mechanism?	**Exercise** **27A.30**

More generally, as we further discuss in Section B, preference revelation mechanisms cannot implement (and fund) fully efficient outcomes if our goal is to have truth telling be a dominant strategy (Nash) equilibrium, but they can do so if we only require truth telling to be a Nash equilibrium strategy. For now, the main point to take away from our discussion is that we *can* think of mechanisms to elicit truthful information about public goods preferences and thereby overcome the incentive to misrepresent preferences in order to free ride on others. However, such mechanisms come at a cost that might make it difficult to implement them in many circumstances. In fact, such mechanisms have only been used on rare occasions to provide public goods.

27A.5.3 Mechanism Design More Generally   Not all mechanisms, however, have as their goal to provide public goods. There are, as we have seen before in this book, many circumstances where some parties have more relevant information than others that would like to acquire some of that information. In such cases, mechanisms can be designed to get individuals to reveal private information knowing what will happen once that information is revealed. Economists, for instance, have had major roles in designing mechanisms by which large public holdings are auctioned in ways that reveal the private valuations by bidders for the public holdings. Economists have also designed mechanisms that, in the absence of market prices, result in optimal "matches" between buyers and sellers. For instance, the mechanism that determines which hospitals are matched with which medical school interns is one that has been designed by economists, as have new mechanisms to match live kidney donors with patients. (The problem in kidney donations is that I might be willing to donate a kidney to my relative and you might be willing to donate your kidney to your relative but neither one of us has the right kidney for the person to whom we are trying to donate. If my kidney is a good match for your relative and yours is a good match for mine, however, there is still a way for our relatives to get donated kidneys if we can find the right mechanisms to determine how such matches are to be made.) In the past few years, economists have also designed large public school choice programs in cities like Boston and New York, programs where parents provide information about their preferences for schools and the mechanism then matches children to schools.[10] While it is beyond the scope of this text, the general area of mechanism design is therefore one of growing interest among economists who aim to achieve more efficient outcomes in the real world when markets on their own cannot get there. It is a fascinating area that you might want to study more.

---

[10]Much of this literature, and efforts to bring its results into the real world, are due to Alvin Roth (1951–), an economics professor at Harvard, and a number of his notable collaborators. Interested students might consider exploring some of Professor Roth's Web site that overviews many recent developments.

27B The Mathematics of Public Goods

We begin our mathematical treatment of public goods in Section 27B.1 by illustrating the basic necessary condition for public good quantities to be optimal. While we do this for a general case with many consumers, we then introduce a simple example involving two consumers with well-defined and identical preferences, and we will use this example throughout the chapter to illustrate the mathematics behind the intuitions developed in Section A. As in our intuitive development of the material, we will demonstrate the free-rider problem as an outgrowth of the presence of positive externalities that individuals generally do not take into account unless their choices are tempered by nonmarket institutions. The direct government policies of public good provision and public good subsidies are introduced in Section 27B.2, and the more indirect "policies" of establishing certain types of markets are discussed in Section 27B.3. Section 27B.4 then considers civil society intervention, particularly in the presence of "warm glow" effects of giving, and Section 27B.5 expands our discussion of preference revelation mechanisms from the simple mechanism discussed in Section A.

27B.1 Public Goods and the Free-Rider Problem

Public goods, as we have seen, give rise to externalities, and we already know from earlier chapters that decentralized market behavior in the presence of externalities often does not result in efficient outcomes. We begin by deriving the necessary condition for optimality of public goods, the condition now quite familiar (from our work in Section A) that the sum of marginal benefits must equal the marginal cost of producing the public good. We then proceed, as we did in Section A, to illustrate the free-rider problem that keeps decentralized market behavior from being efficient.

27B.1.1 The Efficient Level of Public Goods   Suppose x represents a composite private good and y represents the public good. There are N consumers in the economy, with $u^n(x_n, y)$ representing the nth consumer's preferences over his or her consumption of the composite private good x_n and the public good. Suppose further that f represents the technology for producing y from the composite good; i.e., suppose $y = f(x)$. Finally, suppose that the total available level of private good (in the absence of public goods production) is X.

We are first interested in deriving the necessary conditions that have to be satisfied for us to produce an efficient public good level y^*. For a situation to be efficient, we have to set y^* such that nothing can be changed to make one consumer better off without making some consumers worse off. We can therefore calculate this by choosing the consumption levels $(x_1, x_2, \ldots, x_N)$ and y to maximize one consumer's utility subject to holding the others fixed at some arbitrary level and subject to the constraint that $y = f(X - \Sigma x_n)$.

<hr>

Exercise 27B.1   Explain the constraint $y = f(X - \Sigma x_n)$.

<hr>

To cut down a bit on notation as we write down this optimization problem formally, we can define a function $g(\Sigma x_n, y) = y - f(X - \Sigma x_n)$. We can then formally express the optimization problem to derive the necessary conditions for an efficient public good level y^* as

$$\max_{(x_1, \ldots, x_N, y)} u^1(x_1, y) \text{ subject to } u^n(x_n, y) = \bar{u}^n \text{ for all } n = 2, \ldots, N \text{ and } g\left(\sum_{n=1}^{N} x_n, y\right) = 0. \quad (27.1)$$

The Lagrange function for this optimization problem is

$$\mathcal{L} = u^1(x_1, y) + \sum_{n=2}^{N} \lambda_n \left(\bar{u}^n - u^n(x_n, y) \right) + \lambda_1 g\left(\sum_{n=1}^{N} x_n, y \right),$$ (27.2)

where $(\lambda_2, \ldots, \lambda_N)$ are the Lagrange multipliers for the constraints that hold utility levels for consumers 2 through N fixed and λ_1 is the Lagrange multiplier for the production constraint. To get our first order conditions, we differentiate $\mathcal{L}$ with respect to each of the choice variables to get

$$\frac{\partial \mathcal{L}}{\partial x_1} = \frac{\partial u^1}{\partial x_1} + \lambda_1 \frac{\partial g}{\partial x} = 0$$

$$\frac{\partial \mathcal{L}}{\partial x_n} = -\lambda_n \frac{\partial u^n}{\partial x_n} + \lambda_1 \frac{\partial g}{\partial x} = 0 \text{ for all } n = 2, \ldots, N$$ (27.3)

$$\frac{\partial \mathcal{L}}{\partial y} = \frac{\partial u^1}{\partial y} - \sum_{n=2}^{N} \lambda_n \frac{\partial u^n}{\partial y} + \lambda_1 \frac{\partial g}{\partial y} = 0,$$

where we can express $\partial g / \partial x_i$ simply as $\partial g / \partial x$ (since marginal increases in any x_i have the same impact on the first argument of the g function). The first of our first order conditions can be written as $\partial u^1 / \partial x_1 = -\lambda_1 \partial g / \partial x$. We can then divide the first term of the third first order condition by $\partial u^1 / \partial x_1$ and the remaining terms by $-\lambda_1 \partial g / \partial x$. Subtracting the resulting last term from both sides, the last first order condition becomes

$$\frac{\partial u^1 / \partial y}{\partial u^1 / \partial x_1} + \sum_{n=2}^{N} \frac{\lambda_n}{\lambda_1} \frac{\partial u^n / \partial y}{\partial g / \partial x} = \frac{\partial g / \partial y}{\partial g / \partial x}.$$ (27.4)

The second set of first order conditions can be rewritten as

$$\frac{\lambda_n}{\lambda_1} = \frac{\partial g / \partial x}{\partial u^n / \partial x_n} \text{ for all } n = 2, \ldots, N,$$ (27.5)

which, when substituted for λ_n / λ_1 in equation (27.4), yields

$$\frac{\partial u^1 / \partial y}{\partial u^1 / \partial x_1} + \sum_{n=2}^{N} \frac{\partial u^n / \partial y}{\partial u^n / \partial x_n} = \frac{\partial g / \partial y}{\partial g / \partial x}.$$ (27.6)

The first term in this equation can then be brought into the summation in the second term, and the resulting equation can be inverted and multiplied by -1 to yield

$$\sum_{n=1}^{N} -\frac{\partial u^n / \partial x_n}{\partial u^n / \partial y} = -\frac{\partial g / \partial x}{\partial g / \partial y}.$$ (27.7)

Now notice that the left-hand side of the equation is simply the sum of the marginal rates of substitution for all the consumers in the economy, or the sum of the marginal benefits expressed in dollars since we are interpreting x as a dollar-denominated composite good. The right-hand side of the equation can be simplified given that g was defined as $g(\sum x_n, y) = y - f(X - \sum x_n)$, with $\partial g / \partial y = 1$ and $\partial g / \partial x = \partial f / \partial x$. The right-hand side therefore simplifies to $\partial f / \partial x$, which is just the marginal cost (in terms of x) of producing one more unit of y. Equation (27.7) can then simply be written as

$$\sum_{n=1}^{N} MB_y^n = MC_y;$$ (27.8)

i.e., the sum of the marginal benefits of the public good must be equal to the marginal cost of producing it.[11]

27B.1.2 A Simple Example

To make this more concrete in the context of an example we will continue to use in other parts of this section, suppose that we have an economy of two consumers who have identical Cobb–Douglas preferences that can be represented by the utility function

$$u^n(x_n, y) = x_n^\alpha y^{(1-\alpha)}. \qquad (27.9)$$

Suppose further a simple production technology $y = f(x) = x$ that permits us to produce 1 unit of the public good from 1 unit of the composite private good, and suppose the only resources we have are the incomes of the two consumers, I_1 and I_2.

To find the efficient level of the public good y^*, we can then again calculate this by choosing x_1, x_2, and y to maximize one consumer's utility subject to holding the other's fixed at some arbitrary indifference curve $\bar{u}$ and subject to the constraint that only the consumers' incomes can be used to fund the public good; i.e, we can solve the optimization problem

$$\max_{x_1, x_2, y} u^1(x_1, y) \text{ subject to } u^2(x_2, y) = \bar{u} \text{ and } y = (I_1 + I_2 - x_1 - x_2). \qquad (27.10)$$

It is easiest to solve this by taking natural logarithms of the utility function and substituting $y = (I_1 + I_2 - x_1 - x_2)$ into the utility functions for y. We can then write the optimization problem as

$$\max_{x_1, x_2} \alpha \ln x_1 + (1 - \alpha) \ln (I_1 + I_2 - x_1 - x_2) \text{ subject to}$$
$$\alpha \ln x_2 + (1 - \alpha) \ln (I_1 + I_2 - x_1 - x_2) = \bar{u}. \qquad (27.11)$$

Solving the two first order conditions, we get

$$x_1 + x_2 = \alpha(I_1 + I_2), \qquad (27.12)$$

which implies

$$y^* = I_1 + I_2 - x_1 - x_2 = (I_1 + I_2) - \alpha(I_1 + I_2) = (1 - \alpha)(I_1 + I_2). \qquad (27.13)$$

Exercise 27B.2   Verify the outcome of this optimization problem. (*Hint*: Solve the first two first order conditions for λ and use your answer to derive the equation for $(x_1 + x_2)$.)

We can also check that this is the optimal quantity of public goods by adding up demand curves as we did in Section A. We know that Cobb–Douglas preferences represented by $u(x, y) = x^\alpha y^{(1-\alpha)}$ give rise to demand curves for y of the form $y = (1 - \alpha)I/p$. Writing this as an inverse demand curve, consumer n's demand is $p = (1 - \alpha)I_n/y$. If we consider two consumers with identical preferences but different incomes, the (vertical) sum of these is

$$\frac{(1 - \alpha)I_1}{y} + \frac{(1 - \alpha)I_2}{y} = \frac{(1 - \alpha)(I_1 + I_2)}{y}. \qquad (27.14)$$

When the production technology for y takes the simple form $y = f(x) = x$, the marginal cost of producing 1 additional unit of y is $c = 1$. Thus, a social planner who is interested in

----

[11]The optimality condition for public goods is often referred to as the "Samuelsonian" optimality conditions because of their original formal derivation by Paul Samuelson (1915–), the 1970 winner of the Nobel Prize in Economics. Samuelson, an economics professor at MIT, was only the second economist to be awarded a Nobel Prize following the creation of the prize in 1969.

providing the efficient level of the public good would produce y so long as equation (27.14) is greater than marginal cost and would stop when

$$\frac{(1 - \alpha)(I_1 + I_2)}{y} = 1. \tag{27.15}$$

Solving for y, we again get the optimal level of public goods as

$$y^* = (1 - \alpha)(I_1 + I_2). \tag{27.16}$$

What is y^* if there are N rather than 2 consumers of the type described in our example (i.e., with the same Cobb–Douglas tastes but different incomes)? What if everyone's income is also the same?

Exercise 27B.3

27B.1.3 Decentralized Provision of Public Goods

Suppose we now continue with our example and we ask the two consumers to voluntarily contribute to the provision of the public good. In other words, suppose we asked each consumer n to decide on a contribution z_n of his or her income (or the composite good), with each consumer knowing that the public good y will be a function of his or her joint contributions such that

$$y(z_1, z_2) = z_1 + z_2. \tag{27.17}$$

The consumers are then engaged in a simultaneous move game in which they both choose their individual contributions taking the other's contribution as given. To determine consumer 1's best response function to consumer 2 contributing z_2, consumer 1 would solve the problem

$$\max_{x_1, z_1} \ u^1(x_1, y) \ \text{such that} \ I_1 = x_1 + p_1 z_1 \ \text{and} \ y = z_1 + z_2, \tag{27.18}$$

where we have implicitly assumed that the price of x is 1 since x is a dollar-denominated composite good. We have also assumed a "price" p_n for contributing to the public good, where p_n is equal to 1 if no one is subsidizing the contributions of individuals. (We are including the possibility of subsidies in preparation for discussing government subsidies of private giving.)

Explain why $p_1 = p_2 = 1$ for both consumers in the absence of subsidies for giving to the public good.

Exercise 27B.4

Substituting $y = (z_1 + z_2)$ for y and $x_1 = I_1 - p_1 z_1$ for x_1 into the logarithmic transformation of the Cobb–Douglas utility function from equation (27.9), the problem then becomes

$$\max_{z_1} \ \alpha \ln (I_1 - p_1 z_1) + (1 - \alpha) \ln (z_1 + z_2), \tag{27.19}$$

where the first order condition now just involves taking the derivative of the utility function with respect to z_1. Solving this first order condition then gives consumer 1's best response function to z_2 as

$$z_1(z_2) = \frac{(1 - \alpha)I_1}{p_1} - \alpha z_2, \tag{27.20}$$

and doing the same for consumer 2 we can similarly get consumer 2's best response function to z_1 as

$$z_2(z_1) = \frac{(1 - \alpha)I_2}{p_2} - \alpha z_1. \tag{27.21}$$

Exercise 27B.5   Draw the best response functions for the two individuals in a graph similar to Graph 27.3. Carefully label intercepts and slopes.

In a Nash equilibrium to this game, each consumer has to be best responding to the other. Plugging equation (27.21) in for z_2 in equation (27.20), we can solve for consumer 1's equilibrium contribution as

$$z_1^{eq} = \frac{I_1 p_2 - \alpha I_2 p_1}{(1 + \alpha)p_1 p_2} \tag{27.22}$$

and plugging this back into equation (27.21), we get consumer 2's equilibrium contribution as

$$z_2^{eq} = \frac{I_2 p_1 - \alpha I_1 p_2}{(1 + \alpha)p_1 p_2}. \tag{27.23}$$

The sum of the individual contributions, and thus the equilibrium level of the public good under voluntary giving y^v, is therefore

$$y^v(p_1, p_2) = z_1^{eq} + z_1^{eq} = \frac{(1 - \alpha)(I_1 p_2 + I_2 p_1)}{(1 + \alpha)p_1 p_2}. \tag{27.24}$$

Now suppose that consumers in fact do not receive any subsidy to give to the public good, which implies $p_1 = p_2 = 1$. Then equation (27.24) simplifies to

$$y^v(\text{no subsidy}) = \frac{(1 - \alpha)(I_1 + I_2)}{(1 + \alpha)} < (1 - \alpha)(I_1 + I_2) = y^*, \tag{27.25}$$

where the inequality holds for all $\alpha > 0$. Thus, so long as consumers place at least some value on private good consumption, the voluntary contributions result in less than the optimal quantity of the public good as each consumer free rides on the contributions of the other.

Exercise 27B.6   Why do private contributions to the public good result in the optimal level of the public good when $\alpha = 0$?

Table 27.2: $I = 1,000$, $\alpha = 0.5$

	Free Riding as Population Increases					
	$N = 1$	$N = 2$	$N = 5$	$N = 10$	$N = 25$	$N = 100$
y^{eq}	500	666.67	833.33	909.09	961.54	990.10
y^*	500	1,000	2,500	5,000	12,500	50,000
y^{eq}/y^*	1.000	0.667	0.333	0.182	0.077	0.020

Consider the equilibrium public good level as a fraction of the optimal public good level. In our example, what is the lowest this fraction can become, and what is the critical variable?

Exercise
27B.7

You can easily see how this underprovision of public goods under voluntary giving will continue (and in fact get worse) as the number of consumers increases. Suppose, for instance, that everyone is identical in every way, both in terms of their Cobb–Douglas preferences and in terms of their income, and that there is no subsidy for private giving to charity. But now instead of two of us there are N of us. In a symmetric equilibrium (in which all the identical players play the same strategy), we can then simplify equation (27.20) to

$$z = (1 - \alpha)I - \alpha(N - 1)z, \qquad (27.26)$$

where $(N - 1)z$ is the contribution by all $(N - 1)$ players other than the one whose best response function we are working with. Solving this for z, we get

$$z^{eq} = \frac{(1 - \alpha)I}{1 + \alpha(N - 1)}, \qquad (27.27)$$

and the resulting equilibrium level of public good y^{eq} is simply equal to Nz^{eq} or

$$y^{eq} = \frac{N(1 - \alpha)I}{1 + \alpha(N - 1)}. \qquad (27.28)$$

In exercise 27B.3, you should have derived the optimal level of the public good for the N-person case as $y^* = N(1 - \alpha)I$, which means we can rewrite equation (27.28) as

$$y^{eq} = \frac{y^*}{1 + \alpha(N - 1)}. \qquad (27.29)$$

An increase in the number of consumers N of the public good increases the denominator of the right-hand side of this equation, which means that as N increases, the equilibrium quantity of the public good will be a decreasing fraction of the optimal quantity. Put differently, *the free-rider problem gets worse as the number of consumers of the public good increases.*

Table 27.2 demonstrates this dramatically for the case where all consumers have income $I = 1,000$ and $\alpha = 0.5$. The last row of the table reports the equilibrium public good level as a fraction of the optimal public good level. This is 1 when there is only a single consumer (in the first column) and there thus does not exist a free-rider problem. But it falls quickly as we add consumers, already reaching 0.02 at $N = 100$.

As N gets larger, what do y^* and y^{eq} converge to for the example in Table 27.2? What does the equilibrium level of public good as a fraction of the optimal level converge to?

Exercise
27B.8

27B.2 Direct Government Policies to Address Free Riding

As in Section A, we'll consider two direct approaches a government might take to the public goods problem. First, it may itself provide the public good, and second it may use subsidies to make it cheaper for individuals to give to public goods. To result in optimal levels of the public good, both approaches require knowledge of consumer preferences (which governments typically do not have, a topic we take up again in Section 27B.5).

27B.2.1 Government Provision and "Crowd-out"

We have already seen how an efficiency-focused government would calculate the optimal level of public goods, and in end-of-chapter exercise 27.9 you can show how this is affected if we also consider the government needs to raise the necessary revenues to fund public good production when it can only use inefficient taxes. Now suppose the government, either because it does not have sufficient information about preferences or because the political process is not efficient, decides to fund some amount g of the public good (rather than the optimal qantity y^*), and suppose it funds this through a proportional income tax t. Since income is assumed to be exogenous (and not the result of an explicit labor-leisure choice), such a tax would have no deadweight loss in our example. In order to raise sufficient revenues to fund g, it must be that $t(I_1 + I_2) = g$ or, rearranging terms,

$$t = \frac{g}{(I_1 + I_2)}. \tag{27.30}$$

Exercise 27B.9 Can you explain in a bit more detail why the tax in this case is efficient?

Each consumer n then has to determine how much z_n to give to the public good him- or herself *given that the government is contributing g*. Consumer 1 therefore takes as given consumer 2's contribution z_2 as well as the government contribution g, which changes the optimization problem in equation (27.19) to

$$\max_{z_1} \alpha \ln \left((1-t)I_1 - p_1 z_1\right) + (1-\alpha) \ln (z_1 + z_2 + g), \tag{27.31}$$

or, substituting in for t,

$$\max_{z_1} \alpha \ln \left(\frac{(I_1 + I_2 - g)I_1}{I_1 + I_2} - p_1 z_1\right) + (1-\alpha) \ln (z_1 + z_2 + g). \tag{27.32}$$

Solving the first order condition for z_1, we get consumer 1's best response to (z_2, g) as

$$z_1(z_2, g) = \frac{(1-\alpha)I_1(I_1 + I_2 - g)}{(I_1 + I_2)p_1} - \alpha(z_2 + g). \tag{27.33}$$

Similarly, consumer 2's best response to (z_1, g) is

$$z_2(z_1, g) = \frac{(1-\alpha)I_2(I_1 + I_2 - g)}{(I_1 + I_2)p_2} - \alpha(z_1 + g). \tag{27.34}$$

Exercise 27B.10 Demonstrate that these best response functions converge to those in equations (27.20) and (27.21) as g goes to zero.

Substituting consumer 2's best response function into consumer 1's and solving for z_1, we get consumer 1's equilibrium contribution to the public good as a function of the government's contribution

$$z_1^{eq}(g) = \frac{(I_1 + I_2 - g)(I_1 p_2 - \alpha I_2 p_1)}{(1+\alpha)(I_1 + I_2)p_1 p_2} - \frac{\alpha g}{(1+\alpha)}, \tag{27.35}$$

with consumer 2's equilibrium contribution coming to

$$z_2^{eq}(g) = \frac{(I_1 + I_2 - g)(I_2 p_1 - \alpha I_1 p_2)}{(1+\alpha)(I_1 + I_2)p_1 p_2} - \frac{\alpha g}{(1+\alpha)}. \tag{27.36}$$

Adding these individual contributions to the government's, we get the equilibrium public good level $y^{eq}(g)$ as

$$y^{eq}(g) = z_1^{eq}(g) + z_2^{eq}(g) + g$$

$$= \frac{(1 - \alpha)(I_1 p_2 + I_2 p_1)}{(1 + \alpha)p_1 p_2} - g\left[\frac{(1 - \alpha)(I_1 p_2 + I_2 p_1)}{(1 + \alpha)(I_1 + I_2)p_1 p_2} + \frac{2\alpha}{1 + \alpha}\right] + g \quad (27.37)$$

$$= y^v + g - g\left[\frac{(1 - \alpha)(I_1 p_2 + I_2 p_1)}{(1 + \alpha)(I_1 + I_2)p_1 p_2} + \frac{2\alpha}{1 + \alpha}\right],$$

where y^v is our previous voluntary contribution level in the absence of government contributions (from equation (27.29)). When the government contributes $1 to the public good, private contributions therefore decline by an amount equal to the bracketed term in the equation. Government contributions to the public good then crowd out private contributions dollar for dollar if the bracketed term is equal to 1, which, you can check for yourself, occurs when $p_1 = p_2 = 1$. Put differently, when the government is not subsidizing private contributions to the public good (and $1 in contributions costs $1), government contributions to the public good fully crowd out private contributions.

Our perfect crowd-out result holds, however, only to the extent to which consumers are in fact giving to the public good when the government increases its contribution. If a consumer is at a "corner solution" where he or she does not give, then the consumer remains at that corner solution as government contributions rise. Consider, for instance, the simple case where the two consumers have identical incomes I and where the government is not subsidizing individual contributions (i.e., $p_1 = p_2 = 1$). Then equations (27.35) and (27.36) simply become

$$z^{eq}(g) = \frac{(1 - \alpha)I}{1 + \alpha} - \frac{g}{2}. \quad (27.38)$$

This implies that individual contributions are zero when

$$g = \frac{2(1 - \alpha)I}{1 + \alpha}, \quad (27.39)$$

and for government contributions larger than this, there is no crowd-out. (In end-of-chapter exercise 27.8, you can demonstrate that the same crowd-out result holds when the number of individuals is N instead of 2.)

....

Can you tell if there is any crowd-out for the last dollar spent by the government if the government provides the optimal level of the public good in this case?

**Exercise
27B.11**

....

27B.2.2 Tax and Subsidy Policies to Encourage Voluntary Giving

Finally, suppose that the government wanted to offer a subsidy s to reduce the effective price that individuals have to pay in order to contribute to the public good. They may do so directly or, as we discussed in Section A, by making charitable contributions tax deductible. In order to finance this subsidy, the government imposes a tax t on income, and since income is assumed to be exogenous, such a tax would be efficient. By choosing a policy (t, s), the government therefore reduces consumer n's income to $(1 - t)I_n$ and his or her price for contributing to the public good to $(1 - s)$. Substituting these new prices and incomes under policy (t, s) into equation (27.24), we can then write the total amount of giving to the public good as

$$y^v(t, s) = \frac{(1 - \alpha)[(1 - t)I_1(1 - s) + (1 - t)I_2(1 - s)]}{(1 + \alpha)(1 - s)^2}$$

$$= \frac{(1 - \alpha)(1 - t)(I_1 + I_2)}{(1 + \alpha)(1 - s)}. \tag{27.40}$$

But the government can't just pick any combination of t and s because its budget has to balance. Put differently, tax revenues have to be sufficient to pay the subsidy. If the government wants to set subsidies to induce the efficient level of the public good $y^* = (1 - \alpha)(I_1 + I_2)$, it knows it must raise revenues equal to $sy^* = s(1 - \alpha)(I_1 + I_2)$. Its revenues are $t(I_1 + I_2)$, which implies that, for a subsidy s that achieves the optimum level of public good y^*, the government needs to set t such that

$$t(I_1 + I_2) = s(1 - \alpha)(I_1 + I_2), \tag{27.41}$$

which simplifies to $t = s(1 - \alpha)$. Substituting this into equation (27.40), we can write the level of giving as a function of s, assuming the government in fact balances its budget and sets $t = s(1 - \alpha)$; i.e.,

$$y^v(s) = \frac{(1 - \alpha)\left(1 - s(1 - \alpha)\right)(I_1 + I_2)}{(1 + \alpha)(1 - s)}. \tag{27.42}$$

To ensure the optimal level of contributions to the public good, it must then be that $y^v(s) = y^*$, or

$$\frac{(1 - \alpha)\left(1 - s(1 - \alpha)\right)(I_1 + I_2)}{(1 + \alpha)(1 - s)} = (1 - \alpha)(I_1 + I_2). \tag{27.43}$$

With a little algebra, this solves to $s = 1/2$. Thus, the optimal combination of an income tax and a subsidy for giving to the public good is

$$(t^*, s^*) = \left(\frac{1 - \alpha}{2}, \frac{1}{2}\right). \tag{27.44}$$

In exercise 27.1, you can demonstrate that, in the N person case, the optimal subsidy level becomes $s^* = (N - 1)/N$ (and in exercise 27.2 you can explore how the result changes if individuals think more strategically about the balanced budget tax implications of their giving).

Exercise 27B.12 Can you offer an intuitive explanation for why $s^* = 1/2$? How would you expect this to change as the number of consumers increases?

Exercise 27B.13 We previously concluded that the optimal level of the public good is $(1 - \alpha)(I_1 + I_2)$. Can you use our solutions for s^* and t^* to show that this level is achieved through the voluntary contributions of the two individuals when the policy (s^*, t^*) is implemented?

27B.3 Establishing Markets for Public Goods

If we knew individual demands for public goods, we have seen that it would be easy to derive the optimal public good quantity; and, as we saw in Section A, it would also be easy to then derive personalized prices for different consumers, prices under which consumers would in fact choose the optimal public good level that is simultaneously chosen by others (at their personalized prices) as well. This notion of an equilibrium, called a *Lindahl equilibrium*, is the public good analog to a competitive private good equilibrium. It is, in some sense, the mirror image of our notion of a competitive equilibrium where everyone faces the same prices and chooses different quantities because in a Lindahl equilibrium, everyone chooses the same quantities at different prices. In the next section, we will begin by illustrating the mathematics of deriving the Lindahl equilibrium within our two-person example and then briefly move on to the case of local public goods.

27B.3.1 Lindahl Pricing and Markets for Public Good Externalities

Suppose a firm is producing the public good and selling it to consumer n at p_n. The problem is that the firm can only produce a single quantity of y that will be consumed by all consumers, and so it looks for individualized prices such that (1) all consumers would in fact choose to purchase the quantity y that is produced at their individualized price and (2) the producer covers his or her costs. In order for the result to be efficient, it must further be the case that the quantity produced (and demanded by each consumer) is y^*.

Given the simple production function $y = f(x) = x$, the producer faces a constant marginal cost $c = 1$ for each unit of y he or she produces. Thus, to satisfy the condition that the producer's costs are covered (in the absence of fixed costs), it simply has to be the case that

$$p_1 + p_2 = 1. \tag{27.45}$$

We know from our work with Cobb–Douglas preferences that consumers will allocate a fraction of their income to each consumption good, with that fraction being equal to the exponent that accompanies that good in the utility function. Thus, we know that demand for y by consumer n is

$$y_n = \frac{(1 - \alpha)I_n}{p_n}. \tag{27.46}$$

The price p_n^* that will induce consumer n to purchase the optimal public good quantity $y^* = (1 - \alpha)(I_1 + I_2)$ can therefore be determined by simply solving

$$(1 - \alpha)(I_1 + I_2) = \frac{(1 - \alpha)I_n}{p_n} \tag{27.47}$$

for p_n. This gives us

$$p_n^* = \frac{I_n}{I_1 + I_2}. \tag{27.48}$$

With each consumer being charged this price, the sum of the prices is 1 (thus satisfying condition (27.45)) and each consumer chooses $y^* = (1 - \alpha)(I_1 + I_2)$.

What do you think p_n will be in the *N*-person case if everyone shares the same Cobb–Douglas tastes? What if they also all have the same income level?

**Exercise
27B.14**

27B.3.2 Local Public and Club Goods

An alternative "market" solution to (local) public goods provision involves, as we discussed in Section A, having clubs or local communities compete for customers or residents when public goods are excludable. Under conditions we explore further in end-of-chapter exercise 27.4, this results in competition that is analogous to our notion of a competitive equilibrium, with individuals choosing clubs and communities much as they choose supermarkets and shopping centers. The "Tiebout" literature that explores these intuitions is vast, and a detailed mathematical exploration of the properties of Tiebout models is beyond the scope of this text. The interested student should consider taking courses in local public finance and urban economics.

27B.4 Civil Society and the Free-Rider Problem

We noted in Section A that if all we care about is the overall level of the public good but not how that level was arrived at, we should almost never be observed to contribute to more than a single charity. The intuition for this is straightforward: Our contributions to charities are almost always small relative to the size of the public good that is being funded. This means that the marginal impact of our contribution is unlikely to cause a sufficiently large change in the overall public good to warrant switching charities. If charity A was the best charity to give to before I wrote my check, it is still the best charity to give to after I write my check because my check is simply not very big compared to the overall need.

It is not difficult to see this mathematically. Suppose there are three charities called a, b, and c, and before I write my check, they have already received total contributions of Y_a, Y_b, and Y_c. As I consider where to place my contribution, I have come to some judgment about how much these charities add in value to the world, and I can represent this judgment by a function $F(Y_a, Y_b, Y_c)$. If I have an amount D to donate, I will then want to donate in a way that maximizes the impact I have on the world based on my judgment F; i.e., I would like to solve the problem

$$\max_{y_a, y_b, y_c} F(Y_a + y_a, Y_b + y_b, Y_c + y_c) \text{ subject to } D = y_a + y_b + y_c \qquad (27.49)$$

where y_i is my contribution to charity i. When D is small relative to each Y_i, the only way that I will arrive at an "interior solution" where $y_i > 0$ for $i = a, b, c$ is if, prior to my contributions,

$$\frac{\partial F}{\partial Y_a} = \frac{\partial F}{\partial Y_b} = \frac{\partial F}{\partial Y_c}. \qquad (27.50)$$

In that case, I need to make sure that I "balance" my contributions so that this equation continues to hold *after* I have contributed. But if $\partial F / \partial Y_a$ is greater than $\partial F / \partial Y_b$ and $\partial F / \partial Y_c$, then I will solve my optimization problem (27.49) by setting $y_a = D$ and $y_b = y_c = 0$ since it is unlikely that my (relatively) small contribution lowers $\partial F / \partial Y_a$ in any perceptible way. Notice that, to the extent to which I am uncertain about the marginal impact my contributions will have across charities, this is part of the F function that captures my judgments about where my contributions will have their largest impact, and so uncertainty does not undo the argument that people should give only to a single charity if they care only about the impact their contribution has on the world.

Exercise 27B.15   What is different for Bill Gates that might make him rationally contribute to multiple charities?

Exercise 27B.16   Suppose I only give to small local charities. In what way might I then be like Bill Gates and give rationally to more than one?

Exercise 27B.17   Can you explain why it is rational to diversify a private investment portfolio in the presence of risk and uncertainty but the same argument does not hold for diversifying our charitable giving?

Given how often we see individuals give relatively small amounts to many charities, and given that individuals give more than a pure free-rider model would predict, we therefore consider how our predictions change as individuals gain both public and private benefits from giving. Unlike in the analogous section in part A of this chapter, we will forego another discussion of the Coase Theorem (which, due to transactions costs, applies only to "small" public goods and only if informational asymmetries (introduced in Chapter 21) do not impede bargaining) and instead proceed directly to incorporating a warm glow effect into our model of voluntary giving.

27B.4.1 Public Goods and the "Warm Glow" Effect

Suppose, then, that consumers care about their individual contribution itself; that is, suppose consumers get a "warm glow" from giving to the public good in addition to knowing that the overall public good level is higher as a result of their contributions. We could then represent preferences with the Cobb–Douglas utility function

$$u^n(x_n, y, z_n) = x_n^\alpha y^\beta z_n^\gamma = x_n^\alpha \left(z_n + \sum_{j \neq n} z_j \right)^\beta z_n^\gamma, \tag{27.51}$$

where the public good y is simply the sum of all individual contributions. Consumer n's individual contribution z_n therefore enters the utility function twice: once because it contributes to the overall public good level and once because the individual derives utility from writing a check for the public good. As the number of consumers increases, the impact of n's marginal contribution to y diminishes (giving rise to a worsening free-rider problem), but the "warm glow" effect remains unchanged because it is, in essence, a private good.

Consider a simple example in which there are N consumers that are identical both in their incomes I and their preferences (that can be represented as in equation (27.51)). Since all individuals are identical, they will contribute identical amounts z to the public good in equilibrium. Taking everyone else's contribution as given, we can then determine how much z_1 individual 1 will give to the public good by solving the problem

$$\max_{z_1} \quad \alpha \ln (I - z_1) + \beta \ln \left(z_1 + (N - 1)z \right) + \gamma \ln z_1, \tag{27.52}$$

where we have incorporated the individual's budget constraint by expressing $x_1 = I - z_1$ and we have taken the log of the utility function in equation (27.51) to make the derivation of the first order condition a bit less messy. The first order condition (after rearranging a few terms) can be written as

$$(\alpha + \beta + \gamma)z_1^2 + (\alpha + \gamma)(N - 1)zz_1 = (\beta + \gamma)Iz_1 + \gamma(N - 1)Iz. \tag{27.53}$$

Solving this for z_1 would give individual 1's best response to everyone else giving z to the public good. But we know that in equilibrium $z_1 = z$, and so we can simply substitute this into the first order condition and solve for z to get the equilibrium level of contribution by every individual as

$$z^{eq} = \frac{(\beta + \gamma N)I}{\beta + (\alpha + \gamma)N}. \tag{27.54}$$

If you were a social planner choosing z (assuming you constrain yourself to choosing each individual's contribution to be the same as everyone else's), you would set

$$z^* = \frac{(\beta + \gamma)I}{\alpha + \beta + \gamma}. \tag{27.55}$$

Exercise 27B.18

Verify our derivation of z^{eq} and z^*. Then demonstrate that z^{eq} converges to z^* as β goes to zero. Can you make intuitive sense of this?

In Table 27.3, we can then again illustrate how the equilibrium public good level compares to the optimum as population increases. This is similar to our exercise in Table 27.2, where we assumed no warm glow from giving and thus simply saw the free-rider problem at work. In both cases, we are setting the exponent on the private good x equal to the exponent on the public good y, but now we are permitting γ (which was implicitly set to zero in Table 27.2) to be greater than zero

Table 27.3: $I = 1,000$, $\alpha = 0.4$, $\beta = 0.4$, $\gamma = 0.2$

	\multicolumn{6}{c}{"Warm Glow" Free Riding as Population Increases}					
	$N = 1$	$N = 2$	$N = 5$	$N = 10$	$N = 25$	$N = 100$
y^{eq}	600	1,000	2,059	3,750	8,766	33,775
y^*	600	1,200	3,000	6,000	15,000	60,000
y^{eq}/y^*	1.000	0.833	0.686	0.625	0.584	0.563

to introduce a warm glow effect. Notice that the previous prediction that free riding will drive private contributions to zero as population increases now no longer holds because of the private benefit that individuals get from contributing.

27B.4.2 Marketing Public Goods

Civil society institutions that request voluntary contributions clearly attempt to appeal to the warm glow that many of us get when we give to a cause we consider worthwhile. Such institutions may furthermore market their activities in ways that facilitate such a warm glow effect. Consider our example (from Section A) of an international relief agency that assists poor families in the developing world. The alleviation of suffering in developing countries is a public good to the extent that all of us care about it to some degree, and it is a huge public good with huge free-rider problems because it enters so many utility functions. But suppose that the agency can make us think of our individual contributions to this public good as a private good by matching us to specific families that we (and only we, if we believe the marketing) are helping. We can think of this as the marketing branch of our civil society institution telling us to forget about β in our utility function and focus on γ. Put differently, in the Cobb–Douglas example we have been working with where we can think of the exponents as summing to 1, relief agencies—even if they cannot change how much we care about our own private consumption of x (and thus cannot alter α as a fraction of the sum of all the exponents)—might be able to persuade us that γ is large relative to β.

How much does this help? Consider the simple example in Table 27.4. Here, we assume that there are 10,000 identical individuals considering a gift to a public good y. We set $\alpha = 0.4$ and $(\beta + \gamma) = 0.6$ and then ask how each individual's gift will change as the share of $(\beta + \gamma)$ that is a "warm glow" increases (i.e., as γ increases relative to β.) The impact is quite dramatic. If each of us considers our contribution solely to the extent to which it adds to y, we give 15 cents. But if the charitable organization can get us to view even a small portion of what we are giving as a private good, our contributions go up significantly, and they continue going up the more successful the marketing department in the charitable organization is. The total funding for our charity is then given in the second row of the table. The "warm glow" effect can therefore help alleviate the free-rider problem by getting individuals to view their contributions as providing both public and private benefits. However, the effect will never fully overcome the free-rider problem unless we converge to the extreme case you thought about in exercise 27B.18.

Table 27.4: $I = 1,000$, $N = 10,000$, $\alpha = 0.4$, $\beta + \gamma = 0.6$

	\multicolumn{7}{c}{Individual and Total Private Giving with Increasing "Warm Glow"}						
	$\gamma = 0$	$\gamma = 0.1$	$\gamma = 0.2$	$\gamma = 0.3$	$\gamma = 0.4$	$\gamma = 0.5$	$\gamma = 0.6$
z^{eq}	\$0.15	\$200.08	\$333.38	\$428.60	\$500.01	\$555.56	\$600.00
y^{eq}	\$1,500	\$2,000,800	\$3,333,800	\$4,286,000	\$5,000,100	\$5,555,600	\$6,000,000

Suppose the example applies to a pastor whose congregation has 1,000 members who get utility from overall donations y to the church as well as their own individual contribution z_n. Each member makes \$50,000 and tastes are defined as in equation (27.51) with $\alpha = 0.5$, $\beta = 0.495$, and $\gamma = 0.005$. The pastor needs to raise \$1 million for a new church. He can either put his effort into doubling the size of his congregation, or he can put his energy into fiery sermons to his current congregation, sermons that will change γ to 0.01 and β to 0.49. Can you show that these will have roughly the same impact on how much he collects?

Exercise 27B.19

27B.4.3 Civil Society and "Tipping Points"

Now suppose that instead of simply deriving some "warm glow" from knowing that we are contributing to a public good, the size of that warm glow is related to how many of our friends are also giving to the public good. In particular, suppose that the Cobb–Douglas exponent γ depends on the contribution z by others such that

$$\gamma(z) = \delta_1 + \delta_2 \frac{z}{I}. \tag{27.56}$$

Plugging this into the first order condition in equation (27.53), we could again solve for the equilibrium private contribution levels. As you do this, however, you will notice that it has become more difficult to solve for z^{eq} and that we would have to apply the quadratic formula to solve for two rather than one solutions: a low z^{eq}_{low} and a high z^{eq}_{high}.[12] Some parameter choices for δ_1 and δ_2 will make both of these solutions feasible, which implies that we have two different Nash equilibria. Furthermore, since the equilibrium contributions shape preferences by influencing γ, the two equilibria result in different preferences depending on which equilibrium we reach.

In Table 27.5, I calculated the low and high equilibrium contributions for different values of δ_2 just to illustrate how different the multiple equilibria in such settings can be. (The values of the remaining parameters in the model are reported in the table.) Take the middle column where $\delta_2 = 1$ as an example. In the low contributions equilibrium, we contribute not even 3% of what we contribute in the high contribution equilibrium! This is because in the low contributions equilibrium, γ (when α, β, and γ are normalized to sum to 1) is 0.0084, or essentially zero. Thus, we barely derive a private benefit from giving (because all of us are giving so little), and we are essentially just playing the standard free-rider game. In the high contributions equilibrium, on the other hand, the same normalized γ is 0.422, with each of us deriving substantial private benefit from our public giving.

Table 27.5: $I = 1,000$, $N = 10,000$, $\alpha = 0.4$, $\beta = 0.4$, $\delta_1 = -0.01$

	Multiple Equilibria when "Warm Glow" is Endogenous					
	$\delta_2 = 0.6$	$\delta_2 = 0.8$	$\delta_2 = 1.0$	$\delta_2 = 1.2$	$\delta_2 = 1.4$	$\delta_2 = 1.6$
z^{eq}_{low}	\$56.59	\$25.57	\$16.79	\$12.53	\$10.00	\$8.32
z^{eq}_{high}	\$293.34	\$486.88	\$593.17	\$662.44	\$711.40	\$747.90

---

[12]Substituting $\gamma(z)$ into equation (27.54) and cross-multiplying, we get

$$\beta z + \alpha N z + \gamma(z) N z = \beta I + \gamma(z) N I, \tag{27.57}$$

and replacing $\gamma(z)$ with $\delta_1 + \delta_2(z/I)$, we get (after some more rearranging of terms)

$$\frac{\delta_2 N}{I} z^2 + (\beta - (\delta_2 - \alpha - \delta_1)N)z - (\beta + \delta_1 N)I = 0. \tag{27.58}$$

It is to this expression that the quadratic formula can then be applied.

Exercise
27B.20*

Suppose $\delta_2 = 1$. Using $\delta_1 = -0.01$ and the values z_{low}^{eq} and z_{high}^{eq} in the table, derive the implied level of γ in the two equilibria. (Note that these will not match the ones discussed in the text because the table does not normalize all exponents in the utility function to sum to 1.) Then, using the parameters for I, N, α, and β provided in the table, employ equation (27.54) to verify z_{low}^{eq} as well as z_{high}^{eq}.

Nothing in the game theory that we have learned makes one of these equilibria more or less plausible than the other. They are simply two different ways in which individuals might coordinate their behavior if they in fact value their own contribution to public goods more when their friends are also contributing. But if a civil society institution finds itself in a "low contribution" equilibrium, it might find ways to get individuals to coordinate on the "high contribution" equilibrium instead. If it can get sufficiently many individuals to "temporarily" deviate from their low contribution, then this makes it more attractive for others to follow suit. The magnitude of the deviations matter a great deal because if deviations are not sufficiently large, individuals are likely to fall back into the "low contributions" equilibrium. But if the institution can induce sufficiently large deviations, we can cross a "tipping point" where the critical mass has changed their contributions and the natural tendency is now to fall into the "high contribution" equilibrium.

27B.5 Preference Revelation Mechanisms

As we noted in Section A, individuals typically have an incentive to misrepresent their preferences for public goods if their contributions to the public good are linked to their stated preferences for public goods. Economists have therefore thought hard about how to overcome this problem, and they have proposed "mechanisms" that take into account this incentive problem. The general study of creating mechanisms that provide individuals with the incentive to truthfully reveal private information (like their preferences for public goods) is called *mechanism design*. We will begin by introducing the general concept and will then illustrate a more general example of a mechanism (than the one we introduced in Section A) under which individuals reveal their true preferences for public goods to the institution that requests such information.

27B.5.1 Mechanism Design
Suppose that A denotes the set of possible outcomes that we may wish to attain, and let $\{\succsim\}$ denote the set of possible preferences that individuals might have over these outcomes. For instance, in the public goods case, A might denote different levels of public goods and different ways of funding them. An institution like the government might then have in mind some function $f: \{\succsim\}^N \to A$ that would translate the preferences of the N different individuals in the population into the "best" outcome from A according to some criteria captured by the function f. For instance, in the public goods case, the government might wish to implement the efficient level of public goods, which depends on the preferences that people in the population have. If the government knew all the preferences in the population, it could simply do this.

Instead, however, the government needs to request the information about preferences from individuals in the form of "messages" that individuals can send to the government. Let M denote the set of possible messages that individuals are allowed to convey to the government. The government then needs to take all the messages it collects and translate these into an outcome from A; i.e., it needs to define a function $g : M^N \to A$. A *mechanism* is the combination of the definition of the types of messages that individuals are permitted to send and the manner in which the messages are translated into outcomes; i.e., a mechanism is the combination (M, g).

The challenge for the mechanism designer is to define M and g such that the outcome that emerges from the messages sent by individuals is the same that the government would have chosen had it simply been able to observe preferences directly and used the function f to pick outcomes. The mechanism involves "truth telling" if the equilibrium strategy of individuals is to send messages that truthfully reveal the relevant information about their preferences needed by the government *given that individuals know the function g* that the government uses to translate messages into outcomes. The mechanism is said to *implement f* if the outcomes that emerge through the application of g to the equilibrium messages sent by individuals are the same outcomes that would have emerged if f could have been applied directly to the true preferences individuals have. This is depicted graphically in Graph 27.5 where, rather than being able to directly observe $\{\gtrsim\}^N$ and implement f to choose a social outcome from A, a mechanism (M, g) is set up to create a "message game" in which each player chooses what message to send given that messages are translated to outcomes through g.

27B.5.2 The "Groves-Clarke" Mechanism for Public Goods
Suppose then that we consider a world in which N different individuals would benefit from the provision of a public good y that can be produced at constant marginal cost MC. Our objective f is to provide the efficient public good level and raise revenues to pay for the cost of doing so. In order to determine the optimal public good quantity y^*, we need to know individual demands for y, but we typically do not know what these demands are. We therefore need to have the N individuals report their demands to us by defining a set of possible messages M that they can send and devise a scheme g by which we are going to settle on a public good level and a payment to be paid by each of the individuals. The *Groves-Clarke mechanism* is one such mechanism that has been proposed.[13]

The mechanism proceeds as follows, with (1) defining M and (2) and (3) together defining $g: M^N \rightarrow A$:

(1) First, individuals are asked to reveal their (inverse) demands for the public good, with each individual i revealing $RD_i(y)$. Such a revealed demand curve is depicted in panel (a) of Graph 27.6 for consumer i. The set of possible messages M is therefore simply the set of possible downward-sloping demand curves.

(2) The institution that implements the mechanism then determines y^* as if the revealed demands were in fact people's actual demands. The RD_i curves are thus added up, and y^* is set so that the (vertical) sum of revealed demands is equal to the marginal cost MC of producing the public good; i.e.,

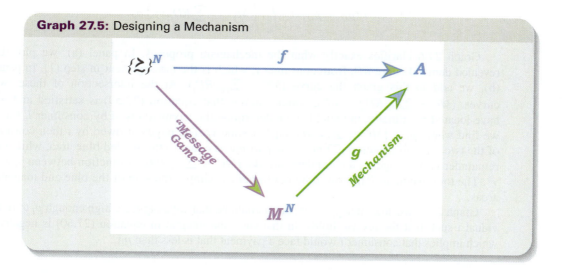

Graph 27.5: Designing a Mechanism

---

[13]The mechanism is named for Theodore Groves (1942–) and Edward Clarke (1939–) who separately developed different versions in the late 1960s and early 1970s. William Vickerey (1914–96) is often credited with having hinted at a similar mechanism in his earlier work on auctions, and some therefore refer to the mechanism as the "Vickery-Groves-Clarke mechanism." Vickery won the Nobel Prize in Economics in 1996 but passed away only three days after the prize was announced.

Graph 27.6: The Groves-Clarke Mechanism

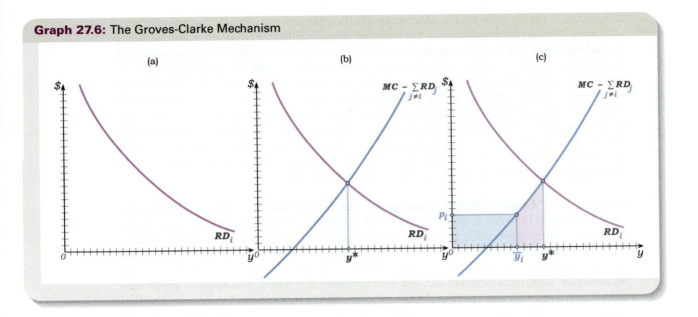

$$\sum_{i=1}^{N} RD_i(y^*) = MC. \tag{27.59}$$

(3) Each individual is assigned a "price" p_i in some arbitrary way that has no relation to what individuals revealed, with the only restriction that the sum of the individual p_i's equals the marginal cost MC; i.e., $\sum p_i = MC$. For each individual i, a quantity $\bar{y}_i$ is then defined such that $p_i = [MC - \sum_{j \neq i} RD_j(y)]$ and the total payment P_i charged to individual i is set to

$$P_i(p_i) = p_i \bar{y}_i + \int_{\bar{y}_i}^{y^*} \left(MC - \sum_{j \neq i} RD_j(y) \right) dy. \tag{27.60}$$

Graph 27.6 clarifies exactly what the mechanism proposes. In panel (a), we plot the revealed demand curve RD_i from consumer i, which is the message sent in step (1). In panel (b), we add to this graph the curve $(MC - \sum_{j \neq i} RD_j)$. At the intersection of these two curves, $(MC - \sum_{j \neq i} RD_j) = RD_i$, which implies that equation (27.59) is satisfied and we have located y^*. Finally, in panel (c) we determine the payment owed by consumer i. First, we find where $p_i = [MC - \sum_{j \neq i} RD_j(y)]$ to define $\bar{y}_i$. The payment owed by i then consists of the two parts in equation (27.60): The part $p_i \bar{y}_i$ is equal to the shaded blue area, while the remainder is the magenta area underneath the $(MC - \sum_{j \neq i} RD_j(y))$ function between $\bar{y}_i$ and y^*. The total payment $P_i(p_i)$ owed by consumer i is simply the sum of the blue and magenta areas.

Graph 27.6c assumes that $\bar{y}_i < y^*$, but it could be that we assigned a high enough p_i to individual i such that the reverse holds. In that case, the integral in equation (27.60) is negative, which implies that consumer i would face a payment that is less than $p_i \bar{y}_i$.

Exercise 27B.21   Illustrate in a graph similar to Graph 27.6 what the payment $P_i(p_i)$ for this individual would be if p_i is sufficiently high such that $\bar{y}_i > y^*$.

27B.5.3 Equilibrium Messages in the Groves-Clarke Mechanism

We can now ask what messages each individual will send in equilibrium under this mechanism. First, notice the following: The payment $P_i(p_i)$ owed by individual i depends on a number of variables, none of which except for one can be influenced by the message that is sent by individual i. To be more precise, the individual has no control over p_i, which is arbitrarily set by the mechanism designer. He furthermore has no control over the marginal cost MC or the messages $RD_j(y)$ sent by others. Since $\bar{y}_i$ is determined from $(MC - \sum_{j\neq i} RD_j)$, he furthermore has no control over $\bar{y}_i$. That leaves only y^* which is actually affected by individual i's message! This is key to making the mechanism work.

Stage 1 of the mechanism, the stage in which individuals send their demand curve messages to the mechanism designer, is a simultaneous move game in which each player settles on a strategy. We can then ask what consumer i's best strategy is given what strategies are played by all other players. And it will turn out that we have defined a simultaneous move game in which each player in fact has a *dominant* strategy; i.e., a strategy that is his best response to any and all messages that others might send.

We can illustrate this by beginning in panel (a) of Graph 27.7 with all the portions of the problem that are not impacted by the message sent by individual i. These are graphed in blue and include the curve $(MC - \sum_{j\neq i} RD_j)$ and the "price" p_i assigned to consumer i. We can then add to this the green demand curve that is consumer i's *true* demand curve (which only he knows). If the individual chooses to tell the truth and reports this as his message, the outcome will be that y^t will be produced, with consumer i charged the shaded (blue and magenta) area.

In panels (b) and (c), we then consider how consumer i will fare if he under- or overreports his demand for the public good. Consider first the case where he reports the magenta curve $RD_i^u(y)$ is panel (b). The charge he will incur will then be equal to the area $(d + e + f)$ rather than the area $(b + c + d + e + f)$ that he would incur if he told the truth. Thus, by under reporting his true demand for the public good, he will save $(b + c)$. But at the same time, his under reporting will cause the public good quantity that is produced to fall from y^t to y^u. If we then use his green true demand as his marginal willingness to pay curve,[14] we can

Graph 27.7: Truth Telling Is Optimal

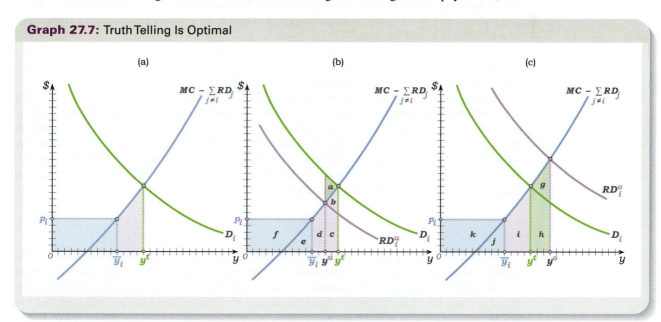

[14]We know from our consumer theory chapters that uncompensated demand curves can be interpreted as marginal willingness to pay (or Hicksian) curves only in the case of quasilinear preferences. For simplicity, we are therefore assuming that underlying preferences are quasilinear. However, while the graphs would get a bit more complex, the analysis holds also for any set of preferences that are not quasilinear.

conclude that this reduction in the public good will cause him to lose area $(a + b + c)$ in value from the lower public good output. While he therefore would save $(b + c)$ in payments, he would lose the equivalent of $(a + b + c)$ in value from the reduced public good, leaving him worse off by area (a). Under reporting his demand for the public good is therefore counterproductive.

In panel (c), we do the analogous exercise for considering whether it might be in the consumer's interest to overreport his demand for the public good by reporting RD_i^o. This will increase the payment he owes from $(i + j + k)$ under truth telling to $(g + h + i + j + k)$ when the consumer overreports his demand, thus increasing his payment by $(g + h)$. But the additional value from the increase in the public good (from y^t under truth telling to y^o when over-reporting) is only h. Thus, sending the message RD_i^o rather than the truth results in a loss of (g). Overreporting is therefore also counterproductive.

Exercise 27B.22 In Graph 27.7, we considered the case in which $\bar{y}_i < y^t$. Repeat the analysis to show that over- and underreporting is similarly counterproductive when p_i is sufficiently high to cause $\bar{y}_i > y^t$.

Since none of our reasoning has assumed anything about whether individuals other than i are reporting their demands truthfully, we can conclude that it is in fact a dominant strategy for consumer i to report his demand for the public good truthfully. And the same reasoning applies to all consumers, implying that *truth telling is a dominant strategy equilibrium* under the Groves-Clarke mechanism. This in turn implies that the mechanism will produce the optimal level y^* of the public good.

27B.5.4 Feasibility of the Groves-Clarke Mechanism

While we now know that individuals, when faced with the incentives of the Groves-Clarke mechanism, will report their demands for public goods truthfully, the mechanism will not be feasible unless it raises sufficient revenues TR for the mechanism designer to actually pay for the total cost (which is equal to $TC = MCy^*$ in the absence of fixed costs) of the public good output level y^* that emerges. It is easy to illustrate that this is in fact the case.

For each of the individuals affected by the mechanism, one of three scenarios will arise depending on what p_i the individual was assigned: (1) $\bar{y}_i < y^*$, (2) $\bar{y}_i = y^*$ or (3) $\bar{y}_i > y^*$. These three cases are graphed in the three panels of Graph 27.8.

In panel (a), $\bar{y}_i < y^*$, which results in $P_i(p_i)$ that is equal to the area $(a + b + c + d)$. This area could be divided into an area $p_iy^* = (a + b + c)$ plus the remaining shaded triangle (d). In panel (c), $\bar{y}_i > y^*$, which results in $P_i(p_i) = (e + f + g + h)$, and this area can similarly be divided into $p_iy^* = (e + f + g)$ plus the shaded area (h). In both cases, we therefore know that we will collect p_iy^* plus some additional revenue. Only in panel (b) where $\bar{y}_i = y^*$ is the payment $P_i(p_i)$ exactly equal to p_iy^*. The total revenue TR we collect from all consumers is then at least $\sum p_iy^*$, and since $\sum p_i = MC$, we can conclude that

$$TR \geq \sum_{i=1}^{N} p_iy^* = MCy^* = TC. \tag{27.61}$$

We can furthermore see from Graph 27.8 that the only way in which the inequality in the equation becomes an equality, i.e., the only way that total revenues will exactly equal total costs, is if the "prices" happened to be assigned in such a way that $\bar{y}_i = y^*$ for all individuals (as illustrated in panel (b) of the graph). In that special case, the "prices" we have assigned are like real prices in the sense that individuals pay exactly price times quantity for the public good. In that special case, it is furthermore true that all individuals would in fact choose the optimal public good level y^* under the per-unit prices they were assigned. In other words, in that special case, p_i is the Lindahl price for all consumers and we have implemented a Lindahl equilibrium. Of course

Graph 27.8: Revenues Exceed Costs under the Groves-Clarke Mechanism

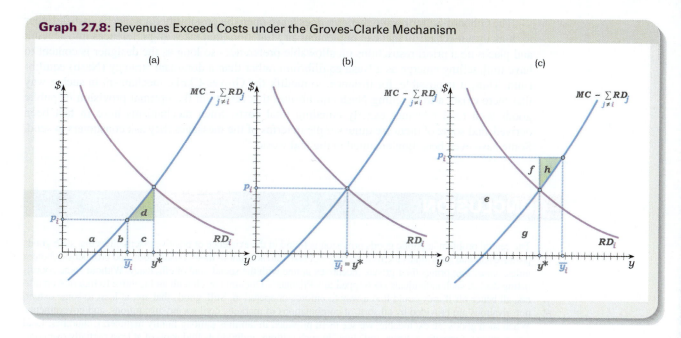

this could only happen accidentally under the Groves-Clarke mechanism because the p_i's are assigned arbitrarily without knowledge of the underlying demands by individuals.

27B.5.5 A Fundamental Problem in Mechanism Design

Our conclusion that the Groves-Clarke mechanism will almost always raise revenues that exceed the cost of providing the optimal level of the public good then creates a problem for us: What do we do with the excess revenue? Remember that we are trying to implement an efficient solution to the public goods problem, which means that throwing away the excess revenue cannot be the answer. After all, if we did throw away the excess revenue, we can easily think of a way of making someone better off without making anyone else worse off: Just give the excess revenue back to one or some or all of the consumers. But that creates another problem: If we return the excess revenues, we would create income effects for consumers unless tastes are quasilinear, which then would mean that we would alter the optimal level of the public good. Put differently, giving back the excess revenue alters y^*, which means our whole previous analysis is thrown out the window. For this reason, the Groves-Clarke mechanism actually can only implement a Pareto optimum under the special assumption that individual preferences are quasilinear, a rather strong assumption to make about preferences we know nothing about at the beginning of the mechanism. But if preferences were quasilinear in the public good, then we could simply return all the excess revenues to individuals without changing y^*.

This is a symptom of a much more general problem faced by mechanism designers, a problem that has become formalized in what is known as the "Gibbard-Satterthwaite Theorem."[15] We will not develop this formally here, but it bears a striking resemblance to another theorem we will develop in Section B of Chapter 28. In essence, the theorem says the following: So long as the f function that the mechanism designer is trying to implement in Graph 27.5 takes into account the tastes of more than one individual, the function *cannot be implemented by any mechanism that makes truth telling a dominant strategy* unless we can restrict the type of preferences that individuals have to begin with. In the Groves-Clarke mechanism, for instance, the only way in which we could implement an efficient outcome was to assume individuals only have quasilinear preferences.

---

[15]The theorem is named for Allan Gibbard (1942–) and Mark Satterthwaite (1945–), who independently developed the basic result in the early 1970s.

The Gibbard-Satterthwaite theorem does leave open the possibility for a mechanism designer to think up a mechanism that can implement an f function (that takes all preferences into account and places no a priori restrictions on allowable preference) so long as the designer is content to have truth telling emerge as a Nash equilibrium rather than a dominant strategy (Nash) equilibrium. Thus, it is possible, for instance, to modify the Groves-Clarke mechanism in such a way that there exists a truth telling Nash equilibrium that results in the optimal provision of public goods with total revenues exactly equaling total costs. Such mechanisms have in fact been derived, and some of them are quite simple in terms of the messages they ask consumers to send. Some have even been implemented in the real world.[16]

CONCLUSION

The central problem in public goods provision is found in the existence of positive externalities that such goods produce and that individuals themselves may not take into account in their consumption and production choices unless *something* brings their private incentives in line with the social goal of efficiency. Without some coordinating device, such individuals are trapped in a Prisoner's Dilemma, each with an incentive to free ride on others, all better off if they could find a way to enforce cooperation. Still, goods that are, at least to some extent, non-rivalrous are provided by all sorts of combinations of markets, civil society institutions, and governments. When such goods are excludable, we see them provided in families (among family members), churches, local communities, competitive firms, and clubs. In such settings, individuals find ways of at least partially overcoming the free-rider problem and its Prisoner's Dilemma incentives, whether through repeated interactions, through government subsidies, through Coasian bargaining, through Tiebout competition, or by responding to "warm glow" elements of their tastes. While in some cases the solution is found solely in voluntary civil society interactions, often such goods are provided through combinations of markets, civil society, and government. As goods become nonexcludable and more non-rivalrous, however, it becomes increasingly difficult to rely on markets or civil society institutions as problems of free riding and incentives to misrepresent preferences become more intense, and the case for central government provision of such goods becomes increasingly compelling.

Governments, of course, have their own challenges to overcome. In the case of public goods, for instance, optimal policy typically requires knowledge of individual preferences that can be aggregated by the government to determine the appropriate level of public goods. Preference revelation mechanisms of the type we have discussed in this chapter offer one way to gather such knowledge, but it has not been one that has, at least thus far, proven terribly practical in most real-world public goods settings. The other natural way in which we attempt to convey our preferences about public goods is through democratic political processes, processes in which we vote either directly (or indirectly through our elected representatives) for or against a proposal.

In Chapter 28, we will therefore take on the challenge of thinking about democratic political processes and the ways in which they gather information on voter preferences and generate policy outcomes from this information. Since voting is (usually) anonymous, we do not run into the problem that individuals have an incentive to misrepresent their tastes for public goods, although we will see that nonanonymous legislators often do have such strategic incentives. We will see, however, that democratic processes give rise to a whole different set of their own peculiar problems.

END-OF-CHAPTER EXERCISES

27.1[†]   We discussed in the text the basic externality problem that we face when we rely on private giving to public projects. In this exercise, we consider how this changes as the number of people involved increases.

   A. Suppose that there are N individuals who consume a public good.

---

[16] The most famous such mechanism was developed in Theodore Groves and John Ledyard, "Optimal Allocation of Public Goods: A Solution to the 'Free Rider' Problem," *Econometrica* 45 (1977), 783–810.
*conceptually challenging
**computationally challenging
†solutions in Study Guide

a. Begin with the best response function in panel (a) of Graph 27.3; i.e., the best response of one person's giving to another person's giving when $N = 2$. Draw the 45-degree line into your graph of this best response function.

b. Now suppose that all N individuals are the same, just as we assumed the two individuals in Graph 27.3 are the same. Given the symmetry of the problem (in terms of everyone being identical), how must the contributions of each person relate to one another in equilibrium?

c. In your graph, replace y_2, the giving by person 2, with y and let y be the giving that each person other than person 1 undertakes (assuming they all give the same amount). As N increases, what happens to the best response function for person 1? Explain, and relate your answer to the free-rider problem.

d. Given your answers to (b) and (c), what happens to person 1's equilibrium contribution as N increases? (*Hint*: Where on the best response function will the equilibrium contribution lie?)

e. When $N = 2$, how much of the overall benefit from his contribution is individual 1 taking into account as she determines her level of giving? How does this change when N increases to 3 and 4? How does it change as N gets very large?

f. What does your answer imply for the level of subsidy s that is necessary to get people to contribute to the efficient level of the public good as N increases? (Define s as the level of subsidy that will cause a \$1 contribution to the public good to cost the individual only \$$(1 - s)$.)

g. Explain how, as N becomes large, the optimal subsidy policy becomes pretty much equivalent to the government simply providing the public good.

B. In Section 27B.2.2, we considered how two individuals respond to having the government subsidize their voluntary giving to the production of a public good. Suppose again that individuals have preferences that are captured by the utility function $u(x, y) = x^\alpha y^{(1-\alpha)}$, where x is dollars worth of private consumption and y is dollars spent on the public good. All individuals have income I, and the public good is financed by private contributions denoted z_n for individual n. The government subsidizes private contributions at a rate of $s \leq 1$ and finances this with a tax t on income.

a. Suppose there are N individuals. What is the efficient level of public good funding?

b. Since individuals are identical, the Nash equilibrium response to any policy (t, s) will be symmetric; i.e., all individuals end up giving the same in equilibrium. Suppose all individuals other than n give z. Derive the best response function $z_n(t, s, z)$ for individual n. (As in the text, this is most easily done by defining n's optimization as an unconstrained optimization problem with only z_n as the choice variable and the Cobb–Douglas utility function written in log form.)

c. Use your answer to (b) to derive the equilibrium level of individual private giving $z^{eq}(t, s)$. How does it vary with N?

d. What is the equilibrium quantity of the public good for policy (t, s)?

e. For the policy (t, s) to result in the optimal level of public good funding, what has to be the relationship between t and s if the government is to cover the cost of the subsidy with the tax revenues it raises?

f. Substitute your expression for t from (e) into your answer to (d). Then determine what level of s is necessary in order for private giving to result in the efficient level of output you determined in (a).

g. Derive the optimal policy (t^*, s^*) that results in efficient levels of public good provision through voluntary giving. What is the optimal policy when $N = 2$? (Your answer should be equal to what we calculated for the two-person case in Section 27B.2.2.) What if $N = 3$ and $N = 4$?

h. Can you explain s^* when N is 2, 3, and 4 in terms of how the externality changes as N increases? Does s^* for $N = 1$ make intuitive sense?

i. What does this optimal policy converge to as N gets large? Interpret what this means.

27.2* In exercise 27.1, we extended our analysis of subsidized voluntary giving from 2 to N people. In the process, we simply assumed the government would set t to cover its costs, and that individuals would take t as given when they make their decision on how much to give. We now explore how the strategic setting changes when individuals predict how their giving will translate into taxes.

A. Consider again the case where N identical people enjoy the public good.

    a.   First, suppose $N = 2$ and suppose the government subsidizes private giving at a rate of s. If individual n gives y_n to the public good, what fraction of the resulting tax to cover the subsidy on his giving will he have to pay?

    b.   Compare the case where the individual does not take the tax effect of his giving into account to the case where he does. What would you expect to happen to n's best response function for giving to the public good in the former case relative to the latter case? In which case would you expect the equilibrium response to a subsidy s to be greater?

    c.   Explain the following true statement: When $N = 2$, a subsidy s in the case where individuals do not take the balanced-budget tax consequence of a subsidy into account will have the same impact as a subsidy $2s$ in the case where they do.

    d.   Given your answer to (c) (and given that the optimal subsidy level when $N = 2$ in exercise 27.1 was 0.5), what do you think s would have to be to achieve the efficient level of the public good now that individuals think about balanced-budget tax consequences?

    e.   Next suppose N is very large. Explain why it is now a good approximation to assume that individual n takes t as given when he chooses his contribution level to the public good (as he did in exercise 27.1).

    f.   *True or False*: The efficient level of the subsidy is the same when $N = 2$ as when N is very large if individuals take into account the tax implication of increasing their giving to the subsidized public good.

    g.   Finally, suppose we start with $N = 2$ and raise N. What happens to the degree to which n's giving decisions impact n's tax obligations as N increases? What happens to the size of the free-rider problem as N increases? In what sense do these introduce offsetting forces as we think about the equilibrium level of private contributions?

B. Consider the same set-up as in exercise 27.1, but now suppose that each individual assumes the government will balance its budget and therefore anticipates the impact his giving has on the tax rate t when the subsidy s is greater than zero.

    a.   The problem is again symmetric in the sense that all individuals are the same, so in equilibrium, all individuals will end up giving the same amount to the public good. Suppose all $(N - 1)$ individuals other than n give z when the subsidy is s. Express the budget-balancing tax rate as a function of s assuming person n gives z_n while everyone else gives z.

    b.   Individual n knows that his after-tax income will be $(1 - t)I$ while his cost of giving z_n is $(1 - s)z_n$. Using your answer from (a), express individual n's private good consumption as a function of s and z_n (given everyone else gives z).

    c.   Set up the utility maximization problem for individual n to determine his best response giving function (given that everyone else gives z). Then solve for z_n as a function of z and s. (The problem is easiest to solve if it is set up as an unconstrained optimization problem with only z_1 as the choice variable, and with utility expressed as the log of the Cobb–Douglas functional form.)

    d.   Use the fact that z_n has to be equal to z in equilibrium to solve for the equilibrium individual contribution z^{eq} as a function of s. (You should be able to simplify the denominator of your expression to $(1 + \alpha(N - 1)(1 - s))$.)

    e.   If everyone gave an equal share of the efficient level of the public good funding, how much would each person contribute? Use this to derive the optimal level of s. Does it depend on N?

    f.   *True or False*: When individuals take into account the tax implications of government-subsidized private giving, the optimal subsidy rate is the same regardless of N and equal to what it is when N gets large for the case when people do not consider the impact of subsidized giving on tax rates (as explored in exercise 27.1).

27.3   **Everyday Application:** *Sandwiches, Chess Clubs, Movie Theaters, and Fireworks*: In the introduction, we mentioned that while we often treat public and private goods as distinct concepts, many goods actually lie in between the extremes because of "crowding."

    A. We can think of the level of crowding as determining the optimal group size for consumption of the good, with optimal group size in turn locating the good on the continuum between purely private and purely public goods.

a.   One way to model different types of goods is in terms of the marginal cost and marginal benefit of admitting additional group members to enjoy the good. Begin by considering a bite of your lunch sandwich. What is the marginal benefit of admitting a second person to the consumption of this bite? What is therefore the optimal "group size," and how does this relate to our conception of the sandwich bite as a private good?

b.   Next, consider a chess club. Draw a graph with group size N on the horizontal axis and dollars on the vertical. With additional members, you'll have to get more chessboards, with the marginal cost of additional members plausibly being flat. The marginal benefit of additional members might initially be increasing, but if the club gets too large, it becomes impersonal and not much fun. Draw the marginal benefit and marginal cost curves and indicate the optimal group size. In what way is the chess club not a pure public good?

c.   Consider the same exercise with respect to a movie theater that has N seats (but you could add additional people by having them sit or stand in the aisles). Each customer adds to the mess and thus the cleanup cost. What might the marginal cost and benefit curves now look like?

d.   Repeat the exercise for fireworks.

e.   Which of these do you think the market and/or civil society can provide relatively efficiently, and which might require some government assistance?

f.   Why do you think fireworks on national holidays are usually provided by local governments, but Disney World is able to put on fireworks every night without government help?

B. Consider in this part of the exercise only crowding on the cost side, with the cost of providing some discrete public good given by the function $c(N) = FC + \alpha N^\beta$ with $\alpha > 0$ and $\beta \geq 0$. Assume throughout that there is no crowding in consumption of the public good.

a.   Derive the marginal cost of admitting additional customers. In order for there to be crowding in production, how large must β be?

b.   Find the group membership at the lowest point of the average cost function. How does this relate to optimal group size when group size is sufficiently small for multiple providers to be in the market?

c.   What is the relationship between α, β, and FC for purely private goods?

d.   Suppose that the good is a purely public good. What value of α could make this so? If $\alpha > 0$, what value of β might make this so?

e.   How does α affect optimal group size? What about FC and β? Interpret your answer.

27.4 **Everyday, Business, and Policy Application:** *Competitive Local Public and Club Good Production*: In exercise 27.3, we considered some ways in which we can differentiate between goods that lie in between the extremes of pure private and pure public goods.

A. Consider the case where there is a (recurring) fixed cost FC to producing the public good y, and the marginal cost of producing the same level of y is increasing in the group size N because of crowding.

a.   Consider again a graph with N, the group size, on the horizontal and dollars on the vertical. Then graph the average and marginal cost of providing a given level of y as N increases.

b.   Suppose that the lowest point of the average curve you have drawn occurs at N^*, with N^* greater than 1 but significantly less than the population size. If the good is excludable, what would you expect the admissions price to be in long-run competitive equilibrium if firms (or clubs) that provide the good can freely enter and/or exit?

c.   You have so far considered the case of firms producing a given level of y. Suppose next that firms could choose lower levels of y (smaller swimming pools, schools with larger class sizes, etc.) that carry lower recurring fixed costs. If people have different demands for y, what would you expect to happen in equilibrium as firms compete?

d.   Suppose instead that the public good is not excludable in the usual sense but rather that it is a good that can be consumed only by those who live within a certain distance of where the good is produced. (Consider, for instance, a public school.) How does the shape of the average cost curve you have drawn determine the optimal community size (where communities provide the public good)?

e.   Local communities often use property taxes to finance their public good production. If households of different types are free to buy houses of different size (and value), why might higher income households (that buy larger homes) be worried about lower income households "free riding"?

f.   Many communities impose zoning regulations that require houses and land plots to be of some minimum size. Can you explain the motivation for such "exclusionary zoning" in light of the concern over free riding?

g.   If local public goods are such that optimal group size is sufficiently small to result in a very competitive environment (in which communities compete for residents), how might the practice of exclusionary zoning result in very homogeneous communities; i.e., in communities where households are very similar to one another and live in very similar types of houses?

h.   Suppose that a court rules (as real-world courts have) that even wealthy communities must set aside some fraction of their land for "low income housing." How would you expect the prices of "low income houses" in relatively wealthy communities (that provide high levels of local public goods) to compare to the prices of identical houses in low income communities? How would you expect the average income of those residing in identical low income housing to compare across these different communities?

i.   *True or False*: The insights from this exercise suggest that local community competition might result in efficient provision of local public goods, but they also raise the "equity" concern that the poor will have less access to certain local public goods (such as good public schools).

B. Consider again the cost function $c(N) = FC + \alpha N^\beta$ with $\alpha > 0$ and $\beta \geq 0$ (as we did in exercise 27.3).

a.   In the case of competitive firms providing this excludable public good, calculate the long-run equilibrium admission price you would expect to emerge.

b.   Consider a town in which, at any given time, 23,500 people are interested in going to the movies. Suppose the per auditorium/screen costs of a movie theater are characterized by the functions in this problem, with $FC = 900$, $\alpha = 0.5$, and $\beta = 1.5$. Determine the optimal auditorium capacity N^*, the equilibrium price per ticket p^*, and the equilibrium number of movie screens.

c.   Suppose instead that a spatially constrained public good is provided by local communities that fund the public good production through a property tax. Economic theorists have shown that, if we assume it is relatively easy to move from one community to another, an equilibrium may not exist unless communities find a way of excluding those who might attempt to free ride. Can you explain the intuition for this?

d.   Would the (unconstitutional) practice of being able to set a minimum income level for community members establish a way for an equilibrium to emerge? How does the practice of exclusionary zoning (as defined in part A of the exercise) accomplish the same thing?

e.   In the extreme, a model with exclusionary zoning might result in complete self-selection of household types into communities, with everyone within a community being identical to everyone else. How does the property tax in this case mimic a per-capita user fee for the public good?

f.* Can you argue that, in light of your answer to A(g), the same might be true if zoning regulations are not uniformly the same within a community?

27.5* **Everyday and Business Application:** *Raising Money for a Streetlight through a "Subscription Campaign":* Sometimes, a civil society institution's goal can be clearly articulated in terms of a dollar value that is needed. Consider, for instance, the problem you and I face when we want to fund a streetlight on our dark cul-de-sac. We know that the total cost of the light will be C, and so we know exactly how much money we need to raise. One way we can raise the money is through what is known as a *subscription campaign*. Here is how a subscription campaign would work: We put a money "pledge jar" in between our two houses, and you begin by pledging an amount x_1^Y. We then agree that we will alternate putting a pledge for a contribution into the jar on a daily basis, with me putting in a pledge x_2^M the second day, then you putting in a pledge x_3^Y the third day, me putting in x_4^M the fourth day, etc. When enough money is pledged to cover the cost C of the streetlight, we pay for the light, with you writing a check equal to the total that you have pledged and me writing a check for the total I have pledged.

EVERYDAY APPLICATION

BUSINESS APPLICATION

A. Suppose you and I each value the light at $1,000 but the light costs $1,750. We are both incredibly impatient people, with $1.00 tomorrow valued by us at only $0.50 today. For simplicity, assume the light can be put up the day it is paid for.

    a.   Suppose it ends up taking T days for us to raise enough pledges to fund the light. Let x_T^i be the last pledge that is made before we reach the goal. What does subgame perfection imply x_T^i is? (*Hint*: Would it be subgame perfect for person j who pledges the day before to leave an amount to be pledged that is less than the maximum person i is willing to pledge on day T?)

    b.   Next, consider person j whose turn it is to pledge on day $(T - 1)$. What is x_{T-1}^i? (*Hint*: Person j knows that, unless she gives the amount necessary for i to finish off the required pledges on day T, she will end up having to give again (an amount equal to what you calculated for x_T^i) on day $(T + 1)$ and have the light delayed by one day.)

    c.   Continue working backward. How many days will it take to collect enough pledges?

    d.   How much does each of us have to pay for the streetlight (assuming you go first)?

    e.   How much would each of us be willing to pay the government to tax us an amount equal to what we end up contributing but to do so today and thus put up the light today?

    f.   What is the remaining source of inefficiency in the subscription campaign?

    g.   Why might a subscription campaign be a good way for a pastor of a church to raise money for a new building but not for the American Cancer Association to raise money for funding cancer research?

B. Now consider the more general case where you and I both value the street light at $\$V$, it costs $\$C$, and $\$1$ tomorrow is worth $\$\delta < 1$ today. Assume throughout that the equilibrium is subgame perfect.

    a.   Suppose, as in A(a), that we will have collected enough pledges on day T when individual i puts in the last pledge. What is x_T^i in terms of δ and V?

    b.   What is x_{T-1}^i? What about x_{T-2}^i?

    c.   From your answers to (b), can you infer the pledge amount x_{T-t} for t ranging from 1 to $(T - 1)$?

    d.   What is the amount pledged today; i.e., in period 0?

    e.   What is the highest that C can be in order for $(T + 1)$ pledges, pledges starting on day 0 and ending on day T, to cover the full cost of the light?

    f.   Recalling that $\sum_{t=0}^{\infty} \delta^t = 1/(1 - \delta)$, what is the greatest amount that a subscription campaign can raise if it goes on sufficiently long such that we can approximate the period of the campaign as an infinite number of days?

    g.   *True or False*: A subscription campaign will eventually succeed in raising the necessary funds so long as it is efficient for us to build the streetlight.

    h.   *True or False*: In subscription campaigns, we should expect initial pledges to be small and the campaign to "show increasing momentum" as time passes, with pledges increasing as we near the goal.

27.6 **Business Application:** *The Marketing Challenge for Social Entrepreneurs*: Social entrepreneurs are entrepreneurs who use their talents to advance social causes that are typically linked to the provision of some type of public good. Their challenge within the civil society is, in part, to motivate individuals to give sufficient funding to the projects that are being advanced. Aside from lobbying for government aid, we can think of two general ways in which social entrepreneurs might succeed in increasing the funding for their organizations. Both involve marketing: one aimed at increasing the number of individuals who are aware of the public good and thus to increase the donor pool, the other aimed at persuading people that they get something real out of giving to the cause.

A. We can then think of the social entrepreneur as using his labor as an input into two different single-input production processes: one aimed at increasing the pool of donors, the other aimed at persuading current donors of the benefits they get from becoming more engaged.

    a.   Suppose that both production processes have decreasing returns to scale. What does this imply for the marginal revenue product of each production process?

    b.   If the social entrepreneur allocates his time optimally, how will his marginal revenue product of labor in the two production processes be related to one another?

    c.   Another way to view the social entrepreneur's problem is that he has a fixed labor time allotment L that forms a time budget constraint. Graph such a budget constraint, with ℓ_1, the time allocated to increasing the donor pool, on the horizontal axis and ℓ_2, the time allocated to persuading existing donors, on the vertical.

d. What do the isoquants for the two-input production process look like? Can you interpret these as the social entrepreneur's indifference curves?

e. Illustrate how the social entrepreneur will optimize in this graph. Can you interpret your result as identical to the one you derived in (b)?

f. Within the context of our discussion of "warm glow" effects from giving, can you interpret ℓ_2 as effort that goes into persuading individuals that public goods have private benefits?

g. How might you reinterpret this model as one applying to a politician (or a "political entrepreneur") who chooses between allocating campaign resources to mass mailings versus political rallies?

h. We discussed in the text that sometimes there is a role for "tipping points" in efforts to get individuals engaged in public causes. If the social entrepreneur attempts to pass such a "tipping point," how might his strategy change as the fundraising effort progresses?

B. Suppose that the two production processes introduced in part A are $f_1(\ell_1)$ and $f_2(\ell_2)$, with $df_i/d\ell_i < 0$ for $i = 1,2$ and with "output" in each process defined as "dollars raised."

a. Assuming the entrepreneur has L hours to allocate, set up his optimization problem. Can you demonstrate your conclusion from A(b)?

b. Suppose $f_1(\ell_1) = A \ln \ell_1$ and $f_2(\ell_2) = B \ln \ell_2$ with both A and B greater than 0. Derive the optimal ℓ_1 and ℓ_2.

c. In equation (27.54), we determined the individual equilibrium contribution in the presence of a warm glow effect. Suppose that this represents the equilibrium contribution level for the donors that the social entrepreneur works with, and suppose $I = 1,000$, $\alpha = 0.4$, and $\beta = 0.6$. In the absence of any efforts on the part of the entrepreneur, $N = 1,000$ and $\gamma = 0.01$. How much will the entrepreneur raise without putting in any effort?

d.** Next, suppose that $N(\ell_1) = 1,000(1 + \ell_1^{1/2})$, and $\gamma(\ell_2) = 0.01(1 + \ell_2^{1/2})$, and suppose that the entrepreneur has a total of 1,000 hours to devote to the fundraising effort. Assume that he will in fact devote all 1,000 hours to the effort, with ℓ_2 therefore equal to $(1,000 - \ell_1)$. Create a table with ℓ_1 in the first column ranging from 0 to 1,000 in 100 hour increments. Calculate the implied level of ℓ_2, N, and γ in the next three columns, and then report the equilibrium level of individual contributions z^{eq} and the equilibrium overall funds raised y^{eq} in the last two columns. (Obviously, this is easiest to do by programming the problem in a spreadsheet.)

e. Approximately how would you recommend that the entrepreneur split his time between recruiting more donors and working with existing donors?

f.** Suppose all the parameters of the problem remain the same except for the following: $\gamma = 0.01(1 + \ell_2^{0.5} + 0.001N^{1.1})$. By modifying the spreadsheet that you used to create the table in part (d), can you determine the optimal number of hours the entrepreneur should put into his two fundraising activities now? How much will he raise?

27.7 Policy Application: *Demand for Charities and Tax Deductibility*: In end-of-chapter exercise 9.9 of Chapter 9, we investigated the impact of various U.S. income tax changes on the level of charitable giving. If you have not already done this exercise, do so now and investigate the different ways that tax policy changes in the United States over the past few decades might have impacted the level of charitable giving.

27.8† Policy Application: *Do Antipoverty Efforts Provide a Public Good?* There are many equity- or fairness-based arguments for government engagement in antipoverty programs, and for general government redistribution programs. But is there an efficiency case to be made for government programs that redistribute income? One such possibility lies in viewing government antipoverty efforts as a public good, but whether or not this is a credible argument depends on how we think contributions to antipoverty efforts enter people's tastes.

A. Suppose there is a set A of individuals that contribute to antipoverty programs and a different set B of individuals that receive income transfers from such programs (and suppose that everyone in the population is in one of these two sets).

a. In considering whether there is an efficiency case to be made for government intervention in antipoverty efforts, do we have to consider the increased welfare of those who receive income transfers?

    b.   How would the individuals who give to antipoverty programs have to view such programs in order for there to be no externality to private giving?

    c.   If your answer to (b) is in fact how individuals view antipoverty efforts, are antipoverty efforts efficient in the absence of government intervention? If the government introduced antipoverty programs funded through taxes on those who are privately giving to such efforts already, to what extent would you expect the government programs to "crowd out" private efforts?

    d.   How would individuals have to view their contributions to antipoverty programs in order for such programs to be pure public goods?

    e.   If the conditions in (d) hold, why is there an efficiency case for government redistribution programs?

    f.   If government redistribution programs are funded through taxes on the individuals who are voluntarily giving to antipoverty programs, why might the government's program have to be large in order to accomplish anything?

    g.   How does your answer to (f) change if there is a third set of individuals that does not give to antipoverty programs or does not benefit from them but would be taxed (together with those who are privately giving to anti-poverty programs) to finance government redistribution programs?

    h.   Some argue that private anti-poverty programs are inherently more effective because civil society anti-poverty programs make use of information that government programs cannot get to. As a result, the argument goes, civil society anti-poverty efforts achieve a greater increase in welfare for the poor for every dollar spent than government redistributive programs. If this is indeed the case, discuss the tradeoffs this raises as one thinks about optimal government involvement in anti-poverty efforts.

B.   Denote individual n's private good consumption as x_n, the government contribution to antipoverty efforts as g and individual n's contribution to antipoverty efforts as z_n. Let individual n's tastes be defined as $u^n(x_n, y, z_n) = x_n^\alpha y^\beta z_n^\gamma$. (Assume that antipoverty efforts are pure transfers of money to the poor.)

    a.   What has to be true for antipoverty efforts to be strictly private goods?

    b.   What has to be true for antipoverty efforts to be pure public goods?

    c.   Suppose the condition you derived in (a) applies (and maintain this assumption until you get to part (g)). Suppose further that there are N individuals who have different income levels, with n's income denoted I_n. Will private antipoverty efforts be funded efficiently when $g = 0$? What will be the equilibrium level of private funding for antipoverty programs when $g = 0$ as N gets large?

    d.   If the government increases g without raising taxes, will private contributions to antipoverty efforts be affected (assuming still that the condition derived in (a) holds)? (*Hint*: How does the individual's optimization problem change?)

    e.   Suppose the government instead levies a proportional tax t on all income and uses the funds solely to fund g. How much private funding for antipoverty programs will this government intervention crowd out? By how much will overall contributions to antipoverty programs (including the government's contribution) change? (Consider again the impact on the individual's optimization problem.)

    f.   Can this government intervention in antipoverty efforts be justified on efficiency grounds?

    g.   Suppose instead that the condition you derived in (b) holds. To simplify the analysis, suppose that the N people who care about antipoverty programs all have the same income level I (as well as the same preferences). What is the equilibrium level of funding for antipoverty programs when $g = 0$?

    h.   What happens to overall funding (both public and private) when the government increases g without changing taxes?

    i.   If the government instead imposes a proportional income tax t and uses the revenues solely to fund g, what happens to overall funding of antipoverty efforts, assuming the N individuals still give positive contributions in equilibrium?

    j.   Under what condition will the balanced budget (t, g) government program raise the overall funding level for antipoverty programs?

27.9 **Policy Application:** *Distortionary Taxes and National Security*: In the real world, government provision of public goods usually entails the use of distortionary taxes to raise the required revenues. Consider the pure public good "national defense," a good provided exclusively by the government (with no private contributions).

A. Consider varying degrees of inefficiency in the nation's tax system.

 a. In our development of the concept of deadweight loss from taxation, we found that the deadweight loss from taxes tends to increase at a rate k^2 for a k-fold increase in the tax rate. Define the "social marginal cost of funds" *SMCF* as the marginal cost society incurs from each additional dollar spent by the government. What is the shape of the *SMCF* curve?

 b. *True or False*: If the public good is defined as "spending on national defense," then the marginal cost of providing $1 of increased funding for the public good is $1 under an efficient tax system.

 c. How does the marginal cost of providing this public good change as the tax system becomes more inefficient?

 d. Use your answer to (c) to explain the following statement: "As the inefficiency of the tax system increases, the optimal level of national defense spending by the government falls."

 e. What do you think of the following statement: "Nations that have devised more efficient tax systems are more likely to win wars than nations with inefficient tax systems."

B. Suppose we approximate the demand side for goods by assuming a representative consumer with utility function $u(x, y) = x^{1/2}y^{1/2}$ and income I, where x is private consumption (in dollars) and y is national defense spending (in dollars).

 a. If the government can use lump sum taxes to raise revenues, what is the efficient level of national defense spending?

 b. Next, suppose that the government only has access to inefficient taxes that give rise to deadweight losses. Specifically, suppose that it employs a tax rate t on income I, with tax revenue equal to $TR = tI/(1 + \beta t)^2$. How does this capture the idea of deadweight loss? What would β be if the tax were efficient?

 c. Given that it has to use this tax to fund national defense, derive the efficient tax rate and level of national defense. (It is easiest to do this by setting up an optimization problem in which t is the only choice variable, with the utility function converted to logs.) How does it compare to your answer to (a)?

 d. Suppose $I = 2,000$. What is national defense spending and the tax rate t when $\beta = 0$? How does it change when $\beta = 0.25$? What if $\beta = 1$? $\beta = 4$? $\beta = 9$?

 e. Suppose next that the government provides two pure public goods: spending on national defense y_1 and spending on the alleviation of poverty y_2 (where the latter is a public good in the ways developed in exercise 27.8). Suppose that the representative consumer's tastes can be described by $u(x, y_1, y_2) = x^{0.5}y_1^{\gamma}y_2^{(0.5-\gamma)}$. Modify the optimization problem in (c) to one appropriate for this setting, with the government now choosing both t *and* the fraction k of tax revenues spent on national defense (versus the fraction $(1 - k)$ spent on poverty alleviation.)

 f. Does the optimal tax rate differ from what you derived before? What fraction of tax revenues will be spent on national defense?

27.10 **Policy Application:** *Social Norms and Private Actions*: In exercise 21.12 of Chapter 21, we investigated the role of social norms in determining the number of "green cars" on a city's streets. Revisit this exercise and relate your conclusions to the idea of tipping points from this chapter.

27.11† **Policy Application:** *The Pork Barrel Commons*: In representative democracies where legislators represent geographic districts in legislative bodies (such as the U.S. House of Representatives), we often hear of "pork barrel spending." Typically, this refers to special projects that legislators include in bills that pass the legislature, projects that have direct benefits for the legislator's district but not outside the district. In this exercise, we will think of these as publicly funded private goods whose benefits are confined to some fraction of residents of the geographical boundaries of the district. (In exercise 27.12, we will consider the case of different types of local public goods.)

A. Suppose that there are N different legislative districts, each with an equal proportion of the population. Suppose for simplicity that all citizens are identical and that tax laws affect all individuals equally.

Suppose further that all projects cost C, and that the total benefits B of a project are entirely contained in the district in which the project is undertaken.

a. How much of the cost of a project that is passed by the legislature do the citizens in district i pay?

b. How much of a benefit do the citizens in district i receive if the project is located in district i? What if it is not?

c. Suppose the possible projects that can be brought to district i range in benefits from $B = 0$ to $B = \overline{B}$ where $\overline{B} > C$. Which projects should be built in district i if the legislature cares only about efficiency?

d. Now consider a legislator who represents district i and whose payoff is proportional to the surplus her district gets from the projects she brings to the district. What projects will this legislator seek to include in bills that pass the legislature?

e. If there is only a single district (i.e., if $N = 1$) is there a difference between your answer to (c) and (d)?

f. How does the set of inefficient projects that the legislator includes in bills change as N increases?

g. In what sense do legislators have an incentive to propose inefficient projects even though all of their constituents would be better off if no inefficient projects were located in any district? Can you describe this as a Prisoner's Dilemma? Can you also relate it to the Tragedy of the Commons (where you treat taxpayer money as the common resource)?

B. Consider the same set of issues modeled slightly differently. Instead of thinking about a number of different projects per district, suppose there is a single project per district but it can vary in size. Let y_i be the size of a government project in district i. Suppose that the cost of funding a project of size y is $c(y) = Ay^\alpha$ where $\alpha > 1$, and suppose that the total benefit to the district of such a project is $b(y) = By^\beta$ where $\beta \leq 1$.

a. What do the conditions $\alpha > 1$ and $\beta \leq 1$ mean? Do they seem like reasonable assumptions?

b. Suppose all districts other than district i get projects of size $\overline{y}$ and district i gets a project of size y_i. Let district i's legislator get a payoff π^i that is some fraction k of the net benefit that citizens within his district get from all government projects. What is $\pi^i(y_i, N, \overline{y})$, assuming that the government is paying for all its projects through a tax system that splits the cost of all projects equally across all districts?

c. What level of y_i will legislator i choose to include in the government budget? Does it matter what $\overline{y}$ is?

d. What level of y^{eq} will all legislators request for their districts?

e. What is the efficient level of y^* per district? How does it differ from the equilibrium level?

27.12 Policy Application: *Local and National Public Goods as Pork Barrel Projects*: Consider again, as in exercise 27.11, the political incentives for legislators that represent districts. In exercise 27.11, we considered pork barrel projects as publicly funded private goods that residents within the targeted districts enjoyed but everyone paid for. This resulted in a "Tragedy of the Commons" where legislators view the pool of taxpayer resources as a common pool that funds their own pet projects for their districts. As a result, such pork barrel projects are overprovided (much as fishermen overfish publicly owned lakes), leading to inefficiently high government spending.

POLICY APPLICATION

A. Now suppose that the projects in question are not private goods but rather *local public* goods; that is, suppose that the benefit B of a project in district i is a benefit that each of the n residents of district i enjoys equally.

a. In what way do your answers to A(a) through A(f) of exercise 27.11 change?

b. Does your basic conclusion from exercise 27.11 still hold?

c. Next, suppose that each project, while located in one district, benefits all Nn citizens of the country equally; i.e., suppose that projects are national public goods without geographic boundaries in which benefits are contained. Does your basic conclusion change now?

d. *True or False*: The extent to which the fraction of projects requested by legislators is inefficient depends on the degree to which the benefits of the project are national rather than local.

B. Now consider the way we modeled these issues in part B of exercise 27.11. Each district gets a project, with the costs and benefits varying with the size of the project. The cost of providing y in a district is again $c(y) = Ay^\alpha$, but the benefit of the project is reaped by each of the n residents of the district; i.e., the benefit is $b(y) = Bny^\beta$. Assume again that $\alpha > 1$ and $\beta \leq 1$.

   a.   Repeat B(b) through B(e) of exercise 27.11 and determine y^{eq} and y^*.

   b.   Are the projects again inefficiently large? How does the inefficiency vary with N?

   c.   Next, suppose that the benefits of each project are spread across all nN citizens. Derive y^{eq} and y^* for this case of each project being a national public good.

   d.   Is there still an inefficiency from having legislators requesting projects for their districts?

Governments and Politics

Throughout this book, we have treated individuals, whether they be consumers or workers or firms, as doing the best they can given their circumstances."[1] What is "best" was typically interpreted as a subjective judgment of the individual, although we have assumed that firms view maximizing their profits as "best." And on a few occasions when we found particular real-world policies to be inefficient (and sometimes inequitable), we hinted that we might want to look at politicians in the same way; that is, we might want to forego idealistic notions of democratic politicians simply implementing "the will of the people" and rather take a more realistic view of the incentives that guide political behavior.

In this chapter, that is precisely what we will do. The motivation for this arises from a famous result by Ken Arrow, an analytic proof of the proposition that, in a sense, there is generally no such thing as "the will of the people." I realize that may sound a bit odd, but it is absolutely true. What Arrow showed (and what we will demonstrate formally in part B of this chapter) is that democratic processes of aggregating voter preferences generally do not result in a rational "social preference order" (that could be called "the will of the people") where social alternatives can be clearly ranked from best to worst. Rather, democratic processes tend to result in social preference rankings that make it possible for politicians, especially those who can set the agenda on which voting takes place, to manipulate the process to their own advantage.

For this reason, economists and political scientists have studied different types of political institutions extensively over the past few decades, because it is the incentives contained in particular political institutions that shape the outcome of government policy in democratic societies. Some such institutions make it more difficult for politicians to manipulate the process; others make it easier. But no matter how well-designed the institution, democracy is a messy business. To put it in the language used throughout this text, *there is no first welfare theorem for politicians*; political competition in democratic institutions does not generally result in efficient outcomes. This is important to realize for economists who give policy advice: Just like markets and civil society institutions face problems, so do governments. Which part of society (if any) should get involved in solving problems then depends in part on which faces the fewest problems in implementing what we would like to ideally see happen.

We will depart in this chapter from our usual practice of having part A sections roughly correspond to part B sections. Rather, the main ideas of political economy that I want to introduce here are not particularly mathematically intensive and can be presented quite easily in an intuitive

---

[1]This chapter requires a basic understanding of consumer theory as developed in Chapters 2 and 4 through 6. While not formally appealing to game theory, a few concepts from Chapter 24 are employed, and some references to oligopolies as covered in Chapters 25 and 26 are made. However, it is relatively straightforward to read the chapter without much knowledge of these.

and graphical framework. The exception to this is an exposition of Arrow's Theorem, which involves a bit of mathematical notation and formal reasoning. We will therefore leave the full development of Arrow's Theorem as the main task of Section B of the chapter.

The Economic Way of Thinking about Politics

While we will not formally go through Arrow's Theorem until Section B, it is important to understand a bit about where Arrow was coming from and how his sweeping theorem has shaped the way we think of government policy formation. For centuries, political philosophers had spoken in terms of phrases such as "the will of the people," and it was often taken for granted that political outcomes are expressions of this "will." In the 2000 presidential election in the United States, for example, the "will of the people" was claimed by both sides as moral justification for each side winning. But what, Arrow asked, do we mean when we use such phrases? Do such phrases even make sense?

I think what most of us have in mind when we use such phrases as "the will of the people" is that political processes are ways of "aggregating" individual preferences over outcomes we all care about: taxes, public goods, regulations on private property, nuclear power, war and peace, abortion, stem cell research, civil liberties, religious freedom, etc. We then refer to the "aggregate preferences" that shape political outcomes as "the will of the people." That is exactly what Arrow had in mind: He viewed democratic processes as ways in which societies attempt to aggregate the preferences of their citizens so that the aggregated or "social" preferences that emerge can be used to make decisions and trade-offs on the important issues of our time. Different democratic processes, however, might lead to different ways in which individual preferences are aggregated to form social preferences, which implies that different democratic processes might lead to different "wills" of the same people. So Arrow wanted to ask what kinds of social preferences, what kinds of "wills of the people," we might expect to see emerge from democratic processes.

What he found was both startling and depressing, and it gave rise to a whole new branch of economics that intersects with political science. If we think of the social preferences that *should* emerge from a democratic process as preferences that respect a minimal level of democracy, that do not violate unanimously held views and that cannot be manipulated by politicians that control the political agenda, *we are out of luck*. There is no such general democratic process! There is, in a very real way, no such thing as "the will of the people." When we speak collectively as "we," there is, in a very real sense, no such thing as "we." While "we" certainly make decisions through political institutions, those decisions are not, Arrow's Theorem implies, guided by anything that can be called "social preferences" or a "will of the people."

Arrow's intention was not, however, to argue against democracy; quite the opposite, it was to get us to begin thinking seriously about how some democratic institutions are better than others and how democracy can be made to work better if we understand it better. What comes out of democratic political processes, Arrow demonstrated, not only depends on precisely how these processes are designed and have evolved but it also often depends a lot on who within politics shapes the agenda over which a subset of citizens vote and how much the political institutions constrain that person from abusing his or her power. As we will see later, we can construct examples where the powers of this "agenda setter" approach those of a dictator despite all appearances of truly underlying democratic processes. But we will also give examples of political institutions, some formal and some informal, that have emerged to restrain political agenda setters. In short, Arrow made the case for the study of political institutions because political institutions and their incentives "matter" when there is no "will of the people" that is magically revealed as we go to the polls to vote.

We will therefore describe in this chapter some of the ways in which political institutions "matter" and how we cannot in general expect democratic political institutions to necessarily result in policies that advance any particular goal consistently, whether that goal be economic efficiency, social equity of some kind, or simply making sure that flowers bloom everywhere all the time. In the process, I hope you will discover some of the ways in which we can think of political actors in much the same way as we have thought of consumers and producers: as actors with preferences trying to do the best they can given their circumstances.

28A.1 Agenda Setting and Manipulation of Policy

We will begin our discussion of political institutions in some very simple settings. First, we will look at how a voting equilibrium can emerge when the set of issues we vote on can be neatly lined up on a single dimension. We can think of this as a single dimensional issue, such as how much we would like to spend on our local public schools given that we have to raise the required revenues through a proportional tax. Political scientists also use such a "single dimensional issue space" as a reduced form way of representing preferences over more complicated sets of issues, with bundles of policies lined up from the political "right" to the political "left." When we can think of the relevant "issue" as lying on such a single dimension, we can derive conditions on voter preferences that result in an equilibrium that bears striking resemblance to the Hotelling model in the absence of price differentiation as introduced in Chapter 26. We will then see how quickly a role for an agenda setter emerges as the underlying model is tweaked slightly, either in terms of the voter preferences that we consider or in terms of the dimensionality of the "issue space."

28A.1.1 Single-Dimensional Politics and the "Median Voter Theorem"   Let's begin then with the following example: Suppose there is a local referendum on public school spending, and suppose for the moment that there exists no such thing as private schools. Every family therefore has to send its children to public schools. Suppose further that spending is all that matters in schools, that every voter has one school-aged child, and that families have preferences over school spending y and a composite private good x. Finally, suppose that families understand that higher school spending has to be financed through a tax, and that any increase in y therefore results in proportionately less x.

In panel (a) of Graph 28.1, we then illustrate the trade-off a particular voter i faces between y and x, a trade-off that looks exactly like our usual budget constraint. What is different is that the slope of the budget constraint is not determined by the relative price of y but rather by tax payments that the consumer has to make in order to finance more y. Furthermore, the consumer does not actually get to choose his or her most preferred bundle but rather is one of many who votes in an election that will determine the bundle he or she gets to consume.

Suppose y is defined as per pupil spending in public schools. If there are N different taxpayers and an equal number of school children, and if all taxpayers share the financing of public schools equally, what is the slope of this "budget line"?

Exercise 28A.1

Suppose instead that y is defined as the overall spending in public schools. What is the slope of the "budget line" under the same conditions as described in exercise 28A.1?

Exercise 28A.2

In panel (b) of the graph, we then illustrate three indifference curves for our voter, with the blue indifference curve giving the consumer's most preferred level of public school spending y_i^*. Each of the other two indifference curves cross the budget line twice, giving a higher and a lower level of public school spending that the voter is indifferent between. Finally, in panel (c) of our graph, we plot the utility level that the consumer attains for different levels of public

Graph 28.1: Single-Peaked Preferences over Public School Spending

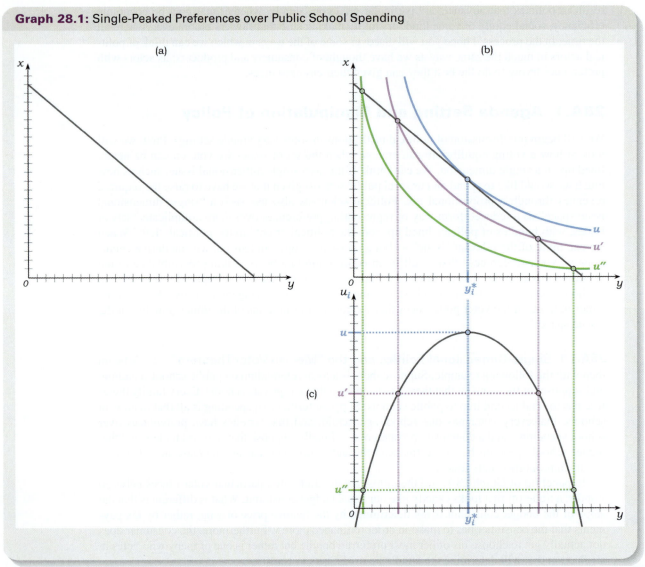

school spending. Notice that the resulting graph is "single-peaked"; that is, the voter has a most preferred public school spending level y_i^*, with utility declining as the actual public school spending level deviates from this ideal in either direction.

Exercise 28A.3 Suppose that tax rates were progressive, implying that the tax rate increases as more tax revenue is being raised. Would preferences over y still be single peaked?

Now imagine there are five school board members who need to come to a decision on the level of per pupil spending, and suppose that the democratic procedure is to subject any proposal that is made to pairwise voting until only one proposal survives. In other words, suppose we begin by voting on two of the proposals, then vote the winner against a third proposal, then the winner against a fourth and so forth. This process will come to a definitive end if there is what political scientists call a "Condorcet winner": a proposal that defeats all other proposals in pairwise voting.[2]

Under the set-up we have described, there is in fact a policy that is the Condorcet winner. Consider the five voters whose single-peaked preferences over per pupil spending are graphed in Graph 28.2. The voter whose "peak" falls in the middle, the voter whose preferences are high-lighted in magenta, is labeled the "median voter." Suppose this median voter's preferred policy, y_m^*, is put up against any proposal that falls to the left of it, i.e., any proposal $y < y_m^*$. Since their ideal point is closer to y_m^* than to y, *any* voter whose ideal point lies to the right of y_m^* will prefer y_m^* to such a y. Thus, voters 4 and 5 will join the median voter in defeating any such proposal. Similarly, any proposal $y' > y_m^*$ will be defeated by voters 1 and 2 together with the median voter when put up against y_m^*. Thus, there does not exist any policy proposal that can beat y_m^*, which makes y_m^* the Condorcet winner.

In the graph, we have depicted all the single peaked preferences as having the same shape and differing only in the placement of the ideal point. Would the same Condorcet winner arise under single peaked preferences that differ in their shapes but not the horizontal location of ideal points?

Exercise 28A.4

The result we just derived for five voters holds for any odd number of voters no matter how many there are. For instance, we could model a presidential election as a contest between two candidates that position themselves along an ideological spectrum that ranges from extreme left to extreme right. Large numbers of voters vote in presidential elections, and we could approximate that large

Graph 28.2: The Median Voter Theorem

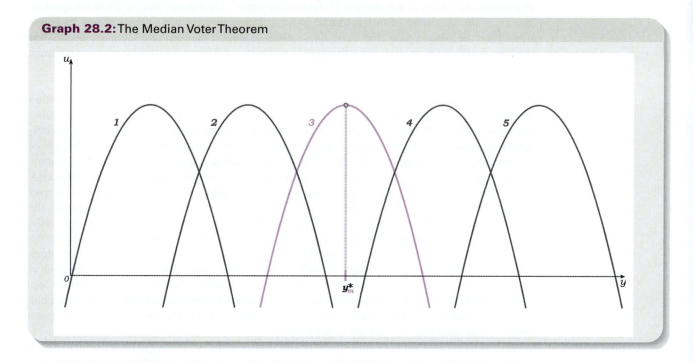

---

[2]The name "Condorcet winner" is in reference to Nicolas de Condorcet (1743–94) who first showed that majority preferences may not be transitive (as we will see shortly). Condorcet was not only a philosopher, mathematician, and political scientist, but he was also an influential figure in the French Revolution, and one of its victims when he died under suspicious circumstances two days after his arrest during Robespierre's "reign of terror."

number with a continuum of consumers whose ideal points are distributed across that spectrum, with each voter becoming worse off the further the elected president's ideological stance is from the voter's. We can then ask where we think the candidates will position themselves, and the model predicts that, if either candidate positions him- or herself at any point other than the median voter's ideal point, the other candidate can defeat the candidate by picking the median voter's position. In equilibrium, we would therefore expect the candidates to both cater to the median voter.

Exercise 28A.5
Can you see how this equilibrium prediction conforms to the equilibrium in the Hotelling model when firms are restricted to charging the same output price (and where the ideological spectrum is replaced by product differentiation)?

Exercise 28A.6
In the United States, prior to running as a party nominee in a presidential election, a potential candidate first has to win primary elections that are restricted to members of the potential candidate's party. For instance, multiple candidates for the Democratic Party's nomination must compete first among only Democrats to earn the party's nomination before competing against the Republican Party's nominee in the general election. Can you use our median voter model to argue that candidates for the Democratic Party's nomination will initially position themselves to the left of the median voter but will then succeed in the general election (against the Republican nominee) only to the extent to which they can "move to the center" in the general election campaign?

The insight from our model thus far can be summarized in what is known as the *Median Voter Theorem*: So long as the issues that are voted on fall on a single-dimensional spectrum and so long as voters have single-peaked preferences over that spectrum, majority rule over pairwise alternatives will result in the election of the median voter's ideal point. Notice the two important caveats in the statement of this theorem: Voter preferences over the issues have to be *single peaked* and the "issue space" has to be *single dimensional*. In the next two sections, we will see just how sensitive the median voter theorem is and how quickly its result disappears as we relax either of these important assumptions.

28A.1.2 Manipulation through Agenda Setting: Non-Single Peaked Preferences

Suppose we relax our model of voting on per pupil spending a bit by allowing for the possibility that some voters will send their children to private schools if public school spending is sufficiently low. For some voters, it may then be the case that their preferences over public school spending are not single-peaked. Think of it this way: If public school spending falls below some critical level, such voters will send their children to private schools. But if they send their children to private schools, they are still paying taxes for the public schools they don't use, so over the range of public school spending where the voter would choose private schools instead, the voter will become better off as public school spending (and thus the voter's tax bill) falls. Graph 28.3 then illustrates the resulting utility for such a voter for different levels of public school spending y: The public school spending level $\underline{y}_i$ is the lowest level of spending at which this voter i will choose public schooling for her child, and for any public school spending below $\underline{y}_i$, she will choose private schools. When she chooses private schools, she would prefer less public school spending over more, resulting in the initial downward relationship between public school spending and utility. But once she sends her children to public schools, she prefers more public school spending until we get to her ideal: y_i^*.

This is then an example of non-single peaked preferences over a single dimensional issue. I give the example simply to illustrate that such preferences are quite plausible even in simple settings where there is only a single issue that is being voted on. But we'll see next that this then implies that no Condorcet winner might exist; i.e., that there does not exist a per pupil spending level that can defeat any alternative proposal someone might make.

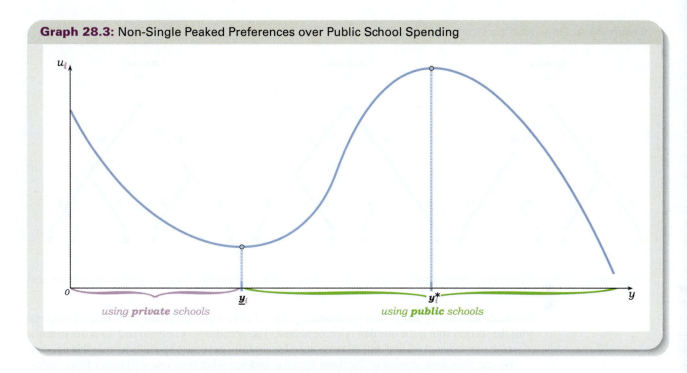

Graph 28.3: Non-Single Peaked Preferences over Public School Spending

Suppose we have three spending levels that are being considered, with $y_1 < y_2 < y_3$. Then suppose there are three voters whose preferences are given by

Voter 1: y_1 preferred to y_2 preferred to y_3

Voter 2: y_2 preferred to y_3 preferred to y_1 (28.1)

Voter 3: y_3 preferred to y_1 preferred to y_2

Which of these voters have single peaked preferences over public school spending?   Exercise
                                                                                               28A.7

Now consider what happens as we put different proposals against one another to see which one would win a majority of votes. In putting y_1 against y_2, we can see from the voter preferences that voters 1 and 3 will vote for y_1, thus defeating y_2. In putting y_2 against y_3, voters 1 and 2 will vote for y_2, thus defeating y_3. Finally, in putting y_3 against y_1, voters 2 and 3 will vote for y_3, thus defeating y_1. This gives the following result under majority rule:

$$y_1 \text{ defeats } y_2 \text{ defeats } y_3 \text{ defeats } y_1. \qquad (28.2)$$

There is no Condorcet winner because each of the three proposals is defeated by one of the others in a pairwise contest. In Arrow's words, social preferences in this case are not rational because they violate transitivity, and when transitivity is violated, it is difficult to make decisions. There is no "will of the people" because "the people" keep defeating each proposal. In our example, we could then easily end up in an endless cycle of votes with no conclusion unless *someone* figures out a rule for how the voting will stop.

We will call that "someone" an *agenda setter*. The agenda setter might be one of the voters, or he might have no vote at all. But he does have the job of determining how we will implement majority rule voting and at what point the voting stops and a decision is made. Graph 28.4 illustrates the three natural voting "agendas" that such an agenda setter might then implement. In panel (a), a decision is

Graph 28.4: Three Possible Voting "Agendas"

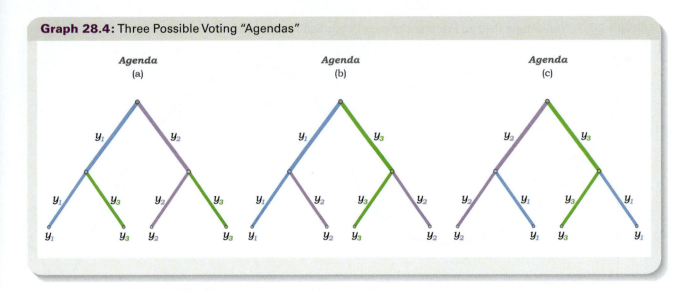

first made between y_1 and y_2, and the winning proposal is then put up against y_3. Whatever proposal wins the second vote is the one that is implemented. The agendas in panels (b) and (c) differ in terms of which pair is voted on first, but all three agendas are fully governed by majority rule throughout.

We can then look at each of the three agendas and see what outcome will result from majority voting. In Graph 28.5, we replicate the three agendas but this time indicate in bold how each of the votes will turn out given what we concluded in expression (28.2). Notice that whoever sets the agenda determines the choice that is made *without even necessarily having a vote to cast himself*. This is the issue with majority rule social preferences when such preferences violate transitivity: The intransitivity makes majority voting subject to manipulation by agenda setters because no Condorcet winner exists. Put differently, when there is no coherent "will of the people," it may be that the result of majority rule is the "will of the agenda setter."

You might look at this and think that the voters must be pretty naive to let an agenda setter manipulate them in this way. And you would be right. But even when voters are not naive, the agenda setter in our example can still get his way. Consider the same three agendas, replicated

Graph 28.5: Voting Outcomes under the Three Agendas

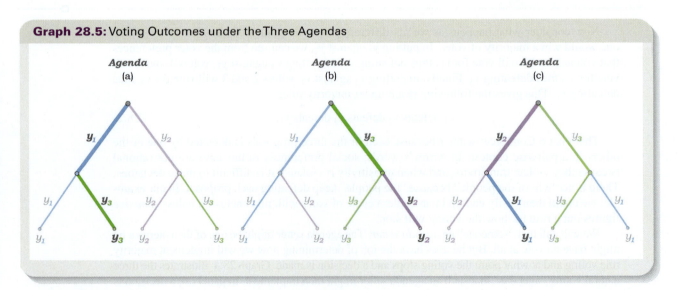

again in Graph 28.6. This time, let's assume that our three voters are "sophisticated"; that is, let's assume voters look down the "voting tree" to see what will happen later as they vote in the first vote. In panel (a) of the graph, we therefore highlight what will be the outcome in the second vote from each of the two possible nodes in the voting tree. If the first node is reached and y_1 is put up against y_3, then we know y_3 will win, and if the second node is reached and y_2 is put up against y_3, we know y_2 will win. Thus, a sophisticated voter that looks ahead to the second vote under the agenda (a) knows that a vote that is framed as a vote of y_1 against y_2 is really a vote of y_3 against y_2, and if the voters are sophisticated, this will mean that y_2 will win the first vote. The crucial voter in this case is voter 1: If she votes her sincere preferences naively, she would vote for y_1 in the first vote since y_1 is her most preferred outcome. But when voter 1 thinks in a sophisticated way, she realizes that a vote for y_1 is really a vote for y_3 since y_1 will lose against y_3 in the next vote. Thus, since y_3 is her least preferred outcome, she will vote strategically for y_2 against y_1 despite y_1 being her most preferred policy.

Legislators (like senators) who run for executive office (like governor or president) are often confronted by the media with votes they have taken in the legislature that seem to contradict their stated positions. Sometimes you will hear politicians respond that their vote against something was actually a vote for something given the sequence of votes that was scheduled. Are they being sly or might they be telling the truth?

Exercise
28A.8

The first agenda in Graph 28.6 therefore results in the outcome y_2 under sophisticated (or strategic) voting while it resulted in outcome y_3 under sincere voting (in Graph 28.5). Repeating the same analysis for the other two agendas, however, means once again that we have one agenda for each outcome that we might want to implement. The agenda necessary to implement a particular outcome is now different if voters are strategic than if they are naive, but the agenda setter can still get any outcome he wants by simply manipulating the agenda.

This is the underlying reason why it matters so much which political party controls each house of the Congress because the party in the majority gets to set the broad agenda. This is generally well understood by most people who follow politics. What is less appreciated is that within an institution like the U.S. House of Representatives, there are important committees whose chair gets to choose sequences of votes within committees, and there is a powerful "Rules Committee" that determines the rules under which legislative proposals come to the floor for votes and

Graph 28.6: Agenda Setting under Sophisticated Voting

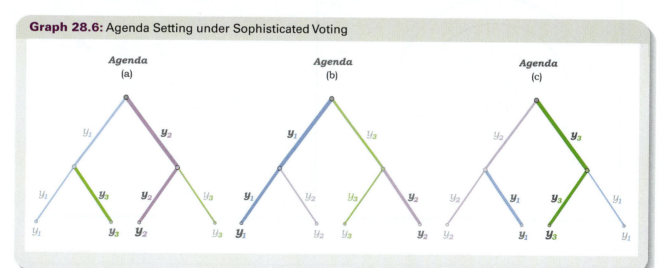

amendments. Such agenda-setting powers are important because they influence outcomes, and they are important even though committee chairs often do not themselves vote on proposals.

28A.1.3 Multidimensional Politics and the "Anything Can Happen" Theorem

The median voter theorem that guarantees a Condorcet winner required (1) single peaked preferences over (2) a single-dimensional issue space. We have just seen what happens when preferences are not single peaked: We lose the guarantee of a Condorcet winner and with that loss introduce power for (non-voting) agenda setters. The same happens, in an even more dramatic way, when we allow the "issue space" to be multidimensional.

Suppose, for instance, that there are two general government budget priorities to set: domestic spending y and military spending z. In panel (a) of Graph 28.7, we illustrate this on a graph with domestic spending on the horizontal axis and military spending on the vertical. We can then think of an individual voter i's preferences within this two-dimensional issue space. Such a voter understands that taxes have to be paid (at least at some point) in order to finance government spending of any kind, and so the voter's preferences cannot satisfy the "more is better" assumption for all levels of y and z. Eventually, the cost of paying additional taxes is too high to want more spending. So somewhere in the (y, z) space, our voter has an "ideal point" that is his or her most preferred. No matter which direction away from this ideal point we move in our two-dimensional issue space, our voter will become worse off. For simplicity, we can for instance assume that how much worse off he or she will be depends solely on the distance of a (y, z) bundle away from the voter's ideal bundle (y_i^*, z_i^*). This allows us to draw circles around the voter's ideal point, with each circle representing an indifference curve and with utility decreasing as the circles get bigger.

Exercise 28A.9 How would ideal points differ for voters who report that they are conservative, liberal, or libertarian?

Graph 28.7: Two-Dimensional Issue Spaces

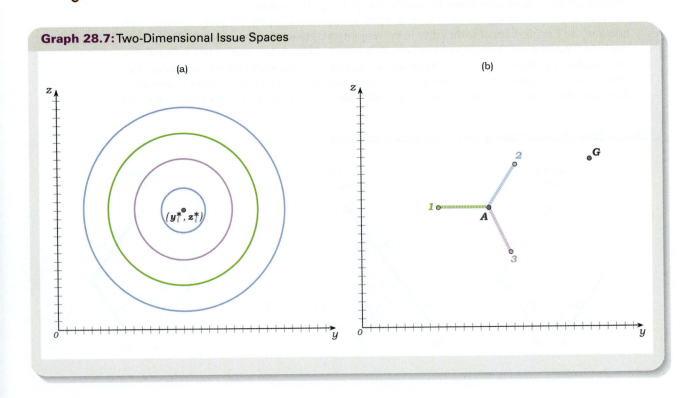

Notice that the preferences we have just drawn are single-peaked over the two-dimensional issue space. If we imagine utility as a third axis, we would get a single utility mountain with one peak. Furthermore, since we have made the simplifying assumption that the only thing that matters in terms of utility is how far a particular policy bundle is away from the voter's ideal point, we literally have all the information we need about preferences when we identify the voter's ideal point. As a result, we can represent the preferences of many voters on a single graph by simply indicating the ideal points of the voters, and we can then pick any two policy bundles and check which way each of the voters will vote depending on how far the two bundles are from each voter's ideal point.

For instance, in panel (b) of Graph 28.7, we illustrate three voters by illustrating three different ideal points labeled 1, 2, and 3. In the same graph, we illustrate a policy labeled A. From each ideal point, we draw a dashed line to the proposal, and we will know that for any proposal B that is put up against proposal A in a vote, each voter will vote for B if and only if the distance from that voter's ideal point to B is smaller than the distance from the ideal point to A. It's immediately clear that there are many policies that could not win against A because A is so centrally located relative to the voters' ideal points. For instance, policy G way to the upper right of the graph would go down to unanimous defeat if put up against A.

But now I will make a bold claim: If you put me in charge of designing an agenda, a sequence of pairwise votes where the winning proposal goes on to face the next proposal in the sequence, I can get the extreme policy G to be the outcome of a majority rule process with these three voters voting to implement G rather than A. In fact, I can get *any* policy in the two-dimensional issue space to be an outcome of a thoughtfully designed agenda that begins with a vote of A against some other policy. More than that, you can start me with *any* policy at the beginning of the sequence of votes, and I can construct a sequence to get us to *any* other policy.

We won't prove this formally here, but I'll at least show you how I can get from A to G when all voters would unanimously send G down to defeat if we simply voted A against G. For our purposes, we will assume that voters vote sincerely, as they would be likely to do if there were many voters of each type. From this simple example you will quickly see how the general theorem, what I am calling the "Anything-Can-Happen Theorem," must in fact be true.[3]

We'll begin in panel (a) of Graph 28.8 where I am proposing policy B as an alternative to A. Notice that although B is much farther from voter 2's ideal point than A, it is just a bit closer to voters 1 and 3. Thus, voters 1 and 3 will vote for B over A. In panel (b) of the graph, we then start with the policy that won in the previous vote—policy B—and I will propose policy C as an alternative in my voting agenda. In selecting C, I gave up on voter 3 and focused on voters 1 and 2, making sure I get as far out as possible while still having C closer than B to those two voters' ideal points. This ensures that voters 1 and 2 will vote for C against B, which in turn ensures that C wins. Next, in panel (c), I write off voter 1 and focus on voters 2 and 3, choosing a policy D that is more extreme but that still lies closer to voters 2 and 3's ideal points than C; this ensures that D will defeat C.

Panels (d) through (f) continue this same process. Each time I think of the next policy in the sequence, I let go of one of the voters that just voted for the previous policy in order to be able to pick a more extreme policy that will win. By the time I get to panel (f), I have reached the policy G I had boldly claimed I could implement through majority rule. No one likes G very much except me, and I didn't even have a vote along the way. But by being the agenda setter, I was able to implement my ideal point while making it look like the process had been fully democratic throughout. I could have of course kept the outward spiraling of policies going and gotten to even more extreme policies if I had wanted.

Can you explain how panels (d) through (f) complete the argument that G can be implemented through a sequence of pair-wise votes?

Exercise 28A.10

[3]The theorem is actually known as the McKelvey Theorem after the political scientist Richard McKelvey (1944–2002) who proved it in "Intransitivities in Multidimensional Voting Models and Some Implications for Agenda Control," *Journal of Economic Theory* 12 (1976), 472–82.

Graph 28.8: The "Anything Can Happen" Theorem

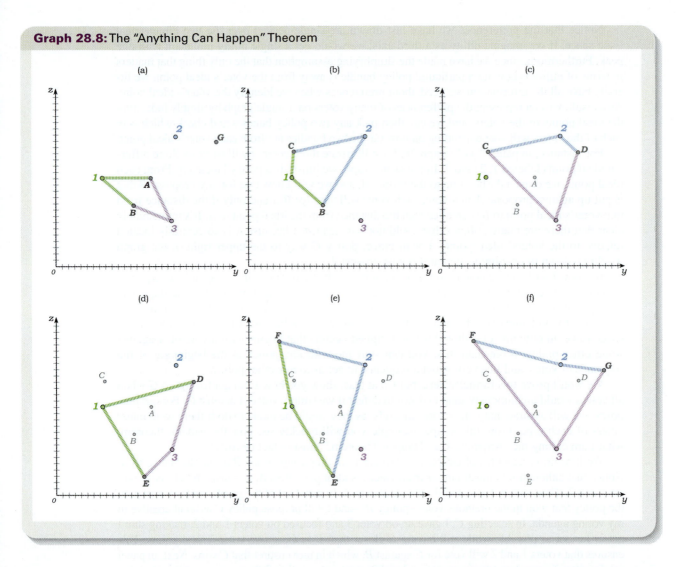

The result is remarkable. It says that, when issues get complicated and can't just be modeled along a single dimension, agenda setters almost always control everything given that voter preferences do not add up to a coherent "will of the people." (In end-of-chapter exercise 28.2, you can explore a special case for which the result does not hold.) We will shortly see how political institutions, rules, and customs constrain this power of the agenda setter. But if you doubt that agenda setters can in principle do what we have just done in Graph 28.8, I encourage you to read a fascinating account of how one of the founding fathers of experimental economics did precisely that in his flight club. To make a long story short, he was put in charge of designing a "democratic" agenda that would lead to an expression of the will of the club members in selecting a new fleet of aircraft for the flight club to purchase. Understanding that there likely was no such thing as the "will of the club members," Charles Plott set off to design an agenda that would implement a very particular outcome he determined in advance, and then he proceeded to document exactly how successful he was in getting the club membership to democratically decide to implement what he determined he wanted at the beginning.[4]

---

[4]Charles Plott (1938–) is Professor of Economics at California Institute of Technology where he established one of the first experimental economics laboratories. His direct experience with agenda setting is reported in an article with Michael Levine: "Agenda Influence and Implications," *Virginia Law Review* 63, no. 4 (1977), 561–604.

28A.2 Institutional Restraints on Policy Manipulation

The world is, of course, not as chaotic as all that. Agenda setters cannot just get anything they want, and they themselves must first get into the position of being able to shape the political agenda (which might mean that their preferences might not be as extreme as mine in our previous example). Nor would a political system that does not find ways of constraining what agenda setters can dictate be among the more successful. So it would therefore not be surprising if a combination of deliberate institutional design with the evolution of institutional features that proved worthwhile has led to a considerable taming of the chaos that could in principle emerge under majority rule voting. Some of these we learn in our middle school civics classes: basic lessons on balance of power between executive, legislative, and judicial branches. We will now break this into some finer detail and consider two particular types of political institutions that tend to play important roles in democratic legislative processes.

28A.2.1 Structure-Induced Voting Equilibria: Breaking Up Complex Issues

One of the ways in which real-world legislative bodies deal with the potential chaos that can arise under democratic processes is to restrict severely the set of proposals that are ever voted on in the full legislature, and to subject that voting process to specific rules. The U.S. Congress, for instance, passes a budget for the government, but the pieces of the budget get produced by committees and subcommittees that deal with much narrower issues. The committee structure in Congress therefore breaks up the multidimensional issue space (in which Congress ultimately chooses policy) into issues that are much closer to the single dimensional issues dealt with in our median voter theorem. There is a committee that deals with military spending, and another that deals with welfare spending, and another that deals with Social Security, etc.

To see how this can tame the process by which I designed an agenda that took us from what looked like a relative consensus policy A to an extreme policy G, consider a legislature in which there are many members who ultimately have to choose a policy pair (y, z) but who rely on committees to come forward with proposals on y and z separately. In panel (a) of Graph 28.9, for instance, we illustrate the ideal points of 10 members of the legislature. We then imagine that the leader of the legislature picks individuals to sit on committees that will forward recommendations on spending levels. Specifically, suppose the members whose ideal points are circled in blue are assigned to the y committee that is charged with recommending a level of spending on y, and the members whose ideal points are encased in magenta squares are assigned to the z committee that is charged with recommending a level of spending on z.

When these committees gather to consider a single dimensional issue y or z, their single-peaked preferences in the two-dimensional issue space translate into single-peaked preferences over the single issue they are considering. As a result, we can simply find the person whose ideal point on the dimension the committee is considering is the median ideal point for the committee, and, by the median voter theorem, this is the proposal that is the Condorcet winner in the committee. In the y committee, for instance, this will result in the median proposal y_m, and in the z committee it will result in the proposal z_m. When these two proposals are then brought to the floor of the legislature and combined, they result in the proposal indicated by the green X in the graph. And the legislature is now asked to take an up or down vote on the proposal X (or is asked to vote X against some status-quo policy that is already in place).

This kind of a voting equilibrium is called a "structure-induced" equilibrium because its outcome is "induced" by the structure of the committees that can produce Condorcet winners within the committees. In panel (a) of our graph, the process results in a proposal that appears to lie very much toward the middle of where all the individual ideal points for members of the legislature are. But that is an artifact of the way we assigned members to committees. In

Graph 28.9: Structure-Induced Voting Equilibria

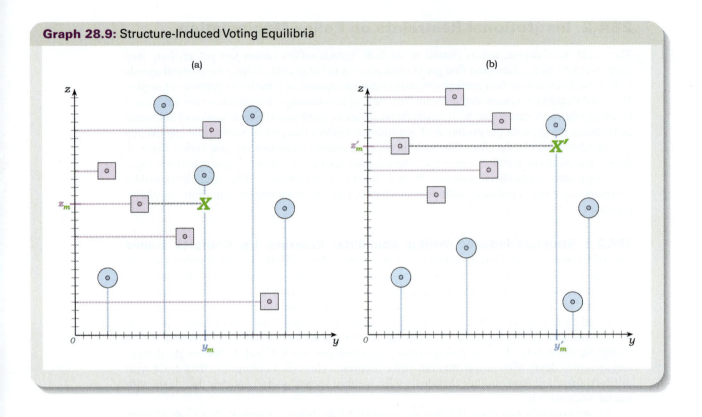

panel (b) of the graph, I reassigned the same members differently between the two committees. The resulting green proposal X' is more extreme than what we produced in panel (a), containing more of y and more of z. Thus, by altering the committee assignments, the agenda setter in the legislature still has quite a bit of influence on how the final proposal looks.

Exercise 28A.11   How would you assign the members to committees if you wanted to get less spending on y and z than we did in panel (a) of Graph 28.9? What if you wanted more of y but less of z?

Notice that "agenda setting" now takes a different form: The leader of the legislature might not be able to cleverly construct sequences of votes like we did in the last section, but he or she can influence the outcome in the legislature by cleverly choosing committee memberships. While this agenda setter therefore retains a great deal of control over the ultimate outcome of the legislative process, you should also notice that the committee system limits how extreme an outcome can arise under democratic voting. In particular, if you found the smallest convex set of policies that contains all the members' ideal points, the policy produced by the committee system has to lie within that set. This was not true in Graph 28.8, where G lies far outside this set.

Committees in legislative bodies have arisen over time as such bodies have tried to figure out procedures that work. They are, in many ways, informal institutions that have emerged rather than having been explicitly designed. Similar institutions, like the rules that govern legislative debate and the rules that can be applied to limit the kinds of amendments that members can offer to bills that reach the floor of the legislature, have emerged and are rarely altered directly. Other institutions have been more deliberately designed. The U.S. founders split the legislature into two separate bodies (the House of Representatives and the Senate) in part to have these institutions put a check on each other. The U.S. Constitution relegated a number of issues to states, which in turn have relegated some issues to local control. Local governments are often split by function, with school districts separate from fire districts and water districts that are in turn separate from municipalities. Sometimes the political process asks voters to vote directly on single issues, such as when referenda are placed in front of voters. All these mechanisms—those that have been formally designed and those that have evolved over time—in part accomplish the task of imposing structure on democratic voting, with that structure helping to determine what outcomes ultimately emerge.

The political economy literature on how different structures under which voting happens result in different outcomes is vast, too vast for us to even begin to crack it here. (You may wish to take a course in political economy to explore the topics in this chapter further.) For now, the main lesson you should take away from what we have done is that when issues of any complexity require political solutions, any voting process will be subject to manipulation by agenda setters, but structured voting can lessen the degree to which such manipulation can result in extreme outcomes.

28A.2.2 Expressing Intensity of Preferences: Vote Trading and Reciprocity

In real-world legislatures, politicians often find ways of lumping together different issues into single pieces of legislation that then receive an up-or-down vote. We explored how this relates to spending on special projects targeted at a legislator's district, or what we called "pork barrel spending," in two Chapter 27 end-of-chapter exercises (which we include as end-of-chapter exercise 28.11 in this chapter). And we found that such spending is often inefficient for reasons that find their roots in the Tragedy of the Commons, with inefficiency rising as the number of legislative districts N increases and each legislator therefore only confronts $1/Nth$ the cost of a project. (This is sometimes referred to as the *Law of* $1/N$). We now think more generally about policies that may not have anything to do with pork barrel spending, again leaving much to be explored in other courses that you may take in the future.

First, note that a lumping together of specific policies in a single piece of legislation is a way for politicians to trade votes, a practice sometimes referred to as *logrolling*. I might decide to join a coalition with you if you agree to include my favorite pet project in a bill that also includes yours even if I don't care at all about your pet project. Second, this process of vote trading can allow us to give expression to not just *whether* we like a particular project but also *how much* we like it. If I really like my pet project, I will be willing to join a coalition that is putting together a piece of legislation that also contains a lot I don't like, whereas if I only like my project a little bit, I will not be willing to join so readily.

Consider the projects A through E listed in Table 28.1. Suppose these projects are being considered in a simple legislature composed of representatives from three districts: voters 1, 2, and 3. The table then indicates the net benefit that each district obtains from each project. You can think of these net benefits in dollar terms, where negative amounts indicate that the tax revenues raised from members of the district for a particular project outweigh the monetary benefits the district would get from the project. Project E, for instance, might be a road that goes through the heart of district 1 and a bit through district 2 but does not affect district 3. Since taxpayers everywhere have to pay for the road, district 3 is made a lot worse off by the project because it would pay taxes in exchange for no benefits, while district 1 gets the largest net benefit since the road goes straight through that district.

First, suppose that only A and B were on the agenda. Neither project could receive a majority of votes since only one voter would in fact vote for each of the projects. But voters 1 and 2 can form a coalition and put the two projects into a single piece of legislation that is voted up or

Table 28.1: Net Benefit of Five Projects for Three Voters

	Vote Trading				
	A	B	C	D	E
Voter 1	−1	3	0	−1	3
Voter 2	3	−1	−4	3	−1
Voter 3	−1	−1	2	−3	−3
Net Social Benefit	1	1	−2	−1	−1

down. This bundled legislation will then receive yes votes from voters 1 and 2, and as a bundle the two projects can therefore be implemented through majority rule. Voters 1 and 2 have, in effect, traded votes, with voter 1 agreeing to trade her vote for project A in exchange for voter 2 trading his vote for project B.

In this case, the outcome is efficient since the net benefit across the three districts of each of the projects is positive. Thus, vote trading has overcome an otherwise inefficient outcome of having two projects that create net social benefits defeated individually. But there is no guarantee that vote trading will in fact result in the implementation of efficient projects. Consider projects D and E whose net benefits are identical to those of A and B for voters 1 and 2 but not for voter 3. For the same reasons as before, D and E cannot be implemented through simply majority rule unless vote trading occurs and the two projects are bundled. But now the overall net benefit of both projects is negative, which implies that vote trading would result in the building of inefficient projects.

And, as in the previous sections, whoever exercises control over the agenda of what can in fact be lumped together also exercises a great deal of power. Suppose, for instance, that projects A and B are currently under consideration and voter 3 suddenly becomes committee chair in charge of setting the agenda of what will be considered by the committee. By introducing C onto the agenda, the new chair will then ensure that the coalition between voters 1 and 2 is broken up and that voter 1 will instead enter a coalition with him to implement projects B and C. The outcome is less efficient: project C has negative net social benefits while project A does not, but the new committee chair likes C and not B.

Bundling different projects into a single piece of legislation is one possible way for legislators to trade votes and thereby implement projects that could not be implemented on their own. There are also other ways for legislators to accomplish this. One such way is through the development of a "norm of reciprocity" that, in essence, is an understood longer-run agreement between legislators that "I'll scratch your back if you'll scratch mine." Since legislators understand that they will interact repeatedly, such norms can easily develop, with voter 1 comfortable voting for project B knowing that this will mean voter 2 will "owe her a favor" and will therefore vote for project A when it comes up for a vote. Thus, even when projects are not explicitly bundled, implicit bundling may well emerge.

28A.3 Rent Seeking, Political Competition, and Government as "Leviathan"

The study of political economy has evolved in different "schools" over the last half century, with different assumptions guiding the development of these different schools and how they view democratic political competition and efficiency. The crucial concern of these schools revolves around the degree to which politicians are able to seek "rents" for themselves through the political process. Rent-seeking politicians have goals of their own that conflict with the goals of voters: They view the political process as a means to attain something equivalent to profit. They are, in some sense, no different than profit maximizing firms. In the case of competitive firms, we have found that competition can reduce, or in the extreme case eliminate, the potential for firms to make profits. It is then natural to ask whether political competition can serve a function similar to market competition, driving political rents to zero just as market competition drives firm profits to zero.

This question is a bit different from what we have analyzed so far. In the previous sections of this chapter, we have simply assumed that politicians have preferences over policy outcomes and we have seen that, in the absence of a Condorcet winner, those who control the political agenda have a great deal of power to shape the policy outcomes to those that conform with their own preferences. To the extent to which the agenda setter is not necessarily concerned about economic efficiency, policy outcomes that are shaped by the agenda setter may therefore deviate substantially from economic efficiency. We now ask a related question: Suppose that the politicians' preferences include preferences for political rents, which could be simply the satisfaction of seeing one's preferred (and quite possibly inefficient) policies implemented, or it could involve more personal rents such as cushy offices, excessively large staffs to supervise, big projects bearing the names of the politician, etc.

One school of political economy, known as the "Chicago School," comes to the conclusion that political competition can in fact serve the same purpose as market competition. Without going into great detail, you can see the intuition for this conclusion from the simple Bertrand model in our study of oligopolies: In that model, even when only two firms competed, they ended up charging a price equal to marginal cost. Similarly, the Chicago School argues, political candidates that compete for votes will be forced to compete by lowering the rents they can obtain once elected, and just as profits fall to zero under Bertrand competition, so political rents fall to zero under political competition.

Another school of political economy, known as the "Virginia School" or the "Public Choice School," is considerably more skeptical that such Bertrand-like competition can effectively restrain political rents. The analogy to our study of Bertrand competition for oligopolistic firms again becomes useful to see the reasons for this skepticism. We found that the Bertrand result is quite crucially dependent on the assumption that firms are producing the same (or perfectly substitutable) products. As soon as we allowed for product differentiation in Chapter 26, Bertrand competition did *not* imply price being competed to marginal cost, with such product differentiation therefore opening the door for positive profits. In exactly the same way, the Chicago efficiency result for political competition holds only if candidates are viewed as perfect substitutes. Just as firms can strategically differentiate their products, political candidates can strategically differentiate themselves (along, for instance, ideological lines or party affiliation), and this (combined with barriers to entry into the "political market place") opens the door for political rents. Under Bertrand competition, it has to furthermore be the case that consumers are aware of the different producers' products, and unawareness can result in positive profits. Similarly, in the political process consumers might simply not be aware of certain issues that have only a marginal impact on their well-being, opening the door for politicians to seek political rents in those areas. In this section, we will therefore briefly discuss a few of the insights that have emerged from this Public Choice School.[5]

28A.3.1 Interest Groups: The Politics of Concentrated Benefits and Diffuse Costs
In some of our discussions of government policies, starting with our discussion of price ceilings and price floors in Chapter 18, we have already asked how economically inefficient

[5]The Public Choice School is most closely identified with 1986 Nobel Laureate James Buchanan (1919–). To get a more detailed sense of his perspective, see G. Brennan and J. Buchanan, *The Power to Tax: Analytic Foundations of a Fiscal Constitution* (Cambridge: Cambridge University Press, 1980). For the alternative Chicago school, see D. Wittman, *The Myth of Democratic Failure: Why Political Institutions Are Efficient* (Chicago: University of Chicago Press, 1995).

policies appear to survive the political process. If price ceilings and price floors create more harm than benefit, how can they be sustained by democratic institutions? If trade on balance produces social surplus, why is it so politically difficult to lower trade barriers? In our previous discussions, we found an answer in a recognition that often the costs and benefits of policies are not evenly distributed. This insight came squarely from the Public Choice School that we have just introduced.

Our basic argument in earlier chapters has been that *when benefits of a policy are concentrated* and *costs are diffuse*, then it is more likely that political interest groups representing those who benefit from the policy will succeed in their attempt to influence policy. Underlying this argument is the assumption that it is costly to organize political interest groups. If this were not the case, then those who lose from the policy would pool their resources to compete against those who win in the political arena, and if those who lose stand to lose more than those who gain stand to gain, one would expect them to be able to succeed in that arena. But if it is sufficiently costly to organize a diffuse 100 million consumers of milk against milk price support policies, it may well be that the concentrated beneficiaries of such policies—a few large dairy farmers, for instance—will apply intense political pressure that does not meet very much of an opposition. Self-interested politicians who need political and financial support of motivated constituencies will then find it easy to listen to (and accept money from) concentrated beneficiaries, secure in their knowledge that the costs of the policy are spread across many consumers who are only partially aware of those costs and who are sufficiently large in number to not be able to organize effectively.

Exercise 28A.12   Relate the idea of concentrated benefits and diffuse costs to the free-rider problem faced by interest groups that represent beneficiaries and victims of policies.

You might notice that this argument is, in some way, similar to Coase's argument about decentralized solutions to externalities. Coase emphasized transactions costs: If those were sufficiently low, then parties to externalities could resolve externalities (so long as property rights were established). If political interest groups play a role in policy making, we might similarly expect efficient policies so long as the transactions costs of organizing such interest groups are low. But if such costs are high (as they are in many circumstances), then policies with concentrated benefits and diffuse costs are likely to win even if such policies produce net social losses.

28A.3.2 Regulatory Capture

The Public Choice School's insights on the role of concentrated benefits and diffuse costs furthermore extends beyond the process of policy *making* to the process of policy *implementation*. Legislatures write broad policies that are then implemented by agencies that are charged to interpret such policies in specific instances. The Federal Communications Commission, for instance, is broadly charged with implementing policy regarding telephone, television, and radio service to consumers, but the commission itself issues large numbers of regulations in the process of implementation and determines when to intervene in the decentralized decisions by private providers of phone, television, and radio services.

Since government agencies are institutions that are not disciplined by market competition, they are natural places where rent-seeking individuals might look to advance careers. In principle, they are overseen by democratic institutions (both on the legislative and the executive sides of the government), but they are also subject to political pressure from those institutions and from outside individuals who have a large stake in what the agencies do. Whether indirectly through politicians that then exert pressure on regulatory agencies, or whether directly through lobbying of the regulatory agency itself, the voice of concentrated beneficiaries is likely to outweigh the voice of more diffuse constituencies that bear the cost.

This, too, is something we have hinted at before, as in our treatment of regulating monopolies or oligopolies. The intent of legislation that creates regulatory agencies to oversee oligopolistic industries is typically to enhance consumer welfare by limiting anticompetitive behavior in the industry. Consumers, then, are the diffuse group that bears the cost of anticompetitive behavior in industry (and reap the benefit of reducing such anticompetitive behavior). Oligopolistic firms, on the other hand, reap concentrated benefits from anticompetitive behavior (and bear concentrated costs of limits to such behavior). Those with the most to gain from being heard in the process of policy implementation by the regulating agency, therefore, are the oligopolists themselves. Public choice theory then raises the possibility that such agencies will in fact be "captured" by those whose behavior is to be regulated, and that regulations in practice are then shaped in accordance with the wishes of the regulated. In public choice theory, this is referred to as *regulatory capture*.

The initial implementation of President Roosevelt's New Deal reforms of industry presents an excellent case study. In Chapter 25, we discussed these reforms that led to the establishment of the National Recovery Administration (NRA) that was to "foster fair competition." In the brief period of its existence (before it was struck down by the Supreme Court), it became clear that industrial leaders themselves were essentially in charge of the regulations that emerged from the NRA and that much of this regulation in fact served the purpose of legally enforcing cartels that restrained competition. Public choice economists have written about numerous other examples where the evidence seems to suggest that, counter to our intuition, the regulated become the biggest supporters of the regulation that is supposed to restrain them.

28A.3.3 (Self-Perpetuating) Bureaucracy as Concentrated Beneficiary Milton Friedman, one of the best known economists of the 20th century and a deep skeptic of government, once said that a government program epitomizes the closest thing to eternal life on earth. This succinctly captures another insight from public choice theory: Once a government program is established, a bureaucracy typically accompanies the program, and individuals in that bureaucracy have an interest in keeping and expanding the program because this keeps and expands career opportunities for these individuals. This is fine if the program works, but if the program does not work, there is nevertheless a powerful constituency that becomes a concentrated beneficiary. Those in the bureaucracy are likely to lobby for additional funding because it benefits them, and they are a concentrated group that can easily organize to make the case. The public choice theory of concentrated benefits and diffuse costs therefore suggests that government bureaucracies will become inefficiently large and will perpetuate programs even if they do not meet the initial expectations of legislators.

28A.3.4 Constitutions and Government Competition to Restrain "Leviathan"
While we have only given some brief descriptions of how public choice theory predicts that political processes will lead to inefficient policy, it should be clear even from this brief description of public choice insights that this theory also predicts the emergence of a government that is inefficiently large. Some have dubbed this the "Leviathan" model of government, where "Leviathan" is a reference to Hebrew images of large (and typically malevolent) monsters. Yet few public choice theories would argue that government should be dispensed with—rather, they, just like Arrow, are interested in institutional constraints on democratic governments—constraints that will restrain the "Leviathan" and make government more "benevolent."

We have already mentioned some such institutional constraints in our discussion of multi-dimensional voting. While the Chicago School of political economy relies on democratic competition to restrain Leviathan, Public Choice theorists typically emphasize two further checks on democratic processes: (1) broad constitutional constraints that limit the scope of government, and (2) the fostering of intergovernmental competition. Note that both of these emphases follow from the Public Choice School's identification of channels that lead to inefficiently large (and self-perpetuating) government activity, activity that emerges from the hypothesized disproportionate emphasis on concentrated beneficiaries of policies over the diffuse costs imposed on society at large.

Public choice theorists often count the founders of the U.S. Constitution, for instance, as intellectual predecessors of the modern school of public choice, especially those that emphasized the need for strong subnational governments (i.e., states) and the need for balance of power among the three branches of the federal government. The modern school of public choice emphasizes precisely such channels as appropriate tools for limiting excesses in legislative and regulatory institutions, with constitutions specifying the areas in which governments can legislate and regulate, and with federalism creating both hierarchical and horizontal competition that can discipline political processes beyond the discipline voters impose at the ballot box.

28B   An Exposition of Arrow's Impossibility Theorem

While the Public Choice School that we have just discussed finds its roots in the writings of political philosophers of centuries ago, much of the more microfoundational modeling of political institutions and processes originates with Arrow's Theorem that we have mentioned throughout. In fact, one of the criticisms often levied against the Public Choice School is that it has not fully linked to these microeconomic foundations and has relied on more informal insights on government behavior. Over the last few decades, however, these different strands of political economy have increasingly merged, with those inspired by Arrow's Theorem increasingly taking up the challenge of adding microfoundations to the insights of modern public choice theory. As a result, an understanding of Arrow's insight is increasingly important.

As we mentioned in the introduction, Arrow's Theorem directly challenges us to use microeconomics to think about political processes and to identify how different political institutions yield different policy outcomes. This would not be necessary if it were the case that democracy itself simply gives expression to a well-defined set of social preferences. But since Arrow demonstrates that such well-defined social preferences do not in general exist, he implicitly is giving us a roadmap for what kinds of trade-offs we face in modeling political institutions, and what kinds of trade-offs democratic institutions must make. Put differently, Arrow tells us that politics matters, that the details of political institutions matter and that we cannot simply assume that democratic institutions will give rise to outcomes that satisfy any particular social goal (like economic efficiency).

Given the importance of Arrow's Theorem in the development of political economy, we therefore devote this section of the chapter to a full exposition of the theorem. That exposition begins with the concept of a *social choice function*, a function that translates individual preferences into aggregate social preferences over outcomes that political institutions are asked to decide. As we will see, Arrow's basic question then asks whether we can expect particular social choice functions to emerge from democratic processes. He then demonstrates that the functions that can emerge under democracy are functions that are subject to manipulation by those who can shape the agenda within political institutions, and that the type of institution will have every bit as much to do with the outcomes we should expect from democratic voting as with the underlying preferences of the voters.

28B.1   Social Choice Functions and the Axiomatic Approach

A *social choice function* is a function f that aggregates individual preferences over social outcomes to a single preference ordering. Let $\{\succsim\}$ denote the set of possible preference relations over a set of possible social outcomes A, and let $N = \{1, 2, \ldots, N\}$ denote the set of N individuals affected by those social outcomes. A social choice function takes the form $f: \{\succsim\}^N \rightarrow \{\succsim\}$ translating any profile of individual preferences $\{\succsim^n\}_{n=1}^N = \left\{\succsim^1, \succsim^2, \ldots \succsim^N\right\}$ into a single preference, ordering $\succsim$.

Arrow then took what is known as an *axiomatic* approach. This approach begins by specifying a set of "axioms" that a social choice function f should satisfy in order to facilitate social decision making. It then investigates how much the set of all possible social choice functions is narrowed down by these axioms. In everything we do in the following sections, we will assume that there are at least two individuals and at least three possible social states, but everything we derive holds for any finite number of individuals and social states larger than that.

28B.2 Arrow's Five Axioms

Arrow began by defining five basic axioms that he thought would be sensible for any social choice function to satisfy. The first three are quite basic and simply require that social choice functions do not restrict individual preferences, respect unanimity, and contain at least some minimal element of democracy. The last two axioms are intended to prohibit the democratic process that is represented by the social choice function from being manipulable by those who control the agenda. We will define each axiom before proceeding to show that no social choice function can satisfy all five axioms at the same time.

28B.2.1 The "Universal Domain" (UD) Axiom
Arrow's starting point is that we cannot dictate to individuals how they feel about social outcomes, which means that we must permit them to have whatever preferences they actually have. We may not like their individual preferences, and we may not pay that much attention to some of them in our social choice function, but we have to let people have the preferences they come with. The only restriction we will permit is that individual preferences must make sense, which, in the language we used in developing consumer preferences at the beginning of the book, simply means that the individual preference relations $\succsim^n$ are complete and transitive (or what we called "rational"). Put slightly more formally, we want the *domain* $\{\succsim\}^N$ of the social choice function $f: \{\succsim\}^N \to \{\succsim\}$ to universally admit all combinations of rational individual preferences. For this reason, we will refer to this axiom as *universal domain* and denote it UD.

28B.2.2 The "Pareto Unanimity" (PU) Axiom
The second requirement Arrow had for social choice functions is that unanimously held views are respected when social decisions are made. Thus, if an alternative $x \in A$ is preferred by *everyone* to an alternative $y \in A$, then the social preference ordering should rank x above y. Put formally, if $x \succsim^n y$ for all $n = 1, 2, \ldots, N$, then $x \succsim y$ for $\succsim = f(\succsim^1, \succsim^2, \ldots \succsim^N)$. Notice that under most preference profiles that actually occur in populations, this axiom would impose no restrictions on the actual outcome of the social choice process because it is presumably rare that *everyone* agrees one thing is better than another. All the axiom says is that *if* everyone happens to like one thing better than another, then the outcome of a social choice process ought to agree with that preference ordering. Arrow originally called this the Pareto Axiom, but since it is not the same as Pareto Optimality, we will call it the *Pareto Unanimity* axiom and denote it as PU.

How does Pareto Optimality as a concept differ from Pareto Unanimity?

Exercise 28B.1

28B.2.3 The "No Dictatorship" (ND) Axiom
Arrow was fundamentally interested in *democratic* social choice processes; that is, social choice processes where the preferences of more than one person matter. So it is natural for him to posit as one of his axioms that the social choice function should not be dictatorial. But his definition of a dictator is a definition of a quite powerful dictator, which differs from our usual conception of a dictator as someone who controls many but not all things. For this reason, the kind of dictator that Arrow is attempting to prohibit from social choice processes is known as an *Arrow Dictator*.

An individual is an Arrow Dictator if, *for every pair* (x, y) of social states, *whenever* everyone else prefers x to y and he is the only one to disagree, the social choice function sides with him in opposition to everyone else. More formally, n is an Arrow dictator if, for all $x \in A$ and all $y \in A$, whenever $x \succsim^j y$ for all $j \neq n$ and $y \succsim^n x$, the social preference ordering $\succsim = f(\succsim^1, \succsim^2, \ldots \succsim^N)$ is such that $y \succsim x$. The *No Dictatorship* axiom, denoted ND, simply states that no individual in society should have such power over the social choice process; that is, the social choice function f should not permit one individual to *always* get his way *whenever* he is a minority of 1. Note that the axiom is not violated if there is an individual who *almost always* gets his way when he is a minority of 1. It just does not allow for an individual to *always* get his way.

Exercise 28B.2
In Section A, we developed the "median voter theorem" that says that when voters' preferences over a single dimensional issue are single peaked, the outcome under majority rule is the outcome preferred by the median voter. If we define that social choice function to be majority rule, does this make the median voter an Arrow Dictator under that rule? (*Hint*: The answer is no.)

Exercise 28B.3
Is the agenda setter in Graph 28.5 an Arrow Dictator? Is the agenda setter in our discussion of the "Anything-Can-Happen" Theorem an Arrow Dictator?

28B.2.4 The "Rationality" (R) Axiom

When we introduced the concept of preferences in consumer theory, we insisted that completeness and transitivity were quite necessary properties in order to make much headway in analyzing consumer choice because without them, it is not clear that a "best" consumption bundle is well defined. Completeness simply meant that, when confronted with two consumption bundles, a consumer must be able to tell us which one she prefers or whether she is indifferent. Transitivity meant that the consumer could not like bundle x better than y, bundle y better than z *and* bundle z better than x. If this were violated, the consumer could end up in an endless cycle, choosing x over y, y over z, z over x, and so forth and thus never actually be able to make a decision. We then lumped the properties of completeness and transitivity together and called it "rationality."

Arrow insists that this basic rationality property must also hold for social preferences. As we have seen in Section A, if it does not (as may be the case under majority rule when preferences over a single dimensional issue are not single-peaked), the door is opened for an "agenda setter" to manipulate the outcome of the social choice process to fit with his own ideal. We therefore require that the social choice function f has the property that, for *all* rational preference profiles $\{\succsim^n\}_{n=1}^N$ that might emerge in the population, the social preferences $\succsim = f(\{\succsim^n\}_{n=1}^N)$ must be rational; i.e., they must satisfy completeness and transitivity. We will call this property *rationality* and denote it as R.

28B.2.5 The "Independence of Irrelevant Alternatives" (IIA) Axiom

Of the five axioms specified by Arrow, the last is the least understood and the most controversial. It says the following: Suppose that, for a particular preference profile in the population, the social choice process results in social preferences that pick x over y. Then it must be the case that the same social choice process results in social preferences that will still pick x over y for all other individual preference profiles that maintain individual rankings of x and y as they were in the original preference profile of the population. Put differently, when "society" chooses between x and y, individual preferences over x and y should be what matters, and not individual preferences over other pairs of social outcomes. This ensures that an "agenda setter" cannot influence social preferences over x and y by adding a social state that is irrelevant for a choice over x and y to what is contained in the set of possible social states A. Note that it does not mean that x is chosen by society as the best outcome regardless of what other alternatives are considered in the set of possible alternatives A; it merely says that, when confronted with a choice solely between x and y, it does not matter what other alternatives are in the set A. It is analogous to saying that consumers should feel the same way about two different consumption bundles that they are asked to compare regardless of what other consumption bundles are in the consumer's budget set.

To put it more formally, we can state the axiom as follows: Suppose f is such that, when individual preferences take the form $\{\succsim^n\}_{n=1}^N$, the social preference ordering $\succsim = f(\{\succsim^n\}_{n=1}^N)$ results in $x \succsim y$. Then *for all* individual preference profiles $\{\succsim'^n\}_{n=1}^N$ where $x \succsim'^n y$ if and only if $x \succsim^n y$, it must be that the new social preferences $\succsim' = f(\{\succsim'^n\}_{n=1}^N)$ result in $x \succsim' y$. When this holds, we will say that the social choice over x and y is *independent* of all other alternatives that are *irrelevant* for the choice between x and y. And when this holds for all pairs of social states, we will say that the *Independence of Irrelevant Alternatives* axiom, denoted as IIA, is satisfied by the social choice process f.

28B.3 "Decisiveness" of Coalitions

As we work our way toward the result that no social choice function f exists that satisfies all five of Arrow's axioms, it becomes useful to define a concept known as the *decisiveness* of a coalition of individuals. A *coalition D* is simply a subset of the set of all individuals; i.e., $D \subseteq N$. You should think of D as just a set of individuals, not individuals with fixed preferences. We will then define a coalition D to be *decisive over the pair* (x,y) *under the social choice function f* if the members of the coalition together have the powers of an Arrow Dictator with respect to the pair (x,y) of social states. In other words, we will say that the members of D are decisive over (x,y) if, *whenever* they all prefer y to x *and* everyone outside the coalition prefers x to y (or if the reverse holds), the coalition's preferences are those respected by the social choice rule f.

We will formalize this notion in two steps. First, we will formally define the limited notion of decisiveness of a coalition, "decisiveness over a pair of social states." We then define a more sweeping version of the concept, "full decisiveness over all pairs of social states." While these will seem quite different concepts of the power that a coalition has, we will demonstrate the surprising fact that, under any social choice function f that satisfies Arrow's axioms, it must be the case that if a coalition is decisive over a pair of social states it is in fact decisive over *all* pairs of social states. Notice that if a coalition D is composed of only a single member and is decisive over all pairs of social states, the single member of that coalition is an Arrow Dictator.

28B.3.1 Limited and Full Decisiveness of Coalitions
We now state our two different notions of the "decisiveness" of a coalition under a social choice function f more precisely. First, suppose there exist two social states, $x \in A$ and $y \in A$, and suppose we have a social choice function f that has the property that, for some $D \subseteq N$,

$$x \succsim^i y \ \forall\, i \in D \text{ and } y \succsim^j x \ \forall\, j \notin D \Rightarrow x \succsim y \tag{28.3}$$

and

$$y \succsim^i x \ \forall\, i \in D \text{ and } x \succsim^j y \ \forall\, j \notin D \Rightarrow y \succsim x, \tag{28.4}$$

where $\succsim = f(\{\succsim^n\}_{n=1}^N)$ (and where the $\forall$ symbol means "for all" and the "$\Rightarrow$" symbol means "implies"). In other words, we have a coalition D for which it is the case that members of the coalition get their choice of x over y under the social choice process f whenever the members of the coalition unanimously agree on their ranking of the pair (x,y) and everyone else disagrees. We will say that such a coalition D is *decisive over* (x,y) *under f*.

This initial definition of decisiveness of a coalition is *limited* to just a pair of social states. When a coalition is decisive over *all* possible pairs of social states in A under the social choice process f, then we will say that the coalition is *fully decisive under f*. Any coalition that is fully decisive is by definition decisive over a pair (x,y), but it does not logically follow that limited decisiveness over a pair of social states implies full decisiveness (over all possible pairs). It turns out, however, that limited decisiveness *does* imply full decisiveness when f is assumed to satisfy all five of Arrow's axioms, a proposition we will show to be true next.

28B.3.2 Limited Decisiveness Implies Full Decisiveness under Arrow's Axioms

Suppose, then, that under some social choice function f that satisfies all five of Arrow's axioms, a coalition $D \subseteq N$ is decisive over a pair (x,y) from the set of all possible social states A. The Universal Domain (UD) axiom implies that the individuals should be able to have any set of rational preferences over the social states in A. Suppose, then, that individual preferences $\{\succsim^n\}_{n=1}^N$ happen to result in preference orderings over alternatives x, y, and z such that

$$x \succsim^i y \succsim^i z \, \forall i \in D$$
$$y \succsim^j z \succsim^j x\text{-} \, \forall j \notin D. \tag{28.5}$$

Then, given that D is decisive over the pair (x, y), it must be the case that the social preference ordering $\succsim = f(\{\succsim^n\}_{n=1}^N)$ picks x over y; i.e.,

$$x \succsim y. \tag{28.6}$$

Exercise 28B.4   Explain why this conclusion follows from the definition of the decisiveness over (x,y) of the coalition D.

Furthermore, since f satisfies the Pareto Unanimity (PU) axiom, it also must be the case that the social preference ordering chooses y over z (since everyone agrees y is better than z); i.e.,

$$PU \Rightarrow y \succsim z. \tag{28.7}$$

Given conclusions (28.6) and (28.7), the Rationality Axiom (R) then implies that the social preference ordering choose x over z; i.e.,

$$R \Rightarrow x \succsim z. \tag{28.8}$$

But this means that the members of the coalition D appear to be decisive over the pair (x, z) as well. After all, only members of D prefer x to z, and everyone else prefers z to x, and we have just concluded that the social preference ordering sides with members of D. Furthermore, the IIA Axiom implies that this social preference ordering over x and z is independent of how people feel about y, which means that the position of y in the individual preference orderings in (28.5) can be switched around without affecting the conclusion $x \succsim z$. Thus, *whenever* the members of D prefer x to z and everyone else prefers z to x, the social preference ordering will choose x over z.

Exercise 28B.5*   By changing the the individual preference orderings in (28.5) and then proceeding through similar steps, can you show that it is similarly true that whenever members of D prefer z over x and everyone else disagrees, the social preference ordering that arises from f must pick z over x as well?

The same reasoning clearly holds for any other social state that appears in the set of possible social states A. Thus, we conclude that *if a coalition D is decisive over a pair of social states under f, then it must in fact be decisive over all social states under f if f satisfies Arrow's five axioms.*

28B.4 Proving Arrow's Theorem

We are now ready to demonstrate Arrow's Theorem that no social choice function f can simultaneously satisfy all five of Arrow's Axioms. The proof is a *proof by contradiction*. Such a proof begins by assuming that the theorem is false, that in fact there *does* exist a social choice function f that satisfies Arrow's five Axioms. It then uses these axioms to show that the assumption that such a function f exists leads to a logical contradiction and therefore cannot in fact be true.

28B.4.1 ND $\Rightarrow$ A Decisive Coalition Exists

One of Arrow's Axioms is the No Dictatorship (ND) Axiom. Recall that this axiom rules out the existence of an Arrow Dictator under the social choice function f; that is, it rules out the existence of a single individual who always gets his or her way in the social preference ordering whenever he or she is a minority of one. So let's define a coalition D that consists of everyone in N other than one person; for instance, let $D = \{2, 3, \ldots, N\}$ (where we have just left out individual 1). Since individual 1 cannot be an Arrow Dictator, there is at least one pair of social states over which individual 1 does not get his or her way in the social preference ordering when he or she feels one way and everyone else feels the opposite. Let that pair of social states be denoted (x, y).[6]

From the previous section, we know that limited decisiveness over a pair of social states actually implies full decisiveness of that coalition over all pairs of social states. Thus, given that our coalition $D = \{2, 3, \ldots, N\}$ is decisive over (x, y), it is also decisive over all other pairs in A.

This reasoning implies that *every* coalition of everyone but one person must be decisive. How can it be that both $D = \{2, 3, \ldots, N\}$ and $D' = \{1, 2, 3, \ldots, N-1\}$ can be decisive?

Exercise 28B.6

28B.4.2 UD, PU, R, and IIA $\Rightarrow$ Decisive Coalitions Contain Smaller Decisive Coalitions

Since we now know that a decisive coalition must always exist under a social choice function that satisfies Arrow's Axioms, let's begin with such a coalition $D \subset N$ where D contains at least two members (since ND rules out a single person being decisive). Now let's partition D into two subsets of individuals; i.e., $B \subset D$ and $C \subset D$ such that $B \cup C = D$ and $B \cap C = \emptyset$. The UD axiom implies that we are not restricting individual preferences, which means that preferences could be such that

$$x \succsim^i y \succsim^i z \; \forall \, i \in B$$

$$z \succsim^j x \succsim^j y \; \forall \, j \in C \qquad (28.9)$$

$$y \succsim^k z \succsim^k x \; \forall \, k \notin D.$$

Since we assume that the social preference ordering that arises from f is complete, it must be that the pair y and z is ranked. So, either $z > y$ or $y \succsim z$.

If $z > y$, then the social choice rule is siding with members of the coalition C in a case where only members of C prefer z to y and everyone else disagrees. By the IIA Axiom, that social preference ordering is preserved for *all* other individual preference profiles under which the pairwise orderings over y and z remains unchanged. Thus, in *every* case in which members of C prefer z to y and everyone else disagrees, the coalition C gets its way; i.e., coalition C is decisive over the pair (y, z), which, because of our result that limited decisiveness implies full decisiveness under Arrow's Axioms, implies that coalition C is fully decisive.

Now suppose instead that $y \succsim z$; i.e., the social choice function chooses y over z under the preference profile in (28.9). Since we started with the assumption that D is decisive, we also know that $x \succsim y$ since everyone in D prefers x to y and everyone outside D disagrees. The transitivity requirement in the R axiom then implies that $x \succsim z$. But this means that, in the

---

[6]Technically, the ND Axiom only requires a single instance of a preference ordering under which individual 1 is in a minority of 1 and does not get his way. But the IIA Axiom implies that if this single instance involves the pair (x, y), individual 1 will not get his way for *any* set of individual preferences where individual 1 feels one way about the pair (x, y) and everyone else disagrees, with the individual preference orderings over other alternatives relative to x and y irrelevant to the social ordering over this pair.

social ranking of x relative to z, the social choice function is siding with members of the coalition B against everyone else, and the IIA axiom implies that this will hold for all other individual preference orderings that maintain individual rankings over the pair (x, z). Thus, *whenever members of B prefer x over z and everyone else disagrees, members of B get their way.* Thus, the coalition B is decisive over the pair (x, z), which, because of our result that limited decisiveness implies full decisiveness under Arrow's Axioms, implies that coalition B is fully decisive.

Notice what we just concluded: Beginning with a decisive coalition D (which we know exists given the ND axiom), we split that coalition into two and found that, one way or another, one of the two subcoalitions will be decisive. Thus, so long as D contains at least two members, *any decisive coalition D (under f that satisfies Arrow's Axioms) can be divided into smaller subcoalitions with one of those subcoalitions again being decisive.*

28B.4.3 Proving Arrow's Theorem

We are now basically done with our proof for Arrow's Theorem. We began by assuming that we have a social choice function f that satisfies all five of Arrow's Axioms. We showed that this implies that there exists a coalition $D \subset N$ that is fully decisive. We then showed that so long as this coalition contains at least two members, it can be divided into two subcoalitions, with one of these being fully decisive. But so long as that subcoalition once again contains at least two members, it can (by the same reasoning) be further divided into two subcoalitions, with one of these once again being fully decisive. We can keep doing this, and sooner or later we will end up with a decisive coalition that only has a single member. And when we reach that point, we will have ended up with an Arrow Dictator, a single individual who, whenever she is a minority of 1, gets her preferences respected by the social preference ranking. But that contradicts our assumption that the social choice function f satisfies Arrow's five axioms. Since assuming that such a social choice function exists leads to a logical contradiction, we can conclude that such a function in fact does not exist.

This allows us to state Arrow's Theorem formally in two different ways. The first phrases the result as a negative one:

Arrow's Impossibility Theorem: In a world in which there are at least two individuals and at least three social states to choose from, there does not exist a social choice process that satisfies UD, ND, PU, R, and IIA.

Alternatively, we can rephrase the theorem as a positive result:

Arrow's Possibility Theorem: In a world in which there are at least two individuals and at least three social states to choose from, there exists a social choice process that satisfies UD, PU, R, and IIA. However, that social choice process violates ND and therefore results in an Arrow Dictator.

CONCLUSION

This chapter concludes our discussion of strategic considerations by economic agents in environments in which they are not "small" relative to their economic environment. Our discussion started in Chapter 23 with monopoly pricing and then turned in Chapter 24 to an introduction to game theory, which is the basic tool that has become the workhorse of economists and other social scientists who think about strategic decision making. We first applied these insights to firms that operate in noncompetitive environments and illustrated how strategic thinking can cause firm behavior to deviate from the socially optimal behavior we derived in a competitive (nonstrategic) environment. We then considered in Chapter 27 how strategic decision making can also play a role in consumer choices as these relate to goods that exhibit externalities. Finally, we concluded in this chapter with a discussion of why strategic decisions by actors in political institutions matter as we think about the crafting and implementation of public policy aimed at correcting situations when private incentives deviate from social goals.

Throughout the text, we have emphasized a view that society consists of three basic pillars of institutions: markets, civil society, and government. Economic incentives play a crucial role in each of these institutions, with particular economic problems sometimes best addressed by one of these pillars or by some combination of the three. We will return to this theme in our concluding chapter (Chapter 30) where I will attempt to pull together the lessons of the book to help you form a big-picture framework of thinking about the relative advantages and disadvantages faced by the different institutions that can address fundamental economic problems. But before we turn back to this big picture, we need to think a bit more explicitly about what it is that we actually wish for these institutions to achieve. We therefore turn in the next chapter to the question of "What is Good"; i.e., what is the "good" that we wish for different institutions to move us toward. The answer to that question will likely differ across individuals, and it will help shape how you take the lessons of microeconomics to construct your own way of thinking about the optimal balance of markets, civil society, and government.

END-OF-CHAPTER EXERCISES

28.1* In Chapter 4, we considered different ways of thinking about single-peaked preferences over two-dimensional issue spaces. We did so in particular in end-of-chapter exercise 4.11, which you can now revisit.

28.2† In the text, we discussed two main conditions under which the median voter's favored policy is also the Condorcet winner.

    A. Review the definition of a *Condorcet winner*.

        a. What are the two conditions under which we can predict that the median voter's position is such a Condorcet winner?

        b. Implicitly, we have assumed an odd number of voters (such that there exists a single median voter). Can you predict a range of possible policies that cannot be beaten in pairwise elections when there is an even number of voters and the conditions of the median voter theorem are otherwise satisfied?

        c. Suppose that the issue space is two-dimensional, as in the case where we have to choose spending levels on military and domestic priorities. Consider the following special case: All voters have ideal points that lie on a downward-sloping line in the two-dimensional space, and voters become worse off as the distance between their ideal point and the actual policy increases. Is there a Condorcet winner in this case?

        d. Revisit the "Anything-Can-Happen" theorem in the text. Suppose that the current policy A in our two-dimensional policy space is equal to the ideal point of the "median voter" along the line on which all ideal points lie. If you are an agenda setter and you can set up a sequence of pairwise votes, which other policies could you implement assuming the first vote in the sequence needs to put up a policy against A?

        e. In our discussion of the "Anything-Can-Happen" theorem, we raised the possibility of single-issue committees as a mechanism for disciplining the political process (and limiting the set of proposals that can come up for a vote in a full legislature). Is such structure necessary in our special case of ideal points falling on the same line in the two-dimensional policy space?

        f. In the more general case where we allow ideal points to lie anywhere, the agenda setter still has some control over what policy alternative gets constructed in a structure induced equilibrium in which single-issue committees play a role. In real-world legislatures, the ability of the agenda setter to name members of committees is often constrained by seniority rules that have emerged over time; i.e., rules that give certain "rights" to committee assignments based on the length of service of a legislator. Can we think of such rules or norms as further constraining the "Anything-Can-Happen" chaos of democratic decision making?

    B. Consider a simple example of how single-peaked and non-single-peaked tastes over policy might naturally emerge in a case where there is only a single dimensional issue. A voter has preferences that can be represented by the utility function $u(x, y) = xy$ where x is private consumption and y is a public good. The only contributor to y is the government, which employs a proportional tax rate t. Suppose $y = \delta t$.

        a. Suppose an individual has income I. Write his utility as a function of t, δ, and I.

        b. What shape does this function have with respect to the policy variable t?

---

*conceptually challenging
**computationally challenging
†solutions in Study Guide

    c.   At what t does this function reach its maximum?

    d.   Suppose that an individual with income I can purchase a perfect substitute to y on the private market at a price of 1 per unit. Determine, as a a function of I, at what level of t an individual will be indifferent between purchasing the private substitute and consuming the public good.

    e.   What does this imply for the real shape of the individual's preferences over the policy variable t, assuming $\delta > I/4$?

28.3 **Everyday Application:** *Why Vote?* Voting is costly. If you vote in person, you have to find your polling place and often stand in line until you get to the voting booth to vote. If you vote by absentee ballot, you have to figure out how to get one and then be sure to mail it in. In both cases, you probably have to do some work figuring out who the candidates are and what the issues are.

A. Many people purposefully choose not to vote, and they often give the following reason: "I don't think it matters." As we will see in this exercise, they might mean one of two things by this, and they appear to be right in at least one sense.

    a.   First, suppose we take the median voter model really seriously and believe it accurately predicts the position of the two candidates from which we choose. How might this justify the excuse given by voters who don't vote?

    b.   In the real world, there are many frictions that keep the median voter model's prediction from fully coming to fruition. For instance, candidates might have to win party nominations first and then run in the general election, which means we tend to end up with right-of-center and left-of-center candidates. In light of this, is it reasonable to think that the excuse given in (a) is justified in the real world?

    c.   Next, consider a different way in which the "it does not matter" statement might be meant: Perhaps a voter recognizes that it matters which candidate wins (in the sense that the world will change differently depending on which one wins), but she believes the candidate who will win will almost certainly win whether any individual voter goes to the polls or not. Do you think this is true in the real world?

    d.   In light of your answer to (c), might it be rational for many people not to vote?

    e.   In the 2008 U.S. presidential election, Barack Obama won by close to 10 million votes. In what sense is the puzzle not so much why more people didn't vote but rather why so many—about 60% of eligible voters—did.

    f.   Suppose we believe that governments are more effective the more voters engage in elections. In what sense does this imply that voters have Prisoner's Dilemma incentives that give rise to free riding?

    g.   In Chapter 27, we suggested that one way charitable organizations overcome free-rider problems among potential donors is to find ways of eliciting within donors a "warm glow" from giving. Can you think of an analogous explanation that can rationalize why so many people vote in large elections?

    h.   Suppose that the voters who do not vote are those who are "disillusioned." What positions might two candidates take on the Hotelling interval [0,1] if the disillusioned voters (who do not vote) are those who cannot find a candidate whose position is within 3/16ths of their ideal point? Could we have an equilibrium where the extreme ends of the political spectrum do not vote? Could we have one where the center does not vote?

B. In the 2000 U.S. presidential election, George W. Bush defeated Al Gore by 537 votes in Florida, and with those 537 votes won the election.

    a.   The close margin in the 2000 election is often cited by politicians as evidence that you should "not believe your vote does not matter." I would argue that it shows the opposite: Even in close elections, it is almost never the case that one vote counts. What do you think?

    b.   Ralph Nader, the Green Party candidate, received nearly 100,000 votes in Florida in the 2000 presidential election. Many believe that had Ralph Nader's name not been on the ballot, Al Gore would have won Florida, and with it the presidency. If so, which one of Arrow's axioms does this suggest is violated by the way the United States elects presidents? Explain.

    c.   Some election systems require the winning candidate to win with at least 50% plus 1 votes, and, if no candidate achieves this, require a run-off election between the top two candidates. Since this seems difficult to implement in the 50 statewide elections that result in electoral college votes that determine the winner of a U.S. presidential election, some have proposed a system of *instant run-off voting*. In such a system, voters rank the candidates from most preferred to least preferred. In the first round of vote counting, each voter's top ranked candidate is considered as having received a vote from that voter, and if one candidate gets 50% plus 1 votes, he or she is declared the winner. If no candidate receives that many votes, the election authorities find which candidate received the lowest first round votes and then reassign that candidate's votes to the candidates who were ranked second by these voters. If one candidate reaches 50% plus 1 votes, he or she wins; otherwise, the election authorities repeat the exercise, this time reassigning the votes of the candidate who initially received the second to last number of first place rankings. This continues until someone gets 50% plus 1 votes. Had Florida used this system in 2000, do you think the presidential election outcome might have been different?

d.* Nader is often referred to as a "spoiler" because of many people's belief that he "spoiled" the election outcome for Gore. *True or False*: It is much less likely that a third candidate plays the role of spoiler in an instant run-off election, but it is still possible if the third candidate is sufficiently strong.

28.4 **Everyday Application:** *"Winner-Take-All" Elections and the U.S. Electoral College*: In the United States, presidential elections are not won by the candidate who wins the popular vote nationally. (If they were won in this way, Al Gore would have become president in 2000.) Rather, each state is given a number of "electors" equal to that state's representation in the U.S. Congress. In almost all states, the candidate who gets the most votes gets all the electors of that state, and the presidency is won by the candidate who collects at least 270 electoral college votes.[7]

A. Consider a simplified version of this system in which there are only two states, with state 1 more than twice the size of state 2 and exactly twice the electoral college votes. Suppose all preferences are single peaked along a "left/right" continuum. Let n_i be the median voter's ideal point in state i, with $n_1 < n_2$. In the event of a statewide tie, assume the electoral college votes for the state are split.

a. If the aim of two presidential candidates is only to win, what position will they take in equilibrium?

b. Suppose instead that there are four states, states 2 and 3 that are small (with 10% of the electoral votes each) and states 1 and 4 that are large (with 40% of the electoral college votes each). Suppose further that the ideal points for median voters in each state are such that $n_1 < n_2 < n_3 < n_4$. What position do you now expect the candidates to take?

c. Explain how this relates to the common observation that most of the U.S. presidential election actually takes place in a subset of states, often called "battleground states," with the rest of the country largely ignored by the candidates.

d. In exercise 28.3, we suggested that one way to view the decision of whether or not to vote is by comparing the marginal benefit of voting to the marginal cost. The marginal benefit of voting includes the probability that one's vote will determine the outcome of the election. If this is a major consideration in people's decision of whether to vote, how would you expect voter participation in presidential elections to differ across states?

e. The electoral college system gives each state two electors outright plus one elector for each representative that the state has in the House of Representatives (where representation in the House is roughly in proportion to population). How would you evaluate the following statement: In such a system, we would expect, all else being equal, disproportionately more resources spent per voter in small states.

f. Some states have considered switching from a statewide winner-take-all system for electing "electors" in presidential races to a system in which electors from the state represent each candidate in proportion to the popular vote received in the state.[8] Which of your answers would be affected by such a change?

---

[7]If no candidate gets 270 electoral college votes because of a 269–269 tie or because of three candidates in the race, the U.S. House of Representatives decides the winning candidate. We will ignore this possibility here.
[8]Often such proposals envision winner-take-all elections at the House of Representatives District level, which comes close to proportional allocation of electors in large states. The states of Maine and Nebraska in fact allocate some of their electors in this way, and Nebraska was the only state in the 2008 election that therefore split its electoral vote.

g. Prior to running in the general election as either the Democratic or the Republican candidate, a politician first needs to win a party's presidential nomination. This is done mainly in earlier "primary" (or "caucus") elections held in each state. In the Republican nomination fight, almost all such primary elections are "winner-take-all" (like the electoral college system in the general election), but on the Democratic side, most primaries allocate votes to each candidate proportionally. In which party would you expect more states to be ignored during the nomination fight?

B. In exercise 28.3, we used the 2000 election and the controversy regarding Ralph Nader's participation to suggest that the way we elect U.S. presidents violates the spirit of Arrow's IIA axiom. Is there any reason to believe that this would be less true if the United States switched to a proportional system of electing its presidents?

28.5 **Everyday Application:** *To Enter or Not to Enter the Race*: Suppose there are three possible candidates who might run for office, and each has to decide whether or not to enter the race. Assume the electorate's ideal points can be defined by the Hotelling line from Chapter 26; i.e., the ideal points are uniformly distributed on the interval [0,1].

A. Let π_i denote the probability that candidate i will win the election. Suppose that the payoff to a candidate jumping into the race is $(\pi_i - c)$ where c is the cost of running a campaign.

a. How high must the probability of getting elected be in order for a candidate to get into the race?

b. Consider the following model: In stage 1, three potential candidates decide simultaneously whether or not to get into the race and pay the cost c. Then, in stage 2, they take positions on the Hotelling line, with voters then choosing in an election where the candidate who gets the most votes wins. *True or False*: If there is a Nash equilibrium in stage 2 of the game, it must be that the probability of winning is the same for each candidate that entered the race in stage 1.

c. Suppose there is a Nash equilibrium in stage 2 regardless of how many of the three candidates entered in stage 1. What determines whether there will be one, two, or three candidates running in the election?

d. Suppose that the probability of winning in stage 2 is a function of the number of candidates who are running as well as the amount spent in the campaign, with candidates able to choose different levels of c when they enter in stage 1 but facing an increasing marginal cost $p(c)$ for raising campaign cash. (The payoff for a candidate is therefore now $(\pi_i - p(c))$.) In particular, suppose the following: Campaign spending matters only in cases where an election run solely on issues would lead to a tie (in the sense that each candidate would win with equal probability). In that case, whoever spent the most wins the election. What might you expect the possible equilibria in stage 1 (where entry and campaign spending are determined simultaneously) to look like?

e. Suppose the incumbent is one of the potential candidates, and he decides whether to enter the race and how much to spend first. Can you in this case see a role for strategic entry deterrence similar to what we developed for monopolists who are threatened by a potential entrant?

f. With the marginal cost of raising additional funds to build up a campaign war chest increasing, might the incumbent still allow entry of another candidate?

B. Consider the existence of a Nash equilibrium in stage 2.

a. What are two possible ways in which three candidates might take positions in the second stage of our game such that your conclusion in A(b) holds?

b. Can either of these be an equilibrium under the conditions specified in part A?

c. Suppose that, instead of voter ideal points being uniformly distributed on the Hotelling line, one third of all voters hold the median voter position (with the remining two thirds uniformly distributed on the Hotelling line). How does your conclusion about the existence of a stage 2 Nash equilibrium with three candidates change? Does your conclusion from A(c) still hold?

28.6* **Everyday Application:** *Citizen Candidates*: Whenever we have modeled political candidates who stand for election, we have assumed that they care only about winning and are perfectly content to change their position in whatever way maximizes the probability of winning. Now consider a different way of thinking about political candidates: Suppose that the citizens again have uniformly distributed ideal points on the Hotelling line [0,1]. Before any election is held, each citizen has to decide whether to pay the cost $c > 0$ to run as a candidate, with the payoff from probability π of winning the election equal to $(\pi - c)$.

A. Assume candidates cannot change their position from their ideal point, and citizens who do not become candidates get payoff equal to minus the distance of the winning candidate position x^* to their own on [0,1]. The highest attainable payoff for a noncandidate is therefore 0. (Candidates who lose get the same payoff as citizens who do not run, except that they also incur cost c from having run.)

    a. For what range of c is the following an equilibrium: A citizen with the median position 0.5 is the only candidate to enter the race and thus wins.

    b. How high does c have to be in order for the following to be a possible equilibrium: A citizen with position 0.25 enters the race as the only candidate and therefore wins. How high must c be for an equilibrium to have a citizen with position 0 be the only candidate to run (and thus win)?

    c. For what range of c will it be an equilibrium for two candidates with position 0.5 to compete in the election?

    d. For what range of c is it an equilibrium for two candidates with positions 0.25 and 0.75 to compete?

    e. For what range of c is it an equilibrium for two candidates with positions 0 and 1 to compete?

B. Consider the same set-up as in part A.

    a. Let $x \in [0,0.5)$. For what range of c is it an equilibrium for a citizen with position x to be the only candidate to run for office? Is your answer consistent with what you derived for A(b)?

    b. For what range of c is it an equilibrium for two candidates to compete, one taking position x and the other taking the position $(1 - x)$? Is your answer consistent with your answers to A(d) and A(e)?

    c. Let ϵ be arbitrarily close to zero. For what range of c will two candidates with positions $(0.5 - \epsilon)$ and $(0.5 + \epsilon)$ be able to run against one another in equilibrium? What does this range converge to as ϵ converges to zero?

    d. How does the range you calculated in (c) compare to the range of c that makes it possible for two candidates with position 0.5 to run against one another in equilibrium (as derived in A(c))?

28.7[†] **Business and Policy Application:** *Voting with Points:* Jean-Charles de Borda (1733–99), a contemporary of Condorcet in France, argued for a democratic system that deviates from our usual conception of majority rule. The system works as follows: Suppose there are M proposals. Each voter is asked to rank these, with the proposal ranked first by a voter given M points, the one ranked second given $(M - 1)$ points, and so forth.[9] The points given to each proposal are then summed across all voters, and the top N proposals are chosen, where N might be as low as 1. This voting method, known as the *Borda Count,* is used in a variety of corporate and academic settings as well as some political elections in countries around the world.

BUSINESS APPLICATION

POLICY APPLICATION

A. Suppose there are five voters denoted 1 through 5, and there are five possible projects $\{A, B, C, D, E\}$ to be ranked. Voters 1 through 3 rank the projects in alphabetical sequence (with A ranked highest). Voter 4 ranks C highest, followed by D, E, B, and finally A. Voter 5 ranks E highest, followed by C, D, B, and finally A.

    a. How does the Borda Count rank these? If only one can be implemented, which one will it be?

    b. Suppose option D was withdrawn from consideration before the vote in which voters rank the options. How does the Borda Count now rank the remaining projects? If only one can be implemented, which one will it be?

    c. What if both D and E are withdrawn?

    d. Suppose I get to decide which projects will be considered by the group and the group allows me to use my discretion to eliminate projects that clearly do not have widespread support. Will I be able to manipulate the outcome of the Borda Count by strategically picking which projects to leave off?

---

[9] There exist other versions of Borda's method, such as assigning (M − 1) points to the top ranked choice and leaving zero for the last ranked. For purposes of this problem, define the method as it is defined in the problem.

B. Arrow's Theorem tells us that any nondictatorial social choice function must violate at least one of his remaining four axioms.

    a.   Do you think the Borda Count violates Pareto Unanimity? What about Universal Domain or Rationality?

    b.   In what way do your results from part A of the exercise tell us something about whether the Borda Count violates the Independence of Irrelevant Alternatives (IIA) axiom?

    c.   Derive again the Borda Count ranking of the five projects in part A given the voter preferences as described.

    d.   Suppose voter 4 changed his mind and now ranks B second and D fourth (rather than the other way around). Suppose further that voter 5 similarly switches the position of B and D in her preference ordering and now ranks B third and D fourth. If a social choice function satisfies IIA, which social rankings cannot be affected by this change in preferences?

    e.   How does the social ordering of the projects change under the Borda Count? Does the Borda Count violate IIA?

28.8 **Policy Application:** *Interest Groups, Transactions Costs, and Vote Buying*: Suppose that a legislature has to vote for one of two mutually exclusive proposals: proposal A or B. Two interest groups are willing to spend money on getting their preferred proposal implemented, with interest group 1 willing to pay up to y^A to get A implemented and interest group 2 willing to pay up to y^B to get proposal B passed. Both interest groups get payoff of zero if the opposing group's project gets implemented. Legislators care first and foremost about campaign contributions and will vote for the proposal whose supporters contributed more money, but they have a weak preference for project B in the sense that they will vote for B if they received equal amounts from both interest groups.

A. To simplify the analysis, suppose that there are only three legislators. Suppose further that interest group 1 makes its contribution first, followed by interest group 2.

    a.   If $y^A = y^B$, will any campaign contributions be made in a subgame-perfect equilibrium?

    b.   Suppose $1.5y^B > y^A > y^B$. Does your answer to (a) change?

    c.   Suppose $y^A > 1.5y^B$. What is the subgame-perfect equilibrium now?

    d.   Suppose that project B is extending milk price support programs while project A is eliminating such programs, and suppose that $y^A > 1.5y^B$ because milk price support programs are inefficient. Interest group 1 represents milk consumers and interest group 2 represents milk producers. Which interest group do you think will find it easier to mobilize its members to give the necessary funds to buy votes in the legislature?

    e.   Suppose $y^A > 3y^B$. It costs interest group 2 exactly \$1 for every dollar in contributions to a legislator, but, because of the transactions costs of organizing its members, it costs interest group 1 an amount \$c per \$1 contributed to a legislator. How high does c need to be in order for the inefficient project to be passed?

    f.   How might the free-rider problem be part of the transactions costs that affect interest group 1 disproportionately?

B. Consider the problem faced by the interest groups in light of results derived in Chapter 27. In particular, suppose that all members of interest group A have tastes $u^A(x, y) = x^\alpha y^{(1-\alpha)}$ where x is private consumption and y is a function of the likelihood that project A is implemented. Members of interest group B similarly have tastes $u^B(x, y) = x^\beta y^{(1-\beta)}$ where y is a function of the likelihood that project B is implemented. Suppose that interest groups have successfully persuaded members to believe y is equal to the sum of their contributions to the interest group. Everyone has income I, and there are N^A members of interest group 1 and N^B members of interest group 2.

    a.   What is the equilibrium level of contributions to the two interest groups?

    b.   Suppose again that B is a renewal of an inefficient government program with concentrated benefits and diffuse costs and A is the elimination of the program. What does this imply about the relationship between N^A and N^B? What does it imply about the relationship between α and β?

    c.   Suppose $N^A = 10{,}000$, $N^B = 6$, $I = 1{,}000$, $\alpha = 0.8$, and $\beta = 0.6$. How much will each interest group raise? How does your answer change if N^A is 100,000 instead? What if it is 1,000,000?

    d.   Suppose that β is also 0.8 (and thus equal to α). If the vote-buying process is as described in part A, will legislation B pass even though there are 1,000,000 members of interest group 1 and only 6 in interest group 2?

    e.   Finally, suppose that there is only a single beneficiary of B. How much will he contribute when $\beta = 0.8$? What if $\beta = 0.6$? Within this example, can even one concentrated beneficiary stop a project that benefits no one other than him?

28.9 **Policy Application:** *Political Coalitions and Public School Finance Policy*: In this exercise, we consider some policy issues related to public support for schools, and the coalitions between income groups that might form to determine the political equilibrium.

  A. Throughout, suppose that individuals vote on only the single dimension of the issue at hand, and consider a population that is modeled on the Hotelling line [0,1] with income increasing on the line. (Thus, individual 0 has the lowest income and individual 1 has the highest income, with individual 0.5 being the median income individual.)

    a.   Consider first the case of public school funding in the absence of the existence of private school alternatives. Do you think the usual median voter theorem might hold in this case, with the public school funding level determined by the ideal point of the median income household?

    b.   Next, suppose private schools compete with public schools, with private schools charging tuition and public schools funded by taxes paid by everyone. How does this change the politics of public school funding?

    c.   Some have argued that political debates on public school funding are driven by "the ends against the middle." In terms of our model, this means that the households on the ends of the income distribution on the Hotelling line will form a coalition with one another, with households in the middle forming the opposing coalition. What has to be true about who disproportionately demands private schooling in order for this "ends against the middle" scenario to unfold?

    d.   Assume that the set of private school students comes from high income households. What would this model predict about the income level of the the new median voter?

    e.   Consider two factors: First, the introduction of private schools causes a change in the income level of the median voter, and second, we now have private school attending households that pay taxes but do not use public schools. In light of this, can you tell whether per pupil public school spending increases or decreases as private school markets attract less than half the population? What if they attract more than half the population?

    f.   So far, we have treated public school financing without reference to the local nature of public schools. In the United States, public schools have traditionally been funded locally, with low income households often constrained to live in public school districts that provide low quality. How might this explain an "ends against the middle" coalition in favor of private school vouchers (that provide public funds for households to pay private school tuition)?

    g.*   In the 1970s, California switched from local financing of public schools to statewide (and equalized) financing of its public schools. Statewide school spending appears to have declined as a result. Some have explained this by appealing to the fact that the income distribution is skewed to the left, with the statewide median income below the statewide mean income. Suppose that local financing implies that each public school is funded by roughly identical households (who have self-selected into different districts as our Chapter 27 Tiebout model would predict), while state financing implies that the public school spending level is determined by the state median voter. Can you explain how the skewedness of the state income distribution can then explain the decline in statewide public school spending as the state switched from local to state financing?

  B.* Suppose preferences over private consumption x, a public good y, and leisure ℓ can be described by the utility function $u(x, y, \ell) = x^{\alpha} y^{\beta} \ell^{\gamma}$. Individuals are endowed with the same leisure amount L and share the same preferences but have different wages. Until part (e), taxes are exogenous.

    a.   Suppose a proportional wage tax t is used to fund the public good y and a tax rate t results in public good level $y = \delta t$. Calculate the demand function for x and the labor supply function. (Note: Since t is not under the control of individuals, neither t nor y are choice variables at this point.)

b. Suppose instead that a per-capita tax T is used to fund the public good; i.e., everyone has to pay an equal amount T. Suppose that a per-capita tax T results in public good level $y = T$. Calculate the demand function for x and the labor supply function.

c. *True or False*: Since the wage tax does not result in a distortion of the labor supply decision while the per-capita tax does, the former has no deadweight loss while the latter does.

d. Calculate the indirect utility function for part (a) (as a function of L, w, and t).

e. Now suppose that a vote is held to determine the wage tax t. What tax rate will be implemented under majority rule? (*Hint*: Use your result from (d) to determine the ideal point for a voter.)

f. Suppose that y is per pupil spending on public education. What does this imply that δ is (in terms of average population income $\bar{I}$, number of taxpayers K, and number of kids N in school)?

g. Now suppose there exists a private school market that offers spending levels demanded by those interested in opting out of public education (and assume that spending is all that matters in people's evaluation of school quality). People attending private school no longer attend public school but still have to pay taxes. Without doing any additional math, what are the possible public school per pupil spending levels y that you think could emerge in a voting equilibrium (assuming that public education is funded through a proportional wage tax)? Who will go to what type of school?

h. Can you think of necessary and sufficient conditions for the introduction of a private school market to result in a Pareto improvement in this model?

i. In (e), you should have concluded that, under the proportional wage tax, everyone unanimously agrees on what the tax rate should be (when there are no private schools). Would the same be true if schools were funded by a per-capita tax T?

28.10[†] **Policy Application:** *Government Competition, Leviathan, and Benevolence*: Suppose governments can spend taxpayer resources on both public goods that have social benefits and political "rents" that are private benefits for government officials. To the extent to which governments emphasize the latter over the former, we have called them "Leviathan," and this exercise investigates to what extent competition between governments can restrain this Leviathan. To the extent to which governments emphasize the former, we will call them "benevolent." In part B of the exercise, we consider competition between such benevolent governments.

A. Consider a collection N of local governments that can employ local property taxes to fund public goods and local political rents. Suppose that local governments are pure Leviathans; i.e., they seek only political rents. For simplicity, suppose also that all households are identical.

a. Begin with a simple demand and supply (for housing) graph for one community. If a local Leviathan government is a political monopolist in the sense that it faces no competitive pressures from other communities, how would it go about setting the tax rate that maximizes its rents?

b. Now consider the case where households are fully mobile across jurisdictional boundaries and thus choose to live where their utility is highest. In equilibrium, how must utility in any jurisdiction i be related to utility in any other jurisdiction j?

c. Suppose that the property tax is zero in all communities. Consider community i's Leviathan mayor. If he raises t_i above zero and uses the revenues only for political rents, what will have to be true about housing prices in community i after the tax is imposed (relative to before it is imposed)? Can you demonstrate how this comes about? (*Hint*: Consider the competitive pressure from household mobility.)

d. *True or False*: So long as housing supply is not perfectly elastic, the Leviathan mayor in part (c) will be able to raise property taxes to fund political rents.

e. Now consider all local governments setting some tax rate t and using revenues for political rents. If t is very low, can a single community's Leviathan's mayor benefit from raising his tax rate? If t is very high, can a single Leviathan mayor benefit from lowering his tax rate?

f. Use your answer to (e) to argue that there must exist some level of Leviathan taxation across competing communities that will be a Nash equilibrium.

g. Evaluate the following statement: "Unless housing supply is perfectly elastic, government competition between Leviathan governments is not sufficient to eliminate political rents, but it restrains the ability of Leviathan government to amass such rents."

h. *True or False*: To the extent to which government behavior is characterized by rent seeking, greater competition between governments enhances efficiency.

B. Next, consider the opposite type of government, i.e., one that is benevolent and raises taxes only to the extent to which it can find worthwhile public goods to finance. Suppose again that there are N such governments that use a local property tax to fund local public goods, and suppose that all public benefits from such public goods are contained within each government's jurisdictional boundaries.

a. Begin, as in A(a), by assuming that there is mobility of consumers across jurisdictions and thus no government faces any competitive pressures. Will they produce the efficient level of local public goods?

b. Next, consider the competitive case. If the projects funded by local governments are truly local public goods, in what sense are taxes imposed by benevolent governments offset by benefits received?

c. Suppose governments are charging low tax rates that result in inefficiently low levels of public goods. If community i raises its tax rate and provides more public goods, will population increase or decrease in community i? Will housing prices go up or down?

d. Consider an equilibrium with benevolent local governments providing efficient levels of local public goods. Can any government raise property values by raising or lowering taxes? *True or False*: Property value maximizing local governments behave like benevolent local governments.

e. Suppose next that local property taxes are paid by both households and firms, but only households benefit from local public goods (like schools). If firms are mobile, in what sense does community i's decision to tax the property of firms give rise to a positive externality for other communities?

f. What does your answer to (e) imply about the spending levels by benevolent local governments as competitive pressures increase in environments such as those described in (e)?

28.11 Policy Application: *The Pork Barrel Commons and the "Law of* $1/N$*"*: If you did not do these in Chapter 27, you can now do end-of-chapter exercises 27.11 and 27.12 to explore the problem of pork barrel projects and the "Law of $1/N$."

**POLICY
APPLICATION**

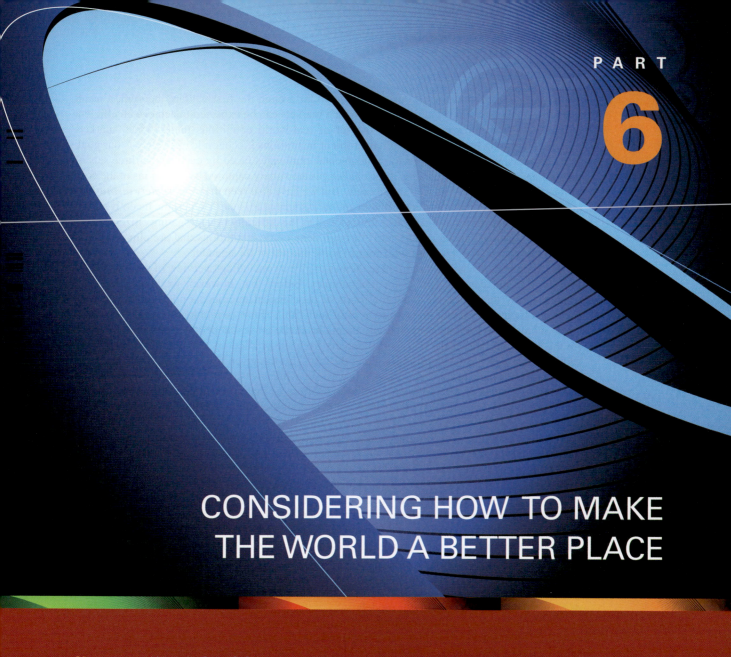

CONSIDERING HOW TO MAKE
THE WORLD A BETTER PLACE

We have organized virtually all our discussion so far around the first welfare theorem, a result that tells us precisely the conditions under which markets can be expected to achieve an efficient outcome and thus implicitly outlines the set of real-world conditions under which markets require fine-tuning by civil society or government institutions if economic efficiency is our goal. In the process, we have also seen the fundamental challenges faced by each of the three sets of institutions in society. For *markets*, these challenges are simply captured by violations of the conditions that underlie the first welfare theorem. But we have also seen that *civil society institutions* are often plagued by the free-rider problem and its associated Prisoner's Dilemma incentives, and *governments* face informational constraints as well as the difficulty of aggregating citizen preferences into coherent "social preferences" through democratic institutions that are almost always subject to manipulation by those who control some aspects of the agenda.

In Chapter 30, we will return to these themes to give a concluding overview of the big-picture lessons from our development of microeconomics. Before that, however, we take a detour in Chapter 29 by thinking a bit about the limits of neoclassical microeconomics and its primary focus on efficiency. We will find two sources of such limits: First, psychologists have compiled a set of anomalies to economic predictions, anomalies in the sense that people's observed behavior (in the laboratory and/or the real world) departs from the predictions that emerge from models such as those we have developed throughout the text. This has given rise to the field of *behavioral economics* in which researchers adapt the ways in which we have modeled preferences and constraints to account for systematic psychological biases that appear to be important in some types of decisions we make. While behavioral economists continue with our basic premise that "people try to do the best they can given their circumstances," their models differ in the sense that "best" and "circumstances" might include psychological elements not present in the standard microeconomics framework.

The work of behavioral economists is potentially important in the sense that it challenges some very basic notions shared by many mainstream economists in regard to answering the question "what is good." The most obvious example of this involves the idea of expanding choice sets, with the typical economist usually arguing that expanding choice sets must be "good" for people (unless some violation of the first welfare theorem is involved). Behavioral economists, however, have shown ways in which psychological biases in decision making might in fact cause us to think of contracted choice sets as "good" under some circumstances. We will explore this and related topics in our discussion of behavioral economics in Chapter 29 before considering in some more depth the idea of "utility" or "happiness" and what it might actually mean to people as opposed to what it means in our models.

This then leads us to the branch of economics known as *normative economics* as distinguished from positive economics that has framed most of our previous chapters. To the extent to which we have implicitly assumed that "efficiency is good" in previous chapters, we have in fact already taken a particular normative position, but one we have repeatedly pointed out is probably in need of further elaboration. The latter part of Chapter 29 does just that, introducing the idea of incorporating various types of ethical criteria into an analysis of what "the good society" might actually look like. While economists are not trained to be philosophers, and philosophers sometimes define economists as "bad philosophers," we will see that this normative branch of economics intersects with particular branches of philosophy. At the same time, we will suggest that philosophers probably think much more deeply about some of the issues that we treat superficially in normative economics, and that there may well be much room for greater dialogue between philosophy and economics.

What Is Good? Challenges from Psychology and Philosophy

As we mentioned at the outset of this text, the human being is considerably more complex than the simplified models used by economists, but the purpose of the models is not to fully represent what it means to be human.[1] Rather, the purpose is to predict and understand individual as well as aggregate behavior and, in many cases, to find ways of improving human welfare as a result of our increased understanding. There is, however, a considerable leap from modeling behavior well to knowing "what is good" for us. If the model does not incorporate all the complexities of who we are, is it useful as we move from considering "what is" to "what is good"?

We have implicitly attempted to do just that in modest ways throughout the text, using notions of consumer surplus and profit to arrive at concepts like deadweight loss and efficiency-enhancing policy. The first welfare theorem has offered us a framework on which to consider how individual incentives might deviate from social goals, particularly when those goals center on achieving outcomes that exploit all possible efficiency gains. But economics is not the only discipline that thinks about human *welfare*, and "human welfare" may well mean more than is captured by the definitions of "surplus" that emerge from within the very models we readily admit are almost grotesque in the simplicity with which they treat the human condition. It is furthermore not the only discipline to investigate human *behavior*, with psychology in particular exposing a number of ways in which such behavior might, under certain circumstances, deviate from what economic models would predict. And philosophers of course think about the human condition in much deeper ways, ways that we will see interact with normative economics. In thinking about the question "what is good," we therefore consider in this chapter how our views might be influenced by insights from other disciplines.

In some of our chapters, we have already done a little of that, as, for example, in our considerations of how cooperation in Prisoner's Dilemmas may emerge for reasons having to do with how we sometimes "bring each other along" to reach tipping points in the presence of network effects. In some end-of-chapter exercises, we have furthermore emphasized the role of social norms, of ideas like "fairness" that might cause us to engage in behavior that might seem against our immediate self-interest while reinforcing our valued "identity" of standing up for "what is right." Some of these topics cross not only into the area of psychology but also of sociology, with economists now more frequently than ever collaborating with sociologists on various topics of mutual interest.

---

[1]This chapter relies on a basic understanding of consumer theory up to and including Chapter 7 as well as the basic idea behind the efficiency-focused first welfare theorem introduced in Chapter 15. The idea of Edgeworth Boxes from Chapter 16 is briefly mentioned but not essential for part A of the chapter. Part B of the chapter also builds on insights of expected utility theory as articulated in the first two sections of Chapter 17.

We will now consider some intersections of economics and two particular disciplines more directly with the aim of illustrating some of the complexities of moving from "what is" to "what is good" while hopefully bringing a bit of clarity to the possible limits of neoclassical economics. To be more precise, we will touch on intersections between economics and psychology, asking whether insights from psychology can in some circumstances not only improve the predictive power of our models but also change the way we think about "what is good" in markets, civil society, and government policy. And we will investigate the intersection of economics with philosophy, asking once again how positive models can help us formulate answers to the question "What is good?"

29A Who Are We Really, and What Is It All About?

The point of this chapter, then, is not to give an answer to the question "What is good?" in the way we might expect to have an answer to the question "What will people do when the price of gasoline doubles?" Rather, it is to provide some lenses through which one might tackle this normative question in light of the positive theory and results that form the core of microeconomics. As we will see, a tilting of economic models toward psychology will suggest that some scenarios that the economist might instinctively conclude are "not good" might in fact be viewed differently when insights from psychology are incorporated into our positive models of behavior. For instance, unless some violation of the first welfare theorem is involved, an individual's choice set A that strictly contains a smaller choice set B would typically be regarded by economists as unambiguously "better" since individuals can always choose not to take advantage of the additional choices available in A and thus cannot be made worse off by them. Yet we do not have to look too far beyond our everyday experience to realize that we sometimes actively seek to limit the choices we will have in cases such as when we throw away the leftover cake to keep ourselves from coming back for more rather than put it in the refrigerator to preserve the option to eat more later. We will see that introducing some psychology insights can explain why we might at times diagnose ourselves as having self-control problems, and why this might cause us to sometimes conclude that fewer options are "better" than more options. We'll also see how little things in life might matter in ways that traditional economic theory will not pick up, and how this too can change how we think about "what is good."

While our treatment of the impact of psychology on economics in Section 29A.1 gets at the question of "what is good" by expanding positive models of economic behavior, the remainder of the chapter then tackles the question from a more normative perspective. We will begin in Section 29A.2 by asking what it is that we really mean by "happiness" and how it might or might not relate to the "good" that we are attempting to define. This will take us into a brief discussion of some survey results on "happiness" and its causes as well as down a more philosophical road, both of which will suggest that the "happiness" modeled by positive economists in their attempts to predict probably lacks the depth that real human beings ascribe to it. With these caveats in mind, we then consider what we will call "consequentialist" approaches to normative economics in Section 29A.3 before concluding in Section 29A.4 with alternative philosophical approaches that rely more on notions of "process justice" rather than "outcome justice."

29A.1 Psychology and Behavioral Economics

Much of the criticism leveled against neoclassical microeconomics comes from perceptions of conflicts between the discipline of economics and the discipline of psychology, and the (often mistaken) notion that economists believe everyone is always rational and selfish in particularly stark ways. But, while tension between the disciplines is undeniable, recent years have also seen increasing synergies between them, synergies that have formed the basis for the new subfield of *behavioral economics* in which insights from psychology are incorporated into economic models (and the even newer subfield of *neuroeconomics* in which neuroscientists and economists jointly investigate how the physiology of the brain impacts decision making under different circumstances).

The impetus for much of this cross-disciplinary collaboration stems from widespread documentations of "behavioral anomalies"—systematic ways in which observed human behavior appears to depart from economic predictions in some circumstances. As evidence on such "anomalies" became empirically compelling, behavioral economists began to explore how psychology-based modifications of traditional neoclassical economic assumptions might lead to new models that better predict behavior. This is not without controversy among economists, some of whom believe that the motivating "anomalies" can just as easily be rationalized through more careful economic modeling that does not borrow from psychology. Competing models, some drawing more on psychology and others relying primarily on expanded neoclassical assumptions, continue to be tested (to see which better fit the available data) as the debate on the degree to which economics and psychology need one another continues. We will not settle this debate here but merely present some of the main anomalies and most compelling behavioral explanations for them in this section.

Before proceeding, we should note that the subfield of behavioral economics is understood differently in different quarters, which is not unexpected given that the merging of economics and psychology is a relatively recent phomonenon. Some scholars who see themselves as behavioral economists specialize in documenting examples of "anomalies" within laboratory settings where people are observed as they make decisions in controlled settings. Such scholars are therefore also practitioners of another relatively recent subfield known as *experimental economics*. Obtaining experimental data through controlled laboratory experiments does not, however, come as naturally to most economists as it does to psychologists, with many economists arguing that the settings can seem artificial and withdrawn from the richness in which real-world decisions are made, that they frequently don't permit for the kind of learning that happens in the real world, and that they so often rely on a very peculiar group (undergraduates) as subjects. There is, in fact, considerable evidence that not all experimental results are robust to repetitions and learning. Still, some experimental evidence, repeatedly replicated under different conditions, is so compelling that it has had an impact on our discipline, usually because we see echos of the same phenomena in data from the real world. We should nevertheless keep in mind, however, that experiments in and of themselves are not what define behavioral economics even if experimental results have often clarified how new features might be usefully included in existing economic models by behavioral economists.

While we will therefore make some occasional reference to experiments, the real meat of behavioral economics for our purposes lies in the conceptual paths it has opened and the ways in which it has allowed us to modify some of our previous models to help explain *real-world* phenomena that are otherwise difficult to reconcile with economic analysis. Behavioral economics *does not* require that we let go of the fundamental approach that ties together all of microeconomics—that people "try to do the best they can given their circumstances." Instead, it highlights for us aspects of what is "best" and what kinds of "circumstances" might matter. Put differently, it helps us think more carefully about features of tastes (in Sections 29A.1.1 and 29A.1.2) and constraints (in Section 29A.1.3) that might be important and that we would probably neglect without the prodding from those pesky psychologists.

29A.1.1 Present-Biased Preferences and Self-Control Problems   Most smokers plan to quit at some point in the future and believe they will in fact quit even though they find it too costly to quit today. We plan to start exercising and eat better—next year. We have every intention of saving more for retirement as we drag home that big-screen TV we just charged to a credit card. And, after staying up several nights in a row to cram for midterms, you vow to not let that happen again during finals week, but first you decide you need a little time to blow off some steam and get away from all that "school stuff." These are all examples of behavior that suggests *time inconsistent* preferences, the kinds of preferences that make us think something in the future will be worthwhile but, without any change other than the passage of time, we change our mind when the future comes. Put differently, such behavior suggests that there is something special about the "present"—the "here and now"—and because the future invariably becomes the present with the passage of time, the future will become similarly "special" when it arrives. Such *present-bias* then leads to *preference reversals* that are of no particular surprise to psychologists who have long studied human *self-control problems*. But they *are* unexpected when viewed through the lens of the standard microeconomist's model of time-consistent intertemporal choice, the kind of choice where people end up doing what they plan to do unless circumstances change.

Consider a simple example in which we suppose that $1 in period $(t + 1)$ is always worth $\$\delta < \$1$ to you in period t. You are currently in period 0 and are thinking about what you will do in period 1 when you can take an action like studying or not smoking or saving that will cost you c but will get you a benefit b in period 2. Looking ahead from period 0, your present discounted value of c one period later is δc and your present discounted value of b in two periods is $\delta(\delta)b = \delta^2 b$. So you'll look ahead and conclude that the costly action in period 1 is worth taking so long as $\delta c < \delta^2 b$, which reduces to $c < \delta b$. Then, when period 1 comes and you actually have to undertake the costly action, you will incur a cost c now and get a benefit b one period later, with the present discounted value of b now equal to δb. Thus you will in fact take the action next period so long as $c < \delta b$. Your view of the action one period in the future is the same as your view when period 1 comes because we have not assumed that there is anything special about the "present" that will cause you to change your mind when the future becomes the present. Your tastes are therefore fully *time consistent*, with your decision rule as to whether or not to invest in period 1 the same when you look ahead from period 0 as when you face the actual choice in period 1. This is illustrated in the first row of Table 29.1.

But suppose that the way we evaluate costs and benefits is a bit different. Instead of evaluating $1 next period as worth $\$\delta$ and $1 two periods from now as $\$\delta^2$, we value the $1 next period at $\$\beta\delta$ and the $1 two periods from now at $\$\beta\delta^2$. Now let's revisit our decision of whether to undertake an action that costs c in period 1 but yields benefit b in period 2. As we think about our decision today (in period 0), we will value c one period from now at $\beta\delta c$ and b two periods from now at $\beta\delta^2 b$, and we will forecast the action in period 1 to be worthwhile so long as $\beta\delta c < \beta\delta^2 b$, which reduces to $c < \delta b$ just as it did before. This is illustrated as the first entry under $t = 0$ for the "$\beta - \delta$ Model" in Table 29.1. But now consider what happens when we actually have to undertake the costly action as we find ourselves in period 1, when period 1 has become the "present": We now face an immediate cost of c and value the benefit b next period at $\beta\delta b$, implying that we will undertake the action so long as $c < \beta\delta$. If $\beta \neq 1$, our decision rule has changed as the future became the present! And if $\beta < 1$, this implies that we might look from period 0 toward period 1 and think the investment worthwhile, but when period 1 rolls around, we may end up concluding that the investment isn't actually such a good idea after all. That's time-inconsistent.

Exercise 29A.1   Suppose $c = 100$, $b = 125$, $\delta = 0.95$, and $\beta = 0.8$. What is the expected value of undertaking the investment c in period 1 when viewed from $t = 0$? What is it when viewed from $t = 1$?

This model, known as the *beta-delta model*, has been adapted from similar models used to explain animal behavior since the mid-1900s and is now used by behavioral economists to explain

Table 29.1: Conditions for Investing c at $t = 1$ to Get b at $t = 2$

	Preference Reversals	
	$t = 0$	$t = 1$
"δ Model"	$c + \delta b > 0$	$c + \delta b > 0$
"$\beta - \delta$ Model"	$c + \delta b > 0$	$c + \beta\delta b > 0$

Chapter 29. What Is Good? Challenges from Psychology and Philosophy

1133

the many empirical findings of individual self-control problems.[2] Notice that it is different from the neoclassical model of intertemporal choice only in the term β, with β appearing before the usual δ discount terms. Since it appears as β in front of δ as well as δ^2, it drops out when we think about trade-offs that are fully contained in the future (as you can see in the first row of Table 29.1 where we are merely contemplating whether we should undertake the investment in period 1 from our vantage point of period 0). But when the future becomes the present, β matters because the model has incorporated the idea that there is always something special about the present moment. *The beta-delta model of time preference therefore simply changes the way we think about the present versus the future, not the way we think about the future versus the more distant future.*

When psychologists offer people the choice of $50 today or $100 next year, they tend to pick the $50 immediately. But when the same people are offered the choice of $50 five years from now or $100 six years from now, they usually pick the $100. Explain how this does not fit into the usual model of intertemporal choice but it does fit into the modified model in the previous paragraph.

Exercise 29A.2

One of the dangers of introducing a present-biased model of this kind is that students often misinterpret the model as giving expression to *impatience* rather than present-bias. Someone is impatient if he or she places a lot more value on consuming now than consuming in the future, which simply means he or she discounts the future a lot and thus will end up investing less and eating more now than someone who is more patient. *But there is nothing time-inconsistent about impatience*: If you are really impatient, you will look forward to period 1 and know that you will not in fact want to pay c to get b one period later (unless b is very large relative to c), and that is precisely what you'll actually decide when period 1 becomes the present. A time-inconsistency problem arises when you plan to do something in the future and then, without anything other than time changing, you can't stick to your plan as the future becomes the present. This inability to stick by what we plan is, in the beta-delta model, caused by "present-bias" that follows individuals through time whether they are patient or not, and it is what defines the self-control problem that we are trying to get at.

Table 29.2 illustrates this distinction between impatience and present-bias. In the first section of the table, we show how much larger the period 2 benefit b has to be than the period 1 investment cost c in order for the investment to be judged worthwhile. We assume that $\delta = 1/1.05 \approx 0.952$; i.e., generally you view $1 in period $(t + 1)$ as equivalent to about $0.95 in period t. But we also assume that you might be present-biased by considering different potential values of β (listed in the very top row). Your future plans are unaffected by the inclusion of β in the way you discount, so when you are in period 0 and you look forward, only the δ discount parameter matters. This implies you will think the investment *will be* worthwhile so long as $(b/c) > 1.05$ (as indicated in the row labeled "Future Plan at $t = 0$"). When $\beta = 1$, the beta-delta model introduces no bias and thus the decision rule at $t = 1$ remains to undertake the investment so long as $(b/c) > 1.05$. But when $\beta < 1$, we have present-bias: For instance, the table tells us that $\beta = 0.5$ implies that when we actually have to make the decision of whether to invest, we will suddenly require $(b/c) > 2.1$ to get us to give up c now in order to get b next period, even though we had initially planned to go through with the investment so long as $(b/c) > 1.05$. In a sense, $\beta = 0.5$ therefore implies we suddenly become impatient in terms of trading off the present for the future when $t = 1$ rolls around, even though we expected to be relatively patient in period 1 when we were looking forward from period 0.

The second part of Table 29.2 then derives the δ that would be necessary (if β were set to 1) to arrive at the same decision rule at $t = 1$ as the present-biased preferences in the first part.

---

[2]The model is most closely associated with the Harvard economist David Laibson (1966–). His beta-delta model is also known as a model of *quasi-hyperbolic discounting*, which is a simplification of the more common *hyperbolic discounting* model previously used in other disciplines (and discussed in a bit more detail in Section B).

Table 29.2: Ratio of b to c Necessary to Justify the Investment

Present Bias versus Impatience							
Time-Inconsistent Beta-Delta Model of Present-Bias (with $\delta = 1/1.05$)							
β	0.50	0.75	0.90	0.95	1.00	1.05	1.10
Future Plan at $t = 0$	1.050	1.050	1.050	1.050	1.050	1.050	1.050
Present Bias at $t = 1$	2.100	1.400	1.167	1.105	1.050	1.000	0.955
Equivalent δ in Time-Consistent Model of Impatience (with $\beta = 1$)							
δ	0.476	0.714	0.857	0.905	0.952	1.000	1.047
Future Plan at $t = 0$	2.100	1.400	1.167	1.105	1.050	1.000	0.955
Decision Rule at $t = 1$	2.100	1.400	1.167	1.105	1.050	1.000	0.955

For instance, $\delta = 0.476$ gives us the same decision rule as the present-biased rule when $\beta = 0.5$. The difference is that, when $\delta = 0.476$, we know that we are impatient and we are OK with that in the sense that our future actions will not contradict our current plans. As a result, our future plan at time 0 is the same as our actual decision rule at time 1 for any level of impatience. But when the same decision rule emerges from $\beta = 0.5$ in the top part of the table, we disagree at time $t = 1$ with the plans we had made at time $t = 0$.

Exercise 29A.3

What does it mean for β to be greater than 1 in the beta-delta model?

Exercise 29A.4

Consider again the example in within-chapter-exercise 29A.2. Suppose $\delta = 1/1.05 \approx 0.952$. What is the highest level of β that could lead to the choices in the example? What would δ have to be now if $\beta = 1$ to lead to the present choice, and why does this not help us explain the dual result described in the example?

We might then ask what implications such a model has for how we think about "what is good" with respect to markets, civil society, and government policy. Some might, for instance, be concerned that impatience causes individuals to underinvest and overconsume, with many philosophers, for instance, seeing no moral justification for anyone discounting the future. Patience is therefore sometimes seen as a moral virtue, though not one easily forced on people. It takes a relatively paternalistic, or patronizing, form of government to use concerns over people's impatience as a basis for a policy that will force individuals to invest more when they would prefer to consume. From an efficiency standpoint, such a policy would in fact be the opposite of a Pareto improvement, with some people being made worse off (as judged by themselves) while others (who would have been patient without being forced) were made no better off. Properly functioning credit markets may constrain the extent to which individuals can act on their impatience by lending only up to a point, but at the same time such markets are also interested in selling now rather than later and thus benefit from consumer impatience. However, a whole host of civil society institutions—parents, families, churches—are engaged in attempting to persuade us to adopt a longer time horizon, to think about tomorrow as we make decisions today, and it seems plausible that such institutions might have a great deal of impact on how individuals make voluntary trade-offs over time. To the extent to which patience is a virtue, it is then often within the civil society that the virtue is fostered, and perhaps a failure of the civil society if impatience gets out of hand.

But present-biased preferences, and the accompanying self-control problems, raise a different set of issues. Individuals who are aware of their self-control problems will in fact search for ways of overcoming these, ways of "binding themselves" in the future so as to avoid the temptation to undo their own plans when the future becomes the present. Put differently, if you know you have a problem with sticking to your plans, you would be willing to expend resources to "fix the problem," to invest in what economists call *commitment devices* that force you to take actions in the future, actions that you rationally predict your future "self" will not want to take even though your present "self" wants the future "self" to do so. In Homer's famous Greek classic *Odyssey*, the hero's 10-year voyage home from the Trojan War takes him past the land of the Sirens whose intoxicating song is known to lure the toughest of warriors into a deadly trap. Odysseus wants to hear the Sirens' song but also does not want to fall under their spell and into their trap. He understands, however, that once he hears the song, he will not have the self-control to keep himself away. He therefore designs a commitment device, asking his shipmates to bind him to the ship's mast while plugging their own ears so that they can hear neither the song nor Odysseus's pleading commands to unbind him. His self-control awareness keeps him from giving in to the present-bias he knows he will have in the future, and the commitment device keeps him from giving in to the temptation he knows is coming.

We have our own ways of constructing commitment devices when we find ourselves in positions analogous to Odysseus. You might commit to your spouse that you will stop smoking in hopes that her disappointment in you when she smells smoke will keep you from violating your commitment. You might start a monthly savings plan that penalizes you for not making regular deposits or "bind" you retirement savings in a 401k plan that penalizes you for early withdrawals. Perhaps you ask your professors to give you homework deadlines rather than trusting that you will pace yourself as the final exam approaches. Many people ceremoniously cut up their credit cards (following their latest buying binge) so as not to be tempted to abuse them again. They invest their savings in "illiquid assets," assets that they cannot easily sell when the itch to consume hits, or they tie them up in a government-designed college fund for their kids. The self-aware addict might take one more dose of cocaine but then checks herself into a rehab center where they will keep her from doing it again, or I might ask my wife to throw away the rest of that incredibly delicious cake so that I won't be tempted to go back for more. For those who are searching for commitment devices to discipline their "future selves," we find many examples of such devices—some sold in the market, some volunteered within the civil society, and some designed by government. Leaving more options open is no longer the optimal strategy for those who believe they can't handle it, and limiting options therefore becomes desirable from the self-aware individual's perspective just as Odysseus was wise to bind himself to the ship's mast and not leave all options open.

Many people buy health club memberships only never to use them. Yet they hold on to them and continue paying their monthly fees for long periods of time. How can the purchase of such memberships be explained, and what does the fact that individuals hold on to their memberships without using them tell us about their awareness of how they are making decisions?

Exercise 29A.5

Some financial advisors recommend that people choose 15-year mortgages with higher monthly payments rather than 30-year mortgages with lower monthly payments even if the interest rates on both mortgages are the same and even if the 30-year mortgages allow people to pre-pay (and thus pay them off in 15 years) if they want to. How does this make sense from a behavioral economist's perspective when it makes less sense when viewed through a traditional economic model?

Exercise 29A.6

Exercise
29A.7

In the period prior to the 2007 housing crisis, it was easy for people to refinance their homes. If people choose 15-year (rather than 30-year) mortgages as a savings commitment device (as suggested in exercise 29A.6), might the ready option to refinance have made self-aware but present-biased people worse off?

But it is probably unreasonable to think that everyone who has self-control problems fully perceives himself to have such problems. And in some instances, it may be that institutions like markets don't have the right incentives to make you aware of your problem. "Another drink? Why certainly, good man," the bartender might say as he feeds the addiction of his alcoholic client, just as the electronics store will gladly supply you with yet another set of gadgets on your nearly maxed-out credit card. At first glance, it may seem that government intervention to assist the unaware reeks of the same paternalism we sensed in government attempts to make us "more virtuous" by getting us to behave less impatiently, and some social commentators have therefore been highly skeptical of drawing policy inferences from the results of behavioral economists who work on present-bias. It turns out, however, many behavioral economists argue for much less threatening types of policy interventions, interventions we will refer to as "libertarian paternalism," which is a form of paternalism that does not presume the government knows best but rather sets up some "nudges" that will get those with self-control problems to do what is ultimately in their best interest (as judged by themselves) while imposing no costs of great significance on those that have no such problems.[3] We will conclude the section on behavioral economics with some examples of such policies after covering a few other major insights from the intersection of economics and psychology that have bearing on what such policies might look like.

29A.1.2 Reference Dependent Preferences, Loss Aversion, and Endowment Effects

You may be aware that at Duke University (where I teach) there is quite a basketball culture. The basketball stadium does not have nearly enough space to accommodate demand, and students often have to jump through all sorts of hoops to get tickets. Even after jumping through these hoops, the quantity demanded sometimes exceeds supply (as when Duke makes it into the NCAA tournament finals), and lotteries are used to determine the ultimate recipients of tickets from those that jumped through all the hoops. In one such instance, a psychologist in the business school at Duke decided to call up students who had won the lottery to try to negotiate a price at which the winners might be willing to sell their tickets. He also called the losers from the lottery, who were just as enthusiastic about Duke basketball as the winners and had shown this by jumping through all the same hoops, to see how much they'd be willing to pay to buy tickets. His claim is that the winners were willing to sell their tickets for an average of about $1,400 while the losers were willing to pay only about $170.[4]

Exercise
29A.8*

True or False: If individual tastes are quasilinear in basketball tickets, the prices people were willing to accept should be identical to the prices they were willing to pay. (*Hint*: You may have done a detailed exercise that is identical to this in end-of-chapter exercise 10.7 of Chapter 10.)

---

[3]I am borrowing the term "nudge" from the title of a delightful recent book on behavioral economics (Richard Thaler and Cass Sunstein, *Nudge* (New Haven, Conn.: Yale University Press, 2008). Richard Thaler (1945–) is one of the pioneers of behavioral economics, and Cass Sunstein (1954–) is a University of Chicago legal scholar who has taken insights from behavioral economics to analyze the law. Sunstein was tapped by Barack Obama to head the White House Office of Information and Regulatory Affairs.

[4]My psychology colleague is Dan Ariely (1968–). He is also the author of the best-seller *Predictably Irrational* (New York: Harper Collins, 2008), an intriguing collection of psychology experiments and their relationship to decision making, with conclusions that are deeply critical of neoclassical economics. While it makes for fascinating reading in many ways, empirical economists would argue with some of Ariely's predictions that appear at times to contradict empirical evidence outside the laboratory. For an example, see within-chapter-exercise 29A.11.

The randomness with which students were selected into "winners" and "losers" suggests that we should be able to assume that their preferences and economic circumstances are on average roughly the same. If we assume this, the only difference between them is that "winners" have a basketball ticket and "losers" do not. Put differently, the only difference between the two is a relatively modest wealth effect, so modest in fact that we would think it should not amount to much of a difference between the marginal willingness to pay on the part of the "losers" and the marginal willingness to accept on the part of the "winners." It is therefore virtually impossible to explain the actual result found by my psychology colleague with the tools of standard neoclassical economics, and this failure of our typical model points to a wider class of phenomena uncovered by psychologists and brought into economics by behavioral economists.

As it turns out, people sometimes seem to evaluate options not in an absolute sense but rather in comparison to a *reference point* that is often (but not always) related to their current endowment.[5] Our decisions are, as a result, sometimes *reference dependent*. In our example, for instance, suppose two students are identical except that student 1 is a "loser" of the basketball lottery and achieves utility level u_1 on his indifference map, and student 2 is the "winner" who achieves utility level $u_2 > u_1$. When called about either selling or buying a ticket, the two students formulate their response with their endowment (of a ticket or no ticket) as a reference point. This means that student 2 will view selling the ticket as "the loss of a ticket" whereas student 1 views buying the ticket as the "gain of a ticket." So far, so good—nothing yet is keeping us from expecting them to come up with roughly similar prices. But there is another feature of tastes that psychologists have found sometimes matters: When we evaluate gains and losses relative to a reference point, we tend to place more weight on losses than on gains. Thus, when student 2 views selling the ticket as "the loss of a ticket," this "loss" is psychologically more painful than the "gain" for student 1 who is considering buying a ticket as pleasurable, even though the ticket was worth exactly the same to both of them when they first started jumping through all the hoops to qualify.

This second insight is known as *loss aversion*, and together with the insight that we evaluate gains and losses relative to a reference point, it can help to explain what behavioral economists call the *endowment effect* (or sometimes the *status quo effect*). This effect essentially says that there is something about *ownership* or the *status quo* that matters in ways not captured by our neoclassical model. We tend to place greater value on what we own after we take ownership than before, and we seem attached to the status quo of our current situation. We will explore how this can change some of the insights from our initial development of consumer theory in end-of-chapter exercise 29.9 within the context of housing markets, where consumers appear to form particular psychological attachments that seem to give rise to such endowment effects. And these endowment and status quo effects, which show up in lots of psychology experiments, can certainly help us explain why the Duke students who won the right to attend a basketball game could not easily be made to give it up, even though identical students who did not have a ticket were not willing to pay all that much to get the right to attend the game. It seems in fact likely that if endowment effects are real, we might expect them to be particularly important when the endowment involves something in which our emotions get tied up, such as our home or the prospect of seeing our team beat their hated rivals.

In end-of-chapter exercise 10.7, we considered a very similar situation in which two individuals are identical except that one has a pizza coupon. We concluded that the two individuals will be able to agree on a price at which to trade the coupon so long as pizza is not a normal good. If there is an endowment effect, will the two people be more or less likely to trade the coupon?

**Exercise
29A.9**

---

[5] This and related insights are closely associated with a theory known as *prospect theory* developed by the psychologists Daniel Kahneman (1934–) and Amos Tversky (1937–1996). For his work in behavioral economics, Kahneman shared the 2002 Nobel Prize in Economics with the experimental economist Vernon Smith (1927–).

The concept of loss aversion can also make sense of one of the most frustrating things that people do, frustrating, that is, from an economist's perspective: No matter how much we preach at people, there are times when they behave as if sunk costs were true economic costs. (Truth be told, my wife has pointed out an occasion or two when I have done so myself, although I continue to insist that she secretly drugged me just to catch me in my own contradictions.) You can probably relate to how this happens by simply thinking of an example we gave earlier in the text: paying for a movie ticket and discovering within the first few minutes that the movie is just terrible. How often have you not walked out of a movie and instead suffered through it just because you paid to get in? Perhaps the reason is that you made your decision to stay with respect to a reference point—the fact that you owned a movie ticket—from which admitting a loss is psychologically painful.

Exercise 29A.10

On several occasions, I have observed one of my colleagues insist on taking a special trip to the movie rental place in order to return a movie that would otherwise be overdue when he could have just waited to the next day and returned the movie on his way to work. The late fee is $1. If I called this same colleague (on a night when he did not have a movie due) with "special information" that there was $1 hidden behind one of the movies in the movie place, and that he can be virtually assured of getting the dollar if he comes by now, he would never think it worth it to take that special trip for $1. Can you explain my colleague's behavior using reference-based preferences with loss aversion?

There are many other implications that emerge from reference-based decision making, some of which—in particular those related to risk—we will touch on in Section B and various end-of-chapter exercises. And there are certainly implications for how an awareness of such decision-making might change some of our conclusions about "what is good." If we are indeed willing to give up more to avoid losses than we are to achieve gains, for instance, taxing wealth—i.e., taxing stuff that people own—might be considerably worse from an efficiency perspective than taxing income, even though a standard model might suggest the opposite. When taxing income, it might furthermore be "better" to withhold taxes from an employee's paycheck (so that she never actually takes ownership of the pre-tax income) rather than asking her to pay taxes all at once at the end of the year (once she has already experienced the pre-tax income). Bankruptcy laws that are comparatively lenient in terms of allowing people to keep their homes might find some genuine justification. And it might alter the way we think about the possible macroeconomic trade-off between smoothing business cycles and fostering growth (as we will explore in end-of-chapter exercise 29.14).

Exercise 29A.11

In his book *Predictably Irrational*, my psychologist colleague Dan Ariely suggests (incorrectly, it turns out) that taxing gasoline may not have much impact on long-run gasoline consumption because, he hypothesizes, people will adjust their reference point and thus will respond primarily in the short run and not that much in the long run. This is exactly the opposite prediction that a neoclassical economist would make. Can you see how he arrives at his prediction?[6]

Reference-based decision making can also, however, raise some deeper ethical issues when the "reference point" is not your own endowment but rather your neighbor's consumption. As we will see in our section on the "happiness literature," some behavioral economists have in fact argued

---

[6] A large number of empirical studies have in fact estimated the short-run price elasticity of demand for gasoline to be approximately -0.25 and the long-run elasticity at approximately -0.60, a result consistent with standard economic theory and inconsistent with the reference-based model's prediction. While psychologists can certainly find "anomalies" to the economist's predictions, economists will similarly point out lots of such "anomalies" relative to the psychologist's predictions!

Chapter 29. What Is Good? Challenges from Psychology and Philosophy

1139

that this is precisely how we evaluate our own position in life, not in an absolute sense (i.e., not "How well am I doing?") but rather in a relative sense (i.e., "Am I doing better than my high school buddy?"). And such a view of human nature is sometimes argued to call for dramatically egalitarian policies, policies that aim to minimize the difference between people, quite possibly at the cost of dramatically reducing everyone's standard of living because of the incentive issues such policies would raise. Few economists take this view, perhaps because we are quite persuaded that human welfare is more likely to be affected by absolute rather than relative factors, or perhaps because there is something unseemly about basing large-scale social policy on what amounts to people's envy of one another. We will return to some related issues in our upcoming section on happiness as well as in end-of-chapter exercise 29.4.

29A.1.3 Some Neglected Constraints: Framing, Bounded Rationality, and More
Suppose you are very environmentally conscious and you have three options: Option 1 replaces an 8-mile-per-gallon (MPG) gas guzzler with a slightly more efficient car that gets 2 more miles to the gallon (for a total of 10 MPG); option 2 replaces a 25 MPG car with car that gets 15 *more* miles to the gallon (for a total of 40 MPG); and option 3 replaces a 50 MPG car with a super-efficient 100 MPG hybrid (that runs mainly on love of nature). Assuming that each car would be driven the same number of miles for the next few years, which option would you pick to maximize the positive impact of less pollution on the environment?

Now suppose I give you three other options to choose from: Option A replaces a car that uses 125 gallons of gas per 1,000 miles with a car that saves 25 gallons of gas per 1,000 miles; option B replaces a car that uses 40 gallons per 1,000 miles with one that saves 15 gallons for every 1,000 miles driven; and option C replaces a car that uses 20 gallons per 1,000 miles with one that saves 10 gallons for every 1,000 miles. Which one would you choose now?

I suspect you are catching on to what I have just done: option 1 is identical to option A; option 2 is identical to option B; and option 3 is identical to option C. Both sets of options give you information on the fuel efficiency of the initial cars and the ones that would replace them, but the first set of options *framed* the choice in terms of "miles per gallon" whereas the second framed it in terms of "gallons per 1,000 miles." The information is the same, but it sure sounds a whole lot different. *Framing*, it turns out, matters in terms of what choices we make, a fact long understood by advertisers and the psychologists who help advertisers manipulate us.[7]

....

Explain how the two sets of options are equivalent.

Exercise 29A.12

....

Some years ago, Congress passed a law permitting stores to charge different amounts to cash customers than they do to credit card customers. When it became clear that the law would pass, the credit card lobby insisted on language that would permit "cash discounts" but not "credit card surcharges." In light of reference-based preferences with loss aversion, can you think of why credit card companies might have lobbied so hard for this?

Exercise 29A.13

....

There are lots of reasons framing matters, and I will leave it to one of your psychology classes to explore this in more depth. In some cases, it matters because our *bounded rationality*, our limited capacity to absorb and process information, has led us to use simple "rules of thumb" instead of really thinking through problems. Such "rules of thumb" may respond differently depending on how something is framed, and they may well have evolved over long periods of time to help us solve problems more easily and more effectively. But as the world has changed

---

[7] The "miles per gallon" versus "gallons per mile" example is borrowed from work by two management professors, Richard Larrick and and Jack Soll, at Duke's Fuqua School of Business.

(and is changing more rapidly than it used to), some evolutionarily effective rules may now be lousy in instances for which they simply were never "intended."

In other cases, psychologists have discovered systematic ways in which we trip ourselves up even in circumstances that require only third-grade math, such as not recognizing the equivalence between miles per gallon and its inverse, gallons per mile. In yet others, psychologists have discovered systematic ways in which individuals have difficulty internalizing some basics about probabilities of random events (as we uncover in some examples in end-of-chapter exercise 29.3). And in the examples such as those offered in end-of-chapter exercise 29.6, the framing impact has literally nothing to do with computational limitations and, in the words of psychologists Kahnemann and Tversky, "resemble perceptual illusions." For instance, unscrupulous pollsters (who are willing to get polling data to say whatever the client wants) know a bit about how to frame polling questions to cause people to answer in one or the other direction. And of course it may well be the case that certain types of decisions are impacted by emotions that find their roots in our complex brain chemistry, a subject that is taken seriously in the collaboration of neuroscientists with economists.

In instances where framing matters, we may then once again see a role for markets, civil society, and government to structure institutions in ways that minimize systematic errors. If, for instance, we indeed understand fuel efficiency better when phrased in terms of gallons per mile rather than miles per gallon, such an awareness might lead car companies, consumer advocacy groups, or government to be proactive in reframing how fuel efficiency data on different automobiles is presented to consumers. In instances where firms are able to lead consumers into making systematic and profit-maximizing errors through marketing and advertising, there may be a role for government to reframe the issue, as perhaps governments worldwide have done by placing scary pictures and apocalyptic warnings on cigarette boxes. And, as we will see next, there may once again be a role for "libertarian paternalism," of which the scary pictures on cigarette boxes might just be one example.

29A.1.4 "Libertarian Paternalism"

Behavioral economics is not foremost about people making mistakes; it's about people exhibiting *systematic biases* that emerge from how the preferences and constraints that encounter one another as we make choices have been shaped by psychological factors. It then becomes tempting to "fix the biases" through policy, which almost instantly invites the question: If human decisions are meaningfully shaped by these biases, why would we not expect human beings who make policy to be similarly shaped by such biases as they legislate and implement such policies? Isn't there something obnoxiously paternalistic in a policy maker telling me he will now force me to do something I don't want to do because he wants to protect me from my biases? But to many behavioral economists, and to many who have casually watched the development of the field, the policy implications are more subtle and less paternalistic. We will illustrate with an example and leave you to consider others on your own.

Consider the case of present-biased individuals who can't carry through on their plans to save for retirement. To the extent to which they are aware of their self-control problem, they might, as we have mentioned, find "commitment devices," but perhaps they are only partially or not at all aware of the problem. Heavy-handed paternalism might lead us to legislating forced savings plans, while libertarian paternalism might simply involve a "nudge" to get people to consider regular monthly saving as their "reference point."

Consider the following: A large number of companies now offer their employees the opportunity to save for retirement through tax-advantaged (401k) plans that deduct some percentage of the employees' paycheck and contribute the deducted amount into the retirement plan. Participation in these plans is entirely voluntary, but some companies enroll employees automatically while giving them an option to discontinue their automatic payroll deductions and opt out of the plan while other companies do not enroll employees unless the employee requests it. In both cases, changing from the default company policy requires little more than a phone call, which means that it really "should not matter" whether the default is for the company to enroll its employees or not. *But it does matter—a lot.* People who are automatically enrolled in such retirement plans are much more

Chapter 29. What Is Good? Challenges from Psychology and Philosophy

1141

likely to stay in those plans than people who are not automatically enrolled are likely to enroll. Libertarian paternalism in the face of evidence on present-biased and reference-based savings decisions would then suggest automatic enrollment of everyone into retirement programs, thereby improving the welfare of those with self-control problems (who also make reference-based decisions) while imposing virtually no cost on those who make decisions in a more conventional way and might want to opt out.

How can reference-based preferences explain the empirical facts on enrollments in retirement programs?

Exercise 29A.14

Note the difference between the type of heavy-handed paternalism that attempts to enforce the "virtue of patience" (as discussed in Section 29A.1.3) and this example of "libertarian paternalism." In the former case, the object of the paternalism is to correct impatience, and in so doing it makes impatient people worse off while not impacting those that are already patient. It might also, of course, lead some who have self-control problems to save, but this form of paternalism offers no real path for a nuanced use of information that distinguishes between the merely impatient and the present-biased. The libertarian paternalism in our example allows for much more subtlety while minimizing the chances that anyone is seriously hurt by the policy. It is most effective if present-biased and reference-biased decision making are correlated, which would imply that those in greatest need of a mechanism to get them to save more are the very ones who will view the automatic enrollment in a retirement program as a relevant "reference point" that will keep them enrolled. But it also allows the impatient who operate without reference-bias to opt out and to indulge their impatient whims (without interfering with their time-consistent plans to live a life full of impatience). Rather than "imposing virtue," libertarian paternalism attempts to nudge people toward solutions they may not themselves be aware of while keeping costs low for those who require no help.

29A.2 Happiness: The Social Sciences versus the Humanities

While they may not always agree on the degree to which neoclassical assumptions of microeconomics require tweaking, both traditional and behavioral economists share the same underlying approach: We think that we can best *predict* behavior by assuming that "people always try to do the best they can given their circumstances." What they might consider "best" may be subject to psychological biases, and their constraints may extend beyond economic constraints to cognitive constraints and framing biases, but in the end we still view individuals as optimizing agents. And the "thing" they are optimizing is something we call "utility," which is usually interpreted to mean "happiness."[8]

There are then two ways in which we can view this thing called "happiness" that we think people are trying to soak in. The first simply defines happiness as whatever "thing" motivates people into action, as a "work-horse" of sorts that helps us understand why people do what they do. In the absence of distinguishing between utility and happiness, this work-horse definition of happiness is what is captured in what we have called tastes that then confront constraints to shape the *behavior* that we can actually observe, study, and predict. We can then quite confidently say that "more money

---

[8] The extent to which "utility," the thing we try to optimize, is the same as what most people call "happiness" is a somewhat open question among economists. Gary Becker (1930–), the 1992 recipient of the Nobel Prize in Economics, has for instance recently argued that what people call "happiness" might more appropriately be viewed as something analogous to a commodity that plays a role in determining an individual's "utility" but is not itself the entirety of what makes up "utility." As such, it would then be possible for someone who is fully rational to be observed undertaking an action that optimizes her utility while at the same time reporting that the action made her less "happy" as she trades off "happiness" against other contributors to "utility."

makes people happy" (because they sure seem to jump into action to pursue it). The economic model, whatever we think about how much to include psychological biases, predicts well in many circumstances precisely because "positive" economists—i.e., economists who seek to predict behavior—deliberately do not try to define a deeper meaning of happiness beyond this work-horse definition. It is a shallow view of happiness, but one whose purpose is quite deliberately not deep.

Yet this does not mean that there isn't some deeper view of happiness, a view deeper even than simply distinguishing between "utility" and "happiness." Such a deeper view is often found in the humanities where attempts are made in all sorts of ways to reconcile the various aspects of the human being, attempts that sometimes give rise to puzzling but quite possibly true statements like "money doesn't make you happy." And if we are ultimately to address the question of "what is good," it is difficult to not at some point confront that deeper meaning of happiness for which the positive economist legitimately has little use in his pursuit of good behavioral predictions.

We will return to a brief pedestrian discussion of this deeper view of happiness in Section 29A.2.3 after briefly touching on some findings from a relatively recent social science "happiness literature" that tries to at least come to terms with what conditions people associate with the state of being "happy" at particular instances in time. This literature uses combinations of surveys and psychological indicators to arrive at measures of "happiness," measures that throughout this book we have shied away from given the modern economist's typical position that happiness is not objectively measurable even if individuals can subjectively experience it. Despite the economist's instinct against "cardinal" or "measurable" utility, and in favor of "ordinal utility" that merely requires people to tell us what is better and what is worse, economists have recently collaborated with other social scientists in this literature that some have labeled "happiness economics."

29A.2.1 The Social Science "Happiness Literature"

Given our maintained position that all we need is some ordinal notion of preferences and not a cardinal—or measurable—happiness scale to predict behavior, it is far from clear that the economist's work-horse notion of happiness is what is measured in data sets that contain a happiness index. At the same time, it is unlikely that the happiness measure in such data sets is what philosophers mean by some deeper meaning of happiness. It is therefore not entirely clear how to interpret empirical findings on how "happiness" quantitatively relates to various types of societal and personal indicators of well-being. Still, the results are intriguing and informative for those striving to move from the question of "what is" to the question of "what is good."

Early on in this literature, two apparently contradictory findings came to be known as the *Easterlin Paradox*.[9] The first finding was that, *within* countries at any given time, the marginal impact of greater income on happiness is positive but diminishes as income increases. Thus, while it is especially true that more money "makes people happier" at low levels of income, this is increasingly less true (although it is never false) as income rises. In terms of language that we have conspicuously avoided throughout this text, we can equivalently say that these findings suggest a positive but diminishing marginal utility of income (and consumption).

Exercise 29A.15   Explain the last sentence.

Exercise 29A.16   In earlier end-of-chapter exercises, we introduced the notion of "compensating differentials" in labor markets—wage differences that emerge because some jobs are inherently less pleasurable or involve more risk, factors that in equilibrium will be reflected in wages. How might the existence of such compensating differentials bias researchers into finding the marginal utility of income to be diminishing when it actually is not?

---

[9] The paradox is named for Richard Easterlin, an economist who first raised it in 1974.

This first finding is not particularly surprising to economists; "more", it seems, is indeed "better" (even if getting more makes less of a difference the more we have). But the Easterlin Paradox emerges from the second set of findings: There appeared to be relatively little relationship between average happiness and average incomes *across* countries (except for the very poorest); and there appeared to be similarly little relationship between average happiness and average income *within countries over time* as average income increases. Thus, it isn't clear that people in richer countries are necessarily happier than those in somewhat poorer countries, nor does it appear that my generation is all that much happier than my grandparents' generation whose material standard of living was less than a third of what I enjoy. In light of our discussion of reference-based preferences in the previous section, a behavioral economics explanation of these seemingly contradictory findings is that happiness (above basic subsistence levels) is primarily driven by *relative income* considerations and not by *absolute income* levels.

Explain how reference-based preferences can provide such an explanation for the two sets of findings.	**Exercise** **29A.17**
If the reference-based preference explanation for the Easterlin Paradox is correct, how would this imply that we are all caught up in a big Prisoner's Dilemma?	**Exercise** **29A.18**

Some more recent work suggests that the second set of findings in the Easterlin puzzle might actually have been overstated, and that there might in fact be less of a puzzle than initially thought. It remains an issue of some debate in the literature. There is, however, wide consensus that happiness (as measured in the "happiness literature") is certainly not *only* produced by (either absolute or relative) income or consumption. Rather, reported happiness is also driven in large part by factors such as feelings of security, connectedness to social networks of friends and family, "being good at something," and being relatively healthy. The typical economic model that bases the bulk of its emphasis on happiness from material consumption certainly seems to result in many good predictions. But its work-horse definition of happiness cannot easily be viewed as the entire answer to the question "What is happiness?" I doubt that this is any more surprising to most economists than it is to most "normal" people, even as economists find the work-horse model of happiness an extremely useful tool for predicting human behavior in a wide variety of settings.

29A.2.2 So Why Does "Work-horse" Happiness Predict Behavior?   With such evidence that our work-horse definition of happiness does not get to the heart of the complexity of what the "good life" is all about, why does the work-horse predict so well? If the happiness literature had concluded that "money doesn't make us happy," we'd have a serious puzzle on our hands. As it stands, however, the literature says that ultimately there are many aspects of life—friends, family, etc.—that matter, and that money appears not as important in producing happiness as these other aspects of life. But money *does* matter, and whether it matters in an absolute or relative sense is not as crucial for the question of why the work-horse model predicts well: In either case, an individual would *act as if* money mattered for his happiness. Still, if material consumption matters *somewhat* in the empirical happiness literature but is modeled as essentially being the *only* thing that matters in most of economics, one is still left with a bit of a disconnect between the predictive power of economics and the importance of so much that we typically don't consider in our models.

If it is true that the work-horse definition of happiness predicts "too well," psychologists have come up with one possible explanation: It seems that our brain remembers the past in a systematically biased way, and we then use this information to determine what to do next. When we strive to get the money together to buy that shiny new car, for instance, we anticipate great utility from ultimately getting the car, with that anticipation motivating us to get there. When we do get there and begin to drive that new car, we often end up disappointed in the sense that the experience does not provide nearly as much pleasure as we thought it would. But when we are asked a year or two later about what it was like to finally get that new car, we report a level of pleasure commensurate with our anticipation of getting the car, not the level we actually enjoyed. Thus, our brain tells us that getting more stuff like the new car will be really great because we "remember" how great it was to get that new car by remembering how great we *thought* it would be to get it! We then "act as if more makes us happy," thus making the positive economist's predictions so accurate, even if we aren't getting all that much more happy as we get more.[10]

Exercise 29A.19   Suppose we consider our brain as the outcome of an evolutionary process aimed at maximizing the survival of our species. How might this be consistent with the memory bias we have just discussed?

Exercise 29A.20   In what sense do you think this memory bias might work in the opposite direction as present-bias discussed earlier?

This might also help to explain why we insist on doing things that happiness researchers suggest make us downright miserable. For instance, one of the most robust findings of the happiness literature in psychology is that having children makes us less happy, with marital bliss maximized just before the arrival of kids in the household and never quite recovering until the little beasts leave the nest (assuming the marriage has survived that long). How is it that most of us still have kids, and even more puzzling, why is it that we wax on retrospectively about how wonderful a thing that was? Psychologists might suggest that the same memory-bias is at play: We "remember" the little darlings fondly when they aren't around or have left the nest, but what we are actually "remembering" is our anticipation of how wonderful it would be to have kids rather than the actual nightmare that we really experienced.

Or, I'd like to think it might be that we really know what we are talking about when we wax on about how having children was the best thing we ever did, and that what we describe as "happiness" in the moment isn't really all that we actually seek in an attempt to live the "good life." The example might then plug into a much deeper notion of happiness, a notion that has little relation to the more hedonistic "work-horse" version but one that gets closer to the heart of what it means to be human.

29A.2.3 *The Matrix*, Philosophy, and the Deeper Meaning of Life

This deeper aspect to the question of "what is happiness" is something the positive economist, behavioral or traditional, never has to confront. But philosophers often confront the question head on by posing the following hypothetical that was loosely adapted as the premise for the Hollywood motion picture *The Matrix* (starring the arguably acting-challenged Keanu Reeves). Imagine being confronted with the following offer: You can step into my office and I will quickly hook you up to a machine that will remove your consciousness from this world and instead stimulate your brain into experiencing a much better world, one in which your desires are quickly met, one in which the machine provides conditions under which you will achieve substantially more utility than you can ever hope to achieve in the world we occupy. Suppose further that once you are hooked up to this machine, you will live out the rest of your life in this artificial world, but all your experiences will feel just as real as they do in this world. You will, in fact, not know that you are anywhere other than the "real" world, but everything will be so much better than it is here. Do you accept my offer?

---

[10]A recent engaging and entertaining book on this is by Harvard psychologist Daniel Gilbert: *Stumbling onto Happiness* (New York Vintage Books, 2005).

If we take the positive economist's work-horse definition of happiness or the more expanded version from the social science "happiness literature" literally, I do not see why you wouldn't. My machine offers you more of this kind of happiness (that explains so much of your behavior) than you could ever attain in life, and happiness, or utility, is what we presume you maximize. The potential discomfort from knowing that you are entering an imaginary world for the few minutes it takes me to hook you up to the machine can't possibly be so great as to cause you to give up such a life of bliss. Since this is a hypothetical thought experiment, we can even dispense with these few minutes and suppose that my machine is instantly hooked up to you. Still, most people say quite definitively that they would not agree to be hooked up to my machine, not even if it takes only a second to hook them up, not even if the machine has been proven 100% flawless and there is no chance that it might ever malfunction.

This silly thought experiment is meant to point out that there must be something deeper than our work-horse definition of happiness that we crave, that there is more to the "good life" than a "happy life," even one that expands the notion of "happiness" to the various components of factors that the happiness literature tells us matter. Even if the desire to achieve such happiness or utility can explain our actions (as positive economists attempt to argue it does to a remarkable extent), the fact that "there is more to life than experiencing happiness" then suggests that we will miss something important if we rely solely on the utility ruler (that helps us predict) to fully evaluate whether social outcomes are "good." The "good" life may not coincide perfectly with the "happy" life even if the happy life is what motivates much of the behavior that is the subject of the analysis of social scientists (including economists).

This is not a book on philosophy, nor am I qualified to write such a book. But, as we now turn to the topic of normative economics, it is difficult to fully avoid the questions philosophers think about when they ask what constitutes the "good." Still, all we can do here is raise these deeper questions because economists ultimately aren't in any special position to fully "answer" them in a satisfactory way. (If we could, we could get rid of philosophy departments.) The main point of raising the questions is therefore simply to suggest that some humility might be in order as we take an economist's, or even a broader social scientist's, predictive models toward a complete picture of defining "what is good." I have little doubt that the economist's framework is quite fundamental to coming to an answer, but it is almost certainly not sufficient in and of itself.

Having raised such a need for humility, we nevertheless now once again resort to simplified models as we consider the interaction of economics with a limited set of different philosophical approaches to answering the question "What is good?"

29A.3 Evaluating Distributions of Outcomes: Philosophy and Normative Economics

We can agree to disagree about whether we think that happiness—or utility—can be measured in some meaningful way, or the extent to which individuals are fully "rational" in the traditional sense or instead riddled with psychological baggage that causes persistent mistakes. None of that, however, has to keep us from engaging in the philosophical question of how we would evaluate different distributions of utility in society if we were able to do so. Some of what we call "normative economics" does precisely that and, in the process, permits economists to engage in larger philosophical debates about "what is good" at an admittedly abstract level. We will begin with a discussion of this abstract debate while linking it to some of the micro foundations we developed earlier in the text in ways that are common in normative economics.

We will also, however, ask what other normative measures we can bring to discussions of policy when such measures need to be based on an assumption that we cannot actually measure utility in practice. This, too, is a part of normative economics, albeit one that is much more loosely tied to philosophy. But both the abstract and the more concrete discussions in this section share one fundamental premise: that what "matters" in thinking about "what is good" is the outcomes (or consequences) that result from how institutions within society are set up. Whether these are outcomes we can actually measure (such as income or consumption) or outcomes we may not be able to measure (such as utility), the focus is on how distributions and levels of outcomes relate to how we think about the "good" in society. The underlying approach, therefore, is what philosophers might call *consequentialist*, which means entirely focused on outcomes rather than processes. It is not the only approach nor necessarily the most common among philosophers, but it is the approach most commonly employed in normative economics. In Section 29A.4, we will briefly discuss an alternative that is implicitly also advocated by many economists, although I suspect at least in part for consequentialist reasons.

29A.3.1 Utility Possibility Frontiers

A *utility possibility set* is a description of all the possible combinations of utilities for individuals that could be achieved in an economy. If there is truth in the notion of "diminishing marginal utility of income" (as suggested by the "happiness" literature), we might expect the boundary of the utility possibility set—known as the *utility possibility frontier*—to take on the general shape depicted in panel (b) of Graph 29.1 for cases where we consider a society made up of only two individuals. Notice that in drawing such a utility possibility frontier, we implicitly assume there are ways of converting individual 2's utility u_2 into individual 1's utility u_1 (and vice versa), but that it becomes increasingly difficult to convert person 2's utility into u_1 the higher u_1 gets. Diminishing marginal utility of income would get us this result if the means by which we convert utility across people is through redistribution of income.

Exercise 29A.21   Suppose the marginal utility of income is constant and we can costlessly redistribute income across individuals. What would that imply for the shape of the utility possibility frontier?

Graph 29.1: Deriving the Utility Possibility Frontier from an Edgeworth Box

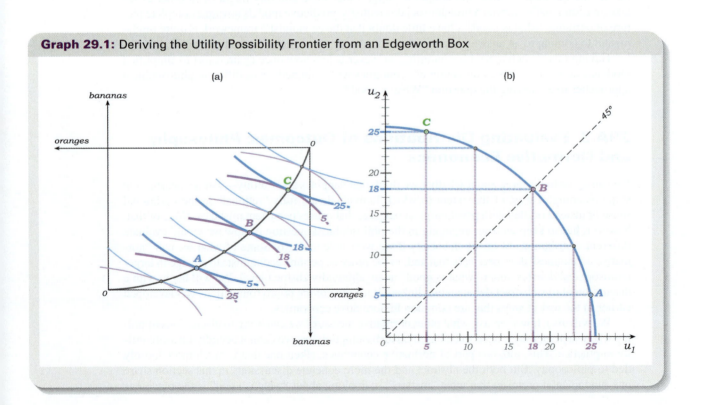

Chapter 29. What Is Good? Challenges from Psychology and Philosophy

1147

If you have read about Edgeworth Boxes in Chapter 16, we can furthermore illustrate how utility possibility frontiers arise from the set of Pareto efficient allocations in a typical neoclassical depiction of an exchange economy. (If you did not cover Chapter 16, you can simply skip this paragraph.) In Graph 16.3b, we traced out what we called the *contract curve* for such an economy—the set of Pareto efficient allocations. In panel (a) of Graph 29.1, we again illustrate such a contract curve, but this time we add utility numbers to some of the indifference curves. In panel (b) of Graph 29.1, we then translate the three highlighted points on the contract curve to a graph that has the utility of individual 1 on the horizontal axis and the utility of individual 2 on the vertical. By doing this for each of the possible points on the contract curve, we derive the utility possibility frontier that forms the boundary of the shaded *utility possibility set*. All combinations of utilities in the shaded set up to and including the frontier are then possible in this Edgeworth Box economy, but combinations of utilities outside this set are not possible.

True or False: Every allocation on the contract curve in panel (a) translates to a point on the utility possibility frontier in panel (b).

**Exercise
29A.22**

Now notice that there exists a logical relationship between the utility allocations on the utility possibility frontier and the set of efficient outcomes: Points on the utility possibility frontier are such that there is no way to move to the northeast in the graph and still remain within the utility possibility frontier; i.e., there is no way to make both people better off. There is similarly no way to move straight up or straight to the right, and thus no way to make one person better off without making anyone else worse off. Thus, by definition, the points on the utility possibility *frontier* represent the set of efficient outcomes for our little two-person society. As we have pointed out before, it is for instance efficient to give everything to one person or the other, but it is also efficient to have them share resources in ways such that there are no further gains from trade. Points inside the utility possibility set are then inefficient because from such points it is possible to move to the northeast within the utility possibility set and thus make everyone better off.

As we will see, it is unlikely that a consequentialist approach to deciding "what is good" within this framework will lead us to choose a point other than one that is located on the efficient utility possibility frontier. Were we to choose a point inside the frontier, we would need to conclude that it is in fact best not to make everyone better off. This then explains our heavy focus on efficiency because efficiency is a *necessary* condition for an optimal outcome under virtually any consequatialist normative approach. It is not, however, a *sufficient condition* for an optimal outcome because we might prefer some outcomes on the utility possibility frontier over others. We will illustrate this formally in Section 29A.3.3 after considering some real-world wrinkles to constructing utility possibility frontiers.

29A.3.2 "First-Best" and "Second-Best" Utility Possibility Frontiers
The utility possibility frontier we derived in Graph 29.1 simply plotted the utility allocations associated with all possible efficient outcomes in an economy. But we paid no attention to whether it is actually *possible* to reach all of these allocations. Within the typical neoclassical economics model, we know that, *so long as the government can use nondistortionary lump sum taxes to redistribute across individuals*, all efficient allocations are indeed feasible equilibrium outcomes for some redistributive government policy. (In Chapter 16, we referred to this as the "second welfare theorem.") But we also know from our treatment of taxes throughout the text that real-world governments often do not have access to lump sum taxes but must instead rely on distortionary taxes that create deadweight losses. And under distortionary taxation, the utility possibility frontier that is *in principle* possible under lump sum taxes is no longer possible *in practice*.

Put differently, we can think of lump sum taxes as a "first-best" redistributive tool for the government, and we can call the utility possibility frontier that emerges from applications of lump sum redistribution as the *first-best utility possibility frontier*. When the government must instead choose from distortionary taxes, we will refer to the best such distortionary tax policy as "second-best" and the resulting utility possibility frontier as a *second-best utility possibility frontier*. We can then similarly distinguish between "first-best" and "second-best" notions of efficiency, in each case referring to the utility allocations along the relevant utility possibility frontier.

Suppose, for instance, that individual 1 is initially endowed with everything in the economy. Then if nothing is done, we would be at the lower right-hand corner of our first-best utility possibility frontier. Now suppose we imagine the government using distortionary taxes to transfer wealth from individual 1 to individual 2. In panel (a) of Graph 29.2, we illustrate a possible (green) "second-best" utility possibility frontier and compare it with the (blue) "first-best" frontier taken from Graph 29.1b. As distortionary taxes are imposed on individual 1, the deadweight loss from taxation results in the second-best utility possibility frontier lying inside the first-best utility possibility set, with the distance between the first- and second-best frontiers increasing as the tax (and its associated deadweight loss) increases.

Exercise 29A.23 Suppose that initial wealth were more equally distributed. Illustrate how the first- and second-best utility possibilities would then be related to one another. What point do they share in common?

Panel (b) of the graph illustrates an even more dramatic possibility. Think back to our development of the Laffer Curve in Chapter 8, a curve that illustrates the impact on labor tax revenues from a tax on wages. We concluded that as the tax on wages increases, there comes a point at which individuals would choose to no longer work. If we imagine individual 1 as the worker and individual 2 as someone unable to work (and unable to consume unless he receives some transfer), we could then imagine the second-best utility possibility frontier in panel (b) emerging. As taxes are levied

Graph 29.2: First-Best and Second-Best Utility Possibility Frontiers

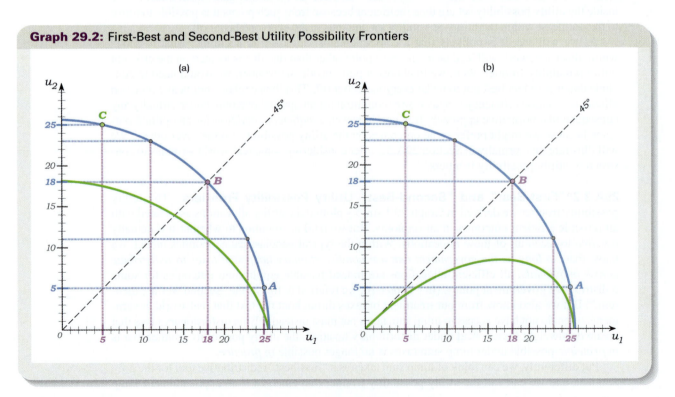

initially on individual 1, there is some deadweight loss but not enough to keep us from being able to transfer some consumption to individual 2. But as the tax on individual 1 increases, there comes a point at which increasing the tax further will reduce how much we raise from him, and thus reduce how much we can transfer to individual 2. From that point forward, both individuals become worse off as the wage tax increases.

29A.3.3 Using Social Indifference Curves to Choose What Is "Best"

Before we can ask which allocation (within an economy like the one represented by an Edgeworth Box) is "best," we have to define a way to measure which allocations are better and which are worse. If all we care about is first-best efficiency, then all the points on the contract curve (and thus all the points on the first-best utility possibility frontier) are "best" since they are all efficient. But I suspect that you would probably say that points that lie toward the middle of the first-best utility possibility frontier are "better" than points that lie toward the ends. This is because you probably think that equality is also a value we should care about.

If panel (b) of Graph 29.1 had goods rather than utilities on the axes and the utility possibility frontier were a budget constraint for a consumer, we would already know how to think about what is better and what is worse. All we would have to do is define the preferences of the individual who is trying to do the best she can, preferences like those for perfect complements or perfect substitutes or something in between. Now, however, we are trying to define social preferences over "utility bundles" rather than personal preferences over consumption bundles, and we would like to define these preferences in line with some ethical criterion.

Suppose, then, that we thought of individual utilities as perfectly substitutable much like we thought of Coke and Pepsi as perfectly substitutable when we analyzed consumer preferences. Our social preferences would then be such that they give rise to social indifference curves that are straight lines with slope -1. Such social indifference maps are often called *Benthamite social prefereces*.[11] Suppose instead that we thought of individual utilities as perfect complements much like we thought of sugar and tea as perfect complements in Chapter 5. In that case, our social indifference curves would take on L-shapes with the corners of the "L" along the 45-degree line. Such social indifference maps are often referred to as *Rawlsian social preferences* after the 20th-century philosopher John Rawls.[12] Or we could think of degrees of substitutability between these extremes, giving rise to social indifference curves that lie in between those of Benthamite straight lines and Rawlsian L-shapes. Graph 29.3 then illustrates how we can choose the "best" allocation of utilities, and thereby the "best" allocation in the Edgeworth Box, using different social indifference curves.

For the particular example illustrated in Graph 29.3, it turns out that each of our sets of social indifference curves picks out the exact same point on the utility possibility frontier. This is because we have assumed that both the utility possibility frontier and the social indifference curves are symmetric. By "symmetric" I mean that if we draw a 45-degree line, both the indifference curves and the utility possibility frontier below the 45-degree line are mirror images of the indifference curves and the utility possibility frontier above the 45-degree line. As we will argue in the next section, it is often natural to assume that social indifference curves are symmetric in this way because that implies that all individuals are treated equally by the ethical criterion we are choosing to evaluate social outcomes. But, as we have already seen in our development of second-best utility possibility frontiers, it is far from obvious why we should assume that utility possibility frontiers are generally symmetric.

---

[11]These are named after the 19th-century utilitarian philosopher Jeremy Bentham (1748–1832), who advocated the "greatest good for the greatest number of people." Whether he would actually have agreed that his preferred social indifference map treated individuals as perfect substitutes is, however, debatable.

[12]John Rawls (1921–2002) was among the most influential 20th-century moral and political philosophers who taught at Harvard for most of his career. His most influential work, in which he argued that society should maximize the welfare of the least well-off, is *A Theory of Justice* (Cambridge, Mass.: Harvard University Press, 1971).

Graph 29.3: Three Sets of Social Indifference Curves

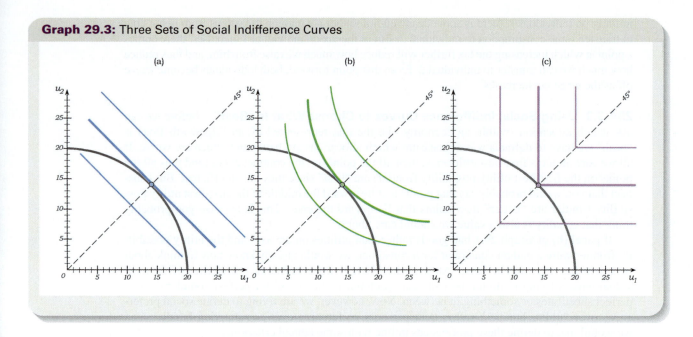

Consider, for instance, two second-best utility possibility frontiers such as those in Graph 29.4. In panel (a), the social preferences represented by (magenta) Rawlsian social indifference curves (that treat utilities as perfect complements) result in point A being optimal, while the social preferences represented by (blue) Benthamite social indifference curves (that treat utilities as perfect substitutes) result in point B being optimal. Panel (b) of Graph 29.4 further illustrates

Graph 29.4: Choosing what Is "Best" with Second-Best Utility Possibility Frontiers

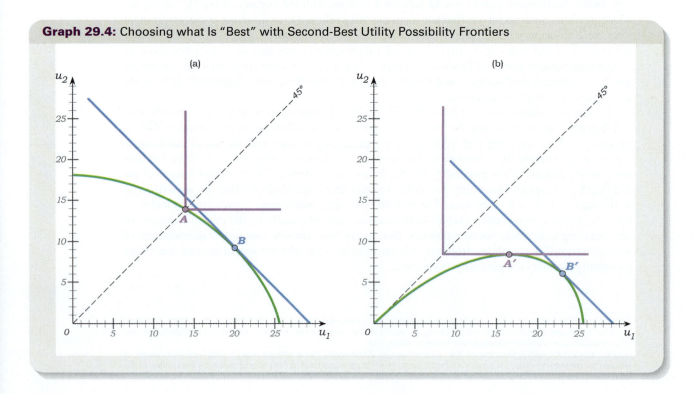

how, when second-best taxation is used for redistribution, the optimal outcome can lie off the 45-degree line even when utilities are perfect complements in the social indifference curves. The disappearance of the symmetry of the first-best utility possibility frontier due to second-best taxation therefore creates a divergence of what we consider optimal depending on how we feel about the relative substitutability of individual utilities.

True or False: Symmetric social preferences that view utilities as somewhat substitutable—i.e., social preferences that give rise to indifference curves between the extremes of perfect complements and perfect substitutes—would result in optimal allocations that lie between *A* and *B* in Graph 29.4a.

Exercise 29A.24

29A.3.4 Choosing Social Indifference Curves from behind a "Veil of Ignorance"

So, given that different social indifference curves give different answers to what is "best," how are we to choose the set of social indifference curves that should guide our policy choices? Given what we know from Arrow's Theorem in Chapter 28, we cannot simply say that social preferences are those that emerge from democratic political processes because Arrow's Theorem tells us that democratic processes do not give rise to well defined social preferences. Rather, the question is fundamentally an ethical question, and the answer therefore involves taking a philosophical stand on what *should* matter to us.

One conceptual approach that philosophers have developed to help us think through this issue is that of imagining that we have to choose an ethical criterion prior to knowing what position in society we actually occupy. Imagine that we are taken out of this world and placed behind a "veil of ignorance" that conceals from us who we are in this world. Behind this veil, in a place that philosophers call "the original position," we do not know whether we are born to rich or poor parents, whether we like Coke or Pepsi, whether we are smart or not so smart, beautiful or not, etc. All we know is the various places that will exist in the world, any one of which we might actually end up occupying. In placing ourselves behind this veil, would we be able to agree on some ethical criterion that should guide how we will agree to evaluate social outcomes once we are born?

In his famous work *A Theory of Justice* (1971), John Rawls argues that we will choose a very particular answer from this position of ignorance—that we will find ourselves desiring a society that maximizes the welfare of the least well off individual. This would imply that, in comparing different social outcomes, we will say that outcome *A* is better than outcome *B* if and only if the least well off individual under *A* is better off than the least well off individual under *B*. Notice that this is analogous to how a consumer who considers *x* and *y* perfect complements evaluates bundles of *x* and *y*. If *x* is tea and *y* is sugar, the individual cares only about how many drinkable beverages she has, and if she has 10 teas and 5 sugars, she only has 5 drinkable beverages. Bundle $A = (x_A, y_A)$ for such a consumer is then better than bundle $B = (x_B, y_B)$ if and only if the lesser of x_A and y_A is greater than the lesser of x_B and y_B. That is exactly how Rawls says we will feel about utility bundles, which is to say that Rawls believes we will want to choose an ethical criterion that can be captured by social indifference curves that treat utilities as perfect complements. This is why we have called such social indifference maps *Rawlsian social preferences*.

But not everyone agrees that this is indeed what we would choose from behind the veil of ignorance. The influential economist John Harsanyi (1920–2000) argued that we would view the choice of an ethical criterion as a choice made in the presence of risk, and that we will choose an ethical criterion that maximizes our *expected utility* once the veil of ignorance is lifted.[13] Rawls dismissed the very possibility that we could assign probabilities to ending up in

---

[13]John Harsanyi (who wrote his dissertation under fellow Nobel Laureate Ken Arrow) shared the 1994 Nobel Prize with his fellow game theorists John Nash and Reinhard Selten. He taught for much of his career at the University of California-Berkeley.

different positions once the veil is lifted, and he therefore dismissed the possibility that we could in fact choose a criterion that maximizes *expected* utility.

But, as we show more formally in part B of this chapter, if we allow for the possibility that individuals in fact know the probability of ending up in different places after the veil is lifted, one can reconcile Rawls's conclusion with Harsanyi's. Rawls's solution—that we will choose social indifference curves that treat individual utilities as perfect complements—will emerge if we assume that we are extremely *risk averse* behind the veil of ignorance. The extreme risk aversion then focuses us entirely on the possibility that we will in fact become the least well off person in society and causes us to choose an ethical criterion that places all the emphasis on the least well off. Under less risk aversion, however, we might choose an ethical criterion that allows for substitutability between individual utility, accepting some risk that we might end up the least well off (and worse off than under Rawls's criterion) in exchange for higher utility if we end up not being so unlucky.

It seems, then, that the conceptual device of imagining a "veil of ignorance" behind which an ethical criterion is chosen does *not* result in unanimous agreement among philosophers (or economists) about the types of social indifference curves that should guide our ethical judgments about "what is good." There are, however, some areas on which there is agreement: First, it seems likely that we would agree to choose a point *on* at least the second best utility possibility frontier, not a point that lies inside the utility possibility set. Furthermore, if the utility possibility frontier takes on a second-best shape such as that in Graph 29.2b, it seems likely that we will *not* choose a point on the upward-sloping part of the frontier, at least not unless we allow envy (discussed more explicitly in end-of-chapter exercise 29.4) to enter the calculation. Put differently, we would almost certainly choose an ethical criterion that satisfies at least some notion of efficiency, even if it is a "second-best" notion of efficiency that accepts some deadweight losses from redistributive taxation. Second, it seems unlikely that, not knowing who we will be in society, we would choose social indifference curves that would value the utility combination (u_a, u_b) more or less than the utility combination (u_b, u_a). Put differently, since I do not know if I will be individual 1 or individual 2, I will choose an ethical criterion that treats individuals 1 and 2 *symmetrically*.

29A.3.5 From Unmeasurable Utility to Measurable Outcomes

Although practitioners in the happiness literature may disagree, most economists would still argue that it is difficult if not impossible to ever arrive at objective measures of utility. This difficulty limits the degree to which we can actually use the philosophical insights discussed thus far to guide actual evaluation of policy. If one is inclined to make ethical judgments that go beyond efficiency in evaluating outcomes from alternative institutional arrangements, one has to therefore look for measurable outcomes on which to base these judgments. Personal income and consumption are two possible candidates for such measurable outcomes.

Rather than putting individual utilities on the axes of our graphs, we could then put individual incomes on the axes, and we could define social indifference maps over income bundles just as we defined social indifference curves over utility bundles. Treating income as perfectly substitutable across individuals would then imply that we have social preferences that cause us to choose policies that maximize *total* income in society. Treating individual incomes as perfect complements, on the other hand, would imply "Rawlsian" social preferences that cause us to maximize the income of the lowest income individual in society. And of course we could again define many social preferences that fall in between these extremes.

Exercise 29A.25

Suppose that government income redistribution programs cause no change in behavior. *True or False*: Then the Rawlsian social indifference curves would imply full redistribution of income; i.e., full income equality after redistribution.

**Exercise
29A.26**

Now suppose that government redistribution programs cause changes in behavior (such as those predicted by the Laffer Curve from Chapter 8). Can you argue that Rawlsian social indifference curves would now imply less than full redistribution; i.e., some income inequality would remain after the Rawlsian redistribution program has been implemented?

Even this approach, despite now being fully based on observable outcomes, is often too involved to make certain kinds of real world comparisons between institutional arrangements. As a result, economists have developed alternative tools to capture the degree of inequality that arises under different circumstances. A full description of these is beyond the scope of this text, and so we offer just one common example known as the *Gini coefficient*.

In Graph 29.5, we illustrate how this Gini coefficient is calculated. The horizontal axis of each of the panels has the cumulative share of individuals from lowest to highest income. For instance, 0.4 on this axis represents the person who has a level of income such that 40% of the population is poorer and 60% is richer. The vertical axis, on the other hand, has the cumulative share of income earned, or the fraction of the society's income that accrues to the different segments of society. For instance, point *B* in panel (a) indicates that the poorest 40% of the population earns just 5% of the total income in society. Point *A* indicates that the poorest 80% earns 50% of total income, or, put differently, the top 20% earn half of all income. For any distribution of income in a society, we can therefore plot such a relationship, which is called the *Lorenz curve*.[14]

Complete equality of income would imply that the poorest individuals earn the same percentage of total income as the richest. Thus, the poorest 5% would earn 5% of total income, the poorest 25% would earn 25% of total income, and the poorest 75% would earn 75%. This implies that full equality would result in a Lorenz curve that lies exactly on the 45-degree line. The sequence of panels in Graph 29.5 then begins with a relatively unequal income distribution and moves toward greater equality.

Graph 29.5: Lorenz Curves

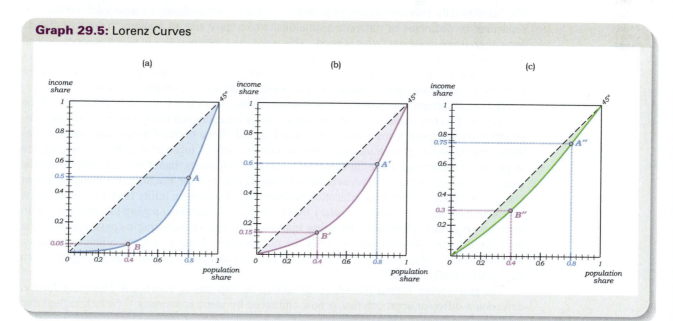

[14]The curve is named after the economist Max Lorenz (1880–1962), who developed the concept as a graduate student unaware of how influential it would become. He did not include it in his doctoral dissertation (which developed a theory of railroad rates).

Exercise
29A.27   Can the relationship in these graphs ever cross the 45-degree line?

Exercise
29A.28   Using the points analogous to *A* and *B* from panel (a) in Graph 29.5, show how panels (b) and (c) represent an increasingly equal income distribution.

The Gini coefficient (named after the Italian statistician Corrado Gini (1884–1965)) is then simply defined as the shaded area between the Lorenz curve and the 45-degree line divided by the area underneath the 45-degree line. Note that this implies that the Gini coefficient will always take on a value in the interval from zero to 1. Under perfect equality, the shaded area is equal to zero, implying a Gini coefficient of zero. Under perfect inequality, a single person would receive all the income in society, leaving us with a Lorenz curve that lies on the axes below the 45-degree line. In that case, the coefficient would be equal to the area below the 45-degree line divided by the same area, which is equal to 1.

The Gini coefficient is convenient in that it summarizes the level of inequality in a single number between 0 and 1. However, for any given society this number changes depending on what precisely we use to measure personal income. For instance, do we measure income before or after taxes, before or after government transfer payments, at one point in time or over the lifetime of individuals? Most developed countries have Gini coefficients in the range of 0.25 to 0.4, with countries that are smaller and more uniform tending to have lower Gini coefficients than countries that are larger and more heterogeneous. Few countries have Gini coefficients larger than 0.6.

29A.4 An Alternative: The "Rules of the Game" Are What Matter

We introduced the previous section by pointing out that we were initially focused solely on the consequences or outcomes of different institutions, which gave rise to a purely "consequentialist" approach to thinking about "what is good." This is the most common way in which economists tend to think of normative questions. We are good at predicting consequences of institutional incentives using the positive economics we have developed throughout the text, and those consequences then form the basis for how most economists think about the desirability of different policies.

But not all economists take this view. Part of the reason for this is the recognition that, in the absence of objective measures of utility that allow for interpersonal utility comparisons, the consequentialist approach loses some of its natural appeal. If we think of measurable outcomes as those that enter social welfare functions, outcomes such as income or consumption, we are implicitly making much more fundamental normative judgments than if we were able to use the more abstract utility-based approach. Individuals with a love for teaching, for instance, might choose lower paying careers in education because they derive more utility from the combination of teaching and the accompanying salary than they would from higher paying jobs that carry with them less personal satisfaction. By using individual income or measurable consumption as the basis for thinking about equity, we miss the nonpecuniary benefits society offers to teachers. Should it really violate our sense of "equity" if a teacher makes less money than an engineer even if they are equally happy?

The philosopher Robert Nozick (1938–2002), in response to Rawls's *A Theory of Justice*, defended a different approach that is now embraced by some economics.[15] Nozick argued that

---

[15]Robert Nozick was John Rawls's colleague at Harvard and is a frequently cited philosopher by those with libertarian ideological leanings. His response to Rawls, titled *Anarchy, State and Utopia*, was published in 1974, three years after Rawls's *A Theory of Justice*.

Chapter 29. What Is Good? Challenges from Psychology and Philosophy

1155

you cannot judge whether an observed distribution of income is "just" by simply observing the distribution; rather, you have to know how the distribution came about. If the "starting point" was just, he viewed the distribution of income (or wealth or utility) that emerges from that starting point as also just so long as the distribution was brought about by free exchange among consenting adults. If I choose to have less income because I love teaching and teachers don't get paid as much in the market, then this does not take away from the justness of the observed distribution because I voluntarily chose to trade off income with teaching satisfaction.

What mattered to Nozick, then, is not how equal or unequal the current distribution of resources in a society is; the Gini coefficient is not relevant because it is simply a summary index of consequences that arose from choices made by people who started at some starting point. The questions that need to be answered to determine whether a society is just are: (1) was the starting point just and (2) did people freely choose their path from that point forward? If the starting point was just, and if the "rules of the game" from then on were such that choices were made voluntarily and freely, there is nothing more to be gleaned from observing the outcome. You may notice that this perspective tends to lead to a decidedly libertarian view of government in society, government as an enforcer of contracts and property rights that allow individuals to engage in free and voluntary exchange.

Under what conditions would Nozick's just society lead to efficient outcomes?

Exercise 29A.29

But the libertarian conclusion on the role of government presumes that the "starting point" was just to begin with. And this raises the question of what we mean by the "starting point" and what conclusions we would draw about the role of government if we judge that starting point to be unjust. Uniform access to quality education, for instance, would seem to many as a necessary condition for the starting point to be truly just, but if parental incomes are vastly unequal, it is unlikely that children from different backgrounds really start at positions that are equitably distributed unless nonmarket institutions ensure access to education that is largely independent of parental income. Nozick's emphasis on starting points may therefore lead to more egalitarian policy prescriptions than might be apparent at first, although the nature of such policies would be more focused on ensuring "equal opportunity" rather than "equal outcomes."

It is likely that economists who take the Nozick "nonconsequentialist" position often do so in part for consequentialist reasons because they conclude from the first welfare theorem that the voluntary exchange in markets is the primary means through which welfare gains arise in a competitive economy. Put differently, one might be a consequentialist in the sense that one in fact takes consequences (rather than starting points and fair rules) as the basis for making moral judgments about "what is good," but at the same time one believes that ensuring equitable starting points and then allowing voluntary exchange to govern the end point is in fact the best means to get to "good" consequences. In that sense, the views articulated by Rawls and Nozick might be at least partially reconciled.

29B Some Tools in the Search for "What Is Good"

In Section A, we have tried to present some challenges to the material covered in the previous chapters in light of the larger question of how one might take some of the insights of this text and move from the positive question "what is" to the normative question "what is good?" We'll make no attempt in Section B to replicate this overview, but we instead go into somewhat greater depth in particular dimensions. There is much to normative economics that this will not touch, but all we aim for is a beginning that you might want to explore further in other courses. Section 29B.1

focuses on expanding our discussion of present-biased and reference point-based decision making in behavioral economics, while Section 29B.2 elaborates on topics raised in our discussion of consequentialist normative economics.

29B.1 Probing Deeper into Aspects of Behavioral Economics

We begin, then, with the challenges economists face from the field of psychology, challenges that, as we have noted, are the central focus of the relatively new subfield known as behavioral economics. As noted in Section A, behavioral economists do not dispense with the basic underlying framework used throughout this book and premised on the assertion that "individuals try to do the best they can given their circumstances." Rather, motivated by behavioral "anomalies" that are not easily explained within the standard microeconomics approach, they find ways of modeling tastes and circumstances with insights from psychology in mind. While it is often the case that there are other ways of "tweaking" standard models to bring their predictions in line with these empirical anomalies, behavioral economics sometimes offers the simplest and intuitively most compelling mechanisms. We focused in Section A especially on present-bias and reference-based decision making, and we now return to these topics in somewhat greater depth.

29B.1.1 Time Inconsistent Tastes and Present-Bias

In Section A, we raised the fact that some individuals appear to have "present-biased" preferences that lead to self-control problems. One way to explain this is that such individuals discount the immediate future more heavily than the more distant future, thus searching for immediate gratification now while intending to "invest for the future" in the future. But if preferences are truly "present biased," then they will be so again in future "presents," resulting in more search for immediate gratification combined with intentions to "invest for the future" in the yet-to-come future.

The model we introduced was the "beta-delta model," a model in which trade-offs between costs and benefits between future periods are made just as they are in standard economic models. *But* trade-offs between future periods and the present are made with a bias toward consuming benefits in the present and postponing costs to the future. And, crucially, the assumption is that the increased discounting of the future from the present is not just a phenomenon linked to the particular period in which we find ourselves but is rather linked to the idea of "present" that moves forward in time and thus changes future discount rates as the future becomes the present.

Extending the beta-delta model to more than three periods is trivial in that it only involves multiplying *all* δ discount terms by β. If we then consider an investment project that costs c in t periods but will create benefit b in $(t + n)$ periods, we would conclude that the investment will be worth undertaking so long as $\beta\delta^{t}c < \beta\delta^{(t+n)}b$ or simply $c < \delta^{n}b$. But when period t becomes period 0 and the future "present" has arrived, we will want to undertake the project only if $c < \beta\delta^{n}b$, which is a different rule than we had planned on using unless $\beta = 1$. Thus, just as in the three-period case, the beta-delta model introduces no bias between future periods, only a bias between now and any future period.

In Section A, we mentioned the danger of confusing the concept of *impatience* in the standard model of discounting with the idea of *present-bias* in the beta-delta model. A second danger (that we did not explicitly address in Section A) is that many believe the model differs from the standard neoclassical model in that it permits discount rates to change. This is not so, with changing discount rates neither problematic for the standard approach nor giving rise to time-inconsistent decision rules. To be sure, economists often assume constant discounting, but they do so more as a matter of convenience than necessity, not because changing discount rates will somehow give rise to time inconsistencies.

For instance, I can plan to discount the future more as I get older, and as I look ahead and try to guess whether some investment will be worthwhile when I am 55, I will come up with exactly the same decision rule as the one I will end up following when I am 55 *as long as the discount rates actually follow the pattern that I anticipate as the future becomes the present.* More generally, suppose that I consider at time $t = 0$ an investment c in period t that results in a benefit b in period $(t + n)$, and suppose that I view \$1 in period i as equivalent to \$$\delta_i$ in period $(i - 1)$, with no restriction on how δ_i relates to δ_j for periods $i \neq j$. Looking ahead from period 0, I will then think the investment in period t worthwhile so long as

$$\delta_1 \delta_2 \dots \delta_t c < (\delta_1 \delta_2 \dots \delta_t) \delta_{t+1} \delta_{t+2} \dots \delta_{t+n} b, \tag{29.1}$$

which simplifies to

$$c < \delta_{t+1} \delta_{t+2} \dots \delta_{t+n} b. \tag{29.2}$$

The latter is then exactly the same as the decision rule I will use to determine whether the investment is worthwhile when I get to period t and actually have to pull the trigger on making (or not making) the investment c. *Time-consistent choice does not require constant discounting.* The key is that the different values of δ are attached to time periods defined in an absolute sense; i.e., each subscript might refer to a specific calendar year or a specific age that I will be in that period, and they are not defined in a relative sense that would imply δ_t is always the relevant discount term t periods from now. Put differently, t refers to a point in time as we allow discount terms to vary, not to a period of delay from the present moment.

In the same way, the beta-delta model does not require a single δ and can be governed by different δ's across *absolute* time so long as β continues to play the same role as before. With deltas as specified, we will then get the same result as before—i.e., the decision rule in equation (29.2)—as we contemplate an investment in the future, but we will get a "less patient" decision rule once t rolls around and becomes the present.

Demonstrate that the last sentence is true.

Exercise 29B.1

The beta-delta model therefore does not add time-varying discount rates to economics; rather, it brings into economics the psychologist's idea that our discounting rule is present-biased, and thus alters our anticipated discount rates as the future becomes the present. It is one simple way to model self-control problems, one that has considerable intuitive appeal.

In within-chapter-exercise 29A.2, we implicitly assumed that δ is constant over time. Would allowing for the possible change in δ over time allow for the standard model to explain what we previously concluded only the beta-delta model can explain?

Exercise 29B.2

Finally, it is worth mentioning that the beta-delta model is also known as a model of "quasi-hyperbolic discounting" because it is a tractable simplification of a previously employed "hyperbolic discounting" model in which the present-bias is not as discrete as it is in the beta-delta model. To be more precise, the beta-delta model assumes that we don't change at all how future periods are traded off against one another, only how the future is being traded off against the present. More general hyperbolic discounting models soften this discreteness in difference between how the future is treated relative to the present versus how the more distant future is treated relative to the more immediate future. As a result, some models of hyperbolic discounting allow the bias to extend beyond the immediate present. In the end, however, it is often most convenient to simply focus on the simplest of all models that captures what we are after, and the beta-delta model is therefore frequently employed over less tractable hyperbolic discounting models for precisely this reason.

29B.1.2 Reference Points, Risk, and Prospect Theory

We mentioned in Section A the idea of reference points and the related notion of loss aversion that arises when we find that incurring losses is particularly difficult psychologically. The underlying theory, known as *prospect theory* and first put forward by Amos Tverski (1937–1996) and Daniel Kahneman (1934–), is actually more general than this and deals in particular with how people confront risks in many situations where the standard neoclassical approach does not predict well.

Suppose you face a gamble in which you will get a payoff of x_1 with probability δ and x_2 with probability $(1 - \delta)$. Prospect theory says that you will evaluate this gamble using the function

$$\pi(\delta)u(x_1 - r) + \pi(1 - \delta)u(x_2 - r) \tag{29.3}$$

where r is a reference point and π is a function that transforms the real underlying probabilities with which the two events are likely to occur. Notice that our standard expected utility formulation of gambles is contained within this equation as a special case, with $\pi(\delta) = \delta$, $\pi(1 - \delta) = (1 - \delta)$, and $r = 0$.

Exercise 29B.3

Explain the last sentence.

For any $r \neq 0$, this formulation of utility in the presence of risk therefore instantly becomes *reference dependent*. The phenomenon of *loss aversion* (as described in Section A) comes about if the utility function u is kinked at the reference point, with losses from the reference point weighted more heavily than gains. For instance, if the reference point is $r = 1,000$ and $(x_1, x_2) = (800, 1200)$, then x_1 is interpreted as a "loss" while x_2 is interpreted as a gain. But, under loss aversion, $-u(-200) > u(200)$. These are the two types of effects that we mentioned in Section A.

Exercise 29B.4

In one set of experiments, individuals were asked how much they would be willing to pay to participate in a gamble in which they receive $8 when a coin comes up heads but owe $5 if it comes up tails. Close to two thirds were not willing to pay anything, which can be explained in the standard expected utility framework only if we are willing to assume a level of risk aversion that is roughly equivalent to such individuals never leaving their house for fear of all the risks they will encounter. Can you rationalize the results of the experiment for a risk averse individual using only the parts of prospect theory that incorporate reference bias and loss aversion?

Our formulation here, however, allows for two additional effects that appear to be important in at least some settings. First, Tversky and Kahnemann hypothesized that the utility function used to evaluate equation (29.3) is concave over gains and convex over losses, giving rise to *diminishing sensitivity* of outcomes as we move farther from the reference point. Consider again $r = 1,000$ and $(x_1, x_2) = (800, 1200)$ and then compare it to the outcome pair $(x_1', x_2') = (600, 1400)$. Diminishing sensitivity implies that this doubling of the distance away from the reference point affects the individual less (in either direction) than the initial deviation from the reference point.

To clarify this further, consider the following famous experiment: Subjects are randomly assigned to two different groups. Individuals in Group 1 are given $1,000 to participate and are then asked to choose between getting Option 1A under which they get $500 more and Option 1B under which a coin toss determines whether they get $1,000 more (if the coin comes up heads) or nothing more (if it comes up tails). Individuals in Group 2 are given $2,000 to participate and are asked to choose between Option 2A that simply involves giving up $500 and Option 2B under which a coin toss determines whether they need to give up $1,000 (if the coin comes up heads) or nothing (if it comes up tails). It turns out that 84% in Group 1 but only 31% in Group 2 chose the "safer" A option.

In panel (a) of Graph 29.6, we illustrate why our standard expected utility theory from Chapter 17 cannot rationalize what happens in this experiment. In the graph, we model a utility/consumption relationship that allows us to express a risk averse individual's utility from taking gambles as an expected utility. Options $1A$ and $2A$ are identical in that the subject in each case faces an equal chance of being able to consume $1,000 (plus whatever other income x he has) and consuming $2,000 (plus whatever other income x he has). Options $1B$ and $2B$ are similarly identical in the sense that the subjects in both cases leave the experiment with $1,500 more consumption than they could get before the experiment. Expected utility theory therefore predicts that $u_{1A} = u_{2A}$ and $u_{1B} = u_{2B}$, implying that approximately the same number of subjects in the two groups should pick option A over option B when subjects are randomly assigned to both groups. But a lot more people in Group 1 end up doing so than in Group 2.

....

Demonstrate that the same conclusion—i.e., that $u_{1A} = u_{2A}$ and $u_{1B} = u_{2B}$—arises when tastes are risk loving. How are the options ranked differently by each group relative to risk aversion?

**Exercise
29B.5**

....

Panels (b) and (c) of Graph 29.6 then illustrate how prospect theory can rationalize the outcome of the experiment *if the subjects use the amount of money they are handed at the outset as a reference point* against which to compare alternatives. Those in Group 1 get $1,000 as they walk into the experiment, and thus the reference point r is $1,000 as in panel (b). Those in Group 2, on the other hand, are handed $2,000 as they walk into the experiment, and thus $r = \$2,000$ for them. In Group 1, everything that follows is interpreted as a "gain," and thus is evaluated by the blue portion of the u function that lies to the right of r (in panel (b)) where the function is concave. In Group 2, on the other hand, everything that follows is interpreted as a "loss," and thus is evaluated on the magenta

Graph 29.6: Prospect Theory versus Standard Expected Utility Theory

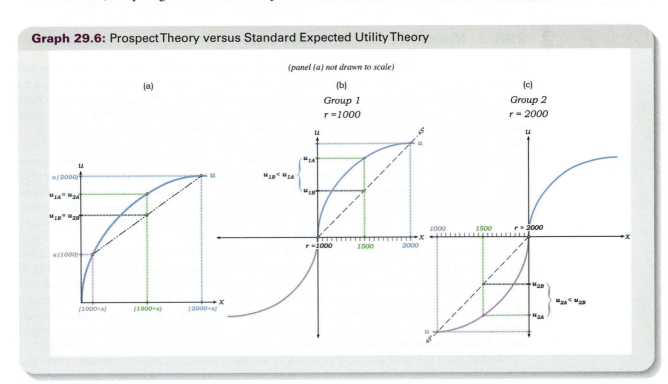

portion of the u function that lies to the left of r (in panel (c)) where the function is convex. As a result, you can see that $u_{1B} < u_{1A}$, implying that prospect theory predicts individuals in Group 1 will choose the safe A option. But in panel (c), $u_{2A} < u_{2B}$, implying that the theory predicts individuals in Group 2 will choose the riskier B option instead. Notice that prospect theory therefore implies *risk aversion when people evaluate gains and risk loving when they evaluate losses.*

Exercise 29B.6

Can you explain how *diminishing sensitivity* gives rise to the switch between risk loving and risk aversion at the reference point?

The second additional effect allowed for in equation (29.3) is known as *probability weighting*. This arises because the equation suggests that individuals might not consider the actual probabilities of events (i.e., δ and $(1 - \delta)$) but rather some transformation π of these probabilities, with experimental and empirical evidence suggesting that π overweights small probabilities and underweights large probabilities. This offers an immediate possible explanation for how otherwise risk averse people (who buy insurance against all sorts of risks in their lives) go out and buy lottery tickets that offer them a tiny probability of winning a large amount (with an expected payoff that is negative). It may also help explain why individuals appear to consistently choose to pay substantially higher than actuarially fair insurance for small and relatively low-probability risks (like small losses in homeowner's insurance policies).

Exercise 29B.7

Explain how probability weighting can make sense of the fact that risk averse individuals play in state lotteries. How can it explain purchases of insurance against small, low-probability risks when insurance policies are priced far from actuarily fair?

29B.2 Normative Economics when Consequences Matter

In Section A, we referred to different ways in which economists and philosophers might approach normative economics in the abstract and in practice, with the most common approach used by economists taking on a highly *consequentialist* flavor. Put differently, economists typically believe that the normative answer to "what is good" will depend a great deal on the positive answer to the question "what is" or "what will be." Thus, knowing the consequences of different options we choose from will assist us in deciding which option is "good" and which isn't. In the abstract treatment of such an approach to normative economics, we can assume that we know the utility consequences of different options for different individuals and then use a *social welfare function* (that acts as a utility functions over utility allocations) to choose what is "good." Thus, the social welfare function embodies within it normative or ethical judgments about distributional issues within societies, with some social welfare functions being more "egalitarian" in their focus on equality and some more "utilitarian" in their focus on overall societal utility.

Of course we cannot typically observe utility in practice, and we have therefore suggested that the abstract engagements of normative economists with philosophy must ultimately give way to the practical issue of what tools will be available to us to make ethical judgments beyond efficiency with the data we actually have. Instead of making the set of utility allocations the domain of social welfare functions, for instance, we could make individual consumption or income levels the domain that is evaluated. Consumption and income are, after all, measurable and, according to the "happiness" literature touched on in Section A, at least somewhat correlated with utility.

We will leave the more practical aspects touched on in Section A largely untouched here and instead illustrate some of the basics of the more abstract approach to normative economics. We will also leave aside some of the deeper questions on the disconnect between our "work-horse" definition of happiness in positive economics with the "real thing" that human beings might experience, taking it for granted that there is probably a gap between these and that factors like security, family, faith, etc., play important roles that we simply ignore here. We will, however, focus toward the end of the chapter on the Rawlsian assertion that, were we to be able to choose from behind a veil of ignorance, we would tend to choose a society governed by Rawlsian social welfare functions and will present an economist's approach to the assertion (and a challenge to it).

29B.2.1 "First-Best" and "Second-Best" Utility Possibility Frontiers

In Section A, we first derived utility possibility frontiers from the contract curve in an exchange economy and then distinguished between "first-best" and "second-best" utility possibility frontiers, with the former assuming the availability of efficient redistributive taxation while the latter constrains governments to using distortionary taxes for redistributing resources. We will leave the derivation of utility possibility frontiers from contract curves as an exercise (in end-of-chapter exercise 29.1) and illustrate here an example of how first-and second-best frontiers differ.

Suppose that consumer 1 is endowed with one normalized unit of leisure time, any fraction of which can be turned into an equal amount of private consumption through labor effort at a wage normalized to 1. Thus, if ℓ denotes her leisure consumption, her private good consumption c_1 in the absence of taxation is $(1 - \ell)$. Suppose further that individual 2 is not able to work and thus unable to earn an income for private good consumption. The only way that individual 2 can consume $c_2 > 0$ is if the government redistributes resources from individual 1 to individual 2. Assume the utility functions are given by

$$u_1 = 2c_1^{1/2}\ell^{1/2} \text{ and } u_2 = c_2. \tag{29.4}$$

Consider first the case of an efficient lump sum tax that is used to redistribute a fraction T of consumer 1's endowment. Under such a non-distortionary tax, individual 1's endowment therefore shrinks from 1 to $(1 - T)$, and her consumption now becomes $(1 - T - \ell)$. We can then solve for consumer 1's optimizing choice of leisure and consumption as $\ell^* = (1 - T)/2$ and $c_1^* = (1 - T)/2$, with consumer 2 simply receiving the lump sum transfer T and thus consuming $c_2 = T = u_2$. Substituting ℓ^* and c_1^* into consumer 1's utility function and then substituting $u_2 = T$, we get

$$u_1 = 2\left(\frac{(1 - T)}{2}\right)^{1/2}\left(\frac{(1 - T)}{2}\right)^{1/2} = (1 - T) = 1 - u_2, \tag{29.5}$$

which gives us the linear first-best utility possibility frontier $u_1 = 1 - u_2$.

Verify the derivation of this first-best utility possibility frontier.

Exercise 29B.8

In Section A, we suggested that the shape of the utility possibility frontier has something to do with our assumptions about the marginal utility of income. Can you apply this insight here to explain the linear utility possibility frontier in our example?

Exercise 29B.9*

Next, suppose instead that the government uses a distortionary tax t levied on individual 1's earnings $(1 - \ell)$. Then, depending on individual 1's leisure choice ℓ, the consumption levels for our two individuals will be

$$c_1 = (1 - t)(1 - \ell) \text{ and } c_2 = t(1 - \ell). \tag{29.6}$$

Solving individual 1's utility maximization problem, we get her optimal choice as $\ell^* = 1/2$ and $c_1^* = (1 - t)/2$, with individual 2 receiving $c_2 = t(1 - \ell^*) = t/2$. Substituting ℓ^* and c_1^* into consumer 1's utility function, we then get

$$u_1 = 2\left(\frac{(1 - t)}{2}\right)^{1/2}\left(\frac{1}{2}\right)^{1/2} = (1 - t)^{1/2}. \tag{29.7}$$

With $c_1 = t/2$, we have $u_2 = t/2$ and can therefore substitute $t = 2u_2$ into our expression for u_1 to get the second-best utility possibility frontier $u_1 = (1 - 2u_2)^{1/2}$.

When we now solve our first- and second-best utility possibility frontiers for u_2, we can also express them as

$$\text{First-Best Utility Possibility Frontier:}\quad u_2 = 1 - u_1$$

$$\text{Second-Best Utility Possibility Frontier:}\quad u_2 = \frac{1 - u_1^2}{2}. \tag{29.8}$$

Exercise 29B.10 Verify the derivation of the second-best utility possibility frontier.

Exercise 29B.11 Can you graph these two utility possibility frontiers and explain their relationship intuitively?

29B.2.2 Social Welfare Functions

A social welfare function is then simply the social planner's utility function over the two consumers' utility levels; i.e., it is a function W that has u_1 and u_2 (instead of the usual two consumption goods) as its arguments. Such a function might, for instance, take the Cobb–Douglas form

$$W = u_1^\alpha u_2^{(1-\alpha)} \tag{29.9}$$

and the social planner's problem would then be to maximize this function subject to the utility possibility constraint. In the case of our first-best constraint, the planner's problem would be

$$\max_{u_1, u_2} W = u_1^\alpha u_2^{(1-\alpha)} \text{ subject to } u_2 = 1 - u_1, \tag{29.10}$$

which, when solved in the usual way, gives us the first best optimum of

$$u_1^{FB} = \alpha \text{ and } u_2^{FB} = (1 - \alpha). \tag{29.11}$$

But if the social planner can only use the distortionary tax t, his problem is instead

$$\max_{u_1, u_2} W = u_1^\alpha u_2^{(1-\alpha)} \text{ subject to } u_2 = \frac{1 - u_1^2}{2} \tag{29.12}$$

and the solution to this problem is

$$u_1^{SB} = \left(\frac{\alpha}{2 - \alpha}\right)^{1/2} \text{ and } u_2^{SB} = \frac{1 - \alpha}{2 - \alpha}. \tag{29.13}$$

Exercise 29B.12 Verify these solutions for the different social welfare functions.

Chapter 29. What Is Good? Challenges from Psychology and Philosophy

1163

Table 29.3: First- and Second-Best Social Welfare Maxima

Cobb–Douglas Social Welfare Function $W = u_1^{\alpha} u_2^{(1-\alpha)}$					
α	0.00	0.25	0.50	0.75	1.00
First Best u_1	0.000	0.250	0.500	0.750	1.000
Second Best u_1	0.000	0.378	0.577	0.775	1.000
First Best u_2	1.000	0.750	0.500	0.250	0.000
Second Best u_2	0.500	0.429	0.333	0.200	0.000

In Table 29.3, we then calculate the first- and second-best utility levels for different α values in the social welfare function, where α is the relative weight the social welfare function places on individual 1's utility. When $\alpha = 0$, for instance, no weight is placed on u_1, implying that the optimum will be zero utility for individual 1, and this holds in both the first- and second-best case. But note that u_2 is only half as large in the second-best case as in the first-best case, a direct consequence of the fact that the second-best utility possibility frontier has a u_2 intercept half as large as the first-best utility possibility frontier. When $\alpha = 1$, on the other hand, the entire social weight is placed on individual 1, who therefore ends up getting all the utility. Now, however, the first- and second-best cases are identical because the social optimum in both cases requires no redistribution (and thus no distortionary tax in the second-best case). In between these extreme values of α, consumer 1 always gets more utility under the second best case and consumer 2 gets less because the social planner will not redistribute as much when the tax is distortionary.

We have implicitly assumed that we can measure individual utilities in order to construct first- and second-best utility possibility frontiers. Suppose instead that we can only measure consumption. What would the first- and second-best consumption possibilities frontiers look like for our example?

Exercise 29B.13

Might a government that derives the first- and second-best consumption possibilities frontiers from exercise 29B.13 mistakenly think that there is no efficiency loss from redistribution? How does your conclusion illustrate our conclusion from earlier chapters that deadweight loss from labor taxes cannot be derived by simply looking at uncompensated labor supply curves?

Exercise 29B.14

If a government used the second-best consumption possibility frontier as if it were the appropriate utility possibility frontier, would it redistribute too much or too little relative to what it would do if it could measure utilities?

Exercise 29B.15

29B.2.3 Rawls versus Bentham   There is, of course, no particular reason to assume a Cobb–Douglas functional form for the social welfare function that gives expression to the ethical criterion we are using to choose socially optimal outcomes from efficient outcomes. For instance, we know from our development of utility functions in Chapter 5 that the Cobb–Douglas specification of utility is a special case of the more general constant elasticity of substitution specification, with perfect complements and perfect substitutes as the two most extreme special cases. In Section A, we similarly introduced the Rawlsian notion of social indifference curves that treat individual utility levels as prefect complements and would thus give rise to a *Rawlsian social welfare function* of the form

$$W = \min\{u_1, u_2\}. \tag{29.14}$$

We also explored the opposite extreme of social indifference curves that treat individual utilities as perfect substitutes. The social welfare function that gives rise to such indifference curves is known as the *Benthamite social welfare function* and takes the form

$$W = u_1 + u_2. \tag{29.15}$$

Since the Rawlsian social welfare function has indifference curves with right angles along the 45-degree line, we know that the social optimum will lie at the intersection of the 45-degree line and the utility possibility frontier (so long as the utility possibility frontier is always downward sloping), which occurs at $u_1 = u_2 = 0.5$ in our first-best example and at $u_1 = u_2 \approx 0.414$ in our second-best example. Alternatively, we can consider the social optimum under the Benthamite function that gives rise to linear indifference curves with slope equal to -1. Since our example has a first-best utility possibility frontier that is also linear with slope -1, all utility allocations on the first-best frontier sum to the same total utility value and are thus all optimal according to this Benthamite social welfare function. In our second-best case, however, the only way to attain this much utility involves no distortionary redistribution, and thus the Benthamite social welfare function would choose the allocation $(u_1, u_2) = (1, 0)$ in the second-best case.

Exercise 29B.16 Can you draw the first- and second-best utility possibility frontiers and indicate how you would graphically arrive at the same results?

Exercise 29B.17 We concluded that the Benthamite, Rawlsian, and Cobb–Douglas social welfare function with $\alpha = 0.5$ all agree that the first-best utility allocation $u_1 = u_2 = 0.5$ is optimal, but we also found that they quite dramatically disagree on what the second-best utility allocation is. Explain why.

29B.2.4 Risk Aversion behind the "Veil of Ignorance" In Section A, we concluded our more abstract treatment of consequentialist normative economics with a discussion of how one might go about choosing the ethical criterion that should shape our social welfare function. Imagine again, as we discussed at more length in Section A, that you are asked to think about this criterion for social welfare from the "original position" behind the "veil of ignorance." You know you will eventually assume one of N possible identities, each with probability $1/N$. There are A possible social states, with social state a giving composite good consumption x_a^n to individual n. Furthermore, if you end up as individual n, you will be endowed with utility function $u^n: \mathbb{R} \to \mathbb{R}$. Thus, under state a you will receive utility $u^n(x_a^n) = u_a^n$.

We mentioned that Rawls in essence argued that the Rawlsian social welfare function would be chosen by anyone from behind the veil of ignorance while the economist Harsanyi argued that which social welfare function is chosen would depend on our assumptions about risk aversion behind the veil. We will now show that Harsanyi's approach in fact results in the Rawlsian social welfare function only if risk aversion is infinite, and that less extreme forms of risk aversion would lead to less extreme social welfare functions. As noted in Section A, Rawls rejected this approach on the grounds that the probabilities one would need to know behind the veil in order to use expected utility theory can simply not be assumed to be knowable behind the veil. In framing the problem in the previous paragraph, however, we have ignored this objection and have assigned probability $1/N$ to each position that might eventually be occupied by a person once he leaves the veil of ignorance behind.

When viewed from the perspective of the model of choice in the presence of risk (from Chapter 17), the "rational" way for you to evaluate the desirability of a particular social state $a \in A$ is then to consider your *expected utility* given by

$$U(a) = \sum_{n=1}^{N} \frac{1}{N} u_a^n = \frac{1}{N} \sum_{n=1}^{N} u_a^n. \tag{29.16}$$

Thus, you would evaluate alternative a as better than b if and only if $U(a) > U(b)$, which, if we multiply each side by N, is equivalent to

$$\sum_{n=1}^{N} u_a^n > \sum_{n=1}^{N} u_b^n. \tag{29.17}$$

This is simply the utilitarian criterion of the Benthamite social welfare function; all that matters is the sum of the utilities of the individuals, with your preferred social welfare function V expressed as

$$V(a) = \sum_{n=1}^{N} u_a^n. \tag{29.18}$$

At this point, it seems that our derivation of social welfare functions from the "original position" does not permit a role for risk aversion. Might it not be that, behind the veil of ignorance, I would want to think about the risk that I might end up as the least well off individual as suggested by Rawls?

Recall that risk aversion in the expected utility framework requires the u functions to be concave. We can then incorporate a role for risk aversion into the analysis by incorporating it directly into the N utility functions that are summed in equation (29.18). Suppose we write n's utility as $v^n(x) = (-u^n(x))^{-\rho}$. So long as $\rho > 0$, this is in fact a positive monotone transformation of u^n.

Verify that this is in fact a positive monotone transformation.

Exercise 29B.18

Note that, as ρ increases, the curvature of the utility function v^n increases, implying that risk aversion is increasing in the parameter ρ, which results in infinite risk aversion as ρ approaches infinity. Equation (29.18) then becomes

$$\overline{V}(a) = \sum_{n=1}^{N} v^n(x_a^n) = -\sum_{n=1}^{N} (u_a^n)^{-\rho}. \tag{29.19}$$

The ordering of social states given by $\overline{V}$ does not change if we subject $\overline{V}$ itself to a positive monotone transformation. Thus, we can express the same utilitarian criterion as

$$W(a) = (-\overline{V}(a))^{-1/\rho} = \left(\sum_{n=1}^{N} (u_a^n)^{-\rho} \right)^{-1/\rho}. \tag{29.20}$$

How is what we have just done a positive monotone transformation?

Exercise 29B.19

Notice that we now have a social welfare function that has the constant elasticity of substitution (CES) form, with elasticity of substitution $\sigma = 1/(1 + \rho)$. We know from our work with CES utility functions in Chapter 5 that σ approaches 0 as ρ approaches ∞. Put differently, as ρ approaches ∞, the social welfare indifference curves approach those of perfect complements. Thus, extreme risk aversion at the individual level results in the Rawlsian social welfare function that treats individual utilities as perfect complements, thus ensuring that use of such a social welfare function will result in maximizing the welfare of the least well off person in society. The Rawlsian social welfare function can then be viewed as a special case of the utilitarian criterion, one that assumes infinite risk aversion as individuals choose a social welfare function from the "original position."

This has a certain intuitive appeal if we indeed think (as Rawls did not) that one can use the expected utility framework to think about what social welfare function would be chosen by individuals from behind the veil of ignorance. If such individuals exhibit extreme risk aversion, they will care only about the risk of being the least well-off person and will thus choose a social welfare function that minimizes that risk. That social welfare function is the one that Rawls argued we would all choose from behind the veil of ignorance. Thus, if we believe we would indeed be extremely risk averse behind the veil, Rawls is right from the perspective of expected utility theory.

CONCLUSION

Although we have in previous chapters often suggested normative interpretations of our conclusions from positive economic analysis, we have not focused until this chapter on the bigger question of which predicted outcomes of our analysis might be considered "good." To be sure, our treatment of the efficiency or inefficiency of outcomes within the context of the first welfare theorem has normative content in the sense that efficient situations have some desirable properties, but this chapter has also clarified that efficiency is unlikely to be the sole goal of a "good" society. In order to get closer to being able to think in more normative terms, we have therefore tried to bring insights from some other disciplines to bear on our economic analysis and have emphasized in particular some intersections between economics on the one hand and psychology and philosophy on the other.

The contribution of psychology to our discussion began with a consideration of how our strictly positive analysis might in some instances be improved through the inclusion of insights on how behavior sometimes deviates from the predictions of traditional economic analysis. It is, as it turns out, easy to come up with a whole host of "anomalies" that might best be explained by such insights from psychologists, and it sometimes becomes tempting to question all of economics because of the existence of some such anomalies. At the same time, one should not lose sight of the fact that traditional economic models have provided powerful insights about the way the world works, insights that have withstood the test of empirical investigations. An honest recognition of the limits of traditional economic models therefore should probably not lead us to throw out the baby with the bath water, as some recent books on behavioral economics have done in chapters with titles like "The Fallacy of Supply and Demand." Not all predictions from economic models hold up under empirical scrutiny, opening up doors for fruitful cross-disciplinary investigations. But it can equally well be said that not all models informed by psychology hold up to such scrutiny, with traditional economic models still often carrying the day. The goal of science—and in particular social science—is to employ those tools that are empirically relevant for the problem at hand, with no particular discipline likely to have full ownership of the "right" tools for every question we face, and with blind allegiance to a single discipline thus decidedly "unscientific." Still, the positive tools of microeconomics remain quite powerful in terms of their ability to predict, despite the legitimate challenges from psychologists.

In terms of our goal to come closer to making informed judgments about "what is good," we have seen that behavioral economics has helped to create some conceptual frameworks to challenge such notions as "more choices are always better," and such frameworks can play an important role in choosing among institutions that take into account aspects of the human condition that would almost certainly be missed by slavish devotion to a single discipline's insights. The same can be said of the role that philosophy can play in digging deeper into the fundamental questions that lie behind the search for the "good," which can seem deceptively simple in the absence of such deeper analysis. Neither this book nor this chapter has all the answers, but the hope is that they have gotten us a little bit closer.

END-OF-CHAPTER EXERCISES

29.1 For students who have read Chapter 16, we have indicated that, for exchange economies, the utility possibility frontier corresponds to utility levels on the contract curve that is contained in the Edgeworth Box.

A. Consider the special two-good case where consumer 1 views the goods x_1 and x_2 as perfect complements, with utility equal to the lower of the quantities of x_1 and x_2 in her basket. Consumer 2, on the other hand, views the goods as perfect substitutes, with utility equal to the sum of the quantities of x_1 and x_2 in his basket.

*conceptually challenging
**computationally challenging
†solutions in Study Guide

    a.   Illustrate the contract curve for these two consumers in the Edgeworth Box assuming the overall endowment of each of the two goods in the economy is e.

    b.   What does the utility possibility frontier that derives from this contract curve look like? Carefully label intercepts and slopes.

    c.   How would the utility possibility frontier be different if the utility of consumer 2 were given by half the sum of the quantities of x_1 and x_2 in his basket?

    d.   Consider the original utility possibility frontier from part (b). Suppose the two individuals are currently endowed with the midpoint of the Edgeworth Box. Locate the point on the utility possibility frontier that corresponds to this allocation of goods.

    e.   Suppose that the government does not have access to efficient taxes for the purpose of redistributing resources. Rather, the government uses distortionary taxes, with the marginal cost of redistributing \$1 increasing with the level of redistribution. What do you think the second-best utility possibility frontier now looks like relative to the first best? Do the two share any points in common?

    f.   Suppose instead that the current endowment bundle lies off the contract curve on the diagonal that runs from the upper left to the lower right corner of the Edgeworth Box. If competitive markets are allowed to operate, do your first- and second-best utility possibility frontiers differ from those you derived so far?

    g.   If markets were not allowed to operate in the case described in (f), where would the second-best utility possibility frontier now lie relative to the first best?

B. Suppose we have an Edgeworth economy in which both individuals have the utility function $u(x_1, x_2) = x_1^\alpha x_2^{(1-\alpha)}$ and where the economy's endowment of each of the two goods is e.

    a.   Set up a maximization problem in which the utility of consumer 1 is maximized subject to the economy-wide endowment constraints and subject to keeping individual 2's utility at $\bar{u}$. (By defining individual 2's consumption of each good as the residual left over from individual 1's consumption, you can write this problem with just a single constraint.)

    b.   Derive the contract curve for this economy.

    c.   Use this to derive the utility possibility frontier. What shape does it have?

    d.   How would your answers change if we had specified the utility function as $u(x_1, x_2) = x_1^\beta x_2^{(0.5-\beta)}$ with $0 < \beta < 0.5$.

    e.   Do the two different utility functions represent the same underlying (ordinal) preferences? If so, explain the difference in the two utility possibility frontiers.

    f.   How could you keep the same (ordinal) preferences but transform the utility function in such a way as to cause the utility possibility set to be non-convex? Explain.

29.2   In the Appendix to Chapter 17, we introduced the *Allais Paradox*. It went as follows: Suppose there are three closed doors with \$5 million, \$1 million, and \$0 behind them. You are first offered a choice between Gamble 1 ($G1$) that will reveal the \$1 million door with certainty and Gamble 2 ($G2$) that will open the \$5 million door with probability 0.1, the \$1 million door with probability 0.89 and the \$0 door with probability 0.01. You get to keep whatever is behind the door that is revealed. Then, you are offered the following choice instead: either Gamble 3 ($G3$) that reveals the \$1 million door with probability 0.11 and the \$0 door with probability 0.89, or Gamble 4 ($G4$) that opens the \$5 million door with probability 0.1 and the \$0 door with probability 0.9.

A. It turns out that most people will pick $G1$ over $G2$ and $G4$ over $G3$.

    a.   Why is this set of choices inconsistent with standard expected utility theory?

    b.   Suppose that people use reference-based preferences to evaluate outcomes when making their choice between gambles. Why might the most reasonable reference point in the choice between $G1$ and $G2$ be \$1 million while the most reasonable reference point in the choice between $G3$ and $G4$ is \$0?

    c.   Can you explain how such reference-based preferences might explain the Allais paradox?

B. Suppose that individuals' reference-based tastes can be described by $u(x, r) = (x - r)^{0.5}$ when $x \geq r$ and by $v(x, r) = -(r - x)^{0.75}$ when $x < r$ (where x is the dollar value of the outcome and r is the reference point).

    a.   Consider the case where the reference points are as described in A(b). What are the utility values associated with the three outcomes when the choice is between $G1$ and $G2$? What are they when the choice is between $G3$ and $G4$?

    b.   Which gamble would be chosen by someone with such preferences in each of the two choices? How does this compare to the choices people actually make?

    c.   Show that the Allais paradox would arise if the reference point were always $0 rather than what you assumed in your resolution to the Allais paradox.

    d.   We mentioned in the text that prospect theory also allows for the possibility of probability weighting. If people overestimate what low probabilities mean, could this also help explain the Allais paradox?

29.3   One topic investigated by behavioral economists but not covered in the text relates to how individuals assess probabilities of random events occurring repeatedly. The *hot-hand fallacy* is the fallacy that a randomly generated event is *more* likely to occur again if it has just been observed to have occurred multiple times. For instance, a poker player that has had a streak of "hot hands" might believe that he is on a winning streak and will again be dealt a "hot hand" in the next game. The *gambler's fallacy*, on the other hand, occurs when people believe that once a randomly generated event has occurred, it is *less* likely to occur again. For instance, a lottery player might observe that a particular number has just won in a lottery and conclude that it is less likely that this number will win in the next run of the same lottery. (Note that neither part A nor part B of this exercise requires any material presented in Section B.)

A.   Both types of fallacies arise, for instance, for naive investors in stocks.

    a.   When a stock falls in value, people often hold on to it based on the argument that "what goes down must come up." What fallacy is this an example of?

    b.   When a stock rises in value, people sometimes hold on to it because "the company must be doing well and will thus continue to rise in value." What fallacy is at play now?

    c.   If you know that lots of other people believe that stocks that have risen in value will rise again in the near future, might this affect your investment choices even if you do not yourself operate under any particular illusion about probabilities of random events?

    d.   In the period leading up to the housing market crash in 2007, housing values were increasing at dramatic rates—by as much as 20% to 25% annually in some markets. Lots of people invested with the expectation that this would continue. Can you use the hot-hand fallacy to explain such financial "bubbles"?

    e.   The empirical evidence suggests that investors generally are less likely to dispose of losing stocks than they are to dispose of winning stocks. Is there another aspect of behavioral economics, one that is explicitly covered in the text, that might explain this (rather than either of the fallacies we have mentioned in this exercise)?

    f.   In lotteries where people guess what number will be chosen, the total money pot gets split between the winners. In light of the fact that the gambler's fallacy appears to be strong among lottery players, why might it be best to choose last week's winning number when playing the lottery this week?

B.   One of my friends had four children, each a boy. She had really been hoping for a girl for some time and reasoned that she should try again. After all, having four boys in a row was an unlikely enough event—what were the chances of the even less likely event of five boys in a row?

    a.   How many possible gender sequences are there for a woman who gives birth to four children? What does this imply for the probability that the sequence will be "all boy"?

    b.   What is the probability that her first five births are all boys?

    c.   What is the probability that the sequence of a woman's first four children is boy-girl-boy-girl? What about any other gender sequence?

    d.   What is the probability that my friend's next (and fifth) child will be a boy? How does it compare to the probability that a woman who has had the boy-girl-boy-girl sequence will have a girl as her fifth child?

    e.   My friend used the evidence that four boys in a row was an unlikely event and five boys in a row would be an even more unlikely event as her reason for why she thought she had a good chance of her fifth child being a girl. What part of her reasoning is correct, and what part is incorrect?[16]

29.4*† Everyday Application: *Reference Points, Happiness, and Envy*: The stylized results from the happiness literature suggest that happiness, at least as reported on surveys, is "reference-based" in the sense that people evaluate how happy they are not exclusively based on how much they have but, at least in part, based on how much they have *relative* to everyone else in their proximity.

EVERYDAY APPLICATION

A. This form of reference-based tastes differs from what we encounter in other settings in the sense that the "reference point" is typically something internal to the individual, such as the individual's current endowment.

    a. Explain how one might interpret the combination of the two empirical claims cited in the text as evidence of such reference-based determinants of happiness. (The two empirical claims are: (1) within countries, happiness is increasing with income; and (2) excluding countries and times of extreme poverty, there appears to be little relationship between average happiness and average income across countries or across time.)

    b. Suppose we have a situation where we have to allocate a fixed amount of money between two individuals. Individual 1 has reference-based preferences, with his happiness increasing only in his own consumption but decreasing in individual 2's consumption. Individual 2, on the other hand, has the usual preferences, with her happiness increasing only in her own consumption. In what sense is individual 1 driven in part by "envy" while individual 2 is not?

    c. Suppose utility for individual 2 is simply equal to dollars of consumption and utility for individual 1 is dollars of own consumption minus some fraction α of dollars of individual 2's consumption. Begin by drawing the utility possibility frontier for the case where $\alpha = 0$. Then show how the utility possibility frontier changes as α increases.

    d. *True or False*: When $\alpha = 0$, equal division of resources between the two individuals is socially optimal for any social indifference map that is symmetric across the 45-degree line, including the Rawlsian, the Benthamite, and any that fall in between these extremes.

    e. Now consider the utility possibility frontier when $\alpha > 0$. How will the Rawlsian and Benthamite social indifference maps now give different optimal divisions of resources? What about in-between social indifference maps that are symmetric across the 45-degree line?

    f. For an equal allocation of utilities when $\alpha > 0$, will resources also be equally allocated?

    g. *True or False*: Envy is rewarded by each of our social indifference maps, but it is increasingly more rewarded as we move from the Rawlsian to the Benthamite extreme.

    h. Can you explain how many might feel discomfort in incorporating such reference-based preferences as a foundation for normative analysis of redistribution?

B. Let x indicate individual 1's consumption (in dollars) and let y indicate individual 2's consumption (in dollars). Suppose that individual 1's utility is given by $u_1(x, y) = x - \alpha y$ and individual 2's utility is given by $u_2(x, y) = y - \beta x$.

    a. If the overall level of consumption to be divided between these two individuals is I, set up the optimization problem that maximizes individual 2's utility subject to individual 1 attaining utility u_1 and subject to the overall resource constraint.

    b. Solve for the allocation (x, y) as a function of u_1; i.e., solve for the optimal allocation of I between the two individuals given that individual 1 gets utility u_1. (*Hint*: You do not need to solve your optimization problem from (a) because the two constraints by themselves determine the solution to the problem.)

    c. Solve for the utility possibility frontier $u_2(u_1, I)$; i.e., a function giving the utility individual 2 can get as a function of u_1 and I (as well as the α and β parameters).

    d. Consider the special case in which $\alpha = 0.5$ and $\beta = 0$. Which of the two individuals now has reference-based preferences, and in what way can you characterize these as being driven by some degree of "envy"?

    e. What allocation of utilities and resources will be chosen if the ethical standard determining the distribution of resources is encompassed in the Benthamite social welfare function $W = u_1 + u_2$? Does the same division of resources hold for any combination of $\alpha > \beta$?

---

[16]In case you are wondering, my friend did recently give birth to a fifth child. And yes, it was another boy.

  f.   Repeat (for the case of $\alpha = 0.5$ and $\beta = 0$) using the Cobb–Douglas social welfare function
       $W = u_1^{\delta} u_2^{(1-\delta)}$ and then using the Rawlsian social welfare function $W = \min\{u_1, u_2\}$.

  g.   Does your conclusion from A(g) hold?

29.5 **Everyday Application:** *Extreme Altruism and Normative Economics*: In exercise 29.4, we considered
the case of two individuals where one had the usual preferences that depend only on his own consumption level and the other had preferences partially characterized by envy. Consider now the opposite case
where individual 2 still has the usual preferences and individual 1 has the same preferences as in
exercise 29.4 except that now $\alpha < 0$. Put differently, individual 1 now derives positive utility from
individual 2's consumption. How do your conclusions now change?

29.6 **Everyday Application:** *Framing the Options: Praying while Smoking, and Fighting Pandemics*: By
framing options for people in particular ways, we can sometimes get them to choose what we'd like
them to choose. One such instance is when tastes are reference based.

  A. When first introducing the topic of "framing," we sometimes tell the story of two priests who wanted
  their bishop's permission to smoke while praying. The first asked the bishop if it would be permissible for him to smoke when praying. The second asked for permission if, during those moments of
  weakness when he smokes, it might be permissible for him to say a prayer.

   a.   The bishop said "definitely not" to one of the priests and "of course, my son" to the other. Can
        you guess which priest got which answer?

   b.   How can reference-based preferences on the part of the bishop explain the different responses
        to what amounts to the same question as to whether or not one can smoke during prayer?

  B. Suppose that a local outbreak of a rare disease will, unless something is done, result in 600 deaths.
  There are two mutually exclusive emergency plans that can be put into place. Under plan *A*, 200
  people will be saved, while under plan *B*, there is a one-third chance that all 600 people will be saved
  and a two-thirds chance that none of them will be saved. When presented with this choice, an
  overwhelming majority of people choose *A* over *B*.

   a.   Do people exhibit risk aversion or risk-seeking preferences when making this choice?

   b.   There is a different way to frame the same two programs: Under plan *C*, 400 people will die,
        and under plan *D*, there is a one-third chance that no one will die and a two-thirds chance that
        600 people will die. Explain how options *A* and *C* are identical and how options *B* and *D* are
        identical.

   c.   Would someone have to be risk seeking or risk averse when choosing *D* over *C*?

   d.   Can you use prospect theory to explain the fact that people prefer *A* to *B* and *D* to *C*? Draw a
        graph to explain your answer.

29.7† **Everyday and Business Application:** *Teaser Rates on Credit Cards and Mortgages*: Credit card
companies often offer "teaser rates" to new customers; i.e., interest rates that are initially very low but
then increase dramatically after a year. Mortgage companies did the same during the subprime mortgage
period prior to the financial crisis of 2007.

  A. Consider present-bias as modeled by the beta-delta framework and the explanation it might offer for
  how students and homeowners end up taking on "too much debt."

   a.   Consider first a college student who receives credit card offers with teaser rates that charge low
        interest until the student graduates. As a high school senior, our student decides on how much
        consumption he will undertake once he gets to college (knowing that he will have access to such
        credit cards). Assuming that δ is the same for present-biased students as it is for students who do
        not have present-bias, will the plans such students make for consumption while in college differ?

   b.   Next, consider the student in his freshman year. How will students deviate in their actual
        consumption from their previous plans if they are present-biased?

   c.   As our student consumes in his freshman year, he plans for consumption in his remaining
        three years in college. Will the present-biased student's plans for consuming over the coming
        years now differ from the nonpresent-biased student (given how each may have deviated from
        their initial plans during the freshman year)?

d. Now consider our student in his sophomore year. Will the present-biased student now take on more debt than he planned as he was contemplating his sophomore year during his time as a freshman?

e. Explain how students might end up with considerably more debt than they had planned to, and how limits on credit card borrowing might improve the welfare of some students.

f. Prior to 2007, mortgage companies offered low teaser interest rates to new home buyers. Home values increased dramatically from 2001 through 2005, allowing homeowners to refinance at new teaser rates throughout. How might behavioral economists explain the explosion of home foreclosures beginning in 2006 and 2007 when home prices began to level off and then fall?

B. Consider a three-period model of a college student in his junior year. Suppose this student has no income in periods 0 and 1 while he is in school but then expects an income I in period 2 after he graduates. Suppose that utility of consumption in period i is given by $u(c_i) = \ln c_i$, where c_i is consumption in period i. Suppose further that the student discounts in accordance with the beta-delta model, with his utility of a consumption stream (c_0, c_1, c_2) given by $U = u(c_0) + \beta\delta u(c_1) + \beta\delta^2 u(c_2)$.

a. The student is unable to consume in periods 0 and 1 unless he borrows on his income from period 2. A credit card company offers him a credit card that charges no interest while he is in school and an interest rate r thereafter. Thus, he pays no interest for consumption he undertakes in periods 0 and 1 until period 2 when he has to pay interest $(1 + r)(c_1 + c_2)$. Set up this student's optimization problem subject to a three-period budget constraint.

b.** Derive his optimal consumption plan c_0, c_1, and c_2 as a function of I, r, β, and δ.

c. Suppose $I = \$100,000$, $r = 0.2$, and $\delta = 0.95$. If the student does not have present-bias, what consumption levels will the student plan to have in each period, and how much credit card debt does the student plan to have when he graduates?

d. Suppose that $\beta = 0.5$. How much credit card debt does the student plan to have when he graduates?

e. Calculate the ratio of his period 1 to period 2 consumption plans in the two scenarios. Why are they the same?

f. How much credit card debt will the student from part (c) actually have when he graduates? What about the student from part (d)?

g. Now consider the student with $\beta = 0.5$ as a sophomore looking ahead to being a junior. He is fully supported by his parents in his sophomore year, but he knows they will no longer support him in his junior year when he is able to get credit. (Assume that credit card companies do not offer cards to sophomores but only to juniors.) As he thinks about how much he will end up borrowing, will his plan differ from the student who is not present-biased? How much more credit card debt will he end up with than he planned to as a sophomore?

h. *True or False*: Regulations that limit the amount of credit card debt that students can take on can improve the welfare of present-biased sophomores.

29.8 **Everyday and Policy Application:** *Impatient versus Present-Biased Students*: In exercise 29.7, we considered how low "teaser" interest rates impact borrowing when college students are present-biased. We now consider the difference in borrowing responses to such teaser rates by impatient versus present-biased students.

EVERYDAY APPLICATION

POLICY APPLICATION

A. Throughout, compare an impatient student without present-bias to a present-biased student assuming both consume (and therefore borrow) the same amount in their junior year. Assume throughout that no credit card offers are made prior to the junior year.

a. When the two student are sophomores, which of the two plans on accumulating more credit card debt by the time he graduates?

b. When the two students are juniors, which plans to accumulate more debt by graduation?

c. In what sense is government regulation to limit student credit card debt more paternalistic when it is motivated by combatting student impatience than it is when it is motivated by combatting present-bias?

B. Consider the same set-up as in part B of exercise 29.7. (You should do exercise 29.7 prior to moving on.)

   a.   In B(d) of exercise 29.7, you should have concluded that $c_0 = \$43,262$ for the present-biased student when $I = 100,000$, $r = 0.2$, $\delta = 0.95$, and $\beta = 0.5$. What level of δ would be required for the nonpresent-biased student to be sufficiently impatient for him to choose the same c_0?

   b.   For such an impatient but nonpresent-biased student, what will consumption levels in periods 1 and 2 be? How much credit card debt will he have when he graduates?

   c.   Compare your answer to the levels of credit card debt our "patient" present-biased student (with $\delta = 0.95$ and $\beta = 0.5$) will have.

   d.   Next, compare the impatient student's level of credit card debt to the level of debt the present-biased student plans for when he is a sophomore. Is it greater or less? What about the levels of credit card debt the present-biased student plans for when he is in his junior year?

   e.   *True or False*: Our present-biased student will have greater credit card debt than the impatient student who borrows the same in the junior year, but the impatient student will accurately predict his credit card debt when he graduates while the present-biased student predicts he will end up with much less debt.

29.9   Everyday and Business Application: *Endowment Effects and Housing Markets*: In end-of-chapter exercises 6.9 and 7.6, we derived the curious prediction that homeowners are made better off by housing price fluctuations regardless of whether housing prices go up or down. This was because, assuming some degree of substitutability between housing and other goods (and no transactions costs), homeowners will sell their homes whenever housing prices change, buying smaller homes and consuming more when price increases and buying larger homes and consuming less when housing prices fall.

A. Revisit the logic behind this conclusion before proceeding.

   a.   One reason that homeowners do not constantly switch homes when housing prices fluctuate arises from the fact that there are moving costs that make switching homes not worthwhile for small price fluctuations. Now consider another explanation rooted in endowment effects uncovered by behavioral economists. Within the context of the model you used in exercises 6.9 and 7.6, how might you be able to model such endowment effects in terms of the shapes of indifference curves for homeowners?

   b.   Next, consider the problem faced by a homeowner who needs to move during a "down" market. Suppose the homeowner originally purchased her home at price p_0, and suppose that this price has become a "reference point" with the homeowner interpreting a sales price above p_0 as a "gain" and a sales price below p_0 as a "loss." Explain how behavioral economists might predict that the level of p_0 will affect the asking price that the homeowner sets.

   c.   Housing economists have uncovered the following empirical fact: During times when housing demand is falling (putting downward pressure on home prices), houses that are for sale typically take longer to sell, resulting in an increase in the number of houses on the market. Can you explain this using reference-based preferences with "loss aversion"?

B. Consider the optimization problem faced by a homeowner who is moving and is determining an asking price for his home. Such a homeowner faces the following trade-off: A higher asking price p means a lower probability of selling the home, but it also means greater utility for the homeowner if the home sells. Suppose that the probability of a sale is given by $\delta(p) = 1 - 0.00001p$. Suppose further that $p_0 = \$100,000$ was the price at which the homeowner had originally bought the home, and his utility from not selling the home is $\bar{u} = (10,000 - \alpha p_0)$. His utility of selling the home depends on the price p and is given by $u(p, p_0) = (p - \alpha p_0)$ when $p \geq p_0$ and $v(p, p_0) = \beta(p - \alpha p_0)$ when $p < p_0$.

   a.   What values do α and β take in a model without reference-based preferences?

   b.   Set up the optimization problem for the homeowner under the assumptions in (a) and solve for the optimal asking price.

   c.   Next, suppose (from here on out) that $\alpha = 1$ and $\beta = 2.25$. Repeat the optimization exercise assuming that the homeowner uses the function u (and not v). What would be the optimal asking price?

   d.   If the homeowner has reference-based preferences as specified by u and v, is the price you calculated in (c) the true optimal asking price?

e. Next, set up the optimization problem again, but this time use v instead of u. What is the optimal asking price you now get? Is this the true optimal asking price for this homeowner? Explain.

f. What is the probability that the home will sell for the price you calculated in (b) and (c), and how does it compare to the probability that the home will sell at the price you calculated in (e)? Can you reconcile this with the empirical fact stated in A(c)?

29.10 **Business Application:** *The Equity Premium Puzzle*: Investments in equities (like stocks) yield substantially higher returns than investment in bonds. By itself, this is no surprise because stocks are riskier than bonds. What is a surprise when viewed through the usual model of risk is the *size* of the premium that equities provide to investors. In a typical year, for instance, bonds might give investors a safe rate of return of 2% while stocks might give a return of between 6% and 8%. Economists who have tried to explain this "equity premium" simply in terms of risk aversion have concluded that the level of risk aversion necessary to explain the premium is simply far beyond what anyone can take seriously. Risk aversion alone therefore cannot explain the equity premium, which raises an "anomaly" known as the *equity premium puzzle*.

A. Consider the equity premium puzzle through the lens of reference-based preferences. In particular, suppose you are investing $1,000 and you know you can get a 2% return on this over 1 year by investing your money in bonds. Alternatively, you can invest the $1,000 in a stock and expect to lose $100 with probability 0.1 and gain $100 with probability 0.9.

a. What is the expected rate of return from a stock investment. What does this imply is the equity premium?

b. Suppose you thought that investors had reference-based preferences. What do you think their reference point might be when comparing the two investments?

c. Can you use the concept of "loss aversion" to explain how behavioral economics might have an explanation for the equity premium puzzle?

d.* In your explanation in (c), you almost certainly thought of the investor as having a one-year horizon. Suppose investors are in it "for the long run," facing a 10% chance of a loss on their stocks each year. Do you think your behavioral economics explanation that relies on reference-based preferences and loss aversion can still explain the equity premium puzzle?

B.* Consider prospect theory (which you implicitly used in part A) a little more closely. Suppose that an investor bases her decision on a one-year investment horizon and evaluates risky gambles relative to a reference point that is equal to the amount she invests. Suppose she invests $1,000, which then becomes her reference point. If invested in risk-free bonds, the $1,000 will be worth $1,022.54 one year from now. If she invests the same amount in stocks, her investment will be worth $900 with probability 0.12 and $1,100 with probability 0.88. The utility of any amount x is evaluated using the function

$$u(x, r) = 100(x - r) - 0.5(x - r)^2 \text{ if } x \geq r \text{ and}$$
$$= 400(x - r) + 2(x - r)^2 \text{ if } x < r, \qquad (29.21)$$

where r is the reference point, and the utility of a gamble that results in x_1 with probability δ and x_2 with probability $(1 - \delta)$ is given by $U = \delta u(x_1, r) + (1 - \delta)u(x_2, r)$.

a. We discussed four features of prospect theory in the text: (1) reference-dependence, (2) loss-aversion, (3) diminishing sensitivity, and (4) probability weighting. Which of these are we modeling here, and which are we not?

b. What is the expected return on investing $1,000 in stocks? What is the equity premium?

c. What utility will this investor get from investing $1,000 in bonds?

d. What utility will she get from investing $1,000 in stocks?

e. If this is a typical investor, is the equity premium explained by our version of prospect theory?

f. Suppose you are a young investor who is investing for retirement in 30 years. For all practical purposes, you can in this case be almost certain that an investment in stocks will result in an average rate of return equal to the expected rate of return. Recalculate the average annual utility from investing $1,000 in bonds versus investing $1,000 in stocks for such an investor.

g. If all investors were like this young investor, could our prospect theory still explain the equity premium puzzle?

29.11 Business and Policy Application: *Increased Liquidity, Procrastination, and National Savings*: Over the past few decades, increasingly sophisticated financial investment possibilities have enabled individuals to place their savings into assets that can be sold instantly if need be as opposed to investments in more "illiquid" assets like land, assets that require time and effort to convert to cash.

A. Consider individual 1 whose intertemporal tastes can be characterized by the beta-delta model versus individual 2 whose intertemporal tastes are characterized in the more usual neoclassical "delta" model. Both individuals just inherited some money and intend to invest this for their retirement.

    a.   Could an increase in the availability of liquid assets for investment purposes make individual 2 better off? Could it make individual 2 worse off?

    b.   Now consider individual 1. Suppose this individual consults an investment planner who has observed this individual's past savings and consumption decisions and recommends an investment strategy. Why might the investment planner recommend a strategy that focuses on illiquid assets?

    c.   If individual 1 is aware of his time-inconsistency problem, will he accept the financial planner's advice? Would he have any reason not to accept it if he is unaware of his self-control problem?

    d.   Suppose that, instead of just having inherited money, the two individuals have just accepted a job in which their company contributes to a 401k retirement plan. The individuals now must choose between two investments for their retirement account: Investment A consists of a mix of stocks and bonds that can be sold easily, while investment B consists of 10-year savings "certificates of deposit" that cannot be cashed out without a substantial penalty. (In both cases, there would be a tax penalty for withdrawing funds from the 401k plan, but, since it is the same for any 401k withdrawal, ignore this feature of 401k plans here.) Assuming identical rates of return on the two investments, which will cause individual 1 to accumulate more savings for retirement? What about individual 2?

    e.   Suppose individual 1 also has reference-based preferences subject to endowment or status quo effects. If the company gets to choose the initial investment strategy but allows individuals to opt into a different strategy if they want to, which investment strategy would the company choose for its workers (assuming it cares about the level of retirement savings that employees undertake)?

    f.   Over the past few decades, there has been a substantial decrease in national savings in the United States. How might a behavioral economist use the idea of procrastination to explain this?

29.12† Policy Application: *First- and Second-Best Rawlsian Income Redistribution*: Most governments raise tax revenues from higher income individuals and distribute them to lower income individuals in an attempt to achieve a more equal distribution of consumption. Such governments face a trade-off that emerges from the competing goals of achieving greater consumption equality while minimizing deadweight losses from taxation.

A. Consider in this exercise a government with Rawlsian goals; i.e., the goal of making the least well off individual the most well off. If the government does not have access to information about people's utilities, it may choose instead to treat people's consumption levels as if these represented utility values. Thus, instead of social indifference curves over utility allocations, the government would use social indifference curves over consumption allocations.

    a.   Suppose individual 1 has income I_1 and individual 2 has income I_2, with $I_1 > I_2$. Draw the "consumption possibilities frontier" assuming that the government can costlessly redistribute income between the individuals. Indicate on your graph the consumption allocation that exists in the absence of government redistribution (and in the absence of any voluntary charitable efforts).

    b.   What consumption allocation on this possibilities frontier would a Rawlsian government choose?

    c.   Now illustrate how the consumption possibilities frontier changes if the government uses an inefficient tax system. Suppose the inefficiency takes the following form: As the tax rate on the rich increases, consumption of the rich decreases as if the tax system were efficient, but the deadweight loss increases at an increasing rate as the tax rate rises, with this loss reducing the amount available for distribution to the poor.

    d.   Illustrate how a Rawlsian government might now not choose to equalize consumption levels between the rich and the poor.

e. Suppose that income differences arise in part from "compensating differentials" in the labor market; i.e., suppose that higher income people make more money in part because they undertake unpleasant activities such as traveling a lot for their job and working long hours. If the government's real goal is to apply its social welfare function to utility allocations instead of consumption allocations, how might the Rawlsian social welfare function applied to consumption allocations lead to excessive redistribution?

f. Suppose instead that the marginal utility of consumption diminishes as consumption increases. Would the application of the Rawlsian goal to consumption distributions now lead to a tax rate that is too high or too low?

B. Suppose again that there are two individuals: one who makes an income I_1 and the other who makes only I_2, where $I_1 > I_2$. Assume that the government would like to redistribute income but does not have information on individual utilities. Thus, instead of applying a social welfare function to choose a utility allocation, the government applies a social welfare function to choose consumption allocations directly. The function it uses is the Rawlsian social welfare function $W = \min\{c_1, c_2\}$.

a. Give an example of a utility function $u(c)$ that would make this equivalent to a social welfare function that chooses utility allocations. What has to be true about the marginal utility of consumption?

b. Suppose that the government uses an income tax t charged to the rich and then transfers the revenues to the poor. Suppose first that this income tax is a lump sum tax; i.e., it raises revenues without deadweight loss. What tax rate t would the government choose?

c. Suppose next that the income tax used by the government is not a lump sum tax. For a tax rate $t < 1$, it is able to transfer the amount $(tI_1 - (ktI_1)^2)$ to individual 2. If the government wants to maximize the amount of transfer it can make, what tax rate will it choose?

d. Suppose $I_1 = \$200{,}000$ and $I_2 = \$10{,}000$. What is the government's "first-best" income tax rate when it can tax individual 1's income without any deadweight loss?

e. Consider next the second-best case and suppose $k = 0.0025$. For the same two income levels as in (d), what is the government's "second-best" income tax rate given that the tax system gives rise to the deadweight losses modeled in (c)?

f. How much consumption does each of the two individuals undertake under the first-best outcome? How about under the second-best outcome?

29.13 Policy Application: *Confirmation Bias, Politics, Research, and Last-Minute Studying*: Individuals have lots of assumptions about the way the world works, assumptions that help frame how they make decisions. These assumptions are often challenged or confirmed by empirical evidence. However, psychologists who have analyzed how people change their assumptions about the world suggest that we tend to seek out evidence that confirms our assumptions and ignore evidence that contradicts our assumptions. This phenomenon is known as *confirmation bias*, and one of the early experiments uncovering this bias is described in part B.

POLICY APPLICATION

A. Over the past few decades, there has been a vast increase in the number of sources that individuals can use to inform themselves about what is going on in the world. For instance, most individuals used to rely on their local newspaper (which often drew its material primarily from a handful of national news outlets) and the evening newscast on one of three networks. Today, on the other hand, there are lots of cable news channels people can choose from throughout the day, and an increasing number of people rely on news from Internet sources.

a. Many observers of public discourse have suggested that the assumptions individuals bring to policy discussions are now often more diametrically opposed than in the past, with different camps often no longer able to hold civil dialogue because they so fundamentally disagree about the underlying "facts." If this is true, how can this be explained by the increased number of news and opinion outlets?

b. In the past, opinion polls often suggested that public disapproval of a U.S. president was in the single digits, but more recently, a president is considered as doing well if his disapproval ratings are in the 20% to 30% range. Can confirmation bias in the more recent news environment explain this?

c. Until the mid-1980s, the Federal Communication Commission in the United States enforced a rule known as the "Fairness Doctrine." This rule required news outlets, particularly on radio and TV, to present opposing viewpoints. It was argued at the time that some media markets only had one or two such news outlets, and thus the Fairness Doctrine was required to allow people to get alternative points of view so that they could then form informed opinions. Since the mid-1980s, the Fairness Doctrine is no longer applied, allowing news outlets to present news and opinions in any way they see fit. It was argued that increased competition has led to competing news outlets in virtually all markets, thus automatically allowing individuals to gather alternative viewpoints to form their own opinions. Now some are arguing for a reinstatement of the Fairness Doctrine but others view it as a violation of free speech and free competition of ideas in the product-differentiated marketplace. Can you argue both sides of this issue?

d. Some have observed an increase in the number of people who believe in a variety of "conspiracy theories," theories such as that the 9/11 attack was orchestrated by the government or that a politician secretly adheres to a religious view that differs from his or her stated view. How might this be explained in light of the fact that most individuals find evidence against such theories conclusive?

e. Empirical social scientists often do econometric regression analysis on real-world data to ascertain the direction and magnitude of people's responses to different policies. As computational analysis has become less costly, such researchers are now able to run literally tens of thousands of different regressions, using combinations of different variables and empirical specifications, whereas in the past they have had to limit themselves to a few regressions. Suppose that researchers have prior beliefs about what an empirical investigation might show. How might you view statistically significant empirical results reported in research papers more skeptically as a result of knowing about confirmation bias?

f. In the final hours before an exam, students often "study" intensely by scanning their notes and focusing on key terms that they have highlighted. Some students find that this dramatically increases their sense of being prepared for the exam, and then find that they do not do nearly as well on the exam as they had thought they would given their last-minute studying. Can you explain this using the idea of confirmation bias?

B. The following experiment, first conducted in the early 1960s, is an illustration of confirmation bias. Suppose that you are given the following sequence of numbers: 2-4-6. You are told that this sequence conforms with a particular rule that was used to generate the sequence and are asked to figure out what the underlying rule is. To do so, you can generate your own three-number sequences and ask the experimenter for feedback on whether your sequence also conforms with the underlying rule. You can do this as often as you need to until you are certain you know what the underlying rule is, at which time you tell the experimenter your conclusion.

a. Suppose that, when you first see the 2-4-6 sequence, you recognize it as a sequence of even numbers and believe that the underlying rule probably requires the even numbers. What is an example of a sequence that you might use to test this assumption if you have confirmation bias?

b. What sequence of numbers might you propose to test your assumption if you did not have confirmation bias and were open to your assumption being incorrect?

c. The underlying rule was simple: In order to comply with the rule, it simply had to be an ascending sequence. Very few subjects correctly identified this rule, instead very confidently concluding that the rule was much more complex. The experimenters concluded that people consistently derived an incorrect rule because they gave examples that would confirm their assumptions rather than attempt to *falsify* them. (A sequence intended to "falsify" an assumption would be one that violates the assumption.) How is this consistent with your answers to (a) and (b)?

29.14† **Policy Application:** *Smoothing the Business Cycle versus Fostering Economic Growth: Psychology Meets Normative Macroeconomics*: It is sometimes argued that there is a policy trade-off between softening the impact of economic recessions and fostering long-run economic growth. Suppose such a trade-off in macroeconomic policy exists. Those who advocate a growth-focused economic policy point out that even a small increase in the long-run growth rate of an economy will generate far greater welfare gains than a substantial softening (or even an elimination) of transitory downturns in the business cycle. Thus, they conclude, to the extent to which there is a trade-off between softening recessions and fostering long-run economic growth, the emphasis should be primarily on long-run growth. (You are asked to show this in a numerical example in part B, which does not presume any Section B material.)

Chapter 29. What Is Good? Challenges from Psychology and Philosophy

1177

A. There is little debate about the relative magnitude of welfare gains from softening recessions versus increasing long-run growth rates. Still, governments expend substantial resources on fighting recessions, often by taking on debt and introducing incentive distortions into the economy, which in turn will harm long-run growth.

    a. Suppose that, instead of taking the usual form, preferences are reference-based and exhibit a high degree of loss aversion. How does this change how we think about the welfare impact of recessions?

    b. Suppose that the happiness literature is onto something, and that happiness is a more relative rather than absolute notion. How is this consistent with the claimed evidence that happiness within societies does not change much with time even as standards of living increase dramatically?

    c. If you wanted to argue in favor of greater emphasis on softening recessions at the cost of accepting less long-run economic growth, how might you do this in light of your answers to (a) and (b)?

B.** The average U.S. growth rate over the past few decades has been in the range of 2.3%, with recessions happening about once every decade. Suppose, then, that we currently have a growth rate of 2.9% during nonrecession years and a negative growth rate of -3.3% during recession years (which averages to about 2.3% if recession years happen once every decade).

    a. Suppose further that, over the next 50 years, we will experience a recession year in years 10, 20, 30, 40, and 50, with the intervening 9 years (beginning in year 1) representing years of economic expansion. If the current average household income is $60,000, what do you project it will be in 50 years (assuming the growth rates of 2.9% and -3.3% in expansion and recession years)? (You can do this by calculating first the increase in average incomes over the first 9 years, then the decrease from the recession in year 10, and so forth. By setting this up in a spreadsheet, you can then easily undertake the policy experiments in parts (b) and (c).)

    b. Now suppose that you have devised a policy that reduces the drop in average income during recessions by nearly 50% from 3.3% to 1.7% at the cost of reducing growth during expansion years by only a little over 10% from 2.9% to 2.6%. What will average household income be in 50 years? What about average income during recession years?

    c. Suppose instead that you have devised a policy that raises the growth rate during expansions by about 10% from 2.9% to 3.2% at the cost of also increasing the severity of recessions by 50% from 3.3% to 5%. What will average household income be in 50 years? What about average income during recession years?

    d. *True or False*: Compared to the status quo as well as the policy experiment in (b), the policy experiment in (c) will result in greater average household income in 50 years *and* during every recession year.

    e. Explain how your answer to (d) may lead economists to favor one policy while psychologists who believe in the importance of prospect theory favor another, despite agreeing on the underlying empirical facts.

30

Balancing Government, Civil Society, and Markets

Do safer cars necessarily result in fewer traffic deaths? Is it sensible to subsidize domestic U.S. oil drilling in an effort to make the United States less dependent on unstable regions of the world? Would outlawing live Christmas trees help to reduce deforestation? Should we impose laws against "price gouging"? Is boycotting companies that use cheap labor abroad a good way to express our outrage at the dismal working conditions in those countries? Would it be better for workers to require their employers to pay their Social Security taxes rather than taxing the workers directly? Should we tax the sales by monopolies so that these companies don't earn such outrageous profits?

We began with this paragraph in Chapter 1, where we suggested that the economist's instinctive answers may differ from the answers given by many noneconomists. Safer cars *might* lead to more deaths if we end up driving more recklessly as a result of knowing that we are less likely to get hurt in an accident. Subsidizing U.S. oil drilling won't make the United States much less dependent on unstable regions in the world since oil is sold in a world market, and what ultimately matters is the world price of oil, which has little to do with how much is produced in the United States. Outlawing live Christmas trees might cause a reduction in forests grown precisely for the purpose of growing Christmas trees, and interfering with competitive prices will lead to non-price rationing that may in fact impose larger costs on the very individuals we aim to protect with "price-gouging" laws. Boycotting companies that use cheap labor abroad reduces foreign demand for low-wage workers, thereby depressing their wages. It should really not matter who pays Social Security taxes—employers or employees—since the economic incidence of such taxes depends on elasticities of labor supply and demand, not on how politicians write laws. And taxing the sales of monopolies will only make the inefficiency of monopoly pricing worse because it will increase already inflated consumer prices.

These are just a few examples of how an economist's perspective on the world differs not because economists are strange or ideologically driven but rather because economists have internalized intuitions about how individual optimizing choices aggregate to result in the economic environments we see. And it is these intuitions that form a basis for how economists and noneconomists alike might develop a framework that allows a reasoned debate on what role we ideally envision for markets, civil society, and government.

Resolvable versus Unresolvable Differences

This in no way implies, however, that everyone will agree on the "right" balance between these different institutions in society. We bring to the table different assumptions about the way the world works as well as different systems of values and beliefs on "what is good." To the extent to which our disagreements are driven by assumptions about the way the world works, the positive economist (and more generally, the positive social scientist) can be of great assistance as he or she brings his or her tool kit to an empirical investigation that can clarify which of our assumptions are correct and which are mistaken. The more we can agree on the underlying assumptions, the less we will typically disagree on what is desirable. But in the end we might still disagree because we take different philosophical positions on points that have nothing to do with empirically falsifiable assumptions. While philosophers can help by clarifying our thinking, it seems unlikely that they will get us all (or even each other) to agree on "what is good." In some instances, we may end up simply having to agree to disagree.

For instance, suppose you and I disagree on "what is good" because I operate under the assumption that people are by and large rational in their decision making (as modeled by economists) and you operate under the assumption that we are riddled with psychological biases that are pervasive and large in magnitude (as suggested by many psychologists). This type of disagreement about assumptions can in principle be resolved through empirical testing, and if you and I are open to the possibility that not all of our assumptions are in fact true, empirical social science research will help us resolve some of our disagreements. This book is not one that develops the means by which we can undertake such empirical investigations, and you should consider taking courses in statistics and econometrics to find out more about how social scientists ultimately do this. For our purposes, however, it is enough to simply recognize that differences in opinion can at least in principle be resolved to the extent to which such differences are rooted in assumptions that can be tested with real-world data. (The biggest obstacle to us resolving such differences might actually lie in a tendency by human beings to seek only evidence that confirms their assumptions to the exclusion of evidence that contradicts them, a topic briefly taken up in end-of-chapter exercise 29.13 of the previous chapter.)

But suppose instead that our disagreements about "what is good" arise from different philosophical positions that stand in at least partial contradiction to one another. You might believe that "justice" is rooted in a respect for "natural rights" and that such deference to natural rights prohibits any type of forced redistribution of income. I, on the other hand, might be a Rawlsian utilitarian, convinced that "justice" requires society to be ordered in such a way as to make the least well off as well off as possible. If the utilitarian consequences of the natural rights position turn out to be in less conflict with my Rawlsian ideal than is immediately apparent, we may still end up converging somewhat by learning from positive social science. Economists have, for instance, demonstrated the power of decentralized markets to generate large social surplus. Generating such surplus is important for utilitarians even if Rawlsian redistribution occurs alongside it. But the enforcement of contracts and property rights required for decentralized markets to generate surplus is precisely what natural law philosophy might tell us a "good" society should do. Positive economics—knowing about "what is"—therefore creates common ground where we might not have seen any in its absence, but it is unlikely that it will remove all our differences. The Rawlsian among us will always view property rights as a means to the end of a society in which the least fortunate do as well as possible, while the natural rights advocate will see the rights themselves as the end. The former is therefore willing to violate what the latter considers untouchable, and there is nothing the positive economist can really add to resolve that particular conflict.

The Three-Legged Stool

To what extent can the material covered in this text then help identify which of our differences are resolvable and which are the types of differences on which we will ultimately have to agree to disagree? Is there a bigger picture framework that emerges, or is it all just a mishmash of models that don't sum to more than their parts?

While much of the focus of the text has been on what markets do well and what they don't do so well, we have emphasized throughout that markets never operate in a vacuum. In fact, markets rely on the protection of contracts and property rights or else are subject to the Tragedy of the Commons, and thus we immediately see a role for nonmarket institutions on whose foundations market transactions rest. While there are certainly anarchist theories about how such protections can in principle exist without governments, we can think of few if any modern examples where this has ever been accomplished. Governments are then defined by their claim to have an exclusive right to initiate the use of force, whether through taxation or regulation that are both backed by mechanisms to punish those who do not comply. We similarly know of no society that has existed without institutions that are governed neither by governments nor by market prices, institutions like families, which exist in a complex web of voluntary associations we have referred to as the civil society. Nor can we think of examples of societies where market forces have not played a role, even if sometimes operating within a "black market" that functions outside the legal framework.

I conclude from all this that it is probably a fair statement to say the following: Virtually everyone agrees that the institutions that make up what we call "society" involve a mix of markets, civil society, and government, a three-legged stool, so to speak, on which all activities in the society unfold. The question is then not *whether* markets, civil society, and government have a role to play; it is rather a question of what the appropriate sphere for each should be in a society that optimally balances these to achieve whatever aims we have set. And while economics has a limited set of insights to contribute to what the *aims* should be, it has a lot to say about what trade-offs we face as we think of the appropriate balance between the three legs of our stool.

Combining the First Welfare Theorem with Other Insights

Our insights begin with the first welfare theorem that forms the underlying connection between all the various subfields in microeconomics. The theorem is so important because it so precisely delineates the admittedly unrealistic conditions for markets to operate in an efficient way assuming that individuals are not subject to psychological biases in decision making. Were the world truly characterized by these conditions, the only question that would remain is whether nonmarket interventions are necessary in order to achieve a better *distribution* of outcomes than what markets achieve or, alternatively, whether the initial allocation of endowments is sufficiently "just" to permit us not to worry about tinkering with the efficient outcome that markets produce. We can then combine the insights of the first welfare theorem with concerns from psychology and issues related to equity or fairness to arrive at the ideal conditions under which markets would achieve our social aims. In a nutshell, these are:

1. All property rights are clear and enforced, with all externalities (including those related to public goods) therefore internalized (Chapters 21 and 27).
2. There are no barriers to market prices governing production and exchange (Chapters 18 through 20).
3. No actors in the market are "large" enough to be able to exercise market power (Chapters 23 and 24 through 26).
4. No actors are asymmetrically informed in ways that allow them to use this informational advantage to exploit those who are less informed (Chapter 22).
5. Everyone is "rational" in the sense that everyone aims to do the best he or she can given his or her circumstances, with neither preferences nor the interpretation of circumstances subject to systematic psychological biases (Chapter 29).

6. Depending on one's philosophical approach, either the initial distribution of endowments is judged to be fair, or the outcomes produced by markets satisfy our ethical criterion for distributional goals (Chapter 29).

The psychology- and philosophy-based concerns (in points (5) and (6)) do not fall by the wayside when we recognize that conditions (1) through (4) in fact often do not hold; they only add to the possible ways in which nonmarket institutions might contribute to the balance of the three-legged stool. But notice that points (1) through (5) fundamentally involve empirically falsifiable conditions, the very conditions that empirical social scientists can in fact test with real-world data to ascertain where nonmarket institutions may in fact hold the most promise for improving human welfare. It is only when we get to condition (6) that we may end at an impasse where certain philosophical premises lead us to disagree despite agreement on those aspects of the question that are empirically testable.

Nonmarket Institutions and their Challenges

The material in this text therefore goes a long way toward clarifying the promises and limits of markets in answering questions regarding the appropriate balance of our three-legged stool, and this framework helps identify circumstances in which nonmarket institutions can *in principle* improve on market outcomes. While clarifying the *promise* of nonmarket institutions, they do not, however, by themselves clarify the *limits* of those institutions. Still, we have investigated these as well, and they essentially boil down to the following:

1. Civil society institutions are fundamentally challenged by the *free-rider problem* that arises when individuals cannot be forced to go against their self-interest despite violations of the first welfare theorem that call for some form of collective action (Chapter 24 and 27).
2. Governments face both *informational constraints* as well as *preference aggregation problems* that result in a different kind of *strategic power* as they employ force to alter human behavior (Chapter 28).

The free-rider problem faced by civil society efforts arises from the fact that civil society institutions, unlike governments, cannot employ the use of force and must therefore rely on persuasion, and this links closely to the externality issues we uncovered in our development of the first welfare theorem. This suggests that voluntary efforts by civil society groups result in Prisoner's Dilemma incentives that will tend to cause such groups to insufficiently mobilize individuals who maximize their self-interested aims. While such institutions often are in possession of considerably more information than governments that seek to address the same problems, the Prisoner's Dilemma incentives result in a lack of the resources necessary to adequately meet the challenges they identify. These are challenges that are not impossible to overcome, with much evidence suggesting that civil society organizations like families and community groups fill gaps that link closely to aspects of human needs not easily included in standard neoclassical economics models. This opens the possibility for civil society institutions to play effective roles when these are not excessively undermined by either market or government forces. Still, the free-rider problem remains a challenge that itself may require non-civil society institutions. Government support of such institutions may take a variety of forms, each intended to address the underlying externality problem that is present in civil society engagements.

But, just like markets and civil society institutions, governments confront two challenges of their own. Even if they are made up of entirely benevolent policy makers, they often lack sufficient information to correct "market failures" or "civil society failures" without introducing distortions and unintended consequences that may create problems greater than the ones they seek to correct. One advantage of markets and, to at least some extent, civil society institutions arises precisely from the more efficient use of individual knowledge that these can make to solve problems. And even if informational asymmetries posed no difficulties for governments, we have found in Chapter 28 that, in the absence of benevolent dictators, democratic governments give rise to institutions that invariably create "strategic power" for concentrated interest groups and agenda setters whose aims may diverge from those we seek to implement. The challenge is then to arrive at a role for government that provides ways for the use of force to achieve desirable social outcomes without that very force being strategically abused by concentrated power within governments. None of this is to suggest that governments cannot play important roles in enhancing social welfare; it only suggests that the mere presence of "market failures" and "civil society failures" no more implies an immediate role for government than a recognition of "government failure" implies no role for government.

Spontaneous Order outside the Market

There is, however, one final insight that a careful study of markets provides for those genuinely concerned about finding the appropriate balance for markets, civil society, and government. In our initial development of the first welfare theorem, we marveled at the way in which order can arise "spontaneously" from the self-interested engagements of individuals who possess no more information than what is naturally contained within each of them. But this idea of a *spontaneous order*, while far from suggesting a "perfect order," is not one that is limited solely to market interactions. And it may therefore lead us to think differently than we otherwise would about *how* interactions between governments, civil society, and markets ought to be structured.

Consider, for instance, the evolution of law, an idea that most of us instinctively associate with the "laws" that are written down in our constitutions and the various legislations and statutes that are written down by the political institutions set up by those constitutions. It naturally comes as a surprise to many that most of "the law" that governs many societies is not in fact derived from "laws" that were at some point written down, just as most of the products produced in the market are not the result of conscious planning by the thousands of market participants that simply did the best they could given their limited information and circumstances. Much of what happens in U.S. or British courtrooms is in fact based on *common law*, a complex system of rules that has "spontaneously" emerged over centuries as different courts laid out basic principles that, when judged to "work well," were then adopted by other courts to evolve into precedents that became universally accepted. Much as the Apple Corporation stumbled on the iPod or a car company first thought of the minivan only to see these ideas revolutionize the way we listen to music or shuttle around our kids, innovations in the law were often driven by solutions to needs of the moment that, when successful, were replicated by others. The same can be said of the evolution of *language* that, particularly in the English language, is rarely centrally directed but rather adapts to new needs and circumstances as societies change. At the same time, just as many crazy inventions in the marketplace quickly fizzle and some language "innovations" turn out to be short-lived fads, certain rules made in courts end up producing "bad" unintended outcomes and thus never make it into the "common law" that is more or less universally accepted (at least in societies based on common law principles).

Or consider our discussion of "structure induced" political equilibria in Chapter 28, equilibria that discipline the chaos that can arise under democratic decision making through rules and conventions that are written down nowhere but accepted as nearly sacred where they are used. The U.S. Constitution does not say anything about setting up lots of committees that produce legislation to be considered by the Congress, nor is there anything in the Constitution about filibuster rules that govern the U.S. Senate or whether the Supreme Court has the power to declare legislation "unconstitutional." While the U.S. Constitution lays out a basic framework in which decisions are to be made, it leaves much to be determined by the "spontaneous order" that would shape the processes by which government actually functions. There is no guarantee that any one of these processes is "good" in some abstract sense any more than there is a guarantee that markets invent only "good" products or the common law never gets us stuck in antiquated ways of thinking or language fads of the moment have any positive lasting impact. But by recognizing the often surprising roles played by spontaneous orders that *can* emerge from the bottom up, we begin to see the usefulness of being open to allowing institutions to change from within as circumstances change.

In our discussion of public goods (in Chapter 27), we also touched on market-like mechanisms that can discipline governments or "clubs" to be less rent-seeking and more responsive to constituent needs than might be apparent at first, much as competition between firms limits the extent to which firms can strategically manipulate price to achieve economic profit. The "Tiebout" model of competing governments, most appropriately applied to local rather than national competition, suggests an admittedly imperfect spontaneous order as citizen choice of where to live impacts what local governments do; and the possibility of excluding from consumption those who do not contribute to some forms of public goods opens ways for market-like competition between firms and clubs that meet a variety of human needs. Once again, the idea of a "spontaneous order" is potentially powerful in helping us understand the purely empirical question of what sorts of "failures" that arise in abstract models may in fact be ameliorated by institutions that emerge or compete within the real-world complexities that we actually face. Models are helpful in clarifying our thinking on where the problems might lie, but they are sometimes limiting if we cannot take insights from one model to the next to see how larger forces shape the societies we are analyzing and seeking to improve.

We have also seen how an appreciation of how markets give rise to spontaneous orders can shape policies that, rather than mandating solutions, create a set of incentives to unleash entrepreneurial efforts aimed at achieving ends that markets themselves would otherwise have no incentive to address. In our treatment of pollution in Chapter 21, for instance, we compared "top-down" approaches of regulation and some forms of "Pigouvian taxation" to examples of pollution voucher systems that create a role for market participants to determine where pollution is most efficiently reduced while providing incentives for new firms to innovate less polluting production processes. Economists therefore often find themselves favoring policies that create the "right" incentives rather than those that presume governments can obtain the necessary information *and* discipline themselves to use this information in ways that directly implement desirable outcomes. This economist-bias toward decentralized solutions based on incentives emerges precisely from an intuitive appreciation of how spontaneous orders can, within the appropriate institutional setting, make use of information and unleash entrepreneurial efforts.

And there may be instances in which we cannot immediately see how civil society institutions can overcome the free-rider problem that can in principle cripple the civil society, and yet we see in many places a rich fabric of such institutions succeeding in all sorts of surprising ways. As we have emphasized from the beginning in our discussion of the Prisoner's Dilemma in Chapter 23, people seem to cooperate more in voluntary ways that appear to run against their narrow self-interest than we would predict in a simple economic model, with ideas like "fairness" and "identity," "tipping points" and the "warm glow" from altruism adding to strictly "rational" forces of trigger strategies and punishment mechanisms that operate in complex ways. Social entrepreneurs often use such insights, some of which are rooted in the very psychological biases that create issues for the first welfare theorem, in effective ways to mobilize the civil society, and successful efforts there can be replicated just as they are elsewhere in governments and markets. Here, too, one can see possibilities for "spontaneous orders" that might be unnecessarily disturbed by attempts to discipline "civil society" or "market" failures without an appreciation of the larger forces at work.

A Beginning, Not an End

If a single course or a single textbook claims to offer all the answers, you should probably be suspicious. The world is too complex, and the underlying trade-offs we face, individually and as a society, are too intricate for simple answers that are often more rooted in ideological presuppositions and subject to "confirmation biases" that keep us from considering evidence that challenges our assumptions. My hope is therefore that this text is a beginning, not an end—a beginning to thinking more clearly about the world around us while being open to challenges that can allow us to change our mind. So many of our heated debates result in little more than shouting matches because we skip steps, cling to presumptions without considering alternatives, and develop the hubris of "knowing" the answer before coming to terms with "the question." Reasoned debate, and reasoned acceptance of differences, can be found only if we discipline ourselves through the use of devices like those that we have tried to develop in the chapters of this text. It also typically results in more nuanced views of the world, views that shy away from "corner solutions" in which we emphasize one aspect of a problem to the exclusion of all others.

Ultimately, I would not be an economist if I were not fundamentally convinced about the value that the economist's lens can bring to a fuller understanding of the world in which to live. But I am not sure I would qualify as a human being if I did not also believe that all answers never rest in one lens. The challenge for anyone who begins the study of economics (or any other discipline that aims to understand the human condition) is to ultimately synthesize its insights into a bigger picture, and it is my hope that this book offers a useful set of tools to do just that.

GLOSSARY

The italics in the glossary indicate that the term is defined elsewhere in the glossary.

actuarily fair insurance Insurance contracts that reduce risk without changing expected values (and earn *zero profit* for insurance companies that serve a random selection of the population).

adverse selection The *asymmetric information* problem that causes higher cost customers to "adversely select" into the market or, alternatively, that causes low quality suppliers to "adversely select" into the market.

agenda setting The sequencing of votes and procedures that govern the process by which democratic institutions choose social outcomes.

aggregate risk Risk that impacts groups rather than randomly impacting individuals; as, for instance, the risk of economic recessions.

antitrust economics Subfield of economics that investigates the impact of government regulation and legal rulings on anticompetitive behavior by firms.

asymmetric information Circumstances in which buyers and sellers do not share the same information relevant to the transaction they are entering into.

average cost *Cost* divided by output.

average expenditure *Expenditure* divided by output.

average variable cost *Variable cost* divided by output.

bandwagon effect A form of *network externality* under which individuals value an item more as consumption of the item by others increases.

barriers to entry A *fixed cost* incurred by a firm if it chooses to enter a market; if sufficiently high, it may prevent market entry by new firms.

battle of the sexes A type of *coordination game* in which two players want to engage in the same activity (rather than engaging in different activities), but they differ over the activity on which they wish to coordinate.

Bayes rule A rule for updating *beliefs* as new information is revealed.

Bayesian Nash equilibrium A *Nash equilibrium* extended to *incomplete information games* in which *beliefs* become part of the equilibrium.

behavioral economics A branch of economics that incorporates insights from psychology into economic models.

beliefs In *game theory*, a probability distribution over the possible types an opposing player might be.

Benthamite social preferences A normative metric for evaluating outcomes by ranking them according to the sum of all individual outcomes; all individuals are given equal weight.

Bertrand competition Strategic competition (by firms) in which firms view price as the strategic variable.

best-response strategy In *game theory*, an individual's *strategy* that results in the highest possible payoff given the strategies played by others in the game.

best-response function A *function* that mathematically summarizes the *best response strategies* to all possible strategies taken by others in a game.

beta-delta model A (*behavioral economics*) model of *present-biased* preferences.

binary relations Mathematical relations that rank pairs of alternatives.

bounded rationality The assumption that individuals are cognitively limited in terms of how much they can compute; often leads to the prediction of the use of "rules of thumb" in complex choice environments.

budget constraint (or budget line) The set of possible alternatives that are affordable when the entire budget is used; i.e., the boundary of the *budget set*.

budget (or choice) set The set of possible alternatives that are affordable.

call option A contract that gives the holder the option of buying some quantity in the future at a predetermined price.

cap-and-trade A policy that caps the overall amount of pollution and requires polluters to purchase *tradable pollution permits* (also called pollution vouchers).

capital A variety of nonlabor inputs into production, including financial capital and physical capital (plant and equipment).

cartel A group of firms that form an agreement to collude (either on price or quantity) in order to raise profit; e.g., OPEC.

certainty equivalent The amount x that would make someone who faces a risky *gamble* indifferent between participating in the gamble versus accepting x.

choice set The set of feasible alternatives.

choice variables The variables that can be chosen (rather than being taken as given) in a constrained or unconstrained *optimization problem*.

circumstances The constraints faced by someone who has to make a choice.

civil society Formal and informal institutions that facilitate cooperation without primarily relying on either prices or government coercion.

club goods *Non-rivalrous, excludable* goods; i.e., excludable *public goods.*

Coase theorem The theorem that states that *externalities* will be fully internalized by the affected parties so long as *transactions costs* are low and property rights are clearly assigned.

Cobb-Douglas function $f(x_1, x_2) = x_1^\alpha x_2^\beta$ (where x_1 and x_2 are consumption goods when f is a *utility function* and production inputs when f is a *production function*).

collusion Explicit or implicit cooperation by firms in order to restrict quantity and raise price.

compensated budget A (typically) hypothetical budget that, following a price change, provides a consumer with just enough income to reach the pre-price change *indifference curve.*

compensated demand A consumer's demand holding utility constant; i.e., a consumer's demand under the assumption that, as prices change, the consumer will always receive just enough income to attain the same *indifference curve.*

compensated supply (of labor or capital) A worker's (or saver's) supply of labor (or capital) assuming utility remains unchanged as prices (i.e., wages and interest rates) change.

competitive equilibrium Prices and resource allocations in which no consumer or firm has an incentive to change what he or she is doing given the prevailing prices (assuming everyone is small relative to the market).

complements Goods that tend to be consumed together by consumers, or inputs that tend to be used together in production.

complete information games Games in which the payoffs of all players are known by all players.

complete tastes Tastes that enable individuals to rank all pairs of alternatives in terms of relative desirability.

composite good An artificial or hypothetical good that takes the place of "all other consumption"; usually denominated in "dollars of other consumption," with price therefore set to 1 by definition.

compound interest The interest in future periods on interest earned this period.

concave functions A function f such that $f(\alpha x + (1 - \alpha)y) \ge \alpha f(x) + (1 - \alpha) f(y)$; in producer theory, concave *production functions* give rise to convex *producer choice sets.*

conditional input demand A cost-minimizing firm's demand for an input (at given input prices) conditional on producing a certain fixed level of output.

constant cost industry A perfectly competitive industry with no *barriers to entry* and identical firms—with a horizontal long-run industry demand curve.

constant elasticity of substitution (CES) Utility or production functions with the same *elasticity of substitution* between goods (or inputs) at all goods (or input) bundles.

constant returns to scale Production technologies under which a *t*-fold increase in all inputs results in a *t*-fold increase in output (when no inputs are wasted).

constrained optimization problem A mathematical problem in which some function is maximized subject to *constraints.*

constraint A limit on the choice set; for consumers the constraint is typically formed by prices and incomes (or endowments); for firms the constraint is typically the technology that limits which production plans are technologically feasible.

consumer surplus The difference between what a consumer would have been willing to pay and what he or she had to pay for the quantity of a good that he or she purchases.

continuous tastes Tastes that are not subject to "sudden jumps."

contract curve The set of *Pareto efficient* allocations of goods in general equilibrium *exchange economies.*

convex combination The weighted average of two bundles (of goods or inputs).

convex set A set of points for which it is the case that any *convex combination* of two points within the set also lies within the set.

convex tastes Tastes under which the *convex combination* of equally preferred bundles is more desirable (or at least no worse) than the "extreme" bundles; the set of bundles that are preferred to a

bundle is a *convex set* when tastes are convex.

convex production sets *Convex sets* of feasible *production plans* that emerge from decreasing (or constant) *returns to scale* production processes (represented by *concave production functions*).

coordination games Games with multiple pure strategy *Nash equilibria* in which players choose the same strategy.

core The set of allocations (of goods) in general equilibrium *exchange economies* such that no coalition of individuals could do better on their own; in two-person exchange economies, this is equivalent to the set of *Pareto efficient* allocations that are mutually preferred to the initial endowments by both players.

corner solution A solution to an *optimization problem* in which zero quantity of at least one of the *choice variables* is chosen.

cost What is given up when a particular activity is chosen; also called *opportunity cost* or *economic cost.*

cost minimization The act of producing a given output level at the minimum economic cost possible (given input prices and given technological constraints).

Cournot competition Strategic competition (by firms) in which firms view quantity as the strategic variable.

cross-price demand curve The curve that relates demand for one good to the price of another good.

crowd-out The tendency of an increase in government spending on a project to lower private contributions for the same project.

deadweight loss A loss in social surplus resulting from a violation of the *first welfare theorem*'s conditions.

decentralized market equilibrium Perfectly competitive equilibrium when everyone is a *price taker.*

decreasing cost industries Industries with downward-sloping long-run industry supply curves.

decreasing returns to scale Production technologies under which a *t*-fold increase in all inputs results in less than a *t*-fold increase in output (when no inputs are wasted).

demand function Function that gives the quantity demanded as a function of the economic circumstances (i.e. prices and incomes) faced by the demander.

diffuse costs Costs spread across large numbers of individuals such that the cost for each individual is small.

diminishing marginal product *Marginal product* (of an input in production) that falls as more of the input is hired (holding all other inputs fixed).

diminishing marginal rate of substitution Property of convex tastes that results in individuals being increasingly less willing to substitute good *x* for good *y* the more *y* they already have.

diminishing sensitivity The hypothesis (in *prospect theory*) that individuals become less sensitive to marginal gains and losses the farther these occur from their reference point.

diminishing technical rate of substitution The property of production processes that implies it becomes increasingly difficult to substitute one input for another and keep output constant.

discounting Valuing $1 in the future at less than $1 now.

disequilibrium An economic environment in which everyone is not doing the best they can given the circumstances they face.

distortionary Usually refers to a policy that alters prices and thus the opportunity costs faced by individuals.

Dixit-Stiglitz utility function A particular utility function that models utility increasing as the variety of available products increases.

dominant strategy A *strategy* that is a *best response* to all possible strategies played by others.

duality The connection between *utility maximization* and *expenditure minimization* (for consumers) and between *profit maximization* and *cost minimization* (for producers).

duopoly An *oligopoly* composed of two firms.

Easterlin paradox The finding that happiness increases with income within countries but not across countries.

econometrics The subfield in economics that investigates how to employ statistical techniques to test economic models.

economic costs *Opportunity costs.*

economically efficient production Cost minimizing production; i.e., production of output at the lowest possible economic cost.

economics of education Subfield of economics that deals with incentive issues related to the provision of primary, secondary, and higher education.

Edgeworth box A graphical way of representing a two-person, two-good *exchange economy.*

efficient A situation that cannot be changed in a way that would make some people better off without making anyone worse off; same as *Pareto efficient.*

elasticity The percentage change in behavior resulting from a 1% change in some aspect of the economic environment.

elasticity of substitution The percentage change in the ratio of goods resulting from a 1% change in the marginal rate of substitution along an *indifference curve.*

endogenous Arising from within the system; e.g., budgets that emerge from the sale of *endowments* at market prices.

endowment Assets that can be sold to generate income for consumption.

Engel curve *Income demand curve.*

entrepreneurial skill Innovative or managerial skills that are often in fixed supply within a firm even as other inputs can change.

entry deterrence The strategic setting of output or price by a firm in an attempt to deter entry of a competing firm into the market.

envelope theorem Mathematical theorem used in the derivation of *Hotelling's Lemma*, *Shephard's Lemma*, and *Roy's Identity.*

equilibrium An economic environment in which everyone is doing the best they can given the circumstances they face (and given what others are doing).

equity premium puzzle The empirical observation of high risk-based returns that are difficult to justify with typical models of risk aversion.

essential goods Goods without which utility from consuming other goods would be the same as the utility of consuming nothing.

exchange economy An economy in which individuals trade existing goods but no new goods are produced.

excludability The property of private goods whose consumption can be restricted to only those who pay a price for consuming.

exit price The output price at which a firm will choose to exit a competitive market.

exogenous Given from outside the system; e.g., budgets that are fixed at some dollar value independent of other economic variables.

expected utility The probability-weighted average of utilities associated with the outcomes of a *gamble.*

expected utility theory The theory that the utility over *gambles* can be expressed as an *expected utility.*

expected value The probability-weighted average of the outcomes of a *gamble.*

expenditure (or expense) The financial outlays of a firm including *economic costs* and *sunk costs.*

expenditure function In consumer theory, the function that gives, for any set of prices and utility level *u*, the minimum income necessary to attain *u*.

expenditure minimization problem Finding the minimum expenditure necessary to attain a particular indifference curve at given prices; also results in *Hicksian demand curves* (or *compensated demand curves*).

experimental economics Subfield of economics that tests economic models through controlled experiments.

exporters Individuals who buy in low priced regions and ship goods to high priced regions in order to make a profit.

extensive form A way of illustrating games using a *game tree.*

externalities The positive or negative impact that individual decisions have on others besides those specifically involved in a market transaction.

financial economics Subfield of economics that investigates financial markets.

first degree price discrimination
Perfect *price discrimination* under which monopolists can identify consumer types, prevent resale, and vary prices across consumers as well as for different units sold to one consumer.

first mover advantage   Sequential move strategic settings in which players who move early can gain an advantage.

first order conditions   In a mathematical optimization problem, the first derivative conditions that represent the *necessary conditions* for a solution to be an optimum.

first-price auction   An auction in which the winner pays the highest bid for the auctioned item.

first welfare theorem   The theorem that states that resource allocations in an economy are *efficient* so long as there are no price distortions, no *externality*, no *asymmetric information*, and no *market power*.

fixed cost   An economic cost that remains unchanged regardless of how much output is produced.

fixed expenditure   An expense that is independent of how much is produced and includes a *sunk cost*.

fixed input   An input that cannot be varied by the firm (usually in the *short run*).

folk theorem   In *game theory*, the theorem that illustrates that a wide range of possible equilibrium outcomes can occur in infinitely *repeated games*.

framing   In *behavioral economics*, the observation that decisions can be impacted by the way that salient features of the decision are presented to the chooser.

free-rider problem   The efficiency problem that emerges in settings where individuals have an incentive to not contribute in some way but rather rely on the contributions of others.

functions   Mathematical rules that assign numbers (typically on the real line) to points.

fundamental non-convexities   *Non-convexities* that arise in the creation of property rights markets aimed at solving *externality* problems.

gains from trade   Increases in welfare for both parties when individuals choose to engage in voluntary trade.

gambler's fallacy   When people erroneously believe that once a randomly generated event has occurred, it is less likely to occur again.

gambles   A way to model choice involving risk when individuals know that different outcomes might happen with some probability.

game theory   Subfield of economics that develops tools for investigating strategic decision making.

game tree   A way of representing games in the form of a "tree" that lays out decision nodes and outcomes.

general equilibrium models   Models that take into account the interaction of markets as prices are formed.

generalized CES production function
The *constant elasticity of substitution (CES) function* generalized to include a parameter specifying *returns to scale*.

Gibbard-Satterthwaite theorem
Theorem that proves the impossibility of designing a mechanism that can implement a function with truth telling as the *dominant strategy*.

Giffen goods   *Inferior goods* with sufficiently small *substitution effects* relative to *income effects* such that the own price demand curve slopes up.

Gini coefficient   Measure of inequality derived from the *Lorenz curve* (usually applied to income or wealth inequality).

Gorman form   The form preferences must take in order for groups of consumers to behave as if they were a single *representative consumer*.

Groves-Clarke mechanism
A mechanism designed to implement the efficient level of a *public good* when preferences are only known to individuals.

head tax   A tax that is levied on everyone (who has a head) equally; example of a *lump sum tax*.

health economics   Subfield of economics that deals with issues related to the health care sector.

Henry George Theorem   A theorem illustrating the efficiency of land taxes.

Hicksian demand   *Compensated demand*; i.e., the demand for a good holding utility constant (and assuming enough income is made available to always reach that utility level).

homogeneous function   A function $f(x, y)$ such that $f(tx, ty) = t^k f(x, y)$ (which is then homogeneous of degree k).

homothetic producer choice set
A *producer choice set* whose map of *isoquants* has the property that the *technical rate of substitution* depends only on the ratio of inputs (and is thus the same along any ray from the origin).

homothetic tastes   Tastes whose map of *indifference curves* has the property that the *marginal rate of substitution* depends only on the ratio of goods (and is thus the same along any ray from the origin).

hot-hand fallacy   Occurs when people erroneously believe that a randomly generated event is more likely to occur again if it has just been observed to have occurred multiple times.

Hotelling model   A two-firm model of product differentiation along a line of possible product characteristics.

Hotelling's Lemma   The derivative of the *profit function* with respect to output price is equal to the supply function; and the derivative of the *profit function* with respect to input price is the negative of the input demand function.

hyperbolic discounting   In *behavioral economics*, a model of *discounting* that incorporates *present* (and near-present) *bias* and leads to *time inconsistent* choices.

image marketing   Advertising aimed at altering the image rather than providing information on the quality or price of a product.

impatience   Intertemporal decisions characterized by heavy *discounting* of the future.

import quota   A legal maximum of how much of a particular good can be imported.

importers   Individuals who have bought elsewhere at a low price and bring products into a high-priced region in order to sell them at a profit.

income demand curve   Curve that illustrates the relationship between the quantity of a good that is demanded with income; also known as an *Engle curve*.

income effect   The change in consumption behavior resulting from a change in income.

income elasticity of demand   The percentage change in the quantity demanded that results from a 1% change in income.

incomplete information games   Games in which players do not know the payoffs of all other players.

increasing cost industries   Competitive industries for which the *long-run* industry supply curve is upward sloping.

increasing returns to scale   Production technologies under which a *t*-fold increase in all inputs results in more than a *t*-fold increase in output (when no inputs are wasted).

incumbent firm   A firm that is already operating in an industry for which there is a large *fixed cost* of entry.

independence axiom   The assumption that underlies *expected utility theory*; states that if a gamble is preferred to another gamble, then the preference ordering does not change when both gambles are mixed with the same third gamble.

indifference curve   A set of consumption bundles that a consumer is indifferent between.

indifference map   A map of *indifference curves* that represents a person's tastes.

indirect utility function   The function that tells us, for any set of economic circumstances, how much utility a person will attain (assuming the person maximizes utility).

industrial organization   Subfield of economics that investigates competition in different types of industry structures.

inefficient   A situation that can be changed in such a way as to make some individuals better off without making anyone worse off.

inferior good   A good whose consumption increases as income falls (and falls as income increases).

information set   The set of decision nodes that an individual knows has been reached along a *game tree*.

informational advertising   Advertising that is aimed at providing information about the quality or price of a product.

innovation   The search for new products or for improvements in existing products.

insurance   A contract that reduces risk by increasing consumption in the "bad" outcome while lowering consumption in the "good" outcome.

interest rate   The price of using financial capital.

interior solution   A solution (to an optimization problem) that has strictly positive values for all choice variables.

intertemporal budget   A budget illustrating consumption trade-offs across time.

isocost curve   A set of input bundles that all cost the same (given current input prices).

isoprofit curve   A set of *production plans* that all result in the same *profit* (given the current input and output prices).

isoquant   A set of input bundles that all result in the same level of output (given the current technological constraint).

labor demand   The demand for labor by firms (as a function of input prices).

labor economics   Subfield of economics that deals with issues related to labor supply and demand (and related issues).

labor supply   The supply of labor by workers (who trade off consumption and leisure).

Laffer curve   Curve illustrating the relationship between tax rates and tax revenues.

Lagrange function   A function, composed of the *objective function* and (λ times) the *constraint* set to zero, used in mathematical *optimization problems*.

Lagrange multiplier   The λ term in the Lagrange function.

land rent   The rental price of a unit of land.

land value   The market price of land, equal to the present discounted value of all future land rents.

law and economics   Subfield of economics dealing with the intersection of law and economics.

law of 1/N   In political science, a rule of thumb predicting the degree of inefficiency of a marginal public project (voted on in legislatures) as a function of the number *N* of legislators.

law of diminishing marginal product   The fact that, for any real-world production process, the *marginal product* of every input must at some point decline.

leisure   Discretionary time not spent working.

Lerner index   A monopolist's mark-up (i.e., price minus marginal cost) divided by price.

Leviathan government   A government that maximizes political rents rather than social goals (such as efficiency).

lexicographic tastes   An example of tastes that satisfy all our five basic assumptions except for continuity.

libertarian paternalism   In *behavioral economics*, the idea that default choices should be set to overcome psychological biases while allowing individuals to choose differently.

Lindahl equilibrium   An equilibrium concept in which individuals pay personalized prices for *public goods* such that their decentralized choices lead to *efficient* public good provision.

Lindahl prices   Individualized prices that result in a *Lindahl equilibrium*.

local non-satiation   A property of tastes that assumes there always exists an alternate consumption bundle close to the one currently consumed such that the consumer would prefer that alternate bundle.

local public finance   Subfield in economics that studies the formation and functioning of local governments and clubs.

local public goods   Locally non-*rivalrous* and non-*excludable* public goods.

logrolling   Legislative deal making in which legislators agree to vote for each other's favorite *pork barrel projects*.

long run   For firms, the period over which all inputs become variable; for industries, the period over which exit/entry of firms is possible.

Lorenz curve   A curve relating the percentiles of the population to percentiles of income or wealth; used to calculate the *Gini coefficient*.

loss aversion   In *prospect theory*, people's tendency to prefer avoiding losses to acquiring gains.

lump sum tax   A non-*distortionary* tax, payment of which cannot be avoided through a change in behavior.

luxury good   A good whose consumption as a percentage of income increases as income increases.

macoreconomics   Subfield in economics that deals with the determination of economic aggregates such as unemployment, inflation, and growth.

marginal   Refers to "one additional" or "the last" of some economic variable.

marginal cost   The change in cost from one additional unit of output; or, equivalently, the change in cost from the last unit of output produced.

marginal rate of substitution   The rate at which a consumer is willing to trade one good for another; also, the negative slope of an *indifference curve*.

marginal revenue   The change in revenue from producing (and selling) one more unit of output, or, equivalently, the change in revenue from the last unit.

marginal technical rate of substitution See *technical rate of substitution*.

marginal utility   The change in utility from one more unit of a good; or, equivalently, the change in utility from the last unit of a good.

marginal willingness to pay   The willingness to pay for one more (or for the last) unit of a consumption good.

market   A structure that permits buyers and sellers to trade.

market power   The power to influence price.

mark-up   Price minus *marginal cost*.

Marshallian demand *Uncompensated demand* (that gives the quantity demanded as a function of prices and income (or wealth)).

Marshallian consumer surplus   The area above price up to the Marshallian demand curve.

matching pennies   A *zero-sum game* in which one player attempts to mimic the other while the other player attempts not to mimic the first player.

McKelvey theorem   Theorem illustrating that, in general, sequences of pairwise majority rule votes can lead to even the most extreme outcomes.

mechanism design   Subfield of economics that develops mechanisms to allocate scarce resources in the absence of market prices.

median voter theorem   Theorem that predicts the median voter's most preferred policy will be implemented under majority rule if the issue space is single-dimensional and preferences are *single-peaked*.

minimum wage   A *price floor*, or minimum legal price, in the labor market.

mixed gambles   *Gambles* that result from gambling over gambles.

mixed strategy   In *game theory*, strategies that place non-zero probability on more than one *pure strategy*.

monopolistic competition   A market structure with relatively low (but non-zero) barriers to entry and (usually) some product differentiation.

monopoly   Market structure with a single firm and high barriers to entry; the firm therefore has *market power*.

monoposony   *Market power* on the demand side.

monotonic tastes   Tastes under which more is better than (or at least as good as) less.

moral hazard   The tendency to change behavior after entering a contract, particularly one that reduces risk.

Nash equilibrium   In *game theory*, equilibrium in which all players play a strategy that is a *best response* to the strategies played by all other players.

natural monopoly   A *monopoly* that is protected from competition by barriers to entry that arise from the nature of the production process that gives rise to declining *average cost* (either because of high *fixed costs* or *increasing returns to scale* over large quantities).

necessary conditions   Conditions that must be satisfied for something (usually an optimum, in our case) to be true.

necessity   A good whose consumption as a percentage of income falls as income increases.

network externality   The effect that one consumer's consumption decision has on the value of a product to others.

neuroeconomics   Subfield that lies at the intersection of economics and neuroscience.

neutral goods   Goods that neither raise nor lower utility.

non-convexity   A property of sets under which one can find two points in the set such that the line connecting those points lies at least partially outside the set.

non-credible threats   In *game theory*, threats that will not be carried out by rational players.

non-excludability   The impossibility of excluding non-paying consumers from consuming certain goods.

non-price rationing   Rationing mechanisms to allocate scarce resources when prices are distorted.

non-rivalry   Property of *public goods* that can be consumed by more than one person at the same time.

norm of reciprocity   A *social norm* that is encapsulated by the saying "I'll scratch your back if you scratch mine."

normal form   In *game theory*, a representation of a game in a *payoff matrix* (rather than a *game tree*).

normal good   A good that is consumed in greater amounts as income increases.

normative economics   Subfield of economics that intersects with philosophy in that it asks "what is good."

numeraire   In general equilibrium models, the good that is assigned a price of 1.

objective function   The function that is being maximized or minimized in a mathematical *optimization problem*.

oligopoly   Market structure in which several large firms compete in the presence of *barriers to entry* that keep other firms out of the market.

opportunity cost   What someone gives up by undertaking an activity; also called *economic cost* or just cost.

optimization problem   A problem in which some variables are chosen in order to maximize or minimize a function.

optimizing   Doing the best one can (given the circumstances).

order-preserving function (or transformation)   A *function* that preserves the ranking of numbers assigned to points.

outsourcing   The practice of producing goods in low-wage markets while selling them in high-wage markets.

own-price demand curves   Curves relating the quantity of a good demanded to that good's price (holding all else equal).

Pareto efficient   Same as *efficient*.

Pareto optimal   Same as *Pareto efficient*.

partial equilibrium model   A model in which one market is analyzed in isolation.

patent   A legal *barrier to entry* established to allow an innovating firm to operate without the threat of entry from other firms for a limited amount of time.

payoff matrix   In two-player games, a matrix that provides each player's payoff for all combination of *strategies*.

perfect Bayesian (Nash) equilibrium   In *incomplete information games*, a set of *strategies* and *beliefs* such that each player's strategy is a best response to all other players' strategies given the player's beliefs.

perfect complements   Goods that produce utility only if consumed together.

perfect price discrimination   *First degree price discrimination*.

perfect substitutes   Goods that are completely substitutable for one another from the consumer's perspective.

perfectly competitive industry   Market structure in which many small firms produce identical products and each acts as a *price taker*.

Pigouvian subsidy   A *subsidy* designed to internalize a positive *externality*.

Pigouvian tax   A tax designed to internalize a negative *externality*.

political economy   Subfield that lies at the intersection of political science and economics in that it investigates the economics of political behavior.

pooling contracts   In insurance markets, when different risk types buy the same insurance contract.

pooling equilibrium   In *incomplete information games*, equilibrium in which some players play *pooling strategies*; in insurance markets, equilibrium with pooling contracts.

pooling strategy   In *incomplete information games*, strategies in which individuals play the same way regardless of what type they are.

pork barrel spending   Government spending targeted at one legislator's district but paid for by everyone.

positive economics   Branch of economics whose purpose is to predict behavior and its equilibrium consequences.

positive monotone transformation   Same as *order preserving transformation*.

preference revelation mechanism   A mechanism designed to get individuals to reveal their true preferences (often for *public goods*).

present-bias   In *intertemporal* decision making, a psychological bias that always treats the "present" as unique; captured in the *beta-delta model*.

price ceiling   A maximum legal price.

price discrimination   The practice of charging different prices to different individuals for the same product.

price elasticity   The percentage change in quantity from a 1% change in price.

price floor   A minimum legal price.

price subsidy   A *subsidy* that lowers the price for consumers.

price-taking   Nonstrategic behavior resulting from individuals rationally treating prices as given (because the individuals are too small relative to the market to impact the prices through their decisions).

price-gouging   A popular term used to denote moral outrage at the charging of high prices during periods of supply disruptions.

Prisoner's Dilemma   In *game theory*, a game in which not cooperating is a *dominant strategy* even though all players would be better off if they all cooperated.

private goods   Goods characterized by *rivalry* and *excludability*.

probability weighting   In *prospect theory*, the tendency of individuals to overweight small probabilities and underweight large probabilities as they make decisions.

producer choice set   The set of *production plans* that are technologically feasible.

producer surplus   The amount a producer would be willing to pay to operate in a market; i.e., economic *profit*.

product differentiation   The practice of differentiating one's product in order to soften competition (and raise *profit*).

production frontier   The boundary of the *producer choice set*; i.e., the production plans that are technologically feasible and that do not waste inputs.

production function   Mathematical characterization of the *production frontier*.

production plan   A list of inputs and outputs.

production possibilities frontier   In a two-good model, a depiction of the highest possible quantity of one good that can be produced given how much of the second good is produced.

profit   The difference between economic revenue and economic cost; also called *producer surplus*.

profit function   The function that gives profit for any set of input and output prices (assuming profit-maximizing behavior by the firm).

profit maximization   The act of finding the *production plan* that yields the largest possible *profit* given the technological and economic *constraints* faced by a firm.

proof by contradiction   A logical proof that begins by presuming that a statement is false and then illustrates that this presumption leads to a contradiction, which then implies that the statement is in fact true.

prospect theory   A *behavioral economics* model of choice in the presence of risk that introduces psychological biases that are at odds with traditional *expected utility theory*.

public economics   Subfield of economics that investigates taxation and government expenditures; also known as public finance.

public goods   Goods that are characterized by *non-rivalry* (and often, but not always, *non-excludability*).

pure strategy   In *game theory*, a *strategy* that plays an action with probability 1 at each *information set*.

put option   A contract that gives the holder the option of selling some quantity in the future at a predetermined price.

quasi-hyperbolic discounting
A special case of *hyperbolic discounting* captured by the *beta-delta model*.

quasi-concave function   A *function* whose level curves give rise to convex *upper-contour sets*.

quasilinear tastes   Tastes under which the *marginal rate of substitution* is independent of the quantity of one of the goods in the consumption bundle; tastes that do not give rise to *income effects*.

rational tastes   Tastes that are *complete* and *transitive*.

rationing   Any process that allocates scarce resources.

Rawlsian social preferences   An ethical rule that favors mechanisms that maximize the welfare of the least well-off person.

Rawlsian social welfare function
A function that represents *Rawlsian social preferences*.

real income   In microeconomics, typically means utility constant income; in macroeconomics (and sometimes in microeconomics) it means inflation-adjusted income.

reference-dependent preferences
In *behavioral economics*, preferences that evaluate choices relative to a status quo or reference point.

regular inferior goods   *Inferior goods* that are not *Giffen goods*.

regulatory capture   The tendency of regulators to be responsive to interests of those who are being regulated.

rent control   A *price ceiling* in the housing rental market.

rental rate   The price for use of *capital* (or land).

repeated game   A game that is played repeatedly, with players observing the outcome of all previous interactions.

representative consumer
A hypothetical consumer used to model the behavior of a group of consumers.

representative producer
A hypothetical produce used to model the behavior of a group of producers.

reservation utility   Utility that is obtainable for an individual in the absence of trading, usually from consumption of the *endowment*.

returns to scale   Property of production technologies describing how output responds to proportional increases in all inputs.

risk aversion   The willingness to pay positive amounts in order to reduce risk while not changing the expected outcome; i.e., tastes where the *certainty equivalent* is less than the *expected value* of a gamble.

risk neutral   Indifference between gambles that have the same expected outcome but different levels of risk.

risk premium   The difference between the *expected value* of a gamble and the *certainty equivalent*.

rivalry   The feature of *private goods* that they can be consumed by only one person.

Robinson Crusoe economy
A *general equilibrium* model of a single individual who acts as both a price taking producer and consumer.

Roy's identity   The mathematical relationship that allows one to derive output demand from *indirect utility functions*.

saving   The difference between current income and current consumption.

screening   In the presence of *asymmetric information*, the practice of expending effort to ascertain information about the individual (or firm) on the other side of a market transaction.

sealed-bid auction   Auctions in which bids are submitted at the same time without other bidders knowing any of the bids.

second-best analysis   Economic analysis that investigates what happens when one or more efficiency conditions cannot be satisfied.

second-degree price discrimination
Price discrimination when firms cannot identify consumer marginal willingness to pay and thus structure nonlinear price schedules to induce consumers to reveal their type in a *separating equilibrium*.

second order condition   Sufficient condition for a solution (derived from *first order conditions*) to an *optimization problem* to be optimal.

second-price auction   Auction in which the winner pays the second highest bid for the item.

second welfare theorem   The theorem that states that any *efficient* allocation of resources in an economy can be achieved through a decentralized market process so long as governments can engage in *lump sum taxation* and redistribution.

secondary market   A market in which goods previously obtained elsewhere are offered for sale.

separating equilibrium   In *incomplete information games*, equilibrium in which all types of players play different strategies (thus revealing information); in insurance markets, equilibrium in which different insurance contracts are sold to different risk types.

separating strategy   In *incomplete information games*, strategies in which individuals play differently depending on what type they are.

sequential move game   A game in which players play in sequence, with later players observing at least some of what previous players have done.

Shephard's lemma   In consumer theory, the derivative of the *expenditure function* with respect to output price is equal to the *Hicksian demand* function; in producer theory, the derivative of the *cost function* with respect to input price is equal to the *conditional input demand* function.

short run   For firms, usually the period over which some inputs are fixed; for industries, the period over which exit/entry of firms is not possible.

shut-down price   The output price at which a firm will choose to stop producing in the *short run*.

signaling   In the presence of *asymmetric information*, the practice of expending effort to provide information about oneself to the individual (or firm) on the other side of a market transaction.

signaling games   Games in which players with private information can reveal their type by adopting particular strategies.

simultaneous move games   Games in which all players choose their action simultaneously.

single-crossing property   Property of classes of tastes that implies indifference curves from two different *indifference maps* only cross once.

single-peaked preferences   In *political economy* models, tastes that have a most preferred bundle, with utility decreasing in the distance from that bundle.

Slutsky equation   The equation that decomposes the consumer response to a price change into the portion that is due to the *income effect* and the portion that is due to the *substitution effect*.

Slutsky substitution   The change in behavior from a price change when the individual is compensated so that he or she can still afford the original bundle.

snob effect   A *network externality* that causes individuals to place higher value on a good the fewer others also consume that good.

social choice function   A function that ranks different social states.

social entrepreneurs   Entrepreneurs who aim to innovate in nonprofit sectors to achieve social change.

social indifference curves   Indifference curves over utility (or income or wealth) allocations across individuals.

social marginal benefit   The sum of all marginal benefits resulting from an action.

social marginal cost   The sum of all marginal costs resulting from an action.

social norms   Behavioral expectations that are largely shared within the *civil society*.

social planner   A hypothetical individual who is in possession of all information and allocates resources with the aim of maximizing some social goal.

social welfare function   A *function* that ranks different utility (or income or wealth) allocations.

speculation   The attempt to make money by trading across time.

speculator   One who engages in *speculation*.

split-rate tax   A property tax that levies a higher rate on building structures than on land.

spontaneous order   An order that emerges without central planning.

spot market   The market in which goods currently trade.

spot price   The price in the *spot market*.

Stackelberg competition   Strategic competition (by firms) in which firms view quantity as the strategic variable and firms move sequentially.

state-contingent assets   Assets that become available if a particular state of the world materializes.

state-contingent consumption   Consumption that is contingent on a particular state of the world materializing.

state-dependent tastes (or utility)   *Expected utility* in the presence of risk, with different functions required to measure utility in different states of the world.

state-independent tastes (or utility)   *Expected utility* in the presence of risk, with a single function used to measure utility in different states of the world.

statistical discrimination   Discrimination that results from *asymmetric information* where the less informed party uses group averages to infer individual characteristics; a form of stereotyping.

status-quo effect   In *prospect theory*, the tendency of the status quo being used to evaluate changes in circumstances.

statutory tax incidence   The legal incidence of tax obligations as written in tax laws (or statutes).

Stone-Geary utility function   A utility function that incorporates subsistence levels of consumption below which utility is not defined.

strategy   In *game theory*, a player's complete plan of action prior to the beginning of the game.

structure-induced voting equilibrium   A voting equilibrium that emerges from institutional restrictions that limit what can be voted on and how.

subgame   Any part of a sequential game that begins at an *information set* consisting of a single node and includes the rest of the game tree from there on, with all information sets following the initial node required to be fully contained in the subgame.

subgame perfect equilibrium   A *Nash equilibrium* that does not rely on any *noncredible threats* (and thus is also a Nash equilibrium in all *subgames*).

subsidy   Government financial assistance that may take the form of a cash payment and/or a *price subsidy*.

substitutability   The degree to which consumption goods can be substituted for one another without changing utility or inputs can be substituted for one another without changing output.

substitution effect   In consumer theory, the portion of a response (to a price change) that is due solely to the change in *opportunity costs*; in producer theory, the change in input bundles that a *cost-minimizing* producer undertakes in response to input price changes (while keeping output constant).

sufficient conditions   Conditions that, if satisfied, guarantee that something (usually an optimum derived from *first order conditions*, in our case) is true.

sunk cost   An expense that is unaffected by the economic choice at hand.

supply curve   A graph that relates quantity supplied to price.

supply function   A function that, for any economic environment, gives the amount that will be supplied.

tariff   A tax on imports.

tastes   A ranking of consumption bundles, also called preferences.

tax base   The value of the activities that are subject to a tax.

tax credit   An amount that can be deducted from a taxpayer's tax obligation prior to tax payment being made.

tax deduction   An amount that can be deducted from a person's taxable income that is used to calculate the person's tax obligation.

tax incidence   The analysis of how the burden of a tax is distributed between individuals.

tax-deferred savings   Savings that are not subject to taxation until withdrawn for consumption (usually in retirement).

technical rate of substitution   The rate at which inputs can be substituted for one another in production without changing output; also, the slope of *isoquants*; sometimes referred to as marginal technical rate of substitution.

technologically efficient production   Production that does not waste inputs.

third-degree price discrimination   *Price discrimination* in which monopolists can identify consumer marginal willingness to pay and can charge different per-unit prices to different consumers.

Tiebout model   Model of *local public finance* in which residents choose locations by taking into account the mix of local taxes and services.

time inconsistency   Intertemporal decisions in which individuals plan for the future in ways that they do not stick to as the future becomes the present.

tipping point   A critical mass of engagement in an activity by individuals such that the activity turns from one undertaken in an initial equilibrium by only a few to one undertaken in a new equilibrium by many due to the presence of *network externalities*.

tit-for-tat strategy   In repeated *Prisoner's Dilemma games*, the strategy that begins by cooperating and then always mimics the opponents action from the last interaction.

total cost   The sum of all economic costs.

total expenditure   The sum of all expenses, including *sunk costs*.

tradable pollution permits   Legal permits (in a *cap-and-trade* system) that entitle the holder to engage in a specified amount of pollution or to sell that right to someone else.

tragedy of the commons   The overuse of commonly held resources due to the *free-rider problem*.

transactions cost   The cost (other than the price paid) incurred by the parties to an economic exchange.

transitive tastes   Tastes such that bundle A being preferred to B and B being preferred to C implies that A is preferred to C.

trigger strategy   In *repeated games*, a *strategy* under which punishments in future interactions are triggered by an opponent's behavior.

two-part tariffs   Nonlinear prices under which consumers are charged a fixed fee as well as a per-unit price.

uncompensated demand   The demand for a good when the individual is not compensated for price changes; same as *Marshallian demand*.

unconstrained optimization problem   An *optimization problem* that is not subject to a *constraint*, sometimes because the constraint has been substituted into the *objective function*.

upper contour set   The set of points above the level curve of a function.

urban economics   Subfield of economics that investigates the functioning of cities.

usury laws   Laws that place *price ceilings* on interest rates.

utility function   A function that represents *tastes* by ranking consumption bundles.

utility maximization   The act of choosing from the *consumer choice set* the consumption bundle that yields the highest level of utility.

utility possibility frontier   In a two-consumer model, a depiction of the highest possible utility attainable by one individual given how much utility is attained by the second individual.

utility possibility set   The *utility possibility frontier* and all utility allocations below this frontier.

utils   Hypothetical measurement unit for utility.

variable cost   Cost that changes as the quantity produced changes.

veil of ignorance   Hypothetical idea of a veil behind which individuals are imagined to choose social systems without knowing their own particular circumstances in life.

von Neumann-Morgenstern expected utility   Same as *expected utility*.

wage   For firms, the price of labor; for workers, the opportunity cost of leisure.

Walras' law   In *general equilibrium* theory, the result that permits us to conclude that supply is equal to demand in the nth market if supply is equal to demand in all other $(n - 1)$ markets.

warm glow effect   The utility one gets from the act of charitable giving (apart from the utility from the difference that is made by the charitable gift).

wealth effect   In models with *endogenous* budgets, the change in behavior (from a price change) that is due to the implicit change in wealth rather than the change in *opportunity costs*.

zero profit   Level of profit expected in *perfectly competitive industries* in the *long run;* implies a firm is doing as well as it could in its next best alternative activity.

zero-sum game   Game in which the winners' winnings are exactly equal to the losers' losses.